Hoover's Handbook of

American Business
2010

HOOVERS™
A D&B COMPANY

Austin, Texas

Hoover's Handbook of American Business 2010 is intended to provide readers with accurate and authoritative information about the enterprises covered in it. Hoover's researched all companies and organizations profiled, and in many cases contacted them directly so that companies represented could provide information. The information contained herein is as accurate as we could reasonably make it. In many cases we have relied on third-party material that we believe to be trustworthy, but were unable to independently verify. We do not warrant that the book is absolutely accurate or without error. Readers should not rely on any information contained herein in instances where such reliance might cause financial loss. The publisher, the editors, and their data suppliers specifically disclaim all warranties, including the implied warranties of merchantability and fitness for a specific purpose. This book is sold with the understanding that neither the publisher, the editors, nor any content contributors are engaged in providing investment, financial, accounting, legal, or other professional advice.

The financial data (Historical Financials sections) in this book are from a variety of sources. Morningstar, Inc., provided selected data for the Historical Financials sections of publicly traded companies. For private companies and for historical information on public companies prior to their becoming public, we obtained information directly from the companies or from trade sources deemed to be reliable. Hoover's, Inc., is solely responsible for the presentation of all data.

Many of the names of products and services mentioned in this book are the trademarks or service marks of the companies manufacturing or selling them and are subject to protection under US law. Space has not permitted us to indicate which names are subject to such protection, and readers are advised to consult with the owners of such marks regarding their use. Hoover's is a trademark of Hoover's, Inc.

10 9 8 7 6 5 4 3 2 1

Publishers Cataloging-in-Publication Data
Hoover's Handbook of American Business 2010

    Includes indexes.

    ISBN: 978-1-57311-136-2

    ISSN 1055-7202

    1. Business enterprises — Directories. 2. Corporations — Directories.

HF3010 338.7

Hoover's Company Information is also available on the Internet at Hoover's Online (www.hoovers.com). A catalog of Hoover's products is available on the Internet at www.hooversbooks.com.

The Hoover's Handbook series is produced for Hoover's Business Press by:

Sycamore Productions, Inc.
5808 Balcones Drive, Suite 205
Austin, Texas 78731
info@syprod.com

Cover design is by John Baker. Electronic prepress and printing are by Sheridan Books, Inc., Ann Arbor, Michigan.

U.S. AND WORLD BOOK SALES

Hoover's, Inc.
5800 Airport Blvd.
Austin, TX 78752
Phone: 512-374-4500
Fax: 512-374-4538
e-mail: orders@hoovers.com
Web: www.hooversbooks.com

EUROPEAN BOOK SALES

William Snyder Publishing Associates
5 Five Mile Drive
Oxford OX2 8HT
England
Phone & fax: +44-186-551-3186
e-mail: snyderpub@aol.com

Hoover's, Inc.

Founder: Gary Hoover
President: Hyune Hand
EVP Marketing and Business Development: Peter Poulin
VP Business Excellence: Jeffrey A. (Jeff) Cross
VP Technology: Mamie Jones
VP Business Development: Heidi Tucker
VP Advertising Sales and Operations: Mark Walters
VP Sales: Tom Wickersham
Leader e-Commerce and Books: Dan Tharp
Leader New Business Acquisitions: Amy Bible
Leader Human Resources: Robin Pfahler

(For the latest updates on Hoover's, please visit: http://hoovers.com/global/corp)

EDITORIAL

Managing Editor: Margaret L. Harrison
Senior Editors: Adrianne Argumaniz, Larry Bills, Jason Cother, Barbara-Anne Mansfield, Greg Perliski, Barbara Redding, Dennis Sutton
Team Leads: Danny Cummings and Matt Saucedo
Editors: Chelsea Adams, Adam Anderson, Jenn Barnier, Victoria Bernard, Alex Biesada, Joe Bramhall, James Bryant, Anthony Buchanan, Ryan Caione, Jason Cella, Catherine Colbert, Tami Conner, Nancy Daniels, Jeff Dorsch, Bobby Duncan, Lesley Epperson, Rachel Gallo, Jenni Gilmer, Chris Hampton, Stuart Hampton, Jim Harris, Laura Huchzermeyer, Chris Huston, Donna Iroabuchi, Ellen Jacobs, Jessica Jimenez, Linnea Anderson Kirgan, Sylvia Lambert, Anne Law, Josh Lower, John MacAyeal, Kathryn Mackenzie, Rebecca Mallett, Erin McInnis, Michael McLellan, Barbara Murray, Nell Newton, Lynett Oliver, Tracey Panek, Peter Partheymuller, Rachel Pierce, David Ramirez, Diane Ramirez, Mark Richardson, Melanie Robertson, Patrice Sarath, Amy Schein, Nikki Sein, Seth Shafer, Lee Simmons, Paula Smith, Anthony Staats, Barbara Strickland, Tracy Uba, Vanessa Valencia, Ryan Wade, Randy Williams, David Woodruff
QA Editors: Carrie Geis, Rosie Hatch, Diane Lee, John Willis
Editorial Customer Advocates: Adi Anand and Kenny Jones

HOOVER'S BUSINESS PRESS

Distribution Manager: Rhonda Mitchell
Customer Support and Fulfillment Manager: Michael Febonio

ABOUT HOOVER'S, INC. – THE BUSINESS INFORMATION AUTHORITY℠

Hoover's, a D&B company, provides its customers the fastest path to business with insight and actionable information about companies, industries, and key decision makers, along with the powerful tools to find and connect to the right people to get business done. Hoover's provides this information for sales, marketing, business development, and other professionals who need intelligence on U.S. and global companies, industries, and the people who lead them. Hoover's unique combination of editorial expertise and one-of-a-kind data collection with user-generated and company-supplied content gives customers a 360-degree view and competitive edge. This information, along with powerful tools to search, sort, download, and integrate the content, is available through Hoover's (http://www.hoovers.com), the company's premier online service. Hoover's is headquartered in Austin, Texas.

Abbreviations

AFL-CIO – American Federation of Labor and Congress of Industrial Organizations

AMA – American Medical Association

AMEX – American Stock Exchange

ARM – adjustable-rate mortgage

ASP – application services provider

ATM – asynchronous transfer mode

ATM – automated teller machine

CAD/CAM – computer-aided design/computer-aided manufacturing

CD-ROM – compact disc – read-only memory

CD-R – CD-recordable

CEO – chief executive officer

CFO – chief financial officer

CMOS – complimentary metal oxide silicon

COO – chief operating officer

DAT – digital audiotape

DOD – Department of Defense

DOE – Department of Energy

DOS – disk operating system

DOT – Department of Transportation

DRAM – dynamic random-access memory

DSL – digital subscriber line

DVD – digital versatile disc/digital video disc

DVD-R – DVD-recordable

EPA – Environmental Protection Agency

EPROM – erasable programmable read-only memory

EPS – earnings per share

ESOP – employee stock ownership plan

EU – European Union

EVP – executive vice president

FCC – Federal Communications Commission

FDA – Food and Drug Administration

FDIC – Federal Deposit Insurance Corporation

FTC – Federal Trade Commission

FTP – file transfer protocol

GATT – General Agreement on Tariffs and Trade

GDP – gross domestic product

HMO – health maintenance organization

HR – human resources

HTML – hypertext markup language

ICC – Interstate Commerce Commission

IPO – initial public offering

IRS – Internal Revenue Service

ISP – Internet service provider

kWh – kilowatt-hour

LAN – local-area network

LBO – leveraged buyout

LCD – liquid crystal display

LNG – liquefied natural gas

LP – limited partnership

Ltd. – limited

mips – millions of instructions per second

MW – megawatt

NAFTA – North American Free Trade Agreement

NASA – National Aeronautics and Space Administration

NASDAQ – National Association of Securities Dealers Automated Quotations

NATO – North Atlantic Treaty Organization

NYSE – New York Stock Exchange

OCR – optical character recognition

OECD – Organization for Economic Cooperation and Development

OEM – original equipment manufacturer

OPEC – Organization of Petroleum Exporting Countries

OS – operating system

OSHA – Occupational Safety and Health Administration

OTC – over-the-counter

PBX – private branch exchange

PCMCIA – Personal Computer Memory Card International Association

P/E – price to earnings ratio

RAID – redundant array of independent disks

RAM – random-access memory

R&D – research and development

RBOC – regional Bell operating company

RISC – reduced instruction set computer

REIT – real estate investment trust

ROA – return on assets

ROE – return on equity

ROI – return on investment

ROM – read-only memory

S&L – savings and loan

SCSI – Small Computer System Interface

SEC – Securities and Exchange Commission

SEVP – senior executive vice president

SIC – Standard Industrial Classification

SOC – system on a chip

SVP – senior vice president

USB – universal serial bus

VAR – value-added reseller

VAT – value-added tax

VC – venture capitalist

VoIP – Voice over Internet Protocol

VP – vice president

WAN – wide-area network

WWW – World Wide Web

Contents

List of Lists vi

Companies Profiled vii

About *Hoover's Handbook of American Business 2010* xi

Using Hoover's Handbooks xii

A List-Lover's Compendium 1

The Companies 25

The Indexes 935

    Index of Companies by Industry 936

    Index of Companies by Headquarters Location 941

    Index of Company Executives 946

List of Lists

HOOVER'S RANKINGS

The 300 Largest Companies by Sales in *Hoover's Handbook of American Business 2010* 2–3
The 300 Most Profitable Companies in *Hoover's Handbook of American Business 2010* 4–5
The 300 Most Valuable Public Companies in *Hoover's Handbook of American Business 2010* 6–7
The 300 Largest Employers in *Hoover's Handbook of American Business 2010* 8–9
The 100 Fastest-Growing Companies by Sales Growth in *Hoover's Handbook of American Business 2010* 10
The 100 Fastest-Growing Companies by Employment Growth in *Hoover's Handbook of American Business 2010* 11
50 Shrinking Companies by Sales Growth in *Hoover's Handbook of American Business 2010* 12
50 Shrinking Companies by Employment Growth in *Hoover's Handbook of American Business 2010* 12

THE BIGGEST AND THE RICHEST

The *FORTUNE* 500 Largest US Corporations.............13–16
The *Forbes* Largest Private Companies in the US......17–19
Top 20 in CEO Compensation...20
Top 20 Most Powerful Women in Business 20
Forbes Greatest US Fortunes 20
Forbes 20 Most Powerful Celebrities 20

MEDIA

Advertising Age's Top 50 Media Companies by Revenue...21

RETAIL

STORES' Top 20 US Retailers 21
Supermarket News' Top 20 Supermarket Companies 21

LEGAL, BUSINESS, AND FINANCIAL SERVICES

Top 20 Bank Holding Companies 22
Top 20 US Law Firms 22
Top 20 Money Managers...22
Top 20 Tax and Accounting Firms.....................................22

THE WORKPLACE

FORTUNE's 100 Best Companies to Work for in America...23
FORTUNE's 10 Most Admired Companies........................23
Top 20 Black-Owned Businesses.......................................24
Top 20 Hispanic-Owned Businesses 24
Top 10 Companies for Female Executives.........................24

Companies Profiled

3M Company 26
A. Schulman 27
A&P 28
Aaron's, Inc. 29
Abbott Laboratories....................................31
ABC, Inc...32
Abercrombie & Fitch 33
ABM Industries...35
Accenture Ltd...36
Ace Hardware 37
Activision Blizzard 38
Adams Resources & Energy.......................39
Administaff, Inc. 40
Adobe Systems...41
Advance Publications 42
Advanced Micro Devices............................43
The AES Corporation 44
Aetna Inc..46
Affiliated Computer Services 47
Aflac Incorporated......................................48
AGCO Corporation 50
Agilent Technologies...................................51
Air Products and Chemicals 52
Airgas, Inc..53
AirTran Holdings...54
AK Steel Holding...55
Alaska Air Group 57
Alberto-Culver 58
Alcoa Inc...59
Allegheny Energy..60
Allegheny Technologies 61
Allergan, Inc. 62
Alliance One International...........................64
Alliant Techsystems 65
The Allstate Corporation.............................66
Altria Group..67
Amazon.com...69
Ambac Financial Group 70
AMERCO 71
Ameren Corporation 72
American Eagle Outfitters 73
American Electric Power Company............75
American Express..76
American Financial Group...........................77
American Greetings 79
American International Group 80
American Water Works 82
AmeriCredit Corp..83
AmeriGas Partners 84
AmerisourceBergen 84
Amgen Inc...85
Amkor Technology 87
AMR Corporation 88
Anadarko Petroleum 89
Analog Devices...90
Anixter International 92
AnnTaylor Stores...93
A. O. Smith...94
Aon Corporation...95
Apache Corporation 96
Apollo Group..98
Apple Inc...99

Applied Industrial Technologies...............100
Applied Materials......................................101
ARAMARK Corporation............................103
Arch Coal 104
Archer Daniels Midland 105
Arrow Electronics 107
ArvinMeritor...108
Ashland Inc...109
AT&T Inc...110
Autodesk, Inc..112
Automatic Data Processing.......................113
AutoNation, Inc...114
AutoZone, Inc..115
Avery Dennison 117
Avis Budget Group 118
Avnet, Inc. 119
Avon Products 120
Baker & McKenzie 122
Baker Hughes..123
Baldor Electric 124
Ball Corporation.......................................125
Bank of America 126
Bank of New York Mellon 128
Barnes & Noble 129
Baxter International...................................130
BB&T Corporation 132
BE Aerospace..133
Beazer Homes USA....................................134
Bechtel Group 135
Beckman Coulter 136
Becton, Dickinson.....................................137
Bed Bath & Beyond 139
Belden Inc. 140
Bemis Company 142
Benchmark Electronics 143
Berkshire Hathaway..................................144
Best Buy..146
Big Lots 147
BJ Services..149
BJ's Wholesale Club 150
Black & Decker...151
Blockbuster Inc...152
BMC Software 154
Bob Evans Farms 155
The Boeing Company................................156
Bon-Ton Stores 157
Borders Group 158
BorgWarner Inc...160
Boston Scientific 161
Boyd Gaming 162
Briggs & Stratton......................................164
Brightpoint Inc..165
Brinker International..................................166
The Brink's Company.................................167
Bristol-Myers Squibb 168
Broadcom Corporation 170
Brown Shoe Company 171
Brown-Forman Corporation......................173
Brunswick Corporation.............................174
Burger King Holdings................................176
Burlington Northern Santa Fe 177
CA, Inc..178

Cablevision Systems..................................179
Cabot Corporation....................................180
CACI International 182
CalPERS 183
Calpine Corporation 184
Campbell Soup 185
Capital One Financial...............................186
Cardinal Health 187
Cargill, Incorporated.................................188
Carlisle Companies 190
Carlson Wagonlit Travel 191
CarMax, Inc. 192
Carnival Corporation 193
Carpenter Technology...............................194
Casey's General Stores 195
Caterpillar Inc...196
CB Richard Ellis Group 197
CBS Corporation.......................................198
CenterPoint Energy 200
Central Garden & Pet................................201
CenturyTel, Inc. 202
Cenveo, Inc...203
Cephalon, Inc. 204
Cerner Corporation...................................205
C.H. Robinson Worldwide.........................207
Champion Enterprises 208
Charles Schwab 209
Charming Shoppes.....................................210
Charter Communications...........................212
The Cheesecake Factory............................213
Chesapeake Energy 214
Chevron Corporation 215
Chiquita Brands International....................216
CHS Inc...217
The Chubb Corporation 218
Church & Dwight.......................................219
CIGNA Corporation...................................221
Cincinnati Financial 222
Cinemark Holdings 223
Cintas Corporation....................................224
Cisco Systems...225
Citigroup Inc...227
Cliffs Natural Resources............................228
The Clorox Company 229
CMS Energy...230
CNA Financial 231
The Coca-Cola Company...........................232
Coca-Cola Enterprises...............................234
Colgate-Palmolive.....................................235
Collective Brands 237
Comcast Corporation 238
Comerica Incorporated 239
Commercial Metals 240
CommScope, Inc..241
Computer Sciences Corporation 242
ConAgra Foods 244
ConocoPhillips 245
Conseco, Inc..246
CONSOL Energy 248
Consolidated Edison 249
Constellation Brands..................................250
Constellation Energy Group......................251

Companies Profiled (continued)

Continental Airlines......................252
Con-way Inc...............................253
Cooper Industries.........................255
Cooper Tire & Rubber......................256
Corning Incorporated......................257
Costco Wholesale..........................259
Covance Inc...............................260
Cox Enterprises...........................261
C. R. Bard, Inc...........................262
Cracker Barrel Old Country Store..........264
Crane Co..................................265
Crown Holdings............................266
CSX Corporation...........................268
Cummins, Inc..............................269
CVS Caremark..............................270
Cytec Industries..........................271
Dana Holding..............................272
Danaher Corporation.......................274
Darden Restaurants........................275
DaVita Inc................................276
Dean Foods................................277
Deere & Company...........................279
Del Monte Foods...........................280
Dell Inc..................................282
Deloitte Touche Tohmatsu..................283
Delta Air Lines...........................284
Deluxe Corporation........................285
Denny's Corporation.......................287
DENTSPLY International.....................288
Devon Energy..............................289
Diamond Offshore Drilling.................290
Diebold, Incorporated.....................291
Dillard's, Inc............................292
DineEquity, Inc...........................294
The DIRECTV Group.........................295
Discovery Communications..................296
DISH Network..............................297
Dole Food.................................298
Dominion Resources........................299
Domino's Pizza............................301
Donaldson Company.........................302
Dover Corporation.........................303
Dow Chemical..............................304
D.R. Horton...............................306
DST Systems...............................307
DTE Energy................................308
Duke Energy...............................309
Dun & Bradstreet..........................310
DuPont....................................311
Dynegy Inc................................312
E. & J. Gallo Winery......................314
EarthLink, Inc............................315
Eastman Chemical..........................316
Eastman Kodak.............................317
Eaton Corporation.........................318
eBay Inc..................................320
Ecolab Inc................................321
Edison International......................322
El Paso Corporation.......................323
Electronic Arts...........................324
Eli Lilly.................................325
EMC Corporation...........................327
EMCOR Group...............................328
Emerson Electric..........................329
ENSCO International........................331
Entergy Corporation.......................332
Enterprise Products Partners..............333
EOG Resources.............................334
Equifax Inc...............................335
Equity Residential........................336
Ernst & Young Global......................337
Estée Lauder..............................338
E*TRADE Financial.........................339
E. W. Scripps.............................340
Exelon Corporation........................342
Exide Technologies........................343
Expeditors International..................344
Express Scripts...........................345
Exxon Mobil...............................346

Family Dollar Stores......................347
Fastenal Company..........................349
Federal-Mogul.............................350
FedEx Corporation.........................351
Ferrellgas Partners.......................353
Fifth Third Bancorp.......................353
The First American Corporation............355
FirstEnergy Corp..........................356
Fiserv, Inc...............................357
Flowers Foods.............................358
Fluor Corporation.........................360
FMC Corporation...........................361
FMR LLC...................................362
Foot Locker...............................363
Ford Motor................................364
Forest Laboratories.......................366
Fortune Brands............................367
Fossil, Inc...............................368
Foster Wheeler............................369
Fox Entertainment.........................371
FPL Group.................................372
Franklin Resources........................373
Freeport-McMoRan Copper & Gold............374
Frontier Communications...................375
Furniture Brands International............376
GameStop Corp.............................378
Gannett Co................................379
The Gap...................................380
General Cable.............................382
General Dynamics..........................383
General Electric..........................384
General Mills.............................386
General Motors............................387
Genuine Parts.............................388
Genzyme Corporation.......................390
Gerdau Ameristeel.........................391
Gilead Sciences...........................392
Global Crossing...........................393
Goldman Sachs.............................395
Goodrich Corporation......................396
Goodyear Tire & Rubber....................397
Google Inc................................399
Green Bay Packers.........................400
Greif, Inc................................401
Guess?, Inc...............................402
Halliburton Company.......................403
Hallmark Cards............................404
H&R Block.................................405
Hanover Insurance.........................407
Harley-Davidson...........................408
Harman International.......................409
Harris Corporation........................411
Hartford Financial Services...............412
Hasbro, Inc...............................413
HCA Inc...................................415
Health Management Associates..............416
Health Net................................417
HealthSouth Corporation...................418
Hearst Corporation........................420
Helmerich & Payne.........................421
Henry Schein..............................422
Herman Miller.............................423
The Hershey Company.......................424
Hertz Global Holdings.....................425
Hess Corporation..........................427
Hewitt Associates.........................428
Hewlett-Packard...........................429
Highmark Inc..............................430
Hill-Rom Holdings.........................432
Hilton Worldwide..........................433
H. J. Heinz Company.......................434
HNI Corporation...........................435
Holly Corporation.........................436
Hologic, Inc..............................437
Home Depot................................439
Honeywell International...................440
Hormel Foods..............................441
Hovnanian Enterprises.....................443
HSN, Inc..................................444

Hub Group.................................445
Humana Inc................................446
Huntington Bancshares.....................447
Hyatt Hotels Corporation..................448
IAC/InterActiveCorp.......................450
IDT Corporation...........................451
IGA, Inc..................................452
Illinois Tool Works.......................453
Imation Corp..............................454
IMS Health................................455
Ingersoll-Rand............................456
Ingram Micro..............................458
Insight Enterprises.......................459
Intel Corporation.........................460
International Business Machines............462
International Flavors & Fragrances.........463
International Game Technology..............464
International Paper........................465
Interpublic Group.........................467
Intuit Inc................................468
Invacare Corporation......................469
Invesco Ltd...............................470
Iron Mountain.............................471
Itron, Inc................................472
ITT Corporation...........................474
Jabil Circuit.............................475
Jack in the Box...........................476
Jacobs Engineering........................477
J.B. Hunt Transport Services..............479
J. C. Penney..............................480
Jefferies Group...........................481
The J. M. Smucker Company.................482
Jo-Ann Stores.............................484
John Wiley & Sons.........................485
Johnson & Johnson.........................486
Johnson Controls..........................488
Jones Apparel.............................489
Jones Lang LaSalle........................491
Joy Global................................492
JPMorgan Chase............................493
Kaiser Foundation Health Plan.............494
Kansas City Southern......................495
KB Home...................................496
Kellogg Company...........................497
Kelly Services............................499
Kennametal Inc............................500
Key Energy Services.......................502
KeyCorp...................................502
Kimberly-Clark............................504
Kindred Healthcare........................505
Kinetic Concepts..........................506
King Ranch................................507
KLA-Tencor................................508
Kmart Corporation.........................510
Koch Industries...........................511
Kohl's Corporation........................512
KPMG International.........................513
Kraft Foods...............................514
The Kroger Co.............................516
L-3 Communications........................517
Lam Research..............................519
Land O'Lakes..............................520
La-Z-Boy..................................521
Legg Mason................................523
Leggett & Platt...........................524
Lennar Corporation........................525
Lennox International......................527
Level 3 Communications....................528
Levi Strauss..............................529
Lexmark International......................530
Liberty Mutual............................531
Limited Brands............................533
Lincare Holdings..........................534
Lincoln Electric Holdings.................535
Lincoln National..........................536
Live Nation...............................537
Liz Claiborne.............................539
Lockheed Martin...........................540
Loews Corporation.........................542

Companies Profiled (continued)

Lowe's Companies....................543
LSI Corporation.......................544
The Lubrizol Corporation.........545
MacAndrews & Forbes.............547
Macy's, Inc.............................548
Magellan Health Services.........549
Manitowoc Company................550
Manpower Inc.........................551
Marathon Oil..........................553
Markel Corporation.................554
Marriott International...............555
Mars, Incorporated.................556
Marsh & McLennan..................558
Martha Stewart Living..............559
Martin Marietta Materials........560
Masco Corporation..................561
Massachusetts Mutual Life Insurance.....563
MasterCard Incorporated.........564
Mattel, Inc.............................565
Maxim Integrated Products......566
MBIA Inc...............................568
McAfee, Inc...........................569
McClatchy Company................570
McCormick & Company.............571
McDermott International...........572
McDonald's Corporation...........573
McGraw-Hill...........................575
McKesson Corporation.............576
McKinsey & Company...............577
MeadWestvaco........................578
Medco Health Solutions...........580
Medtronic, Inc.......................581
Men's Wearhouse....................582
Merck & Co...........................583
MetLife, Inc...........................585
MetroPCS Communications.......586
MGM MIRAGE.........................587
Micron Technology..................588
Microsoft Corporation.............590
Mohawk Industries..................591
Molex Incorporated.................592
Molson Coors Brewing..............593
Monsanto Company.................595
Moog Inc...............................596
Morgan Stanley.......................598
Motorola, Inc.........................599
MPS Group............................600
MSC Industrial Direct..............601
Mylan Inc..............................602
NACCO Industries....................603
Nalco Holding.........................605
NASDAQ OMX Group................606
Nash-Finch Company...............607
National Fuel Gas....................608
National Semiconductor............609
Nationwide Mutual Insurance....610
Navistar International...............611
NBC Television........................613
NBTY, Inc..............................614
NCI Building Systems...............615
NCR Corporation.....................616
NetApp, Inc...........................617
New York Life Insurance...........618
New York Times......................619
Newell Rubbermaid.................620
Newmont Mining.....................622
News Corporation....................623
Nicor Inc...............................625
NIKE, Inc..............................626
NiSource Inc..........................627
Noble Corporation...................628
Nordstrom, Inc.......................629
Norfolk Southern.....................631
Northeast Utilities...................632
Northern Trust.......................633
Northrop Grumman..................634
Northwestern Mutual Life Insurance.....635
Novell, Inc............................636
NRG Energy............................638

NSTAR..................................638
Nucor Corporation..................639
NVIDIA Corporation.................641
NVR, Inc...............................642
NYSE Euronext.......................643
Occidental Petroleum...............644
Office Depot...........................645
OfficeMax..............................647
Olin Corporation.....................648
Omnicare, Inc........................649
Omnicom Group......................650
ONEOK, Inc...........................651
Oracle Corporation..................652
Oshkosh Corporation...............654
Owens & Minor.......................655
Owens-Illinois........................656
PACCAR Inc...........................657
Pall Corporation.....................658
Palm, Inc..............................659
The Pantry.............................660
Parker Hannifin.......................661
Patterson Companies................663
Paychex, Inc..........................664
PC Connection........................665
The Pep Boys.........................666
Pepco Holdings.......................668
Pepsi Bottling Group................668
PepsiAmericas, Inc..................670
PepsiCo, Inc...........................671
PerkinElmer, Inc.....................673
Perot Systems........................674
Perrigo Company....................676
Peter Kiewit Sons'...................677
PetSmart, Inc........................678
Pfizer Inc..............................679
PG&E Corporation...................681
Phillips-Van Heusen.................682
Pinnacle West Capital..............683
Pioneer Natural Resources........684
Pitney Bowes.........................685
Plains All American Pipeline......687
Plexus Corp...........................688
PNC Financial Services.............689
Polaris Industries....................690
Polo Ralph Lauren...................691
PPG Industries........................692
PPL Corporation.....................694
Praxair, Inc...........................695
Precision Castparts.................696
priceline.com.........................698
PricewaterhouseCoopers...........699
Principal Financial...................700
Procter & Gamble...................701
Progress Energy......................703
Progressive Corporation...........704
Protective Life........................705
Prudential Financial.................706
PSS World Medical..................707
Psychiatric Solutions...............708
Public Service Enterprise Group.....709
Publix Super Markets...............711
Pulte Homes..........................712
QUALCOMM...........................713
Quest Diagnostics...................714
Quiksilver, Inc........................716
Qwest Communications............717
RadioShack Corporation...........718
Ralcorp Holdings.....................719
Raymond James Financial.........720
Raytheon Company..................722
Regions Financial....................723
Regis Corporation...................724
Rent-A-Center........................726
Republic Services....................727
Revlon, Inc............................728
Reynolds American..................729
Rite Aid................................731
Robert Half............................732
Rock-Tenn Company................733

Rockwell Automation................734
Roper Industries.....................735
Ross Stores...........................736
Rowan Companies....................738
Royal Caribbean Cruises...........739
RPM International....................740
R.R. Donnelley.......................741
Ryder System.........................742
The Ryland Group....................744
Safeway Inc...........................745
SAIC, Inc...............................746
St. Jude Medical.....................747
Sanderson Farms.....................748
SanDisk Corporation................749
Sanmina-SCI..........................750
Sara Lee...............................751
S.C. Johnson..........................753
SCANA Corporation.................754
ScanSource, Inc......................755
Schlumberger Limited..............756
Schnitzer Steel Industries.........757
Scholastic Corporation.............758
Scotts Miracle-Gro..................760
Seaboard Corporation..............761
SEACOR Holdings....................762
Seagate Technology.................763
Sealed Air Corp......................764
Sealy Corporation...................766
Sears, Roebuck.......................767
Sempra Energy.......................768
Service Corporation.................769
The Shaw Group......................770
Sherwin-Williams....................771
Sigma-Aldrich Corporation........773
Simon Property Group..............774
Skadden, Arps........................775
SkyWest, Inc..........................776
Smithfield Foods.....................777
Snap-on Incorporated..............778
Solutia Inc............................780
Sonoco Products.....................781
Sotheby's..............................782
Southern Company..................783
Southern Union......................784
Southwest Airlines...................785
Southwest Gas.......................787
Spartan Stores.......................787
Spherion Corporation..............788
Sprint Nextel.........................789
SPX Corporation.....................790
Staples, Inc...........................792
Starbucks Corporation..............793
Starwood Hotels & Resorts.......794
State Farm Mutual...................796
State Street Corporation...........797
Steelcase Inc..........................798
Sun Healthcare.......................799
Sunoco, Inc...........................800
SunTrust Banks.......................801
SUPERVALU INC......................803
Symantec Corporation.............804
SYSCO Corporation.................805
T. Rowe Price Group.................807
Target Corporation..................808
TD Ameritrade.......................809
Tech Data Corporation.............810
Telephone & Data Systems.......811
Tellabs, Inc...........................812
Temple-Inland........................813
Tenet Healthcare....................815
Tenneco Inc...........................816
Tennessee Valley Authority.......817
Terex Corporation...................818
Terra Industries......................820
Tesoro Corporation.................821
Tetra Tech.............................821
Texas Instruments...................823
Textron Inc............................824
Thermo Fisher Scientific...........825

Companies Profiled (continued)

Thomas & Betts....................................827
Thor Industries 828
TIAA-CREF 829
Tiffany & Co. 830
The Timberland Company 832
Time Warner 833
The Timken Company...........................834
TJX Companies....................................835
Toll Brothers 837
Torchmark Corporation........................838
The Toro Company...............................839
Total System Services 840
Transocean Inc.....................................841
Travelers Companies 842
Trinity Industries 843
True Value 845
Tupperware Brands 846
Tyco International................................847
Tyson Foods..848
UAL Corporation 850
UGI Corporation..................................851
Union Pacific 852
Unisys Corporation 853
United Natural Foods...........................854
United Parcel Service 855
United Rentals 857
United States Cellular 858
United States Steel 859
United Stationers 860
United Technologies 861

UnitedHealth Group.............................863
Universal Corporation..........................864
Unum Group 865
Urban Outfitters 866
URS 867
US Airways..869
U.S. Bancorp.......................................870
US Postal Service 871
USAA 872
USEC Inc...873
USG Corporation.................................874
Valassis Communications 875
Valero Energy......................................876
The Valspar Corporation.......................877
The Vanguard Group.............................879
VeriSign, Inc..880
Verizon Communications 881
V.F. Corporation 882
Viad Corp 884
Visa Inc 885
Vishay Intertechnology 886
Volt Information Sciences 888
Vulcan Materials..................................888
Wakefern Food 890
Walgreen Co. 890
Wal-Mart Stores 892
The Walt Disney Company.....................893
Warnaco Group 895
Warner Music Group.............................896
Washington Post 897

Waste Management 899
Watsco, Inc...900
Watson Pharmaceuticals.......................901
Watson Wyatt Worldwide......................902
Weatherford International 903
WellPoint, Inc......................................904
Wells Fargo...906
Wendy's/Arby's Group 907
Werner Enterprises 908
WESCO International 909
Westar Energy.....................................910
Western Digital 911
Weyerhaeuser Company 913
Whirlpool Corporation..........................914
Whole Foods Market 915
Williams Companies 917
Williams-Sonoma.................................918
Winn-Dixie Stores................................919
World Fuel Services 920
Worthington Industries 921
W. R. Grace..923
W.W. Grainger 924
Xcel Energy 925
Xerox Corporation...............................926
Xilinx, Inc..927
Yahoo!..929
YRC Worldwide 930
YUM! Brands.......................................931
Zale Corporation 932
Zions Bancorporation 933

About Hoover's Handbook of American Business 2010

In times of great economic turbulence such as we are currently experiencing, knowledge is king. When it's information about companies you need to make business, financial, or employment decisions, we believe that Hoover's Business Press is the place to turn. For our premier Hoover's Handbooks series of guides to businesses, we've done the sorting and sifting of information, leaving you with the facts you need to make the important decisions you face.

This 20th edition of *Hoover's Handbook of American Business,* as it has throughout its history, stands as one of America's respected sources of business information, packed with the information you need.

Hoover's Handbook of American Business is the first of our four-title series of handbooks that covers, literally, the world of business. The series is available as an indexed set, and also includes *Hoover's Handbook of World Business, Hoover's Handbook of Private Companies,* and *Hoover's Handbook of Emerging Companies.* This series brings you information on the biggest, fastest-growing, and most influential enterprises in the world.

HOOVER'S ONLINE FOR BUSINESS NEEDS

In addition to the 2,550 companies featured in our handbooks, comprehensive coverage of more than 40,000 business enterprises is available in electronic format on our Web site, Hoover's Online (www.hoovers.com). Our goal is to provide one site that offers authoritative, updated intelligence on US and global companies, industries, and the people who shape them. Hoover's has partnered with other prestigious business information and service providers to bring you all the right business information, services, and links in one place.

We welcome the recognition we have received as a provider of high-quality company information — online, electronically, and in print — and continue to look for ways to make our products more available and more useful to you.

We believe that anyone who buys from, sells to, invests in, lends to, competes with, interviews with, or works for a company should know all there is to know about that enterprise. Taken together, this book and the other Hoover's products and resources represent the most complete source of basic corporate information readily available to the general public.

This latest version of *Hoover's Handbook of American Business* contains, as always, profiles of the largest and most influential companies in the United States. Each of the companies profiled here was chosen because of its important role in American business. For more details on how these companies were selected, see the section titled "Using Hoover's Handbooks."

HOW TO USE THIS BOOK

This book has four sections:

1. "Using Hoover's Handbooks" describes the contents of our profiles and explains the ways in which we gather and compile our data.

2. "A List-Lover's Compendium" contains lists of the largest, smallest, best, most, and other superlatives related to companies involved in American business.

3. The company profiles section makes up the largest and most important part of the book — 750 profiles of major US enterprises.

4. Three indexes complete the book. The first sorts companies by industry groups, the second by headquarters location. The third index is a list of all the executives found in the Executives section of each company profile.

As always, we hope you find our books useful. We invite your comments via phone (512-374-4500), fax (512-374-4538), mail (5800 Airport Boulevard, Austin, Texas 78752), or e-mail (custsupport@hoovers.com).

The Editors,
Austin, Texas,
October 2009

Using Hoover's Handbooks

SELECTION OF THE COMPANIES PROFILED

The 750 enterprises profiled in this book include the largest and most influential companies in America. Among them are:

- more than 690 publicly held companies, from 3M to Zions Bancorporation
- more than 40 large private enterprises (such as Cargill and Mars)
- several mutual and cooperative organizations (such as USAA and Ace Hardware)
- a selection of other enterprises (such as Kaiser Foundation Health Plan, the US Postal Service, and the Tennessee Valley Authority) that we believe are sufficiently large and influential enough to warrant inclusion.

In selecting these companies, our foremost question was "What companies will our readers be most interested in?" Our goal was to answer as many questions as we could in one book — in effect, trying to anticipate your curiosity. This approach resulted in four general selection criteria for including companies in the book:

1. Size. The 500 or so largest American companies, measured by sales and by number of employees, are included in the book. In general, these companies have sales in excess of $2 billion, and they are the ones you will have heard of and the ones you will want to know about. These are the companies at the top of the *FORTUNE*, *Forbes*, and *Business Week* lists. We have made sure to include the top private companies in this number.

2. Growth. We believe that relatively few readers will be going to work for, or investing in, the railroad industry. Therefore, only a few railroads are in the book. On the other hand, we have included a number of technology firms, as well as companies that provide medical products and services — pharmaceutical and biotech companies, health care insurers, and medical device makers.

3. Visibility. Most readers will have heard of the Hilton Worldwide and Harley-Davidson companies. Their service or consumer natures make them household names, even though they are not among the corporate giants in terms of sales and employment.

4. Breadth of coverage. To show the diversity of economic activity, we've included, among others, a professional sports team, one ranch, the Big Four accounting firms, and one of the largest law firms in the US. We feel that these businesses are important enough to enjoy at least "token" representation. While we might not emphasize certain industries, the industry leaders are present.

ORGANIZATION

The profiles are presented in alphabetical order. This alphabetization is generally word by word, which means that Legg Mason precedes Leggett & Platt. You will find the commonly used name of the enterprise at the beginning of the profile; the full, legal name is found in the Locations section. If a company name is also a person's name, like Walt Disney, it will be alphabetized under the first name; if the company name starts with initials, like J. C. Penney or H.J. Heinz, look for it under the combined initials (in the above examples, JC and HJ, respectively). Basic financial data is listed under the heading Historical Financials; also included is the exchange on which the company's stock is traded if it is public, the ticker symbol used by the stock exchange, and the company's fiscal year-end.

The annual financial information contained in the profiles is current through fiscal year-ends occurring as late as May 2009. We have included certain nonfinancial developments, such as officer changes, through September 2009.

OVERVIEW

In the first section of the profile, we have tried to give a thumbnail description of the company and what it does. The description will usually include information on the company's strategy, reputation, and ownership. We recommend that you read this section first.

HISTORY

This extended section, included for almost all companies in the book, reflects our belief that every enterprise is the sum of its history and that you have to know where you came from in order to know where you are going. While some companies have limited historical awareness, we think the vast majority of the enterprises in this book have colorful backgrounds. We have tried to focus on the people who made the enterprises what they are today. We have found these histories to be full of twists and ironies; they make fascinating reading.

EXECUTIVES

Here we list the names of the people who run the company, insofar as space allows. In the case of public companies, we have shown the ages and total compensation of key officers. In some cases the published data is for the previous year although the company has announced promotions or retirements since year-end. Total compensation is the sum of salary, bonus, and the value of any other benefits, such as stock options or deferred compensation.

Although companies are free to structure their management titles any way they please, most modern corporations follow standard practices. The ultimate power in any corporation lies with the shareholders, who elect a board of directors, usually including officers or "insiders" as well as individuals from outside the company. The chief officer, the person on whose desk the buck stops, is usually called the chief executive officer (CEO). Often, he or she is also the chairman of the board.

As corporate management has become more complex, it is common for the CEO to have a "right-hand person" who oversees the day-to-day operations of the company, allowing the CEO plenty of time to focus on strategy and long-term issues. This right-hand person is usually designated the chief operating officer (COO) and is often the president of the company. In other cases one person is both chairman and president.

A multitude of other titles exists, including chief financial officer (CFO), chief administrative officer, and vice chairman. We have always tried to include the CFO, the chief legal officer, and the chief human resources or personnel officer. Our best advice is that officers' pay levels are clear indicators of who the board of directors thinks are the most important members of the management team.

The people named in the Executives section are indexed at the back of the book.

The Executives section also includes the name of the company's auditing (accounting) firm, where available.

LOCATIONS

Here we include the company's full legal name and its headquarters, street address, telephone and fax numbers, and Web site, as available. The back of the book includes an index of companies by headquarters locations.

In some cases we have also included information on the geographic distribution of the company's business, including sales and profit data. Note that these profit numbers, like those in the Products/Operations section below, are usually operating or pretax profits rather than net profits. Operating profits are generally those before financing costs (interest income and payments) and before taxes, which are considered costs attributable to the whole company rather than to one division or part of the world. For this reason the net income figures (in the Historical Financials section) are usually much lower, since they are after interest and taxes. Pretax profits are after interest but before taxes.

Headquarters for companies that are incorporated in Bermuda, but whose operational headquarters are in the US, are listed under their US address.

PRODUCTS/OPERATIONS

This section lists as many of the company's products, services, brand names, divisions, subsidiaries, and joint ventures as we could fit. We have tried to include all its major lines and all familiar brand names. The nature of this section varies by company and the amount of information available. If the company publishes sales and profit information by type of business, we have included it.

COMPETITORS

In this section we have listed companies that compete with the profiled company. This feature is included as a quick way to locate similar companies and compare them. The universe of competitors includes all public companies and all private companies with sales in excess of $500 million. In a few instances we have identified smaller private companies as key competitors.

HISTORICAL FINANCIALS

Here we have tried to present as much data about each enterprise's financial performance as we could compile in the allocated space. The information varies somewhat from industry to industry and is less complete in the case of private companies that do not release data (although we have always tried to provide annual sales and employment). There are a few industries, venture capital and investment banking, for example, for which revenue numbers are unavailable as a rule.

The following information is generally present.

A 5-year table, with relevant annualized compound growth rates, covers:
- Sales — fiscal year sales (year-end assets for most financial companies)
- Net income — fiscal year net income (before accounting changes)
- Net profit margin — fiscal year net income as a percent of sales (as a percent of assets for most financial firms)
- Employees — fiscal year-end or average number of employees
- Stock price — the fiscal year close
- P/E — high and low price/earnings ratio
- Earnings per share — fiscal year earnings per share (EPS)
- Dividends per share — fiscal year dividends per share
- Book value per share — fiscal year-end book value (common shareholders' equity per share)

The information on the number of employees is intended to aid the reader interested in knowing whether a company has a long-term trend of increasing or decreasing employment. As far as we know, we are the only company that publishes this information in print format.

The numbers on the left in each row of the Historical Financials section give the month and the year in which the company's fiscal year actually ends. Thus, a company with a March 31, 2009, year-end is shown as 3/09.

In addition, we have provided in graph form a stock price history for most public companies. The graphs, covering up to five years, show the range of trading between the high and the low price, as well as the closing price for each fiscal year. Generally, for private companies, we have graphed net income, or, if that is unavailable, sales.

Key year-end statistics in this section generally show the financial strength of the enterprise, including:

- Debt ratio (long-term debt as a percent of shareholders' equity)
- Return on equity (net income divided by the average of beginning and ending common shareholders' equity)
- Cash and cash equivalents
- Current ratio (ratio of current assets to current liabilities)
- Total long-term debt (including capital lease obligations)

- Number of shares of common stock outstanding
- Dividend yield (fiscal year dividends per share divided by the fiscal year-end closing stock price)
- Dividend payout (fiscal year dividends divided by fiscal year EPS)
- Market value at fiscal year-end (fiscal year-end closing stock price multiplied by fiscal year-end number of shares outstanding)

Per share data has been adjusted for stock splits. The data for public companies has been provided to us by Morningstar, Inc. Other public company information was compiled by Hoover's, which takes full responsibility for the content of this section.

In the case of private companies that do not publicly disclose financial information, we usually did not have access to such standardized data. We have gathered estimates of sales and other statistics from numerous sources.

Hoover's Handbook of

American Business

A List-Lover's Compendium

The 300 Largest Companies by Sales in
Hoover's Handbook of American Business 2010

Rank	Company	Sales ($ mil.)	Rank	Company	Sales ($ mil.)	Rank	Company	Sales ($ mil.)
1	Exxon Mobil	477,359	51	Safeway Inc.	44,104	101	Travelers Companies	24,477
2	Wal-Mart Stores	405,607	52	PepsiCo, Inc.	43,251	102	Publix Super Markets	24,110
3	Chevron Corporation	273,005	53	Lockheed Martin	42,731	103	Tech Data Corporation	24,081
4	ConocoPhillips	246,182	54	Kraft Foods	42,201	104	Merck & Co.	23,850
5	General Electric	182,515	55	Wells Fargo	41,897	105	AMR Corporation	23,766
6	General Motors	148,979	56	Hess Corporation	41,165	106	United States Steel	23,754
7	Ford Motor	146,277	57	Kaiser Foundation Health Plan	40,300	107	Nucor Corporation	23,663
8	AT&T Inc.	124,028	58	Cisco Systems	39,540	108	McDonald's Corporation	23,522
9	Valero Energy	119,114	59	Johnson Controls	38,062	109	Oracle Corporation	23,252
10	Hewlett-Packard	118,364	60	The Walt Disney Company	37,843	110	Raytheon Company	23,174
11	Cargill, Incorporated	116,579	61	Intel Corporation	37,586	111	Staples, Inc.	23,084
12	Berkshire Hathaway	107,786	62	SYSCO Corporation	36,853	112	Nationwide Mutual Insurance	22,962
13	McKesson Corporation	106,632	63	Honeywell International	36,556	113	Delta Air Lines	22,697
14	International Business Machines	103,630	64	Sprint Nextel	35,635	114	KPMG International	22,690
15	Koch Industries	100,000	65	FedEx Corporation	35,497	115	Coca-Cola Enterprises	22,381
16	Cardinal Health	99,512	66	Ingram Micro	34,362	116	Fluor Corporation	22,326
17	Verizon Communications	97,354	67	Comcast Corporation	34,256	117	Goldman Sachs	22,222
18	CVS Caremark	87,472	68	Northrop Grumman	33,887	118	Express Scripts	21,978
19	UnitedHealth Group	81,186	69	Apple Inc.	32,479	119	Northwestern Mutual Life Insurance	21,923
20	Procter & Gamble	79,029	70	The Coca-Cola Company	31,944	120	Enterprise Products Partners	21,906
21	The Kroger Co.	76,000	71	DuPont	31,836	121	Google Inc.	21,796
22	US Postal Service	74,932	72	Bechtel Group	31,400	122	Manpower Inc.	21,553
23	Bank of America	72,782	73	Aetna Inc.	30,951	123	Bristol-Myers Squibb	20,597
24	Costco Wholesale	72,483	74	News Corporation	30,423	124	Eli Lilly	20,378
25	Marathon Oil	72,128	75	Motorola, Inc.	30,146	125	Tyco International	20,199
26	Home Depot	71,288	76	Plains All American Pipeline	30,061	126	UAL Corporation	20,194
27	AmerisourceBergen	70,190	77	Mars, Incorporated	30,000	127	Constellation Energy Group	19,818
28	Archer Daniels Midland	69,207	78	Abbott Laboratories	29,528	128	The DIRECTV Group	19,693
29	JPMorgan Chase	67,252	79	The Allstate Corporation	29,394	129	Goodyear Tire & Rubber	19,488
30	Target Corporation	64,948	80	General Dynamics	29,300	130	Kimberly-Clark	19,415
31	Johnson & Johnson	63,747	81	Prudential Financial	29,275	131	Altria Group	19,356
32	State Farm Mutual	61,300	82	Humana Inc.	28,946	132	Massachusetts Mutual Life Insurance	19,301
33	WellPoint, Inc.	61,251	83	Liberty Mutual	28,855	133	NIKE, Inc.	19,176
34	Dell Inc.	61,101	84	Deere & Company	28,438	134	Amazon.com	19,166
35	The Boeing Company	60,909	85	American Express	28,365	135	CIGNA Corporation	19,101
36	Walgreen Co.	59,034	86	Tesoro Corporation	28,309	136	TJX Companies	19,000
37	United Technologies	58,681	87	PricewaterhouseCoopers	28,185	137	Whirlpool Corporation	18,907
38	Microsoft Corporation	58,437	88	Deloitte Touche Tohmatsu	27,400	138	Exelon Corporation	18,859
39	Dow Chemical	57,514	89	Schlumberger Limited	27,163	139	World Fuel Services	18,509
40	Sunoco, Inc.	54,146	90	Alcoa Inc.	26,901	140	J. C. Penney	18,486
41	Citigroup Inc.	52,793	91	Tyson Foods	26,862	141	Halliburton Company	18,279
42	United Parcel Service	51,486	92	Rite Aid	26,289	142	Burlington Northern Santa Fe	18,018
43	Caterpillar Inc.	51,324	93	Accenture Ltd	25,314	143	Union Pacific	17,970
44	Medco Health Solutions	51,258	94	3M Company	25,269	144	Freeport-McMoRan Copper & Gold	17,796
45	MetLife, Inc.	50,989	95	Macy's, Inc.	24,892	145	Xerox Corporation	17,608
46	Pfizer Inc.	48,296	96	International Paper	24,829	146	Southern Company	17,127
47	Lowe's Companies	48,230	97	Emerson Electric	24,807	147	New York Life Insurance	16,830
48	Time Warner	46,984	98	Morgan Stanley	24,739	148	Arrow Electronics	16,761
49	Best Buy	45,015	99	Ernst & Young Global	24,500	149	Computer Sciences Corporation	16,740
50	SUPERVALU INC.	44,564	100	Occidental Petroleum	24,480	150	Aflac Incorporated	16,554

SOURCE: HOOVER'S, INC., DATABASE, SEPTEMBER 2009

The 300 Largest Companies by Sales in
Hoover's Handbook of American Business 2010 (continued)

Rank	Company	Sales ($ mil.)	Rank	Company	Sales ($ mil.)	Rank	Company	Sales ($ mil.)
151	FPL Group	16,410	201	Highmark Inc.	13,002	251	BJ's Wholesale Club	10,027
152	Kohl's Corporation	16,389	202	USAA	12,912	252	Unum Group	9,982
153	Dominion Resources	16,290	203	Sara Lee	12,881	253	Calpine Corporation	9,937
154	Avnet, Inc.	16,230	204	Marriott International	12,879	254	Principal Financial	9,936
155	Kmart Corporation	16,219	205	Progressive Corporation	12,840	255	Terex Corporation	9,890
156	ONEOK, Inc.	16,157	206	Kellogg Company	12,822	256	Lincoln National	9,883
157	The AES Corporation	16,070	207	Jabil Circuit	12,780	257	Seagate Technology	9,805
158	Illinois Tool Works	15,869	208	ConAgra Foods	12,731	258	Weatherford International	9,601
159	PPG Industries	15,849	209	Danaher Corporation	12,698	259	Masco Corporation	9,600
160	Anadarko Petroleum	15,723	210	Transocean Inc.	12,674	260	A&P	9,516
161	Cox Enterprises	15,400	211	Texas Instruments	12,501	261	Eastman Kodak	9,416
162	Eaton Corporation	15,376	212	Smithfield Foods	12,488	262	DTE Energy	9,329
163	Health Net	15,367	213	Dean Foods	12,455	263	Hartford Financial Services	9,219
164	Colgate-Palmolive	15,330	214	Apache Corporation	12,390	264	Progress Energy	9,167
165	Continental Airlines	15,241	215	Williams Companies	12,352	265	SunTrust Banks	9,093
166	Devon Energy	15,211	216	Baxter International	12,348	266	Limited Brands	9,043
167	Amgen Inc.	15,003	217	US Airways	12,118	267	The Pantry	8,996
168	PACCAR Inc	14,973	218	Land O'Lakes	12,039	268	YRC Worldwide	8,940
169	L-3 Communications	14,901	219	Baker Hughes	11,864	269	NiSource Inc.	8,874
170	EMC Corporation	14,876	220	ITT Corporation	11,695	270	Automatic Data Processing	8,867
171	Navistar International	14,724	221	Chesapeake Energy	11,629	271	Reynolds American	8,845
172	General Mills	14,691	222	DISH Network	11,617	272	GameStop Corp.	8,806
173	Carnival Corporation	14,646	223	Marsh & McLennan	11,587	273	Tenet Healthcare	8,663
174	PG&E Corporation	14,628	224	R.R. Donnelley	11,582	274	C.H. Robinson Worldwide	8,579
175	Medtronic, Inc.	14,599	225	Monsanto Company	11,365	275	Nordstrom, Inc.	8,573
176	U.S. Bancorp	14,543	226	CenterPoint Energy	11,322	276	eBay Inc.	8,541
177	The Gap	14,526	227	YUM! Brands	11,279	277	Gerdau Ameristeel	8,529
178	Office Depot	14,496	228	CSX Corporation	11,255	278	Hertz Global Holdings	8,525
179	American Electric Power Company	14,440	229	Jacobs Engineering	11,252	279	AGCO Corporation	8,425
180	Cummins, Inc.	14,342	230	Xcel Energy	11,203	280	Ashland Inc.	8,381
181	Textron Inc.	14,246	231	QUALCOMM	11,142	281	Crown Holdings	8,305
182	AutoNation, Inc.	14,132	232	American International Group	11,104	282	OfficeMax	8,267
183	Edison International	14,112	233	Southwest Airlines	11,023	283	Applied Materials	8,129
184	CBS Corporation	13,950	234	Genuine Parts	11,015	284	Dana Holding	8,095
185	Capital One Financial	13,893	235	Praxair, Inc.	10,796	285	Hilton Hotels	8,090
186	Pepsi Bottling Group	13,796	236	Sempra Energy	10,758	286	Boston Scientific	8,050
187	Bank of New York Mellon	13,652	237	Pepco Holdings	10,700	287	PPL Corporation	8,044
188	FirstEnergy Corp.	13,627	238	State Street Corporation	10,693	288	Weyerhaeuser Company	8,018
189	Consolidated Edison	13,583	239	Avon Products	10,690	289	Peter Kiewit Sons'	8,000
190	Qwest Communications	13,475	240	Norfolk Southern	10,661	290	S.C. Johnson	8,000
191	ARAMARK Corporation	13,470	241	Wakefern Food	10,600	291	Campbell Soup	7,998
192	Waste Management	13,388	242	Thermo Fisher Scientific	10,498	292	Sherwin-Williams	7,980
193	Omnicom Group	13,360	243	Commercial Metals	10,427	293	Advance Publications	7,970
194	Public Service Enterprise Group	13,322	244	Air Products and Chemicals	10,415	294	Whole Foods Market	7,954
195	Loews Corporation	13,247	245	Starbucks Corporation	10,383	295	Owens-Illinois	7,885
196	Ingersoll-Rand	13,227	246	Tennessee Valley Authority	10,382	296	MGM MIRAGE	7,884
197	The Chubb Corporation	13,221	247	Parker Hannifin	10,309	297	Ameren Corporation	7,839
198	Duke Energy	13,207	248	H. J. Heinz Company	10,148	298	CNA Financial	7,799
199	TIAA-CREF	13,187	249	URS	10,086	299	AK Steel Holding	7,644
200	Entergy Corporation	13,094	250	SAIC, Inc.	10,070	300	V.F. Corporation	7,643

The 300 Most Profitable Companies in
Hoover's Handbook of American Business 2010

Rank	Company	Net Income ($ mil.)	Rank	Company	Net Income ($ mil.)	Rank	Company	Net Income ($ mil.)
1	Exxon Mobil	45,220	51	Exelon Corporation	2,737	101	NIKE, Inc.	1,487
2	Chevron Corporation	23,931	52	American Express	2,699	102	TIAA-CREF	1,465
3	General Electric	17,410	53	The Boeing Company	2,672	103	Aon Corporation	1,462
4	Microsoft Corporation	14,569	54	Wells Fargo	2,655	104	Bank of New York Mellon	1,445
5	Procter & Gamble	13,436	55	Comcast Corporation	2,547	105	Williams Companies	1,418
6	Wal-Mart Stores	13,400	56	WellPoint, Inc.	2,491	106	Aetna Inc.	1,384
7	Johnson & Johnson	12,949	57	Dell Inc.	2,478	107	American Electric Power Company	1,380
8	AT&T Inc.	12,867	58	General Dynamics	2,459	108	CSX Corporation	1,365
9	International Business Machines	12,334	59	EOG Resources	2,437	109	Weatherford International	1,354
10	Hewlett-Packard	8,329	60	Emerson Electric	2,412	110	EMC Corporation	1,346
11	Pfizer Inc.	8,104	61	Hess Corporation	2,360	111	FirstEnergy Corp.	1,342
12	Cisco Systems	8,052	62	Union Pacific	2,338	112	Reynolds American	1,338
13	Merck & Co.	7,808	63	Carnival Corporation	2,330	113	PG&E Corporation	1,338
14	Occidental Petroleum	6,857	64	Goldman Sachs	2,322	114	Automatic Data Processing	1,333
15	Verizon Communications	6,428	65	Home Depot	2,260	115	Danaher Corporation	1,318
16	The Coca-Cola Company	5,807	66	Target Corporation	2,214	116	Diamond Offshore Drilling	1,311
17	Oracle Corporation	5,593	67	Lowe's Companies	2,195	117	General Mills	1,304
18	Schlumberger Limited	5,435	68	Medtronic, Inc.	2,169	118	Duke Energy	1,295
19	Intel Corporation	5,292	69	Walgreen Co.	2,157	119	Costco Wholesale	1,283
20	Corning Incorporated	5,257	70	Burlington Northern Santa Fe	2,115	120	Aflac Incorporated	1,254
21	Bristol-Myers Squibb	5,247	71	United States Steel	2,112	121	The Kroger Co.	1,249
22	PepsiCo, Inc.	5,142	72	Deere & Company	2,053	122	The AES Corporation	1,234
23	Berkshire Hathaway	4,994	73	Monsanto Company	2,024	123	Entergy Corporation	1,221
24	Altria Group	4,930	74	Baxter International	2,014	124	Edison International	1,215
25	Abbott Laboratories	4,881	75	Gilead Sciences	2,011	125	Charles Schwab	1,212
26	Apple Inc.	4,834	76	DuPont	2,007	126	Praxair, Inc.	1,211
27	United Technologies	4,689	77	Nationwide Mutual Insurance	1,994	127	Consolidated Edison	1,196
28	Loews Corporation	4,530	78	Colgate-Palmolive	1,957	128	Public Service Enterprise Group	1,188
29	The Walt Disney Company	4,427	79	Texas Instruments	1,920	129	NRG Energy	1,188
30	McDonald's Corporation	4,313	80	Dominion Resources	1,834	130	Campbell Soup	1,165
31	Google Inc.	4,227	81	Nucor Corporation	1,831	131	Cardinal Health	1,152
32	Transocean Inc.	4,202	82	State Street Corporation	1,811	132	ENSCO International	1,151
33	Amgen Inc.	4,196	83	The Chubb Corporation	1,804	133	Kellogg Company	1,148
34	Bank of America	4,008	84	eBay Inc.	1,780	134	Liberty Mutual	1,140
35	JPMorgan Chase	3,699	85	Halliburton Company	1,778	135	Becton, Dickinson	1,127
36	Caterpillar Inc.	3,557	86	Southern Company	1,742	136	Computer Sciences Corporation	1,115
37	Marathon Oil	3,528	87	Norfolk Southern	1,716	137	Sempra Energy	1,113
38	3M Company	3,460	88	Archer Daniels Midland	1,707	138	Medco Health Solutions	1,103
39	Cargill, Incorporated	3,334	89	Morgan Stanley	1,707	139	Publix Super Markets	1,090
40	Anadarko Petroleum	3,261	90	Accenture Ltd	1,692	140	Waste Management	1,087
41	Lockheed Martin	3,217	91	Raytheon Company	1,672	141	Eaton Corporation	1,058
42	CVS Caremark	3,212	92	Kimberly-Clark	1,671	142	SYSCO Corporation	1,056
43	MetLife, Inc.	3,209	93	FPL Group	1,639	143	Precision Castparts	1,045
44	QUALCOMM	3,160	94	Baker Hughes	1,635	144	PACCAR Inc	1,018
45	United Parcel Service	3,003	95	Franklin Resources	1,588	145	Best Buy	1,003
46	UnitedHealth Group	2,977	96	Noble Corporation	1,561	146	Omnicom Group	1,000
47	U.S. Bancorp	2,946	97	Tyco International	1,553	147	Thermo Fisher Scientific	994
48	Travelers Companies	2,924	98	The DIRECTV Group	1,521	148	Johnson Controls	979
49	Kraft Foods	2,901	99	BB&T Corporation	1,519	149	ConAgra Foods	978
50	Honeywell International	2,792	100	Illinois Tool Works	1,519	150	The Gap	967

SOURCE: HOOVER'S, INC., DATABASE, SEPTEMBER 2009

Rank	Company	Net Income ($ mil.)	Rank	Company	Net Income ($ mil.)	Rank	Company	Net Income ($ mil.)
151	Safeway Inc.	965	201	Dow Chemical	579	251	Nordstrom, Inc.	401
152	YUM! Brands	964	202	Allergan, Inc.	579	252	AGCO Corporation	400
153	Applied Materials	961	203	Rockwell Automation	578	253	GameStop Corp.	398
154	Enterprise Products Partners	954	204	Royal Caribbean Cruises	574	254	Allegheny Energy	395
155	PPL Corporation	930	205	J. C. Penney	572	255	Molson Coors Brewing	388
156	L-3 Communications	929	206	Fiserv, Inc.	569	256	St. Jude Medical	384
157	H. J. Heinz Company	923	207	Allegheny Technologies	566	257	Mattel, Inc.	380
158	Air Products and Chemicals	910	208	Unum Group	553	258	Xilinx, Inc.	376
159	DISH Network	903	209	DTE Energy	546	259	Joy Global	374
160	Kohl's Corporation	885	210	PPG Industries	538	260	DaVita Inc.	374
161	PNC Financial Services	882	211	The Clorox Company	537	261	Darden Restaurants	372
162	TJX Companies	881	212	Paychex, Inc.	534	262	CenturyTel, Inc.	366
163	Avon Products	875	213	Foster Wheeler	527	263	Sara Lee	364
164	Adobe Systems	872	214	Cliffs Natural Resources	516	264	Marriott International	362
165	Newmont Mining	853	215	Parker Hannifin	509	265	C.H. Robinson Worldwide	359
166	Progress Energy	830	216	T. Rowe Price Group	491	266	Arch Coal	354
167	McKesson Corporation	823	217	Textron Inc.	486	267	Affiliated Computer Services	350
168	Tennessee Valley Authority	817	218	H&R Block	486	268	Eastman Chemical	346
169	Staples, Inc.	805	219	Northwestern Mutual Life Insurance	483	269	International Game Technology	343
170	Visa Inc	804	220	Invesco Ltd.	482	270	Sigma-Aldrich Corporation	342
171	TD Ameritrade	804	221	Sherwin-Williams	477	271	SCANA Corporation	338
172	McGraw-Hill	800	222	Intuit Inc.	477	272	Starwood Hotels & Resorts	329
173	SunTrust Banks	796	223	Apollo Group	477	273	NASDAQ OMX Group	320
174	Northern Trust	795	224	W.W. Grainger	475	274	Ball Corporation	320
175	ITT Corporation	795	225	Genuine Parts	475	275	Discovery Communications	317
176	Analog Devices	786	226	Western Digital	470	276	Starbucks Corporation	316
177	Solutia Inc.	786	227	Simon Property Group	464	277	ONEOK, Inc.	312
178	Express Scripts	776	228	Helmerich & Payne	462	278	The Hershey Company	311
179	Sunoco, Inc.	776	229	Principal Financial	458	279	IMS Health	311
180	Forest Laboratories	768	230	Torchmark Corporation	452	280	Fortune Brands	311
181	Cummins, Inc.	755	231	SAIC, Inc.	452	281	Dun & Bradstreet	311
182	Chesapeake Energy	723	232	Ecolab Inc.	448	282	Hasbro, Inc.	307
183	Fluor Corporation	721	233	CenterPoint Energy	447	283	Ross Stores	305
184	Apache Corporation	712	234	Harris Corporation	444	284	FMC Corporation	305
185	CA, Inc.	694	235	CONSOL Energy	443	285	Expeditors International	301
186	Agilent Technologies	693	236	Plains All American Pipeline	437	286	Pepco Holdings	300
187	Goodrich Corporation	681	237	Brown-Forman Corporation	435	287	CMS Energy	300
188	Qwest Communications	681	238	McDermott International	429	288	Southern Union	295
189	Harley-Davidson	655	239	Cincinnati Financial	429	289	Interpublic Group	295
190	Humana Inc.	647	240	Rowan Companies	428	290	Black & Decker	294
191	Xcel Energy	646	241	Bed Bath & Beyond	425	291	CIGNA Corporation	292
192	Amazon.com	645	242	Yahoo!	424	292	Roper Industries	287
193	AutoZone, Inc.	642	243	USAA	423	293	Trinity Industries	286
194	Terra Industries	641	244	Genzyme Corporation	421	294	Hormel Foods	286
195	Cooper Industries	632	245	Jacobs Engineering	421	295	DENTSPLY International	284
196	BJ Services	609	246	Equity Residential	420	296	Fastenal Company	280
197	Ameren Corporation	605	247	Pitney Bowes	420	297	Tesoro Corporation	278
198	V.F. Corporation	603	248	Whirlpool Corporation	418	298	Equifax Inc.	273
199	Dover Corporation	591	249	C. R. Bard, Inc.	417	299	Abercrombie & Fitch	272
200	Quest Diagnostics	582	250	Polo Ralph Lauren	406	300	National Fuel Gas	269

The 300 Most Valuable Public Companies in
Hoover's Handbook of American Business 2010

Rank	Company	Market Value* ($ mil.)	Rank	Company	Market Value ($ mil.)	Rank	Company	Market Value ($ mil.)
1	Exxon Mobil	383,646	51	Colgate-Palmolive	34,162	101	MasterCard Incorporated	18,533
2	Microsoft Corporation	211,807	52	Bank of New York Mellon	34,076	102	American Electric Power Company	18,391
3	Wal-Mart Stores	183,609	53	Lockheed Martin	32,317	103	Praxair, Inc.	18,211
4	General Electric	172,155	54	Baxter International	32,299	104	Danaher Corporation	18,100
5	AT&T Inc.	168,150	55	Altria Group	31,139	105	Johnson Controls	18,046
6	Johnson & Johnson	164,880	56	The Boeing Company	30,997	106	eBay Inc.	18,014
7	Berkshire Hathaway	149,897	57	UnitedHealth Group	30,920	107	Genzyme Corporation	17,940
8	Procter & Gamble	149,155	58	Southern Company	30,897	108	The Chubb Corporation	17,845
9	Chevron Corporation	148,348	59	Emerson Electric	30,657	109	BB&T Corporation	17,798
10	Wells Fargo	137,719	60	Costco Wholesale	29,163	110	Automatic Data Processing	17,796
11	Cisco Systems	126,836	61	Devon Energy	29,162	111	Carnival Corporation	17,626
12	JPMorgan Chase	123,994	62	MetLife, Inc.	28,538	112	The Allstate Corporation	17,572
13	Bank of America	121,814	63	Caterpillar Inc.	27,753	113	Hess Corporation	17,543
14	Pfizer Inc.	119,527	64	NIKE, Inc.	27,722	114	Illinois Tool Works	17,530
15	International Business Machines	110,324	65	News Corporation	27,633	115	FedEx Corporation	17,313
16	The Coca-Cola Company	104,911	66	Lowe's Companies	26,976	116	Norfolk Southern	17,297
17	Apple Inc.	101,819	67	Time Warner	26,434	117	Dow Chemical	17,257
18	Oracle Corporation	98,092	68	Burlington Northern Santa Fe	25,743	118	Applied Materials	17,209
19	Google Inc.	97,393	69	Travelers Companies	25,654	119	Archer Daniels Midland	17,187
20	Verizon Communications	96,297	70	Accenture Ltd	25,406	120	Yahoo!	17,121
21	Hewlett-Packard	91,346	71	Apache Corporation	25,023	121	Kellogg Company	16,788
22	PepsiCo, Inc.	85,324	72	Honeywell International	24,690	122	EOG Resources	16,774
23	Abbott Laboratories	82,505	73	Union Pacific	24,106	123	General Mills	16,655
24	Intel Corporation	82,067	74	Target Corporation	23,458	124	Tyco International	16,603
25	ConocoPhillips	76,814	75	DuPont	22,861	125	Halliburton Company	16,393
26	QUALCOMM	71,429	76	PNC Financial Services	22,609	126	Deere & Company	16,309
27	McDonald's Corporation	67,871	77	The DIRECTV Group	22,390	127	Entergy Corporation	16,276
28	Merck & Co.	64,109	78	General Dynamics	22,177	128	Transocean Inc.	15,104
29	Monsanto Company	62,371	79	Amazon.com	22,143	129	Express Scripts	15,087
30	Amgen Inc.	58,644	80	American Express	22,060	130	FirstEnergy Corp.	15,066
31	The Walt Disney Company	57,039	81	Kimberly-Clark	21,860	131	Simon Property Group	14,933
32	United Parcel Service	54,854	82	Aflac Incorporated	21,431	132	Corning Incorporated	14,815
33	Visa Inc	51,968	83	Dominion Resources	21,334	133	Public Service Enterprise Group	14,759
34	Schlumberger Limited	50,704	84	EMC Corporation	21,171	134	SunTrust Banks	14,735
35	United Technologies	50,452	85	Waste Management	20,888	135	YUM! Brands	14,697
36	Occidental Petroleum	48,638	86	FPL Group	20,709	136	The Kroger Co.	14,658
37	Comcast Corporation	48,442	87	WellPoint, Inc.	20,418	137	Nucor Corporation	14,538
38	U.S. Bancorp	47,818	88	Franklin Resources	20,299	138	Capital One Financial	14,509
39	Eli Lilly	46,271	89	Morgan Stanley	20,048	139	Air Products and Chemicals	14,388
40	Gilead Sciences	46,244	90	Raytheon Company	19,874	140	PG&E Corporation	14,349
41	Bristol-Myers Squibb	46,057	91	Medco Health Solutions	19,855	141	Northrop Grumman	14,328
42	CVS Caremark	41,478	92	Texas Instruments	19,577	142	Prudential Financial	13,950
43	Goldman Sachs	40,383	93	Newmont Mining	19,525	143	Thermo Fisher Scientific	13,906
44	3M Company	40,181	94	Duke Energy	19,464	144	SYSCO Corporation	13,286
45	Kraft Foods	39,603	95	State Street Corporation	19,448	145	Campbell Soup	12,745
46	Citigroup Inc.	36,957	96	Marathon Oil	19,363	146	CSX Corporation	12,734
47	Home Depot	36,674	97	Becton, Dickinson	19,213	147	Marsh & McLennan	12,713
48	Exelon Corporation	36,651	98	Anadarko Petroleum	18,910	148	Aetna Inc.	12,620
49	Walgreen Co.	36,152	99	Charles Schwab	18,771	149	Northern Trust	12,587
50	Medtronic, Inc.	35,817	100	Dell Inc.	18,563	150	Aon Corporation	12,538

*Market value at the latest available fiscal year-end

SOURCE: HOOVER'S, INC., DATABASE, SEPTEMBER 2009

Rank	Company	Market Value ($ mil.)	Rank	Company	Market Value ($ mil.)	Rank	Company	Market Value ($ mil.)
151	Allergan, Inc.	12,399	201	Omnicom Group	8,366	251	Western Digital	5,954
152	Loews Corporation	12,233	202	Ecolab Inc.	8,324	252	Electronic Arts	5,885
153	Valero Energy	12,178	203	Eaton Corporation	8,232	253	Coca-Cola Enterprises	5,870
154	Symantec Corporation	12,169	204	TJX Companies	8,231	254	DTE Energy	5,867
155	Adobe Systems	12,159	205	C. R. Bard, Inc.	8,225	255	SCANA Corporation	5,796
156	Best Buy	11,999	206	ConAgra Foods	8,219	256	The Hershey Company	5,783
157	Reynolds American	11,745	207	Diamond Offshore Drilling	8,193	257	Noble Corporation	5,777
158	Boston Scientific	11,668	208	Equity Residential	8,170	258	Cephalon, Inc.	5,751
159	PPL Corporation	11,557	209	CenturyTel, Inc.	8,124	259	Allegheny Energy	5,739
160	Staples, Inc.	11,514	210	Fluor Corporation	8,071	260	Mattel, Inc.	5,737
161	St. Jude Medical	11,469	211	Weatherford International	7,874	261	Lincoln National	5,691
162	Kohl's Corporation	11,211	212	Molson Coors Brewing	7,870	262	Fiserv, Inc.	5,615
163	Progress Energy	11,118	213	The Gap	7,860	263	AmerisourceBergen	5,596
164	Cardinal Health	10,988	214	The Clorox Company	7,769	264	Computer Sciences Corporation	5,589
165	Activision Blizzard	10,986	215	Agilent Technologies	7,619	265	BJ Services	5,588
166	Alcoa Inc.	10,971	216	KeyCorp	7,485	266	Bed Bath & Beyond	5,578
167	Starbucks Corporation	10,961	217	Ford Motor	7,377	267	CBS Corporation	5,551
168	H. J. Heinz Company	10,849	218	AutoZone, Inc.	7,374	268	Ingersoll-Rand	5,536
169	Consolidated Edison	10,705	219	McGraw-Hill	7,293	269	The AES Corporation	5,496
170	Edison International	10,465	220	Principal Financial	7,198	270	El Paso Corporation	5,490
171	Sempra Energy	10,459	221	Ameren Corporation	7,130	271	McAfee, Inc.	5,434
172	PACCAR Inc	10,391	222	NYSE Euronext	7,119	272	Cummins, Inc.	5,394
173	Chesapeake Energy	10,376	223	Expeditors International	7,058	273	Hartford Financial Services	5,388
174	Avon Products	10,260	224	PPG Industries	6,997	274	Goodrich Corporation	5,352
175	Motorola, Inc.	10,168	225	Brown-Forman Corporation	6,981	275	United States Steel	5,332
176	Freeport-McMoRan Copper & Gold	10,064	226	Sherwin-Williams	6,948	276	Rockwell Automation	5,301
177	Progressive Corporation	10,050	227	Xerox Corporation	6,927	277	Cablevision Systems	5,292
178	Baker Hughes	9,938	228	Parker Hannifin	6,896	278	Xilinx, Inc.	5,288
179	Safeway Inc.	9,900	229	Marriott International	6,886	279	Pitney Bowes	5,276
180	Paychex, Inc.	9,872	230	Sara Lee	6,790	280	Sprint Nextel	5,263
181	Apollo Group	9,787	231	Jacobs Engineering	6,730	281	MetroPCS Communications	5,229
182	TD Ameritrade	9,774	232	Forest Laboratories	6,625	282	Seagate Technology	5,182
183	Quest Diagnostics	9,642	233	Fifth Third Bancorp	6,569	283	Fastenal Company	5,176
184	Enterprise Products Partners	9,540	234	Weyerhaeuser Company	6,470	284	CONSOL Energy	5,164
185	Regions Financial	9,458	235	Estée Lauder	6,426	285	DaVita Inc.	5,155
186	Republic Services	9,400	236	Southwest Airlines	6,391	286	Sigma-Aldrich Corporation	5,145
187	McKesson Corporation	9,326	237	Harris Corporation	6,328	287	International Paper	5,107
188	C.H. Robinson Worldwide	9,266	238	Humana Inc.	6,325	288	International Game Technology	5,090
189	CA, Inc.	9,224	239	Qwest Communications	6,275	289	Sunoco, Inc.	5,080
190	T. Rowe Price Group	9,077	240	Analog Devices	6,227	290	H&R Block	5,059
191	Delta Air Lines	8,912	241	Fortune Brands	6,202	291	Darden Restaurants	5,043
192	Intuit Inc.	8,829	242	NRG Energy	6,189	292	Constellation Energy Group	5,034
193	Vulcan Materials	8,697	243	Unum Group	6,164	293	Iron Mountain	5,018
194	W.W. Grainger	8,646	244	NetApp, Inc.	6,140	294	NASDAQ OMX Group	5,010
195	L-3 Communications	8,601	245	Dover Corporation	6,128	295	Hologic, Inc.	4,961
196	Xcel Energy	8,454	246	V.F. Corporation	6,104	296	DISH Network	4,955
197	Williams Companies	8,441	247	BMC Software	6,072	297	Cooper Industries	4,874
198	Broadcom Corporation	8,415	248	MGM MIRAGE	6,070	298	Pepsi Bottling Group	4,850
199	Precision Castparts	8,399	249	Genuine Parts	6,040	299	Maxim Integrated Products	4,802
200	ITT Corporation	8,389	250	Invesco Ltd.	6,008	300	Pall Corporation	4,767

The 300 Largest Employers in
Hoover's Handbook of American Business 2010

Rank	Company	Employees	Rank	Company	Employees	Rank	Company	Employees
1	Manpower Inc.	4,033,000	51	Costco Wholesale	137,000	101	Koch Industries	70,000
2	Wal-Mart Stores	2,100,000	52	KPMG International	136,896	102	Mars, Incorporated	70,000
3	US Postal Service	663,238	53	Ernst & Young Global	135,000	103	Whirlpool Corporation	70,000
4	Kelly Services	650,000	54	Hilton Hotels	135,000	104	Abbott Laboratories	69,000
5	United Parcel Service	426,000	55	Procter & Gamble	135,000	105	State Farm Mutual	68,600
6	McDonald's Corporation	400,000	56	The Gap	134,000	106	Omnicom Group	68,000
7	International Business Machines	398,455	57	H&R Block	133,700	107	Chevron Corporation	67,000
8	Target Corporation	351,000	58	Kmart Corporation	133,000	108	Pepsi Bottling Group	66,800
9	YUM! Brands	336,000	59	TJX Companies	133,000	109	Cisco Systems	66,129
10	Citigroup Inc.	326,900	60	Honeywell International	128,000	110	American Express	66,000
11	The Kroger Co.	326,000	61	Kohl's Corporation	126,000	111	L-3 Communications	65,000
12	General Electric	323,000	62	Hyatt Hotels Corporation	125,000	112	Cracker Barrel Old Country Store	65,000
13	Home Depot	322,000	63	Northrop Grumman	123,600	113	Illinois Tool Works	65,000
14	Hewlett-Packard	321,000	64	Johnson & Johnson	118,700	114	Motorola, Inc.	64,000
15	AT&T Inc.	301,000	65	American International Group	116,000	115	R.R. Donnelley	62,000
16	Wells Fargo	281,000	66	Tyco International	113,000	116	International Paper	61,700
17	ARAMARK Corporation	260,000	67	Caterpillar Inc.	112,887	117	MGM MIRAGE	61,000
18	Berkshire Hathaway	246,000	68	Tyson Foods	107,000	118	Jabil Circuit	61,000
19	Bank of America	243,000	69	Rite Aid	103,000	119	Tenet Healthcare	60,297
20	General Motors	243,000	70	Comcast Corporation	100,000	120	Ingersoll-Rand	60,000
21	Walgreen Co.	237,000	71	ABM Industries	100,000	121	DuPont	60,000
22	Lowe's Companies	229,000	72	Kraft Foods	98,000	122	PNC Financial Services	59,595
23	JPMorgan Chase	224,961	73	Microsoft Corporation	93,000	123	Regis Corporation	59,000
24	Verizon Communications	223,900	74	The Coca-Cola Company	92,400	124	Blockbuster Inc.	58,561
25	United Technologies	223,100	75	General Dynamics	92,300	125	Xerox Corporation	57,100
26	Spherion Corporation	215,000	76	Computer Sciences Corporation	92,000	126	U.S. Bancorp	57,000
27	CVS Caremark	215,000	77	Staples, Inc.	91,125	127	AutoZone, Inc.	57,000
28	Ford Motor	213,000	78	Limited Brands	90,900	128	MetLife, Inc.	57,000
29	PepsiCo, Inc.	198,000	79	Alcoa Inc.	87,000	129	Halliburton Company	57,000
30	Safeway Inc.	197,000	80	Schlumberger Limited	87,000	130	The Brink's Company	56,900
31	Accenture Ltd	186,000	81	Time Warner	87,000	131	Deere & Company	56,700
32	Darden Restaurants	179,000	82	Oracle Corporation	86,000	132	Sprint Nextel	56,000
33	SUPERVALU INC.	178,000	83	Carnival Corporation	85,900	133	Merck & Co.	55,200
34	Starbucks Corporation	176,000	84	Delta Air Lines	84,306	134	News Corporation	55,000
35	Kaiser Foundation Health Plan	167,300	85	AMR Corporation	84,100	135	YRC Worldwide	55,000
36	Macy's, Inc.	167,000	86	Intel Corporation	83,900	136	Marsh & McLennan	54,400
37	Deloitte Touche Tohmatsu	165,000	87	Abercrombie & Fitch	83,000	137	Kindred Healthcare	53,700
38	The Boeing Company	162,200	88	Pfizer Inc.	81,800	138	Kimberly-Clark	53,000
39	Cargill, Incorporated	159,000	89	Exxon Mobil	79,900	139	Whole Foods Market	52,900
40	PricewaterhouseCoopers	155,693	90	3M Company	79,183	140	Smithfield Foods	52,400
41	Best Buy	155,000	91	Dell Inc.	78,900	141	Nordstrom, Inc.	52,000
42	The Walt Disney Company	150,000	92	Cox Enterprises	77,000	142	Parker Hannifin	51,639
43	J. C. Penney	147,000	93	Dole Food	75,800	143	Danaher Corporation	50,300
44	Lockheed Martin	146,000	94	UnitedHealth Group	75,000	144	Wakefern Food	50,000
45	Marriott International	146,000	95	Eaton Corporation	75,000	145	URS	50,000
46	Starwood Hotels & Resorts	145,000	96	Goodyear Tire & Rubber	74,700	146	Weatherford International	50,000
47	Publix Super Markets	144,000	97	Affiliated Computer Services	74,000	147	UAL Corporation	50,000
48	Emerson Electric	140,700	98	Raytheon Company	73,000	148	Dillard's, Inc.	49,000
49	Johnson Controls	140,000	99	Coca-Cola Enterprises	72,000	149	United States Steel	49,000
50	FedEx Corporation	140,000	100	Wendy's/Arby's Group	70,000	150	Baxter International	48,500

SOURCE: HOOVER'S, INC., DATABASE, SEPTEMBER 2009

The 300 Largest Employers in
Hoover's Handbook of American Business 2010 (continued)

Rank	Company	Employees	Rank	Company	Employees	Rank	Company	Employees
151	Union Pacific	48,242	201	RadioShack Corporation	36,800	251	Unisys Corporation	29,000
152	A&P	48,000	202	Colgate-Palmolive	36,600	252	Mattel, Inc.	29,000
153	Morgan Stanley	46,964	203	Jones Lang LaSalle	36,200	253	Dana Holding	29,000
154	V.F. Corporation	46,600	204	Nationwide Mutual Insurance	36,023	254	Humana Inc.	28,900
155	Bob Evans Farms	46,495	205	Avery Dennison	35,700	255	Charming Shoppes	28,700
156	Dow Chemical	46,102	206	Aetna Inc.	35,500	256	State Street Corporation	28,475
157	PetSmart, Inc.	46,000	207	Southwest Airlines	35,499	257	Becton, Dickinson	28,300
158	Waste Management	45,900	208	Pitney Bowes	35,140	258	Archer Daniels Midland	28,200
159	Sanmina-SCI	45,610	209	Apple Inc.	35,100	259	Ryder System	28,000
160	SAIC, Inc.	45,400	210	Republic Services	35,000	260	EMCOR Group	28,000
161	Interpublic Group	45,000	211	Bristol-Myers Squibb	35,000	261	Southern Company	27,276
162	Automatic Data Processing	45,000	212	Thermo Fisher Scientific	34,500	262	Fortune Brands	27,100
163	Liberty Mutual	45,000	213	NIKE, Inc.	34,300	263	Corning Incorporated	27,000
164	PPG Industries	44,900	214	CSX Corporation	34,000	264	Praxair, Inc.	26,936
165	Apollo Group	44,647	215	ConocoPhillips	33,800	265	American Greetings	26,600
166	Family Dollar Stores	44,000	216	Travelers Companies	33,000	266	Con-way Inc.	26,600
167	Bechtel Group	44,000	217	OfficeMax	33,000	267	Ecolab Inc.	26,500
168	Jacobs Engineering	43,700	218	Qwest Communications	32,937	268	McDermott International	26,400
169	Federal-Mogul	43,400	219	Health Management Associates	32,700	269	Monsanto Company	26,400
170	Textron Inc.	43,000	220	H. J. Heinz Company	32,500	270	DISH Network	26,000
171	Office Depot	43,000	221	McKesson Corporation	32,500	271	Avis Budget Group	26,000
172	WellPoint, Inc.	42,900	222	DaVita Inc.	32,500	272	The Shaw Group	26,000
173	Bank of New York Mellon	42,900	223	Kellogg Company	32,400	273	Progressive Corporation	25,929
174	Quest Diagnostics	42,800	224	Dover Corporation	32,300	274	CBS Corporation	25,920
175	Jack in the Box	42,700	225	The First American Corporation	31,411	275	Dean Foods	25,820
176	Continental Airlines	42,490	226	Estée Lauder	31,300	276	Capital One Financial	25,800
177	Fluor Corporation	42,119	227	Mohawk Industries	31,200	277	The Timken Company	25,662
178	EMC Corporation	42,100	228	Cooper Industries	31,200	278	Borders Group	25,600
179	Avon Products	42,000	229	Hartford Financial Services	31,000	279	ConAgra Foods	25,600
180	Volt Information Sciences	42,000	230	The Cheesecake Factory	31,000	280	DineEquity, Inc.	25,248
181	Prudential Financial	41,844	231	Cintas Corporation	31,000	281	Molex Incorporated	25,240
182	Gannett Co.	41,500	232	Collective Brands	31,000	282	The AES Corporation	25,000
183	Burger King Holdings	41,320	233	Regions Financial	30,784	283	Goodrich Corporation	25,000
184	GameStop Corp.	41,000	234	Norfolk Southern	30,709	284	Hertz Global Holdings	24,900
185	Medtronic, Inc.	41,000	235	Sherwin-Williams	30,677	285	Boston Scientific	24,800
186	ITT Corporation	40,800	236	Marathon Oil	30,360	286	Vishay Intertechnology	24,800
187	Eli Lilly	40,500	237	Genuine Parts	30,300	287	Eastman Kodak	24,400
188	Ross Stores	40,000	238	CIGNA Corporation	30,300	288	Universal Corporation	24,000
189	Burlington Northern Santa Fe	40,000	239	Goldman Sachs	30,067	289	Perot Systems	23,100
190	Baker Hughes	39,800	240	General Mills	30,000	290	Psychiatric Solutions	23,000
191	Cummins, Inc.	39,800	241	Williams-Sonoma	30,000	291	Owens-Illinois	23,000
192	Foot Locker	39,758	242	CB Richard Ellis Group	30,000	292	Chiquita Brands International	23,000
193	Masco Corporation	39,000	243	Sun Healthcare	29,845	293	Hewitt Associates	23,000
194	The Allstate Corporation	38,900	244	BB&T Corporation	29,600	294	Micron Technology	22,800
195	Aon Corporation	37,700	245	Cardinal Health	29,600	295	Fifth Third Bancorp	22,423
196	American Eagle Outfitters	37,500	246	Texas Instruments	29,537	296	NCR Corporation	22,400
197	US Airways	37,500	247	SunTrust Banks	29,333	297	Black & Decker	22,100
198	Big Lots	37,000	248	Freeport-McMoRan Copper & Gold	29,300	298	MeadWestvaco	22,000
199	Bed Bath & Beyond	37,000	249	Bon-Ton Stores	29,100	299	BJ's Wholesale Club	22,000
200	Barnes & Noble	37,000	250	Advance Publications	29,100	300	HealthSouth Corporation	22,000

The 100 Fastest-Growing Companies by Sales Growth in
Hoover's Handbook of American Business 2010

Rank	Company	Annual % Change*	Rank	Company	Annual % Change	Rank	Company	Annual % Change
1	Hilton Hotels	225.0%	36	SkyWest, Inc.	31.9%	71	Tesoro Corporation	23.3%
2	NYSE Euronext	71.7%	37	Baldor Electric	31.8%	72	Manitowoc Company	23.1%
3	Freeport-McMoRan Copper & Gold	65.5%	38	Cliffs Natural Resources	31.5%	73	QUALCOMM	22.9%
4	Hologic, Inc.	64.5%	39	URS	31.4%	74	Valassis Communications	22.9%
5	Google Inc.	61.7%	40	WellPoint, Inc.	31.0%	75	SUPERVALU INC.	22.9%
6	NASDAQ OMX Group	61.2%	41	NRG Energy	30.7%	76	The Shaw Group	22.8%
7	Visa Inc	56.7%	42	Kansas City Southern	30.5%	77	Watson Wyatt Worldwide	22.8%
8	Wendy's/Arby's Group	53.5%	43	BE Aerospace	30.2%	78	Sun Healthcare	22.1%
9	Discovery Communications	52.8%	44	Guess?, Inc.	30.2%	79	Urban Outfitters	22.0%
10	Schnitzer Steel Industries	51.7%	45	CVS Caremark	30.0%	80	Humana Inc.	21.9%
11	Transocean Inc.	48.4%	46	Gerdau Ameristeel	29.7%	81	Cinemark Holdings	21.8%
12	Itron, Inc.	47.9%	47	Amazon.com	29.0%	82	Commercial Metals	21.6%
13	GameStop Corp.	47.9%	48	ONEOK, Inc.	28.2%	83	UnitedHealth Group	21.5%
14	Thermo Fisher Scientific	47.7%	49	Enterprise Products Partners	27.4%	84	Valero Energy	21.5%
15	DineEquity, Inc.	45.6%	50	Holly Corporation	27.1%	85	CB Richard Ellis Group	21.4%
16	Diamond Offshore Drilling	44.4%	51	eBay Inc.	27.1%	86	L-3 Communications	21.2%
17	Chesapeake Energy	43.9%	52	Anadarko Petroleum	26.9%	87	State Street Corporation	21.2%
18	Gilead Sciences	41.7%	53	Foster Wheeler	26.7%	88	Bank of New York Mellon	21.2%
19	Apple Inc.	40.7%	54	The Pantry	26.7%	89	Occidental Petroleum	21.1%
20	Mylan Inc.	39.0%	55	Koch Industries	25.7%	90	Allergan, Inc.	21.1%
21	MetroPCS Communications	38.5%	56	Brightpoint Inc.	25.6%	91	Activision Blizzard	21.1%
22	Psychiatric Solutions	38.0%	57	DaVita Inc.	25.3%	92	Adobe Systems	21.1%
23	CommScope, Inc.	36.6%	58	Hess Corporation	25.2%	93	ARAMARK Corporation	20.9%
24	McDermott International	36.0%	59	AirTran Holdings	25.1%	94	NetApp, Inc.	20.8%
25	SEACOR Holdings	35.5%	60	Jacobs Engineering	25.1%	95	Sunoco, Inc.	20.7%
26	Helmerich & Payne	34.6%	61	Bon-Ton Stores	25.0%	96	Cytec Industries	20.6%
27	World Fuel Services	34.5%	62	Joy Global	24.3%	97	Harris Corporation	20.5%
28	Noble Corporation	34.1%	63	Peter Kiewit Sons'	24.3%	98	Genzyme Corporation	20.3%
29	ENSCO International	33.6%	64	Symantec Corporation	24.2%	99	BJ Services	20.2%
30	General Cable	33.3%	65	Fluor Corporation	24.2%	100	Monsanto Company	20.1%
31	Oshkosh Corporation	33.3%	66	Roper Industries	24.2%			
32	EOG Resources	33.1%	67	Schlumberger Limited	24.0%			
33	Rowan Companies	32.9%	68	Precision Castparts	23.7%			
34	Weatherford International	32.3%	69	Apache Corporation	23.5%			
35	AT&T Inc.	32.1%	70	Jones Lang LaSalle	23.3%			

*These rates are compounded annualized increases, and may have resulted from acquisitions or one
time gains. If less than 5 years of data are available, growth is for the years available.

SOURCE: HOOVER'S, INC., DATABASE, SEPTEMBER 2009

The *FORTUNE* 500 Largest US Corporations

Rank	Company	Sales ($ mil.)	Rank	Company	Sales ($ mil.)	Rank	Company	Sales ($ mil.)
1	Exxon Mobil	442,851.0	51	Supervalu	44,048.0	101	Publix Super Markets	24,109.6
2	Wal-Mart Stores	405,607.0	52	PepsiCo	43,251.0	102	Tech Data	24,080.5
3	Chevron	263,159.0	53	Kraft Foods	42,867.0	103	Merck	23,850.3
4	ConocoPhillips	230,764.0	54	Lockheed Martin	42,731.0	104	AMR	23,766.0
5	General Electric	183,207.0	55	Hess	41,094.0	105	United States Steel	23,754.0
6	General Motors	148,979.0	56	Best Buy	40,023.0	106	Nucor	23,663.3
7	Ford Motor	146,277.0	57	Cisco Systems	39,540.0	107	McDonald's	23,522.4
8	AT&T	124,028.0	58	Johnson Controls	38,062.0	108	Raytheon	23,174.0
9	Hewlett-Packard	118,364.0	59	FedEx	37,953.0	109	Staples	23,083.8
10	Valero Energy	118,298.0	60	Walt Disney	37,843.0	110	Wyeth	22,833.9
11	Bank of America Corp.	113,106.0	61	Intel	37,586.0	111	Delta Air Lines	22,697.0
12	Citigroup	112,372.0	62	Sysco	37,522.1	112	Fannie Mae	22,652.0
13	Berkshire Hathaway	107,786.0	63	Honeywell International	36,556.0	113	Oracle	22,430.0
14	International Business Machines	103,630.0	64	Sprint Nextel	35,635.0	114	Fluor	22,325.9
15	McKesson	101,703.0	65	Enterprise GP Holdings	35,469.6	115	Express Scripts	22,022.7
16	J.P. Morgan Chase & Co.	101,491.0	66	GMAC	35,445.0	116	Coca-Cola Enterprises	21,807.0
17	Verizon Communications	97,354.0	67	Ingram Micro	34,362.2	117	Google	21,795.6
18	Cardinal Health	91,091.4	68	Comcast	34,256.0	118	Northwestern Mutual	21,734.4
19	CVS Caremark	87,471.9	69	Northrop Grumman	33,940.0	119	Manpower	21,552.8
20	Procter & Gamble	83,503.0	70	News Corp.	32,996.0	120	Bristol-Myers Squibb	21,366.0
21	UnitedHealth Group	81,186.0	71	Apple	32,479.0	121	Delphi	20,383.0
22	Kroger	76,000.0	72	CHS	32,167.5	122	Eli Lilly	20,378.0
23	Marathon Oil	73,504.0	73	Coca-Cola	31,944.0	123	UAL	20,194.0
24	Costco Wholesale	72,483.0	74	American Express	31,877.0	124	Nationwide	19,848.0
25	Home Depot	71,288.0	75	DuPont	31,836.0	125	Constellation Energy	19,818.3
26	AmerisourceBergen	70,593.5	76	New York Life Insurance	31,416.2	126	DirecTV Group	19,693.0
27	Archer Daniels Midland	69,816.0	77	Aetna	30,950.7	127	Goodyear Tire & Rubber	19,488.0
28	Target	64,948.0	78	Motorola	30,146.0	128	Kimberly-Clark	19,415.0
29	Johnson & Johnson	63,747.0	79	Plains All American Pipeline	30,061.0	129	U.S. Bancorp	19,229.0
30	Morgan Stanley	62,262.0	80	Abbott Laboratories	29,527.6	130	Amazon.com	19,166.0
31	State Farm Insurance Cos.	61,343.4	81	Allstate	29,394.0	131	TJX	19,147.5
32	WellPoint	61,251.1	82	TIAA-CREF	29,362.5	132	Cigna	19,101.0
33	Dell	61,101.0	83	General Dynamics	29,302.0	133	Whirlpool	18,907.0
34	Boeing	60,909.0	84	Prudential Financial	29,275.0	134	Exelon	18,859.0
35	Microsoft	60,420.0	85	Humana	28,946.4	135	Massachusetts Mutual Life Insurance	18,744.6
36	Walgreen	59,034.0	86	Liberty Mutual Insurance Group	28,855.0	136	Nike	18,627.0
37	United Technologies	58,681.0	87	Deere	28,437.6	137	World Fuel Services	18,509.4
38	Dow Chemical	57,514.0	88	HCA	28,374.0	138	Schering-Plough	18,502.0
39	MetLife	55,085.0	89	Tyson Foods	28,130.0	139	J.C. Penney	18,486.0
40	Goldman Sachs Group	53,579.0	90	Alcoa	28,119.0	140	International Assets Holding	18,358.9
41	Sunoco	51,652.0	91	Tesoro	28,031.0	141	Halliburton	18,279.0
41	Wells Fargo	51,652.0	92	Murphy Oil	27,512.5	142	Burlington Northern Santa Fe	18,018.0
43	United Parcel Service	51,486.0	93	Philip Morris International	25,705.0	143	Union Pacific	17,970.0
44	Caterpillar	51,324.0	94	Emerson Electric	25,281.0	144	Avnet	17,952.7
45	Medco Health Solutions	51,258.0	95	3M	25,269.0	145	Capital One Financial	17,868.5
46	Pfizer	48,296.0	96	Macy's	24,892.0	146	Freeport-McMoRan Copper & Gold	17,796.0
47	Lowe's	48,230.0	97	International Paper	24,829.0	147	Xerox	17,608.0
48	Time Warner	46,984.0	98	Occidental Petroleum	24,480.0	148	Illinois Tool Works	17,217.9
49	Sears Holdings	46,770.0	99	Travelers Cos.	24,477.0	149	Southern	17,127.0
50	Safeway	44,104.0	100	Rite Aid	24,417.7	150	Merrill Lynch	16,784.0

SOURCE: *FORTUNE*, MAY 4, 2009

The *FORTUNE* 500 Largest US Corporations (continued)

Rank	Company	Sales ($ mil.)	Rank	Company	Sales ($ mil.)	Rank	Company	Sales ($ mil.)
151	Arrow Electronics	16,761.0	201	Waste Management	13,388.0	251	Commercial Metals	10,764.6
152	AFLAC	16,554.0	202	Omnicom Group	13,359.9	252	Sempra Energy	10,758.0
153	Computer Sciences	16,499.5	203	Chubb	13,221.0	253	Western Refining	10,725.6
154	FPL Group	16,410.0	204	Duke Energy	13,212.0	254	Pepco Holdings	10,700.0
155	Kohl's	16,389.0	205	Entergy	13,093.8	255	Avon Products	10,690.1
156	Bank of New York Mellon Corp.	16,355.0	206	State Street Corp.	12,922.0	256	Norfolk Southern	10,661.0
157	Dominion Resources	16,290.0	207	USAA	12,912.0	257	Liberty Global	10,561.1
158	AES	16,170.0	208	Marriott International	12,880.0	258	Thermo Fisher Scientific	10,498.0
159	Oneok	16,157.4	209	Progressive	12,840.1	259	Dollar General	10,457.7
160	Altria Group	15,957.0	210	Kellogg	12,822.0	260	BB&T Corp.	10,404.0
161	PPG Industries	15,849.0	211	SunTrust Banks	12,800.8	261	Starbucks	10,383.0
162	Anadarko Petroleum	15,723.0	212	Jabil Circuit	12,779.7	262	Huntsman	10,215.0
163	Devon Energy	15,560.0	213	Danaher	12,697.5	263	Harrah's Entertainment	10,127.0
164	Eaton	15,376.0	214	Reliant Energy	12,553.2	264	URS	10,086.3
165	Health Net	15,366.6	215	Texas Instruments	12,501.0	265	Liberty Media	10,084.0
166	Colgate-Palmolive	15,329.9	216	Dean Foods	12,454.6	266	SAIC	10,078.0
167	Continental Airlines	15,241.0	217	Apache	12,389.8	267	H.J. Heinz	10,070.8
168	Amgen	15,003.0	218	Williams	12,357.0	268	Enbridge Energy Partners	10,060.0
169	TRW Automotive Holdings	14,995.0	219	Baxter International	12,348.0	269	BJ's Wholesale Club	10,027.4
170	Paccar	14,972.5	220	Freddie Mac	12,302.0	270	Unum Group	9,982.3
171	L-3 Communications	14,901.0	221	Parker Hannifin	12,145.6	271	Genworth Financial	9,948.0
172	EMC	14,876.2	222	US Airways Group	12,118.0	272	Calpine	9,937.0
173	Textron	14,806.0	223	Knight	12,094.8	273	Principal Financial	9,935.9
174	Loews	14,733.0	224	Land O'Lakes	12,039.3	274	Lincoln National	9,905.0
175	Navistar International	14,724.0	225	Penske Automotive Group	11,917.7	275	Terex	9,889.6
176	PG&E Corp.	14,628.0	226	Coventry Health Care	11,913.6	276	Mosaic	9,812.6
177	Viacom	14,625.0	227	Baker Hughes	11,864.0	277	Masco	9,700.0
178	Gap	14,526.0	228	Circuit City Stores	11,743.7	278	PNC Financial Services Group	9,680.0
179	Office Depot	14,495.5	229	ITT	11,702.5	279	Guardian Life Ins. Co. of America	9,675.0
180	American Electric Power	14,442.0	230	Chesapeake Energy	11,629.0	280	Regions Financial	9,636.6
181	Cummins	14,342.0	231	DISH Network	11,617.2	281	Rohm & Haas	9,575.0
182	AutoNation	14,288.0	232	Marsh & McLennan	11,587.0	282	Visteon	9,544.0
183	Smithfield Foods	14,264.1	233	R.R. Donnelley & Sons	11,581.6	283	Tenet Healthcare	9,494.0
184	Edison International	14,112.0	234	KBR	11,581.0	284	Eastman Kodak	9,416.0
185	Integrys Energy Group	14,047.8	235	Monsanto	11,579.0	285	DTE Energy	9,336.0
186	CBS	13,950.4	236	Weyerhaeuser	11,401.0	286	Energy Transfer Equity	9,293.4
187	Sun Microsystems	13,880.0	237	Energy Future Holdings	11,364.0	287	Hartford Financial Services	9,219.0
188	ConAgra Foods	13,808.7	238	CenterPoint Energy	11,322.0	288	Progress Energy	9,186.0
189	Pepsi Bottling	13,796.0	239	Yum Brands	11,279.0	289	NiSource	9,069.5
190	Public Service Enterprise Group	13,741.0	240	CSX	11,255.0	290	Limited Brands	9,043.0
191	Consolidated Edison	13,725.9	241	Jacobs Engineering Group	11,252.2	291	Global Partners	9,019.1
192	Toys "R" Us	13,724.0	242	Xcel Energy	11,203.2	292	Sanmina-SCI	9,004.9
193	General Mills	13,652.1	243	Community Health Systems	11,156.4	293	YRC Worldwide	8,940.4
194	FirstEnergy	13,627.0	244	Qualcomm	11,142.0	294	Reynolds American	8,845.0
195	Lear	13,570.5	245	American International Group	11,104.0	295	First Data	8,811.3
196	Medtronic	13,515.0	246	Southwest Airlines	11,023.0	296	GameStop	8,805.9
197	Qwest Communications	13,475.0	247	Genuine Parts	11,015.3	297	Automatic Data Processing	8,776.5
198	Aramark	13,470.2	248	Air Products & Chemicals	10,938.6	298	Reliance Steel & Aluminum	8,718.8
199	Sara Lee	13,450.0	249	Praxair	10,796.0	299	Assurant	8,601.2
200	National Oilwell Varco	13,431.4	250	Smith International	10,770.8	300	C.H. Robinson Worldwide	8,578.6

The *FORTUNE* 500 Largest US Corporations (continued)

Rank	Company	Sales ($ mil.)	Rank	Company	Sales ($ mil.)	Rank	Company	Sales ($ mil.)
301	Nordstrom	8,573.0	351	Fortune Brands	7,105.1	401	Affiliated Computer Services	6,160.6
302	Fifth Third Bancorp	8,554.0	352	Discover Financial Services	7,088.0	402	SPX	6,144.0
303	eBay	8,541.3	353	Peabody Energy	7,074.0	403	Ecolab	6,137.5
304	Pilgrim's Pride	8,525.1	354	Goodrich	7,061.7	404	Anixter International	6,136.6
305	Hertz Global Holdings	8,525.1	355	Bed Bath & Beyond	7,048.9	405	Embarq	6,124.0
306	AGCO	8,424.6	356	Smurfit-Stone Container	7,042.0	406	Wesco International	6,110.8
307	Aon	8,406.0	357	Shaw Group	6,998.0	407	Hexion Specialty Chemicals	6,093.0
308	Centex	8,405.7	358	Dillard's	6,988.4	408	Black & Decker	6,086.1
309	Campbell Soup	8,391.0	359	Family Dollar Stores	6,983.6	409	Thrivent Financial for Lutherans	6,060.6
310	Ashland	8,381.0	360	Great Atlantic & Pacific Tea	6,963.8	410	Franklin Resources	6,032.4
311	CarMax	8,318.8	361	Interpublic Group	6,962.7	411	Avis Budget Group	5,984.0
312	Crown Holdings	8,305.0	362	Precision Castparts	6,916.4	412	Harley-Davidson	5,971.3
313	OfficeMax	8,267.0	363	NRG Energy	6,905.0	413	Aleris International	5,968.2
314	PPL	8,206.0	364	Eastman Chemical	6,895.0	414	Corning	5,948.0
315	Applied Materials	8,129.2	365	MeadWestvaco	6,890.0	415	Mattel	5,918.0
316	Dana Holding	8,101.0	366	W.W. Grainger	6,850.0	416	Tenneco	5,916.0
317	Pantry	8,088.6	367	Mohawk Industries	6,826.3	417	Starwood Hotels & Resorts	5,907.0
318	Steel Dynamics	8,080.5	368	Celanese	6,823.0	418	Advanced Micro Devices	5,881.0
319	Western Digital	8,074.0	369	CMS Energy	6,821.0	419	Symantec	5,874.4
320	Boston Scientific	8,050.0	370	Emcor Group	6,785.2	420	Holly	5,867.7
321	Peter Kiewit Sons'	8,012.0	371	Gannett	6,767.7	421	Cameron International	5,848.9
322	Sherwin-Williams	7,979.7	372	CC Media Holdings	6,764.8	422	Owens Corning	5,847.0
323	Targa Resources	7,970.2	373	Hormel Foods	6,754.9	423	Micron Technology	5,841.0
324	Whole Foods Market	7,953.9	374	Darden Restaurants	6,747.2	424	Northeast Utilities	5,800.1
325	Estée Lauder	7,910.8	375	Stryker	6,718.2	425	Agilent Technologies	5,774.0
326	Owens-Illinois	7,884.7	376	Avery Dennison	6,710.4	426	ProLogis	5,772.8
327	Ameren	7,839.0	377	UGI	6,648.2	427	Dr Pepper Snapple Group	5,710.0
328	Synnex	7,768.2	378	D.R. Horton	6,646.1	428	Group 1 Automotive	5,703.3
329	Dole Food	7,732.4	379	AbitibiBowater	6,645.1	429	Rockwell Automation	5,697.8
330	XTO Energy	7,695.0	380	AutoZone	6,522.7	430	Northern Trust Corp.	5,677.9
331	SLM	7,689.4	381	WellCare Health Plans	6,521.9	431	Timken	5,663.7
332	TravelCenters of America	7,658.4	382	KeyCorp	6,499.0	432	Perini	5,660.3
333	Dover	7,653.0	383	Frontier Oil	6,498.8	433	DaVita	5,660.2
334	AK Steel Holding	7,644.3	384	Ross Stores	6,486.1	434	Expeditors International	5,633.9
335	VF	7,642.6	385	Charter Communications	6,479.0	435	SunGard Data Systems	5,596.0
336	Ball	7,561.5	386	Autoliv	6,473.2	436	CH2M Hill	5,589.9
337	Sonic Automotive	7,488.0	387	Newell Rubbermaid	6,470.6	437	Kelly Services	5,517.3
338	Virgin Media	7,439.9	388	American Family Insurance Group	6,431.3	438	BJ Services	5,426.3
339	Owens & Minor	7,337.6	389	Henry Schein	6,407.6	439	Graybar Electric	5,400.2
340	Winn-Dixie Stores	7,281.4	390	Domtar	6,394.0	440	Charles Schwab	5,393.0
341	Quest Diagnostics	7,249.4	391	McGraw-Hill	6,355.1	441	Western & Southern Financial Group	5,391.7
342	Cablevision Systems	7,230.1	392	Omnicare	6,310.6	442	Jarden	5,383.3
343	Atmos Energy	7,221.3	393	Pulte Homes	6,289.5	443	El Paso	5,363.0
344	MGM Mirage	7,208.8	394	Visa	6,263.0	444	Gilead Sciences	5,335.8
345	Yahoo	7,208.5	395	Pitney Bowes	6,262.3	445	Scana	5,319.0
346	ArvinMeritor	7,174.0	396	General Cable	6,230.1	446	NCR	5,315.0
347	Becton Dickinson	7,158.5	397	CIT Group	6,228.9	447	Harris	5,311.0
348	Ameriprise Financial	7,149.0	398	First American Corp.	6,213.8	448	Allegheny Technologies	5,309.7
349	Oshkosh	7,138.3	399	Ryder System	6,203.7	449	Host Hotels & Resorts	5,294.0
350	EOG Resources	7,127.1	400	Newmont Mining	6,199.0	450	Blockbuster	5,287.9

The *FORTUNE* 500 Largest US Corporations (continued)

Rank	Company	Sales ($ mil.)	Rank	Company	Sales ($ mil.)	Rank	Company	Sales ($ mil.)
451	Western Union	5,282.0	471	Lubrizol	5,027.8	491	Brunswick	4,708.7
452	Clorox	5,273.0	472	CVR Energy	5,016.1	492	Nash-Finch	4,703.7
453	BorgWarner	5,263.9	473	MDU Resources Group	5,003.3	493	Leggett & Platt	4,664.7
454	Foot Locker	5,237.0	474	MasterCard	4,991.6	494	Universal American	4,659.2
455	Barnes & Noble	5,235.3	475	United Stationers	4,986.9	495	Broadcom	4,658.1
456	Unisys	5,233.2	476	Auto-Owners Insurance	4,951.8	496	Brightpoint	4,658.0
457	Freescale Semiconductor	5,226.0	477	NYSE Euronext	4,951.0	497	Consol Energy	4,652.4
458	AECOM Technology	5,216.2	478	PepsiAmericas	4,937.2	498	Big Lots	4,645.3
459	Spectra Energy	5,184.0	479	Crosstex Energy	4,915.6	499	Dollar Tree	4,644.9
460	FMC Technologies	5,163.4	480	Manitowoc	4,884.3	500	Legg Mason	4,634.1
461	Advance Auto Parts	5,142.3	481	Polo Ralph Lauren	4,880.1			
462	Mylan	5,137.6	482	Fiserv	4,873.0			
463	Hershey	5,132.8	483	Sealed Air	4,843.5			
464	CB Richard Ellis Group	5,130.1	484	Insight Enterprises	4,834.4			
465	Telephone & Data Systems	5,092.0	485	NuStar Energy	4,828.8			
466	Icahn Enterprises	5,088.0	486	Asbury Automotive Group	4,785.0			
467	Universal Health Services	5,080.9	487	Molson Coors Brewing	4,774.3			
468	PetSmart	5,065.3	488	Rockwell Collins	4,769.0			
469	BlackRock	5,063.9	489	Realogy	4,725.0			
470	Con-way	5,036.8	490	W. R. Berkley	4,708.8			

The *Forbes* Largest Private Companies in the US

Rank	Company	Sales ($ mil.)	Rank	Company	Sales ($ mil.)	Rank	Company	Sales ($ mil.)
1	Cargill	110,630	51	Hexion Specialty Chemicals	5,810	101	Consolidated Elec. Distributors	3,900
2	Koch Industries	98,000	52	Freescale Semiconductor	5,720	102	Manor Care	3,890
3	Chrysler	59,700	53	Gulf States Toyota	5,700	103	Michaels Stores	3,860
4	GMAC Financial Services	31,490	54	Allegis Group	5,600	104	Belk	3,830
5	PricewaterhouseCoopers	28,190	55	Keystone Foods	5,580	105	Roundy's Supermarkets	3,800
6	Mars	27,400	56	RaceTrac Petroleum	5,520	106	Stater Bros.	3,740
7	Bechtel	27,000	57	MBM	5,500	107	Booz Allen Hamilton	3,700
8	HCA	26,860	58	Guardian Industries	5,470	108	Brightstar	3,660
9	Ernst & Young	24,520	59	Bloomberg	5,400	109	Walsh Group	3,600
10	Publix Super Markets	23,190	60	McKinsey & Co.	5,330	110	Tishman Construction	3,560
11	US Foodservice	20,160	61	International Automotive Components	5,310	111	HT Hackney	3,550
12	C&S Wholesale Grocers	19,450	62	Unisource Worldwide	5,300	112	VWR Funding	3,540
13	H.E. Butt Grocery	15,500	63	Graybar Electric	5,260	113	Berry Plastics	3,540
14	Fidelity Investments	14,900	64	Kohler	5,230	114	WinCo Foods	3,520
15	Cox Enterprises	14,590	65	Avaya	5,100	115	Eby-Brown	3,460
16	Flying J	14,320	66	Mansfield Oil	5,100	116	Raley's	3,450
17	Toys "R" Us	13,790	67	Save Mart Supermarkets	5,100	117	InterTech Group	3,450
18	Meijer	13,650	68	Tribune Company	5,060	118	Ashley Furniture Industries	3,430
19	Platinum Equity	13,500	69	Wawa	5,050	119	Burlington Coat Factory	3,420
20	Aramark	13,200	70	Pro-Build Holdings	5,000	120	Schneider National	3,400
21	Enterprise Rent-A-Car	13,100	71	SunGard Data Systems	4,980	121	ServiceMaster	3,360
22	TransMontaigne	12,250	72	Southwire	4,980	122	Structure Tone	3,330
23	JM Family Enterprises	12,200	73	Kinray	4,800	123	Golden State Foods	3,300
24	Tenaska Energy	11,600	74	NewPage	4,660	124	Schwan Food	3,300
25	Love's Travel Stops	11,460	75	OSI Group	4,620	125	Swift Transportation	3,270
26	Reyes Holdings	11,200	76	DeBruce Grain	4,620	126	Black & Veatch	3,200
27	Harrah's Entertainment	10,830	77	Neiman Marcus Group	4,600	127	International Data Group	3,200
28	Capital Group Cos	9,900	78	Charmer Sunbelt Group	4,600	128	Jeld-Wen	3,160
29	Dollar General	9,500	79	Kingston Technology Company	4,500	129	Glazer's Wholesale Drug	3,150
30	Performance Food Group	9,480	80	Wegmans Food Markets	4,500	130	E&J Gallo Winery	3,150
31	SC Johnson & Son	8,750	81	Ergon	4,490	131	Golub	3,140
32	Transammonia	8,340	82	Sheetz	4,410	132	84 Lumber	3,100
33	Southern Wine & Spirits	8,300	83	J.R. Simplot	4,400	133	LPL Investment Holdings	3,100
34	CDW	8,150	84	Hearst	4,380	134	Boise Cascade	3,080
35	Cumberland Farms	8,100	85	CH2M Hill Cos.	4,380	135	JohnsonDiversey	3,040
36	Hilton Hotels	8,090	86	Levi Strauss & Co.	4,360	136	Andersen	3,000
37	QuikTrip	8,090	87	Carlson Cos.	4,360	137	Central National-Gottesman	3,000
38	First Data	8,050	88	Republic National Distributing	4,320	138	Sabre Holdings	3,000
39	Giant Eagle	8,020	89	Perdue	4,300	139	US Oncology	3,000
40	Energy Future Holdings	7,990	90	Scoular	4,300	140	Sports Authority	2,980
41	Advance Publications	7,970	91	Washington Cos.	4,300	141	Gilbane	2,970
42	Murdock Holding Company	7,900	92	Clark Enterprises	4,220	142	Alex Lee	2,920
43	Menard	7,800	93	Hallmark Cards	4,170	143	McCarthy Building Cos	2,900
44	Alticor	7,100	94	Edward Jones	4,150	144	Sammons Enterprises	2,900
45	Sinclair Oil	7,000	95	OSI Restaurant Partners	4,150	145	Schreiber Foods	2,900
46	Gordon Food Service	6,700	96	Global Hyatt	4,000	146	Parsons	2,900
47	Aleris International	6,600	97	Renco Group	4,000	147	General Parts	2,870
48	Hy-Vee	6,270	98	Whiting-Turner Contracting	3,970	148	Medline Industries	2,830
49	Peter Kiewit Sons'	6,240	99	McJunkin Red Man	3,950	149	Cooper-Standard Automotive	2,810
50	Colonial Group	6,200	100	Red Apple Group	3,950	150	Dot Foods	2,810

SOURCE: *FORBES*, NOVEMBER 3, 2009

The *Forbes* Largest Private Companies in the US (continued)

Rank	Company	Sales ($ mil.)	Rank	Company	Sales ($ mil.)	Rank	Company	Sales ($ mil.)
151	Amsted Industries	2,800	201	Houchens Industries	2,290	251	Warren Equities	1,940
152	Vanguard Health Systems	2,790	202	Milliken & Co.	2,270	252	Goodman Manufacturing	1,930
153	Reader's Digest Association	2,790	203	JF Shea	2,260	253	Frank Consolidated Enterprises	1,930
154	Grocers Supply	2,720	204	Baker & Taylor	2,260	254	Barnes & Noble College Booksellers	1,930
155	Flex-N-Gate	2,720	205	ShopKo Stores	2,250	255	JD Heiskell & Co.	1,920
156	Quintiles Transnational	2,700	206	J. M. Smith	2,220	256	Apex Oil	1,910
157	Services Group of America	2,700	207	Anderson Cos.	2,210	257	D&H Distributing	1,900
158	Bass Pro Shops	2,650	208	Brookshire Grocery	2,200	258	Newegg Inc.	1,900
159	JE Dunn Construction Group	2,630	209	UniGroup	2,200	259	Parsons Brinckerhoff	1,900
160	ABC Supply	2,630	210	Young's Market	2,200	260	Conair	1,900
161	Bi-Lo Holdings	2,620	211	US Oil	2,190	261	Drummond	1,890
162	Leprino Foods	2,620	212	Bose	2,180	262	American Tire Distributors Holdings	1,880
163	Rich Products	2,600	213	Skadden, Arps	2,170	263	Shamrock Foods	1,860
164	Hensel Phelps Construction	2,520	214	Heico Cos.	2,170	264	Metals USA	1,860
165	Follett	2,520	215	Bashas'	2,160	265	Rexnord	1,850
166	AMC Entertainment	2,500	216	SAS Institute	2,150	266	Electro-Motive Diesel	1,830
167	Bausch & Lomb	2,500	217	Affinia Group	2,140	267	Merit Energy	1,830
168	Demoulas Super Markets	2,500	218	M. A. Mortenson	2,140	268	Catalent Pharma Solutions	1,830
169	Quality King Distributors	2,500	219	Life Care Centers of America	2,120	269	Crown Equipment	1,830
170	Schnuck Markets	2,500	220	Hunt Consolidated/Hunt Oil	2,120	270	Guthy-Renker	1,800
171	Tower Automotive	2,500	221	Solo Cup	2,110	271	ICC Industries	1,800
172	Truman Arnold Cos.	2,500	222	CompuCom Systems	2,100	272	Koch Foods	1,800
173	World Wide Technology	2,500	223	JM Huber	2,100	273	Rooney Holdings	1,800
174	Graham Packaging Holdings	2,490	224	TIC Holdings	2,100	274	Arctic Slope Regional	1,780
175	Golden Living	2,490	225	Zachry Construction	2,100	275	Great Lakes Cheese	1,780
176	Travelport	2,490	226	Ingram Industries	2,100	276	Hobby Lobby Stores	1,770
177	Ben E. Keith	2,460	227	Fagen	2,080	277	Soave Enterprises	1,770
178	O'Neal Steel	2,440	228	Univision Communications	2,070	278	Red Chamber Group	1,760
179	WinWholesale	2,430	229	Genesis HealthCare	2,070	279	Rooms To Go	1,750
180	W.L. Gore & Associates	2,400	230	Iasis Healthcare	2,070	280	Austin Industries	1,750
181	Maines Paper & Food Service	2,400	231	Academy Sports & Outdoors	2,060	281	Columbia Sussex	1,730
182	Mary Kay	2,400	232	Quad/Graphics	2,050	282	Reynolds and Reynolds	1,730
183	Petco Animal Supplies	2,400	233	Wilbur-Ellis	2,010	283	Kum & Go	1,720
184	Rosen's Diversified	2,400	234	Dresser	2,010	284	Bradco Supply	1,700
185	G-I Holdings	2,380	235	Brasfield & Gorrie	2,010	285	McWane	1,700
186	Biomet	2,380	236	Latham & Watkins	2,010	286	Taylor	1,700
187	NTK Holdings	2,370	237	Foster Farms	2,000	287	Vertis	1,700
188	Asplundh Tree Expert	2,370	238	Holiday Cos.	2,000	288	Duane Reade	1,690
189	Fry's Electronics	2,350	239	Hunt Construction Group	2,000	289	Education Management	1,680
190	West Corp.	2,350	240	Ma Labs	2,000	290	Continental Grain	1,680
191	Software House Intl.	2,330	241	Plastipak Holdings	2,000	291	K-VA-T Food Stores	1,660
192	Delaware North Cos.	2,310	242	Sun Products	2,000	292	Ardent Health Services	1,650
193	Discount Tire	2,310	243	Select Medical	1,990	293	Tang Industries	1,650
194	Boston Consulting Group	2,300	244	Yates Cos.	1,980	294	Carpenter	1,650
195	Ebsco Industries	2,300	245	Day & Zimmermann	1,980	295	Ceridian	1,650
196	Guitar Center	2,300	246	Roll International	1,980	296	Bain & Co.	1,640
197	HP Hood	2,300	247	Vizio	1,970	297	Vought Aircraft Industries	1,630
198	Infor	2,300	248	Sequa	1,960	298	Crowley Maritime	1,620
199	Oxbow	2,300	249	Swinerton	1,960	299	L.L. Bean	1,620
200	Smart & Final	2,300	250	Thorntons	1,940	300	Knowledge Learning	1,620

The *Forbes* Largest Private Companies in the US (continued)

Rank	Company	Sales ($ mil.)	Rank	Company	Sales ($ mil.)	Rank	Company	Sales ($ mil.)
301	The Brock Group	1,620	351	API Group	1,350	401	Mountaire Farms	1,150
302	Weitz	1,610	352	New Balance Athletic Shoe	1,350	402	Williamson-Dickie Manufacturing	1,150
303	SSA Marine	1,610	353	David Weekley Homes	1,340	403	A. G. Spanos Cos.	1,130
304	Camac International	1,600	354	Honickman Affiliates	1,330	404	Remy International	1,130
305	Haworth	1,600	355	Big Y Foods	1,330	405	Marc Glassman	1,130
306	International Specialty Products	1,600	356	Affinion Group	1,320	406	Simmons Bedding	1,130
307	ViewSonic	1,600	357	GSC Enterprises	1,320	407	Central Parking	1,120
308	HealthMarkets	1,600	358	Kirkland & Ellis	1,310	408	Goss International	1,110
309	KAR Holdings	1,590	359	Foodarama Supermarkets	1,310	409	Indalex	1,110
310	CC Industries	1,590	360	Bozzuto's	1,300	410	William Lyon Homes	1,110
311	Sigma Plastics Group	1,580	361	Brookshire Brothers	1,300	411	Blue Tee	1,100
312	Towers Perrin	1,570	362	Dean Health System	1,300	412	Beaulieu of America Group	1,100
313	Suffolk Construction	1,570	363	FHC Health Systems	1,300	413	Booz & Company	1,100
314	Maritz	1,560	364	MWH	1,300	414	Hilmar Cheese	1,100
315	GNC	1,550	365	Schottenstein Stores	1,300	415	National Gypsum	1,100
316	Dart Container	1,540	366	Swagelok	1,300	416	Pliant	1,100
317	Ilitch Holdings	1,520	367	Euramax International	1,300	417	Extended Stay Hotels	1,090
318	Turner Industries Group	1,520	368	The Flintco Companies	1,290	418	McKee Foods	1,090
319	Pinnacle Foods	1,510	369	PC Richard & Son	1,290	419	Crete Carrier	1,080
320	Claire's Stores	1,510	370	NCO Group	1,290	420	Safety-Kleen Systems	1,070
321	Bartlett & Co.	1,510	371	24 Hour Fitness Worldwide	1,280	421	Sutherland Lumber	1,070
322	US Xpress Enterprises	1,510	372	Ash Grove Cement	1,270	422	Orgill	1,070
323	Marsh Supermarkets	1,500	373	SavaSeniorCare	1,270	423	Inserra Supermarkets	1,060
324	Cook Group	1,500	374	Visant	1,270	424	Lifetouch	1,050
325	Interstate Battery System	1,500	375	Beall's	1,270	425	North Pacific Group	1,040
326	The Kraft Group	1,500	376	Forever 21	1,260	426	Stewart's Shops	1,040
327	Pella	1,500	377	Goya Foods	1,260	427	Ryan Companies	1,040
328	Les Schwab Tire Centers	1,480	378	Amscan Holdings	1,250	428	Morgan Lewis & Bockius	1,030
329	Dunavant Enterprises	1,480	379	Pepper Construction Group	1,240	429	Newark Group	1,030
330	Brand Energy	1,480	380	TeamHealth	1,230	430	BrandsMart USA	1,030
331	DPR Construction	1,470	381	Holder Construction	1,230	431	Coastal Pacific Food Distributors	1,020
332	Michael Foods	1,470	382	Associated Materials	1,200	432	Pittsburgh Glass Works	1,010
333	Berwind	1,470	383	Advanced Drainage Systems	1,200	433	Sierra Pacific Industries	1,010
334	Buffets	1,460	384	ASI	1,200	434	ValleyCrest Landscape Cos.	1,010
335	Personal Communications Devices	1,450	385	Barry-Wehmiller Companies	1,200	435	Crescent Electric Supply	1,000
336	Station Casinos	1,450	386	Deseret Management	1,200	436	Davisco Foods International	1,000
337	Jones Day	1,440	387	Henkels & McCoy	1,200	437	Kellwood	1,000
338	Gate Petroleum	1,440	388	Keane	1,200	438	Key Safety Systems	1,000
339	Laureate Education	1,420	389	Topa Equities	1,200	439	MGA Entertainment	1,000
340	Barton Malow	1,400	390	Warren Equipment	1,200	440	Walbridge Aldinger	1,000
341	Micro Electronics	1,400	391	Weil, Gotshal & Manges	1,200	441	Wells' Dairy	1,000
342	Landmark Media Group	1,400	392	Nypro	1,190			
343	Estes Express Lines	1,400	393	MTD Products	1,190			
344	Sidley Austin	1,390	394	Hoffman	1,190			
345	Freeman	1,380	395	Mayer Brown	1,180			
346	White & Case	1,370	396	Ritz Camera Centers	1,180			
347	Dawn Food Products	1,370	397	Sherwood Food Distributors	1,180			
348	Wirtz	1,370	398	Alsco	1,160			
349	MediaNews Group	1,360	399	Gould Paper	1,160			
350	Printpack	1,360	400	Alberici	1,150			

Top 20 in CEO Compensation

Rank	Name	Company	Total Pay* ($ mil.)
1	Lawrence J. Ellison	Oracle	557.0
2	Ray R. Irani	Occidental Petroleum	222.6
3	John B. Hess	Hess	154.6
4	Michael D. Watford	Ultra Petroleum	116.9
5	Mark G. Papa	EOG Resources	90.5
6	William R. Berkley	W. R. Berkley	87.5
7	Matthew K. Rose	Burlington Santa Fe	68.6
8	Paul J. Evanson	Allegheny Energy	67.3
9	Hugh Grant	Monsanto	64.6
10	Robert W. Lane	Deere & Co.	61.3
11	Keith A. Hutton	XTO Energy	54.8
12	Mark V. Hurd	Hewlett-Packard	51.9
13	John H. Hammergren	McKesson	51.3
14	Bradbury H. Anderson	Best Buy	49.3
15	David J. O'Reilly	Chevron	47.6
16	Frederick W. Smith	FedEx	44.5
17	Robert J. Stevens	Lockheed Martin	42.7
18	Ronald E. Hermance Jr.	Hudson City Bancorp	42.3
19	Brian L. Roberts	Comcast	39.3
20	John W. Rowe	Exelon	39.2

*Includes salary, bonus, and long-term compensation

SOURCE: *FORBES*, APRIL 22, 2009

Top 20 Most Powerful Women in Business

Rank	Name	Position
1	Indra Nooyi	Chairman and CEO, PepsiCo
2	Irene Rosenfeld	Chairman and CEO, Kraft Foods
3	Pat Woertz	Chairman and CEO, Archer Daniels Midland
4	Angela Braly	President and CEO, Wellpoint
5	Andrea Jung	Chairman and CEO, Avon Products
6	Oprah Winfrey	Chairman, Harpo
7	Ellen Kullman	CEO, DuPont
8	Carol Bartz	CEO, Yahoo
9	Ursula Burns	CEO, Xerox
10	Brenda Barnes	Chairman and CEO, Sara Lee
11	Ginni Rometty	SVP, Global Sales and Distribution, IBM
12	Safra Catz	Co-president, Oracle
13	Ann Livermore	EVP, Hewlett-Packard
14	Sheri McCoy	Group chairman, Johnson & Johnson
15	Melanie Healey	Group president, Procter & Gamble
16	Anne Sweeney	Co-Chair, Disney Media Networks
17	Heidi Miller	EVP, JPMorgan Chase
18	Carol Meyrowitz	CEO and president, TJX
19	Colleen Goggins	Group Chairman, Johnson & Johnson
20	Judy McGrath	Chairman and CEO, MTV Networks

SOURCE: *FORTUNE*, SEPTEMBER 15, 2009

Forbes Greatest US Fortunes

Rank	Name	Age	Net Worth ($ bil.)	Source
1	William Gates III	53	50.0	Microsoft
2	Warren Buffett	79	40.0	Berkshire Hathaway
3	Lawrence Ellison	65	27.0	Oracle
4	Christy Walton & family	54	21.5	Wal-Mart
5	Jim C. Walton	61	19.6	Wal-Mart
6	Alice Walton	60	19.3	Wal-Mart
7	S. Robson Walton	65	19.0	Wal-Mart
8	Michael Bloomberg	67	17.5	Bloomberg
9	Charles Koch	73	16.0	Manufacturing, energy
9	David Koch	69	16.0	Manufacturing, energy
11	Sergey Brin	36	15.3	Google
11	Larry Page	36	15.3	Google
13	Michael Dell	44	14.5	Dell
14	Steven Ballmer	53	13.3	Microsoft
15	George Soros	79	13.0	Hedge funds
16	Donald Bren	77	12.0	Real estate
17	Paul Allen	56	11.5	Microsoft, investments
17	Abigail Johnson	47	11.5	Fidelity
19	Forrest Edward Mars	78	11.0	Candy, pet food
19	Jacqueline Mars	70	11.0	Candy, pet food
19	John Mars	73	11.0	Candy, pet food

SOURCE: *FORBES*, SEPTEMBER 30, 2009

Forbes 20 Most Powerful Celebrities

Rank	Name	Earnings ($ mil.)
1	Angelina Jolie	27.0
2	Oprah Winfrey	275.0
3	Madonna	110.0
4	Beyonce Knowles	87.0
5	Tiger Woods	110.0
6	Bruce Springsteen	70.0
7	Steven Spielberg	150.0
8	Jennifer Aniston	25.0
9	Brad Pitt	28.0
10	Kobe Bryant	45.0
11	Will Smith	45.0
12	Dr. Phil McGraw	80.0
13	Britney Spears	35.0
14	David Letterman	45.0
15	Coldplay	70.0
16	Adam Sandler	55.0
17	Harrison Ford	65.0
18	Michael Jordan	45.0
19	LeBron James	40.0
20	Tom Cruise	33.0

*Forbes' rankings are based on income and media recognition (Web prominence, magazine covers, radio/TV and newspaper coverage)

SOURCE: *FORBES*, JUNE 3, 2009

Hoover's Handbook of

American Business

The Companies

3M Company

Loath to be stuck on one thing, 3M makes everything from masking tape to asthma inhalers. The company has six operating segments: display and graphics (specialty film, traffic control materials); health care (dental and medical supplies, and health IT); safety, security, and protection (commercial care, occupational health and safety products); electro and communications (connecting, splicing, and insulating products); industrial and transportation (filtration products, tapes, and adhesives); and consumer and office. Well-known brands include Scotchgard fabric protectors, Post-it Notes, Scotch-Brite scouring products, and Scotch tapes.

The company is looking to drive growth both through its core operations and through acquisitions. Indeed, after a relatively slow period of M&A activity in the first half of this decade, 3M has been increasingly active in terms of acquisitions in the latter half. Its first big move was the billion-dollar acquisition of liquid filtration producer CUNO. 3M's own filtration products business — primarily air filters — amounted to more than $1 billion in annual sales before the deal, and the deal added nearly half that. CUNO's filtration products are used in the health care, potable water, and fluid processing markets. Like many other companies 3M expects the provision of clean water to become a huge growth industry as the developing world continues to industrialize.

The company ran through another string of acquisitions in 2007, buying companies such as Unifam, Lingualcare, Innovative Paper Technologies, and Diamond Productions. 3M also purchased Bondo Corp., which makes auto body repair products, from RPM International. A bigger deal was the 2008 purchase of protection products maker Aearo Technologies for $1.2 billion. That company makes a line of hearing and eye protection products for the occupational health and safety market. 3M also bought the Beiersdorf subsidiary Futuro, which makes medical products like wraps, elastic bandages, and compression hosiery.

HISTORY

Five businessmen in Two Harbors, Minnesota, founded Minnesota Mining and Manufacturing (3M) in 1902 to sell corundum to grinding-wheel manufacturers. The company soon needed to raise working capital. Co-founder John Dwan offered his friend Edgar Ober 60% of 3M's stock. Ober persuaded Lucius Ordway, VP of a plumbing business, to help underwrite 3M. In 1905 the two took over the company and moved it to Duluth.

In 1907 future CEO William McKnight joined 3M as a bookkeeper. Three years later the plant moved to St. Paul. The board of directors declared a dividend to shareholders in the last quarter of 1916, and 3M hasn't missed a dividend since. The next two products 3M developed — Scotch-brand masking tape (1925) and Scotch-brand cellophane tape (1930) — assured its future.

McKnight introduced one of the first employee pension plans in 1931, and in the late 1940s he implemented a vertical management structure. 3M introduced the first commercially viable magnetic recording tape in 1947.

In 1950, after a decade of work and $1 million in development costs, 3M employee Carl Miller completed the Thermo-Fax copying machine, which was the foundation of 3M's duplicating division. Products in the 1960s included 3M's dry-silver microfilm, photographic products, carbonless papers, overhead projection systems, and medical and dental products. 3M moved into pharmaceuticals, radiology, energy control, and office markets in the 1970s and 1980s.

A 3M scientist developed Post-it Notes (1980) because he wanted to attach page markers to his church hymnal. Recalling that a colleague had developed an adhesive that wasn't very sticky, he brushed some on paper and began a product line that now generates hundreds of millions of dollars each year.

In 1990 the company bought sponge maker O-Cel-O. But not all of its inventions have brought 3M good news. In 1995, along with fellow silicone breast-implant makers Baxter International and Bristol-Myers Squibb, it agreed to settle thousands of personal-injury claims related to implants. The companies paid an average of $26,000 per claim.

3M spun off its low-profit imaging and data-storage businesses in 1996 as Imation Corp. and closed its audiotape and videotape businesses. In 1997 3M sold its National Advertising billboard business to Infinity Outdoor for $1 billion.

The company created the 3M Nexcare brand for its line of first-aid and home health products in 1998. To regain earnings growth, 3M closed about 10% of its plants in the US and abroad; it also discontinued unprofitable product lines. The next year 3M bought out Hoechst AG's 46% stake in Dyneon LLC, a fluorine elastomer joint venture between the two companies.

3M bought Polaroid's Technical Polarizer and Display Films business and a controlling stake in Germany-based Quante AG (telecom systems) in 2000. In addition, the company decided to stop making many of its Scotchgard-brand repellent products due to research revealing that one of the compounds (perfluorooctane sulfonate) used in the manufacturing process is "persistent and pervasive" in the environment and in people's bloodstreams. As 2000 drew to a close, 3M named GE executive James McNerney to succeed L. D. DeSimone as its chairman and CEO.

3M announced plans to cut 6,000 jobs and authorized a stock buy-back program of up to $2.5 billion in 2001. The company changed its legal name from Minnesota Mining and Manufacturing Company to 3M Company that year. In 2002, 3M restructured its business segments around end uses rather than products or raw materials. By the end of that year, it had cut more than 8,500 jobs, 11% of its total workforce.

CEO McNerney left 3M in 2005 to join Boeing in the same capacity and was replaced by George Buckley, formerly of the Brunswick Corporation.

The company signaled a new strategic direction in 2006 when it broke up its pharmaceutical unit along geographic lines and sold it in pieces. The North and South American business was sold to Graceway Pharmaceuticals, the European unit to Meda AB, and the Asia/Pacific division to Australian private equity firms Ironbridge Capital and Archer Capital. In total, 3M got $2.1 billion for the sale of its pharmaceutical operations.

EXECUTIVES

Chairman, President, and CEO: George W. Buckley, age 62, $12,911,466 total compensation
President and Chief Intellectual Property Counsel, 3M Innovative Properties Co: Gary L. Griswold
EVP International Operations: Inge G. Thulin, age 55, $4,644,199 total compensation
EVP Research and Development and CTO: Frederick J. Palensky, age 59
EVP Electro and Communications: Joaquin Delgado
EVP Industrial and Transportation Business: Hak Cheol (H. C.) Shin, age 51
EVP Health Care Business: Brad T. Sauer, age 49, $3,407,909 total compensation
EVP Consumer and Office: Joe E. Harlan, age 50, $2,686,414 total compensation
EVP Safety, Security, and Protection Services Business: Jean Lobey, age 56
EVP Display and Graphics Business: Michael A. Kelly, age 52
SVP and CFO: Patrick D. (Pat) Campbell, age 56, $3,902,201 total compensation
SVP Legal Affairs and General Counsel: Marschall I. Smith, age 64
SVP Corporate Supply Chain Operations: John K. Woodworth, age 57
SVP Marketing and Sales: Robert D. MacDonald, age 58
SVP Human Resources: Angela S. Lalor, age 43
VP, Corporate Controller, and Chief Accounting Officer: David W. Meline, age 51
VP and Treasurer: Janet L. Yeomans
VP Community Affairs and VP 3M Foundation: Alexander C. Cirillo Jr.
President, Health Information Systems: Nancy A. Larson
Deputy General Counsel and Secretary: Gregg M. Larson
Director Investor Relations: Matt Ginter
Public Relations: Stephanie Sanderson
Auditors: PricewaterhouseCoopers LLP

LOCATIONS

HQ: 3M Company
3M Center, St. Paul, MN 55144
Phone: 651-733-1110 **Fax:** 651-733-9973
Web: www.mmm.com

2008 Sales

	$ mil.	% of total
US	9,179	36
Europe/Africa/Middle East	6,941	28
Asia/Pacific	6,423	25
Latin America/Canada	2,723	11
Other regions	3	—
Total	**25,269**	**100**

PRODUCTS/OPERATIONS

2008 Sales

	$ mil.	% of total
Industrial & Transportation	7,818	31
Health Care	4,293	17
Safety, Security & Protection Services	3,642	14
Consumer & Office	3,448	14
Display & Graphics	3,255	13
Electro & Communications	2,791	11
Corporate	22	—
Total	**25,269**	**100**

Selected Segments and Products

Industrial and Transportation
   Automotive aftermarket products
   Automotive products
   Closures for disposable diapers
   Coated and nonwoven abrasives
   Films
   Filtration products
   Specialty adhesives
   Tapes

Abbott Laboratories

Filling baby bottles and soothing aching joints are a habit for Abbott. Abbott Laboratories is one of the US's top health care products makers. The company's pharmaceuticals include HIV treatment Norvir, rheumatoid arthritis therapy Humira, and obesity drug Meridia. Its nutritional products division makes such well-known brands as Similac infant formula and the Ensure line of nutrition supplements. Abbott's medical devices group makes diagnostic systems, including the FreeStyle diabetes care line, and eye surgery and care products. Its animal health division offers wound care, nutritional supplements, and IV supplies. The company sells its products in about 130 countries through affiliates and distributors.

Abbott's pharmaceuticals division — which focuses on the therapeutic areas of immunology, oncology, neuroscience, metabolic disorders, and infectious disease — brings in more than half of sales. Humira is the division's big hit and considerable R&D and marketing money is dedicated to expanding uses for the drug, as well as for new cholesterol drugs. One such drug is Trilipix, a cholesterol and lipid fibrate therapy, for which it received approval in 2008.

Like all pharmaceutical giants, the company knows the pains of patent expiration. Facing the patent expiration of many of its top sellers between 2011 and 2016 (Aluvia, TriCor, Niaspan, Humira), Abbott is hoping new candidates in its R&D pipeline, as well as expanded uses for drugs like Humira, will make up for any resulting losses. It is also looking to expand its diabetes care offerings.

Though diagnostics (including lab tests for HIV, cancer, and pregnancy) were once the core of Abbott's product line, acquisitions have shifted the company's focus toward pharmaceuticals.

In 2008 Abbott sold off its share of TAP Pharmaceutical Products to Takeda Pharmaceutical. Abbott and Takeda had formed the joint venture in 1977 to market Takeda's drugs in the US. Takeda paid more than $1.5 billion for TAP. Takeda took home best-selling acid-reflux treatment Prevacid and the TAP pipeline of products, while Abbott carried away the rights to oncology drug Lupron and will continue to receive payments on current and future TAP products.

It expanded its vascular division with the 2009 purchase of Advanced Medical Optics for about $2.8 billion. The company, renamed Abbott Medical Optics, is a leading provider of surgical equipment and products for cataract and vision correction procedures, as well as contact lens care products.

Until mid-2009 Abbott was embroiled in a decade-long intellectual property rights lawsuit with Medtronic over certain patents related to coronary stent and stent-delivery systems. Medtronic eventually agreed to pay $400 million to Abbott to settle the lawsuit.

Abbott continues to search for medical technology acquisitions as the global economic downturn has put many smaller companies in financial difficulty.

HISTORY

Dr. Wallace Abbott started making his dosimetric granule (a pill that supplied uniform quantities of drugs) at his home outside Chicago in 1888. Aggressive marketing earned Abbott the American Medical Association's criticism, though much of the medical profession supported him.

During WWI, Abbott scientists synthesized anesthetics previously available only from Germany. Abbott improved its research capacity in 1922 by buying Dermatological Research Laboratories; in 1928 it bought John T. Milliken and its well-trained sales force. Abbott went public in 1929.

Salesman DeWitt Clough became president in 1933. International operations began in the mid-1930s with branches in Argentina, Brazil, Cuba, Mexico, and the UK.

Abbott was integral to the WWII effort; the US made only 28 pounds of penicillin in 1943 before the company began to ratchet up production. Consumer, infant, and nutritional products (such as Selsun Blue shampoo, Murine eye drops, and Similac formula) joined the roster in the 1960s. The FDA banned Abbott's artificial sweetener Sucaryl in 1970, saying it might be carcinogenic, and in 1971 millions of intravenous solutions were recalled following contamination deaths.

Robert Schoellhorn became CEO in 1979; profits increased but research and development was cut. In the 1980s Abbott began selling Japanese-developed pharmaceuticals in the US.

Duane Burnham became CEO in 1989; under his conservative management the company received FDA approvals to market insomnia treatment ProSom (1990), hypertension drug Hytrin for enlarged prostates (1994), and ulcer treatment Prevacid and central nervous system disorder treatment Depakote (1995).

Abbott bought MediSense, a maker of blood sugar self-tests for diabetics, in 1996; it also paid $32.5 million to settle claims by 17 states of infant formula price-fixing. In 1997 FTC action prompted Abbott to stop claiming that doctors recommended its Ensure nutritional supplement for healthy adults. That year the FDA allowed Abbott to use Norvir to treat HIV and AIDS in children, after approving its use in adults in a record 72 days in 1996.

In 1999 Abbott agreed to buy pharmaceutical research company ALZA, but the deal fell through, in part because of FTC antitrust concerns. That year the FDA fined the company $100 million and pulled 125 of its medical diagnostic kits off the market, citing quality assurance problems. In 2000 the FDA approved Gengraf, a drug that fights organ transplant rejection, and Kaletra, a promising protease inhibitor designed to combat AIDS.

Insider Miles White was named chairman and CEO in 2001. That same year Abbott bought Knoll Pharmaceuticals, a pharmaceutical unit of German chemicals giant BASF, and also purchased Vysis, thereby acquiring that company's worldwide distribution network and adding its products for the evaluation and management of cancer, prenatal disorders, and other genetic diseases to its portfolio of diagnostics.

The FDA thwarted the company's launch of new diagnostic products in 2002 by declaring that Abbott's Chicago manufacturing plant was not up to snuff.

In 2004 Abbott spun off its hospital products division, Hospira, into a separate company.

Abbot ceased selling attention deficit drug Cylert in early 2005, citing declining sales, concurrent with a consumer advocacy group's complaint that the drug caused more than 20 cases of liver failure. The FDA withdrew approval for the drug later that year.

EXECUTIVES

Chairman and CEO: Miles D. White, age 54, $28,335,494 total compensation
EVP Finance and CFO: Thomas C. (Tom) Freyman, age 54, $6,847,843 total compensation
EVP Diagnostic Products: Edward L. Michael, age 52
EVP Medical Devices: John M. Capek, age 47, $5,341,407 total compensation
EVP Nutritional Products: Holger A. Liepmann, age 57
EVP Pharmaceutical Products: Olivier Bohuon, age 50
EVP Corporate Development: Richard W. Ashley, age 65
EVP, Secretary, and General Counsel: Laura J. Schumacher, age 45, $5,715,310 total compensation
SVP International Nutrition: Thomas F. Chen, age 59
SVP Human Resources: Stephen R. (Steve) Fussell, age 51
SVP Abbott Vascular: Robert B. (Chip) Hance, age 49
SVP Pharmaceuticals Research and Development: John M. Leonard, age 51
SVP Pharmaceuticals, Manufacturing, and Supply: John C. Landgraf, age 56
SVP U.S. Pharmaceuticals: Mary T. Szela, age 45
SVP Abbott Diabetes Care: Heather L. Mason, age 48
SVP U.S. Nutrition: Donald V. Patton Jr., age 56
SVP Diagnostics: Michael J. Warmuth
VP Investor Relations: John B. Thomas
President, Abbott Biotech Ventures: James L. Tyree, age 55, $6,232,208 total compensation
Auditors: Deloitte & Touche LLP

LOCATIONS

HQ: Abbott Laboratories
100 Abbott Park Rd., Abbott Park, IL 60064
Phone: 847-937-6100   **Fax:** 847-937-9555
Web: www.abbott.com

2008 Sales

	$ mil.	% of total
US	14,495	49
Netherlands	1,753	6
Germany	1,381	5
Japan	1,249	5
Italy	1,089	4
France	977	3
Canada	924	3
Spain	909	3
UK	725	2
Other countries	6,026	20
Total	**29,528**	**100**

PRODUCTS/OPERATIONS

2008 Sales

	$ mil.	% of total
Pharmaceuticals	16,708	57
Nutritionals	4,924	17
Diagnostics	3,575	12
Vascular	2,241	7
Other	2,080	7
Total	**29,528**	**100**

Selected Products

Pharmaceutical
 Aluvia (HIV)
 Biaxin (anti-infective)
 Depakote (epileptic seizures, bipolar disorder, migraines)
 Erythrocin (anti-infective)
 Humira (rheumatoid arthritis, psoriasis, Crohn's disease)
 Kaletra (HIV)
 Meridia (obesity)
 Niaspan (high cholesterol)
 Norvir (HIV)
 Ogastro/Prevacid (ulcers, erosive esophagitis, through TAP Pharmaceutical Products)
 Omnicef (antibiotic)
 Reductil (obesity)
 Synthroid (hyperthyroidism)
 TriCor (dyslipidemia)
 Ultane/Sevorane (anesthesia)
 Vicodin (pain relief)

Diagnostic
  Abbott PRISM (high-volume blood-screening system)
  ARCHITECT c8000 (clinical chemistry system)
  AxSYM (immunoassay system)
  Cell-Dyn (hematology systems and reagents)
  FreeStyle (glucose monitoring meters, test strips, data management software, and accessories)
  i-STAT (point-of-care diagnostics, blood analysis)
  PathVysion (breast cancer diagnostic test)
  UroVysion (bladder cancer)
Nutritional
  AdvantEdge (nutritional supplements)
  Alimentum (infant formula)
  Ensure (adult nutrition)
  Glucerna (nutritional beverage for diabetics)
  Isomil (soy-based infant formula)
  Jevity (liquid food for enteral feeding)
  Myoplex (nutritional supplements)
  Pedialyte (pediatric electrolyte solution)
  PediaSure (children's nutrition)
  Similac (infant formula)
  ZonePerfect (nutritional bars)
Vascular
  Acculink/Accunet (carotid stent)
  Asahi (coronary guidewires)
  Balance Middleweight (coronary guidewire)
  Multi-Link Vision (coronary metallic stent)
  StarClose (vessel closure)
  Xience V (drug-eluting stent)
  Voyager (balloon dilation products)

COMPETITORS

Amgen
AstraZeneca
Bard
Barr Pharmaceuticals
Baxter International
Bayer AG
Becton, Dickinson
Boston Scientific
Bristol-Myers Squibb
Cordis
Eli Lilly
Genentech
GlaxoSmithKline
Johnson & Johnson
Medtronic CardioVascular
Merck
Mylan
Nestlé
Novartis
Pfizer
Roche Holding
Sandoz International GmbH
Sanofi-Aventis
Schering-Plough
Solvay
Teva Pharmaceuticals
Watson Pharmaceuticals
Wyeth

HISTORICAL FINANCIALS

Company Type: Public

Income Statement

FYE: December 31

	REVENUE ($ mil.)	NET INCOME ($ mil.)	NET PROFIT MARGIN	EMPLOYEES
12/08	29,527.6	4,880.7	16.5%	69,000
12/07	25,914.2	3,606.3	13.9%	68,000
12/06	22,476.3	1,716.8	7.6%	66,663
12/05	22,337.8	3,372.1	15.1%	59,735
12/04	19,680.0	3,235.9	16.4%	60,600
Annual Growth	10.7%	10.8%	—	3.3%

2008 Year-End Financials

Debt ratio: 49.8%
Return on equity: 27.7%
Cash ($ mil.): 4,112
Current ratio: 1.47
Long-term debt ($ mil.): 8,713

No. of shares (mil.): 1,546
Dividends
  Yield: 2.6%
  Payout: 44.9%
Market value ($ mil.): 82,505

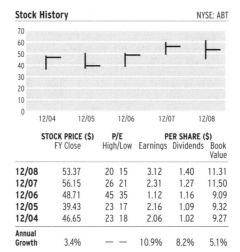

	STOCK PRICE ($) FY Close	P/E High/Low		PER SHARE ($) Earnings	Dividends	Book Value
12/08	53.37	20	15	3.12	1.40	11.31
12/07	56.15	26	21	2.31	1.27	11.50
12/06	48.71	45	35	1.12	1.16	9.09
12/05	39.43	23	17	2.16	1.09	9.32
12/04	46.65	23	18	2.06	1.02	9.27
Annual Growth	3.4%	—	—	10.9%	8.2%	5.1%

ABC, Inc.

Some *Desperate Housewives,* a group of *Lost* plane crash survivors, and doctors schooled in *Grey's Anatomy* call this network home. ABC operates the #3 television network in the US (behind CBS and FOX), with more than 230 affiliates (including 10 corporate-owned stations). ABC also owns ESPN, a leader in cable sports broadcasting with a stable of channels, including ESPN2, ESPN Classic, and ESPN News, as well as its flagship channel. In addition, the company operates mass-market publisher Hyperion. ABC is the cornerstone of Disney-ABC Television Group, the TV division of parent Walt Disney.

ABC has continued to struggle in the race for audience share, having slipped from second to third place among the top broadcast networks during the 2006-07 season. The decline came in part due to a long winter hiatus for hit show *Lost,* as well as the loss of former ratings stalwart *Monday Night Football,* which was picked up for the 2006 NFL season by ESPN. ABC, along with the other networks, was also struck by the Hollywood writers' strike that put most scripted TV shows on ice for several months during the 2007-08 season.

In addition to declining ratings, the network has been hurt by the worsening economy which has slowed ad spending. In an effort to reduce costs, Disney-ABC Television announced hundreds of job cuts early in 2006. The unit also combined its ABC Studio production unit with prime-time programming arm ABC Entertainment in an effort to streamline new production.

The company has been actively trying to exploit new digital distribution channels to reach audiences. In 2009 parent Walt Disney became a partner in video site Hulu with NBC Universal and News Corporation. The deal saw Disney take a 30% stake in the joint venture and made ABC shows available on Hulu. The network was one of the first to distribute full-length episodes on-

line through its own ABC.com site. It also sells episodes through Apple's iTunes store. (Apple head honcho Steve Jobs is the largest shareholder in Disney, with a 7% stake.)

HISTORY

ABC was launched in 1927 by RCA as the Blue Network. A sister network to NBC (now owned by General Electric), Blue Network was sold to Life Savers candy magnate Edward J. Noble in 1943 after an FCC ruling that prohibited ownership of more than one network. Renamed the American Broadcasting Company (ABC) three years later, ABC struggled with just 100 radio stations in its network and no big stars. By 1953 the company had expanded into television with 14 affiliates. That year United Paramount Theatres, led by Leonard Goldenson, bought ABC for $25 million.

To compete with CBS and NBC, Goldenson turned to Hollywood. He signed a $40 million deal with Walt Disney in 1953 that gave ABC access to the Disney film library and an exclusive programming alliance. The network turned to other studios for programming such as *77 Sunset Strip* and *Maverick.* During the 1960s ABC fended off takeover attempts by ITT and Howard Hughes, and in the 1970s it pioneered the long-form mini-series with *Roots* and *Rich Man, Poor Man.* Hit shows, including *Happy Days* and *Charlie's Angels,* helped put the network on top during the 1976 season. In 1984 the company bought cable sports channel ESPN. (It sold 20% of ESPN to Hearst in 1991.) The next year ABC was sold to Capital Cities Communications for $3.5 billion.

Founded by Frank Smith as Hudson Valley Broadcasting, Capital Cities had started out as a bankrupt TV station in Albany, New York. In 1957 it acquired a second station in Raleigh, North Carolina; changed its name; and went public in 1964. Smith died in 1966, and Thomas Murphy took over as chairman and CEO. The company bought magazine publisher Fairchild Publications in 1968 and newspapers such as the *Fort Worth Star-Telegram* and *Kansas City Star* in the 1970s. By the 1980s Capital Cities had revenues of more than $1 billion.

During the early 1990s Capital Cities/ABC saw ratings soar with such hits as *Roseanne* and *Home Improvement.* Robert Iger was appointed president in 1994. Two years later Disney bought the company for $19 billion, selling off its newspapers for $1.65 billion. In 1998 ABC agreed to pay $9.2 billion for National Football League broadcast rights through 2005. In addition, Patricia Fili-Krushel was named president of ABC Television, making her the first woman to head a major broadcast network. Iger was named chairman of ABC in 1999, and ESPN chief Steven Bornstein took over as president.

In 1999 Disney sold ABC's Fairchild magazine unit to Advance Publications for about $650 million. Bornstein left late that year to head Disney's GO.com (now Disney Online). In early 2000 Iger was named president and COO of Disney, leaving broadcast president Robert Callahan in charge. Fili-Krushel later resigned. (Iger became CEO of Disney in 2005.)

Negotiations over rebroadcast rights between Disney and Time Warner Cable went south in 2000 and ABC broadcasts were briefly suspended for about 3.5 million viewers. (Time Warner

Cable was later admonished by the FCC for dropping the stations during sweeps periods.) Despite the interruption, ABC finished #1 in the ratings for the first time in five years. That success was short-lived, however, as the network's audience share eroded the next season and ABC fell to #2.

Callahan resigned from ABC in 2001, and Bornstein returned from Disney Internet to become broadcast group president that year. Later Disney bought the Fox Family Channel, renamed ABC Family, and the international assets of the Fox Kids Network (later rebranded as JETIX) from News Corp. and Haim Saban for $5.2 billion (including debt). The network's start to the 2001-02 season was inauspicious as NBC and CBS scored strong ratings, leaving ABC in the dust.

In 2002 ABC announced an agreement to broadcast NBA games in conjunction with ESPN and AOL Time Warner (now called Time Warner). Bornstein resigned as president in mid-2002. ABC reshuffled management again in 2004, with Anne Sweeny taking over management of all Disney and ABC's television operations, and Stephen McPherson taking over ABC's primetime entertainment duties.

In 2007 Disney spun off the radio broadcasting operations of ABC, including ABC Radio Network (later Citadel Media), which merged with Citadel Broadcasting. The $2.7 billion merger left Disney shareholders owning 57% of the combined company.

EXECUTIVES

Co-Chairman, Disney Media Networks; President, ESPN and ABC Sports: George W. Bodenheimer, age 50
Co-Chairman, Disney Media Networks; President, Disney-ABC Television Group: Anne M. Sweeney
EVP and CFO, ABC Television Network and ABC Television Studios: James L. (Jim) Hedges
EVP Marketing, Advertising, and Promotion: Michael (Mike) Benson
EVP Marketing: Marla Provencio
EVP: Jeffrey D. (Jeff) Bader
EVP Casting, ABC Entertainment Television Group: Keli Lee
EVP Strategy and Research, Disney Media Networks: Peter Seymour, age 41
SVP Human Resources: Jeffrey S. Rosen
SVP Movies and Mini-Series: Lance B. Taylor
SVP Motion Pictures for Television: Quinn Taylor
SVP Business Development: Bruce Gersh
SVP Comedy Development: Samie Kim Falvey
SVP Research: Charles Kennedy
President, ABC News: David Westin
President, Daytime, Disney-ABC Television Group: Brian S. Frons
President, ABC-Owned Television Stations: Walter C. Liss Jr.
President, Broadcast Operations and Engineering: Preston A. Davis
President, Sales and Marketing, ABC Television Network: Mike Shaw
President, ABC Family: Paul Lee
President, ABC Entertainment Group: Stephen (Steve) McPherson
President, Hyperion: Ellen Archer, age 46
Senior Advisor to Office of Co-Chairman: Mark Pedowitz
Auditors: PricewaterhouseCoopers LLP

LOCATIONS

HQ: ABC, Inc.
77 W. 66th St., New York, NY 10023
Phone: 212-456-7777 **Fax:** 212-456-1424
Web: abc.go.com

PRODUCTS/OPERATIONS

Selected Network Shows

20/20
Better Off Ted
Brothers & Sisters
Castle
Cougar Town (Fall 2009)
Dancing With The Stars
The Deep End (Fall 2009)
Desperate Housewives
Eastwick (Fall 2009)
Extreme Makeover: Home Edition
Flash Forward (Fall 2009)
The Forgotten (Fall 2009)
Grey's Anatomy
Hank (Fall 2009)
Happy Town (Fall 2009)
Lost
The Middle (Fall 2009)
Modern Family (Fall 2009)
Private Practice
Scrubs
Shark Tank (Fall 2009)
Ugly Betty
V (Fall 2009)

Television Stations

KABC (Los Angeles)
KFSN (Fresno, CA)
KGO (San Francisco)
KTRK (Houston)
WABC (New York City)
WJRT (Flint, MI)
WLS (Chicago)
WPVI (Philadelphia)
WTVD (Raleigh-Durham-Fayetteville, NC)
WTVG (Toledo, OH)

COMPETITORS

CBS	MyNetworkTV
The CW	NBC
Discovery Communications	Turner Broadcasting
FOX Broadcasting	Univision
MTV Networks	

Abercrombie & Fitch

Trading on its century-old name, Abercrombie & Fitch (A&F) sells upscale men's, women's, and kids' casual clothes and accessories — quite a change from when the company outfitted Ernest Hemingway and Teddy Roosevelt for safaris. A&F operates some 1,125 stores in the US, Canada, and the UK, and also sells via its catalog and online. Its carefully selected college-age sales staff and use of 20-something models imbue its stores with an upscale fraternity house feel. A&F also runs a fast-growing chain of some 515 teen stores called Hollister Co., and a chain targeted at boys and girls ages seven to 14 called abercrombie. RUEHL, a Greenwich Village-inspired concept for the post-college set, is slated for closure.

The decision to shutter all 29 RUEHL stores and related e-commerce operations in 2009 came shortly after A&F conducted a strategic review of the high-end RUEHL business. (RUEHL's same-store sales decreased 34% in the first quarter of the year.) CEO Mike Jeffries said RUEHL, which debuted in 2004, was a casualty of the economy.

A&F's newest brand, Gilly Hicks, launched in early 2008. The just-for-women brand sells "cute" bras, underwear, and personal care products at more than a dozen stores. The company also opened its first Hollister stores in malls in the UK in 2008.

A&F's strategy not to discount in-season products isn't going over well with today's bargain-conscious shoppers. Indeed, after reporting a 24% decline in revenue for the quarter ended May 2009, the retailer reconsidered and announced that it will cut prices to spur sales. Despite falling sales across its three main chains and e-commerce business, the retailer still expects to open 10 mall-based stores in the US and another 10 abroad. Four flagship stores are slated to open in New York, Milan, and Tokyo.

A&F is searching for a new president and COO following the resignation of Robert Singer, after only 15 months with the company. Singer's abrupt departure was due to a disagreement over the company's international expansion strategy.

Abercrombie's e-commerce business, which operates Web sites for all of its store brands, has grown to account for about 9% of net sales.

HISTORY

Scotsman David Abercrombie began selling camping equipment in lower Manhattan in 1892. Joined by lawyer Ezra Fitch, Abercrombie & Fitch (A&F) soon established itself as the purveyor of outdoors equipment for the very rich. A&F supplied Theodore Roosevelt and Ernest Hemingway for safaris and provided gear for Charles Lindbergh and polar explorer Richard Byrd. In 1917 the company moved into a 12-story edifice in Manhattan that included a log cabin (which Fitch lived in) and a casting pool.

A&F thrived through the 1960s. Mounted animal heads adorned its New York store, which offered 15,000 types of lures and 700 different shotguns. However, by the 1970s A&F's core customers were as extinct or endangered as the animals they had hunted, and the company struggled to find new markets. In 1977 A&F filed for bankruptcy. A year later sports retailer Oshman's (now The Sports Authority) bought the company and expanded the number of stores while providing an eclectic assortment of goods. In 1988 clothing retailer The Limited bought A&F, then with about 25 stores, and shifted the company's emphasis to apparel.

Michael Jeffries took over in 1992 and transformed the still money-losing chain into an outfitter for college students. The new *jefe* micromanaged, issuing a 29-page book on everything from how A&F salespeople (who earned around $6 an hour) must look to exactly how many sweaters can be placed in a stack. Draconian perhaps, but the strategy worked, and A&F returned to profitability in fiscal 1995. The company went public in 1996 with more than 110 stores.

In 1998 The Limited spun off its remaining 84% stake. Also that year A&F sued rival American Eagle Outfitters, claiming it illegally copied A&F's clothing and approach (the suit was dismissed in 1999), and it raised the hackles of Mothers Against Drunk Driving with a catalog article entitled "Drinking 101." The company got attention of a different sort in 1999 when the SEC launched an investigation after A&F leaked sales figures to an analyst before they were made available to the public. In 2000 A&F launched its new teen store concept called Hollister Co.

A&F continued to push the envelope with its A&F Quarterly in summer 2001. Under the theme "Let Summer Begin," the catalog featured naked and half-naked models having "wet 'n' wild summer fun" and T-shirts logos that read "I Have a Big One" and "Get on the Stick."

The company pushed a little further in Spring 2002 with a line of T-shirts portraying Asian caricatures. Vocal protests from Asian groups forced A&F to pull the T-shirts from its shelves and issue an apology. Later that spring, A&F may have pushed a little too hard. A line of children's-sized thong underwear bearing sexually suggestive messages caused a furor among family-advocacy groups.

In December 2003 Abercrombie & Fitch toned down further with the discontinuation of its popular and racy A&F Quarterly magazine. Using half-nude models, the publication targeted consumers aged 18-24. In September 2004 it launched a young professionals' brand called RUEHL. The stores target customers aged 22 to 30, traditionally J. Crew and Banana Republic customers, offering hip styles at lower prices.

In May 2005 A&F established a Japanese subsidiary company called ANF. In November the company opened its first RUEHL Accessories store, a tiny (600 sq. ft.) shop on Manhattan's Bleecker Street. Also in November the company opened its first off-mall, flagship store on New York's Fifth Avenue at 56th Street.

In late 2007 the retailer launched an e-commerce site for its RUEHL concept. Soon after, in January 2008 the company launched its newest brand, Gilly Hicks, with a store opening in Natick, Massachusetts. The company also opened its first Hollister stores in malls in the UK in 2008.

EXECUTIVES

Chairman and CEO: Michael S. (Mike) Jeffries, age 64, $15,912,111 total compensation
EVP and CFO: Jonathan E. Ramsden, age 44, $320,915 total compensation
EVP Planning and Allocation: Leslee K. Herro, age 48, $4,386,696 total compensation
EVP Sourcing: Diane Chang, age 53, $4,386,696 total compensation
EVP Female Merchandising: Charles F. (Chad) Kessler, age 36, $3,182,936 total compensation
SVP and CIO: Kristen Blum
SVP Global Real Estate: David L. Leino, age 42
SVP Diversity and Inclusion: Todd Corley
SVP and General Manager: Beverly House
SVP Real Estate: Jeffrey Sinkey
SVP, General Counsel, and Secretary: David S. Cupps, age 72, $698,059 total compensation
SVP Human Resources: Ron Grzymkowski
SVP Store Construction: Abed W. Karaze
SVP Store Operations: Mike P. Rosera
SVP Supply Chain: John A. Singleton
SVP Stores: Amy L. Zehrer
VP Corporate Communications and Public Relations: Thomas D. (Tom) Lennox
VP Finance and Controller: Brian P. Logan, $502,646 total compensation
Auditors: PricewaterhouseCoopers LLP

LOCATIONS

HQ: Abercrombie & Fitch Co.
6301 Fitch Path, New Albany, OH 43054
Phone: 614-283-6500   **Fax:** 614-283-6710
Web: www.abercrombie.com

2009 Stores

	No.
California	140
Texas	103
Florida	77
New York	58
Illinois	50
Pennsylvania	49
New Jersey	42
Ohio	41
Michigan	34
Massachusetts	35
North Carolina	30
Georgia	29
Virginia	28
Indiana	26
Tennessee	24
Washington	24
Missouri	20
Connecticut	22
Minnesota	24
Arizona	17
Alabama	15
Kentucky	14
Louisiana	15
Maryland	20
Wisconsin	16
South Carolina	15
Oregon	15
Oklahoma	10
Colorado	12
Nevada	15
New Hampshire	11
Arkansas	7
Kansas	6
Utah	7
Iowa	8
Hawaii	5
Mississippi	6
Nebraska	6
New Mexico	4
Rhode Island	4
West Virginia	5
Delaware	4
Idaho	4
Maine	4
Montana	3
North Dakota	2
South Dakota	2
Vermont	2
Alaska	1
District of Columbia	1
Canada	11
UK	4
Total	**1,127**

PRODUCTS/OPERATIONS

2009 Stores

	No.
Hollister	515
Abercrombie & Fitch	356
abercrombie	212
RUEHL	28
Gilly Hicks	16
Total	**1,127**

2009 Sales

	$ mil.	% of total
Abercrombie & Fitch	1,531.5	43
Hollister	1,514.2	43
abercrombie	420.5	12
RUEHL	56.2	1
Gilly Hicks	17.9	1
Total	**3,540.3**	**100**

Selected Products

Backpacks	Jackets	Skirts
Belts	Jeans	Sweaters
Caps	Outerwear	Swimwear
Footwear	Pants	Tank tops
Fragrances	Shirts	Underwear
Hats	Shorts	

COMPETITORS

Aéropostale	Lands' End
American Eagle Outfitters	Levi Strauss
Bath & Body Works	L.L. Bean
Benetton	Macy's
Body Shop	Nordstrom
The Buckle	Pacific Sunwear
Dillard's	Polo Ralph Lauren
Express, LLC	Quiksilver
The Gap	Target
Guess?	Tommy Hilfiger
H&M	Urban Outfitters
J. Crew	Victoria's Secret Stores
La Senza	Wet Seal

HISTORICAL FINANCIALS

Company Type: Public

Income Statement

FYE: Saturday nearest January 31

	REVENUE ($ mil.)	NET INCOME ($ mil.)	NET PROFIT MARGIN	EMPLOYEES
1/09	3,540.3	272.3	7.7%	83,000
1/08	3,749.8	475.7	12.7%	99,000
1/07	3,318.2	422.2	12.7%	86,400
1/06	2,784.7	334.0	12.0%	76,100
1/05	2,021.3	216.4	10.7%	62,140
Annual Growth	**15.0%**	**5.9%**	**—**	**7.5%**

2009 Year-End Financials

Debt ratio: 5.4%
Return on equity: 15.7%
Cash ($ mil.): 522
Current ratio: 2.41
Long-term debt ($ mil.): 100
No. of shares (mil.): 88
Dividends
  Yield: 3.9%
  Payout: 23.0%
Market value ($ mil.): 1,569

Stock History

NYSE: ANF

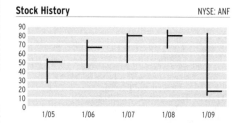

	STOCK PRICE ($) FY Close	P/E High/Low		PER SHARE ($) Earnings	Dividends	Book Value
1/09	17.85	27	4	3.05	0.70	21.00
1/08	79.59	16	13	5.20	0.70	18.42
1/07	79.54	18	11	4.59	0.70	15.99
1/06	66.39	20	12	3.66	0.60	11.32
1/05	50.12	23	12	2.28	0.50	7.62
Annual Growth	**(22.7%)**	**—**		**7.5%**	**8.8%**	**28.9%**

ABM Industries

Many businesses hope to clean up, but diversified facilities services contractor ABM Industries counts on it. Through its primary business unit, ABM Janitorial, the company offers cleaning services to owners and operators of office buildings, hospitals, manufacturing plants, schools, shopping centers, and transportation facilities throughout the US and in Canada and Puerto Rico. Through other units, ABM Industries provides security services and maintains mechanical, electrical, and plumbing systems. Ampco System Parking operates more than 1,600 parking lots and garages, mainly at airports across 40 states, while ABM Security Services provides security officers and security systems monitoring services.

In late 2007 ABM expanded its janitorial segment significantly by acquiring rival facility services company OneSource Services. ABM paid about $390 million for OneSource, which posted revenue of about $825 million for the year ended March 31, 2007. The operations of OneSource, including more than 10,000 commercial accounts in the US, Canada, and Puerto Rico, were integrated into those of ABM Janitorial throughout 2008.

The OneSource purchase was a major deal for ABM Industries, which like other conglomerates in the business services sector, has grown mainly by acquiring local and regional operating companies and their client rosters. ABM can then generate cost savings by centralizing many business functions, such as marketing, sales, and accounting. This strategy also allows ABM to increase sales by more effectively leveraging its diverse portfolio of service offerings.

ABM plans to continue to pursue its strategy of growth via acquisition, not only in the US but also in other countries. In order to focus on its core operations, in late 2008 the company sold the operating assets of its Amtech Lighting Services business to a unit of OSRAM SYLVANIA for about $34 million.

In 2009 ABM kept the acquisition engine running when it snatched up several cleaning and engineering businesses — Control Building Services, Control Engineering Services, and TTF Assets — located primarily in New Jersey and New York. Collectively these businesses generate annual revenues of about $50 million and cater to the commercial, institutional, and pharmaceutical industries.

HISTORY

Morris Rosenberg invested $4.50 in a bucket and cleaning tools and began cleaning San Francisco storefront windows in 1909. Later that year he purchased Chicago Window Cleaning for $300 and, armed with new supplies and a Ford Model T, began offering annual cleaning contracts. He changed the company's name to American Building Maintenance in 1913 to emphasize its broadening services. By 1920 the company had established three west coast offices, and it became the first contractor to clean a major college campus when it signed an agreement with Stanford University in 1921.

The company added cleaning supplies to its offerings in 1927 with the acquisition of Easterday Janitorial Supply Company and continued to grow, even during the Great Depression, by providing cleaning services cheaper than its clients could provide for themselves. ABM expanded to the East Coast in 1932. Morris Rosenberg died in 1935, leaving the company to his oldest son Theodore, who bought electrical services company Alta Electric the following year. During WWII ABM cleaned Navy ships and wired amphibious vehicles called Water Buffaloes. By the end of the war, it operated 17 offices in the US and Canada.

Now called American Building Maintenance Industries, the company went public in 1962 with Theodore serving as chairman and younger brother Sydney as CEO. To diversify its services, ABM Industries stepped up its acquisition pace in the late 1960s, buying Ampco Auto Parks (1967, parking facilities), Commercial Air Conditioning (1968, equipment maintenance), and General Elevator Corporation (1969, elevator maintenance and repair).

ABM Industries continued to expand its business into diverse services and regions through a three-decade buying spree. In 1981 the company combined its air-conditioning, elevator, lighting, and energy services into American Technical Services Company (Amtech) to better focus on the high-growth tech and energy businesses. A management-led buyout of the company failed in 1990 on opposition from the Rosenberg brothers. Although ABM Industries' president stepped down and several lawsuits were filed following the aborted LBO, the company continued to post impressive sales and profit numbers.

The company shortened its name to ABM Industries in 1994, the same year William Steele was named CEO. Sydney Rosenberg retired as chairman in 1997, marking the end of family control. The following year the company formed a Facility Services division to provide one-stop shopping for all of its services. It moved into landscaping services in 1999 with the purchase of Commercial Landscape Systems. The following year Steele stepped down as CEO and Henrik Slipsager, a former executive of Dutch services giant ISS, was tapped as the company's new chief.

In 2001 ABM sold off its Easterday Janitorial Supply subsidiary to AmSan West. ABM acquired six companies in 2001 and 2002, including Lakeside Building Maintenance, a large Midwestern janitorial contractor. In 2003 the company sold its Amtech Elevator Services to Otis Elevator Company for $112 million. Two years later, the company sold its CommAir Mechanical Services unit to Carrier Corp.

In 2005 ABM sold the last of its mechanical operations, divesting its water treatment business to San Joaquin Chemicals. A few years later (in 2008) it also divested its Amtech Lighting Services operations.

EXECUTIVES

Chairman: Maryellen C. Herringer, age 65
President, CEO, and Director: Henrik C. Slipsager, age 54
EVP and CFO: James S. Lusk, age 53
EVP; President, ABM Janitorial Services: James P. (Jim) McClure, age 51
EVP; President, ABM Facility Services and President, Amtech Lighting: Steven M. Zaccagnini, age 47
SVP; Director Business Development, and Chief Marketing Officer: Gary R. Wallace, age 58
SVP, Chief of Staff, and Treasurer: David L. Farwell, age 47
SVP Finance, Chief Accounting Officer, and Controller: Joseph F. Yospe, age 50
SVP Human Resources: Erin M. Andre, age 49
SVP, General Counsel, and Corporate Secretary: Sarah H. McConnell, age 44

VP Corporate Communications: Anthony (Tony) Mitchell
VP and Treasurer: D. Anthony Scaglione
President, Ampco System Parking: Rich Kindorf
President, ABM Engineering Services: Mike Latham
President, American Commercial Security Services and Security Services of America: Larry T. Smith
Auditors: KPMG LLP

LOCATIONS

HQ: ABM Industries Incorporated
551 5th Ave., Ste. 300, New York City, NY 10176
Phone: 212-297-0200   **Fax:** 212-297-0375
Web: www.abm.com

PRODUCTS/OPERATIONS

2008 Sales

	$ mil.	% of total
Janitorial	2,492.3	69
Parking	475.4	13
Security	333.5	9
Engineering	319.8	9
Corporate	2.6	—
Total	**3,623.6**	**100**

COMPETITORS

AlliedBarton Security	ISS A/S
ARAMARK	ServiceMaster
Central Parking	Sodexo USA
Comfort Systems USA	Standard Parking
Guardsmark	Temco Service Industries
Healthcare Services	UGL Unicco
Impark	

HISTORICAL FINANCIALS

Company Type: Public

Income Statement

FYE: October 31

	REVENUE ($ mil.)	NET INCOME ($ mil.)	NET PROFIT MARGIN	EMPLOYEES
10/08	3,623.6	45.4	1.3%	100,000
10/07	2,842.8	52.4	1.8%	107,000
10/06	2,792.7	93.2	3.3%	75,000
10/05	2,587.8	57.9	2.2%	73,000
10/04	2,416.2	30.5	1.3%	70,000
Annual Growth	10.7%	10.5%	—	9.3%

2008 Year-End Financials

Debt ratio: 38.2%	No. of shares (mil.): 51
Return on equity: 7.3%	Dividends
Cash ($ mil.): 1	Yield: 3.1%
Current ratio: 1.76	Payout: 56.8%
Long-term debt ($ mil.): 246	Market value ($ mil.): 838

Stock History

NYSE: ABM

	STOCK PRICE ($) FY Close	P/E High/Low		PER SHARE ($) Earnings	Dividends	Book Value
10/08	16.33	31	14	0.88	0.50	12.54
10/07	23.52	30	18	1.04	0.48	11.80
10/06	19.86	12	9	1.88	0.44	10.54
10/05	19.73	20	16	1.15	0.42	9.27
10/04	20.75	34	25	0.61	0.40	8.61
Annual Growth	(5.8%)	—	—	9.6%	5.7%	9.9%

Accenture Ltd

For Accenture, the accent is on trying to help businesses improve their performance. The world's largest consulting firm, Accenture offers management consulting, information technology and systems integration, and business process outsourcing (BPO) services to customers around the globe. The company divides its practices into five main operating groups — communications and high technology, financial services, public service, products, and resources — that encompass more than 15 industries. Accenture, which is domiciled in Bermuda but headquartered in New York, operates from more than 200 locations in about 50 countries.

Traditional business consulting remains a core function for Accenture, but systems integration and outsourcing have become key growth sectors. The company has been expanding in those areas via tuck-in acquisitions. In addition, Accenture is investing in staff development initiatives designed to more closely integrate the firm's IT-related and strategy-related consulting offerings.

Accenture disperses its advice widely — no single operating group accounts for more than a quarter of the firm's sales. Similarly, Accenture has diversified its operations geographically. Revenue from outside the US makes up a majority of its sales mix, and the company is looking to continue that trend. As with the rest of the outsourcing services industry, Accenture is looking to India, Brazil, China, Japan, and the Philippines as key areas for expansion. Adhering to this strategy, in mid-2008 Accenture acquired ATAN, an industrial and automation services provider based in Brazil that caters to the mining, energy, and utilities sectors. It also snatched up SOPIA, a Tokyo-based consulting firm specializing in Oracle systems integration, earlier that year.

Accenture also added to its transportation and travel services operations (located within its Products Division) in 2008 when it bought AddVal Technology. AddVal provides software and technology used for freight order management, and Accenture plans for the deal to enhance its ability to integrate and simplify its clients' freight management services capabilities. AddVal is based in California and has a software development center in India.

HISTORY

Accenture traces its history back to the storied accounting firm of Arthur Andersen & Co. Founded by Northwestern University professor and accounting legend Arthur Andersen in 1913, the firm's expanding scope of operations led it into forensic accounting and advising clients on financial reporting processes, forming the basis for a management consulting arm. Arthur Andersen led the firm until his death in 1947. His successor, Leonard Spacek, split off the consulting operations as a separate unit in 1954.

The consulting business grew quickly during the 1970s and 1980s, thanks in part to an orgy of US corporate re-engineering. By 1988 consulting accounted for 40% of Andersen's sales. Chafing at sharing profits with the auditors (who faced growing price pressures and a rising tide of legal action due to the accounting irregularities of their clients), the consultants sought more power within the firm. The result was a 1989 restructuring that established Andersen Worldwide (later Andersen) as the parent of two independent units, Arthur Andersen and Andersen Consulting (AC). The growing revenue imbalance between the operations remained unresolved, however, and a year later Arthur Andersen poured gas on the flames by establishing its own business consultancy.

Meanwhile, AC continued to expand during the 1990s by forming practices focused on manufacturing, finance, and government. It addressed the shift from mainframes to PCs by forming alliances with technology heavyweights Hewlett-Packard, Sun Microsystems, and Microsoft. In 1996 AC teamed up with Internet service provider BBN (acquired by GTE in 1997) to form ServiceNet, a joint venture to develop Internet commerce and other systems.

The Andersen family feud took a turn for the worse in 1997 with the retirement of CEO Lawrence Weinbach. A deadlocked vote for a new leader led the board to appoint accounting partner Robert Grafton as CEO, angering the consulting partners. Later that year AC asked the International Chamber of Commerce to negotiate a breakup of Andersen Worldwide. George Shaheen, to whom many attributed the heightened tensions between the units, resigned as CEO of AC in 1999 and was replaced by Joe Forehand.

While the separation dispute dragged on, the consulting business grew and diversified amid increasing consolidation in the industry. In 1999 the company moved into e-commerce venture funding with the formation of Andersen Consulting Ventures, and in 2000 it inked partnership deals with Microsoft (Microsoft system implementation services), Sun Microsystems (for B2B Internet office supply sales), and BT (Internet-based human resources services).

That year an international arbitrator finally approved AC's separation from its parent, ruling that the consultancy must change its name and pay Andersen Worldwide $1 billion (far less than the $15 billion demanded by the accounting partners). Renamed Accenture, the company went public in 2001. While the new name (a made-up word) might have struck some as a marketing challenge, having an identity distinct from that of its former parent proved to be a stroke of luck for Accenture. Andersen broke apart in 2002 after becoming embroiled in the accounting scandals of energy giant Enron.

In 2004 Accenture successfully bid on a $10 billion, 10-year contract to create a system to identify visitors and immigrants coming into the country. Dubbed US-VISIT (United States Visitor and Immigrant Status Indicator Technology), the system was to be employed by the Department of Homeland Security to prevent terrorists from entering the US. However, Accenture's bid nearly ran afoul of congressional critics who tried to pass spending amendments barring firms headquartered outside the US from winning security-related business.

Forehand stepped down as CEO of Accenture in 2004 and was replaced by company veteran William Green. Forehand remained chairman until he retired in 2006, when Green was named to that post, as well.

Accenture acquired Capgemini's North American health practice in 2005 for $175 million in order to strengthen its offerings to hospitals and health care systems. In 2006 the firm expanded its outsourcing operations by buying NaviSys, a leading provider of software for the life insurance industry, along with key assets of Kansas-based accountant Savista.

EXECUTIVES

Chairman and CEO: William D. (Bill) Green, age 56
International Chairman: Diego Visconti
COO: Johan G. Deblaere, age 47
CFO: Pamela J. Craig, age 51
CTO and Managing Director, Technology: Donald J. (Don) Rippert
Chief Strategy and Corporate Development Officer: R. Timothy S. (Tim) Breene, age 59
Chief Risk Officer: Thomas H. (Tom) Pike
Chief Marketing and Communications Officer: Roxanne Taylor
Group Chief Executive, United States: Robert N. Frerichs, age 57
Chief Human Resources Officer: Jill B. Smart
Chief Leadership Officer: Adrian J. Lajtha, age 52
Group Chief Executive, Systems Integration and Technology: Karl-Heinz Floether, age 56
Group Chief Executive, Outsourcing: Kevin M. Campbell, age 48
Group Chief Executive, Management Consulting and Integrated Markets: Mark Foster, age 49
Group Chief Executive, Communications and High Tech: Martin I. (Marty) Cole, age 52
Group Chief Executive, Financial Services: Pierre Nanterme, age 49
SVP Finance: David P. Rowland
Managing Director, US Country: Lisa M. Mascolo, age 48
General Counsel, Secretary, and Compliance Officer: Douglas G. (Doug) Scrivner, age 57
Principal Accounting Officer and Controller: Anthony G. Coughlan, age 51
Senior Director Investor Relations: David Straube
Executive Director, Office of the CEO: Lori L. Lovelace
Auditors: KPMG LLP

LOCATIONS

HQ: Accenture Ltd
1345 Avenue of the Americas, New York, NY 10105
Phone: 917-452-4400   **Fax:** 917-527-9915
Web: www.accenture.com

2008 Sales

	% of total
Europe, the Middle East & Africa	49
Americas	42
Asia/Pacific	9
Total	**100**

PRODUCTS/OPERATIONS

2008 Sales

	% of total
Products	26
Communications & high tech	23
Financial services	22
Resources	17
Government	12
Total	**100**

Selected Practice Areas

Communications and high technology
 Communications
 Electronics and high technology
 Media and entertainment
Products
 Automotive
 Consumer goods and services
 Health and life sciences
 Industrial equipment
 Retail
 Transportation and travel services

Financial services
  Banking
  Capital markets
  Insurance
Resources
  Chemicals
  Energy
  Natural resources
  Utilities
Government

Selected Services

Business consulting
  Customer relationship management
  Finance and performance management
  Human performance
  Strategy
  Supply chain management
Outsourcing
  Application outsourcing
  Business process outsourcing (BPO)
    Customer contact
    Finance and accounting
    Human resources
    Learning
    Procurement
  Infrastructure outsourcing
Systems integration and technology
  Enterprise architecture
  Information management
  Infrastructure consulting
  Intellectual property
  Research and development

COMPETITORS

Bain & Company
BearingPoint
Booz Allen
Boston Consulting
Capgemini
Capgemini US
Charteris
Computer Sciences Corp.
Deloitte Consulting
EDS
IBM
McKinsey & Company
Perot Systems
Siemens AG
Towers Perrin
Unisys

HISTORICAL FINANCIALS

Company Type: Public

Income Statement

FYE: August 31

	REVENUE ($ mil.)	NET INCOME ($ mil.)	NET PROFIT MARGIN	EMPLOYEES
8/08	25,313.8	1,691.8	6.7%	186,000
8/07	21,452.7	1,243.1	5.8%	170,000
8/06	18,228.4	973.3	5.3%	140,000
8/05	17,094.4	940.5	5.5%	123,000
8/04	15,113.6	690.8	4.6%	100,000
Annual Growth	13.8%	25.1%	—	16.8%

2008 Year-End Financials

Debt ratio: 42.8%
Return on equity: 73.5%
Cash ($ mil.): 3,603
Current ratio: 1.34
Long-term debt ($ mil.): 1,088

No. of shares (mil.): 614
Dividends
  Yield: 1.0%
  Payout: 15.8%
Market value ($ mil.): 25,406

Stock History

NYSE: ACN

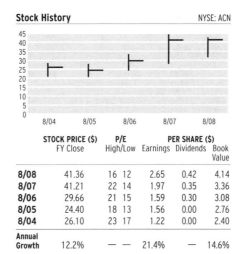

	STOCK PRICE ($) FY Close	P/E High/Low		PER SHARE ($) Earnings	Dividends	Book Value
8/08	41.36	16	12	2.65	0.42	4.14
8/07	41.21	22	14	1.97	0.35	3.36
8/06	29.66	21	15	1.59	0.30	3.08
8/05	24.40	18	13	1.56	0.00	2.76
8/04	26.10	23	17	1.22	0.00	2.40
Annual Growth	12.2%	—	—	21.4%	—	14.6%

Ace Hardware

Luckily, Ace has John Madden up its sleeve. Despite the growth of warehouse-style competitors, Ace Hardware has remained a household name, thanks to ads featuring Madden, a former Oakland Raiders football coach and newly retired TV commentator. By sales the company is the #1 hardware cooperative in the US, ahead of Do It Best. Ace dealer-owners operate more than 4,600 Ace Hardware stores, home centers, and lumber and building materials locations in all 50 US states and about 60 other countries. From about 15 warehouses Ace distributes such products as electrical and plumbing supplies, garden equipment, hand tools, housewares, and power tools. Ace's paint division is a major paint manufacturer in the US.

It also makes its own brand of paint and offers thousands of other Ace-brand products. In addition to its own-brand paints, Ace began offering Benjamin Moore products in its stores in 2006.

Ace additionally provides training programs and advertising campaigns for its dealers. Ace dealers own the company and receive dividends from Ace's profits.

Challenged by big-box chains such as The Home Depot and Lowe's, Ace unveiled its Next Generation store concept, which involves signage with detailed product descriptions and different flooring to set off departments, among other features. The company is also focusing on opening smaller neighborhood stores to entice customers who would rather not drive to edge-of-town big-box chains. In its most ambitious expansion plan to date, Ace Hardware will add 150 to 200 stores.

The company is also increasing the size of its stores. The average store is 10,000 sq. ft., but newer stores are about 14,000 sq. ft. To support store growth in the West, Ace is expanding its distribution center in Prescott Valley, Arizona.

In mid-2007 CEO Ray Griffith sent a letter to Ace's retailers, saying the company was considering changing from a cooperative to a traditional corporation to become more competitive and to better fuel growth.

Shortly after, the company announced a $154 million accounting shortfall uncovered while Ace prepared to convert formats. It then called off the conversion as it researched the error.

Following a review, the company determined that a mid-level employee made the accounting error accidentally. Ace plans to restore equity within two years.

HISTORY

A group of Chicago-area hardware dealers — William Stauber, Richard Hesse, Gern Lindquist, and Oscar Fisher — decided in 1924 to pool their hardware buying and promotional costs. In 1928 the group incorporated as Ace Stores, named in honor of the superior WWI fliers dubbed aces. Hesse became president the following year, retaining that position for the next 44 years. The company also opened its first warehouse in 1929, and by 1933 it had 38 dealers.

The organization had 133 dealers in seven states by 1949. In 1953 Ace began to allow dealers to buy stock in the company through the Ace Perpetuation Plan. During the 1960s Ace expanded into the South and West, and by 1969 it had opened distribution centers in Georgia and California — its first such facilities outside Chicago. In 1968 it opened its first international store in Guam.

By the early 1970s the do-it-yourself market began to surge as inflation pushed up plumber and electrician fees. As the market grew, large home center chains gobbled up market share from independent dealers such as those franchised through Ace. In response, Ace and its dealers became a part of a growing trend in the hardware industry — cooperatives.

Hesse sold the company to its dealers in 1973 for $6 million (less than half its book value), and the following year Ace began operating as a cooperative. Hesse stepped down in 1973. In 1976 the dealers took full control when the company's first Board of Dealer-Directors was elected.

After signing up a number of dealers in the eastern US, Ace had dealers in all 50 states by 1979. The co-op opened a plant to make paint in Matteson, Illinois, in 1984. By 1985 Ace had reached $1 billion in sales and had initiated its Store of the Future Program, allowing dealers to borrow up to $200,000 to upgrade their stores and conduct market analyses. Former head coach John Madden of the National Football League's Oakland Raiders signed on as Ace's mouthpiece in 1988.

A year later the co-op began to test ACENET, a computer network that allowed Ace dealers to check inventory, send and receive e-mail, make special purchase requests, and keep up with prices on commodity items such as lumber. In 1990 Ace established an International Division to handle its overseas stores. (It had been exporting products since 1975.) EVP and COO David Hodnik became president in 1995. That year the co-op added a net of 67 stores, including a three-store chain in Russia. Expanding further internationally, Ace signed a five-year joint-supply agreement in 1996 with Canadian lumber and hardware retailer Beaver Lumber. Hodnik added CEO to his title in 1996.

Ace fell further behind its old rival, True Value, in 1997 when ServiStar Coast to Coast and True Value merged to form TruServ (renamed True Value in 2005), a hardware giant that operated more than 10,000 outlets at the completion of the merger.

Late in 1997 Ace launched an expansion program in Canada. (The co-op already operated distribution centers in Ontario and Calgary.) In

1999 Ace merged its lumber and building materials division with Builder Marts of America to form a dealer-owned buying group to supply about 2,700 retailers. In 2000 Ace gained 208 member outlet stores, but saw 279 member outlets terminated. The next year it gained 220, but lost 255.

Sodisco-Howden bought all the shares of Ace Hardware Canada in February 2003. To better serve international members, Ace opened its first international buying office, in Hong Kong, in April 2004.

In all, the company added 131 new stores in 2005. That year, after 33 years with the company, David F. Hodnik retired as president and CEO of Ace Hardware. He was succeeded by COO Ray A. Griffith.

EXECUTIVES

Chairman: David S. Ziegler
President and CEO: Ray A. Griffith, age 54
CFO: Dorvin D. Lively, age 49
EVP: Rita D. Kahle
SVP International and Paint: David F. (Dave) Myer
SVP Retail Operations: Kenneth L. (Ken) Nichols
SVP, General Counsel, and Secretary:
  Arthur J. (Art) McGivern
VP Merchandising, Marketing, and Advertising:
  Lori L. Bossmann
VP Information Technology: Michael G. (Mike) Elmore
VP Human Resources: Jimmy Alexander
VP Business Development: John Venhuizen, age 37
VP Retail Support: William J. (Bill) Bauman
VP Supply Chain: Daniel C. (Dan) Prochaska
VP Retail Operations: Kane Calamari
Media Contact and Public Relations:
  Christopher Boniface
Auditors: KPMG LLP

LOCATIONS

HQ: Ace Hardware Corporation
  2200 Kensington Ct., Oak Brook, IL 60523
Phone: 630-990-6600   **Fax:** 630-990-6838
Web: www.acehardware.com

COMPETITORS

84 Lumber
Akzo Nobel
Benjamin Moore
Building Materials Holding
Costco Wholesale
Do it Best
Fastenal
Grossman's
Handy Hardware Wholesale
Home Depot
Kmart
Lowe's
McCoy Corp.
Menard
Northern Tool
Orgill
Reno-Depot
Sears
Sherwin-Williams
Stock Building Supply
Sutherland Lumber
True Value
United Hardware Distributing
Wal-Mart

HISTORICAL FINANCIALS
Company Type: Cooperative

Income Statement
FYE: Saturday nearest December 31

	REVENUE ($ mil.)	NET INCOME ($ mil.)	NET PROFIT MARGIN	EMPLOYEES
12/08	3,864.2	85.8	2.2%	4,800
12/07	3,970.6	86.9	2.2%	4,800
12/06	3,770.0	107.4	2.8%	5,000
12/05	3,466.0	100.4	2.9%	4,976
12/04	3,288.7	101.9	3.1%	5,000
Annual Growth	4.1%	(4.2%)	—	(1.0%)

Net Income History

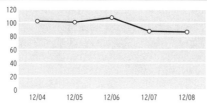

Activision Blizzard

Video game maker Activision Blizzard is a firm believer that action speaks louder than words. The video game publisher is best known for title franchises such as *World of Warcraft, Guitar Hero, Tony Hawk, Doom,* and *Call of Duty*. It also makes games based on licensed properties from LucasArts (*Star Wars*), Marvel (*Spider-Man* and *X-Men*), and DreamWorks Animation (*Shrek*). Its titles are produced for console game systems and handheld devices from Sony, Microsoft, and Nintendo. In 2008 Vivendi acquired a 52% stake in the company in a deal valued at $9.8 billion; Vivendi combined Activision with Vivendi Games (and its Blizzard Entertainment division) to form Activision Blizzard.

Part of Vivendi's strategy behind the Activision purchase was to leverage Activision's existing relationships with movie and media companies, which can lead to profitable video game tie-ins to films and their sequels. Vivendi also was eager to add Activision's prize *Guitar Hero* franchise to its stable of titles.

Activision-Blizzard owns the exclusive rights to develop and publish video games based on Marvel's comic book and film franchises: *Spider-Man, X-Men, Fantastic Four,* and *Iron Man*. It has a similar deal with DreamWorks Animation that grants the company the exclusive rights to publish games based on existing properties, such as *Shrek* and *Madagascar.*

In 2008 Activision-Blizzard sold its game studio Massive Entertainment (publishers of the *World in Conflict* franchise) to UbiSoft. That same year Activision-Blizzard beefed up its music genre offerings through the purchase of Freestyle Games and also strengthened its development capabilities for Nintendo titles through the acquisition of Budcat Creations.

HISTORY

James Levy and four former Atari software designers founded Activision in 1979 to supply game cartridges to Atari. The company went public in 1983. Despite Activision's initial success, Atari's downfall in the 1980s left the company struggling to stay afloat. Levy departed in 1987, and in 1988 new management renamed the company Mediagenic and attempted to transform it into a maker of PC software. Three years later BHK, headed by Robert Kotick, bought a controlling interest in Mediagenic. The company then reorganized under Chapter 11 bankruptcy and changed its name back to Activision.

By 1996 Activision's heavy investment in game development put the company back in the black. The company enhanced its international profile the next year through acquisitions of Take Us! Marketing & Consulting (software for German markets) and UK software distributor CentreSoft. Activision's growth continued in 1998 with its acquisition of Head Games Publishing (sports-oriented CD-ROM games). That year Activision obtained the rights to distribute LucasArts' PC and PlayStation games and expanded its list of game titles through agreements with companies such as Disney, Marvel, and Viacom.

The company's acquisitive streak continued in 1999 with purchases of Expert Software (budget-priced game software) and Elsinore Multimedia (Windows-based games). That year it introduced *Tony Hawk's Pro Skater,* which went on to sell more than 3.5 million copies. Its successes did not keep the company from posting a loss in 2000, however, and as its stock price began sinking, Activision restructured its operations and closed Expert Software. With a focus on its existing brands and other proven properties, including new Tony Hawk titles, the company experienced record growth while the rest of the industry suffered from sluggish sales. Activision also began developing titles for next-generation game systems such as Sony's PlayStation 2 and Microsoft's Xbox.

In 2001 the company bought action and action-sports game developer Treyarch Invention. The following year Activision bought the remaining 60% of Grey Matter Interactive Studios it didn't already own.

In 2002 Activision acquired 30% of Infinity Ward, the developer of *Call of Duty*; in 2003 the company bought the other 70%.

In 2007 the company acquired Bizarre Creations (the company behind the *Project Gotham Racing* and *Geometry Wars* franchises) and Red Octane (*Guitar Hero*). It also purchased network middleware developer DemonWare.

EXECUTIVES

Chairman: Jean-Bernard Lévy, age 54
Co-Chairman: Brian G. Kelly, age 46
Vice Chairman: Bruce L. Hack, age 60
President, CEO, and Director:
  Robert A. (Bobby) Kotick, age 46
CFO and Chief Corporate Officer: Thomas Tippl, age 42
Chief Legal Officer: George L. Rose, age 47
Chief Human Resources Officer: Ann Weiser, age 51
Chief Merger Officer: Jean-Francois Grollemund, age 64
Chief Customer Officer: Brian Hodous, age 45
SVP and Managing Director, European Publishing:
  Thibaud de Saint-Quentin

President and CEO, Red Octane:
Daniel L. (Dan) Rosensweig, age 45
President and CEO, Activision Publishing:
Michael J. Griffith, age 52
President and CEO, Blizzard Entertainment:
Michael (Mike) Morhaime, age 41
Chief Creative Officer, Activision Publishing:
Brad Jakeman
Auditors: PricewaterhouseCoopers LLP

LOCATIONS

HQ: Activision Blizzard, Inc.
3100 Ocean Park Blvd., Santa Monica, CA 90405
Phone: 310-255-2000   **Fax:** 310-255-2100
Web: www.activisionblizzard.com

2008 Sales

	$ mil.	% of total
North America	1,494	49
Europe	1,288	43
Asia/Pacific	227	8
Other	17	—
Total	**3,026**	**100**

PRODUCTS/OPERATIONS

2008 Sales

	$ mil.	% of total
Product sales	1,872	62
Subscription, licensing & other	1,154	38
Total	**3,026**	**100**

COMPETITORS

Capcom
Disney Interactive Studios
Eidos
Electronic Arts
Konami
LucasArts
Microsoft
Midway Games
Namco Limited
Nintendo
SEGA
Sony
Square Enix Holdings Co.
Take-Two
THQ
Ubisoft

HISTORICAL FINANCIALS

Company Type: Public

Income Statement

	REVENUE ($ mil.)	NET INCOME ($ mil.)	NET PROFIT MARGIN	EMPLOYEES
12/08*	3,026.0	(107.0)	—	7,000
3/08	2,898.1	344.9	11.9%	2,640
3/07	1,513.0	85.8	5.7%	2,125
3/06	1,468.0	41.9	2.9%	2,149
3/05	1,405.9	138.3	9.8%	1,728
Annual Growth	**21.1%**	**—**	**—**	**41.9%**

FYE: December 31
*Fiscal year change

2008 Year-End Financials

Debt ratio: —
Return on equity: —
Cash ($ mil.): 2,958
Current ratio: 2.37
Long-term debt ($ mil.): —

No. of shares (mil.): 1,272
Dividends
 Yield: 0.0%
 Payout: —
Market value ($ mil.): 10,986

Stock History   NASDAQ (GS): ATVI

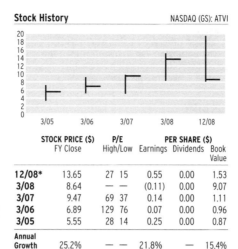

	STOCK PRICE ($) FY Close	P/E High/Low		PER SHARE ($) Earnings	Dividends	Book Value
12/08*	13.65	27	15	0.55	0.00	1.53
3/08	8.64	—	—	(0.11)	0.00	9.07
3/07	9.47	69	37	0.14	0.00	1.11
3/06	6.89	129	76	0.07	0.00	0.96
3/05	5.55	28	14	0.25	0.00	0.87
Annual Growth	**25.2%**	**—**	**—**	**21.8%**	**—**	**15.4%**

*Fiscal year change

Adams Resources & Energy

Bud Adams may have moved his football team to Tennessee years ago, but his Adams Resources & Energy remains a Houston oiler. Subsidiary Gulfmark Energy buys crude oil at the wellhead for transport to refiners and other customers via more than 110 trucks, and the company's Ada Resources subsidiary markets refined petroleum products such as gasoline and diesel fuel. With exploration and production mainly in Texas and Louisiana, Adams Resources boasts proved reserves of 6.4 billion cu. ft. of natural gas and 230,000 barrels of oil. The company's primary operations are all within a 1,000-mile radius of Houston. Chairman and CEO Adams, owner of the NFL's Tennessee Titans, controls 49.3% of the company.

Adams Resources also owns and operates Service Transport, a trucking firm that delivers petroleum products and liquid chemicals to about 400 customers throughout the continental US and Canada.

Adams Resources Exploration Corporation explores for oil and gas, primarily on the Louisiana and Texas Gulf Coast. In 2008 it held stakes in more than 320 wells and operated 40 of them.

Diversifying its geographical coverage, in 2009 the company announced that it had taken a second stake in an oil and gas exploration project in the UK North Sea.

HISTORY

Bud Adams founded Ada Oil in 1947 to explore for and produce oil and gas. These operations, with some real estate holdings, formed the core of what became Adams Resources when the company went public in 1974. An investment in coal in Illinois and Kentucky led to $65 million in losses in 1981 and the closure of those operations. In 1992 Adams Resources bought GulfMark Energy, a crude oil trading company that specialized in oil transport and the marketing of specialty grades of crude.

When intrastate trucking was deregulated in 1995, Adams Resources faced new competition in Texas, where it made 40% of its trucking sales. The company had to cut prices that year, and transportation earnings fell 30%. Adams Resources enjoyed greater production from successful gas wells in the Austin Chalk region in 1996, and the company and partner Nuevo Energy added three wells in Austin Chalk the next year.

Adams Resources completed a 7.5-mile offshore Louisiana crude oil pipeline in 1998, which boosted the company's Gulf of Mexico crude oil throughput by more than 15,000 barrels per day.

The company expanded its operations in 1999 by setting up Adams Resources Marketing as a wholesale purchaser, distributor, and marketer of natural gas. In 2000 it ramped up operations in the US Northeast by forming a regional retail marketing group to sell natural gas and other energy products.

Unusually warm winter weather and charges related to its Enron contracts (Enron had been a major customer) depressed the company's results in 2001. However, Adams Resources & Energy is focusing on niche markets where the company has a strong track record, in order to boost profitability and to reduce the level of price risks associated with its operations. After 2002 results were still below expectations, the company bounced back in 2003.

EXECUTIVES

Chairman and CEO: K. S. (Bud) Adams Jr., age 86, $359,916 total compensation
President, COO, and Director: Frank T. (Chip) Webster, age 60, $508,435 total compensation
VP and CFO: Richard B. (Rick) Abshire, age 56, $348,928 total compensation
Chief Accounting Officer and Treasurer: Sharon Davis
President, Adams Resources Exploration:
James Brock Moore III, age 65
President, Service Transport Company:
Claude H. Lewis, age 65
President, Adams Resources Marketing: Tony A. Gant, age 56
President, GulfMark Energy: Geoffrey L. (Geoff) Griffith
President, Ada Resources: James L. Smith
Secretary: David B. Hurst
Corporate Communications: John Riney
Investor Relations: Willie J. Draves
Auditors: Deloitte & Touche LLP

LOCATIONS

HQ: Adams Resources & Energy, Inc.
4400 Post Oak Pkwy., Ste. 2700, Houston, TX 77027
Phone: 713-881-3600   **Fax:** 713-881-3491
Web: www.adamsresources.com

Adams Resources produces oil and gas in Texas and Louisiana; markets oil and gas products on the Gulf Coast and in New England; and provides energy transportation services throughout the US and Canada.

PRODUCTS/OPERATIONS

Selected Subsidiaries

Ada Crude Oil Company
Ada Mining Corporation
Ada Resources, Inc. (petroleum products marketing)
Ada Resources Marketing, Inc. (wholesale natural gas marketing)
Adams Resources Exploration Corporation
Adams Resources Marketing, Ltd. (natural gas marketing)
Bayou City Pipelines, Inc.
Buckley Mining Corporation
CJC Leasing, Inc.
Classic Coal Corporation
Gulfmark Energy, Inc. (crude oil marketing)
Service Transport Company (liquid chemicals and petroleum products transport)

COMPETITORS

Abraxas Petroleum	Chevron
Anadarko Petroleum	EOG
Apache	Exxon
BP	Pioneer Natural Resources
Cabot Oil & Gas	Royal Dutch Shell

HISTORICAL FINANCIALS

Company Type: Public

Income Statement				FYE: December 31
	REVENUE ($ mil.)	NET INCOME ($ mil.)	NET PROFIT MARGIN	EMPLOYEES
12/08	4,159.7	(5.6)	—	806
12/07	2,636.2	17.1	0.6%	742
12/06	2,246.6	10.5	0.5%	748
12/05	2,364.8	17.6	0.7%	745
12/04	2,069.8	8.6	0.4%	672
Annual Growth	19.1%	—	—	4.7%

2008 Year-End Financials

Debt ratio: 0.0%
Return on equity: —
Cash ($ mil.): 18
Current ratio: 1.33
Long-term debt ($ mil.): 0
No. of shares (mil.): 4
Dividends
  Yield: 2.9%
  Payout: —
Market value ($ mil.): 72

Stock History

NYSE Alternext: AE

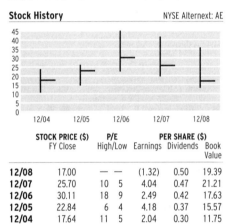

	STOCK PRICE ($) FY Close	P/E High/Low		PER SHARE ($) Earnings	Dividends	Book Value
12/08	17.00	—	—	(1.32)	0.50	19.39
12/07	25.70	10	5	4.04	0.47	21.21
12/06	30.11	18	9	2.49	0.42	17.63
12/05	22.84	6	4	4.18	0.37	15.57
12/04	17.64	11	5	2.04	0.30	11.75
Annual Growth	(0.9%)	—	—	—	13.6%	13.3%

Administaff, Inc.

Administaff handles the payroll so you don't have to. The company is one of the leading professional employer organizations (PEOs) in the US, providing small and midsized companies such services as payroll and benefits administration, workers' compensation programs, personnel records management, and employee recruiting. As a PEO, it is a co-employer of its clients' workers. Administaff also offers Web-based services through its Employee Service Center and operates a business-to-business e-commerce site. Most of its client companies are engaged in the business, financial, and computer services industries.

Administaff has almost 50 sales offices serving more than 20 US markets (expansion plans call for 90 offices in 40 markets). Its business in Texas accounts for about 30% of sales. The company has also opened a fourth service center in Los An-geles. Administaff's long-term goal is to handle human resource services for about 10% of the small and midsized businesses in the US.

The company also focuses on maintaining a consistent client retention rate, which has averaged 79% over the last five years.

HISTORY

Gerald McIntosh and Paul Sarvadi founded Administaff in 1986. The two entrepreneurs saw growth potential in employee leasing, despite the industry's image problems (Sarvadi had worked briefly for James Borgelt, who founded several Dallas-area employee leasing firms and was sentenced to three years in prison in 1996 for stealing from clients).

By 1991 Administaff had become one of the largest employee leasing companies in the US. That year it joined 17 other leasing companies in filing a suit against the Texas State Board of Insurance, which had tried to prohibit leasing companies from buying workers' compensation insurance. Regulators claimed leasing companies were touting their services as a way to avoid high workers' comp premiums. In 1993 a compromise law allowed employee leasing companies to buy workers' comp insurance based on the clients' on-the-job accident history.

With about 1,500 clients, Administaff went public in 1997. The following year the company formed a marketing agreement with American Express, under which the travel and financial services giant refers smaller business clients to Administaff for a fee. It began offering Web-based services during 1999 with Administaff Assistant (now Employee Service Center) and launched Internet portal site bizzport (now My MarketPlace) in 2000. It also began building its fourth service center in Los Angeles (completed in 2002). By the next year the company's client roster had grown to more than 4,000 companies.

In 2002 Administaff acquired the assets of Virtual Growth Incorporated, which provided outsourced accounting services. Also that year it launched (with IBM) HR PowerHouse, a human resources Web site targeting small businesses. In 2005 it bought HRTools.com.

EXECUTIVES

Chairman and CEO: Paul J. Sarvadi, age 52, $2,423,119 total compensation
President and Director: Richard G. Rawson, age 60, $1,505,799 total compensation
EVP Client Services and COO: A. Steve Arizpe, age 51, $1,747,023 total compensation
EVP Sales and Marketing: Jay E. Mincks, age 55, $1,578,390 total compensation
SVP Finance, CFO, and Treasurer: Douglas S. (Doug) Sharp, age 47, $1,229,953 total compensation
SVP Enterprise and Technology Solutions: Samuel G. (Sam) Larson
SVP Strategic Alliances: Randall H. (Randy) McCollum
SVP Client Selection and Pricing: Roger L. Gaskamp
SVP Service Operations: Gregory R. (Greg) Clouse
SVP Corporate Human Resources: Betty L. Collins
SVP Sales: Martin K. (Marty) Scirratt
SVP Strategic Planning: Mark W. Allen
SVP Legal, General Counsel, and Secretary: Daniel D. Herink, age 42
SVP Property and Casualty Products and Services: Ronald M. McGee
Managing Director Marketing and Corporate Communications: Jason Cutbirth
Auditors: Ernst & Young LLP

LOCATIONS

HQ: Administaff, Inc.
19001 Crescent Springs Dr., Kingwood, TX 77339
Phone: 281-358-8986   **Fax:** 281-348-3718
Web: www.administaff.com

2008 Sales

	$ mil.	% of total
Southwest	569.7	33
Northeast	363.3	21
West	345.7	20
Central	249.1	14
Southeast	183.1	11
Other	13.5	1
Total	**1,724.4**	**100**

PRODUCTS/OPERATIONS

Selected Products and Services

Benefits and payroll administration
e-business services
Employee recruiting and selection
Employer liability management
Health insurance programs
Performance management
Personnel records management
Training and development
Workers' compensation programs

COMPETITORS

ADP	Paychex
All Staff HR Group	TeamStaff
CompuPay	TriNet Group
Kelly Services	

HISTORICAL FINANCIALS

Company Type: Public

Income Statement				FYE: December 31
	REVENUE ($ mil.)	NET INCOME ($ mil.)	NET PROFIT MARGIN	EMPLOYEES
12/08	1,724.4	45.8	2.7%	2,060
12/07	1,570.0	47.5	3.0%	117,301
12/06	1,389.5	46.5	3.3%	104,325
12/05	1,169.6	30.0	2.6%	88,780
12/04	969.5	19.2	2.0%	1,350
Annual Growth	15.5%	24.3%	—	11.1%

2008 Year-End Financials

Debt ratio: 0.0%
Return on equity: 22.5%
Cash ($ mil.): 252
Current ratio: 1.28
Long-term debt ($ mil.): 0
No. of shares (mil.): 26
Dividends
  Yield: 2.2%
  Payout: 26.8%
Market value ($ mil.): 554

Stock History

NYSE: ASF

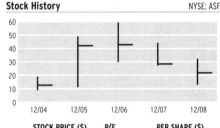

	STOCK PRICE ($) FY Close	P/E High/Low		PER SHARE ($) Earnings	Dividends	Book Value
12/08	21.68	18	7	1.79	0.48	8.17
12/07	28.28	25	16	1.74	0.44	7.78
12/06	42.77	36	18	1.64	0.36	8.95
12/05	42.05	43	10	1.12	0.28	7.14
12/04	12.61	26	13	0.72	0.00	4.96
Annual Growth	14.5%	—	—	25.6%	—	13.3%

Adobe Systems

Adobe Systems' role as a leading desktop publishing software provider is well documented. The company offers the ubiquitous Acrobat Reader (distributed free of charge), a tool that displays portable document format (PDF) files on the Internet. The company's Web and print publishing products include Photoshop, Illustrator, and PageMaker. Adobe's offerings also include print technology geared toward manufacturers, as well as Web design (Dreamweaver) and electronic book publishing software. Its InDesign publishing package provides professional layout and design applications. Adobe's Professional Services group offers implementation, training, and support.

Graphics and Web designers, technical writers, photographers, and other publishing professionals use Adobe's products to create online and print-based documents. The company's largest product segment, creative solutions, accounts for more than half of Adobe's revenues; products in the segment include InDesign, a professional page layout product that competes primarily against Quark's XPress product, as well as its popular Photoshop image editor.

Though products designed for creative professionals remain Adobe's bread and butter, the company continues to expand its market focus. Adobe launched a beta version of Acrobat.com, an online collaboration service for the enterprise market, in 2008. The following year it moved the site to a subscription-based model, charging for shared access to PDF creation applications and other productivity tools.

Though Adobe generates the majority of its sales through Web and print products, the company's activities aren't limited to developing its own software. In addition to direct investments in a handful of high-tech companies, it holds an interest in a venture partnership managed by Granite Ventures. Adobe has investments in more than 30 companies (including Convio and PSS Systems) whose products and services complement its own.

HISTORY

When Charles Geschke hired John Warnock as chief scientist for Xerox's new graphics and imaging lab, he set the stage for one of the world's largest software makers. While at the Xerox lab, the pair developed the PostScript computer language, which tells printers how to reproduce digitized images on paper. When Xerox refused to market it, the duo left that company and started Adobe (named after a creek near their homes in San Jose, California) in 1982.

Their original plan was to produce an electronic document processing system based on PostScript, but the company changed direction when Apple whiz Steve Jobs hired it to co-design the software for his company's LaserWriter printer. A year later Adobe went public. Meanwhile, PostScript was pioneering the desktop publishing industry by enabling users to laser print nearly anything they created on a computer.

In 1987 the company branched into the European market with the establishment of subsidiary Adobe Systems Europe. It also entered the PC market by adapting PostScript for IBM's operating system. Two years later the company began marketing its products in Asia.

Adobe grew throughout the 1990s by acquiring other software firms, including OCR Systems and Nonlinear Technologies (1992), and AH Software and Science & Art (1993). In 1993 the company began licensing its PostScript software to printer manufacturers; it also started marketing its Acrobat software.

Adobe bought Aldus (1994), whose PageMaker software had been instrumental in establishing the desktop publishing market. (PageMaker's success depended on the font software that Adobe made and the two companies had a history of cooperation.) Next the company bought Frame Technology (FrameMaker publishing software, 1995), but that acquisition proved disastrous. Frame sales plummeted, partly the result of Adobe's move to eliminate Frame's technical support operations. Adobe's purchase of Web toolmaker Ceneca Communications that year was more fruitful.

In 1996 Adobe spun off its pre-press applications operations as Luminous. That year its licensing sales suffered a blow when one of its largest customers, Hewlett-Packard, introduced a clone version of PostScript. Also in 1997, for the first time, Adobe's revenues from Windows-based software exceeded those of its once-dominant Macintosh-based software.

In 1998 a takeover bid by competitor Quark proved unsuccessful. Drooping sales that year, which Adobe blamed on the Asian crisis (although some analysts blamed it on Adobe's product strategy), prompted the company to shed a layer of executives, 10% of its workforce, and its Adobe Enterprise Publishing Services and Image Club Graphics units. Its 1999 acquisition of GoLive Systems expanded its Web publishing product line. That year Adobe released professional page layout application InDesign, which immediately spurred the biggest backlog in the company's history.

In December 2000 CEO Warnock passed the reins to president Bruce Chizen. Warnock remained co-chairman along with Geschke. The company boosted its electronic book offerings by acquiring software maker Glassbook.

In early 2003 the company restructured its divisions, creating its Creative Professional segment to replace the Cross-media Publishing division, and its Digital Imaging and Video unit to replace its former Graphics division. This realignment was a part of Adobe's plan to focus on its core market of creative professionals. In order to expand its digital video offerings, the company also acquired the assets of digital audio tools-maker Syntrillium Software that year.

In 2004 the company acquired OKYZ, a Paris-based maker of 3D collaboration software; the acquisition added 3D technology to Adobe's Intelligent Document Platform.

Adobe acquired rival Macromedia for approximately $3.4 billion in stock late in 2005. Macromedia's popular Web site design and animation tools included Dreamweaver and Flash.

Adobe acquired Trade and Technologies France (TTF), a developer of CAD data interoperability software, in 2006.

Adobe acquired publishing software provider Scene7 in 2007. It also purchased online word processing software developer Virtual Ubiquity.

Late in 2007, COO Shantanu Narayen succeeded Chizen as CEO.

EXECUTIVES

Co-Chairman: Charles M. (Chuck) Geschke
Co-Chairman: John E. Warnock, age 68
President, CEO, and Director: Shantanu Narayen, age 46, $8,433,578 total compensation
EVP and CFO: Mark S. Garrett, age 51, $3,009,747 total compensation
SVP and CTO: Kevin M. Lynch, age 43, $3,243,968 total compensation
SVP and CIO: Gerri Martin-Flickinger
SVP and Chief Software Architect, Advanced Technology Labs: Tom Malloy
SVP, General Counsel, and Secretary: Karen O. Cottle, age 60
SVP Corporate Marketing and Communications: Ann Lewnes
SVP and General Manager, Adobe Business Productivity Business Unit: Robert M. (Rob) Tarkoff, age 41
SVP Human Resources: Donna Morris
SVP Creative Solutions Business Unit: John P. (Johnny) Loiacono, $2,499,231 total compensation
SVP Worldwide Sales and Field Operations: Matthew A. (Matt) Thompson, age 50, $2,618,685 total compensation
SVP Print and Classic Publishing Solutions Business Unit; Managing Director, India Research and Development: Naresh Gupta
SVP Engineering Technologies Group: Digby Horner
SVP Corporate Development: Paul Weiskopf
VP Corporate Affairs and Communications: Kevin Burr
VP, Corporate Controller, and Principal Accounting Officer: Richard T. Rowley, age 50
VP Marketing: Andrew F. (Andy) Young, age 49
VP Investor Relations: Mike Saviage
Auditors: KPMG LLP

LOCATIONS

HQ: Adobe Systems Incorporated
345 Park Ave., San Jose, CA 95110
Phone: 408-536-6000   **Fax:** 408-537-6000
Web: www.adobe.com

2008 Sales

	$ mil.	% of total
Americas		
US	1,473.3	41
Other countries	159.5	4
Europe, Middle East & Africa	1,229.2	34
Asia		
Japan	450.8	13
Other countries	267.1	8
Total	**3,579.9**	**100**

PRODUCTS/OPERATIONS

2008 Sales

	$ mil.	% of total
Products	3,396.5	95
Services	183.4	5
Total	**3,579.9**	**100**

2008 Sales

	$ mil.	% of total
Creative solutions	2,072.8	58
Knowledge worker solutions	810.9	23
Enterprise	253.0	7
Print & publishing	211.6	6
Platform	118.5	3
Mobile & device solutions	113.1	3
Total	**3,579.9**	**100**

COMPETITORS

ACD Systems International
Apple Inc.
ArcSoft
Autodesk
Avid Technology
Bare Bones Software
Canon
Citrix Systems
Corel
Dell
Eastman Kodak
Google
Hewlett-Packard
IBM
Interwoven
Lombardi Software
Microsoft
Monotype
Nexaweb
Nikon
Nuance
Oracle
Pegasystems
Pinnacle Systems
Quark
RealNetworks
Sonic Solutions
Sony
Sun Microsystems
TIBCO Software
Ultimus
Vignette
WebEx
Xara
Yahoo!
Zinio Systems

HISTORICAL FINANCIALS

Company Type: Public

Income Statement				FYE: Friday nearest November 30
	REVENUE ($ mil.)	NET INCOME ($ mil.)	NET PROFIT MARGIN	EMPLOYEES
11/08	3,579.9	871.8	24.4%	7,335
11/07	3,157.9	723.8	22.9%	6,959
11/06	2,575.3	505.8	19.6%	6,082
11/05	1,966.3	602.8	30.7%	5,734
11/04	1,666.6	450.4	27.0%	3,142
Annual Growth	21.1%	18.0%	—	23.6%

2008 Year-End Financials

Debt ratio: 7.9%
Return on equity: 19.2%
Cash ($ mil.): 886
Current ratio: 3.59
Long-term debt ($ mil.): 350

No. of shares (mil.): 525
Dividends
Yield: 0.0%
Payout: —
Market value ($ mil.): 12,159

Stock History

NASDAQ (GS): ADBE

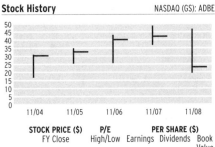

	STOCK PRICE ($) FY Close	P/E High/Low	PER SHARE ($) Earnings	Dividends	Book Value
11/08	23.16	29 12	1.59	0.00	8.40
11/07	42.14	40 31	1.21	0.00	8.86
11/06	40.16	52 31	0.83	0.00	9.81
11/05	32.61	29 22	1.19	0.01	3.55
11/04	30.28	34 19	0.91	0.03	2.71
Annual Growth	(6.5%)	— —	15.0%	—	32.7%

Advance Publications

Advance Publications gets its marching orders from the printed page. A leading US newspaper publisher, Advance owns daily newspapers in some 20 cities around the country, including *The Star-Ledger* (New Jersey), *The Cleveland Plain Dealer*, and its namesake *Staten Island Advance*. It also owns American City Business Journals (more than 40 weekly papers) and Parade Publications (*Parade Magazine* Sunday insert). The company is a top magazine publisher through its Condé Nast unit. Aside from print publishing, Advance is a major online publisher through its Advance Internet network of local news sites; Advance additionally owns television assets. Samuel "Si" Newhouse Jr. and his brother, Donald, own the company.

The company's Condé Nast unit publishes such popular titles as *Allure*, *The New Yorker*, and *Vanity Fair*. Internet properties such as Epicurious (food and dining) and Concierge (travel) are run through its Condé Nast Digital unit. Trade journal publisher Fairchild Fashion Group (*Women's Wear Daily*) is also a division of Condé Nast.

The company has interests in cable television through affiliate Advance/Newhouse Communications, which owns cable systems operator Bright House Networks through a partnership with Time Warner Cable. Advance/Newhouse also controls 33% of Discovery Communications (DCI) after joining with partner Discovery Holding to spin off the cable broadcasting venture to the public.

The company's newspaper operations have been struggling due to sharp declines in advertising brought on by declining readership and the economic recession. Advance Publications shuttered its *Ann Arbor News* (Michigan) and replaced the paper with a local online news publication. The move came shortly after Hearst Newspapers announced a similar strategy for its *Seattle Post-Intelligencer*.

Meanwhile, Advance Publications' *Star-Ledger*, New Jersey's largest newspaper with a daily circulation of 350,000, cut almost half its editorial staff through voluntary buyouts during 2008 as part of a cost-saving effort. The following year the paper joined a consortium of four other papers in New York and New Jersey that will share content in an attempt to cover the news with fewer reporters. The group includes the *Star-Ledger*'s main rival, *The Record*, owned by North Jersey Media Group, and the *Daily News* of New York.

HISTORY

Solomon Neuhaus (later Samuel I. Newhouse) got started in the newspaper business after dropping out of school at age 13. He went to work at the *Bayonne Times* in New Jersey and was put in charge of the failing newspaper in 1911; he managed to turn the paper around within a year. In 1922 he bought the *Staten Island Advance* (founded in 1886) and formed the Staten Island Advance Company in 1924. After buying up more papers, he changed the name of the company to Advance Publications in 1949. By the 1950s the company had local papers in New York, New Jersey, and Alabama.

In 1959 Newhouse bought magazine publisher Condé Nast as an anniversary gift for his wife. (He joked that she had asked for a fashion magazine, so he bought her *Vogue*.) His publishing empire continued to grow with the addition of the *Times-Picayune* (New Orleans) in 1962 and *The Cleveland Plain Dealer* in 1967. In 1976 the company paid more than $300 million for Booth Newspapers, publisher of eight Michigan papers and *Parade Magazine*.

Newhouse died in 1979, leaving his sons Si and Donald to run the company, which encompassed more than 30 newspapers, a half-dozen magazines, and 15 cable systems. The next year Advance bought book publishing giant Random House from RCA. Si resurrected the Roaring Twenties standard *Vanity Fair* in 1983 and added *The New Yorker* under the Condé Nast banner in 1985. The Newhouses scored a victory over the IRS in 1990 after a long-running court battle involving inheritance taxes. Condé Nast bought Knapp Publications (*Architectural Digest*) in 1993 and Advance later acquired American City Business Journals in 1995.

In 1998 the company sold the increasingly unprofitable Random House to Bertelsmann for about $1.2 billion. It later bought hallmark Internet magazine *Wired* (though it passed on Wired Ventures' Internet operations). That year revered *New Yorker* editor Tina Brown, credited with jazzing up the publication's content and increasing its circulation, left the magazine; staff writer and Pulitzer Prize winner David Remnick was named as Brown's replacement.

In 1999 Advance joined Donrey Media Group (now called Stephens Media Group), E.W. Scripps, Hearst Corporation, and MediaNews Group to purchase the online classified advertising network AdOne (later named PowerOne Media). It also bought Walt Disney's trade publishing unit, Fairchile Publications (now Fairchild Fashion Group), for $650 million. In 2000 the company announced it would begin creating Web versions of its popular magazine titles.

In 2001 Condé Nast bought a majority stake in Miami-based Ideas Publishing Group (Spanish language versions of US magazines; its name was later changed to Condé Nast Americas). Also that year Advance bought four golf magazines, including *Golf Digest*, from the New York Times Company for $430 million. Condé Nast picked up *Modern Bride* magazine from PRIMEDIA in 2002 for $52 million.

Richard Diamond, a Newhouse relative who'd been publisher of the *Staten Island Advance* since 1979, died in 2004.

LOCATIONS

HQ: Advance Publications, Inc.
950 Fingerboard Rd., Staten Island, NY 10305
Phone: 718-981-1234   **Fax:** 718-981-1456
Web: www.advance.net

PRODUCTS/OPERATIONS

Selected Operations

Broadcasting and Communications
  Bright House Networks
  Discovery Communications (33%, cable TV channel)
Magazine Publishing
  Condé Nast Publications
    Fairchild Fashion Group
Selected Newspaper Publishing
  American City Business Journals (about 40 weekly
    titles in some 20 states)
    Sporting News
    Street & Smith's Sports Business Group
  Newhouse Newspapers (more than 30 papers across
    the US)
    The Birmingham News (Alabama)
    The Oregonian (Portland)
    The Plain Dealer (Cleveland)
    The Star-Ledger (Newark, NJ)
    Staten Island Advance (New York)
    The Times-Picayune (New Orleans)
  Parade Publications
Selected Online Publishing
  Advance Internet
    al.com (Alabama)
    cleveland.com
    MassLive.com (Massachusetts)
    MLive (Michigan)
    NJ.com (New Jersey)
    NOLA.com (New Orleans)
    OregonLive.com
    PennLive.com (Pennsylvania)
    SILive (New York)
    syracuse.com (New York)
  Condé Nast Digital
    Concierge (travel information)
    Epicurious (recipes and fine dining)
    STYLE.com (fashion and beauty)

COMPETITORS

American Express
American Media
Crain Communications
E. W. Scripps
Essence Communications
F+W Media
Forbes
Freedom Communications
Gannett
Gruner + Jahr
Hearst Corporation
Johnson Publishing
Lagardère Active
Martha Stewart Living
McClatchy Company
Meredith Corporation
New York Times
News Corp.
Newsweek
North Jersey Media
Reader's Digest
Reed Elsevier Group
Rodale
Time Inc.
Tribune Company
Washington Post
Wenner Media

HISTORICAL FINANCIALS

Company Type: Private

Income Statement

FYE: December 31

	ESTIMATED REVENUE ($ mil.)	NET INCOME ($ mil.)	NET PROFIT MARGIN	EMPLOYEES
12/07	7,970.0	—	—	29,100
12/06	7,700.0	—	—	28,000
12/05	7,315.0	—	—	30,000
Annual Growth	4.4%	—	—	(1.5%)

Revenue History

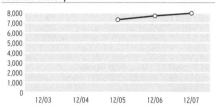

	12/03	12/04	12/05	12/06	12/07
8,000					
7,000					
6,000					
5,000					
4,000					
3,000					
2,000					
1,000					
0					

Advanced Micro Devices

Advanced Micro Devices (AMD) made some advances in its battle against Intel but hasn't capitalized on those gains. AMD ranks #2 in PC and server microprocessors, far behind its archrival. Though Intel commands about three-quarters of the world processor market, AMD at times eroded that market share thanks to the popularity of its Athlon and Opteron processor families. The company also makes embedded processors and other chips for communications and networking applications. Hewlett-Packard is AMD's biggest customer, and Chinese OEMs account for more than 40% of the company's sales. In early 2009 AMD split its operations, spinning off a manufacturing venture.

In 2008 AMD struck a deal with the Advanced Technology Investment Company (ATIC) of Abu Dhabi to form a new semiconductor manufacturing company that took over AMD's wafer fabrication facilities in Germany and the US. ATIC invested $2.1 billion, with $1.4 billion going into the new joint venture and $700 million being paid directly to AMD.

The manufacturing JV, known as GLOBALFOUNDRIES, assumed about $1.1 billion of AMD's debt. At its startup in 2009, GLOBALFOUNDRIES had some 2,800 employees and made its headquarters in Silicon Valley.

Since AMD owns about 34% of GLOBALFOUNDRIES, it retains an ownership interest in its manufacturing. The top two executives of GLOBALFOUNDRIES are executives from AMD. Still, the majority ownership of the spinoff will reside with ATIC, which will be writing the checks to build and upgrade the JV's production facilities. AMD improves its balance sheet and conserves cash with the deal; the loss-ridden chip maker gives up some control over its manufacturing, however. That will leave it at a competitive disadvantage to Intel, which funds and maintains its own worldwide network of wafer fabs.

In 2007 a unit of Mubadala Development Company took an equity stake of about 8% in the chip maker. Mubadala Development is the strategic-investment arm of Abu Dhabi's government, part of the United Arab Emirates. As part of the GLOBALFOUNDRIES spinoff, Mubadala Development boosted its stake to around 20%. It also received a seat on the AMD board.

Seeing sales slow across all business segments in 2008, as have many chip makers, AMD cut about 13% of its global workforce, more than 2,200 employees. The company eliminated another 1,100 jobs in early 2009, 900 through layoffs and the remainder through attrition and the sale of a business unit.

Under new CEO Dirk Meyer, the company agreed in 2008 to sell its digital TV (DTV) chip product line to Broadcom. In early 2009 the company sold graphics and multimedia assets from its handheld electronics business to QUALCOMM.

In 2009 the European Commission fined Intel about $1.44 billion based on complaints brought by AMD, alleging that Intel paid hidden rebates to PC makers to use only Intel processors in their products, and not AMD's processors. Intel is appealing the ruling.

HISTORY

Silicon Valley powerhouse Fairchild Camera & Instrument axed marketing whiz Jerry Sanders, reportedly for wearing a pink shirt on a sales call to IBM. In 1969 Sanders and seven friends started a semiconductor company (just as his former boss, Intel co-founder Robert Noyce, had done a year earlier) based on chip designs licensed from other companies.

Advanced Micro Devices (AMD) went public in 1972. Siemens, eager to enter the US semiconductor market, paid $30 million for nearly 20% of AMD in 1977. (Siemens had sold off its stake by 1991.) In 1982 AMD inked a deal with Intel that let AMD make exact copies of Intel's iAPX86 microprocessors, used in IBM and compatible PCs. By the mid-1980s the company was developing its own chips. In 1987 AMD sued Intel for breaking the 1982 agreement that allowed AMD to second-source Intel's new 386 chips. Intel countersued for copyright infringement when AMD introduced versions of Intel's 287 math coprocessor (1990), 386 chip (1991), and 486 chip (1993).

After a federal jury decided in AMD's favor in the 287 math coprocessor case in 1994, AMD and Intel settled their legal differences in 1995. Each agreed to pay damages, and AMD won a perpetual license to the microcode of Intel's 386 and 486 chips. AMD's K5 microprocessor (a rival of Intel's Pentium) hit the market in 1996 — more than a year late.

In 1996 AMD bought microprocessor developer NexGen Microsystems. AMD unveiled its K6 microprocessor the next year, but had trouble increasing production to meet demand. In 1999 AMD sold programmable logic chip unit Vantis to Lattice Semiconductor. The company debuted its Athlon (K7) chip in 1999 to positive reviews and soon won Compaq Computer and IBM as customers.

Early in 2000 AMD named Hector Ruiz (former head of Motorola's semiconductor operations) president and COO — and thus heir apparent — to Sanders. Improved manufacturing processes, increased sales of high-end Athlons, and a worldwide shortage of flash memory helped AMD turn a profit (and a big one) in 2000, its first since 1995. In the face of a dismal slump in the global chip business, though, AMD cut costs in 2001 by closing two chip plants in Texas and by cutting about 2,300 jobs — 15% of its total workforce — there and in Malaysia.

In 2002 Sanders handed over the CEO reins to Ruiz. In 2003 AMD joined long-time joint-venture partner Fujitsu in forming a new company, called FASL (later renamed Spansion), to pool the two chip makers' flash memory operations. AMD also bought National Semiconductor's Information Appliance unit, which made the Geode line of system-on-a-chip devices.

In 2004 Ruiz succeeded Sanders as chairman as well. AMD filed an antitrust suit against Intel in 2005, alleging that the chip giant had used improper subsidies and coercion to secure sales.

In 2006 AMD acquired ATI Technologies for about $5.4 billion in cash and stock. A year later, the company wrote off $1.3 billion in impaired goodwill on the deal.

After seven consecutive quarters of losses, Hector Ruiz stepped aside as CEO in mid-2008. He remained executive chairman. Dirk Meyer was promoted to CEO to succeed him; Meyer, a 13-year veteran of AMD, was promoted to president and COO of the company in 2006.

EXECUTIVES

Chairman: Bruce L. Claflin, age 57
President, CEO, and Director: Derrick R. (Dirk) Meyer, age 47, $1,914,183 total compensation
EVP, COO, Chief Administrative Officer, and CFO: Robert J. (Bob) Rivet Sr., age 54, $6,726,123 total compensation
EVP Legal, Corporate, and Public Affairs: Thomas M. (Tom) McCoy, age 58, $989,016 total compensation
CIO: Ahmed Mahmoud
SVP and Chief Innovation Officer: William T. (Billy) Edwards, age 51
SVP and Chief Sales Officer: Gustavo A. Arenas
SVP and Chief Marketing Officer: Nigel Dessau, age 44
SVP Human Resources and Chief Talent Officer: Allen Sockwell
SVP and Chief Sales Officer: Emilio Ghilardi, age 51
SVP Products Group: Rick Bergman, age 45
VP Consumer Business: Joseph H. (Joe) Menard
VP Technology Development: Craig Sander
VP Advanced Marketing: Patrick (Pat) Moorhead
VP, Corporate Alliances and Strategic Relations: Robert C. Melendres, age 44
VP; President and General Manager, AMD China: Karen Guo
VP Manufacturing Operations: K. Y. Wong
VP Accelerated Computing: Mike Uhler
VP Public Affairs: Allyson Peerman
President, EMEA: Guiliano Meroni
Secretary: Hollis O'Brien
Manager, Investor Relations: Ruth Cotter
Corporate Fellow: Phil Rogers
Auditors: Ernst & Young LLP

LOCATIONS

HQ: Advanced Micro Devices, Inc.
1 AMD Place, Sunnyvale, CA 94088
Phone: 408-749-4000   **Fax:** 408-982-6164
Web: www.amd.com

Advanced Micro Devices has manufacturing operations in China, Germany, Malaysia, Singapore, and the US. The company has sales offices worldwide.

2008 Sales

	$ mil.	% of total
China	2,553	44
Europe	1,067	18
US	704	12
Japan	207	4
Other countries	1,277	22
Total	**5,808**	**100**

PRODUCTS/OPERATIONS

2008 Sales

	$ mil.	% of total
Computing Solutions	4,559	79
Graphics	1,165	20
Other	84	1
Total	**5,808**	**100**

Selected Products

Computing
    Microprocessors (Athlon, Opteron, Phenom, Sempron, and Turion lines)
    Motherboard reference design kits and chipsets
Graphics
    Embedded graphics processing units for digital TVs and mobile devices
    Macintosh, notebook, and desktop PC graphics processors (Radeon)
    Motherboard chipsets (for AMD and Intel processors)
    PC TV (ATI TV Wonder, ATI Theater)
    Server and workstation graphics processing units
Personal connectivity
    Embedded processors (Geode line)
    Networking chips

COMPETITORS

Analog Devices
Applied Micro Circuits
ARM Holdings
Atmel
Broadcom
Centaur Technology
Epson
Fairchild Semiconductor
Freescale Semiconductor
Hitachi
IBM Microelectronics
Imagination Technologies
Infineon Technologies
Intel Corp.
LSI Corp.
Marvell Technology
Matrox Electronic Systems
MIPS Technologies
NEC Electronics
NVIDIA
NXP
Pixelworks
QUALCOMM
Renesas Technology
Samsung Electronics
SANYO Semiconductor
Sigma Designs
Silicon Image
Silicon Integrated Systems
Sony
STMicroelectronics
Sun Microsystems
Texas Instruments
Toshiba Semiconductor
VIA Technologies

HISTORICAL FINANCIALS

Company Type: Public

Income Statement

	REVENUE ($ mil.)	NET INCOME ($ mil.)	NET PROFIT MARGIN	EMPLOYEES
			FYE: Last Sunday in December	
12/08	5,808.0	(3,098.0)	—	14,700
12/07	6,013.0	(3,379.0)	—	16,420
12/06	5,649.0	(166.0)	—	16,500
12/05	5,847.6	165.5	2.8%	9,860
12/04	5,001.4	91.2	1.8%	15,900
Annual Growth	**3.8%**	**—**	**—**	**(1.9%)**

2008 Year-End Financials

Debt ratio: —   No. of shares (mil.): 668
Return on equity: —   Dividends
Cash ($ mil.): 933   Yield: 0.0%
Current ratio: 1.07   Payout: —
Long-term debt ($ mil.): 4,702   Market value ($ mil.): 1,442

Stock History

NYSE: AMD

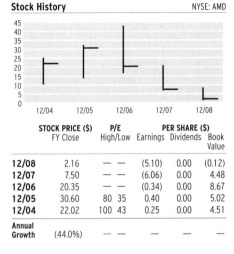

	STOCK PRICE ($) FY Close	P/E High/Low		PER SHARE ($) Earnings	Dividends	Book Value
12/08	2.16	—	—	(5.10)	0.00	(0.12)
12/07	7.50	—	—	(6.06)	0.00	4.48
12/06	20.35	—	—	(0.34)	0.00	8.67
12/05	30.60	80	35	0.40	0.00	5.02
12/04	22.02	100	43	0.25	0.00	4.51
Annual Growth	**(44.0%)**	**—**	**—**	**—**	**—**	**—**

The AES Corporation

The right place at the right time — Is it kismet? No, it's AES, one of the world's leading independent power producers. The company has interests in more than 120 generation facilities in about 30 countries throughout the Americas, Asia, Africa, Europe, and the Middle East that give it a combined net generating capacity of 43,000 MW. AES sells electricity to utilities and other energy marketers through wholesale contracts or on the spot market. AES also sells power directly to customers worldwide through its interests in distribution utilities, mainly in Latin America. In 2009 the company had 3,000 MW of power plants under development in ten countries.

To reduce carbon emissions the company is also developing alternative energy power plants, including wind, hydro, and biomass. In 2005 it began acquiring stakes in wind power generation firms. In 2008 it formed AES Solar Energy, a joint venture with investment firm Riverstone Holdings, to develop solar energy projects.

However, AES is still fond of older methods of power generation: coal-powered plants. AES has earmarked $150 million to build a coal-fueled power plant in El Salvador. The 250 MW plant, estimated to be operational by 2010, will be the first of its kind in the Latin American country. Owning four of the five electricity distribution companies in El Salvador, AES controls nearly 80% of the country's electric distribution utility.

AES has faced controversy in Brazil, where an unstable power market has caused the company to default on debts incurred from its purchases of stakes in local utilities (as well as bankrupt telecom firm Eletronet) in recent years. To restructure its debt with Banco Nacional de Desenvolvimento Economico e Social (BNDES), AES completed a deal in 2007 in which the firm's interests in AES Eletropaulo, AES Uruguaiana, AES Tiete, and AES Sul have been placed into a new holding company (Brasiliana Energia). AES owns 50.1% of the new company, while BNDES holds 49.9%.

HISTORY

Applied Energy Services (AES) was founded in 1981, three years after passage of the Public Utilities Regulation Policies Act, which enabled small power firms to enter electric generation markets formerly dominated by utility monopolies. Co-founders Roger Sant and Dennis Bakke, who had served in President Nixon's Federal Energy Administration, saw that an independent power producer (IPP) could make money by generating cheap power in large volumes to sell to large power consumers and utilities.

AES set about building massive cogeneration plants (producing both steam and electricity) in 1983. The first plant, Deepwater, went into operation near Houston in 1986. By 1989 AES had three plants on line, and it then opened plants in Connecticut and Oklahoma. In 1991 the company, formally renamed AES, went public, but one plant's falsified emissions reports caused AES's stock to plummet in 1992.

Facing environmental groups' opposition to new power plant construction and an overall glut in the US power market, AES bought interests in two Northern Ireland plants in 1992 and began expanding into Latin America in 1993. Also in 1993 AES set up a separately traded subsidiary, AES China Generating Co., to focus on Chinese development projects. AES won a plant development contract with the Puerto Rico Electric Power Authority (1994) and a bid to privatize an Argentine hydrothermal company (1995).

In 1996 AES began adding stakes in electric utility and distribution companies to its portfolio, including interests in formerly state-owned Brazilian electric utilities Light-Servicos de Eletricidade (1996) and CEMIG (1997); one Brazilian and two Argentine distribution companies (1997); and a distribution company in El Salvador (1998).

AES almost doubled its revenues after buying Destec Energy's international operations from NGC (now Dynegy) in 1997. By the next year, prospects in international markets were dimming, so AES turned to the US market again. It bought three California plants from Edison International and arranged for The Williams Companies to supply natural gas to the facilities and market the electricity generated. AES also won a bid to buy six plants from New York State Electric & Gas (now Energy East) affiliate NGE.

Also in 1998, despite black days in many world markets, AES bought 90% of Argentine electric distribution company Edelap and a 45% stake in state-owned Orissa Power Generation in India. Its moves paid off: AES posted a 70% gain in sales that year.

It bought CILCORP, an Illinois utility holding company, in an $886 million deal in 1999. Boosting its presence in the UK, AES bought the Drax power station, a 3,960-MW coal-fired plant, from National Power. It also bought a majority stake in Brazilian data transmission company Eletronet from Brazil's government-owned utility ELETROBRÁS. In 2000 AES increased its interests in Brazilian power distributors. It also gained a 73% stake (later expanded to 87%) in Venezuelan electric utility Grupo EDC in a $1.5 billion hostile takeover.

The next year AES bought IPALCO, the parent of Indianapolis Power & Light, in a $3 billion deal. Also in 2001 AES acquired the outstanding shares of Chilean generation company Gener, in which it previously held a 60% stake.

That year AES moved to take control of CANTV, Venezuela's #1 telecom company. Through Grupo EDC, which already owned 6.9% of CANTV, AES offered to buy 43.2% of the company. But AES withdrew the offer after the CANTV board rejected it. (AES sold Grupo EDC's stake in CANTV the following year.) AES also sold some generation assets in Argentina to TOTAL FINA ELF (now TOTAL) for about $370 million.

In 2002 AES sold its 24% interest in Light Serviços de Eletricidade (Light) to Electricité de France (EDF) in exchange for a 20% stake in Brazilian utility Eletropaulo (increasing its stake in Eletropaulo to 70%). In that same year the company sold its retail energy marketing unit (AES NewEnergy) to Constellation Energy Group for $240 million, and its CILCORP subsidiary, which holds utility Central Illinois Light, to Ameren.

In 2007 the company acquired two 230 MW petroleum coke-fired power generation facilities in Tamuin, Mexico for $611 million. It also bought a 51% stake in Turkish power generator IC ICTAS Energy Group.

EXECUTIVES

Chairman: Philip A. Odeen, age 73
President, CEO, and Director: Paul T. Hanrahan, age 51, $7,074,009 total compensation
EVP and COO: Andrés R. Gluski, age 51, $2,912,844 total compensation
EVP and CFO: Victoria D. Harker, age 44, $2,449,748 total compensation
SVP and CIO: Elizabeth Hackenson, age 48
EVP; President, AES Wind Generation:
Edward (Ned) Hall
EVP; President, Asia and Middle East Region:
Mark E. Woodruff, age 51, $1,556,866 total compensation
EVP, General Counsel, and Secretary: Brian A. Miller, age 43, $1,969,589 total compensation
EVP Business Excellence: Jay L. Kloosterboer, age 48
EVP; President, Latin America: Andrew Vesey
SVP and Managing Director, Biofuels: Sarah Slusser
VP North America Operations Network:
Daniel J. Rothaupt
VP; Group Manager, DR-CAFTA Latin America:
Julian Nebreda
VP Global Risk and Commodity Organization:
Richard Santoroski
VP Tax: Prabu Natarajan
VP; Group Manager, AES Brazil: Britaldo Soares
VP Investor Relations: Ahmed Pasha
VP and Treasurer: Willard C. (Chip) Hoagland III
President and CEO Indianapolis Power & Light Company (IPL): Ann D. Murtlow
CEO, AES Gener: Felipe Ceron
Communications Coordinator: Elizabeth Glasser
Auditors: Deloitte & Touche LLP

LOCATIONS

HQ: The AES Corporation
4300 Wilson Blvd., 11th Fl., Arlington, VA 22203
Phone: 703-522-1315   **Fax:** 703-528-4510
Web: www.aes.com

2008 Sales

	$ mil.	% of total
Latin America		
Utilities	5,911	35
Generation	4,465	26
North America		
Generation	2,234	13
Utilities	1,079	6
Europe & Africa		
Generation	1,160	7
Utilities	782	5
Asia		
Generation	1,264	8
Adjustments	(825)	—
Total	**16,070**	**100**

PRODUCTS/OPERATIONS

2008 Sales

	$ mil.	% of total
Non-regulated	8,298	52
Regulated	7,772	48
Total	**16,070**	**100**

Selected Electric Utilities and Distribution Companies

AES CLESA (64%, electric utility, El Salvador)
AES Edelap (60%, electric utility, Argentina)
AES Eden (60%, electric utility, Argentina)
AES Edes (60%, electric utility, Argentina)
AES Gener (electric generation, Chile)
AES India Private Ltd.
AES SeaWest, Inc.
AES Telasi (75%, electric utility, Georgia)
Brasiliana Energia (50.1%)
   AES Sul Distribuidora Gaucha de Energia SA (AES Sul, electric utility, Brazil)
   AES Tiete (power generation, Brazil)
   AES Uruguaiana (power generation, Brazil)
   Eletropaulo Metropolitana Eletricidade de São Paulo S.A. (AES Electropaulo, 70%, electric distribution, Brazil)
CAESS (75%, electric utility, El Salvador)
   DEUSEM (74%, electric utility, El Salvador)
Companhia Energética de Minas Gerais (CEMIG, 21%, Brazil)
EEO (89%, electric utility, El Salvador)
Grupo La Electricidad de Caracas (EDC, 87%, electric generation and distribution, Venezuela)
IC ICTAS Energy Group (51%, power generation, Turkey)
IPALCO Enterprises, Inc. (holding company)
   Illinois Power & Light Company (IPL, electric utility)

COMPETITORS

Alliant Energy	FPL Group
Bonneville Power	Huadian Power
Calpine	IBERDROLA
CenterPoint Energy	Indeck Energy
CMS Energy	International Power
CPFL Energia	MidAmerican Energy
Duke Energy	Mirant
Dynegy	Nicor
Edison International	NRG Energy
El Paso	PG&E Corporation
Endesa S.A.	Public Service Enterprise
Energias de Portugal	Group
Energy Future	RRI Energy
Enersis	Sempra Energy
Entergy	Siemens AG
E.ON UK	SUEZ-TRACTEBEL
Exelon	Xcel Energy

HISTORICAL FINANCIALS
Company Type: Public

Income Statement

	REVENUE ($ mil.)	NET INCOME ($ mil.)	NET PROFIT MARGIN	EMPLOYEES
12/08	16,070.0	1,234.0	7.7%	25,000
12/07	13,588.0	(95.0)	—	28,000
12/06	12,299.0	240.0	2.0%	32,000
12/05	11,086.0	632.0	5.7%	30,000
12/04	9,486.0	386.0	4.1%	30,000
Annual Growth	14.1%	33.7%	—	(4.5%)

FYE: December 31

2008 Year-End Financials

Debt ratio: 459.6%
Return on equity: 36.1%
Cash ($ mil.): 903
Current ratio: 1.41
Long-term debt ($ mil.): 16,863

No. of shares (mil.): 667
Dividends
Yield: 0.0%
Payout: —
Market value ($ mil.): 5,496

Stock History

NYSE: AES

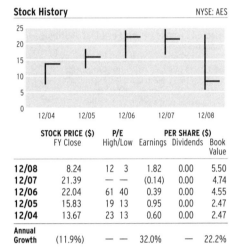

	STOCK PRICE ($) FY Close	P/E High/Low		PER SHARE ($) Earnings	Dividends	Book Value
12/08	8.24	12	3	1.82	0.00	5.50
12/07	21.39	—	—	(0.14)	0.00	4.74
12/06	22.04	61	40	0.39	0.00	4.55
12/05	15.83	19	13	0.95	0.00	2.47
12/04	13.67	23	13	0.60	0.00	2.47
Annual Growth	(11.9%)	—	—	32.0%	—	22.2%

Aetna Inc.

Whether you live or die, Aetna's got an insurance policy to cover it. The company, one of the largest health insurers in the US, also offers life, disability, and long-term care insurance, as well as retirement savings products. Its Health Care division offers managed care plans, health savings accounts, and traditional indemnity coverage, along with dental, vision, behavioral health, and Medicare plans. The division covers nearly 18 million medical members. Aetna's Group Insurance segment sells life, disability, and long-term care insurance nationwide. And its Large Case Pensions segment offers pensions, annuities, and other retirement savings products.

Outside its core medical plan offerings, Aetna provides a number of specialty health insurance products. It is one of the largest dental insurance providers in the country. And through its Aetna Specialty Pharmacy unit, it provides delivery of high-tech medications to patients with chronic diseases. Another subsidiary, The Chickering Group, specializes in health programs for college students.

Aetna has been expanding its health plan offerings, particularly in ways that mitigate rising health care costs and that shift risk and decision-making responsibility onto consumers. Its Aetna HealthFund consumer-directed offerings combine high-deductible plans with medical expense funds that accrue money each year. It has also introduced Web-based access to personal health records, letting users view their medical histories and giving them tools to make health care decisions. Subsidiary ActiveHealth uses technology and data analytics to provide disease management programs, clinical decision support, and other services that identify at-risk plan members and get the right care to patients before they need hospitalization or other expensive procedures.

Though the company primarily provides insurance through large, employer-sponsored programs, it has stepped up its marketing efforts to individuals and small businesses. Another growth area is Medicare plans: It offers Medicare prescription drug coverage (known as Part D) nationwide and has expanded the geographic markets in which it offers privately administered Medicare Advantage health plans. It has also expanded Medicaid services to about a dozen states.

In 2007 the company expanded its health care offerings for expatriates by acquiring Goodhealth, an underwriting agent for international private medical insurance. Aetna continued efforts to expand AGB, signing contracts with the Dubai government in 2008 and inking a deal to work with hospitals in Africa in 2009. It serves about 400,000 customers in more than 100 nations. Aetna positioned the group to take a major leap forward when it set up a representative office in China in mid-2008, the beginning of a two-year process of becoming licensed to sell insurance in the world's largest market.

HISTORY

Hartford, Connecticut, businessman and judge Eliphalet Bulkeley started Connecticut Mutual Life Insurance in 1846. Agents gained control of the firm the following year. Undeterred, Bulkeley and a group of Hartford businessmen founded Aetna Life Insurance in 1853 as a spinoff of Aetna Fire Insurance. Among its offerings was coverage for slaves, a practice for which the company apologized in 2000.

A nationwide agency network fueled early growth at Aetna, which expanded in the 1860s by offering a participating life policy, returning dividends to policyholders based on investment earnings. (This let Aetna compete with mutual life insurers.) In 1868 Aetna became the first firm to offer renewable term life policies.

Eliphalet's son, Morgan, became president in 1879. Aetna moved into accident (1891), health (1899), workers' compensation (1902), and auto and other property insurance (1907) during his 43-year tenure. He served as Hartford mayor, Connecticut governor, and US senator, all the while leading Aetna.

By 1920 the company sold marine insurance, and by 1922 it was the US's largest multiline insurer. Aetna overexpanded its nonlife lines (particularly autos) during the 1920s, threatening its solvency. It survived the Depression by restricting underwriting and rebuilding reserves. After WWII the firm expanded into group life, health, and accident insurance. In 1967 it reorganized into holding company Aetna Life and Casualty.

The 1960s, 1970s, and 1980s were go-go years: The company added lines and bought and sold everything from an oil services firm to commercial real estate. The boom period led to a bust and a 1991 reorganization in which Aetna eliminated 8,000 jobs, withdrew from such lines as auto insurance, and sold its profitable American Reinsurance.

To take advantage of the boom in retirement savings, in 1995 it got permission to set up bank AE Trust to act as a pension trustee. Aetna sold its property/casualty, behavioral managed care (1997), and individual life insurance (1998) businesses. It then expanded overseas and bought U.S. Healthcare and New York Life's NYLCare managed health business (1998).

Controversy marred 1998. Contract terms — including a "gag" clause against discussing uncovered treatments — prompted 400 Texas doctors to leave its system; defections followed in Kentucky and West Virginia. Consumers balked over Aetna's refusal to cover some treatments, including experimental procedures and advanced fertility treatments. One group sued for false advertising.

The American Medical Association that year decried Aetna's plan to buy Prudential's health care unit as anticompetitive; in 1999 the government required Aetna to sell operations, including NYLCare, to gain approval. Also in 1999 Aetna became the second insurer (after Humana) to be sued for misleading clients about treatment decisions; it reached a settlement the next year with the State of Texas over capitation, physician incentives, and other matters.

In 2000 Aetna restated earnings for seven previous quarters at the behest of the SEC. Flagging earnings prompted CEO Richard Huber to resign; William Donaldson, one of the founders of Donaldson, Lufkin & Jenrette, took his place.

John "Jack" Rowe took over the helm as CEO in 2001. In 2002 the company returned to operating profitability after reducing its workforce, raising premiums, and restructuring critical operations. The following year it bought a mail-order pharmacy facility from Eckerd Health Services, and in 2004 formed Aetna Specialty Pharmacy, a joint venture with Priority Healthcare (now CuraScript), to provide mail-order drugs to consumers with chronic diseases.

Ronald Williams succeeded Jack Rowe as CEO in 2006.

EXECUTIVES

Chairman and CEO: Ronald A. (Ron) Williams, age 59, $24,300,112 total compensation
President: Mark T. Bertolini, age 52, $7,869,824 total compensation
EVP, CFO, and Chief Enterprise Risk Officer: Joseph M. Zubretsky, age 52, $5,566,280 total compensation
Chief Medical Officer: Lonny Reisman, age 53, $5,566,280 total compensation
National Medical Director and Chief Clinical Officer, Aetna Pharmacy Management: Edmund J. (Ed) Pezalla
Chief Diversity Officer: J. Raymond Arroyo
Chief Investment Officer: Jean LaTorre
SVP and CIO: Margaret (Meg) McCarthy
SVP Human Resources: Elease E. Wright
SVP and General Counsel: William J. Casazza, age 53, $2,675,841 total compensation
SVP and Deputy General Counsel, Health: Charles H. Klippel
SVP Strategic Marketing and Communications: Robert E. Mead

VP and CTO: Michael G. Mathias, age 50
VP Finance and Treasurer: Alfred P. Quirk Jr.
VP Public Relations: David W. Carter, age 49
VP Investor Relations: Jeffrey Chaffkin
President, Aetna Workers' Comp Access (AWCA):
Patrick J. Scullion
President, Small and Middle Markets, North Central Region: Robert Mendonsa
President, Aetna Global Benefits: Martha Temple
COO Consumer Business Segment: Laurie Brubaker, age 48
COO, Aetna Pharmacy Management: Rob Gallé
Auditors: KPMG LLP

LOCATIONS

HQ: Aetna Inc.
151 Farmington Ave., Hartford, CT 06156
Phone: 860-273-0123   **Fax:** 860-273-3971
Web: www.aetna.com

PRODUCTS/OPERATIONS

2008 Sales

	$ mil.	% of total
Health care	28,775.0	93
Group insurance	1,710.7	5
Large group pensions	465.0	2
Total	**30,950.7**	**100**

Selected Subsidiaries

Active Health Management, Inc.
Aelan Inc.
  Aetna Life & Casualty (Bermuda) Limited
Aetna Health Holdings, LLC
  AET Health Care Plan, Inc.
  Aetna Dental Inc.
  Aetna Health Management, LLC
  Aetna RX Home Delivery, LLC
  Chickering Benefit Planning Insurance Agency, Inc.
  Chickering Claims Administrators, Inc.
  NYLCare Health Plans, Inc.
Aetna Criterion Communications, Inc.
Aetna Financial Holdings, LLC
  Aetna Behavioral Health, LLC
  Aetna Health Information Solutions, Inc.
  Aetna Integrated Informatics, Inc.
  Integrated Pharmacy Solutions, Inc.
  Managed Care Coordinators, Inc.
Aetna Life Insurance Company
  Aetna Government Health Plans, LLC
  AHP Holdings, Inc.
Aetna Health and Life Insurance Company
Aetna Health Insurance Company of New York
Aetna Risk Indemnity Company Limited (Bermuda)
Aetna Specialty Pharmacy, LLC (40%)
ASI Wings, L.L.C.
Luettgens Limited

COMPETITORS

AMERIGROUP
Blue Cross
Caremark Pharmacy Services
Centene
CIGNA
Coventry Health Care
DeCare
Delta Dental Plans
Express Scripts
Guardian Life
Health Net
Humana
Kaiser Foundation Health Plan
Medco Health
MetLife
Molina Healthcare
Principal Financial
Prudential
UnitedHealth Group
USAA
WellPoint

HISTORICAL FINANCIALS
Company Type: Public

Income Statement

FYE: December 31

	REVENUE ($ mil.)	NET INCOME ($ mil.)	NET PROFIT MARGIN	EMPLOYEES
12/08	30,950.7	1,384.1	4.5%	35,500
12/07	27,599.6	1,831.0	6.6%	35,200
12/06	25,145.7	1,701.7	6.8%	30,000
12/05	22,491.9	1,634.5	7.3%	28,200
12/04	19,904.1	2,245.1	11.3%	26,700
Annual Growth	11.7%	(11.4%)	—	7.4%

2008 Year-End Financials

Debt ratio: 44.4%
Return on equity: 15.2%
Cash ($ mil.): 1,180
Current ratio: 0.65
Long-term debt ($ mil.): 3,638

No. of shares (mil.): 443
Dividends
  Yield: 0.1%
  Payout: 1.4%
Market value ($ mil.): 12,620

Stock History

NYSE: AET

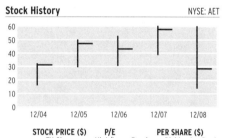

	STOCK PRICE ($) FY Close	P/E High/Low		PER SHARE ($) Earnings	Dividends	Book Value
12/08	28.50	21	5	2.83	0.04	18.49
12/07	57.73	17	11	3.47	0.04	22.67
12/06	43.18	18	10	2.99	0.04	20.65
12/05	47.15	18	11	2.70	0.02	22.82
12/04	31.19	9	5	3.58	0.01	20.51
Annual Growth	(2.2%)	—	—	(5.7%)	41.4%	(2.6%)

Affiliated Computer Services

Affiliated Computer Services (ACS) handles jobs its clients would rather hand off. The company provides business process outsourcing (BPO) services for commercial enterprises and government agencies, focusing on markets such as communications, health care, and transportation. As an outsourcer, ACS handles functions such as administration, including health care claims processing; finance and accounting; human resources; payment processing; sales, marketing, and customer care call centers; and supply chain management. BPO services account for most of the company's sales. In addition, ACS offers information technology and systems integration services.

ACS operates from a network of about 340 offices in the US and about 120 offices in more than 25 other countries.

Along with other BPO companies, ACS has benefited from a cost-conscious mindset at both businesses and government agencies. It draws commercial clients from a wide variety of industries, and its government arm serves federal, state, and local agencies. Handling Medicaid claims for state agencies is a company specialty.

ACS hopes to grow by gaining new clients and by selling new services to existing clients, primarily within its current markets; in addition, it is interested in pursuing acquisitions in hopes of augmenting existing business lines and entering new markets.

In line with that strategy, ACS acquired Argentina-based customer care services provider Grupo Multivoice for an undisclosed amount in late 2008. The combined ACS Multivoice is expected to open the door to further regional growth in South America. The deal also helps expand the diversity of its services, which now includes bilingual capabilities, to customers throughout the Americas and Europe.

In 2009 ACS bought e-Services Group International for $85 million. e-Services, an offshore call center and BPO company, adds 4,000 employees to ACS' ranks whose English language proficiency was cited as a factor in the deal. ACS kept its eye on Europe a few months later when it snatched up UK-based Anix, which specializes in IT consulting, analysis, and design services for the UK market.

Founder and chairman Darwin Deason controls a 44% voting stake in ACS.

HISTORY

In 1967 Darwin Deason took over a company called Affiliated Computer Systems (ACS). Eight years later he sold that company to Dallas-based MTech, but stayed on as its president. Under Deason, MTech became the largest provider of financial data processing in the US. When MTech was bought by General Motors subsidiary Electronic Data Systems in 1988, Deason left to start an entirely new ACS, this one called Affiliated Computer Services.

The new company was created as a financial computer services provider, focused on processing bank transactions. Its 1992 acquisition of Dataplex ushered the company into business process outsourcing, and ACS went public two years later. ACS' 1995 acquisition of The Systems Group extended the company's offerings to include professional services.

The company continued its rapid rate of growth throughout the late 1990s, building a string of acquisitions that included Intelligent Solutions (1997), Computer Data Systems (1997), Betac International (1998), and Canmax's retail systems subsidiary (1998). In 1998 ACS bought the Unclaimed Property Services Division of State Street Corporation. Early the following year it acquired IT services company BRC Holdings. Deason stepped down as CEO (he remained chairman), passing the reins to president Jeffrey Rich, a former Citibank investment banker. Later in 1999 ACS bought Consultec, a provider of IT services for state health programs, from GenAmerica's General American Life subsidiary in a $105 million deal.

In 2000 the company sold its ATM business for about $180 million. It also boosted its government outsourcing capabilities with the acquisition of Intellisource Group. The next year ACS acquired Lockheed Martin's IMS subsidiary, a provider of outsourcing services to municipal and state governments, for $825 million.

In 2002 the company acquired FleetBoston Financial's education services subsidiary, AFSA Data, for about $410 million, and with it a student loan portfolio worth about $85 billion. Also that year COO Mark King assumed the president post from Rich, who remained CEO.

In 2003, moving away from its federal government services business and extending its commercial reach, ACS sold most of its federal government IT services business to Lockheed Martin and bought Lockheed's commercial IT business. The following year the company sold the defense support services portion of its federal government business to ManTech International.

Rich resigned from the company in 2005 and was replaced by King. Also that year ACS moved to expand its business process outsourcing operations through acquisitions. The company bought health care technology services provider Superior Consultant Holdings and formed a new division, ACS Healthcare Solutions. ACS paid about $400 million for Mellon Financial's human resources outsourcing operations (renamed Buck Consultants).

In 2006, however, ACS came under SEC investigation. Later that year, King and CFO Warren Edwards resigned when it was ruled they violated the company's ethics code regarding stock options practices. EVP and COO Lynn Blodgett replaced King as CEO.

Also in 2006 ACS bought INTELLINEX, a provider of outsourced training services, from Ernst & Young. Later in the year, ACS acquired Primax Recoveries, a services provider catering to the health care sector. In 2007 ACS acquired CDR Associates, a maker of auditing and accounting services software geared toward the health care industry.

In the spring of 2007, Deason and investment firm Cerberus Capital Management offered to buy the company for $62 per share, or about $6.2 billion, but Cerberus withdrew its support several months later, citing deteriorating conditions in credit markets. Deason blamed the five independent members of the board, who had sought alternative proposals, for taking too long to make a decision. He demanded and received their resignations in November 2007, but not before considerable back-and-forth sniping.

EXECUTIVES

Chairman: Darwin Deason, age 68,
$2,988,500 total compensation
President, CEO, and Director: Lynn R. Blodgett, age 54,
$4,734,154 total compensation
EVP; COO Government Operations: Tom Burlin, age 51,
$1,991,199 total compensation
EVP; COO Commercial Operations: Tom Blodgett,
age 56, $1,751,614 total compensation
EVP and CFO: Kevin Kyser, age 41,
$1,259,652 total compensation
EVP and Chief People Officer: Lora J. Villarreal, age 65
EVP Corporate Development: John H. Rexford, age 52
EVP; Group President, Commercial: Ann Vezina, age 46
EVP; Group President, ITO Services: Derrell James, age 47
EVP, Corporate Secretary, and General Counsel: Tas Panos, age 53
EVP; Group President, Government Solutions: Joseph P. (Joe) Doherty Jr., age 48
EVP; Group President, Transportation Solutions: David (Dave) Amoriell, age 52
SVP and Chief Accounting Officer: Laura Rossi, age 45
SVP and Chief Information Security Officer:
Christopher (Chris) Leach
CIO: Tasos Tsolakis
Chief Administrative Officer: Skip Stitt
VP Corporate Communications: Kevin Lightfoot
Group President, Business Process Solutions:
Connie Harvey
Auditors: PricewaterhouseCoopers LLP

LOCATIONS

HQ: Affiliated Computer Services, Inc.
2828 N. Haskell Ave., Dallas, TX 75204
Phone: 214-841-6111   **Fax:** 214-821-8315
Web: www.acs-inc.com

2008 Sales

	% of total
US	92
Other countries	8
Total	**100**

PRODUCTS/OPERATIONS

2008 Sales by Market

	$ mil.	% of total
Commercial	3,674.0	60
Government	2,486.5	40
Total	**6,160.5**	**100**

2008 Sales by Service

	$ mil.	% of total
Business process outsourcing	4,792.4	78
Information technology services	1,041.0	17
Systems integration services	327.1	5
Total	**6,160.5**	**100**

Selected Markets

Commercial
  Communications
  Financial services
  Health care
  Higher education
  Insurance
  Manufacturing
  Retail
  Transportation: shipping and logistics
  Travel
Government
  Administration and finance
  Environment
  Federal-US
  Health care
  Human services
  Public safety and justice
  Transportation

Selected Services

Application services
Customer care
Document and data management
Finance and accounting
Human capital management
Information technology

COMPETITORS

Accenture
ADP
Capgemini US
CGI Group
Computer Sciences Corp.
Convergys
Coventry Health Care
EDS
Hewitt Associates
IBM Global Services
Infosys
Keane
ManTech
MAXIMUS
Northrop Grumman
Perot Systems
Unisys
Wipro Technologies

HISTORICAL FINANCIALS

Company Type: Public

Income Statement

FYE: June 30

	REVENUE ($ mil.)	NET INCOME ($ mil.)	NET PROFIT MARGIN	EMPLOYEES
6/08	6,160.5	329.0	5.3%	65,000
6/07	5,772.5	253.1	4.4%	60,000
6/06	5,353.7	358.8	6.7%	58,000
6/05	4,351.2	415.9	9.6%	52,000
6/04	4,106.4	529.8	12.9%	43,000
Annual Growth	**10.7%**	**(11.2%)**	**—**	**10.9%**

2009 Year-End Financials

Debt ratio: 77.9%
Return on equity: 14.2%
Cash ($ mil.): 731
Current ratio: 1.63
Long-term debt ($ mil.): 2,042
No. of shares (mil.): 98
Dividends
  Yield: 0.0%
  Payout: —
Market value ($ mil.): 4,337

Stock History

NYSE: ACS

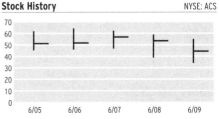

	STOCK PRICE ($) FY Close	P/E High/Low	Earnings	PER SHARE ($) Dividends	Book Value
6/08	53.49	18 12	3.32	0.00	23.65
6/07	56.72	25 19	2.49	0.00	21.17
6/06	51.61	22 16	2.87	0.00	25.17
6/05	51.10	19 14	3.19	0.00	29.08
6/04	52.94	15 11	3.83	0.00	26.54
Annual Growth	**0.3%**	**— —**	**(3.5%)**	**—**	**(2.8%)**

Aflac Incorporated

Aflac's clients may not welcome accidents and illness any more than a visit from Gilbert Gottfried, but at least their coverage will keep them from financial ruin. Aflac (whose popular ads feature a valiant duck voiced by comedian Gottfried) sells supplemental health and life insurance policies that cover special conditions, primarily cancer. It is one of the largest sellers of supplemental insurance in the US and is an industry leader in Japan's cancer-insurance market (with 14 million policies in force). Aflac, which is marketed through and is an acronym for American Family Life Assurance Company, sells policies that pay cash benefits for hospital confinement, emergency treatment, and medical appliances.

The company also offers accident, intensive care, dental, vision, and short-term disability insurance products.

Despite its US roots, Aflac makes more than 70% of its insurance sales in Japan, where its policies fill in gaps not covered by the national health insurance system. Its reliance on Japan has a downside: The company is vulnerable to currency fluctuations between the dollar and yen.

It also faces increased competition due to deregulation of Japan's insurance industry. However, as in the US, Japanese consumers are seeing more health care costs being shifted onto their shoulders, making Aflac's products more attractive.

In Japan, Aflac primarily sells through an agency system in which a corporation forms a subsidiary to sell Aflac insurance to its employees. In the face of Japan's deregulated life insurance industry, the company has also had a marketing alliance with Dai-ichi Mutual Life, the country's second-largest life insurer, since 2000. Changes in regulations now allow the company to sell through banks and post offices, and it has also opened retail shops where consumers can purchase directly from sales associates.

In the US, Aflac sells mainly through the workplace, with employers deducting premiums from paychecks. Building on its strong brand recognition, Aflac has invested in its US business by adding more sales associates and expanding its distribution to include insurance brokers.

To build up its US large-group business, Aflac has announced that it will pay $100 million to purchase Continental American Insurance Company. Continental's payroll-deducted insurance products are distributed through brokers and marketing groups. California, North and South Carolina, Texas, and Virginia account for most of the company's premiums.

Chairman and CEO Dan Amos holds 9% of the company his father and uncles founded.

HISTORY

American Family Life Assurance Company (AFLAC) was founded in Columbus, Georgia, in 1955 by brothers John, Paul, and William Amos to sell life, health, and accident insurance. Competition was fierce, and the little company did poorly. With AFLAC nearing bankruptcy, the brothers looked for a niche.

The polio scares of the 1940s and 1950s had spawned insurance coverage written especially against that disease; the Amos brothers (whose father was a cancer victim) took a cue from that concept and decided to sell cancer insurance. In 1958 they introduced the world's first cancer-expense policy. It was a hit, and by 1959 the company had written nearly a million dollars in premiums and expanded across state lines.

The enterprise grew quickly during the 1960s, especially after developing its cluster-selling approach in the workplace, where employers were usually willing to make payroll deductions for premiums. By 1971 the company was operating in 42 states.

While visiting the World's Fair in Osaka in 1970, John Amos decided to market supplemental cancer coverage to the Japanese, whose national health care plan left them exposed to considerable expense from cancer treatment. After four years the company finally won approval to sell in Japan since the policies did not threaten existing markets and because the Amoses found notable backers in the insurance and medical industries. AFLAC became one of the first US insurance companies to enter the Japanese market, and it enjoyed an eight-year monopoly on the cancer market. Back in the US, in 1973 AFLAC organized a holding company and began buying television stations in the South and Midwest.

The 1980s were marked by US and state government inquiries into dread disease insurance. Critics said such policies were a poor value because they were relatively expensive and covered only one disease. However, the inquiries led nowhere and demand for such insurance increased, bringing new competition. In the 1980s AFLAC's scales tilted: US growth slowed, while business grew in Japan, which soon accounted for most of the company's sales.

In 1990 John Amos died of cancer and was replaced as CEO by his nephew Dan. Two years later the company officially renamed itself Aflac (partly because Dan planned to increase the company's US profile and so many US companies already used the name "American").

Aflac has sought to supplement its cancer insurance by introducing new products and improving old ones to encourage policyholders to add on or trade up. Its Japanese "living benefit" product, which includes lump sum payments for heart attacks and strokes, struck a chord with the aging population.

Connecticut in 1997 repealed its ban on specified-disease insurance; New York eventually followed suit. Also that year Aflac sold its seven TV stations to Raycom Media to focus on insurance.

The company boosted its name recognition in the US from 2% in 1990 to more than 56%, primarily through advertising, including slots during the 1998 Olympic Winter Games and NASCAR races. In 1999 the company signed a three-year cross-selling agreement for its supplemental insurance with what is now HR Logic, a human resources outsourcing firm.

Accident/disability premiums surpassed cancer premiums in the US for the first time in the company's history in 2000. The Aflac duck made its first appearance in a 2001 Japanese commercial for accident insurance. Shortly thereafter it debuted in the US, where it quickly achieved advertising-icon status.

EXECUTIVES

Chairman and CEO: Daniel P. (Dan) Amos, age 57, $9,726,893 total compensation
President, CFO, and Director: Kriss Cloninger III, age 61, $5,460,582 total compensation
EVP and Deputy CFO: Martin A. Durant III, age 58
EVP, General Counsel, and Corporate Secretary: Joey M. Loudermilk, age 55, $2,145,416 total compensation
EVP Corporate Services: Audrey Boone Tillman, age 44
EVP and Chief Administrative Officer, Aflac: Teresa L. White, age 42
SVP Information Technology and CIO: Gerald W. Shields
SVP and Chief Marketing Officer: M. Jeffrey (Jeff) Charney
SVP Investments and Chief Investment Officer: W. Jeremy (Jerry) Jeffery, age 58
SVP Investor Relations: Kenneth S. (Ken) Janke Jr., age 50
SVP Financial Services and Chief Accounting Officer: Ralph A. Rogers Jr., age 60
SVP Governmental Relations: Phillip J. (Jack) Friou
SVP Corporate Learning: Janet P. Baker
SVP and Corporate Actuary: Susan R. Blanck, age 42
VP Media Relations and External Communications: Laura Kane
Chairman, Aflac Japan: Charles D. Lake II, age 47
President and COO, Aflac Japan: Tohru Tonoike, age 56, $2,077,454 total compensation
President, Aflac and COO, Aflac US: Paul S. Amos II, age 33, $2,406,292 total compensation
President and CEO, Communicorp: James C. Woodall
Auditors: KPMG LLP

LOCATIONS

HQ: Aflac Incorporated
    1932 Wynnton Rd., Columbus, GA 31999
Phone: 706-323-3431   **Fax:** 706-324-6330
Web: www.aflac.com

PRODUCTS/OPERATIONS

2008 Revenues

	$ mil.	% of total
Aflac Japan	12,742	72
Aflac US	4,787	27
Corporate	85	1
Realized investment losses	(1,007)	—
Other business	38	—
Adjustments	(91)	—
Total	**16,554**	**100**

Selected Subsidiaries

aflacdirect.com, Limited
American Family Life Assurance Company of Columbus (Aflac)
American Family Life Assurance Company of New York
Communicorp, Incorporated

COMPETITORS

American Fidelity Assurance Company
American National Insurance
Asahi Mutual Life
Conseco
Hartford Life
MetLife
Nationwide Financial Network
Torchmark
Unum Group

HISTORICAL FINANCIALS

Company Type: Public

Income Statement

FYE: December 31

	ASSETS ($ mil.)	NET INCOME ($ mil.)	INCOME AS % OF ASSETS	EMPLOYEES
12/08	79,331.0	1,254.0	1.6%	7,949
12/07	65,805.0	1,634.0	2.5%	8,048
12/06	59,805.0	1,483.0	2.5%	7,411
12/05	56,361.0	1,483.0	2.6%	6,970
12/04	59,326.0	1,299.0	2.2%	6,531
Annual Growth	7.5%	(0.9%)	—	5.0%

2008 Year-End Financials

Equity as % of assets: 8.4%
Return on assets: 1.7%
Return on equity: 16.2%
Long-term debt ($ mil.): 3,454
No. of shares (mil.): 468
Dividends
  Yield: 2.1%
  Payout: 36.6%
Market value ($ mil.): 21,431
Sales ($ mil.): 16,554

Stock History

NYSE: AFL

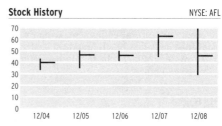

	STOCK PRICE ($) FY Close	P/E High/Low	PER SHARE ($) Earnings	Dividends	Book Value
12/08	45.84	26 11	2.62	0.96	14.20
12/07	62.63	19 14	3.31	0.80	18.81
12/06	46.00	17 14	2.95	0.55	17.84
12/05	46.42	17 12	2.92	0.44	16.96
12/04	39.84	17 13	2.52	0.38	16.20
Annual Growth	3.6%	— —	1.0%	26.1%	(3.2%)

AGCO Corporation

AGCO's annual harvests might be smaller than those of larger rivals John Deere and CNH Global, but it's still able to reap profits worldwide. AGCO manufactures and sells its tractors, combines, hay tools, sprayers, forage equipment, and replacement parts through a global network of more than 2,800 independent dealers and distributors. It also offers lawn and garden and landscaping equipment. Brand names include Massey Ferguson, Challenger, Valtra (Finland-based), and Fendt (German-based). The company offers financing services to customers and dealers through a joint venture with the Netherlands-based Rabobank. AGCO sells its products in more than 140 countries.

AGCO in 2008 introduced a new corporate logo with a new tagline, "Your Agriculture Company," to emphasize the company's focus on "Agriculture" as an industry. The company is focusing on manufacturing technologically advanced equipment to handle the challenges facing the agricultural industry, such as population growth, changing diets, and scarcity of land.

AGCO has increased investments in R&D to provide new products and leading-edge technology. In 2007 it formed Advanced Technology Solutions to develop products incorporating the latest technologies in machine control and management and precision farming. Auto-Guide (Satellite) Navigation and FIELDSTAR offer hands-free steering navigation assistance. SCR technology, e3, injects an organic compound into the exhaust stream that allows engines to run more efficiently and reduces pollution. AGCO Tractors offer high-power PowerMaxx CVT (continuously variable transmission), as well as diesel engines, which improve the efficiency of harvesting and farming equipment.

AGCO partnered with Topcon and Sauer-Danfoss in 2008 to provide steering technology for its professional farming equipment. The company formed a joint venture with one of Russia's leading industrial equipment producers, CTP, to assemble engines. In 2007 it bought Industria Agricola Fortaleza Limitada, a leading Brazilian maker of farm implements, and purchased a 50% stake in Laverda, an Italian harvesting equipment producer, to expand its overseas presence.

AGCO also continues to strengthen its dealer network by setting up three assembly centers in North America to reduce costs and streamline logistics. In June 2008 AGCO partnered with IronPlanet, a leading online auction company for used agricultural equipment, which provides the company's North American dealers a faster, more profitable channel to market and sell used equipment.

HISTORY

In 1861 American Edward Allis purchased the bankrupt Reliance Works, a leading Milwaukee-based manufacturer of sawmills and flour-milling equipment. Under shrewd management, The Reliance Works of Edward P. Allis & Co. weathered financial troubles — bankruptcy in the Panic of 1873 — but managed to renegotiate its debt and recover. By the time Allis died in 1889, Reliance Works employed some 1,500 workers.

The company branched into different areas of manufacturing in the late 19th century, and by the 20th century the Edward P. Allis Co. (as it was then known) was the world leader in steam engines. In 1901 the company merged with another manufacturing giant, Fraser & Chalmers, to form the Allis-Chalmers Company. In the 1920s and 1930s, Allis-Chalmers entered the farm equipment market.

Although overshadowed by John Deere and International Harvester (IH), Allis-Chalmers made key contributions to the industry — the first rubber-tired tractor (1932) and the All-Crop harvester. Allis-Chalmers spun off its farm equipment business in the 1950s, and phased out several unrelated products. The company, with its orange-colored tractors, expanded and prospered from the 1940s through the early 1970s. Then the chaffing farm economy of the late 1970s and early 1980s hurt Allis-Chalmers' sales.

After layoffs and a plant shutdown in 1984, the company was purchased in 1985 by German machinery maker Klockner-Humbolt-Deutz (KHD), who moved the company (renamed Deutz-Allis) to Georgia. In the mid-1980s low food prices hurt farmers and low demand hurt the equipment market. KHD was never able to bring profits up to a satisfactory level, and in 1990 the German firm sold the unit to the US management in a buyout led by Robert Ratliff. Ratliff believed the company could succeed by acquiring belly-up equipment makers, turning them around, and competing on price.

Renamed AGCO, the company launched a buying spree in 1991 that included Fiat's Hesston (1991), White Tractor (1991), the North American distribution rights for Massey Ferguson (1993), and White-New Idea (1993). The bumper crop of product growth enabled AGCO to slice into competitors Deere and Case's market share. AGCO went public in 1992. Its 1994 purchase of the remainder of Massey Ferguson (with 20% of the world market) vaulted AGCO among the world's leading farm equipment makers.

In 1997 AGCO acquired German farm equipment makers Fendt and Dronniberg. It also picked up Deutz Argentina, a supplier of agricultural equipment, engines, and vehicles, in an effort to expand into South America. AGCO entered the agricultural sprayer market in 1998 by acquiring the Spra-Coupe line from Ingersoll-Rand and the Willmar line from Cargill. A worldwide drop in farm equipment sales caused AGCO to cut about 10% of its workforce.

To further overcome stalled sales and slumping profits, in 1999 the company announced it was permanently closing an Ohio plant and would cease production at a Texas plant. The next year AGCO closed its Missouri plant and trimmed its workforce by about 5%.

In 2001 AGCO acquired fertilizer equipment manufacturer Ag-Chem Equipment. In 2002 AGCO suffered a tragic loss when president and CEO John Shumejda and SVP Ed Swingle were killed in an airplane accident in the UK.

In 2004 AGCO added Valtra, a global tractor and off-road engine maker. Also that year chairman Robert Ratliff handed Martin Richenhagen the president and CEO titles he had taken on after the death of Shumejda.

In 2006 AGCO announced a new growth initiative dubbed "Always Growing." The strategy makes some basic assumptions about trends emerging in global agriculture, including the increase in mega-farms, exponential growth in certain developing countries, increased demand for biofuels in developed nations, and increasingly advanced technology.

EXECUTIVES

Chairman, President, and CEO: Martin H. Richenhagen, age 56, $10,571,483 total compensation
SVP and CFO: Andrew H. (Andy) Beck, age 45, $2,352,063 total compensation
SVP Executive Development: Norman L. (Norm) Boyd, age 65
SVP Engineering: Garry L. Ball, age 61
SVP Strategy and Integration and General Manager, Eastern Europe and Asia: Hubertus M. Muehlhaeuser, age 39
SVP Materials Management Worldwide: David L. Caplan, age 61
SVP and General Manager, EAME and Australia/New Zealand: Gary L. Collar, age 52, $2,351,544 total compensation
SVP Global Sales and Marketing and Product Management: Randall G. (Randy) Hoffman, age 57
SVP and General Manager, North America: Robert B. Crain, age 49, $1,948,302 total compensation
SVP and General Manager, South America: André M. Carioba, age 57, $2,041,359 total compensation
SVP Manufacturing and Quality: Hans-Bernd Veltmaat, age 54
SVP Human Resources: Lucinda B. Smith, age 42
VP and CIO: Robert (Bob) Greenberg, age 55
VP Customer Support North America Parts Division: Gretchen DeCoster
VP, Corporate Secretary, and General Counsel: Debra Kuper
Director Investor Relations: Greg Peterson
Auditors: KPMG LLP

LOCATIONS

HQ: AGCO Corporation
4205 River Green Pkwy., Duluth, GA 30096
Phone: 770-813-9200   **Fax:** 770-813-6118
Web: www.agcocorp.com

2008 Sales

	$ mil.	% of total
Europe, Africa & Middle East	4,905.4	58
North America	1,794.3	21
South America	1,496.5	18
Asia/Pacific	228.4	3
Total	**8,424.6**	**100**

PRODUCTS/OPERATIONS

2008 Sales

	$ mil.	% of total
Tractors	5,620.7	67
Replacement parts	1,048.5	12
Combines	481.8	6
Application equipment	363.8	4
Other machinery	909.8	11
Total	**8,424.6**	**100**

Selected Brand Names

AGCO (Tractors and SISU POWER)
Challenger
Fendt
Gleaner
Hesston
Massey Ferguson
RoGator
Spra-Coupe
Sunflower
TerraGator
Valtra
White Planters
Wilmar

COMPETITORS

Caterpillar
CNH Global
Deere
Fiat
Kubota

HISTORICAL FINANCIALS

Company Type: Public

Income Statement

FYE: December 31

	REVENUE ($ mil.)	NET INCOME ($ mil.)	NET PROFIT MARGIN	EMPLOYEES
12/08	8,424.6	400.0	4.7%	15,600
12/07	6,828.1	246.3	3.6%	13,700
12/06	5,435.0	(64.9)	—	12,800
12/05	5,449.7	31.6	0.6%	13,000
12/04	5,273.3	158.8	3.0%	14,300
Annual Growth	12.4%	26.0%	—	2.2%

2008 Year-End Financials

Debt ratio: 34.8%
Return on equity: 20.0%
Cash ($ mil.): 512
Current ratio: 1.52
Long-term debt ($ mil.): 682
No. of shares (mil.): 92
Dividends
  Yield: 0.0%
  Payout: —
Market value ($ mil.): 2,181

Stock History

NYSE: AGCO

	STOCK PRICE ($) FY Close	P/E High/Low		PER SHARE ($) Earnings	Dividends	Book Value
12/08	23.59	17	4	4.09	0.00	21.17
12/07	67.98	28	11	2.55	0.00	22.10
12/06	30.94	—	—	(0.71)	0.00	16.16
12/05	16.57	63	42	0.35	0.00	15.32
12/04	21.89	14	9	1.71	0.00	15.39
Annual Growth	1.9%	—	—	24.4%	—	8.3%

Agilent Technologies

Agilent Technologies keeps scientists on their toes. A leading manufacturer of scientific instruments and analysis equipment, Agilent is the #1 supplier of electronic test and measurement products, including data generators, multimeters, and oscilloscopes. Its life sciences and chemical analysis unit manufactures laboratory equipment and other scientific instruments. Agilent's 30,000 customers include global giants, such as Cisco, Dow Chemical, GlaxoSmithKline, Intel, Merck, and Samsung.

Agilent's electronic test and measurement unit offers a wide range of services, such as consulting on hardware purchases, equipment repair and calibration, and professional engineering.

In fiscal 2009 Agilent broke out its operations into three segments: Electronic Measurement; Bio-analytical Measurement; and Semiconductor & Board Test. The last segment brought together the company's laser interferometer, parametric test, and printed circuit board manufacturing test equipment. Due to poor business results, Agilent is dropping its automated optical inspection and automated X-ray inspection product lines.

Faced with plummeting sales in its Electronic Measurement and Semiconductor & Board Test segments in 2009, Agilent restructured to cut costs by $310 million a year, mostly in Electronic Measurement, its biggest line of business. The company will lay off about 2,700 employees, a reduction in force of around 14%. Spying more promising opportunities in the life sciences, environmental, energy, and materials sectors, Agilent looked to buy Varian for $1.5 billion. Varian expands Agilent's capacity in making scientific instruments for measuring biological and physical attributes.

That Agilent is a leader in the test and measurement equipment industry should come as no surprise — it is the original business started by technology pioneers William Hewlett and David Packard. Hewlett-Packard spun off the business in 1999 so that it could focus on its computer products operations. Being a leader has not spared the company from tough times in the electronics industry, however. Agilent made substantial job cuts and reduced salaries to control costs. It also is outsourcing more of its production and moving manufacturing operations to Asia, in an effort to further lower costs.

HISTORY

Agilent Technologies was formed in 1999 when Hewlett-Packard (HP) split off its measurement business. But Agilent's roots run as deep as HP's — Agilent's core products served as the original business of Stanford-trained electrical engineers William Hewlett and David Packard. The friends started HP in 1939 as a test and measurement equipment maker. Their first product, developed in Packard's garage (Hewlett was living in a rented cottage behind Packard's house) was an audio oscillator for testing sound equipment; Walt Disney Studios bought eight to help make the animation classic *Fantasia*.

Demand for electronic test equipment during WWII pushed sales from $34,000 in 1940 (when HP had three employees and eight products) to nearly $1 million three years later. The company entered the microwave field in 1943, creating signal generators for the Naval Research Laboratory. Its postwar line of microwave test products made it a market leader for signal generation equipment.

Expanding beyond the US in the late 1950s, HP established a plant in West Germany. The company went public in 1957. It entered the medical field in 1961 with the purchase of Sanborn, and the analytical instrumentation business in 1965 with the purchase of F&M Scientific. In the 1970s president Hewlett and chairman Packard began shifting HP's focus toward the computer market. Late in that decade they stepped back from day-to-day management (they would retire in 1987 and 1992, respectively).

Sales hit $3 billion in 1980. In 1991 HP broadened its communications component offerings when it bought Avantek. HP moved into the DNA analysis field in 1994 with pharmaceutical research and health care products. Packard died in 1996. In 1997 HP bought Heartstream, maker of an automatic external defibrillator.

In 1999 HP formed Agilent as a separate company for its test and measurement and other non-computer operations, which by then accounted for 16% of sales. Edward Barnholt, a 30-year HP veteran, was named CEO of the new company. In a move to energize its computer business, HP spun off 15% of Agilent to the public in November 1999. The remainder was distributed to HP shareholders in mid-2000.

In 2000 Philips Electronics agreed to buy Agilent's Healthcare Solutions unit for $1.7 billion. (After lengthy scrutiny from US and European regulators, the deal was completed in mid-2001.)

In a move to bolster its networking business, Agilent completed its $665 million acquisition of network management software maker Objective Systems Integrators in early 2001. The company also implemented cost-cutting measures such as temporary pay cuts. Later that year, in the face of harsh market conditions, Agilent announced two separate layoffs of 4,000 employees each, representing a total staff reduction of about 18%. Hewlett died that same year.

In 2004 Agilent acquired privately held Silicon Genetics (genomics data analysis and management software), broadening its life sciences offerings. Barnholt retired early in 2005; Agilent's COO, Bill Sullivan, was tapped to replace him as president and CEO.

That year Agilent completed the sale of its camera module business to Flextronics and purchased Wavics, a Korean maker of power amplifiers for mobile handsets. The company also acquired Scientific Software, a developer of chromatography data systems and content and business process management applications, and Molecular Imaging, a maker of measurement tools used by nanotechnology researchers.

Later in 2005 Agilent sold its semiconductor operations, which produced such products as application-specific integrated circuits (ASICs), optoelectronic components, and RF chipsets. The semiconductor operations, renamed Avago Technologies, were acquired by two buyout firms — Kohlberg Kravis Roberts & Co. and Silver Lake Partners — for approximately $2.7 billion. Agilent sold its stake in Lumileds Lighting (LEDs) to Philips for $950 million. It also spun off its memory and system-on-a-chip (SoC) test system operations with an IPO in 2006; the new company was called Verigy.

Late in 2007 and into 2008, the company began expanding its product portfolio, primarily to grow its newly created Life Sciences and Chemical Analysis business. Through a series of acquisitions, including Velocity11, TILL Photonics, RVM Scientific, and MTS Systems, Agilent added laboratory robotics, optical microscopy, gas chromatography, and nanoindentation solutions products.

EXECUTIVES

Chairman: James G. Cullen, age 66
President, CEO, and Director: William P. (Bill) Sullivan, age 59
EVP Finance and Administration and CFO: Adrian T. Dillon, age 55
SVP, General Counsel, and Secretary: D. Craig Nordlund, age 59
SVP Human Resources: Jean M. Halloran, age 56
VP and CTO, Agilent Laboratories: Darlene J. Solomon
VP and General Manager, Design Validation Division: David S. Churchill, age 52
VP and General Manager, Wireless Business Unit, Electronic Measurements Group: Ronald S. (Ron) Nersesian, age 48

**VP Corporate Controllership and Tax and Principal
  Accounting Officer:** Didier Hirsch, age 57
VP Corporate Development: Shiela Robertson
**VP and General Manager, Electronic Measurements
  Group Supply Chain:** Shidah Ahmad
VP, Deputy General Counsel, and Assistant Secretary:
  Maria Oh Huber
**VP and General Manager, Electronic Measurement
  Group:** Ron Nersesian, age 49
**VP and Director, Molecular Technology Laboratory,
  Agilent Laboratories:** Neil Cook
VP and Treasurer: Hilliard Terry
Director, Investor Relations: Rodney Gonsalves, age 43
Manager Public Relations: Amy Flores
Auditors: PricewaterhouseCoopers LLP

LOCATIONS

HQ: Agilent Technologies, Inc.
  5301 Stevens Creek Blvd., Santa Clara, CA 95051
Phone: 408-553-7777   **Fax:** 408-345-8474
Web: www.agilent.com

Agilent Technologies has manufacturing and R&D
facilities in Australia, Canada, China, Germany, Japan,
Malaysia, Singapore, South Korea, the UK, and the US,
with marketing centers and sales offices throughout the
world.

2008 Sales

	$ mil.	% of total
US	1,834	32
Japan	663	11
China	642	11
Other countries	2,635	46
Total	**5,774**	**100**

PRODUCTS/OPERATIONS

2008 Sales

	$ mil.	% of total
Electronic measurement	3,239	56
Bio-analytical measurement	2,195	38
Semiconductor & board test	340	6
Total	**5,774**	**100**

2008 Sales by Revenue Type

	$ mil.	% of total
Products	4,804	83
Services & other	970	17
Total	**5,774**	**100**

Selected Products

Test and Measurement
  Automated test equipment
  Electronic component test equipment
  Electronic design automation software
  Fiber-optic test equipment
  General-purpose test equipment
  In-circuit testing equipment
  Network monitoring systems and test equipment
  Optical inspection equipment
  Oscilloscopes
  Precision distance measurement and calibration
    instruments
  Telecom network test equipment
  Wireless communications instruments and systems
Life Sciences and Chemical Analysis
  Bioanalyzers
  Bioinformatic software
  Chromatograph columns, analytical reagents, and
    other consumables
  Gas chromatography systems
  Liquid chromatography systems
  Microarrays

COMPETITORS

Advantest
Aeroflex
Affymetrix
AMETEK
Anritsu
Ansoft
Applied Materials
AWR
Beckman Coulter
Bio-Rad Labs
Bruker
Dionex
EXFO
Fluke Corporation
GE Healthcare
HEIDENHAIN Corp.
IBM Software
Ixia
JDS Uniphase
Keithley Instruments
LeCroy
Life Technologies Corporation
McAfee
MDS
National Instruments
PerkinElmer
Rohde & Schwarz
Shimadzu
Spirent
Tektronix
telent
Teradyne
Thermo Fisher Scientific
Varian
W. R. Grace
Waters Corp.
Yokogawa Electric

HISTORICAL FINANCIALS

Company Type: Public

Income Statement

FYE: October 31

	REVENUE ($ mil.)	NET INCOME ($ mil.)	NET PROFIT MARGIN	EMPLOYEES
10/08	5,774.0	693.0	12.0%	19,600
10/07	5,420.0	638.0	11.8%	19,400
10/06	4,973.0	3,307.0	66.5%	18,700
10/05	5,139.0	327.0	6.4%	21,000
10/04	7,181.0	349.0	4.9%	28,000
Annual Growth	**(5.3%)**	**18.7%**	**—**	**(8.5%)**

2008 Year-End Financials

Debt ratio: 83.0%	No. of shares (mil.): 343
Return on equity: 23.9%	Dividends
Cash ($ mil.): 1,405	Yield: 0.0%
Current ratio: 2.42	Payout: —
Long-term debt ($ mil.): 2,125	Market value ($ mil.): 7,619

Stock History

NYSE: A

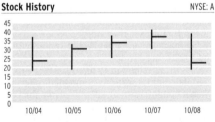

	STOCK PRICE ($) FY Close	P/E High/Low		PER SHARE ($) Earnings	Dividends	Book Value
10/08	22.19	20	10	1.87	0.00	7.41
10/07	36.85	26	19	1.57	0.00	9.37
10/06	35.60	5	4	7.50	0.00	10.57
10/05	32.01	53	31	0.65	0.00	11.82
10/04	25.06	55	27	0.71	0.00	10.34
Annual Growth	**(3.0%)**	**—**	**—**	**27.4%**	**—**	**(8.0%)**

Air Products
and Chemicals

Much like Jumpin' Jack Flash, business at Air
Products and Chemicals is a gas gas gas. The
company provides gases such as argon, hydrogen, nitrogen, and oxygen to manufacturers,
health care facilities, and other industries. Not
all is light and airy, however. It also makes gas
containers and equipment that separates air, pu-
rifies hydrogen, and liquefies gas. The company
distributes industrial gases by building on-site
plants or by shipping by truck for companies
with less extensive needs. It produced chemicals, including catalysts, surfactants, and intermediates derived from vinyl acetate monomer
(VAM) until it sold that unit in 2008.

Air Products sold its amines business to
chemical company Taminco for $210 million in
2006. The company also announced at that time
that it wanted to sell its polymers operations,
which were run through a joint venture with
Wacker-Chemie called Air Products Polymers.
In early 2008 the company finally sold most of
its holdings in the JV to Wacker for $265 mil-
lion. It sold the remaining two facilities that
had belonged to the joint venture to Ashland
Performance Materials later that year.

In 2007 Air Products made a small but strategic move into Eastern Europe. The company
took advantage of Linde's sell-off of some BOC
assets after the German company bought BOC in
2006. Air Products agreed to acquire the Polish
Gazy SP for just under $500 million with the
hopes of moving into the Central and Eastern
European markets to take advantage of the migration of manufacturing to the region.

It created its Air Products Healthcare unit in
1999 and expanded it greatly three years later
when it bought the company American Homecare Supply. The company added to the division
again with the 2005 acquisition of Nightingale
Medical, a homecare supply company that serves
a portion of the American Midwest. Air Products
Healthcare consists of a number of regional
providers of respiratory and rehabilitative products and services. It covers much of the eastern
half of the US. However, the US portion of the
business never performed to the company's expectations, and Air Products announced in 2008
that it wanted to sell the domestic operations of
the health care unit.

The result of these divestitures has been the
continuation of a trend toward the company's international business that started at the beginning of the decade. In 2002 Air Products
achieved only one-third of its total sales from
outside the US; by 2008 that percentage had
risen to more than half.

HISTORY

In the early 1900s Leonard Pool, the son of a
boilermaker, began selling oxygen to industrial
users. By the time he was 30, he was district
manager for Compressed Industrial Gases. In
the late 1930s Pool hired engineer Frank Pavlis
to help him design a cheaper, more efficient oxygen generator. In 1940 they had the design, and
Pool established Air Products in Detroit (initially
sharing space with the cadavers collected by his
brother, who was starting a mortuary science
college). The company was based on a simple,

breakthrough concept: the provision of on-site gases. Instead of delivering oxygen in cylinders, Pool proposed to build oxygen-generating facilities near large-volume gas users and then lease them, reducing distribution costs.

Although industrialists encouraged Pool to pursue his ideas, few orders were forthcoming, and the company faced financial crisis. The outbreak of WWII got the company out of difficulty, as the US military became a major customer. During the war the company moved to Chattanooga, Tennessee, for the available labor.

The end of the war brought with it another downturn as demand dried up. By waiting at the Weirton Steel plant until a contract was signed, Pool won a contract for three on-site generators. Weirton was nearly the company's only customer. Pool relocated the company to Allentown, Pennsylvania, to be closer to the Northeast's industrial market, where he could secure more contracts with steel companies.

The Cold War and the launching of the Sputnik satellite in 1957 propelled the company's growth. Convinced that Soviet rockets were powered by liquid hydrogen, the US government asked Air Products to supply it with the volatile fuel. The company entered the overseas market that year through a joint venture with Butterley (UK), to which it licensed its cryogenic processes and equipment. The company went public in 1961 and formed a subsidiary in Belgium in 1964.

Air Products diversified into chemicals when it bought Houdry Process (chemicals and chemical-plant maintenance, 1962) and Airco's chemicals and plastics operations in the 1970s. The company continued to diversify in the mid-1980s as it built large-scale plants for its environmental- and energy-systems business and added Anchor Chemical and the industrial chemicals unit of Abbott Labs.

In 1995 and 1996 Air Products expanded into China and other countries by winning 20 contracts with semiconductor makers. It bought Carburos Metalicos, Spain's #1 industrial gas supplier, in 1996. To focus on its core gas and chemical lines, the company shed most of its environmental- and energy-systems business.

Expanding further in Europe, Air Products bought the methylamines and derivatives unit of UK-based Imperial Chemical Industries (ICI) in 1997. The company sold its remaining interest in American Ref-Fuel (a waste-to-energy US operation). In 1998 Air Products bought Solkatronic Chemicals and opened a methylamines plant in Florida to complement its ICI purchase.

The next year Air Products sold its polyvinyl alcohol business to Celanese. The company boosted its European presence in 2001 with the acquisition of Messer Griesheim's (Germany) respiratory home-care business and 50% of AGA's Netherlands industrial gases operations.

Air Products was hurt by the slowdown in manufacturing, primarily in the electronics and steel industries, which are major customers for gases. Its chemical revenues also were hurt by pressure on pricing. To improve profits, the company initiated cost cuts, including job cuts (about 10% of its employees) and divestitures such as its US packaged gas business.

The company broadened its health care operations in late 2002 by acquiring American Homecare Supply (now called Air Products Healthcare), which serves the home health care industry with medical gases and related equipment.

EXECUTIVES

Chairman, President, and CEO: John E. McGlade, age 55
SVP and CFO: Paul E. Huck, age 59
SVP Strategic Development and Execution: Scott A. Sherman, age 58
SVP and General Manager, Merchant Gases: Robert D. Dixon, age 50
SVP and General Manager Electronics and Performance Materials: Michael F. Hilton
SVP Human Resources and Communications: Lynn C. Minella, age 51
SVP and General Manager, Tonnage Gases, Equipment, and Energy: Stephen J. Jones, age 48
SVP and General Counsel: John Stanley
VP and CTO: Montgomery (Monty) Alger
VP, Controller, and Chief Accounting Officer: M. Scott Crocco, age 45
VP and Chief Risk Officer: Diane L. Sheridan
VP Energy and Materials: Laurie K. Stewart
VP Strategic Planning Air Products: Norma J. Curby
VP Energy Businesses: David J. Taylor, age 53
VP Global Business Support Services: Wayne M. Mitchell
VP and Treasurer: George G. Bitto
VP Information Technology and CIO: Richard Boocock
VP Corporate Communications: Elizabeth L. (Betsy) Klebe
Europe Region President: Erwin Zwicky
President Air Products Asia: Wilbur W. Mok
Director Investor Relations: Nelson Squires
Auditors: KPMG LLP

LOCATIONS

HQ: Air Products and Chemicals, Inc.
7201 Hamilton Blvd., Allentown, PA 18195
Phone: 610-481-4911 **Fax:** 610-481-5900
Web: www.airproducts.com

2008 Sales

	$ mil.	% of total
US	4,845.1	47
Europe	3,448.0	33
Asia	1,661.3	16
Canada	241.2	2
Latin America	218.9	2
Total	**10,414.5**	**100**

PRODUCTS/OPERATIONS

2008 Sales

	$ mil.	% of total
Merchant Gases	4,192.7	40
Tonnage Gases	3,574.4	35
Electronics & Performance Materials	2,209.3	21
Equipment & Energy	438.1	4
Total	**10,414.5**	**100**

Selected Products and Services

Industrial Gases
  Argon
  Carbon dioxide
  Carbon monoxide
  Helium
  Hydrogen
  Nitrogen
  Oxygen
  Synthesis gas
Equipment and Services
  Air-pollution control systems
  Air-separation equipment
  Hydrogen-purification equipment
  Natural gas-liquefaction equipment

COMPETITORS

Aceto	The Linde Group
Airgas	Messer Group
BASF SE	Praxair
L'Air Liquide	Taiyo Nippon Sanso

HISTORICAL FINANCIALS

Company Type: Public

Income Statement

FYE: September 30

	REVENUE ($ mil.)	NET INCOME ($ mil.)	NET PROFIT MARGIN	EMPLOYEES
9/08	10,414.5	909.7	8.7%	21,100
9/07	10,037.8	1,035.6	10.3%	22,100
9/06	8,850.4	729.6	8.2%	20,700
9/05	8,143.5	711.7	8.7%	19,500
9/04	7,411.4	604.1	8.2%	19,900
Annual Growth	**8.9%**	**10.8%**	**—**	**1.5%**

2008 Year-End Financials

Debt ratio: 69.9%
Return on equity: 17.3%
Cash ($ mil.): 104
Current ratio: 1.29
Long-term debt ($ mil.): 3,515
No. of shares (mil.): 210
Dividends
  Yield: 2.5%
  Payout: 41.0%
Market value ($ mil.): 14,388

Stock History

NYSE: APD

	STOCK PRICE ($) FY Close	P/E High/Low	PER SHARE ($) Earnings	Dividends	Book Value
9/08	68.49	26 16	4.15	1.70	23.95
9/07	97.76	21 14	4.64	1.48	26.16
9/06	66.37	22 17	3.18	1.34	23.44
9/05	55.14	21 17	3.08	1.25	21.78
9/04	54.38	21 17	2.64	1.04	21.15
Annual Growth	**5.9%**	**— —**	**12.0%**	**13.1%**	**3.1%**

Airgas, Inc.

Airgas has floated to the top of the industrial gas distribution industry by buying up more than 400 companies since its founding in 1986. The company's North American network of more than 1,100 locations includes retail stores, gas fill plants, specialty gas labs, production facilities, and distribution centers. Airgas distributes argon, hydrogen, nitrogen, oxygen, welding gases, and a variety of medical and specialty gases, as well as dry ice and protective equipment (hard hats, goggles). Its Merchant Gases unit operates air-separation plants that produce oxygen, nitrogen, and argon. It also sells welding machines, rents industrial gas tanks, and produces acetylene and nitrous oxide.

It is the largest gas distributor in the country, with a 25% market share. Almost all of the company's sales come from distributing bulk gases (nitrogen, oxygen, argon, helium), gas cylinders, and welding equipment. Airgas also distributes dry ice. The industrial manufacturing and repair and maintenance industries account for about a quarter each of the company's sales; customers primarily make fabricated metal products, industrial transportation and equipment, chemical products, and primary metal products. Other industries served include medical and health services, agriculture, mining, repair and maintenance, and wholesale trade.

The company continually strives to grow its business through acquisitions, adding 10-15 companies annually. In 2008 the company acquired 14 companies, including Refron, a US-based reseller and distributor of refrigerants and a provider of technical services and refrigerant reclamation services.

Founder and CEO Peter McCausland and his family control a more than 10% stake in Airgas.

HISTORY

In the early 1980s Peter McCausland was a corporate attorney involved in mergers and acquisitions for Messer Griesheim, a large German industrial gas producer. When the German firm declined McCausland's recommendation in 1982 to buy Connecticut Oxygen, he raised money from private sources and bought it himself. He acquired other distributors and then left Messer Griesheim in 1987 to run Airgas full-time.

Airgas began buying mostly small local and regional gas distributors in the US. By 1994 strategy shifted to purchasing larger "superregional" distributors such as Jimmie Jones Co. and Post Welding Supply of Alabama, which added about $70 million combined to the company's revenues.

Airgas then began "rolling up" additional similar businesses. In 1995 it bought more than 25 companies, and two years later it added more than 20 gas distributors. Also in 1997 Airgas expanded its manufacturing capabilities by building five plants that could fast-fill whole pallets of gas cylinders (the old, manual system rolls cylinders two at a time). By 2000 the company had about 100 cylinder fill plants.

Struggling to integrate acquisitions while dealing with softening markets, Airgas began a companywide realignment in 1998. To that end, it sold its calcium carbide and carbon products operations to former partner Elkem ASA later that year; the company also consolidated 34 hubs into 16 regional companies and sold its operations in Poland and Thailand to Germany-based Linde in 1999.

In 2000 Airgas acquired distributor Mallinckrodt's Puritan-Bennett division (gas products for medical uses) with 36 locations in the US and Canada. The company also acquired the majority of Air Products' US packaged gas business, excluding its electronic gases and magnetic resonance imaging-related helium operations, in 2002.

In 2004 and 2005 it bought units from giants like Air Products and Chemicals, BOC, and LaRoche Industries. In 2006 Airgas continued to build with the purchase of 10 businesses, including Union Industrial Gas, which supplies Texas and much of the Southwest, and then Linde's US bulk gas business for $495 million the next year. Linde, in the process of integrating its 2006 acquisition of BOC, then sold to Airgas a portion of its US packaged gas business for $310 million.

EXECUTIVES

Chairman, President, and CEO: Peter McCausland, age 59, $3,062,832 total compensation
EVP and COO: Michael L. (Mike) Molinini, age 58, $1,059,437 total compensation
SVP and CFO: Robert M. McLaughlin, age 52, $683,013 total compensation
SVP and CIO: Robert A. Dougherty, age 51
SVP Sales: Patrick M. Visintainer, age 45
SVP Human Resources: Dwight T. Wilson, age 53
SVP Sales and Marketing: Ronald J. (Ron) Stark
SVP, Airgas Puritan Medical: Kelly P. Justice
SVP, Airgas Merchant Gases: Thomas S. Thoman
SVP, Specialty Gas and Life Sciences: James A. Muller
SVP Distribution Operations: Michael E. Rohde
SVP Corporate Development: Leslie J. Graff, age 48, $600,876 total compensation
SVP and General Counsel: Robert H. Young Jr., age 58
VP Communications: James S. Ely
VP and Controller: Thomas M. Smyth, age 55
VP Communications and Investor Relations: R. Jay Worley
Division President, Gas Operations and Airgas National Welders: Andrew R. (Andy) Cichocki
Division President, Gas Operations: Ted R. Schulte, age 58
Division President, East: B. Shaun Powers, age 57, $624,436 total compensation
Auditors: KPMG LLP

LOCATIONS

HQ: Airgas, Inc.
259 N. Radnor-Chester Rd., Ste. 100, Radnor, PA 19087
Phone: 610-687-5253   **Fax:** 610-225-3271
Web: www.airgas.com

PRODUCTS/OPERATIONS

2009 Sales

	$ mil.	% of total
Distribution	3,918.4	90
Other operations	457.3	10
Adjustments	(26.2)	—
Total	**4,349.5**	**100**

2009 Sales

	$ mil.	% of total
Gas & rentals	2,665.6	61
Hardgoods	1,683.9	39
Total	**4,349.5**	**100**

Selected Products and Services

Products
  Carbon dioxide
  Dry ice
  Industrial gases
  Argon
  Helium
  Hydrogen
  Liquid oxygen
  Nitrogen
  Nitrous oxide
  Oxygen
  Safety equipment
  Specialty gases
Services
  Container rental
  Welding equipment rental

COMPETITORS

Air Products
American Air Liquide
L'Air Liquide
Lincoln Electric
Matheson Tri-Gas
Praxair Distribution
Valley National Gases
W.W. Grainger

HISTORICAL FINANCIALS

Company Type: Public

Income Statement

FYE: March 31

	REVENUE ($ mil.)	NET INCOME ($ mil.)	NET PROFIT MARGIN	EMPLOYEES
3/09	4,349.5	261.1	6.0%	14,000
3/08	4,017.0	223.3	5.6%	14,500
3/07	3,205.1	154.4	4.8%	11,500
3/06	2,829.6	126.1	4.5%	10,300
3/05	2,411.4	92.0	3.8%	11,000
Annual Growth	**15.9%**	**29.8%**	**—**	**6.2%**

2009 Year-End Financials

Debt ratio: 111.4%   No. of shares (mil.): 82
Return on equity: 17.5%   Dividends
Cash ($ mil.): 47   Yield: 1.7%
Current ratio: 1.66   Payout: 17.9%
Long-term debt ($ mil.): 1,750   Market value ($ mil.): 2,766

Stock History

NYSE: ARG

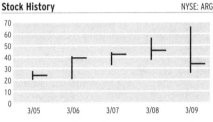

	STOCK PRICE ($) FY Close	P/E High/Low		PER SHARE ($) Earnings	Dividends	Book Value
3/09	33.81	21	8	3.12	0.56	19.21
3/08	45.47	21	14	2.66	0.39	17.27
3/07	42.15	23	17	1.92	0.28	13.75
3/06	39.09	25	13	1.57	0.24	11.58
3/05	23.89	23	17	1.20	0.18	9.95
Annual Growth	**9.1%**	**—**	**—**	**27.0%**	**32.8%**	**17.9%**

AirTran Holdings

The Atlanta airport is one of the world's busiest, and AirTran Holdings is partly responsible. Through its main subsidiary, AirTran Airways, the company offers low-fare passenger transportation, primarily from its hub in Atlanta. AirTran Airways flies to more than 60 cities, mainly in the eastern US. The airline operates a fleet of about 140 Boeing aircraft, including the 717-200 and the 737-700. It is a leading carrier in the Atlanta market, behind Delta, which handles the largest share of the traffic at Hartsfield-Jackson Atlanta International Airport.

The carrier successfully blends a couple of industry models. It often offers lower fares than Delta, but unlike low-fare leader Southwest Airlines, AirTran Airways provides reserved seats and business-class service. In addition, it relies on its Atlanta hub more than Southwest relies on any single airport. Like Southwest, AirTran Airways has been able to maintain a lower cost structure than many of its larger rivals.

AirTran Airways continues to expand its route network, particularly by adding departures from cities other than Atlanta, such as Orlando and Baltimore. From Orlando the carrier has added direct service to several Florida markets. Its fleet of 717s is well-suited to short-haul service. At the same time, AirTran Airways is introducing service to more markets in the western US, in which it can take advantage of the range of its 737s.

The larger aircraft enable AirTran Airways to serve destinations such as San Juan, Puerto Rico, which launched in late 2008 and Cancun, Mexico, which launched in 2009.

The carrier further extends its reach through a marketing partnership with Frontier Airlines, touted as a first among low-fare carriers, in which the carriers refer passengers to each other and credit miles from one another's frequent flier programs. The deal stops short of code-sharing, which involves one carrier selling tickets for another's flights, but potential customers on the AirTran Web site can go to Frontier to book flights to destinations not served by AirTran, and vice-versa.

High fuel prices and a slowing US economy have hurt AirTran, Frontier, and the rest of the airline industry, however, and in May 2008 AirTran announced plans to reduce capacity and to delay delivery of 18 Boeing 737s. The new aircraft, originally scheduled to be delivered from 2009 through 2011, will instead be added to the carrier's fleet in 2013 and 2014.

HISTORY

What became AirTran Holdings began in 1992 when airline veterans Robert Priddy, Maurice Gallagher, and Timothy Flynn founded ValuJet, basing it in Atlanta. By year's end the company operated six aircraft on 34 daily flights to Fort Lauderdale, Jacksonville, Orlando, and Tampa, Florida. By late 1994 it flew 22 jets between 16 cities, mainly in the Southeast. ValuJet continued to expand, linking Washington, DC, to Chicago and Montreal in 1995 and to New York in 1996.

In May 1996 a ValuJet DC-9 crashed in the Florida Everglades, killing all 110 people aboard. The FAA reviewed the company's safety and maintenance procedures after the crash, forcing the airline to shut down for 15 weeks. ValuJet resumed flights in September, offering $19 one-way flights to lure back passengers. Turnaround specialist Joseph Corr, formerly of TWA and Continental Airlines, came aboard in November as CEO to help ValuJet change its course.

To recover passenger bookings, the airline joined the SABRE computer reservation system in 1997, sparking a 60% increase in SABRE bookings. That year ValuJet acquired AirTran Airways through its purchase of Airways Corporation, rebranded itself as AirTran Airlines, kicked off an advertising campaign to overhaul its image, and moved to Orlando. In 1999 Joseph Leonard, a former Eastern Airlines executive, succeeded Corr as CEO. That year AirTran began to replace aging aircraft by taking delivery of new Boeing 717 regional jets, becoming the first airline to use that new aircraft model.

AirTran made an effort to acquire ailing industry giant TWA in 2000, but talks between the two airlines ended shortly after they began. Also that year AirTran transferred to the American Stock Exchange from the Nasdaq.

An effort to acquire Chicago landing slots from bankrupt ATA fell short in 2004 as rival Southwest Airlines outbid AirTran to gain additional space at Midway Airport.

In 2007 AirTran tried to expand by buying smaller rival Midwest Air Group, but its bids were rejected by Midwest's board, which wanted the company to remain independent. Midwest instead accepted an offer from an investment group led by TPG Capital.

That same year President Bob Fornaro was promoted to CEO, succeeding Joe Leonard. Leonard had served as CEO since 1999, the same year Fornaro was hired as president. Fornaro additionally took on the role of chairman in June 2008.

EXECUTIVES

Chairman, President, and CEO, AirTran Holdings and AirTran Airways: Robert L. (Bob) Fornaro, age 56, $1,521,286 total compensation
EVP, Corporate Development, AirTran Airways: Steven A. (Steve) Rossum, age 45, $607,266 total compensation
EVP, Operations and Corporate Affairs, AirTran Airways: Stephen J. Kolski, age 68, $897,383 total compensation
SVP, Customer Service, AirTran Airways: Alfred J. (Jack) Smith III, age 57, $615,640 total compensation
SVP, Finance, Treasurer, and CFO, AirTran Holdings and AirTran Airways: Arne G. Haak, age 41, $703,066 total compensation
SVP and CIO, AirTran Airways: Rocky Wiggins
SVP, Marketing and Planning, AirTran Airways: Kevin P. Healy
SVP, Human Resources and Administration, AirTran Airways: Loral Blinde
SVP, General Counsel, and Secretary: Richard P. Magurno, age 65, $615,034 total compensation
SVP, Operations, AirTran Airways: Klaus Goersch
VP, Marketing and Sales, AirTran Airways: Tad Hutcheson
VP and Chief Accounting Officer, AirTran Airways: Mark W. Osterberg, age 55
VP, Operations, AirTran Airways: Jim Tabor
VP, Maintenance and Engineering, AirTran Airways: Kirk Thornburg
VP, Inflight Service, AirTran Airways: Peggy Sauer-Clark
VP, Flight Operations: Jeff Miller
Director, Corporate Safety, AirTran Airways: Jean-Pierre (J. P.) Dagon
Director, Public Relations, AirTran Airways: Christopher White
Auditors: Ernst & Young LLP

LOCATIONS

HQ: AirTran Holdings, Inc.
9955 AirTran Blvd., Orlando, FL 32827
Phone: 407-318-5600   **Fax:** 407-318-5900
Web: www.airtran.com

PRODUCTS/OPERATIONS

2008 Sales

	$ mil.	% of total
Passenger	2,413.6	95
Cargo	138.9	5
Total	**2,552.5**	**100**

COMPETITORS

AMR Corp.
Continental Airlines
Delta Air Lines
JetBlue
Midwest Air
Northwest Airlines
Southwest Airlines
UAL
US Airways

HISTORICAL FINANCIALS

Company Type: Public

Income Statement

FYE: December 31

	REVENUE ($ mil.)	NET INCOME ($ mil.)	NET PROFIT MARGIN	EMPLOYEES
12/08	2,552.5	(273.8)	—	8,000
12/07	2,310.0	52.7	2.3%	8,500
12/06	1,893.4	15.5	0.8%	7,700
12/05	1,450.5	1.7	0.1%	6,900
12/04	1,041.4	12.3	1.2%	6,100
Annual Growth	25.1%	—	—	7.0%

2008 Year-End Financials

Debt ratio: 388.9%
Return on equity: —
Cash ($ mil.): 315
Current ratio: 0.82
Long-term debt ($ mil.): 957
No. of shares (mil.): 120
Dividends
  Yield: 0.0%
  Payout: —
Market value ($ mil.): 533

Stock History

NYSE: AAI

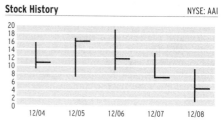

	STOCK PRICE ($) FY Close	P/E High/Low		Earnings	PER SHARE ($) Dividends	Book Value
12/08	4.44	—	—	(2.51)	0.00	2.05
12/07	7.16	23	13	0.56	0.00	3.71
12/06	11.74	111	53	0.17	0.00	3.19
12/05	16.03	835	370	0.02	0.00	2.93
12/04	10.70	111	67	0.14	0.00	2.78
Annual Growth	(19.7%)	—	—	—	—	(7.4%)

AK Steel Holding

Automobile sales help AK Steel's business keep rolling, though it has begun to branch out to the infrastructure and manufacturing industries. The company manufactures carbon, stainless, and electrical steel. It sells hot- and cold-rolled carbon steel to construction companies, steel distributors and service centers, and automotive and industrial machinery producers. AK Steel also sells cold-rolled and aluminum-coated stainless steel to automakers. The company produces electrical steels (iron-silicon alloys with unique magnetic properties) for makers of power transmission and distribution equipment. In addition, it makes carbon and stainless steel tubular products through AK Tube.

The steel industry has been consolidating for years as troubled companies have been snapped up by market leaders. AK Steel was outbid in a couple of major acquisition efforts early in the decade, and analysts have since speculated that the company itself may be an acquisition candidate. AK Steel has maintained its independence, however, in part because of its status as a leading supplier of some high-grade niche products, such as components of stainless steel exhaust systems, for carmakers.

In 2006 the company announced plans to increase production capacity at many of its facilities. Total investments have been about $70 million and have improved AK Steel's electrical and tubular steel output. The company's sales to automobile makers have declined as a percentage of total sales, mostly due to its ability to raise prices for its other products, boosting revenue for those other segments. These capacity increases should only help that trend continue.

Of course, the rapid decline of the domestic auto industry could help, too. In 2008, sales to the auto industry declined to less than a third of AK Steel's total sales. Historically, sales to the industry had made up nearly half of AK Steel's business; in the past GM had been its largest customer, generating 10% of sales.

HISTORY

George Verity, who was in the roofing business in Cincinnati around the turn of the century, often had trouble getting sheet metal, so in 1900 he founded his own steel company, American Rolling Mill. His first plant, in Middletown, Ohio, was followed by a second production facility 11 years later in Ashland, Kentucky. Plant superintendent John Tytus, whose family was in paper milling, applied those rolling techniques to make American Rolling Mill's steel more uniform in thickness.

In 1926 Columbia Steel developed a process to overcome several production problems inherent in the Tytus method, and in 1930 American Rolling Mill bought Columbia Steel. The company changed its name to Armco Steel in 1948.

Armco began diversifying in the 1950s and continued diversifying until the early 1980s. Subsidiaries were involved in coal, oil, and gas-drilling equipment and insurance and financial services, among other things. In 1978 the company changed its name to Armco Inc.

Armco began shedding subsidiaries in the early 1980s. Sales and market share increased as the company approached the billion-dollar mark at the end of the decade. In 1989 Armco formed Armco Steel Company with Japan's Kawasaki Steel Corporation.

Armco's sales reached $1.3 billion in 1991, though the high operating expenses in the steel industry of the 1990s kept profits low. Armco began looking outside the company for help, and in 1992 it persuaded retired steel executive Tom Graham to head the company. Graham brought with him another industry veteran, Richard Wardrop, who would succeed Graham as CEO in 1995. After evaluating the company's holdings, the two divested more than 10 subsidiaries and divisions. Armco also worked on improving quality and customer service, with special emphasis placed on timely delivery.

In 1994 Armco's limited partnership with Kawasaki was altered and AK Steel Holding Corporation was formed, with AK Steel Corporation as its main subsidiary and the Middletown and Ashland plants as its production base. The holding company went public the same year, raising more than $650 million, enabling the company to pay off its debt.

AK Steel Holding moved its headquarters to Middletown, Ohio, in 1995. Despite many naysayers, Graham then pushed a plan to build a state-of-the-art $1.1 billion steel production facility.

Many doubted the wisdom of going into long-term debt so soon after coming out of the hole — especially when a similar facility had produced lackluster results for Inland Steel. Graham stuck by his plant, and in 1997 ground was broken on the facility in Spencer County near Rockport, Indiana (Rockport Works). Graham retired that year, and Wardrop took over as chairman.

In 1998 the company opened its Rockport Works cold-rolling mill and began operating a hot-dip galvanizing and galvannealing line. The next year AK Steel bought former parent Armco for $842 million. AK Steel acquired welded steel tubing maker Alpha Tube Corporation (renamed AK Tube LLC) in 2001. In late 2001 the company took a charge of $194 million for losses in its pension fund, which had been battered by a weak stock market and lowered interest rates.

AK Steel sold its Sawhill Tubular Division to John Maneely Company (Collingswood, NJ) for roughly $50 million in 2002.

AK Steel offered to purchase National Steel, which was operating under Chapter 11 bankruptcy protection. However, AK Steel's bid was trumped in 2003 by one from U.S. Steel that included a ratified labor agreement with the United Steelworkers of America. AK Steel also lost out in an effort to acquire Rouge Industries (later Severstal North America).

Chairman and CEO Wardrop and president John Hritz left their posts in September 2003. CFO James Wainscott was named president and CEO, and Robert Jenkins became chairman. (Wainscott succeeded Jenkins as chairman in January 2006.)

In an effort to reduce its debt, AK Steel in 2004 sold its Douglas Dynamics unit, a maker of snow and ice removal equipment, for $260 million, and its Greens Port Industrial Park, a 600-acre development in Houston, for $75 million.

In 2007 the company moved its corporate headquarters to West Chester, Ohio.

EXECUTIVES

Chairman, President, and CEO:
James L. (Jim) Wainscott, age 52,
$13,233,095 total compensation
SVP Operations: John F. Kaloski, age 59,
$4,036,530 total compensation
SVP, General Counsel, and Secretary: David C. Horn,
age 57, $4,522,462 total compensation
VP Finance and CFO: Albert E. Ferrara Jr., age 60,
$3,336,699 total compensation
VP Human Resources: Lawrence F. Zizzo Jr., age 60
VP Government and Public Relations: Alan H. McCoy,
age 57
VP Sales and Customer Service: Douglas W. Gant,
age 50, $2,710,479 total compensation
VP Labor Relations: Thomas F. McKenna, age 63
Chief Accounting Officer and Controller:
Roger K. Newport
Auditors: Deloitte & Touche LLP

LOCATIONS

HQ: AK Steel Holding Corporation
9227 Centre Pointe Dr., West Chester, OH 45069
Phone: 513-425-5000   **Fax:** 513-425-2676
Web: www.aksteel.com

2008 Sales

	$ mil.	% of total
US	6,376.4	83
Other countries	1,267.9	17
Total	**7,644.3**	**100**

PRODUCTS/OPERATIONS

2008 Sales

	$ mil.	% of total
Carbon steel	4,188.4	55
Stainless & electrical steel	3,234.5	42
Tubular steel & other	221.4	3
Total	**7,644.3**	**100**

2008 Sales

	% of total
Distributors & converters	39
Automotive	32
Industry & manufacturing	29
Total	**100**

COMPETITORS

Dofasco
Nucor
Steel Dynamics
United States Steel
Worthington Industries

HISTORICAL FINANCIALS

Company Type: Public

Income Statement

FYE: December 31

	REVENUE ($ mil.)	NET INCOME ($ mil.)	NET PROFIT MARGIN	EMPLOYEES
12/08	7,644.3	4.0	0.1%	6,800
12/07	7,003.0	387.7	5.5%	6,900
12/06	6,069.0	12.0	0.2%	7,000
12/05	5,647.4	(0.8)	—	8,000
12/04	5,217.3	238.4	4.6%	8,400
Annual Growth	**10.0%**	**(64.0%)**	**—**	**(5.1%)**

2008 Year-End Financials

Debt ratio: 65.4%   No. of shares (mil.): 109
Return on equity: 0.4%   Dividends
Cash ($ mil.): 563   Yield: 2.1%
Current ratio: 2.73   Payout: 500.0%
Long-term debt ($ mil.): 633   Market value ($ mil.): 1,020

Stock History

NYSE: AKS

	STOCK PRICE ($) FY Close	P/E High/Low		PER SHARE ($) Earnings	Dividends	Book Value
12/08	9.32	1,827	130	0.04	0.20	8.85
12/07	46.24	16	5	3.46	0.00	8.00
12/06	16.90	157	69	0.11	0.00	3.81
12/05	7.95	—	—	(0.02)	0.00	2.02
12/04	14.47	7	2	2.18	0.00	1.80
Annual Growth	**(10.4%)**	**—**	**—**	**(63.2%)**	**—**	**48.8%**

Alaska Air Group

Whether you want to capture a Kodiak moment or down a daiquiri by the Sea of Cortez, an Alaska Air Group unit can fly you there. Its primary subsidiary, Alaska Airlines, has a fleet of some 110 Boeing 737 jets serving about 40 cities in Alaska, other western states, and western Canada; it also flies to select major cities elsewhere in the US and about 10 cities in Mexico. Alaska Airlines operates from hubs in Anchorage, Alaska; Portland, Oregon; Los Angeles; and Seattle. Alaska Air Group also owns regional carrier Horizon Air, which flies to another 50 cities in the western US and Canada with a fleet of some 20 jets and 40 turboprops.

Alaska Airlines' leadership in the Alaska air travel market and strong presence on the West Coast have made it an attractive code-sharing partner for airlines such as Air France, American, Continental, Delta, KLM, and Northwest.

Alaska Airlines hopes to grow mainly by increasing the frequency of flights within its existing route structure, but also by adding service to new markets as demand warrants. Alaska Airlines got a boost in 2008 from its freight unit, which broke the $100 million revenue mark for the first time. The healthy cargo business combined with changes to Alaska Airlines' loyalty program gave the carrier a profitable year in 2008 — a novelty among airlines during the economic slowdown.

Like other major US airlines, however, both Alaska Airlines and Horizon Air are working to keep a lid on costs in the face of rising fuel prices and increased competition from low-fare carriers. As part of their cost-control programs, both airlines are moving to one model of aircraft (Alaska Airlines transitioned to an all-737 fleet in 2008 and Horizon Air is moving toward a fleet of Bombardier Q400s by 2010). The airlines have also cut flight frequency and capacity, and revamped some routes.

HISTORY

Pilot Mac McGee started McGee Airways in 1932 to fly cargo between Anchorage and Bristol Bay, Alaska. He joined other local operators in 1937 to form Star Air Lines, which began airmail service between Fairbanks and Bethel in 1938. In 1944, a year after buying three small airlines, Star adopted the name Alaska Airlines.

The company expanded to include freight service to Africa and Australia in 1950. This expansion, coupled with the seasonal nature of the airline's business, caused losses in the early 1970s. Developer Bruce Kennedy gained control of the board, turning the firm around by the end of 1973. But the Civil Aeronautics Board forced the carrier to drop service to northwestern Alaska in 1975, and by 1978 it served only 10 Alaskan cities and Seattle.

Kennedy became CEO the next year. The 1978 Airline Deregulation Act allowed Alaska Air to move into new areas as well as regain the routes it had lost. By 1982 it was the largest airline flying between Alaska and the lower 48 states.

In 1985 the airline reorganized, forming Alaska Air Group as its holding company. The next year Alaska Air Group bought Jet America Airlines (expanding its routes eastward to Chicago, St. Louis, and Dallas) and Seattle-based Horizon Air Industries (which served 30 Northwest cities). When competition in the East and Midwest cut profits in 1987, Kennedy shut down Jet America to focus on West Coast operations.

To counterbalance summer traffic to Alaska, the airline began service to two Mexican resorts in 1988. Fuel prices and sluggish traffic hurt 1990 earnings, but Alaska Air Group stayed in the black, unlike many other carriers. Kennedy retired as chairman and CEO in 1991.

That year the airline began service to Canada and seasonal flights to two Russian cities. Neil Bergt's MarkAir airline declared war, cutting fares and horning in on Alaska Air Group's territory. Alaska Air Group's profits were slashed, and MarkAir went into bankruptcy.

Alaska Air extended Russian flights to year-round in 1994. The airline began service to Vancouver in 1996. That year it became the first major US carrier to use the GPS satellite navigation system. In 1997 it added service to more than a dozen new cities but halted service to Russia because of that country's economic woes in 1998.

Alaska Air Group and Dutch airline KLM agreed to a marketing alliance in 1998 that included reciprocal frequent-flier programs and code-sharing, and in 1999 it added code-sharing agreements with several major airlines, including American and Continental. Alaska Airlines developed an online check-in system, a first among US carriers.

In 2000 an Alaska Airlines MD-83 crashed into the Pacific Ocean near Los Angeles, killing all 88 people on board. A federal investigation of Alaska Airlines' maintenance practices found deficiencies, but the FAA eventually accepted the airline's plan to tighten safety standards.

Like most carriers in the latter part of 2001, Alaska Airlines cut back its flights as a result of reduced demand after the September 11 terrorist attacks. As demand slowly returned in 2002, Alaska Airlines began to add new destinations and increase the number of flights on some established routes.

In 2005 Alaska Airlines announced plans to buy 35 Boeing 737-800s between 2006 and 2011.

EXECUTIVES

Chairman, President, and CEO, Alaska Air Group; Chairman and CEO, Alaska Airlines:
William S. (Bill) Ayer, age 54,
$2,022,664 total compensation
President, Alaska Airlines: Bradley D. (Brad) Tilden, age 48, $924,138 total compensation
President and CEO, Horizon Air Industries:
Jeffrey D. Pinneo, age 52, $852,592 total compensation
EVP Operations and COO, Alaska Airlines:
Benito (Ben) Minicucci, age 42
EVP Finance and CFO, Alaska Air Group and Alaska Airlines: Glenn S. Johnson, age 50,
$1,413,090 total compensation
SVP Alaska, Alaska Airlines: William L. (Bill) MacKay
VP Legal and Corporate Affairs, General Counsel, and Corporate Secretary, Alaska Air Group and Alaska Airlines: Keith Loveless, age 52
VP Safety, Alaska Air Group and Alaska Airlines:
Thomas W. (Tom) Nunn
VP Finance and Controller, Alaska Air Group and Alaska Airlines: Brandon S. Pedersen, age 42
VP Finance and Treasurer: John F. (Jay) Schaefer Jr.
VP Human Resources, Strategy, and Culture and Inclusion, Alaska Airlines: Kelley J. Dobbs, age 42
VP Legal and Administration, Horizon Air:
Arthur E. (Art) Thomas

VP Human Resources and Labor Relations, Alaska Airlines: Dennis J. Hamel
VP Corporate Real Estate, Alaska Airlines:
Edward W. White
VP Flight Operations, Horizon Air:
Eugene C. (Gene) Hahn
VP Marketing, Sales, and Customer Experience, Alaska Airlines: Stephen B. Jarvis
Managing Director, Investor Relations and Corporate Secretary, Alaska Air Group and Alaska Airlines:
Shannon K. Alberts
Managing Director, Brand and Product Marketing, Alaska Airlines: Greg Latimer
Auditors: KPMG LLP

LOCATIONS

HQ: Alaska Air Group, Inc.
19300 International Blvd., Seattle, WA 98188
Phone: 206-392-5040   **Fax:** 206-392-2804
Web: www.alaskaair.com

PRODUCTS/OPERATIONS

2008 Revenues

	$ mil.	% of total
Passenger	3,355.8	92
Freight & mail	103.6	3
Other	160.9	4
Change in loyalty program terms	42.3	1
Total	**3,662.6**	**100**

2008 Revenues

	$ mil.	% of total
Alaska Airlines	3,221.3	81
Horizon Airlines	733.9	19
Other	1.1	—
Adjustments	(293.7)	—
Total	**3,662.6**	**100**

COMPETITORS

ACE Aviation
Aeromexico
Allegiant Travel
AMR Corp.
Continental Airlines
Delta Air Lines
JetBlue
Mesa Air
Northwest Airlines
SkyWest
Southwest Airlines
UAL
US Airways
Virgin America
WestJet

HISTORICAL FINANCIALS

Company Type: Public

Income Statement

	REVENUE ($ mil.)	NET INCOME ($ mil.)	NET PROFIT MARGIN	EMPLOYEES
12/08	3,662.6	(135.9)	—	14,143
12/07	3,506.0	125.0	3.6%	14,710
12/06	3,334.4	(52.6)	—	14,485
12/05	2,975.3	84.5	2.8%	13,768
12/04	2,723.8	(15.3)	—	14,584
Annual Growth	**7.7%**	**—**		**(0.8%)**

FYE: December 31

2008 Year-End Financials

Debt ratio: 241.2%   No. of shares (mil.): 35
Return on equity: —   Dividends
Cash ($ mil.): 283   Yield: 0.0%
Current ratio: 1.11   Payout: —
Long-term debt ($ mil.): 1,596   Market value ($ mil.): 1,027

	STOCK PRICE ($)		P/E		PER SHARE ($)		
	FY Close		High	Low	Earnings	Dividends	Book Value
12/08	29.25		—	—	(3.74)	0.00	18.85
12/07	25.01		14	7	3.09	0.00	29.16
12/06	39.50		—	—	(1.39)	0.00	25.22
12/05	35.72		—	—	(0.01)	0.00	23.57
12/04	33.49		—	—	(0.57)	0.00	18.93
Annual Growth	(3.3%)		—	—	—	—	(0.1%)

Alberto-Culver

From the bathroom to the kitchen to the laundry room, Alberto-Culver has you covered. The company makes products for hair care (Alberto VO5, Nexxus, TRESemmé), skin care (St. Ives), and personal care (FDS); sweeteners and seasonings (Sugar Twin, Mrs. Dash); home care (Kleen Guard); and laundry-care items (Static Guard). Alberto-Culver's products are developed, manufactured, and marketed in the US and in more than 100 other countries. The company also makes beauty products for other US companies under private label. Alberto-Culver sold its Cederroth business, which served Nordic countries, to CapMan in 2008 and then acquired the Noxzema brand from Procter & Gamble (P&G).

Nordic-based private-equity firm, CapMan, purchased Cederroth, a wholly owned subsidiary of Alberto-Culver, in July 2008. Selling off Cederroth has allowed Alberto-Culver to focus on catering to its TRESemmé, Nexxus, Alberto VO5, and St. Ives brands.

In October 2008, Alberto-Culver purchased the worldwide rights and trademarks to the Noxzema brand in the US, Canada, and parts of Latin America. (As part of the agreement, P&G continues to operate the Noxzema business in portions of Western Europe.)

Alberto-Culver has generated sales increases worldwide while some of its rivals logged sales declines in 2008. The company boasts two business segments: US and International. Its US segment, which accounted for 60% of its sales, got a 5% boost in 2008 due to higher sales of TRESemmé items (shampoos, conditioners, and styling products) and multicultural brands. (Its Pro-Line International segment is one of the world's top manufacturers of ethnic hair care items under the Motions, Just Fore Me, TCB, and Soft & Beautiful brand names.)

The company cut off its retail arm a few years ago. Alberto-Culver parted ways with its Sally Beauty unit, the world's #1 beauty supply retailer and distributor to professionals and consumers in 2006.

The Lavin and Bernick families run Alberto-Culver and control about 14% of the voting rights. Bernice Lavin, who founded the company with her husband, Leonard, died in October 2007. Neuberger Berman, LLC, owns about a 7% stake in the company.

HISTORY

Alberto VO5 Conditioning Hairdressing (featuring five vital oils in a water-free base) was developed in the early 1950s by a chemist named Alberto to rejuvenate the coiffures of Hollywood's movie stars from the damage of harsh studio lights. In 1955 36-year-old entrepreneur Leonard Lavin and his wife, Bernice, borrowed $400,000, bought the Los Angeles-based firm that made VO5 from Blaine Culver, and relocated it to Chicago. That year Alberto-Culver implemented a key component of its corporate strategy — aggressive marketing — by running the first television commercial for VO5. Within three years Alberto VO5 led its category. In 1959 the company expanded its product line by buying TRESemmé Hair Color.

Lavin built a new plant and headquarters in Melrose Park, Illinois, in 1960, took the company public in 1961, and formed an international marketing division. A series of product innovations included Alberto VO5 Hair Spray (1961), New Dawn Hair Color (the first shampoo-in, permanent hair color; 1963), Consort Hair Spray for Men (1965), and FDS (1966). Acquisitions in 1969 included low-calorie sugar substitute SugarTwin and 10-store beauty supply chain Sally Beauty Supply.

Alberto-Culver restyled TV advertising in 1972 by putting two 30-second ads in a 60-second spot (it later pioneered the "split 30," back-to-back 15-second ads for two different products). It launched TCB (an ethnic hair care line) in 1975 and Static Guard antistatic spray in 1976.

The firm developed a series of food-substitute products in the 1980s, including Mrs. Dash (1983) and Molly McButter (1987). It also expanded the fast-growing Sally chain to the UK (1987). Lavin's son-in-law Howard Bernick succeeded him as president and COO in 1988.

By 1990 the Sally chain had about 800 stores, many added through the purchases of smaller chains. It bought the bankrupt Milo Beauty & Barber Supply chain (about 90 stores) in 1991. That year Alberto-Culver also bought Cederroth International, a Swedish maker of health and hygiene goods. Bernick became CEO in 1994, though Lavin stayed on as chairman.

In 1995 Lavin's daughter, Carol Bernick, became head of Alberto-Culver USA and led the division to more than $300 million in sales.

The 1,500-store Sally chain opened its first 10 outlets in Japan through a joint venture in 1995 and acquired a small chain in Germany the next year. Also in 1996 Alberto-Culver made its largest acquisition ever, paying $110 million for St. Ives Laboratories, maker of St. Ives Swiss Formula hair and skin care products.

In 1997 the consumer products division cut nearly 25% of its product line to focus on its best-sellers. In 1999 the company bought Argentina-based La Farmaco, a personal care products company, and professional products distributor Heil Beauty Supply. In March Alberto-Culver bought Pro-Line, a maker of personal care products targeting ethnic hair care.

As of November 5, 2003, the company had only one class of common stock outstanding. Previously, it had two publicly traded classes of common stock since 1986. The change was intended to encourage greater trading of the company's shares by institutions and it reduced the voting power of the Lavin and Bernick families to 21% from 27%.

In October 2004 founder and chairman Leonard Lavin stepped down after 49 years as chairman, passing his title to his daughter, Carol Lavin Bernick. Leonard Lavin became chairman emeritus and director of the firm. A director since 1955, Bernice Lavin retired from the board in late January 2005.

Alberto-Culver bought California's Nexxus Products Company in May 2005 and spun off its entire retail operations business, including Sally Beauty and Beauty Systems Group, into a separately traded company in late 2006. As part of the deal, Alberto-Culver spun off its beauty supply business into a standalone company renamed Sally Beauty Holdings, Inc., and paid shareholders a one-time dividend of $25 per share upon completion. Private-equity firm Clayton, Dubilier & Rice bought a 47.5% stake in Sally Beauty for at least $575 million. Alberto-Culver shareholders own the rest.

EXECUTIVES

Chairman: Carol Lavin Bernick, age 56
President, CEO, and Director: V. James Marino, age 58
SVP and CFO: Ralph J. Nicoletti, age 50
SVP Global Operations: Richard Mewborn, age 49
President, Global Brands: Gina R. Boswell, age 63
President, US: Kenneth C. (Casey) Keller Jr., age 47
Auditors: KPMG LLP

LOCATIONS

HQ: Alberto-Culver Company
2525 Armitage Ave., Melrose Park, IL 60160
Phone: 708-450-3000 **Fax:** 708-450-3409
Web: www.alberto.com

2008 Sales

	$ mil.	% of total
US	863.0	60
International	580.5	40
Total	**1,443.5**	**100**

PRODUCTS/OPERATIONS

2008 Sales

	$ mil.	% of total
Beauty care	1,359.0	94
Non-beauty	84.5	6
Total	**1,443.5**	**100**

Selected Brands

Alberto VO5 (hair care products)
Bliw (liquid hand soap, Europe)
Consort (hair care products)
Farmaco (soap, Latin America)
FDS (feminine deodorant spray)
Grumme Tvattsapa (detergent, Europe)
Jordan (toothbrushes, Europe)
Just For Me (ethnic personal care products)
L300 (skin care products, Europe)
Molly McButter (butter-flavored sprinkles)
Motions (ethnic hair care products)
Mrs. Dash (salt-free seasoning)
Nexxus (hair care products)
Noxzema (skin care products)
St. Ives (hair care and skin care products)
Salve (adhesive bandages, Europe)
Samarin (antacids, Europe)
Seltin (salt substitute, Europe)
Soft & Beautiful (ethnic personal care products)
Static Guard (anti-static spray)
SugarTwin (sugar substitute)
Suketter (sugar substitute, Europe)
TCB (ethnic hair care products)
TRESemmé (hair care products)
Veritas (soap, Latin America)

COMPETITORS

Alticor
Avlon
Avon
Bristol-Myers Squibb
Colgate-Palmolive
Combe
Cumberland Packing
Del Laboratories
The Dial Corporation
Estée Lauder
Helen of Troy
Johnson & Johnson
Johnson Publishing
L'Oréal
Mary Kay
McCormick & Company
Nu Skin
Orly International
Procter & Gamble
Regis Corporation
Revlon
Schwarzkopf & Henkel
Shiseido
Unilever

HISTORICAL FINANCIALS

Company Type: Public

Income Statement

FYE: September 30

	REVENUE ($ mil.)	NET INCOME ($ mil.)	NET PROFIT MARGIN	EMPLOYEES
9/08	1,443.5	228.2	15.8%	2,700
9/07	1,541.6	78.3	5.1%	3,800
9/06	3,772.0	205.3	5.4%	3,800
9/05	3,531.2	210.9	6.0%	19,000
9/04	3,258.0	141.8	4.4%	—
Annual Growth	(18.4%)	12.6%	—	(47.8%)

2008 Year-End Financials

Debt ratio: 0.1%
Return on equity: 21.9%
Cash ($ mil.): 445
Current ratio: 3.12
Long-term debt ($ mil.): 1

No. of shares (mil.): 98
Dividends
  Yield: 0.9%
  Payout: 11.0%
Market value ($ mil.): 2,674

Stock History

NYSE: ACV

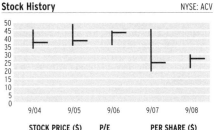

	STOCK PRICE ($) FY Close	P/E High/Low	PER SHARE ($) Earnings	Dividends	Book Value
9/08	27.24	13 10	2.27	0.25	11.32
9/07	24.79	57 25	0.80	0.17	9.92
9/06	43.55	20 16	2.20	0.49	17.62
9/05	38.52	21 16	2.27	0.44	15.60
9/04	37.43	29 22	1.54	0.34	13.38
Annual Growth	(7.6%)	— —	10.2%	(7.4%)	(4.1%)

Alcoa Inc.

Alcoa is among the world's top producers of alumina (aluminum's principal ingredient, processed from bauxite) and aluminum. Its vertically integrated operations include bauxite mining, alumina refining, and aluminum smelting; primary products include alumina and its chemicals, automotive components, and sheet aluminum for beverage cans. The company's non-aluminum products include fiber-optic cables. Major markets include the aerospace, automotive, and construction industries. In 2008 the firm sold its packaging business, which had accounted for more than 10% of sales, to New Zealand private investment firm the Rank Group. In 2009 it sold its wire harness and electrical distribution business to Platinum Equity.

Alcoa has established a presence in China by forming a strategic alliance with Aluminum Corporation of China (Chinalco) and, for a time, taking a small stake in Chinalco, which enabled Alcoa to partake in the world's fastest-growing aluminum market. In 2007 the company sold that stake in a private offering that garnered Alcoa $2 billion. Alcoa stressed its continued commitment to the country though, pointing to its 17 operating locations in China and the expansion of a rolling mill that was completed in 2008. It also joined the Chinese aluminum giant in a bid to obstruct BHP Billiton's takeover of Rio Tinto; in early 2008, Alcoa and Chinalco acquired 9% of Rio Tinto for $14 billion. (Alcoa's portion of that deal was $1.2 billion.)

Its former packaging and consumer businesses included closure systems, Reynolds Wrap, and Reynolds Food Packaging. The Rank Group, which already has significant global holdings in packaging companies, paid Alcoa $2.7 billion for the operations. Alcoa held onto its aluminum sheet for beverage cans operations.

Back in 2007 Alcoa offered to buy what was then the world's #3 aluminum producer, Alcan, for $33 billion but was trumped by Rio Tinto's $40 billion offer. The merger of Russian aluminum giants RUSAL and Sual (along with Glencore's alumina operations) earlier that year briefly created the world's largest aluminum company, pushing Alcoa and Alcan down a notch. With the formation of Rio Tinto Alcan, RUSAL abdicated the title and become the #2 aluminum producer.

Alcoa formed a soft-alloy extrusion joint venture with Sapa Group (part of Orkla) in 2008, called Sapa AB. It is the world's largest aluminum shaper. The two companies also co-owned a joint venture, through Orkla subsidiary Elkem, called Elkem Aluminum. In 2009 Alcoa and Orkla exchanged ownership stakes in the two JVs, with Alcoa taking full ownership of Elkem and Orkla doing the same with Sapa.

HISTORY

In 1886 two chemists, one in France and one in the US, simultaneously discovered an inexpensive process for aluminum production. The American, Charles Hall, pursued commercial applications. Two years later, with an investor group led by Captain Alfred Hunt, Hall formed the Pittsburgh Reduction Company. Its first salesman, Arthur Davis, secured an initial order for 2,000 cooking pots.

In 1889 the Mellon Bank loaned the company $4,000. In 1891 the firm recapitalized, with the Mellon family holding 12% of the stock.

Davis led the business after Hunt died in 1899 and stayed on until 1957 (he died in 1962 at age 95). It introduced aluminum foil (1910) and developed new applications for aluminum in products such as airplanes and cars. It became the Aluminum Company of America in 1907.

By the end of WWI, Alcoa had integrated backward into bauxite mining and forward into end-use production. By the 1920s the Mellons had raised their stake to 33%. The government and Alcoa had debated antitrust issues in court for years since the smelting patent expired in 1912. Finally a 1946 federal ruling forced the company to sell many operations built during WWII, as well as its Canadian subsidiary (Alcan).

In the competitive aluminum industry of the 1960s, Alcoa's lower-cost production helped it seize market share, especially in beverage cans. In the 1970s Alcoa began offering engineered products such as aerospace components, and in the 1980s it invested in research, acquisitions, and plant modernization.

Paul O'Neill (former president of International Paper) arrived as CEO in 1987 and shifted the company's focus back to aluminum. Sales and earnings set records the next two years but plunged afterward, reflecting a weak global economy and record-low aluminum prices. Then the fall of the Soviet Union in the early 1990s led to a worldwide glut as Russian exports soared.

In 1994 Alcoa cut its production as part of a two-year accord with Western and Russian producers. Alcoa formed a joint venture with Shanghai Aluminum Fabrication Plant in China. Alcoa bought #3 US aluminum producer Alumax for $3.8 billion in 1998, but only after divesting its cast-plate operations.

Known by the nickname "Alcoa" since the late 1920s, the company adopted that as its official name in 1999. O'Neill retired as CEO in 1999; COO Alain Belda succeeded him.

In 2000 Alcoa bought aluminum extrusion maker Excel Extrusions from Noranda (now called Falconbridge) and paid $4.5 billion for Reynolds Metals after agreeing to divest some assets — including all of Reynolds' alumina refineries — to satisfy regulators. Late in 2000 President-elect George W. Bush named Alcoa's chairman Paul O'Neill to be treasury secretary. (O'Neill subsequently resigned the post in December 2002.)

Alcoa sold its majority stake in the Worsley alumina refinery (Australia) to BHP Billiton in 2001 for about $1.5 billion as part of its refinery divestments. Treasury Secretary O'Neill completed the sale of his more than $90 million worth of Alcoa stock and options in June.

Late in the year Alcoa agreed to buy an 8% stake in Aluminium Corporation of China (Chalco). The deal gave Alcoa a seat on the board and 27% of Chalco's initial public offering.

In 2003 Alcoa acquired Camargo Correa Group's 41% stake in the South American businesses of Alcoa, including its largest subsidiary in the group — Alcoa Aluminio S.A. (Brazil) — and operations in Argentina, Chile, Colombia, Peru, Uruguay, and Venezuela. Faced with lower aluminum prices in its aerospace, industrial-gas-turbine, and nonresidential construction markets, Alcoa decided to divest under-performing businesses primarily in its automotive, packaging, and specialty chemicals units.

In 2006 the company sold its Home Exteriors unit to Ply Gem Industries; it also sold its aerospace service business to ThyssenKrupp.

EXECUTIVES

Chairman: Alain J. P. Belda, age 66
President, CEO, and Director: Klaus Kleinfeld, age 51
EVP and CFO: Charles D. (Chuck) McLane Jr., age 55
EVP Market Strategy, Technology, and Quality:
 Mohammad A. Zaidi
EVP and Chief Legal and Compliance Officer:
 Nicholas J. DeRoma, age 62
EVP; Group President, Global Primary Products:
 Bernt Reitan, age 60
**EVP; Group President, Engineered Products and
 Solutions:** William F. (Bill) Christopher, age 54
**EVP; President, Global Rolled Products, Hard Alloy
 Extrusions, and Asia:** Helmut Wieser, age 55
EVP Business Development: J. Michael (Mike) Schell,
 age 61
VP, Secretary, and Corporate Governance Counsel:
 Donna C. Dabney, age 58
VP Human Resources: Regina M. Hitchery, age 60
VP; President, European Region:
 Rudolph P. (Rudi) Huber, age 55
VP; President, Alcoa Fastening Systems:
 Olivier M. Jarrault, age 48
VP and General Counsel: Kurt R. Waldo, age 53
VP; President, Latin America and Caribbean:
 Franklin L (Frank) Feder
VP; President, Alcoa Power and Propulsion:
 Raymond B. (Ray) Mitchell
VP; President, Global Primary Products, Australia:
 Alan Cransberg
VP; President, Alcoa Materials Management:
 Kevin J. Anton, age 50
Manager Corporate Communications: Joyce Saltzman
Director Investor Relations: Matthew Garth
Auditors: PricewaterhouseCoopers LLP

LOCATIONS

HQ: Alcoa Inc.
 390 Park Ave., New York, NY 10022
Phone: 212-836-2600   **Fax:** 212-836-2815
Web: www.alcoa.com

2008 Sales

	$ mil.	% of total
US	14,335	53
Australia	3,228	12
Spain	1,733	6
Brazil	1,287	5
The Netherlands	1,263	5
Other countries	5,055	19
Total	**26,901**	**100**

PRODUCTS/OPERATIONS

2008 Sales

	$ mil.	% of total
Flat-rolled Products	9,563	35
Primary Metals	8,021	30
Engineered Products & Solutions	5,602	21
Alumina	2,924	11
Packaging & Consumer	516	2
Corporate	275	1
Total	**26,901**	**100**

Selected Products

Flat-rolled products (light gauge sheet products, such as
 rigid container sheet and foil, for the packaging
 market; sheet and plate mill products for the
 transportation, building, and construction markets)
Primary aluminum (smelted from alumina, which is
 derived from bauxite)
Engineered products and solutions (aluminum wheels,
 forgings, castings, investment castings, fasteners)
Alumina and chemicals (bauxite, alumina, alumina-
 based chemicals, transportation services for bauxite
 and alumina)

Selected Operations

Alcoa Aluminum Deutschland, Inc.
Alcoa Europe S.A.
Alcoa Latin American Holdings Corporation
Alcoa (Shanghai) Aluminum Products Ltd.
Alcoa World Alumina — Atlantic
Alcoa World Alumina and Chemicals — Australia
Cordant Technologies Holding Company
Halco (Mining) Inc. (45%)
Howmet International Inc.
Kawneer Company

COMPETITORS

Aluminum Corporation of China
BHP Billiton
Corus Group
Crown Holdings
Hayes Lemmerz
Hydro Aluminium
Nippon Light Metal
Ormet
Quanex Building Products
Rio Tinto Alcan
RUSAL
Superior Industries

HISTORICAL FINANCIALS

Company Type: Public

Income Statement

FYE: December 31

	REVENUE ($ mil.)	NET INCOME ($ mil.)	NET PROFIT MARGIN	EMPLOYEES
12/08	26,901.0	(74.0)	—	87,000
12/07	30,748.0	2,564.0	8.3%	107,000
12/06	30,379.0	2,248.0	7.4%	123,000
12/05	26,159.0	1,235.0	4.7%	129,000
12/04	23,478.0	1,310.0	5.6%	119,000
Annual Growth	**3.5%**	**—**	**—**	**(7.5%)**

2008 Year-End Financials

Debt ratio: 72.9%
Return on equity: —
Cash ($ mil.): 762
Current ratio: 1.12
Long-term debt ($ mil.): 8,509
No. of shares (mil.): 974
Dividends
 Yield: 6.0%
 Payout: —
Market value ($ mil.): 10,971

Stock History

NYSE: AA

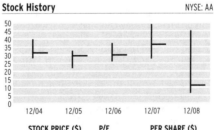

	STOCK PRICE ($) FY Close	P/E High/Low		PER SHARE ($) Earnings	Dividends	Book Value
12/08	11.26	—	—	(0.09)	0.68	12.04
12/07	36.55	17	10	2.95	0.68	16.44
12/06	30.01	14	10	2.57	0.60	15.02
12/05	29.57	23	16	1.40	0.60	13.72
12/04	31.42	26	19	1.49	0.60	13.65
Annual Growth	**(22.6%)**	**—**	**—**	**—**	**3.2%**	**(3.1%)**

Allegheny Energy

Even when the Allegheny Moon isn't shining, Allegheny Energy (AE) can provide plenty of light. The company's Allegheny Power unit provides electricity to almost 1.6 million customers in Maryland, Pennsylvania, West Virginia, and Virginia through regulated utilities Monongahela Power, Potomac Edison, and West Penn Power. Subsidiary Allegheny Energy Supply provides power to AE's utilities and sells electricity to wholesale and retail customers. Subsidiary Allegheny Ventures controls Allegheny Communications Connect (telecommunications) and Allegheny Energy Solutions (energy consulting). It also has transmission line design and management units (Trans-Allegheny Interstate Line Company and PATH, LLC).

About 79% of the company's power output of 9,075 MW from 20 plants comes from coal, which is in abundance in its service area. AE burns nearly 19 million tons of coal annually.

Once focused on expanding its nonregulated generation and marketing businesses, the company now is zeroed in on its core energy delivery operations. In 2007 the company formed the PATH, LLC joint venture with a subsidiary of American Electric Power (AEP) to help finance and manage PATH, a 290-mile, high-voltage transmission line connecting AEP's substation near St. Albans, West Virginia, with a new substation near Kemptown, Maryland.

AE has reduced its wholesale power trading operations due to a downturn in the industry, brought on by #1 energy trader Enron's collapse. Allegheny Energy Supply has exited the western US wholesale energy market and has sold its power supply contract with the California Department of Water Resources to a division of The Goldman Sachs Group.

To further improve its precarious financial situation, AE has been selling noncore assets, including some real estate and power generation holdings. The company has sold Monongahela Power's West Virginia natural gas operations for a reported $217 million. AE also has canceled several power plant developments, and it has postponed plans to spin off up to 18% of a new holding company that would own Allegheny Energy Supply.

HISTORY

American Water Works & Electric Company was one of many utility holding companies created by financiers as the US power industry consolidated in the 1880s. It bought many electric plants and water facilities in the Northeast and united 53 Pennsylvania power companies to form West Penn Power in 1916. It also formed The Potomac Edison Company in 1923, a similar amalgamation of small utilities that supplied power to western Maryland. The next year American Water Works formed Washington County Light & Power Company (later Monongahela Power) to serve customers in West Virginia and Ohio.

In 1925 West Penn Electric Company was born when American Water Works began integrating the systems' power plants, transformers, and lines under that name. The 1929 stock market crash brought the octopus-like holding companies under scrutiny, and in 1935 the Public Utility Holding Company Act restricted utilities' ownership to contiguous regions. American Water Works was dissolved in 1948, and the newly independent West Penn Electric became the owner of the three geographically linked utilities.

The steel industry — which accounted for the largest share of the company's sales — began exiting the region in the 1950s. West Penn was saved because its location was in the middle of one of the richest coal regions in the country. The company divested its nonutility interests, and in 1960 it was renamed Allegheny Power System.

In 1981 Allegheny formed Allegheny Generating Company (AGC), which held 40% of a Virginia hydroelectric station it bought that year. Passage of the Clean Air Act of 1990, which set limits on sulfur dioxide emissions, cost coal-dependent Allegheny an estimated $2 billion.

The Energy Policy Act of 1992 opened the door for deregulation of the energy industry, and Allegheny formed a nonutility holding company (AYP Capital) in 1994. Two years later Pennsylvania approved deregulation legislation, and AYP Capital took over two new subsidiaries: AYP Energy (wholesale power) and Allegheny Communications Connect (telecommunications). In 1997 the company was renamed Allegheny Energy (AE), and it formed Allegheny Energy Solutions to market energy services to Pennsylvania retail customers. It also agreed to buy Pennsylvania utility DQE (now Duquesne Light Holdings), but DQE later backed out.

In 1998 AE entered Pennsylvania's deregulation pilot program. Full competition arrived in Pennsylvania's electricity markets in 1999, and AE formed Allegheny Energy Supply to hold its generation assets, including those of AYP Energy. AYP Capital became Allegheny Ventures, which took charge of AE's telecom unit and Allegheny Energy Solutions.

Expanding its West Virginia operations, the company purchased the West Virginia Power unit of UtiliCorp United (now Aquila) for $75 million, and in 2000 bought natural gas distributor Mountaineer Gas (200,000 customers). AE also entered a communications venture with five other companies; the venture, America's Fiber Network (now Citynet Fiber Network), operates a 13-state fiber-optic network.

Moving to expand Allegheny Energy Supply's power trading operations, AE in 2001 bought Merrill Lynch's Global Energy Markets unit for $490 million and a 2% stake in Allegheny Energy Supply. The company purchased three gas-fired merchant plants (1,700 MW of capacity) in Illinois, Indiana, and Tennessee from Enron for $1 billion that year. AE also purchased two energy services firms (Fellon-McCord & Associates and Alliance Energy Services Partnership), which it sold to Constellation Energy Group the following year.

The company reversed its expansion strategy in 2002 as it began facing financial difficulties due to a downturn in the electricity market; that year the company restructured its management and reduced its workforce by about 10%. Allegheny Energy Supply sold 150,000 retail customer accounts in Pennsylvania and Ohio to Dominion Resources' retail marketing unit that year. Also in 2002 regional transmission organization (RTO) PJM Interconnection began managing AE's regulated transmission assets.

In 2005 AE sold a 512-MW generating station to Cincinnati Gas & Electric (now Duke Energy Ohio) and PSI Energy (now Duke Energy Indiana) for $100 million.

EXECUTIVES

Chairman, President, and CEO; Chairman and CEO, Principal Subsidiaries: Paul J. Evanson, age 67, $10,295,019 total compensation
COO Generation: Curtis H. Davis, age 56, $1,125,417 total compensation
SVP and CFO: Kirk R. Oliver, age 51, $414,582 total compensation
VP and CIO: Richard C. Arthur
VP, Controller, and Chief Accounting Officer: William F. (Rick) Wahl III, age 49
VP Environment, Health, and Safety: David C. Cannon Jr.
VP External Affairs: Loyd (Aldie) Warnock
VP Quality: J. Michael (Mike) Adams
VP Human Resources and Security: Edward (Ed) Dudzinski, age 56, $965,516 total compensation
VP, General Counsel, and Secretary: David M. Feinberg, age 39, $938,760 total compensation
VP and Treasurer: Barry E. Pakenham
VP Corporate Development: Eric S. Gleason, age 42
President, Allegheny Power: Rodney L. Dickens
Executive Director Investor Relations and Corporate Communications: Max Kuniansky
Auditors: PricewaterhouseCoopers LLP

LOCATIONS

HQ: Allegheny Energy, Inc.
800 Cabin Hill Dr., Greensburg, PA 15601
Phone: 724-837-3000 **Fax:** 724-830-5284
Web: www.alleghenyenergy.com

PRODUCTS/OPERATIONS

2008 Sales

	$ mil.	% of total
Delivery & services	2,846.7	58
Generation & marketing	2,279.2	42
Adjustments	(1,740.0)	—
Total	**3,385.9**	**100**

Selected Subsidiaries and Divisions

Allegheny Energy Service Corporation (support services)
Allegheny Energy Supply Company, LLC (AE Supply, electricity generation and energy trading and marketing)
  Allegheny Energy Supply — Marketing and Trading Division (formerly Allegheny Energy Global Markets)
  Allegheny Generating Company (59% owned by AE Supply, 41% owned by Monongahela Power)
Allegheny Power (energy delivery division)
  Monongahela Power Company (electric and gas utility, West Virginia and Ohio)
    Mountaineer Gas Company (gas utility, West Virginia)
  The Potomac Edison Company (electric utility; Maryland, Virginia, and West Virginia)
  West Penn Power Company (electric utility, Pennsylvania)
Allegheny Ventures, Inc.
  Allegheny Energy Solutions, Inc. (energy consulting services, on-site generation)
PATH, LLC (50%, transmission line financing and management)
TrAIL Company (regional transmission planning)

COMPETITORS

AEP	Exelon
Avista	FirstEnergy
CMS Energy	National Fuel Gas
Constellation Energy	NiSource
Delmarva Power	Pepco Holdings
Dominion Peoples	PPL Corporation
Dominion Resources	PSEG Energy Holdings
DPL	TVA
Duke Energy	Vectren
Duquesne Light Holdings	WGL Holdings

HISTORICAL FINANCIALS

Company Type: Public

Income Statement

FYE: December 31

	REVENUE ($ mil.)	NET INCOME ($ mil.)	NET PROFIT MARGIN	EMPLOYEES
12/08	3,385.9	395.4	11.7%	4,455
12/07	3,307.0	412.2	12.5%	4,355
12/06	3,121.5	319.3	10.2%	4,362
12/05	3,037.9	69.0	2.3%	4,460
12/04	2,756.1	(310.6)	—	5,100
Annual Growth	**5.3%**	**—**	**—**	**(3.3%)**

2008 Year-End Financials

Debt ratio: 145.8%
Return on equity: 14.7%
Cash ($ mil.): 362
Current ratio: 1.49
Long-term debt ($ mil.): 4,155
No. of shares (mil.): 169
Dividends
  Yield: 1.3%
  Payout: 19.3%
Market value ($ mil.): 5,739

Stock History

NYSE: AYE

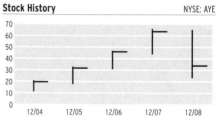

	STOCK PRICE ($) FY Close	P/E High/Low		PER SHARE ($) Earnings	Dividends	Book Value
12/08	33.86	28	10	2.33	0.45	16.82
12/07	63.61	27	18	2.43	0.15	14.96
12/06	45.91	24	17	1.89	0.00	12.27
12/05	31.65	81	46	0.40	0.00	10.00
12/04	19.71	—	—	(1.83)	0.00	7.99
Annual Growth	**14.5%**	**—**	**—**	**—**	**—**	**20.5%**

Allegheny Technologies

Allegheny Technologies, Inc. (ATI) manufactures stainless and specialty steels, nickel- and cobalt-based alloys and superalloys, titanium and titanium alloys, tungsten materials, and such exotic alloys as niobium and zirconium. The company's flat-rolled products (sheet, strip, and plate) account for a great majority of its sales. Its high-performance metals unit produces metal bar, coil, foil, ingot, plate, rod, and wire. Allegheny Technologies' largest markets include aerospace, the chemical process, and oil and gas industries. Three-fourths of its sales are in the US. ATI was formed from the 1996 merger of Teledyne and stainless-steel producer Allegheny Ludlum.

To offset rapidly rising costs in raw materials, energy, health care, and transportation, the company has increased prices on several of its metal grades. Those price increases helped ATI achieve record sales in 2006 and 2007. While the next year did bring a drop in business, the demand in the aerospace and oil and gas industries hasn't decreased too dramatically, and ATI's business with the chemical process industry has actually increased.

HISTORY

Allegheny Ludlum Steel began in 1938 when Allegheny Steel Company (founded in Pennsylvania in 1898) and Ludlum Steel Company (founded in New Jersey in 1854) merged. Allegheny Steel veteran W. F. Detwiler became Allegheny Ludlum Steel's first chairman. During WWII the company developed heat-resisting alloys for aircraft turbine engines.

After the war the focus was on stainless steel and flat-rolled silicon electrical steel used to make electrical transformers. In 1956 the company doubled its capacity for making specialty alloys and installed the industry's first semi-automated system for working hot steel. It expanded outside the US by opening a plant in Belgium in the 1960s.

The company adopted the name Allegheny Ludlum Industries in 1970 and, after diversifying, sold its specialty steel division in a management-led buyout that formed Allegheny Ludlum Steel (1980). In 1986 it became Allegheny Ludlum Corp. It went public in 1987.

Henry Singleton and George Kozmetsky, former Litton Industries executives, invested $225,000 each in 1960 to found Teledyne to make electronic aircraft components. First year sales of $4.5 million grew to nearly $90 million by 1964. Kozmetsky left the firm in 1966.

Under Singleton, Teledyne bought more than 100 successful manufacturing and technology firms in defense-related areas such as engines, unmanned aircraft, specialty metals, and computers. Teledyne also moved into offshore oil-drilling equipment, insurance and finance, and the Water Pik line of oral-care products.

Teledyne spun off its Argonaut Insurance unit in 1986 and left the insurance business entirely with its 1990 spinoff of Unitrin. Its defense businesses were caught in a 1989 fraud probe, and the company paid $4.4 million in restitution. In 1991 Teledyne consolidated its 130 operations into 21 companies. It paid a $13 million fine in 1995 on charges of knowingly selling zirconium to a Chilean arms manufacturer for use in cluster bombs sold to Iraq.

Despite Teledyne's rebuff of holding company WHX's 1994 takeover offer, in 1996 WHX came back with a new proposal that led to the $3.2 billion merger of Teledyne and Allegheny Ludlum in 1997. Also in 1997 CEO William Rutledge was succeeded by former Allegheny Ludlum CEO Richard Simmons. Allegheny and Bethlehem Steel entered into a bidding war for steelmaker Lukens. Bethlehem won but in 1998 granted exclusive access to or sold most of Lukens' stainless-steel operations to Allegheny. The company also bought UK-based Sheffield Forgemaster's Group's aerospace division and titanium producer Oregon Metallurgical.

Allegheny restructured to focus on specialty metals in 1999, changing its name to Allegheny Technologies. The company sold Ryan Aeronautical (aerial drones) to Northrop Grumman, its mining equipment business to Astec Industries, and its lift-truck-making business to Terex. It spun off its consumer oral-hygiene business as Water Pik Technologies and its remaining aerospace businesses as Teledyne Technologies. Lockheed Martin executive Thomas Corcoran became president and CEO in 1999 but abruptly resigned in late 2000. That same year the company bought Baker Hughes' tungsten carbide products unit. VC Robert Bozzone served as chairman and CEO until insider James Murdy was named CEO in 2001.

In order to cut costs, in 2001 Allegheny Technologies closed a plant in Pennsylvania, made workforce cuts, and sold its North American titanium distribution operations to management.

In 2002 the company had another round of workforce cuts (around 275 employees), mostly in its flat-rolled products unit. The following year, Allegheny Technologies formed a joint venture with Russian-based VSMPO AVISMA to make a range of commercially pure titanium products.

Allegheny Technologies purchased J&L Specialty Steel, one of its competitors, for an undisclosed price in 2004. Other buys that year included two plants in Pennsylvania and Ohio from Arcelor. Still it initiated cost-cutting efforts aimed at saving $200 million a year, announcing in 2004 cuts of more than 950 jobs at Allegheny Ludlum. The plants acquired from Arcelor lost more than 300 of their workforce.

EXECUTIVES

Chairman, President, and CEO: L. Patrick (Pat) Hassey, age 63, $10,781,776 total compensation
EVP Finance and CFO: Richard J. (Rich) Harshman, age 52, $3,864,003 total compensation
EVP Human Resources, Chief Legal and Compliance Officer, General Counsel, and Secretary:
Jon D. Walton, age 66, $4,013,770 total compensation
VP, Treasurer, Controller, and Chief Accounting Officer:
Dale G. Reid, age 53
Group President, ATI Primary Metals and Exotic Alloys: Lynn D. Davis, age 62
Group President, ATI Flat-Rolled Products; Business Unit President, ATI Allegheny Ludlum:
Terry L. Dunlap, age 49, $3,003,310 total compensation
Group President, Engineered Products; Business Unit President, ATI Metalworking Products:
David M. Hogan, age 63
President, ATI Long Products; Business Unit President, ATI Allvac Business: Hunter R. Dalton, age 54
Business Unit President, ATI Wah Chang: John D. Sims
Auditors: Ernst & Young LLP

LOCATIONS

HQ: Allegheny Technologies Incorporated
1000 Six PPG Pl., Pittsburgh, PA 15222
Phone: 412-394-2800   **Fax:** 412-394-3034
Web: www.alleghenytechnologies.com

2008 Sales

	$ mil.	% of total
US	3,816.4	72
China	253.9	5
UK	229.2	4
Germany	184.1	3
France	165.2	3
Canada	154.1	3
Japan	96.0	2
Other countries	410.8	8
Total	**5,309.7**	**100**

PRODUCTS/OPERATIONS

2008 Sales

	$ mil.	% of total
Flat-Rolled Products	2,909.1	55
High-Performance Metals	1,944.9	37
Engineered Products	455.7	8
Total	**5,309.7**	**100**

Selected Operations and Products

Flat-Rolled Products
  Allegheny Ludlum (stainless steel, nickel-based alloys, titanium, silicon electrical steels, tool steels, high-tech alloy and titanium plate)
  Allegheny Rodney (stainless steel strip)
  Shanghai STAL Precision Stainless Steel Company Ltd. (60%, precision-rolled strip stainless steel, with Baosteel Group)
  Uniti LLC (50%, industrial titanium maker, owned jointly with Russia's VSMPO-AVISMA)

High-Performance Metals
  Allvac (nickel-based alloys and superalloys, cobalt-based alloys and superalloys, titanium and titanium-based alloys, specialty steel)
  Allvac Ltd. (UK) (nickel-based alloys and superalloys, cobalt-based alloys and superalloys, specialty steel)
  Wah Chang/Oremet (zirconium, zirconium chemicals, hafnium, niobium, tantalum, titanium and titanium-based alloys)
Engineered Products
  Casting Service (large gray iron castings, large ductile iron castings)
  Metalworking Products (cutting tools and tungsten carbide products)
  Portland Forge (carbon forgings, alloy steel forgings, nonferrous forgings)
  Rome Metals (processor of titanium, zirconium, nickel alloy, and other specialty metals)

COMPETITORS

A. M. Castle	Olympic Steel
AK Steel Holding	Ryerson
Corporation	Special Metals
Carpenter Technology	ThyssenKrupp Steel
Eramet	Timken
Kennametal	Titanium Metals
Nippon Steel	United States Steel
Nucor	

HISTORICAL FINANCIALS

Company Type: Public

Income Statement

FYE: December 31

	REVENUE ($ mil.)	NET INCOME ($ mil.)	NET PROFIT MARGIN	EMPLOYEES
12/08	5,309.7	565.9	10.7%	9,600
12/07	5,452.5	747.1	13.7%	9,700
12/06	4,936.6	571.9	11.6%	9,500
12/05	3,539.9	361.8	10.2%	9,300
12/04	2,733.0	19.8	0.7%	9,000
Annual Growth	**18.1%**	**131.2%**	**—**	**1.6%**

2008 Year-End Financials

Debt ratio: 25.2%
Return on equity: 27.0%
Cash ($ mil.): 470
Current ratio: 2.78
Long-term debt ($ mil.): 495
No. of shares (mil.): 98
Dividends
  Yield: 2.8%
  Payout: 12.7%
Market value ($ mil.): 2,504

Stock History

NYSE: ATI

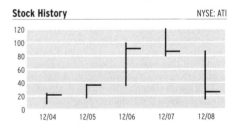

	STOCK PRICE ($) FY Close	P/E High/Low		PER SHARE ($) Earnings	Dividends	Book Value
12/08	25.53	15	3	5.67	0.72	20.00
12/07	86.40	16	11	7.26	0.57	22.67
12/06	90.68	18	6	5.59	0.43	15.22
12/05	36.08	10	5	3.57	0.28	8.16
12/04	21.67	107	39	0.22	0.24	4.34
Annual Growth	**4.2%**	**—**	**—**	**125.3%**	**31.6%**	**46.5%**

Allergan, Inc.

Don't let the name fool you, Allergan can't help you with that runny nose. Instead, the company is a leading maker of eye care, skin care, and aesthetic products, including best-selling pharmaceutical Botox. Originally used to treat muscle spasms (as well as eye spasms and misalignment), Botox has found another, more popular application in diminishing facial wrinkles. Allergan's eye care products include medications for glaucoma, allergic conjunctivitis, and chronic dry eye. Skin care products include treatments for acne, wrinkles, and psoriasis. Allergan also sells implants used in breast augmentation and weight-loss surgery. Its products are sold in 100 countries via direct sales and distributors.

Allergan is focused on acquiring and developing new niche pharmaceuticals, as well as discovering new uses for its existing ones, to expand its market share and replace older products nearing patent expiration. As competition from other anti-wrinkle drugs ramps up, the company is eyeing new possible uses for Botox, including treatments for pain management, neuromuscular conditions, and urology ailments.

A new use for another existing drug came to Allergan's glaucoma drug Lumigan in late 2008. One of the drug's side effects turned out to be eyelash growth, so the company ran it through testing and received FDA approval for that use. Re-formulated for use on eyelashes, the drug was renamed Latisse.

Allergan also received FDA approval for Trivaris, an injectable steroid for the treatment of retinal disease, in 2008. The following year the FDA gave its nod for two more proprietary drugs: Ozurdex, another injectable retinal therapy targeting macular edema (vascular swelling of the eye), and Acuvail, an ophthalmic pain treatment for cataract surgery recovery.

To bolster the ongoing exploration of Botox as a treatment for urinary conditions, the company in 2007 acquired private firm Esprit Pharma, which markets overactive bladder treatment Sanctura through a partnership with Indevus, for $370 million. The following year Allergan entered a collaboration agreement to develop potential bladder cancer treatment EOquin with Spectrum Pharmaceuticals.

Also in 2008 Allergan bought acne gel treatment Aczone from struggling competitor QLT for $150 million; the purchase strengthens Allergan's dermatology portfolio. Aczone is approved for acne treatment in the US and Canada.

The company first entered the surgical products market in 2006 with the acquisition of implant maker Inamed for $3.2 billion. Through the purchase, Allergan gained the Lap-Band treatment for obesity, as well as silicon breast implant products. The next year, Allergan bought obesity implant maker EndoArt.

The company initiated some restructuring measures in early 2009 to combat sluggish sales during recessionary market conditions. Allergan is working to cut costs in its sales and marketing and administrative organizations.

HISTORY

In 1950 Gavin Herbert set up a small ophthalmic business above one of his drugstores in Los Angeles. Chemist Stanley Bly invented the company's first product, antihistamine eye drops called Allergan. The company adopted the name of the eye drops and expanded the business and the product range. Herbert's son Gavin Jr., then a USC student, helped with the business.

By 1960 Allergan was a $1 million company; it moved into the contact lens solution market with its Liquifilm product that year. In 1964 it developed its first foreign distributorship, in Iraq, and the following year it started its first foreign subsidiary, in Canada. International expansion and limited competition for hard contact lens care products sustained sales growth around 20% throughout the 1960s.

Allergan went public in 1971. During the 1970s the company became Bausch & Lomb's contractual supplier of Hydrocare lens solution and enzymatic cleaner for soft contact lenses. By 1975 Allergan had about a third of the hard contact lens care market. When Gavin Sr. died in 1978, Gavin Jr. succeeded him as president and CEO and also became chairman.

SmithKline bought Allergan in 1980 just as the soft contact lens market boomed. In 1984 SmithKline acquired International Hydron, the #2 soft contact lens maker behind Bausch & Lomb; International Hydron became part of Allergan in 1987.

The next year the company acquired the rights to a botulinum toxin product called Oculinum, which would later evolve into Botox. In 1989 SmithKline merged with Beecham and spun off Allergan.

By the early 1990s the contact lens and lens care markets had begun to mature, leading to a company restructuring and a new focus on specialty pharmaceuticals. In 1992 Allergan sold its North and South American contact lens businesses; the rest of its contact lens businesses were sold in 1993.

The company boosted its presence in the intraocular lens market with the 1994 purchase of Ioptex Research. Also in 1994 Allergan and joint venture partner Ligand Pharmaceuticals made their enterprise an independently operating company, Allergan Ligand Retinoid Therapeutics (ALRT). The next year Allergan recalled about 400,000 bottles of contact lens solution because of potential eye irritation.

In 1995 Allergan acquired cataract surgery equipment maker Optical Micro Systems and the contact lens care business of Pilkington Barnes Hind. That year the government probed the company for exporting the botulism toxin in Botox — it feared the product's use in biological weapons — but did not press charges. In 1996 it was discovered that Allergan's Botox could be used to lessen facial wrinkles.

In 1997 Allergan received approval for a handful of new products, including its multifocus eye lens for cataract patients; acne and psoriasis treatment Tazorac; and glaucoma treatment Alphagan. That year Allergan and Ligand acquired the assets of ALRT and formed subsidiary Allergan Specialty Therapeutics to research and develop new drugs. The unit was spun off in 1998, but Allergan bought it back again in 2001.

In 1998 the company restructured, cutting jobs and closing about half of its manufacturing plants. In 2000 Botox was approved by the FDA to treat cervical dystonia.

In 2003, Allergan bought ophthalmic drug company Oculex Pharmaceuticals, which makes the Posurdex implanted drug delivery device, and Bardeen Sciences, which had a complimentary drug pipeline.

Subsidiary Advanced Medical Optics was spun off in 2004.

EXECUTIVES

Chairman and CEO: David E. I. Pyott, age 55, $11,911,106 total compensation
Vice Chairman: Herbert W. Boyer, age 72
President: F. Michael (Mike) Ball, age 53, $3,712,125 total compensation
EVP Finance and Business Development and CFO: Jeffrey L. Edwards, age 48, $2,590,976 total compensation
EVP Global Technical Operations: Raymond H. (Ray) Diradoorian, age 51
EVP, Chief Administration Officer, General Counsel, Secretary, and Chief Ethics Officer: Douglas S. Ingram, age 46, $2,733,453 total compensation
EVP Human Resources: Dianne Dyer-Bruggeman, age 59
EVP Research and Development: Scott M. Whitcup, age 49, $2,834,115 total compensation
SVP Treasury, Risk, and Investor Relations: James M. (Jim) Hindman
SVP and Corporate Controller: James F. Barlow, age 50
VP; President and General Manager, Allergan Medical: Robert E. Grant, age 37
Investor Relations: Joann Bradley
Investor Relations: Emil Schultz
Global Corporate Communications: Caroline Van Hove
Auditors: Ernst & Young LLP

LOCATIONS

HQ: Allergan, Inc.
2525 Dupont Dr., Irvine, CA 92612
Phone: 714-246-4500   **Fax:** 714-246-4971
Web: www.allergan.com

2008 Sales

	$ mil.	% of total
Product sales		
US	2,793.2	64
Europe	881.9	20
Latin America	262.5	6
Asia Pacific	222.3	5
Other regions	168.8	4
Manufacturing operations	11.0	—
Corporate & other	63.7	1
Total	**4,403.4**	**100**

PRODUCTS/OPERATIONS

2008 Sales

	$ mil.	% of total
Specialty pharmaceuticals		
Eye care pharmaceuticals	2,009.1	46
Botox/neuromodulator	1,310.9	30
Skin care	113.7	3
Urologics	68.6	1
Medical devices		
Breast aesthetics	310.0	7
Obesity intervention	296.0	7
Facial aesthetics	231.4	5
Corporate & other revenues	63.7	1
Total	**4,403.4**	**100**

Selected Products

Specialty Pharmaceuticals
Eye Care
Acular (allergic conjunctivitis)
Acuvail (post-surgery pain)
Alocril (allergic conjunctivitis)
Alphagan (glaucoma)
Botox (eye twitching)
Combigan (glaucoma, ocular hypertension)
Elestat (allergic conjunctivitis)
Exocin (ophthalmic anti-infective)
Ganfort (glaucoma)
Lumigan (glaucoma)
Ocuflox (ophthalmic anti-infective)
Oflox (ophthalmic anti-infective)
Optive (chronic dry eye disease)
Ozurdex (macular edema)
Pred Forte (ophthalmic anti-inflammatory)
Refresh (chronic dry eye disease)
Restatis (chronic dry eye disease)
Trivaris (corticosteroid for inflammation)
Zymar (bacterial conjunctivitis)

Neuromodulator
  Botox (neuromuscular disorder treatment)
  Botox Cosmetic (wrinkle reduction)
Skin Care
  Aczone (acne treatment)
  Avage (skin wrinkles or discoloration)
  Azelex (acne treatment)
  Clinique Medical (post-treatment creams)
  Finacea (rosacea)
  Fluoroplex (keratoses)
  M.D. Forte (line of alpha hydroxy acid products)
  Prevage (skin lines or wrinkles and protection)
  Tazorac (treatment for acne and psoriasis)
  Vivite (anti-aging)
Urologics
  Sanctura (overactive bladder)
Medical Devices
  Breast Aesthetics
    CUI (implants)
    Inspira (implants)
    McGhan (implants)
    Natrelle (implants)
    Tissue expanders
  Obesity Intervention
    Orbera (formerly BIB System, stomach implant)
    Lap-Band (stomach implant)
  Facial Aesthetics
    CosmoDerm and CosmoPlast (dermal filler)
    Juvederm (dermal fillers)
    Latisse (eyelash enhancer)
    Zyderm and Zyplast (dermal fillers)

COMPETITORS

Alcon
Astellas
Bausch & Lomb
Bristol-Myers Squibb
CIBA VISION
Cooper Companies
Dermik Laboratories
Galderma Laboratories
GlaxoSmithKline
Hoffmann-La Roche
Ipsen
Johnson & Johnson
L'Oréal
Medicis Pharmaceutical
Merck
Novartis
Pfizer
Procter & Gamble
Sanofi-Aventis
Schering-Plough
Solta Medical
Stiefel Laboratories
Watson Pharmaceuticals

HISTORICAL FINANCIALS

Company Type: Public

Income Statement

FYE: December 31

	REVENUE ($ mil.)	NET INCOME ($ mil.)	NET PROFIT MARGIN	EMPLOYEES
12/08	4,403.4	578.6	13.1%	8,740
12/07	3,938.9	499.3	12.7%	7,886
12/06	3,063.3	(127.4)	—	6,772
12/05	2,319.2	403.9	17.4%	5,055
12/04	2,045.6	377.1	18.4%	5,030
Annual Growth	21.1%	11.3%	—	14.8%

2008 Year-End Financials

Debt ratio: 40.8%
Return on equity: 14.9%
Cash ($ mil.): 1,110
Current ratio: 3.26
Long-term debt ($ mil.): 1,635

No. of shares (mil.): 308
Dividends
  Yield: 0.5%
  Payout: 10.6%
Market value ($ mil.): 12,399

Stock History

NYSE: AGN

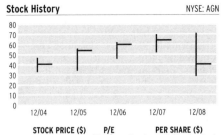

	STOCK PRICE ($) FY Close	P/E High/Low		PER SHARE ($) Earnings	Dividends	Book Value
12/08	40.32	37	15	1.89	0.20	13.04
12/07	64.24	43	32	1.62	0.20	12.16
12/06	59.87	—	—	(0.44)	0.20	10.22
12/05	53.98	37	23	1.50	0.20	5.10
12/04	40.53	33	24	1.41	0.18	3.63
Annual Growth	(0.1%)	—	—	7.6%	2.7%	37.7%

Alliance One International

Alliance One International keeps one eye on the world's tobacco farmers and the other on the cigarette makers. The company is a leading global leaf-tobacco merchant, behind slightly larger rival Universal Corporation. Alliance One buys leaf tobacco directly from growers in more than 45 countries. It also processes flue-cured, burley, and oriental tobaccos and sells them to large multinational cigarette and cigar manufacturers, such as Altria Group, in some 90 countries. Alliance One was formed through the mid-2005 merger of tobacco processor DIMON and Standard Commercial.

Altria and Japan Tobacco, two of Alliance One's largest customers, accounted for nearly 35% and 20%, respectively, of the company's 2007 revenue.

To provide its customers with a less-expensive leaf tobacco, Alliance One has expanded internationally. (Prices in the US are artificially supported by the government, which has driven away foreign buyers.)

Like Universal Corporation, Alliance One has also seen its revenue hurt by the latest trends in tobacco purchasing. While demand for tobacco in the US drops with the decrease in the number of smokers, more cigarette companies are choosing to buy their tobacco directly from farmers or from merchants overseas rather than through domestic auctions.

Alliance One (then DIMON) joined other major cigarette manufacturers in settling a class-action lawsuit from tobacco farmers who alleged the company and others conspired to keep tobacco prices artificially low. The firm made no admission of guilt but agreed to pay $6 million as its share of the $200 million settlement.

In 2007 Brian Harker, chairman, resigned.

HISTORY

DIMON was formed with the 1995 merger of Dibrell Brothers and Monk-Austin, two of the US's leading leaf-tobacco dealers. Founded in 1873 by Alphonso and Richard Dibrell, Dibrell Brothers bought and processed tobacco in the South and sold it in North America, expanding overseas during the 1920s. Early sales were for traditional uses such as chewing tobacco and cigars, and the company began doing business with large US cigarette makers in the early 1930s.

Publicly traded by the end of WWII, Dibrell Brothers diversified in the 1960s and 1970s, adding makers of ice-cream freezers (Richmond Cedar Works) and wooden lamps (Dunning Industries) and a chain of steakhouses (Kentucky Rib-Eye) but exited those businesses by 1990. Throughout the 1970s Dibrell Brothers established operations in Latin America, the Far East, India, and Italy. It moved into Zimbabwe in 1980 and the next year acquired B.V. Tabak Export & Import Compagnie, a Dutch tobacco firm with holdings in Brazil, the Dominican Republic, West Germany, and Zimbabwe.

In another diversification effort, Dibrell Brothers acquired 54% of Florimex Worldwide in 1987 (buying the rest during the next three years). The flower distributor helped boost sales in 1988. In the 1990s the firm's tobacco fortunes picked up with the growing demand for American-blend tobacco from countries in areas such as Eastern Europe, which previously only had access to high-tar cigarettes.

In 1995 Dibrell Brothers reached an agreement to combine with Monk-Austin, the product of a 1990 merger between tobacco firms A.C. Monk and the Austin Company. Founded by A. C. Monk in 1907, A.C. Monk & Company had interests in North Carolina tobacco plants. Subsequent members of the Monk family expanded its operations. It acquired rival Austin Company in 1990 and went public two years later. In 1993 Monk-Austin acquired tobacco trader T.S. Ragsdale; beefed up its operations in Brazil, Malawi, and Zimbabwe; and began building a tobacco processing plant in China. The company won a contract from R.J. Reynolds Tobacco in 1994 to supply all the domestic leaf tobacco that Reynolds requires.

Upon completion of the 1995 merger of Dibrell Brothers and Monk-Austin, Dibrell Brothers CEO Claude Owen became CEO of the newly formed company, DIMON Inc. Also that year the company acquired tobacco operations in Bulgaria, Greece, Italy, and Turkey and reached an agreement to buy and process leaf tobacco for Lorillard Tobacco. DIMON recorded a $30 million loss for the year, largely because of restructuring costs.

The company acquired #4 tobacco merchant Intabex Holdings Worldwide in 1997 for about $246 million. That year the firm extended its relationship with R.J. Reynolds, agreeing to process all of its tobacco. In 1998 DIMON sold Florimex to U.S.A. Floral Products for $90 million, in part to finance debt from the purchase of Intabex. Sales were slowed that year and in 1999 by a worldwide glut of leaf tobacco.

In 1999 DIMON settled a lawsuit it had filed against Intabex's owners and management for allegedly misrepresenting its value; the purchase price was reduced by $50 million. In 2000 the company acquired Greece-based facility operator Austro-Hellenique to expand its operations in that country.

DIMON's sales decreased somewhat over the next year as the company transitioned to direct contract buying (as opposed to buying tobacco at auction).

In May 2005 DIMON and Standard Commercial merged and became Alliance One International.

EXECUTIVES

Chairman, President, and CEO:
Robert E. (Pete) Harrison, age 55
EVP Global Operations: J. Henry Denny, age 59
EVP and CFO: Robert A. Sheets, age 54
EVP Business Strategy and Relationship Management:
J. Pieter Sikkel, age 45
SVP and CIO: William D. Pappas, age 56
SVP, Chief Legal Officer, and Secretary: Henry C. Babb, age 64
SVP Human Resources: Michael K. McDaniel, age 59
VP and Treasurer: Joel L. Thomas
VP Compensation and Benefits: Laura D. Jones
VP International Risk: Dennis A. Paren
VP Corporate Audit Services: B. Holt Ward
VP and Controller: Hampton R. Poole Jr., age 57
Assistant Treasurer: B. Lynne Finney
Assistant General Counsel and Assistant Secretary:
William L. O'Quinn Jr.
Auditors: Deloitte & Touche LLP

LOCATIONS

HQ: Alliance One International, Inc.
8001 Aerial Center Pkwy., Morrisville, NC 27560
Phone: 919-379-4300   **Fax:** 919-379-4346
Web: www.aointl.com

PRODUCTS/OPERATIONS

2009 Sales

	$ mil.	% of total
Belgium	447.5	20
US	322.3	14
China	147.8	6
Netherlands	124.2	6
Indonesia	117.7	5
Russia	115.2	5
Germany	109.3	5
Other	874.2	39
Total	**2,258.2**	**100**

Selected Subsidiaries

Alliance One Brasil Exportadora de Tabacos Ltda.
DIMON Hellas Tobacco S.A.
DIMON International Kyrgyzstan
DIMON Leaf (Thailand) Ltd.
Intabex Netherlands BV
Leaf Trading Company Ltd.
Standard Commercial Tobacco Company (UK) Ltd.
Werkhof GmbH

COMPETITORS

Altadis
British American Tobacco
Japan Tobacco
Universal Corporation

HISTORICAL FINANCIALS

Company Type: Public

Income Statement

FYE: March 31

	REVENUE ($ mil.)	NET INCOME ($ mil.)	NET PROFIT MARGIN	EMPLOYEES
3/09	2,258.2	132.6	5.9%	4,400
3/08	2,011.5	16.9	0.8%	4,700
3/07	1,979.1	(21.3)	—	4,700
3/06	2,112.7	(447.4)	—	5,400
3/05	1,311.4	13.3	1.0%	4,200
Annual Growth	**14.6%**	**77.7%**	**—**	**1.2%**

2009 Year-End Financials
Debt ratio: 199.8%   No. of shares (mil.): 97
Return on equity: 49.3%   Dividends
Cash ($ mil.): 88   Yield: 0.0%
Current ratio: 2.02   Payout: —
Long-term debt ($ mil.): 653 Market value ($ mil.): 373

Stock History

NYSE: AOI

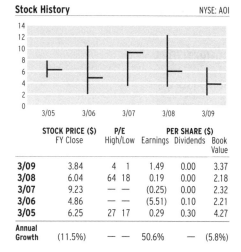

	STOCK PRICE ($) FY Close	P/E High/Low		PER SHARE ($) Earnings	Dividends	Book Value
3/09	3.84	4	1	1.49	0.00	3.37
3/08	6.04	64	18	0.19	0.00	2.18
3/07	9.23	—	—	(0.25)	0.00	2.32
3/06	4.86	—	—	(5.51)	0.10	2.21
3/05	6.25	27	17	0.29	0.30	4.27
Annual Growth	**(11.5%)**	**—**	**—**	**50.6%**	**—**	**(5.8%)**

Alliant Techsystems

Space is not the final frontier for Alliant Techsystems (ATK), as long as its aerospace offerings are paving new paths for the company's technological endeavors. ATK is a leading manufacturer of solid propulsion rocket motors, force protection systems, laser warning systems, and strategic and defense missiles. ATK builds motors for unmanned space launch vehicles such as the Trident II and the Delta II. ATK is also a top supplier of ammunition — from small-caliber rounds to tank ammunition — to the US and its allies. Additional offerings include anti-tank mines, aircraft weapons systems, and high-tech weapons components. The US government and its prime contractors account for over 70% of sales.

ATK is focusing on the research and development of durable, lightweight composite materials to lower the cost and improve performance of aircraft. Its missile and laser warning systems (AN/AAR-47) are being used on military aircraft to prevent attacks. The company is also engaged in transitioning regular aircraft into special mission aircraft to include ISR (Intelligence, Surveillance, and Reconnaissance) systems capabilities. Additionally, ATK is venturing into the production of micro satellites, as well as solar panels and satellite management systems.

For the commercial sector, the company provides its Speer and Federal Premium branded ammunition to law enforcement agencies. It also offers sport shooting accessories through its RCBS and Weaver brands, as well as accessories such as reloading equipment, smokeless powder, and gun care products, among others.

Early in 2009 ATK scored Eagle Industries. The move taps into domestic and international tactical accessories markets serving military and law enforcement customers. Eagle brings its capabilities as a manufacturer of individual operational nylon gear and equipment. The 5,000-plus products include tactical assault vests, load-

bearing equipment, weapon transporting gear, and holsters.

ATK partnered with defense contractors Lockheed Martin and Northrop Grumman in 2008 to develop multi-role weapon systems for the F-22 Raptor and the F-35 Lightning II (both Lockheed Martin aircraft). Also in 2008 ATK offered to pay $1.3 billion for the information systems and geospatial information services division of MacDonald, Dettwiler and Associates. The Canadian government, however, has protested the deal.

ATK got another acquisition in its crosshairs in 2007 when it purchased Swales Aerospace, a provider of satellite components and small spacecraft. Swales' customers include NASA and the US DoD, as well as commercial satellite customers.

HISTORY

Alliant Techsystems (ATK) was formed in 1990 when Honeywell spun off its defense-related businesses to shareholders. Honeywell's roots in the defense business go back to 1941, when it was known as Honeywell-Minnesota. A maker of consumer electronics products such as switches, buttons, and appliances, Honeywell joined the war effort and began producing tank periscopes, turbo engine regulators, automatic ammunition firing control devices, and automatic bomb-release systems.

After WWII Honeywell-Minnesota found that the Cold War provided a reliable and profitable income stream for defense contractors. By 1964 the company had focused on electronics systems. Provisions for the Vietnam War boosted sales, but the fall of Saigon led to downsizing.

When the Iron Curtain fell in the late 1980s, Honeywell's defense operations misfired and ran up huge losses. Honeywell sought to sell its defense businesses as an independent subsidiary, but was unable to obtain an acceptable bid.

Honeywell spun off Alliant Techsystems to shareholders in 1990 under Toby Warson, the CEO of Honeywell's UK subsidiary. A former naval commander, Warson began with about 8,300 employees and lots of bureaucratic layers; he quickly cut about 800 administrative jobs.

Although the Soviet Union and its Eastern Bloc allies had collapsed, a new threat raised its head: Iraq. Cutbacks in the defense budget meant that advanced high-dollar systems were put on the back burner while cheaper alternatives, such as improved ammunition, were moved to the front. During the Gulf War, ATK's ordnance contributions included 120mm uranium-tipped anti-tank shells, 25mm shells for the Bradley Fighting Vehicle, and the 30mm bullets used by Apache helicopters and A-10 Warthog anti-tank planes.

Warson cut another 800 jobs after the Gulf War and reduced the number of management layers from 14 to seven. ATK divested its only non-munitions unit, Metrum Information Storage (data recording and storage devices), in 1992. Metrum had incurred setbacks that caused the company to write off millions of dollars. ATK expanded into additional aerospace markets and achieved vertical integration in propellant production in 1995 with the purchase of the aerospace division of Hercules Incorporated, a maker of space rocket motors, strategic and tactical weapons systems, and ordnance.

ATK refocused on its core operations in 1997 and jettisoned its marine systems group (torpedoes, underwater surveillance systems). The next year the company was awarded a $1 billion contract to make components for Boeing's Delta IV rockets. In 1999 chairman and CEO Dick Schwartz retired from the company and was replaced by retired Navy admiral Paul David Miller.

Miller consolidated plants, improved manufacturing processes, and bought back more than 1.3 million shares of ATK's stock in 2000. While the conventional munitions segment posted slight sales declines that year, primarily due to reduced sales of tactical tank ammunition as the US Army transitioned into the next-generation tank round, Miller's efforts led to greater company profitability. In 2001 ATK acquired Thiokol Propulsion Corp. In September Alliant bought the defense unit of Safety Components International that makes metallic belt links for ammunition. In December the company added another acquisition to the mix with the purchase of the ammunitions unit of Blount International.

In 2003 Dan Murphy became CEO, with Miller remaining as chairman. (Miller retired in 2005 and Murphy assumed that role, as well.)

Acquisitions in 2004 included national security specialist Mission Research Corporation (now ATK Mission Research), and PSI Group, a maker of propellant systems and satellite parts.

In 2006 Alliant sold its lithium battery business to EnerSys for an undisclosed sum.

EXECUTIVES

Chairman and CEO: Daniel J. (Dan) Murphy, age 61, $8,952,576 total compensation
SVP and CFO: John L. Shroyer, age 45, $1,834,322 total compensation
SVP Human Resources and Administrative Services: Paula J. Patineau, age 55
SVP Corporate Strategy: Mark L. Mele, age 52
SVP; President, ATK Space Systems: Blake E. Larson, age 49, $1,694,488 total compensation
SVP; President, ATK Armament Systems: Mark W. DeYoung, age 50, $1,919,238 total compensation
SVP Contracts and Supply Chain Management: Dianne Deering Anton
SVP, General Counsel, and Secretary: Keith D. Ross, age 52
SVP; President, ATK Mission Systems: John J. (Jack) Cronin, age 52, $1,711,727 total compensation
SVP Washington Operations: Steven J. Cortese, age 47
SVP Corporate Communications: Brian P. Cullin
VP, Treasurer, and Investor Relations: Steven P. (Steve) Wold
VP Corporate Development: Michael B. Dolby, age 48
VP Corporate Communications: Bryce Hallowell
Director Investor Relations: Jeff Huebschen
Auditors: Deloitte & Touche LLP

LOCATIONS

HQ: Alliant Techsystems Inc.
7480 Flying Cloud Dr., Minneapolis, MN 55344
Phone: 952-351-3000   **Fax:** 952-351-3009
Web: www.atk.com

PRODUCTS/OPERATIONS

2009 Sales by Segment

	$ mil.	% of total
ATK Armament Systems	1,756.3	37
ATK Mission Systems	1,389.0	29
ATK Space Systems	1,642.3	34
Adjustments	(204.4)	
Total	**4,583.2**	**100**

2009 Sales by Customer

	% of total
US Army	26
NASA	20
US Air Force	12
US Navy	12
Other US Government	6
Commercial & Foreign	24
Total	**100**

COMPETITORS

Aerojet
Allied Defense Group
BAE Systems Inc.
Boeing
DAC Technologies
E'Prime Aerospace
GenCorp
General Dynamics
GIAT Industries
ITT Corp.
Kaman Aerospace
Lockheed Martin
Lockheed Martin Missiles
Metal Storm
Northrop Grumman
Olin
Raytheon
SpaceDev
Teledyne Technologies

HISTORICAL FINANCIALS

Company Type: Public

Income Statement

FYE: March 31

	REVENUE ($ mil.)	NET INCOME ($ mil.)	NET PROFIT MARGIN	EMPLOYEES
3/09	4,583.2	155.1	3.4%	19,000
3/08	4,171.7	222.3	5.3%	17,000
3/07	3,564.9	184.1	5.2%	16,000
3/06	3,216.8	153.9	4.8%	15,200
3/05	2,801.1	153.5	5.5%	14,000
Annual Growth	**13.1%**	**0.3%**	**—**	**7.9%**

2009 Year-End Financials

Debt ratio: 188.7%
Return on equity: 22.9%
Cash ($ mil.): 337
Current ratio: 1.57
Long-term debt ($ mil.): 1,161
No. of shares (mil.): 33
Dividends
Yield: 0.0%
Payout: —
Market value ($ mil.): 2,205

Stock History

NYSE: ATK

	STOCK PRICE ($) FY Close	P/E High/Low		PER SHARE ($) Earnings	Dividends	Book Value
3/09	66.98	25	13	4.56	0.00	18.68
3/08	103.53	19	14	6.32	0.00	22.51
3/07	87.92	17	14	5.32	0.00	16.94
3/06	77.17	19	16	4.11	0.00	19.09
3/05	71.45	19	14	4.03	0.00	20.85
Annual Growth	**(1.6%)**	**—**	**—**	**3.1%**	**—**	**(2.7%)**

The Allstate Corporation

Ya gotta hand it to Allstate. The "good hands" company is the second-largest US personal lines insurer, behind rival State Farm. The company's Allstate Protection segment sells auto, homeowners, property/casualty, and life insurance products in Canada and the US. Allstate Financial provides life insurance through subsidiaries Allstate Life, American Heritage Life, and Lincoln Benefit Life. It also provides investment products, targeting affluent and middle-income consumers. Allstate Motor Club provides emergency road service and, adding to its repertoire, the company also offers the nationwide online Allstate Bank.

Allstate maintains a network of 12,800 exclusive agencies which sell its Allstate-branded insurance products. Independent agencies sell the company's Deerbrook and Encompass-branded products as well as its Allstate lines.

The company has disposed of the majority of its operations outside North America (including Allstate Investments in Japan and the direct auto business in Germany and Italy), focusing on its core markets in Canada and the US.

The 2005 hurricane season with Katrina, Rita, and Wilma combined to account for $5.67 billion in catastrophe losses for Allstate. The comparatively quiet 2006 and 2007 seasons gave the company some respite before being hit in 2008 with $3.34 billion in catastrophe losses, in part from hurricanes Ike and Gustave.

To brace itself for future hurricane seasons, the company has upped its reinsurance and has stopped writing new homeowners policies for properties along the Gulf Coast, Connecticut, Delaware, and New Jersey. The company also aims to reduce its new homeowners policies for coastal parts of New York and has increased its premium rates in Florida. To address the many Allstate Floridian customers whose homeowner policies won't be renewed, the company has struck an agreement with newly formed Royal Palm Insurance Company. Royal Palm offers property policies, sold through Allstate agencies.

In coastal areas of New York, Allstate attempted to limit homeowner policies by only renewing the policies of customers who also held other types of insurance with the company. The New York Insurance Superintendent found the company to be in violation of the state's insurance laws in mid-2007 and pressured Allstate to offer quotes to more than 55,000 former customers who had been dropped.

Customers in earthquake-prone areas now also must look elsewhere for new optional earthquake coverage. Allstate no longer offers it, and is considering doing away with it from its renewable policies as well. It is also pruning its risk exposure to losses from wildfires after taking a loss of $318 million in 2007 from fires in Southern California.

With the US economy weakened, Allstate Financial is suffering alongside its financial services brethren. It took a loss of $1.72 billion in 2008. However, when the US Treasury offered Allstate a piece of the Troubled Asset Relief Program in 2009, the insurer politely turned it down, citing its strong capital and liquidity.

HISTORY

Allstate traces its origins to a friendly game of bridge played in 1930 on a Chicago-area commuter train by Sears president Robert Wood and a friend, insurance broker Carl Odell. The insurance man suggested Sears sell auto insurance through the mail. Wood liked the idea, financed the company, and in 1931 put Odell in charge (that hand of bridge must have shown Wood that Odell was no dummy). The company was named Allstate, after one of Sears' tire brands. Allstate was born just as Sears was beginning its push into retailing, and Allstate went with it, selling insurance out of all the new Sears stores.

Growth was slow during the Depression and WWII, but the postwar boom was a gold mine for both Sears and Allstate. Suburban development made cars a necessity; 1950s prudence necessitated car insurance; and Sears made it easy to buy the insurance at their stores and, increasingly, at freestanding agencies.

In the late 1950s Allstate added home and other property/casualty insurance lines. It also went into life insurance — in-force policies zoomed from zero to $1 billion in six years, the industry's fastest growth ever.

Sears formed Allstate Enterprises in 1960 as an umbrella for all its noninsurance operations. In 1970 that firm bought its first savings and loan (S&L). The insurer continued to acquire other S&Ls and to add subsidiaries throughout the 1970s and 1980s.

This strategy dovetailed with Sears' strategy, which was to become a diversified financial services company. In 1985 Sears introduced the Discover Card through Allstate's Greenwood Trust Company. However, by the late 1980s it was obvious Sears would never be a financial services giant. Moreover, it was losing so much in retailing that by 1987 Allstate was the major contributor to corporate net income. Sears began to dismantle its financial empire in the 1990s.

Allstate also suffered from a backlash against high insurance rates. When Massachusetts instituted no-fault insurance in 1989, Allstate stopped writing new auto insurance there. Later the company had to refund $110 million to customers to settle a suit with California over rate rollbacks required by 1988's Proposition 103.

Allstate went public in 1993, when Sears sold about 20% of its stake. That year it began reducing its operations in Florida to protect itself against high losses from hurricanes. Two years later the retailer sold its remaining interest to its shareholders. Also in 1995 Allstate sold 70% of PMI, its mortgage insurance unit, to the public.

In 1996 Allstate worked to reduce its exposure to hurricane and earthquake losses. (Together, Hurricane Andrew and the Northridge quake helped account for almost $4 billion in casualty losses.) It created a Florida-only subsidiary that would buy reinsurance to protect against losses that could arise from another major hurricane. Also that year Allstate sold its Northbrook (property/casualty) and Allstate Reinsurance operations to St. Paul and SCOR, respectively.

In 1998 Allstate sold its real estate portfolio for nearly $1 billion and opened a savings bank. In 2000 Allstate restructured, adding online and telephone distributions to increase its sales, and buying Provident National Assurance Co. from UNUMProvident. Reducing expenses, Allstate cut some 10% of its staff (some 4,000 jobs) that year and turned its agents into independent contractors. With its purchase of Sterling Collision Centers, Allstate entered the car repair business in 2001.

EXECUTIVES

Chairman, President, and CEO: Thomas J. Wilson II, age 51, $8,343,930 total compensation
SVP and CFO: Don Civgin, age 47, $478,409 total compensation
SVP and CIO, Allstate Insurance: Catherine S. Brune, age 55
SVP Corporate Relations and Interim Chief Marketing Officer, Allstate Insurance: Joan H. Walker, age 61
SVP and Chief Investment Officer: Judith P. (Judy) Greffin, age 48
SVP Claims, Allstate Insurance: Michael J. Roche, age 57
SVP and President Allstate Protection, and Interim President Allstate Financial: George E. Ruebenson, age 60, $4,959,707 total compensation
SVP Human Resources: James D. DeVries
SVP Product Operations, Allstate Insurance: Fredrick F. Cripe, age 51
SVP Protection Distribution, Allstate Insurance: Steven P. Sorenson, age 44
SVP Protection Distribution, Insurance: Joseph J. Richardson Jr., age 48
VP and Controller; Controller, Lincoln Benefit Life Company: Samuel H. (Sam) Pilch, age 62
VP Corporate Relations: Sari L. Macrie
VP Auditing: Kathleen Swain, age 48
VP and General Counsel; SVP and General Counsel, AIC: Michele Coleman Mayes, age 59, $2,861,838 total compensation
VP Procurement: Lori Yelvington, age 50
President, Allstate Workplace Division: David A. Bird
President, Deerbrook Insurance Company: Gregory A. Meyer
President, Sterling Autobody Centers: Allan Robinson
President, Social Networking, Allstate Financial: Desirée Rogers
Secretary: Mary J. McGinn
Auditors: Deloitte & Touche LLP

LOCATIONS

HQ: The Allstate Corporation
2775 Sanders Rd., Northbrook, IL 60062
Phone: 847-402-5000 **Fax:** 847-326-7519
Web: www.allstate.com

PRODUCTS/OPERATIONS

2008 Revenues

	$ mil.	% of total
Property/liability insurance premiums	26,967	78
Net investment income	5,622	16
Life & annuity premiums & contract charges	1,895	6
Realized capital gains & losses	(5,090)	—
Total	**29,394**	**100**

Selected Subsidiaries

Allstate Bank
Allstate Insurance Company of Canada
Allstate Life Insurance Company
Deerbrook Insurance Company
Encompass Insurance Company
Kennett Capital, Inc.
Lincoln Benefit Life Company
Northbrook Indemnity Company
Pafco Insurance Company (Canada)
Pembridge America Inc.
Roadway Protection Auto Club, Inc.
Sterling Collision Centers, Inc.

COMPETITORS

Chubb Corp	Progressive Corporation
Farmers Group	Prudential
GEICO	State Farm
Hanover Insurance	Torchmark
The Hartford	Travelers Companies
MetLife	USAA
Nationwide	

HISTORICAL FINANCIALS

Company Type: Public

Income Statement

FYE: December 31

	ASSETS ($ mil.)	NET INCOME ($ mil.)	INCOME AS % OF ASSETS	EMPLOYEES
12/08	134,798.0	(1,679.0)	—	38,900
12/07	156,408.0	4,636.0	3.0%	38,000
12/06	157,554.0	4,900.0	3.1%	37,900
12/05	156,072.0	1,752.0	1.1%	38,300
12/04	149,725.0	3,356.0	2.2%	38,000
Annual Growth	**(2.6%)**	**—**	**—**	**0.6%**

2008 Year-End Financials

Equity as % of assets: 9.4%
Return on assets: —
Return on equity: —
Long-term debt ($ mil.): 5,659
No. of shares (mil.): 536
Dividends
Yield: 5.0%
Payout: —
Market value ($ mil.): 17,572
Sales ($ mil.): 29,394

Stock History

NYSE: ALL

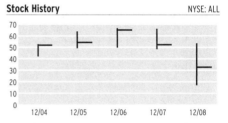

	STOCK PRICE ($) FY Close	P/E High/Low		Earnings	PER SHARE ($) Dividends	Book Value
12/08	32.76	—	—	(3.07)	1.64	23.57
12/07	52.23	8	6	7.77	1.52	40.74
12/06	65.11	8	6	7.84	1.40	40.73
12/05	54.07	24	19	2.64	1.28	37.63
12/04	51.72	11	9	4.54	1.12	40.69
Annual Growth	**(10.8%)**	**—**	**—**	**—**	**10.0%**	**(12.8%)**

Altria Group

The house the Marlboro Man built, Altria Group, is the largest cigarette company in the US. Altria operates its cigarette business through subsidiary Philip Morris USA, which sells Marlboro — the world's best-selling cigarette brand since 1972. Altria controls about half of the US tobacco market. It manufactures cigarettes under the Parliament, Virginia Slims, and Basic cigarette brands. While still firmly hooked on cigarettes, Altria is transitioning from primarily a cigarette manufacturer to a purveyor of a variety of tobacco products, including cigars and smokeless tobacco. To that end, it has made a number of strategic acquisitions, including smokeless tobacco maker UST in 2009.

The all-cash purchase of UST was worth more than $11 billion. Purchasing UST brought popular brands Copenhagen and Skoal into Altria's fold and gave the company a leading position in the smokeless tobacco market. As part of the UST deal, Altria acquired UST's machine-made cigar operation, as well as its Ste. Michelle Wine Estates. (Other liquid holdings include a 28% stake in brewer SABMiller.)

Altria in 2007 bought US cigar maker John Middleton, which specializes in machine-made cigars — most notably the Black & Mild brand. The deal was valued at $2.2 billion.

Altria and its Big Tobacco rivals continue to try to resolve lawsuits over smoking-related illnesses. The industry has reached settlements with US states amounting to nearly $250 billion, and a number of civil suits are pending.

In July 2006 the Florida Supreme Court upheld a lower court's ruling that had overturned a $145 billion award for punitive damages against Big Tobacco defendants, among them Altria's Philip Morris. While the ruling upheld findings that smoking cigarettes causes diseases and nicotine is addictive, it signaled to some investors that the threat of tobacco-related class action lawsuits was lessening.

Historic legislation enacted in June 2009 turned over the regulation of tobacco products to the U.S. Food and Drug Administration, which will now have unprecedented authority to regulate tobacco products, including marketing, labeling, and nicotine content. Altria has pledged to work constructively with the FDA and supported the passage of the legislation.

HISTORY

Philip Morris opened his London tobacco store in 1847 and by 1854 was making his own cigarettes. Morris died in 1873, and his heirs sold the firm to William Thomson just before the turn of the century. Thomson introduced his company's cigarettes to the US in 1902. American investors bought the rights to leading Philip Morris brands in 1919, and in 1925 the new company, Philip Morris & Co., introduced Marlboro, which targeted women smokers and produced modest sales.

When the firm's larger competitors raised their prices in 1930, Philip Morris Companies countered by introducing inexpensive cigarettes that caught on with Depression-weary consumers. By 1936 it was the fourth-biggest cigarette maker.

The firm acquired Benson & Hedges in 1954. It signed ad agency Leo Burnett, which promptly initiated the Marlboro Man campaign. Under Joseph Cullman (who became president in 1957), Philip Morris experienced tremendous growth overseas. After dipping to sixth place among US tobacco companies in 1960, it rebounded at home, thanks to Marlboro's growing popularity among men (Marlboro became the #1 cigarette brand in the world in 1972).

In 1970 Philip Morris bought the nation's seventh-largest brewer, Miller Brewing, and with aggressive marketing it vaulted to #2 among US beer makers by 1980. To protect itself against a shrinking US tobacco market, in 1985 Philip Morris paid $5.6 billion for General Foods (Kool-Aid, Post, Stove Top). In 1988 it bought Kraft (Miracle Whip, Velveeta). The next year Philip Morris joined Kraft with General Foods.

In 1994 Australian Geoffrey Bible became CEO. By late 1998 the company and its rivals had settled tobacco litigation with most states, agreeing to pay about $250 billion over 25 years to receive protection from further state suits.

In 1999 the US government filed a massive lawsuit against Big Tobacco, and Philip Morris admitted — no kidding — that smoking increases the risk of getting cancer and other illnesses. In 2000 Philip Morris vowed to appeal

after a state court awarded $74 billion in punitive damages to Florida smokers. The court later ruled that Philip Morris, Lorillard, and the Liggett Group would pay at least $709 million in the case regardless of the outcome.

In December 2000 Philip Morris completed its purchase of Nabisco Holdings for $18.9 billion. In June 2001 Philip Morris spun off Kraft Foods in what was the second-largest IPO in US history; it retained an 84% stake in the company and 97% of the voting rights.

In April 2002 CFO Louis Camilleri succeeded Bible as CEO; in September Camilleri became chairman upon Bible's retirement. In July 2002, Philip Morris sold Miller Brewing to South African Breweries for $5.6 billion ($3.6 billion in SAB stock and the assumption of $2 billion in Miller debt) in July 2002.

In the ongoing saga of tobacco-related litigation, Philip Morris said it would appeal an October 2002 verdict by a California jury that ordered the company to pay $28 billion in punitive damages (later reduced to $28 million). In January 2003 Philip Morris changed its name to Altria Group in an effort to distance itself from its tobacco litigation. In April a Florida appeals court threw out the state's multibillion-dollar judgment (made in 2000) against Philip Morris USA and four other US tobacco companies.

In March 2003 Philip Morris USA lost an Illinois lawsuit, which claimed the company's use of the word "light" was misleading and violated Illinois consumer fraud laws. The judge ordered Philip Morris USA to pay damages of $10 billion and post a $12 billion bond. The Illinois Supreme Court has lowered the bond to $7 billion and agreed to hear Philip Morris USA's appeal of the original verdict.

In 2005 Altria purchased a $4.8 billion stake in Indonesia's third-largest tobacco firm, PT Hanjaya Mandala Sampoerna.

In mid-2006 Altria unseated Roger Deromedi from Kraft's top spot and appointed Irene Rosenfeld to head the company. The executive realignment was part of Altria's plan to spin off Kraft.

In 2007 Altria completed the spinoff of Kraft Foods to Altria shareholders. A year later Altria spun off its Philip Morris International arm, also to shareholders, and moved its headquarters from New York City's Park Avenue to Richmond, Virginia.

EXECUTIVES

Chairman and CEO: Michael E. Szymanczyk, age 60, $12,023,549 total compensation
EVP and CFO: David R. (Dave) Beran, age 54, $5,539,958 total compensation
EVP and CTO: John R. (Jack) Nelson, age 57, $4,137,107 total compensation
EVP and Chief Compliance and Administrative Officer: Martin J. Barrington, age 55, $3,023,385 total compensation
EVP; President, Phillip Morris USA: Craig A. Johnson, age 56, $4,182,028 total compensation
EVP Strategy and Business Development: Howard A. Willard III, age 45
EVP and General Counsel: Denise F. Keane, age 57, $3,295,985 total compensation
VP and Controller: Linda M. Warren, age 60
VP and Treasurer: William F. Gifford Jr., age 38
VP Taxes: John S. Coccagna
VP Human Resources and Decision Support: Rodger Rolland
President and CEO, Ste. Michelle Wine Estates: Theodor P. Baseler, age 54
President, US Smokeless Tobacco Company: Daniel W. (Dan) Butler, age 49
President and CEO, Philip Morris Capital Corporation: John Mulligan

SVP Marketing, Altria Client Services: Nancy B. Lund, age 56
SVP Litigation and Associate General Counsel, Altria Client Services: Murray Garnick
SVP Human Resources, Altria Client Services: Kevin Benner
VP Corporate Responsibility and Stakeholder Relations, Altria Client Services: Jennifer Hunter
Senior Assistant General Counsel and Secretary: Sean X. McKessy, age 41
Auditors: PricewaterhouseCoopers LLP

LOCATIONS

HQ: Altria Group, Inc.
6601 West Broad St., Richmond, VA 23230
Phone: 804-274-2200   **Fax:** 804-484-8231
Web: www.altria.com

PRODUCTS/OPERATIONS

2008 Sales

	$ mil.	% of total
Cigarettes & other tobacco products	18,753	97
Cigars	387	2
Financial services	216	1
Total	**19,356**	**100**

Selected Subsidiaries

John Middleton Co.
Philip Morris Capital Corp.
Philip Morris USA Inc.
Ste. Michelle Wine Estates
U.S. Smokeless Tobacco Company

COMPETITORS

Altadis
Anheuser-Busch
Anheuser-Busch InBev
British American Tobacco
Constellation Brands
E. & J. Gallo
Foster's Americas
Heineken
Japan Tobacco
Loews
Lorillard
Molson Coors
North Atlantic Trading
Ravenswood Winery
Reynolds American
Sebastiani Vineyards
Swedish Match
Vector Group

HISTORICAL FINANCIALS

Company Type: Public

Income Statement

FYE: December 31

	REVENUE ($ mil.)	NET INCOME ($ mil.)	NET PROFIT MARGIN	EMPLOYEES
12/08	19,356.0	4,930.0	25.5%	10,400
12/07	38,051.0	9,786.0	25.7%	84,000
12/06	70,324.0	12,022.0	17.1%	175,000
12/05	68,920.0	10,435.0	15.1%	199,000
12/04	63,963.0	9,416.0	14.7%	156,000
Annual Growth	(25.8%)	(14.9%)	—	(49.2%)

2008 Year-End Financials

Debt ratio: 259.5%
Return on equity: 46.1%
Cash ($ mil.): 7,916
Current ratio: 1.55
Long-term debt ($ mil.): 7,339

No. of shares (mil.): 2,068
Dividends
  Yield: 11.2%
  Payout: 71.2%
Market value ($ mil.): 31,139

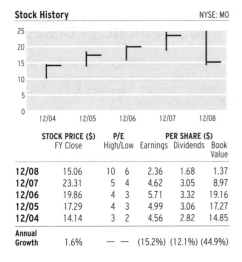

Stock History

NYSE: MO

	STOCK PRICE ($) FY Close	P/E High/Low		PER SHARE ($) Earnings	Dividends	Book Value
12/08	15.06	10	6	2.36	1.68	1.37
12/07	23.31	5	4	4.62	3.05	8.97
12/06	19.86	4	3	5.71	3.32	19.16
12/05	17.29	4	3	4.99	3.06	17.27
12/04	14.14	3	2	4.56	2.82	14.85
Annual Growth	1.6%	—	—	(15.2%)	(12.1%)	(44.9%)

Amazon.com

What started as Earth's biggest bookstore has rapidly become Earth's biggest anything store. Expansion has propelled Amazon.com in innumerable directions. Its main Web site offers millions of books, music, and movies (which still account for most of its sales), not to mention auto parts, toys, electronics, home furnishings, apparel, health and beauty aids, prescription drugs, and groceries. Also, shoppers can download books, games, MP3s, and films to their computers or handheld devices, including Amazon's own portable reader, the Kindle. Amazon also offers services and products, such as self-publishing, online advertising, a Web store platform, and a co-branded credit card.

Amazon plans to pony up some $888 million in stock to acquire Zappos.com, the #1 online shoe seller. The company sees the July 2009 agreement as a way to boost its online sales further, as some of its brick-and-mortar rivals are shuttering their shops due to the economic downturn that began in 2008. For the shoe retailer, being part of the Amazon organization fuels its growth. It's expected that Amazon will retain Zappos.com's management, its name brand, and its headquarters in Las Vegas.

Amazon has logged similar high-dollar purchases during the past couple of years. The company acquired digital audiobooks publisher Audible for about $300 million in 2008. Audible's 80,000 titles (including audiobooks, podcasts, and news publications) further boosts Amazon's digital content offerings, which were expanded in 2007 with the purchase of Brilliance Audio. Amazon also inked a deal in August 2008 to purchase AbeBooks, an online retailer of more than 110 million primarily used, rare, and out-of-print books. Also, Amazon has agreed to acquire Shelfari, a social-networking site for booklovers. (AbeBooks holds an equity stake in Shelfari's main rival, LibraryThing.)

Amazon launched its own electronic book reader, the Kindle, in late 2007. The company underestimated demand for the device, however, and was at first unable to keep up with production. Founder Jeff Bezos apologized for the problems a few months later, adding that the company's manufacturing issues had been fixed. Amazon has an inventory of some 100,000 books in electronic format and sells them in its electronic book store.

Although it still goes toe-to-toe with Barnes & Noble and others in the book business, Amazon faces competition on other fronts. The company plans to continue investing in clothing sales. The firm also allows individuals and companies to sell their wares through Amazon.com — for a price. Hundreds of retailers, including The Gap, Nordstrom, and Lands' End, own and deliver the merchandise listed on Amazon.com, but customers are able to purchase it all in one place.

In 2007 Amazon struck a deal with TiVo, announcing the companies would partner to bring Web content to the television through Amazon's Unbox digital video download service, which debuted in 2006. The company beefed up its digital offerings in 2008 with the launch of Amazon Video On Demand, a service that gives customers the option to stream or download ad-free digital movies and TV shows on Macs or PCs.

Bezos owns about 25% of the firm.

HISTORY

Jeff Bezos was researching the Internet in the early 1990s for hedge fund D.E. Shaw. He realized that book sales would be a perfect fit with e-commerce because book distributors already kept meticulous electronic lists. Bezos, who as a teen had dreamed of entrepreneurship in outer space, took the idea to Shaw. The company passed on the idea, but Bezos ran with it, trekking cross country to Seattle (close to a facility owned by major book distributor Ingram) and typing up a business plan along the way.

Bezos founded Amazon.com in 1994. After months of preparation, he launched a Web site in July 1995 (Douglas Hofstadter's *Fluid Concepts and Creative Analogies* was its first sale); it had sales of $20,000 a week by September. Bezos and his team kept working with the site, pioneering features that now seem mundane, such as one-click shopping, customer reviews, and e-mail order verification.

Amazon.com went public in 1997. Moves to cement the Amazon.com brand included becoming the sole book retailer on AOL's Web site and Netscape's commercial channel.

In 1998 the company launched its online music and video stores, and it began to sell toys and electronics. Amazon.com also expanded its European reach with the purchases of online booksellers in the UK and Germany, and it acquired the Internet Movie Database.

By midyear Amazon.com had attracted so much attention that its market capitalization equaled the combined values of profitable bricks-and-mortar rivals Barnes & Noble and Borders Group, even though their combined sales were far greater than the upstart's. Late that year Amazon.com formed a promotional link with Hoover's, publisher of this profile.

Amazon.com began conducting online auctions in early 1999 and partnered with venerable auction house Sotheby's. In 2000 Amazon.com inked a 10-year deal with Toysrus.com to set up a co-branded toy and video game store. (The partnership came to a bitter end in 2006 after Toys "R" Us sued Amazon.com when it began selling toys from other companies.) Also that year Amazon.com added foreign-language sites for France and Japan.

In 2001 Amazon.com cut 15% of its workforce as part of a restructuring plan that also forced a $150 million charge. In 2002 the firm introduced clothing sales, featuring hundreds of retailers including names such as The Gap, Nordstrom, and Lands' End.

The company launched its Search Inside the Book feature in 2003. The tool allows customers to search the text inside books for more relevant search returns. At launch, the search feature covered more than 120,000 books from over 190 publishers. Amazon.com expanded into China in 2004 with the purchase of Joyo.com. The company acquired shopping site Shopbop.com in 2006, boosting its apparel offerings. In November the Internet book seller introduced an electronic portable book reader called the Kindle ($399).

In May 2008 Amazon invested in The Talk Market, a user-generated TV Shopping Channel. In June the firm launched an online office supplies store and sewed up the acquisition of the online fabrics retailer Fabrics.com.

In June 2009 Amazon agreed to pay Toys "R" Us $51 million to settle a dispute dating back to 2004. The settlement was related to a partnership that gave the toy seller exclusive rights to supply some of the toys on Amazon's site.

EXECUTIVES

Chairman, President, and CEO: Jeffrey P. (Jeff) Bezos, age 45, $1,281,840 total compensation
SVP and CFO: Thomas J. (Tom) Szkutak, age 48, $2,261,393 total compensation
SVP North America Retail: Jeffrey A. (Jeff) Wilke, age 42
SVP International Retail: Diego Piacentini, age 48
SVP Worldwide Operations: Marc Onetto, age 58, $4,598,107 total compensation
SVP Ecommerce Platform: H. Brian Valentine, age 49, $3,877,118 total compensation
SVP, General Counsel, and Secretary: L. Michelle Wilson, age 46
SVP Seller Services: Sebastian J. Gunningham, age 46, $5,044,125 total compensation
SVP Business Development: Jeffrey Blackburn, age 39
SVP Web Services: Andrew Jassy, age 41
SVP Worldwide Digital Media: Steven Kessel, age 43
VP and CTO: Werner Vogels
VP Amazon Services Europe: Eric Broussard
VP Litigation: David Zapolsky
VP Worldwide Controller and Principal Accounting Officer: Shelley L. Reynolds, age 44
VP Music and Movies: Peter Faricy
VP Books: Russell Grandinetti
VP Books: Jeff Belle
CEO, Audible: Donald R. Katz
Auditors: Ernst & Young LLP

LOCATIONS

HQ: Amazon.com, Inc.
    1200 12th Ave. South, Ste. 1200, Seattle, WA 98144
Phone: 206-266-1000
Web: www.amazon.com

2008 Sales

	$ mil.	% of total
North America	10,228	53
Other countries	8,938	47
Total	**19,166**	**100**

PRODUCTS/OPERATIONS

2008 Sales

	$ mil.	% of total
Media	11,084	58
Electronics & other general merchandise	7,540	39
Other	542	3
Total	**19,166**	**100**

Selected Departments

Apparel, shoes, and jewelry
Books
  Fiction and nonfiction
  Kindle books
  Textbooks
  Magazines
Computers and office
  Computers and accessories
  Computer components
  Office products and supplies
  PC games
  Software
Digital downloads
  Amazon shorts
  Game downloads
  Kindle Store
  MP3 downloads
Electronics
  Audio, TV, and home theater
  Camera, photo, and video
  Car electronics and GPS
  Cell phones and service
  Home appliances
  MP3 and media players
  Musical instruments
  Video games
Grocery, health, and beauty
  Beauty
  Gourmet food
  Grocery
  Health and personal care
  Natural and organic
Home and garden
  Bedding and bath
  Furniture and decor
  Home appliances
  Home improvement
  Kitchen and dining
  Patio, lawn, and garden
  Pet supplies
  Sewing, craft, and hobby
  Vacuums and storage
Kindle
  Books
  Blogs
  Magazines
  Newspapers
Movies, music, and games
  Blu-ray
  Movies and TV
  Music
  Musical instruments
  Video games
  Video On Demand
Sports and outdoors
  Action sports
  Camping and hiking
  Cycling
  Exercise and fitness
  Golf
  Team sports
Tools, auto, and industrial
  Automotive
  Home improvement
  Industrial and scientific
  Lighting and electrical
  Motorcycle and ATV
  Outdoor power equipment
  Plumbing fixtures
  Power and hand tools
Toys, kids, and baby
  Apparel (kids and baby)
  Books
  Movies
  Music
  Software
  Toys and games
  Video games

COMPETITORS

AutoNation
AutoZone
Barnes & Noble
barnesandnoble.com
Best Buy
Blockbuster Inc.
Bluefly
Books-A-Million
Borders Group
Build-A-Bear
Buy.com
Columbia House
Corporate Express
eBay
Google
GSI Commerce
Hastings Entertainment
Hollywood Media
Home Depot
HSN
Indigo Books & Music
Lowe's
Netflix
Office Depot
OfficeMax
Overstock.com
PPR SA
Provide Gifts
Sears
shoebuy.com
Staples
Wal-Mart
Yahoo!

HISTORICAL FINANCIALS
Company Type: Public

Income Statement

FYE: December 31

	REVENUE ($ mil.)	NET INCOME ($ mil.)	NET PROFIT MARGIN	EMPLOYEES
12/08	19,166.0	645.0	3.4%	20,700
12/07	14,835.0	476.0	3.2%	17,000
12/06	10,711.0	190.0	1.8%	13,900
12/05	8,490.0	333.0	3.9%	12,000
12/04	6,921.1	588.5	8.5%	9,000
Annual Growth	29.0%	2.3%	—	23.1%

2008 Year-End Financials

Debt ratio: 15.3%
Return on equity: 33.3%
Cash ($ mil.): 2,769
Current ratio: 1.30
Long-term debt ($ mil.): 409
No. of shares (mil.): 432
Dividends
  Yield: 0.0%
  Payout: —
Market value ($ mil.): 22,143

Stock History

NASDAQ (GS): AMZN

	STOCK PRICE ($) FY Close	P/E High/Low		PER SHARE ($) Earnings	Dividends	Book Value
12/08	51.28	62	23	1.49	0.00	6.19
12/07	92.64	90	32	1.12	0.00	2.77
12/06	39.46	108	57	0.45	0.00	1.00
12/05	47.15	60	36	0.84	0.00	0.57
12/04	44.29	42	24	1.39	0.00	(0.53)
Annual Growth	3.7%	—	—	1.8%	—	—

Ambac Financial Group

Ambac Financial Group gives an A+ to those school bonds. Ambac Assurance, the holding company's primary subsidiary, sells financial guarantee insurance and other credit enhancement products for municipal bonds in the US market. In the international market the company insures high-quality infrastructure, structured finance, and utility finance transactions. Its financial services segment, through Ambac Financial Services, offers investment contracts, interest rate swaps, credit swaps, and investment management primarily to states and municipal authorities in connection with their bond financing.

Along with other US bond insurers, including FGIC and MBIA, the US subprime mortgage meltdown has knocked the wind out of Ambac. Its financial guarantee business slowed to a trickle by late 2007 when the company posted losses of $3.5 billion for the last quarter of that year. The large rating houses began sniffing around, endangering Ambac's valuable ratings, and prompting the company to scramble for a plan. Having scrapped one plan to split apart its municipal bond business from its increasingly risky US mortgage securities, the company has decided to raise $1.5 billion through stock sales.

To further steady itself in early 2008 the company took a few deep breaths, quit underwriting certain types of structured finance business (especially asset- and mortgage-backed securities), dropped its dividends down to a penny per share, appointed a Chief Risk Officer, and pinned its future on its public finance business.

Midway through 2008 Ambac went back to its very roots and reactivated a dusty subsidiary dedicated to guaranteeing municipal construction bonds. To get Construction Loan Insurance Company (nicknamed "Connie Lee") ready for its debut, Ambac tucked $850 million of capital into its pocketbook. In 2009 it changed Connie Lee's name to Everspan Financial Guarantee.

Even before the subprime mortgage mess ruptured in the US, Ambac Financial was looking overseas for growth. Spurred by an increase in public/private partnerships in the UK and Western Europe, the company has broadened its presence there. Ambac Assurance UK opened a Milan office in 2005, and provides financial guarantee policies in the UK and EU. While the Japanese market is still slow, an alliance with Sompo Japan will give Ambac access to it as it expands.

HISTORY

Mortgage Guaranty Insurance Corporation (MGIC) in 1971 founded American Municipal Bond Assurance Corporation (Ambac Indemnity) in Milwaukee. That year Ambac wrote the very first municipal bond insurance policy for a bond to fund a medical building and a sewage treatment facility in Juneau, Alaska. New York City's 1975 moratorium on debt payments helped make the new product more attractive. The company wrote the first insurance policies for mutual funds (1977) and secondary market municipal bonds (1983). In 1981 Ambac moved to New York; four years later it became a Citibank subsidiary. It went public in 1991.

In 1995 Ambac and rival MBIA allied to offer bond insurance overseas. Two years later the company formed a UK subsidiary to serve Europe. In recognition of the growing market, the joint venture was amended in 2000 to provide for individual operations by the two partners in Europe, though they continue to reinsure each other there and to work jointly in Japan. Ambac went on a buying spree in 1996 and 1997, buying the investment advisory and broker dealer operations of Cadre and Construction Loan Insurance (renamed Connie Lee Holdings), a guarantor of college bonds and hospital infrastructure bonds.

In 1998 as Ambac lost share in the US municipal bond market because it declined to cut premiums, the company began concentrating on asset-backed securities and international bonds. Two years later, Ambac entered the Japanese market through a joint venture with Yasuda Fire & Marine.

The company sold its Cadre Financial Services and Ambac Securities divisions in 2004.

International expansion served Ambac well: It went on to become one of the world's top guarantors by 2005.

EXECUTIVES

Chairman: Michael A. (Mike) Callen, age 68, $1,651,733 total compensation
President, CEO, and Director: David W. Wallis, age 49, $2,832,065 total compensation
EVP, Ambac Financial and Ambac Assurance; Chairman and CEO, Ambac Assurance UK; CEO Designate, Connie Lee Insurance: Douglas C. Renfield-Miller, age 55
SVP and CFO: Sean T. Leonard, age 44, $1,984,959 total compensation
SVP, Chief Administrative Officer, and Employment Counsel: Gregg L. Bienstock, age 44
Chief Risk Officer: Gregory Raab
SVP and General Counsel: Kevin J. Doyle, age 52, $1,736,164 total compensation
Senior Managing Director, Public Finance East Region, Health Care and Structured Real Estate: Robert G. Shoback, age 49, $1,117,995 total compensation
Senior Managing Director, Structured Finance and International Business: Diana Adams, age 46
Senior Managing Director, Capital Markets and Structured Credit: Thomas J. Gandolfo, age 48
Managing Director and Corporate Secretary: Anne Gill Kelly
Managing Director and Corporate Controller: Robert B. Eisman
Managing Director, Fixed Income Investor Relations: Peter R. Poillon
Managing Director and Director of Tax: Wes Kirchhoff
Managing Director, Marketing: Susan Oehrig
Managing Director and Chief Investment Officer: Rodney D. Kumasaki
Head, Investor Relations: Vandana Sharma
Auditors: KPMG LLP

LOCATIONS

HQ: Ambac Financial Group, Inc.
1 State Street Plaza, New York, NY 10004
Phone: 212-668-0340   **Fax:** 212-509-9190
Web: www.ambac.com

COMPETITORS

ACA Financial Guaranty
Assured Guaranty
Berkshire Hathaway
FGIC
Financial Security Assurance
MBIA
Radian Group
Syncora Holdings

HISTORICAL FINANCIALS

Company Type: Public

Income Statement

FYE: December 31

	ASSETS ($ mil.)	NET INCOME ($ mil.)	INCOME AS % OF ASSETS	EMPLOYEES
12/08	17,256.4	(5,609.2)	—	328
12/07	23,565.0	(3,248.2)	—	367
12/06	20,267.8	875.9	4.3%	359
12/05	19,725.1	751.0	3.8%	354
12/04	18,585.3	724.6	3.9%	360
Annual Growth	(1.8%)	—	—	(2.3%)

2008 Year-End Financials

Equity as % of assets: —
Return on assets: —
Return on equity: —
Long-term debt ($ mil.): 1,869
No. of shares (mil.): 288
Dividends
  Yield: 7.7%
  Payout: —
Market value ($ mil.): 374
Sales ($ mil.): (2,754)

Stock History

NYSE: ABK

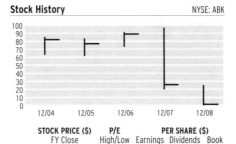

	STOCK PRICE ($) FY Close	P/E High/Low		PER SHARE ($) Earnings	Dividends	Book Value
12/08	1.30	—	—	(22.31)	0.10	(13.15)
12/07	25.77	—	—	(31.56)	0.78	7.93
12/06	89.07	11	9	8.15	0.66	21.51
12/05	77.06	12	9	6.87	0.55	18.68
12/04	82.13	13	10	6.53	0.47	17.47
Annual Growth	(64.5%)	—	—	—	(32.1%)	—

AMERCO

U-Haul, u-work, u-strain, u-hurt . . . u-sure you don't want to spend the extra money for movers? If not, there's AMERCO, whose principal subsidiary, U-Haul International, rents its orange-and-white trucks, trailers, and vehicle tow devices and sells packing supplies to do-it-yourself movers through more than 14,400 independent dealers and 1,400 company-owned centers in the US and Canada. In addition, U-Haul is a leading operator of self-storage facilities, maintaining about 1,100 storage locations in North America.

Established in 1945, AMERCO is 55%-owned by the founding Schoen family. It is led by chairman and president Edward "Joe" Shoen. The firm has been facing mounting losses due to the economic downturn.

To shore up its bottom line, the company is focused on making U-Haul moving rental equipment, storage facilities, and other offerings more accessible and convenient to customers. To this end, the company in 2008 introduced the U-Box service, which provides customers with on-demand storage container delivery and warehousing. It also expanded its truck fleet by about 10% in 2008. (U-Haul's rental fleet consists of about 100,000 trucks, 75,000 trailers, and 35,000

tow devices.) To help customers get on the road, the company's eMove Web site connects users with independent moving and self-storage companies that provide services such as packing, loading, and unloading. The firm aims to improve the capabilities of its eMove.com and uhaul.com sites as the Web has become a major sales force.

U-Haul accounts for about 90% of AMERCO's sales. Other businesses include two insurance companies: Republic Western Insurance provides claims management services and offers property and casualty insurance to U-Haul customers, and Oxford Life reinsures and originates single and group life insurance, disability coverage, and annuities. AMERCO's SAC Holding unit owns self-storage facilities that are managed by U-Haul.

HISTORY

Leonard Samuel (L.S.) Shoen earned his nickname, "Slick," as a poor kid trying to make a buck during the Depression. In 1945, as a Navy veteran, he started U-Haul International in Ridgefield, Washington, to serve long-distance do-it-yourself movers who could not return a truck to its origin. Shoen bought used equipment and hit the road, convincing gas station owners to act as agents.

Shoen and his first wife, Anna Mary, who died in 1957, had six children. In 1958 Shoen remarried and with his second wife, Suzanne, had five children. Shoen bestowed stock on all his offspring but neglected to keep a controlling interest. In the 1960s Shoen brought his sons into the company.

U-Haul moved to Phoenix in 1967. Two years later it bought Oxford Life Insurance Co. Shoen formed AMERCO in 1971 as U-Haul's parent. The oil crunch of the 1970s caused U-Haul's network to shrink as gas stations closed, so the company opened its own agencies. New competitors entered the market, and the company's share of business dropped to below 50%. Shoen took AMERCO into debt to diversify into general consumer rentals. The company also established real estate and insurance subsidiaries.

Shoen's second wife divorced him after the out-of-wedlock birth of his 12th child in 1977. His brief marriage to the mother ended in divorce, and he remarried again (and, later, yet again). Meanwhile, Shoen tapped his eldest son Sam for help in pursuing the diversification strategy. In 1979 sons Edward "Joe" and Mark left the company in dispute. Sam became president.

In 1986 Joe and Mark gained the support of enough siblings to constitute a voting majority and ousted their father and brother. L. S. and Sam almost regained control two years later but were outmaneuvered by Joe, who as chairman issued enough stock to a few loyal employees to shift the balance. Then the outside faction sued the people who had been directors in 1988 over issuance of the stock.

Joe refocused on the self-moving business and began upgrading the fleet, reducing the average age of the equipment from 11 to 5 years. In 1993 AMERCO preferred stock began trading on the NYSE, and the next year its common stock was listed on Nasdaq.

Meanwhile, the lawsuit moved through the courts at a glacial pace. In 1994 the 1988 directors were found to have wrongfully excluded dissenting family members from the board. An initial award of $1.47 billion was later reduced to $462 million, due from the 1988 directors individually. However, they declared bankruptcy, and AMERCO indemnified them for the award. So in 1996 the company issued new stock and sold (and leased back) tens of thousands of vehicles and trailers to fulfill the judgment. In return, the dissenting family faction (including founder L. S.) gave up their 48% stake in the company.

In 1997 AMERCO held its first stockholders' meeting since 1993. The next year Joe lost an appeal to overturn a ruling that he had acted with malice in dealing with family members in the 1988 stock transaction; he was ordered to pay $7 million in punitive damages to relatives, exclusive of the $462 million previously awarded.

In 1999 founder L.S. died at age 83 in a one-car accident believed to be suicide. In 2001 the company debuted its online storage reservation system. AMERCO denied reports published in August 2002 by the Financial Times that the Securities and Exchange Commission was investigating AMERCO's accounts and probing why it dismissed PricewaterhouseCoopers, its auditor of 24 years. The company failed to make a $100 million debt principal payment in October 2002.

AMERCO announced in March 2003 that it had obtained a four-year $865.8 million credit facility. The following month the company filed suit against PricewaterhouseCoopers, alleging negligence and fraud in its audit work. AMERCO disclosed in May that federal securities regulators were investigating its financial statements. (The investigation ended in 2006 with no action being taken against the company.)

Amid its financial difficulties, the company filed for Chapter 11 bankruptcy protection in June 2003. Nine months later, in March 2004, AMERCO emerged from bankruptcy.

EXECUTIVES

Chairman and President: Edward J. (Joe) Shoen, age 60, $764,933 total compensation
Treasurer AMERCO and U-Haul: Gary B. Horton, age 65
Principal Accounting Officer; Chief Accounting Officer, AMERCO: Jason A. Berg, age 36, $205,349 total compensation
President, U-Haul: John C. (JT) Taylor, age 51
EVP U-Haul Field Operations: Ronald C. Frank, age 68
EVP U-Haul Field Operations: Robert R. Willson, age 58
VP U-Haul Business Consultants and Director: James P. Shoen, age 49, $622,141 total compensation
VP U-Haul Business Consultants: Mark V. Shoen, age 58, $625,506 total compensation
President, Republic Western Insurance: Richard M. Amoroso, age 50, $348,010 total compensation
President, Amerco Real Estate: Carlos Vizcarra, age 62
President, Oxford Life Insurance: Mark A. Haydukovich, age 52
President, U-Haul Company of North Shore Chicago: Brandon Blaskowski
Director Investor Relations: Jennifer K. Flachman
General Counsel: Laurence J. (Larry) De Respino, age 48
Auditors: BDO Seidman, LLP

LOCATIONS

HQ: AMERCO
1325 Airmotive Way, Ste. 100, Reno, NV 89502
Phone: 775-688-6300   **Fax:** 775-688-6338
Web: www.amerco.com

2009 Sales

	$ mil.	% of total
US	1,881.7	94
Canada	110.6	6
Total	**1,992.3**	**100**

PRODUCTS/OPERATIONS

2009 Sales

	$ mil.	% of total
Moving & storage	1,733.0	87
Life insurance	109.6	6
Investments & interest	58.0	3
Property & casualty insurance	28.3	1
Property management fees	23.2	1
Other	40.2	2
Total	**1,992.3**	**100**

Selected Operating Units

AMERCO Real Estate Company (real estate)
Oxford Life Insurance Company
Republic Western Insurance Company (property and casualty insurance)
SAC Holding II Corporation (owns self-storage properties managed by U-Haul)
U-Haul International, Inc. (self-moving truck and trailer rental, self-storage unit rental, sales of packing supplies)

COMPETITORS

AIG	Penske Truck Leasing
Allstate	PODS Enterprises
Atlas Van Lines	Prudential
Atlas World Group	Public Storage
Avis Budget	SIRVA
Extra Space	Sovran
The Hartford	UniGroup
MetLife	United Van Lines
Mobile Mini	U-Store-It
National Van Lines	

HISTORICAL FINANCIALS

Company Type: Public

Income Statement

FYE: March 31

	REVENUE ($ mil.)	NET INCOME ($ mil.)	NET PROFIT MARGIN	EMPLOYEES
3/09	1,992.3	13.4	0.7%	17,700
3/08	2,049.2	54.8	2.7%	18,500
3/07	2,085.6	77.6	3.7%	18,000
3/06	2,106.6	108.2	5.1%	17,500
3/05	2,008.1	76.5	3.8%	18,300
Annual Growth	**(0.2%)**	**(35.3%)**	**—**	**(0.8%)**

2009 Year-End Financials

Debt ratio: —
Return on equity: 1.8%
Cash ($ mil.): 241
Current ratio: 0.58
Long-term debt ($ mil.): —
No. of shares (mil.): 20
Dividends
  Yield: 0.0%
  Payout: —
Market value ($ mil.): 657

Stock History

NASDAQ (GS): UHAL

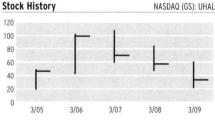

	STOCK PRICE ($) FY Close	P/E High/Low		PER SHARE ($) Earnings	Dividends	Book Value
3/09	33.53	—	—	0.02	0.00	36.60
3/08	57.09	30	17	2.78	0.00	38.68
3/07	69.99	29	16	3.72	0.00	36.62
3/06	98.97	20	8	5.19	0.00	35.48
3/05	46.30	13	5	3.68	0.53	29.21
Annual Growth	**(7.8%)**	**—**	**—**	**(72.8%)**	**—**	**5.8%**

Ameren Corporation

Ameren might be considered amorous when it comes to courting and acquiring midwestern utilities. The holding company, which has been focused on growing its core energy operations, distributes electricity to 2.4 million customers and natural gas to almost 1 million customers in Missouri and Illinois through utility subsidiaries AmerenUE, AmerenCIPS, AmerenCILCO, and AmerenIP. Ameren has a generating capacity of more than 16,500 MW (primarily coal-fired), most of which is controlled by utility AmerenUE and nonregulated subsidiary AmerenEnergy Resources Generating Company. Other nonutility operations include energy marketing and trading, and management and consulting services.

In addition to operating power plants, AmerenEnergy Resources procures natural gas for its affiliated companies, builds new power plants, and provides long-term energy supply contracts. Another subsidiary, Ameren Energy Inc., markets and trades electricity to wholesale and retail customers and provides risk management and other energy-related services.

To comply with FERC requirements, Ameren has transferred control of AmerenCIPS and AmerenUE's transmission assets to the Midwest Independent Transmission System Operator (Midwest ISO). AmerenCILCO and AmerenIP were already members of the Midwest ISO.

In 2007 Ameren subsidiary AmerenUE moved into wind power operations by agreeing to buy 100 MW of wind power from Horizon Wind Energy's Rail Splitter Wind Farm located near Delavan, Illinois.

HISTORY

More than 30 St. Louis companies had built a chaotic grid of generators and power lines throughout the city by 1900. Two years later many of them merged into the Union Company, which attracted national notice when it lit the St. Louis World's Fair in the first broad demonstration of electricity's power. In 1913 the company, by then named Union Electric (UE), began buying electricity from an Iowa dam 150 miles away — the greatest distance power had ever been transmitted in such quantity.

UE pushed into rural Missouri and began buying and building fossil-fuel plants. Despite a slowdown during the Depression, UE built Bagnell Dam on Missouri's Osage River in the early 1930s to gather power for a hydroelectric plant. At the onset of WWII, construction began on new plants with larger generators and lower production costs; however, demand for electricity lagged. In the late 1940s UE compensated by joining a "power pool," a system of utilities with interconnected transmission lines that shared electricity.

Growth in the 1950s came from acquisitions, including Missouri Power & Light (1950) and Missouri Edison (1954). In the 1960s and 1970s, UE built five new plants, including the Labadie plant (2,300 MW), one of the largest coal-fired operations in the US.

UE began producing nuclear energy in 1984 at its Callaway nuke. High costs and the expenses of a scrapped second plant caused UE to battle the Missouri Public Service Commission throughout the 1980s for rate increases.

Charles Mueller became president in 1993 and CEO one year later. He oversaw continued staff reductions and cost cutting through the 1990s in an increasingly competitive market. In 1997 UE expanded into Illinois through its purchase of CIPSCO, which owned utility Central Illinois Public Service Company (CIPS).

CIPS began as a Mattoon, Illinois, streetcar company in the early 1900s. The firm bought Mattoon's electric power plant in 1904 and began growing its power business, buying small electric companies in the 1920s and 1930s. CIPS built five generating units in the 1940s and 1950s and became part-owner (along with UE) of Electric Energy Inc., which built a power plant on the Ohio River. The company bought Illinois Electric and Gas Company in the 1960s and the state's Gas Utilities in the 1980s. To prepare for competition under deregulation, CIPS created holding company CIPSCO in the 1990s to diversify.

UE's purchase of CIPSCO expanded its geographic scope, and the new company was named Ameren in 1997 to reflect its American energy focus. The next year the company committed to adding generating capacity through several natural gas-fired combustion turbines. It joined nine other utilities to form the Midwest Independent System Operator to manage their transmission needs.

In 1999 Ameren bought a 245-mile railroad line between St. Louis and Kansas City to help the area's economic development. Looking for new opportunities in deregulated energy markets, the company purchased Data & Metering Specialties.

In 2000 Ameren created the subsidiary AmerenEnergy Generating to operate its nonregulated power plants and affiliate AmerenEnergy Marketing to sell the generating facilities' power. When deregulation took effect in Illinois in 2002, the company transferred AmerenCIPS' power plants to AmerenEnergy Generating. In 2003 Ameren acquired CILCORP, the holding company for electric and gas utility Central Illinois Light (now operating as AmerenCILCO), from independent power producer AES in a $1.4 billion deal. To further expand its utility operations, Ameren acquired power and gas utility Illinois Power from Dynegy in a $2.3 billion deal in 2004. As part of the agreement, Ameren gained Dynegy's 20% stake in power generator Electric Energy, in which Ameren already held a 60% stake.

EXECUTIVES

Chairman, Ameren and CILCORP: Gary L. Rainwater, age 62, $5,046,122 total compensation
President, CEO, and Director: Thomas R. Voss, age 61, $1,807,004 total compensation
SVP, CFO, and Chief Accounting Officer: Martin J. Lyons, age 42
SVP and Chief Human Resources Officer, Ameren Services: Donna K. Martin, age 61
SVP, General Counsel, and Secretary: Steven R. Sullivan, age 48, $1,487,451 total compensation
SVP AmerenUE: Richard J. Mark, age 53
SVP Ameren Services: Michael L. Moehn, age 39
SVP Communications and Brand Management: Karen Foss, age 64
VP and Treasurer: Jerre E. Birdsong, age 54
VP and Controller: Bruce Steinke
Chairman, President, and CEO, CILCO, CIPS, and IP: Scott A. Cisel, age 55

President and CEO, AmerenUE: Warner L. Baxter, age 47, $1,944,697 total compensation
President and CEO, Ameren Services: Daniel F. Cole, age 55
President, AFS: Michael G. Mueller, age 45
President and Director, Electric Energy; VP Research and Development, Ameren Services: R. Alan Kelley, age 56
Chairman, President, and CEO, Ameren Energy Resources Company; Chairman and President, Ameren Energy Resources Generating Company: Charles D. Naslund, age 56, $1,411,510 total compensation
President, Ameren Energy Marketing Company: Andrew M. Serri, age 47
President, Electric Energy; VP Generation Technical Services, Ameren Services: Robert L. (Bob) Powers, age 57
Auditors: PricewaterhouseCoopers LLP

LOCATIONS

HQ: Ameren Corporation
1901 Chouteau Ave., St. Louis, MO 63103
Phone: 314-621-3222 **Fax:** 314-554-3801
Web: www.ameren.com

PRODUCTS/OPERATIONS

2008 Sales

	$ mil.	% of total
Electric	6,367	81
Gas	1,472	19
Total	**7,839**	**100**

2008 Fuel Mix

	% of total
Coal	85
Nuclear	12
Hydro	2
Natural gas	1
Total	**100**

Selected Subsidiaries

AmerenEnergy, Inc. (power marketing and trading, risk management, and energy services)
AmerenEnergy Resources Company (holding company)
  AmerenEnergy Development Company (power plant development)
  AmerenEnergy Generating Company (nonregulated power generation)
  AmerenEnergy Fuels and Services Company (natural gas procurement)
  AmerenEnergy Marketing Company (retail and wholesale energy marketing, long-term power supply contracts)
Ameren Services Company (provides support services for Ameren and subsidiaries)
Central Illinois Public Service Company (AmerenCIPS, electric and gas utility)
CILCORP Incorporated (holding company)
  Central Illinois Light Company (AmerenCILCO, electric and gas utility)
  AmerenEnergy Resources Generating Company (formerly Central Illinois Generation, nonregulated power generation)
Illinois Power Company (AmerenIP, electric and gas utility)
Union Electric Company (AmerenUE, electric and gas utility)

COMPETITORS

AES	Great Plains Energy
AmerenIP	Laclede Group
Atmos Energy	MidAmerican Energy
CenterPoint Energy	Midwest Generation
Empire District Electric	Nicor
Exelon	Southern Union

HISTORICAL FINANCIALS
Company Type: Public

Income Statement
FYE: December 31

	REVENUE ($ mil.)	NET INCOME ($ mil.)	NET PROFIT MARGIN	EMPLOYEES
12/08	7,839.0	605.0	7.7%	9,524
12/07	7,546.0	618.0	8.2%	9,069
12/06	6,880.0	547.0	8.0%	8,988
12/05	6,780.0	628.0	9.3%	9,136
12/04	5,160.0	530.0	10.3%	9,388
Annual Growth	**11.0%**	**3.4%**	**—**	**0.4%**

2008 Year-End Financials

Debt ratio: 91.6%
Return on equity: 8.7%
Cash ($ mil.): 92
Current ratio: 0.82
Long-term debt ($ mil.): 6,554
No. of shares (mil.): 214
Dividends
 Yield: 7.6%
 Payout: 88.2%
Market value ($ mil.): 7,130

Stock History
NYSE: AEE

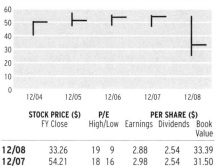

	STOCK PRICE ($) FY Close	P/E High/Low		PER SHARE ($) Earnings	Dividends	Book Value
12/08	33.26	19	9	2.88	2.54	33.39
12/07	54.21	18	16	2.98	2.54	31.50
12/06	53.73	21	18	2.66	2.54	30.71
12/05	51.24	19	16	3.02	2.54	30.60
12/04	50.14	18	14	2.84	2.54	27.97
Annual Growth	**(9.8%)**	**—**	**—**	**0.4%**	**0.0%**	**4.5%**

American Eagle Outfitters

It was once a purveyor of outdoor gear, but American Eagle Outfitters now feathers its nest with polos and khakis. The mall-based retailer sells casual apparel and accessories (shirts, jeans, shorts, sweaters, skirts, footwear, belts, bags) aimed at men and women ages 15-25. Virtually all of the company's products bear its private-label brand names: American Eagle Outfitters, aerie, 77kids, and MARTIN + OSA. The growing chain operates about 1,100 stores in all 50 US states, Puerto Rico, and Canada. Direct sales come from the company's Web site and its *AE* magazine, a lifestyle publication that doubles as a catalog. American Eagle Outfitters opened its first store in 1977 and expanded into Canada in 2001.

The retailer has grown rapidly by opening new stores and launching retail concepts for customers older and younger than its core 15-to-25-year-old audience. The apparel chain's latest online launch — which is slated to make its debut in stores in the near future — is an upscale apparel brand for children ages 2 to 10 called 77kids by American Eagle.

A casual sportswear concept targeting 28-to 40-year-old women and men — called MARTIN + OSA — debuted in 2006 and now operates more than 25 stores. An intimate apparel sub brand called "aerie by American Eagle" also took flight in 2006. The line includes bras, boxers, camis, hoodies, panties, and personal care products targeted at the 15-to-25 female set. Aerie, which competes directly with the PINK line of intimate apparel by Victoria's Secret, is available in about 115 stand-alone aerie by American Eagle stores as well as within AE stores. The company also entered the fragrance game with a pair of scents for men and women, under the American Eagle Real banner, that debuted in AE stores in October 2006.

The retailer added more than 120 stores in 2008 and tripled the number of stand-alone aerie shops in operation. Also, MARTIN + OSA launched an e-commerce site in spring 2008. However, given the dismal outlook for retailers, the chain is taking a more prudent approach to growth in 2009: 17 aerie stores are planned as well as about a dozen new American Eagle stores, including a shop in New York's Times Square. The company also plans to remodel as many as 35 of its existing American Eagle stores.

American Eagle boasts lower prices than its archrival Abercrombie & Fitch (A&F). However, in view of the long recession in the US and double-digit sales declines at A&F, the pricey retailer has reconsidered its no-discount policy and announced that it will cut prices to spur sales.

HISTORY

Retail Ventures, an operator of specialty clothing stores owned by the Silverman family, founded the first American Eagle Outfitters (AE) store in 1977. Another retailing clan, the Schottenstein family (led by Jerome, who died in 1992), bought a 50% stake in Retail Ventures when the Silvermans encountered financial difficulties in 1980. The Schottenstein family had built a retail empire by buying and revamping dying retail chains (holdings include Value City Department and Furniture stores). The retailer returned to financial health and expanded rapidly in the late 1980s.

In 1991 the Schottensteins acquired the remainder of Retail Ventures, and with it, 153 American Eagle Outfitters stores. The company had been running up substantial losses, so the Schottensteins brought in new management and took the company public in 1994 as American Eagle Outfitters, with about 170 stores. AE opened more than 80 stores the following year.

Former president and CEO Sam Forman bought the company's 32-store outlet division in 1995 and attained a license to continue to operate the stores under the American Eagle Outlets name. Two years later AE acquired New York-based Prophecy, an apparel-sourcing firm (the Schottenstein family was Prophecy's majority owner).

In recent years, AE has toned down its rugged, value-conscious image in favor of a collegiate look. One result: In 1998 across-the-mall nemesis Abercrombie & Fitch sued the company claiming AE copied product designs as well as the look of its stores; the suit wound its way up through the courts and was dismissed three times in four years.

In late 2000 the company crossed into Canada with the purchase of 160 Thrifty/Bluenotes and Braemar stores and distribution facilities from Canada's Dylex Limited, all for about $74 million. In 2001 the Braemer stores were converted to American Eagle Outfitters. American Eagle Outfitters opened 81 new US stores in 2001, and it introduced the American Eagle brand to Canada with 46 new stores there.

In November 2003, Jim O'Donnell was named CEO and Roger S. Markfield became vice chairman and president. Previously, the duo had been co-CEOs of the company. About a year later, American Eagle Outfitters sold its Bluenotes apparel chain in Canada to Stitches owner Michael Gold. In 2005 American Eagle Outfitters had nests in all 50 states with the opening of a pair of stores in Alaska.

The fall of 2006 was a busy time for the company with the launch of MARTIN + OSA (a casual sportswear concept targeting 28-to 40-year-old women and men), and the debut of an intimate apparel sub brand called "aerie by American Eagle." The aerie line includes bras, panties, and personal care products for 15-to-25-year-old females. Two years later, the company's new concept for kids ages two to 10 — called 77kids by American Eagle — debuted online in fall 2008.

EXECUTIVES

Chairman: Jay L. Schottenstein, age 54, $878,582 total compensation
Vice Chairman and Executive Creative Director: Roger S. Markfield, age 66
President, CEO. and Director: James V. (Jim) O'Donnell, age 68, $3,796,055 total compensation
EVP and CFO: Joan Holstein Hilson, age 49, $1,015,505 total compensation
EVP and Chief Design Officer: LeAnn Nealz, age 52, $1,385,429 total compensation
EVP Store Operations: Dennis R. Parodi, age 57
EVP Supply Chain and Real Estate: Joseph E. Kerin, age 63
EVP Human Resources: Thomas (Tom) DiDonato, age 50
EVP E-Commerce and AE International: Fredrick W. Grover
EVP and Customs Compliance Officer: Guy Bradford
EVP Blue Star Imports: Hank Shechtman
SVP and COO, MARTIN + OSA: Chuck Chupein
SVP Logistics: Michael J. Fostyk
SVP and Senior Merchandising Officer, AE Brand: Henry Stafford
SVP and Chief Merchandising Officer, aerie: Betsy Schumacher
SVP New Concept Development: Christopher Fiore
VP and CIO: Rick Milazzo
VP, General Counsel, and Secretary: Neil Bulman Jr.
VP Investor Relations: Judy Meehan
VP Public Relations and Corporate Communications: Jani Strand
President, Martin + OSA: Laura Dubin Wander
Auditors: Ernst & Young LLP

LOCATIONS

HQ: American Eagle Outfitters, Inc.
77 Hot Metal St., Pittsburgh, PA 15203
Phone: 412-432-3300   **Fax:** 412-432-3955
Web: www.ae.com

2009 Sales

	$ mil.	% of total
US	2,707.3	90
International	281.6	10
Total	**2,988.9**	**100**

2009 Stores

	No.
US	
California	92
Texas	71
Pennsylvania	67
New York	58
Florida	52
Ohio	41
Illinois	36
Michigan	35
Massachusetts	34
Georgia	33
North Carolina	30
Virginia	30
New Jersey	28
Tennessee	24
Indiana	21
Maryland	21
Minnesota	20
Washington	20
Alabama	19
Connecticut	18
Missouri	18
Wisconsin	18
Arizona	17
Colorado	16
Louisiana	15
South Carolina	15
Kentucky	13
Iowa	12
Oklahoma	12
Utah	12
Oregon	11
Kansas	10
Mississippi	8
West Virginia	9
Arkansas	8
Nebraska	8
New Hampshire	8
Nevada	7
Other states	45
Canada	86
Total	**1,098**

PRODUCTS/OPERATIONS

2009 Stores

	No.
American Eagle Outfitters	954
aerie	116
MARTIN + OSA	28
Total	**1,098**

Selected Products

Accessories
Cargo pants
Footwear
Graphic T-shirts
Khakis
Outerwear
Polo shirts
Rugby shirts
Swimwear

COMPETITORS

Abercrombie & Fitch	J. Crew
Aéropostale	Lands' End
AnnTaylor	Levi Strauss
Bath & Body Works	Liz Claiborne
Benetton	L.L. Bean
The Buckle	Macy's
Calvin Klein	Nautica Apparel
The Children's Place	Nordstrom
Columbia Sportswear	Pacific Sunwear
Dillard's	Polo Ralph Lauren
Eddie Bauer	Reitmans
Fossil, Inc.	Target
The Gap	Tommy Hilfiger
Guess?	Tween Brands
Gymboree	Urban Outfitters
Hot Topic	VF
Hudson's Bay	Victoria's Secret Direct
J. C. Penney	Victoria's Secret Stores

HISTORICAL FINANCIALS

Company Type: Public

Income Statement

	REVENUE ($ mil.)	NET INCOME ($ mil.)	NET PROFIT MARGIN	EMPLOYEES
1/09	2,988.9	179.1	6.0%	37,500
1/08	3,055.4	400.0	13.1%	38,700
1/07	2,794.4	387.4	13.9%	27,600
1/06	2,309.4	294.2	12.7%	23,000
1/05	1,881.2	213.3	11.3%	36,700
Annual Growth	12.3%	(4.3%)	—	0.5%

FYE: Saturday nearest January 31

2009 Year-End Financials

Debt ratio: —
Return on equity: 13.0%
Cash ($ mil.): 473
Current ratio: 2.30
Long-term debt ($ mil.): —
No. of shares (mil.): 207
Dividends
  Yield: 4.4%
  Payout: 46.5%
Market value ($ mil.): 1,863

Stock History

NYSE: AEO

	STOCK PRICE ($) FY Close	P/E High/Low		PER SHARE ($) Earnings	Dividends	Book Value
1/09	9.01	28	8	0.86	0.40	6.83
1/08	22.98	18	9	1.82	0.38	6.50
1/07	32.38	29	15	1.70	0.28	6.87
1/06	26.98	47	15	1.26	0.18	5.60
1/05	50.80	54	20	0.95	0.04	4.67
Annual Growth	(35.1%)	—	—	(2.5%)	77.8%	10.0%

American Electric Power Company

American Electric Power (AEP) takes its slice of the US power pie out of Middle America. The holding company is one of the largest power generators and distributors in the US. AEP owns the nation's largest electricity transmission system, a network of almost 39,000 miles. Its electric utilities serve more than 5 million customers in 11 states and have more than 38,000 MW of largely coal-fired generating capacity. AEP is a top wholesale energy company; it markets and trades electricity, natural gas, and other commodities and has stakes in independent power plants. Other operations include natural gas transportation, storage, and processing, and barge transportation services.

The company will attempt to keep its debt-to-capitalization ratio below 60% and focus its efforts on regulatory activities in Texas. AEP has earmarked $3.7 billion through 2010 for upgrades at its coal-fired generating plants, and an additional $1.5 billion through 2020.

In response to utility deregulation, AEP had been expanding its merchant energy activities; however, due to the collapse of the energy trading industry (spurred by Enron's collapse and the ensuing financial scrutiny of other top marketers), AEP has scaled back its nonregulated operations. The firm has shut down or sold its European trading operations, but it continues to participate in wholesale energy transactions in regions of the US where it owns assets. It has also sold its independent power production operations.

HISTORY

In 1906 Richard Breed, Sidney Mitchell, and Henry Doherty set up American Gas & Electric (AG&E) in New York to buy 23 utilities from Philadelphia's Electric Company of America. With properties in seven northeastern US states, AG&E began acquiring and merging small electric properties, creating the predecessors of Ohio Power (1911), Kentucky Power (1919), and Appalachian Power (1926). AG&E also bought the predecessor of Indiana Michigan Power (1925).

By 1926 the company was operating in Indiana, Kentucky, Michigan, Ohio, Virginia, and West Virginia. In 1935 AG&E engineer Philip Sporn, later known as the Henry Ford of power, introduced its high-voltage, high-velocity circuit breaker. AG&E picked up Kingsport Power in 1938.

Becoming president in 1947, Sporn began an ambitious building program that continued through the 1960s. Plants designed by AG&E (renamed American Electric Power in 1958) were among the world's most efficient, and electric rates stayed 25% to 38% below the national average.

AEP bought Michigan Power in 1967, six years after Donald Cook succeeded Sporn as president. Cook, who refused to attach scrubbers to the smokestacks of coal-fired plants, was criticized in the early 1970s by environmental protesters. AEP's first nuclear plant, named in Cook's honor, went on line in Michigan in 1975. He retired in 1976.

The firm moved from New York to Columbus, Ohio, in 1980 after buying what is now Columbus Southern Power (formed in 1883). It set up AEP Generating in 1982 to provide power to its electric utilities.

AEP began converting its second nuke, Zimmer, to coal in 1984. In 1992 AEP finally began installing scrubbers at its coal-fired Gavin plant in Ohio after being ordered to comply with the Clean Air Act. It also cleaned up its image by planting millions of trees in 1996.

The company formed AEP Communications after the Telecommunications Act of 1996 was approved by Congress. The next year AEP jumped into the UK's deregulated electric market; AEP and New Century Energies (now Xcel Energy) bought Yorkshire Electricity (later Yorkshire Power Group) for $2.8 billion. However, a $109 million UK windfall tax on the transaction — and increased wholesale competition — hurt AEP's bottom line.

As the normally staid electric industry succumbed to merger mania, AEP agreed in 1997 to buy Central and South West (CSW) of Texas in a $6.6 billion deal. AEP's sales would nearly double, and CSW was to bring its own UK utility, SEEBOARD, and other overseas holdings.

In 1998 AEP bought a 20% stake in Pacific Hydro, an Australian power producer, and CitiPower, an Australian electric distribution company. AEP also bought Equitable Resources' Louisiana natural gas midstream operations, including an intrastate pipeline. In 1999 China's Pushan Power Plant (70%-owned by AEP) began operations. Environmental concerns resurfaced that year when the EPA sued the utility, alleging its old coal-powered plants, which had been grandfathered from the Clean Air Act, had been quietly upgraded to extend their lives.

Regulators approved the company's acquisition of CSW in 2000, but AEP had to agree to relinquish control of its 22,000 miles of transmission lines to an independent operator. The deal closed later that year. (However, the SEC's approval of the deal was challenged by a federal appeals court in 2002.)

AEP sold its 50% stake in Yorkshire Power Group to Innogy (now RWE npower) in 2001. AEP became one of the largest US barge operators that year when it bought MEMCO Barge Line from Progress Energy. It also purchased two UK coal-fired power plants (4,000 MW) from Edison Mission Energy, a subsidiary of Edison International, in a $960 million deal.

In 2002 AEP sold its UK utility, SEEBOARD, to Electricité de France in a $2.2 billion deal; it also sold its Australian utility, CitiPower, to a consortium led by Cheung Kong Infrastructure and Hongkong Electric for $855 million. The following year the company sold two of its competitive Texas retail electric providers (WTU Retail Energy and CPL Retail Energy) to UK utility Centrica. It also divested its power plant development subsidiary, AEP Pro Serv, and its stakes in telecom firms C3 Communications and AFN.

The company sold two UK power plants to Scottish and Southern Energy for $456 million in 2004, and it sold a 50% stake in a third UK plant to Scottish Power in a $210 million deal.

In 2006 the company sold its Plaquemine cogeneration plant to Dow Chemical for $64 million. Also that year AEP formed a joint venture company with MidAmerican Energy Holdings to build and own new electric transmission assets within the Electric Reliability Council of Texas.

In 2007 the company settled an eight-year lawsuit with the US Government and agreed to pay more than $4.6 billion to reduce hazardous air pollution from 16 coal-burning power plants.

EXECUTIVES

Chairman, President, and CEO; Chairman, President, and CEO, American Electric Power Service Corporation: Michael G. (Mike) Morris, age 62, $4,019,556 total compensation
COO: Carl L. English, age 62, $1,031,912 total compensation
EVP and CFO: Holly K. Koeppel, age 50, $1,147,617 total compensation
EVP; VP and Director, Southwestern Electric Power and Public Service Company of Oklahoma: Venita McCellon-Allen, age 49
EVP, General Counsel, and Secretary: John B. (Jack) Keane, age 62
EVP Environment, Safety, and Health, and Facilities: Dennis E. Welch, age 57
EVP: Brian X. Tierney, age 44, $1,254,866 total compensation
EVP; VP and Director, American Electric Power Service Corporation: Nicholas K. (Nick) Akins, age 48
CIO: Kevin E. Walker, age 45
SVP, Chief Accounting Officer, and Controller: Joseph M. Buonaiuto
SVP and Chief Nuclear Officer, Cook Nuclear Plant: Joseph N. (Joe) Jensen, age 50
SVP Regulatory and Public Policy: Charles R. Patton, age 49
SVP Investor Relations and Treasurer: Charles E. (Chuck) Zebula, age 49

President, AEP Utilities: Robert P. (Bob) Powers, age 51, $1,071,731 total compensation
President, AEP Transmission, American Electric Power Service Corporation: Susan Tomasky, age 55, $4,453,614 total compensation
President and COO, Kentucky Power: Timothy C. (Tim) Mosher
President and COO, Columbus Southern Power and Ohio Power: Joseph (Joe) Hamrock, age 45
President and COO, Appalachian Power: Dana E. Waldo, age 57
President and COO, Public Service Company of Oklahoma: J. Stuart Solomon, age 47
President and COO, Indiana Michigan Power: Helen J. Murray
President and COO, Southwestern Electric Power: Paul Chodak III, age 45
President and COO, AEP Texas: Pablo A. Vegas, age 36
Principal Communications Consultant, AEP Corporate Communications: David M. Hagelin
Auditors: Deloitte & Touche LLP

LOCATIONS

HQ: American Electric Power Company, Inc.
1 Riverside Plaza, Columbus, OH 43215
Phone: 614-716-1000   **Fax:** 614-716-1823
Web: www.aep.com

PRODUCTS/OPERATIONS

2008 Sales

	$ mil.	% of total
Retail	10,228	71
Wholesale	2,748	19
Other	1,464	10
Total	**14,440**	**100**

Selected Subsidiaries

AEP Energy Services, Inc. (energy marketing and trading)
AEP Generating Co. (electricity generator, marketer)
AEP Retail Energy (retail energy marketing in deregulated territories)
AEP Texas Central Company (formerly Central Power and Light, electric utility)
AEP Texas North Company (formerly West Texas Utilities, electric utility)
AEP Towers (wireless communications towers)
Appalachian Power Company (electric utility)
Columbus Southern Power Company (electric utility)
Indiana Michigan Power Company (electric utility)
Kentucky Power Company (electric utility)
Kingsport Power Company (electric utility)
Ohio Power Company (electric utility)
Public Service Company of Oklahoma (electric utility)
Southwestern Electric Power Company (electric utility)
Wheeling Power Company (electric utility)

Utility Distribution/Customer Service Divisions

AEP Ohio (handles distribution, customer service, and external affairs functions for Columbus Southern Power Company, Ohio Power Company, and Wheeling Power Company)
AEP Texas (handles distribution, customer service, and external affairs functions for AEP Texas Central Company and AEP Texas North Company)
Appalachian Power (handles distribution, customer service, and external affairs functions for Appalachian Power Company and Kingsport Power Company)
Indiana Michigan Power (handles distribution, customer service, and external affairs functions for Indiana Michigan Power Company)
Kentucky Power (handles distribution, customer service, and external affairs functions for Kentucky Power Company)
Public Service Company of Oklahoma (handles distribution, customer service, and external affairs functions for Public Service Company of Oklahoma)
Southwestern Electric Power Company (handles distribution, customer service, and external affairs functions for Southwestern Electric Power Company)

COMPETITORS

Allegheny Energy
BP
Calpine
CenterPoint Energy
CMS Energy
Constellation Energy Group
Delmarva Power
Dominion Resources
DTE
Duke Energy
Dynegy
El Paso
Energy Future
Entergy
Exelon
FirstEnergy
Mirant
NiSource
PG&E Corporation
RRI Energy
Sempra Energy
Southern Company
TVA
UTC Power
Xcel Energy

HISTORICAL FINANCIALS

Company Type: Public

Income Statement

FYE: December 31

	REVENUE ($ mil.)	NET INCOME ($ mil.)	NET PROFIT MARGIN	EMPLOYEES
12/08	14,440.0	1,380.0	9.6%	21,912
12/07	13,380.0	1,192.0	8.9%	20,861
12/06	12,622.0	1,002.0	7.9%	20,442
12/05	12,111.0	1,056.0	8.7%	19,630
12/04	14,057.0	1,210.0	8.6%	19,893
Annual Growth	0.7%	3.3%	—	2.4%

2008 Year-End Financials

Debt ratio: 145.3%
Return on equity: 13.3%
Cash ($ mil.): 497
Current ratio: 0.60
Long-term debt ($ mil.): 15,536
No. of shares (mil.): 553
Dividends
 Yield: 4.9%
 Payout: 48.0%
Market value ($ mil.): 18,391

Stock History

NYSE: AEP

	STOCK PRICE ($) FY Close	P/E High/Low		PER SHARE ($) Earnings	Dividends	Book Value
12/08	33.28	14	7	3.42	1.64	19.46
12/07	46.56	19	15	2.72	1.58	18.35
12/06	42.58	17	13	2.53	1.50	17.03
12/05	37.09	20	16	2.08	1.42	16.56
12/04	34.34	13	10	2.75	1.40	15.52
Annual Growth	(0.8%)	—	—	5.6%	4.0%	5.8%

American Express

American Express makes money even if you do leave home without it. The company is one of the world's largest travel agencies, but it is better known for its charge cards and revolving credit cards. And yes, the company still issues traveler's checks and publishes such magazines as *Food & Wine* and *Travel & Leisure* through its American Express Publishing unit. Its travel agency operations have more than 2,200 locations worldwide, and its Travelers Cheque Group is the world's largest issuer of traveler's checks (it also issues gift cards). But the company's charge and credit cards are its bread and butter; American Express has more than 92 million cards in circulation worldwide.

The company is organized into two business segments: The Global Consumer Group and the Global Business-to-Business Group. Global Consumer offers charge and lending, consumer travel, and stored-value cards. The business group offers business travel services, corporate cards, network and merchant processing services, and point-of-sale, back-office, and marketing services for merchants.

American Express sold the international operations of American Express Bank to Stanchart in 2008. After suffering losses during the economic downturn that year, American Express cut nearly 10% of its work force as a way of reducing costs. The layoffs, coupled with other cost cutting measures, were made in hopes of generating $1.8 billion in savings in 2009. The company was also granted permission by the Federal Reserve to convert to a bank holding company structure. The move afforded American Express access to the US government's $250 billion in bank bailout funds as the company faces increased credit losses and write-offs of nonperforming customer accounts. It received some $3.4 billion from the Troubled Asset Relief Fund (TARP) in early 2009. The restructuring may also make it easier for American Express to merge with another lender.

In 2007, American Express reached a $2.5 billion settlement with Visa and other defendants including JPMorgan Chase, Capital One, U.S. Bancorp, and Wells Fargo, dropping them from a lawsuit that alleged they conspired to block American Express from the bank-issued card business in the US. The following year it reached a $1.8 billion settlement with Mastercard, the final remaining defendant in the suit.

Warren Buffett's Berkshire Hathaway owns about 13% of American Express.

HISTORY

In 1850 Henry Wells and his two main competitors combined their delivery services to form American Express. When directors refused to expand to California in 1852, Wells and VP William Fargo formed Wells Fargo while remaining at American Express.

American Express merged with Merchants Union Express in 1868 and developed a money order to compete with the government's postal money order. Fargo's difficulty in cashing letters of credit in Europe led to the offering of Travelers Cheques in 1891.

During WWI the US nationalized and consolidated all express delivery services, compensating the owners. After the war, American Express incorporated as an overseas freight and financial services and exchange provider (the freight operation was sold in 1970). In 1958 the company introduced the American Express charge card. It bought Fireman's Fund American Insurance (sold gradually between 1985 and 1989) and Equitable Securities in 1968.

James Robinson, CEO from 1977 to 1993, hoped to turn American Express into a financial services supermarket. The company bought brokerage Shearson Loeb Rhoades in 1981 and investment banker Lehman Brothers in 1984, among others. In 1987 it introduced Optima, a revolving credit card, to compete with MasterCard and Visa; with no experience in underwriting credit cards, it was badly burned by losses.

Most of the financial units were combined as Shearson Lehman Brothers. But the financial services supermarket never came to fruition, and losses in this area brought a steep drop in earnings in the early 1990s. Harvey Golub was brought in as CEO in 1993 to restore stability.

The company sold its brokerage operations as Shearson (to Travelers, now Citigroup) and spun off investment banking as Lehman Brothers in 1994. In late 1996 it teamed with Advanta Corp. to allow Advanta Visa and MasterCard holders to earn points in the American Express Membership Rewards program. The move sparked a lawsuit from Visa and MasterCard, which prohibit their member banks from doing business with American Express. This move set off a spate of lawsuits culminating in the US Justice Department filing an antitrust suit against Visa and MasterCard. A federal judge sided with the Justice Department in 2001.

In 1997 Kenneth Chenault became president and COO, putting him in line to succeed Golub. In 2000 the company established a headquarters in Beijing to develop business in China.

In 2001 Chenault replaced Golub as chairman and CEO. American Express was hit hard that year by bad investments in below-investment grade bonds by its money-management unit, which shaved about $1 billion from earnings.

To grow its corporate travel management business, Amex acquired Rosenbluth International, a leading global travel management company with corporate travel operations in 15 countries, in 2003. When Rosenbluth became fully integrated into the organization in mid-2004, American Express announced a relaunch of its corporate travel organization, renamed American Express Business Travel.

American Express underwent a mild shakedown in 2004 when it cut 2.5% of its workforce in a restructuring that included the company's business travel operations; the move also included the sale of its banking operations in Bangladesh, Egypt, Luxembourg, and Pakistan.

In 2004 the company announced a milestone agreement with Industrial and Commercial Bank of China (ICBC), one of the biggest banks in China, to issue the first American Express-branded credit cards in that country.

To focus on its travel and credit card operations, the company in 2005 spun off Ameriprise Financial (formerly American Express Financial Advisors), which provides insurance, mutual funds, investment advice, and brokerage and asset management services.

In separate transactions toward that same end, American Express sold its Tax and Business Services division to H&R Block and its UK-based American Express Financial Services Europe to TD Waterhouse (now part of TD AMERITRADE). Also in 2005 the company sold its equipment leasing business to Key Equipment Finance.

EXECUTIVES

Chairman and CEO: Kenneth I. (Ken) Chenault, age 57, $27,327,318 total compensation
Vice Chairman and CEO, Business-to-Business: Edward P. (Ed) Gilligan, age 49, $15,800,627 total compensation
President: Alfred F. (Al) Kelly Jr., age 50, $11,533,476 total compensation
EVP and CFO: Daniel T. (Dan) Henry, age 59, $5,860,306 total compensation
EVP Corporate Development and CIO: Stephen (Steve) Squeri, age 49, $6,252,701 total compensation
EVP Global Advertising and Brand Management and Chief Marketing Officer: John D. Hayes, age 54
EVP and Chief Risk Officer; President, Risk, Information Management, and Banking: Ashwini (Ash) Gupta, age 55
EVP Corporate Affairs and Communications: Thomas Schick, age 62
EVP and General Counsel: Louise M. Parent, age 58
EVP Merchant Services North America: Kim C. Goodman, age 44
EVP and Comptroller: Joan L. Amble, age 56
EVP Human Resources: L. Kevin Cox, age 44
EVP Global Marketing and Source-to-Settle: Valerie S. Keating
EVP: President, Global Merchant Services: William H. (Bill) Glenn
SVP Investor Relations: Ron Stovall
SVP and Treasurer: David L. Yowan
VP Investor Relations: Gabriella P. Fitzgerald
President, Global Travelers Cheque and Prepaid Services, U.S. Card Services: Valerie (Val) Soranno-Keating
President, American Express Business Travel: Charles Petruccelli
President and CEO, Consumer Services: Judson C. (Jud) Linville, age 51
Secretary: Carol V. Schwartz
Auditors: PricewaterhouseCoopers LLP

LOCATIONS

HQ: American Express Company
World Financial Center, 200 Vesey St.
New York, NY 10285
Phone: 212-640-2000
Web: www.americanexpress.com

PRODUCTS/OPERATIONS

2008 Gross Revenues

	$ mil.	% of total
Discount revenue	15,025	47
Interest & fees on loans	6,159	19
Net card fees	2,150	7
Travel commissions & fees	2,010	6
Other commissions & fees	2,307	8
Net securitization income	1,070	3
Other interest	1,042	3
Other	2,157	7
Total	**31,920**	**100**

COMPETITORS

Advance Publications
Bank of America
Barclays
BCD Travel
Capital One
Citigroup
Discover
Expedia
JPMorgan Chase
JTB Corp.
MasterCard
Ovation Travel Group
Travel Franchise Group
Visa Inc
Western Union

HISTORICAL FINANCIALS

Company Type: Public

Income Statement

FYE: December 31

	ASSETS ($ mil.)	NET INCOME ($ mil.)	INCOME AS % OF ASSETS	EMPLOYEES
12/08	126,074.0	2,699.0	2.1%	66,000
12/07	149,830.0	4,012.0	2.7%	67,700
12/06	127,853.0	3,707.0	2.9%	65,400
12/05	113,960.0	3,734.0	3.3%	65,800
12/04	192,638.0	3,516.0	1.8%	77,500
Annual Growth	(10.1%)	(6.4%)	—	(3.9%)

2008 Year-End Financials

Equity as % of assets: 9.4%
Return on assets: 2.0%
Return on equity: 23.6%
Long-term debt ($ mil.): 60,041
No. of shares (mil.): 1,189
Dividends
Yield: 3.9%
Payout: 30.9%
Market value ($ mil.): 22,060
Sales ($ mil.): 28,365

Stock History

NYSE: AXP

	STOCK PRICE ($) FY Close	P/E High/Low		PER SHARE ($) Earnings	Dividends	Book Value
12/08	18.55	23	7	2.33	0.72	9.96
12/07	52.02	20	15	3.36	0.63	9.27
12/06	60.67	21	17	2.99	0.57	8.84
12/05	51.46	18	15	2.97	0.48	8.87
12/04	49.36	19	15	2.68	0.44	13.47
Annual Growth	(21.7%)	—	—	(3.4%)	13.1%	(7.3%)

American Financial Group

American Financial Group (AFG) insures businessmen in pursuit of the great American Dream. Through the Great American Insurance Group of companies and its flagship Great American Insurance Company, AFG offers commercial property/casualty insurance focused on specialties such as workers' compensation, professional liability, ocean and inland marine, and multiperil crop insurance. The company also provides surety coverage for contractors and risk management services. For individuals and employers AFG provides supplemental medical insurance products, and a wide range of annuities sold through its Great American Financial Resources (GAFRI) subsidiary.

While the company writes some reinsurance for its own companies, and others, it chooses to limit its exposure by purchasing catastrophe reinsurance from other providers. It suffered about $60 million in catastrophe losses in 2008.

AFG is engaged in non-insurance operations, primarily commercial real estate holdings in Cincinnati and Pittsburgh, as well as resorts and hotels in Charleston, South Carolina; George-town, Maryland; Whitefield, New Hampshire; New Orleans; and Palm Beach, Florida.

In 2008 the company purchased 67% of medical malpractice insurer and Lloyd's of London member Marketform Group. It also acquired Louisiana-based workers' compensation provider Strategic Comp Holdings.

Legendary businessman Carl Lindner Jr., who is also part owner of the Cincinnati Reds, retired as CEO in 2005 and was succeeded by two of his sons, Carl Lindner III and Craig Lindner, who share the CEO job. Together, the Lindners own nearly 30% of AFG.

HISTORY

When his father became ill in the mid-1930s, Carl Lindner dropped out of high school to take over his family's dairy business. He built it into a large ice-cream store chain called United Dairy Farmers. Lindner branched out in 1955 with Henthy Realty, and in 1959 he bought three savings and loans. The next year Lindner changed the company's name to American Financial Corp. (AFC). He took it public in 1961, using the proceeds to buy United Liberty Life Insurance (1963) and Provident Bank (1966).

Lindner also formed the American Financial Leasing & Services Company in 1968 to lease airplanes, computers, and other equipment. In 1969 the company acquired Phoenix developer Rubenstein Construction and renamed it American Continental. AFC bought several life, casualty, and mortgage insurance firms in the 1970s, including National General, parent of Great American Insurance Group, later the core of AFC's insurance segment. The company also moved into publishing by buying 95% of the *Cincinnati Enquirer*, paperback publisher Bantam Books, and hardback publisher Grosset & Dunlap.

But the publishing interests soon went back on the block, as Lindner concentrated on insurance, which was then suffering from an industry wide slowdown. In addition to selling the *Enquirer*, AFC spun off American Continental in 1976. American Continental's president was Charles Keating, who had joined AFC in 1972 and whose brother published the *Enquirer*. Keating (who was later jailed, released, then eventually pleaded guilty in connection with the failure of Lincoln Savings) underwent an SEC investigation during part of his time at AFC for alleged improprieties at Provident Bank. The bank was spun off in 1980.

Lindner took AFC private in 1981. That year, following a strategy of bottom-feeding, the company began building its interest in the non-railroad assets of Penn Central, the former railroad that had emerged from bankruptcy as an industrial manufacturer. Later that decade AFC increased its ownership in United Brands (later renamed Chiquita Brands International) from 29% to 45%. Lindner installed himself as CEO and reversed that company's losses. In 1987 AFC acquired a TV company, Taft Communications (renamed Great American Communications), entailing a heavy debt load. To reduce its debt, AFC trimmed its holdings, including Circle K, Hunter S&L, and an interest in Scripps Howard Broadcasting.

Great American Communications went bankrupt in 1992 and emerged the next year as Citicasters Inc. (sold in 1996). In 1995 Lindner created American Financial Group to effect the merger of AFC and Premier Underwriters, of which he owned 42%. The result was American Financial Group (AFG).

Lindner's bipartisan political donations gained publicity when it became known that his gifts to Republicans had brought support in a dispute with the European Union over the banana trade. The next year AFG sold some noncore units, including software consultancy Millennium Dynamics and its commercial insurance operations. In 1999 AFG bought direct-response auto insurer Worldwide Insurance Company as part of its efforts to build depth in the highly commodified auto insurance market.

In 2000 American Financial Group agreed to pay $75 million over the next 30 years to get its name on the Cincinnati Reds' new stadium, known as Great American Ball Park. In 2001 AFG sold its Japanese property/casualty division to Japanese insurer Mitsui Marine & Fire (now Mitsui Sumitomo Insurance).

AFG's results in the 1990s were uneven, and it typically did not make an underwriting profit. In 2003 the company kept operating expenses down (partly by merging two of its holding company subsidiaries into AFG) and swung to a profit even though premium revenue was down.

The company shed some commercial lines to concentrate on its property/casualty and life and annuities businesses. To refine its mix, AFG transferred Atlanta Casualty Company, Infinity Insurance Company, Leader Insurance Company, and Windsor Insurance Company into 40%-owned Infinity Property and Casualty, which went public in 2003. In 2004 the company exchanged its stake in Provident Financial Group for a holding in National City Corporation.

EXECUTIVES

Chairman: Carl H. Lindner, age 89
Co-President, Co-CEO, and Director: S. Craig Lindner, age 54, $4,374,769 total compensation
Co-President, Co-CEO, and Director: Carl H. Lindner III, age 55, $4,361,697 total compensation
SVP and CFO: Keith A. Jensen, age 58, $1,865,299 total compensation
SVP Taxes: Thomas E. Mischell, age 61, $1,514,075 total compensation
SVP, General Counsel, and Director: James E. Evans, age 63, $2,705,857 total compensation
VP and CIO: Piyush K. Singh
VP Taxation: Kathleen J. Brown
VP Investor Relations: Anne N. Watson
VP and Controller: Robert H. Ruffing
VP, Secretary, and Deputy General Counsel: James C. Kennedy
VP and Assistant Secretary: Karl J. Grafe
VP Internal Audit: Robert E. Dobbs
VP: Sandra W. Heimann
VP: Karen Holley Horrell, age 53
VP and Treasurer: David J. Witzgall
Auditors: Ernst & Young LLP

LOCATIONS

HQ: American Financial Group, Inc.
1 E. 4th St., Cincinnati, OH 45202
Phone: 513-579-2121 **Fax:** 513-579-2113
Web: www.amfnl.com

PRODUCTS/OPERATIONS

2008 Sales

	$ mil.	% of total
Premiums		
Property & casualty	2,867.2	61
Life, accident & health	434.6	9
Investment income	1,123.2	24
Realized losses	(426.4)	—
Other income	294.1	6
Total	**4,292.7**	**100**

Selected Subsidiaries

American Money Management Corporation
APU Holding Company
    American Premier Underwriters, Inc.
    Premier Lease & Loan Services Insurance Agency, Inc.
    Premier Lease & Loan Services of Canada, Inc.
    Republic Indemnity Company of America
        Republic Indemnity Company of California
Great American Financial Resources, Inc.
    AAG Holding Company, Inc
        Great American Life Insurance Company
        Loyal American Holding Corporation
        Manhattan National Life Insurance Company
        United Teacher Associates Insurance Company
    Ceres Group, Inc.
GAI Holding Bermuda Ltd.
    GAI Indemnity, Ltd.
    Marketform Group Limited (67%)
        Marketform Holdings Limited
            Lavenham Underwriting Limited
            Marketform Limited
            Sampford Underwriting Limited
Great American Holding, Inc.
    American Empire Surplus Lines Insurance Company
        American Empire Insurance Company
    Mid-Continent Casualty Company
        Mid-Continent Insurance Company
        Oklahoma Surety Company
Great American Insurance Company
    Brothers Property Corporation (80%)
    Farmers Crop Insurance Alliance, Inc.
    GAI Warranty Company
    Great American Alliance Insurance Company
    Great American Assurance Company
    Great American E&S Insurance Company
    Great American Fidelity Insurance Company
    Great American Insurance Company of New York
    Great American Management Services, Inc.
    Great American Protection Insurance Company
    Great American Security Insurance Company
    Great American Spirit Insurance Company
    National Interstate Corporation (53%)
        National Interstate Insurance Company
            National Interstate Insurance Company of Hawaii, Inc.
    Professional Risk Brokers, Inc.
    Strategic Comp Holdings, LLC

COMPETITORS

ACE Limited
AIG
Allianz Life
Arch Capital
Bankers Life and Casualty Company
Chubb Corp
Cincinnati Financial
CNA Financial
The Hartford
HCC Insurance
ING
LSW
Markel
Midland National Life
Mutual of Omaha
Philadelphia Insurance Companies
Travelers Companies
W. R. Berkley
XL Capital
Zenith National

HISTORICAL FINANCIALS

Company Type: Public

Income Statement

FYE: December 31

	ASSETS ($ mil.)	NET INCOME ($ mil.)	INCOME AS % OF ASSETS	EMPLOYEES
12/08	26,427.5	195.8	0.7%	600
12/07	25,807.5	383.2	1.5%	500
12/06	25,101.1	453.4	1.8%	5,200
12/05	22,816.0	206.6	0.9%	6,100
12/04	22,559.5	365.5	1.6%	4,400
Annual Growth	4.0%	(14.4%)	—	(39.2%)

2008 Year-End Financials

Equity as % of assets: 9.4%	Dividends
Return on assets: 0.7%	Yield: 2.2%
Return on equity: 7.1%	Payout: 29.9%
Long-term debt ($ mil.): 1,030	Market value ($ mil.): 2,996
No. of shares (mil.): 131	Sales ($ mil.): 4,293

Stock History

NYSE: AFG

	STOCK PRICE ($) FY Close	P/E High/Low		PER SHARE ($) Earnings	Dividends	Book Value
12/08	22.88	19	8	1.67	0.50	19.01
12/07	28.88	12	8	3.10	0.40	23.26
12/06	35.91	10	7	3.75	0.37	22.37
12/05	25.54	15	11	1.75	0.33	18.77
12/04	20.87	7	6	3.21	0.33	18.56
Annual Growth	2.3%	—	—	(15.1%)	10.9%	0.6%

American Greetings

American Greetings has been building its sturdy house of cards for more than a century. The #2 US maker of greeting cards (behind Hallmark), the company makes American Greetings, Carlton Cards, and Gibson Greetings brand missives. While greeting cards make up more than 60% of sales, the company also produces DesignWare party goods, Plus Mark gift wrap, and DateWorks calendars. The company's AG Interactive subsidiary distributes online greeting cards and other interactive media. American Greetings' products are sold through card and stationery stores, mass merchants, and other retail outlets worldwide. The family of chairman Morry Weiss controls more than 45% of the company.

The company's core business continues to rest on traditional greeting cards, but American Greetings has recognized that technology is changing the way people communicate and interact. In response, the company has been making investments in product development and interactive technologies. Its AG Interactive unit boasts nearly 4 million subscribers who have unlimited access to its e-cards and ringtones. At the same time, American Greetings continues to expand its traditional cards business: In 2009 it acquired Chicago-based Recycled Paper Greetings out of bankruptcy. The deal is designed to help expand American Greetings' line of humor cards.

Looking to capitalize on the popularity of digital photos, the company acquired photo sharing Web site Webshots from CNET Networks for about $45 million in 2007 and followed that in 2008 with the purchase of online photo firm PhotoWorks for nearly $30 million.

American Greetings has been keen to cut costs and divest under-performing or non-core assets. In 2009 the company sold its chain of more than 340 retail stores to California-based Schurman Fine Papers. The divestment will allow American Greetings to focus on its core greeting cards and other media products. Schurman plans to continue operating the stores under the names American Greetings and Carlton, as well as its own Papyrus brand.

The company is also parting ways with some of its branded characters, agreeing in 2008 to sell its Strawberry Shortcake and Care Bears properties to Toronto-based animation giant Cookie Jar Group. Under the terms of the $195 million deal, American Greetings would hold a 10-year license to continue using the characters for its products. The credit crisis that year delayed closing the deal, however, allowing American Greetings to solicit other offers. French animation house MoonScoop offered to acquire the assets for nearly $100 million, with about $20 million going to Cookie Jar. The Canadian animator, however, made a matching counter-offer.

HISTORY

In 1906 Polish immigrant Jacob Sapirstein founded Sapirstein Greeting Card Company and began selling postcards from a horse-drawn wagon. The outbreak of WWI and the resulting separation of families helped spur demand for the company's products. The impact of the war also helped shape the company's future: After an embargo was imposed on cards produced in Germany, Sapirstein decided to begin manufacturing his own cards.

Sapirstein's sons eventually joined the burgeoning company and, in 1940, after adopting the American Greetings Publishers name, the company's sales topped $1 million. The company incorporated as American Greetings in 1944 and went public in 1952. It introduced Hi Brows, a line of funny studio cards, in 1956 and broke ground on a 1.5-million-sq.-ft. headquarters building the same year.

In 1960 Sapirstein's son, Irving Stone (all three Sapirstein sons changed their surname to Stone, a derivative of Sapirstein) was appointed president, and Jacob Sapirstein became chairman. The ubiquitous Holly Hobbie made her first appearance on greeting cards in 1967 (within a decade, she had become the world's most popular licensed female character). In 1968 American Greetings' sales exceeded $100 million.

American Greetings introduced the Ziggy character in 1972 and launched Plus Mark, a maker of seasonal wrapping paper, boxed cards, and accessories six years later. Irving Stone succeeded his father as chairman and CEO in 1978, and Morry Weiss, Irving Stone's son-in-law, was appointed president.

With the success of Holly Hobbie licensing, American Greetings was prompted to create its own licensing division in 1980. In 1982 it introduced the Care Bears, licensed characters that appeared in animated films. Following the death of Jacob Sapirstein in 1987 (at age 102), Morry Weiss became chairman and CEO, and Irving Stone became founder-chairman.

In 1993 the company bought Magnivision (nonprescription reading glasses). It ventured onto the Internet two years later, when it began offering online greeting cards.

Its acquisitions of greeting card companies Camden Graphics and Hanson White in 1998 helped American Greetings double its presence in the UK. As part of an international restructuring plan, in 1999 the company shuttered a Canadian plant, eliminating 650 jobs. Later that year, in an expansion of its existing agreement with America Online (now part of Time Warner), American Greetings' online unit became AOL's exclusive provider of electronic greetings.

Founder-chairman Irving Stone died in early 2000 at the age of 90. Also that year American Greetings paid $175 million for smaller rival Gibson Greetings, along with Gibson's stake in Egreetings Network. The company later expanded its profile in the gift wrap market through its acquisition of CPS Corporation, a supplier of gift wrap and packaging. In 2001 the company bought the remaining shares of Egreetings Network and folded the business into its online business, and later that year did the same with ExciteHome's BlueMountain.com e-mail cards unit.

In 2003 CEO Morry Weiss and president James Spira resigned from the management of the company. Weiss retained his chairman title and Spira remained on the board. Morry's sons, Zev and Jeffrey, became CEO and president, respectively. In late 2004 the company closed one of its plants in Tennessee and laid off 450 people.

The company sold its educational products unit Learning Horizons in 2007 to a portfolio company of Evolution Capital Partners. American Greetings expanded its digital media operations with the 2007 acquisition of photo sharing Web site Webshots from CNET Networks for $45 million. The following year it purchased PhotoWorks for nearly $30 million.

EXECUTIVES

Chairman: Morry Weiss, age 68, $2,886,223 total compensation
CEO and Director: Zev Weiss, age 42, $1,463,808 total compensation
President, COO, and Director: Jeffrey M. (Jeff) Weiss, age 45, $1,091,472 total compensation
SVP and CFO: Stephen J. Smith, age 45, $552,251 total compensation
SVP Human Resources: Brian T. McGrath, age 58
SVP Enterprise Resource Planning: Erwin Weiss, age 60
SVP Executive Sales and Marketing Officer: John W. Beeder, age 49
SVP and Executive Supply Chain Officer: Michael L. Goulder, age 49, $690,595 total compensation
SVP International and Managing Director, UK Greetings: John S.N. Charlton, age 62
SVP, General Counsel, and Secretary: Catherine M. (Cathy) Kilbane, age 46
SVP Creative and Merchandising; President, Carlton Cards Retail: Thomas H. Johnston, age 61
SVP Wal-Mart Team: Robert C. Swellie
SVP and General Manager, AmericanGreetings.com: Sally Babcock

VP and Corporate Controller: Joseph B. Cipollone, age 50
VP Information Services: Douglas W. (Doug) Rommel, age 53
President and CEO, AG Intellectual Property Group: Josef A. Mandelbaum, age 42
CEO, Recycled Paper Greetings: Jude Rake, age 47
Director Investor Relations and Treasurer: Gregory M. Steinberg
Auditors: Ernst & Young LLP

LOCATIONS

HQ: American Greetings Corporation
1 American Rd., Cleveland, OH 44144
Phone: 216-252-7300 **Fax:** 216-252-6778
Web: corporate.americangreetings.com

2009 Sales

	$ mil.	% of total
US	1,235.8	73
UK	222.9	13
Other countries	232.0	14
Total	**1,690.7**	**100**

PRODUCTS/OPERATIONS

2009 Sales

	$ mil.	% of total
Greeting cards		
Everyday products	704.4	42
Seasonal	356.8	21
Gift packaging	240.4	14
Other	389.1	23
Total	**1,690.7**	**100**

2009 Sales

	$ mil.	% of total
Social Expression products		
North America	1,095.4	65
International	270.7	16
Retail stores	178.8	10
AG Interactive	83.4	5
Other	62.4	4
Total	**1,690.7**	**100**

Selected Products and Operations

Greeting cards
  American Greetings
  Carlton Cards
  Gibson
  Just For You
  Papyrus
  Recycled Paper Greetings
  Tender Thoughts
Gift packaging and other
  DateWorks (calendars)
  DesignWare (party goods)
  Plus Mark (gift wrap)
AG Interactive (online and interactive media)
  AmericanGreetings.com
  BlueMountain.com
  eGreetings.com
  Kiwee.com
  PhotoWorks
  Webshots

COMPETITORS

Carte Blanche Greetings
CSS Industries
Eastman Kodak
Hallmark
International Greetings
NobleWorks
Pomegranate Communications
Quotable Cards
Shutterfly
Snapfish
SPS Studios
Taylor Corporation

HISTORICAL FINANCIALS

Company Type: Public

Income Statement

FYE: Last day in February

	REVENUE ($ mil.)	NET INCOME ($ mil.)	NET PROFIT MARGIN	EMPLOYEES
2/09	1,690.7	(227.8)	—	26,600
2/08	1,776.5	83.0	4.7%	27,300
2/07	1,744.6	42.4	2.4%	9,400
2/06	1,885.7	84.4	4.5%	29,500
2/05	1,902.7	95.3	5.0%	26,600
Annual Growth	**(2.9%)**	**—**	**—**	**0.0%**

2009 Year-End Financials

Debt ratio: 73.6%
Return on equity: —
Cash ($ mil.): 60
Current ratio: 1.63
Long-term debt ($ mil.): 389
No. of shares (mil.): 39
Dividends
  Yield: 16.1%
  Payout: —
Market value ($ mil.): 147

Stock History

NYSE: AM

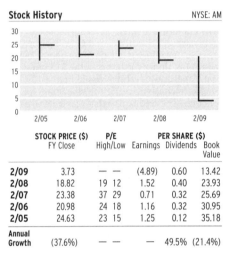

	STOCK PRICE ($) FY Close	P/E High/Low		PER SHARE ($) Earnings	Dividends	Book Value
2/09	3.73	—	—	(4.89)	0.60	13.42
2/08	18.82	19	12	1.52	0.40	23.93
2/07	23.38	37	29	0.71	0.32	25.69
2/06	20.98	24	18	1.16	0.32	30.95
2/05	24.63	23	15	1.25	0.12	35.18
Annual Growth	**(37.6%)**	**—**	**—**	**—**	**49.5%**	**(21.4%)**

American International Group

Even to this day American International Group (AIG) is one of the world's largest insurance firms. While it remains in the spotlight for staggering losses and government bailouts, the company's subsidiaries are still providing insurance. AIG is a leading US provider of property/casualty and specialty insurance to commercial, institutional, and individual customers. Internationally, the company provides reinsurance, life insurance and retirement services, asset management, and financial services (including financing commercial aircraft leasing) in more than 130 countries. The US government holds more than 80% of the company, and its future remains in a state of flux.

While AIG has long been a leader in insuring risk for institutions worldwide, it also led the industry in the practice of investing in murky assets to bring a little zest to the otherwise dull world of insurance. But its riskier investments brought home billions of dollars in losses and the company's liquidity seized up like cold gravy.

By September 2008 AIG was laying out plans to jettison several of its most valuable businesses, such as its domestic auto insurance and annuities units. Despite this desperate scramble to raise capital, the firm's credit ratings were cut.

With insolvency only days away, the US Federal Reserve stepped up with an $85 billion loan. But the company continued to struggle and the Fed restructured and augmented its loans several times over. By March of 2009, amid swirling speculation of a possible bankruptcy, the government, apparently figuring "in for a penny, in for a pound," agreed to give the company access to another $30 billion from its Troubled Asset Relief Program, bringing its total support of AIG to around $182 billion.

AIG is letting go of all its US life insurance, annuity, and consumer finance operations. It will also sell off almost all of its personal insurance lines. If all goes to plan the company will be left with its profitable US and foreign commercial property/casualty businesses. To put a better face on some of its assets (and distance them from their parent's misery), AIG has created a new company, Chartis, to hold the commercial and international property/casualty operations as an independently managed company. AIG has also announced plans to spin off its American International Assurance (AIA), which holds ALICO and the rest of its stable Asian life insurance operations. In mid-2009 it handed the Federal Reserve Bank of New York $25 billion worth of interest in AIA and ALICO to help repay some of its loans.

Martin Sullivan stepped down as CEO in 2008 and chairman Robert Willumstad stepped in to fill that role. However, as part of the government bailout agreement later that year, former Allstate executive Edward Liddy took over both the chairman and CEO titles from Willumstad. Nine months into the job, after leading AIG's first round of restructuring measures, Liddy announced his retirement; Robert Benmosche (a former MetLife executive) replaced Liddy as CEO, while director Harvey Golub was named non-executive chairman.

HISTORY

Former ice cream parlor owner Cornelius Starr founded property/casualty insurer American Asiatic Underwriters in Shanghai in 1919. After underwriting business for other insurers, Starr began selling life insurance policies to the Chinese in 1921 (foreign companies are loath to do so despite the longevity of the Chinese). In 1926 he opened a New York office specializing in foreign risks incurred by American companies. As WWII loomed, Starr moved his base to the US; when the war cut off business in Europe, he focused on Latin America. After a brief postwar return to China, the company was kicked out by the communist government.

In the 1950s the company began providing disability, health, and life insurance and pension plans for employees who moved from country to country. Starr chose his successor, Maurice "Hank" Greenberg, in 1967 and died the next year. Greenberg, who had come aboard in 1960 to develop overseas operations, took over the newly formed American International Group, a holding company for Starr's worldwide collection of insurance concerns. Greenberg's policy of achieving underwriting profits forced the company to use tight fiscal discipline. AIG went public in 1969.

By 1975 AIG was the largest foreign life insurer in much of Asia and the only insurer with global sales and support facilities. AIG's underwriting policies saved it when price wars from 1979 to 1984 brought heavy losses to most insurers. In 1987 AIG became the second US-owned insurer (after Chubb) to enter the traditionally closed South Korean market.

The 1980s saw AIG begin investment operations in Asia, increase its presence in health care, and form a financial services group. The firm resumed its Chinese operations in 1993 after triumphing over stiff opposition from state-owned monopolies.

In 2001 AIG agreed to be the business sponsor for the troubled Chiyoda Mutual Life Insurance Company; it also bought American General, wooing the insurer away from rival suitor Prudential plc to bolster AIG's share of the lucrative US retirement-planning market.

The insurer paid out about $800 million in claims related to the attacks on the World Trade Center. Legal settlements forced the company to take a $1.8 billion charge in 2003 in a move that surprised analysts and sent shock waves throughout the industry, causing other large insurance stocks to plummet.

Legal woes continued to befall AIG in 2004, when two company executives pleaded guilty to charges of involvement in an alleged price-fixing scheme that also involved insurance broker Marsh and insurer ACE. AIG also reached a $126 million settlement with federal regulators in 2004 over allegations the insurer sold products and services used to help customers improve their financial appearance.

In 2004 AIG came under investigation by the Office of the Attorney General for the State of New York, the New York Insurance Department, and the SEC into possible accounting irregularities and the company's use of offshore reinsurers. In early 2005 Greenberg was forced to step down as CEO. Former vice chairman and co-COO Martin Sullivan was named to succeed him. Soon after, Greenberg — the man most associated with the company — was forced to give up his chairman's seat as well.

As a result of the allegations, which included accounting irregularities, fraud, and bid-rigging, and along with acknowledging some wrongdoing, in 2006 the company agreed to pay a $1.6 billion settlement to the three agencies.

EXECUTIVES

Chairman: Harvey Golub, age 70
Vice Chairman and Chief Restructuring Officer: Paula R. Reynolds, age 52
Vice Chairman Legal, Human Resources, Corporate Communications, and Corporate Affairs: Anastasia D. (Stasia) Kelly, age 59
Vice Chairman Transition Planning and Administration; President and CEO, American General Life Companies: Matthew E. (Matt) Winter, age 52
Vice Chairman Global Economic Strategies: Jacob A. Frenkel, age 64
President, CEO, and Director: Robert H. (Bob) Benmosche, age 65
EVP and CFO: David L. Herzog, age 49, $1,939,674 total compensation
EVP; President and CEO, AIG Property Casualty Group: Kristian P. Moor, age 49, $5,984,114 total compensation
EVP, Foreign General Insurance; President and CEO, American International Underwriters: Nicholas C. (Nick) Walsh, age 58
EVP AIG Property Casualty Group; President, AIG Commercial Insurance Group: John Q. Doyle

SVP Financial Services; Interim President and CEO Financial Products: William N. (Bill) Dooley, age 56
SVP and Chief Risk Officer: Robert E. Lewis, age 57
SVP and Chief Human Resources Officer: Andrew J. Kaslow, age 58
SVP and Chief Investment Officer: Monika Machon, age 48
VP and Chief Administrative Officer; SVP and Head Asset Management Restructuring: Jeffrey J. Hurd, age 42
SVP, Secretary, and Deputy General Counsel: Kathleen E. Shannon, age 59
SVP; Chairman, President, and CEO, AIG Companies in Japan and Korea: Robert W. Clyde
VP and Director Investor Relations: Charlene M. Hamrah
Chairman, International Life and Retirement Services; Chairman, American Life Insurance Company, and Chairman, American International Assurance Company Limited: Rodney O. (Rod) Martin Jr., age 56
Chairman and CEO, Global Investment Group: Win J. Neuger, age 59, $6,354,969 total compensation
President and CEO, Domestic Life and Retirement Services: Jay S. Wintrob, age 51
President and CEO, American General Life Companies: Mary Jane B. Fortin
Auditors: PricewaterhouseCoopers LLP

LOCATIONS

HQ: American International Group, Inc.
70 Pine St., New York, NY 10270
Phone: 212-770-7000   **Fax:** 212-509-9705
Web: www.aigcorporate.com

2008 Revenues

	$ mil.	% of total
North America	(33,301)	—
Asia	25,022	56
Other regions	19,383	44
Total	**11,104**	**100**

PRODUCTS/OPERATIONS

2008 Revenues

	$ mil.	% of total
Premiums & other considerations	83,505	87
Net investment income	12,222	13
Net realized capital losses	(55,484)	—
Unrealized market valuation losses	(28,602)	—
Other income or losses	(537)	—
Total	**11,104**	**100**

2008 Revenues

	$ mil.	% of total
General insurance	44,676	94
Life insurance & retirement services	3,054	6
Asset management	(4,526)	—
Financial services	(31,095)	—
Other, consolidation & eliminations	(1,005)	—
Total	**11,104**	**100**

Selected Subsidiaries

Asset Management
AIG SunAmerica Asset Management Corp. (SAAMCo)
AIG Global Asset Management Holdings Corp. (AIGGIG)
AIG Global Real Estate Investment Corp. (AIG Global Real Estate)

Financial Services
International Lease Finance Corporation
AIG Financial Products Corporation
American General Finance, Inc. (AGF)
AIG Consumer Finance Group, Inc. (AIGCFG)
Imperial A.I. Credit Companies

General Insurance
AIU Insurance Company
American Home Assurance Company (American Home)
American International Underwriters Overseas, Ltd. (AIUO)
Lexington Insurance Company (Lexington)
National Union Fire Insurance Company of Pittsburgh, Pa. (National Union)
New Hampshire Insurance Company (New Hampshire)
Transatlantic Reinsurance Company
United Guaranty Residential Insurance Company
Life Insurance & Retirement Services
Domestic
AIG Annuity Insurance Company (AIG Annuity)
AIG SunAmerica Life Assurance Company
American General Life Insurance Company (AIG American General)
American General Life and Accident Insurance Company (AGLA)
The United States Life Insurance Company in the City of New York (USLIFE)
The Variable Annuity Life Insurance Company (VALIC)
Foreign
AIG Star Life Insurance Company, Ltd.
American International Assurance Company (AIA)
American Life Insurance Company (ALICO)
Nan Shan Life Insurance Company, Ltd.
The Philippine American Life and General Insurance Company (Philamlife)

COMPETITORS

ACE Limited
AEGON
Allianz
Aon
AXA
Berkshire Hathaway
Chubb Corp
CNA Financial
GE
General Re
Hanover Insurance
The Hartford
ING
John Hancock Financial Services
Liberty Mutual
Manulife Financial
MetLife
MGIC Investment
Nationwide
New York Life
Northwestern Mutual
Prudential
Tokio Marine
Travelers Companies
Zurich Financial Services

HISTORICAL FINANCIALS

Company Type: Public

Income Statement

FYE: December 31

	ASSETS ($ mil.)	NET INCOME ($ mil.)	INCOME AS % OF ASSETS	EMPLOYEES
12/08	860,418.0	(99,289.0)	—	116,000
12/07	1,060,505.0	6,200.0	0.6%	116,000
12/06	979,414.0	14,014.0	1.4%	106,000
12/05	853,370.0	10,477.0	1.2%	97,000
12/04	798,660.0	9,875.0	1.2%	92,000
Annual Growth	**1.9%**	**—**	**—**	**6.0%**

2008 Year-End Financials

Equity as % of assets: 6.1%
Return on assets: —
Return on equity: —
Long-term debt ($ mil.): 137,667
No. of shares (mil.): 135
Dividends
  Yield: 39.5%
  Payout: —
Market value ($ mil.): 4,226
Sales ($ mil.): 11,104

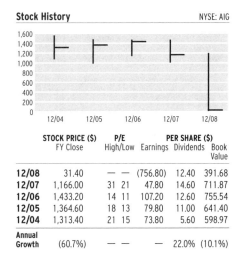

| | STOCK PRICE ($) | P/E | | PER SHARE ($) | |
	FY Close	High/Low	Earnings	Dividends	Book Value
12/08	31.40	— —	(756.80)	12.40	391.68
12/07	1,166.00	31 21	47.80	14.60	711.87
12/06	1,433.20	14 11	107.20	12.60	755.54
12/05	1,364.60	18 13	79.80	11.00	641.40
12/04	1,313.40	21 15	73.80	5.60	598.97
Annual Growth	(60.7%)	— —	—	22.0%	(10.1%)

American Water Works

Water, water, everywhere — and American Water Works wants to own it. The company, once a subsidiary of German utility giant RWE, is by far the largest public water utility in the US. Through its regulated utilities and its contract services division, American Water Works serves about 15 million consumers in 32 US states, plus Ontario. The company also provides wastewater treatment in some of its service areas. Its regulated operations account for nearly 90% of sales. Nonregulated subsidiary American Water Works Service provides contract management services for water and wastewater systems. In 2008 RWE spun off American Water Works, but retained a majority stake, which has since been reduced to about 25%.

In 2007 the company's New Jersey American Water unit acquired S.J. Services Inc., expanding the parent company's service area and customer base deeper into Southern New Jersey. The next year saw its Pennsylvania American Water subsidiary acquire the Claysville-Donegal Joint Municipal Authority water and wastewater systems. Those two states provide almost half of the company's regulated business.

HISTORY

American Water Works was founded in 1886 as the American Water Works & Guarantee Company. By the time it became American Water Works & Electric (AWW&E) in 1914, it ranked among the giant US utility holding companies and owned a bevy of unrelated electric, gas, and water companies, as well as California real estate. While AWW&E was growing, John H. Ware Jr., an eighth-grade dropout, bought water companies nationwide, including Northeastern Water.

After the 1929 stock market crash ruined many utilities, the federal government passed the Public Utility Holding Company Act of 1935 to break up and regulate the powerful trusts that controlled the nation's electric and gas utilities. AWW&E tried to fight the act in the courts (but filed a reorganization plan in 1937, the first utility holding company to do so, and divested its California land holdings). The Supreme Court upheld the act in 1946, and the company put its electric utilities and its highly profitable water properties up for sale as American Water Works Co., Inc.

Ware submitted the only bid in 1947, and his Northeastern Water paid $13 million for a 51% share of a company with assets of more than $180 million. The company went public that year.

A few years after buying American Water Works, Ware spun off its electric holdings. In 1960 Ware retired as chairman and was replaced by his son, John Ware III. Three years later, Northeastern Water and American Water Works merged their operations, and in 1976 the company moved to Voorhees, New Jersey.

The federal government, which had started regulating water quality in 1974, continued to pass tougher and tougher water laws — making it harder for smaller players to survive. After decades of buying and selling small water companies, American Water Works entered a period of consolidation and integration that helped it survive the economic downturn of the late 1960s and 1970s. By 1984, the year John Ware III retired, American had 33 operating units (it had acquired more than 150 companies since the 1930s). Ware was replaced by Philadelphia banker Sam Ballam. In 1987 Marilyn Ware Lewis, daughter of John Ware III, became chairman, bringing the company back into the family's purview.

In 1998 James Barr took over as CEO. Barr, who had started at American Water Works as a 20-year-old records clerk, recognized opportunity in new federal water-quality rules that forced municipalities to upgrade their old and ailing water systems. Lacking the resources to make all the repairs themselves, many were turning to the private sector. That year American Water Works began scouting for acquisitions and completed 22.

The next year the company bought National Enterprises, a family-owned water utility operator that served 1.5 million customers in Missouri, Indiana, Illinois, and New York. The 1999 $700 million acquisition was the largest in the history of the US water utility industry. American Water Works topped it, however, later that year when it agreed to acquire the water and wastewater businesses of Citizens Utilities (now Citizens Communications); the acquisition was completed in 2002 in a $979 million deal.

In 2000 American Water Works agreed to buy California water utility SJW for about $480 million, but the companies terminated the deal in 2001 because of delays in obtaining approval from California regulators.

Unfazed by the collapse of the SJW deal, American Water Works in 2001 bought the North American operations of Enron's Azurix water unit. American Water Works also agreed to sell water utilities in Connecticut, Massachusetts, New York, and New Hampshire to UK-based Kelda Group and its US subsidiary, Aquarion; the deal was completed in 2002 for $224 million.

In September 2001 the company agreed to be acquired by RWE for $4.6 billion in cash and $4 billion in assumed debt; the deal was completed in 2003. Chairman Marilyn Ware Lewis and CEO James Barr both left the company upon completion of the acquisition; Thames Water CEO Bill Alexander inherited both positions. Later in 2003, Thames Water's Jeremy Pelczer took over the chief executive's role as president of American Water Works; Alexander remained chairman.

The company was acquired by RWE in 2003.

EXECUTIVES

Chairman: George MacKenzie Jr., age 60
President, CEO, and Director: Donald L. (Don) Correll, age 58, $2,903,802 total compensation
SVP and CFO: Ellen C. Wolf, age 55, $2,045,329 total compensation
SVP, General Counsel, and Secretary: George W. Patrick, age 66
SVP Corporate and Business Development: William D. (Bill) Patterson, age 54
SVP Corporate Communications and External Affairs: Laura L. Monica, age 52
SVP Human Resources: Sean G. Burke, age 53
SVP Eastern Division; President, Kentucky American Water: Nick O. Rowe, age 51
VP and CIO: Emily Ashworth
VP and Controller: Mark Chesla, age 49
VP and Treasurer: James M. Kalinovich, age 41
VP Investor Relations: Edward D. Vallejo
President American Water Enterprises: Mark F. Strauss, age 57
President, Regulated Operations: Walter J. Lynch, age 46, $1,274,680 total compensation
President, American Water Services and American Water Works Service Company: John S. Young, age 55, $2,243,161 total compensation
President, American Water Resources: Sharon C. Cameron
Auditors: PricewaterhouseCoopers LLP

LOCATIONS

HQ: American Water Works Company, Inc.
1025 Laurel Oak Rd., Voorhees, NJ 08043
Phone: 856-346-8200   **Fax:** 856-346-8440
Web: www.amwater.com

PRODUCTS/OPERATIONS

2008 Sales

	$ mil.	% of total
Regulated	2,082.7	88
Non-regulated	272.2	12
Adjustments	(18.0)	—
Total	**2,336.9**	**100**

Selected Subsidiaries

Arizona American Water
California American Water
Hawaii American Water
Illinois American Water
Indiana American Water
Iowa American Water
Kentucky American Water
Long Island Americam Water
Missouri American Water
New Jersey American Water
New Mexico American Water
Ohio American Water
Pennsylvania American Water
Tennessee American Water
Virginia American Water
West Virginia American Water

COMPETITORS

American States Water
Aqua America
Aquarion
California Water Service
Connecticut Water Service
Indianapolis Water
Memphis Light
Middlesex Water
Severn Trent
SJW
Southwest Water
SRP
United Water Inc.
Utilities, Inc.
Veolia Environnement

HISTORICAL FINANCIALS
Company Type: Public

Income Statement
FYE: December 31

	REVENUE ($ mil.)	NET INCOME ($ mil.)	NET PROFIT MARGIN	EMPLOYEES
12/08	2,336.9	(562.4)	—	7,300
12/07	2,214.2	(342.8)	—	7,000
Annual Growth	5.5%	—	—	4.3%

2008 Year-End Financials
Debt ratio: 113.3%
Return on equity: —
Cash ($ mil.): 10
Current ratio: 0.38
Long-term debt ($ mil.): 4,648

No. of shares (mil.): 175
Dividends
  Yield: 1.0%
  Payout: —
Market value ($ mil.): 3,645

Stock History
NYSE: AWK

	STOCK PRICE ($) FY Close	P/E High/Low	PER SHARE ($) Earnings	Dividends	Book Value
12/08	20.88	— —	(3.52)	0.20	23.52

AmeriCredit Corp.

AmeriCredit gives credit where it's not necessarily due. The company purchases loans made by more than 17,000 franchised and selected independent auto dealers primarily to consumers with less-than-ideal credit histories. It typically finances low-mileage, late-model used cars (about 80% of all loans), and the occasional new automobile. The company then periodically transfers its loans to securitization trusts, retains the servicing, and reinvests the proceeds in new loans. The lender has more than 1 million customers and approximately $15 billion in managed auto receivables. It operates about 25 branches in the US. Investment firm Leucadia owns more than 20% of AmeriCredit.

The company has expanded its traditional operations in the subprime market by acquiring businesses serving prime and near-prime customers. In 2006 AmeriCredit purchased specialty auto lender Bay View Acceptance Corporation (BVAC) from Bay View Capital (later Great Lakes Bancorp) for about $62 million. The following year, it bought indirect near-prime lender Long Beach Acceptance from ACC Capital for some $283 million. Both companies' operations were merged into those of subsidiary AmeriCredit Financial Services.

Going into 2008, AmeriCredit's plans for growth included making more direct-to-consumer loans, adding leasing programs, and expanding in Canada. However, credit market conditions took a nosedive as loan defaults increased, and the company revised its strategies. It raised its minimum credit score requirements for new loans, closed more than half of its credit centers, and eliminated about 1,000 staff positions. AmeriCredit also stopped issuing loans directly to customers, stopped providing lease financing through its dealership network, and discontinued operations in Canada.

HISTORY

AmeriCredit began in 1986 as UrCarco — used car lots offering both sales and financing to customers with poor credit. It was the inspiration of Cash America pawnshop executives Jack Daugherty and Clifton Morris, who financed UrCarco with four other investors and created the nation's first chain of used car lots. The company's 1989 IPO met with great success, but the excitement was short-lived; after quadrupling in size to 20 lots, UrCarco became mired in huge losses from poor underwriting and bad loans on top of declining car sales. In 1991 the company began reinventing itself, completely restructuring after receiving $10 million from Rainwater Management.

In 1992 UrCarco changed its name to AmeriCredit, liquidated its used car business, and expanded its indirect lending services. The company improved its underwriting by adopting a credit-risk scorecard in 1994 (with assistance from credit-scoring industry leader Fair Isaac Corporation). In 1996 AmeriCredit acquired California-based Rancho Vista Mortgage (it became AmeriCredit Corporation of California) and established a home equity lending operation, making and acquiring loans through a network of mortgage brokers.

The late 1990s provided their challenges. AmeriCredit survived the subprime market meltdown of 1997 and faced continuing criticism for its accounting practices. In 1999 it formed an alliance with Chase Manhattan (now JPMorgan Chase) to provide subprime financing to auto dealers who do business with Chase. That year it discontinued its mortgage operations and liquidated its AmeriCredit Corporation of California subsidiary to focus on its auto lending.

In 2001 it teamed with JPMorgan Chase, Wells Fargo, and other finance companies to launch DealerTrack, an online system that allows dealers to submit loan applications electronically to various lenders and receive faster responses.

EXECUTIVES

Chairman: Clifton H. Morris Jr., age 73
President, CEO, and Director: Daniel E. (Dan) Berce, age 55
EVP, CFO, and Treasurer: Chris A. Choate, age 45
EVP, Chief Credit and Risk Officer: Steven P. Bowman, age 41
VP Investor Relations: Caitlin DeYoung
Secretary: J. Michael May
Auditors: Deloitte & Touche LLP

LOCATIONS

HQ: AmeriCredit Corp.
  801 Cherry St., Ste. 3900, Fort Worth, TX 76102
Phone: 817-302-7000   **Fax:** 817-302-7101
Web: www.americredit.com

PRODUCTS/OPERATIONS

2009 Sales

	$ mil.	% of total
Finance charges	1,902.7	91
Other	179.7	9
Total	**2,082.1**	**100**

Selected Subsidiaries
ACF Investment Corp.
AFS Funding Corp.
AFS Funding Trust
AFS SenSub Corp.
AFS Warehouse Corp.
ALC Leasing Ltd.
AmeriCredit Consumer Discount Company
AmeriCredit Consumer Loan Company, Inc.
Americredit Corporation of California
AmeriCredit Finance Canada LP
AmeriCredit Financial Services of Canada Ltd.
AmeriCredit Financial Services, Inc.
AmeriCredit Flight Operations, LLC
AmeriCredit Funding Corp. VII
AmeriCredit Management Trust
AmeriCredit Master Trust
AmeriCredit Repurchase Trust
Bay View Acceptance Corporation
CAR Group, Inc.
Long Beach Acceptance Corp.
Long Beach Acceptance Receivables Corp.

COMPETITORS

Capital One Auto Finance
Consumer Portfolio
Credit Acceptance
First Investors Financial

HSBC Finance
Nicholas Financial
United PanAm Financial
World Acceptance

HISTORICAL FINANCIALS
Company Type: Public

Income Statement
FYE: June 30

	ASSETS ($ mil.)	NET INCOME ($ mil.)	INCOME AS % OF ASSETS	EMPLOYEES
6/09	11,984.2	13.9	0.1%	3,064
6/08	16,547.2	(69.3)	—	3,832
6/07	17,811.0	360.2	2.0%	4,831
6/06	13,067.9	306.2	2.3%	4,025
6/05	10,947.0	285.9	2.6%	3,653
Annual Growth	2.3%	(53.0%)	—	(4.3%)

2009 Year-End Financials
Equity as % of assets: 17.2%
Return on assets: 0.1%
Return on equity: 0.7%
Long-term debt ($ mil.): 554
No. of shares (mil.): 133

Dividends
  Yield: 0.0%
  Payout: —
Market value ($ mil.): 1,806
Sales ($ mil.): 2,082

Stock History
NYSE: ACF

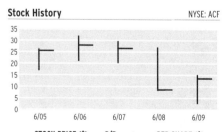

	STOCK PRICE ($) FY Close	P/E High/Low	PER SHARE ($) Earnings	Dividends	Book Value
6/09	13.55	135 26	0.11	0.00	15.48
6/08	8.62	— —	(0.60)	0.00	14.23
6/07	26.55	11 7	2.73	0.00	15.57
6/06	27.92	15 10	2.08	0.00	15.07
6/05	25.50	15 10	1.73	0.00	15.92
Annual Growth	(14.6%)	— —	(49.8%)	—	(0.7%)

AmeriGas Partners

America has a gas with AmeriGas Partners. Purveying propane has propelled the company to its position as one of the top two US retail propane marketers (rivaling Ferrellgas for the #1 slot). It serves 1.3 million residential, commercial, industrial, agricultural, motor fuel, and wholesale customers from about 600 locations in 46 states. AmeriGas also sells propane-related supplies and equipment and exchanges prefilled portable tanks for empty ones. The company stores propane in Arizona, California, and Virginia and distributes its products through an interstate carrier structure that runs across the US and in Canada. Utility holding company UGI owns 43% of AmeriGas.

In a consolidating industry, the fuel supplier has pursued a strategy of growth through acquisitions. In 2007 the company acquired Royal Dutch Shell's US retail propane operations. It also purchased All Star Gas.

In 2008 the company bought Penn Fuel Propane and four other companies, boosting its customer base by 42,000 and its annual propane output by 20 million gallons.

AmeriGas is also growing internally through the expansion of its prefilled propane business (cylinder exchange) located at about 25,000 retail locations in the US.

HISTORY

The forerunner of AmeriGas Partners was set up in 1959, when UGI subsidiary Ugite Gas entered the liquefied petroleum gas market in Maryland and Pennsylvania. By the early 1970s the company had expanded into eight states, and in 1977 AmeriGas was formed to replace Ugite Gas.

In the 1980s UGI began to focus more on propane. AmeriGas became one of the industry's leading players when it acquired Cal Gas in 1987, and three years later UGI merged AmeriGas with AP Propane. In 1993 UGI acquired a stake in propane marketer Petrolane, and the next year it formed AmeriGas Partners to acquire AmeriGas Propane, AmeriGas Propane-2 (another UGI unit), and Petrolane.

In 1995 UGI sold 42% of AmeriGas Partners to the public. AmeriGas Partners acquired Hawaii's Oahu Gas Service, Pur-Gas Service in Florida, and Enderby Gas in Texas the next year. In 1997 it acquired 14 firms in Florida, Georgia, Illinois, Louisiana, Mississippi, and South Carolina. The next year it bought 10 more companies and expanded its prefilled propane tank operations by more than 4,000 locations.

AmeriGas gained retail propane operations in five western states from All Star Gas in 2000. The next year the company paid $202 million for NiSource's Columbia Energy Group propane businesses. In 2003 AmeriGas purchased the propane distribution assets of Active Propane, Rocky Mountain LP, and Noreika Gas; as well as three propane distribution outlets from Suburban Propane Partners. Later that year, the company purchased the retail propane distribution business of Horizon Propane.

EXECUTIVES

Chairman; Chairman and CEO, UGI: Lon R. Greenberg, age 58
Vice Chairman and Director: John L. Walsh, age 53
President, CEO, and Director: Eugene V. N. Bissell, age 55

VP Finance and CFO: Jerry E. Sheridan, age 43
CIO: R. W. Fabrizio
Chief Accounting Officer and Controller: William J. Stanczak, age 53
VP Finance and CFO, UGI: Michael J. Cuzzolina, age 63
VP, General Counsel, and Corporate Secretary: Robert H. Knauss, age 55
VP Human Resources: William D. Katz, age 55
VP and Treasurer: Robert W. Krick
VP Supply and Logistics: David L. Lugar, age 51
VP Sales and Marketing: Carey M. Monaghan, age 57
VP Business Reengineering: John S. Iannarelli
VP Operations Support: Kevin Rumbelow
VP Field Operations: Randy A. Hannigan
Media Relations: Brenda Blake
Auditors: PricewaterhouseCoopers LLP

LOCATIONS

HQ: AmeriGas Partners, L.P.
460 N. Gulph Rd., King of Prussia, PA 19406
Phone: 610-337-7000   **Fax:** 610-992-3259
Web: www.amerigas.com

PRODUCTS/OPERATIONS

2008 Sales

	$ mil.	% of total
Propane		
Retail	2,439.2	87
Wholesale	185.4	6
Other	190.6	7
Total	**2,815.2**	**100**

Selected Subsidiaries

AmeriGas Eagle Finance Corp.
AmeriGas Finance Corp.
AmeriGas Propane, L.P. (99%)
  AmeriGas Eagle Propane, L.P. (99%)
    AmeriGas Eagle Parts & Service, Inc.
  AmeriGas Propane Parts & Service, Inc.
  AmeriGas Eagle Propane, Inc.
    AmeriGas Eagle Holdings, Inc.
      Active Propane of Wisconsin LLC
AP Eagle Finance Corp.

COMPETITORS

Energy Transfer
Ferrellgas Partners
Piedmont Natural Gas
Southern States
Star Gas Partners
Suburban Propane

HISTORICAL FINANCIALS

Company Type: Public

Income Statement

FYE: September 30

	REVENUE ($ mil.)	NET INCOME ($ mil.)	NET PROFIT MARGIN	EMPLOYEES
9/08	2,815.2	158.0	5.6%	5,900
9/07	2,277.4	185.2	8.1%	6,200
9/06	2,119.3	90.2	4.3%	5,900
9/05	1,963.3	60.2	3.1%	6,000
9/04	1,775.9	90.9	5.1%	6,100
Annual Growth	**12.2%**	**14.8%**	**—**	**(0.8%)**

2008 Year-End Financials

Debt ratio: —
Return on equity: —
Cash ($ mil.): 11
Current ratio: 0.80
Long-term debt ($ mil.): 862
No. of shares (mil.): 57
Dividends
  Yield: 8.2%
  Payout: 92.6%
Market value ($ mil.): 1,736

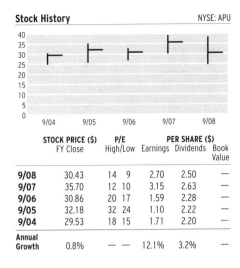

Stock History

NYSE: APU

	STOCK PRICE ($) FY Close	P/E High/Low		Earnings	PER SHARE ($) Dividends	Book Value
9/08	30.43	14	9	2.70	2.50	—
9/07	35.70	12	10	3.15	2.63	—
9/06	30.86	20	17	1.59	2.28	—
9/05	32.18	32	24	1.10	2.22	—
9/04	29.53	18	15	1.71	2.20	—
Annual Growth	**0.8%**	**—**	**—**	**12.1%**	**3.2%**	

AmerisourceBergen

AmerisourceBergen is *the* source for many of North America's pharmacies and health care providers. The company serves as a go-between for drugmakers and the pharmacies, doctors' offices, hospitals, and other health care providers who dispense drugs. Operating primarily in the US and Canada, it distributes generic, branded, and over-the-counter pharmaceuticals, as well as some medical supplies and other products, using its network of about 25 facilities. Its specialty distribution unit focuses on sensitive and complex biopharmaceuticals, such as cancer drugs, vaccines, and plasma products. The company also has some pharmaceutical packaging operations.

The company's main Pharmaceutical Distribution division includes its US and Canadian wholesaling operations, as well as its specialty distribution business and its specialty packaging group, which provides contracting packaging services to drug manufacturers in North America and the UK.

Its specialty distribution operations are growing at a fast clip, outpacing the growth experienced by the rest of the business. The unit delivers drugs for particular diseases (especially cancer) to the doctors who administer them. It also provides marketing and other services to drugmakers, helping them successfully launch new biotech drugs, among other things. The company acquired three specialty services businesses in 2006 and 2007, adding capabilities in infusion services, consulting, and reimbursement support services.

Acquisitions have also helped the company expand its reach to new customer segments and geographic markets. For example, its $180 million purchase of Bellco Health in 2007 increased its presence with independent community pharmacies in the New York City area. (Bellco's operations have since been parceled out under the wholesale and specialty distribution businesses.) In addition, AmerisourceBergen created its Canadian business through several key acquisitions in 2005 and 2006 that made it that country's second largest drug distributor. AmerisourceBergen further cemented its position in Canada in 2009 by acquiring Innomar Strategies for about $14 million. Innomar is a specialty pharmaceutical services company offering logistics management, patient assistance, and clinical research.

In 2007 AmerisourceBergen spun off its PharMerica subsidiary, which delivers pharmaceuticals and provides drug dispensing services in nursing homes and other long-term care institutions. It spun off the business as PharMerica Long-term Care and merged it with Kindred Healthcare's institutional pharmacy unit to form the new PharMerica entity. The combined entity became the second-largest institutional pharmacy operator in the US.

To further narrow its focus on its core operations, AmerisourceBergen sold its PMSI unit, which provided workers' compensation services to insurance companies and other health care payers, in 2008.

HISTORY

In 1977 Cleveland millionaire and horse racing enthusiast Tinkham Veale went into the drug wholesaling business. His company, Alco Standard (now IKON Office Solutions), already owned chemical, electrical, metallurgical, and mining companies, but by the late 1970s the company was pursuing a strategy of zeroing in on various types of distribution businesses.

Alco's first drug wholesaler purchase was The Drug House (Delaware and Pennsylvania); next was Duff Brothers (Tennessee). The company then bought further wholesalers in the South, East, and Midwest. Its modus operandi was to buy small, well-run companies for cash and Alco stock and leave the incumbent management in charge.

By the early 1980s Alco was the US's third-largest wholesale drug distributor and growing quickly (28% between 1983 and 1988) at a time of mass consolidation in the industry (the number of wholesalers dropped by half between 1980 and 1992). In 1985 Alco Standard spun off its drug distribution operations as Alco Health Services, retaining 60% ownership.

Alco Health boosted its sales above $1 billion mostly via acquisitions and expanded product lines. The company offered marketing and promotional help to its independent pharmacy customers (which were beleaguered by the growth of national discounters) and also targeted hospitals, nursing homes, and clinics.

The US was in the midst of its LBO frenzy in 1988, but an Alco management group failed in its attempt. Rival McKesson then tried to acquire Alco Health, but that deal fell through for antitrust reasons. Later in 1988 management turned for backing to Citicorp Venture Capital in another buyout attempt. This time the move succeeded, and a new holding company, Alco Health Distribution, was formed.

In 1993 Alco Health was named as a defendant in suits by independent pharmacies charging discriminatory pricing policies; a ruling the next year limited its liability. To move away from a reliance on independent drugstores, Alco Health began targeting government entities and others.

Alco Health went public as AmeriSource Health in 1995. Throughout the next year, AmeriSource made a series of acquisitions to move into related areas, including inventory

management technology, drugstore pharmaceutical supplies, and disease-management services for pharmacies.

In 1997 AmeriSource acquired Alabama-based Walker Drug for $140 million, adding 1,500 independent and chain drugstores in the Southeast to its customer list. That same year, McKesson once again made an offer to buy AmeriSource, this time for $2.4 billion, while two other major wholesale distributors, Cardinal Health and Bergen Brunswig, reached a similar pact. The deals were scrapped in 1998 when the Federal Trade Commission voted against both pacts, and a federal judge supported that decision.

In 2001 AmeriSource bought Bergen Brunswig, and the combined company renamed itself AmerisourceBergen.

In 2005, the company acquired Trent Drugs (Wholesale), a Canadian pharmaceutical wholesaler, and renamed it AmerisourceBergen Canada. In late 2006 it acquired Canada's Access M.D. (pharmaceutical support services) to expand its specialty services into Canada.

Also in 2006 the company acquired I.G.G. of America, a pharmacy focusing on blood derivative IVIG. It also purchased medical education and analytical research firm Network for Medical Communications & Research, LLC (NMCR). In March of that year, AmerisourceBergen acquired UK-based pharmaceutical packaging manufacturer Brecon Pharmaceuticals.

EXECUTIVES

Chairman: Richard C. Gozon, age 70
President, CEO, and Director: R. David (Dave) Yost, age 71
EVP and CFO; COO AmerisourceBergen Drug Corporation: Michael D. DiCandilo, age 47
EVP; President, AmerisourceBergen Specialty Group: Steven H. Collis, age 47
SVP and CIO; Leader Business Transformation: Thomas H. Murphy
SVP Operations: Denise Shane
SVP Retail Sales and Marketing: David W. (Dave) Neu
SVP Supply Chain: Antonio R. (Tony) Pera, age 51
SVP Strategy and Corporate Development: David M. Senior
SVP Human Resources: Jeanne B. Fisher, age 67
SVP Supply Chain Management: Leonardo (Len) DeCandia
SVP Health Systems Solutions: John Palumbo
SVP, General Counsel, and Secretary: John G. Chou, age 52
VP and Corporate Treasurer: J. F. (Jack) Quinn
VP and Corporate Controller: Tim G. Guttman
VP Corporate and Investor Relations: Michael N. Kilpatric
President, AmerisourceBergen Canada: Antoine Lefaivre
Director Corporate and Investor Relations: Barbara A. Brungess
Auditors: Ernst & Young LLP

LOCATIONS

HQ: AmerisourceBergen Corporation
1300 Morris Dr., Chesterbrook, PA 19087
Phone: 610-727-7000   **Fax:** 610-727-3600
Web: www.amerisourcebergen.com

PRODUCTS/OPERATIONS

2008 Sales

	$ mil.	% of total
Pharmaceutical Distribution	67,518.9	96
Bulk deliveries to customer warehouses	2,670.8	4
Total	**70,189.7**	**100**

Selected Subsidiaries and Units

AmerisourceBergen Drug Corporation
  AmerisourceBergen Canada Corporation
AmerisourceBergen Packaging Group
  Anderson Packaging
  Brecon Pharmaceutical Limited
  American Health Packaging
AmerisourceBergen Specialty Group

COMPETITORS

BioScrip
Cardinal Health
Covance
Covidien
Express Scripts
FFF Enterprises
H. D. Smith Wholesale Drug
Henry Schein
Kinray
McKesson
Owens & Minor
PSS World Medical
Quality King
UPS Logistics Technologies
US Oncology
Watson Pharmaceuticals

HISTORICAL FINANCIALS

Company Type: Public

Income Statement

FYE: September 30

	REVENUE ($ mil.)	NET INCOME ($ mil.)	NET PROFIT MARGIN	EMPLOYEES
9/08	70,189.7	250.6	0.4%	10,900
9/07	66,074.3	469.2	0.7%	11,300
9/06	61,203.1	467.7	0.8%	14,700
9/05	54,577.3	274.8	0.5%	13,400
9/04	53,179.0	468.4	0.9%	14,100
Annual Growth	**7.2%**	**(14.5%)**	**—**	**(6.2%)**

2008 Year-End Financials

Debt ratio: 43.8%	No. of shares (mil.): 297
Return on equity: 8.6%	Dividends
Cash ($ mil.): 878	Yield: 0.8%
Current ratio: 1.06	Payout: 19.5%
Long-term debt ($ mil.): 1,187	Market value ($ mil.): 5,596

Stock History

NYSE: ABC

	STOCK PRICE ($) FY Close	P/E High/Low		PER SHARE ($) Earnings	Dividends	Book Value
9/08	18.83	32	24	0.77	0.15	9.12
9/07	22.67	22	17	1.25	0.10	10.43
9/06	21.93	21	16	1.13	0.05	13.93
9/05	18.75	31	20	0.62	0.03	14.40
9/04	13.03	16	12	1.01	0.03	14.60
Annual Growth	**9.6%**	**—**	**—**	**(6.6%)**	**49.5%**	**(11.1%)**

Amgen Inc.

Amgen is among the biggest of the biotech big'uns, and it's determined to get even bigger. The company uses cellular biology and medicinal chemistry to target cancers, kidney ailments, inflammatory disorders, and metabolic diseases. Anti-anemia drugs Epogen and Aranesp account for more than one-third of its sales. Enbrel, another leading drug, treats rheumatoid arthritis and is one of the best-selling drugs in this multi-billion-dollar market. Amgen has a promising drug pipeline and marketing alliances with Japanese brewer and drugmaker Kirin, Johnson & Johnson, and other pharmaceutical companies.

In addition to being a key player in the rheumatoid arthritis market, top seller Enbrel also treats psoriasis and other related conditions. Enbrel's sales have climbed as the FDA has approved the drug to be used for these larger patient populations. Enbrel is co-marketed in the US and Canada with Wyeth, which also controls international marketing rights.

However, Aranesp's sales decreased by a total of about $1 billion in 2007 and 2008 following damaging reports of adverse effects of the drug on the heart, as well as increased risks for cancer patients. As a result, the FDA required changes in Aranesp's and Epogen's warning labels in early 2007, and Medicare restricted Aranesp's use in chemotherapy patients mid-year.

Amgen announced restructuring plans in 2007 to help absorb the sales losses. The company has cut its workforce by about 13%, rationalized its manufacturing facilities, and reduced R&D efforts. In 2008 it sold two noncore oncology products (Kepivance and Stemgen) and licensed rights to rheumatoid arthritis drug Kineret to Swedish firm Biovitrum for $130 million plus potential milestone payments. It also sold its Japanese unit and formed a co-development partnership with that country's top drugmaker, Takeda Pharmaceutical, in a deal worth up to $1.2 billion. Amgen continues to look for ways to lower capital expenditures.

Although many of the biotech's products enjoy years of patent protection, Amgen continues to launch new products that may best its best-sellers. Pipeline candidate denosumab is awaiting FDA approval for bone loss associated with hormone therapy in breast and prostate cancer patients; it is also being developed to treat osteoporosis. Other R&D efforts target cancer; inflammation; and neurological, metabolic, and bone disorders.

The company has also expanded its product line through acquisitions. A pair of privately held buys came midway through 2007: Ilypsa, a biotech working in renal disease care, and Alantos, which has been working on therapies for rheumatoid arthritis and for Type II diabetes.

HISTORY

Amgen was formed as Applied Molecular Genetics in 1980 by a group of scientists and venture capitalists to develop health care products based on molecular biology. George Rathmann, a VP at Abbott Laboratories and researcher at UCLA, became the company's CEO and first employee. Rathmann decided to develop a few potentially profitable products rather than conduct research. The firm initially raised $19 million.

Amgen operated close to bankruptcy until 1983, when company scientist Fu-Kuen Lin cloned the human protein erythropoietin (EPO), which stimulates the body's red blood cell production. Amgen went public that year. It formed a joint venture with Kirin Brewery in 1984 to develop and market EPO. The two firms also collaborated on recombinant human granulocyte colony stimulating factor (G-CSF, later called Neupogen), a protein that stimulates the immune system.

Amgen joined Johnson & Johnson subsidiary Ortho Pharmaceutical (now Ortho-McNeil Pharmaceutical) in a marketing alliance in 1985 and created a tie with Roche in 1988. Fortunes soared in 1989 when the FDA approved Epogen (the brand name of EPO) for anemia. (It is most commonly used to counter side effects of kidney dialysis.)

In 1991 Amgen received approval to market Neupogen to chemotherapy patients. A federal court ruling also gave it a US monopoly for EPO. The following year Amgen won another dispute, forcing a competitor to renounce its US patents for G-CSF. Amgen hired MCI veteran Kevin Sharer as president in 1992. Neupogen's usage was expanded in 1993 to include treatment of severe chronic neutropenia (low white blood cell count).

In 1993 Amgen became the first American biotech to gain a foothold in China through an agreement with Kirin Pharmaceuticals to sell Neupogen (under the name Gran) and Epogen there. The purchase of Synergen in 1994 added another research facility, accelerating the pace of and increasing the number of products in research and clinical trials. Amgen's new drug Stemgen for breast cancer patients undergoing chemotherapy was recommended for approval by an FDA advisory committee in 1998.

Amgen had to swallow a couple of tough legal pills in 1998. First, a dispute with J&J over Amgen's 1985 licensing agreement with Ortho Pharmaceutical ended when an arbiter ordered Amgen to pay about $200 million. Later that year, however, Amgen won a legal battle with J&J over the rights to a promising anemia drug.

In 2000 the firm won EU and US approval for Aranesp, an updated version of Epogen; Amgen in 2002 teamed with former J&J marketing partner Fresenius to sell Aranesp in Germany and take some market share away from J&J. Meanwhile, an arbitration committee found J&J had breached its contract with Amgen when it sold Procrit to the dialysis market, which Amgen had reserved for itself in their 1985 licensing deal.

In 2003 the company bought leukemia and rheumatoid arthritis drugs maker Immunex. As part of the FTC's blessing on the $10.3 billion union, Amgen and Immunex licensed some technologies to encourage competition. Merck Serono gained access to Enbrel data, and Regeneron Pharmaceuticals licensed some interleukin inhibitor rights.

In 2004 Amgen spent $1.3 billion to purchase the remaining 79% of cancer treatment technology maker Tularik that it did not already own.

In 2006 Amgen acquired Abgenix, a company that manufactures human therapeutic antibodies. Vectibix, Abgenix's treatment for colorectal cancer, was approved by the FDA that year. The company also acquired private company Avidia, a developer of treatments for inflammation and autoimmune diseases.

Romiplostim (Nplate) for autoimmune bleeding disorder ITP, or immune thrombocytopenic purpura, was given FDA approval in 2008.

EXECUTIVES

Chairman, President, and CEO: Kevin W. Sharer, age 61, $14,512,825 total compensation
EVP Operations: Fabrizio Bonanni, age 62, $6,268,960 total compensation
EVP and CFO: Robert (Bob) Bradway, age 46, $4,236,079 total compensation
EVP Research and Development: Roger M. Perlmutter, age 56, $5,343,213 total compensation
EVP Global Commercial Operations: George J. Morrow, age 57, $5,558,363 total compensation
SVP and CIO: Thomas (Tom) Flanagan, age 59
SVP and Chief Compliance Officer: Anna S. Richo, age 48
SVP and International Chief Medical Officer: Willard H. Dere
SVP Manufacturing: Madhavan Balachandran
SVP Research: David L. (Dave) Lacey
SVP Global Government and Corporate Affairs: David W. Beier, age 60
SVP Human Resources: Brian M. McNamee, age 52
SVP Research and Development: Joseph P. (Joe) Miletich, age 57
SVP, General Counsel, and Secretary: David J. Scott, age 56
SVP Global Regulatory Affairs and Safety: Paul R. Eisenberg
VP Finance and Chief Accounting Officer: Michael A. Kelly
VP Global Regulatory Affairs and Corporate Chief Medical Officer: Sean E. Harper
VP Corporate Communications and Philanthropy: Phyllis J. Piano
VP Investor Relations: Arvind K. Sood
President Amgen Foundation: Jean J. Lim
Senior Director Marketing Operations: Jeanne Fitzgerald
Auditors: Ernst & Young LLP

LOCATIONS

HQ: Amgen Inc.
1 Amgen Center Dr., Thousand Oaks, CA 91320
Phone: 805-447-1000   **Fax:** 805-447-1010
Web: www.amgen.com

2008 Sales

	$ mil.	% of total
US	11,772	78
Other countries	3,231	22
Total	**15,003**	**100**

PRODUCTS/OPERATIONS

2008 Sales

	$ mil.	% of total
Product sales		
Enbrel	3,598	24
Neulasta	3,318	22
Aranesp	3,137	21
Epogen	2,456	16
Neupogen	1,341	9
Sensipar	597	4
Other products	240	2
Other	316	2
Total	**15,003**	**100**

Products

Top sellers
  Enbrel (rheumatoid arthritis, psoriasis)
  Neulasta (chemotherapy-induced neutropenia — low white blood cells)
  Aranesp (chemotherapy-induced anemia and chronic renal failure anemia, sustained duration Epogen)
  Epogen (anemia in chronic renal failure)
  Neupogen (neutropenia)
  Sensipar (chronic kidney disease)

Other drugs
  Infergen (hepatitis C, licensed to InterMune)
  Kineret (rheumatoid arthritis, licensed to Biovitrum)
  Nplate (romiplostim for autoimmune bleeding disorder ITP, or immune thrombocytopenic purpura)
  Vectibix (monoclonal antibody for colorectal cancer)

COMPETITORS

Abbott Labs
Affymax
Astellas
AstraZeneca
Barr Pharmaceuticals
Baxter International
Bayer HealthCare Pharmaceuticals
Biogen Idec
Bristol-Myers Squibb
Cephalon
Chugai
Eli Lilly
Genentech
Genzyme
GlaxoSmithKline
Hospira
Human Genome Sciences
Johnson & Johnson
Kyowa Hakko Kirin
MedImmune
Merck
Merck KGaA
Millennium Pharmaceuticals
Novartis
Pfizer
QLT USA
Ratiopharm
Regeneron Pharmaceuticals
Roche Holding
Sanofi-Aventis
Schering-Plough
Shire
Stiefel Laboratories
Takeda Pharmaceutical
Teva Pharmaceuticals
Wyeth

HISTORICAL FINANCIALS

Company Type: Public

Income Statement

FYE: December 31

	REVENUE ($ mil.)	NET INCOME ($ mil.)	NET PROFIT MARGIN	EMPLOYEES
12/08	15,003.0	4,196.0	28.0%	16,900
12/07	14,771.0	3,166.0	21.4%	17,500
12/06	14,268.0	2,950.0	20.7%	20,100
12/05	12,430.0	3,674.0	29.6%	16,500
12/04	10,550.0	2,363.0	22.4%	14,500
Annual Growth	9.2%	15.4%	—	3.9%

2008 Year-End Financials

Debt ratio: 45.0%
Return on equity: 21.9%
Cash ($ mil.): 1,774
Current ratio: 3.12
Long-term debt ($ mil.): 9,176

No. of shares (mil.): 1,015
Dividends
  Yield: 0.0%
  Payout: —
Market value ($ mil.): 58,644

Stock History

NASDAQ (GS): AMGN

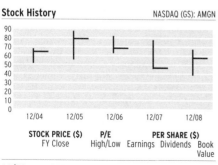

	STOCK PRICE ($) FY Close	P/E High/Low		PER SHARE ($) Earnings	Dividends	Book Value
12/08	57.75	17	10	3.90	0.00	20.08
12/07	46.44	27	16	2.82	0.00	17.60
12/06	68.31	33	26	2.48	0.00	18.67
12/05	78.86	30	19	2.93	0.00	20.14
12/04	64.15	37	29	1.81	0.00	19.40
Annual Growth	(2.6%)	—	—	21.2%	—	0.9%

Amkor Technology

Amkor Technology is more than amicable about lending a helping hand with chip packaging. The company claims a top spot in outsourcing packaging/assembly and testing for semiconductor manufacturers. Packaging includes dicing semiconductor wafers into separate chips, die bonding, wire bonding, and encapsulating chips in protective plastic. Amkor's testing procedures verify function, current, timing, and voltage. The company has hundreds of customers worldwide, including major semiconductor companies and electronics OEMs — Altera, Intel, IBM, LSI Corp., QUALCOMM, Samsung Electronics, STMicroelectronics, Texas Instruments, and Toshiba.

Amkor operates in a naturally competitive, cyclical industry. Its business is established largely on high-volume manufacturing processes and in developing new, tailored packaging and test technologies. Patents associated with packaging computer chips are scrutinized particularly closely. Amkor was hit in 2008 with $61 million in damages when an arbitration panel of the International Chamber of Commerce ruled that the company infringed Tessera's packaging license.

Whipsawed also by the global financial crisis, Amkor wrestles against a significant weakening in the semiconductor industry. The company's 10 largest customers account for approximately 50% of its sales. Spiraling cancellations, deferrals, and a slowdown in orders, plus a downward pressure on prices, drive the company to squeeze operating costs. Lowering headcount in the first three months of 2009 came on the heels of layoffs in 2008, which had eliminated about 1,500 workers, nearly 20% of its workforce.

Amkor has also diversified and expanded its production facilities to China, Japan, the Philippines, Singapore, South Korea, and Taiwan.

Founder and CEO James Kim and his family own about 45% of Amkor Technology. Based on the company's "management succession plan," Kim will become executive chairman, while Ken Joyce, former president and COO, will take over as CEO, effective October 1, 2009.

HISTORY

Kim Joo-Jin (James Kim), the oldest of seven children, came to the US from South Korea in 1955 to study business. A year later his father started electronics firm Anam Industrial, and in 1968 James Kim (chairman and CEO) founded Amkor (short for "American-Korean") Electronics as its US marketing agent.

To lessen its dependence on the volatile semiconductor market, Anam Industrial began diversifying in 1975, first into watch making, and eventually into banking, construction, environmental services, and electronics. (James Kim's wife, Agnes, began selling electronic watches and calculators from a kiosk near the family home in Pennsylvania; the business grew into the Electronics Boutique chain, now part of GameStop.)

James Kim joined the board of California semiconductor maker VLSI Technology (now part of NXP, formerly Philips Semiconductors) in 1982, leading the company into the application-specific integrated circuit market. Anam Industrial, meanwhile, continued to grow along with the semiconductor industry. By 1990 it had 50% of the world's semiconductor package assembly

business, and was only one unit of South Korean *chaebol* (family-run, non-legal conglomerate) Anam Group. That year the group took over a plant in Manila from Advanced Micro Devices and established Amkor/Anam Pilipinas on that site. It also acquired Scotland-based ITEQ Europe Ltd., which was Europe's leading semiconductor assembly contractor.

During the early 1990s Anam Industrial developed the tape-automated bonding manufacturing process. When the senior Kim retired in 1992, James Kim also became head of the Anam Group.

In 1993 Amkor licensed ball-grid array (BGA) packaging technology from Motorola. At the time BGA — in which tiny balls of solder are used for connections, instead of fragile lead wires — was still an emerging standard. By 1995 Amkor had become a leader in BGA packaging. That year the company announced that it would build the US's first independent BGA facility, in Arizona (it opened in 1999).

Anam Industrial began building its fourth semiconductor assembly plant in 1996, this one in the Philippines, with a production goal of 50 million chips per month. In 1997 Amkor opened its complementary metal oxide semiconductor wafer (CMOS) plant near Seoul, using Texas Instruments' technology, as part of a 10-year cooperative agreement. It also created Amkor Industries to consolidate the various Amkor companies. Also that year Amkor/Anam formed an agreement with Acer and Taiwan Semiconductor Manufacturing to build a semiconductor assembly and test facility in Taiwan.

Amkor went public in 1998. That year Anam Industrial changed its name to Anam Semiconductor and announced plans to divest its non-core businesses to focus on chip packaging. In 1999 Amkor opened a support center in France and bought a packaging plant in South Korea from Anam Semiconductor. In 2000 Amkor bought three more plants from Anam Semiconductor — which was still restructuring as its chaebol broke up — and upped its stake in Anam to 42%.

In 2002 Amkor acquired the Japan-based chip assembly business of Citizen Watch. In late 2002 and early 2003 Amkor exited the foundry business when it sold its stake in Anam to South Korean conglomerate (and foundry operator) Dongbu.

Early in 2004, Amkor expanded its capacity by acquiring an assembly and test plant from Taiwan-based FICTA Technology. Later that year, it struck a major agreement with IBM under which Amkor acquired IBM properties in China and Singapore, and will supply the computing giant with assembly and test services.

The US Securities and Exchange Commission in 2004 opened an informal inquiry into stock trading by certain Amkor insiders and other people, covering a period from June 2003 to July 2004. In 2005 the SEC probe was upgraded to a formal inquiry. The former general counsel of the company, who resigned in early 2005, was indicted in Pennsylvania for alleged violations of securities laws.

In mid-2006 Amkor's board created a special committee to review the company's historical practices in granting stock options from May 1998. The committee found, as had been the practice at many other high-tech firms, that the grant dates of certain stock options differed from the recorded dates of the grants and the actual dates of the grants. The company restated eight years of financial results as a result.

The SEC inquiry widened to include the stock-option granting practices.

EXECUTIVES

Chairman and CEO: James J. Kim, age 73,
$1,516,290 total compensation
President and COO: Kenneth T. (Ken) Joyce, age 61,
$1,017,185 total compensation
Corporate VP and CFO: Joanne Solomon, age 42,
$667,129 total compensation
**EVP, Chief Administrative Officer, General Counsel,
and Corporate Secretary:** Gil C. Tilly, age 55,
$912,721 total compensation
EVP Product Management Group: Eric R. Larson,
age 53
EVP Worldwide Sales: Michael J. (Mike) Lamble
EVP Assembly and Test: James (Jim) Fusaro, age 46
SVP Human Resources: Dave Lawton
**SVP Research and Development and Emerging
Technologies:** Tim Olson
VP Advanced Process Development: Miguel Jimarez
VP Business Development: Lee Smith
**President, Amkor Technology Korea and Head
Worldwide Manufacturing:** Jooho Kim
Investor Relations: Claire E. McAdams
Manager Marketing Communication: Shellene Garner
Auditors: PricewaterhouseCoopers LLP

LOCATIONS

HQ: Amkor Technology, Inc.
1900 S. Price Rd., Chandler, AZ 85286
Phone: 480-821-5000   **Fax:** 480-821-8276
Web: www.amkor.com

2008 Sales

	$ mil.	% of total
US	974.3	37
Singapore	657.5	25
Japan	240.8	9
Taiwan	194.3	7
China & Hong Kong	85.7	3
South Korea	126.6	5
Other countries	379.4	14
Total	**2,658.6**	**100**

PRODUCTS/OPERATIONS

2008 Sales

	$ mil.	% of total
Packaging services		
Laminate	1,066	40
Leadframe	753	28
Flip chip & wafer-level processing	526	20
Testing services	314	12
Total	**2,659**	**100**

Products and Services

Chip Packaging
Advanced leadframe (plastic mold with thermal,
electrical characteristics)
Laminate (plastic or tape rather than leadframe
substrate)
Traditional leadframe (plastic mold with metal leads)
Test Services (analog, digital logic, and mixed-signal
chips)

COMPETITORS

Advanced Semiconductor Engineering
ASAT Holdings
ASE Test
ChipMOS
Kingston Technology
PSi Technologies
Siliconware Precision Industries
STATS ChipPAC
Tessera
UTAC

HISTORICAL FINANCIALS

Company Type: Public

Income Statement

FYE: December 31

	REVENUE ($ mil.)	NET INCOME ($ mil.)	NET PROFIT MARGIN	EMPLOYEES
12/08	2,658.6	(456.7)	—	20,500
12/07	2,739.4	219.9	8.0%	21,600
12/06	2,728.6	170.1	6.2%	22,700
12/05	2,099.9	(136.9)	—	24,000
12/04	1,901.3	(37.5)	—	22,033
Annual Growth	**8.7%**	**—**	**—**	**(1.8%)**

2008 Year-End Financials

Debt ratio: 606.7%
Return on equity: —
Cash ($ mil.): 424
Current ratio: 1.55
Long-term debt ($ mil.): 1,439

No. of shares (mil.): 183
Dividends
Yield: 0.0%
Payout: —
Market value ($ mil.): 399

Stock History

NASDAQ (GS): AMKR

	STOCK PRICE ($) FY Close	P/E High/Low		PER SHARE ($) Earnings	Dividends	Book Value
12/08	2.18	—	—	(2.50)	0.00	1.30
12/07	8.53	15	7	1.11	0.00	3.58
12/06	9.34	15	5	0.90	0.00	2.15
12/05	5.60	—	—	(0.78)	0.00	1.23
12/04	6.68	—	—	(0.21)	0.00	2.02
Annual Growth	**(24.4%)**	**—**	**—**	**—**	**—**	**(10.5%)**

AMR Corporation

AMR knows America's spacious skies — and lots of others. Its main subsidiary is American Airlines, one of the largest airlines in the world. Together with sister company American Eagle and regional carriers that operate as American Connection, American Airlines serves some 250 destinations in about 40 countries in the Americas, Europe, and the Asia/Pacific region. The overall fleet exceeds 900 aircraft; American Airlines operates about 625 jets. The carrier extends its geographic reach through code-sharing arrangements. It is part of the Oneworld global marketing alliance, along with British Airways, Cathay Pacific, Iberia, Qantas, and other airlines.

American Airlines hopes to gain revenue by expanding its services to destinations in the Asia/Pacific region, particularly in China, where the number of direct flights from the US is limited by law. The carrier received approval to begin Chicago-to-Beijing service in 2009 but pushed it back to 2010, citing high fuel prices and a weakening global economy.

The carrier also is hoping to strengthen its transatlantic operations, and in August 2008 American Airlines formed an alliance with British Airways and Iberia on flights between North America and Europe. The deal, which

would require approval from antitrust authorities, would go beyond code-sharing and enable the carriers to cooperate in setting prices and schedules. Finnish carrier Finnair and Middle-East carrier Royal Jordanian also are part of the agreement. Air France-KLM, Delta, and Northwest have formed a similar pact.

Unlike peers such as Delta, Northwest, UAL, and US Airways, AMR was able to navigate the airline industry downturn that followed the September 11, 2001, terrorist attacks without making a stop in bankruptcy court. American Airlines reduced its capacity, its fleet, and its workforce and won concessions from its unions; in the meantime, the parent company lost money for five straight years — and piled up debt — before posting profits in 2006 and 2007.

The carrier reduced its domestic capacity by about 12% in late 2008, which was expected to result in the retirement of about 75 aircraft and the elimination of thousands of jobs. In addition, American Airlines imposed new charges for checked luggage, which helped the carrier post more revenues in 2008. In fact, "other revenues" was the biggest growth area for AMR, increasing about 9% or $183 million from 2007. Besides fees for checked baggage, items in the "other" category include services charges, flight change charges, onboard food sales, upgrades to first class on the day of departure, and day-passes to the carrier's Admirals Club lounge.

Even as the company works to cut costs and boost revenue, the carrier has had to address maintenance issues. After an inspection by the Federal Aviation Administration found problems with the way wiring was bundled in aircraft wheel wells, American Airlines canceled more than 3,000 flights over several days in April 2008 in order to re-inspect its fleet of MD-80s. In a separate case, the FAA in August 2008 proposed a $7.1 million fine against American Airlines for allegedly flying airplanes that had not been properly maintained and for allegedly failing to follow drug- and alcohol-testing procedures for employees. The carrier is contesting the agency's findings.

HISTORY

In 1929 Sherman Fairchild created a New York City holding company called the Aviation Corporation (AVCO), combining some 85 small airlines in 1930 to create American Airways. In 1934 the company had its first dose of financial trouble after the government suspended private airmail for months. Corporate raider E. L. Cord took over and named the company American Airlines.

Cord put former AVCO manager C. R. Smith in charge, and American became the leading US airline in the late 1930s. The Douglas DC-3, built to Smith's specifications, was introduced by American in 1936 and became the first commercial airliner to pay its way on passenger revenues alone.

After WWII American bought Amex Airlines, which flew to northern Europe, but another financial crisis prompted Amex's sale in 1950. The airline introduced Sabre, the first automated reservations system, in 1964. Smith left American four years later to serve as secretary of commerce in the Johnson administration.

In 1979, the year after airline industry deregulation, American moved to Dallas/Fort Worth. Former CFO Bob Crandall became president in 1980 (and later, CEO). Using Sabre to track mileage, he introduced the industry's first frequent-flier program (AAdvantage). In 1982

American created AMR as its holding company. After acquiring commuter airline Nashville Eagle in 1987, AMR established American Eagle.

In 1996 AMR spun off nearly 20% of Sabre. Crandall retired in 1998 (after a major airline strike was averted only by President Clinton's intervention) and was replaced by Donald Carty. American also bought Reno Air, and concerns about integrating the smaller airline culminated in American pilots calling in sick for a week in 1999. The union was later ordered to pay almost $46 million in compensation.

To focus on its airlines, AMR sold its executive aviation services, ground services, and call center units in 1999. That year nine people died when an American jet tried to land in Arkansas during a storm and slid off the runway. Also in 2000 AMR spun off the rest of Sabre. In 2001 AMR moved to become a stronger competitor to UAL by buying the assets of troubled rival TWA for $742 million.

Also in 2001 American Airlines lost two aircraft that were used in the September 11 terrorist attacks on the World Trade Center in New York and the Pentagon in Washington, DC. In anticipation of reduced demand for air travel, AMR announced a 20% reduction in flights and layoffs of at least 20,000 employees. Later that year another American Airlines jet crashed in New York, killing all 260 passengers.

In August 2002 the carrier set about reducing its capacity by 9% and reducing its workforce by some 7,000 employees. It also simplified its fleet by retiring its Fokker-100 jets ahead of schedule.

Carty resigned in 2003 after rankling union leaders by failing to disclose executive compensation perquisites during labor negotiations aimed at keeping the airline giant out of bankruptcy. Carty was replaced as CEO by former president and COO Gerard Arpey. Director Edward Brennan, a former chairman and CEO of Sears, Roebuck & Co., was named non-executive chairman. Brennan relinquished the chairman role to Arpey in 2004, but remained a director.

To take advantage of demand for travel to the Asia/Pacific region, American Airlines began nonstop service from Chicago to Shanghai in April 2006.

EXECUTIVES

Chairman, President, and CEO, AMR and American Airlines: Gerard J. Arpey, age 50, $3,419,239 total compensation
EVP Finance and Planning and CFO, AMR and American Airlines: Thomas W. Horton, age 47, $2,231,878 total compensation
EVP Marketing, AMR and American Airlines: Daniel P. Garton, age 51, $2,068,792 total compensation
EVP and President, American Eagle: Peter M. Bowler, age 54
EVP; EVP Operations, American Airlines: Robert W. (Bob) Reding, age 59, $1,928,269 total compensation
SVP Information Technology and CIO, American Airlines: Monte E. Ford, age 49
SVP, General Counsel, and Chief Compliance Officer; SVP and General Counsel, American Airlines: Gary F. Kennedy Sr., age 53, $1,430,746 total compensation
SVP Customer Relationship Marketing and Reservations, American Airlines: Isabella D. (Bella) Goren
SVP Government Affairs, AMR and American Airlines: William K. (Will) Ris Jr.
SVP Airport Services, American Airlines: Thomas R. (Tom) Del Valle
SVP Technical Operations, American Eagle: David L. (Dave) Campbell
SVP International, American Airlines: Craig S. Kreeger

SVP Maintenance and Engineering, American Airlines: Carmine J. Romano
SVP Customer Service, American Eagle: Jonathan D. (Jon) Snook
SVP Human Resources, American Airlines: Jeffery J. Brundage, age 55
VP Corporate Communications and Advertising, American Airlines: Roger C. Frizzell
VP Global Human Resources Services, American Airlines: Denise Lynn
Corporate Secretary: Kenneth W. Wimberly
Auditors: Ernst & Young LLP

LOCATIONS

HQ: AMR Corporation
4333 Amon Carter Blvd., Fort Worth, TX 76155
Phone: 817-963-1234   **Fax:** 817-967-4162
Web: www.aa.com

2008 Revenues

	$ mil.	% of total
US	14,135	59
Latin America	4,927	21
Atlantic	3,671	16
Pacific	1,033	4
Total	**23,766**	**100**

American Airlines Hub Locations

Chicago (O'Hare)
Dallas/Fort Worth
Miami
St. Louis
San Juan, Puerto Rico

PRODUCTS/OPERATIONS

2008 Revenues

	$ mil.	% of total
Passenger		
American Airlines	18,234	77
Regional affiliates	2,486	10
Cargo	874	4
Other	2,172	9
Total	**23,766**	**100**

COMPETITORS

Air France-KLM	Mesa Air
AirTran Holdings	Northwest Airlines
Alaska Air	Pinnacle Airlines
China Southern Airlines	SkyWest
Continental Airlines	Southwest Airlines
Delta Air Lines	UAL
FedEx	UPS
Frontier Airlines	US Airways
Greyhound	Virgin Atlantic Airways
JetBlue	

HISTORICAL FINANCIALS

Company Type: Public

Income Statement

FYE: December 31

	REVENUE ($ mil.)	NET INCOME ($ mil.)	NET PROFIT MARGIN	EMPLOYEES
12/08	23,766.0	(2,071.0)	—	84,100
12/07	22,935.0	504.0	2.2%	85,500
12/06	22,563.0	231.0	1.0%	86,600
12/05	20,712.0	(861.0)	—	88,400
12/04	18,645.0	(761.0)	—	92,100
Annual Growth	6.3%	—	—	(2.2%)

2008 Year-End Financials

Debt ratio: —
Return on equity: —
Cash ($ mil.): 191
Current ratio: 0.63
Long-term debt ($ mil.): 9,001
No. of shares (mil.): 280
Dividends
Yield: 0.0%
Payout: —
Market value ($ mil.): 2,986

Stock History

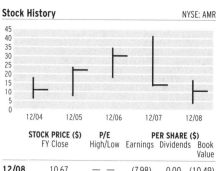

NYSE: AMR

	STOCK PRICE ($) FY Close	P/E High/Low		PER SHARE ($) Earnings	Dividends	Book Value
12/08	10.67	—	—	(7.98)	0.00	(10.49)
12/07	14.03	23	8	1.78	0.00	9.49
12/06	30.23	35	19	0.98	0.00	(2.17)
12/05	22.23	—	—	(5.21)	0.00	(5.28)
12/04	10.95	—	—	(4.74)	0.00	(2.08)
Annual Growth	(0.6%)	—	—	—	—	—

Anadarko Petroleum

Anadarko Petroleum has ventured beyond its original area of operation — the Anadarko Basin — to explore for, develop, produce, and market oil, natural gas, natural gas liquids, and related products worldwide. The large independent company has proved reserves of 1 billion barrels of crude oil and 8 trillion cu. ft. of natural gas, more than 70% of which are located in the Continental US. Other activities include coal, trona, and mineral mining. Anadarko operates seven gas-gathering systems in the mid-continent. Internationally, the company has substantial oil and gas interests in Algeria's Sahara Desert, Venezuela, and western Canada.

In 2008 it spun off midstream unit Western Gas Partners, though it still held onto about 60% of the company. In 2009 it sold $210 million of midstream assets located in the Powder River Basin to Western Gas Partners.

In the years following its acquisitions of Kerr McGee and Western Gas Resources — for which Anadarko spent almost $25 billion in 2006 — the company went on something of a selling spree. Anadarko eventually pocketed more than $15 billion from the sale of assets in Canada, the Gulf of Mexico, the Mid-Continent region of the US, and the Middle East. Those deals greatly helped the company in its quest to lower debt.

HISTORY

In 1959 the Panhandle Eastern Pipe Line Company set up Anadarko (named after the Anadarko Basin) to carry out its gas exploration and production activities. The new company was also formed to take advantage of a ruling by the Federal Power Commission (now the Federal Energy Regulatory Commission) to set lower price ceilings for producing properties owned by pipeline companies.

The company grew rapidly during the early 1960s, largely because of its gas-rich namesake. It bought Ambassador Oil of Fort Worth, Texas, in 1965 — adding interests in 19 states in the US and Canada. The firm also relocated from Kansas to Fort Worth.

Anadarko began offshore exploration in the Gulf of Mexico in 1970 and focused there early in the decade. After moving to Houston in 1974, Anadarko increased its oil exploration activities when the energy crisis led to higher gas prices. A deal with Amoco (now part of BP) led to major finds on Matagorda Island, off the Texas coast, in the early 1980s.

To realize shareholder value, Panhandle spun off Anadarko in 1986 — separating transmission from production. At the time more than 90% of Anadarko's reserves were natural gas. The next year Anadarko made new discoveries in Canada.

Low domestic natural gas prices led Anadarko overseas. It signed a production-sharing agreement with Algeria's national oil and gas firm, SONATRACH, in 1989. The deal covered 5.1 million acres in the Sahara. Two years later Anadarko began operating in the South China Sea and in Alaska's North Slope.

Back home, the company spent $190 million in 1992 for properties in West Texas, and in 1993 Anadarko began divesting noncore assets. Along with some of its partners, the company also discovered oil in the Mahogany Field offshore Louisiana. Production from Mahogany began in 1996.

In 1997 Anadarko added exploration acreage in the North Atlantic and Tunisia. The next year it made two major oil and gas discoveries in the Gulf of Mexico. Anadarko decided to sell some of its noncore Algerian assets in 1999 and teamed up with Texaco (later acquired by Chevron) in a joint exploration program in the Gulf of Mexico, offshore Louisiana. The next year the company acquired Union Pacific Resources in a $5.7 billion stock swap.

Anadarko expanded its presence in western Canada in 2001 by buying Berkley Petroleum for more than $1 billion in cash and assumed debt; a smaller purchase that year, Gulfstream Resources Canada, landed Anadarko in the Persian Gulf and added 70 million barrels of oil equivalent to its reserves.

EXECUTIVES

Chairman Emeritus: Robert J. Allison Jr., age 70
Chairman, President, and CEO: James T. (Jim) Hackett, age 55, $21,336,876 total compensation
SVP and COO: R. A. (Al) Walker, age 52, $6,717,560 total compensation
SVP Finance and CFO: Robert G. Gwin, age 46, $879,686 total compensation
SVP, General Counsel, and Chief Administrative Officer: Robert K. (Bobby) Reeves Sr., age 52, $4,669,974 total compensation
SVP Worldwide Exploration: Robert P. (Bob) Daniels, age 50
SVP Worldwide Operations: Charles A. (Chuck) Meloy Sr., age 49, $6,873,210 total compensation
VP and Chief Information Officer: Mario M. Coll III, age 48
VP, Chief Accounting Officer, and Controller: M. Cathy Douglas, age 53
VP Government Relations: Gregory M. (Greg) Pensabene, age 59
VP Finance and Treasurer: Bruce W. Busmire, age 52
VP, Deputy General Counsel, and Corporate Secretary: David L. Siddall
VP Investor Relations and Communications: John Colglazier
Corporate Controller: Michael C. Pearl, age 36
Auditors: KPMG LLP

LOCATIONS

HQ: Anadarko Petroleum Corporation
1201 Lake Robbins Dr., The Woodlands, TX 77380
Phone: 832-636-1000   **Fax:** 832-636-8220
Web: www.anadarko.com

2008 Sales

	% of total
US	82
Algeria	15
Other countries	3
Total	**100**

PRODUCTS/OPERATIONS

2008 Sales

	$ mil.	% of total
Oil & Gas Exploration & Production	14,270	89
Midstream	1,356	8
Marketing	496	3
Adjustments	(399)	—
Total	**15,723**	**100**

COMPETITORS

Adams Resources	EOG
Apache	Exxon
BP	Hunt Consolidated
Cabot Oil & Gas	Key Energy
Chesapeake Energy	National Fuel Gas
Chevron	Noble Energy
Cimarex	Pioneer Natural Resources
ConocoPhillips	Royal Dutch Shell
Devon Energy	

HISTORICAL FINANCIALS

Company Type: Public

Income Statement

FYE: December 31

	REVENUE ($ mil.)	NET INCOME ($ mil.)	NET PROFIT MARGIN	EMPLOYEES
12/08	15,723.0	3,261.0	20.7%	4,300
12/07	15,892.0	3,781.0	23.8%	4,000
12/06	10,187.0	4,854.0	47.6%	5,200
12/05	7,100.0	2,471.0	34.8%	3,300
12/04	6,067.0	1,606.0	26.5%	3,300
Annual Growth	**26.9%**	**19.4%**	**—**	**6.8%**

2008 Year-End Financials

Debt ratio: 57.8%
Return on equity: 18.6%
Cash ($ mil.): 2,360
Current ratio: 0.97
Long-term debt ($ mil.): 10,867

No. of shares (mil.): 491
Dividends
  Yield: 0.9%
  Payout: 5.2%
Market value ($ mil.): 18,910

Stock History

NYSE: APC

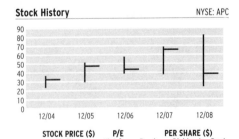

	STOCK PRICE ($) FY Close	P/E High/Low		PER SHARE ($) Earnings	Dividends	Book Value
12/08	38.55	12	4	6.97	0.36	40.87
12/07	65.69	8	5	8.08	0.36	35.58
12/06	43.52	11	4	10.46	0.36	32.43
12/05	94.75	20	12	5.20	0.36	24.03
12/04	64.81	23	15	3.18	0.28	20.19
Annual Growth	**(12.2%)**	**—**	**—**	**21.7%**	**6.5%**	**19.3%**

Analog Devices

Analog Devices, Inc. (ADI) is fluent in both analog and digital. The company is a leading maker of analog (linear and mixed-signal) and digital integrated circuits (ICs), including digital signal processors (DSPs). Its linear ICs translate real-world phenomena such as pressure, temperature, and sound into digital signals. ADI's thousands of chip designs are used in industrial applications, medical and scientific instrumentation, communications equipment, computers, and consumer electronics devices. ADI's chips go into high-tech goods from such companies as Alcatel-Lucent, Dell, Ericsson, Philips, Siemens, and Sony.

Reacting to lower sales, common among semiconductor suppliers in the global economic downturn, ADI aggressively reduced expenses in late 2008 and early 2009. The company plans to consolidate its two US wafer fabrication facilities and was already in the process of consolidating its two fabs in Ireland.

Throughout a brutal years-long market downturn that affected all parts of the semiconductor industry in the early 21st century, ADI continued to keep R&D spending high to promote new product development. The company is among the most consistently profitable ventures in the semiconductor industry.

ADI leveraged its early analog know-how by integrating mixed-signal technology onto DSPs in time to catch the Internet tidal wave. At the same time, the company widened its focus, pioneering tiny silicon devices called micromachines or MEMS, primarily accelerometers used in air bags.

In early 2008 ADI sold the assets of its Othello radio and SoftFone baseband chipset product lines, as well as certain cellular handset baseband support operations, to MediaTek for approximately $350 million in cash. The company will continue to support the wireless handset market through its high-performance analog chips, microelectromechanical systems (MEMS) devices, and programmable DSPs. Also in 2008 ADI sold its CPU voltage regulation and PC thermal monitoring product line to ON Semiconductor for about $184 million.

HISTORY

Ray Stata, an MIT graduate and Hewlett-Packard veteran, and Matthew Lorber founded Analog Devices, Inc. (ADI) in 1965 to make amplifiers for strengthening electrical signals. The company soon expanded into converters used to control machinery and take measurements, and went public in 1968. Lorber left the company that year and went on to found several startups, including Printer Technology, Torque Systems, and Copley Controls.

In 1969 ADI began manufacturing semiconductors. Stata become chairman and CEO in 1973. In 1977 he launched the influential Massachusetts High Technology Council to fight taxes that he felt were restricting the growth of high-tech firms.

During the early 1980s ADI acquired stakes in several technology firms, including Charles River Data Systems (microcomputer hardware and software), Jupiter Systems (color graphics computers), Photodyne (fiber-optics test instruments), and Tau-Tron (high-speed digital instrumentation). In the mid-1980s ADI's profits declined as Japanese competitors acquired market share. In 1990 the company acquired Precision Monolithics, a maker of passive electronic components. The next year ADI introduced the world's first commercial micromachine, an automotive air-bag trigger.

In 1992 ADI formed a joint venture with Hewlett-Packard to develop mixed-signal chips. The company extended its global reach in 1996 by acquiring Mosaic Microsystems, a UK radio-frequency design company. It also formed Washington State-based chip producer WaferTech with Taiwan Semiconductor Manufacturing and others. Also in 1996 company veteran Jerald Fishman became ADI's president and CEO; Stata remained chairman.

In 1998 ADI acquired MediaLight, a Toronto-based developer of digital subscriber line software. ADI also sold its disk drive integrated circuit business to Adaptec for about $27 million. The next year the company bought White Mountain DSP (development software for DSPs) and Edinburgh Portable Compilers (software compilers for embedded applications).

In 2000 and early 2001 ADI completed a string of acquisitions, headlined by the purchases of Ireland-based BCO Technologies ($163 million; wafers for optical components) and Chiplogic ($68 million; broadband networking chips for voice and video). ADI sold its 4% stake in WaferTech to joint venture partner TSMC in 2000.

Ray Stata garnered the chip industry's highest honor in 2001 when he received the Semiconductor Industry Association's Robert N. Noyce Award, which is named after the late industry titan who co-founded Intel and co-invented the integrated circuit.

The Stata Center for Computer, Information, and Intelligence Sciences was opened at MIT in 2004. The distinctive building, designed by Gehry Partners, was built on the site of the institute's legendary "Building 20," a structure put up during WWII that was intended to be temporary but went on to house various programs for 55 years.

In late 2005 ADI and CEO Jerry Fishman tentatively reached a settlement with the US Securities and Exchange Commission on the company's practices in granting stock options from 1998 to 2001. Without admitting or denying the commission's findings from its year-long investigation, the company agreed to pay a civil penalty of $3 million, while Fishman paid $1 million.

Early in 2006 ADI sold its network processor business to Ikanos Communications for $30 million in cash. The product line accounted for about 2% of ADI's sales.

The SEC stock-options probe led to the company receiving a subpoena in 2006 from a federal grand jury in New York investigating backdating and other options abuses. ADI promised to cooperate with the investigation, which targeted numerous other publicly held companies, as well. The company and CEO Jerry Fishman reached a final settlement with the SEC in 2008.

Later in 2006 ADI acquired Integrant Technologies, a Korean company specializing in high-performance analog circuits for reconfigurable radio-frequency signal processing, for about $127 million in cash. Integrant's low-power radio tuners allowed computers, consumer electronics devices, and mobile handsets to receive digital TV and digital radio broadcasts.

EXECUTIVES

Chairman: Ray Stata, age 74
President, CEO, and Director:
Jerald G. (Jerry) Fishman, age 63,
$8,605,574 total compensation
VP and CFO: David A. (Dave) Zinsner, age 40
VP Research and Development and CTO:
Samuel H. Fuller, age 62
VP, Controller, and Chief Accounting Officer:
Seamus Brennan
VP Worldwide Manufacturing: Robert R. (Rob) Marshall, age 54, $1,421,046 total compensation
VP and General Manager, Analog Semiconductor Components: Robert P. (Robbie) McAdam, age 57, $1,390,487 total compensation
VP Worldwide Sales: Vincent Roche, age 48, $1,357,653 total compensation
VP, General Counsel, and Secretary:
Margaret K. (Marnie) Seif, age 47
VP High Speed Signal Processing: John Hussey
VP Precision Signal Processing: Richard (Dick) Meaney
VP Global Accounts: Alex Glass
VP Planning, Logistics, and Quality:
Gerry (Ger) Dundon
VP Power Management Products: Peter Henry
VP Radio Frequency and Networking Components:
Peter Real
VP Human Resources: William (Bill) Matson, age 49
VP Japan Sales; Chairman and President, Analog Devices K.K.: Osamu Mawatari
Treasurer and Director Mergers and Acquisitions:
William A. Martin
Director Corporate Communications: Maria Tagliaferro
Auditors: Ernst & Young LLP

LOCATIONS

HQ: Analog Devices, Inc.
1 Technology Way, Norwood, MA 02062
Phone: 781-329-4700 **Fax:** 781-461-4482
Web: www.analog.com

Analog Devices has facilities in Austria, Belgium, China, Denmark, Finland, France, Germany, Hong Kong, India, Ireland, Israel, Italy, Japan, the Netherlands, the Philippines, Singapore, South Korea, Sweden, Taiwan, the UK, and the US.

2008 Sales

	% of total
Asia/Pacific	
Japan	19
China	16
Other countries	15
Europe	26
Americas	
US	20
Other countries	4
Total	**100**

PRODUCTS/OPERATIONS

2008 Sales

	$ mil.	% of total
Analog signal processing products		
Converters	1,191.0	46
Amplifiers	590.3	23
Other analog	393.8	15
Power management & reference	143.7	6
Digital signal processor products		
General-purpose DSPs	234.9	9
Other DSPs	29.2	1
Total	**2,582.9**	**100**

2008 Sales by Market

	$ mil.	% of total
Industrial	1,274.9	49
Communications	637.3	25
Consumer	544.3	21
Computer	126.4	5
Total	**2,582.9**	**100**

Selected Products

Integrated Circuits (ICs)
  Analog
    Amplifiers
    Analog signal processing devices
    Comparators
    Data converters
    Interface circuits
    Power management ICs
    Voltage references
  Digital signal processing (DSP) devices
  Multifunction mixed-signal devices
Assembled Products
  Hybrid products (mounted and packaged chips and
    discrete components)
  Multichip modules
  Printed circuit board modules
Micromachined Products
  Accelerometers

COMPETITORS

Analogic
Broadcom
Cirrus Logic
Conexant Systems
Custom Sensors & Technologies
DENSO
DSP Group
Fairchild Semiconductor
Freescale Semiconductor
Hittite Microwave
Infineon Technologies
Integrated Device Technology
International Rectifier
Intersil
Linear Technology
Marvell Technology
Maxim Integrated Products
Micrel
Microchip Technology
Microsemi
National Semiconductor
NXP
ON Semiconductor
Panasonic Electronic Devices
Qualcomm CDMA
Robert Bosch
ROHM
Semtech
Silicon Image
Silicon Labs
Siliconix
Skyworks
Standard Microsystems
STMicroelectronics
Texas Instruments

HISTORICAL FINANCIALS

Company Type: Public

Income Statement			FYE: Saturday nearest October 31	
	REVENUE ($ mil.)	NET INCOME ($ mil.)	NET PROFIT MARGIN	EMPLOYEES
10/08	2,582.9	786.3	30.4%	9,000
10/07	2,546.1	496.9	19.5%	9,600
10/06	2,573.2	549.5	21.4%	9,800
10/05	2,388.8	414.8	17.4%	8,800
10/04	2,633.8	570.7	21.7%	8,900
Annual Growth	(0.5%)	8.3%	—	0.3%

2008 Year-End Financials

Debt ratio: —
Return on equity: 33.0%
Cash ($ mil.): 594
Current ratio: 3.67
Long-term debt ($ mil.): —
No. of shares (mil.): 292
Dividends
  Yield: 3.6%
  Payout: 28.7%
Market value ($ mil.): 6,227

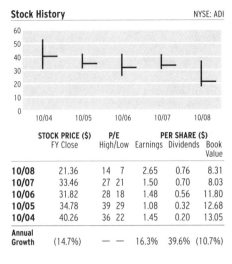

	STOCK PRICE ($) FY Close	P/E High/Low		PER SHARE ($) Earnings	Dividends	Book Value
10/08	21.36	14	7	2.65	0.76	8.31
10/07	33.46	27	21	1.50	0.70	8.03
10/06	31.82	28	18	1.48	0.56	11.80
10/05	34.78	39	29	1.08	0.32	12.68
10/04	40.26	36	22	1.45	0.20	13.05
Annual Growth	(14.7%)	—	—	16.3%	39.6%	(10.7%)

Anixter International

Pssst, need to get wired? Anixter International's got connections. The company is a major global distributor of communication products used to connect voice, video, data, and security systems. It sells more than 400,000 products, including electrical and electronic wire and cable, fasteners, and security system components, through a worldwide network of sales and distribution centers. The company obtains products from more than 5,000 suppliers, and serves such industries as education, government, health care, manufacturing, retail, and transportation. It also supplies contractors and integrators who perform installation and maintenance on communications networks and data centers.

Not content to be a traditional distributor whose sole job is to deliver products to customers, Anixter adds value to its role as a supplier with product application knowledge and quality assurance capabilities.

While the company's growth is primarily driven organically through product expansion and supplier services, it doesn't hesitate to go after niche acquisition opportunities to expand its technical expertise. In 2008 Anixter acquired the assets and operations of Quality Screw & Nut (also known as QSN Industries) and its Quality Screw de Mexico subsidiary for about $80 million. The acquisition augments Anixter's geographic reach, giving it nearly 20 additional facilities.

Later that year the company purchased the assets and operations of World Class Wire & Cable for some $62 million. It also bought France's Sofrasar SA and Germany's Camille Gergen GmbH & Co., KG and Camille Gergen Verwaltungs GmbH for a total of around $40 million in cash and approximately $19 million in assumed debt; the firms are fastener distributors.

Subsidiaries Anixter Fasteners and Anixter Pentacon supply fasteners and aerospace hardware, respectively, to OEMs throughout the world.

Billionaire financier Samuel Zell, Anixter's chairman, holds around 14% of Anixter International. Ariel Capital Management holds another 19% of the company's stock.

HISTORY

Anixter International was founded in 1957 by two brothers, Alan and Bill Anixter, along with a small group of employees in Evanston, Illinois. The company was known as Anixter Brothers at the time and supplied distributors and wholesalers looking for an alternative to buying wire and cable in bulk quantities directly from manufacturers.

In 1967 the company went public on the American Stock Exchange. Anixter became an international company when Anixter United Kingdom was formed in 1972. That decade saw its continued growth throughout North America.

In 1987 holding company Itel bought Anixter, which had since moved into the data communications business to round out its expertise in electrical wire and cable. Itel was led by Chicago financier Samuel Zell, who had become chairman in 1985.

Zell and vice chairman Rod Dammeyer, former Household International CFO, acquired Great Lakes International (marine dredging, 1986), Anixter Bros. (wire and cable, 1986), Pullman (railcars, 1988), and a minority stake in Santa Fe Southern Pacific (railroad, 1988). Other acquisitions included Flexi-Van Leasing (1987), the assets of Evans Asset Holding (railcars, 1987), and B.C. Hydro (rail freight line, 1988). By 1988 Itel was North America's leading railcar leasing company.

In the 1990s Itel repositioned itself, selling its container-leasing business (1990) and its Itel Distribution Systems and Great Lakes Dredge & Deck Co. (1991). When the smoke cleared, Anixter was the company's core operation. Anixter spun off its cable television products subsidiary, ANTEC, in 1993. Also that year Dammeyer replaced Zell as Itel's CEO.

Itel's focus became developing new markets in the burgeoning global communications industry. The company sold its remaining rail leasing interests in 1994. The next year Itel sold its stake in Santa Fe Energy Resources and changed its name to Anixter.

When an ANTEC subsidiary merged with cable TV equipment firm TSX Corp. in 1997, Anixter's ownership in ANTEC was reduced to 19%. That year the company joined with security software maker Check Point Software Technologies to provide network security products in Europe.

Anixter sold its ANTEC holdings in 1998 to finance the repurchase of its common stock, and bought Pacer Electronics, an electrical and data cabling distributor. Also that year, company veteran Robert Grubbs became CEO.

The next year Anixter sold its European network integration business to Persetel Q Data Holdings of South Africa and its data network design and consulting unit to Ameritech for $200 million in cash. It also sold North America Integration and Asia Pacific Integration, completing the dissolution of its integration segment by the close of 1999.

In 2000 Anixter formed a consortium with Panduit, Rockwell Automation, and Siemens for the production of industrially hardened Ethernet connectors. Anixter signed an agreement to distribute network cabling products for IBM in 2001.

In 2002 Anixter was named as a *Forbes* "Platinum 400" company, chosen by the magazine's editors as one of America's "best-performing" corporations by industry. Later that same year it acquired Pentacon (now Anixter Pentacon), a fastener distribution company.

More fastener acquisitions followed: Walters Hexagon in 2003; DDI in 2004; Infast Group in 2005; MFU in 2006; and Eurofast and Total Supply Solutions in 2007.

Robert Grubbs retired as president and CEO in mid-2008. The board designated EVP/COO Robert Eck, a 17-year veteran of Anixter, as his successor.

EXECUTIVES

Chairman: Samuel (Sam) Zell, age 67
President, CEO, and Director: Robert J. Eck, age 50, $2,150,280 total compensation
EVP Finance and CFO: Dennis J. Letham, age 57, $2,489,816 total compensation
VP, General Counsel, and Secretary; General Counsel and Secretary, Anixter Inc.: John A. Dul, age 47, $784,670 total compensation
VP Taxes: Philip F. Meno, age 50
VP and Controller: Terrance A. Faber, age 57, $831,032 total compensation
VP and Treasurer, Anixter International and Anixter Inc.: Rodney A. Shoemaker, age 51
VP Human Resources: Rodney A. Smith, age 51, $481,615 total compensation
VP Internal Audit: Nancy C. Ross-Dronzek, age 48
Auditors: Ernst & Young LLP

LOCATIONS

HQ: Anixter International Inc.
2301 Patriot Blvd., Glenview, IL 60026
Phone: 224-521-8000   **Fax:** 224-521-8100
Web: www.anixter.com

2008 Sales

	$ mil.	% of total
North America		
US	3,602.7	59
Canada	677.4	11
Europe	1,309.4	21
Other regions	547.1	9
Total	**6,136.6**	**100**

PRODUCTS/OPERATIONS

Selected Products and Services

Products
Copper and fiber-optic cable
Electrical/electronic wire and cable
Fasteners and connectors
Video surveillance equipment

Supply chain services
Sourcing
Logistics
Inventory management
Product enhancement and packaging
Deployment
Database tracking

COMPETITORS

Border States Electric
Consolidated Electrical
Crescent Electric Supply
Gexpro
Graybar Electric
Kirby Risk
Lawson Products
Precision Industries
Rexel
Sonepar
WESCO International

HISTORICAL FINANCIALS

Company Type: Public

Income Statement

FYE: Friday nearest December 31

	REVENUE ($ mil.)	NET INCOME ($ mil.)	NET PROFIT MARGIN	EMPLOYEES
12/08	6,136.6	195.7	3.2%	8,645
12/07	5,852.9	253.5	4.3%	8,000
12/06	4,938.6	209.3	4.2%	7,500
12/05	3,847.4	90.0	2.3%	6,800
12/04	3,275.2	73.6	2.2%	5,600
Annual Growth	17.0%	27.7%	—	11.5%

2008 Year-End Financials

Debt ratio: 88.6%
Return on equity: 18.8%
Cash ($ mil.): 65
Current ratio: 2.36
Long-term debt ($ mil.): 918

No. of shares (mil.): 35
Dividends
  Yield: 0.0%
  Payout: —
Market value ($ mil.): 1,063

Stock History

NYSE: AXE

	STOCK PRICE ($) FY Close	P/E High/Low		PER SHARE ($) Earnings	Dividends	Book Value
12/08	30.12	15	4	5.07	0.00	29.34
12/07	62.27	15	9	6.00	0.00	29.68
12/06	54.30	13	8	4.86	0.00	27.25
12/05	39.12	19	14	2.22	0.00	20.01
12/04	35.99	20	13	2.01	0.00	21.61
Annual Growth	(4.4%)	—	—	26.0%	—	7.9%

AnnTaylor Stores

At AnnTaylor, basic black is as appreciated by its customers as its classic styles. The company (named for a fictional person) is a national retailer of upscale women's clothing designed exclusively for its stores. Its AnnTaylor and AnnTaylor LOFT shops offer apparel, shoes, and accessories. Targeting fashion-conscious career women, AnnTaylor operates about 940 stores (500-plus are LOFT outlets) in more than 45 US states, the District of Columbia, and Puerto Rico. Most are located in malls or upscale retail centers. AnnTaylor LOFT stores offer their own label of mid-priced casual apparel, while AnnTaylor Factory and LOFT Outlet stores sell clearance merchandise. AnnTaylor also has its own e-commerce Web site.

Following two consecutive disappointing holiday retail seasons (2007 and 2008) marked by especially weak sales of women's apparel, AnnTaylor announced that it will shutter more than 190 underperforming stores by the end of 2010 and cut its headquarters staff by about 13%. It is also taking a more cautious approach to new store openings: nine LOFT stores are slated to open and no new Ann Taylor stores are planned in 2009. Also, AnnTaylor will delay the test of its new store concept. (The retailer had planned to launch the new format targeting the "modern boomer" in 2008.) The restructuring is expected to generate pretax savings of $50 million by fiscal 2010, with savings of some $20 million to $25 million in fiscal 2008.

In addition to cost cutting, Ann Taylor has appointed a new leadership team to breathe new life into its aging brand. A new merchandising strategy that features core items — such as "the perfect pencil skirt" and "perfect pants" — paired with more frequehtly restocked complmentary companion pieces is helping to keep inventories lean. The retailer hopes to see results beginning with the fall 2009 collection.

Launched in 1999, the fast-growing AnnTaylor LOFT format quickly overtook its more mature sister chain (in terms of the number of outlets) as American women adopted a more casual style of dress. LOFT stores eventually outperformed AnnTaylor stores. However, the deep recession in the US has impacted both chains, with each posting same-store-sales declines in 2008. Overall, the company experienced a decline in sales in excess of 8% in 2008.

AnnTaylor stores are on average 5,300 sq. ft., Loft stores are about 5,900 sq. ft., and the factory stores are around 7,300 sq. ft. About 75% of its core AnnTaylor stores are located in shopping malls and upscale retail centers. The company's three flagship stores are located in Chicago, New York City, and San Francisco. AnnTaylor's products are made in about 15 countries, with about 40% originating in China.

HISTORY

AnnTaylor Stores started out in 1954 as a shop on Chapel Street in New Haven, Connecticut. Founder Robert Liebskind targeted women who would later be called "preppie," using the conservative (and fictitious) Ann Taylor name. The stores proliferated in New England. In 1977 Liebskind sold out to Garfinckel, Brooks Brothers, Miller & Rhodes, which in 1981 was bought by Allied Stores. Under Allied, AnnTaylor was the top performer, thanks in large part to the merchandising savvy of Sally Frame Kasaks, who was president from 1983 to 1985.

Campeau Corporation made a hostile takeover of Allied in 1985. Heavily in debt, and with ill-fated designs on the bigger prize of Federated Department Stores, Campeau mined AnnTaylor for cash and then sold it in 1988 for $420 million to private investors and the division's management. AnnTaylor had suffered from image drift under Campeau, and its new management continued to ignore the company's target career-woman customer; in addition, the chain was slow to see the trend toward more casual career dressing.

In 1991 AnnTaylor went public, but it continued to founder under high debt load and a fuzzy fashion image. Kasaks returned as CEO that year and transformed the store name into a brand name with original designs. She also added shoe stores and a lower-priced apparel concept (Ann Taylor LOFT). The company's fashion sense became a problem again — cropped T-shirts didn't fit in with the workplace attire its customers sought — and AnnTaylor suffered a loss in fiscal 1996. Kasaks was ousted that year.

New CEO Patrick Spainhour and new president Patricia DeRosa quickly led AnnTaylor to another turnaround. They closed the shoe stores in 1997 and refocused the company's designs. The company opened 29 Ann Taylor LOFT stores in 1999 in pursuit of younger, more cost-conscious consumers. In early 2001 DeRosa left the company.

AnnTaylor attempted a short-lived cosmetic line in 2000, which it discontinued in 2001.

In 2004 the company opened five new Ann Taylor stores and 75 Ann Taylor LOFT stores.

In June 2005 the company completed its move to its new headquarters in Times Square Tower in New York City. In August the New York retailer announced it had entered into a trademark licensing agreement with China's Guangzhou Pan Yu San Yuet Fashion Manufactory Ltd. that owns rights to use the Ann Taylor name in China. In September chairman and CEO J. Patrick Spainhour retired and was succeeded as CEO by the company's president Kay Krill. Ronald W. Hovsepian, a director of the company since 1998, became chairman.

In May 2006 COO Laura Weil resigned after less than a year with the company. (Weil had joined AnnTaylor Stores from American Eagle Outfitters in 2005.)

AnnTaylor LOFT's e-commerce site launched in November 2007. Overall in 2007 the company added more than 50 LOFT stores and about a dozen AnnTaylor shops.

In another bid to grow, the apparel and accessories retailer has launched a beauty division that sells fragrances and skin care products. In October 2008 Ann Taylor appointed two top executives — a head designer and an executive over its stores — in its effort to breathe new life into its collections and outlets.

EXECUTIVES

Chairman: Ronald W. (Ron) Hovsepian, age 48, $7,588,393 total compensation
President, CEO, and Director: Katherine L. (Kay) Krill, age 54, $7,844,424 total compensation
EVP, CFO, and Treasurer: Michael J. (Mike) Nicholson, age 43, $1,325,940 total compensation
EVP and Chief Marketing Officer: Robert J. Luzzi
EVP and Chief Supply Chain Officer: Paula J. Zusi
EVP, General Counsel, and Secretary: Barbara K. Eisenberg, age 63
EVP, Human Resources: Mark Morrison
SVP and CIO: Michael Kingston
SVP Finance: Linda M. Siluk, age 51
SVP, Real Estate and Construction: George R. (Buck) Sappenfield, age 58
SVP Production and Sourcing Casual and Outerwear: Philippa Abeles
SVP Sourcing Operations and Strategy: Barbara Fevelo-Hoad
SVP and Director Stores, AnnTaylor Stores: Mary Kay O'Connor-Wente
VP, Corporate Facilities: Darrell DeVoe
VP and Controller: Dominick J. Reis, age 47
President, Ann Taylor LOFT: Gary P. Muto, age 49
President, Corporate Operations: Brian E. Lynch, age 52, $1,971,405 total compensation
President, AnnTaylor Stores: Christine M. Beauchamp
Director Investor Relations: Judith A. Pirro
Auditors: Deloitte & Touche LLP

LOCATIONS

HQ: AnnTaylor Stores Corporation
  7 Times Sq., 15th Fl., New York, NY 10036
Phone: 212-541-3300   **Fax:** 212-541-3379
Web: www.anntaylor.com

PRODUCTS/OPERATIONS

2009 Stores

	No.
AnnTaylor LOFT	510
AnnTaylor	320
AnnTaylor Factory	91
LOFT Outlet	14
Total	**935**

2009 Sales

	$ mil.	% of total
AnnTaylor LOFT	1,088.4	50
AnnTaylor	689.2	31
Other	417.0	19
Total	**2,194.6**	**100**

Selected Store Formats

AnnTaylor (upscale specialty stores selling women's apparel)

AnnTaylor Factory Store (clearance stores for Ann Taylor merchandise)

AnnTaylor LOFT (mid-priced specialty stores selling women's apparel)

LOFT Outlet (clearance stores for and Ann Taylor LOFT merchandise)

COMPETITORS

Banana Republic
Benetton
Bernard Chaus
Brooks Brothers
Caché
Calvin Klein
Chico's FAS
Dillard's
Donna Karan
Ellen Tracy
The Gap
J. Crew
Jones Apparel
Lands' End
Liz Claiborne
Macy's
New York & Company
Nordstrom
Polo Ralph Lauren
Saks
St. John Knits
Talbots
Urban Outfitters

HISTORICAL FINANCIALS

Company Type: Public

Income Statement

FYE: Saturday nearest January 31

	REVENUE ($ mil.)	NET INCOME ($ mil.)	NET PROFIT MARGIN	EMPLOYEES
1/09	2,194.6	(333.9)	—	18,400
1/08	2,396.5	97.2	4.1%	18,400
1/07	2,342.9	143.0	6.1%	17,700
1/06	2,073.1	81.9	4.0%	16,900
1/05	1,853.6	63.3	3.4%	14,900
Annual Growth	**4.3%**	**—**	**—**	**5.4%**

2009 Year-End Financials

Debt ratio: —
Return on equity: —
Cash ($ mil.): 112
Current ratio: 1.39
Long-term debt ($ mil.): —

No. of shares (mil.): 59
Dividends
  Yield: 0.0%
  Payout: —
Market value ($ mil.): 289

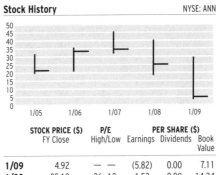

	STOCK PRICE ($) FY Close	P/E High/Low		PER SHARE ($) Earnings	Dividends	Book Value
1/09	4.92	—	—	(5.82)	0.00	7.11
1/08	25.13	26	12	1.53	0.00	14.34
1/07	34.50	23	16	1.98	0.00	17.93
1/06	33.32	31	19	1.13	0.00	17.67
1/05	21.49	36	23	0.88	0.00	15.83
Annual Growth	**(30.8%)**	**—**	**—**	**—**	**—**	**(18.1%)**

A. O. Smith

Aerosmith has a lot of fans — A. O. Smith has a lot of fan motors. The company makes the guts of buildings, i.e. residential and commercial water heaters and electric motors. Its Electrical Products include pump motors for home water systems, swimming pools, and hot tubs; fan motors for furnaces and air conditioners; and hermetic motors for compressors and commercial refrigeration units. The company's Water segment makes residential gas and electric water heaters and commercial water-heating systems. Retail customers include private label relationships with Lowe's and Sears. Customers in the US account for about three-quarters of A. O. Smith's sales. Members of the founding Smith family control the company.

A. O. Smith's profits are driven by roughly 40% of sales from electrical products and 60% from water systems. It peddles most of its electrical products to original equipment manufacturers (82%), with the remainder directed to aftermarket and distribution sales. About a third of electrical sales are dependent upon heating, ventilating, air conditioning, and refrigeration markets.

A. O. Smith's water products are sold through independent wholesale plumbing distributors. Typical end-users are restaurants, hotels, laundries, car washes, and small businesses. Its residential water heaters are moved through retail channels. The company's dual exposure to commercial as well as residential builders has minimized the drag of the US housing slowdown on its bottom line. In addition, with about 10% of the company's sales — driven by commercial water heaters — to China, A. O. Smith's international dealings lend some stability.

Restructuring its family of manufacturing facilities in 2007, residential electric motor plants in Kentucky, North Carolina, and Hungary were shut down with production shifting to plants in Mexico and China. India marks a major expansion for the company. In late 2008 A. O. Smith received approval to construct a plant near Bangalore, the technology capital of India. Production is expected to begin in the first half of 2010.

Smith Investment Company, the firm of the Smith family, owns a control position in A. O. Smith Corporation. In late 2008 the two merged, and Smith Investment became a wholly owned subsidiary of A. O. Smith in a tax-free exchange of stock. As a result, the stockholders of Smith Investment own shares of A. O. Smith directly, rather than through Smith Investment. Family members intend to place their shares in A. O. Smith into a voting trust and refrain for three years from taking any significant action on the ownership of A. O. Smith without the approval of the A. O. Smith board.

HISTORY

Charles Jeremiah Smith founded a machine shop in 1874 to make parts for baby carriages. The business expanded into making bicycles, and by 1895 it was a global leader in bicycle parts. The Smith family sold the firm in 1899. Charles' eldest son, Arthur, began tinkering with car frames, and by 1902 he had a breakthrough design. Arthur bought the company back in 1904 to make car frames and incorporated it as A. O. Smith.

A huge 1906 contract from Ford Motor spurred Arthur to retool the factory, increasing production tenfold. In 1921 A. O. Smith unveiled the first automated assembly line for car frames. Dubbed the Mechanical Marvel, it could produce a frame every eight seconds and did so for the next 40 years.

The firm began production of the first glass-lined residential water heaters in 1939. Acquisitions over the next decade allowed A. O. Smith to enter the electric motor market, and in 1959 it established a plastics unit for its fiberglass pipe.

In 1986 A. O. Smith expanded its electric motor business when it bought Westinghouse's small-motor division. The company doubled the size of its tank business by buying Peabody TecTank (dry storage tanks) the next year. Company veteran Robert O'Toole was named CEO in 1989.

A. O. Smith sold its auto business in 1997 and bought private motor producer UPPCO. The company became the #1 North American maker of compressor motors for the air-conditioning industry with its 1998 purchase of a General Electric subsidiary. The next year it bought Magnetek's electric-motor unit, doubling the size of its pump motor business.

In 2000 the company sold its fluid handling (fiberglass pipe) business to Varco International (Texas). The next year A. O. Smith sold its storage products business to CST Industries (Kansas).

A. O. Smith elected to sell some 3.5 million shares of its common stock in early 2002, with the intention of repaying a portion of its debt. To expand its manufacturing capabilities, the company acquired an electric motor maker in China from the Changheng Group (air-moving motors for the Chinese air-conditioning market). A. O. Smith also pumped up its water systems by acquiring privately held State Industries (water heaters), which contributed about $313 million to its annual net sales. The same year A. O. Smith bought the assets of the Athens Products division of Electrolux.

In 2003 A. O. Smith again expanded its global motor manufacturing business, buying the assets of Taicang Special Motor Co., Ltd., a maker of hermetic electric motors based in China.

In 2005 the company bought another Chinese motor manufacturer, Yueyang Special Electrical Machinery.

O'Toole retired at the end of 2005 and company president Paul Jones was named CEO.

In 2006 A. O. Smith acquired GSW, a Canadian supplier of water heaters, for about $320 million in cash. The acquisition gave A. O. Smith entree as a supplier to home improvement giant Lowe's.

In late 2006 the company sold GSW Building Products, a manufacturer of vinyl rain ware systems, to Euramax International. GSW Building Products employed about 100 people in Barrie, Ontario, and posted 2005 sales of $30 million. A. O. Smith received net proceeds of about $11.3 million from the sale.

EXECUTIVES

Chairman and CEO: Paul W. Jones, age 60, $4,382,669 total compensation
EVP and CFO: Terry M. Murphy, age 60, $1,748,033 total compensation
EVP; President, Water Products: Ajita G. Rajendra, age 57, $1,356,821 total compensation
EVP; President, Electrical Products: Christopher L. (Chris) Mapes, age 47, $1,295,380 total compensation
EVP, General Counsel, and Secretary: James F. Stern, age 46, $841,984 total compensation
SVP and CIO: Randall S. (Randy) Bednar, age 56
SVP Corporate Development: Steve W. Rettler, age 54
SVP Finance, Treasurer, and Controller: John J. Kita, age 53
SVP Human Resources and Public Affairs: Mark A. Petrarca, age 45
VP Corporate Development: Malcolm B. Kinnaird
VP Investor Relations and Treasurer: Patricia K. Ackerman
President and General Manager — A. O. Smith (China) Investment Co.; SVP Asia: Michael J. Cole, age 64
Head of Asia Operations: Wilfried Brouwer
Auditors: Ernst & Young LLP

LOCATIONS

HQ: A. O. Smith Corporation
11270 W. Park Place, Ste. 170,
Milwaukee, WI 53224
Phone: 414-359-4000   **Fax:** 414-359-4115
Web: www.aosmith.com

2008 Sales

	$ mil.	% of total
US	1,711.3	74
Mexico	240.5	11
China	166.7	7
Canada	186.4	8
Total	**2,304.9**	**100**

PRODUCTS/OPERATIONS

2008 Sales

	$ mil.	% of total
Water Products	1,451.3	63
Electrical Products	858.1	37
Adjustments	(4.5)	—
Total	**2,304.9**	**100**

Selected Divisions and Products

Electric Products
  Fractional horsepower electric motors
  Hermetic electric motors
  Integral horsepower A/C and D/C electric motors
Water Products
  Commercial water heaters
  Copper tube boilers
  Residential water heaters

COMPETITORS

AMETEK
AMTROL
Baldor Electric
Bradford White
Emerson Electric
EXX
Franklin Electric
GE
Haier Group
Hayward Industries
Indesit
Kinetek
Lindeteves-Jacoberg
Lochinvar
Paloma Co.
Pentair
RBS Global
Regal Beloit
Tecumseh Products
WEG Electric Motors

HISTORICAL FINANCIALS

Company Type: Public

Income Statement

FYE: December 31

	REVENUE ($ mil.)	NET INCOME ($ mil.)	NET PROFIT MARGIN	EMPLOYEES
12/08	2,304.9	81.9	3.6%	15,350
12/07	2,312.1	88.2	3.8%	16,800
12/06	2,161.3	76.5	3.5%	18,000
12/05	1,689.2	46.5	2.8%	17,650
12/04	1,653.1	35.4	2.1%	16,600
Annual Growth	**8.7%**	**23.3%**	**—**	**(1.9%)**

2008 Year-End Financials

Debt ratio: 49.5%
Return on equity: 11.7%
Cash ($ mil.): 29
Current ratio: 1.55
Long-term debt ($ mil.): 317
No. of shares (mil.): 30
Dividends
  Yield: 2.5%
  Payout: 27.4%
Market value ($ mil.): 890

Stock History

NYSE: AOS

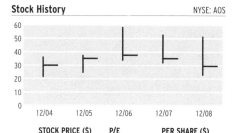

	STOCK PRICE ($) FY Close	P/E High/Low		PER SHARE ($) Earnings	Dividends	Book Value
12/08	29.52	19	9	2.70	0.74	21.26
12/07	35.05	18	11	2.85	0.70	25.13
12/06	37.56	24	14	2.47	0.66	22.70
12/05	35.10	24	16	1.54	0.64	20.32
12/04	29.94	30	18	1.18	0.62	19.59
Annual Growth	**(0.4%)**	**—**	**—**	**23.0%**	**4.5%**	**2.1%**

Aon Corporation

Aon (the name means "oneness" in Gaelic) is one of the world's leading insurance brokerages, as well as a top reinsurance broker. The company operates in two major segments: commercial brokerage and consulting services. The company's Aon Risk Services brokerage unit provides retail property/casualty, liability, workers' compensation, and other insurance products for groups and businesses, as well as risk management services. Aon Benfield handles reinsurance brokerage and analysis services to protect insurers from losses on traditional and specialty property/casualty policies. Aon's consulting unit, Aon Consulting Worldwide, specializes in employee benefits administration.

Aon provides its brokerage and consulting services from more than 500 offices in about 120 countries; the US and Europe are its largest markets. The insurance and reinsurance brokerage operations together account for about 80% of sales. Aon Risk Services provides retail insurance brokerage services to small to large corporations and other professional organizations, as well as to individuals; it also provides risk identification and assessment, cost-control and claims management, and other administrative services.

Aon announced in 2007 that it would take steps to simplify its organization, primarily by slimming down administrative functions and consolidating some European operations. Aon also announced that it would focus on its core brokerage and consulting divisions.

The company then proceeded to exit its older but smaller insurance underwriting segment (including founder W. Clement Stone's original insurance underwriting business, Combined Insurance), which offered supplementary health, accident, and life insurance. Aon in 2008 sold the Combined Insurance unit to ACE Limited for nearly $2.6 billion. The company also completed the sale of its Sterling Life Insurance underwriting unit to Munich Re for $352 million.

Not long after the divestitures were completed, Aon acquired UK-based Benfield Group for $1.75 billion to strengthen its European reinsurance brokerage operations.

HISTORY

Aon's story begins with the birth of W. Clement Stone around the turn of the 20th century. At age six he started working as a paperboy in Chicago. The young Stone devoured the optimistic messages of the 19th-century Horatio Alger novels, which detailed the successes of plucky, enterprising heroes.

Stone's mother bought a small Detroit insurance agency and in 1918 brought her son into the business. Young Stone sold low-cost, low-benefit accident insurance, underwriting and issuing policies on-site. The next year he founded his own agency, the Combined Registry Co. While selling up to 122 policies per day, he recruited a nationwide force of agents.

As the Depression took hold, Stone reduced the company's workforce and improved training. Forced by his son's respiratory illness to winter in the South, Stone followed the sun to Arkansas and Texas. In 1939 he bought American Casualty Insurance Co. of Dallas. It was consolidated with other purchases as the Combined Insurance Co. of America in 1947.

The company grew through the 1950s and 1960s, continuing to sell health and accident policies. In the 1970s Combined expanded overseas despite being hit hard by the recession.

In 1982, after 10 years of stagnant growth under Clement Stone Jr., the elder Stone (then 79) resumed control until the completion of a merger with Ryan Insurance Co. allowed him to transfer power to Patrick Ryan.

Ryan, the son of a Wisconsin Ford dealer, had started his company as an auto credit insurer in 1964. In 1976 the company bought the insurance brokerage units of the Esmark conglomerate. Ryan's less-personal management style differed radically from Stone's rah-rah booster-ism, but the men's shared interest in philanthropy helped seal the deal.

Ryan focused on insurance brokering and added more upscale insurance products. He also trimmed staff and took other cost-cutting measures, and in 1987 he changed Combined's name to Aon. In 1995 the company sold its remaining direct life insurance holdings to focus on consulting. The following year it began offering hostile takeover insurance policies to small and midsized companies.

In 1997 it bought The Minet Group, as well as troubled insurance brokerage Alexander & Alexander Services in a deal that made Aon (temporarily) the largest insurance broker worldwide. The firm made no US buys in 1998, but doubled its employee base with purchases including Spain's largest retail insurance broker, Gil y Carvajal, and the formation of Aon Korea, the first non-Korean firm of its kind to be licensed there.

In 1999 it bought Nikols Sedgwick Group, an Italian insurance firm, and formed RiskAttack (with Zurich US), a risk analysis and financial management concern aimed at technology companies. In 2000 Aon bought Reliance Group's accident and health insurance business, as well as Actuarial Sciences Associates, a compensation and employee benefits consulting company. Later in that year, however, the company decided to cut 6% of its workforce as part of a restructuring effort.

Aon was hit hard by the attacks on the World Trade Center (where it was headquartered) in 2001; the company lost some 175 employees.

Aon teamed up with the Giuliani Group, former New York mayor Rudolph Giuliani's consulting firm, to provide business risk assessment and crisis management services in 2002.

In 2004-2005 Aon, along with other brokers including Marsh & McLennan and Willis Group Holdings, fell under regulatory investigation. At issue was the practice of insurance companies' payments to brokers (known as contingent commissions). The payments were thought to bring a conflict of interest, swaying broker decisions on behalf of carriers, rather than customers.

The bid-rigging investigation resulted in a $190 million settlement with regulators in three states and a shakeup of top management. Ryan stepped down as CEO, but he retained his position as chairman. Ryan was replaced as CEO by McKinsey executive Gregory Case.

Aon then launched a reorganization program. The company sold its wholesale brokerage operations, Swett & Crawford (the largest in the US), to a group of investors led by Hicks, Muse, Tate & Furst (now HM Capital Partners).

Aon also shed its credit, warranty, and property and casualty underwriting operations; it sold its Aon Warranty Group (now named The Warranty Group) division, including Virginia Surety, to Onex for $710 million in late 2006.

EXECUTIVES

Chairman: Lester B. Knight, age 51
President, CEO, and Director: Gregory C. (Greg) Case, age 46, $12,876,647 total compensation
EVP and CFO: Christa Davies, age 37, $3,756,434 total compensation
EVP, Chief Administrative Officer, and Head, Global Strategy: Gregory J. (Greg) Besio, age 51
EVP and General Counsel: Peter Lieb, age 53
EVP; President, Aon Risk Services: Ted T. Devine, age 45, $5,734,776 total compensation
EVP, Middle Market; Head, Aon Risk Services, Southern Region: William M. Choate
Global CTO: Adam Stanley
Global Chief Marketing and Communications Officer: Philip B. Clement
Managing Director and EVP, Aon Construction Services Group: Michael R. Szot
SVP and Head, Human Resources: Jeremy G. O. Farmer, age 59
SVP and Originator, Aon Risk Services: Matt Reese
SVP Global Real Estate: Roy Keller
SVP, Global Controller, and Principal Accounting Officer: Laurel G. Meissner, age 51
VP, Corporate Officer, and Head, Investor Relations: Scott Malchow
VP Global Public Relations: David P. Prosperi
VP, Associate General Counsel, and Secretary: Jennifer L. Kraft
Chairman, Aon Re Global and Aon Benfield Re: Michael D. O'Halleran, age 58
Chairman and CEO, Aon Risk Services: Stephen P. (Steve) McGill, age 50, $7,203,817 total compensation
CEO, Aon Benfield; Chairman, Aon Consulting Worldwide: Andrew M. Appel, age 44, $6,059,028 total compensation
Chairman, Aon Risk Services Americas: Michael D. Rice, age 65
Auditors: Ernst & Young LLP

LOCATIONS

HQ: Aon Corporation
Aon Center, 200 E. Randolph St., Chicago, IL 60601
Phone: 312-381-1000   **Fax:** 312-381-6032
Web: www.aon.com

2008 Sales

	$ mil.	% of total
Americas		
US	2,718	36
Other Americas countries	891	12
Europe, Middle East & Africa		
UK	1,249	16
Other EMEA countries	2,113	28
Asia/Pacific	660	8
Total	**7,631**	**100**

PRODUCTS/OPERATIONS

2008 Sales

	$ mil.	% of total
Risk & insurance brokerage services	6,230	82
Consulting	1,358	18
Other	43	—
Total	**7,631**	**100**

Selected Subsidiaries

Risk and Insurance Brokerage
Aon Benfield Inc. (formerly Aon Re Global, Inc.)
Aon Holdings International BV (Netherlands)
Aon Limited (UK)
Aon Risk Services Companies, Inc.
Aon Specialty (formerly Benfield Corporate Risk)
Cananwill, Inc.

Consulting
Aon Consulting Worldwide, Inc.

COMPETITORS

Alexander Forbes	Meadowbrook Insurance
Arthur Gallagher	National Financial Partners
BB&T	StanCorp Financial Group
Brown & Brown	Towers Perrin
Citigroup	Unum Group
Clark Consulting	USI
Hub International	Watson Wyatt
Jardine Lloyd	Willis Group
Marsh & McLennan	

HISTORICAL FINANCIALS

Company Type: Public

Income Statement

FYE: December 31

	REVENUE ($ mil.)	NET INCOME ($ mil.)	NET PROFIT MARGIN	EMPLOYEES
12/08	7,631.0	1,462.0	19.2%	37,700
12/07	7,471.0	864.0	11.6%	42,500
12/06	8,954.0	719.0	8.0%	43,100
12/05	9,837.0	737.0	7.5%	46,600
12/04	10,172.0	546.0	5.4%	48,000
Annual Growth	**(6.9%)**	**27.9%**	**—**	**(5.9%)**

2008 Year-End Financials

Debt ratio: 35.3%
Return on equity: 25.4%
Cash ($ mil.): 582
Current ratio: 1.13
Long-term debt ($ mil.): 1,872

No. of shares (mil.): 274
Dividends
  Yield: 1.3%
  Payout: 12.3%
Market value ($ mil.): 12,538

Stock History

NYSE: AOC

	STOCK PRICE ($) FY Close	P/E High/Low		PER SHARE ($) Earnings	Dividends	Book Value
12/08	45.68	10	7	4.86	0.60	19.35
12/07	47.69	19	13	2.69	0.60	22.66
12/06	35.34	20	15	2.13	0.60	19.01
12/05	35.95	17	10	2.17	0.60	19.32
12/04	23.86	18	11	1.63	0.60	18.59
Annual Growth	**17.6%**	**—**	**—**	**31.4%**	**0.0%**	**1.0%**

Apache Corporation

There's more than a patch of oil in Apache's portfolio. Apache is an oil and gas exploration and production company with onshore and offshore operations in North America and in Argentina, Australia, Egypt, and the UK (offshore in the North Sea). The company has estimated proved reserves of 2.4 billion barrels of oil equivalent, mostly from five North American regions: the Gulf of Mexico, the Gulf Coast of Texas and Louisiana, the Permian Basin in West Texas, the Anadarko Basin in Oklahoma, and Canada's Western Sedimentary Basin. Of its international operations, Apache's assets in Egypt and the North Sea are the largest.

While the US represents about 40% of the company's production and reserves, Apache is well aware that growth in the region will not be coming from drilling more wells. With that in mind, Apache says that domestic expansion will come largely through acquisitions.

Its international business has been built through acquisitions as well. Though the rate at which it has been making deals has slowed down since 2007, Apache has grown widely through numerous international acquisitions this decade.

Shell is Apache's largest customer, accounting for more than 15% of sales.

In 2009 Apache Corporation founder Raymond Plank retired as chairman of the company. He had been its chief executive from Apache's founding in 1954 until his retirement in 2002, and chairman from then until the beginning of 2009. CEO Steven Farris took up the additional title of chairman at that time.

HISTORY

Originally, Raymond Plank wanted to start a magazine. Then it was an accounting and tax-assistance service. Plank and his co-founding partner, Truman Anderson, had no experience in any of these occupations, but their accounting business succeeded. In the early 1950s Plank and Anderson branched out again, founding APA, a partnership to invest in new ventures, including oil and gas exploration. The partnership founded Apache Oil in Minnesota in 1954. Investors put up the money, and Apache managed the drilling, spreading the risk over several projects.

As problems with government regulations in the oil industry mounted during the 1960s, Apache diversified into real estate. The real estate operations were pivotal in driving a wedge between Plank and Anderson. In 1963 Anderson called a board meeting to ask the directors to fire Plank. Instead, Anderson resigned, and Plank took over.

Apache's holdings soon encompassed 24 firms, including engineering, electronics, farming, and water-supply subsidiaries. Understanding that its fortunes were tied to varying oil and gas prices, the company reassessed its diversified structure in the 1970s. When the energy crisis rocketed oil prices skyward, Apache sold its non-energy operations, which would have been hurt by the price increases.

Apache formed Apache Petroleum in 1981 as an investment vehicle to take advantage of tax laws favoring limited partnerships. Initially the strategy was a success, but it fell victim in the mid-1980s to a one-two punch: Oil prices sank like a rock, and Congress put an end to the tax advantage. After suffering its first loss in 1986, Apache reorganized into a conventional exploration and production company.

Still under Plank's leadership, the company began steadily buying oil and gas properties and companies in 1991. That year it purchased oil and gas sites with more than 100 million barrels of reserves from Amoco and put the wells back into production. By buying Hadson Energy Resources, which operated fields in western Australia, Apache gained entry into the relatively unexplored region in 1993.

In 1995 Apache merged with Calgary, Canada-based DEKALB Energy (later renamed DEK Energy) and continued picking up properties. It bought $600 million worth of US reserves from Texaco (acquired by Chevron in 2001) that year. In 1996 it expanded its Chinese operations and

bought Phoenix Resource Companies, which operated solely in Egypt. A 1998 agreement with Texaco expanded its Chinese acreage thirtyfold. Apache also bought oil and gas properties and production facilities in waters off western Australia from a Mobil unit.

Apache joined with FX Energy and Polish Oil & Gas in 1998 to begin exploratory drilling in Poland. It also worked with XCL and China National Oil & Gas Exploration & Development in Bohai Bay, though the project was slowed by a dispute between Apache and XCL over costs. In 1999 Apache bought Gulf of Mexico assets from a unit of Royal Dutch Shell and acquired oil and gas properties in western Canada from Shell Canada. That year Apache sold its Ivory Coast oil and gas holdings for $46 million.

Still shopping, however, Apache agreed in 2000 to buy assets in western Canada and Argentina with proved reserves of more than 700 billion cu. ft. of natural gas equivalent from New Zealand's Fletcher Challenge Energy. To help pay for the $600 million acquisition, which closed in 2001, Apache sold $100 million in stock to Shell, which acquired other Fletcher Challenge Energy assets. Apache bought the Canadian assets of Phillips Petroleum (later ConocoPhillips) for $490 million in 2000 and acquired the Egyptian assets of Repsol YPF for $410 million in 2001.

Late in 2002 in a move aimed at boosting its natural gas production by more than 10%, Apache acquired 234,000 net acres of land in southern Louisiana for $260 million. That year the company also announced three oil discoveries in the Carnarvon Basin offshore Western Australia.

In 2003 Apache acquired UK and US oil and gas assets from BP for $1.3 billion. The main prize was the Forties field, one of the North Sea's oldest discoveries (dating back to the early 1970s), and its largest.

In 2004 it acquired more than two dozen mature US and Canadian fields from Exxon Mobil for $347 million and Gulf of Mexico properties from Anadarko Petroleum for $525 million. In 2005 Hurricane Katrina destroyed eight of its 241 Gulf rigs.

EXECUTIVES

Chairman and CEO: G. Steven (Steve) Farris, age 60, $10,068,666 total compensation
President: Roger B. Plank, age 52, $673,669 total compensation
Co-COO; President North America: John A. Crum, age 56, $3,850,329 total compensation
Co-COO; President International: Rodney J. Eichler, age 60, $675,265 total compensation
EVP and Technology Officer: Michael S. (Mike) Bahorich, age 52
EVP and General Counsel: P. Anthony Lannie, age 54
EVP: Jon A. Jeppesen, age 60
EVP and Exploration Officer: Floyd R. Price, age 59
EVP Corporate Reservoir Engineering: W. Kregg Olson, age 55
SVP Policy and Governance: Sarah B. Teslik, age 54
VP Information Technology: Aaron Merrick
VP and Treasurer: Matthew W. (Matt) Dundrea, age 55
VP Corporate Services: Robert J. (Bob) Dye, age 53
VP Tax: Jon W. Sauer, age 47
VP Human Resources: Margery M. (Margie) Harris, age 45
VP Planning and Investor Relations: Thomas P. (Tom) Chambers, age 52
VP Oil and Gas Marketing: Janine J. McArdle, age 47
VP and Controller: Rebecca A. (Becky) Hoyt, age 44
Corporate Secretary: Cheri L. Peper, age 54
Auditors: Ernst & Young LLP

LOCATIONS

HQ: Apache Corporation
2000 Post Oak Blvd., Ste. 100, Houston, TX 77056
Phone: 713-296-6000 **Fax:** 713-296-6496
Web: www.apachecorp.com

2008 Sales

	$ mil.	% of total
US	5,083.4	42
Egypt	2,739.3	22
UK (North Sea)	2,103.3	17
Canada	1,650.4	13
Argentina	379.8	3
Australia	371.7	3
Adjustments	61.9	—
Total	**12,389.8**	**100**

PRODUCTS/OPERATIONS

2008 Sales

	$ mil.	% of total
Oil	8,157.3	66
Natural gas	3,964.7	32
Natural gas liquids	205.9	2
Adjustments	61.9	—
Total	**12,389.8**	**100**

Selected Subsidiaries

Apache Canada Ltd.
Apache Energy Limited
Apache International, Inc.
Apache North Sea Limited
Apache Overseas, Inc.
DEK Energy Company

COMPETITORS

Adams Resources
Anadarko Petroleum
BP
Chesapeake Energy
Chevron
Devon Energy
El Paso
EOG
Exxon
Forest Oil
Helmerich & Payne
Hess Corporation
Royal Dutch Shell
Santos Ltd
XTO Energy

HISTORICAL FINANCIALS

Company Type: Public

Income Statement

FYE: December 31

	REVENUE ($ mil.)	NET INCOME ($ mil.)	NET PROFIT MARGIN	EMPLOYEES
12/08	12,389.8	712.0	5.7%	3,639
12/07	9,977.9	2,806.7	28.1%	3,521
12/06	8,288.8	2,552.5	30.8%	3,150
12/05	7,584.2	2,623.7	34.6%	2,805
12/04	5,332.6	1,670.1	31.3%	2,642
Annual Growth	**23.5%**	**(19.2%)**	**—**	**8.3%**

2008 Year-End Financials

Debt ratio: 29.3%
Return on equity: 4.5%
Cash ($ mil.): 1,181
Current ratio: 1.70
Long-term debt ($ mil.): 4,809

No. of shares (mil.): 336
Dividends
  Yield: 0.8%
  Payout: 28.7%
Market value ($ mil.): 25,023

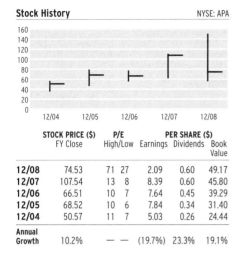

| | 12/04 | 12/05 | 12/06 | 12/07 | 12/08 |

	STOCK PRICE ($) FY Close	P/E High/Low		PER SHARE ($) Earnings	Dividends	Book Value
12/08	74.53	71	27	2.09	0.60	49.17
12/07	107.54	13	8	8.39	0.60	45.80
12/06	66.51	10	7	7.64	0.45	39.29
12/05	68.52	10	6	7.84	0.34	31.40
12/04	50.57	11	7	5.03	0.26	24.44
Annual Growth	10.2%	—	—	(19.7%)	23.3%	19.1%

Apollo Group

Apollo's creed could be that we all deserve the chance to advance. The for-profit group provides educational programs and services through a number of subsidiaries, including online stalwart University of Phoenix, which also has physical campuses in North America and Europe. The largest private university in the US, the University of Phoenix accounts for some 95% of Apollo's sales. Insights Schools offers online high school education for homeschooled students. Western International University offers graduate and undergraduate courses online and through partnerships in China and India. Apollo has more than 360,000 degreed students, or students enrolled in degree programs ranging from associate's to doctoral.

Other subsidiaries include College for Financial Planning Institutes, which offers financial planner certification and graduate programs, and Institute for Professional Development, which consults with schools seeking to expand and develop programs for working adults. Meritus University was established in 2008 to offer online degree programs in Canada.

Apollo Group joined together with private equity firm Carlyle Group in 2007 to create international arm Apollo Global. In Latin America, the unit acquired Chile's Universidad de Artes, Ciencias y Comunicación and Mexico's Universidad Latinoamericana. In 2009 it acquired UK-based BPP, a provider of legal and financial professional training. Apollo Global plans to invest in BPP's growth, enabling it to grow in the UK and throughout Europe. Also in 2009, Apollo Group upped its stake in Apollo Global from 80% to 86%.

Apollo branched out of the world of academia with its 2007 purchase of online advertising network Aptimus for about $48 million. Although the company has said the acquisition will help increase the effectiveness of its online advertising efforts the acquisition might possibly signal a strategic shift to grow the company through a new business line.

Apollo named Gregory W. Cappelli as co-CEO in 2009. Cappelli will share responsibility for the company with Charles "Chas" B. Edelstein, who was appointed CEO in July 2008. As co-CEOs, Edelstein will focus on finance, corporate development, human resources, and legal, while Cappelli will concentrate on operations, strategy, and external communications.

Founder John Sperling and his son Peter (executive and board member) together own about 50% of Apollo.

HISTORY

The son of Missouri sharecroppers, John Sperling had an early interest in higher education for the working class. Following WWII he attended Reed College on the GI Bill and eventually received a PhD in economic history from Cambridge. He started the Institute for Professional Development in 1973 to offer nontraditional programs designed for working adults. Sperling's program was rejected by San Jose State University, where he was a tenured professor, so he took his idea to the University of San Francisco. There he designed a curriculum program for firefighters, police officers, and other workers. Within two years, the program had 2,500 students, but the regional accrediting board accused him of running a diploma mill and yanked his accreditation.

Sperling moved to Arizona (which falls under a different accrediting board), where he founded the University of Phoenix (UOP) in 1976. UOP received accreditation in 1978; its first graduating class had eight students. UOP expanded into new states through the 1980s, and in 1989 it added distance learning to its services using its own dial-up computer network. The company went public as Apollo Group in 1994.

To further expand its reach, Apollo bought Western International University (founded in 1978) in 1995 and the College for Financial Planning from National Endowment of Financial Education in 1997. That year it formed Apollo Learning Group to offer hi-tech training programs. UOP received approval to offer its first doctoral program in 1998, a doctor of management degree. The next year Apollo made its first entry into the northeast US when it was approved by the state of Pennsylvania. It also expanded and upgraded its online operations that year, centralizing its operations in Phoenix.

In 2001 UOP introduced FlexNet, courses that combined classroom and online instruction. The weakening economy in 2001 and 2002 benefited Apollo; as jobs became more scarce, many professionals sought further education as a competitive advantage. In 2003 UOP received state approval to offer courses in New Jersey.

Although it denied the claims, in 2004 Apollo agreed to pay almost $10 million in fines after a US Department of Education inquiry claimed that University of Phoenix recruiters had used unethical or illegal tactics to enroll unqualified students.

Chairman, CEO, and president Todd Nelson resigned in early 2006. Nineteen-year company veteran and president of Apollo's subsidiary, the University of Phoenix, Brian Mueller replaced him as president. Sperling was appointed interim chairman. The company also acquired Insight Schools in 2006, adding operations and expertise in online education for grades K-12.

EXECUTIVES

Executive Chairman: John G. Sperling, age 88
Chairman and Co-CEO: Gregory W. Cappelli, age 41
Vice Chairman and SVP: Peter V. Sperling, age 48
Co-CEO and Director: Charles B. (Chas) Edelstein, age 49
President and COO: Joseph L. (Joe) D'Amico, age 59
EVP External Affairs and Director: Terri Bishop
EVP Marketing and Enrollment: Stan Meyer
EVP University of Phoenix: Dianne Pusch
SVP, CFO, and Treasurer: Brian L. Swartz, age 36
SVP Human Resources: Frederick J. (Fred) Newton III, age 53
SVP and General Counsel: P. Robert (Bob) Moya, age 64
VP Finance: Larry Fleischer
Chief Information Officer: Joe Mildenhall
Chief Accounting Officer: Gregory J. Iverson, age 33
President, University of Phoenix: William (Bill) Pepicello
Provost and SVP, Academic Affairs, University of Phoenix: Adam Honea
Investor Relations: Allyson Pooley
Auditors: Deloitte & Touche LLP

LOCATIONS

HQ: Apollo Group, Inc.
4025 S. Riverpoint Pkwy., Phoenix, AZ 85040
Phone: 480-966-5394   **Fax:** 480-379-3503
Web: www.apollogrp.edu

2008 Sales

	$ mil.	% of total
US	3,122.3	99
Latin America	13.7	1
Other	4.9	—
Total	**3,140.9**	**100**

PRODUCTS/OPERATIONS

2008 Sales

	$ mil.	% of total
Tuition	2,996.1	91
Online course material	184.4	6
Services	77.7	2
Other	43.9	1
Adjustments	(161.2)	—
Total	**3,140.9**	**100**

2008 Sales by Segment

	$ mil.	% of total
University of Phoenix	2,987.7	95
Apollo Global	13.4	1
Insight Schools	7.5	—
Other schools	122.5	4
Other	9.8	—
Total	**3,140.9**	**100**

2008 Enrollment by Age

	% of total
23 to 29	34
30 to 39	31
40 to 49	15
22 and under	14
50 and over	6
Total	**100**

COMPETITORS

Canterbury Consulting	Kaplan
Career Education	Laureate Education
Concorde Colleges	Lincoln Educational
Corinthian Colleges	Services
DeVry	Strayer Education
Education Management	thinkorswim
ITT Educational	UTI

HISTORICAL FINANCIALS

Company Type: Public

Income Statement

FYE: August 31

	REVENUE ($ mil.)	NET INCOME ($ mil.)	NET PROFIT MARGIN	EMPLOYEES
8/08	3,140.9	476.5	15.2%	44,647
8/07	2,723.8	408.8	15.0%	36,418
8/06	2,477.5	414.8	16.7%	36,416
8/05	2,251.5	444.7	19.8%	32,666
8/04	1,798.4	277.8	15.4%	29,913
Annual Growth	15.0%	14.4%	—	10.5%

2008 Year-End Financials

Debt ratio: 17.5%
Return on equity: 64.9%
Cash ($ mil.): 483
Current ratio: 1.35
Long-term debt ($ mil.): 146
No. of shares (mil.): 154
Dividends
  Yield: 0.0%
  Payout: —
Market value ($ mil.): 9,787

Stock History

NASDAQ (GS): APOL

	STOCK PRICE ($) FY Close	P/E High/Low		PER SHARE ($) Earnings	Dividends	Book Value
8/08	63.68	28	13	2.87	0.00	5.43
8/07	58.67	28	14	2.35	0.00	4.12
8/06	50.21	34	18	2.35	0.00	3.93
8/05	78.66	37	26	2.39	0.00	4.60
8/04	78.00	127	79	0.77	0.00	6.23
Annual Growth	(4.9%)	—	—	38.9%	—	(3.4%)

Apple Inc.

Apple aims for nothing short of a revolution, whether in personal computing or digital media distribution. The company's desktop and laptop computers — all of which feature its OS X operating system — include its Mac mini, iMac, and MacBook for the consumer and education markets, and more powerful Mac Pro and MacBook Pro for high-end consumers and professionals involved in design and publishing. Apple scored a runaway hit with its digital music players (iPod) and online music store (iTunes). Other products include mobile phones (iPhone), servers (Xserve), wireless networking equipment (Airport), and publishing and multimedia software. Its FileMaker subsidiary provides database software.

Once the world's top PC maker, Apple has been relegated to relative niche status in a market dominated by Microsoft Windows-based PCs. But the company continues to lead the market in terms of design innovation. Apple's computers run its proprietary UNIX-based operating system, and the company cites the integration and interoperability of its hardware and software as the key advantage over Windows-based PCs.

The uniqueness of Apple's computers is a double-edged sword for the company. The graphical interface and form factor of Apple's computers reflect the aesthetic of co-founder and CEO Steve Jobs, who has long championed the importance of visually attractive, user-friendly design. However, despite market share gains made in recent years, Apple still trails far behind top Window-based PC vendors such as Hewlett-Packard and Dell.

Only Jobs may have expected the level of success the company's music-related products have enjoyed. Since debuting the iPod in 2001, Apple has provided regular feature updates to the line, including touch-screen displays and wireless capabilities. In 2003 Apple announced the launch of an online music service called the iTunes Music Store that lets computer users purchase and download songs for 99 cents each. Apple has since expanded the offerings to include music videos, audiobooks, movies, television shows, and other content. The company has also launched international versions of its music store. In 2008 Apple became the top music retailer by volume in the US market, surpassing Wal-Mart. The following year it rolled out a new demand-based price model (69 cents, 99 cents, $1.29) for music downloads; it also removed the digital rights management (DRM) protection that had essentially restricted the use of iTunes downloads on non-Apple devices.

Early in 2007 the company finally unveiled a long-rumored Apple mobile phone — the iPhone — that combines features of a high-end handset with those of an iPod. Having already captured a significant share of the smart phone market, the iPhone received an update in 2008 that included faster network speed and a lower price tag. Likely looking toward the development of its iPhone, Apple purchased P.A. Semi, a fabless developer of low-power processors, in 2008. iPhones and related products accounted for 6% of Apple's revenues in fiscal 2008.

In an effort to boost brand awareness and its appeal among consumers, the company has opened more than 200 Apple retail stores across the US, and more than 40 more internationally.

HISTORY

College dropouts Steve Jobs and Steve Wozniak founded Apple in 1976 in California's Santa Clara Valley. After Jobs' first sales call brought an order for 50 units, the duo built the Apple I in his garage and sold it without a monitor, keyboard, or casing. Demand convinced Jobs there was a distinct market for small computers, and the company's name (a reference to Jobs' stint on an Oregon farm) and the computer's user-friendly look and feel set it apart from others.

By 1977 Wozniak added a keyboard, color monitor, and eight peripheral device slots (which gave the machine considerable versatility and inspired numerous third-party add-on devices and software). Sales jumped from $7.8 million in 1978 to $117 million in 1980, the year Apple went public. In 1983 Wozniak left the firm and Jobs hired PepsiCo's John Sculley as president. Apple rebounded from failed product introductions that year by unveiling the Macintosh in 1984. After tumultuous struggles with Sculley, Jobs left in 1985 and founded NeXT Software, a designer of applications for developing software. That year Sculley ignored Microsoft founder Bill Gates' appeal for Apple to license its products and make the Microsoft platform an industry standard.

In 1986 Apple blazed the desktop publishing trail with its Mac Plus and LaserWriter printers. The following year it formed the software firm that later became Claris. The late 1980s brought new competition from Microsoft, whose Windows operating system (OS) featured a graphical interface akin to Apple's. Apple sued but lost its claim to copyright protection in 1992.

In 1993 Apple unveiled the Newton handheld computer, but sales were slow. Earnings fell drastically, so the company trimmed its workforce. (Sculley was among the departed.) In 1996 it hired Gilbert Amelio, formerly of National Semiconductor, as CEO, but sales kept dropping and it subsequently cut about 30% of its workforce, canceled projects, and trimmed research costs. Meanwhile Apple's board ousted Amelio and Jobs took the position back on an interim basis.

In 2000, after two-and-a-half years as the semipermanent executive in charge, Jobs took the "interim" out of his title. Apple introduced a digital music player called the iPod in 2001.

In 2002 Apple introduced a new look for its iMac line; featuring a half-dome base and a flat-panel display supported by a pivoting arm, the redesign was the first departure from the original (and, at the time, radical) all-in-one design since iMac's debut in 1998.

Apple announced it would begin incorporating Intel chips into its PC lines in 2005; the transition was completed the following year. Late in 2005 Apple, Motorola, and Cingular Wireless (now AT&T Mobility) announced the debut of a mobile phone with iTunes functionality. In 2006 Apple reached a settlement in a dispute with Creative Technology over technology used in digital music players; Apple agreed to pay the company $100 million in exchange for a license to use Creative's patent related to navigation and organization. Late in 2006 Apple acquired UK-based Proximity, a developer of software used to manage digital audio and video assets.

Apple unveiled a mobile phone offering called the iPhone early in 2007. To reflect the growing breadth of its product portfolio, the company announced it would change its name from Apple Computer to simply Apple.

The company kicked off 2008 with the release of an updated Apple TV device in conjunction with a new iTunes movie rental service.

EXECUTIVES

Chairman: William V. (Bill) Campbell, age 68
CEO and Director: Steven P. (Steve) Jobs, age 54,
  $1 total compensation
COO: Timothy D. (Tim) Cook, age 48,
  $7,423,694 total compensation
SVP and CFO: Peter Oppenheimer, age 46,
  $5,369,447 total compensation
SVP Applications: Sina Tamaddon, age 51
SVP, General Counsel, and Secretary:
  Daniel Cooperman, age 58
SVP Retail: Ronald B. (Ron) Johnson, age 50
SVP Worldwide Product Marketing: Philip W. Schiller,
  age 48
SVP Software Engineering: Bertrand Serlet, age 48
SVP Industrial Design: Jonathan Ive
SVP Devices Hardware Engineering: Mark Papermaster
SVP iPhone Software Engineering and Platform
  Experience: Scott Forstall, age 40
SVP Hardware Engineering: Robert (Bob) Mansfield,
  age 48, $7,111,003 total compensation
Senior Director Marketing Consumer Applications:
  Peter Lowe
Senior Public Relations Manager: Jennifer Bowcock
Manager Worldwide Sales and Services Strategy:
  Jenni Burgess
Investor Relations: Joan Hoover
Auditors: KPMG LLP

LOCATIONS

HQ: Apple Inc.
1 Infinite Loop, Cupertino, CA 95014
Phone: 408-996-1010   **Fax:** 408-974-2113
Web: www.apple.com

2008 Sales

	$ mil.	% of total
US	18,469	57
Other countries	14,010	43
Total	**32,479**	**100**

2008 Sales by Operating Segment

	$ mil.	% of total
Americas	14,573	45
Europe	7,622	23
Retail	6,315	19
Asia/Pacific & Filemaker	2,460	8
Japan	1,509	5
Total	**32,479**	**100**

PRODUCTS/OPERATIONS

2008 Sales

	$ mil.	% of total
Computers		
Portable	8,673	27
Desktop & server	5,603	17
Music-related products		
iPod	9,153	28
iTunes Music Store & other	3,340	10
iPhone & related products and services	1,844	6
Peripherals & other hardware	1,659	5
Software, services & other	2,207	7
Total	**32,479**	**100**

Selected Products

Hardware
  Desktop computers (iMac, Mac mini, Power Macintosh)
  Portable computers (MacBook, MacBook Air, MacBook Pro)
  Displays (Cinema, Studio)
  External hard drives (Time Capsule)
  Keyboards
  Mice (Mighty Mouse)
  Mobile phones (iPhone)
  Portable digital music player (iPod, iPod nano, iPod shuffle)
  Rack-mount servers (Xserve)
  Stereo systems (iPod Hi-Fi)
  Storage systems (Xserve RAID)
  Web cams (iSight)
  Wireless networking systems (AirPort)
Software
  Multimedia (DVD Studio Pro, FinalCut, GarageBand, iDVD, iLife suite, iMovie, iPhoto, iTunes, Quicktime, Soundtrack)
  Networking (Apple Remote Desktop, AppleShare IP)
  Operating system (OS X)
  Personal productivity (AppleWorks, FileMaker, iWork, Keynote, Pages)
  Server (Mac OS X Server)
  Storage area network (SAN) file system (Xsan)
  Web browser (Safari)
Online Services
  .Mac
  Electronic greeting cards (iCard)
  E-mail (Webmail)
  Online multimedia store (iTunes)
  Personal Web page creation (HomePage)
  Remote network storage (iDisk)
  Software (antivirus, backup)
  Technical support

COMPETITORS

Acer	MTV Networks
Adobe Systems	Napster
Amazon.com	NEC
Archos	Netflix
Best Buy	NETGEAR
Blockbuster Inc.	Nokia
Bose	Palm, Inc.
Cisco Systems	Panasonic Corp
Comcast	Philips Electronics
Creative Technology	RealNetworks
Dell	Red Hat
D-Link	Research In Motion
eMachines	Samsung Electronics
eMusic.com	Samsung Group
Ericsson	SanDisk
Fujitsu Technology	SANYO
Solutions	Seagate Technology
Gateway, Inc.	Sharp Electronics
Hewlett-Packard	Sony
High Tech Computer	Sony Ericsson Mobile
IBM	Sun Microsystems
Iriver	Target
Kyocera	Time Warner Cable
Lenovo	Toshiba
Linksys	Wal-Mart
MediaNet Digital	Western Digital
Microsoft	Yahoo!
Motorola, Inc.	

HISTORICAL FINANCIALS

Company Type: Public

Income Statement

FYE: Last Friday in September

	REVENUE ($ mil.)	NET INCOME ($ mil.)	NET PROFIT MARGIN	EMPLOYEES
9/08	32,479.0	4,834.0	14.9%	35,100
9/07	24,006.0	3,496.0	14.6%	21,600
9/06	19,315.0	1,989.0	10.3%	17,787
9/05	13,931.0	1,335.0	9.6%	16,820
9/04	8,279.0	276.0	3.3%	13,426
Annual Growth	**40.7%**	**104.6%**	—	**27.2%**

2008 Year-End Financials

Debt ratio: —
Return on equity: 27.2%
Cash ($ mil.): 11,875
Current ratio: 2.46
Long-term debt ($ mil.): —

No. of shares (mil.): 896
Dividends
  Yield: 0.0%
  Payout: —
Market value ($ mil.): 101,819

Stock History

NASDAQ (GS): AAPL

	STOCK PRICE ($) FY Close	P/E High	P/E Low	PER SHARE ($) Earnings	PER SHARE ($) Dividends	PER SHARE ($) Book Value
9/08	113.66	38	19	5.36	0.00	23.48
9/07	153.47	39	18	3.93	0.00	16.22
9/06	76.98	38	21	2.27	0.00	11.15
9/05	53.61	35	12	1.56	0.00	8.33
9/04	19.38	55	27	0.35	0.00	5.67
Annual Growth	**55.6%**	—	—	**97.8%**	—	**42.7%**

Applied Industrial Technologies

Just imagine getting lost in *that* warehouse. Applied Industrial Technologies distributes millions of parts made by thousands of manufacturers. The short list of products includes bearings, power transmission components, hydraulic and pneumatic components, fabricated rubber products, and linear motion systems. It primarily sells these items through some 450 service centers throughout the US (including Puerto Rico), Canada, and Mexico. The company gets nearly all of its sales in North America. Customers are in the maintenance repair operations (MRO) and OEM markets. Applied also operates regional mechanical, rubber, and fluid power shops that perform services such as engineering design and conveyor belt repair.

In the 21st century Applied has expanded the reach of its distribution and service networks through purchases, especially in Canada and Mexico. In 2008 the company turned on the acquisition faucet and acquired Fluid Power Resource (FPR) for $169 million in cash. Along with FPR comes seven distribution businesses (Bay Advanced Technologies, Carolina Fluid Components, DTS Fluid Power, FluidTech, Hughes HiTech, Hydro Air, and Power Systems) and 19 locations. The acquisition gives Applied additional product scope in the areas of fluid power design and the integration of hydraulics with electronics. It also grows the company's geographic reach throughout North America.

The company relies on a local presence to deliver much of its business. In addition to Applied Industrial Technologies, the service centers operate under the Bearing & Transmission, B&T Rubber, Groupe GLM (Canada), Applied México, and Rafael Benitez Carrillo (Puerto Rico) trade names. The company offers fluid power services through its service centers and from geographic businesses such as Air Draulics, Atelier, and Dees Fluid.

The company's retirement savings plan holds 9% of Applied's shares.

HISTORY

In 1928 founder Joseph Bruening bought the Cleveland office of Detroit Ball Bearing and incorporated his own company as Ohio Ball Bearing. His company acquired a reputation for aggressive acquisitions and maintaining a large inventory. In 1952 the firm bought bearings makers in three other states and changed its name to Bearings Specialists and then to Bearings. By 1973 the company had operations in 25 states. After a serious sales slump in the mid-1980s, former Diamond Shamrock executive John Dannemiller was hired as COO in 1988. He became CEO four years later.

Dannemiller revitalized the company by diversifying its product line, primarily through acquisitions. By 1995 non-bearings technologies accounted for 55% of the company's revenues, up from 35% in 1989. After expanding the company's product lines to include drive systems, rubber products, and fluid power components, it started competing in a broader $21 billion market, rather than the $1.7 billion market for bearings alone.

The company adopted the Applied Industrial Technologies name in 1997. That year it made its largest acquisition to date with the purchase of Invetech, a Detroit distributor with 88 branches in 19 states. It also bought Midwest Rubber and Supply of Denver. Applied broadened its product lines in 1998 by acquiring specialized distributors of bearings and mechanical- and electrical-drive systems. The company closed out the century by shutting down 28 underperforming facilities.

To streamline its businesses, in 2000 Applied reorganized its field sales and service organizations into two product platforms — industrial products and fluid power. It also acquired 21 bearing and power transmission service centers, three rubber fabrication centers, and 15 fluid power facilities from Canada's Dynavest Corp. In 2001 Applied added four facilities in Mexico with its purchase of Baleros Industriales, SA de CV (BISA), a distributor of bearings and power transmission products.

Late in 2002 Applied acquired Canadian industrial parts distributor Industrial Equipment Co., Ltd. Mexico-based Rodamientos y Bandas de la Laguna (industrial product distribution) was acquired the following year for a reported $2.8 million.

In 2006 Applied bought Minnesota Bearing Company, which distributed bearings and power transmission products.

EXECUTIVES

Chairman and CEO: David L. Pugh, age 60
President and COO: Benjamin J. (Ben) Mondics, age 50
VP, CFO, and Treasurer: Mark O. Eisele, age 51
VP and CIO: James T. Hopper, age 64
VP, Chief Administrative Officer, and Government Business: Michael L. Coticchia, age 45
VP Supply Chain Management: Jeffrey A. Ramras, age 53
VP, General Counsel, and Secretary: Fred D. Bauer, age 42
VP Communications and Learning: Richard C. Shaw, age 59
VP Acquisitions and Global Business Development: Todd A. Barlett, age 53
VP Marketing and Strategic Accounts: Thomas E. Armold, age 53
VP Human Resources: Barbara D. Emery, age 49
VP Operational Excellence: Mary E. Kerper, age 57
VP Information Technology: Lonny D. Lawrence, age 45
VP and General Manager, Fluid Power: Warren E. (Bud) Hoffner, age 48
President and COO, Applied Industrial Technologies Ltd., Canada: Ronald A. Sowinski, age 47
Corporate Controller: Daniel T. (Dan) Brezovec, age 47
Manager Public Relations: Julie Kho
Auditors: Deloitte & Touche LLP

LOCATIONS

HQ: Applied Industrial Technologies, Inc.
1 Applied Plaza, Cleveland, OH 44115
Phone: 216-426-4000   **Fax:** 216-426-4845
Web: www.appliedindustrial.com

2009 Sales

	$ mil.	% of total
US	1,674.7	87
Canada	197.8	10
Mexico	50.6	3
Total	**1,923.1**	**100**

PRODUCTS/OPERATIONS

2009 Sales

	$ mil.	% of total
Industrial products	1,422.5	74
Fluid power products	500.6	26
Total	**1,923.1**	**100**

Selected Products

Bearings
  Plane bearings
  Rolling element bearings
    Ball bearings
    Mounted and unmounted bearings
    Roller bearings
Drive Components and Systems
  Electrical components
    Electric motors (AC, DC)
    Motor starters
    Photoelectrics, encoders, sensors
    Variable speed controllers (AC, DC)
    Servo motion controllers
  Mechanical components
    Belt drive components
    Chain drive components
    Clutch/brake mechanicals
    Coupling and U joints
    Material handling products
    Open gears
    Speed reducers and gear motors
Fluid Power
  Accessories (gauges, ball valves, accumulators, subplates, manifold, hose and fittings, hydraulic oil)
  Cylinders
  Filters
  Motors
  Power supplies
  Pumps
  Valves
Linear Technologies
  Bellows
  Cable and hose carriers
  Controls
  Gearheads
  Linear motors
  Precision balls
  Precision mechanical components
  Steps and servo motors
Rubber Products
  Belt drive components
  Conveyor belting and accessories
  Hydraulic hose, fittings, and equipment
  Industrial hose and fittings
  Power transmission belts
  Rubber shop services
Specialty Products
  Analytical tools
  Chemicals (adhesives, lubricants, paints, sealants)
  Fluid sealing products (seals, gaskets)
  General mill supplies
  Maintenance tools
  Precision mechanical components
Shop Services
  Cylinder repair and manufacturing
  Fluid cleanliness consulting
  Hydraulic pump and motor repair
  Hydraulic servo and proportional valve services
  Mechanical repair and maintenance services
  Pneumatic circuit services
  Rubber shop services

COMPETITORS

Commercial Solutions	Kaydon
Dana Holding	Mark IV
DXP Enterprises	McMaster-Carr
Fastenal	Motion Industries
Fenner	MSC Industrial Direct
General Parts	Parker Hannifin
Genuine Parts	Premier Farnell
Hillman Companies	SKF
Horizon Solutions	Tomkins
Ingersoll-Rand	Tuthill
Kaman	W.W. Grainger

HISTORICAL FINANCIALS

Company Type: Public

Income Statement

FYE: June 30

	REVENUE ($ mil.)	NET INCOME ($ mil.)	NET PROFIT MARGIN	EMPLOYEES
6/09	1,923.1	42.3	2.2%	4,673
6/08	2,089.5	95.5	4.6%	4,805
6/07	2,014.1	86.0	4.3%	4,635
6/06	1,900.8	72.3	3.8%	4,683
6/05	1,717.1	55.3	3.2%	4,415
Annual Growth	**2.9%**	**(6.5%)**	**—**	**1.4%**

2009 Year-End Financials

Debt ratio: 14.8%
Return on equity: 8.4%
Cash ($ mil.): 28
Current ratio: 3.36
Long-term debt ($ mil.): 75
No. of shares (mil.): 42
Dividends
  Yield: 3.0%
  Payout: 60.6%
Market value ($ mil.): 834

Stock History

NYSE: AIT

	STOCK PRICE ($) FY Close	P/E High/Low	PER SHARE ($) Earnings	PER SHARE ($) Dividends	PER SHARE ($) Book Value
6/09	19.70	32 14	0.99	0.60	12.01
6/08	24.17	16 10	2.19	0.60	11.86
6/07	29.50	16 11	1.93	0.48	10.66
6/06	24.31	20 13	1.57	0.40	9.80
6/05	21.53	19 10	1.20	0.28	9.29
Annual Growth	**(2.2%)**	**— —**	**(4.7%)**	**21.0%**	**6.6%**

Applied Materials

Today, semiconductor manufacturing; tomorrow, the world — of alternative energy sources. Applied Materials is, by far, the world's largest maker of semiconductor production equipment. With its acquisition of Applied Films, the company moved into the market for equipment used in making solar power cells. Applied's machines vie for supremacy in many segments of the chip-making process, including deposition (layering film on wafers), etching (removing portions of chip material to allow precise construction of circuits), and semiconductor metrology and inspection equipment. More than two-thirds of Applied's sales come from the Asia/Pacific region, with Taiwan leading the way.

Leading customers include Advanced Micro Devices, Freescale Semiconductor, Intel, and Samsung Electronics (16% of sales).

With fiscal 2008 sales falling by about 16% from the previous year, Applied said it would reduce its workforce in fiscal 2009 by around 12%, or 1,800 positions. During fiscal 2008 the company trimmed its worldwide payroll by 1,000 jobs, a 7% cutback.

Applied sees the solar photovoltaic production equipment market increasing from $1 billion in

2006 to more than $3 billion in 2010. Applied added to its PV cells production equipment portfolio in early 2008 by acquiring Baccini SpA, an Italian supplier of material handling automation systems for ultrathin silicon wafers.

As semiconductors are incorporated into more and more products, demand for ever-smaller and more complex chips grows. Just as quickly, chip-making machinery becomes obsolete — which is good news for Applied's sales. To keep up with the chip industry's constant drive toward smaller circuits, larger wafers, and new technologies such as copper interconnects, Applied relies on heavy R&D efforts.

The company has used a combination of acquisitions and internal development to bolster its moves into the few areas of chip manufacturing — such as atomic layer deposition equipment — where it wasn't already a major player. Applied has partnered with specialized construction firms to offer services to speed installation of chip equipment in new plants.

Applied occasionally turned to joint ventures and other collaborative efforts to enter new markets. In 1993 it formed a JV with Komatsu to make LCD production equipment. Applied bought out Komatsu's interest in the JV, Applied Komatsu Technology (AKT), in 1999. Applied has long worked with ASML Holding, the Netherlands-based supplier of photolithography tools, on integrating lithography equipment with other chip-making equipment.

Applied has also formed a joint venture with Dainippon Screen Manufacturing. The JV, Sokudo, combines Screen's wafer track equipment line with cash and technical expertise from Applied.

HISTORY

Applied Materials was founded in 1967 in Mountain View, California, as a maker of chemical vapor deposition systems for fabricating semiconductors. After years of rapid growth, the company went public in 1972. Two years later it purchased wafer maker Galamar Industries.

In 1975 Applied Materials suffered a 45% drop in sales as the semiconductor industry (and the US economy) contracted. Financial and managerial problems plagued the company following the recession, so in 1976 James Morgan, a former division manager for conglomerate Textron, was chosen to replace founder Michael McNeilly as CEO. Two years later Morgan also became chairman.

After selling Galamar (1977) and other non-core units and extending the company's line of credit, Morgan announced a plan to move into Japan. The company's first joint venture, Applied Materials Japan, was set up in 1979.

Morgan's hunch that Japan would become a semiconductor hub paid off. His early arrival, plus his attention to Japanese ways of doing business, put Applied way ahead of its American competitors. Morgan wrote *Cracking the Japanese Market* about his experiences doing business in Japan, which came to account for one-sixth of the company's sales.

When another slump hit the chip industry in 1985, Morgan revved up research and development. With two separate manufacturing technologies poised to compete, Morgan essentially bet on the fast but unproven one-at-a-time,

multiple-chamber method (as opposed to the batch process system). The resulting Precision 5000 series machines revolutionized the industry and catapulted Applied Materials to the top of it. Applied's sales passed the $1 billion mark for the first time in 1993.

Shaking off an industry slump, in 1996 Applied acquired two Israeli companies, Opal (scanning electronic microscopes used in wafer inspection) and Orbot Instruments (wafer and photomask inspection systems), to grab nearly 5% of the crowded chip inspection tools market.

In early 2000 Applied began its move into photolithography — one of the few industry segments in which it didn't operate — by acquiring Etec Systems, a leading maker of semiconductor mask pattern generation equipment, for nearly $2 billion.

A sharp global downturn in the chip industry led the company in early 2001 to take a variety of cost-cutting measures (including executive pay cuts, a voluntary separation plan, and temporary plant shutdowns) that stopped short of layoffs. Later that year, though, Applied let go about 2,000 employees — about 10% of its workforce — in response to continuing poor conditions in the chip market. Late that year the company enacted another 10% layoff, this one affecting 1,700 workers. It repeated the move late in 2002 as the chip industry's worst-ever slump stretched across two full years.

In 2003 longtime Intel executive Michael Splinter succeeded Morgan as CEO; Morgan remained chairman.

In 2006 Applied acquired Applied Films, a supplier of thin-film deposition equipment, for around $464 million. The company delved further into the solar energy market with the 2007 acquisition of HCT Shaping Systems for about $483 million. HCT supplied equipment for making the crystalline silicon wafers that go into producing solar cells.

In 2007 Applied gave up on the ion implantation equipment market, where it was a perennial #3 (behind Varian Semiconductor Equipment Associates and Axcelis Technologies with its SEN Corp. joint venture). The company closed its Applied Implant Technologies operations in Horsham, England, at the end of 2007, with about 270 employees there losing their jobs.

EXECUTIVES

Chairman Emeritus: James C. (Jim) Morgan, age 70
Chairman, President, and CEO:
   Michael R. (Mike) Splinter, age 58
EVP Sales and Marketing: Franz Janker, age 59
SVP; General Manager, Silicon Systems Group:
   Thomas (Tom) St. Dennis, age 56
SVP; General Manager, Applied Global Services:
   Manfred Kerschbaum, age 54
SVP, General Counsel, and Corporate Secretary:
   Joseph J. Sweeney, age 60
SVP and General Manager Strategic Operations:
   Randhir Thakur, age 46
SVP; General Manager Display and Thin Film Solar Products: Gilad Almogy, age 43
SVP and CTO; General Manager, Energy and Environmental Solutions: Mark R. Pinto, age 49
SVP and CFO: George S. Davis, age 51

Group VP and CIO, Global Information Services:
   Ron Kifer, age 57
Group VP and CTO, Silicon Systems: Hans Stork
Group VP and Chief of Staff: Menachem Erad, age 60
Group VP Global Human Resources:
   Jeannette Liebman, age 61
VP and General Manager, Corporate Business Development: Thomas T. Edman, age 46
VP Marketing, Energy and Environmental Solutions:
   John A. Antone
VP Government Affairs: Gary Fazzino
VP and Controller: Yvonne Weatherford, age 57
President, Applied Solar Business: Charles Gay
Managing Director, Global Community Affairs:
   Mark Walker
Auditors: KPMG LLP

LOCATIONS

HQ: Applied Materials, Inc.
   3050 Bowers Ave., Santa Clara, CA 95054
Phone: 408-727-5555   **Fax:** 408-748-9943
Web: www.appliedmaterials.com

Applied Materials has more than 100 facilities in China, France, Germany, India, Israel, Italy, Japan, Malaysia, the Netherlands, Singapore, South Korea, Taiwan, the UK, and the US.

2008 Sales

	$ mil.	% of total
Asia/Pacific		
Taiwan	1,837.1	22
South Korea	1,309.5	16
Japan	1,217.6	15
China & other countries	1,296.0	16
North America	1,519.9	19
Europe	949.1	12
Total	**8,129.2**	**100**

PRODUCTS/OPERATIONS

2008 Sales

	$ mil.	% of total
Silicon	4,005.1	49
Applied Global Services	2,328.9	29
Display	975.6	12
Energy & Environmental Solutions	819.6	10
Total	**8,129.2**	**100**

Selected Products

Chemical mechanical polishing/planarization systems (wafer polishing)
Deposition systems (deposit layers of conducting and insulating material on wafers)
   Dielectric deposition (chemical vapor deposition, or CVD)
   Metal (CVD, electroplating, or physical vapor deposition)
   Silicon and thermal deposition
   Sputtering (physical vapor deposition) for solar cells
   Thin-film silicon solar cells
   Web coating for flexible solar cells
Etch systems (remove portions of a wafer surface for circuit construction)
Inspection systems (defect review for reticles — patterned plates which hold precise images of chip circuit patterns — and wafers)
Ion implant systems (implant ions into wafer surface to change conductive properties)
Manufacturing process optimization software
Metrology systems
   CD-SEM (scanning electron microscope system)
   Optical monitoring systems (for glass or web coating systems)
Rapid thermal processing systems (heat wafers to change electrical characteristics)

HISTORICAL FINANCIALS

Company Type: Public

Income Statement

FYE: Last Sunday in October

	REVENUE ($ mil.)	NET INCOME ($ mil.)	NET PROFIT MARGIN	EMPLOYEES
10/08	8,129.2	960.7	11.8%	15,410
10/07	9,734.9	1,710.2	17.6%	15,328
10/06	9,167.0	1,516.7	16.5%	14,072
10/05	6,991.8	1,209.9	17.3%	12,576
10/04	8,013.1	1,351.3	16.9%	12,960
Annual Growth	0.4%	(8.2%)	—	4.4%

2008 Year-End Financials

Debt ratio: 2.7%
Return on equity: 12.5%
Cash ($ mil.): 1,412
Current ratio: 2.26
Long-term debt ($ mil.): 202

No. of shares (mil.): 1,333
Dividends
  Yield: 1.9%
  Payout: 34.3%
Market value ($ mil.): 17,209

Stock History

NASDAQ (GS): AMAT

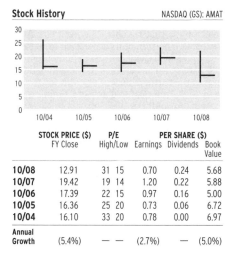

	STOCK PRICE ($) FY Close	P/E High/Low	PER SHARE ($) Earnings	Dividends	Book Value
10/08	12.91	31 15	0.70	0.24	5.68
10/07	19.42	19 14	1.20	0.22	5.88
10/06	17.39	22 15	0.97	0.16	5.00
10/05	16.36	25 20	0.73	0.06	6.72
10/04	16.10	33 20	0.78	0.00	6.97
Annual Growth	(5.4%)	— —	(2.7%)	—	(5.0%)

ARAMARK Corporation

Keeping employees fed and clothed is one mark of this company. ARAMARK is the world's #3 contract foodservice provider (behind Compass Group and Sodexo) and the #2 uniform supplier (behind Cintas) in the US. It offers corporate dining services and operates concessions at many sports arenas and other entertainment venues, while its ARAMARK Refreshment Services unit is a leading provider of vending and beverage services. The company also provides facilities management services. Through ARAMARK Uniform and Career Apparel, the company supplies uniforms for health care, public safety, and technology workers. Founded in 1959, ARAMARK is owned by an investment group led by chairman and CEO Joseph Neubauer.

A leader in its industry, the company continues to look for opportunities to expand not only its client base, but also to expand the number of services it supplies for its existing customers. In 2008 its concessions unit inked a deal with SMG Management to provide food and beverage services at more than 30 concert venues. ARAMARK is also targeting such industry segments as correctional facilities and health care operators.

Keen on international expansion, the company has focused on Europe and Asia, including the burgeoning market in China where it provided foodservices for the 2008 Olympic Games in Beijing. That same year ARAMARK acquired The Patman Group, expanding its reach into India. International markets now account for more than 25% of the company's revenue.

With backing from such investment firms as CCMP Capital, Thomas H. Lee Partners, and Warburg Pincus, Neubauer took the company private in 2007 for $8.3 billion, including the assumption of $2 billion in debt. (The executive already owned 40% of ARAMARK.) The deal marked the second such transaction for the company, having been taken private by Neubauer and a management group in the 1980s.

HISTORY

Davre Davidson began his career in foodservice by selling peanuts from the backseat of his car in the 1930s. He landed his first vending contract with Douglas Aircraft (later McDonnell Douglas, now part of Boeing) in 1935. Through that relationship, Davidson met William Fishman of Chicago, who had vending operations in the Midwest. Davidson and Fishman merged their companies in 1959 to form Automatic Retailers of America (ARA). Davidson became chairman and CEO of the new company; Fishman served as president.

Focusing on candy, beverage, and cigarette machines, ARA became the leading vending machine company in the US by 1961, with operations in 38 states. Despite slimmer profit margins, ARA moved into food vending in the early 1960s. It acquired 150 foodservice businesses between 1959-1963, quickly becoming a leader in the operation of cafeterias at colleges, hospitals, and work sites. The company (which changed its name to ARA Services in 1966) grew so rapidly that the FTC stepped in; ARA agreed to restrict future food vending acquisitions.

ARA provided foodservices at the 1968 Summer Olympics in Mexico City, beginning a long-term relationship with the amateur sports event. The company also diversified into publication distribution that year, and in 1970 it expanded into janitorial and maintenance services. A foray into residential care for the elderly began in 1973 (and ended in 1993 with the sale of the subsidiary). ARA also entered into emergency room staffing services (sold 1997). The company expanded into child care (National Child Care Centers) in 1980.

CFO Joseph Neubauer became CEO in 1983 and was named chairman in 1984. To avoid a hostile takeover shortly thereafter, he led a $1.2 billion leveraged buyout. After the buyout, ARA began refining its core operations. It acquired Szabo (correctional foodservices) in 1986, Children's World Learning Centers in 1987, and Coordinated Health Services (medical billing services) in 1993.

ARA changed its name to ARAMARK in 1994 as part of an effort to raise its profile with its ultimate customers, the public. The company's concession operations suffered from long work stoppages in baseball (1994) and hockey (1995). ARAMARK acquired Galls (North America's #1 supplier of public safety equipment) in 1996, and in 1997 announced plans to become 100% employee-owned.

The following year ARAMARK entered into a joint venture with privately held Anderson News Company, exchanging its magazine distribution operations for a minority stake in the new business. In 2000 the company was on hand to supply foodservices to the Olympic Games in Sydney.

With the new millennium the company was focused on expansion, buying the food and beverage concessions business of conglomerate Ogden Corp. for $236 million. The company penned a 10-year deal with Boeing in 2000 to supply foodservices to about 100 locations, one of the biggest foodservice contracts ever. It also bought Wackenhut's Correctional Foodservice Management division.

ARAMARK continued its expansion with the purchase of ServiceMaster's management services division in 2001 for about $800 million — opening doors in non-food management, groundskeeping, and custodial services. In late 2001 ARAMARK went public.

In 2002 it paid $100 million for Premier, Inc.'s Clinical Technology Services, which maintains and repairs clinical equipment in about 170 hospitals and health care facilities in the US. ARAMARK also completed its acquisition of Fine Host Corporation, which added approximately 900 client locations, for about $100 million.

In 2003 ARAMARK exited the child care business when it sold its Educational Resources unit (operator of Children's World Learning Centers) to Michael Milken's Knowledge Learning Corporation for $225 million. Longtime executive Bill Leonard was named president and CEO that year, with Neubauer taking on the title of executive chairman.

Expanding its Canadian presence in cleanroom services in 2004, ARAMARK acquired Toronto-based Cleanroom Garments. That same year, ARAMARK made its first foray into China by acquiring a 90% stake in Bright China Service Industries, a facilities services firm. After a brief reign, Leonard resigned that year and Neubauer returned to being CEO of the company.

In 2007 Neubauer, with the backing of such investment firms as CCMP Capital, Thomas H. Lee Partners, and Warburg Pincus, took ARAMARK private for $8.3 billion, including the assumption of $2 billion in debt.

EXECUTIVES

Chairman and CEO: Joseph (Joe) Neubauer, age 67
EVP and CFO; Group Executive, ARAMARK Uniform and Career Apparel: L. Frederick Sutherland, age 57
EVP and Chief Globalization Officer; President, ARAMARK International: Ravi K. Saligram, age 52
EVP; Group President, Global Food, Hospitality, and Facilities Services: Andrew C. Kerin, age 45
EVP; President ARAMARK Uniform and Career Apparel (AUCA): Thomas J. (Tom) Vozzo, age 46
EVP Human Resources: Lynn B. McKee, age 53
SVP and Treasurer: Christopher S. (Chris) Holland, age 42
SVP, Controller, and Chief Accounting Officer: Joseph M. (Joe) Munnelly, age 44
Auditors: KPMG LLP

LOCATIONS

HQ: ARAMARK Corporation
ARAMARK Tower, 1101 Market St.
Philadelphia, PA 19107
Phone: 215-238-3000   **Fax:** 215-238-3333
Web: www.aramark.com

2008 Sales

	$ mil.	% of total
US	9,998.0	74
International	3,472.2	26
Total	**13,470.2**	**100**

PRODUCTS/OPERATIONS

2008 Sales

	$ mil.	% of total
Food & support services		
North America	8,924.9	66
International	2,783.0	21
Uniform & career apparel	1,762.3	13
Total	**13,470.2**	**100**

Selected Operations

Food and support services
  ARAMARK Convention Centers
  ARAMARK Correctional Services
  ARAMARK Education
  ARAMARK Facility Services
  ARAMARK Food Services
  ARAMARK Harrison Lodging (conference centers)
  ARAMARK Healthcare
  ARAMARK Higher Education
  ARAMARK Innovative Dining Solutions
  ARAMARK Parks and Destinations
  ARAMARK Refreshment Services (vending services)
  ARAMARK Sports and Entertainment
Uniform and career apparel
  ARAMARK Cleanroom Services
  ARAMARK Uniform & Career Apparel
  Galls (tactical equipment and apparel)

COMPETITORS

ABM Industries
Alsco
Angelica Corporation
Autogrill
Centerplate
Cintas
Compass Group
Delaware North
Elior
G&K Services
Healthcare Services
ISS A/S
Sodexo
UniFirst

HISTORICAL FINANCIALS

Company Type: Private

Income Statement

FYE: Friday nearest September 30

	REVENUE ($ mil.)	NET INCOME ($ mil.)	NET PROFIT MARGIN	EMPLOYEES
9/08	13,470.2	39.5	0.3%	260,000
9/07	12,384.3	30.9	0.2%	250,000
Annual Growth	**8.8%**	**27.8%**	**—**	**4.0%**

Net Income History

Arch Coal

What powers your power company? Perhaps Arch Coal. About half of the electricity generated in the US comes from coal, and Arch Coal is one of the country's largest coal producers, behind industry leader Peabody Energy. Arch Coal produces about 140 million tons of coal a year from about 20 mines in the western US and Central Appalachia; the company has proved and probable reserves of 2.8 billion tons. Steam coal — low-ash coal used by electric utilities to produce steam in boilers — accounts for the vast majority of the company's sales. To store and ship its Appalachian coal, the company operates the Arch Coal Terminal near the Ohio River.

In 2009 the company agreed to acquire Rio Tinto's Jacobs Ranch mine in the Powder River Basin of Wyoming for $760 million. The mine had been included in Rio Tinto spin-off Cloud Peak Energy, though it seems that unit's fate is up in the air at the moment.

HISTORY

Raised in the Oklahoma oil patch, J. Fred Miles founded the Swiss Drilling Company in 1910 and started wildcatting oil wells. Unable to compete against the low prices offered by Standard Oil, Miles moved his company in 1916 to eastern Kentucky and acquired control of 200,000 acres of oil land. With backers such as the Armours of Chicago, Swiss Oil Company soon became one of the leading oil companies in Kentucky.

In the early 1920s the company's oil wells started to play out during a postwar depression. Miles fought back by expanding into refining, buying Tri-State Refining in 1930. The company changed its name in 1936 to Ashland Oil and Refining Company, a business that turned a profit even during the darkest days of the Depression. Miles didn't survive the transition, however. By

1926 Ashland was outperforming its parent, and investors eased Miles out the corporate door.

Pearl Harbor only brought more success to a business the American war machine needed to fuel its ships, planes, and tanks. Although peace brought the inevitable recession, America's postwar love affair with the automobile helped Ashland continue to thrive.

During the 1950s Ashland's refineries ran at near capacity. In 1969 Merle Kelce and Guy Heckman, along with help from Ashland, formed Arch Mineral. Ashland had decided that it needed to diversify and lessen its dependence on oil refining. The Hunt family of Dallas, Texas, put their money into the venture in 1971, and in the following years the company bought Southwestern Illinois Coal Corporation, USX's Lynch Properties, Diamond Shamrock Coal, and Lawson-Hamilton Properties. By the end of 1996, the company owned some 1.5 billion tons of recoverable coal reserves.

Ashland struck out on its own in the coal business in 1975, forming Ashland Coal. Ashland Coal then began a series of acquisitions lasting 15 years. The company bought Addington Brothers Mining (1976), Hobet Mining and Construction (1977), Saarbergwerke (1981), Coal-Mac (1989), Mingo Logan (1990), and Dal-Tex Coal (1992). Growing through that binge of acquisitions, the company went public in 1988.

In 1997 Arch Mineral and Ashland Coal merged into Arch Coal, an entity that consolidated Ashland's coal assets. Ashland kept a 58% stake. In 1998 Arch Coal purchased Atlantic Richfield's (ARCO) US coal operations for $1.14 billion, making itself the second-largest coal producer in the US. That year Arch Coal also created Arch Western Resources, a joint venture in which Arch Coal owns 99% and ARCO owns 1%.

Regulatory pressures and low coal prices in 1999 forced the company to close three mines — the Dal-Tex in West Virginia and two surface mines in Kentucky.

Arch Coal recorded a $346 million loss in 1999. To recover from the profit plunge and benefit from increased demand as utilities complied with Clean Air Act mandates, the company boosted production at its low-sulfur coal Black Thunder mine in Wyoming. In 2000 Ashland reduced its stake in Arch Coal to 12%; it sold the remainder of its stock the next year.

In 2002 Arch Coal and WPP Group formed a partnership, Natural Resource Partners, which went public that October. The next year Arch Coal sold a portion of its stake back to Natural Resource's management for $115 million, and by 2004 Arch Coal had divested its remaining holdings in the partnership.

In 2005 Arch Coal sold four of its mining operations in southern West Virginia to Magnum Coal, a company backed by affiliates of investment firm ArcLight Capital. The sale was part of Arch Coal's strategy of focusing on its core areas, the Central Appalachian Basin and the Powder River Basin. In 2004 the company acquired Triton Coal and its mines in the Powder River Basin. Conversely, Arch Coal dipped its toe into the increasingly important Illinois Basin region with the acquisition of a one-third interest in Knight Hawk Coal.

EXECUTIVES

Chairman and CEO: Steven F. Leer, age 56,
$6,561,609 total compensation
President, COO, and Director: John W. Eaves, age 51,
$4,309,979 total compensation
SVP and CFO: John T. Drexler, age 39,
$1,087,820 total compensation
SVP Law, Secretary, and General Counsel:
Robert G. (Bob) Jones, age 52
**SVP Strategic Development; President, Arch Energy
Resources:** C. Henry Besten Jr., age 60,
$2,381,535 total compensation
SVP Operations: Paul A. Lang, age 48
VP Business Development: David B. Peugh, age 54
VP Marketing and Trading: David N. Warnecke, age 53,
$2,262,756 total compensation
VP Eastern Operations: Robert W. Shanks, age 54
VP and CIO: David E. Hartley
VP and Chief Accounting Officer: John W. Lorson
VP Human Resources: Sheila B. Feldman, age 54
VP Government, Investor, and Public Affairs:
Deck S. Slone, age 45
VP Tax: C. David Steele
VP Safety: Anthony S. Bumbico
VP Market Research: Andy Blumenfeld
Treasurer: James E. Florczak
Corporate Controller: Gregory A. Szczepan
Auditors: Ernst & Young LLP

LOCATIONS

HQ: Arch Coal, Inc.
1 CityPlace Dr., Ste. 300, St. Louis, MO 63141
Phone: 314-994-2700   **Fax:** 314-994-2878
Web: www.archcoal.com

2008 Sales

	$ mil.	% of total
Central Appalachia	1,162.4	39
Powder River Basin	1,162.0	39
Western Bituminous	659.4	22
Total	**2,983.8**	**100**

PRODUCTS/OPERATIONS

Selected Operations

Central Appalachia
 Coal-Mac (West Virginia)
 Lone Mountain (Kentucky)

Western United States
 Arch of Wyoming (Wyoming)
 Black Thunder (Wyoming)
 Coal Creek (Wyoming)
 Dugout Canyon (Utah)
 Skyline (Utah)
 SUFCO (Utah)
 West Elk (Colorado)

Selected Subsidiaries and Affiliates

Arch Coal Terminal
Arch Western Resources, LLC (99%)
 Arch of Wyoming, LLC
 Canyon Fuel Co., LLC
 Mountain Coal Company, LLC
  West Elk mine (Colorado)
 Thunder Basin Coal Company, LLC
  Black Thunder mine (Wyoming)

COMPETITORS

Alliance Resource
Alpha Natural Resources
CONSOL Energy
Drummond Company
International Coal Group
James River Coal
Massey Energy
Peabody Energy
Penn Virginia

HISTORICAL FINANCIALS

Company Type: Public

Income Statement

FYE: December 31

	REVENUE ($ mil.)	NET INCOME ($ mil.)	NET PROFIT MARGIN	EMPLOYEES
12/08	2,983.8	354.3	11.9%	4,300
12/07	2,413.6	174.7	7.2%	4,030
12/06	2,500.4	260.6	10.4%	4,050
12/05	2,508.8	38.1	1.5%	3,700
12/04	1,907.2	113.7	6.0%	4,150
Annual Growth	**11.8%**	**32.9%**	**—**	**0.9%**

2008 Year-End Financials

Debt ratio: 78.3%
Return on equity: 21.7%
Cash ($ mil.): 71
Current ratio: 1.07
Long-term debt ($ mil.): 1,354
No. of shares (mil.): 162
Dividends
 Yield: 2.1%
 Payout: 13.9%
Market value ($ mil.): 2,647

Stock History

NYSE: ACI

	STOCK PRICE ($) FY Close	P/E High/Low		PER SHARE ($) Earnings	Dividends	Book Value
12/08	16.29	32	4	2.45	0.34	10.64
12/07	44.93	37	23	1.21	0.27	9.43
12/06	30.03	31	14	1.80	0.22	8.41
12/05	39.75	235	95	0.17	0.16	7.29
12/04	17.77	22	15	0.89	0.15	6.65
Annual Growth	**(2.2%)**	**—**	**—**	**28.8%**	**22.7%**	**12.5%**

Archer Daniels Midland

Archer Daniels Midland (ADM) knows how to grind and squeeze a fortune out of humble plants. It is one of the world's largest processors of oilseeds, corn, and wheat. Its main offerings include soybean, peanut, and other oilseed products. From corn, it produces syrups, sweeteners, citric and lactic acids, and ethanol, among other products. ADM also produces wheat and durum flour for bakeries and pasta makers; cocoa beans for confectioners; and malt for brewers. It operates one of the world's largest crop origination and transportation networks, through which it connects crops and their markets in more than 60 countries.

With some 240 plants, ADM processes the three largest crops in the US — corn, soybeans, and wheat — for sale to food, beverage, and chemical industries. About one-third of the company's sales come from its oilseed products, including vegetable oils, animal feeds, and emulsifiers. Its 50% joint venture with Golden Peanut Company is a major domestic and foreign supplier of peanuts. ADM also makes vitamin E, textured vegetable protein (TVP), and cotton cellulose pulp (for making paper).

ADM has increased its production of liquid sorbitol due to the increased demand for sugar-free products in the marketplace. Sorbitol is used in the manufacture of items such as toothpaste and chewing gum. It has increased production of ethanol, which can be used as an alternative fuel for automobiles; it also has significant biodiesel operations.

The company continues to introduce value-added products. A line of trans-free fats and oils, NovaLipid, allows the production of margarines, shortenings, and other products with near zero levels of trans-fatty acids. It also makes cholesterol-lowering CardioAid plant steroids, which can be added to such food as sauces, pasta, beverages, and cereals.

Strengthening its European cocoa business, in 2009 the company acquired German chocolate and cocoa-powder maker, Schokinag-Schokolade-Industrie Herrmann.

Already a top producer of ethanol, ADM entered into an alliance with ConocoPhillips in 2007 to develop biofuel, namely to research, develop, and commercialize the process of converting biomass from crops, wood, and switchgrass into biocrude, a non-fossil substance that can be made into fuel.

In 2007 long-time chairman G. Allen Andreas stepped down and was replaced by company CEO and president Patricia Woertz, who, before joining ADM, worked for Chevron.

State Farm Mutual Automobile Insurance Company owns almost 9% of the company.

HISTORY

John Daniels began crushing flaxseed to make linseed oil in 1878, and in 1902 he formed Daniels Linseed Company in Minneapolis. George Archer, another flaxseed crusher, joined the company the following year. In 1923 the company bought Midland Linseed Products and became Archer Daniels Midland (ADM). ADM kept buying oil processing companies in the Midwest during the 1920s. It also started to research the chemical composition of linseed oil.

ADM entered the flour milling business in 1930 when it bought Commander-Larabee (then the #3 flour miller in the US). In the 1930s the company discovered a method for extracting lecithin (an emulsifier food additive used in candy and other products) from soybean oil, significantly lowering its price.

The enterprise grew rapidly following WWII. By 1949 it was the leading processor of linseed oil and soybeans in the US and was fourth in flour milling. During the early 1950s ADM began foreign expansion in earnest.

In 1966 the company's leadership passed to Dwayne Andreas, a former Cargill executive who had purchased a block of Archer family stock. Andreas focused ADM on soybeans, including the production of textured vegetable protein, a cheap soybean by-product used in foodstuffs.

Andreas' restructuring paved the way for productivity and expansion. In 1971 the company acquired Corn Sweeteners (glutens, high-fructose syrups). Other acquisitions included Tabor (grain, 1975) and Colombian Peanut (1981). ADM formed a grain-marketing joint venture with GROWMARK in 1985.

In 1995 the FBI — aided by ADM executive-turned-informer Mark Whitacre — joined a federal investigation of lysine and citric acid price-fixing by the company. The next year ADM agreed to plead guilty to two criminal charges of price-fixing and paid $100 million in penalties, a record at that time for a US criminal antitrust case. Whitacre later lost his immunity when convicted of defrauding ADM out of $9 million. He and two other ADM executives, including onetime ADM heir apparent Michael Andreas, were tried and convicted in 1998 and sentenced to prison in 1999.

Meanwhile, ADM continued to grow. In 1997 it acquired W. R. Grace's cocoa business and, after naming Allen Andreas (Dwayne's nephew) as CEO, bought 42% of Canada-based United Grain Growers. Dwayne turned over the chairman post to Allen in early 1999. In 2000 ADM was again cited for involvement in the price-fixing of lysine and was fined $45 million by the European Commission.

In 2002 ADM acquired Minnesota Corn Processors (MCP), its chief competitor in the ethanol market. In 2003 ADM reached a settlement with the US government regarding violations of the Clean Air Act and agreed to pay approximately $340 million to clean up air pollution at 52 of its midwestern food-processing plants. ADM announced a joint research agreement with Volkswagen AG in 2004 in order to develop next-generation, clean, renewable biodiesel fuels for the auto industry.

In mid-2004 ADM agreed to shell out $400 million to settle a class-action antitrust lawsuit claiming the company conspired to fix the price of high fructose corn syrup between the years of 1991 and 1995. Syrup customers involved in the suit included Coca-Cola and PepsiCo. Faced with potential damage awards of nearly $5 billion, the company chose to settle before going to trial.

In 2006 the company named Patricia Woertz as president, CEO, and director. Woertz joined ADM after having served as an EVP at energy giant Chevron. With her appointment, ADM became the largest publicly traded US company to be headed by a woman.

In 2006 ADM (along with two Dutch companies, Akzo Nobel and Avebe) was found guilty of price fixing in the cleaning agent sodium gluconate sector by an EU court. ADM was fined almost $13 million.

EXECUTIVES

Chairman, President, and CEO: Patricia A. (Pat) Woertz, age 56
President, ADM Alliance Nutrition: Terry Myers
EVP and CFO: Steven R. Mills, age 53
EVP, Secretary, and General Counsel: David J. Smith, age 53
EVP Commercial and Production Division: John D. Rice, age 54
SVP Toepfer and ADM Value Creation Team: Lewis W. Batchelder, age 63
SVP Food and Feed Ingredients: Edward A. Harjehausen, age 58
SVP Human Resources: Michael (Mike) D'Ambrose, age 51
VP Manufacturing and Technical Services: Dennis C. Garceau, age 58
VP Security and Corporate Services: Mark J. Cheviron, age 59
VP Governmental Affairs: John G. Reed Jr., age 75
VP Commodity Risk Management: Kenneth A. Robinson, age 59
VP Compliance and Ethics: Scott A. Roney, age 44
VP Insurance and Risk Management, and President, Agrinational Insurance Company: Michael Lusk, age 59
VP Public Relations: Karla M. Miller
VP Investor Relations: Dwight E. Grimestad
VP and Treasurer: Vikram Luthar, age 41
VP Human Resources: Randall J. (Randy) Moon, age 47
VP and Controller: John Stott, age 41
VP Corporate Communications: Victoria Podesta, age 52
Auditors: Ernst & Young LLP

LOCATIONS

HQ: Archer Daniels Midland Company
4666 Faries Pkwy., Decatur, IL 62525
Phone: 217-424-5200 **Fax:** 217-424-6196
Web: www.admworld.com

2009 Sales

	$ mil.	% of total
US	35,485	51
Germany	7,431	11
Other countries	26,291	38
Total	**69,207**	**100**

PRODUCTS/OPERATIONS

2009 Sales

	$ mil.	% of total
Agricultural services	34,351	47
Oilseeds processing	24,627	34
Corn processing	7,803	11
Other	5,535	8
Adjustment	(3,109)	—
Total	**69,207**	**100**

Selected Products

Animal Feed
    Corn germ meal
    Corn gluten feed
    Corn gluten meal
    Corn oil
    Condensed fermented corn extractives
    Distillers dried grain
    Wet distillers grains
    Whet corn gluten feed
Food
    Acidulants
    Beverage alcohol
    Cocoa and chocolate products
    Edible beans and bean ingredients
    Fiber
    Flour and whole grains
    Lecithin
    Natural-source vitamin E
    Oils and fats
    Plant sterols
    Polyols and gums
    Proteins
    Rice
    Soy isoflavones
    Starches
    Sweeteners
Fuel and Industrial
    Acidulants
    Chemical intermediates
    Emulsifiers and thickeners
    Ethanol
    Industrial oils
    Polymers
    Solvents
    Starches

Selected Services

Agriculture
    Grain merchandising
    Grain milling
    Grain processing
Information
    Billing and invoicing
    Inventory
    Logistics
    Payment
    Product search
Transportation
    Land
    Rail
    Truck
    Water
    Ocean
    River

COMPETITORS

Abengoa Bioenergy	Hain Celestial
Ag Processing	Hershey
AGRI Industries	Intrepid Technology
Agrium	Koch Industries, Inc.
Ajinomoto	Liberty Vegetable Oil
Andersons	Little Sioux
Badger State Ethanol	Corn Processors
Barry Callebaut	Malt Products Corporation
Bartlett and Company	MGP Ingredients
Bayer CropScience	Monsanto Company
Brenntag North America	Nestlé
Buckeye Technologies	Nisshin Oillio
Bunge Limited	Northern Growers
Bunge Milling	Nova Biosource
Cargill	Omega Protein
CHS	Pacific Ethanol
Corn Products	Pioneer Hi-Bred
International	Renewable Energy Group
CP Kelco	Riceland Foods
Danisco A/S	Südzucker
Dow AgroSciences	Scoular
DuPont Agriculture	Syngenta
General Mills	Tate & Lyle
Green Plains	VeraSun

HISTORICAL FINANCIALS

Company Type: Public

Income Statement

FYE: June 30

	REVENUE ($ mil.)	NET INCOME ($ mil.)	NET PROFIT MARGIN	EMPLOYEES
6/09	69,207.0	1,707.0	2.5%	28,200
6/08	69,816.0	1,802.0	2.6%	27,600
6/07	44,018.0	2,162.0	4.9%	27,300
6/06	36,596.1	1,312.1	3.6%	26,800
6/05	35,943.8	1,044.4	2.9%	25,641
Annual Growth	17.8%	13.1%	—	2.4%

2009 Year-End Financials

Debt ratio: 57.8%
Return on equity: 12.6%
Cash ($ mil.): 1,055
Current ratio: 2.18
Long-term debt ($ mil.): 7,800

No. of shares (mil.): 642
Dividends
    Yield: 2.0%
    Payout: 20.4%
Market value ($ mil.): 17,187

Stock History

NYSE: ADM

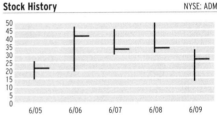

	STOCK PRICE ($) FY Close	P/E High/Low		PER SHARE ($) Earnings	Dividends	Book Value
6/09	26.77	12	5	2.65	0.54	21.03
6/08	33.75	18	11	2.79	0.49	21.01
6/07	33.09	14	9	3.30	0.43	17.53
6/06	41.28	23	10	2.00	0.37	15.27
6/05	21.38	16	9	1.59	0.32	13.14
Annual Growth	5.8%	—	—	13.6%	14.0%	12.5%

Arrow Electronics

Arrow Electronics knows its target market. The company is one of the world's largest distributors of electronic components and computer products, alongside rival Avnet. Arrow sells semiconductors, computer peripherals, passive components, and interconnect products from about 800 suppliers to more than 130,000 OEMs, contract manufacturers, and commercial customers worldwide. The company distributes products made by such manufacturers as 3Com, CA, Freescale Semiconductor, Fujitsu Microelectronics, Hitachi, Intel, and Texas Instruments. Arrow also provides value-added services, such as component design, inventory management, and contract manufacturing. The company gets more than half of its sales outside the US.

Arrow's customers are primarily manufacturers in industries such as aviation and aerospace, computers and office equipment, industrial equipment, medical and scientific devices, and telecommunications equipment, as well as resellers of computer systems. Electronic components account for about two-thirds of sales. The IT business, Arrow Electronic Computing Solutions (ECS), makes up the remainder.

Arrow is expanding its global presence through acquisitions and joint ventures. In 2008 it bought Groupe Open's LOGIX SA subsidiary. LOGIX is a value-added distributor of midrange computer servers, data storage equipment, and software in 11 European countries. That same year Arrow also acquired the electronic components distribution business of Achieva Ltd., a deal that gave it operations in eight Southeast Asian countries.

President/COO Michael Long, an Arrow executive since 1991, was promoted to CEO in 2009, succeeding William Mitchell, who remained as executive chairman. Mitchell, who served as CEO for six years, said he would step down as chairman at the end of 2009.

HISTORY

Arrow Radio began in 1935 in New York City as an outlet for used radio equipment. In the mid-1960s the company was selling various home entertainment products and wholesaling electronic parts. In 1968 three Harvard Business School graduates got Arrow in their sights. Duke Glenn, Roger Green, and John Waddell led a group of investors that acquired the company for $1 million in borrowed money. The three also bought a company that reclaimed lead from used car batteries.

With the money they made in the lead reclamation business, the trio enlarged Arrow's wholesale electronics distribution inventory. The company expanded rapidly during the 1970s, primarily through internal growth, and by 1977 it had become the US's fourth-largest electronics distributor. In 1979 Arrow bought the #2 US distributor, Cramer Electronics. Although the purchase of West Coast-based Cramer was financed with junk bonds and left Arrow deeply in debt, revenues doubled. Arrow went public in 1979.

One year later a hotel fire killed 13 members of Arrow's senior management, including Glenn and Green. Waddell, who had remained at company headquarters to answer questions about a stock split announced that day, was named acting CEO. Company stock fell 19% the first day it

traded after the fire and another 14% before the end of the month. Adding to the company's woes, a slump hit the electronics industry in 1981. That year Arrow's board lured Alfred Stein to leave Motorola and to lead the company's new management team as president and CEO; Waddell remained chairman.

Stein did not mesh with Arrow, and in early 1982 the board fired him and put Waddell in charge again. By 1983 the industry slump was over, and Arrow was temporarily back in the black. However, another industry downturn led to significant losses between 1985 and 1987.

In the mid-1980s Arrow began a major global expansion, acquiring in 1985 a 40% interest in Germany's largest electronics distributor, Spoerle Electronic (Arrow owned the company by 2000). President Stephen Kaufman, a former McKinsey & Company consultant, was named CEO in 1986 (Waddell remained VC). Arrow bought Kierulff Electronics, the fourth-largest US distributor, in 1988, and Lex Electronics, the third-largest, three years later.

Arrow expanded into Asia in 1993 with the acquisition of Hong Kong-based Components Agents and New Zealand's Components+Instrumentation in 1995. The next year Italian subsidiary Silverstar acquired Eurelettronica, one of Italy's biggest semiconductor distributors.

In 1999 Arrow acquired passive components distributor Richey Electronics and the Electronics Distribution Group of Bell Industries. Kaufman stepped down from the CEO post in 2000; company president Francis Scricco was named to the position. Later in 2000 Arrow purchased Wyle Components and Wyle Systems (both North American computer products distributors) from German utility giant E.ON.

Facing a broad downturn in the electronics industry, the company in 2001 laid off 1,500 employees. The next year Arrow sold its Gates/Arrow unit (distribution of PC peripherals and software to North American resellers) to SYNNEX Information Technologies (now just SYNNEX). Also in 2002 Scricco resigned as CEO; Kaufman left his post as chairman to take the reins once again as CEO and director Daniel Duval stepped in as chairman. Later that year Kaufman retired and Duval was named CEO.

Early in 2003 former Solectron executive Bill Mitchell took over as president and CEO; Duval remained chairman. The same year, the company purchased the industrial electronics components division of Agilysys. Late in 2005 Arrow purchased DNSint.com, a German computer distributor. The following year it acquired SKYDATA, the largest distributor of EMC products in Canada.

Also in 2006 Arrow acquired Alternative Technology, a distributor of networking and security products. That same year Arrow acquired the assets of the Specialist Distribution division of InTechnology. InTechnology Distribution specialized in security and data storage products for value-added resellers in the UK.

Mitchell added chairman to his title in 2006 when Duval stepped down from that post (but remained a director).

In 2007 Arrow bought the computer distribution business of Agilysys for $485 million in cash.

That same year Arrow also expanded into Japan for the first time, buying a Tokyo-based distributor of semiconductor and multimedia products, Universe Electron Corp., and establishing a Japanese subsidiary.

EXECUTIVES

Chairman: William E. (Bill) Mitchell, age 65, $7,060,468 total compensation
Vice Chairman: John C. Waddell, age 71
President, CEO, and Director: Michael J. (Mike) Long, age 50, $1,853,815 total compensation
EVP Finance and Operations and CFO: Paul J. Reilly, age 52, $1,456,976 total compensation
Chief Strategy Officer: M. Catherine (Cathy) Morris, age 50
SVP Human Resources: John P. McMahon, age 57, $979,688 total compensation
SVP, General Counsel, and Secretary: Peter S. Brown, age 58, $1,169,643 total compensation
VP; EVP, Arrow Europe, Middle East, Africa, and South America: Jan M. Salsgiver
VP; Chairman, Arrow Europe, Middle East, Africa and South America: Germano Fanelli
VP and CIO: Vincent P. (Vin) Melvin, age 45
VP; President, Global Alliance and Supply Chain, Arrow Global Components: Brian P. McNally
VP; SVP, Global Sales Excellence, Arrow Global Components: Vincent (Vinnie) Vellucci
VP, Legal Affairs, and Chief Compliance Officer: Wayne Brody
President, Arrow Enterprise Computing Solutions: Andrew S. (Andy) Bryant, age 53
President, Global Components: Peter T. Kong
President, Arrow Enterprise Computing Solutions EMEA and LOGIX S.A.: Laurent Sadoun, age 43
Auditors: Ernst & Young LLP

LOCATIONS

HQ: Arrow Electronics, Inc.
50 Marcus Dr., Melville, NY 11747
Phone: 631-847-2000 **Fax:** 631-847-2222
Web: www.arrow.com

Arrow Electronics has more than 300 locations around the world.

2008 Sales

	$ mil.	% of total
North America	8,366.1	50
Europe, Middle East, Africa & South America	5,392.8	32
Asia/Pacific	3,002.1	18
Total	**16,761.0**	**100**

PRODUCTS/OPERATIONS

2008 Sales

	$ mil.	% of total
Electronic components	11,319.5	68
Computer products	5,441.5	32
Total	**16,761.0**	**100**

Selected Products and Services

Computer Products
Communication control equipment
Controllers
Design systems
Desktop computers
Flat-panel displays
Microcomputer boards and systems
Monitors
Printers
Servers
Software
Storage products
System chassis and enclosures
Workstations

Electronic Components
Capacitors
Connectors
Potentiometers
Power supplies
Relays
Resistors
Switches

Services
  Analysis, implementation, and support
  Component design
  Contract manufacturing
  Forecast and order management
  Inventory management

COMPETITORS

Avnet
Bell Microproducts
Digi-Key
ePlus
Future Electronics
Heilind Electronics
Ingram Micro
Newark InOne
N.F. Smith
Nu Horizons Electronics
Premier Farnell
Richardson Electronics
Sager Electrical
SED International
SYNNEX
Tech Data
TTI Inc.
WPG Holdings

HISTORICAL FINANCIALS

Company Type: Public

Income Statement

FYE: December 31

	REVENUE ($ mil.)	NET INCOME ($ mil.)	NET PROFIT MARGIN	EMPLOYEES
12/08	16,761.0	(613.7)	—	12,700
12/07	15,985.0	407.8	2.6%	12,600
12/06	13,577.1	388.3	2.9%	12,000
12/05	11,164.2	253.6	2.3%	11,400
12/04	10,646.1	207.5	1.9%	11,500
Annual Growth	12.0%	—	—	2.5%

2008 Year-End Financials

Debt ratio: 45.7%
Return on equity: —
Cash ($ mil.): 451
Current ratio: 1.80
Long-term debt ($ mil.): 1,224

No. of shares (mil.): 120
Dividends
  Yield: 0.0%
  Payout: —
Market value ($ mil.): 2,254

Stock History

NYSE: ARW

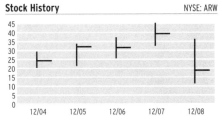

	STOCK PRICE ($) FY Close	P/E High/Low	PER SHARE ($) Earnings	Dividends	Book Value
12/08	18.84	— —	(5.08)	0.00	22.37
12/07	39.28	14 10	3.28	0.00	29.69
12/06	31.55	12 8	3.16	0.00	25.05
12/05	32.03	16 10	2.09	0.00	19.84
12/04	24.30	17 12	1.75	0.00	18.34
Annual Growth	(6.2%)	— —	—	—	5.1%

ArvinMeritor

Whether it is building axles or drum brakes for big rigs and buses, ArvinMeritor's actions are meritorious. Once known as Meritor Automotive, ArvinMeritor was formed in 2000 when Meritor acquired Arvin Industries. The company makes an array of integrated systems, modules, and components primarily for commercial vehicle systems. Its lineup ranges from axles, drivelines, and suspension and braking systems to door and roof systems, and ride control products. ArvinMeritor began divesting its light vehicle aftermarket product businesses, including aftermarket exhaust (North American and European operations), filters, and motion control operations, in 2009. The company makes about 60% of its sales outside North America.

After being slammed by automakers' production cutbacks in 2008 — caused by overcapacity and high costs for fuel and steel — ArvinMeritor started looking for ways to tighten its belt to remain competitive. To that end it is laying off about 2,800 workers (over 10% of the workforce) in North America and Europe and closing or consolidating several of its plants.

In 2008 ArvinMeritor decided to exit the automotive aftermarket business for light vehicles and to focus on commercial, off-highway, and heavy-duty markets for OEM and aftermarket customers in the truck, school bus, and military markets. It announced that it would separate its Light Vehicle Systems (LVS) and Commercial Vehicle Systems (CVS) divisions. CVS would remain with ArvinMeritor, while LVS would be spun off to ArvinMeritor shareholders and renamed Arvin Innovation. Later in the year, ArvinMeritor moved to sell the LVS division.

Unable to attract a buyer due to the credit crisis, ArvinMeritor called off the sale in early 2009, and instead began divesting LVS piece by piece. In the third quarter of 2009 the company shed its wheels business to Brazil-based Iochpe-Maxion, S.A., a maker of wheels and frames for commercial vehicles, and railway freight cars, for about $180 million. The proceeds of the sale will be used to pay down its revolving credit facility as the company struggles to remain in compliance with creditors.

The sale fell on the heels of the divesture of ArvinMeritor's chassis business (Gabriel Ride Control Products North America) to OpenGate Capital, a private-equity firm. Additionally, the company sold its Meritor Suspension Systems Company (MSSC) to its joint venture partner Mitsubishi Steel Mfg. Co., as well as a 51% stake in Gabriel de Venezuela, a manufacturer of shock absorbers, struts, exhaust systems, and suspension modules for the South American market. ArvinMeritor retained its Body Systems business, though the company still plans to sell the division. All told, almost 90% of the LVS division had been divested by September 2009.

ArvinMeritor continues to make investments in the South American region, where production continues to grow in spite of the economic downturn. The company announced plans in 2009 to invest up to $10 million in its Brazilian commercial vehicle business.

Once known as Meritor Automotive, ArvinMeritor was formed in 2000 when Meritor acquired Arvin Industries.

HISTORY

ArvinMeritor's earliest progenitor was the Wisconsin Parts Company, a small axle plant Willard Rockwell bought in 1919 to build a truck axle he had designed himself. In 1953 Rockwell merged Wisconsin Parts with Standard Steel and Spring and Timken-Detroit Axle to form Rockwell Spring and Axle Company. Timken-Detroit was a 1909 spinoff of the Timken Roller Bearing Axle Company, whose buggy springs predated the invention of the automobile.

Rockwell Spring and Axle changed its name in 1958 to Rockwell-Standard Corp. In 1967 Rockwell-Standard took over North American Aviation. North American Aviation needed to improve its public image by burrowing into a reputable company after the Apollo space capsule it had built ignited during a ground test, killing all three astronauts aboard. The new company, called North American Rockwell, was headed by Willard.

North American Rockwell made car and truck parts, tools, printing presses, industrial sewing machines, and electronic flight and navigation instruments. In 1973 North American Rockwell bought Willard Rockwell Jr.'s Rockwell Manufacturing and changed its name once again, to Rockwell International (now Rockwell Automation).

Under Willard Jr.'s leadership, Rockwell bought a number of high-risk businesses. During one period in the early 1970s, the company was losing a million dollars a day. Willard Jr. retired in 1979, and Robert Anderson, who had come to Rockwell in 1968 from Chrysler Corporation, became chairman. Anderson moved the company away from the high-profile consumer market that Willard Jr. had been so keen on. He also required all company divisions to submit profit goals. Under Anderson's management, Rockwell's debt fell dramatically.

In 1986 Rockwell brought out a new line of single-speed and two-speed drive axles for heavy vehicles, and in 1989 it introduced a family of nine- and 13-speed on-highway transmissions. The next year the company's Meritor WABCO unit (a joint venture with American Standard Companies) began supplying antilock brakes for trailers and tractors.

In the 1990s Rockwell's automotive division began growing through acquisitions and overseas expansion. It bought Czech auto parts maker Skoda Miada Boleslav in 1993 and Dura Automotive Systems' window-regulator business in 1995. The next year the division entered into a joint venture with China's Xuzhou Construction Machinery Axle and Case Co.

Rockwell spun off Meritor Automotive in 1997 as an independent, publicly traded company. The new company derived its name from the Latin word "meritum," meaning service, worth, and benefit. In 1999 Meritor bought UK-based LucasVarity's heavy vehicle braking system division; Volvo's heavy-duty truck axle unit; and Euclid Industries, which makes replacement parts for medium- and heavy-duty trucks.

In 2000 Meritor acquired Arvin Industries. Renamed ArvinMeritor, the combined companies formed an automotive systems titan with $7.5 billion in sales. Later that year ArvinMeritor announced that it would reduce its worldwide workforce by about 4% (1,500) because of a slump in the heavy truck industry.

In 2004 the company announced plans to exit the aftermarket business in order to focus on the needs of its OEM customers. That year Arvin-Meritor sold its coil coating operations.

In 2006 ArvinMeritor sold its light vehicle aftermarket Purolator filters business to Robert Bosch and MANN+HUMMEL. Soon afterward the company sold its North American light vehicle aftermarket exhaust business to IMCO (International Muffler Company). The company also sold its light vehicle aftermarket motion control business to AVM Industries LLC.

EXECUTIVES

Chairman, President, and CEO:
Charles G. (Chip) McClure Jr., age 56
EVP and Acting CFO Light Vehicle Systems:
James D. Donlon III, age 63
SVP, CFO, and Acting Controller: Jeffrey A. (Jay) Craig, age 50
SVP and General Counsel: Vernon G. Baker II, age 56
SVP Communications: Linda Cummins, age 62
SVP; President, Commercial Vehicle Systems; COO, ArvinMeritor: Carsten Reinhardt, age 42
SVP Strategic Initiatives: Mary Lehmann, age 51
CIO: Kevin Haskew
VP Human Resources, Light Vehicle Systems:
Bill Fisher
VP Information Technology, Commercial Vehicle Systems: Jay McLean
VP and General Manager, Light Vehicle Chassis Systems: Ed Frutig
VP and General Manager, Commercial Vehicle Systems Trailers Group: Amelia Quelas
VP Purchasing, Commercial Vehicle Systems:
Art Waldowski
VP Sales and Marketing, Light Vehicle Systems:
Sherry Welsh
VP and Corporate Secretary: Barbara Novak
VP and General Manager, Specialty Products:
Christopher Kete
VP and Treasurer: Kevin Nowlan
Senior Director, Corporate Communications and Media Relations: Krista McClure
Senior Director Investor Relations: Brett Penzkofer
Auditors: Deloitte & Touche LLP

LOCATIONS

HQ: ArvinMeritor, Inc.
2135 W. Maple Rd., Troy, MI 48084
Phone: 248-435-1000   **Fax:** 248-435-1393
Web: www.arvinmeritor.com

2008 Sales

	$ mil.	% of total
North America		
US	2,251	32
Mexico	385	5
Canada	287	4
Europe		
France	944	13
Sweden	509	7
Germany	216	3
Other countries	1,063	15
South America	846	12
Asia/Pacific	666	9
Total	**7,167**	**100**

PRODUCTS/OPERATIONS

2008 Sales

	$ mil.	% of total
Commercial Vehicle Systems	4,819	67
Light Vehicle Systems	2,348	33
Total	**7,167**	**100**

Selected Products

Commercial Vehicle Systems
  Axles
  Brakes
  Clutches
  Drivelines
  Exhaust products
  Ride control products
  Suspension systems
  Trailer products (including axles and air suspension products)
Light Vehicle Systems
  Access-control systems
  Door systems
  Roof systems
  Suspension systems
  Wheel products

COMPETITORS

Accuride
AISIN World Corp.
American Axle & Manufacturing
ASC Inc.
AxleTech International
Benteler Group
Boler
BorgWarner
Borla Performance Industries
Carlisle Companies
Dana Holding
Delphi Corp.
Dura Automotive
Eaton
Faurecia
Federal-Mogul
Haldex
Hayes Lemmerz
Magna International
MAN
Metaldyne
Mitsui
NHK Spring
Robert Bosch
SAF-HOLLAND
SOGEFI
Superior Industries
TA Delaware
Tenneco
Titan International
Topy
Trane Inc.
TRW Automotive
Valeo
Visteon
Voith
Westinghouse Air Brake
Williams Controls
ZF Friedrichshafen

HISTORICAL FINANCIALS

Company Type: Public

Income Statement

FYE: September 30

	REVENUE ($ mil.)	NET INCOME ($ mil.)	NET PROFIT MARGIN	EMPLOYEES
9/08	7,167.0	(101.0)	—	19,800
9/07	6,449.0	(219.0)	—	18,000
9/06	9,195.0	(175.0)	—	27,500
9/05	8,903.0	12.0	0.1%	29,000
9/04	8,033.0	(42.0)	—	31,000
Annual Growth	**(2.8%)**	**—**	**—**	**(10.6%)**

2008 Year-End Financials

Debt ratio: 230.1%
Return on equity: —
Cash ($ mil.): 497
Current ratio: 1.15
Long-term debt ($ mil.): 1,063
No. of shares (mil.): 74
Dividends
  Yield: 3.1%
  Payout: —
Market value ($ mil.): 964

	STOCK PRICE ($) FY Close	P/E High/Low	PER SHARE ($) Earnings	Dividends	Book Value
9/08	13.04	— —	(1.40)	0.40	6.25
9/07	16.82	— —	(3.11)	0.40	7.34
9/06	14.24	— —	(2.52)	0.40	12.76
9/05	16.72	134 69	0.17	0.40	11.83
9/04	18.75	— —	(0.61)	0.40	13.36
Annual Growth	**(8.7%)**	**— —**	**—**	**0.0%**	**(17.3%)**

Ashland Inc.

Ashland is built on chemicals and cars. The company consists of five business units. Ashland Distribution, which represents half of its business, buys chemicals and plastics and then blends and repackages them for distribution in Europe and North America. Ashland Performance Materials makes specialty resins, polymers, and adhesives. Ashland Hercules Water Technologies provides chemical and non-chemical products for commercial, industrial, and municipal water treatment facilities. Valvoline runs an oil-change chain and markets Valvoline motor oil and Zerex antifreeze. The last unit is Ashland Aqualon Functional Ingredients, which makes additives for the personal care, food, and pharmaceutical industries.

In 2008 Ashland paid $3.3 billion to buy specialty chemicals company Hercules, which added significantly to its water treatment and resins businesses.

That move was only the latest in a grand reorganization of Ashland. Since 2005 it has sold its former petroleum refining joint venture (with Marathon Oil), now called Marathon Petroleum Company; acquired car cleaning products maker Car Brite for Valvoline; purchased Degussa's water treatment business (operating as Stockhausen); and bought adhesives and coatings company Northwest Coatings, which makes coatings that use ultraviolet and electron beam polymerisation technologies. Another big deal, though, provided a complementary book end to the sale of Marathon Petroleum. In 2006 Ashland sold construction unit APAC (which supplies highway materials, builds bridges, and paves streets) to Oldcastle Materials for $1.3 billion. Oldcastle is the US division of Irish construction company CRH. The move, coming as it did on the heels of the divestiture of MAP, transformed Ashland into solely a chemicals company.

HISTORY

After moving to Kentucky in 1917, Fred Miles formed the Swiss Oil Company. In 1924 Swiss Oil bought a refinery in Catlettsburg, a rough town near sedate Ashland, and created a unit called

Ashland Refining. Miles battled Swiss Oil directors for control, lost, and resigned in 1927.

Swiss Oil bought Tri-State Refining in 1930 and Cumberland Pipeline's eastern Kentucky pipe network in 1931. Swiss Oil changed its name to Ashland Oil and Refining in 1936. After WWII it bought small independent oil firms, acquiring the Valvoline name in 1950 by buying Freedom-Valvoline.

The firm formed Ashland Chemical in 1967 after buying Anderson-Prichard Oil (1958), United Carbon (1963), and ADM Chemical (1967). Ashland Chemical changed its name to Ashland Oil. It added the SuperAmerica convenience store chain (1970) and started exploring for oil in Nigeria after OPEC nations raised oil prices.

Scandal hit in 1975, the year Ashland Coal was formed. CEO Orin Atkins admitted to ordering Ashland executives to make illegal contributions to the 1972 Nixon presidential campaign. Atkins was deposed in 1981 after the company made questionable payments to highly placed "consultants" with connections to oil-rich Middle Eastern governments. In 1988 Atkins was arrested for trying to fence purloined documents regarding litigation between Ashland and the National Iranian Oil Company (NIOC). Ashland, which launched the federal investigation that led to Atkins' arrest, settled with NIOC in 1989. Atkins pleaded guilty and received probation.

Ashland went on a shopping spree in the 1990s. The company bought Permian (crude oil gathering and marketing) in 1991 and merged it into Scurlock Oil. In 1992 Ashland Chemical bought most of Unocal's chemical distribution business, and two years later it bought two companies that produce chemicals for the semiconductor industry. Also in 1994 Ashland made a promising oil discovery in Nigeria.

The company, by then named Ashland Inc., spent $368 million on 14 acquisitions to expand its energy and chemical divisions in 1995. It received a $75 million settlement with Columbia Gas System (now Columbia Energy Group) for abrogated natural gas contracts resulting from Columbia's bankruptcy.

In 1996 president Paul Chellgren became CEO and, with the company under shareholder fire, began a major reorganization. The next year Arch Mineral and Ashland Coal combined to form Arch Coal, with Ashland owning 58%. Also that year Ashland made more than a dozen acquisitions to bolster its chemical and construction businesses. Its exploration unit, renamed Blazer Energy, was sold to Norway's Statoil for $566 million.

Ashland joined USX-Marathon (now Marathon Oil) in 1998 to create Marathon Ashland Petroleum (now called Marathon Petroleum). It bought 20 companies, including Eagle One Industries, a maker of car-care products, and Masters-Jackson, a group of highway construction companies. Ashland reduced its holdings in Arch Coal from 58% to 12% in 2000; it sold the remainder in early 2001.

In 2002 the company was jolted when Chellgren was forced to retire after violating a company policy prohibiting romantic office relationships. James O'Brien replaced Chellgren.

Ashland had a record year in 2001 but was hampered in 2002 by smaller profits from MAP, which was hurt by reduced demand for petroleum products and tighter margins. Ashland Distribution also hurt the bottom line, which led Ashland to reorganize that unit's management and sales teams.

After that record year Ashland came back to earth with much smaller profits in 2002 and the next year; APAC, particularly, was hit hard in 2003. The construction division swung from $120 million in profits in 2002 to a loss of more than $40 million in 2003; the company attributes the decline to unusual weather conditions, which can greatly affect the construction business more than others. (The pendulum swung back into the black in 2004 with more than $100 million in operating income.)

The company sold its interest in Marathon Petroleum to Marathon in the middle of 2005.

EXECUTIVES

Chairman and CEO: James J. (Jim) O'Brien Jr., age 54
SVP and CFO: Lamar M. Chambers, age 55
SVP and General Counsel: David L. Hausrath
VP; President, Ashland Consumer Markets: Samuel J. (Sam) Mitchell Jr., age 48
VP; President, Ashland Water Technologies and Ashland Performance Materials: Frank L. (Hank) Waters
VP Human Resources and Communications: Susan B. Esler, age 48
VP; President, Ashland Global Supply Chain: Michael J. Shannon, age 48
VP and Controller: J. William Heitman, age 55
VP Communications and Corporate Affairs: Martha C. Johnson
VP Information Systems: Kristy J. Folkwein
VP Enterprise Optimization: Rick E. Music
VP International and Canada, Ashland Distribution: Stephen P. Fazakas
VP; President, Ashland China: Dale M. MacDonald
Assistant General Counsel and Corporate Secretary: Linda L. Foss
Treasurer: J. Kevin Willis
General Auditor: John F. Guldig
Manager Public Relations: James E. (Jim) Vitak
Auditors: Ernst & Young LLP

LOCATIONS

HQ: Ashland Inc.
50 E. RiverCenter Blvd., Covington, KY 41012
Phone: 859-815-3333   **Fax:** 859-815-5053
Web: www.ashland.com

2008 Sales

	$ mil.	% of total
US	5,549	66
Other countries	2,832	34
Total	**8,381**	**100**

PRODUCTS/OPERATIONS

2008 Sales

	$ mil.	% of total
Distribution	4,374	51
Valvoline	1,662	19
Performance Materials	1,621	19
Water Technologies	893	11
Adjustments	(169)	—
Total	**8,381**	**100**

COMPETITORS

Aceto	Harcros Chemicals
Arkema	HELM U.S.
BASF SE	Hexion
BP Lubricants USA	Hydrite
Brenntag	Jiffy Lube
Chemtura	SABIC Innovative Plastics
Cytec	Univar
DuPont	

HISTORICAL FINANCIALS

Company Type: Public

Income Statement

FYE: September 30

	REVENUE ($ mil.)	NET INCOME ($ mil.)	NET PROFIT MARGIN	EMPLOYEES
9/08	8,381.0	167.0	2.0%	11,900
9/07	7,834.0	230.0	2.9%	11,700
9/06	7,277.0	407.0	5.6%	11,700
9/05	9,860.0	2,004.0	20.3%	20,900
9/04	8,781.0	378.0	4.3%	21,200
Annual Growth	**(1.2%)**	**(18.5%)**	**—**	**(13.4%)**

2008 Year-End Financials

Debt ratio: 1.4%
Return on equity: 5.3%
Cash ($ mil.): 886
Current ratio: 2.47
Long-term debt ($ mil.): 45

No. of shares (mil.): 74
Dividends
  Yield: 3.8%
  Payout: 41.8%
Market value ($ mil.): 2,176

Stock History

NYSE: ASH

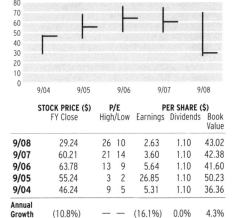

	STOCK PRICE ($) FY Close	P/E High/Low		PER SHARE ($) Earnings	Dividends	Book Value
9/08	29.24	26	10	2.63	1.10	43.02
9/07	60.21	21	14	3.60	1.10	42.38
9/06	63.78	13	9	5.64	1.10	41.60
9/05	55.24	3	2	26.85	1.10	50.23
9/04	46.24	9	5	5.31	1.10	36.36
Annual Growth	**(10.8%)**	**—**	**—**	**(16.1%)**	**0.0%**	**4.3%**

AT&T Inc.

Through its subsidiaries, affiliates, and operating companies, holding company AT&T is the industry-leading provider of wireline voice communications services in the US. Customers in 22 states use AT&T-branded telephone, Internet, IP-voice, and digital video services; key markets include California, Illinois, and Texas. The company's corporate, government, and public sector clients use its extensive range of conferencing, data networking, managed network, and wholesale communications services. Subsidiary AT&T Mobility is the nation's second largest wireless carrier by both sales and subscriptions (after Verizon Wireless). It provides mobile voice and data services to about 77 million subscribers.

Since the purchase of Cingular Wireless and the establishment of AT&T Mobility in 2007, AT&T has pushed its mobile services through increased advertising and marketing efforts (including an exclusive partnership with Apple to carry the iPhone in the US), as well as further acquisitions to make the mobile segment its fastest-growing business. The purchase of Dobson Communications in 2007 added nearly 2 million rural wireless subscribers to the books.

continued buying dealerships and car rental firms at a sizzling rate.

Republic spun off its solid-waste operations to the public in 1998 as Republic Services. That year Republic bought or agreed to buy 181 new-car franchises, opened nine AutoNation USA dealerships, and opened 62 CarTemps USA insurance-replacement locations.

Republic became AutoNation in 1999 and announced plans to spin off its rental division. In September 1999 Mike Jackson, the former president and CEO of Mercedes-Benz USA, was named CEO of AutoNation. In December the company closed most of its poorly performing used-car superstores and laid off about 1,800 employees.

In May 2000 AutoNation acquired AutoVantage, an online car-buying service linking over 900 dealerships, and inked a deal to be America Online's (now a division of Time Warner) exclusive auto retailer. Later the company completed its spinoff of ANC Rental (Alamo, National, and CarTemps, with more than 3,400 rental car locations worldwide), making AutoNation a pure-play auto retailer.

In 2001 AutoNation closed its auto-loan unit to further focus on car sales. Huizenga retired as chairman of the company at the end of 2002. Jackson assumed the chairmanship while continuing in his role as CEO.

In March 2003 AutoNation agreed to pay the IRS about $470 million in relation to the tax treatment of some 1997-1999 transactions. It bought a dealership that accounts for some 10% of Mercedes-Benz USA sales, Glauser Mercedes-Benz in Sarasota, Florida, in May 2004. The dealership is now called Mercedes-Benz of Sarasota.

In 2007 AutoNation sold about 540,000 new and used vehicles. However, the company's revenue declined relative to 2006 as the weak economy, particularly in California and Florida, curtailed sales.

In 2008 the company acquired Don Mackey BMW in Tucson, Arizona, and renamed the dealership BMW Tucson.

EXECUTIVES

Chairman and CEO: Michael J. (Mike) Jackson, age 60, $3,392,797 total compensation
President, COO, and Director: Michael E. (Mike) Maroone, age 55, $4,797,394 total compensation
EVP and CFO: Michael J. (Mike) Short, age 47, $1,461,980 total compensation
EVP, Secretary, and General Counsel: Jonathan P. Ferrando, age 43, $1,869,479 total compensation
SVP Sales: Kevin P. Westfall, age 53, $1,002,396 total compensation
SVP Corporate Communications: Marc Cannon
SVP eCommerce: Gary Marcotte
SVP Regional Operations and Industry Relations: Donna Parlapiano
VP Investor Relations: John M. Zimmerman
VP Information Technology: Joyce Vonada
VP Media Services: Ed Cicale
VP Human Resources: Julie Staub
VP and Treasurer: James J. Teufel
VP and Corporate Controller: Michael J. Stephan, age 46
VP Investor Relations: Derek A. Fiebig
President, Texas Region: Dan Agnew
President, Florida Region: James (Jim) Bender
President, West Central Region: Todd Maul
President, East Central Region: Hank Phillips
Auditors: KPMG LLP

LOCATIONS

HQ: AutoNation, Inc.
110 SE 6th St., Fort Lauderdale, FL 33301
Phone: 954-769-6000   **Fax:** 954-769-6537
Web: corp.autonation.com

PRODUCTS/OPERATIONS

2008 Sales

	$ mil.	% of total
New vehicles	7,756.2	55
Used vehicles	3,364.5	24
Parts & service	2,465.2	17
Finance & insurance	482.6	3
Other	63.4	1
Total	**14,131.9**	**100**

COMPETITORS

Asbury Automotive
Brown Automotive
Burt Automotive
CarMax
Ed Morse Auto
Group 1 Automotive
Hendrick Automotive
Holman Enterprises
JM Family Enterprises
Penske Automotive Group
Penske Motor Group
Potamkin Automotive
Sonic Automotive

HISTORICAL FINANCIALS

Company Type: Public

Income Statement

FYE: December 31

	REVENUE ($ mil.)	NET INCOME ($ mil.)	NET PROFIT MARGIN	EMPLOYEES
12/08	14,131.9	(1,243.1)	—	20,000
12/07	17,691.5	278.7	1.6%	25,000
12/06	18,988.6	316.9	1.7%	26,000
12/05	19,253.4	496.5	2.6%	27,000
12/04	19,424.7	433.6	2.2%	27,000
Annual Growth	**(7.6%)**	**—**	**—**	**(7.2%)**

2008 Year-End Financials

Debt ratio: 55.8%
Return on equity: —
Cash ($ mil.): 111
Current ratio: 1.04
Long-term debt ($ mil.): 1,226
No. of shares (mil.): 178
Dividends
Yield: 0.0%
Payout: —
Market value ($ mil.): 1,759

Stock History

NYSE: AN

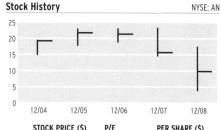

	STOCK PRICE ($) FY Close	P/E High/Low		PER SHARE ($) Earnings	Dividends	Book Value
12/08	9.88	—	—	(6.99)	0.00	12.35
12/07	15.66	17	11	1.39	0.00	19.51
12/06	21.32	17	14	1.38	0.00	20.86
12/05	21.73	12	10	1.85	0.00	26.23
12/04	19.21	12	9	1.59	0.00	23.95
Annual Growth	**(15.3%)**	**—**	**—**	**—**	**—**	**(15.3%)**

AutoZone, Inc.

Imagine that you are in your garage making some weekend car repairs. The wheel cylinders are leaking . . . the brake shoe adjuster nut is rusted solid . . . you're about to enter . . . the AutoZone. With some 4,100 stores in the US and Puerto Rico, AutoZone is the nation's #1 auto parts chain. It has made inroads abroad with about 150 stores in Mexico. AutoZone stores sell hard parts (alternators, engines, batteries), maintenance items (oil, antifreeze), accessories (car stereos, floor mats), and non-automotive merchandise under brand names as well as under private labels, including Duralast and Valucraft. AutoZone also loans tools and sells merchandise and diagnostic and repair advice online.

In addition to auto parts, AutoZone stores also offer diagnostic testing for starters, alternators, and batteries. (The shops do not sell tires or perform general auto repairs.) AutoZone's ALLDATA unit sells automotive diagnostic and repair software.

AutoZone has grown quickly through a series of acquisitions over the past several years but now is focused on internal growth and development. Among the factors AutoZone considers when opening new stores — at a rate of 150 to 200 per year — is how many cars in an area are OKVs or "our kind of vehicle," that is, cars older than seven years and no longer under their manufacturers' warranty. (With the US auto industry in the tank, more and more consumers are driving older cars.) AutoZone is also growing in Mexico, where cars are even older — and in need of more repairs — than in the US.

ESL Partners, controlled by Edward S. Lampert, owns about 40% of the company. In December 2006 Lampert stepped down from AutoZone's board, sparking speculation that ESL might sell its stake in the company. However, Lampert has said that ESL plans to remain a significant shareholder in AutoZone for the foreseeable future. Minority shareholders in the company include investment firms State Street Bank and Trust and D.E. Shaw & Co.

HISTORY

Joseph "Pitt" Hyde took over the family grocery wholesale business, Malone & Hyde (established 1907) in 1968. He expanded into specialty retailing, opening drugstores, sporting goods stores, and supermarkets, but his fortunes began to race on Independence Day 1979, when he opened his first Auto Shack auto parts store in Forrest City, Arkansas.

Using retailing behemoth Wal-Mart as a model, Hyde concentrated on smaller markets in the South and Southeast, emphasizing everyday low prices and centralized distribution operations. He stressed customer service to provide his do-it-yourself customers with expert advice on choosing parts. While a number of retailers have tried to copy Wal-Mart's successful model, Hyde had an inside track: Before starting Auto Shack he served on Wal-Mart's board for seven years.

Auto Shack had expanded into seven states by 1980, and by 1983 it had 129 stores in 10 states. The next year Malone & Hyde's senior management, with investment firm Kohlberg Kravis Roberts (KKR), took the company private in an LBO. Auto Shack continued to expand, reaching 192 stores in 1984.

A year later Auto Shack introduced its Express Parts Service, the first service in the industry to offer a toll-free number and overnight delivery of parts. The following year it introduced another first: a limited lifetime warranty on its merchandise. Also in 1986 Auto Shack introduced its own Duralast line of auto products.

The company was spun off to Malone & Hyde's shareholders in 1987, and Malone & Hyde's other operations were sold. Auto Shack brought its electronic parts catalog online that year. The company changed its name to AutoZone in 1987, in part to settle a lawsuit with RadioShack. By this time it had 390 stores in 15 states.

The company went public in 1991. By the end of that year, it had nearly 600 stores and five distribution centers. The company topped $1 billion in sales in 1992. The next year it opened new distribution centers in Illinois and Tennessee and closed its Memphis operation.

AutoZone began selling to commercial customers such as service stations and repair shops in 1996. It also acquired auto diagnostic software company ALLDATA. Hyde stepped down as CEO that year and as chairman in 1997 and was replaced by COO Johnston (John) Adams.

The company made several key purchases in 1998. It acquired Chief Auto Parts for $280 million, adding 560 stores (most in California) that were converted to AutoZones in 1999. It also purchased Adap and its 112 Auto Palace stores in the Northeast, heavy-duty truck parts distributor TruckPro, and (from Pep Boys) 100 Express stores. Also in 1998 AutoZone opened its first store in Mexico (Nuevo Laredo).

Hyde sold much of his stake by early 1999. Late that year AutoZone expanded its board of directors to 10 members, making room for increasingly active longtime shareholder Edward Lampert.

In January 2001 Steve Odland, formerly COO at supermarket retailer Ahold USA, succeeded Adams as chairman and CEO. In December 2001 AutoZone sold its TruckPro subsidiary to an investor group led by Paratus Capital Management of Boston and New York.

Odland resigned in 2005 to become CEO of Office Depot. He was replaced by Bill Rhodes, an AutoZone EVP.

EXECUTIVES

Chairman, President, and CEO:
William C. (Bill) Rhodes III, age 44
SVP Store Operations: Thomas B. Newbern, age 47
EVP Information Technology and Store Development, CFO, and Treasurer: William T. (Bill) Giles, age 50
EVP, Secretary, and General Counsel:
Harry L. Goldsmith, age 58
EVP Merchandising, Marketing, and Supply Chain:
James A. (Jim) Shea, age 64
EVP Retail Operations, Commercial Operations, and Mexico: Robert D. (Bob) Olsen, age 56
SVP Information Technology and Chief Information Officer: Jon A. Bascom, age 52
SVP Store Operations: Thomas B. Newbern, age 47
SVP Marketing: Lisa R. Kranc, age 56
SVP Commercial: Larry M. Roesel, age 52
SVP and Controller: Charlie Pleas III, age 44
SVP Human Resources: Timothy W. Briggs, age 48
SVP Merchandising: Mark A. Finestone, age 48
SVP Supply Chain: William W. Graves, age 49
President, Mexico: Domingo Hurtado
Auditors: Ernst & Young LLP

LOCATIONS

HQ: AutoZone, Inc.
123 S. Front St., Memphis, TN 38103
Phone: 901-495-6500   **Fax:** 901-495-8300
Web: www.autozone.com

2008 Stores

	No.
US	
Texas	512
California	438
Ohio	211
Illinois	197
Florida	185
Georgia	171
North Carolina	157
Tennessee	150
Michigan	140
Indiana	131
Arizona	116
New York	114
Pennsylvania	107
Louisana	105
Missouri	95
Alabama	90
Mississippi	84
Virginia	82
Kentucky	75
South Carolina	73
Oklahoma	66
Massachusetts	66
Arkansas	59
New Jersey	58
Colorado	58
New Mexico	57
Wisconsin	50
Nevada	48
Washington	48
Kansas	38
Maryland	38
Utah	34
Connecticut	32
Oregon	27
West Virginia	23
Minnesota	23
Iowa	22
Idaho	18
Puerto Rico	17
New Hampshire	16
Rhode Island	15
Nebraska	14
Delaware	10
Other states	22
Mexico	148
Total	**4,240**

PRODUCTS/OPERATIONS

Selected Merchandise

Accessories
  Car stereos
  Floor mats
  Lights
  Mirrors
Hard Parts
  Alternators
  Batteries
  Brake shoes and pads
  Carburetors
  Clutches
  Engines
  Spark plugs
  Starters
  Struts
  Water pumps
Maintenance Items
  Antifreeze
  Brake fluid
  Engine additives
  Oil
  Power steering fluid
  Transmission fluid
  Waxes
  Windshield wipers

Other
  Air fresheners
  Dent filler
  Hand cleaner
  Paint
  Repair manuals
  Tools

Selected Brands

ALLDATA
AutoZone
Duralast
Duralast Gold
Valucraft

COMPETITORS

Advance Auto Parts
CARQUEST
Costco Wholesale
Fisher Auto Parts
Genuine Parts
Goodyear Tire & Rubber
Kmart
O'Reilly Automotive
Pep Boys
Sears
Target
Wal-Mart

HISTORICAL FINANCIALS

Company Type: Public

Income Statement

FYE: Last Saturday in August

	REVENUE ($ mil.)	NET INCOME ($ mil.)	NET PROFIT MARGIN	EMPLOYEES
8/08	6,522.7	641.6	9.8%	57,000
8/07	6,169.8	595.7	9.7%	55,000
8/06	5,948.4	569.3	9.6%	53,000
8/05	5,710.9	571.0	10.0%	52,000
8/04	5,637.0	566.2	10.0%	19,000
Annual Growth	3.7%	3.2%	—	31.6%

2008 Year-End Financials

Debt ratio: 979.6%   No. of shares (mil.): 54
Return on equity: 202.8%   Dividends
Cash ($ mil.): 242   Yield: 0.0%
Current ratio: 1.03   Payout: —
Long-term debt ($ mil.): 2,250   Market value ($ mil.): 7,374

Stock History

NYSE: AZO

	STOCK PRICE ($) FY Close	P/E High/Low	PER SHARE ($) Earnings	PER SHARE ($) Dividends	PER SHARE ($) Book Value
8/08	137.23	14 10	10.04	0.00	4.20
8/07	121.29	16 10	8.53	0.00	7.37
8/06	90.30	14 10	7.50	0.00	8.58
8/05	94.50	14 10	7.18	0.00	7.15
8/04	74.06	16 11	6.56	0.00	3.13
Annual Growth	16.7%	— —	11.2%	—	7.6%

Avery Dennison

Avery Dennison is easy to label: It's a global leader in the making of adhesive labels used on packaging, mailers, and other items. Pressure-sensitive adhesives and materials account for more than half of the company's sales. Under the Avery Dennison and Fasson brands, the company makes papers, films, and foils coated with adhesive and sold in rolls to printers. The company also makes school and office products (Avery, Marks-A-Lot, HI-LITER) such as notebooks, three-ring binders, markers, fasteners, business forms, tickets, tags, and imprinting equipment. Perhaps its most widely used products are the self-adhesive stamps used by the US Postal Service since 1974.

The company, which operates manufacturing facilities and sales offices around the world, has been expanding its international operations through acquisitions, especially in China. The expansion benefitted the company to such an extent that the ratio of Avery Dennison's US sales to its international sales went from 60-40 in 2001 to less than 35-65 in 2008. The company has also expanded in India; its operations in China and India focus on local printers that supply local demand. Avery Dennison has announced plans to expand in Japan, where it is investing in a new distribution center.

In 2007 the company made a major move to expand its Retail Information Services unit, which offers products and services to retailers such as the design and production of labels and tags, as well as supply-chain management services. Avery Dennison spent $1.3 billion to buy Paxar, whose strength in the European market greatly enhances Avery Dennison's own, mostly US business. The next year it acquired the Taiwanese label maker DM Label Group, which operates in five Asian countries, as well as the US.

Avery Dennison said in 2009 that it would cut some 10% of its workforce (about 3,600 jobs).

HISTORY

Avery Dennison was created in 1990 by the merger of Avery International and Dennison Manufacturing. In 1935 Stanton Avery founded Kum-Kleen Products, which would become Avery International. After a fire destroyed the plant's equipment in 1938, Avery, who had renamed the company Avery Adhesives, improved the machinery used in making the labels.

During and after WWII, Avery Adhesives shifted toward the industrial market for self-adhesives. The company incorporated in 1946. At that time Avery Adhesives sold 80% of its production, consisting of industrial labels, to manufacturers that labeled their own products.

The company lost its patent rights for self-adhesive labels in 1952, transforming the firm and the entire industry. As a result, a new division was created — the Avery Paper Company (later renamed Fasson) — to produce and market self-adhesive base materials.

Avery Adhesives went public in 1961. Three years later it had four divisions: label products, base materials, Rotex (hand-operated embossing machines), and Metal-Cal (anodized and etched aluminum foil for nameplates). Renamed Avery International in 1976, the company closed some manufacturing facilities and cut 8% of its workforce in the late 1980s.

In 1990 Avery International merged with Dennison Manufacturing. Dennison was started in 1844 by the father-and-son team of Andrew and Aaron Dennison to produce jewelry boxes. By 1849 Aaron's younger brother, Eliphalet Whorf (E. W.), was running the business and expanding it into tags, labels, and tissue paper. Dennison was incorporated in 1878 with $150,000 in capital.

By 1911 Dennison sold tags, gummed labels, paper boxes, greeting cards, sealing wax, and tissue paper, and it had stores in Boston, Chicago, New York City, Philadelphia, St. Louis, and London. Henry Dennison, E. W.'s grandson, was president from 1917 to 1952.

From the 1960s to the 1980s, Dennison spent heavily on research and development and helped to develop such products as electronic printers and pregnancy test supplies. In the mid-1980s the firm reorganized its operations, selling seven businesses, closing four others, and focusing on stationery, systems, and packaging.

In addition to office products and product identification and control systems, the 1990 merger combined Dennison's office products operations in France (Doret and Cheval Ordex) with Avery International's sizable self-adhesive base materials business.

Avery Dennison sold its 50% interest in a Japanese label converting company, Toppan, in 1996, clearing the way to develop its own businesses in Asia. In 1997 an alliance with Taiwanese rival Four Pillars turned sour when Avery Dennison accused the company of stealing trade secrets. (Two executives at Four Pillars were convicted of espionage in 1999.)

President and COO Philip Neal was promoted to CEO in 1998. (He became chairman in 2000.) In 1999, adhering to its goal of global expansion, Avery Dennison formed office products joint ventures in Germany with Zweckform Buro-Produkte and in Japan with Hitachi Maxell. Record 1998 sales and earnings were dampened by the news of slowing growth, and in 1999 Avery Dennison closed five plants and began laying off workers. Later that year the company bought Stimsonite, a maker of reflective highway safety products.

In early 2000 Avery Dennison began a $40 million expansion of its Chinese manufacturing operations, while eliminating 1,500 jobs worldwide. Later in the year the company agreed to jointly package instant imaging and labeling products with Polaroid. Several acquisitions in 2001 included CD Stomper (CD and DVD labels and software). Avery Dennison continued its acquisitive ways in 2002, acquiring Jackstadt (German maker of pressure-sensitive adhesive materials), RVL Packaging (maker of woven and printed labels and other tags for the apparel and retail industries), and L&E Packaging (key supplier and printer for RVL).

In 2003 the company sold its European package label converting business (including plants in Denmark and France) to label and packaging company CCL Industries. As part of the deal, Avery Dennison began to supply pressure-sensitive base materials to CCL Industries. The divestiture was part of the company's strategy to concentrate its efforts in adhesive materials, office products, and retail information services.

Phillip Neal retired as chairman and CEO in 2005 and was replaced by director Kent Kresa as chairman and by Dean Scarborough as president and CEO.

EXECUTIVES

President, CEO, and Director: Dean A. Scarborough, age 53, $5,831,997 total compensation
EVP Finance and CFO: Daniel R. O'Bryant, age 51, $2,622,374 total compensation
SVP and CIO: Richard W. (Rich) Hoffman
SVP and Chief Human Resources Officer: Anne Hill, age 49
Corporate VP Global Finance and Chief Accounting Officer: Mitchell R. Butier, age 37
SVP Corporate Communications and Advertising: Diane B. Dixon, age 57
SVP Corporate Strategy and Technology: Robert M. Malchione, age 51, $1,594,348 total compensation
SVP, General Counsel, and Secretary: Susan C. Miller
SVP New Growth Platforms: John M. Sallay
VP Global Operations: Stephen A. Mynott
VP and CTO: David N. Edwards
Media Relations: Laurence J. Dwyer
Investor Relations: Cynthia S. Guenther
Auditors: PricewaterhouseCoopers LLP

LOCATIONS

HQ: Avery Dennison Corporation
150 N. Orange Grove Blvd., Pasadena, CA 91103
Phone: 626-304-2000   **Fax:** 626-792-7312
Web: www.averydennison.com

2008 Sales

	$ mil.	% of total
US	2,366.6	35
Europe	2,218.4	33
Asia	1,297.6	19
Latin America	448.0	7
Other regions	379.8	6
Total	**6,710.4**	**100**

PRODUCTS/OPERATIONS

2008 Sales

	$ mil.	% of total
Pressure-Sensitive Materials	3,643.8	54
Retail Information Services	1,548.7	23
Office & Consumer Products	935.8	14
Other specialty converting businesses	582.1	9
Total	**6,710.4**	**100**

Selected Products

Pressure-Sensitive Adhesives and Materials
  Base materials
    Paper and film materials
    Pressure-sensitive coated papers, films, and foils
    Proprietary film face materials
  Graphic products
    Durable cast and reflective films
    Metallic dispersion products
    Proprietary woodgrain film laminates
    Specialty print-receptive films
  Performance polymers products
    Solvent- and emulsion-based acrylic polymer adhesives, top coats, protective coatings
  Specialty tape products
    Single- and double-coated tapes and transfer adhesives

Consumer and Converted Products
  Binder and presentation dividers
  Computer software
  Custom label products (pressure-sensitive and heat-seal labels)
  Inkjet and laser print card and index products
  Label machines (imprinting, dispensing, attaching)
  Labels (copier, data processing, inkjet, and laser printer)
  Markers and highlighters
  Presentation and organizing systems
  Self-adhesive battery labels and postage stamps
  Sheet protectors
  Tags (graphic and bar-coded tags)
  Three-ring binders

Selected Brands
Avery
Avery Dennison
Fasson
HI-LITER
Index Maker
Marks-A-Lot
Stabilo
Zweckform

COMPETITORS
3M
ACCO Brands
Bemis
Bostik
Brady Corporation
Checkpoint Systems
Esselte
Fortune Brands
H.B. Fuller
Newell Rubbermaid
Standard Register
UPM-Kymmene

HISTORICAL FINANCIALS
Company Type: Public

Income Statement

FYE: Saturday nearest December 31

	REVENUE ($ mil.)	NET INCOME ($ mil.)	NET PROFIT MARGIN	EMPLOYEES
12/08	6,710.4	266.1	4.0%	35,700
12/07	6,307.8	303.5	4.8%	37,300
12/06	5,575.9	367.2	6.6%	22,700
12/05	5,473.5	226.4	4.1%	22,600
12/04	5,340.9	279.7	5.2%	21,400
Annual Growth	5.9%	(1.2%)	—	13.6%

2008 Year-End Financials

Debt ratio: 88.3%
Return on equity: 14.2%
Cash ($ mil.): 106
Current ratio: 0.94
Long-term debt ($ mil.): 1,545
No. of shares (mil.): 113
Dividends
Yield: 5.0%
Payout: 60.7%
Market value ($ mil.): 3,690

Stock History

NYSE: AVY

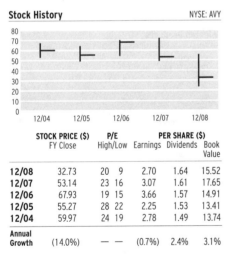

	STOCK PRICE ($) FY Close	P/E High/Low		PER SHARE ($) Earnings	Dividends	Book Value
12/08	32.73	20	9	2.70	1.64	15.52
12/07	53.14	23	16	3.07	1.61	17.65
12/06	67.93	19	15	3.66	1.57	14.91
12/05	55.27	28	22	2.25	1.53	13.41
12/04	59.97	24	19	2.78	1.49	13.74
Annual Growth	(14.0%)	—	—	(0.7%)	2.4%	3.1%

Avis Budget Group

Whether you're a business traveler on an expense account or you're on a family vacation and you're counting every penny, Avis Budget Group has a car rental brand for you. Its Avis Rent A Car unit, which targets corporate and leisure travelers at the high end of the market, has 2,200 locations in the Americas and the Asia/Pacific region. Budget Rent A Car, marketed to those who watch costs closely, rents cars from 1,850 locations in the same regions and trucks from 2,875 dealers in the US. Avis Budget Group, formerly known as Cendant, changed its name in 2006 after spinning off its hotel operations (Wyndham Worldwide) and its real estate division (Realogy) and selling its travel unit (Travelport).

The new Avis Budget Group and its former corporate brethren have signed marketing agreements intended to take advantage of cross-selling opportunities between car rental, hotel, and travel booking businesses. Avis Budget Group stands on its own, though, with its well-known car and truck rental brands. It has formed numerous marketing alliances with hotels and travel agents outside the former Cendant family.

Although Avis and Budget maintain separate brand identities, the companies share a vehicle fleet and an administrative infrastructure. Like several of their rivals, Avis and Budget are working to open more facilities outside airports to compete in the insurance replacement and general use markets, where Enterprise Rent-A-Car has gained a leadership position. Off-airport revenue represents about 20% of Avis Budget Group's overall US car rental business.

Demand for the company's airport rentals is largely dependent on airline passenger volumes, which declined in 2008. As a result, revenue from Avis Budget Group's domestic car rental business was flat in 2008, and its truck rental business declined (largely due to the economic downturn).

HISTORY

Cendant began life through the 1997 merger of CUC International and HFS. A giant in hospitality, HFS was cobbled together as Hospitality Franchise Systems by LBO specialist Blackstone Group in 1992. With brands including Days Inn, Ramada, and Howard Johnson, HFS went public that year. In 1995 HFS bought real estate firm Century 21. The next year it added Electronic Realty Associates (ERA) and Coldwell Banker. Also in 1996, HFS acquired the Super 8 Motels brand as well as car-rental firm Avis. The next year it sold 75% of Avis' #1 franchisee to the public and later bought relocation service firm PHH.

In an attempt to leverage the power of his brands, HFS CEO Henry Silverman began looking at direct marketing giant CUC International. CUC was founded in 1973 as Comp-U-Card America by Walter Forbes and other investors envisioning a computer-based home shopping network. During the 1980s CUC developed as a discount direct marketer and catalog-based shopping club. It went public in 1983 with 100,000 members. CUC saw explosive growth as it signed up 7.6 million members between 1989 and 1993. In 1996 CUC acquired Rent Net, an online apartment rental service, and later bought entertainment software publishers Davidson & Associates and Sierra On-Line. In 1997 CUC bought software maker Knowledge Adventure and launched online shopping site NetMarket.

CUC and HFS completed their $14.1 billion merger in December 1997 with Silverman as CEO and Forbes as chairman. While the name Cendant was derived from "ascendant," the marriage quickly headed in the opposite direction. Accounting irregularities from before the merger that had inflated CUC's revenue and pretax profit by about $500 million were revealed in 1998. Cendant's stock price tumbled, taking a $14 billion hit in one day. Forbes resigned that summer. Silverman quickly took action and began to sell off operations. Cendant Software, National Leisure Group, and Match.com all were sold that year for a total of about $1.4 billion. The company also acquired Jackson Hewitt, the US's #2 tax-preparation firm, and UK-based National Parking.

In 1999 the company sold its fleet business, including PHH Vehicle Management Services, to Avis Rent A Car for $5 billion and sold its Entertainment Publications unit, the world's largest coupon book marketer and publisher, to The Carlyle Group. Cendant later paid $2.8 billion in one of the largest shareholder class action lawsuit settlements. (Accounting firm Ernst & Young also settled with Cendant shareholders for $335 million.)

In 2001 Cendant sought to expand its travel holdings with a slew of acquisitions. Its purchases included timeshare resort firm Fairfield Communities ($690 million); travel services firm Galileo International ($2.4 billion); and online travel reservation service Cheap Tickets ($425 million). In late 2001 Cendant cut some 6,000 jobs to improve its bottom line and announced that during the next year or so it would cut an additional 10,000 jobs and eliminate about 7% of its franchised hotels.

In 2002 the company purchased car-rental company Budget Rent A Car for about $110 million, then slashed costs by closing facilities and laying off more than 450 employees.

In 2004 Cendant's Jackson Hewitt subsidiary filed for its IPO. Also that year, former chairman Walter Forbes and former vice chairman E. Kirk Shelton went to trial on federal fraud and conspiracy charges stemming from pre-merger accounting irregularities that were discovered in 1998. (Shelton was found guilty of multiple counts of fraud in 2005.) CFO Ronald Nelson was named president, taking over for Henry Silverman, who remained chairman and CEO.

In 2004 Cendant acquired online travel firm Orbitz in a deal valued at about $1.25 billion. As 2004 wound to a close Cendant completed the acquisition of the Ramada International Hotels & Resorts brand and franchising operations from Marriott International.

Cendant in 2005 spun off its mortgage operations, PHH Mortgage, and fleet management (PHH Arval) businesses. Also that year Cendant spun off Wright Express (payment processing and information services for fleet management) in an IPO and sold its marketing services division to Apollo Management for about $1.8 billion.

The divestitures that began in 2005 culminated in the unwinding of the Cendant conglomerate the next year. It spun off its hotel and real estate operations and sold its travel services division in 2006, reconfiguring itself around its rental car businesses and renaming itself Avis Budget Group. Silverman became chairman and CEO of the company's real estate business, Realogy, and Nelson took over as chairman and CEO of the slimmed-down Avis Budget Group, which took on its new name in September 2006.

The founder of Avis Rent A Car, Warren Avis, died in April 2007 at the age of 92.

EXECUTIVES

Chairman and CEO: Ronald L. (Ron) Nelson, age 57, $2,265,789 total compensation
President, COO, and Director: F. Robert (Bob) Salerno, age 55, $2,331,474 total compensation
EVP and CFO: David B. Wyshner, $1,473,436 total compensation
SVP and CIO: Mary LeBlanc
EVP and Chief Human Resources Officer: Mark J. Servodidio, age 43, $773,027 total compensation
EVP and General Counsel: Karen Sclafani, age 57
EVP International Operations: Patric Siniscalchi, age 59, $769,006 total compensation
EVP Strategy and Pricing: Scott Deaver, age 57
EVP Sales and Marketing: Thomas M. (Tom) Gartland, age 51
EVP Operations: Larry De Shon, age 49
SVP Fleet Services: Edward Gitlitz
SVP Global Travel and Partnership Sales: Kaye Ceille
SVP Marketing: Becky Alseth
SVP Corporate Sales: Robert (Bob) Lambert
SVP and Chief Accounting Officer: Brett D. Weinblatt, age 40
SVP and Secretary: Jean M. Sera
VP Corporate Communications and Public Affairs: John Barrows
Auditors: Deloitte & Touche LLP

LOCATIONS

HQ: Avis Budget Group, Inc.
   6 Sylvan Way, Parsippany, NJ 07054
Phone: 973-496-3500   **Fax:** 888-304-2315
Web: www.avisbudgetgroup.com

2008 Sales

	$ mil.	% of total
US	5,080	85
Other countries	904	15
Total	**5,984**	**100**

PRODUCTS/OPERATIONS

2008 Sales

	$ mil.	% of total
Domestic car rental	4,695	79
International car rental	904	15
Truck rental	382	6
Corporate & other	3	—
Total	**5,984**	**100**

2008 Sales by Brand

	% of total
Avis	62
Budget	32
Budget Truck	6
Total	**100**

COMPETITORS

AMERCO
Dollar Thrifty Automotive
Enterprise Rent-A-Car
Hertz
Penske Truck Leasing
Ryder System

HISTORICAL FINANCIALS

Company Type: Public

Income Statement

FYE: December 31

	REVENUE ($ mil.)	NET INCOME ($ mil.)	NET PROFIT MARGIN	EMPLOYEES
12/08	5,984.0	(1,124.0)	—	26,000
12/07	5,986.0	(916.0)	—	30,000
12/06	5,689.0	(1,930.0)	—	30,000
12/05	18,236.0	896.0	4.9%	84,800
12/04	19,785.0	2,082.0	10.5%	87,000
Annual Growth	**(25.8%)**	**—**	**—**	**(26.1%)**

2008 Year-End Financials

Debt ratio: 8,401.1%   No. of shares (mil.): 102
Return on equity: —   Dividends
Cash ($ mil.): 258   Yield: 0.0%
Current ratio: 1.78   Payout: —
Long-term debt ($ mil.): 7,813   Market value ($ mil.): 71

Stock History

NYSE: CAR

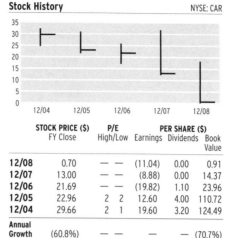

	STOCK PRICE ($) FY Close	P/E High/Low		PER SHARE ($) Earnings	Dividends	Book Value
12/08	0.70	—	—	(11.04)	0.00	0.91
12/07	13.00	—	—	(8.88)	0.00	14.37
12/06	21.69	—	—	(19.82)	1.10	23.96
12/05	22.96	2	2	12.60	4.00	110.72
12/04	29.66	2	1	19.60	3.20	124.49
Annual Growth	**(60.8%)**	**—**	**—**	**—**	**—**	**(70.7%)**

Avnet, Inc.

If you're after an electronic component, Avnet probably has it. The company is one of the world's largest distributors of electronic components and computer products, alongside rival Arrow Electronics. Avnet's suppliers include 300-plus component and systems makers; the company distributes these suppliers' products to some 100,000 manufacturers and resellers. Avnet Electronics Marketing handles semiconductors and other components. Avnet Technology Solutions provides computer products and services for resellers and large end-users, with system-level components, such as motherboards. The company distributes products in more than 70 countries; customers located in the Americas account for about half of sales.

Even in the market's worst troughs, Avnet has continued to expand by buying complementary businesses.

In early 2009 Avnet acquired Abacus Group, a European component distributor based in the UK, for $61 million in cash. The company assumed nearly $81 million in net debt in the transaction. Avnet made Abacus part of Electronics Marketing EMEA. Teaming with Sanko Holding Group, the components distributor picked up over 50% of a joint venture interest in Turkey. The operation, Avnet Technology Solutions Sanayi ve Ticaret A.S., takes the lead as one of the largest IT distributors in Turkey.

The company acquired Horizon Technology Group in mid-2008 for about €98.5 million in cash. Horizon is a distributor and integrator of IT products in Ireland and the UK. It handles products made by EMC, IBM, and Nortel Networks, among others. The group posted 2007 sales of €288 million. Horizon was integrated into Avnet's European Technology Solutions business.

Still hungry for acquisitions, Avnet also purchased Mumbai-based Ontrack Solutions in 2008.

Ontrack, a systems integrator founded in 1993, markets security, networking, and server solutions. Once fully ensconced in the company, Ontrack became part of Avnet Technology Solutions Asia Pacific.

Nearly 60% of Avnet's sales comes from its Electronics Marketing unit, which targets industrial, commercial, and military customers. IBM-made products account for around 14% of sales.

HISTORY

In 1921, before the advent of commercial battery-operated radios, Charles Avnet started a small ham radio replacement parts distributorship in Manhattan, selling parts to designers, inventors, and ship-to-shore radio users on docked ships. The stock market crash in 1929 left the business strapped; it went bankrupt in 1931. A few years later Avnet founded another company, making car radio kits and antennas. But competition got the best of him, and that company also went bankrupt.

During WWII Charles, joined by his sons Lester and Robert, founded Avnet Electronic Supply to sell parts to government and military contractors. After the war the company bought and sold surplus electrical and electronic parts. A contract from Bendix Aviation spurred company growth, and Avnet opened a West Coast warehouse. In 1955 the company incorporated as Avnet Electronics Supply, with Robert as chairman and CEO and Lester as president. Sales reached $1 million that year, although the company lost $17,000. It changed its name to Avnet Electronics in 1959.

In 1960 Avnet made its first acquisition, British Industries, and went public. Acquisitions continued throughout the 1960s with Hamilton Electro (1962), Fairmount Motor Products (1963), Carol Wire & Cable (1968), and Time Electronic Sales (1968).

To acknowledge its diversification into motors and other products, the company again changed its name, to Avnet, Inc., in 1964. Robert Avnet died the next year and Lester took over as chairman; Lester died in 1970.

In 1973 Intel, which had introduced the microprocessor, signed Avnet as a distributor, and by 1979 Avnet's sales had topped $1 billion. A soft 1982 market caused price declines that led Avnet to sell its wire and cable business. The company consolidated many of its operations to its Arizona headquarters in 1987.

During 1991 and 1992 Avnet spent more than $100 million for acquisitions strategic to the European market. In 1993 the company outbid Wyle Laboratories for Hall-Mark Electronics, the US's third-largest distributor; it also acquired Penstock, the top US distributor of microwave radio-frequency products, in 1994. Thanks to its purchases, Avnet was Europe's #2 electronics distributor by 1994, despite having had almost no European operations prior to 1990.

The company continued to expand globally in 1995, acquiring Hong Kong distributor WKK Semiconductor, among others. Also that year it began selling off its non-electronics operations.

In 1998 president and COO Roy Vallee became chairman and CEO. In 1999 Avnet acquired rival Marshall Industries for about $760 million.

In 2000 Avnet acquired IBM midrange server distributor Savoir Technology Group in a $140 million deal, making Avnet the leading distributor of IBM midrange products. Later that year the company acquired a part of Germany-based EBV Group (semiconductor distribution) and RKE (computer products and services), both from German utility giant E.ON, in a cash deal worth about $740 million.

In 2001 Avnet acquired smaller rival Kent Electronics for about $600 million. Also that year the company bought Chinese competitor Sunrise Technology.

In an effort to reduce costs during a global downturn in the electronics industry, Avnet reduced its headcount by about 1,100 people in 2003 and 2004. Also in 2004 the company launched Avnet Logistics as a separate business unit to provide assembly, asset management, distribution, programming, and warehousing services to its customers.

In 2005 the company established Avnet Managed Technologies (AMT) to offer IT services to small and mid-sized businesses. Avnet acquired semiconductor distributor Memec Group Holdings in mid-2005.

In 2007 Avnet acquired Access Distribution, the computer products distribution business of General Electric. Access Distribution specialized in computer hardware made by Sun Microsystems. Also that year Avnet acquired the European Enterprise Infrastructure division of Magirus Group. Avnet also acquired the IT Solutions division of Acal, Acal IT Solutions, which served 2,000 technology resellers and system integrators in Europe; it was integrated into the European operations of Avnet Technology Solutions.

EXECUTIVES

Chairman and CEO: Roy A. Vallee, age 56
SVP and COO: Richard (Rick) Hamada
SVP, CFO, and Assistant Secretary:
Raymond (Ray) Sadowski, age 54
SVP and CIO: Stephen R. (Steve) Phillips
Chief Operational Excellence Officer:
Steven C. (Steve) Church
Chief Human Resources Officer: MaryAnn G. Miller
VP and Chief Tax Officer: Jill Wysolmierski
EVP Business Innovation: Gregory A. (Greg) Frazier
SVP, Secretary, and General Counsel: David R. Birk, age 62
SVP; President, Electronics Marketing Global:
Harley M. Feldberg
SVP and Director Administrative Services:
Patrick Jewett
SVP: Edward B. (Ed) Kamins, age 60
SVP Customer and Supplier Loyalty: Fred J. Cuen
SVP Business Operations and Operational Excellence:
David (Dave) Rapier
SVP and Deputy General Counsel: R. Neil Taylor
SVP; President, Cilicon: Jeffrey (Jeff) Ittel
SVP Operational Excellence: Lisa Hershman
VP and Chief Communications Officer:
Allen W. (Al) Maag
VP and Director, Investor Relations: Vince Keenan
Associate General Counsel and Secretary: Jun Li
Auditors: KPMG LLP

LOCATIONS

HQ: Avnet, Inc.
2211 S. 47th St., Phoenix, AZ 85034
Phone: 480-643-2000 **Fax:** 480-643-7370
Web: www.avnet.com

Avnet has more than 300 locations worldwide.

2009 Sales

	$ mil.	% of total
Americas	7,572.2	47
Europe, Middle East & Africa	5,268.4	32
Asia/Pacific	3,389.3	21
Total	**16,229.9**	**100**

PRODUCTS/OPERATIONS

2009 Sales

	$ mil.	% of total
Avnet Electronics Marketing	9,192.8	57
Avnet Technology Solutions	7,037.1	43
Total	**16,229.9**	**100**

2009 Sales

	$ mil.	% of total
Semiconductors	8,324.0	51
Computer products	6,393.4	39
Connectors	735.2	5
Passives, electromechanical & other	777.3	5
Total	**16,229.9**	**100**

Selected Operations

Avnet Electronics Marketing (component distribution)
Avnet Cilicon (semiconductors)
Analog
Communications
Digital Signal Processors (DSPs)
Discrete
Memory
Microprocessors and microcontrollers
Optoelectronics
Programmable logic
Standard logic
Avnet IP&E (interconnect, passive, and electromechanical devices)
Design Chain Services (integrated circuit and systems-level design services)
Supply Chain Services
Asset management
Demand planning
Information services
Logistics
Order management
Warehousing
Production Supplies & Test (electronics production supplies and test equipment)
Avnet Technology Solutions (computer distribution and information technology services)
Avnet Hall-Mark (computers, software, storage, and services to resellers)
Avnet Applied Computing
Products
Displays
Memory devices
Motherboards
Networking equipment
Peripherals
Point-of-sale
Processors
Software
Storage
Wireless
Supply chain services
Financing
Integration
Logistics
Materials management
Technical service
Avnet Computing Components (microprocessors for systems integrators)

COMPETITORS

Arrow Electronics
Bell Microproducts
Digi-Key
Future Electronics
Heilind Electronics
Ingram Micro
N.F. Smith
Nu Horizons Electronics
Premier Farnell
Richardson Electronics
Sager Electrical
SYNNEX
Tech Data
TTI Inc.
WPG Holdings

HISTORICAL FINANCIALS

Company Type: Public

Income Statement

FYE: Friday nearest June 30

	REVENUE ($ mil.)	NET INCOME ($ mil.)	NET PROFIT MARGIN	EMPLOYEES
6/09	16,229.9	(1,122.5)	—	12,900
6/08	17,952.7	499.1	2.8%	12,800
6/07	15,681.1	393.1	2.5%	11,700
6/06	14,253.6	204.5	1.4%	10,900
6/05	11,066.8	168.2	1.5%	9,800
Annual Growth	**10.0%**	**—**	**—**	**7.1%**

2009 Year-End Financials

Debt ratio: 34.3%
Return on equity: —
Cash ($ mil.): 944
Current ratio: 2.09
Long-term debt ($ mil.): 947

No. of shares (mil.): 151
Dividends
Yield: 0.0%
Payout: —
Market value ($ mil.): 3,177

Stock History

NYSE: AVT

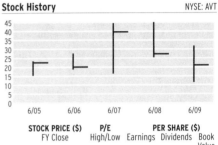

	STOCK PRICE ($) FY Close	P/E High/Low		PER SHARE ($) Earnings	Dividends	Book Value
6/09	21.03	—	—	(7.44)	0.00	18.27
6/08	27.28	14	8	3.27	0.00	27.37
6/07	39.64	17	6	2.63	0.00	22.51
6/06	20.02	20	14	1.39	0.00	18.74
6/05	22.53	17	11	1.39	0.00	13.88
Annual Growth	**(1.7%)**	**—**	**—**	**—**	**—**	**7.1%**

Avon Products

"Avon calling" — calling for a younger crowd, overseas reps, and improved global operational efficiencies. Avon Products, the world's largest direct seller of cosmetics and beauty-related items, is busy building a global brand and enticing customers younger than its typical middle-aged buyers. Direct selling remains the firm's *modus operandi*, but sales also come from catalogs and a Web site. Its products include cosmetics, fragrances, toiletries, jewelry, apparel, home furnishings, and more. Avon boasts about 5.8 million independent representatives with sales operations and distribution in some 110 countries and territories.

Avon's restructuring has involved purging staff, streamlining global manufacturing, and adjusting its supply chain with regard to procurement and distribution. In early 2009 the company announced plans to shut down two plants, one in Ohio and another in Germany. It is also freezing salaries and bolstering its recruitment of sales representatives. By late 2007 the firm had already trimmed its employee ranks by 10% and management by nearly 30%. In early 2008 the firm announced another 4,000 job cuts (about 6% of its workforce). As part of the alignment, Avon in 2007 exited unprofitable operations and product lines. It shuttered its Avon Salon & Spa and its operations in Indonesia, and also discontinued product lines in China and in the US (beComing).

The beauty company also plans to outsource transactional and other services where necessary and to navigate toward countries that offer lower operating costs.

With growth fairly stagnant at home, the company has shed product lines in favor of developing global brands. In March 2008 Avon partnered with Finnish clothing design firm Marimekko in a licensing agreement to create a color collection to sell in the US, Europe, Mexico, and Asia. It also made a Bond Girl 007 fragrance under license. Avon is promoting its image as "The Company for Women" by providing business opportunities for women in countries where fewer choices are available to them.

Despite resistance from China for years, Avon has been trying to get its foot in the country's door. In 1998 China banned direct selling because consumers there found it difficult to distinguish between companies that direct sell and those with pyramid schemes. The beauty firm sees China as an untapped gold mine and in 2005 was given approval from the government to test its direct selling in parts of China, specifically the cities of Beijing and Tianjin and the province of Guangdong.

Avon anticipates driving additional growth based on fragrances (Today, Tomorrow, Always) and skin care (Anew anti-aging) sales. It agreed with French designer Emanuel Ungaro to create two signature fragrances (U by Ungaro for Her and U by Ungaro for Him) that launched in mid-2008. Previous fragrance deals include a partnership with New York Yankee captain Derek Jeter for "Driven" men's fragrance and a personal grooming line of products.

Capital World Investors and Capital Research Global Investors each hold about a 10% interest in Avon Products.

HISTORY

In the 1880s book salesman David McConnell gave small bottles of perfume to New York housewives who listened to his sales pitch. The perfume was more popular than the books, so in 1886 McConnell created the California Perfume Company and hired women to sell door-to-door. (He renamed the company Avon Products in 1939 after being impressed by the beauty of Stratford-upon-Avon in England.) Through the 1950s these women, mostly housewives seeking extra income, made Avon a major force in the cosmetics industry.

From the 1960s until the mid-1980s, Avon was the world's largest cosmetics company, known for its appeal to middle-class homemakers. But the company hit hard times in 1974 — the recession made many of its products too pricey for blue-collar customers, and women were leaving home for the workforce. Discovering that Avon's traditional products had little appeal for younger women, Avon began an overhaul of its product line, introducing the Colorworks line for teenagers with the slogan, "It's not your mother's makeup."

Avon acquired prestigious jeweler Tiffany & Co. in 1979 (sold 1984) to help improve the company's image. To boost profits, it entered the retail prestige fragrance business by launching a joint venture with Liz Claiborne (1985) and buying Giorgio Armani (1987, the Giorgio Beverly Hills retail operations were sold in 1994). But Liz Claiborne dissolved the joint venture when Avon bought competitor Parfums Stern in 1987 (sold 1990). It sold 40% of Avon Japan (started 1969) to the Japanese public that year.

Avon Color cosmetics were introduced in 1988, and sleepwear, preschool toys, and videos followed in 1989. It introduced apparel in 1994 and the next year worked with designer Diane Von Furstenberg to launch a line of clothing. Mattel and Avon joined forces in 1996 to sell toys — Winter Velvet Barbie became Avon's most successful product introduction ever.

Passing over several high-ranking female executives (the company felt they weren't ready), Avon made Charles Perrin its CEO in mid-1998. Andrea Jung, the brain behind the makeover, became president. In 1999 Jung became Avon's first female CEO by replacing the retiring Perrin. Former Goodyear and Rubbermaid CEO Stanley Gault was elected chairman of the board. In March 2000 Avon announced an alliance with Swiss pharmaceutical group Roche to develop a line of women's vitamins and nutritional products (its first) launched in 2001.

In September 2001 Jung was elected chairman of the board. In 2002, as part of a move to improve operating efficiencies, Avon closed its jewelry manufacturing plant in San Sebastian, Puerto Rico. It now outsources its full jewelry line by purchasing finished goods from Asia. In another cost-cutting move, Avon laid off 3,500 employees, or 8% of its workforce, in March 2002. The next month Avon announced the closing of production operations in Northampton, UK, and a shift of these operations to its facility in Garwolin, Poland.

As part of its focus on the younger market, in 2003 Avon launched a new cosmetics line called "mark." — targeted to the 16 to 24 age group. Named for young women making their mark on the world, the line includes 300 products, such as cosmetics, skin care, fragrance, accessories, jewelry, and handbags. In 2004 Avon agreed to acquire a 20% stake in its two Chinese joint ventures with Masson Group.

EXECUTIVES

Chairman and CEO: Andrea Jung, age 50, $11,055,012 total compensation
Vice Chairman, CFO, and Chief Strategy Officer: Charles W. (Chuck) Cramb, age 62, $3,602,029 total compensation
President: Elizabeth A. (Liz) Smith, age 45, $3,349,487 total compensation
SVP and CIO: Donagh Herlihy
EVP, Latin America: Charles M. Herington, age 49, $2,780,514 total compensation
SVP, Western Europe, Middle East & Africa, Asia-Pacific, and China: Bennett R. (Ben) Gallina, age 54, $2,547,985 total compensation
SVP, Global Supply Chain: John F. Owen, age 51
SVP and Global Brand President: Jeri B. Finard, age 49
SVP, Human Resources: Lucien Alziari, age 49
SVP, Global Communications: Nancy Glaser
SVP, General Counsel, and Secretary: Kim K.W. Rucker, age 42

SVP, Central and Eastern Europe: John Philip Higson, age 50
SVP and President, North America: Geralyn R. Breig, age 46
SVP, Global Sales: Srdjan Mijuskovic
VP and Controller: Simon N. R. Harford, age 49
VP, Finance and Global Marketing: Richard S. Foggio, age 49
VP, Associate General Counsel, and Corporate Secretary: Kim K. Azzarelli
Manager Corporate and Media Relations: Sharon Samuel
Auditors: PricewaterhouseCoopers LLP

LOCATIONS

HQ: Avon Products, Inc.
1345 Avenue of the Americas, New York, NY 10105
Phone: 212-282-5000   **Fax:** 212-282-6049
Web: www.avoncompany.com

2008 Sales

	$ mil.	% of total
Latin America	3,884.1	37
North America	2,492.7	23
Central & Eastern Europe	1,719.5	16
Western Europe, Middle East & Africa	1,351.7	13
Asia/Pacific	891.2	8
China	350.9	3
Total	**10,690.1**	**100**

2008 Sales

	$ mil.	% of total
US	2,061.8	19
Brazil	1,674.3	16
All other	6,954.0	65
Total	**10,690.1**	**100**

PRODUCTS/OPERATIONS

2008 Sales

	$ mil.	% of total
Beauty (cosmetics, fragrances, skin care & toiletries)	7,603.7	71
Fashion (fashion jewelry, watches, apparel, footwear & accessories)	1,863.3	17
Home (gift & decorative products, housewares, entertainment & leisure, children's & nutritional products)	1,121.9	11
Other revenue (shipping & handling fees billed to representatives)	101.2	1
Total	**10,690.1**	**100**

Selected Products

Fragrances
Hair Care
Health and Wellness
Skin Care, Bath, and Body

COMPETITORS

Alberto-Culver	Johnson & Johnson
Alticor	Johnson Publishing
Amway China	Kracie
Bath & Body Works	L'Oréal
BeautiControl	LVMH
Beiersdorf	Macy's
Body Shop	Mary Kay
Chanel	Murad, Inc.
Clarins	Nu Skin
Colgate-Palmolive	Perrigo
Coty Inc.	Prestige Cosmetics
Dana Classic Fragrances	Procter & Gamble
Del Laboratories	Revlon
Dillard's	Sara Lee
Elizabeth Arden Inc	Shaklee
Enesco	Shiseido
Estée Lauder	Target
Forever Living	Tupperware Brands
Hanover Direct	Unilever
J. C. Penney	Wal-Mart
Jafra	

HISTORICAL FINANCIALS

Company Type: Public

Income Statement

FYE: December 31

	REVENUE ($ mil.)	NET INCOME ($ mil.)	NET PROFIT MARGIN	EMPLOYEES
12/08	10,690.1	875.3	8.2%	42,000
12/07	9,938.7	530.7	5.3%	42,000
12/06	8,763.9	477.6	5.4%	40,300
12/05	8,149.6	847.6	10.4%	49,000
12/04	7,747.8	846.1	10.9%	47,700
Annual Growth	8.4%	0.9%	—	(3.1%)

2008 Year-End Financials

Debt ratio: 240.8%
Return on equity: 126.3%
Cash ($ mil.): 1,105
Current ratio: 1.22
Long-term debt ($ mil.): 1,625

No. of shares (mil.): 427
Dividends
  Yield: 3.3%
  Payout: 39.2%
Market value ($ mil.): 10,260

Stock History

NYSE: AVP

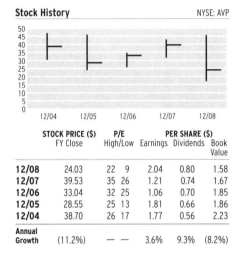

	STOCK PRICE ($) FY Close	P/E High/Low	PER SHARE ($) Earnings	Dividends	Book Value
12/08	24.03	22 9	2.04	0.80	1.58
12/07	39.53	35 26	1.21	0.74	1.67
12/06	33.04	32 25	1.06	0.70	1.85
12/05	28.55	25 13	1.81	0.66	1.86
12/04	38.70	26 17	1.77	0.56	2.23
Annual Growth	(11.2%)	— —	3.6%	9.3%	(8.2%)

Baker & McKenzie

Baker & McKenzie believes big is good and bigger is better. One of the world's largest law firms, it has about 3,900 attorneys practicing from some 70 offices — from Bangkok to Berlin to Buenos Aires — in almost 40 countries. It offers expertise in a wide range of practice areas, including antitrust, intellectual property, international trade, mergers and acquisitions, project finance, and tax law. Baker & McKenzie's client list includes big companies from numerous industries, including banking and finance, construction, and technology, as well as smaller enterprises.

Baker & McKenzie is known for the geographic scope of its practice — some 80% of the firm's attorneys work outside the US. The firm touts its widespread network of offices as an advantage for clients with multinational interests.

The vast scale of Baker & McKenzie's operations increases the firm's exposure to liability, however, and that concern led Baker & McKenzie to reorganize itself as a Swiss Verein in 2004. Under the new structure, which is used by accounting firms such as Deloitte Touche Tohmatsu, Baker & McKenzie's member firms operate as separate entities, insulating the parent firm from liability. Baker & McKenzie was the first international law firm to organize itself under a Verein structure.

HISTORY

Russell Baker traveled from his native New Mexico to Chicago on a railroad freight car to attend law school. Upon graduation in 1925 he started practicing law with his classmate Dana Simpson under the name Simpson & Baker. Inspired by Chicago's role as a manufacturing and agricultural center for the world and influenced by the international focus of his alma mater, the University of Chicago, Baker dreamed of creating an international law practice. He began developing an expertise in international law, and in 1934 Abbott Laboratories retained him to handle its worldwide legal affairs. Baker was on his way to fulfilling his dream.

Baker joined forces with Chicago litigator John McKenzie in 1949, forming Baker & McKenzie. In 1955 the firm opened its first foreign office in Caracas, Venezuela, to meet the needs of its expanding US client base. Over the next 10 years it branched out into Asia, Australia, and Europe, with offices in London, Manila, Paris, and Tokyo. Baker's death in 1979 neither slowed the firm's growth nor changed its international character. The next year it expanded into the Middle East and opened its 30th office in 1982 (Melbourne). To manage the sprawling law firm, Baker & McKenzie created the position of chairman of the executive committee in 1984.

In late 1991 the firm dropped the Church of Scientology as a client, losing an estimated $2 million in business. It was speculated that pressure from client Eli Lilly (maker of the drug Prozac, which Scientologists actively oppose) influenced the decision. In 1992 Baker & McKenzie was ordered to pay $1 million for wrongfully firing an employee who later died of AIDS. (The case became the basis for the 1993 film *Philadelphia*.) The firm fought the verdict but eventually settled for an undisclosed amount in 1995.

In 1994 Baker & McKenzie closed its Los Angeles office (the former MacDonald, Halsted & Laybourne; acquired 1988) amid considerable rancor. Also that year a former secretary at the firm received a $7.1 million judgment for sexual harassment by a partner. (A San Francisco Superior Court judge later reduced the award to $3.5 million.)

John Klotsche, a senior partner from the firm's Palo Alto, California, office, was appointed chairman in 1995. The following year the firm began a major expansion into California's Silicon Valley as part of an initiative to serve technology companies around the world. It also expanded its Warsaw, Poland, office through a merger with the Warsaw office of Dickinson, Wright, Moon, Van Dusen & Freman.

In 1998 Baker & McKenzie formed a special unit in Singapore to deal with business generated by the financial troubles in Asia. The opening of offices in Taiwan and Azerbaijan in 1998 brought the firm's total number of offices to 59. Klotsche stepped down in 1999 as the firm celebrated its 50th anniversary; Christine Lagarde replaced him. In early 2001 Baker & McKenzie created a joint venture practice with Singapore-based associate firm Wong & Leow. Also that year it merged with Madrid-based Briones Alonso y Martin to create the largest independent law firm in Spain.

Lagarde stepped down as executive chairman in 2004, and John Conroy was chosen to lead the firm.

EXECUTIVES

Chairman: John J. Conroy Jr.
COO: Greg Walters
CFO: Robert S. Spencer
Global Director Global Information Systems: Martin Telfer
Chief Global Press Officer: Judith Green
Managing Partner, North American Region and Executive Committee Member: David P. Hackett
Regional Operating Officer, Asia Pacific: Paul Malliate
Regional Operating Officer, Europe, Middle East, and Central Asia: Kate Stonestreet
Regional Operating Officer, Latin America: Leon J. Sacks
Regional Operating Officer, North America: Joseph Plack
Chairman, Australian Offices and Executive Committee Member: David Jacobs
General Counsel: Edward J. Zulkey
Global Director Marketing: David Tabolt
Manager Marketing, North America: Heidi Bouldin
Senior Public Relations Coordinator: Jessica Benzon
Director Communications: Mark Bain

LOCATIONS

HQ: Baker & McKenzie
1 Prudential Plaza, 130 E. Randolph Dr., Ste. 2500, Chicago, IL 60601
Phone: 312-861-8800   **Fax:** 312-861-8823
Web: www.bakernet.com

PRODUCTS/OPERATIONS

Selected Practice Areas

Antitrust and trade
Banking and finance
Corporate
Dispute resolution
Employment
Insurance
Intellectual property
International/commercial
IT/communications
Major projects and project finance
Pharmaceuticals and health care
Real estate, construction, environment, and tourism
Tax

COMPETITORS

Clifford Chance
DLA Piper
Jones Day
Kirkland & Ellis
Latham & Watkins
Mayer Brown
McDermott Will & Emery
Shearman & Sterling
Sidley Austin
Skadden, Arps
Sullivan & Cromwell
Weil, Gotshal & Manges
White & Case

HISTORICAL FINANCIALS

Company Type: Private

Income Statement

FYE: June 30

	REVENUE ($ mil.)	NET INCOME ($ mil.)	NET PROFIT MARGIN	EMPLOYEES
6/09	2,110.0	—	—	9,700
6/08	2,190.0	—	—	9,700
6/07	1,829.0	—	—	9,600
6/06	1,522.0	—	—	9,503
6/05	1,352.0	—	—	8,500
Annual Growth	**11.8%**	**—**	**—**	**3.4%**

Revenue History

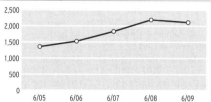

Baker Hughes

Baker Hughes cooks up a baker's dozen of products and services for the global petroleum market. Through its Drilling and Evaluation segment, Baker Hughes makes products and services used to drill oil and natural gas wells. Through its Completion and Production segment, the company provides equipment and services used from the completion phase through the productive life of oil and natural gas wells. The company tests potential well sites and drills and operates the wells; it also makes bits and drilling fluids and submersible pumps, and provides equipment and well services. Baker Hughes' revenues are fairly evenly split between its Drilling and Evaluation and Completion and Production segments.

The Drilling and Evaluation segment consists of Baker Hughes Drilling Fluids (drilling fluids), Hughes Christensen (drill bits), INTEQ (directional drilling, measurement-while-drilling and logging-while-drilling) and Baker Atlas (downhole well logging and services).

Baker Hughes' Completion and Production segment consists of Baker Oil Tools (completion, workover and fishing equipment), Baker Petrolite (oilfield specialty chemicals such as drilling fluids and stimulation additives), Centrilift (electric submersible and progressing cavity pumps), and ProductionQuest (production optimization and permanent monitoring).

While Baker Hughes had made something of a comeback with the increased price of oil — its rig counts had reached a 10-year high in 2008 — the global economic crisis has indeed affected the company adversely. In just the first two months of 2009 its US rig count declined by more than 25%.

In 2006 Baker Hughes divested its 30% stake in seismic services provider WesternGeco, selling out to joint-venture partner Schlumberger.

HISTORY

Howard Hughes Sr. developed the first oil well drill bit for rock in 1909. Hughes and partner Walter Sharp opened a plant in Houston, and their company, Sharp & Hughes, soon had a near monopoly on rock bits. When Sharp died in 1912, Hughes bought his partner's half of the company, incorporating as Hughes Tool. Hughes held 73 patents when he died in 1924; the company passed to Howard Hughes Jr.

It is estimated that between 1924 and 1972 Hughes Tool provided Hughes Jr. with $745 million in pretax profits, which he used to diversify into movies (RKO), airlines (TWA), and Las Vegas casinos. In 1972 he sold the company to the public for $150 million. After 1972 the company expanded into tools for aboveground oil production. In 1974, under the new leadership of chairman James Leach, Hughes bought the oil field equipment business of Borg-Warner.

In 1913 drilling contractor Carl Baker organized the Baker Casing Shoe Company in California to collect royalties on his three oil tool inventions. The firm began to make its own products in 1918, and during the 1920s it expanded nationally, opened global trade, and formed Baker Oil Tools (1928). The company grew in the late 1940s and the 1950s as oil drilling boomed.

During the 1960s Baker prospered, despite fewer US well completions. Foreign sales increased. From 1963 to 1975 Baker bought oil-related companies Kobe, Galigher, Ramsey Engineering, and Reed Tool.

US expenditures for oil services fell between 1982 and 1986 from $40 billion to $9 billion. In 1987 both Baker and Hughes faced falling revenues. The two companies merged to form Baker Hughes. By closing plants and combining operations, the venture became profitable by the end of 1988. The company bought Eastman Christensen (the world leader in directional and horizontal drilling equipment) and acquired the instrumentation unit of Tracor Holdings in 1990.

Baker Hughes spun off BJ Services (pumping services) to the public in 1991 and sold the Eastern Hemisphere operations of Baker Hughes Tubular Services (BHTS) to Tuboscope. It sold the Western Hemisphere operations of BHTS to ICO the following year.

Also in 1992 Baker Hughes bought Teleco Oilfield Services, a pioneer in directional drilling techniques, from Sonat. The next year the company consolidated its drilling-technology businesses into a single unit, Baker Hughes INTEQ.

In 1996 company veteran Max Lukens became CEO. He replaced James Woods as chairman the next year.

Baker Hughes allied with Schlumberger's oil field service operations in 1996. In a move to boost its oil field chemicals business the company bought Petrolite in 1997 and rival Western Atlas for $3.3 billion in 1998, strengthening its land-based seismic data business (#1 in that market) and testing business. A downturn in the Asian economy, disruptions from tropical storms, and slumping oil prices caused oil companies to reduce demand for Baker Hughes' products. The company suffered a big loss in 1998 and in response trimmed its workforce by about 15% in 1999.

In 2000 Lukens stepped down after accounting blunders caused the company to restate earnings. Company director and Newfield Exploration Company CEO Joe Foster replaced him as acting

CEO until Michael Wiley was named to that office. Baker Hughes combined its seismic oil and gas exploration business with that of Schlumberger to create WesternGeco in early 2001.

In 2003 the company formed QuantX, a wellbore instrumentation joint venture company with Expro International. Cornerstone Pipeline Management was acquired in an effort to expand the pipeline inspection services provided by its Baker Petrolite division. Continuing with its acquisition run, Baker Hughes purchased the remaining 10% interest in Compagnie Générale de Géophysique's (CGG) borehole seismic processing business.

In 2004 Baker Hughes exited its Process division when it completed the sale of its Bird Machine subsidiary to Austrian-based machinery manufacturer Andritz. Michael Wiley retired from his position as chairman and CEO of Baker Hughes. Chad Deaton, formerly president and CEO of Hanover Compressor, was named chairman and CEO to replace him.

In late 2005 the company acquired Scotland-based Zeroth Technologies, a company than manufactures expandable metal sealing elements.

In early 2006 Baker Hughes acquired Nova Technology, a Louisiana-based company that supplies monitoring and chemical injection systems for use in offshore gas and oil well operations.

EXECUTIVES

Chairman, President, and CEO: Chad C. Deaton, age 56, $12,710,093 total compensation
SVP and COO: Martin S. Craighead, age 49, $2,428,230 total compensation
SVP and CFO: Peter A. Ragauss, age 51, $4,829,513 total compensation
VP and CIO: Clifton (Clif) Triplett, age 50
VP, Chief Compliance Officer, and Senior Deputy General Counsel: Jay G. Martin, age 57
SVP and General Counsel: Alan R. Crain Jr., age 57, $4,007,686 total compensation
VP and Controller: Alan J. Keifer, age 54
VP; President, Baker Hughes Western Hemisphere Operations: John A. (Andy) O'Donnell, age 60
VP, Corporate Development: David E. Emerson
VP, Tax: John H. Lohman Jr.
VP; President, Baker Oil Tools: Christopher P. (Chris) Beaver, age 51
VP; President, INTEQ: Paul S. Butero, age 52
VP; President, Baker Hughes Drilling Fluids: Richard L. Williams, age 53
VP; President, Baker Hughes Russia: Frank M. (Mike) Davis, age 53
VP; President, Hughes Christensen: Gary G. Rich, age 50
VP, Human Resources: Didier Charreton, age 45
VP; President, Baker Atlas: Stephen K. Ellison, age 50
VP; President Eastern Hemisphere Operations: Belgacem Chariag, age 46
VP; President, Centrilift: Nelson Ney, age 45
VP; President, Products and Technology: Derek Mathieson, age 38
Corporate Secretary: Sandra E. Alford
Director, Investor Relations: Gary R. Flaharty
Auditors: Deloitte & Touche LLP

LOCATIONS

HQ: Baker Hughes Incorporated
  2929 Allen Pkwy., Ste. 2100, Houston, TX 77019
Phone: 713-439-8600   **Fax:** 713-439-8699
Web: www.bakerhughes.com

2008 Sales

	$ mil.	% of total
North America	5,178	44
Europe, Africa, Russia & the Caspian	3,386	29
Middle East & Asia/Pacific	2,173	18
Latin America	1,127	9
Total	**11,864**	**100**

PRODUCTS/OPERATIONS

2008 Sales

	$ mil.	% of total
Drilling & evaluation	6,049	51
Completion & production	5,815	49
Total	**11,864**	**100**

Drilling and Evaluation

Baker Atlas (downhole data acquisition, processing and analysis; pipe recovery)
Baker Hughes Drilling Fluids (drilling fluids)
Hughes Christensen (oil well drill bits)
ITEQ (conventional and rotary directional drilling, measurement-while-drilling and logging-while-drilling)

Completion and Production

Baker Oil Tools (completion, workover, and fishing technologies and services)
Baker Petrolite (specialty chemicals for petroleum, transportation, and refining)
Centrilift (electric submersible pumps and downhole oil/water separation)
ProductionQuest (production optimization and permanent monitoring)

COMPETITORS

Aker Solutions	National Oilwell Varco
BJ Services	Petroleum Geo-Services
CGGVeritas	Precision Drilling
FMC	Schlumberger
Halliburton	Smith International
John Wood Group	Technip
Nabors Industries	Weatherford International
Nalco	

HISTORICAL FINANCIALS

Company Type: Public

Income Statement

FYE: December 31

	REVENUE ($ mil.)	NET INCOME ($ mil.)	NET PROFIT MARGIN	EMPLOYEES
12/08	11,864.0	1,635.0	13.8%	39,800
12/07	10,428.2	1,513.9	14.5%	35,800
12/06	9,027.4	2,419.0	26.8%	34,600
12/05	7,185.5	879.3	12.2%	29,100
12/04	6,103.8	528.6	8.7%	26,900
Annual Growth	18.1%	32.6%	—	10.3%

2008 Year-End Financials

Debt ratio: 26.1%
Return on equity: 24.9%
Cash ($ mil.): 1,955
Current ratio: 2.85
Long-term debt ($ mil.): 1,775
No. of shares (mil.): 310
Dividends
 Yield: 1.7%
 Payout: 10.6%
Market value ($ mil.): 9,938

Stock History

NYSE: BHI

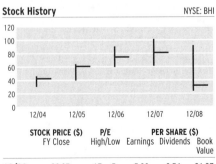

	STOCK PRICE ($) FY Close	P/E High/Low		PER SHARE ($) Earnings	Dividends	Book Value
12/08	32.07	17	5	5.30	0.56	21.97
12/07	81.10	21	13	4.73	0.52	20.35
12/06	74.66	12	8	7.27	0.52	16.92
12/05	60.78	25	16	2.57	0.47	15.16
12/04	42.67	29	20	1.58	0.46	12.57
Annual Growth	(6.9%)	—	—	35.3%	5.0%	15.0%

Baldor Electric

Electricity drives Baldor Electric Company's sales — and its products. The company manufactures industrial AC and DC electric motors, controls, and speed drives that power products ranging from material handling conveyors to fluid handling pumps. Other products include industrial grinders, buffers, polishing lathes, and generators. Baldor Electric sells to OEMs primarily in the agricultural and semiconductor equipment industries and to independent distributors for resale as replacement parts. The company has some 75 sales offices and warehouses in North America and abroad. It maintains manufacturing plants in the US, Canada, Mexico, China, and the UK.

Baldor Electric has been expanding its geographic footprint, particularly in Asia, with acquisitions of Reliance Electric Company from Rockwell Automation in 2007 and Canada-based Poulies Maska in 2008. Both deals gave Baldor manufacturing operations in high-growth China and additional industrial electric motors and mechanical power transmission products. The company is also focused on organic growth through new product development, especially in the area of energy-efficient motors. On average, it releases 250 new products per year.

Not immune to the global economic downturn, Baldor's business was particularly affected in the second half of 2008, causing cost-cutting measures that include an elimination of about 900 jobs (a workforce reduction of about 11%) by mid-2009. The cutbacks are expected to achieve approximately $80 million in cost savings in 2009.

It is also attempting to accelerate the integration of recently acquired businesses. Reliance Electric has been completely absorbed, though Baldor sells its motor products under the Baldor-Reliance brand name.

Lord Abbett & Co. owns about 7% of Baldor Electric. Other institutional investors include Barclays Global Investors and AllianceBernstein, each with roughly a 6% stake.

HISTORY

Electrical engineer Edwin Ballman and master machinist Emil Doerr founded Baldor in 1920 in St. Louis. The company took its name from the last names of the founders. Baldor gained popularity for building fully enclosed motors that included ball bearings. It struggled through the Depression, expanding its line with custom motors, battery chargers, and grinders. After WWII, demand for Baldor's products accelerated. In 1956 the company moved to Fort Smith, Arkansas. It went public in 1976 and built market strength in part through acquisitions, including Lectron (solid-state motor starters, 1986) and Powertron (DC electric motors, 1988).

The company's energy-efficient electric motors sold well in the early 1990s. In 1994 Baldor acquired Grant Gear's line of gear-speed reducers, and in 1997 the company bought Optimised Control (motion controls, UK). Baldor was named one of *FORTUNE*'s 100 Best Companies to Work for in America in 1998. That year Baldor acquired linear-motor maker Northern Magnetics. The next year John McFarland, a 30-year company veteran, was named CEO (a position left vacant since 1997).

In 2000 Baldor acquired Pow'R Gard Generator Corporation, a manufacturer of generators and generator sets, for $40 million. The company closed its drives plant in Plymouth, Minnesota, and consolidated it with its plant in Fort Smith, Arkansas, in 2001. In 2002 Baldor announced plans to acquire the US-based Energy Dynamics, Inc., a manufacturer of industrial generators; the deal was completed in early 2003.

In 2004 the company created Baldor Power Finance, a subsidiary to assist customers with financing and leasing Baldor's larger generators.

In 2005 Baldor acquired the 40% minority interest in Australian Baldor Pty. Ltd. that it did not previously own, making the Australian company a wholly owned subsidiary.

Roland Boreham Jr., the company's CEO from 1978 to 1981 and its chairman from 1981 through 2004, died in early 2006. He had been associated with Baldor Electric for 58 years, first working for his father, a Baldor grinder representative.

In early 2007 Baldor acquired most of Rockwell Automation Power Systems for about $1.8 billion in cash and stock. The company purchased the Reliance Electric motors and motor repair services businesses from Rockwell Automation, along with the Dodge mechanical power transmission products business. Rockwell Automation kept the Reliance Electric and Reliance brand drives business. Baldor exchanged $1.75 billion in cash and 1.58 million shares of its common stock for the Rockwell Automation business segment.

Soon after acquiring the Reliance Electric motor business, Baldor moved to close the Reliance Electric plant in Madison, Indiana, shifting production to plants in Arkansas and Oklahoma. Baldor also sold the Reliance Electric power services business — which maintains, repairs, and supports Reliance motors — to avoid competing with existing customers. Baldor absorbed Reliance Electric, though it sells motor products under the Baldor-Reliance brand name.

EXECUTIVES

Chairman and CEO: John A. McFarland, age 57, $1,511,441 total compensation
President, COO, Secretary, and Director: Ronald E. (Ron) Tucker, age 51, $879,281 total compensation
CFO: George E. Moschner, age 50, $536,949 total compensation
EVP Sales: Randy L. Colip, age 50, $490,784 total compensation
EVP Materials: Gene J. Hagedorn, age 62
EVP Operations: Randal G. (Randy) Waltman, age 59
EVP Business Integration: Edward L. (Ed) Ralston, age 39, $477,357 total compensation
EVP Dodge and International Sales: Michael Cinquemani, age 45
VP Information Services: Mark L. Shackelford, age 49
VP Marketing: Randall P. Breaux, age 46
VP Drives: Roger V. Bullock, age 58
VP Investor Relations: Tracy L. Long, age 43
VP Manufacturing, Reliance: Terry Fulmer
VP Human Resources, Reliance and Dodge: Marvin Ward
VP Engineering: Ronald W. Thurman, age 54
VP Human Resources: Jason W. Green, age 39
VP Materials: Amy Schwan-Burdick
VP Business Integration: Tom Mascari, age 57
Treasurer and Corporate Controller: Bryant G. Dooly, age 47
Auditors: Ernst & Young LLP

LOCATIONS

HQ: Baldor Electric Company
5711 R. S. Boreham, Jr. St., Fort Smith, AR 72901
Phone: 479-646-4711   **Fax:** 479-648-5792
Web: www.baldor.com

2008 Sales

	$ mil.	% of total
US	1,584.6	81
Other countries	370.1	19
Total	**1,954.7**	**100**

PRODUCTS/OPERATIONS

2008 Sales

	% of total
Industrial electric motors	66
Mechanical power transmission products	27
Other (including generators, drives & metal stampings)	7
Total	**100**

Selected Products

Drives
   Linear and rotary servo motors
   Motion control products

Generators
   Emergency & standby generators
   Industrial towable generators
   Mobile light towers
   Peak-shaving generators
   Portable generators
   Prime power generators

Mechanical power transmission
   Bushings
   Conveyor pulleys
   Helical & worm gearings
   Mounted bearings
   Sheaves

Motors
   AC motors (up to 15,000 horsepower)
   DC motors (up to 3,000 horsepower)
   Integral gear motors

COMPETITORS

A. O. Smith	RBS Global
Altra Holdings	Regal Beloit
AMETEK	Rexnord
Bodine Electric	Rockwell Automation
Bosch Rexroth Corp.	Siemens Energy
Converteam	SKF
Emerson Electric	TB Wood's
Franklin Electric	TECO-Westinghouse
GE	TM GE Automation
Johnson Electric	Toshiba
Kinetek	WEG Electric Motors
Magnetek	

HISTORICAL FINANCIALS

Company Type: Public

Income Statement

FYE: Saturday nearest December 31

	REVENUE ($ mil.)	NET INCOME ($ mil.)	NET PROFIT MARGIN	EMPLOYEES
12/08	1,954.7	99.4	5.1%	7,891
12/07	1,824.9	94.1	5.2%	8,083
12/06	811.3	48.1	5.9%	3,950
12/05	721.6	43.0	6.0%	3,841
12/04	648.2	35.1	5.4%	3,814
Annual Growth	**31.8%**	**29.7%**	**—**	**19.9%**

2008 Year-End Financials

Debt ratio: 157.1%
Return on equity: 12.0%
Cash ($ mil.): 13
Current ratio: 2.43
Long-term debt ($ mil.): 1,319
No. of shares (mil.): 47
Dividends
   Yield: 3.8%
   Payout: 31.6%
Market value ($ mil.): 831

Stock History

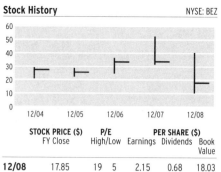

NYSE: BEZ

	STOCK PRICE ($) FY Close	P/E High/Low		Earnings	PER SHARE ($) Dividends	Book Value
12/08	17.85	19	5	2.15	0.68	18.03
12/07	33.66	25	15	2.08	0.68	17.41
12/06	33.42	25	17	1.46	0.67	6.55
12/05	25.65	22	18	1.28	0.62	6.43
12/04	27.53	27	20	1.05	0.57	6.09
Annual Growth	**(10.3%)**	**—**	**—**	**19.6%**	**4.5%**	**31.2%**

Ball Corporation

The well-rounded Ball Corporation pitches packaging to companies producing food, beverage, and household products. Food and beverage packaging includes aluminum and steel cans, and polyethylene terephthalate (PET) plastic containers. A large part of Ball's packaging sales pulls from SABMiller and bottlers of Pepsi-Cola and Coca-Cola brands. Its Aerospace & Technologies segment manufactures remote sensing satellites, telescopes, surveillance, and antenna and video technologies. Contracts funded by agencies such as the US Department of Defense and NASA represent over 90% of this segment's sales.

Operating through five business segments, Ball owes much of its performance to thirsty consumers. Its largest product lines are aluminum and steel beverage cans, which contribute to 75% of Ball's total segment earnings. According to Ball, its Packaging Europe segment is the second largest metal beverage container producer in Europe.

Albeit a core business, Ball's metal beverage packaging has taken a hit from the economic downturn and the ripple effect of reduced product demand. The company has pinched operating costs, cut its workforce, and streamlined its beverage can end manufacturing businesses. In 2008, the company shuttered its metal beverage can plants in Missouri and Puerto Rico, its aluminum beverage can manufacturing plant in Washington, and aerosol can manufacturing plants in California and Georgia. It also exited the custom and decorative tinplate can business in Maryland, and closed a plastic-packaging plant in Ontario. Ball's Australian operation was put on the sale rack too; QinetiQ Group, a British defense company, pocketed it.

The company is delaying completion of a planned beverage can plant in Poland and new construction in India. Ball in 2009 closed its two smallest PET bottle plants, in New York and Wisconsin, and transferred production to other US facilities. However, strategic opportunities are still sought. Ball is establishing a new beverage can plant in Brazil and adding further can capacity in an existing Brazilian plant. Ball also agreed to buy four US beverage can plants from Anheuser-Busch InBev for $577 million.

Before the economy turned south, Ball made several sizeable acquisitions. It acquired US Can's US and Argentinean operations for $550 million. The deal, which included 10 US plants and two Argentinean plants, made Ball the US's largest maker of aerosol cans. Ball also supplemented its plastic bottle manufacturing operations, buying three facilities from Alcan for about $180 million.

HISTORY

The Ball Corporation began in 1880 when Frank Ball and his four brothers started making wood-jacket tin cans to store and transport kerosene and other materials. In 1884 the company switched to tin-jacketed glass containers for kerosene lamps. The lamps, however, were soon displaced by Thomas Edison's electric light bulb.

The Ball brothers then learned that the patent to the original sealed-glass storage container (the Mason jar) had expired. By 1886 the brothers had entered the sealed-jar business and imprinted their jars with the Ball name. In their first year, they made 12,500 jars and sparked a patent war with the two reigning jar producers, who asserted that they controlled the correct patents and threatened to sue. The Ball lawyers proved that the patents had expired, and the jar remained Ball's mainstay for many years.

The company began diversifying, but a 1947 antitrust ruling prohibited it from buying additional glass subsidiaries. Ball decided to take advantage of the space race by buying Control Cells (aerospace science research) in 1957; that operation became Ball Brothers Research Corporation (later Ball Aerospace Systems Division). The Soviets launched Sputnik that year, igniting a massive US scientific effort in 1958, and Ball won federal contracts to make equipment for the US space program.

Ball established its metal beverage-container business in 1969 when it bought Jeffco Manufacturing of Colorado. The operation soon won contracts to supply two-piece cans to Budweiser, Coca-Cola, Dr Pepper, Pepsi, and Stroh's Beer.

John Fisher became president and CEO in 1971. The last company president who was a member of the Ball family, Fisher wanted Ball to diversify. He took the company public in 1972 to fund his efforts. That year he acquired a Singapore-based petroleum equipment company. Next he led Ball into agricultural irrigation systems and prefabricated housing. In 1974 Ball acquired a small California computer firm, which formed the basis of its telecommunications division.

Fisher retired in 1981. Ball's metal-container business suffered in the late 1980s from overcapacity and price wars in its industry. In 1989 the company's aerospace division was hard hit by $10 million in losses on an Air Force contract and by cuts in defense spending.

Ball spun off its Alltrista canning supplies subsidiary to shareholders in 1993 and purchased Heekin Can, a manufacturer for the food, pet food, and aerosol markets. That year Ball's $50 million mirror system corrected the Hubble Space Telescope's blurred vision. The company entered the polyethylene terephthalate (PET) container business in 1995 and placed its glass-container business into a newly formed company, Ball-Foster Glass Container, and the next year sold its stake to its partner, French materials company Saint-Gobain Group.

Ball sold its aerosol-can business to BWAY Corp in 1996. The company popped the top on another big deal in 1998 when it bought Reynolds Metals' aluminum-can business. In 1999 and 2000 the company closed four can plants in an effort to improve an imbalance in supply and demand.

In 2001 Ball and ConAgra Grocery Products formed a joint venture, Ball Western Can Company, to make metal food containers. Also that year subsidiary Ball Aerospace & Technologies landed a $260 million contract with the US Air Force, and Ball's president and COO, David Hoover, was named CEO. That November, Ball entered into a joint venture with Coors Brewing Co. called Rocky Mountain Metal Container to operate Coors' can facilities, making 4.5 billion cans per year.

In 2003, Ball finalized its purchase of German can maker Schmalbach-Lubeca (renamed Ball Packaging Europe) for about $890 million.

EXECUTIVES

Chairman, President, and CEO: R. David Hoover, age 63, $8,111,298 total compensation
EVP and COO: John A. Hayes, age 43, $2,775,393 total compensation
EVP and CFO: Raymond J. Seabrook, age 57, $2,163,256 total compensation
Chief Commercial Officer: Michael D. Herdman, age 59
EVP Administration and Corporate Secretary: David A. Westerlund, age 58, $2,111,237 total compensation
SVP Corporate Relations: Harold L. Sohn, age 62
VP Information Technology: Leroy J. Williams Jr., age 43
VP and Treasurer: Scott C. Morrison, age 46
VP and Controller: Douglas K. Bradford, age 51
VP Administration and Compliance: Lisa A. Pauley, age 47
President, Metal Beverage Packaging, Americas and Asia: John R. Friedery, age 52, $1,893,032 total compensation
President, Plastic Container Operations: Larry J. Green, age 61
President and CEO, Ball Aerospace & Technologies: David L. (Dave) Taylor
Chairman and CEO, Ball Asia Pacific Limited: Terence P. Voce, age 59
President, Ball Metal Food and Household Products Packaging Division, Americas and Director: Michael W. Feldser, age 63
President, Ball Packaging Europe: Gerrit Heske, age 44
General Counsel and Assistant Corporate Secretary: Charles E. Baker, age 51
Media Relations and General Information: Scott McCarty
Investor Relations: Ann Scott
Auditors: PricewaterhouseCoopers LLP

LOCATIONS

HQ: Ball Corporation
10 Longs Peak Dr., Broomfield, CO 80021
Phone: 303-469-3131   **Fax:** 303-460-2127
Web: www.ball.com

2008 Sales

	$ mil.	% of total
US	5,223.8	69
Foreign	2,337.7	31
Total	**7,561.5**	**100**

PRODUCTS/OPERATIONS

2008 Sales

	$ mil.	% of total
Metal beverage packaging, Americas & Asia	2,989.5	40
Metal beverage packaging, Europe	1,868.7	25
Metal food & household products packaging, Americas	1,221.4	16
Plastic packaging, Americas	735.4	9
Aerospace & technologies	746.5	10
Total	**7,561.5**	**100**

Selected Products

Packaging
  Metal
    Two- and three-piece metal food containers
    Two-piece metal beverage containers
  Plastic
    PET plastic food and beverage containers
    Polypropylene food and beverage containers
Aerospace and Technologies
  Products
    Antennas
    Cryogenics
    Laser communications
    Lubrication
    Mirrors
    Pointing and tracking
    Sensors
    Remote sensing
    Video products
    Wireless communications
  Services
    Commercial products and technologies manufacturing
    Global communications and video solutions
    Systems engineering

COMPETITORS

Alcoa
Amcor
Anchor Glass
Boeing
BWAY
CLARCOR
Consolidated Container
Constar International
Crown Holdings
Orbital Sciences
Owens-Illinois
Rexam
Rio Tinto Alcan
Rockwell Collins
Saint-Gobain Containers
Sequa
Silgan
Teledyne Technologies
Tetra Laval

HISTORICAL FINANCIALS

Company Type: Public

Income Statement

FYE: December 31

	REVENUE ($ mil.)	NET INCOME ($ mil.)	NET PROFIT MARGIN	EMPLOYEES
12/08	7,561.5	319.5	4.2%	14,500
12/07	7,389.7	281.3	3.8%	15,500
12/06	6,621.5	329.6	5.0%	15,500
12/05	5,751.2	261.5	4.5%	13,100
12/04	5,440.2	295.6	5.4%	13,200
Annual Growth	**8.6%**	**2.0%**	**—**	**2.4%**

2008 Year-End Financials

Debt ratio: —
Return on equity: —
Cash ($ mil.): —
Current ratio: —
Long-term debt ($ mil.): —

No. of shares (mil.): 94
Dividends
  Yield: 1.0%
  Payout: 12.2%
Market value ($ mil.): 3,914

Stock History   NYSE: BLL

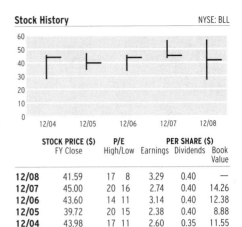

	STOCK PRICE ($) FY Close	P/E High/Low		PER SHARE ($) Earnings	Dividends	Book Value
12/08	41.59	17	8	3.29	0.40	—
12/07	45.00	20	16	2.74	0.40	14.26
12/06	43.60	14	11	3.14	0.40	12.38
12/05	39.72	20	15	2.38	0.40	8.88
12/04	43.98	17	11	2.60	0.35	11.55
Annual Growth	**(1.4%)**	**—**	**—**	**6.1%**	**3.4%**	**7.3%**

Bank of America

Welcome to the machine. One of the largest banks in the US by assets (along with Citigroup and JPMorgan Chase), Bank of America boasts the country's most extensive branch network, with more than 6,100 locations covering some 30 states from coast to coast. Its core services include consumer and small business banking, credit cards, and asset management. In early 2009 Bank of America paid some $29.1 billion in stock for Merrill Lynch, which was crippled by the ongoing credit crisis. The acquisition of the once-mighty investment bank known as "The Bull," beefs up Bank of America's wealth management, investment banking, and international business.

The company later announced it will cut up to 35,000 jobs (approximately 10% of the combined firm's workforce) over three years after the deal's completion. However, the Merrill acquisition made Bank of America one of the world's leading wealth managers with some $1.8 trillion in assets under management. The company also gained a 49% stake (but only 5% of its voting shares) in asset manager BlackRock, which has some $1.3 trillion in assets under management.

The Merrill acquisition proved an unpopular move, though. With the approval of Bank of America leadership, the failed investment bank gave early bonuses worth billions to its executives, prompting angry Bank of America shareholders and lawmakers to cry foul. The Securities and Exchange Commission later slapped Bank of America with a $33 million fine for misleading shareholders about the bonuses. CEO Ken Lewis also came under fire for not disclosing how bleak Merrill Lynch's financial condition was prior to the purchase; Lewis in turn said he had been implicitly pressured by the government to keep the troubles under wraps to prevent the deal from collapsing. A push to oust Lewis at the company's annual meeting in 2009 didn't pass, but shareholders did vote to split the chairman and CEO positions in an effort to provide more accountability to the public. Director Walter Massey was named chairman.

In another instance of Bank of America purchasing a well-known firm that has fallen upon hard times, the company made a $2 billion investment in Countrywide Financial in 2007, then bought the troubled mortgage bank outright early the next year.

The Countrywide purchase made Bank of America the largest residential mortgage lender and servicer in the US. The company also settled a lawsuit contending that Countrywide engaged in deceptive lending practices. Bank of America agreed to pay more than $8 billion toward reductions on interest rates and principals of some 400,000 troubled mortgage accounts.

In an effort to boost the economy and stimulate lending, the US government in 2008 bought some $250 billion worth of preferred shares in the country's top banks. Approximately $45 billion of that was slated for Bank of America ($20 billion more than the original total).

In 2007 Bank of America bought U.S. Trust from Charles Schwab for more than $3 billion and acquired Chicago-based LaSalle Bank from Netherlands-based ABN AMRO for some $21 billion. Prior acquisitions include credit card giant MBNA in 2006, a deal that doubled the bank's credit card customer base and its income from credit card fees.

HISTORY

Bank of America predecessor NationsBank was formed as the Commercial National Bank in 1874 by citizens of Charlotte, North Carolina. In 1901 George Stephens and Word Wood formed what became American Trust Co. The banks merged in 1957 to become American Commercial Bank, which in 1960 merged with Security National to form North Carolina National Bank.

In 1968 the bank formed holding company NCNB, which by 1980 was the largest bank in North Carolina. Under the leadership of Hugh McColl, who became chairman in 1983, NCNB became the first southern bank to span six states.

NCNB profited from the savings and loan crisis of the late 1980s by managing assets and buying defunct thrifts at fire-sale prices. The company nearly doubled its assets in 1988, when the FDIC chose it to manage the shuttered First Republicbank, then Texas' largest bank. The company renamed itself NationsBank in 1991.

A 1993 joint venture with Dean Witter and Discover to open securities brokerages in banks led to complaints that customers were not fully informed of the risks of some investments and that brokers were paying rebates to banking personnel for customer referrals. Dean Witter withdrew from the arrangement in 1994, and SEC investigations and a class-action lawsuit ensued. NationsBank settled the lawsuit for about $30 million the next year. (The company agreed to pay nearly $7 million to settle similar charges in 1998.)

Enter BankAmerica. Founded in 1904 as Bank of Italy, BankAmerica had once been the US's largest bank but had fallen behind as competitors consolidated. The company's board of directors was pondering ways to become more competitive, and in 1998 decided a merger was the best way; NationsBank obliged.

After the merger, the combined firm announced it would write down a billion-dollar bad loan to D.E. Shaw & Co., which followed the same Russian-investment-paved path of descent

as Long-Term Capital Management. David Coulter (head of the old BankAmerica, which made the loan) took the fall for the loss, resigning as president; the balance of power shifted to the NationsBank side in 1999 when Kenneth Lewis took the post. In early 1999 the bank reorganized and reduced overseas operations; it sold its private banking operations in Europe and Asia to UBS. The bank also changed its name to Bank of America.

In 2003 Bank of America's mutual fund chief Robert Gordon was among several employees who left the firm amidst a New York attorney general's investigation into hedge fund client Canary Capital Partners, which allegedly had access to Bank of America's trading platform to make illegal after-hours trades of the company's erstwhile Nations Funds. Bank of America also paid $10 million for failing to provide documents to the SEC during its investigation of the scandal, the largest-ever fine levied by the regulatory body for such an infraction. Meanwhile, the company acquired northeastern banking behemoth FleetBoston for some $50 billion in 2004.

In 2005 the company struck a deal with regulators to implement tighter controls, cut fees charged to investors, exit the mutual fund clearing business, and pay more than $500 million in fines. Also that year, Bank of America remitted another $460 million to settle investor claims that it did not adequately conduct due diligence when underwriting bonds of doomed telecom firm WorldCom in 2001 and 2002.

EXECUTIVES

Chairman: Walter E. Massey, age 71
President, CEO, and Director: Kenneth D. (Ken) Lewis, age 62, $9,959,076 total compensation
CFO: Joe L. Price, $4,021,168 total compensation
Chief Risk Officer: Gregory L. (Greg) Curl, age 60
Chief Marketing Officer: Anne M. Finucane
Chief Administrative Officer: J. Steele Alphin
Chief Accounting Officer: Neil A. Cotty
Head Bank of America Consumer-Mortgage Business: David Sambol, age 49
Head North America Card Services Business: Lance L. Weaver
Head Consumer Banking: Brian T. Moynihan, age 49
President, Bank of America Mortgage, Home Equity and Insurance Services: Barbara J. Desoer, age 56, $7,415,847 total compensation
Head Global Private Client, Institutional, and Investment Management: Keith T. Banks, age 53
Head Global Wealth and Investment Management: Sallie L. Krawcheck, age 44
Head Global Markets and Global Corporate and Investment Banking: Thomas K. (Tom) Montag, age 52
Head Global Commercial Banking: David C. Darnell
Head Private Wealth Management: Frances Aldrich Sevilla-Sacasa
Head Marketing, Global Wealth and Investment Management Division: Claire Huang
Treasurer: Mark Linsz, age 44
Bank Spokesman: Scott Silvestri
Deputy General Counsel and Secretary: Alice A. Herald
General Counsel: Edward O'Keefe, age 54
Auditors: PricewaterhouseCoopers LLP

LOCATIONS

HQ: Bank of America Corporation
100 N. Tryon St., Bank of America Corporate Ctr.
Charlotte, NC 28255
Phone: 704-386-5681 **Fax:** 704-386-6699
Web: www.bankofamerica.com

PRODUCTS/OPERATIONS

2008 Gross Revenues

	$ mil.	% of total
Interest		
Loans & leases, including fees	56,017	45
Debt securities	13,146	11
Trading account assets	9,057	7
Federal funds sold & securities purchased under resale agreements	3,313	3
Other	4,151	3
Noninterest		
Card income	13,314	11
Service charges	10,316	8
Investment & brokerage services	4,972	4
Mortgage banking	4,087	3
Investment banking	2,263	2
Gains on sales of debt securities	1,124	1
Insurance premiums	1,833	2
Equity investments	539	—
Total	**124,132**	**100**

2008 Assets

	$ mil.	% of total
Cash & short-term investments	124,905	7
Trading account assets	159,522	9
Derivative assets	62,252	3
Mortgage-backed securities	229,578	13
Other securities	47,326	2
Net loans & leases	908,375	50
Other	285,985	16
Total	**1,817,943**	**100**

COMPETITORS

American Express
Bank of New York Mellon
BB&T
Capital One
Citigroup
Citizens Financial Group
Goldman Sachs
HSBC Holdings
HSBC USA
JPMorgan Chase
KeyCorp
Morgan Stanley
PNC Financial
Quicken Loans
RBC Financial Group
State Street
SunTrust
UnionBanCal
U.S. Bancorp
Wells Fargo

HISTORICAL FINANCIALS

Company Type: Public

Income Statement

	ASSETS ($ mil.)	NET INCOME ($ mil.)	INCOME AS % OF ASSETS	EMPLOYEES
12/08	1,817,943.0	4,008.0	0.2%	243,000
12/07	1,715,746.0	14,800.0	0.9%	210,000
12/06	1,459,737.0	21,111.0	1.4%	203,425
12/05	1,291,803.0	16,447.0	1.3%	176,638
12/04	1,110,457.0	14,127.0	1.3%	175,742
Annual Growth	13.1%	(27.0%)	—	8.4%

FYE: December 31

2008 Year-End Financials

Equity as % of assets: 7.7%
Return on assets: 0.2%
Return on equity: 2.8%
Long-term debt ($ mil.): 268,292
No. of shares (mil.): 8,652
Dividends
  Yield: 15.9%
  Payout: 407.3%
Market value ($ mil.): 121,814
Sales ($ mil.): 72,782

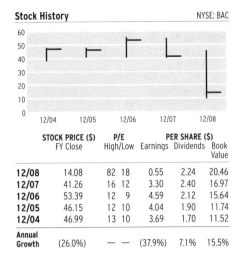

Stock History NYSE: BAC

	STOCK PRICE ($) FY Close	P/E High/Low		PER SHARE ($) Earnings	Dividends	Book Value
12/08	14.08	82	18	0.55	2.24	20.46
12/07	41.26	16	12	3.30	2.40	16.97
12/06	53.39	12	9	4.59	2.12	15.64
12/05	46.15	12	10	4.04	1.90	11.74
12/04	46.99	13	10	3.69	1.70	11.52
Annual Growth	(26.0%)	—	—	(37.9%)	7.1%	15.5%

Bank of New York Mellon

Big Apple, meet Iron City. The Bank of New York cemented its status as one of the world's largest securities servicing firms with the 2007 acquisition of Pittsburgh-based Mellon Financial. The merger also fits in with the company's other areas of focus, including asset management and corporate trust and treasury services. It was The Bank of New York's third attempt to acquire Mellon. Now known as The Bank of New York Mellon (BNY Mellon), the firm has about $20 trillion in assets under custody and some $1 trillion of assets under management. Its Pershing subsidiary is a leading securities clearing firm. BNY Mellon has a presence in about 35 countries.

Subsidiaries BNY Mellon Asset Management and Mellon Capital Management serve institutional investors, while the company's wealth management business courts high-net-worth individuals and families, as well as endowments and foundations. Other operations include mutual fund manager Dreyfus, foreign exchange, investment banking, and issuer services related to American Depository Receipts (ADRs). BNY Mellon also has interests in boutique money managers Standish and UK-based Newton.

BNY Mellon is growing its stable of asset management subsidiaries. In 2009 it announced plans to acquire Insight Investment Management, the investment arm of Lloyds Bank, for $387 million. Insight specializes in liability driven investment management, fixed income, and alternatives. The deal will boost BNY Mellon's assets under management to more than $1 trillion.

The Bank of New York jettisoned much of its traditional banking services for more lucrative fee-based securities and financial services; it swapped its retail branch network for JPMorgan Chase's trust business in 2006. In the deal, the bank swapped virtually its entire branch network in metropolitan New York for JPMorgan Chase's corporate trust business. Both units were valued at more than $2 billion each, and JPMorgan

Chase paid an additional $150 million in cash to make up the difference. The company followed the trade with the sale of Mellon 1st Business Bank to U.S. Bancorp in 2008. The following year, BNY Mellon agreed to sell one of the last remnants of Mellon Financial's banking operations, the Florida-based Mellon United National Bank to Banco de Sabadell.

Also in 2008 BNY Mellon was tapped by the federal government to act as custodian for the US Treasury's $700 million Troubled Asset Relief Program (TARP) meant to provide liquidity to banks.

HISTORY

In 1784 Alexander Hamilton (at 27, already a Revolutionary War hero and economic theorist) and a group of New York merchants and lawyers founded New York City's first bank, The Bank of New York (BNY). Hamilton saw a need for a credit system to finance the nation's growth and to establish credibility for the new nation's chaotic monetary system.

Hamilton became US secretary of the treasury in 1789 and soon negotiated the new US government's first loan — for $200,000 — from BNY. The bank later helped finance the War of 1812 by raising $16 million and the Civil War by loaning the government $150 million. In 1878 BNY became a US Treasury depository for the sale of government bonds.

The bank's conservative fiscal policies and emphasis on commercial banking enabled it to weather economic turbulence in the 19th century. In 1922 it merged with New York Life Insurance and Trust (formed in 1830 by many of BNY's directors) to form Bank of New York and Trust. The bank survived the crash of 1929 and remained profitable, paying dividends throughout the Depression. In 1938 it reclaimed its Bank of New York name.

During the mid-20th century, BNY expanded its operations and its reach through acquisitions, including Fifth Avenue Bank (trust services, 1948) and Empire Trust (serving developing industries, 1966). In 1968 the bank created holding company The Bank of New York Company to expand statewide with purchases such as Empire National Bank (1980).

BNY relaxed its lending policies in the 1980s and began to build its fee-for-service side, boosting its American Depositary Receipts business by directly soliciting European companies and seeking government securities business. The bank bought New York rival Irving Trust in a 1989 hostile takeover and in 1990 began buying other banks' credit card portfolios.

As the economy cooled in the early 1990s, BNY's book of highly leveraged transactions and nonperforming loans suffered, so the company sold many of those loans.

In the mid-1990s BNY bought processing and trust businesses and continued to build its retail business in the suburbs. It pared noncore operations, selling its mortgage banking unit (and in 1998 moved its remaining mortgage operations into a joint venture with Alliance Mortgage); credit card business (1998); and factoring and asset-based lending operations (1999).

The growth of the firm's custody services accelerated in the late 1990s. In 1997 BNY bought operations from Wells Fargo, Signet Bank (now part of First Union), and NationsBank (now Bank of America). Two years later it acquired the trust operations of Royal Bank of Scotland and Barclays Bank.

During this period BNY also built its other operations, largely through purchases. It bought the Bank of Montreal's UK-based fiscal agency business (1998) and Eastbrook Capital Management, which manages assets for businesses and wealthy individuals (1999).

Scandal rocked the firm in 1999 when the US began investigating the possible flow of money related to Russian organized crime; the following year a former bank executive admitted to having laundered about $7 billion through BNY.

In 2000 BNY bought the corporate trust business of Dai-Ichi Kangyo Bank (now part of Mizuho Financial) and Harris Trust and Savings Bank. The next year BNY bought the corporate trust operations of U.S. Trust.

Purchases in 2002 included equity research firm Jaywalk, institutional trader Francis P. Maglio & Co., and a pair of Boston-area asset managers for high-net-worth individuals, Gannet Welsh & Kotler and Beacon Fiduciary Advisors. BNY bought Pershing from Credit Suisse First Boston in 2003.

Fallout from the money laundering scandal lingered. In 2006 the Federal Reserve accused the bank of not tightening its own controls to prevent a recurrence of illegal activity.

EXECUTIVES

Chairman and CEO: Robert P. (Bob) Kelly, age 54, $13,288,556 total compensation
Vice Chairman and CEO, BNY Mellon Asset Management: Ronald P. (Ron) O'Hanley, age 52, $7,758,897 total compensation
Vice Chairman; Co-Head, Integration: Donald R. (Don) Monks, age 58
Senior Vice Chairman; Co-Head, Integration: Steven G. Elliott, age 62, $10,758,878 total compensation
Vice Chairman; VP, The Bank of New York Mellon: David F. (Dave) Lamere, age 48
Vice Chairman; Co-CEO, BNY Mellon Asset Servicing: James P. (Jim) Palermo, age 52
Vice Chairman and EVP: Woody Kerr
President and Director: Gerald L. Hassell, age 57, $7,527,521 total compensation
SEVP and CFO: Thomas P. (Todd) Gibbons, age 50, $5,268,971 total compensation
SEVP and Chief Risk Officer: Brian G. Rogan
Chief Investment Officer, BNY Mellon Wealth Management: Leo P. Grohowski
SEVP and General Counsel: Carl Krasik
SEVP; VP, BNY Mellon: Kurt D. Woetzel
SEVP; CEO, Pershing: Richard F. (Rich) Brueckner
SEVP; EVP, BNY Mellon and VP, Bank of New York Mellon: Lisa B. Peters
SEVP; VP, BNY Mellon: Arthur (Art) Certosimo
SEVP; CEO, Financial Markets and Treasury Services: Karen B. Peetz
SEVP; SVP, BNY Mellon and VP, Bank of New York Mellon: Jonathan M. (Jon) Little
SEVP; VP, BNY Mellon: Torry Berntsen
VP, Corporate Communications: Kevin Heine
Managing Director and Head, Investor Relations: Stephen Lackey
Auditors: KPMG LLP

LOCATIONS

HQ: The Bank of New York Mellon Corporation
1 Wall St., 10th Fl., New York, NY 10286
Phone: 212-495-1784 **Fax:** 212-809-9528
Web: www.bnymellon.com

PRODUCTS/OPERATIONS

2008 Gross Revenues

	$ mil.	% of total
Securities servicing fees		
Asset servicing	3,348	19
Issuer services	1,685	9
Clearing & execution services	1,087	6
Interest	5,638	31
Asset & wealth management fees	3,135	18
Foreign exchange & other trading activities	1,462	8
Treasury services	518	3
Distribution and servicing	421	2
Other	673	4
Total	**17,967**	**100**

Selected Subsidiaries and Business Lines

Alcentra (sub-investment grade debt asset management)
Ankura Capital (Australian equities)
Blackfriars Asset Management (emerging markets and global fixed income)
BNY Mellon Asset Management (institutional asset management)
BNY Mellon Cash Investment Strategies (money market funds)
The Boston Company (equity asset management)
Dreyfus (mutual funds)
EACM Advisors (fund of funds)
Harmon Investment Group (Asian equity management)
Ivy Investment Management (fund of hedge funds management)
Mellon Capital Management
Mellon Global Alternative Investments
Newton (active investment management)
Pershing (securities clearing)
Urdang (global real estate investment management)
Walter Scott (global equity investment management)
WestLB Mellon (European and global fixed income)

COMPETITORS

Bank of America
Barclays
BlackRock
Citigroup
Credit Suisse (USA)
Deutsche Bank
HSBC Holdings
JPMorgan Chase
Northern Trust
PNC Financial
State Street
UBS

HISTORICAL FINANCIALS

Company Type: Public

Income Statement

FYE: December 31

	ASSETS ($ mil.)	NET INCOME ($ mil.)	INCOME AS % OF ASSETS	EMPLOYEES
12/08	237,512.0	1,445.0	0.6%	42,900
12/07	197,656.0	2,219.0	1.1%	42,100
12/06	103,370.0	3,011.0	2.9%	22,961
12/05	102,074.0	1,571.0	1.5%	23,451
12/04	94,529.0	1,440.0	1.5%	23,363
Annual Growth	**25.9%**	**0.1%**	**—**	**16.4%**

2008 Year-End Financials

Equity as % of assets: 10.6%
Return on assets: 0.7%
Return on equity: 5.3%
Long-term debt ($ mil.): 16,620
No. of shares (mil.): 1,203
Dividends
Yield: 3.4%
Payout: 80.0%
Market value ($ mil.): 34,076
Sales ($ mil.): 13,652

Stock History

NYSE: BK

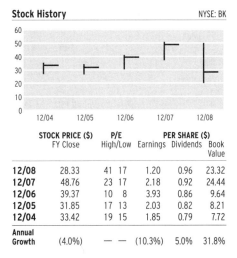

	STOCK PRICE ($) FY Close	P/E High/Low		PER SHARE ($) Earnings	Dividends	Book Value
12/08	28.33	41	17	1.20	0.96	23.32
12/07	48.76	23	17	2.18	0.92	24.44
12/06	39.37	10	8	3.93	0.86	9.64
12/05	31.85	17	13	2.03	0.82	8.21
12/04	33.42	19	15	1.85	0.79	7.72
Annual Growth	**(4.0%)**	**—**	**—**	**(10.3%)**	**5.0%**	**31.8%**

Barnes & Noble

Barnes & Noble does business — big business — by the book. As the #1 bookseller in the US, it operates about 720 Barnes & Noble superstores (selling books, music, movies, and gifts) throughout all 50 US states and Washington, DC. The stores are typically 10,000 to 60,000 sq. ft. and stock between 60,000 and 200,000 book titles. Many of its locations contain Starbucks cafes, as well as music departments that carry more than 30,000 titles. In cyberspace, the firm conducts sales through subsidiary BarnesandNoble.com (BN.com), which accounts for about 10% of total sales.

As book sales continue to sag, Barnes & Noble is looking to explore other revenue streams, including those of the digital sort. The company, which exited the digital book market in 2006, plans to launch an e-bookstore in 2009. To that end, Barnes & Noble acquired electronic bookseller Fictionwise for nearly $16 million in March. It also penned an agreement with Google for users to download free literary works in the public domain. While sales of e-books are still small, they are growing, and electronic offerings have expanded with the success of Amazon.com's Kindle. In another strategic move the bookseller is reuniting with its sister company privately held Barnes & Noble College Booksellers, owned by its chairman Leonard Riggio. The two companies have operated independently since Barnes & Noble went public in 1993. The company will pay $596 million to acquire the 624-store college bookstore chain in a bid to increase its cash flow by acquiring a business that is less vulnerable to economic cycles than its own.

Also on the digital front, BN.com has announced plans to sell subscriptions to more than 1,000 digital and print magazine titles at up to 90% off newsstand cover prices. BN.com is partnering with Zinio, a provider of digital publishing products, to fulfill digital magazine sales.

To stimulate growth in these digital markets, Barnes & Noble is looking to cut its losses in brick-and-mortar operations. In early 2009 the company divested its majority interest in seasonal kiosk retailer Calendar Club. It has also been shutting down its small-format B. Dalton

chain. In 2009 the firm shuttered about 30 B. Dalton locations, bringing total closures to more than 900 since 1989. In 2009, Barnes & Noble had hoped to open as many as 35 superstores, but the company has scaled back and has 15 slated (that will replace existing neighborhood outlets). It also plans to shutter just as many stores that year.

Aiming to trim its costs as the US recession deepens, the company moved its in-house publishing under its Sterling Publishing division. Sterling, which was acquired in 2002, is a leading publisher of general trade books, non-fiction, and illustrated works, offering more than 5,000 titles. All told, Barnes & Noble still controls about 20% of the consumer book market and expects its publishing business to grow to 10% of its revenues by 2010.

In addition to the how-to books, Barnes & Noble courts self-published authors through a stake in publishing portal iUniverse. The online publishing firm offers author support, copy-editing, design, and distribution services.

Chairman Leonard Riggio controls about a third of the company's shares.

HISTORY

Barnes & Noble dates back to 1873 when Charles Barnes went into the used-book business in Wheaton, Illinois. By the turn of the century, he was operating a thriving bookselling operation in Chicago. His son William took over as president in 1902. William sold his share in the firm in 1917 (to C. W. Follett, who built Follett Corp.) and moved to New York City, where he bought an interest in established textbook wholesalers Noble & Noble. The company was soon renamed Barnes & Noble. It first sold mainly to colleges and libraries, providing textbooks and opening a large Fifth Avenue shop. Over the next three decades, Barnes & Noble became one of the leading booksellers in the New York region.

Enter Leonard Riggio, who worked at a New York University bookstore to help pay for night school. He studied engineering but got the itch for bookselling. In 1965, at age 24, he borrowed $5,000 and opened Student Book Exchange NYC, a college bookstore. Beginning in the late 1960s, he expanded by buying other college bookstores.

In 1971 Riggio paid $1.2 million for the Barnes & Noble store on Fifth Avenue. He soon expanded the store, and in 1974 he began offering jaw-dropping, competitor-maddening discounts of up to 40% for best-sellers. Acquiring Marboro Books five years later, the company entered the mail-order and publishing business.

By 1986 Barnes & Noble had grown to about 180 outlets (including 142 college bookstores). Along with Dutch retailer Vendex, that year it bought Dayton Hudson's B. Dalton mall bookstore chain (about 800 stores), forming BDB Holding Corp. (Vendex had sold its shares by 1997.) In 1989 the company acquired the Scribner's Bookstores trade name and the Bookstop/Bookstar superstore chain.

BDB began its shift to superstore format and streamlined its operations to integrate Bookstop and Doubleday (acquired in 1990) into its business. BDB changed its name to Barnes & Noble in 1991. With superstore sales booming, the company went public in 1993 (the college stores remained private).

The bookseller went online in 1997, and in 1998 sold a 50% stake in its Web operation subsidiary to Bertelsmann (which it re-purchased in 2003) in an attempt to strengthen both companies in the battle against online rival Amazon.com.

In 1999 barnesandnoble.com went public and Barnes & Noble bought small book publisher J.B. Fairfax International USA, which included coffee-table book publisher Michael Friedman Publishing Group. Later that year the company bought a 49% stake in book publishing portal iUniverse.com (later reduced to 22%). It also bought Riggio's financially struggling Babbage's Etc., a chain of about 500 Babbage's, Software Etc., and GameStop stores, for $215 million.

The company's Babbage's Etc. subsidiary (renamed GameStop, Inc.) acquired video game retailer Funco for $161.5 million in 2000.

In 2002 the company completed an IPO of its GameStop unit, reducing its ownership interest to about 63%. Leonard also handed over the CEO title to his brother, Steve Riggio.

The company beefed up its self-publishing efforts in 2003 with the purchase of Sterling Publishing, a specialist in how-to and craft books. In addition, Barnes & Noble's half-owned *BOOK* magazine shut down. The next year saw Barnes & Noble exit the video game retailing business when it spun off its remaining shares in GameStop.

EXECUTIVES

Chairman: Leonard S. Riggio, age 68, $752,129 total compensation
Vice Chairman and CEO: Stephen (Steve) Riggio, age 54, $2,978,940 total compensation
COO: Mitchell S. Klipper, age 51, $4,191,511 total compensation
CFO: Joseph J. Lombardi, age 47, $2,048,263 total compensation
VP and CIO: Christopher (Chris) Grady-Troia, age 57
Chief Merchandising Officer: Jaime Carey
EVP Distribution and Logistics: William F. Duffy, age 53
EVP E-Commerce: Thomas P. (Tom) Burke
SVP Corporate Communications and Public Affairs: Mary Ellen Keating, age 52
VP Barnes & Noble Development: David S. Deason, age 50, $1,010,309 total compensation
VP Human Resources: Michelle Smith, age 56
VP Author Relations: Brenda Marsh
VP and Corporate Controller: Allen Lindstrom, age 42
VP and Director of Stores: Mark Bottini, age 48
VP, General Counsel, and Secretary: Jennifer M. Daniels, age 45
President, Barnes & Noble Publishing Group: J. Alan Kahn, age 62, $926,035 total compensation
President, Barnes & Noble.com: William J. Lynch Jr., age 38
Director Corporate Communications: Carolyn J. Brown
Manager Investor Relations: Andy Milevoj
Auditors: BDO Seidman, LLP

LOCATIONS

HQ: Barnes & Noble, Inc.
122 5th Ave., New York, NY 10011
Phone: 212-633-3300   **Fax:** 212-675-0413
Web: www.barnesandnobleinc.com

2009 Stores

	No.
Barnes & Noble	726
B. Dalton	52
Total	**778**

PRODUCTS/OPERATIONS

2009 Sales

	$ mil.	% of total
Barnes & Noble stores	4,525	89
barnesandnoble.com	466	9
B. Dalton stores	68	1
Other	63	1
Total	**5,122**	**100**

COMPETITORS

Amazon.com
Best Buy
Book-of-the-Month Club
Books-A-Million
Borders Group
Buy.com
Costco Wholesale
Half Price Books
Hastings Entertainment
HMV
Hudson News
Wal-Mart

HISTORICAL FINANCIALS

Company Type: Public

Income Statement

FYE: Saturday nearest January 31

	REVENUE ($ mil.)	NET INCOME ($ mil.)	NET PROFIT MARGIN	EMPLOYEES
1/09	5,121.8	75.9	1.5%	37,000
1/08	5,410.8	135.8	2.5%	40,000
1/07	5,261.3	150.5	2.9%	39,000
1/06	5,103.0	146.7	2.9%	39,000
1/05	4,873.6	143.4	2.9%	42,000
Annual Growth	**1.2%**	**(14.7%)**	**—**	**(3.1%)**

2009 Year-End Financials

Debt ratio: —
Return on equity: 7.6%
Cash ($ mil.): 282
Current ratio: 1.17
Long-term debt ($ mil.): —
No. of shares (mil.): 58
Dividends
Yield: 5.5%
Payout: 68.2%
Market value ($ mil.): 956

Stock History

NYSE: BKS

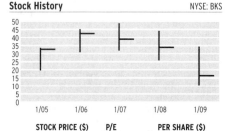

	STOCK PRICE ($) FY Close	P/E High/Low		PER SHARE ($) Earnings	Dividends	Book Value
1/09	16.42	26	8	1.32	0.90	15.84
1/08	33.93	22	13	2.03	0.60	18.47
1/07	38.93	22	15	2.17	0.60	20.02
1/06	42.42	22	15	2.03	0.30	19.18
1/05	32.70	17	10	1.93	0.00	20.04
Annual Growth	**(15.8%)**	**—**	**—**	**(9.1%)**	**—**	**(5.7%)**

Baxter International

Why choose between making drugs and making medical equipment? Baxter International does it all. The company makes a wide variety of medical products across its three divisions, including drugs and vaccines, dialysis equipment, and IV supplies. Its BioScience segment makes protein and plasma therapies to treat hemophilia and immune disorders, as well as vaccines and biological sealants used to close surgical wounds. Baxter is a leading maker of intravenous (IV) supplies and systems via its Medication Delivery segment; the segment also makes infusion pumps and inhaled anesthetics. Baxter's Renal division makes dialyzers and other products for the treatment of end-stage renal disease (ESRD).

Baxter has sold off some underperforming units, including the majority of the services portion of its Renal division. It also spun off its Transfusion Therapies business, which made blood-collection and storage products, into a new company called Fenwal in 2007.

The company's BioScience segment accounts for about 45% of sales, most of which comes from the sale of recombinant proteins and plasma products used to treat hemophilia and immune disorders. Among its products are hemophilia therapy Advate and Aralast NP, a plasma-derived drug for hereditary emphysema that was approved in 2007.

The BioScience unit also makes vaccines for infectious diseases, such as meningitis C and smallpox. It has vaccine products in development for SARS, Lyme disease, and influenza. In 2007 the company inked a deal with the British government to supply the flu vaccine in case of pandemic. Much of the company's R&D efforts are focused in the BioScience segment. It has an ongoing collaboration with Nektar Therapeutics to develop blood-clotting proteins using Nektar's PEGylation technology. And it is working on other products in areas such as regenerative medicine and adult stem cell therapies.

Baxter's Medication Delivery division makes intravenous drug delivery systems, infusion pumps, and anesthesia products. Products include inhaled and injectable anesthetics, as well as premixed drugs and parenteral nutrition products that are administered intravenously.

Along with dialyzers — dialysis equipment used primarily in hospitals or clinics — Baxter's Renal division makes home-use dialyzers that use a technology called peritoneal dialysis. To that end, it entered an agreement with HHD and DEKA Research and Development to produce next generation home dialyzers.

The Renal division is also a leading supplier of heparin, an anticoagulant used during dialysis and in critical care situations such as heart surgery. In 2008 Baxter halted production of heparin, however, after hundreds of bad reactions (including several deaths) occurred in patients using the drug. Subsequent investigations focused on raw heparin supplied to Baxter by a Chinese factory, which may have added a cheaper ingredient into the drug that contaminated it.

With manufacturing operations in more than two dozen countries and sales operations all over the world, Baxter International gets more than half of its revenue outside the US. Continued international expansion is key to the company's growth strategy. It is particularly keen on the possibilities of growing sales of its renal products in developing countries.

HISTORY

Idaho surgeon Ralph Falk, his brother Harry, and California physician Donald Baxter formed Don Baxter Intravenous Products in 1931 to distribute the IV solutions Baxter made in Los Angeles. Two years later the company opened its first plant, located outside Chicago. Ralph Falk bought Baxter's interest in 1935 and began R&D efforts leading to the first sterilized vacuum-type blood collection device (1939), which could store blood for weeks instead of hours. Product demand during WWII spurred sales above $1.5 million by 1945.

In 1949 the company created Travenol Laboratories to make and sell drugs. Baxter went public in 1951 and began an acquisition program the next year. In 1953 failing health caused both Falks to give control to William Graham, a manager since 1945. Under Graham's leadership, Baxter absorbed Wallerstein (1957); Fenwal Labs (1959); Flint, Eaton (1959); and Dayton Flexible Products (1967).

In 1975 Baxter's headquarters moved to Deerfield, Illinois. In 1978 the company debuted the first portable dialysis machine and had $1 billion in sales. Vernon Loucks Jr. became CEO two years later. Baxter claimed the title of the world's leading hospital supplier in 1985 when it bought American Hospital Supply (a Baxter distributor from 1932 to 1962). Offering more than 120,000 products and an electronic system that connected customers with some 1,500 vendors, Baxter captured nearly 25% of the US hospital supply market in 1988. That year it became Baxter International.

In 1993 Baxter pleaded guilty (and was temporarily suspended from selling to the Veterans Administration) to bribing Syria to remove Baxter from a blacklist for trading in Israel.

The company entered the US cardiovascular perfusion services market in 1995 with the purchases of PSICOR and SETA. Baxter, along with two other silicone breast-implant makers, agreed to settle thousands of claims (at an average of $26,000 each) from women suffering side-effects from the implants.

In 1997 Baxter agreed to pay about 20% of a $670 million legal settlement in a suit relating to hemophiliacs infected with HIV from blood products. In response to concerns posed by shareholders, Baxter in 1999 said it would phase out the use of PVC (polyvinyl chloride) in some products by 2010.

In 2000 Baxter withdrew dialysis equipment from Spain and Croatia after patients who used its products died. It also ended production of two types of dialyzers that were sold there. As the number of deaths mounted to more than 50 in seven countries, Baxter began facing lawsuits; it later settled with the families of many of the patients. In September 2002, the FDA issued a warning when several patients died after using Baxter's Meridian dialysis machines.

Robert L. Parkinson, Jr. took over as chairman and CEO in April 2004. Parkinson succeeded Harry M. Jansen Kraemer, Jr. William Graham, who remained on the Baxter board of directors as honorary chairman emeritus after his official retirement in 1996, died in 2006.

In 2005 the FDA seized Baxter's existing inventories of previously recalled 6,000 Colleague Volumetric Infusion Pumps and nearly 1,000 Syndeo PCA Syringe Pumps; the federal agency resorted to these measures after the company did not fix production and design problems with the pumps in a suitable amount of time; the initial recalls had taken place in July of that year.

EXECUTIVES

Chairman and CEO: Robert L. Parkinson Jr., age 58, $16,006,611 total compensation
Corporate VP and CFO: Robert M. Davis, age 42, $3,621,789 total compensation
Corporate VP and CIO: Karenann K. Terrell, age 47
Corporate VP and Chief Scientific Officer: Norbert G. Riedel, age 51
Corporate VP and President, BioScience: Joy A. Amundson, age 54, $4,552,740 total compensation
Corporate VP Manufacturing: James Michael Gatling, age 59
Corporate VP and President, Medication Delivery: Peter J. Arduini, age 44, $3,775,228 total compensation
Corporate VP and General Counsel: Susan R. Lichtenstein, age 52
Corporate VP; President, Asia Pacific: Gerald Lema, age 48
Corporate VP Human Resources: Jeanne K. Mason, age 53
Corporate VP; President, Renal: Bruce McGillivray, age 53
Corporate VP Quality: Cheryl L. White, age 55
Corporate VP and Controller: Michael J. Baughman, age 44
Corporate VP, Deputy Counsel, and Secretary: David P. Scharf, age 40
Corporate VP; President, Baxter Europe: Peter Nicklin
Corporate VP and Treasurer: Robert J. Hombach, age 42
VP Investor Relations: Mary Kay Ladone
Director, External Communications: Deborah Spak
Auditors: PricewaterhouseCoopers LLP

LOCATIONS

HQ: Baxter International Inc.
1 Baxter Pkwy., Deerfield, IL 60015
Phone: 847-948-2000 **Fax:** 847-948-2016
Web: www.baxter.com

2008 Sales

	$ mil.	% of total
US	5,044	41
Europe	4,386	36
Latin America	1,001	8
Canada	473	3
Asia & other regions	1,444	12
Total	**12,348**	**100**

PRODUCTS/OPERATIONS

2008 Sales

	$ mil.	% of total
BioScience	5,308	43
Medication Delivery	4,560	37
Renal	2,306	19
Transition services to Fenwal	174	1
Total	**12,348**	**100**

Selected Products

BioScience
  Advate (hemophilia A)
  Aralast (hereditary emphysema)
  Biosurgical sealants
  IGIV therapies (immune disorders)
  Vaccines
Medication Delivery
  Infusion pumps
  Inhaled anesthesia
  Injectable anesthesia
  IV fluids and medications
  IV tubing and access devices
  Parenteral nutrition products
Renal
  Hemodialysis equipment
  Peritoneal dialysis equipment

COMPETITORS

Abraxis BioScience
APP Pharmaceuticals
Bayer HealthCare
Becton, Dickinson
Biogen Idec
CareFusion
Covidien
CSL Behring
Eli Lilly
Fresenius Medical Care
Gambro AB
Haemacure
Hospira
Johnson & Johnson
Merck
Novartis
Novo Nordisk
Roche Holding
Sanofi Pasteur
Sorin
Talecris
Terumo
Wyeth
ZymoGenetics

HISTORICAL FINANCIALS
Company Type: Public

Income Statement
FYE: December 31

	REVENUE ($ mil.)	NET INCOME ($ mil.)	NET PROFIT MARGIN	EMPLOYEES
12/08	12,348.0	2,014.0	16.3%	48,500
12/07	11,263.0	1,707.0	15.2%	46,000
12/06	10,378.0	1,397.0	13.5%	48,000
12/05	9,849.0	956.0	9.7%	47,000
12/04	9,509.0	388.0	4.1%	48,000
Annual Growth	**6.7%**	**50.9%**	**—**	**0.3%**

2008 Year-End Financials

Debt ratio: 54.0%
Return on equity: 30.6%
Cash ($ mil.): 2,131
Current ratio: 1.97
Long-term debt ($ mil.): 3,362
No. of shares (mil.): 603
Dividends
  Yield: 1.7%
  Payout: 28.8%
Market value ($ mil.): 32,299

Stock History
NYSE: BAX

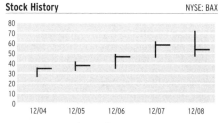

	STOCK PRICE ($) FY Close	P/E High/Low		PER SHARE ($) Earnings	Dividends	Book Value
12/08	53.59	23	15	3.16	0.91	10.33
12/07	58.05	23	18	2.61	0.72	11.47
12/06	46.39	23	16	2.13	0.58	10.41
12/05	37.65	27	22	1.52	0.58	7.13
12/04	34.54	55	42	0.63	0.58	6.15
Annual Growth	**11.6%**	**—**	**—**	**49.7%**	**11.9%**	**13.9%**

BB&T Corporation

Big, Bold & Temerarious? That might be an apt description of BB&T, the banking company that covers the Southeast like kudzu. The company serves consumers, small to midsized businesses, and government entities through more than 1,800 branches. Its flagship subsidiary, Branch Banking and Trust (dba BB&T), is one of North Carolina's oldest banks and a leading originator of residential mortgages in the Southeast. In addition to deposit accounts and loans, the company offers insurance, mutual funds, discount brokerage, wealth management, and financial planning services. Business services include leasing, factoring, and investment banking (through Scott & Stringfellow).

BB&T's bulk allows it to trump smaller competitors, yet the company maintains decentralized regional management of its banks, giving them a community bank feel. Once a serial acquirer of smaller banks throughout the Southeast, BB&T has cooled its jets in recent years amid the sputtering economy. Its only acquisition of 2008 was that of the failed Haven Trust Bank in Georgia in an FDIC-assisted transaction.

In another FDIC-assisted acquisition of a failed bank, albeit on a much larger scale, BB&T assumed ownership of more than 350 bank branches in Alabama, Florida, Georgia, Texas, and Nevada, as well as assets and customer deposits, from Colonial BancGroup, which was shut down by regulators in 2009. BB&T is in talks to sell the Nevada assets from that deal to Global Consumer Acquisition Corp.

BB&T remains an inveterate buyer of small insurance agencies (about 90 acquired since 1990) and asset managers throughout the Southeast, casting itself as a one-stop financial products shop. BB&T has also continued its strategy of purchasing niche financial services companies that offer products that can be sold at its bank branches. Its 2007 purchase of AFCO Credit boosted the insurance premium financing operations of BB&T's specialized lending segment; it also expanded BB&T's reach into Canada for the first time, through AFCO's sister company CAFO. It also acquired Collateral Real Estate Capital, which it folded into its existing commercial mortgage operations and renamed the whole thing Grandbridge Real Estate Capital.

Longtime CEO John Allison stepped down at the end of 2008; he will remain chairman of the company through 2009. Former COO Kelly King was named Allison's successor as CEO. The executive moves capped a five-year executive management transition plan that the company established in 2003.

HISTORY

In 1872 Alpheus Branch, son of a wealthy planter, founded Branch and Company, a mercantile business, in Wilson, North Carolina. He and Thomas Jefferson Hadley, who was organizing a public school system, created the Branch and Hadley bank later that same year. The private bank helped rebuild farms and small businesses after the Civil War.

In 1887 Branch bought out Hadley and changed the bank's name to Branch and Company, Bankers. Two years later Branch secured a state trust charter for the Wilson Banking and Trust Company. He never got the business running, however, and died in 1893. The trust charter was amended to change the name to Branch Banking and Company, and Branch and Company, Bankers, was folded into it in 1900.

In 1907 the bank finally got its trust operations running and began calling itself Branch Banking and Trust Company. In 1922 it opened its first insurance department; the next year it started its mortgage loan activities.

BB&T survived the 1929 stock market crash with the help of the Post Office. Nervous customers withdrew their funds from BB&T and other banks and deposited them in postal savings accounts, unaware that BB&T was the local Post Office's bank and the withdrawn funds went right back to the bank. BB&T opened six more branches between 1929 and 1933.

After WWII consumerism skyrocketed, resulting in more car loans and mortgages. During the 1960s and 1970s the bank embarked on a series of mergers and acquisitions, forming the thin end of a buying wedge that would widen significantly in the coming decades.

By 1994 BB&T was the fourth-largest bank in North Carolina. In 1995 it merged with North Carolina's fifth-largest bank, Southern National Corp., founded in 1897.

With banking regulations loosening to allow different types of operations, BB&T in 1997 made several acquisitions, including banks, thrifts, and securities brokerage Craigie.

BB&T's 1998 activities included three bank acquisitions that pushed it into metro Washington, DC. The company also increased holdings in fields such as insurance sales, venture capital for Southern businesses, and investment banking (through its acquisition of Scott & Stringfellow Financial, the South's oldest NYSE member).

In 1999 Craigie was melded into Scott & Stringfellow. That year BB&T bought several insurance companies and small banks. The company continued its march through the South the following year, buying several Georgia banks and Tennessee's BankFirst. In 2001 BB&T purchased South Carolina's FirstSpartan Financial, multi-bank holding company Century South Banks, Maryland-based FCNB Corporation, and western Georgia's Community First Banking Company. To bolster its presence in the Washington, DC, market, it bought Virginia Capital Bancshares and F&M National.

BB&T purchased Alabama-based Cooney, Rikard & Curtin, a wholesale insurance broker active in 45 states, in 2002. Also that year it added about 100 branches in Kentucky after buying MidAmerica Bancorp and AREA Bancshares, and entered the coveted Florida market following its purchase of Regional Financial, the privately held parent of First South Bank.

Acquisitions continued the following three years, as the bank swallowed First Virginia Banks, among other targets. It took a break in 2005 to assimilate its holdings before joining the acquisition hunt in 2006 with deals for banks in Georgia (Main Street Banks) and Tennessee (First Citizens Bancorp), and in South Carolina (Coastal Financial) in 2007.

EXECUTIVES

Chairman: John A. Allison IV, age 61, $7,464,872 total compensation
President, CEO, and Director: Kelly S. King, age 60, $4,469,299 total compensation
COO: Christopher L. (Chris) Henson, age 48, $1,472,749 total compensation
SEVP and CFO: Daryl Bible, age 47
SEVP and Operations Division Manager: C. Leon Wilson III, age 54
SEVP and Chief Marketing Officer: Steven B. (Steve) Wiggs, age 51
SEVP and Chief Credit Officer: Clarke R. Starnes III, age 50
General Counsel, Corporate Secretary, and Chief Corporate Governance Officer: Frances Jones, age 46
SEVP and Manager, Risk Management and Administrative Group: Robert E. Greene, age 58, $2,314,882 total compensation
SEVP and Manager, Banking Network: Ricky K. Brown, age 53
SEVP and Manager, Electronic Delivery Channels: Barbara F. Duck, age 42
SEVP and Manager, Deposit Services: Donna C. Goodrich, age 46
SEVP and Manager, Operations Division: C. Leon Wilson, age 53, $1,472,749 total compensation
EVP, Capital Planning and Shareholder Reporting: Alan W. Greer
EVP and Corporate Controller: Edward D. (Ed) Vest
EVP, Payments Services: Bennett Bradley
EVP, Acquisitions and Venture Capital: Burney Warren
EVP, Specialized Lending: Jeff McKay
SVP, Executive Communications and Corporate Communications: Robert A. Denham
SVP, Investor Relations: Tamera Gjesdal, age 45
Auditors: PricewaterhouseCoopers LLP

LOCATIONS

HQ: BB&T Corporation
200 W. 2nd St., Winston-Salem, NC 27101
Phone: 336-733-2000 **Fax:** 336-733-2470
Web: www.bbt.com

2008 Branches

	No.
Virginia	392
North Carolina	360
Georgia	162
Maryland	129
South Carolina	117
Florida	107
Kentucky	91
West Virginia	78
Tennessee	58
Washington, DC	12
Alabama	3
Indiana	2
Total	**1,511**

PRODUCTS/OPERATIONS

2008 Gross Revenues

	$ mil.	% of total
Interest		
Loans & leases	6,003	58
Taxable securities	1,056	10
Other	148	1
Noninterest		
Insurance	928	9
Service charges on deposits	673	7
Investment banking & brokerage fees & commissions	354	3
Mortgage banking	275	3
Checkcard fees	201	2
Bankcard fees & merchant discounts	151	1
Trust & investment advisory	147	1
Other nondeposit fees & commissions	189	2
Other	279	3
Total	**10,404**	**100**

2008 Assets

	$ mil.	% of total
Cash & equivalents	3,119	2
Mortgage-backed securities	27,430	18
Other securities	5,789	4
Net loans & leases	97.095	64
Other	18,582	12
Total	**152,015**	**100**

Selected Subsidiaries and Affiliates

BB&T Asset Management, Inc.
BB&T Bankcard Corporation
BB&T Equipment Finance Corporation
BB&T Financial, FSB
BB&T Insurance Services, Inc.
BB&T Investment Services, Inc.
Branch Banking and Trust Company
CRC Insurance Services, Inc.
Grandbridge Real Estate Capital LLC
Lendmark Financial Services, Inc.
McGriff, Seibels & Williams, Inc.
Prime Rate Premium Finance Corporation, Inc.
  AFCO
Regional Acceptance Corporation
Scott & Stringfellow, Inc.
Stanley, Hunt, DuPree & Rhine, Inc.

COMPETITORS

Bank of America	PNC Financial
BankAtlantic	RBC Bank
Capital One	Regions Financial
Fifth Third	SunTrust
First Citizens BancShares	Synovus Financial
First Horizon	United Bankshares
JPMorgan Chase	Wachovia Corp

HISTORICAL FINANCIALS

Company Type: Public

Income Statement
FYE: December 31

	ASSETS ($ mil.)	NET INCOME ($ mil.)	INCOME AS % OF ASSETS	EMPLOYEES
12/08	152,015.0	1,519.0	1.0%	29,600
12/07	132,618.0	1,734.0	1.3%	29,400
12/06	121,351.0	1,528.0	1.3%	29,300
12/05	109,169.8	1,653.8	1.5%	27,700
12/04	100,508.6	1,558.4	1.6%	26,100
Annual Growth	10.9%	(0.6%)	—	3.2%

2008 Year-End Financials

Equity as % of assets: 8.5%
Return on assets: 1.1%
Return on equity: 11.9%
Long-term debt ($ mil.): 18,032
No. of shares (mil.): 648

Dividends
Yield: 8.5%
Payout: 86.0%
Market value ($ mil.): 17,798
Sales ($ mil.): 7,435

Stock History
NYSE: BBT

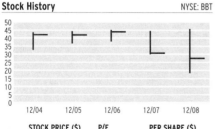

	STOCK PRICE ($) FY Close	P/E High/Low		PER SHARE ($) Earnings	Dividends	Book Value
12/08	27.46	17	7	2.71	2.33	24.74
12/07	30.67	14	10	3.14	1.76	19.49
12/06	43.93	16	14	2.81	1.60	18.12
12/05	41.91	15	12	3.00	1.46	17.17
12/04	42.05	15	12	2.80	1.34	16.78
Annual Growth	(10.1%)	—	—	(0.8%)	14.8%	10.2%

BE Aerospace

BE Aerospace (B/E) ensures that travelers truly enjoy air travel. A leading maker of cabin components for commercial, business jets, and military aircraft, B/E's offerings include aircraft seats, coffeemakers, refrigeration equipment, galley structures, and emergency oxygen systems. In addition to its three business segments — Consumables Management, Commercial Aircraft, and Business Jet — B/E also provides maintenance and repair services for cabin interior products, converts passenger aircraft into freighters, and distributes aerospace fasteners. B/E aftermarket operations and military demand represent approximately 56% of its revenues. B/E sells its products to most major airlines and aviation OEMs.

Consumables Management provides for the distribution of aerospace fasteners and consumables, which includes aircraft food, beverage preparation, and storage equipment. B/E offers a single point of contact for the entire program, a full range of technical capabilities, and turnkey solutions. B/E processes over 8,000 orders daily destined to more than 1,700 locations worldwide. B/E stocks 275,000 parts in 40 locations to serve customers, which include commercial, business jet, and military OEMs, aerospace manufacturers, and aftermarket customers, through its inventory programs.

Commercial Aircraft offers seating products, interior systems, and engineering services for narrow and wide body aircraft. B/E makes aircraft seating for first and premium (including lie-flat seat beds) and economy classes; it also makes spares and replacement parts for aircraft seats. It offers galley equipment, including coffeemakers, water boilers, liquid containers, steam and convection ovens, refrigerators, and freezers. B/E also provides a wide array of interior system components including cabin lighting, passenger and crew oxygen storage and delivery systems, galley chilling systems, and other interior components. In addition, B/E provides engineering, design, integration, installation, and certification services for commercial aircraft passenger cabin interiors, which allows for installation of telecommunications and entertainment equipment, galley relocation, lavatories, overhead bins, and crew rest compartments.

B/E provides complete interior packages for Business Jets, which include seating and divan products for super first class accommodations. B/E also manufactures lighting systems, air valves and oxygen delivery systems along with sidewalls, bulkheads, credenzas, closets, galley inserts, lavatories, and tables, including design services for executive aircraft.

In mid-2008 the company acquired the assets of Honeywell's consumable solutions (HCS) distribution business for $1.15 billion in cash and stock. The consideration in the transaction included about $900 million in cash and 6 million common shares of B/E Aerospace. The HCS business distributes consumables, parts, and supplies to aviation industry manufacturers, airlines, and aircraft repair and overhaul facilities. The combination of HCS and B/E's consumables management segment allows for distribution to every major aerospace fastener manufacturer in the world.

HISTORY

Investors led by Amin Khoury founded BE Aerospace (B/E) in 1987. The name came from the group's first purchase: Bach Engineering. Khoury took B/E public in 1989.

In 1992 B/E bought PTC Aerospace (seats) and Aircraft Products (galley structures and beverage makers) from the Pullman Company; it also acquired the UK's largest maker of aircraft seats, Flight Equipment and Engineering Ltd. The company bought several US firms in 1993.

B/E posted losses in fiscal 1995 and 1996, primarily because of the costs of a writedown related to the introduction of its interactive Multimedia Digital Distribution System (MDDS) as the airline industry was slumping. To compete, B/E focused on broadening its product lines and boosting sales through upgrades, maintenance, and other services.

With the airline industry rebounding, B/E began to recover. In 1998 it acquired companies producing oxygen-delivery systems, aircraft cabin interior products, aircraft cabin interiors, aircraft galley equipment, and aircraft lighting. The next year the company sold a 51% interest in its In-Flight Entertainment business to Sextant Avionique. In late 1999 B/E reported production problems in its seat manufacturing operations, prompting airlines to find other suppliers.

B/E exited the in-flight entertainment business in 2000. Throughout the year, production problems in its seating manufacturing operations impacted earnings, leading to a loss.

The company closed five facilities and cut its workforce by about 20% soon after the terrorist attacks of September 11, 2001, as demand for aircraft cabin interior products slumped drastically. Faced with continued weakness, B/E continued to seek cost savings and consolidation and closed 21 facilities by the end of 2002.

To buffer itself somewhat from the aircraft interior market, B/E acquired aerospace fastener distributor M & M Aerospace Hardware in 2001.

In 2006 the company acquired Draeger Aerospace GmbH from Cobham plc. Draeger is a provider of oxygen delivery systems for commercial and military aircraft. Later that year the company bolstered its fasteners business with the purchase of New York Fasteners Corp., a privately held distributor of aerospace fasteners and hardware. The deal was valued at about $66 million. The acquisitions had the two-fold impact of expanding both B/E's customer base and its product line breadth.

The company expected to gain aftermarket business as airlines refurbished their aircraft interiors in response to increased passenger traffic, increased airline capacity, and stiff competition. A spike in new aircraft orders in 2007 drove demand for BE Aerospace's OEM products. Thanks to these conditions the company enjoyed record sales in 2007.

EXECUTIVES

Chairman and CEO: Amin J. Khoury, age 70, $8,486,190 total compensation
President and COO: Michael B. Baughan, age 49, $1,715,767 total compensation
SVP, CFO, and Treasurer: Thomas P. McCaffrey, age 54, $2,411,362 total compensation
Corporate VP Law, General Counsel, and Secretary: Edmund J. Moriarty, age 65
VP Finance and Controller: Stephen R. Swisher, age 50
VP and General Manager, Consumables Management: Robert A. Marchetti, age 66, $1,326,923 total compensation

VP and General Manager, Business Jet Segment:
Wayne R. Exton, age 45, $801,291 total compensation
VP Human Resources: R. J. Landry
VP and General Manager, Commercial Aircraft
  Products: Werner Lieberherr, age 48,
  $1,120,407 total compensation
VP Investor Relations: Greg Powell
VP Sales and Marketing: Linwood Lewis
Auditors: Deloitte & Touche LLP

LOCATIONS

HQ: BE Aerospace, Inc.
  1400 Corporate Center Way, Wellington, FL 33414
Phone: 561-791-5000   Fax: 561-791-7900
Web: www.beaerospace.com

2008 Sales

	$ mil.	% of total
US	994.4	47
Europe	508.9	24
Asia, Pacific Rim, Middle East & Other	606.7	29
Total	**2,110.0**	**100**

PRODUCTS/OPERATIONS

2008 Sales

	$ mil.	% of total
Commercial Aircraft	1,138.7	54
Consumables Management	697.3	33
Business Jet	274.0	13
Total	**2,110.0**	**100**

COMPETITORS

Alabama Aircraft
Anixter Pentacon
Boeing Commercial Airplanes
DeCrane
EADS
Israel Aerospace Industries
Martin-Baker Aircraft
Seton House Group
TIMCO Aviation
Wesco Aircraft Hardware
Zodiac Aerospace

HISTORICAL FINANCIALS

Company Type: Public

Income Statement

FYE: December 31

	REVENUE ($ mil.)	NET INCOME ($ mil.)	NET PROFIT MARGIN	EMPLOYEES
12/08	2,110.0	(99.4)	—	6,485
12/07	1,677.7	147.3	8.8%	6,298
12/06	1,128.2	85.6	7.6%	5,058
12/05	844.1	84.6	10.0%	3,980
12/04	733.5	(13.7)	—	3,500
Annual Growth	**30.2%**	**—**	**—**	**16.7%**

2008 Year-End Financials

Debt ratio: 88.2%
Return on equity: —
Cash ($ mil.): 168
Current ratio: 3.30
Long-term debt ($ mil.): 1,117

No. of shares (mil.): 101
Dividends
  Yield: 0.0%
  Payout: —
Market value ($ mil.): 778

Net Income History

NASDAQ (GS): BEAV

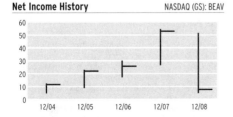

Beazer Homes USA

Beazer Homes USA builds for the middle-class buyer who's ready to make the move into the white-picket-fence scene. Building homes with an average price of about $248,700, the company courts the entry-level, move-up, and active adult markets. Beazer Homes USA focuses on high-growth regions in the Southeast, Mid-Atlantic, and West; it closed on some 7,700 homes in 2008 (down from more than 18,000 in 2006). It also provides title insurance services for some markets. Company design centers offer homebuyers limited customization for such features as appliances, cabinetry, flooring, fixtures, and wall coverings. Like most large home-builders, Beazer subcontracts to build its homes.

Although new construction had been going gangbusters for much of the early part of the 21st century, the housing bubble sprang a leak in 2006 and deflated the following year. Beazer has since struggled to survive amid the housing slump and federal investigations into its dealings. In 2008 Beazer settled with the Securities and Exchange Commission, which had investigated the company for allegedly violating federal securities laws.

There was more bad news: Beazer faced rising mortgage defaults and cancellation rates as the subprime mortgage market collapsed and took the housing market with it. As credit markets around the world froze and foreclosure properties gave qualified home buyers more shopping options, builders like Beazer were forced to survive on plummeting revenues.

The company responded by exiting the mortgage origination business, reorganizing its overhead structure, cutting about 25% of its employees, and exiting some of its land options, as well as markets in Indiana, North Carolina, Ohio, South Carolina, and Tennessee. The company also said it would restate its financial results from 2006 and 2007.

In 2009 Federal authorities agreed not to prosecute Beazer after it agreed to pay up to $55 million in restitution and expenses related to an alleged mortgage fraud scheme in North Carolina. The SEC also returned that year to file a fraud complaint against a former Beazer accounting officer.

Institutional investors own about three-fourths of Beazer Homes USA.

HISTORY

Beazer Homes USA traces its roots to a construction business started in the late 1950s in Bath, England, by the Beazer family. Operations grew to include homebuilding, quarrying, contracting, and real estate. In 1985 Beazer moved into the US and expanded throughout the Southeast through a series of acquisitions.

In 1988 the company bought US aggregates company Koppers in a deal that gave Beazer a presence in US building materials but also left it deep in debt. That debt, plus a recession, had Beazer struggling by 1991, when it was acquired by UK-based Hanson PLC. Hanson spun off the US homebuilding portion of Beazer in 1994 as Beazer Homes USA, which has continued to expand geographically through acquisitions in growth markets. In 1995 it bought Bramalea Homes Texas.

Beazer continued its march across the Sunbelt in 1996, buying homebuilders in Arizona,

Florida, and Texas, and it established Beazer Mortgage. During that year Beazer ran into trouble in Nevada, where cost overruns dragged down the company's 1997 results. That year Beazer acquired Florida homebuilder Calton and formed a joint venture with Mexico's Corporacion GEO to build affordable housing; however, the venture was closed in 2000. The next year it bought Snow Construction of Florida and entered the Mid-Atlantic market by buying Kvaerner's US homebuilding arm, Trafalgar House.

In 2001 the company moved into Colorado by buying Denver-based builder Sanford Homes. The next year Beazer acquired Crossman Communities in a $500 million cash and stock deal, which contributed to a 2% increase in new orders for fiscal 2003. Overall, new orders were up 20% that year, breaking the company's record. The company also had a record 7,426 homes (valued at $1.6 billion) in its backlog. Beazer continued to break its own record through 2004 with annual revenues nearing the $4 billion mark, along with a 36.5% increase in annual earnings. Its backlog that year exceeded 8,400 homes.

In 2005 Beazer entered new markets in California (Fresno), Florida (Sarasota), Georgia (Savannah), Indiana (Ft. Wayne), New Mexico (Albuquerque), and New York (Orange County) and closed on more than 18,100 homes. It ended the year with more than 9,200 homes (worth more than $2.7 billion) in backlog.

EXECUTIVES

Chairman: Brian C. Beazer, age 74
President, CEO, and Director: Ian J. McCarthy, age 56
EVP and COO: Michael H. (Mike) Furlow, age 58
EVP and CFO: Allan P. Merrill, age 43
SVP and CIO: Cindy B. Tierney
SVP and Chief Marketing Officer: Kathi James
SVP, Chief Accounting Officer, and Controller:
  Robert L. Salomon
EVP and General Counsel: Kenneth F. (Ken) Khoury, age 58
SVP Human Resources: Fred Fratto
VP and Treasurer: Jeffrey S. (Jeff) Hoza
Auditors: Deloitte & Touche LLP

LOCATIONS

HQ: Beazer Homes USA, Inc.
  1000 Abernathy Rd., Ste. 1200, Atlanta, GA 30328
Phone: 770-829-3700   Fax: 770-481-2808
Web: www.beazer.com

Beazer Homes USA operates in Arizona, California, Colorado, Delaware, Florida, Georgia, Indiana, Kentucky, Maryland, Nevada, New Jersey, New Mexico, New York, North Carolina, Ohio, Pennsylvania, South Carolina, Tennessee, Texas, and Virginia.

2008 Sales

	$ mil.	% of total
Homebuilding		
West	674.1	32
East	780.4	38
Southeast	354.8	17
Other (including discontinued markets)	260.8	13
Financial services	4.2	—
Total	**2,074.3**	**100**

2008 Homes Closed

	No.
West	2,777
East	2,405
Southeast	1,515
Other	995
Total	**7,692**

PRODUCTS/OPERATIONS

Selected Subsidiaries and Affiliates

April Corporation
Arden Park Ventures, LLC
Beazer Allied Companies Holdings, Inc.
Beazer Clarksburg, LLC
Beazer Commercial Holdings, LLC
Beazer General Services, Inc.
Beazer Homes Capital Trust
Beazer Homes Corp.
Beazer Homes Holdings Corp.
Beazer Homes Indiana Holding Corp.
Beazer Homes Indiana, LLP
Beazer Homes Investments, LLC
Beazer Homes Michigan, LLC
Beazer Homes Sales, Inc.
Beazer Homes Texas Holdings, Inc.
Beazer Homes Texas, LP
Beazer Realty Corp.
Beazer Realty Los Angeles, Inc.
Beazer Realty Sacramento, Inc.
Beazer Realty Services, LLC
Beazer SPE, LLC
Beazer/Squires Realty, Inc.
BH Building Products, LP
BH Procurement Services, LLC
Homebuilders Title Services of Virginia, Inc.
Homebuilders Title Services, Inc.
Paragon Title, LLC
Security Title Insurance Company
Texas Lone Star Title, LP
Trinity Homes, LLC
United Home Insurance Company, *A Risk Retention Group*

COMPETITORS

D.R. Horton
Hovnanian Enterprises
KB Home
Lennar
M.D.C.
Meritage Homes
NVR
Pulte Homes
The Ryland Group
Standard Pacific
Toll Brothers
William Lyon Homes

HISTORICAL FINANCIALS

Company Type: Public

Income Statement

FYE: September 30

	REVENUE ($ mil.)	NET INCOME ($ mil.)	NET PROFIT MARGIN	EMPLOYEES
9/08	2,074.3	(951.9)	—	1,444
9/07	3,490.8	(411.1)	—	2,619
9/06	5,462.0	388.8	7.1%	4,234
9/05	4,995.4	262.5	5.3%	4,578
9/04	3,907.1	235.8	6.0%	3,428
Annual Growth	(14.6%)	—	—	(19.4%)

2008 Year-End Financials

Debt ratio: 447.1%
Return on equity: —
Cash ($ mil.): 584
Current ratio: 27.18
Long-term debt ($ mil.): 1,676

No. of shares (mil.): 39
Dividends
  Yield: 0.0%
  Payout: —
Market value ($ mil.): 235

Stock History

NYSE: BZH

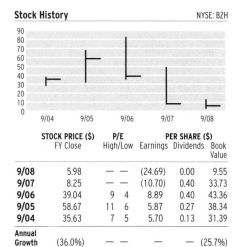

	STOCK PRICE ($) FY Close	P/E High/Low		PER SHARE ($) Earnings	Dividends	Book Value
9/08	5.98	—	—	(24.69)	0.00	9.55
9/07	8.25	—	—	(10.70)	0.40	33.73
9/06	39.04	9	4	8.89	0.40	43.36
9/05	58.67	11	6	5.87	0.27	38.34
9/04	35.63	7	5	5.70	0.13	31.39
Annual Growth	(36.0%)	—	—	—	—	(25.7%)

Bechtel Group

Whether the job is raising an entire city or razing a nuclear power plant, you can bet the Bechtel Group will be there to bid on the business. The engineering, construction, and project management firm was named the US's #1 contractor (ahead of Fluor) by *Engineering News-Record* for 11 consecutive years. It operates worldwide and has participated in such historic projects as the construction of Hoover Dam and the cleanup of the Chernobyl nuclear plant. Bechtel's Oil, Gas & Chemical business unit and Bechtel National, its government contracts group, are its leading revenue producers. The group is in its fourth generation of leadership by the Bechtel family, with chairman and CEO Riley Bechtel at the helm.

Bechtel has made a name for itself by participating in mega-projects. In addition to providing its core project management and design services, it offers such services as environmental restoration and remediation, telecommunications infrastructure (installing cable-optic networks and constructing data centers), and project financing through Bechtel Enterprises.

Bechtel National is the prime contractor for design and construction of the Hanford Vitrification Plant in Washington State, one of the DOE's most complex cleanup projects. The project's aim is to treat 53 million gallons of high-level radioactive waste stored at the Hanford site.

Among Bechtel's more traditional (perhaps notorious) infrastructure projects was its involvement in the "Big Dig," Boston's Central Artery/Tunnel project. Bechtel, in a joint venture with Parsons Brinckerhoff, served as lead contractor on the $14.6 billion project, which was the subject of much dispute over cost overruns and safety issues. After a death occurred in which the ceiling collapsed on a motorist, the National Transportation Safety Board said that Bechtel was partially at fault. Bechtel/Parsons Brinckerhoff paid a $450 million settlement which included a provision removing any criminal liability.

In Europe, the group has expanded its rail business by working on High Speed One, the high-speed rail line connecting London with the Channel Tunnel and the UK's first major new railroad project in a century. It is also managing the upgrade of the UK's West Coast main line and has joined a consortium to renovate part of London's 140-year-old subway. The group provides telecommunications services to US government entities through its Bechtel Federal Telecoms unit.

Bechtel has completed projects in some 50 countries on all seven continents. It was one of the companies that received contracts to help rebuild Iraq's infrastructure beginning in 2003, but it exited that country in 2006 as its contracts expired.

Current projects include a 411-MW combined-cycle power plant in Russia, an Alaska-Canada natural gas pipeline, the Queensland Curtis LNG project in Australia, and the Rio Tinto Alcan aluminum smelter project in British Columbia. The company is also a leading bidder on a pending project to expand the Panama Canal.

HISTORY

In 1898, 25-year-old Warren Bechtel left his Kansas farm to grade railroads in the Oklahoma Indian territories, then followed the rails west. Settling in Oakland, California, he founded his own contracting firm. Foreseeing the importance of roads, oil, and power, he won big projects such as the Northern California Highway and the Bowman Dam. By 1925, when he incorporated his company as W.A. Bechtel & Co., it ranked as the West's largest construction company. In 1931 Bechtel helped found the consortium that built Hoover Dam.

Under the leadership of Steve Bechtel (president after his father's death in 1933), the company obtained contracts for large infrastructure projects such as the San Francisco-Oakland Bay Bridge. Noted for his friendships with influential people, including Dwight Eisenhower, Adlai Stevenson, and Saudi Arabia's King Faisal, Steve developed projects that spanned nations and industries, such as pipelines in Saudi Arabia and numerous power projects. By 1960, when Steve Bechtel Jr. took over, the company was operating on six continents.

In the next two decades, Bechtel worked on transportation projects — such as San Francisco's Bay Area Rapid Transit (BART) system and the Washington, DC, subway system — and power projects, including nuclear plants. After the 1979 Three Mile Island accident, Bechtel tried its hand at nuclear cleanup. With nuclear power no longer in vogue, it focused on other markets, such as mining in New Guinea (gold and copper, 1981-84) and China (coal, 1984). Bechtel's Jubail project in Saudi Arabia, begun in 1976, raised an entire industrial port city on the Persian Gulf.

The US recession and rising developing-world debt of the early 1980s sent Bechtel reeling. It cut its workforce by 22,000 and stemmed losses by piling up small projects.

Riley Bechtel, great-grandson of Warren, became CEO in 1990. After the 1991 Gulf War, Bechtel extinguished Kuwait's flaming oil wells and worked on the oil-spill cleanup. During the decade it also worked on such projects as the Channel tunnel (Chunnel) between England and France, the new airport in Hong Kong, and pipelines in the former Soviet Union.

Bechtel was part of the consortium contracted in 1996 to build a high-speed passenger rail line between London and the Chunnel. International Generating (InterGen), Bechtel's joint venture with Pacific Gas and Electric (PG&E), was chosen to help build Mexico's first private power plant. In 1996 Bechtel bought PG&E's share of InterGen, then sold a 50% stake in InterGen to a unit of Royal Dutch Shell in early 1997.

In 1998 Bechtel joined Battelle and Electricité de France in project management of a long-term plan to stabilize the damaged reactor of the Chernobyl nuclear plant in Ukraine.

The next year Bechtel was hired to decommission the Connecticut Yankee nuclear plant. Bechtel expanded its telecommunications operations in 2001 to provide turnkey network implementation services in Europe, the Middle East, and Asia. In 2002 Bechtel was once again called on to work on the UK's rail system, taking over management of the upgrade of the West Coast main line from financially troubled Railtrack. As part of a consortium with UK facilities management giants Jarvis and Amey, Bechtel began work that year on a project to modernize part of London's aging subway system.

In 2005 Bechtel and joint venture partner Shell Oil sold InterGen, its power production joint venture, to AIG Highstar Capital for about $1.75 billion.

EXECUTIVES

Chairman Emeritus: Stephen D. (Steve) Bechtel Jr., age 84
Chairman and CEO: Riley P. Bechtel, age 54
Vice Chairman, President, and COO: Adrian Zaccaria
CFO and Director: Peter Dawson
CIO and Manager Information Systems and Technology: Geir Ramleth
EVP and Director: Bill Dudley
VP Engineering, Procurement & Construction Functions and Manager, Sigma 6: Carl Rau
EVP Strategy, Marketing, and Business Development, Bechtel Systems and Infrastructure: Craig Weaver
President, Bechtel Systems & Infrastructure, Inc.: Scott Ogilvie
SVP and Principal Deputy Lab Director, Los Alamos National Laboratory: John T. Mitchell
SVP and Manager, Human Resources: Mary Moreton
President, Power Global Business Unit: Jack Futcher
President, Mining and Metals Global Business Unit: Andy Greig
President, Power Global Business Unit and Director: Tim Statton
President, Civil Global Business Unit: Mike Adams
President, Bechtel Nuclear Power: E. James (Jim) Reinsch
President, Oil, Gas, and Chemicals: Jim Jackson
President, Bechtel Federal Telecoms: James F. X. Payne
President, Bechtel National, Inc.: David Walker
Manager, Corporate Media Relations: Jonathan Marshall
General Counsel, Secretary and Director: Judith Miller
Auditors: PricewaterhouseCoopers LLP

LOCATIONS

HQ: Bechtel Group, Inc.
50 Beale St., San Francisco, CA 94105
Phone: 415-768-1234   **Fax:** 415-768-9038
Web: www.bechtel.com

PRODUCTS/OPERATIONS

Selected Services

Construction
Engineering
Financing and development
Procurement
Project management
Safety
Technology

Selected Markets

Civil infrastructure (airports, rail, highways, heavy civil)
Communications (wireless and other telecommunications)
Mining and metals
Oil, gas, and chemicals (Design and construction for chemical, petrochemical, LNG and natural gas plants, and pipelines)
Power electrical (gas, oil, coal, and nuclear power plants)
U.S. Government Services (defense, space, demilitarization, security, nuclear, and environmental restoration and remediation services)

COMPETITORS

Aker Solutions
AMEC
Balfour Construction
Black & Veatch
Bouygues
CH2M HILL
Chiyoda Corp.
EIFFAGE
Fluor
Foster Wheeler
Halliburton
HOCHTIEF
Hyundai Engineering and Construction
ITOCHU
Jacobs Engineering
Kajima
Lummus Technology
Marelich Mechanical
Parsons Corporation
Peter Kiewit Sons'
RWE
Schneider Electric
Shaw Group
Siemens AG
Skanska
SNEF
Technip
Tutor Perini
Uhde
URS
VINCI
Washington Division
Weston

HISTORICAL FINANCIALS

Company Type: Private

Income Statement

FYE: December 31

	REVENUE ($ mil.)	NET INCOME ($ mil.)	NET PROFIT MARGIN	EMPLOYEES
12/08	31,400.0	—	—	44,000
12/07	27,000.0	—	—	42,500
12/06	20,500.0	—	—	40,000
12/05	18,100.0	—	—	40,000
12/04	17,378.0	—	—	40,000
Annual Growth	**15.9%**	**—**	**—**	**2.4%**

Revenue History

Beckman Coulter

Like the nerdiest kid in school, Beckman Coulter never saw a test it didn't love. The company makes more than 600 diagnostic testing systems and supplies, from simple blood tests to complicated genetic diagnostic tools. Its wares are used by hospital and other clinical laboratories to suss out diseases and monitor their progression. Its clinical products include immunoassay, clinical chemistry, and hematology systems, as well as products in the growing field of molecular diagnostics. In addition to its systems for diagnosing patients, Beckman Coulter makes products used by life sciences researchers, including those at academic research centers and drug companies, to understand disease and develop new therapies.

Beckman Coulter has installed more than 200,000 of its systems around the world. Along with instruments, it sells reagents and supplies that provide recurring revenue over the life of a system; nearly 80% of revenue comes from recurring sales, mostly to midsized to large hospitals.

The company counts on developing improved and new systems that cost-effectively perform high volumes of tests for its health care and life sciences clients. In 2007 it introduced a new system (the UniCel DxI 600 Access system) intended for midsized hospitals who want to perform more tests in-house rather than outsourcing them. The next year it launched UniCel DxI 800, a fully automated molecular diagnostics system for high-volume clinical laboratories.

Beckman Coulter has gained new technologies and products through acquisitions as well. Late in 2007 it acquired the flow cytometry business of Danish diagnostics firm Dako, adding two high-end flow cytometry systems to its portfolio of products. In 2009 the company acquired the lab-based diagnostics systems business of Olympus' life sciences unit. The $800 million purchase will allow it to expand its chemistry product lines.

In addition to internal product development and acquisitions, Beckman Coulter's growth strategy focuses on committing resources to developing markets such as China and India and creating a fully integrated molecular diagnostic system.

Beckman Coulter has operations in more than 130 countries, with sales outside the US accounting for nearly half of revenues. The company primarily sells through its own force, but it relies on independent distributors in certain markets. Additionally, Beckman Coulter is the North American distributor of Instrumentation Laboratory's hemostasis products, sold mainly under the ACL brand.

HISTORY

Arnold Beckman created his first chemistry lab as a child in a shed his blacksmith father had built for him. Beckman studied chemical engineering, worked at Bell Labs (now part of Lucent Technologies), and then earned his doctorate in photochemistry in 1928 from the California Institute of Technology. In 1935, while teaching at CalTech and working as a consultant, Beckman created a special ink for the National Postage Meter Company. He formed the National Inking Appliance Company (later National Technical Laboratories), which was 90% owned by National Postage Meter and 10% owned by Beckman.

In 1935 Beckman also created a device for a Southern California citrus processor that measured lemon juice acidity. Beckman's acidity, or pH, meter soon became a standard tool in chemical laboratories. In 1941 he debuted a wavelength spectrum analysis system, a forerunner of today's analytical precision and chemical analysis instruments. That year the company's sales topped $250,000.

The company became Beckman Instruments in 1950 and went public two years later. During that period the company created products for aerospace, military, and industrial markets. However, it increasingly focused on the medical and research niches, and during the 1960s it introduced glucose analyzers and protein peptide sequencers. By 1975 Beckman Instruments' annual sales neared $230 million.

An 82-year-old Beckman sold his company to SmithKline in 1982, creating SmithKline Beckman. In 1988 Louis Rosso, who as president had guided Beckman's move into life sciences and diagnostics, was named CEO. SmithKline Beckman in 1989 merged with UK pharmaceuticals pioneer Beecham Group, becoming SmithKline Beecham. (That company merged with Glaxo Wellcome to become GlaxoSmithKline plc in 2000.) Beckman, operating as a unit within SmithKline Beecham, suffered financially as a result of cuts in health care spending. SmithKline Beecham spun the company off that year as a medical and research market instrument maker.

New products and cost controls returned Beckman Instruments to health. The company restructured in 1993 (taking write-offs in 1993 and 1994), then launched a buying spree. It acquired Genomyx, a maker of DNA sequencing products, in 1996. In late 1997 the company acquired Coulter, which served the same hospitals and medical offices as Beckman — only with hematology products — for $1.2 billion.

Wallace Coulter in 1948 discovered a new technology for blood cell analysis, dubbed the Coulter Principle. With brother Joe, an electrical engineer, Wallace (who died in 1998) began producing the Coulter Counter cell and particle analyzer. The brothers formed Coulter Electronics in 1958. Over the years the private company made tests to detect everything from colon cancer to strep throat, but it became best known for blood cell analysis diagnostic systems.

Beckman Instruments' purchase of Coulter, which led to job cuts (13% of its workforce), caused losses for 1997. The next year the company changed its name to Beckman Coulter. John Wareham, an executive with Beckman since the early 1980s, replaced Rosso as CEO.

The addition of the Coulter product lines enabled the company to win 1999 contracts from several regional health care networks and large purchasing organizations. In 2000 the company initiated some restructuring by closing plants in Argentina, Brazil, and Hong Kong.

In 2005 Beckman Coulter bought Diagnostic Systems Laboratories, a maker of specialty diagnostics in the areas of reproductive endocrinology and cardiovascular risk assessment. It also acquired Agencourt Bioscience, a provider of genomic sequencing and nucleic acid purification services. (Agencourt was combined with Cogenics, a genomic contract research firm acquired from Clinical Data for $17 million in 2009, to form Beckman Coulter Genomics.)

EXECUTIVES

Chairman, President, and CEO: Scott Garrett, age 59, $8,202,631 total compensation
SVP and CFO: Charles P. (Charlie) Slacik, age 54, $1,492,667 total compensation
Corporate VP, Controller, and Chief Accounting Officer: Carolyn D. Beaver, age 51
EVP Worldwide Commercial Operations: Robert W. (Bob) Kleinert Jr., age 57, $1,357,024 total compensation
SVP Strategy, Business Development, Investor Relations, and Communications: Paul Glyer, age 52
SVP Human Resources and Communications: J. Robert Hurley, age 59, $1,340,456 total compensation
SVP, General Counsel, and Secretary: Arnold A. Pinkston, age 50, $1,357,024 total compensation
SVP Supply Chain Management: Pamela A. (Pam) Miller, age 54
SVP Quality and Regulatory Affairs: B. Melina Cimler, age 51
Group VP Chemistry, Discovery, and Automation Business: Scott Atkin, age 45
Group VP Cellular Analysis Business Group: Cynthia Collins, age 50
Group VP High Sensitivity Testing: Richard S. Creager, age 56
Corporate Communications: Mary F. Luthy
Director Investor Relations: Allan D. Harris
Auditors: KPMG LLP

LOCATIONS

HQ: Beckman Coulter, Inc.
4300 N. Harbor Blvd., Fullerton, CA 92834
Phone: 714-871-4848   **Fax:** 714-773-8111
Web: www.beckmancoulter.com

2008 Sales

	$ mil.	% of total
US	1,542.1	50
Europe	687.1	22
Asia Pacific	383.7	12
Eastern Europe, Russia, Middle East, Africa & India	278.3	9
Other	207.7	7
Total	**3,098.9**	**100**

PRODUCTS/OPERATIONS

2008 Sales

	$ mil.	% of total
Clinical Diagnostics		
Cellular analysis	954.2	31
Chemistry & clinical automation	898.6	29
Immunoassay & molecular diagnostics	739.1	24
Life Science	507.0	16
Total	**3,098.9**	**100**

COMPETITORS

Abbott Labs
Agilent Technologies
BD Biosciences
Bio-Rad Labs
Caliper Life Sciences
GE Healthcare
Hitachi High-Technologies
Ortho-Clinical Diagnostics
PerkinElmer
Roche Diagnostics
Shimadzu
Siemens Healthcare Diagnostics
Sysmex Amer
Thermo Fisher Scientific
Waters Corp.

HISTORICAL FINANCIALS

Company Type: Public

Income Statement

FYE: December 31

	REVENUE ($ mil.)	NET INCOME ($ mil.)	NET PROFIT MARGIN	EMPLOYEES
12/08	3,098.9	194.0	6.3%	11,000
12/07	2,761.3	211.3	7.7%	10,500
12/06	2,528.5	186.9	7.4%	10,340
12/05	2,443.8	150.6	6.2%	10,416
12/04	2,408.3	210.9	8.8%	10,200
Annual Growth	**6.5%**	**(2.1%)**	**—**	**1.9%**

2008 Year-End Financials

Debt ratio: 62.4%
Return on equity: 13.5%
Cash ($ mil.): 120
Current ratio: 2.27
Long-term debt ($ mil.): 896
No. of shares (mil.): 69
Dividends
  Yield: 1.5%
  Payout: 22.6%
Market value ($ mil.): 3,012

Stock History

NYSE: BEC

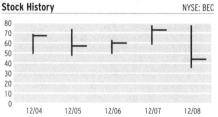

	STOCK PRICE ($) FY Close	P/E High/Low		PER SHARE ($) Earnings	Dividends	Book Value
12/08	43.94	26	12	3.01	0.68	20.95
12/07	72.80	23	18	3.30	0.64	21.03
12/06	59.80	21	17	2.92	0.60	16.84
12/05	56.90	32	21	2.32	0.56	17.43
12/04	66.99	21	15	3.21	0.48	15.96
Annual Growth	**(10.0%)**	**—**	**—**	**(1.6%)**	**9.1%**	**7.0%**

Becton, Dickinson

Don't worry, you'll only feel a slight prick if Becton, Dickinson (BD) is at work. The company's BD Medical segment is one of the top manufacturers of syringes and other injection and infusion devices. BD Medical also makes IV catheters and syringes, self-injection devices for diabetes patients, and surgical instruments (scalpels and anesthesia trays, for instance). BD's Diagnostics segment offers tools for collecting specimens and the equipment and reagents to detect diseases in them. Finally, Becton Dickinson caters to researchers through its BD Biosciences unit, which makes reagents, antibodies, cell imaging systems, and labware used in basic and clinical research.

The company sold what may be one of its more well-known products — ACE brand elastic bandages — in 2009 to 3M. BD first started manufacturing ACE in 1914, but decided to sell the line and its related thermometer product line to focus on other business segments.

BD has manufacturing and distribution operations all over the world. Its main products in international markets are various types of syringes, diagnostics systems, blood collection systems, flow cytometry instruments and reagents, and disposable labware.

BD has been cashing in on the increased emphasis on safety in health care delivery. BD Medical has introduced a number of safety-engineered devices that prevent accidental needlesticks, and thus exposure to infected blood. Additionally, BD Diagnostics makes safety-engineered blood collection equipment, including the BD Vacutainer system.

The Diagnostics segment has also been working on tests that aim to reduce the spread of health care-associated infections, usually infections acquired as the result of a hospital stay. In 2007 BD acquired privately held GeneOhm Sciences, which made molecular diagnostic systems for detecting bacterial infections such as staph and MRSA. And the following year it won FDA approval for the GeneOhm StaphSR assay, a relatively quick, two-hour test that allows health care workers to implement isolation procedures to stop the chain of infection.

Through its BD Biosciences unit, BD makes a variety of research and clinical testing products for drug developers, life sciences researchers, and diagnostics laboratories. Its products include flow cytometry systems, monoclonal antibodies and kits for cellular analysis, and cell culture media. Additionally, BD Biosciences' Discovery Labware segment makes pipettes, tubes, and other basic equipment used in laboratories. In 2008 the company expanded the Biosciences unit with the acquisition of Cytopeia, a maker of flow cytometry instruments.

HISTORY

Maxwell Becton and Fairleigh Dickinson established a medical supply firm in New York in 1897. In 1907 the company moved to New Jersey and became one of the first US firms to make hypodermic needles.

During WWI, Becton, Dickinson (BD) made all-glass syringes and introduced the cotton elastic bandage. After the war, its researchers designed an improved stethoscope and created specialized hypodermic needles. The company supplied medical equipment to the armed forces during WWII. Becton and Dickinson helped establish Fairleigh Dickinson Junior College (now Fairleigh Dickinson University) in 1942. The company continued to develop products such as the Vacutainer blood-collection apparatus, its first medical laboratory aid.

After the deaths of Dickinson (1948) and Becton (1951), their respective sons, Fairleigh Jr. and Henry, took over. The company introduced disposable hypodermic syringes in 1961. BD went public in 1963 to raise money for new expansion. In the 1960s the company opened plants in Brazil, Canada, France, and Ireland and climbed aboard the conglomeration bandwagon by diversifying into such businesses as industrial gloves (Edmont, 1966) and computer systems (Spear, 1968). BD also went on a major acquisition spree in its core fields during the 1960s and 1970s, buying more than 25 medical supply, testing, and lab companies by 1980.

Wesley Howe, successor to Fairleigh Dickinson Jr., expanded the company's foreign sales in the 1970s. Howe thwarted a takeover by the diversifying oil giant Sun Company (now Sunoco) in 1978 and began to sell BD's nonmedical businesses in 1983, ending with the 1989 sale of Edmont. Acquisitions, including Deseret Medical

(IV catheters, surgical gloves and masks; 1986), sharpened the company's focus on medical and surgical supplies.

In the 1990s BD formed a number of alliances and ventures, including a 1991 agreement to make and market Baxter International's Inter-Link needleless injection system, which reduces the risk of accidental needle sticks, and a 1993 joint venture with NeXagen (now part of Gilead Sciences) to make and market in vitro diagnostics. As tuberculosis reemerged in the US as a serious health threat, the firm improved its TB-detection and drug-resistance test systems, which cut testing time from as much as seven weeks to less than two.

In 1996 BD introduced GlucoWatch (a glucose monitoring device developed by Cygnus), and acquired the diagnostic business and brand name of MicroProbe (now Epoch Pharmaceuticals).

Previously known on Wall Street as a homely company that focused on cutting costs, BD changed its image with a string of acquisitions beginning in 1997. The firm acquired PharMingen (biomedical research reagents) and Difco Laboratories (microbiology media), which broadened its product lines.

In 1998 BD bought The BOC Group's medical devices business. The company also settled a lawsuit by a health care worker claiming that BD continued selling conventional syringes that could spread disease through accidental needle sticks instead of promoting safer technology. BD still faced several lawsuits from health workers who had sustained needle sticks.

During 2006 the company acquired GeneOhm Sciences which develops molecular diagnostic testing systems specifically for the rapid detection of bacterial organisms that cause health care-associated infections in hospitalized patients, including MRSA (methicillin resistant *Staphylococcus aureus*) and Group B Strep (rapid testing for bacteria). That same year the company also acquired the 93% of TriPath Imaging that it didn't already own for $350 million. TriPath brought with it a line of cancer management products.

EXECUTIVES

Chairman and CEO: Edward J. (Ed) Ludwig, age 57
Vice Chairman: John R. Considine, age 58
President: Vincent A. Forlenza, age 55
EVP and CFO: David V. Elkins, age 40
SVP and CTO: Scott P. Bruder, age 47
EVP: William A. Kozy, age 57
EVP: Gary M. Cohen, age 50
EVP: A. John Hanson, age 65
SVP Corporate Medical Affairs: David T. Durack, age 64
SVP Corporate Regulatory and External Affairs: Patricia B. Shrader, age 58
SVP and General Counsel: Jeffrey S. Sherman, age 53
SVP Human Resources: Donna M. Boles, age 56
VP Taxes: Mark H. Borofsky
VP and Treasurer: Richard K. Berman
VP, Corporate Secretary and Public Policy: Dean J. Paranicas
Director Corporate Communications: Colleen T. White
Director Investor Relations: Patricia A. Spinella
Auditors: Ernst & Young LLP

LOCATIONS

HQ: Becton, Dickinson and Company
1 Becton Dr., Franklin Lakes, NJ 07417
Phone: 201-847-6800   **Fax:** 201-847-6475
Web: www.bd.com

2008 Sales

	$ mil.	% of total
US	3,184.8	45
Europe	2,489.0	35
Other	1,482.1	20
Total	**7,155.9**	**100**

PRODUCTS/OPERATIONS

2008 Sales

	$ mil.	% of total
BD Medical		
Medical surgical systems	2,004.9	28
Pharmaceutical systems	942.1	13
Diabetes care	775.3	11
Ophthalmic systems	78.7	1
BD Diagnostics		
Preanalytical systems	1,123.5	16
Diagnostic systems	1,036.3	14
BD Biosciences		
Cell analysis		
(immunocytometry systems & Pharmingen)	900.5	13
Discovery Labware	294.6	4
Total	**7,155.9**	**100**

Selected Products

Medical
 Anesthesia needles
 Critical care monitoring systems
 Home health care (ACE bandages, thermometers, insulin self-injection devices)
 Hypodermic needles and syringes
 Intravenous catheters
 Ophthalmic surgical instruments
 Prefillable drug-delivery systems
 Safety needles and syringes
 Surgical blades and scalpels
Diagnostics
 Bar-code systems for patient identification and data capture
 Blood culturing systems
 Cytology systems (for cervical cancer screening)
 Immunodiagnostic test kits
 Microbiology systems (for infectious disease diagnosis)
 Safety-engineered blood collection devices
 Sample collection products
 Specimen management systems
Biosciences
 Cell growth and screening products
 Cellular imaging and analysis systems
 Clinical and research laboratory software
 Labware (tubes, pipettes, Petri dishes, etc.)
 Molecular biology reagents (for study of genes)
 Monoclonal antibodies (for biomedical research)
 Other research reagents
 Rapid molecular diagnostics (GeneOhm)

COMPETITORS

Abbott Labs	Inverness Medical
Accelr8	Innovations
Affymetrix	Johnson & Johnson
B. Braun Medical	Kimberly-Clark Health
Baxter International	Meridian Bioscience
Beckman Coulter	Novo Nordisk
bioMérieux	Retractable Technologies
Bio-Rad Labs	Roche Diagnostics
Boston Scientific	Safety Syringes
Covidien	Siemens Healthcare
Dako	Diagnostics
Gen-Probe	Terumo
Genzyme Diagnostics	Thermo Fisher Scientific
Harvard Bioscience	Third Wave Technologies
Hologic	Trinity Biotech
Hospira	

HISTORICAL FINANCIALS

Company Type: Public

Income Statement

FYE: September 30

	REVENUE ($ mil.)	NET INCOME ($ mil.)	NET PROFIT MARGIN	EMPLOYEES
9/08	7,155.9	1,127.0	15.7%	28,300
9/07	6,359.7	890.0	14.0%	28,018
9/06	5,834.8	752.3	12.9%	26,990
9/05	5,414.7	722.3	13.3%	25,571
9/04	4,934.7	467.4	9.5%	25,005
Annual Growth	9.7%	24.6%	—	3.1%

2008 Year-End Financials

Debt ratio: 19.3%
Return on equity: 24.2%
Cash ($ mil.): 830
Current ratio: 2.55
Long-term debt ($ mil.): 953

No. of shares (mil.): 239
Dividends
  Yield: 1.4%
  Payout: 25.6%
Market value ($ mil.): 19,213

Stock History

NYSE: BDX

	STOCK PRICE ($) FY Close	P/E High/Low	PER SHARE ($) Earnings	Dividends	Book Value
9/08	80.26	21 17	4.46	1.14	20.62
9/07	82.05	24 20	3.49	0.98	18.22
9/06	70.67	24 17	2.93	0.86	16.02
9/05	52.43	22 18	2.77	0.72	13.72
9/04	51.70	31 20	1.77	0.60	12.82
Annual Growth	11.6%	— —	26.0%	17.4%	12.6%

Bed Bath & Beyond

Bed Bath & Beyond (BBB) has everything you need to play "house" for real. It's the #1 superstore domestics retailer in the US with about 930 BBB stores throughout the US and Ontario, Canada. The stores' floor-to-ceiling shelves stock better-quality (brand-name and private-label) goods in two main categories: domestics (bed linens, bathroom and kitchen items) and home furnishings (cookware and cutlery, small household appliances, picture frames, and more). BBB relies exclusively on circulars, mailings, and word-of-mouth for advertising. The company also operates three smaller specialty chains: 50-plus Christmas Tree Shops; 40 Harmon discount health and beauty shops; and 15 buybuy Baby locations.

The retailer's decentralized structure allows store managers to have more control than their peers at other retailers (and the company has less manager turnover). The company cuts costs by locating its stores in strip shopping centers, freestanding buildings, and off-price malls, rather than in pricier regional malls. To cut costs further, BBB's vendors ship merchandise directly to the stores, eliminating the expense of a central distribution center and reducing warehousing costs.

New superstore openings — more than 65 in 2008 — and acquisitions account for much of the firm's growth. The retailer's buybuy Baby format, which sells infant and toddler merchandise, added half a dozen new stores in several new states. However, expansion is likely to slow in 2009 given the deep recession in the US and difficult real estate market.

While its business has suffered of late as a result of the downturn in the economy and liquidation sales at former archrival Linens 'n Things in late 2008, in the long run the demise of Linens 'n Things should provide a major boost for the company in the future.

BBB is branching out into Canada and Mexico. The company opened its first international store in Richmond Hill, Ontario, in late 2007 and now has four stores north of the border. A few months later, BBB entered a joint venture with Mexican retailer Home & More to operate a pair of Home & More stores. BBB's 50% equity stake cost the company about $4 million. BBB anticipates the joint venture will be a springboard for future growth in Mexico.

HISTORY

Warren Eisenberg and Leonard Feinstein, both employed by a discounter called Arlan's, brainstormed an idea in 1971 for a chain of stores offering only home goods. They were betting that customers were, in Feinstein's words, interested in a "designer approach to linens and housewares." The two men started two small linens stores (about 2,000 sq. ft) named bed n bath, one in New York and one in New Jersey.

Expansion came at a fairly slow pace as the company moved only into California and Connecticut by 1985. By then the time was right for such a specialty retailer: Department stores were cutting back on their houseware lines to focus on the more profitable apparel segment, and baby boomers were spending more leisure time at their homes (and more money on spiffing them up). Eisenberg and Feinstein opened a 20,000-sq.-ft. superstore in 1985 that offered a full line of home furnishings. The firm changed its name to Bed Bath & Beyond (BBB) two years later in order to reflect its new offerings.

With the successful superstore format, the company built all new stores in the larger design. BBB grew rapidly; square footage quadrupled between 1992 and 1996. The company went public in 1992. That year it eclipsed the size of its previous stores when it opened a 50,000-sq.-ft. store in Manhattan. (It later enlarged this store to 80,000 sq. ft.; the company's stores now average 42,000 sq. ft.)

BBB's management has attributed its success, in part, to the leeway it gives its store managers, who monitor inventory and have the freedom to try new products and layouts. One example often cited by the company is the case of a manager who decided to sell glasses by the piece instead of in sets. Sales increased 30%, and the whole chain incorporated the practice.

The retailer opened 28 new stores in 1996, 33 in 1997 (its first-ever billion-dollar sales year), and 45 in 1998.

In 1999 the company dipped a toe into the waters of e-commerce by agreeing to buy a stake in Internet Gift Registries, which operates the WeddingNetwork Web site. The company later began offering online sales and bridal registry services. Keeping up its rapid expansion pace, the

company opened 70 stores in 1999, 85 in 2000, and 95 in 2001.

In 2002 BBB acquired Harmon Stores, a health and beauty aid retailer with 29 stores in three states. It acquired Christmas Tree Shops, a giftware and household items retailer with 23 stores in six states, for $200 million in 2003.

In March 2007 BBB acquired buybuy BABY, which operates eight stores on the East Coast, for $67 million. The retailer opened its first Canadian location in Ontario, north of Toronto, in December. In 2008 BBB added three more stores in Canada and its first locations in Mexico, via a joint venture there, under the Home & More banner.

EXECUTIVES

Co-Chairman: Leonard (Lenny) Feinstein, age 72, $4,836,512 total compensation
Co-Chairman: Warren Eisenberg, age 78, $4,774,848 total compensation
CEO and Director: Steven H. (Steve) Temares, age 50, $7,676,442 total compensation
President and Chief Merchandising Officer: Arthur (Art) Stark, age 54, $2,748,459 total compensation
CFO and Treasurer: Eugene A. (Gene) Castagna, age 43, $2,433,398 total compensation
SVP Stores: Matthew Fiorilli, age 52
SVP Investor Relations: Ronald (Ron) Curwin, age 74
VP and CIO: Kevin R. Murphy
VP Legal and General Counsel: Allan N. Rauch
VP Corporate Development; President, Harmon Stores: G. William Waltzinger Jr.
VP Corporate Operations and Chief Strategy Officer; President, BBB Canada: Richard C. (Rich) McMahon
VP Store Operations: Christine R. Pirog
VP Construction and Store Development: Jim Brendle
VP Finance and Principal Accounting Officer: Susan E. Lattmann, age 41
VP Marketing: Rita Little
VP and Corporate Counsel: Michael J. Callahan
VP Human Resources: Concetta Van Dyke
VP and Controller: Robyn M. D'Elia
CEO, Christmas Tree Shops: Charles (Chuck) Bilezikian
Director Public Relations: Bari Fagin
Auditors: KPMG LLP

LOCATIONS

HQ: Bed Bath & Beyond Inc.
  650 Liberty Ave., Union, NJ 07083
Phone: 908-688-0888   **Fax:** 908-688-6483
Web: www.bedbathandbeyond.com

2009 Christmas Tree Shops Stores

	No.
Massachusetts	16
New York	10
Pennsylvania	5
New Jersey	4
Connecticut	4
New Hampshire	4
Rhode Island	2
Maine	2
Delaware	1
Indiana	1
Michigan	1
Ohio	1
Vermont	1
Total	**52**

2009 Harmon Stores

	No.
New Jersey	29
New York	9
Connecticut	2
Total	**40**

2009 Bed Bath & Beyond Stores

	No.
California	104
Texas	73
Florida	70
New York	58
Illinois	39
Ohio	37
New Jersey	35
Pennsylvania	32
Michigan	31
Virginia	30
North Carolina	28
Arizona	25
Georgia	25
Colorado	24
Massachusetts	24
Washington	21
Tennessee	20
Indiana	18
Maryland	17
Connecticut	17
Alabama	14
Missouri	14
South Carolina	13
Utah	12
Louisiana	13
Wisconsin	10
Minnesota	9
Oregon	9
Nevada	8
Iowa	8
New Hampshire	8
Idaho	7
Kansas	7
Kentucky	7
Oklahoma	7
Arkansas	6
Mississippi	6
Maine	5
Montana	5
Nebraska	5
New Mexico	5
Other states	20
Ontario, Canada	4
Total	**930**

2009 buybuy Baby Stores

	No.
New York	5
New Jersey	3
Michigan	2
Florida	1
Illinois	1
Maryland	1
Ohio	1
Virginia	1
Total	**15**

PRODUCTS/OPERATIONS

2009 Stores

	No.
Bed Bath & Beyond	930
Christmas Tree Shops	52
Harmon	40
buybuy Baby	15
Total	**1,037**

Selected Merchandise

Domestics
  Bath accessories
    Hampers
    Shower curtains
    Towels
  Bed linens
    Bedspreads
    Pillows
    Sheets
  Kitchen textiles
    Cloth napkins
    Dish towels
    Placemats
    Tablecloths
    Window treatments

Home Furnishings
  Basic housewares
    Accessories (lamps, chairs, accent rugs)
    General housewares (brooms, ironing boards)
    Small appliances (blenders, coffeemakers, vacuums)
    Storage items (hangers, organizers, shoe racks)
  General home furnishings
    Artificial plants and flowers
    Candles
    Gift wrap
    Picture frames
    Seasonal merchandise
    Wall art
  Kitchen and tabletop items
    Cookware
    Cutlery
    Flatware
    Gadgets
    Glassware
    Serveware

COMPETITORS

Anna's Linens
Art.com
Babies "R" Us
Burlington Coat Factory
The Children's Place
Container Store
Cost Plus
Dillard's
Euromarket Designs
Garden Ridge
Gymboree
IKEA
J. C. Penney
Kmart
Lillian Vernon
Macy's
Pier 1 Imports
Ross Stores
Saks
Sears
Sensational Beginnings
Target
TJX Companies
Tuesday Morning Corporation
Wal-Mart
Williams-Sonoma

HISTORICAL FINANCIALS

Company Type: Public

Income Statement

FYE: Saturday nearest February 28

	REVENUE ($ mil.)	NET INCOME ($ mil.)	NET PROFIT MARGIN	EMPLOYEES
2/09	7,208.3	425.1	5.9%	37,000
2/08	7,048.9	562.8	8.0%	39,000
2/07	6,617.4	594.2	9.0%	35,000
2/06	5,809.6	572.8	9.9%	33,000
2/05	5,147.7	505.0	9.8%	31,000
Annual Growth	**8.8%**	**(4.2%)**	**—**	**4.5%**

2009 Year-End Financials

Debt ratio: 2.9%
Return on equity: 15.3%
Cash ($ mil.): 668
Current ratio: 2.69
Long-term debt ($ mil.): 88

No. of shares (mil.): 262
Dividends
  Yield: 0.0%
  Payout: —
Market value ($ mil.): 5,578

Stock History

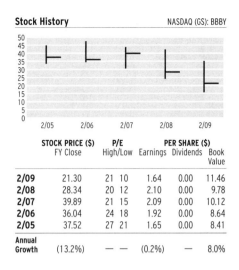

NASDAQ (GS): BBBY

	STOCK PRICE ($) FY Close	P/E High/Low		PER SHARE ($) Earnings	Dividends	Book Value
2/09	21.30	21	10	1.64	0.00	11.46
2/08	28.34	20	12	2.10	0.00	9.78
2/07	39.89	21	15	2.09	0.00	10.12
2/06	36.04	24	18	1.92	0.00	8.64
2/05	37.52	27	21	1.65	0.00	8.41
Annual Growth	**(13.2%)**	**—**	**—**	**(0.2%)**	**—**	**8.0%**

Belden Inc.

Did you get the message? If you didn't, Belden can help. The company designs, makes, and markets thousands of signal transmission products to hook up the entertainment, residential, industrial and security markets. Its equipment includes flat and optical fiber cables, coaxial and multi-conductor cables, connectivity and active components. Connecting access points to area networks, Belden cable is the wire in wireless. It produces connectors, patch panels, and interconnect hardware for end-to-end structured cabling solutions, and industrial and data networking applications. In addition to selling to distributors, Belden garners sales directly from OEMs and systems integrators.

In August 2009 Belden announced a cooperative technology agreement with Byres Security Inc. (BSI), a leader in industrial cyber security for petrochemical and manufacturing sectors. The companies will together launch new products relating to industrial network security. Belden's expertise is in automation, while BSI specializes in protecting companies from cyber and network threats.

Since the company's founding more than a hundred years ago, Belden has focused on market segments that required highly differentiated, high performance products. .

In 2008 the company paid $136 million for Trapeze Networks, a maker of wireless local area networking equipment and software. The deal paid off by opening new competitive frontiers for Belden; Trapeze scored distribution agreements with two of the largest cabling infrastructure distributors in North America.

The purchase comes on the tail of aggressive steps to streamline manufacturing, sales and administrative functions worldwide in an effort to reduce costs. In light of weakening demand, Belden announced plans to consolidate its manufacturing functions, sold its Czech cable assembly operation, and a non-strategic portion of the Hirschmann Automation and Control business. As part of the manufacturing consolidation, the company closed a plant in Midlothian, Virginia, and moved production to the facility in Tijuana, Mexico. The cost-cutting measures include slashing approximately 1,800 jobs, a 20% reduction in staff.

In 2007 the company inked several strategic deals. Belden acquired Hong Kong cable maker LTK Wiring for $195 million. The addition deepens its Asia Pacific presence for launching cable products and internal wiring (used in consumer electronics). On the European shore, it purchased the assets of German connector-maker Lumberg Automation. Lumberg joins in driving the European segment's integrated cable, active component, and connectivity marketing targeting industrial OEMs. Belden also diversified its business with a $260 million deal for Hirschmann. The Germany-based company makes electronic control and safety products, as well as Ethernet connectors.

HISTORY

When Joseph Belden couldn't find the silk-wrapped, magnetic wire needed for telephone coils, he decided to make it himself and founded Belden Manufacturing Company in Chicago in 1902. Thomas Edison was one of the company's early customers. Rubber-covered and enamel-coated wire used by the fledgling electricity industry, and later in radio cars and electrical appliances, spurred the company's growth. During the 1950s Belden began making products for data processing and television.

The company changed its name to Belden Corporation in 1966, and in 1981 it was purchased by Cooper Industries. During that period Belden established its presence in the computer industry. Cooper spun off Belden in 1993. The following year Belden moved its headquarters to St. Louis.

Belden has expanded its product line through acquisitions. Purchases have included American Electric Cordsets and Pope Cable and Wire, BV (a unit of Netherlands-based Philips Electronics) in 1995, Intech Cable (1996), the wire division of Alpha Wire (1997), and Cowen Cable (1997). Belden bought Pacific Dunlop's (now Ansell Limited) Australia-based Olex cable business in 1998. The deal included a factory in Melbourne, Belden's first manufacturing operation in the Asia/Pacific region.

In 2000 Belden won a major contract with SBC Communications for $700 million to supply copper telecommunications cable over the next five years. And to further expand its overseas presence, Belden purchased the metallic communications cable operations division of the UK-based Corning Communications. The following year Belden sold its 70% stake in MCTec (a Netherlands-based company specializing in coatings for medical applications) to STS Biopolymers for $1.4 million. The company also reduced its workforce by nearly 17% during 2001. The trend continued the following year when Belden closed its Kingston, Ontario, plant.

Cable Design Technologies (CDT) was founded as Intercole Automation in 1980 by William Coleman. The company initially made wire and cable and materials-handling systems. In 1988 the company, by then known as CDT, was bought by current chairman Bryan Cressey's investment company. Acquisitions fueled CDT's growth. The company bought Mohawk Wire & Cable, an early developer of wiring for computer and cable networks (1986), and Montrose Products, a maker of specialty electronics cable (1988).

Acquisitive CDT continued its buying trend during the 1990s. In 1991 it bought European cable distributor Anglo-American Cable. CDT went public in 1993, and the following year the company purchased the struggling Nya NEK Kabel AB (cable, Sweden). In 1996 CDT boosted its presence in the telecom market with its $90 million purchase of the communications cable and network wiring products business of Northern Telecom (now Nortel Networks).

CDT gained footholds in the aircraft and wireless communications markets in 1997 with its purchases of specialty cable and wire manufacturers Dearborn Wire & Cable and Barcel Wire & Cable. In 1998 CDT expanded its international reach by buying Örebro (wire and cable, Sweden) and 80% of Germany-based HEW-KABEL (cable). Citing a decline in the telecommunications industry, CDT reduced its workforce by 900 jobs in 2001.

Belden CDT Inc. was born in 2004 when the merger of Cable Design Technologies and Belden was completed. As part of the merger agreement, Belden CDT exited the North American telecommunications market by selling its communications assets to Superior Essex.

The company changed its name from Belden CDT Inc. to Belden Inc. in 2007.

EXECUTIVES

Chairman: Bryan C. Cressey, age 59
President, CEO, and Director: John S. Stroup, age 43, $4,975,870 total compensation
VP Finance and CFO: Gray G. Benoist, age 56, $1,293,557 total compensation
Corporate Controller and Chief Accounting Officer: John S. Norman, age 48
EVP, Asia Pacific Operations: Naresh Kumra, age 38, $1,207,939 total compensation
EVP, Americas Operations and Global Cable Products: Denis Suggs, age 43
SVP, Secretary, and General Counsel: Kevin L. Bloomfield, age 57, $869,719 total compensation
SVP Human Resources: Cathy Odom Staples, age 58
SVP Global Sales and Marketing: Steven R. (Steve) Biegacki, age 50
VP, Treasurer: Stephen H. Johnson, age 59
VP Operations and President, Specialty Products: Louis M. Pace, age 37, $869,784 total compensation
VP Global Manufacturing: Richard (Dick) Kirschner, age 58
VP and General Manager, Belden Asia Pacific: Peter Leung
VP Business Development: Daniel Krawczyk
VP Operations, President Belden EMEA: Wolfgang Babel, age 51
Managing Director, Asia Pacific: Robert Lewis
Manager Marketing Communications and Resource Manager: Frank Stone
Auditors: Ernst & Young LLP

LOCATIONS

HQ: Belden Inc.
7701 Forsyth Blvd., Ste. 800, St. Louis, MO 63105
Phone: 314-854-8000 **Fax:** 314-854-8001
Web: www.beldencdt.com

2008 Sales

	$ mil.	% of total
North America		
US	842.8	42
Canada & Latin America	192.5	10
Europe, Africa & Middle East	570.1	28
Asia/Pacific	400.5	20
Total	**2,005.9**	**100**

PRODUCTS/OPERATIONS

2008 Sales

	$ mil.	% of total
Belden Americas	758.4	38
Europe	678.6	34
Specialty Products	211.6	10
Wireless	13.7	1
Asia/Pacific	343.6	17
Total	**2,005.9**	**100**

Selected Products

Active connectivity products
  Fiber-optic interfaces and media converters
  Industrial Ethernet switches
  Load moment indicators
Composite cables
Connectors
Copper cables
  Coaxial cables
  Ribbon cables
  Shielded and unshielded twisted-pair cables
  Stranded cables
Fiber-optic cables
Heat-shrinkable tubing
Lead and hookup wires
Multiconductor cables
Wire management products

COMPETITORS

ADC Telecommunications
Alcatel-Lucent
AmerCable
Andrew Corporation
Bekaert Corp.
Belkin
Capro
CommScope
Corning
Fujikura Ltd.
Furukawa Electric
General Cable
International Wire
JDS Uniphase
Kalas Manufacturing
Southwire
Sumitomo Electric
Superior Essex
SWCC SHOWA
Tyco
W.L. Gore

HISTORICAL FINANCIALS

Company Type: Public

Income Statement

	REVENUE ($ mil.)	NET INCOME ($ mil.)	NET PROFIT MARGIN	EMPLOYEES
12/08	2,005.9	(361.0)	—	7,500
12/07	2,032.8	137.1	6.7%	9,500
12/06	1,495.8	65.9	4.4%	5,400
12/05	1,352.1	47.6	3.5%	6,100
12/04	966.2	15.2	1.6%	6,750
Annual Growth	**20.0%**	**—**	**—**	**2.7%**

FYE: December 31

2008 Year-End Financials

Debt ratio: 103.4%
Return on equity: —
Cash ($ mil.): 227
Current ratio: 2.32
Long-term debt ($ mil.): 590
No. of shares (mil.): 47
Dividends
  Yield: 1.0%
  Payout: —
Market value ($ mil.): 973

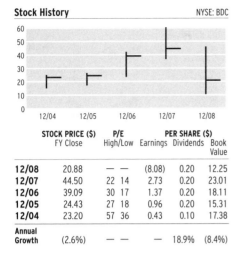

	STOCK PRICE ($) FY Close	P/E High/Low		PER SHARE ($) Earnings	Dividends	Book Value
12/08	20.88	—	—	(8.08)	0.20	12.25
12/07	44.50	22	14	2.73	0.20	23.01
12/06	39.09	30	17	1.37	0.20	18.11
12/05	24.43	27	18	0.96	0.20	15.31
12/04	23.20	57	36	0.43	0.10	17.38
Annual Growth	(2.6%)	—	—	—	18.9%	(8.4%)

Bemis Company

Thanks to companies like Bemis, modern delectables such as potato chips and snack cakes have longer shelf lives than most marriages. Bemis makes a broad line of flexible packaging materials, including polymer films, barrier laminates, and paper-bag packaging that customers in the food industry use to package all manner of edibles. In addition to bags, Bemis also produces pressure-sensitive products ranging from label paper and graphic films to thin-film adhesives. Although Bemis' primary market is the food industry, the company also sells to the agricultural, chemical, medical, personal care, and printing industries.

Broadening its market share in Mexico and South America has been high on this packagemaker's agenda. In mid-2009 Bemis moved to acquire Alcan Packaging Food Americas from mining group Rio Tinto for $1.2 billion. The addition ramps up Bemis' food and beverage packaging expertise in aluminum-foil lamination, and the segment's sales to about 70% of total revenue.

The company also began looking into how it can leverage alliances, and in 2007 it teamed with Australia-based Plantic Technologies, which makes starch-based biopolymers. The point of the partnership is to develop flexible films using renewable resources. The products will be based on Plantic's bioplastic resins and will target flexible packaging for personal care and dry goods.

The Flexible Packaging segment manufactures industrial packaging for food and consumer goods. It also provides carton-sealing tapes and bag-closing materials to package fresh meat, liquids, frozen foods, cereals, condiments, baked goods, pharmaceuticals, and personal care and lawn and garden items, to name a few.

The Pressure Sensitive Materials segment manufactures adhesive coated paper and film substrates and sells it to label, graphic, and technical markets. Primary markets include food and consumer goods, inventory control labels, postage stamps, and shipping labels.

Some major clients include Kimberly-Clark, Procter & Gamble, Sara Lee, Nestlé, Kraft, General Mills, Energizer Batteries, and Hormel Foods. Bemis operates 12 companies and over 56 manufacturing facilities in 10 countries.

HISTORY

Judson Moss Bemis founded J. M. Bemis and Company, Bag Manufacturers, in St. Louis in 1858. The 25-year-old received advice and equipment from cousin Simeon Farwell, who owned an established bag-making factory. St. Louis' role as a trading center supported by major railroads and the Mississippi River helped Bemis' business. The company introduced preprinted and machine-sewn flour sacks to the city's millers, and by the end of its first year it was making about 4,000 sacks a day. In its second year Edward Brown, a relative of Farwell's, became Bemis' partner, and the company was renamed Bemis and Brown.

During the Civil War, Brown opened an office in Boston to make the most of fluctuating exchange rates. Bemis also began trading in raw cotton (priced sky-high because of the war), and it started recycling burlap shipping bags into gunnysacks. The company soon began producing its own burlap sacks from imported jute.

Stephen Bemis, Judson's brother, became a partner in the firm in 1870 and took over its St. Louis operations. Judson joined Brown in Boston, where he could be involved in commodity purchases and financial operations. Soon after, he bought out Brown's share of the firm for an amount considered extravagant at the time — $300,000.

By the early 1880s Bemis Bros. and Co. was the US's #2 bag maker. It opened a second factory in 1881 in Minneapolis, which was home to such companies as General Mills and Pillsbury. During the late 1800s and the early 1900s, Bemis opened plants throughout the US.

Judson retired in 1909, but the company continued to be run by Bemis family members. In 1914 the company entered the emerging industry of paper milling and paper-bag making, but it continued to focus on textile packaging until WWII, when shortages of cotton and jute resulted in an expanded role for paper packaging and led to the development of polyethylene packaging. By the 1950s Bemis' core products were paper and plastic packaging. In 1959 the company opened its own R&D facility. During the late 1950s and 1960s Bemis made several important acquisitions, including Curwood (packaging for medical products) and MACtac (pressure-sensitive materials). The company was renamed Bemis Company in 1965.

Bemis sold more than $100 million of noncore businesses during the 1970s and 1980s. In its effort to become an industry leader, the company began a major capital expansion program. Bemis' sales topped $1 billion in 1988.

Bemis bought candy-packaging producer Milprint, Inc., in 1990; Princeton Packaging's bakery-packaging business in 1993; and Banner Packaging in 1995. In 1996 Bemis introduced the on-battery tester, developed with Eveready. Bemis' medical packaging segment was rejuvenated that year with the purchase of Malaysia-based Perfecseal.

In 1998 Bemis acquired Belgium's Techy International, which became Bemis' base for sales and distribution in Europe. Bemis invested more than $100 million to modernize its packaging manufacturing and printing operations in 1999.

The next year it acquired Arrow Industries' flexible packaging operations, Viskase's plastic-films business, and Kanzaki Specialty Papers' pressure sensitive materials business.

The company opened its pocketbook again in 2002, purchasing the Clysar shrink film business of DuPont (with operations in both the US and Europe) for more than $140 million. The purchase gave Bemis a worldwide reach for its shrink bags, film, and heat-set packaging products.

In 2003 Bemis expanded its operations in Europe through the acquisition of Multi-Fix's pressure sensitive materials business for about $11 million. The next year Bemis acquired flexible packaging assets in Mexico from Masterpak S.A. de C.V. The company also restructured its Pressure Sensitive Materials division, which included the closing of two facilities.

Bemis restructured its operations to reduce costs during 2006; the move primarily consisted of manufacturing facility consolidations that resulted in seven plant closings.

Intent on strengthening its market presence in South America, Bemis bought a majority stake in Brazil-based Dixie Toga, one of the country's largest packaging companies. Bemis had originally purchased a one-third interest in Dixie Toga in 1998.

EXECUTIVES

Executive Chairman and Chairman:
Jeffrey H. (Jeff) Curler, age 58,
$5,545,731 total compensation
President, CEO, and Director: Henry J. Theisen, age 55,
$3,296,731 total compensation
SVP, CFO, and Director: Gene C. Wulf, age 58,
$1,912,075 total compensation
VP and Controller: Stanley A. Jaffy, age 60,
$1,544,106 total compensation
VP Human Resources: Eugene H. (Gene) Seashore Jr.,
age 59, $1,332,809 total compensation
VP, General Counsel, and Secretary: James J. Seifert,
age 52
VP Operations; President and CEO, Morgan Adhesives Company: William F. Austen, age 50
VP Global Sales Development: Chris Martin
VP Investor Relations and Treasurer:
Melanie E. R. Miller, age 45
VP Operations: Robert F. Hawthorne, age 59
VP Operations; President, Curwood:
James W. (Jim) Ransom, age 49
President, Milprint/Banner: Donald E. Nimis
President, Paper Packaging: Gregory J. Derhaag
President, Bemis Flexible Packaging Europe:
Marc Dussart
President, MACtac Europe: Guido Alvino
President, Polyethylene Packaging Division:
Peter R. (Pete) Mathias
President, Perfecseal: Paul R. Verbeten
President, Bemis Mexico: Robert Mescal
President, Dixie Toga: Nelson Fazenda
President, MACtac Americas: James Peruzzi
President, Bemis Clysar: Steve Moore
Public Relations Specialist: Kristi Pavletich
Auditors: PricewaterhouseCoopers LLP

LOCATIONS

HQ: Bemis Company, Inc.
1 Neenah Center, 4th Fl., Neenah, WI 54957
Phone: 920-727-4100   **Fax:** 920-527-7600
Web: www.bemis.com

2008 Sales

	$ mil.	% of total
North America		
US	2,429.4	65
Canada	12.3	—
Europe	656.5	17
South America	582.4	15
Other regions	98.8	3
Total	**3,779.4**	**100**

2009 Stores

	No.
US	1,107
Europe (includes CarphoneWarehouse)	2,465
Canada	200
China	169
Mexico	1
Total	**3,942**

2009 Best Buy US Locations

	No.
California	117
Texas	101
Florida	62
Illinois	57
New York	46
Ohio	38
Virginia	34
Pennsylvania	33
Michigan	32
North Carolina	32
Georgia	30
Arizona	27
Minnesota	27
Massachusetts	27
Wisconsin	23
New Jersey	23
Colorado	22
Maryland	22
Missouri	21
Indiana	20
Washington	20
Tennessee	15
South Carolina	14
Alabama	14
Iowa	13
Louisiana	13
Connecticut	12
Oklahoma	11
Oregon	10
Nevada	10
Kentucky	9
Utah	9
Arkansas	8
Kansas	8
Mississippi	7
Maine	6
Nebraska	6
New Hampshire	6
Other states	34
Puerto Rico	4
Total	**1,023**

2009 Best Buy Mobile Stores

	No.
Connecticut	3
Georgia	4
Illinois	2
Indiana	1
Maryland	5
Minnesota	1
New Jersey	2
New York	4
North Carolina	6
Pennsylvania	5
South Carolina	4
Virginia	1
Total	**38**

2009 Magnolia Audio Video Locations

	No.
California	4
Washington	2
Total	**6**

2009 Sales

	$ mil.	% of total
US	35,070	78
International	9,945	22
Total	**45,015**	**100**

PRODUCTS/OPERATIONS

2009 US Stores

	No.
Best Buy	1,023
Best Buy Mobile	38
Pacific Sales	34
Magnolia Audio Video	6
Geek Squad	6
Total	**1,107**

2009 US Sales

	% of total
Consumer electronics	41
Home office	28
Entertainment software	20
Appliances	5
Services	6
Total	**100**

2009 International Sales

	% of total
Consumer electronics	26
Home office	45
Entertainment software	9
Appliances	10
Services	10
Total	**100**

Selected Products

Consumer Electronics
Audio
Car stereos
Home theater audio systems
MP3 players
Satellite radio systems
Video
Digital cameras and camcorders
DVD players
Televisions
Home Office
Computers
Networking equipment
Office furniture
Printers
Scanners
Supplies
Telephones
Entertainment Software
CDs
Computer software
DVDs
Subscription plans
Video game hardware and software
Appliances
Dishwashers
Microwave ovens
Refrigerators
Stoves and ranges
Vacuum cleaners
Washers and dryers

COMPETITORS

Amazon.com	imeem
Apple Inc.	Lowe's
ARTISTdirect	MediaNet Digital
Audible, Inc.	METRO AG
Barnes & Noble	MSN
Borders Group	MySpace
Brilliant Digital	Office Depot
Entertainment	OfficeMax
Brookstone	RadioShack
Buy.com	RealNetworks
Buzz Media	Sears Holdings
CDNOW	Sony Music
Conn's	Staples
Costco Wholesale	Systemax
Dell	Target
eMusic.com	Trans World Entertainment
Fry's Electronics	Virgin Group
Gateway, Inc.	Wal-Mart
Hastings Entertainment	Yahoo!
Home Depot	

HISTORICAL FINANCIALS

Company Type: Public

Income Statement

FYE: Sat. nearest last day in February

	REVENUE ($ mil.)	NET INCOME ($ mil.)	NET PROFIT MARGIN	EMPLOYEES
2/09	45,015.0	1,003.0	2.2%	155,000
2/08	40,023.0	1,407.0	3.5%	150,000
2/07	35,934.0	1,377.0	3.8%	140,000
2/06	30,848.0	1,140.0	3.7%	128,000
2/05	27,433.0	984.0	3.6%	109,000
Annual Growth	**13.2%**	**0.5%**	**—**	**9.2%**

2009 Year-End Financials

Debt ratio: 24.3%
Return on equity: 22.0%
Cash ($ mil.): 498
Current ratio: 0.97
Long-term debt ($ mil.): 1,126
No. of shares (mil.): 416
Dividends
Yield: 1.9%
Payout: 22.6%
Market value ($ mil.): 11,999

Stock History

NYSE: BBY

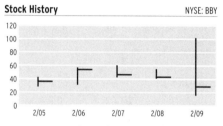

	STOCK PRICE ($) FY Close	P/E High/Low		PER SHARE ($) Earnings	Dividends	Book Value
2/09	28.82	42	7	2.39	0.54	11.15
2/08	43.01	17	13	3.12	0.46	10.77
2/07	46.48	21	16	2.79	0.36	14.89
2/06	53.86	25	14	2.27	0.31	12.63
2/05	36.01	21	15	1.96	0.28	10.69
Annual Growth	**(5.4%)**	**—**	**—**	**5.1%**	**17.8%**	**1.1%**

Big Lots

Big Lots believes that a product's shelf life depends solely on which shelf it's on. The company is the nation's #1 broadline closeout retailer, with some 1,340 Big Lots stores (down from a high of 1,500 in 2005) in 47 states. (More than one-third of its stores are located in California, Florida, Ohio, and Texas.) It sells a variety of brand-name products that have been overproduced, returned, discontinued, or result from liquidations, typically at 20% to 40% below discounters' prices, as well as private-label items and furniture. Its wholesale division, Big Lots Wholesale, sells its discounted merchandise to a variety of retailers, manufacturers, distributors, and other wholesalers.

Big Lots has struggled with declining sales in recent years as it lost sales to dollar and other discount stores. In addition to closing poorly performing locations, the company is testing a new store format — with a racetrack-style center aisle — designed to highlight brand-name products selling for closeout prices. The new prototype is an effort to improve product visibility in Big Lots' often cluttered stores and enhance the shopping experience for its customers. Rather than adding new stores in 2008, Big Lots remodeled some 40 existing locations and focused on improving sales per square foot.

The chain appeared to be turning a corner, with store productivity and profitability on the rise, when recession gripped the US economy. However, the tough market for retailers has created vacancies at attractive terms in the softening commercial real estate market. So for the first time in five years, Big Lots plans to open 45 new stores (and close about 40 others) for an anticipated net gain of about five new stores. Also in 2009 the chain is testing its new store layout at about 60 locations across the US. The new format puts food and other consumables front and center, to capitalize on the trend of shoppers trading down from supermarkets to deep discounters to fulfill their basic needs.

The retailer's merchandise mix includes name-brand and private-label housewares and furniture, electronics, foods, toiletries, tools, toys, and clothing. To stock the shelves of its stores, Big Lots buys truckloads of orphaned bric-a-brac (discontinued, overproduced, and outdated items) at steep discounts from stores and manufacturers.

HISTORY

As a kid growing up in Columbus, Ohio, Russian-born Sol Shenk (pronounced "Shank") couldn't stand to pay full price for anything. His frugality blossomed into a knack for buying low and wholesaling. After a failed effort to make auto parts, Shenk began the precursor to Consolidated Stores in 1967, backed by brothers Alvin, Saul, and Jerome Schottenstein.

The company started by wholesaling closeout auto parts and buying retailers' closeout items to sell to other retailers. By 1971 Shenk had branched into retailing, selling closeout auto parts through a small chain of Corvair Auto Stores.

One of Shenk's sons suggested they devote space in the Corvair stores to closeout merchandise other than car parts. Sales surged, and Shenk decided to sell the Corvair outlets and focus on closeout stores. The first Odd Lots opened in 1982. Consolidated grew more than 100% annually for the next three years. By 1986, the year after it went public, the company was opening two stores a week in midsized markets around the Midwest.

Shenk found that people would buy anything as long as the price was right. Two years after the mania for Rubik's Cubes ended, Odd Lots bought 6 million of the puzzles (once priced at $8) at 8 cents apiece, marked them up 500%, and sold them all.

By 1987 the company had nearly 300 Odd Lots/Big Lots stores. But runaway growth had created massive inventory shortages and losses as disappointed customers stopped browsing the company's sparsely stocked shelves. The woes coincided with a falling-out with the Schottensteins. Shenk retired in 1989.

Apparel and electronics retail executive William Kelley was named chairman and CEO the next year. Kelley returned Consolidated to its closeout roots and increased sales through acquisitions and creating new discount chains.

Consolidated doubled its size in 1996 with the $315 million purchase of more than 1,000 struggling Kay-Bee Toys (now KB Toys) stores from Melville Corp. The expansion continued with the 1998 purchase of top closeout competitor Mac Frugal's Bargains — Closeouts. (Mac Frugal's had nearly bought Consolidated in 1989 before Consolidated board members vetoed the deal.)

The $1 billion acquisition of Mac Frugal's gave Consolidated another 326 western stores under the Pic 'N' Save and Mac Frugal's names.

In 1999 Consolidated combined its online toy sales operations with those of BrainPlay.com to form KBkids.com. In mid-2000 Kelley was ousted as CEO, handing the title over to CFO Michael Potter. In December 2000 the company sold KB Toys (including KBkids.com) to a group led by KB management and global private equity firm Bain Capital for about $300 million. In mid-2001 the company changed its name to Big Lots and began converting all stores to that name to establish a national brand.

In 2002 the company completed converting 434 stores to the Big Lots banner, including 380 stores previously operating under the names of Odd Lots, Mac Frugal's, and Pic 'N' Save. The name changes were part of a larger initiative to broaden the appeal of closeout retailing and to establish a unified national brand.

In 2003 Big Lots continued to remodel stores, opened 86 new locations, and closed 36 others. In 2004 the company opened about 100 new stores and continued to add furniture departments to its existing stores.

Potter stepped down in July 2005. He was succeeded by Steven S. Fishman who became the company's chairman, CEO, and president. Fishman is a veteran of the Pamida, Frank's Nursery & Crafts, and Rhodes Furniture retail chains. Overall, the company shuttered 174 stores in 2005, including 43 Big Lots Furniture stores, and exited the frozen food business.

In late 2006 the company reached tentative settlements of two employee-related class action suits, including one by some 1,400 Big Lots employees in Louisiana and Texas who alleged that they were wrongly classified as managers so that they could be denied overtime pay. The settlements amounted to nearly $10 million. (In February 2004 Big Lots settled a similar suit brought by more than 1,000 California employees by agreeing to pay $10 million.)

EXECUTIVES

Chairman, President, and CEO:
Steven S. (Steve) Fishman, age 57,
$9,025,870 total compensation
SVP Store Operations: Christopher T. Chapin, age 45
SVP and CFO: Joe R. Cooper, age 51,
$1,566,965 total compensation
SVP Merchandise Planning and Allocation and CIO:
Lisa M. Bachmann, age 47,
$1,572,566 total compensation
EVP Human Resources, Loss Prevention, and Risk Management: Brad A. Waite, age 51,
$1,935,754 total compensation
EVP Merchandising: John C. Martin, age 58,
$1,604,316 total compensation
SVP Distribution and Transportation Services:
Harold A. (Hal) Wilson, age 60
SVP Legal and Real Estate, General Counsel, and Secretary: Charles W. Haubiel II, age 43
SVP Big Lots Capital and Wholesale:
Norman J. (Norm) Rankin, age 52
SVP and General Merchandise Manager, Furniture and Home Divisions: Robert Segal, age 54
SVP Marketing: Robert C. Claxton, age 54
VP Loss Prevention: Kevin R. Wolfe
VP Transportation Services: Kathryn A. Keane
VP Divisional Merchandise Manager: Kim Horner
VP Real Estate: Kevin R. Day
VP Store Projects: Gary E. Huber
VP Wholesale: Steven B. Marcus
VP Marketing and Merchandise Presentation:
Richard J. Marsan Jr.
VP Distribution Support Services: Todd A. Noethen
VP Human Resources Services: Jo L. Roney
VP and Treasurer: Jared A. Poff
Auditors: Deloitte & Touche LLP

LOCATIONS

HQ: Big Lots, Inc.
300 Phillipi Rd., Columbus, OH 43228
Phone: 614-278-6800   **Fax:** 614-278-6676
Web: www.biglots.com

2009 Stores

	No.
California	176
Texas	113
Ohio	102
Florida	103
Pennsylvania	61
North Carolina	61
Georgia	57
New York	45
Indiana	44
Tennessee	43
Kentucky	40
Michigan	39
Virginia	36
Illinois	34
Arizona	34
Alabama	28
South Carolina	29
Missouri	23
Louisiana	22
Colorado	21
Washington	19
West Virginia	18
Oklahoma	16
Mississippi	15
Massachusetts	14
New Jersey	13
New Mexico	13
Maryland	12
Nevada	12
Oregon	11
Wisconsin	11
Utah	10
Arkansas	9
Kansas	9
Maine	6
New Hampshire	6
Connecticut	6
Minnesota	5
Idaho	5
Other states	18
Total	**1,339**

PRODUCTS/OPERATIONS

2009 Sales

	$ mil.	% of total
Consumables	1,410.4	30
Home	713.1	15
Furniture	698.3	15
Hardlines	646.6	14
Seasonal	585.0	13
Other	591.9	13
Total	**4,645.3**	**100**

COMPETITORS

99 Cents Only	Michaels Stores
Amazon.com	Quality King
BJ's Wholesale Club	Ross Stores
Costco Wholesale	Salvation Army
Dollar General	Sears
Dollar Tree	Simply Amazing
Family Dollar Stores	Target
Fred's	TJX Companies
Goodwill Industries	Tuesday Morning
J. C. Penney	Corporation
Jo-Ann Stores	Variety Wholesalers
Kmart	Walgreen
Liquidation World	Wal-Mart

HISTORICAL FINANCIALS

Company Type: Public

Income Statement

FYE: Saturday nearest January 31

	REVENUE ($ mil.)	NET INCOME ($ mil.)	NET PROFIT MARGIN	EMPLOYEES
1/09	4,645.3	151.5	3.3%	37,000
1/08	4,656.3	158.5	3.4%	38,153
1/07	4,743.0	124.0	2.6%	38,738
1/06	4,429.9	(10.1)	—	43,985
1/05	4,375.1	23.8	0.5%	46,241
Annual Growth	1.5%	58.8%	—	(5.4%)

2009 Year-End Financials

Debt ratio: 0.0%
Return on equity: 21.4%
Cash ($ mil.): 35
Current ratio: 1.69
Long-term debt ($ mil.): 0
No. of shares (mil.): 83
Dividends
  Yield: 0.0%
  Payout: —
Market value ($ mil.): 1,110

Stock History

NYSE: BIG

	STOCK PRICE ($) FY Close	P/E High/Low	PER SHARE ($) Earnings	Dividends	Book Value
1/09	13.45	19 7	1.85	0.00	9.38
1/08	17.36	23 8	1.55	0.00	7.73
1/07	25.93	24 11	1.11	0.00	13.68
1/06	13.37	— —	(0.09)	0.00	13.06
1/05	11.26	74 51	0.21	0.00	13.03
Annual Growth	4.5%	— —	72.3%	—	(7.9%)

BJ Services

BJ Services keeps the pressure on oil production. Along with Halliburton and Schlumberger, the company is one of the top providers of pressure-pumping services used to protect the oil formation. BJ Services stimulates production through acidizing, cementing, coiled tubing, fracturing, and sand control. Its oilfield services include casing and tubular services, process and pipeline services, production chemicals, completion tools, and completion fluids services. The company operates onshore and offshore in most of the world's major oil and gas producing regions. In a major industry consolidation, in 2009 oil field services giant Baker Hughes agreed to acquire BJ Services for $5.5 billion.

The acquisition promises to expand Baker Hughes' portfolio, adding pressure pumping into its product offering, giving it a stronger platform for international growth, and the ability to better compete for large integrated project contracts.

The bulk of BJ Services' revenues come from pressure pumping, which consists of cementing and stimulation services used during new oil and gas well completion. Its oilfield services include

tubular services (installing casing and tubing to protect the wellbore), pipe connection inspection, and specialty chemical treatments to reduce corrosion and other problems. Through its BJ Chemical Services subsidiary (formerly BJ Unichem), the company provides chemicals used for oil and gas applications such as corrosion and scale inhibitors, emulsion breakers, desalting solutions, microbiocides, and refinery chemicals.

Although BJ Services generates the majority of its revenue from the US and Canada, it also serves the international market through its foreign subsidiaries and joint venture companies. The company has grown internationally by expanding its operations into Central America, Southeast Asia, Africa, New Zealand, and Turkey.

In 2008 it acquired Canadian tool and equipment maker Innicore Subsurface Technologies, which they soon renamed BJ Tool Services. The acquisition allowed BJ Services to add a variety of downhole tools and services to its portfolio.

In 2007 BJ Services began operation of stimulation vessels in India and began fracturing work in Australia.

HISTORY

BJ Services was founded in 1872 as Byron Jackson Company, a pump and equipment maker for the farming and mining industries. The company owned 50% of oil field service firm International Cementers and adopted the Cementers name in 1940. It pioneered practical air-powered drilling and, later, high-pressure power cementing.

In 1951 the company bought out its partners and became BJ Services. Acquired in 1974 by Hughes Tool, it became BJ-Hughes in 1975. Ten years later, Dresser Industries, BJ-Hughes, and Hughes Tool formed a partnership, BJ-Titan Services, which lasted until 1989. The next year the company went public as BJ Services.

Hughes Tool veteran J. W. Stewart was appointed CEO of BJ Services in 1990. Acquisitions were key to BJ Services' growth that decade. In 1995 the company acquired rival Western Company of North America, the #4 pressure-pumping company in the US, and the next year it bought Nowsco Well Service, Canada's #1 pressure-pumping firm.

BJ Services bought Louisiana-based oil field equipment company Top Tool in 1998. The next year it bought another Canadian oil well services company, Fracmaster, and combined it with Nowsco to create Nowsco-Fracmaster, to handle the company's Canadian operations.

In 2001 BJ Services won a major offshore contract to service two North Sea oil fields for global oil giant TOTAL FINA ELF. The following year the company acquired OSCA, a major provider of oil and gas well completion fluids, services, and tools, from Great Lakes Chemical (now Chemtura).

EXECUTIVES

Chairman, President, and CEO: James W. Stewart, age 64
EVP and COO: David D. Dunlap, age 47
SVP Finance and CFO: Jeffrey E. (Jeff) Smith, age 46
VP and CIO: Paul F. Yust, age 55
VP, Treasurer, and Chief Tax Officer: Bret Wells, age 43
VP, Corporate Secretary, and General Counsel: Margaret B. Shannon, age 59
VP and Controller: L. Scott Biar, age 45
VP Human Resources: Susan E. Douget, age 48

VP International Pressure Pumping Services: Alasdair I. Buchanan, age 48
VP Technology and Logistics: Jeff Hibbeler, age 43
VP North America Pressure Pumping Services: Ronald F. Coleman, age 54
VP Human Resources: Susan E. Hill
Auditors: Deloitte & Touche LLP

LOCATIONS

HQ: BJ Services Company
  4601 Westway Park Blvd., Houston, TX 77092
Phone: 713-462-4239   **Fax:** 713-895-5851
Web: www.bjservices.com

2008 Sales

	$ mil.	% of total
US	3,104.9	57
Canada	522.1	10
Other countries	1,799.3	33
Total	**5,426.3**	**100**

PRODUCTS/OPERATIONS

2008 Sales

	$ mil.	% of total
Pressure pumping	4,472.7	82
Other oilfield services	953.6	18
Total	**5,426.3**	**100**

Selected Operations

Acidizing
Casing and tubular services
Cementing
Coiled tubing services
Downhole tools
Fracturing
Nitrogen services
Pipeline testing and commissioning services
Process and pipeline services
Sand control
Specialty chemical services

COMPETITORS

Baker Hughes
CE Franklin
Halliburton
Nabors Industries
Nabors Well Services
Pride International
Schlumberger
Smith International
TETRA Technologies
Tidewater Inc.
Weatherford International
Wenzel Downhole Tools

HISTORICAL FINANCIALS

Company Type: Public

Income Statement

FYE: September 30

	REVENUE ($ mil.)	NET INCOME ($ mil.)	NET PROFIT MARGIN	EMPLOYEES
9/08	5,426.3	609.4	11.2%	18,000
9/07	4,802.4	753.6	15.7%	16,700
9/06	4,367.9	804.6	18.4%	16,000
9/05	3,243.2	453.0	14.0%	13,600
9/04	2,601.0	361.0	13.9%	12,825
Annual Growth	20.2%	14.0%	—	8.8%

2008 Year-End Financials

Debt ratio: 14.5%
Return on equity: 19.4%
Cash ($ mil.): 150
Current ratio: 1.92
Long-term debt ($ mil.): 499
No. of shares (mil.): 292
Dividends
  Yield: 1.0%
  Payout: 9.7%
Market value ($ mil.): 5,588

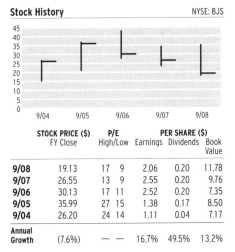

	STOCK PRICE ($) FY Close	P/E High/Low	PER SHARE ($) Earnings	Dividends	Book Value
9/08	19.13	17	9	2.06	0.20	11.78
9/07	26.55	13	9	2.55	0.20	9.76
9/06	30.13	17	11	2.52	0.20	7.35
9/05	35.99	27	15	1.38	0.17	8.50
9/04	26.20	24	14	1.11	0.04	7.17
Annual Growth	(7.6%)	—	—	16.7%	49.5%	13.2%

BJ's Wholesale Club

"Exclusive membership" has never been as common as it is at BJ's Wholesale Club. The firm is the nation's #3 membership warehouse club (behind leaders Costco and SAM'S CLUB) and #1 in New England, with nearly 10 million members and about 180 locations in 15 states, mostly along the Eastern Seaboard. BJ's stores sell some 7,300 products, including canned, fresh, and frozen foods. (Food accounts for about 60% of sales.) It also sells general merchandise, including apparel, housewares, office equipment, small appliances, and gas. BJ's also sells general merchandise, insurance, and other services through its Web site. Unlike its major rivals, BJ's targets individual retail customers rather than small businesses.

In early 2009 COO Laura Sen was named CEO after chairman Herb Zarkin stepped down. As Sen takes the helm during the global economic downturn, BJ's expects its overall sales to flatten because of increased price competition, curbed discretionary spending, and the prospect of deflation. Despite this forecast, the company looks to strengthen its position in food sales heading into 2010. It aims to be customers' first stop for groceries, offering smaller package sizes and lower prices than supermarkets. BJ's is also diversifying its selection with organic produce, fresh and frozen appetizers, desserts, and restaurant-branded items.

Slumping sales at BJ's prompted management changes and a re-evaluation of the chain's merchandising and pricing strategies. In 2007 Zarkin, who led BJ's until 1997, returned as the company's CEO. He trimmed the number of brands and sizes BJ's carried to free up shelf space for a wider assortment of new products, including more luxury items. Fierce price competition between Costco and SAM'S CLUB also pushed BJ's to cut its prices. The changes since Zarkin's arrival helped to boost sales for BJ's. Plus, the economy has brought more traffic to discount warehouses as shoppers pinch pennies. Bucking the trend among retailers to retrench in the face of a worsening economy, BJ's plans to expand by adding six to eight stores in existing markets in 2009.

Like its rivals, BJ's requires membership to its warehouses that span about 110,000 sq. ft. (although it does operate about 20 warehouses that average a mere 70,000 sq. ft. in small cities). To distinguish itself, BJ's employs a liberal membership policy and has added other consumer-minded accoutrements, such as brake and muffler service, food courts with brand-name fast-food restaurants, one-hour photo processing, and optical stores.

It is also upgrading many of its clubs. Planned improvements include upgrading decor, moving expanded health and beauty aids departments to the front of the stores, and improving presentation in its fresh food departments. BJ's operates about 100 gas stations and is planning to add more.

Wellington Management Company owns about 15% of BJ's common stock.

HISTORY

In 1984, with Price Club (now part of Costco) thriving and Wal-Mart Stores' SAM'S CLUB beginning to dot the horizon, Zayre Corp. opened BJ's Wholesale Club, New England's first warehouse club. Zayre, a Massachusetts-based chain of discount department stores, placed the first store in Medford, Massachusetts, and named the operation after top executive Mervin Weich's wife, Barbara Jane. In return for an annual membership fee, customers could buy a mix of goods priced at around 8%-10% above what they cost BJ's.

Zayre's bought the California-based HomeClub chain of home improvement warehouses in 1986 and combined HomeClub with BJ's to form Zayre's warehouse division. Weich was replaced by John Levy the next year.

By mid-1987 BJ's had 15 stores and more than half a billion dollars in annual sales. Over the next few years, the chain expanded into 11 states in the Northeast and Midwest, including stores in the Chicago area. Despite the chain's rapid growth — or because of it — BJ's failed to post profits.

A debt-burdened Zayre began shifting its focus to its moderate-priced chains (including T.J. Maxx and Hit or Miss) during the late 1980s. In 1989 it spun off its warehouse division to shareholders and renamed it Waban (after a nearby Massachusetts town). Zayre was renamed TJX Companies.

Waban cracked the $1 billion sales mark in 1990. During the early 1990s the company moved into the midwestern US, but its stores failed to thrive. In 1991 it closed one of its four Chicago stores and in 1992 turned the other three into HomeBase stores.

Also during those years, BJ's added fresh meats, bakery items, optical departments, and travel agents to its stores. In 1993 Herbert Zarkin, BJ's president, replaced Levy as CEO. That year BJ's had 52 stores and 2.6 million members; its sales reached $2 billion. A new inventory scanning system implemented by the company helped cut costs.

Once again, however, strong sales didn't add up to big profits. In 1993 BJ's per-store profits were far below those of its competitors, primarily due to intense competition and a regional recession. Two years later it became the first warehouse club to accept MasterCard and issued its own store-brand version of that card. BJ's added nine stores in 1995, 10 the next year, and four in 1997.

Meanwhile, Waban was struggling with HomeBase, which was still failing to show a profit due to restructuring charges. In 1997 Waban spun off BJ's Wholesale Club — its star performer — to keep it from being undervalued; Waban then changed its name to HomeBase. Also in 1997 John Nugent was named BJ's CEO. BJ's began adding gas stations at several of its northeastern stores in 1998.

In September 2002 CEO Nugent resigned and was replaced by Michael T. Wedge, formerly an executive vice president of the company. In November two clubs in Columbus, Ohio, and a third in Florida shut down. BJ's entered the Atlanta market in 2002 with four clubs there.

In June 2005 BJ's agreed to settle charges brought by the Federal Trade Commission alleging the company failed to protect information on thousands of its customers. Without admitting guilt the company agreed to implement new security procedures and to periodic audits of those procedures.

In 2006 Mike Wedge resigned as CEO after four years in that position. He was succeeded by chairman Herb Zarkin. In February 2007 BJ's closed its two ProFoods Restaurant Supply stores and discontinued in-store pharmacy sales.

Zarkin stepped down as CEO in early 2009, but retained the chairman's title. President and COO Laura Sen succeeded Zarkin as chief executive of BJ's.

EXECUTIVES

Chairman: Herbert J. (Herb) Zarkin, age 70, $4,328,400 total compensation
President, CEO, and Director: Laura J. Sen, age 52, $2,623,994 total compensation
EVP Club Operations: Thomas F. Gallagher, age 57, $1,744,021 total compensation
EVP and CFO: Frank D. Forward, age 54, $1,979,793 total compensation
SVP and CIO: John A. Polizzi
EVP Merchandising and Logistics: Christina M. (Chris) Neppl, age 48
EVP, General Counsel, and Secretary: Lon F. Povich, age 49, $1,260,972 total compensation
SVP and Director Logistics: Peter Amalfi
SVP and Treasurer: Arthur T. Silk Jr.
SVP and General Manager General Merchandise: Mark S. Titlebaum, age 45
SVP and Director of Marketing and E-Commerce: Michael P. Atkinson
SVP and General Merchandising Manager Consumables and Perishables: Bruce L. Graham, age 56
SVP and Director Sales Operations: Kenneth A. Hayes
SVP Finance: Robert Eddy, age 36
SVP and Director Field Operations: Cornel Catuna
VP Public Relations: Julie Summers
Auditors: PricewaterhouseCoopers LLP

LOCATIONS

HQ: BJ's Wholesale Club, Inc.
1 Mercer Rd., Natick, MA 01760
Phone: 508-651-7400   **Fax:** 508-651-6114
Web: www.bjs.com

2009 Locations

	No.
New York	34
Florida	28
Massachusetts	20
New Jersey	19
Pennsylvania	13
Connecticut	11
Virginia	10
Maryland	9
Georgia	8
North Carolina	8
New Hampshire	6
Ohio	6
Rhode Island	3
Delaware	3
Maine	2
Total	**180**

PRODUCTS/OPERATIONS

2009 Sales

	% of total
Food	64
General merchandise	36
Total	**100**

2009 Sales

	$ mil.	% of total
Merchandise & services	9,802	98
Membership fees	177	2
Other	48	—
Total	**10,027**	**100**

Selected Merchandise

Food
  Baked goods
  Canned goods
  Dairy products
  Dry grocery items
  Fresh produce
  Frozen foods
  Meat and fish
General Merchandise
  Apparel
  Auto accessories
  Books
  Computer software
  Consumer electronics
  Greeting cards
  Hardware
  Health and beauty aids
  Household paper products and cleaning supplies
  Housewares
  Jewelry
  Office equipment
  Office supplies
  Seasonal items
  Small appliances
  Tires
  Toys

COMPETITORS

Aurora Wholesalers
Best Buy
Big Lots
Costco Wholesale
Family Dollar Stores
Hannaford Bros.
IGA
J. C. Penney
Kmart
Office Depot
Pathmark Stores
Penn Traffic
Sam's Club
Sears
Shaw's
Staples
Stop & Shop
Target
Wal-Mart
Weis Markets

HISTORICAL FINANCIALS

Company Type: Public

Income Statement

FYE: Saturday nearest January 31

	REVENUE ($ mil.)	NET INCOME ($ mil.)	NET PROFIT MARGIN	EMPLOYEES
1/09	10,027.4	134.6	1.3%	22,000
1/08	9,005.0	122.9	1.4%	20,800
1/07	8,480.3	72.0	0.8%	21,200
1/06	7,949.9	128.5	1.6%	20,300
1/05	7,375.3	114.4	1.6%	19,600
Annual Growth	**8.0%**	**4.1%**	**—**	**2.9%**

2009 Year-End Financials

Debt ratio: 1.1%	No. of shares (mil.): 56
Return on equity: 13.7%	Dividends
Cash ($ mil.): 51	Yield: 0.0%
Current ratio: 1.18	Payout: —
Long-term debt ($ mil.): 10	Market value ($ mil.): 1,592

Stock History

NYSE: BJ

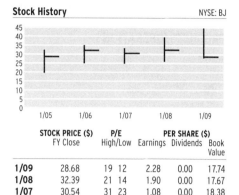

	STOCK PRICE ($) FY Close	P/E High/Low		PER SHARE ($) Earnings	Dividends	Book Value
1/09	28.68	19	12	2.28	0.00	17.74
1/08	32.39	21	14	1.90	0.00	17.67
1/07	30.54	31	23	1.08	0.00	18.38
1/06	32.14	19	14	1.87	0.00	18.30
1/05	28.61	20	12	1.63	0.00	16.92
Annual Growth	**0.1%**	**—**	**—**	**8.8%**	**—**	**1.2%**

Black & Decker

Other toolmakers would like to borrow the power tools, hardware, and home improvement products that Black & Decker has in its shed. Black & Decker is one of the nation's top makers of power tools and accessories, produced mainly under the DEWALT and Black & Decker names. It also makes electric lawn and garden tools, plumbing products (Price Pfister), specialty fastening and assembly systems, security hardware (Kwikset), and cleaning and lighting products (Dustbuster, SnakeLight, Scumbuster). Black & Decker markets its products in more than 100 countries; its largest customers include Home Depot and Lowe's. The company purchased power products maker Vector Products in 2006 for $160 million.

Black & Decker has sorted its business units, more or less, by products and services. It operates three business segments: Power Tools and Accessories (72% of 2008 sales), Hardware and Home Improvement (15%), and Fastening and Assembly Systems (11%).

Black & Decker in 2009 expects to see its revenue dip. Based on a stalled US housing market (that weighed down product sales in 2008) and woes among retailers, the company anticipates that certain retailers may reduce their inventory levels. If so, Black & Decker would expect a double-digit sales decline in 2009.

Thankfully, for the company, sales decreases in its North American business have been offset by a rise in revenue in Europe. Since 2006 Black & Decker has boosted its presence in Europe and now generates 25% of its revenue from the region. During the same time frame, however, the company has steadily logged lower sales in North America, from 64% in 2006 to 60% in 2007 and

55% in 2008. The company attributes a weakness in North American in both the industrial and automotive businesses for its sales declines there. Revenue for the same product segments in Europe rose in 2008. In Asia, sales grew as well.

HISTORY

When Duncan Black and Alonzo Decker opened The Black & Decker Manufacturing Company in Baltimore in 1910 with a $1,200 investment, they began a partnership that would last more than 40 years. Starting with milk-bottle-cap machines and candy dippers, the partners introduced their first major tool in 1916 — a portable half-inch electric drill with patented pistol grip and trigger switch, now on display at the Smithsonian Institution.

In 1917 the company built its first manufacturing plant, which would become its headquarters, in rural Towson, Maryland. Sales passed $1 million in 1919, and the company added a 20,000-sq.-ft. factory. Black & Decker quickly established itself in international markets with sales representatives in Australia, Japan, and Russia that year, and it built a manufacturing plant in England in 1939.

The founders led Black & Decker until they died — Black in 1951 (a year before the company went public) and Decker in 1956; family members took control of operations until the 1970s. Alonzo Decker Jr., the co-founder's only son, was president from 1960 to 1972, chief executive from 1964 to 1975, and chairman from 1968 to 1979, remaining on the board of directors until 2001. (It was Decker Jr. who introduced power tools for home use, and he designed the first cordless drill in the 1960s. He died in March 2002.)

The company acquired the General Electric (GE) housewares operations in 1984, replacing GE's trademark with the Black & Decker hexagonal trademark on such items as toaster ovens, can openers, and irons. Nolan Archibald became Black & Decker's CEO in 1986 and began a major restructuring. Renamed The Black & Decker Corporation, it closed five plants, streamlined distribution systems, consolidated overseas facilities, and cut payroll 10%. Earnings doubled in 1987.

Two years later Black & Decker acquired megaconglomerate Emhart (formerly American Hardware), but the purchase caused earnings to fall. To service its debt, the firm sold off pieces of its acquisition, including Emhart's Bostik adhesives, True Temper Hardware, and North American Mallory Controls.

Black & Decker expanded its international presence in 1995, beginning joint operations in India and China and introducing DEWALT power tools to Europe and Latin America.

The company sold its sluggish household products operations in the US and Latin America (except Brazil) to small-appliance maker Windmere-Durable Holdings (now Applica Incorporated) in 1998. (It kept the more profitable lighting and cleaning lines.) Black & Decker also sold True Temper Sports to Cornerstone Equity Investors and sold Emhart Glass to Bucher Holdings of Switzerland. The sales and restructuring eliminated about 5,000 jobs and allowed the company to focus on its DEWALT brand. The company posted a loss in 1998 due to restructuring and $900 million in goodwill charges.

In 1999 heir apparent and EVP Joseph Galli left; GE veteran Paul McBride replaced him. The company announced in 2002 that it would undergo restructuring that included cutting 2,400 jobs, closing several plants, and transferring some operations from the US and the UK to Mexico, China, and Central Europe.

Also in 2002 the company entered into a cooperative agreement with Tokyo-based Hitachi Koki in their power tools business. That year Home Depot decided to stop selling Black & Decker's plumbing products east of the Rockies.

In 2003 Black & Decker acquired the Baldwin Hardware and Weiser Lock businesses from Masco for about $275 million. Also that year the company closed its plant in Easton, Maryland, eliminating 1,300 jobs there, and leaving the company with virtually no manufacturing presence in its home state.

Black & Decker sold Nemef, a Dutch maker of locks and cylinders, and Corbin, an Italian distributor of cylinders, locks, and padlocks, to ASSA ABLOY in January 2004.

The toolmaker acquired Pentair's Tools Group, which includes Delta, DeVilbiss Air Power, FLEX, Oldham Saw, and Porter-Cable, in 2004. The purchased entity was folded into Black & Decker's Power Tools and Accessories segment. FLEX, the major European component of the Porter-Cable and Delta Tools Group, was sold in November 2005.

In September 2008 Black & Decker acquired Spiralock, a manufacturer of threaded industrial fasteners with sales of approximately $15 million.

EXECUTIVES

Chairman, President, and CEO: Nolan D. Archibald, age 65, $13,653,766 total compensation
SVP and CFO: Stephen F. Reeves, age 49, $1,377,234 total compensation
SVP; President, Worldwide Power Tools and Accessories: Michael D. Mangan, age 52, $4,233,455 total compensation
SVP Human Resources and Corporate Initiatives: Paul F. McBride, age 53
SVP and General Counsel: Charles E. Fenton, age 60, $2,987,109 total compensation
Group VP; President, Industrial Products Group Power Tools and Accessories: John W. Schiech, age 50, $2,692,859 total compensation
Group VP; President, Consumer Products Group Power Tools and Accessories: Bruce W. Brooks, age 44
Group VP; President, Hardware and Home Improvement: James T. (Jim) Caudill, age 41
VP and Controller: Christina M. McMullen, age 53
VP; President, North America Power Tools and Accessories: Les H. Ireland, age 44
VP; President, Asia/Pacific, Power Tools and Accessories: Bhupinder S. (Ben) Sihota, age 50
VP; President Latin America Power Tools and Accessories: Jaime A. Ramirez, age 41
VP; President Europe, Middle East, and Africa Power Tools and Accessories: John H. A. Wyatt, age 50
VP; VP Global Product Development Industrial Products Group Power Tools and Accessories: William S. Taylor
VP; President, Fastening and Assembly Systems: Michael A. (Mike) Tyll, age 52
VP and Corporate Secretary: Natalie A. Shields, age 52
VP Investor Relations and Treasurer: Mark M. Rothleitner, age 50
Auditors: Ernst & Young LLP

LOCATIONS

HQ: The Black & Decker Corporation
701 E. Joppa Rd., Towson, MD 21286
Phone: 410-716-3900   **Fax:** 410-716-2933
Web: www.bdk.com

2008 Sales

	$ mil.	% of total
US	3,358.6	55
Europe	1,516.0	25
Canada	382.3	6
Other regions	829.2	14
Total	**6,086.1**	**100**

PRODUCTS/OPERATIONS

2008 Sales

	$ mil.	% of total
Power tools & accessories	4,371.6	72
Hardware & home improvement	896.6	15
Fastening & assembly systems	700.4	11
Adjustments	117.5	2
Total	**6,086.1**	**100**

2008 Sales by Product Group

	$ mil.	% of total
Consumer & industrial power tools & product service	3,236.1	53
Fastening & assembly systems	740.0	12
Security hardware	649.9	11
Consumer & industrial accessories	452.0	8
Lawn & garden products	377.9	6
Cleaning, automotive, lighting & household products	321.0	5
Plumbing products	309.2	5
Total	**6,086.1**	**100**

COMPETITORS

ASSA ABLOY
Atlas Copco
Cooper Industries
Danaher
Eaton
Electrolux
Emerson Electric
Energizer Holdings
Exmark Manufacturing
Fortune Brands
Hitachi
Illinois Tool Works
Ingersoll-Rand
Jacuzzi Brands
Kohler
Makita
Masco
Panasonic Corp
Robert Bosch LLC
Royal Appliance
Snap-on
Stanley Works
Textron
Toro
Trane Inc.

HISTORICAL FINANCIALS

Company Type: Public

Income Statement

FYE: December 31

	REVENUE ($ mil.)	NET INCOME ($ mil.)	NET PROFIT MARGIN	EMPLOYEES
12/08	6,086.1	293.6	4.8%	22,100
12/07	6,563.2	518.1	7.9%	25,000
12/06	6,447.3	486.1	7.5%	25,500
12/05	6,523.7	543.9	8.3%	27,200
12/04	5,398.4	456.0	8.4%	26,200
Annual Growth	**3.0%**	**(10.4%)**	**—**	**(4.2%)**

2008 Year-End Financials

Debt ratio: 128.4%
Return on equity: 22.7%
Cash ($ mil.): 278
Current ratio: 1.75
Long-term debt ($ mil.): 1,445

No. of shares (mil.): 60
Dividends
  Yield: 4.0%
  Payout: 34.9%
Market value ($ mil.): 2,516

Stock History

NYSE: BDK

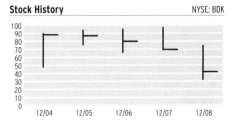

	STOCK PRICE ($) FY Close	P/E High/Low		PER SHARE ($) Earnings	Dividends	Book Value
12/08	41.81	15	7	4.82	1.68	18.69
12/07	69.65	12	9	7.85	1.68	24.24
12/06	79.97	14	10	6.55	1.52	19.34
12/05	86.96	14	11	6.69	1.12	25.32
12/04	88.33	16	9	5.59	0.84	25.91
Annual Growth	**(17.1%)**	**—**	**—**	**(3.6%)**	**18.9%**	**(7.8%)**

Blockbuster Inc.

When it comes to renting movies, this company is a Blockbuster. Blockbuster is the world's largest video rental chain, with more than 7,100 company-owned or franchised stores in more than 20 countries (about 60% are in the US). The chain rents more than 1 billion videos, DVDs, and video games at its Blockbuster Video outlets each year. Customers also can make rentals, purchases, and watch instant downloads through its Web site, Blockbuster Online, which competes head to head with the likes of Netflix. It is closing hundreds of stores and has announced plans to divest its foreign operations (about a third of revenues) and focus on North American business as it navigates toward a digital future.

In early 2009 law firm Kirkland & Ellis stepped in to rescue the sinking video store chain amid the swelling recession. The law firm is working to secure financing that will help keep Blockbuster afloat and avoid filing for bankruptcy protection. Investment bank Rothschild is also advising the company on its restructuring plans. To that end, the chain is accelerating its store closing program. As many as 960 stores (20% of its store base) may be closed and another 250 reduced in size by the end of 2010, as Blockbuster struggles to defend its market from rivals Netflix and Redbox.

Blockbuster is struggling to make the transition from a store-based distribution system to a multi-channel approach to content delivery that includes by-mail, vending, or digital download options. To that end, in January 2009 it created an executive level position to lead its digital entertainment division. In July 2009 the digital entertainment division announced a partnership with Samsung Electronics America that will allow owners of Samsung's next generation high-definition TVs to rent movies with the press of a button on the remote control. The on-demand service is expected to launch in the fall of 2009. An new alliance with TiVo aims to develop and provide a video-on-demand service.

Taking a page from competitor Redbox's strategy book, the company began installing Blockbuster Express-branded DVD kiosks for video rentals via a deal with ATM manufacturer NCR.

The vending machine-style kiosks are set up in supermarkets, convenience stores, and other retail locations. In an effort to expand its online offerings, Blockbuster has announced a partnership with digital media firm Sonic Solutions in 2009. The two companies are working together to offer movies-on-demand for PCs, cell phones, TVs connected to the Internet, and other electronic devices. The companies plan to have streaming and progressive download options available when the service launches. In a earlier move to explore alternative distribution methods, in 2007 Blockbuster acquired Movielink, an online movie-downloading company owned by major Hollywood studios.

In response to the growing popularity of Netflix, Blockbuster launched its Blockbuster Online service where members can rent unlimited DVDs online and have them delivered via postal mail for a monthly fee. Netflix filed suit against Blockbuster in 2006, claiming the video giant's online service violates Netflix's patent on such a video rental system. The two settled their differences in a confidential deal in 2007.)

Blockbuster is also pushing for improved revenue-sharing agreements with film studios and videogame publishers.

Director and activist investor Carl Icahn owns 16% of Blockbuster's Class A shares and nearly 8% of its double-voting Class B shares.

HISTORY

After selling his computing services company, David Cook turned to operating flashy, computerized video rental stores, opening his first in 1985 and adopting the moniker Blockbuster Entertainment in 1986. Entrepreneur Wayne Huizenga took over in 1987, injecting $18 million into Blockbuster and buying the company outright by the end of the year. Huizenga's acquisitions rapidly expanded the number of Blockbuster stores to 130. Other acquisitions (including Major Video, a 175-store chain, and Erol's, the US's third-largest video chain) increased the number of stores to 1,500 by 1990.

Blockbuster became the largest video renter in the UK in 1992 through the purchase of 875-unit Cityvision. It also branched into music retailing that year when it bought the Sound Warehouse and Music Plus chains and created Blockbuster Music. The following year it acquired a majority stake in Spelling Entertainment, then was itself acquired in 1994 by Viacom for $8.4 billion. Viacom took Spelling Entertainment under its wing and formed a division for its new chain of video stores called Blockbuster Entertainment Group. Following the deal, Huizenga left the company.

Over the next few years, Blockbuster experienced a rash of poor business decisions and executive departures, starting with Steven Berrard (CEO after Viacom's 1994 takeover), who resigned in 1996 to head Huizenga's used-car operations. Wal-Mart veteran Bill Fields replaced him and started promoting the retailer as a "neighborhood entertainment center," selling videotapes (instead of renting them), books, CDs, gift items, and music. The company moved its headquarters from Florida to Dallas in 1997, a move many employees refused to make.

Fields resigned later that year and John Antioco replaced him as chairman and CEO. Antioco's reign began with Viacom taking a $300 million charge related to the turmoil at Blockbuster. He immediately started unraveling many of Fields' efforts, especially his focus on non-rental operations. Antioco also set the video rental industry on

its ear in 1997 by forcing the movie studios into a revenue-sharing agreement that replaced the standard practice of buying rental copies for as much as $120 each. By 1999 Viacom spun off a minority stake in Blockbuster.

In 2004 the company launched a $700 million takeover bid for rival Hollywood Entertainment. Hollywood refused to consider the offer and eventually agreed to a purchase by its smaller rival, Movie Gallery, in 2005. In response, Blockbuster launched a hostile bid for Hollywood, raising its offer to $1.3 billion. Hollywood's directors rejected the Blockbuster offer and urged their shareholders to do the same. Blockbuster later abandoned the takeover effort. Movie Gallery completed its purchase of Hollywood later that year, creating a strong #2 in the industry.

Trying to sway customers, Blockbuster eliminated late fees on all of its traditional, in-store rentals in the US and Canada in a promotional plan in 2005. It heavily marketed the plan to the tune of about $60 million and lost more than $500 million in late fee revenues. Shortly after its implementation, however, many Blockbuster franchisors dropped the promotion and returned to charging late fees.

In July 2007 James Keyes, formerly president and CEO of convenience store operator 7-Eleven, joined Blockbuster as chairman and chief executive. He succeeded John Antioco. In September the company laid off 145 employees nationwide, including workers at its corporate headquarters..

In an ill-fated bid to diversify beyond the movie rental industry, Blockbuster in 2008 made a $1.3 billion offer to buy now-defunct Circuit City Stores. The company withdrew the bid in July, however, after reviewing Circuit City's books and announcing that the deal didn't make sense due to market conditions.

EXECUTIVES

Chairman and CEO: James W. (Jim) Keyes, age 54, $8,413,033 total compensation
EVP and CFO: Thomas M. Casey, age 50, $2,447,448 total compensation
CIO: Phillip Keith (Keith) Morrow, $1,054,104 total compensation
EVP, General Counsel, and Secretary: Eric H. Peterson, age 48, $1,391,721 total compensation
SVP Merchandising, Distribution, and Logistics: David (Dave) Podeschi, $1,009,635 total compensation
SVP Digital Entertainment: Kevin Lewis, age 37
VP Studio Relations and New Media: Jeffrey Calman
VP Global Franchise and International Corporate Operations: James W. (Jimmy) Whatley
Senior Director Corporate Communications: Randy Hargrove
Director Investor Relations: Kellie Nugent
Auditors: PricewaterhouseCoopers LLP

LOCATIONS

HQ: Blockbuster Inc.
1201 Elm St., Dallas, TX 75270
Phone: 214-854-3000   **Fax:** 214-854-3677
Web: www.blockbuster.com

2008 Sales

	$ mil.	% of total
Domestic	3,590.8	68
International	1,697.1	32
Total	**5,287.9**	**100**

PRODUCTS/OPERATIONS

2008 Sales

	$ mil.	% of total
Rental revenues	3,865.8	73
Merchandise sales	1,389.4	26
Other revenues	32.7	1
Total	**5,287.9**	**100**

COMPETITORS

Amazon.com
Apple Inc.
Barnes & Noble
Best Buy
Borders Group
CinemaNow
Comcast
DIRECTV
DISH Network Corporation
GameStop
Hastings Entertainment
iN DEMAND
Kroger
Movie Gallery
Netflix
Redbox
Starz Entertainment
Target
Time Warner Cable
Trans World Entertainment
Wal-Mart

HISTORICAL FINANCIALS

Company Type: Public

Income Statement

FYE: December 31

	REVENUE ($ mil.)	NET INCOME ($ mil.)	NET PROFIT MARGIN	EMPLOYEES
12/08	5,287.9	(374.1)	—	58,561
12/07	5,542.4	(73.8)	—	59,643
12/06	5,523.5	54.7	1.0%	67,300
12/05	5,864.4	(588.1)	—	72,600
12/04	6,053.2	(1,248.8)	—	84,300
Annual Growth	**(3.3%)**	**—**	**—**	**(8.7%)**

2008 Year-End Financials

Debt ratio: 950.7%	No. of shares (mil.): 194
Return on equity: —	Dividends
Cash ($ mil.): 155	Yield: 0.0%
Current ratio: 1.00	Payout: —
Long-term debt ($ mil.): 611	Market value ($ mil.): 245

Stock History

NYSE: BBI

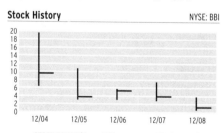

	STOCK PRICE ($) FY Close	P/E High/Low		PER SHARE ($) Earnings	Dividends	Book Value
12/08	1.26	—	—	(2.01)	0.00	1.10
12/07	3.90	—	—	(0.45)	0.00	3.38
12/06	5.29	24	14	0.23	0.00	3.82
12/05	3.75	—	—	(3.20)	0.04	3.25
12/04	9.54	—	—	(6.89)	0.08	5.48
Annual Growth	**(39.7%)**	**—**	**—**	**—**	**—**	**(33.0%)**

BMC Software

BMC doesn't stand for Business Mismanagement Cure, but it could. BMC Software is a leading provider of enterprise management software used for a variety of functions, including recovery and storage management, business process scheduling and integration, service management, and application and database performance management. BMC provides tools designed to manage enterprise servers, speed up and monitor databases, eliminate unplanned outages, and recover system assets. It also provides professional services such as consulting and systems integration. BMC sells directly and through channel partners worldwide.

The company is made up of two primary units: Enterprise Service Management (ESM) and Mainframe Service Management (MSM). ESM primarily provides software for service assurance and automation. Accounting for about half of BMC's revenues in fiscal 2009, ESM also encompasses BMC's professional services unit. MSM provides tools for mainframe database management and monitoring. Geographically, the company's sales are roughly split between US and international customers.

BMC continues to expand past its core expertise in mainframe management and utility software, with an emphasis on its ESM products. The company augmented its ESM offerings with the acquisition of data center automation specialist BladeLogic for about $850 million in 2008. The BladeLogic purchase provided BMC with application release managment, configuration automation and compliance, and server provisioning tools.

The company supports both mainframe and distributed computer systems. It saw its revenues from MSM products drop slightly in fiscal 2009, but mainframe management remains an important part of its business. BMC helps companies in such industries as financial services, telecommunications, and transportation — many of which rely heavily on mainframe computing — to integrate data stored on mainframes with business services.

BMC maintains technology alliances with such companies as Dell, EMC, Sun Microsystems, and Symantec. Its systems integration partners include Accenture, BearingPoint, EDS, and Wipro.

HISTORY

BMC was launched in 1980 by Scott Boulett, John Moores, and Dan Cloer, with their initials giving the company its name. Its first product was designed to improve communications between IBM databases with connected terminals and PCs.

Through an aggressive telemarketing campaign boasted of internally as "telemuscle," the company's utility software was snapped up by a chunk of the *FORTUNE* 500, which used it to boost the performance of wall-sized IBM mainframes and database systems. The company started an international expansion in 1984, opening an office in Germany. BMC went public in 1988.

Two years later COO Max Watson replaced Richard Hosley as president and CEO. Hosley stayed on as vice chairman until 1992, when Watson assumed that title as well. Moores, the only founder who held a position with the company, resigned as chairman that year.

In the early 1990s Watson navigated BMC's transition toward networked PC systems as corporate customers began eschewing mainframes. In 1994 BMC bought PATROL Software, adding a network-based performance optimization product that would later become one of the company's flagship lines.

Using acquisitions to expand, the company in 1996 forged an alliance with Sun Microsystems to develop platform management software. The company bought software specialist DataTools in 1997 and system performance analysis software specialist BGS Systems in 1998.

In 1999 the company doubled its size when it bought rival management software maker Boole & Babbage for about $900 million and Israeli software developer New Dimension Software for about $675 million. Along with these acquisitions came a corporate reinvention that included a new logo and revamped product divisions.

In 2000 BMC increased its e-commerce offerings by acquiring Evity, a provider of Web transaction monitoring services. Early in 2001, Watson brought Robert Beauchamp on board, passing the president and CEO titles to him. Watson later stepped down as chairman as well, and was replaced by Garland Cupp.

The next year the company restructured, trimming its workforce by about 15%.

In 2003 the company purchased the Remedy unit of troubled software provider Peregrine Systems for about $350 million. After investing heavily in developing its storage management software line, BMC exited that business. BMC also expanded its business service management product line through the purchase of IT Masters for about $43 million. It acquired McAfee's (formerly Network Associates) Magic Solutions business unit in 2004.

Also in 2004 BMC acquired Marimba for about $239 million. The following year the company purchased Calendra, a provider of workflow and directory management software, and OpenNetwork Technologies, a maker of Web access management applications.

The company acquired Identify Software, a developer of application problem resolution software, for about $150 million in cash in 2006. The purchase of Identify augmented BMC's transaction management offerings. In 2007 BMC purchased business services management software providers ProactiveNet and Emprisa Networks.

EXECUTIVES

Chairman, President and CEO:
Robert E. (Bob) Beauchamp, age 49,
$9,703,758 total compensation
SVP and CFO: Stephen B. (Steve) Solcher, age 49
VP, Controller, and Chief Accounting Officer:
T. Cory Bleuer, age 40
SVP Worldwide Sales and Services: John D. McMahon,
age 53
SVP Strategy and Corporate Development:
James W. (Jim) Grant, age 60,
$3,294,724 total compensation
SVP, General Counsel, and Secretary: Denise M. Clolery,
age 53
SVP Administration: Michael A. (Mike) Vescuso, age 65
SVP Business Operations: Steve Goddard
President, Enterprise Service Management:
Dev Ittycheria, age 42
President, Mainframe Service Management:
William D. (Bill) Miller, age 59
Director Global Communications: Mark Stouse
Auditors: Ernst & Young LLP

LOCATIONS

HQ: BMC Software, Inc.
2101 CityWest Blvd., Houston, TX 77042
Phone: 713-918-8800   **Fax:** 713-918-8000
Web: www.bmc.com

2009 Sales

	$ mil.	% of total
US	980.0	52
Other countries	891.9	48
Total	**1,871.9**	**100**

PRODUCTS/OPERATIONS

2009 Sales

	$ mil.	% of total
Enterprise Service Management	986.2	53
Mainframe Service Management	741.3	39
Professional services	144.4	8
Total	**1,871.9**	**100**

2009 Sales

	$ mil.	% of total
Maintenance	1,017.8	54
Licenses	709.7	38
Professional services	144.4	8
Total	**1,871.9**	**100**

Selected Products

Enterprise Service Management (ESM)
  Application management
  Database management
  Infrastructure management
  Service management
  Security management
  Transaction management
Mainframe Service Management (MSM)
  Data management
  Infrastructure management
  Enterprise scheduling and output management

COMPETITORS

CA, Inc.
Compuware
Hewlett-Packard
IBM
McAfee
Microsoft
Oracle
SAP
Sun Microsystems

HISTORICAL FINANCIALS

Company Type: Public

Income Statement

FYE: March 31

	REVENUE ($ mil.)	NET INCOME ($ mil.)	NET PROFIT MARGIN	EMPLOYEES
3/09	1,871.9	238.1	12.7%	5,800
3/08	1,731.6	313.6	18.1%	5,800
3/07	1,580.4	215.9	13.7%	6,000
3/06	1,498.4	102.0	6.8%	6,200
3/05	1,463.0	75.3	5.1%	6,905
Annual Growth	**6.4%**	**33.3%**	**—**	**(4.3%)**

2009 Year-End Financials

Debt ratio: 29.9%
Return on equity: 23.3%
Cash ($ mil.): 1,023
Current ratio: 1.17
Long-term debt ($ mil.): 314

No. of shares (mil.): 184
Dividends
  Yield: 0.0%
  Payout: —
Market value ($ mil.): 6,072

EXECUTIVES

Chairman, President, and CEO:
W. James (Jim) McNerney Jr., age 60,
$18,979,604 total compensation
EVP and CFO: James A. Bell, age 60,
$5,905,119 total compensation
VP Information Technology and CIO: John Hinshaw
VP Government Operations and Chief Lobbyist:
David H. Morrison
Chief Investment Officer: Andrew Ward, age 38
SVP; President, Boeing Capital Corporation:
Walter E. (Walt) Skowronski
SVP, International Relations:
Thomas R. (Tom) Pickering
SVP Public Policy: Timothy J. (Tim) Keating, age 47
SVP Business Development and Strategy:
Michael J. (Mike) Cave, age 48
SVP Human Resources and Administration:
Richard D. (Rick) Stephens, age 56
SVP Engineering, Operations and Technology:
John J. Tracy, age 54
SVP and General Counsel: J. Michael Luttig, age 54,
$2,798,962 total compensation
SVP Communications: Thomas J. (Tom) Downey, age 44
SVP, Office of Internal Governance:
Wanda Denson-Low, age 52
VP, Community and Education Relations:
Anne E. Roosevelt
VP Finance and Treasurer: David Dohnalek, age 51
VP International Corporate Communications:
Charlie Miller, age 53
President and CEO, Boeing Commercial Airplanes:
James F. (Jim) Albaugh, age 59,
$5,594,299 total compensation
Auditors: Deloitte & Touche LLP

LOCATIONS

HQ: The Boeing Company
100 N. Riverside Plaza, Chicago, IL 60606
Phone: 312-544-2000   **Fax:** 312-544-2082
Web: www.boeing.com

2008 Sales

	$ mil.	% of total
Americas		
US	37,132	61
Canada	1,849	3
Latin America, Caribbean & other	1,656	3
Asia/Pacific		
China	2,404	4
Other mainland countries	7,913	13
Oceania	989	1
Europe	5,992	10
Middle East	2,568	4
Africa	406	1
Total	**60,909**	**100**

PRODUCTS/OPERATIONS

2008 Sales

	$ mil.	% of total
Commercial Airplanes	28,263	46
Integrated Defense Systems		
Boeing Military Aircraft	13,492	22
Network & Space Systems	11,338	18
Global Services & Support	7,217	12
Boeing Capital Corporation	703	1
Other	567	1
Adjustments	(671)	—
Total	**60,909**	**100**

2008 Sales by Type

	$ mil.	% of total
Products	50,180	82
Services	10,729	18
Total	**60,909**	**100**

Selected Operations

Commercial Airplanes
   737 Next Generation (short-to-medium-range two-
      engine jet)
   747 (long-range four-engine jet)
   767 (medium-to-long-range two-engine jet)
   777 (long-range two-engine jet)
   787 (long-range, super-efficient, 200-250 passenger
      capacity; due in 2008)
Military aircraft and missile systems
   AH-64D Apache helicopter
   AV-8B Harrier II
   C-17 Globemaster III
   C-40 Clipper
   CH-47 Chinook
   F/A-15 Eagle
   F/A-18E/F Super Hornet
   Harpoon Missile
   T-45 Flight Training System
   V-22 Osprey tilt-rotor aircraft
   Various classified projects
   X-45 (Unmanned Combat Air Vehicle — the UCAV is
      an advanced technology demonstrator)
Space and Communications
   737 AEW&C (Airborne Early Warning and Control)
   Global Positioning System satellites (GPS)
   International Space Station (contractor to NASA)
   National Missile Defense Lead Systems Integrator
      (NMDD LSI)
   Space Shuttle
   Various classified projects

COMPETITORS

AgustaWestland
Airbus
BAE SYSTEMS
Bombardier
Cessna
Daimler
Dassault Aviation
EADS
Embraer
Eurocopter
Finmeccanica
GE Aviation
General Dynamics
Goodrich Corp.
Kaman
Lockheed Martin
Northrop Grumman
Panasonic Avionics
Raytheon
Rockwell Collins
Textron
Thales
United Technologies

HISTORICAL FINANCIALS

Company Type: Public

Income Statement

FYE: December 31

	REVENUE ($ mil.)	NET INCOME ($ mil.)	NET PROFIT MARGIN	EMPLOYEES
12/08	60,909.0	2,672.0	4.4%	162,200
12/07	66,387.0	4,074.0	6.1%	159,300
12/06	61,530.0	2,215.0	3.6%	154,000
12/05	54,845.0	2,555.0	4.7%	153,000
12/04	52,457.0	1,872.0	3.6%	159,000
Annual Growth	**3.8%**	**9.3%**	**—**	**0.5%**

2008 Year-End Financials

Debt ratio: —
Return on equity: 69.3%
Cash ($ mil.): 3,268
Current ratio: 0.84
Long-term debt ($ mil.): 6,952

No. of shares (mil.): 726
Dividends
   Yield: 3.7%
   Payout: 43.6%
Market value ($ mil.): 30,997

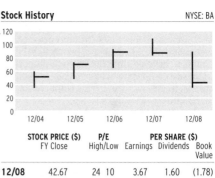

Stock History

NYSE: BA

	STOCK PRICE ($) FY Close	P/E High/Low		Earnings	PER SHARE ($) Dividends	Book Value
12/08	42.67	24	10	3.67	1.60	(1.78)
12/07	87.46	20	16	5.28	1.40	12.39
12/06	88.84	32	23	2.85	1.20	6.52
12/05	70.24	23	15	3.20	1.00	15.22
12/04	51.77	26	16	2.30	0.77	15.54
Annual Growth	**(4.7%)**	**—**	**—**	**12.4%**	**20.1%**	**—**

Bon-Ton Stores

Fashion hounds lost in the wilds from Maine to Montana can take refuge in The Bon-Ton Stores. The company operates about 280 department stores under eight nameplates, including the Bon-Ton, Elder-Beerman, and Carson Pirie Scott banners, in some two dozen states. The stores sell branded (Calvin Klein, Estée Lauder, Liz Claiborne, Nautica, and Waterford) and private-label women's, children's, and men's clothing; accessories; cosmetics; and home furnishings. Bon-Ton acquired the 142-store Northern Department Store Group (NDSG) from Saks in 2006, doubling its store count. The Bon-Ton Stores was founded in 1898 by the Grumbacher family, and today is controlled by its chairman Tim Grumbacher.

Bon-Ton paid about $1.05 billion to Saks for NDSG, which included stores under such brands as Carson Pirie Scott, Bergner's, Boston Store, Herberger's and Younkers, all located throughout more than 10 Midwestern and Great Plains states. The acquisition landed Bon-Ton in second place among regional department store operators (behind Dillard's). The purchase also substantially increased the company's debt load, not long before the US economy entered a deep recession and retail slump. Indeed, in 2008 the retailer's net sale decreased 7% vs. 2007, and sales were flat in 2006.

CEO Bud Bergren, whose employment contract was extended in 2009 to run through 2011, has said about 20 of the company's stores are unprofitable. The weakest-performing stores are in areas affected by layoffs in the auto industry, including central Pennsylvania, Ohio, and Indiana. (The company has announced plans to shutter one store in Ohio in 2009.) To lure shoppers the retailer is shifting its marketing message to emphasize value-priced merchandise. Department store operators have been losing market share to specialty shops and discounters for years.

Bon-Ton has replaced its private-label home brands with those of NDSG's more profitable and upscale lines, including Living Quarters, Laura Ashley, and the Karen Neuberger luxury home collection. In 2008 Bon-Ton partnered with designer Victor Alfaro to create Victor by Victor Alfaro, a private label line with high price points and quality. Exclusive lines of private-label merchandise have become increasingly important to department stores as they struggle to differentiate themselves from their competitors and foster customer loyalty.

The retailer also offers harder-to-find customer services such as free gift wrap and special ordering. Women's clothing accounts for about a quarter of sales.

HISTORY

The Bon-Ton began in York, Pennsylvania, in 1898 when Sam Grumbacher and his son Max opened a one-room millinery and dry goods store, naming it for the French term for good taste. Max's son Tom joined the company — S. Grumbacher & Son — in 1931, assisted his mother and brother in guiding the business through the Depression, and took charge in the early 1940s. A second store opened in 1946, and the company expanded gradually over the next four decades, entering Maryland, New York, and West Virginia.

Tom's son Tim became CEO in 1985. S. Grumbacher & Son bought Pomeroy's, an 11-store Pennsylvania chain, from Allied Stores two years later. With 33 stores and eager to fund further expansion, the company went public in 1991 as The Bon-Ton Stores. It doubled in size in 1994 by buying 35 stores — including 20 Hess stores in Georgia, New Jersey, New York, and Pennsylvania from Crown Holding and 10-store Buffalo, New York-based Adam, Meldrum & Anderson — for about $106 million.

Growing fast but losing money in the process, the chain hired May Department Stores executive Heywood Wilansky as CEO — the first from outside the family — in 1995. To get Bon-Ton back on track, Wilansky closed 10 stores and began upgrading merchandise and using fewer vendors. In 1997 he reaffirmed the company's commitment to stick to smaller markets as it opens new stores.

To celebrate its centennial in 1998, Bon-Ton opened a store in Westfield, Massachusetts, its first location in New England. It opened seven stores in New England and New Jersey the next year. In 2000, following a management restructuring, Tim Grumbacher reassumed the position of CEO when Wilansky retired.

Bon-Ton has been steadily increasing its sales of private-label merchandise from 9.8% in 2000 to nearly 11% in 2002. In October 2003 it bought The Elder-Beerman Stores (67 department stores and two furniture stores in nine states) for $92.8 million.

In July 2005 the company sold its private-label credit card business to HSBC Retail Services for about $316 million (minus $226 million in accounts receivable), closed its corporate credit department, and eliminated about 85 jobs. Under the terms of the deal, HSBC administers the credit card business and pays Bon-Ton a portion of the revenue generated from future credit card sales.

In March 2006 Bon-Ton completed the acquisition of Saks' Northern Department Store Group. As a result, it operated 279 department stores with some $3.4 billion in annual sales. That October the company purchased four Detroit-area Parisian department stores from Belk, which had acquired the chain from Saks.

Late to the online party, Bon-Ton launched an e-commerce sales channel in October 2007.

EXECUTIVES

Executive Chairman: M. Thomas (Tim) Grumbacher, age 69, $2,021,185 total compensation
Vice Chairman, President, Merchandising: Anthony J. (Tony) Buccina, age 58, $1,630,816 total compensation
Vice Chairman, Stores, Distribution, Real Estate and Construction: Stephen R. (Steve) Byers, age 55, $887,649 total compensation
President, CEO, and Director: Byron L. (Bud) Bergren, age 62, $1,931,985 total compensation
EVP, CFO, and Chief Accounting Officer: Keith E. Plowman, age 51, $727,410 total compensation
SVP and CIO: James (Jim) Lance
EVP Human Resources: Dennis R. Clouser, age 56
EVP Stores and Visual Merchandising: Barbara Schrantz, age 50
SVP Stores: John S. Farrell
SVP General Merchandise Manager: Therese Callahan
SVP, Treasurer, Risk Management and Credit: H. Todd Dissinger, age 51
SVP Human Resource Operations: Denise M. Domian, age 44
SVP Distribution and Logistics: James (Jim) Rawlins
SVP Merchandise Planning and Internet Marketing: Jimmy D. Mansker, age 39
VP, General Counsel, and Secretary: Robert E. Stern
VP and Controller: Jeff Miller
VP Public and Investor Relations: Mary Kerr
Auditors: KPMG LLP

LOCATIONS

HQ: The Bon-Ton Stores, Inc.
2801 E. Market St., York, PA 17402
Phone: 717-757-7660   **Fax:** 717-751-3108
Web: www.bonton.com

PRODUCTS/OPERATIONS

2009 Sales

	% of total
Women's apparel	26
Home	18
Men's apparel	13
Cosmetics	13
Accessories	8
Shoes	8
Children's apparel	7
Intimate apparel	4
Juniors' apparel	3
Total	**100**

2009 Stores

	No.
Bon-Ton	69
Elder-Beerman	58
Younkers	49
Herberger's	41
Carson Pirie Scott	34
Bergner's	13
Boston Store	13
Parisian	3
Total	**280**

Selected Private Labels

Breckenridge	Living Quarters
Consensus	Relativity
Cuddle Bear	Ruff Hewn
Karen Neuberger Home	Statements
Kenneth Roberts	Studio Works
Laura Ashley	

COMPETITORS

Belk	Lands' End
Boscov's	Loehmann's
Dillard's	Macy's
The Gap	Sears
J. C. Penney	Target
J. Crew	Wal-Mart
J. Jill Group	Williams-Sonoma
Kohl's	

HISTORICAL FINANCIALS

Company Type: Public

Income Statement

FYE: Saturday nearest January 31

	REVENUE ($ mil.)	NET INCOME ($ mil.)	NET PROFIT MARGIN	EMPLOYEES
1/09	3,225.4	(169.9)	—	29,100
1/08	3,467.7	11.6	0.3%	32,700
1/07	3,455.8	46.9	1.4%	33,000
1/06	1,307.6	26.0	2.0%	33,500
1/05	1,319.6	20.2	1.5%	12,600
Annual Growth	**25.0%**	**—**	**—**	**23.3%**

2009 Year-End Financials

Debt ratio: 856.2%
Return on equity: —
Cash ($ mil.): 20
Current ratio: 2.13
Long-term debt ($ mil.): 1,149

No. of shares (mil.): 19
Dividends
Yield: 14.7%
Payout: —
Market value ($ mil.): 25

Stock History

NASDAQ (GS): BONT

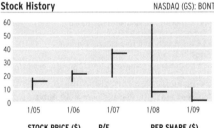

	STOCK PRICE ($) FY Close	P/E High/Low		PER SHARE ($) Earnings	Dividends	Book Value
1/09	1.37	—	—	(10.12)	0.20	7.23
1/08	7.75	85	6	0.68	0.20	19.57
1/07	36.50	14	7	2.78	0.10	18.67
1/06	21.07	15	10	1.57	0.10	15.74
1/05	15.73	14	8	1.24	0.10	14.15
Annual Growth	**(45.7%)**	**—**	**—**	**—**	**18.9%**	**(15.4%)**

Borders Group

If you want John Updike or Janet Jackson to go with your java, Borders is for you. The #2 bookstore operator in the US (after Barnes & Noble), Borders Group runs more than 1,000 retail stores, which include Borders superstores, mall-based Waldenbooks stores, and Paperchase stationery shops. The chain has been divesting its international holdings, selling its Borders (UK) business in 2007 and its 30 Asia/Pacific superstores in 2008, to reduce debt and allow it to focus on domestic operations. Borders stores offer up to 200,000 book, music, and movie titles and regularly host live literary events and musician showcases to lure customers. Borders also set up shop at select US airport and outlet mall locations.

Following a disappointing holiday selling season, ailing Borders replaced its CEO after less than three years on the job. In January 2009 the bookseller named Ron Marshall as CEO, succeeding George Jones. The company cited Marshall's experience turning around troubled companies. Later in the month it appointed Richard "Mick" McGuire to take the reins as chairman, replacing Larry Pollock, who will continue to be a director. McGuire, who joined the board in early 2008, was a partner in hedge fund Pershing Square Capital Management, Borders' largest single shareholder.

Under Marshall, Borders reduced the size of its workforce and implemented cost-cutting initiatives. The company cut almost 1,000 jobs and plans to trim its budget by another $120 million, as sales are expected to continue falling through 2009. Borders also looks to curb spending by shuttering stores, including Waldenbooks outlets.

Trimming its overseas holdings — which included selling Borders stores in Australia, New Zealand, and Singapore to book retailer A&R Whitcoulls Group — gave the company a much-needed cash infusion, as it attempts to reduce debt and streamline core domestic growth.

The divestiture of the bookseller's Asia/Pacific holdings follows the sale of its UK subsidiary to Risk Capital Partners in 2007. The deal, which stipulates that Borders keeps a one-sixth stake in Borders (UK), includes about 70 Borders superstores and Books etc. stores in the UK and Ireland.

Borders is also looking to sell its upmarket UK stationery chain Paperchase Products to raise cash. Paperchase has about 120 stores, primarily in the UK, as well as about 330 Paperchase shops inside select Borders superstores in America.

Noting that growth within the book industry has been on the decline, Borders is looking to stimulate sales by enhancing its Internet offerings. It also developed a store prototype that incorporates "digital centers" for customers to interact with such products as e-books and MP3 players. The first concept store opened in Michigan in early 2008. Borders is also making more exclusive book deals to drive more people into the stores.

HISTORY

Brothers Louis and Tom Borders founded their first bookstore in 1971 in Ann Arbor, Michigan. The store originally sold used books but soon added new books. As titles were added, Louis developed tracking systems for the growing inventory. It's been said that the former MIT student stumbled upon the system while trying to create a software program to predict horse race winners. In the mid-1970s the brothers formed Book Inventory Systems to market the system to other independent bookstores.

Through the late 1970s and early 1980s, the brothers focused on building the service part of their business, but by the mid-1980s they were having trouble finding enough large, independent bookstore customers. Refocusing on retail, they opened their second store (Birmingham, Michigan) in 1985.

They had five stores by 1988 and hired Robert DiRomualdo (president of cheese log chain Hickory Farms) to run Borders and mount a national expansion. Discount retailer Kmart bought Book Inventory Systems (including 19 Borders bookstores) in 1992.

Kmart already owned Waldenbooks, which had been founded in 1933 and named for the Massachusetts pond that inspired Thoreau. Started by Larry Hoyt as a book rental library, Waldenbooks had 250 outlets by 1948. In 1968 the bookseller opened its first all-retail bookstore in Pittsburgh.

By placing stores in the growing number of US shopping malls, Waldenbooks expanded rapidly during the 1970s. In 1979 the company hired former Procter & Gamble executive Harry Hoffman to run the company. Hoffman drew the ire of traditionalists in the book retailing industry because he focused on best sellers instead of literary works. Hoffman also added nonbook items such as greeting cards to the stores' merchandise mix.

In 1981 Waldenbooks became the first bookseller to operate in all 50 states. Kmart acquired the chain three years later. As part of a plan to revive its discount business, in 1995 Kmart spun off Borders Group (which by this time included Waldenbooks, Borders, and part of Planet Music, formerly CD Superstore) to the public. Borders consolidated its three divisions under one roof and bought the rest of Planet Music (closed in 1997). With mall traffic slowing nationally, Borders CEO DiRomualdo steered the company away from Waldenbooks and toward superstores.

Moving beyond its existing borders, the company acquired the UK chain Books etc., opened a store in Singapore in 1997, and entered Australia the next year. Borders finally began offering books, music, and videos through its borders.com Web site in 1998, three years after Amazon.com began selling online.

Philip Pfeffer, a former top executive with publisher Random House and book distributor Ingram (part of Ingram Industries) who succeeded DiRomualdo as CEO in late 1998, was forced out five months later, in part for being slow to address the company's lagging efforts online.

In November 1999 Greg Josefowicz, the former president of Albertson's Jewel-Osco division, was named CEO.

In 2002 DiRomualdo stepped down as chairman, and Josefowicz assumed the role.

International expansion continued in 2005 when Borders boosted its stake in Paperchase Products to 97%. The following year, Josefowicz announced that he planned to retire from the company by the end of 2007. When George Jones was hired in mid-2006 to lead the company, Josefowicz stepped down.

Amid declining sales, Borders replaced CEO Jones in January 2009 with Ron Marshall, a turnaround expert and founder of the private equity firm Wildridge Capital Management.

EXECUTIVES

Chairman: Richard (Mick) McGuire, age 33
President, CEO, and Director: Ron Marshall, age 55, $380,177 total compensation
EVP Finance and CFO: Mark Bierley, age 42, $665,496 total compensation
CIO: Scott Laverty, age 49
SVP and Chief Marketing Officer: Michael A. Tam
EVP, General Counsel, and Secretary: Thomas D. Carney, age 62, $831,595 total compensation
EVP Merchandising and Marketing: Anne Kubek, age 42
SVP Merchandising and Distribution: Larry Norton, age 51
SVP Borders Group Operations: Steve Davis
SVP Children's, Periodicals, Calendars, and Multimedia: Linda Jones
SVP Merchandise Operations and Supply Chain: Mark Palmucci
SVP Merchandise Planning, Replenishment, and Allocation: Anne Frazer
SVP Marketing: Arthur Keeney, age 56
VP Merchandising, Non-Book Products: Michael (Mike) Oprins, age 45
VP Cafe Operations: Chris Nichols
VP Information Technology: Dan Shull
VP Information Technology Delivery Services: Gary E. Baker
VP Creative, Outreach, and Entertainment: Rich Fahle
VP Real Estate: Tony Grant
VP Marketing Revenue: Joanna Goldstein, age 33
Investor Contact: Brenda Rutkey
Auditors: Ernst & Young LLP

LOCATIONS

HQ: Borders Group, Inc.
100 Phoenix Dr., Ann Arbor, MI 48108
Phone: 734-477-1100   **Fax:** 734-477-1285
Web: www.bordersgroupinc.com

2009 Borders Stores

	No.
California	82
Illinois	36
New York	28
Florida	26
Pennsylvania	25
Texas	24
Michigan	19
Ohio	19
Massachusetts	16
New Jersey	15
Georgia	15
Virginia	15
Colorado	14
Indiana	13
Washington	13
Arizona	11
Connecticut	11
Maryland	11
Missouri	11
North Carolina	10
Hawaii	8
Minnesota	7
Nevada	7
Oregon	7
Tennessee	7
Kansas	6
Wisconsin	6
Kentucky	5
New Mexico	5
Iowa	4
New Hampshire	4
Oklahoma	4
District of Columbia	3
Louisiana	3
Maine	3
Montana	3
Nebraska	3
Utah	3
Other states	13
Total	**515**

PRODUCTS/OPERATIONS

2009 Sales

	% of total
Borders	81
Waldenbooks	15
International	4
Total	**100**

COMPETITORS

Amazon.com
Barnes & Noble
Best Buy
Blockbuster Inc.
Book-of-the-Month Club
Books-A-Million
CDNOW
Columbia House
Half Price Books
Hastings Entertainment
HMV
Movie Gallery
Wal-Mart
WHSmith

HISTORICAL FINANCIALS

Company Type: Public

Income Statement

FYE: Saturday nearest January 31

	REVENUE ($ mil.)	NET INCOME ($ mil.)	NET PROFIT MARGIN	EMPLOYEES
1/09	3,275.4	(186.7)	—	25,600
1/08	3,820.9	(157.4)	—	29,500
1/07	4,063.9	(151.3)	—	33,600
1/06	4,030.7	101.0	2.5%	35,500
1/05	3,879.5	131.9	3.4%	32,700
Annual Growth	(4.1%)	—	—	(5.9%)

2009 Year-End Financials

Debt ratio: 2.4%
Return on equity: —
Cash ($ mil.): 54
Current ratio: 1.08
Long-term debt ($ mil.): 6

No. of shares (mil.): 60
Dividends
  Yield: 0.0%
  Payout: —
Market value ($ mil.): 26

Stock History

NYSE: BGP

	STOCK PRICE ($) FY Close	P/E High/Low	PER SHARE ($) Earnings	Dividends	Book Value
1/09	0.44	— —	(3.10)	0.00	4.36
1/08	11.29	— —	(2.68)	0.44	7.92
1/07	20.98	— —	(2.44)	0.41	10.66
1/06	24.62	19 13	1.42	0.37	15.41
1/05	26.25	16 13	1.69	0.33	18.08
Annual Growth	(64.0%)	— —	—	—	(29.9%)

BorgWarner Inc.

If suburbanites need four-wheel-drive vehicles to make it up their steep driveways, that's OK with BorgWarner, a leading maker of power train products for the world's major automotive manufacturers. Its largest customers include Volkswagen (19% of sales), Ford, and Daimler. Its power train products include four-wheel-drive and all-wheel-drive transfer cases (primarily for light trucks and SUVs), as well as automatic transmission and timing-chain systems. BorgWarner operates 60 manufacturing, assembly, and technical facilities worldwide. The company gets more than half of its sales from European customers.

BorgWarner was in high gear. The company was growing profits while many of its peers did well to break even.

Early in 2008 BorgWarner made some rosy predictions for the year's performance. The company said it expected a sales bump of between 8% and 10%. BorgWarner also expected 2008 profit growth of about 25%, based largely on the performance of its European and Asian operations.

The worldwide economic downturn that accelerated in the second half of 2008 obliterated those optimistic projections. The company finished the year with sales off slightly for the 12 months, but

fourth-quarter revenues were down about one-third from the year-ago quarter. It posted a small loss for 2008, its first annual loss since 2002. BorgWarner responded with a variety of cost-cutting measures, including the elimination of about 4,400 jobs (around one-quarter of the worldwide workforce), putting European plants on four-day work weeks, and shutting down all operations for a month at the end of 2008.

BorgWarner was savvy about winning new business from customers outside the US, such as AUDI, Honda, Hyundai, Kia, and VW. The company's strategy is to follow market share as it shifts increasingly away from Detroit and toward Asia and Europe. BorgWarner now generates more business from Volkswagen and Daimler than it does from General Motors, Ford, and Chrysler; sales in Germany now outstrip those in the US.

A part of BorgWarner's global growth strategy is to situate manufacturing operations where its customers reside. The company steadily increased its presence in South Korea (Hyundai and Kia) and expanded operations in China as Western automotive companies scramble to grab market share in that emerging economy, which is threatening to overtake the mature US market as the largest automotive market in the world.

HISTORY

BorgWarner traces its roots to the 1928 merger of major Chicago auto parts companies Borg & Beck (clutches), Warner Gear (transmissions), Mechanics Universal Joint, and Marvel Carburetor. The newly named Borg-Warner Corporation quickly began buying other companies, including Ingersoll Steel & Disc (agricultural blades and discs) and Norge (refrigerators).

The company survived the Depression largely through the contributions of its Norge and Ingersoll divisions. In the latter 1930s, the company purchased Calumet Steel (1935) and US Pressed Steel (1937), along with several other companies.

During the early 1940s Borg-Warner made parts for planes, trucks, and tanks. Between 1942 and 1945 it produced more than 1.6 million automotive transmissions and gained the experience and manufacturing capacity to handle the postwar car boom. Its 1948 contract with Ford Motor to build half of its transmissions resulted in massive growth.

Roy Ingersoll, president of the Ingersoll Steel & Disc division, assumed leadership of Borg-Warner in 1950 and embarked on a major diversification plan. Borg-Warner's 1956 purchases included York, Humphreys Manufacturing, Industrial Crane & Hoist, Dittmer Gear, and the Chemical Process Company, among others. James Bert became president in 1968 and continued diversification.

Borg-Warner entered the security business in 1978 by buying Baker Industries (armored transport under the Wells Fargo name). In 1980 Borg-Warner sold its Ingersoll Products division. It acquired Burns International Security Services in 1982 and spun off York to its shareholders in 1986.

In the face of a 1987 takeover attempt, Merrill Lynch Capital Partners organized an LBO and took the company private, assuming $4.5 billion in debt. Borg-Warner then sold everything but its automotive and security units, including its chemical group to General Electric for $2.3 billion (1988) and its credit unit, Chilton, to TRW for $330 million (1989).

The company went public again in 1993 as Borg-Warner Security; it spun off Borg-Warner Automotive to its shareholders. (Borg-Warner Security changed its name to Burns International Services in 1999.) In 1995 Borg-Warner Automotive formed a joint venture in India (Divgi-Warner) to make transmissions and purchased the precision-forged products division of Federal-Mogul.

To expand its air- and fluid-control business, the company acquired Holley Automotive, Coltec Automotive, and Performance Friction Products from component maker Coltec Industries in 1996. Reduced production of Ford trucks, a weak Asian economy, and a strike at General Motors hurt 1998 sales. The following year the company bought diesel-engine component maker Kuhlman.

In 1999 Borg-Warner Automotive bought the Fluid Power Division (automotive cooling systems) of Eaton for $130 million. The company changed its name to BorgWarner in 2000. Early the next year BorgWarner sold its fuel systems interests to private equity group TMB Industries.

In 2005 BorgWarner purchased a controlling 60% stake in Germany's BERU AG at a price of about $290 million.

Although it attempted to insulate itself from Detroit's woes, few could have predicted the massive 2006 production cuts at Chrysler, Ford, and GM. To adjust, late in 2006 BorgWarner said it would cut about 800 jobs at 19 facilities in the US, Canada, and Mexico — or about 13% of its total North American workforce.

Soon after the job cut announcement, BorgWarner purchased Eaton's European Transmission and Engine Controls product lines for nearly $64 million, net of cash acquired. Products included high-pressure control solenoids for automated transmissions, as well as for rail diesel and gasoline engines.

EXECUTIVES

Chairman and CEO: Timothy M. (Tim) Manganello, age 59, $8,321,617 total compensation
EVP, CFO, Chief Administration Officer, and Director: Robin J. Adams, age 55, $1,784,215 total compensation
CTO: Hans-Peter Schmalzl, age 48
VP and CIO: Jamal M. Farhat
Chief Compliance Officer and Assistant Secretary: Laurene H. Horiszny
VP Global Supply Chain: John J. McGill
VP and Controller: Jeffrey L. Obermayer, age 53
VP; President and General Manager, Transmission Systems: John G. Sanderson, age 56
VP, General Counsel, and Secretary: John J. Gasparovic, age 51
EVP; President and General Manager, BorgWarner Turbo & Emissions Systems: Roger J. Wood, age 46, $1,873,021 total compensation
VP and Treasurer: Anthony D. Hensel, age 50
VP; President and General Manager, BorgWarner Morse TEC and BorgWarner Thermal Systems: Alfred O. Weber, age 51, $1,094,418 total compensation
VP; President and General Manager, BorgWarner TorqTransfer Systems: Daniel J. (Dan) CasaSanta, age 54
VP Business Development and M&A: Christopher H. Vance
VP Human Resources: Angela D'Aversa, age 62
VP; Chairman and CEO, BERU: Thomas Waldhier
VP Marketing, Public Relations, and Internal Communications: Scott Gallett, age 42
Director Investor Relations: Ken Lamb
Director Marketing: Erika Nielsen
Auditors: PricewaterhouseCoopers LLP

LOCATIONS

HQ: BorgWarner Inc.
3850 Hamlin Rd., Auburn Hills, MI 48326
Phone: 248-754-9200   **Fax:** 248-754-9397
Web: www.bwauto.com

2008 Sales

	$ mil.	% of total
US	1,499.6	28
Europe		
Germany	1,948.4	37
Hungary	398.2	8
Other countries	676.1	13
South Korea	251.8	5
Other regions	489.8	9
Total	**5,263.9**	**100**

PRODUCTS/OPERATIONS

2008 Sales

	$ mil.	% of total
Engine	3,861.5	73
Drivetrain	1,426.4	27
Adjustments	(24.0)	—
Total	**5,263.9**	**100**

Selected Products

Engine Group
    Air-control valves
    Chain tensioners and snubbers
    Complete engine induction systems
    Complex solenoids and multi-function modules
    Crankshaft and camshaft sprockets
    Electric air pumps
    Engine hydraulic pumps
    Exhaust gas-recirculation valves
    Fan clutches
    Front-wheel and four-wheel-drive chain and timing-
        chain systems
    Intake manifolds
    On-off fan drives
    Single-function solenoids
    Throttle bodies
    Throttle position sensors
    Turbochargers

Drivetrain Group
    Four-wheel-drive and all-wheel-drive transfer cases
    Friction plates
    One-way clutches
    Torque converter lock-up clutches
    Transmission bands

Selected Joint Ventures

BorgWarner Transmission Systems Korea, Inc. (60%)
Borg-Warner Shenglong (Ningbo) Co. Ltd. (70%, China)
Divgi-Warner Limited (60%, India)
NSK-Warner K.K. (50%, Japan)

COMPETITORS

ArvinMeritor
Dana Holding
Delphi Corp.
DENSO
Eaton
GKN
Honeywell International
IHI Corp.
JTEKT
Kolbenschmidt Pierburg
Magna Powertrain
Mitsubishi Heavy Industries
NGK SPARK PLUG
Renold
Robert Bosch
Schaeffler
Tsubaki Nakashima
Valeo
Visteon

HISTORICAL FINANCIALS

Company Type: Public

Income Statement

FYE: December 31

	REVENUE ($ mil.)	NET INCOME ($ mil.)	NET PROFIT MARGIN	EMPLOYEES
12/08	5,263.9	(35.6)	—	13,800
12/07	5,328.6	288.5	5.4%	17,700
12/06	4,585.4	211.6	4.6%	17,400
12/05	4,293.8	239.6	5.6%	17,400
12/04	3,525.3	218.3	6.2%	14,500
Annual Growth	**10.5%**	**—**	**—**	**(1.2%)**

2008 Year-End Financials

Debt ratio: 22.9%
Return on equity: —
Cash ($ mil.): 103
Current ratio: 1.05
Long-term debt ($ mil.): 460
No. of shares (mil.): 117
Dividends
Yield: 2.0%
Payout: —
Market value ($ mil.): 2,540

Stock History

NYSE: BWA

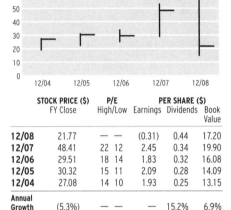

	STOCK PRICE ($) FY Close	P/E High/Low		PER SHARE ($) Earnings	Dividends	Book Value
12/08	21.77	—	—	(0.31)	0.44	17.20
12/07	48.41	22	12	2.45	0.34	19.90
12/06	29.51	18	14	1.83	0.32	16.08
12/05	30.32	15	11	2.09	0.28	14.09
12/04	27.08	14	10	1.93	0.25	13.15
Annual Growth	**(5.3%)**	**—**	**—**	**—**	**15.2%**	**6.9%**

Boston Scientific

Boston Scientific operates under the threat of minimal invasion. The company makes medical supplies used in minimally invasive surgical procedures. Its devices are used to diagnose and treat conditions in a variety of medical fields, including cardiology (cardiovascular group), gynecology and urology (endosurgery group), pain management (neuromodulation), and heart failure and arrhythmia (cardiac rhythm management group). Its 13,000-plus products, made in about 25 factories, include defibrillators, catheters, coronary and urethral stents, pacemakers, biopsy forceps and needles, and urethral slings.

Cardiovascular products account for about 80% of Boston Scientific sales. The cardiovascular segment includes the company's interventional cardiology and cardiac rhythm management businesses. The endosurgery product line is responsible for almost all the rest, addressing the areas of endoscopy, urology, and gynecology. Its newest segment, neuromodulation devices (for the treatment of chronic pain), accounts for a small percentage of revenues.

Despite ongoing controversy over the effectiveness and safety of drug-coated vascular stents (small implantable devices that prop open blood

vessels and arteries), the interventional cardiology business is a top revenue-earner for Boston Scientific. The acquisition of Rubicon Medical in 2007 brought non-invasive stent delivery systems and other less-invasive endovascular devices. In 2008 the company received approval for the Express SD renal stent system used to improve blood flow to the kidneys, which expands its product offerings in the endosurgical market.

Within months of its bitterly fought $28 billion acquisition of Guidant in 2006, Boston Scientific was hit with hundreds of lawsuits over that company's implantable cardioverter defibrillator (ICD) devices. (Guidant recalled over 100,000 faulty defibrillators in 2005.) The number of lawsuits has grown to over 2,000, including more than 70 class-action suits, and the company has paid $240 million in settlement costs; Boston Scientific estimates that legal bills in the matter could total over $700 million.

The company took another hit in 2008 when it received a negative judgment in a patent infringement suit filed by Johnson & Johnson and was fined $700 million by a US District Court. Boston Scientific is appealing the ruling, which involves the company's NIR coronary stent (a product that is no longer sold).

Boston Scientific sold its cardiac surgery and vascular surgery businesses, which make products such as beating-heart bypass systems and vascular grafts and patches, to Swedish firm Getinge for $750 million in cash in early 2008. The company has also sold its fluid management business, which makes products used in angiography and angioplasty procedures, and its venous access business, which makes blood stream access implants, to Avista Capital Partners for $425 million.

In another move designed to reshape its operations, the company named former Zimmer executive Ray Elliott to the post of CEO in mid-2009. Jim Tobin, who held the role for more than 10 years, retired.

Co-founders and board members John Abele and Pete Nicholas (with their families) control about 10% of the company.

HISTORY

Many medical companies start near a hospital, but Boston Scientific's roots sprouted at a children's soccer game where two dads found common ground. John Abele and Peter Nicholas had complementary interests: Wharton MBA Nichols wanted to run his own company; philosophy and physics graduate Abele wanted a job that would help people.

In 1979 the two men founded Boston Scientific to buy medical device maker Medi-Tech. Abele and Nichols had to borrow half a million dollars from a bank and raise an additional $300,000. Medi-Tech's primary product was a steerable catheter, a soft-tipped device that could be maneuvered within the body. The catheter revolutionized gallstone operations in the early 1970s, and Boston Scientific expanded on the success of the product. The company adapted it for a slew of new procedures for the heart, lungs, intestines, and other organs.

Boston Scientific's sales were healthy in 1983, but the firm still lacked funds. It eagerly accepted $21 million from Abbott Laboratories in exchange for a 20% stake. New FDA regulations slowed product introduction and put a crimp in the company's growth. Boston Scientific found a legal loophole in the late 1980s to avoid lengthy delays: The company described its products in the vaguest possible terms so upgraded devices were considered similar enough to predecessors to escape the in-depth scrutiny of the new approval process. Still, Abele and Nicholas had to mortgage their personal properties to stay afloat before this linguistic legerdemain helped to clear government red tape. Boston Scientific returned to profitability in 1991 and went public the next year, buying back Abbott Laboratories' interest in the company as well.

Boston Scientific acquired a bevy of medical device companies in 1995, doubling its sales. Among them were SCIMED Life Systems, which specialized in cardiology products; Heart Technology, a maker of systems to treat coronary atherosclerosis; and Meadox Medicals, which made arterial grafts.

The 1998 purchase of stent maker Schneider Worldwide fattened Boston Scientific's pipeline and payroll; the company in 1999 cut 14% of workers. That year a federal judge ruled that the company's Bandit PTCA catheter infringed on a Guidant patent. In 2000 the company settled with Guidant and the two companies agreed to license products to each other.

Throughout 2003 and 2004 the company's Taxus stent systems were big news, despite recalls of the drug-eluting stent system. (However, controversy over the use of stents began to hurt the product segment's sales in 2006.)

In spite of ongoing patent infringement suits, Boston Scientific has continued to develop new products and acquire smaller companies. The firm bought Advanced Stent Technologies, which develops stents for bifurcated heart vessels (a condition caused by the branching of one vessel into two), in 2005. Boston Scientific also acquired CryoVascular Systems, which produced an angioplasty device used to treat atherosclerotic disease that was distributed by Boston Scientific.

The acquisition of Rubicon Medical later that year brought non-invasive stent delivery systems and other less invasive endovascular devices to the company's product portfolio. Boston Scientific also acquired a portfolio of endoscopic (throat and esophageal) stents from Teleflex subsidiary Willy Rusch GmbH in 2005.

EXECUTIVES

Chairman: Peter M. (Pete) Nicholas, age 67
President, CEO, and Director: J. Raymond (Ray) Elliott, age 59
EVP Operations: Kenneth J. (Ken) Pucel, age 42
EVP Finance and Information Systems and CFO: Samuel R. (Sam) Leno, age 63, $6,321,255 total compensation
SVP, Chief Accounting Officer, and Controller: Jeffrey D. (Jeff) Capello, age 44
EVP and Chief Medical and Scientific Officer: Donald S. Baim, age 59
EVP and Group President, Cardiac Rhythm Management: Fredericus A. (Fred) Colen, age 56, $4,792,585 total compensation
EVP Human Resources: Lucia Luce Quinn, age 55
EVP Strategy and Business Development: James (Jim) Gilbert, age 51
EVP, Secretary, and General Counsel: Timothy A. (Tim) Pratt, age 59
SVP Corporate Communications: Paul Donovan, age 52
SVP and Group President, Endosurgery: Stephen F. (Steve) Moreci, age 57
SVP Sales, Marketing, and Business Strategy, Cardiac Rhythm Management: William F. (Bill) McConnell Jr., age 59, $2,917,490 total compensation

SVP Quality: Brian R. Burns, age 44
SVP and Group President, Interventional Cardiology Group: William H. (Hank) Kucheman, age 59
SVP International: David McFaul, age 52, $3,784,867 total compensation
SVP and President, Neuromodulation: Michael Onuscheck, age 42
SVP and Associate Chief Medical Officer: Ken Stein
VP Investor Relations: Larry Neumann
Director Corporate Communications: Charles Rudnick
Auditors: Ernst & Young LLP

LOCATIONS

HQ: Boston Scientific Corporation
1 Boston Scientific Place, Natick, MA 01760
Phone: 508-650-8000   **Fax:** 508-650-8910
Web: www.bostonscientific.com

PRODUCTS/OPERATIONS

2008 Sales

	$ mil.	% of total
Cardiovascular		
Interventional cardiology	2,879	36
Cardiac rhythm management	2,286	28
Other cardiovascular	1,266	16
Endosurgery	1,374	17
Neuromodulation	245	3
Total	**8,050**	**100**

Selected Products

Cardiovascular
  Interventional Cardiology
    Liberte bare-metal stents
    NexStent carotid stent system
    PolarCath peripheral dilation system
    PROMUS drug-eluting stents
    TAXUS drug-eluting stents
  Cardiac Rhythm Management (CRM)
    ACUITY Steerable left ventricular leads
    COGNIS pulse generator
    CONFIENT ICD (implantable cardiac defibrillator)
    LATITUDE Patient Management System
    LIVIAN CRT-D
  Other cardiovascular
    Cutting Balloon dilation device
    FilterWire EZ embolic protection system
    iLab ultrasound imaging catheter system
    Maverick balloon catheters
Endosurgery
  DuoTome SideLite laser treatment system (prostate intervention)
  Hydro ThermAblator system (excessive uterine bleeding)
  Prolieve Thermodilatation System (prostate intervention)
  Radial Jaw 4 single-use biopsy forceps (gastrointestinal)
  Spyglass direct visualization system (pancreatic system)
Neuromodulation
  Precision Spinal Cord Stimulation system (chronic pain)

COMPETITORS

Abbott Labs
American Medical Systems
Bard
Baxter International
Becton, Dickinson
CONMED Corporation
Cook Group
Covidien
Datascope
Edwards Lifesciences
Johnson & Johnson
Kimberly-Clark Health
Medtronic
St. Jude Medical
ZOLL

HISTORICAL FINANCIALS

Company Type: Public

Income Statement

FYE: December 31

	REVENUE ($ mil.)	NET INCOME ($ mil.)	NET PROFIT MARGIN	EMPLOYEES
12/08	8,050.0	(2,036.0)	—	24,800
12/07	8,357.0	(495.0)	—	27,500
12/06	7,821.0	(3,577.0)	—	28,600
12/05	6,283.0	628.0	10.0%	19,800
12/04	5,624.0	1,062.0	18.9%	17,500
Annual Growth	9.4%	—	—	9.1%

2008 Year-End Financials

Debt ratio: 51.2%
Return on equity: —
Cash ($ mil.): 1,641
Current ratio: 1.69
Long-term debt ($ mil.): 6,743
No. of shares (mil.): 1,507
Dividends
  Yield: 0.0%
  Payout: —
Market value ($ mil.): 11,668

Stock History

NYSE: BSX

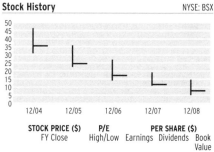

	STOCK PRICE ($) FY Close	P/E High/Low		PER SHARE ($) Earnings	Dividends	Book Value
12/08	7.74	—	—	(1.36)	0.00	8.74
12/07	11.63	—	—	(0.33)	0.00	10.01
12/06	17.18	—	—	(2.81)	0.00	10.15
12/05	24.49	47	30	0.75	0.00	2.84
12/04	35.55	37	25	1.24	0.00	2.67
Annual Growth	(31.7%)	—	—	—	—	34.5%

Boyd Gaming

A key ingredient for Boyd Gaming's success is — or was — stardust. One of the country's leading casino operators, Boyd demolished the iconic Stardust Resort and Casino on the Las Vegas Strip in 2007 to make way for a new development, Echelon Place. Boyd has some 15 properties, which include locations in Las Vegas, as well as in Florida, Indiana, Illinois, Louisiana, and Mississippi; together they have some 22,000 slot machines and 450 table games and typically feature multiple restaurants, lounges, and showrooms. Boyd also owns Coast Casino, as well as 50% of Atlantic City's Borgata Hotel Casino with MGM MIRAGE. Chairman William S. Boyd and his family own more than 35% of Boyd Gaming.

The company's $4.8 billion Echelon Place is planned to be a megacasino, spanning more than 60 acres. The project also includes a hotel joint venture with Morgans Hotel Group. In 2008 the company suspended construction on the project, citing a weak economy. Boyd plans to resume construction once credit markets and consumer spending improves.

The company added a new hotel at its Blue Chip Casino, Hotel & Spa property in Indiana. The expansion, completed in 2009, included a spa and fitness center, additional meeting and event space, and new dining and nightlife venues.

In 2008 Boyd announced plans to develop a casino, resort, and spa within the planned community of Park Highlands in North Las Vegas. The development is a joint venture project with Olympia Gaming, an affiliate of real estate development firm the Olympia Group. After receiving the necessary approvals, construction of the casino is not expected to begin for three to five years.

Boyd's $1.3 billion purchase of Coast Casinos created the fifth-largest gaming company in the US. (Boyd ditched Coast's South Coast Casino due to underperformance.) The company expanded in 2007 with the purchase of a jai alai facility in Dania Beach, Florida. The $152.5 million deal included about 50 acres of related land.

HISTORY

Boyd Gaming patriarch Sam Boyd may have caught the gambling bug early in life: His grandfather reportedly played poker with the outlaw Jesse James. After a stint working on gambling ships during the 1930s, Boyd arrived in Las Vegas in 1941 with less than $100 in his pockets and started running a penny roulette wheel. After years of saving half of what he made, Boyd invested $10,000 for an interest in the Sahara Hotel in 1952. He and his son William purchased the Eldorado Club in Henderson, Nevada, ten years later. Together, they founded Boyd Gaming in 1974 and opened the California Hotel in downtown Vegas the following year. In 1979 they opened Sam's Town on Las Vegas' Boulder Strip.

In 1985 the Boyds bought the Stardust (then a mob-tainted casino on the Las Vegas Strip) and acquired the Fremont Hotel and Casino near their California Hotel. Boyd Gaming was incorporated in 1988 as a holding company, and William was appointed chairman and CEO. Sam Boyd died in 1993, the same year that Boyd Gaming went public.

The company opened three casinos in Mississippi and Louisiana in 1994. That year it began managing the Treasure Chest Casino, a riverboat casino in Louisiana (it also owned a 15% stake). Two years later it acquired the Par-A-Dice Gaming riverboat casino in East Peoria, Illinois. When a federal investigation of Louisiana governor Edwin Edwards pointed toward Robert Guidry, a principal in the Treasure Chest operation, Boyd bought the remaining 85% it didn't already own. (Guidry pleaded guilty in 1998 to making payoffs to Edwards.)

In 1999 the company spent $23 million to renovate the aging Stardust, which later signed Vegas icon Wayne Newton to a 10-year engagement (a contract reportedly worth about $250 million). Boyd Gaming also gained its first foothold in Atlantic City that year when it formed a joint venture with Mirage Resorts (now owned by MGM MIRAGE) to build The Borgata (Italian for "village"), a 2,000-room, $1 billion casino resort. Renovation work at its Sam's Town casinos during 2000 ended Boyd's streak of earnings growth. The next year the company bought the Delta Downs racetrack near Lake Charles, Louisiana. The renamed Delta Downs Racetrack and Casino opened its casino in 2002. That year

the company also purchased Isle of Capri's Tunica, Mississippi, property, adjacent to Sam's Town, for $7.5 million.

In 2004 Boyd acquired Coast Casinos for $1.3 billion. Several Boyd properties in Louisiana were temporarily closed in the wake of Hurricane Katrina, which hit the Gulf Coast in August 2005.

EXECUTIVES

Chairman: William S. (Bill) Boyd, age 77, $4,065,710 total compensation
Vice Chairman and EVP: Marianne Boyd Johnson, age 50
President, CEO, and Director: Keith E. Smith, age 48, $2,904,680 total compensation
EVP and COO: Paul J. Chakmak, age 44, $1,687,866 total compensation
SVP, CFO, Treasurer, and Principal Financial Officer: Josh Hirsberg, age 47, $523,372 total compensation
VP Information Systems: Dennis J. (Denny) Frey
EVP, Secretary, and General Counsel: Brian A. Larson, age 53
SVP and Controller: Jeffrey G. (Jeff) Santoro, age 47
SVP Operations: Christopher R. Gibase
SVP Administration: William J. (Bill) Noonan
VP Strategic Procurement: Richard A. (Rick) Darnold
VP and Director: William R. Boyd, age 49
VP Marketing, Borgata: Dave Coskey
VP Development: Blake Cumbers
VP Government and Community Affairs: Gina B. Polovina
VP Technology and Systems: Paula Eylar, age 46
VP Hospitality, The Water Club: Drew Schlesinger
VP Human Resources: Robert Gerst
VP Internal Audit: Michael Bond
Director; President and CEO, Echelon Resorts: Robert L. (Bob) Boughner, age 55, $2,645,376 total compensation
Auditors: Deloitte & Touche LLP

LOCATIONS

HQ: Boyd Gaming Corporation
3883 Howard Hughes Pkwy, 9th Fl.
Las Vegas, NV 89169
Phone: 702-792-7200 **Fax:** 702-792-7313
Web: www.boydgaming.com

2008 Sales

	% of total
Las Vegas	
Downtown	43
Other	14
Midwest & South	43
Total	**100**

Select Operating Markets and Locations

Las Vegas
California Hotel and Casino
Eldorado Casino
Fremont Hotel and Casino
Gold Coast
Jokers Wild Casino
Main Street Station Casino, Brewery and Hotel
The Orleans
Sam's Town Las Vegas
Suncoast
Other markets
Blue Chip Hotel & Casino (riverboat casino; Michigan City, IN)
Par-A-Dice Hotel and Casino (East Peoria, IL)
Sam's Town Hotel and Gambling Hall (Tunica, MI)
Treasure Chest Casino (riverboat casino; Kenner, LA)
Other operations
Delta Downs (horse racing track; Lake Charles, LA)
Vacations Hawaii (travel agency)

PRODUCTS/OPERATIONS

2008 Sales

	$ mil.	% of total
Gaming	1,477	83
Food & beverage	251	14
Room	141	2
Other	118	1
Adjustments	(206)	—
Total	**1,781**	**100**

COMPETITORS

Ameristar Casinos
Boomtown
Circus and Eldorado
Harrah's Entertainment
Isle of Capri Casinos
Las Vegas Sands
MGM MIRAGE
Pinnacle Entertainment
Rio All-Suite Hotel & Casino
Station Casinos
Tropicana Entertainment
Wynn Resorts

HISTORICAL FINANCIALS

Company Type: Public

Income Statement

FYE: December 31

	REVENUE ($ mil.)	NET INCOME ($ mil.)	NET PROFIT MARGIN	EMPLOYEES
12/08	1,781.0	(223.0)	—	16,000
12/07	1,997.1	303.0	15.2%	16,900
12/06	2,192.6	116.8	5.3%	18,300
12/05	2,223.0	161.0	7.2%	23,400
12/04	1,734.1	111.5	6.4%	19,293
Annual Growth	0.7%	—	—	(4.6%)

2008 Year-End Financials

Debt ratio: 231.5%
Return on equity: —
Cash ($ mil.): 98
Current ratio: 0.61
Long-term debt ($ mil.): 2,647

No. of shares (mil.): 86
Dividends
  Yield: 6.3%
  Payout: —
Market value ($ mil.): 407

Stock History

NYSE: BYD

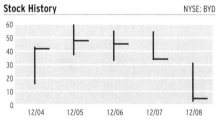

	STOCK PRICE ($) FY Close	P/E High/Low		PER SHARE ($) Earnings	Dividends	Book Value
12/08	4.73	—	—	(2.54)	0.30	13.28
12/07	34.07	16	10	3.42	0.58	16.09
12/06	45.31	42	25	1.30	0.53	12.89
12/05	47.66	37	23	1.60	0.46	12.75
12/04	41.65	30	11	1.42	0.32	10.96
Annual Growth	(41.9%)	—	—	—	(1.6%)	4.9%

Briggs & Stratton

It's no BS, Briggs & Stratton knows outdoor housework. For power equipment, the company is #1 among manufacturers of air-cooled gas engines. Lawn and garden OEMs Husqvarna Outdoor Products, MTD, and Deere are key engine customers; generator, pressure washer, and pump makers are less so. Replacement engines and parts are made for aftermarkets, too. Engines are sold worldwide direct through sales and service arms. Subsidiary Briggs & Stratton Power Products also produces generators, pressure washers, mowers, and other outdoor tools, retailed through Lowes, Home Depot, and Sears, as well as independent dealers. Briggs & Stratton engine and power product facilities dot the US, Europe, Australia, and China.

Publicly held, Briggs & Stratton's manufacturing muscle is tested by weakening demand, precipitated by global economic recession and mounting competition. Its revenue (over 60%) relies upon engine orders from OEMs of outdoor power equipment. Exposed to consumer spending, Briggs & Stratton's power product revenue (about 80% of it) hinges on the health of big-box retailers, such as Wal-Mart and Home Depot. The company has attempted to shore up weaknesses in both engine and outdoor power product markets by branding initiatives that focus on the value and dependability of Briggs & Stratton goods.

Operating costs, which might otherwise chip away at revenues, are vertically contained. Briggs & Stratton integrates manufacture of many of its core components with its engine production. Moreover, because facilities are spread across largely non-union employment regions, wages are less aggressive. Internationally, the company expanded its capacity in 2008 by acquiring Australia's Victa Lawncare, a manufacturer of lawn and garden power equipment. Victa operates as a subsidiary of Briggs & Stratton Australia Pty. Limited, and promises to increase the company's manufacturing might, as well as market share, both in Australia and globally. Domestically however, the company reined in activities in 2008 and 2009. It shuttered two power product facilities in Wisconsin, and one engine facility in Missouri, transferring work to other sites in the US and China.

Spreading out its manufacturing capacity horizontally, Briggs & Stratton has entered into several joint ventures. It makes components for punch presses and rewind starters for Starting Industrial of Japan, and Daihatsu Motor Company, and from its China-based facility, two-cycle engines for The Toro Company. Briggs and Stratton also ties up with Mitsubishi Heavy Industries (MHI) to distribute MHI's air cooled gas engines internationally.

HISTORY

In 1909 inventor Stephen Foster Briggs and grain merchant Harold Stratton gathered $25,000 and founded Briggs & Stratton to produce a six-cylinder, two-cycle engine that Briggs had developed while in college. However, the engine proved too expensive for mass production. A brief foray into the auto assembly business also failed as the company skirted bankruptcy. But in 1910 Briggs received a patent for a single-spark gas engine igniter. It wasn't a runaway success, but the company had found its niche making automotive electrical components. By 1920 Briggs & Stratton was the largest US producer of specialty lights, ignitions, regulators, and starting switches. These specialties accounted for two-thirds of the firm's total business through the mid-1930s.

The company acquired the A. O. Smith Motor Wheel (a gasoline-driven wheel designed to be attached to bicycles) and the Flyer (a two-passenger vehicle similar to a buckboard) in 1919. Neither product was successful and both were soon sold, but the company gained crucial knowledge and experience. In 1923 Briggs & Stratton introduced a stationary version of the Motor Wheel designed to power washing machines, garden tractors, and lawn mowers. The company continued to diversify, moving into the auto lock business in 1924. Its die-cast cylinder lock outsold competitors' brass models, and by the end of the decade, Briggs & Stratton had the lion's share of the market. The company formed BASCO to make auto body hardware. Briggs & Stratton bought Evinrude Outboard Motor Company in 1928, but sold the business within a year.

As with many other industrial manufacturers, Briggs & Stratton benefited by the onset of WWII: The war triggered an insatiable need for the company's products. Its wartime contributions included airplane ignition switches, artillery ammunition, and engines for generators, pumps, compressors, fans, repair shops, emergency hospitals, and mobile kitchens.

After the war Briggs & Stratton focused on small engines for lawn and garden equipment, and soon it dominated the market. In 1953 the company introduced an aluminum die-cast engine that was lighter than competing models and could withstand greater operating temperatures and pressures. Baby boomers' parents fueled sales, and the small market attracted little competition; Briggs & Stratton thrived making air-cooled engines and automobile components, such as locks and switches.

By the end of the 1970s sales had risen to about $590 million and, as the low-cost producer in the industry, the company was without a rival. During the early 1980s, however, Japanese companies (including Honda, Kawasaki, Mitsubishi, and Suzuki) entered the market after motorcycle sales crested. As a result of the strong dollar, these new competitors were able to provide engines to equipment makers at less expense than could Briggs & Stratton; the company suffered a decline in the late 1980s.

The company experienced a resurgence during the early 1990s. Frederick Stratton Jr., grandson of the co-founder, took over as president in 1992, and Briggs & Stratton benefited from a dollar that was weak relative to the yen. In mid-2001 Stratton Jr. stepped down as president (he remained chairman until 2003) and COO John Shiely became president and CEO. Shiely succeeded Stratton as chairman in 2003.

Briggs & Stratton acquired outdoor power equipment manufacturer Simplicity Manufacturing in 2004. Briggs & Stratton acquired the assets of Murray Inc. in early 2005. Murray had once been one of Briggs & Stratton's biggest customers; however, in late 2004 the OEM filed for bankruptcy. Murray operations ceased that year, but Briggs & Stratton continued to make Murray-branded products. The Simplicity and Murray deals significantly boosted the company's top line.

In early 2007 Briggs & Stratton decided to close its engine manufacturing plant in Rolla, Missouri, and to transfer production to facilities in China and elsewhere in the US. Later that year the company elected to shutter its factory in Port Washington, Wisconsin, a facility that was picked up in the 2004 acquisition of Simplicity Manufacturing. Production at Port Washington, where outdoor power equipment was made, was transferred to other facilities.

EXECUTIVES

Chairman and CEO: John S. Shiely, age 56, $4,569,696 total compensation
President, COO, and Director: Todd J. Teske, age 44, $1,293,252 total compensation
SVP and CFO: James E. (Jim) Brenn, age 61, $1,156,779 total compensation
VP Information Technology: Richard L. Kolbe
SVP Sales and Customer Support: William H. Reitman, age 53, $752,571 total compensation
SVP Administration: Thomas R. Savage, age 61, $1,296,626 total compensation
SVP Operations Support: Michael D. Schoen, age 49
SVP and President, Yard Power Products Group: Vincent R. Shiely Jr., age 49
SVP; President, Engine Power Products Group: Joseph C. Wright, age 50
VP Human Resources: Jeffrey G. Mahloch
VP, General Counsel, and Secretary: Robert F. Heath, age 61
VP North American Operations, Engine Power Products Group: David G. Debaets, age 46
VP Customer Experience: Peggy L. Tracy
VP; President, Home Power Products Group: Harold L. Redman, age 45
VP Procurement, Yard Power Products Group: Daniel B (Dan) Kennedy
VP Marketing: Randall R. Carpenter
Managing Director, Briggs & Stratton Australasia: Andrew S. King
Managing Director, Europe: Jerome M. Kozik
Managing Director, Latin America: Joseph M. Spector
Director Corporate Communications: Laura Timm
Auditors: PricewaterhouseCoopers LLP

LOCATIONS

HQ: Briggs & Stratton Corporation
12301 W. Wirth St., Wauwatosa, WI 53222
Phone: 414-259-5333   **Fax:** 414-259-5773
Web: www.briggsandstratton.com

Briggs & Stratton has manufacturing facilities in the US in Alabama, Georgia, Kentucky, Missouri, and Wisconsin, and through joint ventures in China, India, and Japan.

2009 Sales

	$ mil.	% of total
US	1,589.2	76
Other countries	503.0	24
Total	**2,092.2**	**100**

PRODUCTS/OPERATIONS

2009 Sales

	$ mil.	% of total
Engines	1,414.1	61
Power Products	892.9	39
Adjustments	(214.8)	—
Total	**2,092.2**	**100**

Selected Brands and Products

Brands

Briggs & Stratton	John Deere
Brute	Murray
Classic	Simplicity
Craftsman	Snapper
Ferris	Troy-Bilt
Giant Vac	Victa

Products
- Garden tillers
- Generators
- Pressure washers
- Pumps
- Riding lawn mowers
- Snow throwers
- Walk-behind lawn mowers

Power products
- Generators (portable and standby)
- Lawn and garden powered equipment
- Pressure washers
- Snow throwers

COMPETITORS

Aura Systems
Blount International
Campbell Hausfeld
Coleman
Deere
DeVilbiss
Dewey Electronics
Exmark Manufacturing
Generac Power Systems
Graco
Honda
Kawasaki Heavy Industries
Kohler
Kubota Engine America
Metalcraft
Suzuki Motor
Tecumseh Products
Toro
Tradewinds Power

HISTORICAL FINANCIALS

Company Type: Public

Income Statement

FYE: Sunday nearest June 30

	REVENUE ($ mil.)	NET INCOME ($ mil.)	NET PROFIT MARGIN	EMPLOYEES
6/09	2,092.2	32.0	1.5%	—
6/08	2,151.4	22.6	1.1%	7,145
6/07	2,157.2	0.1	0.0%	3,693
6/06	2,542.2	102.3	4.0%	3,874
6/05	2,654.9	116.8	4.4%	4,058
Annual Growth	(5.8%)	(27.7%)	—	20.8%

2009 Year-End Financials

Debt ratio: 40.5%
Return on equity: 4.2%
Cash ($ mil.): 16
Current ratio: 2.86
Long-term debt ($ mil.): 281

No. of shares (mil.): 50
Dividends
  Yield: 5.8%
  Payout: 120.3%
Market value ($ mil.): 667

Stock History

NYSE: BGG

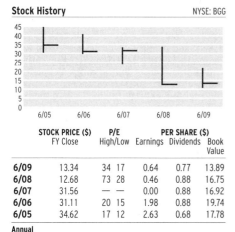

	STOCK PRICE ($) FY Close	P/E High/Low		PER SHARE ($) Earnings	Dividends	Book Value
6/09	13.34	34	17	0.64	0.77	13.89
6/08	12.68	73	28	0.46	0.88	16.75
6/07	31.56	—	—	0.00	0.88	16.92
6/06	31.11	20	15	1.98	0.88	19.74
6/05	34.62	17	12	2.63	0.68	17.78
Annual Growth	(21.2%)	—	—	(29.8%)	3.2%	(6.0%)

Brightpoint Inc.

Brightpoint makes money moving mobiles. The company is a top global distributor of mobile phones and other wireless products, acting as a middleman between manufacturers and wireless service providers. It ships the equipment to companies that sell mobile phones and accessories, including wireless carriers, dealers, and retailers; customers include Vodafone, Best Buy, and Sprint Nextel. Brightpoint also offers a range of services that includes warehousing, product fulfillment, purchasing, contract manufacturing, call center outsourcing, customized packaging, activation, and Web marketing.

Brightpoint's largest suppliers include Nokia (26% of total units handled in 2008), Motorola (21%), and Samsung (15%). Other brands sold by the company include Apple, Sony Ericsson, Kyocera, LG Electronics, and Research In Motion.

The company continues to broaden its selection of services by forming new alliances with telecom and computing equipment makers. Brightpoint has also grown through acquisitions. The company acquired the assets of CellStar's operations serving the US and Latin America for approximately $62 million in cash in 2007. It also purchased Dangaard Telecom, a Danish mobile phone distributor with subsidiaries in 14 countries, for about $385 million in stock.

HISTORY

Robert Laikin started in the portable phone business in 1985, when he established Century Car Phones (later renamed Century Cellular Network). The company grew rapidly but demand grew faster, and by 1989 Laikin's business was having trouble keeping up. That year he and Daniel Koerselman, a salesman for a car phone accessory company, started Wholesale Cellular to supply Century and others with phones. Laikin stepped down as president of Century in 1993. Wholesale Cellular went public a year later and changed its name to Brightpoint in 1995.

That year Brightpoint moved into the foreign market by forming partnerships with UK and India technology companies. It improved its distribution capabilities in North and South America by merging with Philadelphia-based Allied Communications in 1996. The next year Brightpoint further augmented its international operations by acquiring businesses in Hong Kong, Sweden, and Venezuela. It also bought the remaining 20% minority interests of its joint ventures in China, the UK, and Australia. Brightpoint continued its focus on international markets in 1998 with the acquisitions of distributors in the Netherlands and Taiwan.

Facing continuing pressures from resellers, the company in 1999 announced a restructuring plan that curtailed the global expansion, and divested its operations in Argentina, Poland, and the UK; its joint ventures in China; its accessories company in Hong Kong; and its distribution center in the Netherlands. A shareholder lawsuit was filed that summer, charging that Brightpoint withheld news of its mounting troubles in Asia and Latin America from shareholders and institutional investors (the suit was dismissed in 2001).

Despite an extension of the company's US distribution agreement with Nokia, the restructuring helped cause annual losses for Brightpoint in

1999. By 2000 the company had added new pacts and contract extensions on five continents. That year Brightpoint was awarded a patent for its wireless fulfillment system; the company promptly filed a patent infringement suit against chief rival Cellstar.

Late in 2001 Brightpoint announced a joint venture with Hong Kong-based wireless communications company Chinatron; the venture, called Brightpoint China, was established to distribute wireless phones to customers in China. The deal was finalized early in 2002. Within months, however, Brightpoint sold its 50% stake to its joint-venture partner in return for a minority stake in Chinatron. In 2004 Brightpoint sold its operations in Ireland to Celtic Telecom.

In 2006 it purchased fellow wireless product distributor Trio Industries.

EXECUTIVES

Chairman and CEO: Robert J. Laikin, age 45, $3,216,210 total compensation
EVP, CFO, and Treasurer; Interim President Europe, Middle East, and Africa: Anthony W. (Tony) Boor, age 46, $1,080,821 total compensation
EVP and CIO: John Alexander Du Plessis (Jac) Currie, age 44, $1,400,797 total compensation
SVP, Chief Accounting Officer, and Controller: Vincent Donargo, age 48
EVP, General Counsel, and Secretary: Steven E. Fivel, age 48, $1,114,376 total compensation
SVP Human Resources: Annette Cyr
SVP Global Strategy, Investor Relations, and Corporate Communications: Anurag Gupta
President, Asia/Pacific: R. Bruce Thomlinson, age 47, $1,120,204 total compensation
President, Americas: J. Mark Howell, age 44, $1,589,855 total compensation
Director, Shared Services Center: Stephen Babbage
Auditors: Ernst & Young LLP

LOCATIONS

HQ: Brightpoint, Inc.
7635 Interactive Way, Ste. 200
Indianapolis, IN 46278
Phone: 317-707-2355   **Fax:** 317-707-2512
Web: www.brightpoint.com

2008 Sales

	$ mil.	% of total
Europe, Middle East & Africa	2,559.9	55
Asia/Pacific	1,191.2	26
Americas	889.4	19
Total	**4,640.5**	**100**

PRODUCTS/OPERATIONS

2008 Sales

	$ mil.	% of total
Product distribution	4,211.8	91
Logistics services	428.7	9
Total	**4,640.5**	**100**

Suppliers

Audiovox
Kyocera
LG Electronics
Logitech
Motorola
Nokia
Novatel Wireless
Palm
Plantronics
Samsung
SanDisk
Sanyo
Sierra Wireless
Sony Ericsson
UTStarcom

Services

Channel development
  Outbound sales
  Product marketing
  Field training and support
  Merchandising
  Credit determination
  Co-op funds disbursement/tracking
  Commissions management
  Sales incentive programs
  VAR programs
Logistics services
  Inventory management
  Kitting and packaging
  Device programming
  Bulk and end user order processing
  Returns management and processing
  Receivables management
  Credit services
Subscriber services
  Customer contact center
  E-business solutions
  Outbound marketing
  Fulfillment services

COMPETITORS

ATC Technology
Avenir Telecom
BearCom
Brightstar Corp.
Caterpillar Logistics Services
CLST
Ericsson
Euronet
Hello Direct
InfoSonics
Ingram Micro
Kuehne + Nagel International
Kyocera
Motorola, Inc.
Nokia
Panasonic Mobile Communications
PFSweb
Quality Distributors, LLC
SED International
Sony
Tech Data
TESSCO
UPS Supply Chain Solutions

HISTORICAL FINANCIALS

Company Type: Public

Income Statement

FYE: December 31

	REVENUE ($ mil.)	NET INCOME ($ mil.)	NET PROFIT MARGIN	EMPLOYEES
12/08	4,640.5	(342.1)	—	3,032
12/07	4,300.3	47.4	1.1%	3,269
12/06	2,425.4	35.6	1.5%	2,112
12/05	2,140.2	10.4	0.5%	1,683
12/04	1,865.6	16.3	0.9%	1,264
Annual Growth	25.6%	—	—	24.5%

2008 Year-End Financials

Debt ratio: 70.1%
Return on equity: —
Cash ($ mil.): 57
Current ratio: 1.35
Long-term debt ($ mil.): 176
No. of shares (mil.): 82
Dividends
  Yield: 0.0%
  Payout: —
Market value ($ mil.): 357

Stock History

NASDAQ (GS): CELL

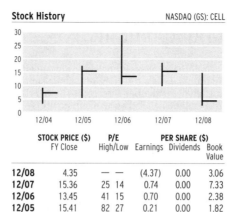

	STOCK PRICE ($) FY Close	P/E High/Low		PER SHARE ($) Earnings	Dividends	Book Value
12/08	4.35	—	—	(4.37)	0.00	3.06
12/07	15.36	25	14	0.74	0.00	7.33
12/06	13.45	41	15	0.70	0.00	2.38
12/05	15.41	82	27	0.21	0.00	1.82
12/04	7.24	28	11	0.31	0.00	1.87
Annual Growth	(12.0%)	—	—	—	—	13.0%

Brinker International

More than a few Chili's heat up this restaurant business. Brinker International is the world's #3 casual-dining operator in terms of revenue (behind Darden Restaurants and OSI Restaurant Partners), with more than 1,650 locations in about 30 countries. Its flagship Chili's Grill & Bar chain boasts more than 1,400 outlets and trails only Applebee's as the largest full-service restaurant chain. Specializing in southwestern-style dishes, Chili's menu features fajitas, margarita grilled chicken, and its popular baby back ribs. Brinker also operates On The Border Mexican Grill & Cantina, a Mexican-themed chain with 160 locations, and Maggiano's Little Italy. More than 650 of the eateries are operated by franchisees.

Brinker has become a leading force in the casual dining industry by successfully developing restaurant brands that appeal to middle America with ethnic-inspired menus and affordable prices. It also spends heavily on marketing to promote its restaurants over rival chains, with limited-time offers and value pricing deals playing key roles in attracting new customers. Brinker's large base of corporate-run locations allows it to have more control over customer service and food quality throughout its chains.

Responding to the recession and weak consumer spending, the company has slowed its pace of expansion in the US, opening about 40 new locations during fiscal 2009, down from about 90 new units the previous year. Most of the new units added were franchised Chili's outlets. More than 50 under-performing locations were closed. Brinker did add more than 40 new dining units outside the US.

Brinker sold an 80% stake in the Romano's Macaroni Grill chain to private equity firm Golden Gate Capital in 2008. The deal, worth more than $130 million, returned cash to the restaurant company for debt payments; it also allowed Brinker to focus on its flagship Chili's banner. The company previously sold its Corner Bakery Cafe and Rockfish Seafood Grill businesses in 2006; the Corner Bakery chain was acquired by upscale restaurant operator Il Fornaio,

while Brinker's 43% stake in Rockfish Grill was sold back to the chain's founders.

The company is named for founder Norman Brinker. A pioneer of the casual-dining industry, he died in 2009 at the age of 78.

HISTORY

Norman Brinker pioneered the so-called "casual-dining" segment in 1966 when he opened his first Steak & Ale in Dallas. In 1971 he took the company public and watched it grow to more than 100 locations by 1976 when Pillsbury bought the chain. After serving as president of Pillsbury Restaurant Group (which included Burger King, Poppin' Fresh Restaurants, and Steak & Ale), Brinker left in 1983 to take over Chili's, a chain of southwestern-styled eateries founded by Larry Lavine in 1975. With plans to develop the company into a major chain, Brinker took Chili's public in 1984.

The company began recruiting joint venture and franchise partners. It also expanded the Chili's menu to include items such as fajitas, staking the company's growth on aging baby boomers who were looking for something more than fast food. Stymied in attempts to regain control of his former S&A Restaurant (later acquired by Metromedia) and to acquire such fast-food chains as Taco Cabana and Flyer's Island Express, Brinker decided to focus on the casual, low-priced restaurant market. In 1989 Chili's acquired Knoxville, Tennessee-based Grady's Goodtimes and Romano's Macaroni Grill, a small Italian chain founded by Texas restaurateur Phil Romano in 1988. Reflecting the expansion of its restaurant offerings, the company changed its name to Brinker International in 1990.

Brinker introduced Spageddies (a casual, lower-priced pasta restaurant) in 1992. With two Italian-cuisine chains in his network, the entrepreneur began to take on rival Olive Garden. Brinker suffered a major head injury in 1993 while playing polo, leaving him comatose for two weeks. Despite the traumatic event and poor early prognosis, he made a rapid recovery and returned to running the company. In 1994 Brinker International expanded to cash in on the popularity of Mexican food. It acquired Cozymel's Coastal Mexican Grill that year and bought the $50 million, 21-unit On The Border Mexican-food chain in 1995.

That year Brinker retired as CEO and was replaced by Ronald McDougall. McDougall sold Grady's and Spageddies to Quality Dining, since they no longer fit the company's overall strategy, and acquired two restaurant concepts (Corner Bakery and Maggiano's Little Italy) from Rich Melman's Lettuce Entertain You Enterprises. With Romano in 1996, the company opened a test location (in Dallas) of eatZi's Market & Bakery, a takeout concept to capitalize on the public's increasing desire not to cook.

In 1999 Brinker began expanding into Guatemala, Saudi Arabia, and Mexico. McDougall was named vice chairman in 1999 and eventually replaced Brinker as chairman the following year.

In 2001 the company gained complete control of Big Bowl and bought a 40% stake in Rockfish Seafood Grill. With an emphasis on company-owned restaurants, Brinker purchased 47 Chili's and On The Border restaurants from New England Restaurant Co. and 39 Chili's restaurants from Sydran Services in 2001. The following year the company sold its chain of eatZi's Market &

Bakery to Romano and investment group Castanea Partners. Brinker later entered its first franchising agreement for Romano's Macaroni Grill.

In 2003 Brinker sold Cozymel's Coastal Mexican Grill to a group that included restaurateur Jack Baum, former Electronic Data Systems president Morton H. Meyerson, and their investment firm 2M Companies. McDougall stepped down from the executive ranks in early 2004, with company president Doug Brooks taking the reins as CEO. (McDougall also retired from the board later that year.)

Brinker reached an historic milestone in 2005 when it opened its 1,000th Chili's location. Company president Wilson Craft resigned that year after only 20 months on the job. The company also began shedding some of its emerging concepts to focus on its core brands, selling Big Bowl Asian Kitchen to Lettuce Entertain You in 2005 and shedding Corner Bakery the following year in a deal with upscale Italian operator Il Fornaio. Also in 2006, Brinker sold its stake in Rockfish Seafood Grill back to that chain's founders.

The company shed a majority of its Romano's chain in 2008, selling an 80% stake in the Italian-themed eatery business to private equity firm Golden Gate Capital.

EXECUTIVES

Chairman, President, and CEO:
Douglas H. (Doug) Brooks, age 56
SVP Global Business Development and COO:
Carin L. Stutz, age 52
EVP and CFO: Charles M. (Chuck) Sonsteby, age 54
SVP Information Solutions: Michael L. Furlow
EVP, Chief Administrative Officer, Secretary, and General Counsel: Roger F. Thomson, age 60
SVP and Chief Marketing Officer; President, Maggiano's Little Italy: Wyman T. Roberts, age 50
EVP and Chief PeopleWorks Officer:
Valerie L. Davisson, age 47
EVP; President of Chili's Grill & Bar and President, On The Border Mexican Restaurant & Cantina:
Todd E. Diener, age 52
EVP Brand Solutions: Michael B. (Happy) Webberman, age 49
SVP and Controller: David R. Doyle
SVP and President Global Business Development:
John Reale, age 55
SVP Finance: Guy J. Constant
VP Design and Architecture:
Richard A. (Rick) McCaffrey
VP Executive Development: Stan A. Fletcher
VP Business Solutions: Laurie A. Gaines
VP Restaurant Development: Jeffry S. Smith
VP PeopleWorks Global Learning and Shared Services:
Jennifer A. Hartley
VP Tax: Kathleen A. Cholette
VP Communications and Corporate Affairs:
Joseph G. (Joe) Taylor
VP Treasury and Investor Relation: Marie L. Perry
Auditors: KPMG LLP

LOCATIONS

HQ: Brinker International, Inc.
6820 LBJ Fwy., Ste. 200, Dallas, TX 75240
Phone: 972-980-9917   **Fax:** 972-770-9593
Web: www.brinker.com

2009 Locations

	No.
US	1,488
International	201
Total	**1,689**

PRODUCTS/OPERATIONS

2009 Locations

	No.
Chili's Grill & Bar	1,485
On The Border Mexican Grill & Cantina	160
Maggiano's Little Italy	44
Total	**1,689**

2009 Locations

	No.
Company-owned	1,024
Franchised	665
Total	**1,689**

COMPETITORS

Carlson Restaurants
Cheesecake Factory
Cracker Barrel
Darden
Denny's
DineEquity
Hooters
OSI Restaurant Partners
Perkins & Marie Callender's
Ruby Tuesday
Steak n Shake
Texas Roadhouse

HISTORICAL FINANCIALS

Company Type: Public

Income Statement

FYE: Last Wednesday in June

	REVENUE ($ mil.)	NET INCOME ($ mil.)	NET PROFIT MARGIN	EMPLOYEES
6/09	3,620.6	79.2	2.2%	77,100
6/08	4,235.2	51.7	1.2%	100,400
6/07	4,376.9	230.0	5.3%	113,900
6/06	4,151.3	212.4	5.1%	110,800
6/05	3,912.9	160.2	4.1%	108,500
Annual Growth	(1.9%)	(16.1%)	—	(8.2%)

2009 Year-End Financials

Debt ratio: 112.4%
Return on equity: 12.8%
Cash ($ mil.): 94
Current ratio: 0.90
Long-term debt ($ mil.): 727

No. of shares (mil.): 102
Dividends
 Yield: 2.6%
 Payout: 57.1%
Market value ($ mil.): 1,740

Stock History

NYSE: EAT

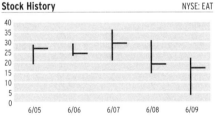

	STOCK PRICE ($) FY Close	P/E High/Low		PER SHARE ($) Earnings	Dividends	Book Value
6/09	17.03	28	5	0.77	0.44	6.33
6/08	18.90	62	30	0.49	0.42	5.83
6/07	29.27	19	11	1.85	0.34	7.88
6/06	24.20	18	14	1.62	0.20	10.53
6/05	26.70	25	17	1.15	0.00	10.77
Annual Growth	(10.6%)	—	—	(9.5%)	—	(12.4%)

The Brink's Company

Teetering on the brink of a security disaster? The Brink's Company can help. The company is a leading operator of armored cars that transport cash for banks and retailers (85% of sales). Brink's also provides other security-related services (such as ATM management, secure long-distance transportation of valuables, and guarding services, including airport security), and has additional government-agency clients. The company serves customers in more than 50 countries. Its operations include some 800 facilities and more than 9,000 vehicles. Brink's completed the spinoff of its home security business in 2008.

About 70% of the company's revenues come from outside North America. The largest seven Brink's operations (Brazil, Colombia, France, Germany, the Netherlands, the US, and Venezuela) account for nearly three-quarters of the company's business.

In 2009 the company expanded its Brazilian operations with the purchase of Sebival for approximately $50 million. Sebival is a leading provider of cash-in-transit (CIT) and payment processing services in midwestern Brazil.

The company previously owned Brink's Home Security (BHS), which installs and monitors alarm systems, and accounted for some 15% of sales. Brink's in 2007 began reviewing shareholder proposals for alternative options for the company and hired consulting firm Monitor Company Group to help in a re-examination of strategic moves. It subsequently spun off BHS into a separate publicly traded company in order to focus on its core secure transportation, cash logistics, and other commercial security services.

HISTORY

The Brink's Company was originally the Pennsylvania Coal Company, founded in 1838 in Pittston, Pennsylvania. In 1901 it was acquired by the Erie Railroad, which itself was purchased by the Alleghany Corp. in 1916.

In the late 1920s intense competition in the coal industry and antitrust concerns prevented Alleghany's expansion. Alleghany created the Pittston Company in 1930 and offered Pittston stock to Alleghany stockholders while retaining a controlling interest. At its founding, Pittston acquired United States Distributing Corp., which owned a trucking firm, warehouses, a wholesale coal distributor, and a Wyoming mining company.

But coal consumption was falling. In 1944 the company began mining bituminous coal (which was increasingly used by industry and utilities), and in the 1950s it entered the fuel oil market. Its trucking and warehousing businesses also expanded, accounting for 43% of net income by 1954. Pittston gained its independence that year: Alleghany purchased a railroad, which raised antitrust concerns and forced the company to sell its 50% stake in Pittston.

Seeking other revenue sources, in 1956 Pittston acquired a 22% stake in (and subsequently control of) the world's largest armored car company, Chicago-based Brink's. Brink's had begun as a delivery company in 1859 and started making payroll deliveries in 1891. Pittston acquired the entire company in 1962.

By the early 1970s Pittston was the #1 exporter of metallurgical coal, used in steel manufacturing. The OPEC oil embargo and the energy crisis of the 1970s increased demand for coal; in 1976 some 90% of company profits were coal-related. However, by the late 1970s labor disputes and a steel industry slump decreased profits dramatically.

Meanwhile, Brink's suffered from rising costs and increased competition in the 1970s. In 1976 a federal grand jury investigated possible antitrust violations in the armored car business. Brink's paid nearly $6 million the following year to settle antitrust charges.

The company diversified further in the 1980s, setting up Brink's Home Security (1984) after selling its warehousing operations. Pittston also entered the highly competitive airfreight express business by purchasing Burlington Air Express (1982).

Pittston began trading as two tracking stocks in 1993: Pittston Services Group (security and transportation) and Pittston Minerals Group (mining). In 1996, to further rationalize its business structure, Pittston split its security and transportation unit into two distinct businesses, each with its own tracking stock: Pittston Brink's Group and Pittston Burlington Group (later BAX Global).

Expanding globally, Brink's formed a transportation venture in 1997 with Switzerland's Zurcher Freilager, a freight-handling company. It also bought out affiliates in the Netherlands and Hong Kong in 1997 and in France and Germany in 1998. In 1999 BHS formed Brink's Mobile Security to provide wireless tracking systems for vehicles.

With its Pittston Minerals unit beset by a growing number of worker-injury lawsuits (black lung and other claims), The Pittston Company in 2000 made plans to exit the coal mining business to minimize future liability. Also that year the company abandoned its tracking stock structure.

In 2002 the company sold some of its coal assets to Braxton-Clay Land & Mineral and Massey Energy, and by the end of the year Pittston had ceased active involvement in the coal business. By 2004 Pittston had sold its remaining natural resources interests, which included natural gas and timber operations.

Also in 2003, the company changed its name to The Brink's Company to reflect its transformation from a conglomerate — with operations in the security, heavy-weight freight transportation, and coal and other natural resource industries — into a company focused solely on security.

In 2006 the company sold its BAX Global unit, which arranges for the delivery of overnight and second-day freight from business to business in more than 120 countries, to Deutsche Bahn for $1.1 billion. The Brink's Company then sold Air Transport International, formerly a part of BAX Global, to Cargo Holdings International. Its Brink's Home Security was spun off in 2008.

EXECUTIVES

Chairman, President, and CEO; CEO, Brink's, Incorporated: Michael T. Dan, age 58, $7,683,903 total compensation
VP and CFO: Joseph W. (Joe) Dziedzic, age 41
VP Risk Management and Insurance: Arthur E. Wheatley, age 66
VP and Chief Administrative Officer: Frank T. Lennon, age 67, $1,664,276 total compensation
VP, General Counsel, and Secretary: McAlister C. Marshall II, age 39

President, Brink's Europe, Middle East and Africa: Michael J. (Mike) Cazer, age 41, $1,603,175 total compensation
Controller: Matthew A. P. Schumacher, age 50
Treasurer: Jonathan A. Leon
Auditors: KPMG LLP

LOCATIONS

HQ: The Brink's Company
1801 Bayberry Ct., Richmond, VA 23226
Phone: 804-289-9600   **Fax:** 804-289-9770
Web: www.brinkscompany.com

2008 Sales

	$ mil.	% of total
Europe, Middle East & Africa	1,359	43
North America	932	30
Latin America	801	25
Asia/Pacific	72	2
Total	**3,164**	**100**

PRODUCTS/OPERATIONS

Selected Clients

Banks
Financial institutions
Government agencies
Jewelers
Mints
Retailers

Selected Services

Automated teller machine (ATM) replenishment and servicing
Cash logistics (supply chain management of cash)
Cash-in-transit (CIT) armored car transportation
Global Services (arranging secure long-distance transportation of valuables)
Guarding services (including airport security)

COMPETITORS

Dunbar Armored
G4S
Garda Cash Logistics
Loomis AB
Prosegur
Rochester Armored Car
Securitas

HISTORICAL FINANCIALS

Company Type: Public

Income Statement

FYE: December 31

	REVENUE ($ mil.)	NET INCOME ($ mil.)	NET PROFIT MARGIN	EMPLOYEES
12/08	3,163.5	183.3	5.8%	56,900
12/07	3,219.0	137.3	4.3%	53,900
12/06	2,837.6	587.2	20.7%	48,700
12/05	2,549.0	147.8	5.8%	45,800
12/04	4,718.1	121.5	2.6%	54,000
Annual Growth	**(9.5%)**	**10.8%**	**—**	**1.3%**

2008 Year-End Financials

Debt ratio: 80.8%
Return on equity: 29.1%
Cash ($ mil.): 251
Current ratio: 1.56
Long-term debt ($ mil.): 173
No. of shares (mil.): 46
Dividends
  Yield: 1.5%
  Payout: 10.2%
Market value ($ mil.): 1,225

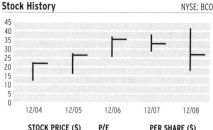

Stock History

NYSE: BCO

	STOCK PRICE ($) FY Close	P/E High/Low		Earnings	PER SHARE ($) Dividends	Book Value
12/08	26.88	10	5	3.93	0.40	4.70
12/07	32.94	13	10	2.92	0.36	22.96
12/06	35.25	3	2	11.64	0.21	16.54
12/05	26.42	11	7	2.50	0.10	18.38
12/04	21.79	10	6	2.20	0.10	14.79
Annual Growth	**5.4%**	**—**	**—**	**15.6%**	**41.4%**	**(24.9%)**

Bristol-Myers Squibb

Pharmaceutical giant Bristol-Myers Squibb (BMS) makes big bucks on matters of the heart. The company's blockbuster cardiovascular lineup includes heart disease drug Plavix, as well as Pravachol (which lowers cholesterol) and Avapro (for hypertension). BMS also makes antipsychotic medication Abilify and drugs in a number of other therapeutic categories, particularly oncology, virology (including HIV), and autoimmune disease. Through its Mead Johnson subsidiary, BMS makes Enfamil infant formula and other nutritional products for children.

As is the case for many of its druggernaut brethren, BMS is faced with aging products losing patent protection. Pravachol used to bring in the big bucks, but its patent expired in 2006 and sales have steadily been eroded by generic copies. Plavix, which accounts for more than 25% of sales, will see its patent expire in 2011.

Lead candidates in the company's pipeline include Apixaban for blood clots and kidney transplant drug Belatacept. Its Onglyza treatment for type 2 diabetes (developed with AstraZeneca) received FDA approval in mid-2009. Other recently approved drugs include Orencia (rheumatoid arthritis), Ixempra (cancer), and Emsam, a treatment for major depressive disorder developed with Somerset Pharmaceuticals.

Collaborations are an integral part of the company's product development and marketing methods. French drugmaker Sanofi-Aventis manufactures and distributes several of the company's products, including Plavix and Avapro. Japanese drug firm Otsuka Pharmaceutical co-promotes the schizophrenia treatment Abilify and diabetes drug Onglyza. BMS and joint venture partner Gilead Sciences began marketing Atripla, an HIV therapy that combines BMS's Sustiva with Gilead's Truvada. It works with Exelixis to develop two anti-cancer drugs.

In mid-2009 BMS acquired one of its development collaborators, Medarex, for about $2.4 billion. The purchase expands the company's development pipeline in the biotech areas of oncology and immunology treatments.

BMS announced in late 2007 that it would place more emphasis on biopharmaceuticals and

HISTORICAL FINANCIALS

Company Type: Public

Income Statement
FYE: Saturday nearest January 31

	REVENUE ($ mil.)	NET INCOME ($ mil.)	NET PROFIT MARGIN	EMPLOYEES
1/09	2,276.4	(133.2)	—	12,400
1/08	2,359.9	60.4	2.6%	13,100
1/07	2,470.9	65.7	2.7%	12,700
1/06	2,292.1	41.0	1.8%	12,800
1/05	1,941.8	43.3	2.2%	12,000
Annual Growth	4.1%	—	—	0.8%

2009 Year-End Financials

Debt ratio: 38.1%
Return on equity: —
Cash ($ mil.): 87
Current ratio: 1.69
Long-term debt ($ mil.): 150

No. of shares (mil.): 43
Dividends
Yield: 6.0%
Payout: —
Market value ($ mil.): 201

Stock History

NYSE: BWS

	STOCK PRICE ($) FY Close	P/E High/Low		PER SHARE ($) Earnings	Dividends	Book Value
1/09	4.69	—	—	(3.21)	0.28	9.19
1/08	17.19	28	9	1.37	0.28	13.02
1/07	36.23	24	13	1.51	0.21	12.21
1/06	20.01	21	14	0.97	0.18	10.12
1/05	12.87	18	11	1.02	0.18	9.12
Annual Growth	(22.3%)	—	—	—	11.7%	0.2%

Brown-Forman Corporation

Don't blame Brown-Forman (B-F) employees if the company Christmas party gets out of control; they have lots to drink on hand. The company's portfolio of some 30 mid-priced to super-premium brands includes such well-known spirits as Jack Daniel's, Canadian Mist, Finlandia, and Southern Comfort. Its wine labels include Fetzer and Korbel. Jack Daniel's is the company's leading brand and is the largest selling American whiskey in the world (by volume). Offering some 30 brands of wines and spirits, the company's beverages are available in 135 countries throughout the world. The founding Brown family, including former chairman Owsley Brown II, controls the company.

Headquartered in Louisville, Kentucky, Brown-Forman has found global success by introducing Jack Daniels and other labels into new markets overseas. The company's principal export markets are Australia, Canada, China, France, Germany, Italy, Japan, Mexico, Poland, Russia, South Africa, Spain, and the UK. In Germany and the UK, it partners with competitor

Bacardi to sell a combined portfolio of both companies' products. And although B-F is an international company, 48% of its sales are generated in the US.

As part of its ongoing review of its offerings, in late 2008 Brown-Forman sold the Italian wine brands Bolla and Fontana to Gruppo Italiano Vini. The decision was in line with the company's strategy of concentrating on opportunities for growth and increasing shareholder value by building its brands and expanding into international markets. However, due to the sluggish worldwide economy, Brown-Forman has switched one of its growth strategies to pushing its markets at home rather than internationally. The faltering economy has also seen the company's sales for its premium beverages slow. Seeing little relief in the global economic situation, B-F has begun devoting more efforts to sell its less expensive labels.

In order to concentrate solely on the alcoholic beverage business, in 2007 B-F sold its remaining non-liquor-related business, jewelry, collectibles, and gift seller Brooks & Bentley. And boosting its presence in the tequila market that year, it acquired Mexican company Grupo Industrial Herradura, which makes several leading higher-priced tequila brands (Herradura and el Jimador), for $876 million in cash.

HISTORY

George Brown and John Forman opened the Brown-Forman Distillery in Louisville, Kentucky, in 1870 to produce Old Forester-brand bourbon. Old Forester sold well through the end of the century, in part because of the company's innovative packaging (safety seals and quality guarantees on the bottles). When Forman died in 1901, Brown bought his interest in the company.

Old Forester continued to be successful under the Brown family. Brown-Forman obtained government approval to produce alcohol for medicinal purposes during Prohibition. In 1923 it made its first acquisition, Early Times, but stored its whiskey in a government warehouse (removed only by permit). The firm went public in 1933 and re-established the Old Forester image as an alcoholic beverage after the repeal of Prohibition.

During WWII the government greatly curtailed alcoholic beverage production (alcohol was needed for the war effort). The company compensated by providing alcohol for wartime rubber and gunpowder production. In 1941 Brown-Forman correctly predicted that the war would be over by the end of 1945 and started the four-year aging process for its bourbon. As a result, Early Times dominated the whiskey market after the war.

In 1956 Brown-Forman expanded beyond Old Forester by purchasing Lynchburg, Tennessee-based Jack Daniel's (sour mash whiskey). The company retained the simple, black Jack Daniel's label and promoted the image of a small Tennessee distillery for the brand.

Brown-Forman continued to expand its alcohol line during the 1960s and 1970s, acquiring Korbel (champagne and brandy, 1965), Quality Importers (Ambassador Scotch, Ambassador Gin, and Old Bushmills Irish Whisky; 1967), Bolla and Cella (wines, 1968), and Canadian Mist (blended whiskey, 1971). In 1979 it purchased Southern Comfort (a top-selling liqueur).

Non-beverage acquisitions included Lenox (a leading US maker of fine china, crystal, gifts, and Hartmann luggage; 1983), Kirk Stief (silver and pewter, 1990), and Dansk International Designs (china, crystal, silver, and the high-quality Gorham line; 1991). Brown-Forman

launched Gentleman Jack Rare Tennessee Whiskey in 1988, the first new whiskey from its Jack Daniels distillery in more than 100 years.

The company acquired Jekel Vineyards in 1991 and the next year bought Fetzer Vineyards. In 1993 Owsley Brown II succeeded his brother Lee as CEO. A year later Moore County, Tennessee, voters approved a referendum that allowed whiskey sales in Lynchburg (home of Jack Daniel's) for the first time since Prohibition. Also in 1995 Brown-Forman formed a joint venture with Jagatjit Industries, India's third-largest spirits producer. In 1997 Brown-Forman bought an 80% stake in Sonoma-Cutrer Vineyards in 1999 (and later bought the rest).

In 2000 Brown-Forman bought 45% of Finlandia Vodka Worldwide for $83 million; Altia (owned by the Finnish government) owns 55%. It became a majority owner of Finlandia in 2004.

The company stirred up fans of Jack Daniel's in 2004 when it announced that it had reduced the alcohol content of Jack Daniel's Black Label whiskey from 90 proof to 80 proof. Brown-Forman also announced in that year plans to close its Dansk outlet stores over a two-year period. Due to a difficult competitive market in the US tabletop and giftware industries, Brown-Forman sold its Lenox subsidiary in 2005 to Department 56 for about $190 million in cash. Brown-Forman introduced the wine label Virgin Vines that year. And finally 2005 saw Paul Varga succeed Owsley Brown as CEO. Brown remained chairman. (Brown retired from the company in 2007, at which time Varga assumed the role of chairman.)

In 2006 the company purchased Chambord Liqueur (a black raspberry liqueur) from Charles Jacquin et Cie for $255 million in cash and it also acquired Australian spirits and winemaker Swift + Moore. The company snapped its suitcase shut that year as well, with the sale of its Hartmann luggage subsidiary to investment firm Clarion Capital Partners.

EXECUTIVES

Chairman and CEO: Paul C. Varga, age 45, $4,579,524 total compensation
Vice Chairman and Executive Director Corporate Affairs, Strategy, Diversity, and Human Affairs: James S. Welch Jr., age 50, $1,609,920 total compensation
EVP and COO: Mark I. McCallum, age 54, $1,288,887 total compensation
EVP and CFO: Donald C. Berg, age 53, $1,432,830 total compensation
Chief Diversity Officer: Ralph de Chabert
EVP Global Business Development: James L. (Jim) Bareuther, age 63, $1,930,551 total compensation
EVP, General Counsel, and Secretary: Matthew E. Hamel, age 49
SVP and Deputy General Counsel: William A. Blodgett Jr.
SVP: Lisa P. Steiner
SVP and Director Finance, Accounting, and Technology: Jane C. Morreau, age 50
SVP Chief of Staff: Philip A. (Phil) Lichtenfels
SVP and Managing Director, Global Production: Jill Jones
VP and Director Tax: Larry W. Perry
VP and Director Corporate Communications: Phil Lynch
Assistant VP and Director Investor Relations: T.J. Graven
VP and Managing Director Western Europe and Africa and Director: G. Garvin Brown IV, age 39
President, North American Region: Michael J. Keyes
Director Corporate Affairs: James A. O'Malley
Auditors: PricewaterhouseCoopers LLP

LOCATIONS

HQ: Brown-Forman Corporation
850 Dixie Hwy., Louisville, KY 40210
Phone: 502-585-1100   **Fax:** 502-774-7876
Web: www.brown-forman.com

2009 Sales

	$ mil.	% of total
US	1,542	48
Europe	892	28
Other regions	758	24
Total	**3,192**	**100**

PRODUCTS/OPERATIONS

2009 Sales

	$ mil.	% of total
Spirits	2,832	89
Wines	360	11
Total	**3,192**	**100**

Selected Products and Brands

Spirits
 Antiguo Tequila
 Canadian Mist Blended Canadian Whisky
 Chambord Liqueur
 Don Eduardo Tequila
 Early Times Kentucky Whisky
 el Jimador Tequila
 Finlandia Vodka
 Gentleman Jack
 Herradura Tequila
 Jack Daniel's Ready-to-Drinks
 Jack Daniel's Single Barrel Whiskey
 Jack Daniel's Tennessee Whiskey
 New Mix Ready-to-Drinks
 Old Forester Bourbon
 Pepe Lopez Tequilas
 Southern Comfort
 Tuaca Liqueur
 Woodford Reserve Bourbon

Wine
 Bel Arbor Wines
 Bonterra Vineyards Wine
 Fetzer
 Five Rivers
 Jekel Vineyards
 Little Black Dress
 Sanctuary
 Sonoma-Cutrer

COMPETITORS

Bacardi
Beam Global Spirits & Wine
Blavod Extreme Spirits
Campari
Castle Brands
Constellation Brands
Corby Distilleries
Diageo
Diageo Chateau & Estate Wines
E. & J. Gallo
Fortune Brands
Foster's Group
Jose Cuervo
Kendall-Jackson
Korbel
LVMH
Paramount Distillers
Pernod Ricard
Rémy Cointreau
Skyy
Smith Bowman Distillery
Suntory Holdings
Taittinger
United Spirits
V&S

HISTORICAL FINANCIALS

Company Type: Public

Income Statement

FYE: April 30

	REVENUE ($ mil.)	NET INCOME ($ mil.)	NET PROFIT MARGIN	EMPLOYEES
4/09	3,192.0	435.0	13.6%	4,100
4/08	3,282.0	440.0	13.4%	4,466
4/07	2,806.0	389.0	13.9%	4,400
4/06	2,444.0	320.0	13.1%	3,750
4/05	2,729.0	308.0	11.3%	6,100
Annual Growth	**4.0%**	**9.0%**	**—**	**(9.5%)**

2009 Year-End Financials

Debt ratio: 28.0%
Return on equity: 24.6%
Cash ($ mil.): 340
Current ratio: 1.88
Long-term debt ($ mil.): 509
No. of shares (mil.): 150
Dividends
 Yield: 2.4%
 Payout: 39.0%
Market value ($ mil.): 6,981

Stock History

NYSE: BFB

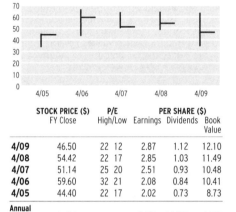

	STOCK PRICE ($) FY Close	P/E High/Low	Earnings	PER SHARE ($) Dividends	Book Value
4/09	46.50	22 12	2.87	1.12	12.10
4/08	54.42	22 17	2.85	1.03	11.49
4/07	51.14	25 20	2.51	0.93	10.48
4/06	59.60	32 21	2.08	0.84	10.41
4/05	44.40	22 17	2.02	0.73	8.73
Annual Growth	**1.2%**	**— —**	**9.2%**	**11.3%**	**8.5%**

Brunswick Corporation

Brunswick's business is everyone else's free time. A global manufacturer of marine, recreation, and fitness products, the company's dominant segment of pleasure boats includes fiberglass and high-performance boats, offshore fishing boats, and pontoons. The company also makes and markets outboard, inboard, and sterndrive engines, and water-jet propulsion systems. Its fitness segment pushes treadmills, total body cross trainers, stair climbers, and stationary bicycles (Life Fitness, ParaBody, and Hammer Strength). Brunswick's bowling and billiards produces the game equipment and operates more than 100 fun centers that feature bowling, billiards, and restaurants.

Brunswick pursues aggressive brand-building activities by acquiring boat brands that establish its presence in almost every possible market. It acquired Cabo Yachts, which builds offshore sports fishing boats, and the Great American Marina near St. Petersburg, Florida, in partnership with Marine-Max Inc. The company also pocketed marine parts and accessories dealer Kellogg Marine, and 51% of Valiant rigid inflatable boats in Europe.

However, since late in 2006, plunging consumer demand and high gas prices have sunk sales across all operations. Brunswick has put itself on a painfully aggressive regimen of cost-cutting, consolidation, and sell-offs. Its heaviest cuts have been made in its boat division. In 2007 the company consolidated its Saltwater Boat Group and Freshwater Boat Group into a new entity, Brunswick Outboard Boat Group. It unloaded its Baja boat business to Fountain Powerboat Industries. In 2008 the company moved to discontinue its Bluewater Marine line of fishing boats. Brunswick also sold off its Brunswick New Technologies business in 2007.

The company planned to slash the number of its boat manufacturing plants from 29 to 17 by the end of 2009. Along with the plant closures, have come reductions to its workforce — total company headcuts of 27%, 40% reaching to 46% for the boat division in 2009.

HISTORY

Swiss immigrant woodworker John Brunswick built his first billiard table in 1845 in Cincinnati. In 1874 he formed a partnership with Julius Balke, and a decade later they teamed with H. W. Collender to form Brunswick-Balke-Collender Company.

Following Brunswick's death, son-in-law Moses Bensinger became president. The company diversified into bowling equipment during the 1880s. Bensinger's son, B. E., followed as president (1904) and led the company into wood and rubber products, phonographs, and records. (Al Jolson recorded "Sonny Boy" on the Brunswick label.) Brunswick went public after WWI.

By 1930 Brunswick focused on bowling and billiards, sports that had seedy reputations during the 1920s and 1930s. When B. E. died in 1935, his son Bob became CEO and launched a massive promotional campaign to make his meal tickets respectable.

Bob's brother Ted succeeded him as CEO in 1954. Bowling equipment rival AMF introduced the first automatic pinsetter in 1952, and Brunswick followed four years later, capturing the lead by 1958. Brunswick diversified, adding Owens Yacht, MacGregor (sporting goods, 1958), Aloe (medical supplies, 1959), Mercury (marine products, 1961), and Zebco (fishing equipment, 1961). The company adopted its present name in 1960.

Bowling sales plummeted in the 1960s, and Brunswick cut costs by selling unprofitable units and focusing on new products such as an automatic scorer. Acquisitions in the 1970s brought Brunswick into the medical diagnostics and energy and transportation markets. CEO Jack Reichert, a former pin boy who became chairman in 1983, cut corporate staff in half and promoted the marine business.

Brunswick sparked an industrywide consolidation trend in 1986 by buying Bayliner and Ray Industries (boats), followed by Kiekhaefer Aeromarine (marine propulsion engines, 1990) and Martin Reel Company (fly reels, 1991). In 1992 Brunswick and Tracker Marine (a Missouri-based boat manufacturer) formed a partnership to build boats and marine equipment. Also that year Brunswick bought the Browning line of rods and reels.

In 1993 Brunswick began selling its businesses in the automotive, electronics, and defense industries. Two years later the company's Brunswick Indoor Recreation division opened family entertainment centers in Brazil, China, Japan, South Korea, and Thailand.

Brunswick expanded its outdoor recreation business in 1996 by purchasing Nelson/Weather Rite (camping equipment) from Roadmaster Industries (later named the RDM Sports Group) along with Roadmaster's bicycle business. Also that year Brunswick acquired the Boston Whaler line of saltwater boats from Meridian Sports. In 1997 the company bought Igloo Holdings (coolers), Bell Sports' (now Easton-Bell Sports) Mongoose bicycle unit, Mancuso's Life Fitness (exercise equipment) unit, Hoppe's gun-cleaning and hunting accessories business, Hammer Strength (fitness equipment), and DBA products (bowling-lane machines and equipment). Brunswick bought ParaBody (fitness equipment) in 1998.

The company lost antitrust lawsuits in 1999 that totaled nearly $300 million. However, all but two cases (with judgments of $65 million) were overturned on appeal.

In early 2001 Brunswick cut some jobs and rolled its bicycle business over to Pacific Cycle. Stung by the US's economic slowdown, the company announced 500 more job cuts in its powerboat division, even as it acquired Princecraft Boats from Outboard Marine. In October the company agreed to buy Hatteras Yachts, a luxury boat maker, from GenMar Holdings.

Early in 2002 Brunswick closed the sale of its European fishing business to Zebco Sports Europe Ltd., a company newly formed by the operation's management. As 2002 came to a close, Brunswick completed the purchase of marine navigation electronics maker Northstar Technologies, Inc, and propeller maker Teignbridge Propellers. Brunswick acquired the Crestliner, Lowe, and Lund lines of aluminum boats from Genmar Holdings for a reported $191 million.

In 2005 Brunswick expanded its offering of offshore sportfishing products with the acquisition of Albemarle Sportfishing Boats Inc. Also that year the company acquired Triton Boat Company, a maker of fiberglass bass and saltwater and aluminum fishing boats.

Brunswick's marina of boat brands continued to grow in 2006 with the purchase of Cabo Yachts of Adelanto, California. Cabo joined Brunswick's Hatteras Collection of sportfishing boat brands.

EXECUTIVES

Chairman and CEO: Dustan E. (Dusty) McCoy, age 59, $3,137,801 total compensation
SVP and CFO: Peter B. Hamilton, age 62, $625,846 total compensation
VP and CIO: William L. Avery
VP and Chief Human Resources Officer: B. Russell (Russ) Lockridge, age 59, $776,659 total compensation
VP and Chief Marketing Officer: George T. Neill, age 42
VP Tax: Judith P. Zelisko, age 57
VP; President, US Marine and Outboard Boats: Andrew E. Graves, age 47, $722,131 total compensation
VP and President, MerCruiser Business Unit of Mercury Marine Group: Kevin S. Grodzki, age 53
VP, Supply Chain Management; President, Latin America Group: William J. Gress
VP and Treasurer: William L. Metzger, age 47
VP Investor and Corporate Relations: Bruce J. Byots, age 50

VP; President, US Marine Division: Stephen M. Wolpert, age 54
VP and President, Life Fitness Division: John E. Stransky, age 57
VP and President, Brunswick Bowling and Billiards: Warren N. Hardie, age 58
VP and Treasurer: William L. Metzger, age 47
VP Investor and Corporate Relations: Bruce J. Byots, age 50
VP Strategy and Corporate Development: Jeffrey M. Kinsey, age 44
VP, General Counsel, and Secretary: Kristin M. Coleman, age 40
Director Public and Financial Relations: Daniel (Dan) Kubera
Auditors: Ernst & Young LLP

LOCATIONS

HQ: Brunswick Corporation
1 N. Field Ct., Lake Forest, IL 60045
Phone: 847-735-4700   **Fax:** 847-735-4765
Web: www.brunswick.com

2008 Sales

	$ mil.	% of total
US	2,650.2	56
Other countries	2,058.5	44
Total	**4,708.7**	**100**

PRODUCTS/OPERATIONS

2008 Sales

	$ mil.	% of total
Marine		
Boat	2,011.9	40
Marine engine	1,955.9	39
Fitness	639.5	12
Bowling & billiards	448.3	9
Adjustments	(346.9)	—
Total	**4,708.7**	**100**

Selected Brands and Products

Boats
  Albermarle
  Aquador
  Arvor
  Askeladden
  Bayliner
  Bella
  Benrock
  Bermuda
  Boston Whaler
  Cabo Yachts
  Crestliner
  Cypress Cay
  Flipper
  Harris FloteBoats
  Hatteras Yachts
  Kayot
  Lowe
  Lund
  Maxum
  Mercury
  Meridian
  Princecraft
  Protector
  Quicksilver
  Rayglass
  Savage
  Sea Ray
  Sealine
  Suncruiser
  Triton
  Trophy
  Uttern
  Valiant
  Wizard
Marine engines
  Mariner
  MerCruiser
  Mercury
  MotoTron
  Quicksilver
  Teignbridge propellers

Fitness
  Hammer Strength
  Life Fitness
  ParaBody
Recreation centers
  Brunswick Zones
Sporting goods
  Brunswick Billiards
  Brunswick Bowling
  Tornado (foosball tables)
  Valley (coin-operated billiards tables)

COMPETITORS

AMF Bowling
Bowl America
Carver Yachts
Cigarette Racing Team
Dave & Buster's
Fountain Powerboat
Genmar Holdings
Giant Manufacturing
Honda
Marine Products Corp.
Yamaha

HISTORICAL FINANCIALS

Company Type: Public

Income Statement

FYE: December 31

	REVENUE ($ mil.)	NET INCOME ($ mil.)	NET PROFIT MARGIN	EMPLOYEES
12/08	4,708.7	(788.1)	—	19,760
12/07	5,671.2	111.6	2.0%	29,920
12/06	5,665.0	133.9	2.4%	28,000
12/05	5,923.8	385.4	6.5%	27,500
12/04	5,229.3	269.8	5.2%	25,600
Annual Growth	**(2.6%)**	**—**	**—**	**(6.3%)**

2008 Year-End Financials

Debt ratio: 99.8%
Return on equity: —
Cash ($ mil.): 318
Current ratio: 1.73
Long-term debt ($ mil.): 729
No. of shares (mil.): 88
Dividends
  Yield: 1.2%
  Payout: —
Market value ($ mil.): 372

Stock History

NYSE: BC

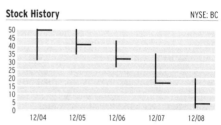

	STOCK PRICE ($) FY Close	P/E High/Low		PER SHARE ($) Earnings	Dividends	Book Value
12/08	4.21	—	—	(8.93)	0.05	8.27
12/07	17.05	28	14	1.24	0.60	21.45
12/06	31.90	30	19	1.41	0.60	21.21
12/05	40.66	13	9	3.90	0.60	22.42
12/04	49.50	18	11	2.77	0.60	19.40
Annual Growth	**(46.0%)**	**—**	**—**	**—**	**(46.3%)**	**(19.2%)**

Burger King Holdings

This king rules a whopper of a fast-food empire. Burger King Holdings operates the world's #2 hamburger chain (behind McDonald's) with more than 11,900 restaurants in the US and more than 70 other countries. In addition to its popular Whopper sandwich, the chain offers a variety of burgers, chicken sandwiches, salads, and breakfast items. More than 1,300 BK locations are company-owned, while the rest are owned and operated by franchisees.

Burger King has experienced growing sales despite the economic slowdown in part because of the company's focus on product development and marketing to its core customers in the 18- to 34-year-old male demographic, the so-called superfans. The fast-food chain has added several premium-priced menu items, such as the Steakhouse Burger made with Angus beef, designed to appeal to hungry foodies. At the same time, though, BK continues to add to its value menu items, typically priced under $1.

Burger King is hoping to boost its breakfast sales through additional marketing and menu items, however it is not looking to take on competitors in the morning coffee business in the way that rival McDonald's has. Burger King has also introduced a new store concept called the Whopper Bar, a smaller outlet where customers can have their burgers made to order.

International expansion has also been a point of emphasis for Burger King, with 80% of its new store openings occurring outside the US. During 2007 Burger King added almost 300 new restaurants worldwide.

Burger King was founded by James McLamore and David Edgerton in 1954. Investment firms TPG Capital, Bain Capital, and Goldman Sachs together own more than 30% of the company.

HISTORY

In 1954 restaurant veterans James McLamore and David Edgerton opened the first Burger King in Miami. Three years later, the company added the Whopper sandwich (which then sold for 37 cents) to its menu of hamburgers, shakes, and sodas. Burger King used television to help advertise the Whopper (its first TV commercial appeared in 1958). During its infancy, Burger King was the first chain to offer dining rooms.

In order to expand nationwide, Burger King turned to franchising in 1959. McLamore and Edgerton took a hands-off approach, allowing franchises to buy large territories and operate with autonomy. Although their technique spurred growth, it also created large service inconsistencies among Burger Kings across the US; this gaffe would haunt the company for years. Having grown to 274 stores in the US and abroad, Burger King was sold to Pillsbury in 1967.

During the early 1970s Burger King continued to add locations. The company did well during this time, launching its successful "Have It Your Way" campaign in 1974 and introducing drive-through service a year later. Yet parent Pillsbury had to fight to rein in large franchisees who argued they could run their Burger Kings better than a packaged-goods company could. In 1977 Pillsbury handed control of Burger King to Donald Smith, a McDonald's veteran, who soon silenced the insurrection. Smith tightened franchising regulations, created 10 regional management offices, and instituted annual visits.

Smith left for Pizza Hut in 1980, and by 1982 Burger King had reached the #2 hamburger chain plateau, trailing only McDonald's. The company struggled through the rest of the 1980s, hurt by high management turnover and a string of unsuccessful ad campaigns (such as the ill-fated 1986 NFL Super Bowl "Herb the Nerd" concept). Pillsbury became the target of a hostile takeover by UK-based Grand Metropolitan, and in 1988 Grand Met acquired Pillsbury along with its 5,500 Burger King restaurants.

Grand Met bolstered Burger King's foreign operations in 1990 by converting about 200 recently acquired UK-based Wimpy hamburger stores into Burger Kings. International expansion increased with new restaurants in Mexico (1991), Saudi Arabia (1993), and Paraguay (1995).

In 1997 Grand Met and Guinness combined their operations to form Diageo, making Burger King a subsidiary. That year Dennis Malamatinas left Grand Met's Asian beverage division to become Burger King's CEO. Malamatinas resigned as CEO and was replaced in 2001 by John Dasburg, former CEO of Northwest Airlines.

An investment group led by Texas Pacific Group (now TPG Capital) acquired Burger King for $1.5 billion in 2002. Earlier that year, Texas Pacific had agreed to pay $2.26 billion but renegotiated amid falling sales and a downturn in the burger market. Shortly after the purchase, Dasburg was ousted and Brad Blum, vice chairman of Darden Restaurants, was named as his replacement.

After just 18 months on the job, Blum resigned his post as CEO in 2004, citing differences with the company's board. He was replaced by Greg Brenneman.

Burger King had consistent sales growth in 2004, and Brenneman's presence was a boost for the company. In addition, that year the company signed a deal (with rancher Luiz Eduardo Batalha) to develop about 50 restaurants in Brazil over a five-year period.

Disregarding the obesity trend in the US and health-officials' advice to citizens to cut down on fat intake, Burger King continues to offer ever-larger, ever-more-fat-laden menu items, such as the MEAT'NORMOUS OMELET SANDWICH, which it introduced in 2005. In 2006 the company ran advertising during the Super Bowl for the first time in 11 years. Brenneman resigned from Burger King that year, shortly before it went public; the company tapped president and CFO John Chidsey as his replacement.

EXECUTIVES

Chairman and CEO: John W. Chidsey, age 46
EVP Global Operations: Julio Ramirez, age 54
EVP and CFO: Ben K. Wells, age 54
EVP, General Counsel, Corporate Secretary, and Chief Ethics and Compliance Officer: Anne Chwat, age 49
SVP and CIO: Rajesh (Raj) Rawal
Chief Concept Officer: Denny Marie Post
EVP and Chief Human Resources Officer: Peter C. (Pete) Smith, age 52
EVP: Peter B. Robinson, age 60
EVP and President, North America: Charles M. (Chuck) Fallon Jr., age 45
SVP Operations, North America: Gladys H. DeClouet
SVP Global Operations Research and Development: John Reckert
SVP Operations and Training, North America: David (Dave) Gagnon, age 61
SVP and President, Asia/Pacific: Peter Tan, age 53
SVP Global Business Intelligence and Strategy: Michael (Mike) Kappitt

SVP Global Product Marketing and Innovation: John Schaufelberger
SVP Development and Franchising: Jonathan (John) Fitzpatrick
SVP Investor Relations and Global Communications: Amy E. Wagner, age 43
President, Global Marketing, Strategy, and Innovation: Russell B. (Russ) Klein, age 50
Auditors: KPMG LLP

LOCATIONS

HQ: Burger King Holdings, Inc.
5505 Blue Lagoon Dr., Miami, FL 33126
Phone: 305-378-3000
Web: www.burgerking.com

2009 Sales

	$ mil.	% of total
US & Canada	1,743.0	69
Europe, Middle East & Asia/Pacific	687.4	27
Latin America	107.0	4
Total	**2,537.4**	**100**

2009 Locations

	No.
US & Canada	7,534
Europe, Middle East & Asia/Pacific	3,313
Latin America	1,078
Total	**11,925**

PRODUCTS/OPERATIONS

2009 Sales

	$ mil.	% of total
Restaurants	1,880.5	74
Franchising	543.4	21
Property	113.5	5
Total	**2,537.4**	**100**

2009 Locations

	No.
Franchised	10,496
Company-owned	1,429
Total	**11,925**

COMPETITORS

AFC Enterprises
Arby's
Chick-fil-A
Church's Chicken
CKE Restaurants
Dairy Queen
Jack in the Box
McDonald's
Quiznos
Subway
Wendy's International, Inc.
YUM!

HISTORICAL FINANCIALS

Company Type: Public

Income Statement

FYE: June 30

	REVENUE ($ mil.)	NET INCOME ($ mil.)	NET PROFIT MARGIN	EMPLOYEES
6/09	2,537.4	200.1	7.9%	41,320
6/08	2,455.0	190.0	7.7%	41,000
6/07	2,234.0	148.0	6.6%	39,000
6/06	2,048.0	27.0	1.3%	37,000
6/05	1,940.0	47.0	2.4%	30,300
Annual Growth	**6.9%**	**43.6%**	**—**	**8.1%**

2009 Year-End Financials

Debt ratio: 84.3%	No. of shares (mil.): 135
Return on equity: 22.0%	Dividends
Cash ($ mil.): 122	Yield: 1.1%
Current ratio: 0.77	Payout: 13.0%
Long-term debt ($ mil.): 821	Market value ($ mil.): 2,328

Stock History

NYSE: BKC

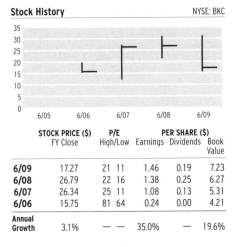

	STOCK PRICE ($) FY Close	P/E High/Low		PER SHARE ($) Earnings	Dividends	Book Value
6/09	17.27	21	11	1.46	0.19	7.23
6/08	26.79	22	16	1.38	0.25	6.27
6/07	26.34	25	11	1.08	0.13	5.31
6/06	15.75	81	64	0.24	0.00	4.21
Annual Growth	3.1%	—	—	35.0%	—	19.6%

Burlington Northern Santa Fe

Over the years the number of major US railroads has dwindled, but Burlington Northern Santa Fe (BNSF) thrives as one of the survivors. Through its primary subsidiary, BNSF Railway, the company is one of the largest railroad operators in the US along with rival Union Pacific. BNSF makes tracks through 28 states in the West, Midwest, and Sunbelt regions of the US and in two Canadian provinces. The company operates its trains over a system of about 32,000 route miles. Along with its rail operations, BNSF generates revenue from its BNSF Logistics unit, a provider of transportation management services. Warren Buffett's Berkshire Hathaway owns about 23% of BNSF.

BNSF's largest revenue generator is its consumer products business, which handles containerized freight and automotive products. The railroad's industrial products business transports building and construction products, chemicals and plastics, food and beverages, and petroleum products.

Despite a strong year in 2008, BNSF is making moves to hedge a sharp drop in traffic and anticipated hardships in 2009. The company said it will lay off about 2,500 workers within the first quarter of 2009 as well as park 700 locomotives and 35,000 rail cars due to slowing freight demand. During the economic slowdown, BNSF will do some updating, spending about $2.7 billion in 2009 on track, signals, rail cars, technology upgrades, and fuel-efficient locomotives.

Economic woes also prompted BNSF to put the brakes on some expansion projects including the planned 500-acre intermodal rail hub near Kansas City, Kansas, a vital point along its busy Chicago-Los Angeles corridor.

HISTORY

Burlington Northern (BN) was largely created by James Hill, who bought the St. Paul & Pacific Railroad in Minnesota in 1878. By 1893 Hill had completed the Great Northern Railway, extending from St. Paul to Seattle. The next year he gained control of Northern Pacific (chartered in 1864), which had been built between Minnesota and Washington. In 1901, with J.P. Morgan's help, Hill acquired the Chicago, Burlington & Quincy (Burlington), whose routes included Chicago-St. Paul and Billings, Montana-Denver-Fort Worth, Texas-Houston. The Spokane, Portland & Seattle Railway (SP&S), completed in 1908, gave Great Northern an entrance to Oregon.

Hill intended to merge Great Northern, Northern Pacific, SP&S, and Burlington under his Morgan-backed Northern Securities Company, but in 1904 the Supreme Court found that Northern Securities had violated the Sherman Antitrust Act. The holding company was dissolved, but Hill controlled the individual railroads until he died in 1916. Hill's railroads produced well-known passenger trains: Great Northern's Empire Builder began service in 1929, and in 1934 Burlington Zephyr was the nation's first streamlined passenger diesel.

After years of deliberation, the Interstate Commerce Commission allowed Great Northern and Northern Pacific to merge in 1970, along with jointly owned subsidiaries Burlington and SP&S. The new company, Burlington Northern (BN), acquired the St. Louis-San Francisco Railway in 1980, adding more than 4,650 miles to its rail network.

The company formed Burlington Motor Carriers (BMC) in 1985 to manage five trucking companies it had acquired. But to focus on its rail operations, BN sold BMC in 1988 and spun off Burlington Resources, a holding company for its other nonrailroad businesses.

A fiery collision between a BN freight train and one operated by Union Pacific in 1995 propelled the rivals to begin joint testing of global positioning satellites for guiding trains. Besides improving safety, the two hoped to end rail bottlenecks. That year BN and Santa Fe Pacific (SFP), founded in 1859, formed Burlington Northern Santa Fe in a $4 billion merger. BN's strength lay in transporting manufacturing, agricultural, and natural resource commodities, and SFP specialized in intermodal shipping (combining train, truck, and ship). SFP (originally the Atchison, Topeka & Santa Fe) had taken the name Santa Fe Pacific in 1989 after its forced sale of Southern Pacific.

The new BNSF acquired Washington Central Railroad in 1996, adding a third connection between central Washington and the Pacific Coast. In 1997 customers protested when BNSF couldn't come up with enough cars and locomotives for grain shipping. A year later UP was in trouble with clogged rail lines: BNSF opened a joint dispatching center in Houston with UP

to help unsnarl traffic. The effort proved successful, and in 1999 BNSF and UP began to combine dispatching in Southern California; the Kansas City, Missouri, area; and Wyoming's Powder River Basin.

In 1999 BNSF announced a $2.5 billion capital improvement program, but later decided to trim spending to $2.28 billion and cut 1,400 jobs.

Later that year BNSF agreed to merge with Canadian National Railway. The companies terminated the deal in 2000, however, after a US moratorium on rail mergers was upheld on appeal. Also in 2000 BNSF began offering intermodal service between the US and Monterrey, Queretaro, and Mexico City, Mexico, its first such US-Mexico service.

In 2001 BNSF became the first US railroad to use the Internet to purchase fuel (via the American Petroleum Exchange). Another milestone followed, albeit a more dubious one: To settle the first federal lawsuit against workplace genetic testing, BNSF agreed to drop its testing program. Without their knowledge, employees who had been diagnosed with carpal tunnel syndrome were tested for genetic defects.

Also in 2001 BNSF announced plans to join with a group of chemical and plastics companies to build a rail-spur southeast of Houston in order to compete with Union Pacific for petrochemical shipping business.

In 2002 BNSF completed the construction of its BNSF Logistics Park in Chicago, designed to integrate direct rail, truck, intermodal, transload services, distribution, and warehousing in a single location.

EXECUTIVES

Chairman, President, and CEO, Burlington Northern Santa Fe Corporation and BNSF Railway: Matthew K. (Matt) Rose, age 50, $15,608,233 total compensation
EVP and COO: Carl R. Ice, age 52, $3,700,325 total compensation
EVP and CFO: Thomas N. Hund, age 55, $3,239,362 total compensation
VP Technology Services and CIO: Jo-ann M. Olsovsky
EVP and Chief Marketing Officer: John P. Lanigan Jr., age 53, $3,369,870 total compensation
EVP Law and Secretary: Roger Nober, age 44, $1,593,647 total compensation
VP and General Tax Counsel: Shelley J. Venick
VP Human Resources and Medical: Linda T. Longo-Kazanova
VP Investor Relations: Linda J. Hurt
VP Network Development: Peter J. Rickershauser, age 60
VP and General Counsel — Regulatory: Richard E. (Rick) Weicher
VP and Corporate General Counsel: James H. (Jim) Gallegos
VP Corporate Audit Services: David W. Stropes
VP and Controller: Paul W. Bischler
VP Government Affairs: Amy Hawkins
VP Corporate Relations: John O. Ambler
VP Finance and Treasurer: Julie A. Piggott
VP and General Counsel: Charles W. Shewmake
General Director Corporate Communications: Patrick (Pat) Hiatte
Director Investor Relations: Mark Bracker
Auditors: PricewaterhouseCoopers LLP

LOCATIONS

HQ: Burlington Northern Santa Fe Corporation
2650 Lou Menk Dr., Fort Worth, TX 76131
Phone: 817-352-1000 **Fax:** 817-352-7171
Web: www.bnsf.com

PRODUCTS/OPERATIONS

2008 Sales

	$ mil.	% of total
Freight		
Consumer products	6,064	34
Industrial products	4,028	22
Coal	3,970	22
Agricultural products	3,441	19
Other	515	3
Total	**18,018**	**100**

COMPETITORS

American Commercial Lines	Kansas City Southern
APL Logistics	Kirby Corporation
Canadian National Railway	Landstar System
Canadian Pacific Railway	Norfolk Southern
CSX	Pacer International
Hub Group	Schneider National
Ingram Industries	Union Pacific
J.B. Hunt	Werner Enterprises

HISTORICAL FINANCIALS

Company Type: Public

Income Statement

FYE: December 31

	REVENUE ($ mil.)	NET INCOME ($ mil.)	NET PROFIT MARGIN	EMPLOYEES
12/08	18,018.0	2,115.0	11.7%	40,000
12/07	15,802.0	1,829.0	11.6%	40,000
12/06	14,985.0	1,887.0	12.6%	41,000
12/05	12,987.0	1,531.0	11.8%	40,000
12/04	10,946.0	791.0	7.2%	38,000
Annual Growth	13.3%	27.9%	—	1.3%

2008 Year-End Financials

Debt ratio: 81.7%	No. of shares (mil.): 340
Return on equity: 19.0%	Dividends
Cash ($ mil.): 633	Yield: 1.9%
Current ratio: 0.73	Payout: 23.7%
Long-term debt ($ mil.): 9,099	Market value ($ mil.): 25,743

Stock History

NYSE: BNI

	STOCK PRICE ($) FY Close	P/E High/Low	PER SHARE ($) Earnings	Dividends	Book Value
12/08	75.71	19 11	6.08	1.44	32.74
12/07	83.23	19 14	5.10	1.14	32.77
12/06	73.81	17 13	5.10	0.90	30.57
12/05	70.82	18 11	4.01	0.74	27.96
12/04	47.31	23 14	2.10	0.64	27.38
Annual Growth	12.5%	— —	30.4%	22.5%	4.6%

CA, Inc.

CA wants to put your information technology under new management. One of the world's largest software companies, CA provides tools for managing networks, databases, applications, storage, security, and other systems. The company's Unicenter enterprise management software is designed to give customers centralized control over network infrastructure. Its applications work across both mainframes and distributed computing environments. The company also offers consulting, implementation, and training services. It markets worldwide to businesses, government agencies, and schools.

CA sells directly and through various resale channels. Software subscriptions and maintenance fees account for the majority of the company's revenues. It generates roughly half of its sales outside the US.

The company primarily focuses on large corporations with the resources to make substantial investments in hardware and software. Target industries include financial services and insurance, government, health care, manufacturing, retail, and technology.

CA's partners include systems integrators such as Accenture and PricewaterhouseCoopers, as well as managed services providers including EDS and IBM. It also maintains technology partnerships to ensure the interoperability of its products with offerings from such companies as Microsoft, SAP, and VMware.

A highly acquisitive company throughout its history, CA continues to expand its application portfolio with strategic purchases. Most recently the company has looked to expand its security offerings. It acquired identity management software developer Eurekify late in 2008, and data loss prevention specialist Orchestria early in 2009. The purchases of Eurikify and Orchestria fit a stated strategy of creating an end-to-end security product portfolio.

CA's internal development efforts have embraced such technology trends as software-as-a-service (SaaS) and virtualization. In 2008 the company began offering its Clarity Project & Portfolio Manager product using the SaaS delivery model. It also began supporting Microsoft virtualization technology across a number of product lines.

Swiss billionaire Walter Haefner owns about a quarter of the company.

HISTORY

Born in Shanghai, Charles Wang fled Communist China with his family in 1952 and grew up in Queens, New York. After working in sales for software developer Standard Data, Wang started a joint venture in 1976 with Swiss-owned Computer Associates (CA) to sell software in the US. He started with four employees and one product, a file organizer for IBM storage systems. It was a great success, and in 1980 Wang bought out his Swiss partners. CA went public in 1981.

Wang realized that a far-flung distribution and service network (continuously fed by new products) was the key to success. Acquiring existing software (and its customers) reduced risky in-house development and moved products to market sooner.

The company expanded its offerings by buying the popular SuperCalc spreadsheet in 1984. The 1987 purchase of chief utilities rival UCCEL gave investor Walter Haefner what remains the largest individual stake in CA.

CA's purchases of mostly struggling software firms made it, in 1989, the first independent software company to reach $1 billion in sales. The $300 million acquisition of Cullinet that year added database and banking applications to CA's product line.

By the early 1990s, CA's acquisition methods had developed a reputation that were seen by some as ruthless — swoop in, gobble up, cut costs, and get rid of employees. As a new owner, CA strongly defended its licensing contracts — often in court.

In 1994 CA promoted EVP of operations Sanjay Kumar to president. Kumar's shift away from older systems to focus on network software was reflected by the acquisitions of ASK Group (1994), Legent (1995), and network management expert Cheyenne Software (1996). CA continued its practice of buying in cash to avoid diluting stock.

Acquisition-related charges caused losses for fiscal 1996. With its lack of a major service operation taking a bite out of potential business, CA made a $9.8 billion hostile takeover offer for consulting firm Computer Sciences Corp. (CSC) in 1998. CA soon dropped its bid in the face of CSC's fierce opposition and later acquired smaller computer service specialist Realogic.

The acquisitions helped cause a drop in profits for fiscal 1999. Later that year CA bought database management software company PLATINUM technology for about $3.5 billion.

In 2000 CA acquired business software specialist Sterling Software in a deal valued at nearly $4 billion. Later that year the company began spinning off some of its promising software businesses; Wang stepped down as CEO to focus on new opportunities for CA as chairman. He handed the CEO reins to Kumar.

Alleging corporate mismanagement, in 2001 Sam Wyly (co-founder of Sterling Software) initiated a proxy fight designed to elect a new board of directors. Wyly's bid failed, however, as it was voted down by shareholders. He initiated a second proxy fight in 2002, but abandoned it after reaching a settlement with the company, which included a $10 million payment. Later in 2002, the board elected Kumar chairman after Wang retired.

An SEC investigation into the company's accounting practices led to the resignation of CA's CFO late in 2003. The investigation continued into 2004, resulting in additional executive resignations. Late in 2004 CA agreed to pay $225 million to shareholders in order to avoid criminal prosecution by the SEC and US Justice Department for fraudulently recording and reporting revenues. Shortly after the settlement was announced, former CEO Sanjay Kumar and former EVP Stephen Richards were indicted on charges of securities fraud, conspiracy, and obstruction of justice. Kumar resigned as chairman, president, and CEO that year (he left the company entirely after a brief stint as chief software architect). IBM veteran John Swainson was named CEO.

In 2005 it acquired network management specialist Concord Communications for about $330 million.

The company purchased application management specialist Wily Technology for $375 million early in 2006. Also in 2006, Computer Associates International officially changed its name to CA.

EXECUTIVES

Chairman: William E. (Bill) McCracken, age 66
Vice Chairman: Russell M. Artzt, age 62
CEO and Director: John A. C. Swainson, age 55
President and COO: Michael J. (Mike) Christenson, age 50
EVP and CFO: Nancy E. Cooper, age 55
EVP and CTO: Alan F. Nugent, age 54
SVP and CIO: David Hansen
EVP and Risk Chief Administrative Officer: James E. Bryant, age 64
Chief Compliance Officer and Chief Counsel Litigation, Law Department: Gary Brown
Chief Ethics Officer, Law Department: Joel Katz
SVP and Chief Marketing Officer: Marianne Budnik
EVP and General Manager, CA Services: Una O'Neill, age 40
EVP Worldwide Human Resources: Andrew (Andy) Goodman, age 50
EVP Products and Technology Group: Ajei S. Gopal, age 47
EVP Global Sales and Marketing: George Fischer
EVP Strategy and Corporate Development: Jacob Lamm, age 44
EVP Worldwide Sales Operations: John Ruthven
EVP and General Counsel: Amy F. Olli, age 45
VP Investor Relations: Joseph (Joe) Doncheski
Auditors: KPMG LLP

LOCATIONS

HQ: CA, Inc.
1 CA Plaza, Islandia, NY 11749
Phone: 800-225-5224   **Fax:** 631-342-6800
Web: www.ca.com

2009 Sales

	$ mil.	% of total
US	2,291	54
Europe	1,265	29
Other regions	715	17
Total	**4,271**	**100**

PRODUCTS/OPERATIONS

2009 Sales

	$ mil.	% of total
Subscriptions & maintenance	3,772	88
Professional services	358	9
Software fees & other	141	3
Total	**4,271**	**100**

Selected Product Groups

Application development and databases
Application performance management
Database management
Infrastructure and operations management
IT service and asset management
Mainframe
Project, portfolio, and financial management
Security management
Storage and information governance

COMPETITORS

BMC Software
Check Point Software
Cisco Systems
Compuware
EMC
Hewlett-Packard
IBM
McAfee
Microsoft
Novell
Oracle
RSA Security
SAP
Sun Microsystems
Sybase
Symantec

HISTORICAL FINANCIALS

Company Type: Public

Income Statement

FYE: March 31

	REVENUE ($ mil.)	NET INCOME ($ mil.)	NET PROFIT MARGIN	EMPLOYEES
3/09	4,271.0	694.0	16.2%	13,200
3/08	4,277.0	500.0	11.7%	13,700
3/07	3,943.0	118.0	3.0%	14,500
3/06	3,796.0	159.0	4.2%	16,000
3/05	3,530.0	11.0	0.3%	15,300
Annual Growth	**4.9%**	**181.8%**	**—**	**(3.6%)**

2009 Year-End Financials

Debt ratio: 29.6%
Return on equity: 17.2%
Cash ($ mil.): —
Current ratio: 1.03
Long-term debt ($ mil.): 1,287
No. of shares (mil.): 524
Dividends
  Yield: 0.9%
  Payout: 12.4%
Market value ($ mil.): 9,224

Stock History

NASDAQ (GS): CA

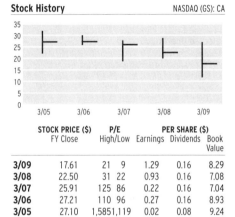

	STOCK PRICE ($) FY Close	P/E High/Low	Earnings	PER SHARE ($) Dividends	Book Value
3/09	17.61	21 9	1.29	0.16	8.29
3/08	22.50	31 22	0.93	0.16	7.08
3/07	25.91	125 86	0.22	0.16	7.04
3/06	27.21	110 96	0.27	0.16	8.93
3/05	27.10	1,585 1,119	0.02	0.08	9.24
Annual Growth	**(10.2%)**	**— —**	**183.4%**	**18.9%**	**(2.7%)**

Cablevision Systems

There's no business like show business for Cablevision, which provides basic cable television to about 3 million customers in the New York City area. More than 2.5 million digital video viewers subscribe to its iO service. Through its Optimum unit, Cablevision serves more than 2 million broadband Internet and 1.5 million computer telephony subscribers. Subsidiary Lightpath provides business communications services. Cablevision also controls sports and entertainment venues Madison Square Garden and Radio City Music Hall, as well as New York sports teams the Knicks and the Rangers. The company owns and manages nationwide and regional cable programming networks and sports channels through Rainbow Media Holdings.

Other properties held by Rainbow Media include cable channels American Movie Classics (AMC), the Independent Film Channel (IFC), and WE: Women's Entertainment. The group also owns Clearview Cinemas which operates about 50 New York-area movie theaters including Manhattan's famous Ziegfeld Theater. Its PVI Virtual Media Services unit provides real-time video insertion of computer-generated images to sporting events and other programming.

Cablevision is using divestitures and acquisitions to fine-tune its portfolio of media and entertainment holdings. The company announced in 2009 that it would spin off its Madison Square Garden business to its stockholders. The assets to be included in the spinoff include the media properties and Knicks and Rangers sports teams, in addition to Madison Square Garden and Radio City Music Hall venues.

In 2008 subsidiary Rainbow Media acquired the Sundance Channel from NBC Universal and Showtime Networks for $496 million. Also that year, Cablevision bought 97% of newspaper Newsday from Tribune Company for $650 million.

The family of founder and chairman Charles Dolan controls nearly 75% of the company.

HISTORY

In 1954 Charles Dolan helped form Sterling Manhattan Cable, which won the cable TV franchise for Lower Manhattan in 1965. It began broadcasting pro basketball and hockey, courtesy of Madison Square Garden (MSG), in 1967. In 1970 Dolan started Home Box Office (HBO), the first nationwide pay-TV channel, and hired Gerald Levin to run it.

Dolan took the company public as Sterling Communications; its partner, media giant Time (now part of Time Warner), came to own 80% of Sterling. Costs mounted, however, and in 1973 Time liquidated Sterling (but kept HBO).

Dolan bought back the New York franchises and formed Long Island Cable Communications Development. He changed its name to Cablevision and expanded around New York and Chicago. In 1980 Cablevision formed Rainbow Programming, which soon included the American Movie Classics and Bravo channels; in 1983 it launched the popular SportsChannel (now Fox Sports New York). Cablevision went public in 1986. It bought two Connecticut cable systems that year and one in Massachusetts the next.

In 1989 Cablevision helped NBC launch the CNBC cable network but sold its interest to NBC in 1991. Cablevision began offering cable phone service to businesses on Long Island — two years before the Telecommunications Act of 1996 was passed. Subsidiary Cablevision Lightpath, a competitive local-exchange carrier, signed a groundbreaking co-carrier agreement with Baby Bell NYNEX (now part of Verizon) in 1995.

To get a grip on NYC entertainment, Cablevision partnered with ITT in 1995 to buy the MSG properties. Three years later Starwood acquired ITT. In late 1996 Charles' son, James, became CEO.

In 1997 Cablevision began dumping cable holdings, which were spread over 19 states, to focus on its New York City area operations and the upgrading of its cable infrastructure.

Cablevision sold 40% of Rainbow's regional sports business to Fox/Liberty (now Fox Sports Net, owned by News Corp.) to create a rival to Disney's ESPN. Fox/Liberty got 40% of MSG, and Cablevision got Fox Sports Net, a chain of 22 regional sports networks. In 1998 Cablevision sold cable systems in 10 states to Mediacom.

In 2001 MGM paid $825 million for a 20% stake in four of Rainbow's national networks. But the recession forced the company to take steps to improve operations, including the elimination of 5,000 jobs.

The next year, the company battled with the Yankees Entertainment & Sports Network (YES Network) over the rights to broadcast New York

Yankees games. The same year, Cablevision sold its Bravo network to NBC, a subsidiary of GE.

Cablevision intended to shut down the financially challenged VOOM satellite service after a plan to spin off Rainbow Media fell apart in early 2005. Charles Dolan unsuccessfully tried to buy VOOM himself but son James, Cablevision's CEO, sided with the board of directors and favored shuttering the unit, resulting in a bit of a family feud. Charles responded to the decision by tossing three Cablevision directors and installing five new ones who were more aligned with his interests. The company gave him more time to come up with the money to make another bid for VOOM, yet the effort turned out to be futile and Cablevision eventually axed the service.

In a move that would have expanded the company's cable systems outside the New York City metro area, Cablevision in 2005 made a failed bid for troubled rival Adelphia's cable systems. The company also wanted to buy Adelphia in an effort to keep rivals Time Warner Cable and Comcast from growing bigger, but the two industry leaders eventually won the bidding war after all.

In 2005 the Dolan family abandoned an offer to take the company private for $7.9 billion, citing an overall decline of value in the communications sector. However, in October of the following year the Dolans made another offer to take the company private for the same amount. In 2007 their bid was raised to $8.9 billion. Both parties finally agreed on a deal worth $10.6 billion that would give the Dolans full control of the company. Shareholders rejected the bid in late 2007.

Also that year Cablevision restructured its Madison Square Garden partnership with News Corporation, resulting in Rainbow Media owning 100% of the sports and entertainment company.

EXECUTIVES

Chairman: Charles F. Dolan, age 82, $13,438,194 total compensation
Vice Chairman; Vice Chairman, Madison Square Garden and Rainbow Media Holdings: Hank J. Ratner, age 50, $11,475,521 total compensation
President, CEO, and Director; Chairman, Madison Square Garden; and Governor, New York Knicks: James L. Dolan, age 53, $13,938,129 total compensation
COO: Thomas M. Rutledge, age 55, $11,736,084 total compensation
EVP and CFO: Michael P. Huseby, age 54, $3,881,727 total compensation
EVP Strategy and Development, Office of the Chairman: Thomas C. Dolan, age 56
EVP and General Counsel: Jonathan D Schwartz, age 47
EVP Cablevision Systems Corporation: Gregg Seibert, age 53
EVP Product Management and Marketing: Patricia Gottesmann
SVP Media and Community Relations: Charles (Charlie) Schueler
SVP and Associate General Counsel and Business Affairs: Lawrence J. Burian
SVP, Deputy General Counsel, and Secretary: Victoria D. Salhus, age 59
SVP Investor Relations: Patricia Armstrong
SVP and Treasurer: Kevin Watson, age 42
SVP Business Development and Strategy: Kim Norris
VP Corporate Communications: Kim Kearns
President and CEO, Rainbow Media: Joshua W. Sapan
Co-President, Office of Strategic Product Development: Wilton (Wilt) Hildenbrand, age 61
President, Cable and Communications: John R. Bickham, age 57
President, Local Media: Tad Smith, age 48
President, MSG Sports: Scott M. O'Neil, age 38
Auditors: KPMG LLP

LOCATIONS

HQ: Cablevision Systems Corporation
1111 Stewart Ave., Bethpage, NY 11714
Phone: 516-803-2300   **Fax:** 516-803-3134
Web: www.cablevision.com

Cablevision Systems operates primarily in the New York City metropolitan area, including parts of Connecticut and New Jersey.

PRODUCTS/OPERATIONS

2008 Sales

	% of total
Telecommuncations services	
Cable television	41
Broadband data	15
Voice-over-Internet-protocol telephony	9
Optimum Lightpath	3
Advertising & other	2
Rainbow Media	14
Madison Square Garden	14
Newsday	2
Total	**100**

Selected Operations

Consumer Services
  CCG Holdings (movie theaters, dba Clearview Cinemas)
  Cable and Communications
    Video
    Consumer Modem
    Consumer Telephone
Business Services
  Cablevision Lightpath (integrated business communications systems)
Programming and Entertainment
  Rainbow Media Holdings
    American Movie Classics (classic films)
    The Independent Film Channel
    Madison Square Garden, L.P.
      FOX Sports Net Chicago
      FOX Sports Net Bay Area (60%)
      FOX Sports Net New England (50%)
      FOX Sports Net New York
      Madison Square Garden
      MSG Arena complex
      MSG Network
      New York Knicks
      New York Liberty
      New York Rangers
      Radio City Music Hall
    Mag Rack (video magazines video-on-demand, formerly Sterling Digital)
    News 12 Networks
    Sportskool (sports and fitness video on demand)
    VOOM HD Networks (80%, high definition cable and satellite entertainment channels)
    WE: Women's Entertainment (entertainment and information for women)
    World Picks (foreign language video on demand programming)

COMPETITORS

A&E Networks
AT&T
Charter Communications
Comcast
Cox Communications
DIRECTV
DISH Network Corporation
Disney
FOX Sports
Liberty Media
NBC
RCN Corporation
Time Warner Cable
Verizon
Viacom

HISTORICAL FINANCIALS

Company Type: Public

Income Statement

FYE: December 31

	REVENUE ($ mil.)	NET INCOME ($ mil.)	NET PROFIT MARGIN	EMPLOYEES
12/08	7,230.1	(227.6)	—	20,105
12/07	6,484.5	218.9	3.4%	22,935
12/06	5,927.5	(125.6)	—	22,075
12/05	5,175.9	94.3	1.8%	20,425
12/04	4,932.9	(668.7)	—	12,270
Annual Growth	**10.0%**	**—**	**—**	**13.1%**

2008 Year-End Financials

Debt ratio: —   No. of shares (mil.): 314
Return on equity: —   Dividends
Cash ($ mil.): 323   Yield: 1.2%
Current ratio: 0.81   Payout: —
Long-term debt ($ mil.): 11,286   Market value ($ mil.): 5,292

Stock History

NYSE: CVC

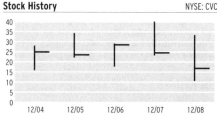

	STOCK PRICE ($) FY Close	P/E High/Low		PER SHARE ($) Earnings	Dividends	Book Value
12/08	16.84	—	—	(0.78)	0.20	(17.06)
12/07	24.50	54	32	0.74	0.00	(16.22)
12/06	28.48	—	—	(0.45)	0.00	(16.99)
12/05	23.47	103	68	0.33	0.00	(7.86)
12/04	24.90	—	—	(2.36)	0.00	(8.37)
Annual Growth	**(9.3%)**	**—**	**—**	**—**	**—**	**—**

Cabot Corporation

Even if it lost money, Cabot still would be in the black. The company is the world's #1 producer of carbon black, a reinforcing and pigmenting agent used in tires, inks, cables, and coatings. It has about 25% of the world market for the product. Cabot also holds its own as a maker of fumed metal oxides such as fumed silica and fumed alumina, which are used as anticaking, thickening, and reinforcing agents in adhesives and coatings. Other products include tantalum (used to make capacitors in electronics) and specialty fluids for gas and oil drilling.

The company is among a small group of carbon black producers with a global presence. (Columbian Chemicals and Evonik Degussa also operate worldwide.) While the US is its single largest market, accounting for more than a quarter of Cabot's total sales, the company is increasing its Chinese business; 2008 marked the first year that country crept past the 10% mark in terms of sales. Much of its carbon black business is done with the top automobile tire makers; Goodyear Tire & Rubber is its largest customer, totaling more than 10% of its entire business.

HISTORY

A descendant of two old-line Boston merchant families, Godfrey Lowell Cabot graduated from Harvard in 1882. His brother had a paint business in Pennsylvania that used coal tars to make black pigment, and the two decided that carbon black — an abundant waste product of the oil fields — would be their business. The brothers built a carbon black plant in Pennsylvania in 1882; five years later Godfrey bought his brother's share in the company. A carbon black glut and the increasing use of natural gas led Godfrey to drill his first gas well in 1888. He took advantage of the glut by buying distressed carbon black factories.

As the Pennsylvania oil fields dried up near the turn of the century, Godfrey moved operations to West Virginia, where he added to his gas holdings and, in 1914, built a natural gas extraction plant. Meanwhile, products such as high-speed printing presses increased the demand for carbon black. The reinforcing and stabilizing properties of the compound became widely known after its use in tires during WWI. The company was incorporated in 1922 as Godfrey L. Cabot, Inc.

The production of carbon black soon moved west, and by 1930 Cabot had eight plants in Texas and one in Oklahoma. Early that decade the company developed dustless carbon black pellets, which, along with gas profits, got Cabot through the Depression. In 1935 Cabot began drilling for oil and gas and processing natural gas in Texas. Soon natural gas accounted for more than half of sales.

WWII led to rubber shortages and temporary government control over the industry. It also led to the construction and improvement (with government assistance) of Cabot plants in Louisiana, Oklahoma, and Texas. The company was the #1 producer of carbon black in 1950 and began its fumed silica operations in 1952. The postwar economic boom allowed Cabot to open carbon black plants in Canada, France, Italy, and the UK by the end of the decade.

In 1960 the company's businesses were united under the Cabot Corporation name. Expansion continued into Argentina, Colombia, Germany, and Spain for the next decade. Godfrey Cabot died in 1962. The next year the company started producing titanium, sold a 12% stake in a public offering, and began experimenting with plastic polymers.

CEO Robert Sharpie used the cash derived from Cabot's chemical businesses during the 1970s for acquisitions — including Kawecki Berylco Industries (tantalum, 1978) and TUCO, Inc. (gas processing and pipeline, 1979) — while its chemical plants deteriorated. The oil crisis early in the decade resulted in the rapid growth of Cabot's energy business. However, when gas prices fell in the 1980s, Cabot's revenue base shrank and its liabilities didn't.

The Cabot family, which owned 30% of the company, replaced Sharpie with Samuel Bodman as CEO in 1987. Bodman invested in the plants and divested many of Cabot's noncore assets, including ceramics, metal manufacturing, and semiconductors. He also exited the energy production and exploration businesses.

In 1996 Cabot formed divisions to make pigment-based inks (inkjet colorants) and drilling fluids (Cabot Specialty Fluids) and sold TUCO. Two years later the company began field testing a drilling fluid (cesium formate) that would halve the drilling time in high-temperature, high-pressure wells. Cabot opened a slurry plant (for semiconductor manufacturing) in Japan in 1999 and completed the second phase of its carbon black plant in China, a joint venture with a Chinese firm. It also spun off 15% of its microelectronics materials business and sold Cabot LNG to Tractebel for around $680 million.

Cabot spun off its remaining stake (about 80%) in Cabot Microelectronics in 2000. The next year Kennett Burnes was named CEO and chairman after Bodman stepped down to become US deputy treasury secretary. (President Bush nominated Bodman to become secretary of energy for his second term, and Bodman was confirmed in early 2005.)

In 2002 Cabot purchased the remainder of Showa Cabot Supermetals (tantalum) from its joint venture partner, Showa Denko, for about $100 million and another $100 million in debt. However, the company experienced lower sales volumes of tantalum because of contract disagreements with some of its customers, including KEMET and AVX.

Cabot continued to develop and expand its newer businesses, including its growing ink jet colorants unit. In late 2002 it launched a new aerogels business (Nanogel), which produces materials for thermal and sound insulating purposes. Cabot sold its 40% stake in Aearo Corporation (maker of safety products like eyewear; formerly called Cabot Safety Holding Corporation) in 2004.

The following year Cabot purchased Showa Denko's interest in another joint venture, Showa Cabot K.K., which marketed carbon black products in Japan.

Early in 2008 BASF executive Patrick Prevost took over the CEO post from Burnes.

EXECUTIVES

Chairman: John F. O'Brien, age 65
President, CEO, and Director: Patrick M. Prevost, age 53
VP and CFO: Eduardo E. Cordeiro, age 41
VP and CIO: Douglas A. Church
EVP and General Manager, Europe: Dirk L. Blevi, age 60
EVP and General Manager, Core Segment and Americas Region: William J. Brady, age 47
VP Engineering: Helmut Lorat
VP Human Resources: Robby D. Sisco
VP and General Counsel: Brian A. Berube, age 46
VP; President, Cabot Supermetals KK: Yasuto Komatsu
VP Research and Development: Yakov Kutsovsky
VP and Treasurer: Irene Sudac
Secretary: Jane A. Bell
Director, Investor Relations: Susannah Robinson
Director, Global Sales: Jose Olivares
Auditors: Deloitte & Touche LLP

LOCATIONS

HQ: Cabot Corporation
  2 Seaport Ln., Ste. 1300, Boston, MA 02210
Phone: 617-345-0100   **Fax:** 617-342-6103
Web: www.cabot-corp.com

2008 Sales

	$ mil.	% of total
US	849	27
Japan	368	11
China	330	10
Other countries	1,644	52
Total	**3,191**	**100**

PRODUCTS/OPERATIONS

2008 Sales

	$ mil.	% of total
Core Segment		
Rubber blacks	1,868	59
Supermetals	195	6
Performance Segment	933	29
Specialty Fluids Segment	68	2
New Business Segment	57	2
Other	70	2
Total	**3,191**	**100**

Selected Products

Core Segment
  Rubber blacks (for tires and industrial products)
  Supermetals
    Niobium
    Tantalum
Performance Segment
  Performance products
    Specialty carbon blacks
    Thermoplastic concentrates
  Metal oxides
    Fumed alumina
    Fumed silica
Specialty fluids (cesium formate drilling fluids)
New Business Segment
  Inkjet colorants
  Nanogel (insulative aerogel materials)
  Superior MicroPowders (business development)

COMPETITORS

Aditya Birla Nuvo
Akzo Nobel
Allegheny Technologies
BASF SE
Clariant
Columbian Chemicals
Dow Chemical
Evonik Degussa
Flint Group
J.M. Huber
MacDermid
Mitsubishi Chemical
SABIC Innovative Plastics
Tokai Carbon
Wacker Chemie

HISTORICAL FINANCIALS

Company Type: Public

Income Statement				FYE: September 30
	REVENUE ($ mil.)	NET INCOME ($ mil.)	NET PROFIT MARGIN	EMPLOYEES
9/08	3,191.0	86.0	2.7%	4,300
9/07	2,616.0	129.0	4.9%	4,300
9/06	2,543.0	90.0	3.5%	4,300
9/05	2,125.0	(48.0)	—	4,400
9/04	1,934.0	124.0	6.4%	4,300
Annual Growth	**13.3%**	**(8.7%)**	**—**	**0.0%**

2008 Year-End Financials

Debt ratio: 46.9%
Return on equity: 7.0%
Cash ($ mil.): 129
Current ratio: 2.34
Long-term debt ($ mil.): 586
No. of shares (mil.): 65
Dividends
  Yield: 2.3%
  Payout: 53.7%
Market value ($ mil.): 2,078

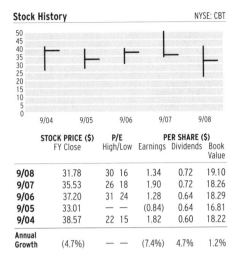

	STOCK PRICE ($) FY Close	P/E High/Low		PER SHARE ($) Earnings	Dividends	Book Value
9/08	31.78	30	16	1.34	0.72	19.10
9/07	35.53	26	18	1.90	0.72	18.26
9/06	37.20	31	24	1.28	0.64	18.29
9/05	33.01	—	—	(0.84)	0.64	16.81
9/04	38.57	22	15	1.82	0.60	18.22
Annual Growth	(4.7%)	—	—	(7.4%)	4.7%	1.2%

CACI International

CACI International doesn't need a lot of clients — just a few with deep pockets. Deriving 95% its revenues from the US government and more than 70% from the US Department of Defense (DOD), CACI is one of the largest government information technology (IT) contractors. The company provides a wide range of technology services including systems integration, network management, knowledge management, and engineering and simulation. Based in the UK, the company's European subsidiary, CACI Limited, accounts for all of its international sales and almost all of its commercial revenue.

The company's plan for securing more business with the DOD is based in part on acquiring companies that already serve the department. In 2007 CACI purchased the Institute for Quality Management, a performance management consultancy and provider of operational support services to the intelligence and homeland security community. It then bought government consulting company Wexford Group, giving it better access to contracts with the US Army. It also acquired government technical and engineering services provider Dragon Development in 2007, as well as Athena Innovative Solutions, a professional services firm serving US intelligence agencies.

CACI generates less than 5% of its revenues from international clients, but the company has made small acquisitions to expand its overseas business. It purchased three UK-based businesses during fiscal 2008: Arete Software and Softsmart (software for local government education authorities), and Invocom (network support for telecom service providers).

HISTORY

In 1962 Harry Markowitz (winner of the 1990 Nobel Memorial Prize in Economic Sciences) and Herb Karr formed California Analysis Center, which provided services related to the SIMSCRIPT programming language. The company went public in 1968 and four years later moved from Santa Monica, California, to the Washington, DC, area. Its name was changed to CACI in the late 1970s. J.P. London, a 12-year company veteran, became CEO in 1984.

Through the 1980s and early 1990s, CACI's dependence on a struggling military sector hurt operations. The company got a big boost in 1991, however, when it won a US Justice Department contract for litigation support services worth $130 million over five years. Profits were revived by 1995. The next year it won a $66 million subcontract to provide information processing support to VGS, a software integration firm charged with building a federal information processing program.

In 1997 CACI gained a foothold in the government and commercial communications services segments when it acquired Infonet Services' Government Systems subsidiary. Also that year it bought AnaData (now CACI Ltd.), a UK-based database marketing software firm. In 1998 the company acquired QuesTech (now CACI Technologies), a computer services contractor to the military and national security segment; CACI began bundling products and services for availability over Internet-based networks.

In 2000 CACI acquired government services specialist XEN Corporation (systems engineering and IT services) and CENTECH (network services and e-commerce) as well as the network services and related assets (Federal Services Business) of net.com.

Continuing its growth strategy, CACI acquired C-CUBED Corporation in October 2003. C-CUBED provides specialized support services known as C4ISR (Command, Control, Communications, Computers, Intelligence, Surveillance, and Reconnaissance) to clients in the Department of Defense, federal, and intelligence communities.

CACI also acquired intelligence contractor Premier Technology Group (PTG) for an undisclosed amount in mid-2003. Prior to PTG, CACI purchased IT service providers Acton Burnell and Digital Systems International, the Government Solutions Division of Condor Technology Solutions, and Applied Technology Solutions of Northern VA.

The company also purchased CMS Information Services, Inc. (CMS) in 2004. That year it also bought American Management Systems' (AMS) Defense Intelligence Group, which performs work for the Department of Defense and government intelligence agencies. The deal, valued at $415 million, happened in 2004 when CGI Group acquired the entirety of AMS, and then sold part of it to CACI.

CACI in 2006 acquired Falls Church, Virginia-based IT firm AlphaInsight. The deal expanded CACI's business with civilian agencies of the federal government including the state and justice department and provided additional contract opportunities with the Department of Homeland Security and the DOD. Also that year, CACI acquired Information Systems Support (ISS), a government systems integrator specializing in communications, IT, and logistics.

In 2007 US operations president Paul Cofoni was named the company's new CEO, replacing London, who retained the title of chairman.

EXECUTIVES

Chairman: J. P. (Jack) London, age 71
President, CEO, and Director: Paul M. Cofoni, age 60
COO, US Operations and Acting EVP, Mission Systems Business Group: Randall C. (Randy) Fuerst, age 53
EVP, CFO, and Treasurer: Thomas A. (Tom) Mutryn, age 54
EVP and CTO: Deborah B. Dunie
EVP and Chief Human Resources Officer: H. Robert (Bob) Boehm
EVP and Chief Resources Officer: Robert B. Turner
Chief Scientist, Advanced Solutions: Stephen T. Makrinos
EVP, Public Relations and Business Communications: Jody A. Brown
EVP and Division Manager, Enterprise Technologies and Services Business Group: Richard W. Mayo
EVP, Transformation Solutions Business Group: Gilbert B. (Gil) Guarino
EVP, Corporate Business Development: Ronald A. (Ron) Schneider
EVP, National Solutions Group: Lowell E. (Jake) Jacoby
EVP, Government Business Operations: Steven H. Weiss
EVP, Security and Intelligence Integration: Albert M. (Bert) Calland III
EVP and Controller, US Operations: Thomas Lex
EVP, Business Development: Dale Luddeke
SVP, Investor Relations: David Dragics
CEO, CACI Limited and President, Information Solutions, United Kingdom: Gregory R. Bradford, age 59
President, US Operations: William M. (Bill) Fairl, age 59
Investor Relations Coordinator: Mary DeClark Peevy
Auditors: Ernst & Young LLP

LOCATIONS

HQ: CACI International Inc
1100 N. Glebe Rd., Arlington, VA 22201
Phone: 703-841-7800   **Fax:** 703-841-7882
Web: www.caci.com

2009 Sales

	$ mil.	% of total
US	2,650.8	97
Other countries	79.4	3
Total	**2,730.2**	**100**

PRODUCTS/OPERATIONS

2009 Sales

	$ mil.	% of total
Department of Defense	2,078.4	76
Federal civilian agencies	542.1	20
Commercial	88.2	3
State & local government	21.5	1
Total	**2,730.2**	**100**

2009 Sales by Contract Type

	$ mil.	% of total
Time & materials	1,310.0	48
Cost reimbursable	875.7	32
Firm fixed-price	544.5	20
Total	**2,730.2**	**100**

Selected Services

Asset management
Automated procurement
Customer database management integration
Electronic commerce
Engineering support
Information management development
Intelligent document management integration
Knowledge management
Litigation support
Logistics support

Marketing and customer database management development
Networking support
Product data and supply-chain management integration
Records management development
Simulation and modeling languages
Software development
Systems integration and reengineering
Weapons systems/equipment configuration management integration

COMPETITORS

Affiliated Computer Services
Alion
Apptis
BAE SYSTEMS
Boeing
Booz Allen
Computer Sciences Corp.
EDS
General Dynamics Information Technology
GTSI
IBM
Jacobs Engineering
L-3 Communications
Lockheed Martin
ManTech
Northrop Grumman
Perot Systems
Raytheon
SAIC
SRA International
Unisys

HISTORICAL FINANCIALS

Company Type: Public

Income Statement

FYE: June 30

	REVENUE ($ mil.)	NET INCOME ($ mil.)	NET PROFIT MARGIN	EMPLOYEES
6/09	2,730.2	95.5	3.5%	12,400
6/08	2,420.5	83.3	3.4%	12,000
6/07	1,938.0	78.5	4.1%	10,400
6/06	1,755.3	84.8	4.8%	10,400
6/05	1,623.1	85.3	5.3%	9,600
Annual Growth	13.9%	2.9%	—	6.6%

2009 Year-End Financials

Debt ratio: 63.2%
Return on equity: 10.0%
Cash ($ mil.): 208
Current ratio: 2.28
Long-term debt ($ mil.): 628

No. of shares (mil.): 30
Dividends
  Yield: 0.0%
  Payout: —
Market value ($ mil.): 1,282

Stock History

NYSE: CACI

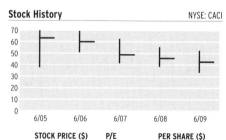

	STOCK PRICE ($) FY Close	P/E High/Low		PER SHARE ($) Earnings	Dividends	Book Value
6/09	42.71	17	11	3.14	0.00	33.09
6/08	45.77	20	14	2.72	0.00	30.58
6/07	48.85	25	17	2.51	0.00	27.11
6/06	60.00	25	19	2.72	0.00	24.83
6/05	63.16	25	14	2.79	0.00	20.39
Annual Growth	(9.3%)	—	—	3.0%	—	12.9%

CalPERS

California's public-sector retirees already have a place in the sun; CalPERS gives them the money to enjoy it. CalPERS is the California Public Employees' Retirement System, the largest public pension system in the US. It manages retirement and health plans for more than 1.5 million beneficiaries (employees, retirees, and their dependents) from more than 2,600 government agencies and school districts. Even though the system's beneficiaries are current or former employees of the Golden State, CalPERS brings its influence to bear in all 50 states and beyond.

With more than $240 billion in assets in its investment funds, CalPERS uses its clout to sway such corporate governance issues as company performance, executive compensation, and even social policy. In the absence of a strong federal effort to purge corporations of corruption, CalPERS has often acted as a force for reform, urging companies to remove conflicts of interest and make themselves more accountable to shareholders, employees, and the public. CalPERS is also a powerful negotiator for such services as insurance; rates established by the system serve as benchmarks for employers throughout the nation.

Most of CalPERS' revenue comes from its enormous investment program: It has interests in US and foreign securities, oil and energy, real estate, and even hedge funds and venture capital activities. CalPERS has steadily increased its investments in private equity, looking to take ownership stakes in more firms.

Fred Buenrostro retired as CEO in 2008. Anne Stausboll, who'd been serving as CalPERS' interim chief investment officer and was previously California's Chief Deputy Treasurer, was named his successor. She is the fund's first female CEO. Shortly after Buenrostro's retirement, CalPERS reported its worst performance in six years, partly due to its investments in undeveloped land earlier in the decade.

During the coming years CalPERS may be forced to sell assets, as it is expected to be hit with a wave of early retirements by middle-aged workers. The fund plans to sell some of its US stocks, which have been declining, in exchange for emerging markets such as India and China.

CalPERS' board consists of six elected and three appointed members as well as four designated members (the director of the state's Department of Personnel Administration, the state controller, the state treasurer, and a member of the State Personnel Board).

HISTORY

The state of California founded CalPERS in 1931 to administer a pension fund for state employees. By the 1940s the system was serving other public agencies and educational institutions on a contract basis.

When the Public Employees' Medical and Hospital Care Act was passed in 1962, CalPERS added health coverage. The fund was conservatively managed in-house, with little exposure to stocks. Despite slow growth, the state used the system's funds to meet its own cash shortfalls.

CalPERS became involved in corporate governance issues in the mid-1980s, when California treasurer Jesse Unruh became outraged by corporate greenmail schemes. In 1987 he hired as

CEO Wisconsin pension board veteran Dale Hanson, who led the movement for corporate accountability to institutional investors.

In the late 1980s CalPERS moved into real estate and Japanese stocks. When both crashed around 1990, Hanson came under pressure. CalPERS was twice forced to take major writedowns for its real estate holdings and turned to expensive outside fund managers, but its investment performance deteriorated and member services suffered.

Legislation in 1990 enabled CalPERS to offer long-term health insurance. Governor Pete Wilson's 1991 attempt to use $1.6 billion from CalPERS to help meet a state budget shortfall resulted in legislation banning future raids. CalPERS made its first direct investment in 1993, an energy-related infrastructure partnership with Enron.

CalPERS suffered in the 1994 bond crash. That year Hanson resigned amid criticism that his focus on corporate governance had depressed fund performance. CalPERS eased its corporate relations stance, creating a separate office to handle investor issues and launching an International Corporate Governance Program. However, the next year CalPERS was uninvited from a KKR investment pool because of criticism of its fund management and fee structure.

In 2000 the system raised health care premiums almost 10% to keep up with rising care costs. It widened the scope of its direct investments with stakes in investment bank Thomas Weisel Partners and asset manager Arrowstreet Capital; it also moved into real estate development, buying Genstar Land Co. with Newland Communities. CalPERS said that year it would sell off more than $500 million in tobacco holdings; it then invested the same amount in five biotech funds, its first foray into the sector.

In 2001 California state controller and CalPERS board member Kathleen Connell successfully sued the system for not following state-sanctioned rules regarding pay increases. CalPERS was forced to cut salaries for investment managers, a move that prompted chief investment officer Daniel Szente to resign.

In 2003 CalPERS agreed to a record $250 million settlement relating to an age-discrimination suit brought by the Equal Employment Opportunity Commission. Also that year CalPERS clamored for (and got) the resignation of New York Stock Exchange (NYSE) chairman Richard Grasso. CalPERS and others claimed Grasso's pay of $140 million a year made it impossible for him to effectively monitor the exchange's member companies for corruption.

CalPERS in 2003 sued the NYSE and several specialist firms, including Bear Wagner Specialists, Fleet Specialist, LaBranche & Co, and Van der Moolen Holding's Van Der Moolen Specialists USA. The suit accused the exchange and the specialists of using the trading system for their own gain at the expense of investors. CalPERS found itself on the receiving end of a corporate governance issue in 2004 when a media group sued, demanding CalPERS make public the fees it pays to venture capital firms and hedge funds. CalPERS settled the suit by disclosing the fees.

Also in 2004 the president of CalPERS' board, Sean Harrigan, was ousted when the State Personnel Board voted to remove him as its representative. Harrigan had drawn the ire of the business community because of his labor ties and because, under his leadership, the board had withheld votes for directors of most of the companies in which CalPERS invests.

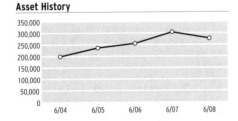
Calpine Corporation

Calpine may get hot, but it also knows how to blow off some steam. The independent power producer and marketer controls more than 24,000 MW of generating capacity through interests in 60 natural gas-fired power plants throughout the US and 15 geothermal power plants in California. Calpine owns 725 MW of capacity at the largest geothermal facility in the US (the Geysers in northern California), where electricity is produced from natural steam. Calpine emerged from bankruptcy in 2008 (having filed for Chapter 11 protection in 2005). Its California and Texas operations account for the great majority of its business.

The company has disposed of most of its natural gas reserves and gathering and transportation assets.

Although Calpine is scaling back on new plant development due to low demand — it has about 1,000 MW under construction — it is building a 775-megawatt power plant in Riverside County, California, for the Inland Empire Energy Center. The plant is based on General Electric's latest gas turbine technology.

Calpine sells electricity to utilities, wholesalers, and end-users, primarily through long-term contracts; the firm also trades power on the wholesale market. Other Calpine operations include construction, consulting, and management services; turbine component manufacturing; and critical power provision for high-tech companies.

EXECUTIVES

Chairman: William J. Patterson
President, CEO, and Director: Jack A. Fusco, age 46,
$7,124,624 total compensation
EVP and CFO: Zamir Rauf, age 49,
$3,119,366 total compensation
Interim EVP Shared Services: Casey L. Gunnell, age 61
SVP and CIO: Dennis Fishback
EVP, Chief Legal Officer, and Secretary:
W. Thaddeus Miller, age 58,
$2,525,917 total compensation
EVP and Chief Commercial Officer:
John B. (Thad) Hill III, age 41,
$3,109,435 total compensation
EVP and Chief Risk Officer: Gary M. Germeroth, age 50
SVP and Chief Accounting Officer: Jim D. Deidiker,
age 53
SVP Government and Regulatory Affairs:
Joseph E. (Joe) Ronan Jr.
SVP Human Resources: Laura D. Guthrie
SVP Commercial Operations: Larry B. Leverett
SVP Renewables Growth: Dennis J. Gilles
SVP Government Affairs and Managing Counsel:
Sarah Novosel
SVP Geothermal Operations: Michael D. (Mike) Rogers,
$4,592,447 total compensation
SVP ERCOT Power Plants: Robert R. (Bob) Regan
VP Corporate Communications: Norma F. Dunn
VP Finance and Investor Relations: Andre K. Walker
Interim Corporate Controller: Kenneth A. (Ken) Graves,
age 43
Auditors: PricewaterhouseCoopers LLP

LOCATIONS

HQ: Calpine Corporation
717 Texas Ave., Ste. 1000, Houston, TX 77002
Phone: 713-830-2000   **Fax:** 713-830-2001
Web: www.calpine.com

PRODUCTS/OPERATIONS

2008 Sales

	$ mil.	% of total
West	4,229	42
Texas	3,891	39
Southeast	1,273	13
North	662	6
Adjustments	(118)	—
Total	**9,937**	**100**

COMPETITORS

AEP
AES
CMS Energy
Covanta
Duke Energy
Edison International
Edison Mission Energy
Energy Future
FPL Group
Indeck Energy
MidAmerican Energy
Mirant
NRG Energy
Ormat
Panda Energy
PG&E Corporation
PSEG Power
RRI Energy
Sempra Energy
Southern Power

HISTORICAL FINANCIALS

Company Type: Public

Income Statement   FYE: December 31

	REVENUE ($ mil.)	NET INCOME ($ mil.)	NET PROFIT MARGIN	EMPLOYEES
12/08	9,937.0	10.0	0.1%	2,049
12/07	7,970.0	2,693.0	33.8%	2,080
12/06	6,705.8	(1,765.4)	—	2,306
12/05	10,112.7	(9,939.2)	—	3,265
12/04	9,229.9	(242.5)	—	3,505
Annual Growth	1.9%	—	—	(12.6%)

2008 Year-End Financials

Debt ratio: 223.2%	No. of shares (mil.): 429
Return on equity: —	Dividends
Cash ($ mil.): 1,657	Yield: 0.0%
Current ratio: 1.34	Payout: —
Long-term debt ($ mil.): 9,756	Market value ($ mil.): 3,121

Stock History   NYSE: CPN

	STOCK PRICE ($) FY Close	P/E High/Low	PER SHARE ($) Earnings	Dividends	Book Value
12/08	7.28	1,168 318	0.02	0.00	10.19

Campbell Soup

Soup means *M'm! M'm! Money!* for the Campbell Soup Company. The company is the world's biggest soup maker; in the US its most popular selections are chicken noodle, tomato, and cream of mushroom soups. The company also makes meal kits, Franco-American sauces and canned pasta, Pace picante sauce, Pepperidge Farm baked goods (yes, the Goldfish crackers you sneak at midnight), and V8 beverages. Its Australian division produces snack foods and its popular "down-under" Arnott's biscuit brand. Campbell products are sold in more than 120 countries. In addition to North America, its principal markets are in France, Germany, Belgium, and Australia.

Campbell is striving to heat up lukewarm sales as consumers seek more convenience in the kitchen and competitors slurp into its market share. The company offers meal kits (just add your own meat) and ready-to-serve soups in pop-top, resealable, and microwaveable containers.

Challenged on quality and in sales by General Mills' Progresso brand soups, Campbell has tried boosting the taste of its products — adding more veggies to its vegetable soup, and making its cream soups creamier. The company's Away From Home unit is following customers out of the kitchen, selling soup and buns to cafeterias, fast-food restaurants, and harried consumers via the supermarket. It has also added microwaveable versions of its Chunky and Select soups.

Meanwhile, Campbell expanded its brand portfolio in 2008 when it acquired the Wolfgang Puck soup label from Country Gourmet Foods. It also inked a licensing deal with Wolfgang Puck Worldwide to use the celebrity chef's name on additional broth and stock products.

In an effort to concentrate on its soup and snacks businesses, the company in 2008 sold its premium chocolate maker, Godiva, to Turkish food company Ülker. Campbell earned $850 million from the sale and said it planned to use the proceeds to repurchase shares. In pursuit of that strategy, the company also divested its French sauce and mayonnaise business, which is marketed under the *Lesieur* brand.

Wal-Mart is the company's largest customer, accounting for 16% of its sales in 2008.

The descendants of John Dorrance, the inventor of condensed soup, own approximately 40% of Campbell.

HISTORY

Campbell Soup Company began in Camden, New Jersey, in 1869 as a canning and preserving business founded by icebox maker Abram Anderson and fruit merchant Joseph Campbell. Anderson left in 1876 and Arthur Dorrance took his place. The Dorrance family assumed control after Campbell retired in 1894.

Arthur's nephew, John Dorrance, joined Campbell in 1897. The young chemist soon found a way to condense soup by eliminating most of its water. Without the heavy bulk of water-filled cans, distribution was cheaper; Campbell products quickly spread.

In 1904 the firm introduced the Campbell Kids characters. Entering the California market in 1911, Campbell became one of the first US companies to achieve national distribution of a food brand. It bought Franco-American, the first American soup maker, in 1915.

The company's ubiquity in American kitchens made its soup can an American icon (consider Andy Warhol's celebrated 1960 print) and brought great wealth to the Dorrance family.

With a reputation for conservative management, Campbell began to diversify, acquiring V8 juice (1948), Swanson (1955), Pepperidge Farm (1961), Godiva Chocolatier (33% in 1966, full ownership in 1974), Vlasic pickles (1978), and Mrs. Paul's seafood (1982). It introduced Prego spaghetti sauce and LeMenu frozen dinners in the early 1980s.

Much of Campbell's sales growth in the 1990s came not from unit sales but from increasing its prices. In 1993 it took a $300 million restructuring charge, and over the next two years it sold poor performers at home and abroad. John Sr.'s grandson, Bennett Dorrance, took up the role of vice chairman in 1993, becoming the first family member to take a senior executive position in 10 years.

Two years later Campbell paid $1.1 billion for Pace Foods (picante sauce) and acquired Fresh Start Bakeries (buns and muffins for McDonald's) and Homepride (popular cooking sauce in the UK).

As part of its international expansion, in 1996 the firm acquired Erasco, a top German soup maker, and Cheong Chan, a food manufacturer in Malaysia. However, back at home it sold Mrs. Paul's. In 1997 Campbell sold its Marie's salad dressing operations and bought Groupe Danone's Liebig (France's leading wet-soup brand). Also that year Dale Morrison, a relative newcomer to the firm, succeeded David Johnson as president and CEO. To reduce costs and focus on other core segments, in 1998 Campbell spun off Swanson frozen foods and Vlasic pickles into Vlasic Foods International. (Vlasic later filed bankruptcy and was snapped up in a leveraged buyout.) In 1999 Campbell redesigned its soup can labels, altering an American icon.

Morrison resigned abruptly as president and CEO in 2000; Johnson returned to the helm during the search for a permanent chief. In early 2001 Douglas Conant, previously of Nabisco Foods, joined Campbell as president and CEO. A fresh plan was introduced to spend up to $600 million on marketing, product development, and quality upgrades (at the expense of shareholder dividends). In 2001 Campbell also bought the Batchelors, Royco, and Heisse Tasse brands of soup, as well as the Oxo brand of stock cubes, from Unilever for about $900 million. The deal made Campbell the leading soup maker in Europe. In 2003 Campbell bought Snack Foods Limited, a leading snack food maker in Australia.

Campbell reorganized its North American business in 2004 into the following units: US Soup, Sauces, and Beverages; Campbell Away From Home, and Canada, Mexico, and Latin America; Pepperidge Farm; and Godiva Worldwide. (In response to dietary trends, the company announced that year that it was removing all transfatty acids from its Pepperidge Farm breads.) The company retired the Franco-American brand in 2004; products which carried the brand (most notably SpaghettiOs) now bear the Campbell brand. Also that year company chairman George M. Sherman retired and was replaced by Harvey Golub.

In 2006 Campbell sold its UK and Irish businesses to Premier Foods for about $870 million. Brands involved in the sale included Homepride sauces, OXO stock cubes, and Batchelors, McDonnells, and Erin soups.

EXECUTIVES

Chairman: Paul R. Charron, age 66
President, CEO, and Director: Douglas R. Conant, age 58
SVP, CFO, and Chief Administrative Officer: B. Craig Owens, age 54
SVP and CIO: Joseph C. (Joe) Spagnoletti, age 44
SVP and Chief Customer Officer; President, Global Sales: Archbold D. (Archie) van Beuren
SVP and Chief Strategy Officer: M. Carl Johnson III, age 60
SVP and Chief Human Resources and Communications Officer: Nancy A. Reardon, age 56
VP and Chief Diversity and Inclusion Officer: Rosalyn T. O'Neale, age 58
SVP Public Affairs: Jerry S. Buckley
SVP Law and Government Affairs: Ellen O. Kaden, age 56
SVP; President, North America Soup, Sauces, and Beverages: Denise M. Morrison, age 55
SVP; President, Campbell International: Larry S. McWilliams, age 52
SVP Global Supply Chain: David R. White, age 53
SVP Global Research and Development and Quality: George Dowdie
VP and Corporate Secretary: John J. Furey
VP Finance and Strategy, North America Soup, Sauces and Beverages: William J. O'Shea, age 51
VP and Controller: Anthony P. DiSilvestro, age 50
VP Investor Relations: Jennifer Driscoll, age 43
VP and Treasurer: Ashok Madhavan, age 47
Auditors: PricewaterhouseCoopers LLP

LOCATIONS

HQ: Campbell Soup Company
1 Campbell Place, Camden, NJ 08103
Phone: 856-342-4800   **Fax:** 856-342-3878
Web: www.campbellsoup.com

2008 Sales

	$ mil.	% of total
US	5,448	68
Australia/Asia Pacific	1,074	13
Europe	770	10
Other countries	706	9
Total	**7,998**	**100**

PRODUCTS/OPERATIONS

2008 Sales

	$ mil.	% of total
US soup, sauces & beverages	3,674	46
Baking & snacking	2,058	26
International soup & sauces	1,610	20
North America foodservice	656	8
Total	**7,998**	**100**

Selected Brand Names

Domestic
  Campbell's (soups)
  Ecce Panis (par-baked artisan breads)
  Pace (Mexican sauces)
  Pepperidge Farm (cookies and crackers)
  Prego (pasta sauces)
  Stockpot (foodservice soups)
  Swanson (broths)
  V8 and V8 Splash (vegetable and fruit juices)
  Wolfgang Puck (soups)

International
  Erasco (soups, Germany)
  Habitant (soups, Canada)
  Heisse Tasse (soups, Germany)
  Royco (soups, France)
  V8 Splash (beverages)

Selected Subsidiaries

Arnott's Biscuits Limited (Australia)
Aulsebrooks Limited (New Zealand)
Continental Foods S.A. (France)
CSC Brands LP
Eugen Lacroix GmbH (Germany)
Grundstuecksverwaltungsgesellschaft GmbH (Germany)
Pepperidge Farm, Incorporated
Players Group Limited (Australia)
Royco Voedingsmiddelenfabrieken B.V. (Netherlands)
Sinalopasta S.A. de C.V. (Mexico)

COMPETITORS

Associated British Foods
Bush Brothers
Canyon Creek Food
ConAgra
Del Monte Foods
Frito-Lay
General Mills
Harry's Fresh Foods
Heinz
Hormel
Kellogg U.S. Snacks
Kraft Foods
Mott's
Nestlé
Ocean Spray
PepsiCo
Reily Foods
Unilever

HISTORICAL FINANCIALS

Company Type: Public

Income Statement

FYE: Sunday nearest July 31

	REVENUE ($ mil.)	NET INCOME ($ mil.)	NET PROFIT MARGIN	EMPLOYEES
7/08	7,998.0	1,165.0	14.6%	19,400
7/07	7,867.0	854.0	10.9%	22,500
7/06	7,343.0	766.0	10.4%	24,000
7/05	7,548.0	707.0	9.4%	24,000
7/04	7,109.0	647.0	9.1%	24,000
Annual Growth	3.0%	15.8%	—	(5.2%)

2008 Year-End Financials

Debt ratio: 123.9%
Return on equity: 89.2%
Cash ($ mil.): 81
Current ratio: 0.70
Long-term debt ($ mil.): 1,633

No. of shares (mil.): 350
Dividends
Yield: 2.4%
Payout: 28.8%
Market value ($ mil.): 12,745

Stock History

NYSE: CPB

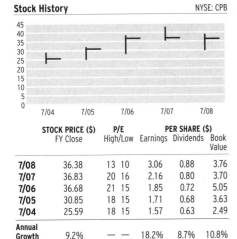

	STOCK PRICE ($) FY Close	P/E High/Low		PER SHARE ($) Earnings	Dividends	Book Value
7/08	36.38	13	10	3.06	0.88	3.76
7/07	36.83	20	16	2.16	0.80	3.70
7/06	36.68	21	15	1.85	0.72	5.05
7/05	30.85	18	15	1.71	0.68	3.63
7/04	25.59	18	15	1.57	0.63	2.49
Annual Growth	9.2%	—	—	18.2%	8.7%	10.8%

Capital One Financial

What's in your mailbox? Probably an offer from Capital One. One of the top credit card issuers in the US, Capital One offers Visa and MasterCard plastic with a variety of rates, credit limits, finance charges, and fees. Products range from platinum and gold cards for preferred customers to secured and unsecured cards for customers with poor or limited credit histories. The company, which boasts more than 44 million cardholders in the US, Canada, and the UK, also provides auto financing, health care finance, and other lending products. In addition, Capital One has more than 700 bank branches, mainly in New York, New Jersey, Louisiana, and Texas; it expanded its franchise by buying Chevy Chase Bank in 2009.

The deal, worth approximately $520 million in cash and stock, added more than 200 locations in the Washington, DC/Baltimore corridor to Capital One's network and made it one of the top banks in the region.

Capital One works hard to keep the *custom* in customer. Cardholders can customize their cards' appearance, rates, and rewards. Card terms run the gamut from secured cards with annual fees (for those with spotty credit) to a low annual percentage rate, no-fee card that offers cash back (for affluent "superprime" customers).

In 2007 Capital One closed wholesale lender GreenPoint Mortgage Funding, acquired as part of its acquisition of North Fork Bancorporation. The unit suffered from the credit woes that have plagued the subprime mortgage industry. Capital One continues to issue mortgages through its bank branches and its Capital One Home Loans division.

In 2008 the company received around $3.5 billion as part of the US government's Troubled Asset Relief Program (TARP).

HISTORY

Capital One Financial is a descendant of the Bank of Virginia, which was formed in 1945. The company began issuing products similar to credit cards in 1953 and was MasterCard issuer #001. Acquisitions and mergers brought some 30 banks and several finance and mortgage companies under the bank's umbrella between 1962 and 1986, when Bank of Virginia became Signet Banking.

Signet's credit card operations had reached a million customers in 1988, when the bank hired consultants Richard Fairbank and Nigel Morris (Fairbank is now chairman and CEO) to implement their "Information-Based Strategy." Under the duo's leadership, the bank began using sophisticated data-collection methods to gather massive amounts of information on existing or prospective customers; it then used the information to design and mass-market customized products to the customer.

In 1991 — after creating an enormous database and developing sophisticated screening processes and direct-mail marketing tactics — Signet escalated the credit card wars, luring customers from its rivals with its innovative balance-transfer credit card. The card let customers of other companies transfer what they owed on higher-interest cards to a Signet card with a lower introductory rate.

The new card immediately drew imitators (by 1997 balance-transfer cards accounted for 85% of credit card solicitations). After skimming off the least risky customers, Fairbank and Morris began going after less desirable credit customers who could be charged higher rates. The result was what they call second-generation products — secured and unsecured cards with lower credit lines and higher annual percentage rates and fees for higher-risk customers.

The credit card business had grown to 5 million customers by 1994, but at a high cost to Signet, which had devoted most of its resources to finding and servicing credit card holders. That year Signet spun off its credit card business as Capital One to focus on banking. (Signet was later acquired by First Union.)

Capital One moved into Florida and Texas in 1995 and into Canada and the UK in 1996; that year it established its savings bank, mainly to offer products and services to its cardholders. In 1997 the company used this unit to move into deposit accounts, buying a deposit portfolio from J. C. Penney. In 1998 the company began marketing its products to such clients as immigrants and high school students (whose parents must co-sign for the card). The company also expanded in terms of products and geography, acquiring auto lender Summit Acceptance and opening a new office in Nottingham, England.

In 1999 the firm's growth continued. The company stepped up its marketing efforts and was rewarded with significant boosts to its noninterest income and customer base. The next year the company launched The Capital One Place, an Internet shopping site. In 2001 the company acquired AmeriFee, which provides loans for elective medical and dental surgery; and PeopleFirst, Inc., the nation's largest online provider of direct motor vehicle loans.

In response to industry-wide concern over subprime lending, Capital One agreed in 2002 to beef up reserves on its subprime portfolio. Also in 2002, the company's UK operations proved profitable for the first time.

The company expanded into banking with the acquisitions of Hibernia (2005) and North Fork Bancorporation (2006). The deals expanded its presence both geographically in the Northeast and in the South and turned the company into one of the top bank holding companies in the US. The $13.2 billion stock-and-cash North Fork deal gave Capitol One more than 300 bank branches in New York, New Jersey, and Connecticut.

The 2005 purchase of New Orleans-based Hibernia, was a stock-and-cash transaction valued at some $5 billion, about 9% less than the originally agreed-upon price. The transaction was delayed, then renegotiated, after Hurricane Katrina devastated Hibernia's home city. Hibernia, which relocated to Houston, adopted the Capital One moniker.

EXECUTIVES

Chairman, President, and CEO:
Richard D. (Rich) Fairbank, age 58,
$9,822,702 total compensation
EVP and CFO: Gary L. Perlin, age 57,
$6,384,574 total compensation
CIO and Head Enterprise Customer Management:
Robert M. Alexander, age 44
EVP and Chief Auditor: James R. Tietjen
EVP and Chief Risk Officer: Peter A. Schnall, age 45,
$3,895,016 total compensation
EVP Brand Management: William J. (Bill) McDonald,
age 52
EVP; President, Banking: J. Herbert (Herb) Boydstun,
age 62

EVP, Corporate Reputation and Governance, General Counsel, and Corporate Secretary:
John G. Finneran Jr., age 59,
$4,147,606 total compensation
EVP Consumer and Private Banking: Carolyn Drexel
EVP and Chief Commercial Credit Risk Officer:
Suzanne Hammett, age 53
SVP Corporate Affairs: Richard Woods
SVP Commercial Real Estate Banking:
Richard (Rick) Lyon
VP Corporate Media: Tatiana Stead
Treasurer: Steve Linehan
Investor Relations: Jeff Norris
Public Relations: Diana Don
Auditors: Ernst & Young LLP

LOCATIONS

HQ: Capital One Financial Corporation
1680 Capital One Dr., McLean, VA 22102
Phone: 703-720-1000   **Fax:** 703-720-2306
Web: www.capitalone.com

PRODUCTS/OPERATIONS

2008 Gross Revenues

	$ mil.	% of total
Interest		
Loans held for investment, including		
past due fees	9,460.4	53
Securities available for sale	1,224.0	7
Other	427.6	2
Noninterest		
Servicing & securitizations	3,384.5	19
Service charges & other customer fees	2,232.4	13
Interchange	562.1	3
Other	565.0	3
Total	**17,856.0**	**100**

COMPETITORS

American Express
AmeriCredit
Bank of America
Citigroup
Credit Acceptance
Discover
HSBC Finance
JPMorgan Chase
PNC Financial
Wells Fargo

HISTORICAL FINANCIALS

Company Type: Public

Income Statement

FYE: December 31

	ASSETS ($ mil.)	NET INCOME ($ mil.)	INCOME AS % OF ASSETS	EMPLOYEES
12/08	165,913.5	(46.0)	—	25,800
12/07	150,590.4	1,570.3	1.0%	17,800
12/06	149,739.3	2,414.5	1.6%	31,800
12/05	88,701.4	1,809.1	2.0%	21,000
12/04	53,747.3	1,543.5	2.9%	14,481
Annual Growth	**32.6%**	**—**	**—**	**15.5%**

2008 Year-End Financials

Equity as % of assets: 14.2%
Return on assets: —
Return on equity: —
Long-term debt ($ mil.): 23,178
No. of shares (mil.): 455
Dividends
Yield: 4.7%
Payout: —
Market value ($ mil.): 14,509
Sales ($ mil.): 13,893

Stock History   NYSE: COF

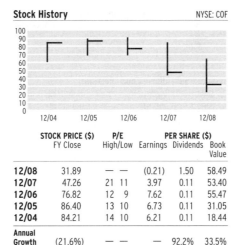

	STOCK PRICE ($) FY Close	P/E High/Low		PER SHARE ($) Earnings	Dividends	Book Value
12/08	31.89	—	—	(0.21)	1.50	58.49
12/07	47.26	21	11	3.97	0.11	53.40
12/06	76.82	12	9	7.62	0.11	55.47
12/05	86.40	13	10	6.73	0.11	31.05
12/04	84.21	14	10	6.21	0.11	18.44
Annual Growth	**(21.6%)**	**—**	**—**	**—**	**92.2%**	**33.5%**

Cardinal Health

Cardinal Health seeks to deliver medicine to all points of the compass. The company is a top distributor of pharmaceuticals and other medical supplies and equipment in the US. Its pharmaceutical division provides supply chain services including prescription and over-the-counter drug distribution, while its medical division parcels out medical, laboratory, and surgical supplies. The divisions also provide logistics, consulting, and data management services. Customers include pharmacies, hospitals, doctor's offices, and other health care businesses. Cardinal Health spun off its medical equipment manufacturing and clinical technologies operations into CareFusion in 2009.

Cardinal Health completed the spinoff of about 81% of CareFusion to its shareholders in August 2009 to maximize shareholder and customer value for all of its businesses. It plans to divest its remaining shares in CareFusion within five years of the spinoff. Former Cardinal chairman and CEO Kerry Clark retired at the time of the spinoff, with George Barrett (the former leader of the distribution operations) taking over Clark's roles.

Pharmaceutical distribution has historically accounted for about 85% of Cardinal Health's sales, with pharmacies accounting for the largest chunk of Cardinal's customer revenues. CVS and Walgreen each account for about 20% of the company's sales. The Cardinal Health Pharmaceutical division operates distribution facilities and nuclear pharmacy labs (for the distribution of medical imaging agents) across the US; it also has limited operations in Mexico (nuclear labs) and the UK (generic drugs). The division also includes the Cardinal Health Pharmacy Management business, the Medicine Shoppe retail pharmacy subsidiary, and a specialty pharmacy unit that distributes plasma and intensive care therapies.

The smaller Cardinal Health Medical distribution division offers branded and private-label supplies, including fluid collection devices, scientific laboratory equipment, and general hospital and physician practice supplies in Canada and the US.

It also assembles procedure kits and makes exam gloves and surgical drapes.

Cardinal has expanded through acquisitions of companies and products within all of its operating segments. Since 1980 it has acquired more than 50 companies. In 2007 Cardinal acquired data management company MedMined, which tracks adverse health events such as the occurrence of deadly infections in hospitals.

On the paring side, the company unloaded its health care marketing services unit and its UK Intercare distribution business in 2007. Even more significantly, Cardinal Health sold its Pharmaceutical Technologies and Services division, which offered drug delivery systems, packaging services, and development services, to The Blackstone Group for $3.3 billion. As part of the deal, Cardinal retained two businesses that complement its generic pharmaceutical operations.

In 2008 Cardinal divested two former VIASYS businesses, Tecomet (orthopedic implants) and MedSystems (feeding tubes).

HISTORY

Cardinal Health harks back to Cardinal Foods, a food wholesaler named for Ohio's state bird. In 1971 Robert Walter, then 26 and with the ink still fresh on his Harvard MBA, acquired Cardinal in a leveraged buyout. He hoped to grow Cardinal by acquisitions but was frustrated when he found that the food distribution industry was already highly consolidated.

In 1980 Cardinal moved into pharmaceuticals distribution with the acquisition of Zanesville. It went public in 1983 as Cardinal Distribution, and Walter began looking for more acquisitions. Cardinal soon expanded nationwide by swallowing other distributors. During the 1980s these purchases included two pharmaceuticals distributors headquartered in New York and a Massachusetts-based pharmaceuticals and food distributor. In 1988 Cardinal sold its food group, including Midland Grocery and Mr. Moneysworth, to Roundy's and narrowed its focus to pharmaceuticals.

Drug distributors joined the rest of the pharmaceutical industry in its rush toward consolidation during the 1990s. Cardinal's acquisitions in those years included Ohio Valley-Clarksburg (1990, the Mid-Atlantic), Chapman Drug Co. (1991, Tennessee), PRN Services (1993, Michigan), Solomons Co. (1993, Georgia), Humiston-Keeling (1994, Illinois), and Behrens (1994, Texas).

One of Cardinal's most important acquisitions during this period was its cash purchase of Whitmire Distribution in 1994. When Cardinal bought it, Whitmire was the US's #6 drug wholesaler; the purchase bumped Cardinal up to #3. At that time the company changed its name to Cardinal Health and Melburn Whitmire became Cardinal's vice chairman.

In 1995 Cardinal made its biggest acquisition yet when it purchased St. Louis-based Medicine Shoppe International, the US's largest franchisor of independent retail pharmacies. Founded by two St. Louis obstetricians in 1970, the Medicine Shoppe had 987 US outlets and 107 abroad at the time of its purchase by Cardinal.

Over the next few years Cardinal continued to grow through acquisitions, including automatic drug-dispensing system maker Pyxis, pharmaceutical packaging company PCI Services, and pharmacy management services company Owen Healthcare (now Cardinal Health Pharmacy Management).

In 1998, however, plans to acquire Bergen Brunswig were blocked by the Federal Trade Commission, along with rival McKesson's bid to buy AmeriSource Health. (AmeriSource later became AmerisourceBergen after boosting itself into the top drug-distributor ranks by purchasing Bergen Brunswig.) This did not deter Cardinal from its strategy; it acquired surgical equipment distribution company Allegiance Healthcare about a year later.

In 2001 Cardinal purchased pharmaceuticals distributor Bindley Western, and it bought contract drug developer Magellan Labs the following year. The company made several acquisitions in 2003, including UK contract manufacturer Intercare Group, radiopharmaceuticals firm Syncor International, and pharmacy franchiser Medicap. It made a $2 billion purchase of IV medication safety products maker Alaris Medical Systems in 2004.

Founder Robert Walter stepped aside as CEO in 2006 to make room for Kerry Clark to take over the role; the following year Clark assumed the founder's chairman role as well. Also in 2006 the company acquired generic drug distributor ParMed Pharmaceuticals.

EXECUTIVES

Chairman, President, and CEO: George S. Barrett, age 54, $2,653,216 total compensation
CFO: Jeffrey W. Henderson, age 43, $3,042,891 total compensation
CIO: Patricia B. (Patty) Morrison, age 50
Chief Human Resources Officer: Carole S. Watkins, age 48
Chief Legal Officer and Secretary: Ivan K. Fong, age 48
Chief Legal and Compliance Officer: Craig S. Morford, age 50
EVP Quality and Regulatory Affairs: Gary D. Dolch, age 61
EVP Global Communications: Shelley Bird
EVP Operations, Healthcare Supply Chain Services: Mike Duffy
President, International: Rudy Mareel, age 46
CEO Medical Segment: Michael Lynch
CEO Pharmaceutical: Michael C. Kaufmann, age 46
President, Integrated Provider Solutions: Mark Rosenbaum
President and General Manager, Specialty and Nuclear Pharmacy Services: John Rademacher
Media Contact: Troy Kirkpatrick
Investor Relations Contact: Jon Lyons
Director, Marketing, Conventional Ventilation: Pete Goulding
Director, Global Strategic Procurement: Meri Stockwell
Auditors: Ernst & Young LLP

LOCATIONS

HQ: Cardinal Health, Inc.
7000 Cardinal Place, Dublin, OH 43017
Phone: 614-757-5000
Web: www.cardinal.com

2009 Sales

	$ mil.	% of total
US	97,849.1	98
International	1,663.3	2
Total	**99,512.4**	**100**

PRODUCTS/OPERATIONS

2009 Sales

	$ mil.	% of total
Healthcare Supply Chain Services	95,717.9	94
Clinical Technologies & Services	4,588.5	5
Other	1,018.3	1
Adjustments	(1,812.3)	—
Total	**99,512.4**	**100**

2009 Healthcare Supply Chain Sales

	% of total
Pharmaceutical distribution	91
Medical distribution	9
Total	**100**

Selected Subsidiaries and Divisions

Cardinal Health Medical (formerly Cardinal Healthcare Supply Chain Services — Medical; Endura, Presource, SP Lab)
Cardinal Health Pharmaceutical (formerly Cardinal Healthcare Supply Chain Services — Pharmaceutical)
Beckloff Associates, Inc.
Cardinal Health Pharmacy Management
Leader Drugstores, Inc.
SpecialtyScripts, LLC
Medicine Shoppe International, Inc.
Medicap Pharmacies Incorporated

COMPETITORS

AmerisourceBergen	Medline Industries
CVS Caremark	Moore Medical
Express Scripts	Omnicare
Franz Haniel	Owens & Minor
H. D. Smith	PharMerica
Wholesale Drug	PSS World Medical
Henry Schein	Quality King
HLTH Corp.	Rite Aid
McKesson	Thermo Fisher Scientific
Medco Health	Walgreen

HISTORICAL FINANCIALS

Company Type: Public

Income Statement

FYE: June 30

	REVENUE ($ mil.)	NET INCOME ($ mil.)	NET PROFIT MARGIN	EMPLOYEES
6/09	99,512.4	1,151.6	1.2%	29,600
6/08	91,091.4	1,300.6	1.4%	47,600
6/07	86,852.0	1,931.1	2.2%	43,500
6/06	81,363.6	1,000.1	1.2%	55,000
6/05	74,910.7	1,050.7	1.4%	55,000
Annual Growth	**7.4%**	**2.3%**	**—**	**(14.3%)**

2009 Year-End Financials

Debt ratio: 37.6%
Return on equity: 14.0%
Cash ($ mil.): 1,848
Current ratio: 1.39
Long-term debt ($ mil.): 3,280
No. of shares (mil.): 360
Dividends
Yield: 1.8%
Payout: 17.6%
Market value ($ mil.): 10,988

Stock History

NYSE: CAH

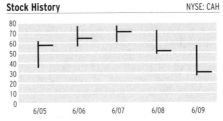

	STOCK PRICE ($) FY Close	P/E High/Low		PER SHARE ($) Earnings	Dividends	Book Value
6/09	30.55	18	9	3.18	0.56	24.26
6/08	51.58	20	14	3.57	0.50	21.54
6/07	70.64	16	13	4.77	0.39	20.51
6/06	64.33	33	24	2.33	0.27	23.61
6/05	57.58	25	15	2.41	0.15	23.89
Annual Growth	**(14.7%)**	**—**	**—**	**7.2%**	**39.0%**	**0.4%**

Cargill, Incorporated

Cargill may be private, but it's highly visible. The US's second-largest private corporation (after Koch Industries), Cargill's diversified operations include grain, cotton, sugar, petroleum, and financial trading; food processing; futures brokering; health and pharmaceutical products; agricultural services such as animal feed and crop protection; and industrial products including biofuels, oils and lubricants, starches, and salt. The company is one of the leading grain producers in the US, and its Excel unit is one of the top US meatpackers. Cargill's brands include Diamond Crystal (salt), Gerkens (cocoa), Honeysuckle White (poultry), Sterling Silver (fresh meats), and Nutrena (dog and cat food).

Being private doesn't mean Cargill is cut off from the world. The agribusiness giant has operations in 67 countries throughout the world. Along with its grain and meatpacking businesses, Cargill is a commodity trader. It is also a global supplier of oils, syrups, flour, and other products used in food processing.

Long the largest private company in the US, it lost the #1 title when conglomerate Koch Industries acquired forest products maker Georgia-Pacific Corp in 2005. But Cargill is still a powerhouse. It is involved in petroleum trading, financial trading, futures brokering, and shipping. To focus on processing, Cargill sold its seed operations and coffee trading business and part of its steel business. It formed a joint venture with Hormel Foods to market fresh beef, along with pork, under the Always Tender brand. Cargill is also a major US supplier for McDonald's, providing the burger behemoth with eggs, oils, sauces, and beef products.

Cargill has a partnership with Coca-Cola to produce and market the sweetener Rebiana, which is said to sweeten without adding calories, while at the same time producing a natural flavor. It is made from the South American herb, stevia. Coke wants to put it in its beverages; Cargill sees uses in yogurt, cereal, ice cream, candy, and, perhaps table-top use. Rebiana received regulatory approval in the US for general use in food and beverages at the end of 2008.

Cargill is looking for additional growth opportunities in the world of bio-plastics. It reclaimed full control of its NatureWorks subsidiary in 2009, acquiring the 50% stake of former joint venture partner Teijin. NatureWorks makes commercial biopolymers, focusing on applications in eco-friendly products.

Long-time CEO Warren Staley retired in 2007. Cargill's board chose 33-year company veteran, president and COO, Gregory Page, to replace Staley. Page stated that he hopes to make Cargill, an historically tight-lipped company, more visible. Later that year, Page was appointed chairman of the company.

HISTORY

William W. Cargill founded Cargill in 1865 when he bought his first grain elevator in Conover, Iowa. He and his brother Sam bought grain elevators all along the Southern Minnesota Railroad in 1870, just as Minnesota was becoming an important shipping route. Sam and a third brother, James, expanded the elevator operations while William worked with the railroads to monopolize transport of grain to markets and coal to farmers.

Around the turn of the century, William's son William S. invested in a number of ill-fated projects. William W. found that his name had been used to finance the projects; shortly afterward, he died of pneumonia. Cargill's creditors pressed for repayment, which threatened to bankrupt the company. John MacMillan, William W.'s son-in-law, took control and rebuilt Cargill. It had recovered by 1916 but lost its holdings in Mexico and Canada. MacMillan opened offices in New York (1922) and Argentina (1929), expanding grain trading and transport operations.

In 1945 Cargill bought Nutrena Mills (animal feed) and entered soybean processing; corn processing began soon after and grew with the demand for corn sweeteners. In 1954 Cargill benefited when the US began making loans to help developing countries buy American grain. Subsidiary Tradax, established in 1955, became one of the largest grain traders in Europe. A decade later, Cargill began trading sugar by purchasing sugar and molasses in the Philippines and selling them abroad.

Cargill made its finances public in 1973 (as a requirement for its unsuccessful takeover bid of Missouri Portland Cement), revealing it to be one of the US's largest companies, with $5.2 billion in sales. In the 1970s it expanded into coal, steel, and waste disposal and became a major force in metals processing, beef, and salt production.

To placate family heirs who wanted to take Cargill public, CEO Whitney MacMillan, grandson of John, created an employee stock plan in 1991 that allowed shareholders to cash in their shares. He also boosted dividends and reorganized the board, reducing the family's control. MacMillan retired in 1995 and non-family member Ernest Micek became CEO and chairman.

The firm bought Akzo Nobel's North American salt operations in 1997, becoming the #2 US salt company. Micek resigned as CEO that year and was replaced by Warren Staley. Also in 1999 Cargill fessed up to misappropriating some genetic seed material from rival Pioneer Hi-Bred, killing the $650 million sale of its North American seed assets to Germany's AgrEvo.

In 2004 the company announced the discovery of genetic markers in cattle that predict whether or not a specific steer will produce good-tasting meat. Also that year Cargill combined its crop-nutrition segment with phosphate fertilizer maker IMC Global to form a new, publicly traded company called Mosaic. Cargill owns about 66% of the company. This is the first time privately held Cargill has ventured into the public sector.

In 2005 Cargill acquired The Dow Chemical Company's interest in the two companies' 50-50 plastics business joint venture, Cargill Dow LLC, and renamed it NatureWorks. It also broke ground for its first oil refinery in Russia.

Cargill introduced Meadowlands Farms ground beef at food retailers throughout the US later in 2007. The introduction marked the company's first foray into the nationally branded hamburger market. However, Cargill was forced to recall meat products twice that year because of *E. coli* contamination. The first involved more than 800,000 pounds of frozen beef patties. More than 1 million pounds of fresh ground beef was involved in the second recall.

In 2008 Cargill added to its sugar business, announcing the construction of its first sugar refinery. The operation is a 50-50 joint venture between Cargill and Louisiana agricultural cooperative Sugar Growers and Refiners.

EXECUTIVES

Chairman and CEO: Gregory R. (Greg) Page, age 57
SVP and CFO: David W. MacLennan, age 50
Corporate VP and CTO: Ronald L. Christenson
Corporate VP and CIO: Rita J. Heise
EVP: David M. Larson
SVP: Richard D. Frasch, age 54
SVP: David W. Rogers
SVP: William A. (Bill) Buckner
SVP: Paul D. Conway
Corporate VP and Controller: Galen G. Johnson, age 62
Corporate VP, Corporate Affairs: Bonnie E. Raquet
Corporate VP, Transportation and Product Assurance: Frank L. Sims, age 58
Corporate VP, Research and Development: Christopher P. (Chris) Mallett
Corporate VP, Human Resources: Peter Vrijsen, age 55
Corporate VP, General Counsel, and Corporate Secretary: Steven C. Euller
President, Value Added Meat: John O'Carroll
President, Cargill Energy, Transportation, and Industrial Group: Tom Intrator
President, Cargill Beef: John Keating
President, Cargill Ag Horizons U.S.: Dan Dye
President, Ocean Transportation: Gert Jan Vandenakker
President, Cargill Meat Solutions and President, Cargill Case Ready Beef: Jody Horner
Auditors: KPMG LLP

LOCATIONS

HQ: Cargill, Incorporated
15407 McGinty Rd. West, Wayzata, MN 55391
Phone: 952-742-7575   **Fax:** 952-742-7393
Web: www.cargill.com

PRODUCTS/OPERATIONS

Selected Products and Services

Agriculture and Animal Nutrition
  Agricultural commodity trading
  Animal nutrition
  Crop production
  Sugar refining
Financial and Risk Management
  Investment
  Risk Management
Food
  Baking and cereals
  Beverages
  Chocolates and confections
  Dairy products
  Health, nutrition, and organic
  Meat and poultry
  Prepared foods
  Salt
  Snacks
Health and Pharmaceutical
  Health, nutrition, and organic
  Pharmaceuticals
Industrial
  Biobased polyols
  Biofuels
  Deicing products and surface overlays
  Fermentation solutions
  Oils and lubricants
  Power and gas
  Salt
  Soy-based candle waxes
  Starches and derivatives
  Steel and ferrous raw materials

Selected Joint Ventures and Operations

Freeman's of Newent Ltd (chicken processing, UK)
Frontier Agriculture (UK)
Horizon Milling
Progressive Baker
Renessen Feed & Processing
Seara (pork and poultry processing, Brazil)
Sun Valley (chicken processing, UK)

COMPETITORS

Abengoa Bioenergy	King Arthur Flour
ADM	Koch Industries, Inc.
Ag Processing	Kraft Foods
Amalgamated Sugar	Lake Area Corn Processors
American Animal Health	Land O'Lakes
American Crystal Sugar	Mars, Incorporated
American Steel	Merisant Worldwide
Asia Food & Properties	Michigan Sugar Company
Aventine	Monsanto Company
Badger State Ethanol	Morton Salt
BASF SE	Nestlé Purina PetCare
Bayer Animal Health	Northern Growers
Beef Products	Nucor
BioFuel Energy	NutraSweet
Blyth	Omega Protein
Bunge Limited	Pacific Ethanol
C&H Sugar	Palm Restaurants
Casco	Perdue Incorporated
Chaparral Energy	Pfizer
CHS	Phibro Animal Health
COFCO	Raeford Farms
Coleman Natural Foods	Rohm and Haas
ConAgra	Royal Canin
ContiGroup	Royal Schouten Group
Corn Products International	Südzucker
Cumberland Packing	Sara Lee Food and Beverage
Danisco A/S	Schering-Plough
Dean Foods	Sime Darby
Del Monte Foods	SMBSC
Dow Chemical	Smithfield Foods
DuPont	Sterling Sugars
Eight in One Pet Products	Sugar Cane Growers
Ellison Meat Company	Cooperative of Florida
Evialis	Sugar Foods
Faultless Starch	Tate & Lyle
Florida Crystals	Teva Pharmaceuticals
General Mills	United Salt
Hershey	United States Steel
Hill's Pet Nutrition	U.S. Microbics
Holly Sugar	U.S. Sugar
Iams	Viterra Inc.
Imperial Sugar	Western Beef
IOI Corporation	Western Sugar Cooperative
JBS	Yankee Candle

HISTORICAL FINANCIALS

Company Type: Private

Income Statement

FYE: May 31

	REVENUE ($ mil.)	NET INCOME ($ mil.)	NET PROFIT MARGIN	EMPLOYEES
5/09	116,579.0	3,334.0	2.9%	159,000
5/08	120,439.0	3,951.0	3.3%	160,000
5/07	88,266.0	2,343.0	2.7%	158,000
5/06	75,208.0	1,537.0	2.0%	149,000
5/05	71,066.0	2,103.0	3.0%	124,000
Annual Growth	13.2%	12.2%	—	6.4%

Net Income History

Carlisle Companies

Commercial manufacturing group Carlisle Companies is nothing if not diverse. Through dozens of subsidiaries, the company makes an array of products that include construction materials, industrial components, foodservice equipment, and aerospace wire and cable assemblies. Representing nearly half of the group's sales, the construction materials segment includes rubber and plastic roofing system products, as well as rigid foam insulation, waterproofing, and protective coatings. Its industrial components segment primarily makes wheels and tires for lawn and garden equipment, all-terrain vehicles, and golf carts.

The group has had to shuffle its operations around in recent years in order to keep its competitive edge. Part of that shuffling has included winding down its heavy-duty braking system manufacturing business — a one-time sales staple for Carlisle that has suffered from declines in sales due to industry forces. In 2007 alone, the company closed facilities in Virginia and Wisconsin in the US and a third facility in Wales. It also began actively reducing its inventory. Two years later the company announced it would exit the on-highway friction and brake shoe business and dissolve its Motion Control Industries subsidiary. (Carlisle is seeking a buyer for its power transmission belt business.)

The remainder of its braking operations, which include a facility in China, were consolidated into the group's specialty products segment. The reason for the realignment was rooted in the combination of higher raw materials costs, mainly steel, and newly implemented emission requirements placed on the heavy-duty trucks that used Carlisle's braking systems. The new requirements led to a massive reduction in the sales of those vehicles.

Carlisle, however, is no stranger to adjusting its operations. The firm has acquired more than 50 companies since 1990, and it continues to grow through bolt-on acquisitions and joint ventures. The group typically focuses on niche markets where it can gain a leading market share, and is constantly tweaking its mix of businesses to optimize value.

In 2007 Carlisle purchased Insulfoam from privately held Premier Industries. Insulfoam, a leading maker of block molded polystyrene insulation products for the construction industry, now operates as part of the company's construction materials segment.

In 2008 Carlisle acquired two more companies, both of which are purported leaders in their respective industries — Dinex International, which makes foodservice equipment used in the health care and other institutional industries, and Carlyle Incorporated, which provides aerospace and network interconnections equipment. Both acquisitions also expand Carlisle's developing applied technologies segment.

HISTORY

Charles Moomy founded Carlisle Tire and Rubber Company in Carlisle, Pennsylvania, in 1917 to make rubber inner tubes for auto tires. The company debuted its full-molded inner tube in 1926. Success followed until the stock market crash of 1929.

Carlisle limped through the Depression with help from the New Deal's Industrial Loan Act.

However, Moomy was forced to turn his stock over to the Federal Reserve Bank of Philadelphia, which became Carlisle's biggest shareholder. Pharis Tire and Rubber Company acquired Carlisle from the Federal Reserve Bank in 1943. Upon Pharis' liquidation in 1949, Carlisle stock was distributed to Pharis stockholders and company officials. Carlisle Corporation was formed, and it bought Dart Truck (mining and construction trucks).

Carlisle continued to diversify. During the 1960s it added jar sealant rings, roofing materials, automotive accessories, and tires for recreational vehicles. It moved to Cincinnati in the 1970s and acquired foodservice product and computer peripherals companies.

In the 1980s, unable to compete with the big car tire makers, Carlisle focused on tires for smaller vehicles (motorcycles and snowblowers), and it sold car tires to the auto aftermarket. The company restructured as Carlisle Companies Incorporated in 1986 and moved to Syracuse, New York, the next year.

Carlisle bought Brookpark Plastics (plastic compression molding) and Off-Highway Braking Systems (from B.F. Goodrich Aerospace) in 1990, gaining factories in Europe and South America. After taking a hit in the early 1990s recession, Carlisle consolidated operations and sold its communications and electronics industries. With its 1993 purchase of Goodyear's roofing products business, Carlisle became the US's top maker of nonresidential roofing products.

Since the mid-1990s Carlisle has increased its acquisitions, buying Sparta Brush (specialty brushes and cleaning tools), Trail King Industries (specialized low-bed trailers), Ti-Brook (dump bodies and trailers), Walker Stainless (trailers and in-plant processing equipment), Intero (steel and aluminum wheel rims), and Unique Wheel (steel wheels).

Carlisle stopped making refrigerated marine shipping containers in 1999, and its Carlisle Tire & Wheel Company subsidiary sold its surfacing products division. Carlisle bought privately owned Johnson Truck Bodies that year to boost its production of insulated dairy trucks.

In 2000 Carlisle bought Damrow Denmark and Damrow USA (cheese-making equipment manufacturers) and Red River Manufacturing (custom trailers and paving equipment). In 2001 the company moved to North Carolina, and the deal-making continued apace with the acquisitions of Wincanton Engineering (food- and beverage-processing equipment) and EcoStar (roofing). Carlisle also bought Mark IV Industries' Dayco industrial power transmission business.

Carlisle sold Carlisle Engineered Products to the Reserve Group in 2005.

Also in 2005 Carlisle announced plans to sell its Carlisle Systems & Equipment operations. The businesses include Carlisle Process Systems (cheese-making and food processing equipment) and the Walker Group (industrial stainless steel storage vessels and trailers). The move was similar to the decision to sell off the former Carlisle Engineered Products business, as the company was looking to strengthen its higher margin businesses. The company failed to find a single buyer for both operations, but late in 2006 Carlisle found a buyer for Carlisle Process Systems, and the sale to Tetra Laval subsidiary Tetra Pak was completed later that year. The Walker Group, including Walker Transport, was sold to private investment firm Insight Equity a short time later.

EXECUTIVES

Chairman, President, and CEO: David A. Roberts, age 61, $5,993,629 total compensation
VP and CFO: Steven J. Ford, age 49, $1,095,348 total compensation
EVP Operating System: Jerry N. Thomsen
Group President, Transportation Products: Fred A. Sutter, age 48
Group President, Construction Materials: John W. Altmeyer, age 49, $2,075,713 total compensation
President, Carlisle Industrial Brake and Friction: D. Christian (Chris) Koch, age 44, $1,401,156 total compensation
President, Asia/Pacific: Kevin G. Forster, age 55
President, Trail King Industries: Carol P. Lowe, age 43, $1,240,869 total compensation
Auditors: Ernst & Young LLP

LOCATIONS

HQ: Carlisle Companies Incorporated
13925 Ballantyne Corporate Place, Ste. 400
Charlotte, NC 28277
Phone: 704-501-1100   **Fax:** 704-501-1190
Web: www.carlisle.com

2008 Sales by Region

	$ mil.	% of total
United States	2,657.5	89
International		
Canada	135.2	5
Europe	101.6	3
Asia	26.4	1
Mexico/Latin America	23.5	1
Middle East	16.7	1
Australia	4.0	—
Africa	4.1	—
Caribbean/other	2.4	—
Total	**2,971.4**	**100**

PRODUCTS/OPERATIONS

2008 Sales

	$ mil.	% of total
Construction materials	1,472.3	49
Transportation products	861.0	29
Applied technologies	464.1	16
Specialty products	174.0	6
Total	**2,971.4**	**100**

Selected Products

Construction Materials
  Roofing accessories (coatings, fasteners, flashings, sealing tapes, and waterproofings)
  Roofing systems (FleeceBack, plastic, and rubber)

Industrial Components
  Pulleys
  Small bias-ply tires
  Stamped and roll-formed wheels
  Tensioners

General Industry
  Commercial and institutional foodservice equipment
  High-performance wire and cable
  Refrigerated truck bodies

Specialty Products
  On- and off-highway motion control systems

Transportation products
  Specialty trailers

COMPETITORS

Atlas Roofing	Johns Manville
Bridgestone	Michelin
CertainTeed	Owens Corning Sales
Dana Holding	Pirelli
Dover Corp.	Southwire
Evergreen Marine	Sumitomo Electric
General Cable	Superior Essex
G-I Holdings	Wabash National
Harvey Industries	

HISTORICAL FINANCIALS

Company Type: Public

Income Statement
FYE: December 31

	REVENUE ($ mil.)	NET INCOME ($ mil.)	NET PROFIT MARGIN	EMPLOYEES
12/08	2,971.4	55.8	1.9%	11,000
12/07	2,876.4	215.6	7.5%	13,000
12/06	2,572.5	258.9	10.1%	11,000
12/05	2,209.6	106.4	4.8%	11,000
12/04	2,227.6	79.6	3.6%	13,677
Annual Growth	7.5%	(8.5%)	—	(5.3%)

2008 Year-End Financials

Debt ratio: 25.0%
Return on equity: 5.0%
Cash ($ mil.): 43
Current ratio: 2.19
Long-term debt ($ mil.): 273

No. of shares (mil.): 61
Dividends
  Yield: 2.9%
  Payout: 65.9%
Market value ($ mil.): 1,268

Stock History

NYSE: CSL

	STOCK PRICE ($) FY Close	P/E High/Low		PER SHARE ($) Earnings	Dividends	Book Value
12/08	20.70	44	18	0.91	0.60	17.86
12/07	37.03	15	11	3.44	0.56	18.27
12/06	39.25	13	10	3.46	0.52	15.38
12/05	34.58	22	17	1.71	0.48	11.92
12/04	32.46	26	21	1.27	0.45	11.40
Annual Growth	(10.6%)	—	—	(8.0%)	7.5%	11.9%

Carlson Wagonlit Travel

Carlson Wagonlit Travel (CWT) is the #2 business travel firm in the world, behind American Express. The company manages business travel through more than 35 subsidiaries and several joint ventures spanning more than 150 countries and territories around the globe. In addition to purchasing travel packages and booking trips online, CWT helps clients customize and assess their own travel programs and also provides travel risk management services. CWT is owned by US-based Carlson Companies, which holds a 55% stake, and JP Morgan affiliate One Equity Partners, which owns 45%. It is descended from Europe's Wagons-Lits (literally, sleeping cars) company and from the US's oldest travel agency chain (Ask Mr. Foster).

In a big move for the travel industry, CWT acquired leading business travel firm Navigant International in 2006. The acquisition (valued at $510 million) doubled CWT's size in North America and added to its presence in other key regions such as Australia and New Zealand. CWT also has been working to expand in regions such as China and India, and in mid-2008, the company acquired the remaining stake in its CWT India joint venture.

CWT's growth agenda is being overseen by a new CEO — Douglas Anderson — the company's former CFO. He replaced Hubert Joly, the company's leader since 2004, who took the reins at parent company Carlson in March 2008.

Although CWT concentrates on business travel management, the Carlson Wagonlit Travel brand has been used for leisure travel operations that have been part of another Carlson unit, Carlson Leisure Group. In 2008, however, Carlson sold the leisure travel business to its management team, and the new owners changed their company's name to Travel Leaders.

HISTORY

Belgian inventor Georges Nagelmackers' first enterprise was adding sleeping compartments to European trains in 1872. Nagelmackers later created the Orient Express. Over the years his Wagons-Lits company expanded its mission to become Wagonlit Travel.

While Nagelmackers was establishing his business in Europe, Ward G. Foster was giving out steamship and train schedules from his gift shop facing the stately Ponce de Leon Hotel in St. Augustine, Florida. As legend has it, hotel patrons with travel questions were directed to Foster's shop with: "Ask Mr. Foster. He'll know." In 1888 he founded Ask Mr. Foster Travel (it became the oldest travel agency in the US). By 1913 the company had offices located in pricey department stores and in the lobbies of upscale hotels and resorts throughout the country. After 50 years at the helm, Foster sold his business in 1937, three years before his death.

After suffering hard times during WWII and into the 1950s, the company changed hands again in 1957 when Donald Fisher and Thomas Orr, two Ask Mr. Foster shareholders, bought controlling interests for $157,000. In 1972 Peter Ueberroth (future Major League Baseball commissioner and Los Angeles Olympic Organizing Committee president) bought the company, then sold it in 1979 to Carlson Companies. In 1990 Ask Mr. Foster became Carlson Travel Network. Also that year Carlson Companies acquired the UK's A.T. Mays, the Travel Agents — a leading UK seller of vacation and tour packages. By 1992 Carlson Companies, besides adding a travel agency a day to the 2,000-plus it already owned, was adding a new hotel every 10 days.

In 1994 Carlson Companies joined with French hotelier Accor to form the joint venture Carlson Wagonlit Travel. (Accor had acquired a majority stake in Wagonlit Travel in 1990.) Under a dual-president ownership, the parent companies owned operations in specific world regions. The two companies began developing new business technology and expanded into new global business markets. Carlson Wagonlit acquired Germany's Brune Reiseburo travel agency and opened a branch office in Moscow. Through 1995 and 1996, acquisitions targeted the Asia/Pacific region, including Hong Kong's and Japan's Dodwell Travel and the corporate travel business of Singapore's Jetset Travel. The joint venture also formed a partnership with Traveland, an Australian travel agency.

In 1997 Carlson and Accor finalized the integration of their travel businesses and named Carlson Travel veteran Travis Tanner global CEO. The following year the new company acquired Florida's Travel Agents International, with more than 300 franchised operations and $600 million in annual sales. Also in 1998 Jon Madonna, formerly KPMG International chairman, was

named CEO of Carlson Wagonlit. In 1999 three travel agencies in eastern Canada consolidated under the Carlson Wagonlit Travel brand, creating the largest travel network in that region. That same year Carlson Companies founder and Carlson Wagonlit Travel chairman Curtis Carlson died.

In 2000 Madonna was replaced as CEO by former European operations chief Herve Gourio. The following year Carlson Wagonlit joined with Japan Travel Bureau (now JTB Corp.) to form JTB Business Travel Solutions, a Japan-based travel management joint venture. The arrangement increased Carlson Wagonlit's presence in Asia while increasing the number of JTB locations in North America. In 2001 Carlson Wagonlit cut jobs because of a slowdown in business travel.

In 2003 the company formed a joint venture with China Air Service, creating China's leading corporate travel management company. In 2004 Gourio stepped down as CEO and was replaced by former Vivendi Universal executive Hubert Joly.

The year 2006 brought about much change for Carlson Wagonlit. During the middle of the year, Accor sold its 50% stake in the company, and by August, Carlson Wagonlit became a joint venture owned by Carlson Companies (55%) and JP affiliate One Equity Partners (45%). In a stunning move, the company also acquired leading travel management firm Navigant International for $510 million that same month. The Navigant acquisition doubled Carlson Wagonlit's size in North America.

In 2008 Hubert Joly became the president and CEO of Carlson Companies, and Carlson Wagonlit replaced him by promoting CFO Douglas Anderson.

EXECUTIVES

President and CEO: Douglas Anderson, age 54
COO Asia/Pacific: Martin Warner
EVP and CFO: Mark Karako
SEVP Central and Eastern Europe: August Gossewisch
EVP Technology and Product Management:
Loren Brown
EVP Human Resources: Philippe Vinay
EVP North America: Scott Guerrero
EVP Traveler and Transaction Services and President Asia/Pacific: Berthold Trenkel
EVP Mediterranean and Latin America: M. Faccini
EVP Global Supplier Management: Mike Koetting
EVP Global Program and Solutions: Cathy Voss
EVP and General Manager, Canada: Bill McLean
EVP Operations, Europe, Middle East, and Africa:
Tony Hopwood
EVP and General Manager North America:
Nick Vournakis
VP Corporate and Marketing Communications:
Isabelle Koch
President Military and Government Markets, North America: Kelly L. Kuhn, age 43
President North America: Jack O'Neill
Director Global Marketing Communications:
Celine Guerton

LOCATIONS

HQ: 701 Carlson Pkwy., Mailstop 8208
  Minneapolis, MN 55305
Phone: 763-212-2197   **Fax:** 763-212-2409
Web: www.carlsonwagonlit.com

COMPETITORS

American Express	Ovation Travel Group
BCD Travel	Thomas Cook
Expedia	Travel Franchise Group
Hotwire, Inc.	Travelocity
JTB Corp.	TUI
Kuoni Travel	Tzell Travel Group

CarMax, Inc.

To the greatest extent possible, CarMax helps drivers find inexpensive autos. The US's largest specialty used-car retailer buys, reconditions, and sells cars and light trucks at about 100 retail units in about 25 US states, mainly in the Southeast and Midwest; CarMax also operates five new-car franchises (all integrated or co-located with the used-car dealers). CarMax sells cars that are generally under six years old with less than 60,000 miles. CarMax also sells used cars through its ValuMax program. ValuMax cars are older than six years or have more than 60,000 miles. The company's Web site lets customers search CarMax outlets nationwide for a particular model. Its CarMax Auto Finance unit offers financing.

The firm also sells wholesale vehicles (more than 194,000 in fiscal 2009) at in-store auctions. Retail sales of used vehicles exceeded 345,000 during the same period.

CarMax's used-vehicle niche acts as a bit of a buffer in today's stormy economy, which has had a negative impact on both new- and used-car sales. Indeed, sales across all of CarMax's vehicle categories (including auctions) were down in fiscal 2009 vs. the year earlier period. To make room for more used-car sales, which account for more than 80% of the company's business, CarMax has divested half of its new-car franchises and may sell more.

CarMax had planned to open about more than a dozen new superstores in fiscal 2009 in new and existing markets. However, the company announced in mid-2008 that it would halt its new store openings and also tighten its staffing, after seeing a dramatic drop-off in sales.

HISTORY

Looking for new retailing channels to conquer, in 1993 Circuit City Stores began test-driving the used-car concept when it opened its first CarMax outlet in Richmond, Virginia. Richard Sharp, who was named Circuit City's CEO in 1986, became the chairman and CEO for CarMax Group as well.

A pioneer in the car industry, CarMax offered computerized shopping, play areas for children, and no-haggle pricing. Competing car dealers criticized CarMax's TV ads, which tarred rivals with a stereotype of sleaze and greed. Some dealers disputed CarMax's low-price claims.

The company extended its geographical reach into North Carolina, Georgia, and Florida in 1995 and 1996. In 1996 CarMax began selling new cars at an Atlanta store.

No longer riding it as a test-drive, Circuit City spun off about 25% of CarMax to the public in 1997. The following year it moved into Illinois.

Also in 1998 CarMax bought a new-car Toyota dealership in Maryland and the multi-make Mauro Auto Mall of Wisconsin. It entered South Carolina that year and added a Georgia Mitsubishi dealership in early 1999. The company acquired two new-car franchises in the competitive Los Angeles market in mid-1999.

In mid-2001 Circuit City reduced its share in CarMax from 75% to about 65%, having sold some stock to help remodel the company's electronics stores. Circuit City then spun off CarMax as an independent company in October 2002. President Austin Ligon took the CEO title at that time (Sharp remained chairman).

CarMax opened five superstores, but sold four new-car dealerships in 2003.

Ligon retired as CEO in June 2006. He was succeeded by EVP Thomas J. Folliard, a 13-year company veteran, who was named president, CEO, and a director of the company.

EXECUTIVES

Chairman: William R. Tiefel, age 75
President, CEO, and Director:
Thomas J. (Tom) Folliard, age 44,
$2,732,482 total compensation
EVP, CFO, Corporate Secretary and Director:
Keith D. Browning, age 56,
$1,940,713 total compensation
SVP and CIO: Richard M. Smith, age 51,
$864,800 total compensation
EVP and Chief Administrative Officer:
Michael K. (Mike) Dolan, age 59,
$1,855,507 total compensation
SVP Marketing and Strategy: Joseph S. Kunkel, age 46,
$1,285,460 total compensation
SVP, General Counsel, and Secretary: Eric M. Margolin, age 55
VP CarMax Auto Finance: Angela Chattin
VP Human Resources: Scott A. Rivas
VP Service Operations: Edwin J. (Ed) Hill
VP Sales: Cliff Wood
VP and Controller: Kim D. Orcutt
VP Advertising: Laura R. Donahue
VP Information Technology: Barbara B. Harvill
VP Consumer Finance: Robert W. (Rob) Mitchell
VP Real Estate: K. Douglass Moyers
VP and Treasurer: Tom Reedy
VP Construction and Facilities: Dan Bickett
VP Marketing: Rob Sorenson
Assistant VP Public Affairs: Lisa Van Riper
Assistant VP Investor Relations: Katherine Kenny
Auditors: KPMG LLP

LOCATIONS

HQ: CarMax, Inc.
12800 Tuckahoe Creek Parkway
Richmond, VA 23238
Phone: 804-747-0422   **Fax:** 804-217-6819
Web: www.carmax.com

2009 Stores

	No
California	13
Texas	12
Florida	10
Illinois	6
North Carolina	8
Virginia	8
Georgia	5
Maryland	4
Tennessee	4
Arizona	3
South Carolina	3
Wisconsin	3
Alabama	2
Connecticut	2
Indiana	2
Kansas	2
Nevada	2
Oklahoma	2
Ohio	2
Colorado	1
Kentucky	1
Mississippi	1
Missouri	1
Nebraska	1
New Mexico	1
Utah	1
Total	**100**

PRODUCTS/OPERATIONS

2009 Sales

	% of total
Used vehicles	82
Wholesale vehicles	11
New vehicles	4
Other	3
Total	**100**

COMPETITORS

Asbury Automotive
AutoNation
Brown Automotive
Danner Company
DriveTime Automotive Group
Ed Morse Auto
Group 1 Automotive
Hendrick Automotive
Holman Enterprises
Internet Brands
JM Family Enterprises
Manheim
McCombs Enterprises
Penske Automotive Group
Serra Automotive
Sonic Automotive

HISTORICAL FINANCIALS

Company Type: Public

Income Statement				FYE: February 28
	REVENUE ($ mil.)	NET INCOME ($ mil.)	NET PROFIT MARGIN	EMPLOYEES
2/09	6,974.0	59.2	0.8%	13,035
2/08	8,199.6	182.0	2.2%	15,637
2/07	7,465.7	198.6	2.7%	13,736
2/06	6,260.0	148.1	2.4%	12,061
2/05	5,260.3	112.9	2.1%	11,175
Annual Growth	7.3%	(14.9%)	—	3.9%

2009 Year-End Financials

Debt ratio: 11.2%
Return on equity: 3.8%
Cash ($ mil.): 141
Current ratio: 2.62
Long-term debt ($ mil.): 178
No. of shares (mil.): 220
Dividends
  Yield: 0.0%
  Payout: —
Market value ($ mil.): 2,077

Stock History

NYSE: KMX

	STOCK PRICE ($) FY Close	P/E High/Low		PER SHARE ($) Earnings	Dividends	Book Value
2/09	9.43	81	21	0.27	0.00	7.23
2/08	18.36	33	19	0.83	0.00	6.76
2/07	26.35	32	16	0.92	0.00	5.66
2/06	15.71	25	18	0.69	0.00	4.36
2/05	16.50	33	17	0.54	0.00	3.64
Annual Growth	(13.1%)	—	—	(15.9%)	—	18.8%

Carnival Corporation

Carnival offers a boatload of fun. The company is the world's #1 cruise operator, operating about a dozen cruise lines and more than 85 ships with a total passenger capacity of nearly 170,000. Carnival operates in North America primarily through its Princess Cruise Line, Holland America, and Seabourn luxury cruise brand, as well as its flagship Carnival Cruise Lines unit. Brands such as AIDA, P&O Cruises, and Costa Cruises offer services to passengers in Europe, and the Cunard Line operates luxury trans-Atlantic liners. Carnival operates as a dual-listed company with UK-based Carnival plc, forming a single enterprise under a unified executive team.

Carnival maintains its top position in the industry by leveraging its cruise lines to penetrate a number of different markets. Carnival Cruises, a leading brand in the US, and Princess both target families, retirees, and other upper middle class customers with competitively priced cruise packages to popular destinations in the Caribbean, along the Mexican Riviera, and in Alaska. P&O Cruises targets similar markets in the UK with trips to the Mediterranean and Scandinavia. (P&O also operates out of Australia and New Zealand.) Holland America is known for its scenic getaways in New England, Canada, and along the Pacific coast. In mid-2006 the company began offering trips to the Asian market through Costa Cruises.

Carnival's Seabourn brand offers luxury cruises targeting upscale travelers with fine food, personalized service, and exotic destinations around the world. Similarly, its Swan Hellenic brand offers premium cruises throughout Europe and in Asia.

Despite fears over terrorism and war, the company has been growing at full steam since its $5.4 billion acquisition of UK-based rival P&O Princess in 2003. The mega deal increased Carnival's presence in the UK and throughout Europe and put it leagues ahead of rival cruising company Royal Caribbean.

Fueled by optimism for the future, Carnival has orders in place for about 17 additional cruise ships, which it will integrate into its fleet by 2012.

In 2007, Carnival entered a partnership with leading Spanish travel firm Orizonia, to form Ibero Cruises. The new cruise line features three Spanish ships sailing from Spain, Brazil, and Portugal.

To fill its expanding inventory of passenger berths, Carnival continues to spend heavily on marketing its cruises, especially to consumers who have never taken to the high seas (about 80% of the population in the US). The company has also expanded the number of ports its ships operate from to put cruising possibilities closer to customers.

Carnival became a dual-listed company after its acquisition of P&O Princess, which was then recast as Carnival plc. The dual-listing structure gives Carnival access to capital markets in both the US and the UK.

CEO Micky Arison and his family own 36% of Carnival Corporation and control a 28% voting stake in the combined entity that consists of Carnival Corporation and Carnival plc. Arison, one of the wealthiest people in Miami, also owns the Miami Heat basketball team.

HISTORY

Israeli emigrant Ted Arison got into the cruise business in the mid-1960s, forming Norwegian Caribbean Lines with shipping magnate Knut Kloster. After their partnership ended in 1971, Arison persuaded old friend Meshulam Riklis to bankroll his $6.5 million purchase of the *Empress of Canada* in 1972. Riklis owned (among other things) the Boston-based American International Travel Service (AITS). Arison set up Carnival Cruise Lines as an AITS subsidiary and renamed his ship the *Mardi Gras*. Unfortunately, she ran aground on her maiden voyage, sending Carnival into red ink for three years.

Arison bought out Riklis in 1974 for $1 and assumed Carnival's $5 million debt. He envisioned a cruise line that would offer affordable vacation packages to young, middle-class consumers, and invented a new type of cruise ship featuring live music, gambling, and other entertainment on board. Carnival was profitable within a month, and by the end of the following year, Arison had paid off Carnival's debt and bought its second ship. Arison's son, Micky, became CEO in 1979. Despite the rising costs of shipbuilding and fuel prices, Carnival continued to add to its fleet. The company grew to become the world's #1 cruise operator, and the Arisons took Carnival public in 1987.

The company acquired luxury cruise business Holland America Line in 1989 and formed a joint venture with Seabourn Cruise Lines in 1992. Carnival changed its name to Carnival Corporation in 1994 to reflect its diversifying operations, and it took a 50% stake in Seabourn the following year. Carnival stepped up its European expansion in 1996 by buying a stake in UK-based Airtours. The next year Carnival and Airtours jointly acquired an interest in European cruise giant Costa Crociere for about $275 million.

Carnival bought a majority interest in the prestigious Cunard Line (*Queen Elizabeth 2*) in 1998, merged it with Seabourn, and bought the remainder of the two cruise lines in 1999. An ugly lawsuit reared its head that year after a woman claimed to have been sexually assaulted while on a Carnival ship. Carnival acknowledged that it had received more than 100 similar complaints against its cruise employees dating back to 1995. (The suit was settled later that year.)

In 2000 Carnival acquired the remaining 50% of Costa Crociere from Airtours. The next year, Carnival sold its 25% stake in Airtours (now known as MyTravel Group).

In an effort to make the airfares sold in connection with cruise packages more competitive, the cruise line announced its plan in 2001 to cut travel agent commissions on the air-travel segment of cruise bookings. Also that year the company countered competitor Royal Caribbean's agreement to merge with P&O Princess Cruises with its own offer of £2.15 billion. P&O shareholders snubbed the offer but later softened and said it would consider a revised offer, leaving the door open for a bidding war between Carnival and Royal Caribbean. That same year, the company pleaded guilty to charges of polluting the ocean and falsifying oil-contaminated discharge records. It agreed to pay $18 million in fines and environmental costs, hire overseers to monitor its ships, and hire an environmental standards officer.

In 2003 Carnival succeeded in wooing P&O away from Royal Caribbean and the two corporations merged operations via a dual-listed company structure. Consequently, P&O changed its name to Carnival plc.

EXECUTIVES

Chairman and CEO; Chairman and CEO, Carnival plc: Micky Arison, age 59, $8,497,576 total compensation
Vice Chairman and COO: Howard S. Frank, age 67, $11,465,567 total compensation
SVP and CFO: David Bernstein, age 51, $1,275,125 total compensation
VP and CIO: Rafael Sanchez
Chief Accounting Officer, VP, and Controller: Larry Freedman, age 57
SVP Shared Services: Richard D. Ames
SVP, General Counsel, and Secretary: Arnaldo Perez, age 48
SVP Corporate Shipbuilding: Bo-Erik Blomqvist
SVP Global Human Resources: Wayne Byers
VP Employee Services: Susan Herrmann
VP Investor Relations: Beth Roberts
VP Public Relations, Carnival Corporation and Carnival PLC: Tim Gallagher
President and CEO, Carnival Cruise Lines: Gerald R. (Gerry) Cahill, age 58, $3,915,043 total compensation
CEO, Carnival Australia: Ann C. Sherry
President and CEO, Princess Cruises: Alan B. Buckelew, age 60
CEO, Carnival UK: David K. Dingle, age 51
Director; Chairman and CEO, Costa Crociere: Pier Luigi Foschi, age 62, $4,685,150 total compensation
President and CEO, Seabourn Cruise Line: Pamela C. Conover
President and Managing Director, Cunard Lines: Peter Shanks
President and CEO, Holland America Line: Stein Kruse, age 50
President, AIDA Cruises: Michael Thamm, age 43
President, Costa Crociere: Gianni Onorato
Director Marketing: Bill Harber
Auditors: PricewaterhouseCoopers LLP

LOCATIONS

HQ: Carnival Corporation & plc
 3655 NW 87th Ave., Miami, FL 33178
Phone: 305-599-2600   **Fax:** 305-406-4700
Web: www.carnivalcorp.com

2008 Revenue

	% of total
North America	55
Europe	37
Other	8
Total	**100**

PRODUCTS/OPERATIONS

2008 Revenue

	% of total
Cruise	
Passenger tickets	76
Onboard & other	21
Other	3
Total	**100**

COMPETITORS

Carlson Companies
Club Med
Disney
NCL
NYK Line
Royal Caribbean Cruises
Saga Group
Star Cruises
TUI

HISTORICAL FINANCIALS
Company Type: Public

Income Statement
FYE: November 30

	REVENUE ($ mil.)	NET INCOME ($ mil.)	NET PROFIT MARGIN	EMPLOYEES
11/08	14,646.0	2,330.0	15.9%	85,900
11/07	13,033.0	2,408.0	18.5%	81,200
11/06	11,839.0	2,279.0	19.2%	74,700
11/05	11,087.0	2,257.0	20.4%	71,200
11/04	9,727.0	1,854.0	19.1%	69,500
Annual Growth	10.8%	5.9%	—	5.4%

2008 Year-End Financials

Debt ratio: 40.5%
Return on equity: 11.9%
Cash ($ mil.): 650
Current ratio: 0.29
Long-term debt ($ mil.): 7,735

No. of shares (mil.): 839
Dividends
Yield: 7.6%
Payout: 55.2%
Market value ($ mil.): 17,626

Stock History
NYSE: CCL

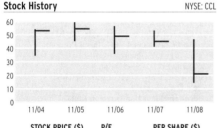

	STOCK PRICE ($) FY Close	P/E High/Low	PER SHARE ($) Earnings	Dividends	Book Value
11/08	21.00	16 5	2.90	1.60	22.75
11/07	45.12	18 14	2.95	1.38	23.78
11/06	48.99	20 13	2.77	1.02	21.70
11/05	54.49	22 17	2.70	0.80	20.22
11/04	53.01	24 16	2.24	0.52	18.78
Annual Growth	(20.7%)	— —	6.7%	32.4%	4.9%

Carpenter Technology

The Tin Man never would have rusted had he been built with metal from Carpenter Technology. The company makes a variety of corrosion-resistant materials; most of its sales come from stainless steel products and alloys that provide special heat- or wear-resistance or special magnetic or conductive properties. Finished products come in billet, bar, rod, wire, and other forms. Carpenter also makes titanium products, engineered ceramic products, and tool and other specialty steels. Customers include companies in the aerospace, automotive, medical, and industrial markets.

In 2005 Carpenter sold its Special Products unit, a manufacturer of precision engineered metal components and assemblies, to investment firm WHI Capital Partners. The former Carpenter Special Products, which serves customers in the aerospace, medical device, and nuclear power generation businesses, was renamed Veridiam. Carpenter continues to supply alloys to its former subsidiary. In 2008 Carpenter also sold its ceramics businesses to Morgan Crucible Co. PLC for about $145 million.

HISTORY

Engineer James Henry Carpenter founded Carpenter Steel in Pennsylvania in 1889. The company began making specialty steels after winning a US Navy contract to develop armor-piercing projectiles. Business declined after Carpenter's death in 1898, but former rival Robert Jennings took over and the company rebounded, thanks to marketing savvy and the development of new steel grades. Carpenter first produced stainless steel in 1917.

The company went public in 1937 and continued to grow. It made huge expansions in its production capacity to meet the demands spawned by WWII. The company changed its name to Carpenter Technology Corporation in 1968.

Carpenter survived the 1981-82 recession largely because of its lucrative niche in specialty steel. Another recession led to a 1991 reorganization. Robert Cardy, a 30-year company veteran, became chairman, president, and CEO the next year.

In 1994 Carpenter established a joint venture in Taiwan with Walsin-Lihwa (a Taiwanese maker of cable and wire). It also acquired Aceros Fortuna (Mexico's largest distributor of specialty steel) and purchased Certech (structural ceramics). In 1997 the company bought Dynamet, a producer of titanium bar and wire. It also purchased about 75% of diversified manufacturer Talley Industries for about $312 million, acquiring the remainder of Talley the next year. Carpenter formed a joint venture with Kalyani Steels in 1999 to make and distribute specialty steels in India.

High natural gas prices forced the company to increase prices for its nickel- and cobalt-based high-temperature alloys in 2001. The following year Carpenter's sales decreased due to lower stainless steel shipments and an overall weakness in the manufacturing industry.

In 2003 Carpenter's president Robert Torcolini was named to the added positions of chairman and CEO after chairman Dennis Draeger's retirement. Because of broad-based demand on its products, Carpenter raised prices primarily on its stainless bar, premium-metal alloys, and high-speed tool steel products in 2004.

Three years after he took on the added roles of chairman and CEO, Torcolini announced his retirement. Carpenter went outside the company to find his replacement, tabbing Ford veteran Anne Stevens to take on all three titles.

EXECUTIVES

Chairman, President, and CEO: Anne L. Stevens, age 60
SVP Finance and CFO: K. Douglas (Doug) Ralph, age 48
SVP Organizational Effectiveness, Strategy, and Corporate Staffs: T. Kathleen Hanley, age 46
VP and Chief Marketing Officer: Sanjay Guglani
VP and Chief Accounting Officer: Thomas F. Cramsey, age 48
SVP Premium Alloys Operations: Michael L. Shor, age 50
SVP Advanced Metals Operations: Mark S. Kamon, age 55
SVP, General Counsel, and Secretary: Oliver C. Mitchell Jr., age 54
VP Forged Bar and Billet Business Group: Russell E. Reber Jr.
VP Integrated Information Systems: William W. (Bill) Beible Jr., age 57
VP Logistics and Operations Planning: Toni M. Brugger
VP Bar Business Group: Michael J. McGarry
VP and Treasurer: Michael A. (Mike) Hajost
VP Human Resources: Barry J. Chapman

President, Dynamet: Andrew McElwee
President, Asia/Pacific and China: Jaime Vasquez
Media Relations and Investor Relations: David A. Christiansen, age 52
Auditors: PricewaterhouseCoopers LLP

LOCATIONS

HQ: Carpenter Technology Corporation
2 Meridian Blvd., Wyomissing, PA 19610
Phone: 610-208-2000   **Fax:** 610-208-3716
Web: www.cartech.com

Carpenter Technology operates manufacturing plants in the US and the UK.

2009 Sales

	$ mil.	% of total
North America		
US	885.3	65
Mexico	72.0	5
Canada	34.2	3
Europe	261.5	19
Asia/Pacific	86.4	6
Other regions	22.9	2
Total	**1,362.3**	**100**

PRODUCTS/OPERATIONS

2009 Sales

	$ mil.	% of total
Special alloys	694.6	51
Stainless steel	460.1	34
Titanium products	141.4	10
Other materials	66.2	5
Total	**1,362.3**	**100**

2009 Sales

	$ mil.	% of total
Advanced Metals	957.4	70
Premium Alloys	413.2	30
Adjustments	(8.3)	—
Total	**1,362.3**	**100**

COMPETITORS

AK Steel Holding Corporation
Allegheny Technologies
Dofasco
Earle M. Jorgensen
Essar Steel Algoma
Gerdau Ameristeel
JFE Holdings
Nucor
Precision Castparts
RTI International Metals
Titanium Metals
United States Steel

HISTORICAL FINANCIALS
Company Type: Public

Income Statement
FYE: June 30

	REVENUE ($ mil.)	NET INCOME ($ mil.)	NET PROFIT MARGIN	EMPLOYEES
6/09	1,362.3	47.9	3.5%	3,200
6/08	1,953.5	277.7	14.2%	3,400
6/07	1,944.8	227.2	11.7%	4,152
6/06	1,568.2	211.8	13.5%	3,990
6/05	1,314.2	135.5	10.3%	4,003
Annual Growth	0.9%	(22.9%)	—	(5.4%)

2009 Year-End Financials

Debt ratio: 41.9%
Return on equity: 6.6%
Cash ($ mil.): 340
Current ratio: 3.78
Long-term debt ($ mil.): 259

No. of shares (mil.): 44
Dividends
Yield: 3.5%
Payout: 66.7%
Market value ($ mil.): 916

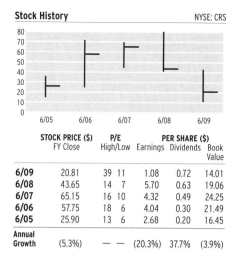

Stock History

NYSE: CRS

	STOCK PRICE ($) FY Close	P/E High/Low	PER SHARE ($) Earnings	Dividends	Book Value
6/09	20.81	39 11	1.08	0.72	14.01
6/08	43.65	14 7	5.70	0.63	19.06
6/07	65.15	16 10	4.32	0.49	24.25
6/06	57.75	18 6	4.04	0.30	21.49
6/05	25.90	13 6	2.68	0.20	16.45
Annual Growth	(5.3%)	— —	(20.3%)	37.7%	(3.9%)

Casey's General Stores

Casey's General Stores makes sure that small towns in the Midwest get their fill of convenient shopping. The company operates about 1,480 company-owned convenience stores, mostly in Illinois, Iowa, and Missouri, but also in Indiana, Kansas, Minnesota, Nebraska, South Dakota, and Wisconsin, all within about 500 miles of its headquarters and distribution center. Towns with 5,000 people or fewer, where rent is low, host about 60% of the chain's stores. Casey's stores sell beverages, gasoline, groceries, and fresh prepared foods, such as donuts, pizza, and sandwiches. Casey's also sells tobacco products, automotive goods, and other nonfood items, including ammunition, housewares, and school and photo supplies.

While sales were down about 3% in fiscal 2009, primarily due to a nearly 9% plunge in gas prices, an increase in grocery and prepared food sales helped to moderate the loss. Indeed, gasoline or gasohol, generally sold under the Casey's name, accounts for about 70% of the company's sales. To fuel the body, nearly all Casey's outlets sell donuts as well as cookies, brownies, Danishes, cinnamon rolls, muffins, and pizza prepared on the premises. Prepared foods return a higher profit margin than fuel sales and so are an attractive and growing business for Casey's. To make more room for food in its stores, in late 2008 the convenience store operator opened its first larger (about 3,800 square feet) "O-shaped" store in Des Moines, Iowa. The new format devotes more space to food and beverages, offering plenty of beer, energy drinks, and other high-margin items. The cashier is located at the center of the store. About 15 such shops opened in fiscal 2009.

Casey's has been expanding in existing markets and broadening its presence by acquiring other midwestern chains. In fiscal 2008 Casey's acquired about a dozen convenience stores. In 2007 it purchased about 50 stores, including 30-plus HandiMart convenience stores and a truck stop in Iowa.

In addition to Casey's General Stores, other banners operated by the chain include Handi-Mart and Just Diesel.

HISTORY

Donald Lamberti, who had run his family's grocery store, founded Casey's General Stores with Kurvin C. "K. C." Fish. The men converted a gas station into the first Casey's convenience store in 1968. To expand and build brand recognition, the company began franchising outlets two years later. By focusing on small towns, the company avoided competition and expensive building and property costs. A significant growth spurt in 1979 took Casey's from 119 stores to 226. Fish retired the following year.

The company went public in 1983 and began to curtail its franchising efforts in favor of more profitable company-owned stores (at the time there were about 190 company-owned stores and about 215 franchised outlets; today only about 130 are franchised). Casey's introduced carry-out pizza in 1984 and sandwiches two years later. Fueled by another stock offering in 1985, the company continued to grow quickly. It opened its 500th store that year and by 1990 had stores in eight states.

By 1996 Casey's had 1,000 stores, and it continued to add about 70 stores a year. After 30 years at the helm, in 1998 Lamberti retired as CEO; president Ronald Lamb took his place. In 2000 Casey's continued to expand at a rate of about 85 stores per year.

The company was accused of charging up to $5 a gallon for gas at 25 Casey's stores in Illinois on September 11, 2001, the day of terrorist attacks in New York City and Washington, DC. Casey's agreed the next month to pay $25,000 to the Red Cross and $5,000 to the state of Illinois. It also agreed to refund customers who were overcharged for gas. In fiscal 2002 the company opened more than 50 company-owned stores.

In fiscal 2003 the company built 15 new stores and purchased another. In April 2003 co-founder Lamberti retired from the company and Ronald Lamb added chairman to his title in May.

In early 2006 the company acquired 51 convenience stores in Nebraska from Gas 'N Shop for about $29 million. In June COO Robert Myers was named CEO of Casey's, succeeding Ronald Lamb, who held onto the chairman's title. In October the company acquired 33 HandiMart convenience stores in Iowa from Nordstrom Oil for about $63 million.

In March 2009 Casey's ended its franchising program begun in the 1970s. (At its peak, Casey's had a total of 230 franchised stores.) As a result, all of its convenience stores are and will be company owned going forward.

EXECUTIVES

Chairman: Ronald M. (Ron) Lamb, age 73
President, CEO, and Director: Robert J. (Bob) Myers, age 62
COO: Terry W. Handley, age 49
SVP and CFO: William J. (Bill) Walljasper, age 44
SVP Logistics and Acquisitions: Sam J. Billmeyer, age 52
VP Marketing: Michael R. (Mike) Richardson
VP Real Estate and Store Development: Cleo R. Kuhns
VP Support Services: Hal D. Brown
VP Food Services: Darryl F. Bacon
VP Human Resources: Julie L. Jackowski
VP and Treasurer: Russell D. Sukut
VP and Corporate Counsel: Eli J. Wirtz
VP Store Operations: Robert C. Ford
Information Systems Administrator: Pat Thomas
Auditors: KPMG LLP

LOCATIONS

HQ: Casey's General Stores, Inc.
1 Convenience Blvd., Ankeny, IA 50021
Phone: 515-965-6100 **Fax:** 515-965-6160
Web: www.caseys.com

PRODUCTS/OPERATIONS

2009 Sales

	$ mil.	% of total
Gasoline	3,321.5	71
Grocery & other merchandise	1,010.1	22
Prepared food & fountain	335.6	7
Other	20.7	—
Total	**4,687.9**	**100**

Selected Merchandise

Ammunition
Automotive products
Beverages
Food
Gasoline (self-service)
Health and beauty aids

Housewares
Pet products
Photo supplies
School supplies
Tobacco products

COMPETITORS

7-Eleven
Chevron
CVS Caremark
Exxon
Holiday Companies
Hy-Vee
IGA

Krause Gentle
Kroger
Kwik Trip
Martin & Bayley
QuikTrip
Royal Dutch Shell
Walgreen

HISTORICAL FINANCIALS

Company Type: Public

Income Statement

FYE: April 30

	REVENUE ($ mil.)	NET INCOME ($ mil.)	NET PROFIT MARGIN	EMPLOYEES
4/09	4,687.9	85.7	1.8%	18,780
4/08	4,827.1	84.9	1.8%	17,983
4/07	4,024.0	61.9	1.5%	17,136
4/06	3,515.1	61.6	1.8%	15,692
4/05	2,810.5	36.8	1.3%	14,440
Annual Growth	13.6%	23.5%	—	6.8%

2009 Year-End Financials

Debt ratio: 23.3%
Return on equity: 12.5%
Cash ($ mil.): 146
Current ratio: 1.29
Long-term debt ($ mil.): 168

No. of shares (mil.): 51
Dividends
  Yield: 1.1%
  Payout: 17.9%
Market value ($ mil.): 1,353

Stock History

NASDAQ (GS): CASY

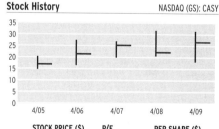

	STOCK PRICE ($) FY Close	P/E High/Low	PER SHARE ($) Earnings	Dividends	Book Value
4/09	26.61	19 11	1.68	0.30	14.18
4/08	22.13	19 12	1.67	0.26	12.73
4/07	25.15	22 17	1.22	0.20	11.25
4/06	21.39	23 14	1.19	0.18	10.29
4/05	16.88	27 21	0.73	0.16	9.22
Annual Growth	12.1%	— —	23.2%	17.0%	11.3%

Caterpillar Inc.

Building more than cocoons, Caterpillar is the world's #1 maker of earthmoving machinery and a leading supplier of agricultural equipment. The company makes construction, mining, and logging machinery; diesel and natural gas engines; industrial gas turbines; and electrical power generation systems. Caterpillar has plants worldwide and sells its equipment globally via a network of 3,500 locations in 180 countries. Caterpillar offers rental services through more than 1,600 outlets worldwide, and it provides financing and insurance for its dealers and customers. Cat Power Ventures invests in power projects that use Caterpillar power generation equipment. Caterpillar Logistics Services offers supply chain services.

Nearly two-thirds of Caterpillar's sales are generated outside the US. The company is investing heavily in China, where the company intends to launch lower-priced equipment, with fewer frills and performance features, under an alternative brand. In developing regions such as China, India, and Indonesia, customers have tended to buy less expensive machinery that doesn't carry the high price of the Caterpillar brand.

Another area of interest is South America. In 2008 Caterpillar acquired MGE Equipamentos & Servicos Ferroviarios, a Brazil-based locomotive component manufacturer.

Like other manufacturers in the industry, Caterpillar is taking steps to reduce costs. Caterpillar is facing increased expenses from retiree pension, health care, and related benefits, and looks to offset most through streamlined operations. The company is also eliminating more than 22,000 workers from its payroll, a reduction in force of nearly 20%. Additional cuts by the heavy equipment maker are planned at five plants in Illinois, Indiana, and Georgia.

Cat and Navistar International are working together to produce Caterpillar-branded heavy-duty vocational trucks for the North American market, and have formed a joint venture to market commercial trucks outside North America. The on-highway vocational trucks will be unveiled in 2010 and will go into production in 2011. The global commercial truck JV initially will target potential customers in Australia, Brazil, China, Russia, South Africa, and Turkey.

HISTORY

In 1904 in Stockton, California, combine maker Benjamin Holt modified the farming tractor by substituting a gas engine for steam and replacing iron wheels with crawler tracks. This improved the tractor's mobility over dirt.

The British adapted the "caterpillar" (Holt's nickname for the tractor) design to the armored tank in 1915. Following WWI, the US Army donated tanks to local governments for construction work. The caterpillar's efficiency spurred the development of earthmoving and construction equipment.

Holt merged with Best Tractor in 1925. The company, renamed Caterpillar (Cat), moved to Peoria, Illinois, in 1928. Cat expanded into foreign markets in the 1930s and phased out combine production to focus on construction and road-building equipment.

Sales volume more than tripled during WWII when Cat supplied the military with earthmoving equipment. Returning GIs touted Cat

durability and quality, and high demand continued. Cat held a solid first place in the industry, far ahead of #2 International Harvester.

Moving beyond US borders, Cat established its first overseas plant in the UK (1951). In 1963 it entered a joint venture with Japanese industrial titan Mitsubishi. Cat bought Solar Turbines (gas turbine engines) in 1981. Fifty consecutive years of profits ended, however, when Cat ran up $953 million in losses between 1982 and 1984 as equipment demand fell and foreign competition intensified. Cat doubled its product line between 1984 and 1989 and shifted production toward smaller equipment.

In 1990 CEO Donald Fites reorganized Cat along product lines. The next year the company clashed with the UAW (United Auto Workers) over wage and health benefits. A strike resulted, and Cat reported its first annual loss since 1984. Most of the striking workers returned to work without a contract by mid-1992.

The firm completed a six-year, $1.8 billion modernization program in 1993 that automated many of its plants. That investment benefited the company when almost two-thirds of Cat's UAW employees at eight plants in Colorado, Illinois, and Pennsylvania went on strike in 1994. The company hired replacement workers and used its foreign factories to help fill orders. In 1995, after two years of record earnings at Cat, the UAW called off the strike. Cat set up a holding company, Caterpillar China Investment Co. Ltd., in 1996 for joint ventures in China.

In 1998 Cat and the UAW (with federal mediation) hammered out their first contract agreement in more than six years. That year Cat paid $1.33 billion for LucasVarity's UK-based Perkins Engines, expanding its capacity to produce small and midsize diesel engines.

Fites retired in 1999; vice chairman Glen Barton succeeded him. Cat cut back its workforce and production after slowdowns in the agricultural, mining, and oil exploration industries reduced machinery orders.

In 2003 the company inked a deal with diversified global resources company BHP Billiton to supply an estimated $1.5 billion in equipment and support to its operations. Additionally, Caterpillar and Eaton Corporation formed joint venture Intelligent Switchgear Organization LLC (Georgia) to produce Cat-branded electrical distribution switching products, with Eaton controlling 51% of the venture and Caterpillar 49%.

In early 2004 Jim Owens became CEO, and Caterpillar increased its stake in A.S.V., Inc. (rubber-tracked, all-purpose crawlers and undercarriages, accessories, and attachments) to roughly 22%. Later that year Caterpillar acquired Swiss industrial gas turbine packager Turbomach S.A. In the same year recreation vehicle manufacturer Fleetwood Enterprises announced that it would equip all of its diesel-powered vehicles with Caterpillar engines by the end of 2005. Williams Technology, a transmission remanufacturing company, was acquired from Remy International in late 2004.

In 2006 Caterpillar bought Progress Rail from One Equity Partners for about $1 billion. Also in 2006, Caterpillar agreed to acquire the rail and non-Cat engine component remanufacturing business of O.E.M. Remanufacturing Company, a subsidiary of Caterpillar distributor Finning.

In 2007 it completed the acquisition of French company Eurenov, which greatly enhanced the remanufacturing division's reach into the European market.

EXECUTIVES

Chairman and CEO: James W. (Jim) Owens, age 63, $17,654,422 total compensation
Group President: Stuart L. Levenick, age 56, $6,571,175 total compensation
Group President: Douglas R. (Doug) Oberhelman, age 55, $6,638,572 total compensation
Group President: Steven H. Wunning, age 57, $5,860,423 total compensation
Group President: Gérard R. Vittecoq, age 60, $6,328,410 total compensation
Group President: Edward J. (Ed) Rapp, age 51, $3,544,374 total compensation
Group President: Richard P. (Rich) Lavin, age 56, $5,467,221 total compensation
VP and CFO: David B. (Dave) Burritt, age 53, $3,064,612 total compensation
VP and CIO: John S. Heller
VP Product Development Center and CTO: Tana L. Utley, age 45
VP and Chief Human Resources Officer: Sidney C. (Sid) Banwart
VP Global Purchasing: Daniel M. (Dan) Murphy
VP Solar Turbines: Stephen A. (Steve) Gosselin
VP Large Power Systems: Gary A. Stroup
VP Latin America: Thomas A. (Tom) Gales, age 60
VP Americas Distribution Services Division: James J. (Jim) Parker
VP Legal Services, General Counsel, and Secretary: James B. (Jim) Buda, age 61
Treasurer: Kevin E. Colgan
Director Investor Relations: Mike DeWalt
Chief Accounting Officer: Jananne A. Copeland, age 46
Auditors: PricewaterhouseCoopers LLP

LOCATIONS

HQ: Caterpillar Inc.
   100 NE Adams St., Peoria, IL 61629
Phone: 309-675-1000   **Fax:** 309-675-1182
Web: www.cat.com

2008 Sales

	$ mil.	% of total
US	17,291	34
Other countries	34,033	66
Total	**51,324**	**100**

PRODUCTS/OPERATIONS

2008 Sales

	$ mil.	% of total
Machinery	31,804	62
Engines	16,240	32
Financial products	3,280	6
Total	**51,324**	**100**

Selected Products

Machinery
   Articulated trucks
   Backhoe loaders
   Log loaders
   Log skidders
   Mining shovels
   Motor graders
   Off-highway trucks
   Paving products
   Pipelayers
   Related parts
   Skid steer loaders
   Telescopic handlers
   Track and wheel excavators
   Track and wheel loaders
   Track and wheel tractors
   Wheel tractor-scrapers
Engines
   Engines for Caterpillar machinery
   Engines for electric power generation systems
   Engines for marine, petroleum, construction, industrial, and agricultural applications
   Engines for on-highway trucks and locomotives

Financing and insurance services
 Financing to customers and dealers
 Insurance to customers and dealers

Selected Brands
Cat
Caterpillar
F.G. Wilson
MaK
Olympian
Perkins
Solar Turbines

COMPETITORS

AGCO
Charles Machine Works
CIT Group
Citibank
CNH Global
Cummins
Daimler
Deere
Detroit Diesel
DHL
Dongfeng Motor
Dresser, Inc.
GE
GENCO Distribution System
Hitachi Construction Machinery
Hyundai Heavy Industries
Ingersoll-Rand
Isuzu
J C Bamford Excavators
JLG Industries
John Deere Credit
John Deere Thibodaux
Kawasaki Heavy Industries
Komatsu
Kubota
Mahindra
MAN
Menlo Worldwide
Mitsubishi Heavy Industries
Multiquip
Navistar International
Rolls-Royce
Sandvik
Scania
Siemens AG
Sumitomo Heavy Industries
Terex
Toyota
UPS Supply Chain Solutions
Volvo
Volvo Financial Services
Wells Fargo Equipment Finance
Woods Equipment

HISTORICAL FINANCIALS
Company Type: Public

Income Statement
FYE: December 31

	REVENUE ($ mil.)	NET INCOME ($ mil.)	NET PROFIT MARGIN	EMPLOYEES
12/08	51,324.0	3,557.0	6.9%	112,887
12/07	44,958.0	3,541.0	7.9%	101,333
12/06	41,517.0	3,537.0	8.5%	94,593
12/05	36,339.0	2,854.0	7.9%	85,116
12/04	30,251.0	2,035.0	6.7%	76,920
Annual Growth	14.1%	15.0%	—	10.1%

2008 Year-End Financials

Debt ratio: 375.1%
Return on equity: 47.5%
Cash ($ mil.): —
Current ratio: 1.21
Long-term debt ($ mil.): 22,834

No. of shares (mil.): 621
Dividends
 Yield: 3.6%
 Payout: 28.6%
Market value ($ mil.): 27,753

Stock History   NYSE: CAT

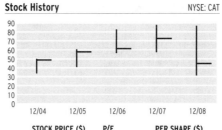

	STOCK PRICE ($) FY Close	P/E High/Low		PER SHARE ($) Earnings	Dividends	Book Value
12/08	44.67	15	6	5.66	1.62	9.80
12/07	72.56	16	11	5.37	1.38	14.30
12/06	61.33	16	11	5.17	1.15	11.04
12/05	57.77	15	10	4.04	0.95	13.57
12/04	48.76	17	12	2.88	0.80	12.02
Annual Growth	(2.2%)	—	—	18.4%	19.3%	(5.0%)

CB Richard Ellis Group

CB Richard Ellis Group (CBRE) is all about location, location, location — not to mention *ubicación, l'emplacement, posizione,* and *Standort.* The world's largest commercial real estate services company and an international powerhouse, CBRE has operations in more than 30 countries. Through subsidiaries Insignia Financial (the acquisition of which made CBRE the largest commercial-property manager in the world) and Trammell Crow, CBRE oversees real estate management, investment, property development, and related operations for top corporations that outsource their real estate requirements. It manages more than 1 billion sq. ft. of commercial space. CBRE also provides asset management and brokerage services.

CBRE has expanded to more than 300 offices; its three geographic segments are the Americas; Europe, the Middle East, and Africa (EMEA); and Asia/Pacific. The Americas division is its largest, accounting for nearly two-thirds of the firm's sales. About 10% of its sales are concentrated in California. CBRE continues to expand its geographic reach globally. In 2008 it opened its first offices in Bahrain and joined forces with Vanke to provide residential property management services in China.

CBRE makes no bones about its acquisition strategy — now that it has acquired firms Insignia Financial and Trammell Crow (purchased in 2006 for $2.2 billion) it continues to seek fill-in acquisitions in regional markets that complement or expand existing operations. Insignia and Trammell Crow represented some of the largest acquisitions for CBRE to date. The additions helped deepen CBRE's outsourcing services (especially project and facilities management) for corporate and institutional clients throughout the US. The company has slowed its strategic acquisitions in light of the current market conditions, but continues to seek such opportunities for growth.

In 2008 the company spun off former subsidiary Realty Finance Corporation after the real estate investment trust continued to post losses in a troubled credit market. The company, which originates and invests in real estate financing, is now managed internally.

Richard Blum and Jane Su each hold a more than 12% stake in CBRE through Blum Strategic Partners.

HISTORY

Colbert Coldwell and Albert Tucker started real estate brokerage Tucker, Lynch, & Coldwell in 1906 in San Francisco. In 1922 the company expanded to Los Angeles, where it began developing real estate in 1933 with a 60-acre subdivision in the burgeoning city.

Having profited from California's rapid growth in the 1950s and 1960s, the firm expanded out of state. The partnership incorporated in 1962 as Coldwell Banker, which went public in 1968. Sears, Roebuck & Co. bought the company in 1981 for 80% above its market price. But by 1991 Sears had abandoned aims to become a financial services giant and sold Coldwell Banker's commercial operations to The Carlyle Group as CB Commercial Real Estate Services Group.

Free of Sears but $56 million in the red, the company didn't return to profitability until 1993. Two years later it embarked on a shopping spree in real estate services, buying tenant representatives Langon Rieder and Westmark Realty. In 1996 the company went public and bought mortgage banker L. J. Melody & Company (now named CBRE | Melody); it purchased Koll Real Estate Services in 1997.

In 1998 the company widened its global scope with the acquisition of REI Limited, the non-UK operations of Richard Ellis; it was renamed CB Richard Ellis Services. CB Richard Ellis also bought Hillier Parker May & Rowden (now operating in the UK as CB Hillier), a London-based provider of commercial property services.

CB Richard Ellis experienced a revenue crunch in 1999 and responded by restructuring its North American operations into three divisions (transaction, financial, and management services) and cutting management ranks by 30%. Growth continued in 1999 with the purchase of Pittsburgh-based Gold & Co., the addition of an office in Venezuela, and a fat contract to manage more than 1,100 locations for Prudential.

In 2000 the company committed significant resources to the Internet, inking a deal to offer the lease management services of MyContracts.com and investing in Canadian real estate transaction tracker RealNet Canada.

A group of investors including then-CEO Ray Wirta, chairman Richard Blum (and his BLUM Capital Partners), and Freeman Spogli took the company private in 2001. Blum Capital Partners bought the 60% of publicly traded CBRE that it did not already own, forming CBRE Holding. Three years later the company went public once again.

In 2003 CBRE merged with top commercial real estate broker and property manager Insignia Financial. The next year the company changed its name to CB Richard Ellis Group and went public. It bought rival Trammell Crow in 2006, as well as a dozen or so other companies as it sought to fill in its holdings.

EXECUTIVES

Chairman: Richard C. Blum, age 73
Vice Chairman: Raymond E. (Ray) Wirta, age 65
President, CEO, and Director: W. Brett White, age 49, $3,068,881 total compensation
Group President and CFO: Robert E. (Bob) Sulentic, age 52, $999,493 total compensation
Global COO: Calvin W. (Cal) Frese Jr., age 52, $1,622,488 total compensation
Global Chief Information Officer: Don Goldstein
EVP Finance, Chief Accounting Officer, and CFO, Americas: Gil Borok, age 41, $788,832 total compensation
Chief Investment Officer, Corporate Finance, Strategy, and Development Services: James R. (Jim) Groch
EVP, General Counsel, Chief Compliance Officer, and Secretary: Laurence H. Midler, age 44
Global Chief Economist: Raymond Torto
EVP Office and Commercial Properties: Jeffrey S. Pion
EVP Brokerage Services: Peter Turchin
SVP Investor Relations: Nick Kormeluk
SVP Global Human Resources: Jennifer Buchholz
President, Investment Properties: Gregory S. Vorwaller
President, Americas Brokerage: Christopher R. Ludeman
Chairman, Global Brokerage Services: Stephen B. (Steve) Siegel, age 64
President, Asia Pacific: Robert (Rob) Blain, age 53, $1,394,300 total compensation
President, EMEA: Michael J. (Mike) Strong, age 61
CEO, CBRE Investors: Vance G. Maddocks
Senior Managing Director Corporate Communications: Steven (Steve) Iaco
Auditors: Deloitte & Touche LLP

LOCATIONS

HQ: CB Richard Ellis Group, Inc.
11150 Santa Monica Blvd., Ste. 1600,
Los Angeles, CA 90025
Phone: 310-405-8900
Web: www.cbre.com

2008 Sales by Segment

	$ mil.	% of total
Americas	3,209.8	63
EMEA	1,080.7	21
Asia/Pacific	558.2	11
Global investment management	161.2	3
Development services	118.9	2
Total	**5,128.8**	**100**

PRODUCTS/OPERATIONS

Selected Subsidiaries

CB Richard Ellis, Inc.
CB Richard Ellis Limited (UK)
CB Richard Ellis Real Estate Services, LLC
CB Richard Ellis Services, Inc
CBRE Melody & Company (commercial mortgage origination)
CBRE Melody of Texas, L.P.
CBRE Real Estate Services, Inc.
Insignia Financial Group, LLC
Relam Amsterdam Holdings B.V. (The Netherlands)
Trammell Crow Company

COMPETITORS

Colliers International	Jones Lang LaSalle
Cushman & Wakefield	Lend Lease
DTZ	Lincoln Property
FirstService	Mitsui Fudosan
Forest City Enterprises	Realia Business
Grubb & Ellis	Realogy
Hines	Shorenstein
Inland Group	Studley
JMB Realty	Tishman

HISTORICAL FINANCIALS

Company Type: Public

Income Statement

FYE: December 31

	REVENUE ($ mil.)	NET INCOME ($ mil.)	NET PROFIT MARGIN	EMPLOYEES
12/08	5,128.8	(1,012.1)	—	30,000
12/07	6,034.2	390.5	6.5%	29,000
12/06	4,032.0	284.7	7.1%	24,000
12/05	2,910.6	210.0	7.2%	14,500
12/04	2,365.1	64.7	2.7%	13,500
Annual Growth	**21.4%**	**—**	**—**	**22.1%**

2008 Year-End Financials

Debt ratio: 1,994.1%
Return on equity: —
Cash ($ mil.): 159
Current ratio: 1.02
Long-term debt ($ mil.): 2,287
No. of shares (mil.): 286
Dividends
Yield: 0.0%
Payout: —
Market value ($ mil.): 1,235

Stock History

NYSE: CBG

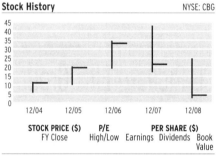

	STOCK PRICE ($) FY Close	P/E High/Low	Earnings	PER SHARE ($) Dividends	Book Value
12/08	4.32	— —	(4.81)	0.00	0.40
12/07	21.55	26 11	1.66	0.00	3.46
12/06	33.20	25 14	1.35	0.00	4.13
12/05	19.62	21 11	0.95	0.00	2.78
12/04	11.18	37 20	0.30	0.00	1.96
Annual Growth	**(21.2%)**	**— —**	**—**	**—**	**(32.7%)**

CBS Corporation

This media conglomerate has its eye focused on the TV. CBS Corporation, one of the leading television broadcasting and production companies in the world, owns CBS Broadcasting, the #1 broadcast network in the US. The corporation also operates about 30 TV stations around the country and owns 50% of The CW Network. On cable, CBS owns movie channel Showtime and sports channel CBS College Sports Network. It creates and distributes programming through CBS Television Distribution Group and CBS Paramount Network Television. In addition to TV, the company owns CBS Radio, CBS Outdoor, and book publisher Simon & Schuster. Chairman Sumner Redstone controls CBS Corp. through his National Amusements movie theater chain.

The company's sprawling collection of media assets not only allows it to reach a mass audience through multiple channels, but to sell time and space to advertisers across those channels. Advertising accounts for more than 65% of sales. CBS also focuses on redistributing its content through multiple outlets and cross-promotion activities.

The economic recession, however, has hurt many ad-supported media businesses as advertisers have reined in spending. In particular, the company's TV and radio stations, which depend on local advertisers for much of their revenue, have borne the brunt of the downturn. In response, CBS has implemented a number of cost-cutting measures, including some layoffs. Its struggling radio division has also been shedding some of its underperforming stations.

In a bold move to expand its online reach, the company purchased online publisher CNET Networks for $1.8 billion in 2008. The deal garnered CBS a collection of popular Web properties, including GameSpot.com (video games), News.com (technology news), and CNET's flagship CNET.com (consumer electronics reviews). In 2009 the company announced a plan to join other TV networks to form an online video subscription offering through a deal with cable operator Comcast.

CBS Outdoor acquired International Outdoor Advertising Group (IOA), a leading billboard operator in South America, for $110 million in 2008. It is also ramping up business in the emerging market of China; it has some 5,700 displays in Beijing.

CBS was once part of the Viacom conglomeration of TV, cable, and film companies, but in late 2005 the media behemoth split into two separate, publicly traded companies: The "new" Viacom and CBS Corporation. Viacom took over the cable and film assets, including Paramount Pictures and MTV Networks, while CBS took on the primarily advertising-supported media assets (television, radio, and Internet operations). Les Moonves, formerly the head of the CBS network, was appointed to lead CBS Corp.

HISTORY

The company that would eventually become CBS Corporation began as Viacom in 1970. It was the result of numerous mergers and acquisitions dating back nearly 90 years, combining everything from a movie studio to a company that made car bumpers. CBS launched Viacom after the FCC ruled that TV networks could not own cable systems and TV stations in the same market. Viacom took over CBS's program syndication division and bought TV and radio stations in the late 1970s and early 1980s. In 1978 it co-founded pay-TV network Showtime. Viacom became full owner in 1982 and combined Showtime with The Movie Channel the following year to form Showtime Networks. Viacom also began producing TV series and bought MTV Networks in 1986.

After a bidding war with renowned financier Carl Icahn and a Viacom management group, Sumner Redstone's National Amusements bought 83% of Viacom in 1987. Viacom bought King's Entertainment (theme parks) shortly thereafter and followed that with two mega-deals in 1994: it bought Paramount Communications for about $10 billion (which included Simon & Schuster) and Blockbuster for $8.4 billion (which included Spelling Entertainment). The next year, along with Chris-Craft, Viacom launched UPN (United Paramount Network), the fifth commercial-broadcast TV network in the US.

Chiseling away at a mountain of debt, Viacom dumped its radio stations and sold its share in USA Networks (now named IAC/InterActiveCorp) to Universal for $1.7 billion in 1997. In 1998 it sold the reference and education publishing divisions of Simon & Schuster to Pearson for

$4.6 billion and unloaded the unprofitable Block-buster Music chain to Wherehouse Entertainment for $115 million.

Viacom created an Internet division (MTV Networks Online) in 1999 to house its MTV, VH1, and Nickelodeon Web sites (later decentralized into The MTVi Group and Nickelodeon Online). Later that year it sold 18% of Blockbuster in an IPO and sold 10% of MTVi to TCI Music (now Liberty Digital) in exchange for the SonicNet Web sites.

Viacom bought Chris-Craft's 50% stake in the struggling UPN Network for a paltry $5 million in 2000 by exercising a buy-sell clause in the contract. BHC Communications (Chris-Craft's 80%-owned subsidiary that actually owned the stake in UPN) filed suit to block Viacom's merger with CBS, claiming that it violated a non-compete clause in the contract, but the New York Supreme Court ruled in Viacom's favor. Its $45 billion merger with CBS went through (reuniting two companies split apart by the government 30 years ago), and Viacom was given one year to sell UPN. However, a federal law prohibiting ownership of more than one TV network was overturned in 2001, allowing Viacom to keep the network.

In 2001 Viacom bought the rest of Infinity Broadcasting that it didn't already own, as well as BET Holdings (the media company targeting African-Americans) for $3 billion.

In 2004 Viacom finally sold its majority stake in Blockbuster, which never really fit in with Viacom's other media properties.

Shortly after its 2005 split, CBS Corp. sold Paramount Parks to Cedar Fair for $1.2 billion. A newly formed network called The CW, a combination of UPN and The WB, debuted in 2006. The following TV season, the CBS network fell from first place in the ratings for the first time in six years. CBS Corp. expanded its online publishing operations in 2008 with the $1.8 billion acquisition of CNET Networks.

EXECUTIVES

Executive Chairman: Sumner M. Redstone, age 85, $12,085,167 total compensation
Vice Chairman: Shari E. Redstone, age 55
President, CEO, and Director: Leslie (Les) Moonves, age 59, $31,962,064 total compensation
EVP and CFO: Joseph R. Ianniello, age 41, $2,539,679 total compensation
SVP, Controller, and Chief Accounting Officer: Susan C. Gordon, age 55
EVP and Chief Communications Officer: Gil Schwartz, age 57
Chief Research Officer; President, CBS Vision: David F. Poltrack
SEVP, CBS Primetime: Kelly Kahl
EVP Investor Relations: Martin M. Shea, age 65
EVP Planning, Policy, and Government Relations: Martin D. Franks, age 58
EVP and General Counsel: Louis J. Briskman, age 60, $5,546,388 total compensation
EVP Human Resources and Administration: Anthony G. Ambrosio, age 48
EVP and General Manager, CBS Records: Larry Jenkins
EVP Investor Relations: Adam Townsend
SVP, Deputy General Counsel, and Secretary: Angeline C. Straka, age 63

President and CEO, Simon & Schuster: Carolyn K. Reidy, age 59
Chairman and CEO, CBS Outdoor: Wally C. Kelly, age 53
President and CEO, CBS Radio: Daniel R. (Dan) Mason
President, CBS Paramount Network Television Entertainment Group: Nancy Tellem
CEO, CBS Interactive: Quincy Smith
President and CEO, CBS Television Stations: Tom Kane
Auditors: PricewaterhouseCoopers LLP

LOCATIONS

HQ: CBS Corporation
51 W. 52nd St., New York, NY 10019
Phone: 212-975-4321   **Fax:** 212-975-4516
Web: www.cbscorporation.com

2008 Sales

	$ mil.	% of total
US	11,704.3	84
Europe		
UK	584.3	4
Other countries	903.5	6
Canada	350.6	3
Other regions	407.7	3
Total	**13,950.4**	**100**

PRODUCTS/OPERATIONS

2008 Sales

	$ mil.	% of total
Advertising	9,239.9	66
TV license fees	1,939.4	14
Affiliate revenue	1,185.1	8
Publishing	857.7	6
Home entertainment	234.0	2
Other	494.3	4
Total	**13,950.4**	**100**

2008 Sales

	$ mil.	% of total
TV	8,991.1	64
Outdoor advertising	2,170.6	16
Radio	1,539.1	11
Publishing	857.7	6
Interactive media	421.7	3
Adjustments	(29.8)	—
Total	**13,950.4**	**100**

Selected Operations

Television
  CBS Broadcasting
  CBS College Sports (cable sports channel)
  CBS Home Entertainment
  CBS Paramount Network Television (production and distribution)
  CBS Television Distribution Group
    CBS Paramount International Television (international distribution)
    CBS Studio (TV production)
  CBS Television Stations
  The CW Television Network (50%)
  Showtime Networks
    FLIX
    The Movie Channel
    Showtime
Outdoor advertising
  CBS Outdoor (outdoor advertising)
  CBS Outernet
  Vendor (Mexico)
Radio
  CBS Radio
  CBS Radio News
  Spanish Broadcasting System (10%)
  Westwood One (8%)

Publishing
  Simon & Schuster
  The Free Press
  Pocket Books
  Scribner
Interactive media
  BNET
  CBS.com
  CBSSports.com
  CNET
  GameSpot
  Last.fm
  TV.com

COMPETITORS

Citadel Broadcasting
Clear Channel
Cox Radio
Cumulus Media
Disney
Google
JCDecaux
Lamar Advertising
NBC Universal
News Corp.
Random House
SIRIUS XM
Time Warner
Yahoo!

HISTORICAL FINANCIALS

Company Type: Public

Income Statement

FYE: December 31

	REVENUE ($ mil.)	NET INCOME ($ mil.)	NET PROFIT MARGIN	EMPLOYEES
12/08	13,950.4	(11,673.4)	—	25,920
12/07	14,072.9	1,247.0	8.9%	23,970
12/06	14,320.2	1,660.5	11.6%	23,654
12/05	14,536.4	(7,089.1)	—	32,160
12/04	22,525.9	(16,149.8)	—	38,350
Annual Growth	(11.3%)	—	—	(9.3%)

2008 Year-End Financials

Debt ratio: 81.1%
Return on equity: —
Cash ($ mil.): 420
Current ratio: 1.08
Long-term debt ($ mil.): 6,975
No. of shares (mil.): 678
Dividends
  Yield: 12.9%
  Payout: —
Market value ($ mil.): 5,551

Stock History

NYSE: CBS

	STOCK PRICE ($) FY Close	P/E High/Low		PER SHARE ($) Earnings	Dividends	Book Value
12/08	8.19	—	—	(17.43)	1.06	12.69
12/07	27.25	21	15	1.73	0.94	31.68
12/06	31.18	15	11	2.15	0.74	34.71
12/05	24.05	—	—	(8.98)	0.56	32.07
12/04	26.85	—	—	(20.38)	0.50	62.01
Annual Growth	(25.7%)	—	—	—	20.7%	(32.7%)

CenterPoint Energy

CenterPoint Energy has made a complete pivot around its core operations. The company, which had evolved from a local utility into a global power provider, has spun off most of its nonregulated operations and has returned to its roots. CenterPoint Energy's regulated utilities distribute natural gas to 3.2 million customers in six US states and electricity to 2 million customers on the Texas Gulf Coast. The company's main stomping ground is Texas, where it has regulated power distribution operations through subsidiary CenterPoint Energy Houston Electric. CenterPoint Energy also operates more than 8,000 miles of interstate gas pipeline, and it has gas gathering and storage operations.

The company's natural gas distribution subsidiaries serve customers in Arkansas, Indiana, Louisiana, Minnesota, Mississippi, Oklahoma, and Texas. CenterPoint Energy also markets natural gas to 9,700 commercial, industrial, and wholesale customers located primarily in the eastern US. It also provides HVAC and other energy-related services through its gas division.

CenterPoint Energy's strategy is focused on enhancing and expanding existing core operations, while acquiring complementary and synergistic businesses.

In 2008 the company expanded its presence in Indiana with the acquisition of Nordic Energy Services' commercial gas accounts.

HISTORY

CenterPoint Energy's earliest predecessor, Houston Electric Lighting and Power, was formed in 1882 by a group including Emanuel Raphael, cashier at Houston Savings Bank, and Mayor William Baker. In 1901 General Electric's financial arm, United Electric Securities Company, took control of the utility, which became Houston Lighting & Power (HL&P). United Electric sold HL&P five years later; by 1922 HL&P ended up in the arms of National Power & Light Company (NP&L), a subsidiary of Electric Bond & Share (a public utility holding company that had been spun off by General Electric).

In 1942 NP&L was forced to sell HL&P in order to comply with the 1935 Public Utility Holding Company Act. As the oil industry boomed in Houston after WWII, so did HL&P.

HL&P became the managing partner in a venture to build a nuclear plant on the Texas Gulf Coast in 1973. Construction on the South Texas Project, with partners Central Power and Light and the cities of Austin and San Antonio, began in 1975. In 1976 Houston Industries (HI) was formed as the holding company for HL&P.

By 1980 the nuke was four years behind schedule and over budget. HL&P and its partners sued construction firm Brown & Root in 1982 and received a $700 million settlement in 1985. (The City of Austin also sued HL&P for damages but lost.) The nuke was finally brought online in 1988, with the final cost estimated at $5.8 billion.

Meanwhile, HI diversified into cable TV in 1986 by creating Enrcom (later Paragon Communications) through a venture with Time Inc. Two years later it bought the US cable interests of Canada's Rogers Communications. HI left the cable business in 1995, selling out to Time Warner.

Developing Latin fever, HI joined a consortium that bought 51% of Argentinean electric company EDELAP in 1992. (However, in 1998 HI sold its stake to AES.) On a roll, HI acquired 90% of Argentina's electric utility EDESE (1995); joined a consortium that won a controlling stake in Light, a Brazilian electric utility (1996); bought a stake in Colombian electric utility EPSA (1997); and bought interests in three electric utilities in El Salvador (1998).

Back in the US, HI acquired gas dealer NorAm for $2.5 billion in 1997. The next year it bought five generating plants in California from Edison International and laid plans to build merchant plants in Arizona (near Phoenix), Illinois, Nevada (near Las Vegas, in partnership with Sempra Energy), and Rhode Island.

In 1999 HI became Reliant Energy and HL&P became Reliant Energy HL&P. That year the company bought a 52% stake in Dutch power generation firm UNA; it bought the remaining 48% the next year. Also in 2000 Reliant Energy paid Sithe Energies (now a part of Dynegy) $2.1 billion for 21 power plants in the mid-Atlantic states. It sold its operations in Brazil, Colombia, and El Salvador that year, and transferred all of its nonregulated operations to subsidiary Reliant Resources. Reliant Energy also announced plans to spin off Reliant Resources that year.

Reliant Energy netted about $1.7 billion in 2001 from the sale to the public of nearly 20% of Reliant Resources. Later that year Reliant Resources announced that it would acquire US independent power producer Orion Power Holdings in a $4.7 billion deal; the deal was completed in 2002. Deregulation took effect in Texas that year, and Reliant Energy transferred its retail power supply business to Reliant Resources.

As the finances of wholesale energy companies came under scrutiny in 2002, the SEC issued a formal investigation into "round-trip" energy trades completed by Reliant Resources. These activities artificially inflated the firm's trading volumes and led it to restate its 1999, 2000, and 2001 financial results; it also reduced its energy marketing and trading workforce by about 35%.

Reliant Energy announced plans in 2001 to form a new holding company (CenterPoint Energy) for itself and Reliant Resources; it completed the name change in 2002.

CenterPoint Energy changed its name in 2002 in preparation for the spinoff of its 83% stake in Reliant Resources (now Reliant Energy), a global independent power producer and energy marketer; the spinoff was completed later that year. (Reliant Resources changed its name to Reliant Energy in 2004.) CenterPoint Energy transferred its nonregulated Texas retail power supply business to Reliant Resources before spinning off the unit.

As part of its corporate reorganization, and in response to Texas' electricity deregulation (which took effect in 2002), CenterPoint Energy separated its Texas power generation and distribution operations. CenterPoint Energy sold Texas Genco to GC Power Acquisition (owned by investment firms The Blackstone Group, Hellman & Friedman, Kohlberg Kravis Roberts, and Texas Pacific Group) for $3.65 billion.

The company has also divested all of its international assets, including its Latin American utility interests.

In 2007 CenterPoint Energy Gas Transmission opened the 172-mile Carthage to Perryville pipeline, enabling the delivery of 1 billion cu. ft. of natural gas a day to pipelines serving end users in the Midwest, Northeast, and Southeast.

EXECUTIVES

Chairman: Milton Carroll, age 58
President, CEO, and Director: David M. McClanahan, age 59, $6,198,934 total compensation
EVP and CFO: Gary L. Whitlock, age 59, $1,771,927 total compensation
SVP and Chief Accounting Officer: Walter L. Fitzgerald, age 51
EVP, General Counsel, and Corporate Secretary: Scott E. Rozzell, age 59, $1,673,770 total compensation
SVP; Group President, Regulated Operations: Thomas R. (Tom) Standish, age 59, $1,883,414 total compensation
SVP; Group President, CenterPoint Energy Pipelines and Field Services: C. Gregory (Greg) Harper, age 44, $235,997 total compensation
Division President, CenterPoint Energy Services: Wayne D. Stinnett, age 58
Division President and COO, CenterPoint Energy Houston Electric: Georgianna E. Nichols, age 60
Division President, CenterPoint Energy Gas Operations: Joseph B. McGoldrick, age 55
Media Contact Corporate and Financial Information: Leticia Lowe
Media Contact Electric, Natural Gas, Pipelines and Field Services Operations: Alicia Dixon
Auditors: Deloitte & Touche LLP

LOCATIONS

HQ: CenterPoint Energy, Inc.
   1111 Louisiana St., Houston, TX 77002
Phone: 713-207-1111   **Fax:** 713-207-3169
Web: www.centerpointenergy.com

PRODUCTS/OPERATIONS

2008 Sales

	$ mil.	% of total
Competitive natural gas sales & services	4,488	40
Natural gas distribution	4,217	37
Electric transmission & distribution delivery	1,916	17
Interstate pipelines	477	4
Field services	213	2
Other	11	—
Total	**11,322**	**100**

COMPETITORS

AEP
AEP Texas Central
AEP Texas North
Ameren
Avista
Cleco
CMS Energy
Constellation Energy Group
Dominion Resources
Duke Energy
El Paso
Energy Future
Entergy
Exelon
Koch Industries, Inc.
Mirant
Mississippi Power
OGE Energy
ONEOK
Progress Energy
Southern Company
Southwestern Electric Power
Southwestern Energy
Williams Companies
Xcel Energy

HISTORICAL FINANCIALS

Company Type: Public

Income Statement

FYE: December 31

	REVENUE ($ mil.)	NET INCOME ($ mil.)	NET PROFIT MARGIN	EMPLOYEES
12/08	11,322.0	447.0	3.9%	8,801
12/07	9,623.0	399.0	4.1%	8,568
12/06	9,319.0	432.0	4.6%	8,623
12/05	9,722.0	222.0	2.3%	9,001
12/04	8,510.4	72.6	0.9%	9,093
Annual Growth	7.4%	57.5%	—	(0.8%)

2008 Year-End Financials

Debt ratio: 499.8%
Return on equity: 23.2%
Cash ($ mil.): 167
Current ratio: 1.07
Long-term debt ($ mil.): 10,181

No. of shares (mil.): 365
Dividends
　Yield: 5.8%
　Payout: 56.2%
Market value ($ mil.): 4,611

Stock History

NYSE: CNP

	STOCK PRICE ($) FY Close	P/E High	P/E Low	PER SHARE ($) Earnings	PER SHARE ($) Dividends	PER SHARE ($) Book Value
12/08	12.62	13	7	1.30	0.73	5.57
12/07	17.13	17	13	1.17	0.68	4.95
12/06	16.58	13	9	1.33	0.60	4.26
12/05	12.85	20	14	0.75	0.40	3.55
12/04	11.30	—	—	(2.48)	0.40	3.03
Annual Growth	2.8%	—	—	—	16.2%	16.5%

Central Garden & Pet

Central Garden & Pet is happy to help with both pets and pests. The company is among the largest US manufacturers and distributors of lawn, garden, and pet supplies, providing its products to pet supplies retailers, home improvement centers, nurseries, and mass merchandisers from approximately 40 manufacturing plants and another 35 distribution centers throughout the US; it also has sales offices in the UK. Central Garden & Pet's proprietary brand lines include AMDRO fire ant bait, Four Paws animal products, Kaytee bird seed, Nylabone dog chews, Norcal pottery, Pennington grass seed and bird seed products, and TFH pet books. Chairman and CEO William Brown controls not quite 50% of the company's voting rights.

Wal-Mart accounts for about 30% of sales; Lowe's and The Home Depot each account for about 15%.

Having built a sizable nationwide distribution network, the company has turned its focus to promoting its existing proprietary brands and adding new products (both through its own innovation and acquisitions). Until the mid-1990s Central Garden & Pet derived almost all of its sales from distributing other manufacturers'

products; in 2008 that figure was about 15% of total sales.

Accordingly, the company is growing through acquisitions; in 2005 it purchased Gulfstream Home & Garden (garden products) and Pets International (small animal and specialty pet supplies). In 2006 Central Garden & Pet acquired animal health product maker Farnam Companies for approximately $285 million. The firm also increased its stake in Tech Pac (supplier of insect control products) from 20% to 80%. It also added pest control maker B2E Corporation, turf grass developer ASP Research, and garden controls manufacturer Matson (of which it had already owned just under 50%).

HISTORY

Central Garden & Pet Company's roots go back to 1955, when it was founded as a small California distributor of lawn and garden supplies. After nearly three decades of unremarkable growth, it was purchased in 1980 by William Brown, a former VP of finance at camera maker Vivitar. The company acquired small distributors but let them operate autonomously. By 1987 Central had sales of $25 million with distribution in California.

The company's first major acquisition was the result of a restructuring of forestry giant Weyerhaeuser, which had diversified into insurance, home building, and diapers, among other products, but was selling noncore divisions to focus solely on timber. It sold Weyerhaeuser Garden Supply to Central in 1990 for $32 million.

Overnight, Central became a national powerhouse with 25 distribution centers serving 38 states. In 1991 sales reached $280 million, of which acquired operations accounted for nearly 70%. The purchase also gave Central 10 high-volume retail customers — including Costco, Kmart, and Wal-Mart — which accounted for half of its business. In 1991 the company also acquired a pet distributor, its first move into pet supplies.

To pay down debt associated with the Weyerhaeuser acquisition, the company (then officially known as Central Garden & Pet Company) went public in 1993 (a 1992 IPO was withdrawn when a warehouse fire damaged inventory). With the capital for growth, Central continued to acquire other distributors (from early 1993 to early 1994 it acquired six distributors with about $70 million in sales).

In 1994 the company's largest supplier, Solaris (then a unit of Monsanto and maker of Ortho and Roundup products), decided to bypass Central as its distributor and sell products directly. Solaris products accounted for nearly 40% of the company's sales, and revenues dipped in 1995. However, that year Solaris decided that self-distribution was too difficult and made Central its exclusive distributor. Total sales increased about 65% in 1996.

Broadening its pet supply distribution network, in 1996 Central paid $33 million for Kenlin Pet Supply, the East Coast's largest pet distributor, and Longhorn Pet Supply in Texas. The following year the company bought Four Paws Products and Sandoz Agro.

In 1997 Central paid $132 million for TFH Publications — one of the nation's largest producers of pet books and maker of Nylabone dog snacks — and Kaytee Products, a maker of bird seed. It added Pennington Seed, a maker of grass and bird seed, in 1998.

The company broadened its scope in 1999 with the purchase of Norcal Pottery Products. It also tried to buy Solaris, but that year Monsanto sold its Solaris unit to grass firm The Scotts Company (now Scotts Miracle-Gro). In a familiar refrain for Central, Scotts then decided to shift partially toward self-distribution, costing Central between $200 million and $250 million in annual sales; Scotts would completely sever distribution ties with Central the following year, leading to countering lawsuits.

Central said in early 2000 it would spin off its lawn and garden distribution business to shareholders, but the company abandoned the plan less than a year later. In March 2000 the company acquired AMDRO fire ant killer and IMAGE, a weed herbicide, from American Home Products (now Wyeth) for $28 million. Later that year Central purchased All-Glass Aquarium Company, a manufacturer and marketer of aquariums and related products.

As a result of no longer being the distributor of Scotts products, Central closed 13 of its distribution centers in 2001. Central announced the next year that it would restate its financial results for 1998 through 2002. The company said the changes would improve fiscal 2001 net results by $2 million, but decrease net results by $1.7 million in 2000, $0.3 million in 1999, and $0.1 million in 1998. Also that year Mars' Kal Kan Division and Arch Chemicals stopped using Central as a distributor.

Remaining with Central as chairman, Brown handed over the CEO reins to president Glenn Novotny in June 2003. The next month Central acquired a 49% stake in E. M. Matson, a lawn and garden manufacturer in the western US.

In 2004 the company completed a menagerie's worth of acquisitions: Kent Marine, an aquarium supplements maker; New England Pottery, which sells decorative pottery and Christmas items (from Heritage Partners); Lawrence plc's pet products division, Interpet; KRB Seed, which does business as Budd Seed (Rebel and Palmer's Pride grass-seed brands); and Energy Savers Unlimited, which distributes aquarium lighting systems and related environmental controls and conditioners.

EXECUTIVES

Chairman and CEO: William E. Brown, age 67
EVP, CFO, and Secretary: Stuart W. Booth, age 58
CIO: John A. Casella
SVP Sales, Garden Group: Paul Duval
SVP Sales and Trade Relations: Tim Vokes
VP Investor Relations and Assistant Secretary:
Paul J. Warburg
VP Corporate Development: Wesley C. (Wes) Davidson
VP, Treasurer, and Assistant Secretary:
Roger J. Fleischmann Jr.
VP Operations Management: Carl Peterson
President, Avian and Small Animal: Chris Mings
President, T.F.H. Publications: Glen Axelrod
President, Business Development: James V. (Jim) Heim, age 54
President, Central Life Sciences:
Kay M. Schwichtenberg
President, Breeder's Choice: Rick Taylor
President, Aquatics: Mark S. Cavanaugh
President, Distribution Pet Products: Jeff Sutherland
President, Central Garden Group: Michael Reed, age 61
President, Garden Décor: Bruce Cazenave
President, Four Paws Products: Allen J. Simon
President, Excel Marketing Garden Group:
Fredric W. Vogelgesang
President, Pet Products: Glen Fleischer
Director Human Resources: Stanley L. Bulger
Auditors: Deloitte & Touche LLP

LOCATIONS

HQ: Central Garden & Pet Company
1340 Treat Blvd., Ste. 600, Walnut Creek, CA 94597
Phone: 925-948-4000   **Fax:** 925-287-0601
Web: www.central.com

PRODUCTS/OPERATIONS

2008 Sales

	$ mil.	% of total
Pet products	897.8	53
Garden products	807.6	47
Total	**1,705.4**	**100**

Selected Products and Brands

Pet products
   Aquatics (All-Glass Aquarium, ESU, Kent Marine, Oceanic)
   Bird and small animal (Canopy Scientific, Kaytee, Super Pet)
   Dog and cat (Four Paws, Interpet, Nylabone, Pet Select, TFH)
   Insect control and animal health (Pre-Strike, Wellmark, Zodiac)
Garden products
   Garden decor and pottery (GKI/Bethlehem Lighting, Matthews Four Seasons, New England Pottery, Norcal Pottery)
   Grass seed (Lofts Seed, Pennington, Rebel)
   Weed, insect, and pest control (AMDRO, Grant's, IMAGE, Lilly Miller, Over'n Out, Sevin)
   Wild bird (Cedar Works, Kaytee, and Pennington)

COMPETITORS

A.C. Graham
Bayer CropScience
Boss Holdings
Dow AgroSciences
Hartz Mountain
Meda Pharmaceuticals
Petmate
Rollins, Inc.
Sara Lee Household and Body Care
Scotts Miracle-Gro
Spectrum Brands
Virbac Corporation

HISTORICAL FINANCIALS

Company Type: Public

Income Statement

FYE: Last Saturday in September

	REVENUE ($ mil.)	NET INCOME ($ mil.)	NET PROFIT MARGIN	EMPLOYEES
9/08	1,705.4	(267.3)	—	4,600
9/07	1,671.1	32.3	1.9%	4,860
9/06	1,621.5	65.5	4.0%	4,865
9/05	1,380.6	53.8	3.9%	4,800
9/04	1,266.5	41.3	3.3%	4,400
Annual Growth	**7.7%**	—	—	**1.1%**

2008 Year-End Financials

Debt ratio: 102.2%
Return on equity: —
Cash ($ mil.): 27
Current ratio: 3.04
Long-term debt ($ mil.): 520

No. of shares (mil.): 70
Dividends
   Yield: 0.0%
   Payout: —
Market value ($ mil.): 415

Stock History

NASDAQ (GS): CENTA

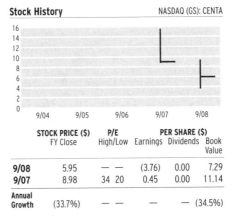

	STOCK PRICE ($) FY Close	P/E High/Low	PER SHARE ($) Earnings	Dividends	Book Value
9/08	5.95	— —	(3.76)	0.00	7.29
9/07	8.98	34 20	0.45	0.00	11.14
Annual Growth	**(33.7%)**	— —	—	—	**(34.5%)**

CenturyTel, Inc.

Bright lights and big cities are not necessarily for CenturyTel. The company mainly provides local telephone services in rural areas, as well as network access to other carriers and businesses. It also offers long-distance and Internet access. It serves about 2 million local voice lines and provides Internet access to about 600,000 subscribers in 23 states throughout the US. CenturyTel's core service areas are located in Alabama, Arkansas, Missouri, Washington, and Wisconsin. Additionally, the company provides paid television service to residential customers through a deal with DISH Network. Its other services include commercial printing, database management, and direct mail.

CenturyTel paid $11.6 billion in stock and debt to buy Overland Park, Kansas-based local phone company Embarq. Shareholders of Embarq own two-thirds of the combined company, while CenturyTel investors control the remaining shares. CenturyTel chief Glen Post remained in the top executive spot.

The purchase gives CenturyTel greater access to the metropolitan and suburban markets where Embarq operates, but it also puts the company up against stiffer competition from other carriers that also vie for customers in those areas. The new name of the combined company will be CenturyLink once regulatory approval for the deal is granted by the FCC; it will have operations in 33 states and serve more than 7 million local exchange accounts and 2 million broadband subscribers.

Looking ahead to new opportunities, in 2008 CenturyTel paid about $150 million to the FCC for wireless spectrum licenses slated for commercial availability during 2009. The company said that it may develop wireless voice and data services to take advantage of these resources in the future.

HISTORY

Today's CenturyTel began in 1930 when Marie and William Clarke Williams bought the Oak Ridge Telephone Company in Oak Ridge, Louisiana. In 1946 they gave the 75-line company as a wedding present to their son, Clarke, who launched a course of growth by acquisition, buying the Marion, Louisiana, telephone exchange in

1950 (Clarke Williams remained active in the company until his death in 2002). The company was renamed Century Telephone Enterprises in 1971; it went public in 1978.

Century bought local-exchange and cellular networks, building regional clusters. States targeted during the early to mid-1990s included Louisiana, Michigan, Mississippi, Ohio, Tennessee, and Texas. Century's biggest purchase came in 1997: It bought Pacific Telecom, Inc. (PTI) from electric utility PacifiCorp for $2.2 billion. Century gained operations in 12 western and Midwestern states and in Alaska, more than doubling its telephone customer base.

Also in 1997 Century merged its Metro Access Networks (MAN) subsidiary into Brooks Fiber and became Brooks' largest shareholder. Brooks' shares rose when WorldCom agreed to buy it, and Century sold 85% of its interest in Brooks.

The company rolled out the CenturyTel brand name in 1998 and bought Ameritech's local-exchange and directory operations in 21 Wisconsin communities. To help pay for the acquisition, the carrier sold its Alaska operations in 1999 to Alaska Communications Systems Holdings, a firm headed by former PTI executives. It also bought the Montana ISP DigiSys.

CenturyTel purchased nearly 500,000 access lines from GTE (now Verizon) in Arkansas, Missouri, and Wisconsin in 2000 and the next year sold its PCS licenses to Leap Wireless.

ALLTEL offered to buy CenturyTel in 2001 for $6.1 billion in cash and stock and $3.3 billion in assumed debt. ALLTEL announced the offer to the public after being told by CenturyTel that the company was not for sale. CenturyTel subsequently sued ALLTEL for releasing information about the company's plans. Tensions eased, however, and in 2002 the two companies reached the agreement that sent CenturyTel's wireless operations, which served more than 800,000 customers in six states, to ALLTEL. The $1.6 billion cash deal enabled the company to expand its fixed-line business, including the acquisition that year of 675,000 switched phone lines in Alabama and Missouri from Verizon Communications for about $2.2 billion.

In 2003 CenturyTel acquired the regional fiber-optic business of bankrupt wholesale transport services provider Digital Teleport in a deal valued at $38 million. It also acquired fiber transport assets in Arkansas, Missouri, and Illinois, from Level 3 Communications in a deal valued at about $16 million.

The company further expanded its network operations with the 2005 acquisition of the fiber-optic network and customer base of KMC Telecom's operations in Monroe and Shreveport, Louisiana, as well as metro fiber networks in 16 additional markets for $75 million in cash.

In 2007 CenturyTel purchased Madison River Communications for $830 million. The acquisition added more than 160,000 rural access lines to its books and gave the company ownership of an additional 2,400 miles of fiber network.

EXECUTIVES

Chairman: William A. (Bill) Owens, age 69
President and CEO: Glen F. Post III, age 56, $11,903,400 total compensation
COO: Karen A. Puckett, age 48, $4,930,398 total compensation
EVP and CFO: R. Stewart Ewing Jr., age 57, $4,890,503 total compensation
Corporate Leader, IT, Network Planning and Engineering, and Product Development: Dennis G. Huber

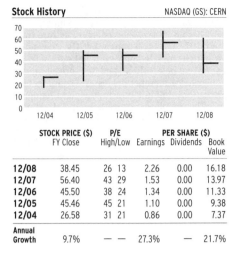

Stock History

NASDAQ (GS): CERN

	STOCK PRICE ($) FY Close	P/E High/Low		PER SHARE ($) Earnings	Dividends	Book Value
12/08	38.45	26	13	2.26	0.00	16.18
12/07	56.40	43	29	1.53	0.00	13.97
12/06	45.50	38	24	1.34	0.00	11.33
12/05	45.46	45	21	1.10	0.00	9.38
12/04	26.58	31	21	0.86	0.00	7.37
Annual Growth	9.7%	—	—	27.3%	—	21.7%

C.H. Robinson Worldwide

C.H. Robinson Worldwide (CHRW) keeps merchandise moving. A third-party logistics provider, the company arranges freight transportation using trucks, trains, ships, and airplanes belonging to other companies. It contracts with some 50,000 carriers. CHRW handles about 7.3 million shipments per year for its 32,000-plus customers, which include companies in the food and beverage, manufacturing, and retail industries. Together with overseeing freight transportation for its customers, it offers supply chain management services through some 225 offices. In addition, CHRW buys, sells, and transports fresh produce throughout the US, and its T-Chek unit provides fuel purchasing management services for motor carriers.

Truckload services are CHRW's primary transportation offering, but the company is endeavoring to diversify by providing more less-than-truckload and freight consolidation services. The company also hopes to sell more supply chain management services to its transportation customers.

Although CHRW does most of its business in the US, the company also has branch offices elsewhere in the Americas and in Europe and Asia. The company has been working to expand — especially outside North America — both through organic growth and through acquisitions.

Along these lines, in mid-2008 CHRW acquired Transera International Holdings, a project forwarding business based in Canada. Transera has office locations in Canada, Dubai, Singapore, and the US and has annual revenues of about $125 million. In addition, CHRW hopes to expand its wholesale produce business by promoting its own brands, "The Fresh 1" and organic line "OurWorld."

HISTORY

In the early 1900s Charles H. Robinson began a produce brokerage in Grand Forks, North Dakota. Robinson entered a partnership in 1905 with Nash Brothers, the leading wholesaler in North Dakota, and the company C.H. Robinson was born.

Robinson became president but soon relinquished control under mysterious circumstances (rumor had it he ran off with Annie Oakley). H. B. Finch took charge, and by 1913 a new company, Nash Finch, became C.H. Robinson's sole owner.

As a subsidiary, C.H. Robinson primarily procured produce for Nash Finch, which helped it expand into Illinois, Minnesota, Texas, and Wisconsin. To avoid FTC scrutiny over preferential treatment, Nash Finch split CHR into two units: C.H. Robinson Co., owned by employees of C.H. Robinson, which sold produce to Nash Finch warehouses; and C.H. Robinson, Inc., owned by Nash Finch.

After WWII the interstate highway system and refrigerated trucks changed the industry. No longer dependent on railroads, C.H. Robinson began charging for truck brokerage of perishables. The two companies formed by the 1940s split reunited under the C.H. Robinson name in the mid-1960s; Nash Finch kept a 25% stake in the company and sold the rest to employees. Not surprisingly, Nash Finch wanted to divert C.H. Robinson profits to its other businesses, so in 1976 C.H. Robinson employees bought out Nash Finch.

The next year D. R. "Sid" Verdoorn was named president and Looe Baker became chairman. They focused on increasing C.H. Robinson's data-processing capability and adding branch offices. In 1980 the Motor Carrier Act deregulated the transportation industry, and C.H. Robinson entered the freight-contracting business, acting as a middleman for all types of goods. The company grew rapidly, from about 30 offices in 1980 to more than 60 in 1990.

As part of its overall effort to become a full-service provider, C.H. Robinson formed its Intermodal Division (more than one mode of transport) in 1988. It also established an information services division (1991) and bought fruit juice concentrate distributor Daystar International (1993). By this time the company was working with more than 14,000 shippers and moving more than 500,000 shipments a year.

Meanwhile, C.H. Robinson had ventured overseas with the launch of its international division in 1989. It entered Mexico in 1990 and added airfreight operations and international freight forwarding through the 1992 purchase of C.S. Green International. In 1993 C.H. Robinson picked up a 30% stake in French motor carrier Transeco (acquiring the rest later) and opened offices in Mexico City, Chile, and Venezuela.

In 1997 the company went public and became C.H. Robinson Worldwide (CHRW); the next year Verdoorn, who was CEO, assumed the additional role of chairman.

The company acquired Argentina's Comexter transportation group in 1998 to gain market share in South America, and it expanded its European operation in 1999 through the purchase of Norminter, a French third-party logistics provider. Much closer to home, CHRW bought Eden Prairie-based Preferred Translocation Systems, a logistics provider to less-than-truckload carriers, and Chicago-based transportation provider American Backhaulers.

CHRW partnered with PaperExchange.com, Inc., in 2000 to provide an exclusive logistics service to members of PaperExchange.com, the global e-business marketplace for the pulp and paper industry.

CHRW continued to expand in 2002 with the purchase of Miami-based Smith Terminal Transportation Services. Verdoorn stepped down as CEO that year, and company president John Wiehoff was promoted to replace him.

The company acquired three US-based produce sourcing and marketing companies — FoodSource, Inc., FoodSource Procurement, and Epic Roots — in 2004 for a reported $270 million. Also that year, CHRW added seven offices in China by acquiring a Dalian-based freight forwarder, and in 2005 it gained operations in Germany, Italy, and the US by buying two freight forwarding companies, Hirdes Group Worldwide and Bussini Transport.

Verdoorn retired at the end of 2006, and Wiehoff succeeded him as chairman.

Also in 2006, CHRW bought US-based freight broker Payne, Lynch & Associates, as well as an India-based freight forwarder, Triune. The next year the company acquired US-based LXSI Services, a specialist in domestic airfreight and expedited ground transportation management that had gross revenue of about $25 million in 2006.

EXECUTIVES

Chairman and CEO: John P. Wiehoff, age 47, $2,784,393 total compensation
SVP and CFO: Chad M. Lindbloom, age 44, $1,103,412 total compensation
VP and CIO: Thomas K. (Tom) Mahlke
SVP: James P. (Jim) Lemke, age 41
SVP Transportation: Mark A. Walker, age 51, $990,293 total compensation
SVP Transportation: Scott A. Satterlee, age 40, $996,992 total compensation
SVP Transportation: James E. (Jim) Butts, age 53, $933,159 total compensation
VP Investor Relations and Public Affairs: Angela K. (Angie) Freeman
VP Human Resources: Laura Gillund
VP International Forwarding: Jeffrey W. Scovill
VP, General Counsel, and Secretary: Ben G. Campbell, age 43
President, T-Chek: Bryan D. Foe
Treasurer, Tax Director, and Assistant Secretary: Troy A. Renner
Auditors: Deloitte & Touche LLP

LOCATIONS

HQ: C.H. Robinson Worldwide, Inc.
14701 Charlson Rd., Eden Prairie, MN 55347
Phone: 952-937-8500 **Fax:** 952-937-6714
Web: www.chrobinson.com

2008 Sales

	% of total
US	90
Other countries	10
Total	**100**

PRODUCTS/OPERATIONS

2008 Sales

	$ mil.	% of total
Transportation	7,129.6	83
Sourcing	1,398.2	16
Information services	50.8	1
Total	**8,578.6**	**100**

COMPETITORS

APL Logistics
Cass Information Systems
CEVA Logistics
Chiquita Brands
Comdata
CorTrans Logistics
DB Schenker
DHL
Dole Food
Expeditors
FedEx Trade Networks
Fresh Del Monte Produce
Greatwide Logistics
Hub Group
Kuehne + Nagel International
Menlo Worldwide
Pacer Transportation Solutions
Panalpina
Penske Truck Leasing
Ryder System
Schneider Logistics
Transplace
UPS Supply Chain Solutions
YRC Logistics

HISTORICAL FINANCIALS

Company Type: Public

Income Statement

FYE: December 31

	REVENUE ($ mil.)	NET INCOME ($ mil.)	NET PROFIT MARGIN	EMPLOYEES
12/08	8,578.6	359.2	4.2%	7,961
12/07	7,316.2	324.3	4.4%	7,332
12/06	6,556.2	266.9	4.1%	6,768
12/05	5,726.9	203.4	3.6%	5,776
12/04	4,375.0	137.3	3.1%	4,806
Annual Growth	18.3%	27.2%	—	13.4%

2008 Year-End Financials

Debt ratio: —
Return on equity: 33.4%
Cash ($ mil.): 495
Current ratio: 1.93
Long-term debt ($ mil.): —
No. of shares (mil.): 168
Dividends
  Yield: 1.6%
  Payout: 43.3%
Market value ($ mil.): 9,266

Stock History

NASDAQ (GS): CHRW

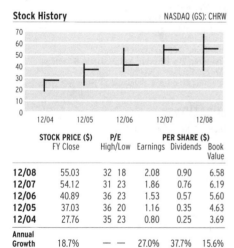

	STOCK PRICE ($) FY Close	P/E High	P/E Low	PER SHARE ($) Earnings	PER SHARE ($) Dividends	PER SHARE ($) Book Value
12/08	55.03	32	18	2.08	0.90	6.58
12/07	54.12	31	23	1.86	0.76	6.19
12/06	40.89	36	23	1.53	0.57	5.60
12/05	37.03	36	20	1.16	0.35	4.63
12/04	27.76	35	23	0.80	0.25	3.69
Annual Growth	18.7%	—	—	27.0%	37.7%	15.6%

Champion Enterprises

Champion Enterprises is constantly jostling to be the #1 builder of manufactured homes in the US, along with rival Palm Harbor. The company sells about 11,000 homes annually. It mainly produces single-family ranch-style homes, but it also makes townhouses, duplexes, and steel-framed modular buildings for commercial use. Sizes range from 400 sq. ft. to 4,000 sq. ft. and retail prices of the homes range from $25,000 to more than $200,000 (averaging $160,000). Champion operates some 30 plants in North American and the UK. Homes are sold through 14 company-owned retail centers in California and through about 1,200 independent retailers, including 725 Champion Home Centers.

Champion spent much of the first half of the decade closing and consolidating plants and retail facilities to eliminate underperforming operations. Once it pared down, it began buying.

Champion made its overseas debut in 2006 with its acquisition of UK manufacturer Calsafe Group and its operating subsidiary Caledonian Building Systems. Its international division now operates five manufacturing plants in the UK and competes in the custom modular industry. Its steel-framed modular buildings are used in prisons, military buildings, and multi-story hotels and residences. Major customers include Her Majesty's Prison Service and the UK Ministry of Defence. Two years later Champion purchased ModularUK Building Systems, which makes steel-framed buildings for the health care, education, and commercial sectors.

Champion followed its expansion into the UK with the purchase of Canada's SRI Homes, a leading producer of homes that operates manufacturing facilities in the provinces of Alberta, British Columbia, and Saskatchewan. That buy gave Champion entry into one of the strongest housing markets in North America, and it continues to report strong growth in that region.

By diversifying its product line and geographic reach Champion was able to weather a major housing slowdown in the US during 2008. While Champion saw a leveling off in some of its markets (especially in the US where it was forced to shut some plants), sales in Canada remained strong. The credit crisis in the UK meant project delays and a lack of project financing for the business, but demand for its product was high.

Wells Fargo is Champion's largest shareholder, with a 19% stake. Other principal owners include Columbia Wanger Asset Management (11%) and First Pacific Advisors (10%).

HISTORY

Champion Home Builders started in 1953, just in time to take advantage of the burgeoning postwar American economy and the passage of a 1956 law allowing mobile homes to be up to 10 feet wide. The increase made mobile homes increasingly popular — by 1960 a majority were "10-wides." The change shifted the main benefit of mobile homes from mobility to affordability. Champion prospered, and it went public in 1962. By the mid-1960s it was one of the leaders in its market.

Part of Champion's success could be attributed to its vertically integrated manufacturing process. Champion made and installed all the components in a home, from plumbing to drapes. This policy increased efficiency, and productivity was twice that of most of its rivals. Despite these advantages, the mid-1970s recession hit the company hard. Industry sales fell about a third from their 1972 peak. Champion felt the recession's brunt in its mobile-home sales, but sales of recreational vehicles (RVs) and low-priced motor homes helped temper the losses. The increase of prices for site-built housing helped Champion and other mobile-home makers out of the slump.

At the start of the 1980s, Champion recovered briefly, but by the mid-1980s the company was again struggling. By 1990 the firm had lost $30 million over the previous five years and was considering bankruptcy proceedings. Walter Young took over that year and quickly revamped the company. To stave off bankruptcy, Young sold some businesses (RV making and component manufacturing) for much-needed cash. Young also gutted the central office and eliminated 248 of 260 jobs.

Champion acquired Dutch Housing in 1994 and Chandeleur Homes and Crest Ridge Homes a year later. It acquired Redman Industries, the #3 US manufactured-housing builder at the time (Champion was #2), in 1996. The acquisition pushed Champion to the top spot in terms of sales that year. In addition, Champion opened five new plants.

In 1998 the company bought manufactured-housing seller The ICA Group, operator of 23 retail outlets. In 1999 Champion bought Care Free Homes (Utah), Central Mississippi Manufactured Housing, Homes of Merit (Florida), and Heartland Homes (Texas).

Although sales increased, Champion's profits nearly halved in 1999 because of bad inventory control, excess retail sites, and tighter consumer financing requirements. In response, the company closed or consolidated eight manufacturing plants and streamlined and upgraded inventory-control processes. Slowing demand and increased competition forced the company to close more than 60 retail outlets and seven of its factories in 2000. The company idled two additional factories and 30 more retail centers in 2001.

The next year Champion closed 12 manufacturing facilities and 126 of its retail sales centers, with a reduction of jobs estimated at 1,500, or 15% of its total workforce.

Champion closed five manufacturing plants (in Arizona, Georgia, Kentucky, North Carolina, and Texas) in 2003 and moved production at a facility in Alabama to an idle plant. The company cut its workforce by 13% (about 1,000 jobs) and shuttered 35 retail centers.

The next year Champion sold its western retail region, which included eight retail sales operations in Colorado, Idaho, Nevada, Utah, and Washington, to Blaser Holding, Inc., for about $4 million. Champion also sold three retail sales centers in Kentucky and one in Texas in 2004.

Champion completed the sale of its traditional retail locations in 2005. The same year, in the aftermath of Hurricane Katrina, Champion received a $60 million order from the Federal Emergency Management Agency (FEMA) to build some 2,000 homes for displaced storm victims. Late in the year Champion acquired New Era Building Systems and its Castle Housing of Pennsylvania and Carolina Building Solutions affiliates. The companies manufacture modular housing in Pennsylvania and North Carolina.

Still on the acquisition track, Champion acquired modular builder Highland Manufacturing for $23 million early in 2006 and Canadian prefab home company SRI Homes in 2007.

EXECUTIVES

Chairman, President, and CEO:
William C. (Bill) Griffiths, age 58,
$899,047 total compensation
EVP, CFO, and Treasurer: Phyllis A. Knight, age 46,
$508,356 total compensation
SVP, General Counsel, and Secretary:
Roger K. Scholten, age 54,
$352,374 total compensation
VP and Controller: Richard P. (Rick) Hevelhorst, age 61,
$237,012 total compensation
VP, Western Region: Don DeHart
VP, Eastern Region: Richard Egger
VP, Investor Relations: Laurie Van Raemdonck
VP, Canadian Region: Kenneth Josuttes
Auditors: Ernst & Young LLP

LOCATIONS

HQ: Champion Enterprises, Inc.
755 W. Big Beaver, Ste. 1000, Troy, MI 48084
Phone: 248-614-8200   **Fax:** 248-273-4208
Web: www.championhomes.net

2008 Sales

	$ mil.	% of total
US	591.1	70
UK	279.7	22
Canada	162.4	8
Total	**1,033.2**	**100**

PRODUCTS/OPERATIONS

2008 Sales

	$ mil.	% of total
Manufacturing	727.3	70
International	279.7	27
Retail	36.5	3
Adjustments	(10.3)	—
Total	**1,033.2**	**100**

Selected Subsidiaries

CBS Monaco Limited
   Calsafe Group Limited
      Caledonian Building Systems Limited
Champion Enterprises Management Co.
Champion Homes of Boaz, Inc.
Dutch Housing, Inc.
Star Fleet, Inc.
Highland Acquisition Corp.
Highland Manufacturing Company, LLC
Homes of Merit, Inc.
Moduline Industries (Canada)
   SRI Homes
New Era Building Systems, Inc.
North American Housing Corp.
Redman Industries, Inc.
   Redman Homes, Inc.
      Western Homes Corporation

COMPETITORS

American Homestar
Cavalier Homes
Cavco
Clayton Homes
Coachmen
Dynamic Homes
Fairmont Homes
Fleetwood Enterprises
Four Seasons Housing
Horton Industries
Liberty Homes
Nobility Homes
Origen Financial
Palm Harbor Homes
Skyline
Southern Energy Homes
Sunshine Homes
Wraith

HISTORICAL FINANCIALS

Company Type: Public

Income Statement   FYE: Saturday nearest December 31

	REVENUE ($ mil.)	NET INCOME ($ mil.)	NET PROFIT MARGIN	EMPLOYEES
12/08	1,033.2	(199.5)	—	4,100
12/07	1,273.5	7.2	0.6%	6,500
12/06	1,364.6	138.3	10.1%	7,000
12/05	1,272.6	37.8	3.0%	7,400
12/04	1,150.2	17.0	1.5%	6,800
Annual Growth	**(2.6%)**	**—**	**—**	**(11.9%)**

2008 Year-End Financials

Debt ratio: 346.5%
Return on equity: —
Cash ($ mil.): 53
Current ratio: 0.80
Long-term debt ($ mil.): 301

No. of shares (mil.): 78
Dividends
Yield: 0.0%
Payout: —
Market value ($ mil.): 44

Stock History   NYSE: CHB

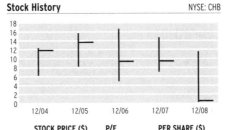

	STOCK PRICE ($) FY Close	P/E High/Low		Earnings	Dividends	Book Value
12/08	0.56	—	—	(2.57)	0.00	1.12
12/07	9.42	162	80	0.09	0.00	4.11
12/06	9.36	9	3	1.78	0.00	3.88
12/05	13.62	32	17	0.48	0.00	1.89
12/04	11.82	58	30	0.21	0.00	0.99
Annual Growth	**(53.3%)**	**—**	**—**	**—**	**—**	**2.9%**

Charles Schwab

The once-rebellious Charles Schwab is all grown up. The discount broker now offers the same traditional brokerage services it shunned some three decades ago. Schwab manages more than $1 trillion in assets for more than 8 million individual and institutional clients. Traders can access its services via telephone, wireless device, the Internet, and through more than 300 US offices. Besides discount brokerage, the firm offers financial research, advice, and planning; investment management; retirement plans; and proprietary Schwab and Laudus mutual funds; in addition to mortgages, CDs, and other banking products through its Charles Schwab Bank unit.

Schwab's primary business remains making trades for investors who make their own decisions. Its services include futures and commodities trading, access to IPOs, and investment educational material. Schwab's OneSource service offers investors access to more than 2,000 no-load funds. The company also provides access to nearly 21,000 bonds, bond funds, and other fixed-income investment products. It provides trading and support services to independent investment advisors, as well.

Through Charles Schwab Bank, the company remains in step with the industrywide movement toward one-stop shopping for financial services. Schwab has also reduced its minimum investment requirement in its brokerage accounts and savings accounts, and instituted a simpler, less-expensive trading fee structure that recalls the company's discount roots.

Growing its service offerings through acquisitions, Schwab acquired The 401(k) Companies from Nationwide Financial Services in 2007. The addition complements the company's existing Charles Schwab Trust subsidiary, which serves as a trustee for employee benefit plans.

Also in 2007 Schwab sold U.S. Trust to Bank of America for some $3.3 billion in cash, and shut down its CyberTrader day trading arm and merged the direct-access brokerage's business with its own.

Charles Schwab owns 18% of his namesake firm. He was succeeded as CEO of the company by president and COO Walter Bettinger II in October 2008. Charles Schwab remained chairman.

HISTORY

During the 1960s Stanford graduate Charles Schwab founded First Commander Corp., which managed investments and published a newsletter. But he failed to properly register with the SEC, and after a hiatus, he returned to the business under the name Charles Schwab & Co. in 1971. Initially a full-service broker, Schwab moved into discount brokerage after the SEC outlawed fixed commissions in 1975. While most brokers defiantly raised commissions, Schwab cut its rates steeply.

From 1977 to 1983 Schwab's client list increased thirtyfold, and revenues grew from $4.6 million to $126.5 million, enabling the firm to automate its operations and develop cash-management account systems. To gain capital, Charles sold the company to BankAmerica (now Bank of America) in 1983. Schwab grew, but federal regulations prevented expansion into such services as mutual funds and telephone trading. Charles bought his company back in 1987 and took it public. When the stock market crashed later that year, trading volume fell by nearly half, from 17,900 per day. Stung, Schwab diversified further, offering new fee-based services. Commission revenues fell from 64% of sales in 1987 to 39% in 1990, but by 1995 the long bull market had pushed commissions to more than 50%.

In 1989 Schwab introduced TeleBroker, a 24-hour Touch-Tone telephone trading service available in English, Spanish, Mandarin, or Cantonese.

Schwab continued to diversify, courting independent financial advisors. Other buys included Mayer & Schweitzer (1991, now Schwab Capital Markets), an OTC market maker that accounted for about 7% of all NASDAQ trades. In 1993 the firm opened its first overseas office in London, but traded only in dollar-denominated stocks until it bought Share-Link (later Charles Schwab Europe), the UK's largest discount brokerage, in 1995. It subsequently sold the British pound sterling brokerage business to Barclays PLC, although it has maintained its US dollar business in the UK.

During the next year Schwab made a concerted effort to build its retirement services by creating a 401(k) administration and investment services unit. In 1997 Schwab allied with J.P. Morgan, Hambrecht & Quist (now J.P. Morgan H&Q), and Credit Suisse First Boston (CSFB) to give its customers access to IPOs; the next year the relationship with CSFB deepened to give Schwab access to debt offerings. In late 1997 and early 1998 Schwab reorganized to reflect its new business lines. The firm also began recruiting talent rather than promoting from within.

Expansion was key at the turn of the century. In 1999 Schwab moved toward more broker-advised investing: It inked a deal (geared toward its retirement products customers) with online financial advice firm Financial Engines, and introduced Velocity, a desktop system designed to make trading easier for fiscally endowed investors. In 2000 Schwab bought online broker CyBerCorp (now CyberTrader), as well as U.S. Trust, which markets to affluent clients.

While Schwab's World Trade Center offices were destroyed by the September 11 terrorist attacks, the company did not lose any of its New York staff.

To pare expenses, Schwab reduced its workforce by about 35% between 2000 and 2003.

Founder and chairman Charles Schwab relinquished his role of co-CEO in early 2003, only to move back into the driver's seat in mid-2004 when former CEO David Pottruck was asked to step down by the company's board.

One of Schwab's first orders of business was to reexamine the company's 2004 acquisition of SoundView Technology Group, which was combined with its Capital Markets operations to form Schwab SoundView Capital Markets. While the purchase was intended to help the company beef up its services for institutional investors, Schwab said that SoundView lacked "synergy" with the company's tradition of supporting the individual investor and sold the business to Swiss bank UBS.

EXECUTIVES

Chairman: Charles R. (Chuck) Schwab, age 71, $6,473,752 total compensation
President, CEO, and Director; President and CEO, Charles Schwab & Co.: Walter W. (Walt) Bettinger II, age 48, $10,114,540 total compensation
EVP and CFO: Joseph R. Martinetto, age 46, $1,888,477 total compensation
EVP Shared Support Services: Jan Hier-King, age 53
EVP and Chief Marketing Officer: Rebecca (Becky) Saeger, age 53, $3,218,103 total compensation
SVP and Chief Investment Strategist, Charles Schwab and Company: Elizabeth Ann (Liz Ann) Sonders
Chief Investment Officer, Charles Schwab Investment Management: Jeffrey Mortimer
EVP, General Counsel, and Secretary: Carrie E. Dwyer, age 58, $4,121,198 total compensation
EVP Investment Management Services: Randall W. Merk, age 53
EVP Shared Strategic Services: John S. Clendening
EVP Institutional Services: James D. McCool, age 50, $2,866,472 total compensation
EVP Investor Services: Benjamin L. Brigeman, age 46
EVP Human Resources and Employee Services: Jay L. Allen, age 52
EVP Schwab Investor Development: Lisa K. Hunt
SVP Investor Relations: Richard G. Fowler
SVP Investor Services, Charles Schwab and Company: Andy Gill
SVP Corporate Public Relations: Greg Gable
President, Schwab Charitable: Kimberly Wright-Violich
Auditors: Deloitte & Touche LLP

LOCATIONS

HQ: The Charles Schwab Corporation
120 Kearny St., San Francisco, CA 94104
Phone: 415-636-7000   **Fax:** 415-636-9820
Web: www.schwab.com

PRODUCTS/OPERATIONS

2008 Sales

	$ mil.	% of total
Asset management & administration fees	2,369.0	46
Interest	1,648.0	32
Trading revenue	1,081.5	21
Other	51.5	1
Total	**5,150.0**	**100**

Selected Subsidiaries

Charles Schwab Bank
Charles Schwab Investment Management, Inc. (mutual fund investment adviser)
Schwab Holdings, Inc.
  Charles Schwab & Co., Inc. (securities broker-dealer)

COMPETITORS

Ameriprise	Morgan Stanley
Bank of America	Principal Financial
Citigroup	Prudential
E*TRADE Financial	Raymond James Financial
Edward Jones	Scottrade
FMR	ShareBuilder
Franklin Resources	TD Ameritrade
John Hancock Financial	UBS Financial Services
Legg Mason	The Vanguard Group

HISTORICAL FINANCIALS

Company Type: Public

Income Statement

FYE: December 31

	REVENUE ($ mil.)	NET INCOME ($ mil.)	NET PROFIT MARGIN	EMPLOYEES
12/08	5,150.0	1,212.0	23.5%	13,400
12/07	4,994.0	2,407.0	48.2%	13,300
12/06	4,309.0	1,227.0	28.5%	12,400
12/05	4,464.0	725.0	16.2%	14,000
12/04	4,202.0	286.0	6.8%	14,200
Annual Growth	**5.2%**	**43.5%**	**—**	**(1.4%)**

2008 Year-End Financials

Debt ratio: 21.7%
Return on equity: 31.1%
Cash ($ mil.): 20,127
Current ratio: —
Long-term debt ($ mil.): 883
No. of shares (mil.): 1,161
Dividends
  Yield: 1.4%
  Payout: 21.0%
Market value ($ mil.): 18,771

Stock History

NASDAQ (GS): SCHW

	STOCK PRICE ($) FY Close	P/E High/Low		PER SHARE ($) Earnings	Dividends	Book Value
12/08	16.17	27	10	1.05	0.22	3.50
12/07	25.55	13	9	1.97	0.20	3.21
12/06	19.34	21	15	0.95	0.14	4.31
12/05	14.67	29	18	0.55	0.09	3.83
12/04	11.96	66	38	0.21	0.07	3.78
Annual Growth	**7.8%**	**—**	**—**	**49.5%**	**33.1%**	**(1.9%)**

Charming Shoppes

Charming Shoppes has got the women's plus-size market covered. The company runs some 2,300 stores (and related Web sites) nationwide at three apparel chains that cater to the amply proportioned: about 900 Fashion Bug stores that sell moderately priced apparel and accessories in girls, juniors, misses, and plus sizes; about 460 Catherines Plus Size stores; and 890 Lane Bryant and Lane Bryant Outlet stores. Across the US, Charming Shoppes serves low- to middle-income women and teens who follow fashion styles rather than set them. The company's purchase of Lane Bryant from Limited Brands in 2001 elevated Charming Shoppes to #1 in the plus-size market. It sold its Crosstown Traders catalog business in 2008.

About half of American women wear size 14 or larger and Americans continue to gain weight, presenting Charming Shoppes with a growth market. (Indeed, plus-size apparel contributes about 80% of the company's sales.) Nevertheless, in today's less-than-charming environment for women's apparel retailers, Charming Shoppes is slimming down. In 2008 the retailer cut jobs, closed more than 100 stores, and sold its misses apparel catalog business Crosstown Traders (acquired in mid-2005) to Orchard Brands for about $35 million. The sale included eight catalog titles and related e-commerce sites, including Old Pueblo Traders, Bedford Fair, Willow Ridge, and Lew Magram, among others. The company also attempted to sell its Figi's gift catalog business but didn't find interested suitors with enough money. Going forward, it plans to shut down its Lane Bryant Woman catalog operation in 2010 to focus on its Lane Bryant retail business.

It's also outsourcing its credit card business to reduce debt. In August 2009 Charming Shoppes inked a deal with Alliance Data Systems Corporation, which will assume operations of the Charming Shoppes-branded credit card programs by the end of 2009. The move involves the purchase of credit card files and service center operations.

The company's restructuring is being led by turnaround specialist James Fogarty, who joined Charming Shoppes as president and CEO in April 2009. Fogarty succeeded chairman Alan Rosskamm, who served as interim chief executive following the resignation of CEO Dorrit Bern in July 2008. Bern left the company under pressure from the board of directors and investors dissatisfied with the retailer's slumping sales and stock performance.

The divestitures, past and pending, leave Charming Shoppes focused on its three core retail brands. The company's stores are primarily located in suburban areas and small towns.

To further expand its Lane Bryant retail channel, Charming Shoppes assumed the leases of 75 Casual Corner outlet stores from Retail Brand Alliance. (RBA sold the Casual Corner chain in 2005 to liquidator Gordon Brothers, which then shut it down.) The stores reopened under the Lane Bryant Outlet banner in mid-2006.

HISTORY

Morris and Arthur Sidewater opened their first women's apparel store, called Charm Shoppes, in Philadelphia in 1940. Morris, a buyer with apparel company Associated Merchandising, and Arthur, who performed as a dancer on tour with

Red Skelton, were challenged from the start: Legal notice came during their first week that the "Charm" name was already taken. The brothers responded by changing the name of the store to Charming Shoppes.

By the end of the 1940s, the brothers began taking on partners to add new stores, with the new partners becoming store managers of the outlets they opened. In 1951 the brothers formed what would become the most significant of their partnerships with a friend of Arthur's, David Wachs, and David's brother Ellis. That year the Sidewater and Wachs brothers opened a store in Norristown, Pennsylvania; later they added another store in Woodbury, New Jersey.

During the 1960s the pairs of brothers moved to follow the steady flight of consumers to malls and large shopping centers, opening new stores in those areas under the Fashion Bug name and renaming old stores. By 1971, the year the company went public, Charming Shoppes operated 21 stores and had a total of 18 partners. As rent at the mall climbed in the mid-1970s, the company began expanding into cheaper strip malls, where rents were less than half those in enclosed malls.

As it entered the 1980s, Charming Shoppes operated nearly 160 stores. That decade marked a period of rapid expansion for the company. Charming Shoppes began opening Fashion Bug Plus stores (and departments within existing stores), featuring sizes for larger women. By 1985 it had more than 500 stores (about 65% of which were located in strip malls).

During the last half of the decade, Charming Shoppes began changing its selection from name brands to private brands. In 1988 David became CEO, replacing Morris, who had served as CEO since the company went public. Although sales had increased unabated for two decades, shrinking profits led the company to curtail expansion, but only slightly. By the end of 1989, it operated more than 900 outlets.

Charming Shoppes continued to grow and increase sales, adding menswear in the early 1990s. With more than 1,400 stores in 1995, the company named Dorrit Bern, a former group VP of apparel and home merchandise at Sears, as CEO.

That year Charming Shoppes reported its biggest loss of $139 million. Bern promptly laid off a third of the company's workforce. She closed nearly 300 poorly performing stores and revamped Charming Shoppes' merchandising strategy, stemming losses in 1996 and bringing the company back to profitability the next year.

In 1998 Charming Shoppes closed another 65 poorly performing stores, replacing them with about 65 new sites. Charming Shoppes bought plus-sized chain Modern Woman and integrated the stores with its acquisition of 436-store Catherines Plus Size chain.

Charming Shoppes positioned itself as a leader in plus-size women's apparel in 2001 with the $335 million purchase of plus-size apparel chain Lane Bryant (with more than 650 stores) from retailer The Limited.

In a move to cut out its biggest drains on capital, the company closed its 80-store Added Dimensions and The Answer plus-size chains, closed 130 Fashion Bug stores, and converted about 45 of its Fashion Bug stores to the more successful Lane Bryant format in 2002.

EXECUTIVES

Chairman: Alan Rosskamm, age 59
President, CEO, and Director: James P. (Jim) Fogarty, age 40
EVP and COO; Interim President, Petite Sophisticate Outlet: Joseph M. (Joe) Baron, age 61, $949,464 total compensation
EVP and CFO: Eric M. Specter, age 51, $824,689 total compensation
SVP and CIO: Denis F. Gingue
EVP Quality Assurance, Control and Technical Design: Erna Zint
EVP, General Counsel, and Secretary: Colin D. Stern, age 60, $850,681 total compensation
EVP Corporate and Labor Relations, and Business Ethics: Anthony A. DeSabato, age 60
EVP Supply Chain Management, Information Technology, and Shared Business Services: James G. (Jim) Bloise, age 65, $678,373 total compensation
EVP Global Sourcing and Business Transformation: Anthony M. (Tony) Romano, age 46
EVP Human Resources: Gale H. Varma, age 58
SVP Real Estate: Jonathon Graub
SVP General Merchandising, Fashion Bug: Rachel A. Ungaro
SVP and Corporate Controller: John J. Sullivan, age 62
SVP Finance, Treasury, and Business Development: Steven R. Wishner, age 57
SVP Business Strategy and Multi-Channel Integration and CFO, Crosstown Traders: Edwin A. Neumann
SVP General Merchandising, Fashion Bug: James A. Ferree
VP Corporate Human Resources: Robert M. (Bob) Chessen
VP Investor Relations: Gayle M. Coolick
VP Corporate Human Resources: Stephen R. Puterbaugh
Auditors: Ernst & Young LLP

LOCATIONS

HQ: Charming Shoppes, Inc.
450 Winks Ln., Bensalem, PA 19020
Phone: 215-245-9100   **Fax:** 215-633-4640
Web: www.charmingshoppes.com

PRODUCTS/OPERATIONS

2009 Stores

	No.
Fashion Bug	897
Lane Bryant & Lane Bryant Outlet	892
Catherines Plus Sizes	463
Petite Sophisticate Outlet	49
Total	**2,301**

2009 Sales

	$ mil.	% of total
Retail	2,292.1	93
Direct-to-consumer	167.6	7
Other	15.2	—
Total	**2,474.9**	**100**

Selected Operations

Catalogs and E-commerce
 Figi's
 Lane Bryant Woman
Retail Stores
 Catherines Plus Sizes
 Fashion Bug
 Lane Bryant
 Lane Bryant Outlet
 Petite Sophisticate Outlet

COMPETITORS

Burlington Coat Factory
Cato
Charlotte Russe Holding
Chico's FAS
Claire's Stores
Coldwater Creek
Deb Shops
dELiA*s
Dress Barn
Foot Locker
The Gap
Hot Topic
J. C. Penney
Kmart
Kohl's
Redcats
Ross Stores
Sears
Stage Stores
Stein Mart
Talbots
Target
TJX Companies
Tween Brands
Wal-Mart

HISTORICAL FINANCIALS

Company Type: Public

Income Statement

FYE: Saturday nearest January 31

	REVENUE ($ mil.)	NET INCOME ($ mil.)	NET PROFIT MARGIN	EMPLOYEES
1/09	2,474.9	(244.2)	—	28,700
1/08	3,010.0	(84.3)	—	30,200
1/07	3,067.5	108.9	3.6%	30,000
1/06	2,755.7	99.4	3.6%	28,000
1/05	2,332.3	64.5	2.8%	27,000
Annual Growth	**1.5%**	**—**	**—**	**1.5%**

2009 Year-End Financials

Debt ratio: 65.6%
Return on equity: —
Cash ($ mil.): 94
Current ratio: 2.40
Long-term debt ($ mil.): 306
No. of shares (mil.): 116
Dividends
 Yield: 0.0%
 Payout: —
Market value ($ mil.): 125

Stock History

NASDAQ (GS): CHRS

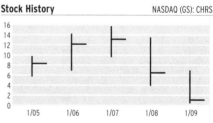

	STOCK PRICE ($) FY Close	P/E High/Low		PER SHARE ($) Earnings	Dividends	Book Value
1/09	1.08	—	—	(2.13)	0.00	4.03
1/08	6.45	—	—	(0.69)	0.00	6.32
1/07	13.12	19	12	0.81	0.00	8.20
1/06	12.15	19	9	0.76	0.00	7.05
1/05	8.30	19	11	0.52	0.00	6.01
Annual Growth	**(39.9%)**	**—**	**—**	**—**	**—**	**(9.5%)**

Charter Communications

Charter Communications is a cable television system operator with about 5 million residential and commercial subscribers in 40 US states, making it the #4 cable company, behind Comcast, Time Warner Cable, and Cox Communications. Not just a leading cable TV player, Charter offers broadband Internet and computer telephony services (it has almost a million phone customers), as well as HDTV. Through agreements with Digeo and Oxygen Media, Charter provides interactive television services. The company also derives a portion of its revenue from the sale of local advertising on such satellite networks as MTV and CNN. Chairman Paul Allen, a co-founder of Microsoft, controls about 90% of Charter's voting power.

Driven by dreams of creating a "wired world," Allen has reportedly poured more than $12 billion into Charter since 1998, and the billionaire has seen most of that investment evaporate. After purchasing a slew of small-town cable assets that needed extensive upgrades, Charter has been mired with subscriber losses and a tremendous debt load (nearly $20 billion). Former CEO Carl Vogel was never able to turn things around during his four years in charge of Charter (he resigned in early 2005 and was replaced later that year by former AOL executive Neil Smit). Throw in several other executive departures and a securities investigation that led to convictions against former COO Dave Barford (sentenced to one year in prison) and former CFO Kent Kalkwarf (14 months in prison), and you've got a rocky road indeed.

Charter, though, is still pursuing the "wired world" strategy and continues to tout its ability to provide voice, Internet access, and other data services as a complete package. It offers an interactive TV service that allows viewers to instantly access Web information related to programming, and works with partners to develop personalized interactive TV services. Charter has seen some success with its push to grow its cable telephony service, which now boasts nearly 1 million customers.

The company, which has skirted bankruptcy for years, filed for Chapter 11 bankruptcy in 2009 in order to reduce its interest expenses and free up funds to put back into the business. The restructuring eliminated about $8 billion in debt, but about $13 billion remains on Charter's books.

HISTORY

Crown Media bought St. Louis-based Cencom Cable in 1992. Rather than relocate to Crown's Dallas home, Cencom CEO Howard Wood joined with fellow executives Barry Babcock and Jerry Kent to form Charter Communications as a cable acquisition and management company in St. Louis. With an investment from Crown, owned by Hallmark Cards, the trio partnered with LEB Communications in 1994 to manage Charter's growth. And grow it did.

In 1994 Charter paid about $900 million for a majority stake in Crown. Charter spent $3 billion on 15 cable acquisitions in its first four years. It had more than 1 million subscribers by early 1997 and began offering high-speed cable Internet access and paging services in some of its markets.

Charter went into acquisition overdrive in 1998 when Microsoft co-founder Paul Allen took control with his $4.5 billion investment. The deal closely followed Allen's $2.8 billion takeover of Dallas-based Marcus Cable; Marcus was merged with Charter. The new Charter, based in St. Louis with Kent as CEO, was the #7 US cable business with 2.5 million subscribers. Also that year the company teamed up with Wink and WorldGate to offer TV Internet services with set-top boxes.

Before the ink was dry on the merger papers, Allen was at it again. The company's 1999 acquisitions included Falcon Communications (1 million cable subscribers) and Fanch Cablevision (more than 500,000); it also bought cable systems from Helicon, InterMedia Partners, Avalon Cable, InterLink Communications, Renaissance Media, and Rifkin. Charter said it would spend $3.5 billion upgrading its systems over three years after raising that amount in a major junk bond sale. Months later the company raised $3.2 billion in its IPO.

In 2000 Charter completed its purchase of Bresnan Communications (700,000 subscribers) and bought a system from Cablevision to form a major cluster in Michigan, Minnesota, and Wisconsin. The next year the company gained 554,000 subscribers by swapping noncore cable systems and $1.8 billion in cash to AT&T Broadband in exchange for systems serving the St. Louis area, parts of Alabama, the Reno area of Nevada, and California. Also in 2001 Kent resigned from the company and its board of directors and was replaced as CEO by former Liberty Media executive Carl Vogel. Vogel stayed on the job until early 2005, at which point he also retired. Former AOL executive Neil Smit replaced Vogel later that year.

The company struck a deal in 2006 to sell nearly $900 million in assets. It sold systems in Illinois and Kentucky to New Wave Communications and systems in West Virginia and Virginia to Cebridge Connections. Shedding more assets, Charter also sold cable TV systems serving nearly 70,000 customers in the western US to subsidiaries of Orange Broadband Holding Company.

EXECUTIVES

Chairman: Paul G. Allen, age 56
President, CEO, and Director: Neil Smit, age 49, $15,384,838 total compensation
EVP and COO: Michael J. Lovett, age 47, $7,204,836 total compensation
EVP and CFO: Eloise E. Schmitz, age 44, $2,066,388 total compensation
EVP and CTO: Marwan Fawaz, age 46, $2,777,679 total compensation
EVP and Chief Administrative Officer: Grier C. Raclin, age 56, $2,408,690 total compensation
Chief Restructuring Officer and General Counsel: Gregory L. (Greg) Doody, age 44
EVP and Chief Marketing Officer: Ted Schremp
VP, Controller, and Chief Accounting Officer: Kevin D. Howard, age 39
SVP Charter Media: James (Jim) Heneghan
SVP Consumer Marketing: Barbara Hedges
SVP Corporate Development: Gregory S. Rigdon

VP Investor Relations and Communications: Mary Jo Moehle
VP, Associate General Counsel, and Corporate Secretary: Richard R. Dykhouse
East Operating Group President: Joshua L. (Josh) Jamison, age 53
Central Division President: Mary L. White, age 46
West Operating Group President: Steve Apodaca
Auditors: KPMG LLP

LOCATIONS

HQ: Charter Communications, Inc.
12405 Powerscourt Dr., Ste. 100
St. Louis, MO 63131
Phone: 314-965-0555　　**Fax:** 314-965-9745
Web: www.charter.com

PRODUCTS/OPERATIONS

2008 Sales

	$ mil.	% of total
Video	3,463	53
High-speed Internet	1,356	21
Telephone	555	9
Commercial	392	6
Advertising sales	308	5
Other	405	6
Total	**6,479**	**100**

Selected Services

Broadband Internet access
Cable TV
Digital TV
High-definition TV
Interactive video programming
Pay-per-view
Telephony
Video-on-demand

COMPETITORS

AOL
AT&T
Cablevision Systems
Comcast
Cox Communications
DIRECTV
DISH Network Corporation
EarthLink
Insight Communications
Mediacom Communications
Suddenlink Communications
Time Warner Cable
Verizon
Xanadoo

HISTORICAL FINANCIALS

Company Type: Public

Income Statement

FYE: December 31

	REVENUE ($ mil.)	NET INCOME ($ mil.)	NET PROFIT MARGIN	EMPLOYEES
12/08	6,479.0	(2,451.0)	—	16,600
12/07	6,002.0	(1,616.0)	—	16,500
12/06	5,504.0	(1,370.0)	—	15,500
12/05	5,254.0	(967.0)	—	17,200
12/04	4,977.0	(3,576.0)	—	15,500
Annual Growth	**6.8%**	**—**	**—**	**1.7%**

2008 Year-End Financials

Debt ratio: —　　　　　　　No. of shares (mil.): 393
Return on equity: —　　　　Dividends
Cash ($ mil.): 960　　　　　　Yield: 0.0%
Current ratio: 0.83　　　　　Payout: —
Long-term debt ($ mil.): 21,586　Market value ($ mil.): 32

	STOCK PRICE ($) FY Close	P/E High/Low		PER SHARE ($)	
			Earnings	Dividends	Book Value
12/08	0.08	— —	(6.56)	0.00	(26.75)
12/07	1.17	— —	(4.39)	0.00	(20.09)
12/06	3.06	— —	(4.13)	0.00	(15.83)
12/05	1.22	— —	(3.13)	0.00	(12.53)
12/04	2.24	— —	(14.47)	0.00	(11.22)
Annual Growth	(56.5%)	— —	—	—	—

The Cheesecake Factory

These restaurants have some industrial strength menus for foodies. The Cheesecake Factory owns and operates more than 140 casual-dining restaurants in 35 states that offer about 200 menu items ranging from sandwiches and salads to steaks and seafood. The highlight of the menu, of course, is cheesecake, which comes in about 40 varieties, including Chocolate Tuxedo Cream and Kahlua Cocoa Coffee. Each restaurant has a unique design, but all have over-the-top opulence and Las Vegas-style glitz. In addition to its flagship concept, the company operates more than a dozen Grand Lux Cafes offering a similar menu. The Cheesecake Factory also sells desserts to grocery stores and foodservice operators.

The company has succeeded in creating a unique brand identity that sets it apart from other operators in the casual-dining sector. The Cheesecake Factory chain enjoys such good return and word-of-mouth business, in fact, that it has had to spend very little on advertising. Waiting times of two hours are not uncommon in some locations. Combined with the large size of its restaurants, that has helped the company generate nearly $10 million in annual sales per location.

During more healthy economic times, The Cheesecake Factory's popularity pushed most of the company's locations to operating capacity, forcing it to rely on expansion for growth. The recession, however, has curtailed consumer spending on things such as dining out and in response The Cheesecake Factory has been slowing its investment in new restaurants. The company opened just half a dozen new locations during 2008 compared to more than 15 openings the previous year. It is also focused on containing food costs.

The Cheesecake Factory is experimenting with a new casual-dining concept called RockSugar Pan Asian Kitchen offering foods from Southeast Asia, including Indonesia, Malaysia, and Thailand. It opened the first location in Los Angeles during 2008.

HISTORY

For 25 years Evelyn Overton made cheesecakes in her basement for friends and bake sales. In 1972 she, her husband Oscar, and their son David founded The Cheesecake Factory in Los Angeles to make cheesecakes and other desserts for local restaurants. David opened a restaurant in Beverly Hills in 1978 to showcase the company's cheesecakes to restaurateurs. The first Cheesecake Factory, which served salads, sandwiches, and a few entrees, was a hit, and a second location was opened in Marina del Rey in 1983.

In the late 1980s the company opened two more outlets in Southern California, and a Washington, DC, location opened in 1991. After going public the next year, The Cheesecake Factory opened one or two restaurants a year (in California and Atlanta in 1993, Maryland in 1994, and Florida in 1994 and 1995). Evelyn Overton died in 1996.

In 1998 the company opened a new bakery/cafe concept called The Cheesecake Factory Express to serve the crowds at Walt Disney's indoor interactive theme park, DisneyQuest, in Orlando. In 1999 it tried another new concept called the Grand Lux Cafe, opening the first in Las Vegas Sands' Venetian Casino Resort.

Continued expansion in 1999 and 2000 helped drive growth in both sales and profits. The following year the company formed The Cheesecake Factory — Oscar and Evelyn Overton Charitable Foundation to help employees participate in local charitable programs and community services.

Despite a gloomy economic outlook, the company accelerated the pace of its expansion, opening nine new Cheesecake Factory locations in 2001. By 2005 the company had exceeded 100 restaurants.

EXECUTIVES

Chairman and CEO: David Overton, age 63, $2,762,072 total compensation
EVP and CFO: W. Douglas Benn, age 54
SVP Information Technology and CIO: James D. Rasmussen
SVP and Chief Marketing Officer: Mark Mears
VP, Controller, and Chief Accounting Officer: Cheryl M. Slomann, age 43, $373,771 total compensation
EVP, Secretary, and General Counsel: Debby R. Zurzolo, age 52, $835,522 total compensation
SVP Bakery Operations: Keith T. Carango
SVP New Restaurant Openings and Operations: Lisa A. McDowell
SVP Purchasing: Ronald S. (Ron) McArthur
SVP Business Planning and Systems Development: William N. (Bill) Lyons
SVP Operations Services: Russell S. Greene
SVP Development: Brian MacKellar
SVP Operations, The Cheesecake Factory Restaurants: David Gordon
SVP Kitchen Operations: Donald C. Moore
SVP Strategic Planning: Matthew E. Clark
VP Culinary Development and Corporate Executive Chef: Robert Okura
VP Investor Relations: Jill Peters
VP Human Resources: Dina R. Barmasse
President, The Cheesecake Factory Bakery: Max S. Byfuglin, age 63, $749,494 total compensation
Auditors: PricewaterhouseCoopers LLP

LOCATIONS

HQ: The Cheesecake Factory Incorporated
26901 Malibu Hills Rd., Calabasas Hills, CA 91301
Phone: 818-871-3000   **Fax:** 818-871-3001
Web: www.thecheesecakefactory.com

2008 Locations

	No.
California	34
Florida	17
Texas	12
New York	9
Massachusetts	7
Arizona	6
Illinois	6
New Jersey	6
Ohio	6
Virginia	6
Maryland	5
Nevada	5
Colorado	4
Georgia	4
Pennsylvania	4
Missouri	3
North Carolina	3
Washington	3
Indiana	2
Oklahoma	2
Wisconsin	2
Alabama	1
Connecticut	1
Hawaii	1
Idaho	1
Iowa	1
Kansas	1
Kentucky	1
Minnesota	1
Nebraska	1
Oregon	1
Rhode Island	1
Tennessee	1
Utah	1
Washington, DC	1
Total	**160**

PRODUCTS/OPERATIONS

2008 Sales

	$ mil.	% of total
Restaurants	1,536.5	93
Bakery	119.5	7
Adjustments	(49.6)	—
Total	**1,606.4**	**100**

COMPETITORS

Applebee's	Houlihan's
Brinker	Johnny Rockets
BUCA	Logan's Roadhouse
California Pizza Kitchen	Lone Star Steakhouse
Carlson Restaurants	Marie Callender
Claim Jumper Restaurants	OSI Restaurant Partners
Cracker Barrel	P.F. Chang's
Darden	Ruby Tuesday
Grill Concepts	Texas Roadhouse

HISTORICAL FINANCIALS

Company Type: Public

Income Statement				FYE: Tuesday nearest December 31
	REVENUE ($ mil.)	NET INCOME ($ mil.)	NET PROFIT MARGIN	EMPLOYEES
12/08	1,606.4	52.3	3.3%	31,000
12/07	1,511.6	74.0	4.9%	29,400
12/06	1,315.3	81.3	6.2%	29,400
12/05	1,177.6	87.5	7.4%	24,700
12/04	969.2	66.5	6.9%	22,200
Annual Growth	13.5%	(5.8%)	—	8.7%

2008 Year-End Financials

Debt ratio: 60.8%	No. of shares (mil.): 60
Return on equity: 10.3%	Dividends
Cash ($ mil.): 80	Yield: 0.0%
Current ratio: 1.02	Payout: —
Long-term debt ($ mil.): 275	Market value ($ mil.): 608

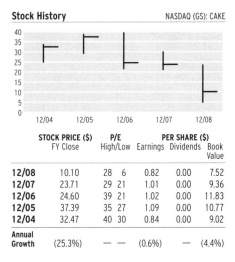

| | 12/04 | 12/05 | 12/06 | 12/07 | 12/08 |
| | | | | | |

	STOCK PRICE ($) FY Close	P/E High/Low		PER SHARE ($) Earnings	Dividends	Book Value
12/08	10.10	28	6	0.82	0.00	7.52
12/07	23.71	29	21	1.01	0.00	9.36
12/06	24.60	39	21	1.02	0.00	11.83
12/05	37.39	35	27	1.09	0.00	10.77
12/04	32.47	40	30	0.84	0.00	9.02
Annual Growth	(25.3%)	—	—	(0.6%)	—	(4.4%)

Chesapeake Energy

Chesapeake Energy knows the peaks and valleys of the oil and gas business, including the 2008-09 oil slump. The exploration and production company concentrates on building natural gas reserves through the acquisition and development of oil and gas assets across the US. The Midcontinent region accounts for more than a third of the company's estimated proved reserves of 12 trillion cu. ft. of natural gas equivalent, but Chesapeake also has assets along the Gulf Coast and in the Permian Basin, Appalachia, and the Ark-La-Tex region. In 2008 it owned or had stakes in 41,200 producing oil and natural gas wells that produced 2.3 billion cu. ft. of natural gas equivalent per day, 92% of which was natural gas.

A national leader in deep vertical and horizontal drilling, Chesapeake (which was named after the childhood Chesapeake Bay haunts of one of its founders) is concentrating on growing its proved reserves through acquisitions. It is also seeking to save costs by owning and operating its own equipment.

Chesapeake is one of the top drillers of natural gas wells in the US, with drilling projects in Arkansas, Kansas, Louisiana, New Mexico, Oklahoma, and Texas.

In 2006 the company expanded, acquiring oil and natural gas assets located in the Barnett Shale, South Texas, Permian Basin, Midcontinent, and East Texas regions for $796 million. It also bought 13 drilling rigs and related assets from Martex Drilling for $150 million. In 2007 Chesapeake began drilling operations at the Dallas/FortWorth Airport, which is located above the productive Barnett Shale formation.

Facing a deepening economic valley as oil prices began to slump, in 2008 the company moved to cut the costs of exploiting its shale assets by selling some of these properties to joint venture partners. In this regard Chesapeake sold 90,000 net acres of natural gas assets in the Arkoma Basin Woodford Shale play for $1.7 billion to BP. It subsequently sold a 25% stake in its Fayetteville Shale assets in Arkansas to BP for $1.9 billion.

In 2008 Chesapeake also teamed up with StatoilHydro to jointly explore unconventional gas opportunities around the world.

HISTORY

Aubrey McClendon (who grew up near Maryland's Chesapeake Bay) and Tom Ward had been nonoperating partners in about 600 wells in Oklahoma before forming their own company in 1989 to develop new fields in Texas and Oklahoma during the 1990s. The firm went public in 1993. In 1995 the company acquired oil and gas acreage in Louisiana, as well as Princeton Natural Gas, an Oklahoma City-based gas marketing firm.

Oil finds in Louisiana and strong production from its Texas and Oklahoma wells helped lift Chesapeake's sales in 1996. That year it acquired Amerada Hess' (later renamed Hess) half of their joint operations in two Oklahoma fields. In 1997 chairman McClendon and president Ward acquired control of Chesapeake.

The company's success was based on its "growth through the drillbit" strategy — developing new wells. But after a 1997 loss, Chesapeake modified its strategy and sought to grow by acquiring other companies. That year it bought energy company AnSon Production. Chesapeake subsequently bought oil and gas explorer-producer Hugoton Energy and energy company DLB Oil & Gas.

In 1998 the company acquired a 40% stake in Canadian oil producer Ranger Oil and paid Occidental Petroleum $105 million for natural gas reserves in the Texas Panhandle. Chesapeake then began to transform itself from a hotshot driller to an acquirer of natural gas properties, almost tripling its proved reserves. The company suffered a huge loss that year, in part from the acquisitions and continuing lower gas prices.

With gas prices soaring again, the company continued its buying spree into 2000, when it agreed to buy midcontinent natural gas producer Gothic Energy for $345 million in stock and assumed debt. The deal closed in 2001. The company also sold its Canadian assets that year, in order to focus on its core US properties.

In 2002 Chesapeake acquired oil and gas producer Canaan Energy for about $118 million. Later that year the company announced plans to sell or trade its Permian Basin assets.

Chesapeake acquired in 2003 a 25% stake in Pioneer Drilling (which it subsequently sold). In 2004 the company acquired Barnett Shale assets from Hallwood Energy for $292 million. That year it also bought privately owned Concho Resources for $420 million. The next year the company acquired privately held BRG Petroleum, which held assets of more than 450 wells with proved reserves of more than 275 billion cu. ft. of natural gas, for $325 million.

In 2005 Chesapeake acquired 20% of Gastar Exploration (reduced to 15% by 2007). That year, in a major move, the company acquired Columbia Natural Resources for $2.2 billion.

EXECUTIVES

Chairman and CEO: Aubrey K. McClendon, age 49, $100,069,200 total compensation
EVP Operations and COO: Steven C. Dixon, age 50, $7,049,745 total compensation
EVP Finance and CFO: Marcus C. (Marc) Rowland, age 56, $9,317,160 total compensation
SVP Information Technology and CIO: Cathlyn L. (Cathy) Tompkins, age 47
SVP Accounting, Chief Accounting Officer, and Controller: Michael A. Johnson, age 43

EVP Exploration: J. Mark Lester, age 56, $7,772,743 total compensation
EVP Acquisitions and Divestitures: Douglas J. Jacobson, age 55, $12,089,727 total compensation
SVP Drilling: Stephen W. Miller, age 52
SVP Corporate Development: Thomas S. Price Jr., age 57
SVP Human and Corporate Resources: Martha A. Burger, age 56
SVP Land and Legal and General Counsel: Henry J. Hood, age 48
SVP, Secretary, and Treasurer: Jennifer M. Grigsby, age 40
SVP Natural Gas Projects; President and COO, Chesapeake Midstream Partners: J. Michael (Mike) Stice, age 50
SVP Production: Jeffrey A. Fisher, age 49
SVP Investor Relations and Research: Jeffrey L. Mobley, age 40
President, Chesapeake Energy Marketing: James C. Johnson, age 51
Director Media Relations: Jim Gipson
Auditors: PricewaterhouseCoopers LLP

LOCATIONS

HQ: Chesapeake Energy Corporation
6100 N. Western Ave., Oklahoma City, OK 73118
Phone: 405-848-8000   **Fax:** 405-843-0573
Web: www.chkenergy.com

2008 Proved Reserves

	% of total
Midcontinent	37
Fort Worth Barnett Shale	24
Appalachian Basin	13
Ark-La-Tex	10
South Texas & Texas Gulf Coast	8
Permian & Delaware Basins	8
Total	**100**

PRODUCTS/OPERATIONS

2008 Sales

	$ mil.	% of total
Exploration & production	7,858	68
Marketing	3,598	31
Service operations	173	1
Total	**11,629**	**100**

COMPETITORS

Adams Resources	ConocoPhillips
Anadarko Petroleum	Devon Energy
Apache	Exxon
Ashland Inc.	Koch Industries, Inc.
Basic Earth Science	Noble Energy
BP	Occidental Petroleum
Cabot Oil & Gas	Pioneer Natural Resources
Chevron	Royal Dutch Shell

HISTORICAL FINANCIALS

Company Type: Public

Income Statement

FYE: December 31

	REVENUE ($ mil.)	NET INCOME ($ mil.)	NET PROFIT MARGIN	EMPLOYEES
12/08	11,629.0	723.0	6.2%	7,600
12/07	7,800.0	1,229.0	15.8%	6,200
12/06	7,325.6	1,904.1	26.0%	4,900
12/05	4,665.3	948.3	20.3%	2,885
12/04	2,709.3	515.2	19.0%	1,718
Annual Growth	43.9%	8.8%	—	45.0%

2008 Year-End Financials

Debt ratio: 89.8%
Return on equity: 5.4%
Cash ($ mil.): 1,749
Current ratio: 1.19
Long-term debt ($ mil.): 14,184

No. of shares (mil.): 642
Dividends
  Yield: 1.8%
  Payout: 25.4%
Market value ($ mil.): 10,376

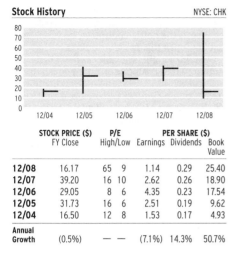

Stock History — NYSE: CHK

	STOCK PRICE ($) FY Close	P/E High/Low		PER SHARE ($) Earnings	Dividends	Book Value
12/08	16.17	65	9	1.14	0.29	25.40
12/07	39.20	16	10	2.62	0.26	18.90
12/06	29.05	8	6	4.35	0.23	17.54
12/05	31.73	16	6	2.51	0.19	9.62
12/04	16.50	12	8	1.53	0.17	4.93
Annual Growth	(0.5%)	—	—	(7.1%)	14.3%	50.7%

Chevron Corporation

Having added Texaco's star (and subsequently Unocal's authority) to its stripes, Chevron can pull rank on its rivals. Among the largest US integrated oil companies, along with Exxon Mobil and ConocoPhillips, it has proved reserves of 11.2 billion barrels of oil equivalent and a daily production of 2.5 million barrels of oil equivalent, and it also owns interests in chemicals, mining, pipelines, and power production businesses. The company, which began to restructure its refinery and retail businesses in 2008, owns or has stakes in 9,700 gas stations in the US that operate under the Chevron and Texaco brands. Outside the US it owns or has stakes in 15,300 gas stations, which also use the Caltex brand.

The company announced plans in 2008 to begin construction on a $3.1 billion natural gas project in the Gulf of Thailand. The project has capacity to meet 14% of Thailand's natural gas needs.

Facing a global recession and a slump in demand for gasoline, Chevron announced that it was considering selling some of its refineries and selling some fuel marketing assets to reduce costs. Ultrapar acquired Chevron's Texaco-branded fuel distribution business in Brazil for $720 million in 2008, and the next year Chevron sold its Nigerian fuel marketing business.

Chevron owns a 50% stake in chemicals producer Chevron Phillips Chemical, a joint venture with ConocoPhillips. It produces coal and molybdenum through Chevron Mining.

HISTORY

Thirty years after the California gold rush, a small firm began digging for a new product — oil. The crude came from wildcatter Frederick Taylor's well located north of Los Angeles. In 1879 Taylor and other oilmen formed Pacific Coast Oil, attracting the attention of John D. Rockefeller's Standard Oil. The two competed fiercely until Standard took over Pacific Coast in 1900.

When Standard Oil was broken up in 1911, its West Coast operations became the standalone Standard Oil Company (California), which was

nicknamed Socal and sold Chevron-brand products. After winning drilling concessions in Bahrain and Saudi Arabia in the 1930s, Socal summoned Texaco to help, and they formed Caltex (California-Texas Oil Company) as equal partners. In 1948 Socony (later Mobil) and Jersey Standard (later Exxon) bought 40% of Caltex's Saudi operations, and the Saudi arm became Aramco (Arabian American Oil Company).

Socal exploration pushed into Louisiana and the Gulf of Mexico in the 1940s. In 1961 it bought Standard Oil Company of Kentucky (Kyso). The 1970s brought setbacks: Caltex holdings were nationalized during the OPEC-spawned upheaval, and the Saudi Arabian government claimed Aramco in 1980.

In 1984 Socal was renamed Chevron and doubled its reserves with its $13 billion purchase of Gulf Corp., which had origins in the 1901 Spindletop gusher in Texas. Gulf became an oil power by developing Kuwaiti concessions but was hobbled when those assets were nationalized in 1975. After Gulf was rocked by disclosures that it had an illegal political slush fund, Socal stepped in. The deal loaded the new company with debt, and it cut 20,000 jobs and sold billions in assets.

Chevron bought Tenneco's Gulf of Mexico properties in 1988 and in 1992 swapped fields valued at $1.1 billion for 15.7 million shares of Chevron stock owned by Pennzoil. It also moved into the North Sea in 1994.

In the 1990s Chevron gave its retailing units a tune-up. It allied with McDonald's (1995) to combine burger stands and gas stations in 12 western states. In addition, the company sold 450 UK gas stations and a refinery to Shell (1997). Meanwhile, Chevron sold its natural gas operation in 1996 for a stake in Houston-based NGC (later Dynegy; sold in 2007), and it signed an onshore exploration contract in China the next year.

Poor economic conditions in Asia and slumping oil prices in 1998 forced Chevron to shed some US holdings, including California properties. Looking for growth overseas, in 1999 it bought Rutherford-Moran Oil, increasing its interests in Thailand, and Petrolera Argentina San Jorge, Argentina's #3 oil company.

Chevron trimmed about 10% of its workforce in 1999 and 2000 in an effort to cut costs. As the rest of the industry consolidated, Chevron discussed merging with Texaco, but the talks collapsed in 1999. Later that year CEO Ken Derr retired, and vice chairman Dave O'Reilly replaced him.

In 2000 Chevron formed a joint venture with Phillips Petroleum (later ConocoPhillips) that combined the companies' chemicals businesses as Chevron Phillips Chemical. That year talks with Texaco were revived and Chevron agreed to acquire its Caltex partner for about $35 billion in stock and about $8 billion in assumed debt. The deal, completed in 2001, formed ChevronTexaco.

Part of the 2001 deal to acquire Texaco required Chevron to sell exclusive rights to the Texaco brand for a period of three years. A division of Royal Dutch Shell owned rights to the Texaco brand until 2004 and changed the name of the service stations to Shell. Once Chevron regained the rights to the Texaco name, it revitalized the brand name by adding about 400 Texaco stations in the western US.

In 2002 ChevronTexaco divested its stakes in US downstream joint ventures Equilon (to Shell) and Motiva (to Shell and Saudi Aramco). It also

sold part of a Gulf of Mexico pipeline and two natural gas plants in Louisiana to Duke Energy, and its 12.5% stake in a natural gas liquids fractionator to Enterprise Products Partners. In 2004 ChevronTexaco sold 150 US natural gas and oil properties to XTO Energy for $912 million. The company changed its name to Chevron Corporation in 2005.

In 2005 Chevron acquired Unocal for more than $16 billion, boosting its proved reserves by about 15%. Equally attractive to Chevron was the strategic position of Unocal's operations; at a time when industries are trying to get a foothold in China, the reserves in Southeast Asia could easily be transported not there but also to a surging India as well. Unocal's other operations easily supplied the US (from the Gulf of Mexico) and Europe (Caspian Sea) with gas and oil. Chevron bought a 5% stake in Indian refiner Reliance Petroleum for about $300 million in 2006. That year a company-led group of exploration firms announced a new successful oil strike in the Gulf of Mexico.

EXECUTIVES

Chairman and CEO: David J. (Dave) O'Reilly, age 62, $19,271,248 total compensation
Vice Chairman: John S. Watson, age 52, $6,986,895 total compensation
VP and CFO: Patricia E. (Pat) Yarrington, age 53
VP and CTO: John W. McDonald, age 57
CIO; President, Chevron Information Technology: Louie Ehrlich
Corporate Secretary and Chief Governance Officer: Lydia I. Beebe, age 56
EVP Technology and Services: John E. Bethancourt, age 57
EVP Upstream and Gas: George L. Kirkland, age 58, $10,610,169 total compensation
EVP Global Downstream: Michael K. (Mike) Wirth, age 48
EVP and General Counsel: Charles A. James, age 54
Corporate VP Human Resources: Joe W. Laymon, age 55
VP San Joaquin Valley Business Unit: Warner Williams
VP and Treasurer: Pierre Breber, age 44
VP Policy, Government, and Public Affairs: Rhonda I. Zygocki, age 51
VP; President Chevron Global Gas: John D. Gass, age 56
VP and General Manager Government Affairs: Lisa Barry
President, Global Marketing: S. Shariq Yosufzai
General Manager Public Affairs: David Samson
Manager Investor Relations: Randy Richards
Auditors: PricewaterhouseCoopers LLP

LOCATIONS

HQ: Chevron Corporation
6001 Bollinger Canyon Rd., San Ramon, CA 94583
Phone: 925-842-1000   **Fax:** 925-842-3530
Web: www.chevron.com

2008 Sales

	$ mil.	% of total
US	133,658	44
Other countries	172,585	56
Adjustments	(33,238)	—
Total	**273,005**	**100**

PRODUCTS/OPERATIONS

2008 Sales

	$ mil.	% of total
Downstream	219,938	71
Upstream	82,318	27
Chemicals	2,170	1
Other	1,817	1
Adjustments	(33,238)	—
Total	**273,005**	**100**

COMPETITORS

Anadarko Petroleum	Koch Industries, Inc.
BP	PEMEX
ConocoPhillips	PETROBRAS
Devon Energy	Petróleos de Venezuela
Eni	Repsol YPF
Exxon	Royal Dutch Shell
Hess Corporation	TOTAL
Imperial Oil	

HISTORICAL FINANCIALS

Company Type: Public

Income Statement

FYE: December 31

	REVENUE ($ mil.)	NET INCOME ($ mil.)	NET PROFIT MARGIN	EMPLOYEES
12/08	273,005.0	23,931.0	8.8%	67,000
12/07	220,904.0	18,688.0	8.5%	65,000
12/06	210,118.0	17,138.0	8.2%	62,500
12/05	198,200.0	14,099.0	7.1%	59,000
12/04	155,300.0	13,328.0	8.6%	56,000
Annual Growth	15.1%	15.8%	—	4.6%

2008 Year-End Financials

Debt ratio: 7.0%
Return on equity: 29.2%
Cash ($ mil.): 9,347
Current ratio: 1.14
Long-term debt ($ mil.): 6,083
No. of shares (mil.): 2,006
Dividends
  Yield: 3.4%
  Payout: 21.7%
Market value ($ mil.): 148,348

Stock History

NYSE: CVX

	STOCK PRICE ($) FY Close	P/E High	P/E Low	Earnings	PER SHARE ($) Dividends	Book Value
12/08	73.97	9	5	11.67	2.53	43.20
12/07	93.33	11	7	8.77	2.26	38.44
12/06	73.53	10	7	7.80	2.01	34.37
12/05	56.77	10	8	6.54	1.75	31.25
12/04	52.51	9	7	6.28	1.53	22.55
Annual Growth	8.9%	—	—	16.8%	13.4%	17.6%

Chiquita Brands International

As one of the world's top banana producers, Chiquita Brands International deals in big bunches. The company grows, procures, markets, and distributes bananas and other fresh fruits and vegetables under the premium Chiquita brand and others. Its products are sold in some 70 countries worldwide. Bananas accounted for 57% of Chiquita's 2008 total sales. Chiquita's other products include whole citrus fruits, melons, grapes, apples, and tomatoes, as well as fresh-cut items, juice, and processed fruit ingredients. The company's Fresh Express unit is the leading seller of packaged ready-to-eat salads in North America.

The company sources its bananas from Colombia, Costa Rica, Ecuador, Guatemala, Honduras, Nicaragua, Panama, and the Philippines. It sold its Ivory Coast operations in 2009.

Serving both the retail and foodservice sectors and offering some 400 different branded products, the company's Fresh Express division supports Chiquita's strategy of providing more convenient healthy food options in order to meet consumers' needs and also makes the company less susceptible to unfavorable EU import regulations.

Increasing its market penetration for Fresh Express products in the northeastern US, Chiquita acquired a regional processor of value-added salads and fruit snacks, Verdelli Farms, in 2007. Available in 10 states from Massachusetts to Virginia, its brand names include Harvest Select and Verdelli Farms.

FMR Corp. owns almost 15% of Chiquita, and Deutsche Bank owns about 10%.

HISTORY

Lorenzo Baker sailed into Jersey City, New Jersey, in 1870 with 160 bunches of Jamaican bananas. Baker arranged to sell bananas through Boston produce agent Andrew Preston and, with the support of Preston's partners, the two formed the Boston Fruit Company in 1885. In 1899 Boston Fruit merged with three other banana importers and incorporated as United Fruit Company. Soon the company was importing bananas from numerous Central American plantations for expanded distribution in the US.

United Fruit entered the Cuban sugar trade with the purchase of Nipe Bay (1907) and Saetia Sugar (1912). It bought Samuel Zemurray's Cuyamel Fruit Company in 1930, leaving Zemurray as the largest shareholder. Zemurray, who had masterminded the overthrow of the Honduran regime in 1905 to establish one favorable to his business, forcibly established himself as United Fruit's president in 1933.

In 1954, when Guatemalan president Jacobo Arbenz threatened to seize United Fruit's holdings, the company claimed he was a communist threat and provided ships to transport CIA-backed troops and ammunition, leading to his ultimate overthrow.

Diversifying in the 1960s, United Fruit purchased A&W (restaurants and root beer, 1966) and Baskin-Robbins (ice cream, 1967). Eli Black, founder of AMK (which included the Morrell meat company), bought United Fruit in 1970 and changed its name to United Brands. Through American Financial Group, Carl Lindner began acquiring large amounts of United Brands' stock in 1973; he became chairman of the company in 1984. During the 1970s and 1980s, United Brands sold many of its holdings, including Baskin-Robbins (1973) and A&W (restaurants, 1982; soft drinks, 1987).

The firm became Chiquita Brands International in 1990. Chiquita acquired Friday Canning two years later. It then began divesting its meat operations, and all were sold by 1995.

In 1993 the European Union (EU) set up trade barriers against banana imports from Latin America, favoring banana-producing former European colonies in the Caribbean. The preference system angered Chiquita, whose bananas come from non-favored countries, although it retained more than 20% of the European market. In 1997 the WTO ruled the EU's trade policy illegal; the battle continued, however, over just how open the market should be.

Chiquita bought vegetable canners Owatonna Canning (1997), American Fine Foods (1997), and Stokely USA (1998) and merged them with Friday Canning in 1998. Also that year Hurricane Mitch destroyed Chiquita plantations in Honduras and Guatemala, costing the company $74 million. Sales were not affected though, as Chiquita was able to turn to growers in Ecuador and Panama. In 2000 the company announced cost-cutting efforts that included job cuts and a reorganization of some divisions.

Beset by a weakened European currency and a banana glut, the company announced in January 2001 that it was unable to pay its public debt. Chiquita also sued the European Commission, demanding $525 million in damages, due to the EU banana trade policy. The EU and the US later reached an agreement modifying quotas and tariffs until 2006, when all such restrictions were set to end. In November 2001 Chiquita filed a debt-restructuring plan under Chapter 11 seeking approval for an agreement the company made with bondholders to change more than $700 million of debt into equity. The plan was approved and the reorganization went into effect in mid-March of 2002 and the company began trading again on the NYSE. That same month, Chiquita announced the resignation of Steve Warshaw as the company president, CEO, and director. Cyrus Freidheim Jr. was named new chairman and CEO.

In a move to further concentrate on its fresh produce business, in 2003 the company sold its subsidiary, Chiquita Processed Foods (vegetable canning), to Seneca Foods. Also that year Chiquita sold its unprofitable Pacific division, located in Panama (Puerto Armuelles Fruit Co.) to a cooperative of banana workers. It sold its interest in a joint venture with The Packers of Indian River, a grapefruit grower and packer, to its joint venture partner. Fernando Aguirre took over the roles of chairman, president, and CEO during 2004.

After Chiquita voluntarily revealed in 2004 that one of its Colombian banana subsidiaries had made protection payments from 1997 though 2004 to terrorist groups, the Justice Department began a criminal investigation, examining the role and conduct of Chiquita and some of its officers in the criminal activity. Chiquita sold the subsidiary in 2004 but owned it at the time of the payments, admitting the payments were improper but that it was trying to ensure the safety of its employees. (In 2007 Chiquita agreed to pay $25 million to settle the case.)

Chiquita acquired Performance Food Group's Fresh Express unit for $855 million in 2005.

EXECUTIVES

Chairman, President, and CEO: Fernando Aguirre, age 51, $3,810,608 total compensation
SVP and CFO: Michael Sims, age 50
VP and CIO: Manjit Singh, age 39
President, Global Innovation and Emerging Markets and Chief Marketing Officer: Tanios E. Viviani, age 47, $1,315,158 total compensation
SVP and Chief People Officer: Kevin R. Holland, age 47
VP and Chief Compliance Officer: Vanessa Vargas
VP, Controller, and Chief Accounting Officer: Lori A. Ritchey, age 45
SVP, General Counsel, and Secretary: James E. Thompson, age 48, $941,373 total compensation

SVP Government and International Affairs and
  Corporate Responsibility Officer: Manuel Rodriguez,
  age 59
SVP Product Supply Organization: Waheed Zaman,
  age 48
VP Taxation: Joseph W. Bradley
VP Logistics, North America: Deverl Masserang
President and COO, Fresh Group Far and Middle
  East/Australia Region: Craig A. Stephen
President, Europe and Middle East: Michel Loeb,
  age 54, $911,264 total compensation
President, North America: Brian W. Kocher, age 39
Manager Corporate Communications and Investor
  Relations: Ed Loyd
Auditors: Ernst & Young LLP

LOCATIONS

HQ: Chiquita Brands International, Inc.
  250 E. 5th St., Cincinnati, OH 45202
Phone: 513-784-8000   Fax: 513-784-8030
Web: www.chiquita.com

2008 Sales

	$ mil.	% of total
US	2,121.4	59
Italy	230.4	6
Germany	191.9	5
Other countries	1,065.7	30
Total	**3,609.4**	**100**

PRODUCTS/OPERATIONS

2008 Sales

	$ mil.	% of total
Bananas	2,060.3	57
Salads & healthy snacks	1,305.0	36
Other produce	244.1	7
Total	**3,609.4**	**100**

Selected Products

Bananas
Other produce
  Fresh cut (packaged salads and fresh-cut fruits,
    including Fresh Express products)
  Fresh whole
    Apples
    Citrus fruit
    Grapes
    Kiwi
    Melons
    Pineapples
    Stonefruit
    Tomatoes

COMPETITORS

Agrial	Monterey Mushrooms
American Fruit & Produce	Moonlight Packing
Bakkavor	National Grape Cooperative
BC Hot House Foods	Naturipe Farms
Bonduelle	Oakshire Mushroom Farm
Calavo Growers	Ocean Spray
C.H. Robinson Worldwide	Oceanside Produce
Del Monte Foods	Orchard House Foods
Dole Food	Pacific Coast Producers
Eastern Fresh Growers	Poupart
Fresh Del Monte Produce	Premier Foods
Fyffes	Ready Pac
Gentile Bros.	Redbridge
Gills Onions	River Ranch Fresh Foods
Giumarra Companies	Seneca Foods
Global Pacific Produce	Sunkist
Grimmway Enterprises	Tanimura & Antle
Jamaica Producers Group	Tropicana
J.G. Boswell Co.	Village Farms
Lykes Bros.	Wilkinson-Cooper Produce
Maui Land & Pineapple	Worldwide Fruit

HISTORICAL FINANCIALS
Company Type: Public

Income Statement
FYE: December 31

	REVENUE ($ mil.)	NET INCOME ($ mil.)	NET PROFIT MARGIN	EMPLOYEES
12/08	3,609.4	(323.7)	—	23,000
12/07	4,662.8	(49.0)	—	24,000
12/06	4,499.1	(95.9)	—	25,000
12/05	3,904.4	131.4	3.4%	25,000
12/04	3,071.5	55.4	1.8%	21,000
Annual Growth	**4.1%**	**—**	**—**	**2.3%**

2008 Year-End Financials

Debt ratio: 171.2%
Return on equity: —
Cash ($ mil.): 77
Current ratio: 1.72
Long-term debt ($ mil.): 766
No. of shares (mil.): 45
Dividends
  Yield: 0.0%
  Payout: —
Market value ($ mil.): 658

Stock History
NYSE: CQB

	STOCK PRICE ($) FY Close	P/E High/Low		PER SHARE ($) Earnings	Dividends	Book Value
12/08	14.78	—	—	(7.40)	0.00	10.05
12/07	18.39	—	—	(1.22)	0.00	20.10
12/06	15.97	—	—	(2.28)	0.20	19.55
12/05	20.01	11	7	2.92	0.40	22.30
12/04	22.06	18	12	1.33	0.10	18.83
Annual Growth	**(9.5%)**	**—**	**—**	**—**	**—**	**(14.5%)**

CHS Inc.

CHS goes with the grain. As one of the US's leading publicly traded, cooperative marketers of grain and oilseed, CHS represents farmers, ranchers, and cooperatives from the Great Lakes to the Pacific Northwest and from the Canadian border to Texas. CHS trades grain and sells supplies to members through its stores. It also processes soybeans for use in food and animal feeds, and grinds wheat into flour used in pastas and bread. Through joint ventures, the company sells soybean oil, and crop nutrient and protection products, and markets grain. In addition, CHS provides insurance and financial and risk-management services, and operates petroleum refineries, marketing Cenex brand fuels, lubricants, and energy products.

CHS's grain trading activities include buying, selling, and arranging for transport. The co-op operates wheat mills to produce flour for pasta and bread, and it provides farm supplies to its approximately 1,650 Cenex/Ampride stores; CHS also processes soybeans for use in margarine, salad dressings, and animal feed. Extending its reach beyond the US, the company formed a joint venture (Multigrain A.G.) with Brazilian agricultural commodities company Multigrain Comercio.

The company's energy division operates oil refineries, and the Country Energy subsidiary sells wholesale propane and other petroleum products. Joint ventures with United Grain Corporation (United Harvest) and Cargill (TEMPCO) operate grain terminals and export grain. CHS also provides ethanol and biodiesel fuel products.

CHS and Land O'Lakes realigned the businesses of their 50-50 joint venture Agriliance in 2007, with CHS acquiring its crop-nutrients wholesale-products business and Land O'Lakes acquiring the crop-protection products business. Canadian ag cooperative La Coop fédérée purchased Agriliance's retail agronomy operation the following year.

Recognizing the growing demand for soy-based food products and, in turn, to increase shareholder value, in 2008 the company acquired Legacy Foods, maker of Ultra Soy and TSP brands of textured soybean products for use by both human food and pet food manufacturers. Legacy's operations are overseen by CHS's oilseed processing division.

On the energy front, in 2008 CHS became the sole owner of Provista Renewable Fuels Marketing by purchasing US BioEnergy's 50% interest in the biofuels maker. (VeraSun Energy bought out US BioEnergy later that year.)

In 2009 CHS acquired Winona River & Rail, including 90,000 tons of dry-fertilizer storage capacity, a dedicated river dock, and a 65-car railroad track capacity. The acquisition of the Minnesota operations bolstered the company's storage capacity and rail access in the midwestern and upper Mississippi River regions.

HISTORY

To help farmers through the Great Depression, the Farmers Union Terminal Association (a grain marketing association formed in 1926) created the Farmers Union Grain Terminal Association (GTA) in 1938. With loans from the Farmers Union Central Exchange (later known as CENEX) and the Farm Credit Association, the organization operated a grain elevator in St. Paul, Minnesota. By 1939 GTA had 250 grain-producing associations as members.

GTA leased terminals in Minneapolis and Washington and then built others in Wisconsin and Montana. It took over a Minnesota flour mill and created Amber Milling. GTA also began managing farming insurance provider Terminal Agency. In 1958 the association bought 57 elevators and feed plants from the McCabe Company.

Adding to its operations in 1960, GTA bought the Honeymead soybean plant. The next year the co-op acquired Minnesota Linseed Oil. In 1977 it acquired Jewett & Sherman (later Holsum Foods), which helped transform the company into a provider of jams, jellies, salad dressings, and syrups.

In 1983 GTA combined with North Pacific Grain Growers, a Pacific Northwest co-op incorporated in 1929, to form Harvest States Cooperatives. Harvest States grew in the early and mid-1990s by acquiring salad dressing makers Albert's Foods, Great American Foods, and Saffola Quality Foods; soup stock producer Private Brands; and margarine and dressings manufacturer and distributor Gregg Foods.

The company started a joint venture to operate the Ag States Agency agricultural insurance company in 1995. The next year the co-op's Holsum Foods division and Mitsui & Co.'s edible oils unit, Wilsey Foods, merged to form Ventura

Foods, a distributor of margarines, oils, spreads, and other food products.

Harvest States merged in 1998 with Minnesota-based CENEX, a 16-state agricultural supply co-op that had been founded in 1931 as Farmers Union Central Exchange. (Among CENEX's major operations was a farm inputs, services, marketing, and processing joint venture with dairy cooperative Land O'Lakes formed in 1987.) CENEX CEO Noel Estenson took the helm of the resulting co-op, Cenex Harvest States Cooperatives, which soon formed a petroleum joint venture called Country Energy with Farmland Industries.

CHS members rejected a proposed merger with Farmland Industries in 1999. Also that year Cenex/Land O'Lakes Agronomy (it became Agriliance in 2000 when Farmland Industries joined the joint venture) bought Terra Industries' $1.7 billion distribution business (400 farm supply stores, seed and chemical distribution operations, partial ownership of two chemical plants).

CHS bought the wholesale propane marketing operations of Williams Companies in 2000. Additionally Estenson retired that year and company president John Johnson took over as CEO.

In 2002 CHS acquired Agway's Grandin, North Dakota-based sunflower business and formed a wheat-milling joint venture (Horizon Milling) with Cargill. In 2003 the company changed its name from Cenex Harvest States Cooperatives to CHS Inc. and began trading on the NASDAQ.

In 2004 CHS purchased all of bankrupt Farmland Industries' ownership of Agriliance, thus giving CHS a 50% ownership of Agriliance (with Land O'Lakes owning the other 50%). With an eye to this growing energy sector, CHS acquired a 28% ownership of ethanol production and marketing company US BioEnergy Corporation in 2005. Also that year it sold off its Mexican foods business and sold 81% of its 20% ownership of crop-nutrient manufacturer CF Industries in an initial public offering. In 2008 it sold off all its remaining shares of CF.

EXECUTIVES

Chairman: Michael Toelle, age 46
First Vice Chairman: Robert Bass, age 54
Second Vice Chairman: James Kile, age 60
President and CEO: John D. Johnson, age 60
EVP and COO, Processing: Jay D. Debertin, age 48
EVP and COO, Energy: Leon E. Westbrock, age 61
EVP and COO, Ag Business: Mark Palmquist, age 51
EVP and CFO: John Schmitz, age 58
VP Information Technology: Beth Nordin
EVP Corporate Administration: Patrick Kluempke, age 60
EVP Business Solutions: Thomas D. (Tom) Larson, age 60
SVP, CHS Europe: Claudio Scarrozza
SVP and General Counsel: David (Dave) Kastelic
SVP, Grain Marketing: Rick Browne
SVP, Energy Sales: Kevin L. Williams
SVP, Oilseed Processing: Dennis Wendland
President, CHS Foundation: William J. Nelson
Secretary, Treasurer, and Director: Bruce Anderson, age 56
Director, Corporate Communications: Lani Jordan
Auditors: PricewaterhouseCoopers LLP

LOCATIONS

HQ: CHS Inc.
5500 Cenex Dr., Inver Grove Heights, MN 55077
Phone: 651-355-6000
Web: www.chsinc.com

PRODUCTS/OPERATIONS

2008 Sales

	% of total
Ag business	61
Energy	35
Processing	4
Total	**100**

Selected Operations

Convenience stores (Cenex)
Farm financing (Fin-Ag, Inc.)
Farm supplies (Agri-Service Centers)
 Crop-protection products
 Fertilizer
 Grain purchasing
 Seeds
Feed manufacturing
Futures and option services (Country Hedging, Inc.)
Grain merchandising (grain purchasing, transportation, and sales)
Petroleum marketing (Country Energy, LLC)
Soybean crushing (soybean conversion into animal feed and crude soybean oil)
Soybean refining (soybean oil conversion into margarine, salad dressings, and baked goods)
Wheat milling (semolina and durum wheat milling for flour)

Selected Subsidiaries

Agriliance LLC (50%, wholesale and retail distribution of agronomy products)
Cenex Pipeline, LLC (finished product transportation)
CHS do Brasil Ltda. (soybean procurement)
Front Range Pipeline, LLC (crude oil transportation)
Horizon Milling, LLC (24%, wheat milling)
Horizon Milling General Partnership (24%, wheat milling, Canada)
Multigrain A.G. (40%, soybean procurement. Brazil)
National Cooperative Refinery Association (75%, petroleum refining)
Provista Renewable Fuels Marketing, LLC (ethanol marketing)
TEMCO, LLC (50%, grain exporting)
United Harvest, LLC (50%, grain exporting)
Ventura Foods, LLC (50%, food manufacturing)

COMPETITORS

ACH Food Companies	GROWMARK
ADM	JR Simplot
Ag Processing	Koch Industries, Inc.
Agrium	Kraft Foods
AmeriGas Partners	Land O'Lakes
Andersons	Land O'Lakes Purina Feed
Bartlett and Company	Louis Dreyfus Group
BP	Marathon Petroleum
Bunge Limited	Marzetti
Bunge Milling	Mosaic Company
Bunge North America	Nestlé
Cargill	Nestlé USA
Carolina Soy	Riceland Foods
Central Soya	Ridley Inc.
C.F. Sauer	Scoular
CITGO	Shell Oil Products
Columbia Grain	Smucker
ConAgra	Terra Industries
ConocoPhillips	Unilever NV
ContiGroup	U.S. Oil
Dakota Growers	US Soy
ExxonMobil Chemical	Valero Energy
Ferrellgas Partners	Wilbur-Ellis

The Chubb Corporation

Here's the skinny on Chubb: The insurer is best known for comprehensive homeowners insurance for the demographic that owns yachts (the company insures those, too). Chubb also offers commercial property/casualty insurance including multiple peril, property and marine, and worker's compensation. Its specialty insurance arm offers professional liability policies for executives across a spectrum of industries and also provides construction and commercial surety bonds. Chubb distributes its products through 8,500 independent agents and brokers in 120 offices across the US and in nearly 30 countries. The company began in 1882 when Thomas Chubb and his son began writing marine insurance in New York City.

Although the US accounts for more than three-fourths of Chubb's direct business, developing its presence in foreign markets through organic growth is an element of the company's strategy. It prefers to target small and midsized public and privately held companies, and has reduced the number of larger public companies in its customer list. It opened a reinsurance subsidiary in Brazil in 2008.

The same year Chubb created the largest private wildfire fighting force in the US when it engaged federal contractor Wildfire Defense Systems, of Montana, to protect customers' homes in 13 Western states. Customers can enroll to use the service at no additional cost.

HISTORY

Thomas C. Chubb and his son Percy formed Chubb & Son in New York in 1882 to underwrite cargo and ship insurance. The company soon became the US manager for Sea Insurance Co. of England and co-founded New York Marine Underwriters (NYMU). In 1901 NYMU became Chubb's chief property/casualty affiliate, Federal Insurance Co.

Chubb expanded in the 1920s, opening a Chicago office (1923) and, just before the 1929 crash, organizing Associated Aviation Underwriters. Growth slowed during the Depression, but Chubb recovered enough by 1939 to buy Vigilant Insurance Co.

The company bought Colonial Life in 1959 and Pacific Indemnity in 1967. That year Chubb Corporation was formed as a holding company, with Chubb & Son designated the manager of the property/casualty insurance businesses. A 1969 takeover attempt by First National City Corp. (predecessor of Citigroup) was foiled by federal regulators.

Chubb acquired Bellemead Development in 1970 to expand its real estate portfolio. Following a strategy of offering specialized insurance, Chubb in the 1970s launched insurance packages for the entertainment industry, including films and Broadway shows. After the Tylenol poisonings of 1982, Chubb developed insurance against product tampering (which it no longer offers). During the 1980s Chubb focused on specialized property/casualty insurance lines; in 1985 it retreated from medical malpractice insurance.

The company combined three subsidiaries into Chubb Life Insurance Co. of America in 1991. The next year Chubb subsidiary Pacific Indemnity settled a suit over Fibreboard Corporation's asbestos liability (Fibreboard was later bought by Owens Corning); the company ultimately paid some $675 million in asbestos-related settlements.

Financial difficulties at Lloyd's of London caused that market to rethink and subsequently relax its rules about doing business with corporate insurance companies. Chubb took advantage of the opportunity and opened an office at Lloyd's in 1993. The next year Chubb's acquisitions included the personal lines business of Alexander & Alexander (now part of Aon Corporation).

Since the 1880s Chubb had maintained an alliance with UK-based Royal & Sun Alliance Insurance Group and its predecessors. Royal & Sun Alliance owned about 5% of Chubb, and Chubb held about 3% of Royal & Sun Alliance. In 1993 the US insurer formed a new joint venture with the British company, with the purpose of extending to the UK Chubb's insurance products targeting the affluent. But in 1996 a major client of Royal & Sun Alliance Insurance Group defected and Chubb ended the agreement.

To focus on the property/casualty market, Chubb in 1997 sold its life and health insurance operations to Jefferson Pilot and parts of its Bellemead real estate business to Paine Webber and Morgan Stanley Dean Witter. (Chubb blamed the real estate market for its lower 1996 earnings.) The next year the commercial lines market tanked and was followed by a drop in Chubb's earnings.

With losses dragging down its otherwise profitable property/casualty segment, Chubb vowed to get tough — raising rates and getting out of unprofitable businesses. It also forged ahead with its overseas plans, buying Venezuelan insurer Italseguros Internacional and creating Chubb Re to offer international reinsurance. In 1999 Chubb bought corporate officer insurer Executive Risk (now with a Chubb prefix) to beef up its executive protection and financial services lines. The next year UK aviation insurer British Aviation Group bought Chubb's Associated Aviation Underwriters.

Severely affected by terrorist strikes on September 11, 2001, and the collapse of Enron, Chubb paid out almost $900 million in claims. In 2002 Chubb took a $700 million charge related to asbestos and toxic waste. The company's property/casualty lines (primarily the commercial segment) had a strong year in 2003, primarily thanks to higher pricing, but this was negatively impacted by large asbestos-related charges.

In 2004 the company sold its post-secondary educational subsidiary, The Chubb Institute.

EXECUTIVES

Chairman, President, and CEO: John D. Finnegan, age 60, $16,823,602 total compensation
Vice Chairman and COO: John J. Degnan, age 64, $6,545,402 total compensation
EVP and CFO: Richard G. Spiro, age 44, $3,218,313 total compensation
EVP and Chief Underwriting Officer: Paul J. Krump, age 49, $2,298,225 total compensation
EVP and Chief Administrative Officer: Dino E. Robusto, age 51, $1,956,849 total compensation
EVP and Chief Global Field Officer:
Harold L. Morrison Jr., age 51, $2,141,304 total compensation
EVP, Chief Domestic Investment Officer:
Ned I. Gerstman
SVP and Chief Accounting Officer: John J. Kennedy, age 52
EVP, Chubb & Son; COO, Chubb Specialty Insurance: Robert C. Cox, age 51
EVP and General Counsel: Maureen A. Brundage, age 52
EVP, Chubb & Son: Steven Pozzi

SVP and Chief International Investment Officer:
Robert M. Witkoff
SVP and Chief Actuary, Chubb & Son: W. Brian Barnes, age 46
VP and Secretary: W. Andrew Macan
VP and Treasurer: Douglas A. Nordstrom
EVP, Chubb & Son; COO, Chubb Personal Insurance:
Andrew A. McElwee Jr., age 54
COO, Worldwide Accident and Health Insurance:
Stuart A. Spencer
Manager, Public Relations: Mark Schussel
Auditors: Ernst & Young LLP

LOCATIONS

HQ: The Chubb Corporation
15 Mountain View Rd., Warren, NJ 07059
Phone: 908-903-2000 **Fax:** 908-903-2027
Web: www.chubb.com

PRODUCTS/OPERATIONS

2008 Sales

	$ mil.	% of total
Property & casualty premiums earned		
Commercial insurance	5,015	38
Personal insurance	3,787	28
Specialty insurance	2,935	22
Reinsurance assumed	91	—
Investment income	1,652	12
Realized investment gains (losses)	(371)	—
Corporate & other	108	—
Other revenues	4	—
Total	**13,221**	**100**

Selected Subsidiaries

Bellemead Development Corporation
Chubb Atlantic Indemnity Ltd.
  DHC Corporation
    Chubb do Brasil Companhia de Seguros (99%, Brazil)
Federal Insurance Company
  Executive Risk Indemnity Inc.
    Executive Risk Specialty Insurance Company
  Great Northern Insurance Company
  Pacific Indemnity Company
    Northwestern Pacific Indemnity Company
    Texas Pacific Indemnity Company
  Vigilant Insurance Company

COMPETITORS

AIG
Allstate
AXA
Berkshire Hathaway
CNA Financial
The Hartford
Liberty Mutual
Safeco
Travelers Companies

HISTORICAL FINANCIALS

Company Type: Public

Income Statement

				FYE: December 31
	ASSETS ($ mil.)	NET INCOME ($ mil.)	INCOME AS % OF ASSETS	EMPLOYEES
12/08	48,429.0	1,804.0	3.7%	10,400
12/07	50,574.0	2,807.0	5.6%	10,600
12/06	50,277.0	2,528.0	5.0%	10,800
12/05	48,060.7	1,825.9	3.8%	10,800
12/04	44,260.3	1,548.4	3.5%	11,800
Annual Growth	2.3%	3.9%	—	(3.1%)

2008 Year-End Financials

Equity as % of assets: 27.7%	Dividends
Return on assets: 3.6%	Yield: 2.6%
Return on equity: 12.9%	Payout: 26.8%
Long-term debt ($ mil.): 3,975	Market value ($ mil.): 17,845
No. of shares (mil.): 350	Sales ($ mil.): 13,221

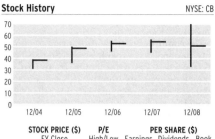

Stock History
NYSE: CB

	STOCK PRICE ($) FY Close	P/E High/Low		PER SHARE ($) Earnings	Dividends	Book Value
12/08	51.00	14	7	4.92	1.32	38.39
12/07	54.58	8	7	7.01	1.16	41.28
12/06	52.91	9	8	5.98	1.00	39.62
12/05	48.83	11	8	4.47	0.86	35.46
12/04	38.45	10	8	4.01	0.78	28.94
Annual Growth	7.3%	—	—	5.2%	14.1%	7.3%

Church & Dwight

Whether you call it saleratus (aerated salt), sodium bicarbonate, or plain old baking soda, Church & Dwight is the world's #1 maker of the powder. Church & Dwight's ARM & HAMMER baking soda, first marketed in 1846, is used as a deodorizer, a cleaner, a swimming pool pH stabilizer, and as leavening. While laundry detergent represents Church & Dwight's top consumer business by sales, the company also makes a variety of other products, such as bathroom cleaners, carpet deodorizer, air fresheners, Brillo scouring pads, toothpaste, antiperspirants, Trojan condoms, industrial-grade carbonates, cat litter, and animal nutrition. It operates in North America, as well as in Australia, Brazil, China, France, and the UK.

The company's business segments are divided into three groups: consumer domestic, consumer international, and specialty products. Church & Dwight's specialty products division. Specialty Products manufactures antacid feed additives for cattle, industrial- and medical-grade sodium bicarbonate (used in kidney dialysis), ammonium bicarbonate, potassium carbonate (used in video monitor glass), and industrial cleaning products. A small subsidiary in the UK produces specialty chemicals for European markets.

Church & Dwight has been investing in its consumer business in the US, where it sells most of these products. Its domestic personal care products segment generated a healthy 37% of its 2008 revenue. To expand its oral care products portfolio, it bought the pharmaceuticals business of Del Laboratories (maker of Orajel) in July 2008 from Coty for about $380 million. Previously, the firm purchased Procter & Gamble's SpinBrush for $75 million plus up to $30 million for performance-related payments. To increase its manufacturing capacity and keep up with growth of its popular laundry segment, Church & Dwight broke ground in September 2008 on a new integrated laundry detergent manufacturing plant and distribution center located in York County, Pennsylvania. (It's slated to be completed by the end of 2009.) The facility replaces its existing laundry detergent plant in North Brunswick, New Jersey. It has also expanded its distribution of ARM & HAMMER laundry and pet care products, as well as Oxiclean and Orange Glo, in North America.

The company continues to concentrate on its international consumer business. Some 82% of its international sales come from Canada, France, Mexico, and the UK. It peddles brands such as Nair in foreign markets and sells Trojan condoms in China and the UK. Since purchasing SpinBrush, the company markets the top US seller in Australia, Canada, China, Japan, and the UK.

Having been appointed president and CEO in mid-2004, James Craigie added the title of chairman in May 2007, when Robert Davies announced he would retire as chairman, but remain on the board.

HISTORY

Chemistry enthusiast Dr. Austin Church and his marketing-driven brother-in-law, John Dwight, founded a company to make bicarbonate of soda for baking in 1846. The ARM & HAMMER trademark — representing Vulcan, the Roman god of fire, and originally used by Church's son James, owner of the Vulcan Spice Mills — was adopted in 1867.

After Church's retirement, his sons ran a separate company until 1896, when they formed Church & Dwight. The company became known for direct marketing and distinctive packaging. Church & Dwight began preaching alternative uses for baking soda in the 1920s and accelerated the effort after WWII, when home baking began to decline.

Dwight Minton, great-great-grandson of Church, was named CEO in 1968. Under his direction the company began appealing to "green" sentiments with new products such as nonphosphate laundry detergent (1970). Church & Dwight went public in 1977.

The Statue of Liberty's inner walls were cleaned with ARM & HAMMER baking soda in 1986 in preparation for its 100th anniversary. New product introductions intensified in the late 1980s and into the 1990s; offerings included toothpaste (1988), carpet deodorizer (1988), and deodorant and other products (1994). The product introductions were badly handled, and a large earnings drop ensued. Minton resigned in 1995 and was replaced by former marketing VP Robert Davies, the first CEO without ties to the founding family.

Broadening its household cleaning products base, the company bought the Brillo soap pad and five other brands from Dial in 1997 and folded Dial's Toss 'N Soft fabric softener business into its laundry basket in 1998. In 1999 it bought the Clean Shower brand (from Clean Shower L.P.) and the Scrub Free and Delicare brands (from Reckitt Benckiser), doubling its household cleaner business.

In 2000 Church & Dwight agreed to combine its laundry detergent business with value-brand cleaning products company USA Detergents. The two companies formed a joint venture, Armkel LLC, before Church & Dwight decided to buy all of USA Detergents in 2001. Several years later, in 2007, Church & Dwight sold USA Detergents to Tital Global Holdings.

Also in 2001 the company acquired Carter-Wallace's consumer products business (Arrid, Trojan, Nair) for $739 million. It bought the US antiperspirant and pet care businesses outright, but the larger part of the deal was made in partnership with private equity firm Kelso & Company. Church & Dwight purchased Unilever's oral care brands in the US and Canada in 2003. Products included in the deal were Mentadent toothpaste and toothbrushes, Pepsodent and Aim toothpaste, and exclusive licensing rights to Close-Up toothpaste. In early 2004 Church & Dwight bought the balance of Kelso & Company's stake for more than $250 million.

In July 2004 chairman and CEO Davies stepped down as CEO, retaining his title as chairman. Former president and CEO of Spalding Sports, James Craigie, took over as president and CEO. He added the title of chairman in mid-2007 when Davies retired.

EXECUTIVES

Chairman Emeritus: Dwight C. Minton
Chairman, President, and CEO: James R. (Jim) Craigie, age 54, $5,132,819 total compensation
EVP Global Operations: Mark G. Conish, age 56, $1,106,525 total compensation
EVP Finance and CFO: Matthew T. Farrell, age 52, $1,906,262 total compensation
EVP and Chief Marketing Officer: Bruce F. Fleming, age 51
VP, Controller, and Chief Accounting Officer: Steven Katz, age 52
EVP Human Resources: Jacquelin J. (Jackie) Brova, age 55
EVP Global New Products Innovation: Steven P. Cugine, age 46
EVP Global Research and Development: Paul A. Siracusa, age 52
EVP Domestic Consumer Sales: Louis H. (Lou) Tursi Jr., age 48
EVP; President and COO, Specialty Products Division: Joseph A. Sipia Jr., age 60, $1,185,404 total compensation
EVP, General Counsel, and Secretary: Susan E. Goldy, age 55
EVP; President, International Consumer Products: Adrian J. Huns, age 61, $1,065,401 total compensation
VP Investor Relations: Maureen K. Usifer
Auditors: Deloitte & Touche LLP

LOCATIONS

HQ: Church & Dwight Co., Inc.
469 N. Harrison St., Princeton, NJ 08543
Phone: 609-683-5900   **Fax:** 609-497-7269
Web: www.churchdwight.com

PRODUCTS/OPERATIONS

2008 Sales

	% of total
Consumer Domestic	
Household	45
Personal care	26
Consumer International	17
Specialty Products	12
Total	**100**

Consumer Domestic Products

Household
    ARM & HAMMER
    Brillo
    Kaboom
    Nice 'N Fluffy
    Orange Glo
    Oxiclean
    Scrub Free
    Xtra

Personal Care
    Aim
    Answer
    ARM & HAMMER
    Arrid
    Close-Up
    First Response
    Nair
    Orajel
    Spinbrush
    Trojan
Specialty Products
    ArmaKleen aqueous cleaner
    Armicarb fungicide
    ARM & HAMMER ammonium bicarbonate
    ARM & HAMMER feed-grade sodium bicarbonate
    ARM & HAMMER sodium bicarbonate
    Armand potassium carbonate
    Armex blast media
    Bio-Chlor
    Fermenten
    MEGALAC rumen bypass fat (animal feed supplement)
    SQ-810 rumen buffer (animal feed supplement)

COMPETITORS

ADM	Johnson & Johnson
Ag Processing	Nestlé Purina PetCare
Alticor	Oil-Dri
Ansell	Procter & Gamble
Cargill	Reckitt Benckiser
CHS	Sara Lee
Clorox	S.C. Johnson
Colgate-Palmolive	SSL International
Dr. Bronner's	Sun Products
FMC	Titan Global
Henkel	Unilever
Inverness Medical	

HISTORICAL FINANCIALS

Company Type: Public

Income Statement

	REVENUE ($ mil.)	NET INCOME ($ mil.)	NET PROFIT MARGIN	EMPLOYEES
12/08	2,422.4	195.2	8.1%	3,500
12/07	2,220.9	169.0	7.6%	3,700
12/06	1,945.7	138.9	7.1%	3,700
12/05	1,736.5	122.9	7.1%	3,700
12/04	1,462.1	88.8	6.1%	3,800
Annual Growth	13.5%	21.8%	—	(2.0%)

FYE: December 31

2008 Year-End Financials

Debt ratio: 58.7%
Return on equity: 16.2%
Cash ($ mil.): 198
Current ratio: 1.72
Long-term debt ($ mil.): 781
No. of shares (mil.): 70
Dividends
    Yield: 0.6%
    Payout: 12.2%
Market value ($ mil.): 3,945

Stock History

NYSE: CHD

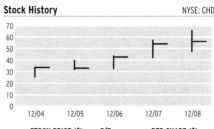

	STOCK PRICE ($) FY Close	P/E High/Low	Earnings	PER SHARE ($) Dividends	Book Value
12/08	56.12	24 17	2.78	0.34	18.94
12/07	54.07	23 17	2.46	0.30	15.37
12/06	42.65	21 16	2.07	0.26	12.29
12/05	33.03	22 18	1.83	0.24	9.91
12/04	33.62	25 19	1.36	0.21	7.97
Annual Growth	13.7%	— —	19.6%	12.8%	24.2%

CIGNA Corporation

One of the top US health insurers, CIGNA covers nearly 12 million people with its various medical plans, which include PPO, HMO, point-of-service (POS), indemnity, and consumer-directed products. CIGNA also offers specialty health coverage in the form of dental, vision, pharmacy, and behavioral health plans, and it sells group accident, life, and disability insurance. Its customers include employers, government entities, unions, Medicare recipients, and other individuals in the US and Canada. Internationally, the company sells life, accident, and supplemental health insurance in parts of Asia and the European Union, and it provides health coverage to expatriate employees of multinational companies.

CIGNA is trying to grow its health care segment by offering new and innovative products, particularly trendy consumer-directed programs such as health savings accounts (through its CIGNA Choice Fund line), health risk assessments, and online tools for comparing coverage options and making sound health care decisions. To that end, CIGNA has jumped on the Medicare Part D bandwagon, offering a Medicare prescription drug benefit program jointly with NationsHealth.

The company's health care operations manage care for its members through a network of some 5,000 hospitals and more than 550,000 providers. CIGNA continually works to strengthen that network of providers, partially through strategic alliances with regional managed care organizations; it has agreements with MVP Health Plan, among others.

CIGNA does much of its business with large employers through direct sales and independent consultants, but it is working to expand its customer base to include more small and midsized businesses, government entities, and seniors. As part of this strategy, it acquired Great-West Healthcare, the health insurance division of Great-West Life & Annuity, in 2008; the acquisition expands CIGNA's range of benefit offerings, particularly in the small and midsized employer market.

CIGNA's disability and life insurance operations offer long- and short-term disability insurance, workers' compensation case management, group life insurance, and accident insurance, among other products. The company sells the policies to employers and employees and to professional associations through brokers and consultants. It covers about 6 million lives with its group life insurance policies.

In addition to its domestic operations, CIGNA is one of the world's largest providers of expatriate health insurance, which covers the overseas employees of multinational corporations. CIGNA also sells life, accident, and supplemental health insurance, primarily through direct marketing channels such as telemarketing.

Chairman and CEO Edward Hanway has announced that he will retire at the end of 2009. President and COO David Cordani will step into the role of CEO while director Isaiah Harris will be named chairman.

HISTORY

The Insurance Company of North America (INA) was founded in 1792 by Philadelphia businessmen. INA was the US's first stock insurance company and its first marine insurer. It later issued life insurance, fire insurance, and coverage for the contents of buildings. In 1808 it began using agents outside Pennsylvania. INA grew internationally in the late 1800s, appointing agents in Canada as well as in London and Vienna in Europe. It was the first US company to write insurance in China, beginning in Shanghai in 1897.

In 1942 INA provided both accident and health insurance for men working on the Manhattan Project, which developed the atomic bomb. It introduced the first widely available homeowner coverage in 1950. In 1978 INA bought HMO International, which was then the largest publicly owned health maintenance organization in the US. INA merged with Connecticut General in 1982 to form CIGNA.

Connecticut General began selling life insurance in 1865 and health insurance in 1912. It wrote its first group insurance (for the *Hartford Courant* newspaper) in 1913 and the first individual accident coverage for airline passengers in 1926. In the late 1930s Connecticut General was a leader in developing group medical coverage. The company offered the first group medical coverage for general use in 1952 and in 1964 added group dental insurance.

After the merger, CIGNA bought Crusader Insurance (UK, 1983; sold 1991) and AFIA (1984). To begin positioning itself as a provider of managed health care, the company sold its individual insurance products division to InterContinental Life in 1988 and its Horace Mann Cos. (individual financial services) to an investor group in 1989. To further its goal, in 1990 CIGNA bought EQUICOR, an HMO started by Hospital Corporation of America (now part of HCA Inc.) and what is now AXA Equitable Life Insurance.

In the early 1990s it began to withdraw from the personal property/casualty business to focus on small and midsized commercial clients in the US, cutting sales overseas and combining them with life and health operations. It also exited such areas as airline insurance and surety bonds.

CIGNA expanded internationally in the mid-1990s, opening a Beijing office in 1993, 43 years after its departure from China.

Reeling from unforeseen environmental liabilities (chiefly related to asbestos), CIGNA in 1995 split its remaining property/casualty business between a healthy segment that continued to write new policies and one for run-off business. Four years later it finally sold these operations (including Cigna Insurance Co. of Europe) to ACE Limited in order to fund internal growth and acquisitions.

In 1997 the company expanded its group benefits operations to India, Brazil, and Poland; at home, it cut its payroll by 1,300 in the US to counter rising costs. It sold its domestic individual life insurance and annuity business in 1998 but began offering investment and pension products in Japan in 1999. In 2000 CIGNA settled a federal lawsuit over Medicare billing fraud. It also sold its reinsurance businesses that year to a subsidiary of Swiss Reinsurance Company.

In 2002 CIGNA formed a joint venture with SDZ, an affiliate of China Merchants Group, to sell life insurance in China. CIGNA sold its retirement division to Prudential in early 2004.

To expand its health care offerings, the company in 2006 bought UK-based vielife, which provides online health management and coaching services, and it acquired Star-HRG, a voluntary health coverage business offering low-cost plans to hourly and part-time workers.

EXECUTIVES

Vice Chairman: Isaiah (Ike) Harris Jr., age 56
Chairman and CEO: H. Edward Hanway, age 57, $12,236,740 total compensation
President and COO: David M. Cordani, age 43, $4,321,161 total compensation
EVP and CFO: Annmarie T. Hagan, age 48
EVP and CIO: Michael D. Woeller, age 56
Chief Marketing Officer: Benjamin (Benjy) Karsch
VP and Chief Accounting Officer: Mary T. Hoeltzel
Chief Medical Officer: Jeffrey L. Kang
Chief Dental Clinical Director: Miles Hall
EVP Human Resources and Services:
John M. Murabito, age 50, $1,951,088 total compensation
EVP and General Counsel: Carol Ann Petren, age 56, $2,184,674 total compensation
SVP and Chief Investment Officer: Richard H. Forde
SVP CIGNA HealthCare: Gary Earl
SVP Service Operations: Brett Browchuk
SVP Sales, Atlanta, Georgia: Tim Vessel
VP Sales, South Texas: Travis H. Brashear
VP Corporate Communications: Christopher Curran
VP, Deputy General Counsel, and Corporate Secretary:
Nicole S. Jones
VP and Treasurer: Thomas McCarthy
VP Investor Relations: Edwin J. (Ted) Detrick
Auditors: PricewaterhouseCoopers LLP

LOCATIONS

HQ: CIGNA Corporation
2 Liberty Place, 1601 Chestnut St.
Philadelphia, PA 19192
Phone: 215-761-1000   **Fax:** 215-761-5515
Web: www.cigna.com

PRODUCTS/OPERATIONS

2008 Sales

	$ mil.	% of total
Net premiums & fees		
Health care	11,615	60
Disability & life	2,562	13
International	1,870	10
Run-off reinsurance & other	156	1
Mail order pharmacy	1,204	6
Net investment income	1,063	6
Realized investment gains (losses)	(170)	—
Other	801	4
Total	**19,101**	**100**

Selected Products and Services

Health care
  Behavioral health care benefits
  CareAllies (disease management and health advocacy)
  CIGNA Choice Fund (consumer-directed products)
  CIGNA Tel-Drug (mail order pharmacy)
  Dental insurance
  Managed care health plans (HMO, PPO, POS)
  Medicare Part D prescription drug coverage)
  Prescription drug coverage
  Stop-loss coverage
  Voluntary plans

Life and disability
  Group disability insurance
  Group term life insurance
  Leave management services
  Workers' compensation case management

International
  Expatriate insurance
  Life, accident, and supplemental health insurance

COMPETITORS

AEGON
Aetna
AIG
Allianz
Allstate
Aon
AXA
Blue Cross
BUPA
Caremark Pharmacy Services
CNA Financial
CVS Caremark
Express Scripts
The Hartford
Health Net
Highmark
Humana
ING
John Hancock Financial Services
Kaiser Foundation Health Plan
MassMutual
Medco Health
MetLife
New York Life
Northwestern Mutual
Principal Financial
Prudential
UnitedHealth Group
Unum Group
WellPoint

HISTORICAL FINANCIALS

Company Type: Public

Income Statement

FYE: December 31

	REVENUE ($ mil.)	NET INCOME ($ mil.)	NET PROFIT MARGIN	EMPLOYEES
12/08	19,101.0	292.0	1.5%	30,300
12/07	17,623.0	1,115.0	6.3%	26,600
12/06	16,547.0	1,155.0	7.0%	27,100
12/05	16,684.0	1,625.0	9.7%	32,700
12/04	18,176.0	1,577.0	8.7%	41,200
Annual Growth	1.2%	(34.4%)	—	(7.4%)

2008 Year-End Financials

Debt ratio: 58.2%
Return on equity: 7.0%
Cash ($ mil.): 1,342
Current ratio: —
Long-term debt ($ mil.): 2,090

No. of shares (mil.): 273
Dividends
  Yield: 0.2%
  Payout: 3.8%
Market value ($ mil.): 4,595

Stock History

NYSE: CI

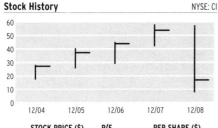

	STOCK PRICE ($) FY Close	P/E High/Low	PER SHARE ($) Earnings	Dividends	Book Value
12/08	16.85	54 8	1.05	0.04	13.17
12/07	53.73	15 11	3.87	0.04	17.41
12/06	43.86	13 9	3.43	0.03	15.88
12/05	37.23	10 6	4.17	0.03	19.65
12/04	27.19	8 5	3.48	0.13	19.08
Annual Growth	(11.3%)	— —	(25.9%)	(25.5%)	(8.8%)

Cincinnati Financial

At Skyline Chili in Cincinnati you can order your chili 3-way, 4-way, or 5-way; at Cincinnati Financial Corporation (CFC) you can order your insurance with plenty of extras as well. The company's flagship Cincinnati Insurance (operating through three subsidiaries) sells commercial property, liability, excess, surplus, auto, bond, and fire insurance; personal lines include home-owners, auto, and liability products. Cincinnati Life sells life, disability income, and annuities. The company's CFC Investment subsidiary provides commercial financing, leasing, and real estate services, and its CinFin Capital Management provides asset management services to businesses, institutions, and not-for-profits.

CFC markets its policies in about 35 states through more than 1,000 independent agencies. The company writes more than 20% of its business in Ohio, and is strong in Illinois, Indiana, and Pennsylvania. Its commercial lines segment targets primarily small to midsized businesses. CFC has tied its growth to expanding the territories it markets in, and increasing the number of new agencies with which it strikes new relationships. Following that strategy it moved into Texas in late 2008.

Also in 2008 CFS netted more than $450 million when it sold about half of its holding in Fifth Third Bancorp. It retained about 6% and will evaluate whether to keep it or dispose of it.

The company formed Cincinnati Specialty Underwriters Insurance Company (CSU), also in 2008, to write commercial surplus and excess coverage for agencies already selling CFC products. It also created CSU Producer Resources as an insurance brokerage offering CSU's products exclusively through Cincinnati Insurance Company agents.

The founding Schiff family owns about 14% of CFC.

HISTORY

Jack Schiff spent three years with the Travelers Company before he joined the Navy in WWII. He returned to Cincinnati to start his own independent insurance agency in 1946 and was joined by his younger brother Robert; both were Ohio State graduates whose affection for the Buckeyes led them in later years to close company banquets with the school fight song. The brothers incorporated Cincinnati Insurance with $200,000 from investors.

Under Harry Turner, the company's first president, the company offered property/casualty insurance to small businesses and homeowners through its network of agents. By 1956 the company had spread into neighboring Kentucky and Indiana. During the next decade Cincinnati Insurance expanded its products and network, adding auto, burglary, and commercial all-risk lines and enlisting agents throughout the Midwest.

In 1963 Turner took the chairman's seat and Jack Schiff became president, introducing a more aggressive leadership style. In 1969 the company reorganized and went public, forming Cincinnati Financial Corporation as a holding company for the insurance operation. CFC used the money to pay off debts and buy new businesses, forming two subsidiaries: CFC Investment Company, in 1970, to deal in commercial real estate and financing; and Queen City Indemnity (later named The Cincinnati Casualty Company), in 1972, to offer direct-bill personal policies.

By 1973 operations included The Life Insurance Company of Cincinnati, Queen City Indemnity, and fellow Cincinnati giant Inter-Ocean Insurance Company. That year Jack Schiff added CEO to his title.

CFC continued to grow throughout the 1970s with a new emphasis on independent investments. In 1982 Cincinnati Financial veteran Robert Morgan became president and CEO. The company's conservative roots and investment base helped it shake off the early-1980s recession and a string of natural disasters that left many other insurers dangling in the wind.

Also during the 1980s, the company started to shift its focus from personal to commercial lines. In 1988 it reorganized its life insurance subsidiaries under the Cincinnati Life banner and formed The Cincinnati Indemnity Company to offer workers' compensation and personal insurance. In 1998 a string of storms (reminiscent of others earlier in the decade) dampened the company's earnings.

Also that year the company — a laggard in the industrywide move into financial services — created CinFin Capital Management. The unit offers the company's in-house asset management skills to corporations, institutions, and wealthy individuals.

In 1999 Jack Schiff Jr. succeeded Morgan as president and CEO. The next year, 96-year-old Harry Turner died. After a 1999 decision by the Ohio Supreme Court that increased exposure on auto policies, CFC set up $110 million in reserves for uninsured motorists claims that year and the following year; the decision was overturned in 2003.

EXECUTIVES

Chairman: John J. Schiff Jr., age 65, $2,072,844 total compensation
Vice Chairman: James E. Benoski, age 70, $1,861,187 total compensation
EVP, CFO, Secretary, Treasurer, Principal Accounting Officer, and Director: Kenneth W. Stecher, age 62, $1,651,689 total compensation
CFO, Treasurer, and Secretary: Steven J. Johnston, age 46, $390,004 total compensation
President and COO, Cincinnati Life Insurance Company: David H. Popplewell, age 65, $985,903 total compensation
VP, Assistant Secretary, Assistant Treasurer, and Principal Accounting Officer; SVP Property Casualty, Cincinnati Insurance Company: Eric N. Mathews, age 53
SVP and Chief Claims Officer, Cincinnati Insurance Co.: Martin J. Mullen
EVP Cincinnati Insurance Company: Jacob F. Scherer Jr., age 56, $1,053,078 total compensation
SVP Operations: Timothy L. Timmel, age 60, $1,616,287 total compensation
SVP Information Technology, Cincinnati Insurance Company: Craig W. Forrester, age 50
SVP Corporate Communications, Cincinnati Insurance Company: Joan O. Shevchik, age 57
SVP; President, Cincinnati Casualty Company: Thomas A. Joseph, age 53, $895,634 total compensation
SVP Excess & Surplus Lines, Cincinnati Insurance Co.: Donald J. Doyle Jr.
SVP, Assistant Secretary, and Assistant Treasurer: Martin F. Hollenbeck
SVP Commercial Lines, Cincinnati Insurance Co.: Charles P. Stoneburner II
VP Personnel, Cincinnati Insurance: Greg Ziegler
Investor Relations Officer: Dennis E. McDaniel
Auditors: Deloitte & Touche LLP

LOCATIONS

HQ: Cincinnati Financial Corporation
  6200 S. Gilmore Rd., Fairfield, OH 45014
Phone: 513-870-2000   **Fax:** 513-870-2911
Web: www.cinfin.com

PRODUCTS/OPERATIONS

2008 Revenues

	$ mil.	% of total
Earned premiums		
Property casualty	3,010	79
Life	126	3
Investment income	537	14
Realized investment gains	138	4
Other	13	—
Total	**3,824**	**100**

COMPETITORS

ALLIED Group
CNA Financial
Erie Indemnity
Farmers Group
Great American Insurance Company
The Hartford
Indiana Insurance
MetLife of Connecticut
Ohio Casualty
OneBeacon
Progressive Corporation
Selective Insurance
Travelers Companies
Westfield Group
Zurich American

HISTORICAL FINANCIALS

Company Type: Public

Income Statement

FYE: December 31

	ASSETS ($ mil.)	NET INCOME ($ mil.)	INCOME AS % OF ASSETS	EMPLOYEES
12/08	13,369.0	429.0	3.2%	4,179
12/07	16,637.0	855.0	5.1%	4,087
12/06	17,222.0	930.0	5.4%	4,048
12/05	16,003.0	602.0	3.8%	3,983
12/04	16,107.0	584.0	3.6%	3,884
Annual Growth	(4.6%)	(7.4%)	—	1.8%

2008 Year-End Financials

Equity as % of assets: 31.3%
Return on assets: 2.9%
Return on equity: 8.5%
Long-term debt ($ mil.): 840
No. of shares (mil.): 163
Dividends
  Yield: 5.4%
  Payout: 59.5%
Market value ($ mil.): 4,728
Sales ($ mil.): 3,824

Stock History

NASDAQ (GS): CINF

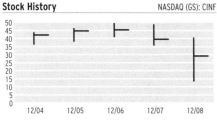

	STOCK PRICE ($) FY Close	P/E High/Low		PER SHARE ($) Earnings	Dividends	Book Value
12/08	29.07	15	5	2.62	1.56	25.71
12/07	39.54	10	7	4.97	1.42	36.46
12/06	45.31	9	8	5.30	1.34	41.86
12/05	44.68	14	11	3.40	1.21	37.42
12/04	42.15	13	11	3.28	1.04	38.42
Annual Growth	(8.9%)	—	—	(5.5%)	10.7%	(9.6%)

Cinemark Holdings

Cinemark Holdings has left its mark on the cinema landscape. The third-largest movie exhibitor in the US (following Regal Entertainment and AMC) has more than 4,700 screens in some 420 theatres in the US, Canada, and Latin America. Cinemark operates its multiplex theaters in smaller cities and suburban areas of major metropolitan markets. Some larger theaters operate under the Tinseltown name; others are "discount" theaters showing no first-run films. The company prefers to build new theaters in mid-sized markets or in suburbs of major cities where the Cinemark theater is the only game in town. In 2007 Cinemark filed to go public.

Despite an economic downturn, people still flocked to the movies, and 2008 hits such as the record-breaking *Dark Knight* were a boon for Cinemark. During 2008 the company continued its expansion by adding some 200 new screens to its holdings. It has commitments to build nearly 150 additional screens by 2012.

Cinemark focuses its efforts on being one of the most modern and technologically advanced movie chains. More than 80% of the company's first-run screens feature stadium seating. Its National CineMedia, a joint venture with Regal Entertainment and AMC Entertainment, delivers digital advertising, pre-recorded concerts, meetings, sporting events, and other non-film entertainment content. In addition, it is planning the continued roll-out of digital cinema through its Digital Cinema Implementation Partners, another joint venture between Cinemark, Regal, and AMC.

In addition to its mainstream theaters, Cinemark operates six art theaters, showing titles such as *Slumdog Millionaire* and *Doubt*, under the CinéArts brand. Internationally, the company has been expanding in Latin America through construction of theaters in growing urban markets. All total, Cinemark operates more than 125 theaters and 1,000 screens in 12 countries in Latin America.

The company is using net proceeds from its 2007 IPO to repay debt. The previous year Cinemark expanded significantly with the acquisition of Century Theatres, the eighth-largest movie-theater operator. The combination added more than 1,000 screens to Cinemark's operations and strengthened its foothold as the third-largest movie-theater operator.

Madison Dearborn Capital Partners owns approximately 45% of Cinemark; Chairman and former CEO Lee Roy Mitchell and the Mitchell Special Trust collectively own about 12%. Members of the Syufy family, the founders of Century Theatres, hold a 8% stake.

HISTORY

Lee Roy Mitchell and partner Paul Broadhead founded Cinemark in 1985, and by the end of 1989, Cinemark had about 660 screens in 18 states. Mitchell set a company goal of 1,000 screens by 1992 and, in addition to constructing its own theaters, Cinemark made acquisitions to achieve its goal.

In 1992 Cinemark built its first megaplex, Hollywood USA — featuring 15 movie screens, a pizzeria, and an arcade. As the multiplex became one of its most profitable theaters, the company added more to its portfolio. Cinemark also

started developing a Latin American presence in 1992, building theaters in Mexico and Chile.

The company formed a joint venture in 1995 to build theaters in Argentina, and in 1996 created three more joint ventures for theaters in Brazil, Ecuador, and Peru.

Meanwhile, Cinemark continued to add megaplexes; it opened 12 theaters with 165 screens (an average of about 14 screens per theater) in 1997. In the first half of 1998, the company added 223 more screens, including 64 in Latin America.

Later that year a group of wheelchair users sued the company, claiming the front-row spaces reserved for them in Cinemark's stadium-seating theaters were uncomfortably close to screens. A US Court of Appeals sided with the theater chain in 2000 and the US Supreme Court refused to hear the plaintiffs' appeal. The company later agreed to modify some theaters and built future theaters in compliance with a court-approved plan.

Cinemark, along with the rest of the movie-theater industry, struggled through the late 1990s as numerous bankruptcies abounded, thanks to overbuilding. The overall decline of the stock market forced the firm to postpone filing an IPO in 2002.

In 2001 Cinemark introduced the electronic gift card for movie ticket and concessions purchases. During 2002, Cinemark opened seven new theaters with 58 screens. The following year the company opened nine new theaters with 77 screens and added three screens to existing theaters.

In 2004 the company brought in investor Madison Dearborn rather than going public, and additional minority investors joined up in the next two years. The following year Cinemark joined Regal Entertainment and AMC Entertainment in National CineMedia, a joint venture that delivers ads and pre-movie entertainment to screens throughout the US and Canada via a private digital network.

In 2006 Cinemark continued its growth with the acquisition of Century Theatres. Also during 2006, the company grew by building 210 screens. In 2007 it again filed an IPO after a brighter year at the box office.

EXECUTIVES

Chairman: Lee Roy Mitchell, age 72,
  $1,780,394 total compensation
CEO: Alan W. Stock, age 48,
  $1,822,416 total compensation
President and COO: Timothy (Tim) Warner, age 63,
  $1,302,295 total compensation
EVP, CFO, Treasurer, and Assistant Secretary:
  Robert D. Copple, age 50,
  $1,251,561 total compensation
EVP and Assistant Secretary: Tandy Mitchell, age 58
SVP Purchasing: Walter Hebert III, age 63
SVP New Technology and Training: Robert F. Carmony, age 50
SVP, General Counsel, and Secretary: Michael Cavalier, age 42, $955,850 total compensation
SVP Film Licensing: Steven (Steve) Bunnell
SVP Real Estate, SVP Development, Director of Real Estate: Tom Owens, age 51
VP Construction: Don Harton, age 51
VP Film Licensing: John Lundin, age 59
VP Marketing and Communications: Terrell Falk, age 58
VP Marketing and Communications: James Meredith, age 40
VP and Director of Theatre Operations: Steve Zuehlke, age 50
President, Cinemark International L.L.C.:
  Valmir Fernandes, age 48
Auditors: Deloitte & Touche LLP

LOCATIONS

HQ: Cinemark Holdings, Inc.
3900 Dallas Pkwy., Ste. 500, Plano, TX 75093
Phone: 972-665-1000   **Fax:** 972-665-1004
Web: www.cinemark.com

2008 US Locations

	Theaters	Screens
Texas	79	1,024
California	64	760
Ohio	20	223
Utah	13	169
Nevada	10	154
Illinois	9	122
Colorado	8	127
Kentucky	8	95
Arizona	7	106
Oregon	7	102
Oklahoma	6	67
Indiana	6	58
Pennsylvania	5	73
Louisiana	5	74
New Mexico	4	54
Virginia	4	52
North Carolina	4	41
Iowa	4	39
Mississippi	3	41
Arkansas	3	30
Florida	2	40
Washington	2	30
Georgia	2	27
New York	2	27
South Carolina	2	22
Kansas	1	20
Michigan	1	16
Alaska	1	16
New Jersey	1	16
Missouri	1	15
South Dakota	1	14
Tennessee	1	14
Wisconsin	1	14
Massachusetts	1	12
Delaware	1	10
West Virginia	1	10
Minnesota	1	8
Montana	1	8
Total	**292**	**3,730**

2008 Foreign Locations

	Theaters	Screens
Brazil	44	368
Mexico	31	300
Chile	12	91
Central America (Costa Rica, El Salvador, Honduras, Nicaragua & Panama)	12	79
Argentina	9	74
Colombia	10	60
Peru	5	43
Ecuador	4	26
Canada	1	12
Total	**128**	**1,053**

2008 Sales

	$ mil.	% of total
US & Canada	1,360	78
Brazil	186	11
Mexico	78	4
Other regions	121	7
Eliminations	(3)	—
Total	**1,742**	**100**

PRODUCTS/OPERATIONS

2008 Sales

	$ mil.	% of total
Admissions	1,127	65
Concession	535	31
Other	80	4
Total	**1,742**	**100**

COMPETITORS

AMC Entertainment
Carmike Cinemas
Clearview Cinemas
Hoyts Cinemas
National Amusements
Pacific Theatres
Regal Entertainment

HISTORICAL FINANCIALS

Company Type: Public

Income Statement

FYE: December 31

	REVENUE ($ mil.)	NET INCOME ($ mil.)	NET PROFIT MARGIN	EMPLOYEES
12/08	1,742.3	(48.3)	—	12,900
12/07	1,682.8	88.9	5.3%	12,300
12/06	1,220.6	0.8	0.1%	13,600
12/05	1,020.6	(25.4)	—	13,600
12/04	790.6	(3.7)	—	—
Annual Growth	**21.8%**	**—**	**—**	**(1.7%)**

2008 Year-End Financials

Debt ratio: 199.0%
Return on equity: —
Cash ($ mil.): 350
Current ratio: 1.74
Long-term debt ($ mil.): 1,614

No. of shares (mil.): 109
Dividends
  Yield: 9.7%
  Payout: —
Market value ($ mil.): 812

Stock History

NYSE: CNK

	STOCK PRICE ($) FY Close	P/E High/Low		PER SHARE ($) Earnings	Dividends	Book Value
12/08	7.43	—	—	(0.45)	0.72	7.42
12/07	17.00	24	17	0.85	0.31	9.32
Annual Growth	**(56.3%)**	—	—	—	**132.3%**	**(20.4%)**

Cintas Corporation

If Cintas had its way, you'd never agonize over what to wear to work. The #1 uniform supplier in the US has about 800,000 clients (Delta Air Lines, DHL) and some 5 million people wear its garb each day. Cintas, which sells, leases, and rents uniforms, operates about 415 facilities across the US and Canada; it leases half of them. In addition to offering shirts, jackets, slacks, and footwear, the company provides cleanroom apparel and flame-resistant clothing. Other products offered by Cintas include uniform cleaning, first aid and safety products, document handling/storage, and cleanroom supplies. CEO Scott Farmer owns about 10% of the firm. His father, Richard, founded the company in 1968.

Uniform rentals generate about 70% of Cintas' sales. The balance of its revenue is logged from uniform sales and its array of other products and services. Although it is the leading renter of corporate uniforms, the company still sees growth potential in this area of its business.

Cintas has been active in building its non-uniform operations, especially its document services unit, through acquisitions. In fiscal 2009 the company purchased about 10 document management businesses in North America. It also made its second acquisition in Europe: Munich, Germany-based Aktenmuehle, which had been the largest independently owned document destruction firm in the country. (Its first European deal was for Certo Information Management in the Netherlands in 2007.) The European acquisitions are in line with Cintas' plans to expand its service offerings in the region. Besides document management firms, Cintas is adding first-aid and fire protection businesses to its portfolio. It acquired three firms in this segment in fiscal 2009. Cintas was particularly active in fiscal 2008, buying up 20 document management services businesses, nine first-aid and fire protection businesses, and one uniform rental business.

Amid the global economic downturn, however, the company is slowing its acquisitive pace and restructuring its business. The US recession and accompanying job losses pushed Cintas in fiscal 2009 to reel in discretionary spending, shut down two manufacturing plants, initiate wage and hiring freezes, and lay off employees. (The firm has slashed more than 10% of its workforce between 2008 and 2009.) The cost-reduction moves saved Cintas about $60 million, but it also took an after-tax charge of about $50 million.

Despite the effects of the turbulent marketplace, Cintas is still recognized as a top company. It was named among the nation's "Most Admired Companies" by Fortune magazine for the ninth consecutive year in 2009. Report on Business magazine also ranked it among Canada's best employers. Cintas employees must wear a Cintas uniform or business suit to work.

HISTORY

In 1929 onetime animal trainer, boxer, and blacksmith Richard "Doc" Farmer started a business of salvaging old rags, cleaning them, and then selling them to factories. Farmer later began renting the rags to his customers. He would pick up the dirty rags, clean them, and return them to the factory. By 1936 the Acme Overall & Rag Laundry had established itself in Cincinnati with plans to convert an old bathhouse into a laundry. Farmer, along with his adopted son Herschell, suffered a setback from flood damage in 1937, but the family rebuilt and continued to grow the business.

Doc Farmer died in 1952, and Herschell assumed command of the company. Five years later Herschell turned the reins over to his 23-year-old son, Richard, who immediately moved Acme into the uniform rental market, and the company blossomed. Throughout the 1960s the company grew enormously, aided by Richard's innovative leadership. (Acme was the first to use a polyester-cotton blend that lasted twice as long as normal cotton work uniforms.) Through a holding company, Richard established a string of uniform plants in the Midwest, starting with a factory in Cleveland in 1968. Four years later the company changed its name to Cintas.

At this time the company began tapping into the new corporate identity market, pushing the idea that uniforms convey a sense of professionalism and present a cleaner, safer image. The company began to custom-design the uniforms, adding logos and distinctive colors. This aspect of the business compelled Cintas to expand to help accommodate its national clients; by 1972 the company had offices throughout Ohio and in Chicago, Detroit, and Washington, DC. By 1975 Cintas was operating in 13 states.

The company went public in 1983. For the rest of the 1980s, Cintas rode the wave of consolidation in the uniform rental industry, making a slew of acquisitions. The company also expanded from its blue-collar base into the service industry and began to supply uniforms to hotels, restaurants, and banks. By the early 1990s Cintas was a presence in most major US cities, and its share of the US market had climbed to about 10%. Farmer turned over the title of CEO to president Robert Kohlhepp in 1995. That year the company acquired Cadet Uniform Services, a Toronto uniform rental business, for $41 million.

Scott Farmer, Richard's 38-year-old son, was named president and COO in 1997. That year Cintas made a number of acquisitions, including Micron-Clean Uniform Service and Canadian firms Act One Uniform Rentals and DW King Services. The company also moved into the first aid supplies industry with its purchase of American First Aid, and added clean room garments to its expanding list of uniform rentals. In 1998 Cintas acquired uniform rental company Apparelmaster, as well as Chicago-based Uniforms To You, a $150 million design and manufacturing company. In an effort to expand its corporate uniform business, the company acquired rival Unitog in 1999 for about $460 million.

As part of the integration of Unitog, in 2000 Cintas closed several of Unitog's uniform rental operations, distribution centers, and manufacturing plants. The company also established first aid supplies and safety equipment unit Xpect. In 2002 Cintas purchased Omni Services, marking its largest acquisition to date.

EXECUTIVES

Chairman: Richard T. (Dick) Farmer, age 73
Vice Chairman: Robert J. (Bob) Kohlhepp, age 64
CEO and Director: Scott D. Farmer, age 49
President and COO: J. Phillip Holloman, age 53
SVP and CFO: William C. Gale, age 52
SVP Global Chain Supply: Kevin Bien
VP, Secretary, and General Counsel:
 Thomas E. Frooman, age 41
VP Human Resources: Michael A. Womack
VP and Treasurer: Michael L. Thompson, age 42
Auditors: Ernst & Young LLP

LOCATIONS

HQ: Cintas Corporation
 6800 Cintas Blvd., Cincinnati, OH 45262
Phone: 513-459-1200   **Fax:** 513-573-4130
Web: www.cintas.com

PRODUCTS/OPERATIONS

2009 Sales

	$ mil.	% of total
Rentals	2,755.0	73
Other services	1,019.7	27
Total	**3,774.7**	**100**

Selected Products and Services

Cleanroom supplies
Document shredding and storage
Entrance mats
Fender covers
Fire protection
First aid and safety products and services
Linen products
Mops
Restroom supplies
Towels
Uniform cleaning
Uniform rental and sales

COMPETITORS

Alsco
Angelica Corporation
ARAMARK
G&K Services
Iron Mountain Inc
NCH
Superior Uniform Group
UniFirst

HISTORICAL FINANCIALS

Company Type: Public

Income Statement

FYE: May 31

	REVENUE ($ mil.)	NET INCOME ($ mil.)	NET PROFIT MARGIN	EMPLOYEES
5/09	3,774.7	226.4	6.0%	31,000
5/08	3,937.9	335.4	8.5%	34,000
5/07	3,706.9	334.5	9.0%	34,000
5/06	3,403.6	327.2	9.6%	32,000
5/05	3,067.3	300.5	9.8%	30,000
Annual Growth	**5.3%**	**(6.8%)**	**—**	**0.8%**

2009 Year-End Financials

Debt ratio: 33.2%
Return on equity: 9.8%
Cash ($ mil.): 130
Current ratio: 4.00
Long-term debt ($ mil.): 786
No. of shares (mil.): 153
Dividends
 Yield: 2.0%
 Payout: 31.8%
Market value ($ mil.): 3,558

Stock History

NASDAQ (GS): CTAS

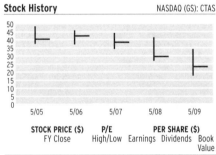

	STOCK PRICE ($) FY Close	P/E High/Low	PER SHARE ($) Earnings	Dividends	Book Value
5/09	23.29	23 12	1.48	0.47	15.49
5/08	29.52	19 13	2.15	0.46	14.75
5/07	38.36	21 17	2.09	0.39	14.19
5/06	42.36	23 19	1.94	0.35	13.67
5/05	40.37	28 22	1.74	0.32	13.77
Annual Growth	**(12.8%)**	**— —**	**(4.0%)**	**10.1%**	**3.0%**

Cisco Systems

Cisco Systems routes packets and routs competitors with equal efficiency. Dominating the market for IP-based networking equipment, Cisco provides routers and switches used to direct data, voice, and video traffic. Other products include remote access servers, IP telephony equipment, optical networking components, Internet conferencing systems, set-top boxes, and network service and security systems. It sells its products primarily to large enterprises and telecommunications service providers, but it also markets products designed for small businesses and consumers through its Linksys division.

Cisco has used acquisitions — more than 120 since 1993 — to broaden its product lines and secure engineering talent in the highly competitive networking sector. Though Cisco remains committed to investments that insure the dominance of its core lines (switches and routers still account for about half of sales), many of the company's recent acquisitions have moved it into new markets.

Among its most significant purchases, the company acquired WebEx Communications, a leading provider of Internet conferencing systems, for approximately $3.2 billion in 2007. The company's acquisition of cable set-top box leader Scientific-Atlanta for approximately $6.9 billion also counted among its most ambitious moves. That deal, which closed early in 2006, was the second largest purchase in its history. (Cisco paid $7 billion for optical networking equipment maker Cerent in 1999.) Cisco has long been an advocate of the convergence of technology behind data, voice, and television networks, and the acquisition of Scientific-Atlanta made it one of the leading providers of the set-top boxes that cable service providers use to deliver advanced features such as movies-on-demand. Looking to build its consumer-oriented business, the company bought camcorder maker Pure Digital Technologies in 2009.

Cisco unveiled a new line of hardware called the Unified Computing System in 2009. Designed to simplify the computing and networking resources in data centers, the product line — which includes blade servers — places Cisco in direct competition with traditional partners such as Hewlett-Packard and IBM.

Its product line far from limited to hardware, Cisco continues to make investments that broaden its technology portfolio. In 2007 it acquired network and e-mail security application developer IronPort Systems for $830 million, as well as policy management software provider Securent. Cisco purchased Pure Networks, a developer of management software for home networks, in 2008. It also acquired e-mail and calendar software maker PostPath.

Cisco has also invested heavily to expand its international presence in recent years. In 2007 it unveiled a $16 billion expansion plan for China, including investments in manufacturing, education programs, and venture capital.

HISTORY

Cisco Systems was founded by Stanford University husband-and-wife team Leonard Bosack and Sandra Lerner and three colleagues in 1984. Bosack developed technology to link his computer lab's network with his wife's network in the graduate business school. Anticipating a market for networking devices, Bosack and Lerner mortgaged their house, bought a used mainframe, put it in their garage, and got friends and relatives to work for deferred pay. They sold their first network router in 1986. Originally targeting universities, the aerospace industry, and the government, the company in 1988 expanded its marketing to include large corporations. Short of cash, Cisco turned to venture capitalist Donald Valentine of Sequoia Capital, who bought a controlling stake and became chairman. He hired John Morgridge of laptop maker GRiD Systems as president and CEO.

Cisco, whose products had a proven track record, had a head start as the market for network routers opened up in the late 1980s. Sales leapt from $1.5 million in 1987 to $28 million in 1989.

The company went public in 1990. That year Morgridge fired Lerner, with whom he had clashed, and Bosack quit. The couple sold their stock for about $200 million, giving most to favorite causes, including animal charities and a Harvard professor looking for extraterrestrials.

With competition increasing, Cisco began expanding through acquisitions. Purchases included networking company Crescendo Communications (1993) and Ethernet switch maker Kalpana (1994). Cisco also surpassed the $1 billion revenue mark in 1994. In 1995 EVP John Chambers succeeded Morgridge as president and CEO; Morgridge became chairman (and Valentine vice chairman).

Cisco entered the service provider market in 1996, when it introduced a line of customer premises equipment (CPE) products. The following year the company broke into the *FORTUNE* 500.

In 1999 Cisco launched a new business line aimed at bringing high-speed Internet access to the consumer market. In its largest acquisition to date, Cisco bought Cerent (fiber-optic network equipment) for $7 billion.

The company's heavy investment in Internet Protocol-based telecommunications equipment proved costly when an industrywide downturn slowed spending among telecom service providers in 2001. Chambers guided Cisco through significant rebuilding measures, including job cuts and a reorganization that aligned its operations around core technologies rather than customer segments.

Key acquisitions over the next few years included home networking specialist Linksys (2003), conferencing systems provider Latitude Communications (2004), and router developer Procket Networks (2004). In mid-2004 the company introduced the CRS-1, a new router designed to compete with high-end offerings from challengers such as Juniper. Featuring an overhauled version of Cisco's Internetwork Operating System (IOS), the CRS-1 resulted from four years of development and an investment of $500 million.

Cisco purchased wireless networking vendor Airespace in 2005. The acquisition provided Cisco with wireless LAN equipment for the enterprise and government sectors.

In 2006 Cisco's advanced technologies unit launched a video messaging product called the Cisco Digital Media System; the system was designed to let companies distribute video messages to employees and customers.

Cisco's 2007 acquisitions included conferencing systems provider WebEx Communications ($3.2 billion), and network security specialist IronPort Systems ($830 million).

EXECUTIVES

Chairman and CEO: John T. Chambers, age 59
EVP and CFO: Frank Calderoni, age 51
SVP and CTO: Padmasree Warrior, age 48
SVP and CIO: Rebecca J. Jacoby
EVP and Chief Marketing Officer, Global Policy and Government Affairs: Susan L. (Sue) Bostrom, age 48
EVP Cisco Services and Chief Globalization Officer: Wim Elfrink, age 56
SVP Corporate Development and Consumer and Small Business Group and Chief Strategy Officer: Ned Hooper
EVP Worldwide Operations and Business Development: Richard J. (Rick) Justice, age 58
EVP Worldwide Operations and Business Development: Robert Lloyd
EVP Operations, Processes, and Systems: Randy Pond, age 54
SVP Human Resources: Brian (Skip) Schipper
SVP Legal Services, General Counsel, and Secretary: Mark Chandler, age 52
SVP Corporate Communications: Blair Christie
SVP and Treasurer: David K. Holland
SVP Global Sales Operations: Bill LePage
SVP Corporate Marketing: Marilyn Mersereau
Investor Relations: Carol Villazon
Auditors: PricewaterhouseCoopers LLP

LOCATIONS

HQ: Cisco Systems, Inc.
170 W. Tasman Dr., Bldg. 10, San Jose, CA 95134
Phone: 408-526-4000 **Fax:** 408-526-4100
Web: www.cisco.com

2008 Sales

	$ mil.	% of total
US & Canada	21,314	54
Europe	8,103	21
Asia/Pacific		
Japan	1,359	3
Other countries	4,254	11
Emerging markets	4,510	11
Total	**39,540**	**100**

PRODUCTS/OPERATIONS

2008 Sales

	$ mil.	% of total
Products		
Switches	13,319	34
Advanced technologies	9,736	25
Routers	7,909	20
Other	2,135	5
Services	6,441	16
Total	**39,540**	**100**

Selected Products

Access servers
Blade servers
Cable modems
Cables and cords
Content delivery devices
Customer contact software
Digital video recorders
Ethernet concentrators, hubs, and transceivers
Interfaces and adapters
Network management software
Networked applications software
Optical platforms
Power supplies
Routers
Security components
Switches
Telephony access systems
Television set-top boxes
Video networking
Virtual private network (VPN) systems
Voice integration applications
Wireless networking

COMPETITORS

3Com	Huawei Technologies
Alcatel-Lucent	IBM
ARRIS	Juniper Networks
Aruba Networks	Meru Networks
Avaya	Microsoft
Belden	Motorola, Inc.
Belkin	MRV Communications
Brocade Communications	NEC
Check Point Software	NETGEAR
Ciena	Nokia Siemens Networks
Dell	Nortel Networks
D-Link	Novell
ECI Telecom	Pace
Enterasys	Polycom
Ericsson	Redback Networks
Extreme Networks	Riverbed Technology
F5 Networks	Sycamore Networks
Force10	Symantec
Fortinet	Tellabs
Fujitsu	THOMSON
Harris Corp.	UTStarcom
Hewlett-Packard	ZTE

HISTORICAL FINANCIALS

Company Type: Public

Income Statement

FYE: Last Sunday in July

	REVENUE ($ mil.)	NET INCOME ($ mil.)	NET PROFIT MARGIN	EMPLOYEES
7/08	39,540.0	8,052.0	20.4%	66,129
7/07	34,922.0	7,333.0	21.0%	61,535
7/06	28,484.0	5,580.0	19.6%	49,926
7/05	24,801.0	5,741.0	23.1%	38,413
7/04	22,045.0	4,968.0	22.5%	34,000
Annual Growth	**15.7%**	**12.8%**	**—**	**18.1%**

2008 Year-End Financials

Debt ratio: 18.6%
Return on equity: 24.5%
Cash ($ mil.): 5,191
Current ratio: 2.58
Long-term debt ($ mil.): 6,393

No. of shares (mil.): 5,768
Dividends
  Yield: 0.0%
  Payout: —
Market value ($ mil.): 126,836

Stock History

NASDAQ (GS): CSCO

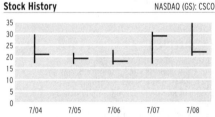

	STOCK PRICE ($) FY Close	P/E High/Low	PER SHARE ($) Earnings	Dividends	Book Value
7/08	21.99	26 16	1.31	0.00	5.96
7/07	28.91	26 15	1.17	0.00	5.46
7/06	17.88	25 19	0.89	0.00	4.15
7/05	19.15	24 20	0.87	0.00	4.02
7/04	20.92	47 28	0.62	0.00	4.48
Annual Growth	**1.3%**	**— —**	**20.6%**	**—**	**7.4%**

Citigroup Inc.

This is the Citi. One of the largest financial services firms known to man, Citigroup (AKA Citi) has some 200 million customer accounts and does business in more than 100 countries. Citigroup offers deposits and loans (mainly through Citibank), investment banking, brokerage, wealth management, alternative investments, and other financial services. Reeling from $90 billion in writedowns and losses on mortgage-related securities and other investments, Citigroup announced plans in early 2009 to split itself in two. The major reorganization will hive off its money-losing assets from its banking divisions.

The two businesses will include Citicorp, which will be made up of the company's retail, investment and private banking units, including Citibank, Citigroup Global Markets, and Citigroup Private Bank. The other business, Citi Holdings, will contain consumer finance segments such as CitiMortgage, CitiFinancial, and Primerica. The move will allow the company to sell or spin off its riskier Citi Holdings assets. It also will allow Citigroup to refocus on its original mission — traditional banking.

The company is combining wealth management units Smith Barney and Quilter with Morgan Stanley's Global Wealth Management Group in a $2.7 billion deal. After the transaction is complete, Citi will own 49% of the new firm, to be called Morgan Stanley Smith Barney (Morgan Stanley will own the other 51%).

The troubles that led to the changes also led to the resignation of CEO Chuck Prince in 2007. He was succeeded by Vikram Pandit, a Morgan Stanley veteran.

As the global credit crisis mounted in 2008, the US government injected some $250 billion into the US banking industry, including a $25 billion investment in Citigroup preferred stock. The government subsequently stepped in again to aid the faltering bank by promising to back some $306 billion in loans and securities and investing another $20 billion in the company. It later announced it would convert the preferred shares into common stock that could amount to a 36% stake in Citigroup.

Meanwhile, the company adopted cost-cutting measures that included reducing its dividends and announcing the elimination of around 15% of its workforce, some 50,000 jobs.

In order to shore up its balance sheet, Citigroup sold some 5% of itself to the Abu Dhabi Investment Authority, a Middle Eastern sovereign fund, for $7.5 billion in 2007. It later raised more than $12 billion by selling preferred shares to investors, including The Government of Singapore Investment Corp., former chairman and CEO Sandy Weill, and Saudi investor Prince Al-Walid bin Talal, who owns a roughly 5% stake in Citigroup.

HISTORY

Empire builder Sanford "Sandy" Weill, who helped build brokerage firm Shearson Loeb Rhoades, sold the company to American Express (AmEx) in 1981. Forced out of AmEx in 1985, Weill bounced back in 1986, buying Control Data's Commercial Credit unit.

Primerica caught Weill's eye next. Its predecessor, American Can, was founded in 1901 as a New Jersey canning company; it eventually expanded into the paper and retail industries before turning to financial services in 1986. The firm was renamed Primerica in 1987 and bought brokerage Smith Barney, Harris Upham & Co.

Weill's Commercial Credit bought Primerica in 1988. In 1993 Primerica bought Shearson from AmEx, as well as Travelers, taking its name and logo. Weill set about trimming Travelers. He sold life subsidiaries and bought Aetna's property/casualty business in 1995. In 1996 he consolidated all property/casualty operations to form Travelers Property Casualty and took it public. In 1997 Travelers bought investment bank Salomon Brothers and formed Salomon Smith Barney Holdings (now Citigroup Global Markets).

Weill sold Citicorp chairman and CEO John Reed on the idea of a merger in 1998, in advance of the Gramm-Leach-Bliley act, which deregulated the financial services industry in the US. By the time the merger went through, a slowed US economy and foreign-market turmoil brought significant losses to both sides. The renamed Citigroup consolidated in 1998 and 1999, laying off more than 10,000 employees.

In 1999 former Treasury Secretary Robert Rubin joined Citigroup as a co-chairman. In 2000 Reed retired. That same year Citigroup bought subprime lender Associates First Capital for approximately $27 billion.

The company parlayed the $4 billion it netted from the 2002 spinoff of 20% of Travelers Property Casualty into a $5.8 billion purchase of California-based Golden State Bancorp, the parent of the then-third-largest thrift in the US, Cal Fed. Also that year Citigroup paid $215 million to settle federal allegations that Associates First Capital made customers unwittingly purchase credit insurance by automatically billing for it.

A landmark ruling by the SEC in 2003 implied that Citigroup issued favorable stock ratings to companies in exchange for investment banking contracts. As part of the ruling, erstwhile star analyst Jack Grubman agreed to pay some $15 million in fines for his overly rosy stock reports and accepted a lifetime ban from working in the securities industry. Citigroup forked over $400 million in fines, the largest portion of a total of some $1.4 billion levied against 10 brokerage firms regarding conflicts of interest between analysts and investment bankers.

Amid the investigations, Citigroup separated its stock-picking and corporate advisory businesses, creating a retail brokerage and equity research unit called Smith Barney. In the SEC's 2003 ruling, such a "Chinese Wall" between bankers and analysts was later made mandatory at all firms.

In 2004 the company — while admitting no wrongdoing — paid $2.65 billion to investors who were burned when WorldCom went bankrupt amid an accounting scandal. (Citigroup was one of the lead underwriters of WorldCom stocks and bonds.) The settlement was one of the largest ever for alleged securities fraud, and compelled Citigroup to set aside an additional $5 billion to cover legal fees for this case and others involving Enron and spinning. The company eventually paid $2 billion in mid-2005 to investors who lost money on publicly traded Enron stocks and bonds, again settling the matter while denying it broke any laws. Enron shareholders had argued that Citigroup helped Enron to set up offshore companies and shady partnerships to exaggerate the energy trader's cash flow.

Weill retired as chairman in 2006 and Prince assumed that title as well. Prince resigned in 2007.

EXECUTIVES

Chairman: Richard D. (Dick) Parsons, age 60
Senior Vice Chairman; Senior International Officer, Citi: William R. (Bill) Rhodes, age 73
Vice Chairman: Edward J. (Ned) Kelly III, age 55
Vice Chairman: Lewis B. (Lew) Kaden, age 67
Vice Chairman: Stephen R. Volk, age 73, $10,532,273 total compensation
CEO and Director: Vikram S. Pandit, age 52, $10,815,263 total compensation
CFO: John C. Gerspach, age 55
Chief Innovation Officer; Managing Director and Senior Advisor, Institutional Clients: Deborah C. (Debby) Hopkins, age 54
Chief Tax Officer: Saul M. Rosen
Chief Auditor: Bonnie L. Howard
Chief Compliance Officer: Cindy Armine
Chief Administrative Officer: Don Callahan, age 52
Chief Risk Officer: Brian Leach, age 49
EVP, Global Government Affairs: Nicholas E. (Nick) Calio
EVP, Global Marketing and Corporate Affairs; Chairman and CEO, Women & Company: Lisa M. Caputo, age 44
EVP, International Customer Franchise and CitiBusiness, Global Consumer Group: Vicky Bindra
SVP, Global Corporate Communications: Kate James
CEO, Citibank, N.A.: Eugene M. (Gene) McQuade, age 60
Head, Global Capital Markets; Markets & Banking; Institutional Clients Group: James A. (Jim) Forese, age 46, $12,855,072 total compensation
General Counsel and Corporate Secretary: Michael S. Helfer, age 63
Head, Human Resources: John L. Donnelly
Treasurer: Eric Aboaf
Auditors: KPMG LLP

LOCATIONS

HQ: Citigroup Inc.
399 Park Ave., New York, NY 10043
Phone: 212-559-1000
Web: www.citigroup.com

PRODUCTS/OPERATIONS

2008 Gross Revenues

	$ mil.	% of total
Interest		
Loans, including fees	62,336	48
Trading account assets	17,489	13
Investments, including dividends	10,718	8
Federal funds sold & securities purchased under resale agreements	9,175	7
Deposits with banks	3,119	2
Other	3,818	3
Noninterest		
Commissions & fees	11,227	9
Administration & other fiduciary fees	8,560	7
Insurance premiums	3,221	3
Other	342	—
Total	**130,005**	**100**

2008 Assets

	$ mil.	% of total
Cash & equivalents	383,717	20
Brokerage receivables	44,278	2
Trading account	377,635	19
Treasury & agency securities	23,965	1
Mortgage-backed securities	29,868	2
Foreign government securities	80,042	4
Debt securities held to maturity	64,459	3
Other securities	57,686	3
Loans		
Consumer	519,673	26
Corporate	174,543	9
Allowance for loan losses	(29,616)	—
Other	212,220	11
Total	**1,938,470**	**100**

COMPETITORS

American Express	HSBC Holdings
Bank of America	JPMorgan Chase
Bank of New York Mellon	Lehman Brothers
Barclays	Mizuho Financial
Capital One	UBS
Deutsche Bank	U.S. Bancorp
FMR	USAA
GE	Wells Fargo
Goldman Sachs	

HISTORICAL FINANCIALS

Company Type: Public

Income Statement

FYE: December 31

	ASSETS ($ mil.)	NET INCOME ($ mil.)	INCOME AS % OF ASSETS	EMPLOYEES
12/08	1,938,470.0	(27,684.0)	—	326,900
12/07	2,187,631.0	3,617.0	0.2%	387,000
12/06	1,884,318.0	21,538.0	1.1%	337,000
12/05	1,494,037.0	24,638.0	1.6%	307,000
12/04	1,484,101.0	17,046.0	1.1%	294,000
Annual Growth	6.9%	—	—	2.7%

2008 Year-End Financials

Equity as % of assets: 3.7%
Return on assets: —
Return on equity: —
Long-term debt ($ mil.): 359,593
No. of shares (mil.): 5,508
Dividends
  Yield: 16.7%
  Payout: —
Market value ($ mil.): 36,957
Sales ($ mil.): 52,793

Stock History

NYSE: C

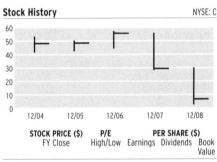

	STOCK PRICE ($) FY Close	P/E High/Low		PER SHARE ($) Earnings	Dividends	Book Value
12/08	6.71	—	—	(5.59)	1.12	25.71
12/07	29.44	77	40	0.72	2.16	20.63
12/06	55.70	13	10	4.31	1.96	21.75
12/05	48.53	11	9	4.75	1.76	20.43
12/04	48.18	16	13	3.26	1.60	19.84
Annual Growth	(38.9%)	—	—	—	(8.5%)	6.7%

Cliffs Natural Resources

Cliffs Natural Resources' favorite period in history? The Iron Age, hands down. The company produces iron ore pellets, a key component of steelmaking, and owns or holds stakes in six iron ore properties that represent almost half of North America's iron ore production. Cliffs' operations, including Northshore Mining and Empire Iron, produce more than 35 million tons of iron ore pellets annually. The company's share is about 65%; the remainder represents the holdings of other mine owners. Cliffs sells its ore primarily in North America but also in Europe and

China. The company also owns Australian iron properties that supply the Asia/Pacific region.

As the North American steel industry struggled early in this decade, Cliffs began to increase its mine ownership by buying up stakes from its steel company partners. The company has continued to buy out the co-owners of the mines it operates even as demand and the greater economy have fluctuated. The latest such deal came in 2008 when it bought Chinese steelmaker Laiwu Steel Group's 30% ownership stake in United Taconite.

In addition, Cliffs has begun to look internationally for new iron ore properties to acquire in order to supply the growing demand for raw materials from the Chinese steel industry. Following the 2005 acquisition of an 80% stake in Australian miner Portman, the company also bought a stake in a venture in Brazil and another in Australia. In the years since its original stake purchase, Cliffs continued to add to its holdings in Portman until it owned the company outright. In early 2009 Portman took on the Cliffs name and identity fully.

In 2007 it acquired PinnOak Resources, a US metallurgical coal producer with operations in West Virginia and Alabama. The deal was for about $600 million in cash and assumed debt. While the acquired company's properties are located in the US, most of its product is slated for export sales.

The next year, it tried to make a much larger move in the same direction with the agreement to buy coal miner Alpha Natural Resources for more than $8 billion. The company soon changed its name from Cleveland-Cliffs. However, the wintry economic climate of late 2008 proved too much for the deal to go through, and the two companies terminated the transaction. Cliffs paid out a $70 million break-up fee as a result.

ArcelorMittal USA accounts for well more than a third of the total sales of Cliffs' North American iron ore pellets.

HISTORY

Samuel Mashers founded the Cleveland Iron Mining Co. in 1846, just five years after the discovery of iron ore in Michigan's Upper Peninsula. To compete in a consolidating market, the company merged with Iron Cliffs Mining in 1891 to form Cleveland-Cliffs. The company offset risks by forming joint ventures with steel companies to own and operate mines. It survived the Depression by selling all its steel and timber operations. The demands of WWII prompted Cleveland-Cliffs to invest in iron mines outside the US — in Canada, Chile, Colombia, Peru, and Venezuela (cut back after WWII to Canada and Australia).

In the 1960s the company rebuffed a takeover bid by Detroit Steel, and in the 1970s it diversified again, acquiring copper, shale oil, timber, and uranium assets. However, Cleveland-Cliffs stumbled financially and sold all its businesses not related to iron ore. The revival of the steel industry in the late 1980s and 1990s lifted Cleveland-Cliff's sales, but the financial struggles of its major customers forced losses on the company.

In 1994 the company bought Cypress Ajax Mineral's Minnesota iron mine (Northshore). In 1996 Cleveland-Cliffs closed its exhausted Australian operations. That year the company formed a joint venture with LTV and Lurgi (of Germany) to make reduced-iron briquettes in Trinidad and Tobago.

Faced with a tide of steel imports from Asia, Brazil, and Russia, the company curtailed production and deferred plans to supply steel minimills with the iron ore pellets needed to produce iron in electric furnaces — the company's planned start-up of its ferrous metallics plant in Trinidad was delayed in 2000 due to mechanical problems. During late 2000 two of Cleveland-Cliffs' mine partners — LTV and Wheeling-Pittsburgh — filed for bankruptcy protection. Cleveland-Cliffs was able to up its stake in the Empire Iron mine, previously co-owned with Wheeling-Pittsburgh, to 35%.

Later that year Canada-based Algoma Steel, co-owner with Cleveland-Cliffs of the Tilden mine, filed for bankruptcy. Also in 2001 Cleveland-Cliffs began production at its ferrous metallics plant in Trinidad; that plant was idled later in the year. In late 2001 the company, along with ALLETE subsidiary Minnesota Power, acquired the iron ore mining and processing facilities of LTV Steel Mining Co., including a rail line and dock facility on Lake Superior. In 2001 Cleveland-Cliffs increased its stake in the Tilden mine to 85%.

In late 2001 the Empire Iron mine was temporarily closed and its operations restructured. The mine reopened in 2002; Cleveland-Cliffs took a $52.7 million charge related to the closure. The following year the company increased its stake in the Empire Iron mine to 79%. In 2003 United Taconite (70% owned by Cleveland-Cliffs) was formed to hold the mining operations it purchased from bankrupt Eveleth Mines.

EXECUTIVES

Chairman, President, and CEO: Joseph A. Carrabba, age 56
EVP and CFO: Laurie Brlas, age 51
CIO: Ronald K. Aderhold, age 46
VP, Corporate Controller, and Chief Accounting Officer: Terrance M. Paradie, age 40
EVP, Commercial North American Iron Ore: William R. Calfee, age 62
EVP Human and Technical Resources: William A. Brake Jr., age 48
SVP Business Development: William C. (Bill) Boor, age 43
SVP; President and CEO, Asia Pacific: Richard R. Mehan, age 53
SVP North American Coal: Duke D. Vetor, age 50
SVP; Managing Director Asia Pacific Iron Ore: Duncan Price
VP Finance: Robert J. Leroux, age 58
VP Public Affairs: Dana W. Byrne, age 59
VP Corporate Planning and Treasurer: Steven Raguz, age 40
VP Sales and Transportation: Terrence R. Mee, age 39
President, North American Business Unit: Donald J. Gallagher, age 56
General Counsel and Secretary: George W. Hawk Jr., age 52
Director Investor Relations and Corporate Communications: Steve Baisden
Auditors: Deloitte & Touche LLP

LOCATIONS

HQ: Cliffs Natural Resources Inc.
  200 Public Sq., Ste. 3300, Cleveland, OH 44114
Phone: 216-694-5700 **Fax:** 216-694-4880
Web: www.cliffsnaturalresources.com

2008 Sales

	$ mil.	% of total
US	1,617.0	45
China	774.2	21
Canada	573.6	16
Japan	263.4	7
Other countries	380.9	11
Total	**3,609.1**	**100**

PRODUCTS/OPERATIONS

2008 Sales

	$ mil.	% of total
North American operations		
Iron	2,369.6	66
Coal	346.3	10
Asian Iron	769.8	21
Other products	123.4	3
Total	**3,609.1**	**100**

Selected Operations

Michigan (Marquette Range)
  Empire Iron Mining Partnership (79%)
  Tilden Mine (85%)
Minnesota (Mesabi Range)
  Hibbing Taconite Company (23%)
  Northshore Mining Company
  United Taconite
Canada
  Wabush Mines (27%, Newfoundland/Quebec)

COMPETITORS

BHP Billiton
Dofasco
Great Northern Iron Ore
International Briquettes
Minerações Brasileiras Reunidas
Rio Tinto Limited
United States Steel
Vale

HISTORICAL FINANCIALS

Company Type: Public

Income Statement

FYE: December 31

	REVENUE ($ mil.)	NET INCOME ($ mil.)	NET PROFIT MARGIN	EMPLOYEES
12/08	3,609.1	515.8	14.3%	5,711
12/07	2,275.2	270.0	11.9%	5,298
12/06	1,921.7	280.1	14.6%	4,189
12/05	1,739.5	272.4	15.7%	4,085
12/04	1,206.7	323.6	26.8%	3,777
Annual Growth	31.5%	12.4%	—	10.9%

2008 Year-End Financials

Debt ratio: 30.0%
Return on equity: 35.4%
Cash ($ mil.): 179
Current ratio: 1.02
Long-term debt ($ mil.): 525
No. of shares (mil.): 114
Dividends
  Yield: 1.4%
  Payout: 7.4%
Market value ($ mil.): 2,913

Stock History

NYSE: CLF

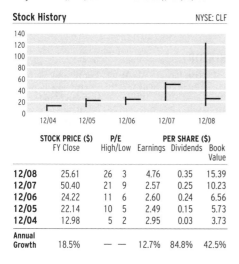

	STOCK PRICE ($) FY Close	P/E High/Low		PER SHARE ($) Earnings	Dividends	Book Value
12/08	25.61	26	3	4.76	0.35	15.39
12/07	50.40	21	9	2.57	0.25	10.23
12/06	24.22	11	6	2.60	0.24	6.56
12/05	22.14	10	5	2.49	0.15	5.73
12/04	12.98	5	2	2.95	0.03	3.73
Annual Growth	18.5%	—	—	12.7%	84.8%	42.5%

The Clorox Company

Bleach is the cornerstone of Clorox. It offers its namesake household cleaning products, where it is a leader worldwide, and reaches beyond bleach. Clorox makes laundry and cleaning items (Formula 409, Pine-Sol, Tilex), dressing/sauce (Hidden Valley, KC Masterpiece), cat litter (Fresh Step, Scoop Away), car care products (Armor All, STP), the Brita water-filtration system (in North America), and charcoal briquettes (Kingsford, Match Light). Its First Brands buy gave Clorox Glad-brand plastic wraps, storage bags, and containers. Clorox entered the natural personal care niche with its acquisition of Burt's Bees in late 2007. Jerry Johnston, former chairman and CEO, retired in May 2006.

Johnston was hospitalized after having suffered a heart attack in March 2006. Clorox named Donald R. Knauss as its chairman and CEO later that year. A former officer in the United States Marine Corps, Knauss began his career as a brand manager for Procter & Gamble. Most recently Knauss was president and CEO of Coca-Cola North America.

While Clorox generated some 84% of its 2008 sales in North America, the company has looked elsewhere for growth potential. The firm sells products in more than 100 countries and makes them in more than two dozen countries. Much of Clorox's foreign growth has been from Latin America and Canada. To secure its foothold there, Clorox bought Latin American and Canadian bleach brands (Javex, Agua Jane, Nevex) from Colgate-Palmolive Company for $126 million plus inventory. The deal, which involved two transactions beginning in December 2006, gave Clorox the license to the Ajax (bleach) brand for a short time in Colombia, the Dominican Republic, and Ecuador. More recently, the company has teamed up with Sara Lee to launch new air freshener products under Clorox's Poett and Mistolin brands in Argentina, Chile, Colombia, Peru, Uruguay, and Venezuela.

It's also inking deals with companies in niche markets to diversify and chase after growing sectors. Enticed by a 9% growth rate and a sector that logs more than $6 billion in annual sales, Clorox purchased the Burt's Bees line of natural skin and hair care products for $925 million in cash in November 2007. Also, in late 2006 Clorox unit The Armor All/STP Products Company signed a licensing agreement with Canada-based Recochem to make and market a line of antifreeze/coolants, windshield washing fluids, and de-icers for sale in North America.

Looking to appeal to a more scrutinizing customer, Clorox in early 2009 announced it is expanding an initiative to disclose and communicate the ingredients it uses in its products. In 2008 Clorox launched the effort with its Green Works line of natural cleaning products.

HISTORY

Known first as the Electro-Alkaline Company, The Clorox Company was founded in 1913 by five Oakland, California, investors to make bleach using water from salt ponds around San Francisco Bay. The next year the company registered the brand name Clorox (the name combines the bleach's two main ingredients, chlorine and sodium hydroxide). At first the company sold only industrial-strength bleach, but in 1916 it formulated a household solution.

With the establishment of a Philadelphia distributor in 1921, Clorox began national expansion. The company went public in 1928 and built plants in Illinois and New Jersey in the 1930s; it opened nine more US plants in the 1940s and 1950s. In 1957 Procter & Gamble (P&G) bought Clorox. The Federal Trade Commission raised antitrust questions, and litigation ensued over the next decade. P&G was ordered to divest Clorox, and in 1969 Clorox again became an independent company.

Following its split with P&G, the firm added household consumer goods and foods, acquiring the brands Liquid-Plumr (drain opener, 1969), Formula 409 (spray cleaner, 1970), Litter Green (cat litter, 1971), and Hidden Valley (salad dressings, 1972). Clorox entered the specialty food products business by purchasing Grocery Store Products (Kitchen Bouquet, 1971) and Kingsford (charcoal briquettes, 1973).

In 1974 Henkel, a large West German maker of cleansers and detergents, purchased 15% of Clorox's stock as part of an agreement to share research. Beginning in 1977, Clorox sold off subsidiaries and brands, such as Country Kitchen Foods (1979), to focus on household goods.

During the 1980s Clorox launched a variety of new products, including Match Light (instant-lighting charcoal, 1980), Tilex (mildew remover, 1981), and Fresh Step (cat litter, 1984). Clorox began marketing Brita water filtration systems in the US in 1988 (adding Canada in 1995). In 1990 it paid $465 million for American Cyanamid's household products group, including Pine-Sol cleaner and Combat insecticide. (It sold Combat and Soft Scrub to Henkel in 2004.)

In 1991 Clorox left the laundry detergent business (begun in 1988) after it was battered by heavyweights P&G and Unilever. Household products VP Craig Sullivan became CEO the next year (stepping down in December 2003).

A string of acquisitions brought the company into new markets as it built on existing brands. Clorox bought Black Flag and Lestoil in 1996 and car care product manufacturer Armor All in 1997. With its 1999 purchase of First Brands — for about $2 billion in stock and debt — Clorox added four more brands of cat litter and diversified into plastic products (Glad).

In 2002 Clorox announced that due to the difficult economic environment in the region, it was selling its Brazil business. In 2003 it jumpstarted a joint venture with Procter & Gamble to take advantage of P&G's manufacturing acumen to improve its Glad products. P&G received a 10% stake in Glad. In late 2004, though, P&G boosted its share in the joint venture (with $133 million) from 10% to 20%, which is the maximum it can invest according to the agreement.

Clorox also sold its Jonny Cat Litter business to Oil-Dri Corporation of America and Black Flag operations in 2003.

In January 2004 Robert Matschullat, the company's nonexecutive chairman, replaced Sullivan upon his retirement. Matschullat stepped down as chairman in January 2005, passing the title to Jerry Johnston, and became a director. Matschullat reclaimed the titles of chairman and CEO on an interim basis when Johnston suffered a heart attack and retired in 2006. Former Coca-Cola executive Donald Knauss was named chairman and CEO in late 2006; Matschullat remained a director.

EXECUTIVES

Chairman and CEO: Donald R. (Don) Knauss, age 58
EVP and CFO: Daniel J. (Dan) Heinrich, age 53
VP and CIO: Robin A. Evitts
SVP and Chief Innovation Officer: Wayne L. Delker, age 55
SVP and Chief Customer Officer: Grant J. LaMontagne, age 53
SVP and Chief Marketing Officer:
Thomas P. (Tom) Britanik, age 51
SVP and Chief Product Supply Officer: James Foster, age 46
EVP Strategy and Growth: Frank A. Tataseo, age 55
EVP and COO, Clorox North America:
Lawrence S. (Larry) Peiros, age 54
EVP International and Natural Personal Care:
Beth (Beth) Springer, age 45
SVP International: Warwick Every-Burns, age 56
SVP and General Manager Specialty Division:
George C. Roeth, age 48
SVP and General Counsel: Laura Stein, age 47
SVP Human Resources and Corporate Affairs:
Jacqueline P. (Jackie) Kane, age 57
SVP and General Manager Cleaning Division:
Benno Dorer, age 45
VP Investor Relations: Steve Austenfeld
VP, Controller, and Chief Accounting Officer:
Thomas D. (Tom) Johnson
VP Marketing: Derek A. Gordon
Auditors: Ernst & Young

LOCATIONS

HQ: The Clorox Company
1221 Broadway, Oakland, CA 94612
Phone: 510-271-7000   **Fax:** 510-832-1463
Web: www.thecloroxcompany.com

2009 Sales

	$ mil.	% of total
North America	4,375	80
International	1,075	20
Total	**5,450**	**100**

PRODUCTS/OPERATIONS

Food-Related Products

Brita
Glad
Glad Press 'n Seal
GladWare
Hidden Valley
K.C. Masterpiece

Household Cleaning Products

Clorox
Clorox 2
Clorox Clean-Up
Clorox Disinfecting Wipes
Clorox FreshCare
Clorox Oxi Magic
Clorox ReadyMop
Clorox Toilet Bowl Cleaner
Formula 409
Formula 409 Carpet Cleaner
Handi-Wipes
Lestoil
Liquid-Plumr
Pine-Sol
S.O.S
Stain Out
Tilex
ToiletWand
Tuffy
Ultra Clorox Bleach

International Products

Agua Jane (bleach, Uruguay)
Ant Rid (insecticides)
Arela (waxes)
Astra (disposable gloves)
Bluebell (cleaners)
Chux (cleaning tools)
Clorisol (bleach)
Clorox Gentle (color-safe bleach)
Glad (containers)
Glad-Lock (reclosable bags)
Guard (shoe polish)
Gumption (cleaners)
Home Mat (insecticides)
Home Keeper (insecticides)
Javex (bleach, Canada)
Mono (aluminum foil)
Nevex (bleach, Venezuela)
OSO (aluminum foil)
Prestone (coolant)
Selton (insecticides)
S.O.S (cleaners)
Super Globo (bleach)
XLO (sponges)
Yuhanrox (bleach)

Specialty Products

Armor All
BBQ Bag
Burt's Bees
EverClean
EverFresh
Fresh Step
Fresh Step Scoop
Kingsford
Match Light
Rain Dance
Scoop Away
Son of a Gun!
STP
Tuff Stuff

COMPETITORS

Alticor	Kiehl's
Avalon Natural Cosmetics	Kiss My Face
Blistex	Kraft Foods
Bonne Bell	McBride plc
CalCedar	Natural Health Trends
Campbell Soup	Nature's Sunshine
Church & Dwight	Newman's Own
Colgate-Palmolive	Oil-Dri
ConAgra	Pactiv
Del Monte Foods	Procter & Gamble
The Dial Corporation	Reckitt Benckiser
Dow Chemical	S.C. Johnson
Dr. Bronner's	Seventh Generation
Estée Lauder	Tree of Life
Forever Living	Turtle Wax
JohnsonDiversey	Unilever

HISTORICAL FINANCIALS

Company Type: Public

Income Statement

FYE: June 30

	REVENUE ($ mil.)	NET INCOME ($ mil.)	NET PROFIT MARGIN	EMPLOYEES
6/09	5,450.0	537.0	9.9%	8,300
6/08	5,273.0	461.0	8.7%	8,300
6/07	4,847.0	501.0	10.3%	7,800
6/06	4,644.0	444.0	9.6%	7,600
6/05	4,388.0	1,096.0	25.0%	7,600
Annual Growth	**5.6%**	**(16.3%)**	**—**	**2.2%**

2009 Year-End Financials

Debt ratio: —
Return on equity: —
Cash ($ mil.): 206
Current ratio: 0.61
Long-term debt ($ mil.): 2,151

No. of shares (mil.): 139
Dividends
  Yield: 3.3%
  Payout: 48.3%
Market value ($ mil.): 7,769

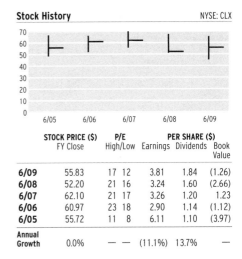
CMS Energy

Michigan consumers rely on CMS Energy. The energy holding company's utility, Consumers Energy, has a generating capacity of 9,600 MW (primarily fossil-fueled) and distributes electricity and natural gas to about 3.5 million customers in Michigan. CMS Enterprises operates the non-utility businesses of CMS Energy, and is a major operator of independent power generating plants; its independent power projects are primarily located in Michigan, but also in California, Connecticut, and North Carolina, and have a gross capacity of 1,200 MW. The company also sells wholesale electricity, natural gas, and other commodities.

Having reined in its international expansion strategy, CMS Energy now focuses solely on the North American market. It has sold nonstrategic assets, including its Latin American electric utilities, as well as its Australian generation and pipeline assets and international power plants and assets in Africa, India, and the Middle East. CMS Energy has also sold its oil and gas exploration and production assets, as well as its domestic gas transportation assets.

HISTORY

In the late 1880s W. A. Foote and Samuel Jarvis formed hydroelectric company Jackson Electrical Light Works in Jackson, Michigan. After building plants in other Michigan towns, Foote formed utility holding company Consumers Power. In 1910 the firm merged with Michigan Light to create Commonwealth Power Railway and Light (CPR&L) and began building a statewide transmission system.

Foote died in 1915, and after nine years of acquisitions, successor Bernard Cobb sold the rail systems and split CPR&L into Commonwealth Power (CP) and Electric Railway Securities. In 1928 Cobb bought Southeastern Power & Light (SP&L) and merged CP with Penn-Ohio Edison to form Allied Power & Light. Commonwealth and Southern (C&S) was then created as the parent of Allied and SP&L.

In 1932 future GOP presidential nominee Wendell Willkie took the helm and became a national political figure by opposing the Public Utility Holding Company Act of 1935, which began 60 years of regulated monopolies. Consumers Power was divested from C&S after WWII.

Consumers brought a nuclear plant on line in 1962 and the next year began buying Michigan oil and gas fields. In 1967 it formed NOMECO (now CMS Oil and Gas) to guide its oil and gas efforts.

The completion of the Palisades nuke in 1971 began a 13-year run of chronic problems and lengthy shutdowns. Cost overruns and an environmental lawsuit killed the firm's third nuke (Midland) in 1984 — after $4.1 billion was spent.

A rate hike and new CEO William McCormick set the firm on a new path in 1985. The new CEO formed a subsidiary to develop and invest in independent power projects in 1986 and created holding company CMS (short for "Consumers") Energy the next year. CMS Gas Transmission was formed in 1989.

Midland Cogeneration Venture (CMS Energy and six partners) completed converting Midland to a natural gas-fueled cogeneration plant in 1990, and CMS Energy wrote off $657 million from its losses at the former nuke. It regained profitability in 1993.

McCormick split the utilities into electric and gas divisions in 1995 and also issued stock for its gas utility and transmission businesses, Consumers Gas Group. The next year CMS Energy formed an energy marketing arm.

In 1996 and 1997 CMS Energy invested in power plants in Morocco and Australia and bought a stake in a Brazilian electric utility. The next year it began developing a gas-fired plant in Ghana and won a bid to build a plant in India. CMS Energy also bought gas gathering and processing firms Continental Natural Gas and Heritage Gas Services in 1998.

Michigan's public service commission (PSC) issued utility restructuring orders in 1997 and 1998, but in 1999 the state Supreme Court ruled that the PSC lacked restructuring authority. Facing less-favorable proposed legislation, CMS Energy and DTE Energy moved to implement competition per the PSC's guidelines.

CMS Energy bought Panhandle Eastern Pipe Line from Duke Energy for $2.2 billion in 1999. It also grabbed a 77% stake in another Brazilian utility and began building its Powder River Basin gas pipeline. In 2000 the company partnered with Marathon Ashland Petroleum (now Marathon Petroleum) and TEPPCO to operate a pipeline transporting refined petroleum from the US Gulf Coast to Illinois. Later that year CMS Energy announced plans for an IPO for its CMS Oil and Gas unit; however, the IPO was withdrawn in 2001.

CMS Energy agreed in 2001 to sell Consumers' high-voltage electric transmission assets to independent transmission operator Trans-Elect for about $290 million; the deal, which was the first of its kind in the US, was completed in 2002. That year the company sold its Equatorial Guinea (West Africa) oil and gas assets to Marathon Oil for about $1 billion. Also that year McCormick stepped down amid controversy over "round trip" power trades that artificially inflated the company's sales and trading volume; CMS Energy later announced that it would restate its 2000 and 2001 financial results to eliminate the effects of the trades.

Later in 2002 the company exited the exploration and production business. It sold CMS Oil and Gas' North American and African assets to private French energy firm Perenco for $167 million, and it sold the unit's Colombian properties to Spanish energy firm Compañía Española de Petróleos (Cepsa) for $65 million. CMS Energy sold its CMS Panhandle companies, which together operated an 11,000-mile pipeline system, to Southern Union for $1.8 billion in 2003.

CMS Energy's nonregulated operations grew to account for more than half of sales in 2001 and 2002; however, as the wholesale power marketing industry has experienced a downturn, the company has refocused on its regulated energy distribution operations. The company has exited the speculative wholesale energy-trading business, which was conducted through its CMS Energy Resource Management (formerly CMS Marketing, Services and Trading) unit; it has sold its wholesale natural gas trading book to Sempra Energy and has sold its electricity trading book to Constellation Energy Commodities Group (formerly Constellation Power Source).

EXECUTIVES

Chairman: Kenneth (Ken) Whipple, age 74
President, CEO, and Director: David W. Joos, age 56, $5,858,785 total compensation
EVP and CFO: Thomas J. (Tom) Webb, age 56, $2,295,106 total compensation
SVP Governmental and Public Affairs and Chief Compliance Officer: David G. Mengebier, age 51
VP and Chief Tax Counsel: Theodore J. Vogel
VP, Controller, and Chief Accounting Officer: Glenn P. Barba, age 43
SVP and General Counsel: James E. Brunner, age 56, $1,639,972 total compensation
SVP Human Resources and Administrative Services: John M. Butler, age 44, $813,636 total compensation
VP Investor Relations and Treasurer: Laura L. Mountcastle
VP and Secretary: Catherine M. Reynolds
President and COO, Consumers Energy: John G. Russell, age 51, $2,046,343 total compensation
Director News and Information: Jeff Holyfield
Director Public Information: Dan Bishop
Auditors: PricewaterhouseCoopers LLP

LOCATIONS

HQ: CMS Energy Corporation
1 Energy Plaza, Jackson, MI 49201
Phone: 517-788-0550   **Fax:** 517-788-1859
Web: www.cmsenergy.com

PRODUCTS/OPERATIONS

2008 Sales

	$ mil.	% of total
Electric utility	3,594	53
Gas utility	2,827	41
Enterprises	379	6
Other	26	—
Total	**6,826**	**100**

Selected Subsidiaries

Consumers Energy Company (electric and gas utility)
CMS Enterprises Company (nonutility holding company)

COMPETITORS

AEP	Edison International
AES	FPL Group
Allegheny Energy	Integrys Energy Group
Alliant Energy	ONEOK
Calpine	SEMCO Energy
CenterPoint Energy	Sempra Energy
Con Edison	SUEZ-TRACTEBEL
DTE	Wisconsin Energy
Duke Energy	Xcel Energy
Dynegy	

HISTORICAL FINANCIALS

Company Type: Public

Income Statement

FYE: December 31

	REVENUE ($ mil.)	NET INCOME ($ mil.)	NET PROFIT MARGIN	EMPLOYEES
12/08	6,826.0	300.0	4.4%	7,970
12/07	6,464.0	(215.0)	—	7,898
12/06	6,810.0	(79.0)	—	8,640
12/05	6,288.0	(84.0)	—	8,713
12/04	5,587.0	123.0	2.2%	8,660
Annual Growth	**5.1%**	**25.0%**	**—**	**(2.1%)**

2008 Year-End Financials

Debt ratio: 253.5%
Return on equity: 13.1%
Cash ($ mil.): 213
Current ratio: 1.52
Long-term debt ($ mil.): 6,243
No. of shares (mil.): 229
Dividends
  Yield: 3.6%
  Payout: 29.3%
Market value ($ mil.): 2,314

Stock History

NYSE: CMS

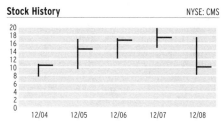

	STOCK PRICE ($) FY Close	P/E High/Low		PER SHARE ($) Earnings	Dividends	Book Value
12/08	10.11	14	7	1.23	0.36	12.01
12/07	17.38	—	—	(1.02)	0.20	10.40
12/06	16.70	—	—	(0.41)	0.00	10.90
12/05	14.51	—	—	(0.44)	0.00	10.14
12/04	10.45	17	12	0.64	0.00	9.05
Annual Growth	**(0.8%)**	**—**	**—**	**17.7%**	**—**	**7.3%**

CNA Financial

CNA Financial is the umbrella organization for a wide range of insurance providers, including Continental Casualty and Continental Assurance. The company primarily provides commercial coverage, with such standard offerings as workers' compensation, general and professional liability, and other products for businesses and institutions. CNA also sells specialty insurance including professional liability for doctors, lawyers, and architects, and vehicle warranty service contracts. The company also offers commercial surety bonds, risk and health care claims management, claims administration, and information services. Its products are sold by independent agents and brokers. Holding company Loews owns about 90% of CNA.

The company has pared its operations to strictly commercial property/casualty. Most of its noncore insurance products are in run-off, including a few remaining annuity and pension products, as well as accident and health insurance.

Like most large insurers, CNA was pinched hard by investment losses and catastrophe losses during industry upheavals in 2008. However, unlike other insurance companies it has the comfort of being held by a good old-fashioned conglomerate. In late 2008 Loews proactively committed up to $1.25 billion of capital injection to CNA to protect the insurer's base.

HISTORY

When merchant Henry Bowen could not find the type of fire insurance he wanted, he began Continental Insurance. Bowen assembled a group of investors and started with about $500,000 in capital. In 1882 Continental Insurance added marine and tornado insurance. Seven years later Francis Moore became president; he was developer of the Universal Mercantile Schedule, a system of assessing fire hazards in buildings.

About the time Continental Insurance was writing the book on fire insurance, several midwestern investors were having trouble assessing risk in their own insurance field — disability. In 1897 this group founded Continental Casualty in Hammond, Indiana. In the early years its primary clients were railroads. Continental Casualty eventually merged with other companies in the field and by 1905 had branch offices in nine states and Hawaii and was writing business in 41 states and territories.

Both Continentals added new insurance lines in 1911: Continental Insurance went into personal auto, and Continental Casualty formed subsidiary Continental Assurance to sell life insurance. By 1915 Continental Insurance had four primary companies; spurred by growing prewar patriotism, they were called the America Fore Group. Both Continentals rose to the challenges presented by the World Wars and the Depression; they entered the 1950s ready for new growth.

In the 1960s the companies began to diversify. Continental Insurance added interests in Diners Club and Capital Financial Services; in 1968 it formed holding company Continental Corp. Meanwhile, Continental Assurance (which had formed its own holding company, CNA Financial) went even farther afield, adding mutual fund, consumer finance, nursing home, and residential construction companies.

By the early 1970s CNA was on the ropes because of the recession and setbacks in the housing business. In 1974 Robert and Laurence Tisch bought most of the company and cut costs ruthlessly. Continental had its own problems in the 1970s, including an Iranian joint venture that got caught up in the revolution.

Both companies suffered losses arising from Hurricane Andrew in 1992, but CNA, which did its housecleaning in the 1970s, was better able to deal with the blow than Continental, which entered the 1990s in need of restructuring.

Rising interest rates in 1994 hurt Continental, whose merger with CNA in 1995 made CNA one of the US's top 10 insurance companies. CNA consolidated the two operations, cutting about 5,000 jobs.

CNA bought Western National Warranty in 1995, followed by managed care provider CoreSource the next year. In 1997 the company spun off its surety business in a deal with Capsure Holdings and formed CNA Surety. Taking advantage of outsourcing trends, CNA created CNA UniSource (payroll and human resources services) and bought its payroll servicer, Interlogic Systems, the next year.

CNA pursued a global strategy, buying majority interests in an Argentine workers' compensation carrier and a British marine insurer, but

with 1998 sales flat and earnings down the tube, the company did more slashing than accumulating. It cut 2,400 jobs and exited such lines as agriculture and entertainment insurance.

The company exited the personal insurance business to focus on the commercial market: It transferred its personal insurance lines, including its auto and homeowners coverage, to Allstate in 1999. Then, in 2000 CNA sold its life reinsurance operations to a subsidiary of Munich Re.

As part of a restructuring effort (the company reshuffled itself into three major segments: property/casualty, life, and group), CNA fired some 10% of its workforce in 2001. In 2002 CNA paid out more than $450 million in claims related to the attacks on the World Trade Center.

CNA Financial restated its earnings in 2002, after being questioned by the SEC over the accounting treatment of investment losses.

Freeing up some much needed capital, CNA sold its group benefits business to The Hartford in 2003 for some $530 million. To better focus on its remaining property & casualty lines, the company sold its individual life insurance segment to Swiss Re Life & Health in 2004.

EXECUTIVES

Chairman and CEO: Thomas F. (Tom) Motamed, age 60
EVP and CFO: D. Craig Mense, age 57, $20,468,596 total compensation
EVP and CIO: John Golden
SVP and Chief Risk Officer: John A. Beckman
EVP and Chief Administration Officer: Thomas (Tom) Pontarelli, age 59
EVP and Chief Actuary: Larry A. Haefner, $1,556,598 total compensation
EVP, General Counsel, and Secretary: Jonathan D. (Jon) Kantor, age 53, $3,191,659 total compensation
EVP Worldwide Property and Casualty Claim: George R. Fay
SVP Specialty Lines Open Brokerage Unit: Daniel S. Fortin
SVP Commercial Insurance: Naveen Anand
SVP Wholesale and Excess and Surplus: John Angerami
SVP Business Insurance: Michael W. (Mike) Coyne
VP Reading, Philadelphia, and Pittsburgh Branches: Michael Smith
VP Small Business: Jim Sinay
VP and Treasurer: Dennis Richard Hemme
Auditors: Deloitte & Touche LLP

LOCATIONS

HQ: CNA Financial Corporation
333 S. Wabash, Chicago, IL 60604
Phone: 312-822-5000 **Fax:** 312-822-6419
Web: www.cna.com

PRODUCTS/OPERATIONS

2008 Sales

	$ mil.	% of total
Net earned premiums		
Property/casualty	6,539	84
Accident & health	611	8
Life	1	—
Net investment income	1,619	21
Realized investment gains (losses)	(1,297)	(17)
Other revenues	326	4
Total	**7,799**	**100**

Selected Subsidiaries

Continental Casualty Company
The Continental Corporation

COMPETITORS

AIG	Nationwide
American Financial Group	Safeco
Chubb Corp	State Farm
The Hartford	Travelers Companies
Liberty Mutual	Zurich Financial Services

HISTORICAL FINANCIALS

Company Type: Public

Income Statement

FYE: December 31

	ASSETS ($ mil.)	NET INCOME ($ mil.)	INCOME AS % OF ASSETS	EMPLOYEES
12/08	51,688.0	(299.0)	—	9,000
12/07	56,732.0	851.0	1.5%	9,400
12/06	60,283.0	1,108.0	1.8%	9,800
12/05	58,786.0	264.0	0.4%	10,100
12/04	62,500.0	441.0	0.7%	10,600
Annual Growth	(4.6%)	—	—	(4.0%)

2008 Year-End Financials

Equity as % of assets: 10.9%	Dividends
Return on assets: —	Yield: 2.7%
Return on equity: —	Payout: —
Long-term debt ($ mil.): 2,058	Market value ($ mil.): 4,423
No. of shares (mil.): 269	Sales ($ mil.): 7,799

Stock History

NYSE: CNA

	STOCK PRICE ($) FY Close	P/E High/Low		PER SHARE ($) Earnings	Dividends	Book Value
12/08	16.44	—	—	(1.18)	0.45	25.56
12/07	33.72	17	10	3.13	0.35	37.73
12/06	40.32	10	7	4.05	0.00	36.31
12/05	32.73	46	34	0.76	0.00	33.27
12/04	26.75	21	15	1.47	0.00	34.22
Annual Growth	(11.5%)	—	—	—	—	(7.0%)

The Coca-Cola Company

Coke is it — *it* being the world's #1 soft-drink company. The Coca-Cola Company owns four of the top five soft-drink brands (Coca-Cola, Diet Coke, Fanta, and Sprite). Its other brands include Barq's, Minute Maid, POWERade, and Dasani water. In North America it sells Groupe Danone's Evian. It also sells brands from Dr Pepper Snapple Group (Crush, Dr Pepper, and Schweppes) outside Australia, Europe, and North America. The firm makes or licenses more than 500 drink products in more than 200 nations. Although it does no bottling itself, Coke owns 35% of Coca-Cola Enterprises (the #1 Coke bottler in the world), 32% of Mexico's bottler Coca-Cola FEMSA, and 23% of European bottler Coca-Cola Hellenic Bottling.

The company's plans to expand its juice operations in China hit a snag in 2009. It was forced to abandon its $2.5 billion offer to buy the Chinese juice company Huiyuan Juice Group after the Chinese government declined to approve the deal on the grounds that it would squeeze out local competition. Coke said that it would, instead, approach expansion in the Chinese market by growing its existing brands and introducing new products.

In 2009 the company began removing the word "Classic" from its prominent place on its flagship US cola products, saying that the reason for the word's being had disappeared. "Classic" was added during the 1980s when the company, having changed the formula for its cola, sought to win back the public, which had soundly rejected the "New Coke." (New Coke was subsequently distributed sparingly by the company and in 2004 quietly dropped.) Although "Classic" is no longer as prominent on the company's cola products, it appears as the phrase "Coke Classic original formula" in a less conspicuous place on product packaging.

Responding to criticism that it sells unhealthy products, in 2009 Coke bought a minority stake of UK smoothie maker Innocent. The €30 million (about $44 million) purchase also furthered Coke's European expansion plans.

Neville Isdell, who came out of retirement in 2004 to help turn the company around, retired as chairman and CEO in 2008. Muhtar Kent, former company president and COO, succeeded Isdell as CEO and retained the title of president. Kent, who was born in New York City, holds dual US and Turkish citizenship, and is known as a skilled tactician, led Coke's 2007 acquisition of Energy Brands, the largest acquisition in company history.

Adding to its non-soda holdings, in 2008 the company acquired a 40% ownership of Honest Tea, a maker of bottled teas and other organic beverages. Another addition to its non-cola offerings took place in 2007, when the company acquired Fuze Beverage, an alternative juice and tea producer, for about $250 million.

The purchase of the maker of smartwater and vitaminwater, Energy Brands (also known as Glacéau), saw Coke forking over some $4 billion in cash in 2007.

Warren Buffett's Berkshire Hathaway owns about 9% of Coca-Cola.

HISTORY

Atlanta pharmacist John Pemberton invented Coke in 1886. His bookkeeper, Frank Robinson, came up with the name based on two ingredients, coca leaves (later cleaned of narcotics) and kola nuts. By 1891 druggist Asa Candler had bought The Coca-Cola Company, and within four years the soda-fountain drink was available in all states; it was in Canada and Mexico by 1898.

Candler sold most US bottling rights in 1899 to Benjamin Thomas and John Whitehead of Chattanooga, Tennessee, for $1. The two designed a regional franchise bottling system that created more than 1,000 bottlers within 20 years. In 1916 Candler retired to become Atlanta's mayor; his family sold the company to Atlanta banker Ernest Woodruff for $25 million in 1919. Coca-Cola went public that year.

The firm expanded overseas and introduced the slogans "The Pause that Refreshes" (1929) and "It's the Real Thing" (1941). To keep WWII

soldiers in Cokes at a nickel a pop, the government built 64 overseas bottling plants. Coca-Cola bought Minute Maid in 1960 and began launching new drinks — Fanta (1960), Sprite (1960), TAB (1963), and Diet Coke (1982).

In 1981 Roberto Goizueta became chairman. Four years later, with Coke slipping in market share, the firm changed its formula and introduced New Coke, which consumers soundly rejected (thus, Coca-Cola Classic was born). In 1986 it consolidated the US bottling operations it owned into Coca-Cola Enterprises and sold 51% of the new company to the public. Goizueta also engineered the purchase of Columbia Pictures in 1982. (Columbia earned Coke a $1 billion profit when it sold the studio to Sony in 1989.)

Goizueta died of lung cancer in 1997; while he was at the helm, the firm's value rose from $4 billion to $145 billion. Douglas Ivester, the architect of Coca-Cola's restructured bottling operations, succeeded him. Ivester resigned in 2000; president and COO Douglas Daft was named chairman and CEO. Coca-Cola began its largest cutbacks ever, slashing nearly 5,000 jobs, and later agreed to pay nearly $193 million to settle a race-discrimination suit filed by African-American workers.

Coca-Cola acquired Mad River Traders (teas, juices, sodas) and Odwalla (juices and smoothies) in 2001. As part of the restructuring initiated by Daft in 2000, another 1,000 employees (half in Atlanta) were laid off in 2003. The company laid off 2,800 employees worldwide in 2003.

Daft retired as Coca-Cola's chairman and CEO in 2004 and former Coca-Cola HBC CEO E. Neville Isdell replaced him. In 2005 Coke bought Danone's 49% stake in their North American bottled-water venture.

Bowing to the public's growing concern about childhood obesity, in 2006 Coke, along with Pepsi, Cadbury Schweppes (whose beverage operations later became Dr Pepper Snapple Group), and the American Beverage Association, agreed to sell only water, unsweetened juice, and low-fat milks to public elementary and middle schools in the US.

In 2006 Coke also joined with Coca-Cola FEMSA to buy top Brazilian juice maker, Jugos del Valle, for $440 million. Still concentrating on Brazil, the next year Coke bought Brazil's bottled tea and beverage maker, Leao Junior. The purchase added more than 60 new products to Coke's Brazilian portfolio.

EXECUTIVES

Chairman, President, and CEO: Muhtar Kent, age 56, $13,990,171 total compensation
EVP and CFO: Gary P. Fayard, age 56, $5,795,404 total compensation
SVP and CIO: Jean-Michel Arès
VP and Chief of Internal Audit: Connie D. McDaniel
EVP and Chief Marketing and Commercial Officer: Joseph V. Tripodi, age 53
EVP and Chief Administrative Officer: Alexander B. (Alex) Cummings Jr., age 52, $5,295,885 total compensation
SVP and Chief Customer and Commercial Officer: Jerry S. Wilson, age 54
EVP; President, Bottling Investments and Supply Chain: Irial Finan, age 51, $6,035,757 total compensation

SVP and General Counsel: Geoffrey J. (Geoff) Kelly, age 64
SVP and Director Human Resources: Cynthia P. McCague, age 58
SVP Corporate Affairs and Productivity: Clyde C. Tuggle
SVP; Head of Global Business and Technology Services: Harry L. Anderson
SVP Global Community Connections; Chairperson, The Coca-Cola Foundation: Ingrid Saunders Jones, age 63
VP and SVP Research and Innovation: Bilal Kaafarani
VP Science: Eddie R. Hays
VP Global Business Services: Ann Taylor
VP and Controller: Kathy N. Waller, age 51
VP Strategic Planning: John M. Farrell
VP and Director Investor Relations: Jackson Kelly
President, Latin America Group: José Octavio Reyes, age 57, $4,712,617 total compensation
Auditors: Ernst & Young LLP

LOCATIONS

HQ: The Coca-Cola Company
1 Coca-Cola Plaza, Atlanta, GA 30313
Phone: 404-676-2121
Web: www.thecoca-colacompany.com

2008 Sales

	$ mil.	% of total
International	23,930	75
US	8,014	25
Total	**31,944**	**100**

PRODUCTS/OPERATIONS

2008 Sales

	% of total
Beverage concentrates & fountain syrups	73
Bottling investments	27
Total	**100**

Selected Brands

Aquarius
Bacardi (mixers and concentrate, licensed)
Barq's
Caffeine free Coca-Cola
Caffeine free Diet Coke
Canada Dry (licensed)
Cherry Coke
Coca-Cola
Coca-Cola Light
Coca-Cola Zero
Coke Zero
Crush
Dasani
Diet Cherry Coke
Diet Coke
Diet Coke Plus
Diet Coke Sweetened with Splenda
Diet Sprite/Sprite Zero/Sprite Light
Evian (licensed)
Fanta
Five Alive
Full Throttle
Fuze
glacéau smartwater
glacéau vitaminwater
Hi-C
Java Monster (distribution in 21 US states, Canada, and six EU countries)
Lost Energy (distribution in 21 US states, Canada, and six EU countries)
Mello Yello
Minute Maid
Monster Energy (distribution in 21 US states, Canada, and six EU countries)
Nestea (Beverage Partners Worldwide, joint venture with Nestlé SA)
Odwalla
Powerade
Rock Star
Schweppes (licensed)
Simply Orange
Sprite
Tab

COMPETITORS

Alamance Foods	Kirin Holdings
American Beverage	Kraft Foods
Aquaterra Corporation	Leading Brands
Britvic Plc	Louis Dreyfus Citrus
Chiquita Brands	Monarch Beverage (GA)
Clearly Canadian	Mountain Valley
Clement Pappas	Naked Juice
Cliffstar	National Beverage
Cool Mountain Beverages	National Grape Cooperative
Cott	Naumes
Cranberries Limited	Nestlé
Danone	Nestlé Waters
Danone Water	New Attitude Beverage
Del Monte Foods	Ocean Spray
Del Monte Pacific	Old Orchard
Dole Food	PepsiCo
Dr Pepper Snapple	Pernod Ricard
Energy Brands	Red Bull
Faygo	Reed's
Ferolito, Vultaggio	Silver Springs
Fiji Water	South Beach Beverage
Florida's Natural	Southern Gardens Citrus
Fresh Del Monte Produce	Sunny Delight
Freshco	Sun-Rype
Gatorade	Suntory Holdings
Goya	Tree Top
Great Western Juice	Tropicana
Hansen Natural	Unilever
Hawaiian Springs	Veryfine
Impulse Energy USA	Welch's
IZZE	Wet Planet Beverages
Jamba	XELR8
Jones Soda	

HISTORICAL FINANCIALS

Company Type: Public

Income Statement

FYE: December 31

	REVENUE ($ mil.)	NET INCOME ($ mil.)	NET PROFIT MARGIN	EMPLOYEES
12/08	31,944.0	5,807.0	18.2%	92,400
12/07	28,857.0	5,981.0	20.7%	90,500
12/06	24,088.0	5,080.0	21.1%	71,000
12/05	23,104.0	4,872.0	21.1%	55,000
12/04	21,962.0	4,847.0	22.1%	50,000
Annual Growth	9.8%	4.6%	—	16.6%

2008 Year-End Financials

Debt ratio: 13.6%	No. of shares (mil.): 2,317
Return on equity: 27.5%	Dividends
Cash ($ mil.): 4,701	Yield: 3.4%
Current ratio: 0.94	Payout: 61.0%
Long-term debt ($ mil.): 2,781	Market value ($ mil.): 104,911

Stock History

NYSE: KO

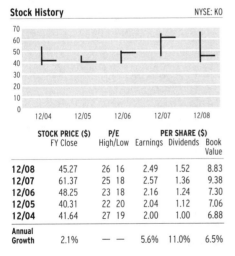

	STOCK PRICE ($) FY Close	P/E High/Low		PER SHARE ($) Earnings	Dividends	Book Value
12/08	45.27	26	16	2.49	1.52	8.83
12/07	61.37	25	18	2.57	1.36	9.38
12/06	48.25	23	18	2.16	1.24	7.30
12/05	40.31	22	20	2.04	1.12	7.06
12/04	41.64	27	19	2.00	1.00	6.88
Annual Growth	2.1%	—	—	5.6%	11.0%	6.5%

Coca-Cola Enterprises

The scientists and the suits at The Coca-Cola Company (TCCC) concoct the secret syrup recipes and market the powerhouse brands, but Coca-Cola Enterprises (CCE) does much of the bottling and distribution of Coke's products. The world's #1 Coke bottler, CCE accounts for 18% of worldwide sales of Coca-Cola's beverages. CCE also bottles and distributes other beverages, including Canada Dry and Dr Pepper (both brands owned by Dr Pepper Snapple Group), Nestea (Nestlé), bottled waters, and juices. It sells soft drinks in nearly every state, the US Virgin Islands, Canada, and six European countries. The company's territories consist of more than 419 million potential customers. The Coca-Cola Company owns 35% of CCE.

An "anchor" bottler for TCCC, CCE continues to increase its share of the Coca-Cola market by acquiring other bottlers in the US, Canada, and Europe. About 54% of the company's North American product and about 42% of its European product are sold in supermarkets. In North America, Wal-Mart is the company's largest customer, accounting for 13% of its 2008 sales.

Boosting its tea offerings, Coca-Cola Enterprises struck an agreement to begin distributing new flavors of AriZona Iced Tea in 2007. That year it also began distributing Campbell fruit and vegetable juice beverages in the US and Canada under an agreement with TCCC.

The company hopes to increase its sales by pursuing growth in its energy drinks, sports drinks, and waters segments, as well as continuing the strong performance of its Coca-Cola Zero brand and the introduction of FUZE, Campbell, and glacéau products.

CCE operates 62 production and 322 distribution sites in North America and 16 production and 31 distribution facilities in Europe. It operates a fleet of approximately 55,000 trucks and owns some 2.4 million coolers, beverage dispensers, and vending machines.

Former CCE chairman Summerfield Johnston Jr. owns about 6% of CCE.

HISTORY

Coca-Cola Enterprises (CCE) was formed in 1986 when The Coca-Cola Company bought its two largest bottlers — JTL Corp. and BCI Holdings — and formed a single corporation. The company went public immediately, though Coca-Cola retained a significant interest in it.

CCE set about acquiring smaller bottling concerns across the US and by 1988 the company had become the #1 bottler in the world. The company centralized operations to boost its slim profit margin.

In 1991 CCE merged with the Johnston Coca-Cola Bottling Group, the #2 US Coca-Cola bottler. The acquisition cost the ailing CCE $125 million, and led a number of disaffected investors to protest. Johnston executives took control when Summerfield Johnston Jr. (whose grandfather had co-founded the first Coke bottling franchisee) assumed the post of CEO, and Henry Schimberg, a former RC Cola route salesman, became president and COO.

In 1992 the bottler was reorganized into 10 US operating regions to allow for better control of individual market dynamics. A $1.5 billion public debt offering occurred that year, and the following year the company began looking outward for growth, acquiring Nederland B.V. (the Coca-Cola bottler of the Netherlands) as well as two Tennessee bottlers. In 1994 CCE recorded its first profitable year since 1990.

CCE bought the 51% stake it didn't already own in Coca-Cola & Schweppes Beverages UK from Cadbury Schweppes for $2 billion in 1997, and it also purchased Coca-Cola's shares in Coca-Cola Beverages Ltd. (Canada's leading bottler) and The Coca-Cola Bottling Company of New York. A half-dozen deals in 1998 included the $1.1 billion purchase of Coke Southwest and other bottling acquisitions in the US and Luxembourg. Schimberg became CEO that year.

Also in 1998 the bottler expanded its vending-machine business, and many distributors and vending-machine owners (who use CCE as a supplier) complained that the firm was charging lower prices in its own machines than independent owners could for the same products.

Bad news came in 1999 when products bottled by CCE in Antwerp, Belgium, and Dunkirk, France, were contaminated by bad carbon dioxide and paint used on wooden pallets to prevent mold. Coca-Cola products were banned or recalled in Belgium, France, and a handful of other European countries for about two weeks, costing the company more than $100 million. Schimberg retired in 1999 and Johnston became CEO again.

In 1999 CCE acquired seven bottlers in the US and one in Europe. European Commission regulators raided various CCE offices in 1999 and 2000 as part of an investigation into anti-competitive marketing programs. In 2001 Johnston stepped down as CEO, but remained chairman. Vice chairman Lowry Kline was named CEO. That same year, the company bought bottlers Hondo and Herbco Enterprises (collectively known as Herb Coca-Cola, the #3 Coke bottler in the US) for about $1.4 billion. The company also announced plans to lay off 2,000 employees as a result of stagnant sales in North America. In 2002 Kline replaced Johnston as chairman.

Having held the position for just one year, president and CEO John Alm left the company in early 2006. Chairman (and former company CEO) Lowery Kline took over temporary leadership until John Brock was appointed president and CEO later in the year. (Brock was formerly CEO of InBev.) Kline continued as chairman.

The company was named (along with the Coca-Cola Company) in a suit brought by independent bottlers in 2006, seeking to bar the two companies from abandoning the tradition in which independent companies that put Coke beverages in bottles and cans also deliver the products to and stack them on the shelves of grocery stores. CCE reached a conditional settlement with Ozarks Coca-Cola and Dr. Pepper Bottling Company.

In addition, a group of shareholders filed a class-action suit against CCE, claiming that the company's practice of channel-stuffing (forcing extra product onto customers in order to boost revenue) affected CCE's financial condition. The suit is ongoing.

The same day that The Coca-Cola Company announced the building of a $45 million plastic recycling plant in 2007, Coca-Cola Enterprises announced the formation of Coca-Cola Recycling. Based at CCE's Atlanta's corporate base, Coca-Cola Recycling will focus on recovering and recycling Coke packaging materials used in North America.

EXECUTIVES

Chairman and CEO: John Franklin Brock, age 61,
$7,066,242 total compensation
EVP and CFO: William W. (Bill) Douglas III, age 48,
$1,758,231 total compensation
SVP and CIO: Esat Sezer, age 47
VP and Chief Customer Officer, North American Group:
Daniel J. Markle, age 52
**VP Business Development, Revenue Growth
Management and Chief Revenue Officer, North
American Group:** Brian E. Wynne, age 44
VP, Controller, and Chief Accounting Officer:
Joseph D. Heinrich, age 53
EVP and President, North American Group:
Steve Cahillane, age 44, $3,785,309 total compensation
EVP; President, European Group: Hubert Patricot,
age 49, $2,374,115 total compensation
SVP and General Counsel: John R. Parker Jr., age 57
SVP Human Resources: Pamela O. (Pam) Kimmet,
age 50
VP Tax: H. Lynn Oliver
VP, Deputy General Counsel, and Assistant Secretary:
Terri L. Purcell
VP and Treasurer: Joyce King-Lavinder
**Vice President and Chief Financial Officer, North
American Group:** Scott Anthony
VP, Secretary, and Deputy General Counsel:
William T. Plybon
VP Retail Industry: Joseph P. Burke
VP Finance, European Group: Charles D. Lischer,
age 40
VP Quality Assurance: Alexander (Alex) Jackson, age 49
VP Internal Audit: Suzanne D. Patterson
Auditors: Ernst & Young LLP

LOCATIONS

HQ: Coca-Cola Enterprises Inc.
2500 Windy Ridge Pkwy., Atlanta, GA 30339
Phone: 770-989-3000   **Fax:** 770-989-3788
Web: www.cokecce.com

2008 Sales

	$ mil.	% of total
North America	15,188	70
Europe	6,619	30
Adjustments (transactions with The Coca-Cola Company)	574	—
Total	**22,381**	**100**

PRODUCTS/OPERATIONS

2008 Sales

	% of total
Coca-Cola products	55
Sparkling flavors & energy products	24
Juices & isotonics	14
Other	7
Total	**100**

Selected Company Brands

North America
  Coca-Cola Classic
  Dasani
  Diet Coke
  POWERade
  Sprite
  smartwater
  vitaminenergy
  vitaminwater
Europe
  Capri-Sun
  Coca-Cola
  Coca-Cola Light
  Coca-Cola Zero
  Diet Coke
  Fanta

Selected Other Company Brands

North America
  A&W
  Ale 8 One
  AriZona Tea
  Big Red
  Canada Dry
  C' plus
  Dannon water
  Dannon water with Flouride
  Diet Ale 8 One
  Diet Big Red
  Diet Canada Dry
  Diet Dr Pepper
  Diet Eas Piranha
  Diet Squirt
  Dr Pepper
  Eas Piranha
  Mendota
  Monster Energy
  Nestea
  Nestea Cool
  Orangina
  Pentric Akers
  Rockstar
  Schweppes
  Spirit
  Squirt
  Vermont Pure
  Yoohoo
Europe
  Appletiser
  Cadbury Schweppes
  Capri-Sun
  Evian
  Fernandes
  Monster Energy
  Rosport
  Viva

COMPETITORS

Britvic Plc
Buffalo Rock
Coca-Cola Bottling Consolidated
Cott
Danone
Danone Water
Eldorado Artesian Springs
Fiji Water
G & J Pepsi-Cola Bottlers
Georgia Crown
Honickman Group
Kraft Foods
Leading Brands
Mountain Valley
National Beverage
Nestlé
Nestlé Waters
Ocean Spray
Palomar Mountain Spring Water
Pepsi Bottling
Pepsi Bottling of Knoxville
Pepsi Bottling Ventures
Pepsi MidAmerica
PepsiAmericas Inc.
PepsiCo
PepsiCo Beverages North America
PepsiCo International
Pepsi-Cola Bottling Company of NY
Pepsi-Cola Bottling of Central Virginia
Pepsi-Cola of Ft. Lauderdale
Snapple
United Water Inc.
Vermont Pure

HISTORICAL FINANCIALS

Company Type: Public

Income Statement

FYE: December 31

	REVENUE ($ mil.)	NET INCOME ($ mil.)	NET PROFIT MARGIN	EMPLOYEES
12/08	22,381.0	(4,394.0)	—	72,000
12/07	20,936.0	711.0	3.4%	73,000
12/06	19,804.0	(1,143.0)	—	74,000
12/05	18,706.0	514.0	2.7%	73,000
12/04	18,158.0	596.0	3.3%	74,000
Annual Growth	**5.4%**	**—**		**(0.7%)**

2008 Year-End Financials

Debt ratio: —
Return on equity: —
Cash ($ mil.): 722
Current ratio: 0.90
Long-term debt ($ mil.): 7,247
No. of shares (mil.): 488
Dividends
Yield: 2.3%
Payout: —
Market value ($ mil.): 5,870

Stock History

NYSE: CCE

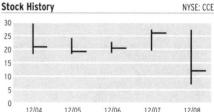

	STOCK PRICE ($) FY Close	P/E High/Low		PER SHARE ($) Earnings	Dividends	Book Value
12/08	12.03	—	—	(9.05)	0.28	(0.06)
12/07	26.03	19	14	1.46	0.24	11.66
12/06	20.42	—	—	(2.41)	0.24	9.28
12/05	19.17	22	17	1.08	0.16	11.56
12/04	20.85	23	15	1.26	0.16	11.02
Annual Growth	**(12.8%)**	**—**	**—**	**—**	**15.0%**	**—**

Colgate-Palmolive

Colgate-Palmolive takes a bite out of grime. The company is a top maker and marketer of toothpaste and a worldwide leader in oral care products (mouthwashes, toothpaste, toothbrushes). Its Hill's Pet Nutrition subsidiary makes Science Diet and Prescription Diet pet foods, while its Tom's of Maine unit covers the natural toothpaste niche. Colgate-Palmolive also makes personal care items (deodorants, shampoos, soaps) and household cleaners (bleaches, fabric softeners, soaps). The company boasts operations in more than 70 countries and sells its products in about 200 countries. Colgate-Palmolive ended its multiyear restructuring plan in late 2008.

To remain competitive, Colgate-Palmolive in late 2004 implemented a four-year restructuring plan. Its three primary objectives were to increase profit, reallocate resources to promising growth areas, and leverage global market efficiencies. It implemented the plan by reducing its global workforce by some 12%, closing about 25 of its 78 factories, and focusing on core units. Colgate-Palmolive also built new state-of-the-art plants to produce toothpaste in the US and

Poland. The company anticipates that its savings, estimated at $500 million altogether, will allow it to fund investments in its key businesses, as well as provide for new product development.

By selling its North American laundry detergent brands in 2005, Colgate-Palmolive is focusing on the high-margin pearly whites (with bite) of its portfolio — oral care and pet care. The company's purchase of natural oral-care products maker Tom's of Maine in 2006 marks its effort to target the natural niche — an industry valued at some $6 billion with a 9% growth rate. It bought some 84% of the firm for about $100 million.

In recent years Colgate-Palmolive brushed up its portfolio by extending its well-known brands into newer product areas. Colgate Simply White teeth whiteners, Motion battery-powered toothbrushes, and Palmolive aromatherapy dishwashing liquids are examples.

While Colgate-Palmolive leads in sales of toothpaste, consumer-goods giant Procter & Gamble (P&G) remains a formidable competitor. With P&G's purchase of Gillette and its greater presence in the industry, Colgate-Palmolive is likely to feel P&G flexing its marketing muscle as it negotiates positions on store shelves and contracts with retailers.

Chairman and CEO Reuben Mark handed over the title of CEO to then president and COO Ian Cook in July 2007 and the title of chairman to Cook in January 2009 as Mark retired at the end of 2008.

HISTORY

William Colgate founded The Colgate Company in Manhattan in 1806 to produce soap, candles, and starch. Colgate died in 1857, and the company was passed to his son Samuel, who renamed it Colgate and Company. In 1873 the company introduced toothpaste in jars, and in 1896 it began selling Colgate Dental Cream in tubes. By 1906 Colgate was making 160 kinds of soap, 625 perfumes, and 2,000 other products. The company went public in 1908.

In 1898 Milwaukee's B. J. Johnson Soap Company (founded 1864) introduced Palmolive, a soap made of palm and olive oils rather than smelly animal fats. It became so popular that the firm changed its name to The Palmolive Company in 1916. Ten years later Palmolive merged with Peet Brothers, a Kansas City-based soap maker founded in 1872. Palmolive-Peet merged with Colgate in 1928, forming Colgate-Palmolive-Peet (shortened to Colgate-Palmolive in 1953). The stock market crash of 1929 prevented a planned merger of the company with Hershey and Kraft.

During the 1930s the firm purchased French and German soap makers and opened branches in Europe. Colgate-Palmolive-Peet introduced Fab detergent and Ajax cleanser in 1947; the brands soon became top sellers in Europe. The company expanded to Asia in the 1950s, and by 1961 foreign sales were 52% of the total.

Colgate-Palmolive introduced a host of products in the 1960s and 1970s, including Palmolive dishwashing liquid (1966), Ultra Brite toothpaste (1968), and Irish Spring soap (1972). During the same time, the company diversified by buying approximately 70 other businesses, including Kendall hospital and industrial supplies (1972), Helena Rubinstein cosmetics (1973), Ram Golf (1974), and Riviana Foods and Hill's Pet Products (1976). The strategy had

mixed results, and most of these acquisitions were sold in the 1980s.

Reuben Mark became CEO of Colgate-Palmolive in 1984. The company bought 50% of Southeast Asia's leading toothpaste, Darkie, in 1985; it changed its name to Darlie in 1989 following protests of its minstrel-in-blackface trademark. Both Palmolive automatic dishwasher detergent and Colgate Tartar Control toothpaste were introduced in 1986. That year Colgate-Palmolive purchased the liquid soap lines of Minnetonka, the most popular of which is Softsoap. In 1992 the company bought Mennen, maker of Speed Stick (the leading US deodorant).

Increasing its share of the oral care market in Latin America to 79% in 1995, Colgate-Palmolive acquired Brazilian company Kolynos (from Wyeth for $1 billion) and 94% of Argentina's Odol Saic. The company also bought Ciba-Geigy's oral hygiene business in India, increasing its share of that toothpaste market. At home, however, sales and earnings in key segments were dismal, so in 1995 Colgate-Palmolive began a restructuring that included cutting more than 8% of its employees and closing or reconfiguring 24 factories in two years.

The company introduced a record 602 products in 1996 and continued to expand its operations in countries with emerging economies. In 1997 Colgate-Palmolive took the lead in the US toothpaste market for the first time in 35 years (displacing P&G).

In 1999 the company sold the rights to Baby Magic (shampoos, lotions, oils) in the US, Canada, and Puerto Rico to Playtex Products, retaining the rights in all other countries. Two years later the company sold its heavy-duty laundry detergent business in Mexico (primarily the Viva brand) to Henkel, one of Europe's leading detergent producers.

In 2002 Colgate-Palmolive introduced a teeth-whitening gel, Simply White, to compete with rival P&G's Crest Whitestrips. The company saw success that year when its Hill's Pet Nutrition subsidiary launched new specialty foods for cats and dogs; one of its dog foods reportedly slows brain aging in canines.

EXECUTIVES

Chairman, President, and CEO: Ian M. Cook, age 56, $15,119,927 total compensation
CFO: Stephen C. Patrick, age 59, $4,167,657 total compensation
VP and CIO: Tom Greene
VP and Chief Ethics and Compliance Officer: Gregory P. Woodson, age 57
VP and Chief Procurement Officer: Manuel Arrese
EVP; President, Colgate-Latin America and Global Sustainability: Fabian T. Garcia, age 49, $3,102,251 total compensation
SVP, General Counsel, and Secretary: Andrew D. Hendry, age 61
SVP Global Information Technology and Business Services: Edmund D. (Ed) Toben, age 60
SVP Global Human Resources: Daniel B. Marsili, age 48
VP Office of the Chairman: John J. Huston, age 54
VP Investor Relations: Delia H. Thompson, age 59
VP Corporate Communications: Jan Guifarro
VP Global Marketing: William H. Lunderman
CEO, Tom's of Maine: Tom O'Brien
President, Global Customer Development: Antonio Caro
President, Global Marketing, Supply Chain, and Technology: Franck J. Moison, age 55, $5,058,159 total compensation
CEO, Hill's Pet Nutrition: Neil Thompson
COO, Colgate-Europe and Greater Asia and Africa: Michael J. Tangney, age 64, $4,997,111 total compensation
Auditors: PricewaterhouseCoopers LLP

LOCATIONS

HQ: Colgate-Palmolive Company
300 Park Ave., New York, NY 10022
Phone: 212-310-2000   **Fax:** 212-310-2475
Web: www.colgate.com

2008 Sales

	$ mil.	% of total
Oral, personal & home care		
Latin America	4,088.0	27
Europe/South Pacific	3,582.7	23
North America	2,851.7	19
Greater Asia/Africa	2,660.0	17
Pet nutrition	2,147.5	14
Total	**15,329.9**	**100**

PRODUCTS/OPERATIONS

2008 Sales

	$ mil.	% of total
Oral, personal & home care	13,182.4	86
Pet nutrition	2,147.5	14
Total	**15,329.9**	**100**

Selected Brands

Personal Care
  Irish Spring
  Mennen
  Palmolive Botanicals
  Softsoap
  Speed Stick

Household Surface Care
  Ajax
  Murphy's oil soap
  Palmolive

Pet Nutrition
  Prescription Diet Canine b/d
  Prescription Diet Feline z/d
  Science Diet

COMPETITORS

Alberto-Culver
Alticor
Avon
Chattem
Church & Dwight
Clorox
Doane Pet Care
Henkel
Johnson & Johnson
L'Oréal USA
Mars, Incorporated
Meda Pharmaceuticals
Nestlé
Nu Skin
Procter & Gamble
Reckitt Benckiser
S.C. Johnson
Unilever

HISTORICAL FINANCIALS

Company Type: Public

Income Statement				FYE: December 31
	REVENUE ($ mil.)	NET INCOME ($ mil.)	NET PROFIT MARGIN	EMPLOYEES
12/08	15,329.9	1,957.2	12.8%	36,600
12/07	13,789.7	1,737.4	12.6%	36,000
12/06	12,237.7	1,353.4	11.1%	34,700
12/05	11,396.9	1,351.4	11.9%	35,800
12/04	10,584.2	1,327.1	12.5%	36,000
Annual Growth	**9.7%**	**10.2%**	**—**	**0.4%**

2008 Year-End Financials

Debt ratio: 205.9%   No. of shares (mil.): 498
Return on equity: 102.2%   Dividends
Cash ($ mil.): 555   Yield: 2.3%
Current ratio: 1.26   Payout: 42.6%
Long-term debt ($ mil.): 3,585   Market value ($ mil.): 34,162

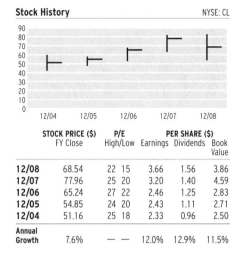

	STOCK PRICE ($) FY Close	P/E High/Low	PER SHARE ($) Earnings	Dividends	Book Value
12/08	68.54	22 15	3.66	1.56	3.86
12/07	77.96	25 20	3.20	1.40	4.59
12/06	65.24	27 22	2.46	1.25	2.83
12/05	54.85	24 20	2.43	1.11	2.71
12/04	51.16	25 18	2.33	0.96	2.50
Annual Growth	7.6%	— —	12.0%	12.9%	11.5%

Collective Brands

Collective Brands is looking to bank on its collective efforts in shoe making and retailing. The holding company boasts a portfolio of premium and moderate footwear and accessories through its Stride Rite unit, a wide reach of about 4,875 Payless ShoeSource and Stride Rite retail outlets, and an established licensing and brand management unit in Collective Licensing. Collective Brands was formed in August 2007, when powerhouse Payless ShoeSource acquired Stride Rite, which is primarily a wholesaler to department stores and operates leased departments at Macy's stores. With brands such as Keds, Saucony, and Robeez, the company operates in the US, Canada, the Caribbean, Central and South America, and Puerto Rico.

The deal to pair Payless ShoeSource with Stride Rite in Collective Brands' closet was valued at $800 million plus an estimated $100 million in debt. As part of the agreement, the businesses operate as separate entities, maintain their current headquarters, and retain their brand identities. A joined Payless ShoeSource, Stride Rite, and Collective Licensing provides numerous competitive advantages for Collective Brands. These include the ability to target a variety of customers at a broader price-point range through multiple channels, such as wholesale, retail, licensing, and e-commerce. Not only did the deal make Collective Brands a top shoe seller worldwide, but it also gave the firm a foothold at the premium and moderate levels of children's shoes.

Payless' 3,900 US stores account for more than 60% of Collective Brands sales. On the international front, in 2009 the company announced plans to expand in Russia through a franchising agreement with M.H. Alshaya. The first Payless stores in Russia are slated to debut in 2010. Alshaya is also Payless' franchise partner in the Middle East, where the shoe seller already operates stores in the UAE, Saudi Arabia, and Kuwait. Other countries in the region, including Bahrain, Egypt, and Lebanon, are on the list for expansion.

Denver-based Collective Licensing, acquired in March 2007 for about $91 million, is a youth-oriented brand development, management, and licensing lifestyle business.

In May 2008 a federal jury in Oregon awarded adidas AG $305 million for trademark violation of its three-stripe design by Collective Brands. The firm is appealing the judgment, which it called "excessive and unjustified."

Matt Rubel, Payless' CEO, also serves as the holding company's top executive. Stride Rite CEO David Chamberlain stepped down as the firm's top executive at the completion of the deal; Richard Thornton was retained as Stride Rite's president and COO.

EXECUTIVES

Chairman, President, and CEO: Matthew E. (Matt) Rubel, age 51, $9,888,006 total compensation
Division SVP, CFO, and Treasurer: Douglas G. (Doug) Boessen, age 46, $456,046 total compensation
SVP and Chief Administrative Officer, Stride Rite: Frank A. Caruso
SVP and Chief Marketing Officer, Payless ShoeSource: Eran Cohen
EVP and Chief Administrative Officer: Douglas J. Treff, age 51, $1,244,487 total compensation
EVP Global Supply Chain, Payless ShoeSource: Darrel J. Pavelka, age 53, $1,832,622 total compensation
SVP, General Counsel, and Secretary: Michael J. Massey, age 44, $1,206,330 total compensation
SVP General Merchandise Manager, Women's, Payless ShoeSource: Theodore O. (Ted) Passig
SVP Retail Operation, Payless ShoeSource: Stephen J. (Steve) Gish
SVP and General Merchandise Manager, Children's, Men's, and Athletics, Payless ShoeSource: Scott Ramsland
SVP Global Sourcing and Product Development: Michael Jeppesen
SVP Human Resources: Betty J. Click, age 47
President and CEO, Collective Licensing International: Bruce Pettet
President and CEO, Payless ShoeSource: LuAnn Via
President and CEO, Stride Rite: Gregg Ribatt, age 40
Corporate Media Relations: Nicole R. (Nikki) Sloup
Auditors: Deloitte & Touche LLP

LOCATIONS

HQ: Collective Brands, Inc.
3231 SE 6th Ave., Topeka, KS 66607
Phone: 785-233-5171   **Fax:** 785-368-7510
Web: www.paylessshoesource.com

2009 Sales

	$ mil.	% of total
US	2,862.0	83
International	580.0	17
Total	**3,442.0**	**100**

PRODUCTS/OPERATIONS

2009 Stores

	No.
Payless domestic	3,900
Payless international	622
Stride Rite retail	355
Total	**4,877**

2009 Sales

	$ mil.	% of total
Payless domestic	2,190.7	64
Payless international	444.7	13
Stride Rite wholesale	591.6	17
Stride Rite retail	215.0	6
Total	**3,442.0**	**100**

Selected Brands

Collective Licensing
  Airwalk
  Dukes
  genetic
  Lamar
  LDT
  Rage
  Sims
  Skate Attack
  Vision Street Wear
  Ultra-Wheels
Payless
  Abaeté for Payless
  ABT for Spotlights
  alice + olivis for Payless
  Airwalk
  American Eagle
  Champion
  Dexter
  Disney
  Dunkman
  Lela Rose for Payless
Stride Rite
  Hind
  Keds
  Pro-Keds
  Robeez
  Saucony
  Sperry Top-Sider
  Stride Rite

COMPETITORS

Aldo	K-Swiss
ASICS	Macy's
Bata	NIKE
Birkenstock Distribution	Nine West
USA	Nordstrom
Brown Shoe	Rack Room Shoes
C&J Clark	Reebok
Cherokee Inc.	Ross Stores
The Children's Place	Sears
Converse	Sears Canada
Crocs	Shoe Carnival
Deckers Outdoor	Shoe Show
Dillard's	Skechers U.S.A.
DSW	Sports Authority
ECCO Sko	Target
Foot Locker	Timberland
The Gap	TJX Companies
Genesco	Vans
Gymboree	Wal-Mart
Iconix Brand Group	Weyco
J. C. Penney	Wolverine World Wide
Kohl's	Zappos.com

HISTORICAL FINANCIALS

Company Type: Public

Income Statement

FYE: Saturday nearest January 31

	REVENUE ($ mil.)	NET INCOME ($ mil.)	NET PROFIT MARGIN	EMPLOYEES
1/09	3,442.0	(68.7)	—	31,000
1/08	3,035.4	42.7	1.4%	31,000
1/07	2,796.7	122.0	4.4%	31,000
1/06	2,667.3	70.5	2.6%	27,550
1/05	2,656.5	(2.0)	—	39,800
Annual Growth	**6.7%**	**—**	**—**	**(6.1%)**

2009 Year-End Financials

Debt ratio: 142.8%
Return on equity: —
Cash ($ mil.): 249
Current ratio: 2.38
Long-term debt (mil.): 888

No. of shares (mil.): 64
Dividends
  Yield: 0.0%
  Payout: —
Market value ($ mil.): 684

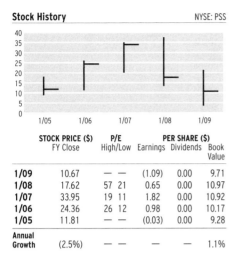

	STOCK PRICE ($) FY Close	P/E High/Low		PER SHARE ($) Earnings	Dividends	Book Value
1/09	10.67	—	—	(1.09)	0.00	9.71
1/08	17.62	57	21	0.65	0.00	10.97
1/07	33.95	19	11	1.82	0.00	10.92
1/06	24.36	26	12	0.98	0.00	10.17
1/05	11.81	—	—	(0.03)	0.00	9.28
Annual Growth	(2.5%)	—	—	—	—	1.1%

Comcast Corporation

Commerce plus broadcasting equals Comcast. The company's core cable division has about 24 million subscribers and is the largest provider in the US (ahead of #2 Time Warner Cable). Comcast Cable derives the bulk of its revenue from television, Internet, and digital phone services offered in 39 states. It has about 15 million subscribers to its broadband Internet service while its Comcast Digital Voice, a Voice over Internet Protocol (VoIP) telephone service, has about 6.5 million customers. Comcast also has programming interests, such as VERSUS and The Golf Channel, and it owns E! Entertainment Television. One-third of Comcast is controlled by CEO Brian Roberts, son of founder and former chairman Ralph Roberts.

The company in 2008 continued to make acquisitions in order to expand its interests in interactive digital content services and to build its media and programming holdings. Comcast acquired social networking company Plaxo and e-mail service provider DailyCandy that year as part of its efforts to tap into new streams of advertising revenue and improve its online social connectivity capabilities. The deals also added new subsets of subscribers (1.5 million and 2.5 million, respectively) to the mix. Comcast has said that it plans to tie these services into other existing properties managed by its Comcast Interactive Media Internet unit such as Fancast.com (online video distribution) and Fandango (online entertainment and movie ticketing) in order to improve user experience and increase customer interactivity.

Other acquisitions included the purchase of additional interest in cable channel Comcast SportsNet Bay Area and the remaining 50% of New England Cable News (NECN) that it did not already own from The Hearst Corp. in 2009; NECN serves about 3 million subscribers in the six New England states.

Comcast's 2008 purchase of Insight Midwest added about 700,000 subscribers in Illinois and Indiana. The company is also branching into wireless broadband and digital telephone services through a partnership with Sprint Nextel-controlled upstart wireless carrier Clearwire.

Through subsidiary Comcast Spectacor, the company owns Philadelphia's pro sports teams, the 76ers and the Flyers, and two arenas in that city. It also manages other venues used for sporting and musical events in Philadelphia.

HISTORY

In 1963 Ralph Roberts, Daniel Aaron, and Julian Brodsky bought American Cable Systems in Tupelo, Mississippi. The company soon expanded throughout the state. In 1969 the company got a new name: Comcast, combining "communications" and "broadcast." Two years later Comcast acquired franchises in western Pennsylvania, and when it went public in 1972, it moved to Philadelphia.

Comcast bought up local operations nationwide through the early 1980s and gained its first foreign cable franchise in 1983 in London (it sold its affiliate there to NTL — now Virgin Media — in 1998). It took a 26% stake in the large Group W Cable in 1986. Roberts also lent financial support that year to a fledgling home-shopping channel called QVC — for "quality, value, and convenience."

A big stride into telecommunications came in 1988 when Comcast bought American Cellular Network, with Delaware and New Jersey franchises. Two years later Roberts' son Brian — who had trained as a cable installer during a summer away from college — became Comcast's president.

In 1992 Comcast bought Metromedia's Philadelphia-area cellular operations and began investing in fiber-optic and wireless phone companies. By then the company was a major QVC shareholder. With an eye toward Comcast's programming needs, Brian persuaded FOX network head Barry Diller to become QVC's chairman. But when Diller tried to use QVC to take over CBS, Comcast bought control of QVC in 1994 to quash the bid, which went against cross-ownership bans. To pay for QVC, Comcast had to sell its 20% stake in cable firm Heritage Communications in 1995. Diller left the company (he now oversees InterActiveCorp, parent of QVC's archrival HSN). Also in 1995 Comcast funded former Disney executive Richard Frank to launch the C3 (Comcast Content and Communication) programming company.

The company agreed to acquire rival MediaOne in 1999, but soon after the $54 billion deal was struck, AT&T weighed in with a $58 billion offer. Comcast dropped its bid for MediaOne when AT&T offered to sell Comcast 2 million cable subscribers. More than a million of those subscribers came from Pennsylvania cable operator Lenfest Communications, which Comcast bought in 2000 from AT&T and the Lenfest family in a $7 billion deal.

In 2001 Comcast completed a systems swap with Adelphia Communications and completed the $2.75 billion purchase of systems in six states from AT&T. Also that year AT&T agreed to sell its cable unit to Comcast for $47 billion in stock and $25 billion in assumed debt. C. Michael Armstrong came from AT&T to Comcast, and was named chairman. Challenged with the task of absorbing AT&T Broadband's assets, Comcast struggled to meet its numbers. About 18 months after the AT&T Broadband deal, Comcast had reduced its headcount by 10,000 people. Also in 2001 Comcast sold its 57% stake in QVC to Liberty Media for about $7.7 billion.

When Armstrong stepped down as chairman in 2004, president and CEO Brian Roberts was named successor. The following year the company joined a consortium that bought film studio MGM.

In 2006 Comcast bought Disney's nearly 40% stake in E! Entertainment Television in a deal valued at nearly $1.25 billion (Comcast already owned 60%).

Comcast had owned a 21% stake in rival Time Warner Cable (TWC), which made for strange bedfellows, but the companies managed to unwind their relationship in mid-2006. The two rivals purchased all of troubled Adelphia Communications' cable television assets. Adelphia shareholders received about $9 billion from TWC and $3.5 billion in cash from Comcast, which also contributed its TWC stake to the deal. Comcast no longer owns any part of TWC.

In 2007 the company expanded its stable of regional sports channels with the purchase of two networks from Cablevision Systems. The $570 million deal included a 60% stake in FSN Bay Area and gave Comcast full ownership of FSN New England which became part of Comcast SportsNet.

EXECUTIVES

Chairman, President, and CEO: Brian L. Roberts, age 49, $23,728,548 total compensation
Chairman Emeritus: Ralph J. Roberts, age 89, $22,683,120 total compensation
Vice Chairman: Julian A. Brodsky, age 75
EVP and COO; President, Comcast Cable: Stephen B. (Steve) Burke, age 51, $20,394,012 total compensation
EVP and CFO: Michael J. Angelakis, age 44, $11,266,720 total compensation
EVP and CTO: Tony G. Werner
SVP, Chief Accounting Officer, and Controller: Lawrence J. Salva, age 52
CIO, Comcast Cable: Andrew Baer
Chief Procurement Officer and SVP, Comcast Cable: Peter Kiriacoulacos
EVP Human Resources, Comcast Cable: Kenneth J. (Ken) Carrig, age 51
EVP National Engineering and Technology Operations, Comcast Cable: John D. Schanz
EVP Marketing and Product Development, Comcast Cable: David A. Juliano
EVP Operations, Comcast Cable: David N. (Dave) Watson
EVP: David L. Cohen, age 53, $8,748,539 total compensation
EVP Content Acquisition, Comcast Cable: Madison (Matt) Bond
EVP Finance and Administration, Comcast Cable: David A. (Dave) Scott
SVP and General Counsel, Comcast Cable: Douglas (Doug) Gaston
SVP Investor Relations: Marlene S. Dooner
SVP, General Counsel, and Secretary: Arthur R. Block, age 53, $3,128,907 total compensation
SVP; President, Comcast Interactive Media: Amy L. Banse
SVP Corporate Communications: D'Arcy Rudnay
Auditors: Deloitte & Touche LLP

LOCATIONS

HQ: Comcast Corporation
1 Comcast Center, Philadelphia, PA 19103
Phone: 215-286-1700
Web: www.comcast.com

PRODUCTS/OPERATIONS

2008 Sales

	$ mil.	% of total
Cable		
Video	18,849	55
High-speed Internet	7,225	21
Phone	2,649	7
Advertising	1,526	4
Franchise fees	911	3
Other	1,283	4
Programming	1,426	5
Other	387	1
Total	**34,256**	**100**

COMPETITORS

AT&T
Cablevision Systems
Charter Communications
Cox Communications
DIRECTV
DISH Network Corporation
ESPN
FOX Sports
Insight Communications
Liberty Media
NBC Universal Cable
RCN Corporation
Time Warner Cable
ValueVision Media
Verizon
Viacom
Xanadoo

HISTORICAL FINANCIALS

Company Type: Public

Income Statement

FYE: December 31

	REVENUE ($ mil.)	NET INCOME ($ mil.)	NET PROFIT MARGIN	EMPLOYEES
12/08	34,256.0	2,547.0	7.4%	100,000
12/07	30,895.0	2,587.0	8.4%	100,000
12/06	24,966.0	2,533.0	10.1%	90,000
12/05	22,255.0	928.0	4.2%	80,000
12/04	20,307.0	970.0	4.8%	74,000
Annual Growth	**14.0%**	**27.3%**	**—**	**7.8%**

2008 Year-End Financials

Debt ratio: 74.6%
Return on equity: 6.2%
Cash ($ mil.): 1,195
Current ratio: 0.42
Long-term debt ($ mil.): 30,178

No. of shares (mil.): 2,870
Dividends
  Yield: 1.5%
  Payout: 29.1%
Market value ($ mil.): 48,442

Stock History

NASDAQ (GS): CMCSA

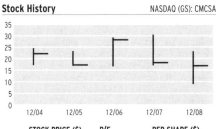

	STOCK PRICE ($) FY Close	P/E High/Low	PER SHARE ($) Earnings	PER SHARE ($) Dividends	PER SHARE ($) Book Value
12/08	16.88	27 11	0.86	0.25	14.10
12/07	18.26	36 21	0.83	0.00	14.41
12/06	28.22	37 21	0.79	0.00	14.34
12/05	17.28	82 61	0.28	0.00	14.01
12/04	22.19	85 61	0.29	0.00	14.43
Annual Growth	**(6.6%)**	**— —**	**31.2%**	**—**	**(0.6%)**

Comerica Incorporated

If you have a cosigner, Comerica will be your copilot. Organized into three business lines, the holding company's Business Bank division focuses on business and asset-based lending to middle-market, large corporate, and government entities; it offers lines of credit and international trade finance, among other services. The Retail Bank provides small business and consumer banking services including deposits, mortgages, small-business loans, and merchant services. The Wealth and Institutional Management arm deals in private banking and asset management, trust products, insurance, and retirement services. Comerica has about 480 branches and other offices, mostly in Arizona, California, Michigan, and Texas.

The company offers trust, loan production, and other financial services in about a dozen states across the US, as well as in Canada, Hong Kong, and Mexico. In 2009 Comerica sold its institutional retirement plan recordkeeping business — which provides services to some 250 retirement plans — to Wells Fargo, signaling the company's move away from ancillary lines.

Comerica has long been a leading commercial lender in the US, catering to garden-variety small and midsized firms, as well as to municipal governments and multinationals. The company remains committed to its core small- and middle-market clientele. (Around half of Comerica's assets are wrapped up in commercial real estate and operating loans.)

HISTORY

Comerica traces its history to 1849, when Michigan governor Epaphroditus Ransom tapped Elon Farnsworth to found the Detroit Savings Fund Institute. At that time Detroit was a major transit point for shipping between Lakes Huron and Erie, as well as between the US and Canada. The bank grew with the town and in 1871 became Detroit Savings Bank.

By 1899 Detroit was one of the top 10 US manufacturing centers and, thanks to a group of local tinkerers and mechanics that included Henry Ford, was on the brink of even greater growth. Detroit Savings grew also, fueled by the deposits of workers whom Ford paid up to $5 a day. Detroit Savings was not, however, the beneficiary of significant business with the auto makers; for corporate banking they turned first to eastern banks and then to large local banks in which they had an interest.

Detroit boomed during the 1920s as America went car-crazy, but after the 1929 crash Detroiters defaulted on mortgages by the thousands. By 1933 Michigan's banks were in such disarray that the governor shut them down three weeks prior to the federal bank holiday. Detroit Savings was one of only four Detroit banks to reopen. None of the major banks associated with auto companies survived.

A few months later Manufacturers National Bank, backed by a group of investors that included Edsel Ford (Henry's son), was founded. Although its start was rocky, Manufacturers National was on firm footing by 1936; around the same time, Detroit Savings Bank renamed itself the Detroit Bank to appeal to a more commercial clientele.

WWII and the postwar boom put Detroit back in gear. In the 1950s and 1960s, both banks thrived. In the 1970s statewide branching was permitted and both banks formed holding companies (DETROITBANK Corp. and Manufacturers National Corp.) and expanded throughout Michigan. As they grew, they added services; when Detroit's economy was hit by the oil shocks of the 1970s, these diversifications helped them through the lean years.

DETROITBANK opened a trust operation in Florida in 1982 to maintain its relationship with retired customers and renamed itself Comerica to be less area-specific. Manufacturers National also began operating in Florida (1983) and made acquisitions in the Chicago area (1987). Comerica went farther afield, buying banks in Texas (1988) and California (1991).

Following the national consolidation trend, in 1992 Comerica and Manufacturers National merged (retaining the Comerica name) but did not fully integrate until 1994, when the new entity began making more acquisitions. To increase sales and develop its consumer business, the company reorganized in 1996. It sold its Illinois bank and its Michigan customs brokerage business and acquired Fairlane Associates to expand its property/casualty insurance line.

As part of its strategy to have operations in all three NAFTA countries, Comerica opened a bank in Mexico in 1997 and one in Canada in 1998. That year it dropped $66 million for the naming rights to the Detroit Tigers' baseball stadium, which opened as Comerica Park in 2000. It also started a Web-based payment system for its international trade business.

To fortify its business lending operations in California, Comerica bought Imperial Bancorp in 2001. At the beginning of 2002, chairman Eugene Miller handed the CEO reins to Ralph Babb, who had been CFO. Later that year, Babb became chairman as well.

EXECUTIVES

Chairman, President, and CEO, Comerica Incorporated and Comerica Bank: Ralph W. Babb Jr., age 60, $6,821,217 total compensation
Vice Chairman, Comerica Incorporated and Comerica Bank: Joseph J. Buttigieg III, age 63, $4,977,212 total compensation
EVP and CFO, Comerica Incorporated and Comerica Bank: Elizabeth S. Acton, age 57, $2,550,804 total compensation
EVP and CIO, Comerica Incorporated and Comerica Bank: John R. Beran, age 56
EVP and Chief Credit Officer; EVP, Comerica Bank: Dale E. Greene, age 62
EVP and Chief Human Resources Officer: Jacquelyn H. Wolf, age 47
EVP, National Business Finance: Ronald P. Marcinelli
EVP; President, Texas Market: Charles L. Gummer, age 62
President and CEO, Western Market: J. Michael Fulton, age 60
EVP Governance, Regulatory Relations and Legal Affairs: Jon W. Bilstrom, age 63
EVP, Middle-Market Banking, Comerica Bank: E. Mark Gregory
EVP; President, Comerica Bank Michigan Market: Thomas D. Ogden, age 60
EVP Comerica Incorporated and Comerica Bank: Mary C. (Connie) Beck, age 63, $2,755,881 total compensation
EVP and General Auditor, Comerica Incorporated and Comerica Bank: David E. Duprey, age 51

EVP Middle Market Midwest, Comerica Bank:
Timothy P. (Tim) Ashley
EVP, Middle Market Midwest, Comerica Bank:
David B. (Dave) Marvin
EVP Wealth and Institutional Management:
Curtis C. Farmer, age 46
SVP, Controller, and Chief Accounting Officer,
Comerica Incorporated and Comerica Bank:
Marvin J. Elenbaas, age 57
SVP; President and CEO, Comerica Securities and
Comerica Insurance: Ross E. Rogers, age 60
SVP Corporate Marketing and Corporate
Communications: Jim Weber
Auditors: Ernst & Young LLP

LOCATIONS

HQ: Comerica Incorporated
Comerica Bank Tower, 1717 Main St.
Dallas, TX 75201
Phone: 214-462-6831
Web: www.comerica.com

PRODUCTS/OPERATIONS

2008 Gross Revenues

	$ mil.	% of total
Interest		
Loans, including fees	2,649	76
Investments	402	5
Noninterest		
Service charges on deposit accounts	229	5
Fees	238	5
Fiduciary income	199	4
Other	227	5
Total	**3,944**	**100**

2008 Assets

	$ mil.	% of total
Commercial loans	27,999	41
Commercial mortgage loans	10,489	16
Investment securities for sale	9,201	13
Real estate construction loans	4,477	7
Short-term investments	2,668	4
Consumer loans	2,592	4
Residential mortgage loans	1,852	3
International loans	1,753	3
Lease financing	1,343	2
Cash & due from banks	913	1
Allowances	(770)	—
Other assets	5,031	6
Total	**67,548**	**100**

Selected Subsidiaries

Cass & Co.
CDVI, Inc.
Comerica Assurance Ltd.
Comerica Bank
Comerica Bank & Trust, National Association
Comerica do Brasil Participacoes e Servicos Ltda.
Comerica Insurance Group
Comerica Preferred Capital
DFP Luxembourg SA
Imperial Capital Trust
Rica & Co., Ltd.
ROC Technologies Inc.
VRB Corp.
WAM Holdings, Inc.
Wilson, Kemp & Associates, Inc.
World Asset Management, Inc. (passively managed index
    portfolios)

COMPETITORS

Bank of America
Citigroup
Cullen/Frost Bankers
Fifth Third
FNB Bancorp (CA)
Huntington Bancshares
Northern Trust
Primerica
SunTrust
SVB Financial
U.S. Bancorp

HISTORICAL FINANCIALS

Company Type: Public

Income Statement

FYE: December 31

	ASSETS ($ mil.)	NET INCOME ($ mil.)	INCOME AS % OF ASSETS	EMPLOYEES
12/08	67,548.0	213.0	0.3%	10,639
12/07	62,331.0	686.0	1.1%	11,337
12/06	58,001.0	893.0	1.5%	11,270
12/05	53,013.0	861.0	1.6%	11,343
12/04	51,766.0	757.0	1.5%	11,514
Annual Growth	**6.9%**	**(27.2%)**	**—**	**(2.0%)**

2008 Year-End Financials

Equity as % of assets: 7.4%
Return on assets: 0.3%
Return on equity: 4.2%
Long-term debt ($ mil.): 15,053
No. of shares (mil.): 151
Dividends
Yield: 11.6%
Payout: 179.1%
Market value ($ mil.): 3,000
Sales ($ mil.): 2,708

Stock History

NYSE: CMA

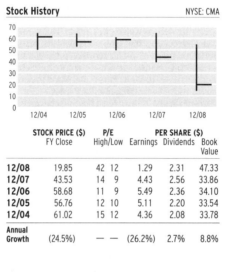

	STOCK PRICE ($) FY Close	P/E High/Low	PER SHARE ($) Earnings	PER SHARE ($) Dividends	PER SHARE ($) Book Value
12/08	19.85	42 12	1.29	2.31	47.33
12/07	43.53	14 9	4.43	2.56	33.86
12/06	58.68	11 9	5.49	2.36	34.10
12/05	56.76	12 10	5.11	2.20	33.54
12/04	61.02	15 12	4.36	2.08	33.78
Annual Growth	**(24.5%)**	**— —**	**(26.2%)**	**2.7%**	**8.8%**

Commercial Metals

Commercial Metals Company (CMC) wants to steel the limelight. CMC's Americas Fabrication and Distribution segment buys and sells primary and secondary metals, fabricated metals, and other industrial metals. The fabrication unit runs a heat treating plant and makes steel fence posts, steel beams, and steel joists. Its Americas Mills segment makes steel products for the construction, energy, petrochemical, and transportation industries, along with copper tubing. CMC's Americas Recycling unit operates 48 secondary metals processing plants that shred, shear, and pulverize scrap metal, which is then sold to steel mills and nonferrous ingot producers.

The marketing and trading segment operates through nearly 20 international trading offices. It brokers industrial products that include primary and secondary metals, fabricated metals, chemicals, and industrial minerals to customers in the steel, non-ferrous metals, metal fabrication, chemical, refractory, and transportation industries.

Expansion is the rule rather than the exception for CMC. In 2007 CMC completed a slew of acquisitions. First it bought Bouras Industries, Inc. for $146 million. The deal included four of

Bouras' operating subsidiaries: United Steel Deck (steel decking), New Columbia Joist (steel joists), ABA Trucking Corporation (delivery services for United Steel Deck and New Columbia Joist), and Nicholas J. Bouras, Inc. (sales, marketing, and engineering for the other three subsidiaries).

Later that year CMC completed two acquisitions in one day. It bought Economy Steel of Las Vegas, which is now called CMC Economy Steel and becomes part of the company's Americas Fabrication and Distribution division. CMC also picked up Valjaonia Cijevi Sisak of Croatia. The company is now called CMC Sisak and is a maker of steel pipe.

Still rolling on the acquisition train, CMC acquired a group of companies in 2008 that included ABC Coating Company (of Texas and Colorado), Banner Rebar, Toltec Steel Services, and Rebar Trucking. The deal also includes a 50% stake in both ABC Coating of North Carolina and ABC Coating of Tennessee. All became part of CMC Americas Fabrication and Distribution.

HISTORY

Russian immigrant Moses Feldman moved to Dallas in 1914 and founded scrap metal company American Iron & Metal the next year. In the 1920s Feldman suffered a heart attack, and his son Jake helped out with the business. Low metal prices hurt the company during the Depression. In 1932 Jake formed a two-man brokerage firm, Commercial Metals Company (CMC), which was combined as a partnership with his father's scrap metal operations. Moses Feldman died in 1937. CMC was incorporated in 1946 and began buying related businesses during the 1950s.

CMC was listed on the American Stock Exchange in 1960. It soon expanded geographically, buying a stake in Texas steelmaker Structural Metals (1963). In 1965 it formed Commercial Metals Europa (the Netherlands), its first overseas subsidiary, and Commonwealth Metal (New York). By 1966 CMC was one of the world's top three scrap metal companies. It bought copper tube manufacturer Howell Metals (Virginia) in 1968, the remainder of Structural Metals, and major stakes in seven affiliated businesses. Over 10 years, CMC opened trading offices around the world. Business continued to grow throughout the 1970s. The company added a small minimill in Arkansas (1971) and certain assets of General Export Iron and Metal in Texas (1976).

CMC began trading on the New York Stock Exchange in 1982. The next year the company bought Connors Steel (Alabama), its third minimill. By the end of 1984 CMC was operating 20 metal recycling plants from Texas to Florida.

The company modernized its minimills in the 1990s. CMC acquired small scrap-metal operations and Shepler's, a concrete-related products business, in 1994. Also that year CEO Stanley Rabin completed the $50 million purchase of Owen Steel (a South Carolina minimill), which expanded CMC's reach into the Mid-Atlantic and Southeast. The company wrapped up a $30 million capital improvement program at its Alabama minimill in 1995 — just in time to ride a strong steel market to record profits.

Although a correction in the steel and metals industry depressed prices in 1996, CMC achieved record sales and profits that fiscal year. However, both dipped the next year, with lower steel and scrap prices widely attributed to an influx of foreign imports. CMC strengthened its vertical integration in 1997 by acquiring Allegheny Heat

Treating (heat treatment services to steel mills) and two auto salvage plants in Florida.

During 1998 CMC moved into the Midwest, buying a metals recycling company in Missouri. It boosted global operations by purchasing a metals trading firm in Australia and entering a joint venture with Trinec, a Czech Republic steel mill, to sell steel products in Germany.

In 2000 CMC picked up three rebar fabricators — two in California (Fontana Steel and C&M Steel), and one in Florida (Suncoast Steel).

In late 2001 the company acquired Florida-based Allform, a maker of concrete-related forms and supplies. The following year Commercial Metals started manufacturing its corrosion-resistant stainless steel-clad products in its facilities in South Carolina.

Marvin Selig, founder and chairman of the company's steel group, retired in 2002 after working for more than 50 years in the steel industry.

In 2003 CMC purchased a 71% stake in Poland-based Huta Zawiercie S.A. for approximately $50 million. CMC purchased the assets of J. L. Davidson Company, a rebar fabricating operation based in California, in 2004.

In 2006 the company acquired Tucson-based concrete products supplier Brost Forming Supply, Inc., and almost all of the assets of Yonack Iron & Metal Co. and Metallic Resources, Inc. Later that year the company bought Cherokee Supply, a provider of tools and supplies for the construction, oilfield, and industrial sectors. The acquisition became part of CMC Construction Services division and operated under the CMC Cherokee name.

Quick on the heels of the Cherokee deal came CMC's purchase of Concrete Formtek Services, a renter of concrete forming and shoring equipment. Concrete Formtek Services was renamed CMC Formtek and became part of CMC Construction Services. In 2008 CMC reorganized its operations under two divisions, CMC Americas and CMC International.

EXECUTIVES

Chairman, President, and CEO: Murray R. McClean, age 60
SVP and CFO: William B. Larson, age 55
VP and Chief Information Officer: Malinda G. Passmore, age 50
EVP; President, CMC Americas: Russell B. (Russ) Rinn, age 50
VP Internal Audit: Manny Rosenfeld
VP Business Development: Devesh Sharma
VP Human Resources: James Alleman
VP, General Counsel, and Secretary: Ann J. Bruder
President, CMC Cometals: Eliezer Skornicki
EVP and Division Manager, CMC Dallas Trading: J. Matthew Kramer
President, CMC Australia: Peter Muller
EVP and Division Manager, Howell Metal: James K. Forkovitch
President, CMC International: Hanns Zoellner, age 60
President, CMC Europe: Ludovit Gajdos
Treasurer: Louis A. Federle, age 60
EVP, Finance and Administration, CMC Americas: Robert (Bob) Unfried
Director Public Relations: Debbie L. Okle
Auditors: Deloitte & Touche LLP

LOCATIONS

HQ: Commercial Metals Company
6565 N. MacArthur Blvd., Ste. 800
Irving, TX 75039
Phone: 214-689-4300 **Fax:** 214-689-5886
Web: www.commercialmetals.com

2008 Sales

	$ mil.	% of total
US	5,833.1	56
Europe	2,399.9	23
Asia	955.8	9
Australia & New Zealand	636.8	6
Other regions	601.8	6
Total	**10,427.4**	**100**

PRODUCTS/OPERATIONS

2008 Sales

	$ mil.	% of total
Fabrication & distribution	6,655.5	56
Mills	3,121.9	26
Recycling	2,189.7	18
Corporate	(1.8)	—
Adjustments	(1,537.9)	—
Total	**10,427.4**	**100**

2008 Sales by Product

	$ mil.	% of total
Steel products	6,594.6	63
Industrial materials	1,247.9	12
Nonferrous scrap	1,006.6	10
Ferrous scrap	861.1	8
Construction materials	327.7	3
Nonferrous products	273.8	3
Other	115.7	1
Total	**10,427.4**	**100**

COMPETITORS

AK Steel Holding Corporation
BHP Billiton
Blue Tee
Connell LP
David J. Joseph
Gerdau Ameristeel
Keywell
Metals USA
Mueller Industries
Nucor
OmniSource
Quanex Building Products
Roanoke Bar Division
Ryerson
Schnitzer Steel
Severstal North America
Simec
Steel Dynamics
Tang Industries
Tube City IMS
United States Steel
Universal Forest Products
Worthington Industries

HISTORICAL FINANCIALS

Company Type: Public

Income Statement

	REVENUE ($ mil.)	NET INCOME ($ mil.)	NET PROFIT MARGIN	EMPLOYEES
8/08	10,427.4	232.0	2.2%	15,276
8/07	8,329.0	355.4	4.3%	12,730
8/06	7,555.9	356.3	4.7%	11,734
8/05	6,592.7	285.8	4.3%	11,027
8/04	4,768.3	132.0	2.8%	10,604
Annual Growth	**21.6%**	**15.1%**	**—**	**9.6%**

FYE: August 31

2008 Year-End Financials

Debt ratio: 73.1%
Return on equity: 14.6%
Cash ($ mil.): 219
Current ratio: 1.86
Long-term debt ($ mil.): 1,198
No. of shares (mil.): 129
Dividends
  Yield: 1.7%
  Payout: 22.8%
Market value ($ mil.): 3,359

Stock History

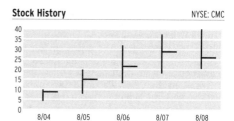

NYSE: CMC

	STOCK PRICE ($) FY Close	P/E High/Low		Earnings	Dividends	Book Value
8/08	26.03	20	11	1.97	0.45	12.69
8/07	28.89	13	6	2.92	0.33	12.00
8/06	21.59	11	5	2.89	0.17	9.45
8/05	14.97	8	4	2.32	0.12	6.97
8/04	8.74	9	4	1.11	0.09	5.12
Annual Growth	**31.4%**	**—**	**—**	**15.4%**	**49.5%**	**25.5%**

CommScope, Inc.

CommScope doesn't need to be coaxed into making cable. The company manufactures coaxial, fiber-optic, and other high-performance cable products for data, voice, and video transmission. Its products include high-bandwidth cable that can provide cable TV, telephone, and Internet access through a single line, primarily for business enterprise applications and broadband service providers. CommScope is also a top provider of coaxial cable for satellite television providers; other applications include cables for LANs and video automation wiring (broadcast and security). The company's customers include Anixter (11% of sales), Alcatel-Lucent, and Comcast. CommScope makes more than half of its sales outside the US.

In 2007 CommScope bought rival Andrew Corporation for $2.65 billion in cash and stock. Andrew Corp. was rechristened Andrew Wireless Solutions following the acquisition.

The transaction trailed a failed acquisition attempt in 2006: CommScope proposed to pay $1.7 billion to acquire Andrew, countering ADC Telecommunications' offer to buy Andrew. Andrew declined both offers and said that it was not for sale. However, it later accepted a higher offer from CommScope, but this time US regulators had a problem with it. They eventually gave the deal the OK on the condition that Andrew sell its 30% stake in Andes Industries. Andrew's stake in Andes would give CommScope excessive control of the coaxial cable market, according to regulators. In 2008 CommScope sold its stake in Andes back to Andes.

Among CommScope's challenges in 2009 are the ongoing integration of Andrew and CommScope, having a limited number of key customers and distributors, similarly having a limited number of key suppliers, relying on contract electronics manufacturers to make the company's products, and intense industry competition, not to mention the global recession and credit crisis.

CommScope is poised to benefit from emerging markets in high-definition and Internet protocol TV, as well as from growing markets for wireless tower and LAN wiring. It is focusing its growth on the enterprise user and communication service provider markets.

In mid-2008 the company reorganized in order to trim costs and to focus its growth. In Europe, the company will consolidate its microwave antenna operations in England down to one facility, while in the Czech Republic the company plans to close its antenna operations. In Scotland it will consolidate its machine shop operations at two plants into one, located in Andrews. Elsewhere, CommScope closed its enterprise cabling operations in Australia early in 2009.

HISTORY

CommScope began as Hickory, North Carolina-based Superior Cable, a maker of telephone cables. The company initiated the CommScope product line of coaxial cables in 1964 and opened its Catawba, North Carolina, manufacturing site two years later.

When Continental Telephone purchased Superior Cable in 1967, CommScope became a division under the new company, Superior Continental. In 1967 Superior sold the CommScope division to a group of Hickory-area investors led by Frank Drendel, CommScope's current chairman and CEO.

In 1980 CommScope became a division of M/A-COM, a cable television equipment company based in Massachusetts. General Instrument, a leading maker of cable television equipment, acquired M/A-COM and CommScope in 1986. As a part of General Instrument's plan to split into three companies, CommScope was spun off in 1997.

In 1998 CommScope sold its aerospace cable business to French telecommunications giant Alcatel (now Alcatel-Lucent) for $13 million. It bought Alcatel's coaxial cable business in 1999.

Expanding into South America in 2000, CommScope purchased a manufacturing facility in Brazil from Motorola. The slowing US economy forced the company to cut about 500 positions — about 13% of its workforce — in 2001. Later that year CommScope acquired an 18% stake in the US-based optical fiber and fiber cable manufacturer OFS BrightWave.

In 2002 the company signed a distribution deal with Hutton Communications to sell and distribute CommScope's wireless products. Not all news was good in 2002, as CommScope was forced to write off more than $20 million due to cable system operator Adelphia Communications' Chapter 11 bankruptcy.

In 2004 CommScope strengthened its core operations with the acquisition of Avaya's connectivity solutions business for $263 million. The acquisition included product groups Exchange-MAX (cable management systems), Integrated Cabinet Solutions (enclosures), and SYSTIMAX (end-to-end cabling solutions for phones, LANs, and workstations).

CommScope acquired Trilogy Communications' 75-ohm trunk and distribution cable television products business in 2006.

EXECUTIVES

Chairman and CEO: Frank M. Drendel, age 64, $4,660,985 total compensation
President and COO: Brian D. Garrett, age 60, $2,363,906 total compensation
EVP and CFO: Jearld L. Leonhardt, age 60, $1,340,231 total compensation
SVP and CIO: Kap K. Kim
EVP and General Manager, Enterprise: Randall W. Crenshaw, age 51
EVP, Coaxial Cable and Antenna Operations: Christopher A. Story, age 49
EVP and General Manager, Antenna, Cable and Cabinets Group: Edward A. Hally, age 59, $1,238,812 total compensation
EVP Broadband Sales and Marketing: James R. (Jim) Hughes, age 48
EVP and General Manager, Wireless Network Solutions: Marvin S. Edwards Jr., age 60, $1,012,197 total compensation
SVP, Human Resources and Environment: James L. Wright
SVP, General Counsel, and Secretary: Frank B. Wyatt II, age 46
SVP and Controller: William R. Gooden, age 67
SVP Investor Relations and Corporate Communications: Philip M. Armstrong Jr.
SVP, Global Enterprise Marketing and Strategic Planning: Mark Peterson
VP and Treasurer: Barry D. Graham
Director Corporate Communications: Rick Aspan
Auditors: Deloitte & Touche LLP

LOCATIONS

HQ: CommScope, Inc.
1100 CommScope Place SE, Hickory, NC 28603
Phone: 828-324-2200   **Fax:** 828-328-3400
Web: www.commscope.com

2008 Sales

	$ mil.	% of total
US	1,903.8	47
Europe, Middle East & Africa	1,112.3	28
Asia/Pacific	628.5	16
Latin America	305.3	7
Canada	66.7	2
Total	**4,016.6**	**100**

PRODUCTS/OPERATIONS

2008 Sales

	$ mil.	% of total
Antenna, Cable & Cabinets Group	1,860.5	46
Enterprise	885.1	22
Wireless Network Solutions	690.9	17
Broadband	590.9	15
Adjustments	(10.8)	—
Total	**4,016.6**	**100**

COMPETITORS

ADC Telecommunications	OFS Fitel
Agilent Technologies	Optical Cable
Alcatel-Lucent	Ortronics
Amphenol	Panduit
ARRIS	Pirelli
Belden	Powerwave Technologies
Comba Telecom	Prysmian
Corning	QUALCOMM
Emerson Electric	Radio Frequency Systems
Ericsson	Sumitomo Electric
General Cable	Superior Essex
Huawei Technologies	SWCC SHOWA
HUBER + SUHNER	TruePosition
KATHREIN-Werke	Tyco Electronics
Nexans	

HISTORICAL FINANCIALS

Company Type: Public

Income Statement

FYE: December 31

	REVENUE ($ mil.)	NET INCOME ($ mil.)	NET PROFIT MARGIN	EMPLOYEES
12/08	4,016.6	(228.5)	—	15,000
12/07	1,930.8	204.8	10.6%	15,500
12/06	1,623.9	130.1	8.0%	4,550
12/05	1,337.2	50.0	3.7%	4,400
12/04	1,152.7	75.8	6.6%	4,300
Annual Growth	**36.6%**	**—**	**—**	**36.7%**

2008 Year-End Financials

Debt ratio: 165.3%   No. of shares (mil.): 94
Return on equity: —   Dividends
Cash ($ mil.): 412   Yield: 0.0%
Current ratio: 1.85   Payout: —
Long-term debt ($ mil.): 1,667   Market value ($ mil.): 1,455

Stock History

NYSE: CTV

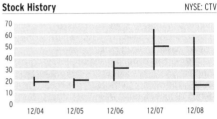

	STOCK PRICE ($) FY Close	P/E High/Low	PER SHARE ($) Earnings	Dividends	Book Value
12/08	15.54	— —	(3.29)	0.00	10.77
12/07	49.21	23 11	2.78	0.00	13.67
12/06	30.48	20 11	1.84	0.00	7.90
12/05	20.13	27 18	0.78	0.00	5.58
12/04	18.90	20 14	1.15	0.00	4.80
Annual Growth	**(4.8%)**	**— —**	**—**	**—**	**22.4%**

Computer Sciences Corporation

CSC has mastered the art and science of computer technology. One of the world's leading providers of systems integration and other technology services, Computer Sciences Corporation (CSC) provides application development, data center management, communications and networking development, and business consulting. It also offers business process outsourcing (BPO) services in such areas as billing and payment processing, customer relationship management (CRM), and human resources. A major government and defense contractor, CSC generates about a third of its revenues from US federal agencies.

CSC divides its offerings into three main service lines: Global Outsourcing Services (GOS), North American Public Sector (NPS), and Business Solutions and Services (BS&S). GOS, which primarily handles large-scale outsourcing contracts, accounts for about 40% of CSC's revenues. NPS, its federal government business, accounts for more than a third of sales. BS&S provides industry-specific consulting and outsourcing services.

The company's government contracts include such tasks as helping the Federal Aviation Administration upgrade and modernize its air traffic control systems, and supporting multiple US Navy programs.

CSC has benefited from an increased interest in outsourcing in the private sector. It has multi-year contracts with such corporations as insurance broker Aon, hospital system Ascension Health, transportation giant Bombardier, computer vendor Sun Microsystems (which is also a business partner), and diversified manufacturer Textron.

In 2007 the company acquired Covansys in a deal valued at $1.3 billion. Covansys specializes in outsourcing services in such industries as financial services, health care, manufacturing, retail, and technology. CSC acquired First Consulting Group, an IT services firm focused on the health care sector, for $352 million in 2008. The acquisitions of Covansys and First Consulting were part of a strategy to expand its offshore capabilities. Covansys operated primarily from development centers in India, and First Consulting added operations in India and Vietnam. The acquisitions were also in line with another CSC growth strategy: focusing on industry-specific offerings for select sectors including chemicals, consumer products, energy, financial services, government, health care, manufacturing, and technology.

HISTORY

Computer Sciences Corporation (CSC) was founded in Los Angeles in 1959 by Fletcher Jones and Roy Nutt to write software for manufacturers such as Honeywell. In 1963 CSC became the first software company to go public. Three years later it signed a $5.5 million contract to support NASA's computation laboratory. Annual sales had climbed to just over $53 million by 1968.

In 1969 CSC agreed to merge with Western Union, but the deal ultimately fell through. When Jones died in a plane crash in 1972, William Hoover, a former NASA executive who had come aboard eight years earlier, became chairman and CEO. Under Hoover, CSC began transforming itself into a systems integrator. In 1986, when federal contracts still accounted for 70% of sales, the company started diversifying into the commercial sector.

In 1991 CSC signed a 10-year, $3 billion contract with defense supplier General Dynamics. In 1995 Hoover, after more than three decades with CSC, stepped down as CEO (remaining chairman until 1997); he was succeeded by president and COO Van Honeycutt. Also that year CSC bought Germany's largest independent computer services company, Ploenzke. In 1996 CSC acquired insurance services provider Continuum Company for $1.5 billion.

In 1998 CSC found itself on the other side of the bargaining table with a $9.8 billion hostile takeover bid from software giant Computer Associates (now CA). After weeks of contentious battle, CA withdrew its bid. That same year the IRS chose CSC to head the PRIME Alliance team that includes IBM, Lucent, and Unisys in a multibillion-dollar project to update the agency's computer system.

That year CSC continued its acquisition spree, buying consulting firms in Europe including Informatica Group (Italy), KMPG Peat Marwick (France), Pergamon (Germany), and SYS-AID

(the Netherlands). In 1999 CSC inked an 11-year, $1 billion deal to manage the back-office functions of energy trading giant Enron's energy services unit. Also in 1999 the company acquired information technology company Nichols Research.

CSC in 2000 boosted its expertise in financial software and services with the cash acquisition of Mynd Corporation (formerly Policy Management Systems) for an estimated $570 million. Also that year CSC signed two large outsourcing contracts — a seven-year, $3 billion deal with telecom equipment maker Nortel Networks that arranged for Nortel to transfer 2,000 employees to CSC, and a $1 billion outsourcing and application development agreement with AT&T.

The company continued to make large deals in 2001, including contracts with the National Security Agency (NSA) and BAE SYSTEMS. The next year saw more of the same: CSC was contracted to operate a central data exchange for the US Environmental Protection Agency, and to collaborate on missile defense systems engineering for the US Army. CSC acquired Defense Department services contractor DynCorp for about $900 million in 2003, doubling the size of its federal services division. (The company sold off various DynCorp units two years later, recouping about $850 million.)

Also in 2003 it won a 10-year, $2.4 billion contract to provide a new network and voice, data, mobile, and Internet services to the UK's Royal Mail. In 2005 it sold some operations connected to its DynCorp Technical Services unit, including DynCorp International and DynMarine, to Varitas Capital for about $850 million. In Asia, CSC acquired the 27% of subsidiary CSA Holdings it didn't already own.

In 2006 CSC acquired Datatrac Information Services, a prime contractor for the US Department of Homeland Security and other federal agencies. President and COO Michael Laphen assumed the CEO's chair in 2007, inheriting the position from Honeycutt. Laphen also became chairman that year.

EXECUTIVES

Chairman, President, and CEO:
Michael W. (Mike) Laphen, age 58,
$7,825,926 total compensation
VP and CFO: Michael J. Mancuso, age 66,
$480,459 total compensation
VP and CIO: David McCue
VP and CTO: John Glowacki
VP and Chief Marketing Officer: Guy Nielsen
VP and Chief Medical Officer, North American Public Sector: Robert Wah
President, Global Business Solutions; VP and Chief Innovation Officer, Office of Innovation:
R. Lemuel (Lem) Lasher
VP Global Legal Compliance: Harvey N. Bernstein, age 62
VP Investor Relations: Bryan Brady
VP: Michael E. Keane, age 53
VP, General Counsel, and Secretary:
William L. (Bill) Deckelman Jr., age 51,
$2,036,328 total compensation
VP and Controller: Donald G. DeBuck, age 51,
$1,521,310 total compensation
VP and Treasurer: Thomas R. Irvin, age 60
VP Human Resources: Nathan G. (Gus) Siekierka,
age 60, $1,691,419 total compensation
VP Corporate Development: Randy E. Phillips, age 50,
$2,137,464 total compensation
Director Office of Communications, North American Public Sector: Chuck Taylor
Director Investor Relations: Stephen Virostek
Auditors: Deloitte & Touche LLP

LOCATIONS

HQ: Computer Sciences Corporation
3170 Fairview Park Dr., Falls Church, VA 22042
Phone: 703-876-1000
Web: www.csc.com

2009 Sales

	$ mil.	% of total
US	10,333.6	62
Europe		
UK	1,890.8	11
Other countries	2,775.4	17
Other regions	1,740.1	10
Total	**16,739.9**	**100**

PRODUCTS/OPERATIONS

2009 Sales

	$ mil.	% of total
Global outsourcing services	6,458.5	38
North American public sector	5,977.4	36
Business solutions & services		
Consulting	2,034.3	12
Financial services	990.8	6
Other	1,384.6	8
Corporate	17.4	—
Adjustments	(123.1)	—
Total	**16,739.9**	**100**

Selected Service Areas

Application outsourcing
Business process outsourcing
Credit services (consumer credit reporting)
Customer relationship management
Data hosting
Enterprise application integration
Knowledge management
Management consulting
Risk management
Security
Supply chain management

COMPETITORS

Accenture	IBM Global Services
ADP	Infosys
Affiliated Computer	Keane
Services	L-3 Titan
Atos Origin	Lockheed Martin
BearingPoint	Logica
Booz Allen	Northrop Grumman
CACI International	Perot Systems
Capgemini	Raytheon
CIBER	SAIC
Cognizant Tech Solutions	Satyam
Convergys	Siemens AG
Deloitte Consulting	Tata Consultancy
EDS	Tech Mahindra Limited
Getronics	Unisys
Honeywell International	Wipro Technologies
HP Technology Solutions	

HISTORICAL FINANCIALS

Company Type: Public

Income Statement				FYE: Friday nearest March 31
	REVENUE ($ mil.)	NET INCOME ($ mil.)	NET PROFIT MARGIN	EMPLOYEES
3/09	16,739.9	1,115.2	6.7%	92,000
3/08	16,499.5	544.6	3.3%	89,000
3/07	14,856.6	388.8	2.6%	79,000
3/06	14,615.6	638.3	4.4%	79,000
3/05	14,058.6	810.2	5.8%	79,000
Annual Growth	**4.5%**	**8.3%**	**—**	**3.9%**

2009 Year-End Financials

Debt ratio: 75.7%
Return on equity: 20.3%
Cash ($ mil.): 2,297
Current ratio: 1.92
Long-term debt ($ mil.): 4,173

No. of shares (mil.): 152
Dividends
Yield: 0.0%
Payout: —
Market value ($ mil.): 5,589

Stock History　　　　　　　　　　　　　　NYSE: CSC

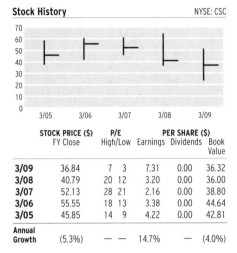

	STOCK PRICE ($) FY Close	P/E High/Low		PER SHARE ($) Earnings	Dividends	Book Value
3/09	36.84	7	3	7.31	0.00	36.32
3/08	40.79	20	12	3.20	0.00	36.00
3/07	52.13	28	21	2.16	0.00	38.80
3/06	55.55	18	13	3.38	0.00	44.64
3/05	45.85	14	9	4.22	0.00	42.81
Annual Growth	(5.3%)	—	—	14.7%	—	(4.0%)

ConAgra Foods

ConAgra Foods fills Americans' refrigerators, freezers, and pantries and, ultimately, their tummies. The company is a US top food producer, offering packaged and frozen foods. ConAgra's brands are a cornucopia of America's well-known foods, including Banquet, Chef Boyardee, Egg Beaters, Healthy Choice, Hunt's, Jiffy, Orville Redenbacher's, PAM, Slim Jim, and Van Camp's. It is also one of the country's largest foodservice suppliers, offering them convenience foods and ingredients. The company has sold off its agricultural segments and a number of non-core brands in order to concentrate on branded and value-added packaged foods.

The company has shifted away from its beginnings as a commodity producer and recast itself as "America's favorite food company." Shedding of nonfood-related businesses have allowed the company to better pay attention to consumer-aimed brands.

In 2009 the company sold its Mexican entree and appetizer Fernando's and El Extremo food-service brands to Foster Poultry Farms.

Three workers were killed and some 40 were injured in an explosion and fire at a company Slim Jim manufacturing plant in Garner, North Carolina, in 2009. It was later determined that the blast was caused by a natural-gas leak.

ConAgra sold its trading and merchandising operations (ConAgra Trade Group) in 2008 to a group of investors that included the Ospraie Special Opportunities Fund for $2.8 billion.

Saying it couldn't give the brand the attention it needs, in 2008 the company sold its Knott's Berry Farm jam and jelly business to J. M. Smucker.

In February 2007 salmonella was found in some of the company's Peter Pan and Great Value (a Wal-Mart product) brands of peanut butter, forcing a nation-wide recall of the peanut butter bearing the product code involved. Salmonella food poisoning was linked to some 600 people in 47 states. No deaths related to the peanut better were confirmed. The recall eventually included products made as far back as October 2004.

ConAgra shut down the Sylvester, Georgia, plant that was involved in the outbreak and re-opened it in August 2007, having spent $15 million on renovation.

Just two months later, the company voluntarily stopped production at the Missouri plant that makes its Banquet and generic brands of frozen turkey and chicken pot pies after learning that the were linked to some 140 cases of salmonella in 30 states. ConAgra did not recall the pies but offered mail-in refunds and store returns. The USDA began an investigation and advised consumers not to eat the pies.

In 2007 the company paid a penalty of $45 million in the wake of SEC charges that alleged the company had misreported its profits for the fiscal years 1999, 2000, and 2001.

HISTORY

Alva Kinney founded Nebraska Consolidated Mills in 1919 by combining the operations of four Nebraska grain mills. It did not expand outside Nebraska until it opened a mill and feed processing plant in Alabama in 1942.

Consolidated Mills developed Duncan Hines cake mix in the 1950s. But Duncan Hines failed to raise a large enough market share, and the company sold it to Procter & Gamble in 1956. Consolidated Mills used the proceeds to expand, opening a flour and feed mill in Puerto Rico the next year. In the 1960s, while competitors were moving into prepared foods, the firm expanded into animal feeds and poultry processing. By 1970 it had poultry processing plants in Alabama, Georgia, and Louisiana. In 1971 the company changed its name to ConAgra (Latin for "in partnership with the land"). During the 1970s it expanded into the fertilizer, catfish, and pet accessory businesses.

Poorly performing subsidiaries and commodity speculation caused ConAgra severe financial problems until 1974, when Mike Harper, a former Pillsbury executive, took over. Harper trimmed properties to reduce debt and had the company back on its feet by 1976. ConAgra stayed focused on the commodities side of the business, but was thus tied to volatile price cycles. In 1978 it bought United Agri Products (agricultural chemicals).

ConAgra moved into consumer food products in the 1980s. It bought Banquet (frozen food, 1980) and within six years had introduced almost 90 new products under that label. Other purchases included Singleton Seafood (1981), Armour Food Company (meats, dairy products, frozen food; 1983), and RJR Nabisco's frozen food business (1986). ConAgra became a major player in the red meat market with the 1987 purchases of E.A. Miller (boxed beef), Monfort (beef and lamb), and Swift Independent Packing.

ConAgra continued with acquisitions of consumer food makers, including Beatrice Foods (Orville Redenbacher's popcorn, Hunt's tomato products) in 1991. In 1997 it agreed to pay $8.3 million to settle federal charges of wire fraud and watering down grain. That year ConAgra named president Bruce Rohde as CEO; he became chairman in 1998.

In 2000 ConAgra acquired major brand holder International Home Foods from HM Capital Partners (known as Hicks, Muse, Tate & Furst at the time) for about $2.9 billion. The company then became ConAgra Foods. During 2001 the company drew SEC attention and was forced to restate earnings for the previous three years due to accounting no-no's in its United Agri Products division.

In 2002 the USDA forced ConAgra to recall 19 million pounds of ground beef because of possible *E. coli* contamination, making it the second-largest food recall in US history.

In 2003 ConAgra agreed to pay $1.5 million in cash and job offers to settle an EEOC lawsuit charging bias against disabled workers at the company's California-based Gilroy Foods plant. The agreement involved the largest disability settlement in the agriculture industry.

In 2005 Rhode retired. His replacement was former chairman and CEO of PepsiCo Beverages and Foods North America, Gary Rodkin. ConAgra agreed to pay a $14 million shareholder settlement in 2005 regarding a lawsuit claiming fictitious sales and mis-reported earnings at its former subsidiary United Agri Products.

Focusing on portfolio trimming, Rodkin sold a large part of ConAgra's refrigerated-meats business. Also that year the company sold its surimi business, including the Louis Kemp brand, to Trident Seafoods and its Singleton Seafood and Meridian Seafood to Singleton Fisheries. It sold its specialty and imported cheese operation Swissrose International to investment company, Fairmount Food Group.

EXECUTIVES

Chairman: Steven F. (Steve) Goldstone, age 63
President, CEO, and Director: Gary M. Rodkin, age 57, $8,830,972 total compensation
EVP and CFO: John F. Gehring, age 48, $1,645,615 total compensation
President, Consumer Foods: André J. Hawaux, age 49, $2,541,391 total compensation
EVP and Chief Marketing Officer: Joan K. Chow, age 48
EVP Human Resources: Peter M. (Pete) Perez, age 55, $1,635,456 total compensation
EVP External Affairs; President, Commercial Foods: Robert F. (Rob) Sharpe Jr., age 57, $3,470,715 total compensation
EVP Supply Chain: Gregory L. (Greg) Smith
EVP Research, Development, Quality, and Innovation: Albert D. (Al) Bolles, age 51
SVP, Treasurer, and Assistant Corporate Secretary: Scott E. Messel, age 50, $1,172,391 total compensation
SVP, General Counsel, and Corporate Secretary: Colleen Batcheler
SVP Enterprise Manufacturing: David J. (Dave) Colo
SVP Procurement: D. K. Singh
SVP Sales and Supply Chain, ConAgra Foods Lamb Weston: Mark Hayden
SVP and Corporate Controller: Patrick D. (Doug) Linehan, age 40
VP Corporate Affairs; President, ConAgra Foods Foundation: Chris Kircher
VP Investor Relations: Christopher W. (Chris) Klinefelter, age 42
VP Corporate Real Estate and Facilities: James D. Doyle
VP Corporate Communication: Teresa Paulsen
Auditors: KPMG LLP

LOCATIONS

HQ: ConAgra Foods, Inc.
　1 ConAgra Dr., Omaha, NE 68102
Phone: 402-595-4000　　　**Fax:** 402-595-4707
Web: www.conagra.com

PRODUCTS/OPERATIONS

2009 Sales

	$ mil.	% of total
Consumer foods	8,031.3	63
Commercial foods	4,699.9	37
Total	**12,731.2**	**100**

Selected Brands

Foodservice and ingredient brands
ConAgra Mills (wheat flour, barley flour)
Eagle Mills (Multi-grain flour)
Gilroy Foods & Flavors (seasonings, flavorings, dehydrated and pureed vegetables)
Lamb Weston (frozen potato-based products)
Lamb Weston Inland Valley (frozen french fries)

Retail brands
Act II microwave popcorn
Andy Capp's salty snacks
Banquet frozen dinners and poultry
Banquet Brown 'N Serve Sausage
Blue Bonnet Margarine
Chef Boyardee canned pasta
Crunch 'N Munch snack mix
DAVID Seeds salted sunflower seeds
Dennison's Chile
Egg Beaters frozen liquid egg substitute
Fiddle Faddle popcorn and caramel snack mix
Fleischmann's Margarine
Gulden's Mustard
Healthy Choice soups, frozen dinners, and pasta sauce.
Hebrew National frankfurters
Hunt's canned tomato products
Jiffy Pop Popcorn
Kid Cuisine frozen meals
La Choy sauces, canned chow mein noodles, canned vegetables, meals, and frozen egg rolls
Libby's canned meats
Luck's Baked Beans
Manwich Sloppy Joe Sauce
Marie Callender's frozen meals and desserts
Orville Redenbacher's Popcorn
Pam non-stick spray
Parkay Margarine
Patio frozen dinners and burritos
Pemmican Beef Jerky
Penrose Pickled Sausage
Peter Pan Peanut Butter
Poppycock Snack Mix
Ranch Style Beans
Reddi-Wip aerosol whipped cream
Ro-Tel canned processed tomatoes
Rosarita Refried Beans
Slim Jim Beef Jerky
Snack Pack shelf-stable pudding
Swiss Miss hit chocolate mix
Van Camp's Pork and Beans
Wesson cooking oil
Wolf Chili

COMPETITORS

American Pop Corn	Kraft Foods
B&G Foods	Link Snacks
Bush Brothers	Malt-O-Meal
Campbell Soup	Manischewitz Company
Clorox	McCain Foods
Del Monte Foods	McIlhenny
Eden Foods	Monterey Gourmet Foods
Frito-Lay	Mott's
General Mills	Nestlé
Gilster-Mary Lee	Newman's Own
Goya	NutriSystem
Hain Celestial	Pinnacle Foods
Hanover Foods	Ralcorp
Heinz	Sara Lee Food and
H.J. Heinz Limited	Beverage
Hormel	Schwan's
Inventure	Seneca Foods
Jenny Craig	Slim-Fast
J-OIL MILLS	smart balance
JR Simplot	Smucker
Kellogg	Snappy Popcorn
Kellogg U.S. Snacks	Weaver Popcorn Company

HISTORICAL FINANCIALS

Company Type: Public

Income Statement

FYE: Last Sunday in May

	REVENUE ($ mil.)	NET INCOME ($ mil.)	NET PROFIT MARGIN	EMPLOYEES
5/09	12,731.2	978.4	7.7%	25,600
5/08	11,605.7	930.6	8.0%	25,000
5/07	12,028.2	764.6	6.4%	24,500
5/06	11,579.4	533.8	4.6%	33,000
5/05	14,566.9	641.5	4.4%	38,000
Annual Growth	**(3.3%)**	**11.1%**	**—**	**(9.4%)**

2009 Year-End Financials

Debt ratio: 73.3%
Return on equity: 19.5%
Cash ($ mil.): 243
Current ratio: 2.12
Long-term debt ($ mil.): 3,461

No. of shares (mil.): 442
Dividends
Yield: 4.1%
Payout: 35.3%
Market value ($ mil.): 8,219

Stock History

NYSE: CAG

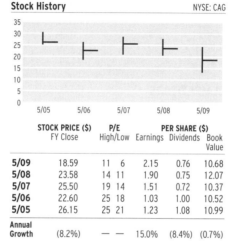

	STOCK PRICE ($) FY Close	P/E High/Low		PER SHARE ($) Earnings	Dividends	Book Value
5/09	18.59	11	6	2.15	0.76	10.68
5/08	23.58	14	11	1.90	0.75	12.07
5/07	25.50	19	14	1.51	0.72	10.37
5/06	22.60	25	18	1.03	1.00	10.52
5/05	26.15	25	21	1.23	1.08	10.99
Annual Growth	**(8.2%)**	**—**	**—**	**15.0%**	**(8.4%)**	**(0.7%)**

ConocoPhillips

Formed by the merger of Conoco and Phillips Petroleum, ConocoPhillips is the #2 integrated oil and gas company in the US, behind Exxon Mobil, and consolidated that position by buying Burlington Resources (for a reported $35 billion). The company explores for oil and gas in more than 30 countries and has proved reserves of 10 billion barrels of oil equivalent (excluding its Syncrude oil sands assets). It has a refining capacity of more than 2.6 million barrels per day and sells petroleum at 8,340 retail outlets in the US under the 76, Conoco, and Phillips 66 brands, and at 1,260 gas stations in Europe. Other operations include chemicals, gas gathering, fuels technology, and power generation.

ConocoPhillps has six operating segments. Exploration and Production; Midstream (gathering and processing of natural gas, and fractionating and marketing natural gas liquids in the US, Canada, and Trinidad); Refining and Marketing of crude oil and petroleum products; LUKOIL Investment (a 20% stake in Russia-based oil giant LUKOIL); Chemicals (manufacturing and marketing petrochemicals and plastics worldwide); and Emerging Businesses (new technologies related to natural gas conversion into

clean fuels, technology solutions, power generation, and emerging technologies).

In 2007 under nationalization pressure from President Hugo Chavez, ConocoPhillips exited Venezuela. In 2008 the company acquired a 50% stake in TransCanada's Keystone Oil Pipeline, which plans to construct a 2,148-mile crude oil pipeline originating in Hardisty, Alberta, with delivery points at Wood River and Patoka, Illinois, and Cushing, Oklahoma.

Also in 2008, in a move to further expand its energy sources, the company and Origin Energy agreed (in an $8 billion deal) to form an Australasian natural gas business focused on coal bed methane production and liquefied natural gas processing and sales.

HISTORY

The roots of ConocoPhillips go back more than a century and run deep into the history of the US oil industry.

Isaac Elder Blake, an Easterner who had lost everything on a bad investment, came to Ogden, Utah, and founded Continental Oil & Transportation (CO&T) in 1875. In 1885 CO&T merged with Standard Oil's operations in the Rockies and was reincorporated in Colorado as Continental Oil. Continental tightened its grip on the Rocky Mountain area and by 1906 had taken over 98% of the western market. Its monopoly ended in 1911 when the US Supreme Court ordered Standard to divest several holdings: Continental was one of 34 independent oil companies created in 1913.

Seeing opportunity in autos, Continental built a gas station in 1914. Two years later it got into oil production when it bought United Oil, and by 1924 it had become fully integrated by merging with Mutual Oil, which owned production, refining, and distribution assets. Continental's biggest merger came in 1929 when it merged with Marland Oil of Oklahoma.

Continental diversified in the 1960s, acquiring American Agricultural Chemicals in 1963 and Consolidation Coal (Consol) in 1966. Restructuring in the 1970s into Conoco Chemical, Consol, and two petroleum divisions, the company ramped up oil exploration and entered ventures to develop uranium. In 1979 it changed its name to Conoco.

In the late 1970s, Conoco began joint ventures with chemical titan DuPont. The companies worked together well, and in 1981 Conoco was acquired by DuPont to forestall hostile takeover attempts by Mobil and Seagram. DuPont sold off $1.5 billion of Conoco's assets and absorbed Conoco Chemical. In 1998, however, DuPont spun off Conoco in what was the US's largest-ever IPO at the time (DuPont had completely divested its 70% stake by the next year).

Conoco expanded its natural gas reserves in 2001 by buying Gulf Canada Resources for $4.3 billion in cash and $2 billion in assumed debt. Also that year Conoco agreed to merge with Phillips Petroleum.

The story of Phillips Petroleum begins with Frank Phillips, a prosperous Iowa barber who married a banker's daughter in 1897 and began selling bonds. When a missionary who worked with Native Americans in Oklahoma regaled him with stories about the oil patch, Phillips migrated to Bartlesville, Oklahoma, and established Anchor Oil in 1903.

Anchor's first two wells were dry, but the next one — the Anna Anderson No. 1 — was the first of a string of 81 successful wells. Phillips and his brother L. E., doubling as bankers in Bartlesville, transformed Anchor into Phillips Petroleum in 1917.

With continued success on Native American lands in Oklahoma, Phillips moved into refining and marketing. In 1927 the company opened its first gas station in Wichita, Kansas. Frank Phillips retired after WWII and died in 1950.

During the 1980s Phillips became a target of takeover attempts. To fend off bids from corporate raiders T. Boone Pickens (1984) and Carl Icahn (1985), Phillips repurchased stock and ran its debt up to $9 billion. It then cut 8,300 jobs and sold billions of dollars' worth of assets; strong petrochemicals earnings kept it afloat.

As part of an industry trend to share costs of less-profitable operations, Phillips and Conoco flirted with the idea of merging their marketing and refining operations in 1996, but the talks failed. Discussions between Phillips and Ultramar Diamond Shamrock about merging the companies' North American oil refining and marketing operations broke down in 1999.

James Mulva took over as CEO in 1999, and Phillips decided to shift its focus to its upstream operations. The company combined its natural gas gathering and processing operations with those of Duke Energy in 2000 and received a minority stake in a new company, Duke Energy Field Services. Also that year Phillips acquired ARCO's Alaska assets for $7 billion and merged its chemicals division with Chevron's.

In 2001, however, Phillips elected to expand its refining and marketing operations rather than spin them off, and the company bought Tosco for about $7.3 billion in stock and $2 billion in assumed debt. Big as it was, the Tosco deal was eclipsed the next year by the merger of Phillips and Conoco.

In 2003, as part of its plan to exit the retail business, the company sold its Circle K gas station chain to Alimentation Couche-Tard.

EXECUTIVES

Chairman and CEO: James J. (Jim) Mulva, age 62, $29,391,988 total compensation
President and COO: John A. Carrig, age 57, $11,243,955 total compensation
SVP Finance and CFO: Sigmund L. (Sig) Cornelius, age 54, $5,746,039 total compensation
SVP and Chief Administrative Officer: Eugene L. (Gene) Batchelder, age 61
EVP: William B. (Bill) Berry, age 56
SVP Corporate Shared Services: Rand C. Berney, age 53, $2,827,862 total compensation
SVP Exploration and Production, Americas: Kevin O. Meyers
SVP Legal, General Counsel, and Corporate Secretary: Janet Langford Kelly, age 51
SVP: Stephen F. (Steve) Gates, age 62
SVP Technology: Stephen R. Brand
SVP Commercial: Gregory J. Goff, age 52
SVP Planning and Strategy: J. W. Sheets, age 50
SVP Government and Public Affairs: Red Cavaney
SVP Refining, Marketing, and Transportation: C. W. (Willie) Chiang, age 48
SVP Exploration and Production, International: Ryan M. Lance, age 46
SVP Project Development: Luc Messier
VP Health, Safety, and Environment: Robert A. (Bob) Ridge, age 60
VP Human Resources: Carin S. Knickel
VP and Treasurer: Frances M. Vallejo
VP and Controller, Finance: Glenda Schwarz
Auditors: Ernst & Young LLP

LOCATIONS

HQ: ConocoPhillips
600 N. Dairy Ashford Rd., Houston, TX 77079
Phone: 281-293-1000
Web: www.conocophillips.com

2008 Sales

	% of total
US	69
UK	12
Canada	2
Norway	1
Australia	1
Other countries	15
Total	**100**

PRODUCTS/OPERATIONS

2008 Sales

	$ mil.	% of total
Refining, marketing & transportation	164,230	68
Exploration & production	69,818	29
Midstream	6,564	3
Emerging businesses	199	—
Chemicals	11	—
Adjustments	5,360	—
Total	**246,182**	**100**

COMPETITORS

Admiral Petroleum
Arabian American Development
Bergesen
BHP Billiton
BP
Chevron
Chevron Products Company
CITGO
CVR
Eni
Exxon
Frontier Oil
George Warren
Hess Corporation
Koch Industries, Inc.
Marathon Oil
Occidental Permian
Occidental Petroleum
Shell Oil Products
Sinclair Oil
Sunoco
TOTAL
Ultra Petroleum
Valero Energy

HISTORICAL FINANCIALS

Company Type: Public

Income Statement				FYE: December 31
	REVENUE ($ mil.)	NET INCOME ($ mil.)	NET PROFIT MARGIN	EMPLOYEES
12/08	246,182.0	(16,998.0)	—	33,800
12/07	192,524.0	11,891.0	6.2%	32,600
12/06	188,523.0	15,550.0	8.2%	38,400
12/05	183,364.0	13,617.0	7.4%	35,600
12/04	136,916.0	8,129.0	5.9%	35,800
Annual Growth	**15.8%**	**—**	**—**	**(1.4%)**

2008 Year-End Financials

Debt ratio: 49.1%
Return on equity: —
Cash ($ mil.): 755
Current ratio: 0.96
Long-term debt ($ mil.): 27,085

No. of shares (mil.): 1,483
Dividends
  Yield: 3.6%
  Payout: —
Market value ($ mil.): 76,814

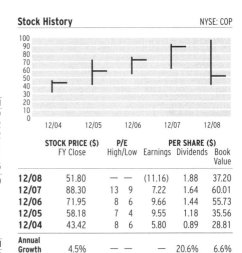

Stock History   NYSE: COP

	STOCK PRICE ($) FY Close	P/E High/Low		PER SHARE ($) Earnings	Dividends	Book Value
12/08	51.80	—	—	(11.16)	1.88	37.20
12/07	88.30	13	9	7.22	1.64	60.01
12/06	71.95	8	6	9.66	1.44	55.73
12/05	58.18	7	4	9.55	1.18	35.56
12/04	43.42	8	6	5.80	0.89	28.81
Annual Growth	**4.5%**	**—**	**—**	**—**	**20.6%**	**6.6%**

Conseco, Inc.

Conseco can see no better way than to serve those whose needs aren't being met. The company offers insurance and related products for middle-income and senior citizens, groups it says are "underserved high growth markets." Its three units include Bankers Life, which markets and distributes Medicare supplement, life, and long-term care insurance and annuities; Conseco Insurance Group, which offers specified disease insurance, as well as Medicare supplement and certain life insurance and annuities; and Colonial Penn, which offers life insurance to consumers through direct selling. Conseco has 4 million customers nationwide, which it serves from three main offices in the Midwest.

About three-quarters of the company's collected premiums come from products sold by its own 5,500 career agents out of 160 branch offices. Independent agents, insurance brokers, marketing organizations, and direct marketing account for the balance of its collected premiums.

In 2008 Conseco agreed to pay a fine of $6.3 million after an investigation determined that its long-term care insurance business Conseco Senior Health had wrongly denied claims and mishandled complaints. The investigation also determined that some sales and marketing practices at Banker's Life did not comply with industry standards.

Ready to be rid of its closed block of long-term care insurance, in late 2008 the company spun off that portion of its business into a new company. The new entity was named Senior Health Insurance Company of Pennsylvania and consists entirely of policies in run-off.

However, the company continues to struggle with accurate internal financial reporting. In 2009, after Conseco admitted the problems — which were confirmed by its auditors — its stock price took a big hit and triggered speculation about bankruptcy. (The company had emerged from Chapter 11 protection in 2003.) It didn't help that the firm, like many of its insurance peers, lost more than $260 million on its investments in 2008.

To conserve capital and reduce complexity, in mid-2009 Conseco announced plans to consolidate three companies within its Conseco Insurance Group segment.

HISTORY

Conseco evolved from Security National, an Indiana insurance company formed in 1979 by Stephen Hilbert. The former encyclopedia salesman and Aetna executive believed most insurance companies were bloated and the industry itself overcrowded, as well as ripe for consolidation by a smart, lean organization.

In 1982 the company began its growth-by-acquisition strategy with the purchase of Executive Income Life Insurance (renamed Security National Life Insurance). The next year it bought Consolidated National Life Insurance and renamed the expanded company Conseco.

The firm went public in 1985, using the proceeds to fund an acquisitions spree that included Lincoln American Life Insurance, Lincoln Income Life (sold 1990), Bankers National Life Insurance, Western National Life Insurance (sold 1994), and National Fidelity Life Insurance.

In 1990 the company formed Conseco Capital Partners (with General Electric and Bankers Trust) to finance acquisitions without seeming to burden the parent company with debt. This device financed the purchase of Great American Reserve and the 1991 acquisition of Beneficial Standard Life.

Conseco bought Bankers Life Insurance in 1992, then sold 67% of it the next year. In 1993 the company formed the Private Capital Group to invest in noninsurance companies.

In 1994 the company tried to acquire the much larger Kemper Corp., but shied away from the debt load that the $2.6 billion deal would have entailed. The aborted deal cost $36 million in bank and accounting fees and spelled the end of the company's relationship with Merrill Lynch, which had underwritten Conseco's IPO, when a Merrill Lynch analyst downgraded Conseco's stock after the fiasco.

Meanwhile, Private Capital's success led Conseco to form Conseco Global Investments. Other investments included stakes in racetrack and riverboat gambling operations in Indiana.

In 1996 and 1997 Conseco absorbed eight life, health, property/casualty, and specialty insurance companies and raised its interest in American Life Holdings to 100%.

Itching to move beyond insurance, in 1998 Conseco bought Green Tree Financial, the US's #1 mobile home financier. Charges of Green Tree's own fuzzy accounting practices helped torpedo Conseco's quest for a federal thrift charter. But the troubles had just begun. The mobile home finance industry took a dive as customers refinanced at lower rates and prepayments slammed Green Tree Financial, reducing Conseco's earnings.

Conseco tried to recoup in 1999 by launching an ad campaign portraying the company as the "Wal-Mart of financial services." It also continued the acquisition spree. But Green Tree Financial (renamed Conseco Finance that year) couldn't stanch the flow of red ink: Buyers grew wary of the quality of the finance unit's loan securities, and changes in accounting methods cost the parent company a $350 million charge against earnings for 1999.

In 2002, due to its financial woes, Gary Wendt stepped down as CEO, the NYSE suspended trading in Conseco, and the company's stock was moved to the OTC. The company also filed for Chapter 11 protection. As part of the reorganization agreement, Conseco agreed to sell Conseco Finance. The company's insurance operations were not subject to the Chapter 11 agreement.

In 2003 Conseco finally unloaded its Conseco Finance unit to CFN Investment Holdings LLC, an investor group, and General Electric Co.'s consumer finance unit for $1 billion. The company emerged from bankruptcy in September 2003.

EXECUTIVES

Chairman: R. Glenn Hilliard, age 66
CEO and Director: C. James (Jim) Prieur, age 58, $2,170,249 total compensation
EVP Technology and Operations:
Russell M. (Russ) Bostick, age 52
EVP and CFO: Edward J. (Ed) Bonach, age 55, $1,070,935 total compensation
SVP and Chief Accounting Officer: John R. Kline, age 51
EVP Human Resources: Susan L. (Sue) Menzel, age 44
EVP Corporate Communications:
Anthony B. (Tony) Zehnder, age 59
EVP Product Management: Christopher J. Nickele, age 52
EVP Government Relations: William (Bill) Fritts
EVP and General Counsel: Matthew J. (Matt) Zimpfer, age 41
SVP and Treasurer: Todd M. Hacker
SVP Financial Planning & Analysis: Thomas D. Barta
SVP and Corporate Actuary: Timothy J. (Tim) Tongson
SVP Operations and Customer Support:
Grace E.M. Cowan, age 49
President, Conseco Insurance Group:
Steven M. (Steve) Stecher, age 48, $883,667 total compensation
President, Bankers Life and Casualty: Scott R. Perry, age 46, $1,065,176 total compensation
Secretary: Karl W. Kindig
Senior Director Investor Relations: Scott Galovic
Auditors: PricewaterhouseCoopers LLP

LOCATIONS

HQ: Conseco, Inc.
11825 N. Pennsylvania St., Carmel, IN 46032
Phone: 317-817-6100   **Fax:** 317-817-2847
Web: www.conseco.com

PRODUCTS/OPERATIONS

2008 Revenues

	$ mil.	% of total
Insurance policy income	3,253.6	73
Net investment income	1,178.8	27
Net realized investment losses	(262.4)	—
Fee revenues & other income	19.7	—
Total	**4,189.7**	**100**

Selected Subsidiaries and Brands
Bankers Life
  Bankers Life and Casualty Company
Colonial Penn Life Insurance Company
Conseco Insurance Group
  Conseco Health Insurance Company
  Conseco Life Insurance Company
  Washington National

COMPETITORS

Aetna
Aflac
AIG American General
American National Insurance
Guardian Life
John Hancock Financial Services
Lincoln Financial Group
MassMutual
MetLife
Monumental Life
Mutual of Omaha
Nationwide Financial Network
New York Life
Northwestern Mutual
Pacific Mutual
Phoenix Companies
Protective Life
Prudential
Securian Financial
Unum Group

HISTORICAL FINANCIALS

Company Type: Public

Income Statement

FYE: December 31

	ASSETS ($ mil.)	NET INCOME ($ mil.)	INCOME AS % OF ASSETS	EMPLOYEES
12/08	28,769.7	(1,126.7)	—	3,700
12/07	33,514.8	(194.0)	—	3,950
12/06	32,717.3	58.5	0.2%	4,000
12/05	31,557.3	324.9	1.0%	4,000
12/04	30,755.5	294.8	1.0%	4,350
Annual Growth	(1.7%)	—	—	(4.0%)

2008 Year-End Financials

Equity as % of assets: 5.6%
Return on assets: —
Return on equity: —
Long-term debt ($ mil.): 2,096
No. of shares (mil.): 185
Dividends
  Yield: 0.0%
  Payout: —
Market value ($ mil.): 958
Sales ($ mil.): 4,190

Stock History

NYSE: CNO

	STOCK PRICE ($) FY Close	P/E High/Low		PER SHARE ($) Earnings	Dividends	Book Value
12/08	5.18	—	—	(6.10)	0.00	8.76
12/07	12.56	—	—	(1.12)	0.00	22.91
12/06	19.98	68	51	0.38	0.00	25.49
12/05	23.17	13	11	1.76	0.00	24.45
12/04	19.95	15	9	1.63	0.00	21.11
Annual Growth	(28.6%)	—	—	—	—	(19.7%)

CONSOL Energy

Consolation prizes don't interest CONSOL Energy. CONSOL is one of the US's largest coal mining companies, along with Peabody Energy and Arch Coal. The company has some 4.5 billion tons of proved reserves, mainly in northern and central Appalachia and the Illinois Basin, and produces about 65 million tons of coal annually. CONSOL primarily mines high BTU coal, which burns cleaner than lower grades. Customers include electric utilities and steel mills. CONSOL delivers coal using its own railroad cars, export terminals, and fleet of towboats and barges. The company also engages in natural gas exploration and production; its proved reserves total 1.4 trillion cu. ft.

Aware that most planned power plants will be gas-fired, CONSOL has diversified its energy holdings by acquiring additional natural gas reserves. In 2005 CONSOL created a new subsidiary, CNX Gas, to handle the company's gas operations. It then sold a minority stake in CNX Gas to a group of institutional investors in a private transaction, and in 2006, CNX Gas went public. CONSOL retained an 82% stake in CNX Gas. The majority-owned subsidiary recovers coalbed methane gas, an increasingly popular fuel for producing electricity.

In early 2008, CONSOL offered to buy back the 18% of CNX it did not already own. CONSOL concluded that it had reached a point where it no longer made sense for CNX to remain majority-owned and publicly traded. Since CONSOL had no desire to divest its interest in CNX, the company made the offer to acquire all of it. After meeting with those institutional investors, CONSOL discovered the move would be too expensive and withdrew its offer. It will retain its controlling stake in CNX.

In addition to its coal and gas businesses, the company distributes mining and industrial supplies through its Fairmont Supply unit. About 40% of Fairmont's business is with its parent. CONSOL also operates a distribution business and runs about 25 towboats and 700 barges.

HISTORY

When Consolidation Coal was formed in Maryland in 1864, coal was just beginning to replace wood as the world's top industrial energy source. In the 1880s Consolidation Coal, like other large coal companies, began operations in the Appalachia region of the US. During the 1920s the company built the Kentucky mining city of Van Lear. (Country music superstar Loretta Lynn's father worked as a Consolidation Coal miner nearby.) In 1945 Consolidation Coal merged with Pittsburgh Coal, and the next year the combined company took over Hanna Coal.

In 1966 Continental Oil, founded in 1875 and later renamed Conoco, bought Consolidation Coal. Two years later 78 workers were killed in a Consolidation Coal mine explosion. Also in 1968 a federal jury found the United Mine Workers (UMW) and the company guilty of conspiring to put Kentucky's South East Coal out of business. In 1971 the UMW and Consolidation Coal paid South East almost $9 million in damages, court costs, and interest. Consolidation Coal became part of DuPont when that company bought Conoco in 1981.

Ten years later the mining unit of German conglomerate RWE, Rheinbraun, bought 50% of Consolidation Coal (later increased to 74%) from DuPont. That year Consolidation Coal and Conoco formed the Pocahontas Gas Partnership to recover coalbed methane gas.

A restructuring in 1992 created CONSOL Energy as a holding company for more than 60 subsidiaries, including principal operating subsidiary Consolidation Coal. The next year the UMW initiated a strike against CONSOL, which was using more and more nonunion workers in its mines. CONSOL opened its ash disposal facility the next year and began developing ways to reuse its plant waste and byproducts.

From 1994 to 1997 the company reduced its workforce by 20% and closed six of its mining complexes. By 1997 about one-third of CONSOL's coal came from nonunion mines. In 1998 the company filed to go public and bought Rochester & Pittsburgh Coal.

CONSOL completed its IPO in 1999. The depressed coal market halved CONSOL's sales that year, and the company scaled back production at some of its smaller, high-cost mines in Pennsylvania and West Virginia. During the winter of 2000 and in early 2001, coal prices improved by 36% and natural gas prices skyrocketed as cold temperatures and an energy crisis in California increased demand for energy sources. Despite the improvement in coal prices, the company continued to shut down high-cost mines.

In 2001 CONSOL acquired Conoco's half of the Pocahontas Gas joint venture. It also bought Windsor Coal, Southern Ohio Coal, and Central Ohio Coal from American Electric Power. In addition, CONSOL bought 50% of the Glennies Creek Mine, its first Australian property.

Also in 2001, CONSOL contracted with Allegheny Energy Supply (an affiliate of largest customer Allegheny Energy) to build an 88-MW electric generating plant in Virginia to be fueled by coalbed methane gas produced by CONSOL.

CONSOL in 2003 sold its Canadian operations (Cardinal River and Line Creek Mines) to Fording. The next year CONSOL sold its Glennies Creek mine interest, thus exiting Australia. Also in 2004, RWE severed ties with CONSOL by selling its remaining 19% stake in the company.

The next year CONSOL created a new subsidiary, CNX Gas, to handle the company's gas operations. It then sold a minority stake in CNX Gas to a group of institutional investors in a private transaction, and in 2006 CNX Gas went public, with CONSOL retaining an 82% stake.

EXECUTIVES

Chairman: John L. Whitmire, age 68
President, CEO, and Director; Chairman and CEO, CNX Gas: J. Brett Harvey, age 58, $8,214,996 total compensation
EVP and COO; President and CEO, CNX Gas: Nicholas J. DeIuliis, age 40, $6,246,083 total compensation
EVP and CFO, CONSOL Energy and CNX Gas: William J. Lyons, age 60, $2,457,490 total compensation
EVP Corporate Affairs, Chief Legal Officer, and Secretary, CONSOL Energy and CNX Gas: P. Jerome Richey, age 59, $1,323,877 total compensation
EVP Energy Sales and Transportation Services, CONSOL Energy and CNX Gas; President, CONSOL Energy Sales: Robert F. Pusateri, age 58
EVP Business Advancement and Support Services, CONSOL Energy and CNX Gas: Robert P. King, age 56

SVP External Affairs: Thomas F. (Tom) Hoffman
SVP Operations Support: Albert A. Aloia
SVP Sales: James J. McCaffrey
Sales, Atlanta: Dennis Duffy
Director Investor Relations: Charles (Chuck) Mazur
Director Public Relations: Joseph A. Cerenzia
Auditors: PricewaterhouseCoopers LLP

LOCATIONS

HQ: CONSOL Energy Inc.
CNX Center, 1000 CONSOL Energy Dr.
Canonsburg, PA 15317
Phone: 724-485-4000
Web: www.consolenergy.com

2008 Sales

	% of total
North America	
US	86
Canada	2
Europe	10
South America	2
Total	**100**

PRODUCTS/OPERATIONS

2008 Sales

	% of total
Coal	76
Gas	16
Other products	8
Total	**100**

COMPETITORS

Alliance Resource
Arch Coal
Devon Energy
EQT Corporation
Massey Energy
Nippon Coke & Engineering
Peabody Energy
Penn Virginia
RAG AG
Rio Tinto Limited
St. Mary Land & Exploration
Westmoreland Coal

HISTORICAL FINANCIALS

Company Type: Public

Income Statement				FYE: December 31
	REVENUE ($ mil.)	NET INCOME ($ mil.)	NET PROFIT MARGIN	EMPLOYEES
12/08	4,486.3	442.5	9.9%	8,176
12/07	3,762.2	267.8	7.1%	7,728
12/06	3,715.2	438.5	11.8%	7,253
12/05	3,810.4	590.3	15.5%	7,257
12/04	2,776.7	115.2	4.1%	6,982
Annual Growth	12.7%	40.0%	—	4.0%

2008 Year-End Financials

Debt ratio: 32.0%
Return on equity: 33.1%
Cash ($ mil.): 139
Current ratio: 0.65
Long-term debt ($ mil.): 468
No. of shares (mil.): 181
Dividends
  Yield: 1.4%
  Payout: 16.7%
Market value ($ mil.): 5,164

Stock History

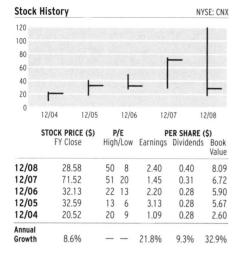

NYSE: CNX

	STOCK PRICE ($) FY Close	P/E High/Low		PER SHARE ($) Earnings	Dividends	Book Value
12/08	28.58	50	8	2.40	0.40	8.09
12/07	71.52	51	20	1.45	0.31	6.72
12/06	32.13	22	13	2.20	0.28	5.90
12/05	32.59	13	6	3.13	0.28	5.67
12/04	20.52	20	9	1.09	0.28	2.60
Annual Growth	8.6%	—	—	21.8%	9.3%	32.9%

Consolidated Edison

Utility holding company Consolidated Edison (Con Edison) is the night light for the city that never sleeps. Con Edison's main subsidiary, Consolidated Edison Company of New York, distributes electricity to more than 3.2 million residential and business customers in New York City; it also delivers natural gas to about 1.1 million customers. Subsidiary Orange and Rockland Utilities serves more than 427,000 electric and gas customers in three states. Con Edison's nonutility operations include retail and wholesale energy marketing, independent power production, and infrastructure project development.

To prepare for deregulation, Con Edison sold almost all of its New York power plants to focus on distribution and transmission. It is expanding its competitive operations and improving its regulated infrastructure assets.

Competitive energy businesses include subsidiary Consolidated Edison Solutions, which markets power and gas to retail customers and provides energy procurement and management services, and Consolidated Edison Energy, which markets and trades wholesale energy. Subsidiary Consolidated Edison Development has interests in power generation facilities in North America, Latin America, and Europe.

In 2008, in order to raise cash to pay down debt and reinvest is core businesses, the company's Consolidated Edison Development unit sold 1,706 MW of generation projects to investment group North American Energy Alliance, LLC for $1.5 billion.

HISTORY

Several professionals, led by Timothy Dewey, formed The New York Gas Light Company in 1823 to illuminate part of Manhattan. In 1884 five other gas companies joined New York Gas Light to form the Consolidated Gas Company of New York.

Thomas Edison's incandescent lamp came on the scene in 1879, and The Edison Electric Illuminating Company of New York was formed in 1880 to build the world's first commercial electric power station (Pearl Street), financed by a group led by J.P. Morgan. Edison supervised the project, and in 1882 New York became the first major city with electric lighting.

Realizing electricity would replace gas, Consolidated Gas acquired electric companies, including Anthony Brady's New York Gas and Electric Light, Heat and Power Company (1900), which joined Edison's Illuminating Company in 1901 to form the New York Edison Company. More than 170 purchases followed, including that of the New York Steam Company (1930), a cheap source of steam for electric turbines.

The Public Utility Holding Company Act of 1935 ushered in the era of regulated, regional monopolies. The next year New York Edison combined its holdings to form the Consolidated Edison Company of New York (Con Ed).

Con Ed opened its first nuclear station in 1962. By then, Con Ed had a reputation for inefficiency and poor service, and shareholders were angry about its slow growth and low earnings. Environmentalists joined the grousers in 1963 when Con Ed began constructing a pumped-storage plant in Cornwall near the Hudson River. Charles Luce, a former undersecretary with the Department of Interior, was recruited to rescue Con Ed in 1967. He added power plants and beefed up customer service.

In the 1970s inflation and the energy crisis drove up oil prices (Con Ed's main fuel source), and in 1974 Luce withheld dividends for the first time since 1885. He persuaded the New York State Power Authority to buy two unfinished power plants, saving Con Ed $200 million. In 1980 Luce ended the Cornwall controversy and donated the land for park use. He retired in 1982.

The utility started buying power from various suppliers and in 1984 began a two-year price freeze, a boon to rate-hike-weary New Yorkers. The New York State Public Service Commission didn't approve another rate increase until 1992.

In 1997 Con Ed, government officials, consumer groups, and other energy firms outlined the company's deregulation plan, which included the formation of the Consolidated Edison, Inc., holding company (known as Con Edison) and a power marketing unit in 1998. The next year Con Edison sold New York City generating facilities to KeySpan, Northern States Power, and Orion Power for a total of $1.65 billion.

Also in 1999 Con Edison bought Orange and Rockland Utilities for $790 million to increase its New York base and expand into New Jersey and Pennsylvania. In an effort to push into New England, the company that year agreed to buy Northeast Utilities (NU) for $3.3 billion in cash and stock and $3.9 billion in assumed debt. But the deal broke down in 2001. NU accused Con Edison of improperly trying to renegotiate terms, while Con Edison accused NU of concealing information about unfavorable power supply contracts.

Con Edison's Indian Point Unit 2 nuclear plant was shut down temporarily in 2000 after a radioactive steam leak; later that year it agreed to sell Indian Point Units 1 and 2 to Entergy for $502 million. The sale was completed in 2001. That year Con Edison also incurred an estimated $400 million in costs related to emergency response and asset damage from the September 11 terrorist attacks on New York City.

After evaluating strategic alternatives for its telecommunications business due to losses at the unit, in 2006 the company sold its Con Edison Communications unit (now RCN Business Solutions) to RCN Corporation for $32 million.

EXECUTIVES

Chairman, President, and CEO; Chairman, CEO, and Trustee, Consolidated Edison of New York: Kevin Burke, age 58, $7,318,517 total compensation
SVP and CFO; SVP and CFO, Consolidated Edison of New York: Robert N. Hoglund, age 47, $1,605,935 total compensation
EVP: John D. McMahon, age 57, $3,208,044 total compensation
SVP Public Affairs, Consolidated Edison of New York: Frances A. Resheske, age 48
SVP Enterprise Shared Services, Consolidated Edison of New York: Luther Tai, age 60
SVP Business Shared Services, Consolidated Edison of New York: JoAnn F. Ryan, age 51
VP Strategic Planning: Gurudatta Nadkarni, age 43
VP and Treasurer; VP and Treasurer, Consolidated Edison of New York: James P. (Jim) O'Brien, age 61
VP and Controller: Robert Muccilo, age 53
President and CEO, Orange and Rockland Utilities: William G. Longhi, age 55
President and COO, Consolidated Edison of New York: Louis L. Rana, age 60, $3,586,566 total compensation
President and CEO, Consolidated Edison Solutions: Jorge J. Lopez
President, Consolidated Edison of New York: Craig S. Ivey, age 46
Director Investor Relations: Jan C. Childress
Secretary; Secretary and Associate General Counsel, Consolidated Edison of New York: Carole Sobin
General Counsel; General Counsel, Consolidated Edison of New York: Charles E. McTiernan Jr., age 64
Manager Investor Relations: Ellen Socolow
Auditors: PricewaterhouseCoopers LLP

LOCATIONS

HQ: Consolidated Edison, Inc.
4 Irving Place, New York, NY 10003
Phone: 212-460-4600 **Fax:** 212-982-7816
Web: www.conedison.com

PRODUCTS/OPERATIONS

2008 Sales

	$ mil.	% of total
Electricity	8,611	63
Gas	2,097	16
Steam	707	5
Other	2,168	16
Total	**13,583**	**100**

Selected Subsidiaries

Consolidated Edison Company of New York, Inc. (utility)
Consolidated Edison Development, Inc. (investments in power generation projects)
Consolidated Edison Energy, Inc. (wholesale energy marketing and trading)
Consolidated Edison Solutions, Inc. (retail energy marketing and services)
Orange and Rockland Utilities, Inc. (utility)

COMPETITORS

Accent Energy
AEP
CH Energy
CMS Energy
Delmarva Power
Duke Energy
Enbridge
Energy East
Green Mountain Energy
National Fuel Gas
National Grid USA
New York Power Authority
Northeast Utilities
NSTAR
PPL Corporation
Public Service Enterprise Group
South Jersey Industries
USPowerGen
Viridis Energy Inc

HISTORICAL FINANCIALS
Company Type: Public

Income Statement
FYE: December 31

	REVENUE ($ mil.)	NET INCOME ($ mil.)	NET PROFIT MARGIN	EMPLOYEES
12/08	13,583.0	1,196.0	8.8%	15,628
12/07	13,120.0	929.0	7.1%	15,214
12/06	12,137.0	737.0	6.1%	14,795
12/05	11,690.0	719.0	6.2%	14,537
12/04	9,758.0	537.0	5.5%	14,096
Annual Growth	8.6%	22.2%	—	2.6%

2008 Year-End Financials
Debt ratio: 95.4%
Return on equity: 12.7%
Cash ($ mil.): —
Current ratio: 1.04
Long-term debt ($ mil.): 9,249
No. of shares (mil.): 275
Dividends
Yield: 6.0%
Payout: 53.5%
Market value ($ mil.): 10,705

Stock History
NYSE: ED

	STOCK PRICE ($) FY Close	P/E High/Low		PER SHARE ($) Earnings	Dividends	Book Value
12/08	38.93	11	8	4.37	2.34	35.27
12/07	48.85	15	12	3.47	2.32	33.78
12/06	48.07	17	14	2.95	2.30	29.88
12/05	46.33	17	14	2.94	2.28	27.36
12/04	43.75	20	16	2.27	2.26	26.43
Annual Growth	(2.9%)	—	—	17.8%	0.9%	7.5%

Constellation Brands

Thinking about alcohol makes this company starry-eyed. Constellation Brands is a leading beer, wine, and spirits maker. It offers more than 200 brands, which it sells in some 150 countries. Its wine division, anchored by its domestic winemaking subsidiary Constellation Wines U.S., is a global leader in wine production, offering brands such as Robert Mondavi and Vendange, as well as such premium labels as Ravenswood and Simi. The company also imports Corona and Tsingtao beers and markets distilled spirits, including Black Velvet whiskey and Svedka vodka. In the UK it produces and distributes cider, wine, and bottled water. CEO Robert Sands and his family control about 65% of Constellation's voting power.

As part of its focus on higher-growth and higher-margin brands, in 2009 Constellation sold its value spirits brands to New Orleans-based Sazerac Company for about $331 million. Some of the brands included in the more-than-40-brand sale were Barton, Sköl, Mr. Boston, Fleischmann's, the 99 schnapps line, the di Amore line, Chi-Chi's pre-mixed cocktail line, and Montezuma Tequila.

In order to eliminate brand duplication and excess production capacity, in 2008 the company sold some of its wine assets to Sonoma Valley-based Eight Estates Fine Wines (dba Ascentai Wine Estates). The sale included the Geyser Peak, Buena Vista, Gary Farrell, Atlas Peak, and XYZin labels, which were acquired from Fortune Brands in 2007; Columbia Winery and Covey Run (including Sunnyside winery) and Ste. Chapelle, all of which were acquired in 2001 from Corus Brands. Proceeds from the sale were used to reduce company debt.

Also that year the company sold the middle-market Almaden and Inglenook wine brands, along with the Paul Masson winery located in Madera, California, to The Wine Group.

HISTORY

Marvin Sands, the son of wine maker Mordecai (Mack) Sands, exited the Navy in 1945 and entered distilling by purchasing an old sauerkraut factory in Canandaigua, New York. His business, Canandaigua Industries, struggled while making fruit wines in bulk for local bottlers in the East. Aiming at regional markets, the company began producing its own brands two years later. Marvin opened the Richards Wine Cellar in Petersburg, Virginia, in 1951 and put his father in charge of the unit. In 1954 Marvin developed his own brand of "fortified" wine — boosted by 190-proof brandy — and named it Richards Wild Irish Rose after his son Richard.

The company slowly expanded, buying a number of small wineries in the 1960s and 1970s. It went public in 1973, changing its name to Canandaigua Wine. A year later the company expanded to the West Coast, thus gaining access to the growing varietal market.

Canandaigua continued to grow through acquisitions and new product introductions in the early 1980s. In 1984, when wine coolers became popular, the company introduced Sun Country Coolers, doubling sales to $173 million by 1986.

The short-lived wine cooler fad made Canandaigua realize that its distribution network could handle more volume, so it began looking for additional brands. The company picked up Kosher wine maker Manischewitz and East Coast wine maker Widmer's Wine Cellars, both in 1987. The company made a major purchase in 1991 when it bought Guild Wineries & Distillers (Cook's champagne) for $60 million.

Richard Sands became CEO in 1993. Subsequent acquisitions included Barton (beer importing, branded spirits; 1993), Vintners International (Paul Masson and Taylor, 1993), Heublein's Almaden and Inglenook (1994), and 12 distilled spirits brands from United Distillers Glenmore (1995). The moves doubled Canandaigua's share of the spirits market, making it the #4 US spirits supplier. After the flurry of acquisitions, the company changed its name in 1997 to Canandaigua Brands.

In 1998 it bought Matthew Clark, a UK-based maker of cider, wine, and bottled water, for $359 million. Further stocking its cabinet, in 1999 Canandaigua bought several whiskey brands (including Black Velvet) and two Canadian production facilities from Diageo. Also in 1999, Canandaigua entered the premium wine business with the purchases of vintners Simi Winery and Franciscan Estates.

Founder Marvin Sands died in 1999. His son, Richard, who had been CEO since 1993, succeeded his father as chairman. In 2000 the firm changed its name to Constellation Brands.

In 2001 Constellation Brands acquired Turner Road Vintners, a division of Sebastiani Vineyards, including the Vendange, Talus, Heritage, Nathanson Creek, La Terre, and Farallon brands of wine, as well as two wineries in California.

Constellation Brands teamed with Australian vintner BRL Hardy in 2001 to form its Pacific Wine Partners joint venture, which targets the mid-priced wine market in the US. That year Constellation Brands also purchased Ravenswood Winery. In 2003 Constellation Brands acquired BRL Hardy. In 2004 the company completed its landmark acquisition of The Robert Mondavi Corporation, further adding to the company's dominance in the wine industry. Also that year Constellation Brands announced plans to buy 40% of Italy's Ruffino.

In 2005 the company acquired Rex Goliath from Hahn Estates and made a number of bids to take over Canada's Vincor International. Vincor's board rejected all offers until 2006, when it accepted an offer of C$1 billion dollars. As part of the integration of Vincor into the company, Constellation eliminated 230 Vincor jobs and renamed the company Vincor Canada.

Constellation Brands formed a 50-50 joint venture with Grupo Modelo in 2006 (Crown Imports) to import and market the Mexican brewer's beer in the US and Guam through a joint venture. The following year Constellation became a 50% owner of UK beverage wholesaler Matthew Clark, with pub operator Punch Taverns.

In addition, in 2007 Constellation added to its premium spirits line with the acquisition of the Swedish vodka label Svedka, along with its New York import operations, Spirits Marque One, for $384 million. In a major boost to its wine division, the company acquired the wine business of Fortune Brands (Beam Wine Estates) for $885 million in cash. The deal added such labels as Clos du Bois, Geyser Peak, and Wild Horse to Constellation's already packed wine cellar. It also included five Sonoma County, California, wineries and vineyards that total 1,500 acres.

Top management changes also took place in 2007. CEO Richard Sands was replaced by Robert (Rob) Sands; Richard Sands remained as chairman. (The men are brothers.)

EXECUTIVES

Chairman: Richard Sands, age 58, $5,536,273 total compensation
President, CEO, and Director: Robert S. (Rob) Sands, age 50, $4,664,120 total compensation
EVP and CFO: Robert (Bob) Ryder, $1,583,418 total compensation
EVP and Chief Administrative Officer: W. Keith Wilson, age 58
EVP and General Counsel: Thomas J. (Tom) Mullin, age 57
EVP Business Development, Corporate Strategy, and International: F. Paul Hetterich, age 46
SVP Compensation and Benefits: L. Denise Watson
VP Investor Relations: Patty Yahn-Urlaub
VP Corporate Communications: Cheryl Gossin
President and CEO, Constellation Wines North America: José F. Fernandez, age 53, $2,152,163 total compensation
President, Europe; President, Wines, Australia: Troy Christensen
President, Constellation Wines Australia Regional Estates: John Grant, age 49
CEO, Constellation New Zealand: Joe Stanton
Director Investor Relations: Bob Czudak
Manager Corporate Communications: Eric Thomas
Auditors: KPMG LLP

LOCATIONS

HQ: Constellation Brands, Inc.
370 Woodcliff Dr., Ste. 300, Fairport, NY 14450
Phone: 585-218-3600   **Fax:** 585-218-3601
Web: www.cbrands.com

2009 Sales

	$ mil.	% of total
US	2,196.3	60
UK	631.7	17
Canada	448.2	12
Australia & New Zealand	351.4	10
Other countries	27.0	1
Total	**3,654.6**	**100**

PRODUCTS/OPERATIONS

2009 Sales

	$ mil.	% of total
Wine		
Branded	3,015.3	83
Wholesale & other	220.6	6
Spirits	418.7	11
Total	**3,654.6**	**100**

Selected Subsidiaries and Operations

Constellation Spirits, Inc.
Constellation Wines U.S.
Crown Imports LLC (50%, joint venture with Grupo
    Modelo, S.A.B. de C.V., beer)
Matthew Clark (50%, joint venture with Punch Taverns
    plc, drinks wholesaler, UK)
Vincor International, Inc. (wine, Canada)

COMPETITORS

Andrew Peller	Kendall-Jackson
Anheuser-Busch InBev	Korbel
Bacardi	LVMH
Beam Global Spirits	MillerCoors
Boston Beer	Patrón Spirits
Bronco Wine Co.	Pernod Ricard
Brown-Forman	Ravenswood Winery
Carlsberg	SABMiller
Diageo	Scheid Vineyards
E. & J. Gallo	Sebastiani Vineyards
Fortune Brands	Taittinger
Foster's Americas	Terlato Wine
Foster's Group	Trinchero Family Estates
GIV	Willamette Valley
Halewood	Vineyards
Heaven Hill Distilleries	Wine Group
Heineken	

HISTORICAL FINANCIALS

Company Type: Public

Income Statement

FYE: Last day in February

	REVENUE ($ mil.)	NET INCOME ($ mil.)	NET PROFIT MARGIN	EMPLOYEES
2/09	3,654.6	(301.4)	—	6,600
2/08	3,773.0	(613.3)	—	8,200
2/07	5,216.4	327.0	6.3%	9,200
2/06	4,603.4	315.5	6.9%	7,900
2/05	4,087.6	266.7	6.5%	7,700
Annual Growth	**(2.8%)**	**—**	**—**	**(3.8%)**

2009 Year-End Financials

Debt ratio: 208.1%   No. of shares (mil.): 221
Return on equity: —   Dividends
Cash ($ mil.): 13   Yield: 0.0%
Current ratio: 1.91   Payout: —
Long-term debt ($ mil.): 3,971   Market value ($ mil.): 2,881

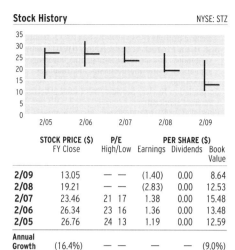
Constellation Energy Group

Constellation Energy Group's leading light is still utility Baltimore Gas and Electric (BGE), which distributes electricity and natural gas in central Maryland. The company trades and markets wholesale energy through subsidiary Constellation Energy Commodities Group, which is one of the top power marketers in North America. Constellation Energy also operates independent power plants with more than 9,100 MW of generating capacity through its Constellation Generation unit, and it competes in retail energy supply through Constellation NewEnergy. In 2007 this unit acquired Cornerstone Energy, creating one of the largest natural gas marketing companies in the US.

Other nonutility operations include a district cooling system in Baltimore, HVAC (heating, ventilation, and air-conditioning) services, appliance sales, and onsite energy system installations; nuclear plant development (through a joint venture); and energy consulting services.

Constellation Energy has been expanding its retail energy supply operations through acquisitions, including its purchase of NewEnergy, the former retail marketing unit of AES. To further expand its nonregulated operations, which have grown to account for the bulk of its sales, the company has purchased a New York nuclear plant for $408 million from Rochester Gas and Electric. In 2008 MidAmerican Energy Holdings agreed to buy Constellation Energy, but the deal was terminated after EDF Development (a subsidiary of EDF) agreed to acquire 50% of Constellation Energy's Constellation Energy Nuclear Group for $4.5 billion.

Overstretched by its rapid expansion, the company has sold noncore assets, including its real estate investments and Latin American power projects. It also sold the Oleander power plant in Cocoa, Florida to fellow utility provider Southern Company.

In 2009, in a move to lessen the risks involved in its business during the economic downturn, the company divested most of its international commodities business and its downstream natural gas unit. In March 2009 it completed the sale of its Houston-based downstream gas unit as well as most of its London-based coal, freight, and international commodities business.

HISTORY

In 1816, back when gas was made out of tar, Rembrandt Peale (an artist and son of painter Charles Willson Peale), William Lorman, and three others formed the US's first gas utility: Gas Light Company of Baltimore; Lorman was president until 1832. The firm soon ran out of money and issued stock to raise capital.

Baltimore's growth outstripped the firm's gas-main capacity, and by 1860 it had a fierce rival in the People's Gas Light Co. In 1871 the two firms divided the city up and then fought a price war with yet another rival. Finally, the three merged as the Consolidated Gas Company of Baltimore City in 1880.

The next year the Brush Electric Light Company and the United States Electric Light and Power Company were established. In 1906 their descendants merged with Consolidated Gas to form the Consolidated Gas Electric Light and Power Co.

As demand for electricity grew, the company turned from hydroelectric power to steam generators in the 1920s. Its revenues increased despite the Depression, and it later set records producing gas and electricity during WWII. Despite a postwar boom in sales, earnings fell as Consolidated spent money on new plants, shifting to natural gas and converting downtown Baltimore from DC to AC.

In 1955 Consolidated was renamed Baltimore Gas and Electric Company (BGE). BGE announced plans in 1967 for Maryland's first nuclear power plant; Calvert Cliffs Unit 1 went on line in 1975, and Unit 2 followed two years later.

BGE began adding to the Safe Harbor Hydroelectric Project in 1981. Over the next two years it sought to form a holding company in order to diversify, but state regulators rejected the request in 1983. Undaunted, the firm formed subsidiary Constellation Holdings in 1985 and began investing in nonutility businesses and pursuing independent power projects.

Both Calvert Cliffs nukes were shut down between 1989 and 1990 for repairs, and BGE had to spend $458 million on replacement power.

The Energy Policy Act fundamentally changed the electric utility industry in 1992 by allowing wholesale power competition in monopoly territories. BGE began expanding its gas division that year, and in 1995 it ventured into Latin America and took a stake in a Bolivian power firm.

BGE formed its power marketing arm that year with Goldman Sachs as its advisor. It teamed up with Goldman Sachs again in 1998 when the duo formed joint venture Orion Power Holdings to buy electric plants in the US and Canada. In 1999 Orion bought plants from Niagara Mohawk, Con Ed, and U.S. Generating.

Meanwhile, Maryland passed deregulation legislation in 1999, and Constellation Energy Group was formed in 1999 as the holding company for BGE and its nonregulated subsidiaries. Competition began in BGE's territory in 2000, and Constellation Energy separated BGE's generation assets from its distribution assets in accordance with the state's deregulation laws.

In 2001 Constellation Energy purchased the Nine Mile Point Nuclear Station Unit 1 and 82% of Unit 2 (most of the holdings were bought from

changed its name to Con-way Truckload in January 2008.

The deal opens up opportunities for Con-way Truckload to strengthen its "through-trailer" service into and out of Mexico through Texas, Arizona, and California. Through-trailer service eliminates the need for transfer and/or storage fees at the border, making delivery faster and reducing transportation costs for customers.

The CFI acquisition is the latest in a series of moves to reshuffle Con-way's business mix. Since 2006 the company has closed its freight forwarding unit, sold its expedited transportation business, and sold Menlo Worldwide's stake in its Vector SCM joint venture to partner General Motors.

Menlo Worldwide, which accounts for about one-third of Con-way's sales, intends to grow by expanding its presence in the Asia/Pacific region. In 2007 the company acquired Singapore-based Cougar Logistics and Shanghai-based Chic Logistics.

HISTORY

What is now Con-way got its start in 1929, when Leland James, co-owner of a bus company in Portland, Oregon, founded Consolidated Truck Lines to serve in the Pacific Northwest. Operations extended to San Francisco and Idaho by 1934 and to North Dakota by 1936. It adopted the name Consolidated Freightways (CF) in 1939.

James formed Freightways Manufacturing that year, making CF the only trucking company to design and build its own trucks (Freightliners). In the 1940s CF extended service to Chicago, Minneapolis, and Los Angeles.

CF went public in 1951 and moved to Menlo Park, California, in 1956. It continued to buy companies (52 between 1955 and 1960) and extended its reach throughout the US and Canada. When an attempt to coordinate intermodal services with railroads and shipping lines failed in 1960, William White became president and exited intermodal operations to focus on less-than-truckload shipping.

In 1966 CF formed CF AirFreight to offer air cargo services in the US. Three years later it bought Pacific Far East Lines, a San Francisco shipping line (now a part of Con-way).

CF sold Freightways Manufacturing to Daimler-Benz in 1981 and started the Con-Way carriers, its regional trucking businesses, in 1983 after the US trucking industry was deregulated. In the 1980s Con-Way moved back into intermodal rail, truck, and ocean shipping.

The company bought Emery Air Freight in 1989 and combined it with CF AirFreight to form Emery Worldwide. Founded in 1946, Emery Air Freight had expanded across the US and overseas, first by using extra cargo space on scheduled airline flights, then by chartering aircraft. Later operating its own air fleet, Emery began having troubles in the 1980s, including difficulties in integrating its 1987 acquisition, Purolator Courier. A 1988 takeover attempt by former FedEx president Arthur Bass further plagued Emery; fending off the takeover resulted in losses of about $100 million in 1989. That year Emery brought CF a deal with the U.S. Postal Service (USPS) to handle its next-day express mail.

Amid the beginning of a three-year profit slump, CF formed Menlo Logistics in 1990 to provide its customers with a range of third-party logistics services. A Teamsters' strike in 1994 that halted union carriers nationwide boosted demand for Con-Way's services, as customers sought nonunion carriers to move their shipments. The next year Con-Way opened 40 service centers and bought another 3,300 tractors and trailers.

In 1996 CF spun off most of its long-haul transportation businesses (including CF MotorFreight, Canadian Freightways, and Milne & Craighead) and renamed the resulting entity Consolidated Freightways. CF then changed its own name to CNF Transportation.

CNF Transportation received a five-year, $1.7 billion contract from USPS in 1997 to sort and transport two-day priority mail in the eastern US. In 2000 CNF Transportation shortened its name to CNF and began renegotiating its money-losing second-day priority mail contract with USPS. (FedEx eventually got the job.) In 2001 CNF's Con-Way Transportation established Con-Way Air Express, an airfreight forwarder that serves the US and Puerto Rico.

Emery grounded its aircraft fleet in 2001 because of maintenance problems discovered by Federal Aviation Administration inspectors. The company hired other carriers in order to continue its airfreight services. In a settlement with the FAA, Emery agreed to pay a $1 million civil fine.

To emphasize its focus on logistics, CNF combined the operations of Emery Worldwide, Menlo Logistics, and Vector SCM into a new company, Menlo Worldwide, effective in January 2002. In 2004 CNF sold its freight forwarding unit, Menlo Worldwide Forwarding and its subsidiary, Menlo Worldwide Expedite, to rival UPS.

As part of an effort to focus on its operating businesses, CNF renamed itself Con-way in 2006. In conjunction with the name change, the businesses of the former Con-Way Transportation Services were split between Con-way Freight and Con-way Transportation LLC (later renamed Con-way Truckload Services). Con-way shut down its Con-way Forwarding subsidiary, which specialized in domestic airfreight forwarding, and sold its expedited freight transportation business to Panther Expedited Services.

EXECUTIVES

Chairman: W. Keith Kennedy Jr., age 65
President, CEO, and Director: Douglas W. Stotlar, age 48, $3,176,566 total compensation
SVP and CFO: Stephen L. (Steve) Bruffett, age 44, $413,814 total compensation
VP and CIO: Jacquelyn (Jackie) Barretta, age 47
VP Communications and Chief Marketing Officer: Thomas (Tom) Nightingale
SVP; President, Menlo Worldwide: Robert L. Bianco Jr., age 44, $1,105,470 total compensation
SVP, General Counsel, and Secretary: Jennifer W. Pileggi, age 44
SVP; President, Con-way Truckload: Herbert J. (Herb) Schmidt, age 53, $1,512,721 total compensation
VP Human Resources: Leslie P. Lundberg, age 51
VP and Treasurer: Mark C. Thickpenny, age 56
VP Investor Relations: Patrick J. (Pat) Fossenier
VP Government Relations and Public Affairs: C. Randal Mullett
VP Global Policy and Economic Sustainability: David L. (Dave) Miller, age 51
VP Culture and Training: Julia P. (Pat) Jannausch
VP Operational Accounting: Kevin C. Schick, age 57, $1,199,388 total compensation
SVP; President Con-way Freight: John G. Labrie, age 42, $1,131,909 total compensation
President, Road Systems: Lynn C. Reinbolt
Director Communications: Gary N. Frantz
Auditors: KPMG LLP

LOCATIONS

HQ: Con-way Inc.
  2855 Campus Dr., Ste. 300, San Mateo, CA 94403
Phone: 650-378-5200   **Fax:** 650-357-9160
Web: www.con-way.com

2008 Sales

	$ mil.	% of total
US	4,707.9	96
Canada	111.3	2
Other countries	217.6	2
Total	**5,036.8**	**100**

PRODUCTS/OPERATIONS

2008 Sales

	$ mil.	% of total
Freight	3,015.9	60
Logistics	1,511.6	30
Truckload	505.2	10
Other	4.1	—
Total	**5,036.8**	**100**

COMPETITORS

APL Logistics
Arkansas Best
Central Freight Lines
CEVA Logistics
C.H. Robinson Worldwide
DHL
Estes Express
Expeditors
FedEx Freight
FedEx Trade Networks
J.B. Hunt
Landstar System
Old Dominion Freight
Pacer Transportation Solutions
Panalpina, Inc.
Ryder System
Saia
Schneider National
Swift Transportation
Transplace
UPS Freight
UPS Supply Chain Solutions
UTi Worldwide
Werner Enterprises
YRC Worldwide

HISTORICAL FINANCIALS

Company Type: Public

Income Statement

FYE: December 31

	REVENUE ($ mil.)	NET INCOME ($ mil.)	NET PROFIT MARGIN	EMPLOYEES
12/08	5,036.8	73.7	1.5%	26,600
12/07	4,387.4	152.9	3.5%	27,100
12/06	4,221.5	270.4	6.4%	21,800
12/05	4,169.6	223.0	5.3%	21,800
12/04	3,712.4	(115.9)	—	26,000
Annual Growth	**7.9%**	**—**	**—**	**0.6%**

2008 Year-End Financials

Debt ratio: 148.1%
Return on equity: 9.6%
Cash ($ mil.): 278
Current ratio: 1.45
Long-term debt ($ mil.): 926
No. of shares (mil.): 49
Dividends
  Yield: 1.5%
  Payout: 28.6%
Market value ($ mil.): 1,304

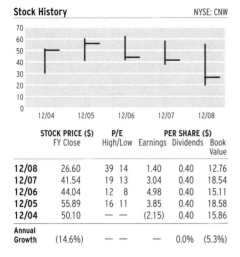
	STOCK PRICE ($) FY Close	P/E High/Low	PER SHARE ($) Earnings	Dividends	Book Value
12/08	26.60	39　14	1.40	0.40	12.76
12/07	41.54	19　13	3.04	0.40	18.54
12/06	44.04	12　8	4.98	0.40	15.11
12/05	55.89	16　11	3.85	0.40	18.58
12/04	50.10	—　—	(2.15)	0.40	15.86
Annual Growth	(14.6%)	—　—	—	0.0%	(5.3%)

Cooper Industries

Cooper Industries likes to keep customers from blowing a fuse. The company's electrical products segment makes circuit protection equipment, as well as lighting fixtures, wiring devices, and other power management and distribution equipment for residential, commercial, and industrial use. Its other main business segment manufactures power tools for the industrial market and hand tools for the do-it-yourself and commercial markets. Major electrical product and tool brands include Buss fuses, Capri conduits, Crescent pliers and wrenches, EMSA power transformers, Plumb hammers, and Weller soldering supplies. Cooper serves markets throughout the Americas, Asia, and Europe, with the US as its largest.

Electrical products account for more than 85% of its sales, and the company has expanded those offerings through several acquisitions. In early 2009, for example, it scored Illumination Management Solutions (IMS), a provider of specialized optics and system design for light-emitting diode (LED) fixtures. The LED tech deal complements previously acquired io Lighting and UK-Based Clarity Lighting. Earlier, Cooper bought electronic instrument and protection equipment maker MTL Instruments for about £144 million (nearly $281 million). MTL joined the Cooper Crouse-Hinds product line. Cooper's acquisitive moves include power engineering software provider Cyme International. The Canadian company was folded into the Cooper Power System's Energy Automation Solutions division.

HISTORY

In 1833 Charles Cooper sold a horse for $50 and borrowed additional money to open a foundry with his brother Elias in Mount Vernon, Ohio. Known as C. & E. Cooper, the company made plows, hog troughs, maple syrup kettles, stoves, and wagon boxes.

C. & E. Cooper began making steam engines in the 1840s for mill and farm use; it later adapted its engines for wood-burning locomotives. In 1868 the company built its first Corliss

steam engine, and in 1875 it introduced the first steam-powered farm tractor. By 1900 C. & E. Cooper sold its steam engines in the US and overseas. The company debuted an internal combustion engine-compressor in 1909 for natural gas pipelines.

In the 1920s the company became the #1 seller of compression engines for oil and gas pipelines. A 1929 merger with Bessemer (small engines) created Cooper-Bessemer, which made diesel engines for power boats.

Diversification began in 1959 with the purchase of Rotor Tools. Cooper adopted its current name in 1965 and moved its headquarters to Houston in 1967. It went on to buy other firms, including Lufkin Rule (measuring tapes, 1967), Crescent (wrenches, 1968), and Weller (soldering tools, 1970).

Cooper's 1979 purchase of Gardner-Denver gave it a strong footing in oil-drilling and mining equipment, and the addition of Crouse-Hinds in 1981 was key to its diversification into electrical materials. The decline in oil prices in the early 1980s caused sales to drop, but Cooper stayed profitable due to its tools and electrical products.

Cooper's electrical segment expanded with the 1985 purchase of McGraw-Edison, a maker of consumer products (Buss fuses) and heavy transmission gear for electrical utilities. Growth continued as it added RTE (electrical equipment, 1988), Cameron Iron Works (oil-drilling equipment, 1989), and Ferramentas Belzer do Brasil (hand-tool maker, 1992).

Expanding into auto parts, Cooper bought Champion Spark Plug (1989) and Moog (auto replacement parts, 1992). From 1991 to 1993, the company divested 11 businesses and bought 13. In 1994 it spun off Gardner-Denver Industrial Machinery (now Gardner Denver), sold Cameron Forged Products, and added Abex Friction Products (brake materials) and Zanxx (lighting components) to its auto parts line.

Cooper spun off Cooper Cameron (petroleum equipment; now Cameron International) in 1995. The next year Cooper bought electrical fuse supplier Karp Electric, tool manufacturer Master Power, and electrical hub maker Myers Electric Products. Company veteran John Riley took over as chairman that year. Cooper added eight acquisitions in 1997, and some, such as Menvier-Swain Group (emergency lights and alarms, UK), helped to bolster its electrical segment. Despite its growth, the company trimmed its workforce by 30% that year.

Cooper completed 11 acquisitions in 1998 and 10 in 1999; among them were the tool business of Global Industrial Technologies (Quackenbush and Rotor Tool brands), Apparatebau Hundsbach (electronic sensors) and Metronix Elektronik (power tool controls), and several lighting firms. In the meantime, the company sold its automotive operations to Federal-Mogul.

In 2000 Cooper acquired B-Line Systems from Sigma-Aldrich for around $425 million. The next year tool maker Danaher offered to acquire Cooper in a deal worth about $5.5 billion. Cooper rejected the initial offer, then Danaher lost interest when Cooper's former automotive unit (sold in 1998) was named in asbestos lawsuits. (Cooper recorded a charge of about $125 million for discontinued operations in 2003 for liability exposure relating to those claims.)

In 2002 the company reincorporated in Bermuda for tax reasons and changed its name from Cooper Industries, Inc., to Cooper Industries, Ltd.

RSA Lighting (commercial lighting fixtures) was purchased in 2004 to expand the architectural lighting product line of its Cooper Lighting division. In 2006 Cooper acquired electrical interconnect maker G&H Technology, which also was integrated into Crouse-Hinds. Its concurrent acquisition of occupancy sensor and accessory manufacturer Novitas expanded its Cooper Wiring Devices division. Cooper also purchased fire safety and emergency communication systems maker Wheelock to bolster its Cooper Menvier operations.

In early 2007 the company acquired WPI Interconnect Products, a manufacturer of custom connectors and cable assemblies for commercial, industrial, and military applications. WPI was added to the Crouse-Hinds division. Cooper paid about $74.5 million for WPI.

Cooper made a $29 million tender offer for Polaron, a UK-based supplier of lighting control products for the non-residential construction market, and acquired the company in early 2007. Cooper also purchased Lighting (fixtures) and Powerline Communications, Inc. (PCI, lighting control panels) for a combined $22 million.

EXECUTIVES

Chairman, President, and CEO: Kirk S. Hachigian, age 49, $10,141,508 total compensation
SVP and CFO: Terry A. Klebe, age 54, $2,704,424 total compensation
VP, Controller, and Chief Accounting Officer: Rick L. Johnson, age 56
SVP, General Counsel, and Chief Compliance Officer: Bruce M. Taten
Chief Marketing Officer: Robert L. Taylor
SVP Business Development: C. Thomas (Tom) O'Grady, age 57, $1,718,129 total compensation
SVP Human Resources: James P. Williams, age 46
VP Operations: Laura K. Ulz, age 46
VP International Operations: Grant L. Gawronski, age 46
VP Internal Audit: David T. Gunther
VP, Taxes: John B. Reed
VP Business Systems: Melissa Scheppele
VP and Treasurer: Tyler Johnson
Group President, Power and Hand Tools: Gary A. Masse, age 46, $1,569,723 total compensation
Group President, Cooper Power Systems: Michael A. (Mike) Stoessl, age 45, $1,557,067 total compensation
Associate General Counsel and Secretary: Terrance V. Helz
Director Investor Relations: Mark Doheny
Auditors: Ernst & Young LLP

LOCATIONS

HQ: Cooper Industries, Ltd.
　　600 Travis St., Ste. 5800, Houston, TX 77002
Phone: 713-209-8400　　　**Fax:** 713-209-8996
Web: www.cooperindustries.com

2008 Sales

	$ mil.	% of total
US	4,480.6	69
Germany	322.8	5
UK	403.8	6
Canada	284.0	4
Mexico	206.5	3
China	173.4	3
Other countries	650.2	10
Total	**6,521.3**	**100**

PRODUCTS/OPERATIONS

2008 Sales

	$ mil.	% of total
Electrical products	5,755.7	88
Tools	765.6	12
Total	**6,521.3**	**100**

Selected Products and Brands

Electrical Products
Architectural recessed lighting (Portfolio)
Architectural and landscape lighting (Lumiere)
Aviation lighting products (Crouse-Hinds)
Current-limiting fuses (Combined Technologies)
Distribution switchgear (Kyle)
Electric fuses (B&S, Edison, Karp, Mercury)
Electrical connectors (Cam-Lok)
Electrical construction materials (CEAG, Crouse-Hinds)
Electrical hubs (Myers)
Electrical outlet and switch boxes (Thepitt)
Emergency alarm systems
Emergency lighting and fire-detection systems (CEAG, JSB, Luminox, Menvier)
Emergency lighting and power systems (Blessing, CSA, Pretronica, Univel)
Enclosures (B-Line)
Exit and emergency lighting (AtLite, Sure-Lites)
Fire-detection systems (Fulleon, Nugelec, Transmould)
Fluorescent lighting (Metalux)
Fasteners (B-Line)
Fuses (Buss, Kearney)
High-abuse, clean room, and vandal-resistant lighting fixtures (Fail-Safe)
Indoor and outdoor HID lighting (McGraw-Edison)
Inductors and transformers (Coiltronics)
Lighting systems (Iris)
Modular wiring systems (MWS)
Plugs and receptacles (Arktite)
Public address systems
Recessed and track-lighting fixtures (Halo)
Relays (Edison and Edison Pro)
Security equipment (Menvier, Scantronic)
Terminal strips and disconnect blocks (Magnum)
Transformer components, cable accessories, and fuses (McGraw-Edison, RTE)
Transient voltage protection devices (TransX)
Wiring devices (Arrow Hart)

Tools and Hardware
Assembly equipment, assembly stations, and transport lines (Assembly Systems, Cooper Automation, DGD/Gardner-Denver, GardoTrans)
Chain products (Campbell)
Cutters and tweezers (Erem)
Farrier tools (Diamond)
Files and saws (Nicholson)
Hammers (Plumb)
Industrial power tools (Airetool, Buckeye, Cleco, Dotco, Quackenbush, Rotor Tool)
Measuring and layout products (Lufkin)
Scissors, shears, and snips (H.K. Porter and Wiss)
Screwdrivers and nutdrivers (Xcelite)
Sockets, screwdriver bits, extensions, and universal joints (Apex, Geta)
Soldering equipment (Weller)
Torque-measuring and control equipment (Utica)
Wrenches and pliers (Crescent)

COMPETITORS

255ABB	Milwaukee Electric Tool
Acuity Brands	Molex
Atlas Copco	Newell Rubbermaid
Bel Fuse	Philips Lighting North
Black & Decker	America
Danaher	Powell Industries
Dover Corp.	Schneider Electric
Eaton	Siemens AG
Emerson Electric	Simpson Manufacturing
GE	SL Industries
Hubbell	Snap-on
Illinois Tool Works	Stanley Works
Ingersoll-Rand	Thomas & Betts
Littelfuse	Tinnerman Palnut
Makita	

HISTORICAL FINANCIALS

Company Type: Public

Income Statement

FYE: December 31

	REVENUE ($ mil.)	NET INCOME ($ mil.)	NET PROFIT MARGIN	EMPLOYEES
12/08	6,521.3	632.2	9.7%	31,200
12/07	5,903.1	692.3	11.7%	31,504
12/06	5,184.6	464.0	8.9%	30,561
12/05	4,730.4	163.9	3.5%	28,903
12/04	4,462.9	339.8	7.6%	26,863
Annual Growth	9.9%	16.8%	—	3.8%

2008 Year-End Financials

Debt ratio: 35.8%
Return on equity: 23.2%
Cash ($ mil.): 259
Current ratio: 1.50
Long-term debt ($ mil.): 933

No. of shares (mil.): 167
Dividends
  Yield: 3.4%
  Payout: 27.8%
Market value ($ mil.): 4,874

Stock History

NYSE: CBE

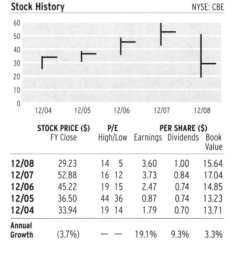

	STOCK PRICE ($) FY Close	P/E High/Low		PER SHARE ($) Earnings	Dividends	Book Value
12/08	29.23	14	5	3.60	1.00	15.64
12/07	52.88	16	12	3.73	0.84	17.04
12/06	45.22	19	15	2.47	0.74	14.85
12/05	36.50	44	36	0.87	0.74	13.23
12/04	33.94	19	14	1.79	0.70	13.71
Annual Growth	(3.7%)	—	—	19.1%	9.3%	3.3%

Cooper Tire & Rubber

Cooper Tire & Rubber is a real wheeler dealer. The company is the fourth largest tire manufacturer in North America (behind the likes of Bridgestone, Michelin, and Goodyear) and among the top 10 in the world. It makes and sells replacement tires mainly for passenger cars and light trucks but also for motorcycles, race cars, and off-road vehicles. Cooper operates eight manufacturing facilities and some 40 distribution centers worldwide. Customers include tire dealers, wholesale distributors, and regional and national tire chains. Unlike some of its rivals, Cooper does not typically sell to automotive OEMs. It divested its tread rubber and retreading operations in 2007 to focus on the replacement tire market.

In addition to its domestic operations, Cooper Tire & Rubber has manufacturing, technical, and distribution centers strategically placed or being developed in such countries as the UK, Mexico, and China.

Its UK operations continue to focus on serving European niche demand for high-performance, racing, and motorcycle tires. It is also steadily increasing its production capabilities and presence in the Asia/Pacific region, with majority stake purchases in two Chinese tire manufacturing

joint ventures and a minority stake in South Korea-based Kumho Tire. The deals are in line with Cooper's strategy of expanding its global footprint through joint ventures and partially owned subsidiaries.

The company hopes manufacturing in lower-cost regions such as Asia and Mexico will also help offset rising raw material costs, a weakened market demand for tires since 2006, and a global recession that began in 2008. Trying to secure its long-term financial health, Cooper announced that year that it would close a manufacturing facility in Georgia by 2010 and a distribution center in New Jersey in 2009 as part of a restructuring.

Dimensional Fund Advisors owns about 8% of Cooper Tire & Rubber. Renaissance Technologies holds another 7% stake.

HISTORY

John Schaefer and Claude Hart (brothers-in-law) bought M and M Manufacturing of Akron, Ohio, in 1914. M and M made tire patches, cement, and repair kits. In 1915 the two bought The Giant Tire & Rubber Company (tire rebuilding). Two years later they moved their business to Findlay, Ohio.

Ira Cooper joined Giant's board in 1917 and soon formed his own company, The Cooper Corporation, which began making tires in 1920. The industry began consolidating in the 1920s, and in 1930 Cooper and Giant merged with Falls Rubber Company (a small tire maker), and Master Tire & Rubber Company was born.

Cooper died in 1941, but the company went on to supply the war effort with tires, pontoons, life jackets, and tank decoys. After WWII the company changed its name to Cooper Tire & Rubber Company. Cooper earned sales and loyalty from retailers and private-brand customers by promising not to open its own sales outlets — a policy continued to this day. The growth of the interstate system in the postwar years meant more cars, tires, and sales. Cooper went public in 1960. In 1964 it established Cooper Industrial Products to make industrial rubber products.

The 1970s brought the radial tire into widespread use. Radials had been around since the late 1940s, but the manufacturing process hadn't been cheap or easy enough to be practical. After undertaking its own research and development, Cooper rolled out its first radial in 1974. Around the same time, it bought a Bowling Green, Ohio, plant that made extruded rubber products and reinforced hose. The plant was quickly adapted to produce rubber parts for cars.

A tire glut in the 1980s (due in part to longer-lasting tires) led to rapid downsizing in the industry. As competitors exited the tire business, Cooper was buying plants and modernizing them for about a third of the cost of building new ones. The company made its first foray outside the US with the acquisition of Rio Grande Servaas (inner tubes, Mexico). Cooper also undertook several projects in the 1980s to upgrade its research capabilities and to improve distribution. By the mid-1980s it could warehouse more than 3 million tires. By the end of the decade Cooper's stock was 68 times its 1980 level. The success came from growth in the replacement market, which was three times the size of the original equipment market.

The benefits of Cooper's capital investments became clear in the 1990s. As the decade began, the company recorded the best margins in the industry (about 33%), and investment continued. It passed the billion-dollar sales mark in 1991 and spent $110 million in capital investments in 1992.

In 1996 Cooper opened an automotive hose plant in Kentucky. The next year it bought Avon Tyres Limited (UK), its first overseas purchase.

Cooper completed its acquisition of Kentucky-based Dean Tire in 1999, expanding its sales of replacement tires for cars and light trucks to 10 countries. Cooper entered joint ventures with Italy's Pirelli in which Cooper sells and distributes Pirelli passenger car and light truck replacement tires in North America, and Pirelli distributes and markets Cooper tires in South America. The company boosted its automotive sealing system business with the purchase of The Standard Products Company in a deal valued at about $750 million.

In 2000 Cooper bought Siebe Automotive, the automotive fluid-handling division of Invensys, and sold Holm Industries (acquired with Standard Products) to an affiliate of Madison Capital Partners. Cooper also sold its automotive plastic trim plant in Winnsboro, South Carolina. Cooper closed several plants and scaled back operations at other facilities during 2001. A class-action lawsuit was settled in late 2002 stemming from claims that the tire maker did not disclose adhesion problems with its steel-belted radial tires; the decision, valued at $1 billion-$3 billion, gives an estimated 40 million consumers an extended warranty. In early 2003 Cooper purchased Max Trac Tire (better known as Mickey Thompson Performance Tires & Wheels). The company introduced the Discoverer H/T Plus (truck and SUV) and the Zeon ZPT (high performance) lines of tires in early 2004.

As 2004 came to a close, Cooper Tire completed the sale of its automotive unit, Cooper Standard Automotive, to Cypress Group and Goldman Sachs Capital Partners. That year the company also sold its inner tube operations.

EXECUTIVES

Chairman, President, and CEO: Roy V. Armes, age 56, $3,990,435 total compensation
VP and CFO: Philip G. (Phil) Weaver, age 56, $444,576 total compensation
SVP Global Human Resources and Communication: Mark W. Krivoruchka, age 54, $467,498 total compensation
VP, General Counsel, and Secretary: James E. Kline, age 67, $430,145 total compensation
VP Strategic Initiatives: James P. (Jim) Keller
VP; President, International Tire Division: Harold C. (Hal) Miller, age 56, $496,615 total compensation
VP, Corporate Purchasing: Linda L. Rennels
VP Sales and Marketing: Phillip D. (Phil) Caris
VP North American Tire Division: Hal Gardner
VP Supply Chain Operations: Fran Brennan
VP and General Manager, Asian Operations: Allen Tsaur
General Director, Cooper Mexico: Jim Smith
Director, Investor Relations: Curtis Schneekloth
Director, Information Technology Infrastructure: Loren Wagner
General Manager, Mickey Thompson Performance Tires & Wheels: Steve Kersh
Director, Corporate Communications: Cathy Hissong
General Manager, Corporacion de Occidente: Jeffrey J. Schumaker
Auditors: Ernst & Young LLP

LOCATIONS

HQ: Cooper Tire & Rubber Company
701 Lima Ave., Findlay, OH 45840
Phone: 419-423-1321   **Fax:** 419-424-4212
Web: www.coopertire.com

2008 Sales

	$ mil.	% of total
North America	2,055.8	71
Europe	303.7	11
Asia	522.3	18
Total	**2,881.8**	**100**

PRODUCTS/OPERATIONS

2008 Sales

	$ mil.	% of total
North American Tire	2,142.1	69
International Tire	975.0	31
Adjustments	(235.3)	—
Total	**2,881.8**	**100**

Selected Products

Light truck tires
Motorcycle tires
Off-road tires
Passenger car tires
Racing tires
Radial medium truck tires

COMPETITORS

Bridgestone
China Enterprises
Continental
Falken Tire
Goodyear
Hankook Tire
Kumho Tire
Michelin
Sumitomo Rubber
Toyo Tire & Rubber
Yokohama Rubber

HISTORICAL FINANCIALS

Company Type: Public

Income Statement

FYE: December 31

	REVENUE ($ mil.)	NET INCOME ($ mil.)	NET PROFIT MARGIN	EMPLOYEES
12/08	2,881.8	(219.4)	—	13,311
12/07	2,932.6	119.6	4.1%	13,355
12/06	2,676.2	(78.5)	—	13,361
12/05	2,155.2	(9.4)	—	8,762
12/04	2,081.6	201.4	9.7%	8,739
Annual Growth	**8.5%**	**—**	**—**	**11.1%**

2008 Year-End Financials

Debt ratio: 110.8%
Return on equity: —
Cash ($ mil.): 248
Current ratio: 1.48
Long-term debt ($ mil.): 326
No. of shares (mil.): 59
Dividends
  Yield: 6.8%
  Payout: —
Market value ($ mil.): 363

Stock History

NYSE: CTB

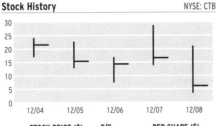

	STOCK PRICE ($) FY Close	P/E High/Low		PER SHARE ($) Earnings	Dividends	Book Value
12/08	6.16	—	—	(3.72)	0.42	4.99
12/07	16.58	15	7	1.91	0.42	13.44
12/06	14.30	—	—	(1.28)	0.42	10.85
12/05	15.32	—	—	(0.15)	0.42	15.92
12/04	21.55	9	6	2.68	0.42	19.85
Annual Growth	**(26.9%)**	**—**	**—**	**—**	**0.0%**	**(29.2%)**

Corning Incorporated

Corning is cookin' up some great technology. Once known mainly for its kitchenware and lab products, the company designs and produces material components for five industries: display technologies (flat-screen televisions, computer monitors, laptops), environmental technologies (mobile emission control systems), telecommunications (optical fiber, cable), life sciences (biosensors for drug research), and specialty materials (semiconductors, optical sensors for aerospace and defense).

When Corning's profits plunged 65% in 2008, the company responded by implementing spending controls and a hiring freeze, adjusting production schedules, and consolidating manufacturing. Corning let its temporary workers go and reduced its regular workforce by around 13% in early 2009.

Later in the year the company acquired Axygen BioScience, a California-based manufacturer and distributor of laboratory plastic ware and benchtop equipment. Corning purchased the company and its subsidiaries from American Capital for about $400 million. The acquisition, which is being integrated into Corning's Life Sciences segment, boosts Corning's portfolio of life sciences products and widens the door to promising global opportunities, channeled through Axygen's two manufacturing locations in Asia.

The company is focusing on emerging technologies. Gorilla Glass, a damage resistant cover glass, was introduced in 2008 for use in mobile phones, notebook computers, and for touch screen technologies. The company's Green Laser technology rivals LED-based solutions by offering improved images on mobile devices. It is developing better silicon on glass (SiOG) technology which adds pure crystalline silicon uniformly to computer chips and devices. The company is also in the early stages of creating a filter that will remove mercury released at coal-fired power plants. Other innovations include the Gen 10 (10th generation) LCD glass, ClearCurve optical fiber, and DuraTrap emissions-control solutions.

Corning is focusing on its display technologies. It has stepped up manufacturing of LCD glass used in computers, televisions, cell phones, and digital camera displays.

The telecommunications segment produces optical fiber and cable, hardware, and equipment for the telecommunications industry. The substitution of fiber over copper lines continues as bandwidth requirements in individual homes grow. The environmental segment products include ceramic technologies and solutions for emissions and pollution control. Future emissions regulations coming into effect in the US, Europe, and Japan could create a demand for heavy-duty emissions controls by 2012. Life sciences produces laboratory products such as coated slides, cell culture dishes, and liquid handling instruments, to name a few.

In 2008 Corning created its fifth operating segment, specialty materials, which includes semiconductors and optical sensors for aerospace and defense.

HISTORY

Amory Houghton started Houghton Glass in Massachusetts in 1851 and moved it to Corning, New York, in 1868. By 1876 the company, renamed Corning Glass Works, was making several types of technical and pharmaceutical glass. In 1880 it supplied the glass for Thomas Edison's first light bulb. Other early developments included the red-yellow-green traffic light system and borosilicate glass (which can withstand sudden temperature changes) for Pyrex oven and laboratory ware.

Joint ventures have been crucial to Corning's success. Early ones included Pittsburgh Corning (with Pittsburgh Plate Glass, 1937, glass construction blocks), Owens-Corning (with Owens-Illinois, 1938, fiberglass), and Dow Corning (with Dow Chemical, 1943, silicones).

By 1945 the company's laboratories had made it the undisputed leader in the manufacture of specialty glass. Applications for its glass technology included the first mass-produced television tubes, freezer-to-oven ceramic cookware (Pyroceram, Corning Ware), and car headlights.

After World War II Corning emphasized consumer product sales and expanded globally. In the 1970s the company pioneered the development of optical fiber and auto emission technology (now two of its principal products).

Seeing maturing markets for such established products as light bulbs and television tubes, Corning began buying higher-growth laboratory services companies — MetPath in 1982, Hazleton in 1987, Enseco in 1989, and G.H. Besse-laar in 1989. Vice chairman James Houghton, the great-great-grandson of Corning's founder, was named chairman and CEO in 1983.

Corning established international joint ventures with Siemens, Mitsubishi, and Samsung. In 1988 the company bought Revere Ware (cookware). The next year Corning dropped Glass Works from its name.

Joint venture Dow Corning, under assault from thousands of women seeking damages because of leaking breast implants, entered Chapter 11 bankruptcy protection in 1995 (and exited Chapter 11 in 2004). The massive losses incurred by Dow Corning due to litigation and a downturn in Corning's lab products sales prompted the company to recast itself. Corning began selling off its well-known consumer brands and putting greater emphasis on its high-tech optical and display products through acquisitions and R&D.

Company veteran Roger Ackerman was named chairman and CEO in 1996, replacing Houghton. He moved quickly to transform the company from a disjointed conglomerate to a high-tech optics manufacturer.

In 1998 Corning sold a majority stake in the housewares unit to Kohlberg Kravis Roberts the next year. In 2000 Corning made more than $5 billion worth of acquisitions to expand its optical fiber and hardware business. It acquired Siemens' optical cable and hardware operations and the remaining 50% of the companies' Siecor joint venture. Corning bought Oak Industries (optical components) for $1.8 billion and NetOptix (optical filters) for $2.15 billion, and purchased the 67% of microelectromechanical systems specialist IntelliSense it didn't already own.

Continuing its spending spree, the company bought part of Pirelli's fiber-optic telecom components business for about $3.6 billion; it also acquired Cisco's 10% stake in the business.

In the first half of 2001, Ackerman retired as chairman and CEO of the company. COO John Loose was named CEO, and Houghton was again appointed chairman.

Slowing demand prompted Corning to lay off about 25% of its staff, shut down plants, and discontinue its glass tubing operations that year. Houghton returned to the position of chief ex-

ecutive after Loose retired in 2002. That year the company made more layoffs, closed plants, and sold several non-core operations.

Corning president Wendell Weeks succeeded Houghton as CEO in 2005. Houghton remained chairman, and retired again in 2006, becoming non-executive chairman. Houghton became chairman emeritus in 2007 and remained on the board as a director. Weeks was elected chairman of the board.

EXECUTIVES

Chairman and CEO: Wendell P. Weeks, age 49, $10,631,753 total compensation
Vice Chairman and CFO: James B. Flaws, age 60, $7,542,950 total compensation
President, COO, and Director: Peter F. Volanakis, age 53, $9,242,087 total compensation
EVP and CTO: Joseph A. (Joe) Miller Jr., age 67, $3,610,179 total compensation
VP and CIO: Kevin J. McManus
SVP Operations Chief of Staff: Pamela C. Schneider, age 54
EVP and Chief Administrative Officer: Kirk P. Gregg, age 49, $4,901,913 total compensation
VP, Deputy General Counsel, and Chief Compliance Officer: Jack H. Cleland
SVP and General Counsel: Vincent P. Hatton, age 58
SVP Worldwide Government Affairs: Timothy J. Regan
SVP and Treasurer: Mark S. Rogus, age 49
SVP Strategy and Corporate Development: Lawrence D. McRae, age 50
SVP and Controller: R. Tony Tripeny, age 50
VP Human Resources: Christine M. Pambianchi
Secretary and Assistant General Counsel: Denise A. Hauselt
Corporate Communications: Daniel F. Collins
Investor Relations: Kenneth C. Sofio
Auditors: PricewaterhouseCoopers LLP

LOCATIONS

HQ: Corning Incorporated
1 Riverfront Plaza, Corning, NY 14831
Phone: 607-974-9000   **Fax:** 607-974-8091
Web: www.corning.com

2008 Sales

	$ mil.	% of total
Asia/Pacific		
Taiwan	1,966	33
Japan	803	13
China	293	5
South Korea	57	1
Other countries	162	3
North America		
US	1,568	26
Canada	113	2
Mexico	50	1
Europe		
Germany	237	4
UK	95	2
France	60	1
Other countries	417	7
Latin America	35	—
Other regions	92	2
Total	**5,948**	**100**

PRODUCTS/OPERATIONS

2008 Sales

	$ mil.	% of total
Display Technologies	2,724	46
Telecommunications	1,799	30
Environmental Technologies	711	12
Specialty Materials	372	6
Life Sciences	326	6
Other	16	—
Total	**5,948**	**100**

Selected Products

Display technologies
  Liquid crystal displays
Telecommunications
  Optical fiber and cable
  Optical networking components
Environmental technologies
  Industrial and stationary emissions products
  Mobile emissions and automotive catalytic converters products
Life sciences
  Genomics and laboratory equipment
Other
  Polarized glass
  Semiconductor materials

COMPETITORS

2573M	IBIDEN
ADC Telecommunications	JDS Uniphase
Alcatel-Lucent	NGK INSULATORS
Amphenol	Nippon Electric Glass
Asahi Glass	Nippon Sheet Glass
Becton, Dickinson	Nortel Networks
Belden	Oerlikon
Carl-Zeiss-Stiftung	Saint-Gobain
CommScope	SCHOTT
Dai Nippon Printing	Shin-Etsu Chemical
Draka Holding	Sumitomo Electric
Fujikura Ltd.	Superior Essex
Furukawa Electric	SWCC SHOWA
General Cable	Thermo Fisher Scientific
Gerresheimer Glass	Thomas & Betts
Heraeus Holding	Toppan Printing
Hoya Corp.	Tyco Electronics

HISTORICAL FINANCIALS

Company Type: Public

Income Statement

FYE: December 31

	REVENUE ($ mil.)	NET INCOME ($ mil.)	NET PROFIT MARGIN	EMPLOYEES
12/08	5,948.0	5,257.0	88.4%	27,000
12/07	5,860.0	2,150.0	36.7%	24,800
12/06	5,174.0	1,855.0	35.9%	24,500
12/05	4,579.0	585.0	12.8%	26,000
12/04	3,854.0	(2,165.0)	—	24,700
Annual Growth	**11.5%**	**—**	**—**	**2.3%**

2008 Year-End Financials

Debt ratio: 11.4%
Return on equity: 45.8%
Cash ($ mil.): 1,873
Current ratio: 2.25
Long-term debt ($ mil.): 1,527

No. of shares (mil.): 1,555
Dividends
  Yield: 2.1%
  Payout: 6.0%
Market value ($ mil.): 14,815

Stock History

NYSE: GLW

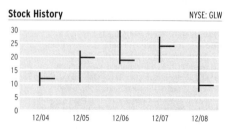

	STOCK PRICE ($) FY Close	P/E High/Low		PER SHARE ($) Earnings	Dividends	Book Value
12/08	9.53	8	2	3.32	0.20	8.65
12/07	23.99	20	14	1.34	0.10	6.11
12/06	18.71	26	15	1.16	0.00	4.66
12/05	19.66	58	28	0.38	0.00	3.61
12/04	11.77	—	—	(1.56)	0.00	2.45
Annual Growth	**(5.1%)**	**—**	**—**	**—**	**—**	**37.0%**

Costco Wholesale

Wal-Mart isn't the biggest in *every* business. Costco Wholesale is the largest wholesale club operator in the US (ahead of Wal-Mart's SAM'S CLUB). The company operates about 555 membership warehouse stores serving more than 53 million cardholders in some 40 US states and Puerto Rico, Canada, Japan, Mexico, South Korea, Taiwan, and the UK, primarily under the Costco Wholesale name. Stores offer discount prices on an average of about 4,000 products (many in bulk packaging), ranging from alcoholic beverages and appliances to fresh food, pharmaceuticals, and tires. Certain club memberships also offer products and services such as car and home insurance, mortgage and real estate services, and travel packages.

To shop at Costco customers must be members — a policy the company believes reinforces customer loyalty and provides a steady source of fee revenue. Costco's card membership renewal rate is 87%.

Facing competition from discounters, including Target, that don't charge a membership fee, as well as from rival SAM'S CLUB, Costco is expanding and retrofitting its warehouses (which average about 141,000 square feet) to accommodate fresh food sections and other ancillary units, such as gas stations, optical departments, pharmacies, and food courts. Costco's foray into grocery sales has been a success. Food and sundries accounted for more than half of Costco's total sales in 2008, making it the third-largest seller of groceries in the US behind Wal-Mart Supercenters and Kroger. Costco is expanding its premium private-label Kirkland Signature line of some 330 items to 500 products by 2011. (It has even struck a deal with Martha Stewart Living Omnimedia for a new line of food products exclusive to Costco, launched in 2008.)

Through its joint venture with Mexico's Controladora Comercial Mexicana, Costco Mexico operates about 30 warehouse stores south of the border. Ultimately, the company envisions as many as 1,000 warehouses worldwide by 2017.

In addition to its stand-alone stores, Costco has begun opening outlets in malls to grow in congested areas, such as Los Angeles.

In what amounts to a black eye for Costco, which enjoys its image as a benevolent employer relative to other retailers (notably Wal-Mart), a federal judge has granted class-action status to a lawsuit filed on behalf of more than 700 female Costco managers. The suit claims the company has discriminated against women seeking promotions to store managers.

HISTORY

From 1954 to 1974 retailer Sol Price built his Fed-Mart discount chain into a $300 million behemoth selling general merchandise to government employees. Price sold the company to Hugo Mann in 1975 and the next year, with son Robert, Rick Libenson, and Giles Bateman, opened the first Price Club warehouse, in San Diego, to sell in volume to small businesses at steep discounts.

Posting a large loss its first year prompted Price Club's decision to expand membership to include government, utility, and hospital employees, as well as credit union members. In 1978 it opened a second store, in Phoenix. With the help of his father, Sol's other son Laurence

began a chain of tire-mounting stores (located adjacent to Price Club outlets on land leased from the company and using tires sold by the Price Clubs).

The company went public in 1980 with four stores in California and Arizona. Price Club moved into the eastern US with its 1984 opening of a store in Virginia and continued to expand, including a joint venture with Canadian retailer Steinberg in 1986 to operate stores in Canada; the first Canadian warehouse opened that year in Montreal.

Two years later Price Club acquired A. M. Lewis (grocery distributor, Southern California and Arizona), and the next year it opened two Price Club Furnishings, offering discounted home and office furniture.

Price Club bought out Steinberg's interest in the Canadian locations in 1990 and added stores on the East Coast and in California, Colorado, and British Columbia. However, competition in the East from ensconced rivals such as SAM'S CLUB and PACE forced the closure of two stores two years later. A 50-50 joint venture with retailer Controladora Comercial Mexicana led to the opening of two Price Clubs in Mexico City, one each in 1992 and 1993.

Price Club merged with Costco Wholesale in 1993. Founded in 1983 by Jeffrey Brotman and James Sinegal (a former EVP of Price Company), Costco Wholesale went public in 1985 and expanded into Canada.

In 1993 Price/Costco opened its first warehouse outside the Americas in a London suburb. Merger costs led to a loss the following year, and Price/Costco spun off its commercial real estate operations, as well as certain international operations as Price Enterprises (now Price Legacy). In 1995 the company launched its Kirkland Signature brand of private-label merchandise. In 1997 the company changed its corporate name to Costco Companies.

Costco began online sales and struck a deal to buy two stores in South Korea in 1998 and opened its first store in Japan in 1999. Under industry-wide pressure over the way members-only chains record fees, Costco took a $118 million charge for fiscal 1999 to change accounting practices. That year the company made yet another name change to Costco Wholesale (emphasizing its core warehouse operations).

In 2000 the company purchased private retailer Littlewoods' 20% stake in Costco UK, increasing Costco's ownership to 80%. Costco began expanding into the Midwest in 2001 as part of plans to open 40 new clubs a year, including ones in China.

During fiscal 2002 Costco opened 29 new warehouse clubs. In December 2002 the retailer opened its first home store — called Costco Home — in Kirkland, Washington, stocked with mostly high-end furniture. A second Costco Home store opened in Tempe, Arizona, in December 2004.

In October 2003, Costco increased its equity interest in Costco Wholesale UK to 100% when it purchased Carrefour Nederland's 20% stake.

In 2006 Costco began offering more than 200 generic prescription medicines (100 count) for $10 or less. The following year Costco.com logged sales in excess of $1 billion.

In July 2009 Costco shuttered its two Costco Home stores, which were located in Washington and Arizona. The retailer cited the weak economy and market for home furnishings, and the fact that the concept didn't fit with its expansion plans, for their closure.

EXECUTIVES

Chairman: Jeffrey H. (Jeff) Brotman, age 67
President, CEO, and Director: James D. (Jim) Sinegal, age 73
SEVP and COO, Global Operations, Distribution and Construction, and Director: Richard D. DiCerchio, age 66
EVP, CFO, and Director: Richard A. Galanti, age 52
SVP Information Systems: Don Burdick
EVP and COO, Eastern and Canadian Divisions: Joseph P. (Joe) Portera, age 55
EVP and COO, Northern and Midwest Divisions: Douglas W. (Doug) Schutt, age 49
EVP Construction and Distribution: Thomas K. Walker, age 69
EVP Real Estate Development: Paul G. Moulton, age 57
EVP and COO, Merchandising: W. Craig Jelinek, age 57
EVP and COO, Southwest Division and Mexico: Dennis R. Zook, age 59
SVP and General Manager, Southeast Region: Roger A. Campbell
SVP Pharmacy: Charles V. Burnett
SVP Merchandising, Foods, and Sundries: Timothy L. Rose
SVP and Corporate Controller: David S. Petterson
SVP Administration and Chief Legal Officer: Joel Benoliel
SVP Human Resources and Risk Management: John Matthews
SVP Administration, Global Operations: Franz E. Lazarus
SVP International Operations: James P. (Jim) Murphy
Auditors: KPMG LLP

LOCATIONS

HQ: Costco Wholesale Corporation
999 Lake Dr., Issaquah, WA 98027
Phone: 425-313-8100
Web: www.costco.com

2008 Locations

	No.
US	398
Canada	75
UK	20
Japan	8
Korea	6
Taiwan	5
Total	**512**

PRODUCTS/OPERATIONS

2008 Sales

	% of total
Sundries (including candy, snacks, beverages, cleaning products & tobacco)	22
Food (dry & institutionally packaged)	20
Hardlines (including major appliances, electronics & office & auto supplies)	19
Fresh food (meat, bakery, deli & produce)	12
Softlines (including apparel, books, cameras & jewelry)	10
Other (including pharmacy, optical, photo & gas stations)	17
Total	**100**

2008 Sales

	$ mil.	% of total
Sales	70,977.5	98
Membership fees	1,505.5	2
Total	**72,483.0**	**100**

Selected Products and Services

Alcoholic beverages
Apparel
Appliances
Automotive insurance products (tires, batteries)
Automobile sales
Baby products
Books
Cameras, film, and photofinishing
Candy
Caskets
CDs
Checks and form printing

Cleaning and institutional supplies
Collectibles
Computer hardware and software
Computer training services
Copying and printing services
Credit card processing
DVDs
Electronics
Eye exams
Flooring
Floral arrangements
Fresh foods (bakery, deli, meats, produce, seafood)
Furniture
Gasoline
Gifts
Glasses and contact lenses
Groceries and institutionally packaged foods
Hardware
Health and beauty aids
Hearing aids
Home insurance
Housewares
Insurance (automobile, small-business health, home)
Jewelry
Lighting supplies
Mortgage service
Office equipment and supplies
Outdoor living products
Payroll processing
Pet supplies
Pharmaceuticals
Plumbing supplies
Real estate services
Snack foods
Soft drinks
Sporting goods
Tobacco
Tools
Toys
Travel packages and other travel services
Video games and systems

COMPETITORS

ALDI	Kohl's
Army and Air Force	Kroger
Exchange	Lowe's
Aurora Wholesalers	Office Depot
AutoZone	PETCO
Barnes & Noble	PetSmart
Best Buy	Safeway
Big Lots	Sam's Club
BJ's Wholesale Club	Smart & Final
CompUSA	Staples
Dollar General	Target
Family Dollar Stores	Toys "R" Us
Home Depot	Trader Joe's
Kmart	Walgreen

HISTORICAL FINANCIALS
Company Type: Public

Income Statement

FYE: Sunday nearest August 31

	REVENUE ($ mil.)	NET INCOME ($ mil.)	NET PROFIT MARGIN	EMPLOYEES
8/08	72,483.0	1,282.7	1.8%	137,000
8/07	64,400.2	1,082.8	1.7%	127,000
8/06	60,151.2	1,103.2	1.8%	127,000
8/05	52,935.2	1,063.1	2.0%	118,000
8/04	48,107.0	882.4	1.8%	113,000
Annual Growth	10.8%	9.8%	—	4.9%

2008 Year-End Financials

Debt ratio: 24.0%
Return on equity: 14.4%
Cash ($ mil.): 2,619
Current ratio: 1.07
Long-term debt ($ mil.): 2,206

No. of shares (mil.): 435
Dividends
  Yield: 0.9%
  Payout: 21.1%
Market value ($ mil.): 29,163

Stock History

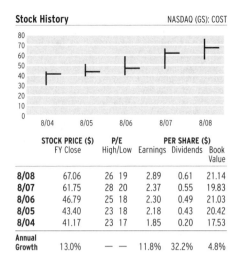

NASDAQ (GS): COST

	STOCK PRICE ($) FY Close	P/E High/Low	PER SHARE ($) Earnings	Dividends	Book Value
8/08	67.06	26 19	2.89	0.61	21.14
8/07	61.75	28 20	2.37	0.55	19.83
8/06	46.79	25 18	2.30	0.49	21.03
8/05	43.40	23 18	2.18	0.43	20.42
8/04	41.17	23 17	1.85	0.20	17.53
Annual Growth	13.0%	— —	11.8%	32.2%	4.8%

Covance Inc.

Behind every great drug company stands a great contract research organization (CRO), and Covance is one of the biggest. Covance helps pharmaceutical and biotech companies develop new drugs, providing preclinical testing services, as well as designing and carrying out human clinical trials to determine if the drugs are safe and effective. Services include toxicology studies, biostatistical analysis, clinical laboratory testing, and post-marketing studies. Among the company's customers are pharmaceutical, biotech, and medical device companies; Covance also offers laboratory testing services to companies in the chemical, agrochemical, and food industries.

Covance is capitalizing on trends toward more and more outsourcing of drug development activities, a practice which generally saves money for drug and medical device companies. It has been expanding its already extensive global presence in order to take advantage of other trends, including the increasing desire of drug companies to test compounds in multiple geographic markets simultaneously. The company has about 50 offices and labs in more than 20 countries (with field operations in many more) in the Americas, Europe, and the Asia/Pacific region. It is expanding its clinical development services, particularly in eastern Europe and Asia; it established new offices in Israel, the Ukraine, and Slovakia in 2009. Covance also beefed up its presence in South and Central America, adding or expanding offices in Argentina, Brazil, Chile, Mexico, and Peru.

The company's revenue is evenly split between Early Development and Late-Stage Development services. It Early Development segment provides preclinical toxicology and chemistry testing that determine a drug's effects on animals and chromosomes and whether its chemical makeup remains stable over time. The division also produces monoclonal antibodies and lab animals used in drug research, and provides early-stage clinical services such as pharmacology testing in humans. Covance has expanded several parts of its Early Development business through acquisitions, as well as by constructing new facilities or renovating existing facilities.

Covance's Late-Stage Development services include central laboratory testing of urine, blood, and tissue samples from patients in drug trials; design and management of clinical trials; and commercialization services, including post-marketing studies and various marketing consulting services.

The company serves about 300 pharmaceutical and biotechnology customers. For its more limited chemical and food industry customers, the company provides services such as testing pesticides for risks to humans and determining nutritional information for food labels.

To expand its capacity and deepen its ties with Eli Lilly, Covance paid $50 million to acquire one of Lilly's early stage drug development facilities in 2008. In return, Lilly awarded Covance with a ten-year, $1.6 billion contract for early and late-stage drug development services.

In 2009 Covance entered into a five-year, $145 million agreement to provide genomics analysis services to Merck & Co. Covance acquired Merck's Seattle-based Gene Expression Laboratory, which had been part of Merck's broken-up Rosetta Inpharmatics group, as part of the deal. The addition of the lab expands Covance's genomic testing and personalized medicine capabilities.

The company has been shedding some non-essential operations. In 2007 it sold its centralized ECG business, which provided cardiac safety monitoring during clinical trials, to eResearchTechnology (eRT). Under the terms of the deal, eRT continues to provide cardiac safety services to Covance's clients. In 2009 the company sold its interactive voice and web response services business to Phase Forward for $10 million. Phase Forward will continue to provide certain electronic data capture and interactive response technology to Covance's clients.

HISTORY

Glassmaker Corning began collecting research organizations in 1987 when it decided to move into laboratory and clinical services. Over the next several years, Corning bought Hazleton (preclinical and clinical trials, 1987), G.H. Besselaar Associates (clinical trials, 1989), PACT (periapproval studies, 1990), and SciCor (clinical laboratory, 1991). It also acquired an interest in Bio-Imaging Technologies in 1994 and National Packaging Systems, a pharmaceutical packaging company, in 1995. Corning moved into health economics and outcomes in 1996 with the purchase of Health Technology Associates and added to its packaging operations with Swiss company Pacamed.

After attempts to sell its laboratory testing division failed, Corning divided the operations into Covance (clinical trials) and Quest Diagnostics (laboratory testing services) and spun them off in late 1996. In 1997 Covance formed an alliance with the China Innovation Center for Life Sciences to develop biopharmaceutical research facilities in China to train Chinese scientists in international research practices and conduct feasibility studies on potential drugs. The next year the firm created a unit to research psychiatric ailments and central nervous system disorders.

In 1999 Covance announced a merger with PAREXEL International, the #3 contract research organization, then canceled it after investors criticized the union.

After a dip in earnings, the firm announced plans to cut its workforce in 2000. It then sold its pharmaceutical packaging services business to Fisher Scientific (which later became Thermo Fisher) in 2001.

To expand its geographical reach, it launched operations in Eastern Europe in mid-2003.

During 2005 and 2006 the company expanded its early development segment by acquiring clinical pharmacology sites of GFI Clinical Services and Radiant Research. It also bought Signet Laboratories to boost its antibody production capabilities.

EXECUTIVES

Chairman and CEO: Joseph L. (Joe) Herring, age 53, $5,410,534 total compensation
EVP and COO: Wendel D. Barr, age 47, $1,765,783 total compensation
SVP, CFO, and Treasurer: William E. Klitgaard, age 55, $1,446,523 total compensation
Corporate VP, Chief Accounting Officer, and Controller: Michele A. Kennedy, age 41
VP and Chief Scientific Officer Global Bioanalytical Services: Steven M. Michael
SVP, General Counsel, and Secretary: James W. Lovett, age 44
SVP Human Resources: Donald Kraft, age 49
SVP; President, Clinical Development: Richard F. Cimino, age 49, $1,538,064 total compensation
SVP; President, Central Laboratory Services: Deborah L. Tanner, age 46, $1,268,764 total compensation
President, Covance Commercialization Services: Luis Gutierrez
President, Labs North America: Mike Lehmann
Auditors: Ernst & Young LLP

LOCATIONS

HQ: Covance Inc.
210 Carnegie Center, Princeton, NJ 08540
Phone: 609-452-4440   **Fax:** 609-452-9375
Web: www.covance.com

2008 Sales

	$ mil.	% of total
Customer revenue		
US	1,038.8	57
UK	227.1	12
Switzerland	215.5	12
Other countries	246.7	13
Other	99.0	6
Total	**1,827.1**	**100**

PRODUCTS/OPERATIONS

2008 Sales

	$ mil.	% of total
Late-Stage Development	883.3	48
Early Development	844.8	46
Other	99.0	6
Total	**1,827.1**	**100**

Selected Services

Early Development
  Preclinical Services
    Bioanalytical services
    Pharmaceutical and nutritional chemistry
    Research products
    Toxicology
  Clinical pharmacology services
Late-Stage Development
  Central laboratory services
  Clinical development services
  Clinical trial support services
    Interactive voice and web response services
  Commercialization services
    Periapproval services
    Market access services

COMPETITORS

Albany Molecular Research
Bioanalytical Systems
Charles River Laboratories
Commonwealth Biotechnologies
Harlan Laboratories
ICON
inVentiv Health
Jackson Laboratory
Kendle
LabCorp
Life Sciences Research
MDS
Medpace
Meridian Bioscience
MPI Research
PAREXEL
Pharmaceutical Product Development
PharmaNet Development Group
PRA International
Quest Diagnostics
Quintiles Transnational
Taconic Farms
WuXi PharmaTech

HISTORICAL FINANCIALS

Company Type: Public

Income Statement

FYE: December 31

	REVENUE ($ mil.)	NET INCOME ($ mil.)	NET PROFIT MARGIN	EMPLOYEES
12/08	1,827.1	196.8	10.8%	9,600
12/07	1,631.5	175.9	10.8%	8,700
12/06	1,406.1	145.0	10.3%	8,100
12/05	1,250.5	119.6	9.6%	7,300
12/04	1,056.4	97.9	9.3%	6,700
Annual Growth	**14.7%**	**19.1%**	**—**	**9.4%**

2008 Year-End Financials

Debt ratio: —
Return on equity: 17.1%
Cash ($ mil.): 221
Current ratio: 1.60
Long-term debt ($ mil.): —
No. of shares (mil.): 64
Dividends
  Yield: 0.0%
  Payout: —
Market value ($ mil.): 2,945

Stock History

NYSE: CVD

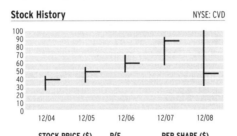

	STOCK PRICE ($) FY Close	P/E High/Low		PER SHARE ($) Earnings	Dividends	Book Value
12/08	46.03	32	10	3.08	0.00	18.68
12/07	86.62	33	21	2.71	0.00	17.35
12/06	58.91	31	22	2.24	0.00	14.43
12/05	48.55	28	19	1.88	0.00	11.44
12/04	38.75	28	17	1.52	0.00	9.97
Annual Growth	**4.4%**	**—**	**—**	**19.3%**	**—**	**17.0%**

Cox Enterprises

Cox Enterprises is a family-owned holding company with operations spanning cable TV, broadcasting, publishing, and auctions. Its flagship subsidiary, Cox Communications, is the #3 cable system operator (behind Comcast and Time Warner Cable) serving more than 6 million customers with TV, Internet, and digital phone services. Its Manheim unit is the largest wholesale vehicle auction company, with some 145 locations. Cox's media operations include Cox Newspapers (10 daily papers), Cox Television (about 15 local stations), and Cox Radio (more than 80 stations). Cox also owns a majority stake in AutoTrader.com, an online used car listing service.

Cox has been focused on beefing up its cable systems operations (which accounts for 55% of sales), expanding such services as digital phone and broadband Internet access, as well as video on demand (VOD) offerings. It is also building a mobile communications network to offer cellular phone service and wireless broadband Internet access to its customers. During 2007 Cox Communications exchanged its 25% stake in cable channel operator Discovery Communications for $1.3 billion in cash. The deal also included the Travel Channel.

The company's vehicle auction business, meanwhile, has been expanding into international markets. In 2007 it launched a joint venture with Shanghai International Commodity Auction Co. to sell cars in several Chinese cities. The following year Manheim expanded its auction business into Turkey.

Looking to capitalize on the growing market for Internet advertising, Cox in 2008 acquired Adify Corporation for $300 million. The online ad network, previously backed by such investors as Venrock Associates, NBC Universal, and Time Warner, serves ads for a number of media Web properties, including sites owned by Forbes, Martha Stewart Living Omnimedia, and The Washington Post Company. Adify joined AutoTrader.com and online search portal Kudzu in Cox's growing digital media portfolio.

Real world publishing, however, has not been so kind to the company. Its Cox Newspapers unit has struggled along with the rest of the newspaper industry with declining readership and advertising revenue. In response, Cox put all but three of its papers up for sale and plans to use the proceeds to pay down debt and new business investments. Its remaining properties, including the *Atlanta Journal-Constitution*, the *Palm Beach Post* (Florida), and the *Dayton Daily News*, plan to boost their online publishing efforts to expand readership. Cox is also selling its Valpak direct mail advertising unit.

Late in 2008, company veteran Jimmy Hayes was tapped to replace James Kennedy as CEO of Cox Enterprises. He was previously head of finance at Cox Communications. Kennedy, who remained chairman, had led the business since 1987; he is the grandson of founder James Cox.

HISTORY

James Middleton Cox, who dropped out of school in 1886 at 16, worked as a teacher, reporter, and congressional secretary before buying the *Dayton Daily News* in 1898. In 1905 he acquired the nearby *Springfield Press-Republican* and then took up politics, serving two terms in the US Congress (1909-1913) and three terms as Ohio governor (1913-1915; 1917-1921). He even ran for president in 1920 (his running mate was future President Franklin Roosevelt) but lost to rival Ohio publisher Warren G. Harding.

Once out of politics, Cox began building his media empire. He bought the *Miami Daily News* in 1923 and founded WHIO (Dayton, Ohio's first radio station). He bought Atlanta's WSB ("Welcome South, Brother"), the South's first radio station, in 1939 and added WSB-FM and WSB-TV, the South's first FM and TV stations, in 1948. Cox founded Dayton's first FM and TV stations (WHIO-FM and WHIO-TV) the next year, and *The Atlanta Constitution* joined his collection in 1950. Cox died in 1957.

The company continued to expand its broadcasting interests in the late 1950s and early 1960s. It was one of the first major broadcasting companies to expand into cable TV when it purchased a system in Lewistown, Pennsylvania, in 1962. The Cox family's broadcast properties were placed in publicly held Cox Broadcasting in 1964. Two years later its newspapers were placed into privately held Cox Enterprises, and the cable holdings became publicly held Cox Cable Communications. The broadcasting arm diversified, buying Manheim Services (auto auctions, 1968), Kansas City Automobile Auction (1969), and TeleRep (TV ad sales, 1972).

Cox Cable had 500,000 subscribers in nine states when it rejoined Cox Broadcasting in 1977. Cox Broadcasting was renamed Cox Communications in 1982, and the Cox family took the company private again in 1985, combining it with Cox Enterprises. The company also invested in upstart cable broadcaster Discover Channel (now part of Discovery Communications) during the 1980s. James Kennedy, grandson of founder James Cox, became chairman and CEO in 1987.

Expansion became the keyword for Cox in the 1990s. The company merged its Manheim unit with the auto auction business of Ford Motor Credit and GE Capital in 1991. It also formed Sprint Spectrum in 1994, a partnership with Sprint, TCI (now part of AT&T), and Comcast to bundle telephone, cable TV, and other communications services (Sprint bought out Cox in 1999). Then, in one of its biggest transactions, Cox bought Times Mirror's cable TV operations for $2.3 billion in 1995 and combined them with its own cable system into a new, publicly traded company called Cox Communications. The following year it spun off its radio holdings into a public company called Cox Radio.

To expand its online presence, the company formed Cox Interactive Media in 1996, establishing a series of city Web sites and making a host of investments in various Internet companies, including Career Path, ExciteHome, iVillage (later acquired by NBC Universal), MP3.com, and Tickets.com (now part of MLB Advanced Media). Cox also applied the online strategy to its automobile auction businesses, establishing AutoTrader.com in 1998 and placing the Internet operations of Manheim Auctions (now just Manheim) into a new company, Manheim Interactive, in 2000.

In 2004, fed up with the demands of running a publicly traded cable company, Cox bought the 38% of Cox Communications that it didn't already own for $8.5 billion.

The company in 2007 exchanged Cox Communications' 25% stake in Discovery Communications for $1.3 billion in cash. The deal also included cable broadcaster the Travel Channel.

EXECUTIVES

Chairman, Cox Enterprises, Cox Communications, and Cox Radio: James C. Kennedy, age 61
Vice Chairman: G. Dennis Berry, age 64
President, CEO, and Director: Jimmy W. Hayes, age 56
EVP and CFO: John M. Dyer, age 54
VP and CIO: Gregory B. (Greg) Morrison
VP Supply Chain Services and Chief Procurement Officer: Michael J. (Mike) Mannheimer
EVP Administration: Timothy W. (Tim) Hughes
SVP Finance: Richard J. Jacobson
SVP Human Resources: Marybeth H. Leamer
SVP Investments and Administration: John G. Boyette
SVP Strategic Investments and Real Estate Planning: Dale Hughes
VP Legal Affairs, General Counsel, and Corporate Secretary: Andrew A. (Andy) Merdek
VP and Treasurer: Susan W. Coker
VP Public Policy and Regulatory Affairs: Alexandra M. Wilson
VP Business Development: J. Lacey Lewis
VP Corporate Communications and Public Affairs: Roberto I. Jimenez
VP Marketing: Deborah E. (Debby) Ruth
President, Cox Communications: Patrick J. (Pat) Esser
President and CEO, Manheim Auctions: Dean H. Eisner
President, Cox Media Group: Sanford H. (Sandy) Schwartz, age 56

LOCATIONS

HQ: Cox Enterprises, Inc.
6205 Peachtree Dunwoody Rd., Atlanta, GA 30328
Phone: 678-645-0000   **Fax:** 678-645-1079
Web: www.coxenterprises.com

PRODUCTS/OPERATIONS

Selected Operations

Cox Communications (cable TV system operations)
 Travel Channel (cable TV channel)

Manheim (wholesale automotive auctions)

Cox Newspapers
 The Atlanta Journal-Constitution
 Austin American-Statesman (Texas)
 Dayton Daily News (Ohio)
 JournalNews (Hamilton, OH)
 Longview News-Journal (Texas)
 The Marshall News Messenger (Texas)
 The Middletown Journal (Ohio)
 Palm Beach Daily News (Florida)
 The Palm Beach Post (Florida)
 Springfield News-Sun (Ohio)

AutoTrader.com (online used vehicle listings)

Cox Television
 KFOX (FOX; El Paso, TX)
 KICU (Ind.; San Jose, CA)
 KIRO (CBS, Seattle)
 KRXI (FOX; Reno, NV)
 KTVU (FOX, San Francisco)
 WAXN (Ind.; Charlotte, NC)
 WFTV (ABC; Orlando, FL)
 WHIO (CBS; Dayton, OH)
 WJAC (NBC; Johnstown, PA)
 WPXI (NBC; Pittsburgh)
 WRDQ (Ind.; Orlando, FL)
 WSB (ABC; Atlanta)
 WSOC (ABC; Charlotte, NC)
 WTOV (NBC; Steubenville, OH)

Cox Radio

COMPETITORS

A. H. Belo	Gannett
Belo Corp.	Hearst Corporation
CBS Corp	McClatchy Company
Clear Channel	Media General
Columbus Fair Auto	New York Times
Auction	Pittsburgh Independent
Comcast	Auto Auction
Cumulus Media	Time Warner Cable
eBay	Tribune Company
Fox Entertainment	Washington Post

HISTORICAL FINANCIALS

Company Type: Private

Income Statement

FYE: December 31

	REVENUE ($ mil.)	NET INCOME ($ mil.)	NET PROFIT MARGIN	EMPLOYEES
12/08	15,400.0	—	—	77,000
12/07	15,033.0	—	—	81,693
12/06	13,200.0	—	—	80,000
12/05	12,000.0	—	—	77,000
12/04	11,552.0	—	—	77,000
Annual Growth	**7.5%**	—	—	**0.0%**

Revenue History

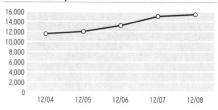

C. R. Bard, Inc.

C. R. Bard is no upstart in the world of medical devices. The company has been in the business for more than a century and introduced the Foley urological catheter (still one of its top sellers) in 1934. Its products fall into four general therapeutic categories: vascular, urology, oncology, and surgical specialties. Among other things, the company makes stents, catheters, and guidewires used in angioplasties and other vascular procedures; urology catheters and products used to treat urinary incontinence; and catheters for delivering chemotherapy treatments. Its line of specialty surgical tools, made by subsidiary Davol, includes devices used in laparoscopic and orthopedic procedures and for hernia repair.

Bard sells its products in more than 100 countries through numerous subsidiaries, joint ventures, and affiliated representatives. Its largest international markets are Europe and Japan. The company focuses marketing programs and expansion efforts on its four key product areas, seeking to provide a diverse and cutting-edge line of offerings to hospitals, doctors' offices, and other health care facilities.

Along with urology catheters, urology products include surgical slings used to treat incontinence, brachytherapy seeds for prostate cancer treatment, and urine monitoring and collection systems. Bard's urology catheter portfolio includes an infection-control catheter (the Bardex IC) that uses a silver coating technology to reduce the risk of urinary tract infection. In 2007 the company introduced a breathing tube (the Agento IC) using the same technology.

The vascular unit makes angioplasty catheters, peripheral vascular stents, biopsy devices, and electrode catheters (used to diagnose and treat heart arrhythmias). The company has expanded the product group through introductions of new products (the Dorado angioplasty catheter in 2007, for instance) and acquisitions. It bought the LifeStent line of peripheral vascular stents from Edwards Lifesciences in 2008. The same year, Bard acquired Specialized Health Products International, which already supplied subsidiary Bard Access Systems with infusion sets for its vascular access lines.

In addition to catheters used in urological and vascular procedures, Bard makes ports and catheters used to deliver chemotherapy in cancer patients. Its oncology segment also includes ultrasound devices and enteral feeding tubes. Its surgical specialty product line focuses on hernia repair products, such as patches and plugs.

HISTORY

When visiting Europe at the turn of the century, silk importer Charles Russell Bard discovered that gomenol, a mixture of olive oil with a eucalyptus extract, offered him relief from urinary problems caused by tuberculosis. He brought gomenol to America and began distributing it.

In 1907 C. R. Bard began selling a ureteral catheter developed by French firm J. Eynard. The company incorporated in 1923 with its present name. When Charles Bard's health declined in 1926, he sold the business to John Willits and Edson Outwin (his sales manager and accountant, respectively).

In 1934 Bard became the sole agent for Davol Rubber's new Foley catheter, which helped the company achieve $1 million in sales by 1948. During the 1950s, sales increased more than 400% when the firm introduced its first pre-sterilized packaged product and expanded its product line to include disposable drainage tubes and an intravenous feeding device.

Bard went public in 1963. In the 1960s the firm expanded both vertically — boosting its manufacturing capabilities (it began making its own plastic tubing) — and through acquisitions. It also established joint ventures with Davol to manufacture and distribute hospital and surgical supplies internationally.

The company diversified into the cardiovascular, respiratory therapy, home care products, and kidney dialysis fields in the 1970s and manufactured the first angioplasty catheter, a nonsurgical device to clear blocked arteries, in 1979.

In 1984 Bard watched its urological business go limp. In response, the company began a buying spree to gain market share in a consolidating hospital products industry. It swallowed up around a dozen companies, including Davol (maker of its best-selling Foley catheter), garnering such products as catheters and other products for angioplasty, diagnostics, and urinary incontinence. In 1988 it faced increasing competition in the coronary catheter market from such giants as Eli Lilly and Pfizer. Bard struck back with innovative products, but it was too little too late — even though the company continued to struggle for 10 more years, it finally pulled out of the cardiovascular market.

Bard agreed in 1993 to pay a then-record $61 million for mislabeling and improperly testing angioplasty catheters blamed for the deaths of two people (and later taken off the market). However, a year later Bard's sales topped $1 billion for the first time, and it purchased catheter-related companies in Canada, France, and Germany.

Purchases in 1995 and 1996 included medical device manufacturers MedChem Products and the Cardiac Assist Division of St. Jude Medical. In 1996 Bard bought a majority stake in Italy-based X-Trode and acquired IMPRA, a leading supplier of vascular grafts (its largest deal ever). That year the ongoing catheter litigation snared

three former Bard executives, who received 18-month prison sentences for conspiring to hide potentially fatal flaws in the products.

In 1998 Bard reorganized along disease-state management lines. Over the next two years, it sold its cardiovascular line after deciding it was going to cost too much time and money to re-establish dominance in that field. Bard built its other fields through purchases, including ProSeed (radiation seed therapy, 1998) and Dymax (ultrasound catheter guidance systems, 1999). The next year Bard partnered with medical device distributor Owens & Minor to launch an online purchasing site.

In the new century, Bard continued to make acquisitions to expand its product lines and its technology base. In 2000 it obtained the Kugel Patch product line with the acquisition of Surgical Sense. In 2003 and 2004 it made several purchases, including a brachytherapy seeds business, a biopsy device, and several hernia repair products. The company added the StatLock line of catheter stabilization products to the urology division with the 2006 acquisition of Venetec International.

EXECUTIVES

Chairman, CEO, and Director: Timothy M. Ring, age 51, $9,159,547 total compensation
President, COO, and Director: John H. Weiland, age 53
President, Asia, Americas: P. R. Curry
President, Bard Canada: J. D. Kondrosky
SVP and CFO: Todd C. Schermerhorn, age 48
VP Information Technology: Vincent J. Gurnari Jr.
SVP and President, Corporate Healthcare Services: James L. Natale, age 62
SVP Science, Technology, and Clinical Affairs: John A. DeFord, age 47
SVP Quality and Regulatory Affairs: Gary D. Dolch, age 61
VP Quality, Environmental Sciences, and Safety: Christopher D. (Chris) Ganser, age 56
VP Operations: Joseph A. (Joe) Cherry
VP Regulatory and Clinical Affairs: Brian R. Barry
VP Government and Public Relations: Holly P. Glass
VP Human Resources: Bronwen K. Kelly, age 54
VP Strategic Planning and Business Development: Robert L. Mellen, age 52
Group VP: Brian P. Kelly, age 50, $2,131,522 total compensation
VP and Treasurer: Scott T. Lowry, age 42
VP Investor Relations: Eric J. Shick
VP, General Counsel, and Secretary: Stephen J. Long, age 43
Auditors: KPMG LLP

LOCATIONS

HQ: C. R. Bard, Inc.
730 Central Ave., Murray Hill, NJ 07974
Phone: 908-277-8000   **Fax:** 908-277-8240
Web: www.crbard.com

2008 Sales

	$ mil.	% of total
US	1,661.3	68
Europe	502.2	20
Japan	121.7	5
Other regions	166.9	7
Total	**2,452.1**	**100**

PRODUCTS/OPERATIONS

2008 Sales

	$ mil.	% of total
Urology	708.5	29
Oncology	646.6	26
Vascular	643.1	26
Surgical specialties	368.2	15
Other	85.7	4
Total	**2,452.1**	**100**

Selected Brands and Products

Urology
Agento IC (infection control endotracheal tube)
Bardex IC Foley (infection control catheter)
Contigen Bard Collagen (stress urinary incontinence implant)
Criticore (urinary output monitor)
Dignicare (fecal incontinence products)
Simetry Brachytherapy Program (prostate cancer treatment products)
StatLock (catheter stabilization products)
Oncology
Hickman & Groshong (venous access catheter)
PowerPICC (vascular access catheter)
PowerPort (implanted IV port)
Precisor Direct Bite (biopsy forceps)
Site-Rite 6 Ultrasound System (for central venous access)
Vascular
Atlas (angioplasty catheter)
Conquest (angioplasty catheter)
Dorado (angioplasty catheter)
E-Luminexx (iliac stent)
Flair (access stent graft)
G2 and G2 Express (vena cava filter)
LifeStent (peripheral vascular stent)
Vacora (biopsy device)
Surgical specialties
Allomax (hernia repair)
Collamend (hernia repair)
PerFex Plug (hernia repair)
Permasorb (fixation device)
Sepramesh (hernia repair)
Ventrio Sperma (hernia repair)
Ventralex (hernia repair)

COMPETITORS

Abbott Labs
American Medical Systems
AngioDynamics
Angiotech Pharmaceuticals
B. Braun Melsungen
Baxter International
Becton, Dickinson
Boston Scientific
CONMED Corporation
Cook Group
Covidien
Datascope
Ethicon
Ethicon Endo-Surgery
HealthTronics
Hologic
I-Flow
Kimberly-Clark Health
Medtronic
Merit Medical Systems
St. Jude Medical
Terumo

HISTORICAL FINANCIALS

Company Type: Public

Income Statement

	REVENUE ($ mil.)	NET INCOME ($ mil.)	NET PROFIT MARGIN	EMPLOYEES	FYE: December 31
12/08	2,452.1	416.5	17.0%	11,000	
12/07	2,202.0	406.4	18.5%	10,200	
12/06	1,985.5	272.1	13.7%	9,400	
12/05	1,771.3	337.1	19.0%	8,900	
12/04	1,656.1	302.8	18.3%	8,600	
Annual Growth	**10.3%**	**8.3%**	**—**	**6.3%**	

2008 Year-End Financials

Debt ratio: 7.6%
Return on equity: 21.8%
Cash ($ mil.): 592
Current ratio: 4.96
Long-term debt ($ mil.): 150
No. of shares (mil.): 98
Dividends
  Yield: 0.7%
  Payout: 15.3%
Market value ($ mil.): 8,225

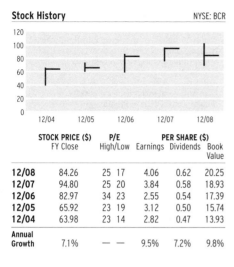

	STOCK PRICE ($) FY Close	P/E High/Low		PER SHARE ($) Earnings Dividends Book Value		
12/08	84.26	25	17	4.06	0.62	20.25
12/07	94.80	25	20	3.84	0.58	18.93
12/06	82.97	34	23	2.55	0.54	17.39
12/05	65.92	23	19	3.12	0.50	15.74
12/04	63.98	23	14	2.82	0.47	13.93
Annual Growth	7.1%	—	—	9.5%	7.2%	9.8%

Cracker Barrel Old Country Store

This company has gotten ahead in the restaurant business by holding on to a bit of the past. Formerly CBRL Group, Cracker Barrel Old Country Store operates more than 580 of its flagship restaurants known for their country kitsch, rustic decor, and down-home cooking. The eateries, located in more than 40 states, offer mostly standard American fare, such as chicken, ham, and roast beef dishes, but they are most popular as breakfast spots. Each Cracker Barrel location features a retail area where patrons can buy hand-blown glassware, cast iron cookware, and woodcrafts, as well as jellies and old-fashioned candies. Most of the restaurants are found along interstate highways and target hungry travelers.

In an effort to confront continued weakness in the economy and slow consumer spending, Cracker Barrel has introduced new menus that spotlight higher-margin items, as well as a revamped selection of breakfast items. It has also been testing a smaller lunch menu to speed service and increase customer turnover.

The company continues to expand its chain, opening nearly 20 new locations during fiscal 2008. Despite rising gasoline prices, Cracker Barrel has not shifted away from building its restaurants along interstate freeways and continues to focus on the traveling public.

While Cracker Barrel's restaurants are popular, its policies and practices have made the company the focus of controversy and lawsuits. The chain drew criticism for its openly anti-gay hiring practices in the early 1990s (the policy was later rescinded) and it has been the target of several racial discrimination lawsuits. (Cracker Barrel has never been found guilty of any discrimination, however.)

HISTORY

Dan Evins opened the first Cracker Barrel Old Country Store in Lebanon, Tennessee, in 1969. As a sales representative for Shell Oil, Evins believed he could sell more gas if he combined gas stations with restaurants. He also envisioned placing his new concept along what was then a relatively new enterprise — the interstate highway system. The company was incorporated in 1970.

Four years later Evins resigned from his job at Shell Oil to give full attention to his burgeoning restaurant chain, which had grown to a dozen locations. The oil embargo of the mid-1970s prompted the company to back away from the sale of gas, and it completely did away with gas pumps by the mid-1980s. Cracker Barrel went public in 1981.

Company sales slumped in 1985, when a plan to force its smaller stores to squeeze out large-store-scale revenue failed. The company rebounded by remodeling the smaller stores to the dimensions of the larger stores and by creating middle management positions to oversee real estate purchasing, gift shop merchandising, and human resource training. It also introduced an incentive program to reward store managers for curbing costs and increasing sales. Between 1980 and 1990, the company added 84 new restaurants to its rapidly expanding chain.

Controversy struck the company during the 1990s when its old country values clashed with present day reality. In 1991 the company issued a statement declaring that it would no longer employ "individuals whose sexual preferences fail to demonstrate normal heterosexual values." Believing that the sexual orientation of such individuals was not in line with the values of its customer base, the company fired more than a dozen employees. Cracker Barrel later rescinded the policy, but the incident deeply scarred the company's image and continued to haunt it throughout the decade. The controversy also spurred changes in SEC regulations — a protest by Cracker Barrel stockholders who opposed the policy eventually led to a 1998 decision permitting stockholders to propose resolutions on employment matters.

As the company expanded its chain of restaurants beyond the southern states, it also began adapting its menus and decor to the tastes and preferences of each region. Cracker Barrel acquired Carmine's Prime Meats (later Carmine Giardini's Gourmet Market), a chain of gourmet food stores, in 1998. With addition of a second chain of stores, the company restructured into a holding company called CBRL Group the following year and later acquired the Logan's Roadhouse steakhouse chain (founded in 1991) for about $180 million.

A group of African-American employees filed a lawsuit against the company in 1999, claiming racial discrimination. Evins resigned his post as CEO in 2001 and was replaced by company veteran Michael Woodhouse.

Even as the racial discrimination suit was pending, the company was hit by a class action discrimination suit by 21 customers claiming that African-Americans were seated in segregated areas, denied service, and served food taken from the garbage. In 2002 a federal court in Georgia ruled against the plaintiffs, claiming that they'd failed to prove that a set of discriminatory circumstances existed to warrant a national class action suit.

That same year the US Justice Department began an investigation into the public accommodations policies of CBRL's Cracker Barrel division. As part of a 2004 settlement with the department, Cracker Barrel agreed to hire an independent auditor to monitor its race-bias policies. Despite this effort, new allegations were brought against the company in 2004 when 10 employees at three Illinois restaurants filed federal charges of sexual harassment and racial discrimination. Later that year CBRL settled a handful of lawsuits at once (while denying any wrongdoing), paying a total of $8.7 million in a variety of southern US courts.

The following year the company dealt with a lawsuit brought on by donations made to a political group called Texans for a Republican Majority, a political action group connected to former congressman Tom DeLay that was alleged to be involved in illegal campaign contributions. CBRL settled their involvement in the case by agreeing to donate money to fund a nonpartisan information program at the University of Texas LBJ School of Public Affairs.

In 2006 CBRL sold its Logan's steakhouse business to a group of private equity firms, including Bruckmann, Rosser, Sherrill & Co., for $486 million. Focused again on its flagship chain, CBRL changed its name in 2008 to Cracker Barrel Old Country Store.

EXECUTIVES

Chairman, President, and CEO; President, Cracker Barrel Old Country Store:
Michael A. (Mike) Woodhouse, age 63
EVP and COO: Douglas E. (Doug) Barber, age 51
EVP and CFO: Sandra B. (Sandy) Cochran, age 50
VP Information Services, Cracker Barrel Old Country Store: Timothy W. (Tim) Mullen
SVP Retail Operations, Cracker Barrel Old Country Store: Terry A. Maxwell, age 49
SVP Human Resources, Cracker Barrel Old Country Store: Robert J. Harig, age 58
SVP Corporate Affairs: Diana S. Wynne, age 53
SVP, Secretary, and Chief Legal Counsel:
N.B. Forrest Shoaf, age 58
SVP Strategic Initiatives: Edward A. Greene, age 53
VP Accounting and Tax and Chief Accounting Officer: Patrick A. Scruggs, age 44
VP Marketing: Peter Keiser
SVP Finance, Cracker Barrel Old Country Store:
P. Doug Couvillion
VP Training and Development, Cracker Barrel Old Country Store: Thomas R. Pate
VP, General Counsel, and Secretary, Cracker Barrel Old Country Store: Michael J. Zylstra
VP Financial Planning and Analysis: Brian R. Eytchison
VP Product Development and Quality Assurance, Cracker Barrel Old Country Store:
Robert F. (Bob) Doyle
Director Corporate Communications: Julie K. Davis
Auditors: Deloitte & Touche LLP

LOCATIONS

HQ: Cracker Barrel Old Country Store, Inc.
    305 Hartmann Dr., Lebanon, TN 37088
Phone: 615-444-5533   **Fax:** 615-443-9476
Web: www.crackerbarrel.com

2008 Locations

	No.
Florida	58
Tennessee	50
Georgia	42
Texas	38
North Carolina	33
Ohio	31
Kentucky	29
Alabama	27
Indiana	27
Virginia	27
Illinois	22
Pennsylvania	21
South Carolina	21
Missouri	17
Michigan	16
Arizona	13
Arkansas	11
Mississippi	11
West Virginia	10
Louisiana	9
New York	8
Oklahoma	7
New Jersey	6
Wisconsin	5
Colorado	4
Kansas	4
Maryland	4
Massachusetts	4
New Mexico	4
Utah	4
Iowa	3
Other states	13
Total	**579**

COMPETITORS

Bob Evans
Brinker
Buffets Holdings
Carlson Restaurants
Darden
Denny's
DineEquity
Hooters
Huddle House
O'Charley's
OSI Restaurant Partners
Perkins & Marie Callender's
Red Robin
Ruby Tuesday
Shoney's
VICORP Restaurants
Waffle House

HISTORICAL FINANCIALS

Company Type: Public

Income Statement

FYE: Friday nearest July 31

	REVENUE ($ mil.)	NET INCOME ($ mil.)	NET PROFIT MARGIN	EMPLOYEES
7/08	2,384.5	65.6	2.8%	65,000
7/07	2,351.6	162.1	6.9%	64,000
7/06	2,643.0	116.3	4.4%	74,031
7/05	2,567.5	126.6	4.9%	75,029
7/04	2,380.9	113.3	4.8%	69,230
Annual Growth	0.0%	(12.8%)	—	(1.6%)

2008 Year-End Financials

Debt ratio: 839.9%
Return on equity: 66.6%
Cash ($ mil.): 12
Current ratio: 0.83
Long-term debt ($ mil.): 779

No. of shares (mil.): 23
Dividends
 Yield: 3.0%
 Payout: 25.7%
Market value ($ mil.): 547

Stock History

NASDAQ (GS): CBRL

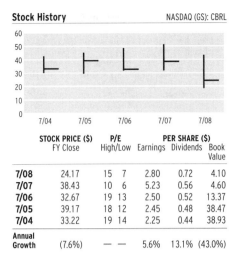

	STOCK PRICE ($) FY Close	P/E High/Low		PER SHARE ($) Earnings	Dividends	Book Value
7/08	24.17	15	7	2.80	0.72	4.10
7/07	38.43	10	6	5.23	0.56	4.60
7/06	32.67	19	13	2.50	0.52	13.37
7/05	39.17	18	12	2.45	0.48	38.47
7/04	33.22	19	14	2.25	0.44	38.93
Annual Growth	(7.6%)	—	—	5.6%	13.1%	(43.0%)

Crane Co.

In many cultures the crane is a symbol of longevity, and this Crane might be as well. Founded in 1855, the company makes a variety of industrial products that are generated by Crane's five business segments: Aerospace & Electronics (sensing and control systems), Engineered Materials (plastic composites, substrates), Merchandising Systems (vending machines), Fluid Handling (valves and pumps), and Controls (diagnostic, measurement, and control devices). Crane products have applications in aerospace, military and defense, recreational vehicle, construction, transportation, automated merchandising, petrochemical, and chemical and power generation industries.

To help strengthen its military and oil and gas customer base, Crane has made several strategic acquisitions to broaden its product portfolio. Crane made two acquisitions in 2008 totaling $79 million in cash: In December the company acquired all of Friedrich Krombach GmbH & Company KG Armaturenwerke and Krombach International GmbH. Krombach manufactures specialty valve flow solutions for the power, oil and gas, and chemical markets, which are complementary to Crane's energy flow solutions unit. In September 2008 Crane acquired Delta Fluid Products (fire safe valves, air vent valves).

The Crane Fund, a charitable trust, owns 13% of Crane. GAMCO Investors holds nearly 8% of the company. Barclays Global Investors has an equity stake of almost 6%.

HISTORY

Crane was founded in 1855 by Richard Teller Crane as a small foundry in a lumberyard owned by his uncle, Martin Ryerson. Crane grew along with Chicago and its railroads. Its first big order was to supply parts to a maker of railroad cars. In 1872 the company began making passenger elevators through the Crane Elevator Company, which was sold in 1895 to a joint venture that became the Otis Elevator Company. Although it had made plumbing materials since 1886, Crane developed a broader line during the 1920s and became a household name. The company remained

under the leadership of the Crane family until Thomas Mellon Evans was elected as chief executive in 1959. Evans diversified the company through acquisitions that included Huttig Sash & Door (1968) and CF&I Steel (1969). Crane also added basic materials with its purchase of Medusa (cement and aggregates) in 1979.

Evans' son, Robert, took over as Crane's chairman in 1984 and began restructuring the company. That year Crane sold its U.S. Plumbing division, and the next year it spun off CF&I Steel to its shareholders. The company then began buying manufacturing companies in the defense, aerospace, fluid controls, vending machine, fiberglass panel, and electronic components markets. Crane expanded its Ferguson Machine business with the purchase of PickOmatic Systems of Detroit (mechanical parts-handling equipment), then boosted its wood building distribution segment with the 1988 acquisitions of Pozzi-Renati Millwork Products and Palmer G. Lewis.

In 1990 Crane acquired Lear Romec (pumps for the aerospace industry) and Crown Pumps' diaphragm pump business. In the early 1990s the company continued its successful strategy of selective buying, adding Jenkins Canada (bronze and iron valves, 1992), Rondel's millwork distributions (1993), Burks Pumps (1993), and Mark Controls (valves, instruments, and controls, 1994).

Crane picked up Interpoint (DC-DC power converters) and Grenson Electronics (low-voltage power conversion components, UK) in 1996. The company's 1998 acquisitions included Environmental Products USA (water-purification systems), Consolidated Lumber Company (wholesale distributor of lumber and millwork products), and the plastic-lined piping products division of Dow Chemical.

In 1999 the company bought Stentorfield (beverage vending machines, UK). Late in the year Crane spun off its distribution subsidiary, Huttig Sash & Door. Huttig sold a 32% stake to UK-based Rugby Group in return for Rugby's US building products business. The combined company was named Huttig Building Products.

In 2001 Crane acquired the industrial flow business of Alfa Laval, Ventech Controls (valve repair), and Laminated Profiles (fiberglass-reinforced panels, UK). In March 2001 the investment firm led by Mario Gabelli increased its stake in Crane to nearly 8%.

Crane continued to add complementary businesses in 2002, purchasing Lasco Composites LP, a Florence, Kentucky, manufacturer of fiberglass-reinforced plastic panels, from Tomkins Industries; the US-based valve and actuator distributor Corva Corporation; and General Technology Corporation, an electronics company (printed circuit boards, customized integrated systems, cables, and wire harnesses) geared for the defense industry.

The buying spree continued in 2003 when Crane completed its announced acquisition of Signal Technology Corporation. Crane bought the pipe couplings and fittings business of Etex Group S.A. the following month.

The next year had hardly begun when Crane acquired P.L. Porter, a maker of motion control products for airline seating. A few days later Crane bought the Hattersley valve brand from Hattersley Newman Hender. Ltd., a subsidiary of Tomkins PLC. At 2004's close Crane announced it had sold the UK-based businesses and intellectual property of Victaulic (Victaulic was a subsidiary of Crane's U.K. subsidiary Crane Limited) to Euro-Victaulic B.V.B.A., a subsidiary of Victaulic Company of America, for $15.4 million.

The company focused on growing its merchandising segment in 2006. Early in the year, Crane acquired CashCode, a company that makes banknote validation, storage, and recycling devices used by the gaming industry as well as vending companies, for $86 million.

Later in 2006 Crane acquired most of the assets of Automatic Products International (APi), which made and distributed vending equipment, for more than $30 million, and it paid $46 million to buy vending-machine maker Dixie-Narco from Whirlpool.

In the fall of 2006 Crane acquired Noble Composites, which made composite panels used to construct RVs, for $72 million. Noble has been combined into the company's Engineered Materials segment. The following year Crane dropped nearly $40 million to acquire another composite panel manufacturer, Fabwel, from Owens Corning.

EXECUTIVES

Chairman: Robert S. Evans, age 64
President, CEO, and Director: Eric C. Fast, age 59, $5,864,652 total compensation
VP Operational Excellence and Acting Group President, Controls: Thomas J. Perlitz, age 40
VP Finance and CFO: Timothy J. MacCarrick, age 43
VP, Controller, and Chief Accounting Officer: Richard A. (Rich) Maue, age 38
VP Taxes: Thomas M. Noonan, age 54
VP Environment, Health, and Safety: Anthony D. Pantaleoni, age 54
VP, General Counsel, and Secretary: Augustus I. duPont, age 57, $1,047,579 total compensation
VP Human Resources: Elise M. Kopczick, age 55
VP Business Development and Strategic Planning: Curtis P. Robb, age 54
VP and Treasurer: Andrew L. Krawitt, age 43
Group President, Crane Merchandising Systems: Bradly L. (Brad) Ellis, age 40
Group President, Aerospace: Gregory A. Ward, age 58
Group President, Fluid Handling: Max H. Mitchell, age 44, $1,485,022 total compensation
Director Investor Relations and Corporate Communications: Richard E. Koch
Auditors: Deloitte & Touche LLP

LOCATIONS

HQ: Crane Co.
100 First Stamford Place, Stamford, CT 06902
Phone: 203-363-7300   **Fax:** 203-363-7295
Web: www.craneco.com

2008 Sales

	$ mil.	% of total
US	1,567.0	60
Canada	306.9	12
Europe	596.8	23
Other regions	133.6	5
Total	**2,604.3**	**100**

PRODUCTS/OPERATIONS

2008 Sales

	$ mil.	% of total
Aerospace & Electronics	638.7	24
Engineered Materials	255.4	10
Merchandising Systems	401.6	15
Fluid Handling	1,161.9	45
Controls	146.7	6
Total	**2,604.3**	**100**

Selected Business Segments and Subsidiaries

Aerospace & electronics
  ELDEC Corporation (sensing and control systems for aircraft)
  General Technology Corporation (GTC, contract manufacturing for military and defense applications)
  Hydro-Aire, Inc. (anti-skid brake control systems)
  Interpoint Corporation (hybrid power converters)
  Lear Romec (lubrication & fuel pumps)
  P. L. Porter (motion control products for airline seating)
  Signal Technology Corporation (STC Microwave Systems, electronic radio frequency components)
Engineered materials
  Crane Composites Inc. (Kemlite, fiberglass-reinforced plastic panels)
  Polyflon (specialty components, substrates for antennas)
Merchandising systems
  Crane Merchandising Systems (Vending Solutions)
  Payment Solutions
    CashCode Co. Inc.
    National Rejectors, Inc. GmbH (coin changers, Germany)
    Telquip Corporation
Fluid handling
  Crane Ltd. (commercial valves, UK)
  Crane Nuclear, Inc. (valve products for the nuclear power industry)
  Crane Pumps & Systems (pumps)
  Crane Supply (distribution)
  Crane Valve Group (valves, pipes, couplings, connectors, actuators)
Controls
  Azonix Corporation (measurement and control systems)
  Barksdale Inc. (pressure switches and transducers)
  Dynalco Controls Corporation (monitoring, diagnostic, and control products)

COMPETITORS

AZKOYEN	Kohler
Chori	KSB AG
CIRCOR International	Kubota
Colfax	Legris Industries Group
Curtiss-Wright	Meggitt Aircraft Braking
Dover Corp.	Parker Hannifin
Eaton	Precision Castparts
Emerson Electric	Standex
Flowserve	Swagelok
Goodrich Corp.	Tuthill
IMI plc	Tyco

HISTORICAL FINANCIALS

Company Type: Public

Income Statement

FYE: December 31

	REVENUE ($ mil.)	NET INCOME ($ mil.)	NET PROFIT MARGIN	EMPLOYEES
12/08	2,604.3	135.2	5.2%	12,000
12/07	2,619.2	(62.3)	—	12,000
12/06	2,256.9	165.9	7.4%	11,870
12/05	2,061.2	136.0	6.6%	10,400
12/04	1,890.3	(105.4)	—	10,500
Annual Growth	**8.3%**	**—**	**—**	**3.4%**

2008 Year-End Financials

Debt ratio: 54.0%
Return on equity: 16.7%
Cash ($ mil.): 232
Current ratio: 1.90
Long-term debt ($ mil.): 398
No. of shares (mil.): 58
Dividends
  Yield: 4.4%
  Payout: 33.9%
Market value ($ mil.): 1,008

Stock History

NYSE: CR

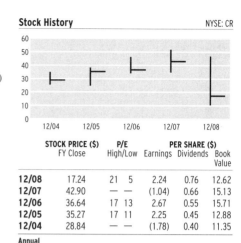

	STOCK PRICE ($) FY Close	P/E High	P/E Low	Earnings	Dividends	Book Value
12/08	17.24	21	5	2.24	0.76	12.62
12/07	42.90	—	—	(1.04)	0.66	15.13
12/06	36.64	17	13	2.67	0.55	15.71
12/05	35.27	17	11	2.25	0.45	12.88
12/04	28.84	—	—	(1.78)	0.40	11.35
Annual Growth	**(12.1%)**	**—**	**—**	**—**	**17.4%**	**2.7%**

Crown Holdings

Crown Holdings knows how to keep a lid on it. The company is a top worldwide producer of consumer packaging; steel and aluminum food and beverage cans and related packaging are the company's primary source of income. Its product portfolio also includes aerosol cans and a wide variety of metal caps, crowns, and closures, as well as specialty packaging, such as decorative novelty containers and industrial paint cans. Additionally, Crown Holdings also manufactures can-making equipment and replacement parts. The company operates 139 plants throughout 41 countries.

Crown Holdings' roster of blue-chip customers includes Coca-Cola, Cadberry Schweppes, Heinz, Nestlé, SC Johnson, Unilever, and Procter & Gamble, which owns Gillette, another customer. The company produces an array of multi-piece beverage cans, ends, and metal bottle caps, which include branded technologies such as Liftoff, SuperEnd, Easylift, and PeelSeam. Ideal Closures and Superplus offer product protection.

Crown Holdings has been focused on improving segment income, reducing debt, and reducing asbestos-related costs. For the segment income task, the company is focusing on targeting promising markets such as Latin America, Asia, and southern and central Europe. It also wants to improve selling rates, reduce costs, and develop unique new products.

In 2008 Crown spent $44 million to build a new beverage can plant in Brazil to meet growing demand in the region. Across the Atlantic, the company invested $32 million into a new production line at its plant in Spain. The investment will nearly double the production capacity at the plant to about 2 billion cans per year. It also opened new facilities in Africa, Cambodia, Vietnam, and the Middle East.

In 2009 the company plans to close two plants in Canada, idling about 175 workers. Affected are the food can facility in Dorval and the beverage can and crown (bottle cap) plant in Montreal.

HISTORY

Formed as Crown Cork & Seal Co. (CC&S) of Baltimore in 1892, the company was consolidated into its present form in 1927 when it merged with New Process Cork and New York Patents. The next year CC&S expanded overseas and formed Crown Cork International. In 1936 CC&S acquired Acme Can and benefited from the movement at the time from home canning to processed canning. The company was the first to develop the aerosol can (1946).

By 1957 heavy debt had CC&S in trouble. Teetering on the brink of bankruptcy, the company hired John Connelly as president. Connelly immediately stopped can production (sending stockpiled inventory to customers), discontinued unprofitable product lines, and reduced costs (25% of employees were laid off in less than two years). He then directed CC&S to take advantage of new uses for aerosol cans (insecticides, hair spray, and bathroom cleaning supplies) and to expand overseas. CC&S obtained "pioneer rights" between 1955 and 1960 from foreign countries that granted it the first crack at new closure and can businesses.

The introduction of the pull-tab pop-top in 1963 hit the can business like an exploding grenade. Connelly embraced pull tabs, but he rejected getting into the production of two-piece aluminum cans (first introduced in the mid-1970s), focusing instead on existing technology for three-piece cans. He also resisted the diversification trend then popular in the can-making industry, which later led to the declining performances of competitors Continental Can and American Can.

In 1970 CC&S moved into the printing end of the industry. It gained the ability to imprint color lithography on its bottle caps and cans after buying R. Hoe.

Connelly kept CC&S debt-free through most of the 1980s, using cash flow to buy back about half of CC&S's stock. In 1989 he picked Bill Avery to succeed him. With Connelly's blessing, Avery started a buying spree that included the purchase of the plants of Continental Can. Connelly died in 1990. Acquisitions continued throughout the 1990s. CC&S's purchases included Constar International, the #1 maker of polyethylene terephthalate (PET) plastic containers (1992), can maker Van Dorn (1993), and the can-manufacturing unit of Tri Valley Growers (1994). California's Northridge earthquake in 1994 ruined the company's plant in Van Nuys.

CC&S bought French packaging company CarnaudMetalbox in 1996. The purchase united CC&S's efficient operations and strong presence in North America with the French company's state-of-the-art manufacturing technology and international marketing experience. That year strikes over contract disputes halted production at eight of the company's plants.

Dropping sales and foreign currency fluctuations in 1998 forced the company to close seven factories and cut 7% of its workforce. CC&S closed more factories in 1999 and sold its composite can (paper cans with metal or plastic ends) business.

CC&S entered into a joint venture with Tempra Technology in 2000 to make and market a self-refrigerating can. The same year Avery announced his retirement; president and COO John Conway succeeded him as CEO in 2001. To reduce debt and move closer to profitability, CC&S sold three product divisions in 2001 and sold its fragrance pump unit to Rexam PLC in 2002. In March 2002 the company sold its Europe-based pharmaceutical packaging business. In May CC&S spun off its PET bottle subsidiary Constar in an IPO offering.

In February 2003 the company completed a refinancing plan and formed a new public holding company, Crown Holdings, Inc.; the CC&S name was retained for the company's operating subsidiary. Crown sold its Global Plastic Closures business to PAI Partners for about $750 million in 2005.

The company's debt reduction plans have called for major asset sales. In line with this plan, Crown Holdings sold its plastics closures business for about $750 million. The company previously had sold several divisions and spun off its PET bottle subsidiary, Constar International. The company then sold its remaining North American and European plastics operations.

EXECUTIVES

Chairman, President, and CEO: John W. Conway, age 63, $18,248,028 total compensation
Vice Chairman: Alan W. Rutherford, age 65, $10,776,037 total compensation
EVP and CFO: Timothy J. Donahue, age 46, $2,166,475 total compensation
EVP; President, European Division: William R. Apted, age 61
EVP, Corporate Technology and Regulatory Affairs: Daniel A. Abramowicz
SVP and Corporate Controller: Thomas A. Kelly, age 49
SVP, General Counsel, and Secretary: William T. Gallagher
VP, Corporate Affairs and Public Relations: Michael F. Dunleavy
VP, Planning and Development: Torsten J. Kreider
VP, Corporate Risk Management: Karen E. Berigan
VP and Assistant Corporate Controller: Kevin C. Clothier
VP and Treasurer: Michael B. Burns
President, Americas Division: Raymond L. McGowan Jr., age 57, $2,380,909 total compensation
President, European Division: Christopher C. Homfray, age 51
President, Asia/Pacific: Jozef Salaerts, age 55
Auditors: PricewaterhouseCoopers LLP

LOCATIONS

HQ: Crown Holdings, Inc.
1 Crown Way, Philadelphia, PA 19154
Phone: 215-698-5100   **Fax:** 215-676-7245
Web: www.crowncork.com

2008 Sales

	$ mil.	% of total
US	2,188	26
UK	817	10
France	733	9
Other regions	4,567	55
Total	**8,305**	**100**

PRODUCTS/OPERATIONS

2008 Sales

	$ mil.	% of total
Metal beverage cans & ends	3,938	47
Metal food cans & ends	2,811	34
Other metal packaging	1,408	17
Plastics packaging	60	1
Other products	88	1
Total	**8,305**	**100**

Selected Products

Metal packaging
  Aerosol cans
  Beverage cans
  Closures and caps
  Crowns
  Ends
  Food cans
Plastics packaging
Specialty packaging (unusual containers)
  Vacuum closures
Other products
  Canmaking equipment and spares

COMPETITORS

Alcoa
Amcor
AptarGroup
Ball Corp.
BWAY
Calmar
Metal Container Corporation
Owens-Illinois
Rexam
Silgan
Sonoco Products
Tetra Laval

HISTORICAL FINANCIALS

Company Type: Public

Income Statement

FYE: December 31

	REVENUE ($ mil.)	NET INCOME ($ mil.)	NET PROFIT MARGIN	EMPLOYEES
12/08	8,305.0	226.0	2.7%	21,300
12/07	7,727.0	528.0	6.8%	21,800
12/06	6,982.0	309.0	4.4%	21,700
12/05	6,908.0	(362.0)	—	24,000
12/04	7,199.0	51.0	0.7%	27,500
Annual Growth	**3.6%**	**45.1%**	**—**	**(6.2%)**

2008 Year-End Financials

Debt ratio: —
Return on equity: —
Cash ($ mil.): 596
Current ratio: 1.19
Long-term debt ($ mil.): 3,247

No. of shares (mil.): 160
Dividends
  Yield: 0.0%
  Payout: —
Market value ($ mil.): 3,074

Stock History

NYSE: CCK

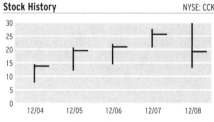

	STOCK PRICE ($) FY Close	P/E High/Low		PER SHARE ($) Earnings	Dividends	Book Value
12/08	19.20	21	10	1.39	0.00	(1.98)
12/07	25.65	9	7	3.19	0.00	0.09
12/06	20.92	12	8	1.82	0.00	(3.40)
12/05	19.53	—	—	(2.18)	0.00	(1.47)
12/04	13.74	47	26	0.30	0.00	1.73
Annual Growth	**8.7%**	**—**	**—**	**46.7%**	**—**	**—**

CSX Corporation

CSX banks on the railway as the right way to make money. Its main subsidiary, CSX Transportation (CSXT), operates a major rail system (some 21,000 route miles) in the eastern US. The freight carrier links 23 states, the District of Columbia, and two Canadian provinces. Freight hauled by the company includes a wide variety of merchandise, coal, automotive products, and intermodal containers.

CSX's rail segment, which accounts for more than 85% of the company's sales, also includes units that operate motor vehicle distribution centers and bulk cargo terminals. Subsidiary CSX Intermodal arranges the transportation of freight by combinations of road and rail carriers. CSXT operates with a fleet of more than 4,000 locomotives and 90,000 railcars. The railroad is concentrating on boosting efficiency by reducing accidents and improving the rate of on-time performance.

Citing fuel prices and environmental efficiency, CSX Intermodal hopes to persuade more shippers to shift freight from trucks to trains, especially for cross-country journeys. CSX announced a $700 million project in 2008 called the National Gateway, which would enable double-stacked railcars to ride three tracks in the eastern US, thus doubling the amount of cargo carried on a single line. CSX agreed to invest $300 million and is working with several states and the federal government to outfit tunnels, bridges, and overpasses to accommodate the taller railcars.

Some investors were displeased by the company's performance in 2008. The Children's Investment Fund Management (TCI) and 3G Capital Partners, leader of a group that owns about 9% of CSX, staged a proxy fight and sought to elect a slate of four directors to the company's board. Two directors from the group's slate were seated in July, and two more joined the board in September after a legal dispute was resolved.

In April 2009, TCI sold all of its shares in CSX, and the fund's managing partner, Christopher Hohn, said he won't stand for re-election to the board. Hohn still personally owns a 4.5% stake in the company.

CSX's other holdings include Total Distribution Services, a storage and distribution company for the automotive industry; Transflo Terminal Services, a logistics company for transferring shipments from rail to truck; and CSX Technology, which provides IT services to the parent company.

In May 2009, CSX sold The Greenbrier resort to investor James Justice for $20.1 million. The purchase came two months after the historic resort in West Virginia filed for Chapter 11 bankruptcy. The Greenbrier's bankruptcy case was dismissed by a federal judge in May. CSX had owned The Greenbrier since 1910.

HISTORY

CSX Corporation was formed in 1980, when Chessie System and Seaboard Coast Line (SCL) merged in an effort to improve the efficiency of their railroads.

Chessie's oldest railroad, the Baltimore & Ohio (B&O), was chartered in 1827 to help Baltimore compete against New York and Philadelphia for freight traffic. By the late 1800s the railroad served Chicago, Cincinnati, New York City, St. Louis, and Washington, DC. Chesapeake & Ohio (C&O) acquired it in 1962.

C&O originated in Virginia with the Louisa Railroad in 1836. It gained access to Chicago, Cincinnati, and Washington, DC, and by the mid-1900s was a major coal carrier. After B&O and C&O acquired joint control of Baltimore-based Western Maryland Railway (1967), the three railroads became subsidiaries of newly formed Chessie System (1973).

One of SCL's two predecessors, Seaboard Air Line Railroad (SAL), grew out of Virginia's Portsmouth & Roanoke Rail Road of 1832. SCL's other predecessor, Atlantic Coast Line Railroad (ACL), took shape between 1869 and 1893 as William Walters acquired several southern railroads. In 1902 ACL bought the Plant System (railroads in Georgia, Florida, and other southern states) and the Louisville & Nashville (a north-south line connecting New Orleans and Chicago), giving ACL the basic form it was to retain until 1967, when it merged with SAL to form SCL.

After CSX inherited the Chessie System and SCL, it bought Texas Gas Resources (gas pipeline, 1983), American Commercial Lines (Texas Gas' river barge subsidiary, 1984), and Sea-Land Corporation (ocean container shipping, 1986). To improve its market value, CSX sold most of its oil and gas properties, its communications holdings (Lightnet, begun in 1983), and most of its resort properties (Rockresorts) in 1988 and 1989. American Commercial Lines acquired Valley Line in 1992.

Sea-Land struck a deal with Danish shipping company Maersk Line in 1996 to share vessels and terminals. That year CSX entered a takeover battle with rival Norfolk Southern for Conrail. Conrail decided to split its assets between the two; CSX paid $4.3 billion for 42%. (The division took place in 1999.)

In 1999 CSX sold Grand Teton Lodge to Vail Resorts for $50 million. Also that year CSX divided Sea-Land into three businesses: international terminal operations (which became CSX World Terminals), domestic container shipping (CSX Lines), and global container shipping. The international shipping business was sold to Denmark's A.P. Møller (parent of Maersk Line) for $800 million.

Rail service disruptions stemming from the integration of Conrail assets were exacerbated by damage from Hurricane Floyd in 1999. The next year a federal audit found defects in CSX track. Service problems related to the Conrail takeover continued, and the company's rail unit underwent a management shake-up.

Later in 2000, CSX, looking to pay down debt, sold its CTI Logistx unit to TNT Post Group for $650 million.

In 2002 CSX established a CSXT office in Europe to focus on international freight and to create partnerships with European freight forwarders and ocean carriers.

CSX sold a controlling stake in its ocean container shipping unit to investment firm Carlyle Group in 2003. The former CSX Lines took the name Horizon Lines. In 2004 Carlyle sold its stake in Horizon Lines to another investment firm, Castle Harlan. The next year CSX sold its CSX World Terminals to Dubai Ports International (later DP World) for $1.14 billion.

In 2004 the two companies reorganized Conrail so that each railroad directly owned the Conrail assets that it operates. (Conrail continued to operate switching facilities and terminals used by both Norfolk Southern and CSX.)

EXECUTIVES

Chairman, President, and CEO; President and CEO, CSX Transportation: Michael J. Ward, age 58, $12,373,346 total compensation
EVP and CFO, CSX Corporation and CSX Transportation: Oscar Munoz, age 50, $3,419,737 total compensation
EVP Sales and Marketing and Chief Commercial Officer, CSX Corporation and CSX Transportation: Clarence W. Gooden, age 57, $4,608,080 total compensation
EVP and COO, CSX Transportation: Tony L. Ingram, age 62, $3,366,297 total compensation
SVP Law and Public Affairs, General Counsel, and Corporate Secretary, CSX Corporation and CSX Transportation: Ellen M. Fitzsimmons, age 48, $2,597,581 total compensation
SVP Human Resources and Labor Relations: Lisa A. Mancini
VP Federal Legislation: Michael J. Ruehling, age 61
VP Strategic Planning: Lester M. Passa, age 55
VP Federal Regulation and General Counsel: Peter J. Shudtz, age 60
VP Tax and Treasurer: David A. Boor, age 55
VP and Controller, CSX Corporation and CSX Transportation: Carolyn T. Sizemore, age 45
President, CSX Intermodal: James R. (Jim) Hertwig
President and Managing Director, The Greenbrier Resort and Club Management Co.: Michael Gordon
President, CSX Real Property: Stephen A. Crosby, age 54
President, CSX Technology Inc.: Frank A. Lonegro
Director Corporate Communications: Gary Sease
Auditors: Ernst & Young LLP

LOCATIONS

HQ: CSX Corporation
500 Water St., 15th Fl., Jacksonville, FL 32202
Phone: 904-359-3200 **Fax:** 904-633-3450
Web: www.csx.com

PRODUCTS/OPERATIONS

2008 Sales

	$ mil.	% of total
Rail		
Coal	3,110	27
Chemicals	1,437	13
Agricultural products	1,011	9
Automotive	784	7
Metals	751	7
Forest products	722	6
Emeging markets (aggregates)	628	6
Phosphates and fertilizers	460	4
Food and consumer	456	4
Other	255	2
Coke and iron ore	175	2
Intermodal		
Domestic	929	8
International	509	5
Other	28	—
Total	**11,255**	**100**

COMPETITORS

APL Logistics
Burlington Northern Santa Fe
Canadian National Railway
Canadian Pacific Railway
Hub Group
J.B. Hunt
Norfolk Southern
Pacer International
Schneider National
Union Pacific

HISTORICAL FINANCIALS

Company Type: Public

Income Statement

FYE: Last Friday in December

	REVENUE ($ mil.)	NET INCOME ($ mil.)	NET PROFIT MARGIN	EMPLOYEES
12/08	11,255.0	1,365.0	12.1%	34,000
12/07	10,030.0	1,336.0	13.3%	35,000
12/06	9,566.0	1,310.0	13.7%	36,000
12/05	8,618.0	1,145.0	13.3%	35,000
12/04	8,020.0	339.0	4.2%	35,847
Annual Growth	8.8%	41.7%	—	(1.3%)

2008 Year-End Financials

Debt ratio: 93.3%
Return on equity: 16.3%
Cash ($ mil.): 669
Current ratio: 0.99
Long-term debt ($ mil.): 7,512
No. of shares (mil.): 392
Dividends
Yield: 2.4%
Payout: 23.1%
Market value ($ mil.): 12,734

Stock History

NYSE: CSX

	STOCK PRICE ($) FY Close	P/E High/Low		PER SHARE ($) Earnings	Dividends	Book Value
12/08	32.47	21	9	3.34	0.77	20.52
12/07	43.98	17	11	2.99	0.54	22.14
12/06	34.43	14	9	2.82	0.33	22.80
12/05	25.39	10	7	2.52	0.22	20.28
12/04	20.04	27	19	0.76	0.20	17.37
Annual Growth	12.8%	—	—	44.8%	40.1%	4.3%

Cummins, Inc.

Cummins is in it for the long haul. The company is the world's leader in the manufacture of large diesel engines. The company's engines also power school buses, medium-duty trucks, pickup trucks (primarily the Dodge Ram), and equipment for mining and construction. Cummins claims just under one-third of the North American market for heavy-duty truck engines. The company also makes power generation products such as its Onan generator sets and Stamford alternators. Other products and brands include Fleetguard (filtration), Kuss (fuel filters), and Holset (turbochargers). Cummins gets more than half of its sales outside the US.

In 2005 Cummins turned in the best year for sales and profits in the company's history. In 2006 Cummins beat that record, and beat it again in 2007. The economic meltdown of 2008, however, forced the company to trim its headcount by some 4,500 people, a reduction in force of more than 10%. Cummins also cut the salaries of its officers by 10% in 2009.

With stricter emission standards on the horizon, Cummins is busy at work designing new, more environmentally friendly technologies. A high pressure fuel system, which was first introduced in 2007 on its mid-range engines, is scheduled to be used on the company's heavy-duty vehicles by 2010.

Cummins is gradually transforming itself from a company focused on North America to one whose strategy is global and aimed at seizing opportunities in emerging markets — chiefly in Brazil, China, India, and Russia. The new strategy aims to eliminate or lessen the cyclical booms and busts that traditionally have been the bane of the heavy-duty truck industry.

The company's strides in emerging markets were made through the nearly 50 joint ventures Cummins formed with overseas partners. As part of its global strategy Cummins also opened purchasing offices in China, India, the Czech Republic, and Brazil. Through these offices Cummins is building purchasing relationships with local manufacturers to secure high-quality, low-cost sourcing. Cummins also opened up a technical center in India.

Cummins plans to stay on top by continuing to invest in high-growth areas, specifically in China and India — Cummins' second- and third-largest customers are located in China and India, respectively.

HISTORY

Chauffeur Clessie Cummins believed that Rudolph Diesel's cumbersome and smoky engine could be improved for use in transportation. Borrowing money and work space from his employer — Columbus, Indiana, banker W. G. Irwin — Cummins founded Cummins Engine in 1919. Irwin invested more than $2.5 million, and in the mid-1920s Cummins produced a mobile diesel engine. Truck manufacturers were reluctant to switch from gas to diesel, so Cummins used publicity stunts (such as racing in the Indianapolis 500) to advertise his engine.

The company was profitable by 1937, the year in which Irwin's grandnephew, J. Irwin Miller, took over the company. During WWII the Cummins engine was used in cargo trucks. Sales jumped from $20 million in 1946 to more than $100 million by 1956. That year Cummins started its first overseas plant in Scotland, and bought Atlas Crankshafts in 1958. By 1967 it had 50% of the diesel engine market.

Cummins diversified in 1970 by acquiring the K2 Ski Company (fiberglass skis) and Coot Industries (all-terrain vehicles), but sold them by 1976. It added turbochargers in 1973 with its acquisition of Holset Engineering. (Founded in 1948 and named for founders W.C. Holmes and Louis Croset, Holset became a subsidiary of BHD Engineering Limited Group in 1952; it 1973 it first was acquired by Hanson Trust in 1973 and later that year by Cummins. Holset changed its name to Cummins Turbo Technologies in 2006.) In the early 1980s Cummins introduced a line of midrange engines developed in a joint venture with J.I. Case (then a subsidiary of Tenneco; now a part of Fiat-controlled CNH Global). To remain competitive, Cummins cut costs by 22%, doubled productivity in its US and UK plants, and spent $1.8 billion to retool its factories.

Having twice repelled unwelcome foreign suitors in 1989, Cummins sold 27% of its stock to Ford, Tenneco, and Kubota for $250 million in 1990. The move raised cash and protected Cummins from future takeover bids.

In 1993 Cummins established engine-making joint ventures with Tata Engineering & Locomotive, India's largest heavy vehicle maker, and Komatsu, a leading Japanese construction equipment maker. Also in 1993 Cummins introduced a natural-gas engine for school buses and formed a joint venture to produce turbochargers in India. The company began Cummins Wartsila, a joint venture with engineering company Wartsila NSD, to develop high-speed diesel and natural gas engines in France and the UK in 1995. It also began restructuring that year, selling plants and laying off workers.

Continuing its strategy of teaming with other manufacturers, Cummins agreed in 1996 to make small and midsize diesel engines with Fiat's Iveco and New Holland (now CNH Global) subsidiaries.

In 1997 subsidiary Cadec Systems signed a license to develop and sell Montreal-based Canadian Marconi's (now BAE SYSTEMS CANADA) fleet-tracking system, which uses satellites and computers. Cummins bought diesel exhaust and air filtration company Nelson Industries for $490 million in early 1998. The company also agreed, without admission of guilt, to pay a $25 million fine and contribute $35 million to environmental programs after the EPA accused Cummins of cheating on emissions tests.

Chairman and CEO James Henderson retired at the end of 1999 and was succeeded by Theodore Solso.

Early in 2001 the company announced that it had signed a long-term deal to supply PACCAR (Peterbilt and Kenworth trucks) with heavy-duty ISX, Signature, N14, ISM, and ISL engines. Cummins also formed a joint venture with Westport Innovations (Cummins Westport Inc.) for the building of low-emission, natural gas engines. Later in 2001 the company shortened its name to Cummins, Inc.

The following year Cummins and Mercury Marine formed a joint venture, Cummins MerCruiser Diesel Marine LLC, to provide diesel engines to the recreational and commercial marine markets.

In 2003 Cummins and Westport Innovations strengthened their joint venture ties by signing a technology partnership agreement that made it easier for the two companies to develop and share alternative fuel technologies.

EXECUTIVES

Chairman and CEO: Theodore M. (Tim) Solso, age 62, $13,275,295 total compensation
President, COO, and Director: N. Thomas (Tom) Linebarger, age 46, $4,327,052 total compensation
VP and CFO: Pat J. Ward, age 45, $1,142,027 total compensation
VP and CTO: John C. Wall, age 57
VP Corporate Quality and Chief Risk Officer: Mark R. Gerstle, age 53
VP and Chief Investment Officer: Richard E. Harris, age 56
EVP Corporate Responsibility; CEO, Cummins Foundation: Jean S. Blackwell, age 54, $3,508,459 total compensation
VP, General Counsel, and Corporate Secretary: Marya M. Rose, age 46
Group VP Emerging Markets and Businesses: Steven M. (Steve) Chapman, age 55
VP; President, Cummins Components Group: Richard J. Freeland, age 51
VP; President, Engine Business: James D. (Jim) Kelly, age 56, $4,099,577 total compensation
VP and General Manager, High-Horsepower Engine Business, Engine Business: Mark Levett
VP, Quality, Heavy-Duty Business, Engine Business: Bob Weimer
VP and President, Power Generation: Tony Satterthwaite, age 49
VP, Corporate Controller, and Principal Accounting Officer: Marsha L. Hunt, age 45
Auditors: PricewaterhouseCoopers LLP

LOCATIONS

HQ: Cummins, Inc.
  500 Jackson St., Columbus, IN 47201
Phone: 812-377-5000   **Fax:** 812-377-3334
Web: www.cummins.com

2008 Sales

	$ mil.	% of total
US	5,817	41
Asia & Australia	3,008	21
Europe	2,586	18
Mexico & Latin America	1,473	10
Africa & Middle East	839	6
Canada	619	4
Total	**14,342**	**100**

PRODUCTS/OPERATIONS

2008 Sales

	$ mil.	% of total
Engines	7,432	52
Power generation	2,601	18
Distribution	2,155	15
Components	2,154	15
Total	**14,342**	**100**

Selected Products

Engines
  Bus engines
  Heavy- and medium-duty truck engines
  Industrial engines for construction, mining,
    agricultural, rail, and marine equipment
  Light, commercial vehicle engines

Power generation
  Generator sets (Onan)

Filtration
  Fleetguard
  Nelson

COMPETITORS

AAF-McQUAY	Mack Trucks
BorgWarner	MAN
Briggs & Stratton Power	Mitsubishi Heavy
Products	Industries
Caterpillar	Navistar International
China Yuchai	Nissan Diesel
CLARCOR	PACCAR
Daimler	Regal Beloit
Detroit Diesel	Renault
DEUTZ	Robert Bosch
Donaldson Company	Scania
Emerson Electric	Tenneco
Hino Motors	ThyssenKrupp
Honeywell International	Tognum
Invensys	Volvo
Isuzu	Weichai Power
Kohler	

HISTORICAL FINANCIALS

Company Type: Public

Income Statement

FYE: December 31

	REVENUE ($ mil.)	NET INCOME ($ mil.)	NET PROFIT MARGIN	EMPLOYEES
12/08	14,342.0	755.0	5.3%	39,800
12/07	13,048.0	739.0	5.7%	37,800
12/06	11,362.0	715.0	6.3%	34,600
12/05	9,918.0	550.0	5.5%	33,500
12/04	8,438.0	350.0	4.1%	28,100
Annual Growth	**14.2%**	**21.2%**	**—**	**9.1%**

2008 Year-End Financials

Debt ratio: 19.5%
Return on equity: 22.7%
Cash ($ mil.): 426
Current ratio: 1.79
Long-term debt ($ mil.): 629
No. of shares (mil.): 202
Dividends
  Yield: 2.2%
  Payout: 15.6%
Market value ($ mil.): 5,394

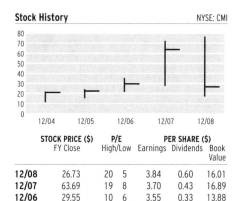

CVS Caremark

CVS Caremark (formerly CVS) interprets the scrawl of more US doctors than anyone. The CVS pharmacy chain fills more prescriptions at more drugstores than any other drugstore operator. With about 7,000 drugstores under the CVS and Longs Drug banners, the company is the nation's largest pharmacy chain (ahead of archrival Walgreen) as a result of a string of acquisitions that included the Eckerd chain, stores from Albertsons, and most recently Longs Drug Stores (2008). In 2007 CVS purchased prescription benefits management (PBM) firm Caremark Rx for about $26.5 billion. Caremark was combined with CVS's PBM and specialty pharmacy unit PharmaCare Management Services to form Caremark Pharmacy Services.

CVS's active acquisition schedule has both greatly expanded the number of retail pharmacies it operates and the range of services it offers to customers, employers, insurance companies, unions, managed care organizations, and other clients. The company is betting that size will make it a more convenient and efficient operator and a preferred provider to health benefit plans attempting to better manage their health care costs.

The Caremark purchase positioned the company as a leading manager of pharmacy benefits in the US. The hard-won deal, launched in November 2006, led to a bidding war between CVS and Caremark rival Express Scripts that forced CVS to up its offer several times.

CVS continues to add MinuteClinic locations in its stores. MinuteClinic (acquired in 2006) operates health clinics inside retail stores. The CVS subsidiary runs about 560 clinics in more than 25 states, most of which are located within CVS stores.

The $2.9-billion purchase of Longs Drug added about 530 retail pharmacies to CVS's store count. Longs operated in the high-growth markets of California, Hawaii, Nevada, and Arizona. It also operated Rx America, a PBM subsidiary that serves more than 8 million members and offers some 450,000 Medicare beneficiaries its prescription drug plan benefits. Through the acquisition, CVS Caremark became the #1 prescription provider in the US (filling or managing more than 1.2 billion prescriptions each year).

An added bonus is Longs' valuable real estate portfolio, estimated at $1 billion. Indeed, Longs' real estate assets became a sticking point in the deal, with several of the company's shareholders saying the CVS bid undervalued the real estate assets. Longs settled the related lawsuits in September 2008, admitting that it did not seek a third party appraisal for its real estate assets.

CVS is drawing fire from consumer groups and the attorneys general of two major states (California and New York) over the alleged sale of expired over-the-counter products in its stores. In June 2009 CVS agreed to pay almost $1 million to settle allegations stemming from the sale of expired OTC medications, infant formula, and dairy products.

HISTORY

Brothers Stanley and Sid Goldstein, who ran health and beauty products distributor Mark Steven, branched out into retail in 1963 when they opened up their first Consumer Value Store in Lowell, Massachusetts, with partner Ralph Hoagland.

The chain grew rapidly, amassing 17 stores by the end of 1964 (the year the CVS name was first used) and 40 by 1969. That year the Goldsteins sold the chain to Melville Shoe to finance further expansion.

Melville had been founded in 1892 by shoe supplier Frank Melville. Melville's son, Ward, grew the company, creating the Thom McAn shoe store chain and later buying its supplier. By 1969 Melville had opened shoe shops in Kmart stores (through its Meldisco unit), launched one apparel chain (Chess King, sold in 1993), and purchased another (Foxwood Stores, renamed Foxmoor and sold in 1985).

In 1972 CVS bought the 84-store Clinton Drug and Discount, a Rochester, New York-based chain. Two years later, when sales hit $100 million, CVS had 232 stores — only 45 of which had pharmacies. The company bought New Jersey-based Mack Drug (36 stores) in 1977. By 1981 CVS had more than 400 stores.

CVS's sales hit $1 billion in 1985 as it continued to add pharmacies to many of its older stores. In 1987 Stanley's success was recognized companywide when he was named chairman and CEO of CVS's parent company, which by then had been renamed Melville.

CVS bought the 490-store Peoples Drug Stores chain from Imasco in 1990, giving it locations in Maryland, Pennsylvania, Virginia, West Virginia, and Washington, DC. CVS created PharmaCare Management Services in 1994 to take advantage of the growing market for pharmacy services and managed-care drug programs. Pharmacist Tom Ryan was named CEO that year.

With CVS outperforming Melville's other operations, in 1995 Melville decided to concentrate on the drugstore chain. By that time Melville's holdings had grown to include discount department store chain Marshalls and furniture chain This End Up, both sold in 1995; footwear chain Footaction, spun off as part of Footstar in 1996, along with Meldisco; the Linens 'n Things chain, spun off in 1996; and the Kay-Bee Toys chain, sold in 1996.

Melville was renamed CVS in late 1996. Amid major consolidation in the drugstore industry, in 1997 CVS — then with about 1,425 stores — paid $3.7 billion for Revco D.S., which had nearly

2,600 stores in 17 states, mainly in the Midwest and Southeast. The next year the company bought Arbor Drugs (200 stores in Michigan, later converted to the CVS banner) for nearly $1.5 billion. Stanley retired as chairman in 1999 and was succeeded by Ryan.

In June 2005 CVS agreed to pay $110 million to settle a shareholders' lawsuit filed in 2001 that alleged the company had made misleading statements to artificially raise its stock price and violated accounting practices. CVS denied the charges and said the settlement was "purely a business decision."

In June 2006 CVS completed the acquisition of some 700 stand-alone Sav-On and Osco drugstores from Albertsons. In March 2007 CVS changed its name to CVS Caremark Corporation. In November CEO Ryan added the chairman's title to his job description following the retirement of Mac Crawford.

In 2008 CVS settled a lawsuit regarding drug-switching allegations for $36.7 million. The company had been accused of switching Medicaid customers to a more expensive capsule form of Zantac from a tablet form; CVS denied the allegations.

EXECUTIVES

Chairman, President, and CEO: Thomas M. (Tom) Ryan, age 56, $24,102,648 total compensation
EVP, CFO, and Chief Administrative Officer: David B. (Dave) Rickard, age 61, $5,096,535 total compensation
SVP and CIO: Stuart M. McGuigan, age 50
EVP and Chief Legal Officer; President, CVS Realty: Douglas A. Sgarro, age 49, $4,348,769 total compensation
EVP and Chief Marketing Officer: Helena B. Foulkes, age 44
EVP and Chief Medical Officer: Troyen A. Brennan, age 54
SVP, Controller, and Chief Accounting Officer: David M. Denton, age 43
SVP and Associate Chief Medical Officer; President and COO, MinuteClinic: Andrew J. (Andy) Sussman
EVP; President, CVS Pharmacy: Larry J. Merlo, age 53, $8,241,994 total compensation
EVP; President, Caremark Pharmacy Services: Howard A. McLure, age 51, $4,462,687 total compensation
EVP Rx Purchasing, Pricing, and Network Relations: Jonathan C. Roberts, age 53
SVP Investor Relations: Nancy R. Christal
SVP Human Resources and Corporate Communications: V. Michael Ferdinandi, age 58
VP and Treasurer: Carol A. DeNale
VP Corporate Communications: Carolyn Castel
President, TheraCom: Chip Phillips
Secretary: Zenon P. Lankowsky
Auditors: Ernst & Young LLP

LOCATIONS

HQ: CVS Caremark Corporation
1 CVS Dr., Woonsocket, RI 02895
Phone: 401-765-1500 **Fax:** 401-762-9227
Web: www.cvs.com

2008 Stores

	No.
California	852
Florida	686
Texas	499
New York	436
Pennsylvania	375
Massachusetts	346
Ohio	311
North Carolina	290
Georgia	296
Indiana	289
New Jersey	258
Michigan	244
Virginia	244
Illinois	235
South Carolina	185
Maryland	169
Alabama	148
Connecticut	133
Arizona	130
Tennessee	128
Nevada	89
Louisiana	88
Rhode Island	59
Kentucky	57
District of Columbia	54
West Virginia	49
Missouri	47
Hawaii	46
Minnesota	37
Mississippi	34
Oklahoma	34
Kansas	31
New Hampshire	31
Wisconsin	28
Other states	62
Total	**7,000**

PRODUCTS/OPERATIONS

2008 Sales

	% of total
Prescription drugs	68
Over-the-counter & personal care	13
Body/cosmetics	4
General merchandise & other	15
Total	**100**

COMPETITORS

A&P	Kmart
Aetna	Kroger
Ahold USA	Medco Health
BioScrip	Prescription Solutions
CIGNA	Rite Aid
drugstore.com	Standard Management
Duane Reade	UnitedHealth Group
Express Scripts	Walgreen
H-E-B	Wal-Mart
Humana	WellPoint
Kerr Drug	

HISTORICAL FINANCIALS

Company Type: Public

Income Statement

FYE: December 31

	REVENUE ($ mil.)	NET INCOME ($ mil.)	NET PROFIT MARGIN	EMPLOYEES
12/08	87,471.9	3,212.1	3.7%	215,000
12/07	76,329.5	2,622.8	3.4%	200,000
12/06	43,813.8	1,355.0	3.1%	176,000
12/05	37,006.2	1,210.6	3.3%	148,000
12/04	30,594.3	904.6	3.0%	145,500
Annual Growth	**30.0%**	**37.3%**	**—**	**10.3%**

2008 Year-End Financials

Debt ratio: 23.4%	No. of shares (mil.): 1,443
Return on equity: 9.8%	Dividends
Cash ($ mil.): 1,352	Yield: 0.9%
Current ratio: 1.23	Payout: 11.9%
Long-term debt ($ mil.): 8,057	Market value ($ mil.): 41,478

Stock History

NYSE: CVS

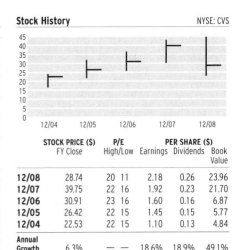

	STOCK PRICE ($) FY Close	P/E High/Low		PER SHARE ($) Earnings	Dividends	Book Value
12/08	28.74	20	11	2.18	0.26	23.96
12/07	39.75	22	16	1.92	0.23	21.70
12/06	30.91	23	16	1.60	0.16	6.87
12/05	26.42	22	15	1.45	0.15	5.77
12/04	22.53	22	15	1.10	0.13	4.84
Annual Growth	**6.3%**	**—**	**—**	**18.6%**	**18.9%**	**49.1%**

Cytec Industries

Cytec Industries covers its business bases. The company produces the building-block chemicals from which it makes engineered materials (composites and adhesives for the aerospace industry), specialty chemicals (resins and coatings for metal, plastic, and wood), and additives used in industrial processes. Cytec also sells its building-block chemicals (acrylonitrile, melamine, and sulfuric acid) to third parties. Cytec Engineered Materials includes aerospace products such as advanced composites and structural adhesives. The Specialty Chemicals unit's products are used in mining, drilling, and the manufacture of pharmaceuticals. The unit combines Cytec's Performance Chemicals and Surface Specialties segments.

Chairman and CEO David Lilley retired at the end of 2008. Cytec Specialty Chemicals president Shane Fleming took his place, having been with the company for a quarter of a century.

HISTORY

Cytec Industries was spun off of parent company American Cyanamid late in 1993. American Cyanamid had focused on agrichemical and pharmaceutical life sciences, while its specialty chemicals operations languished behind its competitors. Cytec was spun off to Cyanamid stockholders, and Darryl Fry, Cyanamid's head of agriculture, became CEO of Cytec. He dumped about $300 million worth of underperforming businesses. Fry overhauled the R&D process by dragging the engineers out of their labs and having them do field work with customers. Fry also encouraged research that focused on creating products with practical applications when he realized that the last breakthrough that translated into a usable product was super glue in the 1970s. The company focused on core areas in which Cytec had expertise. Rather than go for the blockbuster product, the company aimed for an array of smaller, less-profitable but more-accessible products.

By 1996 overseas sales accounted for about 40% of revenues, up from 28% in 1993. Also in

1996 Cytec sold its aluminum sulphate operations. Cost-reduction programs and the company's improved product mix were making themselves felt; though sales were flat between 1995 and 1996, earnings were up.

David Lilley (formerly of American Home Products/Wyeth) was named COO in 1997. That year Cytec completed the sale of its acrylic-fibers business to Sterling Chemicals Holdings. Cytec also acquired Fiberite (excluding its satellite-materials business). Fiberite, a composites maker, was merged with Cytec's advanced composites and aerospace adhesives line to form Cytec Fiberite (now Cytec Engineered Materials).

In 1998 Cytec began Dyno-Cytec, a European coatings joint venture (it bought its partner's stake later in the year). It also bought composite material maker American Materials & Technologies. That year COO Lilley was named CEO; the title of chairman was added in 1999. Also in 1999 Cytec bought Inspec Mining Chemical from the UK's Laporte PLC for $25 million and BIP (amino-coating resins) for $42 million. Later that year the company sold its interest in Fortier Methanol.

The company teamed up with GE Specialty Chemicals and Albemarle in 2000 to form an on-line B2B joint venture to streamline the companies' purchasing. Cytec sold its stake in Criterion Catalyst to its partner CRI International, a subsidiary of Royal Dutch Shell, for $60 million. That November Cytec sold most of its paper chemicals operations, including its sizing and strength business.

In 2001 Cytec added the carbon fiber business of BP and closed up shop on joint venture AC Molding Compounds, which manufactured melamine and urea molding compounds.

With chemical companies at their lowest levels of production in about a decade, Cytec undertook some cost-cutting efforts in 2001-02, including idling an ammonia plant and reducing its staff. Problems associated with the commercial airline industry also squeezed sales.

In June 2003 the company dissolved another of its partnerships, this one with Mitsui Chemicals called Mitsui Cytec (water-treatment chemicals and melamine coating resins). Cytec kept the resins business, while Mitsui held on to the venture's water-treatment operations.

In 2006 the company sold its water treatment chemicals and acrylamide manufacturing operations to Kemira for about $240 million. The divestiture was designed to allow Cytec to pare down its operations and place its focus on core business lines.

David Lilley retired at the close of 2008.

EXECUTIVES

Chairman and CEO: Shane D. Fleming, age 50, $2,185,158 total compensation
CFO: David M. Drillock, age 51, $1,064,441 total compensation
VP Information Technology: Jeffrey C. Futterman
VP Safety, Health, and Environment: Karen E. Koster
VP Corporate and Business Development; President, Cytec Building Block Chemicals: William N. Avrin, age 53
VP Taxes: Richard T. Ferguson
VP, General Counsel, and Secretary: Roy Smith, age 50, $880,903 total compensation
VP Human Resources: Marilyn R. Charles, age 51
President, Cytec Specialty Chemicals: Frank Aranzana
President, Cytec Engineered Materials: Steven C. (Steve) Speak, age 51, $1,182,020 total compensation
Treasurer: Thomas P. Wozniak, age 55
Auditors: KPMG LLP

LOCATIONS

HQ: Cytec Industries Inc.
 5 Garret Mountain Plaza, West Paterson, NJ 07424
Phone: 973-357-3100   **Fax:** 973-357-3065
Web: www.cytec.com

2008 Sales

	$ mil.	% of total
Europe, Middle East & Africa	1,503.4	41
North America	1,322.1	36
Asia/Pacific	508.9	14
Latin America	305.5	9
Total	**3,639.9**	**100**

PRODUCTS/OPERATIONS

2008 Sales

	$ mil.	% of total
Surface Specialties	1,637.7	45
Engineered Materials	748.2	21
Performance Chemicals	742.3	20
Building Block Chemicals	511.7	14
Total	**3,639.9**	**100**

Selected Products

Cytec Surface Specialties
 Liquid coating resins (water- and solvent-borne resins, amino resins)
 Powder coating resins (conventional and ultraviolet powders)
 Radcure resins (oligomers, monomers, and photoinitiators)
Cytec Engineered Materials
 Aerospace materials (structural adhesives, advanced composites)
Performance Chemicals
 Mining chemicals (reagents, polymers)
 Phosphine and phosphine derivatives
 Polymer additives (ultraviolet light absorbers and stabilizers, antioxidants)
Building-block chemicals
 Acrylamide
 Acrylonitrile
 Ammonia
 Melamine
 Sulfuric acid

COMPETITORS

Akzo Nobel
Ashland Inc.
Bayer AG
Ciba Specialty Chemicals
Clariant
Dow Chemical
DSM
DuPont
Georgia Gulf
H.B. Fuller
Hexcel
Lucite
Methanex
Mitsubishi Chemical
Nalco

HISTORICAL FINANCIALS

Company Type: Public

Income Statement

				FYE: December 31
	REVENUE ($ mil.)	NET INCOME ($ mil.)	NET PROFIT MARGIN	EMPLOYEES
12/08	3,639.9	(198.8)	—	6,700
12/07	3,503.8	206.5	5.9%	6,800
12/06	3,329.5	196.1	5.9%	6,700
12/05	2,925.7	59.1	2.0%	7,300
12/04	1,721.3	126.1	7.3%	4,500
Annual Growth	**20.6%**	**—**	**—**	**10.5%**

2008 Year-End Financials

Debt ratio: 54.7%
Return on equity: —
Cash ($ mil.): 55
Current ratio: 2.34
Long-term debt ($ mil.): 806
No. of shares (mil.): 48
Dividends
 Yield: 2.4%
 Payout: —
Market value ($ mil.): 1,029

Stock History

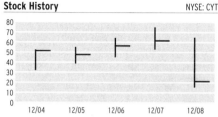

NYSE: CYT

	STOCK PRICE ($) FY Close	P/E High/Low		PER SHARE ($) Earnings	Dividends	Book Value
12/08	21.22	—	—	(4.16)	0.50	30.42
12/07	61.58	18	13	4.20	0.40	39.81
12/06	56.51	16	11	4.01	0.40	32.39
12/05	47.63	43	31	1.27	0.40	25.54
12/04	51.42	18	12	2.84	0.40	18.70
Annual Growth	(19.9%)	—	—	—	5.7%	12.9%

Dana Holding

When it comes to building cars, it starts with the parts. Dana manufactures many of the parts carmakers use to piece together new vehicles. Its core products include axles and driveshafts, as well as sealing, thermal, and structural products. Among its customers are OEMs such as Chrysler, Ford, General Motors, and Toyota. The company also supplies companies that make commercial and off-highway vehicles, such as PACCAR and Navistar. Dana filed for Chapter 11 bankruptcy protection from creditors in 2006 and emerged in 2008. Customers in North America account for around half of Dana's sales.

The woes of the automotive industry weigh heavily on Dana, especially in the US, where new vehicle sales are expected to decline in 2009. The company plans to restructure and reduce the size of its operations in order to cut costs. In 2007 Dana closed 15 manufacturing plants and eliminated post-retirement health care benefits for non-union Dana retirees. During 2008 the company reduced its workforce by 6,000 people, a 17% cutback in employment. Dana intends to close additional facilities in 2009 and 2010.

Having come out of Chapter 11, Dana also is restricted by the financial covenants of its exit financing — restraints that could impede the company as the credit crisis continues. In late 2008 Dana amended some covenants in its exit facility. The company completed the sale of its pump products business to Melling Tool Company in 2008.

Eaton executive James Sweetnam became Dana's president and CEO in mid-2009. His predecessor as CEO, John Devine, continued as executive chairman.

Centerbridge Capital Partners, a private equity firm, invested $790 million in Dana as part of the company's bankruptcy reorganization plan.

HISTORY

Clarence Spicer developed a universal joint and a driveshaft for autos while studying at Cornell University. Leaving Cornell in 1904, he patented his designs, founded Spicer Manufacturing in Plainfield, New Jersey, and marketed the product himself.

The company ran into financial trouble in 1913, and the following year New York attorney Charles Dana joined the firm, advancing Spicer money to refinance. Acquisitions after WWI strengthened Spicer's position in the growing truck industry. The business moved to Toledo, Ohio, in 1929 to be nearer the emerging Detroit automotive mecca. In 1946 the company was renamed in honor of Dana, who became chairman two years later. Sales topped $150 million in the 1950s.

The company entered the replacement-parts market in 1963, and Charles Dana retired that year. Continuing to expand its offerings, Dana acquired the Weatherhead Company (hoses, fittings, and couplings; 1977) and later branched into financial services. In 1989 Dana introduced a nine-speed, heavy-duty truck transmission (developed jointly with truckmaker Navistar), the first all-new design of its type in over 25 years.

Dana sold its mortgage banking business and some other financial services in 1992. It bought Delta Automotive and Krizman, both leading makers and distributors of automotive aftermarket parts. The next year Dana acquired the Reinz Group, a German gasket maker with worldwide operations. Purchases in 1994 included Sige (axles, Italy), Stieber Heidelberg (industrial components, Germany), Tece (auto parts distribution, the Netherlands), and Tremec (transmissions, Mexico).

Acquisitions in 1995 and 1996 included a number of rubber and plastics makers. The company bought Clark-Hurth Components (drivetrains) and the piston ring and cylinder liner operations of SPX Corporation in 1997; it also increased its shares in Wix Filtron (filtration products, Poland).

Dana sold some of its businesses in 1997 as well. These included its sheet-rubber and conveyor-belt business to Coltec Industries, its European warehouse distribution operations to Partco Group, and its Spicer clutch business to Eaton.

In 1998 Dana bought Eaton's heavy-axle and brake business and then paid $3.9 billion for Echlin. Dana then cut 3,500 jobs, or more than 4% of its workforce, and closed 15 plants, mostly former Echlin facilities. It paid $430 million in 1998 for the bearings, washers, and camshafts businesses of Federal-Mogul (auto parts).

In 2000 Dana sold Gresen's hydraulic business to Parker Hannifin and Warner Electric's industrial products business to Colfax. Anticipating a slowdown in North American car production, Dana closed five plants, downsized three, and terminated 1,280 employees.

On the buying side, Dana acquired the auto axle manufacturing and stamping operations of Invensys (UK) in 2000. Also that year president and CEO Joseph Magliochetti, a 33-year Dana veteran, became chairman. Late in 2000 the company announced it would cut 3,000 production jobs.

In 2001 Dana sold its Chelsea Products Division (power take-offs) to Parker Hannifin. Later in the year Dana announced 10,000 more job cuts through plant closings and consolidations.

In November 2002 the company sold Tekonsha Engineering Company (aftermarket electric brake controls), Theodore Bargman Company (exterior lighting, electrical accessories, and locks and latches), and American Electronic Components (sensors, switches, and relays) to leveraged buyout firm The Riverside Company. In mid 2003 Dana sold a significant portion of the Engine Management operations of its Automotive Aftermarket Group to Standard Motor Products for $121 million.

Early in the summer of 2003, ArvinMeritor offered to acquire Dana for $15 per share or about $2.2 billion. By Thanksgiving 2003 the deal fell apart after Dana's board of directors rejected ArvinMeritor's sweetened deal of $2.67 billion. Within weeks of fending off ArvinMeritor, Dana announced it planned to sell all of its aftermarket parts businesses. The deal was finalized in November 2004.

The following year Dana and Dongfeng Motor Ltd. formed 50-50 joint venture Dongfeng Dana Axle Co. Ltd. for the manufacture of commercial vehicle axles in China.

As hard times hit the North American automotive market in 2005, Dana announced it would cut more costs by laying off workers, selling noncore operations, closing plants, and moving more of its manufacturing base to Mexico.

Dana filed for Chapter 11 bankruptcy early in 2006 and exited in 2008.

EXECUTIVES

Chairman: John M. Devine, age 64, $5,853,430 total compensation
Vice Chairman: Gary L. Convis, age 66, $5,096,700 total compensation
President, CEO, and Director: James E. Sweetnam, age 56
President Global Operations: Mark E. Wallace, age 42
EVP and CFO: James A. (Jim) Yost, age 60, $2,117,987 total compensation
VP and CIO: Abdallah F. Shanti, age 48
CTO: George T. Constand, age 50
Chief Administrative Officer: Robert H. Marcin, age 64, $1,082,421 total compensation
Chief Restructuring Officer: Edward J. (Ted) Stenger
VP and Chief Accounting Officer: Richard J. Dyer, age 53
Chief Purchasing Officer: Eric W. Schwarz, age 44
SVP Strategy and Business Development: Jacqueline A. Dedo, age 47
SVP, General Counsel, and Secretary: Marc S. Levin, age 54
President, Global Business Development: Robert A. Fesenmyer
President, Structural Solutions Group, Automotive Systems Group: Gilberto Ceratti
President, Heavy Vehicle Products, Heavy Vehicle Technologies, and Systems Group: Nick L. Stanage, age 50, $677,650 total compensation
President, Engine Products and Thermal Products; President, Dana Europe: Ralf Goettel, age 42, $702,247 total compensation
President, Asia Pacific Operations: Ken J. Cao
President, Torque Products Group, Automotive Systems Group: Margot Hoffman
President, Light Vehicle Driveline: Martin D. Bryant, age 39
Treasurer: Ralph A. Than, age 41
Auditors: PricewaterhouseCoopers LLP

LOCATIONS

HQ: Dana Holding Corporation
4500 Dorr St., Toledo, OH 43615
Phone: 419-535-4500   **Fax:** 419-535-4643
Web: www.dana.com

Dana operates more than 110 manufacturing and engineering facilities worldwide.

2008 Sales

	$ mil.	% of total
North America	3,919	48
Europe	2,393	30
South America	1,103	14
Asia/Pacific	680	8
Total	**8,095**	**100**

PRODUCTS/OPERATIONS

2008 Sales

	$ mil.	% of total
Automotive		
Light axle	2,154	26
Driveshaft	1,179	15
Structures	876	11
Sealing	705	9
Thermal	259	3
Off-Highway	1,727	21
Commercial Vehicle	1,187	15
Other	8	—
Total	**8,095**	**100**

Selected Products

Automotive
  Axles
  Chassis
  Driveshafts
  Engine sealing products
  Steering and suspension components
  Structural products
  Thermal management products
Commercial Vehicle
  Axles
  Brakes
  Chassis and suspension modules
  Driveshafts
  Engine sealing products
  Thermal management products
Off-Highway
  Axles
  Brakes
  Driveshafts
  Electronic controls
  Engine sealing products
  Suspension components
  Transaxles
  Transmissions

COMPETITORS

AISIN World Corp.	Honeywell International
American Axle & Manufacturing	Ingersoll-Rand
ArvinMeritor	ITT Corp.
BorgWarner	LEONI
Capsonic	Magna International
Carraro	Mahle International
Chrysler	Mark IV
Continental AG	Martinrea International
Daimler	Metaldyne
Delphi Corp.	Modine Manufacturing
DENSO	Prestolite Electric
Eaton	Robert Bosch
Emerson Electric	TA Delaware
Federal-Mogul	TRW Automotive
Ford Motor	Valeo
Freudenberg-NOK	Visteon
GKN	Wanxiang
	ZF Friedrichshafen

HISTORICAL FINANCIALS

Company Type: Public

Income Statement

FYE: December 31

	REVENUE ($ mil.)	NET INCOME ($ mil.)	NET PROFIT MARGIN	EMPLOYEES
12/08	8,095.0	18.0	0.2%	29,000
12/07	8,721.0	(551.0)	—	35,000
12/06	8,504.0	(739.0)	—	45,000
12/05	8,611.0	(1,609.0)	—	44,000
12/04	9,056.0	82.0	0.9%	45,900
Annual Growth	(2.8%)	(31.6%)	—	(10.8%)

2008 Year-End Financials

Debt ratio: 95.0%
Return on equity: 7.8%
Cash ($ mil.): 777
Current ratio: 1.89
Long-term debt ($ mil.): 1,181

No. of shares (mil.): 100
Dividends
Yield: 0.0%
Payout: —
Market value ($ mil.): 74

Stock History

NYSE: DAN

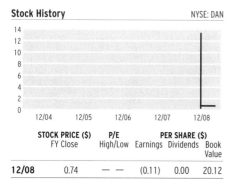

	STOCK PRICE ($) FY Close	P/E High/Low	PER SHARE ($) Earnings	Dividends	Book Value
12/08	0.74	— —	(0.11)	0.00	20.12

Danaher Corporation

If you've ever used Craftsman hand tools or bought something with a bar code on it, then odds are you've been in touch with Danaher's business. Its Professional Instrumentation segment produces environmental and electronic testing technology; Industrial Technologies makes motion control equipment and devices that read bar codes; Medical Technologies makes dental products and medical instrumentation devices; and Danaher's Tools and Components manufactures hand and automotive specialty tools and accessories under brand names like Sears Craftsman. The two Rales brothers, Steven (board chairman) and Mitchell (executive committee chairman), together own approximately 20% of the company.

Danaher derives its sales from the design, manufacture, and marketing of well-known branded medical, industrial, professional, commercial and consumer products, as well as from its proprietary technology. Danaher acquires businesses to augment its product offerings, and it continually assesses the strategic fit of its existing businesses.

In 2009 Danaher announced plans to buy the MDS Analytical Technologies (drug discovery and life sciences research instruments) business of Canada-based MDS for about $650 million; the unit includes a 50% interest in AB SCIEX, which makes mass spectrometry instruments for medical researchers and clinicians. Danaher

plans to buy the remaining shares of AB SCIEX from Life Technologies for about $450 million.

Along with the acquisitions, Danaher announced plans in 2009 to step up its restructuring efforts, including job cuts and plant closings.

HISTORY

Danaher (from the Celtic word *dana* meaning "swift flowing") is named for a fishing stream off the Flat Head River in Montana. The term is also an appropriate description of the spotlight-averse Rales brothers. The two have proven to be fishers not only of trout but also of companies, buying underperforming companies with strong market shares and recognizable brand names.

Once dubbed "raiders in short pants" by *Forbes,* Steven and Mitchell Rales began making acquisitions in their 20s. In 1981 they bought their father's 50% stake in Master Shield, a maker of vinyl building products. The brothers bought tire manufacturer Mohawk Rubber the following year. In 1983 they acquired control of publicly traded DMG, a distressed Florida real-estate firm; the next year they sold DMG's real estate holdings and folded Mohawk and Master Shield into the company, which they renamed Danaher.

Danaher then began taking over low-profile industrial firms that weren't living up to their growth potential. Backed by junk bonds from Michael Milken, it had purchased 12 more companies within two years. Among these early acquisitions were makers of tools (Jacobs, Matco Tools), controls (Partlow, Qualitrol, Veeder-Root), precision components (Allen, maker of the namesake hexagonal wrench), and plastics (A.L. Hyde). With its purchases, Danaher proceeded to cut costs and pay down debt by unloading underperforming assets.

The Rales brothers' takeover efforts weren't always successful. They lost out to Warren Buffett when they tried to buy Scott Fetzer (encyclopedias, vacuum cleaners) in 1985 and INTERCO (furniture, shoes, apparel) in 1988. They did, however, make off with $75 million for their troubles, and INTERCO was driven into dismantlement and bankruptcy in the process.

In 1989 Danaher bought Easco Hand Tools, the main maker of tools for Sears, Roebuck and Co.'s Craftsman line. (The Raleses already controlled Easco Hand Tools; a private partnership they controlled had bought the company from its parent in 1985 and taken it public in 1987.) The deal established the tool division as Danaher's largest, and two years later Sears selected Danaher as the sole manufacturer of Craftsman mechanics' hand tools.

The brothers hired Black & Decker power tools executive George Sherman as president and CEO in 1990. Between 1991 and 1995 Danaher grew through purchases such as Delta Consolidated Industries and Armstrong Brothers Tool. The firm improved its international distribution channels by adding West Instruments (UK, 1993) and Hengstler (Germany, 1994).

Focusing on tools and controls, Danaher sold its automotive components business in 1995. After a lengthy battle, the company bought test maker and controls firm Acme-Cleveland in 1996. Danaher's 1997 purchases included Current Technology and GEMS Sensors. Danaher made its two largest purchases to date in 1998 when it bought Pacific Scientific (motion controls and safety equipment) for $460 million and Fluke (electronic tools) for $625 million.

Boosting its motion-control operations, in 2000 Danaher bought Kollmorgen for about

$240 million and American Precision Industries for $185 million. In 2001 Lawrence Culp, formerly the company's COO, was named president and CEO. Later that year Danaher made a $5.5 billion offer for Cooper Industries (electric products and tools). Cooper rejected the offer and announced that it was exploring other options. Further talks with Cooper followed, but Danaher lost interest when Cooper became embroiled in asbestos lawsuits.

In 2002 Danaher bought Thomson Industries (motion control products), Gilbarco (retail automation and environmental products), and Videojet Technologies (product identification equipment). The next year it expanded its product identification business by acquiring Willett (rigid and flexible packaging labeling) and Accu-Sort Systems (bar code scanners and vision technology).

In 2004 the company acquired Gendex, the dental imaging product manufacturer, from Dentsply International. Danaher's DH-Denmark subsidiary acquired Radiometer, a Denmark-based company that makes blood gas analyzers, later that year. Danaher also acquired a product line of telecom tool and test systems from Harris Corporation in 2004.

The summer of 2005 brought along the acquisition of German optical systems maker Leica Microsystems for about $550 million. Soon after the close of the deal Danaher sold Leica's semiconductor equipment business, which had totaled sales of about $120 million, as a part of a regulatory agreement. It then tried to acquire Leica Geosystems, a company independent of Leica Microsystems, for just under $1 billion. Danaher was in competition with Sweden's Hexagon for Leica Geosystems, however, and lost out to Hexagon.

EXECUTIVES

Chairman: Steven M. Rales, age 57
President, CEO, and Director:
 H. Lawrence (Larry) Culp Jr., age 46,
 $20,525,320 total compensation
EVP and CFO: Daniel L. Comas, age 45,
 $4,182,197 total compensation
VP and Chief Accounting Officer: Robert S. Lutz, age 51
EVP: Philip W. (Phil) Knisely, age 54,
 $4,201,909 total compensation
EVP: Thomas P. Joyce Jr., age 48,
 $3,157,345 total compensation
EVP; President and CEO, Tektronix:
 James A. (Jim) Lico, age 43,
 $3,683,499 total compensation
EVP: William K. (Dan) Daniel II, age 44
SVP Finance and Tax: James H. Ditkoff, age 62
SVP and General Counsel: Jonathan P. Graham, age 48
VP and Group Executive: Richard D. (Rich) McBee, age 46
VP Regulatory Affairs and Quality Assurance:
 Frances B. L. Zee
VP Corporate Development: Daniel A. Raskas, age 42
VP and Group Executive Product Identification:
 Craig B. Purse
VP, Danaher Business System: Brian E. Burnett
VP and Group Executive; President, Danaher Sensors and Control: Alex A. Joseph
VP and Treasurer: Frank T. McFaden
VP; President, Fluke Corporation: Barbara B. Hulit
VP Human Resources: Henk van Duijnhoven, age 45
VP Investor Relations: Matt R. McGrew
Associate General Counsel and Secretary:
 James F. O'Reilly
Auditors: Ernst & Young LLP

LOCATIONS

HQ: Danaher Corporation
2099 Pennsylvania Ave. NW, 12th Fl.
Washington, DC 20006
Phone: 202-828-0850   **Fax:** 202-828-0860
Web: www.danaher.com

2008 Sales

	$ mil.	% of total
US	6,646.6	52
Germany	1,799.4	14
China	771.9	6
UK	485.8	4
Other countries	2,993.8	24
Total	**12,697.5**	**100**

PRODUCTS/OPERATIONS

2008 Sales

	$ mil.	% of total
Professional Instrumentation	4,860.8	38
Medical Technologies	3,277.0	26
Industrial Technologies	3,265.5	26
Tools & Components	1,294.2	10
Total	**12,697.5**	**100**

Selected Operations

Process/Environmental Controls
  Acme-Cleveland Corp.
  Dr. Bruno Lange GmbH (analytical instrumentation
    and reagents, Germany)
  Fluke Corporation (electronic test tools)
  GEMS Sensors, Inc. (level, flow, and pressure sensors)
  Gendex Corporation (dental imaging)
  Hengstler GmbH (force-guided relays, Germany)
  Joslyn Manufacturing Company (pole line hardware)
  Kaltenbach & Voight GmBH (KaVo, Germany)
  Radiometer America Inc. (blood gas analyzers)
  Sybron Dental Specialties, Inc. (orthodontics)
  Videojet Technologies, Inc. (coding and labeling)
  Vision Systems, Ltd. (medical pathology)

Tools and Components
  The Allen Manufacturing Company (wrenches,
    hexagonal keys)
  Armstrong Tools, Inc. (industrial hand tools)
  Delta Consolidated Industries, Inc. (truck boxes and
    industrial gang boxes)
  Hennessy Industries Inc. (wheel-service equipment)
  Holo-Krome Company (fasteners)
  Jacobs Chuck Manufacturing Company (drill chucks
    and tool-holding devices)
  Jacobs Vehicle Systems Inc. (braking systems for
    commercial vehicles)
  Matco Tools Corporation (tools for the automotive
    aftermarket)

COMPETITORS

ABB	Johnson Controls
Baldor Electric	Labfacility
Black & Decker	Makita
Bosch Rexroth Corp.	Mettler-Toledo
Cooper Industries	Parker Hannifin
Datamax-O'Neil	PerkinElmer
Dresser Wayne	Rockwell Automation
Eaton	Schneider Electric
Emerson Electric	Siemens Water
GE	Technologies
Goodrich Corp.	Snap-on
Greenlee Textron	SPX
Hilti Corp.	Stanley Works
Hitachi	Thales Air Defence
Johnson & Johnson	Thermo Fisher Scientific

HISTORICAL FINANCIALS

Company Type: Public

Income Statement

FYE: December 31

	REVENUE ($ mil.)	NET INCOME ($ mil.)	NET PROFIT MARGIN	EMPLOYEES
12/08	12,697.5	1,317.6	10.4%	50,300
12/07	11,025.9	1,369.9	12.4%	50,000
12/06	9,596.4	1,122.0	11.7%	45,000
12/05	7,984.7	897.8	11.2%	40,000
12/04	6,889.3	746.0	10.8%	35,000
Annual Growth	**16.5%**	**15.3%**	**—**	**9.5%**

2008 Year-End Financials

Debt ratio: 26.0%
Return on equity: 13.9%
Cash ($ mil.): 393
Current ratio: 1.53
Long-term debt ($ mil.): 2,553
No. of shares (mil.): 320
Dividends
  Yield: 0.2%
  Payout: 3.0%
Market value ($ mil.): 18,100

Stock History

NYSE: DHR

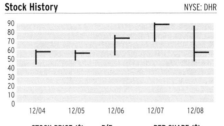

	STOCK PRICE ($) FY Close	P/E High/Low		PER SHARE ($) Earnings	Dividends	Book Value
12/08	56.61	22	12	3.95	0.12	30.68
12/07	87.74	21	16	4.19	0.11	28.42
12/06	72.44	22	16	3.48	0.08	20.78
12/05	55.78	21	18	2.76	0.07	15.89
12/04	57.41	26	19	2.30	0.06	14.45
Annual Growth	**(0.4%)**	**—**	**—**	**14.5%**	**18.9%**	**20.7%**

Darden Restaurants

This company has cornered not one but two dining markets: seafood and "Hospitaliano." Darden Restaurants is the #1 casual-dining operator (in terms of revenue), with more than 1,770 restaurants in the US and Canada. Its flagship chains include seafood segment leader Red Lobster and top Italian-themed concept Olive Garden. Both chains cater to families, with mid-priced menu items, themed interiors, and primarily suburban locations. Darden also operates the LongHorn Steakhouse, chain with more than 320 outlets. In addition, the company operates a small chain of tropical-themed Bahama Breeze restaurants that offer Caribbean-inspired food, along with a casual grill and wine bar concept called Seasons 52.

Darden, unlike rivals such as Brinker (which owns the Chili's Grill & Bar chain) and DineEquity (Applebee's), has reached the top of the casual dining food chain without the use of much franchising. While the strategy involves higher operating and development costs, the company has greater control over food quality and service at its individual eateries.

Many dining chains have suffered as a result of declining consumer spending due to the recession, but Darden's Red Lobster and Olive Garden chains continue to command significant market share thanks in part to heavy marketing efforts centered around new or selected menu items. The company has also used competitive pricing selected discounts to help boost traffic at its restaurants. Its expansion efforts have focused mainly on the Italian-themed Olive Garden, which added nearly 40 new locations during fiscal 2009. Darden has also been investing in efforts to upgrade and modernize its Red Lobster seafood eateries.

Trimming away some of its unprofitable business, the company sold its troubled Smokey Bones Barbeque & Grill concept in 2008 to an affiliate of private equity firm Sun Capital Partners for about $80 million. Smokey Bones managed to grow to almost 130 locations but struggled to find its place in the casual dining sector. The disposal came a year after Darden acquired RARE Hospitality and its LongHorn Steakhouse chain for $1.4 billion, including debt. That deal also included the smaller, upscale Capital Grille, which joined the Bahama Breeze and Seasons 52 chains as part of a new division dubbed the Specialty Restaurant Group.

HISTORY

Nineteen-year-old Bill Darden entered the restaurant business in the late 1930s with a 25-seat luncheonette called the Green Frog in Waycross, Georgia. The restaurant, which featured the slogan "Service with a Hop," was a hit, and his career was born. During the 1950s he owned a variety of restaurants, including several Howard Johnson's, Bonanza, and Kentucky Fried Chicken outlets.

Darden teamed with a group of investors in 1963 to buy an Orlando, Florida, restaurant, Gary's Duck Inn. The restaurant became the prototype for Darden's idea for a moderately priced, sit-down seafood chain. He decided to name the new chain Red Lobster, a takeoff on the old Green Frog.

The first Red Lobster opened in Lakeland, Florida, in 1968 with Joe Lee, who had worked in one of Darden's other restaurants, as its manager. It was such a success that within a month the restaurant had to be expanded. In 1970, when there were three Red Lobsters in operation and two under construction in Central Florida, Betty Crocker's boss, General Mills, bought the chain — keeping Darden on to run it.

Red Lobster was not General Mills' first foray into the restaurant business. The company opened Betty Crocker Tree House Restaurant in 1968 and acquired a fish-and-chips chain and a barbeque chain. But Red Lobster would be its first success. Rather than franchise the Red Lobster name, General Mills chose to develop the chain on its own. Lee was named president of Red Lobster in 1975, and Darden became chairman of General Mills Restaurants.

While General Mills continued to expand Red Lobster, it also sought another restaurant idea to complement the seafood chain. Among concepts tried and discarded were a steak house and Mexican and health-food restaurants. In 1980 the company decided on Italian. After two years of marketing questionnaires and recipe tests, General Mills opened a prototype Olive Garden in Orlando featuring moderately priced Italian food.

General Mills began to add outlets in the mid-1980s, and Olive Garden became another success story of the casual-dining industry.

After testing a new Chinese restaurant concept, General Mills opened its first China Coast in Orlando in 1990. The chain grew rapidly, with more than 45 units opening in a single year. The Olive Garden drive began to cool off in 1993: Same-store sales slid as competitors added Italian items to their menus. The next year Olive Garden increased its advertising budget, introduced new menu items, and began testing new formats, including smaller cafes for malls.

General Mills decided to spin off the restaurant business as a public company in 1995 and focus on consumer foods. The restaurants were renamed Darden Restaurants in honor of Bill Darden (who had died in 1994, the same year that Joe Lee was appointed CEO). That year the company abandoned its China Coast chain.

Darden Restaurants tried again in 1997 with Bahama Breeze, opening a test restaurant in Orlando. Red Lobster's sales flagged in 1997, but the company initiated a turnaround in 1998, in part by revamping Red Lobster's menu. An ill-conceived all-you-can-eat offer at Red Lobster cost Darden in profits (and led to the ousting of chain president Edna Morris after just 18 months). The company dipped into the barbecue sauce in 1999 and opened its inaugural Smokey Bones in Orlando.

The following year Darden Restaurants began expanding its Smokey Bones concept nationally.

With financial results lagging at its Bahama Breeze chain, Darden slowed growth of the concept and expanded its operating hours to include lunch business. The company also promoted former development VP Laurie Burns to lead Bahama Breeze after the unexpected resignation of Gary Heckel in 2002. Clarence Otis Jr. was appointed CEO in 2004, succeeding Joe Lee; the following year Otis added chairman to his title.

The company expanded into the steakhouse market in 2007 with its $1.4 billion (including debt) acquisition of RARE Hospitality. The following year Darden sold its unprofitable Smokey Bones Barbeque & Grill chain to an affiliate of Sun Capital Partners for about $80 million.

EXECUTIVES

Chairman and CEO: Clarence Otis Jr., age 53
President, COO, and Director:
Andrew H. (Drew) Madsen, age 53
SVP and CFO: C. Bradford (Brad) Richmond, age 50
SVP and CIO: Patti Reilly White
SVP Purchasing: Bill Herzig
SVP Supply Chain: Barry B. Moullet, age 51
SVP Human Resources: Daniel M. (Dan) Lyons, age 56
SVP and General Counsel: Paula J. Shives, age 58
SVP and Corporate Controller: Valerie K. (Val) Collins
SVP and Treasurer: Bill White
SVP Group Human Resources: Ronald Bojalad
SVP Government and Community Affairs:
Robert (Bob) McAdam, age 51
SVP; President, Olive Garden: David T. Pickens, age 54
SVP Business Development: James (J. J.) Buettgen, age 49
SVP Strategic Marketing: Roger Thompson
President, Specialty Restaurant Group:
Eugene I. (Gene) Lee Jr., age 47
President, Bahama Breeze: Laurie B. Burns, age 47
President, Red Lobster: Kim A. Lopdrup, age 51
President, LongHorn Steakhouse:
David C. (Dave) George, age 53
President, Seasons 52: Stephen Judge
President, The Capital Grille: John Martin
Auditors: KPMG LLP

LOCATIONS

HQ: Darden Restaurants, Inc.
 5900 Lake Ellenor Dr., Orlando, FL 32809
Phone: 407-245-4000   **Fax:** 407-245-5389
Web: www.dardenrestaurants.com

2009 Locations

	No.
US	
Florida	198
Texas	130
Georgia	114
California	102
Ohio	101
Pennsylvania	85
Illinois	64
Michigan	58
Virginia	56
North Carolina	53
New York	52
Tennessee	50
Indiana	49
New Jersey	46
Missouri	43
Arizona	39
Alabama	38
South Carolina	35
Maryland	34
Colorado	32
Massachusetts	31
Washington	28
Minnesota	25
Kentucky	22
Oklahoma	21
Wisconsin	19
Kansas	16
Utah	16
Iowa	15
Connecticut	14
Louisiana	14
Nevada	14
Arkansas	13
Mississippi	13
Oregon	12
Other states	86
Canada	35
Total	**1,773**

PRODUCTS/OPERATIONS

2009 Locations

	No.
Olive Garden	691
Red Lobster	690
LongHorn Steakhouse	321
The Capital Grille	37
Bahama Breeze	24
Seasons 52	8
Other	2
Total	**1,773**

COMPETITORS

Bob Evans
Brinker
Carlson Restaurants
Cheesecake Factory
Cracker Barrel
Denny's
DineEquity
Hooters
OSI Restaurant Partners
Perkins & Marie Callender's
Ruby Tuesday
Texas Roadhouse

HISTORICAL FINANCIALS

Company Type: Public

Income Statement

				FYE: Last Sunday in May
	REVENUE ($ mil.)	NET INCOME ($ mil.)	NET PROFIT MARGIN	EMPLOYEES
5/09	7,217.5	372.2	5.2%	179,000
5/08	6,626.5	377.2	5.7%	179,000
5/07	5,567.1	201.4	3.6%	157,000
5/06	5,720.6	338.2	5.9%	157,300
5/05	5,278.1	290.6	5.5%	150,100
Annual Growth	8.1%	6.4%	—	4.5%

2009 Year-End Financials

Debt ratio: 105.3%
Return on equity: 24.7%
Cash ($ mil.): 63
Current ratio: 0.51
Long-term debt ($ mil.): 1,691
No. of shares (mil.): 139
Dividends
 Yield: 2.2%
 Payout: 30.2%
Market value ($ mil.): 5,043

Stock History

NYSE: DRI

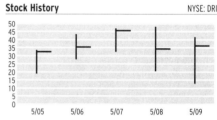

	STOCK PRICE ($) FY Close	P/E High/Low		PER SHARE ($) Earnings	Dividends	Book Value
5/09	36.17	16	5	2.65	0.80	11.52
5/08	34.25	19	8	2.55	0.72	10.11
5/07	45.57	35	24	1.35	0.46	7.85
5/06	35.41	20	13	2.16	0.40	8.82
5/05	32.48	19	11	1.78	0.08	9.13
Annual Growth	2.7%	—	—	10.5%	77.8%	6.0%

DaVita Inc.

DaVita — an Italian phrase that means "gives life" — provides life-sustaining dialysis treatments to patients suffering from end-stage renal disease (also known as chronic kidney failure). As one of the largest chains of outpatient dialysis centers, the company operates or provides administrative services to more than 1,440 centers across the US. The firm also offers home-based dialysis services, as well as inpatient dialysis in some 700 hospitals. DaVita also operates two clinical laboratories that specialize in routine testing of dialysis patients, and its DaVita Clinical Research business conducts research trials with dialysis patients.

Along with its dialysis-based revenue (which accounts for 96% of sales), DaVita offers other services related to kidney disease, including pharmacy services and the operation of chronic kidney disease management programs for employers and health plans. DaVita's Nephrology Partners business provides practice management and administrative services to physicians groups.

Most of DaVita's dialysis patients receive care under Medicare and other government-sponsored programs, and a majority of the company's revenue comes from Medicare.

DaVita decided to try its luck at a broader range of health services in 2007, acquiring a majority stake in HomeChoice Partners, an infusion therapy provider with operations in the southeastern US. The company administers intravenous medications and enteral nutrition to patients with chronic or acute conditions, both in patients' homes and at ambulatory infusion sites.

Nearly all of DaVita's outpatient dialysis centers are either wholly owned or majority-owned by the company. About 20 centers are owned by third-parties, who pay DaVita to perform administrative services.

HISTORY

Hospital chain National Medical Enterprises (NME, now Tenet) formed Medical Ambulatory Care in 1979 to run its in-hospital dialysis centers. The unit bought other centers in NME's markets. In 1994 the subsidiary's management, backed by a Donaldson, Lufkin & Jenrette (now Credit Suisse First Boston (USA)) investment fund, bought the dialysis business and renamed it Total Renal Care (TRC).

To become a leader in its consolidating field, TRC began buying other centers and soon added clinical laboratory and dialysis-related pharmacy services and home dialysis programs. It went public in 1995.

The next year the firm added 66 facilities, 32 from its acquisition of Caremark International's dialysis business. In 1997 TRC expanded abroad, buying UK-based Open Access Sonography (vein care) and partnering with UK-based Priory Hospitals Group.

In 1998 TRC bought Renal Treatment Centers, nearly doubling its size. But the acquisition costs caused a loss that year and sparked shareholder lawsuits (settled in 2000) over alleged misleading statements. The firm also became embroiled in a reimbursement dispute with Florida's Medicare program. Problems continued into 1999 as the company struggled to meld operations. The company took a charge to cover a billing shortfall, and chairman and CEO Victor Chaltiel and COO/CFO John King resigned. New management began improving billing procedures and took other cost-cutting measures.

In 2000 the company changed its name to DaVita, an Italian phrase loosely translated as "he/she gives life." It also sold its international operations to competitor Fresenius.

In 2005 the company acquired Gambro's US dialysis operations for about $3 billion, adding some 565 dialysis clinics to its operations. To meet FTC requirements for the deal, DaVita sold about 70 clinics to RenalAmerica, a company founded by former Gambro Healthcare executive Michael Klein.

EXECUTIVES

Chairman and CEO: Kent J. Thiry, age 53, $11,047,093 total compensation
COO: Dennis L. Kogod, age 49, $2,614,082 total compensation
CFO: Richard K. (Rich) Whitney, age 41
Chief Medical Officer: Allen R. Nissenson, age 62
SVP and Chief People Officer: Laura Mildenberger, age 50
SVP and Chief Compliance Officer: David T. Shapiro, age 39
SVP Communications: Richard A. Grenell

SVP: Thomas O. (Tom) Usilton Jr., age 57
SVP: Georgina Randolph, age 61
SVP: Javier Rodriguez, age 38, $3,260,547 total compensation
SVP Federal Legislative Affairs: John Schaeffler
VP: LeAnne M. Zumwalt, age 50
VP and Controller: James K. (Jim) Hilger, age 47
VP Research: Mahesh Krishnan
Director Marketing and Public Relations: Basak Ertan
Recruiting Manager: Tony Blake
Director Online Marketing: James Walker
Auditors: KPMG LLP

LOCATIONS

HQ: DaVita Inc.
601 Hawaii St., El Segundo, CA 90245
Phone: 310-536-2400   **Fax:** 310-536-2675
Web: www.davita.com

2008 Centers

	No.
California	175
Florida	120
Texas	118
Georgia	93
Pennsylvania	60
North Carolina	56
Ohio	55
Virginia	54
Michigan	52
Maryland	48
Illinois	45
Minnesota	38
Alabama	35
Missouri	35
Tennessee	33
New York	32
Indiana	30
Oklahoma	30
Louisiana	28
Colorado	27
Arizona	24
Kentucky	23
New Jersey	23
South Carolina	22
Connecticut	19
Kansas	17
Nevada	15
Washington	14
Iowa	13
Nebraska	13
Wisconsin	13
Other states	68
Total	**1,428**

PRODUCTS/OPERATIONS

2008 Revenues by Payor

	% of total
Government-based programs	
Medicare & Medicare-assigned HMO plans	59
Medicaid	4
Other government-based programs	2
Commercial	35
Total	**100**

COMPETITORS

Apria Healthcare
Dialysis Clinic Inc
Dialysis Corp.
FMCNA
Fresenius Medical Care
Gentiva
National Renal
Renal Advantage

HISTORICAL FINANCIALS

Company Type: Public

Income Statement

				FYE: December 31
	REVENUE ($ mil.)	**NET INCOME** ($ mil.)	**NET PROFIT MARGIN**	**EMPLOYEES**
12/08	5,660.2	374.2	6.6%	32,500
12/07	5,264.2	381.8	7.3%	31,000
12/06	4,880.7	289.7	5.9%	28,900
12/05	2,973.9	228.6	7.7%	28,000
12/04	2,298.6	222.3	9.7%	15,300
Annual Growth	**25.3%**	**13.9%**	—	**20.7%**

2008 Year-End Financials

Debt ratio: 185.5%
Return on equity: 20.3%
Cash ($ mil.): 411
Current ratio: 1.83
Long-term debt ($ mil.): 3,622
No. of shares (mil.): 104
Dividends
  Yield: 0.0%
  Payout: —
Market value ($ mil.): 5,155

Stock History

NYSE: DVA

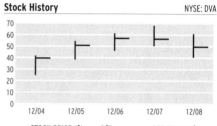

	STOCK PRICE ($) FY Close	**P/E** High/Low		**PER SHARE ($)** Earnings	Dividends	Book Value
12/08	49.57	17	12	3.53	0.00	18.77
12/07	56.35	19	14	3.55	0.00	16.66
12/06	56.88	22	17	2.74	0.00	11.98
12/05	50.64	25	18	2.20	0.00	8.18
12/04	39.53	19	12	2.16	0.00	5.03
Annual Growth	**5.8%**	—	—	**13.1%**	—	**39.0%**

Dean Foods

Dean Foods has become the king of milk by taking over other dairies' thrones. The leading US producer of fluid milk and dairy products, Dean has grown and continues to grow through acquisitions. Its retail and foodservice dairy products are sold under more than 50 regional, private-label, and national brand names, including Borden, Pet, Country Fresh, and Meadow Gold. In addition, the company manufactures coffee creamers, dips and yogurt, ice cream, and specialty dairy products (lactose-free and organic milk, soy milk, flavored milks). Dean Foods owns and operates Horizon Organic, Rachel's Organic, and WhiteWave Foods.

In order to expand its holdings in the dairy-replacement sector, the company acquired the Alpro soy beverage and food operations of Belgium's Vandemoortele for €325 million ($450 million) in 2009. Alpro is Europe's leading soy-based food and beverage business.

Adding to its retail brands, Dean acquired the milk-production plants of Foremost Farms in 2009. The acquistion added the Golden Guernsey and Morning Glory brands of fluid milk to the company roster.

In 2008 Dean entered into a 50-50 joint venture with Swiss company Hero Group, a maker of international fruit and infant-nutrition products. The venture, called Hero/WhiteWave, combines Hero's experience in fruit process engineering with WhiteWave's manufacturing network. The joint venture's first product, a chilled fruit snack called Fruit2Day, was introduced in 2009.

The company has an alliance with Land O'Lakes to market value-added dairy products under their brand, and, through licensing agreements, produces Hershey's flavored milks. In addition, Dean owns approximately 25% of Consolidated Containers (plastic beverage packaging), which supplies Dean with plastic bottles and bottle components, and is one of the US's largest makers of rigid plastic containers.

Wellington Management owns about 7% of Dean; Bank of America owns about 5%.

HISTORY

Investment banker Gregg Engles formed a holding company in 1988 with other investors, including dairy industry veteran Cletes Beshears, to buy the Reddy Ice unit of Dallas-based Southland (operator of the 7-Eleven chain). The company also bought Circle K's Sparkle Ice and combined it with Reddy Ice. By 1990 it had acquired about 15 ice plants.

The company changed its name to Suiza Foods when it bought Suiza Dairy in 1993 for $99 million. The Puerto Rican dairy was formed in 1942 by Hector Nevares Sr. and named for the Spanish word for "Swiss." By 1993 it was Puerto Rico's largest dairy, controlling about 60% of the island's milk market.

Suiza Foods bought Florida's Velda Farms, manufacturer and distributor of milk and dairy products, in 1994. The company went public in 1996, the same year it bought Swiss Dairy (dairy products, California and Nevada) and Garrido y Compañía (coffee products, Puerto Rico).

The company became one of the largest players in the North American dairy industry through its acquisitions in 1997. It paid $960 million for Morningstar (Lactaid brand lactose-free milk, Second Nature brand egg substitute), which — like Suiza Foods itself — was a Dallas-based company formed in 1988 through a Southland divestiture. The company entered the Midwest with its $98 million purchase of Country Fresh and the Northeast with the Bernon family's Massachusetts-based group of dairy and packaging companies, including Garelick Farms and Franklin Plastics (packaging).

Suiza Foods strengthened its presence in the southeastern US in 1998 with its $287 million acquisition of Land-O-Sun Dairies, operator of 13 fluid-dairy and ice-cream processing facilities. Also that year Suiza Foods purchased Continental Can (plastic packaging) for about $345 million and sold Reddy Ice to Packaged Ice for $172 million.

After settling an antitrust lawsuit brought by the US Department of Justice, in 1999 Suiza Foods bought dairy processors in Colorado, Ohio, and Virginia. That year Suiza Foods combined its US packaging operations with Reid Plastics to form Consolidated Containers, retaining about 40% of the new company.

In 2001 Suiza Foods announced it had agreed to purchase rival Dean Foods for $1.5 billion and the assumption of $1 billion worth of debt. Dean Foods had begun as Dean Evaporated Milk, founded in 1925 by Sam Dean, a Chicago evaporated-milk broker. By the mid-1930s it had moved into the fresh milk industry. The company went public in 1961 and was renamed Dean Foods in 1963.

Suiza Foods completed the acquisition and took on the Dean Foods name later in 2001. The new Dean Foods bought out Dairy Farmers of America's interest in Suiza Dairy and merged it with the "old" Dean's fluid-dairy operations to create its internal division, Dean Dairy Group.

Along with the purchase of "old" Dean came a 36% ownership of soy milk maker WhiteWave, and in 2002 Dean Foods purchased the remaining 64%. By the end of the year, Dean had sold off some smaller businesses (boiled peanuts and contract hauling) and its Puerto Rico operations.

During 2003 Dean purchased Michigan milk processor Melody Farms, sold off its frozen non-dairy topping and creamer business to Rich Products, and renamed its Morningstar Foods division Dean Branded Products Group. With an eye on adding organic milk, Dean purchased 13% of Horizon Organic in 2003 and acquired the remainder of the company in 2004. Dean then purchased Michael Foods' dairy products unit Kohler Mix Specialties, including three plants that produce mixes for ice cream and frozen yogurt, soy milk, and coffee creamers; it also acquired Cremora brand non-dairy creamer from Eagle Family Foods.

Dean purchased Milk Products of Alabama and Ross Swiss Dairies of California in 2004. Overseas, Dean acquired Tiger Foods, a dairy processing firm located in Spain.

The next year the company sold Dean's Dips and Marie's Dressings to Ventura Foods. The company spun also off its specialty foods group to its shareholders as TreeHouse Foods in 2005. TreeHouse makes private-label products such as pickles and non-dairy powdered coffee creamers and various regional brands; it also gained several former Dean Foods brands, including Mocha Mix non-dairy creamers and Second Nature egg substitute.

Dean began a concerted marketing campaign in 2006, touting its hormone-free milk sold under the Schepps brand as an alternative to organic milk, which is more expensive.

EXECUTIVES

Chairman and CEO; President, Dairy Group: Gregg L. Engles, age 51
EVP and CFO: John F. (Jack) Callahan Jr., age 50
SVP and CIO: Barbara D. Carlini, age 49
SVP and Chief Accounting Officer: Ronald L. McCrummen
EVP and Chief Supply Chain Officer: Gregg A. Tanner, age 52
EVP Human Resources: Paul T. Moskowitz, age 44
EVP and Chief Strategy and Transformation Officer: Gregory A. (Greg) McKelvey, age 35
EVP, General Counsel, and Secretary: Steven J. Kemps, age 45
EVP Research and Development: Kelly Duffin-Maxwell, age 44
SVP Business Optimization: Rick Fehr, age 57
SVP Government and Industry Relations: Williams C. (Bill) Tinklepaugh
SVP, Sales and COO, Morningstar Operations: John Robinson, age 47
SVP Innovation: Debra B. (Debbie) Carosella, age 52
SVP Corporate Development: Edward F. Fugger Jr.
VP and Treasurer: Timothy A. (Tim) Smith
VP, Corporate Communications: Marguerite Copel
President and CEO, WhiteWave Foods and Morningstar: Joseph E. (Joe) Scalzo, age 50
President, Indulgent Foods: Michael H. (Mike) Keown
President, Horizon Organic: Blaine E. McPeak
President, Fresh DairyDirect: Harrald F. Kroeker, age 51
Auditors: Deloitte & Touche LLP

LOCATIONS

HQ: Dean Foods Company
2515 McKinney Ave., Ste. 1200, Dallas, TX 75201
Phone: 214-303-3400 **Fax:** 214-303-3499
Web: www.deanfoods.com

PRODUCTS/OPERATIONS

2008 Sales

	$ mil.	% of total
DSD Dairy	9,804.6	79
WhiteWave-Morningstar	2,650.0	21
Total	**12,454.6**	**100**

2008 Sales

	% of total
Company brands	52
Private-label products	48
Total	**100**

Selected Brands

Alpro
Alta Dena
Arctic Splash
Barbe's
Barbers
Berkeley Farms
Borden (licensed)
Brown Cow
Brown's Dairy
Bud's Ice Cream
Chug
Country Charm
Country Churn
Country Delite
Country Fresh
Country Love
Creamland
Dairy Fresh
Dean's
Dipzz
Fieldcrest
Foremost (licensed)
Garelick Farms
Golden Guernsey
Hershey's (licensed)
Hygeia
LAND O'LAKES (licensed)
Land-O-Sun
Lehigh Valley Dairy Farms
Mayfield
McArthur
Meadow Brook
Meadow Gold
Mile High Ice Cream
Morning Glory
Mountain High
Nature's Pride
Nurture
Oak Farms
Pet (licensed)
Pog (licensed)
Price's
Purity
Reiter
Saunders
Schenkel's All*Star
Schepps
Sealtest (licensed)
Shenandoah's Pride
Skinny Cow (licensed)
Stroh's
Swiss Dairy
Swiss Premium
Turtle Tracks
Tuscan
Verifine
Viva

COMPETITORS

American Milk Products
Associated Milk Producers
Aurora Organic Dairy
Bel Brands USA
BelGioioso Cheese
Ben & Jerry's
Blistex
Blue Bell
Brewster Dairy
California Dairies Inc.
ConAgra
Crystal Farms Refrigerated Distribution Company
Dairy Farmers of America
Dannon
Danone
Darigold, Inc.
Dreyer's
Ellsworth Cooperative
Foremost Farms
Foster Dairy Farms
Galaxy Nutritional Foods
Great Lakes Cheese
Guida's
Hain Celestial
Hiland Dairy
HP Hood
Kemps, LLC
Kraft Foods
Leprino Foods
Lifeway Foods
Marathon Cheese
Maryland & Virginia Milk Producers
Mayfield Dairy Farms
Morinaga
National Dairy Holdings
Nestlé USA
Northwest Dairy
Organic Valley
Prairie Farms Dairy
Quality Chekd
Rockview Dairies
Saputo Cheese USA Inc.
Springfield Creamery
Stonyfield Farm
Tillamook County Creamery Association
Tofutti Brands
United Dairy Farmers
Vitasoy International
Wells' Dairy

HISTORICAL FINANCIALS

Company Type: Public

Income Statement

FYE: December 31

	REVENUE ($ mil.)	NET INCOME ($ mil.)	NET PROFIT MARGIN	EMPLOYEES
12/08	12,454.6	183.8	1.5%	25,820
12/07	11,821.9	131.4	1.1%	25,585
12/06	10,098.6	225.4	2.2%	26,348
12/05	10,505.6	329.1	3.1%	27,030
12/04	10,822.3	285.4	2.6%	28,610
Annual Growth	3.6%	(10.4%)	—	(2.5%)

2008 Year-End Financials

Debt ratio: 747.7%
Return on equity: 60.3%
Cash ($ mil.): 36
Current ratio: 1.04
Long-term debt ($ mil.): 4,174
No. of shares (mil.): 180
Dividends
  Yield: 0.0%
  Payout: —
Market value ($ mil.): 3,240

Stock History

NYSE: DF

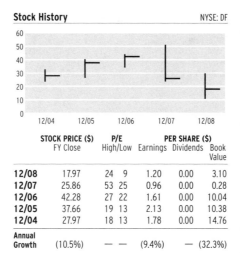

	STOCK PRICE ($) FY Close	P/E High/Low		PER SHARE ($) Earnings	Dividends	Book Value
12/08	17.97	24	9	1.20	0.00	3.10
12/07	25.86	53	25	0.96	0.00	0.28
12/06	42.28	27	22	1.61	0.00	10.04
12/05	37.66	19	13	2.13	0.00	10.38
12/04	27.97	18	13	1.78	0.00	14.76
Annual Growth	(10.5%)	—	—	(9.4%)	—	(32.3%)

Deere & Company

You might say that Deere & Company enjoys having its customers going to seed. The company, one of the world's two largest makers of farm equipment (CNH Global is the other), is also a leading producer of construction, forestry, industrial, and lawn care equipment. It is famous for its "Nothing Runs Like A Deere" brand marketing campaign.

Its farm equipment includes tractors, tillers, harvesting machinery, and soil-preparation machinery. Construction equipment includes backhoes, skid steers, dump trucks, waste equipment, and excavators. For the forestry industry Deere makes harvesters, feller bunchers, and knuckleboom loaders. Deere's other products include residential and commercial lawn care products and equipment, and golf and turf care products.

The drop in new housing starts is having an impact on Deere's Construction & Forestry division. Production was lowered in an effort to clear retail inventories. In 2009 sales of construction and forestry equipment in the US deteriorated even further. Beset, like many manufacturers, by higher costs for basic materials and for transporting products, Deere set plans to close its plant in Welland, Ontario, Canada. The company will transfer production from that facility by the end of 2009 to other plants in Mexico and the US.

In 2008 Deere acquired San Diego-based T-Systems International, which makes a variety of products for the agricultural, nursery, landscape, and greenhouse markets. A month after it acquired T-Systems, Deere bought Israel-based Plastro Irrigation Systems, a leading maker of irrigation system components. The two acquisitions made John Deere Water Technologies one of the top agricultural irrigation companies in the world.

Early in 2008 the company took a 50% ownership in Xuzhou Xuwa Excavator Machinery (XCG), the third-largest maker of excavator equipment in China. Later in 2008 the company signed an agreement with Ashok Leyland of India to make backhoes and four-wheel-drive loaders. As part of the joint venture agreement, Deere will build a manufacturing facility there, with production slated to begin in 2010.

In 2009 Deere named company veteran Sam Allen CEO — only the ninth in the company's history — as part of a planned succession.

HISTORY

Vermont-born John Deere moved to Grand Detour, Illinois, in 1836 and set up a blacksmith shop. Deere and other pioneers had trouble with the rich, black soil of the Midwest sticking to iron plows designed for sandy eastern soils, so in 1837 Deere used a circular steel saw blade to create a self-scouring plow that moved so quickly, it was nicknamed the "whistling plow." He sold only three in 1838, but by 1842 he was making 25 a week.

Deere moved his enterprise to Moline in 1847. His son Charles joined the company in 1853, beginning a tradition of family management. (All five Deere presidents before 1982 were related by blood or marriage.) Charles set up an independent-dealership distribution system and added wagons, buggies, and corn planters to the product line.

Under Charles' son-in-law, William Butterworth (president, 1907-28), Deere bought agricultural equipment companies and developed harvesters and tractors with internal combustion engines. Butterworth's nephew, Charles Wiman, became president in 1928. He extended credit to farmers during the Depression and won customer loyalty. In 1931 Deere opened its first non-US plant in Canada.

William Hewitt, Wiman's son-in-law, became CEO in 1955. Deere passed International Harvester in 1958 to become the #1 US maker of farm equipment; by 1963 it led the world. Deere expanded into Argentina, France, Mexico, and Spain, and it used research and joint ventures abroad (Yanmar, small tractors, 1977; Hitachi, excavators, 1983) to diversify.

Robert Hanson became the first nonfamily CEO in 1982. He poured $2 billion into research and development during the 1980s. Despite an industry-wide sales slump resulting in losses totaling $328 million in 1986-87, Deere was the only major agricultural equipment maker to neither change ownership nor close factories during the 1980s. Instead, Deere cut its workforce 44% and improved efficiency.

In 1989 Deere introduced its largest (at the time) new product offering — the 9000 series of combines. Deere also acquired Funk Manufacturing (powertrain components), and Hans Becherer succeeded Hanson as CEO.

During the 1990s Deere expanded its lawn-care equipment business, mainly in Europe. In 1991 it bought a majority stake in Sabo-Maschinenfabrik (commercial lawn mowers, Germany). After spending most of the early 1990s in the doldrums because of recession and weak farm prices, Deere rebounded.

Deere signed a deal to sell combines in Ukraine (1996), and it formed a joint venture in 1997 to make combines in China. Fading demand for agricultural equipment at home and jeopardized sales contracts from failing economies in Asia, Brazil, and former Soviet states caused layoffs of about 2,400 workers in 1998 and production cutbacks in 1998-99.

In 2000 Deere purchased Finland-based Metso Corporation's Timberjack forestry-equipment business. President and COO Robert Lane succeeded Becherer as chairman and CEO. Deere bought McGinnis Farms — the US's largest horticultural products distributor — in 2001.

That year it cut production due to soft demand. Late in 2001 Deere said it would add to its previously announced job cuts, bringing the total to about 3,000 jobs. Deere also acquired Richton International Corporation; that deal included Richton's landscape irrigation-equipment distributor Century Supply (#1 in the US) and Richton Technology Group (hardware, software, and systems support services).

In 2004 Deere announced that it, along with iRobot, would develop a battlefield vehicle for the US Army. Pilot production began in mid-2005. In 2006 Deere sold John Deere Health Care (now named UnitedHealthcare Services Company of the River Valley, Inc) to UnitedHealth Group for half a billion dollars.

In 2007 Deere added to its barn-full of turf, lawn, and landscape products when it bought LESCO, Inc. The addition of LESCO roughly doubled the number of store locations for Deere's John Deere Landscapes division, with the addition of 345 stores and 114 Stores-on-Wheels.

Looking to address demand for small tractors in a key global market, later in 2007 Deere acquired Ningbo Benye Tractor & Automobile Manufacture, based in southern China.

EXECUTIVES

Chairman: Robert W. (Bob) Lane, age 59
CEO and Director: Samuel R. (Sam) Allen, age 55
SVP and CFO: Michael J. Mack Jr., age 52
VP Information Technology: James R. (Jim) Jabanoski
VP and Chief Compliance Officer: Linda E. Newborn
EVP Strategic Manufacturing and Engineering, Global Tractor and Implement Sourcing (Worldwide Agricultural Equipment): Adel A. Zakaria
EVP Worldwide Parts Services, Global Supply Management and Logistics, Enterprise Information Technology, and Corporate Communications: H. J. Markley, age 58
SVP and General Counsel: James R. Jenkins, age 63
SVP, John Deere Power Systems: Jean Gilles
VP Human Resources: Mertroe B. Hornbuckle
VP Investor Relations: Marie Z. Ziegler, age 51
VP and Treasurer: James A. Davlin
President Water Technologies: Michael McGrady
President, Agricultural Division, North America, Australia, Asia and Global Tractor and Implement Sourcing: David C. Everitt, age 56
President, Worldwide Commercial and Consumer Equipment Division: James M. Field, age 45
President, John Deere Credit: James A. Israel, age 52
President, Agricultural Division, Europe, Africa, and South America and Global Harvesting Equipment Sourcing: Markwart von Pentz, age 45
Secretary and Associate General Counsel: Gregory R. Noe
Auditors: Deloitte & Touche LLP

LOCATIONS

HQ: Deere & Company
1 John Deere Place, Moline, IL 61265
Phone: 309-765-8000 **Fax:** 309-765-5671
Web: www.deere.com

2008 Sales

	$ mil.	% of total
US & Canada	17,065	60
Other countries	11,373	40
Total	**28,438**	**100**

PRODUCTS/OPERATIONS

2008 Sales

	$ mil.	% of total
Agricultural equipment	16,572	58
Construction & forestry	4,818	17
Commercial & consumer equipment	4,413	15
Credit	2,190	8
Other	445	2
Total	**28,438**	**100**

Selected Products and Services

Agricultural Equipment
  Combines
  Cotton harvesting equipment
  Cutters and shredders
  Hay and forage equipment
  Material handling equipment
  Planting and seeding equipment
  Scrapers
  Sprayers
  Tillage
  Tractors
Construction and Forestry Equipment
  Articulated dump trucks
  Backhoe loaders
  Crawler dozers
  Crawler loaders
  Excavators
  Forestry harvesters
  Forklifts
  Landscape loaders
  Log skidders
  Motor graders
  Skid steers
Commercial and Consumer Equipment
  All terrain vehicles
  Golf course equipment
  Lawn and garden tractors
  Riding and walk-behind mowers
  Skid-steer loaders
  Snow equipment
  Trimmers, blowers, and saws
  Utility tractors
  Zero-turn mowers
Credit
  Leasing
  Retail and wholesale financing
Power Systems
  Diesel and natural gas engines
  Powertrain components
  Transmissions

COMPETITORS

AGCO
Black & Decker
Briggs & Stratton
Buhler Industries
Caterpillar
CNH Global
FMC
Foley Machinery
Ford Motor
GE
Great Plains Manufacturing
Honda
Ingersoll-Rand
Komatsu
Kubota
Mahindra
Marubeni-Komatsu
Navistar International
Terex
Toro
Uzel Makina Sanayi
Volvo
Woods Equipment

HISTORICAL FINANCIALS

Company Type: Public

Income Statement

FYE: October 31

	REVENUE ($ mil.)	NET INCOME ($ mil.)	NET PROFIT MARGIN	EMPLOYEES
10/08	28,437.6	2,052.8	7.2%	56,700
10/07	24,082.2	1,821.7	7.6%	52,000
10/06	22,147.8	1,693.8	7.6%	46,500
10/05	21,930.5	1,446.8	6.6%	47,400
10/04	19,986.1	1,406.1	7.0%	46,500
Annual Growth	**9.2%**	**9.9%**	**—**	**5.1%**

2008 Year-End Financials

Debt ratio: 212.8%
Return on equity: 30.0%
Cash ($ mil.): 2,211
Current ratio: 1.95
Long-term debt ($ mil.): 13,899
No. of shares (mil.): 423
Dividends
Yield: 2.7%
Payout: 22.6%
Market value ($ mil.): 16,309

Stock History

NYSE: DE

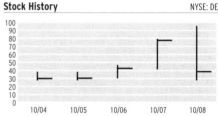

	STOCK PRICE ($) FY Close	P/E High/Low		PER SHARE ($) Earnings	Dividends	Book Value
10/08	38.56	20	6	4.70	1.06	15.45
10/07	77.45	20	11	4.00	0.91	16.92
10/06	42.56	13	9	3.59	0.78	17.71
10/05	30.34	13	10	2.93	0.61	16.20
10/04	29.89	13	10	2.78	0.53	15.11
Annual Growth	**6.6%**	**—**	**—**	**14.0%**	**18.9%**	**0.5%**

Del Monte Foods

How does Del Monte's garden grow? Very well indeed. It is one of the US's largest manufacturers of branded canned fruit, vegetables, and soups and broths. Its flagship products (canned corn, green beans, peas, peaches, pears, and pineapples) are purchased mostly from US growers. The company makes tomato-based foods such as ketchup and tomato sauce. Its retail brands include College Inn, Del Monte, and Contadina. Del Monte makes pets grow too, with a stable of pet-food and -treat brands, including 9Lives, Gravy Train, Milk-Bone, and Meow Mix. The company also makes private-label products and food ingredients for other food manufacturers, and offers products to foodservice operators.

The company sold its seafood operations, including StarKist, to Korean fishery business, Dongwon Industries, for approximately $359 million in 2008. The sale allowed Del Monte to focus on its faster-growing, higher-margin, value-added, branded businesses.

The company has 17 US production and 10 distribution facilities, as well as operations in Mexico and Venezuela. The Del Monte brand is licensed to other companies internationally.

Wal-Mart and SAM'S CLUB accounted for some 34% of Del Monte's 2009 sales.

HISTORY

Fred Tillman adopted the name Del Monte (originally the name of a coffee blend made for the fancy Hotel Del Monte in Monterey, California) in 1891 for use at his newly formed Oakland Preserving Company. Brand-name labeling was becoming a significant marketing tool, and Del Monte ("of the mountain" in Spanish) became known for high value.

In 1899 Oakland Preserving merged into the California Fruit Canners Association (CFCA) with 17 other canneries (half of California's canning industry). The new company, the largest canner in the world, adopted Del Monte as its main brand name. CFCA merged with other California canneries in 1916 to form Calpak, and created national demand for Del Monte products through mass advertising. The company's first ad appeared in the *Saturday Evening Post* in 1917.

Calpak expanded into the Midwest in 1925 by acquiring Rochelle Canneries (Illinois). That year it established British Sales Limited and Philippine Packing Corporation. In later years the company expanded into the Philippines. It weathered slow growth during the Depression, but WWII jump-started Calpak's operations — in 1942 about 40% of the company's products went to feed US troops — and the postwar boom kicked it into high gear.

The company bought control of Canadian Canners Limited, the world's second-largest canner, in 1956, gaining entry into the heavily protected British market. In the 1960s a venture into soft-drink products ended in failure. Calpak changed its name to Del Monte Foods in 1967.

RJR Industries bought Del Monte in 1979 as part of a diversification strategy. In 1989, after its buyout by Kohlberg Kravis Roberts, the newly named, debt-laden RJR Nabisco began selling assets, including Del Monte's Hawaiian Punch line in 1990 and its tropical fruit unit. Merrill Lynch and Del Monte executives bought Del Monte's domestic canning operations in 1990, but the transaction loaded the new company with debt.

To reduce debt, during the 1990s Del Monte sold its dried-fruit operations, its pudding division (to Kraft), and its Mexican subsidiary. Texas Pacific Group, an investment partnership known for recruiting specialists to revive companies, acquired a controlling interest in Del Monte in 1997. It installed Richard Wolford, former president of Dole Packaged Foods, as CEO. That year the company bought Contadina's canned tomato products from Nestlé (which kept the right to use the Contadina brand on refrigerated pasta and sauces).

Interested again in expanding in foreign markets, in 1998 it bought back from Nabisco the rights to the Del Monte brand in South America, and it purchased Nabisco's canned fruits and vegetables business in Venezuela. In 1999 the company completed its IPO. Later that year Del Monte purchased a vegetable processing plant from its competitor Birds Eye Foods and, like all food canners, enjoyed robust sales to Y2K-wary shoppers.

In 2000 Del Monte acquired the Sunfresh brand (citrus and tropical fruits) and a distribution center from The UniMark Group for more than $14 million. Del Monte acquired the S&W brand of canned fruits and vegetables, tomatoes, dry beans, and specialty sauces from bankrupted cooperative Tri Valley Growers for about $39 million in 2001.

Del Monte's 2002 acquisitions from Heinz shifted a mixed bag of stagnant mature brands off Heinz's plate and more than doubled Del Monte's sales. In addition to StarKist tuna, the deal included Heinz's North American pet food business (9Lives, Kibbles 'n Bits), its US baby food business, and College Inn canned broths.

In 2004 Del Monte sold three of its pet-food brands (IVD, Medi-Cal, and Techni-Cal) to French pet-food company Royal Canin. That same year Del Monte acquired Industrias Citricolas de Montemorelos, (ICMOSA), the Mexican subsidiary of The UniMark Group. ICMOSA is a processed tropical and citrus fruit producer and distributor.

The company sold private-label soup and baby food business Nature's Goodness to TreeHouse Foods for about $275 million in 2006. (The TreeHouse deal did not include College Inn broths.)

Later that same year, it purchased the Milk-Bone pet product brand from Kraft for $580 million. In addition, it acquired privately held cat food maker Meow Mix Holdings, Inc., for $705 million. These moves were undertaken in the company's ongoing strategy to focus on higher margin, branded products.

EXECUTIVES

Chairman, President, and CEO: Richard G. Wolford, age 64
COO: Nils Lommerin, age 44
EVP Administration and CFO: David L. Meyers, age 63
SVP Corporate Service Center and Chief Information Officer: Marc Brown, age 49
SVP, Chief Accounting Officer, and Controller: Richard L. French, age 52
SVP and Chief Marketing Officer: William D. (Bill) Pearce, age 46
SVP and Chief Human Resources Officer: Richard W. Muto
EVP Sales: Timothy A. (Tim) Cole, age 52
SVP, General Counsel, and Secretary: James G. Potter, age 52
SVP Operations and Supply Chain: David W. (Dave) Allen, age 48
SVP Finance and Investor Relations: Larry Bodner
investor Relations: Katherine Husseini
Auditors: KPMG LLP

LOCATIONS

HQ: Del Monte Foods Company
1 Market @ The Landmark
San Francisco, CA 94105
Phone: 415-247-3000   **Fax:** 415-247-3565
Web: www.delmonte.com

2009 Sales

	$ mil.	% of total
US	3,420.0	94
Other countries	206.9	6
Total	**3,626.9**	**100**

PRODUCTS/OPERATIONS

2009 Sales

	$ mil.	% of total
Consumer products	1,953.5	54
Pet products	1,673.4	46
Total	**3,626.9**	**100**

Selected Brand Names

Consumer products
 College Inn
 Contadina
 Del Monte
 S&W

Pet products
 9Lives
 Alley Cat
 Canine Carry Outs
 Gravy Train
 Jerky Treats
 Kibbles 'n Bits
 Meaty Bone
 Meow Mix
 Milk-Bone
 Nature's Recipe
 Pounce
 Pup-Peroni
 Snausages
 Wagwells

Selected Products

Canned soup and broth
Canned fruit (apricots, cherries, fruit cocktail, mandarin oranges, mixed and tropical mixed fruit, peaches, pears, pineapples)
Pet food and treats
Sauces (pizza, spaghetti, sloppy joe)
Tomatoes (chunky, crushed, diced, ketchup, stewed, paste, purée, sauce)
Vegetables (asparagus, carrots, corn, mixed and flavored vegetables, peas, potatoes, spinach, zucchini, and green, lima, and wax beans)

COMPETITORS

Bush Brothers
Campbell Soup
Chiquita Brands
Colgate-Palmolive
ConAgra
Dole Food
General Mills
Goya
Hanover Foods
Heinz
Hill's Pet Nutrition
Kraft Foods
Mars, Incorporated
Mars Petcare
Morgan Foods
Nestlé Purina PetCare
Pacific Coast Producers
Pictsweet
Procter & Gamble
Pro-Fac
Royal Canin
Seneca Foods
Unilever

HISTORICAL FINANCIALS

Company Type: Public

Income Statement

FYE: Sunday nearest April 30

	REVENUE ($ mil.)	NET INCOME ($ mil.)	NET PROFIT MARGIN	EMPLOYEES
4/09	3,626.9	172.3	4.8%	5,400
4/08	3,736.8	133.1	3.6%	18,100
4/07	3,414.9	112.6	3.3%	18,200
4/06	2,998.6	169.9	5.7%	16,700
4/05	3,180.9	117.9	3.7%	17,500
Annual Growth	3.3%	9.9%	—	(25.5%)

2009 Year-End Financials

Debt ratio: 95.0%
Return on equity: 11.1%
Cash ($ mil.): 143
Current ratio: 2.26
Long-term debt ($ mil.): 1,526

No. of shares (mil.): 198
Dividends
 Yield: 2.1%
 Payout: 18.4%
Market value ($ mil.): 1,493

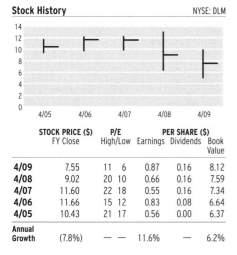

Stock History
NYSE: DLM

	STOCK PRICE ($) FY Close	P/E High/Low		Earnings	PER SHARE ($) Dividends	Book Value
4/09	7.55	11	6	0.87	0.16	8.12
4/08	9.02	20	10	0.66	0.16	7.59
4/07	11.60	22	18	0.55	0.16	7.34
4/06	11.66	15	12	0.83	0.08	6.64
4/05	10.43	21	17	0.56	0.00	6.37
Annual Growth	(7.8%)	—	—	11.6%	—	6.2%

Dell Inc.

Dell wants its name to ring from the desktop to the data center. One of the world's top suppliers of personal computers, the company offers a broad range of technology products for the consumer, education, enterprise, and government sectors. In addition to a full line of desktop and notebook PCs, Dell offers network servers, data storage systems, printers, Ethernet switches, and peripherals such as displays and projectors. It also markets third-party software and hardware. Dell's growing services unit provides infrastructure consulting, systems integration, asset recovery, financing, support, and training.

Michael Dell pioneered the direct-sales model for computers and took the company from his dorm room to the top of the PC heap by keeping it focused on a simple formula: Eliminate the middleman and sell for less. Dell's built-to-order boxes allow for lower inventories, lower costs, and higher profit margins — elements that have served it well through PC price wars and IT spending recessions.

Faced with slowing sales rates in the domestic PC market, Michael Dell has overseen an aggressive campaign to reposition the company for growth. Most significantly Dell has shifted its sales approach. Prior to 2007 Dell had practically no retail presence. Since then the company has partnered with stores such as Best Buy and Wal-Mart, as well as systems integrators, resellers, and distributors worldwide.

The company is looking to international revenue from developing markets such as Brazil, China, India, and Russia to supplant weak sales in the US. The company has also looked overseas to find operational cost-saving opportunities. Based in Singapore, Dell's Asia/Pacific segment includes manufacturing and distribution units in China, India, and Malaysia. The company has made major investments in its call center and development units in India in recent years. Closer to home, the company closed its Austin, Texas-based desktop PC manufacturing facility in 2008. It also shuttered customer care centers in Canada.

Generating about 60% of its sales from desktop and notebook PCs, Dell faces intense competition in the consolidating market it shares with Hewlett-Packard, Acer, and Lenovo. The company's PC sales have followed an industry trend that favors mobile computers; Dell's notebook line, it's largest revenue generator, accounted for almost a third of its sales in fiscal 2009.

The company also provides servers, storage devices, and networking equipment. Dell's storage line includes its PowerVault systems and devices from EMC that it resells. Early in 2008 Dell acquired storage systems provider EqualLogic for $1.4 billion. The purchase expanded Dell's offerings for small and midsized businesses.

The company's software and peripherals segment encompasses Dell-branded displays and printers, as well as third-party peripherals, consumer and enterprise software, digital cameras, printers, and televisions.

Michael Dell owns about 12% of the company.

HISTORY

At age 13 Michael Dell was already a successful businessman. From his parents' home in Houston, Dell ran a mail-order stamp trading business that, within a few months, grossed more than $2,000. At 16 he sold newspaper subscriptions and at 17 bought his first BMW. When Dell enrolled at the University of Texas in 1983, he was thoroughly bitten by the entrepreneurial bug.

Dell started college as a pre-med student but found time to establish a business selling random-access memory (RAM) chips and disk drives for IBM PCs. Dell bought products at cost from IBM dealers, who were required at the time to order from IBM large monthly quotas of PCs, which frequently exceeded demand. Dell resold his stock through newspapers and computer magazines at 10%-15% below retail.

By April 1984 Dell's dorm room computer-components business was grossing about $80,000 a month — enough to persuade him to drop out of college. Soon he started making and selling IBM clones under the brand name PC's Limited. Dell sold his machines directly to consumers rather than through retail outlets, as most manufacturers did. By eliminating the retail markup, Dell could sell PCs at about 40% of the price of an IBM.

The company was plagued by management changes during the mid-1980s. Renamed Dell Computer, it added international sales offices in 1987. In 1988 the company started selling to larger customers, including government agencies. That year Dell went public.

The company tripped in 1990, reporting a 64% drop in profits. Sales were growing — but so were costs, mostly because of efforts to design a PC using proprietary components and reduced instruction set computer (RISC) chips. Within a year Dell turned itself around by cutting inventories and introducing new products.

Dell entered the retail arena by letting Soft Warehouse (now CompUSA) in 1990 and office supply chain Staples in 1991 sell its PCs at mail-order prices, but the computer maker abandoned retail stores in 1994 to refocus on its mail-order origins. It also retooled its troubled notebook computer line and introduced servers.

In 1996 the company started selling PCs through its Web site. The next year Dell entered the market for workstations and strengthened its consumer business by separating it from its small-business unit and launching a leasing program for consumers. In 1998 the company stepped up manufacturing in the Americas and Europe and added a production and customer facility in China.

In 1999 the company made its first acquisition — storage area network equipment maker ConvergeNet. Faced with slumping PC sales in early 2001, the company eliminated 1,700 jobs — about 4% of its workforce. Late that year it expanded its storage offerings when it agreed to resell systems from EMC. Looking to grow its services unit, Dell acquired Microsoft software support specialist Plural in 2002.

The following year the company shortened its name to simply Dell Inc. Dell himself stepped down as CEO in mid-July 2004. Company president Kevin Rollins filled the position, but Dell remained chairman.

In 2007 Rollins resigned as CEO and as a member of the board of directors, and Dell reassumed the top role. Rollins' resignation came as the company struggled with a number of difficult issues, most notably disappointing earnings and an SEC investigation into its finances. (Dell restated several years of financial results after an audit revealed accounting irregularities.)

In mid-2007 the company announced plans to cut its workforce by 10% over the next year.

EXECUTIVES

Chairman and CEO: Michael S. Dell, age 44, $2,125,713 total compensation
Vice Chairman, Operations and Technology: Jeffrey W. (Jeff) Clarke, age 46
SVP and CFO: Brian T. Gladden, age 44, $9,339,626 total compensation
VP and Chief Marketing Officer: Erin Nelson, age 39
SVP, General Counsel, and Secretary: Lawrence P. (Larry) Tu, age 54
SVP Enterprise Product Group: Bradley R. (Brad) Anderson, age 49
SVP; President, Europe, Middle East, and Africa: David A. Marmonti, age 49
SVP Human Resources: Andrew C. (Andy) Esparza, age 50
VP Finance; President, Dell Financial Services: Don Berman
VP Finance; CFO, Dell Financial Services: Gavan Goss
VP Sales and Marketing Consumer Business: Michael Tatelman
VP and General Manager, Small and Medium Business, Dell Americas: Erik Dithmer
President, Public Sector: Paul D. Bell, age 48
President, Global Consumer Group: Ronald G. (Ron) Garriques, age 45, $10,969,558 total compensation
President, Global Large Enterprise: Stephen F. (Steve) Schuckenbrock, age 48, $10,665,312 total compensation
President, Global Small and Medium Business: Stephen J. (Steve) Felice, age 51
Director Global Benefits and Mobility: Kathleen Angel
Media Contact: Venancio Figueroa
Auditors: PricewaterhouseCoopers LLP

LOCATIONS

HQ: Dell Inc.
1 Dell Way, Round Rock, TX 78682
Phone: 512-338-4400   **Fax:** 512-283-6161
Web: www.dell.com

2009 Sales

	$ mil.	% of total
US	31,569	52
Other countries	29,532	48
Total	**61,101**	**100**

2009 Sales

	$ mil.	% of total
Commercial		
Americas	28,614	47
Europe, Middle East & Africa	13,617	22
Asia/Pacific	7,341	12
Consumer	11,529	19
Total	**61,101**	**100**

PRODUCTS/OPERATIONS

2009 Sales

	$ mil.	% of total
Mobility	18,638	31
Desktop PCs	17,244	29
Software & peripherals	10,603	17
Servers & networking	6,275	10
Services	5,715	9
Storage	2,626	4
Total	**61,101**	**100**

Selected Products

Computers
    Desktop (Dimension, OptiPlex, Vostro, XPS)
    Notebook (Adamo, Inspiron, Latitude, Vostro, XPS)
Enterprise systems
    Network servers (PowerEdge)
    Storage (EqualLogic, PowerVault)
    Workstations (Precision)
Ethernet switches (PowerConnect)
Point-of-sale systems
Printers
    Inkjet multifunction
    Laser
Projectors
Refurbished systems
Third-party peripherals and software

COMPETITORS

3Com
Acer
Apple Inc.
ASUSTeK
Brother Industries
Canon
CDW
Cisco Systems
EMC
Enterasys
Epson
Extreme Networks
Fujitsu Technology Solutions
Gateway, Inc.
HCL Infosystems
Hedy Holding
Hewlett-Packard
Hitachi
Hitachi Data Systems
IBM
Insight Enterprises
Lenovo
MPC Computers
NEC
Panasonic Corp
Positivo Informática
Sony
Sun Microsystems
Toshiba
Unisys

HISTORICAL FINANCIALS

Company Type: Public

Income Statement

FYE: Sunday nearest January 31

	REVENUE ($ mil.)	NET INCOME ($ mil.)	NET PROFIT MARGIN	EMPLOYEES
1/09	61,101.0	2,478.0	4.1%	78,900
1/08	61,133.0	2,947.0	4.8%	88,200
1/07	57,420.0	2,583.0	4.5%	90,500
1/06	55,908.0	3,572.0	6.4%	66,100
1/05	49,205.0	3,043.0	6.2%	56,000
Annual Growth	5.6%	(5.0%)	—	8.9%

2009 Year-End Financials

Debt ratio: 44.4%
Return on equity: 61.9%
Cash ($ mil.): 8,352
Current ratio: 1.36
Long-term debt ($ mil.): 1,898

No. of shares (mil.): 1,954
Dividends
    Yield: 0.0%
    Payout: —
Market value ($ mil.): 18,563

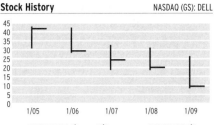

Stock History

NASDAQ (GS): DELL

	STOCK PRICE ($) FY Close	P/E High/Low		Earnings	PER SHARE ($) Dividends	Book Value
1/09	9.50	21	7	1.25	0.00	2.19
1/08	20.04	23	14	1.31	0.00	1.91
1/07	24.22	28	17	1.14	0.00	2.21
1/06	29.31	29	20	1.46	0.00	2.11
1/05	41.76	36	26	1.18	0.00	3.32
Annual Growth	(30.9%)	—	—	1.5%	—	(9.9%)

Deloitte Touche Tohmatsu

This company is "deloitted" to make your acquaintance, particularly if you're a big business in need of accounting services. Deloitte Touche Tohmatsu (dba Deloitte) is one of accounting's Big Four, along with Ernst & Young, KPMG, and PricewaterhouseCoopers. Deloitte operates through four business lines — audit, tax, consulting, and financial advisory services. In addition to audit and fiscal oversight services, Deloitte firms provide human resources and technology services. The group comprises some 150 independent firms in about 140 countries. Units include Deloitte & Touche (the US accounting arm) and Deloitte Consulting. Consulting and tax each account for about a quarter of Deloitte's revenues.

Deloitte's consulting arm grew through acquisition in 2008. Its life sciences unit acquired Recombitant Capital (now operating as Deloitte Recap), which operates a life sciences subscription database and advisory services with 20 years of industry data. The company also acquired the assets of IT consultantcy Solbourne, which served corporate and public clients.

Also in 2008 Deloitte sold its grants and incentives division in the Netherlands and Belgium to PNO Consultants, allowing the group to focus on that region's auditing operations. The following year, Deloitte purchased the North American public services practice of BearingPoint in 2009, which had filed for Chapter 11 bankruptcy protection. The $350 million deal increases Deloitte's presence in the growing government services market.

HISTORY

In 1845 William Deloitte opened an accounting office in London, at first soliciting business from bankrupts. The growth of joint stock companies and the development of stock markets in the mid-19th century created a need for standardized financial reporting and fueled the rise of auditing, and Deloitte moved into the new field.

The Great Western Railway appointed him as its independent auditor (the first anywhere) in 1849.

In 1890 John Griffiths, who had become a partner in 1869, opened the company's first US office in New York City. Four decades later branches had opened throughout the US. In 1952 the firm partnered with Haskins & Sells, which operated 34 US offices.

Deloitte aimed to be "the Cadillac, not the Ford" of accounting. The firm, which became Deloitte Haskins & Sells in 1978, began shedding its conservatism as competition heated up; it was the first of the major accountancy firms to use aggressive ads.

The firm spent the 1980s and 1990s pursuing a strategy of using accountants and consultants in concert to provide seamless service in auditing, accounting, strategic planning, information technology, financial management, and productivity. In 1984 Deloitte Haskins & Sells tried to merge with Price Waterhouse, but the deal was dropped after Price Waterhouse's UK partners objected.

In 1989 Deloitte Haskins & Sells joined the flamboyant Touche Ross (founded 1899) to become Deloitte & Touche. Touche Ross's Japanese affiliate, Ross Tohmatsu (founded 1968) rounded out the current name. The merger was engineered by Deloitte's Michael Cook and Touche's Edward Kangas, in part to unite the former firm's US and European strengths with the latter's Asian presence. Cook continued to oversee US operations, with Kangas presiding over international operations. Many affiliates, particularly in the UK, rejected the merger and defected to competing firms.

As auditors were increasingly held accountable for the financial results of their clients, legal action soared. In the 1990s Deloitte was sued because of its actions relating to Drexel Burnham Lambert junk bond king Michael Milken, the failure of several savings and loans, and clients' bankruptcies.

Nevertheless, in 1995 the SEC chose Michael Sutton, the firm's national director of auditing and accounting practice, as its chief accountant. That year Deloitte formed Deloitte & Touche Consulting to consolidate its US and UK consulting operations; its Asian consulting operations were later added to facilitate regional expansion. Deloitte Consulting became Deloitte's fastest-growing line, offering strategic and management consulting in addition to information technology and human resources consulting services.

Increasingly, Deloitte and its peers came under fire for their combined accounting/consulting operations; regulators and observers wondered whether accountants could maintain objectivity when they were auditing clients for whom they also provided consulting services.

The Asian economic crisis hurt overseas expansion in 1998, but provided a boost in restructuring consulting. In 1999 the firm sold its accounting staffing service unit (Resources Connection) to its managers and Evercore Partners, citing possible conflicts of interest with its core audit business. Also that year Kangas stepped down as CEO to be succeeded by James Copeland.

In 2001 the SEC forced Deloitte & Touche to restate the financial results of Pre-Paid Legal Services. In an unusual move, Deloitte & Touche publicly disagreed with the SEC's findings.

The accountancy put some old trouble to bed in 2003 when it agreed to pay $23 million to settle claims it had been negligent in its auditing of failed Kentucky Life Insurance, a client in the 1980s. Later that year the UK's High Court found

Deloitte negligent in audits related to the failed Barings Bank; however, the ruling was considered something of a victory for the accountancy because it essentially cleared Deloitte of the majority of charges against it and effectively limited its financial liability in the matter.

Copeland retired from the global CEO's office that year and handed the reins over to Bill Parrett, who had formerly served as managing director for the US and the Americas. Parrett was succeeded in 2007 by Jim Quigley, who'd served as CEO of Deloitte's US arm.

EXECUTIVES

Chairman: John P. Connolly
CEO: James H. (Jim) Quigley, age 57
CFO: Jeffrey P. (Jeff) Rohr
Chief Information Officer: Wolfgang Richter
Chief Diversity Officer: James H. (Jim) Wall
Chief Strategy Officer: Mumtaz Ahmed
Chief Knowledge Officer: Tracey Edwards
Global Managing Partner Consulting and Executive Member, US: Ainar D. Aijala Jr.
Executive Member and Country Leader, Germany: Wolfgang Grewe
Executive Member and Country Leader, United States: Barry Salzberg, age 55
Global Managing Partner Regulatory and Risk and Executive Member, US: Jeffrey K. (Jeff) Willemain
Executive Member and Country Leader, United Kingdom: Martin J. A. Eadon
Executive Member and Country Leader, Canada: Alan N. MacGibbon
Executive Member and Country Leader, France: Jean-Paul Picard
Executive Member and Country Leader, Netherlands: Roger J. M. Dassen
Executive Member and Country Leader, Japan: Ryoji Sato
General Counsel: Philip Rotner
Director Global PR and CEO Communications: Madonna Jarrett
Global Brand and Marketing Director: Luis Gallardo
Human Resources Operations: Peter May

LOCATIONS

HQ: Deloitte Touche Tohmatsu
1633 Broadway, New York, NY 10019
Phone: 212-489-1600   **Fax:** 212-489-1687
Web: www.deloitte.com/dtt

PRODUCTS/OPERATIONS

2008 Sales

	% of total
Audit	46
Consulting	23
Tax	22
Financial advisory services	9
Total	**100**

2008 Sales by Industry

	% of total
Financial services	23
Consumer business & transportation	19
Manufacturing	14
Telecommunications, media & technology	12
Energy & resources	8
Public sector	7
Life sciences	7
Real estate	5
Other	5
Total	**100**

Selected Products and Services

Audit
  Auditing services
  Global offerings services
  International financial reporting conversion services
Consulting
  Enterprise applications
  Human capital
  Outsourcing
  Strategy and operations
  Technology integration
Enterprise Risk Services
  Capital markets
  Control assurance
  Corporate responsibility and sustainability
  Internal audit
  Regulatory consulting
  Security and privacy services
Financial Advisory
  Corporate finance
  Forensic services
  Reorganization services
  Transaction services
  Valuation services
Merger and Acquisition Services
Tax
  Corporate tax
  Global tax compliance
  Indirect tax
  International assignment services
  International tax
  M&A transaction services
  Research and development credits
  Tax publications
  Tax technologies
  Transfer pricing

COMPETITORS

Accenture
BDO International
Booz Allen
Boston Consulting
Capgemini
EDS
Ernst & Young Global
Grant Thornton International
KPMG
Marsh & McLennan
McKinsey & Company
PricewaterhouseCoopers
Towers Perrin

HISTORICAL FINANCIALS

Company Type: Partnership

Income Statement

FYE: May 31

	REVENUE ($ mil.)	NET INCOME ($ mil.)	NET PROFIT MARGIN	EMPLOYEES
5/08	27,400.0	—	—	165,000
5/07	23,100.0	—	—	146,600
5/06	20,000.0	—	—	135,000
5/05	18,200.0	—	—	121,283
5/04	16,400.0	—	—	115,000
Annual Growth	13.7%	—	—	9.4%

Revenue History

Delta Air Lines

Just as a delta is a symbol for change in math, Delta Air Lines symbolizes the changing mathematics of the airline industry. Delta became the world's largest airline by traffic after its $2.8 billion October 2008 acquisition of Northwest Airlines. Through its regional carriers (including subsidiary Comair), the combined company serves more than 375 destinations in more than 65 countries, and it operates a mainline fleet of about 775 aircraft. Delta is also part of the SkyTeam marketing and code-sharing alliance (allows airlines to sell tickets on one another's flights and thus extend their networks), which includes carriers such as Air France and KLM.

The SkyTeam alliance extends Delta's reach to more than 900 destinations in almost 170 countries around the globe.

After its acquisition of Northwest, Delta kept its name and continues to be run from its Atlanta headquarters by CEO Richard Anderson (who left Northwest Airlines in 2007 to lead Delta). Although both carriers will eventually merge into one company, they will continue to function as separate airlines until the integration is completed.

Throughout 2008 the deal faced several hurdles, including review by antitrust regulators and initial opposition from Northwest's unionized pilots, who unlike those at Delta were unable to reach agreement on a contract to fly for the combined company before the Delta-Northwest deal was completed. A month after the acquisition was announced, a deal was finally struck, and both sets of pilots were given raises and an equity stake in the combined company.

The combination with Northwest represents a major milestone in Delta's efforts to grow since emerging from Chapter 11 bankruptcy protection in 2007. In its restructuring, Delta worked not only to cut costs but also to boost its international service. Demand for overseas flights has increased as business activity in regions other than the US has picked up, and US carriers typically encounter less price competition on most overseas routes. To expand its service in the Asia/Pacific region, Delta has joined other major airlines in applying for some of the limited number of nonstop routes available between the US and mainland China. The carrier began flights between Atlanta and Shanghai in early 2008.

Delta and Northwest expect to profit from a joint venture with Air France-KLM that covers the carriers' transatlantic flights. The airlines will share revenue and split the cost of transatlantic flights between the US, Canada, Mexico, Europe, the Mediterranean, Africa, the Middle East, India, and Latin America. The effort takes advantage of the Open Skies agreement between the US and Europe, which took effect in 2008 and allows transatlantic service by more airlines between more cities.

To support its growth initiatives, Delta has shifted some of its wide-body jets from domestic to international service. The company at the same time is working to reduce costs in its domestic operations by using smaller aircraft, including regional jets.

Rising fuel prices have caused the carrier to renew its efforts to control costs. In 2008 Delta offered buyout packages to about 30,000 of the company's 55,000 employees, and about 4,000 accepted — twice the number expected.

HISTORY

Delta Air Lines was founded in Macon, Georgia, in 1924 as the world's first crop-dusting service, Huff-Daland Dusters, to combat boll weevil infestation of cotton fields. It moved to Monroe, Louisiana, in 1925. In 1928 field manager C. E. Woolman and two partners bought the service and renamed it Delta Air Service after the Mississippi Delta region it served.

In 1929 Delta pioneered passenger service from Dallas to Jackson, Mississippi. Flying mail without a government subsidy, Delta finally got a US Postal Service contract in 1934 to fly from Fort Worth to Charleston via Atlanta. Delta relocated to Atlanta in 1941. Woolman became president in 1945 and managed the airline until he died in 1966.

Delta added more flights, including a direct route from Chicago to New Orleans with its 1952 purchase of Chicago and Southern Airlines. It offered its first transcontinental flight in 1961. In 1972 the airline bought Northeast Airlines and added service to New England and Canada; it offered service to the UK in 1978, the year that the US airline industry was deregulated.

In 1982 Delta's employees pledged $30 million to buy a Boeing 767 jet, christened *The Spirit of Delta*, as a token of appreciation. In fiscal 1983 the company succumbed to the weak US economy and posted its first loss ever; it quickly became profitable again in 1985. Delta began service to Asia in 1987, the year that longtime employee Ronald Allen became CEO. In 1990 Delta joined TWA and Northwest to form Worldspan, a computer reservation service.

Despite a slump in 1990 earnings, in 1991 Delta bought gates, planes, and Canadian routes from Eastern, as well as Pan Am's New York-Boston shuttle, European routes, and Frankfurt hub. The purchases elevated Delta from a domestic player to a top international carrier, but they also contributed to a $2 billion loss.

Allen began a cost-reduction plan in 1994 that cut many routes and 15,000 jobs over the next three years. However, it also drove down employee morale and Delta's customer service reputation. Allen was let go in 1997 and replaced by Leo Mullin, a former electric utility chief.

Delta bought regional carriers Atlantic Southeast Airlines and Comair. An 89-day pilots' strike led to flight cancellations at Comair in 2001.

In the wake of the September 11, 2001, terrorist attacks on New York and Washington, DC, and the resulting reduction in air travel, Delta cut back its flight schedule and reduced its workforce by about 15% (about 13,000 employees).

In 2003 CEO Leo Mullin resigned and was replaced by Gerald Grinstein, a Delta director. Also in 2003, the federal government approved the largest code-share agreement among US airlines, which included Delta as well as Continental and Northwest.

Delta cut costs significantly during 2005 in an effort to avoid bankruptcy. In a last-ditch bid to raise cash, the company sold its Atlantic Southeast Airlines unit to SkyWest for $425 million in September 2005. Days later, however, the combination of high fuel prices and a string of losses from operations dating back to 2001 finally forced Delta to file for Chapter 11 protection.

A milestone in Delta's journey back to solvency was reached in May 2006, when the company's pilots voted to accept a contract with changes in pay, benefits, and work rules designed to save Delta about $280 million a year. Delta exited Chapter 11 in April 2007 as an independent company.

EXECUTIVES

Non-Executive Chairman: Daniel A. (Dan) Carp, age 60
Non-Executive Vice Chairman: Roy J. Bostock, age 68
CEO and Director: Richard H. Anderson, age 53, $5,888,812 total compensation
President and CEO, NWA: Edward H. (Ed) Bastian, age 51, $8,780,764 total compensation
EVP and COO: Stephen E. Gorman, age 54, $5,410,336 total compensation
SVP and CFO: Hank Halter, age 44, $2,478,215 total compensation
SVP and CIO: Theresa Wise
SVP and Chief Communications Officer: John E. (Ned) Walker, age 56
EVP Human Resources and Labor Relations: Michael H. (Mike) Campbell, age 60, $5,004,133 total compensation
EVP Network Planning and Revenue Management: Glen W. Hauenstein, age 48, $6,007,162 total compensation
EVP and COO, Northwest Airlines: Michael J. (Mike) Becker, age 47
SVP Government Affairs: D. Scott Yohe
SVP International: Laura H. Liu
SVP Finance and Treasurer: Paul A. Jacobson
SVP Finance and Controller: Raymond E. (Ray) Winborne Jr., age 40
SVP Marketing: Tim Mapes
SVP and General Counsel: Richard B. (Ben) Hirst, age 64
SVP Human Resources: Elizabeth (Beth) Johnston
SVP Global Sales and Distribution: Jim Cron
Auditors: Ernst & Young LLP

LOCATIONS

HQ: Delta Air Lines, Inc.
1030 Delta Blvd., Atlanta, GA 30320
Phone: 404-715-2600 **Fax:** 404-715-5042
Web: www.delta.com

2008 Sales

	$ mil.	% of total
North America	15,065	66
Atlantic	5,149	23
Latin America	1,616	7
Pacific	867	4
Total	**22,697**	**100**

PRODUCTS/OPERATIONS

2008 Sales

	$ mil.	% of total
Passenger		
Mainline	15,137	67
Regional affiliates	4,446	20
Cargo	686	3
Other	2,428	10
Total	**22,697**	**100**

COMPETITORS

ACE Aviation
AirTran Holdings
Alaska Air
AMR Corp.
British Airways
Cathay Pacific
Japan Airlines
JetBlue
Lufthansa
Qantas
SAS
Singapore Airlines
Southwest Airlines
UAL
US Airways
Virgin Atlantic Airways

HISTORICAL FINANCIALS

Company Type: Public

Income Statement

FYE: December 31

	REVENUE ($ mil.)	NET INCOME ($ mil.)	NET PROFIT MARGIN	EMPLOYEES
12/08	22,697.0	(8,922.0)	—	84,306
12/07	19,154.0	1,612.0	8.4%	55,044
12/06	17,171.0	(6,203.0)	—	51,300
12/05	16,191.0	(3,818.0)	—	55,700
12/04	15,002.0	(5,198.0)	—	69,150
Annual Growth	**10.9%**	**—**	**—**	**5.1%**

2008 Year-End Financials

Debt ratio: 1,763.3%
Return on equity: —
Cash ($ mil.): 4,255
Current ratio: 0.81
Long-term debt ($ mil.): 15,411

No. of shares (mil.): 778
Dividends
Yield: 0.0%
Payout: —
Market value ($ mil.): 8,912

Stock History

NYSE: DAL

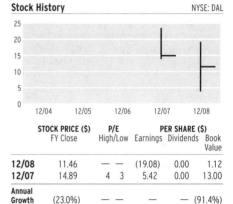

	STOCK PRICE ($) FY Close	P/E High/Low		PER SHARE ($) Earnings	Dividends	Book Value
12/08	11.46	—	—	(19.08)	0.00	1.12
12/07	14.89	4	3	5.42	0.00	13.00
Annual Growth	**(23.0%)**	**—**	**—**	**—**	**—**	**(91.4%)**

Deluxe Corporation

When money can move at the speed of a mouse click, Deluxe wants to do more than keep its revenues in check. The company is a leading printer of checks in the US, serving the nation's banks, credit unions, and financial services companies. Checks and business forms account for the majority of Deluxe's sales; it also sells checkbook covers and address labels, as well as stationery, greeting cards, labels, and packaging supplies online. Deluxe also sells stored-value gift cards. The company's Direct Checks division is the nation's #1 direct-to-consumer seller of personal and business checks under the brands Checks Unlimited and Designer Checks.

Check writing was already on the decline, due to the shift to electronic payment methods, when the recession in the US and turmoil in the financial services industry conspired to depress check volume even more. As a result, Deluxe Corporation's revenue declined more than 7% in 2008 vs. 2007 after falling nearly 2% in the year-earlier period.

To compensate, Deluxe has been shifting its focus from checks to small business services with the aim of becoming a leading supplier of checks, business forms, Web services, marketing materials, and more to these clients. The firm is looking to expand in high-growth areas, including payroll, fraud protection, and Web services. Beefing up its small business offerings, in 2008 the company made several acquisitions, including Web services company Hostopia.com and business social networking company PartnerUp.

In a bid to drive down costs amid decreasing sales, in 2009 Deluxe plans to close five manufacturing facilities. In recent years the firm has closed three other plants. The shutdowns come as the firm moves to expand its use of digital printing processes.

The company was dethroned from the top position in its industry as a result of the 2007 merger of its two primary competitors: check printers John H. Harland and Clarke American to form Harland Clarke.

HISTORY

Deluxe Corporation began in 1915 with the determination of William Hotchkiss, a newspaper publisher turned chicken farmer, to produce one product "better, faster, and more economically than anyone else." From his office in St. Paul, Minnesota, Hotchkiss set out to provide banks with business checks within 48 hours of receiving the order. Deluxe Check Printers made just $23 that year. However, when a new Federal Reserve Bank was established in Minneapolis, the region soon became a major national banking center.

In the 1920s Hotchkiss introduced the most successful product in Deluxe's history: the Handy, a pocket-sized check. During the Depression the company cut employee hours and pay, but not jobs.

George McSweeney, a sales manager, created the Personalized Check Program in 1939 and was named president two years later. During WWII he stabilized the company by printing ration forms for banks. In the 1950s Deluxe was one of the first firms to implement the government's magnetic-ink character-recognition program.

By 1960 the company was selling its printing services to 99% of US commercial banks. Deluxe went public in 1965. The company integrated computers and advanced printing technology into production during the 1970s.

In the following decade Deluxe positioned itself to profit from the increasing automation of transactions, making acquisitions such as Chex-Systems (account verification, 1984), Colwell Systems (medical business forms, 1985), A. O. Smith Data Systems (banking software, 1986), and Current (mail-order greeting cards and checks, 1987). It established a UK base in 1992 with Stockforms Ltd. (computer forms). Deluxe closed about a fourth of its check-printing plants in 1993, the first layoffs in the firm's history.

When Gus Blanchard became president and CEO of Deluxe (the first outsider to do so) the following year, he began a major reorganization. In 1996 he initiated a plan to close more than 20 check-printing plants and eliminate 1,200 jobs (completed 1999). He pursued international business, including a joint venture to provide electronic financial services to India's banking system.

Deluxe bought Fusion Marketing Group (customized database marketing services) in 1997. The next year, through a joint venture with Fair, Isaac and Company (now Fair Isaac Corporation) and Acxiom Corp., Deluxe developed FraudFinder,

a computerized system to rate a merchant's risk in accepting an individual's check or debit card. Increasing its focus on financial services, the company sold off its greeting card, specialty paper, and marketing database businesses. Also in 1998 it began offering check ordering over the Internet and via voice-recognition technology.

The company bought eFunds, which provides the retail and financial sectors with electronic transaction and payment-protection technology. Deluxe also bought the remaining stake of its venture with HCL in 1999, renaming it iDLX and merging it into eFunds. Deluxe spun off the unit in 2000 to focus on paper payment systems.

Also in 2000 Deluxe bought Designer Checks. The next year Deluxe began offering Disney characters on checks, the first time Disney characters have been licensed to appear on personal checks. Also in 2001, Lawrence Mosner was named chairman and CEO of the company.

Looking to grow its small business customer roster, Deluxe purchased Massachusetts-based New England Business Service (NEBS), a provider of business forms and other products to North American small businesses, in 2004. Deluxe combined the operations of NEBS with its former Business Services operations to form its Small Business Services unit.

Mosner retired as chairman and CEO late in 2005. Company president Ronald Eilers succeeded Mosner as CEO on an interim basis; director Stephen Nachtsheim was named chairman. Lee Schram, previously at NCR Corporation, took over the CEO role in 2006. Soon after Schram took over, Deluxe announced cost-cutting measures designed to save the company some $150 million by the end of 2008. The cost-reduction initiatives included consolidating its call-center and check-fulfillment efforts, as well as more efficient manufacturing, supply chain, and shared services.

In August 2008 Deluxe acquired Hostopia.com Inc., a provider of Web services to small businesses with an Internet presence, for C$124 million (about US$96 million).

EXECUTIVES

Chairman: Stephen P. Nachtsheim, age 64
CEO and Director: Lee J. Schram, age 47, $2,260,027 total compensation
SVP and CFO: Richard S. Greene, age 44, $754,617 total compensation
SVP and CIO: Malcolm J. McRoberts, age 44
VP Investor Relations and Chief Accounting Officer: Terry D. Peterson, age 44, $468,560 total compensation
SVP and Chief Sales and Marketing Officer, Financial Institutions and Small Businesses: Luann E. Widener, age 51, $1,662,610 total compensation
SVP, General Counsel, and Secretary: Anthony C. Scarfone, age 47, $696,857 total compensation
SVP; President, Financial Services: Thomas L. (Tom) Morefield, age 46, $402,338 total compensation
SVP Human Resources: Julie M. Loosbrock, age 49
VP Sales and Marketing Direct-to-Consumer: Lynn R. Koldenhoven, age 42
VP Fulfillment: Pete J. Godich, age 44
VP Enterprise Brand, Customer Experience, and Media Relations: Laura L. Radewald, age 48
Corporate and Media Communications: Nicki Gibbs
Auditors: PricewaterhouseCoopers LLP

LOCATIONS

HQ: Deluxe Corporation
3680 Victoria St. North, Shoreview, MN 55126
Phone: 651-483-7111 **Fax:** 651-481-4163
Web: www.deluxe.com

2008 Sales

	$ mil.	% of total
US	1,397.7	95
Foreign, primarily Canada	71.0	5
Total	**1,468.7**	**100**

PRODUCTS/OPERATIONS

2008 Sales

	$ mil.	% of total
Small Business Services	851.1	58
Financial Services	430.0	29
Direct Checks	187.6	13
Total	**1,468.7**	**100**

2008 Sales

	$ mil.	% of total
Checks & related services	960.8	65
Other printed products, including forms	329.0	23
Accessories & promotional products	109.8	7
Packaging supplies & other	69.1	5
Total	**1,468.7**	**100**

Selected Products and Services

Small Business Services (checks, forms, and related products; sold to small offices and home offices)
Financial Services
  Account conversion support
  Check merchandising
  Checks and related products
  Customized reporting
  File management
  Fraud prevention
Direct Checks (checks and related products; sold to consumers)

COMPETITORS

American Banknote
Cenveo
Checks In The Mail
Ennis
Harland Clarke
M & F Worldwide
MDC Partners
Northstar Computer Forms
R.R. Donnelley
Standard Register

HISTORICAL FINANCIALS

Company Type: Public

Income Statement

FYE: December 31

	REVENUE ($ mil.)	NET INCOME ($ mil.)	NET PROFIT MARGIN	EMPLOYEES
12/08	1,468.7	101.6	6.9%	7,172
12/07	1,606.4	143.5	8.9%	7,991
12/06	1,639.7	101.0	6.2%	8,396
12/05	1,716.3	157.5	9.2%	8,310
12/04	1,567.0	198.0	12.6%	8,955
Annual Growth	**(1.6%)**	**(15.4%)**	**—**	**(5.4%)**

2008 Year-End Financials

Debt ratio: 1,458.4%	No. of shares (mil.): 51
Return on equity: 215.8%	Dividends
Cash ($ mil.): 16	Yield: 6.7%
Current ratio: 0.59	Payout: 50.8%
Long-term debt ($ mil.): 774	Market value ($ mil.): 765

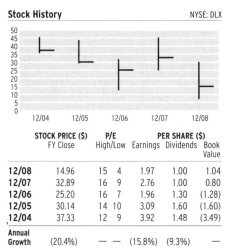

	STOCK PRICE ($)	P/E		PER SHARE ($)		
	FY Close	High/Low		Earnings	Dividends	Book Value
12/08	14.96	15	4	1.97	1.00	1.04
12/07	32.89	16	9	2.76	1.00	0.80
12/06	25.20	16	7	1.96	1.30	(1.28)
12/05	30.14	14	10	3.09	1.60	(1.60)
12/04	37.33	12	9	3.92	1.48	(3.49)
Annual Growth	(20.4%)	—	—	(15.8%)	(9.3%)	—

Denny's Corporation

Feel like getting slammed for breakfast? The home of the Grand Slam Breakfast, Denny's is one of the leading full-service, family-style restaurant chains in the US, with more than 1,500 of its signature eateries located across the country. Its family-style restaurants are typically open 24 hours a day, seven days a week, and serve breakfast, lunch, and dinner. The menu features a variety of breakfast items (which account for the majority of company sales) along with such standard fare as hamburgers, steaks, salads, and desserts. The company owns and operates more than 250 of its restaurants, while the rest are franchised or operate under licensing agreements.

Denny's lives by the adage that says breakfast is the most important meal of the day: Its morning menu has traditionally accounted for a majority of sales. However, the company has been focused on increasing its share of business coming from the lunch and dinner crowd by introducing new menu items and marketing its chain as a nighttime meal destination.

At the same time, Denny's has been contracting its portfolio of corporate-owned restaurants under an initiative to expand its franchising operations. During 2008 it sold nearly 80 restaurants to new and existing franchisees; the company has refranchised more than 200 since starting the initiative in 2007. It hopes the program will attract additional experienced operators while also reducing the company's direct exposure to the sometimes volatile dining business. Franchising and licensing fees account for more than 10% of sales.

HISTORY

Denny's traces its roots to a Lockwood, California, doughnut stand called Danny's Donuts. Opened in 1953 by serial entrepreneur Harold Butler, Danny's was an instant hit and soon began offering coffee and sandwiches along with the doughnuts. Butler changed the name of his business to Danny's Coffee Shop the next year and began expanding. By the end of the decade, Butler had 20 shops in operation. He renamed the chain Denny's in 1959. Concentrated near major highways and freeway exits, Denny's expanded rapidly to more than 80 shops in seven western states. The company went public in 1966.

Denny's pushed eastward with its expansion, reaching about 200 locations by 1968. That year the company acquired other chains such as Sandy's Restaurants and Winchell's Donut Houses. Looking to expand his business into new markets, Butler made an offer to buy Parvin-Dohrmann, the company that owned Las Vegas' landmark Caesar's Palace. The deal soured, however, after government regulators charged Butler had privately sweetened the deal to certain shareholders. Denny's stock tumbled after the scandal and Butler left the company in 1971.

Doughnut mogul Verne Winchell took over as CEO and helped rebuild Denny's fortunes. With a focused expansion plan, the company grew to more than 1,300 outlets by 1977 — about half of them were Denny's Coffee Shops and the other half were Winchell's. That year Denny's introduced its Grand Slam Breakfast. With the addition of the El Pollo Loco grilled-chicken chain in 1983, Denny's operations had expanded to more than 2,000 restaurants, including 1,200 of its signature eateries.

A group led by then president Vern Curtis took the company private for $750 million in 1985. The deal left Denny's saddled with hefty debt, however, and in 1987 the company spun off a 58% stake in its Winchell's business to the public to help raise cash. Later that year, however, Denny's was acquired by TW Services for $830 million in cash and assumed debt.

TW Services owned the hodgepodge of businesses left after Trans World Corporation had spun off its airline, TWA, in 1984. (TWA was later acquired by American Airlines parent AMR Corporation.) Its operations included the Hardee's and Quincy's Family Steakhouse chains, Canteen food and vending business, and American Medical Services. Corporate raider Coniston Partners bought TW Services for $1.7 billion in 1989 and immediately sold off the rest of Winchell's. The medical business was sold the next year. In 1992 Kohlberg Kravis Roberts bought a 47% stake in the remaining food services operations, which began doing business as Flagstar Companies the next year.

Flagstar's history got off to a rough start when patrons who claimed they were denied service because of race filed several lawsuits against its Denny's chain. Most notable was a suit filed by six African-American US Secret Service agents in Maryland. Denny's settled the suits for $54 million in 1994, one of the largest class-action settlements for a hospitality company.

In 1995 chairman and CEO Jerome Richardson stepped down from his executive position to devote more time to his new expansion football franchise, the Carolina Panthers. The company named former Burger King chief James Adamson as the new CEO. (Adamson also became chairman just four months later; in 1996 the NAACP named him Chief Executive of the Year.) It later bought the Coco's, Jojo's, and Carrows chains from Family Restaurants in 1996.

Soft sales and continued losses, however, forced the company to file for Chapter 11 bankruptcy protection in 1997. It emerged from bankruptcy the next year with a new name, Advantica Restaurant Group. That year the company sold its nearly 600 Hardee's fast-food units to CKE Restaurants, the Hardee's franchiser, and its Quincy's chain to Buckley Acquisition. In 1999 the company sold its El Pollo Loco chain to American Securities Capital Partners.

In 2000 Advantica refranchised nearly 150 restaurants that year, and in early 2001 Advantica sold another 28 restaurants to franchisees and added 40 new Denny's locations. Late that year James Adamson retired; director Charles Moran was named chairman and Nelson Marchioli, the former president of El Pollo Loco, was named CEO.

In 2002 Advantica sold its FRD Acquisition subsidiary (now Catalina Restaurant Group), the unit that oversaw Coco's and Carrows. Having shed all its other operations, the company changed its name to Denny's later that year. Moran died in 2004 and was replaced by Robert Marks. The following year Denny's closed several underperforming restaurants and began beefing up its franchising efforts. Debra Smithart-Oglesby was named chairman in 2006 when Marks retired.

EXECUTIVES

Chairman: Debra Smithart-Oglesby, age 54
President, CEO, and Director; President and CEO, Denny's Inc.: Nelson J. Marchioli, age 59, $2,605,941 total compensation
EVP and COO: Janis S. Emplit, age 53, $1,006,207 total compensation
EVP, CFO, and Chief Administrative Officer: F. Mark Wolfinger, age 53, $1,581,805 total compensation
VP Information Technology and CIO, Denny's Corporation and Denny's Inc.: S. Alex Lewis
SVP, General Counsel, Chief Legal Officer, and Assistant Secretary, Denny's Inc.: Timothy E. Flemming
VP, Corporate Controller, and Chief Accounting Officer, Denny's Corporation and Denny's Inc.: Jay C. Gilmore
EVP, Chief Marketing Officer, and Innovation Officer: Mark E. Chmiel, age 54, $752,592 total compensation
SVP Human Resources and Diversity, Denny's Corporation and Denny's Inc.: Louis M. Laguardia, age 60
VP Tax and Treasurer, Denny's Corporation and Denny's Inc.: Ross B. Nell
VP Risk Management and Assets Protection, Denny's Corporation and Denny's Inc.: Michael J. Jank
VP Operations Strategy and Support, Denny's Inc.: Susan L. Mirdamadi
Director Public Relations: Debbie Atkins
Assistant General Counsel, Corporate Governance Officer, and Secretary: J. Scott Melton
Auditors: KPMG LLP

LOCATIONS

HQ: Denny's Corporation
203 E. Main St., Spartanburg, SC 29319
Phone: 864-597-8000   **Fax:** 864-597-8780
Web: www.dennys.com

2008 Locations

US	No.
California	406
Florida	159
Texas	158
Arizona	75
Illinois	52
Washington	51
New York	42
Pennsylvania	36
Indiana	32
Missouri	32
Ohio	32
Nevada	28
Colorado	26
Virginia	24
Maryland	23
New Mexico	23
Oregon	23
Michigan	22
Utah	21
North Carolina	18
Wisconsin	17
Minnesota	15
Georgia	13
South Carolina	13
Kentucky	12
Oklahoma	12
New Jersey	11
Arkansas	9
Connecticut	8
Kansas	8
Hawaii	7
Idaho	7
Other states	53
International	77
Total	**1,541**

PRODUCTS/OPERATIONS

2008 Sales

	$ mil.	% of total
Restaurants	648.3	85
Franchising & licensing	112.0	15
Total	**760.3**	**100**

2008 Locations

	No.
Franchised	1,226
Company-owned	315
Total	**1,541**

COMPETITORS

Bob Evans	Huddle House
Brinker	OSI Restaurant Partners
Buffets Holdings	Perkins & Marie
Carlson Restaurants	Callender's
Cracker Barrel	Ruby Tuesday
Darden	Steak n Shake
DineEquity	VICORP Restaurants
Friendly Ice Cream	Waffle House
Golden Corral	

HISTORICAL FINANCIALS

Company Type: Public

Income Statement
FYE: December 31

	REVENUE ($ mil.)	NET INCOME ($ mil.)	NET PROFIT MARGIN	EMPLOYEES
12/08	760.3	14.7	1.9%	15,000
12/07	939.4	34.7	3.7%	21,000
12/06	994.0	30.1	3.0%	27,000
12/05	978.7	(7.3)	—	27,000
12/04	960.0	(37.7)	—	27,000
Annual Growth	**(5.7%)**	**—**	**—**	**(13.7%)**

2008 Year-End Financials

Debt ratio: —	No. of shares (mil.): 97
Return on equity: —	Dividends
Cash ($ mil.): 21	Yield: 0.0%
Current ratio: 0.50	Payout: —
Long-term debt ($ mil.): 323	Market value ($ mil.): 192

Stock History
NASDAQ (CM): DENN

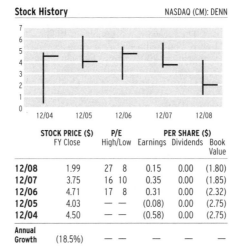

	STOCK PRICE ($) FY Close	P/E High/Low		PER SHARE ($) Earnings	Dividends	Book Value
12/08	1.99	27	8	0.15	0.00	(1.80)
12/07	3.75	16	10	0.35	0.00	(1.85)
12/06	4.71	17	8	0.31	0.00	(2.32)
12/05	4.03	—	—	(0.08)	0.00	(2.75)
12/04	4.50	—	—	(0.58)	0.00	(2.75)
Annual Growth	**(18.5%)**	—	—	—	—	—

DENTSPLY International

Open wider, please, so that DENTSPLY International can fit more of its products in your mouth. The company manufactures a range of dental goods, from anesthetics, pastes, and tooth whiteners to artificial teeth, crown and bridge materials, and implants. DENTSPLY also makes dental equipment, including root canal instruments, ultrasonic polishers, X-ray systems, and orthodontic appliances. The company manufactures its various products under more than 100 brand names. More than half of its products are sold through domestic and international distributors, but DENTSPLY also sells directly to dentists, dental labs, and dental schools in more than 120 countries.

The company's largest customer is distributor Henry Schein, which accounts for more than 10% of sales.

The company's product offerings in various geographic regions reflect the demand of local markets. Developed markets, including the US, Canada, Western Europe, Japan, and Australia, require more technically advanced dental products used in preventive and cosmetic procedures. Less developed countries in Central and South America, Eastern Europe, Africa, and the Middle East typically call for more basic equipment used to fill cavities and finish bridgework. DENTSPLY is focused on supplying products to both ends of this spectrum.

It has invested in new product development through its own internal research centers and collaborations with research institutions and dental schools. DENTSPLY also cites acquisitions as a key part of its growth strategy. In 2008 it acquired a handful of smaller dental companies to further build out its product portfolio, technological capabilities, and geographic breadth.

Barclays Global Investors holds about a 6% stake in DENTSPLY International.

HISTORY

DENTSPLY's roots go back to 1899 when dental business veterans Jacob Frantz, George Whiteley, Dean Osborne, and John Shepherd formed the Dentists' Supply Co. of New York. Facing a competitive market, the four bought a Pennsylvania porcelain teeth manufacturer. One of the company's first innovations was to make ceramic teeth. In 1914 Dentists' Supply introduced different-sized teeth to allow custom fitting for patients.

Between 1920 and 1950 the firm opened factories in Argentina, Australia, Brazil, Germany, Italy, Mexico, and the UK. Facing a mature denture market in the 1950s, Dentists' Supply began investing in other dental technologies. It collaborated with Dr. John Borden in the development of the Borden Airorotor, a high-speed dental drill that revolutionized dental practice. The firm changed its name to DENTSPLY in 1969.

In 1976 the company acquired its worldwide distributor, Amalgamated Dental; it purchased GE's dental X-ray division in 1983. During the 1980s and 1990s DENTSPLY opened operations in China, India, Japan, and Russia as part of its global expansion; it reorganized these operations in the late 1990s to achieve better efficiency. Moving into the information age, DENTSPLY purchased InfoSoft (dental office software). Following a protracted investigation, the Justice Department filed an antitrust suit against DENTSPLY in 1999.

In 2000 DENTSPLY decided to sell its InfoSoft LLC division. The following year, it acquired Friadent, one of Germany's leading makers of dental implants, and it also bought AstraZeneca's dental anesthetic business.

In mid-2006 DENTSPLY sold off its injectable anesthetic manufacturing facility in Chicago. Its supplier Pierrel S.p.A. of Italy agreed to pay $19.5 million for the facility and equipment, with $3 million settled at closing, and the balance to be paid through discounts on future products supplied by Pierrel. The company continues to have contracts with other companies to manufacture the anesthetics.

EXECUTIVES

Chairman and CEO: Bret W. Wise, age 48, $4,078,359 total compensation
President and COO: Christopher T. (Chris) Clark, age 47, $1,820,190 total compensation
SVP and CFO: William R. Jellison, age 51, $1,096,997 total compensation
VP and Chief Clinical Officer: Linda C. Niessen
EVP: James G. (Jim) Mosch, age 51, $1,096,997 total compensation
SVP Global Human Resources: Rachel P. McKinney, age 50
SVP: Robert J. Size, age 50
SVP: Albert Sterkenburg, age 45
VP and Corporate Controller: Timothy S. Warady
VP Tax: Robert J. Winters, age 57
VP, Secretary, and General Counsel: Brian M. Addison, age 54, $956,754 total compensation
VP and Treasurer: William E. Reardon
Auditors: PricewaterhouseCoopers LLP

LOCATIONS

HQ: DENTSPLY International Inc.
221 W. Philadelphia St., York, PA 17405
Phone: 717-845-7511   **Fax:** 717-849-4760
Web: www.dentsply.com

2008 Sales

	$ mil.	% of total
US	865.8	40
Germany	470.8	21
Switzerland	138.1	6
Other foreign countries	719.0	33
Total	**2,193.7**	**100**

PRODUCTS/OPERATIONS

2008 Sales

	$ mil.	% of total
Dental consumable products	680.0	31
Dental laboratory products	558.3	25
Dental specialty products	888.5	41
Non-dental products	66.9	3
Total	**2,193.7**	**100**

Selected Products

Dental consumable products
  Anesthetics
  Bone grafting materials
  High- and low-speed handpieces
  Impression materials
  Infection control materials
  Intraoral light systems
  Prophylaxis paste
  Restorative materials
  Sealants
  Tooth whiteners
  Topical fluoride
  Ultrasonic scalers and polishers

Dental laboratory products
  Computer-aided machining ceramic systems
  Crown and bridge materials
  Dental ceramics
  Precious metal dental alloys
  Prosthetics and artificial teeth

Dental specialty products
  Implants
  Orthodontic appliances and accessories
  Root canal instruments

Non-dental products
  Casting materials (used in jewelry, golf club heads, and certain medical products)

COMPETITORS

AFP Imaging
Align Technology
Astra Tech
Astra Tech (Sweden)
DTI Dental Technologies
Glidewell Laboratories
Henry Schein
National Dentex
Nobel Biocare
Patterson Companies
Sirona
Sybron Dental
Young Innovations

HISTORICAL FINANCIALS

Company Type: Public

Income Statement

FYE: December 31

	REVENUE ($ mil.)	NET INCOME ($ mil.)	NET PROFIT MARGIN	EMPLOYEES
12/08	2,193.7	283.9	12.9%	9,400
12/07	2,009.8	259.7	12.9%	8,900
12/06	1,810.5	223.7	12.4%	8,500
12/05	1,715.1	45.4	2.6%	8,000
12/04	1,694.2	253.2	14.9%	7,700
Annual Growth	**6.7%**	**2.9%**	**—**	**5.1%**

2008 Year-End Financials

Debt ratio: 26.7%
Return on equity: 18.3%
Cash ($ mil.): 204
Current ratio: 2.64
Long-term debt ($ mil.): 424
No. of shares (mil.): 149
Dividends
  Yield: 0.7%
  Payout: 10.2%
Market value ($ mil.): 4,196

Stock History

NASDAQ (GS): XRAY

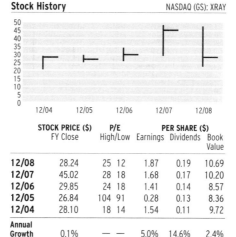

	STOCK PRICE ($) FY Close	P/E High/Low		PER SHARE ($) Earnings	Dividends	Book Value
12/08	28.24	25	12	1.87	0.19	10.69
12/07	45.02	28	18	1.68	0.17	10.20
12/06	29.85	24	18	1.41	0.14	8.57
12/05	26.84	104	91	0.28	0.13	8.36
12/04	28.10	18	14	1.54	0.11	9.72
Annual Growth	0.1%	—	—	5.0%	14.6%	2.4%

Devon Energy

Independent oil and gas producer Devon Energy puts its energy into oil finds far from England's southern coast. It has exploration and production assets in the Gulf of Mexico, North Texas, Oklahoma, Wyoming, Western Canada, and in other major oil patches worldwide such as Azerbaijan, Brazil, and China. In 2008 Devon Energy reported proved reserves of 429 million barrels of oil, 9.9 trillion cu. ft. of natural gas, and 325 million barrels of natural gas liquids. That year the company drilled a record 2,441 gross wells with an overall 98% rate of success. Devon Energy is the largest producer and largest lease holder in the Barnett Shale area of north Texas.

Devon Energy bought its way into the big leagues through a series of multibillion-dollar acquisitions, including Ocean Energy for $3.5 billion and US-based Chief Holdings LLC for $2.2 billion.

Seeking to raise cash to focus its exploration activity on North America, Brazil, and China, in 2007 Devon announced plans to divest all of its assets in West Africa. It sold its oil and gas business in Egypt to Dana Petroleum for $375 million and agreed to sell its Gabon assets for $206 million. In 2008 it sold its oil and gas business in Cote d'Ivoire to Afren plc for $205 million and in Equatorial Guinea for $2.2 billion.

HISTORY

Larry Nichols (a lawyer who clerked for US Supreme Court Chief Justice Earl Warren) and his father, John, founded Devon Energy in 1969. John Nichols was a partner in predecessor company Blackwood and Nichols, an oil partnership formed in 1946.

In 1981 the company bought a small stake in the Northeast Blanco Unit of New Mexico's San Juan Basin. To raise capital, Devon formed the limited partnership Devon Resource Investors

and took it public in 1985. In 1988 Devon consolidated all of its units into a single, publicly traded company.

The firm increased its stake in Northeast Blanco in 1988 and again in 1989, ending up with about 25%. By 1990 Devon had drilled more than 100 wells in the area and had proved reserves of 58 billion cu. ft. of natural gas.

During the 1990s the company launched a major expansion program using a two-pronged strategy: acquiring producing properties and drilling wells in proven fields. In 1990 it bought an 88% interest in six Texas wells; two years later Devon snapped up the US properties of Hondo Oil & Gas. After its 1994 purchase of Alta Energy, which operated in New Mexico, Oklahoma, Texas, and Wyoming, Devon had proved reserves of more than 500 billion cu. ft. of gas.

Between 1992 and 1997 the company also drilled some 840 successful wells. Buoyed by new seismic techniques that raise the odds of finding oil, Devon devoted more resources to pioneering fields in regions where it already had expertise.

Continuing its buying spree, Devon bought Kerr-McGee's onshore assets in 1997. Two years later it bought Alberta, Canada-based Northstar for $775 million, creating a company with holdings divided almost evenly between oil and gas.

Also in 1999 Devon grabbed its biggest prize when it purchased PennzEnergy of Houston in a $2.3 billion stock-and-debt deal that analysts called a bargain. PennzEnergy, spun off from Pennzoil in 1998, dates back to the Texas oil boom after WWII. In addition to new US holdings, the deal gave Devon a number of international oil and gas assets in such places as Azerbaijan, Brazil, Egypt, Qatar, and Venezuela.

On a roll, Devon in 2000 bought Santa Fe Snyder for $2.35 billion in stock and $1 billion in assumed debt. The deal increased Devon's proved reserves by nearly 400 million barrels of oil equivalent.

In 2001 the company agreed to a major deal to supply Indonesian natural gas to Singapore. It also made an unsuccessful bid for rival Barrett Resources that was trumped by a bid from Williams Companies. Undaunted, that year Devon acquired Anderson Exploration for $3.4 billion in cash and $1.2 billion in assumed debt. It also purchased Mitchell Energy & Development for $3.1 billion in cash and stock and $400 million in assumed debt.

As part of its strategy to refocus on core operations, in 2002 the company sold its Indonesian assets to PetroChina for $262 million. By mid-2002 the company had raised about $1.2 billion through the disposition of oil properties worldwide.

EXECUTIVES

Chairman and CEO: J. Larry Nichols, age 66, $38,511,112 total compensation
President and Director: John Richels, age 58, $15,158,560 total compensation
SVP Accounting and Chief Accounting Officer: Danny J. Heatly, age 53, $2,145,651 total compensation
EVP Marketing and Midstream: Darryl G. Smette, age 61, $8,484,641 total compensation
EVP Human Resources: Frank W. Rudolph, age 52
EVP Administration: R. Alan Marcum, age 42
EVP Exploration and Production: David A. (Dave) Hager, age 52
EVP and General Counsel: Lyndon C. Taylor, age 50
EVP Public Affairs: William F. (Bill) Whitsitt

Early in 2002 Diebold acquired voting-systems maker Global Election Systems and renamed the subsidiary Diebold Election Systems, then Premier Election Systems. The voting machine unit made headlines in 2004 when four counties in California banned the use of its terminals after a state advisory board raised concerns about security and reliability. The company responded to the judgment with a statement reaffirming its commitment to election systems development and support. Diebold later agreed to settle a civil action lawsuit brought by the state of California for $2.6 million; the suit accused the company of making false claims about the security and certification of its voting machines.

Diebold bolstered its maintenance and support operations when it acquired TFE Technology Holdings in 2004. That purchase was followed by the acquisition of security systems service provider Antar-Com, and in 2005 Diebold acquired another security systems integrator, TASC Security.

O'Dell resigned as chairman and CEO in 2005; president Thomas Swidarski replaced him as CEO, and director John Lauer was named chairman.

Early in 2006 the company purchased Genpass Service Solutions (GSS), a subsidiary of an ATM service and maintenance company owned by U.S. Bank. It augmented its Diebold Global Security division with the purchase of Actcom, a provider of security systems for government agencies including the US Department of Defense, in mid-2006.

An SEC investigation into Diebold's accounting practices caused the company to delay its annual filing for fiscal 2007. The investigation concerned the reporting of revenue for product shipments (versus delivery) and services.

Seeking to augment its UTC Fire & Security unit, United Technologies made an unsolicited offer to acquire Diebold for $2.6 billion in cash in 2008. Diebold's board of directors issued a statement rejecting the offer, as it had previous overtures from United Technologies. United Technologies later withdrew its offer.

EXECUTIVES

Chairman: John N. Lauer, age 69
President, CEO, and Director: Thomas W. Swidarski, age 50, $4,701,371 total compensation
EVP Global Operations: George S. Mayes Jr., age 50, $1,191,943 total compensation
VP, Corporate Controller, and Interim CFO: Leslie A. Pierce, age 45
VP and CIO: Sean Forrester, age 44
VP and Chief Communications Officer: John D. Kristoff, age 41
VP and Chief Human Resources Officer: Sheila M. Rutt, age 40
VP and Chief Information Security Officer: Scott M. Angelo
VP and Chief Tax Officer: M. Scott Hunter, age 47
SVP Europe, Middle East, and Africa and Asia Pacific Divisions: James L. M. Chen, age 48, $1,391,819 total compensation
SVP Customer Solutions Group: David Bucci, age 57, $1,826,976 total compensation
SVP Global Development and Services: Charles E. (Chuck) Ducey Jr., age 53
VP Corporate Development and Finance: Robert J. Warren, age 62
VP and General Counsel: Warren W. Dettinger, age 55
VP and Treasurer: Timothy J. McDannold, age 46
President, Brazilian Division: Joao Abud Jr., age 52
President, Premier Elections Solutions: Dave Byrd
Director Investor Relations: Christopher (Chris) Bast
Corporate Counsel and Secretary: Chad F. Hesse, age 36
Auditors: KPMG LLP

LOCATIONS

HQ: Diebold, Incorporated
5995 Mayfair Rd., North Canton, OH 44720
Phone: 330-490-4000   **Fax:** 330-490-3794
Web: www.diebold.com

2008 Sales

	$ mil.	% of total
Americas	2,299.6	72
Europe, Middle East & Africa	469.9	15
Asia/Pacific	400.6	13
Total	**3,170.1**	**100**

PRODUCTS/OPERATIONS

2008 Sales

	$ mil.	% of total
Financial self-service		
Products	1,127.1	36
Services	1,113.5	35
Security		
Services	455.9	14
Products	319.5	10
Election systems/lottery	154.1	5
Total	**3,170.1**	**100**

Selected Products

Alarm and monitoring systems
Automated teller machines (ATMs)
Cash dispensers and recyclers
Check imaging
Coin machines
Drive-up banking and pharmacy equipment
Remote bank teller systems
Vaults, safe deposit boxes, locks, and safes
Voting terminals

COMPETITORS

ACI Worldwide, Inc.
ADT Security
De La Rue
Election Systems & Software
Fujitsu
Hart InterCivic
Itautec
NCR
Oki Electric
Sequoia Voting
Siemens AG
Tranax Technologies
Triton
Wincor Nixdorf

HISTORICAL FINANCIALS

Company Type: Public

Income Statement

FYE: December 31

	REVENUE ($ mil.)	NET INCOME ($ mil.)	NET PROFIT MARGIN	EMPLOYEES
12/08	3,170.1	88.6	2.8%	16,658
12/07	2,964.8	39.5	1.3%	16,942
12/06	2,906.2	86.5	3.0%	15,451
12/05	2,587.0	96.7	3.7%	14,603
12/04	2,380.9	184.0	7.7%	14,376
Annual Growth	**7.4%**	**(16.7%)**	**—**	**3.8%**

2008 Year-End Financials

Debt ratio: 62.8%
Return on equity: 8.6%
Cash ($ mil.): 241
Current ratio: 2.19
Long-term debt ($ mil.): 595
No. of shares (mil.): 66
Dividends
  Yield: 3.6%
  Payout: 75.2%
Market value ($ mil.): 1,861

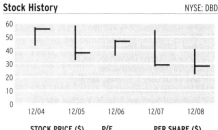

Stock History   NYSE: DBD

	STOCK PRICE ($) FY Close	P/E High/Low		PER SHARE ($) Earnings	Dividends	Book Value
12/08	28.09	30	17	1.33	1.00	14.29
12/07	28.98	92	48	0.59	0.94	16.83
12/06	46.60	37	28	1.29	0.86	16.47
12/05	38.00	43	24	1.36	0.82	17.40
12/04	55.73	22	17	2.54	0.74	19.02
Annual Growth	**(15.7%)**	**—**	**—**	**(14.9%)**	**7.8%**	**(6.9%)**

Dillard's, Inc.

Tradition is trying to catch up with the times at Dillard's. Sandwiched between retail giant Macy's and discount chains, such as Kohl's, Dillard's is being forced to rethink its strategy and trim its store count. The department store chain operates some 315 locations in about 30 states, covering the Sunbelt and the central US. Its stores cater to middle- and upper-middle-income women, selling name-brand and private-label merchandise with a focus on apparel and home furnishings. Women's apparel and accessories account for more than a third of sales. Founded in 1938 by William Dillard, today family members, through the W. D. Company, control nearly all of the company's voting shares and run the company.

Dillard's sales have been declining since 2006, and the company's store count has dipped as it shutters underperforming stores, including the last of its 16 home and furniture stores. Dillard's closed 20 stores in 2008 and plans to close more in 2009. (The company closed its Louisville, Kentucky, distribution center in 2008 to eliminate duplications and cut costs.) In November 2008 Dillard's announced that it was cutting about 500 jobs, including about 60 at headquarters.

Sales across all merchandise categories are falling. To remedy the situation, the department store chain is attempting to move upscale, positioning itself above Macy's and Belk and below high-end chains such as Nordstrom and Bloomingdale's. To attract more customers Dillard's is focusing on adding more fashion, much like J. C. Penney has done in recent years. The firm's new direction is inspired on the success of specialty stores with their edited displays or merchandise in boutique-like settings rather than an endless sea of apparel racks. New stores are smaller (averaging 170,000 sq. ft.) and will be located in open-air lifestyle centers rather than enclosed malls. Dillard's, which is averse to marking down merchandise but has been forced to discount by its lower-end competitors, hopes its move upmarket will stop the markdowns.

Despite these efforts to right itself, same-store sales have continued to decline, and Dillard's has come under fire from disgruntled investors who are demanding the ouster of the family-led management team, including CEO Bill Dillard. The demand comes after Dillard's bowed to pressure from hedge funds Barington Capital Group and Clinton Group and appointed four new directors in April 2008 to avoid a proxy fight.

One of Dillard's strategies is the dual-anchor concept: two locations in the same mall. Currently Dillard's operates about 60 dual-anchor stores. Rather than closing a store when it buys space where it already has a presence, Dillard's uses the additional store, placing women's and children's departments and home furnishings in one location and men's and juniors' departments in the other.

HISTORY

At age 12 William Dillard began working in his father's general store in Mineral Springs, Arkansas. After he graduated from Columbia University in 1937, the third-generation retailer spent seven months in the Sears, Roebuck manager training program in Tulsa, Oklahoma.

With $8,000 borrowed from his father, William opened his first department store in Nashville, Arkansas, in 1938. Service was one of the most important things he had to offer, he said, and he insisted on quality — he personally inspected every item and would settle for nothing but the best. William sold the store in 1948 to finance a partnership in Wooten's Department Store in Texarkana, Arkansas; he bought out Wooten and established Dillard's the next year.

Throughout the 1950s and 1960s, the company became a strong regional retailer, developing its strategy of buying well-established downtown stores in small cities; acquisitions in those years included Mayer & Schmidt (Tyler, Texas; 1956) and Joseph Pfeifer (Little Rock, Arkansas; 1963). Dillard's moved its headquarters to Little Rock after buying Pfeifer. When it went public in 1969, it had 15 stores in three states.

During the early 1960s the company began computerizing operations to streamline inventory and information management. In 1970 Dillard's added computerized cash registers, which gave management hourly sales figures.

The chain continued acquiring outlets (more than 130 over the next three decades, including stores owned by Stix, Baer & Fuller, Macy's, Joske's, and Maison Blanche). In a 1988 joint venture with Edward J. DeBartolo, Dillard's bought a 50% interest in the 12 Higbee's stores in Ohio (buying the other 50% in 1992, shortly after Higbee's bought five former Horne's stores in Ohio).

In 1991 Vendamerica (subsidiary of Vendex International and the only major nonfamily holder of the company's stock) sold its 8.9 million shares of Class A stock (25% of the class) in an underwritten public offering.

A lawsuit filed by the FTC against Dillard's in 1994, claiming the company made it unreasonably difficult for its credit card holders to remove unauthorized charges from their bills, was dismissed the following year.

William retired in 1998 and William Dillard II took over the CEO position, while brother Alex became president. The company then paid $3.1 billion for Mercantile Stores, which operated 106 apparel and home design stores in the South and Midwest. To avoid redundancy in certain regions, Dillard's sold 26 of those stores and exchanged seven others for new Dillard's stores. The assimilation of Mercantile brought distribution problems that cut into earnings for fiscal 1999. In late 2000, with a slumping stock price and declining sales, Dillard's said it would deemphasize its concentration on name-brand merchandise and offer deep discounts on branded items already in stock. Despite these efforts, sales and earnings continued to slide in 2001.

Founder and patriarch William Dillard (the company's guiding force) died in February 2002. Son William II became chairman of the company, which has been family-controlled for half a century.

In November 2004 Dillard's completed the sale of Dillard National Bank, the retailer's credit card portfolio, to GE Consumer Finance for about $1.1 billion (plus debt). Dillard's said it would use the proceeds to reduce debt, repurchase stock, and to achieve general corporate purposes.

In the spring of 2005 Dillard's shuttered the last of 16 home and furniture stores acquired when the department store chain acquired Mercantile Stores Co. in 1998. Hurricanes Katrina, Rita, and Wilma took a toll on Dillard's in 2005, interrupting business in about 60 of the company's stores at various times.

EXECUTIVES

Chairman and CEO; President, Dillard Travel:
William (Bill) Dillard II, age 64,
$2,503,592 total compensation
President and Director: Alex Dillard, age 59,
$1,348,645 total compensation
SVP, CFO, and Director: James I. Freeman, age 59,
$904,079 total compensation
VP and CIO: William L. (Bill) Holder Jr.
EVP; President, Fort Worth Division, and Director:
Drue Corbusier, age 62
EVP; President, Little Rock Division, and Director:
Mike Dillard, age 57, $917,365 total compensation
EVP: Drue Matheny, age 62,
$1,043,822 total compensation
VP; President, Tampa Division: Robin Sanderford,
age 62
VP and General Counsel: Paul J. Schroeder Jr., age 61
VP Shoes: Joseph P. Brennan
VP Merchandising: Bob Thompson
VP Accessories and Intimate Apparel Merchandising:
William Dillard III
Director Investor Relations: Julie J. Bull
Auditors: Deloitte & Touche LLP

LOCATIONS

HQ: Dillard's, Inc.
1600 Cantrell Rd., Little Rock, AR 72201
Phone: 501-376-5200   **Fax:** 501-399-7831
Web: www.dillards.com

2009 Stores

	No.
Texas	59
Florida	46
Arizona	17
North Carolina	16
Ohio	16
Louisiana	14
Georgia	12
Alabama	11
Missouri	11
Tennessee	11
Oklahoma	10
Colorado	9
Virginia	9
Arkansas	8
South Carolina	8
Kansas	7
Kentucky	6
Mississippi	6
New Mexico	6
Utah	6
Iowa	5
Nevada	4
California	3
Illinois	3
Indiana	3
Montana	3
Nebraska	3
Idaho	2
Wyoming	1
Total	**315**

PRODUCTS/OPERATIONS

2009 Sales

	% of total
Women's apparel & accessories	37
Men's apparel & accessories	18
Cosmetics	15
Shoes	13
Juniors' & children's apparel	9
Home & other	7
Construction segment	1
Total	**100**

COMPETITORS

Abercrombie & Fitch	Lands' End
American Eagle Outfitters	Macy's
AnnTaylor	Men's Wearhouse
Bed Bath & Beyond	Neiman Marcus
Belk	Nordstrom
Brown Shoe	Saks
Burlington Coat Factory	Sears
Eddie Bauer llc	Stein Mart
Foot Locker	Talbots
The Gap	Target
J. C. Penney	TJX Companies
J. Crew	Tuesday Morning
Kohl's	

HISTORICAL FINANCIALS

Company Type: Public

Income Statement			FYE: Saturday nearest January 31	
	REVENUE ($ mil.)	NET INCOME ($ mil.)	NET PROFIT MARGIN	EMPLOYEES
1/09	6,988.4	(241.1)	—	49,000
1/08	7,207.4	53.8	0.7%	49,938
1/07	7,636.1	245.6	3.2%	51,385
1/06	7,560.2	121.5	1.6%	52,056
1/05	7,528.6	117.7	1.6%	53,035
Annual Growth	(1.8%)	—	—	(2.0%)

2009 Year-End Financials

Debt ratio: 34.7%
Return on equity: —
Cash ($ mil.): 97
Current ratio: 1.85
Long-term debt ($ mil.): 782
No. of shares (mil.): 74
Dividends
  Yield: 3.7%
  Payout: —
Market value ($ mil.): 321

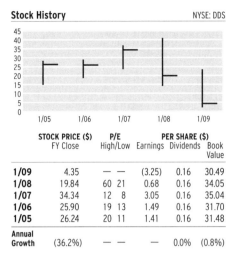
	STOCK PRICE ($) FY Close	P/E High/Low		PER SHARE ($) Earnings	Dividends	Book Value
1/09	4.35	—	—	(3.25)	0.16	30.49
1/08	19.84	60	21	0.68	0.16	34.05
1/07	34.34	12	8	3.05	0.16	35.04
1/06	25.90	19	13	1.49	0.16	31.70
1/05	26.24	20	11	1.41	0.16	31.48
Annual Growth	(36.2%)	—	—	—	0.0%	(0.8%)

DineEquity, Inc.

This company shows an equal bias for breakfast, lunch, and dinner. Formerly IHOP Corp., DineEquity is one of the leading chain restaurant companies in the US, with its two flagship concepts, the International House of Pancakes (IHOP) and Applebee's Neighborhood Grill & Bar. The #3 family-style diner chain behind Denny's and Waffle House, IHOP has more than 1,400 mostly franchised restaurants that are open 24 hours a day. The chain is best known for its breakfast menu, but it also offers standard family fare (sandwiches, burgers, salads) for lunch and dinner. Applebee's is the #1 casual dining chain, with nearly 2,000 locations in about 20 countries offering a wide variety of appetizers and entrees.

DineEquity has traditionally been focused on restaurant franchising, which is seen as a way to insulate the company from the ebbs and flows of the dining business. It generates a steady stream of revenue through fees and royalties paid by local operators. Since acquiring the Applebee's chain in 2007, DineEquity has been keenly focused on selling its estate of corporate-owned casual dining spots to franchisees. During 2008 it refranchised more than 100 locations.

While it strives to remove itself from day-to-day restaurant operation, the company maintains a steady hand on marketing and promoting its dining concepts through a hefty dose of advertising and menu development. Its IHOP chain relies primarily on special offers and limited-time menu items to drive additional traffic. Applebee's, meanwhile, has focused on new menu items and special price offers to attract the dining public.

CEO Julia Stewart plays a key role in efforts to promote both chains, championing new and improved food products to grab the attention of customers. A former executive at Applebee's who left to take over IHOP, she also engineered the $2.1 billion acquisition of the casual dining chain. IHOP changed its name to DineEquity the following year to emphasize its new status as a multi-concept operator.

Early in 2009 the company formed a purchasing co-operative to centralize purchasing of food ingredients and other restaurant supplies. The new co-op is designed to help reduce operating costs for DineEquity's franchisees through bulk purchasing and a more efficient supply chain operation.

Michael Dell, founder and chairman of computer maker Dell, owns more than 10% of DineEquity through MSD Capital.

HISTORY

Al Lapin opened the first International House of Pancakes in Toluca Lake, California, in 1958. Taking inspiration from the Howard Johnson's chain (with its bright orange roof design), Lapin added a blue A-frame roof to the design of his restaurants in 1960. The company went public in 1961 and began acquiring other restaurant chains, and later expanded to businesses outside the restaurant segment. It changed its name to International Industries in 1963. The conglomerate eventually collected about 20 subsidiaries, including eateries such as Orange Julius, Love's Wood Pit Barbecue, and The Original House of Pies, as well as other businesses such as Michael's Artist & Engineering Supplies, Securities Supervisors, Shirt Gallery, and United Rent-All.

While the pancake house chain had grown quickly to more than 1,000 locations, its highly diversified parent ran into debt trouble in the early 1970s. Lapin left, and after a 1976 restructuring, the company was renamed IHOP Corp. and operated just three businesses: Copper Penny Restaurants, Love's Wood Pit Barbecue Restaurants, and International House of Pancakes. Still struggling, IHOP sold out to Swiss company Wienerwald Holding in 1979, and Richard Herzer was made president. After Wienerwald went bankrupt in 1982, creditors sold the Copper Penny and Love's chains. Herzer was named CEO in 1983.

IHOP's expansion remained stunted until 1987, when Herzer and a group of investors bought it, injecting money that allowed it to resume growth. IHOP went public in 1991 with about 500 restaurants and began opening about 65 new sites annually.

The company exceeded $1 billion in systemwide sales for the first time in 1998 and opened about 75 restaurants a year through 2000. In 2001 IHOP created a joint venture with the US Mint to change its Silver Dollar Pancakes to Golden Dollar Pancakes as part of a campaign connected to the release of the new dollar coins. Also that year the company developed 76 new restaurants, and its franchisees developed another 17.

Former Applebee's executive Julia Stewart took over as president and CEO in 2002, and early the next year Herzer retired as chairman (he died later that year). He was replaced by director Larry Kay. That year IHOP began its refranchising effort. The company developed 30 fewer restaurants in the full year, and the number of franchised restaurants increased by four. At the end of 2003 IHOP had 44 company-operated restaurants (compared to 76 at the end of 2002).

In 2004 the company announced that it would ultimately own only a handful of restaurants, franchising the rest. Later in the year IHOP opened its first franchised location in Harlem, New York City, and it quickly became one of the company's top earners. Founder Lapin died the same year.

Larry Kay stepped down as chairman in 2006, and Stewart was appointed to replace him. Kay remained as a board member. The following year the company acquired Applebee's International for about $2.1 billion. (The Applebee's Neighborhood Grill & Bar chain is now operated by Applebee's Services.) IHOP changed its name to DineEquity in 2008.

EXECUTIVES

Chairman and CEO: Julia A. Stewart, age 53, $4,423,795 total compensation
CFO: John F. (Jack) Tierney, age 56
Chief Restaurant Support Officer: Richard C. Celio, age 58, $1,339,917 total compensation
Chief Marketing Officer: Carolyn P. O'Keefe, age 52
SVP Legal, Secretary, and General Counsel: Randi Val Morrison, age 44
SVP Human Resources: John Jakubek, age 56
VP and Corporate Controller: Greggory (Gregg) Kalvin, age 49, $552,642 total compensation
VP, IHOP: Michael Mendelsohn
VP Franchise and Development, IHOP: Jess Sotomayor
President, Applebee's International: Michael J. (Mike) Archer, age 48, $1,572,795 total compensation
Interim President and SVP Operations, IHOP Restaurants: Jim Peros
Executive Director Communications: Patrick J. Lenow
Director Investor Relations: Stacy Roughan
Communications Manager, IHOP: Jennifer Pendergrass
Auditors: Ernst & Young LLP

LOCATIONS

HQ: DineEquity, Inc.
450 N. Brand Blvd., Glendale, CA 91203
Phone: 818-240-6055   **Fax:** 818-637-3131
Web: dineequity.com

PRODUCTS/OPERATIONS

2008 Sales

	$ mil.	% of total
Restaurants	1,103.2	68
Franchising	353.3	22
Rents	131.4	8
Other	25.7	2
Total	**1,613.6**	**100**

2008 Sales

	$ mil.	% of total
Applebee's Neighborhood Grill & Bar	1,236.5	77
International House of Pancakes	377.1	23
Total	**1,613.6**	**100**

2008 Locations

	No.
Applebee's Neighborhood Grill & Bar	
Franchised	1,598
Company-owned	406
International House of Pancakes	
Franchised	1,385
Company-owned	11
Total	**3,400**

COMPETITORS

Bob Evans
Brinker
Carlson Restaurants
Cheesecake Factory
Cracker Barrel
Darden
Denny's
Hooters
OSI Restaurant Partners
Perkins & Marie Callender's
Ruby Tuesday
Waffle House

HISTORICAL FINANCIALS

Company Type: Public

Income Statement

FYE: December 31

	REVENUE ($ mil.)	NET INCOME ($ mil.)	NET PROFIT MARGIN	EMPLOYEES
12/08	1,613.6	(154.5)	—	25,248
12/07	484.6	(0.5)	—	32,300
12/06	349.6	44.6	12.8%	972
12/05	348.0	43.9	12.6%	897
12/04	359.0	33.4	9.3%	1,250
Annual Growth	45.6%	—	—	112.0%

2008 Year-End Financials

Debt ratio: 10,000.0%
Return on equity: —
Cash ($ mil.): 114
Current ratio: 1.41
Long-term debt ($ mil.): 2,333

No. of shares (mil.): 18
Dividends
  Yield: 8.7%
  Payout: —
Market value ($ mil.): 203

Stock History

NYSE: DIN

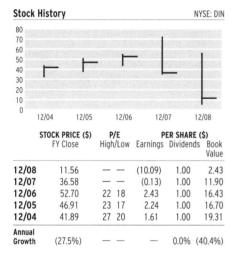

	STOCK PRICE ($) FY Close	P/E High/Low		PER SHARE ($) Earnings	Dividends	Book Value
12/08	11.56	—	—	(10.09)	1.00	2.43
12/07	36.58	—	—	(0.13)	1.00	11.90
12/06	52.70	22	18	2.43	1.00	16.43
12/05	46.91	23	17	2.24	1.00	16.70
12/04	41.89	27	20	1.61	1.00	19.31
Annual Growth	(27.5%)	—	—	—	0.0%	(40.4%)

The DIRECTV Group

DIRECTV takes television straight to the masses — no wires attached. The company operates the largest direct broadcast satellite (DBS) service in the US, ahead of #2 DISH Network, and in direct competition with cable providers Comcast and Time Warner. It provides service to more than 17 million customers in the US and another 5 million or so through its Latin America division. Additionally, regional US phone companies such as Verizon bundle DIRECTV video services with their voice and Internet packages. The company also offers high-definition and video-on-demand (VOD) programming. Liberty Media controls 48% of DIRECTV's voting power and plans to merge the company with its Liberty Entertainment business in 2009.

One of DIRECTV's distinguishing points in terms of programming (relative to cable operators and satellite rival DISH Network) is its status as the only broadcaster authorized to sell NFL Sunday Ticket, which gives subscribers access to most of the Sunday professional football games. DIRECTV's core programming consists of about 2,000 digital video and audio channels, including foreign language, high-definition (HD), and pay-per-view options.

The company made a move in 2008 to entice new customers and pull in additional revenue from existing subscribers with the launch of its DIRECTV-on-Demand service and the expansion of its international programming options. The company in 2009 announced a partnership with AT&T that enables the telephone carrier to market bundled broadband Internet, digital telephone, and DIRECTV video programming to its customers in 22 US states.

Looking to expand its control of the installation and home service network for its products, DIRECTV acquired service provider 180 Connect in 2008. In a related deal, UniTek USA, a provider of communications management and support services, bought 180 Connect's cable television services unit; UniTek transferred satellite TV installation businesses in select markets to DIRECTV in exchange.

Liberty Media in 2008 exchanged its 16% stake in News Corp. for that company's 41% share, held through Fox Entertainment Group, of DIRECTV. It increased its stake in a subsequent share purchase that year. Liberty Media owns 53% of DIRECTV shares, but controls only 48% of its voting rights.

HISTORY

The DIRECTV Group's roots go back to 1932, when Hughes Aircraft was founded to build experimental airplanes for Howard Hughes, who set a number of world airspeed records with the company's H-1 racer. During WWII the company began building a mammoth flying boat to serve as a troop carrier, but the *Spruce Goose* wasn't completed until 1947, when Hughes piloted it for its only flight (to silence critics who claimed it couldn't fly). After WWII the company began moving into the growing defense electronics field. In 1953 it underwent a major shake-up when about 80 of its top engineers walked out, dissatisfied with Hughes, who was becoming distant and difficult.

The US Air Force threatened to cancel the company's contracts because of Hughes' erratic behavior, so he transferred the company's assets to the Howard Hughes Medical Institute (with himself as its sole trustee) and hired former Bendix Aviation executive Lawrence Hyland to run the company. Hyland rebuilt its research staff, and the institute produced the first beam of coherent laser light (1960) and placed the first communications satellite into geosynchronous orbit (1963). The Hughes-built Surveyor landed on the moon in 1966.

When Hughes died in 1976, a board of trustees was created to oversee the institute. In 1984 the Department of Defense canceled several missile contracts, and the firm found it difficult to fund R&D.

The next year the institute sold Hughes Aircraft to General Motors (GM) for $5.2 billion. GM teamed its Delco Electronics auto parts unit with Hughes to form GM Hughes Electronics (GMHE). GMHE acquired General Dynamics' missile business in 1992 and installed former IBM executive Michael Armstrong as CEO. He cut personnel by 25% and refocused the company on commercial electronics.

In 1995 GMHE became Hughes Electronics and launched its DIRECTV satellite service. Hughes bought a majority stake in satellite communications provider PanAmSat in 1996 (PanAmSat was acquired in 2006 by Intelsat).

In 1997 GM sold its defense electronics unit to Raytheon and merged Delco Electronics into GM

subsidiary Delphi Automotive Systems. Armstrong left Hughes to head AT&T and was replaced by Michael Smith, whose brother John Smith was then GM's CEO.

In 1998 Hughes took a public relations hit when several of its satellites failed and temporarily halted most US pager activity. Hughes in 1999 bought United States Satellite Broadcasting and the satellite business of rival PRIMESTAR and folded the businesses into DIRECTV. America Online (now part of Time Warner) invested $1.5 billion in Hughes.

In early 2000 Hughes sold its satellite manufacturing market to Boeing in an effort to focus on its faster-growing communications services businesses. GM also issued a tracking stock for Hughes but retained ownership of all the company's assets. That same year, GM announced that it would try to sell Hughes.

Hughes bought Telocity (renamed DIRECTV Broadband), an ISP that uses DSL (digital subscriber line) technology, in 2001. Later that year Michael Smith retired abruptly amid reports of disputes over the sale of the company. GM's Harry Pearce took over as chairman of Hughes, and Jack Shaw was named CEO.

GM sold its 19.8% interest in Hughes Electronics to News Corp. in 2003. News Corp. acquired another 14.2% from common stockholders, amounting to a 34% stake.

In 2004 Hughes Electronics changed its name to The DIRECTV Group, declaring its focus and commitment to the DIRECTV brand and DTH satellite business. In 2005 the company sold its 80% stake in satellite network operator PanAmSat to a group of private equity firms (KKR, The Carlyle Group, and Providence Equity Partners) in a deal valued at $2.6 billion.

After selling a majority stake in its Mexico-based operations and making acquisitions in Brazil and other areas, DIRECTV restructured its Latin American unit in 2007 to include PanAmericana, Sky Brazil, and Sky Mexico. The segment came fully under DIRECTV's ownership in 2007 when it purchased Darlene Investment's 14% stake.

EXECUTIVES

Chairman: John C. Malone, age 68
Interim CEO; EVP Legal, Human Resources and Administration; General Counsel, and Secretary: Larry D. Hunter, age 58, $3,138,646 total compensation
EVP; President, New Ventures; President and CEO, DIRECTV Latin America: Bruce B. Churchill, age 51, $3,942,999 total compensation
EVP Operations: Michael W. Palkovic, age 51, $2,986,982 total compensation
EVP Finance and CFO: Patrick T. (Pat) Doyle, age 53, $1,688,291 total compensation
EVP and CTO: Romulo Pontual, age 49
EVP and Chief Marketing Officer: Paul Guyardo, age 44
SVP, Controller, and Chief Accounting Officer: John F. Murphy, age 40
EVP Entertainment: Eric Shanks
SVP Strategy and Development, DIRECTV Entertainment Group: Derek Chang, age 40
SVP Advertising Sales: Bob Riordan
SVP Customer Care: Ellen Filipiak
SVP and Treasurer: J. William Little, age 40
SVP Programming Acquisition: Daniel M. Hartman
VP New Business Development: Rich Forester
VP Investor Relations: Jonathan M. (Jon) Rubin
VP Marketing: Randy Satterburg
Auditors: Deloitte & Touche LLP

LOCATIONS

HQ: The DIRECTV Group, Inc.
   2230 E. Imperial Hwy., El Segundo, CA 90245
Phone: 310-964-5000   **Fax:** 310-535-5225
Web: www.directv.com

2008 Sales

	$ mil.	% of total
US	17,310	88
Latin America	2,383	12
Total	**19,693**	**100**

COMPETITORS

Apple Inc.
AT&T
Brasil Telecom
Cablevision Systems
CenturyTel
Charter Communications
Comcast
Cox Communications
DISH Network Corporation
Embarq
Hulu
Netflix
SES AMERICOM
Telefónica
Telmex
Time Warner Cable
Verizon
Windstream

HISTORICAL FINANCIALS

Company Type: Public

Income Statement

FYE: December 31

	REVENUE ($ mil.)	NET INCOME ($ mil.)	NET PROFIT MARGIN	EMPLOYEES
12/08	19,693.0	1,521.0	7.7%	19,600
12/07	17,246.0	1,451.0	8.4%	12,300
12/06	14,755.5	1,420.1	9.6%	11,200
12/05	13,164.5	335.9	2.6%	9,200
12/04	11,360.0	(1,638.7)	—	11,800
Annual Growth	**14.7%**	**—**	**—**	**13.5%**

2008 Year-End Financials

Debt ratio: 129.1%
Return on equity: 27.3%
Cash ($ mil.): 2,005
Current ratio: 1.13
Long-term debt ($ mil.): 6,267

No. of shares (mil.): 977
Dividends
   Yield: 0.0%
   Payout: —
Market value ($ mil.): 22,390

Stock History

NASDAQ (GS): DTV

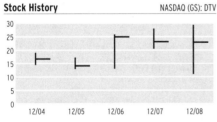

	STOCK PRICE ($) FY Close	P/E High/Low		PER SHARE ($) Earnings	Dividends	Book Value
12/08	22.91	21	8	1.37	0.00	4.97
12/07	23.12	23	17	1.21	0.00	6.45
12/06	24.94	23	12	1.12	0.00	6.84
12/05	14.12	71	55	0.24	0.00	8.12
12/04	16.74	—	—	(1.41)	0.00	7.68
Annual Growth	**8.2%**	**—**	**—**	**—**	**—**	**(10.3%)**

Discovery Communications

This company helps people discover nature and science programming right from their living rooms. Discovery Communications, Inc. (DCI) is a leading operator of cable channels focused primarily on such topics as history, natural and physical science, and technology. Its portfolio is anchored by the Discovery Channel, which reaches nearly 100 million US homes and is broadcast in more than 170 other countries. DCI also runs Animal Planet, the Military Channel, Science Channel, and TLC (The Learning Channel). In addition, the company offers video-on-demand and publishes content online through such Web sites as HowStuffWorks.com.

The broadcaster has carved out its niche in the cable programming world by focusing on non-fiction and reality-based shows that mix entertainment and educational content. Discovery Channel's top shows include *Deadliest Catch* (a reality show focusing on the lives of crab fishermen in Alaska), *MythBusters* (using science — and more than a few explosions — to test modern-day myths and urban legends), and *Man vs. Wild* (survival techniques put to the test). The channel is also home to the popular Shark Week block of programming. DCI's TLC channel, meanwhile, has focused more on personal stories and themes of self-improvement. Its top shows include *Jon & Kate Plus Eight* and *What Not To Wear*.

DCI has been looking to expand its portfolio of cable channels in addition to maintaining its existing outlets. The company joined with talk show host Oprah Winfrey (through her production company Harpo) to form a joint venture channel called OWN: The Oprah Winfrey Network. The channel, which will replace Discovery Health Channel, is slated to launch in 2010. DCI also entered a partnership in 2009 with toy maker Hasbro to launch a new 50%-owned channel aimed at children. The makeover for Discovery Kids, which plans to debut in 2010, will include programming based on many of Hasbro's popular brands, including G.I. Joe, Scrabble, Tonka, and Transformers.

DCI became a public company in 2008 when joint venture partners Advance/Newhouse, an affiliate of Advance Publications, and Discovery Holding Company, controlled by Liberty Media chief John Malone, combined their stakes in the Discovery Channel and Animal Planet. Following the transaction, Advance/Newhouse controls more than 25% of DCI; Malone has more than 30% voting control.

HISTORY

John Hendricks, a history graduate who wanted to expand the presence of educational programming on TV, founded Cable Educational Network in 1982. Three years later he introduced the Discovery Channel. Devoted entirely to documentaries and nature shows, the channel premiered in 156,000 US homes. After dodging bankruptcy (it had $5,000 cash and $1 million in debt to the BBC), within a year the Discovery Channel had 7 million subscribers and a host of new investors, including Cox Cable Communications and TCI (now AT&T Broadband). It expanded its programming from 12 hours to 18 hours a day in 1987.

Discovery continued to attract subscribers, reaching more than 32 million by 1988. The next year it launched Discovery Channel Europe to more than 200,000 homes in the UK and Scandinavia. The company began selling home videos in 1990 and entered the Israeli market. The following year Discovery Communications, Inc. (DCI) was formed to house the company's operations, and it bought The Learning Channel (TLC, founded 1980). The company revamped TLC's programming and in 1992 introduced a daily six-hour commercial-free block of children's programs. The next year it introduced its first CD-ROM title, *In the Company of Whales*, based on the Discovery Channel documentary.

DCI increased its focus on international expansion in 1994, moving into Asia, Latin America, the Middle East, North Africa, Portugal, and Spain. The next year the company introduced its Web site and began selling company merchandise such as CD-ROMs and videos. DCI solidified its move into the retail sector in 1996 with the acquisition of The Nature Company and Scientific Revolution chains (renamed Discovery Channel Store). Also that year it launched its third major cable channel, Animal Planet.

The company continued expanding internationally throughout the mid-1990s, establishing operations in Australia, Canada, India, New Zealand, and South Korea (1995); Africa, Brazil, Germany, and Italy (1996); and Japan and Turkey (1997). DCI also added to its stable of cable channels with the purchase of 70% of the Travel Channel from Paxson Communications (now ION Media Networks) in 1997. (It acquired the remaining 30% interest in 1999.) The company's 1997 original production, "Titanic: Anatomy of a Disaster," attracted 3.2 million US households, setting a network ratings record.

The following year DCI and the BBC launched Animal Planet in Asia through a joint venture and agreed to market and distribute new cable channel BBC America. DCI spent $330 million launching its new health and fitness channel, Discovery Health, in 1999 and formed partnerships with high-speed online service Road Runner (to provide interactive information and services to Road Runner customers) and Rosenbluth Travel (to provide vacation packages based on DCI programming).

In 2002 the company launched a 24-hour high-definition television network called Discovery HD Theater. Two years later founder John Hendricks relinquished his CEO duties (he remained chairman). President Judy McHale replaced him.

DCI started off 2005 by rebranding its aviation-themed Discovery Wings channel as the Military Channel. Later that year former majority owner Liberty Media placed its stake in DCI into a new company called Discovery Holding, which it then spun off to Liberty shareholders.

Early in 2007 former NBC Universal Cable executive David Zaslav was named CEO, replacing McHale. DCI later bought out 25% partner Cox Communications in exchange for $1.3 billion in cash, along with such assets as the Travel Channel and Antenna Audio. It also began shuttering its chain of Discovery Channel Stores as part of a cost-cutting effort.

Joint venture partners Discovery Holding and Advance/Newhouse (an affiliate of Advance Publications) combined their stakes in Discovery Communications in 2008, spinning off DCI as a public company.

EXECUTIVES

Chairman: John S. Hendricks, age 57
President, CEO, and Director: David M. Zaslav, age 49,
 $8,336,781 total compensation
COO: Mark Hollinger
SEVP and CFO: Bradley E. (Brad) Singer, age 41,
 $1,789,518 total compensation
EVP and CIO: David R. Kline
Chief Marketing Officer: Wonya Y. Lucas
EVP Production and Chief Science Editor: Steve Burns
SEVP, General Counsel, and Secretary:
 Joseph A. (Joe) LaSala Jr., age 54,
 $1,207,773 total compensation
SEVP Human Resources: Adria A. Romm
**EVP Advertising Sales and Network Strategies,
 Discovery Networks US:** Evan Sternschein
EVP Sales, Digital Advertising Sales:
 Kathleen (Kathy) Kayse
**EVP and General Manager, Advertising Sales, Discovery
 Networks US:** Scott McGraw
**EVP; President and General Manager, Discovery
 Channel and The Science Channel:** Jane Root
**COO and EVP Discovery Channel and The Science
 Channel:** Tom Cosgrove
EVP Human Resources: Amy Girdwood
EVP Digital Media: Joshua Freeman
EVP Business Strategy and New Media: Doug Coblens
EVP Business Affairs: Clara Kim
SVP Corporate Affairs and Communications:
 David Leavy

LOCATIONS

HQ: Discovery Communications, Inc.
 1 Discovery Place, Silver Spring, MD 20910
Phone: 240-662-2000   **Fax:** 240-662-1868
Web: corporate.discovery.com

PRODUCTS/OPERATIONS

2008 Sales

	$ mil.	% of total
Distribution	1,640	48
Advertising	1,396	40
Other	407	12
Total	**3,443**	**100**

2008 Sales

	$ mil.	% of total
US networks	2,062	60
International networks	1,158	33
Commerce, education & other	196	6
Corporate	27	1
Total	**3,443**	**100**

Selected Operations

Cable channels
 Animal Planet
 Discovery Channel
 Discovery Health
 Discovery Kids
 FitTV
 HD Theater
 Investigation Discovery
 Military Channel
 Planet Green
 Science Channel
 TLC (The Learning Channel)

Commerce and education
 Discovery Education
 DiscoveryStore.com

COMPETITORS

A&E Networks	Fox Entertainment
CBS Corp	NBC Universal
Current Media	PBS
Disney	Scripps Networks
E! Entertainment	Turner Broadcasting
Television	Viacom

HISTORICAL FINANCIALS

Company Type: Public

Income Statement

FYE: December 31

	REVENUE ($ mil.)	NET INCOME ($ mil.)	NET PROFIT MARGIN	EMPLOYEES
12/08	3,443.0	317.0	9.2%	4,000
12/07	707.2	(68.4)	—	3,600
12/06	688.1	(46.0)	—	4,500
12/05	694.5	33.3	4.8%	3,800
12/04	631.2	66.1	10.5%	—
Annual Growth	**52.8%**	**48.0%**	**—**	**1.7%**

2008 Year-End Financials

Debt ratio: 60.2%
Return on equity: —
Cash ($ mil.): 100
Current ratio: 1.04
Long-term debt ($ mil.): 3,331

No. of shares (mil.): 282
Dividends
 Yield: 0.0%
 Payout: —
Market value ($ mil.): 3,992

Stock History

NASDAQ (GS): DISCA

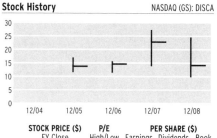

	STOCK PRICE ($) FY Close	P/E High/Low		PER SHARE ($) Earnings	Dividends	Book Value
12/08	14.16	25	10	0.98	0.00	19.64
12/07	22.81	—	—	(0.24)	0.00	15.94
12/06	14.60	—	—	(0.16)	0.00	16.14
12/05	13.74	140	98	0.12	0.00	16.23
Annual Growth	**1.0%**	**—**	**—**	**42.2%**	**—**	**6.2%**

DISH Network

DISH Network serves up fare intended to whet almost everyone's appetite for televised entertainment. The company is the #2 provider of direct broadcast satellite TV service (behind DIRECTV) in the US. The DISH Network provides programming to more than 13 million subscribers; customers include home viewers as well as business customers in such industries as hospitality, restaurants, and retail. DISH also has partnerships with voice and data communications providers including EarthLink, Qwest, and Sprint Nextel to offer bundled services. Co-founder and CEO Charlie Ergen controls about 58% of the voting power of the company through a beneficial ownership stake.

The DISH Network provides a wide range of programming (more than 2,700 digital video and audio channels) and has 14 leased or owned satellites in orbit. It operates digital broadcast operations centers in Arizona and Wyoming. Its subscribers receive service through a small satellite dish, digital set-top receivers, and remote controls.

Deals with telecom providers allow carriers to offer TV, Internet access, and voice as bundled services. The company's Satellite Services unit leases satellite capacity for audio, data, and video services. To thwart increased competition from

regional cable companies, DISH also has deals with local TV affiliates; it offers local channel service to markets in all 50 states.

A distribution agreement with AT&T had been responsible for about 17% of DISH's annual gross subscriber additions, but the deal expired in January 2009, at which point AT&T entered a new deal with chief rival DirecTV. DirecTV is the largest satellite TV provider in the US with more than 17.5 million subscribers.

The company has expanded its offerings to include Sirius Satellite Radio music channels, pay-per-view content, and local and national HD channels. DISH has also paid $712 million to acquire wireless spectrum licenses that the FCC granted to it in February 2009; DISH plans to utilize the additional available spectrum to roll out more bandwidth intensive HD programming in the future.

HISTORY

Charlie Ergen, a former financial analyst for Frito-Lay, founded a Denver company called Echosphere, a retailer of large-dish, C-band satellite TV equipment, with his wife, Cantey, and James DeFranco in 1980. Echosphere evolved into a national manufacturer and distributor, which in 1987 began its move toward the new direct broadcast satellite (DBS) delivery system. It filed for a DBS license and set up subsidiary EchoStar Communications Corporation to build, launch, and operate DBS satellites. In 1992 the FCC granted the company an orbital slot.

By 1994 Echosphere was the US's largest distributor of conventional home satellite equipment, but the future clearly rested with DBS and EchoStar. A 1995 reorganization renamed the firm EchoStar Communications; the Echosphere distributor business became a subsidiary. EchoStar also created the DISH (Digital Sky Highway) Network brand, aiming for an easier-to-remember name than its rivals' "DSS" and "USSB."

The company launched the EchoStar I satellite in 1995, followed a year later by EchoStar II. Commencing DISH Network service in 1996, EchoStar competed against other DBS providers, including DIRECTV, to win 350,000 subscribers by year's end.

In 1997 Rupert Murdoch scrubbed a deal that called for News Corp. to buy half of EchoStar for $1 billion; Ergen sued for $5 billion in damages. EchoStar also went public in 1997 and reached the 1-million-customer mark.

The next year EchoStar tangled again with Murdoch, winning FCC approval to access programming from FX Networks (owned by News Corp. and the former TCI, now AT&T's cable unit), despite FX Networks' claims that it was locked up in exclusive programming agreements with cable companies. That issue and the 1997 lawsuit were put to rest in 1999 when News Corp. and MCI WorldCom (now WorldCom) traded DBS assets, including an orbital slot, for a combined 15% stake in EchoStar.

That year EchoStar and DIRECTV joined forces to successfully lobby for federal legislation allowing local TV signals to be delivered by satellites nationwide. The company entered the Internet business, providing WebTV Internet access via satellite to customers through an agreement with US software giant Microsoft. EchoStar also bought Media4 (now EchoStar Data Networks), which specializes in providing Internet and data transmission over satellite networks.

In 2000, the company reached an agreement to distribute two-way broadband Internet access using technology developed by the Israel-based Gilat Satellite Networks and Microsoft in a joint venture called StarBand Communications. In addition, EchoStar paid $50 million for a 13% stake in startup WildBlue Communications, which has planned to launch two geostationary satellites used to offer the two-way data services. EchoStar later backed out of those alliances.

When Hughes Electronics, at that time the parent of DIRECTV, was put up for sale in 2001, EchoStar expressed interest. After months of negotiations, EchoStar appeared to have given up but instead made an unsolicited offer. Hughes' parent, General Motors, agreed to sell the company to EchoStar after News Corp. dropped out of the bidding. Regulators rejected the deal in 2002, and the companies abandoned their merger plans (To help in the effort to purchase DIRECTV, Vivendi Universal had acquired a 10% stake in EchoStar in a $1.5 billion deal that included a distribution alliance, but it sold the stake back to EchoStar after the merger failed).

In 2007 the company initiated a reorganization that resulted in the spinoff of its broadcast satellite receiver, antennae, and commercial satellite businesses as EchoStar Corporation. The remaining direct satellite subscription service operations became known as DISH Network Corporation. Also in 2007 DISH bought video technology-maker Sling Media for $380 million in order to boost its technology development operations.

In a 2008 federal appeals court decision, a previous patent infringement ruling brought against DISH Network by digital video recorder maker TiVo was upheld. The company was ordered to pay $94 million in damages for violating a software patent held by TiVo that enables viewers to watch one program while recording others.

EXECUTIVES

Chairman, President, and CEO:
Charles W. (Charlie) Ergen, age 56, $829,124 total compensation
COO: Bernard L. (Bernie) Han, age 45, $305,633 total compensation
EVP and CFO: Robert E. Olson, age 50
Chief Marketing Officer: Ira H. Bahr, age 46
EVP and Chief Human Resources Officer:
Stephen W. Wood, age 50
EVP Sales, Distribution, Travel/Events, and Marketing and Director: James DeFranco, age 56, $1,133,979 total compensation
EVP Corporate Development: Thomas A. Cullen, age 49
EVP Commercial and Business Development:
Michael Kelly, age 47, $1,063,774 total compensation
EVP Operations: W. Erik Carlson, age 39
EVP, General Counsel, and Secretary:
R. Stanton Dodge, age 41
SVP Programming: Dave Shull
VP Ad Sales: Michael Finn
Auditors: KPMG LLP

LOCATIONS

HQ: DISH Network Corporation
9601 S. Meridian Blvd., Englewood, CO 80112
Phone: 303-723-1000 **Fax:** 303-723-1999
Web: www.dishnetwork.com

PRODUCTS/OPERATIONS

2008 Sales

	$ mil.	% of total
Subscriber-related revenue	11,455	99
Equipment sales & other	162	1
Total	**11,617**	**100**

COMPETITORS

AT&T	Rainbow Media
Cablevision Systems	RCN Corporation
Charter Communications	Time Warner Cable
Comcast	TiVo
Cox Communications	Verizon
DIRECTV	Xanadoo

HISTORICAL FINANCIALS

Company Type: Public

Income Statement   FYE: December 31

	REVENUE ($ mil.)	NET INCOME ($ mil.)	NET PROFIT MARGIN	EMPLOYEES
12/08	11,617.2	902.9	7.8%	26,000
12/07	11,090.4	756.1	6.8%	23,000
12/06	9,818.5	608.3	6.2%	21,000
12/05	8,425.5	1,514.5	18.0%	21,000
12/04	7,151.2	214.8	3.0%	20,000
Annual Growth	**12.9%**	**43.2%**	—	**6.8%**

2008 Year-End Financials

Debt ratio: —
Return on equity: —
Cash ($ mil.): 99
Current ratio: 0.70
Long-term debt ($ mil.): 4,969

No. of shares (mil.): 447
Dividends
  Yield: 0.0%
  Payout: —
Market value ($ mil.): 4,955

Stock History   NASDAQ (GS): DISH

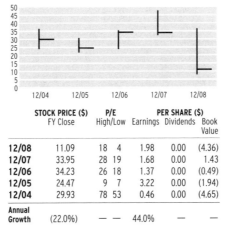

	STOCK PRICE ($) FY Close	P/E High/Low		PER SHARE ($) Earnings	Dividends	Book Value
12/08	11.09	18	4	1.98	0.00	(4.36)
12/07	33.95	28	19	1.68	0.00	1.43
12/06	34.23	26	18	1.37	0.00	(0.49)
12/05	24.47	9	7	3.22	0.00	(1.94)
12/04	29.93	78	53	0.46	0.00	(4.65)
Annual Growth	**(22.0%)**	—	—	**44.0%**	—	—

Dole Food

Fans of bananas and other fresh fruit might find this company to be a-peel-ing. Dole Food is the world's largest producer of fresh fruit and vegetables, known best as the top grower of bananas, pineapples, and other tropical varieties of fruit. The company sources its produce from growers in 25 countries, distributing products under the Dole brand to supermarkets, mass merchandisers, and other customers in about 90 countries. In addition to fresh fruits and vegetables, Dole produces packaged foods such as canned fruit and juices. Tracing its roots to 1851, Dole Food is owned by chairman David Murdock; the company plans to go public through an IPO.

Murdock, who has served as chairman of the company since 1985, took Dole private in 2003 through a $2.5 billion buyout that left the company saddled with substantial debt. Over time,

Dole has been divesting some of its holdings in an effort to pay down that debt, including the sale of its fresh-cut flowers business and some real estate holdings. The company announced plans in 2009 for a public stock offering to raise as much as $500 million, most of which will be used for debt relief.

Dole has become a powerhouse in the fresh produce business thanks to its large-scale sourcing and distribution operation, which allows the company to offer a greater variety of products and which guards against the risk of poor growing seasons in a particular region. It competes on a global scale primarily against such rivals as Chiquita Brands and Fresh Del Monte Produce, though the produce business also includes a large number of local and regional suppliers.

The company is also keen on expanding its value-added and packaged food businesses. Dole has introduced convenience-oriented products such as bagged vegetables, ready-to-eat salads, and individual fruit servings packaged in plastic cups and bowls, as well as niche products such as organic bananas.

Other product development efforts have included a partnership with Monsanto to create vegetables that are more appealing to consumers. With the help of the agriproducts giant, Dole hopes the new plant breeding techniques will result in improved nutritional content, flavor, color, and texture.

HISTORY

James Dole embarked on an unlikely career in a faraway land when he graduated from Harvard College in 1899 and sailed to Hawaii. He bought 61 acres of farmland for $4,000 in 1900 and the next year organized the Hawaiian Pineapple Company, announcing that the island's pineapples would eventually be in every US grocery store.

Others had tried and failed to sell fresh fruit to the mainland. Dole decided he would succeed by canning pineapples. He built his first cannery in 1903 and introduced a national magazine advertising campaign in 1908 designed to make consumers associate Hawaii with pineapples (then considered exotic fruits).

In 1922 Dole expanded his production by buying the island of Lanai, where he set up a pineapple plantation. He financed the purchase by selling a third interest in Hawaiian Pineapple to Waialua Agricultural Company, which was part of Castle & Cooke (C&C). Samuel Castle and Amos Cooke, missionaries to Hawaii, formed C&C in 1851 to manage their church's failing depository, which supplied outlying mission posts with staple goods. In 1858 they entered the sugar business and within 10 years served as agents for several Hawaiian sugar plantations and the ships that carried their cargoes.

C&C gained control of Hawaiian Pineapple in 1932 when it acquired an additional 21% interest in the business. The company began using the Dole name on packaging the next year. Dole became chairman of the board of the reorganized company in 1935 but pursued other business interests until he retired in 1948.

Hawaiian Pineapple was run separately until C&C bought the remainder in 1961. The company started pineapple and banana farms in the Philippines in 1963 to supply markets in East Asia. C&C began importing bananas when it purchased 55% of Standard Fruit of New Orleans in 1964. (It purchased the remainder four years later.)

Heavily in debt and limping from two hostile takeover attempts, C&C agreed in 1985 to merge with Flexi-Van, a container leasing company. The merger brought with it needed capital, Flexi-Van owner David Murdock (who became C&C's CEO), and a fleet of ships to transport produce. Murdock began trimming back, leaving C&C with its fruit and real estate operations. He then decided to end all pineapple operations on Lanai to concentrate on tourist properties. (The company took a $168 million write-off on them in 1995, when it spun off its real estate and resort operations as Castle & Cooke.)

C&C became Dole Food in 1991. The company expanded at home and internationally, adding SAMICA (dried fruits and nuts, Europe, 1992), Dromedary (dates, US, 1994), Chiquita's New Zealand produce operations (1995), and SABA Trading (60%, produce importing and distribution, Sweden, 1998; Dole acquired 100% of SABA in 2005).

In 1995 Dole sold its juice business to Seagram's Tropicana Products division, keeping its pineapple juices and licensing the Dole name to Seagram. (PepsiCo bought Tropicana in 1998.) Dole entered the fresh-flower trade in 1998 by acquiring four major growers and marketers. It is now the world's largest producer of freshly cut flowers.

A worldwide banana glut, Hurricane Mitch, and severe freezes in California hit the company hard in late 1998. The next year Dole launched cost-cutting measures, which by early 2000 had ripened into better earnings. Nonetheless, cutbacks and disposals continued throughout 2001.

In 2002 Murdock made a cash and debt takeover bid for the company worth about $2.5 billion. However, at least one minority shareholder was dissatisfied with the offer and filed a proposal calling for Murdock's resignation. After his offer was rejected, Murdock raised his bid, and the company agreed to the buyout the following year.

In 2004 Lawrence Kern, Dole's president and COO, left the company; chairman, CEO, and sole owner Murdock took over as president. In 2004 CFO Richard Dahl became president. Also in 2004 the company acquired frozen fruit manufacturer J.R. Wood, Inc., which it renamed Dole Packaged Frozen Foods, Inc. It also acquired fresh berry producer Coastal Berry Company (now Dole Berry Company) in 2004, making Dole a top North American strawberry producer.

EXECUTIVES

Chairman: David H. Murdock, age 86
President, CEO, and Director: David A. DeLorenzo, age 62
VP and CFO: Joseph S. Tesoriero, age 56
EVP, Chief of Staff, and Director: Roberta Wieman, age 63
VP, Corporate Controller, and Chief Accounting Officer: Yoon J. Hugh
EVP Corporate Development and Director: Scott A. Griswold, age 56
EVP, General Counsel, Corporate Secretary, and Director: C. Michael Carter, age 66
SVP Worldwide Human Resources and Industrial Relations: Sue Hagen
VP and Director, Dole Nutrition Institute: Jennifer Grossman
VP and Director Worldwide Corporate Social Responsibility: Sylvain Cuperlier
VP New Products and Corporate Development and Director: Justin M. Murdock, age 36
General Manager, Dole Packaged Foods Philippines (Dolefil): Kevin Davis
Manager Corporate Social Responsibility: Roberto Vega
Auditors: Deloitte & Touche LLP

LOCATIONS

HQ: Dole Food Company, Inc.
1 Dole Dr., Westlake Village, CA 91362
Phone: 818-879-6600 **Fax:** 818-879-6615
Web: www.dole.com

2008 Sales

	$ mil.	% of total
US	2,983.0	39
Europe		
Sweden	564.5	7
Germany	551.6	7
UK	242.3	3
Other countries	944.5	12
Japan	723.2	10
Canada	287.7	4
Other regions	1,323.2	17
Total	**7,620.0**	**100**

PRODUCTS/OPERATIONS

2008 Sales

	$ mil.	% of total
Fresh fruit	5,401.1	71
Packaged foods	1,130.8	15
Fresh vegetables	1,086.9	14
Other	1.1	—
Total	**7,620.0**	**100**

COMPETITORS

A. Duda & Sons	Ocean Mist Farms
Bonduelle	Ocean Spray
Calavo Growers	Ready Pac
Chiquita Brands	Seneca Foods
Del Monte Foods	Sunkist
Fresh Del Monte Produce	Sunsweet Growers
Fresh Kist Produce	Tanimura & Antle
Fyffes	Taylor Fresh Foods
Maui Land & Pineapple	Tropicana
National Grape Cooperative	Worldwide Fruit

HISTORICAL FINANCIALS

Company Type: Private

Income Statement		FYE: Saturday nearest December 31		
	REVENUE ($ mil.)	NET INCOME ($ mil.)	NET PROFIT MARGIN	EMPLOYEES
12/08	7,620.0	122.8	1.6%	75,800
12/07	6,931.0	(57.5)	—	87,000
12/06	6,171.5	(89.0)	—	75,000
12/05	5,870.6	—	—	72,000
12/04	5,316.2	—	—	64,000
Annual Growth	**9.4%**	**—**	**—**	**4.3%**

Net Income History

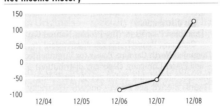

Dominion Resources

And darkness shall have no dominion, as far as Dominion Resources is concerned. Through its Dominion Virginia Power the company transmits and distributes electricity to 2.4 million customers and natural gas to 1.7 million customers in five states. Its Dominion Generation unit manages the company's regulated and nonregulated power plants (27,000 MW of owned or controlled capacity); subsidiary Dominion Energy trades and markets energy, oversees 14,000 miles of natural gas pipelines, and operates underground gas storage facilities (975 billion cu. ft. of capacity). Though it's divested most of its exploration and production operations, Dominion does own 1.2 trillion cu. ft. of natural gas reserves.

In 2007 Dominion sold most of its oil and gas exploration and production assets — excluding its Appalachian operations, because they offer less risk and fit better with the company's gathering and storage systems — for nearly $14 billion. The next year it agreed to sell The Peoples Natural Gas Company and Hope Gas Inc., located in Pennsylvania and West Virginia, to Babcock & Brown for $910 million.

HISTORY

In 1781 the Virginia General Assembly established a group of trustees, including George Washington and James Madison, to promote navigation on the Appomattox River. The group (named the Appomattox Trustees) formed the Upper Appomattox Company in 1795 to secure its water rights. The company eventually began operating hydroelectric plants on the river, and by 1888 it had added a steam-powered plant to its portfolio.

The Virginia Railway and Power Company (VR&P), led by Frank Jay Gould, purchased the Upper Appomattox Company (which had changed its name) in 1909. The next year the firm acquired several electric and gas utilities, as well as some electric streetcar lines.

In 1925 New York engineering company Stone & Webster acquired VR&P. The company became known as Virginia Electric and Power Company (Virginia Power) and was placed under Engineers Public Service (EPS), a new holding company. Virginia Power purchased several North Carolina utilities following its acquisition.

During the 1930s the Depression (and the popularity of the automobile) led the company to exit the trolley business. The Public Utility Holding Company Act of 1935 (repealed in 2005), which ushered in an era of regulated utility monopolies, forced EPS to divest all of its operations except Virginia Power. However, the utility soon merged with the Virginia Public Service Company, thus doubling its service territory.

The company added new power plants to keep up with growing customer demand in the 1950s. Always an innovator, it also built an extra-high-voltage transmission system, the first in the world.

In the 1970s Virginia Power's first nuclear plants became operational. By 1980, however, the firm was near bankruptcy. That year William Berry, who had completed a 23-year rise through the ranks to become president, canceled two other nuclear units. He also became an early supporter of competition in the electric utility industry. In 1983 he formed Dominion Resources as a

HISTORICAL FINANCIALS
Company Type: Public

Income Statement
FYE: Sunday nearest December 31

	REVENUE ($ mil.)	NET INCOME ($ mil.)	NET PROFIT MARGIN	EMPLOYEES
12/08	1,425.1	54.0	3.8%	10,500
12/07	1,462.9	37.9	2.6%	12,500
12/06	1,437.3	106.2	7.4%	13,300
12/05	1,511.6	108.3	7.2%	13,500
12/04	1,446.5	62.3	4.3%	13,500
Annual Growth	(0.4%)	(3.5%)	—	(6.1%)

2008 Year-End Financials

Debt ratio: —	No. of shares (mil.): 58
Return on equity: —	Dividends
Cash ($ mil.): 45	Yield: 0.0%
Current ratio: 1.70	Payout: —
Long-term debt ($ mil.): 1,704	Market value ($ mil.): 271

Stock History
NYSE: DPZ

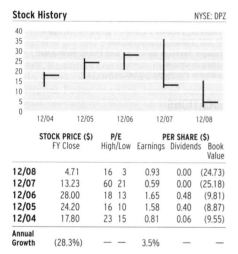

	STOCK PRICE ($) FY Close	P/E High/Low		PER SHARE ($) Earnings	Dividends	Book Value
12/08	4.71	16	3	0.93	0.00	(24.73)
12/07	13.23	60	21	0.59	0.00	(25.18)
12/06	28.00	18	13	1.65	0.48	(9.81)
12/05	24.20	16	10	1.58	0.40	(8.87)
12/04	17.80	23	15	0.81	0.06	(9.55)
Annual Growth	(28.3%)	—	—	3.5%	—	—

Donaldson Company

Grime fighter Donaldson is cleaning up the industrial world. The company makes filtration systems designed to remove contaminants from air and liquids. Donaldson's engine products business makes air intake and exhaust systems, liquid-filtration systems, and replacement parts; products are sold to manufacturers of construction, mining, and transportation equipment, as well as parts distributors and fleet operators. The company's industrial products include dust, fume, and mist collectors and air filtration systems used in industrial gas turbines, computer disk drives, and manufacturers' clean rooms. Donaldson has more than 100 locations worldwide.

The company is pursuing a strategy of growth through the diversification of its products and technologies, and has acquired number of companies to build its global brand base (30 major brands, including Duratek, Formix, PowerCore, Synteq, Tetratex, and Ultrafilter).

In particular, Donaldson is adding to its engine and industrial segment and its first fit-solutions and replacement filters businesses. Acquisitions have included AirCel Corporation, a privately held manufacturer of dryers and purification equipment (2006); Aerospace Filtration Systems, from Westar Aerospace and Defense Group (2007); and Western Filter Corp., a maker of liquid filtration systems and replacement filters (2008).

HISTORY

Frank Donaldson, a salesman for Bull Tractor, invented the first air filter for a combustion engine in 1915 after a tractor he had sold kept breaking down. Noticing a buildup of dirt in the intake manifold, he made a filter out of wire mesh and cloth. The tractor ran, but Donaldson lost his job: His boss did not appreciate his pointing out a defect in the company's products. Donaldson started his own company with his father and his brother Bob to make air filters for tractors. In 1941 the company won a contract to make air filters for US army tanks. Frank Donaldson died in 1945, and John Emblom became president. In 1951 Emblom and a group of senior managers tried to buy the company from the Donaldson family but were rebuffed. Emblom and his allies quit, and Frank Donaldson Jr. became president. The company went public in 1955.

Under Frank Jr. the company expanded, introducing new products (including the first paper filter for the heavy-duty air-cleaner industry) and buying other companies. In 1974 Donaldson bought Torit, which expanded the company into industrial dust collection. Frank Jr. retired as CEO in 1981.

During the 1990s Donaldson continued to expand its product line. In 1998 the company increased its ownership in PT Panata Jaya Mandiri, an Indonesian joint venture, to 30%. The next year it bought AirMaze (industrial compressor filters) and opened a manufacturing facility in China.

Donaldson acquired DCE (dust collection systems, UK) from Invensys in 2000. It then combined DCE with its Torit business to form Donaldson Dust Collection.

In 2002 Donaldson bought German-based ultrafilter international AG — maker of compressed air purification components. The next year the company expanded its hydraulic filters business with the acquisition of LHA Industrial.

In 2004 Donaldson formed an aerospace and defense business unit, merging the operations of its aircraft and defense groups. The company also sold a manufacturing plant located in Stow, Ohio, to Falls Filtration Technology. Later that year Bill Van Dyke stepped down as president and CEO of the company, retaining his position as chairman. SVP Bill Cook was appointed president and CEO to replace him. (Cook was named chairman the next year after Van Dyke retired.) Donaldson closed out 2004 with the acquisition of Canadian liquid filter manufacturer Triboguard Company.

EXECUTIVES

Chairman, President, and CEO: William M. (Bill) Cook, age 55
VP and CFO: Thomas R. (Tom) VerHage, age 57
VP and CTO: Debra L. (Deb) Wilfong, age 53
VP and CIO: Mary Lynne Perushek, age 50
SVP Global Operations: Lowell F. Schwab, age 60
SVP Industrial Products: Charles J. (Charlie) McMurray, age 55
SVP Engine Products: Jay L. Ward, age 44
VP, General Counsel, and Secretary: Norman C. Linnell, age 49

VP Disk Drive and Microelectronic: Peggy A. Herrmann, age 53
VP Human Resources and Communications: Sandra N. Joppa, age 43
VP Europe and Middle East: Tod E. Carpenter, age 50
VP Asia/Pacific: David W. Timm, age 55
VP Global OEM Sales and Customer Service: Dennis D. Jandik, age 55
VP Global Engine Aftermarket Sales: Joseph E. Lehman, age 54
Director Investor Relations: Richard J. (Rich) Sheffer
Auditors: PricewaterhouseCoopers LLP

LOCATIONS

HQ: Donaldson Company, Inc.
1400 W. 94th St., Minneapolis, MN 55431
Phone: 952-887-3131   **Fax:** 952-887-3155
Web: www.donaldson.com

2008 Sales

	$ mil.	% of total
US	888.6	40
Europe	766.8	34
Asia/Pacific	471.3	21
Other regions	105.8	5
Total	**2,232.5**	**100**

PRODUCTS/OPERATIONS

2008 Sales

	$ mil.	% of total
Engine products		
Aftermarket products	657.3	29
Off-road products	448.7	20
Transportation products	123.2	5
Industrial products		
Industrial filtration products	600.5	27
Special application products	213.1	10
Gas turbine products	189.7	9
Total	**2,232.5**	**100**

COMPETITORS

AAF-McQUAY
Cummins
MFRI
Millipore
Pall Corporation
Siemens Water Technologies
Williams Controls

HISTORICAL FINANCIALS
Company Type: Public

Income Statement
FYE: July 31

	REVENUE ($ mil.)	NET INCOME ($ mil.)	NET PROFIT MARGIN	EMPLOYEES
7/08	2,232.5	172.0	7.7%	12,700
7/07	1,918.8	150.7	7.9%	12,000
7/06	1,694.3	132.3	7.8%	11,500
7/05	1,595.7	110.6	6.9%	11,180
7/04	1,415.0	106.3	7.5%	10,400
Annual Growth	12.1%	12.8%	—	5.1%

2008 Year-End Financials

Debt ratio: 23.8%	No. of shares (mil.): 77
Return on equity: 25.2%	Dividends
Cash ($ mil.): 83	Yield: 0.9%
Current ratio: 1.65	Payout: 19.8%
Long-term debt ($ mil.): 176	Market value ($ mil.): 3,481

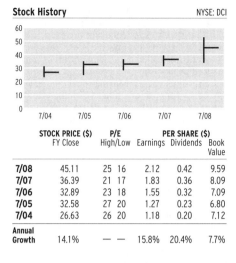

	STOCK PRICE ($) FY Close	P/E High/Low		PER SHARE ($) Earnings	Dividends	Book Value
7/08	45.11	25	16	2.12	0.42	9.59
7/07	36.39	21	17	1.83	0.36	8.09
7/06	32.89	23	18	1.55	0.32	7.09
7/05	32.58	27	20	1.27	0.23	6.80
7/04	26.63	26	20	1.18	0.20	7.12
Annual Growth	14.1%	—	—	15.8%	20.4%	7.7%

Dover Corporation

The "D" in Dover could stand for diversity. Dover manages approximately 40 companies that make equipment ranging from car wash systems to aerospace components. Dover operates in four segments: Electronic Technologies, Engineered Systems, Fluid Management, and Industrial Products. The company maintains a highly decentralized management culture, with a president for each division as well as for each subsidiary company. It has kept up a long-term acquisition and divestment strategy, participating in several transactions per year. The diversification means that while Dover might benefit from some changing economic tides, it may be negatively impacted concurrently by others.

The company is keen on reorganization that yields more defined market segments and greater clarity for shareholders and Wall Street. Dover acquires businesses that manufacture and distribute engineered industrial products that will expand its products portfolio and geographic markets. In 2008 Dover acquired four add-on businesses for an aggregate cost of $104 million: LANTEX Winch & Gear, Brady's Mining & Construction Supply (diamond drill bits for underground mining operations), Neptune Chemical Pump (metering pumps), and Hiltap Fittings (sealing couplings, connectors for petrochemical and nuclear markets).

Dover continues to increase its expansion into international markets, including South America, Asia, and Eastern Europe. Most of its non-US subsidiaries and affiliates are based in Brazil, China, Europe, India, Malaysia, and Mexico. Products are marketed directly to OEMs worldwide and through global dealers and distribution networks to industrial end users.

Robert Livingston was named CEO and elected to the board in late 2008. He took over the reins from Ronald Hoffman, who retired.

HISTORY

George Ohrstrom, a New York stockbroker, formed Dover in 1955 and took it public that year. Originally headquartered in Washington, DC, Dover consisted of four companies: C. Lee Cook (compressor seals and piston rings), Peerless (space-venting heaters), Rotary Lift (automotive lifts), and W.C. Norris (components for oil wells). In 1958 Dover made the first of many acquisitions and entered the elevator industry by buying Shepard Warner Elevator.

Dover continued to diversify throughout the 1960s. Acquisitions included OPW (gas pump nozzles) in 1961 and De-Sta-Co (industrial clamps and valves) the next year. OPW head Thomas Sutton became Dover's president in 1964, and the company moved its headquarters to New York City. Dover acquired Groen Manufacturing (food industry products) in 1967 and Ronningen-Petter (filter-strainer units) the following year.

During the 1970s Dover expanded beyond its core industries (building materials, industrial components, and equipment). In 1975 it acquired Dieterich Standard, a maker of liquid-measurement instruments. Dieterich Standard's president, Gary Roubos, became Dover's president and COO in 1977 and its CEO in 1981. The company sold Peerless in 1977 and acquired electronics assembly equipment manufacturer Universal Instruments in 1979.

Electronics became an increasingly important part of Dover's business during the 1980s. The company bought K&L Microwave, a maker of microwave filters used in satellites and cable TV equipment (1983), Dielectric Laboratories (microwave filter parts, 1985), and NURAD (microwave antennas, 1986). Between 1985 and 1990 Dover bought some 25 companies, including Weldcraft Products (welding equipment, 1985), Wolfe Frostop (salad bars, 1987), Weaver Corp. (automotive lifts, 1987), General Elevator (1988), Texas Hydraulics (1988), Security Elevator (1990), and Marathon Equipment (waste-handling equipment, 1990).

The corporation spun off its DOVatron circuit board assembly subsidiary to shareholders in 1993 after finding that DOVatron was competing with important Dover customers. That year Dover acquired The Heil Company (garbage trucks).

President/COO Thomas Reece succeeded Gary Roubos as CEO in 1994. Dover purchased 10 companies that year, including Hill Phoenix (commercial refrigeration cases) and Koolrad Design & Manufacturing (radiators for transformers). In 1995 it bought France-based Imaje (ink-jet printers and specialty inks) for $200 million. It was the largest purchase in the company's history at the time.

The following year Dover bought Everett Charles Technologies, a maker of electronic testing equipment. In 1998 the company sold its Dover elevator unit — a popular brand, but a management headache — to German steel giant Thyssen (now ThyssenKrupp) for $1.1 billion.

Dover continued its acquisitive ways in 1999 and 2000, picking up 18 and 23 companies, respectively. Notable were Alphasem, which makes semiconductor manufacturing equipment, and Graphics Microsystems, which took Dover into the pressroom equipment market. Dover picked up Triton Systems, a maker of ATMs, in 2000. The following year Dover acquired Kurz-Kasch, a US-based electromagnetic manufacturer with customers in the automotive market.

Dover looked to Asia, and China in particular, as its best hope for near-term growth for its beleaguered telecommunications and electronic assembly businesses; Dover subsidiary Universal Instruments christened a major manufacturing plant in China early in 2003.

In mid-2003 VP Ronald Hoffman, who also served as president and CEO of Dover Resources, was promoted to president and COO of the parent company. Hoffman took over as CEO at the outset of 2005, becoming only the fifth chief executive of Dover Corp.

In 2005 the company aquired Knowles Electronics for $750 million. Knowles makes components for hearing aids and microphones for high-end cell phones. Following that Dover sold Dover Diversified's Tranter, a manufacturer of heat transfer products, to the Swedish equipment maker Alfa Laval.

Among the divestitures in 2006 were Alphasem, Hover-Davis, Universal Instruments, and Vitronics Soltec from the Circuit Assembly and Test Group and Mark Andy from the Product Identification Group.

Also in 2006 Dover acquired Paladin Brands Holding, a manufacturer of attachments and tools for heavy and light mobile construction equipment. Paladin's products were also employed with mobile equipment used in demolition, forestry, material handling, and recycling, among other applications. Dover bought the company from Norwest Equity Partners.

EXECUTIVES

Chairman: Robert W. Cremin, age 68
President, CEO, and Director:
 Robert A. (Bob) Livingston, age 56,
 $4,218,017 total compensation
VP Finance and CFO: Brad M. Cerepak, age 50
VP and Senior Advisor: Robert G. (Rob) Kuhbach,
 age 62, $2,787,133 total compensation
**VP; President and CEO, Dover Electronic
 Technologies:** David R. Van Loan, age 60,
 $4,599,855 total compensation
VP; President and CEO, Dover Industrial Products:
 David J. (Dave) Ropp, age 63,
 $4,394,644 total compensation
VP, General Counsel, and Secretary: Joseph W. Schmidt,
 age 62
VP; Director, Dover Industrial Products:
 Timothy J. (Tim) Sandker, age 60
VP Human Resources: Jay L. Kloosterboer, age 48
VP and Controller: Raymond T. McKay Jr., age 55
VP Taxation: George Pompetzki, age 56
VP; President and CEO, Dover Fluid Management:
 William W. (Bill) Spurgeon, age 50,
 $4,261,847 total compensation
VP; President and CEO, Dover Engineered Systems:
 Raymond (Ray) Hoglund, age 58
VP; President, Fluid Solutions:
 Sivasankaran (Soma) Somasundaram, age 43
VP; President, Material Handling Platform:
 Thomas (Tom) Giacomini, age 43
VP Corporate Development: Stephen R. Sellhausen,
 age 50
Treasurer and Director Investor Relations:
 Paul E. Goldberg, age 45
Auditors: PricewaterhouseCoopers LLP

LOCATIONS

HQ: Dover Corporation
 280 Park Ave., Fl. 34W, New York, NY 10017
Phone: 212-922-1640   **Fax:** 212-922-1656
Web: www.dovercorporation.com

2008 Sales

	$ mil.	% of total
Americas		
US	4,246.8	56
Other countries	642.7	9
Europe	1,544.1	20
Asia	968.2	13
Other regions	167.1	2
Total	**7,568.9**	**100**

PRODUCTS/OPERATIONS

2008 Sales

	$ mil.	% of total
Industrial Products	2,459.5	32
Engineered Systems	2,010.4	27
Fluid Management	1,714.0	23
Electronic Technologies	1,396.1	18
Adjustments	(11.1)	—
Total	**7,568.9**	**100**

Selected Companies

Industrial Products
Material Handling
  DE-STA-CO Industries
  Paladin
  Texas Hydraulics
  Tulsa Winch
  Warn Industries
Mobile Equipment
  Chief Automotive
  Crenlo, LLC
  Heil Environmental
  Heil Trailer International
  Marathon Equipment Co.
  PDQ Manufacturing
  Performance Motorsports
  Rotary Lift
  Sargent

Engineered Systems
Engineered Products
  Belvac Production Machinery
  Hill PHOENIX
  SWEP
  Tipper Tie
  Triton Systems
  Unified Brands
Product Identification
  Datamax Corporation
  Markem-Imaje
  O'Neil Product Development

Fluid Management
Energy
  Energy Products Group
  Gas Equipment Group
  Waukesha Bearings Corp.
Fluid Solutions
  Colder Products Company
  Hydro Systems
  OPW Fluid Transfer Group
  OPW Fueling Components
  Pump Solutions Group

Electronic Technologies
Ceramic Products Group
DEK
Everett Charles Technologies
Knowles Electronics
Microwave Products Group
OK International
Vectron International

COMPETITORS

Carlisle Companies	Navistar
Cookson Group	Oshkosh Truck
Cooper Industries	Paul Mueller
Crane Co.	Power Packaging
Gardner Denver	Sequa
IDEX	Smith Bits
Ingersoll-Rand	Snap-on
Ingersoll-Rand Industrial	Swagelok
Technologies	Tatung
Kaydon	Thermador Groupe
KEMET	Wastequip
KSB AG	Weatherford International
Mark IV	Weston EU
Middleby	

HISTORICAL FINANCIALS

Company Type: Public

Income Statement

FYE: December 31

	REVENUE ($ mil.)	NET INCOME ($ mil.)	NET PROFIT MARGIN	EMPLOYEES
12/08	7,568.9	590.8	7.8%	32,300
12/07	7,226.1	661.1	9.1%	33,400
12/06	6,511.6	561.8	8.6%	33,000
12/05	6,078.4	510.1	8.4%	31,650
12/04	5,488.1	412.8	7.5%	28,100
Annual Growth	**8.4%**	**9.4%**	**—**	**3.5%**

2008 Year-End Financials

Debt ratio: 49.1%
Return on equity: 15.3%
Cash ($ mil.): 547
Current ratio: 2.11
Long-term debt ($ mil.): 1,861
No. of shares (mil.): 186
Dividends
  Yield: 2.7%
  Payout: 28.8%
Market value ($ mil.): 6,128

Stock History

NYSE: DOV

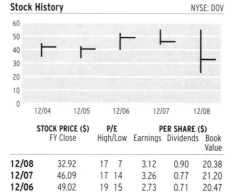

	STOCK PRICE ($) FY Close	P/E High/Low		PER SHARE ($) Earnings	Dividends	Book Value
12/08	32.92	17	7	3.12	0.90	20.38
12/07	46.09	17	14	3.26	0.77	21.20
12/06	49.02	19	15	2.73	0.71	20.47
12/05	40.49	17	14	2.50	0.66	17.89
12/04	41.94	22	17	2.02	0.62	16.75
Annual Growth	**(5.9%)**	**—**	**—**	**11.5%**	**9.8%**	**5.0%**

Dow Chemical

Dow Chemical is a leader in the production of plastics, chemicals, hydrocarbons, and agrochemicals. The largest chemical company in the US and #2 worldwide (ahead of ExxonMobil and behind BASF), Dow also is a leader in performance plastics (engineering plastics, polyurethanes, and materials for Dow Automotive). Other products include polyethylene resins for packaging (such as Styrofoam brand insulation), fibers, and films, as well as performance chemicals like acrylic acid. The company also manufactures commodity chemicals (chlor-alkalies and glycols) and agricultural chemicals. Its last unit, Hydrocarbons and Energy, makes petrochemicals. Dow also owns half of silicone products maker Dow Corning.

Good times for performance products (both performance chemicals and performance plastics) and advanced materials have led the way for Dow, which will focus on growing those segments ahead of old reliables such as basic chemicals. A major move in that direction was the 2007 acquisition of Wolff Walsrode, a maker of cellulose derivatives used in construction materials and personal care products, from the Bayer Group.

In 2007, the company agreed with Chevron Phillips Chemical to combine their respective styrene businesses in the Americas into a 50-50 joint venture. The idea behind the JV is to capitalize on Dow's experience and expertise in the field as well as CPChem's feedstock resources. The venture, called Americas Styrenics, commenced production in 2008.

Continuing the transformational theme, Dow agreed to spend more than $15 billion to buy specialty chemicals maker Rohm and Haas in 2008. Among the largest specialty chemicals makers in the world, Rohm and Haas produces coatings additives, electronics materials, acrylates, and salt products.

The deal encountered trouble, however, as Dow began to move more slowly as the closing date approached. Rohm and Haas then filed suit to try to force Dow to close the acquisition. Eventually the companies were able to work it out, and the deal closed at the beginning of 2009's second quarter. As part of the renewed agreement, and to help pay down debt accumulated from the deal, Rohm and Haas agreed to sell salt-producing subsidiary Morton International to the German company K+S for about $1.7 billion.

HISTORY

Herbert Dow founded Dow Chemical in 1897 after developing a process to extract bromides and chlorides from underground brine deposits around Midland, Michigan. Its first product was chlorine bleach. Dow eventually overcame British and German monopolies on bleach, bromides, and other chemicals.

In the mid-1920s Dow rejected a takeover by DuPont. By 1930, the year of Herbert Dow's death, sales had reached $15 million. Dow started building new plants around the country in the late 1930s.

Dow research yielded new plastics in the 1940s, such as Saran Wrap, the company's initial major consumer product. In 1952 Dow built a plant in Japan (Asahi-Dow), its first subsidiary outside North America. Plastics represented 32% of sales by 1957, compared with 2% in 1940. Strong sales of plastics and silicone products propelled the company into the top ranks of US firms. Dow entered the pharmaceutical field with the 1960 purchase of Allied Labs.

Dow suffered earnings drops from 1981 to 1983 from falling chemical prices. To limit the cyclical effect of chemicals on profits, the company expanded its interests in pharmaceuticals and consumer goods. In 1989 it merged its pharmaceutical division with Marion Labs to create Marion Merrell Dow (it sold its 71% stake to Hoechst in 1995). Also in 1989 it formed DowElanco, a joint venture with Eli Lilly to produce agricultural chemicals.

Following allegations that it had put a breast implant on the market without proper testing, Dow Corning (a joint venture with glassmaker Corning Inc.), the #1 producer of silicone breast implants, stopped making the devices in 1992. In 1995 a federal judge ordered Dow to pay a Nevada woman $14 million in damages — the first breast-implant verdict against the company as a sole defendant. Facing thousands of pending cases, Dow Corning filed for bankruptcy protection. (In 1998 Dow Corning agreed to pay $3.2 billion to settle most breast-implant claims.) Dow Corning finally climbed out of bankruptcy in 2004.

Dow entered the polypropylene and polyethylene terephthalate markets with the 1996 purchase of INCA International. It also bought a stake in seed developer Mycogen.

The company sold its 80% of Destec Energy in 1997 and bought Eli Lilly's 40% stake in DowElanco (renamed Dow AgroSciences, 1998).

In 1998 Dow sold its DowBrands unit — maker of bathroom cleaner (Dow), plastic bags (Ziploc), and plastic wrap (Saran Wrap) — to S.C. Johnson & Son. It also bought the rest of Mycogen, which became part of Dow AgroSciences.

The company paid $600 million in 1999 to purchase ANGUS Chemical (specialty chemicals) from TransCanada PipeLines. Dow also announced it planned to buy rival Union Carbide for $9.3 billion; it completed the acquisition early in 2001 after agreeing to divest some poly-ethylene assets to satisfy regulatory concerns.

In 2000 Michael Parker succeeded William Stavropoulos as president and CEO (Stavropoulos remained chairman). Dow acquired Rohm and Haas' agricultural chemicals (fungicides, insecticides, herbicides) business for $1 billion in 2001.

A weakened economy, high raw material costs, and falling prices took a toll on Dow's sales and profits around the turn of the century. As a result of costs related to the Union Carbide takeover — such as the $830 million charge related to Union Carbide's exposure to asbestos claims — and the sputtering economy, Dow recorded its first annual loss in nearly 10 years in 2001, then reported another loss in 2002. Parker was let go and William Stavropoulos returned to his post as CEO. Stavropoulos went to work cutting jobs and closing plants in an effort to cut at least $1 billion in costs.

From 2002-2004 the company cut nearly 7,000 jobs or better than 13% of its entire workforce. By 2004 those moves, coupled with a rebounding chemicals market, had made Dow profitable again. Stavropoulos felt comfortable enough to relinquish the chief executive title and gave it to president and COO Andrew Liveris.

EXECUTIVES

Chairman, President, and CEO: Andrew N. Liveris, age 54, $16,182,544 total compensation
EVP, CFO, and Director: Geoffery E. (Geoff) Merszei, age 57, $7,705,298 total compensation
EVP Business Services, Chief Sustainability Officer, and CIO: David E. (Dave) Kepler II, age 56
EVP and CTO: William F. (Bill) Banholzer, age 52, $5,189,611 total compensation
Chief Tax Officer and Assistant Secretary: William L. Curry
EVP Manufacturing and Engineering: Michael R. (Mike) Gambrell, age 55, $6,110,482 total compensation
EVP Law and Government Affairs, General Counsel, and Corporate Secretary: Charles J. Kalil, age 57
EVP Health, Agriculture, and Infrastructure Group: Heinz Haller, age 53, $4,986,738 total compensation
EVP Human Resources, Corporate Affairs, and Aviation: Gregory M. Freiwald, age 55
SVP Basic Chemicals Division: Carol Dudley
SVP Performance Products Division: James D. (Jim) McIlvenny, age 51
SVP Hydrocarbons and Basic Plastics Division: Juan R. Luciano
President, Dow Advanced Materials: Jerome A. Peribere
President, India, Middle East, and Africa (IMEA): Earl Shipp
President, Pacific Area: Pat D. Dawson
President and CEO Dow AgroSciences LLC: Antonio Galindez
Auditors: Deloitte & Touche LLP

LOCATIONS

HQ: The Dow Chemical Company
2030 Dow Center, Midland, MI 48674
Phone: 989-636-1000 **Fax:** 989-636-1830
Web: www.dow.com

2008 Sales

	$ mil.	% of total
Europe	21,850	38
US	18,459	32
Other regions	17,205	30
Total	**57,514**	**100**

PRODUCTS/OPERATIONS

2008 Sales

	$ mil.	% of total
Performance Plastics	15,793	27
Basic Plastics	12,974	23
Performance Chemicals	9,229	16
Hydrocarbons & Energy	8,968	15
Basic Chemicals	5,693	10
Agricultural Sciences	4,535	8
Other products	322	1
Total	**57,514**	**100**

Selected Products

Performance Plastics
  Dow Automotive (resins, engineering plastic materials, fluids, adhesives, sealants, acoustical systems)
  Engineering plastics (thermoplastic resins and elastomers, advanced resins, and crystalline polymers)
  Epoxy products and intermediates (acetone, acrylic monomers, epoxy resins, glycerine, and phenol)
  Fabricated products (plastic film, Styrofoam, and Weathermate house wrap)
  Polyurethanes (Great Stuff foam sealant, dispersions, carpet backings, polyurethane gloves, roof adhesives, and fiberboard products)
  Wire and cable compounds (flame-retardant compounds, wire and cable insulation compounds)
Basic Plastics
  Polyethylene (resins, including HDPE, LDPE, and LLDPE grades, and catalysts and process technology)
  Polypropylene (resins and performance polymers)
  Polystyrene (resins and styrenic alloys)
Performance Chemicals
  Custom and fine chemicals (nitroparaffins and nitroparaffin-based specialty chemicals, printing ink distillates, contract manufacturing services)
  Emulsion polymers (synthetic latex)
  Industrial chemicals (biocides, surfactants, and deicing fluids)
  Oxide derivatives (glycol ethers and amines)
  Specialty polymers (acrylic acid/acrylic esters, epoxides, dispersants, vinyl resins, specialty monomers)
  UCAR emulsion systems (water-based emulsions)
  Water-soluble polymers (food gums and material thickeners)
Hydrocarbons and Energy
  Benzene
  Butadiene
  Butylene
  Cumene
  Ethylene
  Propylene
  Styrene
Basic Chemicals
  Caustic soda
  Chlorine
  Ethylene glycol
  Ethylene oxide
  Vinyl chloride monomer
Agricultural Products (Dow AgroSciences)
  Fumigants
  Fungicides
  Herbicides
  Insecticides
Other
  Property and casualty insurance (Liana Limited)

COMPETITORS

Akzo Nobel
BASF SE
Bayer AG
Chevron Phillips Chemical
DuPont
Eastman Chemical
Eni
ExxonMobil Chemical
FMC
Formosa Plastics
Honeywell International
INEOS
Koch Industries, Inc.
LANXESS
Lucite
Mitsui Chemicals
Monsanto Company
Occidental Chemical
Olin Chlor Alkali
PPG Industries
SABIC
Shell Chemicals
Sunoco Chemicals
Syngenta
Wellman

HISTORICAL FINANCIALS

Company Type: Public

Income Statement

FYE: December 31

	REVENUE ($ mil.)	NET INCOME ($ mil.)	NET PROFIT MARGIN	EMPLOYEES
12/08	57,514.0	579.0	1.0%	46,102
12/07	53,513.0	2,887.0	5.4%	45,856
12/06	49,124.0	3,724.0	7.6%	42,578
12/05	46,307.0	4,535.0	9.8%	42,413
12/04	40,161.0	2,797.0	7.0%	43,203
Annual Growth	**9.4%**	**(32.5%)**	**—**	**1.6%**

2008 Year-End Financials

Debt ratio: 59.5%
Return on equity: 3.5%
Cash ($ mil.): 2,800
Current ratio: 1.23
Long-term debt ($ mil.): 8,042
No. of shares (mil.): 1,144
Dividends
  Yield: 11.1%
  Payout: 271.0%
Market value ($ mil.): 17,257

Stock History

NYSE: DOW

	STOCK PRICE ($) FY Close	P/E High/Low		PER SHARE ($) Earnings	Dividends	Book Value
12/08	15.09	70	24	0.62	1.68	11.81
12/07	39.42	16	13	2.99	1.63	16.95
12/06	39.90	12	9	3.82	1.50	14.92
12/05	43.82	12	9	4.62	1.34	13.40
12/04	49.51	18	12	2.93	1.34	10.73
Annual Growth	**(25.7%)**	**—**	**—**	**(32.2%)**	**5.8%**	**2.4%**

D.R. Horton

When this Horton heard a Who, it built the little guy a house. D.R. Horton builds single-family homes designed for the entry-level and move-up markets. Homes range from 1,000 sq. ft. to 5,000 sq. ft., with an average selling price of about $233,500; luxury homes cost up to $900,000. In fiscal 2008 the company sold some 26,000 homes, a 35% drop from the previous year. D.R. Horton operates in about 30 states and provides mortgage financing (through DHI Mortgage) as well as title services. One of the top homebuilders in the US, D.R. Horton has suffered along with its competitors as a result of the housing market bust, the subprime mortgage crisis, the global credit crunch, and years of industrywide overbuilding.

CEO Donald Tomnitz summed it up in 2007 when he said, "I don't want to be too sophisticated here, but '07 is going to suck, all 12 months of the calendar year." Indeed, the company suffered a loss that year and the next, when sales orders declined and cancellation rates rose due to tightened mortgage markets and severe liquidy shortgages. Adding to homebuilders' difficulties, an influx of foreclosed homes on the market brought down the demand for new homes.

D.R. Horton has responded to the downturn by reducing land and housing inventory, controlling construction and inventory costs, and using its cash to reduce debt.

The company saw the first cracks in 2006, when it suffered higher than normal cancellation rates and had to increase sales incentives to buyers. The company also saw a rise in the number of speculative houses. (Speculative or "spec" houses are those that are built before being ordered by a customer.) As a result, D.R. Horton has dramatically reduced the number of speculative homes to be built and is continuing to focus on selling those homes.

Investment giant Fidelity owns a 15% stake in the company.

HISTORY

Donald R. Horton was selling homes in Fort Worth, Texas, when he hit upon a strategy for increasing sales — add options to a basic floor plan. In 1978 he borrowed $33,000 to build his first home, added a bay window for an additional charge, and sold the home for $44,000. Donald soon added floor plans and options that appealed to regional preferences.

The depressed Texas market drove the company to expand beyond the Dallas/Fort Worth area in 1987, when it entered the then-hot Phoenix market. It continued to expand into the Southeast, Mid-Atlantic, Midwest, and West in the late 1980s and early 1990s. By 1991 Horton and his family owned more than 25 companies that were combined as D.R. Horton, which went public in 1992.

D.R. Horton acquired six geographically diverse construction firms in 1994 and 1995. In 1996 the company started a mortgage services joint venture, expanded its title operations, and added three more firms.

In 1998 the company bought four builders, including Scottsdale, Arizona-based Continental Homes. Continental had been expanding beyond its Arizona and Southern California base and had entered the lucrative retirement community market. After the Continental purchase, Donald

Horton stepped down as president, remaining chairman. Richard Beckwitt took over as president, and Donald Tomnitz became CEO. In 1999 the company acquired Century Title and Midwest builder Cambridge Properties.

D.R. Horton sold its St. Louis assets to McBride & Son Enterprises in 2000, after spending five years trying to break into the St. Louis homebuilding market. Tomnitz also took over the duties of president in 2000 when Beckwitt retired.

D.R. Horton gained homebuilding operations in Houston and Phoenix when it bought Emerald Builders in 2001. In February 2002 the company acquired Schuler Homes for $1.2 billion, including debt.

Sales continued to climb in fiscal 2003 and 2004. D.R. Horton experienced its 27th consecutive year of earnings and revenue growth in 2004 and broke records by being the first residential homebuilder to sell more than 45,000 homes in the US in a fiscal year; in fiscal 2005 the company closed 51,172 homes. By 2007, however, it was evident that the heady days were over with a rise in cancellations and a larger value of backlog orders.

EXECUTIVES

Chairman: Donald R. Horton, age 58
Vice Chairman, President, and CEO:
Donald J. (Don) Tomnitz, age 60
EVP, CFO, and Director: William W. (Bill) Wheat, age 42
Director Information Technology: Rick Rawlings
Chief Legal Officer: Ted I. Harbour
EVP Investor Relations and Treasurer: Stacey H. Dwyer, age 41
VP and Regional President, Southwest:
Gordon D. Jones
VP and Assistant Secretary: Thomas Montano
VP and Director, National Accounts: Brad Conlon
President, North Region: George W. Seagraves
President, West Region: Chris Chambers
President, Financial Services:
Randall C. (Randy) Present
President, Central Region: Rick Horton
President, East Region: David Auld
Manager, Human Resources: Paula Hunter-Perkins
Controller: Michael Murray
Auditors: Ernst & Young LLP

LOCATIONS

HQ: D.R. Horton, Inc.
301 Commerce St., Ste. 500, Fort Worth, TX 76102
Phone: 817-390-8200   **Fax:** 817-390-1704
Web: www.drhorton.com

2008 Homes Closed

	Units	% of total
South Central	7,960	30
Southwest	5,309	20
West	5,263	20
Southeast	3,650	14
East	2,309	9
Midwest	1,905	7
Total	**26,396**	**100**

2008 Home Sales

	% of total
West	30
South Central	22
Southwest	18
Southeast	13
East	9
Midwest	8
Total	**100**

PRODUCTS/OPERATIONS

2008 Sales

	$ mil.	% of total
Homebuilding		
Homes	6,164.3	93
Land/lots	354.3	5
Financial services	127.5	2
Total	**6,646.1**	**100**

COMPETITORS

Beazer Homes
Century Homebuilders
David Weekley Homes
Gehan Homes
Hovnanian Enterprises
J.F. Shea
KB Home
Lennar
M.D.C.
Mercedes Homes
Meritage Homes
M/I Homes
NVR
Orleans Homebuilders
Pardee Homes
Pulte Homes
Ryan Building
The Ryland Group
Standard Pacific
Toll Brothers
Weyerhaeuser Real Estate
Woodbridge Holdings

HISTORICAL FINANCIALS
Company Type: Public

Income Statement

	REVENUE ($ mil.)	NET INCOME ($ mil.)	NET PROFIT MARGIN	EMPLOYEES
9/08	6,646.1	(2,633.6)	—	3,800
9/07	11,296.5	(712.5)	—	6,231
9/06	15,051.3	1,233.3	8.2%	8,772
9/05	13,863.7	1,470.5	10.6%	8,900
9/04	10,840.8	975.1	9.0%	7,466
Annual Growth	**(11.5%)**	**—**	**—**	**(15.5%)**

FYE: September 30

2008 Year-End Financials

Debt ratio: —
Return on equity: —
Cash ($ mil.): 1,356
Current ratio: 1.31
Long-term debt ($ mil.): —

No. of shares (mil.): 317
Dividends
  Yield: 3.5%
  Payout: —
Market value ($ mil.): 4,129

Stock History

NYSE: DHI

	STOCK PRICE ($) FY Close	P/E High/Low	PER SHARE ($) Earnings	Dividends	Book Value
9/08	13.02	— —	(8.34)	0.45	8.94
9/07	12.81	— —	(2.27)	0.60	17.62
9/06	23.95	11 5	3.90	0.44	20.35
9/05	36.22	9 4	4.62	0.31	16.90
9/04	24.83	9 6	3.08	0.22	12.49
Annual Growth	**(14.9%)**	**— —**	**—**	**19.6%**	**(8.0%)**

DST Systems

The feeling is mutual at DST Systems. A leading provider of information processing software and services for the mutual fund industry, DST's Financial Services segment processes millions of mutual fund accounts and offers software, systems, and processing services for banks, investment firms, and insurance companies. The company's Output Solutions unit manages statement and bill mailings and customer communications. Its applications and services are used to address a wide range of tasks including business process management, investment management, customer care, and health care claims processing and administration.

The company has historically been very active on the acquisition front, using selective purchases to complement its product line and strategically expand into new geographic areas such as Australia and Asia. DST has balanced its acquisition strategy by purchasing both complementary software and technology providers as well as service providers, with a particular emphasis on buying business process outsourcing and consulting firms.

Recent purchases have included BlueDoor Technologies (an Australia-based provider of funds and savings management software), TASS (shareowner subaccounting services provider), Mosiki (consulting services), and Amisys Synertech (enterprise software and business process outsourcing).

DST Systems bought the 50% of claims processing services and software joint venture Argus Health Systems that it did not already own from partner Financial Holding Corporation in 2009. The purchase was a bid by DST to build its presence in the health care market. Argus provides services and offers custom software to manage and automate such functions as claims processing, rebate administration, and clinical services administration primarily for pharmacy benefits purposes.

HISTORY

After expanding into mutual funds during the early 1960s, Kansas City Southern Industries (KCSI) formed an electronic computer data processing unit to handle its mutual fund transactions, using technology designed originally for tracking railroad cars and their revenues.

In 1968 KCSI incorporated its data processing unit as DST Systems and began offering its services to the financial industry. To establish itself on the East Coast, in 1974 DST formed Boston Financial Data Services, a joint venture with State Street. Also during the 1970s DST entered the insurance market with a system for variable annuity policyholders.

In 1983 KCSI bought a majority stake in Janus Capital, a Denver-based mutual funds company. DST went public later that year; KCSI kept an 86% stake. Thomas McDonnell, president since the early 1970s, was named CEO in 1984.

By the early 1990s DST had a solid position in its markets, and it had begun to increase its service offerings and expand internationally into Canada and Europe. The company bought Vantage Computer to gain a foothold in the life and property insurance software industry, and it established joint ventures with Kemper Financial Services (now part of Zurich Financial Services)

and State Street Boston, thereby pushing into portfolio accounting and stock transfer services.

In 1993 DST sold Vantage to insurance software maker Continuum, gaining a 19% stake in that company. It also bought 50% of client Argus Health Systems as well as a stake in DBS Systems (by 1997 it owned 100%). By the end of 1993 DST was the leader in mutual fund third-party services. In 1995 KCSI sold 51% of DST to the public. Information technology firm Computer Sciences Corporation (CSC) acquired Continuum in 1996, leaving DST with a minority stake in CSC.

In 1998 DST, BankBoston First Chicago Trust, and State Street formed EquiServe, the largest provider of corporate stock transfer services in the US. That year DST bought USCS International, a provider of customer management software and billing services, in an $824 million deal.

DST in 2000 took aim at fund supermarkets operated by Charles Schwab and FMR by launching a service that enabled independent commission-based financial advisers to research and trade funds over the Internet. The company also purchased a controlling stake in EquiServe from the other partners in the joint venture.

In 2001 the company acquired the remainder of EquiServe, and it sold its portfolio accounting systems business to State Street for $75 million. The following year DST bought lock/line, a provider of administrative support services for providers of insurance for telecommunications equipment and event-based debt protection programs.

In 2003 Janus Capital Group sold most of its remaining stake in DST back to the company, in exchange for ownership of DST's commercial printing and graphics design unit; it sold the rest of its stake in 2004.

DST Systems sold its billing and customer management software and services business, including the operations of DST Innovis and DST Interactive, to Amdocs in 2005.

DST's Output Solutions segment, which operates primarily in the US through subsidiary DST Output, expanded its geographic reach through its purchase of DST International, a provider of customer communications and document management services in the UK.

In early 2006 DST merged its lock/line unit (administrative services for telecom carriers) with customer contact and support services provider Asurion Corporation; in 2007 DST sold the majority of the 37% stake it received in Asurion as part of the transaction.

Also in 2006 the company acquired Amisys Synertech, a software developer and applications provider to the commercial health care industry in the US.

EXECUTIVES

CEO and Director: Thomas A. (Tom) McDonnell, age 63, $4,946,838 total compensation
President and COO; Chairman, Boston Financial Data Services: Stephen C. Hooley
VP, CFO, and Treasurer: Kenneth V. Hager, age 58, $1,271,276 total compensation
VP and CIO: Mark C. Prasifka
VP and Chief Accounting Officer: Gregg W. Givens, age 48

EVP US Investment Recordkeeping Solutions: Robert L. Tritt, age 53
EVP, DST Health Solutions and Argus Health Systems: Jonathan J. Boehm, age 48
VP, General Counsel, and Secretary: Randall D. Young, age 52
VP Automated Work Distributor: John C. Vaughn
President, DST Retirement Solutions: Jude C. Metcalfe
President and CEO, DST Output: Steven J. (Steve) Towle, age 51, $1,763,673 total compensation
President and CEO, Boston Financial Data Services: Terry L. Metzger
President, DST Health Solutions: A. Stephan (Steve) Sabino, age 58
CEO, DST International: Thomas R. (Tom) Abraham, age 57, $2,359,232 total compensation
Auditors: PricewaterhouseCoopers LLP

LOCATIONS

HQ: DST Systems, Inc.
   333 W. 11th St., Kansas City, MO 64105
Phone: 816-435-1000   **Fax:** 816-435-8618
Web: www.dstsystems.com

PRODUCTS/OPERATIONS

2008 Sales

	$ mil.	% of total
US Operating Revenues		
Mutual fund/investment management	805	35
Telecommunications, video & utilities	219	10
Health care-related services	212	10
Other	223	10
International Operating Revenues		
Investment management & other financial services	170	7
Telecommunications, video & utilities	31	1
Other	15	—
Out-of-pocket reimbursements	610	27
Total	**2,285**	**100**

Selected Products and Services

DST Output
   Call center management support
   Direct Access (instantaneous online data monitoring)
   Exact View (customer statement replica viewing)
   Info Disc (customer document replica viewing)
   Package configuration and inventory management support
   Rapid Confirm (delivery service for trade confirmations)
   Rapid NetSale (lead management for prospective online brokerage customers)
Financial Services
   eLLITE (fund information access)
   Securities Transfer System (transfer agent support)
   TA2000 (mutual fund shareholder record keeping)
   TRAC-2000 (record keeping for defined contribution plans)
   Vision (Web-based mutual fund processing for independent financial advisers)

COMPETITORS

ACS International	IBM
ADP	Lombardi Software
Advent Software	McKesson
Assurant	Medco Health
Bank of New York Mellon	Misys
Bowne	Pegasystems
Cerner	Perot Systems
CVS Caremark	PNC Global Investment
EDS	Servicing
Express Scripts	RiskMetrics
First Data	Savvion
Fiserv	SS&C
GE Healthcare	State Street
Greenway Medical	SunGard
Technologies	TIBCO Software
HealthPort	TMG Health
HLTH Corp.	TriZetto

HISTORICAL FINANCIALS

Company Type: Public

Income Statement

FYE: December 31

	REVENUE ($ mil.)	NET INCOME ($ mil.)	NET PROFIT MARGIN	EMPLOYEES
12/08	2,285.4	242.9	10.6%	10,900
12/07	2,302.5	874.7	38.0%	11,000
12/06	2,235.8	272.9	12.2%	10,500
12/05	2,515.1	424.6	16.9%	10,500
12/04	2,428.6	222.8	9.2%	11,000
Annual Growth	(1.5%)	2.2%	—	(0.2%)

2008 Year-End Financials

Debt ratio: 586.9%
Return on equity: 34.8%
Cash ($ mil.): 79
Current ratio: 0.85
Long-term debt ($ mil.): 1,392

No. of shares (mil.): 50
Dividends
 Yield: 0.0%
 Payout: —
Market value ($ mil.): 1,888

Stock History

NYSE: DST

	STOCK PRICE ($) FY Close	P/E High/Low		PER SHARE ($) Earnings	Dividends	Book Value
12/08	37.98	18	7	4.28	0.00	4.79
12/07	82.55	7	5	12.35	0.00	23.31
12/06	62.63	17	14	3.78	0.00	11.51
12/05	59.91	12	8	5.39	0.00	9.97
12/04	52.12	20	16	2.59	0.00	15.00
Annual Growth	(7.6%)	—	—	13.4%	—	(24.8%)

DTE Energy

Detroit's economy may be lackluster, but DTE Energy still provides a reliable spark. The holding company's main subsidiary, Detroit Edison, distributes electricity to some 2.2 million customers in southeastern Michigan. The utility's power plants (mainly fossil-fueled) have a generating capacity of more than 11,100 MW. The company's Michigan Consolidated Gas (MichCon) unit distributes natural gas to 1.2 million customers. DTE Energy's nonregulated operations (in 25 US states) include energy marketing and trading; coal transportation and procurement; energy management services for commercial and industrial customers; independent and on site power generation; and gas exploration, production, and processing.

DTE Energy, which is expanding its nonutility businesses, has wholesale power, gas, and coal marketing operations in the Midwest and northeastern US and eastern Canada; it also has merchant generation facilities in Illinois, Indiana, and Michigan.

Clearing out some non-core assets, in 2007 the company sold its Michigan Antrim Shale gas exploration and production assets to Atlas Energy

Resources for about $1.3 billion. That year, due to the expiration of synthetic fuel production tax credits, DTE Energy exited the synfuels business.

As part of its commitment to reduce its carbon footprint, in 2008 DTE Energy announced plans to convert its 800 diesel-fueled trucks and service vehicles to cleaner-burning biodiesel fuel.

HISTORY

DTE Energy's predecessor threw its first switch in 1886 when George Peck and local investors incorporated the Edison Illuminating Company of Detroit. Neighboring utility Peninsular Electric Light was formed in 1891, and both companies bought smaller utilities until they merged in 1903 to form Detroit Edison. A subsidiary of holding company North American Co., Detroit Edison was incorporated in New York to secure financing for power plants.

Detroit's growth in the 1920s and 1930s led the utility to build plants and buy others in outlying areas. Detroit Edison acquired Michigan Electric Power, which had been divested from its holding company under the Public Utility Holding Company Act of 1935, and was itself divested from North American in 1940.

The post-WWII boom prompted Detroit Edison to build more plants, most of them coal-fired. In 1953 it joined a consortium of 34 companies to build Fermi 1, a nuclear plant brought on line in 1963. Still strapped for power, Detroit Edison built the coal-fired Monroe plant, which began service in 1970. In 1972 Fermi 1 had a partial core meltdown and was taken off line.

Detroit Edison began shipping low-sulfur Montana coal through its Wisconsin terminal in 1974, which reduced the cost of obtaining the fuel. The next year it began building another nuke, Fermi 2. The nuke had cost more than $4.8 billion by the time it went on line in 1988. That year the utility began its landfill gas recovery operation (now DTE Biomass Energy).

A recession pounded automakers in the early 1990s, leading to cutbacks in electricity purchases. In 1992 Congress passed the Energy Policy Act, allowing wholesale power competition. In 1993 a fire shut down Fermi 2 for almost two years. Michigan's public service commission (PSC) approved retail customer-choice pilot programs for its utilities in 1994. Detroit Edison and rival Consumers Energy (now CMS Energy) took the PSC to court.

DTE Energy became Detroit Edison's holding company in 1996. The next year it formed DTE Energy Trading (to broker power) and DTE-CoEnergy (to provide energy-management services and sell power to large customers). It also formed Plug Power with Mechanical Technology to develop fuel cells that convert natural gas to power without combustion.

In 1997 and 1998 the PSC, bolstered by state court decisions, issued orders to restructure Michigan's utilities. The transition to retail competition began in 1998. That year DTE Energy and natural gas provider Michigan Consolidated Gas (MichCon) began collaborating on some operations, including billing and meter reading. DTE and GE formed a venture to sell and install Plug Power fuel cell systems.

A higher court shot down the PSC's restructuring orders in 1999, but DTE Energy and CMS Energy decided to implement customer choice using PSC guidelines. That year the US Department of Energy selected DTE Energy to install the world's first super power-cable, which could

carry three times as much electricity as conventional copper. Also in 1999, DTE Energy agreed to acquire MCN Energy, MichCon's parent.

In 2000 DTE Energy formed subsidiary International Transmission (ITC) to hold Detroit Edison's transmission assets; the next year ITC joined the Midwest Independent System Operator, which began to manage ITC's network. It also completed its $4.3 billion purchase of MCN Energy in 2001. Full deregulation of Michigan's electricity market was completed in 2002. International Transmission was sold in 2003 to affiliates of Kohlberg Kravis Roberts and Trimaran Capital Partners for $610 million.

EXECUTIVES

Chairman and CEO: Anthony F. Earley Jr., age 59, $7,528,357 total compensation
President and COO: Gerard M. Anderson, age 50, $3,669,286 total compensation
Group President; President and COO, Michigan Consolidated Gas Company: Gerardo (Jerry) Norcia, age 45, $1,017,659 total compensation
Group President; President and COO, Detroit Edison: Steven E. Kurmas, age 53
EVP and CFO: David E. Meador, age 51, $2,022,947 total compensation
SVP and CIO: Lynne Ellyn, age 57
VP, Controller, and Chief Accounting Officer: Peter B. Oleksiak, age 42
SVP: Ron A. May, age 57
SVP and Assistant to Chairman: Harold Gardner, age 62
SVP and General Counsel: Bruce D. Peterson, age 52, $1,480,645 total compensation
SVP Corporate Affairs: Paul Hillegonds, age 59
SVP Energy Resources; President, DTE Engery Ventures: Knut Simonsen, age 45
VP Corporate Communications: Michael C. Porter, age 55
VP Human Resources: Larry E. Steward, age 56
President, Midwest Energy Resources: Fred L. Shusterich, age 54
President, DTE Coal Services: Matt T. Paul, age 39
President, DTE Biomass Energy: Mark Cousino, age 44
President DTE Gas Storage and DTE Pipeline: Peter Cianci, age 41
President, DTE Energy Trading: Steven (Steve) Mabry
President, DTE Gas Resources: Steven H. Prelipp
Secretary: Sandra K. Ennis, age 52
Auditors: Deloitte & Touche LLP

LOCATIONS

HQ: DTE Energy Company
 2000 2nd Ave., Detroit, MI 48226
Phone: 313-235-4000 **Fax:** 313-235-8055
Web: www.dteenergy.com

PRODUCTS/OPERATIONS

2008 Sales

	$ mil.	% of total
Electric utility	4,874	51
Gas utility	2,152	23
Non-utility operations		
Energy trading	1,388	15
Power & industrial products	987	10
Gas midstream	71	1
Unconventional gas production	48	—
Adjustments	(191)	—
Total	**9,329**	**100**

COMPETITORS

AEP
CMS Energy
CMS Enterprises
Dairyland Power
DPL
Duke Energy
Dynegy
Exelon Energy

Integrys Energy Group
Nicor
Peabody Energy
PG&E Corporation
SEMCO Energy
Southern Company
Wisconsin Energy
Xcel Energy

HISTORICAL FINANCIALS

Company Type: Public

Income Statement

FYE: December 31

	REVENUE ($ mil.)	NET INCOME ($ mil.)	NET PROFIT MARGIN	EMPLOYEES
12/08	9,329.0	546.0	5.9%	10,471
12/07	8,506.0	787.0	9.3%	10,262
12/06	9,022.0	432.0	4.8%	10,527
12/05	9,022.0	540.0	6.0%	11,410
12/04	7,114.0	431.0	6.1%	11,207
Annual Growth	7.0%	6.1%	—	(1.7%)

2008 Year-End Financials

Debt ratio: 129.1%
Return on equity: 9.2%
Cash ($ mil.): 86
Current ratio: 1.10
Long-term debt ($ mil.): 7,741

No. of shares (mil.): 164
Dividends
  Yield: 5.9%
  Payout: 63.1%
Market value ($ mil.): 5,867

Stock History

NYSE: DTE

	STOCK PRICE ($) FY Close	P/E High/Low		PER SHARE ($) Earnings	Dividends	Book Value
12/08	35.67	13	8	3.36	2.12	36.45
12/07	43.96	10	8	5.70	2.12	35.59
12/06	48.41	20	16	2.43	2.08	35.56
12/05	43.19	16	14	3.05	2.06	35.08
12/04	43.13	18	15	2.49	2.06	33.73
Annual Growth	(4.6%)	—	—	7.8%	0.7%	2.0%

Duke Energy

Duke Energy is a John Wayne-sized power business. The company has 4 million electric customers and about 520,000 gas customers in the US South and Midwest. Its US Franchised Electric and Gas unit operates primarily through its Duke Energy Carolinas, Duke Energy Ohio, Duke Energy Indiana and Duke Energy Kentucky regional businesses. The company has 35,000 MW of electric generating capacity in the Midwest and the Carolinas. Duke Energy International has almost 4,000 MW of generation (mostly in Latin America). While it is focused on energy operations, Duke also has stakes in insurance, real estate, and telecom businesses.

In a major industry power move, in 2006 the company bought energy provider Cinergy in a $9 billion stock swap. Reorganizing its business lines to focus on its US power businesses, that year Duke Energy sold its commercial marketing and trading businesses to Fortis, and in 2007 it spun off its natural gas transmission business as Spectra Energy. The company also exited the European energy marketing business; it also left the proprietary (third-party) energy trading business in North America (primarily made up of

Duke Energy North America or DENA, sold to LS Power Equity Partners for a reported $1.5 billion). Duke also wound down its energy-trading joint venture with Exxon Mobil.

In 2008, as part of its refocusing on its energy businesses, the company stopped reporting on its Crescent Resources unit (a joint venture with Morgan Stanley Real Estate Fund which manages land holdings and develops real estate projects).

That year Duke moved to strengthen its alternative energy assets by buying wind energy producer Catamount Energy for about $240 million plus assumed debt. Catamount had about 500MW of renewable energy in operation.

Further pursuing its strategy to develop green energy sources, in 2009 the company agreed to build a second wind power project in Wyoming. That year Duke had more than 500 MW of wind power in operation and another 5,000 MW in development in 14 US states.

HISTORY

Surgeon Gill Wylie founded Catawba Power Company in 1899; its first hydroelectric plant in South Carolina was on line by 1904. The next year Wylie and James "Buck" Duke (founder of the American Tobacco Company and Duke University's namesake) formed Southern Power Company with Wylie as president.

In 1910 Buck Duke became president of Southern Power and organized Mill-Power Supply to sell electric equipment and appliances. He also began investing in electricity-powered textile mills, which prospered as a result of the electric power, and continued to bring in customers. He formed the Southern Public Utility Company in 1913 to buy other Piedmont-region utilities. Wylie died in 1924, the same year the company was renamed Duke Power; Buck Duke died the next year.

Growing after WWII, the company went public in 1950 and moved to the NYSE in 1961. It also formed its real estate arm, Crescent Resources, in the 1960s. Insulating itself from the 1970s energy crises, Duke invested in coal mining and three nuclear plants, the first completed in 1974.

In 1988 Duke began to develop power projects outside its home region, and it also bought neighboring utility Nantahala Power and Light. The next year it formed a joint venture with Fluor's Fluor Daniel unit to provide engineering and construction services to power generators. Mill-Power Supply was sold in 1990.

By the 1990s Duke had moved into overseas markets, acquiring an Argentine power station in 1992. It also tried its hand at telecommunications, creating DukeNet Communications in 1994 to build fiber-optic systems, and in 1996 it joined oil giant Mobil to create a power trading and marketing business. As the US power industry traveled toward deregulation, Duke also sought natural gas operations. It targeted PanEnergy, which owned a major pipeline system in the eastern half of the US. Duke Power bought PanEnergy in 1997 to form Duke Energy Corporation.

Seeing an opportunity in 1998, Duke formed Duke Communication Services to provide antenna sites to the fast-growing wireless communications industry. It also acquired a 52% stake in Electroquil, an electric power generating company in Guayaquil, Ecuador. That year it bought three PG&E power plants to compete in California's deregulated electric utility marketplace.

Duke merged its pipeline business, Duke Energy Trading and Transport, with TEPPCO Partners and acquired gas processing operations from Union Pacific Resources. To further enhance natural gas operations in other regions, Duke bought El Paso's East Tennessee Natural Gas pipeline unit in 2000 and a 20% stake in Canadian 88 Energy; it also purchased $1.4 billion in South American generation assets, including assets from Dominion Resources, and the gas trading operations of Mobil (now Exxon Mobil) in the Netherlands. Also in 2000, Duke and Phillips Petroleum (now ConocoPhillips) merged their gas gathering and processing and NGL operations into Duke Energy Field Services.

In 2001 Duke announced the $8 billion acquisition of Westcoast Energy; the purchase, which was completed in 2002, added more than a million natural gas customers and 6,900 miles of gas pipeline in Canada. That year Duke sold its Duke Engineering & Services unit to Framatome ANP.

Duke set out to sell $1.5 billion in assets in 2003 to focus on core operations. Also that year Duke sold its stake in Foothills Pipe Lines to TransCanada for $181 million, and it sold $300 million in renewable energy facilities to privately owned Highstar Renewable Fuels.

In 2004 the company sold an Indonesian power plant to Freeport-McMoRan in a $300 million deal, and it sold its 30% interest in the Vector Pipeline to Enbridge and DTE Energy for $145 million. It also sold the assets of its merchant finance business (Duke Capital Partners), and its stake in Canadian 88 Energy (now Esprit Exploration). Following this trend in 2005, Duke Energy sold its 620-MW Grays Harbor facility (Washington) to an affiliate of Invenergy for $21 million.

In 2006 Duke sold a 50% stake in its real estate subsidiary, Crescent Resources, to Morgan Stanley Real Estate. That year the company bought an 825-MW power plant in Rockingham County, North Carolina, from Dynegy for $195 million.

EXECUTIVES

Chairman, President, and CEO: James E. (Jim) Rogers, age 61
Group Executive and CFO: Lynn J. Good, age 50, $2,668,134 total compensation
SVP and CIO: A. R. Mullinax, age 54
VP and CTO: David W. Mohler
Group Executive and Chief Administrative Officer: Christopher C. (Chris) Rolfe, age 57
Group Executive, Chief Legal Officer, and Secretary: Marc E. Manly, age 56, $2,959,235 total compensation
Group Executive, Chief Generation Officer, and Chief Nuclear Officer: Dhiaa M. Jamil, age 52
VP Supply Chain and Chief Procurement Officer: Ronald R. Reising, age 48
Chief Human Resources Officer: Jennifer L. Weber
SVP and Chief Communications Officer: Cathy S. Roche
SVP, Treasurer, and Chief Risk Officer: Stephen G. De May, age 46
VP Audit Services and Chief Ethics and Compliance Officer: Jeffery G. Browning
SVP and Controller: Steven K. Young, age 50
SVP Corporate Tax: Keith G. Butler, age 45
Group Executive; President and COO, U.S. Franchised Electric and Gas: James L. (Jim) Turner, age 49, $3,275,761 total compensation
President, Office Nuclear Development: Ellen T. Ruff
President, Duke Energy Ohio and Kentucky: Julia S. (Julie) Janson, age 44
President, Duke Energy Generation Services: Wouter van Kempen
President, Duke Energy Carolinas: Brett C. Carter
President, Duke Energy International: Andrea Bertone
Auditors: Deloitte & Touche LLP

LOCATIONS

HQ: Duke Energy Corporation
526 S. Church St., Charlotte, NC 28202
Phone: 704-594-6200 **Fax:** 704-382-3814
Web: www.duke-energy.com

2008 Sales

	$ mil.	% of total
US	12,022	91
Latin America	1,185	9
Total	**13,207**	**100**

PRODUCTS/OPERATIONS

2008 Sales

	$ mil.	% of total
Regulated electric	9,325	71
Non-regulated electric, natural gas & other	3,092	23
Regulated natural gas	790	6
Total	**13,207**	**100**

Selected Operations

Commercial Power (unregulated power generation)
Duke Energy International (foreign asset development and marketing)
U.S. Franchised Electric and Gas (electric and gas utility)
Other
  Bison Insurance Company Limited
  Crescent Resources (50%, real estate)
  Dukenet (telecom)

COMPETITORS

AEP
AES
Avista
CenterPoint Energy
Constellation Energy Group
Dynegy
El Paso
Energy Future
Entergy
Enterprise Products
Exelon
Koch Industries, Inc.
Mirant
PG&E Corporation
Piedmont Natural Gas
Progress Energy
RRI Energy
SCANA
Southern Company
SUEZ-TRACTEBEL
TVA
Williams Companies

HISTORICAL FINANCIALS

Company Type: Public

Income Statement

FYE: December 31

	REVENUE ($ mil.)	NET INCOME ($ mil.)	NET PROFIT MARGIN	EMPLOYEES
12/08	13,207.0	1,295.0	9.8%	18,250
12/07	12,720.0	1,500.0	11.8%	17,800
12/06	15,184.0	1,863.0	12.3%	25,600
12/05	16,746.0	1,828.0	10.9%	20,400
12/04	22,503.0	1,490.0	6.6%	21,500
Annual Growth	(12.5%)	(3.4%)	—	(4.0%)

2008 Year-End Financials

Debt ratio: 63.1%
Return on equity: 6.1%
Cash ($ mil.): 986
Current ratio: 1.21
Long-term debt ($ mil.): 13,250

No. of shares (mil.): 1,297
Dividends
  Yield: 6.0%
  Payout: 84.1%
Market value ($ mil.): 19,464

Stock History

NYSE: DUK

	STOCK PRICE ($) FY Close	P/E High/Low		PER SHARE ($) Earnings	Dividends	Book Value
12/08	15.01	19	13	1.07	0.90	16.19
12/07	20.17	18	14	1.18	0.86	16.35
12/06	19.33	13	10	1.57	1.26	20.13
12/05	15.98	9	8	1.88	1.17	12.68
12/04	14.75	10	7	1.54	1.10	12.78
Annual Growth	0.4%	—	—	(8.7%)	(4.9%)	6.1%

Dun & Bradstreet

For The Dun & Bradstreet Corporation, there's no business like "know" business. The company, known as D&B, is one of the world's leading suppliers of business information, services, and research. Its database contains statistics on more than 140 million companies in more than 200 countries, including the largest volume of business-credit information in the world. The company's risk management segment sells that information and integrates it into software products and Web-based applications. D&B also offers marketing information and purchasing-support services. The company has broadened its client base with its online offerings; it acquired Hoover's, the publisher of this profile, in 2003.

The Hoover's acquisition signaled a major commitment to provide information via the Internet. D&B strengthened its online presence again in 2007 with the purchases of business information provider Allbusiness.com and First Research, a Web-based provider of editorial-based industry reports aimed at sales people. (After the acquisition, First Research became a wholly owned subsidiary of Hoover's. Allbusiness.com remains a stand-alone brand.) In 2008 Hoover's acquired e-mail connection system Visible Path. All entities are part of D&B's Internet Solutions division, a key company focus.

The company is also making technology investments designed to expand its core businesses. To this end D&B acquired Purisma, a provider of data integration software in 2007. D&B is improving the data capabilities of Risk Management Solutions (which accounts for about two-thirds of sales) and delivering more predictive indicators about credit risks to its customers. Additionally, the company is focused on making investments in and improvements to its Sales and Marketing Solutions division, which supplies lists and related data to direct mail and marketing customers. (In 2008 D&B began managing its Supply Management Solutions segment as a part of its Risk Management business.)

D&B conducts international operations on a market-by-market basis, conducting business through wholly owned subsidiaries, independent correspondents, and strategic partner relationships through its D&B Worldwide Network. As a result, the company offers more international company records to its customers around the world. Altogether, D&B has offices in about 30 countries and correspondents in another 140 countries.

Davis Selected Advisors owns about 16% of the company.

HISTORY

D&B originated as Lewis Tappan's Mercantile Agency, established in 1841 in New York City. One of the first commercial credit-reporting agencies, the Mercantile supplied wholesalers and importers with reports on their customers' credit histories. The company's credit reporters included four future US presidents (Lincoln, Grant, Cleveland, and McKinley). In the 1840s it opened offices in Boston, Philadelphia, and Baltimore, and in 1857 it established operations in Montreal and London.

In 1859 Robert Dun took over the agency and renamed it R.G. Dun & Co. The first edition of the *Dun's Book* (1859) contained information on 20,268 businesses; by 1886 that number had risen to over a million. During this time Dun's was competing fiercely with the John M. Bradstreet Company, founded in 1849 by its namesake in Cincinnati. The rivalry continued until the Depression, when Dun's CEO Arthur Whiteside negotiated a merger of the two firms in 1933; the new company adopted the Dun & Bradstreet name in 1939.

In 1961 Dun & Bradstreet bought Reuben H. Donnelley Corp., a direct-mail advertiser and publisher of the Yellow Pages (first published 1886) and 10 trade magazines. In 1962 Moody's Investors Service (founded 1900) became part of Dun & Bradstreet. The company began computerizing its records in the 1960s and eventually developed the largest private business database in the world. Repackaging that information, the company began creating new products such as Dun's Financial Profiles, first published in 1979.

Dun & Bradstreet continued buying information and publishing companies during the 1970s and 1980s, including Technical Publishing (trade and professional publications, 1978), National CSS (computer services, 1979), and McCormack & Dodge (software, 1983). Later came ACNielsen (1984) and IMS International (pharmaceutical sales data, 1988).

Finding that not all information was equally profitable, Dun & Bradstreet sold its specialty industry and consumer database companies in the early 1990s. Still hoping to cash in on medical and technology information, the company formed D&B HealthCare Information and bought a majority interest in consulting firm Gartner Group. In 1993 the company consolidated its 27 worldwide data centers into four locations. The following year it settled a class-action suit involving overcharging customers for credit reports. After its second earnings decline in three years, management revamped the company in 1996, selling off ACNielsen and Cognizant (consisting of IMS Health and Nielsen Media Research). Volney Taylor was appointed chairman and CEO of Dun & Bradstreet. In 1998 it spun off R. H. Donnelley (formerly Reuben H. Donnelley).

Under pressure from unhappy shareholders, Taylor resigned in late 1999. With director Clifford Alexander Jr. acting as interim CEO, Dun &

Bradstreet announced plans to spin off its Moody's unit. After completing the spinoff the following year, Allan Loren took over as chairman and CEO of Dun & Bradstreet. Loren retired from the company in mid-2005 and president Steven Alesio became chairman and CEO.

The company boosted its risk management business with a $16 million acquisition of online credit management software maker LiveCapital in 2005. A similar lift was given to its Supply Management Solutions unit in 2006 after its $8.3 million purchase of Open Ratings, an Internet-based supply risk management company.

EXECUTIVES

Chairman and CEO: Steven W. (Steve) Alesio, age 54, $11,236,803 total compensation
President, COO, and Director; Head of U.S. Customer Segments: Sara S. Mathew, age 53, $5,122,313 total compensation
SVP and CFO: Anastasios G. (Tasos) Konidaris, age 42, $1,585,219 total compensation
SVP Technology and CIO: Walter S. Hauck III
SVP and Chief Human Resources Officer: Patricia A. Clifford, age 44
SVP, General Counsel, and Corporate Secretary: Jeffrey S. (Jeff) Hurwitz, age 48
SVP US Small Businesses and Sales Operations: Stacy A. Cashman
SVP Asia/Pacific and International Business Development: David J. Emery
SVP Global Sales and Marketing Solutions: James (Jim) Delaney
SVP Strategic Customer Solutions: Joe DiBartolomeo
SVP Global Major Customers: John Cucci
SVP Global Risk Management Solutions: Ajay Mookerjee
SVP Global Reengineering and North America Finance: Richard H. Veldran
President, D&B North America: George I. Stoeckert, age 59
President, Integration Solutions: Byron C. Vielehr, age 45, $2,496,144 total compensation
President, Global Solutions: Charles E. Gottdiener, age 44
President, Hoover's: Hyune Hand
CEO, AllBusiness.com: Kathy Yates
President, Europe, Latin America, and Partnerships: Emanuele A. Conti
Leader External Communications: Joseph M. Jones
Auditors: PricewaterhouseCoopers LLP

LOCATIONS

HQ: The Dun & Bradstreet Corporation
103 JFK Pkwy., Short Hills, NJ 07078
Phone: 973-921-5500   **Fax:** 973-921-6056
Web: www.dnb.com

2008 Sales

	$ mil.	% of total
US	1,321.1	77
Other countries	405.2	23
Total	**1,726.3**	**100**

PRODUCTS/OPERATIONS

2008 Sales by Segment

	$ mil.	% of total
Risk Management Solutions	1,111.0	64
Sales & Marketing Solutions	490.4	29
Internet Solutions	124.9	7
Total	**1,726.3**	**100**

COMPETITORS

Acxiom	Harte-Hanks
Capgemini	infoGROUP
Deloitte Consulting	Information Resources
Equifax	Kreller Business
Experian Americas	Information
Fair Isaac	OneSource
GfK NOP	S&P

HISTORICAL FINANCIALS
Company Type: Public

Income Statement   FYE: December 31

	REVENUE ($ mil.)	NET INCOME ($ mil.)	NET PROFIT MARGIN	EMPLOYEES
12/08	1,726.3	310.6	18.0%	4,900
12/07	1,599.2	298.1	18.6%	4,900
12/06	1,531.3	240.7	15.7%	4,400
12/05	1,443.6	221.2	15.3%	4,350
12/04	1,414.0	211.8	15.0%	4,700
Annual Growth	**5.1%**	**10.0%**	**—**	**1.0%**

2008 Year-End Financials

Debt ratio: —
Return on equity: —
Cash ($ mil.): 164
Current ratio: 0.77
Long-term debt ($ mil.): 904
No. of shares (mil.): 53
Dividends
Yield: 1.6%
Payout: 21.4%
Market value ($ mil.): 4,073

Stock History   NYSE: DNB

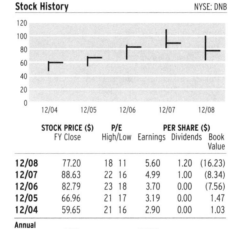

	STOCK PRICE ($) FY Close	P/E High/Low		Earnings	PER SHARE ($) Dividends	Book Value
12/08	77.20	18	11	5.60	1.20	(16.23)
12/07	88.63	22	16	4.99	1.00	(8.34)
12/06	82.79	23	18	3.70	0.00	(7.56)
12/05	66.96	21	17	3.19	0.00	1.47
12/04	59.65	21	16	2.90	0.00	1.03
Annual Growth	**6.7%**	**—**	**—**	**17.9%**	**—**	**—**

DuPont

E. I. du Pont de Nemours wants to cover your house, feed your crops, and coat your car. The #3 US chemical maker (behind Dow and ExxonMobil Chemicals) operates through five business units. These segments produce coatings (automotive finishes and coatings), crop protection chemicals and genetically modified seeds, electronic materials (LCDs, sensors, and fluorochemicals), polymers and resins for packaging and other uses, and safety and security materials (under brand names like Tyvek, Kevlar, and Corian). In this decade, the company has slimmed down, exiting the pharmaceutical business and spinning off its fibers operations, and DuPont is now focusing on biotechnology and safety and protection.

The company gets more than a third of its sales from the US; internationally it operates throughout Europe and Asia as well as in Canada and South America. Though it no longer makes pharmaceutical products, having sold those operations to Bristol-Myers Squibb in 2001, DuPont still receives more than a billion dollars of income from two anti-hypertension drugs, Cozaar and Hyzaar, that are licensed to Merck.

In 2007 the company sold part of its fluoro-chemical products business to Huntsman. The unit sold provides fluoro-products for nonwovens to the textiles industry. They are used to repel water, alcohol, and oil-based fluids in medical, filtration, and automotive applications. Terms were not disclosed.

HISTORY

Eleuthère Irénée du Pont de Nemours fled to America in 1800 after the French Revolution. Two years later he founded a gunpowder plant in Delaware. Within a decade the DuPont plant was the largest of its kind in the US. After Irénée's death in 1834, his sons Alfred and Henry took over. DuPont added dynamite and nitroglycerine in 1880, guncotton in 1892, and smokeless powder in 1894.

In 1902 three du Pont cousins bought DuPont. By 1906 the company controlled most of the US explosives market, but a 1912 antitrust decision forced it to sell part of the powder business. WWI profits were used to diversify into paints, plastics, and dyes.

DuPont acquired an interest in General Motors in 1917; the stake increased to 37% by 1922 (the company surrendered its stake in 1962 due to antitrust regulations). In the 1920s the firm bought and improved French cellophane technology and began producing rayon. DuPont's inventions include neoprene synthetic rubber (1931), Lucite (1937), nylon (1938), Teflon (1938), and Dacron. The last du Pont to head the company resigned as chairman in 1972. DuPont got into the energy business by acquiring Conoco for $7.6 billion in 1981.

In 1991 DuPont and Merck created DuPont Merck Pharmaceutical to focus on non-US markets. After record earnings in 1994, DuPont spent $8.8 billion the next year to buy back shares of the corporation from Seagram. In 1997 DuPont purchased Protein Technologies International (soy proteins) from Ralston Purina and Imperial Chemical's polyester-resins and intermediates operations (1997) and polyester-film business (1998).

DuPont president Chad Holliday became CEO in early 1998. That year DuPont purchased a 20% stake in Pioneer Hi-Bred International (corn seed) for $1.7 billion and Merck's 50% stake in DuPont Merck Pharmaceutical (now DuPont Pharmaceuticals) for $2.6 billion. DuPont's public offering of Conoco in 1998 raised $4.4 billion, the largest US IPO at the time.

In 1999 DuPont bought the Herberts paints and coatings unit from Hoechst. It also bought the remaining 80% of Pioneer Hi-Bred for $7.7 billion and biotechnology research firm CombiChem for $95 million. Making a clean break with its oil business, DuPont sold its remaining 70% stake in Conoco.

In late 2001 Bristol-Myers Squibb bought DuPont's pharmaceutical operations (HIV, heart disease, nerve disorder, and cancer drugs) for $7.8 billion in cash. In early 2002 DuPont initiated a restructuring that included the eventual spin-off of its fibers businesses (now called

INVISTA) and the reorganization of its remaining business units into five segments: Electronics & Communication Technologies, Performance Materials, Coatings & Color Technologies, Safety & Protection, and Agriculture & Nutrition.

Later that year DuPont acquired TOTAL's surface protection and fluoroadditives business to become the largest integrated fluorotelomer protectants maker in both Europe and North America. DuPont also acquired semiconductor chemicals maker ChemFirst and packaging company Liqui-Box in 2002.

Excluding the former pharmaceutical operations, DuPont wasn't profitable for the first few years of the new century. Much of its losses were due to employee severance costs and the write-down of assets. In 2003 the company took a large hit from the separation of INVISTA, among other costs. And so despite a 12% increase in sales, the company saw no real profit.

DuPont announced in late 2003 an initiative that it hoped would deliver $900 million in growth by the end of 2005. In addition to workforce cuts and product consolidation, DuPont also began to shift its focus to emerging markets, by which it meant Asia. The company announced a substantial shift in management in January 2004 to follow up on the initiative, which included appointing a head of global sales for the first time and rearranging its leadership in Asia. The workforce cuts were announced in April; 3,500 jobs were cut in 2004, mostly in the US and Western Europe.

Preparing to separate INVISTA, DuPont reabsorbed DuPont Canada (which had been a separate, public company) into the fold. In early 2004 the company completed the sale of INVISTA; with that, DuPont was completely out of the fibers business.

EXECUTIVES

Chairman: Charles O. (Chad) Holliday Jr., age 61, $8,339,435 total compensation
CEO and Director: Ellen J. Kullman, age 53, $4,443,472 total compensation
EVP and COO: Richard R. Goodmanson, age 61, $4,684,187 total compensation
EVP and CFO: Jeffrey L. Keefer, age 56, $4,286,206 total compensation
Group VP, DuPont Applied BioSciences: Nicholas C. (Nick) Fanandakis, age 52
SVP and Chief Science and Technology Officer: Uma Chowdhry, age 57
VP Information Technology and CIO: Phuong Tram, age 54
EVP and Chief Innovation Officer: Thomas M. (Tom) Connelly Jr., age 56, $3,638,016 total compensation
SVP and Chief Marketing and Sales Officer: David G. Bills, age 47
VP and Chief Sustainability Officer: Linda J. Fisher, age 56
VP, General Auditor, and Chief Ethics and Compliance Officer: Donna H. Grier, age 50
Chief Engineer and VP Engineering and Facilities Services: Jocelyn E. Scott
VP, Associate General Counsel, and Chief Intellectual Property Counsel: P. Michael Walker
SVP Human Resources: W. Donald (Don) Johnson, age 61
SVP Integrated Operations & Engineering: Jeffrey A. Coe, age 56
SVP and General Counsel: Thomas L. Sager, age 59
VP Finance and Treasurer: Susan M. Stalnecker, age 56
VP Investor Relations: Karen A. Fletcher
Manager Business Communications and Media Relations: Lori Captain
Auditors: PricewaterhouseCoopers LLP

LOCATIONS

HQ: E. I. du Pont de Nemours and Company
1007 Market St., Wilmington, DE 19898
Phone: 302-774-1000   **Fax:** 302-999-4399
Web: www.dupont.com

2008 Sales

	% of total
US	36
Europe	31
Asia/Pacific	18
Canada & Latin America	15
Total	**100**

PRODUCTS/OPERATIONS

2008 Sales

	% of total
Agriculture & Nutrition	26
Coatings & Color Technologies	21
Performance Materials	21
Safety & Protection	19
Electronic & Communication Technologies	13
Total	**100**

Selected Operations

Agriculture & Nutrition
  DuPont Crop Protection
  DuPont Nutrition & Health
  DuPont Protein Technologies
  DuPont Qualicon
  Pioneer HiBred International
Coatings & Color Technologies
  DuPont Performance Coatings
  DuPont Titanium Technologies
Performance Materials
  DuPont Dow Elastomers
  DuPont Engineering Polymers
  DuPont Packaging & Industrial Polymers (includes Polyester Resins, formerly part of Polyester)
  DuPont Teijin Films
Safety & Protection
  DuPont Advanced Fiber Systems
  DuPont Chemical Solutions Enterprise
  DuPont Nonwovens
  DuPont Safety Resources
  DuPont Surfaces
Electronic & Communication Technologies
  DuPont Displays Technologies
  DuPont Electronic Technologies
  DuPont Fluoroproducts
  DuPont Imaging Technologies

COMPETITORS

3M
Akzo Nobel
Asahi Kasei
Ashland Inc.
BASF SE
Bayer AG
Cargill
Chevron Phillips Chemical
ConAgra
DIC Corporation
Dow Chemical
Eastman Chemical
Evonik Degussa
FMC
Formosa Plastics
Henkel
Honeywell International
Occidental Chemical
PPG Industries
Reliance Industries
Sherwin-Williams
Shin-Etsu Chemical
Syngenta
W. R. Grace
Wellman

HISTORICAL FINANCIALS

Company Type: Public

Income Statement

FYE: December 31

	REVENUE ($ mil.)	NET INCOME ($ mil.)	NET PROFIT MARGIN	EMPLOYEES
12/08	31,836.0	2,007.0	6.3%	60,000
12/07	29,378.0	2,988.0	10.2%	60,000
12/06	27,421.0	3,148.0	11.5%	59,000
12/05	26,639.0	2,053.0	7.7%	60,000
12/04	27,340.0	1,780.0	6.5%	60,000
Annual Growth	**3.9%**	**3.0%**	**—**	**0.0%**

2008 Year-End Financials

Debt ratio: 110.9%
Return on equity: 22.6%
Cash ($ mil.): 3,645
Current ratio: 1.58
Long-term debt ($ mil.): 7,638

No. of shares (mil.): 904
Dividends
  Yield: 6.5%
  Payout: 74.5%
Market value ($ mil.): 22,861

Stock History

NYSE: DD

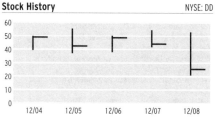

	STOCK PRICE ($) FY Close	P/E High/Low	PER SHARE ($) Earnings	Dividends	Book Value
12/08	25.30	24 10	2.20	1.64	7.89
12/07	44.09	17 13	3.22	1.52	12.32
12/06	48.71	15 11	3.38	1.48	10.43
12/05	42.50	27 18	2.07	1.46	9.86
12/04	49.05	28 23	1.77	1.40	12.59
Annual Growth	**(15.3%)**	**— —**	**5.6%**	**4.0%**	**(11.0%)**

Dynegy Inc.

Power dynamo Dynegy (short for "dynamic energy") provides wholesale power, capacity, and ancillary services to a broad range of customers (utilities, cooperatives, municipalities and other energy operations) in 13 states, in the Midwest, the Northeast, and on the West Coast. The company's power generation portfolio consists of about 30 power plants fueled by coal, fuel oil, and natural gas, and have a generation capacity of more than 13,000 MW. Originally a natural gas trader, the company has refocused in recent years on the wholesale electricity market.

In 2007 Dynegy paid approximately $2 billion in stock for LS Power's power generation facilities, acquiring ten power plants (roughly 8,000 MW) that are primarily natural gas-fired. The addition of these facilities nearly doubled Dynegy's generating capacity, providing it with a stronger foothold in the key Western US region. Dynegy also acquired a 50% interest (alongside LS Power) in a development joint venture, whose focus was on high-return greenfield and brownfield development projects including natural gas, coal, and renewable options. In 2009, citing an uncertain economy, the partners agreed to dissolve the joint venture, and Dynegy returned most of the plants to LS Power. The return of the eight facilities brought back to Dynegy $1 billion in cash and lowered LS Group's holding in Dynegy from 40% to 15%.

In 2007 Dynegy sold its CoGen Lyondell power plant in Texas to a joint venture of PNM Resources and Cascade Investment for approximately $470 million. In 2008 the company sold the Rolling Hills Power Generation Facility, in Wilkesville, Ohio, to an affiliate of Tenaska Capital Management for $368 million.

In 2009 the company agreed to sell the Heard County Power Generation Facility in Georgia to Oglethorpe Power for $105 million.

HISTORY

Dynegy, originally Natural Gas Clearinghouse (NGC), emerged from the deregulation of the natural gas industry. In 1978 the Natural Gas Policy Act reduced interstate pipeline companies' control over the marketplace. Federal Energy Regulatory Commission (FERC) Order 380 (1984) made gas prices on the open market competitive with those of pipeline companies. NGC was founded in late 1984 to match gas buyers and sellers without taking title. Chuck Watson became president and CEO in 1985. The company grew dramatically as deregulation secured larger volumes of gas for independent marketers.

The company developed financial instruments (such as natural gas futures) to provide customers with a hedge against wide fluctuations in natural gas prices. By 1990 NGC was trading natural gas futures on NYMEX. It also branched out by buying gas gathering and processing facilities, and it formed NGC Oil Trading and Transportation to market crude oil.

FERC Order 636 (1992) required most interstate pipeline companies to offer merchant sales, transportation, and storage as separate services, on the same terms that their own affiliates received. With the low-price advantage taken away from pipeline companies, NGC began selling more to local gas utilities.

In 1994 NGC set up partnerships with Canada's NOVA (Novagas Clearinghouse, a natural gas marketer) and British Gas (Accord Energy, an energy marketer), which gave those firms sizable stakes (later reduced) in the company. It also set up an electric power marketing unit, Electric Clearinghouse.

The company changed its name to NGC and went public in 1995 after it bought Trident NGL, an integrated natural gas liquids company. The next year NGC bought Chevron's natural gas business, giving Chevron (which became ChevronTexaco in 2001 and then Chevron again in 2005) a stake in NGC.

In 1997 NGC acquired Destec Energy, a leading independent power producer. Taking the name Dynegy in 1998, the company allied with Florida Power to market wholesale electricity and gas. In 2000 Dynegy paid about $4 billion for utility holding company Illinova.

In November 2001 Dynegy announced an agreement to buy energy trading giant Enron for about $9 billion in stock and $13 billion in assumed debt. Enron had seen its stock price driven down because of controversy over the way it accounted for financial transactions with partnerships controlled by company officers. Later that month, after Enron's stock price continued to plunge, Dynegy canceled the deal and announced that it would exercise its option to buy Enron's Northern Natural Gas (NNG) pipeline for $1.5 billion. Enron then filed for Chapter 11 bankruptcy protection, and the two companies filed lawsuits against each other. In early 2002 Enron let Dynegy take control of the NNG pipeline, and Dynegy agreed to pay Enron $25 million to settle the suits. Dynegy sold the NNG pipeline to MidAmerican Energy Holdings later that year for $928 million plus $950 million in assumed debt.

Also in 2002 the SEC held a formal fraud investigation into how Dynegy accounted for a multi-year natural gas transaction called Project Alpha; the company later restated its 1999-2001 earnings to eliminate a tax benefit and other accounting improprieties related to the transaction. In addition, federal authorities sought information about Dynegy's participation in round-trip energy trades with CMS Energy, which artificially drove up the companies' trading volumes. The company reduced its workforce by 15% that year.

Amid the inquiries, Watson resigned as Dynegy's chairman and CEO. Dynegy later agreed to pay a $3 million fine in relation to the Project Alpha investigation, and in 2003 Jamie Olis was the first former Dynegy executive to be convicted on fraud charges over his involvement in the project. (Olis was sentenced to 24 years in prison in 2004; also that year Dynegy joint venture West Coast Power reached a $280 million settlement — $260 million in lost payments and $20 million in fines — with the FERC over charges of manipulating the California power market during its energy crisis in 2000-01.)

In 2002 and 2003 Dynegy sold its UK gas storage assets to Centrica and Scottish and Southern for a total of $700 million. In 2003 Dynegy sold the utility and its interest in the Joppa power generation facility to Ameren Corporation for $500 million in cash and $1.8 billion in debt in 2004. Dynegy sold off its energy trading unit and its gas processing business in 2005 to Targa Resources for $2.5 billion.

In 2006, it sold its 50% stake in Southern California-based West Coast Power to NRG Energy, and, in a related deal, Dynegy acquired the 50% interest NRG owned in Rocky Road Power, a plant located near Chicago.

EXECUTIVES

Chairman, President, and CEO: Bruce A. Williamson, age 49, $5,944,358 total compensation
EVP Asset Management, Government, and Regulatory Affairs: Lynn A. Lednicky, age 49, $1,494,825 total compensation
EVP Operations: Richard W. (Rich) Eimer, age 60
EVP and CFO: Holli C. Nichols, age 38, $1,903,645 total compensation
CIO and SVP, Technology and Administration: Biren Kumar
EVP Administration and General Counsel: J. Kevin Blodgett, age 37, $1,550,013 total compensation
EVP Commercial and Market Analytics: Charles C. (Chuck) Cook, age 44, $1,022,915 total compensation
SVP and Deputy General Counsel: Kent R. Stephenson, age 58
SVP Commercial Power Operations: Eric Watts
SVP and Treasurer: Carolyn J. Stone, age 36
SVP and Controller: Tracy A. McLauchlin, age 39
VP and General Auditor: James (Jim) Horsch, age 51
VP Midwest Fleet Operations: Keith McFarland
VP Investor and Public Relations: Norelle V. Lundy, age 33
VP Operations, West Region: Daniel P. Thompson
VP Human Resources: Julius Cox, age 35
Senior Director Public Relations: David W. Byford
Auditors: PricewaterhouseCoopers LLP

LOCATIONS

HQ: Dynegy Inc.
1000 Louisiana St., Ste. 5800, Houston, TX 77002
Phone: 713-507-6400   **Fax:** 713-507-6808
Web: www.dynegy.com

2008 Sales

	$ mil.	% of total
Midwest	1,623	46
Northeast	1,006	28
West	925	26
Adjustments	(5)	—
Total	**3,549**	**100**

PRODUCTS/OPERATIONS

2008 Sales

	% of total
MISO	25
NYISO	11
Other customers	64
Total	**100**

COMPETITORS

AEP	Midwest Generation
AES	Mirant
Calpine	NRG Energy
Duke Energy	RRI Energy
Edison International	Sempra Energy
Exelon	Texas New Mexico Power

HISTORICAL FINANCIALS

Company Type: Public

Income Statement

FYE: December 31

	REVENUE ($ mil.)	NET INCOME ($ mil.)	NET PROFIT MARGIN	EMPLOYEES
12/08	3,549.0	174.0	4.9%	2,000
12/07	3,103.0	264.0	8.5%	1,800
12/06	2,017.0	(334.0)	—	1,339
12/05	2,313.0	108.0	4.7%	1,371
12/04	6,153.0	(15.0)	—	2,223
Annual Growth	**(12.9%)**	**—**	**—**	**(2.6%)**

2008 Year-End Financials

Debt ratio: 134.5%
Return on equity: 3.9%
Cash ($ mil.): 693
Current ratio: 1.65
Long-term debt ($ mil.): 6,072

No. of shares (mil.): 845
Dividends
  Yield: 0.0%
  Payout: —
Market value ($ mil.): 1,690

Stock History

NYSE: DYN

	STOCK PRICE ($) FY Close	P/E High/Low		PER SHARE ($) Earnings	Dividends	Book Value
12/08	2.00	50	7	0.20	0.00	5.34
12/07	7.14	31	18	0.35	0.00	5.33
12/06	7.24	—	—	(0.75)	0.00	2.68
12/05	4.84	27	15	0.21	0.00	2.55
12/04	4.62	—	—	(0.10)	0.00	2.21
Annual Growth	**(18.9%)**	**—**	**—**	**—**	**—**	**24.7%**

E. & J. Gallo Winery

E. & J. Gallo Winery brings merlot to the masses. The company is one of the world's largest winemakers, thanks in part to its inexpensive jug and box brands, including Carlo Rossi, Peter Vella, and Boone's Farm brands. The vintner owns seven wineries and about 20,000 acres of California vineyards. It is the leading US exporter of California wine, selling its some 60 brands in more than 90 countries across the globe. Among its premium wines and imports are those of Gallo Family Vineyards Sonoma Reserve and the Italian wine Ecco Domani. For those who prefer a little more kick to their imbibing, Gallo distills several lines of brandy and one gin label.

Gallo once only sold wine in the low-to-moderate price range, but now sells across a wide price range, from alcohol-added wines and wine coolers to upscale varietals that fetch more than $50 a bottle. It has successfully expanded premium wines such as Turning Leaf and Frei Brothers, which don't have the Gallo name on the label. It also imports wines from Argentina, Australia, France, Germany, Italy, New Zealand, South Africa, and Spain.

The company has tried new approaches to marketing its products, such as sponsoring pro volleyball tournaments. It also rebranded its California wines as the "Gallo Family Vineyards" and removed the Ernest & Julio tag from its packaging and advertising. In 2008 it began producing wines under the MARTHA STEWART VINTAGE label. Offering three varieties — chardonnay, cabernet sauvignon, and merlot — the label is a limited-release product consisting of 15,000 cases.

In addition to using its own grapes, Gallo buys the fruit from other Sonoma County growers. Its 2002 purchase of fellow Sonoma County vintner Louis M. Martini Winery marked the first time Gallo bought an entire winery rather than land or wine labels. Gallo invested about $1 million in capital improvements at the winery and ramped up production of cabernet under the Martini label. Along with brewing wine and spirits, Gallo makes its own labels and bottles at its subsidiary, Gallo Glass.

Founded in 1933, the company is still owned and operated by the Gallo family.

HISTORY

Giuseppe Gallo, the father of Ernest and Julio Gallo, was born in 1882 in the wine country of northwest Italy. Around 1900 he and his brother, Michelo (they called themselves Joe and Mike), traveled to America seeking fame and fortune in San Francisco. Both brothers became wealthy growing grapes and anticipating the growth of the market during Prohibition (homemade wine was legal and popular).

Giuseppe's eldest sons, Ernest and Julio, worked with their father from the beginning, but their relationship was strained. The father was reluctant to help his sons, particularly Ernest, in business. However, the mysterious murder-suicide that ended the lives of Giuseppe and his wife in 1933 eliminated that problem: The sons inherited the business their father had been unwilling to share.

From then on, Ernest ran the business end, assembling a large distribution network and building a national brand, while Julio made the wine and Joe Jr., the third, much younger, brother, worked for them. In the early 1940s Gallo opened bottling plants in Los Angeles and New Orleans, using screw-cap bottles, which then seemed more hygienic and modern than corks. Gallo lagged during WWII, when alcohol was diverted for the military. Under Julio's supervision, it upgraded its planting stock and refined its technology.

In an attempt to capitalize on the sweet wines popular in the 1950s, Gallo introduced Thunderbird, a fortified wine (its alcohol content boosted to 20%), in 1957. In the 1960s Gallo spurred its growth by heavily advertising and keeping prices low. It introduced Hearty Burgundy, a jug wine, in 1964, along with Ripple. Gallo introduced the carbonated, fruit-flavored Boone's Farm Apple Wine in 1969, creating short-term interest in "pop" wines.

The company introduced its first varietal wines in 1974. In the 1970s Gallo field workers switched unions, from the United Farm Workers to the Teamsters. Repercussions included protests and boycotts, but sales were largely unaffected. From 1976 to 1982 Gallo operated under an FTC order limiting its control over wholesalers. The order was lifted after the industry's competitive balance changed.

Through the 1970s and 1980s, Gallo expanded its production of varietals; in 1988 it began adding vintage dates to labels. But it also kept a hand in the lower levels of the market, introducing Bartles & Jaymes wine coolers.

Gallo began a legal battle in 1986 with Joe, who had been eased out of the business, over the use of the Gallo name. In 1992 Joe lost the use of his name for commercial purposes. Julio died the next year when his Jeep overturned on a family ranch.

In 1996 rival Kendall-Jackson sued Gallo for trademark infringement over Gallo's new wine brand, Turning Leaf, claiming Gallo copied its Vintner's Reserve bottle and label. A jury ruled in Gallo's favor in 1997; a federal appeals court supported that decision in 1998.

In 2000 Gallo announced plans to promote wine-cooler market leader Bartles & Jaymes with a new advertising campaign, although the category continued to wane. The next year, Gallo expanded the technological end of the wine business. Gallo's research team patented a number of tools licensed to winemakers around the world; one tool, for example, can diagnose a sick vine in a matter of hours, rather than years.

The purchase of Louis M. Martini Winery in Napa Valley in 2002 furthered Gallo's expansion into premium wines. In 2004 it bought the brand name and stocks of San Jose-based wine producer Mirassou Vineyards, one of the oldest wineries in California, and Santa Barbara company Bindlewood Weste Winery. In 2005 Gallo added Grape Links, Inc., maker of Barefoot Cellars, to its stable of holdings.

Ernest Gallo died in 2007 at the age of 97.

EXECUTIVES

Co-Chairman: James E. (Jim) Coleman, age 74
Co-Chairman: Robert J. (Bob) Gallo, age 74
Co-Chairman, President, and CEO:
  Joseph E. (Joe) Gallo, age 65
EVP and General Counsel: Jack B. Owens

VP Operations: Steven (Steve) Kidd
VP Finance: Doug Vilas
VP and CIO: Kent Kushar
VP National Sales: Gary Ippolito
VP Marketing and Chief Marketing Strategist:
  Gerald (Gerry) Glasgow
VP Viticulture: Nick K. Dokoozlian
VP US Sales: Steve Sprinkle
VP Strategic Planning and Public Relations:
  Susan Hensley
VP Sales and Administration: Peter Abate
Director Marketing: Stephanie Gallo, age 36
Senior Manager Public Relations: Michael J. Heintz

LOCATIONS

HQ: E. & J. Gallo Winery
  600 Yosemite Blvd., Modesto, CA 95354
Phone: 209-341-3111
Web: www.gallo.com

PRODUCTS/OPERATIONS

Selected Brands

Spirits
  E. & J. VS Brandy
  E. & J. VSOP Brandy
  E. & J. XO Brandy
  New Amsterdam Gin

Wine
  Anapamu
  André
  Ballatore
  Barefoot Bubbly
  BarefootCellars
  Bartles & Jaymes
  Bella Sera
  Black Swan
  Boone's Farm
  Bridlewood Estate Winery
  Carlo Rossi
  Cask & Cream
  Clarendon Hills
  Dancing Bull
  DaVinci
  Don Miguel Gascon
  Ecco Domani
  Frei Brothers
  Frutézia
  Gallo Family Vineyard Estate
  Gallo Family Vineyard Single Vineyard
  Gallo Family Vineyard Sonoma Reserve
  Gallo Family Vineyard Twin Valley
  Ghost Pines
  Hornsby's
  Indigo Hills
  Liberty Creek
  Livingston Cellars
  Louis M. Martini
  MacMurray Ranch
  Marcelina
  Martn Cõdax
  Maso Canali
  Mattie's Perch
  McWilliam's
  Mirassou
  Peter Vella
  Pölka Dot
  Rancho Zabaco
  Red Bicyclette
  Red Rock Winery
  Redwood Creek
  Sebeka
  Tisdale Vineyards
  Turning Leaf
  Turning Leaf Sonoma Reserve
  Whitehaven
  Wild Vines
  William Hill Estate
  Wycliff Sparkling

COMPETITORS

Asahi Breweries	Newton Vineyard
Bacardi	Pernod Ricard
Bacardi USA	Premier Pacific
Bronco Wine Co.	Ravenswood Winery
Brown-Forman	R.H. Phillips
Concha y Toro	Robert Mondavi Winery
Constellation Wines	Scheid Vineyards
Diageo	Sebastiani Vineyards
Foster's Americas	Sunview Vineyards
Foster's Group	Taittinger
GIV	Terlato Wine
Heaven Hill Distilleries	Trinchero Family Estates
Kendall-Jackson	UST llc
Kirin Holdings Company	Vincor
LVMH	Wine Group

HISTORICAL FINANCIALS
Company Type: Private

Income Statement				FYE: December 31
	ESTIMATED REVENUE ($ mil.)	NET INCOME ($ mil.)	NET PROFIT MARGIN	EMPLOYEES
12/08	2,000.0	—	—	5,000
12/07	3,150.0	—	—	5,000
12/06	2,700.0	—	—	4,600
12/05	2,700.0	—	—	5,000
12/04	3,000.0	—	—	5,000
Annual Growth	(9.6%)	—	—	0%

Revenue History

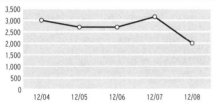

EarthLink, Inc.

As one of the largest ISPs in the US, EarthLink provides Internet connections to about 3 million consumer and small-business subscribers in the US. The company provides premium broadband access to about one third of those customers. It offers such other services as VoIP telephony and Web hosting. Earthlink provides broadband access over cable lines through agreements with companies such as Time Warner Cable, Bright House, and Comcast, while DSL access is made available over lines owned by Covad, AT&T, Verizon, and Qwest. Subsidiary New Edge Networks implements and manages private data networks in addition to providing basic Internet access and Web hosting for small and medium-sized businesses.

As its subscriber continue to decline (2008 numbers were down by about half from 2006) Earthlink took steps to refocus on its core wireline Internet business in 2008 when it sold its stake in mobile virtual network operator HELIO to Virgin Mobile USA in exchange for a small stake in Virgin Mobile USA. Earthlink had announced previously that it would no longer make additional investments in the loss-making joint venture, which it formed in 2005 with South Korea's SK Telecom to market wireless voice and data services in the US.

HISTORY

After his first attempt to log onto the Internet took 80 hours in 1993, a frustrated 23-year-old Sky Dayton had an idea for a new business: an ISP focused on customer service. Dayton, who had already co-founded Los Angeles coffeehouse Cafe Mocha and graphics firm Dayton Walker Design, persuaded investors Reed Slatkin and Kevin O'Donnell to contribute $100,000. EarthLink Network was launched in Glendale, California, in 1994.

Dayton, an Ayn Rand fan who graduated from high school at 16 and never attended college, first tried to do everything — from sales to software — himself. He ultimately decided to concentrate on customer service, correctly betting that such elements as browser software and backbone networks would emerge from other providers. Offering phone help and a flat monthly rate of $19.95, EarthLink sold its first account by the end of 1994.

The next year EarthLink released TotalAccess, a package of leading Internet software that included the popular Netscape Navigator browser and QUALCOMM's Eudora, the oft-used e-mail program. Viacom's Macmillan Publishing agreed to sell TotalAccess disks in its Internet books. EarthLink was to gain similar deals with about 90 other partners.

By 1996 EarthLink had won 30,000 subscribers. The company signed a deal with PSINet giving EarthLink customers dial-up access through PSINet's more than 230 locations in the US and Canada. The next year EarthLink went public.

In 1998 EarthLink teamed with Sprint in a 10-year deal that combined the companies' Internet access services and gave Sprint 29.5% of the firm. As EarthLink passed the 1 million-subscriber mark in 1999, it agreed to offer a co-branded version of America Online's instant messaging service.

EarthLink Network agreed to merge with MindSpring in 1999 in a $1.4 billion deal (closed in 2000). The new company, EarthLink, Inc., moved to MindSpring's Atlanta headquarters. MindSpring founder Charles Brewer took over as chairman, and Dayton remained a director. Brewer left EarthLink later in 2000, however, and Dayton stepped back in as chairman.

Investments in EarthLink during 2000 included $200 million from Apple (which made EarthLink the default ISP on Macintoshes) and another $431 million from Sprint (which boosted its stake after heavy dilution from the MindSpring deal). That year, EarthLink gained 700,000 subscribers by buying OneMain.com, an ISP focused on small cities and rural communities, for $262 million.

EarthLink and Sprint stepped back from their co-branding arrangement in 2001, and Sprint sold about 40% of its stake in the company. That year EarthLink agreed to acquire Cidco, a California-based maker of personal e-mail appliances, in a $5 million deal (completed in 2002). Also in 2002 EarthLink acquired the assets of wireless Internet access provider OmniSky as well as PeoplePC, which used to sell computers with bundled Internet access and now sells value-priced narrowband Internet access (sans computer).

In 2005 Robert Kavner replaced Dayton as EarthLink's chairman of the board. Two years later the company tapped Mpower Communications chairman Rolla Huff as its new president and CEO.

Spurred by mounting costs and dwindling subscribers, Earthlink in 2007 initiated a restructuring plan that included the closure of four offices and workforce cuts of roughly half.

EXECUTIVES

Chairman and CEO: Rolla P. Huff, age 52, $4,390,100 total compensation
COO: Joseph M. (Joe) Wetzel, age 52, $1,706,636 total compensation
CFO: Bradley A. (Brad) Ferguson
Chief Corporate Development Officer: James G. Dole, age 48
Chief People Officer: Stacie Hagan, age 42
VP Products: Kevin F. Brand, age 50
VP Consumer Sales and Marketing: David H.W. Shipps Sr., age 43
President, New Edge Networks: Cardi Prinzi
General Counsel and Secretary: Samuel R. (Sam) DeSimone Jr., age 49, $1,344,630 total compensation
Auditors: Ernst & Young LLP

LOCATIONS

HQ: EarthLink, Inc.
1375 Peachtree St., Atlanta, GA 30309
Phone: 404-815-0770   **Fax:** 404-892-7616
Web: www.earthlink.net

PRODUCTS/OPERATIONS

2008 Sales

	$ mil.	% of total
Consumer services	779.9	82
Business services	175.7	18
Total	**955.6**	**100**

COMPETITORS

AOL
Aplus.net
AT&T
Charter Communications
Comcast
Covad Communications Group
Cox Communications
Google
Internet America
Level 3 Communications
MegaPath
Microsoft
Qwest Communications
ReaLLinx
Sprint Nextel
Time Warner Cable
United Online
Verizon
Vonage
XO Holdings
Yahoo!

HISTORICAL FINANCIALS
Company Type: Public

Income Statement				FYE: December 31
	REVENUE ($ mil.)	NET INCOME ($ mil.)	NET PROFIT MARGIN	EMPLOYEES
12/08	955.6	189.6	19.8%	754
12/07	1,216.0	(135.1)	—	998
12/06	1,301.3	5.0	0.4%	2,210
12/05	1,290.1	142.8	11.1%	1,732
12/04	1,382.2	111.0	8.0%	2,067
Annual Growth	(8.8%)	14.3%	—	(22.3%)

2008 Year-End Financials

Debt ratio: 57.7%	No. of shares (mil.): 106
Return on equity: 53.4%	Dividends
Cash ($ mil.): 487	Yield: 0.0%
Current ratio: 4.52	Payout: —
Long-term debt ($ mil.): 259	Market value ($ mil.): 718

Stock History

NASDAQ (GS): ELNK

	STOCK PRICE ($) FY Close	P/E High/Low		PER SHARE ($) Earnings	Dividends	Book Value
12/08	6.76	6	3	1.71	0.00	4.22
12/07	7.07	—	—	(1.11)	0.00	2.46
12/06	7.10	305	154	0.04	0.00	4.32
12/05	11.11	12	8	1.02	0.00	4.92
12/04	11.52	17	11	0.70	0.00	5.16
Annual Growth	(12.5%)	—	—	25.0%	—	(4.9%)

Eastman Chemical

Eastman Chemical can recall its past through photos — it was once part of film giant Eastman Kodak. The company has developed into a major producer of chemicals, fibers, and plastics. Among Eastman's operating segments are its CASPI (coatings, adhesives, specialty polymers, and inks), Specialty Plastics (engineering polymers), and Fibers (acetate tow and textile fibers) units. Its Performance Polymers segment is the #1 maker of polyethylene terephthalate (PET), a plastic used to make packaging for soft drinks, food, and water. The last segment manufactures Performance Chemicals and Intermediates. Eastman's products go into such items as food and medical packaging, films, and toothbrushes.

Eastman Chemical has operations worldwide, with the US accounting for just more than half of sales. It's expanded internationally by building plants in Asia, Europe, and Latin America. At the end of 2007, however, the company decided to divest its PET facilities in the UK and the Netherlands as well as its Dutch PTA plants. Eastman sold the facilities to Indorama for about $330 million.

In 2009 the company joined with SK Chemicals to form a joint venture that will construct a cellulose acetate tow facility in South Korea. Eastman will own 80% of the JV and operate the plant. The previous year, Eastman had expanded an acetate tow facility it owns in the UK.

Chairman and CEO Brian Ferguson retired in 2009 after nearly seven years as CEO. James Rogers, who had been president of the company and head of the chemicals and fibers group, is his successor, and Ferguson became executive chairman.

HISTORY

Eastman Chemical went public in 1994, but the company traces its roots to the 19th century. George Eastman, after developing a method for dry-plate photography, established the Eastman Dry Plate and Film Company in 1884 in Rochester, New York (the name was changed to Eastman Kodak in 1892).

In 1886 Eastman hired scientist Henry Reichenbach to help create and manufacture new photographic chemicals. As time passed, Reichenbach and the company's other scientists came up with chemicals that were either not directly related to photography or had uses in addition to photography.

Eastman bought a wood-distillation plant in Kingsport, Tennessee, in 1920 and formed the Tennessee Eastman Corporation to make methanol and acetone for the manufacture of photographic chemicals. The company, by this time called Kodak, introduced acetate yarn and Tenite, a cellulose ester plastic, in the early 1930s. During WWII the company formed Holston Defense to make explosives for the US armed forces.

Kodak began to vertically integrate Tennessee Eastman's operations during the 1950s, acquiring A. M. Tenney Associates, Tennessee Eastman's selling agent for its acetate yarn products, in 1950. It also established Texas Eastman, opening a plant in Longview to produce ethyl alcohol and aldehydes, raw materials used in fiber and film production. At the end of 1952, Kodak created Eastman Chemical Products to sell alcohols, plastics, and fibers made by Tennessee Eastman and Texas Eastman. Also that year Tennessee Eastman developed cellulose acetate filter tow for use in cigarette filters. In the late 1950s the company introduced Kodel polyester fiber.

Kodak created Carolina Eastman Company in 1968, opening a plant in Columbia, South Carolina, to produce Kodel and other polyester products. It also created Eastman Chemicals Division to handle its chemical operations.

In the late 1970s Eastman Chemicals Division introduced polyethylene terephthalate (PET) resin used to make containers. It acquired biological and molecular instrumentation manufacturer International Biotechnologies in 1987.

Eastman Chemicals Division became Eastman Chemical Company in 1990. In 1993 it exited the polyester fiber business. When Kodak spun off Eastman Chemical in early 1994, the new company was saddled with $1.8 billion in debt.

Eastman's 1996 earnings were reduced when oversupply lowered prices for PET. Eastman opened plants in Argentina, Malaysia, and the Netherlands in 1998.

Eastman added to its international locations in 1999 by opening a plant in Singapore and an office in Bangkok. It also bought Lawter International (specialty chemicals for ink and coatings) with locations in Belgium, China, and Ireland. In 2000 the company began restructuring into two business segments (chemicals and polymers) and acquired resin and colorant maker McWhorter Technologies.

In 2001 Eastman acquired most of Hercules' resins business. In November the company announced that it had postponed plans to split into two companies (one focusing on specialty chemicals and plastics, the other concentrating on polyethylene, plastics, and acetate fibers) until mid-2002 due to the weak economy. In early 2002 the company announced that it had cancelled those plans altogether and would operate the two as separate divisions.

The following year Eastman announced it would split off part of its coatings, adhesives, specialty polymers, and inks (CASPI) segment. The division had been underperforming and had been hit particularly hard by the high costs of raw materials and a general overcapacity in the marketplace. Eastman sold a portion of CASPI to investment firm Apollo Management for $215 million. Businesses included in the sale were composites, inks and graphic arts raw materials, liquid and powder resins, and textile chemicals. (Apollo called the acquired businesses Resolution Specialty Materials, and then joined RSM with Resolution Performance Products and another of its chemical companies, Borden Chemical, to form the new Hexion Specialty Chemicals in 2005.)

It restructured its divisional alignment in 2006 in an attempt to group together related product groups and technologies. In the process, Eastman disbanded its former Voridian Division.

EXECUTIVES

Chairman: J. Brian Ferguson, age 54, $6,237,656 total compensation
President, CEO, and Director: James P. (Jim) Rogers, age 58, $2,233,878 total compensation
SVP and CFO: Curtis E. Espeland, age 44, $895,782 total compensation
VP and CIO: Jerry Hale
SVP and CTO: Gregory W. Nelson, age 46, $2,241,499 total compensation
SVP, Chief Legal Officer, and Corporate Secretary: Theresa K. Lee, age 56, $1,466,473 total compensation
SVP and Chief Administrative Officer: Norris P. Sneed, age 53
EVP Polymers Business Group and Chief Marketing Officer: Mark J. Costa, age 43, $2,057,602 total compensation
VP, Controller, and Chief Accounting Officer: Scott V. King, age 40
EVP Corporate Strategy and Regional Leadership: Ronald C. Lindsay, age 50
SVP: Richard L. Johnson, age 59
VP and General Manager, Adhesives and Coatings: Damon Warmack
VP Corporate Development and Strategic Planning: Prentice McKibben
VP and Managing Director, Asia/Pacific, Eastman Division: Robert Preston
VP and General Manager, Performance Chemicals: Matthew Stevens
VP and General Manager, Specialty Plastics: Dante Rutstrom
Director Investors Relations: Gregory (Greg) Riddle
Auditors: PricewaterhouseCoopers LLP

LOCATIONS

HQ: Eastman Chemical Company
200 S. Wilcox Dr., Kingsport, TN 37660
Phone: 423-229-2000 **Fax:** 423-229-2145
Web: www.eastman.com

2008 Sales

	$ mil.	% of total
US	3,965	59
Other countries	2,761	41
Total	**6,726**	**100**

PRODUCTS/OPERATIONS

2008 Sales

	$ mil.	% of total
PCI	2,160	32
CASPI	1,524	24
Performance Polymers	1,074	16
Fibers	1,045	16
Specialty Plastics	923	12
Total	**6,726**	**100**

Selected Products

Chemicals
- Adhesives
- Agricultural chemicals
- Food and beverage ingredients
- Inks
- Performance chemicals (chemicals for agricultural products, fibers, food and beverage ingredients, photographic chemicals, pharmaceutical intermediates, polymer compounding)
- Specialty polymers and intermediates

Specialty Plastics
- Polymers
  - Container plastics
  - Specialty plastics
- Fibers
  - Estron acetate tow
  - Estron and Chromspun acetate yarns
  - Estrobond triacetin plasticizers

COMPETITORS

Akzo Nobel	Huntsman Corp
BASF SE	Lonza
Bostik	Nan Ya Plastics
Celanese	NatureWorks
Ciba Specialty Chemicals	Reliance Industries
Clariant	Rhodia
DAK Americas	Rohm and Haas
DIC Corporation	SABIC Innovative Plastics
Dow Chemical	S.C. Johnson
DSM	Sterling Chemicals
DuPont	Teijin
ExxonMobil Chemical	Wellman
Honeywell	

HISTORICAL FINANCIALS

Company Type: Public

Income Statement
FYE: December 31

	REVENUE ($ mil.)	NET INCOME ($ mil.)	NET PROFIT MARGIN	EMPLOYEES
12/08	6,726.0	346.0	5.1%	10,500
12/07	6,830.0	300.0	4.4%	10,800
12/06	7,450.0	409.0	5.5%	11,000
12/05	7,059.0	557.0	7.9%	12,000
12/04	6,580.0	170.0	2.6%	12,000
Annual Growth	0.6%	19.4%	—	(3.3%)

2008 Year-End Financials

Debt ratio: 92.9%
Return on equity: 19.0%
Cash ($ mil.): 387
Current ratio: 1.71
Long-term debt ($ mil.): 1,442

No. of shares (mil.): 73
Dividends
  Yield: 5.6%
  Payout: 38.7%
Market value ($ mil.): 2,304

Stock History

NYSE: EMN

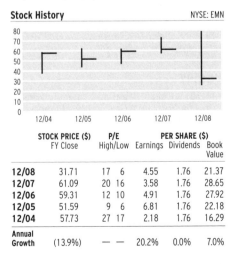

	STOCK PRICE ($) FY Close	P/E High/Low		PER SHARE ($) Earnings	Dividends	Book Value
12/08	31.71	17	6	4.55	1.76	21.37
12/07	61.09	20	16	3.58	1.76	28.65
12/06	59.31	12	10	4.91	1.76	27.92
12/05	51.59	9	6	6.81	1.76	22.18
12/04	57.73	27	17	2.18	1.76	16.29
Annual Growth	(13.9%)	—	—	20.2%	0.0%	7.0%

Eastman Kodak

When Kodak made Brownies, folks began to say cheese. The inventor of the Brownie camera (1900), Kodak has retouched its image from a top maker of photographic film to a provider of imaging technology products and services to the photographic and graphic communications markets. The firm has restructured itself to focus less on film sales and more on sales of digital cameras and imaging systems. It operates through three segments: Consumer Digital Imaging Group; Film, Photofinishing, and Entertainment Group; and Graphic Communications Group. Kodak's shift to become a digital technology business has involved purging some 30,000 employees, with additional plans to eliminate up to 18% of its workforce in 2009.

As a result of Kodak's shift to digital, its iconic Kodachrome color film was discontinued in 2009 due to falling sales.

After posting a 2008 fourth-quarter loss of $137 million, the company announced in January 2009 that it would be cutting up to 4,500 jobs. The plan follows a 2007 restructuring that wiped out about half of Kodak's workforce. That shakeup was intended for the company to retool its offerings and concentrate on digital products and services. Yet slumping sales numbers indicate that Kodak faces a cooling demand for digital cameras, inkjet printers, and flat-panel displays, for which the firm had long-term expansion plans. The global recession in 2008 did not help Kodak's plans of turning its business around.

Its Consumer Digital Imaging segment, which generated 33% of the company's 2008 revenue, is one of the top providers to consumers of digital still cameras, retail printing, and digital picture frames. The company's Kodak Imaging Network, with its 50 million members, is part of this business segment, along with its Kodak All-in-One Inkjet Printing System, which debuted in 2007.

Making and marketing films (including aerial and motion picture), Kodak's Film, Photofinishing, and Entertainment segment serves up traditional photographic products and services for consumers and professionals and brings in some 32% of sales. The company's Graphic Communications segment, accounting for 35% of 2008 revenue, offers software, media, and hardware products for prepress customers and those who do digital and traditional printing.

As the movement toward digital technology continues to transform photography, the company is shooting for a larger share of the digital imaging market (which allows photos to be computer-altered and stored on the Internet). In addition to bundling image-manipulation software with its digital cameras, Kodak offers other computerized products, such as hot-swappable CD writers.

Kodak sold its Health Group in 2007 to an affiliate of Onex Corporation for more than $2 billion. The Health Group, which Onex operates as Carestream Health, generated about a fifth of sales ($2.5 billion) for Kodak in 2006.

Partnerships are giving the company other avenues for revenue growth. Kodak and Motorola inked a 10-year global agreement in 2006 to co-develop camera phones with Kodak sensors. The sensors allow users to integrate with Kodak kiosks, printers, and other services. In 2006 Kodak licensed its passive-matrix organic light emitting diode (OLED) technology to Univision Technology of Taiwan for use in flat panel displays. A cross-licensing deal inked in 2007 with Chi Mei Optoelectronics and Chi Mei EL (CMEL) of Taiwan allows CMEL to use Kodak's technology to make OLED small-panel displays for mobile phones, digital cameras, and portable media players.

In 2009 the company acquired the scanner division of Böwe Bell + Howell. Kodak believes the purchase will help the company to expand its assortment of scanners and complement its business products.

A couple of large acquisitions, in particular, have helped to build a foundation for Kodak's Graphic Communications segment. Kodak in mid-2005 acquired Canada's Creo Inc., the top provider worldwide of workflow software for commercial printers, for about $980 million in cash. It also acquired Sun Chemical's 50% stake in Kodak Polychrome Graphics for about $817 million, paid over several years.

Investment firm Legg Mason Capital Management owns about one-fifth of the company's common stock.

HISTORY

After developing a method for dry-plate photography, George Eastman established The Eastman Dry Plate and Film Company in 1884. In 1888 it introduced its first camera, a small, easy-to-use device that was loaded with enough film for 100 pictures. Owners mailed the camera back to the company, which returned it with the pictures and more film. The firm settled on the name Eastman Kodak in 1892, after Eastman tried many combinations of letters starting and ending with "k," which he thought was a "strong, incisive sort of letter." The user-friendly Brownie camera followed in 1900. Three years later Kodak introduced a home movie camera, projector, and film.

Ailing and convinced that his work was done, Eastman committed suicide in 1932. Kodak continued to dominate the photography industry with the introduction of color film (Kodachrome, 1935) and a handheld movie camera (1951). The company established US plants to produce the chemicals, plastics, and fibers used in its film production.

The Instamatic, introduced in 1963, became Kodak's biggest success. The camera's foolproof film cartridge eliminated the need for loading in the dark. By 1976 Kodak had sold an estimated 60 million Instamatics, 50 million more cameras than all its competitors combined. Subsequent introductions included the Kodak instant camera (1976) and the unsuccessful disc camera (1982).

In the 1980s Kodak diversified into electronic publishing, batteries, floppy disks (Verbatim, 1985, sold 1990), pharmaceuticals (Sterling Drug, sold 1994), and do-it-yourself and household products (L&F Products, sold 1994).

George Fisher, former chairman of Motorola, became Kodak's chairman and CEO in 1993. Fisher began cutting debt by selling noncore assets. Kodak spun off Eastman Chemical in 1994. Sales in 1996 included its money-losing copier sales and services business. Kodak acquired the medical imaging business of Imation in 1998, but it also unloaded more of its noncore operations, including its 450-store Fox Photo chain.

COO Daniel Carp replaced Fisher as CEO in early 2000. Further hits to the economy and Kodak's revenue prompted management in 2001 to eliminate regional divisions and realign the business along product lines. In 2003 the company announced it would cut as many as 6,000 jobs worldwide. This came after reducing as many as 2,200 jobs in the US and Western Europe earlier in the year and cutting as many as 7,000 jobs worldwide in 2002.

In 2004, on the heels of its announcement that it would stop selling film-based cameras in Western markets by year's end, Kodak said it would also stop global production of its Advantix Advanced Photo System (APS) cameras.

In 2005 Kodak said that it would phase out production of black-and-white photographic paper. The firm attributed its exit from the business to a move from chemical-based photography to digital imaging and a 25% decline in demand for black-and-white paper annually. In late 2005 Kodak announced changes related to its 2004 restructuring program that included consolidating color photographic paper manufacturing for North America, closing a Rochester operation that recycles waste to produce Estar polyester film base, and reducing capacity for the production of consumer film products at its Xiamen, China, plant.

Antonio Perez, who took over as president and CEO in mid-2005, added the title of chairman in 2006, when Dan Carp retired. Also that year, Kodak inked an agreement with now-defunct Fischer Imaging Corporation to provide post-sale support (including repair and maintenance) for Fischer's mammography products (such as SenoScan and MammoTest) installed worldwide.

EXECUTIVES

Chairman, President, and CEO: Antonio M. Perez, age 63, $8,636,628 total compensation
President and COO; President, Graphic Communications Group: Philip J. (Phil) Faraci, age 53, $1,797,501 total compensation
EVP and CFO: Frank S. Sklarsky, age 52, $1,938,872 total compensation
VP and CIO: Kim E. VanGelder
VP and CTO: Terry R. Taber, age 54
SVP and Chief Human Resources Officer: Robert L. (Bob) Berman, $869,760 total compensation
VP, Chief Diversity Officer, and Director Community Affairs: Essie L. Calhoun
Board Secretary and Chief Compliance Officer: Patrick M. Sheller, age 47
VP and Chief Marketing Officer: Jeffrey W. (Jeff) Hayzlett, age 48
VP and Chief Intellectual Property Officer: Laura G. Quatela
Chief Marketing Officer and VP, Film, Photofinishing, and Entertainment Group: Ann S. Turner
Chief Accounting Officer and Controller: Eric Samuels, age 41
SVP and General Counsel: Joyce P. Haag, age 58
SVP and President Film, Photofinishing and Entertainment Group: Brad W. Kruchten, age 49
VP and Director Corporate Communications: David T. (Dave) Lanzillo
VP; Chairman and President, North Asia Region; President, Business Development, Asia/Pacific Region: Ying Yeh, age 60
Treasurer: William S. Love
Director Investor Relations: Ann McCorvey
Auditors: PricewaterhouseCoopers LLP

LOCATIONS

HQ: Eastman Kodak Company
343 State St., Rochester, NY 14650
Phone: 585-724-4000   **Fax:** 585-724-1089
Web: www.kodak.com

2008 Sales

	$ mil.	% of total
US	3,834	41
Europe, Middle East & Africa	3,089	33
Asia/Pacific	1,500	16
Canada & Latin America	993	10
Total	**9,416**	**100**

PRODUCTS/OPERATIONS

2008 Sales

	$ mil.	% of total
Graphic Communications Group	3,334	35
Consumer Digital Imaging Group	3,088	33
Film, Photofinishing & Entertainment Group	2,987	32
Other	7	—
Total	**9,416**	**100**

COMPETITORS

3M	Nikon
Agfa	Olympus
Canon	Panasonic Corp
CASIO COMPUTER	Philips Electronics
Dell	PhotoWorks
FUJIFILM	Polaroid
Hewlett-Packard	Procter & Gamble
Konica Minolta	Ricoh Company
Leica Camera	Sharp Corp.
Lexmark	Sony
Nature Vision	Xerox
NEC	

HISTORICAL FINANCIALS

Company Type: Public

Income Statement				FYE: December 31
	REVENUE ($ mil.)	NET INCOME ($ mil.)	NET PROFIT MARGIN	EMPLOYEES
12/08	9,416.0	(442.0)	—	24,400
12/07	10,301.0	676.0	6.6%	26,900
12/06	13,274.0	(601.0)	—	40,900
12/05	14,268.0	(1,305.0)	—	51,100
12/04	13,517.0	556.0	4.1%	54,800
Annual Growth	(8.6%)	—	—	(18.3%)

2008 Year-End Financials

Debt ratio: 130.3%
Return on equity: —
Cash ($ mil.): 2,145
Current ratio: 1.45
Long-term debt ($ mil.): 1,252
No. of shares (mil.): 268
Dividends
Yield: 7.6%
Payout: —
Market value ($ mil.): 1,765

Stock History

NYSE: EK

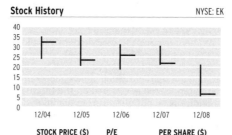

	STOCK PRICE ($) FY Close	P/E High/Low		PER SHARE ($) Earnings	Dividends	Book Value
12/08	6.58	—	—	(1.57)	0.50	3.58
12/07	21.87	13	9	2.35	0.50	11.29
12/06	25.80	—	—	(2.09)	0.50	5.18
12/05	23.40	—	—	(4.73)	0.50	7.33
12/04	32.25	18	12	1.94	0.50	14.21
Annual Growth	(32.8%)	—	—	—	0.0%	(29.1%)

Eaton Corporation

When it comes to diversification, Eaton favors an all-you-can-eat approach. The manufacturer has made dozens of acquisitions (as well as divestitures) over the past few years. The company's product lines include electrical power distribution and control equipment, hydraulic products for use in mobile and industrial applications, aerospace propulsion systems, and truck safety systems. It is also one of the world's largest manufacturers of grips for golf clubs.

Eaton's Electrical division manufactures power distribution and protection equipment such as circuit breakers, switchgear, panelboards, motor controls, and sensors and relays which are used in industrial, institutional, government, utility, and commercial markets.

Hydraulics makes related systems and components for use in mobile and industrial applications. The segment also includes Eaton's Filtration, Golf Grip, and Airflex Industrial clutch and brake businesses. Aerospace designs and manufactures hydraulic, fuel, motion control, and propulsion systems for commercial and military programs. The Truck segment delivers drivetrain and safety systems to fleet owners and freight companies. Automotive develops products to improve fuel economy, emissions, safety, and performance.

Eaton tries to beat economic downturns by adjusting its product mix, keeping a close eye on costs, and making targeted acquisitions. The company bolstered its medium-voltage motor control products offerings in 2007 when it bought SMC Electrical Products. Later that year, the company acquired the small systems business of MGE UPS SYSTEMS from Schneider Electric for $612 million.

Throughout 2008 Eaton filled product gaps in its uninterruptible power supply (UPS) portfolio through joint ventures and acquisitions, spending in excess of $2 billion in the expansion. The majority of the acquisitions focus on the electrical sector, including the Moeller Group (Germany), Phoenixtec (Taiwan), Babco Electric, Pulizzi Engineering, Balmen Electronic (Spain), Power Protection (Prague), and Aphel Technologies. As part of its deal for the Moeller Group, Easton gained a 50% stake in Micro Innovation Holding AG. Micro Innovation is recognized for manufacturing human machine interfaces, programmable logic controllers, and input/output devices. In 2009 Easton scored the remaining 50% ownership of the company.

Barclays Global Investors owns around 10% of the company.

HISTORY

In 1911 Joseph Eaton and Viggo Torbensen started the Torbensen Gear and Axle Company to make an internal-gear rear truck axle that Torbensen had patented in 1902. The company moved from Newark, New Jersey, to Cleveland in 1914. After Republic Motor Truck bought Torbensen (1917), Eaton formed the Eaton Axle Company (1919), repurchased Torbensen (1922), and by 1931 had bought 11 more auto parts businesses. In 1932 it became Eaton Manufacturing.

The Depression flattened auto sales, and Eaton's profits fell. WWII sparked demand that helped the company recover. Joseph Eaton died in 1949. During the 1950s and 1960s, Eaton diversified and expanded geographically. It bought Fuller Manufacturing (truck transmissions,

1958), Dole Valve (1963), and Yale & Towne Manufacturing (locks and forklifts, 1963). Eaton's international business grew, with foreign sales increasing from almost nil in 1961 to 20% of sales by 1966.

Eaton sold its lock business in 1978 and bought Cutler-Hammer (electronics), Kenway (automated storage and retrieval systems), and Samuel Moore (plastics and fluid power). Downturns in the truck and auto industries forced Eaton to close 30 plants and trim 23,000 jobs between 1979 and 1983. The company reported its first loss in 50 years in 1982 and decided to diversify into high technology and to expand operations overseas.

From 1984 to 1993 Eaton spent almost $4 billion in capital improvements and R&D. In 1986 it bought Consolidated Controls (precision instruments), Pacific-Sierra Research (computer and defense systems), and Singer Controls (valves and switches).

Eaton's acquisitions in the 1990s included Nordhauser Ventil (automotive engine valves, Germany), Control Displays (flight-deck equipment), Heinemann Electric (hydraulic-magnetic circuit breakers), and the automotive switch business of Illinois Tool Works. In 1994 Eaton tripled the size of its electrical power and controls operation with its $1.1 billion purchase of Westinghouse's electrical distribution and control business. The next year it bought Emwest Products (electrical switch gear and controls, Australia) and the IKU Group, a Dutch auto-controls firm. It purchased CAPCO Automotive Products (truck transmissions, Brazil) in 1996.

In its repositioning, the company in 1997 sold off its appliance-control business to Siebe PLC and a majority stake in its high-tech defense electronics subsidiary, AIL Systems, to management. Eaton closed and consolidated plants and laid off more than 1,000 workers in its microchip division in 1998.

The company increased its share of the hydraulics market in 1999 by spending $1.7 billion for Aeroquip-Vickers. In 2002 Eaton signed a deal with Volvo to manufacture heavy-duty transmissions for the company's South American truck market.

In 2004 Eaton acquired Powerware, an uninterruptible power supply and power management system manufacturer, from UK-based Invensys. Eaton also made moves to build up its aerospace fluid and air division with two acquisitions late in 2005. First it bought that division of Cobham plc for $270 million, and then it bought a similar operation from PerkinElmer.

In 2006 Eaton continued its string of acquisitions when it purchased Synflex, a maker of thermoplastic tubing and hoses, from materials giant Saint-Gobain. Later that year Eaton bought almost all of China-based Senyuan International Holdings, which makes circuit breakers and other electrical components.

In 2007 Eaton acquired the aerospace business of Argo-Tech for $695 million in cash and assumed debt, a move that will complement the fuel systems business picked up in the acquisition of Cobham Aerospace.

The company continued its international growth through acquisitions, as well. In 2008 it bought the Moeller Group, a German provider of electrical components and industrial controls, for $2.2 billion. A few months after the acquisition Eaton offered about 17 million shares to the public in order to pay down some of it debt and help finance its acquisition of Moeller.

EXECUTIVES

Chairman, President, and CEO:
Alexander M. (Sandy) Cutler, age 57,
$11,217,604 total compensation
Vice Chairman, CFO, and Chief Planning Officer:
Richard H. Fearon, age 52,
$3,797,813 total compensation
Vice Chairman and COO Electrical Sector:
Thomas S. Gross, age 54
Vice Chairman and COO Industrial Sector:
Craig Arnold, age 48, $3,105,890 total compensation
SVP, CTO, and President Europe, Middle East And Africa: Yannis T. Tsavalas, age 52
SVP and CIO: William W. Blausey Jr.
EVP and Chief Human Resources Officer:
Susan J. Cook, age 61
EVP and General Counsel: Mark M. McGuire, age 51
EVP Eaton Business System: Richard D. Holder, age 46
SVP and Controller: Billie K. Rawot, age 57
SVP Taxes: John S. Mitchell
SVP Communications: Donald J. (Don) McGrath
SVP Investor Relations: William C. Hartman
SVP and Secretary: Thomas E. (Tom) Moran, age 44
SVP Public and Community Affairs: William B. Doggett
SVP Environment, Health, and Safety:
John L. Wolfsberger
SVP Corporate Sales and Marketing:
Jeffrey M. Krakowiak
SVP Corporate Development and Treasury:
Kurt McMaken, age 39
Auditors: Ernst & Young LLP

LOCATIONS

HQ: Eaton Corporation
Eaton Ctr., 1111 Superior Ave.
Cleveland, OH 44114
Phone: 216-523-5000   **Fax:** 216-523-4787
Web: www.eaton.com

2008 Sales

	$ mil.	% of total
US	8,775	53
Europe	4,002	24
Asia/Pacific	1,963	12
Latin America	1,455	9
Canada	428	2
Adjustments	(1,247)	—
Total	**15,376**	**100**

PRODUCTS/OPERATIONS

2008 Sales

	$ mil.	% of total
Electrical	6,920	45
Hydraulics	2,523	16
Truck	2,251	15
Automotive	1,871	12
Aerospace	1,811	12
Total	**15,376**	**100**

Selected Brand Names

Electrical
  Cutler-Hammer
  Holec
  MEM
  Powerware
Fluid Power
  Aeroquip
  Boston
  Char-Lynn
  Eaton
  Golf Pride
  Hydro-Line
  Vickers
  Weatherhead
Truck Components
  Eaton
  Fuller
  Roadranger
Automotive Components
  Aeroquip
  Eaton

COMPETITORS

Acushnet
ArvinMeritor
BorgWarner
Callaway Golf
Cummins
Dana Holding
Detroit Diesel
Emerson Electric
Golfsmith
Honeywell International
Hubbell
INTERMET
ITT Corp.
Johnson Controls
Metaldyne
Navistar International
PACCAR
Parker Hannifin
Precision Castparts
Raytheon
Robert Bosch
Rockwell Automation
Sauer-Danfoss
Schneider Electric
Siemens AG
SPX
Thomas & Betts
Trane Inc.
United Technologies
Woodhead Industries
ZF Friedrichshafen

HISTORICAL FINANCIALS

Company Type: Public

Income Statement

FYE: December 31

	REVENUE ($ mil.)	NET INCOME ($ mil.)	NET PROFIT MARGIN	EMPLOYEES
12/08	15,376.0	1,058.0	6.9%	75,000
12/07	13,033.0	994.0	7.6%	64,000
12/06	12,370.0	950.0	7.7%	60,000
12/05	11,115.0	805.0	7.2%	59,000
12/04	9,817.0	648.0	6.6%	55,000
Annual Growth	**11.9%**	**13.0%**	**—**	**8.1%**

2008 Year-End Financials

Debt ratio: 50.5%
Return on equity: 18.4%
Cash ($ mil.): 188
Current ratio: 1.28
Long-term debt ($ mil.): 3,190
No. of shares (mil.): 166
Dividends
  Yield: 4.0%
  Payout: 30.7%
Market value ($ mil.): 8,232

Stock History

NYSE: ETN

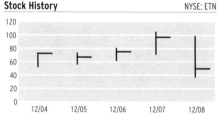

	STOCK PRICE ($) FY Close	P/E High/Low		Earnings	PER SHARE ($) Dividends	Book Value
12/08	49.71	15	6	6.52	2.00	38.15
12/07	96.95	16	11	6.62	1.72	31.23
12/06	75.14	13	10	6.22	1.48	24.79
12/05	67.09	14	11	5.23	1.24	22.81
12/04	72.36	18	13	4.13	0.94	21.78
Annual Growth	**(9.0%)**	**—**	**—**	**12.1%**	**20.8%**	**15.0%**

eBay Inc.

"I got it on eBay" is barreling its way into the lexicon of the new millennium and placing a cyber-grin on the corporate face of online auctioneer extraordinaire eBay. The company offers an online forum for selling merchandise — from fine antiques to the latest video games — hosting about 500,000 e-stores worldwide. eBay, which generates revenue through listing and selling fees and through advertising, boasts about 85 million active users. It also sees gains from its online payments division, composed of PayPal and Bill Me Later, and other e-commerce platforms, including StubHub and Half.com.

In 2009 eBay said it will sell a majority stake in its Skype Internet phone service to an investor group led by the private equity firm Silver Lake for $1.9 billion in cash and a $125 million note. eBay will retain a 35% interest. eBay purchased Skype for nearly $3 billion, but in 2007 it took a write-down for about half that amount.

Because more than half of eBay's revenues are generated outside the US, expanding its international presence has become critical. Overall, eBay and its subsidiaries do business in about 40 markets worldwide. In addition to competition abroad, eBay faces rivals from US-based online powerhouses such as Amazon.com and smaller competitors like Overstock.com.

Looking to diversify its online marketplace operations, eBay has acquired companies with varying objectives. In 2007 it acquired ticket seller StubHub for about $310 million. StubHub joins Rent.com, Shopping.com, and other classified sites within eBay's marketplaces division.

Consumers' use of online payment systems has risen as they have increasingly moved to the Internet for shopping. To get in on the action, eBay expanded its payments department in 2008 with the purchase of Bill Me Later, a firm that processes deferred payments. It joins the auctioneer's PayPal unit, which boasts about 170 million registered users.

Amid the global economic downturn, eBay announced in late 2008 that it would lay off about 10% of its workforce worldwide. The move is part of the firm's plan to simplify its organization and increase competitiveness.

eBay is appealing a French court's ruling that ordered it to pay more than $60 million in damages to the French luxury goods firm LVMH over the sale of counterfeit goods on the Internet. (While eBay polices its site for counterfeit merchandise, the court said it was not doing enough to prevent counterfeit sales.) Just two weeks after the French court ruling, however, a federal judge in New York came to the opposite conclusion in a case over counterfeit goods with jeweler Tiffany & Co. The court ruled in July 2008 that eBay has fulfilled its legal obligation and took adequate precautions to prevent the sale of fake Tiffany jewelry on its site.

Meg Whitman, who led eBay for a decade, stepped down as president and CEO of the company in 2008. She was succeeded by John Donahoe, who previously led the company's highest revenue-producing unit, eBay marketplaces.

eBay chairman and founder Pierre Omidyar owns about 15% of the company.

HISTORY

Pierre Omidyar created a flea market in cyberspace when he launched online auction service Auction Web on Labor Day weekend in 1995. Making a name for itself largely through word of mouth, the company incorporated in 1996, the same year it began to charge a fee to auction items online. That year it enhanced its service with Feedback Forum (buyer and seller ratings).

The company changed the name to eBay in 1997 and began promoting itself through advertising. By the middle of that year, eBay was boasting nearly 800,000 auctions each day and Benchmark Capital came on board as a significant financial backer.

Margaret ("Meg") Whitman, a former Hasbro executive, replaced Omidyar as CEO in early 1998. eBay made a blockbuster debut as a public company later that year. The company moved closer to household name status in 1998 by launching a national ad campaign and inking alliance deals with America Online (now Time Warner) and WebTV.

A bit of the bloom came off the rose in 1999 when online service interruptions (one "brownout" in June persisted for 22 hours) revealed a chink in eBay's armor. The company called its top 10,000 users to convey its apologies and pledged to improve its Web site's performance.

In 2000 the US Department of Justice began an investigation to determine if eBay has violated antitrust laws in its dealing with competitors. In other legal news, a class-action lawsuit was filed against the company claiming that eBay is an auctioneer and therefore must authenticate the items on its site. (A trial court dismissed the case in early 2001.) Also in 2000 the company expanded into Japan through eBay Japan, with computer firm NEC acquiring 30% of the Japanese subsidiary and eBay owning the rest; it also launched Canadian and Austrian sites.

eBay strengthened its European position in 2001 through the purchase of French Internet auction firm iBazar. It also launched sites in Ireland, New Zealand, and Switzerland. It shuttered its eBay Japan operations in 2002 after its dismal performance in that market.

In 2004 eBay took several steps toward diversifying its business. It expanded its international presence through acquisitions in China and India. The company purchased about a 25% stake in online classifieds provider craigslist and announced plans to offer a music downloading service. In 2005 eBay acquired Internet listing site Rent.com. Also that year eBay acquired Shopping.com — a provider of online comparison shopping and consumer reviews with sites in France, the UK, and the US. In mid-October eBay announced it had completed the acquisition of Internet-based telephone services firm Skype, for about $2.6 billion. In November eBay acquired VeriSign's payment gateway business.

In 2008 eBay settled its long-running patent dispute with MercExchange, agreeing to buy the three MercExchange patents it had been accused of violating. MercExchange had sued eBay in 2001, claiming that eBay's "Buy It Now" option infringed on its patent technology.

In June 2008 eBay acquired the California-based visual media company VUVOX Network to further develop rich media capabilities in the eBay marketplace.

EXECUTIVES

Chairman: Pierre M. Omidyar, age 41
President and CEO: John J. Donahoe, age 48, $13,190,170 total compensation
SVP Finance and CFO: Robert H. (Bob) Swan, age 48, $6,798,693 total compensation
SVP Technology: Mark T. Carges, age 47
SVP Legal Affairs, General Counsel, and Secretary: Michael R. Jacobson, age 54
SVP Human Resources: Elizabeth L. (Beth) Axelrod, age 46, $4,342,825 total compensation
SVP Corporate Communications: Alan Marks, age 46
VP and Deputy General Counsel for Government Relations: Tod Cohen
President, Skype: Josh Silverman
President, eBay Marketplaces: Lorrie M. Norrington, age 49, $4,162,130 total compensation
President, PayPal: Scott Thompson, age 51, $5,153,319 total compensation
Auditors: PricewaterhouseCoopers LLP

LOCATIONS

HQ: eBay Inc.
2145 Hamilton Ave., San Jose, CA 95125
Phone: 408-376-7400   **Fax:** 408-376-7401
Web: www.ebay.com

2008 Sales

	$ mil.	% of total
US	3,969.5	46
Germany	1,220.7	14
UK	1,072.9	13
Other countries	2,278.2	27
Total	**8,541.3**	**100**

PRODUCTS/OPERATIONS

2008 Sales

	$ mil.	% of total
Marketplaces	5,586.8	65
Payments	2,403.7	28
Communications	550.8	7
Total	**8,541.3**	**100**

Selected Auction Categories

Antiques
Automobiles
Books
Coins and paper money
Collectibles
Computers
Electronics
Dolls and bears
DVDs and movies
Jewelry and watches
Pottery and glass
Real estate
Sports memorabilia
Toys and hobbies

COMPETITORS

Alibaba.com	OfficeMax
Amazon.com	OnlineAuction
Buy.com	Overstock.com
Christie's	PriceGrabber.com
Collectors Universe	QVC
Costco UK	QVC UK
Costco Wholesale	Rbid
Costco Wholesale Canada	Royal Bank of Scotland
Enable Holdings	Sam's Club
First Data	Sears
Gallery of History	Shopzilla
Google	Sotheby's
Half Price Books	Spectrum Group
HSN	Staples
J. C. Penney	Target
K-tel	Ticketmaster
MasterCard	Tickets.com
Microsoft	Visa Inc
MSN	Walmart.com
NexTag	Yahoo!
Office Depot	

HISTORICAL FINANCIALS

Company Type: Public

Income Statement

FYE: December 31

	REVENUE ($ mil.)	NET INCOME ($ mil.)	NET PROFIT MARGIN	EMPLOYEES
12/08	8,541.3	1,779.5	20.8%	16,200
12/07	7,672.3	348.3	4.5%	15,000
12/06	5,969.7	1,125.6	18.9%	13,200
12/05	4,552.4	1,082.0	23.8%	12,600
12/04	3,271.3	778.2	23.8%	8,100
Annual Growth	27.1%	23.0%	—	18.9%

2008 Year-End Financials

Debt ratio: —
Return on equity: 15.6%
Cash ($ mil.): 3,189
Current ratio: 1.70
Long-term debt ($ mil.): —

No. of shares (mil.): 1,290
Dividends
Yield: 0.0%
Payout: —
Market value ($ mil.): 18,014

Stock History

NASDAQ (GS): EBAY

	STOCK PRICE ($) FY Close	P/E High/Low	PER SHARE ($) Earnings	Dividends	Book Value
12/08	13.96	25 8	1.36	0.00	8.59
12/07	33.19	163 114	0.25	0.00	9.07
12/06	30.07	61 29	0.79	0.00	8.45
12/05	43.22	75 39	0.78	0.00	7.79
12/04	58.17	104 55	0.57	0.00	5.21
Annual Growth	(30.0%)	— —	24.3%	—	13.3%

Ecolab Inc.

Ecolab cleans up by cleaning up. The company offers cleaning, sanitation, pest-elimination, and maintenance products and services to hospitality, institutional, and industrial customers. Its institutional division serves hotels and restaurants, food service and health care facilities, schools, and commercial and institutional laundries. Other divisions focus on products for textile care, water care, fast food, and pest control. Ecolab makes most of its products, although the company sells some products made by other manufacturers. It does about half of its business in the US.

The company has grown through several acquisitions over the years, which have granted Ecolab access to geographic areas as well as business sectors it previously did not have. Ecolab has plans to keep up with its acquisitive ways, and, in 2007, Ecolab made acquisitions in the health care field, buying Microtek Medical Holdings, which makes infection control products for health care facilities. That deal was for about $275 million. The next year it paid $210 million for Ecovation, a company that treats wastewater, solid waste, and air pollution primarily for food and beverage companies.

German consumer products and adhesives giant Henkel had owned more than 25% of Ecolab until it sold that stake through a public offering in 2008. Ecolab itself paid Henkel $300 million for a portion of its stake.

HISTORY

Salesman Merritt Osborn founded Economics Laboratory in 1924 as a specialty chemical maker; its first product was a rug cleaner for hotels. It added industrial and institutional cleaners and consumer detergents in the 1950s. The company went public in 1957. By 1973 it had been organized into five divisions: industrial (cleaners and specialty chemical formulas), institutional (dishwasher products, sanitation formulas), consumer (dishwasher detergent and laundry aids, coffee filters, floor cleaners), food-processing (detergents), and international (run by future CEO Fred Lanners Jr.).

At the time household dishwasher detergent was Economics Laboratory's top seller, second to Procter & Gamble in the US and #1 overseas. The company began offering services and products as packages in the early 1970s, including on-premise laundry services for hotels and hospitals and sanitation and cleaning services for the food industry.

E. B. Osborn, son of the founder, retired in 1978, and Lanners became the company's first CEO outside the Osborn family. Sales of dishwashing detergent had fallen, while the institutional cleaning business had become its primary segment, quadrupling in sales between 1970 and 1980. International sales were growing rapidly. In 1979 the company bought Apollo Technologies (chemicals and pollution-control equipment) to improve its share of the industrial market.

A depressed industrial sector caused Apollo's sales to drop in early 1980. The man expected to save Apollo, Richard Ashley, succeeded Lanners in 1982 but died in a car crash that year. Pierson "Sandy" Grieve became CEO in 1983 and shut down Apollo. Meanwhile, debt was up, the institutional market had shrunk, and the company was slipping in the dishwashing-detergent market. Grieve sold the firm's coffee-filters unit and several plants, laid off employees, and began new packaging processes. The company changed its name to Ecolab in 1986, and in 1987 it sold its dishwashing-detergent unit and bought lawn-service provider ChemLawn. (ChemLawn was sold in 1992.)

As 1990 neared, Grieve introduced what's now known as "Circle the Customer — Circle the Globe," the aim being to become a worldwide leader in core businesses and broaden product offerings. The company concentrated on building its presence in Africa, the Asia/Pacific region, Latin America, and the Middle East. In 1991 Ecolab also began a highly successful joint venture, Henkel-Ecolab, with German consumer-products company Henkel to better exploit European markets.

Ecolab acquired Kay Chemical (cleaning and sanitation products for the fast-food industry, 1994), Monarch (cleaning and sanitation products for food processing, 1996), Huntington Laboratories (janitorial products, 1996), and Australia-based Gibson (cleaning and sanitation products, 1997). In 1995 Grieve stepped down, and president Allan Schuman became CEO. Adding a few more degrees to its circle of services, in 1998 Ecolab bought GCS Service (commercial kitchen equipment repair).

The company further secured footholds in Asia and South America in 2000 by acquiring industrial and institutional cleaning firms Dong Woo Deterpan (South Korea), Spartan de Chile, and Spartan de Argentina. At home, it bought kitchen-equipment companies ARR/CRS and Southwest Sanitary Distributing. Late in 2000 Ecolab sold its Johnson dish machines unit to Endonis and announced a restructuring that was soon followed by the departure of several top executives, including president and COO Bruno Deschamps.

In 2001 Ecolab purchased the 50% of Henkel-Ecolab that it didn't own from Henkel for about $435 million; the move greatly expanded the company's international business.

In mid-2004 Schuman stepped down as CEO (retaining the chairman's role); president Doug Baker took over and became a director in addition to his role as president and CEO. Two years later Allan Schuman retired as chairman, ending his 49-year tenure with Ecolab. The company named Baker to replace Schuman.

EXECUTIVES

Chairman, President, and CEO:
Douglas M. (Doug) Baker Jr., age 50,
$7,625,960 total compensation
CFO: Steven L. Fritze, age 54,
$3,465,383 total compensation
VP and CIO: Robert P. Tabb, age 58
SVP Research, Development, and Engineering and CTO: Larry L. Berger, age 48
EVP, Global Healthcare Sector: Susan K. Nestegard, age 48
President, Industrial and Services, North America Sector: Thomas W. Handley, age 54,
$1,581,268 total compensation
President, International Sector: Phillip J. Mason, age 58
General Counsel and Secretary: Lawrence T. Bell, age 60, $1,947,423 total compensation
SVP Global Supply Chain: Robert K. Gifford, age 51
SVP Global Business Development; General Manager, GCS Service: Michael A. Hickey, age 47
SVP Human Resources: Michael L. Meyer, age 52
VP and Corporate Controller: John J. Corkrean, age 43
VP Marketing: Julie L. Moore
President, EMEA Sector: James H. White, age 44
President, Institutional North America Sector:
James A. Miller, age 52, $1,790,393 total compensation
Auditors: PricewaterhouseCoopers LLP

LOCATIONS

HQ: Ecolab Inc.
370 N. Wabasha St., St. Paul, MN 55102
Phone: 651-293-2233   **Fax:** 651-293-2092
Web: www.ecolab.com

PRODUCTS/OPERATIONS

2008 Sales

	$ mil.	% of total
United States		
Cleaning & Sanitizing	2,661	43
Other services	469	7
International	2,975	49
Other	33	1
Total	**6,138**	**100**

COMPETITORS

3M Health Care	Rentokil Initial
ABM Industries	Rollins, Inc.
Chemed	ServiceMaster
CPAC	STERIS
Healthcare Services	Tranzonic
ISS A/S	UGL Unicco
JohnsonDiversey	Unilever
Medline Industries	Unisource
Reckitt Benckiser (US)	Zep Inc.

HISTORICAL FINANCIALS

Company Type: Public

Income Statement

	REVENUE ($ mil.)	NET INCOME ($ mil.)	NET PROFIT MARGIN	EMPLOYEES
12/08	6,137.5	448.1	7.3%	26,500
12/07	5,469.6	427.2	7.8%	26,050
12/06	4,895.8	368.6	7.5%	23,130
12/05	4,534.8	319.5	7.0%	22,400
12/04	4,184.9	310.5	7.4%	21,300
Annual Growth	10.0%	9.6%	—	5.6%

FYE: December 31

2008 Year-End Financials

Debt ratio: 50.9%
Return on equity: 25.6%
Cash ($ mil.): 67
Current ratio: 1.17
Long-term debt ($ mil.): 799

No. of shares (mil.): 237
Dividends
  Yield: 1.5%
  Payout: 29.4%
Market value ($ mil.): 8,324

Stock History

NYSE: ECL

	STOCK PRICE ($) FY Close	P/E High/Low	PER SHARE ($) Earnings	Dividends	Book Value
12/08	35.15	29 16	1.80	0.53	6.64
12/07	51.21	31 22	1.70	0.47	8.17
12/06	45.20	32 24	1.43	0.41	7.09
12/05	36.27	30 25	1.23	0.36	6.96
12/04	35.13	30 22	1.19	0.33	6.60
Annual Growth	0.0%	— —	10.9%	12.6%	0.1%

Edison International

Although Edison International has been around the world, the company's largest subsidiary is still Southern California Edison (SCE), which distributes electricity to a population of more than 13 million people in central, coastal, and southern California; it is the leading purchaser of renewable energy in the US. The utility's system consists of about 12,000 circuit miles of transmission lines and more than 111,500 circuit miles of distribution lines. SCE also has 5,000 MW of generating capacity from interests in nuclear, hydroelectric, and fossil-fueled power plants. Edison created an international portfolio through Edison Mission Energy (EME), but it has pulled back on most of its international operations.

The pullback is part of Edison International's strategy to focus on the financially more secure US power market. It is investing in upgrading its traditional power infrastructure and expanding its portfolio of solar and wind energy projects, to make the company compliant with increasingly stringent state and federal carbon emission requirements.

After having sold off plants in Asia and Europe, EME now markets energy in only North America and Turkey. This company has interests in 36 power plants in the US and one in Turkey

(Doga project) that give it a net physical generating capacity of more than 11,000 MW.

Edison International also provides consulting, management, and maintenance services for energy projects.

HISTORY

In 1896 a group including Elmer Peck and George Baker organized West Side Lighting to provide electricity in Los Angeles. The next year Baker became president, and the company merged with Los Angeles Edison Electric, which owned the rights to the Edison name and patents in the region. Edison Electric installed the first DC-power underground conduits in the Southwest.

John Barnes Miller took over the top spot in 1901. During his 31-year reign the firm bought many neighboring utilities and built several power plants. In 1909 it took the name Southern California Edison (SCE).

SCE doubled its assets by buying Southern California electric interests from rival Pacific Light & Power in 1917. However, in 1912 the City of Los Angeles had decided to develop its own power distribution system, and by 1922 SCE's authority in the city had ended. A 1925 earthquake and the 1928 collapse of the St. Francis Dam severely damaged SCE's facilities.

SCE built 11 fossil-fueled power stations (1948-1973) and moved into nuclear power in 1963, when it broke ground on the San Onofre plant with San Diego Gas & Electric (brought online in 1968). It finished consolidating its service territory with the 1964 purchase of California Electric Power. In the late 1970s SCE began to build solar, geothermal, and wind power facilities.

Edison Mission Energy (EME) was founded in 1986 to develop, buy, and operate power plants around the world. The next year investment arm Edison Capital was formed, as well as a holding company for the entire group, SCEcorp. EME began to build its portfolio in 1992 when it snagged a 51% stake in an Australian plant and bought hydroelectric facilities in Spain. In 1995 it bought UK hydroelectric company First Hydro; it also began building plants in Italy, Turkey, and Indonesia.

The 1994 Northridge earthquake that cut power to a million SCE customers was nothing compared to the industry's seismic shifts. In 1996 SCEcorp became the more worldly Edison International. California's electricity market opened to competition in 1998, and the utility began divesting SCE's generation assets; it sold 12 gas-fired plants. Overseas EME picked up 25% of a power plant being built in Thailand and a 50% stake in a cogeneration facility in Puerto Rico.

SCE got regulatory approval to offer telecom services in its utility territory in 1999. That year EME snapped up several plants in the Midwest from Unicom for $5 billion. Overseas it purchased two UK coal-fired plants from PowerGen (which it sold to American Electric Power in 2001 for $960 million). The next year EME CEO Edward Muller (who had held the post since 1994) abruptly resigned, and Edison bought Citizens Power from the Peabody Group.

In 2000 SCE got caught in a price squeeze brought on in part by deregulation. Prices on the wholesale power market soared, but the utility was unable to pass along the increase to customers because of a rate freeze. The company gained some prospect of relief in 2001 when California's governor signed legislation to allow a state agency to buy power from wholesalers

under long-term contracts. In addition, the California Public Utilities Commission (CPUC) approved a substantial increase in retail electricity rates, and the Federal Energy Regulatory Commission approved a plan to limit wholesale energy prices during periods of severe shortage in 11 western states.

To reduce debt, Edison International agreed to sell its transmission grid to the state for $2.8 billion. While the California legislature debated the agreement, however, the CPUC announced a settlement in which SCE would be allowed to keep its current high rates in place until its debts are paid off. The settlement, which was approved in 2002, eliminated the need for the sale of the company's transmission grid.

Also in 2001, the company sold most of its Edison Enterprises businesses, including home security services unit Edison Select, which was sold to ADT Security Services.

In 2004 Edison International committed to taking a lead position in developing comprehensive national programs to reduce greenhouse gas emissions, primarily carbon dioxide. In 2006 SCE signed the largest wind energy deal ever completed by a US utility, providing for 1,500 MW of wind power from plants in the Tehachapi area of California.

EXECUTIVES

Chairman, President, and CEO: Theodore F. (Ted) Craver Jr., age 57, $4,213,436 total compensation
EVP, CFO, and Treasurer: W. James (Jim) Scilacci Jr., age 53, $1,401,172 total compensation
SVP and CIO, Edison International; SVP and CIO, Southern California Edison: Mahvash Yazdi, age 57, $1,228,790 total compensation
VP and Chief Ethics and Compliance Officer: Kenneth S. Stewart
VP Safety, Operations Support, and Chief Procurement Officer; VP Safety, Operations Support, and Chief Procurement Officer, Southern California Edison: Cecil R. House, age 47
VP, Associate General Counsel, Chief Governance Officer, and Corporate Secretary; VP, Associate General Counsel, Chief Governance Officer, and Corporate Secretary, Southern California Edison: Barbara E. Mathews
EVP and General Counsel: Robert L. Adler, age 61
EVP, Southern California Edison: Pedro J. Pizzarro, $1,203,579 total compensation
SVP Human Resources; SVP Human Resources, Southern California Edison: Diane L. Featherstone
EVP Public Affairs; EVP Public Affairs, Southern California Edison: Polly L. Gault, $1,447,067 total compensation
VP Investor Relations: Scott S. Cunningham
VP Corporate Communications; VP Corporate Communications, Southern California Edison: Barbara J. Parsky, age 60
VP and Controller: Mark C. Clarke, age 52
VP and General Auditor; VP and General Auditor, Southern California Edison: Megan E. Scott-Kakures
VP Tax; VP Tax, Southern California Edison: Jeffrey L. (Jeff) Barnett
President, Southern California Edison: John R. Fielder, age 63, $2,095,665 total compensation
Chairman and CEO, Southern California Edison: Alan J. Fohrer, age 58, $3,508,108 total compensation
Auditors: PricewaterhouseCoopers LLP

LOCATIONS

HQ: Edison International
  2244 Walnut Grove Ave., Rosemead, CA 91770
Phone: 626-302-2222   **Fax:** 626-302-2517
Web: www.edison.com

PRODUCTS/OPERATIONS

2008 Sales

	$ mil.	% of total
Electric utility	11,248	80
Nonutility power generation	2,811	20
Financial services & other	53	—
Total	**14,112**	**100**

Selected Subsidiaries

Edison Mission Energy (power generation, energy trading and marketing)
Southern California Edison Company (SCE, electric utility)

COMPETITORS

AES	Los Angeles Water
Avista	and Power
Calpine	MidAmerican Energy
CMS Energy	Mirant
Constellation Energy	NRG Energy
Dynegy	NV Energy
Electricité de France	PacifiCorp
Endesa S.A.	PG&E Corporation
Enel	Portland General Electric
Entergy	RRI Energy
FPL Group	Sacramento Municipal
IBERDROLA	Utility
	Sempra Energy

HISTORICAL FINANCIALS

Company Type: Public

Income Statement

FYE: December 31

	REVENUE ($ mil.)	NET INCOME ($ mil.)	NET PROFIT MARGIN	EMPLOYEES
12/08	14,112.0	1,215.0	8.6%	18,291
12/07	13,113.0	1,098.0	8.4%	17,275
12/06	12,622.0	1,180.0	9.3%	16,139
12/05	11,852.0	1,138.0	9.6%	15,838
12/04	10,199.0	916.0	9.0%	15,293
Annual Growth	**8.5%**	**7.3%**	**—**	**4.6%**

2008 Year-End Financials

Debt ratio: 115.1%
Return on equity: 13.5%
Cash ($ mil.): 3,916
Current ratio: 1.10
Long-term debt ($ mil.): 10,950

No. of shares (mil.): 326
Dividends
Yield: 3.8%
Payout: 33.4%
Market value ($ mil.): 10,465

Stock History

NYSE: EIX

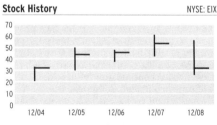

	STOCK PRICE ($) FY Close	P/E High/Low		PER SHARE ($) Earnings	Dividends	Book Value
12/08	32.12	15	7	3.68	1.23	29.21
12/07	53.37	18	13	3.31	1.17	25.92
12/06	45.48	13	11	3.57	1.10	23.66
12/05	43.61	14	9	3.43	1.02	22.51
12/04	32.03	12	8	2.77	0.85	18.96
Annual Growth	**0.1%**	**—**	**—**	**7.4%**	**9.7%**	**11.4%**

El Paso Corporation

Out in the West Texas town of El Paso, this company fell in love with the natural gas industry. Founded in 1928 in its namesake city, El Paso Corp. is primarily engaged in gas transportation and storage, oil and gas exploration and production, and gas gathering and processing. Operator of the largest gas transportation system in the US, El Paso has interests in 42,000 miles of interstate pipeline. Subsidiary El Paso Exploration and Production has estimated proved reserves of 2.3 trillion cu. ft. of natural gas equivalent in Brazil, Egypt, and the US. The company also has interests in global energy projects and markets wholesale energy commodities.

As part of an ongoing sale of non-core assets and eventual divestiture of all of its international power plant operations, in 2009 the company sold its stake in the Porto Velho thermoelectric power plant in Brazil's Rondonia state for about $175 million. It also sold pipelines in South America and is looking to sell a plant in Pakistan as well.

In 2008 El Paso acquired a 50% stake in the Gulf LNG Clean Energy Project, a planned liquefied natural gas terminal in Mississippi.

HISTORY

In 1928 Paul Kayser, a Houston attorney, started the El Paso Natural Gas Company and got the rights to sell natural gas to that West Texas town a year later. Despite the 1929 stock market crash, the company built a 200-mile pipeline, first connecting El Paso, Texas, with natural gas wells in Jal, New Mexico. In 1931 it laid pipe again to reach the copper mines of Arizona and Mexico, and three years later expanded to Phoenix and Tucson.

After World War II the company began a 700-mile pipeline to bring natural gas from Texas' Permian Basin to California. As the Golden State's population exploded, sales soared. El Paso also ventured into new business areas, first chemicals and later textiles, mining, land development, and insurance.

In 1974 the Supreme Court ruled that El Paso had to divest its pipeline holdings north of New Mexico and Arizona. Federal regulators had granted the company the right to buy the holdings two decades earlier but later rescinded. Other operations, such as fiber manufacturing, were posting losses, so the company jettisoned some nongas businesses. El Paso received a boost in 1978 when the Natural Gas Policy Act allowed it more freedom to purchase its own reserves, but later weak demand, coupled with oversupply brought on by the 1970s spike in energy prices, cut into its business by 1982.

Conglomerate Burlington Northern acquired El Paso Natural Gas in 1983. Many of El Paso's operations were spun off when federal regulations required pipeline companies to break apart their sales and transportation businesses and open up interstate pipelines to third parties. El Paso became mainly a gas transportation company.

The company became independent again when Burlington spun it off in 1992. It entered the big leagues in 1996 by buying Tenneco Energy for $4 billion. With some 16,000 miles of pipeline, Tenneco more than doubled El Paso's transportation capacity and gave it the only coast-to-coast natural gas pipeline in the US. El Paso Natural Gas began using the name El Paso Energy and moved from its namesake town to Houston, Tenneco's headquarters. In 1997 it sold Tenneco's oil and gas exploration unit to help pay off debt and bought a 29% stake in Capsa, an Argentine energy concern.

In 1999 El Paso bought Sonat, a natural gas transportation and marketing firm that also had an exploration and production unit, in a $6 billion deal. To gain regulators' approval of the Sonat deal, El Paso sold three pipeline systems in 2000, including East Tennessee Natural Gas (to Duke Energy) and Sea Robin Pipeline (to CMS Energy).

El Paso bought PG&E's natural gas and natural gas liquids businesses for about $900 million in 2000. Also that year the company agreed to buy diversified energy company Coastal in a $24 billion deal, which closed early in 2001. The acquisition helped boost the company's proved reserves to more than 6 trillion cu. ft. of natural gas equivalent. The company changed its name from El Paso Energy to El Paso that year. It expanded its oil and gas exploration and production operations in Canada by buying Velvet Exploration.

Following the collapse of #1 energy trader Enron in 2001, El Paso, along with many other wholesale energy companies, fell under financial scrutiny from investors and regulators. As a result, the company scaled back operations at its El Paso Marketing unit (formerly named El Paso Merchant Energy).

To raise cash to help offset its heavy debt load, the company began selling noncore assets in 2002, including the $782 million sale of midstream oil and gas assets in the Southwest to 27%-owned El Paso Energy Partners (now GulfTerra Energy Partners). The company sold a total of nearly $4 billion in assets in 2002.

In 2003 El Paso was engaged in an unsuccessful proxy contest with dissident shareholders who attempted to replace the company's board of directors. The company reached a $1.7 billion settlement agreement with the California government and the Federal Energy Regulatory Commission over charges of withholding natural gas supplies from the troubled California market in 2000 and 2001, although it admitted no wrongdoing. In addition, the SEC launched an investigation into El Paso's accounting methods for power plant contracts that it restructured in 2002. El Paso sold more than $3 billion in assets that year to further pay down debt, including $500 million in mid-continent gas reserves to Chesapeake Energy; it also sold a 900-MW power plant in New Jersey to The Goldman Sachs Group for $450 million.

The following year, the company sold its Coastal Eagle Point refinery to Sunoco for $246 million and its Aruba refinery to Valero Energy in a $627 million deal. El Paso also sold its Canadian exploration and production assets to BG Group for $346 million. El Paso purchased two natural gas exploration and production facilities, which boosted the company's proven reserves by 124 billion cu. ft. and 29 million cu. ft. per day, in East and South Texas, respectively.

In 2005 El Paso sold its 51% stake in a Montreal chemical manufacturing plant to Petro-Canada. Reversing its trend of selling properties, El Paso acquired the Denver-based Medicine Bow Energy Corporation in late 2005 for a reported $814 million.

EXECUTIVES

Chairman: Ronald L. Kuehn Jr., age 73
President, CEO, and Director:
Douglas L. (Doug) Foshee, age 49,
$6,456,445 total compensation
SVP Operations: Dan Martin
EVP and CFO: David M. (Mark) Leland, age 47,
$2,173,445 total compensation
SVP, Controller, and Principal Accounting Officer:
John R. (J. R.) Sult, age 49
**EVP, Pipeline Group; President, Southern Natural Gas
Company; Chairman and President, Tennessee Gas
Pipeline; Chairman, El Paso Natural Gas; President,
CEO, and Director, El Paso Pipeline GP Company:**
James C. (Jim) Yardley, age 57,
$2,083,536 total compensation
**EVP; President, El Paso Exploration & Production
Company:** Brent J. Smolik, age 47,
$2,307,199 total compensation
EVP and General Counsel: Robert W. Baker, age 52,
$1,999,396 total compensation
**President, Western Pipeline Group; SVP, El Paso
Pipeline GP Company:** James J. Cleary, age 54
SVP Human Resources and Administration:
Susan B. (Sue) Ortenstone, age 52
SVP Pipeline Operations: Daniel B. Martin, age 52
VP Investor and Public Relations: Bruce L. Connery
VP and Corporate Secretary:
Marguerite Woung-Chapman
Auditors: Ernst & Young LLP

LOCATIONS

HQ: El Paso Corporation
El Paso Bldg., 1001 Louisiana St.,
Houston, TX 77002
Phone: 713-420-2600   **Fax:** 713-420-4417
Web: www.elpaso.com

PRODUCTS/OPERATIONS

2008 Sales

	$ mil.	% of total
Exploration & production	2,762	51
Pipelines	2,684	49
Adjustments	(83)	—
Total	**5,363**	**100**

COMPETITORS

Apache	EOG
BP	EQT Corporation
CenterPoint Energy	Exxon
DCP Midstream Partners	Kinder Morgan
Dominion Resources	ONEOK Partners
Duncan Energy	SandRidge Energy
Dynegy	Southern Union
Enbridge	TransCanada
Enron	TransMontaigne
Enterprise Products	Williams Companies

HISTORICAL FINANCIALS

Company Type: Public

Income Statement

FYE: December 31

	REVENUE ($ mil.)	NET INCOME ($ mil.)	NET PROFIT MARGIN	EMPLOYEES
12/08	5,363.0	(823.0)	—	5,344
12/07	4,648.0	1,110.0	23.9%	4,992
12/06	4,281.0	475.0	11.1%	5,050
12/05	4,017.0	(602.0)	—	5,700
12/04	5,874.0	(948.0)	—	6,400
Annual Growth	(2.2%)	—	—	(4.4%)

2008 Year-End Financials

Debt ratio: 390.2%   No. of shares (mil.): 701
Return on equity: —   Dividends
Cash ($ mil.): 1,024   Yield: 2.3%
Current ratio: 0.94   Payout: —
Long-term debt ($ mil.): 12,818   Market value ($ mil.): 5,490

Stock History

NYSE: EP

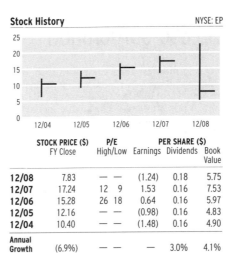

	STOCK PRICE ($) FY Close	P/E High	P/E Low	Earnings	Dividends	Book Value
12/08	7.83	—	—	(1.24)	0.18	5.75
12/07	17.24	12	9	1.53	0.16	7.53
12/06	15.28	26	18	0.64	0.16	5.97
12/05	12.16	—	—	(0.98)	0.16	4.83
12/04	10.40	—	—	(1.48)	0.16	4.90
Annual Growth	(6.9%)	—	—	—	3.0%	4.1%

Electronic Arts

Electronic Arts (EA) has a knack for the craft of creating video games. EA is a leading video game publisher, with popular titles such as *Madden NFL*, *The Sims*, *Need for Speed*, *Spore*, and *Medal of Honor*. It also distributes titles for third-party labels (including *Rock Band*) and publishes games based on Hollywood franchises such as *The Lord of the Rings*, *The Godfather*, *Harry Potter*, and *Batman*. EA develops its games for PCs and console systems and portable devices from Sony, Nintendo, and Microsoft. In early 2008 the company offered $2 billion to purchase Take-Two Interactive, publisher of the *Grand Theft Auto* franchise; Take-Two rejected the offer.

In 2009 the company announced a cost reduction plan that included narrowing its product portfolio, reducing its workforce by about 11%, and closing 10 facilities. As part of that push EA consolidated its operations into three operating segments: EA Games, EA SPORTS, and EA Play.

EA has expanded its target markets to include titles and ringtones for cellular phones and smart phones, including Apple's iPhone. This is part of a broader strategic push of the company into the arena of online delivery of game content and services, a trend that is occurring across the broader video game market as more and more games include multiplayer options over the Internet.

EA's offerings include wholly owned games that it has developed (*Need for Speed*, *The Sims*, *Spore*, *Dead Space*, and *Battlefield*), games that are based on intellectual property that it has licensed (*Madden NFL*, *FIFA Soccer*, and *Tiger Woods PGA Tour*), and games based on popular brands (*Harry Potter*, *The Godfather*, and *Hasbro*.) The company also distributes games from other companies such as MTV Games' *Rock Band* franchise and the Valve Software title *Left 4 Dead*.

Looking to cash in on the market for massively-multiplayer online role-playing games (MMORPG), the company has developed its *Warhammer Online* and *Star Wars: the Old Republic* franchises, which compete with *World of Warcraft* and *EverQuest* in that genre.

HISTORY

After four years with Apple, video game pioneer Trip Hawkins left in 1982, raised $5 million, and founded Electronic Arts to explore the entertainment potential of PCs. The company went public in 1989, and sales exploded the next year when EA began designing games for SEGA's Genesis video game system. Hawkins stepped down as CEO in 1991 and was replaced by president Larry Probst. (Hawkins remained chairman until 1994; he left to devote time to a new game company, 3DO, which later went bankrupt.) The company bought game developer ORIGIN Systems in 1992 and began marketing its games in Japan with partner JVC. By 1995 more than 40% of EA's sales were from outside the US. That year Sony introduced its PlayStation game system in the US.

In 1997 the company bought US publisher Maxis (*SimCity*) for about $215 million. That year ORIGIN introduced *Ultima Online*, an online fantasy game in which players interact with each other. In 1998 EA bought Westwood Studios for $122 million. The next year it established EA.com, an Internet division to develop games for online players. It also agreed to pay America Online (now part of Time Warner) about $80 million to operate AOL's game channel.

In 2000 the company bought DreamWorks Interactive, a joint venture between Microsoft and DreamWorks. It also launched EA.com's Web site, released six titles for Sony's PlayStation 2, and agreed to develop titles for Microsoft's new Xbox game system. In 2001 EA bought online gaming site pogo.com and launched *Majestic* (an interactive, subscription-based game played online) only to terminate the game in 2002 because of its failure to catch on with fans.

EA was banking on the success of the Internet incarnation of its popular Sims franchise, *The Sims Online*, which charges players a monthly subscription fee. The game was launched in late 2002; the response — including negative reviews and sluggish sales — was a letdown. In 2003 EA consolidated its money-losing online unit (EA.com) into its core operations. However, the company continues to experiment with online gaming; it makes some of its titles available for online play via the PlayStation 2 and Xbox systems.

John Riccitiello stepped down as president and COO in April 2004 to start his own private equity business. Also in 2004 EA moved the operations of ORIGIN Systems from Austin, Texas, to Redwood City, California, as part of a larger move toward consolidation of development in California and British Columbia.

When EA suffered a challenge to its popular *Madden NFL* franchise from Take-Two and SEGA (which had joined up to create a set of low-priced, ESPN-branded sports titles), it fired back by procuring a five-year exclusive license to use NFL players and teams in its games as well as acquiring the exclusive rights to the ESPN trademark in 2006. Take-Two retaliated to these challenges with a two-year exclusive license to use MLB teams in its games, essentially putting an end to any new versions of EA's blockbuster hit *MVP Baseball* during that time.

Hardcore video game fans don't just love the company's games, they love the music heard in the games as well. In recognition of this, EA teamed with Nettwerk Music Group in late 2005 in the creation of EA Recordings, a digital-only record label that distributes music from EA's games to popular digital music-downloading services such as Apple's iTunes.

In its most aggressive move to snatch up a portion of the mobile gaming market, the company acquired mobile gaming leader JAMDAT Mobile in 2006 and created a new division, EA Mobile.

In 2007 EA acquired Mythic Entertainment, a developer and publisher of massively multiplayer online role-playing games. Early the next year it purchased VG Holding Corp., the owner of BioWare and Pandemic Studios.

EXECUTIVES

Chairman: Lawrence F. (Larry) Probst III, age 59
CEO and Director: John S. Riccitiello, age 49, $6,365,823 total compensation
COO: John Schappert, age 37
EVP and CFO: Eric F. Brown, age 43, $3,945,027 total compensation
SVP and Chief Accounting Officer:
Kenneth A. (Ken) Barker, age 42
EVP Human Resources: Gabrielle Toledano, age 42
EVP, Western World Publishing: Gerhard Florin, age 50
EVP Business and Legal Affairs: Joel Linzner, age 57
EVP, EA Play Label: Rodney (Rod) Humble, age 43
SVP, General Counsel, and Corporate Secretary:
Stephen G. Bené, age 45
President, EA SPORTS: Peter Moore
President, EA Games Label: Frank D. Gibeau, age 40, $4,069,499 total compensation
President, EA SPORTS Label: Peter R. Moore, age 54, $4,284,366 total compensation
Director Communications: Holly Rockwood
Auditors: KPMG LLP

LOCATIONS

HQ: Electronic Arts Inc.
209 Redwood Shores Pkwy.
Redwood City, CA 94065
Phone: 650-628-1500   **Fax:** 650-628-1422
Web: www.ea.com

2009 Sales

	$ mil.	% of total
North America	2,412	57
Europe	1,589	38
Other regions	211	5
Total	**4,212**	**100**

PRODUCTS/OPERATIONS

2009 Sales

	$ mil.	% of total
Consoles	2,770	66
PC	712	17
Mobile	585	14
Licensing & other	145	3
Total	**4,212**	**100**

Selected Game Titles

Battlefield
Dead Space
FIFA Soccer
Madden NFL
Need for Speed
Spore
The Sims

COMPETITORS

Activision Blizzard	Namco Limited
Atari	NCsoft
Capcom	Nintendo
Eidos	SEGA
Gameloft	Sony Online
Glu Mobile	Entertainment
Konami	Take-Two
LucasArts	THQ
Microsoft	Ubisoft
Midway Games	Valve Corporation

HISTORICAL FINANCIALS

Company Type: Public

Income Statement

	REVENUE ($ mil.)	NET INCOME ($ mil.)	NET PROFIT MARGIN	EMPLOYEES
				FYE: March 31
3/09	4,212.0	(1,088.0)	—	9,100
3/08	3,665.0	(454.0)	—	9,000
3/07	3,091.0	76.0	2.5%	7,900
3/06	2,951.0	236.0	8.0%	7,200
3/05	3,129.0	504.0	16.1%	6,100
Annual Growth	**7.7%**	**—**	**—**	**10.5%**

2009 Year-End Financials

Debt ratio: —	No. of shares (mil.): 324
Return on equity: —	Dividends
Cash ($ mil.): 1,621	Yield: 0.0%
Current ratio: 2.75	Payout: —
Long-term debt ($ mil.): —	Market value ($ mil.): 5,885

Stock History

NASDAQ (GS): ERTS

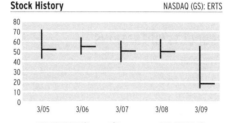

	STOCK PRICE ($) FY Close	P/E High/Low		PER SHARE ($) Earnings	Dividends	Book Value
3/09	18.19	—	—	(3.40)	0.00	9.69
3/08	49.92	—	—	(1.45)	0.00	13.41
3/07	50.36	249	167	0.24	0.00	12.46
3/06	54.72	84	63	0.75	0.00	10.53
3/05	51.78	45	27	1.59	0.00	10.81
Annual Growth	**(23.0%)**	**—**	**—**	**—**	**—**	**(2.7%)**

Eli Lilly

Eli Lilly hopes everything will come up roses for you, healthwise. Although best known for its popular antidepressant Prozac, the company develops medicines for a wide variety of ailments. Its top drugs include neurological therapies Zyprexa (schizophrenia and bipolar disorder) and Cymbalta (depression), cancer treatments Gemzar and Alimta, and endocrinology (hormone-related) products such as Humalog insulin and osteoporosis medication Evista. The company also makes cardiovascular therapies and anti-infective agents, as well as animal health products. Eli Lilly sells its products in some 135 countries.

Eli Lilly knows the value of drug patents: After the company lost its lucrative patent protection for Prozac in August 2001, it saw sales drop dramatically. Lilly's current bestseller Zyprexa, which accounts for nearly a quarter of annual sales, will have patent protection until 2011, but Eli Lilly is avidly seeking new potential blockbusters and has started making "knockoff" versions of its own drugs so it will be less susceptible to generic competition.

The company has some 60 drug candidates in development stages, including treatments for cancer, diabetes, rheumatoid arthritis, cardiovascular thrombosis, and Alzheimer's disease. Biotechnology is increasingly important; the firm completed a $1 billion biotech research facility in Indianapolis in 2008.

Lilly received FDA approval on a top pipeline candidate, blood thinner Effient (or prasugrel, developed with Daiichi Sankyo), in 2009, though the drug will carry heavy warning labels due to fatal bleeding risks. Another promising development candidate is a once-a-week version of diabetes treatment Byetta; the drug is being co-developed with Amylin and Alkermes. The company is also pursuing additional indications for existing drugs; Evista was approved as a breast cancer preventative for postmenopausal women in 2007, and bipolar therapy Symbyax was expanded for treatment-resistant depression indications in 2009.

The company gave its biotech ambitions a big boost through the 2008 acquisition of biotech firm ImClone for about $6.5 billion. ImClone has one blockbuster therapy, Erbitux for colorectal and head/neck cancers, and is developing numerous other cancer therapy candidates.

In 2007 the company acquired development partner ICOS for $2.1 billion; the deal gave Lilly full ownership of Viagra-competitor Cialis.

On the slimming-down side, Lilly announced in late 2007 that it would take additional cost-cutting measures to offset losses from patent expirations, including the attrition of employees.

The power of Zyprexa was diminished in early 2007 when Eli Lilly agreed to settle with patients complaining of side-effects including diabetes, weight gain, and high cholesterol. Total settlement figures have reached $2.6 billion, and in 2009 the company agreed to pay an additional $1.4 billion in government fines to settle allegations over its marketing tactics for Zyprexa.

The Lilly Endowment, a charitable foundation created by the company and the Lilly family in the 1930s, owns 12% of the company.

HISTORY

Colonel Eli Lilly, pharmacist and Union officer in the Civil War, started Eli Lilly and Company in 1876 with $1,300. His process of gelatin-coating pills led to sales of nearly $82,000 in 1881. Later, the company made gelatin capsules, which it still sells. Lilly died in 1898, and his son and two grandsons ran the business until 1953.

Eli Lilly began extracting insulin from the pancreases of hogs and cattle in 1923; 6,000 cattle glands or 24,000 hog glands made one ounce of the substance. Other products created in the 1920s and 1930s included antiseptic Merthiolate, sedative Seconal, and treatments for pernicious anemia and heart disease. In 1947 the company began selling diethylstilbestrol (DES), a drug to prevent miscarriages. Eli Lilly researchers isolated the antibiotic erythromycin from a species of mold found in the Philippines in 1952. Lilly was also the major supplier of Salk polio vaccine.

The company enjoyed a 70% share of the DES market by 1971, when researchers noticed that a rare form of cervical cancer afflicted many of the daughters of women who had taken the drug. The FDA restricted the drug's use and Lilly found itself on the receiving (and frequently losing) end of a number of trailblazing product-liability suits that stretched into the 1990s.

The firm diversified in the 1970s, buying Elizabeth Arden (cosmetics, 1971; sold 1987) and IVAC (medical instruments, 1977). It launched such products as analgesic Darvon and antibiotic Ceclor. Lilly's 1982 launch of Humulin, a synthetic insulin developed by Genentech, made it the first company to market a genetically engineered product. In 1986 Lilly introduced Prozac; that year it also bought biotech firm Hybritech for $300 million (sold in 1995 for less than $10 million).

In 1995 the firm and developer Centocor introduced ReoPro, a blood-clot inhibitor used in angioplasties. The next year it launched antipsychotic Zyprexa, Humalog, and Gemzar, and Prozac was approved to treat bulimia nervosa.

In 1999 a US federal judge found that the firm illegally promoted osteoporosis drug Evista as a breast cancer preventative similar to AstraZeneca's Nolvadex. Lilly halted tests on its variation of heart drug Moxonidine after 53 patients died. Also that year Zyprexa was approved to treat bipolar disorder.

In 2000 the firm began marketing Prozac under the Sarafem name for severe premenstrual syndrome. A federal appeals court knocked more than two years off Prozac's patent, reducing the expected 2003 expiration date to 2001.

While the firm fretted over Prozac and its patents, it continued work to find its next blockbuster. In 2000 Lilly and partner ICOS announced favorable results from a study of erectile dysfunction treatment Cialis, which was approved in Europe in 2002 and in the US in 2004.

In 2002 the company settled with eight states in an infringement-of-privacy case involving the company's accidental disclosure of e-mail addresses for more than 600 Prozac patients.

In late 2004 Lilly announced its attention-deficit disorder drug Strattera had been linked to rare liver problems. The company agreed to add warning labels about the potential side effects to the drug's packaging and advertisements.

After a lengthy lawsuit regarding its patents for its top seller, Zyprexa, a federal judge ruled in Lilly's favor against generic manufacturers IVAX, Dr. Reddy's Laboratories, and Teva Pharmaceutical Industries.

EXECUTIVES

Chairman, President, and CEO: John C. Lechleiter, age 55, $12,978,215 total compensation
SVP and CFO: Derica W. Rice, age 44, $5,206,142 total compensation
VP Information Technology and CIO: Michael C. (Mike) Heim, age 54
VP Medical and Chief Medical Officer: Alan Breier
VP and Chief Procurement Officer: James A. Ward
EVP Global Marketing and Sales: Bryce D. Carmine, $5,962,090 total compensation
EVP, Science and Technology; President, Lilly Research Laboratories: Steven M. Paul, age 58, $6,520,062 total compensation
SVP Corporate Strategy and Business Development: Gino Santini, age 52
SVP and General Counsel: Robert A. Armitage, age 59, $4,458,219 total compensation
SVP Corporate Affairs and Communications: Alex M. Azar II, age 41
SVP Human Resources: Sue Mahony
VP Global Public Policy, Pricing, Reimbursement & Access (PRA), and International Corporate Affairs: Newton F. Crenshaw
VP and General Counsel: Alecia A. DeCoudreaux, age 53
VP Compliance and Enterprise Risk Management and Chief Compliance Officer: Anne Nobles, age 52

VP and Treasurer: Thomas W. Grein, age 57
VP Global Compensation and Human Resources Services: Sharon L. Sullivan
VP Global External Research and Development, Lilly Research Laboratories: Robert W. Armstrong
Secretary and Deputy General Counsel: James B. Lootens
Executive Medical Director: Robert J. Heine
Auditors: Ernst & Young LLP

LOCATIONS

HQ: Eli Lilly and Company
Lilly Corporate Center, 893 S. Delaware
Indianapolis, IN 46285
Phone: 317-276-2000   **Fax:** 317-276-4878
Web: www.lilly.com

2008 Sales

	$ mil.	% of total
US	10,934.4	54
Europe	5,334.9	26
Other regions	4,108.7	20
Total	**20,378.0**	**100**

PRODUCTS/OPERATIONS

2008 Sales

	$ mil.	% of total
Neurosciences	8,371.5	41
Endocrinology	5,890.7	29
Oncology	2,874.5	14
Cardiovascular	1,882.7	9
Animal health	1,093.3	6
Other pharmaceuticals	265.3	1
Total	**20,378.0**	**100**

2008 Sales

	$ mil.	% of total
Zyprexa	4,696.1	23
Cymbalta	2,697.1	13
Humalog	1,735.8	9
Gemzar	1,719.8	9
Cialis	1,444.5	7
Alimta	1,154.7	6
Animal health products	1,093.3	5
Evista	1,075.6	5
Humulin	1,063.2	5
Forteo	778.7	4
Strattera	579.5	3
Other pharmaceuticals	2,339.7	11
Total	**20,378.0**	**100**

Selected Products

Neuroscience
Cymbalta (duloxetine hydrocholoride; depression, anxiety, pain)
Prozac (fluoxetine hydrochloride; depression, panic disorder, obsessive-compulsive disorder)
Strattera (atomoxetine hydrochloride, ADHD)
Symbyax (olanzapine and fluoxetine hydrochloride, bipolar and treatment-resistant depression)
Zyprexa (olanzapine, schizophrenia and bipolar)
Endocrinology (including diabetes)
Actos (pioglitazone hydrochloride, type 2 diabetes)
Byetta (exenatide injection, type 2 diabetes)
Evista (raloxifene hydrochloride, osteoporosis and breast cancer prevention in postmenopausal women)
Forteo (osteoporosis)
Humatrope (somatropin for injection, rDNA origin; growth disorders)
Humulin (human insulin, rDNA origin; diabetes)
Humalog (insulin lispro injection, rDNA origin; diabetes)
Humalog Mix75/25 (75% Insulin lispro protamine suspension, 25% insulin lispro injection, rDNA origin; diabetes)
Humalog Mix50/50 (50% Insulin lispro protamine suspension, 50% insulin lispro injection, rDNA origin; diabetes)
Humalog Pen (insulin lispro, rDNA origin; diabetes)
Humulin Pen (human insulin, rDNA origin; diabetes)

Oncology (cancer)
Alimta (pemetrexed, lung cancer)
Erbitux (colorectal cancer, from ImClone)
Gemzar (gemcitabine hydrochloride; pancreatic, breast, lung, and ovarian cancers)
Cardiovascular
Cialis (tadalafil, erectile dysfunction)
Efient/Effient (atherothrombotic events, approved in the EU and awaiting approval in the US)
ReoPro (percutaneous coronary intervention)
Xigris (activated drotrecogin alfa, sepsis)
Animal Health
Apralan (antibiotic)
Coban, Monteban, and Maxiban (anticoccidal)
Comfortis (flea prevention)
Elector (parasiticide)
Micotil, Pulmotil, and Pulmotil AC (antibiotics)
Paylean, Optaflexx (performance enhancers)
Posilac (protein supplement)
Reconcile (separation anxiety)
Rumensin (feed additive)
Surmax/Maxus (performance enhancer)
Tylan (antibiotic)
Other pharmaceuticals
Ceclor (bacterial infections)
Vancocin (staphylococcal infections)

COMPETITORS

Abbott Labs
Amgen
AstraZeneca
Barr Pharmaceuticals
Baxter International
Bayer AG
Boehringer Ingelheim
Bristol-Myers Squibb
Dr. Reddy's
Elan
Forest Labs
Genentech
GlaxoSmithKline
Johnson & Johnson
Merck
Mylan
Myriad Genetics
Novartis
Novo Nordisk
Pfizer
Ranbaxy Laboratories
Roche Holding
Sanofi-Aventis
Schering-Plough
Shire
Teva Pharmaceuticals
Wyeth

HISTORICAL FINANCIALS

Company Type: Public

Income Statement

FYE: December 31

	REVENUE ($ mil.)	NET INCOME ($ mil.)	NET PROFIT MARGIN	EMPLOYEES
12/08	20,378.0	(2,071.9)	—	40,500
12/07	18,633.5	2,953.0	15.8%	40,600
12/06	15,691.0	2,662.7	17.0%	41,500
12/05	14,645.3	2,001.6	13.7%	42,600
12/04	13,857.9	1,810.1	13.1%	44,500
Annual Growth	**10.1%**	**—**	**—**	**(2.3%)**

2008 Year-End Financials

Debt ratio: 82.0%
Return on equity: —
Cash ($ mil.): 5,497
Current ratio: 0.95
Long-term debt ($ mil.): 5,522

No. of shares (mil.): 1,149
Dividends
  Yield: 4.7%
  Payout: —
Market value ($ mil.): 46,271

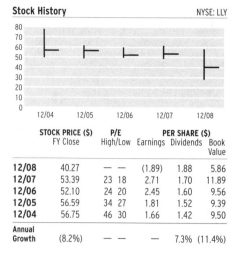

	STOCK PRICE ($) FY Close	P/E High/Low	PER SHARE ($) Earnings	Dividends	Book Value
12/08	40.27	— —	(1.89)	1.88	5.86
12/07	53.39	23 18	2.71	1.70	11.89
12/06	52.10	24 20	2.45	1.60	9.56
12/05	56.59	34 27	1.81	1.52	9.39
12/04	56.75	46 30	1.66	1.42	9.50
Annual Growth	(8.2%)	— —	—	7.3%	(11.4%)

EMC Corporation

EMC bytes data storage problems and swallows every bit. The company is a leading provider of RAID (redundant array of independent disks) storage systems. Banks, manufacturers, Internet service providers, retailers, and government agencies use EMC's systems to store and retrieve massive amounts of information. It also markets a line of network attached storage (NAS) file servers, and a wide array of software designed to manage, protect, and share data. EMC is the majority owner of virtualization specialist VMware, and its RSA division provides security software. It sells its products directly and through distributors and manufacturers. Its biggest resale partner, Dell, sells co-branded EMC systems.

EMC built its storage empire with refrigerator-sized systems used to store data for huge mainframe computers. While the company's high-end Symmetrix and mid-size CLARiiON storage arrays are still EMC's bread and butter, its hardware portfolio has expanded into complementary NAS devices (Celerra). The company's Centera content-addressed storage systems are designed to manage huge archives of fixed data.

CEO Joe Tucci has led an aggressive, multi-year effort to broaden EMC's product portfolio, largely through acquisitions. Much of the company's product expansion has focused on software, and its offerings now encompass a wide range of information lifecycle management applications for storing, managing, protecting, and sharing data. The company acquired content management software developer Document Sciences for about $86 million in 2008. It also grew its consumer-focused hardware portfolio that year, acquiring data storage device maker Iomega for about $213 million. In 2009, EMC acquired Configuresoft, a developer of software that manages server configuration, updates, and compliance issues. EMC, which previously sold Configuresoft's products, is building a software portfolio that can automate storage, server, and network configuration.

In 2009, after a two-month bidding war with rival NetApp, EMC won its bid to acquire Data Domain for $2.4 billion in cash, trumping NetApp's $1.9 billion cash and stock offer. Once the acquisition is complete, the company hopes to improve its disk-based back-up and archiving products by leveraging Data Domain's deduplication technologies.

EMC has kept its head above the competitive waters by leading the development of new storage technologies. It has been at the forefront of the movement away from direct-attached storage configurations, with products optimized for use in storage area networks (SANs). The company has pursued an open-system strategy that encourages greater interoperability with competitors' products.

HISTORY

Former Intel executive Dick Egan and his college roommate, Roger Marino, founded EMC in 1979. (Their initials gave the company its name.) Egan, a feisty entrepreneur whose first job was shining shoes, served as a Marine in Korea and later worked at MIT on the computer system for NASA's Apollo program. Egan also helped found Cambridge Memory Systems (later Cambex).

EMC was started with no business plan, only the idea that Egan and Marino would be better off working for themselves. At first, they sold office furniture, which in short order led to contacts at technology companies and recognition of the niche market for add-on memory boards for minicomputers.

EMC grew steadily throughout the early 1980s and went public in 1986. Two years later Michael Ruettgers, a former COO of high-tech publishing and research company Technical Financial Services, joined the company as EVP of operations. Ruettgers spent his first year and a half at EMC dealing with a crisis that almost ruined the company: Defective disk drives in some of its products were losing customers' files. Ruettgers stepped up quality control and guided EMC through the crisis period. In 1989 he became the company's president and COO.

In the late 1980s EMC expanded into data storage, developing a system that employed small hard disks rather than larger, more expensive disks and tapes used in IBM mainframes. EMC then separated itself from competitors by providing systems with a large cache — a temporary storage area used for quicker data retrieval.

In 1990 EMC pioneered redundant array of independent disks (RAID) storage and eliminated nearly a dozen major product lines, focusing on storage for large IBM computers in a bid to beat Big Blue by undercutting prices. The company introduced its original Symmetrix system, based on the new integrated cached disk array technology that held data from a variety of computer types. Marino left the company in 1990.

Ruettgers became CEO in 1992. The next year the company acquired Epoch Systems, a provider of data management software, and in 1994 it bought storage products company Array Technology and Magna Computer, a leader in tape storage technology for IBM computers. EMC also introduced its first storage product for open systems, the Centriplex series, and its sales passed the $1 billion mark.

EMC increased its presence in this fast-growing data switching and computer connection market with the 1995 acquisition of McDATA. The next year it launched a digital video storage and retrieval system for the TV and film industry and introduced software that let its systems work on networks instead of requiring file servers for data storage management.

EMC bought data storage software provider SOFTWORKS in early 2000. That year EMC took McDATA public; the following year it distributed its majority stake in that company to EMC shareholders. In early 2001 Joe Tucci, who had joined EMC in 2000 as president, added CEO to his title. Ruettgers became chairman and Egan was named chairman emeritus. (Tucci suceeded Ruettgers as chairman at the end of 2005.)

EMC began a major push to expand its software offerings in 2003. The company acquired LEGATO Software for $1.3 billion, and Documentum for approximately $1.5 billion. The following year it purchased server software maker VMware for approximately $625 million. EMC acquired System Management ARTS (SMARTS) for approximately $260 million early in 2005. In 2006 EMC acquired RSA Security for about $2.1 billion.

It bought network configuration and change management specialist Voyence, as well as Berkeley Data Systems, the provider of an online backup and recovery service called Mozy, in 2007.

Co-founder Dick Egan died in 2009, after serving as the US ambassador to Ireland for a brief tenure under President George W. Bush.

EXECUTIVES

Chairman, President, and CEO: Joseph M. (Joe) Tucci, age 61, $12,971,608 total compensation
Vice Chairman: William J. (Bill) Teuber Jr., age 57, $6,086,762 total compensation
EVP and CFO: David I. Goulden, age 49, $5,218,870 total compensation
SVP and CTO: Jeffrey M. (Jeff) Nick
CIO: Sanjay Mirchandani, age 44
SVP and Chief Accounting Officer: Mark A. Link
EVP and General Counsel: Paul T. Dacier, age 51
EVP; President, RSA Security:
Arthur W. (Art) Coviello Jr., age 55
EVP; President, EMC Global Services and Resource Management Software Group: Howard D. Elias, age 51, $6,119,720 total compensation
EVP; President, EMC Content Management and Archiving: Mark S. Lewis, age 46
EVP, Global Marketing and Customer Quality:
Frank M. Hauck, age 49
EVP Office of the Chairman: Harry L. You, age 49
EVP Americas and Global Sales Programs: Bill Scannell
EVP Human Resources: John T. (Jack) Mollen, age 58
EVP Corporate Strategy and Development:
Louise O'Brien
SVP and Treasurer: Irina Simmons
SVP; Co-General Manager, Content Management and Archiving Business: Balaji Yelamanchili
SVP Europe, Middle East, and Africa: Rainer Erlat
SVP and Head of Mergers and Acquisitions:
Thomas (Tom) Heiser
Auditors: PricewaterhouseCoopers LLP

LOCATIONS

HQ: EMC Corporation
176 South St., Hopkinton, MA 01748
Phone: 508-435-1000   **Fax:** 508-555-1212
Web: www.emc.com

2008 Sales

	$ mil.	% of total
US	7,991	54
Europe, Middle East & Africa	4,555	31
Asia/Pacific	1,640	11
Latin America, Mexico & Canada	690	4
Total	**14,876**	**100**

PRODUCTS/OPERATIONS

2008 Sales

	$ mil.	% of total
Systems	6,302	42
Software		
License	3,769	25
Maintenance	2,174	15
Other services	2,631	18
Total	**14,876**	**100**

2008 Sales

	$ mil.	% of total
Information storage	11,632	78
VMware Virtual Infrastructure	1,877	13
Content management & archiving	786	5
RSA Information Security	581	4
Total	**14,876**	**100**

Selected Products and Services

Information Storage Products
  Storage systems
    Content-addressed storage (Centera)
    Data storage arrays (CLARiiON, Symmetrix)
    Fibre Channel switches and directors (Connectrix)
    Network file and media servers (Celerra)
  EMC platform-based software (networked storage system management)
  Services
    Customer education
    Customer service
    Technology solutions
  Multi-platform Software
    Backup and archive
    Content management
    Resource management
  VMware

COMPETITORS

Acronis
CA, Inc.
Dell
Fujitsu
Hewlett-Packard
Hitachi Data Systems
IBM
LSI Corp.
McAfee
Microsoft
NetApp
Oracle
Sun Microsystems
Symantec

HISTORICAL FINANCIALS

Company Type: Public

Income Statement

FYE: December 31

	REVENUE ($ mil.)	NET INCOME ($ mil.)	NET PROFIT MARGIN	EMPLOYEES
12/08	14,876.2	1,345.6	9.0%	42,100
12/07	13,230.2	1,665.7	12.6%	37,700
12/06	11,155.1	1,227.4	11.0%	31,100
12/05	9,664.0	1,133.2	11.7%	26,500
12/04	8,229.5	871.2	10.6%	22,700
Annual Growth	**16.0%**	**11.5%**	**—**	**16.7%**

2008 Year-End Financials

Debt ratio: 26.5%
Return on equity: 10.5%
Cash ($ mil.): 5,844
Current ratio: 2.04
Long-term debt ($ mil.): 3,450

No. of shares (mil.): 2,022
Dividends
  Yield: 0.0%
  Payout: —
Market value ($ mil.): 21,171

Stock History

NYSE: EMC

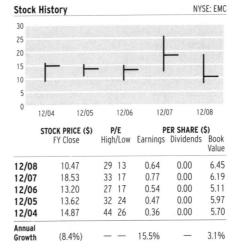

	STOCK PRICE ($) FY Close	P/E High/Low	PER SHARE ($) Earnings	Dividends	Book Value
12/08	10.47	29 13	0.64	0.00	6.45
12/07	18.53	33 17	0.77	0.00	6.19
12/06	13.20	27 17	0.54	0.00	5.11
12/05	13.62	32 24	0.47	0.00	5.97
12/04	14.87	44 26	0.36	0.00	5.70
Annual Growth	**(8.4%)**	**— —**	**15.5%**	**—**	**3.1%**

EMCOR Group

The core of EMCOR Group is electrical and mechanical construction. One of the world's largest specialty construction firms, EMCOR designs, installs, operates, and maintains complex mechanical and electrical systems. These include systems for power generation and distribution, lighting, voice and data communications, plumbing, and heating, ventilation, and air-conditioning (HVAC). It also provides facilities services, including management and maintenance support. Through about 75 subsidiaries and joint ventures, the company serves various commercial, industrial, institutional, and utility customers. EMCOR operates primarily in the US (more than 80% of sales), Canada, and the UK.

EMCOR's mechanical and electrical construction services account for the lion's share of its business. US mechanical and electrical construction services typically account for around 60% of sales; UK and Canadian mechanical and electrical services, more than 10%. Of this business, more than half of revenues are related to new construction. The remainder is derived from renovation or retrofit projects.

Some of EMCOR's largest institutional, industrial, and commercial projects include water treatment plants, hospitals, correctional facilities, research labs, manufacturing plants, oil refineries, data centers, hotels, shopping malls and office buildings. Many of those projects exceed $10 million and can span several years. Clients include Microsoft, the US Department of Veteran Affairs, and Hard Rock Hotel & Casino in Las Vegas.

The company continues to grow and has a strategy to weather the current economic downturn by diversifying its services and expanding geographically. It added to its industrial services operations by acquiring South Carolina-based facilities maintenance provider MOR PPM in 2008. It also has expanded is US fire protection systems business through several acquisitions. In 2009 the company bought LT Mechanical of Charlotte, North Carolina, a leading plumbing and mechanical contractor.

EMCOR is one of the largest union employers, with nearly 70% of its 28,000 employees belonging to various unions.

HISTORY

EMCOR's forerunner, Jamaica Water Supply Co., was incorporated in 1887 to supply water to some residents of Queens and Nassau Counties in New York. In 1902 it bought Jamaica Township Water Co., and by 1906 it was generating revenue — reaching $1.6 million by 1932. Over the next 35 years, the company kept pace with the population of its service area.

In 1966 the enterprise was acquired by Jamaica Water and Utilities, which then bought Sea Cliff Water Co. In 1969 and 1970 it acquired Welsbach (electrical contractors) and A to Z Equipment (construction trailer suppliers); it briefly changed its name in 1974 to Welsbach Corp. before becoming Jamaica Water Properties in 1976.

Diversification proved unprofitable, however, and in 1977, Martin Dwyer and his son Andrew took over the management of the struggling firm. Despite posting million-dollar losses in 1979, it was profitable by 1980.

The Dwyers acquired companies in the electrical and mechanical contracting, security, telecommunications, computer, energy and environmental businesses. In 1985 Andrew Dwyer became president, and the firm changed its name the next year to JWP.

Between 1986 and 1990 JWP acquired more than a dozen companies, including Extel (1986), Gibson Electric (1987), Dynalectric (1988), Drake & Scull (1989), NEECO and Compumat (1990), and Comstock Canada (1990).

In 1991 JWP capped its strategy of buying up US computer systems resellers by acquiring Businessland. It then bought French microelectronics distributor SIVEA. Later that year JWP bought a 34% stake in Resource Recycling Technologies (a solid-waste recycler).

JWP's shopping spree extended the firm's reach, but the company began to struggle when several sectors turned sour. A price war in the information services business and a weak construction market led to a loss of more than $600 million in 1992. That year president David Sokol resigned after questioning JWP's accounting practices. He turned over to the SEC a report that claimed inflated profits.

Cutting itself to about half its former size, the company sold JWP Information Services in 1993. (JWP Information Services later became ENTEX Information Services, which was acquired by Siemens in 2000.) However, JWP continued to struggle, and in early 1994 it filed for bankruptcy. Emerging from Chapter 11 protection in December 1994, the reorganized company took the name EMCOR. That year Frank MacInnis, former CEO of electrical contractor Comstock Group, stepped in to lead EMCOR.

In 1995 the SEC, using Sokol's information, charged several former JWP executives with accounting fraud, claiming they had overstated profits to boost the value of their company stock and their bonuses. EMCOR later reached a nonmonetary settlement with the SEC. The company sold Jamaica Water Supply and Sea Cliff in 1996; it also achieved profitability that year.

Focusing on external growth, EMCOR acquired a number of firms in 1998 and 1999, including Marelich Mechanical Co. and Mesa Energy Systems, BALCO, Inc., and the Poole & Kent group of mechanical contracting companies based in Baltimore and Miami. To meet increased demands for facilities services, in 2000 EMCOR consolidated the operations of three of its mechanical contractors (BALCO, J.C. Higgins, and Tucker

Mechanical) into one company, EMCOR Services, which operates in New England.

That year, about six years after emerging from bankruptcy, EMCOR began trading on the New York Stock Exchange. In 2002 EMCOR bought 19 subsidiaries from its financially troubled rival, Comfort Systems USA, including its largest unit, Shambaugh & Son. Later that year it expanded its facilities services operations with the acquisition of Consolidated Engineering Services (CES), an Archstone-Smith subsidiary that operated in 20 states.

EMCOR broadened its facilities services operations by acquiring the US facility management services unit of Siemens Building Technologies in 2003; in 2005 it added Fluidics, Inc., a mechanical services company based in Philadelphia.

EXECUTIVES

Chairman and CEO: Frank T. MacInnis, age 62, $6,365,864 total compensation
President and COO: Anthony J. (Tony) Guzzi, age 44, $3,616,020 total compensation
EVP and CFO: Mark A. Pompa, age 44, $2,166,504 total compensation
VP and CIO: Joseph A. (Joe) Puglisi
EVP Shared Services: R. Kevin Matz, age 50, $2,049,905 total compensation
EVP, Secretary, and General Counsel: Sheldon I. (Shelly) Cammaker, age 69, $2,463,222 total compensation
VP Risk Management: Rex C. Thrasher
VP Marketing and Communications: Mava K. Heffler
VP Integrated Services: Anthony R. Triano
VP and Controller: William E. Feher
VP Safety and Quality Management: David Copley
President, Site Based Services: Kevin Craig
President, Government Services: Michael W. (Mike) Shelton
President and CEO, EMCOR Construction Services: Michael (Mike) Parry, age 60
President, EMCOR Energy Services: Arthur L. Strenkert
CEO, Comstock Canada: Geoff Birkbeck
President, Mechanical Services: Michael Bordes
Treasurer: Joseph A. Serino
Auditors: Ernst & Young LLP

LOCATIONS

HQ: EMCOR Group, Inc.
301 Merritt Seven Corporate Park, 6th Fl.
Norwalk, CT 06851
Phone: 203-849-7800   **Fax:** 203-849-7900
Web: www.emcorgroup.com

PRODUCTS/OPERATIONS

2008 Sales

	$ mil.	% of total
US mechanical construction & facilities services	2,475.0	37
US electrical construction & facilities services	1,700.5	25
US facilities services	1,519.2	22
UK construction & facilities services	666.0	10
Canada construction & facilities services	424.5	6
Total	**6,785.2**	**100**

Selected Operations

Mechanical and Electrical Construction
  Building plant and lighting systems
  Data communications systems
  Electrical power distribution systems
  Energy recovery
  Heating, ventilation, and air-conditioning (HVAC) systems
  Lighting systems
  Low-voltage systems (alarm, security, communications)
  Piping and plumbing systems
  Refrigeration systems
  Voice communications systems

Facilities Services
  Facilities management
  Installation and support for building systems
  Mobile maintenance and service
  Program development and management for energy systems
  Remote monitoring
  Site-based operations and maintenance
  Small modification and retrofit projects
  Technical consulting and diagnostic services

COMPETITORS

ABM Industries
APi Group
Carrier
CB Richard Ellis
Comfort Systems USA
Dycom
Fluor
Hoffman Corporation
Honeywell International
InfrastruX
Integrated Electrical Services
Jacobs Technology
Johnson Controls
Jones Lang LaSalle
Limbach Facility Services
Linc Facility Services
MasTec
MYR Group
Quanta Services
Schneider Electric
Siemens AG
UGL Unicco

HISTORICAL FINANCIALS

Company Type: Public

Income Statement

FYE: December 31

	REVENUE ($ mil.)	NET INCOME ($ mil.)	NET PROFIT MARGIN	EMPLOYEES
12/08	6,785.2	182.2	2.7%	28,000
12/07	5,927.2	126.8	2.1%	29,000
12/06	5,021.0	86.6	1.7%	27,000
12/05	4,714.5	60.0	1.3%	26,000
12/04	4,747.9	33.2	0.7%	26,000
Annual Growth	**9.3%**	**53.1%**	**—**	**1.9%**

2008 Year-End Financials

Debt ratio: 18.8%
Return on equity: 18.9%
Cash ($ mil.): 406
Current ratio: 1.33
Long-term debt ($ mil.): 196
No. of shares (mil.): 66
Dividends
  Yield: 0.0%
  Payout: —
Market value ($ mil.): 1,478

Stock History

NYSE: EME

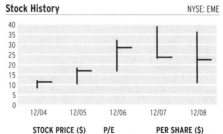

	STOCK PRICE ($) FY Close	P/E High/Low		PER SHARE ($) Earnings	Dividends	Book Value
12/08	22.43	13	4	2.71	0.00	15.84
12/07	23.63	20	12	1.90	0.00	13.43
12/06	28.42	24	13	1.33	0.00	10.78
12/05	16.88	19	11	0.94	0.00	9.34
12/04	11.30	22	16	0.53	0.00	8.54
Annual Growth	**18.7%**	**—**	**—**	**50.4%**	**—**	**16.7%**

Emerson Electric

Ralph Waldo Emerson wrote, "Work and acquire, and thou hast chained the wheel of Chance." Emerson Electric would agree. The company, generally known as just Emerson, makes a host of electrical, electromechanical, and electronic products, many of which are used to control gases, liquids, and electricity. Emerson pursues an active, aggressive acquisition strategy (with select divestitures along the way) in building up its global business with dozens of subsidiaries. The company gathers its 60-plus business units and divisions under eight Emerson Brands. The US accounts for about half of sales. As old Ralph Waldo once said, "Make yourself necessary to somebody," and Emerson Electric follows that adage.

The company may cut its workforce by about 10% during 2009, responding to lower sales and profits due to the worldwide recession. From a high of around 141,000 employees in fiscal 2008, Emerson's headcount fell to approximately 134,000 in early 2009, and the company may finish fiscal 2009 with some 120,000 people.

Emerson serves a wide variety of industries, including commercial refrigeration, computers, food and beverages, health care, heating and air conditioning, home appliances, industrial manufacturing, mining, oil and gas, paper and pulp, petrochemical, pharmaceuticals, municipal utilities, retail, and telecommunications.

In 2008 the company grew its Process Management division with its acquisition of TopWorx. Based in Kentucky, TopWorx makes industrial sensors and controls that monitor valves and other devices. The acquisition gives Emerson access to the discrete instrumentation market.

The company's most famous brand name may be InSinkErator, the popular line of household kitchen disposal units. InSinkErator also provides garbage disposal equipment for professional food service installations and hot-water dispensing systems.

HISTORY

Emerson Electric was founded in 1890 in St. Louis by brothers Alexander and Charles Meston, inventors who developed uses for the alternating-current electric motor, which was new at the time. The company was named after former Missouri judge and US marshal John Emerson, who financed the enterprise and became its first president. Emerson's best-known product was an electric fan introduced in 1892. Between 1910 and 1920 the company helped develop the first forced-air circulating systems.

The Depression and labor problems in the 1930s brought Emerson close to bankruptcy, but new products, including a hermetic motor for refrigerators, revived it. The company's electric motors were adapted for additional uses during WWII, including powering the gun turrets in B-24 bombers.

Emerson suffered in postwar years, having grown dependent on military business. Wallace Persons took over as president in 1954 and reorganized the company's commercial product line, seeking to bring in customers from outside the consumer appliance market.

In the early 1960s the company bought a number of smaller companies to produce thermostats and gas controls, power transmission products, and welding and cutting tools. Emerson's sales increased from $56 million in 1954 to $800 million in 1973. Persons retired in 1974, and Chuck Knight became CEO. Knight took the company into high-tech fields and expanded its hardware segment with six acquisitions between 1976 and 1986.

In 1989 Emerson expanded its electrical offerings by acquiring a 45% stake in Hong Kong-based Astec (power supplies). The company spun off its defense systems, electronics, and other businesses in 1990 as ESCO Electronics.

Emerson bought Fisher Controls International in 1992 and formed S-B Power Tool with Robert Bosch. It also acquired Buehler International (destructive testing equipment). From 1993 through 1995 Emerson expanded globally by targeting the Asia/Pacific market, setting up operations in China and Eastern Europe, and forming joint ventures in China and India.

Bosch bought out Emerson's interest in S-B Power Tool (now Robert Bosch Tool) in 1996. In 1998 Emerson bought CBS Corporation's Westinghouse Process Control division. Through Astec, Emerson pushed into the telecom market by purchasing the Advanced Power Systems (power conversion) business of Northern Telecom (now Nortel Networks).

Early in 2000 Emerson acquired the telecom products division of Jordan Industries for about $980 million and later bought European telecommunications power provider Ericsson Energy Systems from Ericsson for $725 million. Later that year the company dropped "Electric" from its everyday name to reflect its diverse product line.

Also in 2000 Emerson executive David Farr replaced long-time CEO Chuck Knight. In 2004 Farr also assumed the chairmanship as Knight retired and was named chairman emeritus.

Emerson acquired Metran Industrial, a provider of flow products and services in Russia and Eastern Europe, in 2004. Emerson also acquired the US-based outside plant and power systems businesses of Marconi (now telent) for $375 million, which it combined with its Emerson Network Power business.

Emerson acquired process measurement and control equipment maker Solartron Mobrey from the Roxboro Group in 2005. The following year Emerson purchased Knurr, a German manufacturer of racks and enclosures for data centers. Emerson acquired power conversion equipment maker Artesyn Technologies. Emerson sold the wireline test systems business of Emerson Network Power to Tollgrade Communications in 2006. It then acquired Bristol Babcock, a unit of British diversified manufacturer FKI; the purchase added measurement and control products for the energy and utilities markets to Emerson's Process Management segment.

In 2007 the company acquired Stratos International for $83.5 million, net of acquired cash. The purchase expanded the portfolios of the Emerson Network Power and Emerson Connectivity Solutions segments. Stratos made radio-frequency and microwave components, as well as optical subsystems, components, and interconnect products for a variety of applications.

In early 2008 Emerson acquired the Embedded Communications Computing (ECC) business of Motorola for $350 million in cash. The purchase extended Emerson's product portfolio in embedded computing, a niche key to telecommunications industry customers, among others.

EXECUTIVES

Chairman, President, and CEO: David N. Farr, age 54, $12,757,583 total compensation
COO: Edward L. Monser, age 58, $4,524,027 total compensation
SEVP, CFO, and Director: Walter J. Galvin, age 62, $6,917,888 total compensation
SVP and CTO: Randall D. Ledford, age 59
VP and CIO: Stephen C. (Steve) Hassell
VP and Chief Accounting Officer: Richard J. Schlueter, age 55
SEVP and Director: Charles A. Peters, age 54, $3,575,919 total compensation
EVP, Emerson Industrial Automation: Jean-Paul L. Montupet, age 61
EVP, Emerson Motor Technologies and Appliance Solutions: James J. (Jim) Lindemann, age 53
EVP: Patrick J. Sly
EVP, Emerson Network Power Systems Group: Edward K. (Ed) Feeney, age 64
EVP; President, Embedded Computing and Power Group: Jay L. Geldmacher, age 53
EVP, Emerson Climate Technologies: Edgar M. Purvis Jr.
EVP, Emerson Process Management: Steven A. (Steve) Sonnenberg, age 56
SVP Human Resources: Philip A. Hutchison
SVP, Development: James D. Switzer
SVP and Controller: B. N. Eckhardt
SVP, Secretary, and General Counsel: Frank L. Steeves, age 55, $2,465,338 total compensation
VP and Chief Marketing Officer: Katherine Button Bell
VP and Chief Employment Counsel: J. R. Carius
Auditors: KPMG LLP

LOCATIONS

HQ: Emerson Electric Co.
    8000 W. Florissant Ave., St. Louis, MO 63136
Phone: 314-553-2000   **Fax:** 314-553-3527
Web: www.gotoemerson.com

Emerson Electric has approximately 255 manufacturing locations around the world, of which about 165 are outside the US, primarily in Europe and also in Asia, Canada, and Latin America.

2008 Sales

	$ mil.	% of total
US	11,329	46
Europe	5,663	23
Asia	4,480	18
Latin America	1,262	5
Other regions	2,073	8
Total	**24,807**	**100**

PRODUCTS/OPERATIONS

2008 Sales

	$ mil.	% of total
Process management	6,652	26
Network power	6,312	25
Industrial automation	4,852	19
Appliance & tools	3,861	15
Climate technologies	3,822	15
Adjustments	(692)	—
Total	**24,807**	**100**

Selected Products and Services

Process Management
    Measurement and analytical
    Software, services, and systems
    Valves and regulators
Network Power
    AC power systems
    Connectivity
    DC power systems
    Inbound power
    OEM power
    Precision air
    Service

Appliance and Tools
    Appliance controls
    Hand/power tools and wet/dry vacuums
    Motors
    Plumbing products and disposers
Industrial Automation
    Alternators
    Fluid control
    Industrial equipment
    Mechanical power transmission
    Motors and drives
    Power distribution
Climate Technologies
    Compressors
    Flow controls
    Terminal assemblies
    Thermal controls
    Thermostats and valve controls
Storage Solutions
    Bins
    Cabinets
    Display and storage shelving
    Inventory storage racks
    Stock-picking and kitting carts

COMPETITORS

ABB
AMETEK
Black & Decker
Cooper Industries
Cummins
Dana Holding
Danaher
Dresser, Inc.
Eaton
Endress + Hauser
GE
Hitachi
Honeywell International
Illinois Tool Works
Ingersoll-Rand
Interpump
Invensys
Johnson Controls
Kinetek
Lennox
Mark IV
McDermott
NEC
Power-One
Raytheon
Rexnord
Rockwell Automation
Rolls-Royce
Siemens AG
Sino-American Electronic
Snap-on
SPX
Stanley Works
Tecumseh Products
Toshiba
Tripple Manufacturing
Tyco Electronics
United Technologies

HISTORICAL FINANCIALS

Company Type: Public

Income Statement

FYE: September 30

	REVENUE ($ mil.)	NET INCOME ($ mil.)	NET PROFIT MARGIN	EMPLOYEES
9/08	24,807.0	2,412.0	9.7%	140,700
9/07	22,572.0	2,136.0	9.5%	137,700
9/06	20,133.0	1,845.0	9.2%	127,800
9/05	17,305.0	1,422.0	8.2%	114,200
9/04	15,615.0	1,257.0	8.0%	107,800
Annual Growth	**12.3%**	**17.7%**	**—**	**6.9%**

Equifax Inc.

Equifax knows you. Yes, you. One of the US's largest credit reporting agencies (alongside Experian and TransUnion), the company has information on more than 400 million worldwide credit holders. In addition to credit reports, Equifax provides credit card marketing and fraud detection services and offers database marketing, credit risk consulting, and such products as credit scoring software through a host of subsidiaries. Through subsidiary TALX, the company provides human resources and payroll outsourcing. Equifax's customers include financial institutions, retailers, automotive dealers, and mortgage companies. Equifax has operations in North America, South America, and Europe.

With the maturity of its markets (particularly the US), the company has increasingly looked to expand its services and its reach through acquisitions, including TALX (acquired in 2007), direct-marketing firm Naviant (renamed Equifax eMarketing Solutions), and marketing-technology firm BeNOW.

Equifax has been targeting such emerging markets as Latin America, where the infrastructure for consumer credit reporting is nascent, but fast-growing economies have created a need for Equifax's services. It expanded its operations in Peru in 2007 with the acquisition of a rival credit reporting agency. It is also eyeing other markets, including Russia, India, Mexico, and China, where the same conditions apply.

In keeping with those plans, Equifax made a couple of deals in 2008. It acquired a 28% stake in Global Payments Credit Services LLC, a Russian credit information joint venture of Global Payments and Home Credit and Finance Bank of Russia. It also agreed to form a credit information company in India with Tata and CRISIL, an Indian subsidiary of Standard & Poor's.

Equifax's largest shareholder is FMR, which holds a 12% stake in the company.

HISTORY

Brothers Cator and Guy Woolford started Retail Credit Co. in Atlanta in 1899. They compiled credit records of local residents into their Merchants Guide, which they sold to retailers for $25 a year. The brothers extended their services to the insurance industry in 1901, investigating applicants' backgrounds. The company grew steadily and by 1920 had offices across the US and Canada. After several decades, Retail Credit branched into other information sectors, partly through acquisitions of regional credit reporters.

The company came under scrutiny in 1973 when the FTC filed an antimonopoly suit (dropped in 1982) against its consumer credit division and a complaint against its investigative practices (Retail Credit used field investigators to probe people's backgrounds). In 1976 the company became Equifax, short for "equitability in the gathering and presentation of facts."

In the 1980s and 1990s, Equifax continued to buy small businesses in the US and Europe. As the Information Age matured, businesses clamored for its services. By the end of the 1980s, Equifax had passed TRW (now part of Experian) as the largest provider of consumer information.

Receptive to consumer concerns in the late 1980s, the company ended list sales to US direct marketers and scrapped Marketplace, a 1991 joint venture with Lotus Development to compile a database of the shopping habits of 100 million Americans.

During the 1990s Equifax acquired regional credit and collection firms in Florida, Georgia, and Texas. It restructured in 1992, merging its US and Canadian operations, closing field offices, and expanding its international operations.

In 1992 and 1993 it settled cases with several states over intrusive and inaccurate credit and job reference reports. The California State Lottery ended its scratch ticket terminal contract with an Equifax unit, claiming the subsidiary ran substandard operations. The contract was reinstated in 1995 after Equifax threatened to sue, but the lottery business left a bad impression on Equifax. In 1996 it subcontracted most of its contract obligations to GTECH.

Also in 1996 Equifax exited the health care information business; the next year it spun off its insurance services business as Choicepoint. As part of this effort it reassigned CDB Infotek (acquired 1996) to ChoicePoint. After CDB was alleged to have improperly sold voter registration and Social Security number lists, shareholders wondered whether Equifax's management had been unaware of the supposed activities, or if it had bought CDB knowing that it could be assuming legal responsibility for them. Equifax spokespeople gave contradictory explanations. At least partially in response to these woes, Equifax helped launch a self-policing initiative for the industry.

Equifax turned to building its Latin American business, buying the remaining 50% of South American credit company DICOM in 1997. It also bought 80% of Brazil's largest credit information firm, Segurança ao Crédito e Informações (1998), Chilean card processing firm Procard (2000), and one of Uruguay's largest credit information providers, Clearing de Informes (2001).

In 1999 the company entered the UK credit card market with a card-processing contract with IKANO Financial Services. The next year it expanded its direct marketing prowess with its acquisition of R.L. Polk's consumer information database. Also in 2000 the company agreed to pay $500,000 to the FTC for blocking or not responding promptly enough to consumers' phone calls.

In 2001 the company spun off credit-card processing and check-management unit Centegy (since acquired by Fidelity National Information Services) to shareholders, sold its city directory business (acquired in the R.L. Polk acquisition) to infoUSA (now infoGROUP), and underwent a restructuring that included cutting some 700 jobs, primarily outside the US.

In 2005 Equifax acquired APPRO Systems, a provider of automated credit risk management and financial technologies, for approximately $92 million. That year, Richard F. Smith (former COO of GE Insurance Solutions) succeeded Thomas F. Chapman as CEO of the company. Smith also took on the role of chairman when Chapman retired from the firm.

In 2006 Equifax purchased Austin-Tetra, which offers business-to-business data management services.

EXECUTIVES

Chairman and CEO: Richard F. (Rick) Smith, age 49, $9,634,759 total compensation
VP and CFO: Lee Adrean, age 57, $1,862,534 total compensation
VP and Chief Human Resources Officer: Coretha M. Rushing, $1,552,782 total compensation
VP and Chief Legal Officer: Kent E. Mast, age 65, $1,542,860 total compensation
VP and Chief Marketing Officer: Paul J. Springman, age 63
Chief Security and Compliance Officer: Tony Spinelli
SVP, Investor Relations: Jeffrey L. (Jeff) Dodge, age 57
SVP Corporate Development: Joseph M. (Trey) Loughran
SVP Global Operations: Andy S. Bodea
VP, Communications: David Rubinger
SVP and Controller: Nuala M. King, age 54
President, TALX Corporation and Director: William W. (Bill) Canfield, age 70, $1,559,549 total compensation
President, North American Personal Solutions: Steven P. (Steve) Ely, age 52
President, Canadian Operations: Carol J. Gray
President, North America Commercial Solutions: Michael S. Shannon, age 52
President, U.S. Consumer Information Solutions: J. Dann Adams, age 50
President, International: Rodolfo O. Ploder, age 47
President, Enabling Technologies: Rajib Roy, age 42
Office of the Corporate Secretary, Shareholder Services: Kathryn J. Harris
Auditors: Ernst & Young LLP

LOCATIONS

HQ: Equifax Inc.
1550 Peachtree St. NW, Atlanta, GA 30309
Phone: 404-885-8000   **Fax:** 404-885-8988
Web: www.equifax.com

2008 Sales

	$ mil.	% of total
US	1,404.7	73
Canada	136.2	7
UK	141.0	7
Brazil	97.6	5
Other countries	156.2	8
Total	**1,935.7**	**100**

PRODUCTS/OPERATIONS

2008 Sales

	$ mil.	% of total
US consumer information solutions	890.8	46
International	505.7	26
TALX	305.1	16
North America personal solutions	162.6	8
North America commercial solutions	71.5	4
Total	**1,935.7**	**100**

COMPETITORS

Acxiom	Harte-Hanks
ADP	infoGROUP
Aon	Marmon Group
Ceridian	Moody's
Ceridian UK	Paychex
D&B	Right Management
Elavon	SHL Group
Experian	Total System Services
Fair Isaac	TransUnion LLC
First Data	Watson Wyatt

HISTORICAL FINANCIALS
Company Type: Public

Income Statement

	REVENUE ($ mil.)	NET INCOME ($ mil.)	NET PROFIT MARGIN	EMPLOYEES
12/08	1,935.7	272.8	14.1%	6,500
12/07	1,843.0	272.7	14.8%	7,000
12/06	1,546.3	274.5	17.8%	4,960
12/05	1,443.4	246.5	17.1%	4,600
12/04	1,272.8	234.7	18.4%	4,400
Annual Growth	11.1%	3.8%	—	10.2%

FYE: December 31

2008 Year-End Financials

Debt ratio: 90.5%
Return on equity: 20.1%
Cash ($ mil.): 58
Current ratio: 1.11
Long-term debt ($ mil.): 1,187

No. of shares (mil.): 126
Dividends
Yield: 0.6%
Payout: 7.7%
Market value ($ mil.): 3,351

Stock History

NYSE: EFX

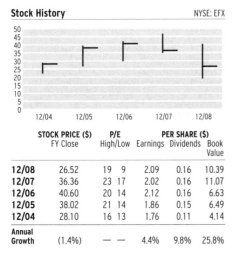

	STOCK PRICE ($) FY Close	P/E High/Low		PER SHARE ($) Earnings	Dividends	Book Value
12/08	26.52	19	9	2.09	0.16	10.39
12/07	36.36	23	17	2.02	0.16	11.07
12/06	40.60	20	14	2.12	0.16	6.63
12/05	38.02	21	14	1.86	0.15	6.49
12/04	28.10	16	13	1.76	0.11	4.14
Annual Growth	(1.4%)	—	—	4.4%	9.8%	25.8%

Equity Residential

The "Grave Dancer" is also the lord of the rents. Sam Zell (whose moniker springs from his buying and turning around moribund properties) is at the head of the conga line at Equity Residential, the nation's #1 apartment owner by sales. Rival AIMCO owns more units, but its affordable-housing focus keeps its revenue more modest. Equity Residential wholly or partially owns some 550 communities with 150,000 units, comprising garden units, mid- and high rises, and military housing. A real estate investment trust (REIT), Equity Residential also provides property leasing, development, managment, and other support operations. The company focuses on fast-growth regions such as Southern California and New York.

In 2006 Equity Residential sold its Lexford Housing Division, reducing its apartment holdings by one third, to companies connected to Empire Group Holdings for $1.09 billion. Through the sale, which reduced its apartment holdings by one third, Equity Residential jettisoned around 300 apartment buildings in slower markets. It acquired around 40 such apartment buildings in both those markets over the next year.

With the housing market showing turmoil in 2007 and 2008, the REIT saw much less turnover

of its apartments, as renters stayed put rather than buy a home. The economic slowdown has also caused the company to lower rates on certain renewals and new rentals, as well as bringing its acquisition activities to a near halt.

Morgan Stanley, The Vanguard Group, and Barclays Global Investors collectively own 20% of Equity Residential.

HISTORY

Sam Zell founded Equity Residential Properties in Chicago in 1969.

When property prices plunged in the early 1990s, Zell earned his "Grave Dancer" nickname: He formed "vulture funds" with Merrill Lynch to buy distressed real estate cheaply. In 1993 Zell created a national apartment company with about 22,000 apartment units, called it Equity Residential Properties Trust, and took it public. Public offerings provided a steady flow of new capital (Equity Residential has had about 15 follow-up offerings since its IPO).

Equity Residential carried on Zell's traditional practice of buying undervalued assets and making them profitable. The REIT began expanding its regional management offices almost immediately. Initially it sought apartment properties or small portfolios, but its appetite grew for ever larger bites, including the acquisitions of entire real estate companies. In 1997 it spent $1 billion each for Wellsford Residential Property Trust and Evans Withycombe Residential, and overall added more than 70,000 units to its portfolio for the year.

The next year Equity Residential went even higher, buying Merry Land & Investment and its nearly 120 properties in the Southeast for $2.2 billion. Expansion continued in 1999, as Equity Residential bought Lexford Residential Trust, bringing Zell's empire to more than 1,000 apartment complexes.

In 2000 the company branched out with the purchase of Globe Business Resources (residential and office furniture) but also kept buying more apartments — this time Grove Property Trust (New England apartments). After taking a loss in the furniture business in 2001, it dumped that venture in 2002, but hung on to Globe's short-term furnished housing business, renaming it Equity Corporate Housing.

In late 2005 Equity Residential bought land in the Lefrak waterfront development in Newport, New Jersey, across from Manhattan. The area is hot, demand for housing is high, and Equity and partner Hovnanian plan to build a 900-unit apartment complex there.

EXECUTIVES

Chairman: Samuel (Sam) Zell, age 67
Vice Chairman: Gerald A. (Gerry) Spector, age 63
President, CEO, and Trustee: David J. Neithercut, age 53, $3,651,075 total compensation
EVP Operations: David Santee, age 50
EVP and CFO: Mark J. Parrell, age 42, $894,918 total compensation
SVP and CTO: Jay Kurtzman
EVP and Chief Investment Officer: Alan W. George, age 51, $1,894,853 total compensation
EVP; President, Property Management: Frederick C. Tuomi, age 54, $1,864,721 total compensation
EVP and General Counsel: Bruce C. Strohm, age 54, $1,304,570 total compensation
EVP Development: Mark N. Tennison, age 48
EVP Human Resources: John Powers, age 61
SVP Development, East Coast: Richard Boales
SVP Development, West Coast: Shyam Taggarsi

SVP Financial Planning and Analysis: John G. Lennox, age 54
SVP, Associate General Counsel, and Secretary: Yasmina Duwe
SVP Acquisitions: Anthony (Tony) Duplisse
Assistant VP, Investor Relations: Marty McKenna
President, Equity Corporate Housing: William (Bill) Hoffman
Auditors: Ernst & Young LLP

LOCATIONS

HQ: Equity Residential
2 N. Riverside Plaza, Chicago, IL 60606
Phone: 312-474-1300   **Fax:** 312-454-8703
Web: www.equityapartments.com

2008 Sales

	% of total
Northeast	29
Southwest	25
Southeast	21
Northwest	19
Other	6
Total	**100**

2008 Properties by Market

	No.
Seattle/Tacoma, WA	49
Phoenix	42
South Florida	39
Los Angeles	38
Boston	37
San Francisco Bay	34
New England (excluding Boston)	32
Atlanta	29
Washington, DC/Northern Virginia	26
Orlando, FL	26
Denver	25
New York City	22
Suburban Maryland	21
Inland Empire, CA	15
Dallas/Ft. Worth, TX	14
San Diego	14
Jacksonville	12
Raleigh/Durham, NC	12
Portland, OR	11
Tampa	11
Orange County, CA	10
Central Valley, CA	8
Other	21
Total	**548**

PRODUCTS/OPERATIONS

2008 Sales

	$ mil.	% of total
Rental income	2,092.5	99
Fees & asset management	10.7	1
Total	**2,103.2**	**100**

2008 Properties

	No. of properties	No. of units
Garden	471	124,850
Mid/high-rise	75	17,685
Military housing	2	4,709
Total	**548**	**147,244**

COMPETITORS

AMLI Residential	Home Properties
Apartment Investment and Management	Irvine Apartment Communities
Archstone	Lend Lease
Associated Estates Realty	Lincoln Property
AvalonBay	Mid-America Apartment Communities
BRE Properties	
Camden Property	Milestone Management
Essex Property Trust	Post Properties
Gables Residential Trust	UDR

E. W. Scripps had previously shuttered *The Albuquerque Tribune* (New Mexico) and the *Cincinnati Post*.

The company spun off its cable TV business as Scripps Networks Interactive in 2008. The new, publicly traded company oversees such channels as Home & Garden Television (HGTV) and the Food Network (70%-owned). By spinning off the new unit, E. W. Scripps hoped to allow shareholders to benefit from the profitable TV operations without the drag imposed by the company's publishing units. Scripps Networks had accounted for more than half the company's revenue.

HISTORY

Edward Willis "E. W." Scripps launched a newspaper empire in 1878 with his creation of *The Penny Press* in Cleveland. While adding to his string of inexpensive newspapers, Scripps demonstrated his fondness for economy by shunning "extras" such as toilet paper and pencils for his employees.

In 1907 Scripps gave the Associated Press a new rival, combining three wire services to form United Press. E. W. Scripps' health began deteriorating in the 1920s, and Roy Howard was named chairman. Howard's contribution to the burgeoning media enterprise soon was acknowledged when the company's name was changed to the Scripps Howard League. E. W. Scripps died in 1926, leaving a newspaper chain second in size only to Hearst.

In the 1930s Scripps made a foray into radio, buying WCPO (Cincinnati) and KNOX (Knoxville, Tennessee). Roy Howard placed his son Jack in charge of Scripps' radio holdings; under Jack's leadership, Scripps branched into TV. Its first TV station, Cleveland's WEWS, began broadcasting in 1947. Scripps also made Charlie Brown a household name when it launched the *Peanuts* comic strip in 1950. By the time Charles Scripps (E. W. Scripps' grandson) became chairman and Jack Howard was appointed president in 1953, the company had amassed 19 newspapers and a handful of radio and TV stations.

United Press merged with Hearst's International News Service in 1958 to become United Press International (UPI). In 1963 Scripps took its broadcasting holdings public as Scripps Howard Broadcasting Company (Scripps retained controlling interest). Scripps Howard Broadcasting expanded its TV station portfolio in the 1970s and 1980s, buying KJRH (Tulsa, Oklahoma; 1971), KSHB (Kansas City; 1977), KNXV (Phoenix; 1985), WFTS (Tampa; 1986), and WXYZ (Detroit; 1986).

With UPI facing mounting losses, Scripps sold the news service in 1982. Under leadership of chief executive Lawrence Leser, Scripps began streamlining, jettisoning extraneous investments and refocusing on its core business lines. In 1988 after decades of family ownership, the company went public as The E. W. Scripps Company (the Scripps family retained a controlling interest).

In 1994 Scripps Howard Broadcasting merged back into E. W. Scripps Company. That year Scripps branched into cable TV when its Home & Garden Television network went on the air. Former newspaper editor William Burleigh became CEO in 1996. Scripps' 1997 purchase of the newspaper and broadcast operations of Harte-Hanks marked the largest acquisition in its history. Scripps promptly traded Harte-Hanks' broadcasting operations for a controlling interest in the Food Network.

Scripps sold television production unit Scripps Howard Productions in 1998. The company sold its Dallas Community Newspaper Group in 1999 and launched the Do It Yourself cable network and affiliated Web site later that year. In 2000 Scripps' financially struggling *Rocky Mountain News* entered into a joint operating agreement with rival *The Denver Post* (owned by MediaNews). The Justice Department approved the agreement in 2001. Scripps launched cable channel Fine Living, aimed at affluent households, in 2002. That year the company shuttered its Scripps Ventures fund, which invested in Internet and online commerce businesses.

In late 2002 the company bought a 70% stake in home shopping network company Summit America Television (owner of the Shop At Home cable network) for $49 million. It bought the remaining 30% of the company in 2004.

Scripps made a foray into online shopping when it acquired comparison shopping site Shopzilla in 2005. The following year Scripps bought UK-based shopping site uSwitch.

The Shop At Home network came to an end in 2006 when Scripps shut down the network after several years of nothing but losses at the channel. Scripps later sold its five Shop At Home affiliate television stations to Multicultural Television Broadcasting for $170 million.

Former chairman Charles Scripps died in 2007. At the end of that year, the company shuttered the *Cincinnati Post*, and the following year it ceased publication of *The Albuquerque Tribune*. E. W. Scripps spun off its cable TV operations as Scripps Networks Interactive later in 2008. It shuttered the *Rocky Mountain News* early in 2009 after attempts to sell the money-losing paper failed.

EXECUTIVES

Chairwoman: Nackey E. Scagliotti, age 63
President, CEO, and Director:
Richard A. (Rich) Boehne, age 52,
$4,283,520 total compensation
SVP, CFO and Corporate Treasurer:
Timothy E. (Tim) Stautberg, age 46,
$1,042,979 total compensation
VP and CIO: Robert A. Carson, age 53
VP, Chief Ethics and Compliance Officer, and Corporate Secretary: Mary Denise Kuprionis, age 53
SVP Newspapers: Mark G. Contreras, age 47,
$1,327,848 total compensation
SVP and General Counsel: William (Bill) Appleton, age 60
SVP Business Development: Sameer Deen
SVP Television: Brian Lawlor, age 41
SVP Human Resources: Lisa Knutson, age 43,
$535,574 total compensation
VP Corporate Communications and Investor Relations: Timothy (Tim) King, age 44
VP and Controller: Douglas F. Lyons, age 51
VP Tax: John E. Viterisi, age 50
VP Audit and Compliance: Michael T. Hales, age 44
President, Scripps Howard Supply; President and CEO, Media Procurement Services: Sharon Hite
President, Home & Garden Television: Jim Samples
President, Shopzilla: William G. (Bill) Glass, age 39
Auditors: Deloitte & Touche LLP

LOCATIONS

HQ: The E. W. Scripps Company
312 Walnut St., Cincinnati, OH 45202
Phone: 513-977-3000   **Fax:** 513-977-3721
Web: www.scripps.com

PRODUCTS/OPERATIONS

2008 Sales

	$ mil.	% of total
Newspapers	568.8	57
Television	326.9	33
Licensing & other	106.1	10
Total	**1,001.8**	**100**

Selected Operations

Newspapers
Abilene Reporter-News (Texas)
Anderson Independent-Mail (South Carolina)
Corpus Christi Caller-Times (Texas)
Evansville Courier & Press (Indiana)
Henderson Gleaner (Kentucky)
Kitsap Sun (Washington)
Knoxville News Sentinel (Tennessee)
Memphis Commercial Appeal (Tennessee)
Naples Daily News (Florida)
Redding Record-Searchlight (California)
San Angelo Standard-Times (Texas)
Stuart News (Florida)
Ventura County Star (California)
Wichita Falls Times Record News (Texas)
Television stations
KJRH (NBC; Tulsa, OK)
KMCI (Ind; Lawrence, KS)
KNXV (ABC, Phoenix)
KSHB (NBC, Kansas City)
WCPO (ABC, Cincinnati)
WEWS (ABC, Cleveland)
WFTS (ABC, Tampa)
WMAR (ABC, Baltimore)
WPTV (NBC; West Palm Beach, FL)
WXYZ (ABC, Detroit)

COMPETITORS

A. H. Belo
CBS
Fox Entertainment
Freedom Communications
Gannett
Hearst Newspapers
Hearst Television
Local TV
McClatchy Company
Media General
Meredith Corporation
New York Times
Raycom Media
Sinclair Broadcast Group
Times Publishing Co.
Tribune Company
Washington Post

HISTORICAL FINANCIALS

Company Type: Public

Income Statement

FYE: December 31

	REVENUE ($ mil.)	NET INCOME ($ mil.)	NET PROFIT MARGIN	EMPLOYEES
12/08	1,001.8	(476.6)	—	6,000
12/07	2,517.1	(1.6)	—	8,500
12/06	2,498.1	353.2	14.1%	9,000
12/05	2,513.9	249.2	9.9%	9,600
12/04	2,167.5	303.8	14.0%	8,900
Annual Growth	(17.5%)	—	—	(9.4%)

2008 Year-End Financials

Debt ratio: 10.3%	No. of shares (mil.): 54
Return on equity: —	Dividends
Cash ($ mil.): 5	Yield: 44.8%
Current ratio: 1.52	Payout: —
Long-term debt ($ mil.): 61	Market value ($ mil.): 120

Stock History

NYSE: SSP

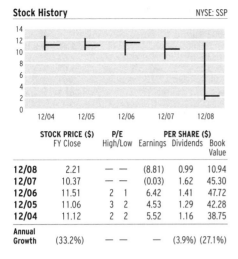

	STOCK PRICE ($) FY Close	P/E High/Low		PER SHARE ($) Earnings	Dividends	Book Value
12/08	2.21	—	—	(8.81)	0.99	10.94
12/07	10.37	—	—	(0.03)	1.62	45.30
12/06	11.51	2	1	6.42	1.41	47.72
12/05	11.06	3	2	4.53	1.29	42.28
12/04	11.12	2	2	5.52	1.16	38.75
Annual Growth	(33.2%)	—	—	—	(3.9%)	(27.1%)

Exelon Corporation

The City of Brotherly Love meets the Windy City in utility holding company Exelon. The company distributes electricity to 5.4 million customers in northern Illinois (including Chicago) and southeastern Pennsylvania (including Philadelphia) through subsidiaries Commonwealth Edison (ComEd) and PECO Energy. PECO also distributes natural gas to 485,000 customers. Subsidiary Exelon Generation holds the company's power plants, whose production capacity is more than 24,800 MW. Exelon Power Team is a top wholesale energy marketer, and Exelon Energy markets retail power and offers other energy-related services.

In 2008, in a move to expand its geographic reach, Exelon made a $6.2 billion bid to buy NRG Energy. Though the offer to buy NRG met with resistance, Exelon has kept up its pursuit of the company. Toward the end of 2008 it announced an exchange offer for NRG's shares. By the expiration date of the offer early the next year, it had acquired just more than 50% of those shares. In addition to announcing another extension of the offer, Exelon said it hoped NRG's Board would allow it to do due diligence and begin negotiations for an acquisition. But an NRG proxy vote rejection in 2009 led Exelon to terminate its offer.

Exelon was formed in 2000 when Philadelphia-based PECO Energy bought Chicago-based Unicom. Both PECO and Unicom were leading nuclear plant operators, and more than two-thirds of Exelon's generating capacity comes from nuclear plants. In 2007 Exelon selected Victoria County as its site in southeast Texas for a federal license application that would allow construction and operation of a new nuclear plant should the company decide to build one.

HISTORY

Thomas Dolan and local investors formed the Brush Electric Light Company of Philadelphia in 1881 to provide street and commercial lighting. Competitors sprang up, and in 1885 Brush merged with the United States Electric Lighting

Company of Pennsylvania to form a secret "electric trust," or holding company. Dolan became president in 1886 and bought four other utilities.

In 1895 Martin Maloney formed Pennsylvania Heat Light and Power to consolidate the city's electric companies. By the next year it had acquired, among other businesses, Columbia Electric Light, Philadelphia Edison, and the electric trust. In 1899 a new firm, National Electric, challenged Maloney by acquiring neighboring rival Southern Electric Light. Before retiring, Maloney negotiated the merger of the two firms, forming Philadelphia Electric in 1902.

Demand rose rapidly into the 1920s, fueled in part by the company's promotion of electric appliances. In 1928, the year after it completed the Conowingo Hydroelectric Station, Philadelphia Electric was absorbed by the much larger United Gas Improvement. United Gas avoided large layoffs during the Depression, but passage of the Public Utility Holding Company Act (PUHCA) in 1935 sounded its death knell. (PUHCA was repealed in 2005.) In 1943 the SEC forced United Gas to divest Philadelphia Electric.

Philadelphia Electric built several plants in the 1950s and 1960s in response to a postwar electricity boom. A small experimental nuclear reactor was completed at Peach Bottom, Pennsylvania, in 1967, and in 1974 the company placed two nuclear units in service at the plant. The Salem (New Jersey) nuke (Unit 1) followed in 1977. The company relied on these plants during the OPEC oil crisis. Another one, Limerick Unit 1, began operations in 1986, and Unit 2 went on line in 1990, but the Peach Bottom plant was shut down from 1989 to 1991 because of management problems (later resolved).

The company began reorganizing in 1993 and changed its name the next year to PECO Energy Company. It also sold Maryland retail subsidiary Conowingo Power, retaining the hydroelectric plant. In 1995 rival PP&L rejected PECO's acquisition bid, citing PECO's nuclear liabilities.

A year later PECO teamed with AT&T Wireless to offer PCS in Philadelphia (service was launched in 1997). EnergyOne, a national venture formed in 1997 by PECO, UtiliCorp United (now Aquila), and AT&T, offered consumers a package of power, phone, and Internet services on one bill. However, the slow deregulation process caused the venture to fail.

PECO also joined with British Energy in 1997 to form AmerGen, hoping to buy nukes at rock-bottom prices from utilities eager to unload them. AmerGen purchased three nuclear facilities in 1999 and 2000: Unit 1 of the Three Mile Island (Pennsylvania) facility; a plant in Clinton, Illinois; and an Oyster Creek (New Jersey) location.

In 1999 PECO announced plans to acquire Chicago's Unicom, the parent company of Commonwealth Edison (ComEd). After the deal was completed in 2000, the combined company took the name Exelon and established its headquarters in Chicago.

Pennsylvania's utility markets were fully deregulated in 2000. To expand its power generation business, Exelon that year bought 49.9% of Sithe Energies for $682 million. In 2001 Exelon agreed to buy two gas-fired power plants (2,300 MW) in Texas from TXU for $443 million; the deal was completed in 2002.

Also in 2002 Exelon purchased Sithe Energies' stakes in six New England power plants with 2,000 MW of capacity (plus 2,400 MW under construction) for $543 million plus the assumption of $1.15 billion in debt. The company also

sold its Philadelphia PCS venture interest to former partner AT&T Wireless Services (now part of AT&T Mobility). Sithe Energies was sold to Dynegy in 2005 for $135 million.

To focus on core utility operations, the firm sold its infrastructure construction business, InfraSource, and its facility and infrastructure management business, Exelon Solutions. Exelon then completed the sale of its interest in telecommunications joint venture PECO TelCove, which provides voice and data services, to its partner TelCove, and sold its district heating and cooling division (Thermal Chicago) to Macquarie Bank. The company plans to sell additional non-core assets.

EXECUTIVES

Chairman and CEO, Exelon Corporation and Exelon Generation; Chairman, PECO: John W. Rowe, age 64, $9,063,496 total compensation
President and COO; President, Exelon Generation: Christopher M. (Chris) Crane, age 50, $5,811,123 total compensation
SVP and CFO; CFO, Exelon Generation: Matthew F. Hilzinger, age 45, $1,626,451 total compensation
SVP and CIO: Dan Hill
EVP and Chief Diversity Officer; President, Exelon Business Services: Ruth Ann M. Gillis, age 54
SVP, Exelon Generation; Chief Nuclear Officer, Exelon Nuclear: Charles M. (Chip) Pardee, age 49
Chairman and CEO, Commonwealth Edison: Frank M. Clark Jr., age 63, $3,197,323 total compensation
EVP Development: Ian P. McLean, age 59, $3,180,995 total compensation
EVP Governmental and Environmental Affairs and Public Policy: Elizabeth Ann (Betsy) Moler, age 60
EVP and General Counsel: Andrea L. Zopp, age 52
EVP Finance and Legal: William A. (Bill) Von Hoene Jr., age 55
EVP; President and CEO, PECO Energy: Denis P. O'Brien, age 48
SVP State, Legislative, and Governmental Affairs, ComEd: John T. Hooker, age 60
SVP; President, Power Team: Kenneth W. (Ken) Cornew, age 43
SVP and CFO, PECO Energy: Phillip S. Barnett, age 45
SVP and COO, PECO Energy: Craig L. Adams, age 56
VP and Controller: Duane M. DesParte, age 45
VP Investor Relations: Chaka Patterson, age 40
President and COO, ComED: Anne R. Pramaggiore, age 50
Senior Communications Specialist: Paul Elsberg
Director Investor Relations and Shareholder Services: Karie Anderson
Auditors: PricewaterhouseCoopers LLP

LOCATIONS

HQ: Exelon Corporation
10 S. Dearborn St., 37th Fl., Chicago, IL 60680
Phone: 312-394-7398   **Fax:** 312-394-7945
Web: www.exeloncorp.com

PRODUCTS/OPERATIONS

2008 Sales

	$ mil.	% of total
Generation	10,754	46
ComEd	6,136	27
PECO	5,567	24
Other	697	3
Adjustments	(4,295)	—
Total	**18,859**	**100**

Major Operating Units, Subsidiaries, and Affiliates

Exelon Energy Delivery
  Commonweath Edison Company (ComEd, electric utility)
  PECO Energy Company (PECO, electric and gas utility)
Exelon Generation Company, LLC
  AmerGen Energy Company, LLC (independent power producer)
  Exelon Energy (nonregulated retail power sales)
  Exelon Nuclear (nuclear power generation)

COMPETITORS

AES
Allegheny Energy
Alliant Energy
Ameren
American Transmission
CenterPoint Energy
Delmarva Power
Dominion Resources
Duke Energy
Duquesne Light Holdings
Dynegy
Entergy
FirstEnergy
FPL Group
Green Mountain Energy
Integrys Energy Group
Nicor
PPL Corporation
RRI Energy
UGI

HISTORICAL FINANCIALS

Company Type: Public

Income Statement

FYE: December 31

	REVENUE ($ mil.)	NET INCOME ($ mil.)	NET PROFIT MARGIN	EMPLOYEES
12/08	18,859.0	2,737.0	14.5%	19,610
12/07	18,916.0	2,736.0	14.5%	17,800
12/06	15,655.0	1,592.0	10.2%	17,200
12/05	15,357.0	965.0	6.3%	17,200
12/04	14,515.0	1,841.0	12.7%	17,300
Annual Growth	6.8%	10.4%	—	3.2%

2008 Year-End Financials

Debt ratio: 114.0%
Return on equity: 25.8%
Cash ($ mil.): 1,271
Current ratio: 1.32
Long-term debt ($ mil.): 12,592

No. of shares (mil.): 659
Dividends
  Yield: 3.7%
  Payout: 49.2%
Market value ($ mil.): 36,651

Stock History

NYSE: EXC

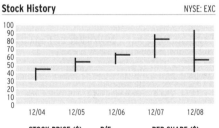

	STOCK PRICE ($) FY Close	P/E High/Low		PER SHARE ($) Earnings	Dividends	Book Value
12/08	55.61	22	10	4.13	2.03	16.76
12/07	81.64	21	15	4.05	1.76	15.38
12/06	61.89	27	22	2.35	1.60	15.13
12/05	53.14	42	31	1.36	1.60	13.98
12/04	44.07	16	11	2.78	1.25	14.43
Annual Growth	6.0%	—	—	10.4%	12.9%	3.8%

Exide Technologies

Exide Technologies hopes you'll get a charge out of its products. The company makes and recycles automotive and industrial batteries for customers — retailers such as Wal-Mart and NAPA and transportation giants such as Fiat and Toyota. The company also makes batteries for hybrid vehicles, boats, farm equipment, golf carts, and wheelchairs. Industrial applications include locomotive, photovoltaic (solar-related), telecommunications, computer, and power plant systems. Classic, Marathon, NASCAR Extreme, Sunlyte, and Super Crank are just some of the company's brand names. Operations outside the US account for more than half of sales.

Though Exide finally eked out a profit in fiscal 2008 (after 11 years of net losses), it again experienced a decline in net sales of about 10% for fiscal 2009, spurring the continuation of restructuring plans, headcount reductions, and reorganization of corporate and divisional functions.

In addition to its internal efforts to improve revenues, the company is pursuing collaborative partnerships and acquisitions to expand its advanced battery technology and product offerings, as well as its global market share. In 2009 the company entered into an exclusive partnership with Advanced Mobil Products (AMP), an automotive products and services company based in Phoenix, Arizona. AMP will market and distribute Exide's lead-acid batteries for the mobile replacement market to customers in Canada and the US. Exide also acquired the principal assets of Mountain Power, a British Columbia firm that makes rechargeable lithium-ion batteries. The acquisition gives the company a greater foothold in the industrial, medical, military, telecom, and utility markets.

India is an investment focus for Exide. The company acquired a controlling interest in Leadage Alloys India, and it expanded capacity at its transportation manufacturing facility in Gujarat. The expansion also included equipment upgrades, production line development, and infrastructure improvements.

Exide emerged from Chapter 11 bankruptcy in 2004 a leaner organization. While in bankruptcy, Exide consolidated manufacturing and distribution facilities, reduced its workforce, and improved its supply chain processes.

Tontine Capital Management owns more than 31% of Exide Technologies.

HISTORY

Exide got its start in 1888 when Thomas Edison founded The Electric Storage Battery Company (ESB) in Gloucester, New Jersey, to develop a backup battery for steam engines and dynamos. By 1890 ESB had installed the first practical battery backup in a Philadelphia utility, and that year it also provided batteries for the US's first streetcars. Sales picked up as the versatility of the battery was recognized, and in 1898 ESB batteries powered the US Navy's first submarine. The company was soon the world's top battery maker.

The Exide brand name (short for "excellent oxide") debuted in 1900, and the firsts kept coming: the first automobile ignition battery (1903), the batteries used in the first transcontinental telephone services (1915), and the batteries used for the first air-conditioned train (1931).

WWII saw the beginning of ESB's vertical integration, with the purchases of a maker of battery chargers and testers (1938) and a maker of battery containers (1946). ESB also developed battery-powered torpedoes used in WWII.

In 1951 Exide batteries assured the continuous operation of many Bell Systems relay stations for the first coast-to-coast wireless telephone network. In 1957 it entered the dry-cell battery business by acquiring the Ray-O-Vac Company. NASA used Exide batteries throughout the Apollo missions of the 1960s and 1970s, including the 1969 moon landing.

Inco Limited of Toronto purchased ESB in 1974. Management reorganized ESB in 1978 as a holding company, ESB Ray-O-Vac. The Exide brand stagnated, losing market share. In 1980 ESB Ray-O-Vac became INCO Electro Energy, with Exide as a subsidiary.

Investors led by the Spectrum Group and First Chicago Investment rescued Exide's North American operations in 1983. In 1985 the company hired ITT executive Arthur Hawkins as CEO and began a turnaround. Exide bought General Battery in 1987 to become #1 in the US auto battery market. The company acquired Speedclip Manufacturing (battery cables, terminals, and accessories; 1989) and Shadwood Industries (automotive battery chargers; fully acquired 1991) and went public in 1993.

Exide expanded into Europe in the mid-1990s, buying firms in France, Spain, and the UK, including two of the continent's largest battery makers. In 1997 it completed its European expansion by buying three battery-making units from Germany's CEAG AG.

Despite market dominance, Exide lost about 75% of its share value from 1996 to 1998. Some shareholders sued management, alleging misrepresentation, and the Florida attorney general and the SEC launched probes into whether the company sold used batteries as new. (In 1999 Exide settled with Florida without admitting wrongdoing, and it also settled with shareholders.) In 1998 management clumsily announced a recapitalization attempt and then changed its mind. Amid these problems, Hawkins resigned as chairman and CEO and former Chrysler exec Robert Lutz replaced him.

In 2001 Exide agreed to a plea deal with federal prosecutors whereby the company would pay out $27.5 million in fines over five years. It admitted to making defective batteries, covering up the defects, and bribing a Sears, Roebuck buyer. Burdened with heavy debt, Exide also announced in 2001 that it planned to issue 20 million new shares in a debt-for-equity deal. That year the company changed its name from Exide Corporation to Exide Technologies.

Early in 2002 Exide filed Chapter 11 bankruptcy as a result of its acquisitions bender and poor conditions in the automotive sector.

Arthur Hawkins, the former CEO of Exide, was convicted in 2002 of fraudulently selling defective batteries to Sears Automotive Marketing Services, a subsidiary of Sears, Roebuck. He was sentenced to 10 years in federal prison; the sentence was upheld in 2005. Three other Exide executives were convicted of various federal charges.

When Exide emerged from Chapter 11 bankruptcy in 2004, the company had cut its debt by a reported 70%. While Exide exited Chapter 11, it still experienced corporate pain — the company continued to lose money, and it shut down its lead-acid battery manufacturing plant in Shreveport, Louisiana, in mid-2006.

EXECUTIVES

Chairman: John P. Reilly, age 65
President, CEO, and Director: Gordon A. Ulsh, age 63, $3,938,791 total compensation
EVP and COO: Edward J. (E.J.) O'Leary, age 53, $1,227,341 total compensation
EVP and CFO: Phillip A. Damaska, age 54, $727,031 total compensation
VP and CIO: Erach S. Balsara
VP, Chief Accounting Officer, and Controller: Louis E. (Lou) Martinez, age 43
EVP Human Resources and Communications: George S. Jones Jr., age 56
EVP and General Counsel: Barbara A. Hatcher, age 54, $716,160 total compensation
VP and Treasurer: Nicholas J. Iuanow
VP Global Engineering and Research: Paul G. Cheeseman, age 48
VP Global Environment, Health, and Safety: Mark W. Cummings
VP US Aftermarket Sales and Branch System: Jeff Barna
VP Global Procurement: Douglas Gillespie
VP Strategic Planning and Business Development: Gary Reinert
President, Industrial Energy Americas: Mitchell S. Bregman, age 55, $800,476 total compensation
President, Transportation Americas: Bruce A. Cole, age 46
President, Asia/Pacific: Luke Lu
President, Industrial Energy Europe: Franz-Josef Dette, age 53
President, Transportation Europe: Michael Ostermann
Auditors: PricewaterhouseCoopers LLP

LOCATIONS

HQ: Exide Technologies
13000 Deerfield Pkwy., Bldg. 200
Alpharetta, GA 30004
Phone: 678-566-9000   **Fax:** 678-566-9188
Web: www.exide.com

2009 Sales

	$ mil.	% of total
US	1,293.3	39
Germany	423.7	13
Spain	260.8	8
France	242.6	7
Italy	209.3	6
Poland	125.4	4
Other	767.2	23
Total	**3,322.3**	**100**

PRODUCTS/OPERATIONS

2009 Sales

	$ mil.	% of total
Transportation	2,044.7	62
Industrial Energy	1,277.6	38
Total	**3,322.3**	**100**

Selected Products

Automotive batteries (for agricultural equipment, buses, commercial trucks, construction equipment, and emergency and passenger vehicles)
Industrial batteries
Motive power batteries (for forklifts, golf carts, and wheelchairs)
Network power batteries (for telecommunication, industrial, and military applications)
Standby/backup batteries (for hospitals, security systems, traffic control, and elevators)

COMPETITORS

C&D Technologies	Hitachi
Crown Battery	Interstate Batteries
Douglas Battery	Johnson Controls
Eagle-Picher	Micro Power Electronics
East Penn Manufacturing	SAFT
EnerSys	Valence Technology
GS Yuasa	

HISTORICAL FINANCIALS

Company Type: Public

Income Statement

FYE: March 31

	REVENUE ($ mil.)	NET INCOME ($ mil.)	NET PROFIT MARGIN	EMPLOYEES
3/09	3,322.3	(69.5)	—	12,081
3/08	3,696.7	32.1	0.9%	13,027
3/07	2,939.8	(105.9)	—	13,862
3/06	2,819.9	(172.7)	—	13,982
3/05	2,690.9	1,281.6	47.6%	14,268
Annual Growth	**5.4%**	**—**	**—**	**(4.1%)**

2009 Year-End Financials

Debt ratio: 198.1%
Return on equity: —
Cash ($ mil.): 70
Current ratio: 1.88
Long-term debt ($ mil.): 646
No. of shares (mil.): 76
Dividends
  Yield: 0.0%
  Payout: —
Market value ($ mil.): 227

Stock History

NASDAQ (GM): XIDE

	STOCK PRICE ($) FY Close	P/E High/Low		PER SHARE ($) Earnings	Dividends	Book Value
3/09	3.00	—	—	(0.92)	0.00	4.32
3/08	13.10	30	11	0.46	0.00	7.21
3/07	8.72	—	—	(2.39)	0.00	4.38
3/06	2.86	—	—	(6.91)	0.00	2.98
3/05	12.90	0	0	50.81	0.00	5.66
Annual Growth	**(30.6%)**	**—**	**—**	**—**	**—**	**(6.5%)**

Expeditors International

Need your goods moved expeditiously? Freight forwarder Expeditors International of Washington can help. As a freight forwarder, the company purchases air and ocean cargo space on a volume basis and resells that space to its customers at lower rates than they could obtain directly from the carriers. The company also acts as a customs broker for air and ocean freight shipped by its customers and offers supply chain management services. Expeditors operates from more than 200 facilities in more than 50 countries worldwide. More than half of the company's sales come from the Asia. Expeditors got its start in 1981 when it focused on airfreight shipments primarily from Taiwan, Singapore, and Hong Kong to the US.

In its rapid development, Expeditors has favored internal growth over expansion by acquisition, and the company continues to open new offices and to invest in its information technology infrastructure. According to Expeditors, this philosophy enables it to stay outside the "trends of consolidation" in order to cope with regional economic downturns.

HISTORY

After leaving the freight forwarding company that became Circle International (later acquired by EGL), Peter Rose used $55,000 in seed money to start his own company, Expeditors International of Washington, in 1979. Two years later Rose met with several fellow shipping veterans to implement their idea of combining freight forwarding and customs clearing services.

Expeditors soon had people beating a path to its door. It grew quickly to become a leading importer of goods made in Asia. Expeditors added export services in 1982 and went public in 1984. The next year it added ocean freight services to its offerings, and in 1986 it entered the European market. As the 1980s ended, the company had offices in 42 countries. Expeditors expanded into the Middle East in 1991 and, despite the economic doldrums of the early 1990s, opened 14 offices in 1992.

Expeditors also diversified with services such as long-term customs brokerage contracts and distribution. In 1997 it added truck and rail border brokerage services for the US, Mexico, and Canada. Expeditors continued to expand rapidly: In 1997 it added 22 offices and in 1999 opened still more, including five in Turkey and others in Greece, Lebanon, and the UK.

In 2000 Expeditors and other freight forwarders urged the US Department of Transportation to allow more dedicated air freighter service for the US-China market.

EXECUTIVES

Chairman, CEO, and Director: Peter J. Rose, age 65, $6,023,859 total compensation
President, COO, and Director: R. Jordan Gates, age 53, $4,548,595 total compensation
CFO and Principal Financial and Accounting Officer: Bradley S. (Brad) Powell, age 48, $354,466 total compensation
SVP and CIO: Jeffrey S. Musser, age 43
EVP, North America: Eugene K. Alger, age 48
EVP, North America: Philip M. Coughlin, age 48
EVP Global Customs: Rosanne Esposito, age 57
SVP and Corporate Controller: Charles J. Lynch, age 48
SVP, Australasia: Jean Claude Carcaillet, age 63
SVP Insurance: Erin M. Thomasson
SVP Air Cargo: Roger A. Idiart, age 55
SVP Ocean Services: Daniel R. Wall, age 40
SVP and Regional Director, South East Asia: Andrew Goh
VP Research and Development: Bret C. Backman
VP, General Counsel, and Secretary: Amy J. Tangeman, age 40
President, Global Sales and Marketing: Timothy C. Barber, age 49
President, Europe, Africa, Near/Middle East, and Indian Subcontinent: Rommel C. Saber, age 51, $4,289,921 total compensation
President, Asia and Director: James L. K. Wang, age 61, $5,683,642 total compensation
President, The Americas: Robert L. Villanueva, age 56, $4,337,840 total compensation
Auditors: KPMG LLP

LOCATIONS

HQ: Expeditors International of Washington, Inc.
1015 3rd Ave., 12th Fl., Seattle, WA 98104
Phone: 206-674-3400   **Fax:** 206-682-9777
Web: www.expeditors.com

2008 Sales

	$ mil.	% of total
Asia	2,974.3	53
North America		
US	1,261.0	22
Other countries	162.7	3
Europe & Africa	789.5	14
Middle East & India	274.1	5
Latin America	90.5	2
Australasia	81.8	1
Total	**5,633.9**	**100**

PRODUCTS/OPERATIONS

2008 Sales

	$ mil.	% of total
Airfreight	2,541.4	45
Ocean freight & ocean services	1,991.0	35
Customs brokerage & other services	1,101.5	20
Total	**5,633.9**	**100**

COMPETITORS

APL Logistics	Mitsui-Soko
CEVA Logistics	Nippon Express
C.H. Robinson Worldwide	Panalpina
DHL	Schenker
FedEx	Sinotrans
Kintetsu World Express	UPS
Kuehne + Nagel	UTi Worldwide

HISTORICAL FINANCIALS

Company Type: Public

Income Statement

FYE: December 31

	REVENUE ($ mil.)	NET INCOME ($ mil.)	NET PROFIT MARGIN	EMPLOYEES
12/08	5,633.9	301.0	5.3%	12,580
12/07	5,235.2	269.2	5.1%	12,310
12/06	4,626.0	235.1	5.1%	11,600
12/05	3,901.8	218.6	5.6%	10,600
12/04	3,317.5	161.2	4.9%	9,400
Annual Growth	**14.2%**	**16.9%**	**—**	**7.6%**

2008 Year-End Financials

Debt ratio: —
Return on equity: 23.2%
Cash ($ mil.): 741
Current ratio: 2.35
Long-term debt ($ mil.): —
No. of shares (mil.): 212
Dividends
  Yield: 1.4%
  Payout: 35.0%
Market value ($ mil.): 7,058

Stock History

NASDAQ (GS): EXPD

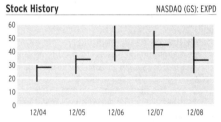

	STOCK PRICE ($) FY Close	P/E High/Low	PER SHARE ($) Earnings	PER SHARE ($) Dividends	PER SHARE ($) Book Value
12/08	33.27	36 18	1.37	0.48	6.44
12/07	44.68	45 32	1.21	0.28	5.78
12/06	40.50	55 31	1.06	0.22	5.04
12/05	33.76	37 24	0.98	0.15	4.31
12/04	27.94	41 25	0.70	0.11	3.81
Annual Growth	**4.5%**	**— —**	**18.3%**	**44.5%**	**14.1%**

Express Scripts

Express Scripts knows its customers like their drugs fast. One of the largest pharmacy benefits management (PBM) companies in North America, Express Scripts administers the prescription drug benefit of millions of health plan members in the US and Canada. Members have access to a network of about 60,000 retail pharmacies, as well as the company's own mail order pharmacies. Express Scripts processes claims for about 500 million prescriptions per year, designs drug plans, and offers such services as disease management programs and consumer drug data analysis. Clients include HMOs and other health insurers, self-insured businesses, and union benefit plans.

Express Scripts is one of the top three players in the PBM industry, the other two being Medco and Caremark. The company and the industry have grown rapidly, as the PBMs strive to save money for their health plan customers by negotiating good deals for prescription drugs with networks of retail pharmacies and by encouraging the use of cheaper generic drugs and home-delivered medications.

The company is moving to become even larger with its pending acquisition of NextRx, the PBM business of Blue Cross Blue Shield (BCBS) licensee WellPoint, for about $4.7 billion. As part of the acquisition, the company will have a 10-year contract to provide PBM services to WellPoint, the nation's largest health insurer. The purchase will increase Express Scripts processing load to more than 750 million prescrptions per year. It will also enhance the company's online, generic drug, and mail delivery service offerings.

In 2008 it expanded its PBM operations with the acquisition of the pharmacy services division of Medical Services Company for $251 million. The acquired business specialized in managing pharmacy benefits for workers' compensation insurers.

Another growing element of Express Scripts' business is its specialty pharmacy division, CuraScript, which provides distribution of injectable biotech drugs to patients' homes, doctors' offices, and other health care providers. Providing the injectable drugs was one thing, but actually providing the infusion therapy was a business that Express Scripts decided it didn't want to be in any longer. It sold off its CuraScript Infusion Pharmacy business, which operated infusion therapy centers in six states, to Walgreen's Option Care subsidiary in 2008.

In 2007 Express Scripts entered the fast-growing world of consumer-directed health plans by acquiring ConnectYourCare, a third-party administrator of such plans, which link a high-deductible with tax-sheltered savings accounts.

Express Scripts owns a minority stake in RxHub, which provides software enabling doctors to write electronic prescriptions and submit them electronically to pharmacies. It also allows pharmacies to communicate electronically with PBMs and health plans. Rivals Caremark and Medco also have stakes in the IT firm.

In addition to its services for health plans and their members, Express Scripts assists pharmaceutical and biotech companies with activities such as delivering marketing samples to doctors and providing customized packaging and logistics services through its Health Bridge division.

HISTORY

In 1986 St. Louis-based drugstore chain Medicare-Glaser and HMO Sanus joined forces to create Express Scripts, which would manage the HMO's prescription program. Express Scripts began managing third-party programs in 1988 and later developed other operations: mail-order prescription, infusion therapy, and vision services. New York Life bought Sanus and picked up the rest of Express Scripts in 1989 when Medicare-Glaser went into bankruptcy.

In 1992 Express Scripts went public. The next year the company formed subsidiary Practice Patterns Science to begin profiling providers and tracking treatment outcomes.

In the late 1990s the company continued to expand, adding customers in Canada (1996) and building operations — with varying success. A 1996 expansion of its eye care management services was abandoned in 1998. Although Express Scripts has traditionally grown through big-ticket contracts, such as its 1997 pact with RightCHOICE Managed Care; it has also bought books of business. In 1998 it purchased Columbia/HCA's (now HCA) ValueRx unit. The next year Express Scripts bought SmithKline Beecham's Diversified Pharmaceutical Services (DPS); however, it lost DPS's largest customer when United Healthcare began moving its more than 8 million enrollees to Merck-Medco in 2000.

The company suffered another setback in 2000 when it wrote down its 20% interest in online pharmacy PlanetRx. It had bought into the company in 1999, when dot-coms were soaring, transferring its own Internet pharmacy operations (YourPharmacy.com) into the fledgling company. In 2001 Express Scripts joined rivals AdvancePCS and Merck-Medco (now Medco Health Solutions) to form RxHub to create technology to allow physicians to file prescriptions electronically.

In 2001 the firm began a bit of an acquisition spree. That year, it bought Phoenix Marketing Group, one of the biggest prescription drug sample fulfillment companies in the US. National Prescription Administrators, a top private pharmacy benefits management company in the US, joined the family in 2002. In 2004 Express Scripts expanded its specialty pharmacy capabilities with CuraScript, a leading specialty pharmacy.

EXECUTIVES

Chairman, President, and CEO: George Paz, age 53, $12,774,367 total compensation
EVP and CFO: Jeffrey L. Hall, age 41, $2,114,000 total compensation
EVP Operations and Technology: Patrick (Pat) McNamee, age 49, $2,769,387 total compensation
EVP and Chief Administrative Officer: Michael R. Holmes, age 50, $2,682,745 total compensation
EVP Sales and Account Management: Edward (Ed) Ignaczak, age 43
EVP, General Counsel, and Secretary: Keith J. Ebling, age 40
SVP Marketing and Corporate Communications: Larry Zarin, age 54
VP Human Resources: Karen Matteuzzi
VP, Controller, and Chief Accouting Officer: Kelley Elliott, age 36
VP Talent Acquisition: Kristi Robinson
President, International Operations: Agnes Rey-Giraud, age 44
Auditors: PricewaterhouseCoopers LLP

LOCATIONS

HQ: Express Scripts, Inc.
1 Express Way, St. Louis, MO 63121
Phone: 314-996-0900
Web: www.express-scripts.com

PRODUCTS/OPERATIONS

2008 Sales

	$ mil.	% of total
Pharmacy Benefits Management (PBM)		
Network	13,039.9	59
Home delivery & other PBM services	5,175.2	24
Specialty & ancillary services	3,762.9	17
Total	**21,978.0**	**100**

Selected Products and Services

PBM
Benefit design consultation
Compliance management programs for members
Drug formulary management
Drug utilization review
Home delivery pharmacy services
Retail drug card programs
Retail network pharmacy management

Specialty and ancillary services
Delivery of specialty biotech drugs (CuraScript)
Sample distribution services
Specialty packaging services
Third-party logistics services

COMPETITORS

Aetna
Argus
BioScrip
Caremark Pharmacy Services
Catalyst Health Solutions
CIGNA
First Health Group
Humana
Medco Health
MedImpact
Omnicare
PharMerica
Prime Therapeutics
Rite Aid
SXC
UnitedHealth Group
Walgreen
Wal-Mart
WellPoint

HISTORICAL FINANCIALS

Company Type: Public

Income Statement

FYE: December 31

	REVENUE ($ mil.)	NET INCOME ($ mil.)	NET PROFIT MARGIN	EMPLOYEES
12/08	21,978.0	776.1	3.5%	10,820
12/07	18,273.6	567.8	3.1%	11,820
12/06	17,660.0	474.4	2.7%	11,300
12/05	16,266.0	400.0	2.5%	11,100
12/04	15,114.7	278.2	1.8%	10,662
Annual Growth	9.8%	29.2%	—	0.4%

2008 Year-End Financials

Debt ratio: 124.3%
Return on equity: 87.5%
Cash ($ mil.): 531
Current ratio: 0.75
Long-term debt ($ mil.): 1,340

No. of shares (mil.): 274
Dividends
  Yield: 0.0%
  Payout: —
Market value ($ mil.): 15,087

Stock History NASDAQ (GS): ESRX

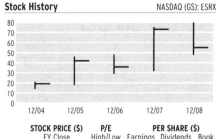

	STOCK PRICE ($) FY Close	P/E High/Low		PER SHARE ($) Earnings	Dividends	Book Value
12/08	54.98	26	16	3.08	0.00	3.93
12/07	73.00	35	15	2.15	0.00	2.54
12/06	35.80	28	18	1.67	0.00	4.10
12/05	41.90	34	14	1.34	0.00	5.34
12/04	19.11	23	16	0.90	0.00	4.36
Annual Growth	30.2%	—	—	36.0%	—	(2.6%)

Exxon Mobil

It's not necessarily the oil standard, but Exxon Mobil is the world's largest integrated oil company (ahead of Royal Dutch Shell and BP). Exxon Mobil engages in oil and gas exploration, production, supply, transportation, and marketing worldwide. It has proved reserves of 12.8 billion barrels of oil equivalent, as well as major holdings in oil sands through Imperial Oil. Exxon Mobil's 37 refineries in 20 countries have a throughput capacity of 6.2 million barrels per day. It supplies refined products to more than 28,600 gas stations in 100 countries. Exxon Mobil is also a major petrochemical producer. The company posted US records for annual corporate earnings in 2005, 2006, 2007, and 2008.

Through ExxonMobil Chemical, the company develops and sells petrochemicals (including ethylene, propylene, and their derivitives, which make up the base of most other petrochemicals and plastics). Another unit mines coal and other minerals. Exxon Mobil also has stakes in electric power plants in China.

With significant oil and gas holdings in Europe, the US, and eastern Canada, the company is looking for new opportunities in West Africa, both onshore and off; in the former Soviet Union; and in South America. It is also investing heavily in deepwater exploration (i.e., in water depths greater than 1,350 feet). Between 2008 and 2010, Exxon Mobil plans to participate in the start up of 19 projects, which collectively will add more than 725,000 oil-equivalent barrels per day to the company's production.

In 2007 President Hugo Chavez expropriated Exxon Mobil's Venezuelan assets, leading to intense international litigation (which remained unresolved in early 2009).

In 2008 the company announced plans to sell to distributors its remaining 820 company-owned US gas stations and another 1,400 outlets operated by dealers.

In response to market demand for cleaner fuels, in late 2008 ExxonMobil announced it will invest more than $1 billion in three refineries to increase the supply of cleaner burning diesel by about six million gallons per day. In 2009 it made its first major investment in developing biofuels,

agreeing to spend $600 million in an algae-to-fuel project with biotech firm Synthetic Genomics.

In 2009 the company signed up to partner with TransCanada to jointly develop the $26 billion Alaska Pipeline Project.

HISTORY

Exxon's 1999 acquisition of Mobil reunited two descendants of John D. Rockefeller's Standard Oil Company. Rockefeller, a commodity trader, started his first oil refinery in 1863 in Cleveland. Realizing that the price of oil at the well would shrink with each new strike, Rockefeller chose to monopolize oil refining and transportation. In 1870 he formed Standard Oil, and in 1882 he created the Standard Oil Trust, which allowed him to set up new, ostensibly independent, companies, including the Standard Oil Company of New Jersey (Jersey Standard); Rochester, New York-based Vacuum Oil; and Standard Oil of New York (nicknamed Socony).

Initially capitalized at $70 million, the Standard Oil Trust controlled 90% of the petroleum industry. In 1911, after two decades of political and legal wrangling, the Supreme Court broke up the trust into 34 companies, the largest of which was Jersey Standard.

Walter Teagle, who became president of Jersey Standard in 1917, secretly bought half of Humble Oil of Texas (1919) and expanded operations into South America. In 1928 Jersey Standard joined in the Red Line Agreement, which reserved most Middle East oil for a few companies. Teagle resigned in 1942 after the company was criticized for a prewar research pact with German chemical giant I.G. Farben.

The 1948 purchase of a 40% stake in Arabian American Oil Company, combined with a 7% share of Iranian production bought in 1954, made Jersey Standard the world's #1 oil company at that time.

Meanwhile, Vacuum Oil and Socony reunited in 1931 as Socony-Vacuum, and the company adopted the Flying Red Horse (Pegasus — representing speed and power) as a trademark. The fast-growing, diversifying company changed its name to Socony Mobil Oil in 1955 and became Mobil in 1976.

Other US companies, still using the Standard Oil name, objected to Jersey Standard's marketing in their territories as Esso (derived from the initials for Standard Oil). To end the confusion, in 1972 Jersey Standard became Exxon, a name change that cost $100 million.

Nationalization of oil assets by producing countries reduced Exxon's access to oil during the 1970s. Though it increased exploration that decade and the next, Exxon's reserves shrank.

Oil tanker *Exxon Valdez* spilled some 11 million gallons of oil into Alaska's Prince William Sound in 1989. Exxon spent billions on the cleanup, and in 1994 a federal jury in Alaska ordered the company to pay $5.3 billion in punitive damages to fishermen and others affected by the spill. (Exxon appealed, and in 2001 the jury award was reduced to $2.5 billion, and in 2008 to $507.5 million).

With the oil industry consolidating, Exxon merged its worldwide oil and fuel additives business with that of Royal Dutch/Shell in 1996. The next year, under FTC pressure, Exxon agreed to run ads refuting claims that its premium gas enabled car engines to run more efficiently. Another PR disaster followed in 1998 when CEO Lee Raymond upset environmentalists by publicly questioning the global warming theory.

Still, Exxon was unstoppable. It acquired Mobil for $81 billion in 1999; the new company had Raymond at the helm and Mobil's Lucio Noto as vice chairman. (Noto retired in 2001.) To get the deal done, Exxon Mobil had to divest $4 billion in assets. It agreed to end its European gasoline and lubricants joint venture with BP and to sell more than 2,400 gas stations in the US. It sold 1,740 East Coast gas stations to Tosco and a California refinery and 340 gas stations to Valero Energy for about $1 billion.

In 2001 Exxon Mobil also announced that it was proceeding with a $12 billion project (with Japanese, Indian, and Russian partners) to develop oil fields in the Russian Far East.

In 2002 Exxon Mobil sold its Chilean copper mining subsidiary (Disputada de Las Condes) to giant Anglo American for $1.3 billion. Exxon Mobil sold its 3.7% stake in China Petroleum & Chemical Corp. (Sinopec) in early 2005. Later that year the company was ordered to pay $1.3 billion to about 10,000 gas station owners for overcharges dating back to 1983; the average amount for each station owner was about $130,000.

EXECUTIVES

Chairman and CEO: Rex W. Tillerson, age 57, $22,414,602 total compensation
SVP and Treasurer: Donald D. (Don) Humphreys, age 61, $11,878,031 total compensation
SVP: Michael J. (Mike) Dolan, age 55
SVP: Andrew P. (Andy) Swiger, age 52
SVP: Mark W. Albers, age 52
VP and General Counsel: Charles W. Matthews Jr., age 64, $9,700,227 total compensation
VP; President, ExxonMobil Fuels Marketing: Harold R. (Hal) Cramer, age 58, $9,273,876 total compensation
VP and Controller: Patrick T. (Pat) Mulva, age 57
VP Human Resources: Lucille J. Cavanaugh
VP Public Affairs: Kenneth P. (Ken) Cohen
VP; President, ExxonMobil Exploration: A. Timothy (Tim) Cejka, age 57
VP; President, ExxonMobil Chemical Company: Stephen D. (Steve) Pryor, age 59, $10,201,644 total compensation
VP; President, ExxonMobil Lubricants and Petroleum Specialties: Allan J. Kelly, age 51
VP; President, ExxonMobil Production Company: R. M. (Rich) Kruger, age 49
VP Investor Relations and Secretary: David S. Rosenthal, age 52
VP; President, ExxonMobil Gas and Power Marketing Company: T. R. (Tom) Walters, age 54
VP; President, ExxonMobil Refining and Supply: Sherman J. Glass Jr., age 61
Chairman, Imperial Oil Limited: Bruce H. March, age 52, $3,264,452 total compensation
President, ExxonMobil Research and Engineering: Richard V. (Rich) Pisarczyk
President, ExxonMobil Development: Neil W. Duffin, age 52
President, ExxonMobil Global Services: Neil A. Chapman
President, ExxonMobil Upstream Research: Steve S.M. Greenlee
Auditors: PricewaterhouseCoopers LLP

LOCATIONS

HQ: Exxon Mobil Corporation
5959 Las Colinas Blvd., Irving, TX 75039
Phone: 972-444-1000   **Fax:** 972-444-1350
Web: www.exxon.mobil.com

Exxon Mobil operates in about 200 countries. Its oil and gas assets are in countries across the globe, including Angola, Argentina, Australia, Azerbaijan, Cameroon, Canada, Chad, Equatorial Guinea, France, Germany, Indonesia, Italy, Japan, Kazakhstan, Malaysia, the Netherlands, Nigeria, Norway, Papua New Guinea, Qatar, Russia, Thailand, the UK, the US (including the Gulf of Mexico), and Yemen.

2008 Sales

	% of total
US	30
Canada	7
Japan	7
UK	6
Belgium	5
Germany	5
France	4
Italy	4
Norway	3
Other countries	29
Total	**100**

PRODUCTS/OPERATIONS

2008 Sales

	% of total
Downstream	83
Upstream	9
Chemicals	8
Total	**100**

Selected Subsidiaries and Affiliates

Aera Energy, LLC (48%)
Al-Jubail Petrochemical Company (50%)
Esso Petroleum Company, Limited (UK)
ExxonMobil Chemical Company
ExxonMobil Pipeline Company
Imperial Oil Limited (69.6%, Canada)

COMPETITORS

7-Eleven
Ashland Inc.
BHP Billiton
BP
Chevron
ConocoPhillips
Costco Wholesale
Dow Chemical
DuPont
Eastman Chemical
Eni
Hess Corporation
Huntsman International
Koch Industries, Inc.
Marathon Oil
Norsk Hydro ASA
Occidental Petroleum
PEMEX
PETROBRAS
Petróleos de Venezuela
Racetrac Petroleum
Repsol YPF
Royal Dutch Shell
Saudi Aramco
Sunoco
TOTAL
Valero Energy

HISTORICAL FINANCIALS

Company Type: Public

Income Statement   FYE: December 31

	REVENUE ($ mil.)	NET INCOME ($ mil.)	NET PROFIT MARGIN	EMPLOYEES
12/08	477,359.0	45,220.0	9.5%	79,900
12/07	404,552.0	40,610.0	10.0%	80,800
12/06	377,635.0	39,500.0	10.5%	82,100
12/05	370,680.0	36,130.0	9.7%	83,700
12/04	298,035.0	25,330.0	8.5%	85,900
Annual Growth	**12.5%**	**15.6%**	**—**	**(1.8%)**

2008 Year-End Financials

Debt ratio: 6.2%	No. of shares (mil.): 4,806
Return on equity: 38.5%	Dividends
Cash ($ mil.): 31,437	Yield: 1.9%
Current ratio: 1.47	Payout: 17.8%
Long-term debt ($ mil.): 7,025	Market value ($ mil.): 383,646

Stock History

NYSE: XOM

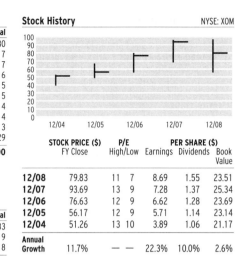

	STOCK PRICE ($) FY Close	P/E High/Low		PER SHARE ($) Earnings	Dividends	Book Value
12/08	79.83	11	7	8.69	1.55	23.51
12/07	93.69	13	9	7.28	1.37	25.34
12/06	76.63	12	9	6.62	1.28	23.69
12/05	56.17	12	9	5.71	1.14	23.14
12/04	51.26	13	10	3.89	1.06	21.17
Annual Growth	**11.7%**	**—**	**—**	**22.3%**	**10.0%**	**2.6%**

Family Dollar Stores

Penny-pinching moms are important to Family Dollar Stores. The nation's #2 dollar store (behind Dollar General) targets women shopping for a family that earns less than $30,000 a year. Family Dollar operates about 6,600 stores in some 45 states and the District of Columbia. Consumables (food, health and beauty aids, and household products) account for about 60% of sales; the stores also sell apparel, shoes, and linens. Family Dollar emphasizes neighborhood stores near its low- and middle-income customers in rural and urban areas. Most merchandise (national brands, Family Dollar private labels, and unbranded items) is less than $10. Family Dollar was founded in 1959 by the father of CEO Howard Levine.

High energy prices, inflation, and rising unemployment hit Family Dollar's low income customers hard in fiscal 2008. They responded by increasing purchases of lower-margin consumables and avoiding higher priced merchandise. The chain, which responded by focusing on consumable categories and controlling costs, got a boost from the government stimulus program in the second half of the year.

In the face of increased competition from mass discounters such as Wal-Mart, the company has shifted to an everyday-low-pricing strategy (as opposed to short-lived promotional advertising), while increasing the number of brand-name goods it carries. It announced in April 2009 that it will roll out some 250 new food items (including Triscuits and Double Stuf Oreos) at its stores to compete head to head with its rivals. Family Dollar Stores is also expanding its food offering to include milk and other perishables, as well as more quick-prep and ready-to-eat products. To keep food fresh, Family Dollar has installed refrigerated coolers in about 5,600 stores. In addition to selling more groceries, the dollar chain has begun accepting food stamps (currently in about 2,400 stores) to attract more low-income customers.

While Family Dollar has been expanding rapidly — adding more than 4,000 new stores in the last 10 years — the pace of new store openings has cooled more recently. Also, the discount chain has been increasing its retail presence in both large and smaller urban areas.

Levine and his family own about 7% of the discount chain.

HISTORY

Leon Levine came from a retailing family. His father, who founded The Hub, a general store-style department store in Rockingham, North Carolina, in 1908, died when Levine was 13. Leon and his older brother Al helped their mother run the store. (Al went on to found the Pic 'n Pay self-service shoe stores in 1957.) In 1959, when he was 25, Levine (with his cousin Bernie) opened his own store in Charlotte, with nothing priced over a dollar, targeting low- and middle-income families. The concept of low prices and small neighborhood stores was immediately popular, and Levine began adding stores. By 1970, when he took Family Dollar Stores public, it had 100 stores in five states. That year Levine brought his cousin Lewis into the business.

Family Dollar's profits plummeted in the mid-1970s as the chain's low-income customers, hit by recession, cut back on spending — even though all merchandise was priced at $3 or less. Such pricing made for tight margins, so the company dropped the policy. Family Dollar also improved inventory controls to make operations more efficient and began moving into other states. Sales picked up, topping $100 million in 1977, and the next year the firm bought the 40-store Top Dollar chain from Sav-A-Stop.

As the 1980s began, Family Dollar had nearly 400 stores in eight southern states; rapidly expanding, it was adding more than 100 stores a year. But in an effort to boost margins, the company had lost its pricing edge to a new threat — Wal-Mart's truckload prices and quick domination of the southern discount retailing market.

After Family Dollar sales were flat in 1986 and dropped 10% in 1987, Levine finally took action. He found his prices were sometimes as much as 10% higher than Wal-Mart's and his stores were often insufficiently stocked with advertised products. He lowered prices, declaring that Family Dollar would not be undersold, and again instituted new inventory controls. But the action had not come quickly enough, argued president and COO Lewis, who left the company in 1987. (He was also upset over a huge salary disparity: Leon — noted for being a hard bargainer with suppliers — was making $1.8 million a year, compared to Lewis's $260,000.) Leon's son Howard, who joined the firm in 1981, also left; he returned to the fold in 1996 and became CEO in 1998.

Family Dollar picked up momentum in the 1990s. It implemented a major renovation of stores and phased out low-margin items such as motor oil and tools in favor of such high-margin items as toys and electronics. The company also accelerated its growth plans, opening stores in a number of new markets and setting up a second distribution center, in Arkansas, in 1994 to support its westward expansion. Also that year Family Dollar began offering everyday low prices and scaled back its sales promotions.

The pace of expansion was steady during the late 1990s, as the company opened hundreds of new stores and more distribution centers and closed underperforming locations. Family Dollar added 165 stores in fiscal 1996, 186 in fiscal 1997, 250 in fiscal 1998, and 366 in fiscal 1999 (its largest single-year increase in stores). It continued adding stores in 2000 and 2001 (although the rate of growth began slowing) and it began emphasizing food, household products, and gift and seasonal items rather than clothing.

Family Dollar increased its presence in urban areas by locating 40% of the 475 stores added in 2002 in cities. Historically about 25% of its stores have been placed in urban markets.

Founder Leon Levine retired in January 2003, 43 years after starting the company. His son Howard (CEO) succeeded him as chairman. In 2003 Family Dollar Stores opened its seventh distribution center and 475 new stores, including its first outlets in Wyoming and North Dakota. In 2004 the chain opened an additional 500 outlets, increasing its store count by about 10%.

In April 2006 an Alabama jury found Family Dollar guilty of violating the Federal Labor Standards Act by misclassifying hourly employees as salaried managers to avoid paying overtime. As a result the company was fined $16.6 million. Also that year Family Dollar opened a new Northeast regional distribution center in Rome, New York, bringing the total to nine centers.

EXECUTIVES

Chairman and CEO: Howard R. Levine, age 49
President and COO: R. James (Jim) Kelly
SVP and CFO: Kenneth T. (Ken) Smith, age 47
SVP and CIO: Joshua R. (Josh) Jewett, age 37
EVP and Chief Merchandising Officer: Dorlisa K. Flur, age 43
EVP, Supply Chain: Charles S. Gibson Jr., age 47
EVP, Store Operations: Barry W. Sullivan, age 42
SVP, Hardlines and Marketing: John J. Scanlon, age 58
SVP, Store Construction and Facility Management: Keith M. Gehl, age 47
SVP, Finance: C. Martin Sowers, age 48
SVP, New Stores: Thomas M. (Tom) Nash
SVP, General Counsel, and Secretary: Janet G. Kelley, age 53
SVP, Planning, Allocation, and Replenishment: Bryan P. Causey
SVP, Human Resources: Bryan E. Venberg, age 40
SVP, Softlines: Mike Kvitko
SVP, General Counsel, and Corporate Secretary: James C. (Jim) Snyder Jr., age 45
VP, Store Operations: Earl C. Bonnecaze
VP, Investor Relations and Communications: Kiley F. Rawlins
VP, Merchandising Strategy and Operations: Boris Zelmanovich
VP, Marketing: Donald G. Smith
Manager, Human Resources Information Systems: Michael Lariosa
Auditors: PricewaterhouseCoopers LLP

LOCATIONS

HQ: Family Dollar Stores, Inc.
10401 Monroe Rd., Matthews, NC 28105
Phone: 704-847-6961   **Fax:** 704-847-0189
Web: www.familydollar.com

2008 Stores

	No.
Texas	821
Ohio	411
Michigan	351
Florida	369
North Carolina	364
Georgia	306
New York	290
Pennsylvania	267
Illinois	238
Louisiana	229
Virginia	214
Tennessee	206
Kentucky	186
South Carolina	199
Indiana	195
Alabama	145
Wisconsin	140
Arizona	131
Oklahoma	128
West Virginia	115
Mississippi	118
Colorado	104
Arkansas	98
Missouri	96
Massachusetts	99
Maryland	92
New Mexico	91
New Jersey	80
Minnesota	71
Utah	60
Connecticut	51
Maine	49
Kansas	35
Iowa	32
Idaho	31
Nebraska	31
Other states	165
Total	**6,598**

PRODUCTS/OPERATIONS

2008 Sales

	% of total
Consumables	61
Home products	14
Apparel & accessories	13
Seasonal & electronics	12
Total	**100**

2008 Sales

	% of total
Nationally advertised brands	44
Family Dollar brands, unlabeled & other	56
Total	**100**

Selected Products

Hardlines
  Automotive supplies
  Candy, snacks, and other foods
  Electronics
  Gifts
  Hardware
  Health and beauty aids
  Household chemical products
  Household paper products
  Housewares
  Seasonal goods
  Stationery and school supplies
  Toys
Soft goods
  Apparel (men's, women's, children's, and infants')
  Domestics (blankets, sheets, and towels)
  Shoes

COMPETITORS

7-Eleven
Big Lots
BJ's Wholesale Club
Costco Wholesale
CVS Caremark
Dollar General
Dollar Tree
Duckwall-ALCO
Fred's
J. C. Penney
Kmart
Kroger
Meijer
Old Navy
Pamida Stores
The Pantry
Retail Ventures
Rite Aid
Sears
ShopKo Stores
Simply Amazing
SUPERVALU
Target
Toys "R" Us
Variety Wholesalers
Walgreen
Wal-Mart

HISTORICAL FINANCIALS

Company Type: Public

Income Statement

FYE: August 31

	REVENUE ($ mil.)	NET INCOME ($ mil.)	NET PROFIT MARGIN	EMPLOYEES
8/08	6,983.6	233.1	3.3%	44,000
8/07	6,834.3	242.9	3.6%	44,000
8/06	6,394.8	195.1	3.1%	44,000
8/05	5,824.8	217.5	3.7%	42,000
8/04	5,281.9	262.7	5.0%	39,000
Annual Growth	7.2%	(2.9%)	—	3.1%

2008 Year-End Financials

Debt ratio: 19.9%
Return on equity: 19.2%
Cash ($ mil.): 159
Current ratio: 1.26
Long-term debt ($ mil.): 250

No. of shares (mil.): 140
Dividends
  Yield: 1.9%
  Payout: 28.9%
Market value ($ mil.): 3,482

Stock History

NYSE: FDO

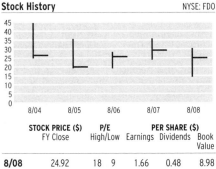

	STOCK PRICE ($) FY Close	P/E High/Low		PER SHARE ($) Earnings	Dividends	Book Value
8/08	24.92	18	9	1.66	0.48	8.98
8/07	29.28	22	15	1.62	0.44	8.41
8/06	25.57	22	15	1.26	0.40	8.65
8/05	19.88	27	15	1.30	0.36	10.22
8/04	26.45	29	16	1.53	0.32	9.74
Annual Growth	(1.5%)	—	—	2.1%	10.7%	(2.0%)

Fastenal Company

Some might say it has a screw loose, but things are really pretty snug at Fastenal. The company operates about 2,350 stores in all 50 US states, Canada, China, Mexico, the Netherlands, Puerto Rico, and Singapore. Its stores stock about 690,000 products in about a dozen categories, including threaded fasteners such as screws, nuts, and bolts. Other sales come from fluid-transfer parts for hydraulic and pneumatic power; janitorial, electrical, and welding supplies; material handling items; metal-cutting tool blades; and power tools. Its customers are typically construction, manufacturing, and other industrial professionals. Fastenal Company was founded by its chairman Bob Kierlin in 1967 and went public in 1987.

Fastenal has been one of the fastest-growing companies in the US — adding about 150 stores annually over the past several years — primarily by selling threaded fasteners, which account for about 45% of sales. Products manufactured by other companies account for about 95% of Fastenal's sales; the remainder comes from items custom-made or modified by Fastenal. Fastenal stores are moving away from their traditional focus on wholesaling. The company's "expected inventory" format seeks to tailor its product offering to specific geographic areas with the goal of being the best industrial and construction supplier in each of the local markets where it does business. Fastenal stores are supplied by about 15 distribution centers throughout North America.

Fastenal believes it has room to continue to grow, but at a slower pace. In 2007 the company began to slow its rate of new store openings, while making stores bigger and increasing staff to boost margins. The onset of the deep recession in the US has slowed new store growth even further as Fastenal's sales — particularly related to its industrial production and nonresidential construction businesses — have suffered. Still, the company is optimistic that when the economy bounces back the North American market can support at least 3,500 of its stores located in small, medium, and large markets.

Fastenal is expanding internationally, most recently into China. Currently about 8% of the company's revenue is generated outside the US.

HISTORY

Peace Corps veteran Robert Kierlin led four friends and Winona Cotter High School classmates in founding Fastenal in 1967 as a distributor of threaded fasteners. (Kierlin's inspiration was customers' inquiries at his father's auto parts store.) The company and its lone store lost money its first two years, but it was able to open another store by 1970. Fastenal then changed its retail focus from regular consumers to contractors and professionals.

The company expanded, locating stores on the outskirts of small and medium-sized cities where real estate and operating costs are lower. By 1987 it had 58 stores. Fastenal went public that year, using some 40% of the IPO proceeds to establish

the Hiawatha Education Foundation to support private high school education, especially the founders' financially troubled alma mater.

Fastenal grew quickly during the early 1990s, from about 100 stores in 1990 to nearly 400 stores in small and large US cities in 1995. It added tool-sharpening services to its stores the next year. The firm also added new product lines as it expanded, including FastTool tools and safety supplies (1993), SharpCut blades and PowerFlow fluid-transfer components (1996), and FastArc welding supplies (1997). In 1997 Fastenal opened its first store in Puerto Rico.

In 1998 the company printed its first catalog and formed a subsidiary to sell its products in Mexico. Fastenal started selling online in 1999. In 2000 the company opened about 90 stores, and the next year opened more than 125, including one in Singapore. In 2002 the company made a move into the retail market through its purchase of the retail fastener and related hardware business of two Textron subsidiaries. The company sold that business, however, to Hillman Companies later that year.

In 2004 Fastenal opened 219 stores (including its first in the Netherlands) compared to 151 new outlets in 2003. In 2005 the company opened its first store in China and added, overall, about 220 stores that year. The following year saw the opening of 225 additional stores.

EXECUTIVES

Chairman: Robert A. (Bob) Kierlin, age 69
President, CEO, and Director:
  Willard D. (Will) Oberton, age 50,
  $2,036,203 total compensation
EVP Internal Operations: James C. (Cory) Jansen,
  age 38, $675,799 total compensation
EVP and CFO: Daniel L. (Dan) Florness, age 46,
  $860,907 total compensation
EVP Human Resources and Director:
  Reyne K. Wisecup, age 46
EVP Sales: Nicholas J. (Nick) Lundquist, age 51,
  $1,071,200 total compensation
EVP Sales: Leland J. (Lee) Hein, age 48,
  $703,818 total compensation
EVP Sales: Steven A. (Steve) Rucinski, age 51
Auditors: KPMG LLP

LOCATIONS

HQ: Fastenal Company
  2001 Theurer Blvd., Winona, MN 55987
Phone: 507-454-5374   **Fax:** 507-453-8049
Web: www.fastenal.com

2008 Stores

	No.
US	2,097
Canada	169
Mexico	33
Puerto Rico	8
Netherlands	2
China	1
Singapore	1
Total	**2,311**

2008 Sales

	% of total
US	92
International	8
Total	**100**

PRODUCTS/OPERATIONS

Selected Brands, Products, and Services

CleanChoice
  Janitorial and paper products
EquipRite
  Material handling and storage products
FastArc
  Welding supplies
Fastenal
  Threaded fasteners (bolts, nuts, screws, and washers)
  Concrete anchors
  Struts
FastTool
  Power tools and accessories
PowerPhase
  Electrical supplies
SharpCut
  Cutting tools

COMPETITORS

Ace Hardware	MSC Industrial Direct
Anixter Pentacon	Noland
Applied Industrial	Park-Ohio Holdings
Technologies	PennEngineering
HD Supply	Production Tool Supply
Home Depot	Snap-on
Lawson Products	True Value
Lowe's	WinWholesale
Menard	W.W. Grainger

HISTORICAL FINANCIALS

Company Type: Public

Income Statement

FYE: December 31

	REVENUE ($ mil.)	NET INCOME ($ mil.)	NET PROFIT MARGIN	EMPLOYEES
12/08	2,340.4	279.7	12.0%	13,634
12/07	2,061.8	232.6	11.3%	12,013
12/06	1,809.3	199.0	11.0%	10,415
12/05	1,523.3	166.8	10.9%	9,306
12/04	1,238.5	131.0	10.6%	7,946
Annual Growth	17.2%	20.9%	—	14.5%

2008 Year-End Financials

Debt ratio: —
Return on equity: 26.0%
Cash ($ mil.): 86
Current ratio: 6.59
Long-term debt ($ mil.): —
No. of shares (mil.): 149
Dividends
  Yield: 1.5%
  Payout: 27.7%
Market value ($ mil.): 5,176

Stock History

NASDAQ (GS): FAST

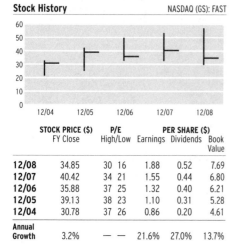

	STOCK PRICE ($) FY Close	P/E High/Low	PER SHARE ($) Earnings	Dividends	Book Value
12/08	34.85	30 16	1.88	0.52	7.69
12/07	40.42	34 21	1.55	0.44	6.80
12/06	35.88	37 25	1.32	0.40	6.21
12/05	39.13	38 23	1.10	0.31	5.28
12/04	30.78	37 26	0.86	0.20	4.61
Annual Growth	3.2%	— —	21.6%	27.0%	13.7%

Federal-Mogul

For Federal-Mogul, the sum of the parts is greater than the whole. The company makes components for cars, trucks, and construction vehicles. Its products include chassis and engine parts, pistons, and sealing systems sold under brand names such as Champion, Federal-Mogul, Fel-Pro, Glyco, and Moog. Federal-Mogul has manufacturing and distribution facilities primarily in the Americas and Europe; major customers include global automakers, such as BMW, General Motors, Ford, and Volkswagen. Federal-Mogul also distributes auto parts to aftermarket customers. The company makes about 60% of its sales outside the US.

The company entered Chapter 11 in 2001 as a result of asbestos claims related to its acquisition of T&N plc. Federal-Mogul exited Chapter 11 in 2007.

Billionaire investor and chairman Carl Icahn previously owned about 25% of the company, after buying more than $1 billion worth of Federal-Mogul's debt. However, in 2008, he exercised his options to buy an additional 50.1 million shares in the company; as a result, Icahn now owns some 75% of Federal-Mogul.

Following six years in bankruptcy, Federal-Mogul became the first leading supplier of auto parts to emerge from Chapter 11. Competitors Dana (exited 2008) and Delphi (still pending) were fast on the company's heels.

While out of bankruptcy reorganization, Federal-Mogul is carrying about $3 billion in debt, a factor that could become critical if the worldwide credit crisis continues and the company needs to refinance its debt.

After more than tripling in size since 1997, Federal-Mogul began to feel the weight of its girth. An ill-advised acquisitions bender, resulting asbestos lawsuits, and falling demand from US automakers forced the company to purge rather than binge.

While it has worked to rebuild its health, the automotive market is still feeling the ill effects of decreased demand. To maintain its flexibility, Federal-Mogul is streamlining its remaining operations. It closed two power train plants in the US and two others in Western Europe, then moved plant capacity to the lower-cost regions of Poland, Turkey, and Mexico. The company reduced the size of its aftermarket division by mothballing five distribution centers in the US, Canada, and Europe. It also is reducing its workforce by about 8,600 people, or 20% of the headcount.

HISTORY

In 1899 J. Howard Muzzy and Edward Lyon formed the Muzzy-Lyon Company, and later, subsidiary Mogul Metal Company. The two modified a printer's typecasting machine and developed a process for making die-cast engine bearings. Their first big order came in 1910, when Buick ordered 10,000 connecting rod bearings for the Buick 10. In 1924 Mogul Metal merged with Federal Bearing and Bushing to become Federal-Mogul Corporation.

In 1941 Federal-Mogul had about 50 factories dedicated to the war effort, and by 1945 sales had doubled from prewar levels. In 1955 the company acquired Bower Roller Bearing Company and changed its name to Federal-Mogul-Bower

Bearings, Inc. By the late 1950s it had nearly 100 distribution centers and sales had quadrupled in 10 years.

The company began investing in foreign manufacturing plants during the 1960s to safeguard against lower US car exports as more foreign cars entered the global market. It changed its name back to Federal-Mogul in 1965 and moved its headquarters from Detroit to Southfield, Michigan, the following year. Following a recession in the mid-1970s, Federal-Mogul realized that it was too dependent on the big automakers and began diversifying. It acquired the Mather Company, a maker of high-performance sealing products, in 1985. The next year it bought Carter Automotive (fuel pumps) and Signal-Stat (lighting and safety components).

In 1989 Dennis Gormley became CEO. He continued the diversification strategy and led the company into the automotive aftermarket. Gormley proposed a push into retail in 1992, and that year Federal-Mogul bought the aftermarket business of TRW Inc. In its effort to become the Pep Boys of the third world, the company sold parts of its manufacturing business to finance its retail ventures. By 1996 it owned about 130 retail stores, primarily in Latin America. The company lost money, and that year Gormley resigned. His successor, Dick Snell, put an immediate end to the retail fiasco.

By 1998 Federal-Mogul had sold all of its retail holdings and was concentrating on providing parts for entire engine systems. That year it made two major acquisitions: Fel-Pro, a domestic maker of gaskets and other sealing products, for $720 million, and T&N plc, a British maker of bearings, pistons, and brake pads, and Europe's largest asbestos maker during the 1980s. T&N was picked up on the cheap, as its stock was depressed by looming asbestos lawsuits. The decision would prove a grave one for Federal-Mogul.

Driving further into the aftermarket, Federal-Mogul paid $1.9 billion for the automotive business of Cooper Industries (Champion spark plugs, windshield wipers, steering and suspension parts, brake parts). UK-based LucasVarity rejected Federal-Mogul's $6.4 billion buyout offer in 1999 in favor of a $7 billion offer from TRW.

In 2000 Federal-Mogul announced plans to close 22 North American replacement parts warehouses and consolidate 18 manufacturing plants in Europe and Asia. Despite the proposed cutbacks aimed at revitalizing the company, CEO Richard Snell stepped down that year. Federal-Mogul director Robert Miller replaced Snell as chairman and became the interim CEO.

In 2001 Frank Macher, a former Ford and ITT Automotive executive, was named CEO. Not long after, in the midst of the economic slowdown, Federal-Mogul announced that it would cut its salaried workforce by almost 9%. In August the company acquired 85% of WSK Gorzyce, a Polish piston maker. Later in 2001 Federal-Mogul filed for Chapter 11 bankruptcy protection as a result of the asbestos lawsuits it inherited from the 1998 acquisition of T&N plc (it emerged from bankruptcy reorganization in 2007).

In 2004 the company sold its large bearing operations in South Africa and Germany, as well as its Dayton, Ohio, transmission operations.

Early in 2005 the company named José Maria Alapont as CEO. Carl Icahn was appointed chairman in 2008 after acquiring an additional 50% stake in Federal-Mogul.

EXECUTIVES

Chairman: Carl C. Icahn, age 73,
$9,604,000 total compensation
President, CEO, and Director: José Maria Alapont,
age 58, $3,314,205 total compensation
VP, Controller, and Chief Accounting Officer:
Alan Haughie, age 45
VP and CIO: Alston German, age 44
SVP Global Vehicle Safety and Protection:
René L.F. Dalleur, age 55,
$1,031,400 total compensation
SVP Aftermarket Products and Services:
Ramzi Y. Hermiz, age 43
SVP Powertrain Bearings and Sealings:
Gérard Chochoy, age 55, $1,135,020 total compensation
SVP Business and Operations Strategy: Jean Brunol,
age 56, $1,411,342 total compensation
SVP Sales and Marketing: William (Steve) Bowers,
age 56
SVP Customer Satisfaction and Global Manufacturing:
Eric McAlexander, age 52
SVP Global Aftermarket: James (Jay) Burkhart, age 51
SVP Global Human Resources and Organization:
Pascal Goachet, age 58
SVP, General Counsel, and Secretary: Robert L. Katz,
age 46
SVP Global Purchasing: Markus Wermers, age 44
VP and Treasurer: David A. Bozynski, age 54
**VP Corporate Communications and Government
Relations:** Steven K. Gaut, age 47
VP Investor Relations: David Pouliot
Auditors: Ernst & Young LLP

LOCATIONS

HQ: Federal-Mogul Corporation
26555 Northwestern Hwy., Southfield, MI 48033
Phone: 248-354-7700   **Fax:** 248-354-8950
Web: www.federal-mogul.com

2008 Sales

	$ mil.	% of total
US	2,597	38
Germany	1,372	20
France	565	8
UK	339	5
Other countries	1,993	29
Total	**6,866**	**100**

PRODUCTS/OPERATIONS

2008 Sales

	$ mil.	% of total
Global Aftermarket	2,637	38
Powertrain energy	2,085	30
Powertrain sealing & bearings	1,048	15
Vehicle safety & protection	717	11
Automotive products	379	6
Total	**6,866**	**100**

Selected Products

Aftermarket
 Bearings and seals
 Camshafts
 Engine bearings
 Friction products (brake drums, linings, pads, and
  rotors)
 Fuel pumps
 Gaskets
 Lighting products
 Oil pumps
 Piston rings
 Pistons
 Spark plugs
 Steering and suspension products
 Timing components
 Valvetrain components
 Wipers

Powertrain Systems
 Camshafts
 Connecting rods
 Engine bearings
 Large bearings
 Piston pins, rings, and liners
 Pistons
 Sintered products
Sealing Systems and Systems Protection Products
 Dynamic seals
 Gaskets
Friction Products
 Brake shoes
 Discs
 Pads

COMPETITORS

Affinia Group
Aisin Seiki
Akebono Brake
ArvinMeritor
ATC Technology
Bendix Commercial Vehicle Systems
Continental AG
Cooper-Standard Automotive
Daido Steel
Dana Holding
Delphi Corp.
Dorman Products
Edelbrock
EnPro
Everett Smith Group
Freudenberg-NOK
Gates Corp.
GKN
Hastings Manufacturing
Honeywell International
Keystone Automotive Industries
Kolbenschmidt Pierburg
Linamar Corp.
LKQ
Mahle International
MAN
MGI Coutier
Miba
Motorcar Parts
NGK SPARK PLUG
Nippon Piston Ring
Prestolite Electric
Remy International
Robert Bosch
SKD Automotive
SPX
Stanadyne
Standard Motor Products
Stant Manufacturing
Sumitomo Metal Industries
Trico Products
TRW Automotive
Turbodyne
Twin Disc
Universal Manufacturing
Valeo
Visteon

HISTORICAL FINANCIALS

Company Type: Public

Income Statement

FYE: December 31

	REVENUE ($ mil.)	NET INCOME ($ mil.)	NET PROFIT MARGIN	EMPLOYEES
12/08	6,865.6	(467.9)	—	43,400
12/07	6,913.9	1,412.3	20.4%	50,000
12/06	6,326.4	(549.6)	—	43,100
12/05	6,286.0	(334.2)	—	—
12/04	6,174.1	(334.0)	—	—
Annual Growth	**2.7%**	**—**	**—**	**0.3%**

2008 Year-End Financials

Debt ratio: 291.0%
Return on equity: —
Cash ($ mil.): 888
Current ratio: 2.07
Long-term debt ($ mil.): 2,768

No. of shares (mil.): 99
Dividends
Yield: 0.0%
Payout: —
Market value ($ mil.): 420

Stock History

NASDAQ (GM): FDML

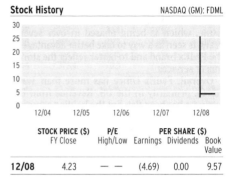

	STOCK PRICE ($) FY Close	P/E High/Low	PER SHARE ($) Earnings	Dividends	Book Value
12/08	4.23	— —	(4.69)	0.00	9.57

FedEx Corporation

Holding company FedEx hopes its package of subsidiaries will keep delivering significant market share. Its FedEx Express unit is the world's #1 express transportation provider, delivering about 3.4 million packages daily to more than 220 countries and territories. It maintains a fleet of about 655 aircraft and more than 51,000 motor vehicles and trailers. To complement the express delivery business, FedEx Ground provides small-package ground delivery in North America, and less-than-truckload (LTL) carrier FedEx Freight hauls larger shipments. FedEx Office stores offer a variety of document-related and other business services and serve as retail hubs for other FedEx units.

FedEx continues to invest in its signature express delivery business, which accounts for about two-thirds of sales. In June 2009, the company inked a deal with OfficeMax to provide express and ground shipping services at all US OfficeMax retail stores (more than 900 locations). Going into effect in late 2009, the deal will fortify FedEx's already vast retail network.

The express unit is also working to expand outside the US, particularly in China and India and in Europe. In 2009 FedEx launched operations at a new Asia/Pacific hub at the Guangzhou Baiyun International Airport in southern China. The hub replaced a smaller one located in the Philippines. In 2007 FedEx Express spent about $430 million to buy out DTW Group (its joint venture partner in China) and acquire DTW Group's domestic delivery network. It also acquired PAFEX, which had provided express delivery service in India under contract with FedEx since 2002, for about $30 million.

In the US, FedEx has been building out the networks of both FedEx Ground and FedEx Freight, which have been the company's fastest-growing units. To boost FedEx Freight's long-haul capabilities, FedEx in 2006 paid about $790 million for LTL carrier Watkins Motor Lines and the assets of Watkins' Canadian unit, Watkins Canada Express. They were renamed FedEx National LTL and FedEx Freight Canada, respectively.

its holdings. In late 2008 Fifth Third took over some $250 million in deposits from Florida's Freedom Bank, which was declared insolvent and placed into receivership by the FDIC earlier that year. The acquisition increases Fifth Third's reach in Florida by adding four branches.

The company is eyeing the sale of some of its noncore operations to help it weather rising mortgage defaults.

Fifth Third operates on an affiliate model, dividing its business operations into separate geographic regions. Each affiliate has considerable autonomy, on the grounds that local executives can make better business decisions applicable to their regions.

In 2009 Fifth Third sold a 51% stake in its processing division to Advent International for $561 million. Fifth Third will retain a 49% stake in First Third Processing Solutions.

Fifth Third traces its unusual name to the 1908 merger of Cincinnati's Fifth National Bank and Third National Bank. Another financial services firm from the company's hometown, insurer Cincinnati Financial Corporation, was once Fifth Third's largest shareholder. CFC sold its entire Fifth Third stake in 2009.

HISTORY

In 1863 a group of Cincinnati businessmen opened the Third National Bank inside a Masonic temple to serve the Ohio River trade. Acquiring the Bank of the Ohio Valley (founded 1858) in 1871, the firm progressed until the panic of 1907. Third National survived, and in 1908 consolidated with Fifth National, forming the Fifth Third National Bank of Cincinnati. The newly organized bank acquired two local banks in 1910.

A second bank consolidation, in 1919, resulted in Fifth Third's affiliation with Union Savings Bank and Trust Company, permitting the bank to establish branches, theretofore forbidden by regulators. The company acquired the assets and offices of five more banks and thrifts that year, operating them as branches.

In 1927 the bank merged its operations with the Union Trust Company, forming the Fifth Third Union Trust. With its combined strength, it weathered the Great Depression and acquired three more banks between 1930 and 1933. However, the Depression also brought massive banking regulations to the industry, limiting Fifth Third's acquisitions.

In the postwar years and during the 1950s and 1960s, the bank expanded its consumer banking services, offering traveler's checks. Under CEO Bill Rowe, son of former CEO John Rowe, the firm emphasized the convenience of its locations and increased hours of operations.

In the 1970s Fifth Third shifted its lending program's emphasis from commercial loans to consumer credit and launched its ATM and telephone banking services. Aware that the bank was technologically unprepared for the onslaught of electronic information, Fifth Third expanded its data processing and information services resources, forming the basis for its Midwest Payment Systems division.

The company formed Fifth Third Bancorp, a holding company, and began to branch within Ohio (branching had previously been limited to the home county) in 1975. Ten years later, more deregulation allowed the bank to move into contiguous states. Focused on consumer banking, and with cautious underwriting policies, Fifth Third weathered the real estate bust and

leveraged-buyout problems of the 1980s and acquired new outlets cheaply by buying several small banks, as well as branches from larger banks. It acquired the American National Bank in Kentucky and moved further afield with its purchase of the Sovereign Savings Bank in Palm Harbor, Florida, in 1991.

The company continued to expand, buying several banks and thrifts in Ohio in 1997 and 1998. In 1999 Fifth Third moved into Indiana in a big way with its purchase of CNB Bancshares, then solidified its position in the state with the acquisition of Peoples Bank of Indianapolis. Fifth Third also moved into new business areas, buying mortgage banker W. Lyman Case, broker-dealer The Ohio Company (1998), and Cincinnati-based commercial mortgage banker Vanguard Financial (1999). The company began to offer online foreign exchange via its FX Internet Trading Web in 2000.

In 2001 Fifth Third bought money manager Maxus Investments and added some 300 bank branches with its purchase of Capital Holdings (Ohio and Michigan) and Old Kent Financial (Michigan, Indiana, and Illinois), its largest-ever acquisition.

Fifth Third exited the property/casualty insurance brokerage business in 2002, selling its operations to Hub International.

Also that year, Fifth Third arranged to enter Tennessee via its planned purchase of Franklin Financial. But the deal was stalled as industry regulators investigated Fifth Third's risk management procedures and internal controls. A moratorium on acquisitions was placed on the bank during the investigation. It was lifted in 2004, and the purchase of Franklin was completed not long afterwards. That opened the door for Fifth Third's acquisition of First National Bankshares of Florida in 2005.

EXECUTIVES

Chairman, Fifth Third Bank, Southern Indiana:
H. Lee Cooper III
Chairman, President, and CEO; President and CEO, Fifth Third Bank: Kevin T. Kabat, age 52, $3,132,787 total compensation
Chairman, Fifth Third Bank, Central Ohio:
Donald B. Shackelford, age 73
Chairman, Fifth Third Bank, Tennessee:
Gordon E. Inman
Chairman, Fifth Third Bank, Northwestern Ohio:
John S. Szuch
Chairman, Fifth Third Bancorp, Central Florida:
Charlie W. Brinkley Jr., age 54
EVP and COO: Greg D. Carmichael, age 47, $1,652,443 total compensation
EVP and CFO: Ross J. Kari, age 50
EVP and CIO: Joseph Robinson
Chief Marketing Officer: Larry S. Magnesen, age 51
EVP and Chief Human Resources Officer:
Nancy R. Phillips, age 41
SEVP; President and CEO, Fifth Third Bank, Cincinnati: Robert A. (Bob) Sullivan, age 54, $1,236,869 total compensation
EVP, Secretary, and General Counsel: Paul L. Reynolds, age 47
EVP and Chief Risk Officer: Mary E. Tuuk, age 35
EVP; President, Fifth Third Processing Solutions:
Charles D. Drucker, age 45, $1,307,434 total compensation
VP Corporate Communications: Debra DeCourcy
Director of Investor Relations and Corporate Analysis:
Jeff Richardson, age 44
Auditors: Deloitte & Touche LLP

LOCATIONS

HQ: Fifth Third Bancorp
38 Fountain Square Plaza, Fifth Third Center
Cincinnati, OH 45263
Phone: 513-579-5300   **Fax:** 513-534-0629
Web: www.53.com

PRODUCTS/OPERATIONS

2008 Gross Revenues

	$ mil.	% of total
Interest		
Loans & leases, including fees	4,935	58
Securities	660	8
Other short-term investments	13	—
Noninterest		
Electronic payment processing revenue	912	11
Service charges on deposits	641	7
Corporate banking	444	5
Investment advisory revenue	353	4
Mortgage Banking	199	2
Other	363	5
Total	**8,640**	**100**

2008 Assets

	$ mil.	% of total
Cash & due from banks	2,739	2
Securities held for sale	12,728	11
Loans held for sale	1,452	1
Net loans & leases	81,356	68
Other	21,489	18
Total	**119,764**	**100**

Selected Subsidiaries

Fifth Third Financial Corporation
  Fifth Third Bank (Ohio)
    Card Management Corporation
    Fifth Third Asset Management, Inc.
    The Fifth Third Company
    Fifth Third Holdings, LLC
    Fifth Third Insurance Agency, Inc.
    Fifth Third International Company
      Fifth Third Trade Services Limited (Hong Kong)
    The Fifth Third Leasing Company
      The Fifth Third Auto Leasing Trust
      Fifth Third Foreign Lease Management, LLC
    Fifth Third Mortgage Company
      Fifth Third Real Estate Investment Trust, Inc.
    Fifth Third Mortgage Reinsurance Company
    Fifth Third Real Estate Capital Markets Company
    Fifth Third Securities, Inc.
  Fifth Third Bank (Michigan)
    Community Financial Services, Inc.
    Fifth Third Auto Funding, LLC
    Fifth Third Funding, LLC
    GNB Management, LLC
      FNB Investment Company, Inc.
      GNB Realty, LLC
    Home Equity of America, Inc.
    Old Kent Mortgage Services, Inc.
  Fifth Third Bank, National Association
  Fifth Third Community Development Corporation
    Fifth Third New Markets Development Co., LLC
  Fifth Third Investment Company
  Fifth Third Reinsurance Company, LTD (Turks and Caicos Islands)
  Fountain Square Life Reinsurance Company, Ltd. (Turks and Caicos Islands)
  Vista Settlement Services, LLC

COMPETITORS

Bank of America	JPMorgan Chase
Cat Financial	KeyCorp
Citigroup	Marshall & Ilsley
Comerica	Metavante
First Data	Northern Trust
FirstMerit	PNC Financial
Harris Bankcorp	U.S. Bancorp
Huntington Bancshares	Wells Fargo

HISTORICAL FINANCIALS

Company Type: Public

Income Statement

FYE: December 31

	ASSETS ($ mil.)	NET INCOME ($ mil.)	INCOME AS % OF ASSETS	EMPLOYEES
12/08	119,764.0	(2,113.0)	—	22,423
12/07	110,962.0	1,076.0	1.0%	22,678
12/06	100,669.0	1,184.0	1.2%	21,362
12/05	105,225.0	1,549.0	1.5%	22,901
12/04	94,456.0	1,525.0	1.6%	21,027
Annual Growth	6.1%	—	—	1.6%

2008 Year-End Financials

Equity as % of assets: 6.5%
Return on assets: —
Return on equity: —
Long-term debt ($ mil.): 13,585
No. of shares (mil.): 795

Dividends
Yield: 9.1%
Payout: —
Market value ($ mil.): 6,569
Sales ($ mil.): 6,460

Stock History

NASDAQ (GS): FITB

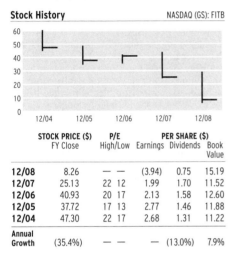

	STOCK PRICE ($) FY Close	P/E High/Low	PER SHARE ($) Earnings	Dividends	Book Value
12/08	8.26	— —	(3.94)	0.75	15.19
12/07	25.13	22 12	1.99	1.70	11.52
12/06	40.93	20 17	2.13	1.58	12.60
12/05	37.72	17 13	2.77	1.46	11.88
12/04	47.30	22 17	2.68	1.31	11.22
Annual Growth	(35.4%)	— —	—	(13.0%)	7.9%

The First American Corporation

The First American Corporation believes that when you're buying real estate, more information is better. Along with good old title insurance from its First American Title subsidiary, the company's financial services arm also provides specialty property/casualty insurance, escrow services, equity loans, and home warranties. First American's information technology arm provides real estate tax monitoring, flood-zone certification, appraisal services, and credit-reporting services for property buyers and mortgage lenders. The company is also making use of extensive databases from its subsidiary First Advantage to offer employee screening and credit reporting for landlords and automotive lenders.

Although First American makes the majority of its money in the US (the company underwrites almost 25% of all title insurance policies in the US), it provides title insurance in countries and territories around the world and has applied extra sales efforts in Australia, Canada, Eastern Europe, South Korea, and the UK. Growth in foreign markets will be key to the company's financial services future as the US housing market remains stagnant in the wake of the subprime lending meltdown.

In 2009 the company moved into Russia, serving Moscow and St. Petersburg to start. It already served Croatia, Serbia, and — through a 38% holding in FU Gayrimenkul Danmanlk — Turkey. The region is overseen by First American's First Title CEE (Central and Eastern Europe), headquartered in Budapest.

Acquisitions and joint ventures have been key to First American's expansion across the real estate services and information technology services industries. Its holdings now include Data Tree, owner of an extensive database of imaged property records; Data Trace Information Services, a joint venture with LandAmerica; and First American Corelogic, a joint venture with Experian. These are helping First American Financial reach its goal: eliminating costly local searches by providing a central source for property titles. However, even with all of the new information services companies, title insurance policies still represent 60% of the company's annual earnings.

As the US housing market first slipped and then slid, First American saw its losses mounting and made plans in early 2008 to split apart, spinning off its insurance segments into a new company to be named First American Financial. However, with sharp cuts to its staff and expenses, the company managed to wrangle an actual income by the middle of 2008 and postponed the planned division.

Chairman emeritus D. P. and chairman and CEO Parker Kennedy are descendants of the founder of the company, C. E. Parker.

HISTORY

In 1889, when Los Angeles was on its way to becoming a real city, the more countrified residents to the south (including the Irvine Company's founding family) formed Orange County, a peaceful realm of citrus groves where land transactions were assisted by title companies Orange County Abstract and Santa Ana Abstract. In 1894 the firms merged under the leadership of local businessman C. E. Parker. For three decades, the resulting Orange County Title limited its business to title searches.

In 1924, as real estate transactions became more complex (in part because of mineral-rights issues related to Southern California's oil boom), Orange County Title began offering title insurance and escrow services. The company remained under Parker family management until 1930, when H. A. Gardner took over and guided it through the Depression. In 1943 the company returned to Parker family control.

In 1957 the company began a major expansion beyond Orange County. The new First American Title Insurance and Trust name acknowledged the firm's expansion into trust and custody operations. Donald Kennedy (C. E. Parker's grandson) took over in 1963 and took the company public the next year.

In 1968 First American Financial was formed as a holding company for subsidiaries First American Title Insurance and First American Trust. This structure facilitated growth as the firm began opening new offices and buying all or parts of other title companies, including Title Guaranty Co. of Wyoming, Security Title & Trust (San Antonio), and Ticore, Inc. (Portland, Oregon), all purchased in 1968.

The 1970s were a quiet time for the company, but it began growing again in the 1980s, as savings and loan deregulation jump-started the commercial real estate market in Southern California. First American diversified into home warranty and real estate tax services. In 1988, on the brink of the California meltdown, the company bought an industrial loan corporation to make commercial real estate loans.

Reduced property sales during California's early 1990s real estate crash and recession rocked company results. Fluctuating interest rates didn't help the tremulous bottom lines. In 1994 Donald Kennedy became chairman; his son Parker became president.

As part of its expansion effort, First American bought CREDCO (mortgage credit reporting) and Flood Data Services (flood zone certification) in 1995.

In 1998 and 1999, First American's acquisitions brought into the company's fold resident-screening services and providers of mortgage loan and loan default management software.

In 2000 the company bought National Information Group, a provider of tax service, flood certification, and insurance tracking for the mortgage industry. That year the company partnered with Transamerica to create the US's largest property database.

Following a Colorado Division of Insurance investigation into the company's First American Title Insurance subsidiary's alleged practice of offering kickbacks in exchange for business, First American reached a settlement in 2005 to pay $24 million back to US consumers affected by such practices, which it has since discontinued.

First American restructured itself a bit during 2005. The company combined its credit information and screening operations into its risk mitigation and business solutions segment. It also moved its credit information group over to risk mitigation and business services firm First Advantage. As part of the deal, First American bumped its stake in First Advantage up to 80%. That year the company also acquired San Francisco-based LoanPerformance, a leading provider of mortgage analytics.

EXECUTIVES

Chairman and CEO; Chairman, First American Title Insurance Company: Parker S. Kennedy, age 61, $3,499,522 total compensation
Vice Chairman; Head of Information Solutions: Frank V. McMahon, age 49, $3,359,181 total compensation
Vice Chairman, First American Real Estate Information Services: Joseph R. Reppert
COO: Dennis J. Gilmore, age 50, $2,685,734 total compensation
CFO and Treasurer: Anthony S. (Buddy) Piszel, age 54
EVP and CIO: Roger S. Hull
CTO: Evan H. Jafa
CIO, Canada, First Canadian Title: Sam Dotson
EVP and CIO Security and Compliance, First American Real Estate Information Services: Laurel B. Geise
SVP and Chief Accounting Officer: Max O. Valdes, age 54
VP and Chief Marketing Officer: Sandra Bell
Chief Actuary: David L. Ruhm
VP and Chief Diversity and Inclusion Officer: Karen J. Collins
Chief Security Officer: Albert B. Kirkpatrick

EVP Title Insurance and Services; Vice Chairman, First
  American Title Insurance Company: Gary L. Kermott,
  age 55
EVP; SEVP and COO, First American Title Insurance
  Company: Curt A. Caspersen, age 53
EVP Technology: John M. Hollenbeck, age 47
SVP Corporate Communications: Jo Etta Bandy
SVP, General Counsel, and Interim Secretary:
  Kenneth D. (Ken) DeGiorgio, age 38
President, Information and Outsourcing Solutions
  Segment: Barry M. Sando, age 49,
  $1,874,933 total compensation
President and CEO, First Advantage Corporation:
  Anand J. Nallathambi, age 47,
  $3,414,121 total compensation
Vice Chairman and President, First American Title
  Insurance: Curt G. Johnson,
  $2,051,021 total compensation
Auditors: PricewaterhouseCoopers LLP

LOCATIONS

HQ: The First American Corporation
  1 First American Way, Santa Ana, CA 92707
Phone: 714-250-3000
Web: www.firstam.com

PRODUCTS/OPERATIONS

2008 Sales

	$ mil.	% of total
Title insurance	3,912.1	62
Risk mitigation & business solutions	782.3	12
Information & outsourcing solutions	739.2	12
Data & analytic solutions	596.0	9
Specialty insurance	297.8	5
Corporate	0.3	—
Adjustments	(113.9)	—
Total	6,213.8	100

COMPETITORS

American Home Shield
Fidelity National Financial
Home Buyers Warranty
Investors Title
LandAmerica Financial Group
North American Title
Old Republic
Stewart Information Services
Ticor Title Co.
Transnation Title Insurance

HISTORICAL FINANCIALS

Company Type: Public

Income Statement

FYE: December 31

	ASSETS ($ mil.)	NET INCOME ($ mil.)	INCOME AS % OF ASSETS	EMPLOYEES
12/08	8,730.1	(26.3)	—	31,411
12/07	8,647.9	(3.1)	—	37,354
12/06	8,224.3	287.7	3.5%	39,670
12/05	7,598.6	485.3	6.4%	35,444
12/04	6,208.4	349.1	5.6%	30,994
Annual Growth	8.9%	—	—	0.3%

2008 Year-End Financials

Equity as % of assets: 30.8%
Return on assets: —
Return on equity: —
Long-term debt ($ mil.): —
No. of shares (mil.): 93
Dividends
  Yield: 3.0%
  Payout: —
Market value ($ mil.): 2,697
Sales ($ mil.): 6,214

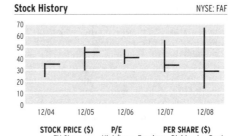

Stock History

NYSE: FAF

	STOCK PRICE ($) FY Close	P/E High/Low		Earnings	PER SHARE ($) Dividends	Book Value
12/08	28.89	—	—	(0.28)	0.88	28.83
12/07	34.12	—	—	(0.03)	0.88	31.97
12/06	40.68	16	12	2.92	0.72	34.30
12/05	45.30	10	6	4.97	0.72	32.20
12/04	35.14	9	6	3.83	0.60	26.39
Annual Growth	(4.8%)	—	—	—	10.0%	2.2%

FirstEnergy Corp.

FirstEnergy's first goal is to deliver power, but
its second goal is to survive deregulation. Its
utilities provide electricity to 4.5 million customers in Ohio, Pennsylvania, and New Jersey,
three states that are ushering in power-industry
competition. The company's domestic power
plants have a total generating capacity of more
than 14,170 MW, most generated by coal-fired
plants. Subsidiary FirstEnergy Solutions trades
energy commodities in deregulated markets
throughout the US, and has more than 120,000
accounts. FirstEnergy's other nonregulated operations include electrical and mechanical contracting and energy planning and procurement.

In response to the deregulation of the US utility market, the company has not only branched
out into new non-utility activities, but it has also
expanded its regulated utility operations into new
territories. FirstEnergy's strategy led to its acquisition of GPU, which made it one of the largest
electric utility holding companies in the US and
nearly doubled its customer count.

As states push to reduce carbon emissions,
FirstEnergy is adding renewable energy to its
plant mix. In 2006 it acquired 34.5 MW of output from the Casselman Wind Power Project
under development in Somerset County, Pennsylvania. In 2009 FirstEnergy announced plans
to reengineer units 4 and 5 at its R.E. Burger
Plant in Shadyside, Ohio, to generate electricity
primarily with biomass. When this plant is completed, FirstEnergy's portfolio of renewable energy will total more than 1,100 MW.

HISTORY

FirstEnergy (as Ohio Edison) came to light in
1893 as the Akron Electric Light and Power
Company. After several mergers, the business
went bankrupt and was sold in 1899 to Akron
Traction and Electric Company, which became
Northern Ohio Power and Light (NOP&L).

In 1930 Commonwealth and Southern (C&S)
bought NOP&L and merged it with four other
Ohio utility holding companies to form Ohio
Edison. The new firm increased sales during the
Depression by selling electric appliances.

The Public Utility Holding Company Act of
1935 (passed to rein in uncontrolled utilities)
caught up with C&S in 1949, forcing it to divest
Ohio Edison. Rival Ohio Public Service was also
divested from its holding company, and in 1950
Ohio Edison bought it.

In 1967, after two decades of expansion, Ohio
Edison and three other Ohio and Pennsylvania
utilities formed the Central Area Power Coordination Group (CAPCO) to share new power-plant
costs, including the construction of the Beaver
Valley nuclear plant (1970-76). Although the
CAPCO partners agreed in 1980 to cancel four
planned nukes, in 1985 Ohio Edison took part in
building the Perry Unit 1 and Beaver Valley Unit
2 nuclear plants.

The federal Energy Policy Act of 1992 allowed
wholesale power competition, and to satisfy new
federal requirements, Ohio Edison formed a six-
state transmission alliance in 1996 with fellow
utilities Centerior Energy, Allegheny Power System, and Dominion Resources' Virginia Power to
coordinate their grids.

Ohio Edison paid about $1.5 billion in 1997 for
Centerior Energy, formed in 1986 as a holding
company for Toledo Edison and Cleveland Electric. Ohio Edison and Centerior, both burdened
by high-cost generating plants, merged to cut
costs, and the expanded energy concern was renamed FirstEnergy Corp.

Looking toward deregulation, FirstEnergy
began buying mechanical construction, contracting, and energy management companies in
1997, including Roth Bros. and RPC Mechanical.
In 1998 it added nine more. FirstEnergy then
ventured into natural gas operations by purchasing MARBEL Energy.

Power marketers Federal Energy Sales and the
Power Co. of America couldn't deliver the juice
to FirstEnergy during the summer of 1998's
hottest days. FirstEnergy later sued Federal Energy for $25 million in damages. The next year
it bought electricity outage insurance.

Pennsylvania began large-scale electric power
competition in 1999, when Ohio lawmakers
passed deregulation legislation. To comply with
state regulation, FirstEnergy agreed to trade
power plants, including Beaver Valley, with DQE
(now Duquesne Light Holdings). That year
brought trouble when the EPA named First-
Energy and six other utilities in a suit that
charged the utility with noncompliance of the
Clean Air Act.

In 2000 FirstEnergy agreed to acquire New
Jersey-based electric utility GPU in an $11.9 bil-
lion deal; it became one of the largest US utilities
in 2001 when it completed the acquisition, which
added three utilities (Jersey Central Power &
Light, Metropolitan Edison, and Pennsylvania
Electric) serving 2.1 million electricity customers.

Following the acquisition, FirstEnergy agreed
to sell an 80% stake in GPU's UK utility, Midlands
Electricity, to UtiliCorp (later Aquila) in a $2 bil-
lion deal, completed in 2002. It also agreed to sell
four Ohio coal-fired plants (2,500 MW) to NRG
Energy for $1.5 billion; however, the deal was
later canceled. To focus on its domestic operations, FirstEnergy sold the international energy
assets gained through the acquisition of GPU, including Australian utility (GasNet) and UK utility (Midlands Electricity). It also exited its
Argentine utility business (Emdersa).

The US-Canada Power System Outage Task
Force, which investigated the massive August
14, 2003, blackout that affected eight states and
a Canadian province, released its interim report
that November and a final report the following

year. The initial report found that FirstEnergy violated four voluntary standards set by the North American Electric Reliability Council and stated that the blackout was largely caused by FirstEnergy's failure to set up proper communication and monitoring procedures for its transmission assets. The report also cited the company's failure to trim trees, which caused several major transmission lines in its service territory to short-circuit during the incident.

FirstEnergy paid a total of $90 million to settle federal lawsuits over its involvement in the blackout, as well as other securities and derivative issues, without admitting any wrongdoing. FirstEnergy faced a formal SEC investigation into financial restatements (in 2003) and an extended nuclear power plant outage (2002-04); the investigation was not related to the blackout and was an extension of an informal SEC inquiry.

To settle with the US Environmental Protection Agency, FirstEnergy agreed in 2005 to pay an estimated $1.1 billion in fines and for anti-pollution devices to be installed at its coal-burning plants in Ohio and Pennsylvania.

EXECUTIVES

Chairman: George M. Smart, age 63
President, CEO, and Director, First Energy Corp and FirstEnergy Service: Anthony J. Alexander, age 57, $13,448,986 total compensation
President and Chief Nuclear Officer, FirstEnergy Nuclear Operating: Joseph J. (Joe) Hagan, age 58
EVP and CFO: Mark T. Clark, age 58, $3,639,120 total compensation
VP and Chief Information Officer FirstEnergy Service Company: Bennett L. Gaines
VP, Controller, and Chief Accounting Officer FirstEnergy Corp and FirstEnergy Service: Harvey L. Wagner, age 56
VP, Corporate Secretary, and Chief Ethics Officer FirstEnergy and FirstEnergy Service: Rhonda S. Ferguson
VP Corporate Risk and Chief Risk Officer: William D. Byrd, age 54
EVP; President FirstEnergy Utilities: Richard R. (Dick) Grigg, age 60, $3,505,709 total compensation
EVP and General Counsel: Leila L. Vespoli, age 49, $3,201,082 total compensation
EVP; President FirstEnergy Generation: Gary R. Leidich, age 58, $4,741,210 total compensation
SVP Human Resources: Lynn M. Cavalier, age 57
SVP: Carole B. Snyder, age 63
SVP Governmental Affairs: David C. Luff, age 61
SVP Energy Delivery and Customer Service, FirstEnergy Solutions: Charles E. (Chuck) Jones, age 53
VP Human Resources: Dennis L. Dabney
Auditors: PricewaterhouseCoopers LLP

LOCATIONS

HQ: FirstEnergy Corp.
76 S. Main St., Akron, OH 44308
Phone: 800-633-4766 **Fax:** 330-384-3866
Web: www.firstenergycorp.com

FirstEnergy serves electricity customers in New Jersey, Ohio, and Pennsylvania.

PRODUCTS/OPERATIONS

2008 Sales

	$ mil.	% of total
Energy delivery services	9,166	67
Ohio transitional generation services	2,902	21
Competitive energy services	1,571	11
Other	72	1
Adjustments	(84)	—
Total	**13,627**	**100**

Electric Utility Subsidiaries

American Transmission Systems, Inc.
The Cleveland Electric Illuminating Company (The Illuminating Company)
Jersey Central Power & Light Company (JCP&L)
Metropolitan Edison Company (Met-Ed)
Ohio Edison Company
Pennsylvania Electric Company (Penelec)
Pennsylvania Power Company (Penn Power)
The Toledo Edison Company

Selected Unregulated Subsidiaries

FirstEnergy Nuclear Operating Co. (nuclear generation facilities)
FirstEnergy Properties, Inc.
FirstEnergy Securities Transfer Company
FirstEnergy Service Company
FirstEnergy Solutions Corp. (retail and wholesale energy marketing and management services)
FirstEnergy Ventures Corp.
GPU Diversified Holdings, LLC
GPU Nuclear, Inc. (nuclear plant management and decommissioning)

COMPETITORS

AEP	Exelon
Allegheny Energy	Exelon Energy
Delmarva Power	Integrys Energy Group
Dominion Resources	Peabody Energy
DPL	PG&E Corporation
Duke Energy	PPL Corporation
Duquesne Light	PSEG Energy Holdings
Duquesne Light Holdings	Public Service Enterprise
Dynegy	Southern Company
EnergySolve	Vectren

HISTORICAL FINANCIALS

Company Type: Public

Income Statement

FYE: December 31

	REVENUE ($ mil.)	NET INCOME ($ mil.)	NET PROFIT MARGIN	EMPLOYEES
12/08	13,627.0	1,342.0	9.8%	14,698
12/07	12,802.0	1,309.0	10.2%	14,534
12/06	11,501.0	1,254.0	10.9%	13,739
12/05	11,989.0	891.0	7.4%	14,586
12/04	12,453.0	878.2	7.1%	15,245
Annual Growth	**2.3%**	**11.2%**	**—**	**(0.9%)**

2008 Year-End Financials

Debt ratio: 109.9%
Return on equity: 15.6%
Cash ($ mil.): 545
Current ratio: 0.43
Long-term debt ($ mil.): 9,100
No. of shares (mil.): 310
Dividends
 Yield: 4.5%
 Payout: 50.2%
Market value ($ mil.): 15,066

Stock History

NYSE: FE

	STOCK PRICE ($) FY Close	P/E High/Low		PER SHARE ($) Earnings	Dividends	Book Value
12/08	48.58	19	9	4.38	2.20	26.71
12/07	72.34	18	14	4.22	2.00	28.95
12/06	60.30	16	13	3.81	1.80	29.13
12/05	48.99	20	14	2.61	1.67	30.22
12/04	39.51	16	13	2.67	1.50	28.78
Annual Growth	**5.3%**	**—**	**—**	**13.2%**	**10.0%**	**(1.8%)**

Fiserv, Inc.

It's 10:30, America. Do you know where your money is? Fiserv does. A leading processor of financial data, Fiserv provides check processing, software development, business support, insurance claims and transaction processing, and other information management services to the financial industry. Its clients include banks, lenders, credit unions, insurance firms, health plan administrators, and leasing companies. The company operates in three business segments: financial institution services, insurance services, and payments and industry products (via its CheckFree business, acquired in 2007). The company has offices in the US and about 15 other countries.

Fiserv hopes to capitalize on the banking industry's increasing reliance on transaction-oriented, fee-based services, which typically demand a large data-processing capability. In 2007 the company paid more than $4 billion for CheckFree, which is a leader in electronic bill payment services. In a smaller deal, it arranged to buy payment processor i_Tech from First Interstate BancSystem the following year.

As it adds new operations, the company in 2009 introduced a new marketing strategy to unify its brands under the Fiserv banner. And though highly acquisitive, the company is not averse to jettisoning businesses that are no longer central to its core operations.

In 2008 it sold most of its health business to UnitedHealth for some $775 million. The sale included Fiserv Health Plan Administration, Fiserv Health Plan Management, Innoviant Pharmacy, Avidyn Health, and other health businesses. Not included were WorkingRx (workers' compensation) and CareGain (technology), which remain with Fiserv.

The company also sold the bulk of its Fiserv ISS business, including advisor services and institutional retirement services, to TD AMERITRADE. In a separate transaction, the newly formed Trust Institution Bank (headed by former Fiserv ISS management) will acquire most of the company's investment administration services business. Fiserv will retain a minority interest in Trust Institution Bank.

The company is also selling a majority stake in Stone River (formerly Fiserv Insurance Services) to Stone Point Capital for some $540 million. Fiserv will retain a 49% stake in the unit, which changed its name to StoneRiver in 2009.

A group of customers of Bernard L. Madoff Securities filed a $1 billion lawsuit against Fiserv in 2009, alleging that the company breached its fiduciary responsibility in handling their pensions or Individual Retirement Accounts. Fiserv had acted as a service provider to Madoff on behalf of some 800 customers. Madoff was charged by federal authorities with running a $50 billion "Ponzi" scheme. Fiserv said the lawsuit had "no merit."

HISTORY

When First Bank System of Minneapolis bought Milwaukee-based Midland Bank in 1984, the head of Midland's data processing operation, George Dalton, bought the unit and then merged that operation with Sunshine State Systems, a newly independent Florida processing company headed by Leslie Muma. Christened Fiserv, the company went public in 1986. It grew by providing outsourcing services to small banks and thrifts.

In the 1990s, Fiserv began targeting larger clients. But industry consolidation sometimes hurt the company, as when the 12-year term of a 1995 contract with Chase Manhattan was reduced to three after Chase and Chemical Bank merged in 1996.

As banks moved into new areas, Fiserv went along. In the late 1990s it acquired BHC Financial and Hanifen, Imhoff Holdings (securities transaction processing). Other purchases that broadened its service list included Automated Financial Technology (credit union software) and Network Data Processing (administrative software for insurance companies). The push into software continued with 1999 purchases in the field of workers' compensation systems.

Also in 1999 Fiserv bolstered its client list by buying QuestPoint's check servicing business. It moved into retirement plan administration with the purchase of a unit from what is now AIG Retirement Services. In 2000 a deal announced a year earlier to provide back-office services for American Express' online Membership Banking unit fell apart, but Fiserv recovered its momentum with enhanced mortgage servicing offerings and an agreement to provide technology services to cahoot, the online banking unit of the UK's Abbey National.

Fiserv continued its acquisitive activities the next year, buying Benefit Planners (a leading employee benefit program administrator with operations in Europe, the Middle East, South America, and the US), Facilities and Services Corporation (a California-based insurance software maker), NCSI (information and services targeting the flood insurance industry), and the bank processing operations of NCR Corporation. The company that year also sold its Human Resources Information Services unit to buyout firm Gores Technology Group.

Fiserv boosted its ATM and EFT (electronic funds transfer) business with the 2002 purchase of Electronic Data Systems' Consumer Network Services unit.

The company sold its securities clearing operations to a unit of FMR in 2005.

EXECUTIVES

Chairman: Donald F. (Don) Dillon, age 69
Vice Chairman: Peter J. (Pete) Kight, age 53,
$1,460,563 total compensation
President, CEO, and Director: Jeffery W. (Jeff) Yabuki, age 48, $6,119,720 total compensation
EVP, CFO, Treasurer, and Assistant Secretary:
Thomas J. Hirsch, age 45,
$1,389,804 total compensation
EVP and CIO: Maryann Goebel
EVP, Chief Administrative Officer, General Counsel, and Secretary: Charles W. Sprague, age 59
EVP and Chief Marketing Officer:
Donald J. (Don) MacDonald, age 47
EVP; Group President, Depository Institution Services:
Stephen (Steve) Olsen, age 48
EVP; Group President, Depository Institution Core Processing: Thomas A. (Tom) Neill, age 60
EVP Corporate Development: James W. Cox, age 45
EVP Depository Institution Services:
Douglas J. (Doug) Craft, age 56

EVP; Group President, Payments and Industry Products: Rahul Gupta, age 51,
$1,219,210 total compensation
EVP Human Resources: Bridie A. Fanning, age 40
EVP; Group President, Financial Institution Services:
Thomas W. Warsop III, age 42,
$1,169,326 total compensation
EVP: Lance F. Drummond, age 55
VP Investor Relations: David Banks
VP Corporate Communications: Judy DeRango Wicks
VP Global Sales and Relationship Management:
Andrew Thompson
President, Originations and Automotive Solutions:
Kevin J. Collins, age 51
Auditors: Deloitte & Touche LLP

LOCATIONS

HQ: Fiserv, Inc.
255 Fiserv Dr., Brookfield, WI 53045
Phone: 262-879-5000   **Fax:** 262-879-5013
Web: www.fiserv.com

PRODUCTS/OPERATIONS

2008 Sales

	$ mil.	% of total
Financial services		
Processing	1,960	41
Products	184	4
Insurance		
Processing	121	3
Products	392	8
Payments		
Processing	1542	32
Products	589	12
Allowances	(49)	—
Total	**4,739**	**100**

Selected Subsidiaries

Bank Intelligence Solutions
Business Analytics for Premier
Corillian Online
Mobile Money
MyMoney
Source Capture Solution

COMPETITORS

Accenture	IBM
BA Merchant Services	Jack Henry
CGI Group	Metavante
Charles Schwab	NCR
Computer Sciences Corp.	Open Solutions
DST	Perot Systems
EDS	SAP
Fidelity National	State Street
Information Services	SunGard
First Data	Total System Services
FMR	Vertafore

HISTORICAL FINANCIALS
Company Type: Public

Income Statement
FYE: December 31

	REVENUE ($ mil.)	NET INCOME ($ mil.)	NET PROFIT MARGIN	EMPLOYEES
12/08	4,739.0	569.0	12.0%	20,000
12/07	3,922.0	439.0	11.2%	25,000
12/06	4,544.2	449.9	9.9%	23,000
12/05	4,059.5	516.4	12.7%	22,000
12/04	3,729.7	377.6	10.1%	22,000
Annual Growth	**6.2%**	**10.8%**	**—**	**(2.4%)**

2008 Year-End Financials

Debt ratio: 148.4%
Return on equity: 22.5%
Cash ($ mil.): 232
Current ratio: 1.05
Long-term debt ($ mil.): 3,850
No. of shares (mil.): 154
Dividends
  Yield: 0.0%
  Payout: —
Market value ($ mil.): 5,615

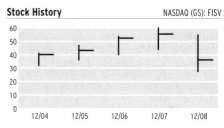

Stock History   NASDAQ (GS): FISV

	STOCK PRICE ($) FY Close	P/E High/Low		Earnings	PER SHARE ($) Dividends	Book Value
12/08	36.37	16	8	3.49	0.00	16.80
12/07	55.49	23	17	2.60	0.00	15.98
12/06	52.42	21	16	2.53	0.00	15.71
12/05	43.27	17	13	2.70	0.00	15.97
12/04	40.19	21	17	1.91	0.00	16.61
Annual Growth	**(2.5%)**	**—**	**—**	**16.3%**	**—**	**0.3%**

Flowers Foods

Look for Flowers Foods in your breadbox, not your garden — the company is one of the largest wholesale bakeries in the US. Its Flowers Bakeries unit produces, markets, and distributes fresh breads, buns, rolls, and bakery goodies to retail and foodservice customers throughout the southern US. The company's brand names include ButterKrust, Cobblestone Mill, and Nature's Own. The company's Flowers Specialty division makes snack cakes and frozen bread products for retail, vending, and co-pack customers nationwide. Flowers Bakeries also rolls out hamburger buns for foodservice chains such as Burger King, Hardee's, Outback Steakhouse, Wendy's, and Whataburger.

Flowers Bakeries makes private-label breads for food retailers. Wal-Mart is the company's largest customer, representing about 21% of its 2008 sales. The company has a long-term strategy of organic and strategic growth that includes developing new products, expanding its distribution system, and acquiring other bakeries. It has completed more than 100 acquisitions in the past 40 years.

Continuing its long-term acquisition strategy, it acquired Holsum Bakers in 2008. Holsum operates two bakeries in the Phoenix area and supplies both retail and foodservice customers with fresh baked goods. Flowers also acquired Lakeland, Florida-based ButterKrust Bakery in 2008. ButterKrust sells its Country Hearth, Rich Harvest, and Sunbeam brands throughout Florida. The acquisition increases Flowers' production capacity, a growing market for the company. That year it also acquired Holsum Bakery in Phoenix, which carries brands including Holsum, Aunt Hatties, and Roman Meal.

Board member J.V. Shields Jr. owns approximately 7% of the company.

HISTORY

Georgia native William Flowers and his brother Joseph opened the Flowers Ice Cream Co. in the winter resort town of Thomasville, Georgia, in 1914 to serve wealthy visitors from the North. Seeing that there was no bakery in the town (the nearest bakery was more than 200 miles away), the brothers opened Flowers Baking Co. in 1919. During the 1920s William took charge of the bakery, while Joseph continued to run the ice-cream operation. In 1928 Flowers moved into the production of sweet rolls and cakes. As its reputation for high-quality baked goods spread, the firm established a regional network of customers. William died in 1934, and his 20-year-old son, Bill, took over.

Amidst the difficult Depression years, Bill led the company in its first acquisition, a bakery in Florida. Flowers operated its bakeries around the clock during WWII to supply military bases in the Southeast. Bill's brother Langdon joined the firm after the war and helped take the company on a major expansion drive in the 1950s and 1960s.

Flowers acquired additional southeastern bakers in the mid-1960s and bought the Atlanta Baking Co. in 1967. The next year the company changed its name to Flowers Industries and went public.

In 1976 the company diversified, entering the frozen-food business by acquiring Stilwell Foods (frozen fruits, battered vegetables) in Oklahoma and its subsidiary, Rio Grande Foods, in Texas. The firm also expanded its fresh bread line, including the Nature's Own brand of variety breads (1978).

During the 1970s and 1980s, the company expanded beyond its southeastern regional base by acquiring bakeries in the Southwest and Midwest. Company veteran Amos McMullian became CEO in 1981 and chairman in 1985, when both Bill and Langdon retired. (Langdon died in 2007 at the age of 85.) In 1989 Flowers bought out Winn-Dixie's bakery operations.

The company launched a $377 million, six-year capital investment program in 1991 to upgrade and automate its bakeries. Flowers began a major expansion strategy with the 1996 acquisition of Mrs. Smith's, the US's top frozen-pie brand, from J.M. Smucker. Later that year, Flowers and joint venture partners Artal Luxembourg and Benmore acquired cookie maker Keebler Foods (which it sold to Kellogg in 2001). In 1997 the company acquired Allied Bakery Products, a baker of frozen bread and rolls for food service customers in the Northeast US. When Keebler went public in 1998, Flowers increased its controlling stake to 55%.

Further acquisitions included Home Baking Company (foodservice buns, 1999) and Kroger's bakery operations in Memphis (2000). Weakened by equipment glitches in newly upgraded Mrs. Smith's facilities, earnings suffered at the end of 1999. Flowers snubbed an acquisition inquiry by Sara Lee in early 2000, but as other mega-food company acquisitions dominoed around it, Flowers agreed to sell Keebler to Kellogg in 2000.

Upon completion of the Keebler/Kellogg deal in 2001, Flowers Industries recreated itself, spinning off its Flowers Bakeries and Mrs. Smith's Bakeries businesses under the Flowers Foods name; it kept the same FLO stock ticker.

To better control costs, the company cut jobs at Mrs. Smiths in 2002 and initiated a restructuring of its operating units. Later that same year, the company acquired family-owned Ideal Baking of Arkansas and the snack-cake maker, Bishop Baking Company.

In 2003 Flowers sold the frozen dessert segment of Mrs. Smith's to The Schwan Food Company for $240 million. Flowers retained the frozen bread and roll dough portion of Mrs. Smith's. That same year, it also introduced a line of snack cakes

under the names Tesoritos and Pan Dulce de Mi Casa, aimed at the Latino and Hispanic markets.

In 2004 the company acquired the Houston operations of the Sara Lee Bakery Group. The terms of the deal were not disclosed. However, the company in 2005 did disclose the settlement of a million-dollar class-action lawsuit brought against the company for producing non-kosher food items on a kosher pie shell line at its production facility in Pembroke, North Carolina. To settle, the company apologized for failing to notify the Orthodox Union for occasions when the error occurred and agreed to donate more than $2 million in cash and bread products to charitable groups.

In 2005 Flowers Foods acquired bankrupt snack maker Royal Cake.

In order to broaden its product line, in 2007 the company began offering flour under its Nature's Own brand. Turning to Americans' dietary concerns, it also introduced a number of 100-calorie products that year such as mini blueberry muffins and mini chocolate cupcakes under the Bluebird and Mrs. Freshley's brands.

EXECUTIVES

Chairman, President, and CEO: George E. Deese, age 63, $4,828,840 total compensation
EVP and COO: Gene D. Lord, age 62, $1,382,228 total compensation
EVP and CFO: R. Steve Kinsey, age 48, $859,456 total compensation
SVP and CIO: Vyto F. Razminas, age 51
EVP and Chief Marketing Officer: Allen L. Shiver, age 53, $1,226,351 total compensation
SVP and Chief Accounting Officer: Karyl H. Lauder, age 52
EVP Corporate Relations: Marta Jones Turner, age 55
EVP, Secretary, and General Counsel: Stephen R. (Steve) Avera, age 52, $1,096,478 total compensation
EVP Supply Chain: Michael A. (Mike) Beaty, age 58
SVP Human Resources: Donald A. Thriffiley Jr., age 55
VP and Treasurer: Kirk L. Tolbert
VP and Corporate Controller: Vandy T. Davis
President, Flowers Bakeries: Bradley K. (Brad) Alexander, age 50
Auditors: PricewaterhouseCoopers LLP

LOCATIONS

HQ: Flowers Foods, Inc.
1919 Flowers Cir., Thomasville, GA 31757
Phone: 229-226-9110 **Fax:** 229-225-3806
Web: www.flowersfoods.com

PRODUCTS/OPERATIONS

2008 Sales

	$ mil.	% of total
Branded retail	1,277.1	53
Store-branded retail	355.3	15
Foodservice & other	782.5	32
Total	**2,414.9**	**100**

Selected Brands
DSD Brands
 BlueBird
 Butter Krust
 Captain John Derst
 Cobblestone Mill
 Dandee
 Evangeline Maid
 Flowers
 Ideal
 Mary Jane
 Nature's Own
 Whitewheat

Regional Franchised Brands
 Aunt Hattie's
 Bunny
 Country Hearth
 Holsum
 Roman Meal
 Sunbeam
Warehouse Delivery Brands
 Broad Street Bakery
 European Bakers
 Mrs. Freshley's
 Snack Away

COMPETITORS

Alpha Baking	Lance Snacks
Atlanta Bread	Lewis Bakeries
Bob's Red Mill Natural Foods	Manischewitz Company
Campbell Soup	McKee Foods
Frito-Lay	Organic Milling
General Mills	Otis Spunkmeyer
George Weston	Panera Bread
Grupo Bimbo	Ralcorp
Heinemann's Bakeries	Rich Products
Interstate Bakeries	Sara Lee Food and Beverage
Kellogg U.S. Snacks	Sterling Foods
King's Hawaiian	Tasty Baking
Kraft Foods	United States Bakery
Kraft North America	

HISTORICAL FINANCIALS
Company Type: Public

Income Statement			FYE: Saturday nearest December 31	
	REVENUE ($ mil.)	NET INCOME ($ mil.)	NET PROFIT MARGIN	EMPLOYEES
12/08	2,414.9	119.2	4.9%	8,800
12/07	2,036.7	98.1	4.8%	7,800
12/06	1,888.7	81.6	4.3%	7,800
12/05	1,715.9	61.2	3.6%	7,500
12/04	1,551.3	50.8	3.3%	7,000
Annual Growth	**11.7%**	**23.8%**	**—**	**5.9%**

2008 Year-End Financials

Debt ratio: 41.6%	No. of shares (mil.): 92
Return on equity: 18.5%	Dividends
Cash ($ mil.): 20	Yield: 2.4%
Current ratio: 1.33	Payout: 44.5%
Long-term debt ($ mil.): 264	Market value ($ mil.): 2,241

Stock History

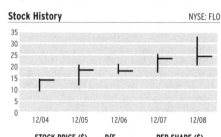

NYSE: FLO

	STOCK PRICE ($) FY Close	P/E High/Low		PER SHARE ($)		
				Earnings	Dividends	Book Value
12/08	24.36	26	16	1.28	0.57	6.90
12/07	23.41	25	17	1.02	0.46	7.13
12/06	17.99	24	20	0.87	0.32	6.12
12/05	18.37	32	19	0.64	0.26	5.57
12/04	14.04	28	19	0.50	0.21	6.19
Annual Growth	**14.8%**	**—**	**—**	**26.5%**	**28.4%**	**2.7%**

Fluor Corporation

Fluor ranks among the leading international design, engineering, and contracting firms. The company oversees construction projects for a range of industrial sectors worldwide, focusing on its core strengths: engineering, procurement, construction, and maintenance. Its projects include designing and building manufacturing facilities, refineries, pharmaceutical facilities, health care buildings, power plants, and telecommunications and transportation infrastructure. Fluor also provides operations and maintenance services for its projects, as well as administrative and support services to the US government.

Fluor's oil and gas segment provides design, engineering, and construction and project management services to markets including upstream oil and gas producers, refiners, petrochemical manufacturers, and producers of specialty and fine chemicals. The unit provides oversight of other contractors and procurement of labor, equipment, and materials. Fluor's oil and gas segment has traditionally been the primary driver for growth in the company.

The company's industrial and infrastructure segment provides design, engineering, procurement, and construction services for pharmaceutical and biotechnology facilities, commercial and institutional buildings, and mining, telecommunications, wind power, and transportation projects. The unit participates in public/private partnerships to oversee financing and management of roadway and railway projects. One recent project is the world's largest offshore wind farm development off the coast of the United Kingdom.

Fluor jumped into the growing outsourcing services market with its global services segment, which provides operations and maintenance support, temporary staffing (through its its TRS Staffing Solutions unit), and asset management. Fluor also provides construction equipment, tools, and fleet outsourcing for construction projects and plant sites worldwide through its American Equipment Company (AMECO) subsidiary. In late 2008 this segment acquired two private engineering companies in Europe — Belgium's UNEC Engineering N.V. and Spain's Europea de Ingenieria y Asesoramiento — for undisclosed amounts.

Fluor's government services segment offers project management primarily to the US Departments of Energy, Defense, and Homeland Security. It provides environmental restoration, engineering and construction, and operations and maintenance services for two former nuclear weapons complexes that are now DOE cleanup sites: the Savannah River site in South Carolina and the Hanford Environmental Management Project in Richland, Washington. Subsidiary Del-Jen provides military base operations and maintenance services and other logistical and infrastructure services around the world.

HISTORY

Fluor's history began in 1890 when three Fluor brothers, immigrants from Switzerland, opened a Wisconsin lumber mill under the name Rudolph Fluor & Brothers. In 1912 John Simon Fluor formed a construction firm in Santa Ana, California. Fluor's company soon began a relationship with Southern California Gas, which led it to specialize in oil and gas construction.

The company, incorporated as Fluor Construction in 1924, later began making engine mufflers. In 1930 it expanded outside of California with a contract to build Texas pipelines.

After WWII, Middle East oil reserves were aggressively developed by Western companies. Fluor cashed in on the stampede, winning major contracts in Saudi Arabia. During the early 1960s it continued to emphasize oil and gas work, establishing a contract drilling unit, and in the 1970s it began work on giant energy projects.

In 1977 Fluor made its biggest purchase: Daniel International, a South Carolina engineering and construction firm with more than $1 billion in annual revenues. The contracting firm, founded by Charles Daniel in 1934, initially did construction work for the textile industry, then later worked for the chemical, pharmaceutical, metal, and power industries.

Flush with cash, Fluor bought St. Joe Minerals in 1981. A drop in oil prices in the 1980s killed demand for the big projects that were its bread and butter. As metal prices fell, St. Joe didn't help the bottom line either. John Robert Fluor, the last of the founding family to head the firm, died in 1984.

When David Tappan stepped in as CEO, he faced a $573 million loss the first year. The white-haired son of missionaries to China, Tappan — known as the Ice Man — dumped subsidiaries and halved the payroll. In 1986 he merged Daniel into Fluor's engineering unit, forming Fluor Daniel.

Leslie McCraw succeeded Tappan as CEO in 1991. McCraw saw Fluor as overly conservative, and three years later he began setting up offices around the world while decentralizing Fluor's structure and adding new business such as temporary staffing and equipment leasing. Fluor also shed some of its commodity companies, including its lead business in 1994. In 1996 Fluor's environmental services unit merged with Groundwater Technology and was spun off as a public company, Fluor Daniel GTI.

Ill with cancer, McCraw stepped down in 1998, and Philip Carroll, who had overhauled Shell Oil, took over as CEO.

Fluor in 1999 cut 5,000 jobs, further streamlined operations, and shifted its focus to growth industries such as biotechnology and telecommunications. The next year the company split its construction and coal mining operations into two separate publicly traded companies, one to concentrate on engineering and construction and one on coal mining. Former Fluor subsidiary A. T. Massey Coal was spun off as Massey Energy.

Carroll, his restructuring job complete, announced in December 2001 that he would retire the following February. That year the company also made plans to dispose of noncore operations of the company's construction equipment and temporary staffing businesses. Alan Boeckmann, who had been president and COO, succeeded Carroll in 2002.

The next year Fluor acquired Del-Jen, a provider of outsourced services to US military bases and to the US Department of Labor. It also picked up five specialty operations and maintenance business groups from Philip Services. And in 2003 the company decided to dissolve its Duke/Fluor Daniel joint venture.

Fluor moved its headquarters from California to Dallas in 2006.

EXECUTIVES

Chairman and CEO: Alan L. Boeckmann, age 60, $14,775,361 total compensation
SVP and CFO: D. Michael (Mike) Steuert, age 60, $5,449,846 total compensation
VP and CIO: Ray F. Barnard, age 50
Chief Legal Officer and Corporate Secretary: Carlos M. Hernandez, age 54
SVP Business Development and Strategy, Infrastructure: Robert (Bob) Prieto
SVP Nuclear Power, Power Group: Ronald E. (Ron) Pitts
SVP Government: James S. Cartner
SVP Construction Services, Health, Safety & Environmental (HSE), Corporate Security: Garry W. Flowers, age 57
SVP Government Relations: David (Dave) Marventano
SVP Human Resources and Administration: Glenn Gilkey
VP Corporate Communications: Lee C. Tashjian
VP Corporate Finance and Investor Relations: Kenneth H. (Ken) Lockwood
Senior Group President, Industrial and Infrastructure and Global Services: Stephen B. Dobbs, age 52, $3,040,159 total compensation
Senior Group President, Energy and Chemicals, Power, and Government Business: David T. Seaton, age 47, $2,493,138 total compensation
Group President, Global Services: Kirk D. Grimes, age 51
Group President, Government Business: Bruce A. Stanski, age 48
Group President, Industrial and Infrastructure: Dwayne A. Wilson, age 50
Group President, Project Operations: David E. Constable, age 47
Group President, Power: David R. Dunning
Group President, Energy and Chemicals: P.W.B. (Peter) Oosterveer
Group Executive Corporate Development: John L. Hopkins, age 55, $3,175,592 total compensation
Auditors: Ernst & Young LLP

LOCATIONS

HQ: Fluor Corporation
6700 Las Colinas Blvd., Irving, TX 75039
Phone: 469-398-7000   **Fax:** 469-398-7255
Web: www.fluor.com

2008 Sales

	$ mil.	% of total
US	11,391	51
Europe	4,338	19
Middle East & Africa	2,169	10
Asia/Pacific	1,991	9
Central & South America	1,429	6
Canada	1,008	5
Total	**22,326**	**100**

PRODUCTS/OPERATIONS

2008 Sales

	$ mil.	% of total
Oil & gas	12,946	58
Industrial & infrastructure	3,470	15
Global services	2,676	12
Power	1,914	9
Government	1,320	6
Total	**22,326**	**100**

Selected Services

Construction management
Design
Engineering, procurement, and construction (EPC)
Operations and maintenance
Program management
Project development and finance
Project management
Staffing

Selected Industries Served

Biotechnology
Chemicals and petrochemicals
Commercial and institutional
Equipment
Gas processing
Government
Manufacturing
Mining
Oil and gas production
Petroleum refining
Pharmaceuticals
Power generation
Telecommunications
Transportation

Selected Subsidiaries

American Construction Equipment Company, Inc.
Fluor Constructors International, Inc.
Fluor Enterprises, Inc.
   Daniel International Corporation
   Del-Jen, Inc.
   ICA-Fluor Daniel, S. de R.L. de C.V. (49%, Mexico)
Fluor Holding Company LLC
TRS Staffing Solutions, Inc.

COMPETITORS

ABB
ARCADIS
Balfour Construction
BE&K
Bechtel
Bilfinger Berger
Black & Veatch
Bouygues
CH2M HILL
Dragados
Earth Tech
Foster Wheeler
Halliburton
Hitachi
Jacobs Engineering
KBR
Marelich Mechanical
McDermott
Michael Baker
Parsons Corporation
POSCO
Raytheon
Shaw Group
Technip
Tetra Tech
Tyco
University Mechanical & Engineering
URS
Vecellio & Grogan
Washington Division
WorleyParsons Corp.

HISTORICAL FINANCIALS

Company Type: Public

Income Statement

FYE: December 31

	REVENUE ($ mil.)	NET INCOME ($ mil.)	NET PROFIT MARGIN	EMPLOYEES
12/08	22,325.9	720.5	3.2%	42,119
12/07	16,691.0	533.3	3.2%	41,260
12/06	14,078.5	263.5	1.9%	37,560
12/05	13,161.1	227.3	1.7%	34,836
12/04	9,380.3	186.7	2.0%	34,799
Annual Growth	24.2%	40.2%	—	4.9%

2008 Year-End Financials

Debt ratio: 0.7%
Return on equity: 29.1%
Cash ($ mil.): 1,834
Current ratio: 1.48
Long-term debt ($ mil.): 18
No. of shares (mil.): 180
Dividends
   Yield: 1.1%
   Payout: 12.7%
Market value ($ mil.): 8,071

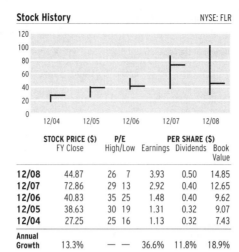

Stock History
NYSE: FLR

	STOCK PRICE ($) FY Close	P/E High/Low		PER SHARE ($) Earnings	Dividends	Book Value
12/08	44.87	26	7	3.93	0.50	14.85
12/07	72.86	29	13	2.92	0.40	12.65
12/06	40.83	35	25	1.48	0.40	9.62
12/05	38.63	30	19	1.31	0.32	9.07
12/04	27.25	25	16	1.13	0.32	7.43
Annual Growth	13.3%	—	—	36.6%	11.8%	18.9%

FMC Corporation

E may = mc2, but FMC = chemicals. Once in areas as diverse as oil field equipment and food machinery, FMC Corporation now focuses on industrial, specialty, and agricultural chemicals. The company's industrial chemicals include soda ash (it's one of the largest producers), hydrogen peroxide, and phosphorus chemicals. The rest of its sales come from agricultural products (insecticides and herbicides) and specialty chemicals (food and pharmaceutical additives). FMC's equation lately has improved after a few years' effort to increase its efficiency, profitability, and credit rating. The company cut costs across the board and refocused on strong growth areas, especially specialty chemicals.

The food and pharmaceutical additives product groups are the areas of choice where FMC sees a real opportunity to improve its fortunes. Product development has been concentrated on specialty chemicals product areas like energy storage (lithium products for batteries) and agricultural products like home and garden pesticides.

To that last point, the company acquired the CB Professional Products line of insecticides from Waterbury Companies in early 2009. CB Professional Products makes an array of aerosol sprays as well as foggers, baits, and other insect control products.

HISTORY

After retiring to California, inventor John Bean developed a pump to deliver a continuous spray of insecticide in 1884. This invention led to the Bean Spray Pump Company in 1904. In 1928 Bean Spray Pump went public and bought Anderson-Barngrover (food-growing and -processing equipment). The company became Food Machinery Corporation the next year. It bought Peerless Pump (agricultural and industrial pumps) in 1933.

During WWII the company began making military equipment. It entered the agricultural chemical field when it bought Niagara Sprayer & Chemical (1943). After the war it added Westvaco Chemical (1948) and changed its name to Food Machinery & Chemical.

The Bean family ran the company until 1956, when John Bean's grandson, John Crummey, retired as chairman. The company extended its product line, buying Oil Center Tool (wellhead equipment, 1957), Sunland Industries (fertilizer and insecticides, 1959), and Barrett Equipment (automotive brake equipment, 1961).

In light of its growing diversification, the company changed its name to FMC Corporation in 1961. Major purchases in the 1960s included American Viscose (rayon and cellophane, 1963) and Link-Belt (equipment for power transmission and for bulk-material handling, 1967).

To be centrally located, FMC moved its headquarters from San Jose to Chicago in 1972. Through the 1970s and early 1980s, the company sold several slow-growing businesses, including its pump and fiber divisions (1976), semiconductor division (1979), industrial packaging division (1980), Niagara Seed Operation (1980), and Power Transmission Group (1981).

It moved into other markets just as quickly. These included a Nevada gold mine (through a 1979 joint venture with Freeport Minerals), Bradley armored personnel carriers (through an early-1980s contract with the US Army), and lithium (by acquiring Lithium Corp. of America, 1985). In a 1986 antitakeover move, FMC gave employees a larger stake in the company.

FMC bought Ciba-Geigy's flame-retardant and water-treatment businesses in 1992 and combined its defense operations with Harsco as United Defense. FMC's 1994 acquisitions included Abex's Jetway Systems Division (aircraft support systems) and Caterpillar's Automated Vehicle Systems group. FMC formed a joint venture with Nippon Sheet Glass and Sumitomo Corporation in 1995 to mine for soda ash.

FMC made a deal with DuPont in 1996 to commercialize new herbicides. The company debuted its composite (nonmetallic) prototype armored vehicle in 1997. In the long shadow of reduced defense budgets, FMC and Harsco sold their stagnant defense operation for $850 million to The Carlyle Group investment firm.

The sale of its defense division didn't protect FMC from a $310 million damage award in a whistleblower suit against the company in 1998. A federal jury found that FMC had misled the Army about the safety of the Bradley armored infantry vehicle. The court later lowered the penalty to about $90 million.

In 1999 the company agreed to combine its phosphorus operations with Solutia to form a joint venture called Astaris. That year FMC sold its process-additives unit to Great Lakes Chemical (now called Chemtura).

FMC bought Northfield Freezing Systems (food processing) in 2000. The following year the company split into separate chemical and machinery companies by spinning off its machinery business as FMC Technologies; FMC Corporation then moved its headquarters from Chicago to Philadelphia. In early 2002 FMC sold its sodium cyanide business to Cyanco Company, a joint venture between Degussa Corporation and Winnemucca Chemicals (a subsidiary of Nevada Chemicals).

In 2005 FMC and Solutia sold Astaris (now called ICL Performance Products) to Israel Chemicals Limited for $255 million.

EXECUTIVES

Chairman, President, and CEO: William G. (Bill) Walter, age 63, $6,870,119 total compensation
SVP and CFO: W. Kim Foster, age 60, $2,225,412 total compensation
VP Government and Public Affairs: Gerald R. Prout, age 54
VP and General Manager, Agricultural Products: Milton Steele, age 60, $2,027,103 total compensation
VP, General Counsel, and Secretary: Andrea E. Utecht, age 60
VP Human Resources and Communications: Kenneth R. Garrett
VP and Corporate Controller: Graham R. Wood, age 55
VP and Treasurer: Thomas C. Deas Jr., age 58
VP and General Manager, Specialty Chemicals: Theodore H. (Ted) Butz, age 50, $1,488,356 total compensation
VP and General Manager, Industrial Chemicals: D. Michael Wilson, age 45, $1,566,433 total compensation
Assistant Treasurer and Director, Tax: Theodore H. Laws Jr.
Director Investor Relations: Brennen Arndt
Media Contact, Food: Olga Drebotij
Media Contact, Pharmaceutical: Melody Evans
Media Relations: Jim Fitzwater
Auditors: KPMG LLP

LOCATIONS

HQ: FMC Corporation
1735 Market St., Philadelphia, PA 19103
Phone: 215-299-6000   **Fax:** 215-299-5998
Web: www.fmc.com

2008 Sales

	$ mil.	% of total
North America		
US	996.2	32
Other countries	68.4	2
Europe/Middle East/Africa	887.0	29
Latin America		
Brazil	478.1	15
Other countries	263.6	9
Asia/Pacific	422.0	13
Total	**3,115.3**	**100**

PRODUCTS/OPERATIONS

2008 Sales

	$ mil.	% of total
Industrial Chemicals	1,296.9	41
Agricultural Chemicals	1,058.7	34
Specialty Chemicals	764.5	25
Adjustments	(4.8)	—
Total	**3,115.3**	**100**

Selected Products

Industrial chemicals
  Hydrogen peroxide
  Phosphorus chemicals
  Soda ash
  Sodium bicarbonate
  Sodium sesquicarbonate

Agricultural products
  Herbicides
  Pesticides

Specialty chemicals
  Cellulose (alginate, carrageenan, and microcrystalline)
  Lithium

COMPETITORS

Agrium	Dow Chemical
Akzo Nobel	DuPont
Arkema	Evonik Degussa
Asahi Glass	PPG Industries
Asahi Kasei	Solvay
BASF SE	SQM
Bayer CropScience	Sumitomo Chemical
Cargill	Syngenta
CP Kelco	Terra Industries

HISTORICAL FINANCIALS

Company Type: Public

Income Statement

FYE: December 31

	REVENUE ($ mil.)	NET INCOME ($ mil.)	NET PROFIT MARGIN	EMPLOYEES
12/08	3,115.3	304.6	9.8%	5,000
12/07	2,632.9	132.4	5.0%	5,000
12/06	2,347.0	132.0	5.6%	5,000
12/05	2,150.2	117.1	5.4%	5,000
12/04	2,051.2	160.2	7.8%	5,100
Annual Growth	**11.0%**	**17.4%**	**—**	**(0.5%)**

2008 Year-End Financials

Debt ratio: 65.7%
Return on equity: 31.0%
Cash ($ mil.): 52
Current ratio: 1.89
Long-term debt ($ mil.): 593
No. of shares (mil.): 72
Dividends
  Yield: 1.1%
  Payout: 11.9%
Market value ($ mil.): 3,243

Stock History

NYSE: FMC

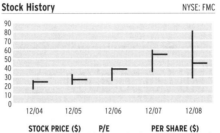

	STOCK PRICE ($) FY Close	P/E High/Low		PER SHARE ($) Earnings	Dividends	Book Value
12/08	44.73	20	7	4.02	0.48	12.45
12/07	54.55	35	21	1.71	0.41	14.68
12/06	38.28	23	15	1.67	0.36	14.06
12/05	26.58	22	15	1.49	0.00	13.23
12/04	24.15	12	8	2.14	0.00	12.09
Annual Growth	**16.7%**	**—**	**—**	**17.1%**	**—**	**0.8%**

FMR LLC

FMR is *semper fidelis* (ever faithful) to its core business. The financial services conglomerate, better known as Fidelity Investments, is one of the world's largest mutual fund firms. Serving more than 24 million individual and institutional clients, Fidelity manages more than 300 funds and has more than $1.4 trillion of assets under management. It also operates a leading online discount brokerage and has more than 100 investor centers in the US and Canada, as well as locations in Europe and Asia. The founding Johnson family controls FMR; Abigail Johnson, CEO Ned Johnson's daughter and perhaps his successor (not to mention one of the richest women in America), is the company's largest single shareholder.

Fidelity's nonfund offerings include life insurance, trust services, securities clearing, and retirement services. It is one of the largest administrators of 401(k) plans, and the firm continues to grow this segment, which includes other services related to benefits outsourcing. The company had been reluctant to give direct investment advice to 401(k) plan participants,

but under pressure from customers struck a formal agreement with Financial Engines, which now provides those services to Fidelity's clients.

FMR has private equity investments in telecommunications firm COLT Telecom Group and transportation company BostonCoach, among others. Like many institutional investors, Fidelity uses its clout to sway the boards of companies in which it has significant holdings. In 2007 the company's Fidelity Equity Partners arm launched a $500 million buyout fund that targets middle-market firms involved in media, software, health care, and service industries in North America and Europe.

FMR also holds about a 15% stake in venerable British investment bank Lazard, which it acquired in 2005.

HISTORY

Boston money management firm Anderson & Cromwell formed Fidelity Fund in 1930. Edward Johnson became president of the fund in 1943, when it had $3 million invested in Treasury bills. Johnson diversified into stocks, and by 1945 the fund had grown to $10 million. In 1946 he established Fidelity Management and Research to act as its investment adviser.

In the early 1950s Johnson hired Gerry Tsai, a young immigrant from Shanghai, to analyze stocks. He put Tsai in charge of Fidelity Capital Fund in 1957. Tsai's brash, go-go investment strategy in such speculative stocks as Xerox and Polaroid paid off; by the time he left to form his own fund in 1965, he was managing more than $1 billion.

The Magellan Fund started in 1962. The company entered the corporate pension plans market (FMR Investment Management) in 1964, and the self-employed individual retirement market (Fidelity Keogh Plan) in 1967. It began serving investors outside the US (Fidelity International) in 1968.

Holding company FMR was formed in 1972, the same year Johnson gave control of Fidelity to his son Ned, who vertically integrated FMR by selling directly to customers rather than through brokers. In 1973 he formed Fidelity Daily Income Trust, the first money market fund to offer check writing.

Peter Lynch was hired as manager of the Magellan Fund in 1977. During his 13-year tenure, Magellan grew from $20 million to $12 billion in assets and outperformed all other mutual funds. Fidelity started Fidelity Brokerage Services in 1978, becoming the first mutual fund company to offer discount brokerage.

In 1980 the company launched a nationwide branch network and in 1986 entered the credit card business. The Wall Street crash of 1987 forced its Magellan Fund to liquidate almost $1 billion in stock in a single day. That year FMR moved into insurance by offering variable life, single premium, and deferred annuity policies. In 1989 the company introduced the low-expense Spartan Fund, targeted toward large, less-active investors.

Magellan's performance faded in the early 1990s, dropping from #1 performer to #3. Most of Fidelity's best performers were from its 36 select funds, which focus on narrow industry segments. FMR founded London-based COLT Telecom in 1993. In 1994 Johnson gave his daughter and possible heir apparent, Abigail, a 25% stake in FMR. She reportedly sold a significant portion of the stake in 2005.

HISTORICAL FINANCIALS

Company Type: Public

Income Statement
FYE: March 31

	REVENUE ($ mil.)	NET INCOME ($ mil.)	NET PROFIT MARGIN	EMPLOYEES
3/09	3,922.8	767.7	19.6%	5,225
3/08	3,501.8	967.9	27.6%	5,211
3/07	3,183.3	454.1	14.3%	5,126
3/06	2,793.9	708.5	25.4%	5,050
3/05	3,052.4	838.8	27.5%	5,136
Annual Growth	6.5%	(2.2%)	—	0.4%

2009 Year-End Financials

Debt ratio: —
Return on equity: 19.6%
Cash ($ mil.): 1,339
Current ratio: 4.63
Long-term debt ($ mil.): —

No. of shares (mil.): 302
Dividends
Yield: 0.0%
Payout: —
Market value ($ mil.): 6,625

Stock History
NYSE: FRX

	STOCK PRICE ($) FY Close	P/E High/Low		PER SHARE ($) Earnings	Dividends	Book Value
3/09	21.96	16	7	2.52	0.00	13.64
3/08	40.01	19	11	3.06	0.00	12.32
3/07	51.44	41	26	1.41	0.00	10.03
3/06	44.63	23	16	2.08	0.00	8.94
3/05	36.95	34	16	2.25	0.00	10.38
Annual Growth	(12.2%)	—	—	2.9%	—	7.1%

Fortune Brands

Execs at Fortune Brands have good reason to meet over a game of golf and a glass of bourbon. The holding company is a leading US producer and distributor of distilled spirits such as Jim Beam, Sauza, DeKuyper, Canadian Club, and Maker's Mark. Its golf equipment company, Acushnet, manufactures and markets brands such as Titleist, Cobra, FootJoy, and Pinnacle. However, Fortune's largest segment is home products and hardware, where its holdings include Moen faucets, MasterBrand Cabinets, Master Lock padlocks, and Therma-Tru doors. All of Fortune Brands' products are sold primarily in the US, Canada, Europe, Australia, and Mexico.

In its less intoxicating businesses, Fortune bolstered its home and hardware division in 2006 when it bought vinyl-framed window replacements maker Simonton Building Products.

As a whole, Fortune Brands' home and hardware division has been suffering losses due to a downturn in the US home products market. And the company does not foresee improvements any time soon. In order to weather the downturn Fortune has reduced its number of manufacturing facilities by 35% and cut jobs at all levels.

In the past few years Fortune has been retooling its spirits division. In 2007 the company shifted its focus on liquor and sold its US wine holdings, including the Clos du Bois, Geyser Peak, and Wild Horse brands, to Constellation Brands for nearly $900 million.

The next year Fortune became embroiled in a lawsuit over the 10% stake in Beam Global Spirits & Wine that it didn't already own. Sweden's V&S Group owned the stake and wanted to transfer it to the Swedish government as part of its 2008 sale to Pernod Ricard. However, Fortune wanted to buy the stake back. After some legal wrangling and negotiating Fortune repurchased the minority stake for some $455 million.

Also in 2008 Fortune paid Pernod Ricard $103 million for Cruzan, one of the fastest growing brands of rum in the US. The following year Fortune Brands continued to stock the bar when it bought the EFFEN vodka brand from Sazerac.

HISTORY

Fortune Brands began in 1864 as W. Duke and Sons, a small tobacco company started by North Carolina farmer Washington Duke. James Buchanan Duke joined his father's business at age 14, and by age 25 was its president. James advertised to expanding markets, bought rival tobacco firms, and by 1904 controlled the industry. That year he merged all the competitive groups as American Tobacco Company. In a 1911 antitrust suit, the US Supreme Court dissolved American Tobacco into its original constituents, ordering them to operate independently.

James left American Tobacco the next year. He established a $100 million trust fund composed mainly of holdings in his power company, Duke Power and Light (now Duke Energy Corporation), for Trinity College. The school became Duke University in 1924.

George Washington Hill became president of American Tobacco in 1925. For the next 19 years until his death, George proved himself a consummate adman, pushing Lucky Strike, Pall Mall, and Tareyton cigarettes to top sales.

Smokers began switching to filter-tipped cigarettes in the 1950s because of health concerns. American Tobacco, however, ignored the trend and continued to rely on its popular filterless brands until the mid-1960s. In 1962 the firm sold J. Wix and Sons (Kensitas cigarettes) to UK tobacco firm Gallaher Group for a stake in Gallaher.

The company remained solely in the tobacco business until 1966, when it purchased Sunshine Biscuits (sold 1988) and Jim Beam Distillery. Reflecting its increasing diversity, the firm became American Brands in 1969. The next year it added Swingline (office supplies) and Master Lock. Meanwhile, American Brands increased its stake in Gallaher, controlling 100% by 1975. In 1976 the company bought Acushnet (Titleist and Bulls Eye); it added FootJoy in 1986.

Threatened with a takeover by E-II Holdings (a conglomerate of brands split from Beatrice), American Brands bought E-II in 1988. It kept five of E-II's companies — Day-Timers, Aristokraft (cabinets), Waterloo (tool boxes), Twentieth Century (plumbing supplies), and Vogel Peterson (office partitions; sold 1995) — and sold the rest (Culligan, Samsonite) to Riklis Family Corporation. Acquisitions in 1990 included Moen (faucets) and Whyte & Mackay (distillers). The company bought seven liquor brands in 1991 from Seagram.

American Brands sold its American Tobacco subsidiary, including the Pall Mall and Lucky Strike brands, to onetime subsidiary B.A.T Industries in 1994. The firm acquired publicly held Cobra Golf in 1996.

The following year American Brands changed its name to Fortune Brands and completed the spinoff of its Gallaher tobacco subsidiary. In 1998 Fortune bought kitchen and bathroom cabinetmaker Schrock from Electrolux, doubling its sales in that category.

Seeking to trim costs, Fortune relocated its headquarters to Lincolnshire, Illinois, in 1999. Also that year Norman Wesley was named chairman and CEO. Also in 1999 the company bought Boone International (presentation products) and NHB Group, a manufacturer of ready-to-assemble kitchen and bath cabinetry.

In 2001 Fortune and Swedish company Vin & Sprit formed Future Brands, a joint venture to distribute Absolut vodka in the US. Fortune bought The Omega Group, a manufacturer of kitchen and bath cabinetry, for $538 million in 2002.

About 20,000 barrels of Fortune's Jim Beam bourbon went up in smoke during a warehouse fire in the summer of 2003. The Bardstown, Kentucky, facility was believed to be the victim of a lighting strike from a passing thunderstorm. Also that year the company expanded its home and hardware division by acquiring privately held doormaker Therma-Tru.

Fortune Brands merged its holdings in General Binding Corporation and office products company ACCO World (Day-Timers, Swingline, Apollo, Kensington) in 2005. It spun off the resulting firm, ACCO Brands Corporation, in order to focus on its Home and Hardware, Spirits, and Golf segments.

That year Fortune spent about $5 billion to acquire more than 20 wine and liquor brands formerly owned by Allied Domecq. First, Pernod Ricard acquired Allied Domecq with Fortune's monetary help; Pernod Ricard then began transferring a group of assets — including Sauza tequila, Canadian Club whiskey, Courvoisier Cognac, Laphroaig single-malt Scotch, and Clos du Bois wines — to Fortune.

Fortune sold its US wine holdings in 2007. Wesley retired in 2008, and was replaced by Bruce Carbonari.

EXECUTIVES

Chairman, President, and CEO: Bruce A. Carbonari, age 53, $4,170,781 total compensation
SVP and CFO: Craig P. Omtvedt, age 59, $1,974,878 total compensation
SVP, General Counsel, and Secretary: Mark A. Roche, age 54, $1,611,209 total compensation
SVP Finance and Treasurer: Mark Hausberg, age 59
SVP Strategy and Corporate Development: Patrick J. Koley
VP and Chief Internal Auditor: Gary L. Tobison
VP Investor Relations: Anthony J. Diaz
VP Corporate Communications and Public Affairs: C. Clarkson Hine
VP Business Development: Allan J. Snape
VP and Associate General Counsel: Lauren S. Tashma
VP and Corporate Controller: Edward A. Wiertel, age 39
VP Taxes: Charles J. Ryan
VP Human Resources: Elizabeth R. Lane
VP Public Affairs: Matt Stanton
VP Strategy: David W. Tanner
Corporate Director, Human Resources: Rosalyn D. Wesley
Auditors: PricewaterhouseCoopers LLP

LOCATIONS

HQ: Fortune Brands, Inc.
520 Lake Cook Rd., Deerfield, IL 60015
Phone: 847-484-4400   **Fax:** 847-478-0073
Web: www.fortunebrands.com

2008 Sales

	$ mil.	% of total
US	5,312.2	70
Canada	549.0	7
UK	435.6	6
Australia	258.4	3
Spain	156.5	2
Other countries	897.2	12
Total	**7,608.9**	**100**

PRODUCTS/OPERATIONS

2008 Sales

	$ mil.	% of total
Home & Hardware	3,759.1	49
Spirits	2,480.9	33
Golf	1,368.9	18
Total	**7,608.9**	**100**

Selected Brands

Golf
  Cobra (clubs)
  FootJoy (shoes and gloves)
  Pinnacle (balls)
  Scotty Cameron (putters)
  Titleist (balls, clubs, bags, and accessories)
Home & Hardware
  Aristokraft (cabinets)
  Master Lock (padlocks)
  MasterBrand (cabinets)
  Moen (faucets)
  Omega (cabinets)
  Schrock (cabinets)
  Waterloo (toolboxes)
Spirits
  Bourbon
    Jim Beam
    Maker's Mark
    Old Grand-Dad
    Old Crow
    Small Batch Bourbon
    Booker's
    Baker's
    Knob Creek
    Basil Hayden's
  Blended Whisky/Whiskey
    Canadian Club
    Teacher's
    Whisky DYC
    Windsor
    Lord Calvert
    Tangle Ridge
    Alberta Springs
    Kessler
    Calvert Extra
    Old Overholt
    Furst Bismarck
  Single Malt Scotch
    Laphroaig
    The Dalmore
    Ardmore
  Tequila
    Sauza
    El Tesoro de Don Felipe
  Cognac
    Courvoisier
    Salignac
  Vodka
    EFFEN
    VOX
    Wolfschmidt
    Kamchatka
    Gilbey's
  Rum
    Cruzan
    Ronrico
  Gin
    Larios
    Gilbey's
    Calvert
  Brandy
    Fundador
    Terry Centenario
    Jacobi 1880
    Tres Cepas
  Cordials
    DeKuyper
    Starbucks Coffee Liqueur
    Kamora
    Kuemmerling
    After Shock
    Leroux
    Castellana
    Sourz
  Pre-Mixed Cocktails
    Jim Beam & Cola
    Jim Beam Black & Cola
    Jim Beam Choice & Dry
  Port
    Cockburn's
  Sherry
    Harveys

COMPETITORS

American Woodmark	Kohler
Armstrong World Industries	Kwikset Corporation
Atrium Companies	Masco
Bacardi USA	Masco Retail Cabinet Group
Black & Decker	Masonite
Bridgestone Sports	Milgard Manufacturing
Brown-Forman	Newell Rubbermaid
Brunswick Corp.	NIKE
Callaway Golf	Pernod Ricard
Cleveland Golf	Reebok
Constellation Brands	Rémy Cointreau
Diageo	Skyy
Eastern Company	Snap-on
Franklin Covey	Stanley Works
Grohe	TaylorMade-adidas Golf
Hampton Affiliates	Trane Inc.
Huffy Corporation	V&S
JELD-WEN	Waxman

HISTORICAL FINANCIALS

Company Type: Public

Income Statement

FYE: December 31

	REVENUE ($ mil.)	NET INCOME ($ mil.)	NET PROFIT MARGIN	EMPLOYEES
12/08	7,608.9	311.1	4.1%	27,100
12/07	8,563.1	762.6	8.9%	31,027
12/06	8,769.0	830.1	9.5%	36,251
12/05	7,061.2	621.1	8.8%	30,298
12/04	7,320.9	783.8	10.7%	31,851
Annual Growth	1.0%	(20.6%)	—	(4.0%)

2008 Year-End Financials

Debt ratio: 100.2%
Return on equity: 6.0%
Cash ($ mil.): 163
Current ratio: 2.91
Long-term debt ($ mil.): 4,689

No. of shares (mil.): 150
Dividends
  Yield: 4.2%
  Payout: 85.1%
Market value ($ mil.): 6,202

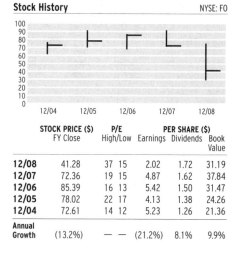

	STOCK PRICE ($) FY Close	P/E High/Low	PER SHARE ($) Earnings	Dividends	Book Value
12/08	41.28	37 15	2.02	1.72	31.19
12/07	72.36	19 15	4.87	1.62	37.84
12/06	85.39	16 13	5.42	1.50	31.47
12/05	78.02	22 17	4.13	1.38	24.26
12/04	72.61	14 12	5.23	1.26	21.36
Annual Growth	(13.2%)	— —	(21.2%)	8.1%	9.9%

Fossil, Inc.

Fossil digs the watch business while unearthing a place in the accessories and apparel niches. A leading mid-priced watchmaker in the US, it generates most of its sales from watches. Brands include its Fossil and Relic watches, as well as licensed names Armani, Michael Kors, adidas, Burberry, and Marc Jacobs, and private-label watches for Target and Wal-Mart. Fossil also distributes fashion accessories, such as leather goods, sunglasses, and apparel. The firm sells through department stores and specialty shops in more than 100 countries and some 200 company-owned stores, as well as through its own catalog and Web site. Brothers and executives Tom and Kosta Kartsotis own about 27% of Fossil.

Like rivals Swatch and Guess?, Fossil has typically targeted those in their teens, 20s, and 30s, i.e., those hip to the latest trends. But Fossil's target audience has become broader to include those who will drop some big green for some bling. Fossil entered the luxury products niche when it acquired Tempus International, which does business as Michele Watches, for about $50 million. The subsidiary launched Michele Jewelry, a collection of 18-karat gold pieces that are sold at Neiman Marcus stores nationwide. During 2008 sales increases among its licensed brands and Michele watches helped to boost the company's wholesale watch shipments in the US, offsetting decreases in sales volume for Fossil's namesake watches.

Fossil has been expanding its number of company-owned stores in recent years. Of its more than 320 company-owned stores, about 305 of them operate under the Fossil banner. In 2009 the company plans to open up to 50 additional Fossil-branded stores. Fossil is focusing its efforts outside the US to peddle its full-price accessories. Building on the Fossil brand name, the company also markets wallets, handbags, and belts. Its products also may be found in gift shops on cruise ships and in airports. The company's wholesale business represented about 80% of its 2008 revenue while its direct to consumer segment generated some 20%.

Fossil has inked several deals that have given the company traction for long-term growth. Fossil has a licensing agreement with Diesel through 2010 and holds the exclusive rights to manufacture, market, and distribute a Diesel jewelry collection. In a move that has placed Fossil at a noteworthy advantage is its deal with retailing behemoth Wal-Mart to design, make, and distribute watches for the retailer's private-label brand George. The company's mass market watch business increased about 40% soon thereafter, more or less attributable to this partnership. Sales of Burberry licensed products and the launch of both Marc by Marc Jacobs and adidas items have helped to boost Fossil's licensing revenue, as well.

The company is watching the clock on its licensing agreements. Its DKNY watch license is set to expire at the end of 2009. During 2008, Fossil negotiated with the owners of the EMPORIO ARMANI brand for a watch licensing agreement that extends through December 31, 2013. Its jewelry agreement with the brand expired at the end of 2008, but Fossil retains the right to distribute EMPORIO ARMANI jewelry while it's in negotiations with the company.

HISTORY

Tom Kartsotis founded a Dallas area import-export company, originally called Overseas Products International, in 1984. He was only 24, and Swatch was the hot watch brand. His brother, Kosta Kartsotis, a department store executive, had told him about high profits from Asian imports. With Lynne Stafford (whom Tom later married) as designer, the company gave its Asian-made Fossil watches a retro image, and sales took off. In 1988 Kosta joined the firm to woo department stores.

Between 1987 and 1989 sales rose from $2 million to $20 million. In 1990 a less-expensive line of watches, Relic, was created for stores such as J. C. Penney and Sears. Tom renamed the company Fossil in 1992 and took it public in 1993. Its product line then included women's accessories (such as belts) and small leather goods for men. Two years later Fossil introduced sunglasses.

The company opened its first US retail outlets in 1996. The next year Fossil signed licensing agreements with Giorgio Armani for the Emporio Armani Orologi watch line and with London Fog to make Fossil outerwear. Through a joint venture with Netherlands-based Capstan Bay, the firm opened its first European store in 1998 in Amsterdam.

In 1999 Fossil entered a joint venture with the American subsidiary of Japanese watchmaker Seiko to produce and market Lorus and Disney character watches. The following year Fossil launched its own Fossil-brand jeans and apparel line to be sold at its approximately 12 new Fossil apparel stores. Fossil acquired UK-based The Avia Watch Company, maker of Avia-brand watches, in mid-2001 to grow its business in the UK, as well as 80% of its Australian distributor FSLA. In November 2001 the company acquired three Swiss watchmakers, Montres Antima SA, Meliga Habillement Horloger SA, and Synergies Horlogères SA. The next year Fossil acquired No-Time (its Swiss distributor) and X-Time (a retailer with three stores in Switzerland).

In 2003 Fossil gave nerds a watch to celebrate. The company developed the Wrist PDA, a line of watches that incorporates a Palm personal digital assistant that synchronizes with a Windows-

based PC. The year 2004 brought a refined version of the Wrist PDA: in a joint effort with Citizen Watch, the companies began production of wrist watches capable of receiving news, weather, and other information, through a subscription-based service provided by Microsoft.

EXECUTIVES

Chairman: Tom Kartsotis, age 49
Vice Chairman: Mark D. Quick, age 60, $1,834,302 total compensation
CEO and Director: Kosta N. Kartsotis, age 55
President, COO, and Director: Michael W. Barnes, age 48, $3,000,979 total compensation
EVP, CFO, and Treasurer: Mike L. Kovar, age 47, $963,632 total compensation
VP Human Resources: Dean Carter
VP Legal: Randy Hyne
VP Internal Audit and Loss Prevention: Christopher King
Managing Director, Fossil (East) and Director: Jal S. Shroff, age 72
President, Retail Division: Jennifer Pritchard, age 50, $1,011,468 total compensation
Integrated Corporate Relations: Allison C. Malkin
Auditors: Deloitte & Touche LLP

LOCATIONS

HQ: Fossil, Inc.
2280 N. Greenville Ave., Richardson, TX 75082
Phone: 972-234-2525 **Fax:** 972-234-4669
Web: www.fossil.com

2008 Sales

	$ mil.	% of total
Europe wholesale	530.0	33
US wholesale	472.7	30
Direct to consumer	309.3	20
Other international wholesale	271.2	17
Total	**1,583.2**	**100**

PRODUCTS/OPERATIONS

2008 Sales

	$ mil.	% of total
Wholesale	1,273.9	80
Direct to consumer	309.3	20
Total	**1,583.2**	**100**

Selected Products

Watches Brands
  Burberry
  Diesel
  DKNY
  Emporio Armani
  Fossil
  Fossil Blue
  Relic
Fashion accessories
  Apparel
  Jewelry
  Leather goods
  Sunglasses

COMPETITORS

Abercrombie & Fitch	Liz Claiborne
American Eagle Outfitters	LVMH
Armitron	Movado Group
Calvin Klein	Nine West
CASIO COMPUTER	Oakley
Citizen	Seiko
Coach, Inc.	Swank
Donna Karan	Swatch
Dooney & Bourke	TAG Heuer
The Gap	Tandy Brands
Gucci	Tandy Leather
Guess?	Timex
Jones Apparel	Tommy Hilfiger
Kenneth Cole	Victorinox Swiss Army

HISTORICAL FINANCIALS

Company Type: Public

Income Statement

FYE: December 31

	REVENUE ($ mil.)	NET INCOME ($ mil.)	NET PROFIT MARGIN	EMPLOYEES
12/08	1,583.2	138.1	8.7%	7,355
12/07	1,433.0	123.3	8.6%	6,000
12/06	1,214.0	77.6	6.4%	7,400
12/05	1,040.5	78.1	7.5%	7,160
12/04	960.0	90.6	9.4%	5,400
Annual Growth	**13.3%**	**11.1%**	**—**	**8.0%**

2008 Year-End Financials

Debt ratio: 0.6%
Return on equity: 17.5%
Cash ($ mil.): 172
Current ratio: 3.69
Long-term debt ($ mil.): 5
No. of shares (mil.): 67
Dividends
  Yield: 0.0%
  Payout: —
Market value ($ mil.): 1,113

Stock History

NASDAQ (GS): FOSL

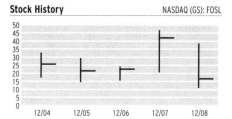

	STOCK PRICE ($) FY Close	P/E High/Low		Earnings	PER SHARE ($) Dividends	Book Value
12/08	16.70	19	6	2.02	0.00	12.03
12/07	41.98	26	12	1.75	0.00	11.58
12/06	22.58	21	14	1.13	0.00	9.03
12/05	21.51	27	14	1.07	0.00	7.89
12/04	25.64	27	14	1.22	0.00	7.86
Annual Growth	**(10.2%)**	**—**	**—**	**13.4%**	**—**	**11.2%**

Foster Wheeler

Even state-of-the-art power plants need facelifts from time to time. That's where Foster Wheeler comes in. The international engineering and construction contractor designs, builds, and upgrades industrial processing facilities and manufactures power equipment through its two business units: Global Engineering & Construction and Global Power. Its Global E&C group serves companies in the oil and gas, chemical, pharmaceutical, and biotechnology markets. The Global Power arm supplies combustion and steam generation equipment for energy and industrial clients. Foster Wheeler also offers construction management, environmental remediation services, and waste-to-energy conversion technologies.

Foster Wheeler has an international bent. It is involved in large gas projects from Saudi Arabia to the Philippines, and it was responsible for building a benchmark liquefied natural gas (LNG) plant for Shell. The company operates from offices in nearly 30 countries in places such as Singapore, Turkey, Chile, France, India, Italy, England, China, and South Africa.

Domestically, it continues to make inroads to the pharmaceutical industry. Its acquisition of US biopharmaceutical company Biokinetics Inc. strengthens Foster Wheeler's position as a major constructor of research, development, and manufacturing facilities in the North American market. To build its upstream oil and gas operations, the company in 2009 acquired the offshore engineering assets of OPE Holdings, active in Houston and Trinidad & Tobago.

The company is continuing to expand its services and heighten its technological offerings. The Global E&C group is involved in the design of facilities in new and development markets sectors such as carbon capture and storage, solid fuel integrated gasification, and biofuels.

Internally, the company — like many of its big construction and engineering peers — is dealing with the legacy of asbestos. Several of its subsidiaries are named as defendants in various US lawsuits stemming from exposure to the toxin. The company forecasts its involvement in such claims to run through 2023.

Foster Wheeler was formed in 1927 from a merger between the Power Specialty Company and the Wheeler Condenser & Engineering Company. The company is run from offices in New Jersey, but is domiciled in Bermuda.

T. Rowe Price owns 10% of Foster Wheeler.

HISTORY

In 1884 Pell and Ernest Foster started Water Works Supply (which became Power Specialty Company in 1900); Ernest hoped to market a European technology that used superheated steam for power. Cousins Frederick and Clifton Wheeler founded Wheeler Condenser & Engineering in New York in 1891 to build condensers and pumps for the marine and power industries.

Power Specialty acquired Wheeler Condenser & Engineering in 1927 and became Foster Wheeler Corporation. That year the company launched a UK subsidiary and in 1928 established a Canadian branch. Foster Wheeler went public in 1929 and bought D. Connelly Boiler in 1931.

US military contracts helped the firm weather the Depression, and the experience won it record business during WWII. After the war Foster Wheeler expanded internationally with subsidiaries in France (1949), Italy (1957), Spain (1965), and Australia (1967).

During the 1960s shortages in many of Foster Wheeler's core industries (energy, fertilizer, and petrochemicals) boosted sales and prompted diversification. In 1967 the company acquired Glitsch International, which made auto and chemical products and electronics.

The company formed Foster Wheeler Energy and Foster Wheeler International in 1973 and acquired Ullrich Copper, a fabricator of industrial copper products. In 1979 it ducked a takeover attempt by McDonnell Douglas.

In the 1980s Foster Wheeler moved into China and Thailand. In 1987 it set up its headquarters in New Jersey and formed Foster Wheeler Constructors to handle Western Hemisphere projects. In the late 1980s it avoided another takeover attempt by New York investor Asher Edelman.

Foster Wheeler opened a Chile subsidiary in 1991 and two years later organized its business into three groups. In 1994 the company acquired Enserch Environmental and formed Foster Wheeler Environmental. It also bought Optimized Process Designs, a construction firm serving the oil industry. That year longtime company executive Richard Swift became CEO.

In 1997 the international builder struggled with the Asian collapse and sold Glitsch to Koch Engineering. It also took a blow on an Illinois waste-to-energy plant (Robbins Resource Recovery) when that state withdrew an interest-free loan and rescinded tax rebates for using that type of energy. The plant cost Foster Wheeler $235 million in charges over the next two years.

Although global sales grew in 1998 (with new contracts in Turkey, Mexico, and China), the oil slump and the Robbins plant hit Foster Wheeler with a $31.5 million loss. That year the company agreed to build a steam generating plant in Ohio and began building Vietnam's first oil refinery.

In 1999 Foster Wheeler formed a recovery plan: It received Chapter 11 bankruptcy protection for the Robbins plant, which it agreed to operate for two years or until sold to a third party, and it filed suit against the State of Illinois. It also cut 1,600 jobs, slashed its quarterly dividend, and closed some facilities. The next year it reorganized its operations, combining the Power Systems Group with the Energy Equipment Group. It also settled a discrimination suit involving about 100 African-American and female employees at the Robbins plant.

In 2001 the company reorganized in Bermuda as Foster Wheeler Ltd. That year Swift retired and was replaced by Raymond Milchovich, a former chairman and CEO of Kaiser Aluminum. To trim down the company, Milchovich launched an aggressive cost-reduction plan in 2002. A decline in the energy sector led subsidiary Foster Wheeler Energy to decide to close its Dansville, New York, manufacturing plant by early 2003. In 2002 the company also consolidated the engineering and construction operations of its New Jersey-based pharmaceutical center under its Reading, UK, office.

The next year Foster Wheeler completed the sale of its environmental management services unit to Tetra Tech for $80 million. In 2004 UK subsidiary Foster Wheeler Energy Limited won a program management contract to provide support for design and construction activities within Iraq's oil sector.

EXECUTIVES

Chairman and CEO: Raymond J. (Ray) Milchovich, age 59, $7,378,313 total compensation
President and COO: Umberto della Sala, age 60, $7,186,197 total compensation
EVP, CFO, and Treasurer: Franco Baseotto, age 50, $1,707,910 total compensation
VP and and Chief Corporate Compliance Officer: Peter D. Rose, age 62
EVP Human Resources: Beth B. Sexton, age 53, $1,038,812 total compensation
EVP, General Counsel, and Secretary: Peter J. Ganz, age 47, $1,637,928 total compensation
EVP Global Sales and Marketing, Global Power Group: David J. Parham
VP Investor Relations and Corporate Communications: W. Scott Lamb, age 54
VP Project Risk Management: David Wardlaw, age 53
Chairman and CEO, Foster Wheeler Energy Limited: Stephen J. (Steve) Davies, age 56
CEO, Foster Wheeler Asia/Pacific (APAC): Franco Anselmi
President and CEO, Foster Wheeler USA Corporation: W. Troy Roder
CEO, Foster Wheeler Iberia: Jesus Cadenas

President and CEO, Foster Wheeler North America; CEO, Power Group Asia: Gary T. Nedelka
CEO, Foster Wheeler Italiana: Marco Moresco
President and CEO, Foster Wheeler France: André Robini
President and CEO, Foster Wheeler Power Group Europe: Tomas Harju-Jeanty
Chief Accounting Officer: Edward (Ed) Carr
Managing Director, Global Sales, Marketing, and Strategic Planning, Global Engineering and Construction: Roberto Penno, age 49
Corporate Communications: Maureen Bingert
Auditors: PricewaterhouseCoopers LLP

LOCATIONS

HQ: Foster Wheeler AG
Perryville Corporate Park, Clinton, NJ 08809
Phone: 908-730-4000 **Fax:** 908-730-5315
Web: www.fwc.com

2008 Sales

	$ mil.	% of total
Australasia	1,745.0	25
Asia	1,575.4	23
Europe	1,451.7	21
North America	1,056.2	15
Middle East	858.6	13
South America	167.4	3
Total	**6,854.3**	**100**

PRODUCTS/OPERATIONS

2008 Sales

	$ mil.	% of total
Engineering & Construction	5,147.2	75
Global Power	1,707.1	25
Total	**6,854.3**	**100**

Selected Operations

Engineering and Construction Group
  Environmental technologies
  Fired heaters
  Licensed technologies to the petrochemical markets
  Process (oil refining) technologies
Global Power Group
  Fluidized-bed, pulverized-coal, and package boilers
  Gasification of biomass
  Heat recovery steam generators
  Specialty products
    Coal pulverizers
    Condensers
    Feedwater heaters
    Selective catalytic reduction

COMPETITORS

ABB	Hitachi
Aker Solutions	HOCHTIEF
ALSTOM	ITOCHU
AMEC	Jacobs Engineering
Babcock & Wilcox	JGC
Barr & Barr	KBR
Bechtel	McDermott
Bilfinger Berger	Mitsubishi Heavy
Black & Veatch	Industries
Bouygues	Parsons Brinckerhoff
Campenon Bernard	Parsons Corporation
Chiyoda Corp.	Saipem
Covanta	Shaw Group
Day & Zimmermann	Skanska
Doosan Babcock	Technip
Doosan Heavy Industries	Tetra Tech
Dresser-Rand	University Mechanical &
Duke Energy	Engineering
Fluor	Washington Division
GE	WorleyParsons Corp.
Halliburton	

HISTORICAL FINANCIALS

Company Type: Public

Income Statement

FYE: Last Friday in December

	REVENUE ($ mil.)	NET INCOME ($ mil.)	NET PROFIT MARGIN	EMPLOYEES
12/08	6,854.3	526.6	7.7%	14,729
12/07	5,107.2	393.9	7.7%	13,859
12/06	3,495.0	262.0	7.5%	11,992
12/05	2,200.0	(109.7)	—	8,953
12/04	2,661.3	(285.3)	—	6,723
Annual Growth	26.7%	—	—	21.7%

2008 Year-End Financials

Debt ratio: 49.2%
Return on equity: 109.3%
Cash ($ mil.): 773
Current ratio: 1.20
Long-term debt ($ mil.): 193
No. of shares (mil.): 126
Dividends
Yield: 0.0%
Payout: —
Market value ($ mil.): 2,956

Stock History

NASDAQ (GS): FWLT

	STOCK PRICE ($) FY Close	P/E High/Low	PER SHARE ($) Earnings	Dividends	Book Value
12/08	23.38	22 4	3.68	0.00	3.10
12/07	77.51	62 17	1.36	0.00	4.52
12/06	27.57	17 9	1.72	0.00	0.50
12/05	18.39	— —	(1.18)	0.00	(2.70)
12/04	7.93	— —	(28.92)	0.00	(4.06)
Annual Growth	31.0%	— —	—	—	—

Fox Entertainment

This Fox has cunning ways to keep TV and movie fans entertained. Fox Entertainment Group (FEG) oversees a broad collection of film and TV entertainment assets owned by media giant News Corporation. Its Fox Filmed Entertainment (FFE) division includes such movie studios as Fox 2000, Fox Searchlight, and its flagship imprint Twentieth Century Fox. FEG also oversees the FOX television network, the upstart MyNetworkTV, and more than 25 broadcasting stations. In addition, it runs a portfolio of cable channels, including FX and the regional sports stations of Fox Sports Net.

Accounting for more than 50% of its parent's revenue, trouble at FEG's film and TV units has hurt the overall performance of News Corporation. Its studios have been hampered by disappointing results at the box office, while FOX television has been hurt by declines in ad spending. In response, News Corporation announced a series of cost-cutting measures early in 2009, including a reduction of hundreds of jobs across its film and TV entertainment operations.

FFE had a difficult time attracting movie audiences during 2008 with lower-than-expected returns from such films as *Australia* and *The Happening*. Those disappointments overshadowed hits such *Marley and Me* and *Slumdog Millionaire*. The studio group rebounded somewhat during the 2009 summer blockbuster season with *X-Men Origins: Wolverine* and the animated *Ice Age: Dawn of the Dinosaurs*. FFE's home entertainment arm has also suffered a decline in DVD sales due to the recession.

The FOX television network fell behind rival CBS in total viewers during the 2008-09 season despite its blockbuster *American Idol* singing contest. (The network is the leader in the all-important 18-49 demographic, however.) It was also hurt that year as advertisers reduced their spending due to the recession. FOX had topped the ratings race the previous season thanks largely to its highly-rated broadcast of the Super Bowl and a Hollywood writers' strike that scotched popular scripted programming on other networks. (FOX had filled the void with reality show *Moment of Truth*.)

MyNetworkTV, Fox's smaller broadcast network, has struggled to find an audience. Originally launched with a schedule heavy on campy, telenovela-style shows, the network announced plans in 2009 to remake itself for the Fall season as a programming service that relies mostly on syndicated programming and second-run movies. It hopes the effort will save on costs by reducing the amount of original programming.

The filmed entertainment and television operations of FEG were reorganized early in 2009 following the resignation of Peter Chernin, who served as president and COO of News Corporation and head of FEG. Chase Carey, previously CEO of DIRECTV, was later named as Chernin's replacement. A longtime Murdoch lieutenant, Carey had served as co-COO with Chernin before taking over the direct satellite service in 2003.

HISTORY

Fox Entertainment Group traces its roots to Hungarian-born immigrant William Fox (originally Wilhelm Fried) who purchased a New York City nickelodeon for $1,600 in 1904. He transformed the failing operation into a success and soon owned (with two partners) 25 theaters across the city. The partners opened a film exchange, The Greater New York Rental Company, and in 1913 began making movies through the Box Office Attraction Company.

Fox became the first to combine film production, leasing, and exhibition when he founded the Fox Film Corporation in 1915. Soon after, he moved the studio to California. One of the first to recognize the value of individual actors, Fox is credited with developing Hollywood's "star system." Fox Film continued to grow through the 1920s, but the company began experiencing trouble in 1927 and by 1930 William Fox was forced out.

In 1935 the company was merged with Twentieth Century Pictures, a studio started two years earlier by Darryl Zanuck, former head of production at Warner Brothers. Under Zanuck's leadership, the studio flourished in the 1930s and 1940s, producing such films as *The Grapes of Wrath* and *All About Eve*. By the early 1950s, however, TV was dulling some of Hollywood's shine. Zanuck left the studio in 1956, only to return in 1962 to help it recover from the disastrously over-budget *Cleopatra*.

The 1960s brought both good (*The Sound of Music*) and bad (*Tora! Tora! Tora!*). By 1971 infighting between Darryl Zanuck and his son Richard, who had been president of the studio, resulted in the resignation of both men. The studio prospered during the 1970s, culminating in 1977 with the release of *Star Wars*, the biggest box office hit in history at that time.

Oilman Marvin Davis bought Twentieth Century Fox for $722 million in 1981. In 1985 the studio changed hands again when it was purchased by Rupert Murdoch. The next year Murdoch bought six TV stations from Metromedia and launched the FOX Broadcasting Company.

Murdoch became CEO in 1995. In 1996 and 1997, respectively, Murdoch created the Fox News Channel and purchased Pat Robertson's International Family Entertainment. The company also joined Liberty Media in 1996 to create a rival to Walt Disney's ESPN sports network.

Fox Entertainment Group went public in November 1998, raising $2.8 billion — one of the largest offerings in American history. In 1999 News Corp. bought the 50% of the Fox/Liberty Networks business that it didn't already own from Liberty Media and transferred ownership to Fox (the operation was renamed FOX Sports Net). The deal gave Liberty Media an 8% stake in News Corp.

In 2001 Fox and partner Saban sold the Fox Family Channel, which they jointly owned, to Walt Disney for about $5.2 billion. It also gained an additional 10 TV stations, when parent News Corp. bought Chris-Craft. In 2003 News Corp. bought 34% of DIRECTV owner Hughes Electronics from General Motors.

In the early part of 2005, News Corp. purchased the rest of Fox Entertainment that it didn't already own for about $6.2 billion. At that time Murdoch passed Fox's top post to president Peter Chernin.

In 2008 News Corp. swapped its 40% stake in DIRECTV, along with three regional sports networks and $625 million in cash, for Liberty Media's 19% stake in News Corp.

Chernin left News Corporation and Fox Entertainment in 2009. He was replaced by former DIRECTV chief Chase Carey.

EXECUTIVES

Deputy Chairman, President, and COO, News Corporation: Chase Carey, age 55
SEVP and CFO: David F. DeVoe, age 62, $7,824,564 total compensation
EVP Sales, Fox Broadcasting: Jean Rossi
EVP Strategic Planning: Preston Beckman
EVP Human Resources: Linda Johns
SVP Diversity Development: Mitsy Wilson
Chairman and CEO Fox Networks: Anthony J. (Tony) Vinciquerra, age 54
Chairman and CEO Fox Filmed Entertainment: Thomas E. (Tom) Rothman
President, Sales, Fox Broadcasting: Jon Nesvig
President, Engineering: Andrew G. (Andy) Setos
Chairman, Entertainment, Fox Broadcasting: Peter Rice
President, FOX National Cable Sports Networks: Robert (Bob) Thompson
President, Fox Sports Net: Randy Freer
President, Fox News Channel: Roger Ailes, age 69, $23,683,140 total compensation
CEO Fox Television Stations Group: Jack Abernethy
President, Digital Media: Dan Fawcett
President, Fox National Cable Networks: Richard (Rich) Battista, age 44
President, Twentieth Century Fox Animation: Vanessa Morrison
President, Twentieth Television: Rick Jacobson
President, 20th Century Fox Films: Jim Gianopoulos
Auditors: Ernst & Young LLP

LOCATIONS

HQ: Fox Entertainment Group, Inc.
10201 W. Pico Blvd., Bldg. 100, Ste. 3220
Los Angeles, CA 90035
Phone: 310-369-1000   **Fax:** 310-969-3300
Web: www.fox.com

PRODUCTS/OPERATIONS

Selected Operations

Cable network programming
 Big Ten Network (49%)
 Fox Business Network
 Fox College Sports
 Fox International Channels
  LAPTV (32%, Latin American pay television)
 Fox Movie Channel
 Fox News Channel
 Fox Pan American Sports (33%)
  Fox Sports en Español
  Fox Sports Latin America
 Fox Reality
 Fox Soccer Channel
 Fox Sports Net
 FUEL TV
 FX
 SPEED
Filmed entertainment
 Feature film production and distribution
  Fox Filmed Entertainment
   Fox 2000
   Fox Atomic
   Fox Searchlight Pictures
   Twentieth Century Fox
   Twentieth Century Fox Animation
  Twentieth Century Fox Home Entertainment
 Television production and distribution
  Fox Television Studios
  Twentieth Century Fox Television
  Twentieth Television
Television
 FOX Broadcasting
 Fox Television Stations
  KCOP (MyNetworkTV, Los Angeles)
  KDFI (FOX, Dallas)
  KDFW (FOX, Dallas)
  KMSP (FOX, Minneapolis)
  KRIV (FOX, Houston)
  KSAZ (FOX, Phoenix)
  KTBC (FOX; Austin, TX)
  KTTV (FOX, Los Angeles)
  KTXH (MyNetworkTV, Houston)
  KUTP (MyNetworkTV, Phoenix)
  WAGA (FOX, Atlanta)
  WDCA (MyNetworkTV; Washington, DC)
  WFLD (FOX, Chicago)
  WFTC (MyNetworkTV, Minneapolis)
  WFXT (FOX, Boston)
  WHBQ (FOX, Memphis)
  WJBK (FOX, Detroit)
  WNYW (FOX, New York City)
  WOFL (FOX; Orlando, FL)
  WOGX (FOX; Gainesville, FL)
  WPWR (MyNetworkTV, Chicago)
  WTTG (FOX; Washington, DC)
  WTVT (FOX, Tampa)
  WTXF (FOX, Philadelphia)
  WUTB (MyNetworkTV, Baltimore)
  WWOR (MyNetworkTV, New York City)
 MyNetworkTV

COMPETITORS

CBS Corp
Discovery Communications
Disney
Liberty Media
MGM
NBC Universal
Sony Pictures Entertainment
Time Warner
Viacom

FPL Group

For a Florida company without any oranges, FPL Group produces a lot of juice. It has operations across the US, including an independent power production business, but most of its revenues are produced by its utility subsidiary, Florida Power & Light (FPL). FPL distributes electricity to 4.5 million customers and about 25,000 MW of generating capacity from interests in nuclear and fossil-fueled power plants. Subsidiary FPL Group Capital owns nonutility businesses, including NextEra Energy Resources, an independent power producer and wholesale energy marketer. Subsidiary FPL FiberNet leases wholesale fiber-optic capacity to telephone, cable, and Internet providers; it operates a 2,745-mile network.

National green power producer NextEra Energy Resources (formerly FPL Energy) gets about 40% of its 16,930 MW generating capacity from wind, solar, hydroelectric, and waste-to-energy facilities; the rest comes from traditional nuclear and thermal plants. The unit owns plants in more than 20 states, and it is expanding its generation portfolio. In 2007 the company acquired the Point Beach Nuclear Plant in Two Rivers from Wisconsin Energy for $924 million.

In 2008 FPL released a 10-year strategic plan for meeting Florida's energy needs. The plan combines additions in generating capacity, while using renewable energy sources and energy efficiency programs to avoid the need to build (the previously proposed) four midsized power plants.

HISTORY

During Florida's land boom of the early 1920s, new homes and businesses were going up fast. But electric utilities were sparse, and no transmission lines linked systems.

In 1925 American Power & Light Company (AP&L), which operated utilities throughout the Americas, set up Florida Power & Light (FPL) to consolidate the state's electric assets. AP&L built transmission lines linking 58 communities from Miami to Stuart on the Atlantic Coast and from Arcadia to Punta Gorda on the Gulf.

FPL accumulated many holdings, including a limestone quarry, streetcars, phone companies, and water utilities, and purchases in 1926 and 1927 nearly doubled its electric properties. In 1927 the company used an electric pump to demonstrate how swamplands could be drained and cultivated.

During the 1940s and 1950s FPL sold its nonelectric properties. The Public Utility Holding Company Act of 1935 forced AP&L to spin off FPL in 1950. The company was listed on the NYSE that year.

FPL grew with Florida's booming population. In 1972 its first nuclear plant (Turkey Point, south of Miami) went on line. In the 1980s it began to diversify with the purchase of real estate firm W. Flagler Investment in 1981, and FPL Group was created in 1984 as a holding company. It subsequently acquired Telesat Cablevision (1985), Colonial Penn Group (1985, insurance), and Turner Foods (1988, citrus groves). FPL Group formed ESI Energy in 1985 to develop nonutility energy projects.

Diversification efforts didn't pan out, and in 1990 the firm wrote off about $750 million. That year, sticking to electricity, the utility snagged its first out-of-state power plant, in Georgia, acquiring a 76% stake (over five years). FPL Group sold its ailing Colonial Penn unit in 1991; two years later it sold its real estate holdings and some of its cable TV businesses.

The utility gave environmentalists cause to complain in 1995. First, the St. Lucie nuclear plant was fined by the NRC for a series of problems. FPL also wanted to burn orimulsion, a cheap, tarlike fuel. (Barred by the governor, the utility gave up the plan in 1998.)

In 1997 FPL Group created FPL Energy, an independent power producer (IPP), out of its ESI Energy and international operations; FPL Energy teamed up with Belgium-based Tractebel the next year to buy two gas-fired plants in Boston and Newark, New Jersey.

FPL Energy built wind-power facilities in Iowa in 1998 and in Wisconsin and Texas in 1999; it also bought 35 generating plants in Maine in 1999. That year FPL Group sold its Turner Foods citrus unit and the rest of its cable TV holdings. By 2000 FPL Energy owned interests in plants in 12 states.

Out of its fiber-optic operations, FPL Group in 2000 created subsidiary FPL FiberNet to market wholesale capacity. That year talks of Spanish utility giant Iberdrola purchasing FPL Group ended when Iberdrola's shareholders objected; in 2001 plans to merge with New Orleans-based Entergy fell through after a series of disagreements. The deal would have created one of the US's largest power companies.

In 2002 FPL Group purchased an 88% interest in the Seabrook Nuclear Generating Station in New Hampshire for $837 million from a consortium of US utilities, including Northeast Utilities and BayCorp Holdings. In 2005 FPL Group acquired Gexa Corp., a Houston-based electric utility.

Late in 2005 FPL agreed to buy rival power concern Constellation Energy Group Inc. in an $11 billion stock deal. However, the companies called the deal off in 2006, citing uncertainty about regulatory approvals.

FPL Energy had agreed to purchase British Energy's 50% stake in nuclear power generation firm AmerGen Energy; however, Exelon, which owns the other half of AmerGen, exercised its right of first refusal and purchased the remainder of AmerGen.

EXECUTIVES

Chairman and CEO; Chairman, Florida Power & Light: Lewis (Lew) Hay III, age 53, $11,540,544 total compensation
Vice Chairman and Chief of Staff: Moray P. Dewhurst, age 53
President and COO: James L. (Jim) Robo, age 46, $9,259 total compensation
EVP Finance and CFO; EVP Finance and CFO, Florida Power & Light: Armando Pimentel Jr., age 46, $1,739,727 total compensation
Controller and Chief Accounting Officer; VP Accounting and Chief Accounting Officer, Florida Power & Light: K. Michael Davis, age 62
EVP Engineering, Construction and Corporate Services; EVP Engineering, Construction and Corporate Services, Florida Power & Light: Robert L. (Bob) McGrath, age 55
EVP Power Generation; EVP Power Generation, Florida Power & Light: Antonio Rodriguez, age 66
EVP and Chief Strategy, Policy, and Business Process Improvement Officer: Christopher A. (Chris) Bennett, age 50
EVP Federal Regulatory Affairs: Joseph T. Kelliher
EVP and General Counsel; EVP and General Counsel, Florida Power & Light: Charles E. Sieving, age 36

EVP Human Resources; EVP Human Resources,
Florida Power & Light: James Poppell Sr., age 58
VP and Corporate Secretary: Alissa E. Ballot
VP Corporate and External Affairs: Pamela M. Rauch
VP Customer Service: Marlene M. Santos
VP Marketing and Communications:
Timothy (Tim) Fitzpatrick
President and CEO, Florida Power & Light:
Armando J. Olivera, age 59,
$3,623,753 total compensation
President, Nuclear Division: John A. Stall, age 54,
$2,934,459 total compensation
Director Investor Relations: Jim von Riesemann
Auditors: Deloitte & Touche LLP

LOCATIONS

HQ: FPL Group, Inc.
700 Universe Blvd., Juno Beach, FL 33408
Phone: 561-694-4000   Fax: 561-694-4620
Web: www.fplgroup.com

PRODUCTS/OPERATIONS

2008 Sales

	$ mil.	% of total
Florida Power & Light	11,649	71
NextEra Energy Resources	4,570	28
Corporate & other	191	1
Total	**16,410**	**100**

Selected Subsidiaries and Divisions

Florida Power & Light Company
    Energy Marketing and Trading
FPL Group Capital Inc.
    NextEra Energy Resources, LLC
        FPL Energy Power Marketing, Inc.
    FPL FiberNet, LLC

COMPETITORS

AES
Bangor Hydro-Electric
Calpine
Chesapeake Utilities
CMS Energy
Delmarva Power
Duke Energy
Edison International
Entergy
Exelon
Florida Public Utilities
JEA
MidAmerican Energy
Mirant
Narragansett
Oglethorpe Power
Progress Energy
Public Service Enterprise Group
SCANA
Seminole Electric
Sempra Energy
Southern Company
TECO Energy

HISTORICAL FINANCIALS

Company Type: Public

Income Statement

FYE: December 31

	REVENUE ($ mil.)	NET INCOME ($ mil.)	NET PROFIT MARGIN	EMPLOYEES
12/08	16,410.0	1,639.0	10.0%	10,700
12/07	15,263.0	1,312.0	8.6%	10,500
12/06	15,710.0	1,281.0	8.2%	10,400
12/05	11,846.0	885.0	7.5%	10,200
12/04	10,522.0	887.0	8.4%	10,000
Annual Growth	**11.8%**	**16.6%**	**—**	**1.7%**

2008 Year-End Financials

Debt ratio: 118.4%
Return on equity: 14.6%
Cash ($ mil.): 535
Current ratio: 0.70
Long-term debt ($ mil.): 13,833

No. of shares (mil.): 411
Dividends
    Yield: 3.5%
    Payout: 43.7%
Market value ($ mil.): 20,709

Stock History

NYSE: FPL

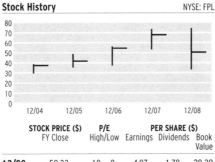

	STOCK PRICE ($) FY Close	P/E High/Low		PER SHARE ($) Earnings	Dividends	Book Value
12/08	50.33	18	8	4.07	1.78	28.39
12/07	67.78	22	16	3.27	1.64	26.09
12/06	54.42	17	12	3.23	1.50	24.13
12/05	41.56	21	16	2.29	1.42	20.66
12/04	37.38	15	12	2.45	1.30	18.32
Annual Growth	**7.7%**	**—**	**—**	**13.5%**	**8.2%**	**11.6%**

Franklin Resources

Franklin Resources believes a penny saved is a penny lost — if it's not invested. Operating as Franklin Templeton Investments, the firm manages a family of more than 300 mutual funds that invest in international and domestic stocks; taxable and tax-exempt money market instruments; and corporate, municipal, and US government bonds. The investment products are sold under the Franklin, Templeton, Mutual Series, Bissett, Darby Overseas, and Fiduciary Trust banners. Franklin Resources also offers separately managed accounts and insurance product funds. Descendants of founder Rupert Johnson Sr. and their families own more than a third of Franklin Resources.

The company, which manages more than $404 billion in assets and more than 20 million shareholder accounts, continues to expand its product portfolio and strengthen its geographic reach. It operates mainly in North America and Europe, but is adding assets under management in South America, Asia, and the Middle East.

Its 2007 acquisition of a 25% stake in Algebra Capital, a Dubai investment firm, is part of its strategy for the region. In 2009 Franklin Resources increased that stake to 40%. All told, Franklin Resources has offices in some 30 countries and offers its products in more than 150.

In addition to its core business, Franklin Resources also provides shareholder services and manages investments for pension plans, trusts, and other institutions. Through banking subsidiaries, it offers such services as lending and deposit accounts. Retail banking, private banking, consumer lending, auto-loan securitization, and trust services are offered through Franklin Templeton Bank & Trust, Franklin Capital, Fiduciary Trust Company International, and other subsidiaries.

HISTORY

Rupert Johnson Sr. founded Franklin Distributors (capitalizing on Benjamin Franklin's reputation for thrift) in New York in 1947; it launched its first fund, Franklin Custodian, in 1948. Custodian grew into five funds, including conservatively managed equity and bond funds. In 1968 Johnson's son Charles (who had joined the firm in 1957) became president and CEO. The company went public in 1971 as Franklin Resources.

In 1973 Franklin bought San Mateo-based investment firm Winfield & Co. and relocated to the Golden State. The buy provided additional products, including the Franklin Gold Fund (made possible by the end of the prohibition in the US against private interests owning commodity gold). With interest rate spikes in the late 1970s and early 1980s, money drained from savings accounts was poured into more lucrative money market mutual funds.

The Franklin Money Fund, launched in 1975, fueled the firm's tremendous asset growth in the 1980s. In 1981 the Franklin Tax-Free Income Fund (introduced in 1977) began investing solely in California municipal bonds. The fund's success led Franklin to introduce 43 tax-free income funds in later years.

In 1985 Franklin bought Pacific Union Bank and Trust (now Franklin Bank), allowing it to offer consumers such services as credit cards and to compete with financial services supermarkets, such as Merrill Lynch. It also bought real estate firm Property Resources (now Franklin Properties).

The 1987 stock crash and the California real estate slump forced Franklin to focus on its funds businesses. In 1992 it bought Bahamas-based Templeton, Galbraith & Hansberger, the manager of Templeton Funds, a major international funds business. The Templeton deal added an aggressive investment management unit to complement the conservatively managed Franklin funds.

In 1940 Sir John Templeton gained control of investment company Templeton, Dobbrow and Vance (TDV). TDV launched Templeton Growth Fund in 1954. In 1969 Templeton sold his interest in TDV but continued to manage the Templeton Growth Fund. John Galbraith became president of Securities Fund Investors (SFI), the distribution company for Templeton Growth Fund, in 1974. In 1977 Galbraith bought SFI from Templeton and began building the Templeton funds broker-dealer network in the US. The Templeton World Fund was formed in 1978. Templeton Investment Counsel was launched to provide investment advice in 1979. In 1986 these companies were combined to form Templeton, Galbraith & Hansberger Ltd.

In 1996 Franklin bought Heine Securities, previous investment adviser to Mutual Series Fund Inc. Max Heine, a leading investor, had established Mutual Shares Corp. in 1949. Heine Securities was formed in 1975. After the purchase, Franklin set up subsidiary Franklin Mutual Advisers as the investment adviser for Mutual Series Fund.

In 1997 the weak Asian economy hurt Templeton's international funds, prompting liquidation of a Japanese stocks-based fund. Franklin cut jobs and shuffled management in 1999; the restructuring acknowledged the clash between the firm's value-investing style and investors' bull-market optimism.

In 2000 the firm gained a foothold in Canada with its purchase of Bissett & Associates Investment Management. Franklin's purchase of Fiduciary Trust the following year gave the firm greater access to institutional investors and affluent individuals.

Franklin Resources boosted its alternative investment offerings with the 2003 acquisition of Darby Overseas, which focuses on private equity, mezzanine, and fixed-income investment products, and specializes in Asian and Latin American fixed-income securities.

Chairman Charles Johnson retired from the CEO's office in 2004, turning the reins over to a new generation; his son Gregory was named CEO. Also that year Franklin Resources agreed to pay $50 million to settle market-timing allegations and reached a $20 million settlement with the SEC and an $18 million settlement with the state of California over commissions paid to brokers for mutual fund sales.

EXECUTIVES

Chairman: Charles B. (Charlie) Johnson, age 75
Vice Chairman: Rupert H. Johnson Jr., age 68
President, CEO, and Director:
Gregory E. (Greg) Johnson, age 47
EVP Technology and Operations:
Jennifer J. (Jenny) Bolt, age 44
EVP, CFO, and Treasurer: Kenneth A. Lewis, age 47
SVP and Chief Administrative Officer:
Norman R. Frisbie Jr., age 41
EVP: Murray L. Simpson, age 71
EVP Alternative Strategies: William Y. Yun, age 50
EVP Portfolio Operations: John M. Lusk, age 50
EVP and General Counsel: Craig S. Tyle, age 48
EVP Global Distribution: Vijay C. Advani, age 48
SVP and Assistant Secretary: Leslie M. Kratter, age 63
VP Human Resources, International: Donna S. Ikeda, age 52
VP Human Resources, US: Penelope S. Alexander, age 48
VP Corporate Communications: Holly E. Gibson Brady, age 42
President, Fiduciary Trust Company International:
Henry P. Johnson
President and CEO, Franklin Templeton Sealand Fund Management: Michael X. Lin
President, Indian Asset Management: Harshendu Bindal
Secretary: Maria Gray
Auditors: PricewaterhouseCoopers LLP

LOCATIONS

HQ: Franklin Resources, Inc.
1 Franklin Pkwy., Bldg. 970, 1st Fl.
San Mateo, CA 94403
Phone: 650-312-2000   **Fax:** 650-312-5606
Web: www.franklintempleton.com

2008 Sales

	$ mil.	% of total
North America		
US	3,828.7	64
Bahamas	844.8	14
Canada	387.1	6
Asia/Pacific & Latin America	667.9	11
Europe, Middle East & Africa	303.9	5
Total	**6,032.4**	**100**

2008 Assets under Management

	% of total
North America	
US	74
Canada	7
Europe, Middle East & Africa	11
Asia/Pacific & Latin America	8
Total	**100**

PRODUCTS/OPERATIONS

2008 Sales

	$ mil.	% of total
Investment management fees	3,683.4	61
Underwriting & distribution fees	2,002.0	33
Shareholder servicing fees	289.4	5
Other	57.6	1
Total	**6,032.4**	**100**

2008 Sales by Segment

	$ mil.	% of total
Investment management & related services	5,995.8	99
Banking/finance	36.6	1
Total	**6,032.4**	**100**

2008 Assets under Management

	% of total
Equity	52
Fixed-income	28
Hybrid	19
Money market	1
Total	**100**

COMPETITORS

AllianceBernstein	Nationwide Financial
American Century	New York Life
AXA Financial	Old Mutual (US)
BlackRock	PIMCO
Capital Group	Pioneer Investment
Citigroup	Principal Financial
FMR	Putnam
Invesco	T. Rowe Price
John Hancock Financial	Torchmark
JPMorgan Chase	USAA
Morgan Stanley	The Vanguard Group

HISTORICAL FINANCIALS

Company Type: Public

Income Statement

FYE: September 30

	ASSETS ($ mil.)	NET INCOME ($ mil.)	INCOME AS % OF ASSETS	EMPLOYEES
9/08	9,176.5	1,588.2	17.3%	8,800
9/07	9,943.3	1,772.9	17.8%	8,700
9/06	9,499.9	1,267.6	13.3%	8,000
9/05	8,893.9	1,057.6	11.9%	7,200
9/04	8,228.1	701.9	8.5%	6,700
Annual Growth	**2.8%**	**22.6%**	**—**	**7.1%**

2008 Year-End Financials

Equity as % of assets: 77.1%
Return on assets: 16.6%
Return on equity: 22.0%
Long-term debt ($ mil.): 118
No. of shares (mil.): 230

Dividends
 Yield: 0.9%
 Payout: 12.0%
Market value ($ mil.): 20,299
Sales ($ mil.): 6,032

Stock History

NYSE: BEN

	STOCK PRICE ($) FY Close	P/E High/Low	PER SHARE ($) Earnings	Dividends	Book Value
9/08	88.13	21 12	6.67	0.80	30.71
9/07	127.50	21 15	7.03	0.60	31.83
9/06	105.75	22 16	4.86	0.48	29.02
9/05	83.96	21 14	4.06	0.40	24.68
9/04	55.76	22 15	2.80	0.34	22.17
Annual Growth	**12.1%**	**— —**	**24.2%**	**23.9%**	**8.5%**

Freeport-McMoRan Copper & Gold

Freeport-McMoRan Copper & Gold (FCX) really digs its profits. Its 91%-owned subsidiary, PT Freeport Indonesia (PT-FI), operates the vast open-pit Grasberg gold, copper, and silver mine in Indonesia, whose government owns the other 9%. FCX controls proved and probable reserves of about 100 billion pounds of copper, 40 million ounces of gold, and 2.5 billion pounds of molybdenum. Copper, in the form of concentrates and in refined products such as cathodes and anodes, accounts for most of FCX's sales. It's the world's #2 copper company behind Codelco. FCX is also engaged in smelting and refining through PT-FI's 25% stake in PT Smelting, which operates a copper smelter and refinery in Indonesia.

Other FCX units include PT Irja Eastern Minerals, which explores for minerals in Indonesia, and Atlantic Copper, which operates a copper smelter in Spain.

Political and environmental controversy in Indonesia has dogged FCX since its major protector, former president Suharto, was forced to resign in 1998 after more than 30 years in power. Terrorism in Indonesia, where FCX is one of the largest employers, also makes the company vulnerable to work stoppages. Anglo-Australian mining giant Rio Tinto is jointly involved with FCX in developing mineral properties in Indonesia's politically and environmentally sensitive Papua region. Too, the company's primary developmental project, the Tenke Fungume copper and gold mine, is located in the Democratic Republic of Congo, which also can be an unstable environment in which to do business. Tenke Fungume is jointly owned with Lundin Mining and the Congolese government.

The 2007 $26 billion acquisition of Phelps Dodge brought that company's global copper, gold, and molybdenum business into the fold. The deal placed Freeport in a position to thrive as a global competitor in the rank just below such metals and mining giants like BHP Billiton, Rio Tinto, and Vale.

A year later Freeport sold the wire and cable business it had acquired in the Phelps Dodge deal, selling the unit to General Cable Corporation for $735 million.

HISTORY

The Freeport Sulfur Company was formed in Texas in 1912 by Francis Pemberton, banker Eric Swenson, and several investors to develop a sulfur field. The next year Freeport Texas was formed as a holding company for Freeport Sulfur and other enterprises.

During the 1930s the company diversified. In 1936 Freeport pioneered a process to remove hydrocarbons from sulfur. The company joined Consolidated Coal in 1955 to establish the National Potash Company. In 1956 Freeport formed an oil and gas subsidiary, Freeport Oil.

Internationally, Freeport formed an Australian minerals subsidiary in 1964 and a copper-mining subsidiary in Indonesia in 1967. The company changed its name to Freeport Minerals in 1971 and merged with Utah-based McMoRan Oil & Gas (formerly McMoRan Explorations) in 1982.

McMoRan Explorations had been formed in 1969 by William McWilliams, Jim Bob Moffett, and Byron Rankin. In 1973 McMoRan formed an exploration and drilling alliance with Dow Chemical and signed a deal with Indonesia to mine in the remote Irian Jaya region. McMoRan went public in 1978.

Moffett became chairman and CEO of Freeport-McMoRan in 1984. Freeport-McMoRan Copper was formed in 1987 to manage the company's Indonesian operations. The unit assumed the Freeport-McMoRan Copper & Gold name in 1991. Two years later Freeport-McMoRan acquired Rio Tinto Minera, a copper-smelting business with operations in Spain.

To support expansion in Indonesia, Freeport-McMoRan spun off its copper and gold division in 1994. In 1995 Freeport-McMoRan Copper & Gold (FCX) formed an alliance with the UK's RTZ Corporation to develop its Indonesian mineral reserves. Local riots that year closed the Grasberg Mine, and FCX's political risk insurance was canceled. Despite these setbacks, higher metal prices and growing sales in 1995 helped the company double its operating income.

An Indonesian tribal leader filed a $6 billion lawsuit in 1996 charging FCX with environmental, human rights, and social and cultural violations. The company called the suit baseless but offered to set aside 1% of its annual revenues, or about $15 million, to help local tribes. Tribal leaders rejected the offer, and in 1997 a judge dismissed the lawsuit.

In 1997 FCX pulled out of Bre-X Minerals' Busang gold mine project, which independent tests later proved to be a fraud of historic proportions. Amid widespread rioting, Indonesia's embattled president Suharto was forced out of office in 1998. The new government investigated charges of cronyism involving FCX.

FCX received permission from the Indonesian government in 1999 to expand the Grasberg Mine and increase ore output up to 300,000 metric tons per day. However, the next year an overflow accident killed four workers in Grasberg and, as a result of the accident, the Indonesian government ordered FCX to reduce its production at the mine by up to 30%. Normal production at the mine resumed in early 2001.

FM Services (administrative, legal, and financial services) was added as a subsidiary in 2002. In 2003 FCX bought an 86% stake in PT Puncakjaya Power, a supplier of power to PT-FI.

EXECUTIVES

Chairman; President Commissioner, PT Freeport Indonesia: James R. (Jim Bob) Moffett, age 70, $25,432,828 total compensation
Vice Chairman: B. M. Rankin Jr., age 79
President, CEO, and Director: Richard C. Adkerson, age 62, $33,386,016 total compensation
EVP, CFO, and Treasurer: Kathleen L. Quirk, age 45, $8,777,300 total compensation
EVP and Chief Administrative Officer: Michael J. Arnold, age 56, $5,116,921 total compensation
SVP, International Relations and Federal Government Affairs: W. Russell King
SVP and General Counsel: L. Richards (Rick) McMillan II, age 61
VP and Controller, Financial Reporting: C. Donald Whitmire Jr.
VP Communications: William L. (Bill) Collier III
President, Atlantic Copper; SVP, FCX (Concentrates): Javier Targhetta
President, Americas Division: Harry M. (Red) Conger, age 76
President, Mining: Richard E. Coleman

President, Climax Molybdenum: David H. (Dave) Thornton
President, PT Freeport Indonesia: Armando Mahler, age 53
President, Africa Division: Phillip S. (Phil) Brumit
Manager Investor Relations: David Joint
Director External Communications: Eric Kinneberg
Auditors: Ernst & Young LLP

LOCATIONS

HQ: Freeport-McMoRan Copper & Gold Inc.
One North Central Ave., Phoenix, AZ 85004
Phone: 602-366-8100
Web: www.fcx.com

2008 Sales

	$ mil.	% of total
US	7,609	43
Japan	2,662	15
Spain	1,872	10
Indonesia	1,420	8
Chile	669	4
United Kingdom	404	2
Other countries	3,160	18
Total	**17,796**	**100**

PRODUCTS/OPERATIONS

2008 Sales

	$ mil.	% of total
Refined copper products	9,575	54
Copper in concentrates	3,954	22
Molybdenum	2,408	14
Gold	1,286	7
Other products	573	3
Total	**17,796**	**100**

Selected Subsidiaries and Affiliates

Atlantic Copper Holding, SA (smelting and refining, Spain)
Chino Mines Company
Climax Molybdenum Company
FM Service Company (administrative and financial services)
Missouri Lead Smelting Company
PT Freeport Indonesia Co. (91%, mining)
    PT Smelting (Gresik) Co. (25%, smelting, Indonesia)
PT Irja Eastern Minerals Corp. (mining, Indonesia)
PT Puncakjaya Power (86%, supplies power to PT Freeport Indonesia)

COMPETITORS

Antofagasta
Barrick Gold
BHP Billiton
Centromin
Chevron Mining
Codelco
Newmont Mining
Rio Tinto Limited
Southern Copper
Vale Inco

HISTORICAL FINANCIALS

Company Type: Public

Income Statement

FYE: December 31

	REVENUE ($ mil.)	NET INCOME ($ mil.)	NET PROFIT MARGIN	EMPLOYEES
12/08	17,796.0	(11,067.0)	—	29,300
12/07	16,939.0	2,977.0	17.6%	25,400
12/06	5,790.5	1,396.0	24.1%	7,000
12/05	4,179.1	995.1	23.8%	26,938
12/04	2,371.9	202.3	8.5%	8,589
Annual Growth	**65.5%**	**—**	**—**	**35.9%**

2008 Year-End Financials

Debt ratio: 447.0%
Return on equity: —
Cash ($ mil.): 872
Current ratio: 1.66
Long-term debt ($ mil.): 9,235
No. of shares (mil.): 412
Dividends
    Yield: 7.4%
    Payout: —
Market value ($ mil.): 10,064

Stock History

NYSE: FCX

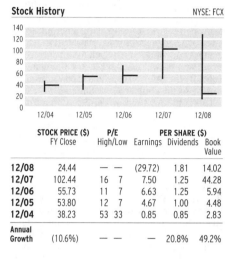

	STOCK PRICE ($) FY Close	P/E High/Low		PER SHARE ($) Earnings	Dividends	Book Value
12/08	24.44	—	—	(29.72)	1.81	14.02
12/07	102.44	16	7	7.50	1.25	44.28
12/06	55.73	11	7	6.63	1.25	5.94
12/05	53.80	12	7	4.67	1.00	4.48
12/04	38.23	53	33	0.85	0.85	2.83
Annual Growth	**(10.6%)**	**—**	**—**	**—**	**20.8%**	**49.2%**

Frontier Communications

Serving city dwellers and country folk alike, Frontier Communications provides local, long-distance, and digital phone services and Internet access to about 3 million primarily residential subscribers in 24 states. The company, formerly known as Citizens Communication, is active mostly in rural and small to midsized markets, where it is the incumbent local-exchange carrier (ILEC) operating under the Frontier Residential brand. Other offerings include satellite television services (offered through a partnership with DISH Network), as well as data, Internet, and telephone packages and equipment for business clients. Frontier had been the company's brand for years; it was adopted as the corporate name in 2008.

The company has been expanding its horizons largely through acquisitions. In 2009 it agreed to buy certain assets (4.8 million access lines) from Verizon Communications for about $8.6 billion in stock. Upon completion of the acquisition, Frontier hopes to begin offering voice and broadband services in rural areas in 14 additional states. The deal is expected to possibly double or triple Frontier's size and give it a healthy boost against other rural communications carriers.

States in which Frontier Communications currently operates include Arizona, California, Illinois, Minnesota, Montana, Nebraska, Nevada, New Mexico, New York, North Dakota, Oregon, Pennsylvania, Tennessee, Utah, West Virginia, and Wisconsin.

HISTORY

Frontier Communications was formed in 1935 as Citizens Utilities Company to acquire Public Utilities Consolidated Corporation, a Minneapolis-based company with interests in electric, gas, water, and telephone utilities throughout the US. From 1950 to 1970 the company bought utilities in rural and suburban areas of Arizona, California, Hawaii, Illinois, Indiana, Ohio, and Pennsylvania. A major acquisition was Hawaii's Kauai Electric Company, in 1969. By the mid-1970s, electric power brought in 40% of the company's revenues.

Leonard Tow, head of Century Communications, was brought on board in 1989 and elected chairman the next year, remaining in that position until 2004. Expanding Citizens through more electric, water, and natural gas acquisitions, he tripled the company's revenues in less than 10 years.

In 1993 Citizens acquired a majority stake in Electric Lightwave, the first competitive local-exchange carrier (CLEC) west of the Mississippi River. Citizens started its long-distance telephone service in 1994. It also acquired 500,000 local access lines in nine states from GTE, quadrupling the size of its operations. By 1995 the telecom group was the fastest-growing segment of the company.

After the Telecommunications Act was passed in 1996, Citizens acquired another 110,000 local access lines and cable systems with more than 7,000 customers from ALLTEL and bought three Southern California cable systems with Century Communications. Citizens aggressively marketed local phone service in neighboring areas to its service territories, but the company didn't see the return it expected and by 1997 had to cut its workforce and tighten cost controls. In light of the cutbacks, bookkeeping troubles, and 1996 threats from Vermont to revoke Citizens' license there for accounting and permit problems, the board voted Tow a pay cut.

The company sold a minority stake in Electric Lightwave to the public in 1997 (Citizens reacquired the stake in 2002 and Electric Lightwave became a wholly owned subsidiary). Citizens continued its buying spree with telecom and gas firms in New York and Hawaii, and a local phone company in Pennsylvania, in 1998.

The next year, Citizens began turning itself into a pure telecom company through a series of transactions. It agreed to pay about $2.8 billion for 900,000 local phone lines owned by U S WEST and GTE. It also sold its cable TV interests and agreed to sell its water and wastewater operations (for $835 million).

Citizens bought more than 1 million local phone lines in 2001 from Global Crossing for about $3.5 billion. Later that year the company canceled its pending acquisition agreements with Qwest, U S WEST's successor, amid a dispute over how much revenue the local lines were producing. The terminated deals, valued at $1.7 billion, would have given Citizens another 540,000 local lines. It later pulled out of a deal to buy an additional 63,000 access lines in Arizona and California from Verizon Communications.

The company also sold part of its natural gas business for $375 million in 2001, the same year it changed its name to Citizens Communications. Although an earlier deal to sell its electric properties fell through, the company completed the sale of its Kauai Electric division in 2002 for $215 million to the Kauai Island Utility Cooperative. That year it also reached an agreement to sell its Hawaiian gas division in a deal valued at $115 million and completed the following year.

In November 2002 two executives of the company's public utilities division were dismissed after an SEC investigation into $7.8 million in payments for services the company did not receive.

Citizens sold its competitive local-exchange carrier (CLEC), Electric Lightwave, to Integra Telecom in mid-2006 in a deal that was valued at $247 million. The next year it acquired Commonwealth Telephone, effectively expanding its access to the Pennsylvania market. Later that year the company then spent $62 million to purchase Global Valley Networks, a California provider of telephone and Internet services, in a move to expand its service area in the Western US.

In 2008 the company took its brand name, Frontier, as its corporate name.

EXECUTIVES

Chairman, President, and CEO:
Mary Agnes (Maggie) Wilderotter, age 54
EVP and COO: Daniel J. McCarthy, age 44
EVP and CFO: Donald R. (Don) Shassian, age 53
SVP and Chief Accounting Officer: Robert J. Larson, age 49
EVP Sales, Marketing, and Business Development: Peter B. (Pete) Hayes, age 51
EVP Human Resources and Call Center Sales and Service: Cecilia K. McKenney, age 46
SVP and General Manager New Business Operations: Melinda M. White, age 49
SVP, General Counsel, and Secretary: Hilary E. Glassman, age 46
SVP and Treasurer: David R. Whitehouse
SVP and General Manager, Southeast Region: Ken Arndt
VP Sales and Distribution: Betty Guy
Auditors: KPMG LLP

LOCATIONS

HQ: Frontier Communications Corporation
   3 High Ridge Park, Stamford, CT 06905
Phone: 203-614-5600   **Fax:** 203-614-4602
Web: www.czn.net

PRODUCTS/OPERATIONS

Selected Subsidiaries

Commonwealth Telephone Company
CTE Telecom
Evans Telephone Holdings
Frontier InfoServices Inc.
Frontier Subsidiary Telco LLC
Frontier Telephone of Rochester, Inc.
Mohave Cellular Limited Partnership
Navajo Communications Company
NCC Systems, Inc.
Ogden Telephone Company
Phone Trends, Inc.
Rhinelander Telecommunications, Inc.

COMPETITORS

AT&T
CenturyTel
Embarq
FairPoint Communications, Inc.
Integra Telecom
Iowa Telecommunications
Qwest Communications
tw telecom
Verizon
Vonage
XO Holdings

HISTORICAL FINANCIALS
Company Type: Public

Income Statement
FYE: December 31

	REVENUE ($ mil.)	NET INCOME ($ mil.)	NET PROFIT MARGIN	EMPLOYEES
12/08	2,237.0	182.7	8.2%	5,671
12/07	2,288.0	214.7	9.4%	5,900
12/06	2,025.4	344.6	17.0%	5,446
12/05	2,162.5	202.4	9.4%	6,103
12/04	2,193.0	72.2	3.3%	6,373
Annual Growth	0.5%	26.1%	—	(2.9%)

2008 Year-End Financials

Debt ratio: 909.7%
Return on equity: 24.1%
Cash ($ mil.): 164
Current ratio: 1.22
Long-term debt ($ mil.): 4,722

No. of shares (mil.): 312
Dividends
   Yield: 11.4%
   Payout: 175.4%
Market value ($ mil.): 2,730

Stock History
NYSE: FTR

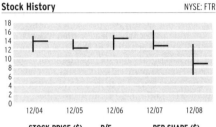

	STOCK PRICE ($) FY Close	P/E High/Low		PER SHARE ($) Earnings	Dividends	Book Value
12/08	8.74	23	11	0.57	1.00	1.66
12/07	12.73	25	19	0.65	1.00	3.19
12/06	14.37	14	11	1.06	1.00	3.39
12/05	12.23	23	20	0.60	1.00	3.34
12/04	13.79	64	50	0.23	0.50	4.36
Annual Growth	(10.8%)	—	—	25.5%	18.9%	(21.4%)

Furniture Brands International

Furniture Brands International runs a furniture-making empire. The company ranks as one of the top US makers of residential furniture. Furniture Brands' subsidiaries offer a lineup of nationally recognized brands, including Broyhill, Lane, Thomasville, and Drexel Heritage, among others. Broyhill makes mid-priced furniture for the bedroom and dining room, as well as other home furnishings. Laneventure (outdoor wicker and teak collections) and Henredon (wood and upholstered pieces) target the premium-priced furniture market. Furniture Brands distributes its products through a network of furniture centers, independent dealers, national and local chains, and department stores.

To weather the US recession, Furniture Brands in December 2008 laid off some 15% of its domestic workforce, amounting to about 1,400 jobs, which included both management and hourly employees. It made further cuts in May 2009 by laying off 250 plant workers. The cuts have primarily affected manufacturing centers in North Carolina and Mississippi. Furniture Brands operates about 20 plants in Mississippi, North Carolina, and Virginia.

Looking for ways to diversify, Furniture Brands announced plans to expand its licensing program. The Thomasville brand has already extended its reach beyond furniture into residential flooring, lighting, and kitchen cabinetry. The company is looking to license its Lane, Broyhill, Drexel Heritage, and Henredon brands.

Samson Holding took a nearly 15% stake in 2007 and indicated that it may seek control of the company or board representation.

To better focus on the residential rather than business furnishings market, Furniture Brands sold its business furniture division, Hickory Business Furniture (HBF), to HNI Corp. for about $75 million in 2008. Furniture Brands also is refocusing its distribution efforts.

In response to financial troubles at major furniture retailers, Furniture Brands is expanding its network of free-standing independently owned stores, such as Thomasville Home Furnishings, which exclusively sell Thomasville products. To strengthen brand awareness and more keenly focus on distribution and sales, Furniture Brands also is boosting its share of Drexel Heritage Home Inspiration Stores.

Due in part to the residential furniture industry trend of shifting to offshore sourcing (primarily to Asia), the company has closed or announced the closing of more than 35 domestic manufacturing facilities since 2001. It has also boosted its manufacturing capacity in Indonesia to capitalize on the low manufacturing costs. It also owns and operates several plants in the Philippines and Indonesia.

CEO Mickey Holliman stepped down in 2008, but kept his position as chairman. His replacement, gum and candy supplier executive Ralph Scozzafava, served as vice chairman and CEO designate for six months before taking on the chief role.

HISTORY

Although already a diversified firm, INTERCO's purchase of Ethan Allen in 1980 took the company in a direction that would eventually become its only business. INTERCO (now Furniture Brands International) traces its roots back to the pairing of two shoe manufacturers and made a name for itself by running men's shoemaker and retailer Florsheim, which it acquired in 1953. It added other operations, including department stores and apparel, beginning in the 1960s. The Ethan Allen purchase gave INTERCO 24 furniture factories and 300 retail outlets.

The company grew its furniture business later in 1980 by purchasing Broyhill Furniture Industries, which was founded by J. E. Broyhill as Lenoir Chair Company in 1926. The Broyhill line first became popular during the 1930s. The Broyhill family built the company into the largest privately owned maker of furniture, with 20 manufacturing facilities when INTERCO purchased it.

In 1986, after acquiring furniture maker Highland House (Hickory), INTERCO made its largest acquisition in the home furnishings and furniture market when it gained control of the Lane Company for approximately $500 million. Founded in 1912 by Ed Lane to make cedar chests, Virginia-based Lane had grown into a full-line maker of furniture with about 15 plants

in operation. The acquisition of Lane lifted furniture and furnishings to 33% of INTERCO's total sales in 1987.

INTERCO added Converse (footwear) in 1986. Richard Loynd, the Converse CEO, served as INTERCO's CEO from 1989 to 1996. In 1988, under a takeover threat by the Rales brothers of Washington, DC, the company retained the investment banking firm of Wasserstein Perella, which advised payment of a $76 special dividend, for which INTERCO borrowed $1.8 billion via junk bonds. To repay the debt, the firm began selling off assets, including its apparel businesses and Ethan Allen. However, the sales yielded low prices and some businesses failed to attract buyers.

After fighting off the hostile takeover, INTERCO filed bankruptcy in 1991 — one of the largest bankruptcy cases in US history. It also filed a malpractice suit against Wasserstein Perella when it emerged from Chapter 11; the suit was settled the following year, and Apollo Investment Fund acquired a large stake in the firm.

INTERCO sold the last of its 80-year-old shoemaking business with the spinoff of its Florsheim and Converse units in 1994. The company acquired Thomasville Furniture from Armstrong World Industries for about $330 million in 1993, a purchase that made it the leading shaker in residential furniture. Founded in 1904, the Finch brothers ran Thomasville until Armstrong acquired it in 1968.

W. G. "Mickey" Holliman became CEO in 1996, and INTERCO's board decided to change the company's name to Furniture Brands International. In 1997 Apollo Investment Fund, its largest shareholder, sold its nearly 40% stake.

In 2000 the company started selling kitchen and bathroom cabinets under the Thomasville brand in Home Depot. In 2001 Furniture Brands bought Drexel Heritage, Henredon, and Maitland-Smith units from LifeStyle Furnishings for $275 million. Thomasville shut down 21 domestic manufacturing facilities in 2003.

Holliman left the company and was replaced by Ralph Scozzafava in January 2008. Scozzafava, who had been an executive at Wm. Wrigley Jr. Co., was elected chairman of the board of Furniture Brands in May.

EXECUTIVES

Chairman and CEO: Ralph P. Scozzafava, age 50, $4,801,847 total compensation
SVP and CFO: Steven G. (Steve) Rolls, age 54, $2,214,067 total compensation
Chief Marketing Officer: Alexander W. (Alex) Hodges
EVP and CFO, HDM Furniture Industries: Bryan Milleson
SVP, General Counsel, and Secretary: Jon D. Botsford, age 54
SVP Global Supply Chain: Raymond J. (Ray) Johnson, age 53
SVP, IT, HDM Furniture Industries: Triche Leander
SVP Human Resources: Mary E. Sweetman, age 45, $1,604,323 total compensation
VP Communications: John S. Hastings
President, Thomasville Furniture Industries: Edward (Ed) Teplitz, age 47
President, Henredon Furniture Industries: Thomas G. (Tom) Tilley Jr., age 59
President and COO, Drexel Heritage: Lenwood Rich
President, Lane Furniture Industries: Gregory P. (Greg) Roy
President, Broyhill Furniture Industries: Jeffrey L. (Jeff) Cook, age 53, $2,321,381 total compensation
President, Designer Group: Dan Bradley, age 52
President, Lane Furniture Industries: Skipper Holliman

Manager of Corporate Communications: Marty Richmond
Controller and Chief Accounting Officer: Richard R. (Rick) Isaak, age 41, $715,518 total compensation
Auditors: KPMG LLP

LOCATIONS

HQ: Furniture Brands International, Inc.
101 S. Hanley Rd., St. Louis, MO 63105
Phone: 314-863-1100 **Fax:** 314-863-5306
Web: www.furniturebrands.com

PRODUCTS/OPERATIONS

Subsidiaries
Broyhill
Drexel Heritage
Henredon
Lane
Laneventure
MaitlandSmith
Pearson
Thomasville

Selected Products
Case Goods Furniture
  Bedroom
  Dining room
  Living room

Occasional Furniture
  Accent items
  Freestanding home entertainment centers
  Home office items
  Wood tables

Stationary Upholstery Products
  Chairs
  Love seats
  Sectionals
  Sofas

Other
  Motion furniture
  Recliners
  Sleep sofas

COMPETITORS

American Leather	Flexsteel
Ashley Furniture	Home Meridian
Bassett Furniture	Hooker Furniture
Berkline BenchCraft	Kimball International
Brown Jordan	Klaussner Furniture
Bush Industries	La-Z-Boy
Chromcraft Revington	Masco
Decorize	Meadowcraft
DMI Furniture	Rowe Fine Furniture
Dorel Industries	Sauder Woodworking
Ethan Allen	Stanley Furniture

HISTORICAL FINANCIALS

Company Type: Public

Income Statement

	REVENUE ($ mil.)	NET INCOME ($ mil.)	NET PROFIT MARGIN	EMPLOYEES
				FYE: December 31
12/08	1,743.2	(385.9)	—	8,100
12/07	2,082.1	(45.6)	—	11,900
12/06	2,418.2	55.1	2.3%	13,800
12/05	2,386.8	61.4	2.6%	15,150
12/04	2,447.4	91.6	3.7%	17,800
Annual Growth	(8.1%)	—	—	(17.9%)

2008 Year-End Financials

Debt ratio: 43.7%	No. of shares (mil.): 49
Return on equity: —	Dividends
Cash ($ mil.): 107	Yield: 5.4%
Current ratio: 3.01	Payout: —
Long-term debt ($ mil.): 160	Market value ($ mil.): 108

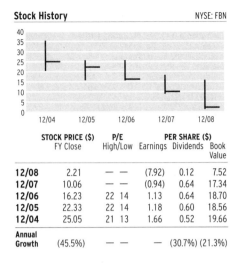

	STOCK PRICE ($)		P/E		PER SHARE ($)		
	FY Close		High/Low	Earnings	Dividends	Book Value
12/08	2.21		— —	(7.92)	0.12	7.52
12/07	10.06		— —	(0.94)	0.64	17.34
12/06	16.23		22 14	1.13	0.64	18.70
12/05	22.33		22 14	1.18	0.60	18.56
12/04	25.05		21 13	1.66	0.52	19.66
Annual Growth	(45.5%)		— —	—	(30.7%)	(21.3%)

GameStop Corp.

GameStop holds the top score in the video game retailing industry. The company is the largest retailer of new and used games, hardware, entertainment software, and accessories. GameStop boasts more than 6,200 stores located in 16 countries, including the US, Canada, Australia, and Europe. A majority of the company's revenue is generated by sales of new and used video games. Retail outlets branded as GameStop and EB Games carry an average of 1,000 new titles and 3,500 used ones. The company also operates e-commerce Web sites (GameStop.com, ebgames.com), publishes *Game Informer*, a video game magazine that reaches more than 3.5 million subscribers, and offers GameStop TV in many of its locations.

The company's purchase of rival Electronics Boutique in 2005 doubled GameStop's size. Prior to buying Electronics Boutique, GameStop had made plans to expand by adding about 400 stores a year. The company exceeded its own expectations with the purchase of its rival. In 2009 it's back to its original store-opening pace.

For store growth, GameStop has set aggressive goals for itself during the past few years and shows no signs of letting up. In the US, where the company generates about 73% of its revenue, it opened 674 new stores in 2008, 586 stores during 2007, and 421 stores in 2006. That's an average of 560 new stores per year. In 2009, despite a recession in the US, the game retailer anticipates opening up to 400 new stores, mostly in strip shops across the US.

Along with its expansion in the US, GameStop has plans to extend its reach further into Canada, Australia, and particularly into Europe, where its revenue rose from 11% in 2008 to 14% in 2009. In 2008 the company struck a major deal to enter European territory with its $629 million purchase of video game retailer Micromania, which brought with it some 330 stores in France. In July 2008 GameStop acquired The Gamesman, the largest independent gaming retailer in New Zealand. The deal included eight Gamesman video game stores and brought GameStop's total store count in the country to 38.

GameStop also plans to continue to target its broad and niche markets to maintain its foothold in new and used gaming. The company chases after the hard-core electronic game enthusiast, as well as those who game on occasion and buy games as gifts at holiday seasons. It allows its customers to trade in used video games for store credits for future purchases.

To better communicate with gamers, the company has announced plans to launch an in-store video network — called GameStop TV — in its 4,000-plus stores via a partnership with CBS Outernet and Reflect Systems. The in-store programming will feature product promotions, game previews, developer interviews, and other customized content, as well as advertising targeted to its customers.

GameStop got a new CEO in 2008 — its first CEO change since the company's inception in 1996. Dick Fontaine gave up the title of chief executive to Daniel DeMatteo, who had served as COO since 1996 and vice chairman of the company since 2004. Also, Paul Raines, formerly of Home Depot, joined the company as COO in September 2008. Fontaine retained the chairman's title and focuses on international operations and acquisitions.

HISTORY

NeoStar Retail Group resulted from the 1994 combination of software retailers Babbage's and Software Etc. Babbage's had been founded by James McCurry and Gary Kusin in 1983. Named for 19th-century mathematician Charles Babbage (considered the father of the computer), it went public in 1988.

Software Etc. began as a division of B. Dalton Bookseller in 1984. Bookstore chain Barnes & Noble and Dutch retailer Vendex acquired B. Dalton two years later. Software Etc. went public in 1992.

Both companies focused on mall retailing: Babbage's on game software, and Software Etc. on a broader variety of PC software. Both saw growth spurred by the rising popularity of Nintendo and Sega game systems and by falling PC prices. The two merged in 1994 in an effort to stave off growing competition from big retail chains such as Best Buy and Wal-Mart. NeoStar opened 122 stores in 1995.

Amid flat sales the following year, several senior executives left. Also in 1996 NeoStar lost its contract to operate software departments at 136 Barnes & Noble sites, and it soon filed for Chapter 11. Late that year a group led by Barnes & Noble's head honcho Leonard Riggio purchased about 460 of NeoStar's 650 stores for $58.5 million and renamed the company Babbage's, Etc. Former Software Etc. chief Dick Fontaine was named CEO.

By 1997 the company began concentrating on popular games and software, and in 1999 it formed its e-commerce site GameStop.com. In late 1999 Barnes & Noble paid Riggio's group $210 million for Babbage's Etc. In June 2000 the company fortified its position and became the #1 US video game retailer with the purchase of rival game retailer Funco (about 400 stores) for $161.5 million. The company changed its name to GameStop in August 2001 and filed to go public, which it accomplished in February 2002. Though public, it was still under the majority control of Barnes & Noble until 2004 when GameStop bought back its shares.

GameStop bought rival Electronics Boutique in 2005, virtually doubling its size from 2,000 to about 4,500 stores. Steven R. Morgan, a former executive with Electronics Boutique, became president of GameStop later that year.

The company appointed COO and vice chairman Daniel DeMatteo as its chief executive while Dick Fontaine retained the title of chairman. Also, Paul Raines, from Home Depot, took over as COO in September 2008.

EXECUTIVES

Chairman: R. Richard (Dick) Fontaine, age 67, $7,008,496 total compensation
CEO and Director: Daniel A. (Dan) DeMatteo, age 61, $6,869,568 total compensation
COO: J. Paul Raines, age 45, $1,713,684 total compensation
EVP and CFO: Catherine R. (Cathy) Smith, age 46
SVP and Chief Accounting Officer: Robert A. Lloyd, age 47
EVP Finance: David W. Carlson, age 46, $2,245,452 total compensation
EVP Merchandising and Marketing: Tony D. Bartel, age 45, $1,895,585 total compensation
SVP Real Estate and Development: Marc Summey
SVP Stores: Mike Dzura
SVP Merchandising: Bob McKenzie
SVP Supply Chain and Refurbishment: Mike Mauler
VP Human Resources: Marissa Andrada
VP Marketing: Mike Hogan
VP Corporate Communications and Public Affairs: Chris Olivera
President Directeur General, Micromania: Pierre Cuilleret
Director Investor Relations: Matt Hodges
Auditors: BDO Seidman, LLP

LOCATIONS

HQ: GameStop Corp.
625 Westport Pkwy., Grapevine, TX 76051
Phone: 817-424-2000   **Fax:** 817-424-2002
Web: www.gamestop.com

2009 Sales

	$ mil.	% of total
US	6,466.7	73
Europe	1,271.0	14
Canada	548.2	7
Australia	520.0	6
Total	**8,805.9**	**100**

2009 Stores

	No.
US	4,331
Europe	1,201
Australia	350
Canada	325
Total	**6,207**

PRODUCTS/OPERATIONS

2009 Sales

	$ mil.	% of total
New video game software	3,685.0	42
Used video game products	2,026.6	23
New video game hardware	1,860.2	21
Other	1,234.1	14
Total	**8,805.9**	**100**

Selected Merchandise

Accessories
    PC entertainment accessories (video cards, joysticks, mice)
    Video game accessories (controllers, memory cards, add-ons)
    Other (strategy guides, magazines, action figures, trading cards)
PC entertainment software and other software
Used video games
Video game hardware
Video game software

COMPETITORS

Amazon.com	GameFly
Best Buy	Hollywood Entertainment
Blockbuster Inc.	Kmart
Borders Group	Movie Gallery
Buy.com	RadioShack
CompUSA	Target
Costco Wholesale	Toys "R" Us
Fry's Electronics	Wal-Mart
GAME Group	Zones

HISTORICAL FINANCIALS

Company Type: Public

Income Statement

FYE: Saturday nearest January 31

	REVENUE ($ mil.)	NET INCOME ($ mil.)	NET PROFIT MARGIN	EMPLOYEES
1/09	8,805.9	398.3	4.5%	41,000
1/08	7,094.0	288.3	4.1%	43,000
1/07	5,318.9	158.3	3.0%	32,000
1/06	3,091.8	100.8	3.3%	42,000
1/05	1,842.8	60.9	3.3%	20,500
Annual Growth	47.9%	59.9%	—	18.9%

2009 Year-End Financials

Debt ratio: 23.7%	No. of shares (mil.): 165
Return on equity: 19.1%	Dividends
Cash ($ mil.): 578	Yield: 0.0%
Current ratio: 1.16	Payout: —
Long-term debt ($ mil.): 546	Market value ($ mil.): 4,079

Stock History

NYSE: GME

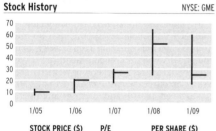

	STOCK PRICE ($) FY Close	P/E High/Low		PER SHARE ($) Earnings	Dividends	Book Value
1/09	24.78	25	7	2.38	0.00	13.97
1/08	51.56	36	14	1.75	0.00	11.31
1/07	26.72	58	36	0.50	0.00	8.36
1/06	20.16	26	12	0.81	0.00	6.77
1/05	9.55	22	14	0.52	0.00	3.30
Annual Growth	26.9%	—	—	46.3%	—	43.5%

Gannett Co.

Gannett satisfies news junkies with a stash of daily US papers. The company is the top newspaper publisher in the US with about 85 daily papers boasting a total circulation of more than 6.5 million. Its flagship *USA TODAY*, with a circulation of more than 2 million, is the nation's largest newspaper. Some other major papers in Gannett's holdings include *The Arizona Republic* and the *Detroit Free Press*. The company also owns about 850 non-daily publications, as well as more than 200 papers in the UK published through subsidiary Newsquest. In addition, Gannett owns 23 television stations in 20 markets, publishes periodicals and inserts (including *USA WEEKEND*), and operates Web sites for many of its papers.

Despite its gargantuan size, Gannett has not been immune to the downturn in advertising and readership affecting the rest of the industry. Its flagship newspaper, in particular, has suffered deep declines in sales due to lower levels of spending on print ads by national advertisers. Newspaper advertising accounts for more than 60% of Gannett's sales.

The company has responded by cutting costs through consolidation of certain business functions within its vast portfolio of newspapers. In the newsroom, Gannett is transforming its papers through an effort to move some content away from the printed page and towards digital delivery. The result of the company's "Information Center" model has been smaller printed editions augmented by more stories appearing online. The operational changes have been accompanied by a 10% reduction in jobs during 2008. Early the following year many Gannett employees were furloughed for a week without pay. Later in 2009 some 1,400 positions were cut at its US community publishing division.

Detroit Media Partnership, a joint operating agency (JOA) that oversees the company's *Free Press* and its rival *Detroit News* (owned by MediaNews Group), cut home delivery of the papers to three times a week in 2009. The move came as a way to reduce expenses at a time when readership and advertising revenue continue to decline. The papers still distribute news online.

The company's television business, which accounts for more than 10% of sales, has also been hurt by the economic recession and lower spending by advertisers. Gannett has responded with job reductions and other cost-cutting measures in an effort to boost the bottom line.

Gannett has also been investing in online media and services to diversify its revenue. It owns comparison shopping site ShopLocal and online advertising company PointRoll, and it has a 50% stake in job site CareerBuilder. Other investments include Classified Ventures (24% stake) and Topix (33%).

HISTORY

In 1906 Frank Gannett started a newspaper empire when he and his associates purchased a stake in New York's *Elmira Gazette*. In 1923 Gannett bought out his associates' interests and formed the Gannett Company. The company's history of technical innovation dates to the 1920s, when Frank Gannett invested in the development of the Teletypesetter; some of his newspapers were printing in color by 1938. The company continued to buy small and midsized dailies in the Northeast, and by Gannett's death in 1957, it had accumulated 30 newspapers.

In the 1960s Gannett expanded nationally through acquisitions. It was not until 1966, however, that it started its own paper, *TODAY* (now *FLORIDA TODAY*), in Cocoa Beach, Florida. Gannett went public in 1967.

The company's greatest period of growth came during the 1970s and 1980s under the direction of Allen Neuharth (CEO from 1973 to 1986). Gannett captured national attention in 1979 when it merged with Phoenix-based Combined Communications Corporation (CCC), whose holdings included TV and radio stations, an outdoor advertising business, and pollster Louis Harris & Associates.

In 1982 Gannett started *USA TODAY*, a national newspaper whose splashy format and mini-stories made it an industry novelty. Critics branded it "McPaper," but circulation passed a million copies a day by the end of 1983. (It wasn't profitable until 1993, however.)

In 1990 declines in newspaper advertising, primarily among US retailers, broke the company's string of 89 consecutive quarters of positive earnings. USA TODAY-On-Demand, a fax news service, began in 1992. Gannett bought Multimedia Inc., a newspaper, TV, cable, and program syndication company, for about $2.3 billion in 1995.

Web site *USA TODAY Online* debuted in 1995. In 1996 Gannett sold Louis Harris & Associates and its outdoor advertising operations and traded six radio stations to Jacor Communications for one Tampa TV station.

Gannett exited the radio industry in 1998 by selling its last five stations. It also sold its Multimedia Security Service. Gannett's integrity took a blow in 1998 when a reporter for one of its newspapers (*The Cincinnati Enquirer*) illegally obtained information for a report accusing Chiquita Brands International of unscrupulous business practices. Gannett retracted the story and settled with Chiquita to the tune of about $14 million.

The company broke new ground in 1999 when Karen Jurgensen was named editor of *USA TODAY* (she was the first woman to head a national newspaper). In early 2000 Gannett sold its cable operations to Cox Communications for $2.7 billion. The company also formed TV and Web venture USA Today Live to produce news stories for its TV stations. Later that year chairman John Curley passed the title of CEO to president Douglas McCorkindale (McCorkindale would become chair the next year).

Also in 2000 Gannett made a slew of acquisitions, including a purchase of the UK's News Communications & Media, *Arizona Republic* publisher Central Newspapers, and 21 newspapers from Thomson Corp. (now Thomson Reuters). The company moved its headquarters in 2001 from Arlington to McLean, Virginia.

In 2004 Gannett purchased more than 30 newspapers and specialty publications from Brown County Publishing in Wisconsin. Jurgensen stepped down as editor of *USA Today* in the fallout of a scandal involving reporter Jack Kelley. Broadcasting chief Craig Dubow took over as president and CEO in 2005. The company boosted its online marketing quotient with its 2005 purchase of Internet advertising technology firm PointRoll. In late 2005 Gannett acquired a TV station in Denver (KTVD-TV).

In 2006 McCorkindale retired and Dubow added chairman to his title. Later that year, the company acquired WATL-TV in Atlanta from the Tribune Company for $180 million.

EXECUTIVES

Chairman, President, and CEO: Craig A. Dubow, age 54, $3,135,469 total compensation
EVP and CFO: Gracia C. Martore, age 57, $3,046,985 total compensation
SVP and Chief Digital Officer: Christopher D. (Chris) Saridakis, age 40, $1,071,969 total compensation
SVP Human Resources: Roxanne V. Horning, age 59
SVP, General Counsel, and Secretary: Todd A. Mayman
VP Planning and Development: Daniel S. Ehrman Jr., age 62
VP and Controller: George R. Gavagan, age 62
VP and Treasurer: Michael A. Hart
VP ContentOne: Tara J. Connell

LOCATIONS

HQ: Gannett Co., Inc.
7950 Jones Branch Dr., McLean, VA 22107
Phone: 703-854-6000   **Fax:** 703-854-2053
Web: www.gannett.com

PRODUCTS/OPERATIONS

2008 Sales

	$ mil.	% of total
Newspapers		
Advertising	4,145.6	61
Circulation	1,216.6	18
Broadcasting	772.5	12
Digital	281.4	4
Other	351.5	5
Total	**6,767.6**	**100**

Selected Operations

Newspapers
The Arizona Republic (Phoenix)
Asbury Park Press (New Jersey)
The Cincinnati Enquirer
The Courier-Journal (Louisville, KY)
The Des Moines Register (Iowa)
Detroit Free Press
The Honolulu Advertiser
The Indianapolis Star
The Journal News (Westchester County, NY)
The News Journal (Wilmington, DE)
Rochester Democrat and Chronicle (New York)
The Tennessean (Nashville)
USA TODAY (McLean, VA)
Broadcasting
KARE-TV (NBC, Minneapolis)
KNAZ-TV (NBC; Flagstaff, AZ)
KPNX-TV (NBC, Phoenix)
KSDK-TV (NBC, St. Louis)
KTHV-TV (CBS; Little Rock, AR)
KTVD-TV (MyNetworkTV, Denver)
KUSA-TV (NBC, Denver)
KXTV-TV (ABC; Sacramento, CA)
WATL-TV (MyNetworkTV, Atlanta)
WBIR-TV (NBC; Knoxville, TN)
WCSH-TV (NBC; Portland, ME)
WFMY-TV (CBS; Greensboro, NC)
WGRZ-TV (NBC; Buffalo, NY)
WJXX-TV (ABC; Jacksonville)
WKYC-TV (NBC; Cleveland)
WLBZ-TV (NBC; Bangor, ME)
WLTX-TV (CBS; Columbia, SC)
WMAZ-TV (CBS; Macon, GA)
WTLV-TV (NBC; Jacksonville)
WTSP-TV (CBS; Tampa)
WUSA-TV (CBS; Washington, DC)
WXIA-TV (NBC; Atlanta)
WZZM-TV (ABC; Grand Rapids, MI)

Other holdings and investments
Army Times Publishing Company (newspapers)
California Newspaper Publishing (19%, community newspapers)
CareerBuilder (51%, online job recruitment)
Classified Ventures (24%, online content publishing)
Clipper Magazine (direct mail advertising)
Gannett Healthcare Group (periodical publishing)
Gannett Offset (commercial printing)
Newsquest plc (newspaper publishing, UK)
Planet Discover (Internet search and advertising)
PointRoll (digital media marketing services)
Ponderay Newsprint (13%)
ShopLocal.com (online shopping portal)
Texas-New Mexico Newspaper Partnership (41%, community newspapers)
Topix.net (34%, news monitoring service)
USA WEEKEND (weekly newspaper insert)

COMPETITORS

Advance Publications	MediaNews
Block Communications	Morris Multimedia
CBS	New York Times
Dispatch Printing	News Corp.
Google	Philadelphia Media
Hearst Newspapers	Sinclair Broadcast Group
Journal Communications	Tribune Company
Lee Enterprises	Washington Post
Local TV	Yahoo!
McClatchy Company	

HISTORICAL FINANCIALS

Company Type: Public

Income Statement

FYE: Last Sunday in December

	REVENUE ($ mil.)	NET INCOME ($ mil.)	NET PROFIT MARGIN	EMPLOYEES
12/08	6,767.6	(6,647.6)	—	41,500
12/07	7,439.5	1,055.6	14.2%	46,100
12/06	8,033.4	1,160.8	14.4%	49,675
12/05	7,598.9	1,244.7	16.4%	52,600
12/04	7,381.3	1,317.2	17.8%	52,500
Annual Growth	**(2.1%)**	**—**	**—**	**(5.7%)**

2008 Year-End Financials

Debt ratio: 361.5%
Return on equity: —
Cash ($ mil.): 99
Current ratio: 1.08
Long-term debt ($ mil.): 3,817

No. of shares (mil.): 235
Dividends
  Yield: 20.0%
  Payout: —
Market value ($ mil.): 1,878

Stock History

NYSE: GCI

	STOCK PRICE ($) FY Close	P/E High/Low		PER SHARE ($) Earnings	Dividends	Book Value
12/08	8.00	—	—	(29.11)	1.60	4.50
12/07	39.00	14	8	4.52	1.42	38.41
12/06	60.46	13	11	4.90	1.20	35.71
12/05	60.57	16	12	5.05	1.12	32.25
12/04	81.70	19	16	4.92	1.04	34.78
Annual Growth	**(44.1%)**	**—**	**—**	**—**	**11.4%**	**(40.0%)**

The Gap

The ubiquitous clothing retailer Gap has been filling closets with jeans and khakis, T-shirts and poplin since the Woodstock era. The company, which operates about 3,150 stores worldwide, built its iconic casual brand on basics for men, women, and children, but over the years has expanded through the urban chic chain Banana Republic and ailing budgeteer Old Navy, launched in 1994. Other brand extensions include GapBody, GapKids, and babyGap; each also has its own online incarnation. All Gap clothing is private-label merchandise made exclusively for the company. From the design board to store displays, Gap controls all aspects of its trademark casual look. Gap was founded by Don and Doris Fisher in 1969.

After four consecutive years of declining sales, failed turnaround attempts, and fashion missteps, the nation's largest specialty apparel retailer is struggling to reverse the trend in a hostile retail environment. CEO Glenn Murphy, who joined Gap in mid-2007 from the Canadian drugstore chain Shoppers Drug Mart, has announced plans to close or consolidate select stores and to reduce the size of others in an attempt to better manage the retailer's vast real estate portfolio. To that end, Gap has trimmed its US store count while expanding cautiously in Asia.

In a bid to regain its merchandising edge, the company has made revamping its Gap-brand women's apparel collection a top priority. To that end, in fall 2008 the company acquired 10-year-old Athleta, a direct-marketer of women's active wear. Gap purchased Athleta as part of its strategy to diversify its brand offerings and upgrade women's apparel. Gap will sell Athleta's merchandise online as the fifth brand in its e-commerce portfolio, which includes its namesake brand, Old Navy, Banana Republic, and Piperlime. Gap has also replaced its chief designer for Gap brand clothing and added petite and tall sizes. The company also redesigned its Spartan look-alike stores in an attempt to win back shoppers with a more homey atmosphere.

In Europe, Gap operates stores in the UK, Ireland, and France. It also has about 140 shops in Japan. Gap is expanding its international footprint through a franchise program launched in 2006. As a result, as of mid-2009, some 100 Gap franchise stores and 30-plus Banana Republic shops are open for business in 17 countries.

Gap dipped its toes into personal care products by signing an agreement with Inter Parfums in mid-2005. As part of the deal, Inter Parfums develops, formulates, manufactures, and packages the products, which are branded under the Gap and Banana Republic names. The Gap markets and sells them in its GapBody stores.

The founding Fisher family owns about a third of Gap Inc.

HISTORY

Donald Fisher and his wife, Doris, opened a small store in 1969 near what is now San Francisco State University. The couple named their store The Gap (after "the generation gap") and concentrated on selling Levi's jeans. The couple opened a second store in San Jose, California, eight months later, and by the end of 1970 there were six Gap stores. The Gap went public six years later.

In the beginning the Fishers catered almost exclusively to teenagers, but in the 1970s they expanded into activewear that would appeal to a larger spectrum of customers. Nevertheless, by the early 1980s The Gap — which had grown to about 500 stores — was still dependent upon its largely teenage customer base. However, it was less dependent on Levi's (about 35% of sales), thanks to its growing stable of private labels.

In a 1983 effort to revamp the company's image, Donald hired Mickey Drexler, a former president of AnnTaylor with a spotless apparel industry track record, as The Gap's new president. Drexler immediately overhauled the motley clothing lines to concentrate on sturdy, brightly colored cotton clothing. He also consolidated the stores' many private clothing labels into the Gap brand.

Also in 1983 The Gap bought Banana Republic, a unique chain of jungle-themed stores that sold safari clothing. The company expanded the chain, which enjoyed tremendous success in the mid-1980s but slumped after the novelty of the stores wore off late in the decade. In response, Drexler introduced a broader range of clothes (including higher-priced leather items) and dumped the safari lines in 1988. By 1990 Banana Republic was again profitable.

The first GapKids opened in 1985 after Drexler couldn't find clothing that he liked for his son. During the late 1980s and early 1990s, the company grew rapidly, opening its first stores in Canada and the UK. In 1990 it introduced baby-Gap in 25 GapKids stores, featuring miniature versions of its GapKids line. The Gap announced in 1991 it would no longer sell Levi's (which had fallen to less than 2% of total sales) and would sell nothing but private-label items.

In 1994 the company launched Old Navy Clothing Co., named after a bar Drexler saw in Paris. Banana Republic opened its first two stores outside the US, both in Canada, in 1995.

Robert Fisher (the founders' son) became the new president of the Gap division (including babyGap and GapKids) in 1997 and was charged with reversing the segment's sales decline. The company refocused its Gap chain on basics (jeans, T-shirts, and khakis) and helped boost its performance with a high-profile advertising campaign focusing on those wares. Later in 1997 the Gap opened an online Gap store.

In late 1999, amid sluggish Gap division sales, Robert Fisher resigned and Drexler took over his duties. Gap misjudged fashion trends in 2000, which resulted in two years of disappointing earnings. After a 10% reduction in its workforce, the company returned to a more conservative fashion approach.

In 2002 Drexler retired and was replaced by Paul Pressler, a veteran of The Walt Disney Company. In 2006 Gap entered into a 10-year non-exclusive services agreement with International Business Machines valued at $1.1 billion.

Stung by allegations in the British press of forced child labor in India being used in the manufacture of apparel for its Gap Kids chain, Gap in 2007 announced a package of measures intended to strengthen its commitment to eradicating the exploitation of children in the garment industry.

In October 2008 Gap acquired Athleta, a direct-marketer of women's active wear. Gap purchased Athleta as part of its strategy to diversify its brand offerings. The company also opened its first Banana Republic and Gap brand factory stores in Canada in late October, extending its outlet business, launched in 1994, to Canada.

EXECUTIVES

Chairman Emeritus: Donald G. (Don) Fisher, age 80
Chairman and CEO: Glenn K. Murphy, age 47, $9,329,170 total compensation
EVP Strategy and Operations; President, Gap Inc. Outlet: Arthur (Art) Peck, age 53, $3,108,594 total compensation
EVP and CFO: Sabrina Simmons, age 46, $2,728,831 total compensation
Chief Creative Designer: Patrick Robinson
SVP, General Counsel, Secretary, and Chief Compliance Officer: Michelle Banks, age 45
EVP Human Resources, Communications, and Corporate Social Responsibility: Eva Sage-Gavin, age 50
SVP Corporate Real Estate: C. David Zoba, age 57
SVP Loss Prevention: Keith White
SVP International Sourcing: Stan Raggio, age 51
SVP Corporate Operations and Logistics: Colin Funnell
SVP and Managing Director: Ron Young
VP Investor Relations: Evan Price
President, Gap Inc. International, Europe: Stephen (Steve) Sunnucks
President, Gap North America: Marka Hansen, age 54, $4,518,064 total compensation
President, Old Navy: J. Tom Wyatt, age 53, $3,698,479 total compensation
President, Banana Republic: Jack Calhoun, age 44
President, Gap Inc. Direct: Toby Lenk
President and CEO, Athleta: Joseph E. (Joe) Teno Jr.
President, GapKids and babyGap: Pamela B. Wallack
Merchandising Director: Karyn Erickson, age 41
Auditors: Deloitte & Touche LLP

LOCATIONS

HQ: The Gap Inc.
2 Folsom St., San Francisco, CA 94105
Phone: 650-952-4400   **Fax:** 415-427-2553
Web: www.gap.com

2009 Sales

	$ mil.	% of total
Retail		
North America	11,768	81
Asia	880	6
Europe	780	5
Other regions	68	1
Direct (US only)	1,030	7
Total	**14,526**	**100**

2009 Stores

	No.
North America	2,833
Europe	176
Asia	140
Total	**3,149**

PRODUCTS/OPERATIONS

2009 Stores

	No.
Gap North America	1,193
Old Navy North America	1,067
Banana Republic North America	573
Gap Europe	173
Gap Asia	113
Banana Republic Asia	27
Banana Republic Europe	3
Total	**3,149**

2009 Sales

	$ mil.	% of total
Gap	5,958	41
Old Navy	5,707	39
Banana Republic	2,636	18
Other	225	2
Total	**14,526**	**100**

Selected Stores and Brands

Athleta (women's activewear)
babyGap (clothing for infants and toddlers)
Banana Republic (upscale clothing and accessories)
Gap (casual and active clothing and body care products)
GapBody (intimate apparel)
GapKids (clothing for children)
Old Navy (lower-priced family clothing)
Piperlime (online shoes)

COMPETITORS

Abercrombie & Fitch	Lands' End
Aéropostale	Levi Strauss
American Eagle Outfitters	L.L. Bean
AnnTaylor	Macy's
Arcadia	Marks & Spencer
Babies "R" Us	Nautica Apparel
Benetton	NIKE
Calvin Klein	Nordstrom
The Children's Place	OshKosh B'Gosh
Dillard's	Phillips-Van Heusen
Eddie Bauer	Polo Ralph Lauren
Express, LLC	Reebok
Fast Retailing	REI
Foot Locker	Retail Brand Alliance
Fruit of the Loom	Ross Stores
Guess?	Saks
Gymboree	Sears
H&M	Talbots
HSN	Target
Inditex	TJX Companies
J. C. Penney	Tommy Hilfiger
J. Crew	VF
Juicy Couture	Wal-Mart
Kohl's	Zappos.com

HISTORICAL FINANCIALS

Company Type: Public

Income Statement

FYE: Saturday nearest January 31

	REVENUE ($ mil.)	NET INCOME ($ mil.)	NET PROFIT MARGIN	EMPLOYEES
1/09	14,526.0	967.0	6.7%	134,000
1/08	15,763.0	833.0	5.3%	150,000
1/07	15,943.0	778.0	4.9%	154,000
1/06	16,023.0	1,113.0	6.9%	153,000
1/05	16,267.0	1,150.0	7.1%	152,000
Annual Growth	**(2.8%)**	**(4.2%)**	**—**	**(3.1%)**

2009 Year-End Financials

Debt ratio: 0.0%
Return on equity: 22.3%
Cash ($ mil.): 1,715
Current ratio: 1.86
Long-term debt ($ mil.): 0
No. of shares (mil.): 697
Dividends
  Yield: 3.0%
  Payout: 25.4%
Market value ($ mil.): 7,860

Stock History

NYSE: GPS

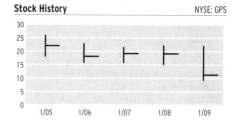

	STOCK PRICE ($) FY Close	P/E High/Low		PER SHARE ($) Earnings	Dividends	Book Value
1/09	11.28	16	7	1.34	0.34	6.30
1/08	19.09	21	14	1.05	0.32	6.13
1/07	19.17	23	17	0.93	0.32	7.43
1/06	18.09	18	13	1.24	0.18	7.79
1/05	22.01	21	15	1.21	0.11	7.08
Annual Growth	**(15.4%)**	**—**	**—**	**2.6%**	**32.6%**	**(2.9%)**

General Cable

General Cable keeps cars running, equipment humming, and information flowing. With a comprehensive line of aluminum, copper, and fiber-optic wire and cable products, it serves a range of industries, from automotive and mining to telecommunications and utilities. Commercial and industrial applications include power distribution and transmission, security and fire systems, and voice, video, and data communications. Brand names include BICC, Carol, and NextGen. The company also manufactures flexible cords for temporary power and custom wire harnesses for any industry using wires and connectors. With more than 45 manufacturing facilities worldwide, General Cable serves customers that include OEMs and distributors.

General Cable acquired cable products and systems provider Gepco International in August 2009. It also purchased Isotec's specialty electronic cable business. The acquisitions expand the company's share in the US market as well as expand its sales structure for global penetration.

Local customer bases around the world are handled through regional operations divided by three geographic segments: North America, Europe and North Africa, and a third consisting of Latin America, Asia/Pacific, sub-Saharan Africa, and the Middle East. Annual revenues are fairly evenly split among the segments, although the company anticipates the third segment will experience better growth over time because of planned investments in electrical infrastructure and electric utility development and construction in places such as Brazil, South Africa, and Thailand.

FMR holds about 9% of General Cable's stock. BlackRock holds another 8%.

HISTORY

General Cable originated from some of the oldest names in the wiring business: Standard Underground Cable (founded by George Westinghouse) and Phillips Wire and Safety Cable Company, both founded in the 1800s. The companies supplied wire for historic events such as Samuel Morse's first telegram between Baltimore and Washington, DC, in 1844, the lighting the Statute of Liberty in 1886, and the first Chicago World's Fair in 1892.

The company's best-known brand of nonmetallic sheathed cable, Romex, was invented at the company's Rome, New York, facility in 1922. Five years later, Phillips Wire and Standard Underground Cable joined to form General Cable Corporation. In 1935 the company's cables were used for power lines connecting the Hoover Dam to Los Angeles.

In the early 1980s the company was purchased by Penn Central Corporation (now known as American Premier Underwriters, part of American Financial Group). Later that decade Penn Central added the Carol brand when it purchased the Carol Cable Company (1989) and bought other wiring companies. The construction industry declined in the early 1990s, leaving wire inventories overstocked. In 1992 Penn Central spun off General Cable to shareholders, but the Lindner family (which owned Penn Central) continued to control most of the stock.

The company also made news in 1992 when it moved its corporate headquarters from Cincinnati to northern Kentucky, representing a win in the battle for companies being waged between the bordering states. That year General Cable also sold its equipment-making subsidiary, Marathon LeTourneau, because it was not directly tied to the wire and cable business.

In 1994 Wassall, a British holding company, bought General Cable, which had lost more than $130 million in the previous two years. (Wassall sold its interest in 1997.) Soon afterward the company hired a new CEO, Stephen Rabinowitz, who had been president of General Electric's electrical distribution and control unit and president of the braking-systems business of AlliedSignal (now Honeywell International). He began integrating the company's many units, which previously had been run separately. He also consolidated the company's distribution sites and closed five manufacturing plants.

General Cable went public in 1997. That year it formed a joint venture with glass company Spectran Corporation (since acquired by Lucent) to create fiber-optic cable under the name General Photonics. In 1999 General Cable bought the energy cable businesses of BICC Plc for $440 million. The deal made General Cable, which operated briefly as BICCGeneral, one of the largest makers of wire and cable in the world.

When its energy cable businesses in Europe, Africa, and Asia failed to perform up to expectations, General Cable agreed to sell some of those businesses (in the UK, Italy, Africa, and Asia) to Italy-based Pirelli for $216 million in 2000. Fearing Pirelli's dominant position, the European Commission opened an in-depth investigation of the takeover, but the deal was approved and completed later that year.

In 2001 General Cable sold its Pyrotenax unit to Raychem HTS Canada, Inc. (a division of Tyco International) for $60 million. The company also freed up $175 million in that same year by selling its building wire interests and exiting the cordset (indoor and outdoor extension cords) business. In early 2002 General Cable acquired the New Zealand-based data cable manufacturer Brand-Rex from Novar plc. Later that same year General Cable sold its building wire operations to Southwire Company.

In Europe it bought Silec in late 2005, which had been the wire and cable business of SAFRAN. The following year the company acquired French power cable maker E.C.N. Cable Group.

The company expanded into China in 2007 with the acquisition of Jiangyin Huaming Specialty Cable, which makes automotive and industrial cables. Later that year it purchased German submarine cable system maker Norddeutsche Seekabelwerke (NSW) from Corning. NSW was part of Corning's Cable Systems unit.

As part of its global expansion into energy and electrical infrastructure markets, the company acquired Phelps Dodge International Corporation, the cable and wire operations of Freeport-McMoRan Copper & Gold Inc., for about $740 million in October 2007. The acquisition gave General Cable a significant foothold in emerging markets, including China, India, and parts of Africa.

The company continued to expand its geographic presence in 2008 when it partnered with the Algerian government to acquire a majority stake in Enica Biskra, a cable manufacturer previously run by the state. Adding to its interest for growing business in Southeast Asia, the company upped its stake in Phelps Dodge Philippines from 40% to 60% that same year.

EXECUTIVES

Chairman: John E. Welsh III, age 58
President, CEO, and Director: Gregory B. Kenny, age 56, $3,710,620 total compensation
EVP, CFO, and Treasurer: Brian J. Robinson, age 40, $1,021,562 total compensation
EVP, General Counsel, and Secretary: Robert J. Siverd, age 60, $1,167,915 total compensation
EVP Global Sales and Business Development: Roderick (Roddy) Macdonald, age 60, $1,046,956 total compensation
EVP; President and CEO, General Cable North America: Gregory J. (Greg) Lampert, age 41, $1,208,182 total compensation
EVP General Cable Rest of World; President and CEO, Phelps Dodge International Corporation: Mathias F. Sandoval, age 48, $2,179,157 total compensation
SVP Human Resources: Peter J. Olmsted
VP Finance, Investor Relations, and Corporate Development: Michael P. Dickerson
EVP; President and CEO, General Cable Europe and North Africa: Domingo Goenaga, age 67, $2,061,028 total compensation
Auditors: Deloitte & Touche LLP

LOCATIONS

HQ: General Cable Corporation
4 Tesseneer Dr., Highland Heights, KY 41076
Phone: 859-572-8000   **Fax:** 859-572-8458
Web: www.generalcable.com

2008 Sales

	$ mil.	% of total
North America	2,178.7	35
Europe & North Africa	2,175.3	35
Other regions	1,876.1	30
Total	**6,230.1**	**100**

PRODUCTS/OPERATIONS

2008 Sales

	$ mil.	% of total
Electric utility	2,120.9	34
Electrical infrastructure	1,626.6	26
Construction	1,439.5	23
Communications	827.5	13
Rod Mill products	215.6	4
Total	**6,230.1**	**100**

Selected Products and Brands

Automotive ignition wire & battery starter cables
Cord, cordsets & portable power cables (Carol)
Data communications cables (GenSPEED)
Electric utility cables (BICC)
Electronic cables for audio/video, computers, microphones & security & fire systems (Carol)
Fiber-optic cables for voice, video & data networks (NextGen)
Industrial instrumentation, power & control cables (FREP, UniShield, VNTC)
Military power, control, signal & communications cable (Brand Rex)
Mining cables (Anaconda)
Nuclear cables (Brand Rex)
Office switchboard & digital transmission cables
Offshore & marine shipboard wire & cables
Telecommunications cables
Transit cables
Wire harnesses & assemblies

COMPETITORS

Andrew Corporation	Kalas Manufacturing
Belden	LEONI
Carlisle Companies	Nexans
Coleman Cable	Owl Wire & Cable
CommScope	Quabbin Wire
Corning	Southwire
Encore Wire	Sumitomo Electric
Hubbell	Superior Essex
Huber + Suhner, Inc.	Volex

HISTORICAL FINANCIALS

Company Type: Public

Income Statement

FYE: December 31

	REVENUE ($ mil.)	NET INCOME ($ mil.)	NET PROFIT MARGIN	EMPLOYEES
12/08	6,230.1	217.2	3.5%	13,000
12/07	4,614.8	208.3	4.5%	11,800
12/06	3,665.1	135.3	3.7%	7,700
12/05	2,380.8	39.2	1.6%	7,300
12/04	1,970.7	37.9	1.9%	6,300
Annual Growth	33.3%	54.7%	—	19.9%

2008 Year-End Financials

Debt ratio: 172.6%
Return on equity: 32.2%
Cash ($ mil.): 283
Current ratio: 1.76
Long-term debt ($ mil.): 1,216

No. of shares (mil.): 52
Dividends
 Yield: 0.0%
 Payout: —
Market value ($ mil.): 919

Stock History

NYSE: BGC

	STOCK PRICE ($) FY Close	P/E High/Low	PER SHARE ($) Earnings	Dividends	Book Value
12/08	17.69	18 2	4.07	0.00	13.63
12/07	73.28	22 11	3.82	0.00	12.53
12/06	43.71	17 8	2.60	0.00	8.36
12/05	19.70	51 27	0.41	0.00	5.64
12/04	13.85	19 9	0.75	0.00	5.80
Annual Growth	6.3%	— —	52.6%	—	23.8%

General Dynamics

Military contractor General Dynamics brings it on by land, air, and sea. The company is the Pentagon's fourth largest prime contractor, following Lockheed Martin, Boeing, and Northrop Grumman. The US government accounts for more than two-thirds of sales. With the war in Iraq starting to wind down as the conflict in Afghanistan heats up, General Dynamics expects the US Department of Defense's budget to moderate in the years ahead, especially as the Obama administration closely examines military procurement programs for their effectiveness. The global economic recession is having a chilling effect on the company's sales of business jets, while revenues from aircraft services are healthily growing.

General Dynamics operates in four areas: Information Systems & Technology (command and control systems), Marine Systems (warships and nuclear submarines), Combat Systems (tanks, amphibious assault vehicles, and munitions), and Aerospace (business jets). General Dynamics' Electric Boat subsidiary builds nuclear submarines (Seawolf, Ohio, Los Angeles classes); Bath Iron Works builds DDG 51 destroyers and LPD 17 landing craft; Land

Systems builds the Abrams M1A1 and M1A2 main battle tanks and Fox reconnaissance vehicles; and Gulfstream Aerospace makes business jets.

The company looks to hook work announced by the Marine Corps in 2009 for a small tactical unmanned aircraft system. To this end, General Dynamics and Elbit Systems of America formed a 50-50 joint venture, UAS Dynamics, to build unmanned aircraft emphasizing surveillance and reconnaissance systems for the military.

Late in 2008 the company acquired Switzerland-based Jet Aviation for $2.3 billion. Jet Aviation, which provides aviation services such as repairs, overhauls, and fixed base operations, maintains facilities in Asia, Europe, the Middle East, and the US. The same year it purchased AxleTech International, a Carlyle Group-owned manufacturer of axles and other suspension components used in military and off-road heavy vehicles. AxleTech's production plants in the US, France, and Brazil joined General Dynamics' Armament and Technical Products division. Subsequently the company inked a deal for Axsys Technologies, Inc. Axsys ramps up General Dynamics' intelligence, surveillance, and reconnaissance lineup with sensor and camera making capabilities.

HISTORY

In 1899 John Holland founded Electric Boat Company, a New Jersey ship and submarine builder. The company built ships, PT boats, and submarines during WWII, but faced with waning postwar orders, CEO John Jay Hopkins diversified with the 1947 purchase of aircraft builder Canadair. Hopkins formed General Dynamics in 1952, merging Electric Boat and Canadair and buying Consolidated Vultee Aircraft (Convair), a major producer of military and civilian aircraft, in 1954.

Electric Boat launched the first nuclear submarine, the Nautilus, in the mid-1950s. In 1955, at the urging of Howard Hughes, Convair began designing its first commercial jetliners. Weakened by the planes' production costs, General Dynamics merged with building-materials supplier Material Service Corporation (1959). Nuclear subs became a mainstay for the company, and it abandoned jetliners in 1961 after losses on the planes reached the staggering sum of $425 million.

During the 1960s General Dynamics developed the controversial F-111 fighter. Despite numerous problems, the aircraft proved financially and militarily successful (F-111s participated in the 1986 US bombing raid on Libya).

In the following years the company won contracts for the US Navy's 688-class attack submarine (1971), liquefied natural gas tankers for Burmah Oil Company (1972), the Trident ballistic-missile submarine (1974), and the F-16 lightweight fighter aircraft (1975). The company sold Canadair in 1976 and bought Chrysler Defense, which had a contract to build the US Army's new M1 tank, in 1982.

The company bought Cessna Aircraft in 1986. The next year it won a contract to design and build the upper stage of the Titan IV space-launch rocket. Facing defense cuts, General Dynamics sold off pieces of the company: In 1992 it sold Cessna Aircraft to Textron and sold its missile operations to Hughes Aircraft; its electronics business was sold to The Carlyle Group in 1993. The company sold its space-systems business to Martin Marietta in 1994.

The next year General Dynamics began a buying spree with the purchase of shipbuilder Bath Iron Works. In 1996 it added Teledyne's combat vehicle unit, followed in 1997 by Lockheed Martin's Defense Systems and Armament Systems units and defense electronics units from Ceridian and Lucent. Also that year Nicholas Chabraja, director of Ceridian and former general counsel for General Dynamics, became CEO.

In 1999 General Dynamics bought business-jet maker Gulfstream Aerospace, which accounts for almost all of the company's commercial-aircraft sales. In 2001 General Dynamics completed the acquisition of munitions maker Primex Technologies. The company also bought Galaxy Aerospace, thus adding midsize aircraft to its Gulfstream lineup. Additionally, General Dynamics acquired Empresa Nacional Santa Bárbara de Industrias Militares (ENSB) of Spain.

General Dynamics sold its space propulsion and fire suppression operations to Aerojet-General in 2002. The next year it acquired General Motors' armored vehicle operations (for about $1.1 billion) and Austria's Steyr Spezialfahrzeug, maker of the Pandur line of wheeled armored vehicles. General Dynamics also acquired government security and intelligence specialist Veridian for about $1.5 billion in 2003.

In 2005 General Dynamics sold its aeronautics services business, which provides aeronautic testing, engineering, and support services, to Wyle Laboratories. Late in 2005 subsidiary Electric Boat said it would cut 2,400 jobs.

The following year General Dynamics acquired the large-caliber artillery and mortar projectile operations of Chamberlain Manufacturing for an undisclosed sum. Chamberlain is a subsidiary of Duchossois Industries. In 2006 General Dynamics also acquired IT specialist Anteon International for $2.1 billion. Anteon specialized in IT systems for defense, homeland security, intelligence units, and other government agencies. Anteon was combined with General Dynamics Network Systems to create a new division, General Dynamics Information Technology.

Early in 2007 General Dynamics acquired SNC Technologies, a Canadian ammunition maker, from SNC-Lavalin Group for about $275 million.

EXECUTIVES

Chairman: Nicholas D. (Nick) Chabraja, age 66, $21,926,640 total compensation
Vice Chairman and CEO: Jay L. Johnson, age 63
SVP and CFO: L. Hugh Redd, age 51, $3,520,638 total compensation
EVP Information Systems and Technology: Gerard J. (Jerry) DeMuro, age 53, $4,027,109 total compensation
EVP and Group Executive, Marine Systems Group: David K. Heebner, age 64
EVP Combat Systems: Charles M. Hall, age 57, $4,444,802 total compensation
EVP Aerospace; President, Gulfstream Aerospace: Joseph (Joe) Lombardo, age 61
SVP, General Counsel, and Secretary: David A. Savner, age 64, $3,766,816 total compensation
SVP Human Resources and Administration: Walter M. Oliver, age 63
SVP Planning and Development: Phebe N. Novakovic, age 51
VP; President, Armament and Technical Products: Michael J. Mulligan, age 44
VP; President, Electric Boat Corporation: John P. Casey, age 54

VP; President, Ordnance and Tactical Systems:
Michael S. Wilson, age 59
VP; President, General Dynamics C4 Systems:
Christopher (Chris) Marzilli, age 49
VP; President, Advanced Information Systems:
Lewis A. Von Thaer, age 48
VP Government Relations and Communications:
Kendell M. Pease, age 61
President, National Steel and Shipbuilding Company:
Frederick J. (Fred) Harris, age 62
President, Bath Iron Works: Jeffrey S. Geiger, age 47
President, Land Systems: Mark C. Roualet, age 50
President, American Overseas Marine Corporation:
Thomas W. Merrell
Auditors: KPMG LLP

LOCATIONS

HQ: General Dynamics Corporation
2941 Fairview Park Dr., Ste. 100
Falls Church, VA 22042
Phone: 703-876-3000   **Fax:** 703-876-3125
Web: www.gendyn.com

2008 Sales

	$ mil.	% of total
North America		
US	24,203	83
Canada	719	2
Other countries	241	1
Europe		
UK	842	3
Spain	662	2
Other countries	1,454	5
Asia/Pacific	545	2
Africa/Middle East	508	2
South America	126	—
Total	**29,300**	**100**

PRODUCTS/OPERATIONS

2008 Sales

	$ mil.	% of total
Information systems & technology	10,038	34
Combat systems	8,194	28
Marine systems	5,556	19
Aerospace	5,512	19
Total	**29,300**	**100**

2008 Sales

	% of total
US government	69
US commercial	14
International defense	9
International commercial	8
Total	**100**

Selected Operations

Information systems and technology
  Actionable intelligence, surveillance, and
    reconnaissance
  Homeland security
  Information assurance
  Integrated space systems
  Maritime combat systems
Combat systems
  Armament Systems
    Advanced materials (composites)
    Detection systems (biological and chemical
      detection systems)
    Gun and munition systems
    Hydra 70 2.75" air-to-ground rocket
  Land systems
    Advanced Amphibious Assault Vehicle (AAAV)
    M1A1 and M1A2 Abrams Main Battle Tank
    Pandur 6x6 and 8x8 wheeled armored vehicles
    Stryker Mobile Gun System
  Ordnance and tactical systems
    Electronic products
    Munitions
    Propellants
    Satellite propulsion systems

Marine systems
  American Overseas Marine (ship-management
    services)
  Bath Iron Works Corp.
    Arleigh Burke class DDG 51 destroyer
    Class DD 21 land attack destroyer
    Class LPD 17 amphibious assault transport
  Electric Boat Corp.
    New Attack submarine (Virginia class)
    Seawolf attack submarine
  General Dynamics Defense Systems, Inc.
  National Steel and Shipbuilding Company
Aerospace
  Gulfstream Aerospace
    G150 (Mid-size, range of 2,950 nautical miles,
      4 passengers)
    G200 (Large-cabin, range of 3,400 nautical miles,
      4 passengers)
    G350 (Large-cabin, range of 3,800 nautical miles,
      8 passengers)
    G450 (Large-cabin, range of 4,350 nautical miles,
      8 passengers)
    G500 (Large-cabin, range of 5,800 nautical miles,
      8 passengers)
    G550 (Large-cabin, range of 6,750 nautical miles,
      8 passengers)

COMPETITORS

Airbus
Alliant Techsystems
BAE SYSTEMS
Boeing
Bombardier
Dassault Aviation
Dewey Electronics
DRS Technologies
DynCorp International
EDS
Goodrich Corp.
Harris Corp.
Harsco
Herley Industries
ITT Corp.
L-3 Communications
Lockheed Martin
Navistar International
Northrop Grumman
Perot Systems
Peugeot
Raytheon
Renco
Rockwell Collins
SAIC
Sperry Marine
Textron
United Technologies
Westwood Corp.

HISTORICAL FINANCIALS

Company Type: Public

Income Statement

FYE: December 31

	REVENUE ($ mil.)	NET INCOME ($ mil.)	NET PROFIT MARGIN	EMPLOYEES
12/08	29,300.0	2,459.0	8.4%	92,300
12/07	27,240.0	2,072.0	7.6%	83,500
12/06	24,063.0	1,856.0	7.7%	81,000
12/05	21,244.0	1,461.0	6.9%	72,200
12/04	19,178.0	1,227.0	6.4%	70,200
Annual Growth	**11.2%**	**19.0%**	**—**	**7.1%**

2008 Year-End Financials

Debt ratio: 31.0%
Return on equity: 22.5%
Cash ($ mil.): 1,621
Current ratio: 1.15
Long-term debt ($ mil.): 3,113
No. of shares (mil.): 385
Dividends
  Yield: 2.3%
  Payout: 21.7%
Market value ($ mil.): 22,177

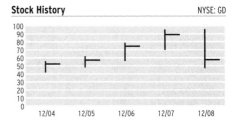
General Electric

From turbines to TV, from household appliances to power plants, General Electric (GE) is plugged in to businesses that have shaped the modern world. The company produces — take a deep breath — aircraft engines, locomotives and other transportation equipment, lighting, kitchen and laundry appliances, generators and turbines, electric distribution and control equipment, and medical imaging equipment. General Electric is also one of the preeminent financial services firms in the US. General Electric Capital, comprising commercial finance, consumer finance, aircraft leasing, real estate, and energy financial services, is its largest segment. Other operations include the NBC television network.

CEO Jeff Immelt is emerging from the considerable shadow of his predecessor, Jack Welch, by not being shy about making sweeping changes. He has diverged somewhat from Welch's slavish obsession with the bottom line and encourages managers to innovate and take more risks. As a result, GE has been growing in such areas as biotech, renewable energy, nanotechnology, and digital technology. Immelt has, however, taken a page from his former boss' playbook by pursuing growth outside the US, particularly in emerging markets like India, China, Eastern Europe, Africa, and the Middle East. More than half of GE's revenues are attributable to activities outside the US.

Immelt set about reshaping GE, spinning off its life and mortgage insurance businesses into a new entity, Genworth Financial, which went public in 2004; it completely divested its remaining stake in Genworth in 2006. Also that year, GE sold off most of its remaining insurance businesses in a sale to Swiss Re. The company kept its US life reinsurance business.

Citing rising commodities costs, GE sold its advanced materials unit, which produced silicone, quartz, and ceramics products, to Apollo Management, and sold its GE Plastics unit (now SABIC Innovative Plastics) to SABIC for more than $11 billion in 2007. Also that year GE shut down the operations of wholesale subprime lender WMC Mortgage.

parts through its Motion Industries subsidiary. To expand its industrial parts business, in 2008 Motion Industries acquired Texas-based Drago Supply Company, Mill Supply Corp., and Monroe Rubber and Plastic Supply. Together the three companies add more than $100 million to Motion Industries' bottom line. More acquisitions are planned for 2009.

GPC also distributes office products through S.P. Richards, one of the oldest office supply wholesalers in the country. The group supplies schools, offices, and other institutions in North America with computer and imaging supplies, office furniture and machines, general office and school supplies, and more. The division has seven proprietary brands including: Sparco, NATURE SAVER, and Compucessory. S.P. Richards sales decreased slightly in 2008 and 2007 as a result of the industry-wide slowdown in office products consumption.

Another subsidiary, EIS, manufactures and distributes electronic and electrical products such as copper foil, magnet wire, and thermal management materials to more than 20,000 electrical and electronic manufacturers in North America. GPC's Rayloc division rebuilds automotive parts.

HISTORY

Genuine Parts Company (GPC) got its start in Atlanta in 1928 when Carlyle Fraser bought a small auto parts store. That year GPC had the only loss in its history. Three years earlier a group that included Fraser had founded the National Automotive Parts Association (NAPA), an organization of automotive manufacturers, remanufacturers, distributors, and retailers.

The Depression was a boon for GPC because fewer new-car sales meant more sales of replacement parts. During the 1930s GPC's sales rose from less than $350,000 to more than $3 million. One tool it developed to spur sales during the Depression was its monthly magazine, *Parts Pups*, which featured pretty girls and corny jokes (discontinued in the 1990s). GPC acquired auto parts rebuilder Rayloc in 1931 and established parts distributor Balkamp in 1936.

WWII boosted sales at GPC because carmakers were producing for the war effort, but scarce resources limited auto parts companies to producing functional parts. GPC went public in 1948.

The postwar boom in car sales boosted GPC's sales in the 1950s and 1960s. It expanded during this period with new distribution centers across the country. GPC bought Colyear Motor Sales (NAPA's West Coast distributor) in 1965 and introduced a line of filters and batteries in 1966 that were the first parts to carry the NAPA name.

GPC moved into Canada in 1972 when it bought Corbetts, a Calgary-based parts distributor. That acquisition included Oliver Industrial Supply. During the mid-1970s GPC began to broaden its distribution businesses, adding S. P. Richards (office products, 1975) and Motion Industries (industrial replacement parts, 1976). In the late 1970s GPC acquired Bearing Specialty and Michigan Bearing as part of Motion Industries.

In 1982 the company introduced its now familiar blue-and-yellow NAPA logo. Canadian parts distributor UAP (formerly United Auto Parts) and GPC formed a joint venture, UAP/NAPA, in 1988, with GPC acquiring a 20% stake in UAP.

During the 1990s GPC diversified its product lines and its geographic reach. Its 1993 acquisition of Berry Bearing made the company a leading distributor of industrial parts. The next year GPC formed a joint venture with Grupo Auto Todo of Mexico.

NAPA formed an agreement in 1995 with Penske Corporation to be the exclusive supplier of auto parts to nearly 900 Penske Auto Centers. GPC purchased Horizon USA Data Supplies that year, adding computer supplies to S. P. Richards' product mix.

A string of acquisitions in the late 1990s increased GPC's industrial distribution business (including Midcap Bearing, Power Drives & Bearings, and Amarillo Bearing).

GPC paid $200 million in 1998 for EIS, a leading wholesale distributor of materials and supplies to the electrical and electronics industries. Late in 1998, after a 10-year joint venture, it bought the remaining 80% of UAP it didn't already own. GPC continued to expand its auto parts distribution network in 1999, acquiring Johnson Industries, an independent distributor of auto supplies for large fleets and car dealers. GPC also acquired Oklahoma City-based Brittain Brothers, a NAPA distributor that serves about 190 auto supply stores in Arkansas, Missouri, Oklahoma, and Texas.

In 2000 the company bought a 15% interest in Mitchell Repair Information (MRIC), a subsidiary of Snap-on Incorporated that provides diagnostic and repair information services. The next year Johnson Industries acquired Coach and Motors, a distribution center in Detroit.

In 2003 GPC acquired NAPA Hawaii, which serves more than 30 independently owned NAPA stores and four company-owned ones in Hawaii and Samoa. President Thomas Gallagher became the company's fourth CEO in more than 75 years when he was named to the position in August 2004. Former CEO Larry Prince remained as chairman until early in 2005 when Gallagher was elected chairman; Prince remains on the board. Also during 2005 the company acquired a 25% interest in Altrom Canada Corp.

GPC subsidiary Motion Industries in mid-2006 acquired Lewis Supply Co., a provider of casters, cutting tools, machinery accessories and other general mill supplies. In October the company merged HorizonUSA Data Supplies, previously a wholly owned subsidiary of S. P. Richards, into S.P. Richards.

In early 2008 the company sold its Johnson Industries subsidiary, which provided automotive supplies to fleets and new car dealers.

EXECUTIVES

Chairman, President, and CEO:
Thomas C. (Tom) Gallagher, age 61,
$4,671,434 total compensation
Vice Chairman, EVP Finance, and CFO: Jerry W. Nix,
age 63, $2,107,859 total compensation
SVP Operations and Logistics: Michael D. Orr
EVP: Robert J. Susor, age 63, $3,356 total compensation
SVP Finance and Corporate Secretary: Carol B. Yancey
SVP and Treasurer: Frank M. Howard
SVP and Corporate Counsel: Scott C. Smith
SVP Human Resources: R. Bruce Clayton, age 61
SVP Technology and Process Improvement:
Charles A. Chesnutt, age 49

VP Planning and Acquisitions: Treg S. Brown
VP Real Estate: Karl J. Koenig
VP Compensation and Benefits: Phillip C. Johnson
VP Investor Relations: Sidney G. (Sid) Jones
Director; Chairman, NAPA Canada/UAP Inc.:
Jean Douville, age 65
President and CEO, Motion Industries:
William J. (Bill) Stevens
Chairman and CEO, S.P. Richards Company:
C. Wayne Beacham
President, U.S. Automotive Parts Group:
Paul D. Donahue, age 52,
$1,004,997 total compensation
Auditors: Ernst & Young LLP

LOCATIONS

HQ: Genuine Parts Company
2999 Circle 75 Pkwy., Atlanta, GA 30339
Phone: 770-953-1700   **Fax:** 770-956-2211
Web: www.genpt.com

PRODUCTS/OPERATIONS

2008 Sales

	% of total
Automotive	48
Industrial	32
Office products	16
Electrical/electronic materials	4
Total	**100**

Selected Operations

Automotive Parts Group
  Altrom Canada Corp. (wholly owned subsidiary;
    distribution of import automotive parts, Canada)
  Balkamp, Inc. (majority-owned subsidiary; distributes
    replacement parts and accessories for cars, heavy-
    duty vehicles, motorcycles, and farm equipment)
  Grupo Auto Todo SA de CV (wholly owned,
    distribution and stores, Mexico)
  UAP Inc. (auto parts distribution, Canada)
Industrial Parts Group
  Motion Industries, Inc.
  Motion Industries (Canada), Inc.
Office Products Group
  S. P. Richards Company (office products)
Electrical/Electronic Materials Group
  EIS, Inc. (products for electrical and electronic
    equipment, including adhesives, copper foil, and
    thermal management materials)

COMPETITORS

Advance Auto Parts	General Motors
Applied Industrial	General Parts
Technologies	Graybar Electric
Arrow Electronics	Hahn Automotive
AutoZone	Ingersoll-Rand
Avnet	Office Depot
CARQUEST	OfficeMax
Coast Distribution	O'Reilly Automotive
D&H Distributing	Staples
Ford Motor	United Stationers

HISTORICAL FINANCIALS

Company Type: Public

Income Statement

FYE: December 31

	REVENUE ($ mil.)	NET INCOME ($ mil.)	NET PROFIT MARGIN	EMPLOYEES
12/08	11,015.3	475.4	4.3%	30,300
12/07	10,843.2	506.3	4.7%	32,000
12/06	10,457.9	475.4	4.5%	32,000
12/05	9,783.0	437.4	4.5%	31,700
12/04	9,097.3	395.6	4.3%	31,200
Annual Growth	4.9%	4.7%	—	(0.7%)

Debt ratio: 21.5%   No. of shares (mil.): 160
Return on equity: 18.9%   Dividends
Cash ($ mil.): 68   Yield: 4.1%
Current ratio: 3.01   Payout: 53.4%
Long-term debt ($ mil.): 500 Market value ($ mil.): 6,040

Stock History   NYSE: GPC

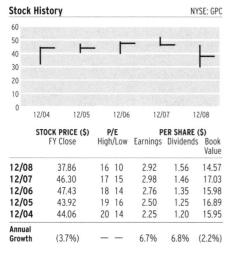

	STOCK PRICE ($) FY Close	P/E High/Low		PER SHARE ($) Earnings	Dividends	Book Value
12/08	37.86	16	10	2.92	1.56	14.57
12/07	46.30	17	15	2.98	1.46	17.03
12/06	47.43	18	14	2.76	1.35	15.98
12/05	43.92	19	16	2.50	1.25	16.89
12/04	44.06	20	14	2.25	1.20	15.95
Annual Growth	(3.7%)	—	—	6.7%	6.8%	(2.2%)

Genzyme Corporation

Genzyme makes big money off small-time diseases. The company's product portfolio focuses on rare genetic disorders as well as kidney disease, cancer, and biosurgery. One of its main products, Cerezyme, is a leading (and pricey) treatment for Gaucher's disease, a rare enzyme-deficiency condition. Founded in 1981, Genzyme also is involved in drug development and genetic testing and other services. In addition, the company develops gene-based cancer diagnosis and treatment products, renal care therapies, and orthopedic biological surgery products. Genzyme's products are sold to health care professionals in some 100 countries, primarily through wholesale distributors.

Cerezyme is one of the most expensive drugs in the world and accounts for nearly one-third of Genzyme's global sales. Genzyme is avidly working to diversify its product line in case competition for Gaucher's disease treatments increases or this radical treatment turns out not to be profitable in the long-term. A shortage in Cerezyme in 2009 due to difficulties at a Genzyme manufacturing plant could harm annual sales of the drug and make room for competitors to elbow their way into the market.

Newer therapies include Myozyme, a treatment for Pompe disease (a genetic disorder caused by a deficiency in the enzymes needed to break down glycogen). The FDA approved Genzyme's Renvela kidney treatment in 2007; Renvela is the next generation of its Renagel kidney disease medicine. In 2008 the company received FDA approval for Mozobil, a treatment for cancer patients undergoing stem cell transplants.

Genzyme's pipeline of potential future drug releases includes therapies for the treatment of multiple sclerosis, kidney disease, osteoarthritis, and leukemia, as well as a new treatment for Gaucher's disease. Genzyme is collaborating with Isis Pharmaceuticals on cholesterol treatment mipomersen and with Osiris Therapeutics on cell therapeutics for cardiovascular, inflammatory, and orthopedic ailments.

Genzyme has been honing in on its cancer treatments and diagnostic testing over the last couple of years. In 2007 it acquired Bioenvision for $345 million, mostly to gain worldwide rights to Bioenvision's acute lymphoblastic leukemia treatment for pediatric patients, clofarabine (sold in the US and Canada under the brand name Clolar and in Europe as Evoltra), which the two companies developed collaboratively. The acquisition bumped up against some disapproval from Bioenvision shareholders but was ultimately approved. Bioenvision was promptly absorbed into Genzyme's other operations, expanding Genzyme's global marketing business in the oncology field. Genzyme plans to expand Clolar's applications to include adult leukemia patients.

HISTORY

From little oaks, mighty biotech companies may grow. In 1981 Tufts professor Henry Blair (now a board member) teamed up with Sherman Snyder and Oak Venture Partners to buy biotech businesses. (The first purchase was an English company that made diagnostic enzymes and had an agreement with the National Institutes of Health to make an enzyme for Gaucher's disease patients.) Armed both with a good therapeutic candidate and a salable product to help fund its development, Genzyme became profitable in 1984 and went public in 1986.

Genzyme diversified through purchases, adding fine chemicals (for use in clinical chemistry testing; exited 1997), diagnostics (such as cholesterol testing), and biotherapeutics. In 1989 the firm bought prenatal testing company Integrated Genetics, which had molecular biology capabilities, and took it public in 1991. Genzyme's development efforts paid off that year when Ceredase was approved to treat Gaucher's disease. The product's protected orphan drug status quickly made it a cash cow. The company later made purchases in such areas as tissue repair (1995), surgical specialties (1996), and cancer treatments (1997).

In 1998 it began selling newly approved Renagel kidney disease treatment (developed with GelTex Pharmaceuticals, which it bought in 2000), as well as Biogen's AVONEX multiple sclerosis drug in Japan. In 1999 the company increased its niche focus by buying Peptimmune, which developed drugs for rare genetic disorders.

In 2000 Genzyme bought Biomatrix and combined it with Genzyme Tissue Repair and Genzyme Surgical Products to form Genzyme Biosurgery. The next year it bought a private Brazilian pharmaceutical company to regain Renagel distribution rights in that key market. In August 2001 its Fabry disease drug Fabrazyme won European approval, marking the firm's entrance into a niche market; Genzyme then geared up to win FDA approval and claim a large share of this limited market.

Looking to capitalize on some R&D, the firm in 2002 created subsidiary Peptimmune to create new therapies for autoimmune and allergy disorders. That year the company settled a 1991 suit with Genentech disputing royalty rights to Genentech's TNKase; Genzyme's buy of Integrated Genetics gave it patents the company alleged were key to TNKase. The FDA helped the company in 2003 expand its product portfolio: The agency approved Fabrazyme and Aldurazyme, another niche drug co-developed with BioMarin. That year it bought antibody drugmaker SangStat Medical.

As part of plans to simplify its structure, Genzyme consolidated its tracking stocks under its primary GENZ ticker in 2003. (However, the consolidation resulted in a $64 million class action lawsuit settlement in 2009 for former Genzyme Biosurgery stockholders over alleged market price manipulations.)

With the 2004 purchase of ILEX Oncology, valued at $1 billion, Genzyme aims to augment its oncology pipeline with two late-stage products and a first-class clinical organization. The next year it bought Verigen, which had developed a cartilage repair cell therapy available in Europe and Australia.

To further expand its oncology operations, Genzyme in 2006 acquired AnorMED, which was developing a treatment for cancer patients undergoing stem cell transplants (Mozobil, approved by the FDA in 2008). AnorMED's operations were integrated into Genzyme's R&D organization. Genzyme also brought to market a new non-small cell lung cancer test for the KRAS gene (and mutations thereof) designed to help doctors determine therapy regimens.

EXECUTIVES

Chairman, President, and CEO: Henri A. Termeer, age 62, $13,773,782 total compensation
EVP Finance and Chief Financial Officer: Michael S. Wyzga, age 53, $3,019,202 total compensation
SVP Biomedical & Regulatory Affairs, and Chief Medical Officer: Richard A. Moscicki, age 56
SVP, General Counsel, and Chief Legal Officer: Thomas J. DesRosier, age 54
SVP Research and Chief Scientific Officer: Alan E. Smith, age 63
EVP Research and Chief Scientific Officer: Sandford D. (Sandy) Smith, age 61, $2,903,746 total compensation
SVP and Chief Human Resources Officer: Zoltan A. Csimma, age 67
SVP Finance, Corporate Controller, and Chief Accounting Officer: Jason A. Amello
EVP Legal and Corporate Development, and Secretary: Peter Wirth, age 58, $3,246,359 total compensation
EVP Cardiovascular, Oncology, and Genetics: Earl M. (Duke) Collier Jr., age 61, $3,135,607 total compensation
EVP Genetic Diseases, Biosurgery & Transplant: David P. Meeker, age 54
SVP Corporate Development: Richard H. Douglas, age 56
SVP Cell and Protein Research and Development: John M. McPherson
SVP Genzyme Diagnostics: David D. Fleming
SVP Corporate Operations and Pharmaceuticals: Mark R. Bamforth, age 46
VP and Treasurer: Gail F. Sullivan
President, Genzyme Oncology: Mark J. Enyedy
President, Genzyme Biosurgery: C. Ann Merrifield, age 56
President, Genzyme Diagnostics: Donald E. (Don) Pogorzelski
Associate Manager, Corporate Communications: Erin Emlock
Investor Relations: Patrick Flanigan
Auditors: PricewaterhouseCoopers LLP

LOCATIONS

HQ: Genzyme Corporation
500 Kendall St., Cambridge, MA 02142
Phone: 617-252-7500   **Fax:** 617-252-7600
Web: www.genzyme.com

2008 Sales

	$ mil.	% of total
US	2,259.1	52
Europe	1,587.3	33
Other regions	758.6	15
Total	**4,605.0**	**100**

PRODUCTS/OPERATIONS

2008 Sales

	$ mil.	% of total
Products		
Genetic diseases	2,226.3	48
Cardiometabolic & renal	955.9	21
Biosurgery	445.7	10
Hematologic oncology	101.2	2
Other products	467.8	10
Services	366.1	8
Research & development	42.0	1
Total	**4,605.0**	**100**

Selected Products

Genetic Diseases (lysosomal storage disorders)
  Aldurazyme (Mucopolysaccharidosis I)
  Cerezyme (Gaucher disease)
  Fabrazyme (Fabry disease)
  Myozyme (Pompe disease)

Cardiometabolic and Renal
  Hectorol (kidney disease)
  Renagel/Renvela (kidney disease)
  Thyrogen (adjunctive diagnostic for thyroid cancer)

Biosurgery
  Carticel (cartilage damage treatment)
  Epicel (severe burn treatment)
  Matrix-induced Autologous Chondrocyte Implantation (MACI, cartilage repair)
  Sepra products (wound healing biomaterials including Seprafilm adhesion barrier)
  Synvisc/Synvisc-One (osteoarthritis pain)

Oncology
  Campath (B-cell chronic lymphocytic leukemia)
  Clolar (clofarabine, acute lymphoblastic leukemia)
  Mozobil (stem cell transplant therapy for non-Hodgkin's lymphoma and multiple myeloma)

Other
  Diagnostic products (infectious disease and cholesterol testing)
  Thymoglobulin (organ rejection)
  WelChol (cholesterol reduction)

COMPETITORS

Abbott Labs	GlaxoSmithKline
ACON Laboratories	Inverness Medical
Actelion	Johnson & Johnson
Amgen	LabCorp
Amicus Therapeutics	Merck
Anika Therapeutics	Novartis
Baxter International	Pfizer
Beckman Coulter	Protalix BioTherapeutics
Becton, Dickinson	QMed
Biogen Idec	Quest Diagnostics
Bristol-Myers Squibb	Roche Holding
Cephalon	Sanofi-Aventis
Chiron	Shire
Ferring Pharmaceuticals	Smith & Nephew
Fresenius	Teva Pharmaceuticals

HISTORICAL FINANCIALS

Company Type: Public

Income Statement FYE: December 31

	REVENUE ($ mil.)	NET INCOME ($ mil.)	NET PROFIT MARGIN	EMPLOYEES
12/08	4,605.0	421.1	9.1%	11,000
12/07	3,813.5	480.2	12.6%	10,000
12/06	3,187.0	(16.8)	—	9,000
12/05	2,734.8	441.5	16.1%	8,200
12/04	2,201.1	86.5	3.9%	7,100
Annual Growth	**20.3%**	**48.5%**	**—**	**11.6%**

2008 Year-End Financials

Debt ratio: 1.7%	No. of shares (mil.): 270
Return on equity: 6.1%	Dividends
Cash ($ mil.): 572	Yield: 0.0%
Current ratio: 2.75	Payout: —
Long-term debt ($ mil.): 124	Market value ($ mil.): 17,940

Stock History NASDAQ (GS): GENZ

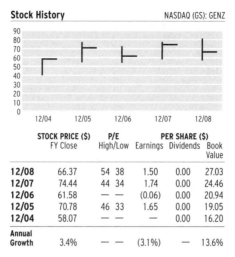

	STOCK PRICE ($) FY Close	P/E High/Low		PER SHARE ($) Earnings	Dividends	Book Value
12/08	66.37	54	38	1.50	0.00	27.03
12/07	74.44	44	34	1.74	0.00	24.46
12/06	61.58	—	—	(0.06)	0.00	20.94
12/05	70.78	46	33	1.65	0.00	19.05
12/04	58.07	—	—	—	0.00	16.20
Annual Growth	**3.4%**	**—**	**—**	**(3.1%)**	**—**	**13.6%**

Gerdau Ameristeel

Gerdau Ameristeel is putting its stamp on the steel business in the US. The company is one of the largest minimill steel makers in North America, producing about 7 million tons of finished steel annually. Through its 20 steel mills (mostly in the US), Gerdau Ameristeel primarily sells to the eastern two-thirds of North America. The company also operates scrap recycling operations, specialty processing centers, and rebar fabricating and coating plants. Its minimills produce beams, flat-rolled steel, merchant bar, rebar, and wire rod primarily used in the automotive, appliance, construction, machinery, and equipment industries. Brazilian steelmaker Gerdau owns approximately two-thirds of the company.

Gerdau Ameristeel's steel mill segment accounts for about 80% of sales, and more than three-fourths of total sales are derived from the US. Recycled scrap metal provides more than 90% of the steel for its minimills, making the company the continent's second largest scrap recycler. Its own scrap operations provide much of the raw material for the minimills. And once the company's minimills produce the steel, the steel product can be sent to its many downstream operations, which include rebar fabrication plants, railroad spike makers, wire and nail operations, and cold drawn plants.

Since its formation the company has quickly grown its geographic presence. It made several acquisitions throughout the Mid-Continent region of the US in the ensuing years, including the $4.2 billion deal for Chaparral Steel, a maker of structural steel products. In 2008 the company added to its downstream operations with the acquisition, through subsidiary Pacific Coast Steel, of structural steel fabricator Century Steel for $150 million and a couple of scrap metal

processors, Metro Recycling and Sand Springs Metal Processing.

Gerdau Ameristeel owns 50% of hot-rolled steel maker Gallatin Steel; Dofasco owns the rest.

HISTORY

Starting in 1955, Gerald Hefferman built up Premier Steel Mills (Alberta, Canada) into a multinational steel producer. Hefferman sold Premier to Stelco in 1962 and soon began building the Lake Ontario Steel Co. (Lasco). In 1970 he formed Co-Steel International Ltd.

Co-Steel borrowed heavily in the late 1970s, targeting $500 million for acquisitions and plant upgrades. In 1972 it bought 63% of UK-based Sheerness Steel, and in 1973 it formed Chaparral Steel with metal and concrete producer Texas Industries. Co-Steel's New Jersey-based Raritan Steel opened in 1980 and changed its name to Co-Steel in 1986. It went public that year to ease its debt; the US steel market was slumping and Japanese steel was abundant.

In 1990 Co-Steel bought the rest of Sheerness. That year Texas Industries completed its purchase of Chaparral Steel from Co-Steel; the deal raised Co-Steel's stake in Texas Industries to 22%. In 1991 Co-Steel merged Sheerness' Raw Materials division with Mayer Newman & Co., forming Mayer Parry Recycling (UK). With a growing international presence, in 1992 Co-Steel reorganized and renamed several operations, including Co-Steel Lasco, Co-Steel Raritan, and Co-Steel Sheerness. Co-Steel formed a partnership with Dofasco in 1993 to build the Gallatin Steel Mill, a $360 million minimill for producing flat-rolled steel in Kentucky.

An industry boom boosted sales in 1994. However, Europe's depressed market kept Sheerness' sales low. By 1995 Co-Steel had sold its stake in Texas Industries and had begun production at Gallatin Steel. Co-Steel experienced its first-ever loss in 1996, related to the Gallatin Steel startup. That year Co-Steel expanded its North American metal-recycling operations by buying Ken Lener & Sons (New York) and Frampton Auto Parts (Ontario). In 1997 it bought Michigan-based recycler Jackson Iron & Metal. Also in 1997 Mayer Parry Recycling formed Hammond Recycling, a joint venture that merged the Irish recycling operations of Mayer Parry (UK), Hammond Lane Metal (Ireland), and European Metal Recycling (UK).

In early 1998 Co-Steel acquired New Jersey Steel (New Jersey Steel was previously 60% owned by Swiss steelmaker Von Roll Group) and changed its name to Co-Steel Sayreville. Minimill firm New Jersey Steel had started as Steel Holdings, formed by the 1976 consolidation of New Jersey Steel, Structural Corp., Capital Steel, and the Fireproof Products Co. The company changed its name to New Jersey Steel in 1978. In 1988 New Jersey Steel bought a third of New Jersey-based reinforcing-rod fabricator A.J. Ross Logistics, which had previously supplied steel for New York City's George Washington Bridge and Jacob Javits Convention Center. When A.J. Ross went bankrupt in 1993, it owed $5.3 million to New Jersey Steel.

Co-Steel sold its money-losing Sheerness plant to UK steelmaker ASW Holdings for a loss in 1999. It also faced losses that year from Russian, Ukrainian, and Indonesian steel firms flooding the US market. Co-Steel and other US steelmakers asked regulators to impose new tariffs or import quotas, but the requests were denied. In 2000 the company sold its 76% stake in steel recycler Mayer Parry (UK).

In 2002 a subsidiary of Brazilian steelmaker Gerdau S.A., called Gerdau North America, bought Co-Steel, changing the company's name to Gerdau Ameristeel. (Ameristeel was an 87%-owned subsidiary that was fully acquired in 2002 and rolled up into the new company.) In 2004 Gerdau Ameristeel grew when it purchased the North Star Steel assets (including steel minimills, recycling facilities, and downstream operations) from Cargill for approximately $300 million. The company began trading on the NYSE that year.

EXECUTIVES

Chairman: Phillip E. Casey, age 67
President, CEO, and Director: Mario Longhi, age 54
VP and COO: Terry A. Sutter
VP, CFO, and Assistant Secretary: Barbara R. Smith, age 49
VP and CIO: Diane Drum
VP Commercial and Downstream Operations: J. Neal McCullohs III, age 52
VP Human Resources: Terry K. Danahy, age 54
VP Raw Materials: Matthew C. (Matt) Yeatman
VP Steel Mill Operations: Michael P. (Mike) Mueller, age 62
VP and General Manager, Sand Spring OK Steel Mill: Robert L. Bullard
VP and General Manager, Whitby Ontario Steel Mill: Roger D. Paiva
VP and General Manager, Gallatin KY Steel Mill: Don B. Daily
VP, General Counsel, and Corporate Secretary: Robert E. Lewis, age 48
VP and General Manager, Beaumont, TX, and Petersburg, VA, Steel Mill: Greg W. Bott
VP and General Manager, St. Paul, MN, Steel Mill: Jerry A. Goodwald
VP Commercial Sales: Jim R. Kerkvliet
Auditors: PricewaterhouseCoopers LLP

LOCATIONS

HQ: Gerdau Ameristeel Corporation
4221 W. Boy Scout Blvd., Ste. 600
Tampa, FL 33607
Phone: 813-286-8383   **Fax:** 813-207-2355
Web: www.gerdauameristeel.com

2008 Sales

	$ mil.	% of total
US	7,300.3	86
Canada	1,228.2	14
Total	**8,528.5**	**100**

PRODUCTS/OPERATIONS

2008 Sales

	$ mil.	% of total
Steel mills	6,769.5	79
Downstream products	1,759.0	21
Total	**8,528.5**	**100**

Selected Subsidiaries

Ameristeel Bright Bar, Inc. (US)
Bradley Steel Processors (50%, Canada)
Canadian Guide Rail Corporation (50%, Canada)
Chaparral Steel Company (US)
Gallatin Steel Company (50%, flat-rolled steel, US)
Gerdau Ameristeel Sayreville Inc. (US)
Ghent Industries (50%, US)

COMPETITORS

AK Steel Holding	Nucor
Allegheny Technologies	Steel Dynamics
ArcelorMittal USA	ThyssenKrupp Steel
Canam Group	United States Steel
Commercial Metals	

HISTORICAL FINANCIALS

Company Type: Public

Income Statement

FYE: December 31

	REVENUE ($ mil.)	NET INCOME ($ mil.)	NET PROFIT MARGIN	EMPLOYEES
12/08	8,528.5	(587.4)	—	10,951
12/07	5,806.6	537.9	9.3%	10,140
12/06	4,464.2	378.6	8.5%	10,140
12/05	3,897.1	295.5	7.6%	7,000
12/04	3,009.9	337.7	11.2%	7,200
Annual Growth	**29.7%**	**—**	**—**	**11.1%**

2008 Year-End Financials

Debt ratio: 105.9%
Return on equity: —
Cash ($ mil.): 483
Current ratio: 5.71
Long-term debt ($ mil.): 3,068

No. of shares (mil.): 433
Dividends
  Yield: 1.3%
  Payout: —
Market value ($ mil.): 2,626

Stock History

NYSE: GNA

	STOCK PRICE ($) FY Close	P/E High/Low		PER SHARE ($) Earnings	Dividends	Book Value
12/08	6.06	—	—	(1.36)	0.08	6.69
12/07	14.22	10	5	1.65	0.08	8.92
12/06	8.92	9	4	1.24	0.08	4.27
12/05	5.64	8	4	0.97	0.08	3.66
12/04	6.76	5	2	1.45	0.00	3.15
Annual Growth	**(2.7%)**	**—**	**—**	**—**	**—**	**20.7%**

Gilead Sciences

Gilead Sciences has biotech balms for infectious diseases, including hepatitis, HIV, and infections related to AIDS. The company's HIV franchise includes blockbuster Truvada, a combination of two of its other drugs, Viread and Emtriva. It co-promotes another HIV treatment, called Atripla, in the US and Europe with Bristol-Myers Squibb. Other products on the market include AmBisome, used to treat systemic fungal infections such as those that accompany AIDS; Vistide, for AIDS-related eye infections; and hepatitis B antiviral Hepsera. Outside of the infectious disease realm, Gilead markets Letairis, a treatment for pulmonary arterial hypertension (PAH), or high pulmonary blood pressure.

The 2007 FDA approval of Letairis was the first big pay-off from Gilead's foray into areas outside of infectious disease. Letairis was gained through the acquisition of Myogen, which also contributed Flolan, an FDA-approved treatment for primary pulmonary hypertension that Gilead now markets in the US under license from GlaxoSmithKline. In 2008 Gilead acquired another potential PAH drug called cicletanine from

Navitas Assets. The off-patent compound is already approved in parts of Europe to treat high blood pressure.

In further matters of the heart, Gilead has acquired CV Therapeutics (since renamed Gilead Palo Alto), which develops and markets therapies for chronic angina (chest pain) and other cardiovascular ailments, as well as cardiac imaging agents. The $1.4 billion acquisition was completed in April 2009 after CV Therapeutics fended off a hostile takeover attempt from marketing partner Astellas Pharma.

Despite its expansion into the areas of cardiovascular and pulmonary diseases, Gilead's main source of revenue continues to be its HIV franchise, which contributes about 85% of product sales. Aside from Atripla, which it co-promotes with Bristol-Myers Squibb (BMS), Gilead promotes its antiviral drugs through its own commercial infrastructure in North America, some European countries, and Australia, and it distributes its products through wholesalers. (US distribution firms Cardinal Health, McKesson, and AmerisourceBergen together account for about half of the company's revenues.)

Increasing international commercialization of Atripla is a major focus area for Gilead. The drug, which is an antiretroviral therapy that combines Bristol-Myers Squibb's Sustiva with Gilead's Truvada, won European Union marketing approval late in 2007; and the two companies are ramping up marketing activities throughout the European territories. The company plans to market Atripla in select Latin American and Asian countries through a partnership with Merck.

Japan Tobacco promotes HIV drugs Truvada, Viread, and Emtriva in Japan. Several of Gilead's other products are marketed in some geographic markets through alliances with other drug firms, such as Astellas Pharma, Dainippon Sumitomo Pharma, and GlaxoSmithKline.

Additionally, Gilead Sciences receives royalties on influenza treatment Tamiflu, which it developed with Roche, and on Macugen, an ophthalmologic drug developed by OSI Pharmaceuticals using technology licensed from Gilead.

HISTORY

Dr. Michael Riordan started Gilead Sciences in 1987, backed by venture capital firm Menlo Ventures. The name was derived from the Biblical phrase "Is there no balm in Gilead?" In 1990 Glaxo Wellcome (now GlaxoSmithKline) agreed to fund Gilead's research into code-blocking treatments for cancer. Gilead went public in 1992.

In 1994 the company formed an alliance with American Home Products' Storz Instruments (now part of Bausch & Lomb) to develop and market a topical treatment for an ophthalmic virus. Two years later Gilead joined forces with Roche to develop treatments for influenza.

Vistide was approved in the US in 1996 and in Europe in 1997. But more-effective HIV therapies brought declining demand for Vistide.

The company bounced back with Tamiflu (the fruit of its Roche partnership), which was approved in 1999. Sales were brisk during that flu season. Also that year Gilead expanded its pipeline and geographic reach with the $550 million, all-stock acquisition of NeXstar Pharmaceuticals, which focused on antifungals, antibiotics, and cancer treatments.

In 2000 Gilead sought approval for Tamiflu in Japan and Europe (it withdrew the European application after regulators there asked for more information) and also sought approval for pediatric uses for the drug, which was granted. The following year it resubmitted Tamiflu for approval in Europe.

Chairman Donald Rumsfeld resigned in 2001 to become US secretary of defense and was replaced by retired Sears, Roebuck executive James Denny. Perhaps the Defense connection has helped: Vistide became one of the many drugs that researchers began studying as possible alternatives to vaccines should a smallpox bio-attack occur in the US.

Also in 2001 Gilead sold its oncology pipeline to OSI Pharmaceuticals to focus on infection-control products and its hepatitis B lead drug candidate. The sale was a smart move — the FDA approved Hepsera less than a year later.

To help alleviate the AIDS epidemic, in 2003 the company announced plans to sell Viread at cost to all African nations and some 15 other impoverished countries striken by the disease. That year Gilead won FDA approval for another weapon to battle AIDS: antiretroviral Emtriva.

Gilead sparred with its Tamiflu partner Roche in 2005, claiming Roche had not put forth enough effort to make the antiviral a blockbuster. The two companies reached a new agreement late that year, with Roche agreeing to a one-time $62.5 million payment and increased royalties.

A 2006 acquisition of Corus Pharma expanded the company's pipeline of investigational drugs outside its core area of infectious disease. Corus Pharma brought a focus on respiratory diseases, adding a late-stage compound that aims to fight cystic fibrosis-related infections.

It also completed a $2.4 billion acquisition of Myogen, which had development programs in the area of cardiovascular disease, including Letairis (approved in 2007).

Gilead Sciences shored up its manufacturing capabilities with a couple of acquisitions in 2006 and 2007. It bought Raylo Chemicals, formerly a Canada-based subsidiary of Degussa (now Evonik Degussa); Raylo is a manufacturer of active pharmaceutical ingredients and other chemicals used in drug development. It also purchased a manufacturing plant in Ireland in 2007.

EXECUTIVES

Chairman and CEO: John C. Martin, age 57, $10,998,006 total compensation
President and COO: John F. Milligan, age 48, $5,187,437 total compensation
SVP and CFO: Robin L. Washington, age 46, $1,166,870 total compensation
EVP Research and Development and Chief Scientific Officer: Norbert W. Bischofberger, age 53, $4,390,994 total compensation
EVP Commercial Operations: Kevin Young, age 51, $4,364,971 total compensation
EVP Corporate and Medical Affairs: Gregg H. Alton, age 43, $2,682,789 total compensation
SVP Pharmaceutical Development and Manufacturing: Taiyin Yang, age 55
SVP Corporate Development: John J. Toole, age 55
SVP Research: William A. Lee, age 53
SVP Manufacturing and Operations: Anthony D. Caracciolo, age 54
SVP Respiratory Therapeutics: A. Bruce Montgomery, age 54
SVP Commercial Operations, North America: James R. Meyers, age 44
SVP International Commercial Operations: Paul Carter
SVP Cardiovascular Therapeutics: Seigo Izumo
SVP Development Operations: Andrew Cheng
VP Human Resources: Kristen M. Metza, age 49
Senior Director Investor Relations: Susan Hubbard
Director Media Relations: Nathan Kaiser
Auditors: Ernst & Young LLP

LOCATIONS

HQ: Gilead Sciences, Inc.
333 Lakeside Dr., Foster City, CA 94404
Phone: 650-574-3000   **Fax:** 650-578-9264
Web: www.gilead.com

2008 Sales

	$ mil.	% of total
US	2,857.5	54
Europe		
France	395.7	7
Spain	356.6	6
UK	297.3	6
Italy	277.4	5
Germany	242.2	5
Switzerland	193.3	4
Other European countries	346.7	6
Other countries	369.1	7
Total	**5,335.8**	**100**

PRODUCTS/OPERATIONS

2008 Sales

	$ mil.	% of total
Antiviral product sales		
Truvada	2,106.7	40
Atripla	1,572.5	29
Viread	621.2	12
Hepsera	341.0	6
Emtriva	31.1	1
Other product sales		
AmBisome	289.6	5
Letairis	112.8	2
Other	9.9	—
Royalties	218.2	4
Contract & other	32.8	1
Total	**5,335.8**	**100**

Selected Products

Approved
   AmBisome (antifungal)
   Atripla (HIV, with Bristol-Myers Squibb)
   Emtriva (HIV)
   Flolan (pulmonary hypertension)
   Hepsera (hepatitis B)
   Letairis (pulmonary arterial hypertension)
   Ranexa (chronic angina)
   Truvada (fixed-dose combination of Viread and Emtriva for HIV)
   Viread (HIV)
   Vistide (AIDS-related cytomegalovirus retinitis)
In development
   Ambrisentan (idiopathic pulmonary fibrosis)
   Aztreonam (cystic fibrosis)
   Darusentan (resistant hypertension)
   Elvitegravir (HIV)

COMPETITORS

Abbott Labs
Actelion
AstraZeneca
Bausch & Lomb
BioCryst Pharmaceuticals
Boehringer Ingelheim
Bristol-Myers Squibb
CIBA VISION
Enzon
Genentech
GlaxoSmithKline
Idenix Pharmaceuticals
InterMune
Merck
Novartis
Pfizer
Roche Holding
Schering-Plough
Shire
Three Rivers Pharmaceuticals
Valeant

HISTORICAL FINANCIALS

Company Type: Public

Income Statement

FYE: December 31

	REVENUE ($ mil.)	NET INCOME ($ mil.)	NET PROFIT MARGIN	EMPLOYEES
12/08	5,335.8	2,011.2	37.7%	3,441
12/07	4,230.0	1,615.3	38.2%	2,979
12/06	3,026.1	(1,190.0)	—	2,515
12/05	2,028.4	813.9	40.1%	1,900
12/04	1,324.6	449.4	33.9%	1,654
Annual Growth	**41.7%**	**45.4%**	**—**	**20.1%**

2008 Year-End Financials

Debt ratio: 32.7%
Return on equity: 52.8%
Cash ($ mil.): 1,459
Current ratio: 3.52
Long-term debt ($ mil.): 1,356

No. of shares (mil.): 904
Dividends
   Yield: 0.0%
   Payout: —
Market value ($ mil.): 46,244

Stock History

NASDAQ (GS): GILD

	STOCK PRICE ($) FY Close	P/E High/Low	PER SHARE ($) Earnings	Dividends	Book Value
12/08	51.14	27 17	2.10	0.00	4.59
12/07	46.01	29 19	1.68	0.00	3.83
12/06	32.47	— —	(1.29)	0.00	2.01
12/05	26.28	33 18	0.86	0.00	3.35
12/04	17.50	39 26	0.50	0.00	2.07
Annual Growth	**30.7%**	**— —**	**43.2%**	**—**	**22.1%**

Global Crossing

Born to bridge the seas, Global Crossing surfs the bandwidth wave. The global Internet protocol (IP)-based telecommunications carrier operates an integrated global system of data networks that reaches about 700 cities in 60 countries. It connects the Americas and Europe, and links to Asia through submarine fiber-cable networks. This fiber stream supports a wide range of services, including Internet access and other data services, for multinational corporations, government agencies, and other telecom service providers. Global Crossing also provides voice calling services over its network. The company operates from offices and facilities throughout Asia, Europe, Latin America, and North America.

Global Crossing's largest single geographic market is the UK, which accounts for about one-quarter of sales. Latin America is another key market, which is overseen by the company's Impsat unit (formerly IMPSAT Fiber Networks, acquired in 2007).

The company in 2008 opened a data hosting center in London in an attempt to provide better service to its European clientele, and another in Miami to fortify connectivity between customers in the US and Latin America. The following year, Global Crossing completed construction of a new section of fiber network in the Brazilian state of São Paulo, and it expanded a data center in Buenos Aires to meet growing demand in the region.

The company primarily uses direct sales to target customers in such key markets as financial services, technology, health care, pharmaceuticals, and transportation.

ST Telemedia, a subsidiary of Singapore-based investment company Temasek Holdings, owns about 63% of Global Crossing.

HISTORY

In glamorous Beverly Hills in 1997, Pacific Capital founder Gary Winnick (who was also a former colleague of ex-junk-bond king Michael Milken) teamed with retired ARCO CEO Lodwrick Cook to form Global Crossing. Their goal was to lay a fiber-optic cable, Atlantic Crossing (AC-1), from the US to Europe. Undersea cables had traditionally been laid by consortia of big telecommunications companies, generally monopolies. AT&T (which wanted to exit the undersea cable laying business and needed fast revenues) agreed to construct AC-1 if Winnick could find $750 million.

Winnick put up $15 million and sold demo videos to lure investors. He also trumpeted his plan to undercut competitors' prices ($20 million per 155 Mbps circuit) by charging only $8 million. Global Crossing soon recouped about half of the $750 million debt.

Telecom veteran Jack Scanlon was tapped as CEO in 1998, and the company mapped out plans for the Pacific Crossing (PC-1) and Mid-Atlantic Crossing (MAC). When AC-1 was finished, Global Crossing went public.

In 1999 Robert Annunziata left AT&T to become CEO of Global Crossing, and he brought visions of transforming the company from wholesale carrier to full-fledged telecom operator. Just 17 days after he arrived, he began acquisition talks with Frontier, which the company agreed to buy in a stock swap.

Global Crossing sweetened the Frontier offer after its share price fell; it wrapped up the deal for $10 billion. Frontier's key assets were its substantial US fiber network and its fast-growing Web hosting unit, GlobalCenter. Global Crossing also bought Cable & Wireless' undersea-cable operations that year, and in 2000 the company bought IPC Communications and its IXnet subsidiary for about $3.8 billion, gaining a suite of Internet-based services for financial institutions.

Cable TV veteran Leo Hindery, who had become CEO of GlobalCenter in 1999, replaced Annunziata in 2000. Hindery stepped down later that year, however, and vice chairman Thomas Casey became the company's fourth CEO since 1998.

Demand for services grew far more slowly than the industry had hoped, and Global Crossing was forced to retrench. To cut costs, the company in 2001 began cutting jobs and looking for noncore assets to sell. It sold GlobalCenter to Exodus Communications in early 2001 for stock that was originally worth $6.5 billion, but whose value later collapsed as Exodus slid toward bankruptcy. Global Crossing sold its local-exchange carrier business (also gained in the Frontier deal) to Citizens Communications for about $3.5 billion in cash.

The next year Global Crossing sought reorganization under Chapter 11 bankruptcy protection. Winnick, who owned 10% of Global Crossing before the bankruptcy filing, was known as a hands-on leader who worked through five CEOs in his company's brief history — three in 2000 alone. However, by the end of 2002 Winnick himself had tendered his resignation in the wake of an investigation into his stock sales, before news had surfaced that the company faced a $1 billion revenue shortfall.

Global Crossing emerged from bankruptcy in 2003 after a lengthy and highly publicized reorganization. Domiciled in Bermuda, Global Crossing moved its operating headquarters from posh surroundings in Beverly Hills, California, to New Jersey. That year Global Crossing completed construction of its core worldwide network and announced plans to cut 2,000 jobs as part of a cost-control effort. Asia Global Crossing CEO John Legere replaced Casey as head of the parent company.

The company reached a bankruptcy court approval to sell a 61.5% majority stake to the telecom unit of Hutchison Whampoa and Singapore Technologies' Telemedia unit. After Hutchison pulled out of the deal, ST Telemedia said it would make good on the $250 million offer on its own, and a nod of approval from the US president seemed to seal the deal.

In 2004, Temasek Holdings, which handles investment business for the Singapore government, acquired Singapore Technologies and its subsidiary ST Telemedia in a corporate restructuring, thereby taking control of Global Crossing.

Also in 2004 Global Crossing sold its Global Marine Systems subsidiary and its 49% stake in the SB Submarine Systems Company joint venture, to Bridgehouse Marine. With the focus on multinationals and other high-capacity clients, the company sold its small business group to Matrix Telecom in 2005.

In 2006 the company acquired UK-based Fibernet Group, enhancing its UK operations with Fibernet's client list of financial, insurance, and retail companies. Later that year it bought Argentina-based IMPSAT Fiber Networks in a deal that expanded Global Crossing's roster of international clients.

EXECUTIVES

Chairman: Lodewijk Christiaan van Wachem, age 77
Vice Chairman: Peter L. H. Seah, age 62
CEO and Director: John J. Legere, age 51
EVP and CFO: John A. Kritzmacher, age 48
EVP and Chief Customer Experience Officer:
  Edward T. (Ted) Higase, age 42
EVP and Chief Marketing Officer:
  David R. (Dave) Carey, age 55
EVP and Chief Administrative Officer:
  Gary Breauninger, age 41
Chief Accounting Officer: Robert A. Klug, age 41
Chief Marketing Officer, EMEA: Niall Anderson, age 42
Chief Security Officer: Marcelo Gimenez
EVP; Managing Director, Global Crossing UK and Europe: Anthony D. Christie, age 47
EVP and General Counsel; Chairman, Global Crossing UK: John B. McShane, age 47
EVP Global Operations: Daniel J. (Dan) Enright, age 49
EVP Global Access Management: John R. Mulhearn Jr., age 58
EVP Enterprise Sales and Collaboration Services:
  Neil Barua, age 31
SVP and Secretary: Mitchell C. Sussis
VP Media Relations and Executive Communications:
  Steve Cross
Senior Manager, Investor Relations: Antonio Suarez
Member Executive Committee: Steven T. (Terry) Clontz, age 58
Member Executive Committee and Director:
  Jeremiah D. Lambert, age 74
Auditors: Ernst & Young LLP

LOCATIONS

HQ: Global Crossing Limited
  Wessex House, 45 Reid St.
  Hamilton HM12, Bermuda
Phone: 441-296-8600
US HQ: 200 Park Ave., Ste. 300
  Florham Park, NJ 07932
US Phone: 973-937-0100   **US Fax:** 973-360-0148
Web: www.globalcrossing.com

2008 Sales

	$ mil.	% of total
US	1,305	50
UK	714	28
Other regions	573	22
Total	**2,592**	**100**

PRODUCTS/OPERATIONS

2008 Sales

	% of total
Data	59
Voice	34
Collaboration	6
Other	1
Total	**100**

Selected Services

Data
  Asynchronous Transfer Mode (ATM)
  Colocation
  Dedicated Internet access
  Frame relay
  Internet dial-up
  Internet Protocol Virtual Private Network (IP VPN) service
  IP transit
  Managed services
    Equipment procurement, provisioning, and installation
    Network monitoring and management
    Pre-sales engineering and customer premises equipment ("CPE") design
  Metro access
  Private lines
  Wavelength services
Voice
  Calling cards
  Commercial managed voice services (UK only)
  Dedicated outbound and inbound domestic and international long-distance traffic
  Switched outbound and inbound domestic and international long-distance traffic
  Toll-free enhanced routing services
Conferencing
  Event call (operator assisted conference calls)
  Ready-Access (audio on-demand, reservation-free audio conferencing service)
  Videoconferencing

COMPETITORS

AT&T	Orange
BT	Premiere Global Services
Cable & Wireless	Qwest Communications
COLT Telecom	Sprint Nextel
Deutsche Telekom AG	Telecom Italia
Equant	Telefónica
France Telecom	Telmex
IDT	Telstra
Intercall	Verizon
Level 3 Communications	XO Holdings

engineered industrial products business as EnPro Industries (completed in 2002). In October Goodrich announced that it was closing 16 plants and cutting its workforce by about 10% because of the slowdown in the aircraft manufacturing business.

Late in 2002 Goodrich paid $1.5 billion in cash for TRW's Aeronautical Systems unit (flight controls, cargo systems, engine control systems, power/utility systems, missile actuation). The company divested its Avionics Systems (integrated flight controls and displays) operations in 2003.

In 2004 Goodrich won a large deal to supply Boeing with thrust reversers, engine coverings, wheels, brake systems, lighting, and cargo handling systems for its upcoming 787 airplane, which could bring Goodrich up to $4 billion in revenue over the life of the contract. The next year Airbus selected Goodrich to supply engine coverings and thrust reversers for its upcoming A350 (which will compete directly with Boeing's 787) in a deal that could be worth $6 billion.

In 2007 Goodrich sold its Goodrich Aviation Technical Services (ATS) subsidiary to Macquarie Bank Limited.

EXECUTIVES

Chairman, President, and CEO: Marshall O. Larsen, age 60, $10,797,108 total compensation
EVP and CFO: Scott E. Kuechle, age 49, $2,160,795 total compensation
EVP Administration and General Counsel: Terrence G. Linnert, age 62, $3,236,354 total compensation
EVP Operational Excellence and Technology: Gerald T. (Jerry) Witowski, age 61
SVP Strategy and Business Development: Stephen R. (Steve) Huggins, age 65
SVP Human Resources: Jennifer Pollino, age 44
VP and Segment President, Actuation and Landing Systems: John J. (Jack) Carmola, age 53, $2,606,562 total compensation
VP Business Development: Joseph F. (Joe) Andolino
VP, Associate General Counsel, and Secretary: Sally L. Geib
VP and Segment President, Nacelles and Interior Systems: Cynthia M. (Cindy) Egnotovich, age 51, $2,499,557 total compensation
VP Corporate Communications: Lisa Bottle
VP Investor Relations: Paul S. Gifford
VP and President, Electronic Systems: Curtis Reusser, age 48
VP and General Manager, Aerostructures: Marc A. Duvall
VP and Controller: Scott A. Cottrill, age 43
VP and General Manager, Lighting Systems: Steve Chalmers
VP Internal Audit: William G. Stiehl
VP and Treasurer: Mike McAuley
VP Tax: Paul Cappiello
VP Acquisitions and Divestitures: Karl Kleiderer
Auditors: Ernst & Young LLP

LOCATIONS

HQ: Goodrich Corporation
Four Coliseum Centre, 2730 W. Tyvola Rd.
Charlotte, NC 28217
Phone: 704-423-7000   **Fax:** 704-423-5540
Web: www.goodrich.com

2008 Sales

	$ mil.	% of total
North America		
US	3,520.7	50
Canada	278.0	4
Europe	2,378.0	34
Asia/Pacific	506.5	7
Other regions	378.5	5
Total	**7,061.7**	**100**

PRODUCTS/OPERATIONS

2008 Sales by Product Group

	$ mil.	% of total
Engine products & services	2,811.1	40
Landing system products & services	1,513.1	21
Electrical & optical products & services	1,205.1	17
Airframe products & services	846.1	12
Safety products & services	567.4	8
Other	118.9	2
Total	**7,061.7**	**100**

2008 Sales by Business Segment

	$ mil.	% of total
Actuation & landing systems	2,614.9	37
Nacelles & interior systems	2,485.6	35
Electronic systems	1,961.2	28
Total	**7,061.7**	**100**

Selected Products

Actuation systems
  Engine and nacelle actuators
  Helicopter main and tail actuators
  Land vehicle actuators
  Precision weapon actuators
  Primary and secondary flight controls
Aircraft wheels and brakes
Engine control systems
  Electronic controls
  Engine health monitoring systems
  Fuel metering controls
  Fuel pumping systems
Intelligence surveillance and reconnaissance systems
  Electro-optical products and services
  Engineered electronics
  Optics
  Shortwave infrared cameras and arrays
Landing gear
Nacelles
Power systems
  Aircraft electrical power systems
Sensor systems
  Cockpit information sensors
  Engine control system sensors
  Flight control sensors

COMPETITORS

AAR Corp.	L-3 Vertex
AeroMechanical Services	Lockheed Martin
Alcoa	LSI Industries
Argo-Tech	Marshall Aerospace
BAE SYSTEMS	Martin-Baker Aircraft
BAE Systems Inc.	Meggitt
Banner Aerospace	Meggitt USA
BE Aerospace	Middle River Aircraft
Boeing	Moog
Breeze-Eastern	Northrop Grumman
Crane Aerospace	Parker Hannifin
Crane Co.	Precision Castparts
Danaher	Raytheon
Ducommun	SAFRAN
EADS	Samsung Group
Esterline	Singapore Technologies
GE	Spirit AeroSystems
General Dynamics	Telair International
Gulfstream Aerospace	Teleflex
Hamilton Sundstrand	Turbine Engine
Héroux-Devtek	Components Technologies
Honeywell International	United Technologies
Hydro-Aire	Vought Aircraft
ITT Corp.	Woodward Governor
Kaman Aerospace	Zodiac Aerospace

HISTORICAL FINANCIALS

Company Type: Public

Income Statement

FYE: December 31

	REVENUE ($ mil.)	NET INCOME ($ mil.)	NET PROFIT MARGIN	EMPLOYEES
12/08	7,061.7	681.2	9.6%	25,000
12/07	6,392.2	482.6	7.5%	23,400
12/06	5,878.3	481.5	8.2%	23,400
12/05	5,396.5	263.6	4.9%	22,600
12/04	4,724.5	156.0	3.3%	21,300
Annual Growth	**10.6%**	**44.6%**	**—**	**4.1%**

2008 Year-End Financials

Debt ratio: 75.7%
Return on equity: 29.2%
Cash ($ mil.): 370
Current ratio: 1.99
Long-term debt ($ mil.): 1,583
No. of shares (mil.): 145
Dividends
  Yield: 2.5%
  Payout: 17.3%
Market value ($ mil.): 5,352

Stock History

NYSE: GR

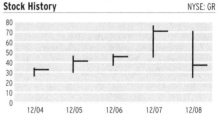

	STOCK PRICE ($) FY Close	P/E High/Low		PER SHARE ($) Earnings	Dividends	Book Value
12/08	37.02	13	5	5.39	0.93	14.47
12/07	70.61	20	12	3.78	0.82	17.84
12/06	45.55	12	10	3.81	0.80	13.67
12/05	41.10	22	14	2.13	0.80	10.19
12/04	32.64	24	19	1.43	0.80	9.29
Annual Growth	**3.2%**	**—**	**—**	**39.3%**	**3.8%**	**11.7%**

Goodyear Tire & Rubber

Despite a worldwide alliance with Sumitomo Rubber Industries designed to dominate the tire industry, The Goodyear Tire & Rubber Company is the #3 tire maker in the world, behind Bridgestone and Michelin. Organized into four geographic segments, the company operates a combined 60 plants worldwide, and has about 1,600 retail tire and auto centers. Goodyear sells tires for the replacement market as well as to the world's automakers. In addition to its own brand of tires, Goodyear makes Dunlop tires for sale in North America and Europe through its alliance with Japan's Sumitomo.

Goodyear experienced a $330 million loss and a 21% decrease in sales for the fourth quarter of 2008. The company cut nearly 4,000 jobs in the second half of 2008 and will cut 5,000 more jobs in 2009, representing a workforce reduction of about 12%. Goodyear is freezing salaries, reducing spending and inventory levels, and looking to sell non-core assets. It also plans to reduce its global tire production capacity by between 15 million and 25 million tires a year over two years, while seeking ways to improve cash flow.

As a strategy to boost sales, Goodyear plans to introduce new product offerings, like the Assurance Fuel Max tire, which is currently used on commercial vehicles, but will soon appear on passenger cars and light-duty trucks, including the Chevrolet Volt electric vehicle.

About two-thirds of the raw materials used by Goodyear in its tire manufacturing are derived from petroleum. The costs of raw materials were up by around 13% in 2008 from the prior year, primarily due to the higher costs for natural and synthetic rubber. The company sees such costs rising another 15%-18% in the first half of 2009, further cutting into the bottom line.

Goodyear sold its Engineered Products division to The Carlyle Group in 2007. The company raised nearly $1.5 billion from the sale of the division, which represented the final act in the company's Capital Structure Improvement Plan (launched in 2003) that was designed overall to restructure the company's debt. So far, it appears its efforts are working. Goodyear is on pace to slash its debt, which peaked at $12 billion in 2006, down to $6 billion in 2008.

For promotional purposes, Goodyear operates three blimps in North America, from bases in California, Florida, and Ohio. Featured in the company's TV commercials, the blimps have represented Goodyear since 1925. A number of other companies have emulated Goodyear's blimp marketing, sending aloft their own fleets of lighter-than-air airships.

HISTORY

In 1898 Frank and Charles Seiberling founded a tire and rubber company in Akron, Ohio, and named it after Charles Goodyear (inventor of the vulcanization process, 1839). The debut of the Quick Detachable tire and the Universal Rim (1903) made Goodyear the world's largest tire maker by 1916.

Goodyear began manufacturing in Canada in 1910, and over the next two decades it expanded into Argentina, Australia, and the Dutch East Indies. The company established its own rubber plantations in Sumatra (now part of Indonesia) in 1916.

Financial woes led to reorganization in 1921, and investment bankers forced the Seiberlings out. Succeeding caretaker management, Paul Litchfield began three decades as CEO in 1926, a time in which Goodyear had emerged to become the world's largest rubber company.

Goodyear blimps served as floating billboards nationwide by the 1930s. During that decade Goodyear opened company stores, acquired tire maker Kelly-Springfield (1935), and began producing tires made from synthetic rubber (1937). After WWII Goodyear was an innovative leader in technologies such as polyester tire cord (1962) and the bias-belted tire (1967).

By 1980 Goodyear had introduced radial tire brands such as the all-weather Tiempo, the Eagle, and the Arriva, as it led the US market.

Thwarting British financier Sir James Goldsmith's takeover attempt in 1986, CEO Robert Mercer raised $1.7 billion by selling the company's non-tire businesses (Motor Wheel, Goodyear Aerospace) and by borrowing heavily.

Recession, overcapacity, and price-cutting in 1990 led to hard times for tire makers. After suffering through 1990, its first money-losing year since the Depression, Goodyear lured Stanley Gault out of retirement. He ceased marketing tires exclusively through Goodyear's dealer network by selling tires through Wal-Mart, Kmart,

and Sears. Gault also cut costs through layoffs, plant closures, and spending reductions and returned Goodyear to profitability in 1991.

The company increased its presence in the US retail market in 1995 when it began selling tires through 860 Penske Auto Centers and 300 Montgomery Ward auto centers. President Samir Gibara succeeded chairman Gault as CEO in 1996. That year Goodyear bought Poland's leading tire maker, T C Debica, and a 60% stake in South African tire maker Contred (acquiring the rest in 1998).

The company acquired Sumitomo Rubber Industries' North American and European Dunlop tire businesses in 1999. The acquisition returned Goodyear to its #1 position in the tire-making industry. Despite record sales in 2000, the company's profits hit some hard road, prompting Goodyear to lay off 10% of its workforce and implement other cost-cutting efforts.

Early in 2001 the company announced that it would close its Mexican tire plant. That same year the company agreed to replace Firestone Wilderness AT tires with Goodyear tires for Ford owners as part of Ford's big Firestone tire recall.

In 2002 the tire maker became embroiled in an age discrimination lawsuit claiming unfair job evaluations for the company's older employees. Blaming a slow US economy, Goodyear announced plans to cut 450 jobs at its Union City, Tennessee, manufacturing plant.

In 2003, as the company was embroiled in a lengthy debate with the United Steelworkers union, it was announced that the Huntsville, Alabama, tire manufacturing plant would be closed. Goodyear also announced that it would cut 500 nonunion salaried employees in North America.

The company announced more job cuts in the non-tire sector in 2004, affecting Goodyear's engineered products and chemical units. In 2005 the company sold its farm tire business to Titan International for $100 million.

In 2005 Goodyear secured the services of J.P. Morgan Securities and Goldman Sachs to help it explore opportunities for the sale of Engineered Products. The company struck a deal for The Carlyle Group in 2007 to buy its Engineered Products division for about $1.5 billion.

EXECUTIVES

Chairman, President, and CEO: Robert J. (Bob) Keegan, age 61, $16,820,764 total compensation
COO; President North American Tire:
Richard J. (Rich) Kramer, age 45, $3,262,027 total compensation
EVP and CFO: Darren R. Wells, age 43, $966,489 total compensation
VP and CIO: Thomas A. (Tom) Connell, age 60
SVP and CTO: Jean-Claude Kihn, age 49
VP and Chief Procurement Officer: Mark Purtilar, age 48
SVP, General Counsel, and Secretary:
C. Thomas Harvie, age 65, $2,488,877 total compensation
SVP Global Sourcing: Christopher W. (Chris) Clark, age 57
SVP, General Counsel, and Secretary:
David L. (Dave) Bialosky, age 51
SVP Global Communications:
Charles L. (Chuck) Sinclair, age 57
SVP Human Resources: Joseph B. (Joe) Ruocco, age 49
SVP Finance and Treasurer: Damon J. Audia, age 38

VP Government Relations: Isabel H. Jasinowski, age 60
VP Business Development: Laura K. Thompson, age 44
VP Consumer Sales, North American Tire:
Jack Winterton
VP Commercial Sales, North American Tire:
Steve McCellan, age 43
VP Marketing, North American Tire: Brett Ponton
VP Global Business Communications: Roger Rydell
Director Human Resource Services and Staffing:
Pat Gorbach
Director Investor Relations: Patrick (Pat) Stobb
Auditors: PricewaterhouseCoopers LLP

LOCATIONS

HQ: The Goodyear Tire & Rubber Company
1144 E. Market St., Akron, OH 44316
Phone: 330-796-2121   **Fax:** 330-796-2222
Web: www.goodyear.com

2008 Sales

	$ mil.	% of total
US	6,662	34
Germany	2,343	12
Other countries	10,483	54
Total	**19,488**	**100**

PRODUCTS/OPERATIONS

2008 Sales

	$ mil.	% of total
North American Tire	8,255	42
Europe, Middle East & Africa Tire	7,316	38
Latin American Tire	2,088	11
Asia/Pacific Tire	1,829	9
Total	**19,488**	**100**

Selected Products

Tires
  Automotive
  Aviation
  Buses
  Earthmoving, mining, and industrial equipment
  Motorcycles
  Trucks

COMPETITORS

AirBoss of America	Pep Boys
Bridgestone	Pirelli
Continental AG	Sime Darby
Cooper Tire & Rubber	SmarTire Systems
Hankook Tire	Titan International
Kumho Tire	Toyo Tire & Rubber
Marangoni	Yokohama Rubber
Michelin	Zeon
Midas	

HISTORICAL FINANCIALS

Company Type: Public

Income Statement

FYE: December 31

	REVENUE ($ mil.)	NET INCOME ($ mil.)	NET PROFIT MARGIN	EMPLOYEES
12/08	19,488.0	(77.0)	—	74,700
12/07	19,644.0	602.0	3.1%	72,000
12/06	20,258.0	(330.0)	—	77,000
12/05	19,723.0	239.0	1.2%	80,000
12/04	18,370.4	114.8	0.6%	84,000
Annual Growth	1.5%	—	—	(2.9%)

2008 Year-End Financials

Debt ratio: 404.3%   No. of shares (mil.): 242
Return on equity: —   Dividends
Cash ($ mil.): 1,894   Yield: 0.0%
Current ratio: 1.75   Payout: —
Long-term debt ($ mil.): 4,132   Market value ($ mil.): 1,444

EXECUTIVES

Chairman: Maurice Marciano, age 60,
$7,867,806 total compensation
Vice Chairman and CEO: Paul Marciano, age 57,
$15,220,426 total compensation
President, COO, and Director: Carlos E. Alberini,
age 53, $3,548,632 total compensation
SVP and CFO: Dennis R. Secor, age 46,
$871,629 total compensation
SVP and CIO: Michael (Mike) Relich, age 48,
$977,590 total compensation
SVP and General Merchandise Manager, Retail Division:
Harriet Sustarsic
SVP General Merchandise: Wendy Klarik
SVP Licensing Products, Guess? Europe:
Stephane Labelle
President, Wholesale: Nancy Shachtman, age 52
President, Guess? Europe: Massimo Macchi
Head, Guess? Business Development, Asia:
Terrence W. Tsang
Director Human Resources: Susan Tenney
Auditors: Ernst & Young LLP

LOCATIONS

HQ: Guess?, Inc.
1444 S. Alameda St., Los Angeles, CA 90021
Phone: 213-765-3100   **Fax:** 213-744-7838
Web: www.guess.com

2009 Stores

	No.
North America	425
International	
Europe	61
Asia	24
Mexico	11
Total	**521**

2009 Sales

	$ mil.	% of total
US	934.2	46
Europe		
Italy	365.2	17
Other countries	364.9	17
Canada	246.8	12
Asia	132.8	6
Mexico	18.9	1
South America	5.0	—
Middle East	14.6	1
Australia	2.7	—
South Africa	4.5	—
Other	3.8	—
Total	**2,093.4**	**100**

PRODUCTS/OPERATIONS

2009 Sales

	$ mil.	% of total
Products		
Retail	978.0	47
Wholesale	296.2	14
European operations	719.0	34
Licensing	100.2	5
Total	**2,093.4**	**100**

2009 North American Stores

	No.
Guess?	192
Guess? Outlet	104
Guess? by MARCIANO	52
G by Guess	43
Guess? Accessories	34
Total	**425**

Licensed GUESS? products

Apparel (kids' and infants')
Eyewear
Fashion accessories
Footwear
Fragrance
Handbags
Jewelry
Leather apparel
Swimwear
Watches

COMPETITORS

Abercrombie & Fitch	The Gap
American Eagle Outfitters	J. Crew
Benetton	Jordache Enterprises
The Buckle	Levi Strauss
Calvin Klein	Liz Claiborne
Diesel SpA	Phillips-Van Heusen
Donna Karan	Polo Ralph Lauren
Esprit Holdings	Tommy Hilfiger
Express, LLC	Urban Outfitters
Fossil, Inc.	VF
French Connection	Warnaco Group
Fruit of the Loom	Wet Seal

HISTORICAL FINANCIALS

Company Type: Public

Income Statement

FYE: Saturday nearest January 31

	REVENUE ($ mil.)	NET INCOME ($ mil.)	NET PROFIT MARGIN	EMPLOYEES
1/09	2,093.4	213.6	10.2%	10,800
1/08*	1,749.9	186.5	10.7%	9,900
12/06	1,185.2	123.2	10.4%	8,800
12/05	936.1	58.8	6.3%	7,300
12/04	729.3	29.6	4.1%	6,800
Annual Growth	**30.2%**	**63.9%**	**—**	**12.3%**

*Fiscal year change

2009 Year-End Financials

Debt ratio: 1.9%
Return on equity: 29.8%
Cash ($ mil.): 294
Current ratio: 2.66
Long-term debt ($ mil.): 15

No. of shares (mil.): 92
Dividends
  Yield: 2.2%
  Payout: 15.8%
Market value ($ mil.): 1,481

Stock History

NYSE: GES

	STOCK PRICE ($) FY Close	P/E High/Low		PER SHARE ($) Earnings	Dividends	Book Value
1/09	16.09	20	5	2.28	0.36	8.43
1/08*	37.31	29	15	1.99	0.28	7.14
12/06	31.72	25	13	1.34	0.00	4.68
12/05	17.80	28	9	0.65	0.00	3.13
12/04	6.28	30	17	0.33	0.00	2.40
Annual Growth	**26.5%**	**—**	**—**	**62.1%**	**—**	**37.0%**

*Fiscal year change

Halliburton Company

One of the largest oilfield services companies in the world, Halliburton serves the upstream oil and gas industry with a complete range of services, from the location of hydrocarbons to the production of oil and gas. Services include providing production optimization, drilling evaluation, fluid services, and oilfield drilling software and consulting. It combines tried-and-true well drilling and optimization techniques with high-tech analysis and modeling software and services. Halliburton works in established oilfields from the North Sea to the Middle East as well as in newer sites in Southeast Asia and Africa.

Oilfield services giant Halliburton is feeling a lot lighter now that it has divested its KBR engineering and military contracts division. Halliburton took KBR public in 2006 by offering a 20% stake in an IPO and later divested the rest, cutting all ties with the company in 2007. It reorganized its management in anticipation of the deal by promoting former KBR CEO Andrew Lane to COO of Halliburton and putting him in charge of all Halliburton subsidiaries. Former CEO of Halliburton's Energy Services Group John Gibson left the company.

Halliburton hoped that spinning off KBR would protect it from the division's declining sales — KBR saw sales fall due to lower government services contracts in the Middle East, the end of fixed-price projects, and the resolution of disputed Iraqi contracts.

In 2006 Halliburton was awarded a multi-million-dollar contract by Saudi Aramco as part of the Khurais oilfield development project, the largest in the region since the 1950s.

The company made headlines in 2007 when it opened a corporate headquarters office in the United Arab Emirates and relocated CEO David Lesar to Dubai. The move allows Halliburton to foster better relations with Middle East oil companies and grow its business in the region.

The past reached out to impact Halliburton in 2009 when, in a settlement with federal authorities, it and its former KBR subsidiary agreed to pay $579 million in fines to settle charges of having bribed Nigerian officials to win billions in construction project contracts.

HISTORY

Erle Halliburton began his oil career in 1916 at Perkins Oil Well Cementing. He moved to oil boomtown Burkburnett, Texas, to start his Better Method Oil Well Cementing Company in 1919. Halliburton used cement to hold a steel pipe in a well, which kept oil out of the water table, strengthened well walls, and reduced the risk of explosions. Though the contribution would later be praised, his technique was considered useless at the time.

In 1920 Halliburton moved to Oklahoma. Incorporating Halliburton Oil Well Cementing Company in 1924, he patented its products and services, forcing oil companies to employ his firm if they wanted to cement wells.

Erle died in 1957, and his company grew through acquisitions between the 1950s and the 1970s. In 1962 it bought Houston construction giant Brown & Root, an expert in offshore platforms. After the 1973 Arab oil embargo Halliburton benefited from the surge in global oil exploration, and later, as drilling costs surged, it became a leader in well stimulation.

When the oil industry slumped in 1982, the firm halved its workforce. Three years later a suffering Brown & Root coughed up $750 million to settle charges of mismanagement at the South Texas Nuclear Project.

In the 1990s Halliburton expanded abroad, entering Russia in 1991 and China in 1993. The next year Brown & Root was named contractor for a pipeline stretching from Qatar to Pakistan. Halliburton drilled the world's deepest horizontal well (18,860 ft.) in Germany in 1995.

Also in 1995 Dick Cheney, a former US defense secretary, became CEO. Brown & Root began providing engineering and logistics services to US Army peacekeeping troops in the Balkans in 1995 and won a major contract to develop an offshore Canadian oil field the next year.

The company nearly doubled in size in 1998 with its $7.7 billion acquisition of oil field equipment manufacturer Dresser Industries. The purchase, coupled with falling oil prices in 1998 and 1999, prompted Halliburton to ax more than 9,000 workers.

Cheney resigned as chairman and CEO that year after he was chosen as George W. Bush's vice presidential running mate. President and COO David Lesar was named to succeed him.

In 2001 a group consisting of investment firms First Reserve and Odyssey Investment Partners and Dresser managers paid $1.55 billion for Dresser Equipment Group. That year a number of multimillion dollar verdicts against Halliburton in asbestos cases sparked rumors that the company was going to file for bankruptcy (flatly denied by Halliburton) and caused the firm's stock price to tumble.

In 2002, in part to protect the company's assets from the unresolved asbestos claims issue, Lesar announced plans to restructure Halliburton into two independent subsidiaries, separating the Energy Services Group from Halliburton's KBR engineering and construction operations.

Halliburton placed its subsidiaries, Dresser Industries and Kellogg Brown & Root, under Chapter 11 bankruptcy protection. Later that year, in an effort to boost its newly formed Energy Services unit, Halliburton purchased Pruett Industries, a fiber optic sensor technology company.

In 2003 Halliburton announced plans to divest its noncore assets in an effort to return its focus to its main operating divisions. In 2004 the company's KBR subsidiary was awarded nearly $1.4 billion worth of contracts to aid in the repair and restoration of Iraq's oil fields during the US-led invasion of Iraq. The US Army Corps of Engineers later withdrew the contracts after allegations that they were awarded to the subsidiary due to Halliburton's relationship to Cheney.

KBR also came under fire when the Pentagon claimed the company overcharged US taxpayers $61 million to supply fuel to Iraq. After an investigation by the US Army Corp of Engineers, Halliburton was cleared of any wrongdoing. The investigation was picked up by the Pentagon's criminal investigative unit and the US State Department. Following an internal audit, Halliburton repaid $6 million after discovering an overcharge from one of its subcontractors.

The company agreed to pay more than $4 billion in cash and stock to settle more than 300,000 asbestos and silica-related personal injury lawsuits filed against its DII Industries and KBR subsidiaries. Halliburton has reorganized its DII and KBR subsidiaries and finalized its asbestos settlements. DII and KBR emerged from Chapter 11 bankruptcy protection in 2005.

EXECUTIVES

Chairman, President, and CEO: David J. (Dave) Lesar, age 55, $17,876,240 total compensation
EVP and CFO: Mark A. McCollum, age 50, $2,420,905 total compensation
EVP Administration and Chief Human Resources Officer: Lawrence J. Pope, age 40
EVP Strategy and Corporate Development: Timothy J. (Tim) Probert, age 57
EVP and General Counsel: Albert O. (Bert) Cornelison Jr., age 59, $3,989,588 total compensation
SVP and Treasurer: Craig W. Nunez, age 47
VP, Corporate Controller, and Principal Accounting Officer: Evelyn M. Angelle, age 41
VP Scandinavia: Jorunn Saetre
VP Investor Relations: Christian A. Garcia
VP and Corporate Secretary: Sherry D. Williams
VP Middle East Region: Gasser El-Badrashini
President, Western Hemisphere: James S. (Jim) Brown, age 54, $2,225,914 total compensation
President, Completion and Production Division: David S. King, age 52
President, Eastern Hemisphere: Ahmed H.M. Lofty, age 54
Director Corporate Affairs: Cathy G. Mann
Senior Representative Public Relations, Trade Media: Zelma Branch
Assistant Secretary: Robert L. Hayter
Auditors: KPMG LLP

LOCATIONS

HQ: Halliburton Company
5 Houston Center, 1401 McKinney St., Ste. 2400
Houston, TX 77010
Phone: 713-759-2600   **Fax:** 713-759-2635
Web: www.halliburton.com

2008 Sales

	$ mil.	% of total
North America	8,340	46
Europe/Africa/CIS	4,346	24
Middle East/Asia	3,168	17
Latin America	2,425	13
Total	**18,279**	**100**

PRODUCTS/OPERATIONS

2008 Sales

	$ mil.	% of total
Completion & production	9,935	54
Drilling & evaluation	8,344	46
Total	**18,279**	**100**

COMPETITORS

Baker Hughes
BJ Services
Saipem
Schlumberger
Technip
Transocean Inc.
Weatherford International

HISTORICAL FINANCIALS

Company Type: Public

Income Statement

FYE: December 31

	REVENUE ($ mil.)	NET INCOME ($ mil.)	NET PROFIT MARGIN	EMPLOYEES
12/08	18,279.0	1,778.0	9.7%	57,000
12/07	15,264.0	3,499.0	22.9%	51,000
12/06	22,576.0	2,348.0	10.4%	104,000
12/05	20,994.0	2,358.0	11.2%	106,000
12/04	20,466.0	(979.0)	—	97,000
Annual Growth	**(2.8%)**	**—**	**—**	**(12.4%)**

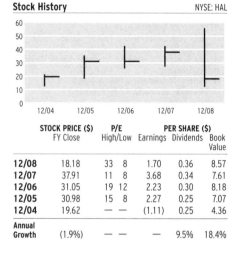

2008 Year-End Financials

Debt ratio: 33.5%
Return on equity: 24.4%
Cash ($ mil.): 1,124
Current ratio: 2.66
Long-term debt ($ mil.): 2,586
No. of shares (mil.): 902
Dividends
Yield: 2.0%
Payout: 21.2%
Market value ($ mil.): 16,393

Stock History

NYSE: HAL

	STOCK PRICE ($) FY Close	P/E High/Low		PER SHARE ($) Earnings	Dividends	Book Value
12/08	18.18	33	8	1.70	0.36	8.57
12/07	37.91	11	8	3.68	0.34	7.61
12/06	31.05	19	12	2.23	0.30	8.18
12/05	30.98	15	8	2.27	0.25	7.07
12/04	19.62	—	—	(1.11)	0.25	4.36
Annual Growth	**(1.9%)**	**—**	**—**	**—**	**9.5%**	**18.4%**

Hallmark Cards

As the #1 producer of warm fuzzies, Hallmark Cards is the Goliath of greeting cards. The company's cards are sold under brand names such as Hallmark, Shoebox, and Ambassador and can be found in more than 43,000 US retail stores. (About 3,500 stores bear the Hallmark Gold Crown name; the majority of these stores are independently owned.) Hallmark also offers electronic greeting cards, gifts, and flowers through its Web site. In addition to greeting cards, the company owns crayon manufacturer Crayola (formerly Binney & Smith), a controlling stake in cable broadcaster Crown Media, and Kansas City's Crown Center real estate development firm. Members of the founding Hall family own two-thirds of Hallmark.

While Hallmark has risen to the top tier in the industry, changes in the ways that people interact and communicate have created new challenges for the company. Sales have been fairly stagnant the past few years, leading Hallmark to continue to downsize its workforce as part of a cost-saving effort; in 2008 it consolidated production at two printing plants in Kansas, eliminating several jobs at plants in Arkansas, Ontario, and at its Sunrise Publications subsidiary in Indiana. The following year the company shuttered *Hallmark Magazine*, a women's lifestyle periodical launched in 2006.

Product development has been key for its traditional card business. Hallmark has had success with a line of musical cards and now sells cards featuring short animated videos. The company has also teamed with DreamWorks Animation to launch interactive cards for children; the cards have flash drives that hold 3 interactive games featuring characters from *Madagascar: Escape 2 Africa*. The high-tech products, along with a new line of humorous cards, have helped boost the traditional card business.

SVP and Chief Marketing Officer, Harley-Davidson Motor Company: Mark Hans Richer, age 42
Chief Accounting Officer: Mark Kornetzke
EVP Corporate Product Planning:
James A. (Jim) McCaslin, age 60,
$2,347,491 total compensation
SVP Manufacturing, Harley-Davidson Motor Company:
Karl M. Eberle, age 60
VP and Treasurer: James M. Brostowitz
VP Communications: Susan Henderson, age 56
VP and Treasurer: Perry A. Glassgow
VP Core Customer Marketing: William J. Davidson
VP and General Counsel: Edward W. Krishok
Director Investor Relations: Amy S. Giuffre
Auditors: Ernst & Young LLP

LOCATIONS

HQ: Harley-Davidson, Inc.
3700 W. Juneau Ave., Milwaukee, WI 53208
Phone: 414-342-4680   **Fax:** 414-343-8230
Web: www.harley-davidson.com

2008 Motorcycle Sales

	$ mil.	% of total
US	4,192.4	70
Europe	907.2	15
Canada	282.0	5
Japan	279.4	5
Australia	168.1	3
Other regions	142.2	2
Total	**5,971.3**	**100**

PRODUCTS/OPERATIONS

2008 Sales and Financial Services

	$ mil.	% of total
Motorcycles	5,594.3	94
Financial services	377.0	6
Total	**5,971.3**	**100**

2008 Unit Shipments

	Units
Harley-Davidson	
Custom motorcycles	140,908
Touring motorcycles	101,887
Sportster motorcycles	60,684
Buell motorcycles	13,119
Total	**316,598**

Selected Motorcycles

Harley-Davidson
Dyna
Fat Bob
Low Rider
Street Bob
Super Glide (and Custom)
Softail
Cross Bones
Fat Boy
Heritage Softail Classic
Night Train
Rocker and Rocker C
Softail (Custom and Deluxe)
Sportster
883 (Low and Custom)
1200 (Custom and Roadster)
Iron 883
Nightster
XR1200
Touring
Electra Glide (Standard, Classic, and Ultra Classic)
Road Glide
Road King (and Classic)
Street Glide
Tri Glide Ultra Classic
VRSC
Night Rod Special
V-Rod (and V-Rod Muscle)

Buell
Adventure
XB12X
XB12XT
Blast
Sportbike
1125R
XB12R
Street
CityX XB9SX
XB12S
XB12Scg
XB12Ss
XB12STT

Selected Operations

Buell Motorcycle Company
Harley-Davidson Financial Services, Inc.
Harley-Davidson Motor Company
MV Agusta

COMPETITORS

American Ironhorse
BMW
BMW of North America
Ducati
Ek Chor China Motorcycle
Honda
Kawasaki Heavy Industries
Polaris Industries
Suzuki Motor
Triumph Motorcycles
Viper Motorcycle
Yamaha Motor

HISTORICAL FINANCIALS

Company Type: Public

Income Statement

FYE: December 31

	REVENUE ($ mil.)	NET INCOME ($ mil.)	NET PROFIT MARGIN	EMPLOYEES
12/08	5,971.3	654.7	11.7%	10,100
12/07	5,726.8	933.8	16.3%	9,775
12/06	5,800.7	1,043.2	18.0%	9,704
12/05	5,673.8	959.6	16.9%	9,700
12/04	5,320.5	889.8	16.7%	9,580
Annual Growth	**2.9%**	**(7.4%)**	**—**	**1.3%**

2008 Year-End Financials

Debt ratio: 102.9%
Return on equity: 29.2%
Cash ($ mil.): 594
Current ratio: 2.07
Long-term debt ($ mil.): 2,176
No. of shares (mil.): 235
Dividends
   Yield: 7.6%
   Payout: 46.2%
Market value ($ mil.): 3,981

Stock History

NYSE: HOG

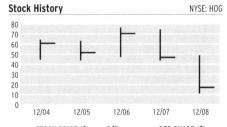

	STOCK PRICE ($) FY Close	P/E High/Low		PER SHARE ($) Earnings	Dividends	Book Value
12/08	16.97	17	4	2.79	1.29	9.02
12/07	46.71	20	12	3.74	1.06	10.13
12/06	70.47	19	12	3.93	0.81	11.75
12/05	51.49	18	13	3.41	0.63	13.15
12/04	60.75	21	15	3.00	0.41	13.72
Annual Growth	**(27.3%)**	**—**	**—**	**(1.8%)**	**33.2%**	**(10.0%)**

Harman International

Harman International Industries is loud and clear. It makes high-end stereo and audio equipment for consumer and professional markets. Its consumer group makes loudspeakers, CD and DVD players, CD recorders, and amplifiers under brands Harman/Kardon, Infinity, Becker, Logic 7, JBL, Mark Levinson, and others. Harman's auto unit sells branded audio systems through several car makers, including Toyota/Lexus and General Motors. Its professional unit makes audio equipment, such as studio monitors, amplifiers, microphones, and mixing consoles for recording studios, cinemas, touring performers, and others.

Harman's automotive products accounted for about 72% of the company's 2008 revenue, with auto makers Daimler and Audi/VW representing 18% and 11%, respectively, of 2008 sales. Harman added another name to its portfolio of premium loudspeaker brands in April 2008 by partnering with B & W Group, which owns the Bowers & Wilkins name. The agreement allows Harman to use Bowers & Wilkins technologies in its automotive unit. UK-based B & W, which outfitted London's Abbey Road Studios, makes and markets products under the Bowers & Wilkins, Classe, and Rotel names for home theater, hi-fi, and multimedia.

To extend its reach, Harman in September 2008 partnered with Wipro Technologies (of Wipro Limited) to launch an engineering center based in India named the Harman India Development Center. The agreement is the foundation for Harman's expansion in India. Harman hopes to employ more than 1,000 people there by 2011.

In its effort to diversify, the high-end audio company moved into the market for other gadgets, including Portable Navigation Devices, with disappointing results. Harman's performance has been hurt by aggressive price cutting by rival TomTom and others.

Feisty namesake and chairman Sidney Harman, the backbone of the company for half a century, has been considered a legend in the audio industry. He owns about 5% of Harman.

Just shy of his 90th birthday, Harman retired from his post as chairman in late 2008. Dinesh C. Paliwal was tapped to take over the position, in addition to continuing his duties as CEO.

HISTORY

Sidney Harman and his partner, Bernard Kardon, left their engineering jobs at a public address system company to found Harman/Kardon in 1953. The two marketed their home audio components to the general public instead of to the traditional audio buff. Their novel concept was to package amplifiers and a tuner in a single unit (called a receiver) that appealed to average consumers.

Kardon cashed out in a 1956 IPO that left Harman with about 33% of the firm. Harman Kardon acquired the respected JBL speaker business in 1969.

Harman was also interested in internal growth. He introduced new management techniques emphasizing workers' quality of life, allowing employees to redesign their jobs and leave work after meeting production quotas. His projects, which had varying degrees of success, attracted the attention of President Carter's administration, which brought Harman on board as undersecretary of commerce in 1977. Harman sold the company to Beatrice Foods that year to avoid a conflict of interest. The company did poorly under the conglomerate, and Harman bought much of it back in 1980, taking it private. He then changed the name to Harman International Industries.

Through acquisitions, he quickly expanded the business into the auto OEM market, acquiring Essex Loudspeaker from United Technologies (1981), then moving into the professional audio equipment market with his purchase of Infinity (1983). In the mid-1980s Harman signed exclusive deals to supply JBL speakers to Ford (ended in 1995) and Chrysler (now DaimlerChrysler), and in 1985 it bought back the Harman/Kardon trade name (Beatrice Foods had sold it to Japanese company Shin Shirasuna). The company went public again the next year.

In 1991 Harman went into a tailspin (losing $20 million, laying off 500) caused by a worldwide recession, poor auto sales, and four soured acquisitions. Harman, who had been living in Washington, DC, with his politician wife, Jane, moved back to California, site of the company's largest plant. President Donald Esters quit in 1992, and Harman set about reorganizing the firm.

The company bought AKG, a leading Austrian microphone maker, in 1993. Signaling its interest in the new digital age, Harman created a new business unit, Harman Interactive, the following year to focus on PC and home theater systems.

It acquired Becker, supplier of audio systems to Mercedes, and high-end equipment manufacturer Madrigal Audio Laboratories in 1995. Harman expanded its customer base by selling to home electronics superstores and specialty stores for audiophiles.

A year later the company began supplying speakers for a Compaq line of computers. In 1997 it boosted its car audio business with new agreements to supply audio systems to certain models of BMW, Toyota, Hyundai, and Peugeot, and it purchased two car loudspeaker makers (Oxford International and Audio Electronic Systems).

In the late 1990s Harman trimmed its consumer product lines from 2,000 to 200. With its sales to Asia down and European sales ailing as well, it closed plants and laid off workers in 1998. That year president Bernard Girod succeeded Harman as CEO. Also in 1998 the company created a remote control with Microsoft and divested several of its international distribution companies to focus on manufacturing and marketing. Harman sold its Orban broadcasting-products business in 1999, and replaced it with Crown International (maker of high-powered amplifiers) in 2000.

In September 2001 Harman sold its Allen & Heath subsidiary, a maker of mixing consoles, to a group consisting of some of the company's top management. In July 2003 Harman acquired Wavemakers, a Canadian developer of processors and software algorithms.

Longtime CEO Bernard Girod, who took the reigns from Sidney Harman in 1998, retired at the end of 2006. Earlier that year Douglas Pertz took over as CEO, but resigned from the company midyear after a short stint.

EXECUTIVES

Chairman and CEO: Dinesh C. Paliwal, age 51
CFO: Herbert K. Parker, age 50
CTO: Sachin Lawande
VP and Chief Human Resources Officer: John Stacey, age 44
VP and Chief Accounting Officer: Jennifer Peter, age 36
SVP Operational Excellence: David Karch, age 48
VP, General Counsel, and Secretary: Todd A. Suko, age 42
VP Corporate Communications: Brad A. Hoffman
VP and Treasurer: Robert C. Ryan
VP Strategy and Investor Relations: Robert V. Lardon
VP Marketing Services: Eric M. Plaskonos
President, Audio Division and VP Corporate Development: David Slump
President, Automotive: Klaus Blickle, age 54
President, Professional Division; Regional Manager, North America: Blake Augsburger, age 46
President and CEO, Harman International Automotive Division: Klaus Blickle
Auditors: KPMG LLP

LOCATIONS

HQ: Harman International Industries, Incorporated
    400 Atlantic St., 15th Fl., Stamford, CT 06901
Phone: 203-328-3500
Web: www.harman.com

2009 Sales

	$ mil.	% of total
Europe		
Germany	1,236.2	43
Other countries	548.3	19
US	577.6	20
Other regions	528.9	18
Total	**2,891.0**	**100**

PRODUCTS/OPERATIONS

2009 Sales

	$ mil.	% of total
Automotive	2,004.8	70
Professional	492.9	17
Consumer	356.5	12
Other	36.8	1
Total	**2,891.0**	**100**

Selected Products

Automotive
    Audio systems
    Information and entertainment systems
Professional
    Audio amplifiers
    Audio headphones
    Broadcasting studio equipment
    Cinema audio systems
    Digital audio workstations
    Equalizers
    Loudspeakers
    Microphones
    Mixing consoles
    Signal processing systems
    Sound reinforcement systems
    Special effects units
    Surround sound systems
Consumer
    Audio amplifiers
    Audio and video receivers
    CD players
    Digital signal processors
    DVD players
    Home theater systems
    Loudspeakers
    PC audio systems

Selected Brands

AKG	JBL
BSS	JBL Professional
Crown	Lexicon
dbx	Mark Levinson
DigiTech	Revel
Harman/Kardon	Soundcraft
Infinity	Studer

COMPETITORS

Aisin Seiki	Macintosh Retail Group
Altec Lansing	Magellan Navigation
Audio Research	Marshall Amplification
Bosch Communications	Meyer Sound
Bose	Mitsubishi Electric
Boston Acoustics	Onkyo
BSH Bosch und Siemens	Panasonic
Creative Technology	Peavey Electronics
D&M	Pioneer Corporation
Delphi Corp.	Polk Audio
Denon Electronics	QSC Audio
DENSO	Sennheiser
Fender	Shure
Foster Electric (U.S.A.)	Sony
JVC KENWOOD	TASCAM
Klipsch	TomTom
Krell	Visteon
Logitech	Yamaha
LOUD Technologies	

HISTORICAL FINANCIALS

Company Type: Public

Income Statement

FYE: June 30

	REVENUE ($ mil.)	NET INCOME ($ mil.)	NET PROFIT MARGIN	EMPLOYEES
6/09	2,891.0	(422.6)	—	9,482
6/08	4,112.5	107.8	2.6%	11,694
6/07	3,551.1	314.0	8.8%	11,688
6/06	3,247.9	255.3	7.9%	11,246
6/05	3,030.9	232.8	7.7%	10,845
Annual Growth	**(1.2%)**	**—**	**—**	**(3.3%)**

2009 Year-End Financials

Debt ratio: 64.6%
Return on equity: —
Cash ($ mil.): 591
Current ratio: 2.03
Long-term debt ($ mil.): 629
No. of shares (mil.): 69
Dividends
    Yield: 0.2%
    Payout: —
Market value ($ mil.): 1,303

Stock History

NYSE: HAR

	STOCK PRICE ($) FY Close	P/E High/Low		PER SHARE ($) Earnings	Dividends	Book Value
6/09	18.80	—	—	(7.19)	0.04	14.05
6/08	41.39	68	21	1.73	0.05	19.33
6/07	116.80	27	16	4.72	0.05	21.55
6/06	85.37	31	21	3.75	0.05	17.71
6/05	81.36	40	21	3.31	0.05	15.30
Annual Growth	**(30.7%)**	**—**	**—**	**—**	**(5.4%)**	**(2.1%)**

Harris Corporation

Hail Harris for a high-flying, high-tech hookup. The company, which develops communications products for government and commercial customers worldwide, makes microwave, satellite, and other wireless network transmission equipment; air traffic control systems; mobile radio systems; and digital network broadcasting and management systems. The company's largest customer is the US government. Harris' commercial clients include radio and TV broadcasters, utilities providers, construction companies, and oil producers. Customers have included Clear Channel Communications, Sony, and Lockheed Martin.

Harris continues to build its line of communications products with acquisitions and adapt technologies created for its government customers to other markets. The company has drawn on its expertise in broadcast, high-frequency, and radio-frequency transmission to build up a portfolio of wireless broadband communications systems in an ongoing effort to expand into commercial markets. Harris' government and defense communications segments still accounts for most of its revenues.

The company invested in broadcast communications with the acquisition of broadcast video systems maker Leitch Technology in 2006. The buy gave Harris a stake in the transition to high-definition digital services. The company also purchased broadcast management software maker Optimal Solutions and the digital video business of Aastra Technologies that year.

In 2007 Harris merged its Microwave Communication Division with its Stratex Networks subsidiary to form Harris Stratex Networks. It initially held a 56% stake in the combined company, but in 2009 Harris spun off its shares of Harris Stratex to its shareholders.

Also in 2009, Harris acquired the wireless systems business of Tyco Electronics (formerly known as M/A-COM) for $675 million in cash. Harris combined the business, which makes wireless communications systems for law enforcement and other public service organizations, with its RF Communications unit. It also bought the air traffic control business of SolaCom Technologies, which included voice and data communications equipment for air traffic control facilities, along with radio systems for communication between air traffic control and in-flight airplanes.

HISTORY

Harris was founded in Niles, Ohio, in 1895 by brothers Alfred and Charles Harris, both jewelers and inventors. Among their inventions was a printing press that became Harris Automatic Press Company's flagship product.

Harris remained a small, family-run company until 1944, when engineer George Dively was hired as general manager. Under Dively the company began manufacturing bindery, typesetting, and paper converting equipment while remaining a leading supplier of printing presses. In 1957 Harris merged with typesetter maker Intertype and changed its name to Harris-Intertype Corporation.

During the 1960s and 1970s Harris-Intertype grew through acquisitions. In 1967 it bought electronics and data processing equipment maker Radiation, a company heavily dependent on government contracts, and relocated to Radiation's headquarters in Melbourne, Florida. The company also bought RF Communications (two-way radios, 1969), General Electric's broadcast equipment line (1972), and UCC-Communications Systems (data processing equipment, 1972).

The company changed its name to Harris Corporation in 1974. In 1980 Harris bought Farinon, a manufacturer of microwave radio systems, and Lanier Business Products, the leading maker of dictating equipment. In 1983 it sold its printing equipment business.

Harris formed a joint venture with 3M, called Harris/3M Document Products, in 1986 to market copiers and fax machines, and in 1989 it acquired the entire operation, which became Lanier Worldwide. Other 1980s acquisitions included Scientific Calculations, a CAD software developer (1986), and General Electric's Solid State group (1988).

Harris won a contract with the FAA in 1992 to modernize voice communications between airports and airplanes. Later that year Harris acquired Westronic, a supplier of automated control systems for electric utilities. In 1994 Harris began installing the world's largest private digital telephone network, along Russia's gas pipeline, and it spun off its computer products division as Harris Computer Systems.

In 1996 Harris became the first company to demonstrate a digital TV transmitter. That year it acquired NovAtel, a maker of cellular and wireless local-loop systems for rural areas, and it bought a stake in the Chile-based phone company Compania de Teléfonos. In 1997 it purchased digital broadcasting specialist Innovation Telecommunications Image and Sound.

The company in 1998 purchased German chemical manufacturer Bayer's Agfa-Gevaert photocopier business, which doubled Lanier's share of the European office equipment market. Hurt by a tough semiconductor market that year, Harris laid off about 8% of its workforce.

Shifting toward a strictly communications-related operation in 1999, Harris sold its semiconductor operation (which now does business as Intersil) in a deal valued at about $600 million and spun off Lanier to shareholders. It also sold its photomask manufacturing unit to Align-Rite.

In 2000 Harris expanded its broadcasting and wireless transmission product lines with the acquisitions of Louth Automation and Wavtrace. That year the company began outsourcing the assembly of its commercial printed circuit boards and folded its telephone switching and alarm management product lines.

The company broadened its communications product portfolio in 2001 with the acquisitions of Exigent, a provider of satellite tracking and control software, and Hirschmann, a maker of digital broadcasting radio transmitters and cable systems. That year Harris sold its minority stakes in two industrial electronics joint ventures to majority owner General Electric.

The company also sold its telecom testing product lines, which accounted for about $30 million in revenue, to Danaher Corporation in mid-2004. Later that year the company bought Encoda, a developer of software and services to customers in the broadcast media industry, for $340 million.

Harris acquired Multimax — a provider of government IT and communication services — for $400 million in 2007.

EXECUTIVES

Chairman, President, and CEO: Howard L. Lance, age 53
EVP and COO: Robert K. Henry, age 61
SVP and CFO: Gary L. McArthur, age 48
VP Information Services and CIO: William H. Miller Jr.
VP Engineering, Government Communications Systems and CTO: R. Kent Buchanan, age 58
VP Investor Relations and Corporate Communications: Pamela (Pam) Padgett
VP Human Resources and Corporate Relations: Jeffrey S. (Jeff) Shuman, age 53
VP Harris Healthcare Solutions: James A. (Jim) Traficant
VP Corporate Development: Ricardo A. (Rick) Navarro, age 58
VP Government Relations: Peter Challan, age 61
VP Corporate Communications: Jim Burke
VP Supply Chain Management and Operations: Leon V. Shivamber
VP, Associate General Counsel, and Corporate Secretary: Scott T. Mikuen, age 46
VP, Counsel, and Director Business Conduct: John D. Gronda, age 48
VP and General Counsel: Eugene S. (Gene) Cavallucci, age 61
VP and Principal Accounting Officer: Lewis A. Schwartz, age 45
Auditors: Ernst & Young LLP

LOCATIONS

HQ: Harris Corporation
1025 W. NASA Blvd., Melbourne, FL 32919
Phone: 321-727-9100   Fax: 321-674-4740
Web: www.harris.com

2008 Sales

	$ mil.	% of total
US	4,621.4	87
Other countries	689.6	13
Total	**5,311.0**	**100**

PRODUCTS/OPERATIONS

2008 Sales

	$ mil.	% of total
Government communications systems	1,999.8	38
Defense communications & electronics	1,975.2	37
Harris Stratex Networks	718.4	13
Broadcast communications	643.1	12
Adjustments	(25.5)	—
Total	**5,311.0**	**100**

2008 Sales

	$ mil.	% of total
Products	4,151.2	78
Services	1,159.8	22
Total	**5,311.0**	**100**

Selected Business Groups

Government communications systems
  Civil programs
  IT services
  National intelligence programs
Defense communications and electronics
  Defense programs
  RF Communications
  Broadcast communicationsInfrastructure and networking
  Media and workflow
  Television and radio transmission systems

HISTORICAL FINANCIALS

Company Type: Public

Income Statement

FYE: Friday nearest June 30

	REVENUE ($ mil.)	NET INCOME ($ mil.)	NET PROFIT MARGIN	EMPLOYEES
6/08	5,311.0	444.2	8.4%	16,500
6/07	4,243.0	480.4	11.3%	16,000
6/06	3,474.8	237.9	6.8%	13,900
6/05	3,000.6	202.2	6.7%	12,600
6/04	2,518.6	132.8	5.3%	10,900
Annual Growth	20.5%	35.2%	—	10.9%

2008 Year-End Financials

Debt ratio: 36.6%
Return on equity: 21.3%
Cash ($ mil.): 370
Current ratio: 2.06
Long-term debt ($ mil.): 832

No. of shares (mil.): 132
Dividends
Yield: 1.3%
Payout: 18.4%
Market value ($ mil.): 6,328

Stock History

NYSE: HRS

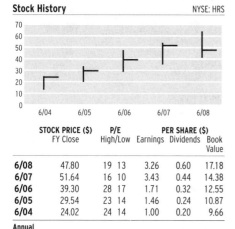

	STOCK PRICE ($) FY Close	P/E High/Low		PER SHARE ($) Earnings	Dividends	Book Value
6/08	47.80	19	13	3.26	0.60	17.18
6/07	51.64	16	10	3.43	0.44	14.38
6/06	39.30	28	17	1.71	0.32	12.55
6/05	29.54	23	14	1.46	0.24	10.87
6/04	24.02	24	14	1.00	0.20	9.66
Annual Growth	18.8%	—	—	34.4%	31.6%	15.5%

Hartford Financial Services

The Hartford Financial Services buck makes bucks by offering a variety of personal and commercial insurance products, including homeowners, auto, and workers' compensation. Through its Hartford Life subsidiary, the company offers individual and group life insurance, annuities, asset management, retirement plans, and mutual funds (managed both in-house and by other groups including Wellington Management). Its property/casualty operations include both personal and business coverage, including specialty commercial coverage for large companies. The Hartford, in business since 1810, sells its products through about 11,000 independent agencies and more than 100,000 registered broker-dealers.

In 2008 European insurer Allianz made a capital investment of about $2.5 billion in the Hartford, in a deal intended to shore up its liquidity position and prevent a ratings downgrade. Allianz is buying both stock and debt, with warrants that allow it to acquire up to 20% of the company.

The Hartford's troubles stem from losses attributed to its investment holdings in Fannie Mae, Freddie Mac, and Lehman Brothers — all of them casualties of the 2008 financial crisis. In mid-2009 the US Treasury stepped in and offered The Hartford and other major life insurers access to its Capital Purchase Program. The Hartford will be eligible to receive as much as $3.4 billion to shore up its capital reserves.

Prior to that announcement, the only hope The Hartford had to get its mitts on any Treasury funds was to transform itself into a bank. In 2009 The Hartford acquired Federal Trust Corporation, a regional bank holding company, for $10 million.

As the baby-boomer generation ages, Hartford Life is targeting the retirement savings market and seeking marketing alliances. The Hartford's property/casualty segment already enjoys such an arrangement with an exclusive agreement to provide auto and homeowners polices to members of AARP (the American Association of Retired Persons).

To better keep track of its offerings, Hartford Life acquired a defined contribution recordkeeping business (Princeton Retirement Group, 2007) and a Web-based technology company to assist with data management (TopNoggin, 2008).

The company has exited virtually all of its international property/casualty operations and is pulling back on its international life insurance. The Hartford has businesses in Brazil, Japan, and the UK but has decided to focus on its domestic businesses.

Chairman and CEO Ramani Ayer had planned on retiring at the end of 2008, but agreed to stay at the helm through 2009.

HISTORY

In 1810 a group of Hartford, Connecticut, businessmen led by Walter Mitchell and Henry Terry founded the Hartford Fire Insurance Co. Frequent fires in America's wooden cities and executive ignorance of risk assessment and premium-setting often left the firm on the edge of insolvency. (In 1835 stockholders staged a coup and threw management out.) Still, each urban conflagration — including the Great Chicago Fire of 1871 — gave the Hartford an opportunity to seek out and pay all its policyholders, thus teaching the company to underwrite under fire, as it were, and to use such disasters to refine its rates.

The company's stag logo was initially a little deer, as shown on a policy sold to Abraham Lincoln in 1861. A few years later, however, Hartford began using the majestic creature (from a Landseer painting) now familiar to customers. By the 1880s Hartford operated nationwide, as well as in Canada and Hawaii.

The company survived both world wars and the Depression but emerged in the 1950s in need of organization. It set up new regional offices and added life insurance, buying Columbian National Life (founded 1902), which became Hartford Life Insurance Co.

In 1969 Hartford was bought by ITT (formerly International Telephone and Telegraph), whose CEO, Harold Geneen, was an avid conglomerateur. Consumer advocate Ralph Nader strongly opposed the acquisition — he fought the merger in court for years and felt vindicated when ITT spun off Hartford in 1995. Others opposed it, too, because ITT had engineered the merger based on an IRS ruling (later revoked) that Hartford stockholders wouldn't have to pay capital gains taxes on the purchase price of their stock.

Insurance operations consolidated under the Hartford Life Insurance banner in 1978. Through the 1980s, Hartford Life remained one of ITT's strongest operations. A conservative investment policy kept Hartford safe from the junk bond and real estate manias of the 1980s.

Hartford reorganized its property/casualty operations along three lines in 1986, and in 1992 it organized its reinsurance business into one unit. The company faced some liability in relation to Dow Corning's breast-implant litigation, but underwriting standards after 1985 reduced long-term risk. In 1994 the company began selling insurance products to AARP members under an exclusive agreement. In 1996 the company finished its spinoff from ITT, which was acquired by Starwood Hotels & Resorts two years later.

To grow its reinsurance operation, Hartford acquired the reinsurance business of Orion Capital (now Royal & SunAlliance USA) in 1996. It posted a loss of $99 million, due in large part to asbestos and pollution liabilities. Late that year the firm changed its name to The Hartford Financial Services Group.

To shore up reserves and fund growth, in 1997 the company spun off 19% of Hartford Life. The Hartford expanded into nonstandard auto insurance in 1998 by buying Omni Insurance Group (since sold in 2006). The company also sold its London & Edinburgh Insurance Group in 1998 to Norwich Union (now part of Aviva, formerly CGNU). In 1999 Hartford acquired the reinsurance business of Vesta Fire Insurance, a subsidiary of Vesta Insurance Group.

In 2000 Hartford bought back the part of Hartford Life it had spun off. Hartford also bought the financial products and excess and surplus specialty insurance lines of Reliance Group Holdings. Assurances Générales de France bought the company's Dutch subsidiary, Zwolsche Algemeene. In 2001 the company bought Fortis Financial, a US subsidiary of Belgian insurer Fortis, and sold Hartford Seguros — its Spanish subsidiary — to Liberty Mutual.

EXECUTIVES

Chairman and CEO; Chairman, Hartford Life:
Ramani Ayer, age 62, $4,470,496 total compensation
EVP and CFO: Lizabeth H. (Liz) Zlatkus, age 50,
$4,316,727 total compensation
SVP and CIO: Brian O'Connell
**EVP and Chief Investment Officer; President, Hartford
Investment Management Co.:** David M. Znamierowski,
age 48
**EVP and Chief Investment Officer; President Hartford
Investment Management Co.:** Greg McGreevey
SVP, Controller, and Chief Accounting Officer:
Beth A. Bombara, age 40
SVP and Enterprise Chief Risk Officer: Robert Paiano
EVP: Neal S. Wolin, age 47,
$3,447,039 total compensation
EVP Group Benefits Division: Ronald R. Gendreau
EVP Human Resources: Eileen G. Whelley, age 54
EVP and General Counsel: Alan J. Kreczko, age 57
**EVP Sales and Distribution, Hartford Property and
Casualty Insurance Operations:** Dan Brown
SVP Marketing and Communications:
Constance K. (Connie) Weaver, age 56
SVP Finance: Michael L. (Mike) Kalen
SVP Investor Relations: Richard G. Costello, age 40
SVP and CIO, Property and Casualty Operations:
Robert C. (Bob) Ingram III
SVP Corporate Finance: Kim Johnson
SVP and Secretary: Ricardo A. Anzaldua
President and COO, Hartford Life: John C. Walters,
age 47, $2,569,565 total compensation
Auditors: Deloitte & Touche LLP

LOCATIONS

HQ: The Hartford Financial Services Group, Inc.
One Hartford Plaza, Hartford, CT 06155
Phone: 860-547-5000   **Fax:** 860-547-2680
Web: www.thehartford.com

PRODUCTS/OPERATIONS

2008 Sales

	$ mil.	% of total
Earned premiums	15,503	61
Fee income	5,135	20
Net investment income		
Securities available-for-sale & other	4,335	17
Equity securities held for trading	(10,340)	1
Net realized capital gains	(5,918)	—
Other revenue	504	1
Total	**9,219**	**100**

COMPETITORS

AEGON USA
AIG
Allstate
Berkshire Hathaway
CNA Financial
ING
Liberty Mutual
MetLife
Nationwide Financial
New York Life
Northwestern Mutual
Prudential
State Farm
TIAA-CREF
Travelers Companies
Zurich Financial Services

HISTORICAL FINANCIALS

Company Type: Public

Income Statement

FYE: December 31

	ASSETS ($ mil.)	NET INCOME ($ mil.)	INCOME AS % OF ASSETS	EMPLOYEES
12/08	287,583.0	(2,749.0)	—	31,000
12/07	360,361.0	2,949.0	0.8%	31,000
12/06	326,710.0	2,745.0	0.8%	31,000
12/05	285,557.0	2,274.0	0.8%	30,000
12/04	259,735.0	2,138.0	0.8%	30,000
Annual Growth	2.6%	—	—	0.8%

2008 Year-End Financials

Equity as % of assets: 3.2%
Return on assets: —
Return on equity: —
Long-term debt ($ mil.): 5,823
No. of shares (mil.): 328
Dividends
  Yield: 11.6%
  Payout: —
Market value ($ mil.): 5,388
Sales ($ mil.): 9,219

Stock History

NYSE: HIG

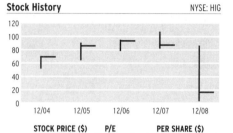

	STOCK PRICE ($) FY Close	P/E High	P/E Low	Earnings	Dividends	Book Value
12/08	16.42	—	—	(8.99)	1.91	28.24
12/07	87.19	11	9	9.24	2.03	58.52
12/06	93.31	11	9	8.69	1.70	57.52
12/05	85.89	12	9	7.44	1.17	46.70
12/04	69.31	10	7	7.12	1.13	43.39
Annual Growth	(30.2%)	—	—	—	14.0%	(10.2%)

Hasbro, Inc.

It's all fun and games at Hasbro, the #2 toy maker in the US (after Mattel) and the producer of such childhood favorites as G.I. Joe, Play-Doh, Tonka toys, Nerf balls, and My Little Pony. Besides toys, Hasbro makes board games under its Milton Bradley (*Scrabble, Candy Land*), Cranium, and Parker Brothers (*Monopoly, Trivial Pursuit*) brands, as well as trading cards such as *Magic: The Gathering* (through its Wizards of the Coast unit) and *Dungeons & Dragons*. Hasbro also makes *Star Wars* action figures and is the licensee of action figures and games for the prequels, as well as toys related to Disney and other movie and TV characters. Hasbro also has a licensing deal with Marvel Entertainment for toys and games.

Hasbro has been busy enlisting more superheroes to bring Barbie and Mattel down a notch. The toy maker has access to some 5,000-odd Marvel characters (such as Fantastic Four, X-Men, Captain America, and Ghost Rider) thanks to a licensing agreement it inked with Marvel in 2006 to sell Marvel-branded toys and games through 2017. In 2008 the company saw a spike in boys' toy sales that coincided with the movie releases of *Ironman* and *Indiana Jones*

and *the Kingdom of the Crystal Skull*. Its Star Wars, Spider-Man, and Transformers offerings were also bolstered by the animated TV series. Hasbro expects to see another spike in sales with the 2009 releases of *G.I. Joe: Rise of the Cobra* and *Transformers: Revenge of the Fallen*.

Hasbro has hopes its other toys, games, and puzzles can stand up to Mattel's Barbie. To this end, the company acquired popular game maker Cranium in January 2008 for more than $75 million. It plans to expand Cranium's popular board games to the international market.

Hasbro's long-term strategy involves extending its brands into the digital world. Hasbro teamed up with Electronic Arts (EA) to create video game versions of some of its classic board games, such as *Monopoly, Scrabble,* and *Yahtzee*. Titles are available for major platforms, including gaming consoles, mobile phones, and PCs.

The company hasn't forgotten about girls' toys, digital or otherwise. In 2008 Hasbro introduced the *Littlest Pet Shop* video game series. The toy maker also saw increased revenues from the redesign of its classic Easy-Bake oven.

In keeping with creative partnerships, Hasbro teamed up with cable programming giant Discovery Communications to form a joint venture for its Discovery Kids channel. The network plans to offer family and educational programming based on Hasbro's brands, including G.I. Joe, My Little Pony, and Scrabble, beginning in 2010. The partners also plan to create a Web site featuring related interactive content. To supply its joint venture with content and programming, the company formed Hasbro Studios.

Hasbro announced some 200 manufacturing and support job cuts at its East Longmeadow, Massachusetts, facility in early 2008. (The cuts represent about 3% of its global workforce.)

Chairman Alan Hassenfeld, the third generation of Hassenfelds to control the company, owns about 10% of Hasbro. Hassenfeld stepped down in May 2008 to make way for Al Verrecchia to become chairman. Brian Goldner, Hasbro's COO, succeeded Verrecchia as chief executive. Hassenfeld remains a director of the company.

HISTORY

Henry and Helal Hassenfeld formed Hassenfeld Brothers in Pawtucket, Rhode Island, in 1923 to distribute fabric remnants. By 1926 the company was manufacturing fabric-covered pencil boxes and shortly thereafter, pencils.

Hassenfeld Brothers branched into the toy industry during the 1940s by introducing toy nurse and doctor kits. The company's toy division was the first to use TV to promote a toy product (Mr. Potato Head in 1952).

Expansion continued in the mid-1960s with the introduction of the G.I. Joe doll, which quickly became its primary toy line. Hassenfeld Brothers went public in 1968 and changed its name to Hasbro Industries. It bought Romper Room (TV productions) the next year.

In the 1970s the toy and pencil divisions, led by different family members, disagreed over the company's finances, future direction, and leadership. The dispute caused the company to split in 1980. The toy division continued to operate under the Hasbro name; the pencil division (Empire Pencil Corporation in Shelbyville, Tennessee, led by Harold Hassenfeld) became a separate corporation.

Hasbro expanded rapidly in the 1980s under new CEO Stephen Hassenfeld. He reduced the number of products by one-third to concentrate on developing a line of toys aimed at specific markets. During that decade the firm released a number of successful toys, including a smaller version of G.I. Joe (1982) and Transformers (small vehicles that transform into robots, 1984). Hasbro acquired Milton Bradley, a major producer of board games (*Chutes and Ladders, Candy Land*), puzzles, and preschool toys (Playskool) in 1984.

The company acquired Cabbage Patch Kids, *Scrabble, Parcheesi,* and other product lines in 1989. Stephen died that year. His brother Alan, who had spearheaded Hasbro's international sales growth in the late 1980s, became CEO.

Hasbro bought Tonka (including the Kenner and Parker Brothers brands) in 1991 and established operations in Greece, Mexico, and Hungary. Hasbro blocked a $5.2 billion hostile takeover attempt by Mattel in 1996, and in 1997 it began cutting about 2,500 jobs (20% of Hasbro's employees) that year.

Expanding in the high-tech toys niche, in 1998 Hasbro made several acquisitions, including Tiger Electronics (Giga Pets), the rights to some 75 Atari home console game titles (*Missile Command, Centipede*), MicroProse (3-D video games for PCs), and Galoob Toys, a fellow *Star Wars* prequel licensee and maker of Micro Machines and Pound Puppies. Tiger Electronics had the hit of the 1998 holiday season: a chattering interactive doll called Furby.

In 1999 Hasbro bought game maker and retailer Wizards of the Coast (maker of *Pokémon* trading cards). In late 1999 the company announced it would can another 19% of its workforce (2,200 jobs), and close two plants in Mexico and the UK. Another 750 job cuts followed in late 2000.

In 2003 Hasbro announced it would close its manufacturing plant in Valencia, Spain, and shift operations to China and Ireland, affecting about 500 employees. In 2004 Hasbro laid off about 125 employees across several departments.

In 2008 Hasbro picked up the intellectual property rights to the Trivial Pursuit brand for $80 million from Horn Abbot Ltd. and Horn Abbot International Ltd.

EXECUTIVES

Chairman: Alfred J. (Al) Verrecchia, age 67, $15,018,011 total compensation
President, CEO, and Director: Brian Goldner, age 46, $6,321,241 total compensation
COO: David D. R. Hargreaves, age 56, $5,177,460 total compensation
CFO: Deborah (Deb) Thomas, age 45
Global Chief Development Officer: Duncan Billing, age 50, $1,350,481 total compensation
Global Chief Marketing Officer:
Johnathan (John) Frascotti, age 49, $890,727 total compensation
SVP and Treasurer: Martin R. Trueb, age 56
SVP Human Resources: Bob Carniaux
SVP Marketing: Ira Hernowitz
SVP Investor Relations: Karen A. Warren
SVP Corporate Communications: Wayne S. Charness
SVP Marketing, Hasbro Games: Mark Blecher
SVP Entertainment and Licensing: Bryony Bouyer
SVP Entertainment and Licensing: Bennett Schneir
VP Entertainment and Licensing: Michael (Mike) Riley
VP Marketing, Hasbro Games: Mark Stark
VP Marketing: Todd Rywolt
VP Community Relations: Karen Davis

President and CEO, Hasbro-Discovery Communications Joint Venture: Margaret A. Loesch, age 60
President, Hasbro Studios: Stephen J. Davis, age 46
CEO, Wizards of the Coast: Greg Leeds
President, Hasbro Properties: Jane Ritson Parsons
Chief Legal Officer and Secretary: Barry Nagler, age 52, $1,862,122 total compensation
Director Corporate Communications: Audrey DeSimone
Auditors: KPMG LLP

LOCATIONS

HQ: Hasbro, Inc.
  1027 Newport Ave., Pawtucket, RI 02862
Phone: 401-431-8697   **Fax:** 401-431-8535
Web: www.hasbro.com

2008 Sales

	$ mil.	% of total
US	2,339.2	58
International	1,682.3	42
Total	**4,021.5**	**100**

PRODUCTS/OPERATIONS

2008 Sales

	$ mil.	% of total
Games & puzzles	1,315.4	33
Boys' toys	1,083.3	27
Girls' toys	790.5	19
Preschool toys	480.7	12
Tweens' toys	270.2	7
Other	81.4	2
Total	**4,021.5**	**100**

Selected Brands and Products

Electronics
  Tiger Electronics
    Furby
    FurReal Friends
    Giga Pets
    Hitclips (micro music systems)
    Luv Cubs
    Thintronix (ultra-thin speakerphone, FM radio)
    VideoNow (personal video player)
Games and Puzzles
  Avalon Hill
    Acquire
    Axis & Allies
    Battle Cry
    Cosmic Encounter
    Diplomacy
    History of the World
    Risk 2210 A.D.
    Stratego Legends
  Jigsaw Puzzles
    Big Ben
    Croxley
    Guild
  Milton Bradley
    Battleship
    Candy Land
    Chutes and Ladders
    Connect Four
    The Game of Life
    Hungry Hungry Hippos
    Jenga
    Mousetrap
    Operation
    PERFALOCK
    Scattergories
    Scrabble
  Tiger Games
    Trouble
    Twister
    Yahtzee
  Parker Brothers
    Boggle
    Clue
    Monopoly
    Ouija
    Risk
    Sorry!
    Trivial Pursuit

Wizards of the Coast
  Dungeons and Dragons
  Harry Potter trading cards
  Magic: The Gathering
  Magic: The Gathering Online
  NeoPets
  Pokémon
  Major League Baseball Showdown
Wrebbit
  PERFALOCK
  PUZZ-3D
Boys' Toys
  BeyBlade spinning tops
  BTR (Built To Rule action building sets)
  Engine Gear spinning tops
  G.I. Joe action figures
  Hard Metal System spinning tops
  Micro Machines
  NakNak (stacking battle figures)
  Star Wars action figures
  Tonka (toy trucks)
  Transformers (small vehicles that transform into robots)
Preschool Toys
  2-in-1 Tummy Time Gym
  Bob the Builder toys
  Busy Ball Popper
  Cool Crew
  First Starts (role-playing products)
  Gloworm
  Go-Bots
  Kick Start Gym
  Major Powers (action figure)
  Mr. Potato Head
  Playskool
  Silly Sports (action games)
  Sit 'N Spin
  Speedstars (race cars and track sets)
  Step Start Walk n' Ride
  Weebles
Creative Play
  Easy-Bake Oven
  Lite-Brite
  Lite-Brite Cube
  Play-Doh
  Spirograph
  Tinkertoys
Girls' Toys
  e-kera (handheld karaoke system)
  Makeup Mindy (dolls)
  My Little Pony
  Raggedy Ann and Raggedy Andy dolls
  Secret Central (dolls)
  TwinkleTwirls Dance Studio
Other
  Nerf (soft play toys)
  Power Air Surfer Sky Wolf (remote control airplane)
  Rave Master (games, action figures, and accessories)
  Shrek 2 (boys, girls, creative play, plush, board games, and puzzles categories)
  Super Soaker water products
  The Incredibles toys
  Wheels on the Bus

COMPETITORS

Build-A-Bear	Playmates Toys Limited
Corgi International	Playmobil
Enesco	Poof-Slinky
The First Years	Radio Flyer
Graco Children's Products	RC2 Corporation
JAKKS Pacific	Sanrio
LeapFrog	Simba Dickie Group
LEGO	Smoby
Marvel Entertainment	Spin Master
Mattel	TakaraTomy
MGA Entertainment	Toy Quest
Nakajima USA	Ty
Namco Bandai	VTech Holdings
Ohio Art	WHAM-O

HISTORICAL FINANCIALS

Company Type: Public

Income Statement

FYE: Last Sunday in December

	REVENUE ($ mil.)	NET INCOME ($ mil.)	NET PROFIT MARGIN	EMPLOYEES
12/08	4,021.5	306.8	7.6%	5,900
12/07	3,837.6	333.0	8.7%	5,900
12/06	3,151.5	230.1	7.3%	5,800
12/05	3,087.6	212.1	6.9%	5,900
12/04	2,997.5	196.0	6.5%	6,000
Annual Growth	7.6%	11.9%	—	(0.4%)

2008 Year-End Financials

Debt ratio: 51.0%	No. of shares (mil.): 140
Return on equity: 22.1%	Dividends
Cash ($ mil.): 630	Yield: 2.6%
Current ratio: 2.14	Payout: 38.0%
Long-term debt ($ mil.): 710	Market value ($ mil.): 4,081

Stock History

NYSE: HAS

	STOCK PRICE ($) FY Close	P/E High/Low		PER SHARE ($) Earnings	Dividends	Book Value
12/08	29.17	21	11	2.00	0.76	9.94
12/07	25.58	17	13	1.97	0.60	9.90
12/06	27.25	21	13	1.29	0.45	10.99
12/05	20.18	21	16	1.09	0.33	12.32
12/04	19.38	24	18	0.96	0.21	11.72
Annual Growth	10.8%	—	—	20.1%	37.9%	(4.0%)

HCA Inc.

The largest for-profit hospital operator in the US, HCA (also known as Hospital Corporation of America) operates about 170 acute care, psychiatric, and rehabilitation hospitals in the US and abroad. It also runs about 100 ambulatory surgery centers, as well as diagnostic imaging, cancer treatment, and outpatient rehab centers that form health care networks in many of the communities it serves. The company has facilities in about 20 states, with about three-quarters of its hospitals located in the southern US (about 70 are in Florida and Texas). The hospital giant's HCA International operates a handful of hospitals and clinics in the UK.

The private investor group that owns HCA includes co-founder Thomas Frist Jr. (the largest shareholder), as well as Bain Capital, Kohlberg Kravis Roberts, the private equity arm of Merrill Lynch, and other members of HCA management.

Most of HCA's hospitals are in high-growth urban and suburban markets, and the vast majority are medical-surgical hospitals. (It has five psychiatric facilities and one rehabilitation hospital.)

The company plans to grow in its selected markets by acquiring hospitals and by luring patients to its existing facilities with high-quality care and a broad range of services. It is particularly interested in expanding its outpatient offerings, as well as specialty services in high-margin fields such as orthopedics and cardiology.

HCA also tries to take advantage of its national scale (and its position as the leading health care provider in many communities) to negotiate advantageous purchasing contracts, as well as favorable deals with managed care companies.

Thirty-year company veteran Jack Bovender Jr. retired as CEO at the end of 2008; he was succeeded by president and COO Richard Bracken. Bovender remains chairman of the board through 2009. Founder Frist relinquished his seat on the board to son William Frist shortly after Bovender announced his retirement.

HISTORY

In 1987 Dallas lawyer Rick Scott and Fort Worth, Texas, financier Richard Rainwater founded Columbia Hospital Corp. to buy two hospitals in El Paso, Texas. The partners eventually sold 40% of the hospitals to local doctors, hoping that ownership would motivate physicians to increase productivity and efficiency.

The company entered the Miami market the next year and by 1990 had four hospitals. After merging with Smith Laboratories that year, Columbia went public and then acquired Sutter Laboratories (orthopedic products). By the end of 1990 it had 11 hospitals.

Columbia moved into Florida in 1992, purchasing several hospitals and other facilities. The next year it acquired Galen Health Care, which operated 73 hospitals and had been spun off from health plan operator Humana earlier in the year. The merger thrust the hospital chain into about 15 new markets.

Columbia bought Hospital Corporation of America (HCA) in 1994. Thomas Frist, his son Thomas Frist Jr., and Jack Massey (former owner of Kentucky Fried Chicken, now part of TRICON) founded HCA in Nashville, Tennessee, in 1968. By 1973 the company had grown to 50 hospitals.

Meanwhile, the medical industry was changing — insurers, Medicare, and Medicaid began scrutinizing payment procedures, while the growth of HMOs (which aimed to restrict hospital admissions) cut hospital occupancy rates. HCA began paring operations in the late 1980s, selling more than 100 hospitals. In 1989 the younger Frist led a $5.1 billion leveraged buyout of the company. He sold more assets and in 1992 took HCA public again, but losses and a tumbling stock price made it a takeover target.

Later in 1994 the newly christened Columbia/HCA acquired the US's largest operator of outpatient surgery centers, Dallas-based Medical Care America. A year later it bought 117-hospital HealthTrust, a 1987 offshoot of HCA. Columbia/HCA was unstoppable in 1996, with some 150 acquisitions.

In 1997 the government began investigating the company's business practices. After executive indictments, the company fired Scott and several other top officers. Frist Jr. became chairman and CEO, pledging to shrink the company and tone down its aggressive approach. Columbia/HCA sold its home care business, more than 100 of its less-desirable hospitals, and almost all the operations of Value Health, a pharmacy benefits and behavioral health care management firm it had recently bought.

The trimming continued in 1998: The company sold nearly three dozen outpatient surgery centers and more than a dozen hospitals. That year Columbia/HCA sued former financial executive Samuel Greco and several vendors, accusing them of defrauding the company of several million dollars. In 1999 it spun off regional operators LifePoint Hospitals (23 facilities) and Triad Hospitals (34) to trim its holdings. The next year it sold some 120 medical buildings to MedCap Properties, a joint venture formed with First Union Capital Partners.

During 2000 the company bought out partner Sun Life and Provincial Holdings' (now AXA UK) interest in several London hospitals and bought three hospitals there from St. Martins Healthcare. It also renamed itself HCA – The Healthcare Company. While continuing a strategy of consolidating and streamlining operations, (and resolving remaining legal matters), in 2001 the company even streamlined its name to simply HCA Inc.

By 2002 HCA began shaking off its past. Profits stabilized, allowing it to reinvest millions into modernizing facilities and equipment at its hospitals and surgery centers. It entered the Kansas City market in 2003 by acquiring a local hospital chain.

During 2003 the company finally closed the books on the numerous government investigations launched in 1997 into its business practices. In the five years leading up to 2003, HCA paid out some $2 billion in settlements for Medicare fraud and other claims. These settlements took their toll on the firm's bottom line.

In 2005 the firm acquired Tampa, Florida's Total I Imaging and its five centers that offer diagnostic services.

The devastating hurricane season of 2005 took a toll on HCA's operations, concentrated as they are in the southern US. When Hurricane Katrina hit, the devastation caused HCA to evacuate its Tulane University Hospital and Clinic (it reopened in early 2006). Hurricane Rita spurred HCA to evacuate three Houston-area hospitals (Mainland Medical Center in Texas City, East Houston Regional Medical Center in Houston, and Clear Lake Regional Medical Center in Webster) and partially evacuate two others.

In 2006 a group of investors — including Thomas Frist Jr., as well as Bain Capital, Kohlberg Kravis Roberts, and the private equity arm of Merrill Lynch — took HCA private in a $30 billion leveraged buyout.

EXECUTIVES

Chairman: Jack O. Bovender Jr., age 64
President, CEO, and Director: Richard M. Bracken, age 56
EVP and CFO: R. Milton Johnson, age 52
SVP and CIO: Noel Brown Williams, age 53
SVP and Chief Ethics and Compliance Officer: Alan R. Yuspeh, age 59
President, Clinical Services Group and Chief Medical Officer: Jonathan B. (Jon) Perlin, age 48
SVP and General Counsel: Robert A. (Bob) Waterman, age 55
SVP Development: V. Carl George, age 64
SVP Finance and Treasurer: David G. Anderson, age 62
SVP: Victor L. Campbell, age 62
SVP Internal Audit Services: Joseph N. (Joe) Steakley, age 54
SVP Human Resources: John M. Steele, age 53
SVP and Controller: Donald W. (Don) Stinnett, age 53
VP and Corporate Secretary: John M. Franck II
VP Investor Relations: Mark Kimbrough

President, Western Group: Samuel N. (Sam) Hazen, age 48
President, Outpatient Services Group: A. Bruce Moore Jr., age 49
President, Shared Services Group: Beverly B. Wallace, age 58
President, Central Group: William P. (Paul) Rutledge, age 54
Auditors: Ernst & Young LLP

LOCATIONS

HQ: HCA Inc.
1 Park Plaza, Nashville, TN 37203
Phone: 615-344-9551 **Fax:** 615-344-2266
Web: www.hcahealthcare.com

2008 Sales

	$ mil.	% of total
Western Group	12,118	43
Eastern Group	8,570	30
Central Group	6,740	24
Corporate & other	946	3
Total	**28,374**	**100**

2008 Locations

	No.
US	
Florida	38
Texas	34
Tennessee	13
Georgia	11
Louisiana	10
Virginia	9
Colorado	7
Missouri	6
Utah	6
California	5
Kansas	4
Nevada	3
South Carolina	3
Idaho	2
Kentucky	2
New Hampshire	2
Oklahoma	2
Alaska	1
Indiana	1
Mississippi	1
UK	6
Total	**166**

PRODUCTS/OPERATIONS

2008 Sales

	% of total
Medicare	24
Uninsured	10
Medicaid	5
Managed Medicare	5
Managed Medicaid	3
Managed care & other insurers	53
Total	**100**

COMPETITORS

Adventist Health
Adventist Health System
Ascension Health
Banner Health
Baptist Hospital
Baylor Health
Catholic Health Initiatives
Catholic Healthcare West
Children's Medical Center of Dallas
CHRISTUS Health
Community Health Systems
Health Management Associates
HealthSouth
Kaiser Permanente
Psychiatric Solutions
SSM Health Care
Tenet Healthcare
Trinity Health (Novi)
Universal Health Services

HISTORICAL FINANCIALS

Company Type: Private

Income Statement

FYE: March 31

	REVENUE ($ mil.)	NET INCOME ($ mil.)	NET PROFIT MARGIN	EMPLOYEES
12/08	28,374	673	2.4%	191,000
12/07	26,858	874	3.3%	186,000
12/06	25,477	1,036	4.1%	186,000
12/05	24,455	—	—	191,100
12/04	21,808	—	—	191,400
Annual Growth	**6.8%**	**(19.4%)**		**(0.1%)**

Revenue History

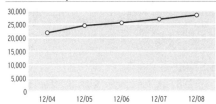

Health Management Associates

William Schoen, chairman of Health Management Associates (HMA) once described his company as the "Wal-Mart of the hospital business" because, like Sam Walton's empire, HMA thrives in small-town America. The company operates a network of about 60 acute care and psychiatric hospitals in 15 mainly southern states (although it also has facilities in Washington and Pennsylvania). Combined, the facilities have about 8,000 beds. HMA's hospitals provide general medical and surgical care, along with outpatient and emergency room services and specialty care in some areas such as cancer care and obstetrics. It also operates about a dozen rural health clinics and outpatient surgery centers.

Because of the smaller markets they serve, HMA's facilities aren't large research hospitals offering highly specialized care (like organ transplants, for instance). However, the company is interested in upgrading its hospitals and broadening the services they offer in order to prevent local populations from traveling to urban medical centers for treatment. To that end, HMA focuses much of its energy on recruiting and retaining qualified primary care doctors and specialists to practice in its communities and affiliate with its hospitals.

HMA has built its portfolio through numerous acquisitions of hospitals that are the primary source of health care in their regions. It has typically looked for underperforming hospitals in nevertheless attractive markets and then worked to upgrade facilities and equipment and increase patient volumes and efficiency.

Though it has historically bought several hospitals each year, the company since mid-2006 has slowed down its acquisition activity and is instead focused on quality and efficiency improvements at its existing facilities. It operates on a decentralized model, with a local CEO, CFO, and Chief Nursing Officer seeing to the daily operations of each hospital. However, the company does maintain central control of finances, purchasing, and other systems.

In addition to new equipment, specialty units, and capacity expansions at existing hospitals, HCA also rebuilt an aging facility, Carlisle Regional Medical Center in Pennsylvania, and built a second hospital in the Naples, Florida, market (Physician Regional Medical Center — Collier Boulevard) in 2007.

HMA is also experimenting with physician joint ventures in some of its markets, allowing doctors to take a minority stake in the hospitals they serve. It instituted two such arrangements in 2007 and formed five joint ventures in 2008. It's looking for other similar opportunities with both doctors' groups and other investors.

One reason for the interest in joint ventures is HMA's need to reduce its long-term debt and offload some underperforming facilities. It has divested or closed several such facilities: In 2008 it closed Mississippi's Gulf Coast Medical Center, which had failed to recover financially from the effects of 2005's devastating Hurricane Katrina; it also shut down a women's specialty hospital in Texas due to financial losses. HMA sold the Southwest Regional Medical Center in Arkansas that year, and in 2007 it sold two Virginia hospitals to Wellmont Health System.

Like most hospital operators, HMA has struggled with debts resulting from treating uninsured patients who can't pay their medical bills. The company is banking on its quality improvements and expansion of services to attract more paying patients to its hospitals.

In 2007 Burke Whitman (formerly the company's president and COO) took the helm as CEO, replacing Joseph Vumbacco. The very next year, however, Whitman resigned and was replaced as CEO by Gary Newsome, a former executive returning to the company after a 10-year stint at Community Health Systems.

HISTORY

From its founding in 1977 by Joseph Greene until 1985, Health Management Associates (HMA) owned only a handful of hospitals, mostly in urban areas. In 1983 CEO Greene brought aboard William Schoen, an ex-Marine who ran a beer company in New York before founding a bank in Florida. Schoen became president and COO that year, took a co-CEO position in 1985, and assumed full leadership in 1986 when Greene retired.

Schoen sold the urban hospitals and refocused on small-town hospitals in underserved, mainly southern communities with growing populations. To finance acquisitions and hospital overhauls, HMA went public in 1986. Two years later Schoen took it private, but it went public again in 1991. In the early 1990s it had a growth spurt, adding 10 hospitals.

HMA continued buying, adding two facilities in 1996, another two in 1997, and five in 1998 (three in Mississippi and two in Florida). The acquisitions continued in 1999 as Medicare cutbacks and costly Y2K computer fixes forced many small hospitals to seek buyers; the company bought facilities in Florida, Mississippi (two), and Pennsylvania. In 2000 HMA continued to be acquisitive, buying three medical centers (in Florida, North Carolina, and Pennsylvania), although it shut down its treatment center for at-risk youth in Kansas due to security concerns. In 2001 HMA bought some hospitals from the financially troubled Clarent Hospital.

Also in 2001, William Schoen resigned as CEO and was replaced by Joseph Vumbacco. Schoen remained as chairman.

In 2003, HMA acquired five hospitals from Tenet and expanded into the US northwest by purchasing two hospitals in Washington. The next year, the company bought Chester County Hospital in South Carolina. In 2005 HMA acquired five hospitals in Florida, Mississippi, and Virginia.

HMA's 2006 acquisitions included Gulf Coast Medical Center in Mississippi (which it later closed) from Tenet Healthcare; Cleveland-Naples Hospital in Florida; and Barrow Community Hospital in Georgia. The same year it sold off two psychiatric hospitals in Florida to Psychiatric Solutions.

EXECUTIVES

Chairman: William J. Schoen, age 73
President, CEO, and Director: Gary D. Newsome, age 51, $1,461,363 total compensation
SVP Operations: Stanley D. McLemore
SVP and CFO: Robert E. Farnham, age 53, $1,003,313 total compensation
SVP MIS: James L. (Jim) Jordan
EVP and Chief Administrative Officer: Kelly E. Curry, age 54, $1,676,951 total compensation
Chief Medical Officer: Ronald N. Riner
EVP Development: Peter M. Lawson, age 47
EVP Hospital Operations and President, Division 2: Jon P. Vollmer, age 52
SVP, General Counsel, and Corporate Secretary: Timothy R. Parry, age 54, $867,336 total compensation
SVP Human Resources: Frederick L. Drow
SVP Reimbursement: Kenneth M. Koopman
SVP Support Services: Johnny A. Owenby
SVP Clinical Affairs: Lisa Gore
SVP and Corporate Treasurer: Joseph C. Meek
Auditors: Ernst & Young LLP

LOCATIONS

HQ: Health Management Associates, Inc.
5811 Pelican Bay Blvd., Ste. 500, Naples, FL 34108
Phone: 239-598-3131   **Fax:** 239-598-2705
Web: www.hma-corp.com

PRODUCTS/OPERATIONS

2008 Revenue by Source

	% of total
Medicare	32
Self pay	9
Medicaid	8
Commercial insurance & other	51
Total	**100**

COMPETITORS

Ascension Health	Greenville Hospital System
Baptist Health Care	HCA
Baptist Memorial Health	Lee Memorial
Catholic Health East	LifePoint Hospitals
Catholic Health Initiatives	Methodist Healthcare
CHRISTUS Health	SSM Health Care
Community Health Corporation	SunLink Health Systems
Community Health Systems	Tenet Healthcare
FirstHealth of the Carolinas	Universal Health Services
	University Health Services

HISTORICAL FINANCIALS

Company Type: Public

Income Statement

FYE: December 31

	REVENUE ($ mil.)	NET INCOME ($ mil.)	NET PROFIT MARGIN	EMPLOYEES
12/08	4,451.6	167.2	3.8%	32,700
12/07	4,392.1	119.9	2.7%	35,645
12/06*	4,056.6	182.7	4.5%	34,500
9/05	3,588.8	353.1	9.8%	31,000
9/04	3,205.9	325.1	10.1%	28,000
Annual Growth	**8.6%**	**(15.3%)**	**—**	**4.0%**

*Fiscal year change

2008 Year-End Financials

Debt ratio: 2,065.4%
Return on equity: 142.1%
Cash ($ mil.): 144
Current ratio: 2.14
Long-term debt ($ mil.): 3,187
No. of shares (mil.): 247
Dividends
  Yield: 0.0%
  Payout: —
Market value ($ mil.): 441

Stock History

NYSE: HMA

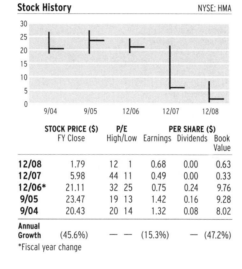

	STOCK PRICE ($) FY Close	P/E High/Low		PER SHARE ($) Earnings	Dividends	Book Value
12/08	1.79	12	1	0.68	0.00	0.63
12/07	5.98	44	11	0.49	0.00	0.33
12/06*	21.11	32	25	0.75	0.24	9.76
9/05	23.47	19	13	1.42	0.16	9.28
9/04	20.43	20	14	1.32	0.08	8.02
Annual Growth	**(45.6%)**	**—**	**—**	**(15.3%)**	**—**	**(47.2%)**

*Fiscal year change

Health Net

Health Net is not another Web site trying to give you health advice, it's a web of health services. The company provides managed health care medical coverage to some 6.7 million members across the US. The company's health plan services unit offers HMO, PPO, Medicare, and Medicaid plans, as well as vision, dental care, and pharmacy benefit programs. The Managed Health Network subsidiary provides behavioral health and employee assistance to nearly 7 million individuals, including traditional health plan customers. Health Net's products are marketed to commercial clients through its sales force and external brokers; individual plans are sold mostly through independent agents.

The company's managed care units focus on providing health plans to about 3.7 million members (including Medicare and Medicaid recipients) across the US. California comprises Health Net's largest health plan market. HN California, Health Net's California HMO, is part of the State Children's Health Insurance Program (known as Healthy Families) and insures some

130,000 children. Other key states include Arizona, Connecticut, New Jersey, New York, and Oregon. Some services, such as Medicare Part D and mental health provisions, are offered in all 50 states.

The company agreed to sell its Northeast subsidiaries (offering HMO, commercial, and Medicaid plans in Connecticut, New Jersey, and New York) to national provider UnitedHealth in mid-2009 in a deal worth up to $630 million. Health Net's 580,000 customers in the Northeast will make a gradual transition over to UnitedHealth's plans. Health Net is divesting the operations so that it can focus on its core health markets in the West (in California, Arizona, and Oregon).

In 2009 the company lost valuable government contracts to provide health care coverage for some 3 million military and other government personnel and their dependents through TRICARE. It had held TRICARE contracts in more than 20 states in the Northeast and Midwest, as well as other Department of Defense and Veterans Affairs contracts. The loss was somewhat mitigated by the fact that Health Net will serve as a subcontractor on some of the contracts awarded to UnitedHealth Group.

Health Net is focusing growth efforts within its commercial health plan segment toward adding new small employer (2 to 50 employees) and mid-market customers. To that end, in 2007 Health Net acquired partner Guardian Life's stake in former joint venture HealthCare Solutions. The company is also concentrating on Medicare growth opportunities.

To settle a pair of lawsuits, in early 2009 Health Net agreed to pay as much as $14 million to former policyholders whose coverage was cancelled after submitting large medical bills. During the suits, it was determined that Health Net had made 1,600 rescissions (dropping customers with large claims) to save some $35.5 million. The payments to customers, combined with other fines and fees will eventually cost the company more than $40 million.

HISTORY

Foundation Health started as the not-for-profit Foundation Community Health Plan in the 1960s. In 1984 it was bought by AmeriCare Health, which had HMOs in six states. The acquisition was a coup: Foundation Health soon accounted for the bulk of AmeriCare's sales.

AmeriCare went public in 1985. The next year it lost to another firm the rights to that name. Redubbed Foundation Health, the company expanded into new states and unrelated businesses: commercial real estate, silk flowers, and furniture. In late 1986 senior management led a $140 million LBO that left Foundation Health hobbled with debt when the industry started to slide. A 1988 Department of Defense (DOD) CHAMPUS contract brightened prospects, but the five-year, $3 billion contract to provide health care to 860,000 military retirees and dependents in California and Hawaii provided little short-term relief against the effects of high debt and rapid growth: The company lost money again.

The CEO slot had been vacant a year when Dan Crowley, a trained accountant with a good turnaround record, came aboard in 1989. He cut staff, slashed budgets, sold unrelated and non-performing units, and kicked off a huge sales effort. To satisfy bankers and the DOD, which was threatening to rescind its contract, Crowley refinanced Foundation's debt. In a little over a year, Foundation Health recorded its best results ever.

In 1990 the company went public.

Back on solid ground, the company expanded its services and markets, buying such firms as Western Universal Life Insurance (renamed Foundation Health Benefit Life Insurance, 1991), Occupational Health Services (employee assistance and substance abuse programs, 1992), and California Compensation Insurance (workers' compensation insurance, 1993).

Foundation Health lost the DOD Hawaii/California contract (almost half its revenues) in 1993, but managed to cope until it regained the business — by then worth $2.5 billion — two years later. Also that year Foundation Health won DOD's five-year, $1.8 billion managed-care contract for Oklahoma and parts of Arkansas, Louisiana, and Texas.

Meanwhile, the company had formed Integrated Pharmaceutical Services and bought CareFlorida Health Systems, Intergroup Healthcare, and Thomas-Davis Medical Centers in 1994.

Renewed discussions with Health Systems International resulted in the companies merging to become Foundation Health Systems in 1997. Crowley — whose aggressive style garnered profits but was denounced as brutal by some critics — resigned after the merger.

In 1998 the company pushed into the Northeast, buying Connecticut-based HMO Physicians Health Services. It then sold its workers' compensation insurance operations.

The financial aftershocks of the companies' merger continued, and FHS pruned its operations in 1999 and 2000, exiting such states as Colorado, New Mexico, and Texas; trimming its Medicare operations; and selling certain non-core administrative business lines. In 2000 the California Medical Association sued the company under RICO statutes, claiming it coerced doctors and interfered in doctor-patient relationships. Later that year the company changed its name to Health Net.

In an effort to further expand its business in the Golden State, the company acquired the health plan assets of Universal Care in 2006, adding another 20,000 Medi-Cal and Healthy Families members to its ranks (as well as some 5,000 Medicare Advantage and 75,000 commercial members).

EXECUTIVES

Chairman: Roger F. Greaves, age 71
President, CEO, and Director: Jay M. Gellert, age 55, $4,425,355 total compensation
EVP and COO: James E. (Jim) Woys, age 50, $1,887,555 total compensation
EVP and CFO: Joseph C. Capezza, age 53, $1,151,797 total compensation
CIO: Duncan Rose
SVP and Chief Regulatory and External Relations Officer: Patricia T. (Pat) Clarey
Chief Actuarial Officer: Joyce Li
SVP and Chief Medical Officer: Jonathan Scheff, age 54
Chief Medical Officer, Health Net Health Plan of Oregon: Brenda Bruns
VP, Chief Compliance Officer, Deputy General Counsel, and Corporate Ethics Officer: Philip G. (Phil) Davis, age 57
COO and President, MHN: Juanell Hefner
Chief Quality Officer: Ray Nan Berry
Chief Government Programs Officer: Scott R. Kelly
SVP Organization Effectiveness: Karin D. Mayhew, age 57
SVP, General Counsel, and Secretary: Linda V. Tiano, age 51
SVP and Controller, Corporate Finance: Bret A. Morris
VP and Treasurer: Jonathan Rollins, age 44
Manager Investor Relations and Corporate Communications: Lori A. Hillman
Auditors: Deloitte & Touche LLP

LOCATIONS

HQ: Health Net, Inc.
21650 Oxnard St., Woodland Hills, CA 91367
Phone: 818-676-6000   **Fax:** 818-676-8591
Web: www.healthnet.com

PRODUCTS/OPERATIONS

2008 Sales

	$ mil.	% of total
Health plan services	12,392.0	81
Government contracts	2,835.3	18
Net investment income	91.0	1
Administrative services fees & other	48.3	—
Total	**15,366.6**	**100**

COMPETITORS

Aetna
Blue Cross Blue Shield of Arizona
Blue Shield Of California
CIGNA
ConnectiCare
EmblemHealth
Horizon Healthcare
Humana
Kaiser Permanente
LifeWise Health Plan of Oregon
Oregon Dental
PacificSource
Providence Health
Regence BlueCross BlueShield
UnitedHealth Group
WellPoint

HISTORICAL FINANCIALS

Company Type: Public

Income Statement

FYE: December 31

	REVENUE ($ mil.)	NET INCOME ($ mil.)	NET PROFIT MARGIN	EMPLOYEES
12/08	15,366.6	95.0	0.6%	9,646
12/07	14,108.3	193.7	1.4%	9,910
12/06	12,908.3	329.3	2.6%	10,068
12/05	11,940.5	229.8	1.9%	9,286
12/04	11,646.4	42.6	0.4%	8,569
Annual Growth	**7.2%**	**22.2%**	**—**	**3.0%**

2008 Year-End Financials

Debt ratio: 37.2%
Return on equity: 5.2%
Cash ($ mil.): 668
Current ratio: 1.60
Long-term debt ($ mil.): 652

No. of shares (mil.): 104
Dividends
  Yield: 0.0%
  Payout: —
Market value ($ mil.): 1,131

Stock History

NYSE: HNT

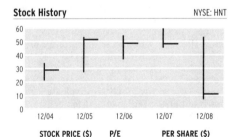

	STOCK PRICE ($) FY Close	P/E High/Low		PER SHARE ($) Earnings	Dividends	Book Value
12/08	10.89	60	8	0.88	0.00	16.87
12/07	48.30	35	27	1.70	0.00	18.06
12/06	48.66	19	13	2.78	0.00	17.13
12/05	51.55	27	14	1.99	0.00	15.30
12/04	28.87	88	57	0.38	0.00	12.26
Annual Growth	**(21.6%)**	**—**	**—**	**23.4%**	**—**	**8.3%**

HealthSouth Corporation

HealthSouth has rebuilt its health care operations to focus on rehabilitation. It has shed its outpatient surgery, outpatient rehab, and diagnostic imaging divisions to focus on its inpatient rehabilitation business, which operates about 100 wholly or jointly owned facilities in 26 states, with the largest concentrations in Alabama, Florida, Pennsylvania, Tennessee, and Texas. Its facilities include rehabilitation hospitals and outpatient centers, as well as long-term acute care facilities that provide nursing and therapy to patients who have experienced significant disabilities as a result of stroke, spinal cord injury, neuromuscular disease, or other conditions.

The company spent 2007 undergoing a massive restructuring, selling off three of its major divisions in order to pay down debt and refocus as a pure-play inpatient rehab provider. It took its first step by selling its outpatient rehabilitation division — which comprised more than 550 facilities in about 35 states — to privately owned Select Medical. It sold its outpatient surgery unit, consisting of more than 135 surgery centers and three surgical hospitals, to private investment firm TPG. And later in the year, it offloaded its diagnostics unit (which provided MRI and other diagnostic imaging services) to private equity firm The Gores Group.

With restructuring largely complete, HealthSouth is focused on providing post-acute care services, including inpatient rehabilitative care. Its remaining operations include 90 inpatient rehab hospitals with about 6,500 beds, 6 long-term acute care hospitals, and a number of outpatient centers located adjacent to or inside of its inpatient facilities. Some of its hospitals also operate home health agencies.

After refocusing its operations, the company has begun to grow the business by building or acquiring new hospitals and expanding capacity at its existing facilities. It acquired facilities in Arizona, New Jersey, and Texas in 2008, and it has plans to build a new hospital in Florida.

Government-funded health programs are the largest source of revenue for HealthSouth; nearly 70% of inpatient revenues are paid by Medicare.

HealthSouth restructuring efforts came as the company was fighting to regain its footing after accounting scandals led the company to the brink of bankruptcy beginning in 2003. It ended up paying $3 million to avoid criminal prosecution by the Justice Department for the accounting fraud. Under terms of the federal agreement, the company accepted responsibility for crimes committed by its executives and is enacting more strict internal controls; it was on probation until 2009. It has also paid out millions in civil litigation settlements with the SEC and stockholders.

HISTORY

A one-time service station worker (when he was a 17-year-old married man with a baby on the way), Richard Scrushy got into the health care industry by working in respiratory therapy; he earned a degree in the subject in 1974. Recruited for a job with a Texas health care management firm, Scrushy saw the convergence of several trends: lowered reimbursements for medical care; a new emphasis on rehabilitation as a way to reduce the need for surgery and get employees back to work faster; and a dearth of brand names in health care. Scrushy decided to establish a national health care brand of rehabilitation hospitals, and in 1984 he and four of his co-workers founded Amcare and built its first outpatient center in Birmingham, Alabama.

From the beginning, Scrushy wanted to make his rehabilitation centers less like hospitals and more like upscale health clubs. He also sought workers' compensation and rehabilitation contracts from self-insured companies and managed care operations. The strategies worked. The company had revenues of $5 million in 1985, the year it became HealthSouth. Other strategies included specializing in specific ailments, such as back problems and sports injuries, and using the same floor plan and furnishings for all HealthSouth locations to save money. The company went public in 1986.

By 1988 HealthSouth had nearly 40 facilities in 15 states and kept shopping for more. A merger with its biggest rival, Continental Medical Systems, fell through in 1992, but HealthSouth became the #1 provider of rehabilitative services the next year with its acquisition of most of the rehabilitation services of National Medical Enterprises (now Tenet Healthcare). (Scrushy and other officers formed MedPartners, a physician management company, in 1993.) Additional acquisitions included the inpatient rehabilitation hospitals of ReLife (1994) and NovaCare (now NAHC) and Caremark's rehabilitation services (1995). HealthSouth became the #1 operator of outpatient surgery centers with its acquisition of Surgical Care Affiliates in 1995. The $1.1 billion stock swap was the company's largest acquisition ever.

In 1997 HealthSouth acquired Horizon/CMS Healthcare, the US's largest provider of specialty health care. After completing the Horizon/CMS deal, HealthSouth sold Horizon's 139 long-term-care facilities, 12 specialty hospitals, and 35 institutional pharmacies to Integrated Health Services; it kept about 30 inpatient and 275 outpatient rehabilitation facilities.

In the late 1990s HealthSouth built its outpatient operations through acquisitions, buying nearly three dozen outpatient centers from what is now HCA — The Healthcare Company; it also bought National Surgery Centers, adding another 40 locations in 1998.

In 2003 the SEC initiated an investigation of HealthSouth's accounting practices which led to the firing of chairman and CEO Richard Scrushy, removal of the company's auditor, and delisting of its stock by the NYSE. Scrushy was brought to trial and eventually acquitted of any wrongdoing. However, several other executives at the company ended up in jail over the scandal, a $2.7 billion, seven-year run of accounting fraud aimed at inflating the company's profits. The scandal and its aftermath brought HealthSouth to the brink of bankruptcy.

Former HCA executive Jay Grinney was appointed as CEO of HealthSouth in 2004. The company began selling off operations to pay down debt from earlier acquisitions and to pay SEC and Justice Department fines from the accounting scandal.

The company divested its last international facility, Australia's Cedar Court Rehabilitation Hospital, late in 2006.

EXECUTIVES

Chairman: Jon F. Hanson, age 72
President, CEO, and Director: Jay Grinney, age 58, $6,645,474 total compensation
EVP Operations: Mark J. Tarr, age 46, $1,379,218 total compensation
EVP and CFO: John L. Workman, age 57, $2,420,811 total compensation
SVP and CIO: Randy Carpenter
EVP, General Counsel, and Corporate Secretary: John P. Whittington, $1,593,160 total compensation
SVP Investor Relations and Corporate Communications: Mary Ann Arico
Inspector General and Senior Vice President, Internal Audit and Controls: Sandra K. Vollman, age 51
SVP and Chief Compliance Officer: Christine Bachrach
SVP Reimbursement: Rob Wisner
SVP Human Resources: Cheryl Levy
SVP and Treasurer: Edmund Fay
SVP Goverment and Regulatory Affairs: Justin Hunter
SVP Tax: Jim McAndrews
SVP Development: Stephen Royal
SVP Real Estate: Art Wilson
President, Diagnostic Division: R. Gregory (Greg) Brophy
President, Texas Region: Laurie English
President, West Region: Jerry Gray
President, Northeast Region: Peter Mantegazza
President, Mid Atlantic Region: Terry Maxhimer
President, Southeast Region: Linda Wilder
Auditors: PricewaterhouseCoopers LLP

LOCATIONS

HQ: HealthSouth Corporation
   3660 Grandview Pkwy., Ste. 200
   Birmingham, AL 35243
Phone: 205-967-7116   **Fax:** 205-969-3543
Web: www.healthsouth.com

PRODUCTS/OPERATIONS

2008 Sales

	$ mil.	% of total
Inpatient	1,659.5	90
Outpatient & other	182.9	10
Total	**1,842.4**	**100**

2008 Revenue Sources

	% of total
Medicare	67
Managed care & other discount plans	19
Other third-party payers	7
Workers' compensation	2
Medicaid	2
Patients	1
Other income	2
Total	**100**

COMPETITORS

Ascension Health
Burke Rehabilitation Hospital
Genesis HealthCare
HCA
Kindred Healthcare
Manor Care
RehabCare
Select Medical
Skilled Healthcare Group
Tenet Healthcare

HISTORICAL FINANCIALS

Company Type: Public

Income Statement

FYE: December 31

	REVENUE ($ mil.)	NET INCOME ($ mil.)	NET PROFIT MARGIN	EMPLOYEES
12/08	1,842.4	252.4	13.7%	22,000
12/07	1,752.5	653.4	37.3%	22,000
12/06	3,000.1	(625.0)	—	33,000
12/05	3,207.7	(446.0)	—	37,000
12/04	3,753.8	(174.5)	—	40,000
Annual Growth	**(16.3%)**	**—**	**—**	**(13.9%)**

2008 Year-End Financials

Debt ratio: —
Return on equity: —
Cash ($ mil.): 32
Current ratio: 0.91
Long-term debt ($ mil.): 1,790
No. of shares (mil.): 88
Dividends
   Yield: 0.0%
   Payout: —
Market value ($ mil.): 968

Stock History

NYSE: HLS

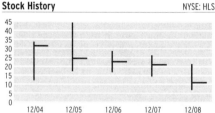

	STOCK PRICE ($) FY Close	P/E High/Low		PER SHARE ($) Earnings	Dividends	Book Value
12/08	10.96	8	3	2.62	0.00	(13.24)
12/07	21.00	4	2	7.10	0.00	(13.22)
12/06	22.65	—	—	(8.14)	0.00	(24.74)
12/05	24.50	—	—	(5.60)	0.00	(17.45)
12/04	31.40	—	—	(2.20)	0.00	(12.56)
Annual Growth	**(23.1%)**	**—**	**—**	**—**	**—**	**—**

Hearst Corporation

Like founder William Randolph Hearst's castle, The Hearst Corporation is sprawling. Through Hearst Newspapers, the company owns some 15 daily newspapers (such as the *San Francisco Chronicle* and the *Houston Chronicle*) and 50 weekly newspapers. Its Hearst Magazines publishes some 15 US consumer magazines (*Cosmopolitan*, *Esquire*) with nearly 200 international editions. Hearst has broadcasting operations through its Hearst Television subsidiary. Its Hearst Entertainment & Syndication unit includes syndication service King Features, newspaper production service Reed Brennan, and stakes in cable networks (A&E, ESPN). The Hearst Corporation is owned by the Hearst family, but managed by a board of trustees.

Hearst publishes information for automotive, electronic, pharmaceutical, and finance industries through its Hearst Business Media segment. Through its Hearst Interactive Media unit, the company makes strategic investments in online properties such as drugstore.com, and Gather. Hearst's top magazine title, *Cosmopolitan*, is published in about 35 languages and sold in more than 100 countries, making it the largest magazine franchise in the world. The company publishes magazines in the UK through subsidiary

The National Magazine Company. Hearst also has interests in over 60 daily and 100 non-daily newspapers owned by MediaNews Group, which include the *Denver Post* and *Salt Lake Tribune.*

In a tough economic climate, especially for the print media world, Hearst has experienced a massive decline in newspaper and magazine advertising and newsstand sales. In 2009 the company published the last print editition of its *Seattle Post-Intelligencer.* It now operates a Web-only version, and is the largest American newspaper to make the leap from print to the exclusively digital format.

However, the company is working hard to offset these challenges by making progress on the digital media front. Hearst in 2008 partnered with MSN to launch online food destination Delish.com. Also that year the company partnered with real estate Web site Zillow.com and other newspaper companies to launch an online real estate advertising network.

The company is also boosting its involvement in television broadcasting; in 2009 it acquired the remaining shares it didn't already own in Hearst Television (formerly Hearst-Argyle). The business operates about 30 TV stations in about two dozen markets. Also in 2009 Hearst announced that its A&E plans to acquire cable network Lifetime Entertainment Services.

CEO Victor F. Ganzi resigned from his position in 2008. Vice chairman (and previous company head) Frank A. Bennack Jr. has reassumed the role of CEO.

Although the company no longer owns Hearst Castle (deeded to the State of California in 1951), it has extensive real estate holdings. Projects include the Hearst Ranch in San Simeon, California, and the Hearst Tower in New York.

Upon his death, William Randolph Hearst left 99% of the company's common stock to two charitable trusts controlled by a 13-member board that includes five family and eight non-family members. The will includes a clause that allows the trustees to disinherit any heir who contests the will.

HISTORY

William Randolph Hearst, son of a California mining magnate, started as a reporter — after being expelled from Harvard in 1884 for playing jokes on professors. In 1887 he became editor of the *San Francisco Examiner,* which his father had obtained as payment for a gambling debt. In 1895 he bought the *New York Morning Journal* and competed against Joseph Pulitzer's *New York World.* The "yellow journalism" resulting from that rivalry characterized American-style reporting at the turn of the century.

Hearst branched into magazines (1903), film (1913), and radio (1928). Also during this time it created the Hearst International News Service (it was sold to E.W. Scripps' United Press in 1958 to form United Press International). By 1935 Hearst was at its peak, with newspapers in 19 cities, the largest syndicate (King Features), international news and photo services, 13 magazines, eight radio stations, and two motion picture companies. Two years later Hearst relinquished control of the company to avoid bankruptcy, selling movie companies, radio stations, magazines, and, later, most of his San Simeon estate. (Hearst's rise and fall inspired the 1941 film *Citizen Kane.*)

In 1948 Hearst became the owner of one of the US's first TV stations, WBAL-TV in Baltimore. When Hearst died in 1951, company veteran Richard Berlin became CEO. Berlin sold off failing newspapers, moved into television, and acquired more magazines.

Frank Bennack, CEO since 1979, expanded the company, acquiring newspapers, publishing firms (notably William Morrow, 1981), TV stations, magazines (*Redbook,* 1982; *Esquire,* 1986), and 20% of cable sports network ESPN (1991). Hearst branched into video via a joint venture with Capital Cities/ABC (1981) and helped launch the Lifetime and Arts & Entertainment cable channels (1984).

In 1992 Hearst brought on board former Federal Communications Commission chairman Alfred Sikes, who quickly moved the company onto the Internet. In 1996 Randolph A. Hearst passed the title of chairman to nephew George Hearst (the last surviving son of the founder, Randolph died in 2000).

The company sold its book publishing operations to News Corp.'s HarperCollins unit in 1999. It also agreed to buy the *San Francisco Chronicle* from rival Chronicle Publishing. That deal was called into question over concerns that the *San Francisco Examiner* would not survive and the city would be left with one major paper. To resolve the issue, the next year Hearst sold the *Examiner* to ExIn (a group of investors affiliated with the Ted Fang family and other owners of the *San Francisco Independent*).

In mid-2002 Victor Ganzi took over as CEO and president following Bennack's retirement from these positions.

Hearst further expanded its potent stable of magazines in 2003 by purchasing *Seventeen* magazine from PRIMEDIA. Hearst also became a major player in yellow page publishing with its 2004 purchase of White Directory Publishers, one of the largest telephone directory companies in the US.

In 2006 Hearst backed MediaNews when that company paid $1 billion to acquire four newspapers (including the *San Jose Mercury News,* the *Contra Costa Times,* and the *St. Paul Pioneer Press)* from McClatchy. The following year Hearst purchased a 31% interest in 47 daily and 37 non-daily newspapers of MediaNews Group.

EXECUTIVES

Chairman: George R. Hearst Jr., age 81
Vice Chairman and CEO: Frank A. Bennack Jr., age 76
SVP and CFO: Ronald J. Doerfler, age 67
SVP, Chief Legal and Development Officer, Director, and Trustee: James M. Asher
SVP and Digital Media, Hearst Newspapers:
  Lincoln Millstein
SVP; President, Hearst Entertainment & Syndication:
  Scott M. Sassa, age 49
SVP Finance, Hearst Newspapers:
  John M. (Jack) Condon
SVP; President, Hearst Newspapers: Steven R. Swartz, age 46
VP; President and CEO, Hearst Magazines International; EVP, Hearst Magazines: George J. Green
VP; EVP and Deputy Group Head, Hearst Business Media: Steven A. Hobbs, age 49
Executive Director Corporate Communications; VP Communications, Hearst Magazines: Paul Luthringer
VP Public Relations, Hearst Magazines:
  Jessica S. Kleiman
VP and Special Assistant to the CEO: Neeraj Khemlani, age 38
Chairman and Editorial Director, SmartMoney:
  Edwin A. Finn Jr.
President, Hearst Magazines: Cathleen P. (Cathie) Black, age 64
President and CEO, Hearst Television: David J. Barrett, age 61
President, Hearst Business Media: Richard P. Malloch
President, Hearst Interactive Media:
  Kenneth A. Bronfin, age 49
President, San Francisco Chronicle / SFGate.com:
  Mark Adkins

LOCATIONS

HQ: The Hearst Corporation
    300 W. 57th St., New York, NY 10019
Phone: 212-649-2000   **Fax:** 212-649-2108
Web: www.hearstcorp.com

PRODUCTS/OPERATIONS

Selected Operations

Hearst Broadcasting
  Hearst Television
Hearst Business Media
  Black Book
  Diversion
  Electronic Products
  First DataBank
  MOTOR Magazine
Hearst Entertainment & Syndication
  A&E Television Networks (joint venture with ABC and NBC)
    A&E
    The Biography Channel
    The History Channel
    History Channel International
  ESPN (20%)
  King Features Syndicate
  Hearst Entertainment (content library and production operations)
  Lifetime Entertainment Services (with Walt Disney Company)
    Lifetime Movie Network
    Lifetime Online
    Lifetime Television
  Reed Brennan Media Associates (production services for newspapers)
Hearst Interactive Media
  Circles (online loyalty marketing programs)
  drugstore.com (online pharmacy site)
  Gather (social networking)
  Hire.com (job site)
Hearst Magazines
  Cosmopolitan
  Country Living
  Esquire
  Good Housekeeping
  Harper's BAZAAR
  House Beautiful
  Marie Claire
  O, The Oprah Magazine (with Harpo)
  Popular Mechanics
  Quick & Simple
  Redbook
  Seventeen
  SmartMoney (with Dow Jones)
  Teen
  Weekend
Hearst Newspapers
  Albany Times Union (New York)
  Houston Chronicle
  Huron Daily Tribune (Michigan)
  Laredo Morning Times (Texas)
  Midland Daily News (Michigan)
  San Antonio Express-News
  San Francisco Chronicle
Other Operations
  Real estate

COMPETITORS

Advance Publications
Andrews McMeel Universal
Bauer Publishing (UK)
Belo Corp.
Bertelsmann
Bloomberg L.P.
Cox Enterprises
Dennis Publishing
Disney
E. W. Scripps
Freedom Communications
Gannett
IPC Group
Lagardère
Liberty Media
McClatchy Company
McGraw-Hill
Meredith Corporation
New York Times
News Corp.
Reader's Digest
Reed Elsevier Group
Rodale
Time Warner
Tribune Company
Viacom
Washington Post
Yellow Book USA

HISTORICAL FINANCIALS

Company Type: Private

Income Statement

	ESTIMATED REVENUE ($ mil.)	NET INCOME ($ mil.)	NET PROFIT MARGIN	EMPLOYEES
12/07	4,380.0	—	—	17,070
12/06	4,520.0	—	—	17,062
12/05	4,550.0	—	—	17,016
12/04	4,000.0	—	—	16,667
12/03	4,100.0	—	—	20,000
Annual Growth	1.7%	—	—	(3.9%)

Revenue History

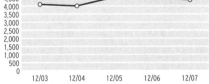

| | 12/03 | 12/04 | 12/05 | 12/06 | 12/07 |

Helmerich & Payne

In the oil and gas industry, Helmerich & Payne knows the drill: The contract driller operates almost 215 land and nine offshore platform rigs, mostly for industry giants such as BP, PDVSA, and Marathon Oil. Its US contract drilling operations are conducted mainly in Louisiana, Oklahoma, Texas, and Wyoming, as well as offshore California, in the Gulf of Mexico, in South America, and in North and West Africa. Helmerich & Payne operates 146 FlexRigs (drilling rigs equipped with new technologies, environmental and safety design, and the capability of simultaneous crew activity). The company also has real estate operations, including a shopping center, residential buildings, and office buildings, in Tulsa.

The bulk of Helmerich & Payne's international contract work is conducted in Venezuela, but the company also operates in Argentina, Bolivia, Chile, Colombia, Ecuador, Equatorial Guinea, and Tunisia.

Helmerich & Payne has grown through the addition of new equipment and the enhancement of its current drilling fleet. In 2005 launched a program to build a total of 127 new FlexRigs. In 2007 the company lost a FlexRig in a well blowout fire.

In order to complement technology used by its FlexRig fleet, in 2008, Helmerich & Payne acquired TerraVici Drilling Solutions, which developed proprietary rotary steerable technology to improve horizontal and directional drilling operations. Through integrating this technology the company hopes to improve drilling productivity and reduce costs to the customer.

In 2009 Helmerich & Payne began to cease operations on its 11 rigs in Venezuela as PDVSA failed to make good on its back payments.

HISTORY

H&P was founded in 1920 by Walt Helmerich and William Payne. The company expanded rapidly over the next two decades. Payne left in 1936 to form his own business, Big Chief Oil. Helmerich's son Walt III joined H&P in the late 1940s. The firm began international operations in Venezuela in 1957 and purchased chemical firm Natural Gas Odorizing in 1960.

Emerging from the 1980s oil slump, H&P focused on offshore drilling in Venezuela, Trinidad, and Papua New Guinea. In 1992 the company landed its largest contract ever, drilling for oil in Colombia for British Petroleum.

In 1995 Shell hired H&P to build two rigs for the deepwater Mars field in the Gulf of Mexico. Refocusing on its core oil and gas businesses, the company sold Natural Gas Odorizing in 1996 to Occidental Petroleum. The next year H&P started to increase its US land rig fleet by about 25%, but in 1998, as petroleum prices dropped, H&P sold a number of its oil and gas properties.

In 1999 H&P expanded its South American presence by placing two rigs in Argentina for contract work.The company also won a contract to manage Exxon Mobil's Jade offshore platform in Equatorial Guinea in 2000, and in 2001 it secured a contract with BP to drill in the Rockies for the first time since 1986.

In 2002 the company spun off its oil and gas exploration and production division and merged it with Key Production to form Cimarex Energy.

EXECUTIVES

Chairman: Walter H. Helmerich III, age 86
President, CEO, and Director: Hans Helmerich, age 50
EVP and CFO: Douglas E. Fears, age 59
EVP, Secretary, and General Counsel: Steven R. Mackey, age 57
EVP, US and International Operations, Helmerich and Payne International Drilling: John W. Lindsay, age 47
EVP, Engineering and Development, Helmerich and Payne International Drilling: M. Alan Orr, age 57
VP and Controller: Gordon K. Helm, age 55
Auditors: Ernst & Young LLP

LOCATIONS

HQ: Helmerich & Payne, Inc.
1437 S. Boulder Ave., Tulsa, OK 74119
Phone: 918-742-5531   **Fax:** 918-742-0237
Web: www.hpinc.com

2008 Sales

	$ mil.	% of total
US	1,687.1	83
Venezuela	167.2	8
Ecuador	55.1	3
Colombia	42.5	2
Other countries	84.6	4
Total	**2,036.5**	**100**

PRODUCTS/OPERATIONS

Selected Subsidiaries

Helmerich & Payne International Drilling Co.
Helmerich & Payne (Africa) Drilling Co.
Helmerich & Payne (Argentina) Drilling Co.
Helmerich & Payne (Australia) Drilling Co.
Helmerich & Payne (Boulder) Drilling Co.
Helmerich & Payne (Colombia) Drilling Co.
Helmerich & Payne de Venezuela, C.A.
Helmerich & Payne del Ecuador, Inc.
Helmerich & Payne Drilling (Bolivia) S.A.
Helmerich & Payne (Gabon) Drilling Co.
Helmerich & Payne Rasco, Inc.
H&P Finco
H&P Invest (dba H&P Yemen Drilling Co.)
Turrum Pty. Ltd. (New Guinea)
Helmerich & Payne Properties, Inc.
The Space Center, Inc.
Utica Square Shopping Center, Inc.
Fishercorp, Inc.

COMPETITORS

Diamond Offshore
ENSCO
Nabors Industries
Noble
Parker Drilling
Patterson-UTI Energy
Pride International
Rowan Companies
Transocean Inc.

HISTORICAL FINANCIALS

Company Type: Public

Income Statement

FYE: September 30

	REVENUE ($ mil.)	NET INCOME ($ mil.)	NET PROFIT MARGIN	EMPLOYEES
9/08	2,036.5	461.7	22.7%	6,198
9/07	1,629.7	449.3	27.6%	6,456
9/06	1,224.8	293.9	24.0%	5,705
9/05	800.7	127.6	15.9%	4,801
9/04	620.9	4.4	0.7%	4,251
Annual Growth	34.6%	220.1%	—	9.9%

2008 Year-End Financials

Debt ratio: 21.0%	No. of shares (mil.): 105
Return on equity: 22.6%	Dividends
Cash ($ mil.): 122	Yield: 0.4%
Current ratio: 2.24	Payout: 4.4%
Long-term debt ($ mil.): 475	Market value ($ mil.): 4,555

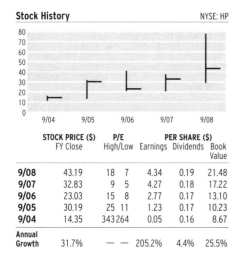

	STOCK PRICE ($) FY Close	P/E High/Low		PER SHARE ($) Earnings	Dividends	Book Value
9/08	43.19	18	7	4.34	0.19	21.48
9/07	32.83	9	5	4.27	0.18	17.22
9/06	23.03	15	8	2.77	0.17	13.10
9/05	30.19	25	11	1.23	0.17	10.23
9/04	14.35	343	264	0.05	0.16	8.67
Annual Growth	31.7%	—	—	205.2%	4.4%	25.5%

Henry Schein

Whether you're in Poughkeepsie or Prague, Henry Schein will help your dentist get those sparkly whites to shine. The company is a leading global distributor of dental supplies and equipment, with operations in North America, Europe, and Australia. Henry Schein provides such items as impression materials, X-ray equipment, and anesthetics. But the company isn't only interested in teeth: It also supplies doctors' offices, veterinarians, and other office-based health care providers with diagnostic kits, surgical tools, drugs, vaccines, and animal health products. Additionally, its technology division offers practice management software and other services to dental, medical, and veterinary offices.

Not content with its more than half a million customers worldwide (and a particularly strong presence in North America), the company aggressively pursues acquisitions to further build its business. The company's purchases have expanded its array of products and its geographic reach. It also operates through affiliates in the Middle East and Iceland. Henry Schein has nine US distribution centers, three in Europe, and one in Canada.

In 2008 the company picked up European veterinary, medical, and dental firms Noviko of the Czech Republic, Medka of Germany, Minerva Dental Limited of the UK, and DNA Anthos Impianti of Italy. The following year it acquired Ortho Organizers, an orthodontic device manufacturer and distributor.

In 2007 Henry Schein bought a New Zealand-based developer of dental practice management software (called Software of Excellence International) in order to add to its technology-related offerings. It also boosted its veterinarian offerings with the purchase of the UK's W&J Dunlop.

HISTORY

For more than 50 years, Henry Schein distributed drugs made by Schein Pharmaceuticals. In 1992 management spun off the drug business and, led by former accountant Stanley Bergman, began acquiring other dental supply companies at a terrific rate: 34 between 1994 and 1996 alone.

The company went public in 1995 and bought more than a dozen businesses. These purchases, which included product marketer Vertex Corporation's distribution unit, moved Henry Schein into the medical and veterinary supply fields. The purchase of Schein Dental Equipment (founded by Marvin Schein) boosted per-customer sales by adding big-ticket merchandise to the product mix.

Acquisitions continued hot and heavy as the company boosted operations abroad. The purchases hit the bottom line; Schein avoided bloat by restructuring operations, closing facilities, and developing new systems. The company consolidated 13 distribution centers into five in 1997. The following year the firm expanded into Canada, and bought a controlling stake in UK direct marketer Porter Nash.

To boost profits, the company announced in 2000 that it would cut 5% of its workforce. It also shut down some facilities and sold its software development business as part of its overall restructuring plan. In 2001 the firm resumed its acquisitions when it bought the dental supply business of drugmaker Zila.

EXECUTIVES

Chairman, President, and CEO: Stanley M. Bergman, age 59, $3,722,320 total compensation
President, COO, and Director: James P. Breslawski, age 55, $2,032,422 total compensation
EVP, CFO, and Director: Steven Paladino, age 52, $1,680,092 total compensation
SVP and CTO; Head, Technology Group: Jim Harding, age 53
EVP, Chief Administrative Officer, and Director: Gerald A. Benjamin, age 56
SVP and Chief Compliance Officer: Leonard A. David, age 60
SVP and Chief Merchandising Officer: Michael Racioppi, age 54
EVP Corporate Business Development Group and Director: Mark E. Mlotek, age 53, $1,671,538 total compensation
SVP and General Counsel: Michael S. Ettinger
VP Corporate Communications: Susan Vassallo
VP Personal Relations: Steven W. Kess
VP Investor Relations: Neal Goldner
President, International Group: Michael Zack, age 56
President, Medical Group: David C. McKinley
Human Resources: Jan Ushioko
Senior Advisor: Stanley Komaroff, age 73, $1,671,538 total compensation
Auditors: BDO Seidman, LLP

LOCATIONS

HQ: Henry Schein, Inc.
135 Duryea Rd., Melville, NY 11747
Phone: 631-843-5500   **Fax:** 631-843-5658
Web: www.henryschein.com

2008 Sales

	$ mil.	% of total
US	3,912.0	61
Germany	671.3	11
Other countries	1,811.6	28
Total	**6,394.9**	**100**

PRODUCTS/OPERATIONS

2008 Sales

	$ mil.	% of total
Health care distribution		
Dental (US & Canadian dental markets)	2,581.5	40
International (non-US dental, medical & animal health markets)	2,221.1	35
Medical (US medical & animal health markets)	1,429.0	22
Technology	163.3	3
Total	**6,394.9**	**100**

Selected Products

Dental products
 Acrylics
 Alloys
 Anesthetics
 Articulators
 Bridges
 Composites
 Crowns
 Gypsum
 Impression materials
 Preventatives
 Surgical equipment
 X-ray equipment
Medical products
 Diagnostic kits
 Office equipment
 Pharmaceuticals (generic & brand-name)
 Surgical tools
 Vitamins
Technology
 Dental practice management software
Veterinary products
 Dental equipment
 Pharmaceuticals
 Surgical tools

COMPETITORS

Allscripts
athenahealth
Benco Dental
Cardinal Health
Darby Dental
IDEXX Labs
McKesson
Moore Medical
MWI Veterinary Supply
NextGen
Omega Pharma
Owens & Minor
Patterson Companies
PSS World Medical
Sybron Dental

HISTORICAL FINANCIALS

Company Type: Public

Income Statement

	REVENUE ($ mil.)	NET INCOME ($ mil.)	NET PROFIT MARGIN	EMPLOYEES
12/08	6,394.9	243.1	3.8%	12,500
12/07	5,920.2	215.2	3.6%	12,000
12/06	5,153.1	163.8	3.2%	11,000
12/05	4,635.9	151.3	3.3%	11,000
12/04	4,060.3	128.2	3.2%	9,600
Annual Growth	12.0%	17.3%	—	6.8%

FYE: Last Saturday in December

2008 Year-End Financials

Debt ratio: 13.8%   No. of shares (mil.): 90
Return on equity: 13.1%   Dividends
Cash ($ mil.): 370   Yield: 0.0%
Current ratio: 1.75   Payout: —
Long-term debt ($ mil.): 267   Market value ($ mil.): 3,309

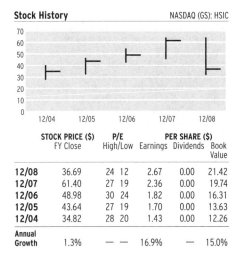

	STOCK PRICE ($) FY Close	P/E High/Low		PER SHARE ($) Earnings	Dividends	Book Value
12/08	36.69	24	12	2.67	0.00	21.42
12/07	61.40	27	19	2.36	0.00	19.74
12/06	48.98	30	24	1.82	0.00	16.31
12/05	43.64	27	19	1.70	0.00	13.63
12/04	34.82	28	20	1.43	0.00	12.26
Annual Growth	1.3%	—	—	16.9%	—	15.0%

Herman Miller

Desk jockeys can ride Herman Miller's products all the way up the corporate ladder and home again. A top US maker of office furniture, it's known for developing designs for corporate, government, home office, leisure, and health care environments. Herman Miller's products include ergonomic devices, filing and storage systems, free-standing furniture, lighting, seating, textiles, and wooden casegoods. It makes products in the UK and the US and sells them worldwide through its sales staff and dealer network, as well as through independent dealers and the Internet. Columbia Wanger Asset Management and Ariel Capital Management each own about a 10% stake in the firm.

Looking to give its health care business a shot in the arm and cater to the sturdy health care construction sector, Herman Miller in June 2009 bought furnishings leader Nemschoff. While Nemschoff's expertise is in making soft seating and furniture for patient care environments, the company also provides complementary products for commercial office and education markets, adding depth to niche markets where Herman Miller already operates.

The furnishings maker is also growing through its Geiger International subsidiary. In early 2009 the commercial furnishings unit acquired North Carolina-based Ruskin Industries, which specializes in making seating, tables, and casegoods for the contract furniture markets. Ruskin has produced carved wood pieces for piano manufacturer Steinway and chair frames for contract furnishings makers HBF and Cabot Wrenn. The addition of Ruskin under the Herman Miller umbrella is expected to boost the company's selection of tables and seating as well as up its design standards.

Herman Miller hopes to see profits from its expanding international customer base, especially in the Asia/Pacific region. In 2008 the company negotiated an international alliance with Hong Kong-based POSH Office Systems, a designer and manufacturer of modern work centers. As part of the alliance, both firms will be able to access the other's product portfolio and distribution network, expanding their range of products and footprint.

During the past few years, the company had been focusing on landing big contracts with major corporations, but it shifted gears to develop new designs to grab medium-sized companies and small startups. It also handled a slowing economy by cutting costs through layoffs and by consolidating some brands and operations.

In addition to its investments in furniture manufacturing, Herman Miller has also developed an interest in energy management. Its Convia subsidiary offers programmable electrical distribution components. In 2009 Wiremold, a leading producer of electrical wiring systems, penned an agreement to have Convia's controls used in its units.

HISTORY

In 1923 Herman Miller lent his son-in-law, D. J. De Pree, enough money to buy Star Furniture, started in 1905 in Zeeland, Michigan. (De Pree renamed the furniture maker after Miller.) Designer Gilbert Rohde led Herman Miller's transformation from traditional to more modern styles in the 1930s.

Rohde designed the company's first office component line, the Executive Office Group (introduced in 1942). Rohde died two years later, and in 1946 George Nelson was named Herman Miller's design director. Nelson brought in a number of notable designers, including Charles Eames and Isamu Noguchi.

Throughout its history, the company has maintained a reputation for being open to suggestions and comments from its workers. This policy dates back to De Pree's learning that one of his millwrights who had died had also been a poet; De Pree began to value his employees for their innate talents rather than just for the work they did for him.

Herman Miller grew, largely unimpeded by national competitors, except for neighboring Steelcase. In 1950 the company adopted the Scanlon plan, an employee participation plan that included bonuses based on helpful participation, such as cost-cutting suggestions.

De Pree retired in 1962 and was succeeded by his son, Hugh. Two years later Herman Miller introduced the Action Office, a collection of panels, work surfaces, and storage units that could be moved about to create custom-designed work spaces within an open-plan office; this line has been the company mainstay ever since.

The firm, which went public in 1970, introduced its Ergon ergonomic chair in 1976. Hugh retired in 1980 and was succeeded by his brother Max, who capped executive salaries at 20 times the average wage of factory-line workers. Max became chairman in 1988 and resigned from day-to-day management duties to pursue teaching opportunities.

Max's successor, 33-year company veteran Richard Ruch, began restructuring to sharpen Herman Miller's focus. Then the commercial real estate market collapsed and, with it, the need for new office furnishings. Earnings tumbled in 1991 and 1992. Ruch retired in 1992 to become vice chairman and was succeeded by first-ever company outsider Kermit Campbell.

In 1994 Herman Miller acquired German furniture company Geneal. Earnings plummeted in 1995 and chairman Campbell was forced out. Despite his commitment to its traditionally employee-friendly corporate culture, CEO Michael Volkema led Herman Miller in a shake-up, cutting 180 jobs and closing underperforming plants. The company introduced its cubicle systems office furniture unit, Miller SQA ("simple, quick, and affordable"), in 1995.

Herman Miller and leading carpet tile maker Interface formed a joint venture in 1997 to provide integrated office furniture and carpeting systems for commercial clients. The next year the company became the first major office furniture maker to target customers over the Internet. Herman Miller acquired wood furniture maker Geiger Brickel in 1999. The company launched a low-cost line of office furniture, dubbed RED, aimed at fledgling Internet-oriented firms in late 2000, shortly before the bubble burst for Web startups.

A slowdown in the US economy prompted cut after cut in 2001; by March 2002 the company had eliminated some 3,900 positions (or 37% of its workforce). The company also phased out its SQA and RED lines that year amidst slowing sales; in 2003, it consolidated two of its manufacturing sites (Holland, Michigan and Canton, Georgia) into existing facilities. President and COO Brian Walker succeeded Volkema as CEO in July 2004. Volkema remains as chairman.

EXECUTIVES

Chairman: Michael A. Volkema, age 53
President, CEO, and Director: Brian C. Walker, age 47
EVP Operations: Kenneth L. Goodson Jr., age 57
EVP and CFO: Gregory J. (Greg) Bylsma, age 44
Chief Development Officer: Gary S. Miller, age 59
EVP; President, Herman Miller Healthcare:
Elizabeth A. (Beth) Nickels, age 47
EVP and Chief Administrative Officer:
Andrew J. (Andy) Lock, age 55
EVP Research, Design, and Development:
Donald D. Goeman, age 52
EVP; President, North American Office and Learning Environments: Curt Pullen
SVP Legal Services and Secretary:
James E. Christenson, age 62
SVP Marketing: Kathy Koch
President, Herman Miller International:
John P. Portlock, age 63
President, Geiger International and Herman Miller for the Home: Steve Gane
Director Seating Products: Jack Schreur
Auditors: Ernst & Young LLP

LOCATIONS

HQ: Herman Miller, Inc.
855 E. Main Ave., Zeeland, MI 49464
Phone: 616-654-3000 **Fax:** 616-654-5234
Web: www.hermanmiller.com

2009 Sales

	$ mil.	% of total
US	1,349.4	83
Other countries	280.6	17
Total	**1,630.0**	**100**

PRODUCTS/OPERATIONS

2009 Sales

	$ mil.	% of total
Systems	511.6	32
International	365.7	22
Seating	361.1	22
Freestanding & storage	260.3	16
Other	131.3	8
Total	**1,630.0**	**100**

Selected Products and Brands

Accessories (Accents, Aalto, Eames)
Freestanding furniture (Passage, Aalto, Abak, Burdick, Eames, Arrio, Kiva)
Health care systems (Ethospace)
Modular systems (Action Office, Ethospace, Q System, Resolve, Vivo Interiors)
Screens (Eames)
Seating (Aeron, Ambi, Equa, Ergon, Mirra, Reaction)
Storage and filing (Meridian, Eames)
Textiles (Ituri, Meinecke)
Wooden casegoods (Geiger)

COMPETITORS

American of Martinsville
CFGroup
Flexsteel
Haworth, Inc.
HMU, LLC
HNI
Inscape corp
Kewaunee Scientific
KI
Kimball International
Knoll, Inc.
MITY
Neutral Posture
Reconditioned Systems
Shelby Williams
Steelcase
TAB Products
Teknion
Virco Mfg.

HISTORICAL FINANCIALS

Company Type: Public

Income Statement

FYE: Saturday nearest May 31

	REVENUE ($ mil.)	NET INCOME ($ mil.)	NET PROFIT MARGIN	EMPLOYEES
5/09	1,630.0	68.0	4.2%	5,229
5/08	2,012.1	152.3	7.6%	6,478
5/07	1,918.9	129.1	6.7%	6,574
5/06	1,737.2	99.2	5.7%	6,242
5/05	1,515.6	68.0	4.5%	6,234
Annual Growth	1.8%	0.0%	—	(4.3%)

2009 Year-End Financials

Debt ratio: 3,780.0%
Return on equity: 433.1%
Cash ($ mil.): 193
Current ratio: 1.59
Long-term debt ($ mil.): 302
No. of shares (mil.): 56
Dividends
  Yield: 2.0%
  Payout: 23.2%
Market value ($ mil.): 795

Stock History

NASDAQ (GS): MLHR

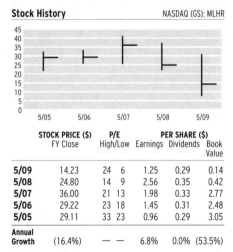

	STOCK PRICE ($) FY Close	P/E High/Low		PER SHARE ($) Earnings	Dividends	Book Value
5/09	14.23	24	6	1.25	0.29	0.14
5/08	24.80	14	9	2.56	0.35	0.42
5/07	36.00	21	13	1.98	0.33	2.77
5/06	29.22	23	18	1.45	0.31	2.48
5/05	29.11	33	23	0.96	0.29	3.05
Annual Growth	(16.4%)	—	—	6.8%	0.0%	(53.5%)

The Hershey Company

The Hershey Company will cover you in Kisses and bring you Almond Joy. The company makes such well-known chocolate and candy brands as Hershey's Kisses, Reese's peanut butter cups, Swizzles licorice, Mounds, York Peppermint Patty, and Kit Kat (licensed from Nestlé). Hershey also makes grocery goods such as baking chocolate, ice-cream toppings, chocolate syrup, cocoa mix, cookies, snack nuts, hard candies, and lollipops. Its products are sold throughout North America and exported overseas. The Hershey Trust — which benefits the Milton Hershey School for disadvantaged children — controls approximately 99% of Hershey's voting power.

President and CEO Richard Lenny left the company in 2007, having been at Hershey's helm since 2001. It is generally thought that Lenny's resignation was due to disagreements between him and the trust regarding the company's business strategies. CFO David J. West was named as Lenny's successor as president and CEO.

Chocolate may be the name of the game but the company is also a growing presence in the hard- and non-chocolate candy markets, offering such brands as Good & Plenty and Jolly Rancher. The company is expanding its products with new versions of old favorites, such as Jolly Rancher lollipops and bite-sized bits of its popular chocolate bars. It introduced sugar-free chocolate and expanded the snack-food and Hispanic markets, as well as producing packaged cookies whose flavors are based on the flavors of its Almond Joy, Reese's, and York products.

Hershey has also been attempting to join the quickly expanding premium chocolate market. It has introduced its own Special Dark, Extra Dark, and Cacao Reserve brands.

Moving from the confectionery market to the snack market, Hershey has been busy introducing such items as cookies (Kisses Mini Cookies), 100-calorie treats (Snacksters), and granola bars (Hershey's SnackBarz).

The company formed a joint venture with South Korean confectioner, Lotte, in 2007 to manufacture and sell Hershey's products in China. Continuing to expand its geographical reach that year, Hershey acquired a 51% interest in the food and beverage operations of the Indian conglomerate, Godrej Industries.

Hershey markets its more than 80 brands in more than 50 countries worldwide.

HISTORY

The Hershey Company is the legacy of Milton Hershey, of Pennsylvania Dutch origin. Apprenticed in 1872 at age 15 to a candy maker, Hershey started Lancaster Caramel Company at age 30. In 1893, at the Chicago Exposition, he saw a new chocolate-making machine, and in 1900 he sold the caramel operations for $1 million to start a chocolate factory.

The factory was completed in 1905 in Derry Church, Pennsylvania, and renamed Hershey Foods the next year. Chocolate Kisses, individually hand wrapped in silver foil, were introduced in 1907. Two years later the candy man founded the Milton Hershey School, an orphanage; the company was donated to a trust in 1918 and for years existed solely to fund the school. Although Hershey went public in 1927, the school still controls the majority of shareholder votes.

The candy firm pioneered mass-production techniques for chocolates and developed much of the machinery for making and packaging its products. At one time Hershey supplied its own sugar cane from Cuba and enlarged the world's almond supply sixfold through nut farm ownership. The Hershey bar became so universally familiar that it was used overseas during WWII as currency. Milton refused to advertise, believing that quality would speak for itself. Even after his death in 1945, the company continued his policy. Then, in 1970, facing a sluggish candy market and a diet-conscious public, the company lost share to Mars and management relented.

During the 1960s and 1970s, Hershey diversified in order to stabilize the effects of changing commodity prices. The company got into the pasta business with its 1966 purchase of San Giorgio Macaroni, and it bought the Friendly Ice Cream chain in 1979 (sold 1988). It expanded candy operations by bringing out large-sized bars (1980) and buying Cadbury's US candy business (Peter Paul, Cadbury, Caramello; 1988).

Kenneth Wolfe was named chairman and CEO in 1994. In 1999 the company sold its pasta business to New World Pasta for $450 million and a 6% interest in that company. Also that year the Hershey Trust, wanting to diversify its holdings, sold $100 million of its stock to Hershey.

In 2001 Nabisco veteran Rick Lenny replaced Wolfe as CEO. Hershey established a manufacturing presence in South America that year by acquiring the chocolate and confectionery business of Brazilian company Visagis. It also cut about 400 salaried positions and closed three plants and a distribution facility.

In 2002 Wolfe retired as chairman and Lenny was selected to replace him. Also that year Hershey settled a bitter six-week factory-worker strike, the longest in company history.

Also in 2002 the Hershey Trust said that to diversify its holdings, it wanted to sell its 77% interest in Hershey. However, the sale was temporarily blocked while the state of Pennsylvania reviewed the impact it would have on the community. Despite the injunction against the sale, the trust continued to look for a buyer and was considering a $12.5 billion offer from chewing gum giant Wm. Wrigley Jr. and a $10.5 billion joint offer from Nestlé and Cadbury Schweppes (now Cadbury).

Amid the community outcry and legal wrangling, the sale was finally called off later in 2002, after 10 of the trust's 17 members changed their minds. Due to the uproar surrounding the proposed sale, the trust board promised to restructure itself. Among the outgoing board members was William Lepley, president and chief executive of the Milton Hershey School.

To expand its sales in the Hispanic market, in 2004 Hershey announced a new line of Latin-inspired candies, including those with chili-based flavors and *dulce de leche* fillings.

The company changed its name to The Hershey Company in 2005, dropping the "Foods" from its name to reflect the company's move away from coffee, pasta, and restaurant businesses and the concentration on confectionery.

In 2006 the company purchased organic chocolate confectioner, Dagoba. The company established the Hershey Center for Health and Nutrition in 2006 in order to research and develop new products that help provide consumers with heart health, weight management, and mental and physical energy.

EXECUTIVES

Chairman: James E. Nevels, age 57
President, CEO, and Director: David J. (Dave) West, age 45, $4,387,178 total compensation
SVP Global Operations: Terence L. O'Day, age 58
SVP and CFO: Humberto P. (Bert) Alfonso, age 51, $1,669,822 total compensation
SVP and CIO: George F. Davis, age 60
SVP and Global Chief Marketing Officer: Michele B. Buck, age 47, $1,430,421 total compensation
VP and Chief Accounting Officer: David W. Tacka, age 55
VP and Global Chief Customer Officer: E. Daniel Vucovich Jr.
SVP and Chief People Officer: Charlene Binder
SVP; President, Hershey North America: John P. (J.P.) Bilbrey, age 52, $2,042,138 total compensation
SVP, General Counsel, and Secretary: Burton H. (Burt) Snyder, age 61, $1,987,158 total compensation
SVP Strategy and Business Development: Javier H. Idrovo
SVP; President, Hershey International: Thaddeus J. (Ted) Jastrzebski, age 47
VP Global Research and Development: C. Daniel Azzara
VP Investor Relations: Mark K. Pogharian
VP Public Affairs: Andy McCormick
VP Global Human Resources: Karen M. Mooney
Treasurer: Rosa C. Stroh
Public Relations: Kirk Saville
Auditors: KPMG LLP

LOCATIONS

HQ: The Hershey Company
100 Crystal A Dr., Hershey, PA 17033
Phone: 717-534-4200
Web: www.thehersheycompany.com

2008 Sales

	% of total
US	86
Other countries	14
Total	**100**

PRODUCTS/OPERATIONS

Selected Brands

Food and beverage enhancers
 Bake Shoppe
 Goodnight Hugs
 Goodnight Kisses
Refreshment products
 Breath Saver
 Bubble Yum
 Ice Breakers
 York
Snack products
 Almond Joy Cookies
 Hershey's Cookies
 Hershey's Granola Bars
 Mauna Loa Macadamia Snack Nuts and Cookies
 Reese's Cookies
 Reese's Granola Bars
 Snacksters Snack Mix
 York Cookies
Confectionery
 Hershey's
  Bliss
  Cookies N' Crème
  Hershey's Milk Chocolate
  Hugs
  Kisses
  Kissables
  Nuggets
  Sticks
 Reese's
  Fast Break
  Nutrageous
  Peanut Butter Cups
  Pieces
  Reesesticks
  Whipps

Other
 5th Avenue
 Almond Joy (worldwide license from Cadbury)
 Cacao Reserve
 Caramello (USA license from Cadbury)
 Chipits (Canada)
 Eat More (Canada)
 Godrej (India)
 Good & Plenty (wordwide license from Huhtamäki)
 Heath (wordwide license from Huhtamäki)
 Jolly Rancher (wordwide license from Huhtamäki)
 Kit Kat (US license from Nestlé)
 Milk Duds (wordwide license from Huhtamäki)
 Mounds (worldwide license from Cadbury)
 Mr. Goodbar
 Payday (wordwide license from Huhtamäki)
 Pelón Pelo Rico (Mexico)
 Pot Of Gold
 Rolo (US license from Nestlé)
 Scharffen Berger
 Skor
 Special Dark
 Symphony
 Take5
 Twizzlers
 Whatchamacallit
 Whoppers (wordwide license from Huhtamäki)
 York (worldwide license from Cadbury)
 Zagnut
 Zero

COMPETITORS

Annabelle Candy
Anthony-Thomas Candy
Asher's Chocolates
Barry Callebaut
Betsy Ann Candies
Cadbury
Chase General
Chocolates à la Carte
Chupa Chups
ConAgra
Endangered Species Chocolate
Enstrom
Farley's & Sathers
Fazer Konfektyr
Ferrero
Ghirardelli Chocolate
Godiva Chocolatier
Goetze's Candy
Green & Black's
Guittard
Harry London Candies
Interstate Bakeries
Jelly Belly Candy
Kellogg
Kraft Foods
Kraft North America
Laura Secord
Lindt & Sprüngli
Madelaine Chocolate
Mars, Incorporated
Nestlé
Otis Spunkmeyer
Perfetti Van Melle
Perfetti Van Melle USA
Purdy's Chocolates
Rocky Mountain Chocolate
Russell Stover
See's Candies
Smucker
Spangler Candy
The Sweet Shop USA
Tasty Baking
Tootsie Roll
Unilever
Warrell Corporation
World's Finest Chocolate
Wrigley
Zachary Confections

HISTORICAL FINANCIALS

Company Type: Public

Income Statement

FYE: December 31

	REVENUE ($ mil.)	NET INCOME ($ mil.)	NET PROFIT MARGIN	EMPLOYEES
12/08	5,132.8	311.4	6.1%	14,400
12/07	4,946.7	214.2	4.3%	12,800
12/06	4,944.2	559.1	11.3%	15,000
12/05	4,836.0	493.2	10.2%	13,750
12/04	4,429.2	590.9	13.3%	13,700
Annual Growth	**3.8%**	**(14.8%)**	**—**	**1.3%**

2008 Year-End Financials

Debt ratio: 473.3%
Return on equity: 68.4%
Cash ($ mil.): 37
Current ratio: 1.06
Long-term debt ($ mil.): 1,506

No. of shares (mil.): 166
Dividends
 Yield: 3.4%
 Payout: 87.5%
Market value ($ mil.): 5,783

Stock History

NYSE: HSY

	STOCK PRICE ($) FY Close	P/E High/Low	PER SHARE ($) Earnings	Dividends	Book Value
12/08	34.74	33 24	1.36	1.19	1.91
12/07	39.40	61 41	0.93	1.13	3.56
12/06	49.80	25 21	2.34	1.03	4.11
12/05	55.25	34 26	1.99	0.93	6.13
12/04	55.54	25 16	2.30	0.83	6.54
Annual Growth	**(11.1%)**	**— —**	**(12.3%)**	**9.4%**	**(26.5%)**

Hertz Global Holdings

If you've ever said, "Don't worry about it, it's just a rental," guess who hurts: Hertz, one of the world's leading car rental firms. On its own and through agents and licensees, Hertz operates about 8,000 rental locations in more than 140 countries worldwide, including some 500 at US airports. Its fleet includes some 500,000 cars from Ford, General Motors, Toyota, and other manufacturers. Hertz also rents a variety of heavy equipment through some 345 locations in North America, Europe, and China. Investment firms Clayton Dubilier & Rice, The Carlyle Group, and Merrill Lynch Global Private Equity own some 55% of Hertz.

The investment firms bought Hertz from Ford in 2005 and took the car rental company public in late 2006.

The recession in the US (and consequent decline in air travel) has led to declining sales at Hertz's airport locations, which account for more than 75% of its rental revenue. To lessen its dependence on the volatile air travel industry, the company has increased the number of off-airport locations it operates by about 20%.

Hertz is also increasing its presence in the online leisure market. To that end, in April 2009

Hertz acquired the assets of Texas-based Advantage Rent A Car for about $33 million. Advantage, which filed for bankruptcy in 2008, operates locations in key US leisure travel markets, including California, Florida, and Hawaii. Advantage also boasts substantial market share on online travel booking sites, such as Expedia, Travelocity, and priceline.com.

To ride out the recession the company is moving to cut costs, mainly in its US car rental operations. Over the past several years, Hertz has consistently whittled down its workforce each year. In early 2009, the firm announced plans to shed 4,000 of the more than 29,000 employees it cited at the end of 2007.

In 2008 Hertz bought one of its franchise partners in the Czech Republic (with its subsidiary in Slovakia), strengthening its ties in Central and Eastern Europe. The company invested in its Connect by Hertz business by acquiring Paris-based Eileo S.A. in April 2009. Eileo specializes in car-sharing technology and buying the company boosts Hertz's operations in London, New York City, and Paris, where it uses its Connect by Hertz service.

To strengthen its fleet sales, the firm acquired the Automoti Group, which created an online marketplace for used vehicles. Hertz hopes the purchase will help to expand its Rent2Buy program, which allows customers to rent a vehicle for up to three days before purchase.

Subsidiary Hertz Equipment Rental Corporation (HERC) is a major renter of industrial and construction equipment, primarily in the US and Canada but also in France, Spain, and now China. HERC's inventory includes earthmoving equipment, material-handling equipment, and aerial and electrical equipment.

HISTORY

In 1918, 22-year-old John Jacobs opened a Chicago car rental business with 12 Model T Fords that he had repaired. By 1923, when Yellow Cab entrepreneur John Hertz bought Jacobs' business, it had revenues of about $1 million. Jacobs continued as top executive of the company, renamed Hertz Drive-Ur-Self System. Three years later General Motors acquired the company when it bought Yellow Truck from John Hertz. Hertz introduced the first car rental charge card in 1926, opened its first airport location at Chicago's Midway Airport in 1932, and initiated the first one-way (rent-it-here/leave-it-there) plan in 1933. The company expanded into Canada in 1938 and Europe in 1950.

Omnibus bought Hertz from GM in 1953, sold its bus interests, and focused on vehicle leasing and renting. The next year Omnibus changed its name to The Hertz Corporation and was listed on the NYSE. Also in 1954 the company purchased Metropolitan Distributors, a New York-based truck leasing firm. In 1961 Hertz began operations in South America.

The company formed its Hertz Equipment Rental subsidiary in 1965. RCA bought Hertz two years later but allowed the company to maintain its board of directors and management. In 1972 it introduced the first frequent traveler's club, the #1 Club, which allowed the rental location to prepare a rental agreement before the customer arrived at the counter. Three years later Hertz began defining the company's image through TV commercials featuring football star/celebrity O. J. Simpson running through

airports. (Hertz canceled Simpson's contract in 1994 after his arrest on murder charges — the TV ads had stopped in 1992.) Frank Olson became CEO in 1977 after serving in the same position at United Airlines.

United Airlines bought Hertz from RCA in 1985, then sold it in 1987 for $1.3 billion to Park Ridge, which had been formed by Hertz management and Ford Motor specifically for the purchase. (Hertz was Ford's largest customer.) In 1988 Ford, which held 80% of Park Ridge, sold 20% to Volvo North America for $100 million. (Ford later reduced its stake to 49% when it sold shares to Volvo.)

Ford bought all the shares of Hertz it didn't already own in 1994. Taking advantage of heightened investor interest in rental car companies, Ford sold 17% of Hertz to the public in 1997.

Hertz acquired several equipment rental companies in 1998, including the Boireau Group (France) and Matthews Equipment (Canada). In 1999 the company's European acquisitions included French car rental franchise SST and German van rental company Yellow Truck.

Olson retired as CEO in 1999, and president Craig Koch was named his successor. Lackluster performance of Hertz stock in 2001 prompted Ford to buy back shares held by the public — once again making the car rental company a wholly owned Ford subsidiary.

As part of an effort to strengthen its balance sheet and focus on its core automotive manufacturing operations, Ford sold Hertz to a group of investment firms — Clayton Dubilier & Rice, The Carlyle Group, and Merrill Lynch Global Private Equity — in December 2005 for $5.6 billion and nearly $10 billion in assumed debt. The firms spun Hertz off to the public in 2006.

Koch stepped down as CEO in 2006 because of a family medical issue. He was named chairman, and Tenneco's Mark Frissora was hired to be CEO. Frissora became chairman upon Koch's retirement in 2007. In July 2007 Hertz acquired Autotravel, a UK-based car-rental business, for an undisclosed sum.

In April 2009 HERC acquired Spain's Rent One, a leading power generation company serving event and media companies throughout Spain.

EXECUTIVES

Chairman and CEO; Chairman and CEO, Hertz:
Mark P. Frissora, age 53, $8,358,766 total compensation
EVP and CFO; EVP and CFO, Hertz: Elyse Douglas, age 53, $1,554,872 total compensation
SVP and CIO; SVP and CIO, Hertz:
Joseph F. (Joe) Eckroth Jr., age 50
SVP and Chief Marketing Officer; SVP and Chief Marketing Officer, Hertz: Michael P. (Mike) Senackerib, age 43
SVP and Chief Human Resources Officer; SVP and Chief Human Resources Officer, Hertz: LeighAnne G. Baker, age 50
EVP; President, Vehicle Rental and Leasing, The Americas and Pacific: Joseph R. Nothwang, age 62, $6,191,270 total compensation
EVP; President, HERC: Gerald A. Plescia, age 53, $2,577,510 total compensation
EVP; President, Hertz Europe: Michel Taride, age 52, $2,630,532 total compensation
EVP Supply Chain Management; EVP Supply Chain Management, Hertz: John A. Thomas, age 44
SVP Quality Assurance and Administration:
Charles L. Shafer
SVP Process Improvement and Project Management; SVP Process Improvement and Project Management, Hertz: Lois I. Boyd, age 55
SVP Global Sales; SVP Global Sales, Hertz:
Robert J. Stuart, age 47

SVP, General Counsel, and Secretary; SVP, General Counsel, and Secretary, Hertz: J. Jeffrey Zimmerman, age 49
SVP Finance and Corporate Controller; SVP Finance and Corporate Controller, Hertz: Jatindar Kapur, age 50
SVP Corporate Affairs and Communications; SVP Corporate Affairs and Communications, Hertz: Richard D. Broome, age 50
VP and Treasurer; VP and Treasurer, Hertz: R. Scott Massengill, age 46
Staff VP Investor Relations: Leslie Hunziker
Manager Public Relations: Paula Rivera
Senior Director Marketing and Advertising: Lisa Diliberto
Auditors: PricewaterhouseCoopers LLP

LOCATIONS

HQ: Hertz Global Holdings, Inc.
225 Brae Blvd., Park Ridge, NJ 07656
Phone: 201-307-2000   **Fax:** 201-307-2644
Web: www.hertz.com

2008 Sales

	$ mil.	% of total
US	5,506.1	65
Other countries	3,019.0	35
Total	**8,525.1**	**100**

PRODUCTS/OPERATIONS

2008 Sales

	$ mil.	% of total
Car rental	6,730.4	80
Equipment rental	1,657.3	20
Corporate & other	137.4	—
Total	**8,525.1**	**100**

COMPETITORS

Avis Budget
Avis Europe
Caterpillar
Dollar Thrifty Automotive
Enterprise Rent-A-Car
HD Supply
Neff
NES Rentals
RSC Equipment Rental
Sixt
Sunbelt Rentals
United Rentals

HISTORICAL FINANCIALS

Company Type: Public

Income Statement

FYE: December 31

	REVENUE ($ mil.)	NET INCOME ($ mil.)	NET PROFIT MARGIN	EMPLOYEES
12/08	8,525.1	(1,206.7)	—	24,900
12/07	8,685.6	264.6	3.0%	29,350
12/06	8,058.4	115.9	1.4%	31,500
12/05	7,469.2	350.0	4.7%	32,200
12/04	6,676.0	365.5	5.5%	31,400
Annual Growth	6.3%	—	—	(5.6%)

2008 Year-End Financials

Debt ratio: 746.1%   No. of shares (mil.): 409
Return on equity: —   Dividends
Cash ($ mil.): 594   Yield: 0.0%
Current ratio: 1.65   Payout: —
Long-term debt ($ mil.): 10,972 Market value ($ mil.): 2,075

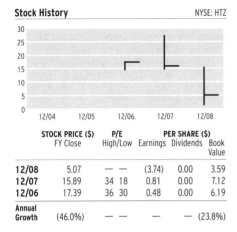
Hess Corporation

Hess Corporation (formerly Amerada Hess) has what it takes. The integrated oil and gas company conducts exploration and production primarily in Algeria, Australia, Azerbaijan, Brazil, Denmark, Egypt, Equatorial Guinea, Gabon, Ghana, Indonesia, Libya, Malaysia, Norway, Peru, Russia, Thailand, the UK, and the US. In 2008 Hess reported proved reserves totaling more than 1.4 billion barrels of oil equivalent. It operates a 50%-owned refinery (HOVENSA) in the US Virgin Islands and a smaller one in New Jersey, and it markets gasoline through about 1,370 HESS gas stations, chiefly in the eastern US. It also provides power to customers in the Northeast and Mid-Atlantic.

On the downstream side, Hess' refinery in the US Virgin Islands is operated as a joint venture with Venezuela's state oil company Petróleos de Venezuela S.A (PDVSA).

Hess' European properties account for more than 30% of its total proved oil and gas reserves. The company is looking to exploit attractive properties in Algeria, Australia, Azerbaijan, and Latin America, as well as Asia (particularly in Malaysia and Thailand) to boost its reserves. In 2007 the company acquired an exploration license covering 780,000 acres in the Carnarvon basin offshore Western Australia.

Although exploration and production is the engine of growth for Hess, the company also seeks opportunities on the refining and marketing side of the business. In late 2008 Hess expanded its electricity marketing business in its core US retail market, acquiring power assets in the northeastern US from RRI Energy.

HISTORY

In 1919 British oil entrepreneur Lord Cowdray formed Amerada Corporation to explore for oil in North America. Cowdray soon hired geophysicist Everette DeGolyer, a pioneer in oil geology research. DeGolyer's systematic methods helped Amerada not only find oil deposits faster but also pick up fields missed by competitors. DeGolyer became president of Amerada in 1929 but left in 1932 to work independently.

After WWII Amerada began exploring overseas and during the 1950s entered pipelining and refining. It continued its overseas exploration through Oasis, a consortium formed in 1964 with Marathon, Shell, and Continental to explore in Libya.

Leon Hess began to buy stock in Amerada in 1966. The son of immigrants, he had entered the oil business during the Depression, selling "resid" — thick refining leftovers that refineries discarded — from a 1929 Dodge truck in New Jersey. He bought the resid cheap and sold it as heating fuel to hotels. Hess also speculated, buying oil at low prices in the summer and selling it for a profit in the winter. He later bought more trucks, a transportation network, refineries, and gas stations and went into oil exploration. Expansion pushed up debt, so in 1962 Leon's company went public as Hess Oil and Chemical after merging with Cletrac Corporation.

Hess acquired Amerada in 1969, after an ownership battle with Phillips Petroleum. During the Arab oil embargo of the 1970s, Amerada Hess began drilling on Alaska's North Slope. Oilman T. Boone Pickens bought up a chunk of Amerada Hess stock during the 1980s, spurring takeover rumors. They proved premature.

Amerada Hess completed a pipeline in 1993 to carry natural gas from the North Sea to the UK. In 1995 Leon Hess stepped down as CEO (he died in 1999), and his son John took the position. Amerada Hess sold its 81% interest in the Northstar oil field in Alaska to BP, and the next year Petro-Canada bought the company's Canadian operations. In 1996 the company acquired a 25% stake (sold in 2002) in UK-based Premier Oil.

The company teamed with Dixons Stores Group in 1997 to market gas in the UK. It also purchased 66 Pick Wick convenience store/service stations.

In 1998 Amerada Hess signed production-sharing contracts with a Malaysian oil firm as part of its strategy to move into Southeast Asia and began to sell natural gas to retail customers in the UK.

To offset losses brought on by depressed oil prices, Amerada Hess sold assets worth more than $300 million in 1999, including its southeastern pipeline network, gas stations in Georgia and South Carolina, and Gulf Coast terminals. It also moved into Latin America, acquiring stakes in fields in offshore Brazil.

In 2000 Amerada Hess acquired Statoil Energy Services, which markets natural gas and electricity to industrial and commercial customers in the northeastern US. It also announced its intention to buy LASMO, a UK-based exploration and production company, before Italy's Eni topped the Amerada Hess offer.

Undeterred, in 2001 the company bought Dallas-based exploration and production company Triton Energy for $2.7 billion in cash and $500 million in assumed debt. Amerada Hess also acquired the Gulf of Mexico assets of LLOG Exploration Company for $750 million. That year, however, stiff competition prompted Amerada Hess to put its UK gas and electricity supply business on the auction block. The unit was sold to TXU (now Energy Future Holdings) in 2002.

In 2003 Amerada Hess sold 26 oil and gas fields in the Gulf of Mexico to Anadarko Petroleum. Amerada Hess was granted permission by the

Equatorial Guinea government in 2004 to develop 29 new wells in that country. That year Amerada Hess acquired a 65% stake in Trabant Holdings International, a Russia-based production and exploration company.

The company re-entered its former oil and gas production operations in the Waha concessions in Libya in 2006. Also that year it changed its name to Hess Corporation.

EXECUTIVES

Chairman, CEO and Director: John B. Hess, age 54, $21,152,340 total compensation
SVP and CFO: John P. Rielly, age 46, $4,171,053 total compensation
VP and CIO: Jeff L. Steinhorn
VP and Chief Risk Officer: J. C. Stein
EVP and Director; President, Marketing and Refining: F. Borden Walker, age 55, $6,273,697 total compensation
EVP, General Counsel, and Director: J. Barclay Collins II, age 64, $5,947,557 total compensation
SVP Global E&P Services: George F. Sandison, age 52
EVP and Director; President, Worldwide Exploration and Production: Gregory P. Hill, age 47
SVP Refining and Marketing Supply and Financial Controls: Lawrence H. Ornstein, age 57
SVP Energy Marketing: John A. Gartman, age 61
SVP Human Resources: Brian J. Bohling, age 48
SVP Global New Business Development: Howard Paver, age 58
SVP Finance and Corporate Development: John J. Scelfo, age 51
SVP Global Exploration and New Ventures: William (Bill) Drennen, age 58
SVP Global Production: Michael R. Turner, age 49
SVP Global Developments: Gary Boubel, age 54
VP, Secretary, and Deputy General Counsel: George C. Barry
VP Investor Relations: Jay R. Wilson
VP and Treasurer: Sachin J. Mehra, age 38
VP Corporate Communications: Jon L. Pepper
VP and General Counsel: Timothy B. Goodell, age 51
Auditors: Ernst & Young LLP

LOCATIONS

HQ: Hess Corporation
    1185 Avenue of the Americas, New York, NY 10036
Phone: 212-997-8500   **Fax:** 212-536-8593
Web: www.hess.com

2008 Sales

	$ mil.	% of total
US	33,233	81
Europe	3,488	8
Africa	3,173	8
Asia & other regions	1,271	3
Total	**41,165**	**100**

PRODUCTS/OPERATIONS

2008 Sales

	$ mil.	% of total
Marketing and Refining	31,304	76
Exploration and Production	9,858	24
Other	3	—
Total	**41,165**	**100**

2008 Sales

	$ mil.	% of total
Refined petroleum products	19,765	48
Natural gas	8,800	21
Crude oil & natural gas liquids	7,764	19
Electricity	2,926	7
Convenience stores & other	1,910	5
Total	**41,165**	**100**

COMPETITORS

BP
CAMAC International
Chevron
Chevron Products Company
CMA CGM
ConocoPhillips
Constellation Energy Group
Continental Energy
Desire Petroleum
Devon Energy
Dominion Resources
Eni
Eni Lasmo
ERHC
Exxon
Getty Petroleum Marketing
Gulf Oil
Koch Industries, Inc.
Marathon Oil
Marathon Petroleum
Norsk Hydro ASA
Occidental Petroleum
PEMEX
PETROBRAS
Petróleos de Venezuela
Royal Dutch Shell
Serica Energy
Sinclair Oil
Sunoco
TOTAL
United Refining

HISTORICAL FINANCIALS

Company Type: Public

Income Statement

FYE: December 31

	REVENUE ($ mil.)	NET INCOME ($ mil.)	NET PROFIT MARGIN	EMPLOYEES
12/08	41,165.0	2,360.0	5.7%	13,500
12/07	31,924.0	1,832.0	5.7%	13,300
12/06	28,720.0	1,916.0	6.7%	13,700
12/05	22,747.0	1,242.0	5.5%	11,610
12/04	16,733.0	977.0	5.8%	11,119
Annual Growth	25.2%	24.7%	—	5.0%

2008 Year-End Financials

Debt ratio: 31.0%
Return on equity: 21.4%
Cash ($ mil.): 908
Current ratio: 0.95
Long-term debt ($ mil.): 3,812

No. of shares (mil.): 327
Dividends
Yield: 0.7%
Payout: 5.5%
Market value ($ mil.): 17,543

Stock History

NYSE: HES

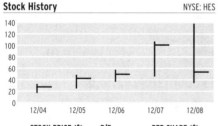

	STOCK PRICE ($) FY Close	P/E High	P/E Low	PER SHARE ($) Earnings	Dividends	Book Value
12/08	53.64	19	5	7.24	0.40	37.63
12/07	100.86	18	8	5.74	0.40	29.89
12/06	49.57	9	6	6.07	0.69	24.80
12/05	42.27	12	7	3.98	0.40	19.22
12/04	27.46	10	6	3.19	0.40	17.11
Annual Growth	18.2%	—	—	22.7%	0.0%	21.8%

Hewitt Associates

If any of a company's resources are human, chances are it'll need the assistance of Hewitt Associates. As one of the primary leaders in its industry, the company provides a variety of HR related services including payroll, organizational change management, talent and reward consulting, and the largest portion of the company's business — benefits outsourcing. Hewitt Associates administers medical, 401(k), and pension plans on an outsourced basis for mainly larger companies with complex benefit programs. The company also provides consulting for the design, implementation, and operation of many of the same human resources programs. Hewitt Associates was founded by Ted Hewitt in 1940 and has 110 offices worldwide.

Hewitt's outsourcing services account for about 50% of its total revenue. The company has expanded its operations internationally through a number of acquisitions over the years. In 2008, international revenue represented about 25% of the company's overall sales — a percentage that has steadily been growing over the past few years. During that year, Hewitt stayed focused on international acquisitions when it bought New Bridge Street Consultants (specialist compensation consultancy in the UK) and CSi - The Remuneration Specialists (a provider of data, analytics, and compensation consulting in Australia and New Zealand). In July 2009 Hewitt took its stake in Germany-based BodeHewitt to full ownership. The acquisition beefs up Hewitt's offerings in pension administration and investment consulting in Germany, which it considers a key market.

In late 2007, Hewitt looked toward the mid-sized health and welfare benefits market when it acquired RealLife HR. A few months later, Hewitt announced it was divesting its Cyborg operations (licensed HR and payroll software services) in order to streamline its HR outsourcing offerings. (Cyborg's software was not core to Hewitt's central outsourcing strategy.)

While the company does look to acquisitions for potential growth, it largely depends on its strong client retention rate, which in any given year typically exceeds 95%.

HISTORY

Edwin "Ted" Hewitt founded Hewitt Associates in 1940 to offer personal estate property and financial services. In the 1950s it became one of the first to measure defined-plan investment performance and offer personalized benefit statements. Hewitt also worked for the government, designing forms for the Welfare and Pension Plans Disclosure Act and serving on the Federal Interagency Task Force from 1964 to 1968.

Hewitt Associates developed the first flexible benefit plans and the Benefit Index (for measuring the competitive value between benefit plans) in the 1970s. It also established its investment consultancy, Hewitt Investment Group, in 1974. The company developed computerized employee benefit program systems and benefits software packages in the 1980s for integrated compensation management, defined contribution administration, pension management, and retirement plan simulation. Hewitt Technologies, its information technology division, became part of the firm in 1988.

In 1992 it created the Defined Contribution Alliance to bundle communication, investment management, record keeping, and trustee services for 401(k) plans. The company's new benefits management center opened near Orlando, Florida, in 1997. The following year Hewitt Associates teamed with online investment adviser Financial Engines to offer its clients Internet-based investment advice. In 2000 the company arranged with investment consulting firm James P. Marshall to establish a new Hewitt venture in Canada. Later that year, the company announced a merger with UK consulting firm Bacon & Woodrow.

After nearly 60 years as a privately held company, the company registered to trade on the New York Stock Exchange in 2002. Hewitt Associates bought HR management software and payroll services provider Cyborg Worldwide in 2003. In 2004 Hewitt Associates acquired Exult, a human resources and consulting firm.

EXECUTIVES

Chairman and CEO: Russell P. (Russ) Fradin, age 53
CFO: John J. Park, age 47
CIO: Bradley A. Anderson, age 47
Global Chief, Consulting Operations: Monica M. Burmeister, age 55
Chief Diversity Officer: Andrés Tapia
SVP Corporate Development and Strategy: Matthew C. (Matt) Levin, age 35
SVP Global Business Services and Technology: Kristi A. Savacool, age 49
SVP, General Counsel, and Corporate Secretary: Steven J. Kyono, age 47
SVP Human Resources: Tracy Keogh, age 47
HR Consulting, Sales, and Client Management Leader: Michael R. Lee
HR Consulting, Global Talent and Organization Practice Leader: John L. Anderson
President, HR Outsourcing: Jay C. Rising, age 52
President, Client and Market Leadership: Julie S. Gordon, age 51
Global Corporate Relations Leader: Julie Macdonald
Global Marketing Leader: Jeff McKay
Investor Relations Leader: Sean McHugh
Auditors: Ernst & Young LLP

LOCATIONS

HQ: Hewitt Associates, Inc.
100 Half Day Rd., Lincolnshire, IL 60069
Phone: 847-295-5000 **Fax:** 847-295-7634
Web: www.hewittassociates.com

2008 Sales

	$ mil.	% of total
US	2,398.3	74
UK	389.1	12
Other countries	440.2	14
Total	3,227.6	100

PRODUCTS/OPERATIONS

2008 Sales

	% of total
Benefits outsourcing	49
Consulting	34
HR business process outsourcing	17
Total	100

Selected Products and Services

Health care
HR, payroll, and benefits outsourcing
Retirement and financial management
Talent and organizational change

COMPETITORS

Accenture	GatesMcDonald
Administaff	Marsh & McLennan
ADP	Mercer
Affiliated Computer	Right Management
BearingPoint	Schloss & Co.
Ceridian	T. Rowe Price
Convergys	Towers Perrin
EDS	The Vanguard Group
Envestnet	Watson Wyatt

HISTORICAL FINANCIALS

Company Type: Public

Income Statement

FYE: September 30

	REVENUE ($ mil.)	NET INCOME ($ mil.)	NET PROFIT MARGIN	EMPLOYEES
9/08	3,227.6	188.1	5.8%	23,000
9/07	2,990.3	(175.1)	—	23,000
9/06	2,857.2	(115.9)	—	24,000
9/05	2,898.4	134.7	4.6%	22,000
9/04	2,262.2	122.8	5.4%	17,000
Annual Growth	9.3%	11.2%	—	7.8%

2008 Year-End Financials

Debt ratio: 100.0%
Return on equity: 22.3%
Cash ($ mil.): 541
Current ratio: 1.37
Long-term debt ($ mil.): 650

No. of shares (mil.): 93
Dividends
  Yield: 0.0%
  Payout: —
Market value ($ mil.): 3,391

Stock History

NYSE: HEW

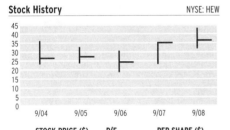

	STOCK PRICE ($) FY Close	P/E High/Low		PER SHARE ($) Earnings	Dividends	Book Value
9/08	36.44	23	17	1.85	0.00	6.99
9/07	35.05	—	—	(1.62)	0.00	11.15
9/06	24.26	—	—	(1.08)	0.00	13.50
9/05	27.28	27	20	1.19	0.00	14.09
9/04	26.46	29	19	1.25	0.00	9.23
Annual Growth	8.3%	—	—	10.3%	—	(6.7%)

Hewlett-Packard

HP wants to be "it" when it comes to IT. Hewlett-Packard provides one of the tech world's most comprehensive portfolios of hardware, software, and services. Its products include personal computers, servers, storage devices, printers, and networking equipment. The company's service unit provides IT and business process outsourcing, application development and management, consulting, systems integration, and other technology services. HP's software products include enterprise IT management, information management, business intelligence, and carrier-grade communications applications. The company markets to consumers, businesses, government agencies, and schools in more than 170 countries.

HP, which already boasted an IT service organization that was among the world's largest, acquired Electronic Data Systems (EDS) for about $13.9 billion in cash in 2008. HP expects the EDS purchase to more than double its revenue from services. It plans to use the EDS brand for the combined services business. HP's services business scored a major contract in 2009 when the company formed a 10-year alliance with telecom equipment maker Alcatel-Lucent.

HP's software offerings include a collection of IT management tools it markets as the HP Business Technology Optimization (BTO) suite (formerly OpenView). Its BTO applications include tools for automating tasks associated with data center and client computer management. HP gave its BTO portfolio a boost when it purchased Opsware, a developer of data center automation software, for approximately $1.6 billion in 2007. Other major software groups include network services (OpenCall), as well as information management and business intelligence. Communications service providers use its OpenCall platform to deploy voice, data, and video services.

HP's Personal Systems Group (PSG) markets desktop and notebook PCs to consumer, businesses, government agencies, and schools. PSG, which jockeys with Dell for PC supremacy, sells both HP and Compaq-branded products. In addition to traditional PCs, PSG provides handheld computers, calculators, televisions, and digital media centers. HP's Voodoo unit provides systems used for gaming and other high-performance applications.

Imaging and Printing Group (IPG) provides inkjet, laser, and large-format printers. Its comprehensive line also includes copiers, digital presses, scanners, multifunction devices, software, and supplies. IPG also oversees HP's digital photo printers and online photo services.

HISTORY

Encouraged by professor Frederick Terman (considered the founder of Silicon Valley), in 1938 Stanford engineers Bill Hewlett and David Packard started Hewlett-Packard (HP) in a garage in Palo Alto, California, with $538. Hewlett was the idea man, while Packard served as manager; the two were so low-key that the company's first official meeting ended with no decision on exactly what to manufacture. Finding good people took priority over finding something to sell. The first product ended up being an audio oscillator. Walt Disney Studios, one of HP's first customers, bought eight to use in the making of *Fantasia*.

Demand for HP's electronic testing equipment during WWII spurred sales growth from $34,000 in 1940 to nearly $1 million just three years later. HP went public in 1957. The company expanded beyond the US during 1959, establishing a marketing organization in Switzerland and a manufacturing plant in West Germany. HP entered the medical field in 1961 by acquiring Sanborn, and the analytical instrumentation business in 1965 with the purchase of F&M Scientific. Chairman Packard in 1969 began serving two years as deputy defense secretary.

In 1972 the company pioneered personal computing with the world's first handheld scientific calculator. Under the leadership of John Young, the founders' chosen successor (named CEO in 1978), HP introduced its first PCs, the first desktop mainframe, and the LaserJet printer. Its initial PCs were known for their rugged build, tailored for factory operations. They were also

more expensive than rival versions and, consequently, didn't enjoy strong sales.

By 1986 a five-year, $250 million R&D project — the company's largest to date — had produced a family of HP computers based on the reduced instruction set computing (RISC) architecture. Hewlett retired in 1987 (he died in 2001); sons of both Hewlett and Packard were named that year to the company's board of directors. HP became a leader in workstations with the 1989 purchase of market pioneer Apollo Computer.

In 1992 Lewis Platt, an EVP since 1987, was named president and CEO. Packard retired in 1993 (he died in 1996). In 1999 HP formed Agilent Technologies for its test and measurement and other noncomputer operations, and spun off 15% of the company to the public. (HP distributed to its shareholders its remaining 85% in mid-2000.) Also in 1999 Platt retired and HP — one of the first major US corporations to be headed by a woman — appointed Lucent executive Carly Fiorina president and CEO. She was named chairman the following year.

In 2001 HP agreed to pay $400 million to Pitney Bowes to settle a 1995 patent-infringement case related to printer technology. HP said in mid-2002 that it was cutting about 6,000 jobs.

Next came the announcement of a blockbuster deal: HP agreed to buy rival Compaq in a stock transaction initially valued at about $25 billion. The highly contentious deal eventually met with shareholder approval in early 2002. At the time of closing, the deal was valued at approximately $19 billion. Integration efforts included a workforce reduction of roughly 10%, as the company eliminated redundant product groups. Fiorina soon had to address the clash of disparate corporate cultures and subsequent morale problems.

Fiorina's differences with HP's board over strategic direction finally came to a head early in 2005, and she stepped down. CFO Robert Wayman was named interim CEO, and director Patricia Dunn took over as non-executive chairman. Mark Hurd, formerly CEO of NCR, was soon named to lead HP.

HP's leadership experienced another shakeup the following year, this time prompted by negative attention related to tactics used in an investigation of boardroom leaks. The company's board came under fire after it was revealed that third-party investigators employed by the company impersonated board members and journalists to obtain their phone records.

Dunn was asked to resign from the board in September 2006, and Hurd replaced her as chairman. HP settled a related dispute with the California Attorney General later that year, agreeing to pay $14.5 million.

EXECUTIVES

Chairman, President, and CEO: Mark V. Hurd, age 52
EVP and CFO: Catherine A. (Cathie) Lesjak, age 48
EVP and CIO: Randall D. (Randy) Mott, age 52
EVP and Chief Strategy and Technology Officer:
Shane V. Robison, age 55
SVP and Chief Marketing Officer: Michael Mendenhall, age 47
EVP and Chief Administrative Officer:
Peter J. (Pete) Bocian, age 54
Chief Learning Officer: Sam Szteinbaum
SVP and Chief Sales Officer:
Donald C. (Don) Grantham, age 51

EVP Enterprise Servers, Storage, and Networking:
David A. Donatelli, age 43
EVP Technology Solutions Group: Ann M. Livermore, age 50
EVP Imaging and Printing Group: Vyomesh (V.J.) Joshi, age 55
EVP Personal Systems Group: R. Todd Bradley, age 50
EVP Human Resources: Marcela Perez de Alonso
EVP, General Counsel, and Secretary:
Michael J. Holston, age 47
SVP Strategy and Corporate Development:
Brian Humphries
SVP and Treasurer: John McMullen, age 50
SVP, Controller, and Principal Accounting Officer:
Jim Murrin, age 48
VP, Assistant Secretary, and Acting General Counsel:
Charles N. Charnas, age 47
VP Human Resources: Mike Paolucci, age 48
Auditors: Ernst & Young LLP

LOCATIONS

HQ: Hewlett-Packard Company
3000 Hanover St., Palo Alto, CA 94304
Phone: 650-857-1501   **Fax:** 650-857-5518
Web: www.hp.com

2008 Sales

	$ mil.	% of total
US	36,932	31
Other countries	81,432	69
Total	**118,364**	**100**

PRODUCTS/OPERATIONS

2008 Sales

	$ mil.	% of total
Products	91,697	78
Services	26,297	22
Financing	370	—
Total	**118,364**	**100**

2008 Sales

	$ mil.	% of total
Technology Solutions Group		
HP Services	22,397	19
Enterprise storage & servers	19,400	16
Software	3,029	3
Personal Systems Group	42,295	35
Imaging & Printing	29,385	24
HP Financial Services	2,698	2
Investments	965	1
Adjustments	(1,805)	—
Total	**118,364**	**100**

Selected Products and Services

Enterprise Systems
  Business technology optimization software
  Networking equipment
  Servers (Linux, Unix, Windows)
    Blade
    Carrier-grade
    Rack-optimized
    Server appliances
    Super-scalable
    Tower
  Storage
    Disks and disk arrays
    Network-attached storage (NAS) devices
    Optical disk drives
    Storage area network (SAN) systems
    Tape drives and libraries
Services
  Consulting
  Design and installation
  Education
  Financing
  Outsourcing
  Printing
  Support and maintenance
  Web hosting

Personal Systems
  Calculators
  Desktop PCs
  Digital entertainment centers
  DVD writers
  Handheld computers
  Notebook computers
  Televisions (LCD, plasma)
  Workstations
Imaging and Printing
  Commercial printing
    Digital presses
    Printers
  Digital imaging
    Projectors
    Scanners
  Personal printing
    All-in-ones (copier, fax, printer, scanner)
    Ink jet printers
    Laser printers
  Shared printing
    Networked inkjet, laser, and multifunction printers
    Office all-in-ones
    Services
  Supplies

COMPETITORS

3Com
Accenture
Acer
ADP
Affiliated Computer Services
Apple Inc.
ASUSTeK
BearingPoint
BMC Software
CA, Inc.
CACI International
Canon
Capgemini
CGI Group
Cisco Systems
Computer Sciences Corp.
Convergys
Dell
Eastman Kodak
EMC
Epson
First Data
Fiserv
Fuji Xerox
Fujitsu
Fujitsu Technology Solutions
Gateway, Inc.
Heidelberger Druckmaschinen
Hewitt Associates
Hitachi
IBM
InfoPrint
Infosys
Konica Minolta
Lenovo
Lexmark
Microsoft
NCR
NEC
NetApp
Océ
Palm, Inc.
Panasonic Corp
Perot Systems
Ricoh Company
Samsung Electronics
Sharp Corp.
Siemens AG
Sony
Sun Microsystems
Symantec
Tata Consultancy
Teradata
Toshiba
Unisys
Wipro Technologies
Xerox

HISTORICAL FINANCIALS

Company Type: Public

Income Statement

FYE: October 31

	REVENUE ($ mil.)	NET INCOME ($ mil.)	NET PROFIT MARGIN	EMPLOYEES
10/08	118,364.0	8,329.0	7.0%	321,000
10/07	104,286.0	7,264.0	7.0%	172,000
10/06	91,658.0	6,198.0	6.8%	156,000
10/05	86,696.0	2,398.0	2.8%	150,000
10/04	79,905.0	3,497.0	4.4%	151,000
Annual Growth	**10.3%**	**24.2%**	**—**	**20.7%**

2008 Year-End Financials

Debt ratio: 19.7%
Return on equity: 21.5%
Cash ($ mil.): 10,153
Current ratio: 0.98
Long-term debt ($ mil.): 7,676

No. of shares (mil.): 2,386
Dividends
  Yield: 0.8%
  Payout: 9.8%
Market value ($ mil.): 91,346

Stock History

NYSE: HPQ

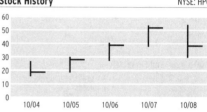

	STOCK PRICE ($) FY Close	P/E High/Low		PER SHARE ($) Earnings	Dividends	Book Value
10/08	38.28	16	9	3.25	0.32	16.32
10/07	51.68	20	14	2.68	0.32	16.14
10/06	38.74	18	13	2.18	0.32	15.98
10/05	28.04	36	23	0.82	0.32	15.58
10/04	18.66	23	14	1.15	0.32	15.74
Annual Growth	**19.7%**	**—**	**—**	**29.7%**	**0.0%**	**0.9%**

Highmark Inc.

Highmark has staked its claim as the largest health insurer in the Keystone state. A licensee of the Blue Cross and Blue Shield Association, the not-for-profit firm covers some 4 million people in central and western Pennsylvania, as well as the Lehigh Valley. It serves another 800,000 customers in West Virginia and other areas of Pennsylvania through affiliations and partnerships with other insurers, and it provides administrative and network-access services nationally. In addition, Highmark sells Medicare Advantage and prescription drug plans to seniors in both states. Other subsidiaries (not operating under the BCBS license) provide dental insurance, vision care, and other products and services nationwide.

Outside of its core Pennsylvania service areas (served through wholly owned subsidiaries Highmark Blue Cross Blue Shield, Keystone Health Plan West, and Highmark Blue Shield), the company manages the benefits of self-insured employers and provides third-party administrative and claims processing services to other BCBS plans.

After nearly two years of planning, Highmark and its Philadelphia-based neighbor Independence Blue Cross cancelled their plans to merge in early 2009, citing concerns that the deal would not receive regulatory approval. The merger would have created a massive health insurer covering more than half of Pennsylvania's population and was the subject of harsh criticism from Pennsylvania politicians, regulators, and other parties concerned that such a mega-company would stifle competition.

Despite the canceled merger plans, Highmark continues to co-market Blue-branded coverage in southeastern Pennsylvania with Independence Blue Cross under a previous collaboration agreement. The company operates similarly in the northeastern part of the state through a partnership with Blue Cross of Northeastern Pennsylvania. It works through affiliate Mountain State Blue Cross Blue Shield (in which it owns a controlling stake) to offer health plans in West Virginia.

Highmark plans to expand its health insurance operations by strengthening partnerships with other insurance companies and by increasing involvement in government health programs such as Medicare. It is also increasing its health plan offerings for individual consumers. The company is experiencing strong growth in its dental and vision care businesses, as well.

Highmark provides an impressive array of specialty services through its non-Blue subsidiaries. In the optical arena, subsidiaries include managed vision care organization Davis Vision, the Eye Care Centers of America chain of retail vision care centers, and eyewear manufacturer Viva. HM Insurance Group offers employer health risk solutions, such as stop-loss insurance and a limited benefit medical plan, while United Concordia Companies provides dental coverage to around 8 million members across the US.

HISTORY

Highmark was created from the merger of Blue Cross of Western Pennsylvania (founded in 1937) and Pennsylvania Blue Shield, created in 1964 when the Medical Service Association of Pennsylvania (MSAP) adopted the Blue Shield name.

The Pennsylvania Medical Society, in conjunction with the state of Pennsylvania, had formed MSAP to provide medical insurance to the poor and indigent. MSAP borrowed $25,000 from the Pennsylvania Medical Society to help set up its operations, and Chauncey Palmer (who had originally proposed the organization) was named president. Individuals paid 35 cents per month, and families paid $1.75 each month to join MSAP, which initially covered mainly obstetrical and surgical procedures.

In 1945 Arthur Daugherty replaced Palmer as president (he served until his death in 1968) and helped MSAP recruit major new accounts, including the United Mine Workers and the Congress of Industrial Organizations. MSAP in 1946 became a chapter of the national Blue Shield association, which was started that year by the medical societies of several states to provide prepaid health insurance plans.

In 1951 MSAP signed up the 150,000 employees of United States Steel, bringing its total enrollment to more than 1.6 million. Growth did not lead to prosperity, though, as the organization had trouble keeping up with payments to its doctors. This shortfall in funds led MSAP to raise its premiums in 1961, at which point the state

reminded the association of its social mission and suggested it concentrate on controlling costs instead of raising rates.

MSAP changed its name to Pennsylvania Blue Shield in 1964. Two years later the association began managing the state's Medicare plan and started the 65-Special plan to supplement Medicare coverage. In the 1970s Pennsylvania Blue Shield again could not keep up with the cost of paying its doctors, which led to more rate increases and closer scrutiny of its expenses. Competition increased in the 1980s as HMOs cropped up around the state. Pennsylvania Blue Shield fought back by creating its own HMO plans — some of which it owned jointly with Blue Cross of Western Pennsylvania — in the 1980s.

After years of slowly collecting noninsurance businesses, Blue Cross of Western Pennsylvania changed its name to Veritus in 1991 to reflect the growing importance of its for-profit operations.

In 1996 Pennsylvania Blue Shield overcame physicians' protests and state regulators' concerns to merge with Veritus. The company adopted the name Highmark to represent its standards for high quality; it took a loss as it failed to meet cost-cutting goals and suffered early-retirement costs related to the merger consolidation. To gain support for the merger, Highmark sold for-profit subsidiary Keystone Health Plan East to Independence Blue Cross in 1997.

In 1999 Highmark teamed with Mountain State Blue Cross Blue Shield to become West Virginia's primary licensee. Rate hikes and investment returns helped propel the company into the black as the decade closed.

As a result of some belt-tightening in 2004, the company shut down its Alliance Ventures (administrative and information services) and Lifestyle Advantage subsidiaries. Highmark sold its Medmark specialty pharmacy unit to Walgreens in 2006, and its HM Insurance subsidiary sold its life and disability insurance operations to Fort Dearborn Life Insurance. The company also acquired Eye Care Centers of America in 2006.

EXECUTIVES

Chairman: J. Robert Baum
President, CEO, and Director: Kenneth R. (Ken) Melani
EVP, CFO, and Treasurer: Michael J. Kincaid, age 51
SVP and Chief Audit Executive: Elizabeth A. Farbacher
EVP Subsidiary Services: Robert C. Gray
EVP Government Services: David M. O'Brien
EVP Health Services: Deborah Rice
SVP, Corporate Secretary, and General Counsel:
Gary R. Truitt
SVP and Corporate Compliance Officer:
Michael A. Romano
SVP Corporate Development and Investments:
Brett C. Moraski
President and CEO, HVHC, Inc. and Eye Care Centers of America: David L. Holmberg, age 50
President Operations, Mountain State Blue Cross Blue Shield: J. Fred Earley II
Chairman and CEO, HM Insurance Group and United Concordia: Daniel J. (Dan) Lebish
CIO, HVHC Inc. and Davis Vision: Michael L. Thibdeau
Auditors: PricewaterhouseCoopers LLP

LOCATIONS

HQ: Highmark Inc.
Fifth Avenue Place, 120 5th Ave.
Pittsburgh, PA 15222
Phone: 412-544-7000   **Fax:** 412-544-8368
Web: www.highmark.com/hmk2

PRODUCTS/OPERATIONS

2008 Revenue

	$ mil.	% of total
Premiums	11,020	84
Vision revenue	1,077	8
Management services	626	5
Net investment income	160	1
Net realized gain (loss) on investments	(79)	—
Other	198	2
Total	**13,002**	**100**

Selected Subsidiaries and Affiliates

Blue Cross Blue Shield Licensee Companies
Highmark Blue Cross Blue Shield (health care plans, western Pennsylvania)
Highmark Blue Shield (health care plans, central Pennsylvania and the Lehigh Valley; also operates through partnerships in northeastern and southeastern Pennsylvania)
Highmark Health Insurance Company (Medicare Advantage plans, West Virginia)
Highmark Senior Resources, Inc. (Medicare Part D prescription drug plans, Pennsylvania and West Virginia)
Keystone Health Plan West, Inc. (HMO and Medicare Advantage plans, western Pennsylvania)
Mountain State Blue Cross & Blue Shield (controlled affiliate; health care plans, West Virginia)
Other Subsidiaries
Davis Vision, Inc. (vision insurance and ophthalmic laboratories)
Eye Care Centers of America, Inc. (retail vision care)
Gateway Health Plan (Medical Assistance coverage)
Highmark Medicare Services, Inc. (Medicare claims administration and financial management)
HM Insurance Group (stop loss insurance, HMO reinsurance, and other health risk solutions)
Industrial Medical Consultants (physician workforce productivity services)
United Concordia Companies, Inc. (dental insurance)

COMPETITORS

Aetna	Geisinger Health System
American United Mutual	Genworth Financial
AmeriChoice	HealthAmerica
Blue Cross of Northeastern	Humana
Pennsylvania	Independence Blue Cross
Capital BlueCross	Independence Holding
CIGNA	LensCrafters
DeCare	National Vision
Delta Dental Plans	Pearle Vision
Dental Benefit Providers	UPMC
DentaQuest	U.S. Vision
Emerging Vision	Wal-Mart

HISTORICAL FINANCIALS

Company Type: Not-for-profit

Income Statement				FYE: December 31
	REVENUE ($ mil.)	NET INCOME ($ mil.)	NET PROFIT MARGIN	EMPLOYEES
12/08	13,002.0	94.1	0.7%	19,000
12/07	12,352.6	375.4	3.0%	18,500
12/06	11,083.8	398.3	3.6%	18,500
12/05	9,847.3	341.6	3.5%	12,000
12/04	9,118.4	310.5	3.4%	11,000
Annual Growth	**9.3%**	**(25.8%)**	**—**	**14.6%**

Net Income History

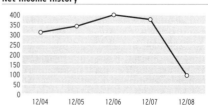

Hill-Rom Holdings

No longer torn between the quick and the dead, Hill-Rom Holdings (formerly Hillenbrand Industries) has cast its lot with the living. In 2008 the holding company spun off its funeral services business Batesville Casket into a separate entity owned by newly created holding company Hillenbrand. That separation left Hill-Rom Holdings focused on its other operating unit, Hill-Rom, which makes, sells, and rents hospital beds and other patient-room furniture and equipment, along with stretchers, surgical table accessories, health care software, and non-invasive equipment for pulmonary and circulatory conditions and wounds. Its customers are acute and long-term care facilities around the world.

In 2007 Hillenbrand announced plans to split its two operating units into separate publicly traded companies, in order to increase value for shareholders and tighten industry focus for each unit. The following year the company spun off Batesville Casket (the leading casket maker in the US) into a new public company; Hill-Rom then became the sole operating unit of what was renamed as Hill-Rom Holdings. To make things a little more confusing, Batesville changed its name to Hillenbrand, with Batesville Casket Company as its operating subsidiary.

Hill-Rom had been considering strategic alternatives for the company since 2006. It had also announced several other strategic initiatives that year, including improving its sales force effectiveness and focusing on product solutions that reduce the side effects of long hospital stays, such as bed sores and infections; it has an ongoing collaboration with Ascension Health to address these issues. Additionally, Hill-Rom kick-started its rental business by cutting costs, improving efficiency, and investing in its out-of-date truck fleet, initiatives that paid off in the form of double-digit growth in that business in fiscal year 2008.

The company also sees room for growth in the post-acute care market (long-term care facilities and home care) and in some international markets. It has been expanding the post-acute care business via new product launches, distribution agreements, and acquisitions. For instance, it acquired Swedish firm Liko, which makes slings and other devices used to move patients from one surface to another, in 2008. And it expanded into Australia with the 2006 acquisition of Medicraft, a maker of hospital beds.

Rolf Classon was the first leader of the company outside the Hillenbrand family when he took on the role of chairman in 2006. At the same time, Peter Soderberg was appointed CEO.

HISTORY

In 1906 John A. Hillenbrand, a banker, newspaperman, and general store owner in Batesville, Indiana, bought the ailing Batesville Casket Company (founded 1884) to save it from bankruptcy. Under Hillenbrand, and later his four sons (John W., who succeeded his father as president of the company; William; George; and Daniel), the casket company flourished.

In 1929 William Hillenbrand established the Hill-Rom Company in Batesville to make hospital furniture. Hill-Rom made its furniture out of wood instead of tubular steel and quickly became a leader in innovative hospital furnishings.

During the following decades George Hillenbrand created several patented products for both Batesville Casket and Hill-Rom. By the 1940s, for example, the company had developed corrosion-, air-, and water-resistant metal caskets. George constantly sought ways to improve manufacturing techniques and product quality, giving the company a competitive edge in sales and productivity.

Daniel, the youngest son, became president of Batesville Casket in 1964 and consolidated Batesville Casket and Hill-Rom into Hillenbrand Industries five years later. Hoping to make the company more competitive nationally (and eventually globally), Daniel took Hillenbrand public in 1971.

The company acquired Dominion Metalware Industries (1972) and luggage maker American Tourister (1978; sold to Astrum International, maker of Samsonite luggage, in 1993). In 1984 it bought Medeco Security Locks (sold 1998) and a year later purchased Support Systems International (SSI), provider of specialty rental mattresses for critically ill and immobile patients. (In 1994 SSI was integrated into Hill-Rom.)

Hillenbrand founded the Forethought Group in 1985 to provide special life insurance to cover prearranged funerals. In 1991 it entered the European market by acquiring Le Couviour, a French maker of hospital beds. The company also bought Block Medical, a maker of home infusion-therapy products, that year. August Hillenbrand, nephew of Daniel, became CEO in 1989.

In 1992 Batesville Casket set out to consolidate its market, buying casket producer Cormier & Gaudet (Canada). It then bought Bridge Casket (New Jersey), Lincoln Casket (Hamtramck, Michigan); and Industrias Arga (Mexico City), all in 1993. That year Hillenbrand also purchased L & C Arnold, one of the biggest and oldest hospital furniture makers in Germany.

With the casket market flat in the mid-1990s, Hillenbrand grew its business by going after market share in cremation products.

As the 20th century drew to a close, Medicare reimbursement cutbacks bit into Hill-Rom's sales. The company cut jobs in both 2000 and 2001. Those years also brought the retirement of both August and Daniel Hillenbrand. Frederick Rockwood became president and CEO in 2000; Ray Hillenbrand (nephew of Daniel) was named chairman in 2001.

Hillenbrand sold its piped medical gas unit (to Beacon Medical Products in late 2003) and the Air-Shields infant care products business of Hill-Rom, since those operations were not key to Hill-Rom's success. It acquired Advanced Respiratory, a maker of airway management equipment, in 2003 and MEDIQ, a company that provides medical equipment outsourcing, asset management, and rentals to the health care industry, in 2004.

To focus on Hill-Rom and Batesville, Hillenbrand sold its Forethought Financial Services subsidiary in July 2004. As its name suggests, Forethought offered funeral prepayment products and services.

Rockwood retired in 2005; Peter Soderberg replaced him the following year.

In 2008, following a review of strategic alternatives, the company split itself in two, spinning off Batesville Casket into a separately, publicly traded company.

EXECUTIVES

Chairman: Rolf A. Classon, age 63
Vice Chairperson: Joanne C. Smith, age 48
President, CEO, and Director; President and CEO, Hill-Rom: Peter H. Soderberg, age 62
SVP and CFO, Hillenbrand Industries and Hill-Rom: Gregory N. Miller, age 45
SVP North America Post-Acute Care and Information Technology, Hill-Rom: Kimberly K. Dennis, age 41
VP, Controller, and Chief Accounting Officer, Hillenbrand Industries and Hill-Rom: Richard G. Keller, age 47
SVP, Chief Administrative Officer, Assistant General Counsel, and Assistant Secretary: Sheri Edison, age 51
SVP, General Counsel, and Secretary: Patrick D. de Maynadier, age 48
SVP Human Resources, Hillenbrand Industries and Hill-Rom: John H. Dickey, age 54
SVP Operations and Product Development: Mark D. Baron, age 57
SVP and CFO, Hillenbrand, Inc.: Cynthia L. (Cindy) Lucchese, age 48
VP and Treasurer: Mark R. Lanning, age 54
VP Investor Relations, Communications, and Global Brand Development, Hillenbrand Industries and Hill-Rom: Blair A. (Andy) Rieth Jr., age 51
VP Business Development and Strategy, Hillenbrand Industries and Hill-Rom: Michael J. Grippo, age 39
President International and Surgical Division: Gregory J. (Greg) Tucholski, age 48
President Acute Care North America: Jeffrey (Jeff) Kao, age 41
Group VP Care Continuum Services: Earl DeCarli, age 53
Auditors: PricewaterhouseCoopers LLP

LOCATIONS

HQ: Hill-Rom Holdings, Inc.
1069 State Rte. 46 East, Batesville, IN 47006
Phone: 812-934-7777   **Fax:** 812-931-3533
Web: www.hillenbrand.com

2008 Sales

	$ mil.	% of total
US	1,180.3	78
Other countries	327.4	22
Total	**1,507.7**	**100**

PRODUCTS/OPERATIONS

2008 Sales

	$ mil.	% of total
North America acute care	934.7	62
International & surgical	381.4	25
North America post-acute care	197.0	13
Adjustments	(5.4)	—
Total	**1,507.7**	**100**

Selected Products and Services

Patient surfaces
  Hospital beds (TotalCare, TotalCare Bariatric)
  Surgical beds (VersaCare, CareAssist, AvantGuard, Evolution156)
  ER and transport beds
  Labor and delivery beds (Affinity)
  Long-term care beds (Resident LTC bed, Gerialit)
Health care information technology
  Clinical communication software (NaviCare)
  Maternal and fetal monitoring software (WatchChild)
Medical equipment management services (equipment rental and asset management)
Therapeutic products
  Pressure redistribution products (Flexicair Eclipse, Silkair Overlay)
  Treatments for pressure sores and burns (Clinitron Rite Hite Air Fluidized Therapy System)
  Wound prevention products (Comfortline, SimpliMatt, Clinisert 2)

HISTORY

Holly was founded in 1947 as General Appliance Corp. to process other companies' crude oil; the current name was adopted in 1952. Holly grew with the number of gas-guzzling cars in the 1950s and 1960s, and in the 1970s it developed its Navajo refinery in New Mexico. In 1981 Holly began producing higher-grade gasoline and started an asphalt company at Navajo.

In 1984 Holly became a partner in Montana Refining and later bought the entire business. It upgraded the Navajo refinery in the early 1990s to meet the demand for unleaded gasoline. In 1995 Amoco, Mapco, and Holly formed a joint venture, the 265-mile Rio Grande Pipeline (completed in 1997), to transport natural gas liquids to Mexico.

Also in 1997, FINA and Holly allied to expand and use Holly's pipelines in the southwestern US. A proposed merger with another southwestern refiner, Giant Industries, died in 1998 because of federal antitrust concerns and a billion-dollar lawsuit filed against Holly by Longhorn Partners Pipeline. Court papers revealed in 2000 that Holly had paid $4 million to fight Longhorn's request for a permit to transport gasoline in its Houston-to-El Paso pipeline. The permit, if approved, would compete with Holly's own interests in western Texas.

Later in 2000 Holly cut its workforce by about 10%, mostly at Navajo Refining. The next year Navajo Refining secured a $122 million contract to provide jet fuel to the Defense Department.

In a move to expand its production capacity, in 2003 Holly acquired ConocoPhillips' Woods Cross refinery and related assets for $25 million. Holly agreed to be acquired by Frontier Oil for about $450 million that year, but the companies terminated the agreement, and litigation between the parties resulted.

In 2004 the company spun off its Navajo refinery-related refined petroleum pipeline and other distribution assets as Holly Energy Partners, L.P., retaining a 45% interest.

In 2005 the Delaware Chancery Court ruled that Frontier Oil had not proved that Holly had repudiated the merger agreement, and awarded Frontier Oil only $1 in damages. Also that year, Holly acquired the remaining 51% of NK Asphalt Producers that it did not already own. The company sold its intermediate feedstock pipelines connecting two refining facilities in Lovington and Artesia, New Mexico to Holly Energy Partners for $81.5 million.

EXECUTIVES

Chairman and CEO: Matthew P. (Matt) Clifton, age 57, $3,541,910 total compensation
President: David L. Lamp, age 51, $1,706,926 total compensation
SVP and CFO: Bruce R. Shaw, age 41, $1,702,208 total compensation
VP Information Technology: Nellson D. Burns
SVP Refinery Operations,, Holly Corporation and Holly Refining and Marketing Company: Gary Fuller
SVP Supply and Marketing, Holly Corporation and Holly Logistic Services: George J. Damiris, age 49, $869,190 total compensation
VP Special Projects, Holly Corporation and Holly Refining & Marketing Company: James G. Townsend, age 54
VP, Controller, and Principal Accounting Officer, Holly Corporation, Holly Refining & Marketing, and Holly Logistic Services: Scott C. Surplus
VP Investor Relations, Holly Corporation and Holly Logistic Services: M. Neale Hickerson, age 56

VP and Treasurer, Holly Corporation, Holly Logistic Services, and Holly Refining & Marketing: Stephen D. Wise
VP Human Resources, Holly Corporation, Holly Refining & Marketing, and Holly Logistic Services: Nancy F. Hartmann
VP Crude Supply, Holly Corporation and Holly Refining & Marketing: Thomas G. Creery
VP, General Counsel, and Secretary, Holly Corporation, Holly Refining & Marketing Company, and Holly Logistic Services: Denise C. McWatters, age 49, $395,865 total compensation
Auditors: Ernst & Young LLP

LOCATIONS

HQ: Holly Corporation
100 Crescent Ct., Ste. 1600, Dallas, TX 75201
Phone: 214-871-3555   **Fax:** 214-871-3560
Web: www.hollycorp.com

PRODUCTS/OPERATIONS

2008 Sales

	$ mil.	% of total
Refining	5,837.5	98
HEP	101.8	2
Adjustments	(71.6)	—
Total	**5,867.7**	**100**

Selected Subsidiaries

Black Eagle, Inc.
Holly Logistics
    Holly Energy Partners, L.P (45%)
Holly Petroleum, Inc.
Navajo Corp.
Navajo Holdings, Inc.
Navajo Pipeline Co.
    Navajo Southern, Inc.
Navajo Refining Co.
    Lorefco, Inc.
        Lea Refining Co.
    Navajo Northern, Inc.
    Navajo Western Asphalt Co.
Woods Cross Refining Co., L.L.C.

COMPETITORS

BP
Crown Central
Exxon
George Warren
Marathon Petroleum
Sunoco
Tesoro
Valero Energy
Western Refining, Inc.
Williams Companies

HISTORICAL FINANCIALS

Company Type: Public

Income Statement

FYE: December 31

	REVENUE ($ mil.)	NET INCOME ($ mil.)	NET PROFIT MARGIN	EMPLOYEES
12/08	5,867.7	120.6	2.1%	978
12/07	4,791.7	334.1	7.0%	909
12/06	4,023.2	266.6	6.6%	859
12/05	3,212.7	167.0	5.2%	881
12/04	2,246.4	83.9	3.7%	845
Annual Growth	**27.1%**	**9.5%**	**—**	**3.7%**

2008 Year-End Financials

Debt ratio: 63.1%
Return on equity: 21.2%
Cash ($ mil.): 41
Current ratio: 1.15
Long-term debt ($ mil.): 342
No. of shares (mil.): 50
Dividends
    Yield: 3.3%
    Payout: 25.2%
Market value ($ mil.): 916

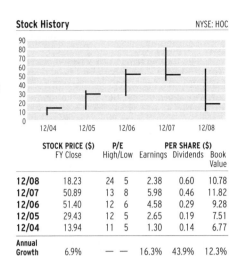

Stock History

NYSE: HOC

	STOCK PRICE ($) FY Close	P/E High/Low		PER SHARE ($) Earnings	Dividends	Book Value
12/08	18.23	24	5	2.38	0.60	10.78
12/07	50.89	13	8	5.98	0.46	11.82
12/06	51.40	12	6	4.58	0.29	9.28
12/05	29.43	12	5	2.65	0.19	7.51
12/04	13.94	11	5	1.30	0.14	6.77
Annual Growth	**6.9%**	—	—	**16.3%**	**43.9%**	**12.3%**

Hologic, Inc.

With its mammography and breast biopsy systems, Hologic puts the squeeze on women to help save their lives. Its mammography products include film-based and digital systems, as well as the workstations and computer-aided detection systems that interpret the images. Additional products include X-ray and ultrasound bone densitometers, which detect and monitor osteoporosis, and breast biopsy collection systems (branded ATEC) sold by its Suros division. With its 2007 merger with women's health firm Cytyc, Hologic gained several other product lines, including tests to screen for cervical cancer. The company markets its products to hospitals, and clinical labs worldwide through distributors and a direct sales force.

Hologic paid more than $6 billion for the larger Cytyc, which, like Hologic, was headquartered in the Boston area. The two companies had been discussing a tie-up off and on since 2004 and create a force to be reckoned with in the women's health sector, with expected annual revenues of $1.7 billion.

Hologic hopes it can take advantage of cross-selling opportunities that arise from combining the two companies' complementary product lines. Cytyc adds products in the areas of cervical cancer screening, prenatal diagnostics, and breast cancer treatment to Hologic's existing portfolio of breast health and osteoporosis products.

Cytyc marketed its ThinPrep cervical cancer screening system as a better alternative to the conventional Pap smear. It also contributed surgical systems to treat excessive menstrual bleeding and radiation therapy products for breast cancer, as well as a preterm birth diagnostic called the FullTerm Fetal Fibronectin Test.

In early 2008 Hologic agreed to sell the marketing rights for Gestiva, an investigational drug for preventing preterm births that it had gained in the Cytyc merger, to K-V Pharmaceutical.

Both Cytyc and Hologic had already been in expansion mode prior to the merger, adding product lines in complementary areas through a number of smaller acquisitions. One such Hologic acquisition in 2007, of California-based

BioLucent, added the MammoPad breast cushion, a pad designed to alleviate the discomfort of getting a mammogram.

In 2008 the company made a move to further expand its diagnostic operations by acquiring Third Wave Technologies for $580 million. The purchase added diagnostics for conditions such as hepatitis C and cystic fibrosis; it also contributed women's health tests for cervical cancer and human papillomavirus (HPV) that bolster Hologic's core product offerings.

In a boost to its gynecological surgical products line, in 2009 the company unveiled its FDA-approved Adiana system for permanent contraception for women. Introduced as an alternative to tubal ligation, the system allows doctors to perform the procedure with only local anesthesia.

In addition to its women's health products, Hologic manufactures and sells photoconductor materials used in electrophotographic devices and small fluoroscopic imaging systems used by orthopedic surgeons on extremities such as hands, feet, and knees. The company is also the US distributor of Esaote's MRI systems designed for use on extremities.

HISTORY

In 1981 S. David Ellenbogen and Jay Stein founded Diagnostic Technology (DTI) and developed a digital angiography product. A Squibb subsidiary bought DTI in 1982, and in 1985 Ellenbogen and Stein founded Hologic.

The firm shipped its first bone scanner in 1987 and went public in 1990. Increased global focus on women's health fueled Hologic's growth in 1994. That year it penetrated the Latin American and Japanese markets, and Medicare patients started receiving reimbursement for bone density examinations. Also in 1994 Hologic partnered with Serex to develop a test to monitor biochemical indicators of bone loss (Ostex International joined the effort in 1996).

Targeting private practices requiring less-expensive equipment, Hologic bought Walker Magnetic Group's ultrasound bone analyzer business and that of European rival Sophia Medical Systems in 1995. That year it purchased FluoroScan Imaging Systems, a maker of X-ray equipment.

In 1998 the company introduced its Sahara Clinical Bone Sonometer in the US. In 1999 Hologic acquired Direct Radiography, another X-ray equipment maker. That year Fleet Business Credit, which had an agreement with Hologic through which it purchased bone densitometers and then leased them to physicians, pulled out of the partnership; sales sank, and Hologic filed a lawsuit against Fleet to recoup losses. Also in 1999 Hologic sold its Medical Data Management division to focus on core operations.

In 2000 the company bought the US operations of medical imaging company Trex Medical Corporation. This acquisition added the Lorad-brand line of mammography and breast biopsy systems, to Hologic's operations. The acquisition was costly, and, to recover, Hologic implemented a restructuring plan in 2001 that led to a reduction of the workforce, a reduction of operating expenses, and phasing out unprofitable units. The company closed its conventional X-ray equipment manufacturing facility in Littleton, Massachusetts and relocated some of the product lines and personnel to Bedford, Massachusetts.

With a renewed appetite for growth, in 2005 Hologic resumed its acquisition strategy, starting with the purchase of Fischer Imaging's SenoScan

digital mammography and MammoTest stereo-tactic breast biopsy systems for $32 million. The following year it acquired R2 Technology for $220 million to gain that company's computer-aided detection (CAD) technology. Also in 2006 it acquired breast biopsy and tissue excision device producer Suros Surgical Systems for $240 million.

EXECUTIVES

Chairman Emeritus and CTO: Jay A. Stein, age 66
Chairman and CEO: John W. (Jack) Cumming, age 63
President, COO, and Director: Robert A. Cascella, age 54
EVP Finance and Administration, CFO, Treasurer, Secretary, and Director: Glenn P. Muir, age 49
SVP and CIO: David M. Rudzinsky
SVP and Chief Accounting Officer: Robert H. Lavallee
SVP Human Resources: David J. Brady
SVP International Sales: Mark A. Duerst
SVP Breast Health: Peter K. Soltani, age 48
SVP Sales and Strategic Accounts: John R. Pekarsky, age 55
SVP Skeletal Health: William Healy
SVP Business Development: Thomas Umbel
SVP GYN Surgical: Stuart A. (Tony) Kingsley, age 45
SVP Customer Service: Roger D. Mills
SVP Diagnostic Products: Howard B. Doran, age 48
SVP, General Counsel, and Assistant Secretary: Mark J. Casey, age 45
SVP Interventional Breast Products: David P. Harding
SVP Diagnostics & GYN Surgical International Products: Douglas Ikeda
VP and Corporate Controller: Karleen Oberton
VP Investor Relations: Deborah R. Gordon
Auditors: Ernst & Young LLP

LOCATIONS

HQ: Hologic, Inc.
　35 Crosby Dr., Bedford, MA 01730
Phone: 781-999-7300　　**Fax:** 781-280-0669
Web: www.hologic.com

2008 Sales

	% of total
US	80
Europe	12
Asia	4
Other regions	4
Total	**100**

PRODUCTS/OPERATIONS

2008 Sales

	$ mil.	% of total
Breast Health	860.8	51
Diagnostics	485.0	29
GYN Surgical	221.1	13
Skeletal Health	107.6	7
Total	**1,674.5**	**100**

Selected Products

Breast Health
　ATEC (Automated Tissue Excision and Collection, breast biopsy system)
　Lorad Affinity (mammography system)
　Lorad M-IV (mammography system)
　MammoPad (mammography breast cushion)
　MammoSite (breast cancer radiation therapy system)
　Selenia (full field digital mammography system)
　StereoLoc (stereotactic breast biopsy systems)
Diagnostic Products
　FullTerm Fetal Fibronectin Test (preterm birth risk assessment)
　Invader molecular diagnostic tests
　ThinPrep System (cervical cancer screening)

GYN Surgical Products
　NovaSure (treatment system for menorrhagia)
Skeletal Health Products
　InSight fluoroscan imaging systems (mini c-arm X-ray imaging devices)
　QDR X-Ray Bone Densitometers (osteoporosis diagnostic devices)
　Sahara Clinical Bone Sonometers (portable ultrasound bone analyzers)
QDR series bone densitometer
Sahara Bone Sonometer (ultrasound-based densitometer)

COMPETITORS

Abbott Labs	Innogenetics
Affymetrix	Intact Medical Corporation
Agfa	Johnson & Johnson
American Medical Systems	Life Technologies
Bard	Corporation
Becton, Dickinson	Luminex
Boston Scientific	Microsulis
Cardinal Health	Philips Healthcare
Carestream Health	QIAGEN
Celera	Roche Diagnostics
Clarient	Sectra
Ethicon	SenoRx
FUJIFILM	Siemens Healthcare
GE Healthcare	Toshiba
Gen-Probe	Varian Medical Systems
iCAD	

HISTORICAL FINANCIALS

Company Type: Public

Income Statement

FYE: Last Saturday in September

	REVENUE ($ mil.)	NET INCOME ($ mil.)	NET PROFIT MARGIN	EMPLOYEES
9/08	1,674.5	(385.6)	—	3,933
9/07	738.4	94.6	12.8%	3,580
9/06	462.7	27.4	5.9%	1,617
9/05	287.7	28.3	9.8%	870
9/04	228.7	12.2	5.3%	761
Annual Growth	**64.5%**	**—**	**—**	**50.8%**

2008 Year-End Financials

Debt ratio: 46.6%
Return on equity: —
Cash ($ mil.): 96
Current ratio: 2.03
Long-term debt ($ mil.): 2,162

No. of shares (mil.): 257
Dividends
　Yield: 0.0%
　Payout: —
Market value ($ mil.): 4,961

Stock History

NASDAQ (GS): HOLX

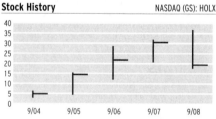

	STOCK PRICE ($) FY Close	P/E High/Low		PER SHARE ($) Earnings	Dividends	Book Value
9/08	19.33	—	—	(1.57)	0.00	18.09
9/07	30.50	37	24	0.86	0.00	3.14
9/06	21.76	101	44	0.28	0.00	2.36
9/05	14.44	48	15	0.31	0.00	0.85
9/04	4.82	42	22	0.14	0.00	0.65
Annual Growth	**41.5%**	**—**	**—**	**—**	**—**	**129.9%**

Home Depot

When embarking on household projects, many start their journey at The Home Depot. As the world's largest home improvement chain and second-largest retailer in the US after Wal-Mart, the firm operates about 2,200 stores across North America, Puerto Rico, and China, as well as an e-commerce site. It targets the do-it-yourself and professional markets with its selection of about 40,000 items, including lumber, flooring, plumbing, gardening supplies, tools, paint, and appliances. The Home Depot also offers carpeting, cabinetry, and other installation services. In response to angry shareholders, the retailer decided in 2008 that it will close its EXPO, THD Design Center, and Yardbirds stores.

The exit, part of a move to satisfy investors calling for a more robust stock price, come amid a deepening recession and a battered housing market. The EXPO, THD Design Center, and Yardbirds stores were part of Home Depot's upscale group of home design and hardware stores targeted at those remodeling their homes. Also in early 2009 the company eliminated about 7,000 jobs, and it plans to shed 2,000 non-store positions and freeze the pay of its officers. The home improvement chain also decided to close 15 stores and curtail its 2010 growth plan by about 50 stores.

The cost-cutting measures turn up as the retailer looks to reposition itself as a bargain-priced DIY store. To spur sales along, the company has slashed prices on its best-selling items, cleaned up stores to attract female customers, and retrained employees in customer service. While The Home Depot does not expect to see results from this approach in 2009, the retailer hopes its sales will rebound with the economy and housing market in the years following.

As the US's #2 retailer works to boost sales at home, it is also aiming to leverage itself in international markets. About 10% of The Home Depot's stores are located in Canada, China, and Mexico. The company operates about a dozen stores in China and about 170 locations in Canada. Home Depot Mexico is the country's #1 do-it-yourself operator with about 70 stores.

Recent years have been difficult for the home improvement chain, marked by the departure of its controversial former CEO Robert Nardelli in 2007, slowing same-store sales, and investor dissatisfaction. Under Nardelli, the company had aggressively expanded its professional services business while critics claimed, the retail side of the business suffered. The downturn in the US housing market also interrupted the company's turnaround plans led by Nardelli's successor, Frank Blake. In late 2007 The Home Depot had cut about 950 jobs when it decided to close three call centers related to its sagging home services business. More job reductions were announced in early 2008, when 500 positions were cut from the company's headquarters, amounting to about 10% of employees there.

HISTORY

Bernard Marcus and Arthur Blank founded The Home Depot in 1978 after they were fired (under disputed circumstances) from Handy Dan Home Improvement Centers. They joined Handy Dan co-worker Ronald Brill to launch a "new and improved" home center for the do-it-yourselfer (DIY). In 1979 they opened three stores in the fast-growing Atlanta area and expanded to four stores in 1980.

Home Depot went public, opened four stores in South Florida, and posted sales of $50 million in 1981. The chain entered Louisiana and Arizona next. By 1983 sales were more than $250 million.

In 1984 Home Depot's stock was listed on the NYSE and the company acquired nine Bowater Home Centers in the South. Through subsequent stock and debenture offerings, Home Depot continued to grow, entering California (Handy Dan's home turf) with six new stores in 1985.

Back on track in 1986, sales exceeded $1 billion in the firm's 60 stores. Home Depot began the current policy of "low day-in, day-out pricing" the following year, achieving Marcus' dream of eliminating sales events. The company entered the competitive northeastern market with stores in Long Island, New York, in 1988 and opened its first EXPO Design Center in San Diego.

Home Depot's sales continued to rise during the 1990-92 recession and the retailer kept opening stores. It entered Canada in 1994 when it acquired a 75% interest in Aikenhead's, a DIY chain that it converted to the Home Depot name (it bought the remaining 25% in 1998).

A series of gender-bias lawsuits plagued the company in 1994 as female workers claimed they were not treated on an equal basis with male employees. Home Depot reached a $65 million out-of-court settlement in 1997, but not before the company was ordered to pay another female employee $1.7 million in a case in California.

In 1997 Blank succeeded Marcus as the company's CEO; Marcus remained chairman. In 2000 the company named General Electric executive Robert Nardelli as its president and CEO. Marcus and Blank were named co-chairmen, but Marcus was named chairman in 2001 after Blank stepped down. Later in the year Marcus retired and Nardelli became chairman.

In mid-2005 Home Depot acquired National Waterworks Holdings (now National Waterworks, Inc.) and Williams Bros. Lumber of Georgia, and folded them both into its The Home Depot Supply business (renamed HD Supply).

The company's direct-to-consumer division launched a pair of high-end catalogs in 2005: 10 Crescent Lane and Paces Trading Company. However, the catalogs, which featured home furnishings and lighting products, were discontinued in 2006 and selected products were folded back into the main Home Depot store catalog and Web site.

In January 2006 Home Depot acquired carpet and upholstery cleaning franchisor Chem-Dry, which it will add to its At-Home Services division. (Chem-Dry has nearly 4,000 franchises worldwide, including 2,500 in the US.) In March the company completed its largest acquisition to date: the construction, repair, and maintenance products distributor Hughes Supply Inc., for $3.2 billion. That purchase was followed in May by the acquisition of Cox Lumber Co., a Tampa-based provider of trusses, doors, and lumber-related products.

In early 2007 Nardelli left the company and vice chairman and EVP Frank Blake took the top spot. Home Depot decided to close its handful of flooring-only stores that year. It also closed a call center in Texas, affecting 550 employees.

The company sold its HD Supply business in 2007 to Bain Capital, Carlyle Group, and Clayton Dubilier & Rice.

LOCATIONS

HQ: The Home Depot, Inc.
2455 Paces Ferry Rd. NW, Atlanta, GA 30339
Phone: 770-433-8211   **Fax:** 770-384-2356
Web: www.homedepot.com

2009 Locations

	No.
US	1,971
Canada	176
Mexico	74
China	12
Total	**2,233**

PRODUCTS/OPERATIONS

2009 Sales

	% of total
Plumbing, electrical & kitchen	30
Hardware & seasonal	29
Building materials, lumber & millwork	22
Paint, flooring & wall covering	19
Total	**100**

Selected Private Labels and Proprietary Brands

Behr Premium Plus (paint)
Hampton Bay (lighting)
Husky (hand tools)
Mill's Pride (cabinets)
Traffic Master (carpet)
Vigoro (fertilizer)

COMPETITORS

84 Lumber	Menard
Abbey Carpet	Northern Tool
Ace Hardware	Pacific Coast Building
Amazon.com	Products
B&Q	Reno-Depot
Best Buy	RONA
Building Materials Holding	Sears
CCA Global	Sherwin-Williams
Costco Wholesale	Stock Building Supply
Do it Best	Sutherland Lumber
F.W. Webb	Target
Guardian Building	Tractor Supply
Products	True Value
Improvement Direct	Wal-Mart
Kelly-Moore	W.E. Aubuchon
Kmart	Wolseley
Lowe's	

HISTORICAL FINANCIALS

Company Type: Public

Income Statement

FYE: Sunday nearest January 31

	REVENUE ($ mil.)	NET INCOME ($ mil.)	NET PROFIT MARGIN	EMPLOYEES
1/09	71,288.0	2,260.0	3.2%	322,000
1/08	77,349.0	4,395.0	5.7%	331,000
1/07	90,837.0	5,761.0	6.3%	364,000
1/06	81,511.0	5,838.0	7.2%	345,000
1/05	73,094.0	5,001.0	6.8%	325,000
Annual Growth	(0.6%)	(18.0%)	—	(0.2%)

2009 Year-End Financials

Debt ratio: 54.4%
Return on equity: 12.7%
Cash ($ mil.): 519
Current ratio: 1.20
Long-term debt ($ mil.): 9,667

No. of shares (mil.): 1,703
Dividends
  Yield: 4.2%
  Payout: 67.2%
Market value ($ mil.): 36,674

Stock History

NYSE: HD

	STOCK PRICE ($) FY Close	P/E High/Low	PER SHARE ($) Earnings	Dividends	Book Value
1/09	21.53	23 13	1.34	0.90	10.44
1/08	30.64	18 10	2.37	0.90	10.40
1/07	40.74	16 12	2.79	0.68	14.69
1/06	40.55	16 13	2.72	0.40	15.80
1/05	41.26	20 14	2.26	0.32	14.18
Annual Growth	(15.0%)	— —	(12.2%)	29.5%	(7.4%)

Honeywell International

Jet engines and thermostats seem worlds apart, but they're Honeywell International's bread and butter. More than a century old, the company is a diverse industrial conglomerate, with automation/control products and aerospace offerings its biggest lines of business. Aerospace is Honeywell's most profitable business, yet the company is bracing for possible changes in the Pentagon budget. Sales to the US government account for about 12% of Honeywell's revenues. The company tends to constantly tweak its unique blend of businesses through acquisitions and divestitures.

The company's largest business segment, Automation and Control, includes home and industrial heating, ventilation, and manufacturing process products. Close behind is Honeywell Aerospace, which makes products such as turbofan and turboprop engines and flight safety and landing systems. Honeywell, through its Specialty Materials segment, also makes performance materials used in semiconductors, polymers for electronics and fibers, and specialty

friction materials. Lastly, the company turns out consumer car care products (Prestone, FRAM brands) through its Transportation Systems segment.

In 2009 Honeywell advanced further into the clean energy market. The company acquired Germany-based RMG Group (RMG Regel + Messtechnik Gmbh) and subsidiaries. A maker of regulating and safety systems, metering and shutoff, and installation services for natural gas businesses, RMG Group builds Honeywell's position in supplying natural gas transmission, storage, and industrial demand. In another arena, Honeywell picked up Norcross Safety Products in 2008 for around $1.2 billion. Norcross expands Honeywell Life Safety, part of Honeywell's Automation and Control Solutions.

Later that year the company sold its Consumable Solutions business to BE Aerospace for $1.15 billion in cash and stock. Consumable Solutions distributes aerospace fasteners and hardware around the world to airlines, distributors, flight service centers, OEMs, and repair shops.

HISTORY

During WWI Germany controlled much of the world's chemical industry, causing dye and drug shortages. In response, *Washington Post* publisher Eugene Meyer and scientist William Nichols organized the Allied Chemical & Dye Corporation in 1920.

Allied opened a synthetic ammonia plant in 1928 near Hopewell, Virginia, and became the world's leading producer of ammonia. After WWII Allied began making nylon, refrigerants, and other products. The company became Allied Chemical Corporation in 1958.

Seeking a supplier of raw materials for its chemical products, in 1962 Allied bought Union Texas Natural Gas. In the early 1970s CEO John Connor sold many of the firm's unprofitable businesses and invested in oil and gas exploration. By 1979, when Edward Hennessy became CEO, Union Texas produced 80% of Allied's income.

Hennessy led the company into the electronics and technical markets. Under a new name, Allied Corporation (1981), it bought the Bendix Corporation, an aerospace and automotive company, in 1983. In 1985 Allied merged with Signal Companies (founded by Sam Mosher in 1922) to form AlliedSignal. The company spun off more than 40 unprofitable chemical and engineering businesses over the next two years.

Larry Bossidy, hired from General Electric in 1991 as the new CEO, began to cut waste and buy growth businesses. Late in 1999 the company acquired Honeywell in a deal valued at $15 billion and changed its name to Honeywell International. Honeywell, after trying to make a go of it in the computer and telecommunications industries, had refocused on its bread and butter — thermostats, security systems, and other automation equipment. The chairman and CEO of the original Honeywell, Michael Bonsignore, took the same titles in the combined company.

In 2000 Honeywell picked up building-security and fire systems company Pittway for $2 billion. Then, amid lower-than-expected earnings, the company announced plans to cut an additional 6,000 jobs on top of the 11,000 cuts already planned.

Late in the year Honeywell was reportedly close to inking a deal to be acquired by United Technologies, but the talks ended when industrial behemoth GE made a better offer. Honeywell then agreed to be acquired by GE in a stock deal worth

about $45 billion. However, the deal collapsed in 2001 when GE — which had offered to sell assets that generate about $2.2 billion a year — balked at demands from European Union regulators that it sell virtually all of Honeywell's avionics operations. The EU formally rejected the acquisition in July, and Honeywell ousted CEO Bonsignore, replacing him with Bossidy.

In September the company said that it would take cost-cutting measures with charges of almost $1 billion and increased the total of previously announced layoffs, cutting about 16,000 jobs (about 13% of its workforce) by year's end. In December Honeywell agreed to pay Northrop Grumman $440 million to settle an antitrust and patent infringement lawsuit filed against it by Litton (now a part of Northrop) in 1990.

In 2002 David Cote (like Bossidy, a former GE executive), the former chairman, president, and CEO of TRW, was named president and CEO of Honeywell, replacing Bossidy (Cote also replaced Bossidy as chairman in July 2002).

Early in 2005 Honeywell acquired UK-based Novar plc for about $1.7 billion. Novar's operations include aluminum products, building control and security systems, and checkbook printing. Late in 2005 Honeywell sold its US nylon fibers business to Shaw Industries and its Clarke American Checks (check printing) business to M&F Worldwide for $800 million. It also bought Dow Chemical's 50% stake in UOP, their energy refining joint venture, for $825 million.

Honeywell sold Novar's Indalex Aluminum Solutions operations to Sun Capital Partners for $425 million early in 2006. Not long after, Honeywell completed the acquisition of First Technology PLC, a maker of gas sensing, automotive, and safety equipment, for $718 million.

In mid-2007 Honeywell acquired Dimensions International, a provider of logistics support to the US military and other defense agencies.

In late 2007 Honeywell bought Hand Held Products Inc., a maker of automatic identification and data collection (AIDC) equipment.

EXECUTIVES

Chairman and CEO: David M. Cote, age 56, $30,312,456 total compensation
SVP Technology and Operations: Larry E. Kittelberger, age 60
SVP and CFO: David J. (Dave) Anderson, age 59, $8,442,355 total compensation
SVP Energy Strategy: Adriane M. Brown, age 50
SVP Human Resources and Communications: Mark James, age 47
SVP and General Counsel: Katherine L. (Kate) Adams
VP, Strategy and Business Development: Rhonda G. Germany
VP, Secretary, and Deputy Corporate Counsel: Thomas F. Larkins
VP and Controller: Kathleen A. Winters, age 41
President and CEO, Aerospace: Robert J. (Rob) Gillette
President and CEO, Automation and Control Solutions: Roger Fradin, age 55, $13,453,516 total compensation
President and CEO, Specialty Materials: Andreas Kramvis
President and CEO, Transportation Business: Alexandre (Alex) Ismail, age 44
Auditors: PricewaterhouseCoopers LLP

LOCATIONS

HQ: Honeywell International Inc.
  101 Columbia Rd., Morristown, NJ 07962
Phone: 973-455-2000   **Fax:** 973-455-4807
Web: www.honeywell.com

	$ mil.	% of total
US	22,291	61
Europe	9,484	26
Other regions	4,781	13
Total	**36,556**	**100**

PRODUCTS/OPERATIONS

2008 Sales

	$ mil.	% of total
Automation & Control Solutions	14,018	38
Aerospace	12,650	35
Specialty Materials	5,266	14
Transportation Systems	4,622	13
Total	**36,556**	**100**

COMPETITORS

3M	Jeppesen Sanderson
ABB AG	John Deere Thibodaux
Air Products	Johnson Controls
Akebono Brake	KVH Industries
Akzo Nobel	Kyocera
Anixter International	L-3 Communications
Arch Chemicals	Lockheed Martin
Arkema	Lonza
ArvinMeritor	LSI Industries
Asahi Glass	Meggitt Aircraft Braking
Astronautics	Systems
Autoliv	Merck KGaA
Avecia	Mexichem
Avnet	Mine Safety Appliances
BAE Systems Inc.	Modine Manufacturing
Ball Aerospace	Motorola, Inc.
BASF SE	NavCom Technology
Bayer AG	NGK SPARK PLUG
BE Aerospace	Northrop Grumman
Beaulieu Group	Old World Industries
Bechtel	Parker Hannifin
BorgWarner	Pelco
Carrier	Raytheon
CLARCOR	Riken Corporation
Clariant	Robert Bosch
Computer Sciences Corp.	Rockwell Automation
Daikin	Rolls-Royce
Dana Holding	Süd-Chemie
Delphi Corp.	SAFRAN
Dow Chemical	SAIC
DSM	Sauer-Danfoss
DuPont	Schneider Electric
DynCorp International	Shinko Electric
Eastman Chemical	Siemens AG
Eaton	Sigma-Aldrich
Emerson Electric	Solvay
Endress + Hauser	TAT Group
Evonik Degussa	Teijin
Exxon Mobil	Tenneco
Federal-Mogul	Textron
Foxconn International	Thales
Garmin	Thermo Fisher Scientific
GE	Trimble Navigation
Goodrich Corp.	Tyco
Hella	United Technologies
Hexcel	Unitika
INEOS	Universal Avionics
Ingersoll-Rand	Valeo
Intermec	Wesco Aircraft Hardware
Invensys	Yokogawa Electric
ITT Corp.	ZF Electronics

HISTORICAL FINANCIALS

Company Type: Public

Income Statement

FYE: December 31

	REVENUE ($ mil.)	NET INCOME ($ mil.)	NET PROFIT MARGIN	EMPLOYEES
12/08	36,556.0	2,792.0	7.6%	128,000
12/07	34,589.0	2,444.0	7.1%	122,000
12/06	31,367.0	2,083.0	6.6%	118,000
12/05	27,653.0	1,676.0	6.1%	116,000
12/04	25,601.0	1,281.0	5.0%	109,000
Annual Growth	**9.3%**	**21.5%**	**—**	**4.1%**

2008 Year-End Financials

Debt ratio: 81.6%
Return on equity: 34.0%
Cash ($ mil.): 2,065
Current ratio: 1.08
Long-term debt ($ mil.): 5,865
No. of shares (mil.): 752
Dividends
  Yield: 3.4%
  Payout: 29.3%
Market value ($ mil.): 24,690

Stock History

NYSE: HON

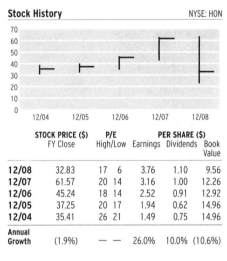

	STOCK PRICE ($) FY Close	P/E High/Low		Earnings	Dividends	Book Value
12/08	32.83	17	6	3.76	1.10	9.56
12/07	61.57	20	14	3.16	1.00	12.26
12/06	45.24	18	14	2.52	0.91	12.92
12/05	37.25	20	17	1.94	0.62	14.96
12/04	35.41	26	21	1.49	0.75	14.96
Annual Growth	**(1.9%)**	**—**	**—**	**26.0%**	**10.0%**	**(10.6%)**

Hormel Foods

Now that Hormel Foods has stocked its pantry with ethnic convenience foods, can we look forward to SPAM soufflé, SPAM enchiladas, or SPAM curry? Along with its famous canned "spiced ham," SPAM, Hormel is a top US turkey processor and a major pork processor, making Jennie-O turkey products, Cure 81 hams, and Always Tender fresh pork, as well as canned Stagg chili and Dinty Moore beef stews. Hormel has branched out into convenience, ethnic, and frozen foods, offering brands such as Chi-Chi's Mexican, Patak's Indian, and House of Tsang Asian products. Hormel also has a significant foodservice operation.

Hormel's action plan is expansion; it has joint ventures across the globe, including ones in Australia, Canada, China (the world's biggest market for pork), Japan, and the Philippines. Back home, the company has a 51% joint venture (Precept Foods) with Cargill that markets case-ready fresh beef and pork under the Always Tender brand. In 2009 it formed another joint venture, this time with Herdez Del Fuerte to market Mexican foods in the US. Called MegaMex Foods, it is headquartered in Chino, California, and is part of Hormel's plan to diversify its portfolio.

The company's specialty foods segment packages and sells various sugar and sugar-substitute products, salt and pepper, liquid-portion products, dessert mixes, ready-to-drink products, gelatin products, and private-label canned meats to retail and foodservice customers. The segment also makes nutritional food products and supplements for hospitals, nursing homes, and other marketers of nutritional products.

Hormel acquired Burke Corporation, a maker of pizza toppings and other fully cooked meat items in 2007. The acquisition allowed Hormel to extend its pizza-topping operations into the foodservice sector. The following year, it acquired Boca Grande Foods, a maker of Poco Pac branded jams, jellies, and pancake syrup portion-control products.

The Hormel Foundation, a charitable trust formed during WWII, owns about 47% of the company's stock.

HISTORY

George Hormel opened his Austin, Minnesota, slaughterhouse in an abandoned creamery in 1891. By 1900 Hormel had modernized his facilities to compete with larger meat processors. In 1903 the enterprise introduced its first brand name (Dairy Brand) and a year later began opening distribution centers nationwide. The scandal that ensued after the discovery in 1921 that an assistant controller had embezzled over $1 million almost broke the company, causing Hormel to initiate tighter controls. By 1924 it was processing more than a million hogs annually. Hormel introduced canned ham two years later.

Jay Hormel, George's son, became president in 1929; under his guidance Hormel introduced Dinty Moore beef stew (1936) and SPAM (1937). A Hormel executive won a contest, and $100, by submitting the name, a contraction of "spiced ham." During WWII the US government bought over half of Hormel's output; it supplied SPAM to GIs and Allied forces.

In 1959 Hormel introduced its Little Sizzlers pork sausage and sold its billionth can of SPAM. New products rolled out in the 1960s included Hormel's Cure 81 ham (1963). By the mid-1970s the firm had more than 750 products.

The company survived a violent, nationally publicized strike triggered by a pay cut in 1985. In the end only 500 of the original 1,500 strikers returned to accept lower pay scales.

Sensing the consumer shift toward poultry, Hormel purchased Jennie-O Foods in 1986. Later acquisitions included the House of Tsang and Oriental Deli (1992), Dubuque (processed pork, 1993) and Herb-Ox (bouillon and dry soup mix, 1993). After more than a century as Geo. A. Hormel & Co., the company began calling itself Hormel Foods in 1993 to reflect its expansion into non-pork foods. Former General Foods executive Joel Johnson was named president and CEO that year (and chairman two years later).

Hormel proved it could take a joke with the 1994 debut of its tongue-in-cheek SPAM catalog, featuring dozens of SPAM-related products. But when a 1996 Muppets movie featured a porcine character named Spa'am, Hormel sued Jim Henson Productions; a federal court gave Spa'am the go-ahead.

Earnings fell in 1996, due in part to soaring hog prices. The company was hit hard again in 1998 when production contracts with hog growers meant it wound up paying premium rates, despite a market glut. In 1998 the Smithsonian Institution accepted two cans of SPAM (one from

1937, the other an updated 1997 version) for its History of Technology collection.

SPAM sales soared in 1999 as nervous consumers stockpiled provisions for the millennium. To build its growing HealthLabs division, Hormel acquired Cliffdale Farms (2000) and Diamond Crystal Brands nutritional products (a division of Imperial Sugar) in 2001 — boosting its share of the market for easy-to-swallow foods sold to hospitals and nursing homes.

In early 2001 Hormel acquired family-owned The Turkey Store for approximately $334 million and folded it into its Jennie-O division. Hormel produced its 6 billionth can of SPAM in 2002.

To further diversify, in 2003 Hormel acquired food manufacturer Century Foods International (whey-based protein powders, beverages, and nutrition bars) and added it to its burgeoning specialty foods group.

In 2004 Hormel bought Southern California's Clougherty Packing for about $186 million. The pork processor's facilities help extend Hormel's capacity for further-processed foods in the southwestern US.

Responding to the growing trend of the US population to dine out, Hormel expanded its foodservice segment (which it refers to as its specialty foods business) with the 2005 purchase of foodservice food manufacturer and distributor Mark-Lynn Foods.

Johnson retired in 2006; company veteran Jeffrey Ettinger was tapped to be the new chairman and CEO.

Adding to its grocery product offerings, in 2006 the company acquired canned, ready-to-eat chicken producer Valley Fresh Foods for $78 million. It also bought pepperoni and pasta maker Provena Foods, and sausage and sliced meat maker Saag's Products.

It added another to its list of countries in which it has joint ventures in 2006, when it formed a JV with San Miguel to raise and market hogs and animal feed in Vietnam. The JV is 49%-owned by Hormel.

EXECUTIVES

Chairman, President, and CEO: Jeffrey M. Ettinger, age 50
SVP, CFO, and Director: Jody H. Feragen, age 52
EVP Grocery Products: Ronald W. Fielding, age 55
VP; SVP Consumer Products Sales: Kurt F. Mueller, age 52
VP; SVP Consumer Products Sales: Douglas R. Reetz, age 54
SVP Supply Chain: William F. Snyder, age 51
SVP Foodservice: Thomas R. Day, age 50
SVP External Affairs and General Counsel: James W. Cavanaugh, age 58
VP; SVP Consumer Products Sales: Daniel A. Hartzog, age 57
Group VP; President, Hormel Foods International: Richard A. Bross, age 57
Group VP Refrigerated Products: Steven G. Binder, age 51
Group VP Consumer Products Sales: Larry L. Vorpahl, age 45
VP and Controller: James N. Sheehan, age 53
VP Finance and Treasurer: Roland G. Gentzler, age 54
VP Corporate Communications: Julie H. Craven, age 53
VP Research and Development: Phillip L. (Phil) Minerich, age 55
VP Human Resources: David P. Juhlke, age 49
Corporate Secretary and Senior Attorney: Brian D. Johnson, age 48
Auditors: Ernst & Young LLP

LOCATIONS

HQ: Hormel Foods Corporation
1 Hormel Place, Austin, MN 55912
Phone: 507-437-5611 **Fax:** 507-437-5129
Web: www.hormel.com

2008 Sales

	$ mil.	% of total
US	6,408.3	95
Foreign	346.6	5
Total	**6,754.9**	**100**

PRODUCTS/OPERATIONS

2008 Sales

	$ mil.	% of total
Refrigerated foods	3,521.7	52
Jennie-O Turkey Store	1,268.0	19
Grocery products	947.2	14
Specialty foods	777.7	11
Other	240.3	4
Total	**6,754.9**	**100**

Selected Brands

Deli
  HORMEL Deli Beef
  HORMEL Deli Dry Sausage
  HORMEL Deli Ham
  HORMEL Deli Turkey
  HORMEL Party Trays
Ethnic
  BUFALO Authentic Mexican Products
  CARAPELLI Olive Oils
  CHI-CHI'S Mexican Products
  DOÑA MARÍA Authentic Mexican Products
  EL TORITO Mexican Products
  HERDEZ Authentic Mexican Products
  HOUSE OF TSANG Asian Sauces and Oils
  MANNY'S Tortilla Products
  MARRAKESH EXPRESS Mediterranean Products
  PATAK'S Indian Products
  PELOPONNESE Mediterranean Products
Pantry
  DINTY MOORE Products
  HERB-OX Bouillon
  HORMEL Bacon Toppings
  HORMEL Chili
  HORMEL Chunk Meats
  HORMEL Dried Beef
  HORMEL Hash
  HORMEL KID'S KITCHEN Microwave Meals
  HORMEL Microwave Meals and Soups
  HORMEL Microwave Trays
  NOT-SO-SLOPPY-JOE Sloppy Joe Sauce
  SPAM Family of Products
  STAGG Chili
  VALLEY FRESH Premium Canned Poultry Products
Refrigerated
  HORMEL ALWAYS TENDER Flavored Pork and Beef
  HORMEL Bacon
  HORMEL CURE 81 Ham
  HORMEL Fully Cooked Entrees
  HORMEL NATURAL CHOICE Deli Lunch Meats
  HORMEL OLD SMOKEHOUSE Summer Sausage
  HORMEL Pepperoni
  HORMEL WRANGLERS Smoked Franks
  JENNIE-O TURKEY STORE Turkey Products
  LITTLE SIZZLERS Pork Sausage
  LLOYD'S BBQ Products

COMPETITORS

B&G Foods
Boar's Head
Bob Evans
Bridgford Foods
Bush Brothers
Butterball
Campbell Soup
Cargill
ConAgra
Cooper Farms
The Dial Corporation
Eberly Poultry
Foster Farms
Gusto Packing
H.J. Heinz Limited
JBS USA
Kraft Foods
Perdue Incorporated
Pilgrim's Pride
Pinnacle Foods
Plainville Farms
Sanderson Farms
Sara Lee Food and Beverage
Seaboard
Smithfield Foods
Tyson Foods

HISTORICAL FINANCIALS

Company Type: Public

Income Statement

FYE: Last Saturday in October

	REVENUE ($ mil.)	NET INCOME ($ mil.)	NET PROFIT MARGIN	EMPLOYEES
10/08	6,754.9	285.5	4.2%	19,100
10/07	6,193.0	301.9	4.9%	18,500
10/06	5,745.5	286.1	5.0%	18,100
10/05	5,414.0	253.5	4.7%	17,600
10/04	4,779.9	231.7	4.8%	15,600
Annual Growth	**9.0%**	**5.4%**	**—**	**5.2%**

2008 Year-End Financials

Debt ratio: 17.4%
Return on equity: 14.7%
Cash ($ mil.): 155
Current ratio: 1.84
Long-term debt ($ mil.): 350
No. of shares (mil.): 134
Dividends
  Yield: 2.6%
  Payout: 35.6%
Market value ($ mil.): 3,794

Stock History

NYSE: HRL

	STOCK PRICE ($) FY Close	P/E High/Low		PER SHARE ($) Earnings	Dividends	Book Value
10/08	28.26	21	13	2.08	0.74	14.95
10/07	36.48	18	14	2.17	0.60	14.04
10/06	36.11	19	15	2.05	0.56	13.43
10/05	31.80	18	16	1.82	0.52	11.73
10/04	28.11	19	15	1.65	0.45	10.42
Annual Growth	**0.1%**	**—**	**—**	**6.0%**	**13.2%**	**9.4%**

Hovnanian Enterprises

Gimme shelter. Hovnanian Enterprises designs, builds, and markets single-family detached homes, condominiums, and townhomes for first-time, move-up, and luxury buyers as well as for empty-nesters and active adults. Hovnanian delivered about 11,000 homes in fiscal 2008 (down from more than 20,000 in 2006), with base prices ranging from $36,000 to $2.5 million and averaging about $300,000. The company operates in some 300 communities in about 20 states, primarily operating along the East Coast and in the Midwest, California, and Texas. Its K. Hovnanian American Mortgage unit offers mortgage financing and title services. Members of the Hovnanian family control more than 90% of Hovnanian Enterprises.

The company builds homes under the K. Hovnanian, Brighton, CraftBuilt, Matzel and Mumford, Oster, Parkwood Builders, and Town & Country names, among others.

Like its peers, Hovnanian has been hit hard by the housing downturn and credit crunch, resulting in its building fewer homes, declines in sales, and increased cancellations. An influx of foreclosed homes on the market has also decreased demand for new housing. The company reduced its workforce some 60% between 2006 and 2008.

HISTORY

After fleeing revolution in his home of Iraq in the 1950s, Kevork Hovnanian came to America and began building homes in New Jersey in 1959 with his three brothers (including brother Vahak, later to become founder of Internet service provider SPEEDUS.COM). His firm incorporated as K. Hovnanian Enterprises in 1967, and Kevork's son Ara came on board in 1979. (Ara became president in 1988 and CEO in 1997.) The company's 1983 IPO helped Hovnanian take advantage of New Jersey's strong housing market, which peaked in 1986. However, the boom had declined dramatically by 1990, and Hovnanian landed in the red.

Responding to the setback, Hovnanian expanded geographically in the 1990s. It moved into the Washington, DC, area in 1992 and into Southern California in 1994. But the new markets did not add much to the bottom line, thanks to a slowdown in North Carolina and a recession in California.

Hovnanian crews traveled to Armenia in 1988 to help rebuild the country after devastating earthquakes had rumbled though, wreaking havoc. The trip convinced Kevork, an Armenian who grew up in Iraq, to expand Hovnanian operations into the emerging economies of Eastern Europe. Because of its relatively more advanced real estate and mortgage laws, Poland was chosen, and Hovnanian began constructing townhouses there in 1996.

In 1997 Hovnanian began to divest itself of commercial holdings to focus on housing; by 1998 the company had exited the investment properties business.

With cash to plow into homebuilding, Hovnanian strengthened its Washington, DC, operations in 1998 by acquiring Virginia's P.C. Homes. The next year the builder purchased New Jersey luxury homebuilder Matzel & Mumford and entered Texas with the purchase of Dallas-based Goodman Family of Builders. In 2001 Hovnanian bought Washington Homes, which operated primarily in North Carolina and the Washington, DC, metropolitan area.

In early 2002 Hovnanian acquired the homebuilding assets of The Forecast Group, increasing Hovnanian's presence in California. The company was listed that year as one of the 100 fastest-growing companies in the US by *FORTUNE* magazine. Also that year Hovnanian expanded its presence in Texas, entering the Houston homebuilding market with its purchase of Parkside Homes.

Hovnanian initiated plans in 2003 to stop selling homes in Poland and to liquidate its homebuilding operations in the Mid-South US. On the expansion side, the company acquired Brighton Homes to strengthen its position in the Houston area. It also acquired Great Western Homes, expanding its market into the Phoenix area and the Southwest, and Tampa, Florida-based Windward Homes, expanding its southeastern US market into Florida. In 2004 Hovnanian expanded its metro DC presence by acquiring the homebuilding assets of McLean, Virginia-based Rocky Gorge Homes for an undisclosed amount.

In 2005 Hovnanian entered the Chicago market by acquiring homebuilder Town and Country Homes. It also entered the Orlando market and expanded its operations in Florida and Minnesota by acquiring Cambridge Homes. Hovnanian also acquired Oster Homes (Ohio) and First Home Builders (Florida) in 2005.

EXECUTIVES

Chairman: Kevork S. Hovnanian, age 85, $2,127,971 total compensation
President, CEO, and Director: Ara K. Hovnanian, age 51, $10,255,501 total compensation
SVP Corporate Operations: Mark S. Hodges
EVP, CFO, and Director: J. Larry Sorsby, age 53, $2,589,019 total compensation
VP and CIO: John F. Ulen
SVP and Chief Accounting Officer: Paul W. Buchanan, age 58, $664,943 total compensation
SVP and General Counsel: Peter S. Reinhart, age 58, $635,829 total compensation
SVP Finance and Treasurer: Kevin C. Hake, age 49
SVP Human Resources: Robyn T. Mingle
VP Finance: David G Valiaveedan, age 42
Group President, Landover Group: Thomas J. Pellerito
Group President: John R. (Bobby) Ray
President, Houston Division — Brighton Homes: David Orlando
Co-President, Tampa Division: Chad Horne
Co-President, Tampa Division: David Nader
President, Minnesota Area, K. Hovnanian Homes: Thomas (Tom) Standke
Group President, Edison Group: Joseph F. (Joe) Riggs
President, Ohio Area, K. Hovnanian Homes: Francis (Fran) Saltalamacchia
President, Houston Division — Parkside Homes: Mark Kaufman
President, Eastern Title Agency: Michael P. Kehoe
President, K. Hovnanian American Mortgage: Dan A. Klinger
Director, Investor Relations: Jeffrey T. (Jeff) O'Keefe
Auditors: Ernst & Young LLP

LOCATIONS

HQ: Hovnanian Enterprises, Inc.
110 W. Front St., Red Bank, NJ 07701
Phone: 732-747-7800   **Fax:** 732-747-6835
Web: www.khov.com

2008 Home Sales

	$ mil.	% of total
Northeast	679.5	21
Southeast	624.1	20
Southwest	603.5	19
West	552.0	17
Mid-Atlantic	509.0	16
Midwest	209.8	7
Total	**3,177.9**	**100**

2008 Homes Delivered

	No.	% of total
Southwest	2,616	23
Southeast	2,572	23
West	1,764	16
Northeast	1,412	12
Mid-Atlantic	1,248	11
Midwest	965	9
Joint ventures	704	6
Total	**11,281**	**100**

PRODUCTS/OPERATIONS

2008 Sales

	$ mil.	% of total
Homebuilding		
Sale of homes	3,177.9	96
Land sales & other	78.0	2
Financial services	52.2	2
Total	**3,308.1**	**100**

Selected Trade Names

Brighton Homes
CraftBuilt Homes
Forecast Homes
K. Hovnanian Homes
K. Hovnanian Homes Built On Your Lot
K. Hovnanian Homes Metro Living
K. Hovnanian's Four Seasons (active-adult communities)
Matzel and Mumford
Oster Homes
Parkwood Builders
Town & Country Homes
Windward Homes

COMPETITORS

Beazer Homes
D.R. Horton
KB Home
Lennar
M/I Homes
NVR
Orleans Homebuilders
Pulte Homes
Rottlund
The Ryland Group
Toll Brothers
Weyerhaeuser Real Estate

HISTORICAL FINANCIALS

Company Type: Public

Income Statement

FYE: October 31

	REVENUE ($ mil.)	NET INCOME ($ mil.)	NET PROFIT MARGIN	EMPLOYEES
10/08	3,308.1	(1,124.6)	—	2,816
10/07	4,798.9	(637.8)	—	4,318
10/06	6,148.2	138.9	2.3%	6,239
10/05	5,348.4	469.1	8.8%	6,084
10/04	4,160.4	348.7	8.4%	3,837
Annual Growth	**(5.6%)**	**—**	**—**	**(7.4%)**

2008 Year-End Financials

Debt ratio: 305.0%
Return on equity: —
Cash ($ mil.): 848
Current ratio: —
Long-term debt ($ mil.): 595
No. of shares (mil.): 77
Dividends
  Yield: 0.0%
  Payout: —
Market value ($ mil.): 331

Stock History

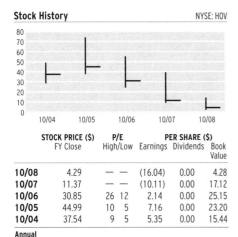

Stock History   NYSE: HOV

	STOCK PRICE ($)	P/E		PER SHARE ($)		
	FY Close	High/Low		Earnings	Dividends	Book Value
10/08	4.29	—	—	(16.04)	0.00	4.28
10/07	11.37	—	—	(10.11)	0.00	17.12
10/06	30.85	26	12	2.14	0.00	25.15
10/05	44.99	10	5	7.16	0.00	23.20
10/04	37.54	9	5	5.35	0.00	15.44
Annual Growth	(41.9%)	—	—	—	—	(27.5%)

HSN, Inc.

There's no need to worry about normal business hours when shopping from this retailer. HSN (known to night owls and from-the-couch shoppers as Home Shopping Network) operates a home shopping television network that reaches more than 90 million US homes. HSN offers computers; electronics; fashion items; home and kitchen goods; jewelry; and health, beauty, and fitness products. HSN operates its business through two segments — namesake HSN and Cornerstone Brands — and peddles products through HSN.com and under several catalog titles. The firm also operates shopping channels in China and Japan. Founded in 1977, HSN was a subsidiary of Barry Diller's IAC/InterActiveCorp until August 2008, when it was spun off.

The deep recession in the US made for rocky going in 2008. Cornerstone Brands, whose product mix is weighted toward apparel and luxury items, was harder hit than the home shopping business, with sales falling 15%. (Cornerstone, which mailed about 325 million catalogs in 2008, generates about 30% of HSN's revenue.) HSN posted a modest gain in net sales of 3%, which included a 16% increase in sales at HSN.com. HSN's flexible business model, which enables the retailer to quickly change its merchandise mix to meet customer demand, was credited for the success. Also, in recent years the company has focused on marketing HSN-exclusive items, which is a marketing strategy that has worked well for the company. Under former NIKE executive Mindy Grossman, who joined HSN in 2006 to boost sales, the company has ditched hour-long programs that focus on one product — such as a treadmill — and pared down its celebrity-driven product pitches.

HSN's sales are increasingly coming from its Web site, as well. HSN.com accounts for more than a third of the company's sales (up from about a quarter not long ago). As of August 2009 shoppers can purchase merchandise from HSN.com using Apple's iPhone.

HSN, which accounted for about half of IAC's revenue prior to the separation, was one of four businesses spun off by Diller so that they could trade and operate as separate entities. Liberty Media Corporation, an investor in HSN's former parent IAC, owns about 30% of HSN's shares following the spin off, which it opposed as it diluted its control. In return for ultimately agreeing to the spin off of HSN (and other IAC companies), Liberty was awarded representation on HSN's board of directors.

HISTORY

Lowell Paxson, who had spent years working in radio, owned an AM radio station in Clearwater, Florida, in the mid-1970s that began losing listeners to its FM competitors. Paxson began selling merchandise over the air in 1977. He bought distressed and overstocked merchandise from local merchants and sold it on his Suncoast Bargaineers program. The show was a hit, and Paxson began giving it more airtime.

By the early 1980s the Clearwater area was wired for cable, and Paxson teamed with Roy Speer, a Florida assistant attorney general, to found the Home Shopping Club in 1982. They soon expanded to other cable services in the Tampa Bay area. In 1985 the jump was made to become a national network. The company's name was changed to Home Shopping Network, which offered live 24-hour shopping on cable services across the nation.

The network was a success, as viewers embraced the bargain-basement prices coupled with game-show-type entertainment. Products were displayed one at a time, for 2-10 minutes, and could be bought only while on screen. Shoppers never knew what was going to come up next, so some of the more rabid fans stayed riveted for hours just to see what would come up for sale. The network's rotating collection of hosts gained cult followings.

Home Shopping Network went public in 1986 in one of the hottest IPOs of the year. That year the company moved into broadcast TV, paying $226 million for 12 UHF stations. The deal gave it broadcast and cable programming in several major markets, including New York, Los Angeles, and Boston.

The luster began to wear off when a host of competitors entered the TV retail fray. The network's competitors were given a boost when the Home Shopping Network's phone system became overloaded in 1987. Home Shopping Network sued GTE for $1.5 billion, claiming it lost half of its incoming calls because of the phone problems.

The company, led by CEO Speer, made unsuccessful attempts to diversify into other businesses, including financial services and mail-order pharmaceuticals, but in 1989 decided to focus solely on electronic retailing. That year the network lost its case against GTE, and it was forced to pay $4.5 million in legal fees and damages from a countersuit for libel.

Despite these setbacks, its core shopping business continued to grow, and by 1990 it reached $1 billion in sales. Also that year Paxson retired as president. Then in 1992, Home Shopping Network spun off its television stations unit, HSN. Speer sold his controlling interest in the company the next year to Liberty Media. He left the company amid allegations of corruption, including vendor kickbacks, but the investigation was dropped in 1994.

In 1995 Hollywood mogul Barry Diller acquired HSN. Diller (who built the Fox network) and TCI chief John Malone were named that year to the company's board. Also in 1995 the network and Sumitomo Corp., one of Japan's largest trading companies, agreed to start a television shopping business in Japan. That company, Silver King Communications, changed its name to HSN, Inc. in 1996, after buying the much larger Home Shopping Network and Savoy Pictures Entertainment.

In 1998 HSN formed a 50-50 joint venture with Scandinavian Broadcast System to operate a home shopping network (HSN-SBS) in Italy. HSN changed its name to USA Networks Inc. Also that year it purchased Ticketmaster.

In 1999 HSN launched its e-commerce website, HSN.com, which reached profitability within three months and has since been redesigned to be integrated with the HSN television network. That same year, HSN also acquired Ingenious Designs, a producer of consumer products, as a direct source for HSN products.

During the next few years, the company made several smaller acquisitions in its home shopping business, while expanding its entertainment sector. Then in 2002 USA Networks sold all of its entertainment assets to Vivendi Universal and became a holding company, USA Interactive (now IAC/InterActiveCorp), with HSN as its strong arm. That same year HSN entered into an agreement with network ABC to cross-market products associated with selected ABC soap operas. Susan Lucci Intimates, a lingerie line based on the actress' All My Children character — vixen Erica Kane — launched in 2004.

IAC acquired catalog retailer Cornerstone Brands in 2005 for about $720 million. IAC later merged HSN's catalog operations into the acquired business. As a benefit from the deal, HSN began to offer many of Cornerstone's upscale lifestyle products through its television and Web operations, with hopes that the product mix would lead to high margins for the shopping channel. Mindy Grossman was named CEO of IAC Retailing, which oversees HSN, in 2006.

In April 2007, citing increasing cable and satellite distribution costs, HSN shut down America's Store, a home shopping network that reached about 14.3 million households in 2006. In May the company laid off 60 workers, primarily in operations at its St. Petersburg TV production and customer service campus. In June the company sold Home Shopping Europe for about $216.5 million.

Along with several other subsidiaries, HSN was spun off from parent IAC in August 2008 and began trading on NASDAQ.

EXECUTIVES

Chairman: Arthur C. Martinez, age 69
President, CEO, and Director: Mindy Grossman, age 51, $3,238,665 total compensation
EVP and COO: Mark Ethier, $1,775,423 total compensation
EVP and CFO: Judy Schmeling, $1,852,671 total compensation
Director, Technology: Gerard Johnson
EVP and General Counsel: Steve Armstrong
EVP Merchandising: Barbara Lynne Ronon
EVP Human Resources: Lisa Letizio
EVP HSN Affiliate Relations Group: Peter Ruben
EVP Programming, Advanced Services, Marketing, and Business Development: Bill Brand
EVP HSN.com and Advanced Services: Brian S. Bradley, age 38
EVP Television and Executive Creative Director, HSN: Andrew Sheldon
SVP Investor Relations and Strategy: Felise Glantz Kissell
VP Business Development: John McDevitt
President, Ingenious Designs LLC: Joy Mangano
Director, Public Relations and Events: Brad Bohnert
Auditors: Ernst & Young LLP

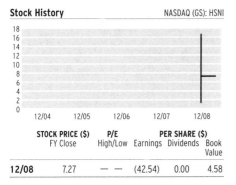
Hub Group

Hub Group helps its clients by handling the hubbub of freight movement throughout North America. An intermodal marketing company, Hub Group specializes in arranging the transportation of freight by a combination of rail and truck. A customer's freight is loaded into a container or trailer and transported by rail from one Hub Group operating center to another, then taken to its destination by a local trucking company, which in some cases is operated by a Hub Group unit. The company also provides truck brokerage and logistics services. It operates from about 20 main offices, each located near one or more railheads. The family of the company's late founder, Phillip Yeager, owns a controlling stake in Hub Group.

As part of its intermodal business, the company provides drayage (local trucking) services in key markets through subsidiaries Quality Services and Comtrak Logistics, which collectively operate a fleet of about 320 tractors and 600 trailers.

Hub Group's truck brokerage business, known as Hub Highway Services, matches shippers' loads with carriers' capacity. The unit manages the transportation of refrigerated and other specialty cargo, as well as standard dry freight.

To spur the growth of its logistics unit, Unyson, Hub Group has invested in technology and enhanced its online presence. Unyson arranges the transportation of cargo not handled by other Hub Group units, such as parcels, freight requiring expedited delivery, and less-than-truckload freight.

Hub Group markets its services to customers in a wide range of industries, including consumer products, durable goods, and retail. Much of the company's business comes from long-term clients, but it is also considering acquisitions that would add to its mix of services as a key to its growth prospects.

HISTORY

Phillip Yeager and his wife, Joyce, founded the first Hub City Terminal in 1971. At the time, intermodal transport was neither efficient nor widely used, and the enterprise grew slowly. The deregulation of the trucking and rail industries in the early 1980s and the passage of the GATT and NAFTA trade agreements in the early 1990s spurred intermodal growth.

Hub Group launched Hub Group International in 1994 to market intermodal services to shippers, forwarders, and shipping lines moving international cargo. The company was incorporated as Hub Group in 1995; it went public the next year. At the time, the 26 existing hubs were separately held corporations; the money from the IPO was used to buy out hubs and purchase a controlling interest in the logistics arm (Hub Group Distribution Services, or HGDS), whose ownership had been shared by the individual hubs.

In 1997, while struggling with the railroads' congestion problems, the company continued buying the remaining interests in its Los Angeles, New Orleans, and San Francisco hubs. The next year Hub Group bought Quality Intermodal (intermodal and truck brokerage service), and in 1999 the company teamed up with Norfolk Southern to serve the rail company's customers in the eastern and southeastern US. Norfolk Southern had acquired more than half of Conrail, but problems resulting from the split-up of Conrail and integration of its assets caused some

of Hub Group's intermodal customers to switch from rail to truck.

The company's HGDS unit began offering home delivery services in 2000 for Internet retailers. Hub Group came under fire from investors in 2002 when it announced it had overstated $3.4 million of HGDS revenues for 1999 and 2000. Later that year the company said it had received proposals from potential purchasers but had declined to pursue any of them.

Also in 2002 Hub Group bought out the remaining 35% partnership interest in HGDS to take full ownership of the unit. In 2004 HGDS transferred its pharmaceutical-sample delivery business to the parent company. Two years later Hub Group sold the remaining assets of HGDS to the unit's president.

Hub Group reorganized in 2004 in an effort to recover market share that had been lost to trucking companies, many of which had begun providing intermodal services. Each hub had been managed essentially as a stand-alone business while Hub Group oversaw railroad relations, financial services, and information systems support. Under the new system, responsibility for key sales functions was centralized at company headquarters, along with the other administrative functions.

The company expanded its drayage operations in March 2006 when it paid about $40 million for Memphis-based Comtrak, which was renamed Comtrak Logistics.

Founder and chairman Phillip Yeager died in 2008 at age 80.

EXECUTIVES

Chairman and CEO: David P. Yeager, age 55, $1,318,483 total compensation
Vice Chairman, President, and COO: Mark A. Yeager, age 44, $1,011,380 total compensation
EVP, CFO, and Treasurer: Terri A. Pizzuto, age 50, $650,291 total compensation
EVP Information Services: Dennis R. Polsen, age 55
Chief Intermodal Officer: Christopher R. (Chris) Kravas, age 43, $579,797 total compensation
Chief Marketing Officer: David L. Marsh, age 41, $631,478 total compensation
EVP Logistics: Donald G. Maltby, age 54
EVP Customer Service: Stephen P. Cosgrove, age 49
EVP Sales: James B. (Jim) Gaw, age 58
EVP Highway: Dwight C. Nixon, age 46
VP, Secretary, and General Counsel: David C. Zeilstra, age 39
Auditors: Ernst & Young LLP

LOCATIONS

HQ: Hub Group, Inc.
3050 Highland Pkwy., Ste. 100
Downers Grove, IL 60515
Phone: 630-271-3600   **Fax:** 630-964-6475
Web: www.hubgroup.com

PRODUCTS/OPERATIONS

2008 Sales

	$ mil.	% of total
Intermodal	1,329.4	71
Brokerage	372.3	20
Logistics	158.9	9
Total	**1,860.6**	**100**

COMPETITORS

APL Logistics	Menlo Worldwide
C.H. Robinson Worldwide	Pacer International
J.B. Hunt	Transplace
Landstar System	UPS

HISTORICAL FINANCIALS

Company Type: Public

Income Statement

FYE: December 31

	REVENUE ($ mil.)	NET INCOME ($ mil.)	NET PROFIT MARGIN	EMPLOYEES
12/08	1,860.6	59.2	3.2%	1,420
12/07	1,658.2	59.8	3.6%	1,412
12/06	1,609.5	48.7	3.0%	1,513
12/05	1,531.5	32.9	2.1%	1,184
12/04	1,426.8	17.3	1.2%	1,172
Annual Growth	6.9%	36.0%	—	4.9%

2008 Year-End Financials

Debt ratio: —
Return on equity: 20.9%
Cash ($ mil.): 86
Current ratio: 1.70
Long-term debt ($ mil.): —

No. of shares (mil.): 38
Dividends
  Yield: 0.0%
  Payout: —
Market value ($ mil.): 1,003

Stock History

NASDAQ (GS): HUBG

	STOCK PRICE ($) FY Close	P/E High/Low	PER SHARE ($) Earnings	Dividends	Book Value
12/08	26.53	28 13	1.58	0.00	8.33
12/07	26.58	26 15	1.53	0.00	6.63
12/06	27.55	25 15	1.19	0.00	6.84
12/05	17.67	26 15	0.80	0.00	6.40
12/04	13.06	30 11	0.46	0.00	6.00
Annual Growth	19.4%	— —	36.1%	—	8.6%

Humana Inc.

Medicare has made Humana a big-time player in the health insurance game. One of the country's largest Medicare providers and a top health insurer, Humana provides Medicare Advantage plans and prescription drug coverage to more than 4.5 million members in all 50 states and Puerto Rico. It also administers managed care plans for other government programs, including Medicaid plans in Florida and Puerto Rico and TRICARE (a program for military personnel) in 10 southern states. Additionally, Humana offers health plans and some specialty products (group life and disability insurance, for example) to commercial employers and individuals. All told, it covers more than 11 million members in the US.

The company has been aggressive in signing up Medicare recipients for prescription drug coverage under Medicare Part D. It has also been expanding the geographic reach of its Medicare Advantage plans and now offers its private fee-for-service version of the plans in every state in the US. (It offers HMO and PPO versions in select markets.)

In 2008 Humana acquired about 25,000 Medicare Advantage members in Nevada from UnitedHealth. Later that year it acquired Florida-based Medicare Advantage provider Metcare Health Plans from Metropolitan Health Networks.

More than two-thirds of Humana's sales come from government program premiums, and more than half come from Medicare-related premiums alone. The company's reliance on its government business has brought it significant growth, but also leaves it vulnerable to cuts in reimbursement rates.

Humana is also working to bolster its commercial business, which offers health coverage to employer groups on a fully-insured basis or with an "administrative services only" model to self-funded groups. Its products include HMO, PPO, and fee-for-service plans, as well as consumer-directed products such as health savings accounts.

The company has grown its commercial membership and diversified its product line through a number of acquisitions and internal initiatives. It expanded its portfolio of individual health plans in 2007, adding a consumer-driven plan and an employer-style, full-coverage plan.

It further grew its product line with the 2007 acquisition of Atlanta-based CompBenefits, a provider of dental and vision benefits to nearly 5 million members. The acquisition gave Humana a full-service vision offering and expanded its dental benefits operations. Later that year the company bought KMG America, a life and health insurer and third-party administrator for more than 1 million members.

Also in 2008 the company acquired OSF HealthPlans, an Illinois-based managed care company belonging to OSF Healthcare. The company also acquired Tennessee-based PHP Companies (which does business as Cariten Healthcare) from Covenant Health.

HISTORY

In 1961 Louisville, Kentucky, lawyers David Jones and Wendell Cherry bought a nursing home as a real estate investment. Within six years their company, Extendicare, was the largest nursing home chain in the US (with only eight homes).

Faced with a glutted nursing home market, the partners noticed that hospitals received more money per patient per day than nursing homes, so they took their company public in 1968 to finance hospital purchases (one per month from 1968 to 1971). The company then sold its 40 nursing homes. Sales rose 13 times over in the next five years, and in 1973 the firm changed its name to Humana.

By 1975 Humana had built 27 hospitals in the South and Southwest. It targeted young, privately insured patients and kept its charity caseload and bad-debt expenses low. Three years later #3 for-profit hospital operator Humana moved up a notch when it bought #2 American Medicorp.

In 1983 the government began reimbursing Medicare payments based on fixed rates. Counting on its high hospital occupancy, in 1984 the company launched Humana Health Care Plans, rewarding doctors and patients who used Humana hospitals. However, hospital occupancy dropped, and the company closed several clinics. When its net income fell 75% in 1986, the firm responded by lowering premiums to attract employers.

In 1991 co-founder Cherry died. With hospital profits down, in 1993 Jones spun off Humana's 76 hospitals as Galen Healthcare, which formed the nucleus of what is now HCA — The Healthcare Company. The next year Humana added 1.3 million members when it bought EMPHESYS, and the company's income, which had stagnated since the salad days of the late 1980s and early 1990s, seemed headed in the right direction.

In the mid-1990s cutthroat premiums failed to cover rising health care costs as members' hospital use soared out of control, particularly in the company's new Washington, DC, market. Profits dropped 94%, and Humana's already tense relationship with doctors and members worsened. President and COO Wayne Smith and CFO Roger Drury resigned as part of a management shake-up, and newly appointed president Gregory Wolf offered to drop the company's gag clause after the Florida Physicians Association threatened to sue.

A reorganized Humana rebounded in 1997. The company pulled out of 13 unprofitable markets, including Alabama (though it did not drop TRICARE, its military health coverage program, in that state) and Washington, DC. Refocusing on core markets in the Midwest and Southeast, Humana bought Physician Corp. of America (PCA) and ChoiceCare, a Cincinnati HMO. Wolf replaced Jones as CEO in 1997.

Humana did everything *but* party in 1999. The company faced RICO charges for allegedly overcharging members for co-insurance; it agreed to repay $15 million in Medicare overpayments to the government; and it became the first health insurance firm to be slapped with a class-action suit over its physician incentives and other coverage policies.

Humana sold PCA in 2000, saying that it had paid too much for the company. That year Humana also sold its underperforming Florida Medicaid HMO to Well Care HMO, and agreed to pay more than $14 million to the government for submitting false Medicare payment information.

Expanding its holdings in the southeast, Humana acquired Louisiana's Ochsner Health Plan in 2004.

EXECUTIVES

Chairman: David A. Jones Jr., age 51
President, CEO, and Director:
  Michael B. (Mike) McCallister, age 56,
  $4,764,309 total compensation
COO: James E. (Jim) Murray, age 55,
  $2,467,361 total compensation
SVP, CFO, and Treasurer: James H. (Jim) Bloem,
  age 58, $1,772,851 total compensation
SVP and Chief Service and Information Officer:
  Bruce J. Goodman, age 67,
  $1,588,048 total compensation
SVP and Chief Human Resources Officer:
  Bonita C. (Bonnie) Hathcock, age 60
SVP and Chief Strategy Officer: Paul B. Kusserow
SVP and Chief Innovation and Marketing Officer:
  Raja Rajamannar
SVP Corporate Communications:
  Thomas J. (Tom) Noland Jr.
SVP and General Counsel: Christopher Todoroff, age 46
SVP Senior Products: Thomas J. (Tom) Liston, age 47
SVP Government Relations: Heidi S. Margulis, age 55
**SVP, National Contracting; President, ChoiceCare
  Network:** Bruce Perkins
VP Investor Relations: Regina C. Nethery
VP and Controller, Principal Accounting Officer:
  Steven E. McCulley, age 47
VP and Acting General Counsel: Kathleen Pellegrino
Auditors: PricewaterhouseCoopers LLP

LOCATIONS

HQ: Humana Inc.
500 W. Main St., Louisville, KY 40202
Phone: 502-580-1000 **Fax:** 502-580-3677
Web: www.humana.com

PRODUCTS/OPERATIONS

2008 Sales

	$ mil.	% of total
Government		
Premiums		
Medicare Advantage	13,778.0	48
Medicare stand-alone PDP	3,380.4	12
Military services	3,218.3	11
Medicaid	591.5	2
Administrative services fees	85.9	—
Investment income	115.2	1
Other income	1.8	—
Commercial		
Premiums		
Fully insured	6,169.4	21
Specialty	927.2	3
Administrative services fees	366.0	1
Investment income	105.0	—
Other income	207.7	1
Total	**28,946.4**	**100**

2008 Membership

	No.
Government	
Medicare stand-alone PDP	3,066,600
Medicare Advantage	1,435,900
Military services	1,736,400
Military administrative services only (ASO)	1,228,300
Medicaid	385,400
Medicaid ASO	85,700
Commercial fully-insured	1,978,800
Commercial ASO	1,642,000
Total	**11,559,100**

Selected Products and Services

Government
  Medicaid managed care plans
  Medicare Advantage plans
  Medicare prescription drug plans
  TRICARE (military personnel)
Commercial
  Administrative services only
  Health care spending accounts
  HMO plans
  Humana Classic (traditional indemnity plan)
  HumanaOne (individual insurance)
  POS (point-of-service) plans
  PPO plans
  Specialty products
    Dental insurance
    Life insurance
    Short-term disability insurance

COMPETITORS

Aetna
AMERIGROUP
Blue Cross
Caremark Pharmacy Services
Centene
CIGNA
Express Scripts
HCSC
Health Net
Kaiser Foundation Health Plan
Medco Health
Molina Healthcare
UnitedHealth Group
WellCare Health Plans
WellPoint

HISTORICAL FINANCIALS

Company Type: Public

Income Statement

FYE: December 31

	REVENUE ($ mil.)	NET INCOME ($ mil.)	NET PROFIT MARGIN	EMPLOYEES
12/08	28,946.4	647.2	2.2%	28,900
12/07	25,290.0	833.7	3.3%	25,000
12/06	21,416.5	487.4	2.3%	22,300
12/05	14,418.1	308.5	2.1%	18,700
12/04	13,104.3	280.0	2.1%	13,700
Annual Growth	**21.9%**	**23.3%**	**—**	**20.5%**

2008 Year-End Financials

Debt ratio: 43.5%
Return on equity: 15.3%
Cash ($ mil.): 1,970
Current ratio: —
Long-term debt ($ mil.): 1,937
No. of shares (mil.): 170
Dividends
  Yield: 0.0%
  Payout: —
Market value ($ mil.): 6,325

Stock History

NYSE: HUM

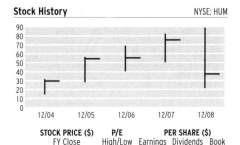

	STOCK PRICE ($) FY Close	P/E High/Low		PER SHARE ($) Earnings	Dividends	Book Value
12/08	37.28	23	6	3.83	0.00	26.27
12/07	75.31	17	10	4.91	0.00	23.75
12/06	55.31	24	14	2.90	0.00	18.00
12/05	54.33	30	15	1.87	0.00	14.58
12/04	29.69	18	9	1.72	0.00	12.32
Annual Growth	**5.9%**	**—**	**—**	**22.2%**	**—**	**20.8%**

Huntington Bancshares

Huntington Bancshares is the holding company for The Huntington National Bank, which operates more than 600 offices, mainly in Ohio and Michigan, but also in Indiana, Kentucky, Pennsylvania, and West Virginia. Huntington Bancshares operates in two other segments besides regional banking. Its Dealer Sales unit finances auto sales and leases through more than 3,000 car dealerships throughout the Midwest and other states, while its Private Financial and Capital Markets Group provides asset management, private banking, and brokerage services to wealthy customers. Huntington Bancshares also offers trust and insurance services.

In 2007 the company entered the Pennsylvania market with the acquisition of Sky Financial, which offered banking and other financial services at some 330 branches in the Keystone State, as well as in Indiana, Michigan, Ohio, and West Virginia.

Huntington survived the 2008 economy but did post a moderate loss at the end of the year. Early in 2009, management announced a plan to eliminate bonuses and other incentive programs

for all employees, and initiated additional cost-cutting measures designed to save one-time expenses. The bank also cut its staff by 4 percent and cut its quarterly dividend to 1 cent per share.

Chairman, president, and CEO Thomas Hoaglin retired in 2009, after serving eight years in those positions. Former Citizens Financial Group CEO Stephen Steinour was named Hoaglin's successor.

HISTORY

Pelatiah Webster (P. W.) Huntington, descendant of both a Revolutionary War leader and a Declaration of Independence signer, went to work at sea in 1850 at age 14. He returned to go into banking, and in 1866 founded what would become Huntington National Bank of Columbus. As the business grew, he conscripted four of his five sons. The bank took a national charter in 1905 and became The Huntington National Bank of Columbus. It survived the hard times of 1907 and 1912 through the Huntington philosophy of sitting on piles of cash.

P. W. died in 1918 and his son Francis became president. Francis expanded the company into trust services. Unlike many bankers in the 1920s, he refused to make speculative loans based on the stock market. Francis died in 1928 and was succeeded by brother Theodore. By 1930 Huntington's trust assets accounted for more than half of the total. The family's conservative philosophy helped the bank sail through the 1933 bank holiday, although when it reopened the amount of cash it could pay out was restricted to 10% of deposits.

P. W.'s son Gwynne chaired the bank during its post-WWII expansion. His death in 1958 ended the Huntington family reign. The bank began opening branches and adding new services, such as mortgage and consumer loans. In 1966, in order to expand statewide, the corporation formed a holding company, Huntington Bancshares. In the 1960s and 1970s, the corporation added new operations, including mortgage and leasing companies and an international division to help clients with foreign exchange.

In 1979 the company consolidated its 15 affiliates into The Huntington National Bank. Three years later the company bit off more than it could chew with the acquisitions of Reeves Banking and Trust Company of Dover and Union Commerce Corporation of Cleveland. The latter purchase loaded the company with debt. Nevertheless, it continued to expand, particularly after 1985 when banking regulations allowed interstate branch banking, and it soon had operations in Florida, Indiana, Kentucky, Michigan, and West Virginia.

Huntington Bancshares was largely insulated from the real estate problems of the late 1980s and early 1990s, thanks to its continuing conservative lending policies. But the company was at risk from the nationwide consolidation of the banking industry, which made it a potential takeover target. It increased its service offerings and bolstered its place in the market through acquisitions. In 1996 Huntington Bancshares bought life insurance agency Tice & Associates and began cross-selling bank and insurance products. Important banking acquisitions in 1997 included First Michigan Bank and several Florida companies.

Also in 1997 the company took advantage of deregulation to consolidate its interstate operations (except for The Huntington State Bank) into a single operating company. In 1998 Huntington

Bancshares continued to build its Huntington insurance services unit with the acquisition of Pollock & Pollock. In 1999 the bank launched a mortgage program aimed at wealthy clients and sold its credit card receivables portfolio to Chase Manhattan (now JPMorgan Chase & Co.). In 2000 the company bought Michigan's Empire Banc Corporation.

Former BANK ONE executive Thomas Hoaglin was named president and CEO in 2001. Later that year he became chairman when Frank Wobst retired after leading the company for 20 years.

In 2002 the company consolidated some branches in the Midwest to cut costs and exited the retail banking market in Florida, selling some 140 retail branches there to SunTrust. After the mid-2007 acquisition of Sky Financial, Sky's CEO Marty Adams became president and COO of Huntington Bancshares. He retired at the end of 2007, and Hoaglin resumed the president's role until his own retirement in 2009; Stephen Steinour then took the helm.

EXECUTIVES

Chairman, President, and CEO:
Stephen D. (Steve) Steinour, age 50
EVP, CFO, and Treasurer: Donald R. Kimble, age 49, $668,597 total compensation
SVP and Chief Risk Officer: Kevin M. Blakely
SEVP and Senior Trust Officer:
Daniel B. (Dan) Benhase, age 49, $629,441 total compensation
SEVP and Group Manager, Dealer Sales, The Huntington National Bank: Nicholas G. (Nick) Stanutz, age 54
Regional Banking Group President; SEVP The Huntington National Bank: Mary W. Navarro, age 53, $660,390 total compensation
SEVP and Director Commercial Banking; Regional President, West Michigan: James E. (Jim) Dunlap
SEVP and Director Strategy and Business Segment Performance: Mark E. Thompson
SEVP; Director Commercial Real Estate:
Randall G. Stickler
EVP and Human Resources Director:
Melinda S. Ackerman, age 61
General Counsel and Secretary; EVP, General Counsel, Secretary, and Cashier, The Huntington National Bank: Richard A. Cheap, age 57
EVP and Chief Auditor: Eric N. Sutphin
EVP Customer Experience, The Huntington National Bank: Neeli Bendapudi, age 45
EVP and Manager, Business Banking, The Huntington National Bank: Jeff Rosen
EVP and Chief Credit Officer: Richard (Dick) Witherow, age 59
EVP Commercial Banking, The Huntington National Bank: Mark Maiberger
Media: Jeri Grier
Controller: Thomas P. Reed, age 51
Auditors: Deloitte & Touche LLP

LOCATIONS

HQ: Huntington Bancshares Incorporated
Huntington Center, 41 S. High St.
Columbus, OH 43287
Phone: 614-480-8300   **Fax:** 614-480-5284
Web: www.huntington.com

PRODUCTS/OPERATIONS

2008 Gross Revenues

	$ mil.	% of total
Interest	2,798.3	76
Noninterest		
Service charges on deposit accounts	308.0	8
Brokerage & insurance	137.8	4
Trust services	126.0	3
Electronic banking	90.2	2
Bank-owned life insurance	54.8	1
Automobile lease income	39.9	1
Mortgage banking	9.0	1
Other	138.8	4
Total	**3,702.8**	**100**

2008 Assets

	$ mil.	% of total
Cash & equivalents	1,137.2	2
Trading account securities	88.7	—
Investment securities	4,384.5	8
Loans held for sale	390.4	—
Loans & leases		
Commercial & industrial	13,540.8	25
Commercial real estate	10,098.2	19
Automobile loans	3,900.9	7
Automobile leases	563.4	1
Home equity	7,556.4	13
Residential mortgage	4,761.4	10
Other consumer	671.0	1
Allowance for loan losses	(900.2)	
Other assets	7,804.5	14
Total	**54,352.9**	**100**

COMPETITORS

Bank of America
Bank of Kentucky Financial
Citigroup
Comerica
Fifth Third
FirstMerit
JPMorgan Chase
KeyCorp
NorthWest Indiana Bancorp
Ohio Valley Banc
PNC Financial
Regions Financial
U.S. Bancorp

HISTORICAL FINANCIALS

Company Type: Public

Income Statement

FYE: December 31

	ASSETS ($ mil.)	NET INCOME ($ mil.)	INCOME AS % OF ASSETS	EMPLOYEES
12/08	54,352.9	(113.8)	—	10,951
12/07	54,697.5	75.2	0.1%	11,925
12/06	35,329.0	461.2	1.3%	8,081
12/05	32,764.8	412.1	1.3%	7,602
12/04	32,565.5	398.9	1.2%	7,812
Annual Growth	**13.7%**	**—**	**—**	**8.8%**

2008 Year-End Financials

Equity as % of assets: 9.8%
Return on assets: —
Return on equity: —
Long-term debt ($ mil.): 6,871
No. of shares (mil.): 569
Dividends
Yield: 8.6%
Payout: —
Market value ($ mil.): 4,359
Sales ($ mil.): 2,239

Stock History   NASDAQ (GS): HBAN

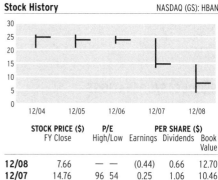

	STOCK PRICE ($) FY Close	P/E High/Low		PER SHARE ($) Earnings	Dividends	Book Value
12/08	7.66	—	—	(0.44)	0.66	12.70
12/07	14.76	96	54	0.25	1.06	10.46
12/06	23.75	13	12	1.92	1.00	5.30
12/05	23.75	14	12	1.77	0.85	4.49
12/04	24.74	15	12	1.71	0.75	4.46
Annual Growth	**(25.4%)**	**—**	**—**	**—**	**(3.1%)**	**29.9%**

Hyatt Hotels Corporation

Travelers interested in luxury lodgings can check in for the Hyatt touch. The company is one of the world's top operators of full-service luxury hotels and resorts with more than 400 managed, franchised, and owned properties in some 45 countries. Its core Hyatt Regency brand offers hospitality services targeted primarily to business travelers and upscale vacationers. The firm also operates properties under the names Grand Hyatt, Park Hyatt, Hyatt Place, Hyatt Summerfield Suites, Hyatt Resorts, and Andaz. Although Hyatt Hotels was formed in 2004, the Hyatt chain traces its roots back to 1957. It is majority-owned by the wealthy Pritzker family of Chicago. In 2009 the company filed an IPO.

While the timing of the public offering is questionable, with the hotel industry suffering from decreased demand in the midst of a global recession, Hyatt's IPO has been years in the making as a way for the Pritzker family to raise cash. The family is splitting up its assets among 11 adult cousins, a process that it hopes to complete by 2011.

As part of an effort to focus on its growth luxury hotel businesses and international expansion, the company sold its U.S. Franchise Systems subsidiary in 2008 to Wyndham Worldwide. The unit, acquired in 2000, operated the smaller Hawthorn Suites and Microtel Inns & Suites chains. Future hotels are planned for India (Hyatt Regency Pune and Park Hyatt Hyderabad), Mexico (Park Hyatt Mexico City), United Arab Emirates (Park Hyatt Abu Dhabi), and China (Grand Hyatt Shenzhen), all of which are set to open in 2010.

Hyatt Hotels has been busy investing in its Hyatt Place banner, a new brand designed to attract younger travelers with wireless Internet access, flat screen televisions, and contemporary interiors. The limited-service chain was rebranded from AmeriSuites, a banner Hyatt acquired in 2005 from Prime Hospitality. The company is also growing its Hyatt Summerfield Suites chain, an upscale all-suite/extended-stay brand previously known as Summerfield Suites (acquired from The Blackstone Group in 2006). Hyatt launched Andaz, its newest luxury hotel brand, in 2007. Andaz Wall Street is set to open in New York City in 2009, while Andaz Fifth Avenue, also in New York, has a 2010 launch date.

As part of an ongoing effort to restructure H Group Holding, the holding company that oversees the Pritzker's various business enterprises, Hyatt Hotels, was formed to consolidate the family's hospitality interests. The reorganization brought together the operations of Hyatt Hotels Corporation (domestic hotels), Hyatt International (international hotels), Hyatt Equities (hotel ownership), and Hyatt Vacation Ownership (timeshares) under one umbrella, called Global Hyatt. In 2009 the company changed its name from Global Hyatt to Hyatt Hotels.

The Pritzkers hold an 85% stake in the company, while Goldman Sachs Group has a nearly 8%, and Madrone Capital Partners holds about 6%. (Madrone is affiliated with Wal-Mart chairman and heir Rob Walton.)

HISTORY

Nicholas Pritzker left Kiev for Chicago in 1881, where his family's ascent to the ranks of America's wealthiest families began. His son A. N. left the family law practice in the 1930s and began investing in a variety of businesses. He turned a 1942 investment (Cory Corporation) worth $25,000 into $23 million by 1967. A. N.'s son Jay followed in his father's wheeling-and-dealing footsteps. In 1953, with the help of his father's banking connections, Jay purchased Colson Company and recruited his brother Bob, an industrial engineer, to restructure a company that made tricycles and US Navy rockets. By 1990 Jay and Bob had added 60 industrial companies, with annual sales exceeding $3 billion, to the entity they called The Marmon Group.

The family's connection to Hyatt hotels was established in 1957 when Jay Pritzker bought a hotel called Hyatt House, located near the Los Angeles airport, from Hyatt von Dehn. Jay added five locations by 1961 and hired his gregarious youngest brother, Donald, to manage the hotel company. Hyatt went public in 1967, but the move that opened new vistas for the hotel chain was the purchase that year of an 800-room hotel in Atlanta that both Hilton and Marriott had turned down. John Portman's design, incorporating a 21-story atrium, a large fountain, and a revolving rooftop restaurant, became a Hyatt trademark.

The Pritzkers formed Hyatt International in 1969 to operate hotels overseas, and the company grew rapidly in the US and abroad during the 1970s. Donald Pritzker died in 1972, and Jay assumed control of Hyatt. The family decided to take the company private in 1979. Much of Hyatt's growth in the 1970s came from contracts to manage Hyatt hotels built by other investors. When Hyatt's earnings on those contracts shrank in the 1980s, the company launched its own hotel and resort developments under Nick Pritzker, a cousin to Jay and Bob. In 1988, with US and Japanese partners, it built the Hyatt Regency Waikoloa on Hawaii's Big Island for $360 million — a record at the time for a hotel.

The Pritzkers took a side-venture into air travel in 1983 when they bought bedraggled Braniff Airlines through Hyatt subsidiaries as it emerged from bankruptcy. After a failed 1987 attempt to merge the airline with Pan Am, the Pritzkers sold Braniff in 1988.

Hyatt opened Classic Residence by Hyatt, a group of upscale retirement communities, in 1989. The company joined Circus Circus (now part of MGM MIRAGE) in 1994 to launch the Grand Victoria, the nation's largest cruising gaming vessel. The next year, as part of a new strategy to manage both freestanding golf courses and those near Hyatt hotels, the company opened its first freestanding course: an 18-hole, par 71 championship course in Aruba.

President Thomas Pritzker, Jay's son, took over as Hyatt chairman and CEO following his father's death in early 1999. In 2000 the Pritzker family that year led a buyout of U.S. Franchise Systems (sold to Wyndham Worldwide in 2008).

In 2004 the Pritzker family consolidated its hospitality holdings to form Global Hyatt Corporation. The following year the company bought the AmeriSuites limited-service hotel chain from Prime Hospitality.

Mark Hoplamazian, president of The Pritzker Organization, a merchant-banking firm serving the family's business activities, took over as president and CEO in 2006; Thomas Pritzker remained chairman.

EXECUTIVES

Executive Chairman: Thomas J. (Tom) Pritzker, age 59
President, CEO, and Director: Mark S. Hoplamazian, age 45
COO North America: H. Charles (Chuck) Floyd, age 49
COO International Operations: Rakesh Sarna, age 52
CFO: Harmit J. Singh, age 46
Chief Human Resources Officer: Robert W. K. Webb, age 53
EVP Global Real Estate and Development: Stephen G. (Steve) Haggerty, age 41
SVP, General Counsel, and Secretary: Susan T. Smith, age 53
SVP Brand Communication, Hyatt Hotels and Resorts: Amy Curtis-McIntyre
VP Marketing, Hyatt Hotels: Amy Weyman
Global Head Marketing and Brand Strategy: John Wallis, age 56

LOCATIONS

HQ: Hyatt Hotels Corporation
71 S. Wacker Dr., 12th FL., Chicago, IL 60606
Phone: 312-750-1234   **Fax:** 312-750-8550
Web: www.hyatt.com

2008 Sales

	$ mil.	% of total
US	3,064.4	80
International	772.3	20
Total	**3,836.7**	**100**

PRODUCTS/OPERATIONS

2008 Sales

	$ mil.	% of total
Owned & leased hotels	2,138.6	54
North American management & franchising	1,474.8	37
International management & franchising	225.4	6
Corporate & other	104.5	3
Eliminations	(106.6)	—
Total	**3,836.7**	**100**

2008 Properties by Type

	No. of properties
Managed	186
Franchised	100
Owned	96
Vacation ownership	15
Residential properties	10
Total	**407**

Selected Brands

Andaz (simple, sophisticated luxury hotels)
Grand Hyatt Hotels (large-scale luxury format)
Hyatt Regency Hotels (core hotel format)
Hyatt Resorts (local culture, including spas and cuisine)
Hyatt Summerfield Suites (extended stay)
Hyatt Vacation Ownership (timeshares)
Park Hyatt Hotels (smaller-scale luxury hotels)

Selected Properties

Andaz West Hollywood
Grand Hyatt New York
Grand Hyatt San Antonio
Grand Hyatt San Francisco
Grand Hyatt Seattle
Grand Hyatt Tampa Bay
Hyatt Place Atlanta/Perimeter Center
Hyatt Place Baltimore/Owings Mills
Hyatt Place Birmingham/Inverness
Hyatt Place Boise/Towne Square
Hyatt Place Charlotte Airport/Tyvola Road
Hyatt Place Chicago/Hoffman Estates
Hyatt Place Chicago/Itasca
Hyatt Place Chicago/Lombard/Oak Brook
Hyatt Place Cincinnati Northeast
Hyatt Regency Atlanta
Hyatt Regency Baltimore
Hyatt Regency Bellevue
Hyatt Regency Boston
Hyatt Regency Buffalo
Hyatt Regency Cincinnati
Hyatt Regency Cleveland at The Arcade
Hyatt Regency Coconut Point Resort & Spa
Hyatt Summerfield Suites Boston/Waltham
Hyatt Summerfield Suites Denver Tech Center
Hyatt Summerfield Suites Miami Airport
Hyatt Summerfield Suites Parsippany/Whippany
Hyatt Summerfield Suites Morristown
Park Hyatt Chicago
Park Hyatt Philadelphia at Bellevue
Park Hyatt Toronto
Park Hyatt Washington

COMPETITORS

Accor	LXR Luxury Resorts
Carlson Hotels	Marriott
Club Med	Millennium & Copthorne
Four Seasons Hotels	Sonesta International
Hilton Hotels	Starwood Hotels
InterContinental Hotels	Wyndham Worldwide

HISTORICAL FINANCIALS

Company Type: Private

Income Statement

FYE: December 31

	REVENUE ($ mil.)	NET INCOME ($ mil.)	NET PROFIT MARGIN	EMPLOYEES
12/08	3,836.7	170.0	4.4%	125,000
12/07*	3,738.0	271.0	7.2%	90,000
1/06	3,471.0	329.0	9.5%	85,000
1/05	3,200.0	—	—	70,000
1/04	5,812.0	—	—	—
Annual Growth	(9.9%)	(28.1%)	—	21.3%

*Fiscal year change

Net Income History

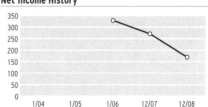

IAC/InterActiveCorp

IAC/InterActiveCorp (IAC) satisfies inquisitive minds who want to explore local hot spots, meet the right partner, find a contractor, and maybe even host a party or two. The Internet conglomerate owns more than 35 Web companies, including search engine Ask.com, local guide Citysearch, dating site Match.com, home service provider network ServiceMagic, and online-invitation firm Evite. Formerly a jumble of disparate assets that included cable-TV networks, travel services, and mortgage lending, the company has slimmed down to focus on the online search and content market. To achieve this goal, it split into five public companies in 2008, with IAC retaining the Web properties. IAC is controlled by CEO Barry Diller.

Diller spun off HSN, Ticketmaster, Tree.com, and Interval Leisure Group in order to address shareholder frustration at a cluttered business model. The split has undone years of acquisitions by IAC that positioned it as a big player in e-commerce, but also created a complex corporate structure that confused investors. (Previously, IAC had spun off its online travel subsidiary Expedia amid a slowdown in the online travel business. The spinoff included other travel-related businesses, such as Hotels.com and travel-advice site TripAdvisor.com, among others.)

The newly organized IAC consists of units devoted to Media & Advertising, Match, Emerging Businesses, and ServiceMagic. Its Ask.com (formerly Ask Jeeves) is the company's flagship search engine that falls under Media & Advertising, along with Citysearch and Evite. Media & Advertising makes money by selling ads on IAC-owned Web sites. The unit has struck a deal with Google — worth an estimated $3.5 billion through 2012 — granting Google the right to sell ads on Ask.com and other IAC sites. In 2008 Google acounted for some 40% of revenues.

Emerging Businesses includes some of the company's more recent purchases, such as its majority stake in Connected Ventures, the parent company of racy college entertainment site CollegeHumor.com. Other Emerging Businesses include ReserveAmerica, Internet videogame firm InstantAction, shoe site Shoebuy.com, and general e-commerce service Pronto.com. Its personal finance site FiLife.com, launched in 2008, is a joint venture with Dow Jones. In addition, the company has set his sights on China, where IAC plans to invest about $100 million to create services for local users there. To that end, IAC plans to introduce its Ask.com search engine in China by 2010.

Diller's breakup plan for IAC overcame stiff resistance from John Malone's Liberty Media, which owned about 30% of IAC's equity and about 60% of the voting power due to a two-tier share structure, although through an agreement with Malone, Diller had controlled Liberty's votes. Malone initially opposed the spinoffs because the new companies have a single-tier voting structure, shrinking Liberty's power. A 2008 court ruling siding with Diller allowed the breakup plan to proceed. After filing an appeal to the court's decision, Liberty Media later dropped it in exchange for the power to appoint several board members to the new spinoff companies. The agreement with Malone also gives Liberty Media about 30% voting power in each of the companies.

HISTORY

TV networks aren't built in a day; but if anyone could do it, it's probably Barry Diller. Since dropping out of UCLA in 1958 to work in the mailroom at the William Morris talent agency (he was promoted to agent in 1961), Diller has been all over Tinseltown. He got into television in 1968 as the VP of programming for ABC, where he developed the concepts of the mini-series and the made-for-TV movie. Diller's next step took him into movies as chairman of Paramount Pictures in 1974. His 10-year Paramount stint produced films including *Raiders of the Lost Ark*. But Diller's biggest claim to fame is his tenure at FOX. Beginning in 1984, Diller led the brash television network from joke to jewel. After a scrape with FOX boss Rupert Murdoch in 1992, he moved on to home shopping as head of QVC in 1993.

Diller built a company of his own in 1995 after leaving QVC. With financial backing from TCI (later bought by AT&T Broadband), Diller took over the Home Shopping Network (now HSN) and its separately traded distribution unit, Silver King Communications. In 1997 HSN bought Microsoft co-founder Paul Allen's 47% interest in Ticketmaster. Diller followed that up with the $4 billion purchase of USA Networks in 1998.

USA Networks dates back to 1977, when Kay Koplovitz founded the all-sports Madison Square Garden Network cable channel. In 1980 she sold the channel (now USA Network) to Time, MCA, and Paramount. By 1988 Paramount (later bought by Viacom) and MCA had become equal owners in USA. (Universal bought out Viacom's interest in 1997.)

Diller bought USA Networks and Vivendi UNIVERSAL Entertainment's TV production and US distribution business as well. The deal gave Seagram a 45% stake in HSN, which changed its name to USA Networks. USA Networks bought the remainder of Ticketmaster in 1998, then purchased online entertainment guide publisher Citysearch, merging it with Ticketmaster Online.

In 1999 Diller bought parts of PolyGram Filmed Entertainment and independent film companies Gramercy and October from Seagram, renaming them Focus. In 2000 French utility and media firm Vivendi (now Vivendi UNIVERSAL) bought Seagram, gaining Seagram's 43% stake in USA Networks.

In 2001 USA Networks agreed to sell its TV stations to Univision for $1.1 billion. At the end of 2001 Diller decided to shift USA Interactive's focus entirely to retailing. He agreed to sell USA Networks' entertainment assets to Vivendi UNIVERSAL for $10.3 billion. The deal was completed in 2002, and the company changed its name to USA Interactive with Diller retaining his voting control of the firm.

In 2003 the company completed its acquisition of the outstanding shares of Hotels.com and Expedia that it didn't already own. The same day of the Expedia deal, IAC completed its acquisition of online financial services company LendingTree (now Tree.com).

In 2004 the company changed its name to IAC/InterActiveCorp. In 2005 it completed the acquisition of Cornerstone Brands, a portfolio of leading print catalogs and online retailing sites. Later that year IAC completed the spinoff to IAC shareholders of its travel businesses.

In 2007 IAC sold its German TV and Internet retailer, HSE Germany. In 2007 IAC struck a deal with online video syndication firm Brightcove to create and distribute video for IAC's brands.

EXECUTIVES

Chairman and CEO: Barry Diller, age 67, $13,174,733 total compensation
Vice Chairman: Victor A. Kaufman, age 65, $6,213,285 total compensation
EVP and CFO: Thomas J. (Tom) McInerney, age 44, $9,414,810 total compensation
Chief Administrative Officer: Jason Stewart
EVP; CEO, Match.com: Gregory R. (Greg) Blatt, age 40, $7,464,789 total compensation
SVP Corporate Development: Mark J. Stein
SVP and Deputy General Counsel: Joanne Hawkins
SVP and General Manager, Evite: Rosanna McCollough
SVP Mergers and Acquisitions and Strategy: Shana Fisher
SVP Tax: Greg Morrow
SVP and Controller: Michael H. Schwerdtman
SVP Publishing, Citysearch: Kara Nortman
SVP Mergers and Acquisitions and Finance: Joey Levin
SVP and General Counsel: Gregg Winiarski
VP Finance, IAC Advertising: Roger Clark
VP Corporate Communications: Stacy Simpson
CEO, Mindspark Interactive Network: John Park
Associate Director Corporate Communications: Leslie Cafferty
Senior Advisor: Michael Jackson
Auditors: Ernst & Young LLP

LOCATIONS

HQ: IAC/InterActiveCorp
555 West 18th St., New York, NY 10011
Phone: 212-314-7300
Web: www.iac.com

2008 Sales

	$ mil.	% of total
US	1,169	81
Other countries	276	19
Total	**1,445**	**100**

PRODUCTS/OPERATIONS

2008 Sales

	$ mil.	% of total
Media & advertising	779	53
Match	365	25
Emerging businesses	197	13
Service Magic	124	9
Adjustments	(20)	—
Total	**1,445**	**100**

Selected Properties

Ask.com
Citysearch
CollegeHumor.com
The Daily Beast
Evite
FiLife.com
Gifts.com
InstantAction.com
Match.com
Pronto.com
ReserveAmerica
RushmoreDrive.com
ServiceMagic
Shoebuy
VeryShortList.com

COMPETITORS

AOL
CBS Interactive
Cox Enterprises
craigslist
Disney Online
Facebook
Fox Interactive
Google
Hearst Interactive Media
MSN
Yahoo!

HISTORICAL FINANCIALS

Company Type: Public

Income Statement

	REVENUE ($ mil.)	NET INCOME ($ mil.)	NET PROFIT MARGIN	EMPLOYEES
12/08	1,445.1	(156.2)	—	3,200
12/07	6,373.4	(144.1)	—	21,000
12/06	6,277.6	192.6	3.1%	20,000
12/05	5,753.7	806.0	14.0%	28,000
12/04	6,192.7	164.9	2.7%	26,000
Annual Growth	(30.5%)	—	—	(40.8%)

FYE: December 31

2008 Year-End Financials

Debt ratio: 11.3%
Return on equity: —
Cash ($ mil.): 1,745
Current ratio: 7.65
Long-term debt ($ mil.): 499

No. of shares (mil.): 132
Dividends
  Yield: 0.0%
  Payout: —
Market value ($ mil.): 2,083

Stock History

NASDAQ (GS): IACI

	STOCK PRICE ($) FY Close	P/E High/Low		PER SHARE ($) Earnings	Dividends	Book Value
12/08	15.73	—	—	(1.08)	0.00	33.44
12/07	23.49	—	—	(1.00)	0.00	64.83
12/06	32.42	28	17	1.20	0.00	66.23
12/05	24.70	5	4	4.92	0.00	69.72
12/04	26.76	42	23	0.80	0.00	110.31
Annual Growth	(12.4%)	—	—	—	—	(25.8%)

IDT Corporation

IDT keeps a corporate finger in several pies. The company makes most of its money through IDT Telecom, which provides retail domestic and international long-distance access mainly in the US, as well as wholesale voice and data services. IDT also offers wireless service and prepaid calling cards. The company's international business consists of calling card sales to customers primarily in Europe. IDT's other operations include a capital division, which acquires and manages media and broadcast properties; an energy services unit that resells natural gas and electric power in New York state; and IDT Carmel, which provides debt collection services. Founder and chairman Howard Jonas controls IDT with 40% ownership.

IDT pioneered international callback technology, sometimes known as call reorigination, which allows international phone callers to bypass overseas carriers (and their high rates) by rerouting calls through less expensive US exchanges. IDT now operates a network that includes switches in Europe and the US to connect callers around the globe. The company leases additional capacity from other carriers, including 14 undersea fiber-optic cables that connect to the facilities of IDT's partners in Asia, Europe, and Latin America.

In 2006 the company acquired the remaining 60% of Net2Phone that it did not already own. Net2Phone, which was a leading provider of global hosted VoIP services for service providers, is a success story in IDT's telecom industry investment strategy. The acquired company became a privately held subsidiary of IDT.

In 2007 the company sold its IDT Entertainment unit, now known as Starz Media, to Liberty Media. In the deal, IDT received all of Liberty Media's shareholdings in IDT, including a 5% stake in IDT Telecom, plus $186 million in cash and some assumed debt. With that deal, the company cashed in on a unit that it built through multiple acquisitions. IDT Entertainment had been the company's second-largest unit. It included animation and live-action production studios and a home entertainment distribution business.

In 2008 the company bought a 75% controlling stake in EGL Oil Shale in a move to expand its energy sector holdings. EGL holds leases from the US Bureau of Land Management to explore for oil shale in western Colorado. The business was later renamed American Shale Oil Corporation (AMSO).

HISTORY

Howard Jonas started a trade publishing business in 1978; when he ran up an $8,000 phone bill establishing a sales office in Israel, the 33-year-old entrepreneur bought $300 worth of components and rigged up a callback device. That feat of ingenuity led Jonas to start International Discount Telecommunications (IDT) in 1990. The next year the company began selling its international call reorigination services, which took advantage of cheaper US rates. By 1993 it had more than 1,000 customers in some 60 countries and had begun reselling long-distance services to its US customers.

In 1994 IDT added Internet access to its service portfolio. Jonas renamed the company IDT Corporation in 1995. That year IDT took advantage of the volume of callers that used its callback services and began reselling to other long-distance carriers. The company went public the next year and also acquired the Genie online service. Continuing to experiment with telephony services, IDT formed Net2Phone in 1997 to provide long-distance phone service over the Internet.

The company dropped its rates in 1998, offering long-distance rates of five cents per minute in some markets. It introduced Net2Fax, which routes faxes over the Internet, and Click2Talk, which connects Web-surfing customers directly to live customer service representatives. Also in 1998 it acquired InterExchange, a debit card firm that complemented IDT's calling card services.

The next year IDT spun off Net2Phone, then sold a stake in the former subsidiary to AT&T. It formed a joint venture with Spain's Terra Networks (spun off from Telefónica) to provide Internet products and services to the US Hispanic population. Also in 1999 Chattle, IDT's wholly owned subsidiary, joined with Westmintech to provide high-speed voice and data services, cable TV, and Internet access worldwide.

In 2000 IDT reorganized into two divisions: IDT Telecom, with its international retail and wholesale telecom services, and IDT Ventures and Investments, to pursue other opportunities, including branded wireless services using the Sprint PCS network. That year Liberty Media bought a stake in IDT. In addition, the company raised $1.1 billion by selling most of its remaining stake in Net2Phone to AT&T.

When its joint venture with Terra Networks crumbled in 2001, IDT launched a lawsuit. That year the company bought the debit card business of PT-1 Communications (part of STAR Telecommunications) and invested $1.2 million in STAR. Still flush with cash, IDT traded some of its own stock to Liberty Media for stakes in struggling competitive local-exchange carriers ICG and Teligent. It regained control of its Net2Phone spinoff that year when it took the lead in a consortium with AT&T and Liberty Media that holds a 49% stake in Net2Phone and controls about 64% of the voting power (AT&T later sold its stake to the other two).

In 2003 IDT was outbid in a plan to offer $255 million to acquire fiber-optic network operator Global Crossing. It also entered discussions over acquiring ITXC after dropping a hostile stock offer valued at about $60 million. ITXC, however, rejected the buyout offer (ITXC has since been acquired by Teleglobe).

IDT could, at times, stand for "Invest in Distressed Telecom" companies: It has pieced together remnants of struggling competitive carriers Teligent, ICG Communications, and long-distance firm STAR Telecommunications. It once offered to buy parts of WorldCom (MCI). But the company's investments have sometimes provided mixed results. It hoped to repeat the success of Net2Phone with the spinoff of IDT Spectrum, but it discontinued IDT Spectrum instead in 2006. The company has also written off or sold its stakes in money-losing firms Teligent and ICG.

The company in 2006 sold operating subsidiaries Winstar Communications, Winstar Government Solutions, and Winstar Wireless, entities that provide telecom services under US government contracts, to Detroit-based GVC Networks.

EXECUTIVES

Chairman: Howard S. Jonas, age 52
Vice Chairman and CEO: James A. (Jim) Courter, age 67
President: Ira A. Greenstein, age 48
EVP, CFO, and Treasurer: Bill Pereira, age 43
Chief Tax Officer: Douglas W. (Doug) Mauro, age 66
Controller and Chief Accounting Officer: Mitch Silberman, age 40
Chief Legal Officer: Elliot Rothstein, age 41
EVP, General Counsel, and Secretary: Joyce J. Mason, age 49
EVP: Marc E. Knoller, age 47
EVP: Liore Alroy, age 40
CEO, IDT Internet Mobile Group: Morris Berger
CFO, IDT Telecom: Marcelo Fischer
COO, IDT Telecom: Yona Katz
External Affairs: Bill Ulrey
Auditors: Ernst & Young LLP

LOCATIONS

HQ: IDT Corporation
520 Broad St., Newark, NJ 07102
Phone: 973-438-1000   **Fax:** 973-482-3971
Web: www.idt.net

PRODUCTS/OPERATIONS

2008 Sales

	$ mil.	% of total
Wholesale telecommunications services	1,062.6	47
Prepaid products	778.4	34
IDT Energy	248.9	11
Consumer phone services	88.0	4
IDT Capital	55.0	2
IDT Carmel	45.6	2
Adjustments	(400.5)	—
Total	**1,878.0**	**100**

COMPETITORS

Arbinet
AT&T
Blackhawk Network
Coinstar
Con Edison
France Telecom
KDDI
National Fuel Gas
National Grid
Orange & Rockland Utilities
Qwest Communications
Rochester Gas and Electric
Sprint Nextel
Telefónica
Verizon

HISTORICAL FINANCIALS

Company Type: Public

Income Statement

FYE: July 31

	REVENUE ($ mil.)	NET INCOME ($ mil.)	NET PROFIT MARGIN	EMPLOYEES
7/08	1,878.0	(224.3)	—	1,850
7/07	2,012.7	58.6	2.9%	2,360
7/06	2,226.4	(178.7)	—	3,000
7/05	2,468.5	(43.8)	—	5,951
7/04	2,216.9	(95.7)	—	4,989
Annual Growth	(4.1%)	—	—	(22.0%)

2008 Year-End Financials

Debt ratio: 32.5%
Return on equity: —
Cash ($ mil.): 169
Current ratio: 1.10
Long-term debt ($ mil.): 111

No. of shares (mil.): 24
Dividends
  Yield: 0.0%
  Payout: —
Market value ($ mil.): 127

Stock History

NYSE: IDT

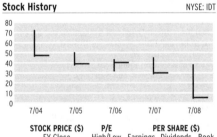

	STOCK PRICE ($) FY Close	P/E High/Low	PER SHARE ($) Earnings	Dividends	Book Value
7/08	5.31	— —	(8.85)	0.00	14.34
7/07	29.94	21 14	2.13	1.13	26.39
7/06	40.14	— —	(5.58)	0.00	33.64
7/05	38.97	— —	(1.35)	0.00	43.48
7/04	47.25	— —	(3.27)	0.00	41.51
Annual Growth	(42.1%)	— —	—	—	(23.3%)

IGA, Inc.

IGA grocers are independent, but not alone. The world's largest voluntary supermarket network, IGA has about 4,000 stores, including members in some 45 US states and more than 40 other countries on six continents. Collectively, its members are among North America's leaders in terms of supermarket sales. IGA (for either International or Independent Grocers Alliance, the company says) is owned by about 35 worldwide distribution companies, including SUPERVALU. Members can sell IGA brand private-label products (over 2,300 items) and take advantage of joint operations and services, such as advertising and volume buying. Some stores in the IGA alliance, which primarily caters to smaller towns, also sell gas.

About two-thirds of IGA's total stores are located outside the US. As the first US grocer in China and Singapore, the company has plans for some 1,000 IGA-affiliated stores in China. IGA is also present in Europe, with operations in Poland and Spain.

In 2006 the company reorganized by splitting itself into three companies: IGA USA, IGA Global, and the IGA Coca-Cola Institute. All three operate under IGA, Inc. As a result of the reorganization, Thomas Haggai became chairman and CEO of IGA International and Mark Batenic — formerly of Clemens Markets — joined the company as chairman, president, and CEO of IGA USA. (Previously, IGA realigned its corporate structure in 2001.)

By separating IGA's domestic stores from its stores overseas the company hopes to improve communications among IGA's US retailers.

One of Batenic's first moves was to establish a presence for IGA in San Francisco with the acquisition of eight supermarkets there from Ralphs Grocery.

IGA claims that it doesn't try to fight large chains such as Wal-Mart and Publix, instead preferring to keep the focus on its own niche of hometown and family-owned grocery stores.

HISTORY

IGA was founded in Chicago in 1926 by a group led by accountant Frank Grimes. During the 1920s chains began to dominate the grocery store industry. Grimes, an accountant for many grocery wholesalers, saw an opportunity to develop a network of independent grocers that could compete with the burgeoning chains. Grimes and five associates — Gene Flack, Louis Groebe, W. K. Hunter, H. V. Swenson, and William Thompson — created IGA.

Their idea was to "level the playing field" for independent grocers and chain stores by taking advantage of volume buying and mass marketing. IGA originally acted as a purchasing agent for its wholesalers but eventually passed that duty to the wholesalers. The group's first members were Poughkeepsie, New York-based grocery distributor W. T. Reynolds Company and the 69 grocery stores it serviced.

IGA focused on adding distributors and retailers, and it soon added wholesaler Fleming-Wilson (now Fleming Companies) and Winston & Newell (now SUPERVALU). In 1930 it hired Babe Ruth as a spokesman; other celebrity endorsers during the period included Jackie Cooper, Jack Dempsey, and Popeye. IGA also sponsored a radio program called the *IGA Home Town Hour*.

In 1945 the company introduced the Foodliner format, a design for stores larger than 4,000 sq. ft. The next year IGA introduced the 30-ft.-by-100-ft. Precision Store — designed so customers had to pass all the other merchandise in the store to get to the dairy and bread sections.

Grimes retired as president in 1951. He was succeeded by his son, Don, who continued to expand the company. Don was succeeded in 1968 by Richard Jones, head of IGA member J. M. Jones Co.

Thomas Haggai was named chairman of the company in 1976. A Baptist minister, radio commentator, and former CIA employee, Haggai had come to the attention of Grimes in 1960 when he praised Christian Scientists in one of his radio broadcasts. Grimes, a Christian Scientist, asked Haggai to speak at an IGA convention and eventually asked him to join the IGA board. Haggai, who became CEO in 1986, tightened the restrictions for IGA members, weeding out many of the smaller, low-volume mom-and-pop stores making up much of the group's network.

Haggai also began a push for international expansion. In 1988 the organization signed a deal with Japanese food company C. Itoh (now ITOCHU) to open a distribution outlet in Tokyo.

The 1990s saw expansion into Australia, Papua New Guinea, the Caribbean, China, Singapore, South Africa, and Brazil. IGA also expanded outside the continental US when it entered Hawaii. In 1993 IGA began an international television advertising campaign, a first for the supermarket industry. The next year the company launched its first line of private-label products for an ethnic food market, introducing several Mexican food products. In 1998 the group developed a new format for its stores that included on-site gas pumps.

SUPERVALU signed 54 independent grocery stores (primarily in Mississippi and Arkansas, and Trinidad in the Caribbean) to the IGA banner in August 1999.

With more than 60% of sales from international operations, IGA realigned its corporate structure in 2001, setting up IGA North America, IGA Southern Hemisphere/Europe/Caribbean, and IGA Asia, each with its own president.

IGA suffered the loss of Fleming (one of the grocery chain's principal wholesale distributors) and 300 stores in 2003. On the plus side, four Julian's Supermarkets on the Caribbean island of St. Lucia converted to IGA, giving IGA a presence in 45 countries worldwide.

EXECUTIVES

Chairman and CEO: Thomas S. Haggai
VP Finance and CFO: John Collins
VP Information Technology: Nick Liakopulos
President, IGA Coca-Cola Institute: Paulo Goelzer
SVP Retail and Business Development: Doug Fritsch
SVP Procurement and Private Brands: David S. Bennett
VP Communications and Events: Barbara G. Wiest
CEO, IGA USA: Mark K. Batenic
National Accounts Manager: Jim Collins
Senior Director Marketing, Branding, and Business Development, IGA USA: Jim Walz
New Area Director, Western US: Terry Carr
Manager Marketing and Retail Programs: Heidi Huff
Director Private Brands: Wayne Altschul
Editor, IGA Grocergram Quarterly: Ashley M. Page
Liaison: Richard Lukeman

LOCATIONS

HQ: IGA, Inc.
8725 W. Higgins Rd., Chicago, IL 60631
Phone: 773-693-4520   **Fax:** 773-693-4532
Web: www.igainc.com

PRODUCTS/OPERATIONS

Selected Joint Operations and Services

Advertising
Community service programs
Equipment purchase
IGA Brand (private-label products)
IGA Grocergram (in-house magazine)
Internet services
Marketing
Merchandising
Red Oval Family (manufacturer/IGA collaboration on
   sales, marketing, and other activities)
Volume buying

COMPETITORS

A&P	H-E-B
Albertsons	Ito-Yokado
Associated Wholesale	Kroger
Grocers	Meijer
BJ's Wholesale Club	Penn Traffic
C & S Wholesale	Publix
Carrefour	Roundy's Supermarkets
Casino Guichard	Royal Ahold
Coles Group	Safeway
Daiei	Spartan Stores
Dairy Farm International	Wakefern Food
Delhaize	Wal-Mart
George Weston	Winn-Dixie
Hannaford Bros.	

Illinois Tool Works

Don't let the name fool you — Illinois Tool Works (ITW) hammers out a lot more than just tools, and it operates well beyond the Land of Lincoln. With more than 800 separate operations in about 50 nations, ITW makes a range of products used in the automotive, construction, electronics, food and beverage, paper products, and pharmaceuticals industries. The company's engineered products segment offers fasteners, nail guns, industrial adhesives, and automotive transmission components. Its specialty systems segment drives products such as paint application equipment and welding machines.

ITW's operating strategy typically resembles something like mergers-and-acquisitions therapy. The multinational manufacturer often buys small, niche companies and turns them into more efficient producers. In 2006 the acquisitive company set a record for itself, buying more than 50 companies at a cost of around $1.7 billion. The following year, ITW's buying spree accumulated another 52 firms.

Hit by deteriorating markets and accelerated cash burn in 2008, ITW has taken steps to free its operations from fickle consumer and small business buying and focus on businesses that it can make more efficient. The company looked to divest its Click Commerce, a business with a buffet of industrial software applications, but dim opportunities for growth. In mid-2009 private equity firm Marlin Equity Partners bought three software divisions from Requisite Technology (formerly Click Commerce). The deal raked in Service

Network Solutions, Research and Healthcare Solutions, and Contract Service and Management operations, as well as the Click Commerce name.

ITW also pushed to unload an automotive components business, on the sale rack since 2007. The business was classified instead as discontinued, along with an automotive machinery business, and two consumer packaging businesses. Its consumer products holdings (appliances and cookware, exercise equipment, and ceramic tile acquired with Premark International) also went by the wayside. In a surprise move, ITW's decorative surfaces segment, which could not find a buyer, was reclassified as a continuing business.

By contrast, ITW has sought to acquire ventures that pump up its industrial and technology mix. Trymer was a solid catch in 2008; the maker of rigid foam products expands ITW's mechanical insulation segment. Its product applications run from mechanical and panel insulation to floral arrangements and crafts.

Heading into 2009, customer efforts to slash inventories — or "destock" — amid sliding demand have added significantly to the uncertainties facing ITW. With clients sharply reducing orders, and deciding to shutter their factories, the company has been driven to ratchet back production. The decline has also caused the company to trim jobs at some of its operations. Even amid the downslide, the company in 2009 purchased Ride Rite, an inflatable paper dunnage (packing) bag manufacturer, from KapStone Paper and Packaging. Terms of the transaction were not disclosed.

HISTORY

In the early years of the 20th century, Byron Smith, founder of Chicago's Northern Trust Company, recognized that rapid industrialization was outgrowing the capacity of small shops to supply machine tools. Smith encouraged two of his four sons to launch Illinois Tool Works (ITW) in 1912. Harold C. Smith became president of ITW in 1915 and expanded its product line into automotive parts.

ITW developed the Shakeproof fastener, the first twisted-tooth lock washer, in 1923. When Harold C. died in 1936, the torch passed to his son Harold B., who decentralized the company and exhorted salesmen to learn customers' businesses so they could develop solutions even before the customers recognized the problems. Smith plowed profits back into research as WWII spurred demand.

In the 1950s the company began exploring plastics and combination metal and plastic fasteners, as well as electrical controls and instruments, to become a leader in miniaturization. Its major breakthrough came in the early 1960s with the development of flexible plastic collars to hold six-packs of beverage cans. This item, under a new division called Hi-Cone, was ITW's most-profitable offering.

Silas Cathcart became CEO in 1970. Smith's son, another Harold B., was president and COO until 1981 (he remained on the board of directors and served as chairman of the board's executive committee). By the early 1980s ITW had become bureaucratic and susceptible to foreign competition. It was forced to lower prices to hold on to customers. Wary after the 1982 recession, ITW hired John Nichols as CEO.

Nichols broadened the company's product line, introduced more-effective production methods, and doubled ITW's size by buying 27

companies, the largest being Signode Industries, bought for $524 million (1986). Nichols broke Signode into smaller units to speed development of 20 new products.

ITW purchased Ransburg Corporation (electrostatic finishing systems, 1989) and the DeVilbiss division of Eagle Industries (1990) and merged the two to form its Finishing Systems and Products division. Through a stock swap, ITW acquired ownership of the Miller Group (arc welding equipment and related systems) in 1993.

In 1995 ITW named president James Farrell as CEO. He replaced Nichols as chairman in 1996. ITW acquired Hobart Brothers (welding products) and Medalists Industries (industrial fasteners) in 1996 and made 28 acquisitions and joint ventures in 1997.

In 1999 ITW paid $3.5 billion for Premark International (consumer products, which it began selling off in 2002). Early in 2001 the company added to its welding operations by buying four welding component businesses from Dover Corporation. In early 2002 the company's board of directors gave its stamp of approval for the divestiture of ITW's consumer products segment. That decision led to the sale of its Precor fitness equipment business to Finland's Amer Sports.

Farrell retired as CEO, though he remained chairman, in 2005; he was replaced by president David Speer. Farrell retired as chairman in 2006 and was succeeded by Speer in that post.

In early 2005 ITW purchased the Wynn Oil segment of industrial products maker Parker Hannifin. Wynn Oil manufactures chemical car care products and maintenance technology for the auto industry.

In early 2006 ITW bought Alpine Engineered Products, a maker of connectors, design software, and related machinery from Stonebridge Partners. In mid-2006 ITW bought BagCo (plastic recloseable packaging) and Kester (solder and related materials). In late 2006 ITW purchased Speedline Technologies, a manufacturer of printed circuit board assembly and semiconductor packaging equipment.

In 2007 ITW acquired the assets of Avery Berkel, a venerable manufacturer of retail scales and other food processing equipment, from Avery Weigh-Tronix.

EXECUTIVES

Chairman, President, and CEO: David B. Speer, age 57,
   $10,193,503 total compensation
Vice Chairman: Thomas J. (Tom) Hansen, age 60,
   $4,337,533 total compensation
Vice Chairman: E. Scott Santi, age 47
SVP and CFO: Ronald D. (Ron) Kropp, age 43,
   $1,470,367 total compensation
VP and Chief Accounting Officer:
   Randall J. (Randy) Scheuneman, age 41
EVP: Philip M. (Phil) Gresh Jr., age 60
EVP: Jane L. Warner, age 62
EVP: Steven L. (Steve) Martindale, age 52
EVP: Craig A. Hindman, age 54
EVP: Robert E. Brunner, age 51
EVP: David C. Parry, age 55
EVP: Roland M. Martel, age 54
EVP: Juan Valls, age 47
EVP: Timothy Gardner, age 54
SVP Taxes and Investments: Allan C. (Al) Sutherland,
   age 45
SVP Human Resources: Sharon M. Brady, age 58
SVP, General Counsel, and Secretary:
   James H. Wooten Jr., age 60
VP Investor Relations: John L. Brooklier
VP Patents and Technology: Mark W. Croll
**VP Research and Development and Head, Technology
   Center:** Lei Z. Schlitz
Auditors: Deloitte & Touche LLP

LOCATIONS

HQ: Illinois Tool Works Inc.
3600 W. Lake Ave., Glenview, IL 60026
Phone: 847-724-7500   **Fax:** 847-657-4261
Web: www.itw.com

2008 Sales

	$ mil.	% of total
North America		
US	6,517.5	41
Other countries	944.9	6
Europe	5,423.0	34
Asia	1,583.2	10
Australia & New Zealand	764.8	5
Other regions	636.0	4
Total	**15,869.4**	**100**

PRODUCTS/OPERATIONS

2008 Sales

	$ mil.	% of total
Industrial Packaging	2,591.1	16
Power Systems & Electronics	2,356.9	15
Transportation	2,347.7	15
Food Equipment	2,133.2	13
Construction Products	1,990.7	13
Polymers & Fluids	1,255.9	8
Other	3,248.1	20
Adjustments	(54.2)	—
Total	**15,869.4**	**100**

Selected Products

Specialty Systems
   Arc welding equipment
   Food-preparation equipment
   Industrial adhesive-application equipment
   Paint application equipment
   Recyclable ring packaging
   Steel and plastic strapping systems

Engineered Products
   Adhesives
   Fasteners and assemblies
   Fastening tools
   Laminates

COMPETITORS

3M	Manitowoc
BASF SE	Marmon Group
Black & Decker	NCH
Cooper Industries	Nordson
DuPont	Park-Ohio Holdings
Emerson Electric	PennEngineering
Entegris	Snap-on
ESAB	Stanley Works
Federal Screw Works	Textron
GE	Thermadyne
Graco	TriMas
IBIDEN	TRW Automotive
Ingersoll-Rand	Tyco
Koch Enterprises	W. R. Grace
Lincoln Electric	

HISTORICAL FINANCIALS

Company Type: Public

Income Statement

FYE: December 31

	REVENUE ($ mil.)	NET INCOME ($ mil.)	NET PROFIT MARGIN	EMPLOYEES
12/08	15,869.4	1,519.0	9.6%	65,000
12/07	16,170.6	1,869.9	11.6%	60,000
12/06	14,055.0	1,717.7	12.2%	55,000
12/05	12,921.8	1,494.9	11.6%	50,000
12/04	11,731.4	1,338.7	11.4%	49,000
Annual Growth	**7.8%**	**3.2%**	**—**	**7.3%**

2008 Year-End Financials

Debt ratio: 16.2%	No. of shares (mil.): 500
Return on equity: 17.9%	Dividends
Cash ($ mil.): 743	Yield: 3.4%
Current ratio: 1.21	Payout: 40.5%
Long-term debt ($ mil.): 1,244	Market value ($ mil.): 17,530

Stock History

NYSE: ITW

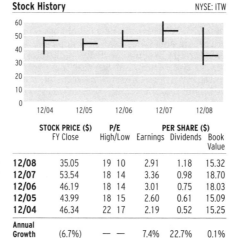

	STOCK PRICE ($) FY Close	P/E High/Low		PER SHARE ($) Earnings	Dividends	Book Value
12/08	35.05	19	10	2.91	1.18	15.32
12/07	53.54	18	14	3.36	0.98	18.70
12/06	46.19	18	14	3.01	0.75	18.03
12/05	43.99	18	15	2.60	0.61	15.09
12/04	46.34	22	17	2.19	0.52	15.25
Annual Growth	**(6.7%)**	**—**	**—**	**7.4%**	**22.7%**	**0.1%**

Imation Corp.

Imation wants to start fresh with a blank disk. The company is one of the world's top makers of media used to capture, process, store, and distribute information on computers and other electronic devices. Its removable data storage media products include optical disks (CD-R, CD-RW, DVD) and magnetic storage tapes. It also offers flash memory drives. Imation sells its products directly and through distributors to customers ranging from personal computer owners to large corporations. Imation has used acquisitions to dramatically expand its recording media product lines.

It purchased rival Memorex for $329 million in 2006. The following year Imation acquired TDK's brand and recording media sales operations for $300 million in cash and stock. (TDK owns 20% of Imation.) The company then acquired the assets of Memcorp, a manufacturer of Memorex-branded electronics, for $60 million. The Memcorp purchase included products such as LCD televisions, iPod accessories, and digital cameras. In 2008 Imation expanded its line of accessories for Apple products when it bought Xtreme Accessories for $9 million.

Imation has traditionally been a leader in magnetic diskettes, but in recent years the company has turned its focus to optical media. Optical products now make up about half of Imation's sales. Magnetic media products accounted for about 30% of revenues in 2008. More than half of Imation's sales are to customers outside the US.

HISTORY

Imation's ancestry stretches back to 1902, when five businessmen founded Minnesota Mining and Manufacturing (3M) in Two Harbors, Minnesota, to sell corundum to manufacturers

for grinding wheels. Faced with stiff competition and the realization that its mining holdings contained the nearly worthless igneous rock anorthosite instead of corundum, the company shifted gears and began making sandpaper and abrasive wheels.

In a research-fueled corporate culture, 3M's engineers thrived, launching a long line of culturally implanted products including Scotch masking tape, the dry-printing photocopy process, Post-it adhesive notepads, and, in 1947, the first commercially viable magnetic recording tape. This ancestor of the cassette tape would mark 3M's leap into the business that later helped make Imation.

The genesis of Imation's other lines continued in the 1950s and 1960s when 3M ventured into photographic products. It jumped into color proofing systems and X-ray and other medical imaging technologies in the 1970s. When its diskette manufacturing business faced intense global competition in the 1980s, 3M expanded its efforts in the data storage products market.

Imation — a name taken from the words "imaging" and "information" — was born in 1996 when 3M spun off its low-performing data storage, imaging, and printing businesses. The move was part of a broader 3M reorganization that saw it retain its industrial and consumer and life science units, while discontinuing its audio- and videotape business. About 75% of 3M's data storage and medical imaging employees made the move; the rest opted for early retirement. That year William Monahan, who began his career in the early 1970s selling 3M data storage products on Wall Street and rose to serve as VP of the company's Electro and Communication Group, was named chairman and CEO.

In 1996 Imation also unveiled the LS-120 diskette for a drive that used both standard floppy disks (1.44 MB) and 120-MB, 3.5-in. disks. Hitachi, Panasonic, and Mitsubishi made products based on the technology. Also that year the company bought Seattle-based prepress software company Luminous Corp., and was awarded its first non-3M patent for a mini-cartridge design.

While Imation struggled in an intensely competitive market with plummeting product prices, industry watchers questioned the company's commitment to new technology. Imation intensified restructuring efforts to pare operations and sharpen its focus. In 1997 it stepped up a new technology push by acquiring digital medical imaging specialist Cemax-Icon, as well as Internet service provider Imaginet, resulting in the creation of Imation Internet Studio. (The unit was sold in 1999 to Gage Marketing Group when its strategies conflicted with Imation's.)

More losses piled up in 1997 despite a slew of new products and features. So in 1998 Imation tried to turn around its financial results by slashing 3,400 jobs. The company also sold its CD-ROM services unit to optical media company Metatec and its medical imaging systems to Eastman Kodak for about $520 million, partly to settle an intellectual-property lawsuit. In 1999 Imation sold its Photo Color Systems business (photographic film, single-use cameras) to Schroder plc affiliate Schroder Ventures.

In early 2000 Imation introduced Verifi — technology that lets online shoppers verify the accuracy of colors on their monitors. The following year the company agreed to sell its color proofing and color software businesses to Kodak Polychrome Graphics (a joint venture between

Kodak and Dainippon Ink and Chemicals subsidiary Sun Chemical); the deal closed in early 2002. Later that year Imation sold its North American Digital Solutions and Services (DSS) operations to DecisionOne, and closed DSS operations outside of North America.

Monahan retired from Imation in 2004. Bruce Henderson, a former chief executive for Invensys Control Systems, replaced him.

In 2005 the company sold its specialty papers business, which generated about 4% of its sales, to Nekoosa Coated Products for $17 million, plus possible future consideration. Nekoosa is a new company formed by Dunsirn Partners and PS Capital Partners, two investment firms.

Henderson resigned due to health reasons in 2007. President Frank Russomanno, who had served as acting CEO since 2006, replaced him.

EXECUTIVES

Chairman: Linda W. Hart, age 68
Vice Chairman and CEO: Frank P. Russomanno, age 61, $1,952,300 total compensation
President and COO: Mark E. Lucas, age 54
SVP and CFO: Paul R. Zeller, age 48
SVP Global Commercial Business and CTO:
Subodh K. Kulkarni, age 44, $609,163 total compensation
Chief Accounting Officer and Corporate Controller:
Scott J. Robinson, age 42
VP and Chief Marketing Officer: Stephen F. Moss, age 52
SVP, Secretary, and General Counsel: John L. Sullivan, age 54, $845,690 total compensation
VP Investor Relations: Bradley D. (Brad) Allen, age 58
VP Human Resources: Jacqueline A. (Jackie) Chase, age 55, $735,824 total compensation
VP Global Operations: Peter A. Koehn, age 48
VP Japan Consumer Business: Nancy Tan
VP Strategy and Mergers and Acquisitions:
James C. Ellis, age 51
VP Americas Consumer Business: Thomas (Tom) Lally
VP Japan Consumer Business: Kuniyoshi Matsui
VP Global Marketing and Product Management:
Jeffrey Meredith
Director Global Communications: Mary Rawlings-Taylor
Auditors: PricewaterhouseCoopers LLP

LOCATIONS

HQ: Imation Corp.
1 Imation Place, Oakdale, MN 55128
Phone: 651-704-4000   **Fax:** 651-704-4200
Web: www.imation.com

2008 Sales

	$ mil.	% of total
US	905.0	42
Other countries	1,249.6	58
Total	**2,154.6**	**100**

PRODUCTS/OPERATIONS

2008 Sales

	$ mil.	% of total
Optical	1,025.2	48
Magnetic	644.4	30
Flash	99.2	4
Other	385.8	18
Total	**2,154.6**	**100**

Selected Products

Optical
　CD-R
　CD-RW
　DVD
Magnetic
　Audio and video tape
　Data storage tape media
　Floppy diskettes
Flash (primarily Memorex)
　Flash cards
　USB flash drives
Other
　CD and DVD cleaning, labeling, and storing products
　Electronic products (primarily Memcorp consumer electronics)

COMPETITORS

FUJIFILM
Griffin Technology
Hitachi Maxell
Iomega
Kingston Technology
LaCie
Lexar
Philips Electronics
PNY Technologies
Quantum Corporation
SanDisk
Seagate Technology
Sony
THOMSON
Verbatim Corp.
Western Digital

HISTORICAL FINANCIALS

Company Type: Public

Income Statement

FYE: December 31

	REVENUE ($ mil.)	NET INCOME ($ mil.)	NET PROFIT MARGIN	EMPLOYEES
12/08	2,154.6	(33.3)	—	1,570
12/07	2,062.0	(50.4)	—	2,250
12/06	1,584.7	76.4	4.8%	2,070
12/05	1,258.1	87.9	7.0%	2,100
12/04	1,219.3	29.9	2.5%	2,550
Annual Growth	**15.3%**	—	—	**(11.4%)**

2008 Year-End Financials

Debt ratio: 0.0%
Return on equity: —
Cash ($ mil.): 97
Current ratio: 1.94
Long-term debt ($ mil.): 0
No. of shares (mil.): 38
Dividends
　Yield: 4.1%
　Payout: —
Market value ($ mil.): 516

Stock History

NYSE: IMN

	STOCK PRICE ($) FY Close	P/E High/Low		PER SHARE ($) Earnings	Dividends	Book Value
12/08	13.57	—	—	(0.89)	0.56	24.82
12/07	21.00	—	—	(1.36)	0.62	27.69
12/06	46.43	23	17	2.17	0.54	24.86
12/05	46.07	18	12	2.54	0.46	22.47
12/04	31.83	53	34	0.84	0.38	20.67
Annual Growth	**(19.2%)**	—	—	—	**10.2%**	**4.7%**

IMS Health

IMS Health has the dope on drugs. The company is a leading provider of sales management and market research services to clients in the pharmaceutical and health care industries. It tracks not only the sale of prescription drugs and over-the-counter products but also the productivity of individual sales representatives that work for its client companies. It offers market forecasts and surveys physicians and hospitals about drugs they are prescribing to patients. In addition, IMS Health offers consulting and other professional services. The company serves clients worldwide and operates through about 100 offices in more than 75 countries.

Being a dominant player in its market, IMS Health sees acquisitions or joint ventures as a major part of its growth strategy. In 2008 the company acquired five companies: Australia-based Robinson and James Research, a health care and pharmaceutical marketing research company; UK-based Fourth Hurdle Consulting, a health economics and outcomes research firm; US-based Health Benchmarks, a health services research company; Russia-based RMBC Pharma, specializing in pharmaceutical market intelligence and analytics; and the services practice group of Canada-based Skura Corporation.

In 2008 IMS Health cut its workforce by 10% — part of the company's ongoing strategy to minimize its operating structure, cut down on costs, and increase efficiency.

IMS Health's most lucrative business segment remains its Sales Force Effectiveness operations, which track sales of not only prescription drugs but also over-the-counter products. Clients can access the data electronically or they can get hardcopy reports. IMS Health also provides decision support software (Sales Insight) to make the data more useful for its clients.

IMS Health comprises two additional operating segments: Portfolio Optimization specializes in identifying and developing pharmaceutical product portfolios. Launch, Brand Management and Other offers clients consulting and brand planning tools and services during each step of the pharmaceutical brands marketing process.

HISTORY

IMS Health (IMS is short for International Marketing Services) was founded in 1954 by Ludwig Wilhelm Frohlich, who headed the New York-based prescription drug advertising agency L.W. Frohlich (founded in the 1930s) and was considered one of the fathers of the drug marketing business. As the post-WWII prescription drug industry grew, drug manufacturers turned to market research to monitor promotions and sales. Frohlich created IMS in 1954 to extend the drug marketing business internationally.

IMS expanded into market research in 1957 under research chief David DuBow, who completed the first syndicated study of the pharmaceutical market. By 1966 IMS had operations throughout Europe. IMS expanded through purchases of research firms RA Gosselin & Co., Lea Associates, and Medical Data Service, and went public in 1972.

Dun & Bradstreet (D&B) bought IMS in 1988, one of several data and publishing companies it added during the 1970s and 1980s. But D&B reversed its growth strategy soon after, and in 1996 it split into three corporations: Cognizant

(IMS's parent), ACNielsen, and Dun & Bradstreet Corporation.

IMS continued expanding internationally in 1997. The following year *Advertising Age* identified IMS as the #1 research company in terms of US revenue. The same year Cognizant announced it would split into two entities: Nielsen Media Research and IMS Health. Cognizant chairman and CEO Robert Weissman became IMS's chairman and CEO. IMS continued to grow, buying Walsh International, a developer of sales force automation for pharmaceutical companies; ChinaMetrik, a pharmaceutical tracker focusing on the Chinese market; and the non-US assets of Pharmaceutical Marketing Services. Also in 1998 IMS formed a joint venture with Institut fur Marktanalysen to enhance health care information services in Switzerland.

In 1999 IMS launched I2 (I-squared), an Internet portal for pharmaceutical companies. Victoria Fash became CEO that year (Weissman remained as chairman). IMS also spun off its interest in IT research and consulting firm Gartner Group. The following year IMS agreed to be acquired by The TriZetto Group, an Internet portal developer for the health care industry, for about $8 billion. However, the companies soon called off the deal, and IMS instead sold its Erisco Managed Care Technologies unit to TriZetto in a stock swap deal valued at $255 million that gave IMS a 33% stake in TriZetto. IMS also spun off its Strategic Technologies and Clark-O'Neill divisions as SYNAVANT (later acquired by Dendrite International). In late 2000 former IBM executive David Thomas took over as CEO. The following year IMS sold its DataEdge unit, a provider of clinical trial databases, to clinical trial services firm Fast Track Systems.

IMS also became involved in a bitter dispute with European competition authorities in 2000. The European Union ordered IMS to license its system that tracks drug sales in Germany to competitors, claiming the dominance of IMS in that market prevented anyone from entering or staying in the business. IMS Health won its appeal in 2001, and a European Commission ended its probe into IMS in 2002 after finding that IMS no longer engaged in activities adverse to competition.

In early 2003 IMS Health sold its stake in Cognizant Technology Solutions, leaving the company with pharmaceutical sales management and market research services as its primary businesses. David Carlucci, who joined the company as president in 2002, was named CEO when Thomas stepped down from the chief executive position in 2005.

A proposed deal for the company to be acquired by marketing research firm VNU was scrapped in 2005 after several large VNU shareholders expressed opposition. Also that year IMS Health acquired PharMetrics, a provider of health care market data.

EXECUTIVES

Chairman, President, and CEO:
 David R. (Dave) Carlucci, age 54,
 $5,663,183 total compensation
EVP and COO: Gilles V. J. Pajot, age 59,
 $3,925,624 total compensation
SVP and CFO: Leslye G. Katz, age 54,
 $1,074,133 total compensation
Chief Privacy Officer, Americas:
 Kimberly S. (Kim) Gray

SVP Payer and Government Solutions:
 John R. (Jack) Walsh, age 54
SVP Healthcare Insight: Murray L. Aitken
SVP Customer Delivery and Development:
 Kevin S. McKay, age 55
SVP Business Line Management: Kevin C. Knightly,
 age 48, $1,408,012 total compensation
SVP Human Resources: Karla L. Packer, age 49
VP Investor Relations: Darcie Peck
VP and Treasurer: Jeffrey J. Ford, age 44
President, IMS Japan: Tatsuyuki Saeki
President, IMS Americas: William J. Nelligan, age 48
President, IMS Europe, Middle East, and Africa:
 Adel Al-Saleh, age 45
Director Communications and Public Relations,
 Americas: Gary Gatyas
Auditors: PricewaterhouseCoopers LLP

LOCATIONS

HQ: IMS Health Incorporated
 901 Main Ave., Ste. 612, Norwalk, CT 06851
Phone: 203-845-5200   **Fax:** 203-845-5304
Web: www.imshealth.com

2008 Sales

	$ mil.	% of total
Americas	1,017.4	44
Europe, Middle East & Africa	984.4	42
Asia/Pacific	327.7	14
Total	**2,329.5**	**100**

PRODUCTS/OPERATIONS

2008 Sales

	$ mil.	% of total
Sales Force Effectiveness	1,057.0	45
Portfolio Optimization	653.6	28
Launch, Brand & Other	618.9	27
Total	**2,329.5**	**100**

2008 Sales

	$ mil.	% of total
Information & analytics revenue	1,786.7	77
Consulting & services revenue	542.8	23
Total	**2,329.5**	**100**

Selected Products and Services

Market research
 Hospital audits (product sales to hospitals)
 Medical audits (physician surveys)
 MIDAS (data analysis tools)
 Pharmaceutical audits (product sales to pharmacies)
 Prescription audits (product sales by pharmacies)
 Promotional audits (promotional campaign
  effectiveness)
Sales management
 Consumer health (market share and pricing of over-
  the-counter drugs and personal care products)
 Prescription tracking reporting
 Sales territory reporting
Other services
 Consulting
 Market trend reports

COMPETITORS

Advisory Board
Alteer
Cegedim
GfK AG
GfK NOP
GfK U.S. Healthcare
Information Resources
Ipsos
The Nielsen Company
SDI Health
TNS Custom
Wolters Kluwer

HISTORICAL FINANCIALS

Company Type: Public

Income Statement

FYE: December 31

	REVENUE ($ mil.)	NET INCOME ($ mil.)	NET PROFIT MARGIN	EMPLOYEES
12/08	2,329.5	311.3	13.4%	7,500
12/07	2,192.6	234.0	10.7%	7,950
12/06	1,958.6	315.5	16.1%	7,400
12/05	1,754.8	284.1	16.2%	6,900
12/04	1,569.0	285.4	18.2%	6,400
Annual Growth	**10.4%**	**2.2%**	**—**	**4.0%**

2008 Year-End Financials

Debt ratio: —
Return on equity: —
Cash ($ mil.): 216
Current ratio: 1.43
Long-term debt ($ mil.): 1,404

No. of shares (mil.): 182
Dividends
 Yield: 0.8%
 Payout: 7.1%
Market value ($ mil.): 2,765

Stock History

NYSE: RX

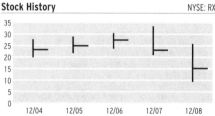

	STOCK PRICE ($) FY Close	P/E High/Low		PER SHARE ($) Earnings	Dividends	Book Value
12/08	15.16	15	6	1.70	0.12	(1.40)
12/07	23.04	28	18	1.18	0.12	(0.22)
12/06	27.44	20	16	1.53	0.12	0.19
12/05	24.92	23	18	1.22	0.08	2.28
12/04	23.21	23	17	1.20	0.08	1.40
Annual Growth	**(10.1%)**	**—**	**—**	**9.1%**	**10.7%**	**—**

Ingersoll-Rand

Ingersoll-Rand's heavy machinery helped carve the faces of Mount Rushmore, but more recently the company is raising its profile as a market-leading commercial products manufacturer. Its stable of commercial and industrial brands includes Club Car golf carts, Hussmann refrigeration equipment, Schlage security locks, Thermo King temperature control equipment, and Trane air conditioning systems and services. Pumps, tools, air compressors, and material handling equipment are also made under the Ingersoll-Rand brand. The company sells its products both directly and through distributors to customers in about 200 countries around the world. It has manufacturing plants in the Americas, Asia, and Europe.

Ingersoll-Rand made a key acquisition in 2008, with the addition of Trane for about $9.6 billion. The deal is expected to more than triple the size of Ingersoll-Rand's climate control technologies business and give it a more consistent revenue stream through economic cycles. Later that year the company initiated a restructuring to streamline the group's manufacturing operations and cut general and administrative costs, moves that should result in savings of more than $100 million in 2010. In early 2009 IR closed 34 facilities, including 12 factories and 14 warehouses, in its cost-cutting program.

Further reorganizational plans involved moving the company's tax residency from Bermuda to Ireland in mid-2009. Ingersoll-Rand plc, an Irish incorporated company, replaced Ingersoll-Rand Company Limited as the group's ultimate parent. The company already has manufacturing, sales, and corporate operations on the Emerald Isle, which makes the location a good fit.

HISTORY

Simon Ingersoll invented the steam-driven rock drill in New York City in 1871. In 1874 he sold the patent to Jose Francisco de Navarro, who financed the organization of the Ingersoll Rock Drill Company. Three years later it merged with Sergeant Drill, a company created by Henry Clark Sergeant, Navarro's former foreman.

Meanwhile, the Rand brothers were also establishing a drill company. The companies merged in 1905 to become Ingersoll-Rand.

Ingersoll-Rand initially produced air compressors and a basic line of rock drills. In 1912 the company added centrifugal compressors and turbo blowers. Later, portable air tools were added. After WWII Ingersoll-Rand, which had mostly served US mining operations, expanded internationally. From the 1960s on, the company diversified into specialized machinery and products. Acquisitions in the 1970s and 1980s made Ingersoll-Rand the largest US manufacturer of bearings.

The company also developed small air compressors and water-jet systems capable of cutting steel and concrete. In 1986 Ingersoll-Rand formed a joint venture with Dresser Industries called Dresser-Rand to produce gas turbines, compressors, and similar equipment. Ingersoll-Rand and Dresser Industries combined pump operations to form another joint venture, Ingersoll-Dresser Pump, in 1992.

In 1993 16-year Ingersoll-Rand veteran James Perrella became CEO. That year the company bought the German needle- and cylindrical-bearing business of FAG Kugelfischer Georg Schafer; it also sold its underground coal-mining machinery business (to Long-Airdox), as well as its domestic jet-engine bearing operation. ECOAIR, a unit of MAN GHH, was among several 1994 acquisitions.

Ingersoll-Rand acquired Clark Equipment for $1.5 billion in 1995 in a deal that included the businesses of Bobcat (skid-steer loaders), Clark-Hurth Components (axles and transmissions, sold 1997), Club Car (golf cars), and Blaw-Knox Construction Equipment (asphalt-paving equipment). In 1996 Ingersoll-Rand bought Metaldyne's (formerly Mascotech) Steelcraft Division (steel doors). In 1997 Ingersoll-Rand bought Newman Tonks Group (UK) and technology from the Master Lock unit of Fortune Brands, which boosted its architectural hardware line and extended its distribution in Europe and Asia. That year Ingersoll-Rand bought Thermo King from Westinghouse (now CBS) for $2.6 billion.

In 1999 Ingersoll-Rand bought Harrow Industries (access controls, architectural hardware, decorative bath fixtures). The company's industrial production equipment was enhanced when it struck a deal with Cadence Design Systems, a world-leading supplier of electronic design and automation software. James Perrella stepped down as CEO that year; Herbert Henkel, formerly of Textron, succeeded him.

In 2000 Ingersoll-Rand bought Halliburton's stake in its joint ventures with Dresser-Rand and Ingersoll-Dresser Pump. Ingersoll-Rand then sold Ingersoll-Dresser Pump to Flowserve for about $775 million and bought Neal Manufacturing, which makes compact road-paving equipment. It also acquired Hussmann International (refrigeration equipment) for about $1.8 billion. That same year, Ingersoll-Rand sold the reciprocating gas compressor packaging and rental business of its Dresser-Rand unit to Hanover Compressor Company for $190 million.

The company closed 20 plants and laid off more than 3,900 employees the next year. But acquisitions continued. Ingersoll-Rand's 2001 purchases included refrigeration company National Refrigeration Services and lock maker Kryptonite Corporation (originator of the U-shaped bicycle lock), as well as companies in the Czech Republic, France, the Netherlands, and Turkey.

Ingersoll-Rand reincorporated in Bermuda in late 2001; the move could save the company nearly $40 million in US taxes every year.

The company sold its Torrington Co. unit (bearings and motion-control components) to The Timken Co. for $840 million in 2003. It then sold its drilling business to Atlas Copco for $225 million. A bigger divestment came in late 2004 with the sale of Dresser-Rand to private equity group First Reserve Corporation for about $1.2 billion.

Early in 2007 Ingersoll-Rand sold its road construction equipment division to AB Volvo for $1.3 billion in cash. Later that year the company said it was exploring options for Bobcat and its other construction equipment businesses, citing the fact that these operations no longer complement its core business. Ingersoll-Rand found a buyer later in 2007 in a teaming of two sister companies of the Doosan Group — Doosan Infracore and Doosan Engine. The two companies paid $4.9 billion for the businesses, which essentially made up Ingersoll-Rand's construction division — Bobcat, utility equipment, and attachments.

EXECUTIVES

Chairman and CEO: Herbert L. (Herb) Henkel, age 60, $14,947,879 total compensation
President and COO; President, Trane Commercial Systems: Michael W. (Mike) Lamach, age 45, $1,995,122 total compensation
SVP and CFO: Steven R. (Steve) Shawley, age 56, $6,907,007 total compensation
VP and CIO: Barry Libenson
SVP, General Counsel, and Director: Patricia Nachtigal, age 62, $2,944,082 total compensation
SVP and President, Trane Residential Systems: David R. (Dave) Pannier, age 58
SVP; President, Construction Technologies: Christopher P. (Chris) Vasiloff, age 57
SVP and President, Industrial Technologies: James R. (Jim) Bolch, age 51, $1,678,836 total compensation
SVP Human Resources and Communications: Marcia J. Avedon, age 47
SVP Enterprise Services: William B. (Bill) Gauld, age 55
SVP; President, Compact Vehicle Technologies: Richard F. (Dick) Pedtke, age 60
SVP and President, Climate Control Technologies Sector: Didier Teirlinck
SVP; President, Security Technologies Sector: John W. Conover IV
VP Investor Relations and Treasurer: Barbara L. Brasier
VP Finance: Richard (Rich) Randall, age 58
VP Corporate Governance and Secretary: Barbara A. Santoro
VP, Principal Accounting Officer, and Controller: Richard J. (Rick) Weller, age 52

Director Investor Relations: Joseph P. (Joe) Fimbianti
Director Public Relations: Paul Dickard
Auditors: PricewaterhouseCoopers LLP

LOCATIONS

HQ: Ingersoll-Rand plc
170/175 Lakeview Dr., Airside Business Park
Swords, Dublin, Ireland
Phone: 353-1-870-7400
US HQ: 1 Centennial Ave., Piscataway, NJ 08854
US Phone: 732-652-7000
Web: www.irco.com

2008 Sales

	$ mil.	% of total
US	7,709.4	58
Other countries	5,518.0	42
Total	**13,227.4**	**100**

PRODUCTS/OPERATIONS

2008 Sales

	$ mil.	% of total
Air conditioning systems & services	4,401.3	33
Climate control technologies	3,356.8	26
Industrial technologies	2,938.3	22
Security technologies	2,531.0	19
Total	**13,227.4**	**100**

Selected Business Segments, Products, and Brands

Air Conditioning Systems and Services
Building controls (Trane)
Chillers (Trane)
Heating, ventilation and air conditioning equipment (Trane)
OEM compressors (Trane)

Climate Control Technologies
Refrigerated display cases (Koxka)
Transport temperature control units (Thermo King)
Walk-in storage coolers and freezers (Hussmann)

Industrial Technologies
Air compressors (Ingersoll-Rand)
Evaporative condensers (Ingersoll-Rand)
Fluid handling equipment (Ingersoll-Rand)
Golf carts and utility vehicles (Club Car)
Lifting and material handling equipment (Ingersoll-Rand)
Pumps and dispensing equipment (Ingersoll-Rand)
Tools (Ingersoll-Rand)
Winches and hoists (Ingersoll-Rand)

Security Technologies
Bathroom fittings (Normbau)
Biometric technologies (Schlage)
Decorative and security hardware (Ives)
Door hardware (Legge)
Door holders, stops, and latches (Glynn-Johnson, LCN)
Electronic access control (Bricard)
Exit devices (Von Duprin)
Locks (Bricard, CISA)
Portable lock chains and cables (Kryptonite)
Safes (CISA)
Steel doors and frames (Steelcraft)
Wireless security access technologies (Schlage)

COMPETITORS

ASSA ABLOY
Black & Decker
Carrier
Cooper Industries
Dover Corp.
Emerson Electric
E-Z-GO
Gardner Denver
Illinois Tool Works
ITT Corp.
Johnson Controls
Snap-on
SPX
Stanley Works
Textron
Tyco

HISTORICAL FINANCIALS

Company Type: Public

Income Statement

	REVENUE ($ mil.)	NET INCOME ($ mil.)	NET PROFIT MARGIN	EMPLOYEES
12/08	13,227.4	(2,624.8)	—	60,000
12/07	8,763.1	3,966.7	45.3%	35,560
12/06	11,409.3	1,032.5	9.0%	43,000
12/05	10,546.9	1,054.2	10.0%	40,000
12/04	9,393.6	1,218.7	13.0%	36,000
Annual Growth	8.9%	—	—	13.6%

FYE: December 31

2008 Year-End Financials

Debt ratio: 41.6%
Return on equity: —
Cash ($ mil.): 550
Current ratio: 0.98
Long-term debt ($ mil.): 2,774

No. of shares (mil.): 319
Dividends
Yield: 4.1%
Payout: —
Market value ($ mil.): 5,536

Stock History

NYSE: IR

	STOCK PRICE ($) FY Close	P/E High/Low	PER SHARE ($) Earnings	Dividends	Book Value
12/08	17.35	— —	(8.73)	0.72	20.88
12/07	46.47	4 3	13.43	0.72	24.78
12/06	39.13	15 11	3.20	0.68	16.94
12/05	40.37	14 11	3.09	0.57	18.06
12/04	40.15	12 8	3.47	0.44	17.97
Annual Growth	(18.9%)	— —	—	13.1%	3.8%

Ingram Micro

There's nothing micro about Ingram. Ingram Micro is the world's largest wholesale distributor of computer products. It provides thousands of products — desktop and notebook PCs, servers, storage devices, monitors, printers, and software — to 170,000 reseller customers around the globe. The company also provides a wide range of services for its resellers and suppliers, including contract manufacturing and warehousing, customer care, financing, logistics, outsourcing management, and enterprise network support services. Customers include resellers such as CompUSA, Wal-Mart.com, Staples, and Office Depot.

Though it remains primarily focused on computer-related products, Ingram Micro has expanded into such markets as automatic identification and data capture (AIDC), point-of-sale (POS) systems, and consumer electronics. The company cites the breadth of its product offerings as some protection against demand volatility.

The company also continues to expand its managed and professional services. Its Ingram Micro Services Division offers managed services such as network security, application hosting, and remote monitoring under the Seismic brand.

The unit's professional services include consulting and staffing, and it also provides warranty contract management. Another division, Ingram Micro Logistics, handles fulfillment, order management, transportation, and warehousing.

With more than 100 distribution centers around the globe, the company sells to customers in more than 150 countries. Ingram generates about 60% of its sales outside North America.

HISTORY

Micro D was founded in Fountain Valley, California, in 1979 by husband-and-wife entrepreneurs Geza Csige and Lorraine Mecca. As the company grew, Mecca sought to merge the computer distributor with a partner that could take over daily operations. She relinquished control of Micro D to Linwood "Chip" Lacy in 1986 and sold her 51% share of the company to minority shareholder Ingram Distribution Group.

Sales bottomed out for Micro D that year. Lacy tightened Micro D's belt and took huge charges for outdated inventory it sold at a discount and overdue payments from customers that had gone bankrupt.

At the same time, Ingram Industries was busy merging recently acquired Ingram Software Distribution Services of Buffalo, New York, with Compton, California-based Softeam. The merger made the company one of the nation's largest wholesale distributors of computer software. Lacy saw Ingram's purchase of Micro D shares as a conflict of interest, but he was too busy returning Micro D to profitability — centralizing its marketing and distribution functions, cutting costs, and expanding its market to include more small retailers, which provided higher margins. Micro D went from the fourth-largest distributor of microcomputer products to #1 in just one year.

The surging PC market in the late 1980s fueled Micro D's growth. By 1988 the firm had expanded outside the US for the first time, acquiring Canadian company Frantek Computer Products.

Ingram Industries offered to acquire the 41% of outstanding Micro D stock it did not own in 1988, but Lacy resisted, preferring to let Ingram wait. Though Ingram owned a majority of Micro D stock, it only controlled three of seven seats on the board. Ingram was forced to play Lacy's game and finally acquired the company at a higher cost in 1989. The new company, which controlled 20% of the computer distribution market, was called Ingram Micro D. The merger was anything but smooth, and several Micro D executives jumped ship.

As the PC took hold in the US in the 1990s, Ingram Micro D became the dominant industry player, but relations between Lacy and the Ingram family never improved. The company shortened its name to Ingram Micro in 1991, and two years later, as it was hitting stride, Lacy announced plans to leave. To keep him, Ingram Industries CEO Bronson Ingram (much to his distaste) promised to let Lacy take the company public.

Bronson Ingram died in 1995, and the next year his widow, Martha, forced Lacy's resignation. Lacy was replaced by Jerre Stead, formerly CEO of software maker LEGENT (bought by Computer Associates), who devised a compensation package for himself consisting solely of stock options (no salary) and listed "Head Coach" on his business card. Ingram went public a few months after Stead took over.

In 1998 Ingram Micro forged a distribution alliance with Japanese computer giant SOFTBANK and bought a majority stake in German computer products distributor Macrotron. It also expanded into build-to-order PC manufacturing. Amid softer PC sales industrywide, Ingram Micro in 1999 terminated nearly 600 employees as part of a worldwide realignment and signed a deal (worth an estimated $10 billion) with CompUSA to be its primary PC manufacturer and distributor.

Later in 1999 Stead — with Ingram Micro's sales slipping and its stock slumping — made plans to step down as CEO. The search ended in 2000 when the company named GTE veteran Kent Foster to the post.

Ingram Micro expanded its portfolio of services for enterprises and began offering more extensive network and product support services. The company outsourced certain IT infrastructure operations, along with the related personnel, to Affiliated Computer Services (ACS) in late 2002. Ingram Micro continued to expand international operations that year, acquiring the 49% of a Singapore exporter it did not previously own, and purchasing operations in Belgium and the Netherlands. In a move to expand its presence in the Asia/Pacific region, Ingram acquired Australian distributor Tech Pacific in 2004.

Company president Greg Spierkel replaced Foster as CEO in 2005. It also acquired select assets of consumer electronics distributor AVAD. The following year it expanded its reach in Northern Europe when it purchased the assets of SymTech Nordic. It also formed a new North American services division focused on professional IT services, warranty contract management, and managed services. Ingram purchased consumer electronics distributor DBL Distributing for $96 million in 2007.

EXECUTIVES

Chairman: Dale R. Laurance, age 63
CEO and Director: Gregory M.E. (Greg) Spierkel, age 52, $1,442,062 total compensation
President and COO: Alain Monié, age 58
EVP and CFO: William D. Humes, age 44, $668,219 total compensation
SVP and CIO: Mario F. Leone, age 53
Chief Strategy and Communications Officer: Ria Marie Carlson, age 47
EVP; President, Ingram Micro North America: Keith W. F. Bradley, age 45, $1,224,746 total compensation
EVP Ingram Micro Asia-Pacific; President, Ingram Micro Asia-Pacific: Shailendra Gupta, age 46, $1,405,076 total compensation
SVP Human Resources: Lynn Jolliffe, age 56
SVP, General Counsel, and Secretary: Larry C. Boyd, age 56
SVP Legal Services, Ingram Micro US: Mark K. Slater
SVP and General Manager, Strategic Divisions, Ingram Micro North America: John Soumbasakis
SVP and Global Human Resources Leader: Tom Kraabel
President, Ingram Micro Europe, Middle East, and Africa: Alain Maquet, age 57, $1,296,618 total compensation
Senior Manager, Corporate Communications: Rekha Parthasarathy
Auditors: PricewaterhouseCoopers LLP

LOCATIONS

HQ: Ingram Micro Inc.
1600 E. St. Andrew Place, Santa Ana, CA 92799
Phone: 714-566-1000   **Fax:** 714-566-7900
Web: www.ingrammicro.com

2008 Sales

	$ mil.	% of total
North America	14,192.0	41
Europe, Middle East & Africa	11,535.0	34
Asia/Pacific	6,904.6	20
Latin America	1,730.6	5
Total	**34,362.2**	**100**

PRODUCTS/OPERATIONS

Selected Products

IT Peripheral/CE/AIDC/POS/Mobility and Others
  Printers
  Barcode/card printers
  Cell phones
  Components
  Digital cameras
  Digital signage products
  Digital video disc players
  Game consoles
  Mass storage
  Projectors
  Scanners
  Supplies and accessories
  Televisions
Networking
  Network interface cards
  Storage
  Switches, hubs, and routers
  Wireless local area networks
Software
  Business application software
  Developer software tools
  Entertainment software
  Middleware
  Operating system software
  Security software
  Storage software
Systems
  Desktops
  Personal digital assistants
  Portable personal computers
  Rack, tower, and blade servers

COMPETITORS

Agilysys
Arrow Electronics
ASI Computer Technologies
Avnet
Bell Microproducts
Black Box
Computacenter
D&H Distributing
DHL
Digiland
Digital China
Flextronics
Intcomex
Menlo Worldwide
New Age Electronics
Redington Group
ScanSource
SED International
Softmart
Software House
Supercom
SYNNEX
Tech Data
United Stationers
UPS Supply Chain Solutions
Westcon

HISTORICAL FINANCIALS

Company Type: Public

Income Statement				FYE: Saturday nearest December 31
	REVENUE ($ mil.)	NET INCOME ($ mil.)	NET PROFIT MARGIN	EMPLOYEES
12/08	34,362.2	(394.9)	—	14,500
12/07	35,047.1	275.9	0.8%	15,000
12/06	31,357.5	265.8	0.8%	13,700
12/05	28,808.3	216.9	0.8%	13,000
12/04	25,462.1	219.9	0.9%	13,600
Annual Growth	7.8%	—	—	1.6%

2008 Year-End Financials

Debt ratio: 13.4%
Return on equity: —
Cash ($ mil.): 763
Current ratio: 1.65
Long-term debt ($ mil.): 357
No. of shares (mil.): 163
Dividends
  Yield: 0.0%
  Payout: —
Market value ($ mil.): 2,183

Stock History

NYSE: IM

	STOCK PRICE ($) FY Close	P/E High/Low		PER SHARE ($) Earnings	Dividends	Book Value
12/08	13.39	—	—	(2.37)	0.00	16.29
12/07	18.04	14	11	1.56	0.00	21.02
12/06	20.41	14	11	1.56	0.00	17.91
12/05	19.93	16	11	1.32	0.00	14.96
12/04	20.80	15	8	1.38	0.00	13.74
Annual Growth	(10.4%)	—	—	—	—	4.3%

Insight Enterprises

With this company around, the end of your technology woes could be in sight. Insight Enterprises is a top distributor of computer hardware and software in North America, carrying thousands of products from major manufacturers, such as Hewlett-Packard, IBM, and Microsoft. It uses direct telesales and field sales agents to reach customers in business, government, and education. Insight, which has boosted its services unit, also sells products through catalogs and its Web site. Outside North America, it serves customers in 15 countries in Europe, the Middle East, Africa, and the Asia/Pacific region. It bought software and mobile solutions firm Software Spectrum, as well as Calence, a networking and communications company.

To stay ahead of the competition and broaden its revenue streams, the company has been focused on expanding its technology services business. To that end, Insight Enterprises in April 2008 purchased Arizona-based Calence, one of the largest Cisco providers in the US. The purchase of Calence, at $125 million (plus an additional $35 million through 2012 if Calence hits its set performance targets), gave the company a leg up in several US regions (Southwest, Northwest, and Midwest), as well as strategic states New York, Texas, and North Carolina. Insight Enterprises also added Calence's managed services, security, and technological expertise to its menu of services. As part of the deal, the company retained Calence CEO Michael Fong.

To fund its expansion into the services sector, Insight Enterprises has been offloading other units. The company sold the PC Wholesale division (acquired in 2002) of its subsidiary Insight Direct USA Inc. to Synnex Corp. in 2007 for about $10 million, plus approximately $20 million for net assets acquired. Insight Enterprises

in 2006 also sold its business process outsourcing (BPO) division, Direct Alliance, to TeleTech Holdings for $46 million.

The deep recession in the US has slowed technology purchases by businesses and put the squeeze on Insight's sales. To control expenses in a difficult environment, the company has cut more than 500 jobs (over 10% of its workforce) since late 2008 and taken other measures to control costs. Still the company is forging ahead with its plans under the leadership of former IBM executive Richard Fennessy, who was appointed in 2004 to replace co-founder Tom Crown as CEO. Crown, now chairman of the company, started Insight with his brother, Eric (now chairman emeritus). To grow its international business the company teamed up with Google Enterprise in May 2009 to bring Google Apps' online application to customers outside the US.

As part of its marketing strategy, Insight sponsors the Insight Bowl, a college football bowl game.

HISTORY

Eric Crown worked for a small computer retail chain in the mid-1980s before leaving to market PCs. In 1986 he and his brother, Tim, pooled $2,000 from credit cards and $1,300 in savings and, anticipating a drop in hard drive prices, placed an ad for low-cost hard drives in a computer magazine. The ad pulled in $20,000 worth of sales and, since costs did indeed drop, the profit was enough to start a new company, Hard Drives International. In 1988 they changed the name to Insight Enterprises; by 1991 the Crowns also sold Insight-branded PCs, software, and peripherals (discontinued in 1995). The company passed the $100 million revenue mark in 1992.

Insight shifted its marketing focus to catalogs in 1993 and had a circulation of more than 7 million by 1995. The company went public that year and entered an alliance with Computer City (acquired by CompUSA in 1998) to handle its mail-order fulfillment. It also launched its Web site. The next year subsidiary Insight Direct began to offer on-site service warranties, and in 1997 retailing subsidiary Direct Alliance was chosen to provide product fulfillment for Internet software firm Geo Publishing. That year the company began sponsoring the Copper Bowl, a college football game played in Arizona, which was renamed the Insight.com Bowl (and later the Insight Bowl).

Looking beyond the US, in 1998 Insight established operations in Canada and acquired direct marketers Choice Peripherals (UK) and Computerprofis Computersysteme (Germany). At home it added direct marketer Treasure Chest Computers. Sales passed the billion-dollar mark that year.

The company formed an alliance with Daisytek International in 1999 that expanded its product line by more than 10,000. Soon thereafter, Insight walked away from a merger with UK-based computer wholesaler Action Computer Supplies when Action's profits slumped.

Insight withdrew its planned IPO and spinoff of Direct Alliance in 2001 due to poor market conditions. Also that month Eric became chairman and Tim became CEO (they had previously shared the title of co-CEO). Insight ended up buying Action Computer Supplies in 2001. It also shut down its German operations and acquired computer direct marketers in both the UK and Canada in late 2001.

In April 2002 Insight acquired Comark, a leading private reseller of computers, peripherals, and computer supplies in the US, and began integrating its operations into Insight North America's existing operational structure.

Tim stepped down as president and CEO and became chairman in late 2004, while Eric assumed the title of chairman emeritus. The company appointed IBM veteran Richard Fennessy to the position of president and CEO. That year Insight spun off its UK-based Internet service provider PlusNet.

Insight sold its outsourcing subsidiary, Direct Alliance, in 2006 to TeleTech for about $46 million and bought services firm Software Spectrum the same year. In early 2008 Insight Enterprises purchased Calence to extend its reach into the services sector once again. Soon after that purchase the company realigned its US sales organization and in November laid off some 240 employees.

EXECUTIVES

Chairman: Timothy A. (Tim) Crown, age 45
President, CEO, and Director: Richard A. Fennessy, age 44
CFO: Glynis A. Bryan, age 50, $1,021,351 total compensation
CIO: Stephen A. Speidel, age 44
Chief Administrative Officer, General Counsel, and Secretary: Steven R. Andrews, age 56
SVP Investor Relations and Treasurer: Helen K. Johnson, age 40
SVP Strategic Partnerships and Marketing: Dave Casillo
President, Insight EMEA: Stuart A. Fenton, age 40, $1,211,000 total compensation
Senior Manager Marketing: Shana Diana
Auditors: KPMG LLP

LOCATIONS

HQ: Insight Enterprises, Inc.
1305 W. Auto Dr., Tempe, AZ 85284
Phone: 480-902-1001   **Fax:** 480-902-1157
Web: www.insight.com

2008 Sales

	$ mil.	% of total
North America	3,362.5	70
Europe, Middle East & Africa	1,309.4	27
Asia/Pacific	153.6	3
Total	**4,825.5**	**100**

PRODUCTS/OPERATIONS

Selected Products

Computer memory and processors
Desktop computers
Displays
Laptop computers
Networking equipment
Servers
Software
Storage devices

Selected Services

Business process outsourcing
  Collections
  Credit card processing
  Customer support
  Direct marketing
  Fulfillment
  Inbound and outbound call handling
  Supply chain management

Information technology
  Consulting
  Help desk support
  Maintenance
  Managed services
  Network administration
  Project management
  Systems integration
  Security

COMPETITORS

Amazon.com	Micro Electronics
Best Buy	Microsoft
Buy.com	ModusLink
CDW	Office Depot
CompuCom	OfficeMax
Convergys	PC Connection
Dell	PC Mall
Digital River	PFSweb
DSG International	RadioShack
EDS	Softchoice
Fry's Electronics	Software House
Gateway, Inc.	Staples
Hewlett-Packard	Systemax
IBM	Zones
Lenovo	

HISTORICAL FINANCIALS

Company Type: Public

Income Statement

FYE: December 31

	REVENUE ($ mil.)	NET INCOME ($ mil.)	NET PROFIT MARGIN	EMPLOYEES
12/08	4,825.5	(239.7)	—	4,763
12/07	4,800.4	77.8	1.6%	4,763
12/06	3,817.1	76.8	2.0%	4,568
12/05	3,261.1	55.3	1.7%	3,967
12/04	3,082.7	114.5	3.7%	5,000
Annual Growth	**11.9%**	**—**	**—**	**(1.2%)**

2008 Year-End Financials

Debt ratio: 54.0%
Return on equity: —
Cash ($ mil.): 49
Current ratio: 1.34
Long-term debt ($ mil.): 228
No. of shares (mil.): 46
Dividends
  Yield: 0.0%
  Payout: —
Market value ($ mil.): 316

Stock History

NASDAQ (GS): NSIT

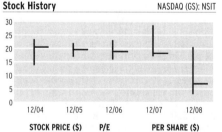

	STOCK PRICE ($) FY Close	P/E High/Low		PER SHARE ($) Earnings	Dividends	Book Value
12/08	6.90	—	—	(5.15)	0.00	9.20
12/07	18.24	18	11	1.56	0.00	16.90
12/06	18.87	14	10	1.58	0.00	15.05
12/05	19.61	19	15	1.12	0.00	12.34
12/04	20.52	14	9	1.64	0.00	12.20
Annual Growth	**(23.9%)**	**—**	**—**	**—**	**—**	**(6.8%)**

Intel Corporation

Intel is still #1 in semiconductors, but profits and chip demand are shrinking. The company holds about 80% of the market share for microprocessors that go into desktop and notebook computers, and also into computer servers. Archrival AMD ate into Intel's market share for a time, but the big guy fought back with faster processors and advanced manufacturing technology. Intel also makes embedded semiconductors for the industrial equipment and networking gear markets. While most computer makers use Intel processors — PC giants Dell (18% of sales) and Hewlett-Packard (20%) are the company's largest customers — computer sales are plummeting.

The world's largest semiconductor manufacturer was humbled by a series of events, including slumping demand for PCs, increased competition in its core chip business, temporary shortages of chipsets, and unsuccessful forays into niche markets. The global financial crisis hasn't helped. As a result of drastically falling profits, Intel announced plant closures in China, Malaysia, the Philippines and the US, which may eliminate up to 8,000 jobs.

The company's long-running battle with AMD heated up when that company's successful Athlon processor took market share away from Intel's Pentium models. AMD pulled off its coup through timely introductions of high-performance chips during a period in the early 21st century when Intel experienced uncharacteristic component shortages and manufacturing glitches. Intel struck back with rounds of price cuts and an unusually aggressive schedule for introducing faster Pentium models.

AMD filed an antitrust suit against Intel, alleging that its rival used improper subsidies and coercion to secure sales. In 2008 the Federal Trade Commission upgraded an informal inquiry on Intel's practices in the microprocessor market to a formal investigation, issuing subpoenas to AMD, Intel, and other companies.

In 2009 the European Commission levied a record fine against Intel — more than €1 billion or about $1.44 billion. The antitrust regulators alleged that Intel paid hidden rebates to PC manufacturers to only use Intel's microprocessors in their computers. Intel is appealing the ruling and fine, stating it took "strong exception" to the decision and denying that consumers were harmed by its business practices.

In 2009 the company acquired Wind River Systems, a supplier of software for embedded electronics, for about $884 million in cash. While Intel is well known as a chip manufacturer, the company has a substantial software development organization, turning out tools that help smooth the integration of its parts into system designs.

Intel decided in 2007 to build a 300mm wafer fabrication plant in Dalian, a city in northeast China. The $2.5 billion project, dubbed Fab 68, will be the company's first wafer fab in Asia.

Paul Otellini is only the fifth CEO in the company's four-decade history, and the first non-engineer. His predecessor, Craig Barrett, retired as chairman in 2009.

HISTORY

In 1968 three engineers from Fairchild Semiconductor created Intel in Mountain View, California, to develop technology for silicon-based chips. ("Intel" is a contraction of "integrated electronics.") The trio consisted of Robert Noyce (who co-invented the integrated circuit, or IC, in 1958), Gordon Moore, and Andy Grove.

Intel initially provided computer memory chips such as DRAMs (1970) and EPROMs (1971). These successes funded the microprocessor designs that revolutionized the electronics industry. In 1971 Intel introduced the 4004 microprocessor, promoted as "a microprogrammable computer on a chip."

In 1979 Moore became Intel's chairman and Grove its president. (Grove became CEO in 1987.) When Intel's 8088 chip was chosen for IBM's PC in 1981, Intel secured its place as the microcomputer standard-setter.

Cutthroat pricing by Japanese competitors forced Intel out of the DRAM market in 1985; in a breathtaking strategy shift that became the subject of countless business school case studies, the company refocused on microprocessors. It licensed its 286 chip technology to Advanced Micro Devices (AMD) and others in an effort to create an industry standard. Reacting to AMD's escalating market share (which stood at more than half by 1990), Intel fiercely protected the technology of its 386 (1985) and 486 (1989) chips; AMD sued for breach of contract.

Grove handed the CEO reins to president Craig Barrett in 1998; Grove replaced Moore as chairman, while Moore became chairman emeritus. (Thanks to a mandatory retirement age he helped set, Moore retired from Intel's board in 2001.) Also in 1998 Intel unveiled its low-end Celeron chip. Late in 1999 the company began shipping prototypes of its Itanium 64-bit processor; Itanium's general release was delayed repeatedly, ultimately into mid-2001.

A string of other problems beset Intel in 2000. The company recalled hundreds of thousands of its motherboards that were distributed with a defective chip, and later cancelled development of a low-cost microprocessor for budget PCs.

In 2004 it announced plans to spend $2 billion to add a cutting-edge production plant in Ireland. The following year Intel unveiled plans for its second plant in Israel. The company also announced plans to invest more than $1 billion to expand its operations in India.

In 2005 Grove retired from the board, Barrett retired as CEO and succeeded Grove as chairman, and Otellini succeeded Barrett as CEO.

Intel announced in 2005 that it would join with Micron Technology to form a new company devoted to NAND flash memory. Each contributed roughly $1.3 billion to create IM Flash Technologies, which will manufacture memory exclusively for Micron and Intel.

Responding to reports of lost market share and other problems, Intel announced in 2006 it would cut 1,000 management jobs to trim costs in the face of stiff competition and lower demand for PCs. The company then said it would reduce its headcount by 10,500 jobs by mid-2007, through attrition and workforce reductions, particularly in management, marketing, and IT functions.

In 2006 Intel sold its communications and application processor line to Marvell Technology for $600 million in cash.

EXECUTIVES

Chairman: Jane E. Shaw, age 70
President, CEO, and Director: Paul S. Otellini, age 58, $12,722,600 total compensation
VP and CFO: Stacy J. Smith, age 46, $2,542,200 total compensation
VP, Director Corporate Technology Group, and CTO: Justin R. Rattner, age 59
VP and Co-CIO: John N. Johnson, age 56
VP and Co-CIO: Diane M. Bryant, age 47
VP Digital Enterprise Group and Chief Architect, Hybrid Parallel Computing: David R. Ditzel, age 52
EVP and Chief Sales and Marketing Officer: Sean M. Maloney, age 52, $5,259,100 total compensation
EVP Finance and Enterprise Services and Chief Administrative Officer: Andy D. Bryant, age 59, $5,502,900 total compensation
Chief Virtualization Architect: Richard A. Uhlig
EVP; President, Intel Capital: Arvind Sodhani, age 54
EVP; General Manager, Mobility Group: David (Dadi) Perlmutter, age 56, $4,724,300 total compensation
SVP and Director Human Resources: Patricia Murray
SVP; General Manager, Technology and Manufacturing Group: Robert J. (Bob) Baker, age 53
SVP; General Manager, Ultra Mobility Group: Anand Chandrasekher, age 46
SVP; General Manager, Digital Enterprise Group: Patrick P. (Pat) Gelsinger, age 47
SVP; General Manager, Technology and Manufacturing Group: William M. (Bill) Holt, age 56
SVP and General Counsel: D. Bruce Sewell, age 50
SVP; General Manager, Digital Home Group: Eric B. Kim, age 54
VP and Director Finance: Leslie S. Culbertson
Auditors: Ernst & Young LLP

LOCATIONS

HQ: Intel Corporation
2200 Mission College Blvd., Santa Clara, CA 95054
Phone: 408-765-8080   **Fax:** 408-765-3804
Web: www.intel.com

Intel has manufacturing plants in China, Costa Rica, Ireland, Israel, Malaysia, the Philippines, and the US, and sales offices in more than 40 countries worldwide.

2008 Sales

	$ mil.	% of total
Asia/Pacific		
Taiwan	9,868	26
China	4,974	13
Japan	3,983	11
Other countries	4,202	11
Americas		
US	5,462	15
Other countries	1,981	5
Europe	7,116	19
Total	**37,586**	**100**

PRODUCTS/OPERATIONS

2008 Sales

	$ mil.	% of total
Digital Enterprise Group		
Microprocessors	16,078	43
Chipsets, motherboards & other	4,554	12
Mobility Group		
Microprocessors	11,439	30
Chipsets & other	4,209	11
Other	1,306	4
Total	**37,586**	**100**

Selected Products

Chipsets (consumer electronics, desktop, embedded, laptop, modem, server, workstation)
Communication infrastructure components
  Network processors
  Networked storage products
Flash memory (embedded, wireless)
Microprocessors (control plane, desktop, embedded, laptop, network, server, wireless, workstation)
  Celeron
  Core Duo
  Core Quad
  Itanium
  Pentium
  Xeon
Motherboards
Wired and wireless connectivity components

COMPETITORS

AMD
Analog Devices
Applied Micro Circuits
ARM Holdings
Atmel
Broadcom
Centaur Technology
Cisco Systems
Conexant Systems
Creative Technology
Freescale Semiconductor
Fujitsu Microelectronics
IBM Microelectronics
Infineon Technologies
Integrated Device Technology
Intersil
LSI Corp.
Marvell Technology
Maxim Integrated Products
Microchip Technology
MIPS Technologies
Mitsubishi Electric
National Semiconductor
NEC Electronics
NVIDIA
NXP
Opnext
PMC-Sierra
QUALCOMM
Samsung Electronics
SANYO Semiconductor
Seagate Technology
Silicon Integrated Systems
STMicroelectronics
Sun Microsystems
Texas Instruments
Toshiba Semiconductor
Transmeta
VIA Technologies

HISTORICAL FINANCIALS

Company Type: Public

Income Statement

FYE: Last Saturday in December

	REVENUE ($ mil.)	NET INCOME ($ mil.)	NET PROFIT MARGIN	EMPLOYEES
12/08	37,586.0	5,292.0	14.1%	83,900
12/07	38,334.0	6,976.0	18.2%	86,300
12/06	35,382.0	5,044.0	14.3%	94,100
12/05	38,826.0	8,664.0	22.3%	99,900
12/04	34,209.0	7,516.0	22.0%	85,000
Annual Growth	**2.4%**	**(8.4%)**	**—**	**(0.3%)**

2008 Year-End Financials

Debt ratio: 4.8%
Return on equity: 12.9%
Cash ($ mil.): 3,350
Current ratio: 2.54
Long-term debt ($ mil.): 1,886

No. of shares (mil.): 5,598
Dividends
  Yield: 3.7%
  Payout: 59.8%
Market value ($ mil.): 82,067

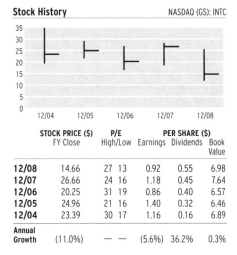
	STOCK PRICE ($)	P/E		PER SHARE ($)		
	FY Close	High/Low	Earnings	Dividends	Book Value
12/08	14.66	27 13	0.92	0.55	6.98
12/07	26.66	24 16	1.18	0.45	7.64
12/06	20.25	31 19	0.86	0.40	6.57
12/05	24.96	21 16	1.40	0.32	6.46
12/04	23.39	30 17	1.16	0.16	6.89
Annual Growth	(11.0%)	— —	(5.6%)	36.2%	0.3%

International Business Machines

Big Blue? Try Huge Blue. International Business Machines (IBM) is the world's top provider of computer products and services. Among the leaders in almost every market in which it competes, the company focuses primarily on its growing services business, which accounts for more than half of sales. Though perhaps still best known for its hardware, its IT and business services units are among the largest in the world and serve customers across most industries. IBM is also one of the largest providers of both business software (ranking #2, behind Microsoft) and semiconductors. The company's computing hardware legacy lives on in the form of its industry-leading enterprise server and storage products lines.

In July 2009 the company announced it was purchasing analytics provider SPSS for about $1.2 billion in cash, a move designed to further its "Information Agenda" initiative that is geared towards helping customers make full use of their business information and processes.

Among the 15 purchases made by the company in 2008 was software developer Cognos. IBM paid about $5 billion for Cognos in a bid to increase its portfolio of so-called business process optimization applications. The deal was intended to help the company gain ground against enterprise software industry leaders Oracle and SAP specifically in the areas of business intelligence and performance management.

IBM's other most notable acquisition that year was the purchase of business process optimization and embedded systems software specialist Telelogic. The deal was intended to complement the embedded systems capabilities of IBM's Rational Software unit in order to meet potential demand for such technology in sectors including auto manufacturing.

IBM's international business has become increasingly important to the bottom line. With clients in about 170 countries, overseas sales account for about two thirds of total revenues. The company's businesses in Brazil, China, India, and Russia accounted for the most notable overseas growth in 2008. IBM management has said that it will continue to seek opportunities outside of the mature markets of North America, Europe, and Japan.

IBM's research and development programs consistently lead the tech industry in patent awards. It is at the forefront of such diverse fields as nanotechnology and quantum computing.

HISTORY

In 1914 National Cash Register's star salesman, Thomas Watson, left to rescue the flagging Computing-Tabulating-Recording (C-T-R) Company, the pioneer in US punch card processing that had been incorporated in 1911. Watson aggressively marketed C-T-R's tabulators, supplying them to the US government during WWI and tripling company revenues to almost $15 million by 1920. The company became International Business Machines (IBM) in 1924 and soon dominated the global market for tabulators, time clocks, and electric typewriters. It was the US's largest office machine maker by 1940.

IBM perfected electromechanical calculation (the Harvard Mark I, 1944) but initially dismissed the potential of computers. When Remington Rand's UNIVAC computer (1951) began replacing IBM machines, IBM quickly responded.

The company unveiled its first computer in 1952. With its superior research and development and marketing, IBM built a market share near 80% in the 1960s and 1970s. Its innovations included the STRETCH systems, which eliminated vacuum tubes (1960), and the first compatible family of computers, the System/360 (1964). IBM also developed floppy disks (1971) and the first laser printer for computers (1975). The introduction of the IBM PC in 1981 ignited the personal computer industry, sparking a barrage of PC clones. Through it all IBM was the subject of a 12-year government antitrust investigation that ended in 1982.

The shift to smaller, open systems, along with greater competition in all of IBM's segments, caused wrenching change. Instead of responding to the market need for cheap PCs and practical business applications, IBM stubbornly stuck with mainframes, and rivals began capitalizing on Big Blue's technology. After posting profits of $6.6 billion in 1984, the company began a slow slide. It sold many noncomputer businesses, including its copier division to Kodak in 1988 and its Lexmark typewriter business in 1991. Closing the book on its heritage, IBM shuttered the last of its punch card plants that year.

In 1993 CEO John Akers was replaced by Louis Gerstner, the first outsider to run IBM. He began to turn the ailing, antiquated company around by slashing costs and nonstrategic divisions, cutting the workforce, shaking up entrenched management, and pushing services. His $1 billion R&D budget cut caused an exodus of IBM scientists and created an operation geared more toward quick turnaround than lengthy research. In 1994 Big Blue reported its first profit in four years. It also began making computer chips that year.

A pioneer in server operating system software, IBM made an early move into messaging and network management software with its acquisitions of spreadsheet pioneer Lotus Development in 1995. Hoping to turn around its ailing PC business, IBM in 1999 axed manufacturing staff and halted sales of its PCs through US retailers. The following year the head of its server business, Samuel Palmisano, was named president and COO; the change fueled speculation that IBM's emperor had found his heir.

In a move intended to bolster its data management division, IBM in 2001 purchased the database software unit of Informix for $1 billion.

IBM acquired PricewaterhouseCoopers' consulting and IT services unit, PwC Consulting, for an estimated $3.5 billion in 2002. While presenting IBM with a significant integration challenge, the transaction served the dual purpose of augmenting IBM's standard array of outsourcing, maintenance, and integration services, while moving the company into high-end management consulting. Palmisano succeeded Gerstner as CEO that year.

In 2003 IBM acquired development tool maker Rational Software for $2.1 billion. The company in 2005 sold its PC business to Lenovo. That year it expanded the presence of its service arm in the health care market when it acquired Healthlink. Also in 2005 it acquired Ascential Software for about $1.1 billion. In 2006 IBM bought FileNet, a maker of content management software, for $1.6 billion.

EXECUTIVES

Chairman, President, and CEO: Samuel J. Palmisano, age 57, $28,542,392 total compensation
SVP and CFO: Mark Loughridge, age 55, $7,873,186 total compensation
VP and CIO: Mark J. Hennessy
VP Regulatory Affairs and Chief Privacy Officer: Harriet P. Pearson
VP ISC Global Procurement and Chief Procurement Officer: John Paterson
Chief Scientist, Entity Analytic Solutions, Software Group and Distinguished Engineer: Jeff Jonas
SVP Human Resources: J. Randall (Randy) MacDonald, age 60
SVP Marketing and Communications: Jon C. Iwata, age 46
SVP Research and Intellectual Property: John E. Kelly III, age 55
SVP Global Technology Services: Michael E. (Mike) Daniels, age 54, $7,669,780 total compensation
SVP Global Business Services: Virginia M. (Ginni) Rometty, age 50, $7,091,697 total compensation
SVP Development and Manufacturing, IBM Systems and Technology Group: Rodney C. (Rod) Adkins, age 50
SVP Systems and Technology Group: Robert W. (Bob) Moffat Jr., age 52
SVP Enterprise On Demand Transformation: Linda S. Sanford, age 56
SVP Software Group: Steven A. (Steve) Mills, age 57, $7,466,746 total compensation
SVP Global Business Services: Frank Kern, age 55
SVP Legal and Regulatory Affairs and General Counsel: Robert C. Weber, age 58
SVP Services Delivery: Timothy S. Shaughnessy, age 51
VP Investor Relations: Patricia Murphy
Auditors: PricewaterhouseCoopers LLP

LOCATIONS

HQ: International Business Machines Corporation New Orchard Road, Armonk, NY 10504
Phone: 914-499-1900   **Fax:** 800-314-1092
Web: www.ibm.com

2008 Sales

	$ mil.	% of total
Americas	42,807	41
Europe, Middle East & Africa	37,020	36
Asia/Pacific	21,111	20
OEM	2,692	3
Total	**103,630**	**100**

PRODUCTS/OPERATIONS

2008 Sales

	$ mil.	% of total
Global technology services	39,264	38
Software	22,089	21
Global business services	19,628	19
Systems & technology	19,287	19
Global financing	2,559	2
Other	803	1
Total	**103,630**	**100**

Selected Services

Business services
  Application management
  E-business
  Strategic consulting
  Systems integration

Financing

Technology services
  Business process outsourcing
  Infrastructure
  Maintenance
  Outsourcing
  Software integration
  Systems management
  Web hosting

Training

Selected Products

Microelectronics
  Application-specific integrated circuits (ASICs)
  Foundry services
  Memory chips
  Microprocessors and embedded processors
  Packaging and interconnect products and services

Printing systems

Servers

Software
  Application development
  Database and data management
  E-commerce
  Graphics and multimedia
  Groupware
  Networking and communication
  Operating systems
  Product life cycle management
  Security
  Speech recognition
  System management
  Transaction system
  Web application servers

Storage
  Hard drive systems
  Optical libraries
  Storage networking
  Tape drives, systems, and libraries

Selected Software Brands

Lotus
Rational
Tivoli
WebSphere

COMPETITORS

Accenture	McKinsey & Company
Alcatel-Lucent	Microsoft
BearingPoint	Motorola, Inc.
CA, Inc.	NEC
Canon	Novell
Capgemini	NTT DATA
Computer Sciences Corp.	Oracle
Dell	Panasonic Corp
Deloitte Consulting	Ricoh Company
EDS	SAP
EMC	Siemens AG
Epson	Sony
Ericsson	Sun Microsystems
Fujitsu	Texas Instruments
Hewlett-Packard	Toshiba
Hitachi	TSMC
Intel Corp.	Unisys
Lexmark	Xerox

HISTORICAL FINANCIALS

Company Type: Public

Income Statement

FYE: December 31

	REVENUE ($ mil.)	NET INCOME ($ mil.)	NET PROFIT MARGIN	EMPLOYEES
12/08	103,630.0	12,334.0	11.9%	398,455
12/07	98,786.0	10,418.0	10.5%	426,969
12/06	91,424.0	9,492.0	10.4%	355,766
12/05	91,134.0	7,970.0	8.7%	366,345
12/04	96,293.0	8,430.0	8.8%	369,277
Annual Growth	**1.9%**	**10.0%**	**—**	**1.9%**

2008 Year-End Financials

Debt ratio: 168.5%
Return on equity: 58.8%
Cash ($ mil.): 12,741
Current ratio: 1.15
Long-term debt ($ mil.): 22,689

No. of shares (mil.): 1,311
Dividends
  Yield: 2.3%
  Payout: 21.3%
Market value ($ mil.): 110,324

Stock History

NYSE: IBM

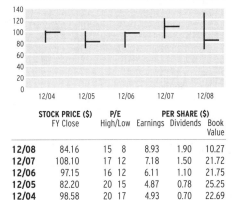

	STOCK PRICE ($) FY Close	P/E High/Low		PER SHARE ($) Earnings	Dividends	Book Value
12/08	84.16	15	8	8.93	1.90	10.27
12/07	108.10	17	12	7.18	1.50	21.72
12/06	97.15	16	12	6.11	1.10	21.75
12/05	82.20	20	15	4.87	0.78	25.25
12/04	98.58	20	17	4.93	0.70	22.69
Annual Growth	**(3.9%)**	**—**	**—**	**16.0%**	**28.4%**	**(18.0%)**

International Flavors & Fragrances

Iff you've got a taste for the sweet and the salty, then International Flavors & Fragrances (IFF) is your kind of company. It's one of the world's leading creators and manufacturers of artificial aromas and flavors, producing fragrances used in the manufacture of perfumes, cosmetics, soaps, and other personal care and household products. The company has more than 15% of the world market, placing it among Givaudan and Firmenich as the top flavor and fragrance maker. IFF sells its flavors principally to makers of prepared foods, dairy foods, beverages, confections, and pharmaceuticals. The company sells its fragrances and flavors in solid and liquid forms in amounts that range from a few pounds to several tons.

The company has manufacturing, sales, and distribution facilities in more than 30 countries. Sales outside North America account for nearly 70% of revenues. The compounds used in IFF's products are made both synthetically and from natural ingredients such as flowers and fruits.

It operates about 30 fragrance and flavor laboratories in more than 20 countries. While IFF's flavor products represent 60% of the total production volume, fragrances contribute more than half of the company's sales. IFF continues to introduce new products and to invest heavily in product development; R&D spending amounts to about 10% of sales.

HISTORY

International Flavors & Fragrances (IFF) began in 1929 when Dutch immigrant and perfumer A. L. van Ameringen (who originally came to the US to work for an agent of the Dutch firm Polak & Schwarz, later leaving to form his own business) and William Haebler formed a fragrance company, van Ameringen-Haebler, in New York City.

The company produced the fragrance for Youth Dew, Estée Lauder's first big cosmetics hit, in 1953. One biographer of Estée Lauder linked her romantically with van Ameringen after her 1939 divorce (she later remarried Joseph Lauder). The business association with van Ameringen's company endured, and by the late 1980s it had produced an estimated 90% of Estée Lauder's fragrances.

In 1958 the company changed its name to International Flavors & Fragrances after it bought Polak & Schwarz. The US market for fragrances grew as consumers bought items such as air fresheners, and manufacturers began adding fragrances to household cleaning items.

Henry Walter, who became CEO when van Ameringen retired in 1963, expanded IFF's presence overseas. Walter boasted, "Most of the great soap fragrances have been ours." So have many famous French perfumes, but most perfume companies wanted to cultivate product mystique, preventing IFF from taking credit for its scents.

Most of IFF's products were made for manufacturers of consumer goods. But under Walter's direction in the 1970s, IFF's R&D team experimented to find scents for museum exhibits and participated in Masters & Johnson research on the connection between sex and smell. Said Walter, "Our business is sex and hunger."

During the early 1980s IFF conducted fragrance research for relieving stress, lowering blood pressure, and alleviating depression. In 1982 IFF researchers developed a way to bind odors to plastic, a process used by makers of garbage bags and toys. Walter retired in 1985 and Eugene Grisanti became CEO. After a three-year slump in new creations, IFF developed fragrances for several prestigious perfumes (Eternity and Halston) in 1988.

IFF enhanced its position in dairy flavors with its 1991 purchase of Wisconsin-based Auro Tech. In 1993 IFF's Living Flower process successfully synthesized the fragrance of growing flowers for perfumes.

IFF inaugurated its flavor and fragrance facility in China (Guangzhou) and formed a joint venture with China's Hangzhou Xin'anjiang Perfumery Factory. The company reasserted its leadership in the US fragrance market in 1996 with the launch of two IFF-developed fragrances: Elizabeth Taylor's Black Pearls and Escada's Jardin de Soleil.

Sales and profits dipped in 1997, prompting IFF to consolidate production. Asia's economic crisis and turmoil in Russia continued to hurt profits in 1998, and in 1999 IFF was hit by the devaluation of Brazil's currency, weak demand for aroma chemicals, and the US dollar's strength against the euro.

In 2000 Unilever executive Richard Goldstein was appointed chairman and CEO. Boosting its natural ingredients operations, IFF bought Laboratoire Monique Remy (France). The same year IFF acquired rival fragrance and flavor maker Bush Boake Allen in a deal worth about $1 billion. The acquisition led to a company-wide reorganization, including the closing of some manufacturing, distribution, and sales facilities worldwide.

In 2001 the company sold its US and Brazilian formulated fruit and vegetable preparation businesses and its aroma chemicals business in the UK. Continuing its product development strategy, in 2003 IFF launched a high-intensity cooling technology (CoolTek) for use in the food, beverage, and pharmaceutical industries that does not use the traditional mint-based technology. The following year it opened a new culinary and baking center to support customers' product development programs.

IFF sold its fruit preparations operations in Switzerland and Germany in August 2004 to Israel's Frutarom. The deal was for $36.5 million. Later that year, it sold the remainder of its fruit preparations business (located in France) to Frutarom. It also closed its Canadian manufacturing facility and its plant in Dijon, France.

Chairman and CEO Goldstein retired in 2006. Former Sears chairman and CEO Arthur Martinez, an IFF director, took over on an interim basis until International Paper's Robert Amen was named chairman and CEO.

EXECUTIVES

Chairman and CEO: Robert M. (Rob) Amen, age 59, $6,817,139 total compensation
EVP and CFO: Kevin Berryman, age 50
EVP and Head Supply Chain: Beth E. Ford, age 45
SVP, General Counsel, and Secretary: Dennis M. Meany, age 61, $1,853,798 total compensation
SVP Human Resources: Steven J. Heaslip, age 51
VP Corporate Development: Richard A. (Rich) O'Leary, age 49, $570,192 total compensation
VP and General Manager Fragrance Ingredients Business: Robert J. M. (Rob) Edelman
Global VP Creation, Application, and Innovation, Flavors: Jesse Wolff
VP Global Manufacturing: Francisco Fortanet
VP Research and Development: Mike Popplewell
VP Global Manufacturing: Todd Hand
Group President, Fragrances: Nicolas Mirzayantz, age 46, $1,576,910 total compensation
Group President, Flavors: Hernan Vaisman, age 50, $1,428,491 total compensation
Controller: Kimberly A. Hendricks, age 45
Director Corporate Communications: Yvette Rudich
Auditors: PricewaterhouseCoopers LLP

LOCATIONS

HQ: International Flavors & Fragrances Inc.
521 W. 57th St., New York, NY 10019
Phone: 212-765-5500 **Fax:** 212-708-7132
Web: www.iff.com

2008 Sales

	$ mil.	% of total
Europe, Africa & Middle East	898	38
North America	601	25
Greater Asia	556	23
Latin America	334	14
Total	**2,389**	**100**

PRODUCTS/OPERATIONS

2008 Sales

	$ mil.	% of total
Fragrances	1,296.8	54
Flavors	1,092.6	46
Total	**2,389.4**	**100**

Selected Applications for IFF's Products

Fragrance chemical uses
Aftershave lotions
Air fresheners
All-purpose cleaners
Colognes
Cosmetic creams
Deodorants
Detergents
Hair care products
Lipsticks
Lotions
Perfumes
Powders
Soaps
Flavor chemical uses
Alcoholic beverages
Baked goods
Candies
Dairy products
Desserts
Diet foods
Drink powders
Pharmaceuticals
Prepared foods
Snacks
Soft drinks

COMPETITORS

Ajinomoto
BASF SE
Bayer AG
Danisco A/S
Firmenich
Frutarom
Givaudan
Henkel
Human Pheromone Sciences
International Specialty Products
Kerry Group
M & F Worldwide
McCormick & Company
Newly Weds Foods
PCAS
Robertet
Sensient
Symrise
Takasago International
Wrigley

HISTORICAL FINANCIALS

Company Type: Public

Income Statement

	REVENUE ($ mil.)	NET INCOME ($ mil.)	NET PROFIT MARGIN	EMPLOYEES
12/08	2,389.4	229.6	9.6%	5,300
12/07	2,276.6	247.1	10.9%	5,315
12/06	2,095.4	226.5	10.8%	5,087
12/05	1,993.4	193.1	9.7%	5,160
12/04	2,033.7	196.1	9.6%	5,212
Annual Growth	**4.1%**	**4.0%**	**—**	**0.4%**

FYE: December 31

2008 Year-End Financials

Debt ratio: 201.3%
Return on equity: 38.6%
Cash ($ mil.): 178
Current ratio: 2.57
Long-term debt ($ mil.): 1,154
No. of shares (mil.): 79
Dividends
Yield: 3.2%
Payout: 33.4%
Market value ($ mil.): 2,348

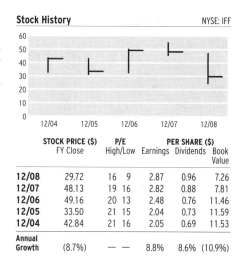

Stock History

NYSE: IFF

	STOCK PRICE ($) FY Close	P/E High/Low		Earnings	Dividends	Book Value
12/08	29.72	16	9	2.87	0.96	7.26
12/07	48.13	19	16	2.82	0.88	7.81
12/06	49.16	20	13	2.48	0.76	11.46
12/05	33.50	21	15	2.04	0.73	11.59
12/04	42.84	21	16	2.05	0.69	11.53
Annual Growth	**(8.7%)**	**—**	**—**	**8.8%**	**8.6%**	**(10.9%)**

International Game Technology

International Game Technology (IGT) has hit the jackpot in the casino gaming business. The company is the world's largest gaming machine manufacturer, with a product portfolio that includes traditional reel slot machines, video slots and video poker, and progressive payout machines. IGT also makes casino management software systems for tracking activity on the casino floor, as well as multiplayer game software and customer relationship management (CRM) systems. It sells products mostly in North America, but it also serves international customers in about 10 other countries.

IGT generates just over 50% of its revenue through product sales and service agreements under which the company collects recurring fees, some of which are based on the amount of money wagered on its machines. The rest of its business comes from more traditional sales and service contracts. IGT is working to increase the number of customers paying under recurring revenue contracts.

The company invests heavily in product development to make games that will attract attention on the crowded casino floor. It has about 1,000 different game themes designed to appeal to game players, including several based on licensed brands and entertainment properties such as popular game shows *Wheel of Fortune* and *The Price is Right*. IGT has also introduced a multigame slot system (MultiPlay) that allows gamblers to play up to four slot games at once with progressive payouts. In addition, the company is putting emphasis on developing and expanding its casino information management systems and server-based gaming platforms that help operate multiple gaming machines.

To help maintain its leadership in the industry, IGT has made several strategic acquisitions and investments in other gaming machine companies. In 2009 the company acquired the global operations of Progressive Gaming International. Complementing its current technology, the acquisition increased IGT's system-install base, providing the company with a more complete product offering.

IGT appointed Patti Hart to replace T.J. Matthews as CEO in 2009. The move was prompted by Matthews' resignation that year. Hart previously served as CEO of software maker Pinnacle Systems.

HISTORY

International Game Technology (IGT) was formed in 1980 by William "Si" Redd, a veteran of the slot machine industry. Lady Luck was good to Redd for five years before turning fickle. Rather than fold, Redd dealt himself a king (hiring Charles Mathewson, a retired top executive from investment firm Jefferies & Co.). Mathewson flushed top management, cinched IGT's belt, and dealt new managers a fresh hand (stock options rather than cash). IGT developed its Telnaes patent-based slot machine — a reel-type slot with higher payouts and higher odds — featuring flashy themes, fewer breakdowns, and improved reporting systems. Slots went from a nickel-and-dime game to a major source of casino revenue.

In 1997 IGT debuted Mega$ports, which accepts unique wagers on sports (such as which quarterback will throw the most yards in a game). That year IGT's vast new headquarters became fully operational (five plants and seven warehouses were moved under one roof). In 1998 IGT beefed up its Australian operations with the $114 million acquisition of Olympic Amusements, a Melbourne-based supplier of gaming equipment and services. IGT also bought the UK-based Barcrest gaming machine business from Bass (which later split into Mitchells & Butlers and InterContinental Hotels) for $70 million.

In 1999 the company acquired Sodak Gaming, a supplier of gaming machines to Native American casinos and other clients. In 2001 IGT bought rivals Silicon Gaming (for about $45 million) and Anchor Gaming. The latter buy was part of the company's strategy of expanding into the lottery business. The following year it created a new division, IGT Lottery, to house its lottery operations, including the former Anchor companies AWI, United Tote, and VLC, and its own Oregon lottery route operations and SAMS lottery system.

IGT purchased gaming software development company Acres Gaming for $130 million in 2003. The company also sold its online lottery operations to Scientific Games for $143 million. That same year, Thomas (T.J.) Matthews was named CEO. In late 2004 IGT created its IGT-Canada unit with the acquisition of Canadian gaming equipment provider Hi-Tech Gaming. It also expanded into online gaming that same year through the purchase of WagerWorks.

Acquisitions continued in 2007 when IGT purchased a stake in electronic table game maker DigiDeal. It also expanded into the Chinese gaming market by investing in Hong Kong-based LotSynergy. Former Pinnacle Systems chief Patti Hart replaced Matthews as CEO in 2009.

EXECUTIVES

Chairman: Thomas J. (T.J.) Matthews, age 43
President, CEO, and Director: Patti S. Hart, age 52
EVP and CFO: Patrick W. (Pat) Cavanaugh, age 48
CTO: Chris Satchell
EVP Operations: Anthony Ciorciari, age 61
EVP Product Strategy: Richard J. (Rich) Schneider, age 51

EVP, General Counsel, and Secretary:
David D. (Dave) Johnson, age 56
EVP Sales and Marketing, North America: Eric Tom
SVP Sales: Ron Rivera
VP Native American Development: Knute Knudson Jr.
VP Human Resources: Tami Corbin
VP Corporate Law and Assistant Secretary:
J. Kenneth Creighton
VP Marketing: Ed Rogich
VP Corporate Finance and Investor Relations:
Craig Billings
President, Global Business Development:
Paulus Karskens, age 56
Treasurer: Daniel R. Siciliano, age 40
Director Marketing: Julie Brown
Auditors: Deloitte & Touche LLP

LOCATIONS

HQ: International Game Technology
9295 Prototype Dr., Reno, NV 89521
Phone: 775-448-7777   **Fax:** 775-448-0719
Web: www.igt.com

2008 Sales

	$ mil.	% of total
North America	1,912.4	76
International	616.2	24
Total	**2,528.6**	**100**

PRODUCTS/OPERATIONS

2008 Sales

	$ mil.	% of total
Gaming	1,337.9	53
Products	1,190.7	47
Total	**2,528.6**	**100**

Selected Products

Amusement with prize machines (limited-payout skill games)
Casino gaming machines
  Progressive payout machines
  Reel and video slot machines
  Video poker
Casino information systems
  Customer relationship management (CRM) software
  Electronic table games
  Multiplayer game management systems
Electronic bingo games
Pachisuro (slot-style gaming machines in Japan)
Video lottery terminal

COMPETITORS

Aristocrat Leisure	Multimedia Games
Aruze Corp.	Novomatic
Bally Technologies	Scientific Games
John Huxley	Shuffle Master
Konami Gaming	WMS Industries
Lottomatica	

HISTORICAL FINANCIALS

Company Type: Public

Income Statement

FYE: September 30

	REVENUE ($ mil.)	NET INCOME ($ mil.)	NET PROFIT MARGIN	EMPLOYEES
9/08	2,528.6	342.5	13.5%	5,900
9/07	2,621.4	508.2	19.4%	5,400
9/06	2,511.7	473.6	18.9%	5,200
9/05	2,379.4	436.5	18.3%	5,000
9/04	2,484.8	488.7	19.7%	4,900
Annual Growth	0.4%	(8.5%)	—	4.8%

2008 Year-End Financials

Debt ratio: 247.2%	No. of shares (mil.): 296
Return on equity: 29.0%	Dividends
Cash ($ mil.): 266	Yield: 3.3%
Current ratio: 2.00	Payout: 50.9%
Long-term debt ($ mil.): 2,247	Market value ($ mil.): 5,090

Stock History

NYSE: IGT

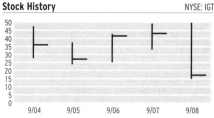

	STOCK PRICE ($) FY Close	P/E High/Low		PER SHARE ($) Earnings	PER SHARE ($) Dividends	PER SHARE ($) Book Value
9/08	17.18	45	14	1.10	0.56	3.07
9/07	43.10	32	22	1.51	0.53	4.90
9/06	41.50	32	19	1.34	0.50	6.89
9/05	27.00	31	20	1.20	0.49	6.43
9/04	35.95	35	21	1.34	0.42	6.67
Annual Growth	(16.9%)	—	—	(4.8%)	7.5%	(17.7%)

International Paper

For International Paper (IP) life is a paper chase. The world's largest forest products company produces uncoated paper, industrial and consumer packaging, and pulp. Together, paper and packaging account for nearly two-thirds of the company's sales. IP also distributes printing, packaging, and graphic-art supplies in North America through subsidiary xpedx and in Europe through multiple subsidiaries. Slimming down, the company has sold its specialty chemicals operations, the majority of its lumber and wood products business, and most of the 6.3 million acres of US forestland it once owned. It retains 300,000 acres of US land and owns or has harvesting rights to nearly 250,000 acres of forestland in Brazil.

IP is creating a partnership with American Timberlands Fund by divesting approximately 143,000 acres in the southeastern US. The land is valued at approximately $275 million, and in exchange IP will receive a 20% interest in the partnership. Like other US paper makers, IP is taking advantage of the federal alternative fuel tax credit, a program that encourages use of alternative fuels for meeting energy needs. The company qualifies by blending diesel with a substance known as "black liquor," a by-product of producing pulp. In the first quarter of 2009, the tax credit has boosted net income by over 90% from a year earlier.

During 2008 IP purchased the containerboard, packaging, and recycling business of rival Weyerhaeuser for $6 billion in cash. The new operations include 10 specialty packaging plants, four kraft bag and sack locations, as well as 19 recycling facilities. The Weyerhaeuser business gives IP the leading market share in the North American containerboard market.

IP has also increased prices; however, the benefits of higher average sales dollars have been more than offset by higher raw material and energy costs, higher freight costs, lower sales volumes, and increased lack-of-order downtime.

Internationally, IP aims to improve its position by adding globally cost-competitive paper mills, expanding the company's uncoated free sheet capacity, and opening up additional growth opportunities. In Brazil, IP exchanged an in-progress pulp mill project and certain forestland operations for Votorantim Celulose e Papel's (VCP) Luiz Antonio uncoated paper and pulp mill plus forestlands in the state of São Paulo. Across the globe in China, IP completed construction of its third containerboard facility, which allows the company to meet growing demand for packaging in that country, as well as other customers in the region.

HISTORY

In 1898, 18 northeastern pulp and paper firms consolidated to lower costs. The resulting International Paper had 20 mills in Maine, Massachusetts, New Hampshire, New York, and Vermont. The mills relied on forests in New England and Canada for wood pulp. When Canada enacted legislation to stop the export of pulpwood in 1919, International Paper formed Canadian International Paper.

In the 1920s International Paper built a hydroelectric plant on the Hudson River. Between 1928 and 1941 the company called itself International Paper & Power. It entered the market for kraft paper (paper sacks) in 1925 with the purchase of Bastrop Pulp & Paper (Louisiana).

During the 1940s and 1950s, the company bought Agar Manufacturing (shipping containers, 1940), Single Service Containers (Pure-Pak milk containers, 1946), and Lord Baltimore Press (folding cartons, 1958). It diversified in the 1960s and 1970s, buying Davol (hospital products, 1968; sold to C. R. Bard, 1980), American Central (land development, 1968; sold to developers, 1974), and General Crude Oil (gas and oil, 1975; sold to Mobil Oil, 1979).

In the 1980s International Paper modernized its plants to focus on less-cyclical products. After selling Canadian International Paper in 1981, the company bought Hammermill Paper (office paper, 1986), Arvey (paper manufacturing and distribution, 1987), and Masonite (composite wood products, 1988). International Paper entered the European paper market in 1989 by buying Aussedat Rey (France), Ilford Group (UK), and Zanders (West Germany). In 1990 it bought Dixon Paper (distributor of paper and graphic arts supplies), Nevamar (laminates), and the UK's Cookson Group (printing plates).

International Paper expanded in the early 1990s with acquisitions such as Scaldia Papier (the Netherlands, 1991) and Western Paper (1992) and through investments in Carter Holt Harvey (New Zealand) and Scitex (Israel), a leading maker of electronic prepress systems. In 1994 International Paper formed a Chinese packaging joint venture and bought two Mexican paper-distributing companies.

After recording a loss in 1997, International Paper began downsizing: It sold $1 billion in marginal assets and cut its workforce by 10%. Branching its US box-making operations into the South and Midwest, International Paper bought Weston Paper & Manufacturing in 1998; it also bought Mead's distribution business. Then the company announced that it would close 25 plants in the combined enterprise.

International Paper paid $7.9 billion in 1999 for rival Union Camp, and it acquired Champion for about $9.6 billion. In 2001 International Paper sold its Masonite operations to Premdor for $500 million. The company also began cutting 10% (3,000 jobs) of its US workforce as part of a restructuring program.

International Paper closed its mill in Natchez, Mississippi, and exited the Chemical Cellulose pulp business in 2003. (The Natchez plant is the world's second-largest producer of acetate pulps.) Layoffs affected about 600 workers, or 6% of International Paper's workforce.

At the close of 2004 International Paper completed the sale of its Weldwood of Canada, Ltd. subsidiary to West Fraser Timber Co. Ltd. of Vancouver, Canada, for about $950 million.

The company also sold its 50.5% stake in Carter Holt Harvey for $1.14 billion.

Other divestitures between 2000 and 2006 included its retail and flexible packaging operations, its Zanders European coated papers business, its oriented strand board business, its decorative products business, and more than 5 million acres of forestland.

IP followed with a joint-venture deal with Ilim Pulp by forming a JV with Ilim Holding. The company bought in 2007 50% of Ilim Holding for about $650 million. The JV, Ilim Group, will operate pulp and paper mills in the European and Siberian regions of Russia. The JV agreement calls for the partnering companies to invest around $1.5 billion over five years in Ilim Group's four mills.

EXECUTIVES

Chairman and CEO: John V. Faraci Jr., age 59, $5,865,772 total compensation
SVP and CFO: Timothy (Tim) Nicholls, age 47, $1,736,100 total compensation
SVP and CIO: John N. Balboni, age 60
SVP, General Counsel, and Secretary: Maura Abeln Smith, age 53
SVP Corporate Development: C. Cato Ealy, age 52
SVP Human Resources: Jerome N. (Jerry) Carter, age 60
SVP Consumer Packaging: Michael J. (Mike) Balduino, age 58
SVP Printing and Communication Papers: H. Wayne Brafford, age 58, $1,577,291 total compensation
SVP; President, IP Asia: Thomas E. (Tom) Gestrich, age 62
SVP; President, IP Brazil: Maximo Pacheco, age 56
SVP Industrial Packaging: Carol L. Roberts, age 49, $2,170,884 total compensation
SVP; President, xpedx: Thomas G. (Tom) Kadien, age 52
SVP; President, European Operations: Mary A. Laschinger, age 48
SVP Supply Chain: Mark S. Sutton, age 47
SVP Manufacturing and Technology: Tommy S. Joseph
VP Finance and Controller: Robert J. Grillet, age 53
VP Investor Relations: Thomas A. Cleves, age 47
VP Internal Audits: Terri L. Herrington, age 53
Manager Investor Relations: Ann-Marie Donaldson
Director Ethics and Business Practice: James D. (Jim) Berg
Auditors: Deloitte & Touche LLP

LOCATIONS

HQ: International Paper Company
6400 Poplar Ave., Memphis, TN 38197
Phone: 901-419-7000   **Fax:** 901-214-9682
Web: www.ipaper.com

2008 Sales

	$ mil.	% of total
Americas		
US	19,501	79
Other countries	1,324	5
Europe	3,177	13
Pacific Rim	827	3
Total	**24,829**	**100**

PRODUCTS/OPERATIONS

2008 Sales

	$ mil.	% of total
Distribution	7,970	31
Printing papers	6,810	26
Industrial packaging	7,690	30
Consumer packaging	3,195	12
Forest products	200	1
Adjustments	(1,036)	—
Total	**24,829**	**100**

Selected Operations and Products

Printing Papers
  Commercial printing papers
  Office and consumer papers
Distribution
  Business products for copiers and computers
  Food service disposables
  Graphic arts equipment and supplies
  Industrial packaging and supplies
  Printing papers
Industrial Packaging
  Containerboard
Consumer Packaging
  Bleached board
  Food service packaging

COMPETITORS

Alcoa	NewPage
Amcor	Nippon Paper
Cascades Inc.	OfficeMax
Domtar	Packaging Corp.
ENCE	Potlatch
Environmental Mill &	Pratt Industries USA
Supply	Sappi
Georgia-Pacific	Smurfit-Stone Container
Louisiana-Pacific	Temple-Inland
McFarland Cascade	UPM-Kymmene
MeadWestvaco	Weyerhaeuser
Myllykoski Paper	

HISTORICAL FINANCIALS

Company Type: Public

Income Statement				FYE: December 31
	REVENUE ($ mil.)	NET INCOME ($ mil.)	NET PROFIT MARGIN	EMPLOYEES
12/08	24,829.0	(1,282.0)	—	61,700
12/07	21,890.0	1,168.0	5.3%	51,500
12/06	21,995.0	1,050.0	4.8%	60,600
12/05	24,097.0	1,100.0	4.6%	68,700
12/04	25,548.0	(35.0)	—	80,000
Annual Growth	(0.7%)	—	—	(6.3%)

2008 Year-End Financials

Debt ratio: 269.8%   No. of shares (mil.): 433
Return on equity: —   Dividends
Cash ($ mil.): —   Yield: 8.5%
Current ratio: 1.55   Payout: —
Long-term debt ($ mil.): 11,246 Market value ($ mil.): 5,107

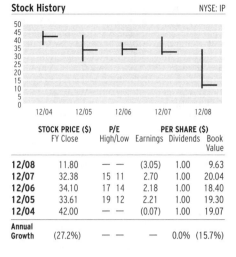
Interpublic Group

Subsidiaries of this company come between brands and the general public. The Interpublic Group of Companies is the world's third-largest advertising and marketing services conglomerate (behind Omnicom Group and WPP Group), operating through offices in more than 100 countries. Its flagship creative agencies include McCann Worldgroup, DraftFCB, and Lowe & Partners, while such firms as Campbell-Ewald, Deutsch, and Hill, Holliday are leaders in the US advertising business. Interpublic also offers direct marketing, media services, and public relations through such agencies as Initiative and Weber Shandwick. Its largest clients include General Motors, Johnson & Johnson, Microsoft, and Unilever.

Interpublic's strategy involves simplifying its operating structure while also acquiring controlling stakes in what it deems emerging markets. Along these lines, in 2006 Interpublic integrated direct marketer Draft, Inc. with advertising agency Foote, Cone & Belding (forming DraftFCB). A year later it restructured its vast network of media brands to report under a single management structure (Mediabrands).

Interpublic has also been keeping its eye on one of the world's fastest-growing economies — India. In mid-2007 it bought all the shares of FCB Ulka, a top-five ad agency in India that operated from six offices. Interpublic integrated the Indian agency with its DraftFCB operations. At the same time, it acquired the remaining 51% stake it didn't hold in Lintas India Private Limited at a cost of $50 million in cash, and integrated it into its Lowe Worldwide network.

In 2008 Interpublic upped its stake to 51% in Middle East Communication Networks, a marketing services company headquartered in Dubai, operating out of 60 offices across almost 15 countries. All in all, the company made 10 acquisitions in 2008.

HISTORY

Standard Oil advertising executive Harrison McCann opened the H. K. McCann Company in 1911 and signed Standard Oil of New Jersey (later Exxon) as his first client. McCann's ad business boomed as the automobile became an integral part of American life. His firm merged with Alfred Erickson's agency (created 1902) in 1930, forming the McCann-Erickson Company. At the end of the decade, the firm hired Marion Harper, a top Yale graduate, as a mailroom clerk. Harper became president in 1948.

Harper began acquiring other ad agencies, and by 1961 controlled more than 20 companies. That year he unveiled a plan to create a holding company that would let the ad firms operate separately, allowing them to work on accounts for competing products, but giving them the parent firm's financial and information resources. He named the company Interpublic Inc. after a German research company owned by the former H. K. McCann Co. The conglomerate continued expanding and was renamed The Interpublic Group of Companies in 1964. Harper's management capabilities weren't up to the task, however, and the company soon faced bankruptcy. In 1967 the board replaced him with Robert Healy, who saved Interpublic and returned it to profitability. The company went public in 1971.

The 1970s were fruitful years for Interpublic; its ad teams created memorable campaigns for Coke ("It's the Real Thing" and "Have a Coke and a Smile") and Miller Beer ("Miller Time" and Miller Lite ads). After Philip Geier became chairman in 1980, the company gained a stake in Lowe Howard-Spink (1983; later The Lowe Group) and purchased Lintas International (1987). Interpublic bought the rest of The Lowe Group in 1990.

Interpublic bought Western International Media (now known as Initiative), and Ammirati & Puris (which was merged with Lintas to form Ammirati Puris Lintas) in 1994. As industry consolidation picked up in 1996, Interpublic kept pace with acquisitions of PR company Weber Group and DraftWorldwide. Interpublic bought a majority stake in artist management and film production company Addis-Wechsler & Associates (now Industry Entertainment) in 1997 and later formed sports marketing and management group Octagon.

Interpublic acquired US agencies Carmichael Lynch and Hill, Holliday, Connors, Cosmopulos in 1998. It also boosted its PR presence with its purchase of International Public Relations (UK), the parent company of public relations networks Shandwick and Golin/Harris. Interpublic strengthened its position in the online world in 1999 when it bought 20% of Stockholm-based Internet services company Icon Medialab International. That year the company merged agencies Ammirati and Lowe & Partners Worldwide to form Lowe Lintas & Partners Worldwide (in 2002 they changed the name to just Lowe & Partners Worldwide).

Interpublic bought market research firm NFO Worldwide for $580 million in 2000 and merged Weber Public Relations with Shandwick International to form Weber Shandwick Worldwide, one of the world's largest PR firms. Later that year the company bought ad agency Deutsch for about $250 million. John Dooner took the position of chairman and CEO at the end of the year after Geier resigned. His first move proved a big one: Interpublic acquired True North Communications for $2.1 billion in stock in 2001.

The honeymoon was short lived; facing a recession, the mounting debt from its buying spree, and with the revelation of accounting discrepancies at McCann-Erickson WorldGroup (renamed McCann Worldgroup in 2004), Dooner stepped aside as chairman and CEO in 2003. Interpublic chose vice chairman David Bell (former CEO of True North) as Dooner's replacement. After almost two years of work to improve Interpublic's balance sheet, Bell was replaced by former MONY Group chief Michael Roth.

In 2005 Roth was tasked with straightening out Interpublic's financial controls and improving its balance sheet. Later that year, the company revealed extensive bookkeeping problems, primarily in its overseas operations, leading to a financial restatement going back to 2000.

EXECUTIVES

Chairman and CEO: Michael I. Roth, age 63, $10,843,080 total compensation
EVP and CFO: Frank Mergenthaler, age 48, $4,520,687 total compensation
SVP and CIO: Joseph W. (Joe) Farrelly, age 64
EVP and Chief Human Resources Officer: Timothy A. Sompolski, age 56, $2,231,678 total compensation
SVP and Chief Risk Officer: Thomas A. (Tom) Dowling, age 57
SVP, Controller, and Chief Accounting Officer: Christopher F. Carroll, age 42
SVP and Chief Diversity and Inclusion Officer: Heide Gardner
EVP Emeritus: Barry R. Linsky
EVP Strategy and Network Operations; CEO, Lowe Worldwide: Stephen J. (Steve) Gatfield
EVP Strategy and Corporate Relations: Philippe Krakowsky, age 46, $2,568,175 total compensation
SVP and Managing Director: Terry D. Peigh
SVP, General Counsel, and Secretary: Nicholas J. (Nick) Camera, age 62
SVP Investor Relations: Jerome J. (Jerry) Leshne
SVP Business Development: David I. Weiss
SVP and Treasurer: Ellen T. Johnson
SVP Leadership and Organizational Development: Frank Guglielmo
SVP Finance and Development: Jonathan B. (Jon) Burleigh
SVP and Managing Director: Peter Leinroth
Auditors: PricewaterhouseCoopers LLP

LOCATIONS

HQ: The Interpublic Group of Companies, Inc.
1114 Avenue of the Americas, New York, NY 10036
Phone: 212-704-1200   **Fax:** 212-704-1201
Web: www.interpublic.com

2008 Sales

	$ mil.	% of total
US	3,786.3	54
Europe		
UK	612.9	9
Other countries	1,150.4	17
Asia/Pacific	657.3	9
Latin America	353.4	5
Other regions	402.4	6
Total	**6,962.7**	**100**

PRODUCTS/OPERATIONS

2008 Sales

	$ mil.	% of total
Integrated Agency Network	5,870.7	84
Constituency Management Group	1,092.0	16
Total	**6,962.7**	**100**

Selected Operations

Advertising and marketing services
Advertising agencies
Austin-Kelly
Avrett Free Ginsberg
Campbell-Ewald
Campbell Mithun
Carmichael Lynch
Dailey & Associates
Deutsch
Gotham
Hill, Holiday
Jay Advertising
Lowe & Partners (UK)
The Martin Agency
McCann Erickson Worldwide
Mullen
Tierney Communications
TM Advertising
Marketing agencies
DraftFCB
The Hacker Group
MRM Partners
Momentum
Rivet
Translation Consulting + Brand Imaging
Media services
Initiative Media
MAGNA Global
Universal McCann
Public relations and corporate communications
DeVries Public Relations
MWW Group
Weber Shandwick

COMPETITORS

Aegis Group
Dentsu
Hakuhodo
Havas
Omnicom
Publicis Groupe
WPP

HISTORICAL FINANCIALS

Company Type: Public

Income Statement

FYE: December 31

	REVENUE ($ mil.)	NET INCOME ($ mil.)	NET PROFIT MARGIN	EMPLOYEES
12/08	6,962.7	295.0	4.2%	45,000
12/07	6,554.2	167.6	2.6%	43,000
12/06	6,190.8	(31.7)	—	42,000
12/05	6,274.3	(262.9)	—	43,000
12/04	6,387.0	(538.4)	—	43,700
Annual Growth	2.2%	—	—	0.7%

2008 Year-End Financials

Debt ratio: 91.6%
Return on equity: 15.7%
Cash ($ mil.): 2,107
Current ratio: 1.09
Long-term debt ($ mil.): 1,787

No. of shares (mil.): 486
Dividends
Yield: 0.0%
Payout: —
Market value ($ mil.): 1,925

Stock History

NYSE: IPG

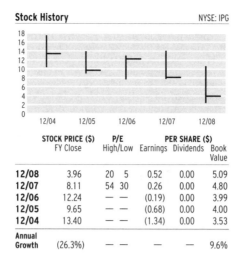

	STOCK PRICE ($) FY Close	P/E High	P/E Low	Earnings	Dividends	Book Value
12/08	3.96	20	5	0.52	0.00	5.09
12/07	8.11	54	30	0.26	0.00	4.80
12/06	12.24	—	—	(0.19)	0.00	3.99
12/05	9.65	—	—	(0.68)	0.00	4.00
12/04	13.40	—	—	(1.34)	0.00	3.53
Annual Growth	(26.3%)	—	—	—	—	9.6%

Intuit Inc.

Intuit knows that good accounting takes more than a pocket calculator. The company is a leading provider of personal finance (Quicken), small business accounting (QuickBooks), and consumer tax preparation (TurboTax) software for consumers, accountants, and small businesses. Other software offerings include industry-specific accounting and management applications for construction, real estate, retail, and wholesale distribution organizations. Intuit also provides payroll services, financial supplies, and software for professional tax preparation.

Intuit has used a string of acquisitions to expand its product lines and services beyond the consumer finance and accounting markets, adding offerings for small and midsized businesses and industry-specific accounting and management applications.

Acquisitions to further that strategy have included its June 2009 purchase of PayCycle (online payroll services) for $170 million, as well as the 2008 purchase of Electronic Clearing House (ECHO), a provider of transaction processing services, for about $131 million. Previous deals included the acquisitions of online banking software provider Digital Insight for about $1.35 billion and e-commerce and Web site software maker Homestead Technologies for about $170 million.

Due to the nature of Intuit's tax preparation products, the company's financial results are very seasonal. Its net revenue is usually highest in the company's second quarter ending January 31 and third quarter ending April 30, with losses typically reported in its first quarter ending October 31 and fourth quarter ending July 31.

HISTORY

After earning his MBA from Harvard, Scott Cook spent three years in marketing at Procter & Gamble and four years with consultancy Bain & Company before founding Intuit in 1983. Research showed that consumers wanted an easy-to-use personal finance software package. Quicken was introduced in 1984.

Intuit was near collapse in 1986 when it received its first big order from software retailer Egghead.com. Intuit released QuickBooks in 1992 and went public in 1993. The next year Intuit acquired a number of firms, including tax preparation software developer ChipSoft, which brought TurboTax onboard. Cook stepped down as CEO in 1994, as former Apple executive William Campbell took the helm.

In 1995 Microsoft's $2 billion bid to buy Intuit was halted by a Justice Department antitrust lawsuit. Also in 1995 Intuit launched an online banking service and forged its first ties with the Web by bundling a browser and free Internet access with Quicken.

Intuit sold its online banking and bill presentation business to CheckFree in 1997. The next year Campbell became chairman, passing the CEO torch to EVP William Harris (formerly COO of ChipSoft). Also in 1998 the company bought Lacerte Software, a provider of software and services to tax professionals.

In 1999 Intuit bought Computing Resources, which had been providing the company's online payroll services, for about $200 million. The company also purchased Rock Financial, an online consumer mortgage company, for about $370 million and renamed it Quicken Loans. Harris resigned and Campbell took over as interim CEO, remaining chairman.

Stephen Bennett, a former GE Financial Services executive, replaced Campbell as CEO in 2000. Later that year Intuit sold its Quicken-Insurance business to InsWeb, an online insurance service. Intuit also bought small business services provider EmployeeMatters for $39 million in stock from FrontLine Capital Group.

Moving to boost its small business offerings, in 2001 the company expanded its QuickBooks software to include industry-specific versions designed for retailers and accountants, and it acquired OMware, a provider of business management software for the construction industry.

In 2002 the company completed a string of acquisitions, purchasing American Fundware (public-sector accounting software), Management Reports (property management software), Eclipse (business management software), CBS Payroll (outsourced payroll services), and Blue Ocean Software (information technology asset management software).

In late 2002 the company sold its Quicken Loans mortgage operation, followed by the sale of its wholly owned Japanese subsidiary Intuit KK in 2003.

Intuit continued to pare down its product line over the next few years in order to focus on its core products, selling its Intuit Public Sector Solutions and Intuit Information Technology Solutions businesses in 2005, as well as its Master Builder operations in 2006.

EXECUTIVES

Chairman: William V. (Bill) Campbell, age 68
Chairman, Executive Committee and Director: Scott D. Cook, age 56
President, CEO, and Director: Brad D. Smith, age 45
SVP and CFO: R. Neil Williams, age 55
SVP and CIO: Ginny Lee
VP Corporate Affairs and Chief Public Policy Officer: Bernard F. (Bernie) McKay
Chief Growth Officer: Justin S. Kitch
Chief Innovation Officer: Per-Kristian (Kris) Halvorsen, age 57
Chief Communications Officer: Harry Pforzheimer
EVP and General Manager, Small Business Ecosystem Division: Kiran M. Patel, age 60

SVP Sales: Caroline F. Donahue, age 46
SVP Human Resources: Sherry Whiteley
SVP Product Development, Small Business Division:
Richard W. (Bill) Ihrie, age 58
SVP and General Manager Small Business Group:
Rick W. Jensen, age 49
SVP; General Manager, Quicken Health Group:
Peter J. Karpas, age 39
SVP, General Counsel, and Corporate Secretary:
Laura A. Fennell, age 47
SVP; President, Digital Insight: Sasan K. Goodarzi,
age 40
SVP Strategy and Corporate Development; President,
Global Business Division: Alexander M. (Alex) Lintner,
age 46
SVP; General Manager, Consumer Tax Group:
Daniel R. (Dan) Maurer, age 52
Auditors: Ernst & Young LLP

LOCATIONS

HQ: Intuit Inc.
2632 Marine Way, Mountain View, CA 94043
Phone: 650-944-6000   Fax: 650-944-3699
Web: www.intuit.com

Intuit has offices in Canada, France, Germany, the UK,
and the US.

PRODUCTS/OPERATIONS

2008 Sales

	$ mil.	% of total
Consumer Tax products & services	929.5	30
QuickBooks products & services	621.8	20
Payroll & Payments products & services	560.8	18
Accounting Professionals products & services	326.7	11
Financial Institutions products & services	298.5	10
Other businesses	333.7	11
Total	**3,071**	**100**

2008 Sales

	$ mil.	% of total
Services	1,574.3	51
Products	1,496.7	49
Total	**3,071**	**100**

Selected Software and Services

Small Business
  Check forms, tax forms, and other supplies
  QuickBooks (accounting software)
    QuickBooks Basic
    QuickBooks Credit Check Services (for access to
      credit reports)
    QuickBooks Enterprise Solutions Business
      Management Software (for businesses with up to
      250 employees)
    QuickBooks Merchant Account Service (for enabling
      credit card payments)
    QuickBooks Online Billing (for enabling electronic
      billing and customer payments)
    QuickBooks Point of Sale (for retail businesses)
    QuickBooks Premier (for small businesses)
    QuickBooks Premier: Accountant Edition (for
      professional accountants)
    QuickBooks Pro (for up to five simultaneous users)
Consumer Tax
  TurboTax (desktop tax preparation software for
    individuals and small businesses)
  TurboTax for the Web (Internet-based tax preparation
    and filing service)
  TurboTax Premier (tax preparation software for
    investors and rental property owners)
Professional Accounting Solutions
  EasyACCT Professional Accounting Series (software for
    helping accountants prepare financial statements
    and tax forms)
  IntuitAdvisor (subscription-based information and
    tools for accounting business growth)
  Lacerte (professional tax preparation software)
  Lacerte Tax Planner (tax planning service software for
    accountants)
  ProSeries (professional tax preparation software)

Personal Finance
  Quicken (desktop personal finance software)
  Quicken Brokerage (online and phone-based securities
    brokerage service powered by Siebert)
  Quicken Financial Planner (retirement planning)
  Quicken Lite
  Quicken Premier (Quicken with added investment and
    tax planning tools)
  Quicken.com (online personal finance information and
    tools)

COMPETITORS

ADP
CA, Inc.
CCH Incorporated
Deluxe Corporation
First Data
Fiserv
H&R Block
Jackson Hewitt
Microsoft Dynamics
MYOB
Online Resources
Paychex
S1 Corp.
Sage Group
SAP

HISTORICAL FINANCIALS

Company Type: Public

Income Statement

FYE: July 31

	REVENUE ($ mil.)	NET INCOME ($ mil.)	NET PROFIT MARGIN	EMPLOYEES
7/08	3,071.0	476.8	15.5%	8,200
7/07	2,672.9	440.0	16.5%	8,200
7/06	2,342.3	417.0	17.8%	7,500
7/05	2,037.7	381.6	18.7%	7,000
7/04	1,867.7	317.0	17.0%	6,700
Annual Growth	**13.2%**	**10.7%**	**—**	**5.2%**

2008 Year-End Financials

Debt ratio: 48.1%
Return on equity: 23.2%
Cash ($ mil.): 413
Current ratio: 1.21
Long-term debt ($ mil.): 998
No. of shares (mil.): 323
Dividends
  Yield: 0.0%
  Payout: —
Market value ($ mil.): 8,829

Stock History

NASDAQ (GS): INTU

	STOCK PRICE ($) FY Close	P/E High/Low		PER SHARE ($) Earnings	Dividends	Book Value
7/08	27.33	23	18	1.41	0.00	6.42
7/07	28.64	29	22	1.24	0.00	6.30
7/06	30.87	27	18	1.16	0.00	5.38
7/05	24.00	24	18	1.01	0.00	5.25
7/04	18.72	34	23	0.79	0.00	5.64
Annual Growth	**9.9%**	**—**	**—**	**15.6%**	**—**	**3.3%**

Invacare Corporation

Invacare's modern wheelchair design is the Ferrari to its predecessors' old Model T. Invacare is a leading maker of wheelchairs worldwide. It makes medical equipment for the home health and extended care markets. Products include crutches, bed systems, respiratory devices, and motorized scooters. It manufactures and sells its own products to more than 25,000 home health care and medical equipment dealers in North America, Europe, and the Asia/Pacific region, as well as to government agencies and distributors. Invacare also distributes other companies' equipment and disposable products such as home diabetic and wound care items.

Invacare makes other home care durables such as bathing equipment, cushions, and slings. Its institutional products group sells beds and furnishings to the non-acute, long-term care facility market.

Invacare continues to benefit from a population that is getting older and living longer, as well as from an increase in home care provision. It has been placing emphasis on product development, launching numerous new products each year. The company is also emphasizing manufacturing outsourcing to China and India, as well as the consolidation of manufacturing and supply facilities, to reduce costs.

Chairman and CEO Malachi Mixon owns about 20% of the company. Joseph Richey, a company executive and board member, owns about 10%.

HISTORY

Invacare traces its roots to the Worthington Company, which began making vehicles for the disabled in 1885. Worthington's successor, Invacare, became a subsidiary of medical equipment maker Technicare in 1971. When Johnson & Johnson bought Technicare in 1978, it put Invacare up for sale; a group led by A. Malachi Mixon, then Technicare's VP of marketing, bought the company. Mixon cut unprofitable lines and pushed product innovation. In 1982 Invacare put out the first motorized wheelchair with computer controls. The company went public in 1984 and entered the European market by purchasing a UK firm. Invacare introduced some 50 new products in 1990, and in 1991 began selling directly to consumers.

In the 1990s Invacare focused on acquisitions, such as makers of personal care products, beds and patient-room furniture, and bathing equipment and lifts. Profits dipped in 1997 as many of its larger customers reduced orders in response to federally legislated Medicare reimbursement cuts. In 1998 it acquired medical supplies wholesaler Suburban Ostomy Supply; in 1999 it bought medical supplies maker Scandinavian Mobility International.

To enhance consumer brand recognition, in 1999 Invacare began a retail merchandising program and brought its acquired products under the Invacare brand name.

After integration with Invacare, Suburban Ostomy Supply was renamed Invacare Supply Group in 2000. Invacare bought Carroll Healthcare, which makes beds and furniture for the long-term care market, in 2003. In 2004 the company acquired Domus, a manufacturer of complementary products such as bath lifts and walking aids. Invacare bought Medical Support Systems Holdings Limited in 2005.

EXECUTIVES

Chairman and CEO: A. Malachi Mixon III, age 68, $3,500,312 total compensation
President, COO, and Director: Gerald B. Blouch, age 62, $2,683,200 total compensation
SVP and CFO: Robert K. (Rob) Gudbranson, age 45, $973,977 total compensation
SVP Global Marketing: Louis F. J. Slangen, age 61, $1,216,416 total compensation
SVP Electronics and Design Engineering and Director; President, Invacare Technologies: Joseph B. Richey II, age 72, $897,316 total compensation
SVP Human Resources: Joseph S. (Joe) Usaj, age 57
SVP, General Counsel, and Secretary: Anthony C. LaPlaca, age 50
Auditors: Ernst & Young LLP

LOCATIONS

HQ: Invacare Corporation
1 Invacare Way, Elyria, OH 44036
Phone: 440-329-6000   **Fax:** 440-366-9008
Web: www.invacare.com

PRODUCTS/OPERATIONS

2008 Sales

	$ mil.	% of total
North America/Home Medical Equipment	741.5	42
Europe	553.8	32
Invacare Supply Group	265.8	15
Institutional Products Group	99.7	6
Asia/Pacific	94.9	5
Total	**1,755.7**	**100**

Selected Products

North America/Home Medical Equipment
  Rehabilitative
    Back supports
    Custom manual wheelchairs
    Power wheelchairs
    Scooters
    Seat cushions
  Respiratory
    Nebulizer compressors
    Oxygen concentrators
    Sleep therapy products
  Standard
    Canes
    Commodes
    Crutches
    Grab bars
    Home care beds and accessories
    Manual wheelchairs
    Mattress overlays
    Patient lifts and slings
    Shower chairs
    Walkers
Invacare Supply Group (distributed products)
  Incontinence care products
  Ostomy care products
  Urology care products
  Wound care products
Institutional Products Group
  Health care furnishings
  Related accessories

Selected Subsidiaries

Adaptive Switch Laboratories, Inc.
Dynamic Controls Ltd. (New Zealand)
Garden City Medical, Inc.
Invatection Insurance Company
Scandinavian Mobility International ApS
SCI Des Hautes Roches (France)

COMPETITORS

Amigo Mobility
Bruno Independent
  Living Aids
Covidien
Electric Mobility
Getinge
Golden Technologies
Graham-Field Health
Hill-Rom Holdings
Joerns
Kinetic Concepts
Medline Industries
Pride Mobility Products
Respironics
Span-America Medical
Sunrise Medical
Vital Signs

HISTORICAL FINANCIALS

Company Type: Public

Income Statement

	REVENUE ($ mil.)	NET INCOME ($ mil.)	NET PROFIT MARGIN	EMPLOYEES
FYE: December 31				
12/08	1,755.7	38.6	2.2%	6,100
12/07	1,602.2	1.2	0.1%	5,700
12/06	1,498.0	(317.8)	—	6,000
12/05	1,529.7	48.9	3.2%	6,100
12/04	1,403.3	75.2	5.4%	6,100
Annual Growth	**5.8%**	**(15.4%)**	**—**	**0.0%**

2008 Year-End Financials

Debt ratio: 95.8%
Return on equity: 7.5%
Cash ($ mil.): 48
Current ratio: 1.93
Long-term debt ($ mil.): 460
No. of shares (mil.): 32
Dividends
  Yield: 0.3%
  Payout: 4.1%
Market value ($ mil.): 499

Stock History

NYSE: IVC

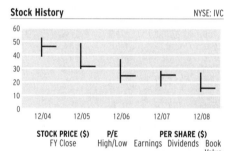

	STOCK PRICE ($) FY Close	P/E High/Low	PER SHARE ($) Earnings	Dividends	Book Value
12/08	15.52	22 11	1.21	0.05	14.96
12/07	25.20	694 431	0.04	0.05	17.24
12/06	24.55	— —	(10.00)	0.05	15.11
12/05	31.49	32 20	1.51	0.05	23.43
12/04	46.26	22 17	2.33	0.05	23.45
Annual Growth	**(23.9%)**	**— —**	**(15.1%)**	**0.0%**	**(10.6%)**

Invesco Ltd.

Invesco (formerly AMVESCAP) is AIMing for the topmost position on the investment heap. One of the world's largest asset managment companies, the firm manages investments for individuals, corporations, foundations, endowments, and government institutions under the Invesco AIM (in the US), Invesco (Europe and Asia), Invesco Perpetual (UK), and Trimark (Canada) brands. Subsidiary Atlantic Trust serves high-net-worth individuals and families. Invesco also offers managed accounts, separate accounts, and college investment plans. The company spreads its operations wide, with nearly 40 offices in some 20 countries. It has approximately $350 billion of assets under management.

In 2007 the company moved its headquarters from London to Atlanta after the proportion of its US-based shareholders exceeded 50%; a substantial chunk of its business had already come from the States. The company also moved its stock listing from the London Stock Exchange to the New York Stock Exchange based on similar reasoning.

Invesco tightened up its operations in 2008 due to the turmoil in the global markets. Its operating margins dropped that year, even though Invesco took steps to streamline its operations and cut discretionary spending.

HISTORY

In the mid-1960s Charles Brady created the investment advisory arm of Atlanta bank Citizens & Southern (now part of Bank of America). At the time, it was one of the first bank-run investment counseling businesses in the country, and Brady built it into a nationwide investment presence.

Brady spun off the investment division in 1979 as INVESCO Inc. In 1986 Montagu Investment Management (MIM), formerly part of banking firm Samuel Montagu, bought INVESCO. MIM later merged with Britannia Arrow, forming Britannia MIM, and INVESCO was folded into the mix in 1988. Brady stayed in charge of the American operations.

In 1993 INVESCO was fined by regulators for its part in a pension scandal involving media titan Robert Maxwell. After a boardroom struggle, Brady took over the CEO spot, cleaning house and slimming down the bloated firm. The troubles didn't end, however. In 1994 the company fired its top fund manager for violating personal trading rules.

INVESCO acquired AIM Management in 1997. Founded in 1976 by a trio including Charles "Ted" Bauer (who retired as vice chairman in 2000), AIM had a strong distribution network in the US, giving INVESCO an instant stronghold in that lucrative market. AIM's stock funds also complemented INVESCO's offerings. The new company was initially named AMVESCO, but was changed to AMVESCAP after a similarly named company cried foul.

In 1998 AMVESCAP bought global fund company LGT Asset Management from Prince Philipp of Liechtenstein and integrated it into INVESCO's European and Asian operations. The next year the company made plans to expand insurance and investment services in Poland. In 2000 the company bought Canada's Trimark Financial and merged it into its AIM Funds Management subsidiary. Later that year it bought British rival Perpetual for more than £1 billion.

The company bought Boston-based asset manager Pell Rudman & Co. in 2001 from South Africa's Old Mutual. The INVESCO Retirement unit changed its name to AMVESCAP Retirement in 2003.

In 2004 the company and some of its US subsidiaries agreed to a settlement with the SEC and some states' attorneys general over allegations of improper trading practices. All told, AMVESCAP paid out some $450 million in penalties. The following year the company sold AMVESCAP Retirement, Inc. Shareholders voted to change the company's name to Invesco in 2007.

EXECUTIVES

Chairman: Rex D. Adams, age 69
President, CEO, and Director:
  Martin L. (Marty) Flanagan, age 48,
  $13,484,901 total compensation
Senior Managing Director and CFO: Loren M. Starr,
  age 47, $2,521,931 total compensation
**Senior Managing Director and Chief Administrative
  Officer:** Colin D. Meadows, age 38
**Managing Director and CEO, Invesco Continental
  Europe:** Jean-Baptiste de Franssu, age 42
**Senior Managing Director and CEO, Invesco Asia
  Pacific:** Andrew T. S. Lo, age 48,
  $2,878,325 total compensation
**Senior Managing Director and Director; CEO, Invesco
  Perpetual and Continental Europe:** James I. Robertson,
  age 51
**Senior Managing Director; CEO, North American
  Retail:** Philip A. (Phil) Taylor, age 54,
  $4,281,344 total compensation
Managing Director and Head, Worldwide Fixed Income:
  Karen D. Kelley, age 47
Managing Director US Consultant Relations:
  Brian M. Baskir
**Senior Managing Director; Chief Investment Officer,
  Invesco Perpetual:** Robert J. (Bob) Yerbury, age 62,
  $7,120,326 total compensation
**Senior Managing Director and Head of Sales,
  Marketing, and Client Service for US Institution:**
  John S. (Jack) Markwalter Jr., age 49
**Senior Managing Director; CEO, Worldwide
  Institutional:** G. Mark (Mark) Armour, age 55,
  $2,850,249 total compensation
**Managing Director and President & CEO, Investco
  Trimark Investments:** Peter Intraligi
Senior Managing Director and General Counsel:
  Kevin M. Carome, age 52
Managing Director Corporate Communications:
  Doug Kidd
Senior Director and Head of Investor Relations:
  Aaron Uhde
Managing Director and Head of Human Resources:
  Washington Dender
CEO, Invesco Real Estate: David A. Ridley, age 54
Auditors: Ernst & Young LLP

LOCATIONS

HQ: Invesco Ltd.
  2 Peachtree Pointe, 1555 Peachtree St., NE
  Atlanta, GA 30309
Phone: 404-479-1095   **Fax:** 404-439-4911
Web: www.invesco.com

2008 Sales

	$ mil.	% of total
US	1,479.9	45
UK & Ireland	1,196.5	36
Canada	516.6	16
Europe & Asia	114.6	3
Total	**3,307.6**	**100**

PRODUCTS/OPERATIONS

2008 Sales

	$ mil.	% of total
Investment management fees	2,617.8	79
Service & distribution fees	512.5	16
Performance fees	75.1	2
Other	102.2	3
Total	**3,307.6**	**100**

COMPETITORS

AllianceBernstein Holding
American Century
Ashmore Group
Aviva
AXA Financial
Barclays
BNP Paribas Asset Management
Capital Group
Charles Schwab
CI Financial
Clerical Medical
Columbia Management Group
Deutsche Bank
Dundee Corp.
Eaton Vance
Edward Jones
FMR
Franklin Resources
Gartmore Group
HSBC Holdings
Janus Capital
Legal & General Group
Lloyds Banking Group
M&G
Mackenzie Financial
Man Group
Neuberger Berman
Old Mutual (US)
Schroders
T. Rowe Price
Van Kampen Investments
The Vanguard Group

HISTORICAL FINANCIALS

Company Type: Public

Income Statement   FYE: December 31

	ASSETS ($ mil.)	NET INCOME ($ mil.)	INCOME AS % OF ASSETS	EMPLOYEES
12/08	9,756.9	481.7	4.9%	5,325
12/07	12,925.2	673.6	5.2%	5,475
12/06	9,292.0	490.1	5.3%	5,574
12/05	7,577.6	212.2	2.8%	5,798
12/04	7,501.1	(332.1)	—	6,693
Annual Growth	**6.8%**	**—**	**—**	**(5.6%)**

2008 Year-End Financials

Equity as % of assets: 58.3%
Return on assets: 4.2%
Return on equity: 7.8%
Long-term debt ($ mil.): 862
No. of shares (mil.): 416
Dividends
  Yield: 3.6%
  Payout: 43.0%
Market value ($ mil.): 6,008
Sales ($ mil.): 3,308

Stock History   NYSE: IVZ

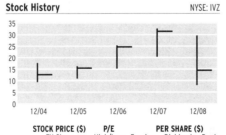

	STOCK PRICE ($) FY Close	P/E High/Low		PER SHARE ($) Earnings	Dividends	Book Value
12/08	14.44	24	7	1.21	0.52	13.67
12/07	31.38	20	13	1.64	0.37	15.84
12/06	24.65	21	13	1.20	0.34	10.28
12/05	15.39	31	21	0.52	0.33	8.68
12/04	12.56	—	—	(0.83)	0.32	8.60
Annual Growth	**3.5%**	**—**	**—**	**—**	**12.9%**	**12.3%**

Iron Mountain

You think you have a mountain of paperwork to deal with? Iron Mountain is one of the largest records storage and information management companies in the world. The company stores paper and digital documents, computer disks, tapes, microfilm and microfiche, audio and videotapes, film, X-rays, and blueprints for more than 120,000 corporate customers. It provides such services as records filing, digital conversion, database management, packing, transportation, disaster recovery, and information destruction. Its COMAC unit stores, builds, and mails information packets for companies. Iron Mountain traces its paper trail back to when it was established — in 1951.

The company sees acquisitions and joint ventures as a key business strategy when it comes to expansion. In 2008 Iron Mountain acquired Colorado-based DocuVault Group, the owner of five records management firms, and bought up the remaining interest of its Brazilian partner. Iron Mountain's significant purchases of 2007 included data storage and services firms ArchivesOne, RMS Services-USA, and Stratify.

The company has pushed into digital markets and has plans to expand its business overseas. By offering customers its secure shredding, online back-up, and electronic discovery services, Iron Mountain looks to strengthen its position in Germany, Japan, and the Middle East.

The company also looks to capitalize on the transition to electronic records in the healthcare industry. In 2008 Iron Mountain introduced a medical records management tool and a digital file storage system for X-rays, CT scans, and other medical images.

Richard Reese stepped down as CEO in 2008, and he was succeeded by Bob Brennan, who joined the company in 2004 as president of North American operations.

Investment firm Davis Selected Advisors owns about 20% of Iron Mountain. Vincent Ryan, on the board of directors, owns about 10%.

HISTORY

Leo W. Pierce founded L.W. Pierce in 1957. Based in Philadelphia, the company sold filing systems and other storage equipment. In 1969 Pierce made the move into document storage, keeping other companies' records in his basement. Off-site document storage caught on during the 1980s, when a depressed economy forced managers to find creative ways to reduce costs.

The company doubled its size in 1990 by paying $36 million to buy Leahy Business Archives. The first corporate records storage firm, Leahy was founded in the 1950s in New York City. Pierce Leahy went public in 1997.

Pierce Leahy's sales increased in the mid-1990s, aided by acquisitions. The company was intent on consolidating the records management market, grabbing up as many smaller firms as it could. Pierce Leahy bought two more data storage companies, Archive (Canada) and Amodio (Connecticut), in 1998. The company made several acquisitions in 1999, including Datavault, a UK records management company, and ImageMax, a digital imaging company.

In early 2000 Pierce Leahy was acquired by its primary competitor, Iron Mountain, for $1.2 billion. Pierce Leahy was the surviving entity of the reverse merger, taking the Iron Mountain name.

Richard Reese, chairman of the former Iron Mountain, became chairman and CEO of the new company. The company acquired Canadian record management company FACS Records Centre in late 2000.

In 2004 Iron Mountain created a new business unit — Iron Mountain Intellectual Property Management — by combining its DSI Technology Escrow and Arcemus subsidiaries. The new unit extended the Iron Mountain brand name to services such as online trademark protection, management of domain name records, and technology escrow. Iron Mountain also purchased Mentmore's interest in joint venture Iron Mountain Europe in 2004, making the company a wholly owned subsidiary. That year Iron Mountain acquired Connected Corp., a maker of data storage and recovery software. The next year the company bought Pickfords Records Management, the Australian and New Zealand operations of SIRVA, for $87 million.

In 2006 Iron Mountain cast its eye on the Pacific Rim when it bought Australia-based DigiGuard, an off-site data storage provider. It also expanded its Asia/Pacific presence later that year when it entered a joint venture with Transnational Company, a provider of information storage services headquartered in Singapore.

In November 2007 Iron Mountain expanded its film and sound archive services business with the purchase of Xepa Digital, a converter of analog and outmoded digital audio and video tapes to high-resolution digital file formats for archiving and distribution. Other domestic acquisitions that year included ArchivesOne, a smaller rival serving more than 8,500 customers; Michigan-based RMS Services USA, which it will integrate into its health information services unit; and Stratify, a software developer and electronic document services provider, for about $160 million.

EXECUTIVES

Chairman: C. Richard Reese, age 63, $3,222,943 total compensation
President, CEO, and Director: Robert T. (Bob) Brennan, age 49, $3,676,458 total compensation
EVP and CFO: Brian P. McKeon, age 47, $1,796,804 total compensation
CIO: William (Bill) Brown, age 53
SVP and Chief Security Officer: Joseph DeSalvo
EVP Corporate Development: John F. Kenny Jr.
EVP Human Resources and Administration: Linda Rossetti
SVP, General Counsel, and Secretary: Ernest W. Cloutier, age 35
VP Investor Relations: Stephen P. Golden
President, North America: Harold E. (Harry) Ebbighausen, age 54, $1,172,157 total compensation
President, Iron Mountain Digital: John Clancy, age 41, $944,986 total compensation
Group President, Asia/Pacific: Robert G. (Bob) Miller, age 48
Group President, Latin America; President, Iron Mountain Fulfillment Services: Ross Engelman
President, International: Marc A. Duale, age 57, $1,551,576 total compensation
Senior Public Relations Manager: Laura Sudnik
Auditors: Deloitte & Touche LLP

LOCATIONS

HQ: Iron Mountain Incorporated
745 Atlantic Ave., Boston, MA 02111
Phone: 617-535-4766   **Fax:** 617-350-7881
Web: www.ironmountain.com

2008 Sales

	$ mil.	% of total
US	2,074.9	68
UK	383.0	13
Canada	197.0	6
Other countries	400.2	13
Total	**3,055.1**	**100**

PRODUCTS/OPERATIONS

2008 Sales

	$ mil.	% of total
Records management	2,146.3	70
Data protection & discovery	612.1	20
Information destruction	296.7	10
Total	**3,055.1**	**100**

Selected Services

Archiving
Consulting
Conversion
Database management
Disaster recovery
Electronic vaulting
Fulfillment
Information destruction
Packing
Shredding
Transportation

COMPETITORS

Administaff
Anacomp
Cintas
DataBank IMX
IPSA
Recall Corporation
Shred-it International
SOURCECORP
TAB Products
Venyu
Xerox

HISTORICAL FINANCIALS

Company Type: Public

Income Statement

FYE: December 31

	REVENUE ($ mil.)	NET INCOME ($ mil.)	NET PROFIT MARGIN	EMPLOYEES
12/08	3,055.1	82.0	2.7%	21,000
12/07	2,730.0	153.1	5.6%	20,100
12/06	2,350.3	128.9	5.5%	18,600
12/05	2,078.2	116.6	5.6%	15,800
12/04	1,817.6	94.2	5.2%	14,500
Annual Growth	**13.9%**	**(3.4%)**	**—**	**9.7%**

2008 Year-End Financials

Debt ratio: 177.9%
Return on equity: 4.6%
Cash ($ mil.): 278
Current ratio: 1.34
Long-term debt ($ mil.): 3,207
No. of shares (mil.): 203
Dividends
  Yield: 0.0%
  Payout: —
Market value ($ mil.): 5,018

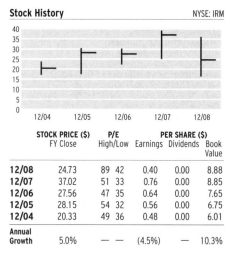

Stock History   NYSE: IRM

	STOCK PRICE ($) FY Close	P/E High/Low		PER SHARE ($) Earnings	Dividends	Book Value
12/08	24.73	89	42	0.40	0.00	8.88
12/07	37.02	51	33	0.76	0.00	8.85
12/06	27.56	47	35	0.64	0.00	7.65
12/05	28.15	54	32	0.56	0.00	6.75
12/04	20.33	49	36	0.48	0.00	6.01
Annual Growth	**5.0%**	**—**	**—**	**(4.5%)**	**—**	**10.3%**

Itron, Inc.

Itron aims to make meter reading a desk job. The company is a global supplier of wireless data acquisition and communication products for electric, gas, and water utilities. Itron makes radio- and telephone-based automatic meter reading (AMR) systems, handheld meter reading computers, and meter data acquisition and analysis software. Its systems are installed at more than 2,000 utilities worldwide — many using more than one Itron product. The company also provides consulting, project management, and outsourcing services. Customers include BC Hydro, Ford, Electrabel, Old Dominion Electric Cooperative, and Progress Energy. Europe is Itron's biggest market, closely followed by North America.

Itron targets the electric utility, water and public power, and natural gas markets.

Among the company's challenges in 2009 are the global recession, long and unpredictable sales cycles in the utility industry, the assimilation of acquisitions, the availability and regulation of radio spectrum (some of its products use radio frequencies for communication), and increasing competition.

Itron continues to grow by acquisitions, acquiring nine companies since the end of 2002.

In 2007 the company acquired Luxembourg-based Actaris Metering Systems for €800 million in cash, plus the assumption of about €445 million in debt, valuing the transaction at about $1.7 billion. Actaris was profitable on 2006 sales of around $1 billion. A former division of Schlumberger that went through an LBO in 2001, Actaris primarily operates in Europe, offering AMR equipment and related services. It has operations in Africa, the Asia/Pacific region, Australia, and South America.

President and COO Malcolm Unsworth in 2009 succeeded LeRoy Nosbaum as CEO of Itron. Nosbaum will remain on the board and serve as its executive chairman until the end of 2009. Unsworth's promotion is part of a leadership succession plan that the board developed.

HISTORY

Itron was formed by a group of engineers in 1977 with financial backing from utility Washington Water Power (now Avista). In 1992 Itron acquired EnScan, a maker of mobile automatic meter reading (AMR) systems. The company went public in 1993. During 1994 and 1995 it installed the largest AMR system in the world for the Public Service Company of Colorado (now New Century Energies).

Itron in 1996 won a major contract from Pittsburgh-based Duquesne Light Co. Itron acquired Utility Translation Services (commercial and industrial AMR systems) that year and Design Concepts (outage detection, quality monitoring, and AMR systems that communicate over telephone lines) in 1997. Also that year Itron and UK Data Collections Services (meter reading services) formed joint venture STAR Data Services to provide meter reading and billing services.

Restructuring charges related to cost-cutting efforts contributed to a loss in 1998. The next year Itron won an 11-year pact to provide meter reading services for Southern California Edison's 350,000 customers — a deal worth at least $20 million. During mid-1999 new CEO Michael Chesser led another restructuring — including layoffs and factory closures. Charges led to a loss for the year.

In 2000 Itron spun off part of its manufacturing operations as contract electronics manufacturer Servatron. That year COO LeRoy Nosbaum replaced Chesser as CEO, and was later named chairman.

In 2002 Itron bolstered its energy consulting and software business through the acquisition of several privately held companies: LineSoft (consulting and software for utility transmission and distribution systems) for about $42 million, Regional Economic Research (energy consulting and software) for $14 million, and eMobile Data Corporation (wireless utility workforce management software) for about $6 million. The following year Itron acquired Silicon Energy (enterprise energy management software) for about $71 million.

In 2004 Itron acquired the Electricity Metering business unit of Schlumberger for $256 million. Schlumberger Electricity Metering became the company's Electricity Metering business.

A major restructuring that year — including the replacement of leading executives, the layoff of 15% of its workforce, and the spinoff of its manufacturing operations as Servatron — repositioned Itron to take advantage of new technologies and industry deregulation.

In 2004 Itron reorganized its market segments from five business units to two main segments: hardware and software. Within the hardware segment, the business was broken down into two lines of business, meter data collection and electricity metering.

In 2006 the company expanded into South America's biggest market with the acquisition of ELO Sistemas e Tecnologia, a Brazilian firm that was distributing Itron products since late 2004 and manufacturing Itron's CENTRON meters since mid-2005. ELO Tecnologia had offices and a manufacturing assembly facility in Campinas and São Paulo, Brazil, and in Chile, employing about 80 people. Itron paid about $2 million in cash for the Brazilian firm.

Purchases during 2006 included Flow Metrix, a manufacturer of leak detection systems for underground pipelines, and Quantum Consulting, an energy consulting firm.

EXECUTIVES

Chairman: LeRoy D. Nosbaum, age 62, $2,617,287 total compensation
President, CEO, and Director: Malcolm Unsworth, age 59, $1,942,012 total compensation
SVP and COO, North America: Philip C. Mezey, age 49, $1,091,619 total compensation
SVP and CFO: Steven M. (Steve) Helmbrecht, age 46, $1,089,913 total compensation
VP Information Technology and CIO: Chuck McAtee
SVP, General Counsel, and Secretary: John W. Holleran, age 54, $1,031,776 total compensation
VP Competitive Resources: Jared P. Serff, age 41
VP Marketing: Russell E. (Russ) Vanos
VP Investor Relations and Corporate Communications: Deloris Duquette
SVP and COO, Actaris: Marcel Regnier, age 52
Communications and Marketing: Kim Papich
Auditors: Ernst & Young LLP

LOCATIONS

HQ: Itron, Inc.
2111 N. Molter Rd., Liberty Lake, WA 99019
Phone: 509-924-9900   **Fax:** 509-891-3355
Web: www.itron.com

Itron has facilities in California, Massachusetts, Minnesota, North Carolina, South Carolina, and Washington, and sales offices in Australia, Brazil, Canada, France, Mexico, the Netherlands, Qatar, Taiwan, and the US.

2008 Sales

	$ mil.	% of total
Europe	916.3	48
North America	648.0	34
Other regions	345.3	18
Total	**1,909.6**	**100**

PRODUCTS/OPERATIONS

2008 Sales

	$ mil.	% of total
Actaris	1,281.4	67
Itron North America	628.2	33
Total	**1,909.6**	**100**

Selected Products

Automatic meter reading (AMR) systems and products
  Meter modules (utility meter attachments that transmit data to remote receivers)
  Mobile AMR (transportable systems for mounting on vehicles)
  Network AMR (utility-automated meter readers)
  Off-site meter reading units (remote reading of radio-equipped meters)
  Telephone-based technology (programmable modules for data collection over telephone lines)
Commercial and industrial meters
Forecasting, research, and analysis software
Handheld systems and products (electronic meter reading — EMR — handheld systems)
Surveying software
Workforce automation software (Service-Link)

Services

Engineering consulting
Forecasting services
Installation
Outsourcing
Project management
System design and installation
Training

COMPETITORS

ABB
Accenture
Badger Meter
Bentley Systems
Capgemini
Comverge
ConneXt
Cooper Industries
DeltaTRAK
Diehl Stiftung
Dresser, Inc.
Echelon Corporation
Electric & Gas Technology
Elster American Meter
Emerson Electric
eMeter
E-MON
EnerNOC
Equitrac
ESCO Technologies
GE
Honeywell International
IBM
Invensys
Landis & Gyr
Logica
Oracle
Pointer Telocation
Power Measurement
PowerSecure International
Roper Industries
SAP
Schneider Electric
Siemens AG
Ventyx

HISTORICAL FINANCIALS

Company Type: Public

Income Statement

FYE: December 31

	REVENUE ($ mil.)	NET INCOME ($ mil.)	NET PROFIT MARGIN	EMPLOYEES
12/08	1,909.6	28.1	1.5%	8,700
12/07	1,464.0	(16.1)	—	8,400
12/06	644.0	33.8	5.2%	2,400
12/05	552.7	33.1	6.0%	2,000
12/04	399.2	(5.3)	—	2,100
Annual Growth	**47.9%**	**—**	**—**	**42.7%**

2008 Year-End Financials

Debt ratio: 115.3%	No. of shares (mil.): 40
Return on equity: 3.1%	Dividends
Cash ($ mil.): 144	Yield: 0.0%
Current ratio: 1.69	Payout: —
Long-term debt ($ mil.): 1,194	Market value ($ mil.): 2,549

Stock History

NASDAQ (GS): ITRI

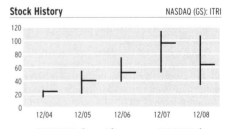

	STOCK PRICE ($) FY Close	P/E High/Low		PER SHARE ($) Earnings	Dividends	Book Value
12/08	63.74	133	43	0.80	0.00	25.89
12/07	95.97	—	—	(0.55)	0.00	18.97
12/06	51.84	58	31	1.28	0.00	9.78
12/05	40.04	41	16	1.33	0.00	7.94
12/04	23.91	—	—	(0.25)	0.00	4.61
Annual Growth	**27.8%**	**—**	**—**	**—**	**—**	**53.9%**

ITT Corporation

ITT doesn't get defensive when you associate its name with fluid motion. The company has three primary segments: defense electronics (combat radios, night vision devices, airborne electronic warfare systems), fluid technology (pumps, mixers, heat exchangers, and valves for water and wastewater systems), and motion and flow control (connectors, boat pumps, shock absorbers, friction pads for communication and transportation applications). ITT, which traces its corporate roots back nearly 90 years to the old ITT phone empire, also provides repair and maintenance services for the products it manufactures.

As the Obama administration takes a closer look at the Pentagon budget, ITT may lose out if certain military programs are reduced or eliminated; the defense electronics segment gets 94% of its revenues from the US government. The company will also keep an eye on controlling costs in general as the credit crisis and recession continue around the world.

The company was fined $100 million in 2007 for illegally providing classified night vision equipment to foreign countries, including China. ITT pleaded guilty to felony charges under the Arms Export Control Act after an extensive investigation by the US Departments of Defense and Justice.

Later that year the company sold its switches business to private equity firm Littlejohn & Co. LLC. The switches business made switches, interface controls, and keypads for use by a number of industries, including automotive, computer, and mobile communications.

In late 2007 ITT acquired International Motion Control (IMC) of Buffalo, New York, for about $395 million. The addition of IMC complements the product mix and global footprint of ITT's motion and flow control business. Buying IMC gave ITT 11 new plants — five of them overseas (three in the Asia/Pacific region and two in Europe).

Still later in 2007 ITT bought EDO Corporation in a transaction valued at about $1.7 billion. EDO is a provider of a wide range of aerospace and defense products, including electronic warfare systems, sonar systems, reconnaissance and surveillance systems, and flight line products.

International growth is a major focus for the company, evidenced from its branding initiative, and emerging markets are a big part of that plan. Nearly 10% of the company's product development engineers are in Asia serving customers in China, the Middle East, and, its most recent foreign investment, India.

Going into 2008 the company was aggressive in working to win military contracts. It inked three lucrative contracts in the first quarter totaling a little more than $100 million. The deals include providing electronic jammers for improvised explosive devices for the US Navy, image tubes used for night vision goggles for the US Army, and electronic warfare systems used in F-16 fighter jets for Pakistan's military.

HISTORY

Colonel Sosthenes Behn founded International Telephone and Telegraph (ITT) in 1920 to build a global telephone company. After three small acquisitions, Behn bought International Western Electric (renamed International Standard Electric, or ISE) from AT&T in 1925, making ITT an international maker of phone equipment. In the late 1920s ITT bought Mackay, a US company that made telegraph, cable, radio, and other equipment.

In the 1930s sales outside the US made up two-thirds of revenues. To increase US opportunities during WWII, Behn arranged for a Mackay subsidiary, Federal AT&T Telegraph (later Federal Electric), to become part of ITT. Behn took charge of Federal and created Federal Telephone & Radio Laboratories. Meanwhile, ISE scientists who fled war-torn Europe gravitated to ITT's research and development operations and laid the foundation for its high-tech electronics business.

ITT became a diverse and unwieldy collection of companies by the 1950s. In mid-decade ISE, its biggest unit, developed advanced telephone-switching equipment.

During the 1960s and 1970s, ITT added auto-part makers such as Teves (brakes, West Germany), Ulma (trim, Italy), and Altissimo (lights and accessories, Italy). ITT's electronics acquisitions included Cannon Electric (electrical connectors) and National Computer Products (satellite communications). It also bought Bell & Gossett (the US's #1 maker of commercial and industrial pumps). When ITT bought Sheraton's hotel chain in 1968, it also got auto-parts supplier Thompson Industries. By 1977 its Engineered Products division consisted of nearly 80 automotive and electrical companies. In 1979 ITT began selling all or part of 250 companies, including the last of its telecom operations.

In the 1980s ITT became a major supplier of antilock brakes and, with the 1988 purchase of the Allis-Chalmers pump business, a global force in fluid technology. Its Defense & Electronics unit earned contracts to make equipment used in the Gulf War. In 1994 ITT Automotive purchases solidified its position as the world's top maker of electric motors and wiper systems.

ITT split into three independent companies in 1995: ITT Corporation (hospitality, entertainment, and information services; now part of Starwood Hotels & Resorts), ITT Hartford (insurance; now Hartford Financial Services), and ITT Industries (auto parts, defense and electric systems, and fluid-control products).

In 1997 ITT Industries acquired Goulds Pumps, establishing it as the world's largest pump maker. After the $815 million takeover, that year the company sold its automotive electrical systems unit to Valeo for $1.7 billion and its brake and chassis unit to Germany's Continental for about $1.9 billion.

In 2004 ITT acquired the Remote Sensing Systems business of Eastman Kodak Company for $725 million. The acquisition of WEDECO through 2004 and 2005 share purchases gave ITT the world's largest manufacturer of ultraviolet disinfection and ozone oxidation systems, a tool that is increasingly seen as a better alternative than chlorine treatment. The company further added to its water treatment business with the 2005 acquisition of Ellis K. Phelps & Company, which for years has been the #1 distributor of ITT's Flygt brand for the wastewater pumping and treatment industry, and the 2006 purchase of F.B. Leopold, a provider of pretreatment filtration technologies.

Early in 2006 ITT exited the automotive tubing (steel and plastic tubing for fuel and brake lines) business by selling those operations to Cooper-Standard Automotive for $205 million.

In mid-2006 the company changed its name from ITT Industries to ITT Corporation.

EXECUTIVES

Chairman, President, and CEO: Steven R. Loranger, age 57, $15,988,683 total compensation
SVP and CFO: Denise L. Ramos, age 52, $3,028,378 total compensation
VP and CIO: Carol J. Zierhoffer, age 48
VP, Chief Accounting Officer, and Assistant Secretary: Janice M. Klettner, age 48
VP Corporate Responsibility: Ann D. Davidson, age 56
SVP and Chief Communications Officer: Angela A. Buonocore, age 50
Chief Inclusion and Diversity Officer: Robert Ellis, age 57
VP and Chief Learning Officer: Nancy Lewis, age 56
SVP and Director Human Resources: Scott A. Crum, age 52
SVP and Treasurer: Donald E. Foley, age 57
SVP and Director; President, Fluid and Motion Control: Gretchen W. McClain, age 46, $2,627,479 total compensation
SVP and Director Strategy and Corporate Development: Aris C. Chicles, age 47
VP, Secretary, and Associate General Counsel: Kathleen S. Stolar
VP Finance: Robert J. (Bob) Pagano Jr., age 46
VP and General Counsel: Frank R. Jimenez, age 44
VP; President, Defense Electronics and Services: David F. Melcher, age 54
President, Residential and Commercial Water, Fluid Technology: John P. Williamson, age 48
President, Interconnect Solutions: William E. Taylor, age 55
President, Space Systems Division: Chris Young
Director Public Relations: Andy Hilton
Director Investor Relations: Thomas (Tom) Scalera
Auditors: Deloitte & Touche LLP

LOCATIONS

HQ: ITT Corporation
1133 Westchester Ave., White Plains, NY 10604
Phone: 914-641-2000   **Fax:** 914-696-2950
Web: www.itt.com

2008 Sales

	$ mil.	% of total
US	7,998.0	68
Western Europe	2,098.3	18
Asia/Pacific	603.6	5
Other regions	994.9	9
Total	**11,694.8**	**100**

PRODUCTS/OPERATIONS

2008 Sales

	$ mil.	% of total
Defense Electronics & Services	6,282.3	54
Fluid Technology	3,840.6	33
Motion & Flow Control	1,583.4	13
Adjustments	(11.5)	—
Total	**11,694.8**	**100**

2008 Sales by Type

	$ mil.	% of total
Products	9,181.2	79
Services	2,513.6	21
Total	**11,694.8**	**100**

Selected Products

Defense Electronics
  Aircraft armament systems
  Electronic warfare systems
  Imaging and navigation systems
  Night vision devices
  Tactical communications equipment
Fluid Technology
  Controls
  Heat exchangers
  Mixers
  Pumps
  Treatment systems
  Valves

Motion and Flow Control
  Aerospace controls
  Cable assemblies
  Connectors
  Friction pads
  Interconnects
  Precision valves
  Pumps for boat and spa baths
  Shock absorbers

COMPETITORS

Alliant Techsystems	KSB AG
BAE SYSTEMS	L-3 Communications
Dana Holding	Lockheed Martin
Delphi Corp.	Marmon Group
DENSO	Molex
Dresser, Inc.	Northrop Grumman
DynCorp International	Oilgear
Eaton	Parker Hannifin
Ebara	Raytheon
Flowserve	Robert Bosch
GE	Roper Industries
GenCorp	Siemens AG
General Dynamics	SPX
Goodrich Corp.	Swagelok
Harris Corp.	Thomas & Betts
Honeywell International	Tyco
IDEX	Watts Water Technologies
Ingersoll-Rand	Woodward Governor
Interpump	

HISTORICAL FINANCIALS
Company Type: Public

Income Statement
FYE: December 31

	REVENUE ($ mil.)	NET INCOME ($ mil.)	NET PROFIT MARGIN	EMPLOYEES
12/08	11,694.8	794.7	6.8%	40,800
12/07	9,003.3	742.1	8.2%	39,700
12/06	7,807.9	581.1	7.4%	37,500
12/05	7,427.3	366.0	4.9%	40,900
12/04	6,764.1	432.3	6.4%	44,000
Annual Growth	14.7%	16.4%	—	(1.9%)

2008 Year-End Financials

Debt ratio: 15.3%	No. of shares (mil.): 182
Return on equity: 22.7%	Dividends
Cash ($ mil.): 965	Yield: 1.5%
Current ratio: 1.01	Payout: 16.2%
Long-term debt ($ mil.): 468	Market value ($ mil.): 8,389

Stock History
NYSE: ITT

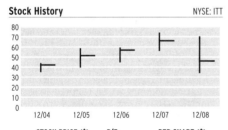

			STOCK PRICE ($)	P/E		PER SHARE ($)		
			FY Close	High/Low	Earnings	Dividends	Book Value
12/08			45.99	16	8	4.33	0.70	16.78
12/07			66.04	18	14	4.03	0.56	21.63
12/06			56.82	19	15	3.10	0.44	15.71
12/05			51.41	30	21	1.91	0.36	14.93
12/04			42.22	19	16	2.29	0.34	12.85
Annual Growth			2.2%	—	—	17.3%	19.8%	6.9%

Jabil Circuit

Jabil Circuit takes more than a jab at contract electronics manufacturing. The company is one of the leading providers of electronics manufacturing services (EMS) in the world. Parts made by Jabil on a contract basis are used in communications products, computers and computer peripherals, and automobiles. Services range from product design and component procurement to order fulfillment and supply chain management. The company is rapidly expanding into Asian and Eastern European markets through acquisitions and new plants. Top customers include Cisco Systems (16% of sales), Hewlett-Packard (11%), Nokia, and Philips. The Americas provide about 40% of sales.

Bringing a more specialized approach to its customer base, Jabil reorganized into two divisions, Consumer Electronics and EMS. Consumer Electronics makes cell phones and other mobile electronic products, TVs, set-top boxes, and computer peripherals. The EMS division essentially manufactures everything else, from electronic components to printed circuit boards, serving both traditional and emerging markets. The company also derives a small portion of its annual revenues from repair and warranty services for the products it makes.

To compete in a rapidly consolidating industry, Jabil provides global parallel production and uses a "workcell" approach, in which semi-autonomous business units are dedicated to individual customers. The company continues to add services and to expand globally through acquisitions, including deals to acquire manufacturing operations from Lucent Technologies (now Alcatel-Lucent), NEC, and Philips.

The 2008-09 economic recession, and the company's shift into low cost developing countries for manufacturing has squeezed operations in the US. In 2009 Jabil began shutting down a Massachusetts plant, laying off more than 300 workers. Simultaneously, the company raised the bar on assisting its workforce by encouraging neighboring companies to court its employees, pairing up workers with training and recruiting programs, and donating space and equipment at the plant.

Earlier Jabil acquired the manufacturing assets of two plants in Italy from Nokia Siemens Networks, an established customer. In 2007 Jabil leased the two plants, which together employ more than 600 people, from Nokia Siemens Networks. The companies sweetened the deal by signing a long-term manufacturing services agreement. The facility in Cassina de Pecchi makes microwave devices for wireline and wireless networks, while the site in Marcianise produces equipment for GSM and EDGE radio access wireless communications networks.

Chairman William Morean and his family own about 14% of Jabil Circuit.

HISTORY

Jabil Circuit was named for founders James Golden and Bill Morean. The duo, who originally ran an excavation business, started Jabil in suburban Detroit in 1966 to provide assembly and reworking services to electronics manufacturers. Jabil incorporated in 1969 and began making printed circuit boards for Control Data Corporation (later renamed Control Data Systems) that year.

William D. Morean, the founder's son who had worked summers at Jabil while in high school, joined the company in 1977. The next year the younger Morean took over Jabil's day-to-day operations. The company entered the automotive electronics business in 1976 through a $12 million contract with General Motors.

During the 1980s Jabil began building computer components, adding such customers as Dell, NEC, Sun Microsystems, and Toshiba. Jabil moved its headquarters to St. Petersburg, Florida, in 1983. William Morean became Jabil's chairman and CEO in 1988.

Production design accounted for most of Jabil's sales for the first time in 1992. The next year the company went public and also opened a factory in Scotland. A major laptop computer manufacturing contract from Epson soured when, in 1995, cracks appeared in the casings of the laptops, and Epson balked at paying its tab.

By 1997 Jabil had successfully diversified beyond low-margin PC manufacturing, becoming one of the top US circuit board manufacturers, while adding higher-margin products such as networking hardware.

In 1999 the company expanded into China when it acquired electronics manufacturing services provider GET Manufacturing. The next year William Morean stepped down as CEO (he remained chairman); he was succeeded by president Timothy Main.

In 2001 Jabil announced it would cut about 3,000 jobs, or about 10% of its staff. Also in 2001 it signed an agreement with chip titan Intel under which Jabil would acquire an Intel plant in Malaysia and supply Intel with parts for three years.

In 2002 Jabil acquired most of the assets of Lucent Technologies of Shanghai, a joint venture among Lucent (now Alcatel-Lucent) and three Chinese partners. Also that year the company bought Philips Contract Manufacturing Services, an arm of the Dutch electronics giant, for around $210 million.

In late 2004 Jabil began expanding its manufacturing capacity in Asia by breaking ground on new plants in India and China. The facilities represented the company's second plant in India and its fourth in China.

In early 2005 the company paid about $195 million to acquire the contract manufacturing business of Varian, Inc., the instrument vendor. Together with Carl Zeiss, Jabil created a joint venture in early 2006 to manufacture optical modules for computer displays and other applications.

In 2006 Jabil exercised a purchase option to acquire Celetronix International, an India-based electronics manufacturer, which had operations in India, the UK, and the US.

Late in the year Jabil started building a new facility in Uzhgorod, Ukraine. The plant was its second in the former Soviet republic and joined other Eastern European facilities in Hungary and Poland.

In 2007 Jabil acquired Taiwan Green Point Enterprises, a contract manufacturer with plants in China, Malaysia, and Taiwan. Green Point specialized in plastic parts for cell phones and other portable electronics products. Jabil planned to operate Green Point as an autonomous subsidiary, hiring about 30,000 employees and keeping the company's management in place.

Further expanding into Asian markets, Jabil opened a facility in Vietnam in mid-2007.

EXECUTIVES

Chairman: William D. Morean, age 53
Vice Chairman: Thomas A. Sansone, age 59
President, CEO, and Director: Timothy L. Main, age 51
COO: Mark T. Mondello, age 44
CFO: Forbes I. J. Alexander, age 48
CIO: David Couch
EVP and CEO, Consumer Division: John P. Lovato, age 48
EVP and CEO, EMS Division: William D. (Bill) Muir Jr., age 40
SVP Tools, Systems, and Training:
 Wesley B. (Butch) Edwards, age 56
SVP Human Resources: William E. (Bill) Peters, age 45
SVP Global Business Units: Joseph A. (Joe) McGee, age 46
SVP Worldwide Operations: Teck Ping Yuen, age 53
SVP Global Business Units: Courtney J. Ryan, age 39
SVP After-Market Services: Hartmut Liebel
SVP: Hai Hwai (HH) Chiang
VP Communications and Investor Relations:
 Beth A. Walters, age 48
VP Corporate Development: Donald J. Myers
VP,Human Resources: Thomas T. (Tom) O'Connor
CEO India Business Ventures: Sirjang L. Tandon
General Counsel and Secretary: Robert L. Paver, age 52
Senior Advisor, Europe: Michel Charriau, age 66
Auditors: KPMG LLP

LOCATIONS

HQ: Jabil Circuit, Inc.
 10560 Dr. Martin Luther King Jr. St. North,
 St. Petersburg, FL 33716
Phone: 727-577-9749   **Fax:** 727-579-8529
Web: www.jabil.com

Jabil Circuit has design, manufacturing, repair, and warehouse operations in Austria, Belgium, Brazil, China, France, Hungary, India, Ireland, Italy, Japan, Malaysia, Mexico, the Netherlands, Poland, Singapore, Taiwan, Ukraine, the UK, the US, and Vietnam.

2008 Sales

	$ mil.	% of total
China	2,841.4	22
US	2,605.1	20
Mexico	2,042.8	16
Malaysia	996.0	8
Poland	972.6	8
Hungary	755.8	6
Brazil	419.4	3
Other countries	2,146.6	17
Total	**12,779.7**	**100**

PRODUCTS/OPERATIONS

2008 Sales

	$ mil.	% of total
Electronics manufacturing services	8,217.9	64
Consumer electronics	3,895.1	31
Aftermarket services (repair & warranty)	666.7	5
Total	**12,779.7**	**100**

2008 Sales by Market

	% of total
Electronics manufacturing services	
Networking	21
Instrumentation & medical	18
Computing & storage	13
Telecommunications	6
Automotive	4
Other	2
Consumer electronics	
Mobility products	12
Peripherals	12
Display products	7
Aftermarket services	5
Total	**100**

Services

Component selection, sourcing, and procurement
Design and prototyping
Engineering
Printed circuit board assembly
Repair and warranty services
Systems assembly
Test development

COMPETITORS

ASUSTeK
Benchmark Electronics
BenQ
Celestica
Compal Electronics
CTS Corp.
Elcoteq
Flextronics
Hon Hai
Inventec
Key Tronic
LaBarge
Merix
Nam Tai
Plexus
Sanmina-SCI
SMTC Corp.
Sparton
Suntron
SYNNEX
Sypris Solutions
Universal Scientific
Venture Corp.
Viasystems
Wistron

HISTORICAL FINANCIALS

Company Type: Public

Income Statement

FYE: August 31

	REVENUE ($ mil.)	NET INCOME ($ mil.)	NET PROFIT MARGIN	EMPLOYEES
8/08	12,779.7	133.9	1.0%	61,000
8/07	12,290.6	73.2	0.6%	61,000
8/06	10,265.4	164.5	1.6%	49,000
8/05	7,524.4	231.8	3.1%	40,000
8/04	6,252.9	166.9	2.7%	34,000
Annual Growth	19.6%	(5.4%)	—	15.7%

2008 Year-End Financials

Debt ratio: —
Return on equity: 5.2%
Cash ($ mil.): 773
Current ratio: 1.36
Long-term debt ($ mil.): —
No. of shares (mil.): 214
Dividends
 Yield: 1.7%
 Payout: 43.1%
Market value ($ mil.): 3,602

Stock History

NYSE: JBL

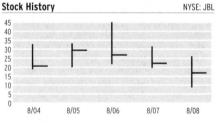

	STOCK PRICE ($) FY Close	P/E High/Low		PER SHARE ($) Earnings	Dividends	Book Value
8/08	16.86	40	14	0.65	0.28	12.71
8/07	22.20	89	57	0.35	0.28	11.44
8/06	26.83	58	29	0.77	0.14	10.74
8/05	29.44	29	18	1.12	0.00	9.99
8/04	20.63	40	24	0.81	0.00	8.52
Annual Growth	(4.9%)	—	—	(5.4%)	—	10.5%

Jack in the Box

Led by an affable "CEO" with a ping-pong ball for a head, Jack in the Box is among the leading quick-service restaurant businesses in the US. The company operates and franchises about 2,200 of its flagship hamburger outlets in California, Texas, and about 15 other states. Jack in the Box offers such standard fast-food fare as burgers, fries, and soft drinks, as well as salads, tacos, and breakfast items. More than 1,250 locations are company-owned, while the rest are franchised. In addition to its mainstay burger business, the company runs a chain of about 500 Qdoba Mexican Grill fast-casual eateries through its Qdoba Restaurant Corporation subsidiary.

Jack in the Box continues to lean on quirky marketing efforts and an almost constant stream of new menu items to help compete with such larger rivals as McDonald's and Burger King. Its advertising campaign featuring the company's off-kilter, fictional CEO, Jack, strikes a balance somewhere between the family friendly image of the Golden Arches and the marketing efforts of BK, which skews more toward the young male demographic. Meanwhile, Jack in the Box is working to upgrade many of its outlets with modern interior designs, complete with flat-screen televisions and ceramic tile floors.

The company's expansion efforts have focused mostly in its core markets, with more than 20 new corporate-owned locations opening during fiscal 2008. It also sold more than 100 units to franchisees that year.

Looking to gobble up more market share in the still-growing quick-casual dining segment, Jack in the Box's Qdoba chain added about 60 locations (mostly franchised stores) during 2008. The concept, acquired in 2003, is the #2 fast-casual Mexican chain behind Chipotle Mexican Grill (spun off from McDonald's in 2006).

The company is selling its Quick Stuff convenience store chain, with more than 60 locations, in order to focus on its dining business.

HISTORY

Robert Peterson founded his first restaurant, Topsy's Drive-In, in 1941 in San Diego. He soon renamed it Oscar's (his middle name) and began to expand the restaurant. By 1950 he had four Oscar's drive-in restaurants. That year he changed the name again to Jack in the Box and in 1951 opened one of the country's first drive-through restaurants, which featured a speaker mounted in the chain's signature clown's head.

The drive-through concept took off, and by the late 1960s the company, renamed Foodmaker, operated about 300 Jack in the Box restaurants. In 1968 Peterson sold Foodmaker to Ralston Purina (now Nestlé Purina PetCare). To differentiate itself from competitors, Foodmaker added new food items, including the first breakfast sandwich (1969). The company continued to expand during the 1970s, and by 1979 it had more than 1,000 restaurants. That year it decided to concentrate on the western and southwestern US, selling 232 restaurants in the East and Midwest.

To attract more adult customers, in 1980 Foodmaker began remodeling its stores and adding menu items geared toward adult tastes. The company ran a series of TV ads showing its trademark clown logo being blown up. The ads were meant to show that Jack in the Box was not just for children anymore, but they drew protests from parents worried about the violence in the advertisements.

In 1985 Foodmaker's management acquired the company in a $450 million LBO. The company went public in 1987, but management took it private again the next year. Led by then-CEO Jack Goodall, Foodmaker expanded its number of franchises. (Unlike most of its competitors, the company had previously owned almost all of its restaurants.) By 1987 about 30% of the company's 900 stores were owned by franchisees.

The next year Foodmaker paid about $230 million for the Chi-Chi's chain of 200 Mexican restaurants. It made its first move outside the US in 1991, opening restaurants in Mexico and Hong Kong. The company went public again the following year.

In 1993 four people died, and more than 700 became ill, after eating *E. coli*-tainted hamburgers from Jack in the Box restaurants in several states, the largest such contamination in US history. Customers, shareholders, and franchisees sued Foodmaker, which in turn sued meat supplier and supermarket chain Vons and Vons' suppliers. Foodmaker's stock and profits plummeted, and the company subsequently enacted a stringent food safety program, which became a model for the fast-food industry and won kudos from the FDA.

Foodmaker sold its Chi-Chi's chain to Family Restaurants (later renamed Prandium, which dissolved in 2004) in 1994 for about $200 million and briefly held a stake in that company. In 1996 Goodall retired as CEO, and Robert Nugent succeeded him. The next year Foodmaker announced a major expansion to add 200 Jack in the Box restaurants, primarily in the western US.

Foodmaker put the *E. coli* episode farther behind it in 1998 when it accepted a $58.5 million settlement from Vons and others. In 1999 the company began building units in selected southeastern markets. Also that year Foodmaker dropped its generic moniker and renamed the firm Jack in the Box. The following year it got a nice break from Uncle Sam in the form of a nearly $23 million tax benefit related to the 1995 selling of its stake in Family Restaurants Inc. The company also opened 120 new stores, many in the southeastern US.

In 2001 Goodall stepped down from the board and was replaced by Nugent as chairman. With same-store sales down amidst a sagging economy and fewer tourist dollars, the company scaled down its expansion plans. In 2002 it built 100 new locations (down from 126 the previous year), including about 30 in the Southeast.

Following the lead of its competitors, Jack in the Box acquired fast-casual restaurant operator Qdoba Restaurant Corporation in 2003 for about $45 million.

In 2004 the company announced it would restate earnings dating back to 2002 as a result of adjustments in its accounting practices. The following year Nugent retired and was replaced by company president Linda Lang.

EXECUTIVES

Chairman and CEO: Linda A. Lang, age 50
President and COO: Paul L. Schultz, age 54
EVP and CFO: Jerry P. Rebel, age 51
VP and CIO: Stephanie E. Cline, age 63
SVP and Chief Development Officer: Charles E. Watson
SVP and Chief Marketing Officer: Terri F. Graham, age 43

SVP Human Resources and Strategic Planning: Carlo E. Cetti, age 64
SVP, General Counsel, and Corporate Secretary: Phillip H. (Phil) Rudolph, age 50
VP Financial Strategy: John F. Hoffner, age 61
VP Investor Relations and Corporate Communications: Carol A. DiRaimo, age 47
Division VP Advertising & Marketing Communications: Greg Joumas
Division VP Corporate Communications: Brian Luscomb
Division VP Menu Marketing and Promotions: Tammy Bailey
Corporate VP Human Resources: Mark Blankenship, age 44
President and CEO, Qdoba Restaurant Corporation: Gary J. Beisler, age 52
Manager, Corporate Communications: Kathleen Finn
Auditors: KPMG LLP

LOCATIONS

HQ: Jack in the Box Inc.
9330 Balboa Ave., San Diego, CA 92123
Phone: 858-571-2121   **Fax:** 858-571-2101
Web: www.jackinthebox.com

PRODUCTS/OPERATIONS

2008 Sales

	$ mil.	% of total
Restaurants	2,101.6	83
Distribution	275.2	11
Franchising	162.8	6
Total	**2,539.6**	**100**

2008 Locations

	No.
Company-owned	1,457
Franchised	1,155
Total	**2,612**

2008 Locations

	No.
Jack in the Box	2,158
Qdoba Mexican Grill	454
Total	**2,612**

COMPETITORS

AFC Enterprises	Fresh Enterprises
American Dairy Queen	In-N-Out Burgers
Burger King	McDonald's
Checkers Drive-In	Quiznos
Chick-fil-A	Sonic Corp.
Chipotle	Subway
Church's Chicken	Wendy's/Arby's Group, Inc.
CKE Restaurants	Whataburger
Del Taco	YUM!
FOCUS Brands	

HISTORICAL FINANCIALS

Company Type: Public

Income Statement

FYE: Sunday nearest September 30

	REVENUE ($ mil.)	NET INCOME ($ mil.)	NET PROFIT MARGIN	EMPLOYEES
9/08	2,539.6	119.3	4.7%	42,700
9/07	2,876.0	126.3	4.4%	42,500
9/06	2,765.6	109.1	3.9%	44,300
9/05	2,507.2	91.5	3.6%	44,600
9/04	2,322.4	74.7	3.2%	45,000
Annual Growth	**2.3%**	**12.4%**	**—**	**(1.3%)**

2008 Year-End Financials

Debt ratio: 112.9%
Return on equity: 27.4%
Cash ($ mil.): 48
Current ratio: 1.11
Long-term debt ($ mil.): 516
No. of shares (mil.): 74
Dividends
　Yield: 0.0%
　Payout: —
Market value ($ mil.): 1,560

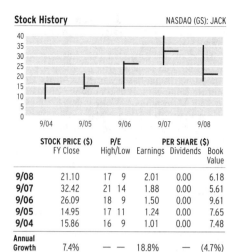

	STOCK PRICE ($) FY Close	P/E High/Low		PER SHARE ($) Earnings	Dividends	Book Value
9/08	21.10	17	9	2.01	0.00	6.18
9/07	32.42	21	14	1.88	0.00	5.61
9/06	26.09	18	9	1.50	0.00	9.61
9/05	14.95	17	11	1.24	0.00	7.65
9/04	15.86	16	9	1.01	0.00	7.48
Annual Growth	**7.4%**	**—**	**—**	**18.8%**	**—**	**(4.7%)**

Jacobs Engineering

Jacobs climbs its ladder of success by keeping it professional. Jacobs Engineering Group provides professional, technical, and construction services for the industrial, commercial, and government sectors. It provides a wide range of services, including project design and engineering, construction, operations and maintenance, and consultation. Engineering and construction projects for the chemical, petroleum, and pharmaceutical and biotech industries generate much of the group's revenues. US government contracts, chiefly for aerospace and defense, also add significantly to Jacobs' bottom line. The company has more than 160 offices around the world, primarily in North America, Europe, Asia, and Australia.

US government agencies involved in defense and aerospace programs have been pivotal to the company's growth. The Air Force's Arnold Engineering Development Center (AEDC) has been a key client for 50 years, almost as long as the engineering firm itself has existed. Jacobs Engineering Group helped design and build modifications of test cells used in performance testing of the F-35 aircraft. Another long-term client is NASA, for which the company has a 40-year history of contract work. It provides design and construction support for the Propulsion Research Laboratory, which studies new propulsion concepts for future space travel.

The group also participates in the environmental restoration of former weapons production and defense sites. Its strategy to speed up environmental cleanup at the Department of Energy's Oak Ridge site has earned it contracts to help accelerate cleanup at other major DOE facilities. The company has also been providing services for the Air Force Center for Environmental Excellence (AFCEE) to help the agency with its environmental cleanup goals since 1991.

Jacobs Engineering Group grows by entering new markets and services lines via strategic mergers and acquisitions, allowing it to offer one-stop services. In 2004 Jacobs acquired Scottish engineering firm Babtie Group (now Jacobs U.K.). Three years later its acquisition of

Carter & Burgess added that company's expertise in transportation, water infrastructure, and land development.

The company expanded its Middle East operations in 2008 by acquiring a 60% interest in the Saudi Arabia–based Zamel & Turbag Consulting Engineers. It also bought a 30% stake in AWE Management Limited, which allows it to partner with Lockheed Martin and Serco to manage the Atomic Weapons Establishment for the UK government.

Investment behemoth Fidelity owns some 14% of Jacobs Engineering Group.

HISTORY

Joseph Jacobs graduated from the Polytechnic Institute of Brooklyn in 1942 with a doctorate in engineering. He went to work for Merck, designing processes for pharmaceutical production. Later he moved to Chemurgic Corp. near San Francisco, where he worked until 1947, when he founded Jacobs Engineering as a consulting firm. Jacobs also sold industrial equipment, avoiding any apparent conflict of interest by simply telling his consulting clients.

When equipment sales outstripped consulting work by 1954, Jacobs hired four salesmen and engineer Stan Krugman, who became his right-hand man. Two years later the company got its first big chemical design job for Kaiser Aluminum. Jacobs incorporated his sole proprietorship in 1957.

In 1960 the firm won its first construction contract to design and build a potash flotation plant, and Jacobs Engineering became an integrated design and construction firm. In 1967 it opened its first regional office but kept management decentralized to replicate the small size and hard-hitting qualities of its home office. Three years later Jacobs Engineering went public.

The firm merged with Houston-based Pace Companies, which specialized in petrochemical engineering design, in 1974. Also that year the firm became Jacobs Engineering Group and began building its first major overseas chemical plant in Ireland.

By 1977 sales had reached $250 million. A decade of lobbying paid off that year when the firm won a contract for the Arab Potash complex in Jordan. Jacobs began to withdraw from his firm's operations in the early 1980s, but the 1982-83 recession and poor management decisions pounded earnings. Jacobs returned from retirement in 1985, fired 14 VPs, cut staff in half, and pushed the firm to pursue smaller process-plant jobs and specialty construction.

After abandoning a 1986 attempt to take the company private, Jacobs began making acquisitions to improve the firm's construction expertise. In 1992 he relinquished his role as CEO to president Noel Watson. The next year the company expanded its international holdings by acquiring the UK's H&G Process Contracting and H&G Contractors.

The firm's $38 million purchase of CRS Sirrine Engineers and CRSS Constructors in 1994 was the company's largest buy to that point and added new markets in the paper and semiconductor industries. By 1995 Jacobs Engineering was working on a record backlog.

Continuing its acquisition drive, the company bought a 49% interest in European engineering specialist Serete Group in 1996; it bought the rest the next year. Also in 1997 it gained control of Indian engineering affiliate Humphreys & Glasgow (now Jacobs H&G), increasing its 40%

stake to 70%, and bought CPR Engineering, a pulp and paper processing specialist. It also formed a joint venture with Krupp UHDE to provide design, engineering, and construction management services in Mexico.

In 2000 Jacobs Engineering purchased half of Dutch firm Stork Engineering's business (it acquired the rest in 2001).

After being accused of overcharging the US government, the company settled a whistle-blower lawsuit (for $35 million) in 2000 while continuing to deny the allegations. However, the next year Jacobs continued to receive federal contracts, including contracts for boosting security at the US Capitol complex and providing logistics to the US Special Operations Command.

After acquiring airport consulting firm Leigh Fisher Associates in 2003, Jacobs announced that it planned a larger acquisition. Jacobs then went on a shopping spree, acquiring a controlling stake in Finland's largest engineering firm, Neste Engineering, and picking up Glasgow-based engineering firm Babtie Group.

In 2004 the group's founder and chairman died at the age of 88. He was succeeded as chairman by Watson, who retained the CEO post until 2005.

EXECUTIVES

Chairman: Noel G. Watson, age 72
President, CEO, and Director: Craig L. Martin, age 60
EVP Operations: Thomas R. (Tom) Hammond, age 57
EVP Finance, Administration, and Treasurer: John W. Prosser Jr., age 63
SVP Information Technology: Cora L. Carmody, age 51
EVP Operations: Gregory J. Landry, age 60
EVP Operations: George A. Kunberger Jr., age 56
SVP and Controller: Nazim G. Thawerbhoy, age 61
SVP Acquisitions and Strategy: John McLachlan, age 62
SVP Operations: Laurence R. Sadoff, age 62
SVP, General Counsel, and Secretary: William C. Markley III, age 63
SVP Global Sales: Andrew F. (Andy) Kremer, age 51
SVP: Martin G. Duvivier, age 56
SVP Global Human Resources: Patricia H. Summers, age 51
SVP Quality and Safety: Robert G. Norfleet, age 45
SVP Public Sector Sales: William J. Birkhofer, age 61
President Jacobs Technology: Rogers F. Starr, age 66
Auditors: Ernst & Young LLP

LOCATIONS

HQ: Jacobs Engineering Group Inc.
1111 S. Arroyo Pkwy., Pasadena, CA 91105
Phone: 626-578-3500   **Fax:** 626-578-6916
Web: www.jacobs.com

Jacobs Engineering Group operates worldwide from more than 160 offices.

2008 Sales

	$ mil.	% of total
US	6,998.2	62
Europe	2,323.3	21
Canada	1,593.0	14
Asia	290.0	3
Other regions	47.7	—
Total	**11,252.2**	**100**

PRODUCTS/OPERATIONS

2008 Sales

	$ mil.	% of total
Downstream energy & refining	3,687.8	33
National government programs	1,976.2	18
Chemicals & polymers	1,409.9	12
Upstream oil & gas	1,102.7	10
Pharmaceuticals & biotechnology	978.9	9
Infrastructure	935.3	8
Buildings	708.1	6
Industrial & other	453.3	4
Total	**11,252.2**	**100**

2008 Sales

	$ mil.	% of total
Technical professional services		
Project services	5,128.5	45
Consulting	770.2	7
Field services		
Construction	4,239.5	38
Operations & maintenance	1,114.0	10
Total	**11,252.2**	**100**

COMPETITORS

AECOM
Aker Solutions
AMEC
BE&K
Bechtel
CH2M HILL
Computer Sciences Corp.
Day & Zimmermann
Earth Tech
Fluor
Foster Wheeler
HDR
HNTB Companies
HOK
Honeywell International
KBR
Lockheed Martin
Louis Berger
Parsons Brinckerhoff
Parsons Corporation
Peter Kiewit Sons'
Raytheon
SAIC
Shaw Group
Technip
Tetra Tech
Turner Construction
URS
Washington Division
Weston

HISTORICAL FINANCIALS

Company Type: Public

Income Statement

	REVENUE ($ mil.)	NET INCOME ($ mil.)	NET PROFIT MARGIN	EMPLOYEES
FYE: September 30				
9/08	11,252.2	420.7	3.7%	43,700
9/07	8,474.0	287.1	3.4%	36,400
9/06	7,421.3	196.9	2.7%	31,700
9/05	5,635.0	151.0	2.7%	38,600
9/04	4,594.2	129.0	2.8%	24,000
Annual Growth	**25.1%**	**34.4%**	**—**	**16.2%**

2008 Year-End Financials

Debt ratio: 2.5%
Return on equity: 20.6%
Cash ($ mil.): 604
Current ratio: 1.74
Long-term debt ($ mil.): 56
No. of shares (mil.): 124
Dividends
  Yield: 0.0%
  Payout: —
Market value ($ mil.): 6,730

NYSE: JEC

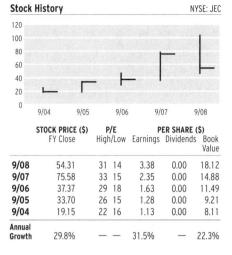

	STOCK PRICE ($) FY Close	P/E High/Low		PER SHARE ($) Earnings	Dividends	Book Value
9/08	54.31	31	14	3.38	0.00	18.12
9/07	75.58	33	15	2.35	0.00	14.88
9/06	37.37	29	18	1.63	0.00	11.49
9/05	33.70	26	15	1.28	0.00	9.21
9/04	19.15	22	16	1.13	0.00	8.11
Annual Growth	29.8%	—	—	31.5%	—	22.3%

J.B. Hunt Transport Services

When it comes to hauling freight, J.B. Hunt Transport Services is a leader of the pack. Its intermodal unit, the company's largest, maintains some 2,100 tractors and 39,000 containers and moves customers' cargo by combinations of truck and train. J.B. Hunt's dedicated contract services unit supplies customers with drivers and equipment; it operates about 4,400 company-controlled trucks. The company's truckload transportation unit, which has a fleet of about 2,500 tractors, provides dry van freight transportation service in the US, Canada, and Mexico. A fourth business segment, integrated capacity solutions (ICS), manages freight transportation via third-party carriers as well as J.B. Hunt equipment.

Formerly part of J.B. Hunt's truckload transportation segment, ICS began to have its results reported separately in 2007. The business often arranges specialty trucking services, such as transporting freight that requires the use of flatbed or refrigerated trailers. J.B. Hunt also is engaged in transportation management through its 37% stake in Transplace, a company formed from the logistics units of several truckload carriers.

J.B. Hunt hopes to grow by concentrating on its operating segments as separate, but overlapping, businesses and by selling more value-added services to its customers. It has seen strong growth in its intermodal unit, which has partnerships with several major North American railroads. To emphasize higher-margin offerings, J.B. Hunt has been shifting resources away from truckload transportation, and during 2008 the company repaid about $280 million in outstanding debt and reduced its overall equipment fleet.

Freight transported by J.B. Hunt includes automotive parts, building materials, chemicals, food and beverages, forest and paper products, and general merchandise. The company's top customer is its Arkansas neighbor, Wal-Mart, which accounted for 12% of sales in 2007 and 9% in 2008.

The family of founder J.B. Hunt, who retired as senior chairman in 2004 and died in 2006, owns 28% of the company. His son, Bryan Hunt, is a board member. Company chairman Wayne Garrison holds a 5% stake.

HISTORY

Johnnie Bryan (J.B.) Hunt's life was a classic tale of rolling from rags to riches — with a little help from a Rockefeller.

Hunt grew up in a family of sharecroppers during the Depression, and he left school at age 12 to work for his uncle's Arkansas sawmill. In the late 1950s, after driving trucks for more than nine years, Hunt noticed that the rice mills along his eastern Arkansas route were burning rice hulls. Believing the hulls could be used as poultry litter, Hunt got a contract to haul away the hulls and began selling them to chicken farmers.

In 1961 he began the J.B. Hunt Company with help from future Arkansas governor Winthrop Rockefeller, who owned Winrock grass company, where Hunt bought sod for one of his side businesses. Hunt developed a machine to compress the rice hulls, which made their transportation profitable, and within a few years the company was the world's largest producer of rice hulls for poultry litter.

Still looking for new opportunities, Hunt bought some used trucks and refrigerated trailers in 1969, though the company continued to focus on its original business. In the 1970s it found that the ground rice hulls made a good base for livestock vitamins and medications. Buyers of the ground hulls included Pfizer and Eli Lilly. J.B. Hunt, with Pfizer's backing, soon began selling a vitamin premix to feed companies.

In the 1980s J.B. Hunt's trucking division grew dramatically and became lucrative as the trucking industry was being deregulated. In 1981-82 the Hunt trucking business had higher margins than most trucking firms. In 1983, when J.B. Hunt Transport Services went public, Hunt sold the rice hull business to concentrate on trucking.

By 1986 J.B. Hunt was the US's third-largest irregular-route trucking company. The time was ripe to expand, and it began trucking in Canada (1988) and Mexico (1989). It also formed an alliance in 1989 with Santa Fe Pacific Railroad (now Burlington Northern Santa Fe) to provide intermodal services between the West Coast and the Midwest.

The company began adding computers to its trucks in 1992 to improve data exchange and communication on the road. J.B. Hunt also formed a joint venture with Latin America's largest transportation company, Transportación Marítima Mexicana. Founder Hunt retired in 1995 and became senior chairman.

J.B. Hunt tried hauling automobiles in 1996 but abandoned the idea when it found that cars were easily dented on intermodal trailers. More in line with the trucking company's long-term goals was an effort to stabilize its roster of drivers. It raised wages by one-third in 1997 to counteract driver shortages and high turnover. That year J.B. Hunt sold its underperforming flatbed-trucking unit (renamed Charger Inc.).

In 1998 the company reaped the benefit of greater profits from its efforts to retain drivers. The next year it began testing a satellite system from ORBCOMM Global to track empty trailers.

The company combined its J.B. Logistics (JBL) unit with the logistics businesses of five other truckers in 2000 to form Transplace.com (later

known as Transplace). Also that year J.B. Hunt inked a $100 million deal with Wal-Mart to increase its full-truckload services to the retailer by 50%.

In 2002 J.B. Hunt bought a 10% stake in Transplace from Werner Enterprises, increasing its stake in the logistics company to 37%.

Founder Hunt stepped down from the company's board in 2004. He died in 2006.

EXECUTIVES

Chairman: Wayne Garrison, age 56, $2,403,420 total compensation
President, CEO, and Director: Kirk Thompson, age 55, $1,838,548 total compensation
EVP Operations and COO: Craig Harper, age 51, $801,610 total compensation
EVP Finance and Administration and CFO:
Jerry W. Walton, age 62, $1,027,381 total compensation
SVP Tax and Risk Management and Corporate Secretary: David G. Mee, age 48
EVP and CIO: Kay J. Palmer, age 45
EVP and Chief Marketing Officer; President, Intermodal: Paul R. Bergant, age 62, $907,329 total compensation
SVP Finance, Controller, and Chief Accounting Officer: Donald G. Cope, age 58
EVP; President, Dedicated Contract Services:
John N. Roberts III, age 44
EVP Equipment and Properties: Bob D. Ralston, age 62
EVP Sales and Marketing: Terrence D. Matthews, age 50
SVP; President, Integrated Capacity Solutions:
Shelley Simpson, age 38
VP and Treasurer: David N. Chelette, age 45
Auditors: Ernst & Young LLP

LOCATIONS

HQ: J.B. Hunt Transport Services, Inc.
615 J.B. Hunt Corporate Dr., Lowell, AR 72745
Phone: 479-820-0000 **Fax:** 479-820-3418
Web: www.jbhunt.com

PRODUCTS/OPERATIONS

2008 Sales

	$ mil.	% of total
Intermodal	1,952	52
Dedicated contract services	927	25
Trucking	676	18
Integrated capacity solutions	209	5
Adjustments	(32)	—
Total	**3,732**	**100**

COMPETITORS

APL Logistics
Burlington Northern Santa Fe
Canadian National Railway
Con-way Inc.
CSX
Hub Group
Kansas City Southern
Landstar System
Norfolk Southern
Pacer International
Ryder System
Schneider National
Swift Transportation
Union Pacific
U.S. Xpress
Werner Enterprises
YRC Worldwide

HISTORICAL FINANCIALS

Company Type: Public

Income Statement

FYE: December 31

	REVENUE ($ mil.)	NET INCOME ($ mil.)	NET PROFIT MARGIN	EMPLOYEES
12/08	3,731.9	200.6	5.4%	14,667
12/07	3,489.9	213.1	6.1%	15,795
12/06	3,328.0	220.0	6.6%	5,916
12/05	3,127.9	207.3	6.6%	16,367
12/04	2,786.2	146.3	5.3%	15,850
Annual Growth	7.6%	8.2%	—	(1.9%)

2008 Year-End Financials

Debt ratio: 97.4%
Return on equity: 46.0%
Cash ($ mil.): 2
Current ratio: 0.97
Long-term debt ($ mil.): 515
No. of shares (mil.): 127
Dividends
  Yield: 1.5%
  Payout: 25.6%
Market value ($ mil.): 3,332

Stock History

NASDAQ (GS): JBHT

	STOCK PRICE ($) FY Close	P/E High/Low	PER SHARE ($) Earnings	Dividends	Book Value
12/08	26.27	26 13	1.56	0.40	4.17
12/07	27.55	21 14	1.55	0.36	2.71
12/06	20.77	18 13	1.44	0.32	5.99
12/05	22.64	20 14	1.28	0.24	6.44
12/04	22.42	26 14	0.88	0.05	6.79
Annual Growth	4.0%	— —	15.4%	68.2%	(11.5%)

J. C. Penney

An old name in retailing, J. C. Penney has been busy reinventing itself to bring style to Middle America's department store shoppers. The company's chain of about 1,090 JCPenney department stores in the US and Puerto Rico has found itself squeezed between upscale competitors and major discounters (Kohls, Target, Wal-Mart). Following the sale of its ailing Eckerd drugstore chain to The Jean Coutu Group and CVS for $4.5 billion in 2004, the retailer has focused firmly on fashion. The firm runs one of the top catalog operations in the US. J. C. Penney Corporation is a wholly owned subsidiary of holding company J. C. Penney Company (created in 2002), which is the publicly traded entity.

CEO Myron Ullman, an experienced retail veteran and former chief executive of archrival Macy's, has focused on fashion in his attempt to reshape Penney's. Indeed, in a direct challenge to his former employer, in 2009 Penney's opened its first Manhattan store — boasting some 150,000 sq. ft. — on Sixth Avenue near Macy's flagship location on Herald Square. Ullman has also been aggressively expanding its private-label brand offerings with the proceeds from the Eckerd sale (formerly 45% of Penney's sales) and

the sale of Penney's stake in the Renner department store chain in Brazil.

Ullman's latest move is also the biggest in Penney's 107-year history. The launch of the new American Living collection — developed exclusively for Penney by Polo Ralph Lauren's Global Brands Concepts — includes men's, women's and children's clothing; shoes; handbags; bedding; towels; window treatments; luggage; furniture; and swimwear. Ullman has high hopes for American Living, which he expects to eventually ring up about $1 billion in sales annually. The American Living collection launched in 2008 in some 600 Penney stores, as well as online and in catalogs. The retailer is building separate American Living shops within many of its stores. On the home front, Penney introduced its Linden Street home collection in 2008 and more recently the Cindy Crawford Style collection in 2009.

Sales from Penney's 25-plus proprietary brands now account for more than half of total department store merchandise. Penney is hoping that its leadership in private-label apparel and other merchandise will carry it through the recession.

In a bid to attract younger and more affluent shoppers, Penney has teamed up with beauty purveyor Sephora USA, which operates more than 100 Sephora ministores inside Penney's department stores.

HISTORY

In 1902 James Cash Penney and two former employers opened the Golden Rule, a dry goods store, in Kemmerer, Wyoming. Penney bought out his partners in 1907 and opened stores that sold soft goods in small towns. Basing his customer service policy on his Baptist heritage, he held employees (called "associates") to a high moral code.

The firm incorporated in Utah in 1913 as the J. C. Penney Company, with headquarters in Salt Lake City, but it moved to New York City the next year to improve buying and financial operations. It expanded to nearly 1,400 stores in the 1920s and went public in 1929. The company grew during the Depression with its reputation for high quality and low prices.

J. C. Penney rode the postwar boom, and by 1951 sales had surpassed $1 billion. It introduced credit plans in 1958 and entered catalog retailing in 1962 with its purchase of General Merchandise Co. The next year the stores added hard goods, which allowed them to compete with Sears and Montgomery Ward.

The company formed J. C. Penney Insurance in the mid-1960s and bought Thrift Drug in 1969. The chain continued to grow, and in 1973, two years after Penney's death, there were 2,053 stores. Also in the 1970s J. C. Penney began its ill-fated foray overseas by buying chains in Belgium and Italy in hopes of duplicating its US formula — giant department stores.

It bought Delaware-based First National Bank in 1983 (renamed J. C. Penney National Bank in 1984) to issue MasterCard and Visa cards. Stores refocused on soft goods during the 1980s and stopped selling automotive services, appliances, paint, hardware, and fabrics in 1983. It discontinued sporting goods, consumer electronics, and photographic equipment in 1987.

The next year J. C. Penney Telemarketing was formed to take catalog phone orders and provide telemarketing services for other companies. Also in 1988 the company moved its headquarters to

Plano, Texas. J. C. Penney tried to move upmarket in the 1980s, enlisting fashion designer Halston. The line failed, however, so the company developed its own brands.

James Oesterreicher was named CEO in 1995. Facing a slow-growing department store business back home, it then bought 272 drugstores from Fay's Inc. and 200 more from Rite Aid. In 1997 it acquired Eckerd (nearly 1,750 stores) for $3.3 billion, converting its other drugstores to the Eckerd name. The company also sold its $740 million credit card portfolio of J. C. Penney National Bank to Associates First Capital in 1997.

With its stock value falling, J. C. Penney announced in 1999 it would sell 20% of Eckerd in the form of a tracking stock, but it postponed the IPO three times. That year it also sold its private-label credit card operations to GE Capital and sold its store in Chile to department store chain Almacenas Paris.

In 2000 Oesterreicher retired and was replaced by Allen Questrom, who was hired because of the work he did turning around Federated Department Stores and Barneys New York.

In 2001 the company shuttered about 50 more department stores and drugstores. Also that year Dutch insurer AEGON acquired J. C. Penney's Direct Marketing Services (DMS) unit, including its life insurance subsidiaries, for $1.3 billion. The company changed its name to J. C. Penney Corporation in January 2002 and formed a holding company under its former name.

Despite a major initiative to remodel hundreds of Eckerd stores and centralize the drugstore chain's distribution and merchandising systems, sales gains continued to lag behind rivals. Ultimately J.C. Penney sold its drugstores operations to The Jean Coutu Group and CVS for $4.5 billion in cash in August 2004.

In 2004 Questrom stepped down and was succeeded by Myron E. "Mike" Ullman III.

In July 2005 J. C. Penney's Brazilian subsidiary, J. C. Penney Brazil, sold its controlling stake in the 60-store Brazilian department store chain through an IPO, which generated net proceeds of about $260 million.

EXECUTIVES

Chairman and CEO: Myron E. (Mike) Ullman III, age 62, $10,023,947 total compensation
EVP and CFO: Robert B. Cavanaugh, age 57, $2,261,007 total compensation
EVP and CIO: Thomas M. Nealon, age 48, $2,094,888 total compensation
EVP and Chief Marketing Officer: Michael J. (Mike) Boylson
EVP, Chief Human Resources and Administration Officer: Michael T. Theilmann, age 44, $2,412,439 total compensation
EVP and President, JCPenney Direct: John W. Irvin
EVP, General Counsel, and Secretary: Janet L. Dhillon, age 47
EVP and General Merchandise Manager, Home and Custom Decorating: Jeffrey J. Allison
EVP and Director Product Development and Sourcing: Peter M. McGrath
EVP and General Merchandise Manager, Women's Apparel: Elizabeth H. (Liz) Sweney
EVP and Director, JCPenney Stores: Michael W. Taxter
EVP and Director Planning and Allocation: Clarence Kelley
EVP and General Merchandise Manager, Men's Division: Steven (Steve) Lawrence

SVP and COO, JCPenney Direct: Bernard D. Feiwus
SVP and Director Brand Marketing: Ruby Anik, age 51
SVP and Director Property Development:
  Michael P. Dastugue
SVP and Director Supply Chain Management; President
  JCP Logistics LP: Marie Lacertosa
VP and Director Investor Relations:
  Phillip (Phil) Sanchez, age 48
Senior Public Relations Manager: Quinton Crenshaw
Auditors: KPMG LLP

LOCATIONS

HQ: J. C. Penney Corporation, Inc.
  6501 Legacy Dr., Plano, TX 75024
Phone: 972-431-1000   Fax: 972-431-1362
Web: www.jcpenney.net

2009 Stores

	No.
Alabama	21
Arizona	22
Arkansas	16
California	79
Colorado	21
Connecticut	10
Florida	59
Georgia	30
Illinois	42
Indiana	30
Iowa	20
Kansas	18
Kentucky	22
Louisiana	16
Maryland	17
Massachusetts	13
Michigan	45
Minnesota	26
Mississippi	17
Missouri	25
Nebraska	12
New Hampshire	10
New Jersey	17
New Mexico	10
New York	42
North Carolina	36
Ohio	47
Oklahoma	18
Oregon	14
Pennsylvania	41
South Carolina	18
Tennessee	25
Texas	89
Virginia	27
Washington	23
Wisconsin	25
Other states	83
Puerto Rico	7
Total	**1,093**

PRODUCTS/OPERATIONS

2009 Sales

	% of total
Women's apparel	24
Home	20
Men's apparel & accessories	19
Children's apparel	11
Women's accessories	10
Family footwear	6
Fine jewelry	5
Services & other	5
Total	**100**

Major Product Lines

Accessories
Family apparel
Home furnishings
Jewelry
Shoes

Selected Private and Exclusive Labels

Ambrielle (intimate apparel)
American Living (apparel and home furnishings)
a.n.a. (casual women's apparel)
Crazy Horse by Liz Claiborne (exclusive third-party
  brand)
Decree
east5th
Every Day Matters
Hunt Club
J. Ferrar
Jacqueline Ferrar
JCPenney Home Collection (bedding, furniture, window
  coverings)
Linden Street
nicole by Nicole Miller
Okie Dokie
St. John's Bay
Stafford
The Chris Madden for JCPenney Home
The Original Arizona Jean Co.
USA Olympic
Worthington

COMPETITORS

Bed Bath & Beyond
Belk
Bon-Ton Stores
Brown Shoe
Costco Wholesale
Dillard's
Dress Barn
Eddie Bauer llc
Foot Locker
The Gap
J. Crew
J. Jill Group
Kmart
Kohl's
Lands' End
Macy's
Nine West
Nordstrom
Otto GmbH & Co KG
Ross Stores
Saks
Sears
Signet
Stage Stores
Target
TJX Companies
Wal-Mart
Zale

HISTORICAL FINANCIALS

Company Type: Subsidiary

Income Statement

	REVENUE ($ mil.)	NET INCOME ($ mil.)	NET PROFIT MARGIN	FYE: Saturday nearest January 31 EMPLOYEES
1/09	18,486.0	572.0	3.1%	147,000
1/08	19,860.0	1,111.0	5.6%	155,000
1/07	19,903.0	1,153.0	5.8%	155,000
1/06	18,781.0	1,088.0	5.8%	151,000
1/05	18,424.0	524.0	2.8%	151,000
Annual Growth	**0.1%**	**2.2%**	**—**	**(0.7%)**

Net Income History

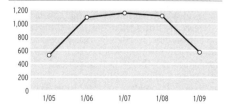

Jefferies Group

Because smaller companies need hostile-takeover advice, too. Through various operating units, Jefferies Group raises capital, performs securities trading and research, and provides advisory services for small and midsized companies in the US through its Jefferies & Company subsidiary. Serving about 2,000 institutional clients worldwide, the company also trades derivatives and commodities and makes markets for some 5,000 US and international equities. Jefferies Group also oversees approximately $3.5 billion on behalf of investors and private clients. The company has about 25 offices in North America, Europe, and Asia.

Its Jefferies Quarterdeck unit specializes in mergers and acquisitions (M&A) advice for the aerospace and defense sectors, while Jefferies Randall & Dewey serves the energy industry and Jefferies Broadview focuses on technology. Jefferies Group acquired the financial services investment banking business of Putnam Lovell (now Jefferies Putnam Lovell) from National Bank of Canada in 2007. Two years later it acquired First Albany Securities, which specializes in municipal capital markets, from DEPFA.

Jefferies Group had been focused on expanding into Latin America and the Middle East, but the economic downturn has put the kibosh on those plans, as Jefferies Group announced in late 2008 that it would cut more than 10% of its workforce and close offices in Dubai, Singapore, and Tokyo.

Chairman Richard Handler owns about 8% of the company.

HISTORY

Former cowboy and stock exchange clerk Boyd Jefferies founded Jefferies & Company in 1962. The firm referred customers to brokers in exchange for cuts of their commissions. In 1969 mutual fund giant Investors Diversified Services (IDS) acquired the upstart. Because IDS was not a broker, Jefferies was kicked off the NYSE and increased its off-exchange activities.

Boyd Jefferies bought back his company in 1973 and took it public in 1983. Because the SEC had less control over off-exchange trades, Jefferies was a popular stop for greenmailers amassing stock for hostile takeovers. By 1986 the firm was in Japan, Switzerland, and the UK.

After 1987's "Black Monday" stock crash it was revealed that Jefferies had illegally "parked" stocks for Ivan Boesky. Boyd Jefferies pleaded guilty to SEC rules violations, resigned, and sold his interest in the company. New CEO Frank Baxter launched subsidiary Investment Technology Group (ITG). When Michael Milken's Drexel Burnham Lambert failed in 1990, Baxter hired scores of former Drexelites.

During the 1990s ITG grew along with demand for off-exchange trading. In 1999 Jefferies merged ITG into a separate company, spinning off its other operations as the new Jefferies Group. Jefferies formed an alliance with Crédit Lyonnais' US brokerage subsidiary and bought a stake in online bond trading system LIMITrader.com, which had mostly ceased operations by 2001.

At the end of 2000 Baxter retired as CEO but stayed on as chairman until 2002. He was succeeded in both capacities by Jefferies Group veteran Richard Handler. Also in 2000, Jefferies bought The Europe Company to boost its international operations.

The company's Helfant Group subsidiary (which was renamed Jefferies Execution Services in 2004) was created from the 2002 merger of Lawrence Helfant and W&D Securities.

Jefferies Group enhanced its capital-raising capabilities by acquiring Helix Associates, a UK-based private equity fund placement firm, in 2005. Jefferies & Company was fined $5.5 million by the NASD and $4.2 million by the SEC in 2006 for giving nearly $2 million worth of improper gifts to equity traders at Fidelity.

EXECUTIVES

Chairman and CEO, Jefferies Group and Jefferies & Company: Richard B. Handler, age 47, $8,279,996 total compensation

EVP and CFO: Peregrine C. de M. (Peg) Broadbent, age 44, $8,279,996 total compensation

EVP, General Counsel, and Secretary: Lloyd H. Feller, age 66, $1,536,902 total compensation

EVP and Co-Head of Investment Banking: Chris M. Kanoff, age 50

SVP, Investment Banking Technology, Jefferies & Company: Omer Soykan

SVP and Global Head of Compliance: Robert J. (Bob) Albano

SVP and Equity Research Analyst, Jefferies & Company: Jonathan A. Schildkraut

SVP, Private Client Services Department, Jefferies & Company: Michael W. Hyde

SVP, MBS and ABS Sales, Chicago: Elizabeth Harper

SVP, Par Loan Trading: John Gally

Vice Chairman and Co-Head of Investment Banking, Jefferies & Company: Andrew R. Whittaker, age 44

Chairman, Randall & Dewey: Ralph Eads III

Chairman, Investment Banking, Jefferies & Company: Benjamin D. (Ben) Lorello

Controller; EVP and CFO, Jefferies & Company: Maxine Syrjamaki, age 64

Treasurer: Charles J. (Chuck) Hendrickson, $1,132,515 total compensation

Director, Marketing Communications: Thomas E. (Tom) Tarrant

Auditors: KPMG LLP

LOCATIONS

HQ: Jefferies Group, Inc.
520 Madison Ave., 12th Fl., New York, NY 10022
Phone: 212-284-2300   **Fax:** 212-284-2111
Web: www.jefco.com

PRODUCTS/OPERATIONS

2008 Gross Revenues

	$ mil.	% of total
Interest	749.6	43
Commissions	444.3	26
Investment banking	425.9	24
Principal transactions	87.3	5
Other	28.6	2
Total	**1,735.7**	**100**

COMPETITORS

Arlington Asset Investment	Lehman Brothers
Banc of America Securities	Lincoln International
Collins Stewart (US)	Merrill Lynch
Cowen Group	N M Rothschild & Sons
Deutsche Bank	Piper Jaffray
Alex. Brown	RBC Wealth Management
Goldman Sachs	Robert W. Baird & Co.
Houlihan Lokey	Thomas Weisel Partners
JPMorgan Chase	UBS Financial Services
KBW	Wedbush Morgan
Lazard	WR Hambrecht

HISTORICAL FINANCIALS

Company Type: Public

Income Statement

FYE: December 31

	REVENUE ($ mil.)	NET INCOME ($ mil.)	NET PROFIT MARGIN	EMPLOYEES
12/08	1,021.8	(536.1)	—	2,270
12/07	1,568.1	144.7	9.2%	2,568
12/06	1,457.6	204.1	14.0%	2,254
12/05	1,204.7	157.4	13.1%	2,045
12/04	1,198.6	131.4	11.0%	1,783
Annual Growth	**(3.9%)**	**—**	**—**	**6.2%**

2008 Year-End Financials

Debt ratio: 83.2%
Return on equity: —
Cash ($ mil.): 2,446
Current ratio: —
Long-term debt ($ mil.): 1,764
No. of shares (mil.): 173
Dividends
Yield: 1.8%
Payout: —
Market value ($ mil.): 2,426

Stock History

NYSE: JEF

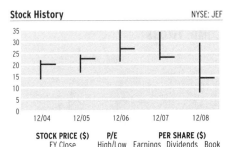

	STOCK PRICE ($) FY Close	P/E High/Low		Earnings	PER SHARE ($) Dividends	Book Value
12/08	14.06	—	—	(3.23)	0.25	12.29
12/07	23.05	35	23	0.97	0.50	10.21
12/06	26.82	25	15	1.42	0.45	9.16
12/05	22.49	21	14	1.16	0.25	7.46
12/04	20.14	21	13	1.03	0.18	6.02
Annual Growth	**(8.6%)**	**—**	**—**	**—**	**8.6%**	**19.5%**

The J. M. Smucker Company

The J. M. Smucker Company is best known for the sweet and sticky fruity stuff, but hopes coffee will fatten its bottom line. The #1 US producer of jams, jellies, and preserves also makes dessert toppings, juices, and specialty fruit spreads under names such as Smucker's, Laura Scudder's, and Knott's Berry Farm. The company is home to the #1 coffee brand in the US — Folgers. Many of its brands, including Folgers, Smucker's, Jif, and Crisco, are market leaders. Smucker's roster also includes baking-goods brands Hungry Jack, Pillsbury, and Eagle and PET evaporated milk products. The company has manufacturing and processing facilities in the US and Canada.

Never forgetting what "butters" its bread on the bottom line, in 2008 Smucker acquired the jam and jelly business, Knott's Berry Farm, from ConAgra. Later that year, it purchased The Folger Coffee Company from Procter & Gamble in an all-stock transaction valued at some $3 billion. Smucker assumed some $350 million of Folger's

debt. Both deals are in line with company strategy to offer top name brands. As part of the Folgers deal, the company gained operations in Cincinnati, New Orleans, Kansas City, and Sherman, Texas, as well as some 1,250 employees (its pre-deal employee number was about 3,500).

The Folger's purchase has paid off particularly well. Coffee (which is new to Smucker) appeared at the top of its segment sales in 2009, accounting for 25% of the company's total sales for the year.

Further adding to its baking offerings and accompanying its PET milk products, Smucker acquired sweetened condensed and evaporated milk producer, Eagle Family Foods Holdings in 2007, paying $133 million in cash and $115 in assumed debt. Given Smucker's size and subsequent bargaining power with food retailers (including Wal-Mart, *the* giant in US food retailing) and Eagle's domination of the North American canned-milk sector (it is the largest producer of evaporated and sweetened condensed milk in the US and Canada), the pairing of the two companies was a sensible move for both.

Adding to its list of leading North American brands in 2007, Smucker also acquired the Carnation Milk brand in Canada from Nestlé. The deal fit well with Smucker's Eagle Sweetened Condensed Milk brand. The next year, it continued its growth strategy by acquiring Canadian company, Europe's Best, maker of the best-selling frozen fruit and vegetables in that country.

Wal-Mart accounted for about 24% of the company's sales for its 2009 fiscal year.

HISTORY

Jerome Smucker began operating a steam-powered cider mill in 1897 for farmers in Orrville, Ohio, but he found that his biggest business was selling apple butter made using a secret Smucker family recipe. By the 1920s The J. M. Smucker Company had begun producing a full line of preserves and jellies, and in 1935 it acquired its first fruit-processing operations.

Under Jerome's grandson, Paul Smucker, the company gained widespread national distribution by the mid-1960s. Tim Smucker succeeded his father, Paul, as president in 1981, then as chairman in 1987, when his brother Richard became president.

The company's growth has been enhanced through the development of its industrial fruit fillings business and acquisitions of domestic natural juice and peanut butter companies, including Knudsen & Sons (1984), After the Fall (1994), and Laura Scudder's (from National Grape Co-op, 1994). It has gradually expanded internationally through acquisitions. In 1993 it acquired the jam, preserves, and pie-filling unit of Canada's Culinar. In a 1998 deal Smucker purchased Australia's Allowrie jam and Lackersteens marmalade lines.

Smucker sold its flagging Mrs. Smith's frozen pie business to Flowers in 1997, less than two years after buying the unit from Kellogg. It bought Kraft's domestic fruit spread unit in 1997 and in 1999 purchased the northwestern Adams peanut butter business from Pro-Fac Cooperative. Smucker kept the Adams name but shifted packaging to its Pennsylvania peanut butter plant.

Spreading into retail, the company opened a store in 1999 in its hometown of Orrville and then launched online and catalog sales. Also that year Smucker bought a fruit filling plant in Brazil from Groupe Danone, a major customer. During

2000 the company's Henry Jones Foods subsidiary (Australia) purchased Taylor Foods (sauces, marinades).

Smucker acquired International Flavors & Fragrances' formulated fruit and vegetable preparation businesses in 2001. Moving beyond its stronghold in natural peanut butter brands, the next year Smucker purchased the Jif peanut butter and Crisco cooking oil and shortening brands from Procter & Gamble. The $670 million purchase price for Jif and Crisco included shifting 53% of Smucker stock into the hands of P&G shareholders.

A decision to concentrate on North America led to the $37 million sale of Australian subsidiary Henry Jones Foods in 2004. Also that year, Smucker sold its operations in Brazil to Cargill and closed down two fruit processing plants in California and Oregon. Its purchase of International Multifoods that year added an array of US brands to the Smucker family, including Pillsbury flour, baking mixes, and ready-to-spread frostings; Hungry Jack pancake mixes, syrup, and potato side dishes; Martha White baking mixes and ingredients; and PET evaporated milk brands. Canadian brands included Robin Hood flour and baking mixes, Bick's pickles and condiments, and Golden Temple flour and rice.

To further its strategy of concentrating on its core retail brands, in 2005 Smucker sold its US foodservice and bakery business and the Canadian operations of Gourmet Baker (all part of its International Multifoods acquisition) to Value Creation Partners. The following year, the company sold its Canadian grain-based foodservice operations and industrial businesses to Cargill and CHS Inc. The operations were integrated into leading US flour miller Horizon Milling (which is jointly owned by Cargill and CHS). Adding to its name-brand offerings in 2006, Smucker acquired the White Lily brand of flours, baking mixes, and frozen biscuits from C.H. Guenther.

EXECUTIVES

Executive Chairman, President, and Co-CEO:
Richard K. Smucker, age 60,
$5,592,717 total compensation
Chairman of the Board and Co-CEO:
Timothy P. (Tim) Smucker, age 65,
$4,832,870 total compensation
VP, CFO, and Treasurer: Mark R. Belgya,
$1,042,163 total compensation
VP Information Services and CIO: Andrew G. Platt, age 53
SVP Corporate and Organization Development:
Barry C. Dunaway, age 46
VP and General Manager, Smucker Quality Beverages:
Julia L. Sabin, age 49
VP, General Counsel, and Secretary: M. Ann Harlan, age 49
VP and Controller: John W. Denman, age 52
VP Quality Assurance: Albert W. Yeagley, age 61
VP Customer Development: John F. Mayer, age 53
VP Marketing Services: Christopher R. Resweber, age 47
VP Logistics and Operations Support:
Dennis J. Armstrong, age 54
VP Alternate Channels: Kenneth A. Miller, age 60

President, Coffee Strategic Business Area; Director:
Vincent C. Byrd, age 54, $1,754,872 total compensation
President, Consumer Strategic Business Area:
Steven T. Oakland, age 48,
$1,205,511 total compensation
President, Special Markets; Director: Mark T. Smucker, age 39
President, Oils and Baking; Director: Paul S. Wagstaff, age 39
Director Corporate Communications:
Maribeth Badertscher
Director Corporate Finance and Investor Relations:
Sonal P. Robinson
Auditors: Ernst & Young LLP

LOCATIONS

HQ: The J. M. Smucker Company
1 Strawberry Ln., Orrville, OH 44667
Phone: 330-682-3000   **Fax:** 330-684-6410
Web: www.smucker.com

2009 Sales

	$ mil.	% of total
US	3,353.4	89
Canada	356.3	10
Other countries	48.2	1
Total	**3,757.9**	**100**

PRODUCTS/OPERATIONS

2009 Sales

	% of total
Coffee	25
Peanut butter	14
Shortening & oils	11
Fruit spreads	9
Baking mixes & frostings	8
Canned milk	7
Flour & baking ingredients	7
Portion control	4
Juices & beverages	3
Toppings & syrups	3
Uncrustables brand frozen sandwiches	3
Other	6
Total	**100**

Selected Brands

Adams (peanut butter)
After The Fall (juice beverages)
Bick's (pickles and condiments, Canada)
Crisco (cooking oils, shortening)
Crosse & Blackwell (chutneys, jellies, relishes, meat and seafood sauces)
Dickinson's (fruit spreads)
Double Fruit (fruit spreads, Canada)
Eagle Brand (canned milk products, dessert kits)
Europe's Best (frozen fruits and vegetables, Canada)
Folgers (coffee)
Golden Temple (flour and rice)
Hungry Jack (pancake mix, syrup, and potato side dishes)
Jif (peanut butter)
Knott's Berry Farm (jams, jellies, preserves)
Laura Scudder's (peanut butter)
Martha White (baking mixes and ingredients)
Magnolia (sweetened condensed milk)
Millstone (coffee)
PET (canned milk products)
Pillsbury (flour, frostings, and refrigerated doughs)
Red River (hot cereal mix, Canada)
Rocket Juice (juice beverages)
Robin Hood (flour and baking mixes, Canada)
R.W. Knudsen (juice beverages)
Santa Cruz Organic (juice beverages)
Smucker's (dessert topping, jam, jelly, preserves, peanut butter)
Smucker's Goober (peanut butter)
Smucker's Simply Fruit (fruit spreads)
Smucker's Uncrustables (frozen peanut-butter-and-jelly sandwiches)
White Lily (flour)

Selected Subsidiaries

Eagle Family Foods, Inc.
Fantasia Confections, Inc.
The Folger Coffee Company, LLC
Juice Creations Co.
King Kelly, LLC
Knudsen & Sons, Inc.
Martha White Foods, Inc.
Mary Ellen's, Incorporated
Millstone Coffee, Inc.
Milnot Company
RHM Corporation (Canada)

COMPETITORS

B&G Foods	Hansen Natural
Birds Eye	Hershey
Boyd Coffee	H.J. Heinz Limited
Bucks County Coffee	Kraft Foods
Caribou Coffee	National Grape Cooperative
Chiquita Brands	Nestlé
Coca-Cola	Ocean Spray
Coca-Cola North America	PepsiCo
Community Coffee	Pinnacle Foods
ConAgra	Ralcorp
Cranberries Limited	Rowland Coffee Roasters
Darigold, Inc.	Sara Lee Food and
Dean Foods	Beverage
Diedrich Coffee	Spectrum Organic
Dole Food	Products
E.D. Smith	Starbucks
General Mills	Tree Top
Glanbia Foods	Tropicana
Goya	Unilever
Green Mountain Coffee	Welch's

HISTORICAL FINANCIALS

Company Type: Public

Income Statement

				FYE: April 30
	REVENUE ($ mil.)	**NET INCOME** ($ mil.)	**NET PROFIT MARGIN**	**EMPLOYEES**
4/09	3,757.9	266.0	7.1%	4,700
4/08	2,524.8	170.4	6.7%	3,250
4/07	2,148.0	157.2	7.3%	3,025
4/06	2,154.7	143.4	6.7%	3,500
4/05	2,043.9	129.1	6.3%	3,700
Annual Growth	16.4%	19.8%	—	6.2%

2009 Year-End Financials

Debt ratio: 18.4%	No. of shares (mil.): 119
Return on equity: 7.9%	Dividends
Cash ($ mil.): 457	Yield: 3.2%
Current ratio: 1.32	Payout: 41.0%
Long-term debt ($ mil.): 910	Market value ($ mil.): 4,686

Stock History

NYSE: SJM

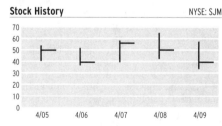

	STOCK PRICE ($) FY Close	P/E High/Low	PER SHARE ($) Earnings	Dividends	Book Value
4/09	39.40	18 11	3.12	1.28	41.54
4/08	49.88	21 14	3.00	1.20	15.13
4/07	55.82	21 14	2.76	1.12	15.10
4/06	39.26	21 15	2.45	1.08	14.53
4/05	49.62	24 18	2.24	1.00	14.22
Annual Growth	(5.6%)	— —	8.6%	6.4%	30.7%

Jo-Ann Stores

Jo-Ann Stores has sewn up the leadership of the fabric store market. The company is the #1 fabric retailer in the US, well ahead of Hancock Fabrics. Jo-Ann Stores sells fabrics and sewing supplies, craft materials, decorating and floral items, and seasonal goods in more than 45 US states. Most of the company's roughly 555 stores, located mainly in strip shopping centers, operate under the Jo-Ann Fabrics and Crafts name. The company also operates about 210 Jo-Ann superstores and an e-commerce site Joann.com. Jo-Ann Stores has closed more than 150 shops in response to weak sales in recent years and is luring non-sewers with arts and crafts and home-decorating items.

The recession in the US may bode well for the company's business, which saw a small uptick in sales of sewing products last year and a modest increase in its sales overall. Changes in consumer behavior, including families spending more time together and making their own gifts and clothes, should help Jo-Ann Stores in the long run.

The chain is pinning its hopes for future growth on its 38,000-sq.-ft. Jo-Ann superstores — more than twice the size of the company's 14,700-sq.-ft. traditional stores. The superstores offer an expanded and more complete assortment of products than the smaller stores. (The company decreased the size of its superstore format from 45,000 sq. ft. to 38,000 sq. ft. in 2003.) In fiscal 2009 the company opened 11 superstores and 10 traditional stores. In fiscal 2010 the retailer's growth is expected to match the previous year.

The retailer is also partnering with celebrities, most recently Christie Brinkley, to raise its profile and spur sales. In spring 2009 the company launched the Christie Brinkley Home collection of organic cotton and other ecologically friendly fabrics.

HISTORY

Jo-Ann Stores' predecessor began in 1943 when the German immigrant Rohrbach family started Cleveland Fabric with the help of fellow immigrants, the Reichs. Alma, daughter of the Rohrbachs, worked at the store and was joined by Betty Reich in 1947.

Betty's and Alma's respective husbands, Martin Rosskamm and Freddy Zimmerman, also joined the company. At the urging of Martin (who eventually became chairman), Cleveland Fabric opened more stores, mainly in malls. As it moved beyond Cleveland, it adopted a new store name — Jo-Ann — devised from the names of Alma and Freddy's daughter Joan and Betty and Martin's daughter Jackie Ann. It changed its name to Fabri-Centers of America in 1968 and went public the following year.

The very postwar boom that brought Alma and Betty into the workforce worked against the company in the 1970s, as women tucked away their sewing baskets in favor of jobs outside their homes. As department stores responded to the trend and stopped offering sewing supplies, specialty fabric stores found a niche. But they soon faced competition from fabric superstores and heavily discounted ready-made clothing.

Martin and Betty's son Alan took over as president and CEO in 1985 and began to modernize the company and the stores. Trained in real estate law, he began focusing on opening larger stores in strip shopping centers, which offered cheaper leases than malls. The company had about 625 stores by mid-1989.

As its industry consolidated, Fabri-Centers held on, despite missteps such as its 1984 launch of the Cargo Express housewares chain (the money-losing venture, with about 40 stores at its peak, ended in 1994). The firm became the nation's #1 fabrics and crafts chain in 1994 when it bought 300-plus Cloth World stores. At the close of that deal, Fabri-Centers had nearly 1,000 stores, with locations in every state except Hawaii.

In 1995 Fabri-Centers opened a store on its home turf in Hudson, Ohio, that offered not only a range of fabric and craft items, but also home decorating merchandise, furniture, craft classes, and day care. At three times the size of its other stores, the Jo-Ann etc superstore helped the company pull in non-sewers looking for art supplies, picture frames, and decorating ideas. Jo-Ann etc became the focus of the company's growth.

Fabri-Centers paid $3.8 million in 1997 to settle SEC charges that it had overstated its profits during a 1992 debt offering. In 1998 it paid nearly $100 million for ailing Los Angeles-based fabric and craft company House of Fabrics, adding about 260 locations and strengthening its West Coast presence. Fabri-Centers then renamed itself Jo-Ann Stores and began placing all of its stores under the Jo-Ann name.

Jo-Ann continued relocating traditional stores and opening new shops while snipping underperforming locations. In 1999 the company signed a pact with Martha Stewart Living Omnimedia to sell fancy decorating fabrics under the Martha Stewart Home name. (As of 2003 the company no longer offers Martha Stewart's fabrics.)

Jo-Ann invested in and partnered with Idea Forest, an Internet-based arts and crafts retailer, in 2000 to run Jo-Ann's e-commerce site. In 2001 the company reported a $13.2 million loss (only the second in its history), in part because of inventory and distribution problems. As a result, Jo-Ann closed more than 90 underperforming stores and reduced the number of items carried in the shops.

In 2003 Jo-Ann Stores bought three stores in the Dallas-Fort Worth area from bankrupt MJDesigns. Those stores had a combined revenue of $16 million during the last fiscal year they operated under the former name.

In September 2005 CFO Brian P. Carney left the firm to join supermarket operator BI-LO.

In January 2006 Jo-Ann Stores eliminated 75 administrative jobs. In April the company completed construction of its new 700,000-sq.-ft. distribution center in Opelika, Alabama. The facility was designed to support growth in the South, specifically in Florida, Georgia, and Texas. Jo-Ann Stores operates two other distribution centers in California and Ohio. In July, Alan Rosskamm stepped down as chairman, president, and CEO (although he remains a director of the company) when Darrell Webb, formerly with Fred Meyer, was appointed to the positions. James Kerr became CFO in August. Previously, Kerr was the retailer's VP, controller, and chief accounting officer.

In 2007 the company acquired full ownership of the Web site Joann.com from IdeaForest.com.

EXECUTIVES

Chairman, President, and CEO: Darrell D. Webb, age 51, $2,151,077 total compensation
COO and EVP Merchandising and Marketing: Travis Smith, age 36, $1,065,206 total compensation
EVP and CFO: James C. Kerr, age 46, $826,214 total compensation
EVP Human Resources: Rosalind Thompson
EVP Store Operations: Ken Haverkost, age 52, $1,152,390 total compensation
SVP, General Counsel, and Secretary: David B. Goldston
VP Controller: Christopher Beem
Regional VP: Edward Dann
VP and General Merchandise Manager, Sewing and Seasonal: Michelle Christensen
Store Development and Facilities: Richard Chapman
Regional VP Mid-Atlantic Region: Kris Christian
Auditors: Ernst & Young LLP

LOCATIONS

HQ: Jo-Ann Stores, Inc.
5555 Darrow Rd., Hudson, OH 44236
Phone: 330-656-2600 **Fax:** 330-463-6675
Web: www.joann.com

2009 Stores

	No.
California	83
Ohio	55
Florida	51
Michigan	46
Pennsylvania	43
New York	38
Texas	36
Illinois	35
Washington	30
Indiana	26
Oregon	24
Massachusetts	23
Virginia	22
Minnesota	20
Wisconsin	18
Maryland	17
Arizona	15
Colorado	14
New Jersey	12
Georgia	12
Missouri	11
Connecticut	10
Iowa	10
Utah	10
Idaho	9
Kansas	8
New Hampshire	8
Montana	7
North Carolina	7
Alaska	6
New Mexico	6
Maine	5
Nevada	5
West Virginia	5
Other states	37
Total	**764**

PRODUCTS/OPERATIONS

2009 Sales

	% of total
Sewing products	51
Non-sewing products	49
Total	**100**

Selected Products

Softlines
  Fabrics
    Apparel fabrics used in the construction of garments (cottons, linens, wools, fleece, and outerwear)
    Craft fabrics (for quilting, craft, and holiday projects)
    Home-decorating fabrics (for window treatments, furniture, and bed coverings)
    Printed fabrics (juvenile designs, seasonal designs, National Football League logo prints, and proprietary print designs)
    Special-occasion fabrics (satins, metallics, and other fabrics for evening wear and bridal gowns)
  Patterns
  Sewing machines
  Sewing notions
    Buttons
    Cutting implements
    Elastics
    Pins
    Ribbons
  Tapes
  Threads
  Trims
  Zippers
Hardlines
  Accessories for arranging flowers and making wreaths
  Craft materials (for making stencils, dolls, jewelry, wood projects, wall décor, rubber stamps, memory books, and plaster)
  Custom floral arrangements
  Decorations
  Fine art materials
    Brushes
    Canvas
    Easels
    Paints (pastels, water colors, oils, and acrylics)
  Floral products line
  Framed art
  Full-service framing
  Gifts
  Hobby items
  Holiday supplies
  Home accessories
    Baskets
    Candles
    Potpourri
  Needlecraft items
  Needles
  Paint-by-number kits
  Paper
  Photo albums
  Picture-framing materials (custom frames, mat boards, glass, and backing materials)
  Plastic model kits and supplies
  Ready-made frames
  Seasonal products
  Silk, dried, and artificial flowers
  Wooden model kits and supplies
  Yarns and threads (for knitting, needlepoint, embroidery, cross-stitching, crocheting, and other stitchery)

COMPETITORS

A.C. Moore
Burnes Home Accents
Garden Ridge
Hancock Fabrics
Hobby Lobby
Kirkland's
Kmart
Martha Stewart Living
Michaels Stores
Pier 1 Imports
Target
Wal-Mart

HISTORICAL FINANCIALS

Company Type: Public

Income Statement

FYE: Saturday nearest January 31

	REVENUE ($ mil.)	NET INCOME ($ mil.)	NET PROFIT MARGIN	EMPLOYEES
1/09	1,901.1	21.9	1.2%	21,708
1/08	1,878.8	15.4	0.8%	21,707
1/07	1,850.6	(2.9)	—	22,280
1/06	1,882.8	(23.0)	—	24,060
1/05	1,812.4	46.2	2.5%	22,251
Annual Growth	1.2%	(17.0%)	—	(0.6%)

2009 Year-End Financials

Debt ratio: 34.0%
Return on equity: 4.8%
Cash ($ mil.): 81
Current ratio: 2.19
Long-term debt ($ mil.): 163
No. of shares (mil.): 26
Dividends
  Yield: 0.0%
  Payout: —
Market value ($ mil.): 338

Stock History

NYSE: JAS

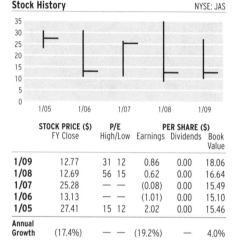

	STOCK PRICE ($) FY Close	P/E High/Low		Earnings	PER SHARE ($) Dividends	Book Value
1/09	12.77	31	12	0.86	0.00	18.06
1/08	12.69	56	15	0.62	0.00	16.64
1/07	25.28	—	—	(0.08)	0.00	15.49
1/06	13.13	—	—	(1.01)	0.00	15.10
1/05	27.41	15	12	2.02	0.00	15.46
Annual Growth	(17.4%)	—	—	(19.2%)	—	4.0%

John Wiley & Sons

John Wiley & Sons might not adorn its books with shirtless hunks, but with such titles as *Patty's Industrial Hygiene and Toxicology*, who needs Fabio? The company publishes scientific, technical, and medical works, including journals and reference works such as *Current Protocols* and *Kirk-Othmer Encyclopedia of Chemical Technology*. All total, it publishes more than 1,500 journal titles. It also produces professional and nonfiction trade books, and is a publisher of college textbooks. The firm publishes the *For Dummies* how-to series, the travel guide brand *Frommer's*, and *CliffsNotes* study guides, as well. Wiley has publishing, marketing, and distribution centers in North America, Europe, Asia, and Australia.

The company's Higher Education division publishes textbooks and other educational materials. The division expanded in 2009, when it acquired the rights to publish a list of business and modern language textbooks from Cengage Learning. The purchase reflects the company's growth strategy of making acquisitions that complement its existing businesses, as the Cengage titles compliment Wiley's existing programs in business and modern language.

Wiley boosted its academic and professional holdings with the acquisition of Blackwell Publishing for $1 billion in 2007, the largest purchase in the company's history. Blackwell subsequently became Wiley-Blackwell, a part of the company's Scientific, Technical, Medical and Scholarly (STMS) division. STMS accounts for about 60% of the company's business. The division's Wiley InterScience is a Web site that gives its journal subscribers online access to most of its periodical titles. It also offers online professional and education exam reviews and other interactive materials, as well as a mobile wireless service.

In addition to STMS and Higher Education, the company operates through its Professional/Trade division (about 25% of sales), which includes titles published under the *For Dummies, Frommer's, Betty Crocker, Weight Watchers, CliffsNotes*, and *Webster's New World* brands.

Wiley's publications are sold throughout the world, and approximately 50% of the company's revenue comes from outside the US.

The Wiley family controls the majority of voting stock through a trust.

HISTORY

Charles Wiley founded a bookstore when he was 25 years old in 1807 and began printing and marketing books for local authors in return for a share of the profits. Soon, prominent writers began meeting in the store's back room (known as "The Den"), which attracted more attention to the business. By the end of the Civil War, the firm (renamed John Wiley & Sons, after Charles' son) had become an established publisher of books on science and technology. Wiley pioneered technical textbooks that became industry standards. In 1899 it published Charles Davenport's *Statistical Methods* and in 1947 Hans Liepmann's *Aerodynamics of a Compressible Fluid,* among others. The company went public in 1962.

In 1989, Wiley acquired Alan R. Liss, a publisher of scientific journals. Four years later Bradford Wiley II took over as chairman of the company. Wiley sold its Canadian high school and Australian primary school textbook subsidiaries the next year and bought the professional computer book line of QED Information Services and UK-based science publisher Belhaven. Wiley teamed with publisher Adweek Magazines in 1995 to print media and marketing books under the name Adweek Books. Also that year the company purchased the publishing operations of Executive Enterprises.

In 1996 Wiley acquired a 90% stake in Germany's VCH Publishing Group, boosting the company's presence in the scientific and technical journal markets. The company increased its Teutonic knowledge base in 1998 by buying German scientific book publisher Huthig Publishing. In addition, it bought the publishing business of Chronimed (which included about 80 titles), a provider of health care products and pharmacy services. Also that year Wiley started working with various online publishers on interactive quizzes in accounting and other educational fields.

In 1999 the company bought a number of college textbook titles from Pearson for $58 million, and later bought San Francisco-based business publisher Jossey-Bass from the same UK company for $82 million.

In 2001 the company bought Hungry Minds, publisher of the *For Dummies* series of how-to books, for about $185 million. The acquisition was the largest in the company's history at that time. It also bought Frank J. Fabozzi Publishing, a finance title publisher based in Pennsylvania. In 2002 the company moved its headquarters from New York to Hoboken, New Jersey. That year the company acquired 250 teacher education titles from Prentice Hall Direct, part of Pearson Education, for $6.5 million.

In 2005 the company sold Chronimed to MIM Corporation (now BioScrip). Wiley expanded in 2007 with the acquisition of Blackwell Publishing.

EXECUTIVES

Chairman: Peter Booth Wiley, age 66
President, CEO, and Director: William J. (Will) Pesce, age 58
EVP and COO: Stephen M. (Steve) Smith, age 54
EVP, CFO, and Operations Officer: Ellis E. Cousens, age 57
SVP Information Technology and CIO:
Warren C. Fristensky
VP, Corporate Controller, and Chief Accounting Officer:
Edward J. Melando, age 53
EVP; President, Professional and Trade Publishing:
Stephen A. Kippur, age 62
SVP Scientific, Technical, Medical, and Scholarly:
Eric A. Swanson, age 61
SVP Higher Education: Bonnie E. Lieberman, age 61
SVP Planning and Development: Timothy B. King, age 69
SVP Human Resources: William J. Arlington, age 60
SVP Corporate Communications: Deborah E. Wiley, age 63
SVP Customer Service and Distribution: Clifford Kline
SVP and General Counsel: Gary M. Rinck, age 57
VP and Corporate Secretary:
Josephine A. Bacchi-Mourtziou, age 62
VP and Treasurer: Vincent Marzano, age 46
Auditors: KPMG LLP

LOCATIONS

HQ: John Wiley & Sons, Inc.
111 River St., Ste. 2000, Hoboken, NJ 07030
Phone: 201-748-6000 **Fax:** 201-748-6088
Web: www.wiley.com

2009 Sales

	$ mil.	% of total
US	812.4	50
Asia	220.1	14
UK	126.2	8
Germany	88.3	6
Canada	67.2	4
Australia	65.1	4
Other regions	232.1	14
Total	**1,611.4**	**100**

PRODUCTS/OPERATIONS

2009 Sales

	$ mil.	% of total
STMS	969.2	60
Professional trade	412.7	26
Higher education	229.5	14
Total	**1,611.4**	**100**

Selected Products

Educational textbooks
Electronic publications
Instructional materials
Online content
Professional books
Scientific, technical, and medical titles
Trade books

Selected Imprints

Betty Crocker
Capstone
CliffsNotes
Current Protocols
For Dummies
Frommer's
InfoPOEMs
Interscience
Jacaranda
J.K. Lasser
Jossey-Bass
Pfeiffer
Webster's New World
Weight Watchers
Wiley
WileyPLUS
Wiley-Blackwell
Wiley Interscience
Wiley-Liss
Wiley/MOAC
Wiley-VCH
Wiley Desktop Editions

COMPETITORS

Bertelsmann
Flat World Knowledge
Goodheart-Willcox
HarperCollins
Houghton Mifflin Holding Company
IHS
Lonely Planet
McGraw-Hill
National Academies Press
O'Reilly Media
Pearson plc
Random House
Reader's Digest
Reed Elsevier Group
Scholastic
Simon & Schuster
Sterling Publishing
Thomson Reuters
Time Inc.
Wolters Kluwer
W.W. Norton

HISTORICAL FINANCIALS

Company Type: Public

Income Statement

FYE: April 30

	REVENUE ($ mil.)	NET INCOME ($ mil.)	NET PROFIT MARGIN	EMPLOYEES
4/09	1,611.4	128.3	8.0%	5,100
4/08	1,673.7	147.5	8.8%	4,800
4/07	1,234.9	99.6	8.1%	4,800
4/06	1,044.2	110.3	10.6%	3,600
4/05	974.0	83.8	8.6%	3,400
Annual Growth	**13.4%**	**11.2%**	—	**10.7%**

2009 Year-End Financials

Debt ratio: 147.0%
Return on equity: 21.3%
Cash ($ mil.): 103
Current ratio: 0.74
Long-term debt ($ mil.): 755
No. of shares (mil.): 58
Dividends
  Yield: 1.5%
  Payout: 24.2%
Market value ($ mil.): 1,979

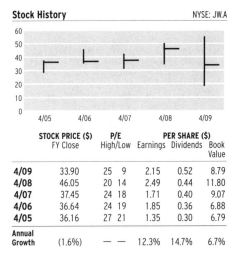

Stock History

NYSE: JW.A

	STOCK PRICE ($) FY Close	P/E High/Low		PER SHARE ($) Earnings	Dividends	Book Value
4/09	33.90	25	9	2.15	0.52	8.79
4/08	46.05	20	14	2.49	0.44	11.80
4/07	37.45	24	18	1.71	0.40	9.07
4/06	36.64	24	19	1.85	0.36	6.88
4/05	36.16	27	21	1.35	0.30	6.79
Annual Growth	**(1.6%)**	—	—	**12.3%**	**14.7%**	**6.7%**

Johnson & Johnson

It's nearly impossible to get well without Johnson & Johnson (J&J). The diversified health care giant operates in three segments through more than 250 operating companies located in some 60 countries. Its Pharmaceuticals division makes drugs for an array of ailments, such as neurological conditions, blood disorders, autoimmune diseases, and pain. Top sellers are schizophrenia medication Risperdal and psoriasis drug Remicade. J&J's Medical Devices and Diagnostics division offers surgical equipment, monitoring devices, orthopedic products, and contact lenses, among other things. Its Consumer segment makes over-the-counter drugs and products for baby care, skin care, oral care, first aid, and women's health.

J&J prides itself on its decentralized operating structure, with the management teams of its myriad and far-flung operating units having wide latitude to make decisions. Each company belongs to one of J&J's three broad divisions.

The company's Pharmaceuticals segment is its largest, accounting for about 40% of sales. Operating companies in the division include Centocor Ortho Biotech, Ortho-McNeil, Janssen, and Noramco. Along with Risperdal and Remicade (which treats Crohn's disease and rheumatoid arthritis in addition to psoriasis), key drugs are epilepsy medicine Topamax, attention deficit drug Concerta, and anti-infectives Floxin and Levaquin.

J&J has confidence that its drug development pipeline will produce some additional winners. The company put antibacterial Doribax and antiretroviral Prezista on the market in 2007 and won approval for HIV drug Intelence in 2008. J&J announced in 2007 plans to seek FDA approval for around 10 new investigational compounds by 2010 in areas including immunology, pain, cardiology, infectious disease, and neurology.

The company's push for R&D growth is driven by the drug industry's biggest challenge: patent expiration. Global blockbusters Risperdal and Topamax lost patent protection in 2008 and thus face competition from cheaper generics. Safety concerns and bad publicity have inflicted wounds on a couple of other J&J brands. Its anemia drug Procrit, which is prescribed for dialysis and chemotherapy patients, came under fire in 2007 after some studies indicated that patients on the drug were at higher risk for strokes, blood clots, heart attacks, and death, as well as possible worsening of their cancer. Another product, contraceptive patch Ortho Evra, is facing lawsuits over claims that the product creates a greater risk for blood clots than do birth control pills.

In response to challenges in its Pharmaceuticals and Medical Device divisions, J&J in 2007 announced a major restructuring aimed at trimming costs in some areas and re-investing in others. The restructuring included job cuts amounting to about 4% of J&J's global workforce.

The restructuring did not preclude expansion in some areas of the business, however. In late 2008, for example, J&J acquired biosurgical products maker Omrix Biopharmaceuticals for $438 million, and in early 2009 it paid about $1.1 billion for Mentor Corporation, a maker of medical products for aesthetic procedures.

Also in 2009 the company paid $885 million for an 18% stake in Irish drug maker Elan. J&J also gained control of Elan's portion of an Alzheimer's disease treatment partnership with Wyeth. J&J has incorporated the Alzheimer's Immunotherapy Program (AIP) into a new company (Janssen Alzheimer Immunotherapy), in which Elan owns a nearly 50% equity interest. J&J will invest up to $500 million toward further development of the drugs in the AIP Program, including lead candidate bapineuzumab, a late-stage antibody (protein) therapy thought to slow the progression of Alzheimer's disease.

A bright spot for J&J has been its Consumer segment, which expanded substantially through the 2006 acquisition of Pfizer's consumer health business. The combined offerings include consumer brands Benadryl, Listerine, Lubriderm, Neutrogena, Rolaids, Splenda, Sudafed, Tylenol, and (of course) Johnson's.

HISTORY

Brothers James and Edward Mead Johnson founded their medical products company in 1885 in New Brunswick, New Jersey. In 1886 Robert joined his brothers to make the antiseptic surgical dressings he developed. The company bought gauze maker Chicopee Manufacturing in 1916. In 1921 it introduced two of its classic products, the Band-Aid and Johnson's Baby Cream.

Robert Jr. became chairman in 1932 and served until 1963. A WWII Army general, he believed in decentralization; managers were given substantial freedom, a principle still used today. Product lines in the 1940s included Ortho (birth control products) and Ethicon (sutures). In 1959 Johnson & Johnson bought McNeil Labs, which launched Tylenol (acetaminophen) as an OTC drug the next year. Foreign acquisitions included Switzerland's Cilag-Chemie (1959) and Belgium's Janssen (1961). The company focused on consumer products in the 1970s, gaining half the feminine protection market and making Tylenol the top-selling painkiller.

J&J bought Iolab, a developer of intraocular lenses used in cataract surgery, in 1980. Trouble struck in 1982 when someone laced Tylenol capsules with cyanide, killing eight people. The

company's response is now a damage-control classic: It immediately recalled 31 million bottles and totally redesigned its packaging to prevent future tampering. The move cost $240 million but saved the Tylenol brand. The next year prescription painkiller Zomax was linked to five deaths and was pulled.

New products in the 1980s included ACUVUE disposable contact lenses and Retin-A. The company bought LifeScan (blood-monitoring products for diabetics) in 1986. In 1989 it began a joint venture with Merck to sell Mylanta and other drugs bought from ICI Americas.

The firm continued its acquisition and diversification strategy in the 1990s. After introducing the first daily-wear, disposable contact lenses in 1993, it bought skin-care product maker Neutrogena (1994) to enhance its consumer lines. To diversify its medical products and better compete for hospital business, it bought Mitek Surgical Products (1995) and heart disease product maker Cordis (1996).

In 1997 J&J bought the OTC rights to Motrin from Pharmacia (now Pfizer). In response to numerous negative events in 1998 — several drugs in late development fell through, rights to an anemia drug were lost, and the company's share of the coronary stent market fell — the firm cut jobs and consolidated plants worldwide to control inventory and improve service.

In 1999 the Ethicon Endo-Surgery unit settled three patent-infringement suits with Tyco International's U.S. Surgical.

After more than 80 deaths were linked to its use, J&J pulled heartburn drug Propulsid from the US market in 2000. The company made headlines in 2002 with its INDEPENDENCE iBOT, a robotic wheelchair capable of climbing staircases and traversing rough terrain, made by subsidiary Independence Technology.

In 2006 the company paid $16.6 billion to acquire Pfizer's consumer products business, which added about 40 brands to J&J's offerings. In order to clear some FTC hurdles, J&J sold US marketing rights for Pfizer's Zantac to Boehringer Ingelheim Pharmaceuticals. J&J also sold five brands (Act mouthwash, Unisom sleep aid, Cortizone anti-itch treatment, Kaopectate antidiarrhea medication, and Balmex for diaper rash) to Chattem.

In 2009 J&J broke into the growing flu vaccine development market by making an investment in Dutch biotech firm Crucell, buying an 18% stake for $443 million and forming a collaboration with Crucell to develop influenza therapies and vaccines based on Crucell's monoclonal antibody technology.

EXECUTIVES

Chairman and CEO: William C. (Bill) Weldon, age 60, $29,392,224 total compensation
VP Finance and CFO: Dominic J. Caruso, age 51, $3,921,028 total compensation
VP and CIO: Laverne H. Council
VP, General Counsel, and Chief Compliance Officer: Russell C. Deyo, age 59, $8,062,240 total compensation
Chief Science and Technology Officer, Device and Diagnostic Unit: Harlan Weisman
VP Investor Relations: Louise Mehrotra
VP Science and Technology: Theodore J. Torphy
VP Human Resources: Kaye I. Foster-Cheek, age 49
VP Public Affairs and Corporate Communications: Raymond Jordan

Worldwide Chairman, Surgical Care Group: Alex Gorsky, age 48
Worldwide Chairman, Consumer Group: Colleen A. Goggins, age 54, $8,490,272 total compensation
Group President, Research and Development: Jay P. Siegel
Worldwide Chairman, Pharmaceuticals Group: Sherilyn S. McCoy, age 50
Worldwide Chairman, Comprehensive Care: Donald M. Casey Jr., age 49
President, Merck Consumer Pharmaceuticals Co.: Calvin Schmidt
President, Ortho Biotech and Centocor: Kim Taylor
Treasurer: John A. Papa
Group Chairman, Pharmaceutical Research and Development: Paul Stoffels
Associate General Counsel and Secretary: Steven M. Rosenberg
Auditors: PricewaterhouseCoopers LLP

LOCATIONS

HQ: Johnson & Johnson
1 Johnson & Johnson Plaza
New Brunswick, NJ 08933
Phone: 732-524-0400   Fax: 732-214-0332
Web: www.jnj.com

2008 Sales

	$ mil.	% of total
US	32,309	51
Europe	16,782	26
Asia/Pacific & Africa	9,483	15
Western Hemisphere, excluding US	5,173	8
Total	**63,747**	**100**

PRODUCTS/OPERATIONS

2008 Sales

	$ mil.	% of total
Pharmaceuticals		
Remicade	3,748	6
Topamax	2,731	4
Procrit/Eprex	2,460	4
Risperdal	2,126	3
Levaquin/Floxin	1,591	2
Risperdal Consta	1,309	2
Concerta	1,247	2
Aciphex/Pariet	1,158	2
Durasesic/Fentanyl transdermal	1,036	2
Other	7,161	11
Medical Devices & Diagnostics		
DePuy	4,989	8
Ethicon Endo-Surgery	4,286	7
Ethicon	3,840	6
Cordis	3,135	5
Diabetes care (LifeScan)	2,535	4
Vision care (Vistakon)	2,500	4
Ortho-Clinical Diagnostics	1,841	3
Consumer		
OTC pharmaceuticals & nutritionals	5,894	9
Skin care	3,381	5
Baby care	2,214	3
Women's health	1,911	3
Oral care	1,624	3
Wound care & other	1,030	2
Total	**63,747**	**100**

COMPETITORS

3M	Forest Labs
Abbott Labs	Genzyme
Affymetrix	GlaxoSmithKline
Alberto-Culver	Kimberly-Clark
Alcon	L'Oréal USA
Alkermes	Medicis Pharmaceutical
Allergan	Medtronic
Amgen	Mentholatum Company
ArthroCare	Merck
AstraZeneca	Mylan
Bard	Novartis
Barr Pharmaceuticals	NutraSweet
Bausch & Lomb	Par Pharmaceutical
Baxter International	Companies
Bayer AG	Perrigo
Beckman Coulter	Pfizer
Becton, Dickinson	Procter & Gamble
Biogen Idec	Roche Holding
Boehringer Ingelheim	Sanofi-Aventis
Boston Scientific	Schering-Plough
Bristol-Myers Squibb	Shire
Chattem	Smith & Nephew
Colgate-Palmolive	St. Jude Medical
Cook Incorporated	Terumo
Covidien	Teva Pharmaceuticals
The Dial Corporation	UCB
Dr. Reddy's	Unilever
Edwards Lifesciences	Watson Pharmaceuticals
Elan	Wyeth
Eli Lilly	

HISTORICAL FINANCIALS

Company Type: Public

Income Statement

FYE: Sunday nearest December 31

	REVENUE ($ mil.)	NET INCOME ($ mil.)	NET PROFIT MARGIN	EMPLOYEES
12/08	63,747.0	12,949.0	20.3%	118,700
12/07	61,095.0	10,576.0	17.3%	119,200
12/06	53,324.0	11,053.0	20.7%	122,200
12/05	50,514.0	10,411.0	20.6%	115,600
12/04	47,348.0	8,509.0	18.0%	109,900
Annual Growth	7.7%	11.1%	—	1.9%

2008 Year-End Financials

Debt ratio: 19.1%
Return on equity: 30.2%
Cash ($ mil.): 10,768
Current ratio: 1.65
Long-term debt ($ mil.): 8,120

No. of shares (mil.): 2,756
Dividends
  Yield: 3.0%
  Payout: 39.2%
Market value ($ mil.): 164,880

Stock History

NYSE: JNJ

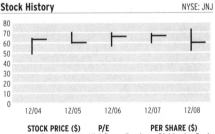

	STOCK PRICE ($) FY Close	P/E High/Low	PER SHARE ($) Earnings	Dividends	Book Value
12/08	59.83	16 11	4.57	1.79	15.43
12/07	66.70	19 16	3.63	1.62	15.72
12/06	66.02	19 15	3.73	1.46	14.27
12/05	60.10	20 17	3.46	1.27	13.74
12/04	63.42	23 17	2.84	1.10	11.54
Annual Growth	(1.4%)	— —	12.6%	12.9%	7.5%

Johnson Controls

Johnson Controls wants to put you in the driver's seat — an environmentally conscious one. The company makes car batteries and interior parts for passenger and hybrid electric vehicles, as well as energy-efficient HVAC systems for commercial buildings. Car interior products include seating, instrument panels, and electronics. Major OEM customers include GM, Daimler, Chrysler, and Ford. The battery unit makes car batteries for retailers such as Advance Auto, AutoZone, Pep Boys, and Wal-Mart. The building efficiency division makes, installs, and services mechanical equipment that controls HVAC, lighting, security, and fire systems in non-residential buildings. The unit also offers on-site facility management.

Responding to lower vehicle production levels in Europe and North America, the company is closing 10 plants, with workforce reductions resulting. Johnson Control first began restructuring its businesses in late 2008, aimed at saving $495 million in costs, then initiated another round of cuts in 2009.

Like most automotive suppliers, Johnson Controls is beefing up its presence in China to be near its customers' greatest geographic growth. Johnson Controls opened its first Chinese factory in 1997, and has since added 11 more to command the largest share of the Chinese seating market. The company is expanding capacity at its Shanghai seat plant to meet increased demand. The company also plans to expand its component offerings beyond seating in China by entering the interior electronics, overhead systems, and cockpits markets. Johnson Controls' purchase of Delphi's global auto battery operations also increased its footprint in Asia, particularly in China.

As increasing numbers of consumers seek out fuel-efficient, low-emission vehicles, Johnson Controls is broadening its expertise in green energy through both acquisitions and collaborations. The year 2008 saw the company's acquisition of PWI Energy, an independent provider of energy and greenhouse gas management services. Johnson Controls also opened the world's first lithium-ion hybrid vehicle battery production facility, which is supplying batteries for a test fleet of Ford Escape plug-in hybrid vehicles, in Nersac, France.

Johnson Controls-Saft, the joint venture between the company and France's SAFT, set plans in 2009 to build a plant for making lithium-ion hybrid batteries in Holland, Michigan.

HISTORY

Professor Warren Johnson developed the electric telethermoscope in 1880 so that janitors at Whitewater, Wisconsin's State Normal School, could regulate room temperatures without disturbing classrooms. His device, the thermostat, used mercury to move a heat element that opened and shut a circuit. Milwaukee hotelier William Plankinton believed in the invention and invested $150,000 to start production.

The two men formed Johnson Electric Service Company in 1885. They sold the marketing, installation, and service rights to concentrate on manufacturing. Johnson also invented other devices such as tower clocks, and he experimented with the telegraph before becoming intrigued with the automobile and beginning

production of steam-powered cars. He won the US Postal Service's first automotive contract, but never gained support within his own company. Johnson continued to look elsewhere for financing until his death in 1911.

The renamed Johnson Services regained full rights to its thermostats in 1912 and sold its other businesses. During the Depression it produced economy systems that regulated building temperatures. Johnson Services became a public company in 1940. During WWII it aided the war effort, building weather-data gatherers and test radar sets.

In the 1960s Johnson Services began developing centralized control systems for temperature, fire alarm, lighting, and security regulation. The company was renamed Johnson Controls in 1974; it acquired automotive battery maker Globe-Union in 1978.

Johnson Controls bought auto seat makers Hoover Universal and Ferro Manufacturing in 1985. It expanded its controls business through the purchases of ITT's European controls group (1982) and Pan Am World Services (1989).

The company sold its car-door components business in 1990 and bought battery maker Varta's Canadian plant. The next year Johnson Controls purchased several car-seat component makers in Europe, and in 1992 it bought a Welsh plastics manufacturer and a Czech seat-cover producer.

The battery unit faced a major setback in 1994, when Sears dropped the company as its battery maker. Two years later, however, the battery business was recharged by an exclusive supply contract with Target stores.

In 1996 Johnson Controls bought most of Roth Frères (auto components) and Prince Automotive (interior systems), becoming a major interior-systems integrator.

Late in 2000 the company bought a 15% stake in Donnelly Corporation (automotive components). In 2001 Johnson Controls paid $435 million in cash for the automotive electronics business of France's Sagem (now SAFRAN). It added the automotive battery operations of Varta AG (Germany) in 2002 and Borg Instruments (automotive electronics) in 2003.

In 2005 Johnson Controls sold its engine electronics division (engine management systems and components) to France's Valeo for about $437 million. The company also sold its Johnson Controls World Services subsidiary to IAP Worldwide Services for about $260 million.

The company's controls division was complemented by Johnson Controls' late 2005 acquisition of York International, the US's third-largest supplier of heating, ventilation, air-conditioning, and refrigeration equipment. The deal was valued at $3.2 billion.

In 2006 Johnson Controls bought Environmental Technologies Inc., a supplier of HVAC equipment. In mid-2006 Johnson Controls announced it would take an estimated after-tax charge of between $130 and $140 million in the third quarter for restructuring. The revamping was aimed at reducing costs at its automotive interiors and facilities management businesses. The plan included the cutting of 5,000 jobs and the closure of 16 plants over one year.

The Building Efficiency division also grew in 2007 with the acquisition of Skymark International, a provider of indoor packaged HVAC equipment. Skymark's self-contained units are used in both new construction and retrofit markets.

Johnson Controls bought financially strapped Plastech Engineered Products' automotive interiors operations in 2008.

EXECUTIVES

Chairman, President, and CEO: Stephen A. Roell, age 58
EVP and CFO: R. Bruce McDonald, age 48
VP Information Technology and CIO: Colin Boyd, age 49
EVP Human Resources: Susan F. Davis, age 55
VP, Secretary, and General Counsel: Jerome D. Okarma, age 56
VP; President, Building Efficiency:
C. David (Dave) Myers, age 45
VP and Treasurer: Frank A. Voltolina, age 48
VP and President, Interior Experience:
Beda-Helmut Bolzenius, age 52
VP and Corporate Controller: Susan M. Kreh, age 46
VP Communication: Jacqueline F. Strayer, age 54
VP; President, Power Solutions: Alex A. Molinaroli, age 49
VP; VP Building Efficiency: Jeffrey G. Augustin, age 46
VP Diversity and Public Affairs: Charles A. Harvey, age 56
VP and General Manager Europe, Automotive Experience: Johannes Roters, age 49
VP and General Manager, Hybrid Systems; CEO, Johnson Controls-Saft Advanced Power Solutions: Mary Ann Wright
VP and General Manager Asia, Building Efficiency:
Wilson Sun
VP and General Manager, Global WorkPlace Solutions:
Guy Holden
VP Government Affairs: Mark Wagner
VP and General Manager, North American Operations:
John Moulton
Auditors: PricewaterhouseCoopers LLP

LOCATIONS

HQ: Johnson Controls, Inc.
5757 N. Green Bay Ave., Milwaukee, WI 53209
Phone: 414-524-1200   **Fax:** 414-524-2077
Web: www.johnsoncontrols.com

2008 Sales

	$ mil.	% of total
US	13,372	35
Europe		
Germany	4,009	10
Other countries	10,956	29
Other regions	9,725	26
Total	**38,062**	**100**

PRODUCTS/OPERATIONS

2008 Sales

	$ mil.	% of total
Automotive experience	18,091	48
Building efficiency	14,121	37
Power solutions	5,850	15
Total	**38,062**	**100**

Selected Products

Automotive experience
Electronics
Body electronics
Driver information
Energy management
Infotainment and connectivity
Interiors
Cockpits and instrument panels
Door panels and systems
Floor consoles
Overhead systems and modules
Seating
Climate systems
Foam
Front seats
Metal structures and mechanisms
Rear seats
Safety systems
Trim

Building efficiency
Building automation and control systems
Fire life safety products
HVAC products
Refrigeration
Safety and security products
Snowmaking equipment
York equipment
Power solutions
Batteries
Plastic battery containers

COMPETITORS

A123 Systems
Addison
Alcatel-Lucent
Ansell
Carrier
Comfort Systems USA
Danaher
Delphi Corp.
DENSO
Eagle-Picher
East Penn Manufacturing
Eaton
Emerson Electric
Exide
Faurecia
GE
General Motors
Goodman Global
GS Yuasa
Hitachi
Honeywell International
Invensys
Johnson Electric
Lear Corp.
Lennox
Magna International
Paloma Co.
Rieter Automotive North America
Robert Bosch
Siemens AG
SPX
Textron
Trane Inc.
Tyco
Valeo
Visteon
Yazaki North America

HISTORICAL FINANCIALS

Company Type: Public

Income Statement

FYE: September 30

	REVENUE ($ mil.)	NET INCOME ($ mil.)	NET PROFIT MARGIN	EMPLOYEES
9/08	38,062.0	979.0	2.6%	140,000
9/07	34,624.0	1,252.0	3.6%	140,000
9/06	32,235.0	1,035.0	3.2%	136,000
9/05	27,479.4	909.4	3.3%	114,000
9/04	26,553.4	815.7	3.1%	123,000
Annual Growth	**9.4%**	**4.7%**	**—**	**3.3%**

2008 Year-End Financials

Debt ratio: 34.0%
Return on equity: 10.7%
Cash ($ mil.): 384
Current ratio: 1.09
Long-term debt ($ mil.): 3,201
No. of shares (mil.): 595
Dividends
Yield: 1.7%
Payout: 31.9%
Market value ($ mil.): 18,046

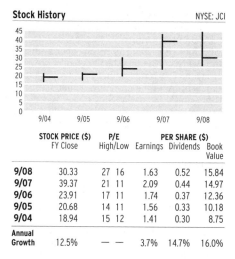

Stock History   NYSE: JCI

	STOCK PRICE ($) FY Close	P/E High/Low	Earnings	PER SHARE ($) Dividends	Book Value
9/08	30.33	27 16	1.63	0.52	15.84
9/07	39.37	21 11	2.09	0.44	14.97
9/06	23.91	17 11	1.74	0.37	12.36
9/05	20.68	14 11	1.56	0.33	10.18
9/04	18.94	15 12	1.41	0.30	8.75
Annual Growth	**12.5%**	**— —**	**3.7%**	**14.7%**	**16.0%**

Jones Apparel

While some are busy keeping up with the Joneses, Jones Apparel Group is too busy taking stock in its portfolio of brands to take notice. It provides a wide range of women's and men's clothing and shoes. Jones owns and operates about 1,015 outlet and specialty stores. Its brands include Jones New York and Evan-Picone, among many others. Subsidiary Nine West Group designs shoes under the names Easy Spirit, Enzo Angiolini, Bandolino, and Gloria Vanderbilt. Gloria Vanderbilt and l.e.i. design twill and denim casualwear, swimwear, and accessories. The company sold its luxury fashion retailer Barneys New York in 2007 to focus on its other brands.

A significant portion of the company's sales are to retailers, who peddle their products in the US and Canada. Macy's, alone, generated about 21% of the company's 2008 gross revenue. Hoping to benefit from the breadth of uber retailer Wal-Mart, Jones inked a deal with the company in February 2008 to make Wal-Mart the exclusive retailer of the l.e.i. brand.

Jones's products are manufactured — mainly by third parties — in Asia (mostly), the Middle East, and Africa. Footwear is made in China. The company also licenses its Jones New York and Evan-Picone brand names to other makers of women's and men's apparel and accessories. The company reached the Asian market in June 2008 by purchasing a 10% equity interest in GRI, an international brand-management firm that concentrates on accessories and apparel, as well as retail distribution. Jones's more than $20 million investment had secured its foothold in Asia, as GRI operates in a dozen countries and is the exclusive licensee for several Jones brands, such as Nine West, Easy Spirit, and Enzo Angiolini, among others. Looking to strengthen its commitment to Asia, Jones in June 2009 increased its ownership interest in GRI to 25%.

During the past several years, Jones has been restructuring various parts of its businesses to reduce excess capacity and decrease its dependency on licensed wholesale products. To that end, the company sold its luxury department store chain Barneys in late 2007 for $945 million. Previously, the firm sold its Polo Jeans Company apparel business to Polo Ralph Lauren in 2006.

Despite a downturn in the economy worldwide, Jones is keeping its eye on opportunities to grow when consumers start to spend more readily again. The company in 2008 jumped into a joint venture with Rachel Roy, Damon Dash, and TSM Capital to market Roy's New York-based fashion brand. Jones Apparel holds a 50% stake in the venture, as it continues to invest in the global designer business.

HISTORY

When diversifying chemical firm W. R. Grace & Co. began a brief foray into the fashion world in 1970, it hired Sidney Kimmel to run the show. Kimmel had worked in a knitting mill in the 1950s and served as president of women's sportswear maker Villager in the 1960s. He and his companion, designer Rena Rowan, created Grace's fashionable but moderately priced Jones New York line.

Kimmel and Grace's accountant, Gerard Rubin, bought Grace's fashion division in 1975, incorporating it as Jones Apparel Group. Jones expanded quickly by bringing out new labels and licensing others, such as Christian Dior. Talks to sell the company to underwear maker Warnaco fell through in 1981.

Tapping into two trends of the early 1980s, Jones Apparel offered the sweatsuit fashions of Norma Kamali and in 1984 acquired the license for the Gloria Vanderbilt line from Murjani. Swan-adorned Gloria Vanderbilt jeans had been must-haves early in the decade, but the deal turned into an ugly duckling as costs beyond Jones Apparel's control pushed the company into the red. (Meanwhile, Kimmel produced the films *9 1/2 Weeks* and *Clan of the Cave Bear* and led a group that briefly controlled the Famous Amos Cookie Co.)

Creditors forced Jones Apparel to unload most of its brands — all but Jones New York, Saville, and Christian Dior — and cut jobs, and by 1988 it was profitable again. Kimmel bought Rubin's interest in the company in 1989 and took it public in 1991, retaining about half of the stock.

In the early 1990s, as recession-minded shoppers looked for bargains and the American workplace became more casual, Jones again took off. The company expanded with new lines, such as Rena Rowan (inexpensive suits) and Jones & Co. (career casuals). Jones Apparel moved into women's accessories with the 1993 purchase of the Evan-Picone brand name.

Two years later the company struck its first licensing agreement with Polo Ralph Lauren, for the Lauren by Ralph Lauren line of women's sportswear. Propelled by the new line, Jones reached $1 billion in sales in 1996.

Jones Apparel licensed Ralph by Ralph Lauren, a lower-priced juniors' line, in 1998. That year it purchased Sun Apparel, picking up the rights to Todd Oldham and Polo jeans, and in 1999 it bought the remaining clothing, footwear, cosmetics, and apparel rights to the youth-oriented Oldham name.

The firm then made its biggest acquisition by far when it paid $1.4 billion for shoe designer and retailer Nine West Group (Easy Spirit, Enzo Angiolini, Bandolino, Amalfi).

With the Nine West purchase, Jones Apparel inherited an FTC investigation into the footwear designer's pricing policies. The company closed several Nine West facilities in 1999, cutting about 1,900 jobs, followed by the sale of its retail operations in Canada (1999), Asia (2000), and the UK (2001).

Continuing its acquisition spree, the company agreed to purchase Gloria Vanderbilt Apparel in March 2002. In May president Peter Boneparth was named CEO after Kimmel stepped down (he remains as chairman). Jones Apparel bought RSV Sport, maker of l.e.i. jeanswear for girls, in August 2002.

In 2003 Jones announced plans to close some of its manufacturing facilities, cut jobs, and convert most of its Angiolini shoe stores into more successful Bandolino stores.

The company shut down its Rena Rowan business in 2004; meanwhile, Jones closed the Barneys New York deal for about $400 million.

The company has held the exclusive license to produce Lauren-branded apparel in Canada, Mexico, and the US for the Polo Ralph Lauren Corp. The deal, however, spurred litigation over control of the brand. In 2006 Jones and Polo Ralph Lauren agreed to a settlement. Polo Ralph Lauren paid Jones some $355 million for the Jones Sun Apparel subsidiary that operates the brand and for a controlling ownership of the brand in the US.

EXECUTIVES

Chairman: Sidney Kimmel, age 81, $1,329,225 total compensation
President, CEO, and Director: Wesley R. Card, $5,482,687 total compensation
COO: Cynthia (Cindy) DiPietrantonio
CFO: John T. McClain, age 47, $1,437,496 total compensation
EVP and CTO: Paul Lanham
EVP, Chief Accounting Officer, and Controller: Christopher R. Cade, age 41
EVP Human Resources: Aida Tejero-DeColli
EVP Corporate Quality and Production: Ronald Harrison, age 61
EVP, General Counsel, and Secretary: Ira M. Dansky, age 63, $1,169,163 total compensation
EVP Marketing: Stacy Lastrina
EVP Production, Better Sportwear Divisions: Douglas (Doug) Means, age 43
EVP Distribution Operations: Mike Kauffman
EVP Management Information Services: Norman (Norm) Veit
SVP Product Development, Jeanswear: Mehmet Tangoren
SVP Corporate Taxation and Risk Management and Treasurer: Joseph Donnalley
SVP Merchandising, Nine West Accessories: Tobi Snyder
CEO Wholesale Footwear and Accessories: Andrew (Andy) Cohen, age 59, $2,201,834 total compensation
Auditors: BDO Seidman, LLP

LOCATIONS

HQ: Jones Apparel Group, Inc.
1411 Broadway, New York, NY 10018
Phone: 212-642-3860   **Fax:** 215-785-1795
Web: www.jny.com

2008 Sales

	$ mil.	% of total
US	3,279.0	91
International	337.4	9
Total	**3,616.4**	**100**

PRODUCTS/OPERATIONS

2008 Sales

	$ mil.	% of total
Wholesale better apparel	1,098.7	30
Wholesale footwear & accessories	938.3	26
Wholesale jeanswear	796.5	22
Retail	730.2	20
Licensing & other	52.7	2
Total	**3,616.4**	**100**

2008 Sales

	$ mil.	% of total
Net sales	3,562.6	99
Licensing	52.1	1
Service & other revenues	1.7	—
Total	**3,616.4**	**100**

2008 Stores

	No.
Outlet	644
Specialty retail	373
Total	**1,017**

Selected Brand Affiliates

Jones New York
Nine West
Anne Klein
Gloria Vanderbilt
Kasper
Bandolino
Easy Spirit
Evan-Picone
l.e.i.
Energie
Enzo Angiolini
Joan & David
Mootsies Tootsies
Sam & Libby
Napier
Judith Jack
Le Suit
Givenchy (costume jewelry licensed from Givenchy Corporation)
Dockers Women (footwear licensed from Levi Strauss & Co.)

COMPETITORS

AnnTaylor	Hampshire Group
Bally	Iconix Brand Group
bebe stores	IT Holding
Berkshire Hathaway	J. Jill Group
Bernard Chaus	Kenneth Cole
Bill Blass	Levi Strauss
Brown Shoe	Liz Claiborne
Caché	Nordstrom
Calvin Klein	Phillips-Van Heusen
Chico's FAS	Polo Ralph Lauren
Coach, Inc.	Salvatore Ferragamo
Coldwater Creek	Skechers U.S.A.
Collective Brands	St. John Knits
Donna Karan	Steven Madden
Ellen Tracy	Talbots
Etienne Aigner Group	VF
Gucci	

HISTORICAL FINANCIALS

Company Type: Public

Income Statement				FYE: December 31
	REVENUE ($ mil.)	NET INCOME ($ mil.)	NET PROFIT MARGIN	EMPLOYEES
12/08	3,616.4	(765.4)	—	7,925
12/07	3,848.5	311.1	8.1%	8,450
12/06	4,742.8	(146.0)	—	16,485
12/05	5,074.2	274.3	5.4%	18,430
12/04	4,649.7	301.8	6.5%	17,260
Annual Growth	**(6.1%)**	**—**	**—**	**(17.7%)**

2008 Year-End Financials

Debt ratio: 44.7%
Return on equity: —
Cash ($ mil.): 338
Current ratio: 2.13
Long-term debt ($ mil.): 529

No. of shares (mil.): 85
Dividends
Yield: 9.6%
Payout: —
Market value ($ mil.): 500

Stock History

NYSE: JNY

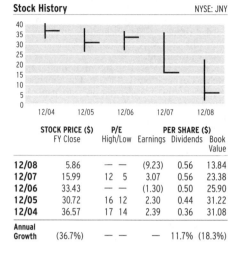

	STOCK PRICE ($) FY Close	P/E High/Low		PER SHARE ($) Earnings	Dividends	Book Value
12/08	5.86	—	—	(9.23)	0.56	13.84
12/07	15.99	12	5	3.07	0.56	23.38
12/06	33.43	—	—	(1.30)	0.50	25.90
12/05	30.72	16	12	2.30	0.44	31.22
12/04	36.57	17	14	2.39	0.36	31.08
Annual Growth	(36.7%)	—	—	—	11.7%	(18.3%)

Jones Lang LaSalle

Borders mean little to Jones Lang LaSalle. The giant real estate services company helps its customers buy, sell, and manage property in more than 60 countries on five continents. It offers property and project management, leasing, and tenant representation for a variety of properties including offices, hotels, retail, industrial, residential, hospital, and entertainment venues. Jones Lang LaSalle's financial services include investment banking and corporate and real estate financing. The firm also offers real estate investment management services to pension funds, insurance firms, and money managers. It has nearly $50 billion in assets under management and a total portfolio of 1.4 billion sq. ft. worldwide.

During the past several years, Jones Lang LaSalle has completed more than 25 strategic acquisitions intended to expand its capabilities in certain service areas and gain share in key markets. These deals have been completed in Australia, England, Finland, France, Germany, Hong Kong, Japan, Scotland, Spain, Sweden, and the US.

With the acquisition of Spaulding & Slye, Jones Lang LaSalle increased its expertise in leasing, project management, investment sales, and consulting and development. It also increased its footprint in the lucrative New England region, Spaulding & Sly's home territory, and retained the Spaulding brand under the names Spaulding & Slye Investments and Spaulding & Slye Construction.

Jones Lang LaSalle increased its presence in key US markets when it merged with The Staubach Company in 2008. The company paid $613 million for the rival real estate services firm, which was founded by football legend and former Dallas Cowboys quarterback Roger Staubach.

Another one of its more interesting deals occurred in 2007 when it bought a 45% interest in the former Trammell Crow Meghraj, one of the largest private real estate services companies in India. (It has agreed to acquire the remaining interests in 2010 and 2012.) The new company operates as Jones Lang LaSalle Meghraj in 10 cities and has some 44 million sq. ft. under management.

Although Jones Lang LaSalle has been on a shopping spree, the company expects much of its acquisition activity will be curtailed at least through 2009 as it tries to maintain a healthy balance sheet in tumultuous market conditions.

Ariel Capital Management owns about 14% of the company, down from more than 20% in 2006.

HISTORY

Jones Lang Wootton had roots in London's Paternoster Row auction houses in 1783. LaSalle Partners, originally known as IDC Real Estate, was founded in El Paso, Texas, in 1968. The two companies could not have started out in a more disparate fashion, yet their combined force is now one of the largest real estate services firms in the world.

Richard Winstanley opened an auction house in 1783, and his son James joined him in that business in 1806. In 1840, the Joneses entered the picture — the Winstanleys created a partnership with one James Jones. The business moved to King Street (in the Guildhall section of London) in 1860 and remained in that location for some 100 years in various incarnations — James' son Frederick took over the business, renaming it Frederick Jones and Co. When James retired in 1872, the firm was again renamed, to Jones Lang and Co., and was controlled by C. A. Lang. Jones Lang merged with Wootton and Son in 1939, becoming Jones Lang Wootton and Sons.

Jones Lang Wootton was active in redrawing the property lines in London after the Blitz. In 1945, the firm began contacting small landowners and by combining small parcels of land, secured development, leasing, and/or purchase contracts. When the rebuilding of London began in 1954, Jones Lang Wootton was in a secure place to be right at the forefront of that new development. The firm began engaging in speculative development in the West End and in the City of London.

1958 saw the expansion of Jones Lang Wootton into Australia; the firm had offices throughout the Asia Pacific region by 1968. Further expansion took place closer to home in Scotland (1962) and Ireland (1965), and the first continental European office in Brussels (also 1965). The firm moved into the Manhattan market in 1975.

On the other side of the story, IDC Real Estate (the name change to LaSalle Partners came in 1977) was a group of partnerships, initially focused on investment banking, investment management, and land. The firm began offering development management services in 1975; it moved into property management, leasing, and tenant representation in 1978 and facility management operations in 1980.

It built market share by buying other firms, including Kleinwort Benson Realty Advisors Corp. (1994) and UK-based investment adviser CIN Property Management (1996).

The firm leveraged its experience and long-term client base to pursue an acquisition strategy, taking advantage of trends shaping commercial real estate — globalization, consolidation, and merchant banking. LaSalle went public in 1997, amalgamating the Galbreath Company (a property and development management firm with which it merged that year) with its other partnerships and becoming a corporation.

In 1998 it acquired the project management business of Satulah Group and two retail management business units from Lend Lease, and took real estate investment trust LaSalle Hotel Properties public. In 1999 the firm strengthened its world position by merging with Jones Lang Wootton; the company was renamed Jones Lang LaSalle.

The merger with Jones Lang Wootton combined Wootton's strength in Asia and Europe with LaSalle Partners' large presence in North America to create a worldwide real estate services firm.

EXECUTIVES

Chairman: Sheila A. Penrose, age 63
President, CEO, and Director: Colin Dyer, age 56, $3,187,065 total compensation
EVP, COO, CFO, and Director: Lauralee E. Martin, age 58, $3,578,406 total compensation
CIO: David A. Johnson
EVP and Chief Human Resources Officer: Nazneen Razi, age 56
Chief Marketing and Communications Officer: Charles J. Doyle, age 48
EVP, Global General Counsel, and Corporate Secretary: Mark J. Ohringer, age 50
EVP and Manager Global Finance Operations: Stanley (Stan) Stec, age 50
EVP: David Hendrickson
EVP and Global Controller: Mark K. Engel, age 37
Chairman, LaSalle Investment Management: Lynn C. Thurber, age 62
President, Global Client Services: John G. Minks, age 53
Chairman, Asia Pacific and Jones Lang Lasalle Hotels: Peter A. Barge, age 59, $2,505,088 total compensation
Chairman, Corporate Solutions: John Phillips
Executive Chairman, Americas; Director: Roger T. Staubach, age 67
CEO, Capital Markets: Earl E. Webb, age 46
CEO, LaSalle Investment Management: Jeff A. Jacobson, age 47, $3,514,435 total compensation
CEO, Americas: Peter C. Roberts, age 48, $2,269,407 total compensation
CEO, Asia Pacific: Alastair Hughes, age 43, $1,722,185 total compensation
International Director: Robert S. Orr, age 45
Auditors: KPMG LLP

LOCATIONS

HQ: Jones Lang LaSalle Incorporated
200 E. Randolph Dr., Chicago, IL 60601
Phone: 312-782-5800 **Fax:** 312-782-4339
Web: www.joneslanglasalle.com

PRODUCTS/OPERATIONS

2008 Sales

	$ mil.	% of total
Investor and occupier services	2,340.3	87
Investment management	351.8	13
Adjustments	5.5	—
Total	**2,697.6**	**100**

Selected Services

Investor services
  Agency leasing
  Property management
  Valuations and consulting
Occupier services
  Facilities management
  Project and development services
  Tenant representation
Construction management
Capital markets
Energy and sustainability services
Hotel advisory
Money management
Strategic consulting

COMPETITORS

CB Richard Ellis	Lend Lease
Colliers International	Realogy
Cushman & Wakefield	Shorenstein
Grubb & Ellis	Studley
Hines	Trammell Crow Company
Inland Group	

HISTORICAL FINANCIALS

Company Type: Public

Income Statement
FYE: December 31

	REVENUE ($ mil.)	NET INCOME ($ mil.)	NET PROFIT MARGIN	EMPLOYEES
12/08	2,697.6	84.9	3.1%	36,200
12/07	2,652.1	257.8	9.7%	32,700
12/06	2,013.6	175.2	8.7%	25,500
12/05	1,366.8	103.3	7.6%	22,000
12/04	1,167.0	64.2	5.5%	19,300
Annual Growth	23.3%	7.2%	—	17.0%

2008 Year-End Financials

Debt ratio: 45.3%	No. of shares (mil.): 42
Return on equity: 8.2%	Dividends
Cash ($ mil.): 46	Yield: 2.7%
Current ratio: 1.01	Payout: 30.7%
Long-term debt ($ mil.): 484	Market value ($ mil.): 1,157

Stock History
NYSE: JLL

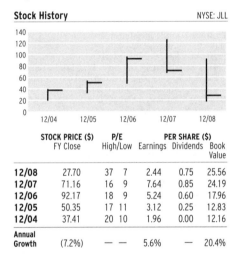

	STOCK PRICE ($) FY Close	P/E High/Low		PER SHARE ($) Earnings	Dividends	Book Value
12/08	27.70	37	7	2.44	0.75	25.56
12/07	71.16	16	9	7.64	0.85	24.19
12/06	92.17	18	9	5.24	0.60	17.96
12/05	50.35	17	11	3.12	0.25	12.83
12/04	37.41	20	10	1.96	0.00	12.16
Annual Growth	(7.2%)	—	—	5.6%	—	20.4%

Joy Global

Joy Global is pretty peppy for a company that builds equipment that is destined to spend the majority of its life down in a hole. The company makes heavy equipment for the mining industry through two subsidiaries. Its Joy Mining Machinery subsidiary makes underground coal-mining equipment that includes armored face conveyors, roof supports, longwall shearers, and shuttle cars. Subsidiary P&H Mining Equipment makes draglines, blasthole drills, and other equipment used by surface miners; it also provides parts and services to mines through its P&H MinePro Services group. Joy Global, which operates manufacturing and service facilities worldwide, makes more than half of its sales outside the US.

In early 2008 Joy Global acquired Continental Global Group (now known as Continental

Crushing & Conveying), a maker of conveyor systems and material handling machinery used in mining and other industrial applications. The deal, valued at about $270 million, complements Joy Global's surface and underground mining equipment offerings in international markets for iron ore, copper, coal, and oil sands. Also in 2008 the company expanded its position in China with the acquisition of Wuxi Shengda, which makes longwall shearing machines used by mining firms.

HISTORY

In the mid-1880s German immigrant Henry Harnischfeger and partner Alonzo Pawling started Pawling and Harnischfeger (P&H), a small machine and pattern shop, in Milwaukee. The company shipped its first overhead electric crane in 1888. After a fire destroyed its main shop in 1903, P&H built a new plant in West Milwaukee the following year that became the world's leading manufacturer of overhead cranes. The company became Harnischfeger Corporation after Pawling died in 1914. In remembrance of Pawling, Harnischfeger kept its P&H trademark.

The highly cyclical heavy-equipment industry encountered a big upswing with WWI. After the war, Harnischfeger began selling excavating and mining equipment to help weather downturns in the industry. Harnischfeger died in 1930, and his son Walter became president. The Depression was hard for the company, as it lost money every year from 1931 to 1939. Harnischfeger diversified into welding equipment, diesel engines, and prefabricated houses during the 1930s and 1940s.

WWII and the postwar period boosted the company, and Harnischfeger was listed on the AMEX in 1956. Walter became chairman in 1959, and his son Henry became president. Harnischfeger streamlined operations in the 1960s, keeping its construction and mining division and its industrial and electrical division.

Harnischfeger was listed on the NYSE in 1971. After the 1973 oil embargo, its machinery sales increased with the opening of coal reserves and the construction of oil pipelines and mass transit systems. By the end of the 1970s, however, recession and high interest rates took their toll on the company.

On the verge of bankruptcy in the early 1980s, Harnischfeger revived itself by trimming down, diversifying, and making key acquisitions. It formed Harnischfeger Engineering in 1984 (sold in the early 1990s), and in 1986 the company bought Beloit (papermaking equipment) and formed Harnischfeger Industries as a holding company.

Harnischfeger began moving away from systems handling in the early 1990s. It bought underground mining equipment maker Joy Technologies (now Joy Mining Machinery) in 1994 and Longwall International (through the acquisition of Dobson Park Industries) in 1995. The next year Harnischfeger bought Ingersoll-Rand's pulp machinery division. In 1997 the company's $631 million bid for Giddings & Lewis (machine tools) was thwarted when Giddings & Lewis agreed to be acquired by Thyssen (now ThyssenKrupp AG).

After the Asian economic crisis and other factors weakened demand for its papermaking and mining equipment, Harnischfeger announced in 1998 it would be laying off about 20% of its workforce — about 3,100 jobs. Harnischfeger also sold an 80% stake in P&H Material Handling to Chartwell Investments for $340 million that year.

In 1999 Harnischfeger rearranged the terms of $500 million in loans and obtained an additional $250 million term loan. CEO Jeffery Grade, also chairman since 1993, stepped down. Grade spearheaded the company's aggressive growth strategy, which was stymied by slips in demand for the company's machinery due to weak prices for metal and paper. President John Hanson succeeded Grade as CEO. Unable to keep up with its debt, the company filed for Chapter 11 bankruptcy protection.

Creditors accepted a $160 million offer from Metso Corporation in 2000 to buy Beloit's assets, including its roll cover division, paper machine aftermarket assets, and related paper machine technology. Harnischfeger emerged from bankruptcy and changed its name to Joy Global Inc. in 2001.

Orders for new equipment were soft in 2002, although limited sales were offset by paced revenue growth through the company's operations in China. In 2003 Joy Global completed the purchase of the remaining 25% interest in P&H-Australia (surface mining equipment) that it didn't already own.

P&H sold its subsidiary The Horsburgh & Scott Co., a manufacturer of industrial gears and mechanical gear drives, in November 2005. The following year Joy Global purchased the Stamler business of Oldenburg Group, Inc. for $118 million. Stamler's products, used in underground and surface coal mining, included feeder breakers, battery haulers, and continuous haulage systems.

Also in 2006 EVP Michael Sutherlin succeeded John Hanson as president and CEO; Hanson remained chairman. Sutherlin previously served as president and COO of Joy Mining Machinery for three years.

EXECUTIVES

Chairman: John N. Hanson, age 67
President, CEO, and Director: Michael W. Sutherlin, age 62
EVP; President and COO, Joy Mining Machinery: Edward L. (Ted) Doheny II, age 47
EVP, CFO, and Treasurer: Michael S. (Mike) Olsen, age 57
EVP, Human Resources: Dennis R. Winkleman, age 58
EVP, General Counsel, and Secretary: Sean D. Major, age 44
President and COO, Continental Crushing & Conveying and EVP, Joy Global Inc.: Terry Nicola
VP, Investor Relations and Corporate Communications: Sara Leuchter Wilkins, age 54
Auditors: Ernst & Young LLP

LOCATIONS

HQ: Joy Global Inc.
100 E. Wisconsin Ave., Ste. 2780
Milwaukee, WI 53202
Phone: 414-319-8500   **Fax:** 414-319-8520
Web: www.joyglobal.com

2008 Sales

	$ mil.	% of total
US	1,632.5	48
Australia	470.5	14
Europe	363.2	10
Other regions	952.7	28
Total	**3,418.9**	**100**

PRODUCTS/OPERATIONS

2008 Sales

	$ mil.	% of total
Underground mining equipment	1,736.5	51
Surface mining equipment	1,431.4	42
Crushing & conveying	251.0	7
Total	**3,418.9**	**100**

Selected Products

Underground mining machinery
  Armored face conveyors
  Complete longwall mining systems
  Continuous chain haulage systems
  Continuous miners
  Feeder breakers
  Flexible conveyor trains
  Longwall shearers
  Roof bolters
  Roof supports
  Shuttle cars
Surface mining equipment
  Electric mining shovels
  Rotary blasthole drills
  Walking draglines

COMPETITORS

Bucyrus	Marmon Group
Caterpillar	Metso
Hitachi	Multi-Shifter
Howle Holdings	Rowan Companies
Ingersoll-Rand	Sandvik
Jervis B. Webb	Sime Darby
Komatsu	Terex

HISTORICAL FINANCIALS

Company Type: Public

Income Statement

FYE: Saturday nearest October 31

	REVENUE ($ mil.)	NET INCOME ($ mil.)	NET PROFIT MARGIN	EMPLOYEES
10/08	3,418.9	374.3	10.9%	11,800
10/07	2,547.3	279.8	11.0%	9,200
10/06	2,401.7	414.9	17.3%	8,900
10/05	1,927.5	148.0	7.7%	7,900
10/04	1,432.2	55.3	3.9%	7,700
Annual Growth	24.3%	61.3%	—	11.3%

2008 Year-End Financials

Debt ratio: 101.6%	No. of shares (mil.): 102
Return on equity: 59.6%	Dividends
Cash ($ mil.): 202	Yield: 2.2%
Current ratio: 1.52	Payout: 18.3%
Long-term debt ($ mil.): 541	Market value ($ mil.): 2,963

Stock History

NASDAQ (GS): JOYG

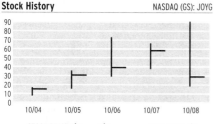

	STOCK PRICE ($) FY Close	P/E High/Low		PER SHARE ($) Earnings	Dividends	Book Value
10/08	28.98	26	6	3.45	0.63	5.21
10/07	58.06	26	15	2.51	0.60	7.08
10/06	39.11	21	9	3.38	0.41	9.00
10/05	30.58	29	13	1.20	0.28	6.53
10/04	15.02	35	18	0.46	0.12	4.42
Annual Growth	17.9%	—	—	65.5%	51.4%	4.2%

JPMorgan Chase

JPMorgan Chase was born with a silver spoon in its mouth but that hasn't stopped it. One of the largest financial services firms in the US, the company has more than 5,000 bank branches in some two dozen states (and growing) and is also among the nation's top mortgage lenders and credit card issuers. Active in some 60 countries, it also boasts formidable investment banking and asset management operations. The company's subsidiaries include the prestigious JPMorgan Private Bank and institutional investment manager JPMorgan Asset Management (with some $1.5 trillion in assets under supervision). In 2008 JPMorgan Chase bought Bear Stearns and followed that up with Washington Mutual (WaMu).

JPMorgan Chase made a bargain-basement offer of $270 million (around $2 a share) for its struggling rival, Bear Stearns, although it later raised its offer to around $10 a share, or some $1.2 billion. The high-profile deal came after the Fed extended a $30 billion lifeline to Bear Stearns, which had been drowning in subprime mortgage investment debt.

It also stepped in to buy WaMu when that bank failed and was seized by regulators later that year. JPMorgan paid $1.9 billion for the bank and assumed some $31 billion in losses. JPMorgan is combining WaMu's branches with its own retail network, but plans to close about 10% of the total 5,400 branches in some markets where there is overlap. In late 2008 JPMorgan also announced that it would cut 9,200 WaMu jobs — about 20% of its workforce.

As part of a plan to stimulate the economy, the US government invested in JPMorgan Chase and other banks. The bank got $25 billion of the $700 billion taxpayer-funded bailout package that was approved in late 2008. The investment came with restrictions on executive pay and other rules, and JPMorgan returned the money the following year, saying it was doing just fine without it.

Among other operations, JPMorgan Chase owns private equity firm One Equity Partners and 44% of mutual fund company American Century. In 2008 it assumed full ownership of payments processor Chase Paymentech Solutions, which had been a joint venture with First Data. First Data assumed 49% of Chase Paymentech's assets and clients in the deal.

In 2009 JPMorgan Chase acquired full ownership of hedge fund Highbridge Capital Management, which has some $21 billion in assets under management.

HISTORY

JPMorgan Chase & Co.'s roots are in The Manhattan Company, created in 1799 to bring water to New York City. A provision buried in its incorporation documents let the company provide banking services; investor and future US Vice President Aaron Burr brought the company (eventually the Bank of Manhattan) into competition with The Bank of New York, founded by Burr's political rival Alexander Hamilton. JPMorgan Chase still owns the pistols from the notorious 1804 duel in which Burr mortally wounded Hamilton.

In 1877 John Thompson formed Chase National, naming it for Salmon Chase, Abraham Lincoln's secretary of the treasury and the architect of the national bank system. Chase National

merged with John D. Rockefeller's Equitable Trust in 1930, becoming the world's largest bank and beginning a long relationship with the Rockefellers. Chase National continued growing after WWII, and in 1955 it merged with the Bank of Manhattan. Christened Chase Manhattan, the bank remained the US's largest into the 1960s.

When soaring 1970s oil prices made energy loans attractive, Chase invested in Penn Square, an obscure oil-patch bank in Oklahoma and the first notable bank failure of the 1980s. (The legal aftereffects of Penn Square's 1982 failure dragged on until 1993.) Losses following the 1987 foreign loan crisis hit the company hard, as did the real estate crash. In 1995 the bank went looking for a partner. After talks with Bank of America, it settled on Chemical Bank.

Chemical Bank opened in 1824 and was one of the US's largest banks by 1900. As with Chase, Chemical Bank began as an unrelated business (New York Chemical Manufacturing) in 1823, largely in order to open a bank (it dropped its chemical operations in 1844). Chemical would merge with Manufacturers Hanover in 1991.

After its 1996 merger with Chase, Chemical Bank was the surviving entity but assumed Chase's more prestigious name. In 1997 Chase acquired the credit business of The Bank of New York and the corporate trustee business of Mellon Financial.

In 2001 it closed its $30 billion buy of J.P. Morgan and renamed itself JPMorgan Chase & Co. The new firm eliminated some 10% of its combined workforce as a result of the merger. Chairman Sandy Warner (who ran J.P. Morgan) retired at year-end and was replaced by former Chase Manhattan leader CEO William Harrison.

JPMorgan Chase had more than $1 billion in exposure to Enron, but in 2003 recovered some $600 million after a court battle with the failed energy trader's insurers.

In 2004 JPMorgan Chase and its investment banking arm, JPMorgan Securities, avoided a trial by paying some $2 billion to settle claims from investors who lost money on bonds that the firm underwrote in 2000 and 2001 for scandal-ridden WorldCom (now MCI).

On the heels of its massive BANK ONE buy in 2004, JPMorgan Chase got the go-ahead from the FTC and bought Kohl's $1.6 billion credit card portfolio.

Enron continued to haunt the company: in 2005 it forked over $2.2 billion to settle part of an investor class-action suit over fraud charges related to the Enron debacle and paid another $350 million to the infamous energy trading firm, which asserted that JPMorgan Chase and about 10 other banks aided and abetted the company's collapse. However, the next year the company got some good news regarding its alleged involvement with the collapse of Enron when the class action suit against it was dismissed.

In 2006 the bank was quick to settle its part of a class-action lawsuit brought by investors claiming they were cheated in the dot-com IPO boom. JPMorgan Chase paid $425 million to settle that case. William Harrison retired as chairman at the end of 2006; he was succeeded by president and CEO Jamie Dimon (former CEO of BANK ONE).

As one of the largest mortgage and home equity providers in the country, JPMorgan Chase was hurt by the subprime mortgage crisis and subsequent fall in home values in 2007. It had to write off more than $500 million in home equity loans that year.

EXECUTIVES

Chairman, President, and CEO: James (Jamie) Dimon,
age 53, $19,651,556 total compensation
CFO: Michael J. Cavanagh, age 43,
$8,945,887 total compensation
CIO: Guy Chiarello
Chief Risk Officer: Barry L. Zubrow, age 56
Chief Administrative Officer: Frank J. Bisignano,
age 51, $10,192,946 total compensation
**Chief Investment Officer, Europe, Middle East, and
Africa:** Achilles O. Macris
CFO, Treasury and Securities Services Unit, New York:
Claudia Slacik
EVP; CEO, Treasury and Securities Services:
Heidi G. Miller, age 56
EVP, Global Government Relations and Public Policy:
Peter L. Scher
Co-CEO, Investment Bank: Steven D. Black, age 56
Co-CEO, Investment Bank: Carlos M. Hernandez,
age 47
Co-CEO, Investment Bank: William T. (Bill) Winters,
age 47
CEO, Retail Financial Services:
Charles W. (Charlie) Scharf, age 43,
$13,031,844 total compensation
CEO, Asset Management: James E. (Jes) Staley, age 53
CEO, Card Services: Gordon A. Smith, age 50,
$12,232,483 total compensation
Secretary: Anthony J. Horan
General Counsel: Stephen M. (Steve) Cutler, age 47
Head Strategy and Business Development:
Jay Mandelbaum, age 46
Director Human Resources: John L. Donnelly
Chief Investment Officer: Ina R. Drew, age 52
Corporate Communications: Joseph M. Evangelisti
Auditors: PricewaterhouseCoopers LLP

LOCATIONS

HQ: JPMorgan Chase & Co.
270 Park Ave., New York, NY 10017
Phone: 212-270-6000   **Fax:** 212-270-1648
Web: www.jpmorganchase.com

PRODUCTS/OPERATIONS

2008 Gross Revenues

	$ mil.	% of total
Interest income		
Loans	38,347	34
Trading assets	17,236	15
Securities	6,344	6
Federal funds sold & securities purchased		
under resale agreements	5,983	5
Securities borrowed	2,297	2
Other	2,811	3
Noninterest income		
Asset management, administration		
& commissions	13,943	12
Credit cards	7,419	7
Investment banking fees	5,526	5
Lending & deposit-related fees	5,088	5
Mortgage fees & related income	3,467	3
Other	3,729	3
Total	**112,190**	**100**

2008 Assets

	$ mil.	% of total
Cash & equivalents	368,149	17
Securities borrowed	124,000	6
Trading assets	509,983	23
Securities	205,943	10
Net loans	721,734	33
Other	245,243	11
Total	**2,175,052**	**100**

COMPETITORS

American Express	Deutsche Bank
Bank of America	Goldman Sachs
Barclays	HSBC Holdings
Capital One	Morgan Stanley
CIBC	RBC Financial Group
Citigroup	UBS
Credit Suisse (USA)	Wells Fargo

HISTORICAL FINANCIALS

Company Type: Public

Income Statement				FYE: December 31
	ASSETS ($ mil.)	NET INCOME ($ mil.)	INCOME AS % OF ASSETS	EMPLOYEES
12/08	2,175,052.0	3,699.0	0.2%	224,961
12/07	1,562,147.0	15,365.0	1.0%	180,667
12/06	1,351,520.0	14,444.0	1.1%	174,360
12/05	1,198,942.0	8,470.0	0.7%	168,847
12/04	1,157,248.0	4,414.0	0.4%	160,968
Annual Growth	**17.1%**	**(4.3%)**	**—**	**8.7%**

2008 Year-End Financials

Equity as % of assets: 6.2%
Return on assets: 0.2%
Return on equity: 2.9%
Long-term debt ($ mil.): 384,494
No. of shares (mil.): 3,933

Dividends
  Yield: 4.8%
  Payout: 110.9%
Market value ($ mil.): 123,994
Sales ($ mil.): 67,252

Stock History

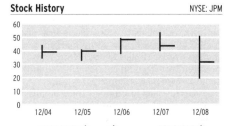

NYSE: JPM

	STOCK PRICE ($) FY Close	P/E High/Low		PER SHARE ($) Earnings	Dividends	Book Value
12/08	31.53	37	14	1.37	1.52	42.44
12/07	43.65	12	9	4.38	1.48	31.33
12/06	48.30	12	9	4.04	1.36	29.44
12/05	39.69	17	14	2.38	1.36	27.26
12/04	39.01	28	22	1.55	1.36	26.87
Annual Growth	**(5.2%)**	**—**	**—**	**(3.0%)**	**2.8%**	**12.1%**

Kaiser Foundation Health Plan

Kaiser Foundation Health Plan aims to be the emperor of the HMO universe. With more than 8.5 million members in nine states and the District of Columbia, it is one of the largest not-for-profit managed health care companies in the US. Kaiser has an integrated care model, offering both hospital and physician care through a network of hospitals and physician practices operating under the Kaiser Permanente name. Members of Kaiser health plans have access to hospitals and some 400 other health care facilities operated by Kaiser Foundation Hospitals and Permanente Medical Groups, associations consisting of about 14,000 doctors.

California is the company's largest market, accounting for some 75% of its members. It also operates in Colorado, Georgia, Hawaii, Maryland, Ohio, Oregon, Virginia, Washington, and the District of Columbia.

Kaiser's strategy for growth and profitability consists of strengthening its integrated care model via increased use of technology and construction of new health care facilities.

HISTORY

Henry Kaiser — shipbuilder, war profiteer, builder of the Hoover and Grand Coulee dams, and founder of Kaiser Aluminum — was a bootstrap capitalist who did well by doing good. A high school dropout from upstate New York, Kaiser moved to Spokane, Washington, in 1906 and went into road construction. During the Depression, he headed the consortium that built the great WPA dams.

It was in building the Grand Coulee Dam that, in 1938, Kaiser teamed with Dr. Sidney Garfield, who earlier had devised a prepayment health plan for workers on California public works projects. As Kaiser moved into steelmaking and shipbuilding during WWII (turning out some 1,400 bare-bones Liberty ships — one per day at peak production), Kaiser decided healthy workers produce more than sick ones, and he called on Garfield to set up on-site clinics funded by the US government as part of operating expenses. Garfield was released from military service by President Roosevelt for the purpose.

After the war, the clinics became war surplus. Kaiser and his wife bought them — at a 99% discount — through the new Kaiser Hospital Foundation. His vision was to provide the public with low-cost, prepaid medical care. He created the health plan — the self-supporting entity that would administer the system — and the group medical organization, Permanente (named after Kaiser's first cement plant site). He then endowed the health plan with $200,000.

This health plan, the classic HMO model, was criticized by the medical establishment as socialized medicine performed by "employee" doctors. But the plan flourished, becoming California's #1 medical system. In 1958 Kaiser retired to Hawaii and started his health plan there. But physician resistance limited national growth; HMOs were illegal in some states well into the 1970s.

As health care costs rose, Congress legalized HMOs in all states. Kaiser expanded in the 1980s; as it moved outside its traditional geographic areas, the company contracted for space in hospitals rather than build them. Growth slowed as competition increased.

Some health care costs in California fell in the early 1990s as more medical procedures were performed on an outpatient basis. Specialists flooded the state, and as price competition among doctors and hospitals heated up, many HMOs landed advantageous contracts. Kaiser, with its own highly paid doctors, was unable to realize the same savings and was no longer the best deal in town. Its membership stalled.

To boost membership and control expenses, Kaiser instituted a controversial program in 1996 in which nurses earned bonuses for cost-cutting. Critics said the program could lead to a decrease in care quality; Kaiser later became the focus of investigations into wrongful death suits linked to cost-cutting in California (where it has since beefed up staffing and programs) and Texas (where it has agreed to pay $1 million in fines).

In 1997 Kaiser and Washington-based Group Health Cooperative of Puget Sound formed Kaiser/Group Health to handle administrative services in the Northwest. Kaiser also tried to boost membership by lowering premiums, but the strategy proved *too* effective: Costs linked to an unwieldy 20% enrollment surge brought a loss in 1997 — Kaiser's first annual loss ever.

A second year in the red in 1998 prompted Kaiser to sell its Texas operations to Sierra Health Services. It also entered the Florida market via an alliance with Miami-based AvMed Health Plan. In 1999 Kaiser announced plans to sell its unprofitable North Carolina operations (it closed the deal the following year).

In 2000 Kaiser announced plans to charge premiums for its Medicare HMO, Medicare Advantage, to offset the shortfall in federal reimbursements. Kaiser also responded to rising costs by selling its unprofitable operations in North Carolina (2000) and Kansas (2001). In 2001 the company's hospital division bought the technology and assets of defunct Internet grocer Webvan in an effort to increase its distribution activity. Also that year the son of a deceased anthrax victim sued a Kaiser facility for failing to recognize and treat his father's symptoms.

EXECUTIVES

Chairman and CEO: George C. Halvorson
EVP Strategic Planning and CFO: Kathy Lancaster
SVP and CIO: Philip (Phil) Fasano
SVP and Chief Human Resources Officer: Paul Records
SVP and Chief Diversity Officer: Ronald Knox
EVP Health Plan Operations: Arthur M. Southam
EVP Health Plan and Hospital Operations:
  Bernard J. Tyson
SVP Research and Policy Development:
  Robert M. Crane
SVP Brand Strategy, Communications, and Public Relations: Diane Gage Lofgren
SVP, Community Benefit, Research, and Health Policy; CEO, KP Cal: Raymond J. (Ray) Baxter
SVP, Quality and Clinical Systems Support:
  Louise L. Liang
SVP and General Counsel: Steven (Steve) Zatkin
SVP and Managing Director, Kaiser Permanente's Venture Capital and Corporate Development Group: Chris Grant
VP, Clinical Information System (CIS) Project:
  Bruce Turkstra
VP and Treasurer: Tom Meier
Executive Director, The Permanente Federation:
  John H. Cochran Jr.
Chief Compliance Officer and Director:
  Daniel P. (Dan) Garcia
SVP and COO, The Permanente Federation:
  Harold F. Wolf III
Auditors: KPMG LLP

LOCATIONS

HQ: Kaiser Foundation Health Plan, Inc.
  1 Kaiser Plaza, Oakland, CA 94612
Phone: 510-271-5800   **Fax:** 510-271-6493
Web: www.kaiserpermanente.org

2008 Membership

	No. of members
Northern California	3,285,068
Southern California	3,281,915
Mid-Atlantic States (Virginia, Maryland & Washington, DC)	485,401
Colorado	479,980
Northwest (Oregon & Washington)	472,555
Georgia	269,802
Hawaii	222,594
Ohio	137,669
Total	**8,634,984**

COMPETITORS

Aetna
AMERIGROUP
Blue Shield Of California
CareFirst
CIGNA
Community Health Plan of Washington
Coventry Health Care
First Choice Health
Group Health Cooperative (Puget Sound)
Hawaii Medical Service Association
Health Net
Humana
Molina Healthcare
Oregon Dental
Premera Blue Cross
Regence
Sharp Health Plan
UnitedHealth Group
WellCare Health Plans
WellPoint

HISTORICAL FINANCIALS

Company Type: Subsidiary

Income Statement

FYE: December 31

	REVENUE ($ mil.)	NET INCOME ($ mil.)	NET PROFIT MARGIN	EMPLOYEES
12/08	40,300.0	—	—	167,300
12/07	37,800.0	—	—	159,766
12/06	34,400.0	—	—	156,000
12/05	31,100.0	—	—	—
12/04	28,000.0	—	—	—
Annual Growth	**9.5%**	—	—	**3.6%**

Revenue History

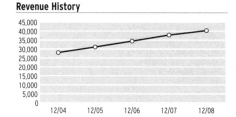

Kansas City Southern

Kansas City Southern (KCS) rides the rails of a 6,000-mile network that stretches from Missouri to Mexico. The company's Kansas City Southern Railway (KCSR) owns and operates more than 3,200 miles of track in the midwestern and southern US. KCS offers rail freight service in Mexico through Kansas City Southern de México (KCSM, formerly TFM), which maintains more than 2,600 miles of track and serves three major ports. Another KCS unit, Texas Mexican Railway, connects the KCSR and KCSM systems. The KCS railroads transport such freight as industrial and consumer products, agricultural and mineral products, and chemical and petroleum products.

Through its own system and marketing agreements with other railroads, KCS can arrange to have its customers' freight carried throughout much of Canada, Mexico, and the US, thus capitalizing on business generated by the North American Free Trade Agreement (NAFTA).

KCS sees traffic at the Port of Lázaro Cárdenas, on Mexico's Pacific coast, as a key source of new business. The railroad is building intermodal hubs in Lázaro Cárdenas; Mexico City; Rosenberg, Texas (southeast of Houston); and Kansas City, Missouri. It's also expanding and renovating existing hubs in Dallas and Jackson, Mississippi. KCS picks up intermodal containers arriving from Asia at the port in Mexico and hauls them into the US through Texas, offering Asian shippers an alternative to busier ports in California.

Within the US, KCS is working with railroad operator Norfolk Southern to boost capacity on the Meridian Speedway, a 320-mile line between Shreveport, Louisiana, and Meridian, Mississippi, that has become a key rail link between the southeastern and southwestern US.

In addition to its main rail system, KCS owns a 50% stake in the Panama Canal Railway Company, which transports passengers and cargo over a 48-mile railroad between the Atlantic and Pacific oceans.

KCS has a railcar and locomotive leasing business with GATX Rail called Southern Capital Corporation LLC. The partnership company leases more than 2,800 railcars and about 300 locomotives to KCSR.

HISTORY

Arthur Edward Stilwell founded the Kansas City Southern Railway (KCSR) in 1887 to transport commodities for local meatpackers and granaries. By 1891 Stilwell had expanded the line southward to Fort Smith, Arkansas. Two years later he extended the line to the Gulf of Mexico to give the heartland's agricultural producers an outlet to the sea. Stilwell decided to route his lines to Lake Sabine, Texas, seven miles inland from the Gulf and relatively protected from hurricanes. He built a port on the lake and then dredged a canal to the Gulf. Subsequently named Port Arthur, the site became the second-largest grain port after New York.

In the 1920s and 1930s Leonore Loree, Stilwell's successor, guided the company through the Depression and beyond with sound financial management. In 1939 KCSR bought the Louisiana and Arkansas Railways to extend its lines to New Orleans and Dallas. That year General Motors chose the railroad to test its first passenger-service diesel-electric locomotive.

Kansas businessmen wrested control of the company from its eastern owners in 1944 and appointed William Deramus as president. With a new leader and operating strategy in place, the railroad focused on expanding its business into territories that were experiencing a post-WWII industrial boom.

In the 1950s KCSR developed a computerized data-processing system for its businesses. During the mid-1950s Deramus and his son, William Deramus III (then president of the Chicago Great Western and Katy Railway), were heavily involved in building the Mid-America Pipeline (MAPCO) along their railroads' rights-of-way, though KCSR's interest ended by the early 1980s.

In 1961 William Deramus III joined his father in senior management at the company. Kansas City Southern Industries (KCSI) was incorporated as a holding company for the purpose of diversification in the face of growing competition from airlines and the trucking industry. As the company's data-processing and information management needs increased, KCSI capitalized on its early data-processing experience by forming DST Systems.

Growth during the 1980s resulted from an increase in coal transport and additional freight traffic. In 1983 KCSI bought a majority stake in Janus Capital, a Denver-based mutual funds company. By the late 1980s the company's transportation and financial management divisions were prospering because of higher coal volume and the growth of the mutual funds industry.

KCSI increased its mutual funds holdings by buying Berger and Associates in 1992. In 1997 the company formed Kansas City Southern Lines, a holding company for its transportation segments, to streamline its corporate structure and refocus on its core businesses.

The next year KCSI created FAM Holding Company to house its financial asset management subsidiaries, including Janus Capital, Berger Associates, and DST Systems, and it expanded its financial operations with the acquisition of 80% of UK-based Nelson Money Managers. Also in 1998, with partner Mi-Jack Products (a maker of intermodal equipment), KCSI was awarded the Panama Canal railroad concession by the government of Panama.

The company's founder returned in spirit in 1999 when KSCI announced plans to spin off its financial services businesses to shareholders as a new company, Stilwell Financial. Although executives at Janus, then one of the hottest US mutual fund managers, lobbied for their company to be spun off separately, Janus was part of Stilwell when Stilwell began trading in 2000. (Janus and Stilwell were combined in 2003 to form Janus Capital Group.)

KCSI completed reconstruction of the Panama Canal Railway in 2001 and reopened the railroad for freight and passenger transport. Two years after the Stilwell spinoff, KCSI shortened its name to Kansas City Southern (KCS) to reflect its renewed focus on transportation.

KCS completed its purchase of Grupo TMM's stake in Grupo TFM in 2005. Later in 2005, the settlement of a tax dispute that involved KCS, TFM, Grupo TFM, Grupo TMM, and the Mexican government resulted in KCS receiving the 20% stake in TFM held by the government and thus gaining full ownership of the railroad. In return, KCS and Grupo TMM gave up their claim to a tax refund the companies had been seeking.

EXECUTIVES

Chairman and CEO: Michael R. (Mike) Haverty, age 64, $3,504,351 total compensation
President and COO; President and CEO, Kansas City Southern Railway: David L. Starling, age 59
EVP and CFO: Michael W. (Mike) Upchurch, age 47, $645,846 total compensation
Chief Operations Support, Mexico: Jacobo Jacome
SVP and Chief Legal Officer: W. James (Jim) Wochner, age 61
VP and Chief Mechanical Officer: John Foster
VP and Chief Engineer: John S. Jacobsen
SVP and Chief Accounting Officer: Mary K. Stadler, age 49
EVP Corporate Affairs: Warren K. Erdman, age 50
EVP and Assistant to the Chairman: Larry M. Lawrence, age 46
EVP Sales and Marketing: Patrick J. (Pat) Ottensmeyer, age 51, $1,344,692 total compensation
SVP, Finance and Treasurer, Kansas City Northern and Kansas City Southern Railway: Paul J. Weyandt, age 55
SVP International Engineering: Jerry W. Heavin
SVP Human Resources: John E. Derry, age 41

VP Investor Relations: William (Bill) Galligan
President and Executive Representative, Kansas City Southern de Mexico, S.A. de C.V.:
Jose G. Zozaya Delano
President and Director General, Panama Canal Railway Company: Thomas H. (Tom) Kenna
Assistant VP Corporate Communications and Community Affairs: C. Doniele Kane
Associate General Counsel and Corporate Secretary:
Brian P. Banks
Auditors: KPMG LLP

LOCATIONS

HQ: Kansas City Southern
427 W. 12th St., Kansas City, MO 64105
Phone: 816-983-1303   **Fax:** 816-983-1108
Web: www.kcsi.com

2008 Sales

	$ mil.	% of total
US	1,033.6	56
Mexico	818.5	44
Total	**1,852.1**	**100**

PRODUCTS/OPERATIONS

2008 Sales

	$ mil.	% of total
Industrial & consumer products	508.6	27
Agriculture & minerals	455.0	25
Chemical & petroleum	347.8	19
Coal	203.7	11
Intermodal	160.6	9
Automotive	105.6	6
Other	70.8	3
Total	**1,852.1**	**100**

COMPETITORS

American Commercial Lines
Burlington Northern Santa Fe
Canadian National Railway
Canadian Pacific Railway
Crowley Maritime
CSX
Grupo Carso
Grupo México
Ingram Industries
J.B. Hunt
Kirby Corporation
Norfolk Southern
Schneider National
Union Pacific
Werner Enterprises

HISTORICAL FINANCIALS

Company Type: Public

Income Statement

FYE: December 31

	REVENUE ($ mil.)	NET INCOME ($ mil.)	NET PROFIT MARGIN	EMPLOYEES
12/08	1,852.1	183.9	9.9%	6,400
12/07	1,742.8	134.0	7.7%	6,485
12/06	1,659.7	89.4	5.4%	6,470
12/05	1,352.0	100.9	7.5%	3,060
12/04	639.5	24.4	3.8%	2,680
Annual Growth	**30.5%**	**65.7%**	—	**24.3%**

2008 Year-End Financials

Debt ratio: 76.0%
Return on equity: 10.1%
Cash ($ mil.): 230
Current ratio: 0.63
Long-term debt ($ mil.): 1,449

No. of shares (mil.): 95
Dividends
  Yield: 0.0%
  Payout: —
Market value ($ mil.): 1,807

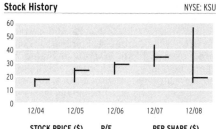

Stock History   NYSE: KSU

	STOCK PRICE ($) FY Close	P/E High/Low		Earnings	PER SHARE ($) Dividends	Book Value
12/08	19.05	30	8	1.86	0.00	20.15
12/07	34.33	27	18	1.57	0.00	18.20
12/06	28.98	28	20	1.08	0.00	16.68
12/05	24.43	23	15	1.10	0.00	15.03
12/04	17.73	72	50	0.25	0.00	10.80
Annual Growth	1.8%	—	—	65.2%	—	16.9%

KB Home

For a dwelling done your way, you might turn to KB Home. KB Home builds mainly for first-time, trade-up, and active adult buyers primarily in the southern, western, and southwestern US. The company markets homes under its Built to Order brand, allowing buyers to customize their homes through KB Home Studio. The program lets customers choose from thousands of options to be included in the construction of their new homes. The company also has branding deals with Martha Stewart and the Walt Disney Company. KB Home offers financing, mortgage assistance, and home insurance through Bank of America.

KB Home's financial problems continued in 2008, as revenues fell 47%. The company delivered 12,438 homes in 2008, down 48% from 2007, at an average selling price of $236,000. The company was hit hard by a glut of available housing due to a high rate of foreclosures coupled with overbuilding and tight credit. Sales remain slow despite record low mortgage rates.

By comparison, KB delivered around 23,700 homes in 2007, down substantially from the 32,000 homes it delivered in 2006. Average selling price also dropped, to $261,000 from $288,000, and the company's revenues were slashed by about 40% as well.

KB Home continued to retrench its operations in 2008, cutting staff, abandoning markets, and working to move products to generate cash flow and manage debt. In late 2008, KB announced it was leaving the Atlanta market.

Key to its strategy for surviving the downturn is its ability to turn out cheaper and smaller houses. In 2009 KB announced a product line called "Open Series" that allows homebuyers to control such specifications as square footage or how many rooms they want. More than 25 percent of KB's communities are offering this new product.

In a measure to stem the bleeding, in 2007 KB Home sold its 49% stake in French subsidiary Kaufman & Broad to PAI Partners for about $800 million, thus exiting all international operations. The sale enabled it to reduce its outstanding debt by about $1 billion.

HISTORY

Kaufman and Broad Building Co. was founded in Detroit in 1957 by Eli Broad and Donald Kaufman. Broad, an accountant, parlayed an initial $25,000 investment into sales of $250,000 on the first weekend of business. By the end of its first year, Kaufman and Broad was posting revenues of $1.7 million.

The company expanded rapidly and went public in 1961. A year later it was the first homebuilder to be listed on the NYSE. Kaufman and Broad moved into California in 1963. Through acquisitions, it rapidly became a top US homebuilder, expanding into New York, San Francisco, and Chicago. In 1965 it formed a mortgage subsidiary to arrange loans for its customers.

In the early 1970s the firm entered Europe and Canada. Sales passed the $100 million mark in 1971 and the company diversified, buying Sun Life Insurance. Housing operations were renamed Kaufman and Broad Development Group (KBDG).

In 1980 the flamboyant Bruce Karatz, who had joined the firm in 1972, was appointed president. Karatz steered the company through the recession of the early 1980s, focusing on California, France, and Canada. KBDG acquired Bati-Service, a major French developer of affordable homes, in 1985.

The company was renamed Kaufman and Broad Home Corporation in 1986. In 1989 it reorganized into two separate billion-dollar companies: Broad Inc. (now SunAmerica), an insurance firm with Eli Broad as its chairman and CEO; and Kaufman and Broad Home, with Karatz as CEO (and later chairman), which was spun off to shareholders in 1989.

When the California real estate market crashed in 1990, earnings plummeted. Karatz diversified by buying up strong regional builders. Kaufman and Broad entered Arizona, Colorado, and Nevada in 1993 and Utah in 1994. Profits dropped in 1995-96 because of weakness in the California and Paris markets and the company's winding down of Canadian operations. But expansion continued, including the acquisition of Rayco, a Texas builder, in 1996.

Borrowing from the methods of Rayco, Kaufman and Broad began surveying homebuyers for suggestions to incorporate into new designs. In 1998 the company began to build its New Home Showrooms. The corporation continued its expansion drive that year when it paid about $165 million for Dover/Ideal, PrideMark, and Estes, privately held builders based in Houston, Denver, and Tucson, respectively. In 1999 Kaufman and Broad bought Lewis Homes, a major California builder and the #1 builder in Las Vegas, for about $545 million.

In 2001 the company changed its name again, shortening it to KB Home.

KB Home launched a division in Tampa and expanded operations into Central Florida in 2002 by acquiring Orlando-based American Heritage Homes for about $74 million. It also expanded in other markets, which included Tucson (by acquiring assets of New World Homes, gaining more than 1,600 lots in 12 new home communities there) and the Rio Grande Valley of Texas (by opening a division in the fast-growing McAllen region, about four miles from the Mexican border).

KB Home continued to build its empire in 2003 by acquiring Atlanta-based Colony Homes, one of the Southeast's largest privately owned homebuilders, with principal operations in Atlanta, Raleigh, and Charlotte, which are among the largest markets in the Southeast for new-home permits. The company also moved into the Midwest with the $33 million purchase of privately held homebuilder Zale Homes (Chicago). KB Home also added to its French holdings by acquiring Euro Immobilier.

In 2004 KB Home expanded its operations in the Southeast by acquiring South Carolina-based Palmetto Traditional Homes, which builds in the state's largest metropolitan areas: Charleston, Columbia, and Greenville-Spartanburg-Anderson. It also acquired Indianapolis builder Dura Builders and two French builders, Groupe Avantis and Foncier Investissement.

KB Home sold its KB Home Mortgage subsidiary to Countrywide Home Loans in 2005, and then formed its Countrywide KB Home Loans joint venture to serve KB customers.

When charges of fraud surrounding company stock options were leveled against Karatz in 2006, the chairman and president retired from KB Home; former COO Jeff Mezger was then named president and CEO.

EXECUTIVES

Chairman: Stephen F. Bollenbach, age 66
President, CEO, and Director: Jeffrey T. (Jeff) Mezger, age 53, $9,624,932 total compensation
SVP and Chief Accounting Officer: William R. (Bill) Hollinger, age 50, $955,211 total compensation
EVP, General Counsel, and Corporate Secretary: Wendy C. Shiba, age 58, $1,250,186 total compensation
SVP Studios: Lisa M. Kalmbach
SVP Tax: Cory F. Cohen
SVP Sales, Marketing, and Communications: Wendy Marlett
SVP Human Resources: Thomas F. (Tom) Norton, age 38
SVP and Treasurer: Kelly Masuda, age 41, $702,448 total compensation
SVP KBnxt Group: Glen Barnard, age 64, $887,060 total compensation
President, New Mexico Division: Marcia Dillon
Auditors: Ernst & Young LLP

LOCATIONS

HQ: KB Home
10990 Wilshire Blvd., 7th Fl.
Los Angeles, CA 90024
Phone: 310-231-4000   **Fax:** 310-231-4222
Web: www.kbhome.com

PRODUCTS/OPERATIONS

2008 Sales

	$ mil.	% of total
Construction	3,023.2	99
Financial Services	10.7	1
Total	**3,033.9**	**100**

COMPETITORS

Beazer Homes	Meritage Homes
Capital Pacific	NVR
David Weekley Homes	Pulte Homes
D.R. Horton	The Ryland Group
Highland Homes	Shapell Industries
Hovnanian Enterprises	Standard Pacific
Lennar	Toll Brothers
M.D.C.	Weyerhaeuser Real Estate
Mercedes Homes	William Lyon Homes

HISTORICAL FINANCIALS

Company Type: Public

Income Statement

FYE: November 30

	REVENUE ($ mil.)	NET INCOME ($ mil.)	NET PROFIT MARGIN	EMPLOYEES
11/08	3,033.9	(976.1)	—	1,600
11/07	6,416.5	(929.4)	—	3,100
11/06	11,003.8	482.4	4.4%	5,100
11/05	9,441.7	842.4	8.9%	6,700
11/04	7,052.7	480.9	6.8%	6,000
Annual Growth	**(19.0%)**	**—**	**—**	**(28.1%)**

2008 Year-End Financials

Debt ratio: —
Return on equity: —
Cash ($ mil.): 1,135
Current ratio: 1.16
Long-term debt ($ mil.): —
No. of shares (mil.): 127
Dividends
Yield: 7.0%
Payout: —
Market value ($ mil.): 1,476

Stock History

NYSE: KBH

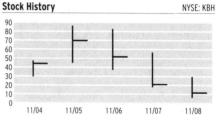

	STOCK PRICE ($) FY Close	P/E High/Low		PER SHARE ($) Earnings	Dividends	Book Value
11/08	11.63	—	—	(12.59)	0.81	6.55
11/07	20.89	—	—	(12.04)	1.00	14.59
11/06	51.69	14	7	5.82	1.00	23.03
11/05	69.77	9	5	9.53	0.75	22.47
11/04	43.94	8	5	5.70	0.50	16.20
Annual Growth	**(28.3%)**	**—**	**—**	**—**	**12.8%**	**(20.3%)**

Kellogg Company

Kellogg is in a constant battle for the #1 spot in the US cereal market with its main rival, General Mills. (In 2008 both held a 29.8% market share, so we'll call it a tie for now.) Among Kellogg's well-known brands are Frosted Flakes, Corn Pops, and Rice Krispies. And while the company fills many a cereal bowl every morning, it buffs up its bottom line with snacks and cookies (Keebler and Famous Amos), along with convenience foods such as Eggo waffles and Nutri-Grain cereal bars. The private charity the W. K. Kellogg Foundation owns 25% of the company. The George Gund Foundation owns 16%. The Gund family, which sold its coffee business (later Sanka) to Kellogg in 1927, owns 9% of the company.

Although Kellogg snaps under the pressure of its ongoing cereal war with General Mills, it also crackles under fierce competition from Ralcorp, which acquired the Post cereal operations of Kraft Foods in 2008. And Kellogg pops with continued pursuit of new markets, one acquisition being Worthington Foods, owner of the Morningstar Farms meat alternative brand. It added to its meatless menu with its 2007 acquisition of Wholesome & Hearty Foods, the maker of Gardenburger. It also acquired Bear Naked, a small seller of natural granola, in 2007.

Expanding its international presence, in 2008 the company acquired Chinese cookie and cracker manufacturer Zhenghang Food Company (dba Navigable Foods). Also that year Kellogg acquired The United Bakers Group, a top cracker, biscuit, and breakfast cereal manufacturer, as well as Specialty Cereals, an Australian cereal manufacturer.

The company wrapped up 2008 in a sweet fashion by purchasing the recipes and trademarks from the bankrupt (but popular in the western US) Mother's Cake & Cookie Co. Kellogg added the brands, which include Chips Deluxe, Fudge Shoppe, and Sandies, to its snacks business unit and hopes to expand their distribution.

The company's largest customer is Wal-Mart, which accounted for about 20% of Kellogg's 2008 sales.

HISTORY

Will Keith (W. K.) Kellogg first made wheat flakes in 1894 while working for his brother, Dr. John Kellogg, at Battle Creek, Michigan's famed homeopathic sanitarium. While doing an experiment with grains (for patients' diets), the two men were interrupted; by the time they returned to the dough, it had absorbed water. They rolled it anyway, toasted the result, and accidentally created the first flaked cereal. John sold the flakes via mail order (1899) in a partnership that W. K. managed. In 1906 W. K. started his own firm to produce corn flakes.

As head of the Battle Creek Toasted Corn Flake Company, W. K. competed against 42 cereal companies in Battle Creek (one run by former patient C. W. Post) and roared to the head of the pack with his innovative marketing ideas. A 1906 *Ladies' Home Journal* ad helped increase demand from 33 cases a day earlier that year to 2,900 a day by year-end. W. K. soon introduced Bran Flakes (1915), All-Bran (1916), and Rice Krispies (1928). International expansion began in Canada (1914) and followed in Australia (1924) and England (1938). Diversifying a little, the company introduced the Pop-Tart in 1964 and acquired Eggo waffles in the 1970s. By the early 1980s Kellogg's US market share dipped, due to strong competition from General Mills and other rivals. The company pitched new cereals to adults and aggressively pursued the fast-growing European market.

Kellogg spent the mid-1990s reengineering itself, creating the USA Convenience Foods Division and selling such noncore assets as its carton container and Argentine snack-food makers (1993). It teamed with ConAgra in 1994 to create a cereal line sold under the latter's popular Healthy Choice label.

In 1997-98 the company expanded operations in Australia, the UK, Asia, and Latin America, and it slashed about 25% of its salaried North American workforce and hiked prices on about two-thirds of its cereals. Several top officers left in 1998-99, and Cuban-born president and COO Carlos Gutierrez became CEO.

The company sold the disappointing Lender's division to Aurora Foods in 1999 for just $275 million. (Aurora later merged with Pinnacle Foods to become Pinnacle Foods Group — now Pinnacle Foods Finance and owned by Blackstone.) Kellogg took another crack at non-breakfast foods when it bought Worthington Foods (Morningstar Farms meat alternatives, Harvest Burgers) for $307 million.

By the beginning of 2000, cereal competitor General Mills had closed the gap with Kellogg in US market share (in 2001 it passed Kellogg as the #1 cereal maker). In 2001 Kellogg bulked up its snacks portfolio by acquiring Keebler Foods for $4.5 billion. In the aftermath of the acquisition, the company trimmed jobs at Keebler and its own headquarters.

To boost enthusiasm among kids for breakfast, in 2002 Kellogg launched new cereals featuring Disney characters Buzz Lightyear, Mickey Mouse, and Winnie the Pooh — the first such alliance for The Walt Disney Company. That move, combined with better marketing and General Mills being distracted by its purchase of Pillsbury, helped Kellogg grab back the top spot in the US.

In 2004 Kellogg sold the Athens repackaging business of Keebler to Total Logistics. Later that year, Kellogg reached an agreement with then New York Attorney General Eliot Spitzer to stop using promotional toys identified as a possible environmental risk in its cereal products. In addition the company agreed to phase out the sale or distribution of promotional products containing mercury by the end of 2004, recycle mercury batteries returned by consumers, and educate consumers as to the need to dispose of mercury properly.

Continuing its integration of Keebler Foods, in 2004 the company did some geographic juggling: The US snack division was relocated from Elmhurst, Illinois, to Kellogg's main headquarters in Battle Creek, Michigan. The Food Away From Home (FAFH) business unit and the Information Technology Center remained in Elmhurst.

In 2005 Gutierrez resigned from Kellogg to become secretary of the Department of Commerce in the George W. Bush administration. He was succeeded at the cereal behemoth by advertising executive and Kellogg board member James Jenness. In 2006 David Mackay was appointed Kellogg's CEO, replacing Jenness who remained as chairman.

The company began using oils derived from genetically modified soybeans in some of its products in 2006 in order to lower their fat content.

EXECUTIVES

Chairman: James M. (Jim) Jenness, age 62
President, CEO, and Director: A. D. David Mackay, age 53, $12,344,889 total compensation
EVP, COO, and CFO: John A. Bryant, age 43, $4,095,169 total compensation
SVP Global Information Technology and CIO: Brian S. Rice
SVP Global Nutrition and Corporate Affairs and Chief Sustainability Officer: Celeste A. Clark, age 55
VP and Global Chief Marketing Officer: Mark Baynes, age 48
VP and Chief Ethics and Compliance Officer: Neil Nyberg
SVP; President, Kellogg Specialty Channels: David (Dave) Pfanzelter
SVP Corporate Development, General Counsel, and Secretary: Gary H. Pilnick, age 44
SVP; EVP, Kellogg International; President, Kellogg Europe: Timothy P. Mobsby, age 53, $2,813,599 total compensation
SVP; President, Kellogg International: Paul Norman, age 44, $3,028,784 total compensation
SVP; President, Kellogg North America: Bradford J. (Brad) Davidson, age 48, $3,510,698 total compensation
SVP Global Human Resources: Kathleen Wilson-Thompson, age 51
SVP; President, U.S. Morning Foods: Juan Pablo Villalobos, age 43
VP Treasury and Investor Relations: Joel R. Wittenberg, age 46
VP; President, Kellogg U.S. Snacks: Todd Penegor, age 44
VP Corporate Development: Michael J. Libbing, age 39
Auditors: PricewaterhouseCoopers LLP

LOCATIONS

HQ: Kellogg Company
1 Kellogg Sq., Battle Creek, MI 49016
Phone: 269-961-2000 **Fax:** 269-961-2871
Web: www.kelloggcompany.com

2008 Sales

	$ mil.	% of total
North America	8,457	66
Europe	2,619	20
Latin America	1,030	8
Asia/Pacific	716	6
Total	**12,822**	**100**

PRODUCTS/OPERATIONS

2008 Sales

	$ mil.	% of total
Cereal	6,585	51
Snacks	3,960	31
Frozen & specialty foods	1,459	12
Convenience foods	818	6
Total	**12,822**	**100**

Selected US Cereal Brands

All-Bran
Apple Jacks
Bran Buds
Cinnamon Crunch
Cocoa Krispies
Complete Bran Flakes
Complete Wheat Flakes
Corn Pops
Cracklin' Oat Bran
Crispix
Crunch
Cruncheroos
Froot Loops
Frosted Krispies
Frosted Mini-Wheats
Just Right
Kellogg's Corn Flakes
Kellogg's Frosted Flakes
Kellogg's Low Fat Granola
Kellogg's Raisin Bran
Mueslix
Pops
Product 19
Raisin Bran
Rice Krispies
Smacks/Honey Smacks
Smart Start
Special K
Special K Red Berries

Selected Other Products

Cereal Bars and Granola
  All-Bran
  Bear Naked
  Choco Krispies
  Froot Loops
  GoLean
  Kashi

Convenience Foods
  Cheez-It
  Chips Deluxe
  Club
  Croutettes Croutons
  E. L. Fudge
  Famous Amos
  Fudge Shoppe
  Hi-Ho
  Keebler
  Kellogg's Corn Flake Crumbs
  Pop-Tarts
  Ready Crust
  Rice Krispies Squares
  Rice Krispies Treats
  Sandies
  Soft Batch
  Sunshine
  Toasteds
  Town House
Frozen Waffles and Pancakes
  Eggo
  Froot Loops
  Nutri-Grain
  Special K
Water and Water Mixes
  Special K
  Special K2O
Meat and Egg Alternatives
  Gardenburger
  Loma Linda
  Morningstar Farms
  Natural Touch
  Worthington

COMPETITORS

Amy's Kitchen
Barbara's Bakery
Bob's Red Mill Natural Foods
Boca Foods
Campbell Soup
ConAgra
Frito-Lay
General Mills
Gilster-Mary Lee
Hain Celestial
Interstate Bakeries
J & J Snack Foods
Kraft Foods
Lance Snacks
Malt-O-Meal
McKee Foods
Nestlé
Patty King
Pinnacle Foods
PowerBar
Ralcorp
Ralston Food
Weetabix
Wessanen
Weston Foods

HISTORICAL FINANCIALS

Company Type: Public

Income Statement
FYE: December 31

	REVENUE ($ mil.)	NET INCOME ($ mil.)	NET PROFIT MARGIN	EMPLOYEES
12/08	12,822.0	1,148.0	9.0%	32,400
12/07	11,776.0	1,103.0	9.4%	26,000
12/06	10,906.7	1,004.1	9.2%	26,000
12/05	10,177.2	980.4	9.6%	25,600
12/04	9,613.9	890.6	9.3%	25,000
Annual Growth	7.5%	6.6%	—	6.7%

2008 Year-End Financials

Debt ratio: 280.9%
Return on equity: 57.8%
Cash ($ mil.): 255
Current ratio: 0.71
Long-term debt ($ mil.): 4,068

No. of shares (mil.): 383
Dividends
  Yield: 3.0%
  Payout: 43.5%
Market value ($ mil.): 16,788

Stock History
NYSE: K

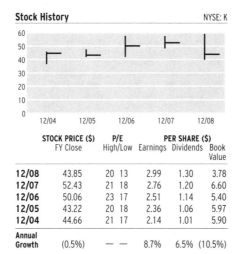

	STOCK PRICE ($) FY Close	P/E High/Low		PER SHARE ($) Earnings	Dividends	Book Value
12/08	43.85	20	13	2.99	1.30	3.78
12/07	52.43	21	18	2.76	1.20	6.60
12/06	50.06	23	17	2.51	1.14	5.40
12/05	43.22	20	18	2.36	1.06	5.97
12/04	44.66	21	17	2.14	1.01	5.90
Annual Growth	(0.5%)	—	—	8.7%	6.5%	(10.5%)

Kelly Services

These days a lot of "Kelly Girls" are men. Once a business that supplied only female clerical help, Kelly Services has expanded to include male and female employees in light industrial, technical, and professional sectors, including information technology specialists, engineers, and accountants. It also places lawyers (Kelly Law Registry), scientists (Kelly Scientific Resources), substitute teachers (Kelly Educational Staffing), nurses and other medical staff (Kelly Healthcare Resources), and teleservices personnel (KellyConnect). Overall, Kelly Services provides some 650,000 employees through about 2,500 offices in more than 35 countries. Chairman Terence Adderley owns a controlling stake in the company.

Kelly Services continues to grow by opening new offices in target markets across the US and abroad. The company provides additional personnel in areas such as automotive (Kelly Automotive Services Group), electronics (Kelly Electronic Assembly Services), merchandising (Kelly Marketing Services), and catering (Kelly Catering and Hospitality).

During economic downturns, Kelly Services says many companies reduce the number of temporary workers used before laying off full-time employees. Kelly is not immune — the company plans to drop 350 workers from its payroll in 2009. To sidestep the widening weak economy, Kelly plans to focus on contracting with large corporate clients to provide temporary workers.

In order to augment its portfolio of career transition services and business effectiveness consulting, Kelly Services bought New York-based The Ayers Group. It also expanded its reach to the Czech Republic and Poland with the buyout of executive search firm Talents Technology in 2007.

Its presence in Japan grew when it acquired all the shares of former joint venture Tempstaff Kelly in 2007. Looking to China, Hong Kong, and Singapore, Kelly Services acquired executive search and HR outsourcing services firm P-Serv. In 2008 the company entered a new market with the acquisition of all the Portuguese subsidiaries of global staffing powerhouse Randstad Holding.

Kelly expanded its offering in specialized accounting and finance recruiting by purchasing UK-based Toner Graham in 2008.

At the same time, the company shed some non-core operations. Kelly Services sold its Home Care Services unit to Res-Care in 2007 and sold its staff leasing operations to Oasis Outsourcing Holdings the year before. in 2007 Kelly Services closed 22 underperforming branches in the UK.

HISTORY

William Russell Kelly, a college dropout and former car salesman, went to Detroit after WWII to seek his fortune. An owner of modern business equipment, he set up Russell Kelly Office Service in 1946 to provide copying, typing, and inventory services for other businesses; first-year sales from 12 customers totaled $848.

Although companies began to acquire their own machines, Kelly knew that they still needed people to work at their offices. He reincorporated his rapidly expanding business as Personnel Service in 1952 and opened the company's first branch office in Louisville, Kentucky, in 1955; by the end of that year, he had 35 offices throughout the US. In 1957 the company was renamed Kelly Girl Service to reflect its all-female workforce.

In the 1960s Kelly ventured beyond office services and began placing convention hostesses, blue-collar workers, data processors, door-to-door marketers, and drafters, among others. Kelly Girl went public in 1962, boasting 148 branches at the time. In 1966 the company adopted the name Kelly Services. It opened its first non-US office in Toronto in 1968, and one in Paris followed in 1972.

A tough US economy in the 1970s saw a surge in corporate interest in temporary employees. Employers saw the benefits of hiring "Kelly Girls" to meet seasonal needs and special projects. In 1976 Kelly Services acquired a modest health care services company and used it to form Kelly Home Care. In the 1980s this division abandoned the Medicaid and Medicare markets and shifted to private-sector care. Renamed Kelly Assisted Living Services in 1984 (and later known as Kelly Home Care Services), the unit offered aides to perform household duties and nurses to conduct home visits for the elderly and disabled. Also in the 1980s Kelly Services began hiring retired people as part of its ENCORE Program.

In 1988 Kelly began a program of international expansion that would see the company add operations in the Asia/Pacific region and in Europe.

The company developed specialty services in the US in the 1990s. It acquired ComTrain (testing and training software products) and Your Staff (an employee-leasing firm providing companies with entire human resources departments, including benefits and payroll services) in 1994. The following year it bought the Wallace Law Registry (renamed Kelly Law Registry), a provider of lawyers, paralegals, and clerks. Kelly also established Kelly Scientific Resources to place science professionals. In 1996 that subsidiary acquired Oak Ridge Research Institute, which provided scientists to the defense and energy industries.

William Kelly died at the age of 92 in 1998, and the company named president and CEO Terence Adderley, his adopted son, to replace him as chairman. (Adderley relinquished the title of president in late 2001.) The next year the company made four additions to its staffing services:

Kelly Healthcare Resources, Kelly Financial Resources, Kelly Educational Staffing (substitute teachers), and KellyConnect (teleservices).

In 2000 the company made three acquisitions: Extra ETT in Spain (automotive staffing), ProStaff Group in the US (general staffing), and Business Trends Group in Singapore (general staffing). Kelly Services continued with its acquisition strategy the following year, purchasing the engineering services business of Compuware, among others. In 2002 the company opened new offices in the US, Europe, and Canada. In 2003 Kelly Services launched Kelly FedSecure, which provides professionals with security clearances to companies and government contractors.

Citing medical reasons, Adderley stepped down as chairman and CEO in 2006. President and COO Carl Camden took over as CEO, but by May 2006 Adderley had recovered and was named chairman again.

EXECUTIVES

Chairman: Terence E. (Terry) Adderley, age 75
President, CEO, and Director: Carl T. Camden, age 54, $2,035,324 total compensation
EVP and COO: George S. Corona, age 50, $787,065 total compensation
EVP and CFO: Patricia Little, age 49, $958,800 total compensation
SVP and CIO: Joseph Drouin
EVP and Chief Administrative Officer: Michael L. Durik, age 60, $1,102,614 total compensation
SVP and Chief Accounting Officer: Michael E. Debs, age 51, $500,635 total compensation
EVP Global Sales, Service, and Marketing: Michael S. Webster, age 53, $767,766 total compensation
SVP International and Outsourcing and Consulting Group: Rolf E. Kleiner, age 54
SVP Outsourcing and Consulting Group, Global Administration: James H. Bradley
SVP Global Marketing: Michael S. Morrow
SVP Outsourcing Consulting Group, Europe, Middle East, and Africa: Bernard Tommasini
SVP Information Technology: Allison M. Everett
SVP, General Counsel, and Corporate Secretary: Daniel T. Lis, age 62
SVP Central Operations and Businesses: Jonathan D. Means
SVP Human Resources: Nina M. Ramsey, age 54
SVP Technical Services Group: Steve S. Armstrong
SVP Global Solutions and Services: Pamela M. Berklich
SVP Global Service: Teresa S. Carroll
SVP Global Client Relationships: Peter W. Quigley
Auditors: PricewaterhouseCoopers LLP

LOCATIONS

HQ: Kelly Services, Inc.
999 W. Big Beaver Rd., Troy, MI 48084
Phone: 248-362-4444   **Fax:** 248-244-4360
Web: www.kellyservices.com

PRODUCTS/OPERATIONS

2008 Revenues

	$ mil.	% of total
Americas		
Commercial	2,502.6	45
PT	911.4	17
International		
Commercial	1,598.2	29
PT	198.8	4
Outsourcing/consulting	246.6	4
Other	59.7	1
Total	**5,517.3**	**100**

Selected Services

KellyConnect (call center staffing)
KellyDirect (permanent placement service)
KellySelect (temporary-to-hire service)
Kelly Automotive Services Group
Kelly Catering and Hospitality (chefs, porters)
Kelly Educational Staffing (substitute teachers)
Kelly Electronic Assembly Services
Kelly Engineering Resources (engineers)
Kelly Financial Resources (accounting, analysts)
Kelly Government Solutions (US federal government staffing)
Kelly Healthcare Resources (nurses, medical technicians)
Kelly Information Technology Resources
Kelly Law Registry
Kelly Light Industrial
Kelly Management Services
Kelly Marketing Services
Kelly Office Services (clerical staffing)
Kelly Scientific Resources (science staffing)

COMPETITORS

Adecco
Administaff
Allegis Group
ATC Healthcare
Gevity HR
Manpower
MPS
On Assignment
Randstad Holding
Robert Half
Spherion
TAC Worldwide
TrueBlue
Volt Information

HISTORICAL FINANCIALS

Company Type: Public

Income Statement

FYE: Sunday nearest December 31

	REVENUE ($ mil.)	NET INCOME ($ mil.)	NET PROFIT MARGIN	EMPLOYEES
12/08	5,517.3	(82.2)	—	650,000
12/07	5,667.6	61.0	1.1%	760,000
12/06	5,605.8	63.5	1.1%	750,000
12/05	5,289.8	39.3	0.7%	708,600
12/04	4,984.1	22.1	0.4%	8,400
Annual Growth	**2.6%**	**—**	**—**	**196.6%**

2008 Year-End Financials

Debt ratio: 12.3%
Return on equity: —
Cash ($ mil.): 118
Current ratio: 1.71
Long-term debt ($ mil.): 80
No. of shares (mil.): 35
Dividends
   Yield: 4.2%
   Payout: —
Market value ($ mil.): 455

Stock History

NASDAQ (GS): KELYA

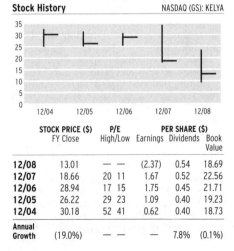

	STOCK PRICE ($) FY Close	P/E High/Low		PER SHARE ($) Earnings	Dividends	Book Value
12/08	13.01	—	—	(2.37)	0.54	18.69
12/07	18.66	20	11	1.67	0.52	22.56
12/06	28.94	17	15	1.75	0.45	21.71
12/05	26.22	29	23	1.09	0.40	19.23
12/04	30.18	52	41	0.62	0.40	18.73
Annual Growth	**(19.0%)**	**—**	**—**	**—**	**7.8%**	**(0.1%)**

Kennametal Inc.

Kennametal welcomes cutting-edge remarks. The company offers a host of metal-cutting tools, mining and highway construction equipment, and engineering services through its two divisions: Metalworking Solutions and Services Group and Advanced Materials Solutions Group. Its products include cutting, milling, and drilling tools used in metalworking; drums, bits, and accessories used in mining; and bits, grader blades, and snowplow blades used in construction.

Kennametal and its subsidiaries sell products worldwide under the Cleveland, Conforma Clad, Drill-Fix, Fix-Perfect, Greenfield, Kendex, Kenloc, Kennametal, and Kyon brand names. Customers outside the US account for more than half of sales.

In 2007 the company acquired the metal-cutting tool business of Federal Signal for about $67 million. The business comprised Manchester Tool Company, ClappDiCO Corporation, and On Time Machining Company (OTM). The company saw the purchase as a "bolt-on" acquisition that was easily integrated into its Metalworking Solutions and Services Group. In 2008 Kennametal sold OTM to Kyocera Industrial Ceramics Corp., a subsidiary of Kyocera International. Kyocera Industrial Ceramics made the unbolted OTM part of its US Cutting Tool Division.

Kennametal's bottom line was hurt in the early 21st century by weak demand in the oil and gas industries, the agricultural market, and the overall depressed market. In response the company cut costs by reducing its salaried workforce and consolidated eight North American warehouses to a single, central location near Cleveland. The company believes these moves will help bolster future profits.

Kennametal also decided to make its Advanced Materials Solutions Group (AMSG) represent half of its revenue. To that end, it purchased Tricon Metals & Services (not to be confused with Tricon Industries) in 2008, renamed it Kennametal Tricon Metals & Services, and placed it under the AMSG umbrella.

In 2009 Kennametal agreed to sell its high-speed steel drills, related product lines, and assets to Top-Eastern Drills. The proposed transaction involves four sites in North America, employing about 400 people.

HISTORY

In 1832 Irish immigrant and coppersmith Robert McKenna came to Pittsburgh and opened a copper works. His three sons took over the business after he died in 1852. In 1900 Robert's grandson, A. G. McKenna, developed a revolutionary cutting tool made of steel and tungsten (and later, of vanadium). The family set up Vanadium Alloys Steel Co. in 1910.

In 1938 Philip McKenna, A. G.'s son, formed a new business called Kennametal, based on a tungsten-titanium carbide alloy for cutting tools. The family incorporated the company as Kennametal in 1943. WWII and the Korean War brought strong US military demand for the company's products. Kennametal expanded overseas during the 1960s and 1970s and went public in 1977. During the 1980s Kennametal bought Bristol Erickson (UK), as well as companies in Belgium, Canada, France, and the Netherlands.

The company was accused of illegally selling equipment to an Iraqi-controlled firm in the UK in 1991, in violation of a trade embargo imposed by the first Bush Administration in 1990. While the US Department of Justice ultimately concluded that no export laws had been broken by Kennametal, the company settled the case in 1997 by paying a fine of $13,457, without admitting any wrongdoing.

The firm bought J & L Industrial Supply, a Detroit-based catalog supplier of metalwork tools, in 1991, and continued to grow by buying a majority stake in German toolmaker Hertel (1993) and by forming a marketing alliance with industrial supplies distributor W.W. Grainger (1994). During fiscal 1995 Kennametal invested in Asia, Mexico, and Poland. The next year William Newlin became the first outsider to become chairman. He succeeded Quentin McKenna, a nephew of Philip McKenna, who had been chairman for 13 years.

Kennametal added JLK Direct Distribution to its supply operations in 1997 and then spun off the unit, retaining about 80% ownership. It also bought rival toolmaker Greenfield Industries. Weak product demand caused by slumps in the oil and paper industries and Asian economic woes contributed to Kennametal's job cuts (about 5% of its workforce) and its plans for plant closures in 1998 and 1999.

Markos Tambakeras succeeded Robert Mc-Geehan as president and CEO in mid-1999. McGeehan had served 10 years as president of Kennametal, and was the first person outside the McKenna family to hold that post.

In 2001 Kennametal announced that it would cut between 6% and 8% of its salaried workforce. Newlin stepped down as chairman, remaining on the board as lead director, and was succeeded by Tambakeras as chairman in 2002.

In 2003 the company named its global technology center in Latrobe the Quentin C. McKenna Technology Center, after its former chief executive, who died that year at the age of 76. After being named president of Kennemetal in 1978 and CEO a year later, Quentin McKenna built the company from a regional toolmaker into a *FORTUNE* 500 company.

In early 2005 Kennametal added Pennsylvania-based Extrude Hone, which provides engineered component process technologies to a variety of industries, in a deal valued at $137 million.

In 2006 the company made a move to narrow its focus, selling its distribution subsidiary, J & L Industrial Supply, to MSC Industrial Direct for about $350 million. With the closing of the J & L sale, Kennametal exited the distribution business completely.

EVP/COO Carlos Cardoso was promoted to president and CEO at the outset of 2006, after one year as chief of manufacturing operations. Markos Tambakeras remained as executive chairman following the management transition.

In mid-2006 the company acquired Sintec Group of Germany, a manufacturer of ceramic engineered components for the aerospace, medical, and metalizing markets. Tambakeras served one year as executive chairman before leaving the board at the end of 2006. Larry Yost, the former chairman and CEO of ArvinMeritor and a Kennametal director since 1987, was elected to succeed Tambakeras as chairman.

In late 2007 the board selected president/CEO Carlos Cardoso to serve in the additional post of chairman. Larry Yost was picked to serve as the board's lead director.

EXECUTIVES

Chairman, President, and CEO: Carlos M. Cardoso, age 51
VP and CFO: Frank P. Simpkins, age 46
VP and CTO: John R. Tucker
VP and CIO: Steven R. (Steve) Hanna
Chief Marketing Officer: John H. Jacko Jr., age 52
VP and Chief Human Resources Officer: Kevin R. Walling, age 44
VP Finance and Corporate Controller: Wayne D. Moser, age 56
VP; Director, Kennametal Distribution Services: P. Mark Schiller, age 57
VP and Treasurer: Lawrence J. Lanza, age 60
VP, Mergers and Acquisitions: James E. Morrison, age 58
VP, Secretary, and General Counsel: David W. Greenfield, age 59
VP, Value Business System and Lean Enterprise: Philip H. Weihl, age 53
VP; President, Advanced Materials Solutions Group: Gary W. Weismann, age 54
VP; President, Metalworking Solutions Services Group: Paul DeMand, age 44
Assistant Treasurer and Director, Tax: Brian E. Kelly, age 42
Assistant Secretary and Assistant General Counsel: Kevin G. Nowe, age 52
Director, Manufacturing, Europe: Brendan Drummond
Director, Sales and Service, Europe: Gerald Goubau
Director, Marketing, Europe: Doug Phillips
Auditors: PricewaterhouseCoopers LLP

LOCATIONS

HQ: Kennametal Inc.
 1600 Technology Way, Latrobe, PA 15650
Phone: 724-539-5000   **Fax:** 724-539-6657
Web: www.kennametal.com

2009 Sales

	$ mil.	% of total
North America		
US	908.0	46
Canada	47.3	2
Europe		
Germany	360.6	18
UK	59.7	3
Asia	266.7	13
Other regions	357.6	18
Total	**1,999.9**	**100**

PRODUCTS/OPERATIONS

2009 Sales

	$ mil.	% of total
Metalworking Solutions & Services	1,191.8	60
Advanced Materials Solutions	808.1	40
Total	**1,999.9**	**100**

Selected Products

Metalworking Tools
 Boring tools
 Combination tools
 Metal-cutting inserts
 Milling kits
 Tool management software
Mining, Construction, and Other Equipment
 Agricultural implements
 Auger tooling and drilling products
 Face and roof augers
 Motor grader blades
 Pining-rod systems
 Scraper and grader blades
 Snowplow blades
 Soil stabilization tooling
 Two-prong bits

Industrial Supply
 Bandsaws
 Boring bars
 Calipers
 Dies
 Drills and drill bits
 Lathes
 Milling cutters
 Reamers
 Safety wear and equipment
 Taps

Selected Brand Names

Block Style K
Chicago Latrobe
Cleveland
Conforma Clad
Drill-Fix
Ecogrind
Erickson
Fix-Perfect
Greenfield
Heinlein
Hertel
Kendex
Kenloc
KennaMAX
Kennametal
Kennametal Hertel
KM
KM Micro
Kyon
RTW
Top Notch
Widia
Widma

COMPETITORS

Actuant
Allegheny Technologies
Atlas Copco
Flow International
Giddings & Lewis
GILDEMEISTER
Hardinge
Jore
L. S. Starrett
Sandvik
Seco Tools
WALTER

HISTORICAL FINANCIALS

Company Type: Public

Income Statement

FYE: June 30

	REVENUE ($ mil.)	NET INCOME ($ mil.)	NET PROFIT MARGIN	EMPLOYEES
6/09	1,999.9	(119.7)	—	11,600
6/08	2,705.1	167.8	6.2%	13,673
6/07	2,385.5	174.2	7.3%	13,947
6/06	2,329.6	256.3	11.0%	13,300
6/05	2,304.2	119.3	5.2%	14,000
Annual Growth	**(3.5%)**	**—**	**—**	**(4.6%)**

2009 Year-End Financials

Debt ratio: 35.0%
Return on equity: —
Cash ($ mil.): 70
Current ratio: 2.31
Long-term debt ($ mil.): 437

No. of shares (mil.): 81
Dividends
 Yield: 2.5%
 Payout: —
Market value ($ mil.): 1,559

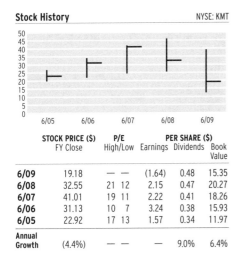

	STOCK PRICE ($) FY Close	P/E High/Low		PER SHARE ($) Earnings	Dividends	Book Value
6/09	19.18	—	—	(1.64)	0.48	15.35
6/08	32.55	21	12	2.15	0.47	20.27
6/07	41.01	19	11	2.22	0.41	18.26
6/06	31.13	10	7	3.24	0.38	15.93
6/05	22.92	17	13	1.57	0.34	11.97
Annual Growth	(4.4%)	—	—	—	9.0%	6.4%

Key Energy Services

Energy is the key to growth for Key Energy Services, one of the US's largest well-servicing and workover companies. The company provides maintenance, workover, and recompletion of wells, primarily for onshore drilling. It also provides services such as contract drilling, well completion and abandonment, oil field fluid transportation, production testing, and storage and disposal services to major and independent oil companies. Key Energy Services has a fleet of 924 well service rigs, which operate primarily in the US, as well as in Argentina, Canada, and Mexico. It also has minority stakes in a Canada-based drilling and production services company and a Russia-based drilling and workover services firm.

Key Energy Services is active in major onshore oil and gas regions of the US, including the Four Corners area, the Gulf Coast, the midcontinent area, the Rocky Mountains, and the Appalachian, Permian, and San Joaquin basins.

To complement its core drilling contracting business the company makes strategic acquisitions to expand its product lines and geographic coverage. In 2007 it acquired well services company Moncla Companies. In 2008 the company expanded its shale play assets in the US through the acquisition of Leader Energy Services Ltd. $34.6 million. That year it also acquired drilling and services firms Tri-Energy Services, Western Drilling, and Hydra-Walk.

HISTORY

Yankee Oil & Gas was formed by Paul Montle in 1977 to run a mix of energy and financial businesses. By 1987 it was fighting for its financial life. Steep dips in oil and gas prices devastated its energy businesses (including flagship Yale E. Key), and its Yankee Bank for Finance and Savings went into receivership in 1988.

The company restructured around its oil and gas businesses while acquiring an asbestos-abatement firm, a sludge treatment unit, and Toxic Clean up Systems. After Montle stepped down as CEO in 1989, Francis John took over as the company struggled to stay afloat. The firm sold its environmental services unit and declared

bankruptcy in 1992. It also adopted the name Key Energy Group that year.

Buoyed by an oil industry recovery, John turned the company (which he had pared down to a small West Texas oil and gas well service firm) into a major consolidator in the highly fragmented industry. In 1993 Key Energy Group acquired Odessa Exploration (which it subsequently sold) and picked up Clint Hurt Drilling in 1995. That year it also acquired a 58% stake in Orbitron, a firm with 24 gas wells in West Texas, and added 58 well service rigs in 1996 by buying WellTech.

Key Energy Group acquired or agreed to acquire more than two dozen companies in 1997, including two well service operations with more than 100 rigs from Nabors Industries. In 1998 it bought Dawson Production Services, nearly doubling its assets, and changed its name to Key Energy Services, amid a major reorganization. Rising oil prices in 1999 stimulated exploration, prompting increased demand for Key Energy's services.

In 2000 Key Energy added three rigs to the seven it is operating in Argentina. The company expanded its domestic well service operations in 2002 by buying closely held Q Services.

Financial discrepancies forced the company to delay its 2003, 2004, and 2005 annual SEC filings, and to write down assets. In 2005 it sold US land drilling operations (35 rigs) to Patterson-UTI.

EXECUTIVES

Chairman, President, and CEO: Richard J. (Dick) Alario, age 54, $6,197,213 total compensation
EVP and COO: Newton W. (Trey) Wilson III, age 58, $2,011,705 total compensation
SVP and CFO: T.M. (Trey) Whichard III, age 50
SVP Administration and Chief People Officer: Kim B. Clarke, age 53, $1,409,429 total compensation
SVP Western Division: Jim D. Flynt, age 64
SVP Product Development, Strategic Planning, and Quality: Don D. Weinheimer, age 50, $1,092,019 total compensation
SVP Eastern Region: Phil G. Coyne, age 57
SVP and General Counsel: Kimberly R. (Kim) Frye
VP Corporate Development: Blake Hutchinson
Group VP Drilling and International Operations, Houston: Steven A. (Steve) Richards
VP and Treasurer: J. Marshall Dodson, age 38
VP Business Development: Tommy Pipes
VP Health, Safety, Security, and Environmental: Ken Houston
VP Pressure Pumping: John Carnett
VP and Controller: Ike Smith, age 34
Auditors: Grant Thornton LLP

LOCATIONS

HQ: Key Energy Services, Inc.
1301 McKinney St., Ste. 1800, Houston, TX 77010
Phone: 713-651-4300   **Fax:** 713-652-4005
Web: www.keyenergy.com

2008 Sales

	$ mil.	% of total
US	1,800.2	91
Argentina	118.8	6
Mexico	47.2	3
Canada	5.9	—
Total	**1,972.1**	**100**

PRODUCTS/OPERATIONS

2008 Sales

	$ mil.	% of total
Well servicing	1,509.8	77
Pressure pumping	345.0	17
Fishing & rental services	117.3	6
Total	**1,972.1**	**100**

COMPETITORS

Allis-Chalmers
Basic Energy Services
BJ Services
Halliburton
Helmerich & Payne
Nabors Industries
Pride International
Schlumberger
Weatherford International

HISTORICAL FINANCIALS

Company Type: Public

Income Statement

	REVENUE ($ mil.)	NET INCOME ($ mil.)	NET PROFIT MARGIN	EMPLOYEES
				FYE: December 31
12/08	1,972.1	84.1	4.3%	8,582
12/07	1,662.0	169.3	10.2%	9,820
12/06	1,546.2	171.0	11.1%	9,400
12/05	1,190.4	45.7	3.8%	9,400
12/04	987.7	(32.2)	—	9,400
Annual Growth	18.9%	—	—	(2.3%)

2008 Year-End Financials

Debt ratio: 73.6%
Return on equity: 9.6%
Cash ($ mil.): 93
Current ratio: 2.05
Long-term debt ($ mil.): 634
No. of shares (mil.): 124
Dividends
Yield: 0.0%
Payout: —
Market value ($ mil.): 547

Stock History   NYSE: KEG

	STOCK PRICE ($) FY Close	P/E High/Low		PER SHARE ($) Earnings	Dividends	Book Value
12/08	4.41	31	5	0.67	0.00	6.94
12/07	14.39	16	10	1.27	0.00	7.17
12/06	15.65	15	10	1.28	0.00	5.89
12/05	13.47	44	28	0.34	0.00	4.47
12/04	11.80	—	—	(0.24)	0.00	4.08
Annual Growth	(21.8%)	—	—	—	—	14.2%

KeyCorp

Financial services giant KeyCorp has the clout of mean Henry Potter of Bedford Falls, but wants to be the sweet George Bailey of bankers. With a focus on relationship banking and retail operations, flagship subsidiary KeyBank operates more than 985 branches (KeyCenters) in more than a dozen states. Its operations are divided into two groups: community banking offers local banking services including deposits, loans, and financial planning, while national banking provides real estate capital, equipment financing, and capital markets services to large corporate clients. Non-bank subsidiaries offer insurance, brokerage, investment banking, and credit card processing for small businesses.

KeyCorp was not immune to the 2008 credit crisis. It was one of several banks that took part in the $250 billion government bailout, which was aimed at increasing the flow of financing to

US businesses and consumers. KeyCorp recieved some $2.5 billion that year by issuing shares of preferred stock to the US Treasury.

KeyCorp has been paring away some of its nonbanking subsidiaries to focus on its core consumer and corporate businesses. As part of this focus on local banking, the company sold Champion Mortgage, which specializes in high-risk customers, to HSBC Holdings (which bought Champion's mortgage loan portfolio) and Nationstar Mortgage (acquired Champion's loan origination operations). KeyCorp also sold its financial services unit McDonald Investments to UBS Financial Services.

In addition to exiting the subprime mortgage business other areas of business also are being cut as a way to curb risky lending. KeyCorp is exiting retail inventory lending to dealers of marine and recreational vehicles. It also is limiting educational loans to those backed by the government and it plans to quit offering loans to homebuilders.

The company's community banking group continues to perform well, despite the economic turmoil. It built upon its banking division when it bought U.S.B. Holding Co. and its 31-branch Union State Bank subsidiary for some $550 million in early 2008. The deal nearly doubled KeyCorp's footprint in the Hudson River Valley region.

It also acquired Tuition Management Systems, which provides outsourced tuition billing, accounting, and counseling services for schools and colleges, in 2007. It merged the new unit into its Key Education Resources operations.

HISTORY

KeyCorp predecessor Commercial Bank of Albany was chartered in 1825. In 1865 it joined the new national banking system and became National Commercial Bank of Albany. After WWI National Commercial consolidated with Union National Bank & Trust as National Commercial Bank and Trust, which then merged with First Trust and Deposit in 1971.

In 1973 Victor Riley became president and CEO. Under Riley, National Commercial grew during the 1970s and 1980s through acquisitions. Riley sought to make the company a regional powerhouse but was thwarted when several New England states passed legislation barring New York banks from buying banks in the region.

As a result, the company, renamed Key Bank in 1979, turned west, targeting small towns with less competition. Thus situated, it prospered, despite entering Alaska just in time for the 1986 oil price collapse. Its folksy image and small-town success earned it a reputation as the "Wal-Mart of banking."

Meanwhile, in Cleveland, Society for Savings followed a different path. Founded as a mutual savings bank in 1849, the institution succeeded from the start. It survived the Civil War and postwar economic turmoil and built Cleveland's first skyscraper in 1890. It continued to grow even during the Depression and became the largest savings bank outside the Northeast in 1949.

In 1955 the bank formed a holding company, Society National. Society grew through the acquisitions of smaller banks in Ohio until 1979,

when Ohio allowed branch banking in contiguous counties. Thereafter, Society National opened branches, as well. In the mid-1980s and the early 1990s, the renamed Society Corporation began consolidating its operations and continued growing.

A 1994 merger of National Commercial with Society more than doubled assets for the surviving KeyCorp; compatibility of the two companies' systems and software simplified consolidation. KeyCorp sold its mortgage-servicing unit to NationsBank (now Bank of America) in 1995 and over the next year bought investment management, finance, and investment banking firms.

In 1997 KeyCorp began trimming its branch network, divesting 200 offices, including its 28-branch KeyBank Wyoming subsidiary. It expanded its consumer lending business that year by buying Champion Mortgage. In cooperation with USF&G (now part of The St. Paul Travelers Companies) and three HMOs, KeyCorp began offering health insurance to the underserved small-business market.

In 1998 the company bought Leasetec, which leases computer storage systems globally through its StorageTek subsidiary; it also bought McDonald & Company Investments (now McDonald Investments; sold in 2007), with an eye toward reaching its goal of earning half of its revenues from fees. Also in 1998, KeyCorp began offering business lines of credit to customers of Costco Wholesale, the nation's largest wholesale club.

As part of a restructuring effort, KeyCorp sold 28 Long Island, New York, branches to Dime Bancorp in 1999. The next year the company sold its credit card portfolio to Associates First Capital (now part of Citigroup) and bought National Realty Funding, a securitizer of commercial mortgages. In 2001 it acquired Denver-based investment bank The Wallach Company.

The company expanded further in the Denver area with its 2002 purchase of Union Bankshares. Two years later KeyCorp bought Seattle-area bank EverTrust Financial Group.

EXECUTIVES

Chairman, President, and CEO: Henry L. Meyer III, age 59, $4,860,595 total compensation
Vice Chairman, Chief Administrative Officer, and Director: Thomas C. (Tom) Stevens, age 59, $1,517,872 total compensation
Vice Chair: Beth E. Mooney, age 53, $1,374,380 total compensation
Vice Chair; President, Key National Banking: Peter D. Hancock, age 50, $1,280,288 total compensation
SEVP and CFO: Jeffrey B. Weeden, age 52, $1,549,025 total compensation
EVP and CIO: Stephen E. (Steve) Yates, age 61
Chief Accounting Officer: Robert L. Morris, age 56
EVP, Chief Risk Review Officer, and General Auditor: Kevin T. Ryan
EVP Investor Relations: Vernon L. (Vern) Patterson
EVP and Chief Human Resources Officer: Thomas E. (Tom) Helfrich, age 56
EVP Wealth Management Group: Timothy J. (Tim) Lathe, age 53
EVP and Director Corporate Diversity and Philanthropy: Margot J. Copeland
EVP KeyBank; President, Community Development Banking: Bruce D. Murphy

EVP Global Treasury Management, Global Trade Services: Pamela A. (Pam) Carson
EVP, General Counsel, and Secretary: Paul N. Harris, age 50
EVP and Chief Risk Officer: Charles S. (Chuck) Hyle, age 57
EVP Client Services Group: Michael P. (Mike) Barnum
EVP Bank Capital Markets, Key Corporate and Investment Bank: Richard W. Owens
EVP Corporate Development and Strategic Planning: Andrew R. (Andy) Tyson
EVP and Treasurer: Joseph M. Vayda
EVP and Head Credit Portfolio Management: Jeffery J. (Jeff) Weaver
Auditors: Ernst & Young LLP

LOCATIONS

HQ: KeyCorp
127 Public Sq., Cleveland, OH 44114
Phone: 216-689-6300   **Fax:** 216-689-0519
Web: www.key.com

PRODUCTS/OPERATIONS

2008 Gross Revenues

	$ mil.	% of total
Interest		
Loans	4,048	61
Securities	440	7
Other investments	141	2
Noninterest		
Trust & investment services	538	8
Service charges on deposits	365	5
Operating lease income	270	4
Letter of credit & loan fees	183	3
Other	673	10
Total	**6,658**	**100**

COMPETITORS

Associated Banc-Corp
Bank of America
Bank of New York Mellon
Citigroup
Citizens Financial Group
Comerica
Fifth Third
Flagstar Bancorp
HSBC USA
Huntington Bancshares
JPMorgan Chase
M&T Bank
Marshall & Ilsley
Northern Trust
PNC Financial
Sovereign Bank
U.S. Bancorp
Wells Fargo

HISTORICAL FINANCIALS

Company Type: Public

Income Statement

FYE: December 31

	ASSETS ($ mil.)	NET INCOME ($ mil.)	INCOME AS % OF ASSETS	EMPLOYEES
12/08	104,531.0	(1,468.0)	—	18,095
12/07	99,983.0	919.0	0.9%	18,934
12/06	92,337.0	1,050.0	1.1%	20,006
12/05	93,126.0	1,129.0	1.2%	19,485
12/04	90,739.0	954.0	1.1%	19,576
Annual Growth	3.6%	—	—	(1.9%)

2008 Year-End Financials

Equity as % of assets: 7.1%
Return on assets: —
Return on equity: —
Long-term debt ($ mil.): 14,995
No. of shares (mil.): 879
Dividends
Yield: 11.7%
Payout: —
Market value ($ mil.): 7,485
Sales ($ mil.): 4,279

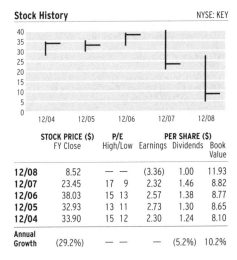
	STOCK PRICE ($) FY Close	P/E High/Low		PER SHARE ($) Earnings	Dividends	Book Value
12/08	8.52	—	—	(3.36)	1.00	11.93
12/07	23.45	17	9	2.32	1.46	8.82
12/06	38.03	15	13	2.57	1.38	8.77
12/05	32.93	13	11	2.73	1.30	8.65
12/04	33.90	15	12	2.30	1.24	8.10
Annual Growth	**(29.2%)**	—	—	—	**(5.2%)**	**10.2%**

Kimberly-Clark

Nobody knows noses and diapering babies better than Kimberly-Clark, the world's top maker of personal paper products. It operates under four business segments: personal care, consumer tissue, K-C Professional, and health care. Under brand names such as Cottonelle, Kleenex, and Scott, Kimberly-Clark makes facial and bathroom tissues, paper towels, and other household items. Its personal care products include Huggies, Kotex, and Depend. The company also makes WypAll and Kimwipes commercial wipes. It spun off its paper (Neenah Paper, Technical Paper), pulp, and timber operations to create Neenah Paper. The firm kicked off a multiyear reorganization in 2005 and bought Germany's Microcuff GmbH.

The company also makes specialty and technical papers. Products, such as its Huggies Little Swimmers disposable swimpants and Depend and Poise incontinence care products, have helped fuel the company's sales growth. In its ongoing battle with Procter & Gamble's rival Pampers for dominance of the diaper market, Huggies introduced new diapers to replace its Huggies Supreme line. Wal-Mart has represented 13% of Kimberly-Clark's sales consistently since 2004.

Best known for its consumer products, Kimberly-Clark has seen wealth in the health and medical sectors. The company has been expanding into medical products and is now a leading US maker of disposable medical goods. Kimberly-Clark also has been adding products for the health care market through acquisitions. The firm makes sterilization wrap, face masks, surgical drapes and gowns, and closed-suction respiratory products.

While it balances its mix of products and reacts to the slowdown in the global economy, Kimberly-Clark has been restructuring its operations. In mid-2009 the company announced plans to reduce its worldwide workforce by about 1,600 primarily salaried positions by the end of the year. The cuts follow the purging in 2008 of about 10% of the firm's employees (some 6,000 employees) worldwide. Kimberly-Clark has also closed or sold more than 20 plants (representing about 17% of its manufacturing facilities).

Kimberly-Clark is extending its reach overseas. In early 2009 the company acquired the remaining 31% of its Bogota, Colombia-based subsidiary Colombiana Kimberly Colpapel (CKC). In late 2006 the company bought the remaining 30% stake in its Kimberly-Clark Kenko Industria e Comercio Ltda, based in Brazil, from Alsercom Comercio De Produtos Texteis e Plasticos Ltda. In 2008 Kimberly-Clark announced plans to purchase the remaining stake (about 50%) in its Kimberly-Clark of South Africa unit from The Lion Match Company, a subsidiary of FASIC Investment Corporation. Kimberly-Clark and other companies have operated the South African joint venture since 1955.

HISTORY

John Kimberly, Charles Clark, Havilah Babcock, and Frank Shattuck founded Kimberly, Clark & Company in Neenah, Wisconsin, in 1872 to manufacture newsprint from rags. The company incorporated as Kimberly & Clark Company in 1880 and built a pulp and paper plant on the Fox River in 1889.

In 1914 the company developed cellu-cotton, a cotton substitute used by the US Army as surgical cotton during WWI. Army nurses used cellu-cotton pads as disposable sanitary napkins, and six years later the company introduced Kotex, the first disposable feminine hygiene product. Kleenex, the first throwaway handkerchief, followed in 1924. Kimberly & Clark joined with The New York Times Company in 1926 to build a newsprint mill (Spruce Falls Power and Paper) in Ontario, Canada. Two years later the company went public as Kimberly-Clark.

The firm expanded internationally during the 1950s, opening plants in Mexico, Germany, and the UK. It began operations in 17 more foreign locations in the 1960s.

CEO Guy Minard, who retired in 1971, sold the four mills that handled Kimberly-Clark's unprofitable coated-paper business and entered the paper towel and disposable diaper markets. Minard's successor, Darwin Smith, introduced Kimbies diapers in 1968, but they leaked and were withdrawn from the market. An improved version came out in 1976, followed by Huggies, a premium-priced diaper with elastic leg bands, two years later.

The company formed Midwest Express Airlines from its corporate flight department in 1984 (a business it exited in 1996). Smith moved Kimberly-Clark's headquarters from Neenah to Irving, Texas, the following year.

In 1991 Kimberly-Clark and The New York Times Company sold Spruce Falls Power and Paper. Smith retired as chairman in 1992 and was succeeded by Wayne Sanders, who was largely responsible for designing Huggies Pull-Ups (introduced in 1989). Kimberly-Clark entered a joint venture to make personal care products in Argentina in 1994 and also bought the feminine hygiene units of VP-Schickedanz (Germany) and Handan Comfort and Beauty Group (China).

Kimberly-Clark bought Scott Paper in 1995 for $9.4 billion. The move boosted its market share in bathroom tissue from 5% to 31% and its share in paper towels from 6% to 18%, but led to some headaches as the company absorbed Scott's operations.

In 1997 Kimberly-Clark sold its 50% stake in Canada's Scott Paper to forest products company Kruger and bought diaper operations in Spain and Portugal and disposable surgical face masks maker Tecnol Medical Products. A tissue

price war in Europe bruised the company's bottom line that year and the company began massive job cuts. (By the end of 1999, nearly 4,000 jobs, mostly in the tissue-based businesses, had been axed.)

In part to focus on its health care business, which it entered in 1997, the company in 1999 sold some of its timber interests and its timber fleet to Cooper/T. Smith Corp. Augmenting its presence in Germany, Switzerland, and Austria, in 1999 the company paid $365 million for the tissue business of Swiss-based Attisholz Holding. Adding to its lineup of medical products, the company bought Ballard Medical Products in 1999 for $744 million and examination glove maker Safeskin in 2000 for about $800 million.

Also in 2000 the company bought virtually all of Taiwan's S-K Corporation; the move made Kimberly-Clark one of the largest manufacturers of consumer packaged goods in Taiwan and set the stage for expanded distribution in the Asia/Pacific region.

In 2002 Kimberly-Clark purchased paper-packaging rival Amcor's stake in their Kimberly-Clark Australia joint venture.

EXECUTIVES

Chairman, President, and CEO: Thomas J. (Tom) Falk, age 50, $7,236,831 total compensation
SVP and CFO: Mark A. Buthman, age 48, $2,198,177 total compensation
SVP and Chief Human Resources Officer: Lizanne C. (Liz) Gottung, age 52
SVP and Chief Marketing Officer: Anthony J. Palmer, age 49, $1,765,034 total compensation
SVP Law, Government Affairs, and Chief Compliance Officer: Thomas J. (Tom) Mielke, age 50
SVP and Chief Strategy Officer: Christian A. (Chris) Brickman, age 44
VP Communications and Public Relations, Korea, Northern Asia Pacific: E.W. Lee
Group President, North Atlantic Consumer Products: Robert E. Abernathy, age 54, $2,772,825 total compensation
Group President, Developing and Emerging Markets: Robert W. (Bob) Black, age 49, $1,629,376 total compensation
President, Global Health Care: Joanne B. Bauer, age 53
President, Global K-C Professional: Jan B. Spencer, age 53
Director Corporate Communications: David J. (Dave) Dickson
Auditors: Deloitte & Touche LLP

LOCATIONS

HQ: Kimberly-Clark Corporation
351 Phelps Dr., Irving, TX 75038
Phone: 972-281-1200 **Fax:** 972-281-1490
Web: www.kimberly-clark.com

2008 Sales

	$ mil.	% of total
US	10,143	50
Asia, Latin America & other	5,942	29
Europe	3,679	18
Canada	574	3
Adjustments	(923)	—
Total	**19,415**	**100**

PRODUCTS/OPERATIONS

2008 Sales

	$ mil.	% of total
Personal care products	8,272	43
Consumer tissue	6,748	35
K-C Professional & other	3,174	16
Health care	1,224	6
Corporate & other	79	—
Adjustments	(82)	—
Total	**19,415**	**100**

Selected Products and Brands

Medical
- Closed-suction respiratory products
- Examination gloves (Safeskin)
- Face masks
- Infection-control products
- Scrub suits and apparel
- Sterile wrap (Kimguard)
- Surgical drapes and gowns

Personal Care
- Baby wipes (Huggies)
- Disposable diapers (Huggies, Pull-Ups)
- Feminine hygiene products (Kotex, New Freedom, Lightdays)
- Incontinence products (Depend, Poise)
- Swimpants (Little Swimmers)

Tissue-Based
- Bathroom tissue (Cottonelle, Scott)
- Commercial wipes (Kimwipes, WypAll)
- Facial tissue (Kleenex)
- Paper napkins (Scott)
- Paper towels (Kleenex, Scott, Viva)

COMPETITORS

3M	Energizer Holdings
Ansell	Georgia-Pacific
Becton, Dickinson	Johnson & Johnson
Bristol-Myers Squibb	Medline Industries
Cardinal Supply Chain Medical	Nice-Pak Products Potlatch
CCA Industries	Procter & Gamble
DSG International Ltd	SSI Surgical Services

HISTORICAL FINANCIALS

Company Type: Public

Income Statement
FYE: December 31

	REVENUE ($ mil.)	NET INCOME ($ mil.)	NET PROFIT MARGIN	EMPLOYEES
12/08	19,415.0	1,671.0	8.6%	53,000
12/07	18,266.0	1,822.9	10.0%	53,000
12/06	16,746.9	1,499.5	9.0%	55,000
12/05	15,902.6	1,580.6	9.9%	57,000
12/04	15,083.2	1,800.2	11.9%	60,000
Annual Growth	6.5%	(1.8%)	—	(3.1%)

2008 Year-End Financials

Debt ratio: 125.9%
Return on equity: 36.7%
Cash ($ mil.): 505
Current ratio: 1.22
Long-term debt ($ mil.): 4,882

No. of shares (mil.): 414
Dividends
  Yield: 4.4%
  Payout: 57.4%
Market value ($ mil.): 21,860

Stock History
NYSE: KMB

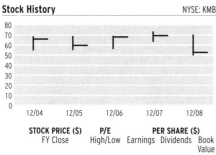

	STOCK PRICE ($) FY Close	P/E High/Low	PER SHARE ($) Earnings	Dividends	Book Value
12/08	52.74	17 12	4.04	2.32	9.36
12/07	69.34	18 16	4.09	2.12	12.60
12/06	67.95	21 17	3.25	1.96	14.71
12/05	59.65	21 17	3.28	1.80	13.41
12/04	65.81	19 15	3.61	1.60	15.99
Annual Growth	(5.4%)	— —	2.9%	9.7%	(12.5%)

Kindred Healthcare

Kindred Healthcare is one of the largest long-term health care providers in the US. Kindred operates some 230 nursing homes and more than 80 long-term acute care hospitals located in about 35 states. Its facilities have a combined capacity of about 35,000 beds. The company owns some of its facilities, but operates most of them under lease agreements with Ventas and other third parties. Kindred also operates a contract rehabilitation therapy business, which serves its own and other long-term care facilities, through its People*first* Rehabilitation division.

In 2007 Kindred spun off its Kindred Pharmacy Services unit, which distributed drugs to long-term care facilities. The unit was combined with the institutional pharmacy unit of AmerisourceBergen to form a new entity named PharMerica. The deal created the #2 institutional pharmacy nationwide (behind Omnicare). Kindred Pharmacy Services contributed more than 40 institutional pharmacies in 26 states to the combined company.

Kindred's health services division, which accounts for more than 40% of sales, operates nursing home facilities and provides specialized treatment for certain diseases such as Alzheimer's. It also provides rehabilitative care, often through contracts with Kindred's own rehabilitation division. (About 75% of the rehab unit's sales come from such contracts.)

The company's hospital division includes both freestanding hospitals and "hospitals-within-hospitals," which are co-located with short-term acute care facilities and sometimes receive patients as they are discharged from the host facility. All of Kindred's hospitals care for patients with complex medical conditions: those who are recovering from major surgery, are experiencing multiple organ failure, or have brain or spinal cord injuries, for instance.

Providing high quality care, recruiting qualified medical personnel, and improving operating efficiencies are key to Kindred's strategy across all its divisions. The company also wants to capitalize on marketing opportunities within "cluster markets" where it has multiple facilities.

Medicare and Medicaid reimbursements make up nearly three-fourths of Kindred's revenue, and the company is looking for ways to increase admissions (particularly in its hospital division) of patients with commercial insurance, which reimburses at higher rates.

Additionally, Kindred tries to manage its portfolio of facilities to rid itself of underperforming assets and acquire or build new ones. It divested about 30 unprofitable nursing homes and one long-term acute care hospital in 2007 and 2008. Looking to add more profitable facilities, the company entered lease agreements for eight nursing homes in San Francisco in 2007. In addition, Kindred has a handful of new freestanding hospital facilities under development.

Investment advisory firm Franklin Mutual Advisers (FMA) owns about 20% of Kindred.

HISTORY

After a stint as Kentucky's commerce secretary in the 1980s, Bruce Lunsford was approached by respiratory therapist Michael Barr with the idea of establishing long-term hospitals for ventilator-dependent patients. Barr said these hospitals would be cheaper to run than full-service facilities, which require additional equipment. Lunsford (who became chairman, president, and CEO) and Barr (who was COO) founded Vencare in 1983 with backing from Gene Smith (a wealthy political associate of Lunsford). They bought a money-losing, 62-bed Indiana hospital and soon turned the operation around.

Vencare expanded into Florida and Texas and, by the end of the 1980s, operated more than 420 beds in seven facilities. Revenues jumped from less than $1 million in 1985 to $54 million by 1989, the year it changed its name to Vencor.

During the early 1990s Vencor added facilities in Arizona, California, Colorado, Georgia, and Missouri. Vencor ran 29 facilities by the end of 1993, the same year it launched its Vencare respiratory care program.

Vencor acquisitions in 1995 included hospital respiratory and cardiopulmonary departments in seven states. Later that year it bought the much-larger Hillhaven, the US's #2 nursing home operator at that time. (In 1990 Hillhaven had been spun off from what is now Tenet Healthcare.) When Vencor bought it, Hillhaven owned 310 nursing homes, 60 pharmacies, and 23 retirement communities. The buy furthered Lunsford's vision of creating a network of long-term-care facilities and services. Vencor also debuted VenTouch, an electronic-pad-based record-keeping system for its facilities, in 1995.

In 1996 Vencor spun off its assisted and independent living properties as Atria Communities; as part of the Hillhaven assimilation, it also consolidated its MediSave pharmacy unit into its hospital operations and sold 34 nursing homes to Lennox Healthcare.

Vencor's 1997 buys included TheraTx (216 rehabilitation centers, 28 nursing centers, 16 occupational health clinics), and Transitional Hospitals (long-term acute care hospitals).

In 1998 the company split into Ventas (real estate) and Vencor (operations). It also sold most of its remaining interest in an assisted living company (now called Atria Senior Quarters) it had spun off in 1996. To attract wealthier residents, it also launched a program in 1998 to turn away — and turn out — Medicaid patients. Vencor soon abandoned the plan amid heated attacks from advocacy groups. (Welcoming back the evictees didn't stop Florida regulators from fining Vencor.) Several other states and the federal government also began probing Vencor's practices; in 1999 the affair prompted Congressional action designed to protect Medicaid patients. Lunsford and Barr were ousted in the turmoil. The government also demanded that Vencor return $90 million in overpayments over 60 months ($2 million a month) or risk losing Medicare payments.

The company filed for Chapter 11 bankruptcy later in 1999. Despite bankruptcy protection, the Justice Department in 2000 filed claims for more than $1 billion from Vencor for Medicare fraud since 1992. In 2001 Vencor settled the majority of these claims. The company emerged from bankruptcy in April 2001 and changed its name to Kindred Healthcare. In 2003 the company sold all of its Texas and Florida nursing center operations. Kindred Healthcare began operating its contract rehabilitation business as a separate division in 2004.

In 2006 the company bought the long-term care operations of Commonwealth Communities Holdings, gaining six long-term acute care hospitals and 11 nursing homes in Massachusetts.

EXECUTIVES

Chairman: Edward L. (Eddie) Kuntz, age 63, $1,904,045 total compensation
President, CEO, and Director: Paul J. Diaz, age 47, $4,440,979 total compensation
COO: Frank J. Battafarano, age 58, $2,230,246 total compensation
EVP and CFO: Richard A. (Rich) Lechleiter, age 50, $1,177,484 total compensation
EVP, CIO, and Chief Administrative Officer: Richard E. Chapman, age 60
SVP and Chief Compliance Officer: Kim Martin
EVP; President, Health Services Division: Lane M. Bowen, age 58, $1,299,458 total compensation
EVP Central Region, Hospital Division: Steven L. (Steve) Monaghan
EVP; President, Hospital Division: Benjamin A. Breier, age 37
SVP and General Counsel: M. Suzanne Riedman, age 57
SVP Strategy and Public Policy: William M. Altman, age 49
SVP Operational Reimbursement, Health Services Division: Dennis J. Hansen
SVP Clinical and Residential Services, Health Services Division: Barbara L. Baylis
SVP Corporate Legal Affairs and Corporate Secretary: Joseph L. Landenwich, age 44
SVP Corporate Development and Financial Planning: Gregory C. (Greg) Miller, age 39
SVP Finance and Corporate Controller: John J. Lucchese
SVP Human Resources, Hospital Division: Jeffrey B. (Jeff) Reeves
VP Communications: Susan E. Moss
President, Peoplefirst Rehabilitation Division: Christopher M. (Chris) Bird, age 44
Auditors: PricewaterhouseCoopers LLP

LOCATIONS

HQ: Kindred Healthcare, Inc.
680 S. 4th St., Louisville, KY 40202
Phone: 502-596-7300   **Fax:** 502-596-4170
Web: www.kindredhealthcare.com

2008 Nursing Home Locations

	No.
Massachusetts	41
California	24
Indiana	24
North Carolina	19
Kentucky	13
Ohio	13
Wisconsin	12
Maine	8
Idaho	8
Tennessee	8
Washington	7
Connecticut	6
Arizona	5
Utah	5
Georgia	4
Colorado	4
Virginia	4
Wyoming	4
Alabama	3
New Hampshire	3
Missouri	2
Montana	2
Nevada	2
Oregon	2
Rhode Island	2
Vermont	2
Pennsylvania	1
Total	**228**

2008 Hospital Locations

	No.
Texas	11
California	10
Florida	9
Massachusetts	7
Pennsylvania	7
Illinois	5
Arizona	4
Missouri	3
Nevada	3
New Jersey	3
Ohio	3
Indiana	2
Kentucky	2
Oklahoma	2
Tennessee	2
Colorado	1
Georgia	1
Louisiana	1
New Mexico	1
North Carolina	1
South Carolina	1
Virginia	1
Washington	1
Wisconsin	1
Total	**82**

PRODUCTS/OPERATIONS

2008 Sales

	$ mil.	% of motal
Health services division	2,155.4	49
Hospital division	1,837.4	41
Rehabilitation division	427.3	10
Adjustments	(268.7)	—
Total	**4,151.4**	**100**

2008 Sales by Payor

	$ mil.	% of total
Medicare	1,755.3	40
Medicaid	1,107.5	25
Other third parties	1,557.3	35
Adjustments	(268.7)	—
Total	**4,151.4**	**100**

COMPETITORS

Ascension Health	HealthSouth
Catholic Healthcare Partners	Life Care Centers
	Manor Care
Covenant Care	National HealthCare
Ensign Group	RehabCare
Extendicare REIT	SavaSeniorCare
Five Star Quality Care	Select Medical
Genesis HealthCare	Skilled Healthcare Group
Golden Horizons	Sun Healthcare
HCA	Tenet Healthcare

HISTORICAL FINANCIALS

Company Type: Public

Income Statement

FYE: December 31

	REVENUE ($ mil.)	NET INCOME ($ mil.)	NET PROFIT MARGIN	EMPLOYEES
12/08	4,151.4	36.3	0.9%	53,700
12/07	4,220.3	(46.9)	—	38,200
12/06	4,266.7	78.7	1.8%	55,000
12/05	3,924.0	144.9	3.7%	51,600
12/04	3,531.2	70.6	2.0%	50,700
Annual Growth	**4.1%**	**(15.3%)**	**—**	**1.4%**

2008 Year-End Financials

Debt ratio: 38.2%
Return on equity: 4.1%
Cash ($ mil.): 141
Current ratio: 1.76
Long-term debt ($ mil.): 349
No. of shares (mil.): 39
Dividends
  Yield: 0.0%
  Payout: —
Market value ($ mil.): 508

Stock History

NYSE: KND

	STOCK PRICE ($) FY Close	P/E High/Low		PER SHARE ($) Earnings	Dividends	Book Value
12/08	13.02	36	9	0.93	0.00	23.44
12/07	24.98	—	—	(1.17)	0.00	22.09
12/06	19.47	13	8	1.92	0.00	25.51
12/05	19.86	10	6	3.20	0.00	22.30
12/04	23.09	14	10	1.67	0.00	18.44
Annual Growth	**(13.3%)**	**—**	**—**	**(13.6%)**	**—**	**6.2%**

Kinetic Concepts

Kinetic Concepts makes its bed and has no problems lying in it. The company's products include hospital beds, specialized mattresses, and pressure relief and pulmonary care systems. Such "therapeutic surfaces" treat and prevent complications associated with patient immobility, such as pressure sores and buildup of fluid in the lungs. Kinetic Concepts also makes vacuum-assisted wound care systems and critical care therapy systems, which rotate immobilized patients to reduce the incidence of pulmonary complications and pressure sores. Customers include acute and long-term care facilities, home health agencies, wound care clinics, and individuals in the US and abroad.

The company's bariatric care products include surfaces (tables, beds, wheelchairs) which can accommodate patients weighing between 300 and 1,000 pounds. Such specialized products help health care workers move and treat such patients with a reduced risk of injury to themselves and the patients.

Kinetic Concepts markets and distributes it products through its own sales force in the US. The company also maintains an in-house team of some 200 specialists who help customers negotiate the paperwork of Medicare and private insurance. Internationally, the company distributes its products directly, and through local distributors.

The company acquired regenerative tissue maker LifeCell Corporation in 2008 for $1.7 billion to create a new biosurgery division. LifeCell's products are primarily marketed in the US for general surgical and periodontal surgical applications. Kinetic Concepts' plan is to expand the division with additional negative-pressure products designed for use during surgery. As part of that strategy, the company in 2009 acquired the patents and intellectual property rights of Hill-Rom's negative wound pressure therapy business. The deal included both US and foreign patents.

The firm's customers include more than just hospitals and long-term care facilities around the world. Its largest customer is Novation, a group purchasing organization that accounts for 10% of revenue.

Founder and chairman emeritus James Leininger holds 12% of the company's shares.

HISTORY

As a doctor, James Leininger was disturbed to see patients survive intense physical trauma only to die from complications caused by immobility. In 1975 he and his wife bought a troubled hospital bed maker, renaming it Kinetic Concepts (KCI). Leininger bought the rights to the RotoRest, which KCI began renting and selling. The firm's first decade was marked by slow, painful growth; its 1984 introduction of the KinAir bed boosted sales and put the company on firm fiscal ground. KCI went public in 1988.

In 1992 KCI sued its biggest rival Hillenbrand (now Hill-Rom Holdings) for patent infringement on its rotating bed. Two years later Hillenbrand settled with KCI for $84.8 million. In 1995 KCI sued Hillenbrand again, this time filing an antitrust suit for more than $200 million.

KCI went on a binge in 1997, buying five medical equipment firms. Among them was Colorado's RIK Medical, which made non-electric beds that could be used in prisons and psychiatric wards. In 1998 KCI was taken private again when two investment concerns, Richard C. Blum & Associates and Fremont Partners, offered it a deal worth about $850 million. That year KCI introduced the miniV.A.C., a lightweight, mobile, vacuum-assisted wound-closure device that lets convalescing patients move about. Legal woes surfaced that year when the company was sued over injuries allegedly caused by one of its beds. In 1999 KCI formed Wound Works, a wound management joint venture, with Georgia company Coloplast.

With a broader base of products and solid growth record, Kinetic Concepts was taken public again in 2004.

EXECUTIVES

Chairman: Ronald W. (Ron) Dollens, age 62
President, CEO, and Director: Cathy (Cathy) Burzik, age 58, $5,654,935 total compensation
EVP and CFO: Martin J. (Marty) Landon, age 49, $1,454,261 total compensation
SVP and CIO: David H. Ramsey, age 39
SVP Research and Development, CTO, and Chief Medical Officer: Todd M. Fruchterman, age 39, $1,375,885 total compensation
EVP, Chief Administrative Officer, and General Counsel: Stephen D. Seidel, age 52, $1,556,467 total compensation
SVP Global Operations: Michael Schneider, age 59
SVP Human Resources and Corporate Communications: R. James Cravens, age 45
SVP Corporate Development: Rohit Kashyap, age 38
SVP U.S. VAC Therapy Sales and Marketing: Michael J. DelVacchio Jr., age 41
President, LifeCell: Lisa N. Colleran, age 51
President, Europe, Middle East, and Africa: TLV Kumar, age 54
Global President, Therapeutic Support Systems: Lynne D. Sly, age 48, $1,322,064 total compensation
President, Asia/Pacific: Patrick Loh, age 41
Global President, Wound Therapy: Michael (Mike) Genau
Investor Relations: David Holmes
Media Relations: Kristie Madara
Director Manufacturing: Bob Buckley
Auditors: Ernst & Young LLP

LOCATIONS

HQ: Kinetic Concepts, Inc.
8023 Vantage Dr., San Antonio, TX 78230
Phone: 210-524-9000   **Fax:** 210-255-6998
Web: www.kci1.com

2008 Revenue

	$ mil.	% of total
North America	1,270.9	68
Other	450.2	24
LifeCell (primarily US)	156.8	8
Total	**1,877.9**	**100**

PRODUCTS/OPERATIONS

2008 Revenues

	$ mil.	% of total
V.A.C. therapy products		
Rentals	925.5	49
Sales	468.4	25
Therapeutic support system products		
Rentals	274.3	15
Sales	52.9	3
LifeCell sales	156.8	8
Total	**1,877.9**	**100**

Selected Products

BariAir Therapy System (convertible hospital bed/cardiac chair for obese patients)
BariMaxx II (hospital bed for obese patients)
KinAir MedSurg (pressure sore prevention overlay)
PlexiPulse (vascular therapy products)
RotoProne Therapy System (rotating bed)
TheraPulse (wound care beds)
TriaDyne Proventa Therapy System (rotating bed)
V.A.C. Freedom System (portable wound healing system)
V.A.C. Instill System (wound therapy equipment)

COMPETITORS

Gaymar
Getinge
Hill-Rom
Medela
Osteotech
RTI Biologics
Smith & Nephew
Span-America Medical
Stryker
Wright Medical Group

HISTORICAL FINANCIALS

Company Type: Public

Income Statement

FYE: December 31

	REVENUE ($ mil.)	NET INCOME ($ mil.)	NET PROFIT MARGIN	EMPLOYEES
12/08	1,877.9	173.9	9.3%	6,900
12/07	1,609.9	237.1	14.7%	6,400
12/06	1,371.6	195.5	14.3%	6,300
12/05	1,208.6	122.2	10.1%	5,735
12/04	992.6	30.9	3.1%	4,980
Annual Growth	**17.3%**	**54.0%**	**—**	**8.5%**

2008 Year-End Financials

Debt ratio: 193.5%
Return on equity: 23.4%
Cash ($ mil.): 248
Current ratio: 1.98
Long-term debt ($ mil.): 1,569
No. of shares (mil.): 71
Dividends
  Yield: 0.0%
  Payout: —
Market value ($ mil.): 1,363

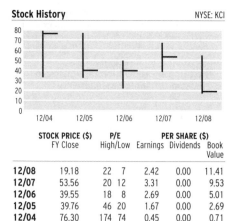

Stock History   NYSE: KCI

	STOCK PRICE ($) FY Close	P/E High/Low		PER SHARE ($) Earnings	Dividends	Book Value
12/08	19.18	22	7	2.42	0.00	11.41
12/07	53.56	20	12	3.31	0.00	9.53
12/06	39.55	18	8	2.69	0.00	5.01
12/05	39.76	46	20	1.67	0.00	2.69
12/04	76.30	174	74	0.45	0.00	0.71
Annual Growth	**(29.2%)**	**—**	**—**	**52.3%**	**—**	**99.9%**

King Ranch

Meanwhile, back at the ranch . . . the sprawling King Ranch, to be exact. Founded in 1853, King Ranch's operations extend beyond its original 825,000 Texan cattle-raising acres. The ranch is still home to cattle and horses, of course. However, King Ranch oversees considerable farming interests in its home state and elsewhere (cotton, sorghum, sod, citrus, pecans, vegetables, and cane sugar). It also has varied retail operations (hardware, designer saddles and other leather goods, publishing and printing). In addition, King Ranch also beefs up revenues with tourist dollars from birdwatchers, hunters, and sightseers who visit its Texas ranch lands. The descendants of founder Richard King own King Ranch.

Considered the birthplace of the American ranching industry, King Ranch introduced the highly fertile breed of beef cattle, the King Ranch Santa Cruz, which is one-fourth Gelbvieh, one-fourth Red Angus, and one-half Santa Gertrudis. Raising animals isn't the only thing King Ranch cottons to — this sprawl of four noncontiguous ranches is also one of the US's largest cotton producers and a significant producer of shelled pecans. In addition to its cattle, King Ranch has about 300 quarter horses. Its quarter horse and thoroughbred programs can be traced back to Richard King and his son-in-law, Robert Kleberg Sr.

The company owns the Kingsville Publishing Company, which offers printing services and publishes several local newspapers, including the *Kingsville Record* and *Bishop News*. It also owns the Robstown Hardware Company.

In order to expand and diversify its agricultural operations, in 2006 King acquired North Carolina's Young Pecan Company. Young Pecan grows no nut crops of its own but, with state-of-the-art laser operations, it is one of the world's largest pecan shellers, selling its products to food manufacturers as ingredients as well as as to retail retail food purveyors as snacks and for baking.

According to CEO Jack Hunt, King sought a company in the nut sector for acquisition because the nut industry isn't involved in farm subsidy programs and the sector also has little or no competition from foreign markets.

The company's operations are managed from its Houston corporate headquarters.

HISTORY

King Ranch was founded in 1853 by former steamboat captain Richard King and his wife Henrietta, the daughter of a Brownsville, Texas, missionary. On the advice of his friend Robert E. Lee, King used his steamboating profits and occasional strong-arm tactics to buy land — miles of flat, brush-filled coastal plain and desert south of Corpus Christi, Texas, valued at pennies an acre.

The next year King relocated the residents of an entire drought-ravaged village to the ranch and employed them as ranch hands, known ever after as *kineños* ("King's men"). The Kings built their homestead in 1858 at a site recommended by Lee.

King Ranch endured attacks from Union guerrillas during the Civil War and Mexican bandits after the war. Times were tough, but King was up to the challenge, always traveling armed and with outriders.

In 1867 the ranch used its famed Running W brand for the first time. After King's death in 1885, Robert Kleberg, who married King's daughter Alice, managed the 1.2 million-acre ranch for his mother-in-law. Henrietta died in 1925 and left three-fourths of the ranch to Alice. Before Robert's death in 1932, control of the ranch passed to sons Richard and Bob. In 1933 Bob negotiated an exclusive oil and gas lease with Houston-based Humble Oil, which later became part of Exxon.

While Richard served in Congress, Bob ran the ranch. He developed the Santa Gertrudis, the first breed of cattle ever created in the US, by crossing British shorthorn cattle with Indian Brahmas. The new breed was better suited to the hot, dry South Texas climate.

Bob made King Ranch a leading breeder of quarter horses, which worked cattle, and Thoroughbreds, which he raced. He bought Kentucky Derby winner Bold Venture in 1936 and a Kentucky breeding farm in 1946; that year a King Ranch horse, Assault, won racing's Triple Crown.

When Bob died in 1974, the family asked James Clement, husband of one of the founders' great-granddaughters, to become CEO and bypassed Robert Shelton, a King relative and orphan whom Bob had raised as his own son. Shelton severed ties with the ranch in 1977 over a lawsuit he filed against Exxon, and partially won, alleging underpayment of royalties.

Under Clement, King Ranch became a multinational corporation. In 1980 it formed King Ranch Oil and Gas (also called King Ranch Energy) to explore for and produce oil and gas in five states and the Gulf of Mexico. In 1988 Clement retired, and Kimberly-Clark executive Darwin Smith became the first CEO not related to the founders. Smith left after one year, and the reins passed to petroleum geologist Roger Jarvis and then to Jack Hunt in 1995.

With the help of scientists in the 1990s the company developed a leaner, more fertile breed of the Santa Gertrudis called the Santa Cruz.

In 1998 Stephen "Tio" Kleberg, the only King descendant still actively working the ranch, was pushed from the saddle of daily operations to a seat on the board. King Ranch sold its Kentucky horse farm in 1998 and teamed up with Collier Enterprises that year to purchase citrus grower Turner Foods from utility holding company FPL Group. In 2000 King Ranch sold King Ranch Energy to St. Mary Land and Exploration Co. for $60 million.

Like a good western movie, some things ride into the sunset at King Ranch. By 2000 the company had sold its 670-acre Kentucky Thoroughbred breeding and racing farm, most of its foreign ranches, and its primary oil and gas subsidiary.

EXECUTIVES

Chairman: James H. Clement Jr., age 54
President and CEO: Jack Hunt, age 64
CFO: William J. (Bill) Gardiner
Chief Wildlife Biologist: Mickey W. Hellickson
VP Audit: Richard Nilles
VP Livestock and Ranch Operations: Paul Genho
VP Farming Operations: Robert J. Underbrink
Director Human Resources: Martha McGee
Secretary and General Counsel: Frank Perrone
Director Security and Wildlife: Butch Thompson

LOCATIONS

HQ: King Ranch, Inc.
   3 River Way, Ste. 1600, Houston, TX 77056
Phone: 832-681-5700   **Fax:** 832-681-5759
Web: www.king-ranch.com

Selected Farming Operations

Florida
   3,100 acres (St. Augustine sod)
   12,000 acres (sugar cane)
   40,000 acres (orange and grapefruit groves)
Texas
   60,000 acres (cotton and grain)
   825,000 acres (cattle)

PRODUCTS/OPERATIONS

Selected Operations

Caesar Kleberg Wildlife Research Institute
Consolidated Citrus L.P.
Kingsville Publishing
King Ranch — Florida
King Ranch — Texas
King Ranch Cattle
King Ranch Citrus
King Ranch Feeding
King Ranch Institute of Ranch Management
King Ranch Museum
King Ranch Nature Tour Program
King Ranch Quarter Horses
King Ranch Saddle Shop
King Ranch Sod
King Ranch Sugar Cane
Robstown Hardware Company
Young Pecan Company

COMPETITORS

A. Duda & Sons	Laura's Lean Beef Co.
Ace Hardware	Lowe's
Alico	Lykes Bros.
AzTx Cattle	M A Patout
Bartlett and Company	Maverick Ranch
Blue Diamond Growers	Meridian Nut Growers
Cactus Feeders	ML Macadamia Orchards
Chiquita Brands	Niman Ranch
Coleman Natural Foods	Organic Valley
ContiGroup	Pederson's
Dakota Beef	SMBSC
Diamond Foods	Southern States
Dole Food	Sugar Cane Growers
Golden Peanut	Cooperative of Florida
Golden West Nuts	Sun Growers
Green Valley Pecan	Sun-Maid
Home Depot	Texoma Peanut
King Nut Companies	

KLA-Tencor

KLA-Tencor is hard-core when it comes to hunting down flaws in chips. The company — one of the world's largest makers of semiconductor equipment — offers yield management systems that monitor and analyze wafers at various stages of chip production, inspecting reticles (which make circuit patterns) and measuring crucial microscopic layers. The systems' feedback allows flaws to be corrected before they can ruin the costly wafers. KLA-Tencor has long dominated the market for equipment that inspects semiconductor photomasks and reticles.

As chip makers generally stopped buying capital equipment in the worldwide financial meltdown, KLA-Tencor initiated a cost reduction program that included a 15% reduction in workforce, laying off about 900 employees by mid-2009. The company seeks to reduce operating expenses by more than $660 million a year through the cost-cutting measures.

Seeing no improvement in business conditions in 2009, KLA-Tencor said it would lay off another 10% of its global workforce, consolidate facilities, schedule additional forced time off, and reduce employee stock purchase plan benefits.

The company's software includes products for factorywide yield management and for test floor automation and control. KLA-Tencor's systems are used by most of the world's major semiconductor makers, as well as by silicon wafer and data storage product manufacturers.

KLA-Tencor is the undisputed leader in its niche; it tries to position itself as a one-stop shop for its customers' yield management needs, particularly by complementing its technology offerings with consulting services.

In mid-2008 the company acquired ICOS Vision Systems, a leading supplier of inspection equipment for semiconductor packaging and interconnects, photovoltaic solar cells, and light-emitting diodes (LEDs), for about $466 million, net of cash. The acquisition widens KLA-Tencor's offerings in inspection, following its earlier purchase of ADE Corp. and its failed attempt to buy August Technology.

Entities affiliated with The Capital Group Companies own more than 44% of KLA-Tencor.

HISTORY

In the semiconductor industry's early years, chip defects rendered about half of some product runs unusable. Silicon Valley entrepreneurs Kenneth Levy — who helped develop image processing equipment pioneer Computervision (later merged into Parametric Technology) — and Robert Anderson founded KLA Instruments in 1975. ("KLA" originally stood for Kenneth Levy Associates.) Their goal was to develop inspection equipment to improve semiconductor factory yields. In 1978 KLA introduced a first-of-its-kind inspection system that employed advanced optical and image processing technology to test the templates used to etch circuit designs onto silicon wafers. It cut inspection time from eight hours to about 15 minutes.

KLA went public in 1980; within two years it had introduced wafer inspection and wafer metrology systems. As chip yields jumped, so did KLA's sales, shooting past $60 million by mid-decade. When increased competition left US demand faltering, Levy began targeting markets in Europe and Asia. By 1987, 40% of KLA's sales came from those two regions.

Levy named former Hewlett-Packard executive Kenneth Schroeder president in 1991 to take more day-to-day control of the company. Anderson by then had given up his executive duties; he retired in 1994.

Seeking an edge in an increasingly splintered market, the company merged with Tencor Instruments (and changed its name to KLA-Tencor) in 1997. The $1.3 billion deal created a company with the broadest line of wafer inspection equipment, film measurement systems, and yield management software in the industry.

Czechoslovakian Karel Urbanek had started Tencor in 1976 to make semiconductor measurement and test instruments. Tencor's first product was the Alpha-Step, a film layer profiler, but the company became known for a system that detected and analyzed wafer defects measuring as small as 1/100,000th the width of a human hair. Tencor went public in 1993.

Following the merger, Levy gave up his CEO duties (he remained chairman) to top Tencor executive Jon Tompkins. The two switched titles in 1998 to better reflect their strengths.

Tompkins retired as chairman in 1999 but remained on the board. Levy resumed the chairmanship, and Schroeder became CEO.

Kenneth Schroeder retired as CEO at the end of 2005 and became a special advisor to the company. His successor, COO Richard Wallace, had joined KLA in 1988.

KLA-Tencor in 2006 acquired competitor ADE Corporation in a transaction valued at approximately $474 million. Following a special board committee's review of historical practices in granting stock options, co-founder Ken Levy retired from the board in late 2006 and was named chairman emeritus. Edward Barnholt, a director since 1995 and the former CEO of Agilent Technologies, was named non-executive chairman to succeed Levy. The company repriced all outstanding retroactively priced stock options held by Levy and other executives following the probe, which resulted in KLA-Tencor restating financial results from mid-1997 to mid-2002 and taking a non-cash charge of $370 million for stock-based compensation expenses.

KLA-Tencor also "terminated all aspects of its employment relationship" with former CEO and director Kenneth Schroeder after the conclusion of the options probe and canceled all options held by Schroeder. The former CEO contested the company's actions. Stuart Nichols, the company's general counsel for six years, resigned his post. Other top executives were exonerated of wrongdoing by the board committee. Former chairman and CEO Jon Tompkins resigned from the board just before the end of 2006.

KLA-Tencor nearly put an end to the stock-options mess in mid-2007, reaching a settlement with the SEC. The company consented to a permanent injunction against violations of federal securities laws on books and records, internal controls, and reporting. KLA-Tencor wasn't required to pay any fine, penalty, or monetary damages to settle the case.

Kenneth Schroeder didn't get off as easy, however; the SEC charged him with fraud, accusing the former CEO of backdating more than $200 million worth of stock options.

In early 2008 the company agreed to pay $65 million in cash to settle a class-action shareholder lawsuit over backdated stock-option grants, brought by the City of Philadelphia Board of Pensions and other plaintiffs.

EXECUTIVES

Chairman: Edward W. (Ned) Barnholt, age 65
CEO and Director: Richard P. (Rick) Wallace, age 48
CFO: Mark P. Dentinger, age 50
EVP and CTO: Benjamin B.M. Tsai, age 50
SVP, General Counsel, and Secretary: Brian M. Martin, age 47
VP, Corporate Controller, and Chief Accounting Officer: Virendra Kirloskar, age 45
Chief Engineer and Group VP, PSG, Rapid, and Ebeam: Zain Saidin
Senior Director Corporate Communications: Kyra Whitten
Manager Investor Relations: Wentsong Lin
Senior Director Corporation Communications: Meggan Powers
Director Global Public Relations: Charles Lewis
Auditors: PricewaterhouseCoopers LLP

LOCATIONS

HQ: KLA-Tencor Corporation
1 Technology Dr., Milpitas, CA 95035
Phone: 408-875-3000   **Fax:** 408-875-4144
Web: www.kla-tencor.com

KLA-Tencor has manufacturing facilities in Israel, Singapore, and the US. It also has offices in China, France, Germany, India, Italy, Japan, Malaysia, Singapore, South Korea, Taiwan, the UK, and the US.

2009 Sales

	$ mil.	% of total
US	372.9	24
Europe & Israel	162.7	11
Japan	437.1	29
Taiwan	181.4	12
Korea	187.6	12
Asia/Pacific	178.5	12
Total	**1,520.2**	**100**

PRODUCTS/OPERATIONS

Selected Products

Metrology systems
    Critical dimension scanning electron microscopes (SEMs)
    Film and film stress measurement
    Optical overlay measurement
    Surface profiling

Reticle (circuit pattern mask) inspection systems
Wafer inspection systems
    Automated defect classification
    Defect analysis software
    In-line monitoring
    Optical and SEM defect review
    Process tool performance monitoring
Yield management software
    Factorywide yield management software
    Test floor automation/control software

COMPETITORS

Applied Materials
Camtek
Carl Zeiss
Cascade Microtech
Cognex
Dainippon Screen
Electroglas
FEI
Hitachi High-Technologies
Keithley Instruments
Nanometrics
Nova Measuring
Orbotech
PDF Solutions
Rudolph Technologies
Veeco Instruments
Zygo

HISTORICAL FINANCIALS

Company Type: Public

Income Statement

FYE: June 30

	REVENUE ($ mil.)	NET INCOME ($ mil.)	NET PROFIT MARGIN	EMPLOYEES
6/09	1,520.2	(523.4)	—	4,900
6/08	2,521.7	359.1	14.2%	6,000
6/07	2,731.2	528.1	19.3%	6,000
6/06	2,070.6	380.5	18.4%	5,900
6/05	2,085.2	466.7	22.4%	5,500
Annual Growth	**(7.6%)**	**—**	**—**	**(2.8%)**

2009 Year-End Financials

Debt ratio: 34.1%
Return on equity: —
Cash ($ mil.): 525
Current ratio: 4.25
Long-term debt ($ mil.): 745

No. of shares (mil.): 171
Dividends
    Yield: 2.4%
    Payout: —
Market value ($ mil.): 4,309

Stock History

NASDAQ (GS): KLAC

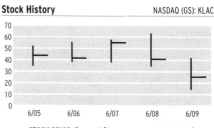

	STOCK PRICE ($) FY Close	P/E High/Low		PER SHARE ($) Earnings	Dividends	Book Value
6/09	25.25	—	—	(3.07)	0.60	12.80
6/08	40.71	32	18	1.95	0.60	17.47
6/07	54.95	22	15	2.61	0.48	20.80
6/06	41.57	30	21	1.86	0.48	20.91
6/05	43.68	22	15	2.32	0.12	17.84
Annual Growth	**(12.8%)**	**—**	**—**	**—**	**49.5%**	**(8.0%)**

Kmart Corporation

Attention Kmart shoppers: Kmart is the #3 discount retailer in the US, behind Wal-Mart and Target. It sells name-brand and private-label goods (including its Joe Boxer, Jaclyn Smith, and Martha Stewart labels), mostly to low- and mid-income families. It runs about 1,365 off-mall stores (including more than 45 Supercenters) in 49 US states, Puerto Rico, Guam, and the US Virgin Islands. About 290 Kmart stores sell home appliances (including Sears' Kenmore brand) and more than 1,025 locations house in-store pharmacies. The company also operates the kmart.com Web site. Kmart is a subsidiary of Sears Holdings Corp., formed by the 2005 combination of ailing Sears, Roebuck and Kmart.

The combination of Sears and Kmart was intended to leverage the strengths of both chains and to make their products, brands, and services available through more locations and customer distribution channels. Sears, which has long sought a way to diversify away from the shopping mall, was attracted to Kmart's off-mall locations. But so far the combination has proved disappointing. Both retailers are suffering from falling same-store sales as they fail to attract customers. Indeed, about 15 underperforming Kmart stores closed in early 2009 following another bad year in 2008, capped by a dismal holiday retail season.

Shortly after Sears Holdings announced in early 2008 a restructuring of its retail operations, Aylwin Lewis left the company. Lewis, who since 2005 has served as CEO of Sears Holdings, and Kmart before that, was replaced on an interim basis by EVP W. Bruce Johnson, while the company searches for a permanent replacement.

In a bid to move its Sears chain out of the mall, Sears Holdings wasted no time converting about 400 of Kmart's stand-alone stores to Sears outlets. Sears is also taking advantage of cross-selling opportunities by offering proprietary Sears brands, including Craftsman, Diehard, and Kenmore products, in Kmart stores. The sale of Kenmore brand appliances is meant to help Kmart differentiate itself from its larger rivals, Wal-Mart and Target, which stock a more limited range of appliances.

HISTORY

Sebastian Kresge and John McCrorey opened five-and-dime stores in Memphis and Detroit in 1897. When the partners split two years later, Kresge got Detroit and McCrorey took Memphis. By the time Kresge incorporated as S. S. Kresge Company in 1912, it had become the second-largest dime store chain in the US, with 85 stores. Kresge expanded rapidly in the next several decades, forming S. S. Kresge, Ltd., in 1929 to operate stores in Canada. In the late 1920s and 1930s, the company opened stores in suburban shopping centers. By the 1950s Kresge was one of the largest general merchandise retailers in the US.

A marketing study prompted management to enter discount retailing in 1958, and three unprofitable locations were transformed into Jupiter Discount stores in 1961. The company judged this a success and opened the first Kmart discount store in Detroit in 1962; by 1966 the company had more than 160 Kmart stores. Kresge formed a joint venture with G. J. Coles & Coy (later Coles Myer) to operate Kmart stores in Australia (1968; sold in 1994). The company expanded the Kmart format swiftly in the 1970s, opening more than 270 stores in 1976 alone. With about 95% of its sales coming from Kmart stores, the company changed its name to Kmart in 1977.

Kmart diversified during the 1980s and early 1990s, adding various retailers, including Walden Book Company, then the #1 US bookstore chain, and Builders Square (formerly Home Centers of America) in 1984; PayLess Drug Stores Northwest in 1985; PACE Membership Warehouse in 1989; The Sports Authority in 1990; a 90% stake in OfficeMax by 1991; and the Borders bookstore chain in 1992.

In 1994 and 1995, amid falling earnings, the company began shedding operations, spinning off or selling OfficeMax, The Sports Authority, PACE, its US automotive service centers (to Penske, which still runs them), and Borders. In 1995 CEO Joseph Antonini — architect of the diversification strategy — was replaced by Floyd Hall. More than 200 US stores were closed.

The company then sold Kmart Mexico, a joint venture with El Puerto de Liverpool, and an 87.5% stake in Kmart Canada in 1997 (it sold the rest in 1998). Also in 1997 it unveiled the new Big Kmart format. The company also sold woebegone 162-store Builders Square to Leonard Green & Partners (owners of the Hechinger chain) for a mere $10 million, but retained a $761 million liability for the stores' lease obligations. (Hechinger filed for bankruptcy in 1999, and Kmart assumed the obligations of 115 stores.)

In May 2000 Hall was replaced by former CVS president and COO Charles Conaway. In July 2001 Kmart said it would close 72 stores (in about 30 states) in locations that did not fit with expansion plans.

In a management shakeup that followed downgrades in Kmart's credit rating in January 2002, director James Adamson replaced Conaway as chairman. Soon after, key vendors suspended shipments to the troubled discounter saying Kmart failed to make regular weekly payments. Kmart filed for Chapter 11 bankruptcy protection that month. Soon after, Adamson was also named CEO. After filing for bankruptcy Kmart closed 283 stores, resulting in 22,000 job losses. It announced additional job cuts, including about 400 corporate positions, in August. Nearly a year after filing for bankruptcy, Kmart's shares were delisted in December after 84 years on the New York Stock Exchange.

In January 2003 Adamson was succeeded as CEO by Julian Day, president and COO of Kmart. Later in the month Kmart won final approval from the bankruptcy court to close another 316 stores and proceed with a $2 billion exit financing package.

In May 2003, 15 months after filing Chapter 11, Kmart emerged from bankruptcy protection with the help of its largest shareholder, ESL Investments.

Aylwin Lewis, a 13-year veteran of YUM! Brands, succeeded Day as president and CEO of Kmart Holding Corp. in 2004. In August 2005 two former Kmart executives (Conaway and ex-CFO John McDonald) were accused by the Securities and Exchange Commission of misleading investors about the company's finances prior to its 2002 bankruptcy filing.

EXECUTIVES

Interim President and Interim CEO: W. Bruce Johnson, age 57, $1,166,293 total compensation
EVP Operating and Support Businesses: Scott J. Freidheim, age 43, $1,060,606 total compensation
SVP and CFO: Michael D. (Mike) Collins, $618,593 total compensation
SVP, Controller, and Chief Accounting Officer: William K. Phelan, age 46
EVP and Chief Administrative Officer: William C. Crowley, age 51
EVP Store Operations: Kevin R. Holt, age 50, $2,248,833 total compensation
SVP Marketing: Richard Gerstein, $1,215,636 total compensation
SVP and General Manager, Kmart Retail: Donald J. Germano
SVP Human Resources, General Counsel, and Corporate Secretary: William R. Harker, age 36
SVP Supply Chain and Operations: James P. (Jim) Mixon, age 64
Auditors: Deloitte & Touche LLP

LOCATIONS

HQ: Kmart Corporation
3333 Beverly Rd., Hoffman Estates, IL 60179
Phone: 847-286-2500   **Fax:** 847-286-5500
Web: www.kmartcorp.com

PRODUCTS/OPERATIONS

2009 Stores

	No.
Kmart discount stores	1,321
Kmart Supercenters	47
Total	**1,368**

Selected Private Labels

Craftsman (tools)
DieHard (car batteries)
Jaclyn Smith (ladies' apparel)
Joe Boxer (men's and women's apparel)
Kenmore (appliances)
Martha Stewart Everyday (home fashions, kitchenware)
Route 66 (casual wear and shoes)

Retail Divisions

Kmart discount store (general merchandise/small grocery section)
Kmart Supercenter (general merchandise/supermarkets)

COMPETITORS

Bed Bath & Beyond
Best Buy
Big Lots
BJ's Wholesale Club
Costco Wholesale
CVS Caremark
Dollar General
Family Dollar Stores
J. C. Penney
Kohl's
Kroger
Office Depot
PETCO
Rite Aid
Ross Stores
ShopKo Stores
Staples
Target
TJX Companies
Toys "R" Us
Walgreen
Wal-Mart

spread. In 1930 Kraft was bought by National Dairy, but its operations were kept separate. New and notable products included Miracle Whip salad dressing (1933), macaroni and cheese dinners (1937), and Parkay margarine (1940). In the decades that followed, Kraft expanded into foreign markets.

National Dairy became Kraftco in 1969 and Kraft in 1976, hoping to benefit from its internationally known trademark. To diversify, Kraft merged with Dart Industries in 1980; Dart's subsidiaries (including Duracell batteries) and Kraft kept separate operations. With non-food sales sagging, Dart & Kraft split up in 1986. Kraft kept its original lines and added Duracell (sold 1988); the rest became Premark International. Tobacco giant Philip Morris Companies bought Kraft in 1988 for $12.9 billion. The next year Philip Morris joined Kraft with another unit, General Foods.

General Foods began when Charles Post, who marketed a wheat/bran health beverage, established the Postum Cereal Co. in 1896; he expanded the firm with such cereals as Grape-Nuts and Post Toasties. The company went public in 1922. Postum bought the makers of Jell-O (1925), Baker's chocolate (1927), Log Cabin syrup (1927), and Maxwell House coffee (1928), and in 1929 it acquired control of General Foods (owned by frozen vegetable pioneer Clarence Birdseye) and changed its own name to General Foods.

Its later purchases included Perkins Products (Kool-Aid, 1953) and Kohner Brothers (toys, 1970). Most of its non-food lines proved unsuccessful and were sold throughout the years. General Foods bought Oscar Mayer, the US's #1 hot dog maker, in 1981. Philip Morris bought General Foods for $5.6 billion in 1985.

The 1989 combination of Kraft and General Foods (the units still ran independently) created the largest US food maker, Kraft General Foods. To streamline management, Philip Morris integrated Kraft and General Foods in 1995.

In 2000 parent Philip Morris (which renamed itself the Altria Group in 2003) outbid Danone and Cadbury Schweppes (now Cadbury) and agreed to buy Nabisco Holdings. It completed the deal that December for $18.9 billion and began integrating those operations into Kraft Foods and Kraft Foods International. Then Philip Morris created a holding company for the newly combined food operations under the Kraft Foods Inc. name in 2001. The original Kraft Foods was renamed Kraft Foods North America.

Kraft Foods International CEO Roger Deromedi was appointed co-CEO of the new holding company, along with Betsy Holden. Kraft Foods Inc. was spun off by Altria in 2001 in what was the US's second-largest IPO ever at the time. Kraft cut 7,500 jobs in 2002 as a result of the integration of Nabisco operations.

Deromedi was named sole CEO in 2003. As part of his plan to refashion Kraft's product lineup, in 2005 the company sold its Altoids breath mints, LifeSavers and CremeSavers candies brands. Wm. Wrigley Jr. Company paid about $1.4 billion for the popular brands.

Despite his efforts to improve the bottom line, Deromedi was shown the door in 2006. He was replaced by Frito-Lay's CEO Irene Rosenfeld. Rosenfeld is a former long-time top Kraft executive who was instrumental in the company's acquisition and integration of Nabisco. She returned to Kraft, having been CEO of Pepsico's Frito-Lay since 2004.

EXECUTIVES

Chairman and CEO: Irene B. Rosenfeld, age 55, $16,998,852 total compensation
EVP Operations and Business Services: David A. (Dave) Brearton, age 48
EVP and CFO: Timothy R. (Tim) McLevish, age 53, $3,464,683 total compensation
EVP and Chief Marketing Officer: Mary Beth West, age 46
EVP: Richard G. (Rick) Searer, age 55, $3,835,087 total compensation
EVP Reseach, Development, and Quality: Jean E. Spence, age 51
EVP Global Human Resources: Karen J. May, age 51
EVP Global Supply Chain: Franz-Josef H. Vogelsang, age 58
EVP Corporate and Legal Affairs and General Counsel: Marc S. Firestone, age 49, $2,869,151 total compensation
EVP; President, International Commercial: Sanjay Khosla, age 57, $3,242,097 total compensation
EVP Strategy: Michael Osanloo, age 42
SVP Health and Wellness and Sustainability: Lance Friedmann
SVP and Controller: Pamela E. King, age 46
SVP Sales, International Commercial: Franco Suardi
SVP Corporate Affairs: Perry Yeatman
SVP Corporate Affairs, Business Units: Nancy Daigler
SVP Global Integrated Marketing and Communications: Carole Irgang
VP Finance and Investor Relations: Christopher M. (Chris) Jakubik
VP and Corporate Secretary: Carol J. Ward
Senior Director Corporate External Communications: Michael Mitchell
Auditors: PricewaterhouseCoopers LLP

LOCATIONS

HQ: Kraft Foods Inc.
3 Lakes Dr., Northfield, IL 60093
Phone: 847-646-2000   **Fax:** 847-646-6005
Web: www.kraft.com

2008 Sales

	$ mil.	% of total
US	21,436	51
Europe	13,139	31
Other countries	7,626	18
Total	**42,201**	**100**

PRODUCTS/OPERATIONS

2008 Sales

	$ mil.	% of total
Snacks	15,914	38
Beverages	8,481	20
Cheese	7,462	18
Convenient meals	6,173	14
Grocery	4,171	10
Total	**42,201**	**100**

Selected North American Brands

Beverages
  Country Time
  Crystal Light
  General Foods International
  Kool-Aid
  Maxwell House
  Sanka
  Tang
  Tassimo
  Yuban
Cheese
  Cheez Whiz
  Cracker Barrel
  Deli Deluxe
  Knudsen
  Kraft
  Philadelphia
  Velveeta

Convenient Meals
  Boca
  Deli Creations
  DiGiorno
  Louis Rich
Grocery
  A.1.
  Back to Nature
  Bull's-Eye
  Cool Whip
  Easy Cheese
Snacks
  Cheese Nips
  Chips Ahoy!
  Honey Maid Grahams
  Newtons
  Nilla
  Nutter Butter
  Oreo
  Planters

  Lunchables
  Oscar Mayer
  Stove Top
  Tombstone

  Grey Poupon
  Jell-O
  Miracle Whip
  Shake N' Bake

  Premium
  Ritz
  SnackWell's
  Teddy Grahams
  Toblerone
  Triscuit
  Wheat Thins
  Velveeta

COMPETITORS

ADM
Amy's Kitchen
Associated British Foods
Bob Evans
Cadbury
Campbell Soup
Cargill
Caribou Coffee
Cheesemakers, Inc.
Coca-Cola
Cold Stone Creamery
Community Coffee
ConAgra
Dairy Crest
Dairy Farmers of America
Danone
Dean Foods
Del Monte Foods
Dr Pepper Snapple Group
Eden Foods
Farmland Dairies
Fehr Foods
Ferolito, Vultaggio
Folger
Frito-Lay
Fromageries Bel
Galaxy Nutritional Foods
Gaspar's Sausage
General Mills
George Weston
Goya
Great Lakes Cheese
Green Mountain Coffee
Hain Celestial
Heinz
Hershey
Hormel
Interstate Bakeries
J & B Sausage
Jenny Craig
Johnsonville Sausage
Kellogg
Kellogg U.S. Snacks
Kerry Group
Lactalis
Lance Snacks
Land O'Lakes
Lindt & Sprüngli
Manischewitz Company
Manischewitz Food
  Products

Maple Leaf Foods
Marathon Cheese
Mars, Incorporated
McCain Foods
Michael Foods, Inc.
Mott's
Mrs. Fields
Naked Juice
Nestlé
Nestlé USA
Newman's Own
Northern Foods
NutriSystem
Oberto Sausage Company
Odwalla
Old Home Foods
Old Orchard
Otis Spunkmeyer
Parmalat Canada
Pepperidge Farm
PepsiCo
Procter & Gamble
Ralcorp
Rich Products
Salton
Saputo
Sara Lee Food and
  Beverage
Sargento
Schwan's
Seneca Foods
Slim-Fast
smart balance
Smucker
Snapple
Starbucks
Stonyfield Farm
Sweet Leaf Tea
Tofutti Brands
Tropicana
Tyson Foods
Unilever
Uniq
United Biscuits
Voortman Cookies
Weight Watchers
  International
Welch's
WhiteWave
Williams Sausage

HISTORICAL FINANCIALS

Company Type: Public

Income Statement
FYE: December 31

	REVENUE ($ mil.)	NET INCOME ($ mil.)	NET PROFIT MARGIN	EMPLOYEES
12/08	42,201.0	2,901.0	6.9%	98,000
12/07	37,241.0	2,590.0	7.0%	103,000
12/06	34,356.0	3,060.0	8.9%	90,000
12/05	34,113.0	2,632.0	7.7%	94,000
12/04	32,168.0	2,665.0	8.3%	98,000
Annual Growth	7.0%	2.1%	—	0.0%

2008 Year-End Financials

Debt ratio: 83.7%
Return on equity: 11.7%
Cash ($ mil.): 1,244
Current ratio: 1.03
Long-term debt ($ mil.): 18,589

No. of shares (mil.): 1,475
Dividends
Yield: 4.2%
Payout: 58.3%
Market value ($ mil.): 39,603

Stock History
NYSE: KFT

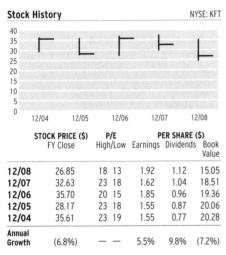

	STOCK PRICE ($) FY Close	P/E High/Low	PER SHARE ($) Earnings	Dividends	Book Value
12/08	26.85	18 13	1.92	1.12	15.05
12/07	32.63	23 18	1.62	1.04	18.51
12/06	35.70	20 15	1.85	0.96	19.36
12/05	28.17	23 18	1.55	0.87	20.06
12/04	35.61	23 19	1.55	0.77	20.28
Annual Growth	(6.8%)	— —	5.5%	9.8%	(7.2%)

The Kroger Co.

Kroger is the nation's #1 pure grocery chain, but it still must watch out for falling prices; Wal-Mart has overtaken Kroger as the largest seller of groceries in the US. While Kroger has diversified through acquisitions, adding jewelry and general merchandise to its mix, food stores still account for about 85% of sales. The company operates about 3,550 stores, including some 2,480 supermarkets and multi-department stores, under about two dozen banners, in about 30 states. It also runs 685 convenience stores under names such as Quik Stop and Kwik Shop. Kroger's Fred Meyer Stores subsidiary (acquired in 1999) operates about 125 supercenters, which offer groceries, general merchandise, and jewelry, in the western US.

In response to intense price competition and aggressive supercenter expansion from non-traditional grocery sellers, such as Wal-Mart Supercenters and Costco Wholesale (the #1 and #3 sellers of groceries in the US, respectively), Kroger has been cutting prices while improving service and product selection to hang on to customers, with some success; sales were up in 2008 despite the downturn in the economy. Wal-Mart operates supercenters in more than half of Kroger's markets.

Private-label products help to differentiate supermarket chains from their competitors and foster customer loyalty. They are a pillar of Kroger's merchandising strategy. To keep its shelves stocked with its own store brands, Kroger operates 40 food processing plants, including 18 dairies and 10 deli or bakery plants, that supply its supermarkets with a growing stable of some 14,000 private-label products (accounting for about 25% of its grocery sales), including Naturally Preferred, Kroger's own brand of natural and organic products. Digging deeper into the organics market, Kroger has launched a second line of some 60 organic items (including pasta, tea, waffles, peanut butter, snacks, and milk) called "Organics for Everyone." The new line, which targets mainstream consumers, is priced lower than Kroger's Naturally Preferred brand.

Kroger is also a major pharmacy operator, with pharmacies in about 80% of its food stores. Kroger pharmacies, as well as those in Ralphs, Fred Meyer, QFC, City Market, and King Soopers stores, began offering a $4 generic prescription drug program in 2008. To complement its pharmacy operation, Kroger has begun adding walk-in medical clinics to some stores. To that end, in mid-2008 the company acquired a significant stake in The Little Clinic, which operates about 25 in-store clinics for Kroger.

Kroger's 1999 acquisition of Fred Meyer not only added three supermarket chains (Ralphs, Smith's Food & Drug Centers, and QFC), it gave the company several new retailing formats: multi-department stores (Fred Meyer), price-impact warehouse outlets (Food 4 Less and Foods Co.), and jewelry stores (under the Barclay, Fred Meyer, and Littman names). The purchase gave Kroger a significant presence in the western US.

HISTORY

Bernard Kroger was 22 when he started the Great Western Tea Company in 1883 in Cincinnati. Kroger lowered prices by cutting out middlemen, sometimes by making products such as bread. Growing to 40 stores in Cincinnati and northern Kentucky, the company became Kroger Grocery and Baking Company in 1902. It expanded into St. Louis in 1912 and grew rapidly during the 1910s and 1920s by purchasing smaller, cash-strapped companies. Kroger sold his holdings in the company for $28 million in 1928, the year before the stock market crash, and retired.

The company acquired Piggly Wiggly stores in the late 1920s and bought most of Piggly Wiggly's corporate stock, which it held until the early 1940s. The chain reached its largest number of stores — a whopping 5,575 — in 1929. (The Depression later trimmed that total.) A year later Kroger manager Michael Cullen suggested opening self-service, low-price supermarkets, but company executives demurred. Cullen left Kroger and began King Kullen, the first supermarket. If he was ahead of his time at Kroger, it wasn't by much; within five years, the company had 50 supermarkets.

During the 1950s Kroger acquired companies with stores in Texas, Georgia, and Washington, DC. It added New Jersey-based Sav-on drugstores in 1960 and it opened its first SupeRx drugstore in 1961. The company began opening larger supermarkets in 1971; between 1970 and 1980 Kroger's store count grew just 5%, but its selling space nearly doubled.

In 1983 the grocer bought Kansas-based Dillons Food Stores (supermarkets and convenience stores) and Kwik Shop convenience stores. Kroger sold most of its interests in the Hook and SupeRx drug chains (which became Hook-SupeRx) in 1987 and focused on its food-and-drugstores. (It sold its remaining stake to Revco in 1994.) The next year it faced two separate takeover bids from the Herbert Haft family and from Kohlberg Kravis Roberts. The company warded off the raiders by borrowing $4.1 billion to pay a special dividend to shareholders and to buy shares for an employee stock plan.

Joseph Pichler became CEO in 1990. Kroger sold its Time Saver Stores in 1995. In 1999 Kroger acquired Fred Meyer, operator of about 800 stores mainly in the West, in a $13 billion deal.

In late 2001 Kroger said it would cut 1,500 jobs. Kroger acquired 17 supermarkets (16 in the Houston area) from Albertson's (now Albertsons LLC) and another seven stores from Winn-Dixie in the Dallas/Fort Worth area in 2002.

In June, Joseph Pichler stepped down as CEO (but remained chairman) and was succeeded by David B. Dillon.

A four-and-a-half-month-long strike by grocery workers at Kroger's Ralphs chain in Southern California ended in March 2004. The dispute pitted workers' demands for continued generous health care benefits against management's call to control costs in the face of increasing non-union competition.

Pichler retired as chairman in June 2004 and was succeeded by Dillon.

In August 2006 Kroger sold 11 Cala Foods and Bell Markets in the San Francisco Bay area to DeLano Retail Partners, headed by Hartley DeLano, the former president of the Cala chain, for an undisclosed sum.

In July 2007 Kroger bought 20 Farmer Jack stores in the Detroit area from A&P. Also in 2007 the firm purchased 18 Scott's Food & Pharmacy stores in Indiana from rival SUPERVALU for an undisclosed amount. Kroger retained the Scott's banner and incorporated the business into its Indianapolis-based Central division.

EXECUTIVES

Chairman and CEO: David B. Dillon, age 58, $8,031,721 total compensation
President and COO: W. Rodney McMullen, age 48, $3,341,698 total compensation
President, COO, and Director: Don W. (Donnie) McGeorge, age 54, $3,935,319 total compensation
SVP and CFO: J. Michael Schlotman, age 51, $1,786,766 total compensation
SVP and CIO: Christopher T. (Chris) Hjelm, age 47
Chief Diversity Officer: Carver L. Johnson, age 59
EVP, Secretary, and General Counsel: Paul W. Heldman, age 57
EVP Merchandise: Donald E. Becker, age 60, $3,019,747 total compensation
SVP Retail Operations: Paul J. Scutt, age 60
SVP: R. Pete Williams, age 54
SVP: M. Marnette Perry, age 57
Group VP Corporate Affairs: Lynn Marmer, age 56
Group VP Perishables Merchandising and Procurement: Joseph A. Grieshaber Jr., age 51
Group VP Human Resources: Della Wall, age 57
Group VP Logistics: Kevin M. Dougherty, age 56
VP and President, Manufacturing: Calvin Kaufman, age 46
VP and Controller: M. Elizabeth Van Oflen, age 51
VP and Treasurer: Scott M. Henderson, age 53
Director, Investor Relations: Carin Fike
Media Relations: Meghan Glynn
Auditors: PricewaterhouseCoopers LLP

LOCATIONS

HQ: The Kroger Co.
1014 Vine St., Cincinnati, OH 45202
Phone: 513-762-4000   **Fax:** 513-762-1160
Web: www.kroger.com

PRODUCTS/OPERATIONS

2009 Stores

	No.
Supermarkets & multi-department stores	2,481
Convenience stores	684
Jewelry	385
Total	**3,550**

2009 Sales

	$ mil.	% of total
Food stores	63,795	84
Food store fuel sales	7,464	10
Other stores & manufacturing	4,741	6
Total	**76,000**	**100**

2009 Supermarkets

	No.
Combo stores	2,169
Price-impact warehouse stores	146
Multi-department stores	124
Marketplace stores	42
Total	**2,481**

Selected Kroger Stores

Multi-department Stores
  Fred Meyer
Supermarkets
  Baker's
  City Market Food & Pharmacy
  Dillon Food Stores
  Fry's Food & Drug Stores
  Gerbes Supermarkets
  Hilander Food Stores
  Jay C Food Stores
  King Soopers
  Kroger
  Kroger Fresh Fare
  Owen's
  Pay Less Super Markets
  Quality Food Centers (QFC)
  Ralphs
  Scott's Food & Pharmacy
  Smith's Food & Drug Centers
Warehouse Stores
  Food 4 Less
  FoodsCo
Convenience Stores
  Kwik Shop
  Loaf 'N Jug
  Quik Stop Markets
  Tom Thumb Food Stores
  Turkey Hill Minit Markets
Jewelry Stores
  Barclay Jewelers
  Fox's Jewelers
  Fred Meyer Jewelers
  Littman Jewelers

Selected Private-Label Brands

Bath & Body Therapies (body and bath)
Banner brands (Kroger, Ralphs, King Soopers)
Everyday Living (kitchen gadgets)
FMV (For Maximum Value)
HD Design (upscale kitchen gadgets)
Moto Tech (automotive)
Naturally Preferred (premium quality natural and
  organic brand)
Office Works (office and school supplies)
Private Selection (premium quality brand)
Splash Spa (body and bath)
Splash Sport (body and bath)

COMPETITORS

7-Eleven
99 Cents Only
A&P
Ahold USA
Albertsons
Costco Wholesale
CVS Caremark
Delhaize America
Dollar General
Family Dollar Stores
Giant Eagle
H-E-B
Hy-Vee
IGA
Kmart
Marsh Supermarkets
Meijer
Publix
Raley's
Randall's
Rite Aid
Safeway
Save Mart
Stater Bros.
Sterling Jewelers
SUPERVALU
Target
Walgreen
Wal-Mart
Wegmans
Whole Foods
Winn-Dixie
Zale

HISTORICAL FINANCIALS

Company Type: Public

Income Statement

FYE: Saturday nearest January 31

	REVENUE ($ mil.)	NET INCOME ($ mil.)	NET PROFIT MARGIN	EMPLOYEES
1/09	76,000.0	1,249.0	1.6%	326,000
1/08	70,235.0	1,181.0	1.7%	323,000
1/07	66,111.0	1,115.0	1.7%	310,000
1/06	60,553.0	958.0	1.6%	290,000
1/05	56,434.0	(100.0)	—	289,000
Annual Growth	**7.7%**	**—**	**—**	**3.1%**

2009 Year-End Financials

Debt ratio: 145.0%
Return on equity: 24.8%
Cash ($ mil.): 894
Current ratio: 0.94
Long-term debt ($ mil.): 7,505

No. of shares (mil.): 651
Dividends
  Yield: 1.6%
  Payout: 18.9%
Market value ($ mil.): 14,658

Stock History

NYSE: KR

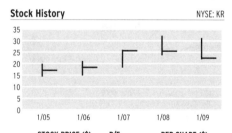

	STOCK PRICE ($) FY Close	P/E High/Low		PER SHARE ($) Earnings	Dividends	Book Value
1/09	22.50	16	12	1.90	0.36	7.95
1/08	25.45	19	14	1.69	0.30	7.54
1/07	25.60	17	12	1.54	0.26	7.56
1/06	18.40	16	12	1.31	0.00	6.74
1/05	17.10	—	—	(0.14)	0.00	5.43
Annual Growth	**7.1%**	**—**	**—**	**—**	**—**	**10.0%**

L-3 Communications

L-3's good defense is its best commercial offense. L-3 Communications Holdings makes secure and specialized systems for satellite, avionics, and marine communications. The US government (primarily the Department of Defense) accounts for about 80% of the company's business, but L-3 is using acquisitions to expand its commercial offerings. As a government contractor, the company is subject to the whims of the Pentagon and other government agencies; L-3 also faces potential cuts in military programs by the Obama administration. The company makes most of its sales in North America.

Commercial products include flight recorders (black boxes), display systems, and wireless telecom gear. L-3 added to its aircraft repair, overhaul, and technical services with the 2001 purchase of Spar Aerospace and what are now L-3 Communications Integrated Systems, L-3 Communications Vertex Aerospace, and L-3 Communications Cincinnati Electronics.

In 2007 L-3 acquired Global Communications Solutions, a maker of portable satellite communications equipment, for $152 million. Global Communications Solutions, which was renamed L-3 GCS, had annual sales of about $90 million. L-3 GCS now operates as part of L-3's Specialized Products segment.

In early 2008 the company realigned several businesses in the Specialized Products segment to form a Marine and Power Systems Group. Gathered into the $1.2 billion group are the Power and Control, Automation, Navigation, Undersea Warfare, and Offshore businesses. Later in the year it added new acquisition Chesapeake Sciences Corp. (CSC) to the group. CSC, a manufacturer of anti-submarine warfare systems, has annual sales of about $70 million.

Also in 2008 the company acquired Electro-Optical Systems from Northrop Grumman. L-3 paid $178 million for the night vision technology developer which it renamed L-3 EOS.

It also added some government training late in the year when it picked up International Resources Group for $58 million.

All those acquisitions left L-3 with a substantial debt load of $4.55 billion, a figure that may grow difficult to manage if the credit crisis continues.

HISTORY

In the early 1970s Frank Lanza caught defense giant Lockheed's eye by building Loral Corporation into an aerospace industry contender through acquisitions of smaller defense technology firms. Lockheed (now Lockheed Martin) eventually bought Loral in 1996 and made Lanza the head of defense electronics. Looking for more action, Lanza formed L-3 Communications Holdings in 1997 by convincing Lockheed Martin's CEO to spin off a group of 10 communications technology units and put him at the helm. The operations were units from General Electric and Loral acquired by Lockheed Martin in 1993 and 1996, respectively.

In charge were two of the L's in the L-3 name: 20-year Loral executives Lanza (chairman and CEO, by then old enough to retire) and Robert LaPenta (president and CFO). The third L stood for major backer Lehman Brothers. The company embarked on an acquisition binge (just as Loral had originally done) in 1997. L-3 targeted strapped independent companies and the potential noncore operations resulting from large corporate mergers.

Much as he had during his tenure at Loral, Lanza remained a hands-off executive, a surprising approach in a red tape-wrapped industry. As a result, L-3's divisions developed an entrepreneurial freedom. In 1998, the year L-3 went public, it purchased the Ocean Systems unit of AlliedSignal (now Honeywell International; sonar products), ILEX Systems (information technology and support for the US government), SPD Technologies (electronics and power products), and the satellite transmission systems unit of California Microwave.

In 2000 L-3 sold its network security software division to Symantec. The next year L-3 sued Raytheon for not disclosing material liabilities before the sale of the division. The company later dropped the lawsuit, saying it intended to improve its relations with Raytheon to benefit the Defense Department following September 11.

In 2002 L-3 made its largest acquisition to date, buying Raytheon's Aircraft Integration Systems unit for $1.13 billion in cash.

L-3 acquired Vertex Aerospace, a company that provides technical services for government agencies, for about $650 million in 2003.

The acquisition roll continued in 2005 as L-3 acquired the Marine Controls division (shipboard control systems) of CAE, the Propulsion Systems business unit (transmissions, engines, suspensions, and turret drives) of General Dynamics, and most of Boeing's Electron Dynamic Devices, Inc. business, including the space and military traveling wave tubes, traveling wave tube amplifiers, passive microwave devices, and electric propulsion operations. L-3 also acquired Mobile-Vision Inc., a maker of video surveillance systems used in police cars.

Early in 2006 L-3 completed its $150 million acquisition of SAM Electronics, a German naval electronics company. Not long afterwards it added CyTerra Corp.(military and homeland security sensors) and SafeView Inc. (security systems).

Later that year the company acquired Germany's Magnet-Motor GmbH, a maker of high-tech electric and energy systems for propulsion of commercial and combat vehicles, and marine vessels. The company was renamed L-3 Communications Magnet-Motor; terms of the deal were not disclosed. Later that year L-3 acquired radio and satellite communications systems maker TRL Electronics PLC of the UK for about $176 million.

L-3 then kept the 2006 acquisitions spree going with the agreement to purchase Crestview Aerospace Corporation (airframe assemblies and military aircraft modifications) for $135 million. Crestview became part of L-3's Aircraft Modernization and Maintenance division when the transaction closed in late 2006. L-3 also bought SSG Precision Optronics, a maker of optics, telescopes, and optical subsystems for government, defense, and commercial customers.

In June 2006 Lanza died suddenly. Shortly after Lanza's death, L-3 completed its acquisition of Nautronix Defence Group, a provider of mine warfare and anti-submarine systems.

Speculation sparked immediately that Lanza's death might spur rivals such as BAE SYSTEMS to seek to acquire L-3 — either as a whole or in parts. Within days of Lanza's death L-3 CFO Michael Strianese was named interim CEO. Board member Robert Millard was named chairman. Overtures by potential suitors, however, never materialized.

EXECUTIVES

Chairman, President, and CEO: Michael T. Strianese, age 52, $10,050,828 total compensation
SVP Business Operations: David T. Butler III, age 52
VP and CFO: Ralph G. D'Ambrosio, age 41, $1,981,893 total compensation
VP and Chief Information Officer: Vincent T. Taylor
VP and Chief Technology Officer: A. Michael Andrews II
VP Science and Technology; CTO, Homeland Security Group: Paul De Lia
VP Chief Patent Counsel: David Kinsinger
EVP Corporate Strategy and Development: Curtis Brunson, age 61, $2,094,258 total compensation
SVP; President, Products Group: Charles J. Schafer, age 61
SVP: Robert W. RisCassi, age 73
SVP Washington DC Operations: Jimmie V. Adams, age 72
SVP and General Counsel Mergers and Acquisitions: Christopher C. Cambria
SVP; President, Sensors and Simulation Group: James W. Dunn, age 65, $2,487,821 total compensation
SVP; President, Marine and Power Systems Group: Steven (Steve) Kantor, age 64
SVP, Corporate Secretary, and General Counsel: Steven M. (Steve) Post, age 56
SVP and President, Integrated Systems Group: John C. McNellis, age 56
SVP; President, L-3 Services Group: Carl E. Vuono, age 74, $2,482,464 total compensation
SVP and Senior Counsel: Kathleen E. Karelis, age 48
VP; President, Communication Systems East: Gregory B. Roberts
VP Corporate Communications: Karen C. Tripp
VP Human Resources: John Hill
Controller and Principal Accounting Officer: Dan Azmon, age 45
Auditors: PricewaterhouseCoopers LLP

LOCATIONS

HQ: L-3 Communications Holdings, Inc.
600 3rd Ave., New York, NY 10016
Phone: 212-697-1111   **Fax:** 212-805-5477
Web: www.l-3com.com

2008 Sales

	$ mil.	% of total
US	12,815	86
Germany	324	2
Canada	308	2
UK	212	1
Australia	147	1
South Korea	140	1
Italy	93	1
New Zealand	42	—
Other countries	820	6
Total	**14,901**	**100**

PRODUCTS/OPERATIONS

2008 Sales

	$ mil.	% of total
Specialized products	5,373.8	36
Government services	4,303.0	29
Aircraft modernization & maintenance	2,657.4	18
Command, control & communications (C3), intelligence, surveillance & reconnaissance	2,566.9	17
Total	**14,901.1**	**100**

2008 Sales by Customer

	$ mil.	% of total
US government agencies	12,126	81
Commercial	1,676	14
Allied foreign governments	1,099	5
Total	**14,901**	**100**

Selected Operations

Specialized Products
  Acoustic undersea warfare products
  Forward looking infrared sensors, laser range finders, illuminators, and designators
  Fusing products
  Naval power distribution, conditioning, switching, and protection equipment
  Ruggedized displays
  Telemetry, instrumentation, space, and navigation products
  Training simulators
  Video surveillance and display systems
Government Services
  Acquisition management and staff augmentation
  Battlefield and weapon simulation
  Communication software support
  Information management and IT systems support and software design, development, and systems integration
  Information technology systems
  Linguistic interpretation, translation, and analysis services
  Network and enterprise administration and management
  Surveillance systems and products, installation, logistics, and support
  System support and concept operations
  Systems acquisition and advisory support and comprehensive operational support services
  Systems engineering, operations analysis, research and technical analysis
  Weapons training
Aircraft Modernization & Maintenance
  Aircraft maintenance and modification services
  Airborne traffic and collision avoidance systems
  Ruggedization of displays, computers, and electronics
  Voice recorders, flight data recorders, and maritime hardened voyage recorders
Command, Control & Communications & Intelligence, Surveillance, and Reconnaissance
  Airborne, space, and surface data link terminals, ground stations, and transportable tactical SATCOM systems
  Fleet management of special mission aircraft
  Ground-based satellite communications terminals and payloads
  Prime mission systems integration, sensor development, and operations and support
  Satellite command and control sustainment and support
  Satellite communication and tracking systems
  Secure communication terminals and equipment, and secure network encryption products
  Shipboard communications

COMPETITORS

AeroMechanical Services	JPS Communications
BAE SYSTEMS	Lockheed Martin
CACI International	Meggitt
CAE Inc.	Motorola, Inc.
Cubic Corp.	Northrop Grumman
DIRECTV	Orbital Sciences
DRS Technologies	Oshkosh Truck
DynCorp International	Raytheon
Ericsson	Rockwell Collins
GE	Sierra Nevada Corp
General Dynamics	telent
Harris Corp.	Thales
Herley Industries	Trimble Navigation
Honeywell International	United Technologies
ITT Corp.	

HISTORICAL FINANCIALS

Company Type: Public

Income Statement

FYE: December 31

	REVENUE ($ mil.)	NET INCOME ($ mil.)	NET PROFIT MARGIN	EMPLOYEES
12/08	14,901.0	929.0	6.2%	65,000
12/07	13,960.5	756.1	5.4%	64,600
12/06	12,476.9	526.1	4.2%	63,700
12/05	9,444.7	508.5	5.4%	59,500
12/04	6,897.0	381.9	5.5%	44,200
Annual Growth	21.2%	24.9%	—	10.1%

2008 Year-End Financials

Debt ratio: 78.1%
Return on equity: 15.7%
Cash ($ mil.): 867
Current ratio: 1.83
Long-term debt ($ mil.): 4,556

No. of shares (mil.): 117
Dividends
 Yield: 1.6%
 Payout: 15.5%
Market value ($ mil.): 8,601

Stock History

NYSE: LLL

	STOCK PRICE ($) FY Close	P/E High/Low		PER SHARE ($) Earnings	Dividends	Book Value
12/08	73.78	15	8	7.72	1.20	50.02
12/07	105.94	19	13	5.98	1.00	51.37
12/06	81.78	21	16	4.22	0.75	45.51
12/05	74.35	20	15	4.20	0.50	38.52
12/04	73.24	23	15	3.33	0.40	32.59
Annual Growth	0.2%	—	—	23.4%	31.6%	11.3%

Lam Research

It's not uncommon for chip makers in need of critical manufacturing equipment to go on the Lam. Lam Research is a top maker of semiconductor processing equipment. The company's products address two key steps in the chip-making process. Its plasma etch machines are used to create tiny circuitry patterns on silicon wafers. Lam also makes cleaning equipment that keeps unwanted particles from contaminating processed wafers. The company's customers include many large chip makers, such as Hynix Semiconductor, Samsung Electronics (about 19% of sales), STMicroelectronics, and Toshiba (13%). About three-quarters of the company's sales are to customers in the Asia/Pacific region, primarily in South Korea and Taiwan.

In response to a slump in the chip business at the end of the 1990s, Lam restructured its operations, staked a claim on its niche markets, and showed itself quick to introduce equipment designed to process latest-generation 300mm wafers. When the chip industry climbed again, Lam's sales rode high; but as the roller-coaster industry went back into steep decline from 2001-2003, the company implemented cost-cutting

measures, including two rounds of layoffs that together reduced Lam's workforce by about 20%.

In confronting poor business conditions in 2008, due to the credit crisis and the subsequent global financial meltdown, Lam reacted as many other suppliers of semiconductor equipment did. It kicked off a corporate restructuring that included the layoff of about 600 people, a 15% reduction in force.

With business worsening in 2009, the company laid off around 375 employees, a 10% reduction, and planned to close some facilities. The majority of the layoffs were in North America.

In 2008 Lam acquired the SEZ Group for about $568 million in cash. Net of cash acquired, the purchase is valued at around $447 million. SEZ made wafer-cleaning equipment. The Swiss company became the Spin Clean division of Lam.

HISTORY

Chinese immigrant David Lam started Lam Research in 1980 to use plasma chemistry to improve processes for making semiconductors. The company introduced its first product, AutoEtch, in 1982 and went public in 1984. David Lam left the company in 1985. Roger Emerick became Lam Research's CEO in 1982 and continued in that post until 1997, presiding over the company's growth into an industry leader.

Lam Research introduced its Rainbow line of dry-etch equipment in 1987 and its Transformer Coupled Plasma technology in 1992. The company signed a development agreement in 1994 with the U.S. Display Consortium to develop equipment for making advanced circuits for flat-panel displays. Lam posted its first "gigabuck" year, with annual revenues of $1.25 billion, in fiscal 1996. Since then, the company's revenues have yo-yoed up and down in response to cyclicality in the semiconductor equipment industry.

In 1997 Lam acquired OnTrak Systems, a maker of chemical mechanical planarization (CMP) wafer cleaning equipment. OnTrak's chairman and CEO, James Bagley, a former Applied Materials executive, became Lam's CEO and, in 1998, the company's chairman.

In 1998 Lam formed a pact with National Semiconductor to develop aluminum etch systems. That year a steep downturn in the global semiconductor industry, fed by the Asian economic crisis, led the company to close plants and cut its workforce by more than a quarter. Lam also exited the market for deposition equipment (which applies thin layers of material onto silicon wafers), and shuttered its flat-panel display operations.

With the chip industry rebounding in 1999, Lam won major orders from big chip makers, including AMD and STMicroelectronics. Lam posted strong profits in 2000 after three years of losses.

In 2001 the chip industry braked sharply. Lam responded with various cost-cutting measures, including two rounds of layoffs.

As the company (and the chip industry) rebounded in 2004, Lam discontinued its line of chemical mechanical planarization (CMP) products to focus on its offerings of etching and cleaning equipment.

In mid-2005 Bagley was succeeded as CEO by Stephen Newberry, who had been Lam's COO since 1997. Bagley remained as executive chairman. Like Bagley, Newberry had a long tenure at Applied Materials before joining Lam.

In late 2006 Lam acquired the silicon-growing and fabrication assets of Bullen Ultrasonics, a manufacturer of precision machined components, for approximately $175 million in cash. Bullen had been a supplier to Lam since 1991, providing silicon materials used in the process chambers of Lam's etching equipment. The business was renamed Bullen Semiconductor, a division of Lam.

EXECUTIVES

Chairman: James W. (Jim) Bagley, age 70
President, CEO, and Director:
 Stephen G. (Steve) Newberry, age 55
EVP and COO: Martin B. Anstice, age 42
SVP and CFO: Ernest E. Maddock, age 50
Group VP Human Resources and Chief Legal Officer:
 Sarah A. O¿Dowd
EVP Products: Nicolas J. (Nick) Bright, age 52
Group VP and General Manager Etch Products:
 Richard A. (Rick) Gottscho, age 57
Group VP Customer Support Business Group:
 Abdi Hariri, age 48
VP, General Counsel, and Secretary:
 George M. Schisler Jr.
VP Global Field Operations: Thomas J. Bondur, age 41
Investor Relations: Julie Cimino
Corporate Relations Manager: Shawn Lynch
Auditors: Ernst & Young LLP

LOCATIONS

HQ: Lam Research Corporation
 4650 Cushing Pkwy., Fremont, CA 94538
Phone: 510-572-0200   **Fax:** 510-572-2935
Web: www.lamrc.com

Lam Research has manufacturing plants in Austria and the US. It has offices in China, France, Germany, Ireland, Israel, Italy, Japan, Malaysia, the Netherlands, Singapore, South Korea, Switzerland, Taiwan, and the US.

2009 Sales

	$ mil.	% of total
Asia/Pacific		
South Korea	239.9	21
Japan	234.1	21
Taiwan	208.0	19
Other countries	141.4	13
US	171.4	15
Europe	121.2	11
Total	**1,116.0**	**100**

PRODUCTS/OPERATIONS

Selected Products

Plasma ("dry") wafer-etching equipment
Wafer residue cleaning tools

COMPETITORS

Applied Materials
Dainippon Screen
Ebara
Hitachi High-Technologies
Hitachi Kokusai Electric
Intevac
Mattson Technology
Novellus
Plasma Etch
Süss MicroTec
Semitool
Surface Technology
Tegal
Tokyo Electron
ULVAC
Veeco Instruments

HISTORICAL FINANCIALS

Company Type: Public

Income Statement

FYE: Last Sunday in June

	REVENUE ($ mil.)	NET INCOME ($ mil.)	NET PROFIT MARGIN	EMPLOYEES
6/09	1,115.9	(302.1)	—	2,711
6/08	2,474.9	439.3	17.8%	3,800
6/07	2,566.6	685.8	26.7%	3,000
6/06	1,642.2	335.8	20.4%	2,430
6/05	1,502.5	299.3	19.9%	2,200
Annual Growth	(7.2%)	—	—	5.4%

2009 Year-End Financials

Debt ratio: 2.8%
Return on equity: —
Cash ($ mil.): 374
Current ratio: 3.51
Long-term debt ($ mil.): 41

No. of shares (mil.): 127
Dividends
Yield: 0.0%
Payout: —
Market value ($ mil.): 3,293

Stock History

NASDAQ (GS): LRCX

	STOCK PRICE ($) FY Close	P/E High/Low	PER SHARE ($) Earnings	Dividends	Book Value
6/09	26.00	— —	(2.41)	0.00	11.47
6/08	36.15	18 10	3.47	0.00	14.04
6/07	51.40	12 8	4.85	0.00	9.29
6/06	46.72	23 12	2.34	0.00	11.02
6/05	28.94	15 9	2.10	0.00	8.42
Annual Growth	(2.6%)	— —	—	—	8.0%

Land O'Lakes

Land O'Lakes butters up its customers, and shows you what life is like if everyone cooperates. Owned by and serving more than 7,000 dairy farmer members and 1,300 community cooperatives, Land O'Lakes is one of the largest dairy co-ops in the US (along with Dairy Farmers of America and California Dairies). It provides its members with wholesale fertilizer and crop protection products, seed, and animal feed. Its oldest and best known product, LAND O' LAKES butter, is the top butter brand in the US. Land O'Lakes also produces packaged milk, margarine, sour cream, and cheese. The co-op's animal-feed division, Land O'Lakes Purina Feed, is a leading animal and pet food maker.

In line with its strategy to concentrate on its crop protection products, in 2009 the company sold nine Agriliance retail stores to Agri-AFC and 11 more to the Tennessee Farmers Cooperative.

In 2007 the company sold its international cheese and protein operations (known as CPI) to Saputo Cheese USA for about $216 million. The sale included the Golden Valley Dairy Products cheese manufacturing and cut-and-wrap operations. The deal also included a long-term milks agreement, such that Land O'Lakes is the sole milk supplier for CPI.

Also in 2007 Land O'Lakes and CHS realigned the businesses of their 50-50 joint venture Agriliance in 2007, with CHS acquiring its crop-nutrients wholesale-products business and Land O'Lakes acquiring the crop-protection products business. The following year, Canadian ag cooperative La Coop fédérée purchased Agriliance's remaining retail agronomy operation.

Land O'Lakes also owns egg producer MoArk. (MoArk sold its liquid egg products operations to Golden Oval Eggs in 2006.) In addition, the company's subsidiary, Land O'Lakes Finance, provides financing services for beef, dairy, pork, and poultry producers.

Outside of the US, Land O'Lakes has taken aim at the largest emerging market: China, where the company is working to establish the Land O'Lakes brand of cheese and cultured dairy products in supermarkets.

The company operates 10 dairy-product manufacturing facilities throughout the US.

HISTORY

In the old days, grocers sold butter from communal tubs and it often went bad. Widespread distribution of dairy products had to await the invention of fast, reliable transportation. By 1921 the necessary transportation was available. That year about 320 dairy farmers in Minnesota formed the Minnesota Cooperative Creameries Association and launched a membership drive with $1,375, mostly borrowed from the US Farm Bureau.

The co-op arranged joint shipments for members, imposed strict hygiene and quality standards, and aggressively marketed its sweet cream butter nationwide, packaged for the first time in the familiar box of four quarter-pound sticks. A month after the co-op's New York sales office opened, it was ordering 80 shipments a week.

Minnesota Cooperative Creameries, as part of its promotional campaigns, ran a contest in 1924 to name that butter. Two contestants offered the winning name — Land O'Lakes. The distinctive Indian Maiden logo first appeared about the same time, and in 1926 the co-op changed its name to Land O'Lakes Creameries. By 1929, when it began supplying feed, its market share approached 50%.

During WWII civilian consumption dropped, but the co-op increased production of dried milk to provide food for soldiers and newly liberated concentration camp victims.

In the 1950s and 1960s, Land O'Lakes added ice cream and yogurt producers to its membership and fought margarine makers, yet butter's market share continued to melt. The co-op diversified in 1970 through acquisitions, adding feeds and agricultural chemicals. Two years later Land O'Lakes threw in the towel and came out with its own margarine. Despite the decreasing use of butter nationally, the co-op's market share grew.

Land O'Lakes formed a marketing joint venture, Cenex/Land O'Lakes Agronomy, with fellow co-op Cenex in 1987. As health consciousness bloomed in the 1980s, Land O'Lakes launched reduced-fat dairy products. It also purchased a California cheese plant, doubling its capacity. Land O'Lakes began ramping up its international projects at the same time: It built a feed mill in Taiwan, introduced feed products in Mexico, and established feed and cheese operations in Poland.

In 1997 the co-op bought low-fat cheese maker Alpine Lace Brands. Land O'Lakes took on the eastern US when it merged with the 3,600-member Atlantic Dairy Cooperative (1997), and it bulked up on the West Coast when California-based Dairyman's Cooperative Creamery Association joined its fold (1998).

During 2000 the co-op sold five plants to Dean Foods with an agreement to continue supplying the plants with raw milk. Also in 2000 Land O'Lakes combined its feed business with those of Farmland Industries to create Land O'Lakes Farmland Feed, LLC, with a 69% ownership. That same year, Land O'Lakes and CHS joined their agronomy operations to create a 50-50 joint venture, Agriliance LLC.

In late 2001 the company spent $359 million to acquire Purina Mills (pet and livestock feeds). Purina Mills was folded into Land O'Lakes Farmland Feed and, as part of the purchase, Land O'Lakes increased its ownership of the feed business to 92%. In 2004 it purchased the remaining 8%.

To take advantage of its nationally recognized brand, Land O'Lakes formed an alliance with Dean Foods in 2002 to develop and market value-added dairy products.

Exiting the meat business, Land O'Lakes sold its swine operations in 2005 to private pork producer Maschhoff West LLC for an undisclosed sum. That same year, it sold its interest in fertilizer manufacturer CF Industries. Long-time president and CEO Jack Gherty retired that year; he was replaced by Chris Policinski. In 2006 the company acquired 100% ownership of MoArk.

EXECUTIVES

Chairman: Peter (Pete) Kappelman, age 46
First Vice Chairman: Ronnie Mohr, age 60
President and CEO: Chris Policinski, age 50
SVP and CFO: Daniel E. (Dan) Knutson, age 52
EVP; COO, Dairy Foods Industrial: Alan Pierson, age 58
EVP; COO, Feed: Fernando J. Palacios, age 49
EVP Ag Business Development and Member Services: David L. (Dave) Seehusen, age 62
EVP; COO, Dairy Foods Value-Added: Steve Dunphy, age 51
EVP; COO, Seed Division: Mike Vande Logt, age 54
EVP; COO, Crop Protection Products: Rodney (Rod) Schroeder, age 53
SVP Public Affairs and Business Development: James D. (Jim) Fife, age 59
SVP Human Resources: Karen Grabow, age 59
SVP and General Counsel: Peter S. Janzen, age 49
SVP Corporate Marketing Strategy: Barry C. Wolfish, age 52
SVP Corporate Strategy and Business Development: Jean-Paul (JP) Ruiz-Funes, age 51
VP Quality Assurance and Regulatory Affairs: Sara Mortimore
Secretary and Director: Douglas (Doug) Reimer, age 58
Director Corporate Communications: Lydia Botham
Director Sourcing and Procurement: Chuck Compton
Auditors: KPMG LLP

LOCATIONS

HQ: Land O'Lakes, Inc.
  4001 Lexington Ave., North, Arden Hills, MN 55112
Phone: 651-481-2222   **Fax:** 651-481-2000
Web: www.landolakesinc.com

PRODUCTS/OPERATIONS

2008 Sales

	$ mil.	% of total
Dairy foods	4,136.4	34
Feed	3,857.4	32
Agronomy	2,335.3	19
Seed	1,185.0	10
Layers	606.2	5
Eliminations	(81.0)	—
Total	**12,039.3**	**100**

Selected Brands and Products

Agronomy
  Winfield Solutions (wholesale crop protection
    products — adjuvants, fungicides, herbicides,
    insecticides and seed treatments)
  Origin (micronutrients)

Animal feed
  Land O'Lakes Purina Feed

Bulk ingredients for manufacturers
  Non-fat dry milk powder
  Cheese
  Whey

Cheese
  Alpine Lace
  LAND O'LAKES
    New Yorker

Eggs
  Eggland's Best
  LAND O"LAKES All-Natural Farm Fresh Eggs

Other consumer dairy foods
  LAND O' LAKES

Seed
  CROPLAN GENETICS (alfalfa, corn, and soybean seed)
  FORAGE FIRST SEED (brassica, forage sorghum,
    grasses, herb, legume, and pasture mix seeds)
  Land O'Lakes Seed (alfalfa, canola, corn, grain
    sorghum, soybean, sugar beet, turf grass, and wheat
    seed)
  HYTEST SEED (alfalfa and corn seed)

Selected Dairy Foods

Butter
  Blends
  Flavored
  Light
  Salted
  Spreadable
  Whipped
  With Canola Oil
  Unsalted

Canola oil

Cheese
  American
  Cheddar
  Monterey Jack
  Mozzarella
  Parmesan
  Provolone
  Romano

Eggs
  All-natural
  Cage-free
  Nutritionally enhanced
  Organic
  Regular

Margarine

COMPETITORS

ADM
Agrium
Associated Milk Producers
Barkley Seed
Blue Seal Feeds
Breeder's Choice
California Dairies Inc.
Cal-Maine Foods
Cargill
ConAgra
Dairy Farmers of America
Darigold, Inc.
Dean Foods
Fonterra
Foremost Farms
Frontier Agriculture
Harris Moran
Hartz Mountain
Hill's Pet Nutrition
HP Hood
Iams
Keller's Creamery
Kent Feeds
Kraft Foods
Latham Seed Company
Mars Petcare
Michael Foods Egg Products
Michael Foods, Inc.
Monsanto Company
MSC
National Dairy Holdings
NC+ Hybrids
Nestlé Purina PetCare
Nestlé USA
Northwest Dairy
Pfister Hybrid Corn
Pioneer Hi-Bred
Prairie Farms Dairy
Rose Acre Farms
Royal Canin
Sakata Seed
Saputo
Sargento
Schreiber Foods
Syngenta Seeds
Unilever
Wilbur-Ellis

HISTORICAL FINANCIALS

Company Type: Cooperative

Income Statement

FYE: December 31

	REVENUE ($ mil.)	NET INCOME ($ mil.)	NET PROFIT MARGIN	EMPLOYEES
12/08	12,039.3	159.6	1.3%	9,100
12/07	8,924.9	163.8	1.8%	8,700
12/06	7,274.9	88.7	1.2%	8,500
12/05	7,556.7	128.9	1.7%	7,500
12/04	7,676.5	21.4	0.3%	8,000
Annual Growth	**11.9%**	**65.3%**	**—**	**3.3%**

Net Income History

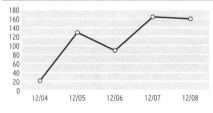

La-Z-Boy

The kickback that La-Z-Boy gives its customers is perfectly legal. The top US maker of upholstered furniture, La-Z-Boy sells its ubiquitous recliners, plus chairs, sofas, tables, and modular seating units. One recliner has sported a drink cooler, phone, and massage and heat system. La-Z-Boy sells through about 70 company-owned stores, some 250 independent La-Z-Boy Furniture Galleries, and about 220 in-store galleries at furniture dealers, department stores, and other outlets. La-Z-Boy also makes wood furniture (desks, cabinets, and bedroom items) and licenses its name for use on furniture for the health care industry. Its brands include La-Z-Boy, Bauhaus USA, Hammary, American Drew/Lea, and Kincaid.

A few factors have made life for La-Z-Boy a little less laid back. An influx of new cost-conscious competitors, such as Costco, IKEA, and Home Depot, has eroded La-Z-Boy's revenue. The weakening US housing market also has led to a decline in sales at the furniture maker, particularly through its upholstered products segment. The business segment's sales dropped from 75% of La-Z-Boy's overall revenue in 2008 to 73% in 2009. Compounding the problem, IKEA's and Costco's alternative distribution and rivals who offer online furniture shopping have lured some customers away from traditional furniture retail outlets and brick-and-mortar shopping. To this end, the company has no new stores slated for 2010, as well, although La-Z-Boy anticipates remodeling up to 10 of its New Generation-format stores during fiscal 2010. These stores typically boast more square footage and an updated appearance.

In response to the increased pressure, La-Z-Boy has made a number of strategic moves to stay competitive and maintain a profitable portfolio. During 2009 the company is reducing its overall workforce by about 10%. Also, it shuttered some 20 mostly dealer-owned La-Z-Boy Furniture Galleries stores in early 2009 and has been significantly reducing its fiscal 2009 capital expenditures and overall discretionary expenses and inventories.

La-Z-Boy's also streamlining its manufacturing operations. In late 2008 the furniture maker adopted a restructuring plan to consolidate all its cutting and sewing operations at five US plants into one centralized facility in Mexico. (The firm began production in Mexico in January 2009 and is hiring about 1,200 employees to staff the plant there.) Also, in mid-2009 the firm combined two of its plants in North Carolina that make hardwood furniture into one.

HISTORY

Carpenter Edward Knabusch repaired and built furniture in his family's garage in Monroe, Michigan, in the early 1920s. When people began clamoring for Knabusch's repair expertise, he quit his job, hired his cousin, Edwin Shoemaker, and in 1927 formed Floral City Furniture.

The duo specialized in new designs, including a telephone stand with seat that they dubbed "the Gossiper." Their first recliner, a wooden porch chair that shaped itself to body contours, was developed in 1928. Positive response prompted family and friends to raise money (Shoemaker's dad mortgaged the farm) for a manufacturing plant. At a customer's urging, the pair upholstered the chair, and Knabusch drummed up even more interest with a contest to name the new piece. Entries included Slack-Back, Sit-N-Snooze, and the moniker that would help define an industry, La-Z-Boy.

In the midst of the Depression, the company thrived, turning the bottom factory floor into a showroom and offering entertainment and circus tents stuffed with merchandise to attract out-of-state visitors. The cousins amassed a petting zoo of farm animals collected, instead of money, from cash-strapped customers.

To separate manufacturing and a burgeoning retail operation, La-Z-Boy Chair was incorporated in 1941. Production stopped during WWII while Knabusch and Shoemaker made tank seats and crash pads.

Its one-of-a-kind product styles helped to distinguish the company through the 1950s and 1960s. Its reputation grew, thanks to products such as a love seat fashioned in the form of a car seat, replete with lights, horns, fins, and tires (1959), and a chair that both rocked and reclined (1961). La-Z-Boy also began what would become a long-lived marketing campaign by using such celebrity spokesmen as football player Joe Namath and talk-show host Johnny Carson.

Sales reached nearly $53 million in 1971, and La-Z-Boy went public the next year. It diversified through the late 1970s into sleeper sofas (1977) and other products. Knabusch's adopted son Charles became chairman in 1985 and vowed to increase female clientele. La-Z-Boy also began making business furniture and began a continuing buying binge, including table maker Hammary Furniture (1986) and dining room and bedroom furniture specialist Kincaid Furniture (1988). Knabusch died in 1988, and the company's largest investor, Prescott Investors, made a failed takeover bid in 1989. That year La-Z-Boy opened its first superstore gallery.

The company changed its name to La-Z-Boy in 1996. Charles Knabusch, Edward's son and company CEO, died in 1997; COO Gerald Kiser was made president. (He was later named CEO in July 2001.) The next year co-founder Shoemaker, who still held the EVP of engineering and VC titles, died in his recliner at the age of 90. Acquisitions continued, including mid-priced furniture maker Bauhaus USA (1999) and LADD Furniture (2000).

In 2003 three casegoods manufacturing facilities were shut down, resulting in the elimination of an additional 400 positions. In 2004 production facilities in Pennsylvania, North Carolina, and Mississippi were shut down, putting about 650 La-Z-Boy employees out of work.

The company exited the office furniture manufacturing industry in mid-2005 so it could focus on the home furnishings business. In a move that further emphasized the company's realignment to the consumer market, it sold its La-Z-Boy Contract Unit, which manufactures furnishings used in commercial and health care settings, to the owners of Best Home Furnishings in 2005.

In July 2006 the company sold American of Martinsville, a maker of furniture for the hospitality industry, to private equity firm Hancock Park Associates for an undisclosed sum.

As it reevaluated its products portfolio, La-Z-Boy sold off its Sam Moore Furniture unit to Hooker Furniture in May 2007. The La-Z-Boy unit specialized in making upscale fabric-to-frame occasional chairs. Having acquired Sam Moore in 1998, La-Z-Boy chose to refocus on functional upholstered furniture.

EXECUTIVES

Chairman: James W. Johnston, age 70
President, CEO, and Director: Kurt L. Darrow, age 54
SVP and CFO: Louis M. (Mike) Riccio Jr., age 46
CIO: Daniel F. DeLand, age 46
VP and Chief Marketing Officer: Doug Collier, age 41
Chief Retail Officer: Mark S. Bacon, age 45
VP, Chief Accounting Officer, and Corporate Controller: Margaret L. (Peg) Mueller, age 40
SVP, Operations, Residential: David A. (Dave) Layman
SVP, Sales and Merchandising: Gregory D. (Greg) White
SVP; President, Casegoods Product and Kincaid Furniture Company: Steven M. (Steve) Kincaid, age 60
SVP; President, Non-Branded Upholstery Product and England: Otis S. Sawyer, age 51
SVP, Retail Operations, Kincaid: Todd Hady
VP, Corporate Human Resources: Steven P. (Steve) Rindskopf, age 45
VP, Corporate Fabric Procurement: Mark R. Hellwig, age 47
VP, Real Estate Development: David Baratta
VP, Brand Marketing: Jennifer (Jen) Sievertsen
VP, Process Improvement: Roger L. Miller
Secretary and General Counsel: James P. Klarr
Director of Investor Relations and Corporate Communications: Kathy Liebmann
Auditors: PricewaterhouseCoopers LLP

LOCATIONS

HQ: La-Z-Boy Incorporated
1284 N. Telegraph Rd., Monroe, MI 48162
Phone: 734-242-1444   **Fax:** 734-457-2005
Web: www.lazboy.com

2009 Sales

	% of total
US	89
Canada & other countries	11
Total	**100**

PRODUCTS/OPERATIONS

2009 Sales

	$ mil.	% of total
Upholstery	899.2	73
Casegoods	178.0	14
Retail	160.8	13
Adjustments	(11.3)	—
Total	**1,226.7**	**100**

Selected Products

Bedroom furniture
Chairs
Dining room furniture
Entertainment units
Leather furniture
Love seats
Modular seating groups
Recliners
Reclining sofas
Sleep sofas
Sofas
Tables
Wall systems
Youth furniture

Divisions and Brands

Upholstery Group
  Bauhaus USA (upholstered furniture, convertible sofas)
  England (mid-priced upholstered and motion furniture for living, family rooms)
  La-Z-Boy (residential and health care furniture)
Casegoods Group
  American Drew (wood furniture for bedroom, dining room, occasional use)
  Hammary (tables, entertainment units, wall units, and upholstered furniture for living, family rooms)
  Kincaid (wood furniture)
  Lea (bedroom furniture)

COMPETITORS

Art Van Furniture
Ashley Furniture
Bassett Furniture
Berkline BenchCraft
Bernhardt Furniture
Brown Jordan International
Chromcraft Revington
Costco Wholesale
DFS Furniture
Ethan Allen
Flexsteel
Furniture Brands International
Herman Miller
HNI
Home Depot
Home Meridian
Hooker Furniture
IKEA
KI
Kimball International
Klaussner Furniture
Natuzzi
Palliser Furniture
Rooms To Go
Rowe Fine Furniture
Sam's Club
Shelby Williams
Stanley Furniture
Steelcase
Target
Thomasville Furniture
Universal Furniture
W. S. Badcock
Wal-Mart

HISTORICAL FINANCIALS

Company Type: Public

Income Statement

FYE: Last Saturday in April

	REVENUE ($ mil.)	NET INCOME ($ mil.)	NET PROFIT MARGIN	EMPLOYEES
4/09	1,226.7	(121.3)	—	7,730
4/08	1,450.9	(13.5)	—	10,057
4/07	1,617.3	4.1	0.3%	11,729
4/06	1,916.8	(3.0)	—	13,404
4/05	2,048.4	35.1	1.7%	14,822
Annual Growth	**(12.0%)**	**—**	**—**	**(15.0%)**

2009 Year-End Financials

Debt ratio: 17.1%
Return on equity: —
Cash ($ mil.): 17
Current ratio: 2.76
Long-term debt ($ mil.): 52
No. of shares (mil.): 51
Dividends
  Yield: 3.8%
  Payout: —
Market value ($ mil.): 137

Stock History

NYSE: LZB

	STOCK PRICE ($) FY Close	P/E High/Low	PER SHARE ($) Earnings	Dividends	Book Value
4/09	2.66	— —	(2.36)	0.10	5.94
4/08	6.37	— —	(0.26)	0.40	8.75
4/07	11.69	205 141	0.08	0.48	9.43
4/06	15.32	— —	(0.06)	0.44	9.91
4/05	11.84	30 17	0.71	0.44	10.24
Annual Growth	**(31.2%)**	**— —**	**—**	**(31.0%)**	**(12.7%)**

Legg Mason

Legg Mason's feats include wealth management and mutual fund management. The financial services firm has several subsidiaries that offer asset management, trust services, and annuities to retail and institutional investors. The company manages more than 150 mutual funds under the Legg Mason, Legg Mason Partners, Western Asset, and The Royce Funds banners. Other offerings include closed-end funds and separately managed accounts. Legg Mason distributes its products through its own offices, retirement plans, and financial intermediaries, as well as through an agreement with Citigroup. The company operates primarily in North America and the UK, but sells its funds in about two dozen other countries.

Legg Mason offers wealth management services to affluent clients through several subsidiaries, including New York-based Barrett Asssociates, Cincinnati's Bartlett & Co., and Legg Mason Investment Counsel & Trust.

In 2008 Legg Mason named Mark Fetting, who had led the company's mutual fund and managed account business, as chairman and CEO, succeeding founder Raymond "Chip" Mason, the only chief executive in the company's 38-year history. Also that year the company cut jobs at its Baltimore headquarters and at its money-management subsidiaries by about one-third. The rocky economy prompted many clients to pull out large amounts of money from their mutual funds, which created losses for the company.

Legg Mason has more than $600 million of client assets under management, about a third less than it had as recently as 2006. More than half of that figure is invested in fixed-income products.

HISTORY

George Mackubin and G. Clem Goodrich formed brokerage firm Mackubin & Goodrich in 1899. The next year John Legg joined the company as a "board boy," employed to chalk stock prices on a small blackboard.

The 1904 Baltimore fire destroyed the firm's offices, and it temporarily had to move to two rooms owned by Legg's dentist until it could rebuild. Legg became a partner in 1905. The firm was hit hard by the halt in trading due to WWI and was reduced to brokering mortgages for a local homebuilder. In 1925 the company started what may have been the first real estate investment trust, National Union Mortgage Company. The company established a new department in 1930 devoted exclusively to women investors and hired A. Catherine Overbeck to run it.

The 1929 stock market crash and Depression devastated the firm, and in 1930 the partners liquidated their own portfolios to inject cash into the company. After Goodrich died in 1932, the firm was renamed Mackubin, Legg & Co. It lost its other founder in 1942 when Mackubin argued with Legg and left to join a competitor. The firm became John C. Legg & Co.

The company flourished in the postwar boom. In 1962 Raymond "Chip" Mason founded his own brokerage in Virginia and eight years later merged it with Legg to form Legg Mason & Co.

In 1973 the firm acquired New York broker-dealer Wood Walker & Co. and became Legg Mason Wood Walker.

The company introduced a money market mutual fund in 1979 and its first equity fund in 1982. Between those two events, it established Legg Mason, Inc. as a holding company for its growing list of subsidiaries; it went public in 1983. During the 1980s and 1990s, the firm added to its straight brokerage business by buying a string of asset management companies.

Targeting wealthy individuals, in 1999 the company obtained a national thrift charter, allowing it to take on trust business outside Maryland. Expanding outside the US at century's end, it bought UK investment firm Johnson Fry Holdings and Canadian pension fund manager Perigee; both acquisitions were ultimately rebranded under the Legg Mason name. Also that year, the company merged Howard, Weil, Labouisse, Friedrichs into Legg Mason Wood Walker.

Legg Mason bought New York-based investment manager Barrett Associates in 2000 and purchased Private Capital Management and Royce & Associates the following year.

In 2004 Legg Mason was one of several companies that settled NASD and SEC charges of failing to pay mutual fund customers discounts to which they were entitled.

Legg Mason swapped its brokerage and capital markets operations for most of the mutual fund and asset management business of Citigroup in a $3.7 billion deal in 2005. The company also bought 80% of The Permal Group, a large funds-of-hedge-funds administrator.

Legg Mason announced the latter agreement the same day it unveiled the unusual Citigroup transaction. These two significant deals allowed Legg Mason to focus solely on asset management and made it one of the largest such companies in the US. The acquisitions also significantly increased the company's assets under management overseas.

In 2006 Legg Mason changed the name of the former Citigroup Asset Management US Equity Group to ClearBridge Advisors. The Smith Barney funds, also acquired in the Citi deal, were renamed Legg Mason Partners Funds.

EXECUTIVES

Chairman, President, and CEO: Mark R. Fetting, age 54, $4,703,699 total compensation
SVP, Treasurer, and CFO: Charles J. Daley Jr., age 47, $2,294,100 total compensation
Chairman and Chief Investment Officer, Legg Mason Capital Management: William H. (Bill) Miller III
SVP and Chief Investment Strategist, Legg Mason Funds: Michael Mauboussin
Managing Director, Chief Investment Officer, and Senior Portfolio Manager, ClearBridge Advisors: Harry D. (Hersh) Cohen
SEVP and Chief Administrative Officer: Joseph A. Sullivan, age 51
SVP and General Counsel: Thomas P. Lemke
SVP; Head Specialized Managers: Jeffrey A. Nattans
SVP and Head, Amercian Division: David R. Odenath, age 52
President and CEO, ClearBridge Advisors: Peter E. Sundman, age 50
CEO, Western Asset Management: James W. (Jim) Hirschmann III, age 48
President and CEO, Legg Mason Investment Counsel: Harry O'Mealia

COO, ClearBridge Advisors: Terrence J. Murphy
Managing Director; Head Institutional Business, Americas: Kimberly M. Mustin
Managing Director and Head of Retail, Americas: Matt Schiffman
EVP Research, Risk Management and New Product Initiatives, Legg Mason Capital Management: Jennifer Murphy
Managing Director and Head of Investor Relations and Corporate Communications: Alan F. Magleby, age 53
Auditors: PricewaterhouseCoopers LLP

LOCATIONS

HQ: Legg Mason, Inc.
100 Light St., Baltimore, MD 21202
Phone: 410-539-0000   **Fax:** 410-454-4923
Web: www.leggmason.com

2009 Sales

	$ mil.	% of total
Americas	2,290.5	68
International	1,066.9	32
Total	**3,357.4**	**100**

PRODUCTS/OPERATIONS

2009 Sales

	$ mil.	% of total
Investment advisory fees		
Funds	1,836.4	55
Separate accounts	1,017.2	30
Performance fees	17.4	1
Distribution & service fees	475.0	14
Other	11.4	—
Total	**3,357.4**	**100**

Selected Subsidiaries and Affiliates

3040692 Nova Scotia Company (Canada)
  Legg Mason Canada Holdings Ltd.
    Legg Mason Canada Inc.
Bartlett & Co.
Batterymarch Financial Management, Inc.
Brandywine Global Investment Management, LLC
ClearBridge Advisors, LLC
Clearbridge Asset Management Inc.
Global Currents Investment Management, LLC
Legg Mason & Co., LLC
Legg Mason Capital Management, Inc.
Legg Mason Fund Adviser, Inc.
Legg Mason Funding, Corp.
Legg Mason International Holdings, LLC
  LM International Holding LP (Cayman Islands)
    Legg Mason International Equities Limited (UK)
    Legg Mason International Equities (Singapore) Pte. Ltd.
    Legg Mason Investments (Hong Kong) Limited
    LM Holdings Limited (UK)
      Legg Mason (UK) Holdings Plc
      Legg Mason Investments Holdings Limited (UK)
      Legg Mason Investments Limited (UK)
    Western Asset Management Company Pte. Ltd. (Singapore)
    Western Asset Management (UK) Holdings Ltd.
      Western Asset Management Company Limited (UK)
Legg Mason Investment Counsel & Trust Company, National Association
  Barrett Associates, Inc.
  Legg Mason Investment Counsel, LLC
Legg Mason Investor Services, LLC
Legg Mason Partners Fund Advisor, LLC
Legg Mason Private Portfolio Group, LLC
Legg Mason Properties, Inc.
Legg Mason Real Estate Investors, Inc.
PCM Holdings I, Inc.
  Carnes Capital Corporation
  Private Capital Management, L.P.
Permal Group Ltd.
Royce & Associates, LLC
  Royce Fund Services, Inc.
  Royce Management Company, LLC
Western Asset Management Company

HISTORICAL FINANCIALS

Company Type: Public

Income Statement

FYE: March 31

	ASSETS ($ mil.)	NET INCOME ($ mil.)	INCOME AS % OF ASSETS	EMPLOYEES
3/09	9,321.4	(1,947.9)	—	3,890
3/08	11,830.4	267.6	2.3%	4,220
3/07	9,604.5	646.8	6.7%	4,030
3/06	9,302.5	1,144.2	12.3%	3,800
3/05	8,219.5	408.4	5.0%	5,580
Annual Growth	3.2%	—	—	(8.6%)

2009 Year-End Financials

Equity as % of assets: 47.8%
Return on assets: —
Return on equity: —
Long-term debt ($ mil.): 2,965
No. of shares (mil.): 144

Dividends
Yield: 6.0%
Payout: —
Market value ($ mil.): 2,286
Sales ($ mil.): 3,357

Stock History

NYSE: LM

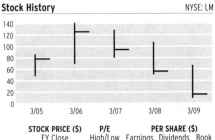

	STOCK PRICE ($) FY Close	P/E High/Low	PER SHARE ($) Earnings	Dividends	Book Value
3/09	15.90	— —	(13.85)	0.96	30.98
3/08	55.98	57 28	1.86	0.96	46.04
3/07	94.21	28 18	4.48	0.81	45.49
3/06	125.33	16 8	8.80	0.69	40.68
3/05	78.14	24 14	3.53	0.55	15.95
Annual Growth	(32.8%)	— —	—	14.9%	18.1%

Leggett & Platt

That spring in your step after a good night's sleep may be there courtesy of Leggett & Platt (L&P) — the pioneer of coiled bedsprings. Primarily using aluminum and steel, the company makes residential furnishings (innersprings, bed frames) and commercial fixtures (store displays, shelving). It also produces industrial materials (wire, steel tubing) and specialized items (quilting machinery, automotive seating and equipment, docking stations for electronic devices). Customers include furniture retailers, telecommunications firms, and manufacturers of automobiles, construction-related products, furniture and bedding, and garden and yard equipment. The company operates about 20 businesses in as many countries.

L&P, which has acquired more than 100 companies since 1996, has reversed course to become a seller, rather than a buyer, of businesses. As part of its revised strategy to only operate in areas where it can be a market leader, L&P has shed about one-fifth of its business portfolio in an effort to generate some $1.2 billion and enhance shareholder value.

The unloading of the company's die-cast aluminum products segment in mid-2008 accounted for its largest divestiture. (It generated nearly $500 million in sales in 2007.) L&P also sold its divisions in prime foam, wood products and fibers, plastics, and the dealer portion of commercial vehicle products. While the economic downturn has slowed plans to pare its portfolio heading into 2009, L&P has continued talks to unload its coated fabrics and storage products divisions.

The company purchased just three companies in 2007: an office furniture component manufacturing business in China, a coated wire products producer, and a designer and assembler of docking stations for computer components in vehicles. In the past L&P had boosted its profitability and grown through acquisitions, strengthening its presence in the residential and commercial furnishings and specialized product markets.

HISTORY

Carthage, Missouri, resident J. P. Leggett, an inventor with several patents, took his coiled bedspring to his businessman/manufacturer brother-in-law, C. B. Platt, in 1883. The two formed a partnership and began selling bedsprings (patented in 1885) to retailers who incorporated them into their mattresses (previous mattresses were made of cotton, horsehair, or feathers). They had two plants when they incorporated as Leggett & Platt Spring Bed & Manufacturing in 1901.

Leggett was president until 1921, when Platt took over. Leggett's son got the nod in 1929, and though he headed the company for only three years, he initiated the production of both innerspring mattress springs (the original coiled spring had been the company's sole product) and coiled springs for upholstered furniture.

By this time L&P was selling to manufacturers rather than retailers, and sales and profits took off along with the innerspring market, though the conservative company didn't open another plant until 1942. Another plant opening in 1947 was its last expansion until 1960. That year CEO Harry Cornell (grandson of J. P. Leggett), who joined the company in 1950, took the reins. By then

L&P had three plants and nearly $10 million in annual sales.

Cornell envisioned the company as a national low-cost supplier of furnishings components. He acquired a woodworking plant in 1960, giving the firm the ability to make wooden bed frames. Acquisitions steadily increased the company's range of products and its geographic scope, and by the early 1970s (the company went public in 1967) L&P had nearly 20 plants and annual sales of around $50 million. The increasing size of the company, along with vertical integration (it began making its own wire in 1970), gave it economies of scale and cost advantages in the fragmented industry.

In 1970 bedding components accounted for about 70% of sales; just four years later — as L&P focused on finished furniture and furniture components — they accounted for about 45%. The company also made investments in new plants, equipment, and products. By 1980 it had about 60 plants and sales of more than $250 million. L&P introduced its continuous coil innerspring — which contributed to the company's good performance in an otherwise slumping industry — around the middle of the decade.

The recession at the beginning of the 1990s hurt the company's sales, but L&P bounced back with the economy and had more than $1 billion in sales in 1992. The next year the company added to its 135 plants the acquisitions of Hanes Holding Company and VWR Textiles & Supplies (bedding and furniture fabrics).

About 75% of the company's 1995 sales increase resulted from acquisitions. The following year L&P acquired almost 15 companies, including Pace Holdings (aluminum die-cast components). Cornell's nearly 50-year-old strategy continued through 1998 as the company purchased more than 40 businesses (about 30 furnishings-related) with aggregate annual sales of about $560 million.

President Felix Wright added CEO to his duties in 1999, and Cornell remained chairman. Throughout 1999 L&P bought 29 companies with a combined revenue of about $480 million. In 2000 the company kept up its buying habit, purchasing about 20 companies. By 2001, however, the firm began to reverse that trend, closing or selling off facilities it deemed unprofitable.

In 2005 L&P bought the assets of Ikex; the membership interests of Jarex Distribution, a Jiajiang, China, furniture mechanism facility; Toronto-based Westex International; and Mississippi's Everwood Products. Also, it purchased a Shanghai, China, fixtures facility.

L&P's acquisition of America's Body Company (ABC) in 2005 gave the company a leg up in the commercial truck equipment segment of the industry and spurred the firm to restructure its operations. ABC makes bodies for vans, flatbed trucks, utility work vehicles, and dump trucks, as well as interiors for vans and equipment for snow and ice control.

Cornell became chairman emeritus in May 2006, when Wright resigned as CEO and took the title of chairman. President David Haffner became CEO as part of the succession.

Following a restructuring announced in 2007, L&P sold its Pace business of aluminum products for some $300 million. It also sold its L&P Plastics unit (a maker of components for the furniture, medical device, power tool, and automotive industries) to Monomoy Capital Partners in September 2008.

EXECUTIVES

Chairman: Richard T. Fisher, age 70
President, CEO, and Director: David S. (Dave) Haffner, age 56, $3,233,029 total compensation
EVP, COO, and Director: Karl G. Glassman, age 50, $1,806,001 total compensation
SVP and CFO: Matthew C. (Matt) Flanigan, age 47, $1,026,264 total compensation
VP Information Technology: Michael Blinzler
VP, Corporate Controller, and Chief Accounting Officer: William S. Weil, age 50
Chief Procurement Officer: Peter W. Connelly
Group EVP Sales and Marketing, Bedding: Mark Quinn
SVP; President, Specialized Products: Jack D. Crusa, age 54
SVP, General Counsel, and Secretary: Ernest C. Jett, age 63
SVP Human Resources: John A. Hale
SVP Operations: Dick Ralston
SVP; President, Industrial Materials: Joseph D. Downes Jr., age 64, $877,827 total compensation
SVP; President, Commercial Fixturing and Components: Dennis S. Park, age 54
SVP; President, Residential Furnishings: Paul R. Hauser, age 57, $856,861 total compensation
VP and Treasurer: Sheri L. Mossbeck
VP Public Affairs and Government Relations: Lance G. Beshore
VP Strategy and Investor Relations: David M. (Dave) DeSonier, age 50
VP Corporate Affairs and Human Resources: John G. Moore, age 48
Director Investor Relations: Susan R. McCoy
Auditors: PricewaterhouseCoopers LLP

LOCATIONS

HQ: Leggett & Platt, Incorporated
No. 1 Leggett Rd., Carthage, MO 64836
Phone: 417-358-8131   **Fax:** 417-358-5840
Web: www.leggett.com

2008 Sales

	$ mil.	% of total
North America		
US	3,025.4	74
Canada	247.4	6
Mexico	75.7	2
Europe	409.0	10
China	267.2	7
Other regions	51.4	1
Total	**4,076.1**	**100**

PRODUCTS/OPERATIONS

2008 Sales

	$ mil.	% of total
Residential furnishings	2,102.3	52
Commercial fixturing & components	696.9	17
Industrial materials	658.2	16
Specialized products	618.7	15
Total	**4,076.1**	**100**

Selected Products

Residential Furnishings
  Finished products
    Adjustable electric beds
    Bed frames
    Bunk beds
    Carpet underlay
    Daybeds
    Fashion beds
    Headboards
    Non-slip products
  Innerspring and box spring units
  Springs and seating suspensions (chairs, sofas)
  Steel mechanisms and hardware (reclining chairs, sleeper sofas)

Commercial Furnishings
  Finished products
    Point-of-purchase displays
    Storage products
    Store counters, carts, fixtures, and shelving
Industrial Materials
  Drawn steel wire
  Steel tubing
Specialized Products
  Quilting machinery
  Seating suspension, lumbar support, and control cable systems (automobile industry)

Selected Trademarks

Gribetz and Porter (quilting and sewing machines)
Hanes (fiber materials)
Lifestyles, S-cape, and Adjustables by Leggett & Platt (adjustable electric beds)
Mira-Coil, Verticoil, Lura-Flex, and Superlastic (mattress innersprings)
No-Sag (wire forms used in seating)
Quietflex and Masterack (equipment and accessories for vans and trucks)
Schukra, Pullmaflex, and Flex-O-Lator (automotive seating products)
Semi-Flex and Semi-Fold (boxspring components and foundations)
Spuhl (mattress innerspring manufacturing machines)
Super Sagless (motion and sofa sleeper mechanisms)
Tack & Jump and Pattern Link (quilting machines)
Wall Hugger (reclining chairs)

COMPETITORS

Advance Auto Parts
Alcoa
AutoZone
Diam International
Flexsteel
FXI — Foamex Innovations
Genuine Parts
Holophane
Keystone Consolidated
Knape & Vogt
Louisville Bedding
Lozier
Wal-Mart

HISTORICAL FINANCIALS

Company Type: Public

Income Statement

FYE: December 31

	REVENUE ($ mil.)	NET INCOME ($ mil.)	NET PROFIT MARGIN	EMPLOYEES
12/08	4,076.1	104.4	2.6%	20,600
12/07	4,306.4	(11.2)	—	24,000
12/06	5,505.4	300.3	5.5%	32,828
12/05	5,299.3	251.3	4.7%	33,000
12/04	5,085.5	285.4	5.6%	33,000
Annual Growth	**(5.4%)**	**(22.2%)**	**—**	**(11.1%)**

2008 Year-End Financials

Debt ratio: 51.5%
Return on equity: 5.5%
Cash ($ mil.): 165
Current ratio: 2.49
Long-term debt ($ mil.): 851
No. of shares (mil.): 156
Dividends
  Yield: 6.6%
  Payout: 161.3%
Market value ($ mil.): 2,372

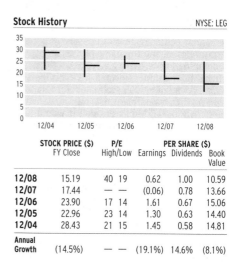

	STOCK PRICE ($) FY Close	P/E High/Low	PER SHARE ($) Earnings	Dividends	Book Value
12/08	15.19	40 19	0.62	1.00	10.59
12/07	17.44	— —	(0.06)	0.78	13.66
12/06	23.90	17 14	1.61	0.67	15.06
12/05	22.96	23 14	1.30	0.63	14.40
12/04	28.43	21 15	1.45	0.58	14.81
Annual Growth	**(14.5%)**	**— —**	**(19.1%)**	**14.6%**	**(8.1%)**

Lennar Corporation

Lennar is one of the largest homebuilding, land-owning, loan-making leviathans in the US, along with D.R. Horton and Pulte Homes. The company primarily builds single-family attached and detached homes in 16 states under brand names including Lennar, Cambridge, NuHome, and Greystone. Lennar targets first-time, move-up, and active adult buyers and markets its homes as "everything included." The company also provides financial services including mortgage financing, title, and closing services. In fiscal 2008 Lennar delivered some 16,000 homes at an average price of $270,000 — a steep drop from the 33,000 homes delivered the previous year. CEO Stuart Miller controls 47% of the company.

Along with the rest of the homebuilding industry, Lennar started to see trouble in 2006 as interest rates rose and years of overbuilding began taking their toll. Fallout from the subprime mortgage crisis and global credit crunch further slowed the market. Lennar's average price per home fell by $40,000 and the number of homes delivered fell by more than 26,000 (in 2008 as compared with fiscal 2005) .

In addition to lowering home prices, Lennar responded to the market downturn by buying fewer homesites. It also reduced its workforce by some 40% and tightened its lending standards to reduce its exposure to loan defaults.

In early 2007 Lennar and its spun-off LNR Properties reduced their stakes in LandSource, a joint venture that invests in raw land (among the riskiest of real estate investments, particularly vulnerable to market downturns). MW Housing Partners, an investment vehicle of the California Public Employees' Retirement System, bought 68% of LandSource for $900 million in cash and property; Lennar lowered its stake from 50% to 16%. The sale proved to be fortuitous for Lennar: Not only did it bring the company much-needed cash, but it also reduced Lennar's exposure to the debt-laden LandSource, which filed for Chapter 11 bankruptcy protection one year later.

In 2009, Lennar agreed to buy back a portion of the Newhall Ranch project from CalPERS by reacquiring LandSource.

HISTORY

Lennar is the creation of Leonard Miller and Arnold Rosen, and the name of the company is a combination of their given names. Rosen, a Miami homebuilder, formed F&R Builders in 1954. A year later Miller graduated from Harvard with no firm career plans. Having worked summers in Florida, Miller decided it would be a good place to make his fortune, and the 23-year-old began selling real estate there.

With $10,000 earned from commissions, Miller bought 42 lots and in 1956 entered a joint venture with Rosen to build homes on the lots. They worked well together, and Miller soon joined F&R. The operation grew, emphasizing marketing and concentrating on low- and medium-priced single-family homes for first-time buyers and retirees.

After expanding into commercial real estate in the late 1960s, the duo folded F&R into a new company — Lennar Corporation — in 1971 and went public. During the 1970s and 1980s, the company hawked Jacuzzi tubs and designer homes (such as the Calvin and the Liz) and promised customers "$10,000 worth of extras" free at Midnight Madness shopping mall sales. Lennar also began expanding, acquiring land and builders in the Phoenix area in 1973. Rosen retired in 1977.

Spurred by a recession, Lennar began to offer mortgage services nationwide in 1981, keeping the potentially lucrative servicing for itself and selling its mortgages to Fannie Mae, Ginnie Mae, and Freddie Mac, among others. In 1984 it dissolved its construction operations and began subbing out its work (a practice that it continues today). Lennar was relatively unscathed by the recession of the late 1980s, in part because Miller had foreseen a slump and had cut corporate debt and overhead. When other builders were overextending themselves by buying land in good times, Miller had used profit to pay down debt so he would have the resources to buy land cheap when bad times arrived.

During the 1990s Lennar targeted other Sun Belt markets and began buying portfolios of distressed property in partnership with heavy hitters like Morgan Stanley. Although Miller had looked at Texas as a development site since 1987, it was not until 1991 that Lennar entered the state, beginning in Dallas.

The company bought up the secured debt of Bramalea Homes in Southern California in 1995 and entered Northern California with its acquisition of Renaissance Homes. Lennar's acquisition of Village Homes and Exxon's Friendswood Development in 1996 made it Houston's top home builder.

In 1997 Stuart Miller became president and CEO (Leonard, his father, remained chairman). That year Lennar also spun off its commercial real estate operations as LNR Property.

The following year the company strengthened its position in the western US, acquiring three California homebuilders: Winncrest Homes (Sacramento), ColRich Communities (San Diego), and Polygon Communities (Southern California and Sacramento).

In 2000 Lennar bought fellow builder U.S. Home for about $1.1 billion in a deal that expanded its operations into 13 states. The company acquired the North and South Carolina operations of The Fortress Group in late 2001. It also added Maryland-based Patriot Homes and assets of California homebuilders Pacific Century Homes and Cambridge Homes in 2002 to bring its homebuilding operations to 16 states.

In July 2002 Leonard Miller died of liver cancer. Stuart Miller continued to lead the company as its president and CEO.

Lennar continued to acquire in 2003, adding Seppala Homes and Coleman Homes, expanding its positions, respectively, in South Carolina and the Central Valley of California.

In mid-2003 an entity jointly owned by Lennar and LNR Property Corporation (real estate investment, finance, and management) agreed to acquire The Newhall Land and Farming Company (California master-planned communities) for about $1 billion. In 2004 Lennar's Texas operations grew with its cash purchase of San Antonio-based Connell-Barron Homes.

Lennar continued to acquire regional builders, mortgage operations, and title and closing businesses. During 2005 Lennar entered the Boston, New York City, and Reno markets; it also expanded its Jacksonville operations by acquiring Admiral Homes. The condo and apartment buildings in New York and Boston were valued at more than $2 billion.

EXECUTIVES

President, CEO, and Director: Stuart A. Miller, age 51, $4,424,596 total compensation
VP and COO: Jonathan M. (Jon) Jaffe, age 49, $3,922,840 total compensation
VP and CFO: Bruce E. Gross, age 50, $3,446,520 total compensation
CIO: John R. Nygard III
Chief Investment Officer, Lennar Land and Homebuilding: Emile Haddad
EVP: Richard Beckwitt, age 49, $3,063,593 total compensation
EVP, Lennar Financial Services, LLC, and President, North American Title Group, Inc.: Linda L. Reed
VP Investor Relations: Marshall H. Ames, age 64
VP and Treasurer: Diane J. Bessette, age 48, $1,826,308 total compensation
VP Taxation: Michael Petrolino
Regional President, Lennar Land and Homebuilding: Jeff Roos
President, Lennar Communications Ventures: David J. Kaiserman
President, Universal American Mortgage Company: James T. Timmons
President, Eagle Home Mortgage, Inc.: Gary E. Carlson
President, East Operations: Laureen Ramsey
President, West Operations: Eric Sergi
Director Communications: Kay L. Howard
Secretary and General Counsel: Mark Sustana, age 47
Controller: David M. Collins, age 39
Director Culture: Andrea Berenfeld
Auditors: Deloitte & Touche LLP

LOCATIONS

HQ: Lennar Corporation
700 NW 107th Ave., Ste. 400, Miami, FL 33172
Phone: 305-559-4000   **Fax:** 305-229-6453
Web: www.lennar.com

2008 Homes Delivered

	Units (No.)	% of total
East (FL, MD, NJ & VA)	4,957	31
West (CA & NV)	4,031	26
Houston	2,736	17
Central (AZ, CO & other TX)	2,442	16
Other (IL, MN, NY, NC & SC)	1,569	10
Total	**15,735**	**100**

PRODUCTS/OPERATIONS

2008 Sales

	$ mil.	% of total
Homebuilding		
Home sales	4,150.7	91
Land sales	112.3	2
Financial services	312.4	7
Total	**4,575.4**	**100**

Selected Brands

Cambridge
Greystone
Lennar
NuHome
Patriot
U.S. Home
Village Builders

Selected Subsidiaries

Eagle Home Mortgage, LLC
Lennar Homes of California, Inc.
Universal American Mortgage Company, LLC

COMPETITORS

Beazer Homes
D.R. Horton
Hovnanian Enterprises
KB Home
M.D.C.
NVR
Pulte Homes
The Ryland Group
Standard Pacific
Toll Brothers
Weyerhaeuser Real Estate

HISTORICAL FINANCIALS

Company Type: Public

Income Statement

FYE: November 30

	REVENUE ($ mil.)	NET INCOME ($ mil.)	NET PROFIT MARGIN	EMPLOYEES
11/08	4,575.4	(1,109.1)	—	4,704
11/07	10,186.8	(1,941.1)	—	6,934
11/06	16,266.7	593.9	3.7%	12,605
11/05	13,867.0	1,355.2	9.8%	13,687
11/04	10,504.9	945.6	9.0%	11,796
Annual Growth	(18.8%)	—	—	(20.5%)

2008 Year-End Financials

Debt ratio: —
Return on equity: —
Cash ($ mil.): 1,091
Current ratio: 24.12
Long-term debt ($ mil.): —
No. of shares (mil.): 175
Dividends
  Yield: 7.3%
  Payout: —
Market value ($ mil.): 1,246

Stock History

NYSE: LEN

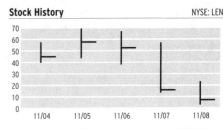

	STOCK PRICE ($) FY Close	P/E High/Low		PER SHARE ($) Earnings	Dividends	Book Value
11/08	7.11	—	—	(7.00)	0.52	14.97
11/07	15.84	—	—	(12.31)	0.64	21.81
11/06	52.50	18	10	3.69	0.64	32.53
11/05	57.68	8	5	8.23	0.57	29.97
11/04	44.93	10	7	5.70	0.51	23.13
Annual Growth	(36.9%)	—	—	—	0.5%	(10.3%)

Lennox International

Lennox International makes products so cool they're hot, and vice versa. The company makes heating, ventilation, air conditioning, and refrigeration products for residential and commercial uses. It sells furnaces, heat pumps, fireplaces, and air conditioners under such brands as Lennox, Armstrong Air, and Aire-Flo; chillers and condensing units are sold under the Bohn and Larkin names. Its products are sold to some 7,000 independent dealers in the US and Canada. The company also owns and operates 120 service and installation centers. Lennox has operations in Asia, Australia, Europe, and South America. Named after inventor Dave Lennox, the company in 1904 was sold to newspaper publisher D.W. Norris.

Lennox has felt the ripple effects of the residential market downturn, which has softened demand for home heating and cooling appliances. In response, the company has worked to improve efficiency at certain manufacturing facilities while divesting and consolidating others. The company transferred its Iowa-based air conditioning operations to a new manufacturing facility it opened in Mexico so that it may more effectively compete, particularly in the Sunbelt region. It also closed a commercial refrigeration manufacturing plant in Illinois, an HVAC plant in South Carolina, and a fireplace manufacturing plant in California, resulting in hundreds of employee layoffs.

HISTORY

Inventors Ernest Bryant and Ezra Smith developed and patented a riveted-steel sheet metal coal furnace in Marshalltown, Iowa, in the 1890s. The cast iron furnaces in use at the time tended to warp with usage; their sheet metal furnace did not. The inventors hired machine shop operator Dave Lennox to build the manufacturing equipment necessary to produce the new furnace. They were underfunded, however, and Lennox took over the patents in lieu of payment and redesigned the furnace. Lennox didn't warm to the furnace business and sold out to D. W. Norris, the local newspaper publisher, and three other people for $40,000 in 1904.

Norris, the company's first president, incorporated the business as Lennox Furnace Company and sold about 600 units the first year. Norris soon established the company's method of selling and delivering directly to authorized dealers. Lennox built a manufacturing plant in New York in 1925 and acquired Armstrong Furnace, a steel coal furnace plant in Ohio, in 1927. That year John Norris, D. W.'s son, joined the company after graduating from MIT. The younger Norris pushed for new innovations such as oil burners, gas furnaces, and blowers. He set up a research department in the 1930s and soon developed a line of gas- and oil-burning furnaces. The company opened another Ohio plant in 1940 and bought a machine shop there in 1942 to make bomb and aircraft parts for WWII. John Norris became president after the death of his father in 1949.

The company established Lennox Industries (Canada) Ltd. in 1952. Norris began developing an air conditioner the same year, after shopping the idea around to his dealers. Soon the company was turning out residential, commercial, and industrial air conditioners and compressors. In 1955 the company's name was changed to Lennox Industries Inc. to reflect its broader product range. The international division was created in 1962. Soon manufacturing facilities were established outside London and other offices were opened in the Netherlands and West Germany.

Lennox acquired Heatcraft, a maker of heating and cooling components, in 1973. Headquarters were moved to Dallas in 1978; in 1980 John Norris Jr. was named CEO. Lennox International Inc. (LII) was formed as the parent company for Heatcraft and Lennox Industries in 1986. The company reacquired Armstrong Air Conditioning (which it had owned in the 1920s and sold in the mid-1950s) in 1988.

LII underwent restructuring in 1989 and 1991, leading to the consolidation of production to four locations and the grouping of the sales, management, product ordering, and marketing teams at its headquarters in Dallas. In 1995 the company formed Lennox Global and rededicated itself to international expansion through joint ventures with foreign companies. LII formed HCF-Lennox, a joint venture with France's Brancher group, in 1996. The company agreed in 1998 to pay $6.2 million to settle an age bias lawsuit filed by 11 former employees. LII went public in 1999 and began buying HVAC dealers.

In 2000 the company more than doubled its number of owned retail outlets with the $300 million acquisition of Service Experts, an HVAC installation and sales business with 120 locations. However, the acquisition disappointed, and some of the locations were later closed.

COO Robert Schjerven succeeded John W. Norris Jr. as CEO in early 2001; Norris remained as chairman. Every operating segment but its commercial segment saw significant sales declines in 2001. The company restructured its service experts operations and some of its manufacturing and distribution operations that year. LII closed plants in Canada and Australia and closed retail centers to cut costs.

In 2002 LII continued restructuring its non-core heat transfer engineering business and made moves to focus on its core operations. That year it formed a joint venture with Outokumpu Oyj (Finland), selling 55% of its former heat transfer business segment in the US and Europe to Outokumpu. (In 2005 Outokumpu exercised its option to buy the remainder of the venture, however.) LII also sold its 50% interest in its underperforming commercial HVAC joint venture in Argentina. Sales overall continued to decline, although slight increases were made in the residential heating and cooling segment and in the refrigeration segment.

EXECUTIVES

Chairman: Richard L. (Rich) Thompson, age 69
CEO and Director: Todd M. Bluedorn, age 46,
  $4,097,772 total compensation
VP Operations: Michael Blatz
VP, Controller, Chief Accounting Officer, and Interim CFO: Roy A. Rumbough Jr., age 53
EVP and CTO: Prakash Bedapudi
EVP, Chief Legal Officer, and Secretary: John D. Torres, age 50
EVP and Chief Human Resources Officer:
  Daniel M. Sessa, age 44, $1,243,258 total compensation
EVP; President and COO, Service Experts:
  Scott J. Boxer, age 58, $2,470,511 total compensation
EVP; President and COO, Worldwide Refrigeration:
  David W. Moon, age 47
EVP; President and COO, LII Commercial Heating & Cooling: Harry J. Bizios, age 59
EVP; President and COO, LII Residential Heating & Cooling: Douglas L. (Doug) Young, age 46,
  $1,604,483 total compensation
VP and Treasurer: Richard A. (Rick) Pelini, age 50
VP Investor Relations: Steve L. Harrison
Managing Director, Australia and New Zealand, Lennox International Worldwide Refrigeration: Bill Moltner
Associate General Counsel: Kenneth C. Fernandez
Director Communications and Public Relations:
  Ozzie Buckler
Auditors: KPMG LLP

LOCATIONS

HQ: Lennox International Inc.
  2140 Lake Park Blvd., Richardson, TX 75080
Phone: 972-497-5000   **Fax:** 972-497-5292
Web: www.lennoxinternational.com

2008 Sales

	$ mil.	% of total
US	2,442.3	70
Canada	391.1	11
Other countries	648.0	19
Total	**3,481.4**	**100**

PRODUCTS/OPERATIONS

2008 Sales

	$ mil.	% of total
Residential heating & cooling	1,493.4	42
Commercial heating & cooling	835.3	23
Service experts	626.6	18
Refrigeration	618.2	17
Adjustments	(92.1)	—
Total	**3,481.4**	**100**

Selected Products and Brand Names

Heating and cooling
  Residential products
    Air conditioners
    Free-standing stoves
    Furnaces
    Heat pumps
    Indoor air quality equipment
    Packaged heating and cooling systems
    Prefabricated fireplaces
  Brand names
    Advanced Distributor Products (ADP)
    AireEase
    Aire-Flo
    Armstrong Air
    Concord
    Country Stoves
    Ducane
    Lennox
    Magic-Pak
    Security Chimneys
    Superior
    Whitfield
  Commercial products
    Unitary heating and air conditioning equipment and
      applied systems
  Brand names
    Allied Commercial
    Lennox

Service experts
  Installation
  Maintenance
  Repair

Refrigeration
  Products
    Air-cooled condensers
    Air handlers
    Chillers
    Condensing units
    Fluid coolers
    Unit coolers
  Brand names
    Bohn
    Chandler Refrigeration
    Climate Control
    Friga-Bohn
    Frigus-Bohn
    Heatcraft Worldwide Refrigeration
    HK Refrigeration
    Kirby
    Larkin
    Lovelocks

HISTORICAL FINANCIALS

Company Type: Public

Income Statement

FYE: December 31

	REVENUE ($ mil.)	NET INCOME ($ mil.)	NET PROFIT MARGIN	EMPLOYEES
12/08	3,481.4	122.8	3.5%	13,500
12/07	3,749.7	169.0	4.5%	15,000
12/06	3,671.1	166.0	4.5%	16,000
12/05	3,366.2	150.7	4.5%	16,000
12/04	2,982.7	(134.4)	—	15,000
Annual Growth	3.9%	—	—	(2.6%)

2008 Year-End Financials

Debt ratio: 90.2%
Return on equity: 19.4%
Cash ($ mil.): 122
Current ratio: 1.62
Long-term debt ($ mil.): 414

No. of shares (mil.): 56
Dividends
  Yield: 1.7%
  Payout: 26.5%
Market value ($ mil.): 1,802

Stock History

NYSE: LII

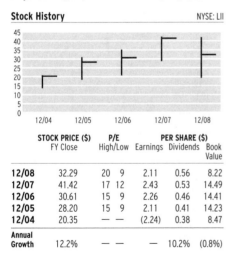

	STOCK PRICE ($) FY Close	P/E High/Low		PER SHARE ($) Earnings	Dividends	Book Value
12/08	32.29	20	9	2.11	0.56	8.22
12/07	41.42	17	12	2.43	0.53	14.49
12/06	30.61	15	9	2.26	0.46	14.41
12/05	28.20	15	9	2.11	0.41	14.23
12/04	20.35	—	—	(2.24)	0.38	8.47
Annual Growth	12.2%	—	—	—	10.2%	(0.8%)

Level 3 Communications

Level 3 Communications owns the communications networking market, or at least a piece of it. The company operates one of the world's largest Internet protocol (IP)-based fiber-optic networks. Its services include broadband and dial-up Internet access, wholesale voice origination and termination, enterprise voice, content distribution, broadband transport, and colocation. Its wholesale customers include ISPs, telecom carriers, cable TV operators, wireless service providers, and the federal government. It markets directly to businesses, state agencies, and schools. Its content delivery unit targets video distribution companies, Web portals, online gaming and software companies, and social networking sites.

Level 3's core network services accounted for more than 70% of its revenues in 2008. Its core network services include transport and infrastructure, IP and data services, local and enterprise voice services, and Level 3 Vyvx broadcast services. Its transport and infrastructure group encompasses point-to-point connections of fixed bandwidth, dark fiber leasing, colocation sites, and transatlantic cable transport. Its IP and data services include high-speed Internet access, dedicated Internet access, ATM and frame relay, VPN, and content delivery services. Vyvx provides transport services for audio and video programming. In 2008 Level 3 sold the advertising portion of it Vyvx content distribution unit to DG FastChannel for $129 million.

The company's wholesale business accounted for almost 20% of its revenues in 2008. Its wholesale services include domestic and international voice termination and toll free services.

Besides its communications network, Level 3 owns a coal-mining company, KCP, with a 50% stake in two mines in Montana and Wyoming.

HISTORY

Thoroughly modern Level 3 Communications was the brainchild of an Omaha, Nebraska, construction company that traces its roots to 1884 — the multinational Peter Kiewit Sons'. With cash to invest in the 1980s, Kiewit acquired Metropolitan Fiber Systems, which built fiber-optic networks for phone companies. In 1986 Kiewit executive James Crowe convinced CEO Walter Scott that Kiewit should build some phone circuits of its own, and by 1987 Kiewit had created MFS Communications, headed by Crowe, to build networks in business districts. Kiewit slated $500 million for the project in 1989.

By 1995 MFS had gone public and was the biggest of the competitive local-exchange carriers (CLECs). That year Crowe and Scott heard Bill Gates speak on the power of the Internet to destroy traditional phone traffic. MFS launched "Project Silver" to decide how to respond. The answer: buy UUNET. In 1996 MFS acquired the giant ISP and Internet backbone operator, and in the process made itself an acquisition target. WorldCom bought MFS for $14 billion by year's end.

Within a month Crowe walked away from WorldCom (with several MFS execs in tow) to head Kiewit Diversified Group, with holdings in telecommunications, technology, and energy.

In 1998 Kiewit split into the Peter Kiewit Sons' construction group, headed by Ken Stinson, and a diversified company called Level 3 Communications, headed by Crowe. Level 3 kept stakes in telecom companies RCN and C-TEC (now Commonwealth Telephone Enterprises). The Level 3 name came from the seven-layer Open Systems Interconnect (OSI) network model: the company saw its field of play in the bottom three levels — the physical plant, data link, and network layers.

Kiewit provided Crowe with a $2.5 billion grubstake; Level 3 went public and sold its oil interests and Michigan cable TV operation. It retained its coal-mining and toll-road interests to help fund the buildout of a new fiber-optic network to be based on Internet protocol (IP) technology instead of the old circuit-switching system.

Level 3 secured rights-of-way from Burlington Northern and Union Pacific. The company found a new angel in Craig McCaw, whose INTERNEXT agreed to plunge $700 million into the Level 3 network in return for capacity. By year's end the company had begun local networks in 25 US cities and had completed gateway sites in 17.

In 1999 Level 3 moved from Omaha to Broomfield, Colorado, deciding that it could grow faster in the Rockies. Level 3 hired Tyco International to develop an Atlantic undersea cable and agreed to participate in the building of the Japan-US Cable Network across the Pacific.

Fellow fiber baron Global Crossing agreed to buy a 50% interest in the transatlantic cable in 2000. In early 2001 the company announced the completion of its network construction and said it would expand its European network to eight additional markets despite cutting about 6% of its workforce.

For Level 3, as for many of its rivals, demand for bandwidth capacity and services failed to reach expected levels and the company in 2001 scaled back its revenue estimates and cut almost 25% of its workforce. It also sold its Asian operations, including its Tiger network and its capacity on a Japan-US submarine cable and backhaul network, to Reach, the wholesale carrier partnership of Telstra and PCCW.

In 2002 Level 3 acquired Massachusetts-based software distributor CorpSoft and Software Spectrum, a business software distributor based in Texas. The companies were combined and Level 3 soon derived much of its revenues from software distribution, which provided relief from the telecom sector's hard times.

In 2003 the company teamed up with PanAmSat, combining the two companies' network capabilities to form a hybrid fiber-optic and satellite delivery system for entertainment content and information to cable and TV broadcasters, ISPs, and others (PanAmSat was acquired in 2006 by Intelsat). In a separate deal, Level 3 agreed to provide Internet access through its satellite platform to the 500,000 Internet access customers of Hughes Electronics' DIRECTV unit. Vyvx was acquired in 2005 when Level 3 bought WilTel Communications Group from Leucadia National.

Level 3 made a number of acquistions in 2006, including Progress Telecom, TelCove, metro transport services provider Looking Glass Networks, and the rest of ICG Communications.

The company acquired Broadwing, a provider of voice and data communications services, for $254 million in early 2007. Level 3 also completed its purchase of SAVVIS's content delivery network (CDN) services business for approximately $132 million, and it bought online video management firm Servecast for $45 million.

Limited Brands

Limited Brands is as much of a shopping-mall mainstay as food courts and teenagers. The company operates about 3,000 stores throughout North America under the Victoria's Secret, Bath & Body Works (BBW), and La Senza (in Canada only) banners, as well as corresponding Web sites. Originally focused on apparel, Limited Brands sold its ailing Limited Stores and Express chains — leaving the company free to focus on two core brands: Victoria's Secret and BBW. Limited Brands also owns apparel importer MAST Industries, luxe department store operator Henri Bendel, and The White Barn Candle Co. The company is controlled by founder and chairman Leslie Wexner.

Wexner announced in mid-2006 that he wanted to see Victoria's Secret blossom into a $10 billion brand. Despite the lofty goal (Victoria's Secret generates a little more than $5.1 billion in sales), the company began to integrate its operations and pool top management. By 2009 Limited Brands had integrated its Intimate Brands subsidiary into its operations. Limited Brands grouped Victoria's Secret Stores, Victoria's Secret Beauty, Victoria's Secret Direct, and PINK under one entity (Victoria's Secret Megabrand and Intimate Apparel) led by president and CEO Sharen Jester Turney (recruited from Victoria's Secret Direct).

In response to the ailing economy, which caused its net sales to tumble about 11% in 2008, Limited Brands planned to lower capital spending by as much as 40% in 2009 and trimmed expansion plans. Still, the firm planned to open about 20 new BBW stores in Canada in 2009, after opening half a dozen stores there in 2008.

In 2007 Limited Brands completed its acquisition of lingerie maker and retailer La Senza, based in Montreal, for about $600 million. With more than 320 company-owned stores in Canada and independently owned La Senza stores in some 45 countries, La Senza is key to Wexner's goal to enhance its lingerie holdings internationally. The Canadian retailer operates under the banners La Senza, La Senza Express, La Senza Spirit, and La Senza Girl.

To speed product development in its beauty business, Limited Brands has formed Beauty Avenues, a personal care sourcing and production company. The in-house division is charged with creating personal care and beauty brands for BBW and Victoria's Secret Beauty, and La Senza.

Limited Brands is expanding Henri Bendel, which currently operates five specialty stores that feature fashion and accessories, and cosmetics. Henri Bendel opened a Bendel-branded accessories-only shop in Boca Raton, Florida, in fall 2008 and two similar stores in Florida and San Diego later in the year.

HISTORY

After a disagreement with his father in 1963 over the operation of the family store (Leslie's), Leslie Wexner, then 26, opened the first Limited store in Columbus, Ohio, with $5,000 borrowed from his aunt. The company was named from Wexner's desire to do one product line well — moderately priced fashionable attire for teenagers and young women.

When The Limited went public in 1969, it had only five stores, but the rapid development of large, covered malls spurred growth to 100 stores by 1976. Two years later The Limited acquired MAST Industries, an international apparel purchasing and importing company. The company opened Express in 1980 to serve the teen market.

The Limited grew with acquisitions, including the 1982 purchases of Lane Bryant (large sizes) and Victoria's Secret (lingerie). That year it formed the Brylane fashion catalog division and acquired Roaman's, a bricks-and-mortar and catalog merchandiser of plus sizes.

Wexner bought The Lerner Stores (budget women's apparel) and Henri Bendel (high fashion) in 1985, sportswear retailer Abercrombie & Fitch (A&F) in 1988, and London-based perfumer Penhaligon's in 1990 (sold in 1997). The Limited introduced several in-store shops, including Cacique (French lingerie) in 1988 and Limited Too (girls' fashions), which were later expanded into stand-alone stores. It also launched Structure (men's sportswear) in 1989 and Bath & Body Works shops in 1990. All of these stores were in malls, often strategically clustered together.

The company closed many The Limited and Lerner stores in 1993 and sold 60% of its Brylane catalog unit to Freeman Spogli (Brylane went public in 1997). It opened four Bath & Body Works stores in the UK (its first non-US stores) to compete with British rival The Body Shop.

The company began spinning off its businesses while keeping controlling stakes; it spun off Intimate Brands (Victoria's Secret, Cacique, and Bath & Body Works) in 1995 and A&F in 1996. (The Limited sold its remaining 84% in A&F in 1998.)

The Limited closed more than 100 of its women's apparel stores in 1997 and Intimate Brands shuttered the Cacique chain; the next year The Limited closed nearly 300 more companywide (excluding the Intimate Brands chains) and the majority of its Henri Bendel stores. In 1999 the company spun off Limited Too, its most successful chain, as Too, Inc.

In 2001 The Limited sold its Lane Bryant unit to Charming Shoppes for $335 million. The Limited bought back the remaining shares of Intimate Brands it did not already own in March 2002. In May 2002 the company changed its name to Limited Brands from The Limited. Later that year Limited Brands sold off its remaining stake in Lerner New York.

Limited Brands in 2004 sold 1.6 million shares of the plus-size United Retail Group Inc. and it acquired New York-based Slatkin & Co. (a prestige home fragrance company). Later that year Limited Brands laid off 25% of the headquarters workforce of its Express division — including managers and support personnel, but not store employees or warehouse workers — in the face of slipping earnings.

In January 2007 Limited Brands completed its acquisition of lingerie maker and retailer La Senza, based in Montreal, for about $600 million. La Senza is a specialty retailer offering lingerie and sleepwear for women age 18 to 35, as well as apparel for girls in the 7-14 age group. In July Limited Brands sold a 75% interest in its Express chain to affiliates of Golden Gate Capital for about $425 million. In a similar transaction completed in August, Limited Brands sold a 75% stake in its 251-store Limited Stores business to Sun Capital Partners.

Former vice chairman and COO Len Schlesinger retired in September 2007 after eight years with the firm. Wexner and administrative executive Martyn Redgrave took over Schlesinger's responsibilities.

In 2008 BBW opened its first stores in Canada.

EXECUTIVES

Chairman and CEO: Leslie H. Wexner, age 71, $7,534,428 total compensation
EVP and CFO: Stuart B. Burgdoerfer, age 46, $2,147,791 total compensation
EVP and Chief Administrative Officer:
Martyn R. Redgrave, age 56, $3,969,911 total compensation
EVP Business Integration: Peter Z. Horvath, age 51
EVP Human Resources: Jane L. Ramsey, age 51
EVP Retail Real Estate: Jamie Bersani
EVP International: Martin Waters
SVP Law, Policy and Governance, and Secretary: Samuel P. Fried
SVP and Counsel Company Affairs: Bruce A. Soll, age 51
SVP and General Merchandise Manager Fashion, Henri Bendel: Scott Schramm
SVP and General Counsel: Douglas L. Williams
VP Treasury, Mergers and Acquisitions: Timothy J. Faber
VP External Communication: Tammy Roberts Myers
VP Marketing and Media: Pattie Glod
VP Investor Relations: Amie Preston
CEO, Bath & Body Works: Diane L. Neal, age 52, $2,500,126 total compensation
President and CEO, Victoria's Secret Group:
Sharen J. Turney, age 52, $8,818,050 total compensation
Director Community Relations: Janelle N. Simmons
Auditors: Ernst & Young LLP

LOCATIONS

HQ: Limited Brands, Inc.
3 Limited Pkwy., Columbus, OH 43216
Phone: 614-415-7000   **Fax:** 614-415-7440
Web: www.limitedbrands.com

PRODUCTS/OPERATIONS

2009 Stores

	No.
Victoria's Secret	
Victoria's Secret Stores	1,043
La Senza	322
Bath & Body Works US	1,638
Bath & Body Works Canada	6
Henri Bendel	5
Total	**3,014**

2009 Sales

	$ mil.	% of total
Victoria's Secret Stores	3,590	40
Victoria's Secret Direct	1,523	17
La Senza	491	5
Bath & Body Works	2,374	26
Other (includes Henri Bendel, Mast & BBW Canada)	1,065	12
Total	**9,043.0**	**100**

Selected Retail Brands

Bath & Body Works
C.O. Bigelow
Henri Bendel
La Senza
Pink
The White Barn Candle Company
Victoria's Secret

COMPETITORS

Abercrombie & Fitch
American Eagle Outfitters
Avon
Bergdorf Goodman
Body Shop
CVS Caremark
Dillard's
Estée Lauder
Frederick's of Hollywood
Fruit of the Loom
The Gap
Hanesbrands
J. C. Penney
Jockey International
Kiehl's
Macy's
Mary Kay
Nordstrom
Revlon
Saks
Sephora USA
Shiseido Cosmetics
Target
Ulta
VF
Wal-Mart
Warnaco Group

HISTORICAL FINANCIALS

Company Type: Public

Income Statement — FYE: Saturday nearest January 31

	REVENUE ($ mil.)	NET INCOME ($ mil.)	NET PROFIT MARGIN	EMPLOYEES
1/09	9,043.0	220.0	2.4%	90,900
1/08	10,134.0	718.0	7.1%	97,500
1/07	10,671.0	675.0	6.3%	125,500
1/06	9,699.0	666.0	6.9%	110,000
1/05	9,408.0	705.0	7.5%	115,300
Annual Growth	(1.0%)	(25.3%)	—	(5.8%)

2009 Year-End Financials

Debt ratio: 154.6%
Return on equity: 10.8%
Cash ($ mil.): 1,173
Current ratio: 2.28
Long-term debt ($ mil.): 2,897
No. of shares (mil.): 322
Dividends
Yield: 7.6%
Payout: 92.3%
Market value ($ mil.): 2,547

Stock History — NYSE: LTD

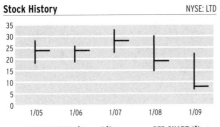

	STOCK PRICE ($) FY Close	P/E High/Low		PER SHARE ($) Earnings	Dividends	Book Value
1/09	7.92	34	11	0.65	0.60	5.83
1/08	19.07	16	8	1.89	0.60	6.90
1/07	27.94	19	14	1.68	0.60	9.19
1/06	23.66	15	11	1.66	0.60	7.68
1/05	23.70	19	12	1.47	0.48	7.26
Annual Growth	(24.0%)	—	—	(18.5%)	5.7%	(5.3%)

Lincare Holdings

Lincare Holdings doesn't take breathing for granted. With more than 1,000 offices across the US, the company helps some 700,000 patients with chronic obstructive pulmonary diseases (including emphysema and severe asthma) by providing oxygen therapy services. Through its local service centers, Lincare delivers oxygen equipment to patients in their homes, and it trains them and monitors their use of the equipment. The company offers positive airway pressure machines for patients with sleep apnea and supplies other home medical equipment. In some markets the company also provides home infusion services, such as chemotherapy, pain management, parenteral nutrition, and other procedures.

Lincare's oxygen and respiratory therapy services account for more than 90% of sales; the company derives about half of its sales from Medicare and Medicaid reimbursements. A series of changes to Medicare rules from 2005 to 2007 have lowered reimbursement rates for many of the company's services, including some inhalation drug therapies and oxygen equipment.

Despite those changes, the company has so far managed to expand its customer base and geographic reach through acquisitions and internal growth. Lincare prefers to acquire smaller regional home respiratory service providers to enter into new markets and increase its market share in existing geographic markets.

HISTORY

Linde Homecare Medical Systems was formed in 1972 as part of Union Carbide's industrial gases division (now Praxair). Under threat of a hostile takeover bid, Union Carbide in 1987 decided to raise cash by spinning off Linde Homecare's operations as Lincare Inc. In 1990 investors helped the spinoff's management buy out the company, renamed Lincare Holdings.

The company went public that year. Flush with cash from the IPO, Lincare Holdings went on an acquisition spree, spreading by targeting existing companies in new markets. It also benefited from new regulations; in 1993 the government set up an expensive and complicated claims process that forced out smaller competitors. In 1994 the company bought Wyoming-based Home Oxygen Plus Equipment and Colorado-based Meridian Medical. A merger attempt the following year between Lincare Holdings and competitor Coram Healthcare failed.

The buying frenzy, however, continued in 1996, when the company inhaled 17 competitors, and again in 1997, when it acquired 24 more. In 1998 Lincare Holdings received government warnings about inadequate testing of liquid medical oxygen at several manufacturing plants. Expansion continued in 1999 and 2000, with purchases of home nursing services firm Healthcor Holdings and of home respiratory provider United Medical. In 2001 Lincare acquired 18 competitors. The company's legal woes also continued: The federal Department of Health and Human Services subpoenaed Medicare billing records for certain local operations in 1999 and a federal grand jury launched an investigation in 2000. One part of the investigations focused on possible inappropriate gifts given to doctors, while other parts focused on whether Lincare sought inappropriate reimbursement from Medicare.

Lincare settled the investigations in 2006 with a $12 million payment to the government and signed a corporate integrity agreement with the Office of Inspector General.

EXECUTIVES

Chairman and CEO: John P. Byrnes, age 50, $6,548,749 total compensation
President and COO: Shawn S. Schabel, age 44, $4,656,605 total compensation
CFO and Secretary: Paul G. Gabos, age 43, $3,271,107 total compensation
Human Resources Manager: Shelia Dilley
Marketing and Development: Mickey McKenzie
Auditors: KPMG LLP

LOCATIONS

HQ: Lincare Holdings Inc.
19387 US 19 North, Clearwater, FL 33764
Phone: 727-530-7700 **Fax:** 727-532-9692
Web: www.lincare.com

PRODUCTS/OPERATIONS

2008 Sales

	$ mil.	% of total
Oxygen & other respiratory therapy	1,526.8	92
Home medical equipment & other	137.8	8
Total	**1,664.6**	**100**

2008 Sales by Payer

	% of total
Medicare & Medicaid programs	52
Private insurance	39
Direct payment	9
Total	**100**

Selected Subsidiaries

Alpha Respiratory Inc.
Caring Responders LLC
ConvaCare Services Inc.
Health Care Solutions at Home Inc.
Home-Care Equipment Network Inc.
Healthlink Medical Equipment LLC
Med4Home Inc.
PulmoRehab LLC

COMPETITORS

Accredo Health
Amedisys
American HomePatient
Apria Healthcare
BioScrip
Critical Homecare Solutions
Gentiva
Option Care
Rotech Healthcare
Trinity HomeCare

HISTORICAL FINANCIALS

Company Type: Public

Income Statement — FYE: December 31

	REVENUE ($ mil.)	NET INCOME ($ mil.)	NET PROFIT MARGIN	EMPLOYEES
12/08	1,664.6	237.2	14.2%	9,957
12/07	1,596.0	226.1	14.2%	9,450
12/06	1,409.8	213.0	15.1%	9,070
12/05	1,266.6	213.7	16.9%	8,258
12/04	1,268.5	273.4	21.6%	7,857
Annual Growth	7.0%	(3.5%)	—	6.1%

2008 Year-End Financials

Debt ratio: 56.7%
Return on equity: 27.9%
Cash ($ mil.): 73
Current ratio: 1.71
Long-term debt ($ mil.): 550

No. of shares (mil.): 68
Dividends
Yield: 0.0%
Payout: —
Market value ($ mil.): 1,827

Stock History

NASDAQ (GS): LNCR

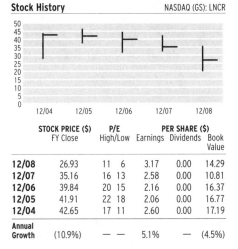

	STOCK PRICE ($) FY Close	P/E High/Low		PER SHARE ($) Earnings	Dividends	Book Value
12/08	26.93	11	6	3.17	0.00	14.29
12/07	35.16	16	13	2.58	0.00	10.81
12/06	39.84	20	15	2.16	0.00	16.37
12/05	41.91	22	18	2.06	0.00	16.77
12/04	42.65	17	11	2.60	0.00	17.19
Annual Growth	(10.9%)	—	—	5.1%	—	(4.5%)

Lincoln Electric Holdings

With this thing, I thee weld. Lincoln Electric is a global manufacturer of welding and cutting products, including arc welding power sources, consumable electrodes, fluxes, fume extraction equipment, robotic welding systems, and wire feeders. Other welding products include regulators and torches. In North America, which geographically accounts for more than half of its sales, products are sold primarily through a network of industrial distributors. Outside of North America, the company has manufacturing facilities and an international sales organization that serve customers in Asia/Pacific, Europe, and South America.

Major end users of its welding and cutting products include metal fabricators, offshore oil and gas explorers, power generation facilities, shipbuilding and automotive industries, and structural steel construction companies.

Lincoln Electric is growing both in terms of products and geography through acquisition. Several deals in South America and China expanded its product base and local manufacturing capabilities, and thereby enabled it to reach customers directly in those regions. Its Asian subsidiary, The Lincoln Electric Company (Asia Pacific) Pte., Ltd., improved its welding consumables business in China by inking a deal in early 2009 with Jinzhou Jin Tai Welding and Metal Co., a welding wire business, to make Jin Tai a wholly owned subsidiary of Lincoln Electric. Aiming to advance into key energy and infrastructure markets, Lincoln Electric acquired pipe-cutting equipment maker Vernon Tool Company in late 2007.

However, the severity of global economic conditions forced the company to initiate a series of cost-cutting moves in 2008, including a reduction

in its worldwide workforce of more than 10%, salary cuts for executives, and a hiring freeze.

Former director David C. Lincoln owns about 5% of Lincoln Electric.

HISTORY

John Lincoln founded The Lincoln Electric Company in 1895 to make and repair electric motors. By the time his younger brother James joined Lincoln as a salesman in 1907, John had expanded into rechargeable batteries and had also begun researching arc welding. John dedicated himself to research and left James to handle management.

In the workplace, James formed an advisory board made up of elected employee representatives from each department. Its twice-monthly meetings became a cornerstone of the company's Incentive Management System, which Lincoln based on six tenets: people as assets, Christian ethics, principles, simplicity, competition, and customer satisfaction. As part of the system, piecework pay and group life insurance (unusual at the time) were begun in 1915. Meanwhile, John perfected the electric arc welding machine that soon became the company's chief product, and in 1917 he formed The Lincoln Electric Welding School.

In 1934 workers offered to work longer hours during the Depression in exchange for a share of the company's profits; that year bonuses averaged 30% of pay. By the 1940s Lincoln was the world's #1 maker of arc-welding equipment, with subsidiaries in Australia, Canada, and the UK and licensees in Argentina, Brazil, Canada, and Mexico. Lincoln added a pension plan and an internal promotion program during WWII as ship manufacturing fueled demand for its products.

William Irrgang, a German engineer with 26 years at the company, succeeded James Lincoln as president in 1954 (James became chairman). Under Irrgang and Lincoln the company practiced conservative policies: It prohibited capital spending projects with paybacks lasting more than one year. Irrgang became chairman in 1965 and was named CEO (a new title) in 1972, the same year George Willis, a Harvard MBA and devotee of the Incentive Management System, became president. Willis was constrained by Irrgang's conservatism and the economic woes of the early 1980s. Sales dropped and though Lincoln's policy of not laying off workers was strained, workers shifted jobs into maintenance or sales work.

Irrgang died in 1986, leaving Willis in control. Willis quickly expanded product lines and geographic coverage. Soon the company's offerings included robotic and gas-based welding products. When he retired the next year, Willis left a legacy of expansion and debt. Though sales had doubled and the company's international presence had grown to 15 countries, debt had risen from about $18 million in 1988 to $222 million in 1993. Lincoln also had trouble exporting its incentive system to other countries. It returned to profitability in 1994, cutting jobs and closing factories in Europe and Latin America and adding jobs in the US.

Anthony Massaro became CEO in 1996. He looked overseas for opportunities, including deals in China, Indonesia, and Italy. In 1997 Lincoln consolidated production at its European plants and agreed to settle some of the lawsuits alleging that a type of its welding wire contributed to building damage in California's 1994 Northridge earthquake.

In 1998 the company acquired Indalco, a Canada-based maker of aluminum welding wire, and Germany-based Uhrhan & Schwill, which made pipe-welding systems. It also obtained a 50% stake in Turkish welding company AS Kaynak and opened a distribution center near Johannesburg, South Africa.

In 2000 Lincoln bought a 35% stake in Kuang Tai Metal Industrial, a Taiwan-based company that made mild and stainless-steel welding wires. It then went after UK-based welding-equipment maker Charter plc, but was unable to complete the transaction after the US Federal Trade Commission ruled it would require Lincoln to divest certain operations if it acquired Charter. In 2001 the company opened a new research facility in Cleveland; the next year it acquired 85% of Polish welding equipment maker Bester S.A.

In 2004 John Stropki replaced Anthony Massaro as president and CEO of Lincoln Electric. Stropki also became chairman when Massaro retired near the end of 2004.

In 2005 Lincoln Electric purchased brazing and soldering alloys manufacturer J.W. Harris Co. J.W. Harris was merged with Harris Calorific to form The Harris Products Group.

In 2006 the company purchased Metrode Products, a UK-based firm that made specialty consumables for the process and power generation industries.

EXECUTIVES

Chairman, President, and CEO: John M. Stropki Jr., age 58, $4,618,628 total compensation
SVP, CFO, and Treasurer: Vincent K. Petrella, age 48, $1,465,525 total compensation
SVP; President North America: George D. Blankenship, age 46
SVP Global Marketing and Automation: Richard J. Seif
SVP, General Counsel, and Secretary: Frederick G. Stueber, age 55, $1,784,862 total compensation
SVP; President International: David M. LeBlanc, age 44, $1,022,333 total compensation
SVP Human Resources and Compliance: Gretchen A. Farrell, age 46
VP Machine Division: Ronald A. Nelson
VP; President, Lincoln Electric Canada: Joseph G. Doria
VP; Group President, Brazing, Cutting, and Retail Subsidiaries: David J. (Dave) Nangle
VP Sales, North America: Michael S. Mintun
VP Mergers, Acquisitions, and Investor Relations: Earl L. Ward, age 56
VP; President, Lincoln Electric Asia Pacific: Thomas A. (Tom) Flohn, age 48, $1,270,260 total compensation
VP and Controller: Gabriel Bruno
VP Corporate Tax: Michele R. Kuhrt
VP Global Operations Development: Vinod K. Kapoor
VP Strategy and Business Development: Steven B. Hedlund
General Manager, Automation Division: Christopher A. Bailey
Auditors: Ernst & Young LLP

LOCATIONS

HQ: Lincoln Electric Holdings, Inc.
22801 St. Clair Ave., Cleveland, OH 44117
Phone: 216-481-8100   **Fax:** 216-486-1751
Web: www.lincolnelectric.com

Lincoln Electric Holdings has manufacturing facilities in Australia, Brazil, Canada, China, Colombia, France, Germany, India, Indonesia, Italy, Mexico, the Netherlands, Poland, Portugal, Spain, Taiwan, Turkey, the UK, the US, Venezuela, and Vietnam.

2008 Sales

	$ mil.	% of total
North America	1,566.0	59
Europe	602.6	23
Other regions	461.4	18
Adjustments	(150.9)	—
Total	**2,479.1**	**100**

PRODUCTS/OPERATIONS

Selected Products

Advanced process welders
Commercial and industrial engine drives
Computer-controlled pipe cutting equipment
Fluxes
Fume extractors
Industrial welders
MIG wires
Multi-process welders
Pipe welding consumables
Plasma cutting equipment
Power sources
Robotic welders
Stainless, nickel, and high alloy consumables
Stick electrodes
Submerged arc and automatic equipment
TIG welders
Welding guns and torches
Wire feeders

COMPETITORS

Airgas
Charter International
ESAB
FANUC
Flow International
Illinois Tool Works
Indel
Kobe Steel
KUKA
Schumacher Electric
Shinsho
Thermadyne
Uniweld Products

HISTORICAL FINANCIALS

Company Type: Public

Income Statement

FYE: December 31

	REVENUE ($ mil.)	NET INCOME ($ mil.)	NET PROFIT MARGIN	EMPLOYEES
12/08	2,479.1	212.3	8.6%	9,329
12/07	2,280.8	202.7	8.9%	8,992
12/06	1,971.9	175.0	8.9%	8,430
12/05	1,601.2	122.3	7.6%	7,485
12/04	1,333.7	80.6	6.0%	6,835
Annual Growth	**16.8%**	**27.4%**	**—**	**8.1%**

2008 Year-End Financials

Debt ratio: 9.2%
Return on equity: 20.4%
Cash ($ mil.): 284
Current ratio: 2.87
Long-term debt ($ mil.): 92
No. of shares (mil.): 43
Dividends
  Yield: 2.0%
  Payout: 20.7%
Market value ($ mil.): 2,166

Stock History

NASDAQ (GS): LECO

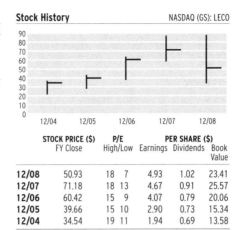

	STOCK PRICE ($) FY Close	P/E High/Low		PER SHARE ($) Earnings	Dividends	Book Value
12/08	50.93	18	7	4.93	1.02	23.41
12/07	71.18	18	13	4.67	0.91	25.57
12/06	60.42	15	9	4.07	0.79	20.06
12/05	39.66	15	10	2.90	0.73	15.34
12/04	34.54	19	11	1.94	0.69	13.58
Annual Growth	**10.2%**	**—**	**—**	**26.3%**	**10.3%**	**14.6%**

Lincoln National

Who better to trust with your nest egg than the company that took its name from Honest Abe? Lincoln National, which operates as Lincoln Financial Group, provides retirement planning and life insurance to individuals and employers in the form of annuities, 401K savings plans, and a variety of life, dental, and disability insurance products. It does business through such subsidiaries as Lincoln National Life Insurance and Lincoln Life & Annuity Company of New York. The company is also active in the investment management business, offering individual and institutional clients such financial services as pension plans, trusts, and mutual funds through its subsidiaries.

Lincoln National sells products through its own system of financial advisors, as well as through a variety of third parties (brokerages, independent financial advisors, and institutions). It also provided retirement products and financial services in the UK through subsidiary Lincoln National (UK), but the company sold that subsidiary in 2009 in order to focus on its US-based businesses. Canada-based Sun Life Financial bought the UK arm for C$359 million (US$317 million).

The company also agreed to sell its asset management subsidiary, Delaware Management Holdings, later in 2009 to Australian financial services firm Macquarie Group for nearly $430 million. Lincoln National is divesting the investment business to focus on its insurance and retirement operations. Delaware Management will continue to manage some of Lincoln National's insurance assets following the sale.

As the economic waters turned murky and cold, in 2008 Lincoln Financial sought relief under the US Treasury's TARP program. As the TARP was originally structured to assist banks, Lincoln's earliest efforts were focused on making itself more eligible by acquiring regional banking company Newton Country Loan & Savings of Goodland, Indiana. The Office of Thrift Supervision now recognizes the company as a savings and loan holding company. However, while Lincoln Financial was still waiting for approval to participate in the Capital Purchase

Programs as a bank, in 2009 the feds instead decided to extend its funds to major life insurers, including Lincoln Financial. The company received approval for $2.5 billion in Treasury funds to shore up its capital.

Its subsidiary Lincoln Financial Media owns and operates some 15 radio stations — a legacy from its 2006 acquisition of Jefferson-Pilot. However it is exiting the media business gradually. In early 2008 the company sold off three television stations and a sports syndication business to Raycom Media for $548 million, and it sold three radio stations to Greater Media for a total of $100 million.

HISTORY

Wilbur Wynant, a sort of Johnny Appleseed of shady fraternal benefits societies, arrived in Fort Wayne, Indiana, in 1902. He persuaded several respected businessmen and professionals to help him found the Fraternal Assurance Society of America, an assessable mutual organization in which surviving members contributed to the death benefits of deceased members. Wynant absconded within a couple of years, and the local organizers restructured the society's remains as a stock company in 1905. To clean up the organization's reputation, they obtained permission from Abraham Lincoln's son Robert to use his father's name and image.

In 1905, when the company wrote its first policy, it had three agents, including its leading executive, Arthur Hall. By 1911 the company had 106 agents. Careful risk assessment was an early hallmark of the company and allowed it to accept business that other companies rejected based on more superficial analysis.

From a very early period, the company grew through acquisitions. WWI increased claims, but not as much as the global flu epidemic that followed the war. Organic growth continued in the 1920s.

Death and disability claims increased abnormally during the Depression, and the company's underwriting became more stringent. Lincoln National used the financial turmoil of the period to buy other troubled insurers. Reinsurance became the firm's primary line until after WWII.

The company bought up other firms in the 1950s and 1960s, and in 1968 it formed holding company Lincoln National. Soon it began diversifying, buying Chicago Title and Trust (1969; sold 1985) as well as more life and reinsurance companies. Lincoln National also went into the health benefits business, setting up its own HMO and investing in EMPHESYS (which it took public in 1994, divesting the remainder of its stock in 1995).

The collapse of the real estate market in many areas nicked results in the late 1980s, and in 1990 the company accepted an infusion of cash from Dai-Ichi Mutual Life Insurance. Property/casualty results were hurt in the early 1990s by an unprecedented string of natural disasters.

With the growth of retirement savings from baby boomers hitting their 50s, the company shifted gears into wealth management. In 1995 Lincoln National expanded its investment management capacities by purchasing Delaware Management Holdings and Laurentian Financial Group. In 1997 it bought Voyageur Fund Managers, a tax-free-bond fund business. It sold its 83% interest in property/casualty firm American States Financial in 1996.

Lincoln National bought CIGNA's annuity and individual life insurance business and Aetna's

US individual life insurance operations in 1998. It reorganized that year to help it absorb these businesses, causing earnings to take a substantial hit.

In 1999, after nearly a century in the heartland, Lincoln National moved its headquarters to Philadelphia. Other transformations included the sale of its individual disability income business in 1999. In 2001 it sold its reinsurance operations to Swiss Re to re-focus on wealth and asset accumulation products and services. The reshaping continued in 2002 when the company acquired employee benefits record-keeping firm The Administrative Management Group.

Lincoln National completed a merger/acquisition of Jefferson-Pilot in early 2006. The $7.5 billion deal combined the Lincoln Financial Group with the Jefferson Pilot Financial group (the operating brand for Jefferson-Pilot Corporation) and created a new company, operating as Lincoln Financial Group. Led by management from both former organizations, the new group expanded insurance and financial products offerings and national retail and wholesale distribution platforms.

EXECUTIVES

Chairman: J. Patrick Barrett, age 72
President, CEO, and Director: Dennis R. Glass, age 59, $7,325,265 total compensation
COO: Thomas P. O'Neill
EVP and CFO: Frederick J. (Fred) Crawford, age 45, $1,723,701 total compensation
EVP and Chief Administrative Officer: Charles C. (Chuck) Cornelio, age 49
SVP and Chief Marketing Officer: Heather C. Dzielak, age 40
SVP and Chief Human Resources Officer: Lisa Bettinger-Buckingham, age 43
SVP, Sales and Marketing, Lincoln Employer Markets: Len Cavallaro
SVP and General Counsel: Dennis L. Schoff, age 49
SVP, Strategic Investment Relationships and Initiatives, Delaware Investments: David P. O'Connor
SVP, Distribution for Retirement, Executive Benefits and Group Protection, Lincoln Employer Markets: Don Roberson
VP and Treasurer: Duane L. Bernt
VP, Corporate Development: Lisa Marie DeSimone
President, Retirement and Insurance Solutions: Mark E. Konen, age 49, $1,590,707 total compensation
President and Managing Director, Lincoln National (UK): Michael Tallett-Williams, age 55
President and CEO, Lincoln Financial Advisors: Robert W. (Bob) Dineen, age 59, $2,248,881 total compensation
President, Lincoln National Investment Company, Inc. and Delaware Management Holdings, Inc: Patrick P. (Pat) Coyne, age 45, $3,295,639 total compensation
President and CEO, Lincoln Financial Distributors: Wilford H. Fuller, age 38
Secretary: C. Suzanne Womack
Chief Risk Officer and Treasurer: Randy Freitag
Auditors: Ernst & Young LLP

LOCATIONS

HQ: Lincoln National Corporation
 150 N. Radnor Chester Rd., Radnor, PA 19807
Phone: 484-583-1400   **Fax:** 484-583-1421
Web: www.lfg.com

PRODUCTS/OPERATIONS

2008 Revenues

	$ mil.	% of total
Insurance		
Life insurance	4,250	40
Group protection	1,640	15
Retirement		
Annuities	2,610	25
Defined contribution	936	9
Investment management	438	4
Lincoln UK	327	3
Other operations	442	4
Realized loss	(760)	—
Total	**9,883**	**100**

2008 Sales

	$ mil.	% of total
Net investment income	4,208	40
Insurance fees	3,229	31
Insurance premiums	2,096	20
Investment advisory fees	268	3
Realized loss	(537)	—
Amortization of deferred gain on indemnity reinsurance	76	1
Other revenues & fees	543	5
Total	**9,883**	**100**

COMPETITORS

AEGON
AIG
AXA
Guardian Life
The Hartford
Hartford Life
ING
John Hancock Financial Services
MassMutual
MetLife
Nationwide Financial
New York Life
Northwestern Mutual
Pacific Mutual
Principal Financial
Prudential
Prudential plc
TIAA-CREF
Torchmark
Unum Group

HISTORICAL FINANCIALS

Company Type: Public

Income Statement

FYE: December 31

	ASSETS ($ mil.)	NET INCOME ($ mil.)	INCOME AS % OF ASSETS	EMPLOYEES
12/08	163,136.0	57.0	0.0%	9,696
12/07	191,435.0	1,215.0	0.6%	10,870
12/06	178,494.0	1,316.0	0.7%	10,744
12/05	124,787.6	831.1	0.7%	5,259
12/04	116,219.3	731.5	0.6%	5,441
Annual Growth	**8.8%**	**(47.2%)**	**—**	**15.5%**

2008 Year-End Financials

Equity as % of assets: 4.9%
Return on assets: 0.0%
Return on equity: 0.6%
Long-term debt ($ mil.): 4,731
No. of shares (mil.): 302
Dividends
 Yield: 9.9%
 Payout: 850.0%
Market value ($ mil.): 5,691
Sales ($ mil.): 9,883

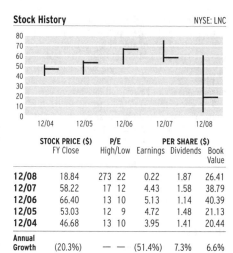

Stock History
NYSE: LNC

	STOCK PRICE ($) FY Close	P/E High/Low		PER SHARE ($) Earnings	Dividends	Book Value
12/08	18.84	273	22	0.22	1.87	26.41
12/07	58.22	17	12	4.43	1.58	38.79
12/06	66.40	13	10	5.13	1.14	40.39
12/05	53.03	12	9	4.72	1.48	21.13
12/04	46.68	13	10	3.95	1.41	20.44
Annual Growth	**(20.3%)**	**—**	**—**	**(51.4%)**	**7.3%**	**6.6%**

Live Nation

Live Nation holds center stage as the world's largest producer and promoter of live entertainment. The firm owns or operates some 150 venues in North America and Europe. Annually, more than 57 million people attend some 22,000 Live Nation events. Live Nation also owns House of Blues venues through HOB Entertainment. Through a deal with pop star Madonna, Live Nation owns a stake in the Material Girl's music, including albums, tours, and merchandise. It has similar deals with other artists, and has expanded into ticketing services. Once a part of radio giant Clear Channel, in 2005 Live Nation was spun off. The company in 2009 announced plans to acquire Ticketmaster, creating a powerful live-music conglomerate.

The all-stock merger between Live Nation and Ticketmaster, said to be worth some $2.5 billion, will create a giant in the music industry that will control concert promotion, ticketing services, and artist-management, all under one roof. The new company is to be called Live Nation Entertainment; the deal awaits approval by the Justice Department's antitrust division in order to clear.

Live Nation stunned the music business with its success in luring away Madonna from her deal with traditional record label Warner Bros. Records in 2007. The 10-year pact gave Madonna a mix of cash and stock worth some $120 million in exchange for the rights to sell three studio albums, promote concert tours, sell merchandise, and license her name. The Madonna deal was the first in a series of moves by Live Nation to expand beyond staging live events as it diversifies into other areas of the music business. Part of this strategy included the $79 million purchase of concert T-shirt seller Signatures Network, as well as the acquisitions of UltraStar Entertainment and MusicToday, which run fan-club and e-commerce Web sites for musicians.

Live Nation in 2008 signed deals with Irish rock band U2 and hip-hop star Jay-Z, similar to its deal with Madonna, giving the promoter exclusive rights to produce the artists' concerts, manufacture and sell their merchandise, license their images, and run their Web sites and online fan clubs. Such activities operate under the company's newly formed Artist Nation business. Spearheaded by former chairman and Live Nation Artists chief Michael Cohl, the deals led to an internal power struggle with CEO Michael Rapino, who wanted to slow the pace of such agreements. Cohl resigned later that year.

The company continues to divest itself of its noncore assets. In 2008 the small portion of Live Nation's operations that was devoted to specialized motor sports (such as monster truck shows and motorcycle racing) and sports representation was sold to Feld Entertainment for some $175 million. The firm also that year sold its North American theatrical business, which produced touring Broadway shows.

HISTORY

Robert Sillerman began his career teaching advertisers how to reach young consumers. He started investing in radio and TV stations and founded SFX Broadcasting (named for a scrambling of his initials) in 1992. In early 1997 the firm entered the live entertainment field with the formation of SFX Concerts and the purchase of concert promoter Delsener/Slater.

When SFX Broadcasting agreed to be bought in 1997 by Capstar Broadcasting, 87% controlled by investment firm Hicks, Muse, Tate & Furst (now HM Capital), SFX Entertainment was formed to house the live entertainment operations (it was spun off in 1998). In 1998 the company continued its rapid acquisition rate with the purchases of sports marketing and management team FAME, New England concert promoter Don Law, and national concert producer PACE Entertainment.

In 1999 the company bought concert promoter The Cellar Door Companies (which almost doubled SFX's size), sports marketing firm Integrated Sports International, sporting event management company The Marquee Group, sports talent agency Hendricks Management, 50% of urban-music producer A.H. Enterprises, and troubled theatrical producer Livent. SFX also made its first foray abroad through its purchase of Apollo Leisure, a UK-based live entertainment firm. The company rolled all of its sports talent and marketing businesses into a new division, SFX Sports Group, that year.

In 2000 SFX jumped on the other side of the acquisition train when it was bought by radio station owner Clear Channel Communications for about $4 billion. Sillerman stepped down as chairman and CEO and was replaced by Clear Channel EVP Brian Becker. Later that year SFX acquired Philadelphia-based concert promoter and venue operator Electric Factory Concerts; Core Audience Entertainment, Canada's second-largest concert promoter and events marketer; and the Cotter Group, a North Carolina-based motorsports marketing agency.

In 2001 SFX acquired a majority interest in the International Hot Rod Association. It also bought professional golf talent agency Signature Sports Group. Later that year the company changed its name to Clear Channel Entertainment.

While operating as Clear Channel Entertainment, Live Nation spent nearly $2 billion on acquisitions (Pace Entertainment, Livent), almost single-handedly consolidating the live entertainment industry.

Before being spun off in 2005, the company changed its name to Live Nation. Also that year

Randall Mays became chairman and Michael Rapino replaced Becker as CEO. As part of the Clear Channel spinoff, the company relocated from Houston to headquarters in tony Beverly Hills. It trimmed the fat by shutting down operating divisions such as museum exhibitions and music publishing (and laying off about 400 employees in the process).

In 2006 the company acquired rival HOB Entertainment. Live Nation used the acquisition to expand its presence in the midsize venue business and fill in geographic gaps in its existing amphitheater network. As part of the deal, it gained high profile House of Blues-branded music venues such as San Francisco's Fillmore Auditorium, Jones Beach in New York, and London's Apollo Theatre and Wembley Arena.

Through its North American Music segment, in 2007 Live Nation promoted or produced some 10,000 live music events, including tours for Van Halen, Dave Matthews Band, and Kenny Chesney. International Music operations for the year included Cirque De Soleil's *Delirium*, as well as UK's *Reading Festival*. Also in 2007 the company produced global tours for legends such as The Police, The Rolling Stones, Genesis, and The Who, and it presented some 5,000 theatrical performances, such as the UK touring production of *Chicago*.

EXECUTIVES

Chairman: Randall T. Mays, age 43,
$2,611,602 total compensation
President, CEO, and Director: Michael (Mike) Rapino, age 43
EVP and CFO: Kathy Willard, age 42
SVP Interactive Technology: Dave Kochbeck
Chief Strategic Officer: Robert Peters
President and Chief Creative Officer, Merchandising; CEO and Creative Director, TRUNK: Brad Beckerman
SVP and Chief Accounting Officer: Brian Capo
Chief Marketing Officer, Global: Seth Matlins
EVP; Executive Producer, Interactive Products: Scott Fedewa
EVP Direct Marketing and Research: Jeff Schroeder
EVP and General Manager, LiveNation.com: Noah Maffitt
EVP Mergers and Acquisitions and Strategic Finance: John Hopmans, age 50
SVP Corporate Finance: Lee Ann Gliha
SVP Pan Asia: Colleen Ironside
SVP Touring: Bruce Kapp
VP Communications: John Vlautin
Chairman, Global Touring and Global Music: Arthur Fogel, age 55
Chairman, Global Theatrical: David Ian
CEO, International Music Division: Alan Ridgeway, age 42
CEO, Global Music: Jason Garner, age 56
General Counsel and Secretary: Michael G. Rowles, age 43
Auditors: Ernst & Young LLP

LOCATIONS

HQ: Live Nation, Inc.
9348 Civic Center Dr., Beverly Hills, CA 90210
Phone: 310-867-7000   **Fax:** 310-867-7001
Web: www.livenation.com

2008 Sales

	$ mil.	% of total
US	2,662	64
UK	557	13
Other countries	948	23
Total	**4,167**	**100**

PRODUCTS/OPERATIONS

2008 Sales

	$ mil.	% of total
North American Music	2,236	53
International Music	1,183	28
Artist Nation	664	16
Ticketing	22	1
Other	88	2
Eliminations	(26)	—
Total	**4,167**	**100**

Selected Artist Rights Agreements

U2
Jay-Z
Madonna
Nickelback
Shakira

Selected Concerts

Aerosmith
Jimmy Buffett
Cher
Kenny Chesney
Dave Matthews Band
Genesis
Josh Groban
Toby Keith
Linkin Park
Madonna
Bette Midler
The Police
The Rolling Stones
Barbra Streisand
Sting
Van Halen
The Who

Selected Music Venues

Austin Music Hall
Cynthia Woods Mitchell Pavilion (Houston)
The Fillmore (San Francisco)
The Fillmore Detroit
Orpheum Theatre-Boston
Roseland Ballroom (New York)
Rosemont Theatre (Chicago)
Verizon Wireless Amphitheatre (Los Angeles)

COMPETITORS

Anschutz Entertainment
Dodger Stage Holding Theatricals
Feld Entertainment
Gaylord Entertainment
IMG
Jujamcyn Theaters
Nederlander Producing Company
Octagon
On Stage Entertainment
Shubert Organization
SMG Management
TBA Global
Westwood One

HISTORICAL FINANCIALS

Company Type: Public

Income Statement

FYE: December 31

	REVENUE ($ mil.)	NET INCOME ($ mil.)	NET PROFIT MARGIN	EMPLOYEES
12/08	4,166.8	(231.8)	—	4,700
12/07	4,185.0	(11.9)	—	4,700
12/06	3,691.6	(31.4)	—	4,400
12/05	2,936.8	(130.6)	—	3,000
12/04	2,806.1	16.3	0.6%	—
Annual Growth	**10.4%**	**—**	**—**	**16.1%**

2008 Year-End Financials

Debt ratio: 134.5%
Return on equity: —
Cash ($ mil.): 200
Current ratio: 0.83
Long-term debt ($ mil.): 837

No. of shares (mil.): 86
Dividends
Yield: 0.0%
Payout: —
Market value ($ mil.): 493

Stock History

NYSE: LYV

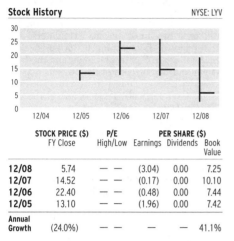

	STOCK PRICE ($) FY Close	P/E High/Low	PER SHARE ($) Earnings	Dividends	Book Value
12/08	5.74	— —	(3.04)	0.00	7.25
12/07	14.52	— —	(0.17)	0.00	10.10
12/06	22.40	— —	(0.48)	0.00	7.44
12/05	13.10	— —	(1.96)	0.00	7.42
Annual Growth	(24.0%)	— —	—	—	41.1%

Liz Claiborne

Liz Claiborne is dressed for success as a leading US seller of clothes and accessories for women. It markets its products as designer items but prices them for a broader market. Its brands — including Liz & Co., Concepts by Claiborne, Kate Spade, Juicy Couture, and Lucky Brand Jeans — are sold worldwide in department stores, in more than 440 specialty stores, in about 365 outlets, and among numerous brand Web sites. Liz Claiborne also makes men's clothing and licenses its name for shoes, sunglasses, swimwear, formalwear, home furnishings, and stationery. In 2008 the company cut jobs and completed a strategic review of its operations that involved repurposing its stores and catering to its top brands.

Liz Claiborne's reorganization involved purging some 8% of its global workforce, or 700 positions, as well as shuttering or rebranding about 20 retail locations. Most staff reductions involved senior-level positions. The company says that the move was necessary to make it more nimble, to increase operating efficiencies, and to provide for more growth opportunities.

As part of the restructuring, Liz Claiborne separated its power brands — brands the company defines as having the most potential — from its other brand names. Its power brands include direct-to-consumer names Juicy Couture and Lucky Brands and these are the operations that receive the most attention and funding. Liz Claiborne also has decided to keep the contemporary brands Kensie and Mac & Jac, and licensed its Dana Buchman line to Kohl's.

Liz Claiborne has been pulling the plug on retail formats that don't have the potential to support a minimum of 100 stores and trimming its stable of brands. The company sold eight of its 16 brands, including Ellen Tracy and prAna men's and women's lines. Other brands sold include Laundry By Design and C&C California. The company also closed its remaining 54 Sigrid

Olsen stores in 2008. The company closed its three Laundry retail stores in New York and California to focus on Laundry's wholesale business.

Liz Claiborne also scaled back in Europe by shuttering its wholesale business in Germany, Russia, and Sweden in late 2007. In 2008 the company refocused its efforts on France, Belgium, Portugal, and Spain, where the Liz Claiborne brand is strongest overseas.

In a major move to revitalize its name, the company hired high fashion designer Isaac Mizrahi to design and market Liz Claiborne apparel and accessories. His Liz products hit stores in early 2009.

The firm has a history of increasing its product offerings by licensing or acquiring new brands. In December 2006 the apparel giant acquired handbag and accessories maker kate spade from Neiman Marcus for some $124 million. The purchase gives Liz Claiborne a strong foothold in the handbag business, which is one of the hottest segments of the accessories sector.

William McComb, formerly with Johnson & Johnson, succeeded retiring CEO Paul Charron in 2006.

HISTORY

In 1975 Liz Claiborne, a dress designer in Jonathan Logan's Youth Guild division, had a vision of stylish, sporty, affordable clothes for working women. Unable to sell the concept to her employer, Claiborne quit and, with husband Arthur Ortenberg and partners Jerome Chazen and Leonard Boxer, founded Liz Claiborne in 1976 with $250,000.

Born just as women were beginning to flood the workforce, Liz Claiborne became an immediate success by rescuing them from drab business suits. Making money its first year, Liz Claiborne remained the fastest-growing, most profitable US apparel maker in the 1980s. In 1981 it went public and by 1986 had made the *FORTUNE* 500, with sales topping $800 million.

The company expanded into men's clothing (Claiborne, 1985), cosmetics (Liz Claiborne, a 1986 joint venture with Avon; in 1988 it acquired full rights to the line), women's plus sizes (Elisabeth, 1989), and knit sportswear (Liz & Co., 1989). Higher-priced sportswear by in-house designer Dana Buchman was introduced in 1987. Liz Claiborne moved into retailing the following year, opening First Issue boutiques.

Claiborne and Ortenberg began withdrawing from the business side in 1989 and left the board the next year. About this time the retail business began to slow down as a recession loomed. In addition, baby boomers' clothing tastes began to shift toward comfort and versatility.

Liz Claiborne acquired the Crazy Horse, Russ Togs, Villager, and Red Horse brand names in 1992 and took over 16 outlet stores from bankrupt Russ Togs.

In response to slow sales, Liz Claiborne brought in VF veteran Paul Charron as COO. Named CEO in 1995, Charron closed the First Issue stores and moved production from US union plants to foreign factories. In 1996, as sales picked up, the company began selling its repositioned First Issue line through Sears. It launched Emma James (moderately priced career separates) in 1997.

In response to sagging sales, the company took a $27 million charge in 1998 to close 30 retail stores and cut 400 jobs.

Charron set out to give Liz Claiborne a broader appeal. In 1999 the company bought

trendy Laundry (women's sportswear and dresses), an 85% stake in women's sportswear firm Segrets (Sigrid Olsen), teen-targeted Lucky Brand Dungarees, and a minority stake in Kenneth Cole Productions.

By 2000 about 20% of Liz Claiborne's sales came from non-Liz lines. Increasing that percentage even further, the company bought fashion jeweler Monet Group for about $40 million.

In 2003 the company bought Travis Jeans (now named Juicy Couture), maker of Juicy Couture upscale casualwear and jeans.

In 2005 and 2006 the firm extended its reach across North America. It acquired California-inspired men's and women's apparel maker C&C California. In 2006 Liz Claiborne picked up Vancouver, Canada-based Westcoast Contempo Fashions Limited and Mac and Jac Holdings Limited.

Company namesake Liz Claiborne died at the age of 78 in mid-2007.

Trimming its stable of brands, Liz Claiborne sold the Laundry By Design and C&C California labels to Perry Ellis International in February 2008. It also sold prAna to that company's management in April 2008.

In October 2008 the company sold the Enyce brand to Sean "Diddy" Combs, a music artist and fashion designer who runs Sean John Clothing.

EXECUTIVES

Chairman: Kay Koplovitz, age 63
CEO and Director: William L. McComb, age 46, $5,499,489 total compensation
EVP and CFO: Andrew C. (Andy) Warren, age 42, $1,345,400 total compensation
SVP and CIO: Evon L. Jones, age 45
Chief Creative Officer: Timothy (Tim) Gunn
EVP, General Counsel, and Secretary: Nicholas Rubino, age 47
EVP Partnered Brands: David McTague, age 46, $1,179,060 total compensation
SVP Real Estate and Construction: Trent Merrill
SVP and Managing Director Market Development: Jeff Fardell
SVP Business Development, Legal, and Corporate Affairs: Roberta Schuhalter Karp, age 50
SVP Global Sourcing: Peter Warner
VP, Corporate Controller, and Chief Accounting Officer: Elaine H. Goodell
VP Finance and Treasurer: Robert J. Vill
VP Corporate Communications: Jane Randel
VP Planning and Research: Lori O'Rourke
VP and General Manager, Juicy Couture Retail: Beth Cohn
VP International/SIS Store Design and Construction: Brad Lenz
VP E-commerce: Suzanne Norris
Director Investor Relations: Elizabeth Schwartz
Auditors: Deloitte & Touche LLP

LOCATIONS

HQ: Liz Claiborne, Inc.
1441 Broadway, New York, NY 10018
Phone: 212-354-4900   **Fax:** 212-626-3416
Web: www.lizclaiborne.com

2008 Sales

	$ mil.	% of total
Partnered Brands	1,574.6	40
Domestic-based Direct Brands	1,207.4	30
International-based Direct Brands	1,202.9	30
Total	**3,984.9**	**100**

PRODUCTS/OPERATIONS

2008 US Specialty Retail Stores

	No.
Lucky Brand Jeans	182
Juicy Couture	61
Kate Spade	46
Jack Spade	2
Total	**291**

2008 Foreign Specialty Retail Stores

	No.
Mexx Europe	96
Mexx Canada	40
Lucky Brand Jeans Canada	11
Monet Europe	4
Juicy Couture Europe	1
Total	**152**

2008 US Outlet Stores

	No.
Liz Claiborne	97
Lucky Brand Jeans	39
Juicy Couture	33
Kate Spade	28
DKNY Jeans	14
Kensie	1
Total	**212**

2008 Foreign Outlet Stores

	No.
Mexx Canada	54
Mexx	46
Liz Claiborne Canada	45
Liz Claiborne Europe	8
Total	**153**

COMPETITORS

AnnTaylor
AZ3
bebe stores
Benetton
Bernard Chaus
Calvin Klein
Chico's FAS
Coach, Inc.
Cole Haan
Diesel SpA
Donna Karan
Esprit Holdings
French Connection
The Gap
Guess?
H&M
Hartmarx
Inditex
J. Crew
J. Jill Group
Jones Apparel
Lands' End
Limited Brands
Marc Jacobs International
michael kors
Nautica Apparel
NEXT
Polo Ralph Lauren
Roc Apparel
Sean John
St. John Knits
Talbots
Tommy Hilfiger
Tory Burch
True Religion Apparel
Urban Outfitters
Warnaco Group
Zara

HISTORICAL FINANCIALS

Company Type: Public

Income Statement — FYE: Saturday nearest December 31

	REVENUE ($ mil.)	NET INCOME ($ mil.)	NET PROFIT MARGIN	EMPLOYEES
12/08	3,984.9	(951.8)	—	15,000
12/07	4,577.3	(372.8)	—	16,500
12/06	4,994.3	254.7	5.1%	17,000
12/05	4,847.8	317.4	6.5%	15,400
12/04	4,632.8	313.6	6.8%	14,500
Annual Growth	**(3.7%)**	**—**	**—**	**0.9%**

2008 Year-End Financials

Debt ratio: 125.8%
Return on equity: —
Cash ($ mil.): 25
Current ratio: 1.69
Long-term debt ($ mil.): 633

No. of shares (mil.): 95
Dividends
  Yield: 8.7%
  Payout: —
Market value ($ mil.): 247

Stock History — NYSE: LIZ

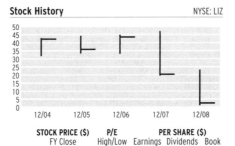

	STOCK PRICE ($) FY Close	P/E High/Low	PER SHARE ($) Earnings	Dividends	Book Value
12/08	2.60	— —	(10.17)	0.23	5.30
12/07	20.35	— —	(3.74)	0.23	15.94
12/06	43.46	18 14	2.46	0.23	22.40
12/05	35.82	15 11	2.94	0.23	21.06
12/04	42.21	15 11	2.85	0.23	19.05
Annual Growth	**(50.2%)**	**— —**	**—**	**0.0%**	**(27.4%)**

Lockheed Martin

Lockheed Martin moves product in times of crisis — the company is the world's #1 military contractor (ahead of Boeing and Northrop Grumman). Lockheed is firmly on the defense/government side of the aerospace industry; in fact, the US government accounts for about 85% of sales. This reliance on the US government is a double-edged sword: Lockheed can largely avoid turbulence in the commercial aerospace sector, but the company is vulnerable to military spending cuts.

Its business segments include Aeronautics, which makes the F-16 and F-22 fighters, and the upcoming F-35 Joint Strike Fighter (Lightning II); Electronic Systems, encompassing everything from missiles and submarine warfare systems to homeland security systems, radar, and postal automation systems; Space Systems, which supplies satellites, strategic missiles, and airborne defense systems; and Information Systems & Global Services, which provides IT services, mission systems, and command, control, and communication systems and reconnaissance/surveillance systems.

The conflicts in Afghanistan and Iraq, along with increased spending on homeland security,

buoyed the company's sales, but looming military program cuts may affect some of Lockheed's largest programs. The Obama administration, while maintaining some continuity with the re-appointment of incumbent Defense Secretary Robert Gates, is examining the Pentagon budget to set priorities.

Lockheed is the prime contractor for the US military's two most recent jet fighters, the $200 billion F-35 Lightning II (formerly called the Joint Strike Fighter) program and the F-22 Raptor, but one or both of the projects may be scaled back due to budget constraints. The F-22 Raptor was a particular target of former Defense Secretary Donald Rumsfeld, who directed that the Raptor program be cut from the 277 planes already approved to 180 planes. The US Air Force countered that it would rather cut F-35 Lightning IIs than Raptors, but the request went unheeded. Despite its uncertain future, the Raptor was approved for full-scale production in 2005 and was rated "mission capable" in 2006. Lockheed delivered 23 Raptors during 2008, for a total of 133 produced; at the end of 2008, there were 62 F-22s on backlog. The inaugural flight of the F-35 Lightning II took place in late 2006.

The company teamed up with rivals Northrop Grumman and Alliant Techsystems in 2008 to develop multi-role weapons for Lockheed's F-22 Raptor and its F-35 Lightning II.

The company's Maritime Systems & Sensors unit incorporates Aculight, an industrial laser manufacturer that counts the US Department of Defense, US Air Force, and US Navy as customers. Meanwhile, Lockheed's Simulation, Training and Support division is taking over Universal Systems & Technology, Inc. (UNITECH), which provides interactive training and simulation to major US and international military and national defense agencies. Lockheed Martin's acquisition of UNITECH closed in early 2009.

HISTORY

Brothers Allan and Malcolm Loughead (pronounced "Lockheed") joined Fred Keeler in 1926 to form Lockheed Aircraft. John Northrop (who later founded Northrop Corporation) designed Lockheed's first airplane, the Vega (flown by Amelia Earhart).

Robert Gross, Carl Squier, and Lloyd Stearman bought Lockheed in 1932. The company produced such aviation classics as the P-38 Lightning fighter, the U-2 spy plane, and the SR-71 Blackbird spy plane. It also produced submarine-launched ballistic missiles (Polaris, 1958), military transports (C-5 Galaxy, 1968), and the L-1011 TriStar airliner (1971).

Lockheed suffered from the cancellation of its Cheyenne attack helicopter, the C-5A cost-overrun scandal, and financial problems with the L-1011. Government loans saved the firm from bankruptcy in 1971.

In the late 1970s Lockheed was at the center of a corporate bribery scandal that overturned governments in Japan and Italy and led to tougher US anti-bribery laws. During the 1970s and 1980s, Lockheed developed the Hubble Space Telescope and the F-117A stealth fighter. Lockheed merged with Martin Marietta in 1995 to form Lockheed Martin.

Glenn Martin started Martin Marietta in 1917. Martin Marietta made the first US-built bombers, as well as military and commercial flying boats. During the 1950s Martin Marietta made missiles, electronics, and nuclear systems. In 1961 it merged with American-Marietta Company (construction materials and chemical products).

In 1996 Lockheed Martin sold its Defense Systems and Armament Systems units to General Dynamics and bought most of Loral Corporation (advanced electronics). In 1997 it partly spun off 10 noncore technology units as L-3 Communications Holdings. In 1999 it acquired a 49% stake in COMSAT, a satellite network company that is the centerpiece of Lockheed Martin's communications business.

A series of launch failures in 1999 destroyed about $4 billion in rockets and payloads and led to an inquiry that blamed poor management oversight and quality-control problems.

In 2000 the Pentagon bailed out Lockheed Martin by agreeing to buy 24 C-130J transports. The company also won a $3.97 billion contract from the Pentagon to develop the Theater High-Altitude Area Defense (THAAD) anti-missile defense system. Lockheed sold some defense electronics units, including its Sanders unit (aerial electronic warfare and countermeasure systems), to UK-based BAE SYSTEMS for around $1.67 billion; in a separate deal it also sold its Lockheed Martin Control Systems unit to BAE. That year Lockheed Martin purchased the 51% of COMSAT it didn't already own.

In 2001 Lockheed Martin (along with TRW) was awarded a $2.7 billion contract for the US military's next-generation communications satellite system. In 2002 the company was awarded a $12.7 billion US defense contract (spread out over 23 years) to provide support work for single-seat F-16s flown by 16 different countries.

In 2005 the US Navy selected Lockheed (prime contractor) and AgustaWestland to build a new fleet of 23 Presidential Marine One helicopters in a deal worth about $6.1 billion. In 2006 Lockheed bought Pacific Architects and Engineers Incorporated (PAE), a provider of services that support military readiness, peacekeeping missions, and disaster relief.

Also in 2006, Lockheed got a bonanza of business when NASA awarded the company with the coveted Orion manned lunar spaceship contract.

EXECUTIVES

Chairman, President, and CEO: Robert J. Stevens, age 57, $26,521,848 total compensation
EVP and CFO: Bruce L. Tanner, age 49, $3,161,160 total compensation
EVP Information Systems and Global Services: Linda R. Gooden, age 55, $5,454,383 total compensation
Acting Controller and Chief Accounting Officer: Mark R. Bostic
EVP Electronic Systems: Christopher E. Kubasik, age 47, $6,059,224 total compensation
EVP Aeronautics: Ralph D. Heath, age 60, $5,526,101 total compensation
EVP and General Manager, F-35 Program: Daniel J. (Dan) Crowley
EVP Space Systems: Joanne M. Maguire, age 54
SVP, Human Resources: Kenneth J. Disken
SVP and General Counsel: James B. Comey, age 48
SVP Finance: Mary Margaret (Meg) VanDeWeghe, age 49
SVP Washington Operations: Gregory R. (Greg) Dahlberg, age 57
VP and Controller: Martin T. Stanislav, age 44
VP Navigation Systems: Donald G. (Don) DeGryse
VP Cyber Security Solutions: Charles E. (Charlie) Croom Jr.
VP Mergers & Acquisitions: Jeffery D. MacLauchlan

VP; Head of Center for Cyber Security Innovation: Lee Holcomb
VP Corporate International Business Development: Patrick M. (Pat) Dewar
VP Solar Energy Programs: Chris Myers
VP Radar Systems: Carl Bannar
Auditors: Ernst & Young LLP

LOCATIONS

HQ: Lockheed Martin Corporation
6801 Rockledge Dr., Bethesda, MD 20817
Phone: 301-897-6000   **Fax:** 301-897-6704
Web: www.lockheedmartin.com

2008 Sales

	$ mil.	% of total
US	36,831	86
Other countries	5,900	14
Total	**42,731**	**100**

PRODUCTS/OPERATIONS

2008 Sales

	$ mil.	% of total
Electronic Systems	11,620	27
Information Systems & Global Services	11,611	27
Aeronautics	11,473	27
Space Systems	8,027	19
Total	**42,731**	**100**

2008 Sales by Customer

	$ mil.	% of total
US government	36,050	84
Foreign governments	5,487	13
Commercial & other	1,194	3
Total	**42,731**	**100**

Selected Products and Services

Aeronautics
  C-5 (strategic airlift aircraft)
  C-130J (tactical airlift aircraft)
  F-2 (Japanese combat aircraft)
  F-16 (multi-role fighter)
  F-22 (air-superiority fighter)
  F-35 Joint Strike Fighter (next-generation multi-role fighter)
  Special mission and reconaissance aircraft (S-3 Viking, U-2, P-3 Orion)
  T-50 (Korean advanced trainer)
Electronic Systems
  Advanced aviation management
  Air and theater missile defense systems
  Anti-submarine and undersea warfare systems
  Avionics and ground combat vehicle integration
  Homeland security systems
  Missiles and fire control systems
  Platform integration systems
  Postal automation systems
  Radars
  Security and information technology solutions
  Simulation and training systems
  Surface ship and submarine combat systems
  Surveillance and reconnaissance systems
Information Systems & Global Services
  Aircraft and engine maintenance and modification services
  Application development
  Command, control, and communication systems
  Computer system design and service
  Engineering, science, and information services for NASA
  Engineering, science, and technology services
  Enterprise solutions
  Government technology services
  Information technology integration and management
  Intelligence
  Launch, mission, and analysis services for military, classified, and commercial satellites
  Nuclear operations and materials management (Oak Ridge, Tennessee, and other locations)
  Operation, maintenance, training, and logistics support for military, homeland security, and civilian systems
  Surveillance

Space Systems
  Airborne defense systems
  Defensive missiles
  Missile launch vehicles
  Satellites (for commercial and government use)
  Satellite launch services
  Strategic missiles

COMPETITORS

Alcatel-Lucent
Alliant Techsystems
Arianespace
BAE SYSTEMS
Boeing
CACI International
Daimler
DynCorp International
EADS
Finmeccanica
GE
General Dynamics
Goodrich Corp.
Herley Industries
Honeywell International
ITT Corp.
L-3 Communications
Northrop Grumman
Orbital Sciences
Raytheon
Saab AB
SAIC
Siemens AG
Textron
Thales
United Technologies
URS

HISTORICAL FINANCIALS

Company Type: Public

Income Statement

	REVENUE ($ mil.)	NET INCOME ($ mil.)	NET PROFIT MARGIN	EMPLOYEES
				FYE: December 31
12/08	42,731.0	3,217.0	7.5%	146,000
12/07	41,862.0	3,033.0	7.2%	140,000
12/06	39,620.0	2,529.0	6.4%	140,000
12/05	37,213.0	1,825.0	4.9%	135,000
12/04	35,526.0	1,266.0	3.6%	130,000
Annual Growth	**4.7%**	**26.3%**	**—**	**2.9%**

2008 Year-End Financials

Debt ratio: 124.4%
Return on equity: 50.8%
Cash ($ mil.): 2,168
Current ratio: 1.01
Long-term debt ($ mil.): 3,563
No. of shares (mil.): 384
Dividends
  Yield: 2.2%
  Payout: 23.3%
Market value ($ mil.): 32,317

Stock History

NYSE: LMT

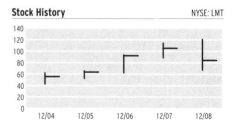

	STOCK PRICE ($) FY Close	P/E High/Low		PER SHARE ($) Earnings	Dividends	Book Value
12/08	84.08	15	9	7.86	1.83	7.45
12/07	105.26	16	13	7.10	1.47	25.51
12/06	92.07	16	11	5.80	1.25	17.91
12/05	63.63	16	13	4.10	1.05	20.47
12/04	55.55	22	15	2.83	0.91	18.27
Annual Growth	**10.9%**			**29.1%**	**19.1%**	**(20.1%)**

Loews Corporation

This diversified holding company not only drills deep and makes the bed — it'll insure others that do, too. Loews' main interest is insurance through publicly traded subsidiary CNA Financial, which offers commercial property/casualty coverage. Other wholly owned and partially owned holdings include hotels in the US and Canada through its Loews Hotels subsidiary. Its energy holdings include contract oil-drilling operator Diamond Offshore Drilling (which operates nearly 50 offshore oil rigs), interstate natural gas transmission pipeline systems operator Boardwalk Pipelines, and HighMount Exploration & Production (also natural gas).

Despite Loews' eclectic collection of businesses, its flagship unit CNA Financial still accounts for more than half of the corporation's revenues. CNA's affiliates include The Continental Insurance Company and Continental Assurance Company.

While commercial insurance is generally stable stuff, during 2008 CNA was faced with the same investment losses of all big insurers. To make sure CNA would have enough cash on hand to pay any claims that might arise, Loews committed to inject up to $1.25 billion. Shortly thereafter, the company announced it would invest up to $500 million in Boardwalk Pipeline to help it complete pipeline expansion projects.

Tobacco was long a staple in Loews' portfolio until the company kicked the habit. Prior to quitting, the company kept its 62% ownership of Lorillard rolled up as Carolina Group and traded it as a tracking subsidiary. Lorillard, which included the Kent, Newport, and True US cigarette brands, accounted for more than 20% of Loews' revenues. However, after a steady stream of tobacco-related litigations, the company spun Lorillard off into an independent public company in 2008, eliminating the Carolina Group, and exiting the industry.

That disposition was fully in keeping with the Loews strategy of acquiring what can be turned around, letting go of what can't be turned around, and the wisdom to know the difference. The company spent $4 billion in 2007 to acquire oil and gas exploration operator HighMount Exploration & Production. And, while accessories make the outfit, in early 2008 Loews slipped its Bulova subsidiary off of its wrist and handed it to competitor Citizen Watch for $250 million.

Members of the Tisch family, including co-chairmen cousins Andrew and Jonathan Tisch, CEO James Tisch, and their mothers, control more than 20% of the company's stock.

HISTORY

In 1946 Larry Tisch, who earned a business degree from New York University at age 18, dropped out of Harvard Law to run his parents' New Jersey resort. Younger brother Bob joined him in creating a new entity, Tisch Hotels. The company bought two Atlantic City hotels in 1952, quickly making them profitable. Later Tisch purchased such illustrious hotels as the Mark Hopkins, The Drake, the Belmont Plaza, and the Regency.

Moving beyond hotels, the brothers bought money-losing companies with poor management. Discarding the management along with underperforming divisions, they tightened operational control and eliminated such frills as fancy offices, company planes, and even memos.

In 1960 Tisch Hotels gained control of MGM's ailing Loew's Theaters to take advantage of their desirable city locations. The company then began demolishing more than 50 stately movie palaces and selling the land to developers. In 1968 the company bought Lorillard, the oldest US tobacco company; it shed Lorillard's unprofitable pet food and candy operations and reversed its slipping tobacco market share.

Taking the Loews name in 1971, the company bought CNA Financial in 1974. The Tisch method turned losses of more than $200 million to profits of more than $100 million the very next year. It bought Bulova Watch in 1979, and guided by Larry's son Andrew, it gradually returned to profitability.

In the early 1980s Loews entered the energy business by investing in oil supertankers. The company sold its last movie theaters in 1985. Then in 1987 Loews helped CBS fend off a takeover attempt by Ted Turner and ended up with about 25% of the company. Larry became president of the broadcaster.

In 1989 Loews acquired Diamond M Offshore, a Texas drilling company, and with the acquisition of Odeco Drilling in 1992, the company amassed the world's largest fleet of offshore rigs. The next year Loews grouped its drilling interests as Diamond Offshore Drilling.

In 1994 CNA expanded its insurance empire, buying The Continental Corp. The next year Loews sold its interest in CBS, and the following year Diamond Offshore Drilling merged with Arethusa (Off-Shore) Limited.

As deft as the Tisch brothers had been in accumulating their riches, Larry's bearish investment strategy (short-selling stocks) cost Loews in the late 1990s (more than $900 million alone during 1997's bull market). Larry and Bob retired as co-CEOs at the end of 1998; Larry's son James, already president and COO, became CEO.

That year Lorillard signed on to the 46-state tobacco lawsuit settlement; the first payment cost the company $325 million (payments continue until 2025). Facing a softened insurance market, CNA sold unprofitable lines to focus on commercial insurance; in 1999 it transferred its auto and homeowners lines to Allstate (it continues writing and renewing these policies) and put its life and life reinsurance units up for sale in 2000. Also that year Lorillard was hit with $16 billion of a record-breaking $144 billion punitive damage award in a smokers' class-action suit in Florida. CNA Financial paid out over $450 million in 2001-02 for claims related to the attacks on the World Trade Center.

In 2004 the company continued to expand its natural resource offerings when its subsidiary Boardwalk Pipelines (formerly known as TGT Pipeline) acquired Gulf South Pipeline, which operates natural gas pipeline and gathering systems in Texas, Louisiana, Mississippi, Alabama, and Florida, including several major supply hubs. Loews had acquired gas pipeline operator Texas Gas Transmission in 2003. Texas Gas operates natural gas pipeline systems reaching from the Louisiana Gulf Coast and East Texas north through Louisiana, Arkansas, Mississippi, Tennessee, Kentucky, Indiana, and into Ohio and Illinois.

Larry Tisch died at the age of 80 in 2003. Chairman Bob Tisch died of cancer in late 2005. Tisch also was co-owner of the New York Giants of the National Football League.

EXECUTIVES

Co-Chairman, Office of the President, and Chairman, Executive Committee: Andrew H. Tisch, age 59, $5,356,347 total compensation
Co-Chairman and Office of the President; Chairman and CEO, Loews Hotels: Jonathan M. Tisch, age 55, $5,496,930 total compensation
President, CEO, Office of the President, and Director: James S. Tisch, age 56, $1,808,312 total compensation
SVP and CFO: Peter W. Keegan, age 64, $3,433,976 total compensation
VP and Chief Investment Officer: Richard W. Scott, age 54
SVP: Herbert C. Hofmann, age 66
SVP: Arthur L. Rebell, age 68
SVP: David B. Edelson, age 49, $4,053,777 total compensation
SVP Tax: Susan Becker
SVP, General Counsel, Secretary: Gary W. Garson, age 62
VP Human Resources: Alan Momeyer
VP Internal Audit: Robert F. Crook
VP Corporate Development: Jonathan Nathanson
VP Risk Management: Audrey A. Rampinelli
Treasurer: John J. Kenny
Controller: Mark S. Schwartz, age 50
Investor Relations: Darren Daugherty
Auditors: Deloitte & Touche LLP

LOCATIONS

HQ: Loews Corporation
667 Madison Ave., New York, NY 10065
Phone: 212-521-2000   **Fax:** 212-521-2525
Web: www.loews.com

PRODUCTS/OPERATIONS

2008 Sales

	$ mil.	% of total
Insurance premiums	7,150	49
Contract drilling revenues	3,476	24
Net investment income	1,581	11
Gain on issuance of subsidiary stock	2	—
Investment gains (losses)	(1,296)	—
Other	2,334	16
Total	**13,247**	**100**

2008 Sales

	$ mil.	% of total
CNA Financial	7,799	54
Diamond Offshore	3,487	24
Boardwalk Partners	848	6
HighMount	770	5
Loews Hotels	380	3
Corporate & other	1,227	8
Adjustments	(1,264)	—
Total	**13,247**	**100**

Selected Subsidiaries

Boardwalk Pipeline Partners, LP (74%)
CNA Financial Corporation (90%)
  The Continental Corporation
    Continental Casualty Company
Diamond Offshore Drilling, Inc. (50%)
HighMount Exploration & Production LLC
Loews Hotels Holding Corporation

COMPETITORS

ACE Limited	Hyatt
AIG	Marriott
American Financial Group	Ritz-Carlton
Apache	Safeco
Berkshire Hathaway	Starwood Hotels & Resorts
Chubb Corp	StatoilHydro
Cincinnati Financial	Travelers Companies
Four Seasons Hotels	Wyndham Worldwide
The Hartford	XL Capital
Hilton Hotels	

HISTORICAL FINANCIALS

Company Type: Public

Income Statement

	ASSETS ($ mil.)	NET INCOME ($ mil.)	INCOME AS % OF ASSETS	EMPLOYEES
12/08	69,857.0	4,530.0	6.5%	19,100
12/07	76,079.0	2,489.0	3.3%	21,700
12/06	76,880.9	2,491.3	3.2%	21,600
12/05	70,675.6	1,211.6	1.7%	21,600
12/04	73,749.5	1,231.3	1.7%	22,000
Annual Growth	(1.3%)	38.5%	—	(3.5%)

FYE: December 31

2008 Year-End Financials

Equity as % of assets: 18.8%
Return on assets: 6.2%
Return on equity: 29.5%
Long-term debt ($ mil.): 8,187
No. of shares (mil.): 433
Dividends
Yield: 0.9%
Payout: 2.8%
Market value ($ mil.): 12,233
Sales ($ mil.): 13,247

Stock History

NYSE: L

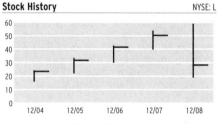

	STOCK PRICE ($) FY Close	P/E High/Low		PER SHARE ($) Earnings	Dividends	Book Value
12/08	28.25	6	2	9.05	0.25	30.31
12/07	50.34	15	11	3.65	0.25	40.62
12/06	41.47	11	8	3.75	0.24	38.11
12/05	31.62	19	13	1.72	0.20	30.23
12/04	23.43	13	9	1.88	0.20	28.14
Annual Growth	4.8%	—	—	48.1%	5.7%	1.9%

Lowe's Companies

No longer a low-profile company, Lowe's Companies has evolved from a regional hardware store operator into a nationwide chain of home improvement superstores bent on international expansion. The #2 US home improvement chain (after The Home Depot), Lowe's has about 1,640 superstores in 50 states and about a dozen outlets in Canada. The company's stores sell about 40,000 products for do-it-yourselfers and professionals for home improvement and repair projects, such as gardening products, home fashion items, lumber, millwork, plumbing and electrical supplies, and tools, as well as appliances and furniture. Lowe's is the second-largest US home appliance retailer after Sears.

In the past, Lowe's concentrated on small and medium-sized markets, but that trend is changing. The hardware chain is expanding in large metro areas (with populations of 500,000 or more). But it's not forgetting its traditional customer base either. About 20% of the new stores Lowe's plans to open will be smaller stores in rural markets. Overall, the company sees potential in the North American market for up to 2,500 Lowe's locations.

Outside of North America Lowe's has set its sights on the land down under. In a partnership

with Australia's top retailer Woolworths Ltd., Lowe's plans to begin opening its big-box hardware stores in Australia beginning in 2011. Woolworths will own two-thirds of the joint venture, which plans to open more than 150 sites over the next five years.

Lowe's continues to expand to gain market share. The company had been adding about 150 stores each year, but slowed the pace in 2008 to just 115 new outlets in response to the dismal housing market. In 2009 it expected to open between 60 and 70 new stores, including its first stores in Monterrey, Mexico. (Rival Home Depot is Mexico's #1 do-it-yourself operator with more than 55 stores there.) The hardware chain will also continue to grow in Canada, where it opened its first outlets in 2007.

Lowe's is also trying to attract more female customers, who, the company claims, call the shots on about 80% of home improvement decisions. To make its big-box stores appealing the company makes effective use of lighting and signage and cater to women and baby boomers with an attractive store design. In addition, Lowe's has been increasing exclusive product arrangements with suppliers. Like Home Depot, Lowe's is putting more emphasis on services, offering installation service in more than 40 categories, such as flooring and cabinet installation.

HISTORY

Lowe's Companies was founded in 1921 as Mr. L. S. Lowe's North Wilkesboro Hardware in North Wilkesboro, North Carolina. A family operation by 1945, Mr. Lowe's store (which also sold groceries, snuff, and harnesses) was run by his son Jim and his son-in-law H. Carl Buchan. Buchan bought Lowe's share of the company in 1956 and incorporated as Lowe's North Wilkesboro Hardware; he wanted Lowe's as part of the company name because he liked the slogan "Lowe's Low Prices." The chain expanded from North Carolina into Tennessee, Virginia, and West Virginia. By 1960 Buchan had 15 stores and sales of $31 million — up $4 million from a decade before.

Buchan planned to create a profit-sharing plan for Lowe's employees, but in 1960 he died of a heart attack at age 44. In 1961 Lowe's management and the executors of Buchan's estate established the Lowe's Employees Profit Sharing and Trust, which bought Buchan's 89% of the company (later renamed Lowe's Companies). That year they financed the transaction through a public offering, which diluted the employees' stock. Lowe's was listed on the NYSE in 1979.

Robert Strickland, who had joined the company in 1957, became chairman in 1978. Revenues increased from $170 million in 1971 to more than $900 million, with a net income of $25 million, in 1979. Traditionally, the majority of Lowe's business was in sales to professional homebuilders, but in 1980 housing starts fell, and company profits dropped. Concurrently, The Home Depot introduced its low-price warehouse concept. Instead of building warehouse stores of its own, Strickland changed the stores' layouts and by 1982 had redesigned half of the 229 stores to be more oriented toward do-it-yourself (DIY) consumers. The new designs featured softer lighting and displays of entire room layouts to appeal to women, who made up over half of all DIY customers. In 1982 Lowe's made more than half of its sales to consumers for the first time in its history.

Although Lowe's had more than 300 stores by 1988, its outlets were only about 20,000 sq. ft.

(one-fifth the size of Home Depot's warehouse stores). By 1989 Lowe's, which had continued to target contractors as well as DIYers, was overtaken by Home Depot as the US's #1 home retail chain.

Since 1989 the company has focused on building larger stores, taking a charge of $71 million in 1991 to phase out smaller stores and build warehouse outlets. In 1993 Lowe's opened 57 large stores (half were replacements for existing stores), almost doubling its total floor space.

The retailer opened 29 new stores in 1995. During 1996 Lowe's added a net of 37 stores, and in 1997 it opened 42 stores in new markets. Also that year president and CEO Leonard Herring retired and was replaced by former COO Robert Tillman, who also took the post of chairman when Strickland stepped down in 1998.

Also in 1998 the company entered a joint venture to sell an exclusive line of Kobalt-brand professional mechanics' tools produced by Snap-on and, to better serve commercial customers, began allowing them to special order items not stocked in stores. In addition, Lowe's announced it would spend $1.5 billion over the next several years on a 100-store push into the western US. Lowe's westward expansion was fueled when it purchased Washington-based, 38-store Eagle Hardware & Garden in 1999 in a stock swap deal worth $1.3 billion. The company gradually converted the Eagle stores into Lowe's.

In 2001 Lowe's opened more than 100 new stores and more than 110 new stores in 2002.

Robert Niblock was promoted from CFO to president in 2003. Lowe's sold its some 30 outlets operating as The Contractor Yard to The Strober Organization in 2004. Also that year it opened its first predominantly urban-oriented store, suited to the needs of city dwellers and building superintendents, in Brooklyn.

Chairman and CEO Robert Tillman retired in January 2005. He was succeeded by president Robert Niblock.

EXECUTIVES

Chairman and CEO: Robert A. Niblock, age 46, $7,876,339 total compensation
President and COO: Larry D. Stone, age 57, $4,295,060 total compensation
EVP and CFO: Robert F. (Bob) Hull Jr., age 44, $2,751,161 total compensation
SVP and CIO: Steven M. Stone, age 47
SVP and Chief Risk Officer: Marshall A. Croom, age 48
SVP and Chief Accounting Officer: Matthew V. Hollifield, age 42
SVP, General Counsel, and Chief Compliance Officer: Gaither M. Keener Jr., age 59
EVP Merchandising: Charles W. (Nick) Canter Jr., age 58, $2,599,328 total compensation
EVP Business Development: Gregory M. (Greg) Bridgeford, age 54, $2,579,190 total compensation
EVP Store Operations: Michael K. (Mike) Brown, age 45
EVP Logistics and Distribution: Joseph M. (Mike) Mabry Jr., age 46
SVP Human Resources: Maureen K. Ausura, age 53
SVP Product Development; President, Global Sourcing: Michael K. Menser, age 53
SVP, Real Estate, Engineering and Construction: David E. Shelton, age 60
SVP, Marketing and Advertising: Robert J. Gfeller Jr., age 45
SVP Logistics: Eric D. Sowder, age 52
SVP, General Counsel, and Secretary: Ross W. McCanless, age 51
SVP Corporate Affairs: N. Brian Peace, age 43
President, Canada: Don T. Stallings
Investor Relations Specialist: Vicki C. Heitman
Auditors: Deloitte & Touche LLP

LOCATIONS

HQ: Lowe's Companies, Inc.
1000 Lowe's Blvd., Mooresville, NC 28117
Phone: 704-758-1000   **Fax:** 336-658-4766
Web: www.lowes.com

2009 Stores

	No.
US	1,638
Canada	11
Total	**1,649**

PRODUCTS/OPERATIONS

Selected Brands

National
  Bosch
  DeWalt
  Electrolux
  John Deere
  KitchenAid
  Kohler
  Owens Corning
  Pella
  Porter-Cable
  Samsung
  Troy-Bilt
  Werner
  Whirlpool
  Valspar
Proprietary
  Harbor Breeze
  Kobalt
  Premier Living
  Portfolio
  Top-Choice
  Utilitech

COMPETITORS

84 Lumber
Abbey Carpet
Ace Hardware
Best Buy
CCA Global
Do it Best
E.N. Beard Hardwood Lumber
F.W. Webb
Guardian Building Products Distribution
HD Supply
Home Depot
McCoy Corp.
Menard
Northern Tool
Sears
Sherwin-Williams
Sutherland Lumber
True Value
Wal-Mart
Wolseley

HISTORICAL FINANCIALS

Company Type: Public

Income Statement

FYE: Friday nearest January 31

	REVENUE ($ mil.)	NET INCOME ($ mil.)	NET PROFIT MARGIN	EMPLOYEES
1/09	48,230.0	2,195.0	4.6%	229,000
1/08	48,283.0	2,809.0	5.8%	216,000
1/07	46,927.0	3,105.0	6.6%	210,000
1/06	43,243.0	2,771.0	6.4%	185,000
1/05	36,464.0	2,176.0	6.0%	162,000
Annual Growth	**7.2%**	**0.2%**	**—**	**9.0%**

2009 Year-End Financials

Debt ratio: 27.9%
Return on equity: 12.9%
Cash ($ mil.): 245
Current ratio: 1.15
Long-term debt ($ mil.): 5,039

No. of shares (mil.): 1,477
Dividends
  Yield: 1.8%
  Payout: 22.8%
Market value ($ mil.): 26,976

Stock History

NYSE: LOW

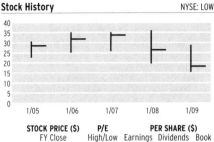

	STOCK PRICE ($) FY Close	P/E High/Low		PER SHARE ($) Earnings	Dividends	Book Value
1/09	18.27	19	11	1.49	0.34	12.23
1/08	26.43	19	11	1.86	0.29	10.90
1/07	33.71	18	13	1.99	0.18	10.65
1/06	31.77	20	15	1.73	0.11	9.71
1/05	28.50	22	17	1.36	0.08	7.81
Annual Growth	**(10.5%)**	**—**	**—**	**2.3%**	**43.6%**	**11.9%**

LSI Corporation

LSI doesn't stand for Lotta Semiconductors International. The fabless semiconductor developer provides standard integrated circuits (ICs) and custom-designed application-specific ICs (ASICs), focusing on broadband and wireless communications, data storage, and networking markets. LSI was a pioneer of system-on-a-chip (SoC) devices, which combine elements of an electronic system — especially a microprocessor, memory, and logic — onto a single chip. LSI also provides hardware and software for storage area networks.

LSI's top customers include Hewlett-Packard, IBM (16% of sales), and Seagate (17%). The Asia/Pacific region accounts for more than half of the company's sales.

LSI not only contends with the highly cyclical nature of the semiconductor industry, but — like other chip makers — it faces a downturn in sales of electronic products, and consequently semiconductors, pushed by the worldwide economic crisis.

The company has reframed its product portfolio through a series of acquisitions and divestitures. In 2008 Infineon Technologies sold the assets of its hard-disk drive (HDD) semiconductor business to LSI. Customers for the HDD chip line include Hitachi Global Storage Technologies. The following year LSI acquired the 3ware RAID adapter business of Applied Micro Circuits; the 3ware business joined the LSI Engenio Storage Group. LSI's lineup of network-attached and unified storage solutions was further expanded in mid-2009. The company moved to acquire ONStor, Inc., a provider of clustered network-attached storage (NAS) tools, enabling enterprises to consolidate, protect, and manage unstructured data.

HISTORY

Wilfred (Wilf) Corrigan, an engineer and former CEO of Fairchild Camera & Instrument (the original parent company of Fairchild Semiconductor), founded LSI Logic in 1981. (Its name is the acronym for large-scale integration, describing a chip that has up to 100,000 transistors.) LSI Logic went public in 1983 with a $152 million

IPO, a record for its time. That year the company introduced regional design centers — where customers could design chips using LSI Logic equipment and facilities — in Massachusetts and the UK. It established affiliates in Japan and Germany in 1984.

By 1985 LSI Logic had won big military and aerospace customers and, with sales of $140 million, was the US's leading application-specific integrated circuit (ASIC) maker. By the end of the 1980s, however, LSI Logic was foundering after heavy investment in factories (it had geared up for a boom that failed to materialize). In 1992 the company began developing its CoreWare mix-and-match standardization technology.

A trimmer, smarter LSI Logic emerged in 1993 — the year it introduced the 0.5-micron CMOS ASIC chip. Also that year LSI Logic penned 10-year technology sharing agreements with electronic design automation leaders Synopsys and Cadence Design Systems. LSI Logic passed the $1 billion sales mark in 1995.

LSI Logic paid $804 million to acquire Symbios, a US electronics subsidiary of cash-strapped Hyundai, in 1998. It also entered a DVD development joint venture with SANYO.

In 1999 the company bought SEEQ Technology, a maker of data communications semiconductor products. That year LSI Logic won a lucrative contract to make chips for Sony's PlayStation consoles, and teamed up with Hitachi to develop embedded hybrid chips.

In 2001 the company purchased C-Cube Microsystems (chips for digital set-top boxes and DVDs) in a deal valued at about $850 million. Also in 2001 LSI Logic bought a business unit of American Megatrends that makes hardware and software for redundant array of independent disks (RAID) systems used in networking and storage applications. Early in 2002 the company shed two product lines and cut 1,400 positions in an effort to return to profitability.

Intel veteran Abhi Talwalkar succeeded Wilf Corrigan as CEO in 2005. Corrigan remained chairman of the board. In 2006, however, LSI Logic's founder retired from the board of directors, officially ending his 25-year association with the company. James Keyes, the former CEO of Johnson Controls and an LSI Logic director since 1983, succeeded Corrigan as non-executive chairman.

Late in 2005 the company announced plans to sell its Oregon-based manufacturing facility and transition to a fabless model, under which the company contracted out its manufacturing chores. In 2006 LSI sold the Oregon fab to ON Semiconductor for about $105 million in cash. Among other agreements between the companies, LSI committed to paying ON Semi around $100 million a year for two years for ON to make chips for LSI.

In 2006 LSI said it would sell its ZSP digital signal processor business. It had acquired ZSP seven years earlier, in 1999. ZSP's assets were acquired by VeriSilicon Holdings, an ASIC design house based in China, for $13 million in cash and stock. Most of the ZSP workforce was hired by VeriSilicon.

In late 2006 LSI acquired StoreAge Networking Technologies, a developer of network storage management and data protection software, for around $50 million in cash. The company hired all of StoreAge's employees.

In early 2007 LSI Logic completed its $4 billion acquisition of rival Agere Systems and changed its name to LSI Corporation. Also that year Gregorio Reyes became non-executive chairman.

Softness in business during the first half of 2007 led LSI to eliminate approximately 900 jobs, a 10% reduction for the combined Agere-LSI workforce. As part of a general corporate restructuring in 2007, LSI sold its consumer products business to Magnum Semiconductor, a venture-funded chip company.

Later in 2007 LSI sold its division that made semiconductors and software for mobile telephones to Infineon Technologies for $450 million in cash. The company also sold its assembly and test operations in Pathumthani, Thailand, to STATS ChipPAC for approximately $100 million. LSI phased out assembly and test operations in Singapore and Wichita, Kansas, in 2008, turning over those facilities to contract manufacturers.

Capping off a busy year of acquisitions and divestitures, LSI bought networking chip developer Tarari for about $85 million in cash. The purchase added content processing capabilities to LSI's product portfolio, especially in the areas of network security and control, helping to block computer viruses and spam e-mail from enterprise networks.

EXECUTIVES

Chairman: Gregorio Reyes, age 68
President, CEO, and Director:
Abhijit Y. (Abhi) Talwalkar, age 44,
$7,479,345 total compensation
EVP, CFO, and Chief Administrative Officer:
Bryon Look, age 55, $1,744,466 total compensation
EVP, General Counsel, and Secretary: Jean F. Rankin, age 50
EVP and General Manager, Engenio Storage Group:
Philip W. (Phil) Bullinger, age 44
EVP Worldwide Manufacturing Operations:
Andrew Micallef, age 44, $2,700,635 total compensation
EVP and General Manager, Semiconductor Solutions Group: D. Jeffrey (Jeff) Richardson, age 44,
$2,374,616 total compensation
SVP Corporate Planning and Marketing:
Philip G. Brace, age 38
VP Human Resources: Jon R. Gibson, age 62
Auditors: PricewaterhouseCoopers LLP

LOCATIONS

HQ: LSI Corporation
1621 Barber Ln., Milpitas, CA 95035
Phone: 408-433-8000   **Fax:** 408-954-3220
Web: www.lsi.com

LSI has operations in Australia, Austria, Canada, China, France, Germany, Hong Kong, India, Ireland, Israel, Italy, Japan, Russia, Singapore, South Korea, Spain, Sweden, Taiwan, the United Arab Emirates, the UK, and the US.

2008 Sales

	$ mil.	% of total
Asia/Pacific	1,359.8	51
North America	737.2	27
Europe & Middle East	580.1	22
Total	**2,677.1**	**100**

PRODUCTS/OPERATIONS

2008 Sales

	$ mil.	% of total
Semiconductors	1,795.1	67
Storage systems	882.0	33
Total	**2,677.1**	**100**

Selected Semiconductor Products and Markets

Broadband and wireless networking (analog and digital chip cores, ASICs, and baseband processors)
Wide-area network (WAN) equipment
Wireless local-area network (LAN) equipment
Broadband entertainment (analog and digital chip cores, ASICs, and software)
Digital set-top boxes
DVD players
Home video games
Satellite and terrestrial television broadcasting
Networking infrastructure
Analog equipment (Ethernet physical-layer devices)
Digital equipment (ARM- and MIPS-based microprocessors, Ethernet controllers, and high-speed content-addressable memory)
Storage components (ASICs, software, and standard input/output components)
Fibre Channel (host adapters and adapter boards, physical-layer components, protocol controllers, SAN switches, and transceivers)
Hard disk drives and tape peripherals (controllers)

COMPETITORS

3PAR
Adaptec
Altera
Applied Micro Circuits
Atmel
Avago Technologies
Broadcom
Cirrus Logic
Compellent Technologies
Conexant Systems
Dot Hill
EMC
Epson
Freescale Semiconductor
Fujitsu Microelectronics
Hitachi Data Systems
IBM Microelectronics
Integrated Device Technology
Isilon Systems
Marvell Technology
MediaTek
NEC Electronics
NetApp
NetLogic Microsystems
NXP
PMC-Sierra
QLogic
Samsung Electronics
STMicroelectronics
Texas Instruments
Xilinx
Xiotech
Xyratex

HISTORICAL FINANCIALS

Company Type: Public

Income Statement

FYE: December 31

	REVENUE ($ mil.)	NET INCOME ($ mil.)	NET PROFIT MARGIN	EMPLOYEES
12/08	2,677.1	(622.3)	—	5,488
12/07	2,603.6	(2,486.8)	—	6,193
12/06	1,982.1	169.6	8.6%	4,010
12/05	1,919.3	(5.6)	—	4,322
12/04	1,700.2	(463.5)	—	4,414
Annual Growth	12.0%	—	—	5.6%

2008 Year-End Financials

Debt ratio: 37.7%
Return on equity: —
Cash ($ mil.): 829
Current ratio: 2.26
Long-term debt ($ mil.): 544

No. of shares (mil.): 652
Dividends
  Yield: 0.0%
  Payout: —
Market value ($ mil.): 2,145

Stock History

NYSE: LSI

	STOCK PRICE ($) FY Close	P/E High/Low	PER SHARE ($) Earnings	Dividends	Book Value
12/08	3.29	— —	(0.96)	0.00	2.21
12/07	5.31	— —	(3.87)	0.00	3.81
12/06	9.00	28 18	0.42	0.00	2.91
12/05	8.00	— —	(0.01)	0.00	2.50
12/04	5.48	— —	(1.21)	0.00	2.48
Annual Growth	(12.0%)	— —	—	—	(2.9%)

The Lubrizol Corporation

Lubrizol is a smooth operator — the company is the world's #1 maker of additives for lubricants and fuels. Its Lubrizol Additives segment includes engine oil additives that fight sludge buildup, viscosity breakdown, and component wear; fuel additives designed to control deposits and improve combustion; and additives for paints, inks, greases, metalworking, and other industrial markets. Lubrizol's Advanced Materials segment sends its products to the personal care and rubber and plastics markets. The company markets nearly 3,000 products in more than 100 countries. Lubrizol operates research facilities and testing labs in Europe, Asia, and North America. More than half of its sales come from outside the US.

After a few years where Lubrizol concentrated on slimming down and developing its core operations, by 2007, the company was in the mood to build its business back up a bit. Toward the end of the year it acquired Croda's refrigeration lubricants operations. Then, at the end of 2008, the company bought DuPont's thermoplastic polyurethane business, which will fit in with Lubrizol's Estane Engineered Polymers unit.

HISTORY

The company that eventually became Lubrizol was founded in 1928 by the Smith (Kelvin, Kevin, and Vincent) and Nason (Alex and Frank) brothers, along with their friend, Thomas James. Chemistry was in the Smiths' blood; all three had worked at Dow Chemical, a company their chemist father helped start. Known originally as The Graphite Oil Products Company, Lubrizol's first product, Lubri-graph, was a suspended graphite and oil product designed to keep car springs quiet. Following the success of their anti-squeak product, the principals turned their attention to the gunk that built up from the mineral oil used in car engines. Cars of the era overheated often and pistons frequently became stuck from excessive heat or sludge build-up. Graphite Oil chemists discovered that the addition of chlorine to lubricants solved the overheating problem. The new product (and later the company) was named Lubrizol.

Alex Nason went to Detroit in 1935 and convinced General Motors to add Lubrizol to its list of recommended products. Following that success Lubrizol was used extensively during WWII by the military, which established performance standards. During the war the company stopped producing lubricants and concentrated solely on additives, including rust inhibitors, detergents, and chemicals to slow oil breakdown.

After WWII performance standards for cars were set, and Lubrizol cleaned up, having patented many ingredients and processes used to manufacture lubricants. By the 1950s the privately held corporation was the #1 petroleum additive company in the world. It was during this time that the company made its first acquisition, R.O. Hull Company, a rustproofing chemicals manufacturer (it has since been sold). Lubrizol went public in 1960.

The company benefited as environmental regulations grew, since unleaded gas and catalytic converters required new additives. Lubrizol also benefited from the oil crisis in the early 1970s because the more fuel-efficient cars that resulted required new transmission fluids, fuel additives, and gear lubricants. Even the recession helped the slippery company, as industrial companies relied more on quality lubricants and additives to protect costly machinery.

Lubrizol purchased lithium battery maker Althus Corporation in 1979 and moved into biotechnology soon afterward. In 1985 the firm bought Agrigenetics Corporation and focused its biotechnology efforts on genetically altered plants. Biotechnology seemed to offer vast patent potential, whereas additives had become so effective that growth opportunities there seemed limited in comparison. However, after seven costly years, Lubrizol sold a controlling interest in Agrigenetics, which had become the sixth-largest seed company in the US, to Mycogen (acquired by Dow Chemical in 1998).

Lubrizol continued divesting noncore interests, and by 1996 it was back to being an additives company. Despite the turmoil in Asia, the company formed two joint ventures in China in 1997. The next year Lubrizol acquired the Adibis unit of BP Chemicals (now called BP Petrochemicals) and five other companies, adding a few additional percentage points to its share of the additives market. Shrinking profits caused the company to cut production by approximately 20% and its workforce by 11% between 1999 and 2000.

In 2000 Lubrizol bought RPM's Alox metalworking additive business. The next year it acquired ROSS Chem, a privately held maker of antifoam and defoaming agents used by the coatings, inks, textile, food, and metalworking industries. The company's 2002 acquisitions have included Kabo International (defoaming products), Chemron (specialty surfactants), and Lambent Technologies (silicone defoamers).

Over the next year and a half the company continued to buy when the mood struck. Lubrizol bought the additives business of Avecia in 2004. The former Avecia unit makes pigment and color dispersants for inks and coatings under the brand names Solsperse, Solplus, and Solthix. Later that year it bought up the formerly private company Noveon, which had announced its intention to go public. Noveon makes polymers and additives used in food and pharmaceuticals. The total price Lubrizol paid for the company

was $1.85 billion. The deal triggered a restructuring that resulted in Lubrizol's two main operating segments: its former activities called Lubricant Additives and Noveon's operations making up the Specialty Chemicals segment.

In the summer of 2005 the company announced its intention to divest noncore operations. The first move came later that year with the sale of Lubrizol Performance Systems to the Dutch medical and industrial technology company Delft Instruments. The following year brought the sale of Noveon's consumer specialties line of chemical products to Sun Capital Partners. The unit provided chemicals and performance materials to the food and beverage, personal care, and textiles industries. Lubrizol then sold the active pharmaceutical ingredients and intermediate compounds business of Noveon to German private equity firm Auctus Management. The move was the last in the planned divestiture of its non-core businesses. It then ceased to use the Noveon name for its specialty chemicals business.

EXECUTIVES

Chairman, President, and CEO: James L. Hambrick, age 54, $8,357,685 total compensation
SVP and COO: Stephen F. (Steve) Kirk, age 59, $2,937,436 total compensation
SVP, CFO, and Treasurer: Charles P. Cooley, age 53, $1,787,502 total compensation
VP Information Systems: Patrick H. Saunier, age 53
VP Global Risk Management and Chief Ethics Officer: Gregory R. (Greg) Lewis, age 50
Chief Tax Officer: Jeffrey A. Vavruska, age 48
VP and General Counsel: Joseph W. Bauer, age 55, $1,346,594 total compensation
VP Human Resources: Mark W. Meister, age 54
VP, Finance, Lubricant Additives: Gregory P. Lieb, age 54
VP; President Lubrizo Additives: Dan Sheets, age 51
VP Operations: Larry Norwood, age 58
VP Research and Development: Bob Graf, age 50
VP; President Lubrizol Advanced Materials: Eric Schnur, age 42
VP, Driveline and Specialty Additives: Val A. Pakis
VP, Corporate Planning, Development, and Communications: Gregory D. Taylor, age 50
VP Human Resources: C. Lawrence Miller, age 52
Corporate Secretary and Counsel: Leslie M. Reynolds, age 48
SVP and COO, Lubrizol Advanced Materials: Julian M. Steinberg, age 54
Corporate Controller: W. Scott Emerick, age 44
Manager, Public Affairs: David L. Cowen, age 56
Director, Investor Relations and Corporate Communications: Mark Sutherland
Manager, Communications — Trade Media Relations: Gail Norris
Strategic Account Manager, Paints, Coatings, and Adhesives, Performance Coatings: Mark Ruch
Auditors: Deloitte & Touche LLP

LOCATIONS

HQ: The Lubrizol Corporation
29400 Lakeland Blvd., Wickliffe, OH 44092
Phone: 440-943-4200   **Fax:** 440-943-5337
Web: www.lubrizol.com

2008 Sales

	$ mil.	% of total
North America		
US	1,710.1	34
Other countries	184.8	4
Europe	1,576.7	31
Asia/Pacific & Middle East	1,176.8	23
Latin America	379.4	8
Total	**5,027.8**	**100**

PRODUCTS/OPERATIONS

2008 Sales

	$ mil.	% of total
Lubrizol Additives	3,541.5	70
Lubrizol Advanced Materials	1,486.3	30
Total	**5,027.8**	**100**

Selected Products and Services

Lubrizol Additives
  Compression lubricants
  Corrosion control products
  Fuel additives
    E-diesel products (non-petroleum based)
  Lubricant additives
    Engine oils
    Driveline lubricants
    Industrial lubricants
    Viscosity modifiers
  Metalworking additives
  Refinery and oilfield products
  Specialty surfactants
  Terminals
  Toll manufacturing
  Warehousing
Lubrizol Advanced Materials
  Engineered Polymers
    Chlorinated polyvinyl chloride (TempRite)
    Foam control additives
    Reactive liquid polymers (Hycar)
    Specialty monomers
    Thermoplastic polyurethane (Estane)
  Performance Coatings
    Acrylic-based coatings for textiles
    Dye thickeners and binders
    Emulsions for specialty paper
    Glyoxal and glyoxal resins
    Ink additives
      Dispersants
      Ink vehicles
      Waxes
      Paints and coatings
      Polymers for inks and packaging
  Consumer Specialties
    Food and Beverage
      Benzoates (sodium and potassium)
      Flavor and fragrance enhancers
      Intermediates (phenol, benzaldehyde, benzyl alcohol, and benzoic acid)
      Natural colors and pigments
    Personal care and pharmaceuticals
      Acrylic thickener (Carbopol)
      Advanced intermediates
      Amino acid-based actives
      Cassia gum
      Colorants
      Polymeric emulsifier (Pemulen)
      Polymers for cosmetics and skin care products (Avalure)
      Resins for hair styling (Fixate)
      Specialty silicones

COMPETITORS

Afton Chemical
Avecia
BASF SE
Bayer MaterialScience
Chevron Oronite
Cognis
CP Kelco
Dow Chemical
DSM
FUCHS
Infineum
Reichhold
Rhodia
Rohm and Haas
Symrise

HISTORICAL FINANCIALS
Company Type: Public

Income Statement
FYE: December 31

	REVENUE ($ mil.)	NET INCOME ($ mil.)	NET PROFIT MARGIN	EMPLOYEES
12/08	5,027.8	(66.1)	—	6,970
12/07	4,499.0	283.4	6.3%	6,900
12/06	4,040.8	105.6	2.6%	6,700
12/05	4,042.7	189.3	4.7%	7,500
12/04	3,159.5	93.5	3.0%	7,800
Annual Growth	12.3%	—	—	(2.8%)

2008 Year-End Financials

Debt ratio: 62.7%
Return on equity: —
Cash ($ mil.): 186
Current ratio: 1.66
Long-term debt ($ mil.): 955

No. of shares (mil.): 68
Dividends
  Yield: 3.4%
  Payout: —
Market value ($ mil.): 2,461

Stock History
NYSE: LZ

	STOCK PRICE ($) FY Close	P/E High/Low	PER SHARE ($) Earnings	Dividends	Book Value
12/08	36.39	— —	(0.97)	1.23	22.53
12/07	54.16	17 12	4.05	1.16	28.85
12/06	50.13	33 25	1.52	1.04	25.25
12/05	43.43	16 13	2.75	1.04	23.17
12/04	36.86	22 18	1.67	1.04	22.53
Annual Growth	(0.3%)	— —	—	4.3%	0.0%

MacAndrews & Forbes

Through MacAndrews & Forbes Holdings, financier Ron Perelman is focused on cosmetics and cash. The holding company has investments in an array of public and private firms, most notably cosmetics giant Revlon and M&F Worldwide, which deals in licorice flavors and financial products. It also has an influential role in entertainment, with significant stakes in Panavision, the top provider of cameras for movies and TV shows, and Deluxe Entertainment Services Group, the largest processor of motion picture film. MacAndrews & Forbes' other holdings include biotech firm SIGA Technologies, lottery system and gaming developer Scientific Games, and AM General, maker of Humvee and HUMMER vehicles.

Perelman is intent on reversing the fortunes of Revlon, which he has controlled since 1985. The company in 2009 offered to buy out all of Revlon's minority shareholders, a move intended to slash the cosmetics maker's debt. The deal would forgive $75 million of a nearly $110 million loan from MacAndrews & Forbes and leave the holding company in control. Later in the year Revlon rolled out an exchange offer to holders of its Class A stock. The exchange offer is slated to close in September. MacAndrews &

Forbes owns about 60% of Revlon's Class A stock and all of its Class B stock.

Adding more companies to the mix, MacAndrews & Forbes acquired the data management business of Pearson for $225 million in 2008. As part of the agreement, the business is operated by MacAndrews & Forbes' Scantron testing unit. The data management business deal follows the company's 2007 acquisition of John H. Harland for nearly $2 billion, which was paired with its Clarke American unit.

Also in 2008 MacAndrews and Forbes unloaded its security services assets. It struck a deal with private equity firm Blackstone Group to take over its Allied Security business for $750 million.

HISTORY

Ron Perelman grew up working in his father's Philadelphia-based conglomerate, Belmont Industries, but he left at the age of 35 to seek his fortune in New York. In 1978 he bought 40% of jewelry store operator Cohen-Hatfield Industries. The next year Cohen-Hatfield bought a minority stake in MacAndrews & Forbes (licorice flavoring). Cohen-Hatfield acquired MacAndrews & Forbes in 1980.

In 1984 Perelman reshuffled his assets to create MacAndrews & Forbes Holdings, which acquired control of Pantry Pride, a Florida-based supermarket chain, in 1985. Pantry Pride then bought Revlon for $1.8 billion with the help of (convicted felon) Michael Milken. After Perelman acquired Revlon, he added several other cosmetics vendors, including Max Factor and Yves Saint Laurent's fragrance and cosmetic lines.

In 1988 MacAndrews & Forbes agreed to invest $315 million in five failing Texas savings and loans (S&Ls), which Perelman combined and named First Gibraltar (sold to BankAmerica, now Bank of America, in 1993). The next year MacAndrews & Forbes bought The Coleman Company, a maker of outdoor equipment.

With a growing reputation for buying struggling companies, revamping them, and then selling them at a higher price, Perelman bought Marvel Entertainment Group (Marvel Comics) in 1989 and took it public in 1991. That year he sold Revlon's Max Factor and Betrix units to Procter & Gamble for more than $1 billion.

MacAndrews & Forbes acquired 37.5% of TV infomercial producer Guthy-Renker and SCI Television's seven stations and merged them to create New World Television. That company was combined with TV syndicator Genesis Entertainment and TV production house New World Entertainment to create New World Communications Group, which Perelman took public in 1994. That year MacAndrews & Forbes and partner Gerald J. Ford bought Ford Motor's First Nationwide, the US's fifth-largest S&L at that time.

Subsidiaries Mafco Worldwide and Consolidated Cigar Holdings merged with Abex (aircraft parts) to create Mafco Consolidated Group in 1995. Following diminishing comic sales, Perelman placed Marvel in bankruptcy in 1996 and subsequently lost control of the company.

In 1997 First Nationwide bought California thrift Cal Fed Bancorp for $1.2 billion. In addition, Perelman sold New World to Rupert Murdoch's News Corp.

In 1998 Perelman orchestrated a $1.8 billion deal in which First Nationwide merged with Golden State Bancorp to form the US's third-largest thrift. Sunbeam Corp. (now American

Household) bought Perelman's stake in Coleman that year, making Perelman a major American Household shareholder. Also in 1998 MacAndrews & Forbes bought a 72% stake in Panavision (movie camera maker, later increased to 91%), invested in WeddingChannel.com (sold in 2006), and sold its 64% stake in Consolidated Cigar to French tobacco giant Seita (netting Perelman a smoking $350 million profit).

Perelman's stock in American Household was rendered worthless when the company initiated bankruptcy proceedings in February 2001. He also was sued by angry shareholders after the board of M&F Worldwide, the licorice company he controls, bought Perelman's stock in Panavision at more than five times its market value. In order to settle the litigation surrounding the purchase, in 2002 M&F agreed to return Perelman's 83% stake in Panavision to Mafco. Golden State Bancorp also left the MacAndrews fold in 2002 when it was acquired by Citigroup.

MacAndrews & Forbes Holdings acquired Allied Security, the largest independent provider of contract security services and products in the US, from Gryphon Investors in 2003.

Perelman's sale of The Coleman Company — in the late 1990s — helped the investor improve his cash flow later on. In his suit against Morgan Stanley, Perelman alleged that the investment bank withheld its knowledge of Sunbeam's accounting fraud when Perelman sold The Coleman Company to Sunbeam in 1998 for about $1.5 billion. Perelman's investment (he held 14.1 million shares of Sunbeam stock as part of the sale) later tanked as news broke of the accounting irregularities. Despite an attempt to settle the dispute with Morgan Stanley in 2003 for $20 million, Perelman took the bank to court and was awarded more than $1.5 billion in damages by a Florida jury in mid-2005.

It bought Deluxe Entertainment Services Group from The Rank Group for some $750 million in 2006. The purchase complements its majority stake in Panavision, the top provider of cameras for shooting movies and TV shows.

EXECUTIVES

Chairman and CEO: Ronald O. (Ron) Perelman, age 65
Executive Vice Chairman and Chief Administrative Officer: Barry F. Schwartz, age 59
EVP and CFO: Paul G. Savas
SEVP: David L. Kennedy, age 62, $2,990,891 total compensation
EVP Life Sciences; CEO, SIGA Technologies: Eric Rose
SVP Corporate Communications: Christine Taylor
President and CEO, Panavision: William C. (Bill) Bevins, age 63
President, Harland Financial Solutions: Raju M. Shivdasani
CEO, Scientific Games: Joseph R. (Joe) Wright Jr., age 70, $4,179,645 total compensation
CEO, Deluxe Entertainment Services Group: Cyril Drabinsky
President, Scantron: William D. (Bill) Hansen, age 49
President and CEO, TransTech Pharma: Adnan M. Mjalli, age 45
President and COO, AM General: Paul J. Kern, age 63
CEO, Harland Clarke: Charles T. (Chuck) Dawson, age 60, $2,492,336 total compensation
CEO, Revlon: Alan T. Ennis, age 39, $1,009,976 total compensation
CEO, Mafco Worldwide: Stephen Taub
CEO, Faneuil: Joseph (Joe) Ahearn

LOCATIONS

HQ: MacAndrews & Forbes Holdings Inc.
35 E. 62nd St., New York, NY 10065
Phone: 212-572-8600   **Fax:** 212-572-8400
Web: www.macandrewsandforbes.com

PRODUCTS/OPERATIONS

Selected Holdings

AM General (majority stake, multipurpose and military vehicles)
Deluxe Entertainment Services Group (film processing)
M&F Worldwide (minority stake, licorice extract and financial products)
Revlon (majority stake, cosmetics and personal care products)

COMPETITORS

Alberto-Culver	iRobot
Alticor	Johnson & Johnson
Avon	Kellwood
BAE Systems	Lockheed Martin
Body Shop	L'Oréal USA
Boeing	LVMH
Chattem	Mary Kay
Colgate-Palmolive	Procter & Gamble
The Dial Corporation	Ulta
Estée Lauder	Unilever
General Dynamics	

Macy's, Inc.

The nation's #1 department store chain has adopted the name of its most famous brand and cash cow: Macy's. Macy's, Inc., operates more than 840 stores in 45 states, the District of Columbia, Guam, and Puerto Rico under the Macy's and Bloomingdale's banners that ring up some $25 billion in annual sales. The stores sell men's, women's, and children's apparel and accessories, cosmetics, and home furnishings, among other things. The company also operates macys.com and bloomingdales.com. Macy's flagship store in Manhattan's Herald Square is the world's largest. The Macy's Thanksgiving Day Parade, started in 1924, is an annual rite. Macy's (formerly Federated Department Stores) began as a dry goods store 150 years ago.

The road to success has been a bumpy one for Macy's since its 2005 purchase of May Department Stores. The deep recession in the US and retail slump have only made matters worse. Following a difficult 2008 holiday selling season, which contributed to a 59% plunge in fourth-quarter earnings, Macy's has announced plans to close 11 underperforming stores in nine states in 2009. The retailer expects to open three new Macy's stores and one replacement store in 2009.

In April 2009 the company reorganized yet again, this time around its "My Macy's" localization initiative launched on a limited basis in 2008. (The initiative is designed to better focus on local markets, boost same-store sales, and reduce expenses.) The restructuring resulted in the elimination of some 7,000 jobs across the company as Macy's consolidated its four regional divisions (Macy's East, Macy's Central, Macy's West, and Macy's Florida).

CEO Terry Lundgren is on a mission to reinvent the American department store by making it more relevant to younger consumers, who tend to shop elsewhere. In fact, the plan for Macy's is to promote it as "America's department store." To that end, the company has hired a chief marketing officer away from Citibank to help build the Macy's brand.

To further court a younger audience as well as one that prefers instant gratification, Macy's in May 2008 made products such as iPods, Canon and Samsung digital cameras, and Bang & Olufsen headphones available through a deal with ZoomSystems. The products will be sold through e-Spot automated shops, which are akin to using an ATM, in as many as 400 Macy's stores.

Looking toward entirely new regions, Macy's is exploring opportunities for international expansion of both the Macy's and Bloomingdale's brands. To that end, the first Bloomingdale's store outside the US is slated to open in Dubai, United Arab Emirates, in early 2010. The twin apparel and accessories and home stores will anchor The Dubai Mall.

HISTORY

In 1929 Fred Lazarus, who controlled Columbus, Ohio's giant F&R Lazarus department store and the John Shillito Company (the oldest department store west of the Alleghenies; 1830), met with three other great retailers on a yacht in Long Island Sound: Walter Rothschild of Brooklyn-based Abraham & Straus; Louis Kirstein of Boston-based Filene's; and Samuel Bloomingdale, head of Manhattan's Bloomingdale's. Lazarus, Rothschild, and Kirstein agreed to merge their stores into a loose federation. Bloomingdale joined the next year.

Though Federated set up headquarters in Cincinnati in 1945, it continued to be run by powerful merchants in each city where it operated. Under Lazarus' leadership, it was among the first to see the coming growth of the Sunbelt, acquiring Foley's (Houston, 1945), Burdines (Miami, 1956), Sanger's (Dallas, 1958), Bullock's and I. Magnin (California, 1964), and Rich's (Atlanta, 1976).

Federated's growth stalled after Lazarus' son Ralph stepped down in 1981. The company faced stiffer competition from rival department store operators and chains, including May Department Stores, Nordstrom, and Dillard's. By 1989 Federated was no longer a leader, although it was still financially strong.

Years before, when Federated was leader of the department store industry, Allied Stores was #2. Allied was made up mostly of stores that were in small towns or were #2 in their market, with a few leaders (Maas Brothers, The Bon Marché, Jordan Marsh). It had a mediocre track record until Thomas Macioce took the helm in 1971. He closed unprofitable stores, downsized others, and went on an acquisition spree (Brooks Brothers, Ann Taylor).

Campeau Corporation bought Allied and Federated in 1988. Saddled with more than $8 billion in debt from the purchase, both companies declared bankruptcy in 1990. Allen Questrom became Federated's CEO, and in 1992 the companies emerged from bankruptcy as Federated Department Stores.

The next year, after being rebuffed in a bid to merge with Macy's, Federated purchased 50% of Macy's unsecured debt, setting the stage for Federated's 1994 acquisition of the respected department store.

Rowland Macy opened a store under his name in Manhattan in 1858. After Macy's death, the Strauses, a New York china merchant family, bought the department store in 1896 and expanded it across the US. In 1986 chairman Edward Finkelstein led a $3.5 billion buyout of

Macy's and took it private. Its debt load increased into the early 1990s, and Macy's entered bankruptcy proceedings in 1992.

Questrom quit (under longstanding tensions with Federated) in 1997, succeeded by president James Zimmerman.

In July 2002 Federated sold $1.2 billion in Fingerhut credit card receivables to credit card company CompuCredit and other Fingerhut assets to FAC Acquisitions, of which former Fingerhut CEO Thomas Fedders and business partner Theodore Deikel are principals.

In 2003 COO Terry J. Lundgren succeeded Zimmerman as CEO of the company. Lundgren took on the chairman title in 2004. On August 30, 2005, Federated completed its $11 billion acquisition of rival May Department Stores.

In 2006 Federated completed the first of two transactions in its sale of the May Company's credit card receivables to Citigroup, for about $753 million. The second transaction was completed in mid-July for $1 billion. In October Federated completed the sale of its 48-store Lord & Taylor department store chain to NRDC Equity Partners LLC for nearly $1.1 billion.

Adopting the name of its most famous brand, Federated changed its corporate name to Macy's, Inc., in June 2007.

EXECUTIVES

Chairman, President, and CEO: Terry J. Lundgren, age 57, $5,441,441 total compensation
CFO: Karen M. Hoguet, age 52, $2,437,915 total compensation
President and CIO, Macy's Systems and Technology: Larry A. Lewark
Chief Administrative Officer: Thomas L. (Tom) Cole, age 60, $2,319,433 total compensation
Chief Stores Officer: Ronald (Ron) Klein, age 59
Chief Marketing Officer; Chairman and CEO, macys.com: Peter R. Sachse, age 51
Chief Private Brand Officer: Timothy M. (Tim) Adams, age 54
Chief Merchandise Planning Officer: Julie Greiner, age 55
Chief Merchandising Officer: Jeffrey (Jeff) Gennette, age 47
SVP Human Resources: David W. Clark, age 52
SVP, General Counsel, and Secretary: Dennis J. Broderick, age 60
SVP Property Development: Amy Hanson, age 50
VP Corporate Communications and External Affairs: James A. (Jim) Sluzewski, age 49
Chairman, Bloomingdale's: Michael (Mike) Gould
Vice Chair, Department Store Divisions: Susan D. Kronick, age 57, $2,694,102 total compensation
Chairman and CEO, Macy's Central: Edwin J. (Ed) Holman, age 62
Vice Chair, Merchandising, Private Brand and Product Development; Chairman and CEO, Macy's Merchandising Group (MMG): Janet E. Grove, age 58, $2,283,700 total compensation
Vice Chairman and Director Stores, Macy's West: Rudolph J. Borneo, age 68
Vice Chair, Legal, Human Resources, Internal Audit and External Affairs: Thomas G. Cody, age 67
Auditors: KPMG LLP

LOCATIONS

HQ: Macy's, Inc.
7 W. 7th St., Cincinnati, OH 45202
Phone: 513-579-7000   Fax: 513-579-7555
Web: www.federated-fds.com

2009 Stores

	No.
Mid-Atlantic	107
North	68
Northeast	118
Northwest	139
Southeast	119
Southwest	129
Midwest	105
South Central	62
Total	**847**

PRODUCTS/OPERATIONS

2009 Sales

	% of total
Women's accessories, intimate apparel, shoes & cosmetics	36
Women's apparel	27
Men's & children's	22
Home & miscellaneous	15
Total	**100**

2009 Stores

	No.
Macy's	807
Bloomingdale's	40
Total	**847**

Store Chains

Bloomingdale's
Macy's

Other Selected Operations

bloomingdales.com
macys.com

Selected Private Labels

Alfani (women's and men's apparel)
American Rag Cie. (casual sportswear for juniors and
 young men)
The Cellar (housewares and related home merchandise)
Charter Club (women's and men's apparel, home
 furnishings)
First Impressions (infant and layette apparel)
Greendog (children's apparel)
Hotel Collection (sheets, towels, tabletop, and barware)
I.N.C (casual and career fashions for men and women)
ML/Material London (men's sportswear, suits, shoes)
Style & Co. (sportswear & casual apparel)
Tasso Elba (menswear)
Tools of the Trade (cookware, bakeware, cutlery, and
 kitchen gadgets)

COMPETITORS

AnnTaylor
Bed Bath & Beyond
Belk
Bon-Ton Stores
Brown Shoe
Burlington Coat Factory
Dillard's
Eddie Bauer Holdings
Foot Locker
The Gap
J. C. Penney
J. Crew
Jos. A. Bank
Kohl's
Lands' End
Limited Brands
Lord & Taylor
Men's Wearhouse
Neiman Marcus
Nine West
Nordstrom
Polo Ralph Lauren
Saks
Sears
Stage Stores
Talbots
Target
TJX Companies
Wal-Mart
Zale

HISTORICAL FINANCIALS

Company Type: Public

Income Statement

FYE: Saturday nearest January 31

	REVENUE ($ mil.)	NET INCOME ($ mil.)	NET PROFIT MARGIN	EMPLOYEES
1/09	24,892.0	(4,803.0)	—	167,000
1/08	26,313.0	893.0	3.4%	182,000
1/07	26,970.0	995.0	3.7%	188,000
1/06	22,390.0	1,406.0	6.3%	232,000
1/05	15,630.0	689.0	4.4%	112,000
Annual Growth	**12.3%**	**—**	**—**	**10.5%**

2009 Year-End Financials

Debt ratio: 188.0%
Return on equity: —
Cash ($ mil.): 1,306
Current ratio: 1.31
Long-term debt ($ mil.): 8,733
No. of shares (mil.): 421
Dividends
 Yield: 5.9%
 Payout: —
Market value ($ mil.): 3,764

Stock History

NYSE: M

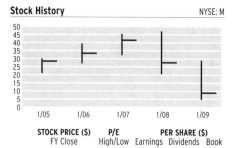

	STOCK PRICE ($) FY Close	P/E High/Low		PER SHARE ($) Earnings	Dividends	Book Value
1/09	8.95	—	—	(11.40)	0.53	11.05
1/08	27.62	24	11	1.97	0.52	23.56
1/07	41.49	25	18	1.81	0.51	29.14
1/06	33.31	12	8	3.23	0.38	32.14
1/05	28.40	15	11	1.93	0.26	14.66
Annual Growth	**(25.1%)**	**—**	**—**	**—**	**19.5%**	**(6.8%)**

Magellan Health Services

Magellan Health Services has charted its course to become one of the largest managed behavioral health care companies in the nation. The company manages mental health plan, employee assistance, and work/life programs through its nationwide third-party provider network that consists of about 70,000 behavioral health professionals. Magellan also provides specialty pharmaceutical management and radiology benefits management. Overall the company serves some 60 million members through contracts with federal and local government agencies, insurance companies, and employers. Its services include administration, billing, claims handling, technology programs, and coordination of care.

Magellan's managed care operations for public sector programs make up more than half of the company's sales. These programs generally provide behavioral health benefits to Medicaid recipients through contracts with state and local authorities.

The firm is expanding by developing new products and purchasing other companies. Through acquisitions in 2006 Magellan entered two new service categories, radiology benefits management and specialty pharmaceutical management, which have grown to account for about 20% of the company's sales. These services are provided through subsidiaries National Imaging Associates (NIA), which manages benefits for diagnostic imaging facilities, and ICORE Healthcare, which manages coverage of specialty drugs to treat cancer and other serious diseases.

In addition to growing its existing operations, the company plans to diversify into new specialty areas to provide a one-stop shopping point for outsourced managed care services. To that end, Magellan agreed in 2009 to pay $110 million to acquire First Health Services from Coventry Health Care. The acquisition marked Magellan's entry into the pharmacy benefits management market, as well as expanded its breadth of Medicaid offerings.

HISTORY

William Fickling, once a star basketball player at Auburn University, started his career in his father's real estate office in Georgia. In 1969 Fickling founded Charter Medical as a holding company for the family's six nursing homes and one hospital. The company went public in 1971 as an owner/manager of general acute care hospitals. By the mid-1980s it had focused on psychiatric facilities and was adding addiction treatment centers to its portfolio. Charter had 63 psychiatric and 13 acute care hospitals by 1987, when Fickling engineered a $1.4 billion LBO, largely funded by the company's employee stock ownership plan (ESOP), which ended up owning 68% of the company, with Fickling owning the rest.

By 1989 Charter was in trouble. Not only was it dogged by Medicare and Medicaid fraud probes, but Fickling was accused of cheating the ESOP, which had purchased another 13% of the company from him at allegedly inflated prices. (A month after that sale, Fickling announced accounting errors that cut operating income by $26 million and the ESOP's stake plummeted.) In 1992 the Medicare fraud charges were settled for $1.9 million; a suit related to the ESOP stock sale was settled for $82 million.

But Charter's problems ran deeper — the industry itself was in flux. New treatments and managed care restrictions reduced the average stay for psychiatric patients from 26 days to 20 by 1991. Stories of abuses in the psychiatric industry surfaced, and payers were demanding fewer hospitalizations and more outpatient care. Undaunted, but deeply in debt, Charter continued to build inpatient facilities, bringing losses.

The company went into Chapter 11 in 1991, emerging in 1992 with a plan to focus on behavioral health care; it also went public again. The next year Fickling left Charter and was eventually replaced by E. Mac Crawford. As part of its plan, Charter sold its general hospitals and bought 40 psychiatric hospitals from National Medical Enterprises (now Tenet Healthcare) in 1994; it also began offering outpatient and home care services. That year Charter relocated to Atlanta.

As part of its reorganization, Charter in 1995 bought Magellan Health Services and took that name. It also bought 51% of Green Spring Health Services, a managed care company specializing in mental health and substance abuse. (It bought the rest in 1998.)

Reorganization costs and corporate cutbacks on mental health benefits brought losses until 1996, when it posted its only profit of the decade amid the increasing privatization of government psychiatric care. Seeing fast growth in managed care, Magellan sold its psychiatric hospitals to Crescent Operating in 1997, using the money to buy two more managed behavioral care companies. Magellan and Crescent created joint venture Charter Behavioral Health Systems (CBHS) to run the psychiatric facilities under the Charter name.

In 1998 Crawford was succeeded by Henry Harbin, a founder of Green Spring. In 1999 Magellan sold its European operations, and relocated to Columbia, Maryland. With CBHS flailing, Magellan gave Crescent all but 10% of the hospital firm, which filed for bankruptcy in 2000. While making plans to sell its specialty managed health care segment, Magellan also agreed to sell human services segment National Mentor, which offered at-home care for sufferers of chronic disorders, in a management buyout. The National Mentor sale closed in 2001, when Magellan also began its exit from its stake in CBHS. The company then became engaged in the managed behavioral health care business only.

In 2003, weak earnings and high debt prompted Magellan to file for Chapter 11 bankruptcy. In January 2004, Magellan emerged from Chapter 11 bankruptcy.

The company expanded through the acquisition of National Imaging Associates (NIA), a provider of radiology benefits management services, in 2006. Specialty pharmaceutical management firm ICORE Healthcare was also added to the fold that year.

EXECUTIVES

Chairman and CEO: René Lerer, age 53, $5,151,381 total compensation
President: Karen S. Rohan, age 46
EVP and CFO: Jonathan N. (Jon) Rubin, age 46, $294,828 total compensation
Chief Human Resources Officer: Caskie Lewis-Clapper, $1,111,999 total compensation
Chief Medical Officer: Anthony M. (Tony) Kotin, age 55
SVP Public Relations: Erin S. Somers
SVP Public Sector Behavioral Health: Anne McCabe
CEO, National Imaging Associates: Tina M. Blasi, age 51
President and CEO, ICORE: Alan Lotvin, age 47
General Counsel: Daniel N. Gregoire, age 53, $1,059,199 total compensation
Auditors: Ernst & Young LLP

LOCATIONS

HQ: Magellan Health Services, Inc.
55 Nod Rd., Avon, CT 06001
Phone: 860-507-1900   **Fax:** 860-507-1990
Web: www.magellanhealth.com

PRODUCTS/OPERATIONS

2008 Sales

	$ mil.	% of total
Public sector	1,451.9	55
Commercial	649.7	25
Radiology benefits management	295.3	11
Specialty pharmaceutical management	228.5	9
Total	**2,625.4**	**100**

COMPETITORS

American Imaging Management
APS Healthcare
CareCore
Caremark Pharmacy Services
CIGNA Behavioral Health
Comprehensive Care
ComPsych
Express Scripts
FHC Health Systems
First Health Group
Horizon Health
HSG Health Systems
Medco Health
Mental Health Network
Psychiatric Solutions
Schaller Anderson Inc
UBH
US Oncology

HISTORICAL FINANCIALS

Company Type: Public

Income Statement

FYE: December 31

	REVENUE ($ mil.)	NET INCOME ($ mil.)	NET PROFIT MARGIN	EMPLOYEES
12/08	2,625.4	86.2	3.3%	5,200
12/07	2,156.0	94.2	4.4%	5,600
12/06	1,690.3	86.3	5.1%	3,900
12/05	1,808.0	130.6	7.2%	3,900
12/04	1,795.4	88.4	4.9%	4,300
Annual Growth	**10.0%**	**(0.6%)**	**—**	**4.9%**

2008 Year-End Financials

Debt ratio: 0.0%
Return on equity: 9.5%
Cash ($ mil.): 212
Current ratio: 2.20
Long-term debt ($ mil.): 0
No. of shares (mil.): 35
Dividends
 Yield: 0.0%
 Payout: —
Market value ($ mil.): 1,382

Stock History

NASDAQ (GS): MGLN

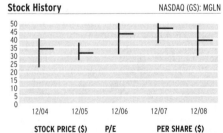

	STOCK PRICE ($) FY Close	P/E High/Low	PER SHARE ($) Earnings	Dividends	Book Value
12/08	39.16	22 14	2.16	0.00	25.73
12/07	46.63	21 16	2.36	0.00	25.73
12/06	43.22	22 14	2.23	0.00	21.63
12/05	31.45	11 8	3.46	0.00	17.94
12/04	34.16	16 10	2.43	0.00	14.08
Annual Growth	**3.5%**	**— —**	**(2.9%)**	**—**	**16.3%**

Manitowoc Company

The Manitowoc Company makes foodservice equipment, such as ice-making, beverage-dispensing, and refrigerating products, as well as cranes and related products. Its ice-making and beverage-dispensing machines serve the restaurant, hospitality, and convenience store markets. Manitowoc sells its boom cranes, tower cranes, telescopic cranes, and related equipment to companies in the construction and mining industries. The company, which began at the turn of the 20th century as a shipbuilder, sold its shipbuilding and ship repair business to Fincantieri Cantieri Navali Italiani in 2008 for about $120 million in cash.

Having sold its marine division, Manitowoc can now focus on building its crane and foodservice businesses, as well as use transaction proceeds to retire corporate debt.

The company tends to be acquisitive. In 2008 Manitowoc embarked on its largest acquisition by purchasing rival Enodis plc for $2.7 billion. A bidding war ensued between Manitowoc and Illinois Tool Works (ITW), but Manitowoc topped ITW's offer by about 5% and won the auction. The acquisition of Enodis looked to allow Manitowoc to equip entire commercial kitchens, and the company believes that synergies created by combining the two businesses will result in $60 million in annual savings by 2010.

As part of the Enodis acquisition, Manitowoc agreed with the European Commission and the US Department of Justice to divest most of its ice machine business to satisfy anti-competition concerns. (In 2009 the company unloaded the Enodis ice machine business to an affiliate of Warburg Pincus Private Equity for $160 million. The transaction included the Scotsman, Ice-O-Matic, Simag, Barline, and other ice machine businesses).

Also in 2008 the company formed a 50% joint venture with China-based TaiAn Dongyue Heavy Machinery. The purpose of the venture is to build mobile and truck-mounted hydraulic cranes. Manitowoc hopes the deal will give it a foothold in the rapidly growing Chinese construction equipment market. If successful, Manitowoc plans to form similar partnerships in other Chinese provinces, starting with major port cities.

In 2007 it picked up the Carrydeck line of mobile industrial cranes from privately held Marine Travelift. The move enhanced Manitowoc's position in industrial cranes with the addition of six models. Later in 2007 the company bolstered its international presence with the purchase of India's Shirke Construction Equipments, a maker of tower cranes.

Manitowoc Crane Group has two of its largest manufacturing facilities in the US, and other operations and facilities in 27 countries worldwide.

Foodservice equipment now includes primary cooking, warming, and warewashing equipment, as well as food preparation equipment and kitchen utensils and tools. The Manitowoc Education and Technology Center in Florida offers a test kitchen for hands-on testing of new products and kitchen design services. It also provides training for its customers, marketing representatives, service providers, industry consultants, dealers, and distributors.

HISTORY

Manitowoc began in 1902 when naval architect Charles West and shipbuilder Elias Gunnell bought a shipyard. The company grew during WWI, but the government canceled its contracts at war's end. After feuding with Gunnell, West bought Manitowoc (he would run it until his death in 1957) and diversified into industrial equipment. Crane manufacturing helped Manitowoc survive the Depression. During WWII Manitowoc built submarines and landing craft. After the war the company branched out into freezers and dry-cleaning machines.

A recession and oil-patch bust in the 1980s caused Manitowoc's sales to plummet. By the decade's end, aging product lines had stalled earnings growth. CEO Fred Butler ended the company's shipbuilding operations and focused it on repairing vessels instead. It also modernized its cranes and broadened its product line through acquisitions in 1990. From 1994 to 1998 the company grew six-fold, largely through acquisitions.

In 1998 Manitowoc improved earnings by buying boom truck and forklift maker Powerscreen USC and by expanding into Europe with a 50% stake in Italy-based ice-machine maker F.A.G. That year Butler retired and Terry Growcock, president of subsidiary Manitowoc Ice, became CEO.

Manitowoc bought Purchasing Support Group, a beverage equipment distributor with broad US regional reach, in 1999. The next year Manitowoc boosted its cranes and related equipment business by acquiring Pioneer Holdings (hydraulic boom trucks). It also acquired Harford Duracool, a maker of walk-in refrigerators and freezers in the eastern US, and Marinette Marine, a Great Lakes shipyard (which added a significant shipbuilding business to its marine repair operations).

In 2001 the company bought Legris Industries' Potain tower crane unit. Manitowoc then added mobile cranes to its crane business in 2002 by acquiring Grove Worldwide for about $270 million. In 2002 Terry Growcock, the company's CEO, was also named as chairman, a post that had been vacant for 10 years.

In early 2003 Manitowoc sold its Manitowoc Boom Trucks unit to Quantum Heavy Equipment, LLC. The company sold this unit in order to satisfy an order set by the Justice Department to complete the acquisition of Grove Worldwide.

In 2004 the company sold its Delta Manlift subsidiary to JLG Industries, exiting the aerial platform business. The following year it sold its Diversified Refrigeration, Inc. (DRI) subsidiary to a subsidiary of GE.

In 2006 Manitowoc attempted to make a $1.8 billion bid for the UK commercial foodservice concern Enodis; the offer was rebuffed. Enodis then warmed to the idea after Manitowoc said informally that any future bid would be higher. Enodis granted Manitowoc due-diligence access to its books, but after a period of looking more closely at each others' operations, the two companies walked away from discussions. In 2008 Illinois Tool Works (ITW) then made an offer to buy Enodis for about $2 billion in cash, an offer initially accepted by the Enodis board. Manitowoc answered by bumping up its bid, topping the ITW offer by about 5% and valuing Enodis at around $2.1 billion. The Enodis board recommended the higher Manitowoc offer to shareholders.

EXECUTIVES

Chairman, President, and CEO: Glen E. Tellock, age 48, $4,751,527 total compensation
SVP, CFO, and Treasurer: Carl J. Laurino, age 47, $4,631,329 total compensation
SVP Human Resources and Administration: Thomas G. Musial, age 57, $2,048,144 total compensation
SVP, Secretary, and General Counsel: Maurice D. Jones, age 49, $1,688,789 total compensation
SVP; President, Foodservice Segment: Mike Kachmer, age 50
SVP; President, Manitowoc Crane Group: Eric Etchart
VP Finance and Treasurer: Dean J. Nolden, age 40
VP Corporate Development: Mary Ellen Bowers, age 52
VP Global Procurement: Robert E. Ward
VP Business Development: Paul A. Boggs
VP Sales, North America: David (Dave) Hull
Director Investor Relations and Corporate Communications: Steven C. Khail
Auditors: PricewaterhouseCoopers LLP

LOCATIONS

HQ: The Manitowoc Company, Inc.
2400 S. 44th St., Manitowoc, WI 54221
Phone: 920-684-4410   **Fax:** 920-652-9778
Web: www.manitowoc.com

2008 Sales

	$ mil.	% of total
North America		
US	1,896.6	42
Other countries	127.7	3
Europe	1,444.2	32
Asia	395.0	9
Middle East	314.0	7
Central & South America	117.4	3
Australia	111.8	2
Africa	82.8	2
South Pacific & Caribbean	13.5	—
Total	**4,503.0**	**100**

PRODUCTS/OPERATIONS

2008 Sales

	$ mil.	% of total
Cranes & Related Products	3,882.9	86
Foodservice Equipment	620.1	14
Total	**4,503.0**	**100**

Selected Brands

Cranes & Related Products

Crane CARE	National
Dongyue	Potain
Grove	Shuttlelift
Manitowoc	

Foodservice Equipment

Cleveland	Kysor Panel Systems
Convotherm	Kysor/Warren
Delfield	Lincoln
Frymaster	Manitowoc
Garland	Merrychef
Jackson	Multiplex
Kolpak	SerVend

COMPETITORS

Aga Rangemaster	Hitachi
Altec Industries	Ingersoll-Rand
American Panel	Instant UpRight
Carrier	Kobelco
Caterpillar	Komatsu
CLARK Material Handling	Lancer
Deere-Hitachi	Scotsman Group
Delfield	Terex
Furukawa	Vulcan-Hart

HISTORICAL FINANCIALS

Company Type: Public

Income Statement

FYE: December 31

	REVENUE ($ mil.)	NET INCOME ($ mil.)	NET PROFIT MARGIN	EMPLOYEES
12/08	4,503.0	(10.7)	—	18,400
12/07	4,005.0	336.7	8.4%	10,500
12/06	2,933.3	166.2	5.7%	9,500
12/05	2,254.1	65.8	2.9%	8,000
12/04	1,964.1	39.1	2.0%	7,600
Annual Growth	**23.1%**	**—**	**—**	**24.7%**

2008 Year-End Financials

Debt ratio: 190.3%
Return on equity: —
Cash ($ mil.): 173
Current ratio: 1.32
Long-term debt ($ mil.): 2,473

No. of shares (mil.): 131
Dividends
  Yield: 0.9%
  Payout: —
Market value ($ mil.): 1,131

Stock History

NYSE: MTW

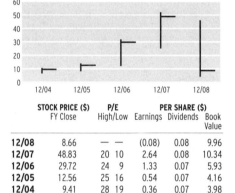

	STOCK PRICE ($) FY Close	P/E High/Low		PER SHARE ($) Earnings	Dividends	Book Value
12/08	8.66	—	—	(0.08)	0.08	9.96
12/07	48.83	20	10	2.64	0.08	10.34
12/06	29.72	24	9	1.33	0.07	5.93
12/05	12.56	25	16	0.54	0.07	4.16
12/04	9.41	28	19	0.36	0.07	3.98
Annual Growth	**(2.1%)**	**—**	**—**	**—**	**3.4%**	**25.8%**

Manpower Inc.

Millions of men (and women) have helped power this firm to the upper echelon of the staffing industry. Manpower is one of the world's largest providers of temporary employees (behind Adecco and Randstad), placing about 4 million people in office, industrial, and professional positions every year. It has some 4,400 owned or franchised offices in 80 countries and territories (mainly France, Italy, the UK, and the US). The company also provides employee testing, training, and other contract services. Its Global Learning Centers give employees access to training materials over the Internet.

The staffing giant offers its products and services across five primary brands: Manpower, Manpower Professional, Elan, Jefferson Wells, and Right Management. The Jefferson Wells segment provides consulting and staffing services to the financial services industry, while its Manpower UK branch operates through a network of about 115 offices. Another segment, Brook Street Bureau, targets the UK as well, operating across some 115 branch offices. Elan is an IT staffing company in 16 countries, the largest being in the UK.

Manpower, which generates about 75% of its sales overseas, supplies temporary employees to businesses on an as-needed basis. The company generates most of its sales from office and light-industrial placements, but its professional placement division is the fastest-growing area.

In 2007 Manpower obtained a temporary staffing business license in China, the first global staffing corporation to be offered such an opportunity. (The company has provided permanent staffing in China for over a decade.) Two years later, it became the first company to obtain a permanent staffing license in Vietnam, making it the 14th Asian country where Manpower has operations. Emerging market revenue grew by almost 50% in 2008.

Manpower made four acquisitions in 2008 before the US credit crisis hit in the later part of the year. In January it bought professional recruitment provider Clarendon Parker Middle East, which had been its partner in that region. The deal gave Manpower its own operations in Bahrain, Kuwait, Qatar, Saudi Arabia and the United Arab Emirates. In March it bought Dutch professional recruitment provider Vitae and Los-Angeles based business process outsourcer CRI, Inc. By August, Jefferson Wells acquired The Gelber Organization, a state and local tax consulting firm.

HISTORY

Milwaukee lawyers Elmer Winter and Aaron Scheinfeld founded Manpower in 1948. It originally concentrated on supplying temporary help to industry during the first few years of the post-war boom. In the next few years, the company expanded, and in 1956 it began franchising. During the 1960s Manpower opened franchises in Europe, Asia, and South America. Unlike many of its competitors, however, it continued to emphasize blue-collar placements.

Manpower embarked on a series of acquisitions in the 1970s and began to shift its emphasis from industrial to clerical placements. It was Mitchell Fromstein, Manpower's advertising account executive in the 1960s, who orchestrated the company's growth into a powerhouse. Fromstein joined the board in 1971 and became president and CEO in 1976.

Mid-decade, with Scheinfeld deceased and Winter eager to sell, the Parker Pen Company came along. Parker Pen, also based in Wisconsin, was trying to re-energize its fading fortunes after the arrival of the disposable pen. Parker Pen bought Manpower in 1976, sold the pen business 10 years later, and became Manpower Inc. Fromstein continued as president and CEO, with a 20% interest in the company.

In the late 1970s Manpower entered the computer age, instituting a computer training program for its temporary employees. The company grew as the character of employment in the US changed from career-long employment with one company to a series of shorter-term jobs with many employers. In addition to providing short-term workers, Manpower began offering hiring and training services for permanent employees, thus saving companies in-house recruitment and training costs.

Blue Arrow, a temporary-employment agency based in the UK, acquired the firm in 1987. The combined companies operated as Manpower, and almost immediately tensions arose between Fromstein and his new boss, Antony Berry, who accused Fromstein of obstructing efforts to unite the two companies. Fromstein was fired in 1988.

Manpower's worldwide franchisees revolted against Berry, and the UK began an investigation of how the acquisition of Manpower was financed — a $1.5 billion stock sale by UK bank NatWest (now Royal Bank of Scotland Group). Berry was ousted in 1989, and Fromstein regained control. A push by US interests changed the US composition of the company's ownership during that year from just 9% in January to over 60% by the end of the year. This gave Fromstein the support he needed to move Manpower back to Wisconsin in 1991.

Fromstein then worked to disentangle the two companies by selling off all Blue Arrow holdings not related to employment. During the mid-1990s the company opened hundreds of new offices in the US and abroad. It spent more than $15 million in 1995 to upgrade its computerized worker-to-job matching system. An alliance with Drake Beam Morin the following year gave the company access to more than 200,000 new clients.

Manpower began two pilot programs in 1997 — one to place inner-city welfare recipients in the workforce, and one offering free technology-related training to company applicants via the Internet. In 1998 the company acquired Australia's Kirby Contract Labour, which added 15 branches to the 55 already operating in Australia and New Zealand. The following year Fromstein retired after leading Manpower for 23 years. Jeffrey Joerres took over as CEO (and added chairman to his title in 2001).

Later in 1999, Manpower changed the name of its Manpower Technical division to Manpower Professional to better indicate the variety of disciplines it supported and compete in an increasingly tight market for professional workers. In 2001 the company bought financial services provider Jefferson Wells International. Manpower started a program that provides internships for high school students in 2002. In 2003 the company launched its Business Resource Center, which offers online human resources information for small and midsized businesses. Manpower acquired Right Management in 2004.

EXECUTIVES

Chairman, President, and CEO: Jeffrey A. (Jeff) Joerres, age 49, $5,743,775 total compensation
EVP and CFO: Michael J. (Mike) Van Handel, age 49, $1,959,560 total compensation
VP and Global Chief Information Officer: Denis Edwards
EVP Global Strategy and Talent: Mara E. Swan, age 49
EVP; President, Asia-Pacific and Middle East Operations: Darryl E. Green, age 48, $1,276,323 total compensation
EVP; CEO, Right Management Consultants and Jefferson Wells International: Owen J. Sullivan, age 51, $1,529,034 total compensation
EVP; President, Europe, Middle East, and Africa: Barbara J. Beck, age 48
EVP; President, The Americas: Jonas Prising, age 43, $1,282,352 total compensation
EVP; President, France: Françoise Gri, age 51, $798,043 total compensation
SVP Workforce Strategy: Tammy Johns
SVP and President Corporate and Government Affairs: David Arkless
SVP Global Marketing: Emma van Rooyen
SVP, General Counsel, and Secretary: Kenneth C. Hunt, age 59

VP and General Manager, Manpower North America: Mike Steinmetz
VP of Work Solutions, Manpower North America: Melanie Holmes
President and COO, Jefferson Wells: Michael E. (Mike) Touhey
Managing Director Manpower Professional: Jason Kobrin
CEO, Manpower Norway: Maalfrid Brath
Director Global Communications: Tracy Shilobrit
Auditors: Deloitte & Touche LLP

LOCATIONS

HQ: Manpower Inc.
  100 Manpower Place, Milwaukee, WI 53212
Phone: 414-961-1000   **Fax:** 414-906-7985
Web: www.manpower.com

PRODUCTS/OPERATIONS

2008 Sales

	$ mil.	% of total
France	6,935.6	32
Italy	1,519.5	7
Other Europe, Middle East & Africa	7,437.7	35
US	1,945.4	9
Right Management	449.7	2
Jefferson Wells	291.0	1
Other operations	2,973.9	14
Total	**21,552.8**	**100**

Selected Services

Staffing
Industrial trades
Manpower Professional
  Engineering
  Finance
  Information technology
  Telecommunications
Office and clerical

Other Services

Brook Street (office and light industrial staffing in the UK)
Elan Group (IT staffing in UK)
Global Learning Center (online employee testing and training)
Jefferson Wells (financial services)
Right Management Consultants (career consulting)

COMPETITORS

Adecco	Randstad Holding
Kelly Services	Robert Half
Korn/Ferry	Spherion
Michael Page	TrueBlue
MPS	Volt Information

HISTORICAL FINANCIALS

Company Type: Public

Income Statement

FYE: December 31

	REVENUE ($ mil.)	NET INCOME ($ mil.)	NET PROFIT MARGIN	EMPLOYEES
12/08	21,552.8	218.9	1.0%	4,033,000
12/07	20,500.3	484.7	2.4%	5,033,000
12/06	17,562.5	398.0	2.3%	4,030,000
12/05	16,080.4	260.1	1.6%	4,027,000
12/04	14,930.0	245.7	1.6%	2,027,100
Annual Growth	9.6%	(2.8%)	—	18.8%

2008 Year-End Financials

Debt ratio: 33.7%
Return on equity: 8.5%
Cash ($ mil.): 874
Current ratio: 1.61
Long-term debt ($ mil.): 837
No. of shares (mil.): 78
Dividends
  Yield: 2.2%
  Payout: 26.9%
Market value ($ mil.): 2,664

Stock History

NYSE: MAN

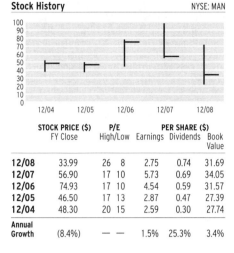

	STOCK PRICE ($) FY Close	P/E High/Low		PER SHARE ($) Earnings	Dividends	Book Value
12/08	33.99	26	8	2.75	0.74	31.69
12/07	56.90	17	10	5.73	0.69	34.05
12/06	74.93	17	10	4.54	0.59	31.57
12/05	46.50	17	13	2.87	0.47	27.39
12/04	48.30	20	15	2.59	0.30	27.74
Annual Growth	(8.4%)	—	—	1.5%	25.3%	3.4%

Marathon Oil

In the long-running competition for profits in the oil and gas industry, Marathon Oil is keeping up a steady pace. Through its Marathon Oil Company subsidiary, the company explores for and produces oil and gas primarily in Angola, Canada, Equatorial Guinea, Libya, Norway, Indonesia, the UK, and the US. It has net proved reserves of 1.2 billion barrels of oil equivalent and 299 million barrels of bitumen (oil sands). Marathon Oil's Marathon Petroleum operates seven refineries with a total capacity of 1 million barrels of crude oil a day. Marathon Petroleum supplies about 4,600 Marathon-branded US retail gas outlets. Marathon Oil also services 1,620 Speedway SuperAmerica gas stations.

As a way to expand its hydrocarbon asset base the company is investing heavily in nonconventional exploration and production areas. In 2006, as part of a five-year $1.5 billion investment, the company announced plans to drill as many as 225 new wells in western North Dakota in the Bakken Oil Formation (tight shale layers) over a five-year period. The following year Marathon Oil expanded into the Canadian oil sands market through the acquisition of Western Oil Sands for about $5.8 billion.

In a move to focus on its core businesses, in 2008 the company announced it would sell $2 billion-$4 billion in non-core assets. In 2009 Marathon Oil sold its 50% stake in truck stop chain Pilot Travel Centers LLC to the joint venture's partner, Pilot Corp., for $700 million. It also sold its Irish exploration and production subsidiary for $180 million. In 2009 the company agreed to sell 20% of its 30% stake in its Angola-based oil and gas operations to CNOOC and Sinopec in order to raise about $1.3 billion.

In late 2008 Marathon Oil began looking at splitting the company's two main businesses into separate public entities. Marathon Oil's Houston operations would retain the exploration, oil-sands mining, and natural gas businesses, while its Findlay, Ohio, operations would keep the marketing, refining, pipeline, and transportation functions.

HISTORY

Marathon Oil was founded in 1887 in Lima, Ohio, as The Ohio Oil Company by 14 independent oil producers to compete with Standard Oil. Within two years Ohio Oil was the largest producer in the state. This success did not go unnoticed by Standard Oil, which proceeded to buy Ohio Oil in 1889. In 1905 the company moved to Findlay, Ohio, where it remained until it relocated to Houston in 1990.

When the US Supreme Court broke up Standard Oil in 1911, Ohio Oil became independent once again and expanded its exploration activities to Kansas, Louisiana, Texas, and Wyoming.

In a 1924 attempt to drill three wells west of the Pecos River in Texas, Ohio Oil mistakenly drilled three dry holes to the east. The company was on the verge of abandoning the project until a geologist reported the error. Ohio Oil drilled in the right area and the wells flowed. That year the company bought Lincoln Oil Refining — its first venture outside crude oil production.

Ohio Oil continued its expansion into refining and marketing operations in 1927. Following WWII the company began international exploration. Through Conorada Petroleum (later Oasis), a partnership with Continental Oil (later Conoco and then ConocoPhillips) and Amerada Hess, the company explored in Africa and South and Central America. Conorada's biggest overseas deal came in 1955, when it acquired concessions on more than 60 million acres in Libya.

In 1962 the company acquired Plymouth Oil and changed its name to Marathon Oil Company; it had been using the Marathon name in its marketing activities since the late 1930s. Marathon added a 200,000-barrel-a-day refinery in Louisiana to its operations in 1976 when it acquired ECOL Ltd.

After a battle with Mobil, U.S. Steel acquired Marathon in 1982 for $6.5 billion. U.S. Steel changed its name to USX in 1986 and acquired Texas Oil & Gas. That year the US government introduced economic sanctions against Libya, putting Marathon's Libyan holdings in suspension.

USX consolidated Texas Oil and Marathon in 1990. After a protracted struggle with corporate raider Carl Icahn, USX split Marathon and U.S. Steel into two separate stock classes in 1991. A third offering, USX-Delhi Group (the pipeline operator division), followed the next year. (Koch Industries bought USX-Delhi in 1997.)

A consortium led by USX-Marathon signed an agreement with the Russian government in 1994 to develop oil and gas fields off Sakhalin Island (although USX-Marathon sold its stake in the project in 2000). In 1996 Marathon formed a venture, ElectroGen International, with East Coast utility DQE to develop power generation projects in the Asia/Pacific region.

In 1998 Marathon and Ashland merged their refining and retail operations, creating Marathon Ashland Petroleum (MAP), with Marathon owning 62%. That year Marathon, in a deal that boosted its reserves by 18%, acquired Calgary-based Tarragon Oil and Gas.

As part of a restructuring drive, in 1999 MAP sold its crude oil gathering business, Scurlock Permian, to Plains All American Pipeline. With oil prices rebounding, Marathon ramped up its oil exploration in 2000, buying more deepwater leases in the Gulf of Mexico and acquiring an interest in an oil and gas play offshore the Republic of Congo.

The company bought Pennaco Energy, a Colorado-based producer of coalbed methane gas, for about $500 million in 2001, and it agreed to buy CMS Energy's Equatorial Guinea

(West Africa) oil and gas assets in a $993 million deal that was completed in 2002. At the end of 2001, USX spun off U.S. Steel and changed the name of the remaining company to Marathon Oil Corporation. In 2002 Marathon acquired Globex Energy, a privately held exploration and production company with assets in West Africa, for $155 million.

In 2005 Ashland sold its 38% stake in Marathon Ashland to Marathon Oil for about $3.7 billion.

In addition to acquiring MAP, Marathon Oil also obtained Ashland's maleic anhydride business, a share of its Valvoline Instant Oil Change business in Michigan and Ohio, and other assets.

In 2006 the company sold its oil and gas assets in the Khanty-Mansiysk autonomous region of western Siberia to LUKOIL for $787 million. Also that year Marathon Oil announced a $3.2 billion plan to expand the crude oil refining capacity of its refinery in Garyville, Louisiana.

EXECUTIVES

Chairman: Thomas J. Usher, age 66
President, CEO, and Director: Clarence P. Cazalot Jr., age 58, $3,975,950 total compensation
EVP and CFO: Janet F. Clark, age 54, $3,125,897 total compensation
CIO: Thomas K. Sneed
EVP Down Stream: Gary R. Heminger, age 55, $5,343,480 total compensation
EVP Upstream: David E. (Dave) Roberts Jr., age 48, $3,604,426 total compensation
SVP Marketing Marathon Pipe Line LLC: Mary Ellen Peters
SVP Corporate Affairs: Jerry Howard, age 60
SVP Exploration: Annell R. Bay
VP Corporate Compliance and Ethics: Daniel J. Sullenbarger, age 53
VP, General Counsel, and Secretary: William F. (Bill) Schwind Jr., age 64
VP Human Resources: Eileen M. Campbell, age 47
VP Finance and Treasurer: Paul C. Reinbolt, age 53
VP Emerging Technology: Linda A. Capuano
VP Accounting and Controller: Michael K. Stewart, age 51
VP Investor Relations and Public Affairs: Howard J. Thill, age 50
VP Strategic Planning and Portfolio Management: Robert E. Estill
VP Natural Gas and Crude Oil Sales: Patrick J. Kuntz
VP and General Counsel: Sylvia J. Kerrigan, age 44
Auditors: PricewaterhouseCoopers LLP

LOCATIONS

HQ: Marathon Oil Corporation
   5555 San Felipe Rd., Houston, TX 77056
Phone: 713-629-6600   **Fax:** 713-296-2952
Web: www.marathon.com

2008 Sales

	$ mil.	% of total
US	69,034	96
Other countries	8,159	4
Adjustments	(5,065)	—
Total	**72,128**	**100**

PRODUCTS/OPERATIONS

2008 Sales

	$ mil.	% of total
Refining, marketing & transportation	64,272	83
Exploration & production	11,906	16
Oil sands mining	922	1
Integrated gas	93	—
Adjustments	(5,065)	—
Total	**72,128**	**100**

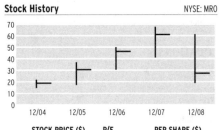
Markel Corporation

Have you ever thought about who insures the manicurist or an antique motorcycle? Markel Corporation takes on the risks its competition won't touch, from amusement parks to thoroughbred horses and summer camps. Coverage is also available for one-time events, such as golf tournaments and auto races. Markel's commercial excess and surplus subsidiaries include Essex Insurance and Markel Shand Professional/Products Liability, while its specialty admitted segment includes Markel Insurance, which covers groups ranging from martial arts schools to dude ranches. Markel International provides specialty insurance internationally from its base in the UK.

Excess insurance kicks in when a company's regular insurance fizzles out. For example, a regular policy might pay up to $100,000 on claims, but the excess policy could then pay any amounts over $100,000 and up to $1 million. Surplus insurance is coverage that no regular insurance company can offer and typically comes with a higher level of risk and higher-priced premiums.

Higher premium volume (primarily in its excess and surplus segment) and improved results by its previously struggling international business have helped to increase Markel's underwriting profits. Rather than sit on its hands while its investment portfolio tanked during 2008, Markel chose to sell off portions of its investments and take substantial write downs that year.

Unlike standard insurers (whose rates are generally regulated), specialty insurers can charge the rates they consider reasonable. To that end, after taking significant losses from the 2005 hurricane season (Katrina, Rita, Wilma), and additional hits from the 2008 season (Gustav, Ike), the company decided to raise the rates on its catastrophe-exposed businesses.

The company moved to expand its specialty property/casualty operations in 2009 by agreeing to acquire Elliott Special Risks, a Canadian general agent providing underwriting services for non-standard policies, for $75 million. The purchase will expand Markel's operations in North America.

President Anthony Markel and his cousin vice chairman Steven Markel control about 8% of the company.

HISTORY

In the 1920s Sam Markel formed a mutual insurance company for "jitneys" (passenger cars refurbished as public transportation buses). In 1930 he founded Markel Service to expand nationally. To keep up with industry growth, the company revamped itself as a managing general agent and independent claims service organization in the late 1950s. In 1978 Markel began covering taverns, restaurants, and vacant buildings. It created excess and surplus lines underwriter Essex Insurance in 1980.

Markel went public in 1986. The next year it invested in Shand Morahan and Evanston Insurance (specialty coverage, including architects, engineers, and lawyers professional liability; officers and directors insurance; errors and omissions; and medical malpractice). It bought summer camp insurer Rhulen Agency in 1989.

In the 1990s Markel began buying insurers with their own offbeat niches. In 1990 it bought the rest of Shand Morahan and Evanston Insurance. In 1995 it bought Lincoln Insurance (excess and surplus lines) from media giant Thomson (now Thomson Reuters). The next year the company bought Investors Insurance Holding (excess and surplus lines). Markel, which already owned nearly 10% of Gryphon Holdings (commercial property/casualty), bought the rest in 1999.

Expanding internationally, Markel bought Bermuda-based Terra Nova Holdings, a reinsurer and a Lloyd's managing agency, in 2000. The company experienced heavy losses in 2001, not only related to the events of September 11 but also to its slumping international business (the company took a $100 million charge).

EXECUTIVES

Chairman and CEO: Alan I. Kirshner, age 73, $720,073 total compensation
Vice Chairman: Anthony F. (Tony) Markel, age 67, $689,671 total compensation
Vice Chairman: Steven A. Markel, age 60, $686,709 total compensation
VP Marketing: Brenda Phillips
President and COO: Paul W. Springman, age 57, $979,507 total compensation
SVP and CFO: Richard R. Whitt III, age 45, $760,402 total compensation
CIO: David Egbert
EVP and Chief Investment Officer: Thomas S. Gayner, age 47, $962,102 total compensation
Chief Administrative Officer and Chief Corporate Actuary: Brad Kiscaden
Chief Administrative Officer: Britton (Britt) Glisson
SVP and Chief Underwritting Officer: Gerard Albanese Jr., age 56
EVP Midwest: Henry Lopez
VP Human Resources: Pam Perrott
VP Investor Relations: Bruce Kay
VP Marketing: Letha Heaton
Secretary: D. Michael Jones
Auditors: KPMG LLP

LOCATIONS

HQ: Markel Corporation
    4521 Highwoods Pkwy., Glen Allen, VA 23060
Phone: 804-747-0136   Fax: 804-965-1600
Web: www.markelcorp.com

PRODUCTS/OPERATIONS

2008 Revenues

	$ mil.	% of total
Earned premiums		
Excess & surplus lines	1,090.0	47
London insurance market	615.8	27
Specialty admitted	315.7	14
Other	0.6	—
Net investment income	283.7	12
Net realized investment losses	(407.5)	—
Total	**1,898.3**	**100**

Selected Subsidiaries

Essex Insurance Company
Gryphon Holding Inc.
    Associated International Insurance Company
    Deerfield Insurance Company
Markel American Insurance Company
Markel Insurance Company
Shand/Evanston Group, Inc.
    Evanston Insurance Company
Terra Nova (Bermuda) Holdings Ltd.
    Markel International Limited (UK)
        Markel International Insurance Company Limited
Markel Capital Limited (UK)

HISTORICAL FINANCIALS

Company Type: Public

Income Statement

FYE: December 31

	ASSETS ($ mil.)	NET INCOME ($ mil.)	INCOME AS % OF ASSETS	EMPLOYEES
12/08	9,477.7	(58.8)	—	2,000
12/07	10,134.4	405.7	4.0%	2,000
12/06	10,088.1	392.5	3.9%	1,897
12/05	9,814.1	147.9	1.5%	1,866
12/04	9,397.6	165.4	1.8%	1,834
Annual Growth	0.2%	—	—	2.2%

2008 Year-End Financials

Equity as % of assets: 23.0%
Return on assets: —
Return on equity: —
Long-term debt ($ mil.): 689
No. of shares (mil.): 10

Dividends
Yield: 0.0%
Payout: —
Market value ($ mil.): 2,935
Sales ($ mil.): 1,898

Stock History

NYSE: MKL

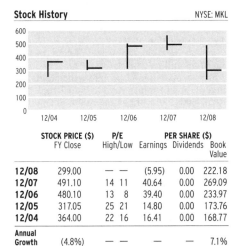

	STOCK PRICE ($) FY Close	P/E High/Low	PER SHARE ($) Earnings	Dividends	Book Value
12/08	299.00	— —	(5.95)	0.00	222.18
12/07	491.10	14 11	40.64	0.00	269.09
12/06	480.10	13 8	39.40	0.00	233.97
12/05	317.05	25 21	14.80	0.00	173.76
12/04	364.00	22 16	16.41	0.00	168.77
Annual Growth	(4.8%)	— —	—	—	7.1%

Marriott International

Marriott International signs in at the top of the lodging industry. The company is one of the world's leading hoteliers with some 3,000 operated or franchised properties in more than 65 countries. Marriott's hotels include such full-service brands as Renaissance Hotels and its flagship Marriott Hotels & Resorts, as well as select-service and extended-stay brands Courtyard and Fairfield Inn. It also owns the Ritz-Carlton luxury chain and resort and time-share properties operated by Marriott Vacation Club International. Marriott additionally provides more than 2,000 rental units for corporate housing and manages 45 golf courses. The Marriott family, including CEO J. W. Marriott Jr., owns about 30% of the firm.

Marriott operates more than 1,000 of its hotels and gets most of its revenue through lease agreements and management fees collected from property owners. It has more than 2,000 franchised hotels that pay the company fees and royalties as well as a percentage of their food and beverage revenue. While the bulk of its hotels are located in the US, about 14% of its properties are international. The company has long-term management agreements with properties that are owned or leased by Host Hotels & Resorts, a major customer that accounts for about 20% of Marriott's sales.

Marriott is keen to increase its share of the extended-stay and select-service market, which typically has higher margins since those hotels offer fewer amenities. The company has benefited from a weak US dollar that continues to drive international travelers to the US. In 2007 the company added some 200 properties to its holdings. Also that year it announced plans to develop a boutique chain (small, upscale, stylish hotels in prime locations) called Edition, designed by Ian Schrager, the hotelier behind hip properties such as Manhattan's Morgans Hotel. The first Edition hotel is slated to open in 2010.

In response to the declining economy, the company instituted a restructuring of its Timeshare segment, which included the reduction and consolidation of sales channels in the US, and closing down certain operations in Europe. In early 2009 Marriott cut more than 1,000 jobs.

Later that year the company announced plans to purchase The Greenbrier, a resort in White Sulpher Springs, West Virginia. The Greenbrier's roots go back to the 18th century; its noted guests have included President Eisenhower, and Monaco's Prince Rainier and Princess Grace. However, in recent years The Greenbrier has posted losses, and Marriott is buying the resort — a National Historic landmark — just as it announced it is filing for bankruptcy.

HISTORY

The company began in 1927 as a Washington, DC, root beer stand operated by John and Alice Marriott. Later they added hot food and named their business the Hot Shoppe. In 1929 the couple incorporated and began building a regional chain. Hot Shoppes opened its first hotel, the Twin Bridges Marriott Motor Hotel, in Arlington, Virginia, in 1957.

When the Marriotts' son Bill became president in 1964 (CEO in 1972, chairman in 1985), he focused on expanding the hotel business. The company changed its name to Marriott Corp. in 1967. With the rise in airline travel, Marriott built several airport hotels during the 1970s. By 1977 sales had topped $1 billion.

Marriott became the #1 operator of airport food, beverage, and merchandise facilities in the US with its 1982 acquisition of Host International, and it introduced moderately priced Courtyard hotels in 1983. Acquisitions in the 1980s included a time-share business, food service companies, and competitor Howard Johnson. (Marriott later sold the hotels but kept the restaurants and turnpike units.)

The company entered three new market segments in 1987: Marriott Suites (full-service suites), Residence Inn (moderately priced suites), and Fairfield Inn (economy hotels). It also began developing "life-care" communities, which provide apartments, meals, and limited nursing care to the elderly, in 1988.

Marriott split its operations into two companies in 1993: Host Marriott to own hotels, and Marriott International primarily to manage them. However, Marriott International still owned some of the properties, and in 1995 it bought 49% of the Ritz-Carlton luxury hotel group.

In 1997 the firm expanded overseas operations with its purchase of the 150-unit Hong Kong-based Renaissance Hotel Group, a deal that included branding rights to the Ramada chain.

In 1998, after splitting its lodging and food distribution services, the new Marriott International then began trading as a separate company. That year Marriott also acquired the rest of Ritz-Carlton.

Marriott entered the corporate housing business in 1999 through its acquisition of ExecuStay Corporation (renamed ExecuStay by Marriott), which provides fully furnished and accessorized apartments for stays of 30 days or more. The following year the company set up a $3.7 billion investment fund with Ripplewood Holdings (Marriott owns about 20%) that would buy Japanese hotels to operate under Marriott management. It also agreed to pay $400 million to settle a lawsuit brought by stockholders who contended the company defrauded them. Marriott also announced plans in 2000 to join rival Hyatt in launching a joint venture to provide an electronic procurement network serving the hospitality industry. The following year it joined Italy's Bulgari, the world's #3 jeweler, in a $140 million venture of luxury hotels sporting the Bulgari name.

Marriott refocused its operations on the lodging market in 2003 when it exited both the senior living and distribution services businesses. It sold Marriott Distribution Services (food and beverage distribution) to Services Group of America, and sold Marriott Senior Living Services to Sunrise Assisted Living and CNL Retirement Properties (nine communities). The following year Marriott sold the international branding rights to the Ramada and Days Inn chains to Cendant (now Avis Budget Group).

In 2005 Marriott acquired about 30 properties from CTF Holdings (an affiliate of Hong Kong-based New World Development) for nearly $1.5 billion. It sold 14 properties immediately to Sunstone Hotel Investors and Walton Street Capital. The deal put an end to an ongoing legal battle between Marriott and CTF Holdings, which alleged that the hotelier had pocketed kickbacks and fees from outside vendors.

The firm renovated and upgraded many of its Courtyard and Residence Inn locations in 2006.

EXECUTIVES

Chairman and CEO: J. W. (Bill) Marriott Jr., age 76, $9,989,268 total compensation
Vice Chairman: John W. Marriott III, age 48
President and COO: Arne M. Sorenson, age 50, $4,687,117 total compensation
EVP and CFO: Carl T. Berquist, age 57
EVP and CIO: Carl Wilson
EVP Lodging Development: James M. Sullivan, age 65, $4,170,211 total compensation
EVP Finance and Global Treasurer: Carolyn B. Handlon
EVP Finance, International Lodging: Linda A. Bartlett
EVP Development/Owner and Franchise Services, The Americas: Stephen P. Joyce, age 49, $820,831 total compensation
EVP Project Finance: Michael E. Dearing
EVP Owner and Franchise Services: Joel M. Eisemann
EVP Global Brand Strategy and Innovation: Michael E. (Mike) Jannini
EVP Development, Planning, and Feasibility: Scott E. Melby
EVP Lodging Development, Select-Service and Extended-Stay Brands: Daryl A. Nickel
EVP Global Human Resources: David A. Rodriguez, age 50
EVP and General Counsel: Edward A. (Ed) Ryan, age 55
EVP Global Communications and Public Affairs: Kathleen Matthews
SVP Investor Relations: Laura E. Paugh
SVP Global Sales: Stephanie Linnartz
VP, Senior Counsel, and Corporate Secretary: Bancroft S. Gordon
President, North American Lodging Operations and Global Brand Management: Robert J. (Bob) McCarthy, age 55, $3,025,642 total compensation
President and COO, Ritz-Carlton Hotel Company: Simon F. Cooper, age 63
President, Marriott Leisure: Robert A. (Bob) Miller, age 63
Auditors: Ernst & Young LLP

LOCATIONS

HQ: Marriott International, Inc.
Marriott Drive, Washington, DC 20058
Phone: 301-380-3000   **Fax:** 301-380-3969
Web: www.marriott.com

2008 Locations

	No.
Americas	
US	2,748
Other countries	122
Europe	
UK & Ireland	61
Other countries	106
Asia	99
Middle East & Africa	34
Australia	8
Total	**3,178**

PRODUCTS/OPERATIONS

2008 Sales

	$ mil.	% of total
Lodging		
North American full-service	5,631	44
North American limited-service	2,233	17
Timeshare	1,750	14
Luxury	1,659	13
International	1,544	12
Other	62	—
Total	**12,879**	**100**

Selected Operations and Brands

International lodging
  Courtyard by Marriott
  Fairfield Inn by Marriott
  JW Marriott Hotels & Resorts
  Marriott Executive Apartments
  Marriott Hotels & Resorts
  Ramada International
  Renaissance Hotels & Resorts
  Residence Inn by Marriott

Luxury hotels
  Bulgari Hotels & Resorts
  The Ritz-Carlton
North American full-service hotels
  JW Marriott Hotels & Resorts
  Marriott Conference Centers
  Marriott Hotels & Resorts
  Renaissance ClubSport
  Renaissance Hotels & Resorts
North American limited-service hotels
  Courtyard by Marriott
  Fairfield Inn by Marriott
  Marriott ExecuStay
  Residence Inn by Marriott
  SpringHill Suites by Marriott
  TownePlace Suites by Marriott
Timeshare resorts
  Grand Residences by Marriott
  Horizons by Marriott Vacation Club International
  Marriott Vacation Club International
  The Ritz-Carlton Club

COMPETITORS

Accor
Best Western
Carlson Hotels
Choice Hotels
Club Med
Fairmont Raffles
Four Seasons Hotels
Hilton Hotels
HVM
Hyatt
InterContinental Hotels
Loews Hotels
LXR Luxury Resorts
Starwood Hotels & Resorts

HISTORICAL FINANCIALS

Company Type: Public

Income Statement

	REVENUE ($ mil.)	NET INCOME ($ mil.)	NET PROFIT MARGIN	EMPLOYEES
			FYE: Friday nearest December 31	
12/08	12,879.0	362.0	2.8%	146,000
12/07	12,990.0	696.0	5.4%	151,000
12/06	12,160.0	717.0	5.9%	150,600
12/05	11,550.0	669.0	5.8%	143,000
12/04	10,099.0	596.0	5.9%	133,000
Annual Growth	**6.3%**	**(11.7%)**	**—**	**2.4%**

2008 Year-End Financials

Debt ratio: 215.6%
Return on equity: 25.8%
Cash ($ mil.): 134
Current ratio: 1.33
Long-term debt ($ mil.): 2,975
No. of shares (mil.): 357
Dividends
  Yield: 1.7%
  Payout: 33.7%
Market value ($ mil.): 6,886

Stock History

NYSE: MAR

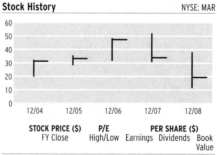

	STOCK PRICE ($) FY Close	P/E High/Low		PER SHARE ($) Earnings	Dividends	Book Value
12/08	19.31	38	12	0.98	0.33	3.87
12/07	33.93	30	18	1.74	0.29	4.01
12/06	47.37	34	23	1.40	0.24	7.34
12/05	33.24	24	20	1.43	0.20	9.12
12/04	31.26	26	16	1.23	0.16	11.44
Annual Growth	**(11.3%)**	**—**	**—**	**(5.5%)**	**19.8%**	**(23.7%)**

Mars, Incorporated

Mars knows chocolate sales are nothing to snicker at. The company makes such worldwide favorites as M&M's, Snickers, and the Mars bar. Its other confections include 3 Musketeers, Dove, Milky Way, Skittles, Twix, and Starburst candy; Combos and Kudos snacks; Uncle Ben's rice; and pet food under the names Pedigree, Sheba, and Whiskas. It also owns the world's largest chewing gum maker, the Wm. Wrigley Jr. Company. The Mars family (including siblings and retired company CEO Forrest Mars Jr., chairman John Franklyn Mars, and VP Jacqueline Badger Mars) owns the highly secretive firm, making the family one of the richest in the US.

Sweet deals are the name of the game in the confectionery sector and Mars' 2008 takeover of chewing gum giant Wrigley (valued at some $23 billion) brought together two iconic US companies, both of which already have a substantial worldwide presence. Mars acquired such well known brands as Altoids, Life Savers, and Creme Savers, along with the best-selling chewing gum brands Spearmint, Juicy Fruit, Doublemint, and a host of others. Together, the companies benefit from greater global marketing and distribution muscle, as well as cost-savings in raw materials.

The deal, which took Wrigley private and left it a stand-alone subsidiary of Mars, was partially financed by Warren Buffett's Berkshire Hathaway, which owns a stake in Wrigley as a result.

Two weeks after the aquisition was final, Mars yanked Wrigley CEO and president, William Perez, and replaced him with a Mars 19-year veteran, Dushan "Duke" Petrovich. Petrovich carries the title of president, Mars having eliminated the CEO position at Wrigley. Perez received a severance package of some $25 million (including $10.5 million in cash).

Mars makes non-chocolate confections including breath mints such as AquaDrops, and snack foods like Combos and Kudos. It swallows a large bite of the pet-food market with its Royal Canin, Pedigree, and Whiskas brands. Pedigree has introduced a product called Wisdom Panel, which is a DNA test kit for dogs that determined the breed mix of pets. Mars' other brands include Uncle Ben's rice, Seeds of Change organic food, and the Klix and Flavia Beverage Systems.

Mars stays virtually debt-free and uses its profits for expansion. It has more than 130 factories in 75 countries and sells its products in more than 100.

HISTORY

Frank Mars invented the Milky Way candy bar in 1923 after his previous three efforts at the candy business left him bankrupt. After his estranged son, Forrest, graduated from Yale, Mars hired him to work at his candy operation. When Forrest demanded one-third control of the company and Frank refused, Forrest moved to England with the foreign rights to Milky Way and started his own company (Food Manufacturers) in the 1930s. He made a sweeter version of Milky Way for the UK, calling it a Mars bar. Forrest also ventured into pet food with the 1934 purchase of Chappel Brothers (renamed Pedigree). At one point he controlled 55% of the British pet food market.

During WWII Forrest returned to the US and introduced Uncle Ben's rice (the world's first brand-name raw commodity) and M&M's (a joint venture between Forrest and Bruce Murrie, son of Hershey's then-president). The idea for M&M's was borrowed from British Smarties, for which Forrest obtained rights (from Rowntree Mackintosh) by relinquishing similar rights to the Snickers bar in some foreign markets. The ad slogan "Melts in your mouth, not in your hand" (and the candy's success in non-air-conditioned stores and war zones) made the company an industry leader. Mars introduced M&M's Peanut in 1954. It was one of the first candy companies to sponsor a television show — Howdy Doody in the 1950s.

Forrest merged his firm with his deceased father's company in 1964, after buying his dying half-sister's controlling interest. (He renamed the business Mars at her request.) The merger was the end of an alliance with Hershey, who had supplied Frank with chocolate since his Milky Way inception.

In 1968 Mars bought Kal Kan. In 1973 Forrest, then 69 years old, delegated his company responsibilities to sons Forrest Jr. and John. Five years later the brothers, looking for snacks to offset dwindling candy resulting from a more diet-conscious America, bought the Twix chocolate-covered cookie brand. During the late 1980s they bought ice-cream bar maker Dove Bar International and Ethel-M Chocolates, producer of liqueur-flavored chocolates, a business their father had begun in his retirement.

Hershey in 1988 surpassed Mars as the largest candy maker in the US when it acquired Mounds, Almond Joy, and other US brands from Cadbury Schweppes (now Cadbury). In response to the success of Hershey's Symphony Bar, Mars introduced its dark-chocolate Dove bar in 1991.

The company entered the huge confectionery market of India in 1989 by building a $10 million factory there. In 1996 the company opened a confectionery processing plant in Brazil.

Forrest Sr. died in 1999, spurring rumors that Mars would go public or be sold. Instead, the company dismantled most of its sales force, opting to use less costly food brokers. Forrest Jr. retired the same year, leaving brother John Franklyn as president and CEO.

In 2000 the company established a subsidiary, Effem India, to market Mars' products in India. In 2003 Mars acquired French pet food producer Royal Canin. That year its Mexican subsidiary, Effem México SA de CV, merged with Mexican confectioner Grupo Matre to form a partnership to produce candy for Hispanic markets.

In 2004 the company appointed two co-presidents, Peter Cheney and Paul Michaels, leaving John Franklyn Mars as chairman. Cheney retired in 2005.

The company sold off its payment-processing subsidiary, MEI Conlux (which has headquarters in Pennsylvania and Japan) in 2006 to investment firms Bain Capital and Advantage Partners for more than $500 million.

Adding to its fast-growing pet-products sector, in 2006 Mars purchased dog-treat manufacturer S&M Nu Tec. Still barking up the pet-product tree, Mars acquired private-label dry pet food manufacturer Doane Pet Care Company that year as well. Doane's products are sold in the US and Europe.

The company discontinued brands in 2006, including Pop'ables and Cookies &, for an estimated $300 million savings, which it invested in advertising. The company introduced new Dove varieties and a dark chocolate version of M&Ms that year as well.

EXECUTIVES

Chairman: John F. Mars
President and CEO: Paul S. Michaels
Chief Science Officer: Harold Schmitz
VP and General Manager, Mars Direct: Jim Cass
VP Small Outlet Sales, Masterfoods USA: Larry Lupo
VP Research and Development, U.S. Food: Mike Wilson
President, Wm. Wrigley Jr. Company:
  Dushan (Duke) Petrovich, age 55
President, Masterfoods Western Europe: Pierre Laubies
President, Mars Snackfoods USA: Todd R. Lachman
President, Snackfoods, Masterfoods Europe:
  Andy Weston-Webb
President, Mars Nutrition for Health and Well-Being:
  James (Jamie) Mattikow
General Manager and CTO, Mars Botanical:
  Mary Wagner
President Mars Drinks: Grant Reid
Global President, Mars Food: Brian Camastral
EVP, Mars Nutrition for Health and Well-Being:
  Joseph (Joe) Perello
Director Corporate Communications: Alison Clark
Global Director, Scientific Affairs: Catherine Woteki
Global Director, Plant Science: Howard-Yana Shapiro
Global Leadership Development Director: Andre Martin

LOCATIONS

HQ: Mars, Incorporated
  6885 Elm St., McLean, VA 22101
Phone: 703-821-4900   **Fax:** 703-448-9678
Web: www.mars.com

PRODUCTS/OPERATIONS

Selected Products and Brands

Mars chocolate
  Dove
  Galaxy
  M&Ms
  Mars
  Milky Way
  Skittles
  Snickers
  Starburst
  Twix
Mars drinks
  Flavia
  Klix
Mars foods
  Dolmio
  Ebly
  Masterfoods
  Seeds of Change
  Uncle Ben's
Mars pet care
  Cesar
  Pedigree
  Royal Canin
  Sheba
  Whiskas
Mars symbioscience
  Cocoapro
  MX
  Seramis
  Wisdom Panel
Wrigley
  Altoids
  Crème Savers
  Doublemint
  Extra
  Freedent
  Hubba Bubba
  Juicy Fruit
  Life Savers
  Orbit
  Skittles
  Starburst
  Winterfresh

COMPETITORS

American Italian Pasta
Barilla
Barry Callebaut
Breeder's Choice
Cadbury
Caribou Coffee
Chupa Chups
Colgate-Palmolive
ConAgra
Ezaki Glico
Farley's & Sathers
Fazer Konfektyr
Ferrara Pan Candy
Ferrero
General Mills
Ghirardelli Chocolate
Godiva Chocolatier
Green Mountain Coffee
Guittard
HARIBO
Harry London Candies
Heinz
Hershey
Hill's Pet Nutrition
Iams
Jelly Belly Candy
Kent Gida
Kraft Foods
Lindt & Sprüngli
Meiji Holdings
Nestlé
Nestlé Purina PetCare
Perfetti Van Melle
PETCO
Riviana Foods
Rocky Mountain Chocolate
Royal Cup Coffee
Russell Stover
S&D Coffee
Sara Lee Foodservice
Sara Lee International Beverage and Bakery
Smucker
Starbucks
SweetWorks
Tootsie Roll
Topps Company
Unilever
Upper Deck

HISTORICAL FINANCIALS

Company Type: Private

Income Statement

	REVENUE ($ mil.)	NET INCOME ($ mil.)	NET PROFIT MARGIN	EMPLOYEES
12/08	30,000.0	—	—	70,000
12/07	25,000.0	—	—	48,000
12/06	21,000.0	—	—	40,000
12/05	18,000.0	—	—	40,500
12/04	18,000.0	—	—	39,000
Annual Growth	13.6%	—	—	15.7%

FYE: December 31

Revenue History

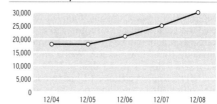

Marsh & McLennan

Marsh & McLennan Companies is the ultimate middleman. The company is one of the world's largest insurance brokers. Through core insurance subsidiary Marsh, the company provides a broad array of insurance and risk management services; its reinsurance business is handled by subsidiary Guy Carpenter. Kroll is Marsh & McLennan's risk consulting and technology services arm. The company also owns Mercer, which provides human resources and financial consulting services to customers worldwide, and Oliver Wyman, which provides management consulting services.

Citing such recent high profile natural disasters as tsunamis and hurricanes as well as international terrorism, Marsh & McLennan plans to expand its role as a risk consultant; its paring of other operations is part of a greater plan to focus on this business sector.

In 2007 the company sold its money management operation, Putnam Investments, to Power Financial Corporation subsidiary Great-West Lifeco for $3.9 billion.

Meanwhile, the company's Marsh insurance subsidiary is restyling itself as a strategic risk adviser while maintaining its primary mission as a broker. In 2007 the company replaced about a third of the subsidiary's office managers nationwide, losing a substantial number of customers as a result but feeling that price to be worth the growth it expects in the long-run.

Late in 2007, the company ousted CEO Michael Cherkasky, who had served in the position since 2004 and shepherded the company through its legal crisis with the New York state attorney general's office. He was unable to lead a recovery of the company following the bid-rigging scandals, however, and the board later hired insurance executive Brian Duperreault, formerly of ACE Limited, to replace Cherkasky. Duperreault has since restructured the operating divisions of its insurance brokerage unit and has shaken up other areas of the MMC management structure.

In 2008 MMC divested Kroll's Corporate Advisory and Restructuring division, and in 2009 it sold the Kroll Government Services business. MMC also intends to divest Kroll Factual Data (services for mortgage lenders). At the same time, the division's more profitable operations have been growing through acquisitions and organically. In early 2009 the company announced plans to grow Mercer's investment consulting division by acquiring rival Callan Associates.

HISTORY

Marsh & McLennan Companies dates back to the Dan H. Bomar Company, founded in 1871 after the Great Chicago Fire. In 1885 a plucky Harvard dropout named Henry Marsh joined the company, then known as R.A. Waller and Company. When Robert Waller died in 1889, Marsh and fellow employee Herbert Ulmann bought a controlling stake and renamed the company Marsh Ulmann & Co. Marsh pioneered insurance brokering and in 1901 set up U.S. Steel's self-insurance program.

In 1904 different directors at Burlington Northern Railroad promised their account to Marsh Ulmann, as well as Manley-McLennan of Duluth (railroad insurance), and D.W. Burrows (a small Chicago-based railroad insurance firm).

Rather than fight over it, the firms joined forces to form the world's largest insurance brokerage. When Burrows retired in 1906, the firm became Marsh & McLennan.

In the early 20th century, Marsh won AT&T's business and McLennan landed the account of Armour Meat Packing.

In 1923 Marsh & McLennan became a closely held corporation. Marsh sold out to McLennan in 1935. The company weathered the Depression without major layoffs by cutting pay and branching into life insurance and employee-benefits consulting after passage of the Social Security Act (1935).

The firm grew through acquisitions in the 1950s, went public in 1962, and in 1969 formed a holding company that became Marsh & McLennan Companies. In the 1970s it diversified, buying Putnam Management (investment management). It set up subsidiary William M. Mercer's employee-benefits consulting business in 1975, and in 1980 it acquired a foothold in the UK with C.T. Bowring Reinsurance. In 1982 Marsh & McLennan formed Seabury & Smith to manage its insurance group programs.

As the insurance business slowed in the 1980s, financial and consulting fields grew. In 1992 the firm formed Mercer Consulting Group as an umbrella for its various consulting companies.

In 1995 Marsh & McLennan opened global brokering centers to centralize its insurance placement services to mid-market businesses. In 1998 the company bought Sedgwick Group, a UK-based insurance services firm.

The next year the firm named Jeffrey Greenberg, the son of AIG chairman Hank Greenberg, to replace chairman and CEO A. J. C. Smith.

With offices in the World Trade Center, the company lost some 300 employees in the September 11 terrorist attacks. Following the attacks on the World Trade Center, Marsh & McLennan launched a new subsidiary (AXIS Specialty) to deal with the capacity shortage in the insurance industry.

Two major Marsh & McLennan units came under legal fire in probes of the mutual fund and insurance brokerage industries, respectively. In 2003 Putnam agreed to settle securities fraud charges with the SEC and reimburse investors; many of Putnam's top officers were replaced and its compliance procedures were restructured.

The following year, Marsh found itself at the center of a price-fixing investigation that involved several insurance companies, including AIG and ACE Limited. At least nine employees of Marsh and AIG pled guilty to criminal charges. Jeffery Greenberg, the son of outspoken AIG CEO Maurice Greenberg, who had served as Marsh & McLennan's chairman and CEO, resigned in 2004 as a result of the allegations.

Strengthening its risk management operations, Marsh & McLennan acquired risk consulting company Kroll for about $2 billion in 2004.

Michael Cherkasky was named as Greenberg's successor. Before entering the insurance industry, Cherkasky had headed the investigations unit of the New York County district attorney's office. Cherkasky guided the company during Marsh's alleged bid-rigging investigation, which ended with an $850 million settlement agreement in early 2005. Following the settlement, the company slashed its dividends and cut jobs.

As part of an effort to relieve possible conflicts of interest following the investigation, MMC divested its US-based wholesale insurance brokerage Crump Group in late 2005.

EXECUTIVES

Chairman: Stephen R. Hardis, age 73
President, CEO, and Director: Brian Duperreault, age 61, $13,317,091 total compensation
EVP and CFO: Vanessa A. Wittman, age 42, $963,773 total compensation
SVP and CIO: William P. (Bill) Krivoshik
SVP and Chief Compliance Officer: E. Scott Gilbert, age 53
EVP and General Counsel: Peter J. Beshar, age 47, $3,917,812 total compensation
SVP Human Resources: Orlando D. Ashford, age 40
SVP International and Client Development: David R. Frediani
Chairman and CEO, Mercer: M. Michele Burns, age 51, $3,934,812 total compensation
President and CEO, Kroll: Ben F. Allen, age 44
President and CEO, Oliver Wyman: John P. Drzik, age 47
Chairman and CEO, Marsh Inc.: Daniel S. (Dan) Glaser, age 49, $9,786,259 total compensation
President and CEO, Guy Carpenter: Peter Zaffino, age 42
Vice Chairman, Office of the CEO: David A. Nadler, age 60
Director Government Relations: Erick Gustafson
Auditors: Deloitte & Touche LLP

LOCATIONS

HQ: Marsh & McLennan Companies, Inc.
1166 Avenue of the Americas, New York, NY 10036
Phone: 212-345-5000   **Fax:** 212-345-4808
Web: www.marshmac.com

2008 Sales

	$ mil.	% of total
US	5,398	46
Europe		
UK	1,984	17
Other European countries	2,064	18
Other regions	2,209	19
Adjustments	(68)	—
Total	**11,587**	**100**

PRODUCTS/OPERATIONS

2008 Sales

	$ mil.	% of total
Risk & insurance services		
Marsh	4,632	40
Guy Carpenter	834	7
Consulting		
Mercer	3,642	31
Oliver Wyman Group	1,554	13
Risk consulting & technology	993	9
Adjustments	(68)	—
Total	**11,587**	**100**

Selected Subsidiaries

Kroll Inc.
Marsh Inc.
  Guy Carpenter & Company, LLC
  Seabury & Smith, Inc.
  Sedgwick Group Limited
MMC Securities Corp.
Mercer Consulting Group, Inc.
  Mercer LLC
  Oliver Wyman, Inc.
  National Economic Research Associates, Inc. (NERA)

COMPETITORS

Accenture
ADP Screening and Selection
AIG
Allianz
Aon
Arthur Gallagher
AXA
Bain & Company
Booz Allen
Brown & Brown
FTI Consulting
General Re
Hewitt Associates
Hub International
ING
Jardine Lloyd
Lloyd's
McKinsey & Company
Morgan Stanley
Towers Perrin
USI
Watson Wyatt
Wells Fargo Insurance Services
Willis Group

HISTORICAL FINANCIALS

Company Type: Public

Income Statement

FYE: December 31

	REVENUE ($ mil.)	NET INCOME ($ mil.)	NET PROFIT MARGIN	EMPLOYEES
12/08	11,587.0	(73.0)	—	54,400
12/07	11,350.0	2,475.0	21.8%	56,000
12/06	11,921.0	990.0	8.3%	55,200
12/05	11,652.0	404.0	3.5%	55,000
12/04	12,159.0	176.0	1.4%	61,800
Annual Growth	(1.2%)	—	—	(3.1%)

2008 Year-End Financials

Debt ratio: 55.8%
Return on equity: —
Cash ($ mil.): 1,685
Current ratio: 1.41
Long-term debt ($ mil.): 3,194

No. of shares (mil.): 524
Dividends
Yield: 3.3%
Payout: —
Market value ($ mil.): 12,713

Stock History

NYSE: MMC

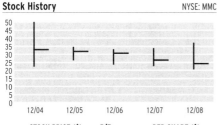

	STOCK PRICE ($) FY Close	P/E High/Low		PER SHARE ($) Earnings	Dividends	Book Value
12/08	24.27	—	—	(0.14)	0.80	10.92
12/07	26.47	7	5	4.53	0.76	14.93
12/06	30.66	19	14	1.76	0.68	11.11
12/05	31.76	46	36	0.74	0.68	10.23
12/04	32.90	151	69	0.33	0.99	9.65
Annual Growth	(7.3%)	—	—	—	(5.2%)	3.1%

Martha Stewart Living

If anyone could turn a stay in jail into a good thing, it's legendary lifestyle maven Martha Stewart. Following the completion of her sentence on federal criminal charges related to insider trading, Stewart has not shied away from the limelight. Rather, she and her company, Martha Stewart Living Omnimedia (MSLO), have embraced the spotlight. The company has its fingers in many money-making pies: publishing (magazines and books), broadcasting (TV programs, satellite radio), Internet, and merchandising. The bulk of MSLO's business comes from its publishing activities, which are driven by its flagship magazine *Martha Stewart Living*. Stewart controls about 50% of MSLO's stock and about 90% of voting stock.

Her recipe: Mix equal parts Julia Child, Miss America, and P. T. Barnum; stir in liberal amounts of ambition and chutzpah; and serve with a flourish to a public hungry for a more gracious existence. Topics covered by the media empire include cooking, entertainment, home, craft, holidays, weddings, organizing, and gardening.

MSLO's recent activities includes its 2008 purchase of the media and licensed properties of popular TV chef Emeril Lagasse. Included in the deal are rights to the TV show *The Essence of Emeril*, syndicated episodes of the *Emeril Live* show on the Food Network, and a dozen cookbooks, as well as Emeril-branded spices, marinades, coffee, and other food products.

Magazines such as *Martha Stewart Living*, *Everyday Food*, and *Martha Stewart Weddings*, and a series of more than 60 books (*Entertaining*, *Martha Stewart's Christmas*) illustrate MSLO's reach into publishing (58% of sales).

MSLO's syndicated daytime show *The Martha Stewart Show* has garnered solid ratings. A TV series based on MSLO's *Everyday Food* magazine airs on PBS. In 2008, the company added a spin-off companion show, *Everyday Baking from Everyday Food*, which also airs weekly on PBS. Broadcasting operations also include the satellite radio channel *Martha Stewart Living Radio*, found on SIRIUS XM Radio.

Retail partnerships with companies such as Kmart, Macy's, Costco, and 1-800-Flowers.com, fall into MSLO's merchandising division. And in 2008 Wal-Mart began selling a line of Martha Stewart-branded craft products (such as scrapbooks and jewelry-making kits).

The scandal around Stewart's sale of ImClone stock, allegedly based on an insider trading tip, briefly rocked Stewart's seemingly perfect world — she was convicted for lying to investigators and obstruction of justice, and her persona (which had been her most successful recipe to date) suffered a hit. While serving less than six months in jail, she saw her company struggle: its stock price dropped, her TV show was put on hold, and for a time executives carefully tried to de-emphasize the "Martha-ness" of its products. The star's jail and home confinement sentence ended in 2005, and her reputation has since recovered. As part of her settlement with the SEC, in 2006 Stewart agreed to a five-year ban from serving as a director of MSLO (and any other public company) and paid a $5 million fine.

HISTORY

A former model and stockbroker, Martha Stewart's entry into the commerce of gracious living can be traced to 1972 when she launched a catering business in Westport, Connecticut. Culling her experiences as a caterer, Stewart published her first book, *Entertaining*, in 1982.

The resounding success of *Entertaining* (the book has gone into 30 printings) propelled Stewart into the public spotlight. Kmart appointed Stewart as its lifestyle consultant in 1987, and in 1991 her notoriety led media giant Time Inc. to begin publishing the *Martha Stewart Living* magazine. Though beautiful to look at, the publication was expensive to produce; it did not achieve profitability until 1996.

Stewart rode the coattails of her magazine's success into a variety of other ventures. Dipping a toe into merchandising, she teamed with Sherwin Williams in 1992 to create a line of paints. Her syndicated TV show, *Martha Stewart Living*, debuted the following year. Expanding further into merchandising, Stewart introduced Martha by Mail, a direct-mail catalog business, in 1995. Frustrated with what she perceived as Time's inability to keep pace with the growth of her burgeoning empire and desirous of a hefty equity stake in her collection of companies, Stewart wrested her operation (then called Martha Stewart Enterprises) away from Time in 1997. Her friend Sharon Patrick negotiated a buyout valuing the company at about $53 million.

Christening her new undertaking Martha Stewart Living Omnimedia (MSLO), Stewart wasted no time in expanding the company. MSLO soon entered into an alliance with Kmart to market the Martha Stewart Everyday line of merchandise.

When MSLO went public in 1999, Stewart greeted harried Wall Street traders with a breakfast of brioches stuffed with scrambled eggs.

Stewart resigned as CEO and chairman in 2003 after being indicted on insider trading charges related to a bio-tech stock. She remained on the board and was given a new title, chief creative officer. Stewart was replaced by COO and president Sharon Patrick as CEO, and managing partner of ValueAct Capital Partners Jeffrey Ubben as chairman.

Stewart was found guilty on all charges in 2004. Shortly after her conviction, Stewart stepped down as chief creative officer and director. Patrick stepped down in 2004 and was replaced by director Susan Lyne, a former ABC television executive. Ubben served as chairman until July 2004 when board member Thomas Siekman was named as his replacement. Charles Koppelman took over as chairman in 2005.

Stewart completed her prison sentence in March 2005 and then served another five months of house arrest. That year the company announced a four-year deal with Sirius Satellite Radio (later SIRIUS XM Radio) to create a 24-hour radio channel featuring cooking, gardening, and entertainment shows aimed at women.

MSLO piled on another deal in 2005, announcing several television programs in development with Discovery Communications. The company also that year began working on a new brand not starring Stewart, called "Petkeeping with Marc Marrone." Marrone has a TV show and other plans include a magazine, newspaper columns, and merchandising.

Lyne left the company in 2008. MSLO tapped former president of media Wenda Harris Millard and president of merchandising Robin Marino to the positions of co-CEO. Millard left the company in 2009; Marino remains as sole CEO.

EXECUTIVES

Executive Chairman; President, Media:
Charles A. Koppelman, age 69,
$3,951,223 total compensation
Director; President and CEO: Robin Marino, age 54,
$1,634,171 total compensation
Founder: Martha Stewart, age 68,
$5,441,519 total compensation
EVP and CFO: Kelli Turner, age 38
Chief Creative Officer: Gael Towey, age 57,
$759,218 total compensation
VP Information Technology: Jeff Frasure
EVP Merchandising: Patsy Pollack
EVP and General Manager, Broadcasting: Bernie Young
EVP Media Sales and Marketing: Janet Balis
SVP Integrated Marketing: Lee Heffernan, age 46
**SVP and Founding Publisher, Martha Stewart
  Weddings:** Marcia E. Miller
SVP Corporate Communications: Elizabeth J. Estroff
SVP Consumer Marketing: Richard P. Fontaine
SVP Publisher and Managing Director, Body + Soul:
  Janesse Bruce
SVP Corporate Communications and Media Relations:
  Diana Pearson
SVP Human Resources: Beth Silver
VP Marketing and Promotion: Jill Boulet-Gercourt
President, Broadcasting: Sheraton Kalouria, age 43
General Counsel: William Stern, age 45
Secretary: Maggie Drucker
Auditors: Ernst & Young LLP

LOCATIONS

HQ: Martha Stewart Living Omnimedia, Inc.
  11 W. 42nd St., New York, NY 10036
Phone: 212-827-8000   **Fax:** 212-827-8204
Web: www.marthastewart.com

PRODUCTS/OPERATIONS

2008 Sales

	$ mil.	% of total
Publishing	163.5	58
Merchandising	57.9	20
Broadcasting	47.3	17
Internet	15.6	5
Total	**284.3**	**100**

Selected Operations

Publishing
  Body + Soul (healthy living magazine)
  Everyday Food (magazine)
  Martha Stewart's Baking Handbook (book)
  Martha Stewart Living (magazine)
  Martha Stewart Weddings (magazine)
  *Martha Stewart's Homekeeping Handbook: The
    Essential Guide to Caring for Everything in Your
    Home* (book)

Merchandising
  Martha Stewart Collection at Macy's
  Martha Stewart Colors at Lowe's
  Martha Stewart at Costco
  Martha Stewart Everyday at Kmart & Sears Canada
  Martha Stewart Furniture with Bernhardt

Broadcasting
  Everyday Food
  Everyday Baking from Everyday Food
  Martha Stewart Living Radio (on SIRIUS XM Radio)
  The Martha Stewart Show

Internet
  MarthaStewart.com

COMPETITORS

Bertelsmann	The Knot
Condé Nast	Lagardère Active
DailyCandy	Lifetime
Disney	Meredith Corporation
Dwell, LLC	News Corp.
Harpo	Oxygen Media
Hearst Magazines	Reader's Digest
iVillage	Time Warner

HISTORICAL FINANCIALS
Company Type: Public

Income Statement   FYE: December 31

	REVENUE ($ mil.)	NET INCOME ($ mil.)	NET PROFIT MARGIN	EMPLOYEES
12/08	284.3	(15.7)	—	645
12/07	327.9	10.3	3.1%	760
12/06	288.3	(17.0)	—	755
12/05	209.5	(75.8)	—	656
12/04	187.4	(59.6)	—	480
Annual Growth	11.0%	—	—	7.7%

2008 Year-End Financials

Debt ratio: 12.9%	No. of shares (mil.): 55
Return on equity: —	Dividends
Cash ($ mil.): 50	Yield: 0.0%
Current ratio: 1.92	Payout: —
Long-term debt ($ mil.): 20	Market value ($ mil.): 142

Stock History   NYSE: MSO

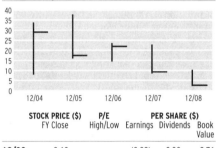

	STOCK PRICE ($) FY Close	P/E High/Low		PER SHARE ($) Earnings	Dividends	Book Value
12/08	2.60	—	—	(0.29)	0.00	2.76
12/07	9.27	112	44	0.20	0.00	2.84
12/06	21.90	—	—	(0.33)	0.00	2.39
12/05	17.43	—	—	(1.49)	0.00	2.94
12/04	29.02	—	—	(1.20)	0.00	3.43
Annual Growth	(45.3%)	—	—	—	—	(5.3%)

Martin Marietta Materials

Martin Marietta Materials (MMM) is a rock star. The company is the #2 US producer (behind Vulcan Materials) of aggregates for highway, infrastructure, commercial, and residential construction. Its Martin Marietta Aggregates division (representing 90% of sales) produces more than 150 million tons of granite, gravel, limestone, and sand annually. Magnesia Specialties produces magnesia-based chemicals for industrial, environmental, and agricultural uses, as well as fiber-reinforced composite materials used for transportation and military applications. MMM serves customers in 30 countries through about 300 quarries, plants, mines, and distribution facilities in the US, Canada, and the Bahamas.

MMM makes more than half of its sales from customers in five key states: Florida, Georgia, Iowa, North Carolina, and Texas.

Over the last decade MMM has expanded geographically via acquisitions, focusing on businesses near rail facilities or navigable waterways. The company believes its lower transportation costs give it a competitive advantage locally,

---

while allowing it to economically ship aggregates to more distant customers.

The company also continues to divest underperforming operations, such as road-paving businesses in Arkansas and Louisiana and the refactories business of the specialty products segment. Its composite materials segment may be next on the chopping block, as the company reported that this product line has not generated any profit since its inception.

With the overall downturn in the residential construction market and the global credit crunch, demand for products in that sector has declined. However, the company expects to see an increase in sales to the infrastructure sector due to an economic stimulus plan signed into law in early 2009.

HISTORY

Aerospace giant Martin Marietta Corporation kept its aggregates business out of the fray during the industry's acquisition binge of the 1980s, during which quarry prices became inflated. When recession hit at the beginning of the 1990s, the company was able to pick up quarries at fire-sale prices before spinning off the group as Martin Marietta Materials (MMM) in 1993. An initial public offering of 19% was completed in 1994.

The next year the company acquired Dravo Corporation's aggregates business for about $121 million, a move that added production and distribution operations in nine states and the Bahamas, as well as new distribution methods (by barge) and nonconstruction markets. Lockheed Martin Corporation (formed by the merger of Martin Marietta and Lockheed in 1995) owned 81% of the company until 1996, when it spun off its stake to shareholders.

In 1997 MMM shelled out $242 million for American Aggregates Corporation to add distribution and production facilities in Indiana and Ohio. The company extended its reach to Arkansas, Louisiana, and Texas the next year with the acquisition of Hot Springs, Arkansas-based Mid-State Construction & Materials. It also acquired Texas-based Redland Stone Products for $272 million from France's Lafarge. Other 1998 purchases included a 14% interest in Meridian Aggregates Company.

Rival Vulcan Materials sued MMM in 1999; Vulcan claimed it had rights to some of the leased reserves MMM had acquired in its purchase of Redland Stone Products. (The suit was dropped in 2000.) Also in 1999 MMM bought another Texas aggregates company, Marock.

In 2000 MMM completed four deals that added three asphalt plants and an aggregate company in Texas, as well as limestone operations in Ohio and West Virginia. The next year MMM bought Brauntex Materials, a limestone facility in Texas, and the part of Meridian Aggregates Company it didn't already own. Also in 2001 MMM sold its Magnesia Specialties refractories business to Minerals Technologies.

From 2002 to 2005, while continuing to pursue strategic acquisitions, the company divested several noncore and underperforming operations, as well as two nonstrategic magnesia business lines. In 2002 MMM began selling noncore aggregates businesses; it also made acquisitions in key markets, including quarries in Texas and North Carolina and an asphalt plant in Texas. It sold facilities in Illinois, Iowa, Ohio, Oklahoma, Tennessee, and Virginia.

The company sold additional noncore aggregate assets in 2003 and 2004. In 2005 it divested underperforming asphalt operations in Arkansas and Texas and closed aggregates plants in North Carolina and Ohio.

EXECUTIVES

Chairman and CEO; Chairman, Magnesia Specialties; President, Aggregates: Stephen P. (Steve) Zelnak Jr., age 64, $8,803,286 total compensation
President and COO: C. Howard (Ward) Nye, age 46, $2,552,607 total compensation
EVP, CFO, and Treasurer: Anne H. Lloyd, age 48, $1,865,255 total compensation
EVP; President, Martin Marietta Materials West: Bruce A. Vaio, age 48
EVP; EVP, Aggregates: Philip J. (Phil) Sipling, age 61, $3,176,842 total compensation
EVP; CEO, Magnesia Specialties: Daniel G. (Dan) Shephard, age 50, $2,084,285 total compensation
SVP, General Counsel, and Corporate Secretary: Roselyn R. Bar, age 50
SVP Human Resources: Jonathan T. (Jon) Stewart, age 60
Auditors: Ernst & Young LLP

LOCATIONS

HQ: Martin Marietta Materials, Inc.
2710 Wycliff Rd., Raleigh, NC 27607
Phone: 919-781-4550   **Fax:** 919-783-4695
Web: www.martinmarietta.com

PRODUCTS/OPERATIONS

2008 Sales by Segment

	$ mil.	% of total
Aggregates		
West	762.2	36
Mideast	620.6	29
Southeast	550.5	26
Specialty Products	186.8	9
Total	**2,120.1**	**100**

2008 Sales by Product Line

	$ mil.	% of total
Aggregates	1,808.8	85
Asphalt	54.0	2
Ready-mixed concrete	37.0	2
Road paving	14.2	1
Other aggregates	19.3	1
Specialty products	186.8	9
Total	**2,120.1**	**100**

Selected Operations

Aggregates Division
  Aggregates (granite, gravel, limestone, and sand)
  Asphalt
  Ready-mixed concrete
  Road paving
Specialty Products Division
  Magnesia Specialties (dolomitic lime, magnesia-based chemicals)
  Structural Composite Products (fiber-reinforced polymer composites)

COMPETITORS

Aggregate Industries	Holcim
Ashland Inc.	Lafarge North America
BPB	Lehigh Hanson
Carmeuse Lime & Stone	MDU Resources
CEMEX	Minerals Technologies
Chemical Lime	Ready Mix USA
Cookson Group	Rogers Group
CRH	ShengdaTech
CSR Limited	Trinity Industries
Eagle Materials	TXI
Florida Rock	Vulcan Materials
Giant Cement	

HISTORICAL FINANCIALS
Company Type: Public

Income Statement

FYE: December 31

	REVENUE ($ mil.)	NET INCOME ($ mil.)	NET PROFIT MARGIN	EMPLOYEES
12/08	2,120.1	176.3	8.3%	4,860
12/07	2,207.1	262.7	11.9%	5,255
12/06	2,206.4	245.4	11.1%	5,500
12/05	2,004.2	192.7	9.6%	5,754
12/04	1,759.6	129.2	7.3%	5,778
Annual Growth	**4.8%**	**8.1%**	**—**	**(4.2%)**

2008 Year-End Financials

Debt ratio: 112.8%
Return on equity: 17.9%
Cash ($ mil.): 38
Current ratio: 1.91
Long-term debt ($ mil.): 1,152

No. of shares (mil.): 45
Dividends
  Yield: 1.5%
  Payout: 35.5%
Market value ($ mil.): 4,324

Stock History

NYSE: MLM

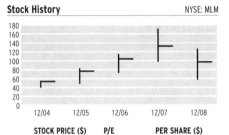

	STOCK PRICE ($) FY Close	P/E High	P/E Low	Earnings	Dividends	Book Value
12/08	97.08	30	14	4.20	1.49	22.94
12/07	132.60	28	16	6.06	1.24	21.24
12/06	103.91	21	14	5.29	1.01	28.16
12/05	76.72	20	12	4.08	0.86	26.35
12/04	53.66	20	16	2.66	0.76	25.90
Annual Growth	**16.0%**	**—**	**—**	**12.1%**	**18.3%**	**(3.0%)**

Masco Corporation

Masco's ideal customer is a home improvement junkie with a thing for cabinets — and a hand-washing fetish. The company is a leading manufacturer of a variety of home improvement and building products. Its cabinet and plumbing products businesses account for more than half its sales. Cabinet brands include KraftMaid, Quality Cabinets, and Merillat in the US and The Moores Group and Tvilum-Scanbirk in Europe. Faucets and bath and shower accessories are sold under the Delta and Peerless brands in the US and Bristan and Hansgrohe in Europe. Masco also makes BEHR paints and stains, windows, doors, staple guns, locksets, and HVAC products. If you're more comfortable on the couch, Masco provides installation services.

Masco's products and services are offered through home builders, retail chains, and wholesale outlets. It has capitalized on the popularity of home-center retail chains such as The Home Depot and Lowe's by offering a single source for a wide range of home improvement products. The Home Depot alone accounts for about 20% of Masco's sales.

In past years Masco has added to its products and services by acquiring companies. It added to its core offerings by purchasing companies that

make hand tools and stains, varnishes, and paints, including BEHR Process. The company's installations services segment also was expanded significantly with the purchase of insulation installer BSI Holdings in the early 2000s. The division, which sells and installs insulation, gutters, roofing, and fireplaces, was hurt by the economic downturn. Since 2006 Masco has been forced to close more than 80 locations formerly operated by its installations arm.

In 2008 the company merged its Mill's Price brand with KraftMaid to form the Masco Retail Cabinet Group. It also merged Merillat and Quality Cabinets to form Masco Builder Cabinet Group. The downturn in home building and home improvement in 2008 forced Masco to shutter several cabinet and window plants and cut jobs. The company is now focused on lean manufacturing principals and has plans to manufacture a common cabinet base that can be used for a variety of applications.

HISTORY

Masco founder Alex Manoogian moved to the US at age 19 in 1920. He wound up in Detroit, and with partners Harry Adjemian and Charles Saunders, he started Masco (the first letters of their last names plus "co" for "company") Screw Products Company eight days before the crash of 1929. Manoogian's partners left within the year.

Largely reliant on Detroit's auto industry, Masco grew slowly during the Depression, making custom parts for Chrysler, Ford, and others. With sales of $200,000 by 1937, it went public on the Detroit Stock Exchange. During WWII Masco focused on defense, and in 1942 sales passed $1 million. A new plant opened in 1948 in Dearborn, Michigan, as Masco resumed peacetime business, mainly in the auto industry.

In 1954 Masco began selling Manoogian's one-handle kitchen faucet (Delta). Sales of faucets passed $1 million by 1958, and Masco opened a new faucet factory in Indiana.

Under Manoogian's son Richard — whose dinner was often delayed while his father used the stove to test the heat tolerance of new faucet parts — Masco Corporation (so renamed in 1961) diversified. From 1964 to 1980 it bought more than 50 companies, concentrating on tool and metal casting, energy exploration, and air compressors. In 1984 the firm split. Masco Corporation pursued the course set by its successful faucet sales, expanding its interests in home improvement and furnishings. The industrial products business was spun off as Masco Industries, a separate public corporation (later Metaldyne) in which Masco maintained a sizable stake.

Masco Corporation became the #1 US furniture maker in the late 1980s by buying Lexington Furniture (1987) and Universal Furniture (1989), both of North Carolina. In 1990 Masco acquired KraftMaid cabinets.

Two years later the company sold its interests in Mechanical Technology, Payless Cashways, and Emco Limited of Canada (Masco bought back 40% of Emco in 1997). Masco reduced its stake in Metaldyne from 47% to 35% in 1993.

Masco sought to establish itself in Europe, and in 1994 it bought a German cabinetmaker and a UK producer of handheld showers. In 1996 founder Manoogian died, but the company flowed on. It added a UK cabinetmaker, a German shower manufacturer, and a German insulation firm. The same year Masco sold its troubled furniture unit to a group of investors and executives (who renamed the unit LifeStyle Furnishings International) for about $1 billion and further reduced its stake in Metaldyne to less than 20% (and later sold it all).

Acquisitions in 1997 included cabinetmakers Texwood Industries of Texas and Liberty Hardware Manufacturing of Florida. Masco made 13 acquisitions from 1999 through early 2000, including Heritage Bathrooms (bathroom equipment, UK), Faucet Queens (plumbing and hardware supply), BEHR Process (coatings), and Mill's Pride (cabinets).

In late 2000 and early 2001 it acquired two US-based installation services companies, Davenport Insulation Group and BSI Holdings, respectively.

During 2002 Masco acquired home improvement products and service companies that included Bristan Ltd. (kitchen and bath faucets and shower and bath accessories), Cambrian Windows Ltd. (vinyl window frames), Duraflex Ltd. (extruded vinyl frame components), SCE Unlimited (siding, shutters, gutters; Illinois), IDI Group (fireplaces, garage doors, shower enclosures; Atlanta), and Service Partners LLC (insulation and other building products, Virginia).

In 2003, Masco increased its ownership interest in Hansgrohe AG (kitchen and bath faucets, hand-held and fixed showerheads, luxury shower systems, and steam showers; Germany) to 64% from 27%. The company established Color Solutions Centers in more than 1,500 Home Depot stores throughout the US. Acquisitions in 2003 included PowerShot Tool Company, Inc. (fastening products, New Jersey) and several small installation service companies for a combined $63 million.

In 2004 Masco sold its Jung Pumpen (pumps), The Alvic Group (kitchen cabinets), Alma Kuchen (kitchen cabinets), E. Missel (acoustic insulation), and SKS Group (shutters and ventilation systems) businesses for $199 million. Masco continued its business review in 2005, selling two operating companies that made and distributed cabinets, vanities, medicine cabinets, shower rods, and bath accessories.

EXECUTIVES

Chairman: Richard A. Manoogian, age 72, $11,763,037 total compensation
President, CEO, and Director: Timothy (Tim) Wadhams, age 60, $5,516,905 total compensation
EVP and COO: Donald J. DeMarie Jr., age 45, $3,249,340 total compensation
VP, CFO, and Treasurer: John G. Sznewajs, age 41, $1,705,706 total compensation
VP and CIO: Timothy J. Monteith
VP, General Counsel, and Secretary: Barry J. Silverman, age 59
VP Sales and Marketing: Karen R. Mendelsohn
VP and Controller: William T. Anderson, age 61, $1,594,266 total compensation
VP Corporate Affairs: Sharon J. Rothwell
VP Investor Relations and Communications: Maria C. Duey
VP Finance, Retail and Wholesale, North America: Jai Shah
VP Human Resources: Charles F. Greenwood, age 61
VP Finance, North America Builder: Timothy J. LaRouere
VP and Controller, Corporate Accounting: John P. Lindow
VP Innovation and Sustainability: Gary L. Yezbick
Group President, North America Builder: W. Timothy (Tim) Yaggi
President, Masco Europe: Thomas Voss
Group President, Retail and Wholesale, North America: Jerry Volas
Manager Corporate Communications: Sue Sabo
Auditors: PricewaterhouseCoopers LLP

LOCATIONS

HQ: Masco Corporation
21001 Van Born Rd., Taylor, MI 48180
Phone: 313-274-7400   **Fax:** 313-792-6135
Web: www.masco.com

2008 Sales

	$ mil.	% of total
North America	7,482	78
International, principally Europe	2,118	22
Total	**9,600**	**100**

PRODUCTS/OPERATIONS

2008 Sales

	$ mil.	% of total
Plumbing products	3,118	33
Cabinets & related products	2,276	24
Installation & other services	1,861	19
Decorative architectural products	1,629	17
Other specialty products	716	7
Total	**9,600**	**100**

Selected Brand Names

Cabinets and Related Products
  KraftMaid
  Merillat
  Moores
  Quality Cabinets
  Tvilum-Scanbirk
  Woodgate
Plumbing Products
  Alsons
  American Shower & Bath
  Aqua Glass
  Axor
  BrassCraft
  Brasstech
  Breuer
  Bristan
  Brizo
  Caldera
  Damixa
  Delta
  Glass
  Hansgrohe
  Heritage
  Hot Spring
  HÜPPE
  BrassCraft
  Mirolin
  Newport Brass
  Peerless
  Pharo
  Plumb Shop
Decorative Architectural Products
  BEHR
  Decor Bathware
  Expressions
  Franklin Brass
  Kilz
  Liberty
Other Specialty Products
  Arrow
  Brugman
  Cambrian
  Duraflex
  Griffin
  Milgard Windows
  Powershot
  Premier
  Superia
  Thermic
  Vasco

COMPETITORS

Akzo Nobel Paints
American Woodmark
Armstrong World Industries
Benjamin Moore
Black & Decker
Columbia Pipe
Elkay Manufacturing
Fortune Brands
Furniture Brands International
Gerber Plumbing Fixtures
Grohe
Helen of Troy
Home Solutions of America
Ingersoll-Rand Security Technologies
Jacuzzi Brands
Jones-Blair
Kohler
Marmon Group
Master Lock
MasterBrand Cabinets
Moen
Nordyne
NTK Holdings
Omega Cabinets
PPG Industries
Price Pfister
Republic National Cabinet
Richelieu Hardware
RSI Holding Corporation
Sherwin-Williams
Simpson Manufacturing
Simpson Strong-Tie
Spear & Jackson
Stanley Works
Trane Inc.
US Home Systems
Valspar
Waxman

HISTORICAL FINANCIALS

Company Type: Public

Income Statement

FYE: December 31

	REVENUE ($ mil.)	NET INCOME ($ mil.)	NET PROFIT MARGIN	EMPLOYEES
12/08	9,600.0	(391.0)	—	39,000
12/07	11,770.0	386.0	3.3%	52,000
12/06	12,778.0	491.0	3.8%	57,000
12/05	12,642.0	940.0	7.4%	62,000
12/04	12,074.0	893.0	7.4%	62,000
Annual Growth	**(5.6%)**	**—**	**—**	**(10.9%)**

2008 Year-End Financials

Debt ratio: 137.6%   No. of shares (mil.): 359
Return on equity: —   Dividends
Cash ($ mil.): 1,028   Yield: 8.3%
Current ratio: 2.13   Payout: —
Long-term debt ($ mil.): 3,915   Market value ($ mil.): 3,998

Stock History

NYSE: MAS

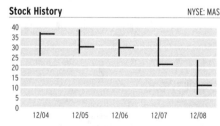

	STOCK PRICE ($) FY Close	P/E High/Low		PER SHARE ($) Earnings	Dividends	Book Value
12/08	11.13	—	—	(1.11)	0.93	7.92
12/07	21.61	34	20	1.03	0.91	11.21
12/06	29.87	28	21	1.22	0.86	12.45
12/05	30.19	18	12	2.19	0.78	13.50
12/04	36.53	19	13	1.96	0.66	15.10
Annual Growth	**(25.7%)**	**—**	**—**	**—**	**9.0%**	**(14.9%)**

LOCATIONS

HQ: MasterCard Incorporated
    2000 Purchase St., Purchase, NY 10577
Phone: 914-249-2000   **Fax:** 914-249-4206
Web: www.mastercard.com

2008 Sales

	% of total
US	47
Inernational	53
Total	**100**

PRODUCTS/OPERATIONS

2008 Sales

	$ mil.	% of total
Net operations fees	3,759	76
Net assessments	1,233	24
Total	**4,992**	**100**

COMPETITORS

American Express
Discover
Fifth Third
First Data
JCB International
NYCE Payments Network
PULSE Network
Total System Services
Visa Inc
Visa International

HISTORICAL FINANCIALS

Company Type: Public

Income Statement

FYE: December 31

	REVENUE ($ mil.)	NET INCOME ($ mil.)	NET PROFIT MARGIN	EMPLOYEES
12/08	4,991.6	(253.9)	—	5,500
12/07	4,067.6	1,085.9	26.7%	5,000
12/06	3,326.1	50.2	1.5%	4,600
12/05	2,937.6	266.7	9.1%	4,300
12/04	2,593.3	238.1	9.2%	4,000
Annual Growth	17.8%	—	—	8.3%

2008 Year-End Financials

Debt ratio: 1.0%
Return on equity: —
Cash ($ mil.): 1,505
Current ratio: 1.44
Long-term debt ($ mil.): 19
No. of shares (mil.): 130
Dividends
    Yield: 0.5%
    Payout: —
Market value ($ mil.): 18,533

Stock History

NYSE: MA

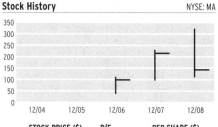

	STOCK PRICE ($) FY Close	P/E High/Low	PER SHARE ($) Earnings	Dividends	Book Value
12/08	142.93	— —	(1.95)	0.75	14.86
12/07	215.20	28 12	8.00	0.54	23.35
12/06	98.49	294 109	0.37	0.09	18.23
Annual Growth	20.5%	— —	—	188.7%	(9.7%)

Mattel, Inc.

Barbie is the platinum blonde in power at Mattel, the #1 toy maker in the world. Its products include Barbie dolls, Fisher-Price toys, Hot Wheels and Matchbox cars, American Girl dolls and books, and various *Sesame Street, Barney, Ferrari,* and other licensed items. Mattel also produces action figures and toys based on Walt Disney movies. To satisfy techie kids, Mattel has accessorized Barbie with interactive games, software, and a line of Barbie MP3 players. The company has even licensed the Barbie name for eyewear. Mattel is trying to reduce its reliance on its biggest customers — Wal-Mart, Toys "R" Us, and Target — through its own catalog and Internet sales.

Mattel is capitalizing on its core brands, particularly with licensing deals. REM Eyewear developed a line of Barbie eyewear for girls, and in 2007 a line of Barbie MP3 players, called Barbie Girls, went on sale. Other licensing deals include a plethora of purple playthings featuring TV's Barney character for its littlest customers; toys based on Warner Bros. characters, including Looney Tunes, Batman, and Superman; and Innovo Group adult apparel and accessories under the Hot Wheels brand. The company was awarded new toy licenses for WWE Wrestling, Thomas and Friends, and Disney/Pixar's *Toy Story* in 2008.

Mattel seems to have won a long-fought legal battle against Bratz doll maker MGA Entertainment. In 2005 MGA filed a lawsuit against Mattel, alleging that Mattel is engaging in unfair competition by copying the Bratz dolls' design with its "My Scene" version of Barbie. In late 2006 Mattel said it had legal claim to the Bratz doll because it had employed the designer and freelancer (Carter Bryant) who created the initial sketches for the doll. In the meantime, Mattel applied for copyright protection for many of those early sketches. In 2008 a federal court ruled that MGA had interfered with Bryant's contract, and the dolls were designed while he was employed by Mattel. A federal jury awarded Mattel $100 million in damages in the dispute. In 2009 the court placed MGA in federal receivership and later appointed a judge to monitor the transfer of Bratz to Mattel, which plans to launch its own Bratz products in spring 2010.

A spate of recalls in 2007, spurred by Chinese-made products considered harmful, were expensive both for Mattel's pocketbook (it estimates its losses at nearly $50 million in product returns and related expenses) and its image. The company had to recall over 2 million Chinese-made toys in 2007, after learning that they may contain hazardous levels of lead paint. Mattel also recalled more than 18 million toys due to potentially hazardous small magnets.

In December 2008 the company agreed to pay $12 million to 39 states to settle an investigation into lead-tainted toys and to lower acceptable levels of lead in imported toys. A class action suit related to the recalls has also been filed against Mattel on behalf of parents who bought the toys.

In response to hard economic times, in late 2008 Mattel cut 1,000 jobs (less than 5% of its worldwide workforce), reducing its professional and management ranks by nearly 10%.

Janus Capital Management and Franklin Mutual Advisors each maintain about a 5% stake in the company.

HISTORY

A small California toy manufacturer began operating out of a converted garage in 1945, producing dollhouse furniture. Harold Matson and Elliot Handler named their new company Mattel, using letters from their last and first names. Matson soon sold his share to Handler and his wife, Ruth, who incorporated the business in 1948.

By 1952 the company's toy line had expanded to include burp guns and musical toys, and sales exceeded $5 million. Sponsorship of Walt Disney's *Mickey Mouse Club* (debuted 1955), a first in toy advertising, was a shrewd marketing step for Mattel, providing direct, year-round access to millions of young potential customers.

In 1959 Mattel introduced the Barbie doll, named after the Handlers' daughter, Barbara, and later introduced Ken, named after their son. Barbie, with her fashionable wardrobe and extensive line of accessories, was an instant hit and eventually became the most successful brand-name toy ever sold.

Mattel went public in 1960, and within two years sales had jumped from $25 million to $75 million. It launched the popular Hot Wheels miniature cars line in 1968.

The Handlers were ousted from management in 1974 after an investigation by the SEC found irregularities in reports of the company's profits. The new management moved into non-toy businesses, adding Western Publishing (Golden Books) and the Ringling Brothers-Barnum & Bailey Combined Shows circus in 1979.

By the 1980s Mattel was a high-volume business with heavy overhead expenses and high development costs. By 1984, in an effort to recapitalize, the company had sold all its non-toy assets. Sales were more than $1 billion in 1987, but Mattel lost $93 million. Toying with bankruptcy, newly appointed chairman John Amerman cut Mattel's manufacturing capacity by 40% and fired 22% of its corporate staff.

The early 1990s saw several acquisitions — Fisher-Price (toys for preschoolers), and Kransco (battery-powered ride-on vehicles).

Amerman relinquished his roles as chairman and CEO in 1997 and was replaced by COO Jill Barad, who had enlivened the Barbie brand. Also in 1997 the company bought #3 US toy maker Tyco Toys (Tickle Me Elmo and Matchbox cars).

Barad started restructuring Mattel in 1999, closing plants and laying off 3,000 workers. The company entered unfamiliar territory in 1999, paying $3.6 billion for leading educational software maker The Learning Company in a deal that would be Barad's downfall. Losses followed, and Barad left in 2000. Mattel named Kraft Foods veteran Bob Eckert chairman and CEO.

Co-founder Ruth Handler, credited with the creation of the Barbie doll, died in April 2002. Mattel and two former employees agreed in December 2002 to pay $477,000 in fines for making political donations in other people's names, the third-largest fine imposed by the Federal Election Commission. Also that year the company closed its Kentucky manufacturing and distribution facilities and in early 2003 consolidated two of its manufacturing facilities in Mexico.

Looking to further its presence in the electronic toys business, Mattel acquired Hong Kong-based Radica Games for $230 million in 2006. The products appeal to children older than Mattel's typical consumer, as well as adults. Also that year Mattel selected Activision Blizzard in a multiyear deal to be the exclusive worldwide distributor for Barbie-branded video games.

EXECUTIVES

Chairman and CEO: Robert A. Eckert, age 54, $6,999,051 total compensation
EVP Worldwide Operations: Thomas A. Debrowski, age 58, $2,078,420 total compensation
CFO: Kevin M. Farr, age 51, $1,713,182 total compensation
EVP Mattel and President, American Girl: Ellen L. Brothers, age 53
SVP Human Resources: Alan Kaye, age 55
SVP Operations Finance and Strategy: Douglas E. Kerner, age 49
SVP and Corporate Controller: H. Scott Topham, age 48
SVP, General Counsel, and Secretary: Robert (Bob) Normile, age 49
SVP Investor Relation, and Treasurer: Dianne Douglas, age 52
SVP Radica: Jim Wagner
SVP Worldwide Quality Assurance: Jim Walter
SVP Mattel Brands: Jerry Bossick
SVP and General Manager Girls Business: Chuck Scothon
SVP Inventor Relations, Licensing, and New Business Fisher-Price Brands: Stan Clutton
SVP and General Manager Fisher-Price: David Allmark
SVP Corporate Responsibility: Geoff Massingberd, age 51
VP Corporate Communications: Lisa Marie Bongiovanni
President, Mattel Brands: Neil B. Friedman, age 61, $3,240,346 total compensation
President, International: Bryan G. Stockton, age 55, $2,447,421 total compensation
Director Investor Relations: Joleen Jackson
Auditors: PricewaterhouseCoopers LLP

LOCATIONS

HQ: Mattel, Inc.
333 Continental Blvd., El Segundo, CA 90245
Phone: 310-252-2000   **Fax:** 310-252-2179
Web: www.mattel.com

2008 Sales

	$ mil.	% of total
US	3,319.2	51
International		
Europe	1,689.7	26
Latin America	978.8	16
Asia/Pacific	286.1	4
Other regions	212.2	3
Adjustments	(568.0)	—
Total	**5,918.0**	**100**

PRODUCTS/OPERATIONS

2008 Sales

	$ mil.	% of total
Domestic		
Fisher-Price Brands US	1,437.9	22
Mattel Girls & Boys Brands US	1,418.2	22
American Girl Brands	463.1	7
International	3,166.8	49
Adjustments	(568.0)	—
Total	**5,918.0**	**100**

Selected Brands

Boys
Batman
DC Universe
Hot Wheels
Kung Fu Panda
Magic 8 Ball
Masters of the Universe
Matchbox
Mattel
Max Steel
Nickelodeon *Rugrats*
Radica
Scrabble (International)
Speed Racer
Tyco Radio Control
Yu-Gi-Oh!

Girls
American Girl
Barbie
Bitty Baby
Boom-O
Cabbage Patch Kids
Coconut
Disney
Diva Starz
ello
Fashion Avenue
Flavas
High School Musical
Just Like You
Little Mommy
Polly Pocket!
Infant and preschool
BabyGear
Barney
Blue's Clues
Disney
Dora the Explorer
Fisher-Price
Geo Trax
Go-Diego-Go!
Little People
Matchbox Kids
Mickey Mouse
Pixter
Power Wheels
See 'n Say
Sesame Street
UNO
View-Master
Winnie the Pooh

COMPETITORS

Electronic Arts
Hasbro
JAKKS Pacific
LeapFrog
LEGO
Marvel Entertainment
MGA Entertainment
Motorsports Authentics
Namco Bandai
Ohio Art
Playmobil
Radica Games
Radio Flyer
RC2 Corporation
Sanrio
Simba Dickie Group
TakaraTomy
Toy Quest
Ty
VTech Holdings

HISTORICAL FINANCIALS

Company Type: Public

Income Statement				FYE: December 31
	REVENUE ($ mil.)	NET INCOME ($ mil.)	NET PROFIT MARGIN	EMPLOYEES
12/08	5,918.0	379.6	6.4%	29,000
12/07	5,970.1	600.0	10.1%	31,000
12/06	5,650.2	592.9	10.5%	32,000
12/05	5,179.0	417.0	8.1%	26,000
12/04	5,102.8	572.7	11.2%	25,000
Annual Growth	**3.8%**	**(9.8%)**	**—**	**3.8%**

2008 Year-End Financials

Debt ratio: 35.4%
Return on equity: 17.2%
Cash ($ mil.): 618
Current ratio: 1.89
Long-term debt ($ mil.): 750

No. of shares (mil.): 359
Dividends
  Yield: 4.7%
  Payout: 71.4%
Market value ($ mil.): 5,737

Stock History

NYSE: MAT

	STOCK PRICE ($) FY Close	P/E High/Low		PER SHARE ($) Earnings	Dividends	Book Value
12/08	16.00	21	10	1.05	0.75	5.90
12/07	19.04	19	12	1.54	0.75	6.43
12/06	22.66	16	10	1.53	0.65	6.79
12/05	15.82	21	14	1.01	0.50	5.86
12/04	19.49	15	12	1.35	0.45	6.65
Annual Growth	**(4.8%)**	**—**	**—**	**(6.1%)**	**13.6%**	**(2.9%)**

Maxim Integrated Products

Maxim's maxim? Invent! Maxim Integrated Products makes more than 5,700 kinds of analog and mixed-signal integrated circuits (ICs), including more than 4,500 of its own invention. Maxim's chips — which include amplifiers, data converters, and timing and switching ICs — translate physical data such as temperature, pressure, and sound into digital signals for electronic processing. The company's products are used by thousands of electronics manufacturers in products including computers and peripherals, industrial controls, telecommunications and networking equipment, military systems, medical devices, instrumentation, and video displays. Four-fifths of sales are from outside the US.

In early 2009 Maxim acquired two product lines from ZiLOG. The company purchased ZiLOG's Wireless Control business in concert with Universal Electronics. Maxim received the hardware portion of the business, microcontrollers and related intellectual property, and will combine those products with its ultra-low-power infrared microcontroller family. On its own, Maxim bought ZiLOG's Secure Transaction product line, with its Zatara line of 32-bit MCUs used in consumer payment terminals. The acquisition dovetails with Maxim's earlier purchase of a French firm, Innova Card, in providing chips for the financial transaction terminal market.

The company's famously no-nonsense founder, Jack Gifford, fostered a work atmosphere built around total candor, high expectations, and high performance. Despite the notorious roller-coaster ups and downs of the chip industry, Maxim recorded large annual profits for more than a decade running.

A stock-options backdating case forced Gifford's retirement after 23 years with the company. Management looked at all options grants given between July 1994 and June 2006, and found many were misdated on when they were actually granted, greatly skewing the compensation expenses Maxim should have taken against profits in that period. As a result, the company took a pre-tax adjustment to income from operations of about $838 million, including more than $773 million for stock-based compensation expenses.

Maxim also implemented a number of corporate reforms, such as new corporate governance guidelines, formal procedures for the granting of stock options and other equity awards, and a more comprehensive insider trading policy.

HISTORY

Jack Gifford, a former UCLA baseball star who began his career at Fairchild Semiconductor and later headed the Intersil subsidiary (later divested) of General Electric, founded Maxim in 1983. Gifford focused on analog chips, which were less vulnerable to Japanese competition than digital integrated circuits (ICs), had a longer product life, and cost less to make. Maxim went public in 1988.

From the beginning, Maxim emphasized research and development: Gifford's 1983 business plan set the ambitious goal of developing at least 15 new products each quarter. The company developed 479 new products between 1993 and 1996.

In 1994 Maxim bought Tektronix's IC business, and the two companies formed the Maxtek joint venture, a maker of multichip modules and hybrid circuits. For the rest of the decade Maxim focused on expanding and modernizing its manufacturing. It opened offices in Hong Kong, South Korea, and Singapore in 1996, and added factories in the Philippines and California in 1997.

Maxim released 250 new products in fiscal 1998, including breakthrough chips for portable computers, flat-panel displays, and paging. Maxim sold its half of Maxtek to Tektronix in 2000. That year it also introduced a record 383 products, and broke ground for a testing facility in Thailand.

In 2001 Maxim acquired specialty IC maker Dallas Semiconductor for about $2.5 billion. It also continued its "product proliferation" strategy as it topped itself once again by introducing 500 new products. Fiscal 2001 also saw the company expand its facilities in California, Thailand, and the Philippines.

Maxim bought a Texas chip fabrication plant from Philips Semiconductors (now NXP) in 2003.

For health reasons, Jack Gifford retired as CEO at the end of 2006; he also left the board of directors. Tunc Doluca, a group president and 22-year veteran of Maxim, was named president and CEO effective at the beginning of 2007. Director B. Kipling Hagopian, a member of the board since 1997, was elected interim chairman to succeed Gifford.

Gifford's sudden departure came while the company was still investigating its past practices in granting stock options, a subject that came to dominate his last year with Maxim. A shareholder derivative lawsuit challenging Maxim's practices in stock-option grants was filed in May 2006. While the company publicly dismissed the complaint as without merit, the SEC soon after opened an informal inquiry on the subject.

The board's special committee wrapped up its review in early 2007, concluding that there were instances from 2000 to 2006 where the recorded price of certain stock-option grants did not reflect the fair market value of the shares on the actual measurement dates. As a result, Jack Gifford retired from his part-time advisory position and CFO Carl Jasper resigned from the company.

Near the end of 2007, Maxim reached a settlement with the SEC on options backdating, agreeing to a permanent injunction against violations of federal securities laws and anti-fraud statutes. The SEC didn't assess any fines or penalties against the company under the settlement. The regulators brought civil charges against Gifford and Jasper for their roles in backdating options.

Gifford settled his case with the SEC, agreeing to return more than $650,000 in bonuses and to pay a penalty of $150,000. Jasper contested the charges, however.

In 2008 the company settled the shareholder derivative lawsuit over the misdated stock options for $28.5 million.

Gifford died in early 2009 at the age of 67.

EXECUTIVES

Chairman: B. Kipling (Kip) Hagopian, age 67
President, CEO, and Director: Tunc Doluca, age 50
CFO: Bruce E. Kiddoo, age 48
SVP Administration and General Counsel:
 Charles G. Rigg, age 64
SVP: Vivek Jain, age 37
VP and Senior Counsel: Edwin Medlin, age 52
VP Worldwide Sales: Matthew J. Murphy, age 35
Group President: Pirooz Parvarandeh, age 48
Group President: Vijay Ullal, age 49
Executive Director Investor Relations: Paresh Maniar
Senior Public Relations Specialist: Drew Ehrlich
Auditors: Deloitte & Touche LLP

LOCATIONS

HQ: Maxim Integrated Products, Inc.
 120 San Gabriel Dr., Sunnyvale, CA 94086
Phone: 408-737-7600 **Fax:** 408-737-7194
Web: www.maxim-ic.com

Maxim Integrated Products has facilities in California, Massachusetts, Oregon, and Texas, and overseas in the Philippines and Thailand.

2009 Sales

	$ mil.	% of total
Asia/Pacific		
China	496.1	30
South Korea	229.8	14
Japan	120.8	7
Other countries	169.2	10
US	302.6	19
Europe	291.5	18
Other regions	36.0	2
Total	**1,646.0**	**100**

PRODUCTS/OPERATIONS

Selected Products

Amplifiers and comparators
 Audio amplifiers
 Operational amplifiers
Analog switches and multiplexers
Data converters, sample-and-hold devices, and voltage references
Digital potentiometers
Display drivers and display power devices
Fiber and communications devices
 Circuits for fiber and cable data transmission
 Framers
 Transceivers
Filters
High-frequency application-specific integrated circuits (ASICs)
Hot-swap and power switching circuits
Interface and interconnect devices

Memories
 Electrically erasable programmable read-only memories (EEPROMs)
 Erasable programmable read-only memories (EPROMs)
 Non-volatile static random-access memories (SRAMs)
 Non-volatile timekeeping RAMs
Microcontrollers
Microprocessor supervisors and non-volatile RAM controllers
Power supplies and battery management devices
 DC-to-DC power supplies
 Low-dropout linear regulators
 Power metal oxide semiconductor field-effect transistor (MOSFET) drivers
Protection and isolation circuits
Sensors, sensor conditioners, and thermal management devices
Timing devices
 Counters and timers
 Oscillators and waveform generators
 Real-time clocks (RTCs)
Wireless and radio-frequency (RF) products
 Downconverters and upconverters
 Low noise amplifiers
 Power amplifiers
 Transmitters and transceivers

COMPETITORS

Altera	Monolithic Power Systems
Analog Devices	National Semiconductor
Analogic Technologies	NXP
Applied Micro Circuits	O2Micro
Atmel	ON Semiconductor
Conexant Systems	PMC-Sierra
Exar	QUALCOMM
Fairchild Semiconductor	RF Micro Devices
Freescale Semiconductor	Ricoh Company
Fujitsu Microelectronics	ROHM
Infineon Technologies	Seiko
Intel Corp.	Semtech
International Rectifier	Silicon Labs
Intersil	Siliconix
Linear Technology	Skyworks
Marvell Technology	STMicroelectronics
Micrel	Texas Instruments
Microchip Technology	Vishay Intertechnology
Mitsubishi Corp.	Vitesse Semiconductor
Mitsui	Volterra Semiconductor

HISTORICAL FINANCIALS

Company Type: Public

Income Statement

FYE: Last Saturday in June

	REVENUE ($ mil.)	NET INCOME ($ mil.)	NET PROFIT MARGIN	EMPLOYEES
6/09	1,646.0	10.5	0.6%	8,765
6/08	2,052.8	317.7	15.5%	9,810
6/07	2,009.1	286.2	14.2%	10,136
6/06	1,856.9	386.1	20.8%	9,096
6/05	1,671.7	540.8	32.4%	7,980
Annual Growth	**(0.4%)**	**(62.7%)**	**—**	**2.4%**

2009 Year-End Financials

Debt ratio: 4.8%
Return on equity: 0.4%
Cash ($ mil.): 709
Current ratio: 5.90
Long-term debt ($ mil.): 125

No. of shares (mil.): 306
Dividends
 Yield: 5.1%
 Payout: 2,666.7%
Market value ($ mil.): 4,802

Stock History

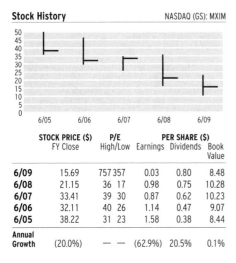

NASDAQ (GS): MXIM

	STOCK PRICE ($) FY Close	P/E High/Low		PER SHARE ($) Earnings Dividends		Book Value
6/09	15.69	757	357	0.03	0.80	8.48
6/08	21.15	36	17	0.98	0.75	10.28
6/07	33.41	39	30	0.87	0.62	10.23
6/06	32.11	40	26	1.14	0.47	9.07
6/05	38.22	31	23	1.58	0.38	8.44
Annual Growth	(20.0%)	—	—	(62.9%)	20.5%	0.1%

MBIA Inc.

MBIA will make sure that bonds get paid, no matter what. Through its independent subsidiary, National Public Finance Guarantee Corporation, MBIA is a leading provider of insurance for municipal bonds and stable corporate bonds (such as utility bonds). Separate from its municipal bond business, MBIA also manages assets for public-sector clients, guarantees bank deposits for government entities, and insures insurance companies' guaranteed investment contracts. Other lines of business include tax compliance services and buying and servicing municipal real estate tax liens. It operates from three US offices and three in Europe as well as ones in Mexico City, Tokyo, and Sydney.

MBIA was one of the largest providers of insurance to asset and mortgage-based securities, which made it vulnerable when the US housing market imploded in 2007. The company posted losses of $2.3 billion the last quarter of 2007, a result of its investments in subprime mortgage-backed securities. In response, MBIA escorted its CEO Gary Dunton to the door and welcomed back his predecessor, Joseph Brown. MBIA and its similarly afflicted competitors, FGIC and Ambac Financial, all scrambled to protect their ratings. MBIA then laid out a plan to split apart its public, structured, and asset management businesses to separate the stable from the unstable. In the interim, the company set in place some drastic changes to reduce its exposure to any single risk. In early 2008 it stopped writing structured finance for six months, and quit insuring credit derivative transactions.

The big change came in early 2009: MBIA split its municipal bond insurance business off into an independent subsidiary named National Public Finance Guarantee Corporation. It receives a credit rating separate from the rest of MBIA's riskier structured-finance businesses.

Before the meltdown, MBIA had expanded internationally for long-term growth although while still writing more than 60% of its business in the US. The company's international business consists primarily of guarantees on privately issued bonds for public projects.

Private equity firm Warburg Pincus owns about a third of the company.

HISTORY

In 1974 such insurers as Aetna, CIGNA, Fireman's Fund (now part of Allianz), and Continental (now part of CNA) formed consortium Municipal Bond Insurance Association. The insurance was intended to reduce investor risk and to boost ratings and cut costs for bond issuers. Holding company MBIA was incorporated and went public in 1986. Three years later it absorbed rival Bond Investors Group.

As bond insurance gained wide acceptance, MBIA moved into coverage of investment-grade corporate bonds, and asset- and mortgage-backed bonds. It also began offering institutional brokerage services and money market funds to municipal customers. But with acceptance came competition, forcing MBIA to take on riskier bond issues. It joined forces with Ambac Indemnity in 1995 to offer bond insurance abroad; the decision pricked MBIA three years later when a Thai company defaulted.

It began investing in real estate tax lien and tax compliance companies in 1996 and picked up asset-backed bond insurer CapMAC Holdings in 1998, despite that company's exposure in Asia. The same year MBIA formed an alliance with Japan's Mitsui Marine & Fire (now Mitsui Sumitomo Insurance) and bought 1838 Investment Advisors, which oversees assets of $6 billion.

The following year the company inked a deal to be the exclusive insurer of municipal bonds on Trading Edge's BondLink trading service. MBIA also sold its bond administration and consulting firm, MBIA MuniFinancial, saying it no longer fit with company strategy.

In 2000 MBIA's venture with Trading Edge opened for online business. That year the company exited its alliance with Mitsui Sumitomo Insurance. Due to its decision to discontinue equity advisory services operations, MBIA sold subsidiary 1838 Investment Advisors to that company's management in 2004; MBIA then focused its advisory services on fixed-income asset management.

EXECUTIVES

Chairman: Daniel P. Kearney, age 69
CEO and Director: Joseph W. (Jay) Brown, age 60, $2,215,651 total compensation
President, CFO, and Chief Administrative Officer: C. Edward (Chuck) Chaplin, age 52, $2,766,623 total compensation
President and COO: William C. (Bill) Fallon, age 49, $2,263,485 total compensation
VP and Chief Risk Officer: Ruth M. Whaley, age 52
EVP, Chief Legal Officer, and Secretary: Ram D. Wertheim, age 54, $1,906,105 total compensation
Chief Compliance Officer and Media Contact: Willard I. Hill Jr.
EVP and Chief Investment Officer; President, MBIA Asset Management: Clifford D. Corso, age 47
EVP and Chief Portfolio Officer: Mitchell I. Sonkin, age 56, $2,760,327 total compensation
Head of Global Public Finance: Thomas G. (Tom) McLoughlin, age 48
Managing Director and Head of International: Christopher E. (Chris) Weeks, age 48
Investor Relations: Greg Diamond
Managing Director and Treasurer, MBIA and MBIA Insurance: Fred C. Pastore
Auditors: PricewaterhouseCoopers LLP

LOCATIONS

HQ: MBIA Inc.
113 King St., Armonk, NY 10504
Phone: 914-273-4545 **Fax:** 914-765-3163
Web: www.mbia.com

PRODUCTS/OPERATIONS

Selected Subsidiaries

CAH Asset Holdings, Inc.
Capital Markets Assurance Corporation
CapMAC Asia Ltd.
CapMAC Financial Services, Inc.
CapMAC Holdings Inc.
CapMAC Investment Management, Inc.
Colorado Investor Services Corporation
Euro Asset Acquisition Limited
KOP Management LLC
MBIA Insurance Corporation
MBIA U.K. (Holdings) Limited
MBIA UK Insurance Limited
Meridian Funding Company, LLC
Municipal Issuers Service Corporation
Municipal Tax Collection Bureau, Inc.
Triple-A One Funding Corporation

COMPETITORS

Ambac
Assured Guaranty
FGIC
Financial Security Assurance
Radian Asset Assurance
Syncora Holdings

HISTORICAL FINANCIALS
Company Type: Public

Income Statement

	ASSETS ($ mil.)	NET INCOME ($ mil.)	INCOME AS % OF ASSETS	EMPLOYEES
12/08	29,657.1	(2,672.7)	—	420
12/07	47,415.1	(1,921.9)	—	486
12/06	39,763.0	819.3	2.1%	492
12/05	34,561.4	711.0	2.1%	626
12/04	33,027.4	815.3	2.5%	623
Annual Growth	(2.7%)	—	—	(9.4%)

FYE: December 31

2008 Year-End Financials

Equity as % of assets: 3.4%
Return on assets: —
Return on equity: —
Long-term debt ($ mil.): 10,527
No. of shares (mil.): 208
Dividends
  Yield: 0.0%
  Payout: —
Market value ($ mil.): 847
Sales ($ mil.): (857)

Stock History

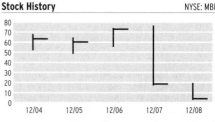

NYSE: MBI

	STOCK PRICE ($) FY Close	P/E High/Low		PER SHARE ($) Earnings Dividends		Book Value
12/08	4.07	—	—	(12.29)	0.00	4.78
12/07	18.63	—	—	(15.17)	1.36	17.58
12/06	73.06	12	9	5.99	1.24	34.64
12/05	60.16	12	9	5.18	1.12	31.69
12/04	63.28	12	9	5.63	0.96	31.63
Annual Growth	(49.6%)	—	—	—	—	(37.6%)

McAfee, Inc.

McAfee puts a virtual padlock on IT resources. The company provides security products that protect computers, networks, and mobile devices. Its software and hardware protect users from viruses, spam, and spyware. Other offerings include data loss prevention, mobile security, host intrusion prevention, encryption, and e-mail security tools. McAfee also provides consulting, support, and training services. The company sells its products directly and through resellers and distributors to consumers, corporate clients, service providers, and government agencies worldwide.

McAfee generates about half of its revenues from services. Its sales are roughly split between North America and other regions.

After a series of divestitures designed to help it focus on anti-virus applications (culminating with the 2004 sale of its Sniffer network protection assets to Network General), McAfee reversed course and has since been on an acquisition tear that has significantly broadened its portfolio of protection tools.

Among its recent purchases was the 2008 acquisition of ScanAlert, the creators of the HACKER SAFE Web site security certification service, for $51 million (with the potential to earn another $24 million if certain performance targets are met). It also purchased data loss prevention specialist Reconnex. It paid $465 million to acquire network security gateway provider Secure Computing in 2008. The purchase of Secure Computing made McAfee one of the world's largest network security software providers. Secure Computing boasted more than 20,000 customers located in over 100 countries.

McAfee also acquired IT infrastructure protection specialist Solidcore in June 2009. Solidcore's products prevent the installation of unauthorized applications on servers and workstations. The purchase gives McAfee a foothold in new markets, as Solidcore's products are also used in such devices as ATMs, point-of-sale systems, and multifunction printers.

HISTORY

John McAfee, a former systems consultant for Lockheed, started McAfee Associates in 1989 to sell his antivirus software. Normal retail channels were too difficult for a small entrepreneur to crack, so he marketed his product on computer bulletin boards as shareware, depending on the honesty of users to pay for the product if they found it useful. Enough of them did, and the success was compounded as satisfied individual users recommended it for their companies' systems.

McAfee Associates went public in 1992. The next year former Apple and Sun Microsystems marketer William Larson became CEO. He built a suite of products through more than a dozen acquisitions, bundled them to reap higher returns, and stretched the company's sales and marketing efforts.

From 1994 to 1997 sales grew to more than $600 million. Following a failed bid to acquire Cheyenne Software in 1996, McAfee bought network management specialist Network General in 1997 and changed its name to Network Associates. It also bought software encryption company Pretty Good Privacy (PGP) that year.

The company continued to pursue acquisitions in 1998, seeking to convert the company from an antivirus leader into a network security and desktop management specialist rivaling CA. (Larson chose the company's Santa Clara headquarters partly because its offices towered over CA's across the highway.) Network Associates moved into firewalls (Trusted Information Systems), intrusion detection (Secure Networks), more antivirus technology (UK-based Dr Solomon's), and diagnostic software (CyberMedia).

That year the SEC began examining the large amount of acquisition-related charges Network Associates had written off. Also in 1998 the company formed subsidiary McAfee.com, a Web site from which consumers could buy software and access PC maintenance and other hosted services. In 1999 Network Associates was forced to restate its 1998 results, resulting in a number of shareholder lawsuits. Also that year Network Associates sold a 15% stake in McAfee.com to the public. Acquisition charges left the company suffering a loss for 1999.

The company's myCIO.com subsidiary began operations at the start of 2000, offering hosted network security services over the Internet for businesses. Late in 2000 a surprise earnings warning was followed by the departure of several top executives, including Larson.

Early the next year Network Associates named George Samenuk, former head of online exchange company Tradeout, CEO and chairman.

In 2002 the company sold its firewall security unit to Secure Computing. Network Associates also repurchased the publicly traded shares of McAfee.com, as part of a broad effort to streamline its product lines.

In 2003 Network Associates entered the intrusion detection market with the acquisitions of Entercept Security Technologies and IntruVert Networks. The company also restated its financial results for fiscal years 1998-2000 after investigations by the SEC and Department of Justice.

The company purchased vulnerability management software provider Foundstone for about $86 million in 2004. McAfee sold its Magic Solutions business unit, which provided help-desk software, to BMC for about $47 million in 2004. Later in 2004 the company announced it was exiting the network software business and focusing on its anti-virus products. It sold its Sniffer product line to Silver Lake Partners and Texas Pacific Group for $235 million and changed its name to McAfee. (With the sale of the Sniffer line Network General was resurrected.)

It acquired security software maker Wireless Security in 2005.

Early in 2006 McAfee reached a settlement with the SEC, agreeing to pay $50 million to end a long-running investigation into its accounting practices. Later that year Samenuk resigned as chairman and CEO; board members Charles Robel and Dale Fuller were named chairman and interim CEO, respectively. Also in 2006, it purchased Web site test and rating specialist SiteAdvisor, as well as data protection service provider Onigma.

In 2007 David DeWalt, formerly a top executive at storage vendor EMC, was named CEO. That year McAfee acquired SafeBoot, a developer of security software for mobile devices, for $350 million.

EXECUTIVES

Chairman: Charles J. (Chuck) Robel, age 59
President, CEO, and Director: David G. (Dave) DeWalt, age 44, $7,528,127 total compensation
COO and CFO: Albert A. (Rocky) Pimentel, age 54, $1,365,843 total compensation
VP and Chief Technology Evangelist: Carl E. Banzhof, age 39
SVP and CIO: Mark Tonnesen
EVP and Chief Marketing Officer: David B. Milam, age 53
Chief Security Officer: Martin Carmichael
SVP Finance and Chief Accounting Officer: Keith Krzeminski, age 47, $831,181 total compensation
EVP Worldwide Channel Operations: Roger J. King
EVP Corporate Strategy and Business Development: Gerhard Watzinger, age 48
EVP, General Counsel, and Corporate Secretary: Mark D. Cochran, age 50, $1,658,568 total compensation
EVP and General Manager, Consumer, Mobile, and Small Business: Todd Gebhart
EVP Worldwide Sales Operations: Michael P. DeCesare, age 44, $3,106,228 total compensation
EVP Human Resources: Joseph P. (Joe) Gabbert, age 57
SVP Worldwide Marketing: Chris Kenworthy
VP Corporate Communications: Michael Busselen
VP Investor Relations: Kelsey Doherty
Auditors: Deloitte & Touche LLP

LOCATIONS

HQ: McAfee, Inc.
   3965 Freedom Cir., Santa Clara, CA 95054
Phone: 408-988-3832   **Fax:** 408-970-9727
Web: www.mcafee.com

2008 Sales

	$ mil.	% of total
North America	844.9	53
Europe, Middle East & Africa	502.9	31
Asia/Pacific		
Japan	116.6	7
Other countries	81.1	5
Latin America	54.6	4
Total	**1,600.1**	**100**

PRODUCTS/OPERATIONS

2008 Sales

	$ mil.	% of total
Service & support	805.5	50
Subscriptions	661.6	42
Products	133.0	8
Total	**1,600.1**	**100**

COMPETITORS

3Com	Kaspersky Lab
Barracuda Networks	Lumension
Blue Coat	Microsoft
CA, Inc.	nCircle
Check Point Software	Novell
Cisco Systems	Panda Security
Comodo	Qualys
EMC	Sophos
Fortinet	Sourcefire
F-Secure	Symantec
Google	TippingPoint
Hauri	Trend Micro
IBM Internet Security	Websense
Juniper Networks	Yahoo!

Income Statement

FYE: December 31

	REVENUE ($ mil.)	NET INCOME ($ mil.)	NET PROFIT MARGIN	EMPLOYEES
12/08	1,600.1	172.2	10.8%	5,600
12/07	1,308.2	167.0	12.8%	4,250
12/06	1,145.2	137.5	12.0%	3,700
12/05	987.3	138.8	14.1%	3,290
12/04	910.5	225.1	24.7%	2,950
Annual Growth	15.1%	(6.5%)	—	17.4%

2008 Year-End Financials

Debt ratio: —
Return on equity: 9.4%
Cash ($ mil.): 483
Current ratio: 1.06
Long-term debt ($ mil.): —

No. of shares (mil.): 157
Dividends
 Yield: 0.0%
 Payout: —
Market value ($ mil.): 5,434

Stock History

NYSE: MFE

	STOCK PRICE ($) FY Close	P/E High/Low	PER SHARE ($) Earnings	Dividends	Book Value
12/08	34.57	38 23	1.08	0.00	11.15
12/07	37.50	41 27	1.02	0.00	12.12
12/06	28.38	36 23	0.84	0.00	9.08
12/05	27.13	41 25	0.82	0.00	9.26
12/04	28.93	26 11	1.31	0.00	7.64
Annual Growth	4.6%	— —	(4.7%)	—	9.9%

McClatchy Company

This company has gotten its clutches on quite a few newspapers. The McClatchy Company is the #3 newspaper business in the US (behind *USA TODAY* publisher Gannett and Tribune Company), with 30 daily papers boasting a combined circulation of more than 2.5 million. Its portfolio includes *The Kansas City Star, The Miami Herald, The Sacramento Bee* (California), and the *Star-Telegram* (Fort Worth, Texas). McClatchy also operates about 50 non-daily newspapers in eight states and operates online news sites in conjunction with many of its papers. In addition, it has a 49% stake in The Seattle Times Company. The McClatchy family controls the company.

Unlike some of its rivals, McClatchy has not diversified into other media businesses such as television stations or publishing, which has left the company to face the full force of the downturn in the newspaper industry. The continuing decline in advertising revenue has left many of its papers struggling to survive while readers turn to other forms of media to get their news.

In response, McClatchy has been focused on reducing costs throughout its publishing operations mostly through significant job reductions.

The company cut its workforce by about 20% during 2008 and announced a further 15% reduction in jobs early the following year. It has also moved to freeze or cut wages. Meanwhile, McClatchy has been investing in Internet publishing to try and boost revenue. Online advertising accounts for about more than 10% of its total advertising sales. In addition to its own Web sites, McClatchy has stakes in CareerBuilder (less than 15%) and Classified Ventures (more than 25%).

McClatchy has also been burdened by mounting debt, most of which accrued from its 2006 acquisition of Knight-Ridder for $4.5 billion in cash and the assumption of $2 billion in debt. In an effort to try and pay down those debts, McClatchy in 2008 sold its stake in SP Newsprint to White Birch Paper Co. as part of a $350 million disposal along with former partners Cox Enterprises and Media General. It also sold the online directory Real Cities Network (purchased as part of the Knight-Ridder acquisition) to online media buyer Centro.

HISTORY

In the 1840s James McClatchy was a reporter for Horace Greeley's *New York Tribune*. When Greeley exhorted young men to go west, McClatchy went. He worked for several newspapers in Sacramento before co-founding *The Bee* (named to liken reporters to industrious insects) in 1857. The paper gained a reputation as a crusader and was known for its antislavery stance. During the 1920s the company expanded with sister *Bees* in Fresno and Modesto, California.

The McClatchy family bought out the other owners, and the company grew under its watch. Granddaughter Eleanor McClatchy ran the company from 1936 until 1978. It went public in 1988.

McClatchy bought three South Carolina dailies from The News and Observer Publishing Co. in 1990. Five years later, it bought the Raleigh-based publisher — giving it a toehold in North Carolina's fast-growing Research Triangle area — as well as Nando.net (renamed Nando Media in 1998), its Internet publishing company. In 1996 and 1997 the company sold five of its community newspapers. Also in 1996 Gary Pruitt, who joined the company in 1984, was named CEO.

In 1997 McClatchy became the surprise winner in the bidding for Cowles Media Company (*Star Tribune*), for which it paid $1.4 billion. In 1998 the company sold Cowles' magazine and book publishing divisions. The company also changed its name from McClatchy Newspapers to The McClatchy Company.

The company made several Web-related investments in 2000; it took equity stakes in StreamSearch.com (a now defunct online audio and video search engine) and BrightStreet.com (online loyalty programs). McClatchy continued to focus on the Internet in 2001 even as it cut costs to combat a slump in ad spending.

In 2003 the company sold its Newspaper Network unit in two parts to news service Associated Press and ad services company Vertis (now called Vertis Communications). The McClatchy Company acquired six California newspapers, including the *Merced Sun-Star*, for $41 million in early 2004. The following year Nando changed its name once again when it became McClatchy Interactive.

Former chairman and patriarch of the family James McClatchy, great-grandson of the company's founder, died in 2006 at the age of 85.

McClatchy briefly became the second-largest newspaper publisher in the US that year after it purchased rival Knight-Ridder for $4.5 billion in cash and the assumption of $2 billion in debt. Following the deal, the company sold several of the newly acquired newspapers, as well as the *Star Tribune*.

EXECUTIVES

Chairman, President, and CEO: Gary B. Pruitt, age 51, $2,767,306 total compensation
VP Finance and CFO: Patrick J. (Pat) Talamantes, age 44, $760,339 total compensation
VP, General Counsel, and Corporate Secretary: Karole Morgan-Prager, age 46
VP Operations: Robert J. (Bob) Weil, age 58, $939,413 total compensation
VP Operations: Frank R. J. Whittaker, age 58, $998,724 total compensation
VP Interactive Media: Christian A. Hendricks, age 46
VP Human Resources: Heather L. Fagundes, age 40
Corporate VP Advertising: Stephen Bernard
Treasurer: R. Elaine Lintecum
Director Communications: Peter Tira
Auditors: Deloitte & Touche LLP

LOCATIONS

HQ: The McClatchy Company
2100 Q St., Sacramento, CA 95816
Phone: 916-321-1846 **Fax:** 916-321-1964
Web: www.mcclatchy.com

PRODUCTS/OPERATIONS

2008 Sales

	$ mil.	% of total
Advertising	1,568.8	83
Circulation	265.6	14
Other	66.1	3
Total	1,900.5	100

Selected Newspapers

Anchorage Daily News (Alaska)
The Beaufort Gazette (South Carolina)
Belleville News-Democrat (Illinois)
The Bellingham Herald (Washington)
The Bradenton Herald (Florida)
Centre Daily Times (Pennsylvania)
Charlotte Observer (North Carolina)
El Nuevo Herald (Spanish-language, Miami)
The Fresno Bee (California)
The Herald (Rock Hill, SC)
Idaho Statesman (Boise)
The Island Packet (Hilton Head, SC)
The Kansas City Star
Ledger-Enquirer (Columbus, GA)
Lexington Herald-Leader (Kentucky)
Merced Sun-Star (California)
The Miami Herald
The Modesto Bee (California)
The News Tribune (Tacoma, WA)
The News & Observer (Raleigh, NC)
The Olympian (Olympia, WA)
The Sacramento Bee (California)
Star-Telegram (Fort Worth, TX)
The State (Columbia, SC)
Sun Herald (Biloxi, MS)
The Sun News (Myrtle Beach, SC)
The Telegraph (Macon, GA)
The Tribune (San Luis Obispo, CA)
The Wichita Eagle (Kansas)
Tri-City Herald (Kennewick, WA)

COMPETITORS

A. H. Belo	Morris Publishing
Dow Jones	New York Times
Gannett	Paxton Media
Hearst Newspapers	Tribune Company
Lee Enterprises	Washington Post
Media General	

HISTORICAL FINANCIALS

Company Type: Public

Income Statement
FYE: Sunday nearest December 31

	REVENUE ($ mil.)	NET INCOME ($ mil.)	NET PROFIT MARGIN	EMPLOYEES
12/08	1,900.5	(4.0)	—	12,100
12/07	2,260.4	(2,736.0)	—	15,748
12/06	1,675.2	(155.6)	—	16,791
12/05	1,186.1	160.5	13.5%	8,948
12/04	1,163.4	155.9	13.4%	9,171
Annual Growth	13.1%	—	—	7.2%

2008 Year-End Financials

Debt ratio: 3,886.7%
Return on equity: —
Cash ($ mil.): 5
Current ratio: 1.60
Long-term debt ($ mil.): 2,038

No. of shares (mil.): 84
Dividends
  Yield: 67.5%
  Payout: —
Market value ($ mil.): 67

Stock History
NYSE: MNI

	STOCK PRICE ($) FY Close	P/E High/Low		PER SHARE ($) Earnings	Dividends	Book Value
12/08	0.80	—	—	(0.05)	0.54	0.62
12/07	12.52	—	—	(33.37)	0.72	5.06
12/06	43.30	—	—	(2.41)	0.72	36.92
12/05	59.10	22	16	3.42	0.67	18.62
12/04	71.81	22	20	3.33	0.50	16.93
Annual Growth	(67.5%)	—	—	—	1.9%	(56.2%)

McCormick & Company

This company offers more than just the flavor of the month — McCormick is the world's #1 spice maker. It makes a tasty assortment of herbs, spices, seasonings, marinades, flavorings, sauces, and extracts. The company distributes its own products, which are sold to consumers under brands including Club House, Ducros, McCormick, and Schwartz, as well as private labels. Its customers include food retailers, the foodservice industry, and industrial food processors worldwide. McCormick has operations in the Americas, Europe, Asia, and Africa.

Ever-expanding its well-known brand roster, McCormick acquired the Lawry's brand of marinades and spice blends from Unilever for $605 million in 2008. In order to buy Lawry's, the company was required by the FTC to sell its Season-All business, which it did — to Morton International. Continuing its brand-name acquisition strategy, the company also purchased Canada's largest honey business, Billy Bee Honey Products, in 2008. McCormick paid $75 million for the name-brand producer.

The company's foodservice customers include Darden Restaurants, Doctor's Associates, McDonald's, Wendy's, and YUM! Brands. PepsiCo is McCormick's largest customer, accounting for about 10% of its 2008 sales.

McCormick is known for scenting its annual reports with one of its more aromatic products, such as vanilla or Chinese five-spice. For 2008 it was cinnamon.

Robert Lawless, who held the position for 11 years, retired as CEO in 2008. COO and president Alan Wilson, who oversaw a $50 million cost-saving restructuring program at the company, was named his replacement. In 2009 Lawless stepped down as chairman and Wilson succeeded him.

An employee profit-sharing plan owns about 24% of McCormick; Lawless owns about 10%.

HISTORY

McCormick & Company was founded in 1889 by 25-year-old Willoughby McCormick, who crafted fruit syrups, root beer, and nerve and bone liniment in his Baltimore home. He employed three assistants to hawk his wares door-to-door. His company soon expanded its product line to include food coloring, cream of tartar, and blood purifier. By 1894 McCormick was exporting, and two years later it acquired the F.G. Emmett Spice Company of Philadelphia, firmly committing itself to the spice industry. By the turn of the century, McCormick was trading around the world.

Willoughby's nephew, Charles McCormick, joined the company as a part-time shipping clerk in 1912. When Willoughby died in 1932, Charles succeeded him as CEO. He increased employee wages, shortened the workweek, and established the Multiple Management system (still an integral part of the company's management structure), which solicited employee input. By 1933 McCormick was on a growth track that continued unabated through the 1930s. In 1938 Charles wrote a book expounding his participative management philosophy.

The company opened its first international office in 1940 and achieved coast-to-coast distribution seven years later with the acquisition of A. Schilling & Co., producers of spices and extracts. In 1959 McCormick purchased Gorman Eckert & Co., Canada's largest spice business and the precursor to Club House Foods. It acquired Gilroy Foods in 1961 and rival Baker Extract in 1962. From 1962 until its sale in 1988 McCormick ran a real estate subsidiary, Maryland Properties (renamed McCormick Properties, 1979).

Charles died in 1970. Though the years following his death were characterized by acquisitions and joint venture agreements in the US and abroad, profits slumped until his son, Charles "Buzz" McCormick, took over as CEO in 1987.

In 1989 Australia's Burns, Philp began challenging McCormick by buying up spice companies in the US and Europe, including the Spice Islands and Durkee French brands. Buzz — succeeded twice as CEO in the mid-1990s, only to return when one successor died and the other left for health reasons — responded with a bruising battle for shelf space that led to Burns, Philp's near-collapse in 1997. The company also sold garlic and onion processing subsidiary Gilroy Foods, Minipack Systems (UK), and several smaller, non-core operations. In 1997 Buzz yielded the CEO's post — for good — to Robert Lawless.

The company's earnings were erratic in the 1990s, partly because of a price war with then-rival Burns, Philp, but also due to the decline of home cooking in the US. McCormick countered with increased advertising and a growing emphasis on industrial sales to flavor the foods eaten outside the home. McCormick also has been expanding internationally through its Decors spice business and operations in China.

Economic woes in Venezuela caused McCormick to cease manufacturing operations there in 1998. In 1999 Lawless succeeded Buzz as chairman. In June 1999 the company announced it would cut costs by eliminating 300 jobs (mostly overseas) and closing a British plant.

McCormick's sweet victory over Burns, Philp was soured by an FTC investigation into its alleged practice of offering some grocery chains low prices in exchange for up to 90% of their shelf space for spices. The investigation brought scrutiny on a common supermarket practice known as slotting fees. McCormick settled with the FTC in 2000, agreeing not to illegally discriminate against retailers in its pricing. Also that year the company bought France-based Ducros (spices, herbs, dessert aid products) from Béghin-Say for about $380 million.

In 2003 McCormick's UK subsidiary acquired condiment maker Uniqsauces, adding the Beswicks and Hammonds, as well as the licensed Newman's Own brands to its European product line. Acquisitions continued in 2004 with McCormick's purchase of C.M. van Sillevoldt B.V. and its Silvo brand of spices, herbs, and seasonings, which is sold in the Netherlands and Belgium.

About 39% of McCormick's sales came from its international operations in 2005. The year was not the company's best, however, as a drop in vanilla prices and the effects of Hurricane Katrina both cut into sales.

Continuing its expansion via acquisitions, the company purchased Dessert Products International (DPI) in 2006. DPI markets the Vahine brand dessert toppings in Europe. It also purchased Simply Asia Foods that year for $97.6 million in cash. Simply Asia manufactures products under the Thai Kitchen and Simply Asia brands; its products include noodle and soup bowls, meal kits, coconut milk, and sauces and pastes.

EXECUTIVES

Chairman, President, and CEO: Alan D. Wilson, age 51, $5,991,109 total compensation
VP Corporate Operations: James Radin
EVP and CFO: Gordon M. Stetz Jr., age 48, $1,286,010 total compensation
VP Supply Chain, and CIO: Jeryl (Jerry) Wolfe
SVP Finance and Treasurer: Paul C. Beard, age 54
VP and Controller: Kenneth A. Kelly Jr., age 54
VP Strategic Sourcing: Stephen J. Donohue
VP Research and Development: Hamed Faridi
VP Quality Assurance: Roger T. Lawrence
VP Financial Shared Services: Sharon H. Mirabelle
VP USIG Food Service: Phillip M. Kafarakis
VP Corporate Communications and Community Relations: John G. McCormick
VP Tax: Paul Nolan
VP Human Resources: Cecile K. Perich, age 57
VP Investor Relations: Joyce L. Brooks
President, North American Consumer Foods: Mark T. Timbie, age 54, $3,109,173 total compensation
President, Asia Pacific and Chairman, McCormick Canada: Keith Gibbons
President, U.S. Industrial Group: Charles T. (Chuck) Langmead, age 51
President, International: Lawrence E. Kurzius, age 51, $2,807,360 total compensation
General Counsel and Secretary: W. Geoffrey (Geoff) Carpenter, age 56
Director Consumer Communications: Laurie Harrsen
Auditors: Ernst & Young LLP

LOCATIONS

HQ: McCormick & Company, Incorporated
18 Loveton Cir., Sparks, MD 21152
Phone: 410-771-7301 **Fax:** 410-771-7462
Web: www.mccormick.com

2008 Sales

	$ mil.	% of total
US	1,846.5	58
Europe	767.4	24
Other countries	562.7	18
Total	**3,176.6**	**100**

PRODUCTS/OPERATIONS

2008 Sales

	$ mil.	% of total
Consumer products	1,850.8	58
Industrial & foodservice products	1,325.8	42
Total	**3,176.6**	**100**

Selected Brands

Billy Bee
Club House
Ducros
Lawry's
McCormick
Schwartz
Silvo
Simply Asia
Thai Kitchen
Vahine
Zatarain's

Selected Products

Coating systems
  Batters
  Breaders
  Glazes
  Marinades
  Rubs
Compound flavors
  Beverage flavors
  Confectionery flavors
  Dairy flavors
Condiments
  Flavored oils
  Jams and jellies
  Ketchup
  Mustards
  Salad dressings
  Sandwich sauces
  Seafood cocktail sauces
Ingredients
  Extracts
  Essential oils and oleoresins
  Fruit and vegetable powders
  Honey
  Spices and herbs
  Tomato powder
Processed flavors
  Meat flavors
  Savory flavors
Seasonings
  Sauces and gravies
  Salty snack seasonings
  Seasoning blends
  Side dish seasonings

COMPETITORS

A.A. Sayia
ACH Food Companies
Adams Extract & Spice
Alberto-Culver
Associated British Foods
B&G Foods
Bolner's Fiesta Products
D. D. Williamson
Danisco A/S
Denali Flavors
First Spice Mixing
Flavormatic Industries
Flayco Products
Givaudan
Goya
The Great Spice Company
Heinz
International Flavors
Kerry Group
La Flor
M & F Worldwide
Magic Seasoning Blends
Main Street Ingredients
Newly Weds Foods
Nielsen-Massey
Northwestern Flavors
Ottens Flavors
Penzeys
RFI Ingredients
Sensient
Sterling Extract
Tone's

HISTORICAL FINANCIALS

Company Type: Public

Income Statement

FYE: November 30

	REVENUE ($ mil.)	NET INCOME ($ mil.)	NET PROFIT MARGIN	EMPLOYEES
11/08	3,176.6	255.8	8.1%	7,500
11/07	2,916.2	230.1	7.9%	7,500
11/06	2,716.4	202.2	7.4%	7,500
11/05	2,592.0	214.9	8.3%	8,000
11/04	2,526.2	214.5	8.5%	8,000
Annual Growth	**5.9%**	**4.5%**	**—**	**(1.6%)**

2008 Year-End Financials

Debt ratio: 83.9%
Return on equity: 23.9%
Cash ($ mil.): 39
Current ratio: 0.94
Long-term debt ($ mil.): 885
No. of shares (mil.): 131
Dividends
  Yield: 3.0%
  Payout: 46.4%
Market value ($ mil.): 3,890

Stock History

NYSE: MKC

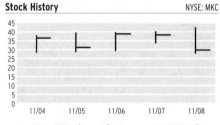

	STOCK PRICE ($) FY Close	P/E High/Low		PER SHARE ($) Earnings	Dividends	Book Value
11/08	29.77	22	15	1.94	0.90	8.08
11/07	38.21	23	20	1.73	0.82	8.30
11/06	38.72	26	20	1.50	0.74	7.14
11/05	31.22	25	19	1.56	0.66	6.12
11/04	36.45	25	19	1.52	0.56	6.81
Annual Growth	**(4.9%)**	**—**	**—**	**6.3%**	**12.6%**	**4.4%**

McDermott International

Whether you are in deep water or all fired up, it's all in a day's work for McDermott International, a global engineering and construction firm active in offshore oil and gas construction, power generation systems, and government contracting. The company's offshore business segment includes subsidiary J. Ray McDermott, which builds deepwater and subsea oil and gas facilities. Its power segment is led by Babcock & Wilcox (B&W) and builds fossil-fuel, nuclear, and other generation systems. B&W subsidiary B&W NPG is the driving force in the company's government segment, which provides nuclear components and services to US government agencies (accounting for about 13% of the parent company's business).

McDermott often looks for acquisitions as a way to grow the company and expand geographically. In 2008 B&W NPG acquired Nuclear Fuel Services, which provides services to the US military and converts Cold War-era stockpiles of enriched uranium into commercial nuclear reactor fuel. The move strengthened its operations in nuclear manufacturing and services for government and commercial markets.

McDermott has operations in more than 20 countries around the world. It operates a fleet of marine vessels and has several fabrication and manufacturing facilities in Indonesia, Mexico, Canada, the United Arab Emirates, and the US.

FMR owns 6% of McDermott International.

HISTORY

When R. Thomas McDermott won a contract to supply drilling rigs to a Texas wildcatter in 1923, he started J. Ray McDermott & Co., named after his father. Following the oil industry's expansion into Louisiana, J. Ray McDermott made New Orleans its headquarters in the 1930s. When the company incorporated in 1946, it supplied services for oil and natural gas production.

After WWII McDermott became a pioneer in the construction of offshore drilling platforms. Spurred by increased demand for oil in the 1960s and by price inflation in the 1970s, the company's offshore business boomed. McDermott supplied the US Navy and the salvage and subsea markets.

In 1978 McDermott diversified. That year it bought Babcock & Wilcox (B&W), which had been founded as a boilermaker in 1867, then later focused on nuclear energy and built the reactor for the first nuclear-powered merchant ship. It made major contributions to the US Navy's nuclear program during the 1950s.

J. Ray McDermott became McDermott Inc. in 1980, and in 1983, McDermott International, Inc. Unprepared for industry changes of the 1980s, McDermott had to shrink its workforce 57% by selling its insulation, controls, trading, and seamless-tube operations.

In a sweeping reorganization, McDermott consolidated its marine construction operations into a subsidiary, J. Ray McDermott, which in 1995 merged with Offshore Pipeline; McDermott owned a majority stake in the resulting company. A consortium including McDermott won a $275 million power plant contract with Huaneng International Power Development, the largest independent power producer in China, in 1996.

In 1986 McKesson narrowed its focus to the health industry by selling its liquor and chemical distributors. It acquired Canadian drug distributor Medis by halves in 1990 and 1991, and a 23% stake in Mexican drug distributor Nadro in 1993.

McKesson sold PCS, the US's #1 prescription claims processor (acquired in 1970), to Eli Lilly in 1994. In 1996 the firm bought bankrupt distributor FoxMeyer Drug and sold its stake in Armor All (auto and home cleaning products) to Clorox.

In 1997 the company purchased General Medical, the US's largest distributor of medical surgical supplies, for about $775 million. McKesson began to focus on health care, selling its Millbrook Distribution Services unit (health and beauty products, general merchandise, and specialty foods).

Under new CEO Mark Pulido, it agreed to buy drug wholesaler AmeriSource Health (now AmerisourceBergen), but withdrew the offer in 1998, facing FTC opposition. Instead, McKesson moved into information systems, paying $14 billion for health care information top dog HBO & Company and forming McKesson HBOC. HBO, a high-flyer in the high-growth health information systems segment, balanced its rather dowdy drug and medical distribution operations.

But just months after the deal closed, accounting inconsistencies at HBO prompted McKesson to restate fourth-quarter results for fiscal 1999 twice, triggering shareholder lawsuits and a housecleaning of top brass. Five ex-HBO executives, including McKesson HBOC chairman Charlie McCall (who was later indicted for securities fraud), were canned for using improper accounting methods. McKesson's veteran CEO Pulido and CFO Richard Hawkins were forced to resign for not seeing the problems coming.

The company changed its name to McKesson Corporation in 2001. The National Health Services Information Authority entered into an agreement with McKesson to develop a human resources and payroll system for use at the over 600 NHS locations throughout the UK.

To catch former #1 pharmaceutical distributor Cardinal Health, McKesson built up its core areas in 2003 and 2004, while trimming away some of the dead weight (Abaton.com, Amysis Managed Care Systems, and ProDental Corp.). The company bought PMO, a specialty mail order prescription business. It also acquired Canadian firm A.L.I. Technologies, which provided systems for managing medical images.

EXECUTIVES

Chairman, President, and CEO: John H. Hammergren, age 50, $34,218,964 total compensation
EVP and Group President; President, McKesson Supply Solutions: Paul C. Julian, age 54, $15,800,835 total compensation
EVP and CFO: Jeffrey C. (Jeff) Campbell, age 49, $15,800,835 total compensation
EVP, CIO, and CTO: Randall N. (Randy) Spratt, age 58
EVP Human Resources: Jorge L. Figueredo
EVP Corporate Strategy and Business Development: Marc E. Owen, age 50, $5,780,455 total compensation
EVP; Group President, McKesson Technology Solutions: Patrick (Pat) Blake, age 45
EVP, General Counsel, and Secretary: Laureen E. Seeger, age 48, $4,862,134 total compensation
SVP and General Manager, Revenue Cycle, McKesson Provider Technologies: Loren Buysman
SVP and President, Health Mart: Tim Canning

VP and Treasurer: Nicholas A. Loiacono
VP and Controller: Nigel A. Rees
VP Investor Relations: Ana Schrank
VP Corporate Communications and Brand: Andy Burtis
President, McKesson Health Solutions: Emad Rizk
President, RelayHealth Buiness Unit: Jim Bodenbender
Director Corporate Public Relations: James Larkin
Auditors: Deloitte & Touche LLP

LOCATIONS

HQ: McKesson Corporation
1 Post St., San Francisco, CA 94104
Phone: 415-983-8300 **Fax:** 415-983-7160
Web: www.mckesson.com

2009 Sales

	$ mil.	% of total
US	98,194	92
Other countries	8,438	8
Total	**106,632**	**100**

PRODUCTS/OPERATIONS

2009 Sales

	$ mil.	% of total
Distribution Solutions		
US pharmaceutical distribution	92,685	87
Canada pharmaceutical distribution & services	8,225	8
Medical-surgical distribution & services	2,658	2
Technology Solutions		
Services	2,337	2
Software & software systems	572	1
Hardware	155	—
Total	**106,632**	**100**

COMPETITORS

Accredo Health
AmerisourceBergen
athenahealth
Cardinal Health
CuraScript
GE Healthcare
H. D. Smith Wholesale Drug
Kinray
Medline Industries
Owens & Minor
PSS World Medical
Quality King
Siemens Healthcare
Surgical Express

HISTORICAL FINANCIALS
Company Type: Public

Income Statement
FYE: March 31

	REVENUE ($ mil.)	NET INCOME ($ mil.)	NET PROFIT MARGIN	EMPLOYEES
3/09	106,632.0	823.0	0.8%	32,500
3/08	101,703.0	990.0	1.0%	32,900
3/07	92,977.0	963.0	1.0%	31,800
3/06	88,050.0	751.0	0.9%	26,400
3/05	80,514.6	(156.7)	—	25,200
Annual Growth	**7.3%**	**—**	**—**	**6.6%**

2009 Year-End Financials

Debt ratio: 37.0%
Return on equity: 13.4%
Cash ($ mil.): 2,109
Current ratio: 1.20
Long-term debt ($ mil.): 2,290
No. of shares (mil.): 266
Dividends
 Yield: 1.4%
 Payout: 16.3%
Market value ($ mil.): 9,326

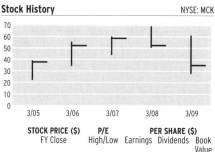

Stock History NYSE: MCK

	STOCK PRICE ($) FY Close	P/E High/Low		PER SHARE ($) Earnings	Dividends	Book Value
3/09	35.04	20	10	2.95	0.48	23.27
3/08	52.37	21	15	3.32	0.24	23.00
3/07	58.54	20	15	2.99	0.24	23.57
3/06	52.13	23	15	2.38	0.24	22.20
3/05	37.75	—	—	(0.53)	0.24	19.82
Annual Growth	**(1.8%)**	**—**	**—**	**—**	**18.9%**	**4.1%**

McKinsey & Company

One of the world's top management consulting firms, McKinsey & Company has about 90 offices in more than 50 countries around the globe. The company advises corporate enterprises, government agencies and institutions, and foundations on a variety of issues. It groups its practices into seven main areas: business technology, corporate finance, marketing and sales, operations, organization, risk, and strategy. McKinsey serves clients in numerous industry sectors, from automotive to high tech to telecommunications. Founded by James McKinsey in 1926, the company is owned by its partners.

McKinsey takes advantage of its global reach to gain business from multinational companies that want help in harmonizing their diverse operations. Toward that end, the firm aims to work collaboratively across its own organization, bringing together the work of multiple offices and practices on behalf of a single client.

In addition to being one of the oldest consulting firms, McKinsey is considered one of the most prestigious (along with Boston Consulting Group and Bain) as measured in surveys of aspiring consultants. Contributing to McKinsey's allure as an employer is the firm's network of 18,000-plus alumni, many of whom have been tapped for C-level jobs in the course of their careers. Alumni running companies, in turn, represent a potential source of business for the firm.

In July 2009 managing director Ian Davis stepped down as Dominic Barton, the firm's regional leader in Asia, was elected to the post by McKinsey's 400 or so senior partners. Davis served two terms as managing director, the maximum allowed under McKinsey's policy.

HISTORY

McKinsey & Company was founded in Chicago in 1926 by University of Chicago accounting professor James McKinsey. The company evolved from an auditing practice of McKinsey and his partners, Marvin Bower and A.T. Kearney, who began analyzing business and industry and offering advice. McKinsey died in 1937; two years later, Bower, who headed the New York office, and Kearney, in Chicago, split the firm. Kearney renamed the Chicago office A.T. Kearney & Co. (later acquired by Electronic Data Systems), and Bower kept the McKinsey name and built up a practice structured like a law firm.

Bower focused on the big picture instead of on specific operating problems, helping boost billings to $2 million by 1950. He hired staff straight out of prestigious business schools, reinforcing the firm's theoretical bent. Bower implemented a competitive up-or-out policy requiring employees who are not continually promoted to leave the firm.

The firm's prestige continued to grow during the booming 1950s along with demand for consulting services. Before becoming president in 1953, Dwight Eisenhower asked McKinsey to find out exactly what the government did. By 1959 Bower had opened an office in London, followed by others in Amsterdam; Dusseldorf, Germany; Melbourne; Paris; and Zurich.

In 1964 the company founded management journal *The McKinsey Quarterly*. When Bower retired in 1967, sales were $20 million, and McKinsey was the #1 management consulting firm. During the 1970s it faced competition from firms with newer approaches and lost market share. In response, then-managing director Ronald Daniel started specialty practices and expanded foreign operations.

The consulting boom of the 1980s was spurred by mergers and buyouts. By 1988 the firm had 1,800 consultants, sales were $620 million, and 50% of billings came from overseas.

The recession of the early 1990s hit white-collar workers, including consultants. McKinsey, scrambling to upgrade its technical side, bought Information Consulting Group (ICG), its first acquisition. But the corporate cultures did not meld, and most ICG people left by 1993.

In 1994 the company elected its first managing director of non-European descent, Indian-born Rajat Gupta. Two years later the traditionally hush-hush firm found itself at the center of that most public 1990s arena, the sexual discrimination lawsuit. A female ex-consultant in Texas sued, claiming McKinsey had sabotaged her career (the case was dismissed).

In 1998 McKinsey partnered with Northwestern University and the University of Pennsylvania to establish a business school in India. The following year graduating seniors surveyed in Europe, the UK, and the US named the company as their ideal employer.

Also in 1999 the company created McKinsey to help "accelerate" Internet startups. The next year it increased salaries and offered incentives to better compete with Internet firms for employees. In 2001 the company expanded its branding business with the acquisition of Envision, a Chicago-based brand consultant.

Like its rivals in the consulting industry, McKinsey took a hit from the dot-com bust and the economic downturn of 2001 and 2002, as many companies were slower to sign up for costly long-term strategy consulting engagements and mergers and acquisitions work dried up.

In 2003 Ian Davis was elected as managing director of the firm, succeeding Gupta, who had served as McKinsey's top executive for nine years. Davis had previously served as the head of the firm's UK office. Davis stepped down in July 2009 to make way for Dominic Barton, who was the firm's regional leader in Asia.

EXECUTIVES

Managing Director: Dominic Barton, age 46
Chairman, Americas: Michael Patsalos-Fox
Chairman, Europe, Middle East, and Africa:
Robert Reibestein
Global Director Communications: Michael Stewart, age 59
Director External Relations, UK:
Andrea Minton Beddoes
Director External Relations, North and South America:
Simon London
Director External Relations, Germany: Kai Peter Rath
Director External Relations, Europe, Middle East, and Africa: Andrew Whitehouse

LOCATIONS

HQ: McKinsey & Company
55 E. 52nd St., 21st Fl., New York, NY 10022
Phone: 212-446-7000   **Fax:** 212-446-8575
Web: www.mckinsey.com

PRODUCTS/OPERATIONS

Selected Industry Practices

Automotive and assembly
Chemicals
Consumer packaged goods
Electric power and natural gas
Financial services
Health care payor and provider
High tech
Media and entertainment
Metals and mining
Petroleum
Pharmaceuticals and medical products
Private equity
Public sector
Pulp and paper
Retail
Social sector
Telecommunications
Travel infrastructure logistics

COMPETITORS

Accenture	EDS
A.T. Kearney	ESource
Bain & Company	IBM
BearingPoint	Mercer
Booz	Monitor Group
Booz Allen	Oliver Wyman
Boston Consulting	PA Consulting
Capgemini	Perot Systems
Computer Sciences Corp.	PRTM Management
Deloitte Consulting	Roland Berger

HISTORICAL FINANCIALS

Company Type: Private

Income Statement

FYE: December 31

	ESTIMATED REVENUE ($ mil.)	NET INCOME ($ mil.)	NET PROFIT MARGIN	EMPLOYEES
12/07	5,330.0	—	—	15,600
12/06	4,370.0	—	—	14,190
12/05	3,800.0	—	—	12,900
12/04	3,150.0	—	—	12,100
12/03	3,000.0	—	—	11,500
Annual Growth	15.5%	—	—	7.9%

Revenue History

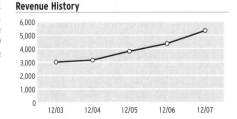

MeadWestvaco

Things do not pass for what they are, most things — MeadWestvaco (MWV) might say — are judged by their package. MWV's packaging operation (folding cartons, corrugated boxes, and printed plastics) pulls in nearly three-fourths of its sales. MWV wraps up health care, personal and beauty care, food, tobacco, and home and garden goods. It also makes school supplies (Mead, Five Star, Trapper Keeper), consumer office products (AT-A-GLANCE, Cambridge), and specialty chemicals (activated carbons, asphalt emulsifiers, tall oil). In 2005 MWV decided it would rather box than shuffle paper; it sold its Papers business — which made labels, book/catalog/magazine papers, and business forms — to Cerberus Capital Management.

Facing the global economic downturn, higher raw materials costs, and lower volumes in consumer and office products, the largest producer of paperboard in North America has made several hard choices. MWV set plans to close or restructure more than a dozen of its factories, and cut about 2,000 jobs, or 10% of its work force, by year end 2009.

The company has been taking aggressive steps over the years to reshape its operations around its packaging, consumer, and specialty chemicals businesses, and move away from forest products. As part of this effort, MWV has sold off large tracts of timber and divested noncore assets. The company reached a deal to sell 228,000 acres, plus another 95,000 acres worth of harvesting rights, to Wells Timberland REIT for $400 million in mid-2007. Later that year, MWV sold 62,000 acres to Penn Virginia Resource Partners for $93 million.

Unloading its Papers segment in 2005 marked a particularly strategic step toward global leadership in premium packaging. Papers accounted for a little less than 30% of MWV's sales prior to the deal, but the segment had been a consistent money pit. (Cerberus set up the divested business as an independent company, NewPage Holding Corporation.) Subsequently MWV reorganized its packaging operations into two groups, Packaging Resources and Consumer Solutions. Striving to play a role in its customers' packaging process rather than just a supplier, the company established a packaging research facility in collaboration with North Carolina State University in Raleigh, North Carolina, and moved its headquarters to Richmond, Virginia. Under the new structure, Packaging Resources specializes in paperboard products and Consumer Solutions tackles consumer packaging products.

Expanding its effort to streamline operations and cut costs, MWV sold its kraft paper mill in North Charleston, South Carolina, to KapStone Paper and Packaging for $485 million. Its packaging plant in Warrington, Pennsylvania, was shuttered as well, and its specialty paper mill in Potsdam, New York, was sold to Potsdam Specialty Paper.

MWV also prepares for weaker demand in some of its markets by ramping up development of products made from materials other than paperboard. The company burned through $714 million to acquire Saint-Gobain Calmar (now MeadWestvaco Calmar) from Compagnie de Saint-Gobain. The French packager specializes in plastic dispensing systems for consumer applications. MWV also grabbed Netherlands-based

Keltec Dispensing Systems and California-based Hayes Products. Tapping new markets, the company partnered with India-based Bilcare to acquire pharmaceutical package-maker International Labs. In late 2008 MWV formed a joint venture with Wadco Packaging, an Indian manufacturer of corrugated boxes. The JV, of which MWV owns 51%, turns out packaging to protect fresh produce as it is transported from field to market.

MWV has looked to save money by tightening its supply chain for paper processing too. MWV's Specialty Chemicals division acquired Eastman Chemical Company's pine chemical products. The chemicals are used in the production of paper, as well as paints, coatings, and other building materials. In 2007 the company completed a successful trial with CSX Transportation and Lydall, to distribute paper to the Port of Virginia by rail. The switch to rail reduces the number of trucks used by more than 400 per week, saving on fuel costs for MWV as well as reducing emissions associated with truck transportation.

HISTORY

Late in August 2001 Mead agreed to merge with Westvaco to form MeadWestvaco. Together, the two companies had combined annual sales of about $7 billion and a market capitalization of some $6 billion; their combined debt tallied at $4.4 billion. The combined company — 50.2%-owned by former Mead shareholders — had an equally split board. Westvaco executives occupied the new CEO, CFO, and transition officer positions, while the new corporate headquarters were Westvaco's Connecticut offices. The two companies merged as MeadWestvaco Corporation in January 2002.

To quickly expand its production capability in Europe, MeadWestvaco also bought Kartoncraft Limited, near Dublin, Ireland, a leading pharmaceutical packaging producer. In July 2002 the company reported that it had eliminated 2,100 jobs of the 2,500 it expected to cut by the end of the year. As part of its plan to divest 950,000 non-strategic acres, the company sold 95,500 acres of forest land in West Virginia for $50 million; the purchase was made through The Forestland Group LLC for Heartwood Forestland Fund IV Limited Partnership in December 2002.

In 2003 the company bought AMCAL, a maker of stationery products including journals, notepads, decorative calendars, and holiday cards.

Sticking with its consolidation and realignment strategy, in mid-2004 MeadWestvaco eliminated some 600 jobs by closing both its Garland, Texas, and St. Joseph, Missouri, facilities. Also in 2004 MeadWestvaco acquired Brazilian-based Tilibra S.A. Produtos de Papelaria, a maker of office products.

MeadWestvaco sold its papers business to Cerberus Capital Management in January 2005. The deal included mills in Kentucky, Maine, Maryland, Michigan, and Ohio and about 900,000 acres of forest land in Illinois, Kentucky, Michigan, Missouri, Ohio, and Tennessee.

EXECUTIVES

Chairman and CEO: John A. Luke Jr., age 60, $6,720,087 total compensation
President: James A. Buzzard, age 54, $3,179,237 total compensation
SVP and CFO: E. Mark Rajkowski, age 50, $1,871,225 total compensation
SVP Technology: Mark T. Watkins, age 55
SVP, Secretary, and General Counsel: Wendell L. Willkie II, age 57, $1,574,620 total compensation
SVP Emerging Markets and Innovation: Bruce V. Thomas, age 52
SVP Human Resources and Communications: Linda V. Schreiner, age 49
SVP MWV Packaging: Mark S. Cross, age 52, $1,220,266 total compensation
SVP; President, Community Development and Land Management Group: Kenneth T. Seeger, age 58
President, Global Business Services: Mark V. Gulling, age 55
President, Tobacco, Paperboard SBUs and Operations: Robert A. (Bob) Feeser, age 46
President, Center for Packaging Innovation: Jack C. Goldfrank, age 64
President, Consumer & Office Products Group: Neil A. McLachlan, age 52
President, MWV Healthcare: Ted Lithgow, age 55
President, Specialty Chemicals: Robert K. Beckler, age 47
President, Tobacco: Peter Doodeman
President, Media and Entertainment Folding Carton: Stephen R. Scherger, age 44
President, Personal & Beauty Care and Home & Garden: Thomas Jonas, age 39
Treasurer: Robert E. Birkenholz, age 48
Director Public Relations: Alison von Puschendorf
Auditors: PricewaterhouseCoopers LLP

LOCATIONS

HQ: MeadWestvaco Corporation
   11013 W. Broad St., Glen Allen, VA 23060
Phone: 804-327-5200   **Fax:** 404-897-6383
Web: www.meadwestvaco.com

PRODUCTS/OPERATIONS

2008 Sales

	$ mil.	% of total
Packaging		
Packaging resources	2,285	34
Consumer solutions	2,509	38
Consumer & office products	1,063	16
Specialty chemicals	547	8
Community development & land management	128	2
Corporate & other	105	2
Total	**6,637**	**100**

Selected Products

Packaging
   Packaging resources
      Bleached paperboard
      Consumer products packaging (media, beverage and dairy, cosmetics, tobacco, pharmaceuticals, health care)
      Kraft paperboard
      Linerboard
   Consumer solutions
      Multi-pack cartons (beverages and tobacco)
      Plastic dispensing and spraying systems
      Printed plastic packaging
Consumer and office products
   School and office products (AT-A-GLANCE, AMCAL, Cambridge, COLUMBIAN, Day Runner, Five Star, Mead, Trapper Keeper)
Specialty chemicals
   Activated carbon
   Emulsifiers
   Printing ink resins

COMPETITORS

3M
ACCO Brands
Alcoa
Amcor
Anglo American
Ball Corp.
Bemis
Boise Cascade
Canal Corp.
Cascades Inc.
Disc Graphics
Georgia-Pacific
Graphic Packaging Holding
Iggesund Paperboard
International Paper
Pratt Industries USA
Smurfit-Stone Container
Sonoco Products
Temple-Inland
UPM-Kymmene
Weyerhaeuser

HISTORICAL FINANCIALS

Company Type: Public

Income Statement

FYE: December 31

	REVENUE ($ mil.)	NET INCOME ($ mil.)	NET PROFIT MARGIN	EMPLOYEES
12/08	6,637.0	90.0	1.4%	22,000
12/07	6,906.0	285.0	4.1%	24,000
12/06	6,530.0	93.0	1.4%	24,000
12/05	6,170.0	28.0	0.5%	22,200
12/04	8,227.0	(349.0)	—	29,400
Annual Growth	**(5.2%)**	**—**	**—**	**(7.0%)**

2008 Year-End Financials

Debt ratio: 77.8%
Return on equity: 2.7%
Cash ($ mil.): 549
Current ratio: 1.70
Long-term debt ($ mil.): 2,309
No. of shares (mil.): 171
Dividends
   Yield: 8.2%
   Payout: 176.9%
Market value ($ mil.): 1,915

Stock History

NYSE: MWV

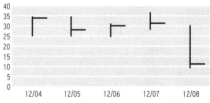

	STOCK PRICE ($) FY Close	P/E High/Low	PER SHARE ($) Earnings	PER SHARE ($) Dividends	PER SHARE ($) Book Value
12/08	11.19	58 18	0.52	0.92	17.34
12/07	31.30	23 18	1.56	0.92	21.67
12/06	30.06	59 48	0.52	0.92	20.65
12/05	28.03	245 179	0.14	0.92	20.35
12/04	33.89	— —	(1.73)	0.92	25.23
Annual Growth	**(24.2%)**	**— —**	**—**	**0.0%**	**(8.9%)**

Medco Health Solutions

Administering some 580 million prescriptions each year, Medco Health Solutions is the country's top pharmacy benefits management company and, through its Accredo Health unit, its top specialty pharmacy as well. The company assists health plans in managing drug costs by designing drug formularies, negotiating discounts with pharmaceutical companies, and processing claims. Members may fill their prescriptions through a network of about 60,000 pharmacies, a mail-order program, or the company's Internet pharmacy. Medco Health Solutions manages drug benefits for clients that include unions, corporations, HMOs, insurance companies, and federal employees.

Customer cost containment is the cornerstone of the company's business strategy. Medco Health Solutions is able to control costs through the use of technology to process prescription claims, automation to fill and distribute prescriptions, and volume purchasing of pharmaceuticals. It also encourages the use of its mail order pharmacies and of generic equivalents in place of more expensive brand name drugs.

Medco's mail order business is a big part of this cost reduction strategy. With nine mail order pharmacies scattered across the country, the company dispenses more than 100 million prescriptions a year. It uses this scale to get better deals from suppliers and to force stricter compliance with health plan formularies.

Within its mail order pharmacies, Medco has instituted what it calls Medco Therapeutic Resource Centers, which are specialized groups of pharmacists who are focused on certain chronic or complex diseases. The company's $1.5 billion acquisition in 2007 of PolyMedica, a mail-order distributor of blood-glucose monitors to diabetes patients, strengthened its Therapeutic Resource Center model, giving it resources dedicated to diabetes patients. Under a previous agreement, Medco had been supplying diabetes drugs to PolyMedica's patients.

Medco continues to operate the diabetes supply business under PolyMedica's former Liberty Medical brand. The company further enhanced the Liberty division when it bought the diabetes distribution assets of Owens & Minor subsidiary Access Diabetic Supply for $63 million in 2009.

Another key component of the company's strategy is the growth of Accredo Health, which dispenses sensitive biotechnology drugs, usually injectable or infusion drugs, to patients with serious diseases such as cancer. Accredo delivers medications and related supplies either to patient homes or clinical sites from three main distribution centers in Tennessee and Pennsylvania.

Medco grew its Accredo unit in 2007 with the acquisition of Critical Care Systems, a national provider of infusion services either in the home or at outpatient infusion sites.

Medco has also been trying to take advantage of the Medicare Part D prescription drug benefit, by tailoring some services to clients offering Part D programs or other drug coverage to their Medicare-eligible members. It has also contracted with the Centers for Medicare & Medicaid Services to offer a Medicare Part D drug plan of its own.

Medco went international in 2008, agreeing to buy a majority stake in privately held Dutch firm Europa Apotheek Venlo, which provides mail order pharmacy and other health care services in the Netherlands and Germany. Earlier the same year, the company partnered up with Apoteket, the Swedish government agency that oversees retail pharmacy operations in that country, to develop an automated prescription-review system.

Also in 2008 the company began construction of a third pharmacy fulfillment center, located in Indiana.

HISTORY

Medco Health Solutions (AKA Medco Containment Services) was started in 1983 by former Wall Street investment banker Martin Wygod. Wygod believed that a mail order pharmacy could improve efficiency, increase sales volume, and reduce prescription costs. Medco Containment Services became a publicly traded company in 1984. The firm acquired retail pharmacy management company, PAID Prescriptions, in 1985. As a result, the company became the first pharmacy in the nation to provide its customers with both retail and mail order pharmacy services.

Wygod's vision proved to be right on target as the company exceeded $1 billion in sales in 1990 and had more than 25 million members by 1991. In 1993 the company was acquired by Merck & Co. and changed its name to Medco Health.

For Medco Health, 1996 proved to be a breakthrough year. The firm received a contract to provide pharmacy benefit management services to a purchasing group consisting of *FORTUNE* 500 companies. As a result, Medco Health managed more than 200 million prescriptions.

In the late 1990s the company used the Internet to improve its efficiency and cut costs. The firm opened its Internet pharmacy and formed partnerships with Healtheon (now part of WebMD Health), CVS, and Reader's Digest.

In 2000 the company acquired ProVantage Health Services, a health care information and benefits management company. The acquisition increased the company's customer base by 5 million members. The next year Medco Health became the first Internet pharmacy to exceed $1 billion in prescription sales.

Accounting issues with parent Merck delayed the planned 2002 spin-off of Medco. The next year, however, the deal was completed; Merck retained no ownership stake in Medco.

In 2005 Medco became the country's leading specialty pharmacy by acquiring Accredo Health. The two companies had formed an alliance in 2004 to deliver biopharmaceuticals to Medco's clients.

EXECUTIVES

Chairman and CEO: David B. Snow Jr., age 54, $13,134,243 total compensation
President and COO: Kenneth O. Klepper, age 54, $4,984,655 total compensation
SVP Finance and CFO: Richard J. Rubino, age 50, $1,736,664 total compensation
SVP Medical and Analytical Affairs and Chief Medical Officer: Robert S. Epstein, age 52
SVP and Chief Marketing Officer: Jack A. Smith, age 60
SVP, Controller, and Chief Accounting Officer: Gabriel R. Cappucci
SVP Human Resources: Karin Princivalle, age 51
President, Liberty Medical and SVP Channel and Generic Strategy: Laizer Kornwasser, age 38
SVP Pharmaceutical Strategies and Solutions, General Counsel, and Secretary: Thomas M. Moriarty
Group President, Health Plans: Brian T. Griffin, age 49

Group President, Key Accounts: Glenn C. Taylor, age 56
Group President, Employer Accounts:
  Timothy C. Wentworth, age 47, $3,254,998 total compensation
President, New Markets: John P. Driscoll, age 48, $3,224,636 total compensation
Group President, Retiree Solutions: Mary T. Daschner, age 50
Auditors: PricewaterhouseCoopers LLP

LOCATIONS

HQ: Medco Health Solutions, Inc.
  100 Parsons Pond Dr., Franklin Lakes, NJ 07417
Phone: 201-269-3400   Fax: 201-269-1109
Web: www.medcohealth.com

PRODUCTS/OPERATIONS

2008 Sales

	$ mil.	% of total
Products		
Retail	28,613.5	56
Mail order	21,962.7	43
Services		
Client & other	502.2	1
Manufacturer	179.6	—
Total	**51,258.0**	**100**

Selected Subsidiaries

Accredo Health, Incorporated
BioPartners In Care, Inc.
Critical Care Systems, Inc.
Hemophilia Resources of America, Inc.
Liberty Healthcare Group, Inc.
medcohealth.com, L.L.C.
PolyMedica Corporation
Systemed, L.L.C.

COMPETITORS

Aetna
AmerisourceBergen
BioScrip
Catalyst Health Solutions
CIGNA
CVS Caremark
drugstore.com
Express Scripts
Humana
McKesson
MedImpact
Rite Aid
UnitedHealth Group
Walgreen
Wal-Mart
WellPoint

HISTORICAL FINANCIALS

Company Type: Public

Income Statement

FYE: December 31

	REVENUE ($ mil.)	NET INCOME ($ mil.)	NET PROFIT MARGIN	EMPLOYEES
12/08	51,258.0	1,102.9	2.2%	21,800
12/07	44,506.2	912.0	2.0%	20,800
12/06	42,543.7	630.2	1.5%	15,700
12/05	37,870.9	602.0	1.6%	15,300
12/04	35,351.9	481.6	1.4%	13,500
Annual Growth	**9.7%**	**23.0%**	**—**	**12.7%**

2008 Year-End Financials

Debt ratio: 67.2%
Return on equity: 17.2%
Cash ($ mil.): 938
Current ratio: 1.22
Long-term debt ($ mil.): 4,003
No. of shares (mil.): 474
Dividends
  Yield: 0.0%
  Payout: —
Market value ($ mil.): 19,855

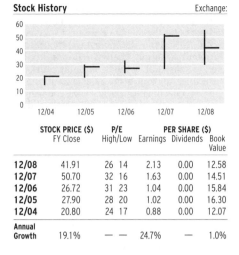

Stock History

Exchange:

	STOCK PRICE ($) FY Close	P/E High/Low		PER SHARE ($) Earnings	Dividends	Book Value
12/08	41.91	26	14	2.13	0.00	12.58
12/07	50.70	32	16	1.63	0.00	14.51
12/06	26.72	31	23	1.04	0.00	15.84
12/05	27.90	28	20	1.02	0.00	16.30
12/04	20.80	24	17	0.88	0.00	12.07
Annual Growth	19.1%	—	—	24.7%	—	1.0%

Medtronic, Inc.

Sometimes the best medicine is a short, sharp shock; that's why Medtronic's products reside in its customers' hearts and minds (among other places). A leading maker of implantable biomedical devices, the company makes defibrillators and pacemakers that shock the heart to help it beat normally. Subsidiary Medtronic Sofamor Danek makes spinal implant devices, and its neurological division makes neurostimulation devices and products that treat urinary incontinence. Medtronic CardioVascular produces catheters, stents, valves, and surgical ablation technologies used to treat vascular and heart disease. Medtronic also makes devices for diabetes; ear, nose, and throat (ENT) conditions; and emergency medicine.

Medtronic got its start treating heart diseases (it was a leader in the development of pacemakers in the 1950s), and a majority of its revenue still comes from sales of products used to treat heart or vascular conditions. Its Cardiac Rhythm Disease Management, or CRDM, division makes pacemakers, defibrillators, heart monitors and other products used to keep the heart beating properly.

In 2008 the company expanded its CRDM division with the acquisition of Canada-based CryoCath Technologies, a maker of cryotherapy products to treat cardiac arrhythmias (irregular heartbeats), for about $374 million. Medtronic further expanded the division in 2009 by purchasing Ablation Frontiers, a maker of ablation therapies for cardiac rhythm disorders.

Medtronic's second largest division manufactures spinal devices and implants, and surgical instruments used in spine surgery. Its also offers bone grafting tissue used in spinal, dental, and oral surgical procedures. The company built up its spinal surgery business in 2007 with the acquisition of Kyphon, a maker of orthopedic medical devices used to treat compression fractures of the spine. The following year, Medtronic settled federal allegations that Kyphon had defrauded Medicare, agreeing to pay a $75 million fine.

The company's CardioVascular division offers drug-eluting stents (to prevent re-clogging of arteries), heart valves, and surgical ablation systems. The company further bolstered this unit with the 2009 acquisitions of CoreValve and Ventor Technologies. Both companies brought in technologies to facilitate aortic valve replacements using catheters instead of traditional surgical methods.

In 2008 Medtronic purchased Restore Medical, adding that company's soft palate implant system, which treats sleep breathing disorders such as snoring and obstructive sleep apnea, to its ENT lineup. Later that year it purchased a similar product line for the treatment of sleep-breathing disorders from InfluENT Medical.

The company's Neuromodulation division accounts for about 10% of total sales and makes electrical stimulation devices and drug delivery systems that help control chronic pain, tremors, and urinary incontinence.

Medtronic has expanded into the growing China market through a joint venture with a Chinese company (51% owned by Medtronic) to market its spine and orthopedics products. The arrangement is Medtronic's first venture in Asia, though it had previously sold pacemakers in China and has manufacturing facilities there.

HISTORY

In 1949 electrical engineer Earl Bakken and brother-in-law Palmer Hermundslie founded Medtronic in Minneapolis as a medical equipment repair outfit. After branching into custom-made products, Bakken made history in 1957 by crafting the world's first external, battery-powered cardiac pacemaker. In 1960 Medtronic began making and selling the first implantable pacemakers; the company quickly claimed about 80% of the market.

In the late 1960s and early 1970s Medtronic acquired other medical devices companies. Calamity struck in 1976 when the firm had to recall more than 35,000 Xytron pacemakers (some of which were already in patients) because body moisture was seeping into the battery chamber. Market share plunged to about 35%.

Medtronic recruited former Pillsbury COO Winston Wallin as chairman and CEO in 1985. The next year Medtronic released its Activitrax pacemaker, which snagged about 20% of the market. Under Wallin (who retired in 1996), the firm opened facilities in Europe and Asia and resumed acquisitions, adding companies in Italy, the Netherlands, and the US.

In the early 1990s Medtronic sought to expand its position in the vascular market. Its 1990 purchase of Bio-Medicus made the company the world's top maker of centrifugal blood pumps; it also entered the lucrative cardiac defibrillator market (1992) and increased other lines with the purchase of a maker of blood recycling devices and a company that produced disposable tubing and detection kits for breast and prostate cancer.

Using its expertise in implant devices, the company developed (and in 1997 received FDA approval for) devices aimed at the growing tremor control and incontinence markets.

In the late 1990s Medtronic undertook a flurry of acquisitions, both to solidify its leadership in the cardiovascular market and to broaden its operations. These purchases included external defibrillator maker Physio-Control International, as well as a maker of power instruments for neurological, bone, and plastic surgery procedures in 1998. The next year Medtronic bought #1 spinal implant product maker Sofamor Danek to boost its neurosurgical business. The company took one more stab at the stent market, buying market-leader Arterial Vascular Engineering. Its share of the market fell after it was acquired, however, so Medtronic closed five facilities. Later that year the company bought Xomed Surgical Products (renamed Medtronic Xomed), a maker of products for ear, nose, and throat specialists.

In 2000 the company announced a partnership with health care companies — including Johnson & Johnson and GE Medical Systems — to provide online product ordering. Medtronic also partnered with WebMD (now WebMD Health) to provide health care information on the Internet.

The following year the firm bought medical device makers MiniMed and Medical Research Group and combined them to form Medtronic MiniMed. In 2002 Medtronic bought VidaMed to grow its urology offerings.

In 2007 the company's CRDM division suspended sales of one of its defibrillator leads (the wires that connect the device to the heart), after determining that a flaw in the wire may have contributed to several deaths. The lead, called Sprint Fidelis, had been implanted in more than 200,000 patients.

EXECUTIVES

Chairman, President, and CEO: William A. (Bill) Hawkins III, age 55, $7,512,626 total compensation
SVP, CFO, and Treasurer: Gary L. Ellis, age 52, $3,323,976 total compensation
SVP and Chief Regulatory Officer: Susan Alpert, age 63
VP and Chief Ethics and Compliance Officer: Kathy E. DiGiorno
SVP and Chief Talent Officer: Martha G. Aronson
EVP Healthcare Policy and Regulatory: Stephen H. (Steve) Mahle, age 63, $3,349,088 total compensation
SVP; President, Surgical Technologies: Bob Blankemeyer, age 62
SVP; President, Cardiac Rhythm Disease Management: James Patrick (Pat) Mackin, age 42
SVP; President, CardioVascular: Scott R. Ward, age 49
SVP Strategy and Innovation: Catherine M. (Katie) Szyman, age 42
SVP Quality and Operations: H. James Dallas, age 50, $2,921,608 total compensation
SVP Medicine and Technology: Stephen N. (Steve) Oesterle, age 58
SVP; President, Medtronic International: Jean-Luc Butel, age 52, $3,611,055 total compensation
SVP, General Counsel, and Corporate Secretary: D. Cameron Findlay, age 49
SVP; President, Neuromodulation: Richard E. (Rick) Kuntz, age 52
SVP; President, Diabetes: Christopher J. (Chris) O'Connell, age 42
SVP; President, Spinal and Biologics: Stephen (Steve) LaNeve, age 50
VP International Public Relations and Communications: Yvan Deurbroeck
Director Investor Relations: Jeff Warren
Senior Director Corporate Communications: Steven I. Cragle
Auditors: PricewaterhouseCoopers LLP

LOCATIONS

HQ: Medtronic, Inc.
710 Medtronic Pkwy., Minneapolis, MN 55432
Phone: 763-514-4000   **Fax:** 763-514-4879
Web: www.medtronic.com

2009 Sales

	$ mil.	% of total
US	8,997	62
Europe	3,564	24
Asia/Pacific	1,558	11
Other regions	480	3
Total	**14,599**	**100**

PRODUCTS/OPERATIONS

2009 Sales

	$ mil.	% of total
Cardiac rhythm disease management (CRDM)	5,014	34
Spinal	3,400	23
CardioVascular	2,437	17
Neuromodulation	1,434	10
Diabetes	1,114	8
Surgical Technologies	857	6
Physio-Control	343	2
Total	**14,599**	**100**

Selected Products

CRDM
  Cardiac resynchronization therapy devices
  Implantable defibrillators
  Pacemakers, pacing systems, leads and monitors
  Patient management tools

Spinal
  Bone graft proteins
  Minimal access retractor systems

Cardiovascular
  Cardiac surgery instruments
  Coronary stents
  Drug-eluting stents
  Embolic protection systems
  Endovascular stent grafts
  Heart stabilizers
  Heart valves
  Peripheral vascular stents
  Surgical ablation systems

Neuromodulation
  Deep brain stimulation systems
  Implantable neurostimulation devices
  Implantable drug delivery systems
  Urology and gastroenterology stimulation therapies

Diabetes
  Blood glucose meters
  Glucose monitoring systems
  Insulin pumps

Surgical Technologies
  Computer-assisted surgery guidance systems
  Ear ventilation tubes
  Hydrocephalus shunts
  Middle ear prostheses
  Nerve integrity monitors
  Palatal implants
  Sinus micro-endoscopy systems

Physio-Control
  Automated external defibrillators

COMPETITORS

Abbott Labs
American Medical Systems
ATS Medical
Boston Scientific
Cardiac Science Corporation
Cook Incorporated
Cyberonics
Datascope
DexCom
Edwards Lifesciences
Gyrus ACMI
Integra LifeSciences
Johnson & Johnson
NuVasive
Olympus
Philips Electronics
Sorin
St. Jude Medical
Stryker
Synthes
Terumo Medical Corporation
Transoma Medical
Urologix
Welch Allyn
W.L. Gore
Zimmer Holdings
ZOLL

HISTORICAL FINANCIALS

Company Type: Public

Income Statement

FYE: Last Friday in April

	REVENUE ($ mil.)	NET INCOME ($ mil.)	NET PROFIT MARGIN	EMPLOYEES
4/09	14,599.0	2,169.0	14.9%	41,000
4/08	13,515.0	2,231.0	16.5%	40,000
4/07	12,299.0	2,802.0	22.8%	38,000
4/06	11,292.0	2,546.7	22.6%	36,000
4/05	10,054.6	1,803.9	17.9%	33,000
Annual Growth	**9.8%**	**4.7%**	**—**	**5.6%**

2009 Year-End Financials

Debt ratio: 52.7%
Return on equity: 17.8%
Cash ($ mil.): 1,271
Current ratio: 2.37
Long-term debt ($ mil.): 6,772
No. of shares (mil.): 1,119
Dividends
  Yield: 2.3%
  Payout: 38.9%
Market value ($ mil.): 35,817

Stock History

NYSE: MDT

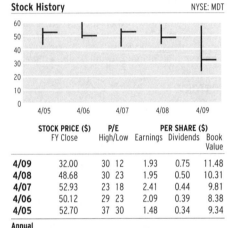

	STOCK PRICE ($) FY Close	P/E High/Low	PER SHARE ($) Earnings	Dividends	Book Value
4/09	32.00	30 12	1.93	0.75	11.48
4/08	48.68	30 23	1.95	0.50	10.31
4/07	52.93	23 18	2.41	0.44	9.81
4/06	50.12	29 23	2.09	0.39	8.38
4/05	52.70	37 30	1.48	0.34	9.34
Annual Growth	**(11.7%)**	**— —**	**6.9%**	**21.9%**	**5.3%**

Men's Wearhouse

With a business strategy tailored for growth, The Men's Wearhouse has made alterations even a haberdasher would be hard-pressed to follow. It's one of the largest discount retailers of men's business and formal attire with more than 1,200 stores. Its primary operations are Men's Wearhouse, which has about 580 stores, Moores Clothing in Canada, and some 490 stores that sell and rent tuxedos. Men's Wearhouse sells discounted tailored suits, as well as shoes, formal wear, and casual clothes. Its K&G unit caters to thriftier shoppers and sells women's careerwear in most of its 100-plus stores. The firm in mid-2009 bid for Filene's Basement at auction and had won until the judge reopened the auction to others.

Soon after The Men's Wearhouse agreed to purchase Filene's Basement, suitors Syms and Crown FB LLC protested and the judge ruled that The Men's Wearhouse was prematurely declared the winner. The next week, Syms purchased the assets of Filene's Basement alongside Vornado Realty in a deal valued at $65 million.

The Men's Wearhouse had extended a bid of $67 million for the 100-year-old Filene's Basement chain, which had filed for Chapter 11 bankruptcy protection in May 2009 for a second time in a decade. The deal involved the Basement name, most of its 25 stores, all inventory, and leases for the Filene's Basement headquarters in Burlington, its Auburn warehouse, and the retailer's flagship location in Boston. The bid required approval by the bankruptcy court.

Declines in same store sales and an inhospitable retail climate had caused the company to trim its growth plans for 2009. After adding more than 40 stores in 2008, The Men's Wearhouse slashed its expansion plans in half. Also, about 80 of the company's K&G stores are slated for makeovers.

In addition to its retail chains, The Men's Wearhouse also operates a corporate apparel and uniform program (Twin Hill) serving about 10 contract customers, as well as 30-plus MW Cleaners dry cleaning and laundry facilities in the Houston area. (Together they account for less than 3% of the company's net sales.) One new dry cleaning plant is due to open in 2009.

The company has finished renaming — again — all of the After Hours Formalwear and Mr. Tux stores (acquired from Macy's, Inc. in 2007) as Men's Wearhouse and Tux (formerly MW Tux shops). The acquisition landed Men's Wearhouse in first place in the tuxedo rental business in North America. The tux rental business attracted Men's Wearhouse because it attracts men younger than the retailer's typical customer. The newly-renamed Men's Wearhouse and Tux stores carry an expanded selection of merchandise, including suit separates, denim, and sportswear targeted at younger men.

Moores Clothing for Men is a chain of more than 115 stores in 10 Canadian provinces. Moores stores also offer tuxedo rentals and "big and tall" merchandise.

Tailored clothing accounts for more than half of sales, although the firm is selling more casual apparel, shoes, and accessories. The Men's Wearhouse stresses attentive, low-pressure customer service to attract the man with little knowledge of buying suits.

HISTORY

George Zimmer, an apparel industry veteran at 23, founded The Men's Wearhouse in fast-growing Houston in 1973 with his father, Robert Zimmer, and college buddy Harry Levy. By the time George debuted on TV in 1986 with his now popular "I guarantee it" motto, the company had 25 stores. It went public in 1992 and continued to grow at a slower but more sustainable pace than its competitors, some of which went bankrupt as a result of overexpansion.

In 1997, through its newly formed Value Price Clothing division, The Men's Wearhouse bought C & R Clothiers, adding 17 stores and a new, lower-priced segment to its operations. The division added four Suit Warehouse stores in the Detroit area the next year.

An on-again-off-again deal to grow into Canada was back on (for good) in early 1999 when The Men's Wearhouse paid $127 million for the Montreal-based Moores Retail Group. The company later began offering tuxedo rentals at some of its Men's Wearhouse stores. Also that year, The Men's Wearhouse bought K&G Men's Center, operator of 34 superstores in 16 states. In 2000 it combined its other discount operations with K&G, renaming most of the stores K&G Men's Center. After 2001's economic downturn hit the company hard, CEO Zimmer announced a return to focusing on the suits, rather than casualwear, and not carrying anything priced more than $500.

In 2002 the company acquired TwinHill, which became its global uniform and corporate apparel division. TwinHill supplies uniforms for clients in the transportation, hospitality, foodservice, banking, retail, security, and entertainment industries. The same year, The Men's Wearhouse purchased the Wilke-Rodriguez brand and became its sole distributor. Plans to launch a 100-store chain catering to Latino men under the Eddie Rodriguez name were abandoned in 2005.

On the lookout for complementary products and services, the company entered the dry-cleaning business in December 2003 when it bought Nesbit's Cleaners and Craig's Cleaners of Houston.

In April 2007 Men's Wearhouse acquired After Hours Formalwear from Federated Department Stores (now Macy's, Inc.) for about $100 million.

Citing the strengthening of the Canadian dollar, Men's Wearhouse closed its manufacturing facility in Montreal (Golden Brand Clothing), which supplied its Moores Clothing stores, in mid-2008. In early 2009 the firm changed the name of its MW Tux stores to Men's Wearhouse and Tux.

EXECUTIVES

Chairman and CEO: George Zimmer, age 60, $1,709,012 total compensation
Vice Chairman: David H. Edwab, age 54, $973,699 total compensation
President and COO: Douglas S. Ewert, age 45, $1,648,813 total compensation
EVP, CFO, Treasurer, and Principal Financial Officer: Neill P. Davis, age 52, $877,729 total compensation
SVP and CIO: William Melvin
EVP Distribution, Logistics, Tuxedo Operations, and Chief Compliance Officer: Gary G. Ckodre, age 59
SVP, Chief Accounting Officer, and Principal Accounting Officer: Diana M. Wilson, age 61
EVP Employee Relations and Chief Legal Officer: Carole Souvenir, age 48
EVP Marketing and Human Resources: Charles Bresler, age 60, $747,592 total compensation
EVP Manufacturing: William C. (Will) Silveira, age 51
SVP Merchandising: James E. Zimmer, age 57
SVP Marketing: Jayme Maxwell
SVP Tuxedo Distribution: Jamie R. Bragg
SVP Real Estate: Thomas L. Jennings
VP Human Resources, Houston: Claudia Pruitt
President, Moores Retail Group: Pasquale De Marco, age 48
President, MW Cleaners: Michael Nesbit
President, TwinHill: Howard Wecksler
President, K&G Fashion Superstore: Mary Beth Blake
President, Moores Retail Store Operations: Dave Starrett
Secretary: Michael W. Conlon
Auditors: Deloitte & Touche LLP

LOCATIONS

HQ: The Men's Wearhouse, Inc.
6380 Rogerdale Rd., Houston, TX 77072
Phone: 281-776-7200
Web: www.menswearhouse.com

2009 Stores

	Men's Wearhouse	K&G	Moores
US			
California	89	1	—
Texas	56	13	—
Florida	41	6	—
New York	30	4	—
Illinois	27	6	—
Michigan	20	7	—
Pennsylvania	24	5	—
Ohio	19	5	—
Georgia	17	6	—
Virginia	18	3	—
Massachusetts	15	5	—
Maryland	14	7	—
Colorado	14	3	—
Washington	14	3	—
New Jersey	16	8	—
North Carolina	13	4	—
Arizona	14	—	—
Missouri	11	2	—
Tennessee	12	2	—
Minnesota	9	2	—
Wisconsin	9	1	—
Oregon	9	—	—
Connecticut	9	2	—
Indiana	9	3	—
Louisiana	7	4	—
Utah	7	—	—
Oklahoma	5	2	—
Alabama	5	1	—
Nevada	6	—	—
Kansas	5	1	—
Kentucky	3	1	—
South Carolina	5	1	—
New Mexico	4	—	—
Iowa	4	—	—
Other states	20	—	—
Canada (Moores Clothing)	—	—	117
Total	**580**	**108**	**117**

PRODUCTS/OPERATIONS

Selected Merchandise

Accessories
Dress shirts
Formal wear
Outerwear
Shoes
Slacks
Sport coats
Sport shirts
Suits

Selected Store Names and Operations

K&G Men's Center
K&G Men's Superstore
K&G Suit Warehouse
K&G Superstore
Men's Wearhouse
Men's Wearhouse and Tux (formerly MW Tux)
Moores Clothing for Men
Moores Vetements Pour Hommes
MW Cleaners (dry cleaning)
Twin Hill Corporate Apparel

COMPETITORS

ARAMARK	Jos. A. Bank
Astor & Black	Kohl's
Brooks Brothers	Macy's
Burlington Coat Factory	Neiman Marcus
Casual Male Retail Group	Nordstrom
Cintas	Ross Stores
Dillard's	S&K Famous Brands
Eddie Bauer Holdings	Saks
G&K Services	Sears
Hudson's Bay	Syms
J. Crew	

HISTORICAL FINANCIALS

Company Type: Public

Income Statement

FYE: Saturday nearest January 31

	REVENUE ($ mil.)	NET INCOME ($ mil.)	NET PROFIT MARGIN	EMPLOYEES
1/09	1,972.4	58.8	3.0%	16,200
1/08	2,112.6	147.0	7.0%	18,400
1/07	1,882.1	148.6	7.9%	14,900
1/06	1,724.9	103.9	6.0%	13,800
1/05	1,546.7	71.4	4.6%	13,200
Annual Growth	6.3%	(4.7%)	—	5.3%

2009 Year-End Financials

Debt ratio: 7.5%
Return on equity: 7.1%
Cash ($ mil.): 87
Current ratio: 2.87
Long-term debt ($ mil.): 63

No. of shares (mil.): 70
Dividends
  Yield: 2.4%
  Payout: 24.8%
Market value ($ mil.): 818

Stock History

NYSE: MW

	STOCK PRICE ($) FY Close	P/E High/Low		PER SHARE ($) Earnings	Dividends	Book Value
1/09	11.65	24	7	1.13	0.28	11.99
1/08	25.49	21	6	2.73	0.23	11.62
1/07	42.94	16	11	2.71	0.20	10.74
1/06	34.17	20	12	1.88	0.00	8.94
1/05	22.18	18	12	1.29	0.00	8.10
Annual Growth	(14.9%)	—	—	(3.3%)	—	10.3%

Merck & Co.

Merck's medicine bag helps asthmatics breathe easier and allows hypertension patients to relax a little. In addition to blockbuster asthma treatment Singulair, the pharmaceutical company's top sellers include cardiovascular drugs ranging from hypertension fighters Cozaar and Hyzaar to cholesterol combatants Vytorin, Zetia, and Zocor. Merck makes drugs in a broad range of other therapeutic areas as well: Januvia is a therapy for type 2 diabetes, Fosamax fights osteoporosis, and Cosopt and Trusopt treat eye disease. In addition to pharmaceuticals, the company makes childhood and adult vaccines for such diseases as measles, mumps, hepatitis, and shingles. Merck has agreed to acquire Schering-Plough for $41 billion.

The merger will create a stronger portfolio of marketed and development-stage pharmaceuticals in areas including cardiovascular, oncology, respiratory, neurology, and women's health. The company anticipates that integration efforts will result in a 15% workforce reduction.

On the drug development front, Merck has enjoyed a string of successes, including the 2006 FDA approval of its cervical cancer vaccine Gardasil, the world's first anti-cancer vaccine. HIV drug Isentress and diabetes drug Janumet got the FDA nod in 2007, and injectable drug Emend, which treats chemotherapy-related nausea and vomiting, was approved in 2008. Adding these new marketed products largely offsets the losses associated with generic competition for Zocor (which started facing generic competition in 2006) and other drugs. Gardasil, in particular, has been a huge success, reaching blockbuster status ($1 billion in sales) within its first nine months on the market.

However, Merck has encountered a number of setbacks in its pipeline— failures that led the company to announce a cut of more than 10% of its global workforce (including one-quarter of Merck executives) later that year. In addition to medical study releases that brought Vytorin's effectiveness into question, the company suffered blows that year when the FDA rejected cholesterol pill Cordaptive and a combination asthma drug, as well as from the loss of patent protection on its blockbuster osteoporosis drug Fosamax. The FDA rejected Arcoxia, a Cox-2 painkiller that Merck hoped would replace its disgraced Vioxx, in 2007. Merck also halted development of an insomnia drug, gaboxadol, and an AIDS vaccine after getting disappointing results on both in clinical trials.

To improve its R&D productivity, it has decided to focus on key therapeutic areas including Alzheimer's disease, atherosclerosis, cardiovascular disease, diabetes, vaccines, obesity, cancer, pain management, and sleep disorders. It has several drugs in late stages of development.

Though the company's troubles over pain drug Vioxx have receded somewhat, Merck is still feeling the effects of its ordeal with the drug, which it withdrew from shelves in 2004 after Vioxx was linked to increased risk of stroke and heart attack. Merck has faced thousands of personal injury lawsuits over Vioxx (some of them class action suits). The company's initial strategy was to aggressively defend each Vioxx case, but in 2007 it announced it would settle after all, agreeing to pay $4.85 billion to plaintiffs in order to resolve the vast majority of the claims.

HISTORY

Merck was started in 1887 when German chemist Theodore Weicker came to the US to set up a branch of E. Merck AG of Germany. George Merck (grandson of the German company's founder) came in 1889 and formed a partnership with Weicker. At first the firm imported and sold drugs and chemicals from Germany, but in 1903 it opened a plant in Rahway, New Jersey, to make alkaloids. Weicker sold out to Merck the next year and bought a controlling interest in competitor Squibb. During WWI, Merck gave the US government the 80% of company stock owned by family in Germany (George kept his shares). After the war, the stock was sold to the public.

The firm acquired Powers-Weightman-Rosengarten of Philadelphia (a producer of antimalarial quinine) in 1927. Merck opened a research lab in 1933; Merck scientists there developed the first steroid, cortisone, in 1944. Five Merck scientists received Nobel Prizes in the 1940s and 1950s. In 1953 Merck bought drugmaker Sharp & Dohme of Philadelphia, which brought with it a strong sales force.

The 1958 introduction of Diuril (antihypertensive) and several other drugs in the early 1960s was followed by a 10-year dry spell. John Horan, who took over in 1976, accelerated R&D to create new products. By the late 1970s Merck had produced Clinoril (antiarthritic), Flexeril (muscle relaxant), and Timoptic (for glaucoma).

Biochemist Roy Vagelos, who became CEO in 1985, continued the commitment to R&D. Merck introduced 10 major new drugs in the 1980s, including Mevacor (high cholesterol) and Vasotec (high blood pressure).

In 1990 the company bought the nonprescription drug segment of ICI Americas; products from the purchase are marketed through a joint venture with Johnson & Johnson.

Merck bought pharmacy benefits manager Medco Containment Services in 1993. The following year Merck established subsidiaries in Cyprus, Germany, the Netherlands, Peru, and South Korea and began a joint venture in China to make and sell its products. The firm brought eight new drugs to market in 1995 and 1996, including Cozaar (for reducing hypertension) and Pepcid AC (antacid).

In 1997 Merck and Rhône-Poulenc (now part of Sanofi-Aventis) merged their animal health units to form Merial; Merck sold its insecticide and fungicide business to Novartis that year. In 1998 DuPont bought out Merck's 50% stake in a drug-marketing joint venture formed by the two firms in 1991.

In 1999 the FDA approved Merck's preservative-free hepatitis B vaccine, Recombivax HB. In 2000 Merck's Fosamax, already in use for female osteoporosis, became the first FDA-approved male osteoporosis treatment. The firm lost patent protection for its hypertension drug Vasotec, high-cholesterol drug Mevacor, and ulcer drug Pepcid in 2001.

In 2004 Merck pulled its blockbuster pain medication Vioxx off the market after studies linked the drug to increased risks of strokes and heart attacks.

Merck announced restructuring plans in 2005 to reduce its workforce by more than 10%. The announcement was the first major move by CEO Richard Clark, a long-time Merck executive who had replaced Raymond Gilmartin as president and CEO earlier that year. Between 2005 and 2008, the company eliminated more than 10,000 jobs and closed a handful of manufacturing plants.

EXECUTIVES

Chairman, President, and CEO: Richard T. (Dick) Clark, age 62, $19,906,430 total compensation
EVP and CFO: Peter N. Kellogg, age 53, $3,819,080 total compensation
EVP Global Services and CIO: J. Chris Scalet, age 50
VP and Chief Communications Officer:
  Adele D. Ambrose, age 52
EVP; President, Global Human Health:
  Kenneth C. (Ken) Frazier, age 54, $5,549,838 total compensation
EVP; President, Merck Research Laboratories:
  Peter S. Kim, age 49, $4,222,822 total compensation
EVP; President, Merck Manufacturing Division:
  Willie A. Deese, age 53
EVP and General Counsel: Bruce N. Kuhlik, age 52, $2,623,241 total compensation
EVP Global Human Resources:
  Miriam M. Graddick-Weir, age 54

SVP, Secretary, and Assistant General Counsel:
  Celia A. Colbert, age 52
SVP Franchise Head: Stephen H. Friend
SVP Finance and Global Controller: John Canan, age 52
SVP Business Development and Corporate Licensing:
  Richard N. Kender, age 53
SVP and Managing Director, France: Guy Eiferman
SVP and Oncology Franchise Head, Merck Research Laboratories: D. Gary Gilliland, age 54
VP Investor Relations: Eva C. Boratto
VP Global Public Policy and Corporate Responsibility:
  Geralyn S. Ritter
President, Global Vaccines and Infectious Diseases:
  Margaret G. (Margie) McGlynn, age 50
President, Global Pharmaceuticals: Adam H. Schechter, age 44
Auditors: PricewaterhouseCoopers LLP

LOCATIONS

HQ: Merck & Co., Inc.
  1 Merck Dr., Whitehouse Station, NJ 08889
Phone: 908-423-1000   **Fax:** 908-735-1253
Web: www.merck.com

2008 Sales

	$ mil.	% of total
US	13,370.5	56
Europe, Middle East & Africa	5,773.8	24
Japan	1,823.5	8
Other regions	2,882.5	12
Total	**23,850.3**	**100**

PRODUCTS/OPERATIONS

2008 Sales

	$ mil.	% of total
Pharmacueticals		
Singulair	4,336.9	18
Cozaar/Hyzaar	3,557.7	15
Fosamax	1,552.7	7
Januvia	1,397.1	6
Cosopt/Trusopt	781.2	3
Zocor	660.1	3
Maxalt	529.2	2
Propecia	429.1	2
Arcoxia	377.3	2
Vasotec/Vaseretic	356.7	1
Janumet	351.1	1
Proscar	323.5	1
Emend	263.8	1
Other pharmaceutical	2,278.9	10
Vaccines/infectious disease		
Gardasil	1,402.8	6
ProQuad/M-M-R II/Varivax	1,268.5	5
Primaxin	760.4	3
RotaTeq	664.5	3
Cancidas	596.4	2
Isentress	361.1	2
Zostavax	312.4	1
Crixivan/Stocrin	275.1	1
Invanz	265.0	1
Hepatitis vaccines	148.3	1
Other vaccines & infectious disease	370.1	2
Other	230.4	1
Total	**23,850.3**	**100**

Selected Products

Cardiology
  Cozaar (hypertension)
  Hyzaar (hypertension)
  Vasotec (hypertension/heart failure)
  Vytorin (elevated cholesterol)
  Zetia (elevated cholesterol)
  Zocor (elevated cholesterol)

Endocrinology
  Fosamax (osteoporosis)
  Propecia (male pattern hair loss)
  Proscar (benign prostate enlargement)

Gastrointestinal
  Pepcid (ulcers, marketed with Johnson & Johnson)

Infection
  Cancidas (antifungal)
  Crixivan (HIV)
  Invanz (antibacterial)
  Primaxin (antibiotic)
  Stocrin (HIV)
Metabolic
  Janumet (diabetes)
  Januvia (diabetes)
Neurological
  Maxalt (migraine)
Ophthalmic
  Cosopt (glaucoma)
  Trusopt (glaucoma)
Respiratory
  Singulair (asthma and allergic rhinitis)
Vaccines
  Comvax (hepatitis B)
  Gardasil (cervical cancer caused by HPV virus)
  M-M-R II (measles, mumps, and rubella)
  Pneumovax (pneumococcal disease)
  ProQuad (measles, mumps, rubella, varicella)
  Recombivax HB (hepatitis B)
  RotaTeq (rotavirus gastroenteritis)
  Vaqta (hepatitis A)
  Varivax (chicken pox)
  Zostavax (shingles)

COMPETITORS

Abbott Labs
Alcon
Allergan
Amgen
AstraZeneca
Barr Pharmaceuticals
Bausch & Lomb
Baxter International
Bayer AG
Boehringer Ingelheim
Bristol-Myers Squibb
Eli Lilly
Forest Labs
Genzyme
Gilead Sciences
GlaxoSmithKline
Johnson & Johnson
King Pharmaceuticals
Mylan
Novartis
Novo Nordisk
Pfizer
Roche Holding
Sandoz International GmbH
Sanofi-Aventis
Shire
Teva Pharmaceuticals
Watson Pharmaceuticals
Wyeth

HISTORICAL FINANCIALS

Company Type: Public

Income Statement

FYE: December 31

	REVENUE ($ mil.)	NET INCOME ($ mil.)	NET PROFIT MARGIN	EMPLOYEES
12/08	23,850.3	7,808.4	32.7%	55,200
12/07	24,197.7	3,275.4	13.5%	59,800
12/06	22,636.0	4,433.8	19.6%	60,000
12/05	22,011.9	4,631.3	21.0%	61,500
12/04	22,938.6	5,813.4	25.3%	63,000
Annual Growth	1.0%	7.7%	—	(3.3%)

2008 Year-End Financials

Debt ratio: 21.0%
Return on equity: 42.3%
Cash ($ mil.): 4,368
Current ratio: 1.35
Long-term debt ($ mil.): 3,943

No. of shares (mil.): 2,109
Dividends
  Yield: 5.0%
  Payout: 41.8%
Market value ($ mil.): 64,109

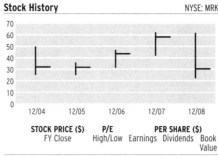

Stock History

NYSE: MRK

	STOCK PRICE ($) FY Close	P/E High/Low		PER SHARE ($) Earnings	Dividends	Book Value
12/08	30.40	17	6	3.64	1.52	8.89
12/07	58.11	41	28	1.49	1.52	8.62
12/06	43.60	23	16	2.03	1.52	8.33
12/05	31.81	17	12	2.10	1.52	8.50
12/04	32.14	19	10	2.61	1.50	8.20
Annual Growth	(1.4%)	—	—	8.7%	0.3%	2.1%

MetLife, Inc.

Part of its name may stand for "metropolitan," but the company is found in villages, towns, and huge cities coast-to-coast and then some. MetLife is the US's largest life insurer; its flagship insurance subsidiary is Metropolitan Life Insurance Company. MetLife's Institutional segment offers group benefits products (life and disability insurance, dental, vision, retirement products, prepaid legal plans); its Individual segment offers consumers many of the same types of products, while its International segment offers the same to groups and individuals in the Asia/Pacific region, Europe, and Latin America. MetLife's Auto & Home segment works through subsidiary Metropolitan Property and Casualty Insurance (MPC).

MetLife also provides FDIC-insured individual banking services online through MetLife Bank.

Policies and other products are sold through a vast network of targeted marketing and sales forces, agency distribution groups, independent agents, affiliated broker-dealers, and direct marketing. In addition, MetLife sells some products through affinity groups and through employers.

MetLife is focusing on emerging markets, increasing its already strong presence in the Asia/Pacific region and in Latin America. The company acquired Adonto, a dental insurance company, in 2008. Adonto has a network of 4,000 dentists serving 300 Brazilian cities. MetLife also launched individual medical plans in Mexico to complement its existing group plans.

Until 2008 the company participated in reinsurance by holding 52% of Reinsurance Group of America. However, MetLife sold off its shares that year to focus on its core activities.

The same year the company purchased dental plan provider SafeGuard, the reverse mortgage business of EverBank, and the mortgage business of First Tennessee Bank.

While MetLife is primarily known as an insurance company, it also holds a solid real estate portfolio valued at more than $10 billion. However, the company has sold off some of its largest properties, including Chicago's Sears Tower (divested in 2004, the tower was renamed Willis

Tower in 2009) and its own landmark headquarters in New York (in 2005 for $1.5 billion). It also sold the Peter Cooper and Stuyvesant Town housing complexes that it helped build with government funding in 1947. Tishman Speyer Properties and BlackRock paid $5.4 billion for the property in late 2006; the sale boosted MetLife's 2006 net income to a record $6.29 billion.

HISTORY

New York merchant Simeon Draper tried to form National Union Life and Limb Insurance to cover Union soldiers in the Civil War, but investors were scared away by heavy casualties. After several reorganizations and name changes, the enterprise emerged in 1868 as Metropolitan Life Insurance (MetLife), a stock company.

Sustained at first by business from mutual assistance societies for German immigrants, MetLife went into industrial insurance with workers' burial policies. The firm was known for its aggressive sales methods. Agents combed working-class neighborhoods, collecting small premiums. If a worker missed one payment, the company could cancel the policy and keep all premiums paid, a practice outlawed in 1900.

MetLife became a mutual company (owned by its policyholders) in 1915 and began offering group insurance two years later.

After a period of conservative management under the Eckers family from 1929 to 1963, MetLife began to change, dropping industrial insurance in 1964. It started offering auto and homeowners insurance in 1974.

To diversify, the company bought State Street Research & Management (1983), Century 21 Real Estate (1985, sold 1995), London-based Albany Life Assurance (1985), and Allstate's group life and health business (1988). In 1987 it took over the annuities segment of the failed Baldwin United Co., and expanded into Spain and Taiwan in 1988. During the early 1990s, MetLife reemphasized insurance, adding such new products as long-term-care insurance.

In 1993 MetLife was charged with improper sales practices in 13 states. Legal fees, fines, and refunds in these cases exceeded $100 million; bad publicity had a chilling effect on sales. MetLife in turn instituted new training and sales practices. (In 1998 it agreed to pay an additional $25 million civil penalty to settle the federal investigation.)

In 1996 MetLife bought New England Mutual Life Insurance, expanding its customer base to include wealthier middle-class customers (it also sought to obliterate its 1995 loss by retroactively restating results on combined sales).

MetLife's problems continued with a suit over its sales of insurance to Americans in Europe and an investigation in Florida related to churning (agents inducing customers to buy more expensive policies).

In 1997 MetLife sold its UK insurance operations and its Canadian business, then cut 10% (about 1,900) of its administrative employees.

In 1999 MetLife followed the industry trend of buying and selling single product lines rather than whole companies. Also in 1999, the company agreed to pay $1.7 billion to settle policyholder lawsuits related to churning allegations.

MetLife saw numerous changes in 2000. Most notably, it went public, bought fellow insurer GenAmerica, and purchased Grand Bank, a one-office nationally chartered bank in New Jersey, which was renamed MetLife Bank. Plans to use

Grand Bank as a ticket into the financial services arena met with opposition from community and consumer groups concerned about how MetLife's ownership would comply with the Community Reinvestment Act. The Federal Reserve Board approved the acquisition in 2001.

To trim expenses, MetLife cut employees and consolidated some offices and in 2001 it exited the large-market 401(k) business and sold asset manager Conning to Swiss Re.

Solidifying its position as a major group benefits provider, MetLife bought John Hancock's group life insurance operations in 2003.

MetLife in 2005 exited the asset management business when it sold State Street Research to BlackRock. That same year it acquired The Travelers Insurance Company and The Travelers Life and Annuity Company, from Citigroup in a cash and equity deal valued at $11.8 billion. The deal, which included Citigroup's international insurance businesses, made MetLife the largest individual life insurer in North America. In 2006 it changed the acquired business' name to MetLife Insurance Company of Connecticut and MetLife Life and Annuity Company of Connecticut, and in 2007 it merged the latter into the former.

EXECUTIVES

Chairman, President, and CEO:
C. Robert (Rob) Henrikson, age 61,
$24,484,380 total compensation
EVP and CFO: William J. (Bill) Wheeler, age 47,
$4,319,257 total compensation
EVP and CIO: Steven L. Sheinheit
SVP and CIO, Corporate Systems: Georgette A. Piligian, age 43
EVP and Chief Administrative Officer: Ruth A. Fattori, age 57
EVP and Chief Investment Officer:
Steven A. Kandarian, age 56,
$3,930,868 total compensation
Chief Accounting Officer: Peter M. (Pete) Carlson, age 45
EVP and General Counsel: James L. Lipscomb, age 62
EVP Metropolitan Life Insurance:
Michael K. (Mike) Farrell, age 55
EVP MetLife Agency Distribution: Mike Vietri
EVP Technology and Operations: Maria R. Morris, age 46
SVP and Secretary: Gwenn L. Carr
VP Institutional Marketing: William J. Raczko
VP Public Relations: John Calagna
VP Investor Relations: Conor Murphy
President, Individual Business: Lisa M. Weber, age 46
President, International: William J. Toppeta, age 60,
$5,239,471 total compensation
President, Institutional Business, MetLife and Metropolitan Life: William J. Mullaney, age 49
President, MetLife Bank: Donnalee A. DeMaio
President, MetLife Auto & Home: William D. Moore
Auditors: Deloitte & Touche LLP

LOCATIONS

HQ: MetLife, Inc.
200 Park Ave., New York, NY 10166
Phone: 212-578-2211   **Fax:** 212-578-3320
Web: www.metlife.com

PRODUCTS/OPERATIONS

2008 Sales

	$ mil.	% of total
Premiums		
Institutional	14,964	29
Individual	4,481	9
International	3,470	7
Auto & home	2,971	6
Corporate & other	28	—
Net investment income	16,296	32
Univeral life & investment-type product policy fees	5,381	11
Net investment gains (losses)	1,812	3
Other	1,586	3
Total	**50,989**	**100**

Business Segments

Auto & Home (auto, home, boat, RV, mobile home, and personal liability insurance)
Banking (mortgage, online consumer savings products, reverse mortgage)
Individual (annuities; life, disability, and long-term care insurance; mutual funds)
International (annuities; life, accident, and health insurance; savings and retirement products; property and casualty insurance)
Institutional (group insurance; retirement and savings products; administrative services)

COMPETITORS

AEGON USA	John Hancock Financial
Aetna	Liberty Mutual
Aflac	Lincoln Financial Group
AIG	MassMutual
AIG American General	Mutual of Omaha
Allianz	Nationwide
Allstate	New York Life
Aon	Northwestern Mutual
AXA	Pacific Mutual
CIGNA	Principal Financial
CNA Financial	Prudential
COUNTRY Financial	State Farm
GEICO	TIAA-CREF
Guardian Life	USAA
The Hartford	Zurich Financial Services
ING	

HISTORICAL FINANCIALS

Company Type: Public

Income Statement

FYE: December 31

	ASSETS ($ mil.)	NET INCOME ($ mil.)	INCOME AS % OF ASSETS	EMPLOYEES
12/08	501,678.0	3,209.0	0.6%	57,000
12/07	558,562.0	4,317.0	0.8%	49,000
12/06	527,715.0	6,293.0	1.2%	47,000
12/05	481,645.0	4,714.0	1.0%	65,500
12/04	356,808.0	2,844.0	0.8%	54,000
Annual Growth	**8.9%**	**3.1%**	**—**	**1.4%**

2008 Year-End Financials

Equity as % of assets: 4.7%
Return on assets: 0.6%
Return on equity: 10.9%
Long-term debt ($ mil.): 18,617
No. of shares (mil.): 819
Dividends
  Yield: 2.1%
  Payout: 17.9%
Market value ($ mil.): 28,538
Sales ($ mil.): 50,989

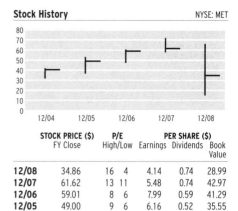

Stock History   NYSE: MET

	STOCK PRICE ($) FY Close	P/E High/Low		PER SHARE ($) Earnings	Dividends	Book Value
12/08	34.86	16	4	4.14	0.74	28.99
12/07	61.62	13	11	5.48	0.74	42.97
12/06	59.01	8	6	7.99	0.59	41.29
12/05	49.00	9	6	6.16	0.52	35.55
12/04	40.51	11	9	3.65	0.46	27.88
Annual Growth	**(3.7%)**	**—**	**—**	**3.2%**	**12.6%**	**1.0%**

MetroPCS Communications

MetroPCS Communications is marching to the beat of a different drummer. The regional wireless service provider offers use of its phone networks, which use CDMA (code division multiple access) technology, without chaining its customers to long-term contracts. Unlike other providers that charge by the minute, MetroPCS offers monthly unlimited usage flat-rate plans for local and domestic long distance services to its approximately 5.4 million customers. It operates in eight states in such major metropolitan areas as Atlanta, Dallas/Ft. Worth, Detroit, Los Angeles, Miami, Sacramento, and San Francisco. CEO Roger Linquist and CTO Malcolm Lorang founded MetroPCS in 1994.

In 2009 MetroPCS expanded its service to the New York and Boston metropolitan areas.

In late 2008 the company entered into a national roaming agreement with Leap Wireless (which MetroPCS unsuccessfully tried to acquire in 2007), as well as agreeing to settle outstanding litigation between the two companies. The pact also included a spectrum exchange agreement which saw Leap acquiring from MetroPCS 10 MHz of spectrum in San Diego, Fresno, Seattle and other Washington and Oregon markets, and MetroPCS acquiring from Leap an additional 10 MHz of spectrum in Dallas/Ft. Worth and other markets in Louisiana and Florida.

MetroPCS has strategically focused on serving densely populated markets, which creates efficiencies for the company in regard to network deployment and product distribution. The company has access to a wireless spectrum coverage area of about 150 million people in the US, including nine of the top 12 US metropolitan areas.

HISTORY

CEO Roger Linquist and CTO Malcolm Lorang founded General Wireless in 1994 to bid on PCS licenses being auctioned by the US government. Linquist was formerly CEO of PacTel Personal Communications (later called AirTouch and now part of the Vodafone Group) and founded PageMart Wireless (now WebLink Wireless). In 1996 Japanese trading house Mitsui and audio-equipment maker Kenwood agreed to invest $10 million in General Wireless. The US electronics unit of Hyundai also made a substantial financial commitment, and Lucent Technologies said it would provide $300 million in vendor financing to build the networks.

Also in 1996, the firm successfully bid $1 billion for 14 PCS licenses. But before the licenses were awarded, the FCC held another auction where similar licenses sold for far less. General Wireless scrapped its IPO in 1997 because of poor market conditions. A year later it filed for Chapter 11 bankruptcy protection and sought to reduce the price of its licenses. The next year a federal bankruptcy court ruled that the licenses were worth only $166 million and that the company could reorganize and keep the licenses. The FCC launched an appeal but the bankruptcy court's decision was upheld in 1999 by a Texas district court. The FCC then lobbied the US Congress to reclaim the licenses, but the resulting bill was blocked.

After emerging from bankruptcy protection, the firm changed its name to MetroPCS Communications. The legal wrangling continued into 2000 when the FCC appealed the decision to the 5th US Circuit Court of Appeals in New Orleans, which ruled in favor of the company. The next year the Supreme Court denied a review of the case, upholding the lower court's decision. MetroPCS then began rolling out operations in its major markets.

In 2007 the company went public and bought $1.4 billion in spectrum licenses, covering regions such as Boston, New York, and Philadelphia, during the federal government's auction.

Also in 2007, the company's more than $5 billion bid to acquire Leap Wireless was rejected. MetroPCS had hoped to significantly expand its service area in order to better compete with nationwide carriers like Sprint Nextel and AT&T Mobility through a merger with Leap.

EXECUTIVES

Chairman, President, and CEO: Roger D. Linquist, age 70, $10,682,652 total compensation
COO: Thomas C. Keys, age 50, $3,895,024 total compensation
EVP and CFO: J. Braxton Carter, age 50, $2,838,984 total compensation
SVP and CTO: Malcolm M. Lorang, age 75
VP and CIO: John J. Olsen, age 52
VP, Chief Accounting Officer, and Controller: Christine B. Kornegay, age 45
EVP, General Counsel, and Secretary: Mark A. Stachiw, age 47, $2,089,221 total compensation
SVP Market Operations, West: Herbert (Chip) Graves IV, age 53
SVP Corporate Operations: Douglas S. (Doug) Glen, age 51
SVP Engineering and Network Operations: Ed Chao
VP Corporate Marketing: Phillip R. Terry
VP Finance, and Treasurer: Keith D. Terreri, age 44
VP Network Operations: David Walker
Auditors: Deloitte & Touche LLP

LOCATIONS

HQ: MetroPCS Communications, Inc.
2250 Lakeside Boulevard, Richardson, TX 75082
Phone: 214-570-5800 **Fax:** 214-570-5859
Web: www.metropcs.com

PRODUCTS/OPERATIONS

2008 Sales

	% of total
Service revenues	89
Equipment revenues	11
Total	**100**

Selected Offerings

Local and long distance wireless calling services
Voice and data services (text messaging, games, and ringtones)

COMPETITORS

AT&T
AT&T Mobility
Boost Mobile
Comcast Cable
Cox Communications
Leap Wireless
Sprint Nextel
Time Warner Cable
T-Mobile USA
TracFone
Verizon
Virgin Mobile
Vonage
XO Holdings

HISTORICAL FINANCIALS

Company Type: Public

Income Statement

FYE: December 31

	REVENUE ($ mil.)	NET INCOME ($ mil.)	NET PROFIT MARGIN	EMPLOYEES
12/08	2,751.5	149.4	5.4%	3,200
12/07	2,235.7	92.7	4.1%	2,498
12/06	1,546.9	29.0	1.9%	2,046
12/05	1,038.4	198.7	19.1%	—
12/04	748.3	86.4	11.5%	861
Annual Growth	**38.5%**	**14.7%**	**—**	**38.8%**

2008 Year-End Financials

Debt ratio: 150.3%
Return on equity: 7.7%
Cash ($ mil.): 698
Current ratio: 1.41
Long-term debt ($ mil.): 3,058
No. of shares (mil.): 352
Dividends
Yield: 0.0%
Payout: —
Market value ($ mil.): 5,229

Stock History

NYSE: PCS

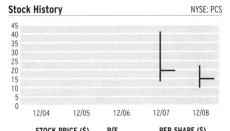

	STOCK PRICE ($) FY Close	P/E High/Low		PER SHARE ($) Earnings	Dividends	Book Value
12/08	14.85	52	24	0.42	0.00	5.78
12/07	19.45	146	49	0.28	0.00	5.25
Annual Growth	**(23.7%)**	**—**	**—**	**50.0%**	**—**	**10.0%**

MGM MIRAGE

It's not your imagination — MGM MIRAGE is one of the world's largest gaming firms. The company's 20 partially or wholly owned properties include Las Vegas' MGM Grand, Luxor, Bellagio, The Mirage, New York-New York, and the Monte Carlo. It also owns casinos elsewhere in Nevada (Reno, Jean, and Henderson), as well as in Illinois (50%-owned), Michigan, and Mississippi. In addition, the company operates the Borgata casino in Atlantic City through a joint venture with Boyd Gaming. MGM MIRAGE shot to the top of the gaming world in 2005 when it acquired rival Mandalay Resort Group for $7.9 billion. However, Harrah's surpassed MGM MIRAGE after it merged with Caesars. Founder Kirk Kerkorian owns about 40% of the firm.

MGM MIRAGE embarked on its most ambitious development plan to date with the announcement of plans to build a mega-resort in Las Vegas on a 66-acre site between the company's Bellagio and Monte Carlo casinos. The site, dubbed CityCenter, was originally designed to feature a 4,000-room casino resort, two 400-room boutique hotels, 425,000 sq. ft. of retail space, restaurants and entertainment venues, and a 2,700-unit condominium complex. However, as a result of the devastated tourism industry amid the economic recession, in early 2009 the company announced plans to scale back the project, reducing its budget and delaying the opening of certain stages of development. In 2009 developers reached an agreement with lenders to complete the $8.5 billion project (which was initially worth some $11 billion) by the end of that year.

In late 2008 chairman and CEO J. Terrence Lanni resigned from his executive positions (he remains on the board of directors). James J. Murren, former president and COO, was appointed his replacement. At the end of 2008 MGM MIRAGE agreed to sell its Treasure Island Hotel & Casino on the Las Vegas Strip to Ruffin Acquisition LLC for $775 million in order to lighten its debt (worth a staggering $14 billion); the deal closed in 2009. The troubled company is also mulling over a possible sale of the Bellagio.

MGM MIRAGE also owns 50% of a hotel and casino resort in Macau, China. The joint venture with private Macau casino developer Pansy Ho Chiu-king developed MGM Grand Macau, which opened in 2007. In 2009 New Jersey regulators issued a report declaring that Ho is an "unsuitable" business partner for MGM, a finding that could jeopardize MGM MIRAGE's license for its casino in Atlantic City.

The company's lavish Beau Rivage casino in Biloxi, Mississippi, includes a barge-bound gambling floor with a waterside compound of restaurants, bars, a hotel, and convention center. MGM MIRAGE has additionally announced a $5 billion project for a new resort in Atlantic City, New Jersey to be completed in 2012 called MGM Grand Atlantic City. That project has also been put on hold. In addition, the busy company in 2009 created a hotel division, MGM MIRAGE Hospitality, to brand and manage hotels from third party developers.

Dubai World, a holding company for the Persian Gulf state that manages the government of Dubai's business projects, owns about 9% of the company's total outstanding shares.

HISTORY

Billionaire Kirk Kerkorian purchased a stake in famed movie studio Metro-Goldwyn-Mayer (MGM; formed in 1924) for just over $80 million in 1970. Around the same time, he began acquiring property in Las Vegas and started construction on the city's largest hotel.

Financial difficulties led Kerkorian to sell his new hotel, as well as many of MGM's assets in the early 1970s. But he kept the MGM name and used it for MGM Grand hotels in Las Vegas and Reno, Nevada. In 1986 Kerkorian sold MGM Grand Hotels to Bally, but he retained the rights to the MGM Grand name and logo. That year Kerkorian founded MGM Grand, Inc. and took the company public in 1987. He set about snapping up Las Vegas property in the late 1980s and early 1990s.

In 1993 Kerkorian and company unveiled Las Vegas' MGM Grand, a $1.1 billion complex featuring a 33-acre theme park and, at the time, the largest casino on the planet (171,500 sq. ft.). The project was a success ($742 million in revenues its first year) and spawned expansion plans.

The 1990s proved a challenge for MGM Grand, however, as attendance figures at the theme park dropped off and the company struggled to maintain profitability. In 1996 MGM Grand began planning for an Atlantic City casino and signed on as developer and manager for gaming company Tsogo Sun, which was opening casinos in South Africa. The following year, through its joint venture with Primadonna Resorts, it opened the 2,035-room hotel and casino New York-New York. In 1998 MGM Grand narrowly won its bid to become one of three groups to build casinos in Detroit. (The MGM Grand Detroit opened the following year and pulled in $4.8 million in its first three days.)

In 1999 the company bought Primadonna Resorts, which gave MGM Grand complete ownership of New York-New York. The company appointed co-CEOs John Redmond and Daniel Wade to their posts in late 1999. (Both Redmond and Wade moved to other positions in the company when Terrence Lanni became CEO in 2001.)

In a landmark deal, MGM Grand bought rival Mirage Resorts for $6.4 billion (including $2 billion in debt) in 2000 and became one of the top gaming companies in the world.

The purchase of Mirage Resorts allowed MGM Grand to add a string of opulent casinos to its collection. Among the casinos the deal brought to the MGM Grand fold were Las Vegas strip properties Bellagio, a luxurious European-style casino, and The Mirage, a tropical-themed casino. The Mirage Resorts acquisition also put Las Vegas' Treasure Island, the Golden Nugget, and Monte Carlo (50%-owned with Mandalay Resort Group) under the MGM Grand umbrella. Mirage Resorts' Beau Rivage in Biloxi, Mississippi, and the Golden Nugget in Laughlin, Nevada, also became MGM Grand properties.

Steven Wynn, who had propelled Mirage Resorts from a single casino (the Golden Nugget) to its spot as one of the world's leading gaming companies, opted not to join the merged firm. Later in 2000 MGM Grand changed its name to MGM MIRAGE. MGM MIRAGE laid off over 6,700 employees after declining guest numbers in the wake of the September 11th terrorist attacks.

In 2004 the company sold its Golden Nugget properties in Las Vegas and Laughlin to a private investment firm. Also in 2004 MGM MIRAGE sold its MGM Grand Hotel and Casino in Darwin, Australia.

EXECUTIVES

Chairman and CEO: James J. (Jim) Murren, age 47, $3,066,604 total compensation
EVP and CFO: Daniel J. D'Arrigo, age 40, $1,593,741 total compensation
Chief Marketing Officer: William J. (Bill) Hornbuckle
Chief Design and Construction Officer and Director: Robert H. Baldwin, age 59, $2,951,732 total compensation
EVP and Chief Accounting Officer: Robert C. Selwood, age 53
EVP and Chief Administrative Officer: Aldo Manzini, age 45, $1,443,651 total compensation
SVP and Senior Counsel: Phyllis A. James, age 56
SVP Public Affairs: Alan Feldman, age 50
SVP Corporate Diversity and Community Affairs: Punam Mathur, age 48
SVP Taxes: Shawn T. Sani, age 43
SVP Human Resources: Miriam Hammond
SVP and Treasurer: Cathryn Santoro, age 40
SVP, Assistant General Counsel, and Assistant Secretary: John M. McManus
VP Diversity, Communications, and Community Affairs: Debra Nelson
VP Strategic Sourcing: Mark Stolarczyk
VP Legal Affairs: Troy E. McHenry
President Corporate Strategy, General Counsel, Secretary, and Director: Gary N. Jacobs, age 63, $1,590,955 total compensation
Auditors: Deloitte & Touche LLP

LOCATIONS

HQ: MGM MIRAGE
3600 Las Vegas Blvd. South, Las Vegas, NV 89109
Phone: 702-693-7120   **Fax:** 702-693-8626
Web: www.mgmmirage.com

PRODUCTS/OPERATIONS

2008 Sales

	$ mil.	% of total
Casino		
Slots	1,795	23
Table games	1,079	14
Other	102	1
Non-casino		
Rooms	1,907	24
Food & beverage	1,582	20
Entertainment, retail & other	1,419	18
Total	**7,884**	**100**

Selected Properties

Bellagio (Las Vegas)
Beau Rivage (Biloxi, MS)
Boardwalk Hotel & Casino (Las Vegas)
Borgata (50%; Atlantic City, NJ)
Circus Circus (Las Vegas)
Circus Circus Reno (Nevada)
The Colorado Belle Hotel and Casino (Laughlin, NV)
The Edgewater Hotel and Casino (Laughlin, NV)
Excalibur (Las Vegas)
Gold Strike (Tunica County, MS)
Gold Strike Hotel and Gambling Hall (Jean, NV)
Luxor (Las Vegas)
Mandalay Bay Resort & Casino (Las Vegas)
MGM Grand (Las Vegas)
MGM Grand Detroit
MGM Grand Macau (50%; Macau, China)
The Mirage (Las Vegas)
Monte Carlo (Las Vegas)
Nevada Landing Hotel and Casino (Jean)
New York-New York (Las Vegas)
Railroad Pass Hotel & Casino (Henderson, NV)
Silver Legacy (50%; Reno, NV)
Slots-A-Fun (Las Vegas)

COMPETITORS

Boyd Gaming	Star City
Harrah's Entertainment	Station Casinos
Las Vegas Sands	Stratosphere
Pinnacle Entertainment	Trump Resorts
Riviera Holdings	Wynn Resorts
SJM	

HISTORICAL FINANCIALS

Company Type: Public

Income Statement

FYE: December 31

	REVENUE ($ mil.)	NET INCOME ($ mil.)	NET PROFIT MARGIN	EMPLOYEES
12/08	7,884.2	(855.3)	—	61,000
12/07	7,691.6	1,584.4	20.6%	67,400
12/06	7,176.0	648.3	9.0%	70,000
12/05	6,482.0	443.3	6.8%	66,500
12/04	4,238.1	412.3	9.7%	40,000
Annual Growth	**16.8%**	**—**	**—**	**11.1%**

2008 Year-End Financials

Debt ratio: 323.5%
Return on equity: —
Cash ($ mil.): 296
Current ratio: 0.51
Long-term debt ($ mil.): 12,857
No. of shares (mil.): 441
Dividends
  Yield: 0.0%
  Payout: —
Market value ($ mil.): 6,070

Stock History

NYSE: MGM

	STOCK PRICE ($) FY Close	P/E High/Low	PER SHARE ($) Earnings	Dividends	Book Value
12/08	13.76	— —	(3.06)	0.00	9.01
12/07	84.02	19 11	5.31	0.00	13.74
12/06	57.35	27 15	2.22	0.00	8.73
12/05	36.67	31 22	1.50	0.00	7.33
12/04	36.37	26 13	1.42	0.00	6.28
Annual Growth	**(21.6%)**	**— —**	**—**	**—**	**9.4%**

Micron Technology

Don't let Micron Technology's name mislead you: The circuits on its chips are well under one micron across, but the company is one of the biggest semiconductor makers in the world. Micron is among the largest memory chip makers in the semiconductor industry. It makes DRAMs, flash memory chips, and memory modules, as well as image sensor chips. The company sells to customers in imaging, networking, and telecommunications, but the bulk of its sales are in the computer market. Dell and Hewlett-Packard are leading customers.

In 2009 the company entered the microdisplay market through its acquisition of Displaytech, a designer of display panels and modules based on ferroelectric liquid crystal on silicon technology, which is manufactured with a CMOS process on a single chip. The microdisplays now being marketed by Micron can be used in head-mounted display products or embedded in mobile phones to work as small projectors. The company touts the integrated approach taken with the product, which doesn't require any companion devices, as digital micromirror devices do.

Also that year Micron agreed to sell the majority interest in its Aptina Imaging business to Riverwood Capital and TPG Capital. The company would keep a 35% equity stake in Aptina, which accounted for $653 million in sales for fiscal 2008. Micron said the transaction would allow Aptina and Micron to focus on their respective core businesses while retaining their ties in manufacturing, marketing, and product development.

Micron CEO Steve Appleton, who is known to fly stunt jets for fun, has steered Micron through the wild cycles of the memory chip market with an intense focus on cost control.

Those volatile cycles hit another painful downturn in 2008. Responding to rapidly falling prices for DRAMs and NAND flash memory devices, due to oversupply in the global market and declining customer demand, Micron said it would reduce the workforce in its memory operations by about 15% over two years.

As the worldwide economic downturn deepened in early 2009, Micron phased out production on 200mm silicon wafers in Boise, eliminating at least 500 jobs and possibly up to 2,000 positions, on top of the previously announced workforce reduction. The company will continue to operate its 300mm R&D fabrication facility at the Boise site.

Micron joined with Intel to form a company devoted to NAND flash memory. Each contributed roughly $1.2 billion to create IM Flash Technologies, which manufactures memory exclusively for Micron and Intel. Apple prepaid $250 million to each company. Apple uses flash memory in some of its iPod digital music players. Intel accounts for 19% of sales, primarily for IM Flash products.

HISTORY

Micron Technology was founded in 1978 by twins Joe and Ward Parkinson and colleague Doug Pitman in the basement of a dentist's office. They started it as a semiconductor design firm but dreamed of manufacturing their own chips. In 1980 they persuaded several local businessmen, including J. R. Simplot and Allen Noble, to provide financial backing. They built their own production facility and in 1982 sold their first DRAM products.

Micron went public in 1984. The following year Japanese chip makers began dumping chips on the US market to capture market share, causing huge losses for US DRAM makers. Micron filed an antidumping petition with the International Trade Commission, and in 1986 the US and Japan agreed to a semiconductor trade pact to curb dumping.

By 1988 a shortage of memory chips had developed, and Micron cashed in. The company began to diversify into SRAM (static random-access memory) chips and other add-in memory products for PCs. (The company wound down its SRAM product line in 2003 in the face of a dire industry slump.)

In the 1990s Micron expanded into PC manufacturing, in part to soften the impact of the volatile cycles of the memory chip industry. It bought PC manufacturer ZEOS in 1995, merging it with two other Micron units to form Micron Electronics, which it took public that year.

Also in 1995 Micron CEO and co-founder Joe Parkinson left the company after a clash with Simplot. Steve Appleton, who had started as a production operator in 1983, became the new CEO. In early 1996 an internal power struggle triggered by longtime director Noble resulted in Appleton's ouster. But within a few days, as several executives

loyal to Appleton threatened to revolt, Simplot wooed the CEO back. Noble resigned.

In 2001 the company acquired full ownership of Japan-based DRAM maker KMT Semiconductor when it bought out joint venture partner Kobe Steel for about $350 million. (KMT was subsequently renamed Micron Japan, Ltd.)

Also that year the company acquired Photobit, a small developer of CMOS image sensors, an image-capturing chip that would become widely used in camera phones and digital still cameras, among other uses. The acquisition launched Micron into a new semiconductor business line that would help the company withstand the volatile cycles of the memory chip business.

At the end of 2001 Micron struck a surprise deal with Toshiba to acquire the Japanese giant's Dominion Semiconductor unit in Virginia. (The deal was closed in 2002; Micron paid about $300 million in cash and stock for Dominion.)

The company used a strong balance sheet to grow capacity during the steep industry swoon of the early 21st century, but also stumbled a bit with slow product introductions. Micron surprised the industry in 2002 by announcing an agreement to buy the DRAM operations of Toshiba. The Toshiba purchase, which cost Micron about $300 million in cash and stock, saddled Micron with too much production capacity in the midst of an especially soft DRAM market. Micron rose on improved industry conditions after the chip industry slump ended in 2003, and returned to black ink by 2004.

In 2004 Intel made a $450 million investment in Micron, giving the chip giant rights to a 5% ownership stake in the company.

In mid-2006 Micron acquired flash memory maker Lexar Media for about $850 million. The Lexar acquisition bolstered Micron's position in NAND flash memory.

In late 2006 Micron bolstered its product portfolio in CMOS image sensors, chips that are used in camera phones, digital still cameras, and other applications, by acquiring the imaging sensor business of Avago Technologies.

EXECUTIVES

Chairman and CEO: Steven R. (Steve) Appleton, age 49
President and COO: D. Mark Durcan, age 47
VP Finance and CFO: Ronald C. (Ron) Foster, age 58
VP Information Systems: James E. (Ed) Mahoney
EVP, MeiYa Technology Corporation, A Micron and Nanya Joint Venture: Michael W. Sadler, age 50
VP Operations: Jay L. Hawkins, age 48
VP Investor Relations: Kipp A. Bedard, age 49
VP Legal Affairs, General Counsel, and Corporate Secretary: Roderic W. Lewis, age 53
VP Memory System Development: Dean A. Klein
VP Imaging Group: Robert J. (Bob) Gove, age 54
VP Worldwide Wafer Fabrication: Brian J. Shields
VP Memory: Brian M. Shirley
VP DRAM Development: John F. Schreck
VP NAND Development: Frankie F. Roohparvar, age 44
VP Worldwide Sales: Mark W. Adams
VP Human Resources: Pat Otte
VP Process Research and Development: Scott J. DeBoer
Treasurer: Norman L. Schlachter
Director Global Media Relations: Daniel Francisco
Director Federal Government Affairs: Melika D. Carroll, age 35
Auditors: PricewaterhouseCoopers LLP

LOCATIONS

HQ: Micron Technology, Inc.
  8000 S. Federal Way, Boise, ID 83716
Phone: 208-368-4000   **Fax:** 208-368-4617
Web: www.micron.com

Micron Technology has manufacturing facilities in Italy, Japan, Puerto Rico, Singapore, the UK, and the US. It has sales and marketing offices in more than a dozen countries worldwide.

2008 Sales

	$ mil.	% of total
US	1,486	25
Asia/Pacific		
China	1,372	23
Japan	441	8
Other countries	1,696	29
Europe	559	10
Other regions	287	5
Total	**5,841**	**100**

PRODUCTS/OPERATIONS

2008 Sales

	$ mil.	% of total
Memory	5,188	89
Imaging	653	11
Total	**5,841**	**100**

Semiconductor Products

Dynamic random-access memories (DRAMs)
  Direct Rambus DRAMs (RDRAMs)
  Synchronous DRAMs (SDRAMs)
  Double data rate synchronous DRAMs (DDR SDRAMs)
Flash memory devices
Image sensors
Memory modules

Selected Operations

Aptina Imaging (CMOS image sensors)
Crucial Technology (memory module upgrade supplier)
IM Flash Technologies, LLC (joint venture with Intel; NAND flash memory devices)
Lexar Media, Inc. (memory cards, USB flash drives)
MP Mask Technology Center, LLC (joint venture with Photronics; photomask production)
TECH Semiconductor Singapore Pte. Ltd. (joint venture with Canon and others; wafer fabrication)

COMPETITORS

Atmel
Cypress Semiconductor
Elpida Memory
Hitachi Global Storage
Hynix
Integrated Device Technology
Kingston Technology
MagnaChip
Mosel Vitelic
Nanya
Numonyx
OmniVision Technologies
Panasonic Corp
PNY Technologies
Qimonda
Quantum Corporation
Rambus
Samsung Electronics
SanDisk
Seagate Technology
Sharp Corp.
SMART Modular Technologies
Sony
Spansion
Toshiba Semiconductor
Viking InterWorks
Western Digital

HISTORICAL FINANCIALS

Company Type: Public

Income Statement

FYE: Thursday nearest August 31

	REVENUE ($ mil.)	NET INCOME ($ mil.)	NET PROFIT MARGIN	EMPLOYEES
8/08	5,841.0	(1,619.0)	—	22,800
8/07	5,688.0	(320.0)	—	23,500
8/06	5,272.0	408.0	7.7%	23,500
8/05	4,880.2	188.0	3.9%	18,800
8/04	4,404.2	157.2	3.6%	17,900
Annual Growth	7.3%	—	—	6.2%

2008 Year-End Financials

Debt ratio: 39.7%
Return on equity: —
Cash ($ mil.): 1,243
Current ratio: 2.36
Long-term debt ($ mil.): 2,451

No. of shares (mil.): 847
Dividends
  Yield: 0.0%
  Payout: —
Market value ($ mil.): 3,591

Stock History

NYSE: MU

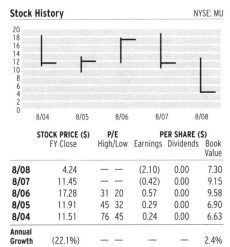

	STOCK PRICE ($) FY Close	P/E High/Low		PER SHARE ($) Earnings	Dividends	Book Value
8/08	4.24	—	—	(2.10)	0.00	7.30
8/07	11.45	—	—	(0.42)	0.00	9.15
8/06	17.28	31	20	0.57	0.00	9.58
8/05	11.91	45	32	0.29	0.00	6.90
8/04	11.51	76	45	0.24	0.00	6.63
Annual Growth	(22.1%)	—	—	—	—	2.4%

Microsoft Corporation

Microsoft's ambitions are anything but small. The world's #1 software company provides a variety of products and services, including its ubiquitous Windows operating systems and Office software suite. Microsoft has expanded into markets such as video game consoles, customer relationship management applications, server and storage software, and digital music players. The company has also used selective acquisitions to bulk up its presence in markets such as online advertising, mobile devices, and enterprise software. In 2008 Microsoft made repeated efforts to acquire Yahoo! but was ultimately rebuffed by that company's board of directors.

Microsoft's bid to acquire Yahoo! in early 2008 would have marked the company's largest acquisition in its history, as Microsoft has typically avoided pursuing huge deals in preference for smaller, selective purchases. Yahoo!'s board of directors refused multiple offers from Microsoft (including proposals to buy certain parts of Yahoo!), insisting that the offers undervalued the company.

Microsoft's primary interest in acquiring Yahoo! was to bulk up its search offerings, where the company has struggled to gain ground on Google. Amid persisting rumors that Yahoo! still might give in and sell its search business to the company, in 2009 Microsoft overhauled and rebranded its own search business as a new search engine called bing.com, replacing its Live Search product. Shortly after the launch of bing.com, Yahoo! and Microsoft finally came to terms on a 10-year agreement for Microsoft to take over the search engine responsibilities on Yahoo!.

Competition between Microsoft and Google stands to heat up even further; in mid-2009 Google announced plans to launch an operating system targeted toward netbooks that will compete directly with Microsoft's OS software.

The company has also partnered with mobile devices makers such as Hewlett-Packard and Motorola to develop handheld computers and mobile phones that utilize Microsoft Windows Mobile and Windows Media software. As part of this push, it acquired ScreenTonic, a provider of mobile advertising products and services.

While desktop applications and platforms remain the cornerstone of its operations, Microsoft has expanded its product lines, which include video game consoles, its MSN division, digital media players, enterprise software, computer peripherals, and software development tools. By transforming itself from a traditional software provider to a broader technology services and media company, Microsoft hopes to position its operating systems, software, and services as a de facto standard for accessing, communicating, and doing business over the Internet.

Bill Gates owns about 10% of Microsoft; CEO Steve Ballmer owns nearly 4%.

HISTORY

Bill Gates founded Microsoft (originally named Micro-soft) in 1975 after dropping out of Harvard at age 19 and teaming with high school friend Paul Allen to sell a version of the programming language BASIC. While Gates was at Harvard, the pair wrote the language for Altair, the first commercial microcomputer. The company was born in an Albuquerque, New Mexico, hotel room and grew by modifying BASIC for other computers.

Gates moved Microsoft to his native Seattle in 1979 and began developing software that let others write programs. The modern PC era dawned in 1980 when IBM chose Microsoft to write the operating system for its new machines. Although hesitant at first, Gates bought QDOS, short for "quick and dirty operating system," for $50,000 from a Seattle programmer, renaming it the Microsoft Disk Operating System (MS-DOS).

Allen fell ill with Hodgkin's disease and left Microsoft in 1983. In the mid-1980s Microsoft introduced Windows, a graphics-based version of MS-DOS that borrowed from rival Apple's Macintosh system. The company went public in 1986, and Gates became the industry's first billionaire a year later. Microsoft introduced Windows NT in 1993 to compete with the UNIX operating system, popular on mainframes and large networks.

The early 1990s brought monopoly charges from inside and outside the industry. In 1995 antitrust concerns scotched a $1.5 billion acquisition of personal finance software maker Intuit.

When the Internet began transforming business practices, holdout Gates at last embraced the medium; the Microsoft Network (MSN) debuted in 1995. That year Microsoft introduced its Internet Explorer Web browser. It also launched Expedia, an online travel site.

The US Justice Department, backed by 18 states, filed antitrust charges in 1998 against the software giant, claiming that it stifled Internet browser competition and limited consumer choice. Gates turned over the president's job to longtime Microsoft executive Steve Ballmer.

In 1999 Microsoft agreed to invest $5 billion for a minority stake in AT&T as part of that company's move to acquire cable operator MediaOne. In addition, Microsoft bought Windows-based technical drawing software specialist Visio for $1.3 billion.

Gates named Ballmer CEO in 2000. Gates remained chairman and added the title of chief software architect. A federal judge's ruling later that year that Microsoft used its monopoly powers to violate antitrust laws left the prospect of two (smaller) Microsofts, a decision the company aggressively appealed. (The initial ruling to split Microsoft into two companies was later struck down, leading to a settlement between the company and the US Justice Department.)

Netscape Communications filed suit in 2002 against Microsoft, seeking unspecified damages and injunctions against the company's alleged antitrust actions. Microsoft settled the suit with Netscape in 2003, agreeing to pay AOL $750 million as part of a larger settlement that includes AOL licensing Microsoft's Internet Explorer browser and its digital media technology.

In 2003 the company declared its first ever dividend for common stock. Microsoft also eliminated stock options, instead moving to a system of distributing shares of its stock directly to employees.

In an attempt to keep pace with Google and other competitors in a consolidating online advertising and search market, the company acquired aQuantive for about $6 billion in 2007. Later in the year Microsoft reached an agreement to acquire a minority stake in social networking site Facebook for $240 million.

Microsoft put many of its legal woes from antitrust issues behind it from 2004-2008, reaching major settlement agreements with Sun Microsystems ($1.6 billion in addition to royalty payments on certain technologies); Novell ($536 million to settle a suit tied to Novell's NetWare software); Gateway ($150 million); IBM ($775 million and extending $75 million in credit toward Microsoft software deployment); and RealNetworks ($761 million in cash and promotions).

EXECUTIVES

Chairman: William H. (Bill) Gates III, age 53
CEO and Director: Steven A. (Steve) Ballmer, age 53
COO: Brian Kevin Turner, age 44
SVP Finance and Administration and CFO:
  Christopher P. (Chris) Liddell, age 48
Chief Experience Officer and CTO, Entertainment and Devices: J Allard
VP and CIO: Tony Scott, age 57
Chief Research and Strategy Officer: Craig J. Mundie, age 60
Chief Software Architect: Ray Ozzie
SVP Interactive Entertainment Business, Entertainment and Devices Division: Don A. Mattrick
SVP, Windows Core Operating System Division:
  Jon S. DeVaan, age 47
SVP, Windows Business: Bill Veghte
SVP, Unlimited Potential Group: Orlando Ayala, age 52
SVP Research: Richard F. (Rick) Rashid, age 56

SVP and President, Microsoft International:
Jean-Philipe Courtois, age 49
SVP Technical Strategy: Eric D. Rudder
SVP Developer Division:
Sivaramakichenane (Soma) Somasegar
SVP, Consumer Strategy and Partnerships:
Henry P. (Hank) Vigil, age 50
SVP Human Resources: Lisa E. Brummel, age 49
SVP, General Counsel, and Corporate Secretary, Legal and Corporate Affairs: Bradford L. (Brad) Smith, age 50
VP and Treasurer: George Zinn
VP Corporate Communications: Larry Cohen
Auditors: Deloitte & Touche LLP

LOCATIONS

HQ: Microsoft Corporation
1 Microsoft Way, Redmond, WA 98052
Phone: 425-882-8080   **Fax:** 425-936-7329
Web: www.microsoft.com

Microsoft has offices in more than 80 countries.

2009 Sales

	$ mil.	% of total
US	33,052	57
Other countries	25,385	43
Total	**58,437**	**100**

PRODUCTS/OPERATIONS

2009 Sales

	$ mil.	% of total
Microsoft Business	18,902	32
Client	14,414	25
Server & Tools	14,135	24
Entertainment & Devices	7,753	13
Online Services	3,088	5
Unallocated & other	145	1
Total	**58,437**	**100**

Selected Products

Desktop Applications
   Access (relational database management)
   Excel (integrated spreadsheet)
   FrontPage (Web site publishing)
   MS Office (business productivity software suite)
   Outlook (messaging and collaboration)
   PowerPoint (presentation graphics)
   Project (project scheduling and resource allocation)
   Word (word processing)

Enterprise Software
   BackOffice (server software suite)
   Content Management Server (content management)
   Exchange Server (messaging server)
   Proxy Server (Internet gateway)
   Site Server (Web site management)
   SQL Server (database and data analysis management)
   Systems Management Server (centralized management)
   Visio (visualization and diagramming suite)

Consumer Software, Services, and Devices
   Flight Simulator (flight simulation software)
   Xbox (video game console)
   Zune (digital media player)

COMPETITORS

Adobe Systems	Novell
Apple Inc.	Oracle
CA, Inc.	Red Hat
EMC	salesforce.com
Google	SAP
Hewlett-Packard	Sony
IBM	Sun Microsystems
Logitech	Symbian
Nintendo	Yahoo!
Nokia	

HISTORICAL FINANCIALS

Company Type: Public

Income Statement

FYE: June 30

	REVENUE ($ mil.)	NET INCOME ($ mil.)	NET PROFIT MARGIN	EMPLOYEES
6/09	58,437.0	14,569.0	24.9%	93,000
6/08	60,420.0	17,681.0	29.3%	91,000
6/07	51,122.0	14,065.0	27.5%	79,000
6/06	44,282.0	12,599.0	28.5%	71,000
6/05	39,788.0	12,254.0	30.8%	61,000
Annual Growth	**10.1%**	**4.4%**	**—**	**11.1%**

2009 Year-End Financials

Debt ratio: 9.5%
Return on equity: 38.4%
Cash ($ mil.): 6,076
Current ratio: 1.82
Long-term debt ($ mil.): 3,746
No. of shares (mil.): 8,911
Dividends
   Yield: 2.1%
   Payout: 30.9%
Market value ($ mil.): 211,807

Stock History

NASDAQ (GS): MSFT

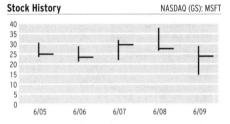

	STOCK PRICE ($) FY Close	P/E High/Low		PER SHARE ($) Earnings	Dividends	Book Value
6/09	23.77	18	9	1.62	0.50	4.44
6/08	27.51	20	14	1.87	0.43	4.07
6/07	29.47	22	16	1.42	0.39	3.49
6/06	23.30	24	18	1.20	0.34	4.50
6/05	24.84	27	21	1.12	0.32	5.40
Annual Growth	**(1.1%)**	**—**	**—**	**9.7%**	**11.8%**	**(4.8%)**

Mohawk Industries

Mohawk Industries doesn't mind being trampled under foot. The company is the second-largest maker of commercial and residential carpets, rugs, and other floor coverings in the US (after Shaw Industries) and one of the largest carpet makers in the world. It produces woven and tufted broadloom carpets and rugs under such names as Mohawk, Aladdin, Durkan, Karastan, and Bigelow. Mohawk's Dal-Tile International division is one of the US's largest makers of ceramic tile and stone flooring. Laminate, wood, and vinyl flooring round out Mohawk's operations. The company sells its wares to about 40,000 customers, including carpet retailers, home centers, mass merchandisers, department stores, and dealers.

Once focused exclusively on carpets and rugs, Mohawk has evolved, adapting itself to changing customer tastes. Its makeover has resulted in a full-service operation, offering popular alternatives to carpet such as hardwood, laminate, and ceramic tile. The company has also rolled out a do-it-yourself flooring lineup that mimics the elegant look of materials like marble or limestone, without the coldness, chipping, or costly installation of real stone.

Hooking up with faster-growing, higher-margin businesses has helped the company diversify its goods; Mohawk bought Dal-Tile, the largest manufacturer and distributor of ceramic and porcelain tile in the US, and Belgium-based Unilin Holding, a laminate-flooring specialist. With the acquisition of Unilin, Mohawk gains a stronger presence in the developing laminate market, both in the US and internationally. In 2007 Mohawk added the wood flooring assets of Columbia Forest Products. The deal included three plants in the US and one in Malaysia.

Mohawk's business faces exposure to rising energy and raw material costs — the carpet maker uses oil-based textiles — and slumping residential builder and homeowner remodeling markets. In 2008 the cost of key raw materials jumped as much as 50%, and customers traded down to lower-quality offerings. The flooring company was forced to shutter a plant that made yarn for carpeting and employed 137 people in Dahlonega, Georgia. Its Dal-Tile segment cut close to 40% of its workforce at its Gettysburg, Pennsylvania, plant.

Investment firm Ruane, Cunniff & Goldfarb, Inc. controls close to 20% of the company. Chairman, president, and CEO Jeffrey Lorberbaum owns about 17%, and Aladdin Partners, L.P. over 10%.

HISTORY

Mohawk Carpet was an ailing unit of Mohasco until 1988, when division president David Kolb led an LBO to separate Mohawk from its parent and became CEO of the new company. Mohawk traces its origins to the Shuttleworth family who founded the company in Amsterdam, New York, in 1878, setting up their business with 14 second-hand looms imported from England. The company was incorporated as Shuttleworth Brothers in 1902. It introduced the popular Karnak carpet design in 1908.

The firm acquired carpet maker McLeary, Wallin and Crouse and began to consolidate the fragmented carpet industry in the Northeast. The company renamed itself Mohawk Carpet Mills and was the only maker of a complete line of domestic carpets, under the Wilton, Axminster, Velvet, and Chenille styles. Over the next three decades the company pioneered a number of industry firsts: the first texture design (Shuttlepoint), the first sculptured weave (Raleigh), and the first knitted carpet (Woven Interlock).

Mohawk Carpet Mills, like the rest of the industry, moved into synthetics such as nylon and acrylics during the late 1940s and early 1950s. The company merged with Alexander Smith in 1956 to form Mohasco Industries, the largest carpet maker in the world at the time.

By 1980 the company was facing a fiercely competitive market. Mohasco had failed to keep up with changing fashions and was no longer the leading carpet maker. Allied Fibers veteran David Kolb was brought in to turn Mohasco's unprofitable Mohawk division around. He moved the company's headquarters to the carpet-making center of the US, Georgia. Kolb began modernizing equipment and refocused the company on its high-margin carpet products and emphasized direct sales to retailers.

Kolb took Mohawk public in 1992 and began acquiring other carpet makers, including Horizon Industries (carpet mills, 1992), American Rug Craftsmen (household rugs and mats, 1993), and Fieldcrest Cannon's Karastan and Bigelow divisions (carpets and rugs, 1993).

In 1994 Mohawk bought Aladdin Mills, then the fourth-largest carpet maker in the US. Jeffrey Lorberbaum, son of Aladdin founder Alan Lorberbaum, became Mohawk's president and COO.

The company's spending spree continued, acquiring Galaxy Carpet Mills in 1995. In 1996 Mohawk added capacity at all its plants: The acquisition of Fiber One boosted Mohawk's annual polypropylene extrusion capacity by 40 million pounds, and in 1997 Mohawk added approximately 100 million pounds of annual polypropylene extrusion capacity by acquiring certain assets of Diamond Rug. In 1998 Mohawk purchased American Weavers and floorcoverings maker World Carpets.

In 1999 the company paid $232 million for Image Industries, a unit of Maxim Group that makes residential polyester carpet from recycled plastic bottles, and $98 million for commercial carpet supplier Durkan Patterned Carpets. Mohawk entered the market for hardwood floors by introducing a product line in 2000. Also that year the company purchased the Wovens Division of Crown Crafts (woven throws, bedspreads, and coverlets). Lorberbaum succeeded Kolb as CEO in 2001.

Early in 2002 Mohawk acquired ceramic tile maker Dal-Tile International for $1.5 billion. Dal-Tile added nearly $1 billion in sales (or nearly a quarter of Mohawk's total revenues) and gave the company an automatic stronghold in the hard flooring business. Mohawk followed that up by acquiring bankrupt Burlington Industries' carpet division, Lees Carpet, for about $350 million in 2003. In 2005 Mohawk acquired Unilin Holding NV, a European manufacturer of laminate flooring. The purchase price for Unilin, which has about $1 billion in annual sales, was $2.6 billion.

EXECUTIVES

Chairman, President, and CEO: Jeffrey S. Lorberbaum, age 54, $1,707,822 total compensation
COO and Director: W. Christopher (Chris) Wellborn, age 53, $2,671,840 total compensation
VP Finance and CFO: Frank H. Boykin, age 53, $1,109,735 total compensation
VP and General Counsel: James T. Lucke, age 48
President, Dal-Tile: Harold G. Turk, age 62
President, Mohawk Flooring: Frank T. Peters, age 60, $1,557,362 total compensation
President, Unilin: Bernard P. Thiers, age 53
Secretary: Barbara M. Goetz
Corporate Controller and Principal Accounting Officer: James F. Brunk, age 44
Auditors: KPMG LLP

LOCATIONS

HQ: Mohawk Industries, Inc.
160 S. Industrial Blvd., Calhoun, GA 30701
Phone: 706-629-7721   **Fax:** 706-624-3825
Web: www.mohawkind.com

2008 Sales

	$ mil.	% of total
North America	5,776.7	85
Other regions	1,049.6	15
Total	**6,826.3**	**100**

PRODUCTS/OPERATIONS

2008 Sales

	$ mil.	% of total
Mohawk	3,628.2	53
Dal-Tile	1,815.3	26
Unilin	1,465.2	21
Adjustments	(82.4)	—
Total	**6,826.3**	**100**

Selected Operations

Mohawk
  Bath rugs
  Blankets
  Carpet
  Ceramic tile
  Decorative throws and pillows
  Doormats
  Hardwood flooring
  Laminate flooring
  Resilient flooring
  Rugs
  Woven and tufted rugs
  Woven bedspreads
Dal-Tile
  Ceramic tile
  Glazed floor tile
  Glazed wall tile
  Glazed and unglazed ceramic mosaic tile
  Porcelain tile
  Quarry tile
  Stone products
Unilin
  Insulated roofing
  Laminate flooring
  Wood paneling

Selected Brand Names

Mohawk
  Aladdin
  Bigelow Commercial
  Durkan
  Horizon
  Karastan
  Lees
  Merit
  Mohawk
  Mohawk Home
  Ralph Lauren
Dal-Tile
  American Olean
  Dal-Tile
Unilin
  Century Flooring
  Columbia Flooring
  Mohawk
  Quick-Step
  Universal Flooring

COMPETITORS

Armstrong	Interface, Inc.
Beaulieu Group	Mannington Mills
Couristan	Perstorp
Dixie Group	Shaw Industries
Formica	Tarkett Inc.
Guilford Mills	Wilsonart International
Hollander Home Fashions	

HISTORICAL FINANCIALS

Company Type: Public

Income Statement

FYE: December 31

	REVENUE ($ mil.)	NET INCOME ($ mil.)	NET PROFIT MARGIN	EMPLOYEES
12/08	6,826.3	(1,458.2)	—	31,200
12/07	7,586.0	706.8	9.3%	36,200
12/06	7,905.8	455.8	5.8%	37,100
12/05	6,620.1	358.2	5.4%	37,700
12/04	5,880.4	368.6	6.3%	34,300
Annual Growth	**3.8%**	**—**	**—**	**(2.3%)**

2008 Year-End Financials

Debt ratio: 59.0%
Return on equity: —
Cash ($ mil.): 94
Current ratio: 2.56
Long-term debt ($ mil.): 1,860

No. of shares (mil.): 68
Dividends
  Yield: 0.0%
  Payout: —
Market value ($ mil.): 2,941

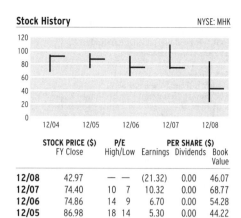

	STOCK PRICE ($) FY Close	P/E High/Low		PER SHARE ($) Earnings	Dividends	Book Value
12/08	42.97	—	—	(21.32)	0.00	46.07
12/07	74.40	10	7	10.32	0.00	68.77
12/06	74.86	14	9	6.70	0.00	54.28
12/05	86.98	18	14	5.30	0.00	44.22
12/04	91.25	17	13	5.46	0.00	38.95
Annual Growth	**(17.2%)**	**—**	**—**	**—**	**—**	**4.3%**

Molex Incorporated

Molex makes mountains out of connections. The company is one of the world's largest makers of plugs and other electrical connectors. It makes more than 100,000 kinds of electronic, electrical, and fiber-optic connectors and switches. Its miniature plugs, jacks, and other complex connectors are used in a wide variety of products, including automobiles, computers, consumer electronics, home appliances, industrial machinery, and telecommunications equipment. Molex sells directly to manufacturers, including Cisco, Dell, Ford, General Motors, Hewlett-Packard, IBM, Motorola, Nokia, and Panasonic. Asian customers, primarily in China and Japan, account for more than half of sales.

New product development is vital in a highly competitive industry like electronic components, where rapid advances in technology are required to keep pace with customer demand. Even in a challenging economic environment, Molex continues to develop new products internally and through acquisitions; in 2009 nearly a quarter of sales came from new products.

Like many electronics manufacturers, Molex has seen sales slump due to lower-than-expected demand in the mobile phone, consumer electronics, and data networking equipment markets, where single devices like the smartphone increasingly offer more broad-based functionality. Some large customers also continue to burn off excess inventory, further reducing demand.

Molex has responded with corporate reorganizations and a variety of cost-cutting measures — including layoffs and plant closures — as well as moving manufacturing operations to lower cost regions outside the US, such as China, Eastern Europe, and Mexico. As the global recession has deepened, Molex has consolidated smaller plants and reorganized its product divisions to improve efficiency and make better use of assets. The company reduced its global workforce by more than 20% in 2009, primarily through closing plants in Europe and Asia.

The Krehbiel family, including co-chairmen Fred and John Jr., grandsons of Molex's founder, owns a controlling interest in the company. Through ownership of Molex's Class B common shares, the family controls nearly 59% of Molex.

HISTORY

In 1938 Frederick Krehbiel, the son of Swiss Mennonites, on a lark began mixing waste substances coal tar and asbestos. The result was a thick, black plastic material that he called Molex, combining a reference to its "mol"-ded state with the modern-sounding "ex." That year he founded Molex Products Company in Brookfield, Illinois. Soon Molex was being used to make everything from flower pots and salt shakers to moisture-resistant bushings and radiator controls.

Frederick's son, John Sr. (known simply as Senior), joined the company in the 1940s and, recognizing the material's electrical insulating properties, expanded its uses to include coatings for US Army land mines (masking them from enemy detectors) and sheathing for electrical components. Senior also shifted the company's focus to connectors that linked electronic components. Because it was still unproven by the start of WWII, Molex was one of the few plastic substances not restricted to use by the war effort; manufacturers flocked to it as a substitute. (The original Molex product later became obsolete due to newer materials, such as nylon.)

By the 1950s and 1960s, Molex, under Senior's leadership, had targeted its connector sales toward manufacturers of televisions, ranges, washer-dryers, and other consumer electronics and appliances.

When Senior asked his son Frederick to use his foreign experience (he had attended school in England) to the company's advantage, Molex began an international expansion in the late 1960s. Frederick thought it wise to build plants overseas to lower costs and be closer to customers; in 1970 the company opened its first non-US factory, in Japan. Molex went public in 1972 and relocated its headquarters to Lisle, Illinois. Senior's older son, John Krehbiel Jr., was named president in 1975.

By the 1980s Molex was the world's tenth-largest maker of electronic connectors. Long cautious in dealings, the company in the late 1980s went on a spending spree. Molex bought stakes in a variety of small companies to position itself in such lucrative locations as China. In 1989 the company bought an 85% interest in Ulti Mate and gained a stronger connector presence in the military market. Fred Krehbiel was named CEO in 1988.

Chairman John Sr. died in 1993. Molex, which more than doubled its global manufacturing capacity in the 1990s, opened new factories in China and Puerto Rico in 1997. In 1999 Fred and John Jr. became co-chairmen and co-CEOs.

In 2000 Molex reported record sales thanks to a wide variety of new products and strong growth in its telecommunications and automotive offerings. Fred and John Jr. handed over the CEO reins to Joseph King in 2001 (Fred and John Jr. remained co-chairmen).

Facing dismal conditions across its target markets in 2001-02, Molex instituted a variety of cost-cutting measures including reductions in executive pay, shortened work-weeks, and a small number of plant closures and layoffs. Molex closed facilities in Puerto Rico, Slovakia,

the UK, and the US. In 2004 Molex acquired France-based Connecteurs Cinch SA, adding manufacturing facilities in France, Portugal, India, and China.

An accounting irregularity in inventory calculations — and the resulting request by company auditors for a management representation letter from a different CFO — led Molex to name an acting CFO in late 2004, make adjustments to 2004 financial results, and delay filing its quarterly SEC report. The auditors also asked that both the CEO and CFO no longer serve as officers of the company and requested additional disclosures; Molex initially refused, and auditor Deloitte & Touche resigned. Late in 2004, however, Molex announced King's resignation and Fred Krehbiel's assumption of the CEO post. (Krehbiel served as CEO until mid-2005, when Martin Slark was named to the position.) Ernst & Young was appointed as auditor.

In 2006 Molex acquired Woodhead Industries (network and electrical infrastructure products) for about $256 million in cash, one of the biggest acquisitions the company had ever attempted.

In 2008 Molex acquired AFlextech, a Taiwan-based flexible circuit manufacturer. AFlextech's products are found in cell phones, computer peripherals, and automobiles. The deal not only gave Molex a bigger piece of the flexible circuit pie, but an additional foothold in Asia.

EXECUTIVES

Co-Chairman: John H. Krehbiel Jr., age 71
Co-Chairman: Frederick A. (Fred) Krehbiel, age 67
Vice Chairman and CEO: Martin P. Slark, age 53
President and COO: Liam G. McCarthy, age 52
EVP, CFO, and Treasurer: David D. Johnson, age 52
CIO: Gary Matula
EVP; President, Transportation Products Division: James E. Fleischhacker, age 64
EVP; President, Global Sales and Marketing Division: Graham C. Brock, age 54
EVP; President, Commercial Products Division: Dave B. Root, age 55
EVP; President,Global Micro Products Division: Katsumi Hirokawa, age 61
SVP; President, Global Integrated Products Division: J. Michael Nauman, age 46
SVP; President, Global Automation and Electrical Products Division: Hans A. van Delft, age 53
President, Connector Products, Americas and Director: Frederick L. (Fred) Krehbiel, age 43
Director, Employee Communications and Public Relations: Susan Armitage
Marketing Communications Director, Americas: Sam Cremin
Secretary: Mark R. Pacioni
Auditors: Ernst & Young LLP

LOCATIONS

HQ: Molex Incorporated
  2222 Wellington Ct., Lisle, IL 60532
Phone: 630-969-4550   **Fax:** 630-968-8356
Web: www.molex.com

2009 Sales

	% of total
Asia/Pacific	54
Americas	27
Europe	19
Total	**100**

PRODUCTS/OPERATIONS

2009 Sales

	$ mil.	% of total
Connector	1789.1	69
Custom & electrical	790.6	31
Corporate & other	2.1	—
Total	**2,581.8**	**100**

2009 Sales by Market

	% of total
Telecommunications	26
Data	21
Consumer	21
Industrial	15
Automotive	14
Other	3
Total	**100**

COMPETITORS

3M	Kyocera
Alps Electric	Methode Electronics
Amphenol	Northrop Grumman
Cooper Industries	Oki Electric
Hirose Electric	Parlex
Hon Hai	Radiall
Hosiden	Thomas & Betts
Innovex	Tyco Electronics
ITT Corp.	Viasystems

HISTORICAL FINANCIALS

Company Type: Public

Income Statement

FYE: June 30

	REVENUE ($ mil.)	NET INCOME ($ mil.)	NET PROFIT MARGIN	EMPLOYEES
6/09	2,581.8	(321.3)	—	25,240
6/08	3,328.3	215.4	6.5%	32,160
6/07	3,265.9	240.8	7.4%	33,200
6/06	2,861.3	237.0	8.3%	32,400
6/05	2,548.7	154.4	6.1%	27,525
Annual Growth	**0.3%**	**—**	**—**	**(2.1%)**

2009 Year-End Financials

Debt ratio: 1.5%	No. of shares (mil.): 173
Return on equity: —	Dividends
Cash ($ mil.): 425	Yield: 3.9%
Current ratio: 2.03	Payout: —
Long-term debt ($ mil.): 30	Market value ($ mil.): 2,696

Stock History

NASDAQ (GS): MOLX

	STOCK PRICE ($) FY Close	P/E High/Low		PER SHARE ($) Earnings	Dividends	Book Value
6/09	15.55	—	—	(1.84)	0.61	11.89
6/08	24.41	26	17	1.19	0.45	15.44
6/07	30.01	31	21	1.30	0.30	14.55
6/06	33.57	31	19	1.26	0.22	13.15
6/05	26.04	39	30	0.81	0.15	12.50
Annual Growth	**(12.1%)**	**—**	**—**	**—**	**42.0%**	**(1.2%)**

Molson Coors Brewing

Molson Coors Brewing Company drinks with the big boys: The company is among the largest brewers by volume in the world, producing more than 42 million barrels of beer. With a portfolio of Molson branded beers, led by the popular Molson Canadian, it dominates the Canadian beer market, accounting for 42% of the beer sold in that country. In the US, Molson Coors operates through joint venture MillerCoors (42%-owned with SABMiller), which markets Coors, Coors Light, and Molson products. It operates in Canada through Molson Canada and in the UK and other European markets through Coors Brewers Limited.

Struggling to compete against the US beer juggernaut Anheuser-Busch, Molson Coors joined with UK-based SABMiller to form MillerCoors in 2008. The joint venture was formed to gain market share by combining both company's popular brands, while at the same time, boosting profits by centralizing their US marketing, sales, and distribution operations. MillerCoors boasts more than half a dozen breweries including Molson Coors' plant in Golden, Colorado, the world's largest single-site brewery.

Also in 2008 Molson Coors and GRUPO MODELO established a joint venture, Modelo Molson Imports ("MMI"), to import, distribute, and market the Corona and Modelo beer brands in Canada. The company also has an agreement with Heineken N.V. to import, market, and sell Heineken products in Canada and with Miller Brewing (a US subsidiary of SABMiller) to brew, market, and sell several Miller brands and to distribute and sell imported Miller brands. It also contract brews Asahi for the US market.

Outside North America, the company competes in the UK beer market with its flagship Coors brands, as well as Grolsch, which is produced and distributed through a joint venture with SABMiller's Royal Grolsch. Coors Brewers also markets beers and other beverages (mainly its Zima and Coors brands) in Asia.

In 2009 the company formed a joint venture with the Billimoria family (owners of Cobra Beer) whereby Molson Coors will own 50.1% of Cobra's UK operations. Neither partner can exit the deal for ten years. Cobra Beer is stocked in more than 6,000 restaurants and in all major supermarkets in the UK.

The Coors family owns about 12% of the company through the Adolph Coors Jr. Trust.

HISTORY

Adolph Coors landed in Baltimore in 1868, a 21-year-old stowaway fleeing Germany's military draft. He worked his way west to Denver, where he bought a bottling company in 1872 and became partners with Jacob Schueler, a local merchant, in 1873. The partners built a brewery in Golden, Colorado, a small town in the nearby Rocky Mountain foothills. Coors became sole owner of the Adolph Coors Company in 1880.

For most of its history, Coors confined its sales to western states. The cost of nationwide distribution was prohibitive because the company used a single brewery, natural brewing methods, and no preservatives; Coors beer was made, transported, and stored under refrigeration, with a shelf life of only one month.

The brewer survived Prohibition by making near beer and malted milk and by entering cement and porcelain chemical ware production. The Coors family built a vertically integrated company that did everything from growing brewing ingredients to pumping the oil that powered its breweries. By 1929, when Adolph died, son Adolph Jr. was running the company. After repeal of the 18th Amendment, beer sales grew steadily in the company's 11-state market.

By the 1960s Coors beer had achieved cult status. Another result of the company's national reputation was that the Coors family had become notoriously private. In 1960 Adolph III was kidnapped and murdered, sending the clan into an even deeper state of secrecy.

Adolph Jr. died in 1970; his son Bill was named chairman and started the country's first aluminum-recycling program. Coors beer was the top seller in 10 of its 11 state markets by 1975, when the company went public. However, sales began to decline as Miller Brewing and Anheuser-Busch introduced new light and super-premium beers. Coors responded by introducing its own light and super-premium brands and expanding its market area to 16 states.

In the late 1970s and 1980s, the company began rapid expansion while enduring boycotts and strikes due to alleged discriminatory labor practices. The brewer eventually developed progressive employment policies.

It spun off its packaging and ceramics firm ACX Technologies in 1992. Also that year it introduced Zima, a clear, malt-based brew. Leo Kiely became the first president of the company's brewing operations from outside the Coors family in 1993. The company also cut its workforce by nearly 700 positions; the severance program cost $70 million and resulted in its first loss in more than 10 years.

The company formed a partnership with Molson Breweries and Foster's in 1997 to manage the distribution of its brands in Canada. (Foster's later sold its stake to Molson.)

In 2000 Peter Coors (Adolph's great-grandson) was named president and CEO of Adolph Coors Company and chairman of Coors Brewing Company. In 2001 the brewer formed a joint venture with Molson to distribute Molson's beers in the US. In 2002 Belgium's Interbrew (now known as Anheuser-Busch InBev) sold the Carling division of its Bass Brewers holding to Coors for nearly $1.8 billion. The purchase led to the creation of Coors Brewers Limited, which makes the Carling, Worthington's, and Jaffrey's beer brands, as well as Grolsch (under license).

The company announced in 2003 that it would cut the workforce at its Memphis brewery by 20%. In 2004 chairman Peter Coors failed to capture a seat in the US Senate. Coors was replaced by Eric Molson as chairman upon the company's merger with Molson. Kiely remained as CEO. Following the merger, 11 top executives left the company, including CFO David Barnes.

Molson signed a contract with the NFL in 2005, making its subsidiary Coors Brewing Company the "Official Beer Sponsor" of the league through the 2010 football season.

With the 2005 merger of Coors and Molson to form Molson Coors, the company added control of three more well-known brands: Coors Light, Carling, and Molson Canadian.

The company sold a 68% stake in its Brazilian brewing operation to FEMSA Cerveza for $68 million in 2006.

EXECUTIVES

Chairman: Peter H. (Pete) Coors, age 62, $6,811,902 total compensation
President and CEO: Peter Swinburn, age 56, $6,032,199 total compensation
CFO: Stewart Glendinning, $1,098,155 total compensation
Chief People Officer: Ralph P. Hargrow, age 56
Global Chief Supply Chain Officer: Gregory L. Wade, age 60
Chief Supply Chain Officer, Molson Canada: Cathy Noonan, age 52
Chief Legal Officer and Corporate Secretary: Samuel D. Walker, age 50
Controller and Chief Accounting Officer: William G. Waters, age 40
Chief Legal Officer, Molson Canada: Kelly Brown, age 38
Chief Public Affairs Officer, Molson Canada: Ferg Devins, age 50
VP Global Alcohol Policy and Corporate Responsibility: Bart Alexander
Global VP, Treasury, Tax, and Strategic Finance; CFO, Molson Canada: Jay Wells, age 46
CEO, MillerCoors: W. Leo Kiely III, age 62, $5,226,719 total compensation
President and CEO, Molson Canada: David (Dave) Perkins, age 55
President and CEO, Coors Brewers: Mark Hunter, age 46, $2,298,656 total compensation
Director Shareholder Services: Meg Beck
Investor Relations: Julie Frye
Chief Integration Officer, MillerCoors: Timothy V. (Tim) Wolf, age 55, $3,553,140 total compensation
Auditors: PricewaterhouseCoopers LLP

LOCATIONS

HQ: Molson Coors Brewing Company
1225 17th St., Ste. 3200, Denver, CO 80202
Phone: 303-279-6565 **Fax:** 303-277-5415
Web: www.molsoncoors.com

2008 Sales

	$ mil.	% of total
Canada	1,804.6	38
US	1,565.7	33
UK	1,311.3	27
Other countries	92.7	2
Total	**4,774.3**	**100**

PRODUCTS/OPERATIONS

Selected Brands

Canada
  Company-owned
    Canadian
    Carling
    Coors Light
    Creemore
    Export
    Molson Dry
    Pilsner
    Rickard's Red
  Joint venture
    Corona (joint venture with GRUPO MODELO)
    Coronita (joint venture with GRUPO MODELO)
    Negra Modelo (joint venture with GRUPO MODELO)
    Pacifico (joint venture with GRUPO MODELO)
  Licensed
    Amstel (licensed from Amstel Brouwerij B.V.)
    Asahi (licensed from Asahi Breweries, Ltd.,)
    Foster's (licensed from Foster's Group Limited)
    Heineken (licensed from Heineken Brouwerijen B.V.)
    Miller Genuine Draft (licensed from Miller Brewing Company)
    Miller Lite (licensed from Miller Brewing Company)
    Milwaukee's Best (licensed from Miller Brewing Company)
    Milwaukee's Best Dry (licensed from Miller Brewing Company)
    Murphy's (licensed from Heineken Brouwerijen B.V.)
    Tiger (license from Asia Pacific Breweries Limited)

President and COO, Discover Financial Services:
Roger C. Hochschild, age 44,
$6,929,415 total compensation
President and COO, Global Wealth Management Group:
Ellyn A. McColgan, age 56
Co-Head, Global Capital Markets: Ted Pick
Chairman, Morgan Stanley Asia:
Stephen S. (Steve) Roach
Global Head of Human Resources: Karen C. Jamesley
Global Controller and Principal Accounting Officer:
Paul C. Wirth
Treasurer: Alan Scheuer
Auditors: Deloitte & Touche LLP

LOCATIONS

HQ: Morgan Stanley
1585 Broadway, New York, NY 10036
Phone: 212-761-4000 **Fax:** 212-761-0086
Web: www.morganstanley.com

PRODUCTS/OPERATIONS

2008 Gross Revenues

	$ mil.	% of total
Interest & dividends	40,725	61
Asset management, distribution & administration fees	5,660	9
Principal transactions	5,452	8
Commissions	4,463	7
Investment banking	4,092	6
Other	6,062	9
Total	**66,454**	**100**

COMPETITORS

Brown Brothers Harriman
Charles Schwab
CIBC
Citigroup
Citigroup Global Markets
Deutsche Bank
FMR
Franklin Resources
Goldman Sachs
JPMorgan Chase
Lehman Brothers
Marsh & McLennan
Merrill Lynch
MF Global
Nomura Securities
Oppenheimer Holdings
Raymond James Financial
State Street
T. Rowe Price
TD Bank
UBS
Wells Fargo Securities, LLC

HISTORICAL FINANCIALS

Company Type: Public

Income Statement

	REVENUE ($ mil.)	NET INCOME ($ mil.)	NET PROFIT MARGIN	EMPLOYEES
11/08	24,739.0	1,707.0	6.9%	46,964
11/07	28,026.0	3,209.0	11.5%	48,256
11/06	33,858.0	7,472.0	22.1%	55,310
11/05	26,778.0	4,890.0	18.3%	53,218
11/04	23,765.0	4,486.0	18.9%	53,284
Annual Growth	1.0%	(21.5%)	—	(3.1%)

FYE: December 31

2008 Year-End Financials

Debt ratio: 516.0%
Return on equity: 5.5%
Cash ($ mil.): 78,654
Current ratio: —
Long-term debt ($ mil.): 163,437

No. of shares (mil.): 1,359
Dividends
  Yield: 7.3%
  Payout: 74.5%
Market value ($ mil.): 20,048

Stock History

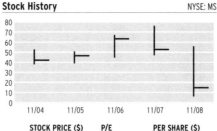

NYSE: MS

	STOCK PRICE ($) FY Close	P/E High/Low		PER SHARE ($) Earnings	Dividends	Book Value
11/08	14.75	38	5	1.45	1.08	37.40
11/07	52.72	25	16	2.98	1.08	23.01
11/06	63.22	9	6	7.07	1.08	26.02
11/05	46.51	11	9	4.57	1.08	21.47
11/04	42.13	13	10	4.06	1.00	20.75
Annual Growth	(23.1%)	—	—	(22.7%)	1.9%	15.9%

Motorola, Inc.

Down but not out, Motorola is still a top choice for mobile phone users worldwide despite flagging handset sales. The company is the #3 manufacturer of wireless telephone handsets (behind leaders Nokia and Samsung) and it also sells wireless network infrastructure equipment such as cellular transmission base stations and signal amplifiers. Motorola's home and broadcast network products include set-top boxes, digital video recorders, and network equipment used to enable video broadcasting, IP telephony, and high-def television. Its products for business and government customers consist mainly of wireless voice and broadband data systems used to build private networks and public safety communications systems.

Motorola has struggled in recent years to regain the momentum it once held in the wireless handset market, with its woes intensifying in the slumping global economy of 2008-2009. Motorola and its competitors have been hit hard by both slowing growth in emerging markets and lower replacement sales as consumers sharply curtail their spending. The company has responded by embarking on a series of restructuring moves in 2008-2009, including announcing a series of job cuts to eliminate about 8,000 jobs, a plan to limit executive compensation, and a freeze on pension plans.

The originator of the clamshell handset, Motorola had its biggest hit with the RAZR phone model (originally introduced in 2003), which has sold more units than any other wireless handset in history, but subsequent designs have been unable to keep pace or generate much excitement among consumers. Competitors such as Nokia and Samsung have been more than happy to take up the slack in terms of market share as Motorola's handset business continues to decline. Motorola is hoping that new smartphones it is developing based on the Google Android operating system will help to bolster its handset sales.

A leading supplier of cell phones to the burgeoning markets of China and Mexico, the company does about half of its handset business outside the US.

The woes of its mobile devices business have often overshadowed its success in its other two major operating businesses: home and networks mobility and enterprise mobility solutions. Confirming rumors of a split, the company announced in 2008 that it would divide its business into two independent public companies in order to separate its handset division from its broadband, network, and public safety products divisions. It also raised the possibility of selling its handset business, although no suitors emerged.

Motorola has embarked upon a string of acquisitions made in an effort to diversify and strengthen other product lines. It expanded its broadcast products division with the purchase of privately held TV-on-demand services provider Broadbus Technologies. The company also bought Symbol Technologies, a manufacturer of bar-code scanners and other devices, for about $3.9 billion.

Motorola also acquired a mobile devices R&D facility (located in the "Danish Silicon Valley" at Aalborg, Denmark) from BenQ Mobile, UK-based mobile phone software and chip maker TTP Communications, and wireless software developer Good Technology. (Motorola would later sell Good Technology to Visto in 2009.)

HISTORY

Born entrepreneur Paul Galvin started his first business as a popcorn vendor when he was 13. In 1928, at age 33, he founded Galvin Manufacturing in Chicago to make battery eliminators, so early radios could run on household current instead of batteries. The following year Galvin began making car radio receivers and trying to develop a mobile radio for the police. In 1940 the company developed the first handheld two-way radio for the US Army.

In 1947 Galvin renamed the company Motorola, after its car radios. In the late 1950s Motorola started making integrated circuits and microprocessors, stepping outside its auto industry mainstay. When Galvin died in 1959, his son Robert became CEO. The firm's purchase that year of a hospital communications systems maker led it to produce some of the first pagers.

Motorola began to change focus in the 1970s. The company invested in the data communications hardware market by acquiring Codex (1977) and Universal Data Systems (1978). In 1977 Motorola began developing its first cellular phone system. By 1985 sales of its cellular systems had taken off. In 1987 Motorola made its last car radio.

In 1990 Motorola organized the 66-satellite Iridium communication system (which went online in 1998). In 1996 China adopted Motorola's technology as its national paging standard.

The founder's grandson, Christopher Galvin, took over as CEO in 1997 on the heels of a major drop in profits — the result of increasing competition in the cellular phone market and a downturn in semiconductor sales. He began a restructuring that included the sale of noncore assets and the layoffs of 15,000 employees.

In 2000 Motorola acquired General Instrument in a deal valued at $17 billion. Also that year Motorola agreed to outsource about 15% of its manufacturing to Flextronics. As part of the $30 billion deal, Motorola took a small stake in Flextronics. In early 2001 Motorola cut more than 30,000 jobs amid slow sales of semiconductors and mobile phones. Motorola also cut back on its manufacturing outsourcing and sold its stake in Flextronics back to that company.

Faced with continuing weak sales, the company continued to make layoffs through 2002.

Motorola ceased production of pagers in 2002 to focus on the development of new wireless handsets, but continued to license its pager technology to other manufacturers.

After disagreeing with the board of directors about Motorola's future in late 2003, Chris Galvin retired as chairman and CEO, and Ed Zander, the former head of Sun Microsystems, took over in 2004, becoming the first person from outside the Galvin family to lead the company.

In 2004 Motorola spun off its semiconductor operations as Freescale Semiconductor, a publicly traded company. Motorola's other restructuring efforts included selling some IT services units, shifting some production to contractors, and using extensive layoffs to reduce costs. The company also sold its automotive products unit to German auto supplier Continental in 2006.

In 2007 activist investor Carl Icahn bought up Motorola shares, about 6% in total, in a successful attempt to obtain seats on the company's board of directors.

Early in 2008 Zander was replaced by COO and communications industry veteran Greg Brown; Zander stayed on as chairman. Former AT&T CEO David Dorman was named chairman upon Zander's retirement in mid-2008, and Sanjay Jha joined Brown as co-CEO that same year.

EXECUTIVES

Chairman: David W. Dorman, age 55
President, Co-CEO, and Director; CEO, Broadband Mobility Solutions: Gregory Q. (Greg) Brown, age 48, $11,344,324 total compensation
Co-CEO and Director; CEO, Mobile Devices: Sanjay K. Jha, age 45, $17,271,676 total compensation
Acting CFO, SVP, and Corporate Controller: Edward J. Fitzpatrick, age 42
SVP and CIO: Leslie Jones
Chief Marketing Officer, Mobile Devices: William (Bill) Ogle
EVP, General Counsel, and Secretary: A. Peter Lawson, age 62, $2,191,677 total compensation
EVP; President, Enterprise Mobility Solutions: Eugene A. (Gene) Delaney, age 52
EVP; President, Home and Networks Mobility: Daniel M. (Dan) Moloney, age 49, $3,556,737 total compensation
SVP Human Resources: Gregory A. (Greg) Lee, age 59, $1,547,689 total compensation
SVP Mobile Devices: Alain Mutricy
SVP and General Manager, Digital Video Solutions: John Burke
SVP Home & Networks Mobility: Fred Wright
SVP Public Affairs and Communications: Karen P. Tandy
SVP and General Manager: John Cipolla
SVP Worldwide Radio Solutions, Enterprise Mobility Solutions: Bob Schassler
VP Global Marketing and Technology: Eduardo Conrado
Auditors: KPMG LLP

LOCATIONS

HQ: Motorola, Inc.
1303 E. Algonquin Rd., Schaumburg, IL 60196
Phone: 847-576-5000 **Fax:** 847-576-5372
Web: www.motorola.com

2008 Sales

	% of total
US	49
Latin America	14
Europe	13
Asia	
China	7
Other countries	10
Other regions	7
Total	**100**

PRODUCTS/OPERATIONS

2008 Sales

	% of total
Mobile Devices	40
Home & Networks Mobility	33
Enterprise Mobility Solutions	27
Total	**100**

Business Segments

Mobile Devices (wireless handsets and accessories)
Home and Networks Mobility (video and Internet products, systems for consumers and carriers)
Enterprise Mobility (radio, voice, data communications products for businesses and government customers)

COMPETITORS

Alcatel-Lucent	LG Group
ARRIS	M/A-Com
Cisco Systems	NEC
Delphi Corp.	Nokia
DENSO	Nokia Siemens Networks
EADS	Nortel Networks
Ericsson	Robert Bosch
Harmonic	Samsung Group
Huawei Technologies	Sony Ericsson Mobile
Intermec	Visteon
Kenwood	ZTE

HISTORICAL FINANCIALS

Company Type: Public

Income Statement

FYE: December 31

	REVENUE ($ mil.)	NET INCOME ($ mil.)	NET PROFIT MARGIN	EMPLOYEES
12/08	30,146.0	(4,244.0)	—	64,000
12/07	36,622.0	(49.0)	—	66,000
12/06	42,879.0	3,661.0	8.5%	66,000
12/05	36,843.0	4,578.0	12.4%	69,000
12/04	31,323.0	1,532.0	4.9%	68,000
Annual Growth	**(1.0%)**	**—**	**—**	**(1.5%)**

2008 Year-End Financials

Debt ratio: 43.0%
Return on equity: —
Cash ($ mil.): 3,064
Current ratio: 1.63
Long-term debt ($ mil.): 4,092
No. of shares (mil.): 2,295
Dividends
 Yield: 4.5%
 Payout: —
Market value ($ mil.): 10,168

Stock History

NYSE: MOT

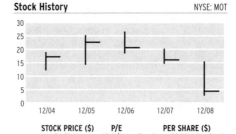

	STOCK PRICE ($) FY Close	P/E High/Low		PER SHARE ($) Earnings	Dividends	Book Value
12/08	4.43	—	—	(1.87)	0.20	4.14
12/07	16.04	—	—	(0.02)	0.20	6.73
12/06	20.56	18	13	1.46	0.19	7.47
12/05	22.59	14	8	1.81	0.16	7.26
12/04	17.20	29	19	0.64	0.16	5.81
Annual Growth	**(28.8%)**	**—**	**—**	**—**	**5.7%**	**(8.1%)**

MPS Group

MPS Group believes in the power of the people. The company (formerly Modis Professional Services) is a staffing specialist, providing personnel to clients throughout Europe, the Asia/Pacific region, and North America. Its offerings also include IT consulting and design services, application development, and project support. MPS Group operates primarily through two divisions: IT services (under the names Modis, Beeline, and Idea Integration) and professional services (using the Accounting Principals and Entegee names, among others). In addition, Badenoch & Clark represents MPS' European professional services operations. MPS Group operates through a network of more than 220 offices around the world.

Other key subsidiaries include Soliant Health, a staffing company catering to hospitals and health care providers, and Special Counsel, a temporary and full time staffer of attorneys and legal professionals. MPS Group continues to focus on internal growth through cross-selling and other techniques, as well as growth through acquisitions. In late 2006, its Beeline unit acquired Integrated Performance Systems, a designer of training software and technology geared toward employers. It also boosted its presence in a key geographic area when it bought Garelli Wong & Associates, a Chicago-centric recruiting and executive search business, the same year.

In 2007 Beeline bought Employer Services Corporation, a firm specializing in recruitment process outsourcing. All in all, MPS Group made seven acquisitions in 2007, with the purchases contributing almost $80 million to its overall 2007 revenue stream. The next year that number dropped to four acquisitions, contributing $46 million.

HISTORY

MPS Group's origins begin with ATS Services, a temporary staffing service founded in 1978 by Delores Kesler (then Delores Pass) in Jacksonville, Florida. The creation of ATS coincided with a nationwide upswing in the temporary services industry, and by 1987 Kesler (who, after growing up poor on a poultry farm, worked her way through college on a tuition reimbursement program) saw ATS become one of the fastest-growing companies in the US.

As the temporary staffing industry evolved, Kesler recognized that consolidation with other firms would be necessary to stay competitive, and in 1992 she merged ATS with three smaller staffing companies (Abacus Services, BSI Temporaries, and Metrotech) to form AccuStaff. As with ATS, the launch of AccuStaff was perfectly timed — the US economy was climbing out of a recession and the temporary staffing industry was once again surging.

Between 1992 and 1994 the company focused on integrating the operations of the four units from which it was formed. It also began distinguishing itself from other staffing firms by offering specialized workers in fields such as information technology (IT) and engineering. In 1994 Kesler stepped down from her position as CEO, and Derek Dewan (a CPA with Coopers and Lybrand who had managed the 1992 merger to create AccuStaff) was appointed to replace her. The company went public later that year.

Following its IPO, AccuStaff wasted no time in building its reputation for aggressive growth. Its 10 acquisitions in 1995 were followed by 39 more in 1996. Its 1996 merger with Career Horizons was one of the largest acquisitions in the staffing industry and doubled AccuStaff's revenue. Kesler resigned as chairman in 1996, and Dewan assumed the chairmanship along with his position as CEO. That year AccuStaff formed its IT services unit.

AccuStaff's 28 acquisitions in 1997 gave the company an international profile. AccuStaff created MindSharp Learning Centers to offer training services, and its buy of Manchester Inc. extended the company's services into outplacement and career development.

In 1998 AccuStaff began narrowing its focus to IT consulting and professional services staffing. Following the sale of its Health Force health care division, the company placed its commercial staffing businesses into the newly formed subsidiary Strategix. AccuStaff had begun the process of taking the subsidiary public when Dutch staffing services firm Randstad approached with an offer. The company withdrew the planned IPO of Strategix and sold the subsidiary to Randstad; AccuStaff changed its name to Modis Professional Services (MPS) after the completion of the deal.

When its stock performance languished, MPS announced in 1999 that it would divide its staffing empire into separate companies. IT services subsidiary Modis, Inc., created e-services unit Idea Integration in early 2000, and MPS later filed to take Idea Integration public. The firm cancelled those plans, as well as plans for spinoff of Modis, Inc., later the same year.

In 2001 Modis announced a reorganization in which COO George Bajalia left the company (the COO job was eliminated) and shifted the focus of its future sales growth to Europe. That same year Timothy Payne succeeded Dewan as CEO. In addition, the company sold its Scientific Staffing unit to Kforce and acquired Kforce's legal staffing division.

The company began 2002 with a name change — the MPS acronym became its legal name. That same year MPS bought Elite Medical (now Soliant Health), a health care staffing firm. In 2003 the company sold its Manchester executive development and career transition unit to Right Management.

EXECUTIVES

Chairman: Derek E. Dewan, age 53
President, CEO, and Director: Timothy D. Payne, age 50, $2,887,533 total compensation
SVP, CFO, Treasurer, and Director: Robert P. Crouch, age 39, $1,408,303 total compensation
SVP and CIO: Jon D. Kerner, $837,517 total compensation
SVP, Chief Legal Officer, and Secretary: Gregory D. Holland, $762,067 total compensation
SVP Corporate Development: Tyra H. Tutor, $619,181 total compensation
SVP Human Resources: Thomas M. Burke
President, Special Counsel: John L. Marshall III
President, Beeline: Richard L. White, $916,176 total compensation
President, Modis: John P. (Jack) Cullen
President, Entegee: Robert L. Cecchini
President, Modis International: James D. (Jim) Albert
President, Soliant Health: David K. Alexander
Auditors: PricewaterhouseCoopers LLP

LOCATIONS

HQ: MPS Group, Inc.
  1 Independent Dr., Ste. 2500
  Jacksonville, FL 32202
Phone: 904-360-2000   **Fax:** 904-360-2350
Web: www.mpsgroup.com

2008 Sales

	$ mil.	% of total
North America	1,340.2	60
International	882.1	40
Total	**2,222.3**	**100**

PRODUCTS/OPERATIONS

2008 Sales

	$ mil.	% of total
Professional services	1,279.8	58
IT services	942.5	42
Total	**2,222.3**	**100**

Selected Operations

IT services
  Beeline
  Modis, Inc.
IT solutions
  Idea Integration
Professional services
  Accounting Principals (accounting and finance staff)
  Badenoch & Clark (recruiting specialist)
  Entegee (engineering and technical staff)
  Gazelle Wong & Associates (recruiting specialist)
  Special Counsel (legal and document management staffing)

COMPETITORS

Adecco
Aerotek
AMN Healthcare
CDI
CIBER
COMSYS IT Partners
Hays plc
Hudson Highland Group
Keane
Kelly Services
Kforce
Michael Page
On Assignment
Resources Global Professionals
Robert Half
Robert Walters
Spherion
TEKsystems

HISTORICAL FINANCIALS

Company Type: Public

Income Statement

FYE: December 31

	REVENUE ($ mil.)	NET INCOME ($ mil.)	NET PROFIT MARGIN	EMPLOYEES
12/08	2,222.3	(236.0)	—	16,900
12/07	2,171.8	87.1	4.0%	22,200
12/06	1,876.6	75.2	4.0%	20,100
12/05	1,684.7	59.6	3.5%	19,400
12/04	1,426.8	35.4	2.5%	18,900
Annual Growth	**11.7%**	**—**	**—**	**(2.8%)**

2008 Year-End Financials

Debt ratio: 1.2%
Return on equity: —
Cash ($ mil.): 91
Current ratio: 2.29
Long-term debt ($ mil.): 7
No. of shares (mil.): 93
Dividends
  Yield: 0.0%
  Payout: —
Market value ($ mil.): 701

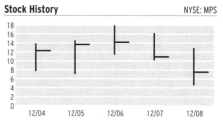

Stock History

NYSE: MPS

	STOCK PRICE ($) FY Close	P/E High/Low		PER SHARE ($) Earnings	Dividends	Book Value
12/08	7.53	—	—	(2.64)	0.00	6.35
12/07	10.94	19	12	0.86	0.00	10.48
12/06	14.18	25	16	0.72	0.00	10.34
12/05	13.67	26	13	0.56	0.00	9.41
12/04	12.26	42	24	0.33	0.00	8.97
Annual Growth	**(11.5%)**	**—**	**—**	**—**	**—**	**(8.3%)**

MSC Industrial Direct

Let's be direct about MSC Industrial Direct's business: The company distributes tools and industrial supplies, such as fasteners, measuring instruments, cutting tools, and plumbing supplies. It stocks more than 500,000 products from some 2,200 suppliers. The company sells to 371,000 customers — mainly small and mid-sized firms — through its "Big Book" master catalog (which runs to several thousand pages) and supplemental publications, as well as via telemarketing and the Internet. Chairman Mitchell Jacobson controls MSC. The company gets almost all of its sales in the US, with a small portion in the UK.

MSC expanded its product line (including name brands and generic offerings) and uses targeted direct-mail marketing and e-commerce in its effort to build its customer base. MSC publishes its master catalog and more than 120 other titles annually.

In 2006 MSC expanded its operations when it acquired J & L Industrial Supply (now MSC/J&L Metalworking) from Kennametal for $350 million. The acquisition gave MSC a solid presence in the central US. The company also opened branches in Fresno, Los Angeles, Oakland, Salt Lake City, San Diego, and Seattle as part of its West Coast expansion strategy. MSC has about 100 branch offices across the US.

Chairman Mitchell Jacobson owns about 21% of MSC Industrial Direct's Class A common shares and around 61% of the company's Class B common shares, giving him nearly half of the voting control. Marjorie Gershwind, Jacobson's sister, holds more than 8% of the Class A shares and almost 19% of the Class B shares, giving her voting power of approximately 15%. Other members of their family have voting power of about 11% in total, and a family trust holds voting power of 5%.

HISTORY

Sidney Jacobson and his brother founded Sid Tool Co. in a Manhattan storefront in 1941. In the late 1950s the company bought Manhattan Supply Co., which became its distribution arm.

Fresh out of law school, son Mitchell Jacobson joined the company's ranks in 1976; he took over from his father as president and CEO in 1982. In 1990, with profits declining, Mitchell reorganized the enterprise following Japanese management techniques to retrain and empower employees. The company restructured in 1995, forming MSC as a holding company for Sid Tool, and went public that year.

MSC expanded its business geographically through acquisitions. In 1996 it bought DTC Tool (Florida), wholesaler Swiss Precision Instruments (California), and distributors Cut-Rite Tool (Florida) and Brooks Precision Supplies (Massachusetts). MSC also broadened its distribution by opening a center in Elkhart, Indiana. In 1997 MSC bought Cleveland-based Discount Tool and Supply.

Continuing to buy complementary lines, MSC acquired distributors in Delaware, Mississippi, Tennessee, and Wisconsin in 1998. The company ventured into the Southwest the next year, opening a distribution center in Reno, Nevada. MSC also added plumbing equipment, pumps and pneumatics equipment, and process instrumentation to its product line. Acquisitions that year included Direct Line (New York) and Corbin Corporation (Ohio).

EXECUTIVES

Chairman: Mitchell Jacobson, age 57
President, CEO, and Director: David Sandler, age 51
EVP, CFO, and Director: Charles A. (Chuck) Boehlke Jr., age 52
VP and CIO: Charles Bonomo, age 43
EVP Sales: Thomas Cox, age 47
SVP Supply Chain Management: Douglas Jones, age 44
SVP Human Resources: Eileen McGuire, age 43
SVP Product Management and Marketing:
  Erik Gershwind, age 37
VP Finance and Accounting: Shelley M. Boxer, age 61
VP Plant and Equipment and Corporate Secretary:
  Thomas R. Eccleston, age 60
Auditors: Ernst & Young LLP

LOCATIONS

HQ: MSC Industrial Direct Co., Inc.
  75 Maxess Rd., Melville, NY 11747
Phone: 516-812-2000   **Fax:** 516-349-1301
Web: www.mscdirect.com

2008 Sales

	$ mil.	% of total
US	1,734.7	97
UK	45.1	3
Total	**1,779.8**	**100**

PRODUCTS/OPERATIONS

Selected Products

Abrasives and files
Carbide inserts and indexable tooling
Drills, reamers, and counterbores
Electrical, HVAC, and plumbing products
Endmills, saws, cutters, tool bits, and band saws
Flat stock, drill rod, and raw materials
Hand/power tools and hardware
Machinery, accessories, knurls, Digital Readouts (DRO), and Electrical Discharge Machining (EDM) products
Material-handling, storage, packaging, shipping, and janitorial products
Measuring instruments
Paints, adhesives, labeling, fluids, and lubes
Pneumatics, hydraulics, and power transmission
Pumps, hose and tubing, process equipment, and pumps
Safety, communication, soldering, and welding products
Taps, dies, and other threading equipment
Tooling components and fasteners

COMPETITORS

Alleghany Corporation
Anixter Pentacon
Applied Industrial Technologies
C. C. Dickson
Communications Supply
DoALL
DXP Enterprises
Etna Supply
Famous Distribution
Fastenal
Hagemeyer North America
Hajoca Corporation
Hillman Companies
Horizon Solutions
Industrial Distribution Group
Kaman Industrial Technologies
L. S. Starrett
Lab Safety Supply
McMaster-Carr
Park-Ohio Holdings
Precision Industries
Production Tool Supply
Redlon & Johnson
Simpson Manufacturing
Strategic Distribution
Turtle & Hughes
Würth Group
WinWholesale
Wolseley
W.W. Grainger

HISTORICAL FINANCIALS

Company Type: Public

Income Statement

FYE: Saturday nearest August 31

	REVENUE ($ mil.)	NET INCOME ($ mil.)	NET PROFIT MARGIN	EMPLOYEES
8/08	1,779.8	196.2	11.0%	4,261
8/07	1,688.2	173.9	10.3%	3,952
8/06	1,317.5	136.4	10.4%	3,775
8/05	1,099.9	112.3	10.2%	3,087
8/04	955.3	81.2	8.5%	2,912
Annual Growth	**16.8%**	**24.7%**	**—**	**10.0%**

2008 Year-End Financials

Debt ratio: 13.8%
Return on equity: 27.3%
Cash ($ mil.): 43
Current ratio: 2.48
Long-term debt ($ mil.): 98
No. of shares (mil.): 63
Dividends
  Yield: 1.5%
  Payout: 24.3%
Market value ($ mil.): 3,188

Stock History

NYSE: MSM

	STOCK PRICE ($) FY Close	P/E High/Low	PER SHARE ($) Earnings	Dividends	Book Value
8/08	50.93	18 11	3.04	0.74	11.37
8/07	51.80	22 14	2.59	0.64	11.63
8/06	39.36	28 16	2.00	0.54	10.21
8/05	35.00	25 16	1.61	0.44	8.47
8/04	31.07	29 17	1.17	0.29	9.88
Annual Growth	**13.2%**	**— —**	**27.0%**	**26.4%**	**3.6%**

Mylan Inc.

Mylan (formerly Mylan Laboratories) knows you may not recognize the names of its drugs, but it hopes you'll appreciate their prices. Through Mylan Pharmaceuticals, Generics (UK), and other subsidiaries, the company is a top global manufacturer of prescription generic drugs. Mylan's pharmaceutical cabinet is full of products such as antibiotics, antidepressants, anti-inflammatories, and laxatives. The company's customers include wholesalers, distributors, retail drugstore chains, and government agencies. Another Mylan division, Matrix, is a top producer of active pharmaceutical ingredients (APIs) for generic drugs. Mylan makes branded specialty pharmaceutical products through its Dey division.

The company's Mylan Technologies subsidiary develops and manufactures generic transdermal patch products. Another unit, UDL Laboratories, puts generic drugs into unit dose packaging for hospital and institutional use.

A key piece of Mylan's strategy is to be the first to file with the FDA to manufacture generic versions of popular drugs as they become fair game. Being first in line gives a manufacturer a three-month window of exclusivity while its competitors have to wait before they can produce an equivalent product.

Mylan is involved in proprietary drug development through subsidiary Somerset Pharmaceuticals, which had operated as a 50/50 joint venture co-owned with Watson Pharmaceuticals. However, in 2008 Mylan bought out Watson's share of the venture, and Somerset became a wholly owned subsidiary. Somerset Pharmaceuticals' primary products are Eldepryl, a drug for the treatment of Parkinson's disease; and Emsam, a transdermal patch for major depressive disorder that is marketed by Bristol-Myers Squibb.

With an eye on global expansion, Mylan acquired control of India's Matrix Laboratories in 2007 and created a new division to hold it. With 10 manufacturing facilities, it is one of the largest companies in India and is the world's largest supplier of generic antiretroviral pharmaceutical ingredients used to treat HIV. By having its own API producer in-house, Mylan hopes to gain an edge over its competitors who must obtain their ingredients from outside manufacturers.

In its biggest deal yet, Mylan spent $6.7 billion in late 2007 to acquire Generics (UK) Ltd. from Merck. Mylan won out in a bidding war that included its major rivals Actavis Group and Teva, with the prize being a business almost twice its size. Following the acquisition, the company changed its name from Mylan Laboratories to just plain Mylan. Akin to a frog swallowing a salmon, Mylan estimates it will take two to three years to fully realize the benefit of the deal.

In 2009 Mylan formed a partnership with Indian biotech firm Biocon to expand into the growing field of generic biotech drugs. The two companies will co-develop and market biologic therapies in numerous countries.

HISTORY

Milan Puskar and a colleague founded Milan as a drug distributor in 1961 and shifted to vitamin manufacturing in 1965. It added generic penicillin in 1966 and tetracycline in 1968. The next year Parke-Davis (now part of Pfizer) became the first major drug company to purchase

Milan's products. Puskar left in 1972 after a management dispute, and the company changed its name to Mylan. The company went public in 1973. Chairman Roy McKnight brought Puskar back as president in 1976 when the two bought control of Mylan. In 1984 the company launched its first proprietary drug. Mylan became the #1 independent drugmaker in the US in 1985, specializing in generics.

In 1988 Mylan formed research joint venture Somerset Pharmaceuticals with Circa Pharmaceuticals (later bought by Watson Pharmaceuticals). The venture helped produce the successful anti-Parkinson's disease drug Eldepryl. The firm absorbed dermatological products maker Dow Hickam Pharmaceuticals in 1991 and drug-delivery specialist Bertek in 1993.

Puskar became chairman and CEO after McKnight died in 1993. Mylan launched cimetidine, a generic ulcer drug, in 1994, and by the following year it held 39% of the market for all new cimetidine prescriptions. Mylan got FDA approval for Etodolac, a generic version of arthritis drug Lodine, in 1997. The next year it bought Penederm Inc., maker of topical antifungal treatment Mentax.

In 2000 Mylan paid $135 million to settle price-fixing and antitrust charges relating to popular antianxiety drugs lorazepam and chlorazepate (generic versions of Ativan and Tranxene). On a happier note that year, the FDA approved the sale of Mylan's generic version of GlaxoSmithKline's Wellbutrin antidepressant. The following year, the company's generic version of Merck's cholesterol drug Mevacor was approved by the FDA, and in 2002 its version of Eli Lilly's Prozac won FDA approval.

The company's proposed acquisition of troubled King Pharmaceuticals rankled investor Carl Icahn, a minority stakeholder in Mylan. In late November 2004, Icahn made a buyout offer of Mylan to end its bid to buy King. That bid became moot after asset manager Perry Corp., led by Richard Perry, increased its stake in Mylan just enough to edge out Icahn as largest shareholder. However, Icahn filed suit against the company and Perry Corp., making charges of hedging to allow Mylan to complete its acquisition of King. The scuffle between shareholders was for naught. At the end of February 2005, Mylan and King terminated their deal, and Perry announced plans to unload his entire near-10% stake in the company. Ichan dropped his lawsuit against Perry, and then re-set his sights on a hostile buyout of Mylan. In retaliation, the company bought back 25% of its stock and closed its Mylan Bertek division — the branded drug unit that would have benefited most from the King Pharmaceuticals acquisition. In the end, Mylan incurred $22.9 million in expenses related to the fizzled plan during its 2005 fiscal year.

EXECUTIVES

Chairman and CEO: Robert J. Coury, age 48, $12,475,094 total compensation
Vice Chairman: Rodney L. (Rod) Piatt, age 56
President: Heather Bresch, age 40, $2,973,426 total compensation
COO: Rajiv Malik, age 48, $2,872,966 total compensation
EVP and CFO: Jolene L. Varney, age 42
SVP and Global CIO: Gregory L. Sheldon
SVP and Chief Compliance Officer: M. Fabiana Lacerca
SVP and Corporate Controller: Daniel C. Rizzo Jr., age 46
SVP and Global Head Biologics: Patrick Vink
SVP Strategic Corporate Development: Timothy B. (Tim) Sawyer

SVP and Global Head Human Resources: David A. Lillback
SVP and Global General Counsel: Joseph F. Haggerty
SVP and Treasurer: Brian Byala
President Specialty: Carolyn Myers, age 51
VP Global Business Development: Andrew G. (Drew) Cuneo
President, North America: Harry A. (Hal) Korman, age 51
President, Europe, Middle East, and Africa: Didier Barret, age 44, $2,153,833 total compensation
President, Asia/Pacific: John Montgomery
Secretary and Special Counsel (in the Office of the CEO): Stuart A. Williams, age 55
Investor and Public Relations: Stacey Chiodo
Auditors: Deloitte & Touche LLP

LOCATIONS

HQ: Mylan Inc.
1500 Corporate Dr., Canonsburg, PA 15317
Phone: 724-514-1800   **Fax:** 724-514-1870
Web: www.mylan.com

2008 Revenues

	$ mil.	% of total
Americas		
US	2,075.3	40
Other American countries	163.5	3
Europe	1,755.8	34
Asia	636.6	13
Other revenues	506.4	10
Total	**5,137.6**	**100**

PRODUCTS/OPERATIONS

2008 Revenues

	$ mil.	% of total
Generics	3,909.3	76
Matrix	444.8	9
Specialty (Dey)	417.3	8
Other	366.2	7
Total	**5,137.6**	**100**

Selected Generic Products

Albuterol (Proventil, Ventolin)
Alprazolam (Xanax)
Cimetidine (Tagamet)
Diazepam (Valium)
Diltiazem Hydrochloride (Cardizem)
Estradiol (Estrace)
Fentanyl (Duragesic)
Fluoxetine (Prozac)
Haloperidol (Haldol)
Lorazepam (Ativan)
Lovastatin (Mevacor)
Metformin hydrochloride (Glucophage)
Naproxen (Naprosyn)
Nifedipine (Procardia)
Omeprazole (Prilosec)
Propanolol hydrochloride (Inderal)
Selegiline hydrochloride (Eldepryl)
Sertraline hydrochloride (Zoloft)
Tizanidine hydrochloride (Zanaflex)

COMPETITORS

Abbott Labs	Perrigo
Barr Pharmaceuticals	Pfizer
Bayer AG	Roche Holding
Bristol-Myers Squibb	Roxane Laboratories
Dr. Reddy's	Sandoz International
Eli Lilly	GmbH
GlaxoSmithKline	Schering-Plough
Johnson & Johnson	Teva Pharmaceuticals
King Pharmaceuticals	Watson Pharmaceuticals
Novartis	Wyeth
Par Pharmaceutical	

HISTORICAL FINANCIALS

Company Type: Public

Income Statement

FYE: December 31

	REVENUE ($ mil.)	NET INCOME ($ mil.)	NET PROFIT MARGIN	EMPLOYEES
12/08*	5,137.6	(181.2)	—	15,000
3/07	1,611.8	217.3	13.5%	6,400
3/06	1,257.2	184.5	14.7%	2,900
3/05	1,253.4	203.6	16.2%	3,000
3/04	1,374.6	334.6	24.3%	2,800
Annual Growth	**39.0%**	**—**	**—**	**52.1%**

*Fiscal year change

2008 Year-End Financials

Debt ratio: 191.1%
Return on equity: —
Cash ($ mil.): 557
Current ratio: 2.06
Long-term debt ($ mil.): 5,165

No. of shares (mil.): 305
Dividends
  Yield: 0.0%
  Payout: —
Market value ($ mil.): 3,020

Stock History

NASDAQ (GS): MYL

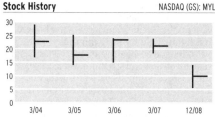

	STOCK PRICE ($) FY Close	P/E High/Low		PER SHARE ($) Earnings	Dividends	Book Value
12/08*	9.89	—	—	(1.05)	0.00	8.85
3/07	21.14	24	19	0.99	0.24	5.40
3/06	23.40	30	19	0.79	0.24	2.58
3/05	17.72	34	19	0.74	0.12	6.05
3/04	22.73	24	14	1.21	0.10	5.44
Annual Growth	**(18.8%)**	**—**	**—**	**—**	**—**	**13.0%**

*Fiscal year change

NACCO Industries

An unlikely combination of coal mines, toasters, and forklifts propels NACCO Industries. The holding company's independent operating subsidiaries do business in a diverse set of industries. North American Coal mines lignite coal in the US and sells it to utilities. NACCO Materials Handling Group makes Hyster and Yale lift trucks and parts. Its Hamilton Beach (formerly Hamilton Beach/Proctor-Silex) and Kitchen Collection subsidiaries are leading US producers of small kitchen appliances and housewares. NACCO Industries got its start back in 1913 as The Cleveland & Western Coal Company and has since diversified its business through acquisitions.

Although it got its start in mining, that segment of NACCO is now the company's smallest. Today a majority of NACCO's sales come from its lift trucks. Its housewares unit accounts for about 20% of sales.

With such diversified interests, the company regularly reorganizes and consolidates manufacturing operations, such as it has done in the US, Mexico, and Europe.

NACCO's chairman, president, and CEO, Alfred Rankin Jr., controls about 12% of the company.

HISTORY

King Coal ruled the early part of the 20th century, and Frank Taplin was ready to be a loyal subject. In 1913 the 38-year-old Cleveland native, formerly an office boy for John D. Rockefeller and later a VP at Standard Oil Company, formed distributor Cleveland & Western Coal. Four years later, spurred by WWI, the company bought three mines and began producing coal. It incorporated in 1925 as North American Coal Corporation (NACCO).

Taplin continued building his company until his death in 1938. Henry Schmidt took over as chairman in 1942, just as the company's sluggish sales began to rise, buoyed by demand for coal during WWII.

When home-heating coal sales declined, NACCO targeted electric utilities, signing its first long-term utility sales contract in 1951 with Ohio Edison. By 1952 NACCO had four underground coal-mining subsidiaries. During this time, strip mining became more common because of its efficiency and low cost. NACCO went public in 1956, and a year later bought its first lignite field for strip mining.

Profits stayed healthy in the 1980s despite frequent strikes and strict mine-safety laws. Pollution issues dimmed coal's prospects, and concerns about a potential buyout led Frank Taplin's heirs (sons Frank and Thomas, daughter Clara, son-in-law Alfred Rankin Sr., and grandson Alfred Rankin Jr.) to okay anti-takeover measures in the mid-1980s. NACCO became a holding company in 1986 and was renamed NACCO Industries. It sold some of its mines and began to diversify and to target simply made products that held top market positions.

During a two-year period beginning in 1988, NACCO bought electrical appliance specialist WearEver-ProctorSilex (it sold off the WearEver pots and pans operation in 1989), appliance factory outlet store chain The Kitchen Collection, and US maker of forklift trucks, Hyster Company. The Hyster buy doubled NACCO's sales and bolstered the company's 1985 purchase of forklift maker Yale Materials Handling. This purchase made NACCO a power in the growing forklift industry. Yale University graduate Alfred Jr., who had been the COO of Eaton, was named president in 1989 (and CEO in 1991).

In 1990 Proctor-Silex bought a majority stake in blender and mixer maker Hamilton Beach (it bought the remainder in 1996). The kitchen appliance foes merged to become a US market leader. By 1990 coal made up less than 15% of NACCO's sales.

Expanding geographically, the firm bought the warehouse-equipment business of Ormic (hand-and-reach trucks, Italy) in 1996. In 1997 NACCO reduced its US activities when it began production at a Hamilton Beach/Proctor-Silex plant in Mexico. Construction began in 1998 on NACCO's 25%-owned Red Hills lignite mine near Ackerman, Mississippi.

In 1999 the company's Netherlands-based unit, NMH Holding, bought Van Eijle BV, a Dutch importer/exporter of forklift trucks. NACCO also opened a forklift plant in China. (It agreed to buy the forklift division of Nissan Motors as well, but the deal fell apart the next year.) The same year NACCO's Hamilton Beach/Proctor Silex subsidiary secured a deal to supply Wal-Mart stores with a new line of GE-brand small appliances. In 2000 NACCO's National American Coal unit purchased from Phillips Coal the remaining assets of the Mississippi Lignite

Mining Company and the Red River Mining Company that it did not already own.

As a part of the company's restructuring plan, NACCO laid off about 150 employees from its Danville, Illinois, auto parts plant in 2001. In 2002 NACCO decided to phase out its Lenoir, North Carolina, lift truck component facility (by 2004) and restructure its Irvine, Scotland, lift truck assembly and component unit (by 2006). The company's Hamilton Beach/Procter-Silex unit also closed its Sotec plant in Juarez, Mexico, and its El Paso warehouse in 2004.

In 2006 NACCO said it would spin off its Hamilton Beach/Proctor-Silex business to shareholders. Upon completion of the spin-off, Hamilton Beach/Proctor-Silex planned to merge with Applica. The newly created entity was to be named Hamilton Beach, Inc., and Applica shareholders would have owned 25% of it. A wrinkle formed in the Applica merger plan late in 2006 when Harbinger Capital Partners made a competing offer. Applica then called off talks with NACCO, which prompted NACCO to file suit against Applica. NACCO later upped its original bid of $175 million to more than $187 million, but Harbinger eventually acquired Applica in 2007. Harbinger is Applica's largest shareholder, with about a 40% stake.

Also in 2006 NACCO's The Kitchen Collection subsidiary acquired Le Gourmet Chef, Inc., a kitchen goods retailer. Le Gourmet Chef operates nearly 80 retail stores across the US.

EXECUTIVES

Chairman, President, and CEO: Alfred M. Rankin Jr., age 67, $1,966,167 total compensation
VP and Controller: Kenneth C. Schilling, age 49, $348,762 total compensation
VP Law and Administration and Secretary, NAC: Thomas A. (Tom) Koza, age 62
VP Consulting Services: Lauren E. Miller, age 54
VP, General Counsel, and Secretary: Charles A. Bittenbender, age 59
VP Corporate Development and Treasurer: J. C. Butler Jr., age 48
VP and Chief Marketing Officer, NMHG: Victoria L. Rickey, age 56
VP Human Resources, NMHG: James M. Phillips, age 60
VP and COO, NMHG: Colin Wilson, age 54
VP Special Projects: Gregory J. Dawe, age 60
VP Finance and Information Systems, and CFO, NMHG: Michael K. Smith, age 64
VP Financial Services: Bob D. Carlton, age 51
VP Global Product Development: Rajiv K. Prasad, age 45
VP Engineering and Eastern Operations, NAC: Douglas L. Darby, age 57
VP Southern Operations and Human Resources, NAC: Michael J. Gregory, age 61
VP Northern Operations, NAC: Dan W. Swetich, age 63
VP Global Supply Chain: Michael E. Rosberg, age 59
President and CEO, Hamilton Beach Brands, Inc.: Michael J. Morecroft, age 67, $1,531,331 total compensation
President and CEO, The Kitchen Collection: Randolph J. Gawelek, age 61
President and CEO, NMHG: Michael P. Brogan, age 58, $725,287 total compensation
President and CEO, North American Coal: Robert L. (Bob) Benson, age 59, $1,248,043 total compensation
Auditors: Ernst & Young LLP

LOCATIONS

HQ: NACCO Industries, Inc.
5875 Landerbrook Dr., Ste. 300
Cleveland, OH 44124
Phone: 440-449-9600   **Fax:** 440-449-9607
Web: www.nacco.com

2008 Sales

	$ mil.	% of total
US	1,938.9	53
Europe, Africa & Middle East	921.8	25
Other	819.6	22
Total	**3,680.3**	**100**

PRODUCTS/OPERATIONS

2008 Sales

	$ mil.	% of total
Materials handling group		
Wholesale	2,740.1	74
Retail	175.4	4
Adjustments	(91.2)	—
Housewares		
HBB	528.7	14
KC	202.3	5
Adjustments	(5.5)	—
NACoal	130.5	3
Total	**3,680.3**	**100**

Selected Subsidiaries

Materials Handling
Hyster-Yale Materials Handling, Inc.
NACCO Materials Handling, BV (The Netherlands)
NACCO Materials Handling Group, Inc.
NACCO Materials Handling Group, Ltd. (UK)
NACCO Materials Handling Group, Pty., Ltd. (Australia)
NACCO Materials Handling, Spa (Italy)
NHMG Mexico SA de CV
NHMG Oregon, Inc.

Housewares
Hamilton Beach/Proctor-Silex de Mexico, SA de CV
Hamilton Beach/Proctor-Silex, Inc.
The Kitchen Collection, Inc.
Proctor-Silex Canada, Inc.

Coal Mining
The Coteau Properties Company
The Falkirk Mining Company
Mississippi Lignite Mining Company
The North American Coal Corporation
The North American Coal Royalty Company
Oxbow Property Company LLC
Red River Mining Company
The Sabine Mining Company

COMPETITORS

Arch Coal
Cascade Corp.
Caterpillar
CLARK Material Handling
CNH Global
Crown Equipment
Deere
Doosan Infracore
Gehl
Jungheinrich
Komatsu
Nissan Forklift
Peabody Energy
Salton
Toyota Material Handling
Whirlpool

HISTORICAL FINANCIALS

Company Type: Public

Income Statement

FYE: December 31

	REVENUE ($ mil.)	NET INCOME ($ mil.)	NET PROFIT MARGIN	EMPLOYEES
12/08	3,680.3	(437.6)	—	5,500

2008 Year-End Financials

Debt ratio: 112.2%	No. of shares (mil.): 8
Return on equity: —	Dividends
Cash ($ mil.): 138	Yield: 5.5%
Current ratio: 1.69	Payout: —
Long-term debt ($ mil.): 401	Market value ($ mil.): 310

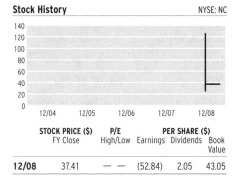

12/08	37.41	— —	(52.84)	2.05	43.05

	STOCK PRICE ($) FY Close	P/E High/Low	PER SHARE ($) Earnings	Dividends	Book Value

Nalco Holding

Dirty water? Wastewater? Process-stream water? Nalco treats them all. The company is the world's largest maker of chemicals used in water treatment and for industrial processes (in front of #2 GE Water and Process Technologies). Nalco's Energy Services segment is also #1 worldwide, ahead of Baker Petrolite; it provides fuel additives, oilfield chemicals, and flow assurance services to energy companies. The company's chemicals help clarify water, conserve energy, prevent pollution, separate liquids from solids, and prevent corrosion in cooling systems and boilers. Its top-ranked Industrial and Institutional Services segment has a 20% market share, and Nalco's pulp and paper unit is #3 behind Ashland and Ciba.

Customers include municipalities, hospitals, and makers of electronics, chemicals, paper, petroleum, and steel. Nalco also provides water management services and, through its Industrial Solutions unit, maintenance of water treatment operations.

Its Nalco Mobotec unit provides services to fight air pollution. It was formed after Nalco acquired Mobotec USA in 2007. Nalco Mobotec announced in 2009 a joint venture with Sonic Technology Solutions that will develop processes to use fly ash from coal-fired power stations as an ingredient in the manufacture of a cement substitute or concrete additives.

HISTORY

Nalco Chemicals got its start because, as its chief chemist would say, "You can put water in your stomach that you dare not put in a boiler." In the early 1920s Herbert Kern founded Chicago Chemical Company, and Wilson Evans started Aluminate Sales Corporation. Both companies sold liquid sodium aluminate, which is used to soften water — Chicago Chemical for water used in industrial boilers, and Aluminate Sales for steam locomotives. In 1928 Chicago Chemical, Aluminate Sales, and Alcoa's sodium aluminate unit merged to form National Aluminate Corporation.

In 1930 the company acquired Paige-Jones Chemical Company of New York, and with it the capability to supply its water-treatment products in the form of "ball briquettes." During the 1930s

it began making gel-type water-softening agents at the urging of one of its chemists, Emmett Culligan. (Culligan left to start his own water-treatment firm in 1935.)

In WWII Chicago Chemical was revived for a three-year stint making catalytic products for aviation fuel. At war's end, it again became a division of National Aluminate, bringing expertise in petroleum cracking and ion exchange materials. In 1947 National Aluminate went public. The postwar era brought a major challenge as railroads converted from steam to diesel locomotives; the changeover cost the company half its business in just a few years. In response, the company developed diesel catalysts and additives, cooling system treatments, and weed-control chemicals for the railroads. In the 1950s National Aluminate expanded into Europe and Latin America and added new customers such as papermakers and nuclear power plant operators. The company changed its name to Nalco Chemical Company in 1959.

In 1962 Nalco and UK-based Imperial Chemical Industries (ICI) formed Catoleum Pty. Ltd. in Australia. Later in the decade the company established Nalfloc in the UK and Katalco in the US (sold to joint venture partner ICI in 1986).

Nalco set up regional water-analysis laboratories throughout the US during the 1970s and continued overseas expansion. The company established itself as a star during a decade of dismal US stock performance. Nalco continued to acquire in the 1980s and moved into new markets such as chemicals for the electronics and auto industries. By 1989 Nalco's sales topped $1 billion.

To combat the recession of the early 1990s, Nalco sold some operations, increased its sales force, and continued to innovate, creating a process to detoxify crude oil sludge. Nalco's 1996 acquisitions included Molson Companies' water-treatment operations and UK-based chemicals firm Albright & Wilson. It soaked up the Netherlands-based International Water Consultants Beheer BV and the assets of Nutmeg Technologies in 1997. Nalco added more water-treatment companies in 1998, including Trident Chemicals, Dutch company USF Houseman Waterbehandling, and three Malaysian firms.

Nalco bought more water-treatment companies in Brazil, Finland, Italy, Sweden, the UK, and the US in 1999. That year French utility Suez bought Nalco for $4.1 billion in cash. In 2000 Suez tapped Nalco to integrate and control the operations of Calgon, Aquazur, and other group water-treatment companies.

Early in 2001 Suez added the Ondeo (on-DAY-o) name to all of its water operations to build brand identity; Nalco Chemical became Ondeo Nalco. (Ondeo was derived from the word "water" in several languages.) The company also purchased GEO Specialty Chemicals' paper chemical business later in 2001.

Suez sold Nalco to a group of private equity firms — the Blackstone Group, Apollo Management, and Goldman Sachs Capital Partners — in 2003 for more than $4 billion. The acquiring group dropped the "Ondeo" from the company's name and hired former Hercules CEO William Joyce to take over as chairman and CEO. Until a secondary offering of shares in mid-2005 the consortium's ownership stake still had been well above the 50% mark. Joyce retired in 2008 and was replaced by J. Erik Fyrwald, who had been president of DuPont Agriculture & Nutrition.

EXECUTIVES

Chairman, President, and CEO: J. Erik Fyrwald, age 49, $4,008,217 total compensation
EVP, CFO, and Treasurer: Bradley J. (Brad) Bell, age 56, $866,131 total compensation
CTO: Manian Ramesh, age 51
Chief Marketing Officer: Mary Kay Kaufmann, age 49
EVP; President: Eric G. Melin, age 48
EVP; President, Water and Process Services: David E. Flitman, age 44, $789,060 total compensation
EVP; President, Energy Services Division: Stephen M. (Steve) Taylor, age 46, $905,039 total compensation
EVP; President, Europe, Africa, and Middle East Operations: David Johnson, age 49, $1,245,420 total compensation
SVP Supply Chain and Safety, Health, and Environment: Scott C. Mason, age 49
VP, General Counsel, and Corporate Secretary: Stephen N. (Steve) Landsman, age 49
VP and Tax Officer: Richard J. O'Shanna
Division VP Communications and Investor Relations: Mike Bushman
VP Human Resources: Mary T. Manupella
Group VP Business Optimization: John P. Yimoyines, age 60
Group VP Water Marketing and Development: Rich Bendure, age 40
VP Energy Services Supply Chain: Mark R. Stoll, age 52
General Manager and Director, Russia: Vaclav Harant
Senior Manager External Communications: Charlie Pajor
General Marketing Manager, Innovation: Bob Duguay
Auditors: Ernst & Young LLP

LOCATIONS

HQ: Nalco Holding Company
    1601 W. Diehl Rd., Naperville, IL 60563
Phone: 630-305-1000   **Fax:** 630-305-2900
Web: www.nalco.com

2008 Sales

	$ mil.	% of total
The Americas		
US	1,884.1	46
Other countries	559.5	13
Europe/Middle East/Africa	1,154.8	27
Asia/Pacific	614.0	14
Total	**4,212.4**	**100**

PRODUCTS/OPERATIONS

2008 Sales

	$ mil.	% of total
Industrial & Institutional Services	1,813.4	43
Energy Services	1,506.4	36
Paper Services	776.9	18
Other	115.7	3
Total	**4,212.4**	**100**

Selected Products

Lubricants and functional fluids
Process chemicals
Water-treatment chemicals

Selected Markets

Automobile industry
Chemical industry
Commercial buildings (hospitals, hotels)
Electronic industry
Food-processing industry
Paper industry
Petroleum industry
Steel industry
Water-treatment plants

COMPETITORS

Arch Chemicals	Cytec
Ashland Hercules	Eka Chemicals
Baker Petrolite	GE Water
BASF Corporation	LANXESS
Champion Technologies	Rockwood Holdings

HISTORICAL FINANCIALS

Company Type: Public

Income Statement

FYE: December 31

	REVENUE ($ mil.)	NET INCOME ($ mil.)	NET PROFIT MARGIN	EMPLOYEES
12/08	4,212.4	(342.6)	—	11,770
12/07	3,912.5	129.0	3.3%	11,560
12/06	3,602.6	98.9	2.7%	11,100
12/05	3,312.4	47.8	1.4%	10,900
12/04	3,033.3	(138.8)	—	10,500
Annual Growth	8.6%	—	—	2.9%

2008 Year-End Financials

Debt ratio: 795.7%
Return on equity: —
Cash ($ mil.): 62
Current ratio: 1.89
Long-term debt ($ mil.): 3,130

No. of shares (mil.): 138
Dividends
Yield: 1.2%
Payout: —
Market value ($ mil.): 1,594

Stock History

NYSE: NLC

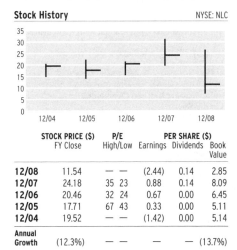

| | 12/04 | 12/05 | 12/06 | 12/07 | 12/08 |

	STOCK PRICE ($) FY Close	P/E High/Low		PER SHARE ($) Earnings	Dividends	Book Value
12/08	11.54	—	—	(2.44)	0.14	2.85
12/07	24.18	35	23	0.88	0.14	8.09
12/06	20.46	32	24	0.67	0.00	6.45
12/05	17.71	67	43	0.33	0.00	5.11
12/04	19.52	—	—	(1.42)	0.00	5.14
Annual Growth	(12.3%)	—	—	—	—	(13.7%)

NASDAQ OMX Group

NASDAQ OMX isn't a place; it's a state of mind. OK, that's not exactly true, but NASDAQ OMX *is* the leader in floorless exchanges and has surpassed NYSE Euronext as the world's largest stock exchange. The group was formed in 2008 when the NASDAQ Stock Market merged with OMX, the owner of Northern Europe's largest securities marketplace. NASDAQ OMX trades in more than 3,900 companies, including Exchange-Traded Funds (ETFs), equities, options, futures, derivatives, commodities, and structured products. The group's market services segment, which includes quotations, order execution, and reporting services, accounts for about 90% of sales.

Its issuer services segment includes shareholder services, newswire services, and such financial products and derivatives as ETFs and the Nasdaq-100 Index. The market technology segment, which accounts for less than 5% of revenues, offers systems integration, advisory, and other support services for exchanges.

NASDAQ bolstered its status in the US by going head-to-head with the venerable New York Stock Exchange; the younger exchange successfully lured a number of companies to dual-list with both competitors (or, in some cases, to move totally to NASDAQ). It launched a trading platform to handle dual-listed companies, as well as all NYSE-listed stocks and ETFs. The exchange also aggressively courted IPOs and foreign company listings, with international firms accounting for some 10% of its total companies.

Close on the heels of NASDAQ's successful domestic strategy, however, was an international push that had more than its share of ups and downs. After a failed attempt to acquire the London Stock Exchange (LSE) in 2006, NASDAQ became the European exchange's largest shareholder, acquiring more than 25% of the LSE in several separate transactions. When NASDAQ's 2007 hostile takeover bid for the LSE also failed, the disappointment was particularly bitter in the face of domestic and transoceanic hookups being carried out by NASDAQ's rivals (including the vaunted deal that created NYSE Euronext). In a peculiar turn of events, NASDAQ in 2007 sold its interests in LSE.

Nasdaq finally caught a break later that year, inking an agreement to acquire OMX. As part of the deal, Borse Dubai, which acquired NASDAQ's stake in LSE, also acquired some 20% (later raised to about 30%) of NASDAQ OMX Group.

Other 2006 international moves included cooperation agreements with exchanges in China, Japan, and Korea. (Earlier foreign forays — including Nasdaq Europe and Nasdaq Japan — proved unsuccessful and were shuttered or sold to joint-venture partners.)

In terms of service offerings, the exchange has used acquisitions (BRUT, Shareholder.com, Instinet, and PrimeNewswire (now GlobeNewswire) to strengthen its positions or add capabilities in such areas as electronic trading platforms, shareholder services, and newswire services. NASDAQ OMX used technology obtained in the Instinet acquisition to move into the options business by launching an options exchange. In 2007 NASDAQ purchased Directors Desk, which helps companies conduct daily communications.

Also in 2008 the company acquired the Philadelphia Stock Exchange (now NASDAQ OMX PHLX), which carries about 15% of the US options market, in a $652 million deal. NASDAQ OMX Group then acquired the Boston Stock Exchange in a deal providing additional trading licenses and clearing licenses. It used the platform to launch a second cash equities market in the US, the NASDAQ OMX BX. Also in 2008 the company launched NASDAQ OMX Commodities, which offers energy and carbon derivatives products.

Traditionally a heavy trader in smaller companies and tech stocks, NASDAQ OMX Group unveiled a tier structure in 2006. Elite stocks are traded on the NASDAQ Global Select Market, which represents more than a third of all listed firms; the other tiers are the NASDAQ Global Market and the NASDAQ Capital Market.

Former parent NASD spun off NASDAQ through a series of private sales, finally divesting its remaining 15% stake in the company in 2006. Shareholders with significant stakes in NASDAQ include the aforementioned Bourse Dubai and Horizon Asset Management (around 13%). Private equity firm Hellman & Friedman sold its stake of more than 15% in 2007.

EXECUTIVES

Chairman: H. Furlong Baldwin, age 77
CEO and Director: Robert (Bob) Greifeld, age 51, $11,507,016 total compensation
EVP Corporate Strategy and Global Data Products and CFO: Adena T. Friedman, age 39
EVP Global Software Development and CIO: Anna M. Ewing, age 48, $2,791,709 total compensation
EVP, General Counsel, and Chief Regulatory Officer: Edward S. Knight, age 58
EVP Worldwide Marketing and Financial Products: John L. Jacobs, age 50
EVP Corporate Client Group: Bruce E. Aust, age 45
EVP Transaction Services, Nordic: Hans-Ole Jochumsen, age 51
EVP Transaction Services US and UK: Eric W. Noll, age 47
SVP Global IT Services: Carl-Magnus Hallberg, age 43
SVP Corporate Communications: Bethany Sherman
SVP Global Human Resources: William H. Morgan
SVP, Controller, and Principal Accounting Officer: Ronald Hassen, age 57
SVP Market Technology: Lars Ottersgård
VP Investor Relations: Vince Palmiere
Associate VP Corporate Communications: Silvia Davi
President, NASDAQ OMX PHLX: Thomas A. (Tom) Wittman
President, NASDAQ OMX Europe: Charlotte Crosswell
Auditors: Ernst & Young LLP

LOCATIONS

HQ: The NASDAQ OMX Group, Inc.
1 Liberty Plaza, 165 Broadway, 50th Fl.
New York, NY 10006
Phone: 212-401-8700   **Fax:** 212-401-1024
Web: www.nasdaqomx.com

2008 Sales

	$ mil.	% of total
US	3,092.0	85
Other countries	556.7	15
Total	**3,648.7**	**100**

PRODUCTS/OPERATIONS

2008 Sales By Segment

	$ mil.	% of total
Market Services	3,207.3	88
Issuer Services	330.6	9
Market Technology	106.1	3
Other	4.7	—
Total	**3,648.7**	**100**

Selected Subsidiaries

Carpenter Moore Insurance Services, Inc.
GlobeNewswire (formerly PrimeNewswire, Inc.)
International Derivatives Clearing Group (81%)
Nasdaq Execution Services, LLC
NASDAQ OMX Commodities
NASDAQ Options Services, LLC
Shareholder.com, Inc.
The FINRA/NASDAQ Trade Reporting Facility

COMPETITORS

Citigroup
CME
Deutsche Börse
Investment Technology
Knight Capital
London Stock Exchange
NYSE Amex
NYSE Euronext
PHLX
TRADEBOOK

HISTORICAL FINANCIALS

Company Type: Public

Income Statement

FYE: December 31

	REVENUE ($ mil.)	NET INCOME ($ mil.)	NET PROFIT MARGIN	EMPLOYEES
12/08	3,648.7	319.9	8.8%	2,507
12/07	2,436.6	518.4	21.3%	891
12/06	1,657.8	127.9	7.7%	898
12/05	879.9	61.7	7.0%	917
12/04	540.4	11.4	2.1%	784
Annual Growth	61.2%	130.2%	—	33.7%

2008 Year-End Financials

Debt ratio: 54.1%
Return on equity: 9.9%
Cash ($ mil.): 566
Current ratio: 1.07
Long-term debt ($ mil.): 2,294

No. of shares (mil.): 203
Dividends
  Yield: 0.0%
  Payout: —
Market value ($ mil.): 5,010

Stock History

NASDAQ (GS): NDAQ

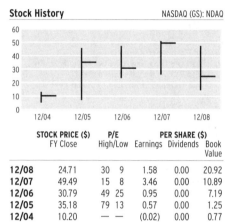

	STOCK PRICE ($) FY Close	P/E High/Low		PER SHARE ($) Earnings	Dividends	Book Value
12/08	24.71	30	9	1.58	0.00	20.92
12/07	49.49	15	8	3.46	0.00	10.89
12/06	30.79	49	25	0.95	0.00	7.19
12/05	35.18	79	13	0.57	0.00	1.25
12/04	10.20	—	—	(0.02)	0.00	0.77
Annual Growth	24.8%	—	—	—	—	128.1%

Nash-Finch Company

Nash-Finch knows what's in store for food retailers. One of the largest US wholesale grocery distributors, the company supplies food and general merchandise to about 1,600 retail grocery stores in more than 25 states. It operates more than 15 distribution centers in the Midwest, the Great Lakes region, and the Southeast. The company is also one of the leading suppliers to the the US armed forces, distributing goods to more than 200 military bases and commissaries both in the US and abroad. In addition to its food distribution businesses, Nash-Finch operates nearly 60 of its own supermarkets under such banners as Econofoods and Sun Mart.

Nash-Finch has been mostly focused on improving efficiencies within its warehouse and distribution system in order to cut costs and boost the bottom line. It has also been working to expand its military supply operations, acquiring three distribution centers from GSC Enterprises during 2008. Serving the armed services accounts for about 30% of sales. Meanwhile, Nash-Finch has been investing in a start-up retail grocery brand called AVANZA, designed to appeal to Hispanic consumers.

HISTORY

Vermont farmers Warren and Mary Nash operated a small country store in the mid-1800s. In 1884 their son Fred followed the homesteading rush to the Dakota Territory, where the next year he opened a small confectionery and tobacco shop in railroad boomtown Devils Lake. His brothers Edgar and Willis soon joined him, and by 1887 there was a Nash Brothers store in Devils Lake and another in Grand Forks.

Two years later North Dakota entered the Union, and the Nash brothers bought an unclaimed boxcar of peaches and turned it into a quick profit. That year the company hired 14-year-old Harry Finch to sort lemons for $4 a week, a job he took to support his ailing father. Also in 1889 Edgar moved to California, where he established ties between the Nashes' wholesale business and California produce growers. He died in 1896; Finch became a manager that year.

Acquisitions expanded the company in the late 1890s and early 1900s. It partnered with local produce brokerage C. H. Robinson in 1905; Nash Brothers controlled it by 1913.

Over the next several decades, Nash Brothers expanded its growing, packaging, and shipping operations, forming companies in California and Texas. It started the Nash Coffee Company and fruit and vegetable packager Nash DeCamp in 1916. Three years later the company moved its headquarters to Minneapolis. Nash Brothers' 60-plus companies incorporated as Nash-Finch in 1921. When Fred died in 1926, Finch became president. During the 1930s the company introduced its own brand, Our Family.

Nash-Finch returned to retailing in the 1950s with 17 supermarkets in Nebraska. Finch, by then a partner, retired in 1953 after 64 years with the company. During the 1960s the FTC limited C. H. Robinson's role with Nash-Finch, and the grocer sold its remaining stake in the broker in 1976. The company reached $1 billion in sales in 1981 and was the US's 10th-largest grocery wholesaler by the mid-1980s.

It made acquisitions throughout the 1990s, including a division of military distributor B. Green & Co. (Maryland, 1992); Easter Enterprises, a 16-store Iowa chain (1993); and 23 Food Folks stores (1994). In 1994 chairman Harold Finch, grandson of Harry, died in an auto accident. President Alfred Flaten became chairman and CEO and separated the wholesale and retail divisions.

The company sold two convenience store subsidiaries (Thomas & Howard and T&H Service Merchandisers) in 1995. In 1996 Nash-Finch bought Military Distributors of Virginia, a distributor of groceries to military bases in the eastern US and Europe, and grocery wholesalers T. J. Morris and Super Food Services.

A year later it bought most of the assets of Nebraska-based grocery distributor United-A.G. Cooperative. Former Pathmark executive Ron Marshall succeeded Flaten as CEO in 1998.

In ensuing years it replaced most of its management team, consolidated distribution centers, and sold produce and dairy subsidiaries to focus more on retailing. In 1999 Nash-Finch sold its Nash DeCamp produce unit to Agriholding, sold Gillette Dairy and Nebraska Dairies to Royal Wessanen, reduced its number of store banners, and closed unprofitable warehouses and stores.

It purchased retailer Erickson's Diversified (18 stores in Minnesota and Wisconsin) and in 2000 bought Hinky Dinky Supermarkets (12 locations in Nebraska). In 2001 Nash-Finch announced

that it would sell its North and South Carolina supermarkets as it continued on the market in the Midwest. To that end, it acquired U Save Foods (14 supermarkets in Nebraska, Kansas, and Colorado) in mid-2001; most of the stores were renamed Sun Mart.

In 2003 the company purchased five Sunshine Food stores in South Dakota and converted some of those to the Econofoods banner. It also started two specialty retail food operations: Buy·n·Save (aimed at low-income customers) and AVANZA (aimed at the Hispanic market). Nash-Finch closed about 20 underperforming retail food stores in 2004, including all of its Buy·n·Save locations and several AVANZA stores.

In the midst of an investigation into internal trading practices in 2006, Marshall stepped down as CEO. Alec Covington, formerly North American chief for Dutch food distributor Koninklijke Wessanen, was named as his replacement.

EXECUTIVES

Chairman: William R. Voss, age 55
President, CEO, and Director: Alec C. Covington, age 52, $5,001,958 total compensation
EVP, CFO, and Treasurer: Robert B. (Bob) Dimond, age 47, $1,405,170 total compensation
EVP and CIO: Calvin S. (Cal) Sihilling, age 59, $1,189,392 total compensation
EVP Supply Chain Management: Jeffrey E. (Jeff) Poore, age 50, $1,021,878 total compensation
EVP Food Distribution: Christopher A. Brown, age 46, $1,547,848 total compensation
SVP Merchandising: Howard Befort
SVP Military: Edward L. Brunot, age 45
SVP, Secretary, and General Counsel: Kathleen M. Mahoney, age 54
VP Sales and Business Development: Gary Bickmore
Auditors: Ernst & Young LLP

LOCATIONS

HQ: Nash-Finch Company
7600 France Ave. South, Minneapolis, MN 55440
Phone: 952-832-0534   **Fax:** 952-844-1237
Web: www.nashfinch.com

PRODUCTS/OPERATIONS

2008 Sales

	$ mil.	% of total
Food distribution	2,740.5	58
Military	1,360.7	29
Retail	602.5	13
Total	**4,703.7**	**100**

2006 Retail Locations

	No.
Sun Mart	22
Econofoods	19
Family Thrift Center	5
AVANZA	4
Pick n' Save	2
Family Fresh Market	1
Food Bonanza	1
Prairie Market	1
Wholesale Food Outlet	1
Other	1
Total	**57**

COMPETITORS

Alex Lee
Associated Wholesale Grocers
C & S Wholesale
Certified Grocers Midwest
Coastal Pacific Food Distributors
Core-Mark
Hy-Vee

Kroger
McLane
Purity Wholesale Grocers
Spartan Stores
SUPERVALU
UniPro Foodservice
United Natural
Wal-Mart

HISTORICAL FINANCIALS

Company Type: Public

Income Statement
FYE: Saturday nearest December 31

	REVENUE ($ mil.)	NET INCOME ($ mil.)	NET PROFIT MARGIN	EMPLOYEES
12/08	4,703.7	36.2	0.8%	7,410
12/07	4,532.6	38.8	0.9%	7,475
12/06	4,631.6	(23.2)	—	8,227
12/05	4,555.5	41.3	0.9%	9,487
12/04	3,897.1	14.9	0.4%	8,658
Annual Growth	4.8%	24.8%	—	(3.8%)

2008 Year-End Financials

Debt ratio: 80.8%
Return on equity: 11.1%
Cash ($ mil.): 1
Current ratio: 1.57
Long-term debt ($ mil.): 272

No. of shares (mil.): 13
Dividends
Yield: 1.6%
Payout: 26.2%
Market value ($ mil.): 576

Stock History
NASDAQ (GS): NAFC

	STOCK PRICE ($) FY Close	P/E High/Low		PER SHARE ($) Earnings	Dividends	Book Value
12/08	44.89	17	11	2.75	0.72	26.17
12/07	35.28	18	9	2.84	0.72	24.58
12/06	27.30	—	—	(1.72)	0.72	22.92
12/05	25.48	14	8	3.13	0.68	25.12
12/04	37.76	34	15	1.18	0.54	21.33
Annual Growth	4.4%	—	—	23.6%	7.5%	5.2%

National Fuel Gas

National Fuel Gas doesn't cover the nation, but it does touch all the bases in its industry: The company explores for, produces, stores, transmits, and distributes natural gas. The diversified energy concern's public utility, National Fuel Gas Distribution, accounts for most of its sales and distributes gas to about 730,000 customers in New York and Pennsylvania. National Fuel Gas has gas exploration, production, storage, and transportation operations; the company also engages in energy marketing, timber processing, independent power, and methane gas production. In 2008 oil and gas subsidiary Seneca Resources reported proved reserves of 225.9 billion cu. ft. of natural gas and 46.2 million barrels of oil.

The unit explores for, develops, and purchases natural gas and oil reserves in the Gulf Coast, Appalachia, the Southwest, and California. In 2007, in order to focus on its US oil and gas operations, Seneca Resources sold its Canadian unit.

Another subsidiary, National Fuel Gas Supply, owns about 30 underground gas storage facilities and a 3,000-mile pipeline that runs from southwestern Pennsylvania to the New York-Canada border. In 2007 the company received the go ahead by federal regulators to extend the Empire State Pipeline by building a 78-mile stretch from near Rochester to Corning (completed in late 2008). In 2008 the company proposed building a new gas pipeline, the Appalachian Lateral, that will provide transportation and storage services to major Northeast market interconnects.

Energy deregulation has changed the rules in recent years, and the firm's utility customers can now choose their own supplier. In response, National Fuel Gas has set up a gas marketing unit (National Fuel Resources) to compete for customers in the northeastern US.

HISTORY

The roots of National Fuel Gas go back to the 1820s in northwestern New York. The early days of natural gas exploitation were marked by varied uses of the fuel and creative transport methods. In 1821 Iroquois Gas (later a National Fuel Gas unit) laid lead pipe from a source beneath Canadaway Creek in New York to light street lamps in the village of Fredonia. Fifty years later an investor group tried (and failed) to pipe gas from Bloomfield, New York, to Rochester, some 25 miles away, using hollow logs connected by iron bands.

A more successful attempt was made in 1886 with an 87-mile iron pipeline that carried gas from McKean County, Pennsylvania, to Buffalo, New York. The Buffalo pipeline was bought by United Natural Gas, a predecessor of National Fuel Gas, and portions of it remained in use well into the 20th century.

Incorporated in 1902, National Fuel Gas bought smaller gas firms in the Buffalo area in the early 1900s and stretched its pipeline network into Pennsylvania. In 1916 Iroquois Gas established the US's first underground gas storage unit.

As gas reserves in the Appalachian region became depleted in the 1930s, the company joined other utilities to develop reserves in the Southwest and connect them through pipelines. Growth exploded in the 1940s, sparked by WWII increases in coal and oil prices, and in the 1950s, when home heating shifted to gas.

The industry was in a feast-or-famine period from the 1960s to the 1980s. The gas market matured in the 1960s, but the 1970s energy crisis increased demand, forcing National Fuel Gas to restrict new customer hookups. The next decade an aggressive industrywide development program glutted the market and prices plummeted. In response, National Fuel Gas diversified, moving away from retail and into storage and transport. In 1986 it bought Utility Constructors to build pipelines.

National Fuel Gas began looking beyond its utility business in 1991, when it set up gas marketing subsidiary National Fuel Resources. The next year the company cut staff and formed a joint venture with Citizens Gas Supply of Boston to purchase, transport, and sell gas to other utilities.

As part of the energy industry's globalization trend, National Fuel Gas established operations in China and the Czech Republic in 1996. The next year oil and gas exploration unit Seneca Resources bought interests in wells in California and Wyoming.

Also in 1997, as the oil and gas industry boomed, National Fuel Gas' exploration and pipeline operations were hampered by a scarcity of drilling rigs because of high demand. The petroleum industry slump in 1998 eliminated the rig shortage, and Seneca increased development drilling. The firm more than doubled its proved reserves in 1998 by acquiring energy exploration and production firms HarCor Energy, Bakersfield Energy, and M.H. Whittier.

The next year National Fuel Gas expanded its Czech Republic holdings and added timber and mineral rights in New York and Pennsylvania to its portfolio. Its National Fuel Resources moved into the electricity marketing business; it also bought a cogeneration plant in New York.

In 2000 the company increased its reserves 30% by acquiring Canada's Tri Link Resources. The next year it formed a joint venture with Canadian company Talisman Energy to explore in the Appalachian Basin. Subsidiary Seneca Resources also acquired another Canadian company, Player Petroleum.

EXECUTIVES

Chairman: Philip C. (Phil) Ackerman, age 64, $3,146,798 total compensation
President and CEO National Fuel: David F. Smith, age 56, $3,231,064 total compensation
CFO and Treasurer; President, National Fuel Gas Supply: Ronald J. (Ron) Tanski, age 57, $2,612,916 total compensation
SVP National Fuel Gas Supply: John R. Pustulka, age 56, $888,355 total compensation
SVP National Fuel Gas Distribution: James D. Ramsdell, age 53
SVP Distribution: Carl M. Carlotti, age 54
VP Business Development: Donna L. DeCarolis, age 49
President, National Fuel Gas Distribution: Anna Marie Cellino, age 55, $950,493 total compensation
President, Seneca Resources: Matthew D. Cabell, age 50, $1,555,640 total compensation
Principal Accounting Officer and Controller; Controller, National Fuel Gas Distribution and National Fuel Gas Supply: Karen M. Camiolo, age 49
Secretary and General Counsel: Paula M. Ciprich, age 48
Director, Investor Relations: Margaret M. Suto
Auditors: PricewaterhouseCoopers LLP

LOCATIONS

HQ: National Fuel Gas Company
6363 Main St., Williamsville, NY 14221
Phone: 716-857-7000   **Fax:** 716-857-7195
Web: www.natfuel.com

National Fuel Gas distributes natural gas in western New York and northwestern Pennsylvania. The company's pipeline network runs from southwestern Pennsylvania to the New York-Canada border. Its oil and gas exploration and production unit operates in the Appalachian region; California; the Gulf Coast regions of Alabama, Louisiana, and Texas; and Wyoming. National Fuel Gas markets energy and timber in the northeastern US.

PRODUCTS/OPERATIONS

2008 Sales

	$ mil.	% of total
Utility	1,194.7	50
Energy marketing	549.9	23
Exploration & production	466.8	19
Pipeline & storage	135.1	6
Timber	49.5	2
Corporate & other	4.4	—
Total	**2,400.4**	**100**

Selected Subsidiaries

Empire State Pipeline (natural gas transportation)
Highland Forest Resources, Inc. (timber processing)
Horizon Energy Development, Inc. (foreign and domestic energy investment, wholesale electricity generation)
Horizon Power, Inc. (wholesale electricity generation)
National Fuel Gas Distribution Corporation (natural gas utility)
National Fuel Gas Supply Corporation (natural gas transportation and storage)
National Fuel Resources, Inc. (energy marketer and broker for utilities and retail customers)
Seneca Resources Corporation (natural gas and oil exploration and production)

COMPETITORS

Allegheny Energy	Energy Future
Anadarko Petroleum	Exelon
Belden & Blake	Niagara Mohawk
Cabot Oil & Gas	ONEOK
Castle Oil	Petroleum Development
Con Edison	PPL Corporation
Duke Energy	Rochester Gas and Electric
Dynegy	Southern Union
El Paso	Southwestern Energy
Enbridge	TransCanada
Energy East	UGI

HISTORICAL FINANCIALS

Company Type: Public

Income Statement

FYE: September 30

	REVENUE ($ mil.)	NET INCOME ($ mil.)	NET PROFIT MARGIN	EMPLOYEES
9/08	2,400.4	268.7	11.2%	1,943
9/07	2,039.6	337.5	16.5%	1,952
9/06	2,311.7	138.1	6.0%	1,993
9/05	1,923.5	189.5	9.9%	2,044
9/04	2,031.4	166.6	8.2%	2,918
Annual Growth	4.3%	12.7%	—	(9.7%)

2008 Year-End Financials

Debt ratio: 62.3%
Return on equity: 16.6%
Cash ($ mil.): 68
Current ratio: 1.33
Long-term debt ($ mil.): 999
No. of shares (mil.): 80
Dividends
 Yield: 3.0%
 Payout: 39.9%
Market value ($ mil.): 3,384

Stock History

NYSE: NFG

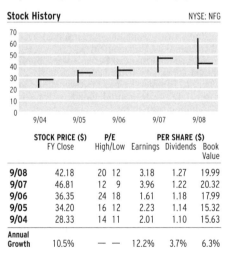

	STOCK PRICE ($) FY Close	P/E High/Low	PER SHARE ($) Earnings	Dividends	Book Value
9/08	42.18	20 12	3.18	1.27	19.99
9/07	46.81	12 9	3.96	1.22	20.32
9/06	36.35	24 18	1.61	1.18	17.99
9/05	34.20	16 12	2.23	1.14	15.32
9/04	28.33	14 11	2.01	1.10	15.63
Annual Growth	10.5%	— —	12.2%	3.7%	6.3%

National Semiconductor

National Semiconductor has an international reputation for semiconductors. The pioneering chip maker offers a variety of integrated circuits (ICs), especially analog and mixed-signal (blending analog and digital functions) chips. Its varied offerings reflect its focus on analog chips, which transform physical information — light, sound, pressure, even radio waves — into data that a computer can use. National's chips are used in a host of communications, consumer electronics, networking, automotive, and aerospace applications. Belying its name, National derives about three-quarters of sales from customers outside the US, largely to contract manufacturers that serve its ultimate OEM customers.

With the worldwide semiconductor industry downturn hitting National as hard as other chip makers, the company will consolidate facilities in 2009 and idle about 1,725 workers, more than a quarter of its worldwide workforce. National will close its assembly and test facility in Suzhou, China, and its wafer fabrication facility in Arlington, Texas.

In 2009 the company acquired Act Solar, a privately held solar energy company. The acquisition expands National's portfolio of power optimization technologies, diagnostics, and panel monitoring capabilities for solar arrays.

Act Solar's PowerString product, which boosts the efficiency of solar modules in an array, joins a burgeoning solar power product line for National. The company has hundreds of products in its PowerWise line for power and thermal management, among other applications. National also markets the SolarMagic power optimizers, which help photovoltaic solar arrays lose less energy due to shading and array mismatch problems.

HISTORY

National Semiconductor was founded as a transistor maker in 1959 by eight engineers from Sperry Rand Corporation. The company was established in Danbury, Connecticut. In 1966, as the company was struggling with only $7 million in annual sales, Peter Sprague (heir to the Sprague Electric fortune) took over as chairman. The next year he hired manufacturing expert Charles Sporck away from Fairchild Semiconductor to be National's CEO.

Sporck transferred company headquarters to Silicon Valley (the Danbury facility closed in 1989), halved the company's transistor workforce, and plowed the savings into developing linear and digital logic chips. During the 1970s National's mass manufacturing of low-cost chips made the company the leading US semiconductor maker for a time; its no-frills management approach led to its employees being dubbed "the animals of Silicon Valley."

The company bought National Advanced Systems (NAS), a distributor and servicer of Hitachi mainframes, in 1979 and Data Terminal Systems, which made point-of-sale terminals, in 1983; the two were combined to form Datachecker. When Japanese manufacturers dumped memory chips on the market in 1984 and 1985, National pulled out of the memory business.

Sporck moved to transform his low-cost commodity chip maker into a higher-margin supplier of niche products. National bought troubled Fairchild in 1987 for its logic chip designs and the custom linear circuits it made for the US military.

With mounting mainframe competition from IBM and Amdahl, in 1989 National sold Datachecker. National left the high-speed, high-density static random-access memory (SRAM) business, and in early 1991 Sporck retired. Former Rockwell International (now Rockwell Automation) executive Gilbert Amelio became CEO and undertook another restructuring.

By 1993 National had shifted production to Arlington, Texas. In 1995 the company purchased SiTel Sierra, a Netherlands-based supplier of cellular and wireless products.

When Amelio joined Apple Computer (now just Apple) in 1996, National chose Intel veteran and LSI Logic EVP Brian Halla as its new leader. Halla consolidated National's operations and resurrected the Fairchild name for its commodity chip business. Soon after Halla's arrival, about 600 jobs were cut, two COOs left, and 14 of 56 VPs resigned or were fired.

In 1997 National sold Fairchild. It bought Cyrix (microprocessors for inexpensive computers) in 1997 and ComCore Semiconductor (communications ICs) in 1998. That year National cut another 10% of its workforce in the face of an industry slump.

Things looked up in late 1998 when heavy hitters IBM, Compaq, and Packard Bell signed on to use Cyrix chips. However, Intel's low-cost Celeron chip hammered Cyrix's sales, and National exited the PC chip market. National sold its flat-panel display operations to Three-Five Systems, and Cyrix to Taiwan's VIA Technologies. Write-offs and acquisition costs in the face of a tough market led to a $1 billion loss for the year.

Also in 1999 National unveiled its Geode system-on-a-chip, targeting the handheld computer market. In 2000 the Geode processor debuted in a TV set-top box made by Philips Electronics for America Online's AOLTV service.

In 2001 the company cut 1,100 jobs — about 10% of its workforce — in response to another, particularly brutal, dropoff in the global chip market. In 2003 the company shuttered a unit that made baseband chips for wireless communications applications and sold the Geode processor line to AMD.

As the semiconductor industry recovered from its meltdown in the early years of the 21st century, National set plans in early 2004 to expand its wafer fabrication plant in South Portland, Maine. The same year National opened its semiconductor assembly and test plant in the Suzhou Industrial Park, located outside of Shanghai, and employing about 400 people.

Among other restructuring moves set in early 2005, National Semi said it would sell its assembly and testing facility in Singapore. Four months later, the company said it would close the facility and transfer its equipment to plants in China and Malaysia.

In mid-2006 the company supplied video iPods to all of its 8,500 employees, celebrating National's success in the previous year. The company supplied analog chips that went into the popular MP3 music player from Apple. The iPods were not, however, gifts from the company to the employees. When National laid off 35 employees from its wafer fab in Arlington, Texas, later the same month, those employees were told to turn in their iPods as company property.

EXECUTIVES

Chairman and CEO: Brian L. Halla, age 62,
$1,956,259 total compensation
President and COO: Donald Macleod, age 60,
$1,513,618 total compensation
SVP Finance and CFO: Lewis Chew, age 46,
$1,454,521 total compensation
SVP Manufacturing Services and CIO: Ulrich J. Seif,
age 51
VP and CIO: Julie Wong
SVP Worldwide Human Resources: Edward J. Sweeney,
age 52
SVP, General Counsel, and Secretary:
Todd M. DuChene, age 44
SVP Analog Signal Path Products Group:
Suneil V. Parulekar, age 61
SVP Power Management Products Group:
Detlev J. Kunz, age 58, $996,387 total compensation
SVP Worldwide Manufacturing: C.S. Liu,
$1,396,645 total compensation
SVP Technology Support: Mohan Yegnashankaran
VP Amplifier Division and Acting VP Audio Division:
Michael S. Polacek
VP Operations, South Portland: Paul Edmonds
VP Web Business: Phil Gibson
VP Worldwide Distribution and Customer Support:
Jennifer J. Bleakney
Media Contact: Meaghan Karabatsos
Treasurer: Robert E. DeBarr
Marketing Director, Communication Infrastructure
Products: Stephen Kempainen
Staff Scientist and Dean, Analog University: Bob Pease
Controller: Jamie E. Samath
National Fellow and CTO, Labs: Ahmad Bahai
National Fellow and CTO, Analog: Dennis Monticelli
Global Sales Channel Manager, Renewable Energy:
Aaron Thurlow
Auditors: KPMG LLP

LOCATIONS

HQ: National Semiconductor Corporation
2900 Semiconductor Dr., Santa Clara, CA 95052
Phone: 408-721-5000
Web: www.national.com

2009 Sales

	$ mil.	% of total
China	462.3	32
US	341.1	23
Germany	310.1	21
Singapore	231.5	16
Japan	115.4	8
Total	**1,460.4**	**100**

PRODUCTS/OPERATIONS

2009 Sales

	$ mil.	% of total
Analog	1,334.9	91
Other	125.5	9
Total	**1,460.4**	**100**

Selected Products

Aerospace and military integrated circuits (ICs)
Amplifiers and regulators
Audio circuits
Automotive ICs
Data acquisition circuits
Display circuits for monitors
Ethernet and Fast Ethernet digital signal processing
devices
Interface circuits
Microcontrollers (automotive, communications, and
industrial applications)
Power management circuits
Temperature sensors
Wireless circuits (radio and other functions)

COMPETITORS

Analog Devices
Atmel
Broadcom
Cypress Semiconductor
Fairchild Semiconductor
Freescale Semiconductor
IBM Microelectronics
Infineon Technologies
Intel Corp.
International Rectifier
Intersil
Linear Technology
Marvell Technology
Maxim Integrated Products
Micrel
Microchip Technology
Microsemi
NEC Electronics
NXP
ON Semiconductor
Qualcomm CDMA
Samsung Electronics
Sanken Electric
SANYO
Sensata
Sharp Corp.
STMicroelectronics
Texas Instruments
Toshiba Semiconductor

HISTORICAL FINANCIALS

Company Type: Public

Income Statement

FYE: Last Sunday in May

	REVENUE ($ mil.)	NET INCOME ($ mil.)	NET PROFIT MARGIN	EMPLOYEES
5/09	1,460.4	73.3	5.0%	5,800
5/08	1,885.9	332.3	17.6%	7,300
5/07	1,929.9	375.3	19.4%	7,600
5/06	2,158.1	449.2	20.8%	8,500
5/05	1,913.1	415.3	21.7%	8,500
Annual Growth	(6.5%)	(35.2%)	—	(9.1%)

2009 Year-End Financials

Debt ratio: 693.4%
Return on equity: 44.1%
Cash ($ mil.): 700
Current ratio: 3.94
Long-term debt ($ mil.): 1,227
No. of shares (mil.): 234
Dividends
Yield: 2.0%
Payout: 90.3%
Market value ($ mil.): 3,249

Stock History

NYSE: NSM

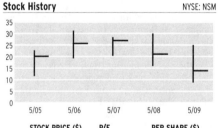

	STOCK PRICE ($) FY Close	P/E High/Low		Earnings	PER SHARE ($) Dividends	Book Value
5/09	13.88	80	29	0.31	0.28	0.76
5/08	21.05	24	13	1.26	0.20	0.66
5/07	26.92	25	18	1.12	0.14	7.47
5/06	25.68	25	15	1.26	0.10	8.23
5/05	20.12	20	11	1.11	0.04	8.78
Annual Growth	(8.9%)	—	—	(27.3%)	62.7%	(45.8%)

Nationwide Mutual Insurance

Call it truth in advertising — Nationwide Mutual Insurance Company has offices throughout the US. The company is a leading US property/casualty insurer that also provides life insurance through its Nationwide Financial Services subsidiary. In addition to personal and commercial property/casualty coverage, life insurance, and financial services, Nationwide also offers such specialty lines as professional liability, workers' compensation, agricultural insurance and loss-control, pet insurance, and other coverage. The company sells its products through such subsidiaries as ALLIED Group, GatesMcDonald, Nationwide Agribusiness Insurance, and Scottsdale Insurance.

As the US insurance industry has been mature for a long time, Nationwide has sought growth by moving into assorted niches, including specialty auto coverage, and financial services. The company launched its Nationwide Better Health program in 2006, and has grown it through acquisitions to provide health, productivity, and disease management services to employers.

Nationwide Financial Services received approval to expand its services to include full-service online and telephone banking in 2006. Operating as Nationwide Bank, the business has added deposit products and ATM access for its insurance, mortgage, and financial services customers. The company also established its Nationwide Advantage Mortgage business, which provides both mortgages and home equity loans. Consumers can access its services online and through Nationwide agents.

Nationwide Mutual sold off the London-based arm of its Gartmore Investment Management subsidiary to Gartmore's management and Hellman & Friedman LLC in 2006. Nationwide retained the US-based retail mutual-fund part of the business, changed its name to Nationwide Funds Group (NFG), and moved it under Nationwide Financial. However, in 2008 the company transferred NFG's active asset management business (with some 26 mutual funds) over to Aberdeen Asset Management.

Nationwide Financial Services was a publicly traded subsidiary from 1997 until early 2009 when, to simplify the group's ownership structure, Nationwide Mutual took it private in a $2.4 billion transaction.

Shortly after the Nationwide Financial transaction was completed, Nationwide Mutual named president and COO Steve Rasmussen as CEO, replacing Jerry Jurgensen, who left the company by mutual agreement with the board after nine years of service as chief executive.

HISTORY

In 1919 members of the Ohio Farm Bureau Federation, a farmers' consumer group, established their own automobile insurance company. (As rural drivers, they didn't want to pay city rates.) To get a license from the state, the company, called Farm Bureau Mutual, needed 100 policyholders. It gathered more than 1,000. Founder Murray Lincoln headed the company until 1964.

The insurer expanded into Delaware, Maryland, North Carolina, and Vermont in 1928 and began selling auto insurance in 1931 to city folks. It expanded into fire insurance in 1934 and life insurance the next year.

During WWII growth slowed, although the company had operations in 12 states and Washington, DC, by 1943. It diversified in 1946 when it bought a Columbus, Ohio, radio station. By 1952 the firm had resumed expansion and changed its name to Nationwide.

The company was one of the first auto insurance companies to use its agents to sell other financial products, adding life insurance and mutual funds in the mid-1950s. Nationwide General, the country's first merit-rated auto insurance firm, was formed in 1956.

Nationwide established Neckura in Germany in 1965 to sell auto and fire insurance. Four years later the company bought GatesMcDonald, a provider of risk, tax, benefit, and health care management services. It organized its property/casualty operations into Nationwide Property & Casualty in 1979.

The company experienced solid growth throughout the 1980s by establishing or purchasing insurance firms, among them Colonial Insurance of California (1980), Financial Horizons Life (1981), Scottsdale (1982), and, the largest, Employers Insurance of Wausau (1985). Wausau wrote the country's first workers' compensation policy in 1911.

Earnings were up and down in the 1990s as the company invested in Wausau and in consolidating office operations. Nationwide set up an ethics office in 1995, a time of increased scrutiny of insurance industry sales practices, and made an effort to hire more women as agents. In 1996 the Florida Insurance Commission claimed the company discriminated against customers on the basis of age, gender, health, income, marital status, and location. Nationwide countered that the allegations originated from disgruntled agents.

In 1997 the company settled a lawsuit by agreeing to stop its redlining practices (it avoided selling homeowners' insurance to urban customers with homes valued at less than $50,000 or more than 30 years old, which allegedly discriminated against minorities). It also dropped a year-old sales quota system that was under investigation.

As the century came to a close, Nationwide began to narrow its focus on its core businesses. It spun off Nationwide Financial Services so the unit could have better access to capital, and it expanded both at home and abroad through such purchases as ALLIED Group (multiline insurance), CalFarm (agricultural insurance in California), and AXA subsidiary PanEuroLife (asset management in Europe). The company's discrimination woes came back to haunt it in 1999, and it created a $750,000 fund to help residents of poor Cincinnati neighborhoods buy homes.

In 2001 Nationwide's expansion in Europe continued with the purchase of UK fund manager Gartmore Investment Management.

Nationwide and several other insurance companies were named in a series of lawsuits stemming from the aftermath of 2005's Hurricane Katrina. One suit alleged that prior to the natural disaster, insurance agents dissuaded their clients from purchasing flood insurance, and that the companies did not offer the full settlement amount to clients whose homes had been damaged by the storm surge of water. In one of the first lawsuits to be decided, the judge ruled in favor of Nationwide.

EXECUTIVES

President and CEO: Stephen S. (Steve) Rasmussen, age 56
EVP and CFO: Lawrence A. (Larry) Hilsheimer, age 51
EVP and CIO: Michael C. Keller, age 49
SVP and Chief Investment Officer: Gail G. Snyder, age 54
EVP, Chief Legal and Governance Officer: Patricia R. (Pat) Hatler, age 54
EVP and Chief Administrative Officer: Terri L. Hill, age 49
EVP and Chief Marketing Officer: James R. (Jim) Lyski, age 46
VP Investor Relations: Mark Barnett
President and COO, Nationwide Financial Services, Inc.: Mark R. Thresher, age 52
President and COO, Scottsdale Insurance: Michael D. (Mike) Miller
Interim CEO, NWD Investment Group: John Grady
President, Nationwide Better Health: Holly Snyder
Global CFO, Gartmore Group: M. Eileen Kennedy, age 51
Treasurer: Harry H. Hallowell, age 48
Chief Privacy Officer, Assistant VP, and Associate General Counsel: Kirk Herath
Chief Medical and Science Officer, Nationwide Better Health: Neil Gordon
Assistant VP Corporate Communications: Joe Case
Chief Diversity Officer: Candice R. Barnhardt
Auditors: KPMG LLP

LOCATIONS

HQ: Nationwide Mutual Insurance Company
1 Nationwide Plaza, Columbus, OH 43215
Phone: 614-249-7111   **Fax:** 614-854-3676
Web: www.nationwide.com

PRODUCTS/OPERATIONS

Selected Subsidiaries and Affiliates

Property and casualty
  American Marine Underwriters, Inc.
  CalFarm Insurance Agency
  Colonial County Mutual Insurance Company
  DVM Insurance Agency, Inc.
  Farmland Mutual Insurance Company
  Nationwide Agribusiness Insurance Company
  Scottsdale Insurance Company
  Titan Insurance Company
  Veterinary Pet Insurance Company
  Victoria National Insurance Company
Life insurance and financial services
  Nationwide Financial Services, Inc.
  Nationwide Life Insurance Company
  Nationwide Bank
  Nationwide Retirement Solutions, Inc.
  Pension Associates, Inc.
  TBG Insurance Services Corp.
Asset management
  Nationwide Asset Management Holdings, LTD.
    Audenstar Limited
    NWD Investment Management, Inc.
Strategic investments
  GatesMcDonald & Company
  Nationwide Advantage Mortgage Company

COMPETITORS

AIG	MassMutual
Allstate	MetLife
American Financial	New York Life
AXA Financial	Northwestern Mutual
Citigroup	Pacific Mutual
CNA Financial	Principal Financial
GEICO	Prudential
Guardian Life	State Farm
The Hartford	Travelers Companies
John Hancock Financial	USAA
Liberty Mutual	

HISTORICAL FINANCIALS

Company Type: Mutual company

Income Statement

FYE: December 31

	ASSETS ($ mil.)	NET INCOME ($ mil.)	INCOME AS % OF ASSETS	EMPLOYEES
12/08	161,090.0	1,994.0	1.2%	36,023
12/07	161,090.0	1,994.0	1.2%	36,000
12/06	160,009.0	2,113.0	1.3%	36,000
12/05	158,258.0	1,149.0	0.7%	35,000
12/04	157,371.0	1,010.0	0.6%	32,933
Annual Growth	0.6%	18.5%	—	2.3%

2008 Year-End Financials

Equity as % of assets: —
Return on assets: 1.2%
Return on equity: —
Long-term debt ($ mil.): —
Sales ($ mil.): 22,962

Net Income History

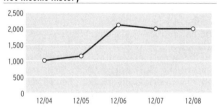

	12/04	12/05	12/06	12/07	12/08

Navistar International

Navistar's gonna roll its truckin' convoy 'cross the USA and beyond. The company manufactures its products under brand names such as International (commercial trucks and military vehicles); MaxxForce (diesel engines); IC (school and commercial buses); and Workhorse (chassis for motor homes). It also designs and manufactures diesel engines for the pickup truck, van, and SUV markets. Navistar's parts group supplies engine parts, and its financial sector offers sales and lease financing for its dealers and customers.

In 2009 Navistar and Ford settled a long legal battle over an engine contract, essentially closing one chapter in their 30-year relationship. The companies will end their current diesel engine supply agreement earlier than planned, with Ford paying an undisclosed amount to Navistar. The companies will continue to collaborate on the existing Blue Diamond Truck and Parts joint venture, which offers medium-duty trucks, as well as parts support for a variety of Ford products, to dealers and customers. The companies will also continue their diesel engine supply relationship in South America. A reduction in Ford production schedules brought about 400 layoffs at the Indianapolis engine plant in 2008.

In 2009 Navistar bought the recreational vehicle manufacturing assets of Monaco RV, which had filed for Chapter 11 bankruptcy protection earlier in the year, for about $47 million.

Navistar partnered with Mumbai-based Mahindra & Mahindra in 2007 to produce light commercial vehicles as well as medium- and heavy-duty diesel engines (targeted to India) under the Mahindra brand. Caterpillar and Navistar are working on an alliance to build Cat-branded construction trucks for the US market beginning in 2010, as well as commercial trucks and engines for overseas markets. In 2008 Navistar partnered to manufacture public and commercial buses with Brazilian bus body maker San Marino Ônibus e Implementos Ltda., which sells internationally under the Neobus brand.

Navistar launched the energy-efficient International ProStar and LoneStar long-haul trucks in 2007 to the US, Canada, and Mexico. It plans to expand modified versions throughout Latin America and other world markets. The company's MaxxForce engine, built to current U.S. emissions standards, has been modified for use in Brazil and Mexico, and ultimately for China, India, and Russia. Navistar continues to expand its global truck business into new markets like the Middle East and South Africa.

Navistar secured more than $1.6 billion in contracts with the US armed forces for military vehicles used to protect troops from roadside bombs in Iraq. The US government accounts for more than 25% of sales.

The company is also stepping up in hybrid technology by partnering with the EPA, UPS, and Eaton to develop a diesel "series" hydraulic urban delivery vehicle. The vehicle uses hydraulic pumps and hydraulic storage tanks to capture and store energy. Navistar is making school buses and mid-size commercial vehicles with hybrid-electric powertrains, as well.

Three trusts for employees and retirees of International Truck and Engine together own about 10% of Navistar International.

HISTORY

Virginia-born inventor Cyrus McCormick perfected the reaper in 1831 and moved west to open a factory in Chicago in 1846. Before his death in 1884, McCormick had implemented such innovations as installment plans, written guarantees, and factory-trained repairmen. In 1902, with help from banker J. P. Morgan, the company merged with Deering Harvester (agricultural machinery) and several smaller companies to form International Harvester (IH); it soon controlled 85% of US harvester production.

IH set up its first overseas plant in 1905 in Sweden. It entered the tractor industry in 1906, and in 1907 it began making the forerunner of the truck — the Auto Buggy. By 1910 IH was making 1,300 trucks and 1,400 tractors annually and had exceeded $100 million in sales.

Cyrus Jr. borrowed $5 million from John D. Rockefeller in 1913 and took control of IH. In 1924 IH introduced the Farmall, the first all-purpose tractor. IH began making heavy trucks in 1928, and by 1937 it was the top US producer of medium and heavy trucks.

Overextended and underfinanced after WWII, IH's market share declined. It produced more trucks than agricultural equipment for the first time in 1955. By 1958 Deere had taken over the lead in farm equipment. IH lost its medium-duty industry sales lead to Ford in the 1960s, and its construction equipment business faltered as well.

A six-month strike by the UAW in 1980, coupled with a recession, sent IH to the edge of bankruptcy. Over the next two years IH lost $2.3 billion. In 1982 IH sold its construction equipment unit, and in 1985 it sold its agricultural equipment business and the International Harvester name. Employee numbers had dropped 85% by 1986, and plants decreased from 48 worldwide to six in North America.

The company was renamed Navistar International in 1986. It redesigned 85% of its truck line by 1987. In 1989 Navistar introduced a nine-speed heavy-truck transmission — its first all-new design in more than 25 years. In 1991 Navistar raised its stake in truck maker Dina Camiones (Mexico) to 17% and inked OEM deals for its engines with Perkins Group (UK) and its North American distributor, Detroit Diesel.

A boom in demand for heavy trucks in 1992 and 1993 resulted in Navistar's retail deliveries rising nearly 33%. Navistar unveiled an engine for vans and trucks in 1994 that was the cleanest burning of its kind, increasing the company's share of the diesel engine market. Company veteran John Horne became CEO in 1995.

In 1999 Navistar bought half of Maxion Motores, Brazil's largest maker of diesel engines. The joint venture was renamed Maxion International Motores. Maxion provided diesel engines to Ford and GM factories in South America.

In 2001 Navistar and Ford announced the formation of a 50-50 joint venture to produce commercial trucks in Mexico. The venture, named Blue Diamond Truck, began operation in 2002. In late 2003 the company created an operating unit for the sole purpose of conducting business with the US military.

An agreement to supply the US Postal Service with 1,700 medium-duty trucks was signed in early 2004. The following year, through subsidiary International Truck and Engine, Navistar bought Workhorse Custom Chassis for an undisclosed sum from Grand Vehicle Works Holdings Corporation, a Carlyle Group company.

EXECUTIVES

Chairman, President, and CEO: Daniel C. (Dan) Ustian, age 59
SVP Corporate Finance, Interim CFO, and Principal Financial Officer: Andrew J. Cederoth, age 44
VP and CIO: Donald C. (Don) Sharp, age 41
SVP, General Counsel, and Chief Ethics Officer: Steven K. (Steve) Covey, age 58
EVP and Chief Risk Officer: William A. (Bill) Caton, age 57
Chief Designer: Dave Allendorph
SVP Sales Operations, North America: James L. Hebe, age 60
SVP; President and CEO, Navistar Financial: David Johanneson
SVP and General Manager, Parts Division: Phyllis E. Cochran, age 58
SVP Human Resources and Administration: Gregory W. (Greg) Elliott, age 48
VP Investor Relations: Heather Kos, age 38
VP and Corporate Controller: John P. Waldron, age 44
VP Corporate Communication: John F. Harmon
VP and Treasurer: James M. (Jim) Moran
President Truck Group International: Deepak T. (Dee) Kapur, age 56
President North American Truck Operations: John J. (Jack) Allen
President Navistar Defense: Archie Massicotte
Corporate Secretary: Curt A. Kramer, age 41
Director Global Logistics: Ed Melching
Auditors: KPMG LLP

LOCATIONS

HQ: Navistar International Corporation
4201 Winfield Rd., Warrenville, IL 60555
Phone: 630-753-5000   **Fax:** 630-753-2303
Web: www.navistar.com

2008 Sales

	$ mil.	% of total
North America		
US	10,318	70
Canada	1,830	13
Mexico	1,337	9
Brazil	1,234	8
Other countries	5	—
Total	**14,724**	**100**

PRODUCTS/OPERATIONS

2008 Sales

	$ mil.	% of total
Trucks	10,314	70
Engines	2,499	17
Parts	1,586	11
Financial services	325	2
Total	**14,724**	**100**

COMPETITORS

BAE SYSTEMS
BAE Systems Inc.
BAE Systems Land & Armaments
Blue Bird
Caterpillar
Cummins
Cummins Westport
Daimler
Daimler Trucks North America
Detroit Diesel
Eaton
Fleetwood Enterprises
Force Protection
Ford Motor
Freightliner Custom Chassis
General Dynamics
General Dynamics Land Systems
General Motors
Hino Motors
Isuzu
Leyland Trucks
Mitsubishi Fuso Truck & Bus
Nissan Diesel
Oshkosh Truck
PACCAR
Scania
Spartan Motors
Volvo
Winnebago

HISTORICAL FINANCIALS

Company Type: Public

Income Statement

	REVENUE ($ mil.)	NET INCOME ($ mil.)	NET PROFIT MARGIN	EMPLOYEES
10/08	14,724.0	134.0	0.9%	17,800
10/07	12,295.0	(120.0)	—	17,200
10/06	14,200.0	301.0	2.1%	18,200
10/05	12,124.0	139.0	1.1%	18,600
10/04	9,724.0	247.0	2.5%	15,600
Annual Growth	**10.9%**	**(14.2%)**	**—**	**3.4%**

FYE: October 31

2008 Year-End Financials

Debt ratio: —
Return on equity: —
Cash ($ mil.): 861
Current ratio: 1.43
Long-term debt ($ mil.): 5,409

No. of shares (mil.): 70
Dividends
  Yield: 0.0%
  Payout: —
Market value ($ mil.): 2,117

Stock History

NYSE: NAV

	STOCK PRICE ($) FY Close	P/E High/Low	PER SHARE ($) Earnings	Dividends	Book Value
10/08	30.12	43 12	1.82	0.00	(21.27)
10/07	63.00	— —	(1.70)	0.00	(10.44)
Annual Growth	**(52.2%)**	**— —**	**—**	**—**	**—**

NBC Television

This company is hoping TV viewers will share in a little water cooler talk at *The Office* with a group of *Heroes*. The flagship broadcast network of media conglomerate NBC Universal, NBC Television Network operates the #4 broadcast network NBC, which reaches millions of viewers through more than 200 affiliate stations including 10 that are company-owned or -operated. Its schedule is anchored by such shows as *The Office*, *Heroes*, and the *Law & Order* franchise. The Peacock network operates as part of NBC Television Group alongside TV production unit Universal Media Studios and Spanish-language broadcaster Telemundo. NBC Universal is 80%-owned by General Electric; French telecom operator Vivendi owns the rest.

A major shakeup occurred in 2009 when entertainment chief Ben Silverman departed the network after two years. The founder of Reveille Productions had come to NBC in 2007 and embarked on a 52-week programming strategy designed to reduce the number of repeats and increase the number of replacement shows during the year. Jeff Gaspin, who also leads NBC Universal Cable was promoted to chairman of NBC Universal Television Entertainment. From that position he heads all of NBCU's cable and broadcast operations.

NBC is banking part of its primetime schedule for the 2009-10 season on the popularity of comedian Jay Leno: The longtime *Tonight Show* host will be hosting an hour-long talk show each weekday night. This latest wrinkle in NBC's schedule is designed to reduce the network's dependence on more expensive scripted programming and to provide a larger audience lead-in for local newscasts.

Where NBC has been more successful is in sports programming. It airs National Football League games on Sunday nights through a broadcasting rights agreement that pays the league about $600 million each year through the 2013 season. Among its other high-profile sports properties, NBC has a long-term deal to air coverage of the Olympics through 2012. (The company ponied up more than $5.5 billion in 2000 for the rights to air both the summer and winter games.) In 2008 the company acquired a controlling stake in World Championship Sports Network, a cable and online sports broadcaster focused on Olympic sporting events. Together, the companies launched Universal Sports to expand NBC's coverage of the Summer Games in Beijing.

NBC also has national broadcasting rights to National Hockey League regular season and playoff games through the 2010-11 season. Unique in sports, the deal is structured as a partnership in which the network and the league share advertising revenue.

The network, meanwhile, is making big investments in online programming to promote and supplement its traditional broadcasting operations. NBC distributes its shows over the Internet through its Web site, where it has also launched some online-only shows that offer a tie-in to its primetime schedule. Parent NBCU is also a joint venture partner in video streaming site Hulu along with News Corporation and Walt Disney.

HISTORY

In 1919 General Electric and Westinghouse formed Radio Corporation of America (RCA). Five years later RCA pioneered television with the transmission of the first radio-photo. Led by inventor-cum-entrepreneur David Sarnoff, RCA set up the National Broadcasting Company (NBC) in 1926 to develop quality radio programs.

The demand for radio network programming grew rapidly. The company split its programming into two networks to give listeners a choice of formats. In 1941 the Federal Communications Commission (FCC) ruled that companies could own only one network. NBC subsequently sold one of its networks, which formed the nucleus of rival American Broadcasting Company (ABC).

Sarnoff also pursued the development of TV. In 1939 NBC began the first regular TV service with coverage of President Roosevelt inaugurating the New York World's Fair. In 1941 NBC obtained a commercial TV license from the FCC, and its WBNT-TV (New York) became the world's first commercial TV station. NBC launched current affairs program *Meet the Press* in 1947. The company won FCC approval for its color TV system in 1953 and presented the first nationwide color broadcast that year.

During the 1970s NBC's ratings slumped, as did its radio business. Led by NBC Entertainment's young president Brandon Tartikoff, the network staged a comeback in the 1980s with an unparalleled string of hits, including *Miami Vice*, *The Cosby Show*, and *Cheers*.

In the midst of the network's resurrection, GE bought RCA for $6.4 billion in 1986. That year Robert Wright was named president and CEO of the NBC network. Despite a number of attempts to revive radio's popularity, the company decided to exit the business. It sold seven of its eight stations in 1988.

In 1990 Tartikoff aide Warren Littlefield took over as head of entertainment. In 1993 the network fell to third in the ratings, had to apologize to General Motors for a fraudulent news demonstration, and lost late-night's David Letterman to rival CBS. But NBC bounced back with a slew of new programs (led by *ER*) in 1994 and 1995 to win back the top ratings spot. Littlefield left in 1998 and was replaced by Scott Sassa. NBC also ended its 33-year affiliation with the National Football League.

In 2002 NBC purchased Telemundo Communications, owner of the second-largest Spanish-language television network in the US, for about $2.6 billion.

In 2004 GE and Paris-based Vivendi Universal (now Vivendi) came together to merge their film and TV business, forming NBC Universal. The media conglomerate, 80%-owned by GE, encompassed broadcast and cable television networks, along with film and TV production studios. Wright was named chairman and CEO of NBCU.

Entertainment head Jeff Zucker was named CEO of NBC Universal Television in 2004, taking on responsibility for the NBC network, as well as NBCU's many cable outlets.

In 2007 Wright announced his departure from NBCU after 20 years leading first the NBC network and later the entertainment conglomerate. Zucker was appointed his successor. Later that year, entertainment chief Kevin Reilly was ousted from his position due to NBC's sagging ratings; TV producer Ben Silverman was tabbed to lead the entertainment division. After two largely unsuccessful years, however, Silverman left NBC and was replaced by NBC Universal Cable chief Jeff Gaspin.

EXECUTIVES

Chairman, NBC Universal Television Entertainment: Jeff Gaspin
SVP and CFO, CNBC: Satpal Brainch
EVP NBC Sports: Jonathan D. (Jon) Miller
EVP Program Planning and Scheduling, NBC Universal: Mitch Metcalf
EVP Affiliate Relations: John Damiano
EVP, NBC Strategic Partnership Group: Jay Linden
EVP Entertainment Strategy and Programs: Ted Frank
EVP Casting, NBC Universal Television: Marc Hirschfeld
EVP Late Night and Primetime Series, NBC Entertainment: Rick Ludwin
EVP NBC Universal Television Group Publicity: Rebecca Marks
EVP Business Affairs, NBC Universal Entertainment and Cable Entertainment: Beth Roberts
EVP Current Series, NBC Entertainment: Erin Gough
EVP Studios and Broadcast Operations: Derek Bond
EVP, NBC Olympics; Executive Producer, NBC Sports: David Neal
EVP Advertising and Promotion, The NBC Agency: Frank Radice
EVP Alternative Programming: Paul Telegdy
SVP Human Resources: Thomas Cairns
President, Telemundo: Donald (Don) Browne
President, Primetime Entertainment: Angela Bromstad
Chairman, NBC Entertainment and Universal Media Studios: Marc Graboff
President, NBC News: Steve Capus
Auditors: KPMG LLP

LOCATIONS

HQ: The NBC Television Network
30 Rockefeller Plaza, New York, NY 10112
Phone: 212-664-4444   **Fax:** 212-664-4085
Web: www.nbc.com

PRODUCTS/OPERATIONS

Selected Shows

NBC News
  Dateline NBC
  Meet the Press
  Today
NBC Entertainment
  30 Rock
  The Biggest Loser
  Chuck
  Community (Fall 2009)
  Friday Night Lights
  Heroes
  The Jay Leno Show (Fall 2009)
  Law & Order
  Law & Order: Special Victims Unit
  The Office
  Parenthood (Fall 2009)
  Parks and Recreation
  Saturday Night Live
  Southland
  Trauma (Fall 2009)
  Tonight Show with Conan O'Brien
NBC Sports
  Football Night in America
  Sunday Night Football

COMPETITORS

ABC, Inc.
CBS
The CW
Discovery Communications
FOX Broadcasting
MTV Networks
MyNetworkTV
Turner Broadcasting
Univision

NBTY, Inc.

NBTY draws upon nature's bounty to cash in on the market for preventive and alternative health care. As the largest vertically integrated source of nutritional supplements in the US, the company manufactures, wholesales, and retails more than 25,000 products including vitamins, minerals, herbs, and sports drinks. Brands include Ester-C, Nature's Bounty, Solgar, and Sundown. NBTY has manufacturing facilities in Canada, the UK, and the US and is able to produce and package capsules, tablets, powders, softgels, and liquids. The company sells its goods through pharmacies, wholesalers, supermarkets, and health food stores and serves customers in more than 85 countries around the world.

In North America it operates more than 400 Vitamin World stores in the US and some 80 Le Naturiste stores in Canada. In the UK the company operates more than 900 Holland & Barrett, GNC, and Julian Graves stores. In the Netherlands the company operates more than 70 De Tuinen retail stores.

In addition to its retail stores, NBTY operates Puritan's Pride, which sells nutritional products through catalogs and over the Internet. Puritan's Pride boasts some 4 million customers.

Unlike many of its competitors that rely upon third-party manufacturers, the company actually manufactures 90% of the nutritional supplements that it sells and also serves as a third-party manufacturer of private-label products for retailers.

NBTY has grown big and strong as the entire natural products industry has boomed, but a steady diet of acquisitions has supplemented its growth. In recent years the highly acquisitive company has bought Canadian vitamin manufacturer and distributor SISU (2005), Wyeth's premium-brand supplement maker Solgar Vitamin and Herb (2005), and Zila Nutraceuticals (2006, formerly a division of Zila). Zila Nutraceuticals was then renamed The Ester-C Company to reflect the business' primary product. In 2008 the company bought the assets of Leiner Health Products, a bankrupt maker of nutritional supplements and over-the-counter drugs, for $371 million. That purchase brought increased manufacturing capacity to support further growth.

To secure its spot as the UK's largest supplement retailer, NBTY paid $25 million to acquire natural foods retail chain Julian Graves in 2008. The purchase bumped the company's spread from 640 stores to more than 900 stores. However it also caught the attention of the UK's Office of Fair Trading, which launched an investigation to determine if the purchase is likely to unfairly reduce competition. In mid-2009 the acquisition was cleared by the Office of Fair Trading. NBTY operates Julian Graves business separately from its existing UK business.

Chairman and CEO Scott Rudolph owns nearly 9% of the company his father founded.

HISTORY

Arthur Rudolph founded NBTY in his garage in the early 1960s. Then called Nature's Bounty, the company went public in 1971 to market nutritional supplements. Rudolph was chairman and CEO until his 1993 resignation, when son Scott succeeded him.

Without so much as a glass of water, Nature's Bounty swallowed the mail-order business of General Nutrition Companies in 1989, and vitamin distributor Prime Natural Health Laboratories in 1993.

In 1995 the company agreed to settle Federal Trade Commission charges that it made deceptive claims about the effectiveness of 26 nutrient supplements. That year Nature's Bounty changed its name to that of its stock symbol, NBTY (the symbol changed to NTY in 2003 when the company moved to the NYSE).

In 1997 NBTY bought leading UK health foods chain Holland & Barrett, which operated more than 400 stores. The acquisition more than doubled NBTY's store count. After the buy, NBTY started stocking Holland & Barrett's shelves with its products. In 1998 the company bought a group of privately held vitamin companies and made a major push to open more Vitamin World stores in the US. In 1999 NBTY acquired Nutrition Warehouse, further bolstering its retail, e-commerce, and mail-order operations. Also that year it bought network marketer Dynamic Essentials to broaden its distribution channels.

Acquisitions continued into the 21st century: SDV Vitamins, a division of Rexall Sundown, joined the family in 2000, and in 2001 NBTY bought the Knox NutraJoint and Knox for Nails nutritional supplement business from Kraft Foods for about $4 million, along with NatureSmart from Whole Foods Market. The company's Holland & Barrett subsidiary bought a chain of 12 vitamin retail stores (Nature's Way) in Ireland. To expand its wholesale business, NBTY in 2002 purchased a line of nutritional supplements sold under the Synergy Plus trademark, a well-known brand among health food aficionados.

A big move came in 2003. NBTY bought Rexall Sundown from Royal Numico N.V. that year. Also that year, the company disbanded its Dynamic Essentials subsidiary after receiving a letter of inquiry by the FTC regarding a weight-loss product marketed by Dynamic Essentials. In addition, the company ceased production of all weight-loss products that contained ephedra, prior to the FDA's eventual ban on the herb.

EXECUTIVES

Chairman and CEO: Scott Rudolph, age 51
President and CFO: Harvey Kamil, age 64
SVP Operations and Corporate Secretary: Hans Lindgren, age 48
SVP Marketing and Advertising: James P. Flaherty, age 51
SVP Wholesale Business: John D. Leahy, age 55
Auditors: PricewaterhouseCoopers LLP

LOCATIONS

HQ: NBTY, Inc.
2100 Smithtown Ave., Ronkonkoma, NY 11779
Phone: 631-567-9500   **Fax:** 631-567-7148
Web: www.nbty.com

PRODUCTS/OPERATIONS

2008 Sales

	$ mil.	% of total
Wholesale	1,160.5	53
Retail		
Europe & UK	600.5	28
North America	208.0	9
Direct response	210.5	10
Total	**2,179.5**	**100**

Selected Retail Operations
DeTuinen (the Netherlands)
GNC (UK)
Holland & Barrett (UK)
Le Naturiste (Canada)
Nature's Way (Ireland)
Nutrition Warehouse (US)
Vitamin World (US)

Selected Brands
American Health
Body Fortress
Ester-C
Flex-A-Min
Good 'N Natural
Knox
MET-Rx
Natural Wealth
Nature's Bounty
Osteo-Bi-Flex
Physiologics
Pure Protein
Puritan's Pride
Rexall
SISU
Solgar
Sundown
Worldwide Sport Nutrition

COMPETITORS

Bactolac Pharmaceutical	Nutraceutical International
GeoPharma	Perrigo
GNC	Pharmavite LLC
Herbalife Ltd.	Schiff Nutrition
Integrated BioPharma	Sunrider
Inverness Medical	Vitacost
Natrol	VS Holdings
Nature's Sunshine	Whole Foods

HISTORICAL FINANCIALS

Company Type: Public

Income Statement

FYE: September 30

	REVENUE ($ mil.)	NET INCOME ($ mil.)	NET PROFIT MARGIN	EMPLOYEES
9/08	2,179.5	153.2	7.0%	13,760
9/07	2,014.5	207.9	10.3%	10,800
9/06	1,880.2	111.8	5.9%	10,900
9/05	1,737.2	78.1	4.5%	11,200
9/04	1,652.0	111.8	6.8%	10,000
Annual Growth	**7.2%**	**8.2%**	**—**	**8.3%**

2008 Year-End Financials

Debt ratio: 53.9%	No. of shares (mil.): 62
Return on equity: 14.9%	Dividends
Cash ($ mil.): 90	Yield: 0.0%
Current ratio: 2.76	Payout: —
Long-term debt ($ mil.): 538	Market value ($ mil.): 1,827

Stock History

NYSE: NTY

	STOCK PRICE ($) FY Close	P/E High/Low		PER SHARE ($) Earnings	Dividends	Book Value
9/08	29.52	18	9	2.33	0.00	16.13
9/07	40.60	18	9	3.00	0.00	17.07
9/06	29.27	20	10	1.62	0.00	13.57
9/05	23.50	26	17	1.13	0.00	11.57
9/04	21.56	24	12	1.62	0.00	10.34
Annual Growth	**8.2%**	**—**	**—**	**9.5%**	**—**	**11.8%**

NCI Building Systems

NCI Building Systems is a group of companies making engineered building systems, metal components (doors, roofs, walls, and trim), and steel coil coating for the North American industrial and construction markets. It sells its products under brand names such as A & S Building Systems, Ceco Building Systems, and Mid-West Steel Building Company. Customers include contractors, developers, and builders; its NCI Metal Depot retail stores sell components to consumers in Texas and New Mexico. Manufacturers of a variety of such items as water heaters and office furniture use NCI's coated coils. The group has some 40 manufacturing facilities in the US, an additional facility in Mexico, and a sales office in Canada.

NCI has grown by buying up other companies and consolidating its growing operations. Since 2006 it has acquired metal building maker Robertson-Ceco and Garco Building Systems, purchases which gave NCI Building Systems access to growth markets in the West.

However, the downturn in the economy and the construction industry has affected NCI's sales. To help offset losses, the company has cut costs, including cutting about 20% of its workforce and closing some manufacturing plants.

The company is shutting down the production of residential overhead doors, a noncore division of its metal components segment.

HISTORY

NCI Building Systems' founder Johnie Schulte Jr. began his career in the mid-1950s when he landed a job punching and shearing metal building pieces in Houston. In 1984 he founded NCI. The enterprise made only metal building components until 1987, when it began making metal buildings. That year NCI had sales of about $2 million. The company went public in 1992, and a year later its sales had reached more than $130 million. While competitors were shuttering plants in the soft market of the early 1990s, NCI was buying companies — including its 1992 purchase of A&S Building Systems, a metal building maker based in Caryville, Tennessee. NCI later expanded its product line to include self-storage buildings. It entered the market for roll-up steel overhead doors in 1995 when it bought Doors & Building Components (also a maker of interior steel parts) and started its own line of steel-frame homes.

NCI continued to make acquisitions in 1996, picking up a metal stud plant in Texas from Alabama Metal Industries, the equipment of Carlisle Engineered Metals, and Mesco Metal Buildings. The next year it bought the rest of Carlisle, including a manufacturing plant in Alabama, and began a 51%-owned joint venture in Mexico to manufacture framing systems. NCI bought the US metal building components business of UK-based BTR in 1998 for $593 million, doubling its size and adding painting and coating capabilities. The company spent 1999 integrating the large business.

NCI bought out Consolidated System's share in their DOUBLECOTE metal coil-coating joint venture for $26 million in 2000. Later that year NCI bought Midland Metals, a maker of metal building components. The move strengthened NCI's presence in the Midwest.

In 2001 NCI sold its 50% interest in Midwest Metal Coatings to its joint venture partner. The company closed five manufacturing facilities during the first quarter of fiscal 2002. NCI launched into direct selling to the public by opening a series of NCI Metal Depot retail factory stores that offer commercial and residential metal components (metal roof and wall panels, light structural and tubing shapes, and accessories) and a variety of small metal building packages (carports, storage sheds, and other metal buildings).

The company opened two retail stores in Texas in fiscal 2003. Also that year, NCI entered the residential garage door market by acquiring Texas-based Able Manufacturing and Wholesale Garage Door Company for about $3.3 million. NCI shortened the company's name to Able Door Manufacturing. Able operates distribution centers in the Dallas, Texas area; Atlanta, Georgia; Oklahoma City, Oklahoma; and Ontario, California.

Founder, president, and CEO Johnie Schulte Jr. retired as an executive in November 2003 and retired as a director the next year; he was succeeded by A. R. Ginn. The following year NCI filed a suit against Schulte, alleging he had violated non-competitive agreements. Schulte filed a countersuit; an undisclosed settlement was reached in 2005.

To expand its retail and builder distribution channels for its small engineered buildings, NCI bought North Little Rock, Arkansas-based Heritage Building Systems and Steelbuilding.com for approximately $30 million in 2004. NCI also acquired the 49% minority stake held by its partners in its manufacturing plant in Monterey, Mexico.

The next year NCI bought the intellectual property rights of metal building and components maker STEELOX Systems of Ohio, gaining the patents and trademarks, copyrights, common law rights, names, logos, Web sites, and customer lists of the established (by more than 70 years) company.

In 2006 NCI paid $370 million in cash for metal buildings maker Robertson-Ceco Corporation and its Robertson Building Systems, Ceco Building Systems, Star Building Systems, and Steelspec divisions. Late that year Ginn stepped down as CEO, with president and COO Norm Chambers becoming president and CEO. The next year Chambers assumed the chairmanship.

EXECUTIVES

Chairman, President, and CEO: Norman C. (Norm) Chambers, age 59, $2,970,546 total compensation
EVP and COO: Mark W. Dobbins, age 50
EVP, CFO, and Treasurer: Mark E. Johnson, age 42
EVP and CIO: Eric J. Brown
EVP, General Counsel, and Secretary: Todd R. Moore, age 49
VP Corporate Development: Mark T. Golladay, age 47
VP Finance and Corporate Controller: Richard W. Allen, age 33
President, Metal Components Division: Charles W. Dickinson, age 57
President, NCI Buildings: Bradley D. (Brad) Robeson, age 46
President, Metal Coil Coatings: John L. Kuzdal
Auditors: Ernst & Young LLP

LOCATIONS

HQ: NCI Building Systems, Inc.
10943 N. Sam Houston Pkwy. West
Houston, TX 77064
Phone: 281-897-7788   **Fax:** 281-477-9674
Web: www.ncilp.com

NCI Building Systems operates some 40 manufacturing facilities in the US and Mexico and additional sales offices in Canada.

PRODUCTS/OPERATIONS

2008 Sales

	$ mil.	% of total
Engineered building systems	1,110.5	52
Metal components	715.3	34
Metal coil coating	305.7	14
Adjustments	(367.3)	—
Total	**1,764.2**	**100**

Selected Products and Services

Metal building components and complete buildings (carports, utility buildings, etc.)
Metal cladding and accessories
Mini-storage buildings
Modular offices
Residential and commercial garage doors
Roll-up doors, partitions, and panels

Selected Brands

A&S Building Systems
ABC (American Building Components)
Able Door Manufacturing
Ceco Building Systems
DBCI
Heritage Building Systems
MBCI
Mesco Building Solutions
Metal Coaters
Metal Depots
Metal Prep
Metallic Building Company
Mid-West Steelbuilding Company
Robertson Building Systems

Selected Subsidiaries

Building Systems de Mexico, S.A. de C.V.
NCI Group, Inc.
Robertson Building Systems Limited (Canada)
Robertson-Ceco II Corporation
Steelbuilding.com, Inc.

COMPETITORS

American Buildings
Berger Building Products
Berlin Steel
Butler Manufacturing
Design Components
G-I Holdings
Gibraltar Industries
Horton Homes
Johns Manville
Nucor
Overhead Door
Varco Pruden Buildings
Williams Scotsman

HISTORICAL FINANCIALS

Company Type: Public

Income Statement			FYE: Saturday nearest October 31	
	REVENUE ($ mil.)	NET INCOME ($ mil.)	NET PROFIT MARGIN	EMPLOYEES
10/08	1,764.2	78.9	4.5%	5,394
10/07	1,624.3	63.7	3.9%	5,721
10/06	1,570.5	73.8	4.7%	6,010
10/05	1,130.1	56.0	5.0%	3,800
10/04	1,084.9	44.9	4.1%	3,800
Annual Growth	**12.9%**	**15.1%**	**—**	**9.2%**

2008 Year-End Financials

Debt ratio: 75.9%
Return on equity: 13.6%
Cash ($ mil.): 68
Current ratio: 1.98
Long-term debt ($ mil.): 473
No. of shares (mil.): 20
Dividends
  Yield: 0.0%
  Payout: —
Market value ($ mil.): 372

Stock History

NYSE: NCS

	STOCK PRICE ($)	P/E		PER SHARE ($)		
	FY Close	High/Low		Earnings	Dividends	Book Value
10/08	18.61	10	4	4.05	0.00	31.21
10/07	39.18	20	12	3.06	0.00	27.00
10/06	59.85	20	12	3.45	0.00	24.94
10/05	41.06	16	11	2.68	0.00	22.22
10/04	32.15	16	10	2.24	0.00	20.07
Annual Growth	(12.8%)	—	—	16.0%	—	11.7%

NCR Corporation

Want to find NCR? Follow the money. A leading maker of automatic teller machines (ATMs), the company also makes point-of-sale (POS) terminals and bar code scanners. Other retail and financial systems offerings include self-service kiosks for such applications as gift registries; paper, ink, and other consumable media; and check image processing systems. NCR's services unit provides maintenance and support, as well as professional services such as systems integration and managed services. The company's target markets include entertainment, financial services, health care, public sector, retail and hospitality, travel and gaming, and technology services.

With a direct sales force handling about 90% of its sales, NCR markets its products worldwide; about two-thirds of its sales were to customers outside the US in 2008. The company reorganized its operational structure in 2008, shifting from product-based business units to geographic divisions. The restructuring allowed NCR to reduce redundancies and process inefficiencies.

NCR has come a long way since it was known as National Cash Register, and the company continues to broaden it product line and move into new markets. It has targeted such industries as entertainment, gaming, health care, and travel for expansion of its self-service systems. Examples of such systems include self-checkout kiosks in hotels and casinos, as well as ordering and payment systems for restaurants.

In 2009 the company acquired TNR Holdings, an operator of DVD rental kiosks. NCR made the purchase to expand its SelfServ Entertainment line, and it plans to install the units in supermarkets and convenience stores nationwide. The kiosks will operate under the Blockbuster Express brand. NCR's alliance with Blockbuster began in 2008 with a pilot kiosk program.

HISTORY

John Patterson bought control of a Dayton, Ohio, cash register factory in 1882 and founded National Cash Register (NCR). Colonel Edward Deeds (who later became chairman) joined NCR in 1889, and hired inventor Charles Kettering in 1904 to develop an electric cash register. (The duo also developed an electric car ignition system and left NCR to start Dayton Engineering Laboratories Co., or Delco.)

By the 1920s NCR controlled 90% of the cash register market. That decade NCR introduced accounting machines, which became almost as important to the company as cash registers. NCR's stock dropped from $154 to $6.87 in the crash of 1929, but by 1936 the company had fully recovered.

Responding to the commercialization of computers following WWII, NCR bought computer developer Computer Research in 1952. During the 1960s the company introduced mainframe computers, opened data processing centers, established microelectronics research facilities, and introduced disk-based computers. However, NCR failed to automate its primary products — cash registers and accounting machines. In 1969 the company had record profits of $50 million; by 1971 they had plunged to $2 million.

William Anderson, who became president in 1972, is credited with saving NCR. He slashed its Dayton workforce by 75% and focused the company on computing, with an emphasis on retail scanners and ATMs.

In the early 1980s NCR moved from proprietary to UNIX operating systems and introduced networking equipment. In 1990 it began developing parallel processing technologies with database management specialist Teradata. That year the company won a contract to supply workstations to JCPenney stores.

Hoping to become one of the world's top PC makers, in 1991 AT&T bought NCR in a $7.4 billion hostile takeover. AT&T also acquired Teradata and merged the two companies as Global Information Systems (GIS). Lars Nyberg, a Swede who had led a divisional turnaround at electronics giant Philips, took over GIS in 1995 and began a reorganization that would eventually cut 11,000 jobs. When he joined GIS, it was losing $2 million a day.

In 1996 AT&T spun off the company (renamed NCR); it had suffered losses totaling nearly $4 billion during its years with AT&T. Nyberg jettisoned NCR's financially draining PC operations but beefed up the company's ATM and retail automation business by acquiring Compris Technologies (grocery automation and management products) and Dataworks (check processing software).

But losses prompted NCR to restructure in 1997, and the company slimmed down its 130-country network of independent operating units into a handful of global business units. The next year the company announced a partnership with Microsoft to further integrate NCR's Teradata systems with Microsoft's server technology, making it easier for companies to create data warehouses. Also in 1998 NCR sold factories in Ireland and the US to contract manufacturer Solectron, which agreed to produce NCR's hardware products for the next five years.

The following year, with a narrowed focus on ATM, banking, retail, and data warehousing systems, the company acquired IBM's financial self-service operations and financial industry automation software company Gaspar.

In 2000 NCR bought Ceres Integrated Solutions, a provider of customer relationship management software, and it acquired information technology and outsourcing service provider 4Front Technologies for $250 million. In 2003 Nyberg handed the CEO reins to NCR president and former Teradata head Mark Hurd. Nyberg retained his chairmanship.

In 2004 NCR acquired Kinetics, a provider of self-service check-in systems for airlines and hotels; Kinetics' products also included systems for restaurant preordering and event ticketing.

Early in 2005 Hurd resigned to become CEO of Hewlett-Packard; NCR director Jim Ringler was appointed chairman and interim CEO. Soon after former Symbol Technologies CEO Bill Nuti was named CEO of NCR.

NCR agreed to acquire the ATM business of Tidel Technologies in 2005; the deal closed early the following year. NCR also acquired the assets of IDVelocity, a developer of RFID infrastructure and process management software in 2006.

The company purchased Touch Automation, a developer of kiosks used to distribute DVDs, in 2007. NCR also spun off its Teradata unit that year.

EXECUTIVES

Chairman, CEO, and Director: William R. (Bill) Nuti, age 45, $12,856,018 total compensation
SVP Global Operations and COO: Peter A. Dorsman, age 53, $1,688,079 total compensation
SVP and CFO: Anthony J. (Tony) Massetti, age 49, $1,823,649 total compensation
EVP Industry Solutions Group: John G. Bruno, age 43
SVP, NCR Services: Christine W. (Chris) Wallace, age 56
SVP and General Manager, Systemedia: Daniel (Dan) Bogan, age 53
SVP Human Resources: Andrea Ledford, age 43
SVP Worldwide Sales: Peter Leav, age 38
VP Worldwide Channels: Tushar Kothari
VP North American Channels: Juliann Larimer
VP European Channels: Dawn Calderbank
VP and General Manager NCR Entertainment Solutions: Alex C. Camara
Auditors: PricewaterhouseCoopers LLP

LOCATIONS

HQ: NCR Corporation
1700 S. Patterson Blvd., Dayton, OH 45479
Phone: 937-445-5000   **Fax:** 937-445-5541
Web: www.ncr.com

2008 Sales

	$ mil.	% of total
Americas		
US	1,787	34
Other countries	482	9
Europe, Middle East & Africa	2,066	39
Asia/Pacific		
Japan	352	6
Other countries	628	12
Total	**5,315**	**100**

PRODUCTS/OPERATIONS

2008 Sales

	$ mil.	% of total
Products	2,861	54
Services	2,454	46
Total	**5,315**	**100**

Selected Products and Services

Customer service
  Maintenance
  Professional and installation-related
Financial Self Service
  Automated teller machines (ATMs)
  Support services
Retail Store Automation
  Consulting, implementation, and maintenance
    services
  Electronic shelf labels
  Point-of-sale workstations and scanners
  Software
  Web-enabled kiosks
NCR Consumables
  Ink
  Paper
  Printer cartridges
Payment and Imaging
  Consulting, outsourcing, and support services
  Transactions processing systems

COMPETITORS

ACI Worldwide, Inc.
Acxiom
BancTec
Coinstar
Cummins-American
Datalogic Scanning
De La Rue
Dell
Diebold
EDS
Fujitsu
Gilbarco
Hewlett-Packard
Hypercom
IBM
Ingenico
Metavante
MICROS Systems
Motorola, Inc.
Oki Electric
Optimal Group
PAR Technology
Radiant Systems
Retalix
SANYO
SITA
Toshiba TEC
Tranax Technologies
Triton
Unisys
VeriFone
Wincor Nixdorf

HISTORICAL FINANCIALS

Company Type: Public

Income Statement

FYE: December 31

	REVENUE ($ mil.)	NET INCOME ($ mil.)	NET PROFIT MARGIN	EMPLOYEES
12/08	5,315.0	228.0	4.3%	22,400
12/07	4,970.0	274.0	5.5%	23,200
12/06	6,142.0	382.0	6.2%	28,900
12/05	6,028.0	529.0	8.8%	28,200
12/04	5,984.0	290.0	4.8%	28,500
Annual Growth	(2.9%)	(5.8%)	—	(5.8%)

2008 Year-End Financials

Debt ratio: 1.6%
Return on equity: 20.8%
Cash ($ mil.): 711
Current ratio: 1.51
Long-term debt ($ mil.): 7

No. of shares (mil.): 159
Dividends
  Yield: 0.0%
  Payout: —
Market value ($ mil.): 2,247

Stock History

NYSE: NCR

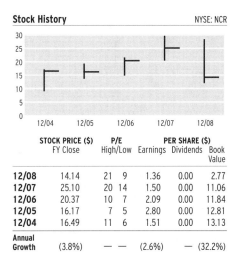

	STOCK PRICE ($) FY Close	P/E High/Low		PER SHARE ($) Earnings	Dividends	Book Value
12/08	14.14	21	9	1.36	0.00	2.77
12/07	25.10	20	14	1.50	0.00	11.06
12/06	20.37	10	7	2.09	0.00	11.84
12/05	16.17	7	5	2.80	0.00	12.81
12/04	16.49	11	6	1.51	0.00	13.13
Annual Growth	(3.8%)	—	—	(2.6%)	—	(32.2%)

NetApp, Inc.

NetApp (formerly Network Appliance) knows storage backwards and forwards. The company is a leading vendor of network-attached storage (NAS) systems designed for midsized to large enterprises; its filers can also be deployed in Fibre Channel and IP-based storage area network (SAN) configurations. NetApp's NearStore line of disk-based devices is designed for backup and archiving. It also provides operating system, data management, and content delivery software. NetApp sells directly and through channel partners to organizations in the communications, energy, financial services, government, health care, media, manufacturing, and technology sectors. Customers include Deutsche Telekom, Yahoo!, and Boeing.

NetApp took an early lead in the NAS market, but the rise in popularity of the relatively inexpensive devices attracted a host of competitors. Never content to cede market share for any storage offering, industry leader EMC sells NAS products. Companies such as Sun Microsystems have used acquisitions to crack the market, and even Dell, which once resold NetApp products, now makes its own NAS devices (Dell is one of a number of companies that make Microsoft Windows-based NAS products).

However, NetApp has expanded beyond the role of pure-play NAS vendor. Responding to customer demand, it expanded the functionality of its storage filers to work within more complex SAN configurations. The company also provides data security appliances and controllers for storage virtualization. At the beginning of 2008 NetApp acquired storage resource management specialist Onaro. The purchase gave NetApp software that enterprises use to optimize storage service levels.

In 2009 NetApp made a failed attempt to acquire storage system maker Data Domain. After a two-month-long bidding war, rival EMC eventually won the battle after offering $2.4 billion in cash for the company. NetApp had previously won the bid with a $1.9 billion cash and stock offer but subsequently backed out after EMC's counteroffer was approved by Data Domain's board.

HISTORY

David Hitz and James Lau (both EVPs) along with Michael Malcolm founded Network Appliance (NetApp) in 1992. The trio saw a market for file servers, hardware that takes the storage duties out of high-performance UNIX-based computers and speeds data flow.

Donald Valentine of Sequoia Capital invested in Network Appliance in 1994, and was named chairman. He promptly brought on board as CEO Daniel Warmenhoven, the top executive of telecommunications company Network Equipment Technologies. (It was the return of a favor — Warmenhoven had given Valentine a tip on investing in a late-1980s fledgling named Cisco.) Warmenhoven ditched the company's network of resellers and built an in-house sales and marketing unit. Network Appliance went public in 1995.

The company in 1996 forged a deal with Microsoft to let Network Appliance's file servers support the software giant's Internet-based network file storage standard. The beefed-up sales emphasis helped the company turn its first profit in fiscal 1996. The next year it bought online caching software specialist IMC. Acquisition costs dropped earnings for fiscal 1997.

Network Appliance furthered its inroads into Europe the next year when it sold data storage and retrieval equipment to UK-based Internet service provider Demon Internet. In 1999 the company introduced servers that transmitted audio and video data streams.

Network Appliance acquired two software companies in 2000: Orca Systems (Windows NT and UNIX systems clustering) and WebManage Technologies (data management and distribution). Responding to a slumping economy the following year, the company announced a restructuring plan that included job cuts.

Early in 2004 it acquired Spinnaker Networks for approximately $300 million in stock. The following year it acquired tape emulation software maker Alacritus for about $11 million in cash, and network security appliance maker Decru for $272 million in cash and stock.

In 2006 Network Appliance sold its NetCache content delivery business to Blue Coat Systems. Late in 2006 Network Appliance acquired data management software developer Topio for about $160 million in cash.

In 2008 Network Appliance officially changed its name to NetApp.

EXECUTIVES

Chairman: Daniel J. (Dan) Warmenhoven, age 57, $5,907,776 total compensation
Vice Chairman: Thomas F. (Tom) Mendoza, age 58, $2,403,321 total compensation
President, CEO, and Director: Thomas (Tom) Georgens, age 49, $2,917,819 total compensation
EVP Finance and CFO: Steven J. (Steve) Gomo, age 57, $1,360,004 total compensation
SVP and CIO: Marina Levinson
SVP and CTO: Brian Pawlowski
EVP and Chief Strategy Officer: James K. Lau, age 50
SVP and Chief Scientist: Steve Kleiman
Chief Marketing Officer: John A. (Jay) Kidd
EVP: David Hitz, age 46
EVP, NetApp Global Services: Ed Deenihan
EVP Field Operations: Robert E. (Rob) Salmon, age 48, $2,762,119 total compensation

SVP Worldwide Sales: D. Patrick (Pat) Linehan
SVP Operations: Mark Jon Bluth
SVP Product Operations: Manish Goel
SVP Human Resources: Gwendolyn (Gwen) McDonald
SVP Business Operations: Tom Gerstenberger
SVP Tax and Legal, Secretary, and General Counsel:
  Andrew Kryder
SVP Americas Sales: Eric Mann
Director Corporate Public Relations: Jodi Baumann
Senior Director Investor Relations: Tara Dhillon
Auditors: Deloitte & Touche LLP

LOCATIONS

HQ: NetApp, Inc.
  495 E. Java Dr., Sunnyvale, CA 94089
Phone: 408-822-6000   Fax: 408-822-4501
Web: www.netapp.com

2009 Sales

	$ mil.	% of total
US	1,753.6	51
Germany	357.6	11
Other countries	1,295.2	38
Total	**3,406.4**	**100**

PRODUCTS/OPERATIONS

2009 Sales

	$ mil.	% of total
Products	2,152.7	61
Services	764.1	22
Software entitlements & maintenance	618.3	17
Adjustments	(128.7)	—
Total	**3,406.4**	**100**

Selected Products

Hardware
  Fabric-attached storage (FAS)
  Near-line (NearStore)
  Security (DataFort)
  Virtualized (V-Series)
Software
  Data protection and management
  Operating system (Data ONTAP)

COMPETITORS

Data Domain
Dell
EMC
Hewlett-Packard
Hitachi Data Systems
IBM
Isilon Systems
LSI Corp.
Microsoft
Quantum Corporation
Sun Microsystems
Xiotech

HISTORICAL FINANCIALS

Company Type: Public

Income Statement

FYE: April 30

	REVENUE ($ mil.)	NET INCOME ($ mil.)	NET PROFIT MARGIN	EMPLOYEES
4/09	3,406.4	86.5	2.5%	7,976
4/08	3,303.2	309.7	9.4%	7,645
4/07	2,804.3	297.7	10.6%	6,635
4/06	2,066.5	266.5	12.9%	4,976
4/05	1,598.1	225.8	14.1%	3,801
Annual Growth	**20.8%**	**(21.3%)**	**—**	**20.4%**

2009 Year-End Financials

Debt ratio: 76.1%   No. of shares (mil.): 336
Return on equity: 5.1%   Dividends
Cash ($ mil.): 1,494   Yield: 0.0%
Current ratio: 2.05   Payout: —
Long-term debt ($ mil.): 1,265   Market value ($ mil.): 6,140

Stock History

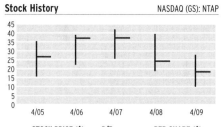

NASDAQ (GS): NTAP

	STOCK PRICE ($) FY Close	P/E High/Low		Earnings	PER SHARE ($) Dividends	Book Value
4/09	18.30	106	40	0.26	0.00	4.95
4/08	24.20	45	22	0.86	0.00	5.07
4/07	37.21	54	34	0.77	0.00	5.93
4/06	37.07	56	33	0.69	0.00	5.73
4/05	26.67	59	27	0.59	0.00	4.95
Annual Growth	**(9.0%)**	**—**	**—**	**(18.5%)**	**—**	**0.0%**

New York Life Insurance

New York Life Insurance has been in the Big Apple since it was just a tiny seed. The company (the top mutual life insurer in the US) is adding products but retaining its core business: life insurance and annuities. New York Life has added such products and services as mutual funds for individuals. It also offers its investment management services to institutional investors. Other lines of business include long-term care insurance and special group policies sold through AARP and other affinity groups or professional associations. The company, through New York Life International, is also reaching out geographically, targeting areas such as Mexico and India where the life insurance markets are not yet mature.

After state legislators rejected a proposed company restructuring, New York Life announced it would not follow its rivals in demutualizing for fear of being gobbled up in a merger.

The insurer instead uses its considerable war chest to further expand its international operations — Asia and Latin America are major expansion targets, and sales growth in both regions has been rapid. It is also expanding its investment management operations through its New York Life Investment Management (mutual funds, group and individual retirement plans, college savings products).

While other big-name insurers in the mature US market are only aiming for high net-worth individual customers, New York Life is also casting its nets a bit lower to catch middle-income consumers and creating products to lure younger families.

HISTORY

In 1841 actuary Pliny Freeman and 56 New York businessmen founded Nautilus Insurance Co., the third US policyholder-owned company. It began operating in 1845 and became New York Life in 1849.

By 1846 the company had the first life insurance agent west of the Mississippi River. Although the Civil War disrupted southern business, New York Life honored all its obligations and renewed lapsed policies when the war ended. By 1887 the company had developed its branch office system.

By the turn of the century, the company had established an agent compensation plan that featured a lifetime income after 20 years of service (discontinued 1991). New York Life moved into Europe in the late 1800s but withdrew after WWI.

In the early 1950s the company simplified insurance forms, slashed premiums, and updated mortality tables from the 1860s. In 1956 it became the first life insurer to use data-processing equipment on a large scale.

New York Life helped develop variable life insurance, which featured variable benefits and level premiums in the 1960s; it added variable annuities in 1968. Steady growth continued into the late 1970s, when high interest rates led to heavy policyholder borrowing. The outflow of money convinced New York Life to make its products more competitive as investments.

The company formed New York Life and Health Insurance Co. in 1982. It acquired MacKay-Shields Financial, which oversees its MainStay mutual funds, in 1984. The company's first pure investment product, a real estate limited partnership, debuted that year. (When limited partnerships proved riskier than most insurance customers bargained for, investors sued New York Life; in 1996 the company negotiated a plan to liquidate the partnerships and reimburse investors.)

Expansion continued in 1987 when New York Life bought a controlling interest in a third-party insurance plan administrator and group insurance programs. The company also acquired Sanus Corp. Health Systems.

New York Life formed an insurance joint venture in Indonesia in 1992; it also entered South Korea and Taiwan. The next year it bought Aetna UK's life insurance operations.

In 1994 New York Life grew its health care holdings, adding utilization review and physician practice management units. Allegations of churning (agents inducing customers to buy more expensive policies) led New York Life to overhaul its sales practices in 1994; it settled the resulting lawsuit for $300 million in 1995. Soon came claims that agents hadn't properly informed customers that some policies were vulnerable to interest-rate changes and that customers might be entitled to share in the settlement. Some agents lashed out, saying New York Life fired them so it wouldn't have to pay them retirement benefits.

As health care margins decreased and the insurance industry consolidated, New York Life in 1998 sold its health insurance operations and said it would demutualize — a plan ultimately foiled by the state legislature.

The company bought two Mexican insurance firms in 2000, including the nation's #2 life insurer, Seguros Monterrey. It received Office of Thrift Supervision permission to open a bank, New York Life Trust Company. Also that year the company created a subsidiary to house its asset management businesses and entered the Indian market through its joint venture with Max India. In 2002 New York Life entered into a joint life insurance venture with China's Haier Group.

EXECUTIVES

Chairman, President, and CEO:
Theodore A. (Ted) Mathas, age 42
Vice Chairman and Chief Investment Officer;
Chairman, New York Life Investment Management:
Gary E. Wendlandt, age 58
EVP and CFO: Michael E. Sproule
SVP and CIO: Eileen T. Slevin
SVP Corporate Information and CTO: Sue Ericksen
EVP, Chief Legal Officer, and General Counsel:
Sheila K. Davidson
EVP and Chief Administrative Officer: Frank M. Boccio
First VP and Chief Diversity Officer: Katherine O'Brien
SVP and Chief Actuary: Gary Scofield
EVP; Chairman and CEO, New York Life International:
Richard L. (Dick) Mucci, age 58
EVP; President and CEO, New York Life Investment Management: John Y. Kim, age 43
EVP US Life Insurance and Agency: Mark W. Pfaff
EVP and COO, New York Life International:
Russell G. Bundschuh
EVP and Chief Distribution Officer, New York Life International: Eric B. Campbell
SVP, General Auditor, and Chief Privacy Officer:
Thomas J. Warga
SVP, Deputy General Counsel, and Secretary:
Susan A. Thrope
SVP, Controller, and Chief Accounting Officer:
John A. Cullen
SVP and Senior Advisor to the President:
Solomon Goldfinger
SVP and General Cousel, New York Life International:
Maria G. Gutierrez
First VP Human Resources: Dorothea Rodd
Auditors: PricewaterhouseCoopers LLP

LOCATIONS

HQ: New York Life Insurance Company
51 Madison Ave., New York, NY 10010
Phone: 212-576-7000   **Fax:** 212-576-8145
Web: www.newyorklife.com

PRODUCTS/OPERATIONS

2008 Sales

	$ mil.	% of total
Premiums	10,647	52
Investment income	7,918	39
Fees	960	5
Investment losses	(3,496)	—
Other	801	4
Total	**16,830**	**100**

COMPETITORS

AIG American General
Allstate
American National Insurance
CIGNA
CNA Financial
Guardian Life
The Hartford
John Hancock Financial Services
MassMutual
MetLife
Mutual of Omaha
Northwestern Mutual
Principal Financial
Prudential
T. Rowe Price
TIAA-CREF
UBS Financial Services

HISTORICAL FINANCIALS

Company Type: Mutual company

Income Statement   FYE: December 31

	ASSETS ($ mil.)	NET INCOME ($ mil.)	INCOME AS % OF ASSETS	EMPLOYEES
12/08	188,908.0	(1,016.0)	—	15,000
12/07	198,383.0	1,497.0	0.8%	14,847
12/06	182,343.0	2,298.0	1.3%	13,580
12/05	168,865.0	855.0	0.5%	13,180
12/04	159,888.0	1,294.0	0.8%	12,650
Annual Growth	**4.3%**	**—**	**—**	**4.4%**

2008 Year-End Financials

Equity as % of assets: —   Long-term debt ($ mil.): —
Return on assets: —   Sales ($ mil.): 16,830
Return on equity: —

Net Income History

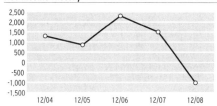

New York Times

"All the News That's Fit to Print, Broadcast, or Post Online" would be a more accurate motto for this media titan. The New York Times Company publishes one of the world's most respected newspapers, *The New York Times* (more than 1 million weekday circulation), as well as large Massachusetts papers *The Boston Globe* and the *Worcester Telegram & Gazette*. It also owns International Herald Tribune, which publishes its eponymous newspaper for English readers in 180 countries. The New York Times Company publishes news online through NYTimes.com and other sites, and it owns online content portal About Group. Chairman Arthur Sulzberger and his family control the company through a trust.

Owning one of the most venerated mastheads in the newspaper business has not spared The New York Times Company from the downward trends in readership and advertising that plague the rest of the industry. Circulation has been down at its flagship paper and its mainstay Boston paper for the past few years while ad sales have been flat to declining across the board. In order to keep revenue from spiraling downward, the company has increased its cover prices and subscription rates.

In order to make ends meet, however, The New York Times Company has had to cut costs and dispose of some non-core assets. The company shuttered its distribution subsidiary that delivered more than 220 publications throughout the greater New York area. The New York Times Company also agreed in 2009 to sell its WQXR classical music station to Hispanic broadcaster Univision Communications. In an effort to cut costs at *The Boston Globe,* the company let go more than 10% of that paper's news staff in 2009.

The crisis that hit the credit markets in 2008 forced The New York Times Company to scramble for needed capital. The company mortgaged its Manhattan headquarters building that year, borrowing about $225 million. The *Times* also started selling banner ads on its front page and the company is looking to sell its nearly 20% stake in New England Sports Ventures, a joint venture that owns the Boston Red Sox baseball team and 80% of cable channel New England Sports Network.

The company raised $250 million from Carlos Slim Helú in 2009 through Inmobiliaria Carso (his family-controlled trust) and Grupo Financiero Inbursa. The deal made the Mexican billionaire the third-largest shareholder in the company after Sulzberger and Harbinger Capital Partners. Carlos Slim and his family control Mexico's #1 telecommunications provider Teléfonos de México (Telmex) and retail holding company Grupo Carso.

The company has also been making investments in digital media. Its primary news destination, nytimes.com, serves a growing audience of about 20 million visitors and online revenue has increased rapidly thanks to its 2005 acquisition of About from PRIMEDIA for $410 million. The company has been adding more video content and social media features to its Web operations to help drive additional traffic.

HISTORY

In 1851 George Jones and Henry Raymond, former *New York Tribune* staffers, started *The New York Times*. The politically minded paper lost ground to the yellow journalism of Hearst and Pulitzer and was bought in 1896 by Tennessee newspaperman Adolph Ochs, who continued to encourage hard news and business coverage. Ochs coined the newspaper's now-famous slogan, "All the News That's Fit to Print."

Ochs' son-in-law Arthur Hays Sulzberger, who ran the paper from 1935 to 1961, diversified the company with the 1944 purchase of two New York City radio stations. In 1963 Ochs' grandson Arthur Ochs "Punch" Sulzberger took control of the company.

In the 1960s declining ad revenues and a newspaper strike sent the company into the red. To regain strength, Punch built the largest news-gathering staff of any newspaper. The *Times'* coverage of the Vietnam War helped change public sentiment, and the newspaper won a Pulitzer Prize in 1972 for publishing the Pentagon Papers. In the meantime Punch had taken the company public (1967), although the family retained solid control. In the late 1960s and 1970s the company began co-publishing the *International Herald Tribune* (1967, with The Washington Post) and bought magazines, publishing houses, TV stations, smaller newspapers, and cable TV systems. In the 1980s the *Times* added feature sections to compete with suburban papers. The company bought *Golf World* in 1988, and the next year sold its cable systems.

Arthur Ochs Sulzberger Jr. succeeded his father as *Times* publisher in 1992. The next year The New York Times bought Affiliated Publications, owner of *The Boston Globe,* for $1.1 billion. In 1997 chairman and CEO Punch Sulzberger retired from executive duties but remained on the board as chairman emeritus. He was replaced by his son as chairman, and non-family member Russell Lewis as CEO.

Journalistic integrity took a nosedive at *The Boston Globe* in mid-1998: Within a span of two months the newspaper demanded the resignations of reporter Patricia Smith after she admitted to making up people and quotes for several stories, and columnist Mike Barnicle after he included jokes from a book by George Carlin in his column without attribution.

In 2001 the company was part of a group of investors calling themselves New England Sports Ventures, which bought the Boston Red Sox, Fenway Park, and cable network New England Sports Network.

Punch Sulzberger retired from the company's board in 2001, but he retained the titles of chairman emeritus of The Times Company and of co-chairman of the *International Herald Tribune*. His daughter, Cathy J. Sulzberger, replaced him on the board.

At the close of the company's 2004 fiscal year, Lewis announced his retirement as president, CEO, and director; former COO Janet Robinson was named his successor.

In 2005 the company acquired online information portal About.com from PRIMEDIA, and it bought a 49% stake in free daily paper *Metro Boston* (owned by Metro International). About 200 employees were laid off to help contain costs in the face of declining newspaper ad revenue. A further 250 jobs were cut the next year.

Also in 2006, The New York Times Company acquired entertainment industry information provider Baseline StudioSystems from Hollywood Media Corp. The New York Times Company further trimmed its non-core assets the following year, selling nine TV stations to Oak Hill Capital Partners for $575 million.

EXECUTIVES

Chairman; Publisher, The New York Times: Arthur O. Sulzberger Jr., age 57, $2,415,874 total compensation
Vice Chairman: Michael Golden, age 59, $1,613,639 total compensation
President, CEO, and Director: Janet L. Robinson, age 58, $5,578,451 total compensation
SVP and CFO: James M. Follo, age 49, $853,571 total compensation
SVP and CIO: Joseph N. Seibert, age 49
SVP Corporate Communications: Catherine J. Mathis
SVP Process Engineering: Stuart P. (Stu) Stoller
SVP, General Counsel, and Secretary: Kenneth A. (Ken) Richieri, age 57
SVP Corporate Development: James C. Lessersohn
SVP Digital Operations: Martin A. Nisenholtz, age 53
SVP Finance and Corporate Controller: R. Anthony (Tony) Benten, age 45
SVP Human Resources: David K. Norton, age 53
SVP Marketing and Circulation, New York Times Media Group: Yasmin Namini, age 49
VP Research and Development Operations: Michael Zimbalist
VP and Treasurer: Laurena L. Emhoff, age 39
VP Human Resources: Michael (Mike) Valentine
President and General Manager, The New York Times: Scott H. Heekin-Canedy, age 57, $2,130,990 total compensation
Publisher, The Globe: P. Steven Ainsley, age 56, $1,947,195 total compensation
Auditors: Ernst & Young LLP

LOCATIONS

HQ: The New York Times Company
620 8th Ave., New York, NY 10018
Phone: 212-556-1234   **Fax:** 212-556-7389
Web: www.nytco.com

PRODUCTS/OPERATIONS

2008 Sales

	$ mil.	% of total
Advertising	1,779.7	60
Circulation	910.2	31
Other	259.0	9
Total	**2,948.9**	**100**

2008 Sales

	$ mil.	% of total
New York Times Media Group	1,925.6	65
New England Media Group	523.6	18
Regional Media Group	384.4	13
About Group	115.3	4
Total	**2,948.9**	**100**

Selected Operations

The New York Times Media Group
  International Herald Tribune (Paris)
  The New York Times
  NYTimes.com
  Other
    Digital Archive Distribution (database licensing)
    The New York Times Index
    The New York Times News Services (news syndication)
    WQXR-FM (New York City)
New England Media Group
  Newspapers
    The Boston Globe
    Worcester Telegram & Gazette (Massachusetts)
  Online content
    Boston.com
    Telegram.com
Regional Media Group
  The Courier (Houma, LA)
  Daily Comet (Thibodaux, LA)
  The Dispatch (Lexington, NC)
  The Gadsden Times (Alabama)
  The Gainesville Sun (Florida)
  Herald-Journal (Spartanburg, SC)
  The Ledger (Lakeland, FL)
  Petaluma Argus-Courier (weekly, California)
  The Press Democrat (Santa Rosa, CA)
  Sarasota Herald-Tribune (Florida)
  Star-Banner (Ocala, FL)
  Times-News (Hendersonville, NC)
  The Tuscaloosa News (Alabama)
  Wilmington Star-News (North Carolina)
About Group (online content)

Other operations and investments
  Donohue Malbaie (49%, newsprint manufacturing, Canada)
  Madison Paper Industries (40%, Maine)
  Metro Boston (49%, fee daily newspaper)
  New England Sports Ventures (17%)
    Boston Red Sox (Major League Baseball franchise)
    Fenway Park (sports stadium)
    New England Sports Network (80%, regional cable broadcasting)
    Roush Fenway Racing (50%, NASCAR racing team)

COMPETITORS

Advance Publications
Agence France-Presse
BBC
Daily News
Financial Times
Gannett
Hearst Newspapers
Herald Media
MSN
News Corp.
Newsday
Tribune Company
Washington Post
Wikimedia Foundation
Yahoo!

HISTORICAL FINANCIALS

Company Type: Public

Income Statement

FYE: Last Sunday in December

	REVENUE ($ mil.)	NET INCOME ($ mil.)	NET PROFIT MARGIN	EMPLOYEES
12/08	2,948.9	(57.8)	—	9,346
12/07	3,195.1	208.7	6.5%	10,231
12/06	3,289.9	(543.4)	—	11,585
12/05	3,372.8	265.6	7.9%	11,965
12/04	3,303.6	292.6	8.9%	12,300
Annual Growth	**(2.8%)**	**—**	**—**	**(6.6%)**

2008 Year-End Financials

Debt ratio: 115.2%
Return on equity: —
Cash ($ mil.): 57
Current ratio: 0.60
Long-term debt ($ mil.): 580
No. of shares (mil.): 144
Dividends
Yield: 10.2%
Payout: —
Market value ($ mil.): 1,059

Stock History

NYSE: NYT

	STOCK PRICE ($) FY Close	P/E High/Low		PER SHARE ($) Earnings	Dividends	Book Value
12/08	7.33	—	—	(0.40)	0.75	3.49
12/07	17.53	19	11	1.45	0.87	6.77
12/06	24.36	—	—	(3.76)	0.69	5.67
12/05	26.45	23	15	1.78	0.65	10.49
12/04	40.80	25	20	1.96	0.61	9.69
Annual Growth	**(34.9%)**	**—**	**—**	**—**	**5.3%**	**(22.5%)**

Newell Rubbermaid

Newell Rubbermaid wants to get its products into your drawers, your kitchen cabinets, and your workbench. It makes housewares (Rubbermaid plastic products, Calphalon cookware), hardware (Amerock cabinet hardware, IRWIN and Lenox hand tools), home furnishings (Levolor blinds), juvenile products (Graco), hair products (Goody), and office products (DYMO, Sanford, Sharpie). Newell Rubbermaid sells its products primarily to mass retailers and home and office supply stores. The firm bought label product maker DYMO from Esselte Corporation in 2005 and sold Newell Cookware Europe to Arc in 2006.

The company's reorganization plan, referred to as Project Acceleration (PA), is being expanded and is expected to be fully implemented in 2010. PA aims to strengthen and transform the consumer products maker's portfolio. Citing rising resin costs, Newell Rubbermaid is targeting resin-intensive products for downsizing or elimination. Actions taken under PA have included cutting some 5,000 employees from its workforce of 31,000 and shuttering a third of its 80 factories. Newell Rubbermaid also sold portions of its Home Decor Europe business to window-coverings giant Hunter Douglas. The sale included businesses in Portugal and the Nordic, Central, and Eastern European regions. (Previously, the company sold its Home Decor operations in the UK.)

Another facet of the restructuring is to boost spending significantly on specific areas of its business, including marketing (and building its brands), R&D (developing new products), and "international growth opportunities" (strengthening its business portfolio). To serve the latter purpose, the company in April 2008 acquired Technical Concepts, an Illinois-based firm that makes restroom hygiene systems for the away-from-home (AFH) market. The deal strengthens Newell Rubbermaid's commercial products business and boosts its position worldwide in the AFH washroom category.

In recent years Newell Rubbermaid has been whittling down its businesses and concentrating on core competencies. The company sold its pre-school toys business, Little Tikes, to MGA Entertainment (maker of the Bratz line of dolls) in late 2006. It also sold off three of its businesses (Anchor Hocking Glass, Burnes Picture Frame, and Mirro Cookware) to Global Home Products, LLC, for an estimated $320 million, as well as its Curver division (European indoor organization and home storage business) to Jardin International Holding.

HISTORY

Businessmen in Ogdensburg, New York, advanced curtain rod maker W.F. Linton Co. $1,000 to relocate from Rhode Island in the early 1900s. Local wholesaler Edgar Newell signed off on the loan; when the company went bankrupt in 1903, he was forced to take over. The company, renamed Newell Manufacturing, set up plants in Canada and Freeport, Illinois, to ease shipping costs and speed delivery.

Production expanded into towel racks, ice picks, and other items; Woolworth's decision to carry Newell's products turned the company into a national supplier. Edgar Newell died in 1920. The company made its first acquisition in 1938, window treatment specialist Drapery Hardware.

The Newell companies were consolidated in the mid-1960s into a single corporation. Daniel Ferguson was named president in 1965 and served alongside his CEO father Leonard, one of Newell's original employees. During his tenure, Daniel hitched the company's future to the growing dominance of large discount stores. Newell went from a $14 million family business to a global, multiline conglomerate by acquiring products that it distributed to these big buyers. The company went public in 1972 and bought paint applicator maker EZ Paintr the next year. By 1978 sales reached $100 million.

Newell moved into housewares with the acquisitions of Mirro (cookware, 1983) and the much larger Anchor Hocking (glassware, 1987). It then bought office supply companies W.T. Rogers and Keene Manufacturing in 1991 and Sanford (writing instruments) in 1992. That year Daniel bowed out of active management.

The company began a global push with its purchase of Corning's European Consumer Products business (1994), and it kept busy at home by buying Insilco's Rolodex unit and Rubbermaid's office products business (both 1997). William Sovey succeeded Daniel as chairman in 1997, and

John McDonough became CEO. Its 1998 acquisitions included Calphalon (upscale cookware), Panex (Brazil, bakeware), and Rotring Group (Germany, writing instruments).

Originally a balloon maker in the 1920s, by the mid-1930s Ohio's Wooster Rubber had acquired the Rubbermaid product line of rubber housewares. It went public in 1955 and two years later changed its name to Rubbermaid. During the 1980s the company enjoyed a decade of phenomenal growth. However — despite product innovations — increased material costs, a competitive retail climate, and weak customer service began dulling Rubbermaid's luster. Profits plunged even as it reached record sales.

Newell's $6 billion purchase of Rubbermaid in 1999 sealed its biggest deal yet and resulted in a name change: Newell Rubbermaid. Also that year Newell Rubbermaid bought the consumer products division of McKechnie (window furnishings and cabinet hardware) and three French firms: Ateliers 28 (drapery hardware), Reynolds (pens and pencils), and Ceanothe Holdings (picture frames).

In late 2000 CEO McDonough resigned and Sovey replaced him. In 2001 Newell Rubbermaid acquired Gillette's stationery business, including the Parker, Paper Mate, Liquid Paper, and Waterman brands. The same month Joseph Galli succeeded Sovey as CEO; Sovey reassumed his position as chairman (and left in mid-2004).

In 2003 Newell Rubbermaid acquired American Saw & Manufacturing for $450 million in cash, and then sold its Cosmolab business to CSI East, an affiliate of Cosmetic Specialties. The same year Newell Rubbermaid moved its corporate headquarters from Illinois to Alpharetta, Georgia (relocated again in 2004 to Atlanta).

In April 2004 Newell sold its Anchor Hocking Glass, Burnes Picture Frame, and Mirro Cookware divisions to Global Home Products, LLC.

To add depth to its office products portfolio the company acquired the DYMO brand from Esselte in late 2005 for $730 million.

CEO Joseph Galli resigned in October 2005. A board member with three decades of experience at Procter & Gamble, Mark Ketchum stepped in as interim CEO. He was made permanent in February 2006.

In a move that expanded the company's juvenile products business and positioned it to expand in Asia, Newell Rubbermaid acquired Japan's Aprica Kassai, a maker of strollers, car seats, and other children's gear, in April 2008.

EXECUTIVES

Chairman: William D. Marohn, age 69
President, CEO, and Director; Interim President Cleaning, Organization, and Decor: Mark D. Ketchum, age 59, $5,903,527 total compensation
EVP and CFO: J. Patrick (Pat) Robinson, age 53, $1,688,967 total compensation
SVP Program Management and CIO: Gordon Steele, age 57
VP, Corporate Controller, and Chief Accounting Officer: John B. Ellis
EVP Human Resources and Corporate Communications: James M. (Jim) Sweet, age 56
SVP, General Counsel, and Corporate Secretary: Dale L. Matschullat, age 63
SVP Marketing and Brand Management: Ted Woehrle, age 48
Group VP Finance, Tools and Hardware: Ronald L. Hardnock, age 37
VP Investor Relations: Nancy O'Donnell
VP Global Licensing: Nathaniel S. (Nat) Milburn, age 36

VP Supply Chain, Home and Family Group: Chris Van Dyke
VP Business Planning and Analysis: Rick T. Dillon
VP Marketing, Food Service Products Global Business Unit: Steve Pawl
VP E-Business and Interactive Marketing: Bert DuMars
VP Corporate Communications: David Doolittle
President, Asia Pacific and EMEA: Magnus R. Nicolin, age 52, $1,487,217 total compensation
Auditors: Ernst & Young LLP

LOCATIONS

HQ: Newell Rubbermaid Inc.
3 Glenlake Pkwy., Atlanta, GA 30328
Phone: 770-418-7000   **Fax:** 770-407-3970
Web: www.newellrubbermaid.com

2008 Sales

	$ mil.	% of total
US	4,447.2	70
Canada	413.4	6
Europe	996.0	15
Central & South America	275.4	4
Other regions	338.6	5
Total	**6,470.6**	**100**

PRODUCTS/OPERATIONS

2008 Sales

	$ mil.	% of total
Cleaning, organization & décor	2,147.3	33
Office products	2,005.8	31
Tools & hardware	1,200.3	19
Home & family	1,117.2	17
Total	**6,470.6**	**100**

Selected Brands and Trade Names

Cleaning, Organization, and Decor
  Brute
  Kirsch
  Levolor
  Roughneck
  Rubbermaid
  TakeAlongs
  TC

Office Products
  Accent
  Berol
  DYMO
  Eberhard Farber
  Expo
  Liquid Paper
  Paper Mate
  Parker
  rotring
  Sharpie
  Uni-Ball (under license)
  Vis-à-vis
  Waterman

Tools and Hardware
  Amerock
  BernzOmatic
  Bulldog
  Irwin
  Lenox
  Quick-Grip
  Marathon
  Shur-Line
  Strait-Line
  Unibit
  Vise-Grip

Home and Family
  Ace
  Aprica
  Calphalon
  Calphalon One
  Cooking with Calphalon
  Goody
  Graco
  Katana
  Kitchen Essentials
  Solano
  Teutonia

HISTORICAL FINANCIALS

Company Type: Public

Income Statement

FYE: December 31

	REVENUE ($ mil.)	NET INCOME ($ mil.)	NET PROFIT MARGIN	EMPLOYEES
12/08	6,470.6	(52.3)	—	20,400
12/07	6,407.3	467.1	7.3%	22,000
12/06	6,201.0	385.0	6.2%	23,500
12/05	6,342.5	251.3	4.0%	27,900
12/04	6,748.4	(116.1)	—	31,100
Annual Growth	(1.0%)	—	—	(10.0%)

2008 Year-End Financials

Debt ratio: 131.2%
Return on equity: —
Cash ($ mil.): 275
Current ratio: 1.09
Long-term debt ($ mil.): 2,118

No. of shares (mil.): 278
Dividends
  Yield: 8.6%
  Payout: —
Market value ($ mil.): 2,716

Stock History

NYSE: NWL

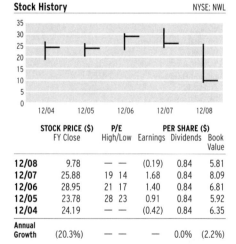

	STOCK PRICE ($) FY Close	P/E High/Low	PER SHARE ($) Earnings	Dividends	Book Value
12/08	9.78	— —	(0.19)	0.84	5.81
12/07	25.88	19 14	1.68	0.84	8.09
12/06	28.95	21 17	1.40	0.84	6.81
12/05	23.78	28 23	0.91	0.84	5.92
12/04	24.19	— —	(0.42)	0.84	6.35
Annual Growth	(20.3%)	— —	—	0.0%	(2.2%)

Newmont Mining

Newmont Mining certainly goes for the gold. The company is among the world's top gold producers (with Barrick ahead of AngloGold Ashanti and Gold Fields), following acquisitions in Canada, Bolivia, and Australia. Newmont produces some 6 million ounces of gold annually; it has proved and probable reserves of more than 85 million ounces of gold. Other metals that the company mines include copper, silver, and zinc. Operations in North America and South America account for about half of Newmont's production. It also has mining facilities in Australia, Indonesia, New Zealand, and Uzbekistan.

The company's North American operations include mines in Nevada's Carlin Trend, one of the largest gold-mining areas in North America. The company also has stakes in gold mines in Peru, Mexico, Uzbekistan, and Indonesia (Batu Hijau, a 45%-owned mine that produces both copper and gold). In 2008 it bought Canadian gold producer Miramar Mining for about $1.5 billion. The move came a few years after an initial acquisition of a 10% stake in Miramar, whose primary mining focus is the Nunavut Territory in far northern Canada. It also bought, in 2009, Anglogold Ashanti out of its one-third stake in the Australian Boddington mine for about $1 billion. The deal gave Newmont 100% of the Boddington project, Australia's largest gold mining property.

To weather price fluctuations, Newmont has tried to keep production costs low. The company has put off discretionary spending and remains largely unhedged, which enables it to profit from gold price increases but offers little protection from falling gold prices.

Once the clear #1 gold producing company in the world, Newmont now ranks behind Barrick following that company's 2006 acquisition of Placer Dome. In 2007 Newmont spun off its royalty assets as Franco-Nevada Corporation. Those assets had been acquired in 2002 and been operating since then as Newmont Mining Corporation of Canada. The spinoff was designed to allow the company to get the most value out of those investments as well as to concentrate on its in-progress mining operations.

Newmont's operations in Ghana consist of one operating mine and a development project; it sees the country as the site of its next big operating district.

HISTORY

Colonel William Boyce Thompson, a flamboyant trader, founded the Newmont Co. in 1916 to trade his various oil and mining stocks. The Newmont name was a combination of New York and Montana, where Thompson grew up. The company was renamed Newmont Corporation in 1921 and Newmont Mining Corporation in 1925, when it went public. Thompson died five years later. During its first 10 years, Newmont focused on investing and trading stocks in promising mineral properties, including US copper and gold mines.

Newmont's gold mines bolstered the company throughout the Depression. During the 1940s its focus shifted to copper and Africa. It bought Idarado Mining in 1943 and Newmont Oil in 1944 (sold 1988). The company grew during the 1950s by acquiring stakes in North American companies involved in offshore oil drilling, nickel mining, and uranium oxide production. It also bought stakes in copper mines in South Africa and South America.

Newmont started producing gold from the Carlin Trend in Nevada in the mid-1960s. It bought a one-third stake in Foote Mineral (iron alloys and lithium) in 1967; by 1974 it controlled 83% of the company (sold 1987). In 1969 Newmont merged with Magma Copper, one of the US's largest copper companies. A Newmont-led consortium bought Peabody Coal, the US's largest coal producer, from Kennecott Copper in 1977 (sold 1990).

After its 1980 discovery of one of the century's most important gold stakes, Gold Quarry in the Carlin Trend, Newmont spent a decade fending off takeover attempts. The company began selling off noncore operations to focus on gold. Magma Copper was spun off to stockholders in 1988.

A proposed merger with American Barrick Resources, a major stockholder, collapsed in 1991. Former Freeport-McMoRan VP Ronald Cambre became CEO in 1993, and that year the company began mining in Peru. A 1994 action by the French government, one of Newmont's partners in Peru's Yanacocha Mine, kicked off a protracted battle over the property's ownership. The claim was upheld in 1998, raising Newmont's stake to more than 50%. Reflecting its increasing interest in Indonesia, in 1996 Newmont and Japan's Sumitomo formed a joint venture to exploit gold reserves on Sumbawa Island. In 1997 the company increased its gold reserves and territory by acquiring Santa Fe Pacific Gold for about $2.1 billion.

For years Newmont and Barrick Gold Corporation operated interlocked mining claims in Nevada's Carlin Trend, which prevented optimal exploitation by either company. In 1999 both companies agreed to a mutually advantageous land swap in the region.

In 2000 an Indonesian court ordered the closure of the Minahasa mine over a local tax dispute; the company's joint venture agreed to pay a $500,000 penalty to settle the matter. Newmont was fined $500,000 after a mercury spill at its Yanacocha mine. That year Newmont settled the lingering ownership dispute over the Yanacocha.

Company president Wayne Murdy became CEO early in 2001 (he replaced Cambre as chairman in 2002). Newmont acquired Battle Mountain Gold in 2001 for nearly $600 million. Late that year Newmont moved to acquire Australia's top gold producer, Normandy Mining (setting off a bidding war with AngloGold), as well as Canadian gold miner France-Nevada Mining Corp. AngloGold bowed out of the "battle for Normandy" in early 2002, but later completed a three-way deal, in which it acquired Normandy and Franco-Nevada.

In 2003 Newmont reduced its stake in Kinross Gold from 14% to 5%, and it mulled selling off the Ghanaian interests it had gained in the Normandy merger. However, in 2004 Newmont literally discovered a gold mine in Ghana — a major district with some 16 million equity ounces of gold.

Murdy retired in 2007; taking the helm was former CEO Richard O'Brien. The next year the company acquired Miramar Mining, which controls the Hope Bay Project — a nearly 400 sq. mi. project that includes one of the largest undeveloped gold projects in North America.

EXECUTIVES

Chairman: Vincent A. Calarco, age 66
President, CEO, and Director: Richard T. O'Brien, age 53, $5,819,737 total compensation
EVP Operations: Brian Hill
EVP and CFO: Russell D. Ball, age 40, $1,720,767 total compensation
Controller and Chief Accounting Officer: Roger Johnson
EVP Development: Guy Lansdown, $1,739,678 total compensation
EVP Strategic Development: Randy Engel, $1,488,545 total compensation
EVP Legal and External Affairs: Alan R. Blank
SVP Human Resources: Darla Caudle
VP Environmental Affairs and Sustainable Development: David A. Baker
VP Exploration Business Development: Jeffrey R. Huspeni
VP North American Operations: Brant Hinze
VP South American Operations: Carlos E. Santa Cruz
VP and Treasurer: Thomas P. Mahoney
VP and Secretary: Sharon E. Thomas
VP Communications: Stephen P. Gottesfeld
VP Tax and Accounting: David V. Gutierrez
VP Technical Services: Gordon R. Nixon
VP Corporate Development: David R. Faley
General Counsel: Blake M. Rhodes
Auditors: PricewaterhouseCoopers LLP

LOCATIONS

HQ: Newmont Mining Corporation
6363 S. Fiddler's Green Cir.
Greenwood Village, CO 80111
Phone: 303-863-7414   **Fax:** 303-837-5837
Web: www.newmont.com

2008 Production

	% of total
US	31
Peru	26
Australia/New Zealand	17
Indonesia	16
Ghana	7
Other	3
Total	**100**

PRODUCTS/OPERATIONS

2008 Sales

	$ mil.	% of total
Gold	5,447	88
Copper	752	12
Total	**6,199**	**100**

Selected Operations

Empresa Minera Inti Raymi, SA (88%, Bolivia)
  Kori Kollo mine
Golden Giant mine (Canada)
Golden Grove (Australia)
Holloway mine (Canada)
La Herradura mine (44%, with Industriales Peñoles; Mexico)
Minera Yanacocha (51%, with Compañía de Minas Buenaventura and others; Peru)
Newmont Gold Co. (California and Nevada)
  Lone Tree mine
  Mesquite mine
  Midas mine
  Twin Creeks mine
Pajingo (Australia)
  Kalgoorlie
  Tanami
  Vera/Nancy mine (Australia)
  Yandal
P.T. Newmont Nusa Tenggara
  Batu Hijau mine (45% copper, Indonesia)
Zarafshan-Newmont (50%, with Uzbek government entities; Uzbekistan)

COMPETITORS

AngloGold Ashanti	Goldcorp
Barrick Gold	Harmony Gold
BHP Billiton	Hecla Mining
Freeport-McMoRan	Kinross Gold
Gold Fields	Rio Tinto Limited

HISTORICAL FINANCIALS

Company Type: Public

Income Statement

FYE: December 31

	REVENUE ($ mil.)	NET INCOME ($ mil.)	NET PROFIT MARGIN	EMPLOYEES
12/08	6,199.0	853.0	13.8%	15,450
12/07	5,526.0	(1,886.0)	—	15,000
12/06	4,987.0	791.0	15.9%	15,000
12/05	4,406.0	322.0	7.3%	15,000
12/04	4,524.2	490.5	10.8%	14,000
Annual Growth	**8.2%**	**14.8%**	**—**	**2.5%**

2008 Year-End Financials

Debt ratio: 47.5%
Return on equity: 11.6%
Cash ($ mil.): 435
Current ratio: 1.48
Long-term debt ($ mil.): 3,373
No. of shares (mil.): 480
Dividends
  Yield: 1.0%
  Payout: 21.4%
Market value ($ mil.): 19,525

Stock History

NYSE: NEM

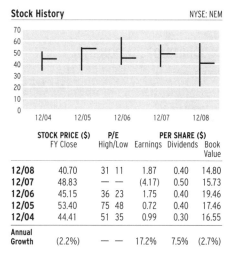

	STOCK PRICE ($) FY Close	P/E High/Low		PER SHARE ($) Earnings	Dividends	Book Value
12/08	40.70	31	11	1.87	0.40	14.80
12/07	48.83	—	—	(4.17)	0.50	15.73
12/06	45.15	36	23	1.75	0.40	19.46
12/05	53.40	75	48	0.72	0.40	17.46
12/04	44.41	51	35	0.99	0.30	16.55
Annual Growth	**(2.2%)**	**—**	**—**	**17.2%**	**7.5%**	**(2.7%)**

News Corporation

This News is heard, seen, and read all around the world. The world's #3 media conglomerate (behind Time Warner and Walt Disney), News Corporation has operations spanning film, television, and publishing. It produces and distributes movies through Fox Filmed Entertainment, while its FOX Broadcasting network boasts more than 200 affiliate stations in the US. The company also owns and operates more than 25 TV stations, as well as a portfolio of cable networks. Its publishing businesses include newspaper publishers Dow Jones (*The Wall Street Journal*) and News International (*The Times*, London), and book publisher HarperCollins. In addition, News Corporation owns about 40% of British Sky Broadcasting.

While the recession has put a damper on many advertising-supported media businesses, News Corporation has borne the brunt of the downturn due to its exposure to the weakened newspaper business. Its papers including *The Times* and the *New York Post* have been struggling for several years as readership and advertising have declined, but the company expanded its holdings in 2007 when it acquired Dow Jones for $5.6 billion. In response to the losses, News Corporation has been focused on cost-cutting measures throughout its newspaper operations, including layoffs and wage freezes.

The one bright spot among its mastheads has been *The Wall Street Journal*, which continues to show strong circulation figures in defiance of industry trends. A newspaper man at heart, Murdoch doggedly pursued Dow Jones and its controlling Bancroft family through a lengthy — and at times contested — negotiation process primarily to get his hands on the flagship title.

The recession has also been unkind to News Corporation's film and television units. Movies such as *Australia* and *The Happening* failed to score at the box office during 2008, undermining hits such as *Marley & Me* and *Slumdog Millionaire*. The company's studios managed to rebound during the 2009 summer blockbuster season with the *X-Men Origins: Wolverine* and animated *Ice Age: Dawn of the Dinosaurs*.

On television, News Corporation's FOX network finished second overall to CBS in the ratings for the 2008-09 season but was the most watched network among the all-important 18-49 age demographic. Despite the big ratings, FOX and the company's local TV stations have been hurt by declining ad revenue. The financial woes led News Corporation to start cutting production budgets and reducing jobs across its Fox Entertainment units during 2009.

News Corporation unloaded its 40% stake in direct broadcast satellite provider DIRECTV as part of a $10.1 billion asset swap with John Malone's Liberty Media holding company in 2008. The company traded the stake in DIRECTV along with three regional cable sports channels and $625 million for Liberty's 19% stake in News Corporation.

The company has also made significant investments to expand its digital and online media operations, including its more than 30% stake in video streaming site Hulu, a partnership with NBC Universal and Walt Disney. Most famously, though, was the company's acquisition of Intermix Media and its social networking site MySpace in 2005 for $580 million.

HISTORY

In 1952 Rupert Murdoch inherited two Adelaide, Australia, newspapers from his father. After launching the *Australian,* the country's first national daily, in 1964 Murdoch moved into the UK market. He bought tabloid *News of the World,* a London Sunday paper, in 1968, and London's *Sun* the next year. In 1973 Murdoch hit the US, buying the *San Antonio Express-News* and founding the *Star* tabloid. He followed this up in 1976 by buying the *New York Post.* Murdoch formed News Corporation in Australia in 1979.

Moving upmarket in 1981, Murdoch bought the London *Times* and 40% of Collins Publishers, a London book publisher. After buying the *Chicago Sun-Times* in 1983 (sold 1986), Murdoch bought 13 US travel, hotel, and aviation trade magazines from Ziff-Davis, as well as film studio Twentieth Century Fox in 1985. In 1986 Murdoch bought six Metromedia stations and launched FOX Broadcasting, the first new US TV network since 1948.

Print was not forgotten, however, and in the late 1980s News Corp. picked up US book publisher Harper & Row as well as Triangle Publications (*TV Guide* and other magazines). It also bought textbook publisher Scott, Foresman and the rest of Collins Publishers. (Harper & Row was later merged with Collins to form HarperCollins.)

In 1996 Murdoch launched the FOX News Channel, an all-news cable channel. In 1998 the company bought the Los Angeles Dodgers and stakes in the new Los Angeles-area Staples Center sports arena. (It sold its stake in the Staples Center in 2004.) Also that year News Corp. spun off part of Fox Entertainment in one of America's largest IPOs, raising $2.7 billion.

That year News Corp. sold *TV Guide* to Tele-Communications Inc.'s United Video Satellite Group (now Gemstar-TV Guide International) for $800 million in cash and a 21% stake. The company also bought the 50% of FOX/Liberty Networks (now FOX Sports Net) it didn't own and transferred ownership to Fox Entertainment. The deal gave John Malone's Liberty Media holding company an 8% stake (later 19%) in News Corp.

In 2001, along with partner Haim Saban, News Corp. sold the Fox Family Channel to Disney for about $5.2 billion. That year the FCC approved the company's $4.8 billion purchase of TV station group Chris-Craft. The deal gave News Corp. an additional 10 TV stations.

News Corp. in 2003 finally realized its dream of owning a chunk of DIRECTV when it bought 34% of Hughes Electronics, the satellite television company's parent, from General Motors. The following year, in an effort to make its stock more attractive to US investors, News Corp shifted its incorporation from Australia to the US. It also purchased the rest of Fox Entertainment that it didn't already own for $6.2 billion.

The company made another splash in the television industry when it launched MyNetworkTV in 2006. The startup network was established in response to rivals WB and UPN merging to form The CW Television Network. The following year News Corp. acquired newspaper giant Dow Jones and its flagship paper *The Wall Street Journal* for $5.6 billion.

EXECUTIVES

Chairman and CEO: K. Rupert Murdoch, age 77, $19,887,610 total compensation
Deputy Chairman, President, and COO: Chase Carey, age 55
SEVP, CFO, and Director; SEVP and CFO, News America and Fox Entertainment: David F. DeVoe, age 62, $7,824,564 total compensation
Chairman and CEO Digital Media and Chief Digital Officer: Jonathan F. (Jon) Miller, age 52
Chief Human Resources Officer: Beryl Cook, age 47
Chief Security Officer, News Corporation and MySpace.com: Hemanshu (Hemu) Nigam
SVP, Deputy General Counsel, and Chief Compliance and Ethics Officer: Genie Gavenchak
SEVP and Group General Counsel: Lawrence A. Jacobs, age 54
EVP Content: Anthea Disney, age 64
EVP Global Marketing and Corporate Affairs: Gary L. Ginsberg, age 47
EVP Government Affairs: Michael Regan
EVP Office of the Chairman: Jeremy Philips
SVP Investor Relations: Reed Nolte

Chairman and CEO, Europe and Asia and Director; Chairman, British Sky Broadcasting Group and News International: James R. Murdoch, age 36, $9,216,184 total compensation
CEO, Dow Jones; Publisher, The Wall Street Journal: Leslie F. (Les) Hinton
Chairman, FOX Sports Networks; President, DIRECTV Entertainment: David Hill
Chairman and CEO, Fox Networks: Anthony J. (Tony) Vinciquerra, age 54
Co-Chairman, Fox Filmed Entertainment: Thomas E. (Tom) Rothman
Co-Chairman, Fox Filmed Entertainment: James N. (Jim) Gianopulos
Chairman and CEO, News Limited: John Hartigan
Chairman and CEO, FOX News Channel; Chairman, Fox Television Stations and Twentieth Television: Roger Ailes, age 69, $23,683,140 total compensation
Auditors: Ernst & Young LLP

LOCATIONS

HQ: News Corporation
1211 Avenue of the Americas, New York, NY 10036
Phone: 212-852-7000   **Fax:** 212-852-7147
Web: www.newscorp.com

2009 Sales

	$ mil.	% of total
US & Canada	16,686	55
Europe	9,331	31
Australia, Asia & other regions	4,406	14
Total	**30,423**	**100**

PRODUCTS/OPERATIONS

2009 Sales

	$ mil.	% of total
Filmed entertainment	5,936	20
Newspapers & inserts	5,858	19
Cable network programming	5,580	18
Television	4,602	15
Direct broadcast satellite	3,760	12
Magazines & inserts	1,168	4
Book publishing	1,141	4
Other	2,378	8
Total	**30,423**	**100**

Selected Operations

Filmed entertainment
  Feature film production and distribution
    Fox Filmed Entertainment
      Fox Searchlight Pictures
      Twentieth Century Fox
      Twentieth Century Fox Animation
      Twentieth Century Fox Home Entertainment
  Television production and distribution
    Fox Television Studios
    Twentieth Century Fox Television
    Twentieth Television
Newspapers
  Dow Jones
    Consumer media
      Barron's
      The Wall Street Journal
    Dow Jones Local Media Group
      Dow Jones Financial Information Services
      Dow Jones Indexes (stock market data)
      Dow Jones Licensing Services
      Dow Jones Newswires
      Factiva (news and business research)
  New York Post
  News International Limited (UK)
    News of the World
    The Sun
    The Sunday Times
    The Times
  News Limited (Australia)

Cable network programming
  Big Ten Network (49%)
  Fox Business Network
  Fox College Sports
  Fox International Channels
    LAPTV (32%, Latin American pay television)
  Fox Movie Channel
  Fox News Channel
  Fox Pan American Sports (33%)
  Fox Sports Net
  FUEL TV
  FX
  National Geographic Channel (67%, cable channel)
  SPEED
Television
  FOX Broadcasting
  Fox Television Stations
  MyNetworkTV
  Star Group (international televison broadcasting, Asia)
Direct broadcast satellite
  British Sky Broadcasting (39%, UK)
  Sky Deutschland (40%, Germany)
  SKY Italia
Magazines and inserts
  Magazine publishing
  News America Marketing Group (insert publications and in-store marketing)
Book publishing
  HarperCollins Publishers
Other operations and investments
  Fox Interactive Media
    Fox.com
    FoxSports.com
    MySpace.com
    Scout.com
  FOXTEL (25%, cable television system, Australia)
  Hulu (32%, online video)
  NDS Group (49%, pay-TV technology and software, UK)
  News Outdoor Group (outdoor advertising)
  SkyNZ (44%, direct broadcast satellite service, New Zealand)

COMPETITORS

Advance Publications	New York Times
Bertelsmann	Pearson plc
Bloomberg L.P.	Reed Elsevier Group
CBS Corp	Sony Pictures
Disney	Thomson Reuters
Gannett	Time Warner
Hearst Corporation	Tribune Company
MGM	Viacom
NBC Universal	Washington Post

HISTORICAL FINANCIALS

Company Type: Public

Income Statement

FYE: Sunday nearest June 30

	REVENUE ($ mil.)	NET INCOME ($ mil.)	NET PROFIT MARGIN	EMPLOYEES
6/09	30,423.0	(3,378.0)	—	55,000
6/08	32,996.0	5,387.0	16.3%	64,000
6/07	28,655.0	3,426.0	12.0%	53,000
6/06	25,327.0	3,327.0	13.1%	47,300
6/05	23,859.0	2,128.0	8.9%	—
Annual Growth	**6.3%**	**—**	**—**	**5.2%**

2009 Year-End Financials

Debt ratio: 52.5%
Return on equity: —
Cash ($ mil.): 6,540
Current ratio: 1.49
Long-term debt ($ mil.): 12,204

No. of shares (mil.): 2,614
Dividends
  Yield: 1.1%
  Payout: —
Market value ($ mil.): 27,633

Stock History

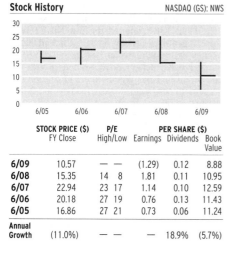

	STOCK PRICE ($) FY Close	P/E High/Low		PER SHARE ($) Earnings	Dividends	Book Value
6/09	10.57	—	—	(1.29)	0.12	8.88
6/08	15.35	14	8	1.81	0.11	10.95
6/07	22.94	23	17	1.14	0.10	12.59
6/06	20.18	27	19	0.76	0.13	11.43
6/05	16.86	27	21	0.73	0.06	11.24
Annual Growth	(11.0%)	—	—	—	18.9%	(5.7%)

Nicor Inc.

Nicor heats the hearths of the Heartland and carries cargo in the Caribbean. The holding company's principal subsidiary, gas utility Northern Illinois Gas (doing business as Nicor Gas), has 34,000 miles of mains and service pipes that distribute natural gas to about 2.2 million residential, commercial, and industrial customers in Illinois, excluding the city of Chicago; it obtains its supply through long-term contracts and on the spot market. Nicor Gas also operates the Chicago Hub, which provides natural gas storage and transmission-related services to marketers and other gas distribution companies. Nicor also ships container cargo through its Florida-based Tropical Shipping subsidiary.

In response to electric utility deregulation in Illinois and nearby states and to hedge its bets by diversification beyond its natural gas utility base.

Its Tropical Shipping unit owns or charters 17 ships that primarily transport freight between Florida and about 30 Caribbean locations; it also has routes to other locations in the Americas, Europe, and Asia.

Nicor has been pursuing other non-utility businesses. Subsidiary Nicor Enerchange markets and trades wholesale gas; other Nicor subsidiaries offer energy-related retail services and pipeline operations. The company sold its 50% stake in construction services firm EN Engineering, L.L.C. in 2009 in order to focus on its other businesses.

HISTORY

Nicor's history dates back to the 1850s, when one of its predecessors lit the Lincoln-Douglas debates by transporting gas through hollowed-out logs. By the early 1900s, it was transporting gas over longer distances in northern Illinois. Over the next half-century, the region's gas and electric companies were united in the Public Service Co. of Northern Illinois.

Utility Commonwealth Edison bought the company in 1953 and the next year created subsidiary Northern Illinois Gas to operate the gas business. In 1955 Northern Illinois Gas was spun off, and it immediately purchased Union Gas &

Electric. A few years later, it built the world's largest underground storage system.

The utility enlarged its service area in the 1960s and began drilling for its own gas with mediocre results. When the energy crisis of the early 1970s began affecting the firm's gas deliveries, it increased gas production and built a synthetic gas plant. A 1974 general rate increase (the company's first in two decades), coupled with cost-cutting measures, helped relieve financial pressures.

To diversify beyond the utility business, Northern Illinois Gas formed holding company Nicor in 1976. Over the next few years Nicor bought coal reserves, oil leases, a drilling company, an inland barge business, and an offshore drilling services company. Nicor also acquired Caribbean shipper Tropical Shipping in 1982. When the energy bust of the 1980s hit, Nicor's diversification program lost its momentum; the company unloaded most of its purchases but kept Tropical Shipping.

The company took another, more cautious, stab at diversifying in 1992, when it began Nicor Energy Services to maintain and repair heating and air-conditioning equipment. In 1993 Northern Illinois Gas and gas wholesaler NGC (later named Dynegy) formed the Chicago Hub to provide various services to sellers and buyers of natural gas.

Nicor formed Nicor Technologies in 1994 to offer energy-related consulting services. Lower prices in the increasingly competitive natural gas market caused sales to fall. Nicor and NGC joined Pacific Enterprises (now Sempra Energy) and National Fuel Gas in 1995 to form Enerchange, to manage the Chicago Hub and others in California and the Northeast.

Northern Illinois Gas was granted a 2.8% rate increase in 1996, its first in 14 years. That year Tropical Shipping expanded into the Cayman Islands, Jamaica, and Puerto Rico by purchasing Thompson Shipping. In 1997 Nicor and NGC formed Nicor Energy, which offered energy services to industrial and commercial customers in the US Midwest. Nicor also joined TransCanada PipeLines to build a pipeline between Illinois and Manitoba, Canada; however, the project was later scrapped. That year Northern Illinois Gas began doing business as Nicor Gas.

Nicor and Dynegy teamed up in 1998 to build natural gas-fired electric power plants in six Midwestern states; however, Nicor bailed out on its first joint project in 1999. Utility deregulation arrived in Illinois in 1999, and by early 2000 Nicor had more than 100,000 users in its customer choice program. Also that year Nicor announced plans with Texas-based pipeline company Kinder Morgan to build a 74-mile pipeline in Illinois, and construction activities commenced in 2001. (The pipeline was completed in 2002.)

Also in 2001 Nicor formed a pipeline engineering joint venture with A. Epstein & Sons, and Tropical Shipping acquired the container operations of Canadian firm Kent Line International.

Retail gas competition was implemented for all customers in Illinois in 2002.

Nicor and former partner Dynegy liquidated the assets of their Nicor Energy joint venture, which marketed gas and electricity to retail customers in the Midwest, due to heavy losses at the unit. (Several former Nicor Energy officers were indicted on charges of inflating the unit's 2001 earnings.)

Thomas Fisher stepped down as CEO in early 2005 and was replaced by Russ Strobel.

EXECUTIVES

Chairman, President, and CEO, Nicor and Nicor Gas: Russ M. Strobel, age 56, $2,922,617 total compensation
EVP and CFO, Nicor and Nicor Gas: Richard L. (Rick) Hawley, age 59, $1,203,014 total compensation
VP, Information Technology, Nicor and Nicor Gas: Barbara A. Zeller, age 54
EVP Diversified Ventures: Daniel R. Dodge, age 55, $843,740 total compensation
EVP Operations, Nicor Gas: Rocco J. D'Alessandro, age 50
SVP, Human Resources and Corporate Communications, Nicor and Nicor Gas: Claudia J. Colalillo, age 59, $793,238 total compensation
SVP, General Counsel, and Secretary, Nicor and Nicor Gas: Paul C. Gracey Jr., age 49
SVP Finance and Strategic Planning: Gerald P. O'Connor, age 57
VP and Treasurer, Nicor and Nicor Gas: Douglas M. Ruschau, age 50
VP Controller: Karen K. Pepping, age 44
VP Human Resources: Becky Bacidore
President and CEO, Tropical Shipping: Rick Murrell, age 60, $1,101,379 total compensation
Senior Manager Corporate Communications: Annette Martinez
Public Relations Manager: Richard Caragol
Director Investor Relations: Kary D. Brunner
Auditors: Deloitte & Touche LLP

LOCATIONS

HQ: Nicor Inc.
1844 Ferry Rd., Naperville, IL 60563
Phone: 630-305-9500 **Fax:** 630-983-9328
Web: www.nicor.com

Nicor subsidiary Nicor Gas distributes gas in northern Illinois, excluding the city of Chicago but including its suburbs. Subsidiary Tropical Shipping primarily transports freight between Florida and about 30 Caribbean locations; it also has routes to other locations in Asia, Europe, Latin America, and North America.

PRODUCTS/OPERATIONS

2008 Sales

	$ mil.	% of total
Gas distribution	3,206.9	83
Shipping	425.2	11
Other energy ventures	230.3	6
Adjustments	(85.8)	—
Total	**3,776.6**	**100**

Major Operations

Northern Illinois Gas Company (operates as Nicor Gas, gas utility)
Tropical Shipping (freight transportation between Florida and the Caribbean)

Other Selected Operations

Horizon Pipeline Co. LLC (50%, pipeline company, joint venture with Kinder Morgan)
Nicor Enerchange (energy trading)
Nicor Energy Services Company (Nicor Services, maintenance and repair for gas piping and HVAC equipment)
Nicor Solutions (energy-related financial and billing services)

COMPETITORS

AES	Duke Energy
Alliant Energy	Evergreen Marine
Ameren	Exelon
AmerenCILCO	Integrys Energy Group
AmerenIP	MidAmerican Energy
Commonwealth Edison	NiSource
Crowley Maritime	NRG Energy
DTE	Seaboard

HISTORICAL FINANCIALS

Company Type: Public

Income Statement

FYE: December 31

	REVENUE ($ mil.)	NET INCOME ($ mil.)	NET PROFIT MARGIN	EMPLOYEES
12/08	3,776.6	119.5	3.2%	3,900
12/07	3,176.3	135.2	4.3%	3,900
12/06	2,960.0	128.3	4.3%	3,900
12/05	3,357.8	136.3	4.1%	3,700
12/04	2,739.7	75.1	2.7%	3,600
Annual Growth	8.4%	12.3%	—	2.0%

2008 Year-End Financials

Debt ratio: 46.0%
Return on equity: 12.5%
Cash ($ mil.): 26
Current ratio: 0.80
Long-term debt ($ mil.): 448

No. of shares (mil.): 45
Dividends
 Yield: 5.4%
 Payout: 70.7%
Market value ($ mil.): 1,571

Stock History

NYSE: GAS

	STOCK PRICE ($) FY Close	P/E High/Low	PER SHARE ($) Earnings	Dividends	Book Value
12/08	34.74	20 12	2.63	1.86	21.52
12/07	42.35	18 13	2.99	1.86	20.90
12/06	46.80	17 13	2.87	1.86	19.30
12/05	39.31	14 12	3.07	1.86	17.94
12/04	36.94	23 19	1.70	1.86	16.57
Annual Growth	(1.5%)	— —	11.5%	0.0%	6.8%

NIKE, Inc.

Nike, the Greek goddess of victory, helped others succeed in times of war. NIKE, the world's #1 shoemaker, does more dominating than assisting, to capture a hefty share of the US athletic shoe market. It designs and sells shoes for a variety of sports, including baseball, cheerleading, golf, volleyball, hiking, tennis, and football. NIKE also sells Cole Haan dress and casual shoes, as well as athletic apparel and equipment. In addition, NIKE operates NIKETOWN shoe and sportswear stores, NIKE factory outlets, and NIKE Women shops, and sells its shoes and apparel online. Overall, it sells its sportswear in some 675 NIKE-owned retail stores in the US and abroad.

Nike acquired soccer star Umbro in 2008. The purchase of the UK-based global soccer brand, for about $576 million, provides NIKE with a firm foundation in soccer in the US and England and positions the company for growth in emerging soccer markets such as China, Russia, and Brazil. Umbro, which sells directly and through licensees, brings to the table high-profile sports marketing agreements with soccer players, teams, and leagues and offers its own global reach. NIKE operates Umbro as a separate brand.

Image-savvy NIKE sells its products through more than 23,000 retail accounts in the US and through independent distributors and licensees in other countries. In addition to Cole Haan, Converse (known for its classic and retro-style shoes, including the Chuck Taylor brand), and Umbro, other NIKE subsidiaries include Hurley International (sports apparel for skateboarding, snowboarding, and surfing). More than a dozen years after acquiring Bauer NIKE Hockey, NIKE sold the hockey unit in 2008 to a group of investors, including Kohlberg & Company and W. Graeme Roustan, for $200 million.

While the US accounts for about a third of NIKE's total revenue, domestic sales growth has slowed in recent years. To make sure it doesn't slip from its #1 spot atop the athletic shoe and apparel market, NIKE in 2009 adopted a new business model centered around six geographies: North America, Western Europe, Central/Eastern Europe, Greater China, Japan, and Emerging Markets. The company also slashed its global workforce by about 5% in a bid to streamline its operations.

Sales in the Asia/Pacific region grew to 17% of NIKE's total sales in 2009 (up from 15% in 2008), as a result of time and design dollars spent in an effort to woo Asian consumers — especially the Chinese — and localize its products there. A long-established sourcing market for NIKE, China has become a key growth market for the company's products, as well. The 2008 Olympic Games in Beijing helped to boost sales there, and NIKE is looking to surpass the $1 billion mark in sales in that country.

NIKE is led by Mark Parker, a longtime brand executive with the company, who was named president and CEO in 2006. Parker succeeded short-lived CEO Bill Perez, who replaced NIKE co-founder Philip Knight in 2005. Chairman Knight owns about 19% of the company.

HISTORY

Phil Knight, a good miler, and Bill Bowerman, a track coach who tinkered with shoe designs, met at the University of Oregon in 1957. The two men formed Blue Ribbon Sports in 1962 in an effort to make quality American running shoes. The next year they began selling Tiger shoes, manufactured by Japanese shoe manufacturer Onitsuka Tiger. They sold the running shoes out of cars at track meets.

The company became NIKE in 1972, named for the Greek goddess of victory. The NIKE "Swoosh" logo was designed by a graduate student named Carolyn Davidson, who was paid $35. The same year NIKE broke with Onitsuka in a dispute over distribution rights.

At the 1972 Olympic Trials in Oregon, Knight and Bowerman persuaded some of the marathoners to wear NIKE shoes. When some of these runners placed, the two advertised that NIKEs were worn by "four of the top seven finishers."

Bowerman tested a new sole in 1974 by stuffing a piece of rubber into a waffle iron. The result was the waffle sole, which NIKE added to its running shoes. NIKE grew as running's popularity surged in the 1970s. (NIKE even offered a red-and-silver shoe for disco dancing.) By 1979 it had 50% of the US running shoe market. NIKE went public the next year.

NIKE expanded with shoes for other sports, introducing the Air Jordan basketball shoe in 1985 (named for basketball star Michael Jordan) and the Cross Trainer two years later. NIKE's famous "Just Do It" slogan was introduced in 1988, the same year it bought dress-shoe maker Cole Haan.

In 1992 NIKE opened its first NIKETOWN store. It acquired Canstar Sports, which included hockey equipment maker Bauer, in 1995 (now Bauer NIKE Hockey). NIKE signed 20-year-old golf phenom Tiger Woods to a $40 million endorsement contract that year. Also in 1995 NIKE acquired a license to place its logo on NFL uniforms. (Reebok took over this license in 2002.)

NIKE launched a Jordan-branded athletic footwear and apparel division in 1997. Prompted by falling sales in Asia, NIKE cut 1,200 jobs in 1998 (about 5% of its workforce) to cut costs. With demand for athletic shoes weakening, in 1999 NIKE reported its first drop in sales since 1994. Also in 1999 the company began opening JORDAN store-within-a-store boutiques. Bowerman died in 1999; NIKE released a line of running shoes in his honor.

In 2000 the company launched a line of athletic electronics, including MP3 players, heart monitors, and two-way radios. A full year before Tiger Woods' contract expired, NIKE in 2000 signed the golfer to a five-year contract. The company said the new contract represented a "substantial raise" from his previous $40 million deal.

NIKE opened its first NIKEgoddess store in Newport Beach, California, in October 2001. The company acquired Hurley International, a distributor of action sports apparel, in April 2002.

In September 2003 NIKE acquired competitor Converse and left it as a separate operating unit to keep the Converse name intact. In October Bauer NIKE Hockey announced the closing of its hockey stick factory in Ontario and a staff reduction at its Quebec facilities.

In early 2008 NIKE bought international football star Umbro.

EXECUTIVES

Chairman: Philip H. Knight, age 71
President, CEO, and Director: Mark G. Parker, age 53, $7,306,694 total compensation
VP and CFO: Donald W. Blair, age 51, $2,908,953 total compensation
VP Global Human Resources, Infrastructure, and Shared Services: Oscar Cardona, age 49
VP Global Sales: Roland P. Wolfram, age 49
VP Merchandising and Product: Eric D. Sprunk, age 45
VP Global Brand and Category Management: Trevor Edwards, age 46, $2,815,548 total compensation
VP Creative Design: Tinker Hatfield, age 57
VP Brand Marketing: Joaquin Hidalgo, age 48
VP Global Retail: Elliott Hill, age 45
VP Investor Relations: Pamela Catlett, age 43
VP and Corporate Controller: Bernard F. (Bernie) Pliska, age 47
VP Marketing North America: Ken Dice
VP Global Operations and Technology: Hans van Alebeek, age 44
VP and Treasurer: Bob Woodruff
VP Global Apparel: Jill Stanton, age 46
President, Global Operations: Gary M. DeStefano, age 52, $3,008,870 total compensation
President, NIKE Brand: Charles D. (Charlie) Denson, age 53, $5,899,548 total compensation
Auditors: PricewaterhouseCoopers LLP

LOCATIONS

HQ: NIKE, Inc.
 1 Bowerman Dr., Beaverton, OR 97005
Phone: 503-671-6453   **Fax:** 503-671-6300
Web: www.nikebiz.com

2009 Sales

	$ mil.	% of total
US	6,542.9	34
Europe, Middle East & Africa	5,512.2	29
Asia Pacific	3,322.0	17
Americas	1,284.7	7
Other	2,514.3	13
Total	**19,176.1**	**100**

PRODUCTS/OPERATIONS

2009 Sales

	$ mil.	% of total
Footwear	10,306.7	54
Apparel	5,244.7	27
Equipment	1,110.4	6
Other	2,514.3	13
Total	**19,176.1**	**100**

Selected Products

Athletic Shoes
  Aquatic
  Auto racing
  Baseball
  Basketball
  Bicycling
  Cheerleading
  Cross-training
  Fitness
  Football
  Golf
  Running
  Soccer
  Tennis
  Volleyball
  Wrestling
Athletic Wear and Equipment
  Accessories
  Athletic bags
  Bats
  Caps
  Fitness wear
  Gloves
  Headwear
  Jackets
  Pants
  Running clothes
  Shirts
  Shorts
  Skirts
  Snowboards and snowboard apparel
  Socks
  Sport balls
  Timepieces
  Uniforms
  Unitards

Selected Subsidiaries

Cole Haan Holdings Inc. (footwear and accessories)
Converse Inc. (footwear)
Hurley International LLC (action sports apparel)

COMPETITORS

Acushnet	Phoenix Footwear
adidas	Polo Ralph Lauren
Amer Sports	PUMA AG
ASICS	Quiksilver
Brown Shoe	R. Griggs
Callaway Golf	Rawlings Sporting Goods
Columbia Sportswear	Rollerblade
Deckers Outdoor	Russell Corporation
Fila Korea	Saucony
Fruit of the Loom	Skechers U.S.A.
FUBU	Stride Rite
Hanesbrands	Timberland
Juicy Couture	Timex
K-Swiss	Tommy Hilfiger
Levi Strauss	Under Armour
Mizuno	VF
New Balance	Victoria's Secret Stores
Oakley	Wolverine World Wide

HISTORICAL FINANCIALS

Company Type: Public

Income Statement

FYE: May 31

	REVENUE ($ mil.)	NET INCOME ($ mil.)	NET PROFIT MARGIN	EMPLOYEES
5/09	19,176.1	1,486.7	7.8%	34,300
5/08	18,627.0	1,883.4	10.1%	32,500
5/07	16,325.9	1,491.5	9.1%	30,200
5/06	14,954.9	1,392.0	9.3%	28,000
5/05	13,739.7	1,211.6	8.8%	26,000
Annual Growth	**8.7%**	**5.2%**	**—**	**7.2%**

2009 Year-End Financials

Debt ratio: 5.0%
Return on equity: 18.0%
Cash ($ mil.): 2,291
Current ratio: 2.97
Long-term debt ($ mil.): 437
No. of shares (mil.): 486
Dividends
  Yield: 1.7%
  Payout: 32.3%
Market value ($ mil.): 27,722

Stock History

NYSE: NKE

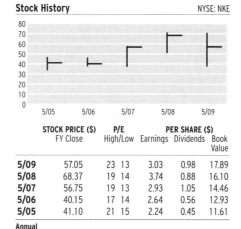

	STOCK PRICE ($) FY Close	P/E High/Low		PER SHARE ($) Earnings	Dividends	Book Value
5/09	57.05	23	13	3.03	0.98	17.89
5/08	68.37	19	14	3.74	0.88	16.10
5/07	56.75	19	13	2.93	1.05	14.46
5/06	40.15	17	14	2.64	0.56	12.93
5/05	41.10	21	15	2.24	0.45	11.61
Annual Growth	**8.5%**	**—**	**—**	**7.8%**	**21.5%**	**11.4%**

NiSource Inc.

NiSource is the main energy source for re-sourceful Americans living in the Midwest, the South, and New England. The company's utility subsidiaries distribute natural gas to about 3.3 million customers in seven states over 57,000 miles of pipeline. NiSource also generates, transmits, and distributes power to some 457,000 customers in 20 counties in its home state through its largest subsidiary, Northern Indiana Public Service Company (NIPSCO). NiSource owns one of the largest natural gas transmission and underground storage systems in the US (capable of storing 629 billion cu. ft. of natural gas), including a 16,000-mile interstate pipeline system.

NiSource's other utilities distribute natural gas in Kentucky, Maryland, Massachusetts, Ohio, Pennsylvania, and Virginia.

Several of NiSource's utilities participate in customer choice programs in states with deregulated energy markets. NiSource also has non-utility subsidiaries that market energy and provide asset management services; however, the company is scaling back on these operations.

NiSource is selling noncore assets to focus on its core electric and natural gas operations. In 2008 Unitil acquired Northern Utilities, Inc. and

Granite State Gas Transmission, Inc. from NiSource for about $202 million. It also sold its Whiting Clean Energy facility to BP Alternative Energy North America for $217 million.

HISTORY

NiSource's earliest ancestor was the South Bend (Indiana) Gas Light Company, founded in 1868 by the Studebaker brothers (of later auto fame) to supply gas. In 1886 a natural-gas discovery near Kokomo, Indiana, led to a boom in northern Indiana's use of the fuel. By 1900 steel plants and other industries had set up shop along Lake Michigan in northwestern Indiana and in Illinois.

Another NiSource ancestor was formed in 1901 as Hammond Illuminating, but it changed its name to South Shore Gas and Electric. In 1909 Northern Indiana Gas and Electric was founded by merging South Shore with other regional utilities. The next year Northern Indiana acquired South Bend.

A third NiSource predecessor, Calumet Electric (founded in 1912), had acquired several utilities by the early 1920s when utility magnate Samuel Insull bought it to add to his huge Midland Utilities holding company. In 1923 Insull bought Northern Indiana Gas and Electric, which merged three years later with Calumet to form Northern Indiana Public Service Company (NIPSCO). NIPSCO acquired its current service territory in 1930 when it swapped some areas with another Midland subsidiary.

The Public Utility Holding Company Act of 1935, beginning the regulation of regional monopolies, forced Midland to divest NIPSCO in 1947. In the 1950s and 1960s NIPSCO built two power plants and tripled its natural gas supply through a contract with a Houston gas company.

Responding to rising demand, NIPSCO in 1970 applied to build a nuclear unit at its Bailly plant, estimated to cost $180 million. In 1981 the nuke was abandoned after its cost rose to $2.1 billion. Reorganizing in 1987, NIPSCO became part of holding company NIPSCO Industries.

The Energy Policy Act of 1992 ushered in wholesale-power competition. That year NIPSCO acquired Kokomo Gas and Fuel, and in 1993 it picked up Northern Indiana Fuel and Light and Crossroads Pipeline.

To prepare for oncoming retail competition, NIPSCO in 1993 divided the electric and gas utilities into competing units and increased NIPSCO's marketing force. In 1997 NIPSCO branched out, buying water utility holding company IWC Resources, and the next year it began a customer choice program for its natural gas customers (all gas was delivered through its distribution lines, however).

The company changed its name to NiSource in 1999 but did not alter its acquisition strategy. NiSource entered the US Northeast's gas market, where deregulation plans were under way, by purchasing New England utility Bay State Gas. A unit of Bay State Gas, EnergyUSA, bought natural gas marketer TPC, and NiSource began integrating its nonregulated operations into EnergyUSA.

After launching a hostile takeover, which it later withdrew, NiSource purchased natural gas giant Columbia Energy Group for $6 billion in 2000. NiSource then sold its salt cavern gas storage and pipeline construction subsidiaries, as well as certain Columbia electric generation and LNG facilities. In 2001 NiSource sold its Columbia Propane unit to AmeriGas Partners; it also agreed to sell water company IWC Resources (and its utility subsidiary Indianapolis Water) to the City of Indianapolis (the sale was completed in 2002).

In 2002 NiSource teamed up with the merchant services unit of Aquila (formerly UtiliCorp) to form an energy marketing and trading joint venture; however, NiSource later backed out of the partnership due to instability in the energy trading industry. It also shut down its coal-fired Mitchell Generating Station, and sold its SM&P Utility Resources subsidiary to The Laclede Group.

The following year NiSource sold its Columbia Transmission Communications (Transcom) subsidiary to Neon Communications (which itself was acquired by Globix in 2005).

EXECUTIVES

Chairman: Ian M. Rolland, age 75
President, CEO, and Director:
  Robert C. (Bob) Skaggs Jr., age 54,
  $2,664,531 total compensation
EVP and CFO: Stephen P. (Steve) Smith, age 47,
  $1,003,240 total compensation
SVP and CIO: Violet G. Sistovaris
VP and Chief Accounting Officer:
  Jeffrey W. (Jeff) Grossman, age 57
EVP and Chief Legal Officer: Carrie J. Hightman,
  age 51
EVP: Michael W. (Mike) O'Donnell, age 64,
  $1,725,281 total compensation
EVP; Group CEO, Gas Distribution Segment:
  Jimmy D. Staton, age 45, $976,207 total compensation
**EVP; Group CEO, NiSource Gas Transmission and
  Storage:** Christopher A. (Chris) Helms, age 54,
  $1,428,006 total compensation
**EVP; Group CEO, NiSource Indiana Business
  Segment:** Eileen O'Neill Odum, age 54,
  $940,399 total compensation
SVP and Environmental Counsel:
  Arthur E. (Art) Smith Jr.
SVP Corporate Affairs: Glen L. Kettering
SVP Human Resources: Robert D. (Rob) Campbell,
  age 49
VP Administration and Corporate Secretary:
  Gary W. Pottorff
VP and Treasurer: David J. (Dave) Vajda
President, Bay State Gas and Northern Utilities:
  Stephen H. (Steve) Bryant
**President, Columbia Gas of Maryland and Columbia
  Gas of Pennsylvania:** Terrence J. Murphy
President, Columbia Gas of Ohio:
  John W. (Jack) Partridge Jr.
President, Columbia Gas of Virginia (Columbia):
  Carl Levander
President, Columbia Gas of Kentucky:
  Herbert A. Miller Jr.
Auditors: Deloitte & Touche LLP

LOCATIONS

HQ: NiSource Inc.
  801 E. 86th Ave., Merrillville, IN 46410
Phone: 219-647-5990   **Fax:** 219-647-5589
Web: www.nisource.com

NiSource distributes energy in Indiana, Kentucky, Maine, Maryland, Massachusetts, New Hampshire, Ohio, Pennsylvania, and Virginia.

PRODUCTS/OPERATIONS

2008 Sales

	$ mil.	% of total
Gas distribution	5,171.3	58
Electric	1,357.0	15
Gas transmission & storage	1,132.4	13
Other	1,213.5	14
Total	**8,874.2**	**100**

Selected Subsidiaries

Utility Operations
  Bay State Gas Company (natural gas utility)
  Columbia Gas of Kentucky, Inc. (natural gas utility)
  Columbia Gas of Maryland, Inc. (natural gas utility)
  Columbia Gas of Ohio, Inc. (natural gas utility)
  Columbia Gas of Pennsylvania, Inc. (natural gas
    utility)
  Columbia Gas of Virginia, Inc. (natural gas utility)
  Kokomo Gas and Fuel Company (natural gas utility)
  Northern Indiana Fuel and Light Company, Inc.
    (NIFL, natural gas utility)
  Northern Indiana Public Service Company (NIPSCO,
    electric and natural gas utility, electric generation)
Gas Transmission and Storage Operations
  Columbia Gas Transmission Corporation
  Columbia Gulf Transmission Company
  Crossroads Pipeline Company
Other Operations
  EnergyUSA-TPC (energy marketing and asset
    management)
  NiSource Energy Technologies (distributed power
    generation technologies)

COMPETITORS

AEP	IPALCO Enterprises
Allegheny Energy	National Grid USA
Atmos Energy	New Jersey Resources
Baltimore Gas and Electric	Nicor
Constellation Energy	Northeast Utilities
Dominion Resources	NSTAR
Duke Energy	RGC Resources
El Paso	Southern Union
E.ON U.S.	Unitil
EQT Corporation	Vectren

HISTORICAL FINANCIALS

Company Type: Public

Income Statement

FYE: December 31

	REVENUE ($ mil.)	NET INCOME ($ mil.)	NET PROFIT MARGIN	EMPLOYEES
12/08	8,874.2	79.0	0.9%	7,981
12/07	7,939.8	321.4	4.0%	7,607
12/06	7,490.0	281.8	3.8%	7,439
12/05	7,899.1	306.8	3.9%	7,822
12/04	6,666.2	436.3	6.5%	8,628
Annual Growth	7.4%	(34.8%)	—	(1.9%)

2008 Year-End Financials

Debt ratio: 125.7%
Return on equity: 1.6%
Cash ($ mil.): 21
Current ratio: 0.74
Long-term debt ($ mil.): 5,944

No. of shares (mil.): 275
Dividends
  Yield: 8.4%
  Payout: 317.2%
Market value ($ mil.): 3,020

Stock History

NYSE: NI

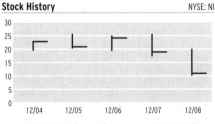

	STOCK PRICE ($) FY Close	P/E High/Low		PER SHARE ($) Earnings	Dividends	Book Value
12/08	10.97	68	36	0.29	0.92	17.17
12/07	18.89	22	15	1.17	0.92	18.44
12/06	24.10	24	19	1.03	0.92	18.21
12/05	20.86	23	18	1.12	0.92	17.92
12/04	22.78	14	12	1.64	0.92	17.39
Annual Growth	(16.7%)	—	—	(35.2%)	0.0%	(0.3%)

Noble Corporation

Noble Corporation may be heir to a fortune as demand increases for deepwater oil and gas contract drilling services. The company, with operations in waters off the coasts of five continents, has a fleet of 63 offshore drilling units: three submersibles, four dynamically positioned drillships, 13 semisubmersibles, and 43 jack-up rigs. Many of its rigs are capable of operating in depths greater than 5,000 feet. About 85% of the company's drilling fleet is deployed in international markets, primarily in the Middle East, India, Mexico, the North Sea, Brazil, and West Africa. Noble (which is domiciled in Switzerland) also provides labor contract drilling, well site, and project management services.

The group, which derives most of its revenues from offshore contracts, has positioned itself to ride a global trend toward deepwater exploration. Through acquisitions and equipment upgrading, Noble has been expanding its geographical reach and increasing its ability to drill in deeper offshore locations.

It has converted five drilling units into company-designed EVA-400 semisubmersible rigs that can drill to depths of more than 5,000 feet. It has also purchased two additional jack-up rigs from a unit of Schlumberger, and it plans to purchase two more from Danish maritime giant A.P. Møller that are now deployed off the coast of Iran. Nine of the company's drilling units (one semisubmersible and eight jackups) are capable of operating in harsh environments.

With the oil services industry consolidating, Noble is looking to pick up new assets or form alliances. Noble has moved four jackup rigs from the Gulf of Mexico to Mexico for a long-term drilling contract with PEMEX, the country's state-owned oil company. In 2008 the company sold its North Sea platform drilling business to Seawell Holding UK Ltd. for $35 million. That year Noble signed a memorandum of understanding for drilling contracts worth $4 billion with PETROBRAS.

In 2009 the company sought a more financially advantageous position by relocating its place of incorporation from the Cayman Islands to the even more corporate-tax-friendly Switzerland.

HISTORY

Lloyd Noble and Art Olsen founded Noble-Olsen Oil in 1921 with one rig in Oklahoma. In 1929 Noble-Olsen ventured outside the US to perform contract drilling services in Canada. The next year Olsen left the firm, and the new Noble Oil formed subsidiary Noble Drilling to operate its contract drilling business. The firm began drilling along the Gulf Coast in 1933.

Oil was discovered in the UK in 1939, and Noble was called to Washington, DC, to discuss the best way to develop the fields. During WWII Noble crews completed more than 100 wells for the British as a contribution toward the war effort. The company also drilled wells in Canada's Northwest Territories near the Arctic Circle in the 1940s. Lloyd Noble died in 1950.

The company built its first jack-up rig in 1955 and began air drilling in 1958. In the mid-1960s, new discoveries in North Dakota kept the firm busy, and it was also able to take advantage of increased drilling activity in the US caused by the Arab oil embargo of the early 1970s. Noble

Drilling's parent, which had become Noble Affiliates, went public in 1972.

In the midst of the 1980s oil bust, Noble Affiliates spun off Noble Drilling, which went public in 1985. The contract driller began acquiring rigs that were being divested at a discount because of the suffering oil industry. Noble bought six offshore rigs and 20 land rigs in 1988. Three years later it bought 12 more offshore rigs. In 1994 the firm acquired Triton Engineering Services, and the next year Noble bought two more jack-up rigs and began operating in the Middle East.

The company added deepwater and harsh-environment capabilities to its fleet with the 1996 acquisition of Neddrill's oil and gas drilling division. Noble also announced that it had successfully completed studies on the conversion of submersibles into semisubmersibles with deepwater drilling capabilities.

As part of its focus on deepwater drilling, Noble sold 12 shallow-water rigs in 1997. That year and in 1998, the firm won contracts for its converted rigs from Shell Oil, PETROBRAS, and Amerada Hess (later renamed Hess), among others. One of the converted rigs, Noble Paul Wolff, set a new world record in 1999 for water depth drilling at more than 8,000 feet off the coast of Brazil.

In 2000 Noble formed a joint venture with Lime Rock Partners to acquire a North Sea jack-up rig for $32.7 million. The company upgraded its technology options in 2001 with the acquisition of Houston-based Maurer Engineering, which it planned to integrate with its drilling technology subsidiary, Noble Engineering and Development.

The company boosted its fleet with the acquisition of two drilling rigs from Ocean Rig ASA, and two from Transocean's Sedco Forex in 2002. The company also purchased two additional jack-up rigs, the Trident III and Dhabi II, from a subsidiary of Schlumberger for about $95 million. It also expanded its technology assets by acquiring WELLDONE Engineering. Later that year Noble Drilling changed its name to Noble Corporation.

In 2005 Noble Corporation increased its stake in offshore drilling contractor Smedvig asa (Norway) to more than 39% by purchasing Smedvig family shares for about NOK 4.6 billion ($687.7 million), but sold its interests in 2006.

EXECUTIVES

Chairman, President, and CEO: David W. Williams, age 51
SVP Operations: Donald E. (Don) Jacobsen
SVP, CFO, Treasurer, and Controller:
Thomas L. Mitchell, age 48
EVP and Corporate Secretary: Julie J. Robertson, age 52
SVP and General Counsel: William E. Turcotte, age 45
VP Investor Relations and Planning: Lee M. Ahlstrom
Director Investor Relations: Brook Wootton
Director, Corporate Communications: John S. Breed
Executive Assistant: Sue Ann Martin
Auditors: PricewaterhouseCoopers LLP

LOCATIONS

HQ: Noble Corporation
13135 S. Dairy Ashford, Ste. 800
Sugar Land, TX 77478
Phone: 281-276-6100   **Fax:** 281-491-2092
Web: www.noblecorp.com

2008 Sales

	$ mil.	% of total
Mexico	678.0	20
US	676.2	20
Qatar	438.7	12
Nigeria	304.8	9
The Netherlands	303.3	9
UK	285.9	8
Brazil	268.8	8
United Arab Emirates	186.6	5
Other countries	304.2	9
Total	**3,446.5**	**100**

PRODUCTS/OPERATIONS

2008 Sales

	$ mil.	% of total
Contract drilling services	3,298.9	96
Reimbursables	90.8	3
Labor contract drilling services	55.1	1
Engineering, consulting & other	1.7	—
Total	**3,446.5**	**100**

Selected Products and Services

Contract drilling (land and offshore drilling for the oil and gas industry)
Turnkey services
  Consulting
  Contract engineering
  Drilling and completion planning and design
  Drilling project management
  Specialized drilling tools and services
Labor contract drilling (drilling and workover personnel)
Engineering services
  Offshore equipment
  Recertification of oil field equipment

COMPETITORS

Acergy
Atwood Oceanics
Baker Hughes
Diamond Offshore
ENSCO
Helmerich & Payne
McDermott
Nabors Industries
Parker Drilling
Pride International
Rowan Companies
Schlumberger
Transocean Inc.
Weatherford International

HISTORICAL FINANCIALS

Company Type: Public

Income Statement

FYE: December 31

	REVENUE ($ mil.)	NET INCOME ($ mil.)	NET PROFIT MARGIN	EMPLOYEES
12/08	3,446.5	1,561.0	45.3%	6,000
12/07	2,995.3	1,206.0	40.3%	6,600
12/06	2,100.2	731.9	34.8%	6,000
12/05	1,382.1	296.7	21.5%	5,600
12/04	1,066.2	146.1	13.7%	5,300
Annual Growth	**34.1%**	**80.8%**	**—**	**3.1%**

2008 Year-End Financials

Debt ratio: 14.2%
Return on equity: 32.5%
Cash ($ mil.): 513
Current ratio: 1.83
Long-term debt ($ mil.): 751
No. of shares (mil.): 262
Dividends
  Yield: 0.7%
  Payout: 2.7%
Market value ($ mil.): 5,777

Stock History

NYSE: NE

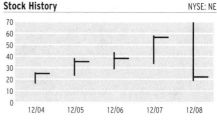

	STOCK PRICE ($) FY Close	P/E High/Low		PER SHARE ($) Earnings	Dividends	Book Value
12/08	22.09	12	3	5.85	0.16	20.23
12/07	56.51	13	8	4.48	0.12	16.47
12/06	38.08	16	11	2.66	0.08	12.35
12/05	35.27	35	22	1.08	0.05	10.44
12/04	24.87	46	31	0.55	0.00	9.12
Annual Growth	**(2.9%)**	**—**	**—**	**80.6%**	**—**	**22.0%**

Nordstrom, Inc.

Service with a smile is a part of Nordstrom's corporate culture. One of the nation's largest upscale apparel and shoe retailers, Nordstrom sells clothes, shoes, and accessories through about 110 Nordstrom stores and about 60 outlet stores (Nordstrom Rack) in more than 25 states. It also operates a pair of "Last Chance" clearance stores, two Jeffrey luxury boutiques, and sells goods online and through catalogs. The retailer has sold its Façonnable boutiques. With its easy-return policy and touches such as thank-you notes from employees, Nordstrom has earned a reputation for top-notch customer service. Members of the Nordstrom family, who own more than 15% of the company's stock, closely supervise the chain.

Nordstrom, along with other upscale department stores chains, is suffering from the effects of reduced consumer spending, which took a heavy toll on the company's sales in the second half of 2008. As a result, the retailer is curtailing its expenses in 2009 by reducing the number of stores it remodels and delaying or canceling plans for several new Nordstrom department stores. Still, plans call for the opening of three new Nordstrom stores and 10 Rack stores in 2009. The cautious approach to new store openings is a retreat from Nordstrom's previously stated five-year growth plan, which called for opening about 30 new or relocated Nordstrom department stores and remodeling some 30 others annually.

The family-run company has consolidated its catalog and Internet businesses into one unit called Nordstrom Direct, which accounts for less than 10% of sales. The firm also owns its own bank, Nordstrom fsb, through which it offers a private-label credit card, as well as two co-branded Nordstrom VISA cards.

HISTORY

In 1901 John Nordstrom, a lumberjack and successful gold miner, used his Alaska Gold Rush money to open Wallin & Nordstrom shoe store in Seattle with shoemaker Carl Wallin. Nordstrom retired in 1928 and sold his half of the business, which included a second store, to his sons Everett and Elmer. Wallin sold his share to the brothers after retiring the following year. A third Nordstrom son, Lloyd, joined in 1933. The shoe chain thrived and incorporated as Nordstrom's in 1946.

By 1963 Nordstrom's was the largest independent shoe chain in the country. The company diversified by acquiring Best Apparel's stores in Seattle and Portland, Oregon. Three years later Nordstrom's bought Portland's Nicholas Ungar, a fashion retailer, and merged it with one of its shoe stores in Portland under the name Nordstrom Best.

Renaming itself Nordstrom Best in 1966, the company went public in 1971 and changed its name again in 1973 to Nordstrom. The retailer grew steadily throughout the 1970s, opening new stores, boosting sales in existing stores, and diversifying. In 1976 Nordstrom started Place Two, featuring apparel and shoes in smaller stores than its traditional department layouts. It moved into Southern California (Orange County) two years later. Buoyed by almost $300 million in new sales, Nordstrom executives planned an aggressive expansion.

Nordstrom opened its first store on the East Coast in 1988 in Virginia. The chain continued to expand, opening stores in Northern California and in the affluent Washington, DC, suburbs.

The 1989 San Francisco earthquake, along with a national downturn, hurt retail sales significantly. Nordstrom's much-touted focus on customer service had a downside: The company was investigated in 1990 for not paying employees for customer services they performed, including delivery of merchandise on their own time. (Three years later Nordstrom set aside $15 million to pay back wages to employees who had performed off-the-clock services.)

The company continued to expand in the East and Midwest, opening its first store in the New York City area in 1991. In 1993 the retailer opened a men's boutique in New York (Façonnable). Looking for new ways to attract customers, Nordstrom introduced a mail-order catalog the next year.

Following the family's business tradition, six members of Nordstrom's fourth generation began running the company in 1995. Third-generation members James Nordstrom, John Nordstrom, Bruce Nordstrom, and Jack McMillan retired as co-chairmen and were replaced by non-family members Ray Johnson and John Whitacre. (Johnson retired in 1996.)

In 1999 Nordstrom created Nordstrom.com, a partnership with Benchmark Capital and Madrona Investment Group, to consolidate its catalog and Internet operations.

In early 2000, amid slumping sales, the company dissolved the co-presidency. Less than a year later, however, the Nordstroms were back in charge. Chairman and CEO Whitacre resigned and Blake Nordstrom took over running the company as president. His father, Bruce, came out of retirement to take the chairman's role. Later the company bought the French design company Façonnable, which supplies the products for its Façonnable boutiques.

In 2002 the company bought out Benchmark's and Madrona's minority stake in Nordstrom.com. In 2005 Nordstrom bought a majority interest in luxury specialty stores Jeffrey New York and Jeffrey Atlanta. Terms of the agreement were not disclosed. The Jeffrey stores had about $35 million in sales in 2004. Also in 2005 the company

opened stores in Atlanta; Dallas; Irvine, California; and San Antonio.

In late 2007 Nordstrom sold its four US Façonnable boutiques and 37 European locations to Lebanon-based M1 Group for about $210 million. Overall in 2007, Nordstrom opened three full-line department stores and a single Rack store.

In early 2008 Nordstrom opened its first full-line department store in Hawaii. In October, amid economic gloom, the retailer opened a store in Pittsburgh. Overall, the retailer opened eight new Nordstrom stores and half a dozen Rack outlets in 2008.

EXECUTIVES

Chairman: Enrique (Rick) Hernandez Jr., age 53
President and Director: Blake W. Nordstrom, age 48, $1,558,770 total compensation
EVP and CFO: Michael G. Koppel, age 49, $1,518,232 total compensation
EVP and Chief Administrative Officer: Daniel F. (Dan) Little, age 47, $999,834 total compensation
EVP and Director; President, Merchandising: Peter E. (Pete) Nordstrom, age 47, $1,244,565 total compensation
EVP Marketing: Linda Toschi Finn, age 61
EVP and Director; President, Stores: Erik B. Nordstrom, age 45, $1,264,085 total compensation
EVP, General Counsel, and Corporate Secretary: Robert B. Sari, age 53
EVP; Chairman and CEO, Nordstrom FSB; President, Nordstrom Credit: Kevin T. Knight, age 53
EVP Human Resources and Diversity Affairs: Delena M. Sunday, age 48
EVP and General Merchandise Manager, Cosmetics Division: Laurie M. Black, age 50
EVP and President, Nordstrom Direct: James F. (Jamie) Nordstrom Jr., age 34
EVP and General Merchandise Manager, Shoe Division: Jack H. Minuk, age 54
EVP and General Merchandise Manager, Men's and Kidswear Divisions: David Whitman, age 50
EVP and General Merchandise Manager, Accessories and Women's Specialized Divisions: Margaret Myers, age 62
EVP; President, Nordstrom Rack: Scott Meden, age 46
EVP and General Merchandise General Merchandise Manager, Women's Apparel Division: Loretta Soffe, age 42
VP Investor Relations and Treasurer: Robert E. Campbell, age 53
VP Corporate Communications: Brooke White
Auditors: Deloitte & Touche LLP

LOCATIONS

HQ: Nordstrom, Inc.
   1617 6th Ave., Seattle, WA 98101
Phone: 206-628-2111   **Fax:** 206-628-1795
Web: www.nordstrom.com

PRODUCTS/OPERATIONS

2009 Stores

	No.
Full-line	109
Rack & other	62
Total	**171**

2009 Sales

	% of total
Women's apparel	34
Shoes	21
Men's apparel	16
Women's accessories	12
Cosmetics	11
Children's apparel	3
Other	3
Total	**100**

Selected Retail Operations

Jeffrey (boutiques)
Last Chance (clearance stores)
Nordstrom (specialty stores selling apparel, shoes, and accessories for women, men, and children)
Nordstrom Direct (catalogs and online ordering)
Nordstrom Rack (outlets selling merchandise from Nordstrom specialty stores and manufacturers)

COMPETITORS

AnnTaylor
Astor & Black
Barneys
Benetton
Bloomingdale's
Brooks Brothers
Brown Shoe
Caché
Dillard's
Donna Karan
Eddie Bauer llc
The Gap
J. C. Penney
J. Crew
Jones Apparel
Lands' End
Loehmann's
Macy's
Men's Wearhouse
Neiman Marcus
Saks Fifth Avenue
Talbots
Tiffany & Co.
Von Maur

HISTORICAL FINANCIALS

Company Type: Public

Income Statement

FYE: January 31

	REVENUE ($ mil.)	NET INCOME ($ mil.)	NET PROFIT MARGIN	EMPLOYEES
1/09	8,573.0	401.0	4.7%	52,000
1/08	8,828.0	715.0	8.1%	55,000
1/07	8,560.7	678.0	7.9%	57,400
1/06	7,722.9	551.3	7.1%	51,400
1/05	7,131.4	393.5	5.5%	49,700
Annual Growth	**4.7%**	**0.5%**	**—**	**1.1%**

2009 Year-End Financials

Debt ratio: 183.0%
Return on equity: 34.5%
Cash ($ mil.): 72
Current ratio: 2.01
Long-term debt ($ mil.): 2,214
No. of shares (mil.): 216
Dividends
   Yield: 5.0%
   Payout: 35.0%
Market value ($ mil.): 2,746

Stock History

NYSE: JWN

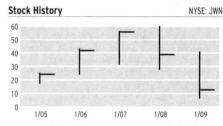

	STOCK PRICE ($) FY Close	P/E High/Low		PER SHARE ($) Earnings	Dividends	Book Value
1/09	12.69	22	4	1.83	0.64	5.59
1/08	38.85	21	10	2.88	0.54	5.15
1/07	55.71	22	12	2.55	0.42	10.02
1/06	41.72	22	12	1.98	0.32	9.67
1/05	24.13	18	13	1.38	0.24	8.27
Annual Growth	**(14.8%)**	**—**	**—**	**7.3%**	**27.8%**	**(9.3%)**

Norfolk Southern

Transportation titan Norfolk Southern is one big train that could. The company's main subsidiary, Norfolk Southern Railway, transports freight over a network consisting of more than 21,000 route miles in 22 states in the eastern US and in Ontario, Canada. The rail system is made up of more than 16,000 route miles owned by Norfolk Southern and about 5,000 route miles of trackage rights, which allow the company to use tracks owned by other railroads. Norfolk Southern transports coal and general merchandise, including automotive products and chemicals. The company also offers intermodal services (freight transportation by a combination of train and truck) through its Triple Crown Services unit.

Demand for rail freight transportation is increasing because of increased fuel prices, highway congestion, regulatory changes in the trucking industry, and a demand for transportation options with less environmental impact.

To meet the increased demand and make better use of its rail network, Norfolk Southern has repaired infrastructure, increased track capacity, and upgraded crossing signals. Targets of the company's investment included $250 million for the Heartland Corridor, between Chicago and Norfolk, Virginia; and the Meridian Speedway, a joint venture with Kansas City Southern between Shreveport, Louisiana, and Meridian, Mississippi, that helps connect southeastern and southwestern markets. Norfolk Southern is also investing $140 million with Pan Am Railways to improve the 436 miles of track in the northeast US known as the Patriot Corridor.

In 2009 Norfolk Southern announced alongside CN the MidAmerica Corridor, a partnership created for the railroads to share track from Chicago to a new coal gateway in Corinth, Mississippi.

By far its biggest project is the Crescent Corridor, a proposed $2 billion improvement and expansion of rail line from New Jersey to Louisiana. Norfolk Southern is heralding the railroad as a solution to environmental and infrastructure concerns, saying it would take up to 1 million trucks off the interstate highway system every year. The company is still in the process of raising capital, some of which will come from state governments.

HISTORY

Norfolk Southern Corporation resulted from the 1982 merger of two US rail giants — Norfolk & Western Railway Company (N&W) and Southern Railway Company — which had emerged from more than 200 and 150 previous mergers, respectively.

N&W dates to 1838, when one track connected Petersburg, Virginia, to City Point (now Hopewell). This eight-miler became part of the Atlantic, Mississippi & Ohio (AM&O), which was created by consolidating three Virginia railways in 1870.

In 1881 Philadelphia bank E.W. Clark bought the AM&O, and renamed it the Norfolk & Western. N&W rolled into Ohio by purchasing two other railroads (1892, 1901).

The company took over the Virginian Railway, a coal carrier with track paralleling much of its own, in 1959. In 1964 N&W became a key railroad in the Midwest by acquiring the New York,

Chicago & St. Louis Railroad and the Pennsylvania Railroad's line between Columbus and Sandusky, Ohio. It also leased the Wabash Railroad, with lines from Detroit and Chicago to Kansas City and St. Louis.

Southern Railway can be traced back to the South Carolina Canal & Rail Road, a nine-mile line chartered in 1827 and built by Horatio Allen to win trade for Charleston's port. It began operating the US's first regularly scheduled passenger train in 1830 and became the world's longest railway when it opened a 136-mile line to Hamburg, South Carolina (1833).

Soon other railroads sprang up in the South, including the Richmond & Danville (Virginia, 1847) and the East Tennessee, Virginia & Georgia (1869), which were combined to form the Southern Railway System in 1894. Southern eventually controlled more than 100 railroads, forging a system from Washington, DC, to St. Louis and New Orleans.

The 1982 merger of Southern and N&W created an extensive rail system throughout the East, South, and Midwest. Norfolk Southern (a holding company created for the two railroads) also bought North American Van Lines in 1985. Triple Crown Services, the company's intermodal subsidiary, was started in 1986. The company also made a failed attempt to take over Piedmont Aviation the next year.

Norfolk Southern revived North American Van Lines by selling its refrigerator truck operation, Tran-star (1993), and suspending its commercial trucking line. But it later sold the rest of the motor carrier (1998) to focus on rail operations.

When CSX announced its plans to buy Conrail in 1997, Norfolk Southern's counteroffer led to a split of the former Northeastern monopoly, between Norfolk Southern (58%) and CSX (42%). Problems with integrating Conrail's assets hurt Norfolk Southern's results. But by 2000 it had regained some of the traffic it had lost to service problems, and its intermodal shipping business also gained speed. In 2004 Norfolk Southern and CSX reorganized Conrail to give each parent company direct ownership of the portion of Conrail's assets that it operates. Conrail still operates switching facilities and terminals used by both Norfolk Southern and CSX.

Norfolk Southern got hit in the wallet in 2001: The company agreed to pay $28 million to settle a racial discrimination lawsuit brought by black employees in 1993. Norfolk Southern began rounds of layoffs and closed redundant depots and facilities in 2001.

In 2005 nine people died in South Carolina when chlorine gas leaked from a ruptured car on a Norfolk Southern freight train. The car was ruptured when the train crashed into a company-owned locomotive and two train cars that were parked on a siding.

EXECUTIVES

Chairman, President, and CEO:
Charles W. (Wick) Moorman IV, age 57, $14,226,049 total compensation
EVP and COO: Mark D. Manion, age 56, $4,356,618 total compensation
EVP Finance and CFO: James A. (Jim) Squires, age 47, $2,378,713 total compensation
EVP Planning and CIO: Deborah H. (Debbie) Butler, age 55, $2,723,561 total compensation
EVP and Chief Marketing Officer:
Donald W. (Don) Seale, age 56, $4,289,988 total compensation
EVP Law and Corporate Relations:
James A. (Jim) Hixon, age 55, $5,934,328 total compensation

EVP Administration: John P. Rathbone, age 56, $4,284,816 total compensation
SVP Energy and Properties: Daniel D. (Danny) Smith, age 56
VP Corporate Affairs: H. Craig Lewis
VP Industrial Products: David T. Lawson
VP Human Resources: Cindy C. Earhart
VP Law: William A. Galanko
VP Government Relations: Bruno Maestri
VP Business Development: Robert E. Martínez
VP Automotive and Intermodal Marketing:
Michael R. McClellan
VP Transportation: Michael J. Wheeler
VP Audit and Compliance: Joseph C. Dimino
VP and Treasurer: Marta R. Stewart, age 51
Corporate Secretary: Howard D. McFadden
Auditors: KPMG LLP

LOCATIONS

HQ: Norfolk Southern Corporation
3 Commercial Place, Norfolk, VA 23510
Phone: 757-629-2600 **Fax:** 757-664-5069
Web: www.nscorp.com

PRODUCTS/OPERATIONS

2008 Sales

	$ mil.	% of total
Coal	3,111	29
Intermodal	2,058	19
General Merchandise		
Agriculture, consumer products & government	1,282	12
Metals/construction	1,251	12
Chemical	1,238	12
Paper, clay & forest	898	8
Automotive	823	8
Total	**10,661**	**100**

COMPETITORS

American Commercial Lines
APL Logistics
Burlington Northern Santa Fe
Canadian National Railway
Canadian Pacific Railway
CSX
Hub Group
Ingram Industries
J.B. Hunt
Kansas City Southern
Kirby Corporation
Landstar System
Pacer International
Schneider National
Union Pacific
Werner Enterprises

HISTORICAL FINANCIALS

Company Type: Public

Income Statement

FYE: December 31

	REVENUE ($ mil.)	NET INCOME ($ mil.)	NET PROFIT MARGIN	EMPLOYEES
12/08	10,661.0	1,716.0	16.1%	30,709
12/07	9,432.0	1,464.0	15.5%	30,806
12/06	9,407.0	1,481.0	15.7%	30,541
12/05	8,527.0	1,281.0	15.0%	30,294
12/04	7,312.0	923.0	12.6%	28,475
Annual Growth	9.9%	16.8%	—	1.9%

2008 Year-End Financials

Debt ratio: 64.4%
Return on equity: 17.8%
Cash ($ mil.): 618
Current ratio: 0.95
Long-term debt ($ mil.): 6,183
No. of shares (mil.): 368
Dividends
Yield: 2.6%
Payout: 27.0%
Market value ($ mil.): 17,297

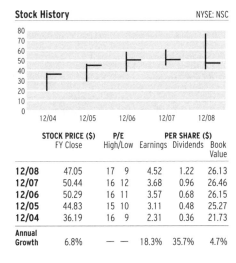

	STOCK PRICE ($)	P/E		PER SHARE ($)		
	FY Close	High/Low	Earnings	Dividends	Book Value
12/08	47.05	17 9	4.52	1.22	26.13
12/07	50.44	16 12	3.68	0.96	26.46
12/06	50.29	16 11	3.57	0.68	26.15
12/05	44.83	15 10	3.11	0.48	25.27
12/04	36.19	16 9	2.31	0.36	21.73
Annual Growth	6.8%	— —	18.3%	35.7%	4.7%

Northeast Utilities

Northeast Utilities (NU) uses a little Yankee ingenuity (and a number of power generation plants) to keep its customers powered up. The largest utility in New England, NU supplies power to about 1.9 million customers in Connecticut, New Hampshire, and Massachusetts through subsidiaries Connecticut Light and Power, Public Service Company of New Hampshire, and Western Massachusetts Electric. The company's power grid encompasses about 3,100 circuit miles of overhead transmission lines and approximately 34,900 pole miles of distribution lines. NU's Yankee Gas utility provides natural gas to 200,000 customers in Connecticut.

Once a more diverse collection of businesses, in the mid-2000s NU decided to focus its future growth on its regulated power and gas distribution and transmission operations. As a result, it subsequently divested most of its non-regulated units (commercial plumbing, electrical, mechanical, telecommunications, contracting operations, wholesale energy marketing and energy services).

In 2006 NU sold nonregulated subsidiary Select Energy, which marketed and traded energy to wholesale and retail customers, to Hess Corporation. That year the company also sold its competitive generation assets in Connecticut and Massachusetts to Energy Capital Partners for $1.34 billion.

In 2007 Connecticut Light and Power Company completed the installation of electric service to Yankee Gas Services Company's new liquefied natural gas facility in Waterbury.

To better serve its customers, in 2008 NU announced plans to relocate its headquarters from Berlin, Connecticut, to a larger building in downtown Hartford.

HISTORY

In 1966 three old, intertwined New England utilities merged. One was The Hartford Electric Light Company (HELCO), founded in 1883 by Austin Dunham in Hartford, Connecticut. In 1915 the company signed the first power exchange agreement in the US with Connecticut Power (CP), which HELCO acquired in 1920.

The second, founded in 1886, was Western Massachusetts Electric (WMECO), which merged with Western Counties in the 1930s to become WMECO. The third was Connecticut Light and Power (CL&P). Founded as Rocky River Power in 1905, it took the CL&P name in 1917. In 1929 it built the US's first large-scale pumped-storage hydroelectric plant.

In the 1950s HELCO formed Yankee Atomic Electric with CL&P, WMECO, and others to build an experimental nuclear reactor. In 1965 members of the group began jointly building the Connecticut Yankee nuke (on line in 1968). After years of cooperation, CL&P, HELCO, and WMECO merged in 1966, and Northeast Utilities (NU) was born. It was the first multistate utility holding company created since the Public Utility Holding Company Act of 1935 had broken up the old utility giants. Holyoke Water Power joined NU the following year.

The 1970s energy crisis spurred NU to continue building nukes, including Maine Yankee, Vermont Yankee, and two Millstone units. But by the 1980s, construction delays had raised the cost of the final unit, Millstone 3.

Regulators forced CL&P to spin off its gas utility, Yankee Energy System, in 1989. The next year NU acquired bankrupt utility Public Service Company of New Hampshire (PSNH) and its new Seabrook nuke. (PSNH emerged from bankruptcy in 1991.)

The 1995 shutdown of Millstone 1 began NU's nuclear troubles. In 1996 regulators closed all of its nukes except Seabrook because of safety concerns, and NU mothballed Connecticut Yankee. The next year Michael Morris replaced CEO Bernard Fox, who left after federal regulators ordered NU to comply with regulations and fix management problems — NU managers had routinely retaliated against whistleblowers — the first time a utility had been given such an order. New managers came in, including a former whistleblower, but NU couldn't avoid a record-setting $2.1 million fine. NU received permission to restart the Millstone units in 1998-99. But it had to absorb the $1 billion in power replacement associated with the shutdown.

Meanwhile, as deregulation loomed, NU created a retail marketer (now Select Energy) and a telecommunications arm (Mode 1 Communications) in 1996. Two years later retail competition began in Massachusetts and deregulation legislation was passed in Connecticut (deregulation went into effect there in 2000).

In 1999 NU sold its Massachusetts plants to New York's Consolidated Edison and auctioned off its non-nuclear plants in Connecticut to its subsidiary, Northeast Generation, and Northern States Power (now Xcel Energy). NU agreed to plead guilty to 25 federal felony counts and pay $10 million in penalties for polluting water near Millstone and lying to regulators.

That year Consolidated Edison agreed to buy NU for $3.3 billion in cash and stock and $3.9 billion in assumed debt. The deal broke down in 2001, however; Con Edison charged NU with misrepresenting information about power-supply contracts, and NU charged Con Edison with improperly attempting to renegotiate the terms of the acquisition.

Bringing an old family member home, NU bought Yankee Energy System for $679 million in 2000. Later that year Dominion Resources, which had helped NU restart Millstone 2 and Millstone 3 (Millstone 1 had been taken out of service), agreed to buy the Millstone complex for $1.3 billion. The sale closed in 2001.

Also in 2001 NU subsidiary Select Energy bought Niagara Mohawk's energy marketing unit; NU sold the distribution business of its Holyoke Water Power utility to the City of Holyoke for $18 million; and retail electric competition began in New Hampshire. NU agreed to sell CL&P's 10% stake in the Vermont Yankee nuclear facility to Entergy in 2001; the deal was completed the following year. In 2002 NU sold its 40% interest in the Seabrook Nuclear Generating facility to FPL Group.

EXECUTIVES

Chairman, President, and CEO: Charles W. (Chuck) Shivery, age 63, $8,094,288 total compensation
EVP and COO; EVP and COO, Northeast Utilities Service Co.; CEO, CL&P, PSNH, WMECO, and Yankee Gas: Leon J. (Lee) Olivier, age 60, $2,133,507 total compensation
EVP and CFO: David R. McHale, age 48, $2,190,205 total compensation
SVP and General Counsel: Gregory B. Butler, age 51, $1,711,666 total compensation
VP Human Resources, Northeast Utilities Service Company: Jean M. LaVecchia, $867,091 total compensation
VP and Treasurer: Randall A. (Randy) Shoop
VP Accounting and Controller: Jay S. Buth, age 39
President and COO, Connecticut Power and Light Co.: Jeffrey D. (Jeff) Butler, age 53
President, Yankee Gas: Rodney O. (Rod) Powell, age 56
President, Western Massachusetts Electric Co.: Peter J. Clarke, age 47
Secretary and Deputy General Counsel: Samuel K. Lee
Auditors: Deloitte & Touche LLP

LOCATIONS

HQ: Northeast Utilities
107 Selden St., Berlin, CT 06037
Phone: 800-286-5000   **Fax:** 860-665-5418
Web: www.nu.com

Northeast Utilities operates primarily in Connecticut, western Massachusetts, and New Hampshire.

PRODUCTS/OPERATIONS

2008 Sales

	$ mil.	% of total
Utilities		
Electric	4,716.1	75
Gas	577.4	9
Transmission	424.8	7
NU Enterprises	114.1	2
Other	416.6	7
Adjustments	(448.9)	—
Total	**5,800.1**	**100**

Selected Subsidiaries

The Northeast Utilities System (regulated utilities)
Connecticut Light and Power Company (CL&P, electric utility)
Public Service Company of New Hampshire (PSNH, electric utility)
Western Massachusetts Electric Company (WMECO, electric utility)
Yankee Energy System, Inc. (natural gas utility, Connecticut)
Yankee Gas Services Company (retail natural gas service)
Other Operations
Northeast Utilities Service Company (administrative services for NU subsidiaries)
NU Enterprises, Inc. (nonutility operations)

COMPETITORS

AEP	National Grid USA
Bangor Hydro-Electric	NiSource
Central Vermont	NSTAR
Public Service	PG&E Corporation
Con Edison	Public Service Enterprise
Energy East	Southern Company
Green Mountain Power	UIL Holdings
Massachusetts Municipal	Unitil
Wholesale Electric	USPowerGen

HISTORICAL FINANCIALS

Company Type: Public

Income Statement
FYE: December 31

	REVENUE ($ mil.)	NET INCOME ($ mil.)	NET PROFIT MARGIN	EMPLOYEES
12/08	5,800.1	260.8	4.5%	6,189
12/07	5,822.2	250.9	4.3%	5,869
12/06	6,884.4	470.6	6.8%	5,869
12/05	7,397.4	(252.5)	—	6,879
12/04	6,686.7	122.1	1.8%	7,079
Annual Growth	(3.5%)	20.9%	—	(3.3%)

2008 Year-End Financials

Debt ratio: 135.9%	No. of shares (mil.): 188
Return on equity: 8.8%	Dividends
Cash ($ mil.): 90	Yield: 3.4%
Current ratio: 0.88	Payout: 49.1%
Long-term debt ($ mil.): 4,103	Market value ($ mil.): 4,529

Stock History
NYSE: NU

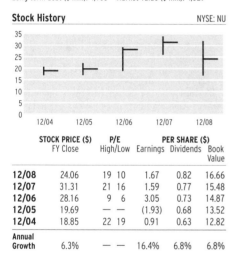

	STOCK PRICE ($) FY Close	P/E High/Low		PER SHARE ($) Earnings	Dividends	Book Value
12/08	24.06	19	10	1.67	0.82	16.66
12/07	31.31	21	16	1.59	0.77	15.48
12/06	28.16	9	6	3.05	0.73	14.87
12/05	19.69	—	—	(1.93)	0.68	13.52
12/04	18.85	22	19	0.91	0.63	12.82
Annual Growth	6.3%	—	—	16.4%	6.8%	6.8%

Northern Trust

Since its founding in 1889, Northern Trust Corporation has been working hard to keep clients' trusts. Flagship subsidiary The Northern Trust Company — along with other units bearing the Northern Trust name — provides banking and trust services to the affluent and to financial institutions and corporations from 85 offices in nearly 20 states and about a dozen countries. Operating in two segments, Corporate and Institutional Services and Personal Financial Services, the corporation is a leading personal trust manager in the US, specializing in master trust services and catering to corporate pension plans and institutional clients.

Northern Trust's Corporate and Institutional Services division administers assets for fund managers, foundations and endowments, and insurance companies. The Personal Financial Services segment offers trust and investment management, banking, mortgages, and other services for small and midsized companies, executives, retirees, and the well-to-do. Subsidiary Northern Trust Global Investments oversees portfolio management, investment research, and other investment products, including the firm's proprietary mutual funds.

Abroad, Northern Trust has branches in Australia, Canada, Ireland, Luxembourg, the Netherlands, and the UK. The company is targeting Asia for growth, where it has offices in China, Hong Kong, India, Japan, and Singapore. All told, Northern Trust has approximately $3 trillion of assets under custody and more than $550 billion under management.

Northern Trust received nearly $1.6 billion from the US government's Troubled Asset Relief Program (TARP), but later said it would return the money after the public funds brought increased scrutiny, particularly over client perks and the company's sponsorship of a golf tournament.

Board member Harold Smith of the founding Smith family owns around 5% of Northern Trust.

HISTORY

When banker Byron Smith took time off to handle family concerns in 1885, friends turned to him for advice on trust and estate matters. It occurred to him that there was a market for such services within a banking framework.

Smith tested new Illinois banking and trust laws by arranging for state banking authorities to reject his charter application for Northern Trust. As Smith had hoped, the charter was upheld by the Illinois Supreme Court.

Northern Trust opened in 1889 in one of Chicago's new skyscrapers, the Rookery. With $1 million in capital — about 40% from Smith and the rest from the likes of Marshall Field (retailing), Martin Ryerson (steel), and Philip Armour (meatpacking) — the bank attracted $138,000 in deposits its first day.

By 1896 the bank was firmly established; Smith began taking a salary and the company issued its first dividend. Ten years later the firm built its solid granite edifice, the "Gray Lady of LaSalle Street," where it still resides.

The bank began buying commercial paper in 1912, joined the Federal Reserve System in 1917, and became a custodian for expropriated German assets during WWI. Byron Smith died in 1914 and was succeeded by his son, Solomon.

Northern Trust rejected the get-rich-quick ethos of the 1920s. It was so strong during the Depression that after the 1933 bank holiday people actually clamored to make deposits. The bank administered the Depression-era scholarship fund that helped Ronald Reagan attend college. By 1941 almost half of Northern Trust's commercial deposits originated outside of Chicago area. The bank kept growing during and after WWII.

Solomon Smith retired in 1963; his son Edward took over and launched the company's expansion overseas (Northern Trust International was formed in 1968) and out of state (Florida in 1971, Arizona in 1974). The firm's business was helped by the 1974 passage by Congress of ERISA, which required company retirement plans to be overseen by an outside custodian. Edward retired in 1979.

Northern Trust expanded locally when Illinois legalized intrastate branch banking in 1981. In 1987 the company lost money, due in part to defaults on loans made to developing countries. It moved into California in 1988 and Texas in 1989.

Northern Trust navigated the early 1990s recession, expanded geographically in the mid-1990s, and added services through acquisitions. In 1995 the company became the first foreign trust company to operate throughout Canada. That year it bought investment management service RCB International (now Northern Trust Global Advisors). It expanded in the Sunbelt with such acquisitions as Dallas' Metroplex Bancshares and was made first custodian for the Teacher Retirement System of Texas (1997).

In 1998 the company expanded into Michigan and broke into the Cleveland and Seattle markets in 1999. Northern Trust entered cyberspace as well, launching a Web site for its mutual funds. In 2000 the company opened locations in Nevada and Missouri and bought Florida-based investment adviser Carl Domino Associates (renamed Northern Trust Value Investors). Also that year the bank bought Ireland's Ulster Bank Investment Services.

In 2004 Northern Trust bought the fund management, custody, and trust operations of Baring Asset Management from Amsterdam-based ING Groep.

EXECUTIVES

Chairman: William A. Osborn, age 61, $8,886,698 total compensation
President, CEO, and Director, Northern Trust Corporation and Northern Trust Company: Frederick H. (Rick) Waddell, age 55, $7,987,831 total compensation
EVP and President, Worldwide Operations and Technology: Jana R. Schreuder, age 50
EVP and CFO, Northern Trust Corporation and Northern Trust Company: Steven L. (Steve) Fradkin, age 47, $2,375,109 total compensation
EVP and CTO, Northern Trust Company: Nirup N. Krishnamurthy
Chief Investment Officer: Robert P. (Bob) Browne, age 43
Chief Investment Strategist: James D. (Jim) McDonald
EVP and Head Asia Pacific Businesses: Gregg D. Behrens, age 56
EVP, Credit Policy: John P. Grube
EVP and Head of Human Resources and Administration, Northern Trust Corporation and Northern Trust Company: Timothy P. Moen, age 56
EVP, General Counsel, Assistant Secretary, and Head of Risk Management, Northern Trust Corporation and Northern Trust Company: Kelly R. Welsh, age 56
EVP, Northern Trust Corporation and Northern Trust Company; Co-President, Personal Financial Services: Sherry S. Barrat, age 59, $2,787,418 total compensation
EVP, Northern Trust Corporation and Northern Trust Company; Co-President, Personal Financial Services: William L. Morrison, age 58, $2,704,282 total compensation
EVP, Northern Trust Corporation and Northern Trust Company; President, Corporate and Institutional Services: Timothy J. Theriault, age 48
EVP, The Northern Trust Company: Patrick J. McDougal
EVP and Head of Corporate Risk Management: Joyce St. Clair, age 50
EVP, Northern Trust Company: Lloyd A. Wennlund
EVP and Controller: Aileen B. Blake, age 41
SVP and Director, Investor Relations: Beverly J. (Bev) Fleming
SVP Technology Operations: James Scholefield
VP, Public Relations: Richard Jurek
Auditors: KPMG LLP

LOCATIONS

HQ: Northern Trust Corporation
50 S. La Salle St., Chicago, IL 60603
Phone: 312-630-6000 **Fax:** 312-630-1512
Web: www.northerntrust.com

PRODUCTS/OPERATIONS

2008 Sales

	$ mil.	% of total
Interest income	1,079.1	25
Noninterest income		
Trust, investment & other servicing fees	2,134.9	50
Foreign exchange trading	616.2	14
Gain on Visa share redemption	167.9	4
Other	280.4	7
Total	**4,278.5**	**100**

2008 Assets

	$ mil.	% of total
Cash & due from banks	2,648.2	3
Time deposits with banks	16,721.0	20
Federal Reserve & other interest-bearing deposits	9,403.8	11
Securities	15,570.8	19
Residential mortgages	10,381.4	13
Commercial & other loans	20,374.0	25
Reserve for credit losses	(229.1)	—
Other assets	7,183.5	9
Total	**82,053.6**	**100**

COMPETITORS

Bank of America
Bank of New York Mellon
Barclays
Bessemer Group
Brown Brothers Harriman
Citigroup
Deutsche Bank
Fifth Third
FMR
Harris Bankcorp
JPMorgan Chase
Morgan Stanley
State Street
Wells Fargo
Wilmington Trust

HISTORICAL FINANCIALS

Company Type: Public

Income Statement
FYE: December 31

	ASSETS ($ mil.)	NET INCOME ($ mil.)	INCOME AS % OF ASSETS	EMPLOYEES
12/08	82,053.6	794.8	1.0%	12,200
12/07	67,611.2	726.9	1.1%	10,918
12/06	60,712.2	665.4	1.1%	9,726
12/05	53,413.8	584.4	1.1%	9,008
12/04	45,276.7	505.6	1.1%	8,022
Annual Growth	**16.0%**	**12.0%**	**—**	**11.1%**

2008 Year-End Financials

Equity as % of assets: 6.0%
Return on assets: 1.1%
Return on equity: 16.9%
Long-term debt ($ mil.): 4,623
No. of shares (mil.): 241
Dividends
Yield: 2.1%
Payout: 32.3%
Market value ($ mil.): 12,587
Sales ($ mil.): 4,279

Stock History
NASDAQ (GS): NTRS

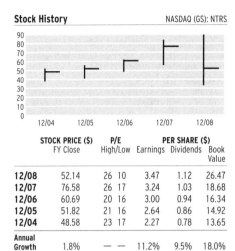

	STOCK PRICE ($) FY Close	P/E High/Low		PER SHARE ($) Earnings	Dividends	Book Value
12/08	52.14	26	10	3.47	1.12	26.47
12/07	76.58	26	17	3.24	1.03	18.68
12/06	60.69	20	16	3.00	0.94	16.34
12/05	51.82	21	16	2.64	0.86	14.92
12/04	48.58	23	17	2.27	0.78	13.65
Annual Growth	**1.8%**	**—**	**—**	**11.2%**	**9.5%**	**18.0%**

Northrop Grumman

Avast there! The acquisitions of Litton Industries, Newport News, and TRW made Northrop Grumman the world's #1 shipbuilder and the #3 military contractor (behind Lockheed Martin and Boeing). It operates through five sectors: Aerospace Systems (combining the former Integrated Systems and Space Technology segments), Electronic Systems (radar, navigation, and communications), Information Systems (combining the former Information Technology and Mission Systems segments), Shipbuilding (military/commercial ships, nuclear submarines, and aircraft carriers), and Technical Services (systems support and training and simulation).

Northrop Grumman expects that the increased military emphasis on information gathering, surveillance, battle management, and precision munitions will lead to heavy government spending on advanced electronics systems and software in the coming years. On the other hand, the company's surface ships and submarines are prime targets for the budget axe as the military looks to cut costs.

Northrop Grumman and EADS were awarded a $35 billion contract to build refueling tankers for the US Air Force, but Boeing filed a protest in early 2008 claiming the bidding process was problematic. The US Government Accountability Office (GAO) reviewed the case and found flaws in the process. As a result of the GAO's findings, the contract will go through the bidding process for the third time in seven years.

Also in 2008, the company partnered with defense contractor rivals Lockheed Martin and Alliant Techsystems to develop weapons systems for Lockheed's F-22 Raptor and F-35 Lightning II. The partnership is designed to pool their technological know-how in order to build the most comprehensive systems for fighters.

In 2009 Northrop Grumman settled two decade-old lawsuits with the US government. It agreed to pay $325 million to resolve allegations that it provided defective military satellite parts to the National Reconnaissance Office. The second lawsuit was filed by Northrop Grumman against the US government for uncompensated costs incurred as a result of the cancellation of the Tri-Service Standoff Attack Missile program. The settlement amounts for the two matters were equal and offset each other.

In 2009 Ronald Sugar announced plans to step down as chairman and CEO at the end of the year, in preparation for his retirement in June 2010. He will stay on the board as chairman emeritus. Wesley Bush, currently president and COO, will take over as CEO on January 1, 2010, as part of a planned succession. Bush, an electrical engineer by training, has been with the company since 1987.

HISTORY

Jack Northrop co-founded Lockheed Aircraft in 1927 and designed its record-setting Vega monoplane. He founded two more companies — Avion Corporation (formed in 1928 and bought by United Aircraft and Transportation) and Northrop Corporation (formed in 1932 with Douglas Aircraft, which absorbed it in 1938) — before founding Northrop Aircraft in California in 1939.

During WWII Northrop produced the P-61 fighter and the famous Flying Wing bomber, which failed to win a production contract. In the 1950s Northrop depended heavily on F-89 fighter and Snark missile sales. When Thomas Jones succeeded Jack Northrop as president (1959), he moved the company away from risky prime contracts in favor of numerous subcontracts and bought Page Communications Engineers (telecommunications, 1959) and Hallicrafters (electronics, 1966) to reduce its dependence on government contracts.

In the early 1970s Northrop was hit with a bribery scandal and the disclosure of illegal payments to Richard Nixon's 1972 campaign fund; Jones was eventually fined for an illegal contribution. As a result, a shareholder lawsuit forced Jones to resign as president (he was allowed to remain as chairman). In 1981 the company won the B-2 bomber contract. Jones retired as chairman in late 1990, and under the leadership of Kent Kresa (who became CEO in early 1990 and chairman when Jones retired), Northrop pleaded guilty to 34 counts related to fudging test results on some government projects; it was fined $17 million. In a related shareholders' suit, Northrop paid $18 million in damages in 1991.

Northrop and private investment firm The Carlyle Group bought LTV's Vought Aircraft in 1992. In 1994 it paid $2.1 billion for Grumman Corporation, a premier electronic systems firm, and changed its name to Northrop Grumman.

In 1929 Roy Grumman, Jake Swirbul, and Bill Schwendler founded Grumman; within three months it had a contract to design a US Navy fighter. Grumman completed its first commercial aircraft (the Grumman Goose) in 1937 and went public in 1938. It soared during WWII on the wings of its Wildcat and Hellcat fighter planes.

Grumman built its first corporate jet (the Gulfstream) in 1958, and in 1963 began work on the Lunar Module for the Apollo space program. It was near bankruptcy during the 1970s due to costs related to its F-14 Tomcat fighter project. The company rebuilt its military business in the 1980s, achieving its greatest success in electronic systems.

In 1998 Northrop Grumman began a restructuring that cut 10,500 defense and aircraft jobs. In 2000 the company sold its underperforming commercial aerostructures business to The Carlyle Group in a $1.2 billion transaction in order to focus on its growing defense electronics and information technology segments.

In 2001 the company completed the deal to acquire Litton Industries for $3.8 billion, plus $1.3 billion in debt. While its wallet was open, the company agreed to match the $2.6 billion that General Dynamics had agreed to pay for submarine and aircraft carrier builder Newport News — a move that the US Defense Department endorsed. In December Honeywell agreed to pay Northrop Grumman $440 million to settle an antitrust and patent infringement lawsuit that Litton had filed against Honeywell in 1990.

The deal to buy Newport News was completed in early 2002. Northrop Grumman then made a hostile $6 billion bid for conglomerate TRW when TRW's stock plunged following the sudden departure of its CEO David Cote to Honeywell. In the wake of Northrop Grumman's spurned initial bid, Raytheon, General Dynamics, and BAE SYSTEMS made offers for TRW's aerospace and defense assets. Finally, though, TRW accepted a sweetened $7.8 billion offer from Northrop Grumman in July 2002.

Northrop sold 80.4% of TRW Automotive to Blackstone Group in February 2003. In April of the same year, Kresa stepped down as president and CEO, and Ronald Sugar took over those roles; Sugar added the chairmanship to his title when Kresa retired in October.

Early in 2005 Northrop reduced its stake in TRW Automotive to 9.9%.

In 2006 Northrop Grumman agreed to buy Essex Corporation — a provider of signal, image, and information processing for defense and intelligence customers in the US.

EXECUTIVES

Chairman and CEO: Ronald D. Sugar, age 60, $17,028,776 total compensation
President and COO: Wesley G. (Wes) Bush, age 47, $7,855,945 total compensation
VP and CFO: James F. (Jim) Palmer, age 60, $4,627,405 total compensation
Corporate VP and CTO: Alexis C. Livanos, age 60
VP and CIO: Bernard P. (Bernie) McVey Jr.
VP and Chief Human Resources and Administrative Officer: Ian V. Ziskin, age 50
VP, Controller, and Chief Accounting Officer: Kenneth N. Heintz, age 62
VP and Chief Information Security Officer: Tim McKnight
Corporate VP; President, Northrop Grumman Shipbuilding: C. Michael (Mike) Petters, age 49
Corporate VP Business Development and Government Relations: Robert W. Helm, age 57
Corporate VP and General Counsel: Stephen D. (Steve) Yslas, age 61
Corporate VP; President, Information Systems: Linda A. Mills, age 59
Corporate VP; President, Aerospace Systems: Gary W. Ervin, age 51
Corporate VP; President, Northrop Grumman Electronic Systems: James F. Pitts, age 57, $5,113,866 total compensation
Corporate VP; President, Technical Services Sector: James L. Cameron, age 51
Corporate VP and Treasurer: Mark A. Rabinowitz, age 47
Corporate VP; President, Information Technology: James R. O'Neill, age 55, $4,137,512 total compensation
Corporate VP, Secretary, and Deputy General Counsel: Joseph Coyne, age 53
VP Corporate and International Communications: Brandon R. (Randy) Belote
VP Investor Relations: Paul O. Gregory
Auditors: Deloitte & Touche LLP

LOCATIONS

HQ: Northrop Grumman Corporation
  1840 Century Park East, Los Angeles, CA 90067
Phone: 310-553-6262 **Fax:** 310-556-4561
Web: www.northropgrumman.com

PRODUCTS/OPERATIONS

2008 Sales

	$ mil.	% of total
Information & Services		
Mission Systems	5,640	16
Information Technology	4,518	13
Technical Services	2,296	6
Aerospace		
Integrated Systems	5,504	16
Space Technology	4,336	12
Electronics	7,090	20
Ships	6,145	17
Adjustments	(1,642)	—
Total	**33,887**	**100**

2008 Sales

	$ mil.	% of total
US government	30,892	91
Other customers	2,995	9
Total	**33,887**	**100**

COMPETITORS

Aerojet
BAE SYSTEMS
Boeing
EADS
Elbit Systems
Finmeccanica
GE
GenCorp
General Dynamics
Hamilton Sundstrand
Hanjin Heavy Industries & Construction
Herley Industries
Honeywell Aerospace
ITT Defense
Lockheed Martin
Meggitt
Raytheon
Rockwell Collins
ThalesRaytheonSystems
Todd Shipyards

HISTORICAL FINANCIALS

Company Type: Public

Income Statement

FYE: December 31

	REVENUE ($ mil.)	NET INCOME ($ mil.)	NET PROFIT MARGIN	EMPLOYEES
12/08	33,887.0	(1,262.0)	—	123,600
12/07	32,018.0	1,790.0	5.6%	122,600
12/06	30,148.0	1,542.0	5.1%	122,200
12/05	30,721.0	1,400.0	4.6%	123,600
12/04	29,853.0	1,084.0	3.6%	125,400
Annual Growth	**3.2%**	**—**	**—**	**(0.4%)**

2008 Year-End Financials

Debt ratio: 28.9%
Return on equity: —
Cash ($ mil.): 1,504
Current ratio: 0.97
Long-term debt ($ mil.): 3,443
No. of shares (mil.): 318
Dividends
  Yield: 3.5%
  Payout: —
Market value ($ mil.): 14,328

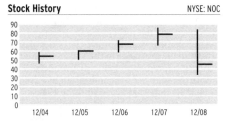

Stock History NYSE: NOC

	STOCK PRICE ($) FY Close	P/E High/Low	PER SHARE ($) Earnings	Dividends	Book Value
12/08	45.04	— —	(3.77)	1.57	37.47
12/07	78.64	17 13	5.12	1.48	55.60
12/06	67.70	16 14	4.37	1.16	52.23
12/05	60.11	16 13	3.85	1.01	52.90
12/04	54.36	20 16	2.97	0.89	52.50
Annual Growth	**(4.6%)**	**— —**	**—**	**15.2%**	**(8.1%)**

Northwestern Mutual Life Insurance

Even The Quiet Company has to toot its own horn. As one of the largest US life insurers, Northwestern Mutual Life holds more than $1 trillion in individual policies in force. Northwestern Mutual's 7,000 agents and financial professionals sell a lineup of life, disability, long-term care, and health insurance. It also offers retirement products, including fixed and variable annuities and mutual funds, to a clientele of small businesses and prosperous individuals. Other lines of business include institutional asset manager Frank Russell Company, known for the Russell 2000 stock index, and brokerage and trust services through its investment services and wealth management subsidiaries.

Northwestern Mutual would "enter the 21st century as we left the 19th," according to former chairman and CEO James D. Ericson (who retired in mid-2001).

Well, not exactly. Although the company has resisted the industry trend of demutualizing and remains committed to ownership by its more than 3 million policyholders, Northwestern Mutual has reorganized to highlight its wealth management products. Life insurance still accounts for the majority of the company's revenue, though. The company targets wealthy individuals over 55.

In late 2008, the company agreed to pay as much as $92 million to settle a class action lawsuit filed in 2004. The plaintiffs alleged that the company's sales materials were misleading regarding certain term life and disability insurance policies. Northwestern Mutual maintained that it had acted fairly, but settled the case to limit its exposure to additional litigation expenses.

HISTORY

In 1854, at age 72, John Johnston, a successful New York insurance agent, moved to Wisconsin to become a farmer. Three years later Johnston returned to the insurance business when he and 36 others formed Mutual Life Insurance (changed to

Northwestern Mutual Life Insurance in 1865). From the beginning, the company's goal was to become better, not just bigger.

The company continued to offer level-premium life insurance in the 1920s, while competitors offered new types of products. This failure to rise to new demands brought a decline in market share that lasted into the 1940s.

Northwestern Mutual automated in the late 1950s. In 1962 it introduced the Insurance Service Account, whereby all policies owned by a family or business could be consolidated into one monthly premium and paid with pre-authorized checks. In 1968 Northwestern Mutual inaugurated Extra Ordinary Life (EOL), which combined whole and term life insurance, using dividends to convert term to paid-up whole life each year. EOL soon became the company's most popular product.

Suffering from a low profile, in 1972 the insurer kicked off its "The Quiet Company" ad campaign during the summer Olympics. Public awareness of Northwestern Mutual jumped. But even in advertising, the company was staid; a revamped Quiet Company campaign made a return Olympic appearance 24 years later in another effort to raise the public's consciousness.

In the 1980s Northwestern Mutual began financing leveraged buyouts, gaining direct ownership of companies. Investments included two-thirds of flooring maker Congoleum (with other investors); it also bought majority interests in Milwaukee securities firm Robert W. Baird (1982) and mortgage guarantee insurer MGIC Investment (1985; later divested).

The firm stayed out of the 1980s mania for fast money and high-risk diversification. Instead, it devoted itself almost religiously to its core business, despite indications that it was a shrinking market.

In the early 1990s new life policy purchases slowed and the agency force declined — ominous signs, since insurers make their premium income on retained policies, and continued sales are crucial to growth. Northwestern Mutual reversed the trend, adding administrative support for its agents, using database marketing to target new customers, and increasing the cross-selling of products among existing customers. The result was a record-setting 1996.

With the financial services industry consolidating, Northwestern Mutual in 1997 moved into the mutual fund business by setting up its Mason Street Funds.

In the 1990s many large mutuals sought to demutualize, and in 1998 Northwestern Mutual, politically influential in Wisconsin, successfully lobbied for legislation to permit demutualization, citing the need to be able to move quickly in shifting markets.

The next year the company acquired Frank Russell Company, a pension management firm. The acquisition gave Northwestern Mutual a foothold in global investment management and analytical services (the Russell 2000 index).

In 2001 the firm opened Northwestern Mutual Trust, a wholly owned personal trust services subsidiary.

In 2004 the employees of Robert W. Baird completed a buyback of Northwestern Mutual's stake in the firm.

EXECUTIVES

Chairman and CEO: Edward J. Zore, age 64
President and Trustee: John E. Schlifske, age 49
SVP Enterprise Operations: Jean M. Maier, age 54
VP and CFO: Michael G. Carter, age 47
CIO: Timothy G. Schaefer
SVP and Chief Actuary: William C. Koenig, age 61
SVP and Chief Investment Officer: Mark G. Doll, age 59
EVP, Chief Risk Officer, and Trustee: Gary A. Poliner, age 55
EVP, Chief Administrative Officer, and Chief Compliance Officer: Marcia Rimai, age 53
EVP Insurance and Technology: Gregory C. Oberland, age 51
SVP Life Product: Meridee J. Maynard, age 53
SVP Agency Services: Christina H. Fiasca, age 54
SVP Real Estate: David D. Clark, age 57
SVP Securities: Jeffrey J. Lueken, age 48
SVP Agencies: Todd M. Schoon
VP Human Resources: Susan A. Lueger, age 55
VP Information Systems: Martha M. Valerio, age 62
VP Government Relations: Michael L. Youngman, age 57
VP Corporate Affairs, and President's Assistant: Gloster B. Current Jr., age 63
VP Marketing: Conrad C. York
Auditors: PricewaterhouseCoopers LLP

LOCATIONS

HQ: The Northwestern Mutual Life Insurance Company
720 E. Wisconsin Ave., Milwaukee, WI 53202
Phone: 414-271-1444
Web: www.nmfn.com

PRODUCTS/OPERATIONS

2008 Sales

	$ mil.	% of total
Premiums	13,551	62
Investment Income	7,835	36
Other Income	537	2
Total	**21,923**	**100**

Selected Subsidiaries

Frank Russell Company
Northwestern Long Term Care Insurance Company
Northwestern Mutual Investment Services, LLC
Northwestern Mutual Wealth Management Company

COMPETITORS

AEGON USA
AIG
AIG American General
AllianceBernstein Holding
Allianz
AXA Financial
CIGNA
Citigroup
CNA Financial
Conseco
FMR
Genworth Financial
Guardian Life
The Hartford
ING
John Hancock Financial Services
Liberty Mutual
MassMutual
Merrill Lynch
MetLife
Morgan Stanley
MSCI
Mutual of Omaha
Nationwide
New York Life
Pacific Mutual
Principal Financial
Prudential
Sun Life
T. Rowe Price
TIAA-CREF

HISTORICAL FINANCIALS

Company Type: Mutual company

Income Statement

FYE: December 31

	ASSETS ($ mil.)	NET INCOME ($ mil.)	INCOME AS % OF ASSETS	EMPLOYEES
12/08	155,154.0	483.0	0.3%	5,000
12/07	156,547.0	1,000.0	0.6%	4,983
12/06	145,102.0	829.0	0.6%	4,800
12/05	133,057.0	924.0	0.7%	4,800
12/04	123,957.0	817.0	0.7%	4,700
Annual Growth	**5.8%**	**(12.3%)**	**—**	**1.6%**

2008 Year-End Financials

Equity as % of assets: —
Return on assets: 0.3%
Return on equity: —
Long-term debt ($ mil.): —
Sales ($ mil.): 21,923

Net Income History

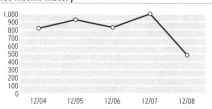

Novell, Inc.

Novell is a firm believer in the power of networking. The company's flagship NetWare network server operating system connects desktop computers to corporate networks, integrating directories, storage systems, printers, servers, and databases. Novell also provides a version of the Linux operating system, and applications including network management software, collaborative tools, and directory services products. In addition, it offers a variety of services such as IT consulting, implementation, support, and training. Novell's strategic partners include CA, Dell, Intel, Microsoft, and SAP. It sells through a direct sales force, as well as through distributors, resellers, and systems integrators.

The company has identified Linux, identity management software, and systems and resource management applications as its growth products. Novell has pursued strategic acquisitions to expand those lines. It built its Linux-based offerings with the acquisitions of Ximian (2003), SuSE Linux (2004), and Immunix (2005). Novell's identity and access management division got a boost from the 2006 purchase of enterprise security software developer e-Security for $72 million. The following year Novell acquired endpoint security management specialist Senforce Technologies, which bolstered its systems and resource management offerings. Novell further expanded its systems and resource management portfolio with two purchases in 2008: data center software developer PlateSpin, and business service management software provider Managed Objects.

Novell reported revenue increases in all of its growth lines in fiscal 2008. Its traditional Workgroup products, which still account for more than 40% of its sales, saw a slight decline.

The company forged an unlikely partnership with rival Microsoft late in 2006. The terms of the deal included a reseller agreement that has Microsoft distributing subscriptions to Novell's SuSE Linux software, the conducting of joint research and development operations, the payment of royalties by Novell to Microsoft, and an agreement by Microsoft not to file patent-infringement charges.

HISTORY

Novell was woven from the remnants of Novell Data Systems, a maker of disk operating systems founded in 1980. (The name was chosen for its suggestion of newness.) High-tech investment firm Safeguard Scientifics bought a controlling stake in the venture in 1981. In 1983 Safeguard incorporated the company and shortened its name to Novell. It also recruited CEO Raymond Noorda, an experienced engineer and marketer who invested $125,000 of his own money.

Under Noorda, Novell focused on developing PC networking systems that designated one machine (the file server) to manage the network and control access to shared devices, such as disk drives and printers. In 1983 Novell introduced NetWare, the first networking software based on file server technology.

Safeguard sold half of its 51% stake to the public two years later and gradually sold off the rest. Novell began acquiring other companies to expand its product line, including Santa Clara Systems (microcomputer workstations, 1987) and Excelan (networking software and equipment, 1989). In 1988 Novell halted production of most hardware.

By the early 1990s Novell dominated the networking market with a nearly 70% share. Wanting to undermine Microsoft's dominant position, Noorda bought the rights to AT&T's UNIX operating system (1992), top word-processing software maker WordPerfect (1994), and Borland's spreadsheet business, Quattro Pro (1994). Novell in 1994 also transferred its database products (NetWare SQL, Xtrieve) to Btrieve Technologies (now Pervasive Software). The acquisitions failed to dent Microsoft's market share.

Noorda retired in 1994 and was succeeded by Hewlett-Packard executive Robert Frankenberg, who began to streamline the company and divest itself of units such as WordPerfect.

Frankenberg was ousted in 1996 after Novell posted flat sales for several consecutive quarters. Temporary CEO John Young began to focus the company's development efforts on the burgeoning Internet market, a push that was intensified when Young was replaced in 1997 by former Sun Microsystems engineer Eric Schmidt.

In 1997 Novell laid off 1,000 workers (18% of its workforce, including nearly half of its 66 VPs) and became the subject of IBM takeover rumors. The next year it shifted its focus to directory services and introduced a version of NetWare designed exclusively for Internet and intranet applications.

Novell bought Netoria, a privately held maker of software for computer network administrators, in 1999. Compaq and Dell began shipping servers with Novell's Internet caching software, which linked PCs to host Internet sites for delivery of content to corporate intranets. That year the company invested $100 million in information technology services provider Whittman-Hart (which went bankrupt under the name marchFIRST in 2001).

In 2001 Novell (along with minority partners Nortel Networks and Accenture) announced the creation of Volera, a caching and content networking company. It also bought Cambridge Technology Partners in a deal valued at about $266 million; Cambridge CEO Jack Messman assumed the role of chief executive at Novell.

The company acquired SilverStream Software in 2002 for about $210 million. It also purchased Accenture and Nortel's stakes in Volera as part of a plan to integrate it into Novell's product lines.

In 2004 Novell agreed to accept a $536 million cash settlement from Microsoft in regards to possible antitrust action relating to Netware products. The following year the company announced a restructuring plan that included a 10% workforce reduction.

Messman was replaced as CEO by company president Ronald Hovsepian in mid-2006.

Novell sold off its management consulting firm Celerant Consulting for $77 million in mid-2006; the buyout group included Celerant management and Caledonia Investments.

EXECUTIVES

Chairman: Richard L. (Rick) Crandall, age 66
President, CEO, and Director:
Ronald W. (Ron) Hovsepian, age 48,
$7,588,393 total compensation
SVP and CFO: Dana C. Russell, age 47,
$2,056,857 total compensation
EVP and CTO: Jeffrey M. (Jeff) Jaffe, age 54,
$2,265,064 total compensation
VP and COO: José Almandoz
SVP and Chief Marketing Officer: John Dragoon, age 48
SVP and General Manager, Identity and Security Management Solutions: James P. (Jim) Ebzery, age 49
SVP, General Counsel, and Secretary: Scott N. Semel, age 51
SVP and General Manager, Workgroup Solutions: Kent Erickson
Acting General Manager and SVP, Open Platform Solutions (OPS) Group: Markus Rex
SVP Services: Colleen O'Keefe, age 52
SVP and General Manager, Systems and Resource Management: Joe Wagner
VP and General Manager, Global Strategic Alliances: Susan Heystee
SVP Strategic Development: Roger Levy
VP Finance: Bill Smith
President and General Manager, Novell Americas: Timothy M. (Tim) Wolfe
CEO, Salmon Ltd.: Christopher C. (Chris) Harvey
Auditors: PricewaterhouseCoopers LLP

LOCATIONS

HQ: Novell, Inc.
404 Wyman St., Ste. 500, Waltham, MA 02451
Phone: 781-464-8000   **Fax:** 781-464-8100
Web: www.novell.com

2008 Sales

	$ mil.	% of total
Americas		
US	461.4	48
Other countries	70.5	7
Europe, Middle East & Africa	343.3	36
Asia/Pacific	81.3	9
Total	**956.5**	**100**

PRODUCTS/OPERATIONS

2008 Sales

	$ mil.	% of total
Maintenance & subscriptions	613.1	64
Software licenses	189.6	20
Services	153.8	16
Total	**956.5**	**100**

2008 Sales

	$ mil.	% of total
Workgroup	414.4	44
Identity & security management	194.0	20
Systems & resource management	193.2	20
Open platform solutions	154.9	16
Total	**956.5**	**100**

COMPETITORS

Avocent
CA, Inc.
Cisco Systems
Hewlett-Packard
IBM
McAfee
Microsoft
Oracle
Red Hat
Sun Microsystems
Symantec
VMware

HISTORICAL FINANCIALS

Company Type: Public

Income Statement			FYE: Last Saturday in October	
	REVENUE ($ mil.)	NET INCOME ($ mil.)	NET PROFIT MARGIN	EMPLOYEES
10/08	956.5	(8.7)	—	4,000
10/07	932.5	(44.5)	—	4,100
10/06	967.3	19.6	2.0%	4,549
10/05	1,197.7	372.6	31.1%	5,066
10/04	1,165.9	57.2	4.9%	6,000
Annual Growth	(4.8%)	—	—	(9.6%)

2008 Year-End Financials

Debt ratio: 0.0%
Return on equity: —
Cash ($ mil.): 680
Current ratio: 1.54
Long-term debt ($ mil.): 0

No. of shares (mil.): 345
Dividends
Yield: 0.0%
Payout: —
Market value ($ mil.): 1,609

Stock History

NASDAQ (GS): NOVL

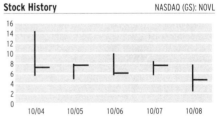

	STOCK PRICE ($) FY Close	P/E High/Low		PER SHARE ($) Earnings	Dividends	Book Value
10/08	4.66	—	—	(0.02)	0.00	3.15
10/07	7.56	—	—	(0.13)	0.00	3.36
10/06	6.00	197	115	0.05	0.00	3.20
10/05	7.62	9	6	0.86	0.00	4.02
10/04	7.19	178	70	0.08	0.00	2.79
Annual Growth	(10.3%)	—	—	—	—	3.1%

NRG Energy

A company so nice they named it twice is doubling its efforts to deliver power. NRG Energy, a leading power producer with an operational generating capacity of more than 24,000 MW, is moving onward and upward. The vast majority of NRG's power plants are in North America, but it also has one in Australia and two in Germany. The company's global portfolio includes 189 generation units at 48 power plants. It also markets natural gas, oil, and other commodities and invests in district heating and cooling and alternative energy projects. In 2008, in a move to expand its geographic reach, Exelon made a $6.2 billion bid to acquire NRG, but NRG rebuffed the offer as inadequate, and in 2009 Exelon withdrew its bid.

Though NRG resisted Exelon's offer, that company has kept up its pursuit. Toward the end of 2008 it announced an exchange offer for NRG's shares. By the expiration date of the offer, early the next year, it had acquired just more than 50% of those shares. In addition to announcing another extension of the offer, Exelon said it hoped NRG's Board would allow it to do due diligence and begin negotiations for an acquisition. Failing that, Exelon said it would nominate its own members for election to NRG's Board.

Like other power wholesalers, the company has been looking to buy similar businesses to increase its market share. In 2006 NRG acquired power generator NRG Texas for $5.8 billion and rejected a takeover bid from Mirant. It submitted an application to build two nuclear reactors in South Texas the following year, and in 2008 it bid $11 billion to acquire Calpine, which Calpine rejected. NRG is also pursuing new power plant initiatives in renewable sources such as wind and solar energy, and in the use of nuclear and clean coal-powered facilities.

It has pulled back on international exposure though, in favor of the less risky North American market. In 2008 NRG sold its power plant in Brazil.

In 2009, in a move to expand its share of the Texas retail market, NRG acquired the Texas retail business of the former Reliant Energy (now called RRI Energy) for about $285 million. NRG also acquired the Reliant Energy trade name in the deal.

Responding to government demands for utilities to increase their use of renewables, in 2009 the company announced plans to develop solar power plants in California and New Mexico.

EXECUTIVES

Chairman: Howard E. Cosgrove, age 65
President, CEO, and Director: David W. Crane, age 50
EVP and COO: John W. Ragan, age 49
EVP and CFO: Robert C. Flexon, age 50,
  $2,134,887 total compensation
EVP and Chief Administrative Officer:
  Denise M. Wilson, age 49
VP and Chief Accounting Officer: James J. Ingoldsby
**EVP and Chief Development Officer, Low-Carbon
  Technology:** Michael Liebelson
EVP; Regional President, Texas: Kevin T. Howell,
  age 51, $2,840,799 total compensation
EVP; Regional President, Northeast:
  J. Andrew (Drew) Murphy, age 48
EVP Strategy: Jonathan Baliff

SVP Commercial Operations: Mauricio Gutierrez
SVP and General Counsel: Michael Bramnick
VP Investor Relations: Nahla A. Azmy
President, Nuclear Innovation North America:
  Steven C. (Steve) Winn, age 43
President and CEO, Padoma Wind Power: Jan C. Paulin
President, Reliant Energy; SVP, NRG Retail: Jason Few,
  age 43
President, NRG Retail: Christopher S. Sotos
Investor Relations: Erin Gilli
Auditors: KPMG LLP

LOCATIONS

HQ: NRG Energy, Inc.
  211 Carnegie Center, Princeton, NJ 08540
Phone: 609-524-4500   **Fax:** 609-524-4501
Web: www.nrgenergy.com

2008 Sales

	$ mil.	% of total
Texas	4,026	58
Northeast	1,630	24
South Central	746	11
West	171	3
International	158	2
Other	154	2
Total	**6,885**	**100**

PRODUCTS/OPERATIONS

2008 Sales

	$ mil.	% of total
Energy	4,519	66
Capacity	1,359	19
Risk management	418	6
Contract amortization	278	4
Thermal	114	2
Other	197	3
Total	**6,885**	**100**

Selected Subsidiaries

NEO Corporation (distributed generation; landfill gas,
  hydroelectric, and other renewable generation)
NRG Power Marketing, Inc. (power sales)
NRG Resource Recovery (waste-to-energy facilities)
NRG Texas LLC (power generation)
NRG Thermal Corporation (district heating and cooling,
  combined heat and power facilities)
Texas Genco LP (power generation)
West Coast Power, LLC (power generation)

COMPETITORS

AEP
AES
Alliant Energy
Calpine
Cogentrix
Duke Energy
Dynegy
Edison International
El Paso
Energy Future
Entergy
E.ON UK
International Power
MidAmerican Energy
Mirant
Nicor
PG&E Corporation
PSEG Power
RRI Energy
Sempra Generation
Tenaska

HISTORICAL FINANCIALS

Company Type: Public

Income Statement

FYE: December 31

	REVENUE ($ mil.)	NET INCOME ($ mil.)	NET PROFIT MARGIN	EMPLOYEES
12/08	6,885.0	1,188.0	17.3%	3,526
12/07	5,989.0	586.0	9.8%	3,412
12/06	5,623.0	621.0	11.0%	3,217
12/05	2,708.0	84.0	3.1%	3,682
12/04	2,361.4	185.6	7.9%	2,644
Annual Growth	**30.7%**	**59.1%**	**—**	**7.5%**

2008 Year-End Financials

Debt ratio: 123.1%
Return on equity: 21.9%
Cash ($ mil.): 1,494
Current ratio: 1.29
Long-term debt ($ mil.): 7,704
No. of shares (mil.): 265
Dividends
Yield: 0.0%
Payout: —
Market value ($ mil.): 6,189

Stock History

NYSE: NRG

	STOCK PRICE ($) FY Close	P/E High/Low		PER SHARE ($) Earnings	Dividends	Book Value
12/08	23.33	11	3	4.29	0.00	26.80
12/07	43.34	23	14	2.01	0.00	20.75
12/06	28.00	15	10	2.04	0.00	21.33
12/05	23.56	66	40	0.38	0.00	8.41
12/04	18.02	20	10	0.93	0.00	10.15
Annual Growth	**6.7%**	**—**	**—**	**46.6%**	**—**	**27.5%**

NSTAR

A giant star in the deregulation firmament, NSTAR was formed by the 1999 merger of BEC Energy and Commonwealth Energy System. NSTAR has responded to energy deregulation in Massachusetts by cutting its rates and selling most of its regulated electric generation assets. The utility holding company transmits and distributes electricity to 1.1 million homes and businesses and serves some 300,000 natural gas customers in Massachusetts. The company also markets wholesale electricity, operates liquefied natural gas (LNG) processing and storage facilities, and provides district heating and cooling services.

NSTAR's power utilities — Boston Edison, Cambridge Electric Light, and Commonwealth Electric — merged as NSTAR Electric in 2007; the new company serves customers in more than 80 Massachusetts communities, including Boston. Subsidiary NSTAR Gas is present in about 50 communities in central and eastern Massachusetts.

Among its other, non-utility businesses are the LNG storage division and a telecom services unit. The latter owns and operates a wholesale transport network for other telecom service providers in the Boston area. These unregulated businesses provide NSTAR with about 5% of its total sales.

HISTORY

NSTAR got its start in 1886 as the Edison Electric Illuminating Company of Boston. The company pushed the use of electricity (promoting and selling appliances in its early days) and helped to develop the first electric vehicles. In the 1920s the company launched radio stations WTAT and WEEI. It changed its name to Boston Edison in 1937.

In the 1970s Boston Edison's fortunes soured as it endured a three-month strike in 1971. In 1972 its nuclear-generated power plant, Pilgrim Station, went online, just in time for the OPEC oil embargo. The company spent about $300 million in the 1980s to fix problems at Pilgrim, which had been heavily fined by the Nuclear Regulatory Commission.

Utility deregulation began gaining momentum in the Northeast in the 1990s, and Boston Edison responded by selling its fossil-fueled power plants, reducing rates, and creating a holding company (BEC Energy) for new, unregulated businesses. In 1996 BEC Energy and the Williams Companies formed a power-marketing joint venture (Williams later took over). It also formed a joint venture with telecommunications company RCN to provide bundled telephone, cable, and Internet access over BEC Energy's fiber-optic networks in Boston.

BEC Energy sold its fossil fuel-generated plants to Sithe Energies in 1997. Still shedding assets in 1999, the company sold its Pilgrim nuke to Entergy. It then merged with Commonwealth Energy System to form NSTAR. In 2000 the new holding company organized its three electric utilities under one brand name, NSTAR Electric, and renamed its gas unit NSTAR Gas.

In 2002 NSTAR sold its 3% interest in the Vermont Yankee nuclear plant to Entergy. That year the company sold its 4% interest in the Seabrook nuclear plant to FPL Group and exchanged its 23% interest in joint venture RCN-BecoCom for an 11% stake in the venture's parent, RCN Corporation. Due to low market value, NSTAR wrote off its investment in RCN in 2005.

NSTAR and Evergreen Solar, a maker of solar power products, formed an alliance in 2007 designed to increase the role of solar power in eastern Massachusetts.

EXECUTIVES

Chairman, President, CEO, and Trustee:
Thomas J. (Tom) May, age 61,
$7,054,168 total compensation
SVP Operations: Werner J. Schweiger, age 49,
$1,683,362 total compensation
SVP and CFO: James J. (Jim) Judge, age 52,
$1,956,128 total compensation
SVP Information Technology: Eugene J. (Gene) Zimon, age 60
VP, Chief Accounting Officer, and Controller:
Robert J. (Bob) Weafer Jr., age 61
SVP Strategy, Law, and Policy; Secretary; and General Counsel: Douglas S. (Doug) Horan, age 59,
$1,944,568 total compensation
SVP Customer and Corporate Relations:
Joseph R. (Joe) Nolan Jr., age 45,
$1,049,908 total compensation
SVP Human Resources: Christine M. (Chris) Carmody

VP Gas Operations: Philip B. Andreas
VP Energy Supply and Supply Chain Management:
Ellen K. Angley
VP Customer Care: Penelope M. (Penni) Conner
VP Financial Strategic Planning and Policy:
Geoffrey O. Lubbock
VP Electric Operations: Paul D. Vaitkus
VP Engineering: Lawrence J. Gelbien
Treasurer: Philip J. (Phil) Lembo
Manager Investor Relations: John F. Gavin
Auditors: PricewaterhouseCoopers LLP

LOCATIONS

HQ: NSTAR
800 Boylston St., Boston, MA 02199
Phone: 617-424-2000   **Fax:** 781-441-8886
Web: www.nstaronline.com

PRODUCTS/OPERATIONS

2008 Sales

	$ mil.	% of total
Electric utility	2,639.6	79
Gas utility	553.7	16
Unregulated operations	152.1	5
Total	**3,345.4**	**100**

Selected Subsidiaries

Advanced Energy Systems, Inc. (district heating and cooling)
Hopkinton LNG Corp. (liquefied natural gas services)
NSTAR Communications, Inc. (wholesale broadband network)
NSTAR Electric Company (electric utility)
NSTAR Gas Company (natural gas utility)

COMPETITORS

Bay State Gas
Con Edison
Energy East
Green Mountain Power
National Grid USA
NiSource
Northeast Utilities
PG&E Corporation
Unitil
USPowerGen

HISTORICAL FINANCIALS

Company Type: Public

Income Statement

	REVENUE ($ mil.)	NET INCOME ($ mil.)	NET PROFIT MARGIN	EMPLOYEES
12/08	3,345.4	237.5	7.1%	3,250
12/07	3,261.8	223.5	6.9%	3,150
12/06	3,577.7	204.8	5.7%	3,100
12/05	3,243.1	194.2	6.0%	3,050
12/04	2,954.3	188.5	6.4%	3,100
Annual Growth	**3.2%**	**5.9%**	**—**	**1.2%**

FYE: December 31

2008 Year-End Financials

Debt ratio: 112.5%
Return on equity: 13.6%
Cash ($ mil.): 22
Current ratio: 0.80
Long-term debt ($ mil.): 2,012

No. of shares (mil.): 107
Dividends
  Yield: 3.9%
  Payout: 64.0%
Market value ($ mil.): 3,897

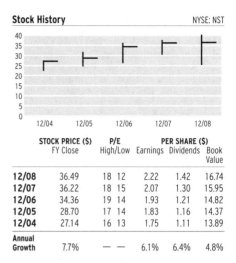

Stock History   NYSE: NST

	STOCK PRICE ($) FY Close	P/E High/Low	PER SHARE ($) Earnings	Dividends	Book Value
12/08	36.49	18 12	2.22	1.42	16.74
12/07	36.22	18 15	2.07	1.30	15.95
12/06	34.36	19 14	1.93	1.21	14.82
12/05	28.70	17 14	1.83	1.16	14.37
12/04	27.14	16 13	1.75	1.11	13.89
Annual Growth	**7.7%**	**— —**	**6.1%**	**6.4%**	**4.8%**

Nucor Corporation

Nucor continues to electrify the steel industry with a simple concept: The minimill is mighty. At its various minimills, Nucor produces about 25 million tons of steel annually, including hot- and cold-rolled steel, steel joists, and metal buildings. A major recycler of scrap metal, Nucor produces steel by melting scrap in electric arc furnaces. Most of its products are sold to steel service centers, manufacturers, and fabricators. Divisions such as Vulcraft — one of the US's largest producers of steel joists, girders, and decking — use the balance of the steel. The company has added greatly to its operations through acquisitions since 2006, including spending $1 billion to buy The David J. Joseph Company.

Nucor has dominated the minimill industry for more than two decades, but competitors in the sector are increasing. The company continues to expand its steel mills, add new facilities, and pursue acquisition opportunities. In the latter half of this decade, it acquired the former Connecticut Steel, a maker of bar product steel like wire rod, rebar, and wire mesh; Verco Manufacturing, which makes steel flooring and roof decking; and Canadian steel products maker Harris Steel, which like Connecticut Steel had been a customer and partner of Nucor for years. Harris produces rebar, wire, and grating and will operate as a separate, wholly owned subsidiary. Harris itself made an acquisition in 2008, when it bought rebar fabricator and distributor Ambassador Steel.

Nucor expanded its downstream operations with the 2007 acquisition of building systems maker MAGNATRAX for $280 million. That company emerged from Chapter 11 bankruptcy protection in 2004 and was owned by creditors prior to the deal. Not long after that, it again acquired a company it has worked with for years. David J. Joseph is a scrap metal broker that had supplied Nucor's minimills for 40 years; it continues to operate as a Nucor subsidiary. It also acquired Metal Recycling Services, a scrap metals services company that will operate as a unit within David J. Joseph, and scrap processer Galamba Metals.

The company has always operated primarily in the US, but in 2008 it moved into the international market with the formation of a European joint venture with Duferco. The JV will produce steel beams and merchant bar products from manufacturing locations in Italy and serve the European and North African markets.

Even though Nucor continues to face stiff domestic and foreign competition as well as pronounced economic difficulties, it has not laid off any employees in more than 30 years. The company's SOP is to modulate its output — and its employees' pay — according to demand; in a downturn the company will produce less steel and its employees will make less than they do during stronger economic times.

HISTORY

Nucor started as the second carmaking venture of Ransom Olds, who built his first gasoline-powered car in 1897. Two years later, Samuel Smith, a Detroit copper and lumber magnate, put up $199,600 to finance Olds Motor Works. A fire destroyed the company's Detroit plant in 1901, so Olds moved production to Lansing, Michigan, where he built America's first mass-produced car — the Oldsmobile. In 1904 Olds left Olds Motor Works, which was bought by General Motors (GM) in 1908, and formed Reo Car Company (renamed Reo Motor Car in 1906). In addition to cars, it eventually made trucks and buses.

By the end of the Depression, Ford, GM, and Chrysler commanded over 85% of the US passenger car market. Reo stopped making cars in 1936 and sold its truck manufacturing operations in 1957. Meanwhile, it had formed Reo Holding, which in 1955 merged with Nuclear Consultants to form Nuclear Corporation of America. The new company offered services such as radiation studies and made nuclear instruments and electronics.

In 1962 Nuclear bought steel joist maker Vulcraft and gained the services of Kenneth Iverson. The diverse company was unprofitable, losing $2 million on $22 million in sales in 1965. That year Iverson took over as CEO, moved headquarters to Charlotte, North Carolina, and shut down or sold about half of the company's businesses. By focusing on its profitable steel joist operations, the firm ended 1966 in the black. Because the company depended on imports for 80% of its steel needs, Iverson decided to move into steel production. Nuclear Corporation built its first minimill in 1969.

The company was renamed Nucor in 1972. It started making steel deck (1977) and cold-finished steel bars (1979). Production tripled and sales more than doubled between 1974 and 1979.

Nucor began to diversify, adding grinding balls (used in the mining industry to process ores, 1981); steel bolts, steel bearings, and machined steel parts (1986); and metal buildings and components (1987). Nucor and Japanese steelmaker Yamato Kogyo formed Nucor-Yamato and built a mill in 1988 to produce wide-flange beams (for heavy construction). The following year Nucor opened a state-of-the-art mill in Crawfordsville, Indiana, and another mill near Hickman, Arkansas, in 1992.

Iverson turned over his CEO duties to company veteran John Correnti in 1996. The next year Nucor began building a steel beam mill in South Carolina and added a galvanizing facility to its Hickman mill.

In 1998 Nucor announced plans to build its first steel plate mill, which became operational in 2000. The company slashed prices twice in 1998 to compete against low-cost imports from Russia, Japan, and Brazil. Differences with the board prompted Correnti to resign in 1999; chairman David Aycock assumed his duties. In September 2000 Aycock resigned from the company and Daniel R. DiMicco, formerly an EVP, was named CEO.

In 2002 Nucor teamed up with Companhia Vale do Rio Doce (Vale), a Brazilian producer and exporter of iron-ore pellets, to develop low-cost iron-based products. In late 2002 Nucor bought financially troubled Birmingham Steel for $615 million in cash and debt.

Its Vulcraft unit saw an increase in non-residential building construction in 2004, which boosted sales of joist girders, steel deck, and steel joists. Nucor bought Corus Tuscaloosa (now called Nucor Tuscaloosa) in mid-2004, a producer of coiled plate with an annual capacity of around 700,000 tons.

The company named CEO DiMicco chairman in 2006.

EXECUTIVES

Chairman, President, and CEO:
Daniel R. (Dan) DiMicco, age 58
COO Steelmaking Operations: John J. Ferriola, age 56, $2,793,492 total compensation
EVP, CFO, and Treasurer: Terry S. Lisenby, age 57, $2,515,157 total compensation
EVP Flat Rolled Products: Ladd R. Hall, age 52
EVP Business Development: Joseph A. Rutkowski, age 54, $2,775,304 total compensation
EVP Bar Products: D. Michael Parrish, age 56
EVP Fabricated Construction Products:
Hamilton Lott Jr., age 59
EVP: Keith B. Grass, $2,264,776 total compensation
EVP Beam and Plate Products: R. Joseph Stratman, age 52
VP; President, Vulcraft and Verco Group:
James R. Darsey
VP; President, Nucor Buildings Group: Harry R. Lowe
VP Human Resources: James M. Coblin, age 64
VP and Corporate Controller: James D. Frias
VP; President, Nucor Building Systems:
Jeffrey B. (Jeff) Carmean
General Manager and Secretary: A. Rae Eagle
Corporate IT Manager: Scott Messenger
General Manager, Business Development and Strategic Planning: Stephen D. Laxton
General Manager, Coporate Legal Affairs:
Douglas R. Gunson
Auditors: PricewaterhouseCoopers LLP

LOCATIONS

HQ: Nucor Corporation
1915 Rexford Rd., Charlotte, NC 28211
Phone: 704-366-7000   **Fax:** 704-362-4208
Web: www.nucor.com

PRODUCTS/OPERATIONS

2008 Sales

	$ mil.	% of total
Steel mills	16,477.9	70
Steel products	4,339.5	18
Raw Materials	2,403.1	10
All other	442.8	2
Total	**23,663.3**	**100**

Selected Products

Alloy steel
  Cold-drawn steel bars
  Finished hex caps
  Hex-head cap screws
  Locknuts
  Structural bolts and nuts
Carbon steel
  Angles
  Beams
  Channels
  Cold-drawn steel bars
  Finished hex nuts
  Flats
  Floor plate
  Galvanized sheet
  Grinding balls
  Hexagons
  Hot-rolled sheet
  Reinforcing bars
  Structural bolts and nuts
  Wide-range beams
Engineered products
  Composite floor joists
  Floor deck
  Joists
  Joist girders
  Pre-engineered metal buildings
  Roof deck
  Special-profile steel trusses
Stainless steel
  Cold-rolled steel
  Hot-rolled steel
  Pickled sheet

COMPETITORS

AK Steel Holding
ArcelorMittal USA
BlueScope Steel
Commercial Metals
Corus Group
Gerdau Ameristeel
Renco
Steel Dynamics
United States Steel

HISTORICAL FINANCIALS

Company Type: Public

Income Statement

FYE: December 31

	REVENUE ($ mil.)	NET INCOME ($ mil.)	NET PROFIT MARGIN	EMPLOYEES
12/08	23,663.3	1,831.0	7.7%	21,700
12/07	16,593.0	1,471.9	8.9%	18,000
12/06	14,751.3	1,757.7	11.9%	11,900
12/05	12,701.0	1,310.3	10.3%	11,300
12/04	11,376.8	1,121.5	9.9%	10,600
Annual Growth	**20.1%**	**13.0%**	**—**	**19.6%**

2008 Year-End Financials

Debt ratio: 38.9%
Return on equity: 28.1%
Cash ($ mil.): 2,355
Current ratio: 3.45
Long-term debt ($ mil.): 3,086

No. of shares (mil.): 315
Dividends
  Yield: 3.3%
  Payout: 25.3%
Market value ($ mil.): 14,538

Stock History

NYSE: NUE

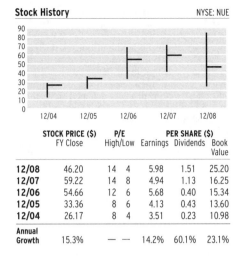

	STOCK PRICE ($) FY Close	P/E High/Low		PER SHARE ($) Earnings	Dividends	Book Value
12/08	46.20	14	4	5.98	1.51	25.20
12/07	59.22	14	8	4.94	1.13	16.25
12/06	54.66	12	6	5.68	0.40	15.34
12/05	33.36	8	6	4.13	0.43	13.60
12/04	26.17	8	4	3.51	0.23	10.98
Annual Growth	15.3%	—	—	14.2%	60.1%	23.1%

NVIDIA Corporation

NVIDIA keeps staging new graphics chip invasions. The fabless semiconductor company designs high-definition 2-D and 3-D graphics processors for gaming and industrial-design applications. Its graphics chips, especially the flagship GeForce line, are used by major PC makers, such as Apple, Dell, Gateway, and Hewlett-Packard, as well as in add-in boards and motherboards produced by ASUSTeK Computer and other companies. NVIDIA also provides complementary graphics driver software, as well as graphics chipsets — clusters of components with integrated graphics functions that aid the operation of PC microprocessors. The company gets about three-quarters of its sales in Asia, primarily in China and Taiwan.

In 2008 NVIDIA acquired AGEIA Technologies, a developer of physics processing software for gaming. AGEIA's PhysX software is used in dozens of games for the Microsoft Xbox 360, Nintendo Wii, and Sony PlayStation 3 game consoles, and for PCs.

In 2007 the company purchased PortalPlayer, a supplier of chips that go into Apple's iPods, SanDisk's Sansa MP3 music players, and other portable electronics.

AMD's 2006 acquisition of NVIDIA's archrival, ATI Technologies, complicated a number of relationships in the semiconductor industry. AMD and NVIDIA previously collaborated on making sure AMD's microprocessors and NVIDIA's graphics processors worked smoothly together; AMD cultivated a similar relationship with ATI Technologies prior to the acquisition. The purchase put AMD and NVIDIA in the awkward position of being both collaborators and competitors, as AMD is developing a new set of "Fusion" processors that meld the capabilities of the AMD and ATI product lines.

AMD and Intel are NVIDIA's biggest competitors. Intel is preparing a multiple-core architecture, code-named Larrabee, that may compete with various NVIDIA products. Intel's Atom processor for low-end PCs also presents a challenge to the company.

The biggest challenge for NVIDIA, of course, is the global recession that is depressing sales of consumer electronics and dampening the revenues of chip makers worldwide.

Adding to industry anxiety was an investigation into the graphics processor market by the Antitrust Division of the US Department of Justice. AMD and NVIDIA received subpoenas in 2006 from the Justice Department for materials related to competitive practices in the business for graphics processing units and cards. The Justice Department also has a longstanding antitrust case in the DRAM device market, which resulted in several industry executives going to prison and vendors paying hundreds of millions of dollars in fines for fixing prices on memory parts, and separate investigations into the static random-access memory (SRAM) and NAND flash memory device markets.

The Department of Justice concluded the antitrust investigation into graphics processing units and cards in late 2008 without taking any action against AMD or NVIDIA.

President and CEO Jen-Hsun Huang owns about 5% of NVIDIA.

HISTORY

Taiwan-born and Stanford-trained engineer Jen-Hsun Huang was already a veteran of Advanced Micro Devices and LSI Logic (now just LSI) when he decided to start his own company at age 30. He co-founded NVIDIA in 1992 with fellow engineers and industry veterans Chris Malachowsky (SVP) and Curtis Priem (former CTO). It was incorporated in 1993.

After its first try at a graphics chip failed miserably in 1995, NVIDIA hit the big time in 1997 when it introduced a graphics processor that set a new industry standard for speed. Good product timing and flawless execution kept the company growing in the years to come: After turning its first profit in 1998, NVIDIA crossed the $100 million, $300 million, and $700 million sales thresholds in successive years.

The company made its IPO in 1999. The following year Microsoft chose NVIDIA to supply the graphics chips for its Xbox video game console. Also in 2000 the company overtook archrival ATI Technologies in market share for desktop PC graphics chips.

Late in 2000 the company announced that it would acquire the assets of erstwhile rival 3dfx in a deal initially valued at $110 million. The transaction was completed in mid-2001 for $70 million in cash and a potential earnout payment of 1 million shares of NVIDIA common stock. In 2002 the company came under review by the SEC for potential accounting irregularities; when the company restated earnings a few months later, though, its financial results for the three-year period in question improved slightly.

Later in 2002 NVIDIA bought privately held 3-D software company Exluna, which was founded by veterans of Pixar. The following year NVIDIA acquired MediaQ, whose handheld graphics and media products were rebranded as GoForce, for about $70 million. In 2004 NVIDIA acquired assets of privately held iReady Corp., primarily consisting of the intellectual property and patents related to its TCP/IP and iSCSI Ethernet technologies.

Early in 2006 the company acquired Taiwanese circuit designer ULi Electronics for about $52 million. The company also acquired Hybrid Graphics, a developer of embedded graphics software for handheld devices, that same year.

EXECUTIVES

President, CEO, and Director: Jen-Hsun Huang, age 46, $4,010,370 total compensation
EVP Operations: Debora C. Shoquist, age 54, $1,988,101 total compensation
EVP and CFO: David L. White, age 53
CIO: Ranga Jayaraman
Chief Scientist and VP, NVIDIA Research: Bill Dally
EVP, General Counsel, and Secretary: David M. Shannon, age 53, $1,762,050 total compensation
EVP Worldwide Sales: Ajay K (Jay) Puri, age 54, $2,020,535 total compensation
SVP Human Resources: Scott P. Sullivan
SVP Marketing: Daniel F. (Dan) Vivoli, age 48
SVP Engineering and Operations: Chris A. Malachowsky, age 50
SVP GPU Business Unit: Jeffrey D. (Jeff) Fisher, age 50
SVP Investor Relations and Communications: Michael W. Hara
SVP Software Engineering: Dwight Diercks
SVP Consumer Electronics Engineering: Frank Fox
SVP GPU Engineering: Jonah M. Alben
SVP VLSI Engineering: Joseph D. (Joe) Greco
SVP MCP Engineering: Gary Hicok
VP Corporate Communications: Robert (Bob) Sherbin, age 51
Director Public Relations: Derek Perez
Auditors: PricewaterhouseCoopers LLP

LOCATIONS

HQ: NVIDIA Corporation
2701 San Tomas Expwy., Santa Clara, CA 95050
Phone: 408-486-2000   **Fax:** 408-486-2200
Web: www.nvidia.com

NVIDIA has design centers, laboratories, and offices in Australia, China, Finland, France, Germany, Hong Kong, India, Japan, Russia, South Korea, Taiwan, the UK, and the US.

2009 Sales

	$ mil.	% of total
Asia/Pacific		
China	1,087.7	32
Taiwan	974.1	28
Other countries	601.5	18
Americas		
US	309.6	9
Other countries	130.9	4
Europe	321.1	9
Total	**3,424.9**	**100**

PRODUCTS/OPERATIONS

2009 Sales

	$ mil.	% of total
GPU Business	1,912.3	56
Professional Solutions Business	693.4	20
Media & Communications Processor	655.6	19
Consumer Products Business	136.3	4
Other	27.3	1
Total	**3,424.9**	**100**

Selected Products

Graphics processing unit (GPU) chips for PCs and workstations (GeForce, NVIDIA Quadro)
Media and communications processors (MCP) for PCs, workstations, and servers (nForce)
Consumer electronics processors for video game consoles and other devices
Handheld GPUs for handheld computers and mobile phones (GoForce)

COMPETITORS

AMD
ARM Holdings
Broadcom
Creative Technology
Epson
Freescale Semiconductor
Fujitsu
Imagination Technologies
Intel Corp.
Marvell Technology
Matrox Electronic Systems
MediaTek
NEC
QUALCOMM
Renesas Technology
Samsung Electronics
Silicon Integrated Systems
STMicroelectronics
Texas Instruments
Toshiba America Electronic Components
VIA Technologies

HISTORICAL FINANCIALS

Company Type: Public

Income Statement

	REVENUE ($ mil.)	NET INCOME ($ mil.)	NET PROFIT MARGIN	EMPLOYEES
1/09	3,424.9	(30.0)	—	5,420
1/08	4,097.9	797.6	19.5%	4,985
1/07	3,068.8	448.1	14.6%	4,083
1/06	2,375.7	302.6	12.7%	2,737
1/05	2,010.0	100.4	5.0%	2,101
Annual Growth	14.3%	—	—	26.7%

FYE: Last Saturday in January

2009 Year-End Financials

Debt ratio: 1.1%
Return on equity: —
Cash ($ mil.): 418
Current ratio: 2.78
Long-term debt ($ mil.): 26
No. of shares (mil.): 548
Dividends
  Yield: 0.0%
  Payout: —
Market value ($ mil.): 4,355

Stock History

NASDAQ (GS): NVDA

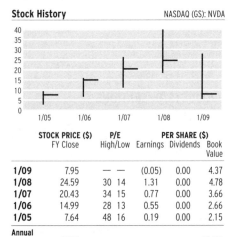

	STOCK PRICE ($) FY Close	P/E High/Low	PER SHARE ($) Earnings	Dividends	Book Value
1/09	7.95	— —	(0.05)	0.00	4.37
1/08	24.59	30 14	1.31	0.00	4.78
1/07	20.43	34 15	0.77	0.00	3.66
1/06	14.99	28 13	0.55	0.00	2.66
1/05	7.64	48 16	0.19	0.00	2.15
Annual Growth	1.0%	— —	—	—	19.4%

NVR, Inc.

From finished lot to signed mortgage, NVR offers homebuyers everything — including the kitchen sink. The company builds single-family detached homes, townhomes, and condominiums, mainly for first-time and move-up buyers, primarily in the eastern US. NVR markets its homes as Ryan Homes, Fox Ridge Homes, Rymarc Homes, and NVHomes. Its largest markets, the Washington, DC, and Baltimore areas, account for about 45% of sales. NVR sells about 15,000 homes annually. Sizes range from 900 sq. ft. to 7,300 sq. ft., and prices range from $60,000 to $2.5 million, averaging about $338,000. Subsidiary NVR Mortgage Finance offers mortgage and title services to its customers. It is about the 10th largest homebuilder in the US.

NVR's Ryan Homes, Fox Ridge Homes, and Rymarc Homes divisions primarily market to first-time buyers. Ryan Homes operates in more than 20 metropolitan areas along the Eastern Seaboard and in Kentucky, Ohio, Pennsylvania, and West Virginia. Fox Ridge Homes is dedicated to the Nashville, Tennessee, market, and Rymarc Homes operates solely in Columbia, South Carolina. NVHomes caters to upscale buyers and builds primarily in the Baltimore, Philadelphia, and Washington, DC, metro areas, as well as on Maryland's Eastern Shore.

Like other big homebuilding companies, NVR continues to weather a slumping housing market. Sales have dipped slightly, but it is faring better than some of its competitors — including D.R. Horton, Pulte, and Lennar — in part because of its conservative land acquisition strategy. To control capital risk, it does not develop land, but instead buys option contracts on finished building lots from developers. The company also has remained profitable by lowering its prices and focusing on locations where it has a high market share.

HISTORY

NVR got its start when Dwight Schar founded NVHomes, Inc., in 1980. Schar had worked for Ryan Homes (founded in 1948) since 1969. NVHomes, like Ryan, specialized in single-family homes around Washington, DC. The strong economy of the 1980s and the deregulation of lending institutions — coupled with favorable partnership and real estate tax laws passed by the Reagan administration — resulted in rapid growth. The company was clearing income of more than $1 million a year by 1983 and soon branched into building townhomes and condos.

In 1986, when the company was reorganized as a limited partnership (NVH L.P.), income was up to $14 million. The new entity soon acquired a controlling interest in Ryan Homes; it completed its acquisition of that company in 1987. NVH reorganized as a holding company (NVRyan L.P.), and 1988 profits reached $33.5 million. Over the years the company formed or acquired almost 100 subsidiaries that were involved in all aspects of homebuilding — from land acquisition and construction to home finance and investment advice. It had also branched out into California, Florida, Indiana, Kentucky, North Carolina, Ohio, Pennsylvania, and Virginia.

Following an economic recession in 1989, demand for new housing dropped off in the US. The company shortened its name to NVR L.P., and its inventory of unsold land and houses started to grow. The situation was exacerbated by changes in the tax code that made real estate less attractive as an investment; sales from development and construction projects dropped from more than $1 billion in 1988 to about $600 million in 1991. NVR posted a $260 million loss in 1990 as sales and the value of its inventory nose-dived.

NVR reorganized in 1990 and 1991. Focused on eight mid-Atlantic states, it put homebuilding under one management structure, consolidated its finance activities, exited its land-development businesses, and offered its mortgage services to customers who weren't NVR homebuyers. It also organized its business into two product lines: upscale (NVHomes) and moderately priced (Ryan Homes) homes. Despite the reorganization and introduction of innovative marketing, NVR and several of its subsidiaries filed for Chapter 11 bankruptcy relief in 1992. That year the CFO of NVR's thrift (NVR Savings Bank) went on the lam to Malta after embezzling more than $750,000.

The company emerged from bankruptcy as NVR, Inc., in 1993 with less debt, new owners, and a new line of credit; it also had its IPO that year. The next year NVR sold NVR Savings Bank, which had four branches in northern Virginia. The robust mid-1990s economy aided NVR; as home sales rose, the company entered new markets, including the Cleveland and Nashville areas, in 1995. To reduce its vulnerability to downturns in the mid-Atlantic area, it continued its expansion outside that region, buying Fox Ridge Homes (the #2 builder in Nashville) in 1997.

In 1999 it merged its homebuilding subsidiary, NVR Homes, and mortgage banking holding company, NVR Financial Services, into NVR. It also acquired Rockville, Maryland-based First Republic Mortgage that year, but closed the subsidiary's retail operations in 2000 and realigned its mortgage banking business to serve NVR customers exclusively.

From 1994 through 2003 the company benefited from increased housing activity, recording steady increases in unit sales, backlog, and profits for nine years.

EXECUTIVES

Chairman: Dwight C. Schar, age 67
President and CEO: Paul C. Saville, age 53, $4,144,707 total compensation
SVP, CFO, and Treasurer: Dennis M. Seremet, age 53, $1,836,616 total compensation
VP Business Planning: Dan Malzahn
VP and Controller: Robert W. Henley, age 42, $632,756 total compensation
President, NVR Mortgage Finance: William J. Inman, age 61, $1,583,876 total compensation
Auditors: KPMG LLP

LOCATIONS

HQ: NVR, Inc.
  Plaza America Tower 1, 11700 Plaza America Dr.
  Ste. 500, Reston, VA 20190
Phone: 703-956-4000   **Fax:** 703-956-4750
Web: www.nvrinc.com

PRODUCTS/OPERATIONS

2008 Sales

	$ mil.	% of total
Homebuilding		
Mid-Atlantic	2,161.8	58
Mideast	659.6	18
Southeast	470.0	13
Northeast	347.4	9
Mortgage Banking	54.3	1
Other income	21.0	1
Total	**3,714.1**	**100**

COMPETITORS

Beazer Homes
Brookfield Homes
Champion Enterprises
David Weekley Homes
D.R. Horton
Hovnanian Enterprises
John Wieland Homes
KB Home
Lennar
M.D.C.
M/I Homes
Orleans Homebuilders
Pulte Homes
The Ryland Group
Toll Brothers

HISTORICAL FINANCIALS

Company Type: Public

Income Statement

FYE: December 31

	REVENUE ($ mil.)	NET INCOME ($ mil.)	NET PROFIT MARGIN	EMPLOYEES
12/08	3,714.1	100.9	2.7%	2,845
12/07	5,156.4	334.0	6.5%	4,119
12/06	6,134.1	587.4	9.6%	4,548
12/05	5,177.7	697.6	13.5%	5,401
12/04	4,319.7	523.2	12.1%	4,407
Annual Growth	(3.7%)	(33.7%)	—	(10.4%)

2008 Year-End Financials

Debt ratio: 12.1%	No. of shares (mil.): 6
Return on equity: 8.1%	Dividends
Cash ($ mil.): 1,148	Yield: 0.0%
Current ratio: 2.77	Payout: —
Long-term debt ($ mil.): 166	Market value ($ mil.): 2,651

Stock History

NYSE: NVR

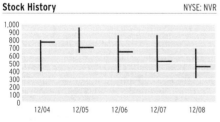

	STOCK PRICE ($) FY Close	P/E High/Low		PER SHARE ($) Earnings	Dividends	Book Value
12/08	456.25	40	19	17.04	0.00	236.47
12/07	524.00	16	7	54.14	0.00	194.40
12/06	645.00	10	4	88.05	0.00	198.31
12/05	702.00	11	7	89.61	0.00	116.56
12/04	769.40	12	6	66.42	0.00	143.73
Annual Growth	(12.2%)	—	—	(28.8%)	—	13.3%

NYSE Euronext

NYSE Euronext is one of the world's largest exchange groups, boasting trades totaling more than a third of the global cash equities volume. It operates such esteemed exchanges as the New York Stock Exchange (NYSE), one of the oldest and largest markets in the world; Euronext, the first cross-border exchange, with markets in Paris, Brussels, Amsterdam, and Lisbon; NYSE Liffe, a leading international derivatives markets with daily trading values exceeding $2.7 trillion; and NYSE Amex, formerly the American Stock Exchange. In 2007 NYSE acquired Euronext and its derivatives and futures markets (including Liffe) for some $10 billion to create the first trans-Atlantic exchange. The following year it bought rival AMEX.

NYSE Euronext agreed to acquire trading efficiency solutions provider NYFIX in 2009.

Continuing its international aspirations, NYSE Euronext in 2007 purchased a 5% stake in India's largest stock exchange, Mumbai-based National Stock Exchange. NYSE Euronext also bought 20% of the Qatar Exchange (formerly Doha Securities Market) for $200 million; the government of Qatar owns the rest. It's the largest investment NYSE Euronext has made in a foreign exchange. The joint venture creates an international market for cash and derivatives.

Also in 2007 the NYSE merged its regulatory body with the National Association of Securities Dealers (NASD). The combined entity, known as the Financial Industry Regulatory Authority (FINRA), is the largest non-governmental regulator of securities firms in the US.

To better compete with electronic exchanges such as archrival NASDAQ OMX, the NYSE broke from its tradition of operating as an auction exchange in 2006 and adopted a hybrid system permitting automated trading. To fuel the transformation, it bought electronic communications network (ECN) Archipelago. Through the acquisition, the NYSE added stock options and fixed-income products and took control of the Archipelago Exchange, now NYSE Arca.

Member-owned and not-for-profit for more than 200 years since its founding, the NYSE became a publicly traded company as part of the $10 billion transaction. NYSE stockholders got about 70% of the firm, while shareholders of Archipelago got the other 30%. However, some traders became wary that the combination might lead to the extinction of the open-outcry floor auctions (where stock prices are set largely by a throng of traders on the exchange floor) that characterize the NYSE.

The NYSE lists some 2,450 companies, including most of the largest US corporations; it also recruits foreign firms seeking the greater liquidity available in US markets. Euronext lists some 1,100 companies and is a leading market for European IPOs. The NYSE Amex, the group's market for emerging US companies, has some 500 listings. NYSE Arca is a fully electronic exchange with more than 1,000 exchange-traded fund, exchange-traded vehicle, and exchange-traded note listings and certificates.

HISTORY

To prevent a monopoly on stock sales by securities auctioneers, 24 New York stockbrokers and businessmen agreed in 1792 to avoid "public auctions," to charge a commission on sales of stock, and to "give preference to each other" in their transactions. The Buttonwood Agreement, named after a tree on Wall Street under which they met, established the first organized stock market in New York. The Bank of New York was the first corporate stock traded under the Buttonwood tree.

Excluded traders continued dealing on the streets of New York until 1921 and later formed the American Stock Exchange.

In 1817 the brokers created the New York Stock & Exchange Board, a stock market with set meeting times. The NYS&EB began to require companies to qualify for trading (listing) by furnishing financial statements in 1853. Ten years later the board became the New York Stock Exchange.

Stock tickers began recording trades in 1867, and two years later the NYSE consolidated with competitors the Open Board of Brokers and the Government Bond Department. Despite repeated panics and recessions in the late 1800s, the stock market remained unregulated until well into the 20th century.

In the 1920s the NYSE installed a centralized stock quote service. Postwar euphoria brought a stock mania that fizzled in the crash of October 1929. The subsequent Depression brought investigation and federal regulation to the securities industry.

The NYSE registered as an exchange in 1934. In 1938 it reorganized, with a board of directors representing member firms, nonmember brokers, and the public; it also hired its first full-time president, member William McChesney Martin. As a self-regulating body, the NYSE policed the activities of its members.

The NYSE began electronic trading in the 1960s; in 1968 it broke 1929's one-day record for trading volume (16 million shares). It became a not-for-profit corporation in 1971.

Despite upgrades, technology was at least partly to blame for the crash of 1987: A cascade of large sales triggered by computer programs fueled the market's fall. NYSE's income suffered, leading to a $3 million loss in 1990.

In 1995 Richard Grasso became the first NYSE staff employee named chairman. The NYSE followed the other US stock markets in 1997 by switching trade increments from one-eighth point to one-sixteenth point (known as a "teenie" by arbitrageurs).

In 1999 the exchange named Karen Nelson Hackett as its first woman governor.

In the wake of the terrorism attacks that shook Wall Street and the nation, the NYSE and Nasdaq in 2001 began discussing a disaster plan that would see the two cooperating should a future incident cripple either market. Also that year the NYSE moved entirely to decimal pricing in accordance with SEC mandates.

Grasso, who earned a reputation as something of a hero in the months following the 2001 terrorist attacks on New York City, resigned under fire two years later when his $187 million pay package was revealed. During the furor over Grasso's pay, the SEC launched an investigation, and many officials — including the heads of top pension funds — called for his resignation.

Former Citigroup chairman John Reed was named interim chairman and CEO following Grasso's departure; former Goldman Sachs president John Thain was subsequently tapped for the CEO role in 2004.

The company acquired ECN Archipelago in 2006 and finally went public. Its 2007 acquisition of Euronext made it the largest global market.

EXECUTIVES

Chairman: Jan-Michiel (J.M.) Hessels, age 67
Deputy Chairman: Marshall N. Carter, age 69
CEO and Director: Duncan L. Niederauer, age 49
Deputy CEO, Head of Strategy, and Director:
Jean-François Théodore, age 62
CFO and Group EVP: Michael S. Geltzeiler, age 50
Group Executive Vice President and Head of US Execution and Global Technology:
Lawrence (Larry) Leibowitz, age 49
Chief Regulatory Officer: James J. (Jim) Draddy Jr., age 49
Group EVP and Head of Global Derivatives:
Hugh R. Freedberg, age 63
Group EVP and Head of European Execution:
Roland Bellegarde, age 47
Group EVP, General Counsel, and Secretary:
John K. Halvey, age 49
EVP Human Resources: Dale B. Bernstein, age 54
EVP Market Data Services: Ronald Jordan, age 45
EVP, Member Firm Regulation and NYSE Regulation:
Grace B. Vogel
EVP and Chief of Enforcement, NYSE Regulation:
Susan L. Merrill
Group EVP and Global Head of Human Resources:
Philippe Duranton, age 48
EVP and Head Corporate Communications:
Joost van der Does de Willebois, age 50
EVP Regulation: John F. Malitzis, age 37
VP Investor Relations: Stephen Davidson
CEO, NYSE Regulation: Richard G. (Rick) Ketchum, age 58
Auditors: PricewaterhouseCoopers LLP

LOCATIONS

HQ: NYSE Euronext
11 Wall St., New York, NY 10005
Phone: 212-656-3000 **Fax:** 212-656-2126
Web: www.nyse.com

2008 Sales

	$ mil.	% of total
US operations	2,970	63
Europe operations	1,760	37
Adjustments	(27)	—
Total	**4,703**	**100**

PRODUCTS/OPERATIONS

2008 Sales

	$ mil.	% of total
Cash trading	2,387	51
Derivatives trading	919	20
Market data	429	9
Listing	395	8
Activity assessment	229	5
Software & technology services	160	3
Regulatory	49	1
Other	135	3
Total	**4,703**	**100**

COMPETITORS

CBOE
Deutsche Börse
E*TRADE Financial
Hong Kong Exchanges
Investment Technology
Knight Capital
Liquidnet
London Stock Exchange
MarketAxess
NASDAQ OMX
NYMEX Holdings
Singapore Exchange
TRADEBOOK

HISTORICAL FINANCIALS

Company Type: Public

Income Statement

FYE: December 31

	REVENUE ($ mil.)	NET INCOME ($ mil.)	NET PROFIT MARGIN	EMPLOYEES
12/08	4,703.0	(738.0)	—	3,757
12/07	4,158.0	643.0	15.5%	3,083
12/06	2,375.9	205.0	8.6%	2,578
12/05	1,717.6	40.7	2.4%	1,975
12/04	541.3	68.9	12.7%	234
Annual Growth	**71.7%**	**—**	**—**	**100.2%**

2008 Year-End Financials

Debt ratio: 27.3%
Return on equity: —
Cash ($ mil.): 777
Current ratio: 0.78
Long-term debt ($ mil.): 1,787
No. of shares (mil.): 260
Dividends
Yield: 4.2%
Payout: —
Market value ($ mil.): 7,119

Stock History

NYSE: NYX

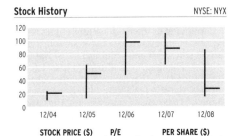

	STOCK PRICE ($) FY Close	P/E High/Low	PER SHARE ($) Earnings	Dividends	Book Value
12/08	27.38	— —	(2.78)	1.15	25.22
12/07	87.77	41 24	2.70	0.75	36.09
12/06	97.20	82 36	1.36	0.00	6.42
12/05	50.00	183 41	0.34	0.00	3.07
12/04	20.97	17 8	1.38	0.00	1.77
Annual Growth	**6.9%**	**— —**	**—**	**—**	**94.2%**

Occidental Petroleum

Harnessing its heritage of Western technical know-how, Occidental Petroleum engages in oil and gas exploration and production and makes basic chemicals, plastics, and petrochemicals. In 2008 the oil giant reported proved reserves of 3 billion barrels of oil equivalent in the US, the Middle East, North Africa, and Latin America. Subsidiary Occidental Chemical (OxyChem) produces acids, chlorine, and specialty products; it also owns OxyVinyls, the #1 producer of polyvinyl chloride (PVC) resin in North America. Occidental Petroleum's midstream and marketing operations gather, treat, process, transport, store, trade, and market crude oil, natural gas, NGLs, condensate, and CO_2, and they generate and market electricity.

Occidental is investing heavily in the Middle East and North Africa. It has begun to import Libyan oil (after a 20-year absence from the US market). In addition to its existing assets in Qatar and Yemen, the company is also developing new fields in Oman and Abu Dhabi.

Occidental has reworked its business and created two divisions, eastern and western hemispheres, for its oil and gas operations. To finance its purchase of the US government's 78% interest in California's historic and underused Elk Hills oil field, the company has divested its natural gas pipeline and marketing operation, MidCon, and sold off noncore oil and gas properties in the US, Venezuela, and the Netherlands. All told, Occidental has shed assets producing some 46,000 barrels of oil per day and let go about a quarter of its workforce.

In 2008 the company agreed spend $5 billion in capital investment to increase gross production in Libya to more than 300,000 barrels per day from the current level of 100,000 barrels per day.

In North America that same year it also bought a 15% stake in the Joslyn Oil Sands project for nearly $500 million. That project is based in Alberta, Canada, and operated by Total. It also acquired $1.2 billion of assets in the Permian and Piceance basins in the US from Plains Exploration & Production.

HISTORY

Founded in 1920, Occidental Petroleum struggled until 1956, when billionaire industrialist Dr. Armand Hammer sank $100,000 into the company, then worth $34,000. It drilled two wells, and both came in. Hammer eventually gained control of the company.

Occidental's discovery of California's second-largest gas field (1959) was followed by a concession from Libya's King Idris (1966) and the discovery of a billion-barrel Libyan oil field. In 1968 Occidental bought Signal Oil's European refining and marketing business as an outlet for the Libyan oil. It also diversified, buying Island Creek Coal and Hooker Chemical.

In 1969 Occidental sold 51% of its Libyan production to the Libyan government under duress (after Idris was ousted). It soon began oil exploration in Latin America (1971) and in the North Sea (1972-73), where it discovered the lucrative Piper field. Other projects included a 20-year fertilizer-for-ammonia deal with the USSR (1974) and a coal joint venture with China (1985).

During the 1980s Occidental sold some foreign assets and bought US natural gas pipeline firm MidCon (1986). It also bought Iowa Beef Processors (IBP) for stock worth $750 million (1981) and then spun off 49% of it in 1987 for $960 million.

In 1983 Hammer hired Ray Irani to revive Occidental's ailing chemicals business (losses that year: $38 million). Irani integrated operations to ensure higher margins during industry downturns and purchased Diamond Shamrock Chemicals (1986), Shell's vinyl chloride monomer unit (1987), a DuPont chloralkali facility (1987), and Cain Chemical (1988). OxyChem's profits reached almost $1.1 billion by 1989.

Hammer died in 1990, and Irani became CEO. In 1991, to reduce debt, Occidental exited the Chinese coal business and sold the North Sea oil properties. Occidental also spun off IBP, the largest US red-meat producer, to its shareholders.

Occidental paid Irani $95 million in 1997 to buy out his employment contract; instead, his compensation (a minimum of $1.2 million a year) was tied to the company's fortunes. That year Occidental's $3.65 billion bid won the US government's auction of its 78% stake in California's Elk Hills petroleum reserve, one of the largest in the continental US.

To help pay for Elk Hills, the company sold MidCon to K N Energy for $3.1 billion in 1998. Occidental traded its petrochemical operations to Equistar Chemicals, a partnership between Lyondell and Millennium Chemicals, for $425 million and a 29.5% stake.

In a venture with The Geon Company, Occidental in 1999 formed Oxy Vinyls, the #1 producer of polyvinyl chloride (PVC) resin in North America. That year also brought a windfall: Chevron agreed to pay Occidental $775 million to settle a lawsuit stemming from the 1982 withdrawal by Gulf (later acquired by Chevron) of an offer to buy Cities Service (later acquired by Occidental).

In 2000 Occidental sold its 29% stake in Canadian Occidental back to the company for $828 million to help fund the purchase of oil and gas producer Altura Energy, a partnership of BP and Shell Oil, for $3.6 billion. Later that year the company sold some Gulf of Mexico properties to Apache for $385 million.

Occidental acquired a new exploration block in Yemen in 2001.

The company sold its 29.5% of Equistar Chemicals to Lyondell Chemical in 2002 in exchange for a 21% stake in Lyondell (Occidental now owns 14%). In 2005 it acquired a stake in a gas and oil production site located in Texas' Permian Basin from ExxonMobil for a reported $972 million. Occidental closed the acquisition of Vintage Petroleum for a reported $3.8 billion in early 2006.

In 2006 the government of Ecuador seized Occidental Petroleum's Ecuadorian assets as part of a nationalization drive. That year Plains Exploration and Production sold non-core oil and gas properties to Occidental for $865 million.

Also in 2006, Occidental reduced its stake in Lyondell Chemical from 12% to 8%. The following year Occidental sold its remaining Lyondell shares on the open market.

EXECUTIVES

Chairman and CEO: Ray R. Irani, age 74, $60,467,848 total compensation
President and CFO: Stephen I. (Steve) Chazen, age 62, $23,008,044 total compensation
VP and CIO: Donald L. Moore Jr.
EVP; President, Oil and Gas, Western Hemisphere: John W. Morgan, age 55, $7,028,261 total compensation
EVP, General Counsel, and Secretary: Donald P. de Brier, age 68, $6,995,948 total compensation
EVP; President, Oil and Gas International: R. Casey Olson, age 55, $5,403,951 total compensation
EVP Finance and Planning: James M. Leinert, age 56
EVP Human Resources: Martin Cozyn, age 48
VP Investor Relations: Christopher G. (Chris) Stavros
VP, Controller, and Principal Accounting Officer: Roy Pineci, age 46
VP Communications and Public Affairs: Richard Kline
VP; President International Production, Oil and Gas: Edward A. (Sandy) Lowe, age 57
VP and President, Oxy Oil and Gas, USA: William E. Albrecht, age 57
President, Occidental Chemical: B. Chuck Anderson, age 49
Auditors: KPMG LLP

LOCATIONS

HQ: Occidental Petroleum Corporation
10889 Wilshire Blvd., Los Angeles, CA 90024
Phone: 310-208-8800   **Fax:** 310-443-6690
Web: www.oxy.com

2008 Sales

	% of total
US	63
Qatar	14
Colombia	7
Oman	5
Yemen	4
Libya	3
Argentina	2
Other countries	2
Total	**100**

PRODUCTS/OPERATIONS

2008 Sales

	$ mil.	% of total
Oil & gas	18,187	73
Chemicals	5,112	21
Midstream, marketing & other	1,598	6
Adjustments	(417)	—
Total	**24,480**	**100**

Selected Subsidiaries

Occidental Chemical Corp. (OxyChem; chemicals, polymers, and plastics)
Occidental Energy Marketing, Inc. (energy marketing)
Occidental Exploration and Production Company (exploration and production)
OxyVinyls, LP (76%, polyvinyl chloride)

COMPETITORS

Apache	Huntsman International
Ashland Inc.	Imperial Oil
BP	J.M. Huber
ConocoPhillips	Koch Industries, Inc.
Devon Energy	Marathon Oil
Dow Chemical	Olin
DuPont	PEMEX
Eastman Chemical	Royal Dutch Shell
Exxon Mobil	Sunoco
Hess Corporation	TOTAL

HISTORICAL FINANCIALS

Company Type: Public

Income Statement

FYE: December 31

	REVENUE ($ mil.)	NET INCOME ($ mil.)	NET PROFIT MARGIN	EMPLOYEES
12/08	24,480.0	6,857.0	28.0%	10,400
12/07	20,013.0	5,400.0	27.0%	9,700
12/06	18,160.0	4,182.0	23.0%	8,886
12/05	15,208.0	5,278.0	34.7%	8,017
12/04	11,368.0	2,568.0	22.6%	7,209
Annual Growth	**21.1%**	**27.8%**	**—**	**9.6%**

2008 Year-End Financials

Debt ratio: 7.5%
Return on equity: 27.4%
Cash ($ mil.): 1,777
Current ratio: 1.17
Long-term debt ($ mil.): 2,049
No. of shares (mil.): 811
Dividends
  Yield: 2.0%
  Payout: 14.5%
Market value ($ mil.): 48,638

Stock History

NYSE: OXY

	STOCK PRICE ($) FY Close	P/E High/Low		PER SHARE ($) Earnings	Dividends	Book Value
12/08	59.99	12	5	8.35	1.21	33.67
12/07	76.99	12	7	6.44	0.94	28.15
12/06	48.83	11	8	4.86	0.80	23.66
12/05	39.94	7	4	6.45	0.64	18.54
12/04	29.18	9	6	3.20	0.55	13.01
Annual Growth	**19.7%**	**—**	**—**	**27.1%**	**21.8%**	**26.8%**

Office Depot

Paper clips are big money; just ask Office Depot. Operating the world's #2 chain of office supply stores (behind Staples), the company sells office supplies through about 1,160 company-owned and licensed locations throughout North America and at about another 160 locations worldwide. The big-box retail stores sell to both consumers and small and medium-sized businesses. In addition to typical office supplies, its stores offer computer hardware and software, office furniture, art and school supplies, and printing and copying services. Office Depot also sells goods through catalogs and call centers, the Internet, and a contract sales force. Amid the softening economy, Office Depot is shutting stores.

While the company's sales had begun to slow even before the financial crisis hit, 2008 was a discouraging year for the office products retailer. In response to the dismal business climate, the company closed more than 120 underperforming stores in North America in 2009. Six of Office Depot's 30-plus distribution centers will also be shut down, as the company faces decreasing demand for office supplies as the economy craters. Also part of the move, the company plans to shed some 2,200 employees. Farther from home, Office Depot plans to close its 27 retail stores in Japan in 2009.

Overall, Office Depot's international operations contribute a growing percentage of its revenues. To extend its reach into India, Office Depot in April 2008 partnered with Reliance Retail, a unit of India's Reliance Industries, in a joint venture to sell office products and services to business customers in India. The US office products giant sells to customer in about 50 countries, including France, Hungary, Israel, South Korea, and now Sweden. Through its joint venture (formed in 1994) in Mexico, Office Depot de Mexico operates about 185 stores there, and in Costa Rica, El Salvador, Guatemala, Honduras, and Panama.

In a bid to increase sales by making shopping easier for its customers, Office Depot has adopted a new store format, called Millennium2 (M2), used in all new store openings and remodels. The new format minimizes construction costs and strategically locates products to encourage sales consultation. The company also is hoping to attract more environmentally-conscious shoppers with its new Office Depot Green line of products, including supplies with 30% or more recycled content, launched in 2008.

Office Depot's business solutions division includes catalog and online sales, as well as its contract sales business. The company boosted this segment with its 2006 purchase of Allied Office Products (AOP), the largest independent dealer of office products and services in the US. To capture a larger share of the small business audience, Office Depot partnered with Google in 2008 to roll out an online Business Resource Center, which includes Google AdWords, Google Apps, and Google Local Business Center. The latter offers free online business listings that appear on Google search and Google Maps.

HISTORY

Pat Scher, Stephen Dougherty, and Jack Kopkin opened the first Office Depot, one of the first office supply superstores, in Lauderdale Lakes, Florida, in 1986. Scher was selected as chairman.

By the end of the year the fledgling company had opened two more stores (both in Florida).

Office Depot opened seven more stores in 1987. When Scher died of leukemia that year, the company recruited David Fuente, former president of Sherwin-Williams' Paint Store Division, as chairman and CEO. Office Depot continued its breakneck expansion under Fuente. In 1988 — the year the company went public — it opened 16 stores and broke into new markets in four states.

The chain stepped up its pace, and by 1990 it had expanded into several other areas, including the South and Midwest. Office Depot also added computers and peripherals and opened its first delivery center.

In 1991 the company became North America's #1 office products retailer and expanded its presence in the West through the acquisition of Office Club, another warehouse-type office supply chain with 59 stores (most in California). Fuente remained chairman and CEO, while former Office Club CEO Mark Begelman became president and COO. (Begelman, who left in 1995 and eventually formed the MARS music chain, had founded the first Office Club in 1987 in Concord, California; he took it public in 1989.)

The company entered the international market with its 1992 purchase of Canada's H. Q. Office International and through licensing agreements in 1993 (in Colombia and Israel). Office Depot created its business services division by acquiring various contract stationers, including Eastman Office Products (the West Coast's #1 contract office supplier), in the mid-1990s, and added locations in Mexico and Poland; it established a joint venture in France with retailer Carrefour in 1996.

Also in 1996 Office Depot announced a $3.4 billion agreement to be acquired by Staples, which would have created a company with more than 1,100 stores. However, the government blocked the purchase on antitrust grounds in 1997 and the agreement dissolved.

In 1998 Office Depot acquired Viking Office Products in a $2.7 billion deal. With more than 60% of its sales coming from outside the US, Viking augmented Office Depot's already strong delivery network and international expansion. Office Depot acquired the remaining 50% of its French operations from Carrefour in 1998, and the remaining 50% of its Japanese operations from Deo Deo in 1999.

In July 2000 Bruce Nelson, CEO of Viking, replaced Fuente as CEO of Office Depot. Citing weak computer sales and high warehouse prices, the company closed about 70 stores and cut its workforce. In 2002 Nelson was named chairman as well as CEO after Fuente stepped down.

Office Depot sold its Australian operations to Officeworks, a unit of Coles Myer, in January 2003. Also that year the company acquired the retail operations of French office supplier Guilbert from Pinault-Printemps-Redoute, a move that doubled the company's business in Europe.

Nelson left the company and Neil Austrian served as interim head. Office Depot named AutoZone leader Steve Odland as CEO and chairman in 2005. During 2005 the company shuttered its Viking Office Products brand in the US, consolidating its catalog sales under the Office Depot banner.

In mid-2008 the company acquired 13 stores in Sweden through the acquisition of AGE Kontor & Data AB, a contract and retail office supply company operating there.

EXECUTIVES

Chairman and CEO: Steve Odland, age 50, $9,361,424 total compensation
EVP and CFO: Michael D. Newman, age 52, $675,272 total compensation
SVP and CIO: Timothy (Tim) Toews
EVP Information Technology: Monica Luechtefeld, age 60
EVP Human Resources: Daisy L. Vanderlinde, age 57
EVP Supply Chain: Kevin A. Peters, age 49
EVP and Managing Director, Europe: Dirk Collin
EVP, General Counsel, and Corporate Secretary: Elisa D. Garcia, age 51
EVP Corporate Operations: Brad Bacon
EVP Merchandising: Steve Mahurin
SVP and Chief Compliance Officer: Robert Brewer
SVP Retail Operations: George Hill
SVP Marketing: Jeff Herbert
VP Investor Relations: Brian Turcotte
President, North American Business Solutions Division: Steven M. (Steve) Schmidt, age 54, $2,126,006 total compensation
President, International: Charles E. Brown, age 55, $2,332,300 total compensation
President, North American Retail: Carl (Chuck) Rubin, age 49, $2,030,161 total compensation
Director Public Relations: Mindy Kramer
Auditors: Deloitte & Touche LLP

LOCATIONS

HQ: Office Depot, Inc.
6600 North Military Trail, Boca Raton, FL 33496
Phone: 561-438-4800   **Fax:** 561-438-4001
Web: www.officedepot.com

2008 International Retail Stores

	No.
France	48
Israel	44
Japan	27
Hungary	17
South Korea	13
Sweden	13
Total	**162**

PRODUCTS/OPERATIONS

2008 Sales

	% of total
Office supplies	62
Technology	25
Furniture & other	13
Total	**100**

2008 Sales

	$ mil.	% of total
North American Retail	6,112.3	42
North American Business Solutions	4,142.1	29
International	4,241.1	29
Total	**14,495.5**	**100**

Selected Products

Office furniture
  Armoires
  Bookcases
  Carts and stands
  Chair mats and floor mats
  Chairs
  Desks
  Filing cabinets
  Lamps and light bulbs
  Office furnishings
  Panel systems
  Tables
  Workstations

Office supplies
  Basic supplies and labels
  Binders and accessories
  Breakroom and janitorial supplies
  Business cases
  Calendars and planners
  Desk accessories
  Executive gifts
  Filing and storage
  Paper and envelopes
  Pens, pencils, and markers
  School supplies
Technology products
  Audiovisual equipment and supplies
  Cameras
  Computers and related accessories (including monitors and printers)
  Copiers
  Data storage supplies
  Fax machines
  Networking supplies
  PDAs
  Software

COMPETITORS

Best Buy	OfficeMax
BJ's Wholesale Club	RadioShack
CDW	School Specialty
Costco Wholesale	Staples
FedEx Office	Systemax
Fry's Electronics	Unisource
IKON	United Stationers
Insight Enterprises	Wal-Mart
Mail Boxes Etc.	

HISTORICAL FINANCIALS

Company Type: Public

Income Statement

FYE: Saturday nearest December 31

	REVENUE ($ mil.)	NET INCOME ($ mil.)	NET PROFIT MARGIN	EMPLOYEES
12/08	14,495.5	(1,478.9)	—	43,000
12/07	15,527.5	395.6	2.5%	49,000
12/06	15,010.8	516.1	3.4%	52,000
12/05	14,278.9	273.8	1.9%	47,000
12/04	13,564.7	335.5	2.5%	47,000
Annual Growth	**1.7%**	—	—	**(2.2%)**

2008 Year-End Financials

Debt ratio: 50.5%
Return on equity: —
Cash ($ mil.): 156
Current ratio: 1.19
Long-term debt ($ mil.): 689

No. of shares (mil.): 281
Dividends
  Yield: 0.0%
  Payout: —
Market value ($ mil.): 836

Stock History

NYSE: ODP

	STOCK PRICE ($) FY Close	P/E High/Low		PER SHARE ($) Earnings	Dividends	Book Value
12/08	2.98	—	—	(5.42)	0.00	4.86
12/07	13.91	28	9	1.43	0.00	10.99
12/06	38.17	26	17	1.79	0.00	9.30
12/05	31.40	37	19	0.87	0.00	9.76
12/04	17.36	18	13	1.06	0.00	11.48
Annual Growth	**(35.6%)**	—	—	—	—	**(19.4%)**

OfficeMax

This company is taking the office supply business to the max. OfficeMax (formerly Boise Cascade) is the #3 office products retailer in North America (behind Staples and Office Depot), with some 1,025 superstores in the US, Mexico, Puerto Rico, and the US Virgin Islands. The stores offer about 10,500 name-brand and OfficeMax-branded products, including paper, pens, forms, and organizers, as well as office furniture and a wide range of technology products. OfficeMax also provides printing and document services through its ImPress store-within-a-store. In addition to its retail outlets, the firm's contract division sells directly to business and government customers through field agents, telesales, and catalogs.

The recession in the US is hitting both OfficeMax's contract and retail store sales. To control costs amid slumping sales, in late 2008 the firm announced that it will eliminate about 245 corporate staff and field management positions in North America. (OfficeMax hired defunct Circuit City's former CFO Bruce Besanko, who also worked in finance at Yankee Candle, in early 2009.) Plans to grow its store base in 2009 or remodel existing stores have been put on hold until the economic outlook in the US brightens.

In late 2008 OfficeMax formed an alliance with the French stationery and office-supply giant Lyreco to supply customers in Europe and Asia through Lyreco and allowing Lyreco to supply customers in the US and Mexico through OfficeMax. OfficeMax is likely to face increased competition in Europe and the US as a result of rival Staples' acquisition of Corporate Express NV in 2008. Corporate Express is a major office products wholesaler, with more than half of its sales in the US through Corporate Express US.

OfficeMax has launched a small-format store called Ink-Paper-Scissors that abandons the warehouse-style format and instead highlights small- and home-office solutions in a warmer atmosphere. The company opened three Ink-Paper-Scissors stores in 2008.

HISTORY

Boise Cascade got its start in 1957 with the merger of two small lumber companies — Boise Payette Lumber Company (based in Boise, Idaho) and Cascade Lumber Company (Yakima, Washington). The business diversified in the 1960s under the leadership of Robert Hansberger, moving into office-products distribution in 1964. A number of acquisitions followed, including Ebasco Industries (1969), a consulting, engineering, and construction firm. By 1970 Boise Cascade had made more than 30 buys to diversify into building materials, paper products, real estate, recreational vehicles (RVs), and publishing.

In the early 1970s the company suffered a timber shortage as its access to public timberlands dwindled. Its plans to develop recreational communities in California, Hawaii, and Washington met opposition from residents, causing Boise Cascade to scrap all but six of the 29 projects.

In 1972 high costs related to the remaining projects left the company in debt. John Fery replaced Hansberger as president that year and sold companies not directly related to the company's core forest-product operations.

In the late 1980s and early 1990s, Boise sold more nonstrategic operations, including its Specialty Paperboard Division in 1989. It sold more than half of its corrugated-container plants in 1992 to focus on manufacturing forest products and distributing building materials and office supplies.

Boise Cascade also sold its wholesale office-product business in 1992 to focus on direct sales to big buyers such as IBM and Boeing. The company sold off its Canadian subsidiary, Rainy River Forest Products, during 1994 and 1995. Resurgent paper prices resulted in a profit in 1995, Boise Cascade's first since 1990.

Also in 1995, in a move into the international paper market, Boise Cascade signed a joint venture agreement with Shenzhen Leasing to form Zhuhai Hiwin Boise Cascade, a Chinese manufacturer of carbonless paper. That year it sold a minority stake in Boise Cascade Office Products (BCOP) to the public.

The company sold its coated-papers business to paper and packaging heavyweight Mead in 1996 for $639 million. The following year Boise began harvesting its first quick-growth cottonwood trees (specially grown to cut the cost of harvesting from traditional slow-growth hardwood plantations). Also in 1997 BCOP bought Jean-Paul Guisset, an office-products direct marketer in France. Although this acquisition boosted sales and increased the company's European presence, company profits suffered that year because of weak paper prices.

The low price of paper in 1998 prompted the company to close four sawmills and a research and development center. Restructuring costs associated with the closures and a fire at the company's Medford, Oregon, plywood plant led to a net income loss for the year.

In 1999 Boise bought Wallace Computer Services, a contract stationer business, and broadened its building-supply distribution network nationwide by acquiring Furman Lumber, a building-supplies distributor. In 2000 Boise Cascade completed the purchase of the 19% of Boise Office Solutions that it didn't already own. The company also sold its European office products operations for $335 million and then turned around and purchased the Blue Star Business Supplies Group of US Office Products in Australia and New Zealand for about $115 million.

Because of the decline in federal timber sales, in 2001 the company closed its plywood mill and lumber operations in Emmett, Idaho, and a sawmill in Cascade, Idaho. In 2002 lagging profits prompted Boise to implement cost-cutting procedures. In 2003 the company pinned its hopes for growth on the office product segment with the acquisition of OfficeMax for nearly $1.2 billion in cash and stock. The deal put Boise Cascade's office products business on par with industry leaders Staples and Office Depot.

The company sold its paper, forest products, and timberland assets to investment firm Madison Dearborn Partners for $3.7 billion in October 2004. That same year the company changed its name to OfficeMax and tagged Christopher Milliken, a former Boise Cascade executive, as CEO, but he resigned after only four months on the job. Former ShopKo Stores CEO Sam Duncan was tapped as his replacement.

In August 2006 the company moved its headquarters from Itasca, Illinois, to nearby Naperville. Looking to improve its balance sheet, OfficeMax announced a major restructuring effort in 2006 that saw the company close about 110 underperforming locations in the US.

EXECUTIVES

Chairman, President, and CEO: Sam K. Duncan, age 57, $1,886,986 total compensation
Director: Rakesh Gangwal, age 55
EVP and COO: Samuel M. (Sam) Martin III, age 52, $1,183,722 total compensation
EVP and CFO: Bruce H. Besanko, age 51
CIO: Randy G. Burdick
SVP Finance and Chief Accounting Officer: Deborah A. (Deb) O'Connor, age 46, $273,178 total compensation
EVP Merchandising and Retail: Steven S. (Steve) Embree
EVP Human Resources: Perry S. Zukowski
EVP Merchandising: Ryan T. Vero, age 39, $824,509 total compensation
EVP, General Counsel, and Secretary: Matthew R. (Matt) Broad, age 49
EVP Supply Chain: Reuben E. Slone
SVP and Managing Director, Australasian Operations: David Kelly
SVP Marketing and Advertising: Bob Thacker
VP Diversity and Inclusion: Carolyn Brooks
VP Global Loss Prevention and Chief Security Officer: John Voytilla
VP Investor Relations and Treasurer: Tony Giuliano, age 50
VP and Secretary: Susan Wagner-Fleming
Auditors: KPMG LLP

LOCATIONS

HQ: OfficeMax Incorporated
    263 Shuman Blvd., Naperville, IL 60563
Phone: 630-438-7800
Web: www.officemax.com

2008 Sales

	$ mil.	% of total
US	6,728.5	81
Other countries	1,538.5	19
Total	**8,267**	**100**

PRODUCTS/OPERATIONS

2008 Sales

	$ mil.	% of total
OfficeMax, Contract	4,310	52
OfficeMax, Retail	3,957	48
Total	**8,267**	**100**

2008 Contract Sales

	% of total
Office supplies & paper	58
Technology products	30
Office furniture	12
Total	**100**

2008 Retail Sales

	% of total
Technology products	52
Office supplies & paper	39
Office furniture	9
Total	**100**

COMPETITORS

Best Buy	Office Depot
BJ's Wholesale Club	RadioShack
CDW	SAM'S CLUB
Container Store	Staples
Costco Wholesale	Systemax
FedEx Office	Unisource
IKON	United Stationers
Insight Enterprises	Wal-Mart
Mail Boxes Etc.	

HISTORICAL FINANCIALS

Company Type: Public

Income Statement

FYE: December 31

	REVENUE ($ mil.)	NET INCOME ($ mil.)	NET PROFIT MARGIN	EMPLOYEES
12/08	8,267.0	(1,657.9)	—	33,000
12/07	9,082.0	207.4	2.3%	36,000
12/06	8,965.7	91.7	1.0%	36,000
12/05	9,157.7	(73.8)	—	35,000
12/04	13,270.2	173.1	1.3%	41,000
Annual Growth	(11.2%)	—	—	(5.3%)

2008 Year-End Financials

Debt ratio: 711.3%
Return on equity: —
Cash ($ mil.): 171
Current ratio: 1.55
Long-term debt ($ mil.): 1,760

No. of shares (mil.): 76
Dividends
Yield: 5.9%
Payout: —
Market value ($ mil.): 583

Stock History

NYSE: OMX

	STOCK PRICE ($) FY Close	P/E High/Low		PER SHARE ($) Earnings	Dividends	Book Value
12/08	7.64	—	—	(21.90)	0.45	3.80
12/07	20.66	21	8	2.66	0.60	29.87
12/06	49.65	44	21	1.19	0.60	26.03
12/05	25.36	—	—	(0.99)	0.60	22.75
12/04	31.38	21	16	1.77	0.60	34.22
Annual Growth	(29.8%)	—	—	—	(6.9%)	(42.3%)

Olin Corporation

The making of bleach and bullets is all in a day's work for Olin. Olin Chlor Alkali Products manufactures chemicals used to make bleach, water purification and swimming pool chemicals, pulp and paper processing agents, and PVC plastics. The unit makes Olin the #3 chlor-alkali producer in North America behind Dow and OxyChem. Olin also makes Winchester-branded ammunition. US customers account for the great majority of Olin's sales, and company's manufacturing facilities are located primarily in the US, though it also has plants in Australia and Canada.

In 2007 Olin sold its former Metals unit to investment group KPS Capital Partners for almost $400 million. The Metals unit — which had accounted for about two-thirds of sales — made copper and copper alloy sheets, clad metal, foil, and stainless-steel strips. KPS Capital Partners, which is the manager of the KPS Special Situation Funds, has said that it will set up the operations as a new company called Global Brass and Copper Holdings.

HISTORY

Vermont-born engineer Franklin Olin founded Equitable Powder in East Alton, Illinois, in 1892 to make blasting powder for midwestern coal fields. By 1898 the company, called Western Cartridge, was also making small arms ammunition.

When WWI increased demand for military cartridges, Western Cartridge built a brass mill. After the war it began making custom brass and other copper alloys for industrial customers. The company bought Winchester Repeating Arms, maker of the famous Winchester Model 1876 repeating rifles, in 1931. During WWII Western Cartridge developed the US carbine and M-1 rifles.

The various businesses of Western Cartridge merged as Olin Industries in 1944. Franklin then retired, handing the company to sons John and Spencer.

Enriched by the war effort, Olin Industries grew. In 1949 it began making cellophane, and in 1951 it acquired Frost Lumber Industries and Ecusta Paper, a maker of cigarette papers. Olin Industries merged with Mathieson Chemical in 1954 to form Olin Mathieson Chemical, the fifth-largest US chemical company.

The Mathieson Alkali Works was founded in Saltville, Virginia, in 1892 to produce alkalis using a process acquired from English chemical firm Neil Mathieson. By 1909 the company began producing liquid chlorine, and in 1923 it built one of the earliest plants for producing synthetic ammonia. During WWII Mathieson manufactured chlorine for water purification and alkali chemicals for sanitation. In 1952 Mathieson acquired drugmaker Squibb.

Olin Mathieson continued to diversify in the mid-1950s, buying Blockson Chemical (industrial phosphates) and Brown Paper Mill (kraft paper bags and corrugated cardboard containers). Frost Lumber and Brown Paper Mill formed the Forest Products Division, later dubbed Olinkraft. In 1956 Olin Mathieson entered the aluminum business via a joint venture — just in time for a drop in aluminum demand.

In the 1960s the company began making urethane chemicals. It also created Olin-American, a subsidiary that built houses, and spun off Squibb. In 1969 it shortened its name to Olin Corporation and moved to Stamford, Connecticut.

The 1970s saw Olin reining in its diverse businesses. It spun off Olinkraft and sold its aluminum operations. During the 1980s Olin sold its sporting-arms business (but kept Winchester ammunition), as well as its paper, housing, and cellophane units. John Olin died in 1982. The company acquired Rockcor, which included Rocket Research, Pacific Electro Dynamics, and Physics International, in 1985.

Olin moved its headquarters to Norwalk, Connecticut, in 1995, the same year Spencer Olin died. In 1996, as the earnings potential of its ordnance and aerospace operations lagged, Olin spun them off as Primex Technologies. It also sold its isocyanate (used in plastics and adhesives) and other cyclical businesses. Olin bought the remaining 50% of its Niachlor chlor alkali joint venture from DuPont in 1997 after considering putting Niachlor up for sale.

Aspiring to become a leading basic-materials company, Olin spun off its specialty chemical business in early 1999 under the name Arch Chemicals. Citing regulatory issues, Olin cancelled plans in 2000 to form a chlor alkali joint venture with Occidental's OxyChem subsidiary. Olin acquired Monarch Brass & Copper Corp. for about $49 million in 2001. The next year it bought brass rod maker Chase Industries. Olin closed its copper and copper alloy sheet plant in Indianapolis in 2003.

EXECUTIVES

Chairman, President, and CEO: Joseph D. Rupp, age 58, $4,756,987 total compensation
VP and CFO: John E. Fischer, age 53, $1,449,942 total compensation
VP; President, Chlor Alkali Products Division: John L. McIntosh, age 54, $1,375,232 total compensation
VP, General Counsel, and Secretary: George H. Pain, age 58
VP and Treasurer: Stephen C. Curley, age 57
VP Strategic Planning: G. Bruce Greer Jr., age 48
VP and Controller: Todd A. Slater, age 45
VP; President, Winchester: Richard M. (Dick) Hammett, age 62
Investor Relations: Larry P. Kromidas
Media Relations: Elaine Patterson
Auditors: KPMG LLP

LOCATIONS

HQ: Olin Corporation
190 Carondelet Plaza, Ste. 1530, Clayton, MO 63105
Phone: 314-480-1400   **Fax:** 314-862-7406
Web: www.olin.com

2008 Sales

	$ mil.	% of total
US	1,573.4	89
Other countries	191.1	11
Total	**1,764.5**	**100**

PRODUCTS/OPERATIONS

2008 Sales

	$ mil.	% of total
Chlor Alkali Products	1,275.4	72
Winchester	489.1	28
Total	**1,764.5**	**100**

Selected Products

Chlor Alkali Products
  Caustic soda
  Chlorine
  Hydrochloric acid
  Sodium hydrochlorite (Industrial and institutional cleaning products)
  Sodium hydrosulfite (bleaching)
Winchester
  Ammunition (shot-shell, small-caliber, and rimfire)
  Government-owned arsenal operation (maintenance for the US Army)
  Industrial cartridges (eight-gauge loads and powder-actuated tool loads for the construction industry)

COMPETITORS

Alliant Techsystems
Arch Chemicals
Blount International
Dow Chemical
FMC
Formosa Plastics USA
Georgia Gulf
Herstal
Honeywell Specialty Materials
Mitsubishi Chemical
Occidental Chemical
PPG Industries
Remington Arms
Sterling Chemicals
Sumitomo Chemical

HISTORICAL FINANCIALS

Company Type: Public

Income Statement

FYE: December 31

	REVENUE ($ mil.)	NET INCOME ($ mil.)	NET PROFIT MARGIN	EMPLOYEES
12/08	1,764.5	157.7	8.9%	3,600
12/07	1,276.8	(9.2)	—	3,600
12/06	3,151.8	149.7	4.7%	6,000
12/05	2,357.7	139.7	5.9%	5,900
12/04	1,997.0	55.0	2.8%	5,800
Annual Growth	(3.0%)	30.1%	—	(11.2%)

2008 Year-End Financials

Debt ratio: 35.8%
Return on equity: 23.0%
Cash ($ mil.): 247
Current ratio: 1.64
Long-term debt ($ mil.): 252

No. of shares (mil.): 78
Dividends
　Yield: 4.4%
　Payout: 38.6%
Market value ($ mil.): 1,414

Stock History

NYSE: OLN

	STOCK PRICE ($) FY Close	P/E High/Low		PER SHARE ($) Earnings	Dividends	Book Value
12/08	18.08	15	6	2.07	0.80	9.01
12/07	19.33	—	—	(0.12)	0.80	8.48
12/06	16.52	11	7	2.06	0.80	6.94
12/05	19.68	14	9	1.86	0.80	5.45
12/04	22.02	29	19	0.80	0.80	4.55
Annual Growth	(4.8%)	—	—	26.8%	0.0%	18.6%

Omnicare, Inc.

With operations across the US, Omnicare strives to be omnipresent. The firm is the country's largest institutional pharmacy services provider, dispensing drugs to nursing homes, assisted-living centers, and other long-term care facilities in the US and parts of Canada. It also provides clinical and financial software and consulting services to long-term care facilities, as well as infusion and respiratory therapy products and services for nursing home residents and hospice patients. The company has more than 200 pharmacy locations across the US and services more than 1.4 million patient beds.

The highly acquisitive Omnicare made more than 30 small acquisitions in 2007 and 2008. The company has had to be nimble to absorb its many acquisitions, however, and keep up its level of service without losing customers. It has also been fighting lower reimbursements on drugs, particularly from health insurer UnitedHealth

Group. Omnicare sued UnitedHealth over reimbursements on its Medicare Part D prescription drug coverage in 2006, but a summary judgment by an Illinois federal court dismissed the lawsuit in 2009; Omnicare has appealed on the ruling. Other market trends, such as the rising use of cheaper generics, have also hurt the company.

Omnicare has responded with a number of customer retention efforts and restructuring initiatives aimed at improving quality and efficiency. The company has been reorganizing its operations into a "hub-and-spoke" model, moving more administrative activities, as well as some routine prescription refilling, to larger regional hubs where scale, centralization, and automation can produce greater efficiency. Smaller local pharmacies (the "spokes") in turn focus on activities requiring direct customer interaction.

Omnicare's Pharmacy Services division, which includes its institutional pharmacy operations, brings in nearly all the company's revenue. In addition to its institutional pharmacy services, the division also operates some retail, mail-order, and home care pharmacies.

A second division (called Omnicare Clinical Research) provides contract clinical drug research and development services to pharmaceutical, biotech, and medical device companies. Its Clinimetrics unit focuses on biotechnology clients. Another unit specializes in assisting drug companies with the development of new treatments for the elderly.

HISTORY

In 1981 W. R. Grace subsidiaries Daylin and Chemed merged some health care units to form Omnicare, which was then spun off. Omnicare began a restructuring process in 1985 that reshaped the firm around pharmacy services for long-term care facilities. It acquired 17 long-term care pharmacies in 1993 alone.

As the baby boomers age, the company will continue to have a growing market for the long run. Using economies of scale to keep costs down, Omnicare began pursuing an aggressive acquisition strategy.

In 1994 the company teamed with Health Care and Retirement Corp., one of the US's largest nursing home operators. It acquired 17 pharmacy units in 1996, including those of Revco and several other retailers. In 1997 Omnicare expanded its operations by targeting assisted living providers and small rural hospitals. It continued acquiring pharmacy service providers (20 in 1997 — including its largest deal up to that time, American Medserve — and CompScript in 1998), and it leveraged its treatment outcomes database with the addition of contract research organizations (Coromed, 1997; IBAH, 1998).

In 1998 Omnicare settled a lawsuit that alleged a company pharmacy had repackaged and resold unused medications originally sold to nursing homes (and paid for by Medicaid). That year the company acquired Extendicare's pharmacy operations. In 1999 Omnicare expanded its services for the drug development industry with the purchase of a German clinical research organization; the company also acquired the pharmaceutical division of nursing home operator Life Care Services of America.

Omnicare consolidated its three clinical research organizations in 2000 into Omnicare Clinical Research.

In 2003 the company acquired NCS HealthCare and Sun Healthcare's SunScript Pharmacy business in a move designed to strengthen its position as the largest supplier of pharmacy services to long-term care facilities in the US.

After a year-long pursuit, the company acquired NeighborCare in a hostile takeover in 2005. The deal, valued at nearly $2 billion, brought with it 300,000 patient beds and took Omnicare's annual revenue to more than $6 billion. Following the acquisition, Omnicare consolidated about 30 pharmacy locations. It also lost some nursing home customers who complained about bad service.

The same it year it won NeighborCare, Omnicare also bought RxCrossroads, a mail-order specialty pharmaceutical company that specializes in providing pricey drugs used to treat chronic conditions, and excelleRx, a distributor of pharmaceuticals and related products to hospice agencies in 47 states.

EXECUTIVES

Chairman: John T. Crotty, age 71
President, CEO, and Director: Joel F. Gemunder, age 69, $28,753,588 total compensation
EVP and COO: Patrick E. Keefe, age 63, $5,056,412 total compensation
SVP and CFO: David W. (Dave) Froesel Jr., age 57, $3,028,717 total compensation
SVP and CIO: Stephen S. Brown
SVP Professional Services; President, Omnicare Senior Health Outcomes: W. Gary Erwin, age 56
SVP Strategic Planning and Development: Tracy Finn, age 49
SVP and Secretary: Cheryl D. Hodges, age 56, $3,282,774 total compensation
SVP Pharmacy Operations: Jeffrey M. Stamps, age 49, $1,533,217 total compensation
SVP Sales and Customer Development: Beth A. Kinerk, age 40
VP Financial Services and Treasurer: Thomas R. Marsh
VP Management Information Systems: D. Michael Laney
VP Public Affairs: Paul W. Baldwin
VP Government Affairs: Timothy L. Vordenbaumen Sr.
VP and General Counsel: Mark G. Kobasuk, age 51
President and CEO, excelleRx: Gary W. Kadlec
General Manager, RxCrossroads: Cindy M. Padgett
President and CEO, Advanced Care Scripts: Jeffrey P. Spafford
President and CEO, Clinimetrics: Matthew P. Smith
Auditors: PricewaterhouseCoopers LLP

LOCATIONS

HQ: Omnicare, Inc.
　1600 RiverCenter II, 100 E. RiverCenter Blvd.
　Covington, KY 41011
Phone: 859-392-3300　　**Fax:** 859-392-3333
Web: www.omnicare.com

2008 Sales

	$ mil.	% of total
US	6,238.3	99
Other countries	72.3	1
Total	**6,310.6**	**100**

PRODUCTS/OPERATIONS

2008 Sales

	$ mil.	% of total
Pharmacy services	6,107.3	97
CRO services	203.3	3
Total	**6,310.6**	**100**

2008 Sources of Revenue

	% of total
Private pay, third-party & facilities	44
Federal Medicare programs	42
State Medicaid programs	10
Other sources	4
Total	**100**

COMPETITORS

Accredo Health
AmerisourceBergen
Cardinal Health
Covance
Covenant Care
Express Scripts
The Harvard Drug Group
Kendle
Life Sciences Research
McKesson
Option Care
PAREXEL
Pharmaceutical Product Development
PharMerica
Quintiles Transnational
Standard Management

HISTORICAL FINANCIALS

Company Type: Public

Income Statement

FYE: December 31

	REVENUE ($ mil.)	NET INCOME ($ mil.)	NET PROFIT MARGIN	EMPLOYEES
12/08	6,310.6	156.1	2.5%	17,200
12/07	6,220.0	114.1	1.8%	17,800
12/06	6,493.0	183.6	2.8%	17,100
12/05	5,292.8	226.5	4.3%	17,900
12/04	4,119.9	236.0	5.7%	12,900
Annual Growth	**11.2%**	**(9.8%)**	**—**	**7.5%**

2008 Year-End Financials

Debt ratio: 79.8%
Return on equity: 4.7%
Cash ($ mil.): 215
Current ratio: 3.70
Long-term debt ($ mil.): 2,731

No. of shares (mil.): 119
Dividends
  Yield: 0.3%
  Payout: 6.8%
Market value ($ mil.): 3,313

Stock History

NYSE: OCR

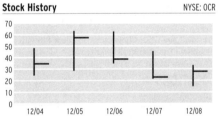

	STOCK PRICE ($) FY Close	P/E High/Low		PER SHARE ($) Earnings	Dividends	Book Value
12/08	27.76	25	12	1.32	0.09	28.67
12/07	22.81	48	23	0.94	0.09	27.58
12/06	38.63	41	24	1.50	0.09	26.50
12/05	57.22	30	14	2.10	0.09	24.65
12/04	34.62	22	12	2.17	0.09	16.15
Annual Growth	**(5.4%)**	**—**	**—**	**(11.7%)**	**0.0%**	**15.4%**

Omnicom Group

While it might not be omnipotent, Omnicom Group can create advertising that is omnipresent. The company ranks as the world's #1 corporate media services conglomerate, with advertising, marketing, and public relations operations serving some 5,000 clients in more than 100 countries. It serves global advertising clients through its agency networks BBDO Worldwide, DDB Worldwide, and TBWA Worldwide, while such firms as GSD&M's Idea City, Merkley + Partners, and Zimmerman Advertising provide services for regional and national clients. More than 160 other firms in its Diversified Agency Services division, including Fleishman-Hillard, Integer, and Rapp, provide public relations and other marketing services.

Despite an economic downturn and a more cost-cautious approach on the part of advertisers, Omnicom has continued to grow both domestically and internationally. The company's fortunes have been buoyed in part by its agency networks and their consistently strong creative work (traditional media advertising accounts for more than 40% of revenue), but the bulk of its growth has come from such areas as customer relationship management (CRM) and specialty communications. Omnicom sees continued growth being tied to its ability to provide an ever expanding menu of services to its largest clients.

Following a long period of consolidation and acquisitions, Omnicom is slowly and quietly beginning to reorganize itself into a new kind of holding company. Longtime CEO John Wren sees the company's agency networks becoming more full-service communications firms and is looking to integrate (or in some cases reintegrate) Omnicom's specialized services units into its global agencies. Throughout 2008, Omnicom made 12 acquisitions.

Omnicom has also been focused on expanding its media planning and buying operations. OMD Worldwide is a leading media specialist firm (behind Publicis' Starcom MediaVest), but Omnicom still trails WPP Group, Publicis, and Interpublic in total media services billings. To help close the gap, OMD launched Full Circle Entertainment, a branded entertainment production unit that works with clients like DIRECTV and Pier 1. In addition, Omnicom's Prometheus Media Services unit is its third media specialist, alongside OMD Worldwide and PHD Media Limited.

HISTORY

Omnicom Group was created in 1986 to combine three leading ad agencies into a single group capable of competing in the worldwide market. BBDO Worldwide, founded in New York in 1928 as Batten, Barton, Durstine & Osborn, had a huge PepsiCo account and developed the Pepsi Generation campaign. Doyle Dane Bernbach Group (DDB), which had created the *fahrvergnügen* ads for Volkswagen, had strong ties in Europe. And Needham Harper Worldwide, which had served up the "You Deserve a Break Today" commercials for McDonald's, had connections in Asia. BBDO remained separate, but DDB and Needham Harper were merged to form DDB Needham Worldwide. The business services units (public relations firms and direct marketers) of each of these companies were tucked under the Diversified Agency Services (DAS) umbrella.

Bruce Crawford, a previous chairman of BBDO who had just finished a stint running New York's Metropolitan Opera, became chairman and CEO in 1989. He transformed DAS from a chaotic group of shops into an integrated marketing giant, and ran Omnicom as a holding company of independent operating units working together through cross-referrals. By keeping costs low, especially interest expenses, Omnicom survived the 1990-91 recession with little pain. The company acquired Goodby, Berlin & Silverstein (now Goodby, Silverstein & Partners) in 1992. The next year TBWA Advertising (founded in Paris in 1970 by American Bill Tragos) was added to Omnicom's roster.

The merger spree continued in 1994 when Omnicom purchased WWAV Group, the largest direct-marketing agency in the UK. In 1995 Omnicom fused TBWA with Chiat/Day (founded in 1968 by Jay Chiat and Guy Day) to form TBWA International Network. Omnicom also acquired Michigan-based Ross Roy Communications (later Interone Marketing Group). In 1997 DDB Needham won back its McDonald's account after a 15-year hiatus. That year Crawford stepped down as CEO (though he remained chairman) and John Wren took control of Omnicom.

In 1998 the company acquired PR firm Fleishman-Hillard, adding to the PR clout it established with the acquisition of Ketchum Communications (now Ketchum) in 1996. Omnicom also acquired GGT Group of London for $235 million. (GGT's New York office, Wells BDDP, had lost a large Procter & Gamble account that year.) It merged GGT's BDDP Worldwide with TBWA to form TBWA Worldwide. BBDO landed a $200 million account with PepsiCo's Frito-Lay that year.

Omnicom's position in Europe was boosted in 1999 when it bought the Abbot Mead Vickers (now Abbot Mead Vickers BBDO) shares it didn't already own. That year TBWA founder William Tragos retired from the company (replaced by Lee Clow) and DDB Needham changed its moniker to DDB Worldwide Communications Group. Omnicom also bought market research firm M/A/R/C for about $95 million, and invested $20 million in pharmaceutical clinical trials company SCIREX. In 2000 BBDO scored a major coup over rival FCB Worldwide (now part of Interpublic) by landing the $1.8 billion DaimlerChrysler account. The next year it formed Seneca Investments to hold its stakes in several i-services shops, including Agency.com and Organic. (Omnicom acquired the interactive agencies outright in 2003.)

EXECUTIVES

Chairman: Bruce Crawford, age 80
Vice Chairman: Peter W. Mead, age 69
Vice Chairman; CEO, Omnicom Asia-Pacific, India, Middle East, and Africa (APIMA): Tim Love, age 59
President, CEO, and Director: John D. Wren, age 56, $2,953,384 total compensation
EVP and CFO: Randall J. Weisenburger, age 50, $2,771,754 total compensation
SVP Finance and Controller: Philip J. Angelastro, age 44
SVP and Corporate Director of Public Affairs: Pat Sloan
SVP, General Counsel, and Secretary: Michael J. O'Brien, age 47
Chairman, TBWA Worldwide: Jean-Marie Dru
Chairman and CEO, GSD&M's Idea City: Roy M. Spence Jr., age 60
President, CEO, and Director, BBDO Worldwide: Andrew Robertson, age 48, $1,855,490 total compensation

Chairman and CEO, Diversified Agency Services:
Thomas L. Harrison, age 61,
$2,289,293 total compensation
President and CEO, DDB Worldwide:
Charles E. (Chuck) Brymer, age 49,
$1,871,579 total compensation
Chairman and Chief Creative Officer DDB Worldwide:
Bob Scarpelli
Chairman and CEO, Omnicom Media Group:
Daryl D. Simm, age 48
Treasurer: Dennis E. Hewitt
Tax Counsel: Philip J. George
Auditors: KPMG LLP

LOCATIONS

HQ: Omnicom Group Inc.
437 Madison Ave., New York, NY 10022
Phone: 212-415-3600 **Fax:** 212-415-3530
Web: www.omnicomgroup.com

2008 Sales

	$ mil.	% of total
US	6,890.0	52
Europe		
UK	1,325.4	10
Other countries	2,985.6	22
Other regions	2,158.9	16
Total	**13,359.9**	**100**

PRODUCTS/OPERATIONS

2008 Sales

	$ mil.	% of total
Traditional media advertising	5,731.8	42
Customer relationship management	5,084.9	38
Specialty communications	1,275.8	10
Public relations	1,267.4	10
Total	**13,359.9**	**100**

Selected Operations

Global advertising networks
 BBDO Worldwide
 DDB Worldwide
 TBWA Worldwide

National advertising agencies
 Goodby, Silverstein & Partners (San Francisco)
 GSD&M's Idea City (Austin, TX)
 Martin|Williams (Minneapolis)
 Merkley + Partners (New York City)
 Zimmerman Partners Advertising (Fort Lauderdale, FL)

Marketing and consulting agencies

Direct response
 Interbrand (brand identity)
 M/A/R/C Research (market research)
 Rapp (direct marketing)
 Targetbase (direct marketing)

Promotional marketing
 CPM (field marketing)
 The Integer Group (retail marketing)
 Kaleidoscope (sports and event marketing)
 Millsport (sports and event marketing)

Public relations
 Brodeur Partners
 Clark & Weinstock
 Cone
 Fleishman-Hillard
 Gavin Anderson & Company
 GPC International
 Ketchum
 Porter Novelli International
 Smythe Dorward Lambert

Specialty communications
 Adelphi Group (health care)
 Corbett Accel Healthcare (health care)
 Dieste Hamel & Partners (multicultural marketing)
 Doremus (business-to-business advertising)
 SafirRosetti (security and intelligence)

Media services
 Icon International
 Novus Print Media
 OMD Worldwide
 PHD Network

COMPETITORS

Aegis Group	Interpublic Group
Dentsu	Publicis Groupe
Hakuhodo	WPP
Havas	

HISTORICAL FINANCIALS

Company Type: Public

Income Statement

FYE: December 31

	REVENUE ($ mil.)	NET INCOME ($ mil.)	NET PROFIT MARGIN	EMPLOYEES
12/08	13,359.9	1,000.3	7.5%	68,000
12/07	12,694.0	975.7	7.7%	70,000
12/06	11,376.9	864.0	7.6%	66,000
12/05	10,481.1	790.7	7.5%	62,000
12/04	9,747.2	723.5	7.4%	61,000
Annual Growth	**8.2%**	**8.4%**	**—**	**2.8%**

2008 Year-End Financials

Debt ratio: 86.7%
Return on equity: 26.3%
Cash ($ mil.): 1,097
Current ratio: 0.88
Long-term debt ($ mil.): 3,054
No. of shares (mil.): 311
Dividends
 Yield: 2.2%
 Payout: 18.9%
Market value ($ mil.): 8,366

Stock History

NYSE: OMC

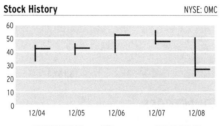

	STOCK PRICE ($) FY Close	P/E High/Low		Earnings	PER SHARE ($) Dividends	Book Value
12/08	26.92	16	7	3.17	0.60	11.34
12/07	47.53	19	16	2.95	0.57	13.17
12/06	52.27	21	16	2.49	0.50	12.46
12/05	42.56	21	17	2.18	0.46	12.70
12/04	42.16	23	17	1.94	0.45	13.12
Annual Growth	**(10.6%)**	**—**	**—**	**13.1%**	**7.5%**	**(3.6%)**

ONEOK, Inc.

One okey-dokey company, ONEOK (pronounced "one oak") is branching out across the energy industry. The company's regulated utilities, Oklahoma Natural Gas, Kansas Gas Service, and Texas Gas Service, distribute natural gas to more than 2 million customers. Through its 47.7%-owned ONEOK Partners, it operates 14,300 miles of gas-gathering pipeline and 6,920 miles of transportation pipeline, as well as gas processing plants and storage facilities. The unit also owns one of the US's top natural gas liquids (NGL) systems. ONEOK's energy services operation focuses on marketing natural gas and related services throughout the US. ONEOK also operates a parking garage and leases office space in Tulsa.

ONEOK's strategy is to deliver consistent growth and sustainable earnings via its ONEOK Partners, Distribution, and Energy Services segments through both internal growth and strategic acquisitions.

In 2006 ONEOK sold its gathering and processing, natural gas liquids, pipelines, and storage businesses to Northern Border Partners (renamed ONEOK Partners) for $3 billion and became that company's general partner.

In 2008 ONEOK Partners announced plans to build a 78-mile natural gas liquids gathering pipeline to connect two processing plants in the Woodford Shale area in southeast Oklahoma.

HISTORY

In 1906 Oklahoma Natural Gas (ONG) was founded to pipe natural gas from northeastern Oklahoma to Oklahoma City. A 100-mile pipeline was completed the next year. In 1921 ONG created two oil companies to pump out the oil it found as a result of its natural gas exploration.

In the 1920s ONG changed hands many times, ending up with utility financier G. L. Ohrstrom and Company, which milked it dry by brokering acquisitions (purchasing gas properties and then selling them to ONG) and collecting fees. Stock sales drove revenues, inflating the stock's price, and the inflated price triggered more stock sales. The bubble burst on October 29, 1929. A series of leadership changes ensued, and in 1932 the company was dissolved and reincorporated. Under president Joseph Bowes, ONG recovered, wooing back dissatisfied customers and upgrading its pipelines.

In the late 1930s the company pioneered a type of underground storage that injected gas into depleted gas reservoirs in the summer and withdrew it during winter's peak use times.

The 1950s and 1960s saw the company expand. In 1962 it created its first subsidiary, Oklahoma Natural Gas Gathering Company, selling gas out of state and therefore subject to federal regulation.

In the lean 1970s ONG was not affected by federal laws that kept wellhead prices low for gas transported across state lines because its main operations were confined to Oklahoma. Congress deregulated wellhead prices in 1978, spurring exploration but causing great price fluctuations in the 1980s. In 1980 ONG changed its name to ONEOK.

In the 1980s ONEOK signed take-or-pay contracts, which forced it to pay for gas offered by its suppliers even if it had no customers. When recession in the 1980s caused demand to drop, ONEOK had to pay for high-priced natural gas it couldn't sell. In 1988 the company was ordered to pay some $50 million to supplier Forest Oil of Denver. A year later ONEOK was sued for allegedly failing to tell stockholders about the take-or-pay agreements (settled in 1993 for $5.5 million). It later sold more than half of its oil and gas reserves to Mustang Energy for $52 million to finance the Forest Oil court award. The company was still settling lawsuits over the agreements into the 1990s; it settled the last of the claims by 1998.

ONEOK began buying gas transmission and production facilities in Oklahoma and creating drilling alliances in the 1990s. In 1997 ONEOK bought the natural gas assets of Westar Energy, formerly Western Resources, for $660 million and ONEOK stock worth $800 million. The acquisition doubled the number of ONEOK's customers and increased its gas marketing, gathering, and transmission operations.

In 1998 the company sold oil and gas reserves, processing plants, and gathering systems in Kansas, Louisiana, and Oklahoma to Duke Energy. With gas utility deregulation looming, ONEOK purchased producing oil and gas properties, primarily in Oklahoma and Texas.

Also in 1998 it agreed to buy Southwest Gas of Las Vegas for $863.6 million. Southern Union offered $976 million for Southwest Gas in 1999, but Southwest Gas agreed instead to a $912.3 million deal with ONEOK. Southern Union sued Southwest Gas, alleging that it had conspired with ONEOK to block the Southern Union bid. In 2000 the legal action made ONEOK cancel the Southwest Gas deal.

President and COO David Kyle took over as chairman and CEO in 2000 after Larry Brummett died of cancer. In 2001 the company established a new unit, ONEOK Power, with the startup of a new power plant northwest of Oklahoma City.

Westar Energy reduced its stake to approximately 15% by selling shares back to ONEOK and to the public in mid-2003; it sold its remaining shares to Cantor Fitzgerald later that year.

ONEOK has been juggling assets to focus on profitable businesses. The firm, which gets a large slice of its revenues from its gas distribution, gathering, and processing operations, sold about 70% of its oil and gas production assets in Kansas, Oklahoma, and Texas to Chesapeake Energy for $300 million in 2003. Later that year, shifting its production focus to the Texas market (and focusing on development rather than exploration), it acquired oil and gas reserves and related gathering systems in East Texas from Wagner & Brown for about $240 million.

The company also acquired Southern Union's Texas natural gas distribution business (540,000 customers), as well as Southern Union's stake in a Mexican gas utility and its propane distribution, gas marketing, and gas transmission operations in the southwestern US, for $420 million.

ONEOK acquired Northern Plains Natural Gas, a general partner of pipeline operator Northern Border Partners (later renamed ONEOK Partners), from CCE Holdings (a joint venture of Southern Union and GE Commercial Finance) for $175 million in 2004.

In 2005 the company bought Koch Industries' natural gas liquids assets for $1.35 billion. That year ONEOK sold properties to TXOK Acquisition Inc. for $645 million, and some Texas natural gas assets to Eagle Rock Energy for $528 million to help pay down debt.

EXECUTIVES

Chairman: David L. Kyle, age 56
CEO and Director; Chairman and CEO, ONEOK Partners: John W. Gibson, age 57, $6,571,790 total compensation
President: James C. (Jim) Kneale, age 58, $4,497,809 total compensation
COO: Robert F. (Rob) Martinovich, age 51
SVP, CFO, and Treasurer: Curtis L. Dinan, age 41, $1,280,587 total compensation
VP and CIO: Kevin L. Burdick, age 44
EVP; COO, ONEOK Partners: Terry K. Spencer, age 50
EVP, Northern Plains Gas Company: Christopher R. (Chris) Skoog, age 45
SVP and Special Counsel to the Chairman: John A. Gaberino Jr., age 67
SVP Administrative Services: David E. Roth, age 54
SVP Compliance: D. Lamar Miller, age 49

SVP Technical and Corporate Services: Stephan R. (Steve) Guy, age 54
SVP Corporate Planning and Development: Caron A. Lawhorn, age 48
SVP, General Counsel, and Assistant Secretary: John R. Barker, age 61, $1,476,272 total compensation
VP Communications and Investor Relations: Dandridge (Dan) Harrison, age 53
President, Kansas Gas Service: Bradley O. (Brad) Dixon, age 56
President, Oklahoma Natural Gas: Roger N. Mitchell, age 57
President, Texas Gas Service: Gregory A. (Greg) Phillips, age 46
President, Energy Services: Patrick J. (Pat) McDonie, age 48
Auditors: PricewaterhouseCoopers LLP

LOCATIONS

HQ: ONEOK, Inc.
100 W. 5th St., Tulsa, OK 74103
Phone: 918-588-7000   **Fax:** 918-588-7960
Web: www.oneok.com

ONEOK operates primarily in Kansas, Oklahoma, and Texas.

PRODUCTS/OPERATIONS

2008 Sales

	$ mil.	% of total
Energy Services	7,001.3	43
ONEOK Partners	6,975.3	43
Distribution	2,177.6	14
Adjustments	3.2	—
Total	**16,157.4**	**100**

COMPETITORS

Adams Resources
AEP
Atmos Energy
BP
CenterPoint Energy
CMS Energy
Duncan Energy
Dynegy
Energen
Energy Future
EQT Corporation
Exxon Mobil
FirstEnergy
Hess Corporation
National Fuel Gas
OGE Energy
Southern Union
Southwest Gas
Williams Companies

HISTORICAL FINANCIALS

Company Type: Public

Income Statement
FYE: December 31

	REVENUE ($ mil.)	NET INCOME ($ mil.)	NET PROFIT MARGIN	EMPLOYEES
12/08	16,157.4	311.9	1.9%	4,742
12/07	13,477.4	304.9	2.3%	4,555
12/06	11,896.1	306.3	2.6%	4,536
12/05	12,676.2	546.5	4.3%	4,558
12/04	5,988.1	242.2	4.0%	4,627
Annual Growth	**28.2%**	**6.5%**	**—**	**0.6%**

2008 Year-End Financials

Debt ratio: 196.9%
Return on equity: 15.4%
Cash ($ mil.): 510
Current ratio: 0.81
Long-term debt ($ mil.): 4,113

No. of shares (mil.): 105
Dividends
  Yield: 5.4%
  Payout: 52.9%
Market value ($ mil.): 3,069

Stock History

NYSE: OKE

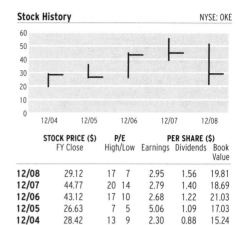

	STOCK PRICE ($) FY Close	P/E High/Low		PER SHARE ($) Earnings	Dividends	Book Value
12/08	29.12	17	7	2.95	1.56	19.81
12/07	44.77	20	14	2.79	1.40	18.69
12/06	43.12	17	10	2.68	1.22	21.03
12/05	26.63	7	5	5.06	1.09	17.03
12/04	28.42	13	9	2.30	0.88	15.24
Annual Growth	**0.6%**	**—**	**—**	**6.4%**	**15.4%**	**6.8%**

Oracle Corporation

According to Oracle, consolidation in the business software industry is the wisest move. The enterprise software giant provides a range of tools for managing business data, supporting business operations, and facilitating collaboration and application development. Oracle also offers business applications for data warehousing, customer relationship management, and supply chain management. In recent years the company has aggressively used acquisitions to expand its product lines, including the purchases of PeopleSoft, Siebel Systems, BEA Systems, and Hyperion Solutions. In April 2009 the company announced plans for its most ambitious acquisition to date, the purchase of Sun for about $7.4 billion.

The proposed Sun acquisition would not only be one of the larger deals Oracle has undertaken, but would also mark its first significant foray into the world of hardware and chips. Oracle hopes to extend its software expertise to Sun's servers, Solaris operating system, and SPARC chips, enabling Oracle to offer customers an integrated offering of both hardware and software (much like Oracle rivals IBM and Hewlett Packard do).

In recent years the company has faced a similar pleasurable dilemma encountered by its rival Microsoft: what to do with a mountain of cash. Oracle's dominant position in the lucrative world of databases produces a steady stream of cash flow and profits, but it also has generated pressure from shareholders to put the company's cash hoard to use. In response the company has embarked on an extended spending spree with one primary goal: to expand its business applications product line and market share through acquisitions, both large and small.

The first blockbuster acquisition Oracle undertook was the purchase of PeopleSoft, a $10.3 billion deal. The company then acquired Retek, as well as a host of smaller deals including identity management software developer Oblix; data management software maker TimesTen; retail inventory management software developer ProfitLogic; and logistics software provider Global Logistics Technologies.

Not content to rest on its acquisitive laurels, Oracle initiated another blockbuster deal, purchasing Siebel Systems for $5.85 billion. It also acquired Portal Software for about $220 million, in addition to purchasing TelephonyWork. Next up was business intelligence software provider Hyperion Solutions for about $3.3 billion and Agile Software for about $495 million.

In October 2007 the company made an offer to purchase BEA Systems for $6.7 billion. BEA rejected the offer, insisting it would only start negotiations at a price of more than $8 billion, and Oracle withdrew its bid. In early 2008 BEA accepted a second offer from Oracle valued at $8.5 billion.

Collectively, the company has spent more than $30 billion on acquisitions in 2004-2008.

HISTORY

Larry Ellison, Robert Miner, Bruce Scott, and Edward Oates founded System Development Laboratories in 1977 to create a database management system according to theoretical specifications published by IBM. Ellison had studied physics at the University of Chicago but dropped out in the 1960s to seek his fortune in Silicon Valley. Working first for Ampex and then Amdahl (now Fujitsu IT Holdings), he was part of the team that developed the first IBM-compatible mainframe. Miner, an experienced programmer, was the main developer of Oracle's database manager, which was able to run on many computer brands and was introduced in 1979. The company also changed its name that year to Relational Software.

In 1983 the company changed its name again, this time to Oracle, in order to more closely align itself with its primary product. Oracle went public in 1986 and within two years had a 36% share of Uncle Sam's PC database market. It also added financial management, graphics, and human resource management software.

Oracle's rapid growth came at a great cost. It gained notoriety as a leader in vaporware — that is, announced products that actually had not yet been developed. When the company's software was released, it was sometimes bug-ridden and lacking promised features. Duplicate billings and the booking of unconsummated sales inflated revenues.

Oracle recorded a loss for fiscal 1991, accompanied by a downward restatement of earnings for past years. Its stock nosedived. The company laid off 400 employees and revised its growth estimates. Ellison stabilized the company with $80 million in financing from Nippon Steel.

Thanks to Oracle7 (launched 1992), the company within two years became the #1 database management software maker. Sales for fiscal 1994 hit $2 billion. Ellison by that time had developed a reputation as an extravagant adventurer (his hobbies included yacht racing and piloting disarmed fighter planes).

Oracle formed affiliate Network Computer Inc. in 1997 to market Internet appliances (with no disk drive and local memory) that Ellison envisioned would strip Microsoft of its operating system ubiquity. Oracle and Netscape (now owned by Time Warner) merged joint venture Navio Communications one year later into Network Computer (renamed Liberate Technologies, redesigned around interactive software, and spun off in 1999).

In 1999 the company bought three niche front-office software specialists and took its Oracle Japan subsidiary public. The next year it partnered with rival Commerce One to provide software and support for a giant online venture merging the Web-based procurement exchanges of General Motors, Ford Motor, and Daimler.

Oracle continued to expand its portfolio of business applications in 2001, introducing warehouse, supply chain, and customer relationship management software, as well as software suites targeted at small businesses.

The company launched a hostile takeover bid for PeopleSoft in 2003, just days after the rival software maker had disclosed plans to acquire J.D. Edwards. PeopleSoft's board unanimously rejected the initial all-cash offer of $5.1 billion, deeming the unsolicited bid inadequate and citing antitrust concerns. After bitter negotiations that included a number of rejected bids, Oracle finally reached an agreement to acquire PeopleSoft for $10.3 billion in December 2004; the deal closed the following month.

Soon after the PeopleSoft deal closed, Oracle again pursued a takeover. Rival SAP had announced plans to acquire retail software developer Retek for about $500 million. After a brief bidding war Oracle purchased Retek for about $670 million.

EXECUTIVES

CEO and Director: Lawrence J. (Larry) Ellison, age 64
Co-President and Director: Safra A. Catz, age 47
Co-President and Director:
 Charles E. (Chuck) Phillips Jr., age 49
SVP; President and CEO Oracle, Japan: Takao Endo
EVP and CFO: Jeffrey E. Epstein, age 52
SVP and CIO: Mark E. Sunday, age 54
Chief Corporate Architect: Edward Screven
Chief Security Officer: Mary Ann Davidson
Chief Marketing Officer and SVP: Judith Sim
VP and Chief Technologist, SOA: Dave Chappell
Chief Customer Officer: Jeb Dasteel
EVP Japan Sales and Consulting: Derek H. Williams
EVP Product Development: Charles A. (Chuck) Rozwat
EVP North America Sales and Consulting:
 Keith G. Block, age 47
EVP Oracle Customer Services: Juergen Rottler, age 40
EVP Oracle Latin America: Luiz Meisler
EVP Oracle Europe, Middle East, and Africa:
 Loïc le Guisquet
SVP Oracle University: John L. Hall
SVP and General Manager, Oracle Retail:
 Duncan B. Angove
SVP Human Resources: Joyce Westerdahl
SVP Office of the CEO: Ken Glueck
SVP, General Counsel, and Secretary: Dorian Daley
Auditors: Ernst & Young LLP

LOCATIONS

HQ: Oracle Corporation
 500 Oracle Pkwy., Redwood City, CA 94065
Phone: 650-506-7000   **Fax:** 650-506-7200
Web: www.oracle.com

Oracle has offices in more than 60 countries.

2009 Sales

	$ mil.	% of total
US	10,190	44
UK	1,587	7
Japan	1,189	5
Germany	956	4
France	856	4
Canada	737	3
Other countries	7,737	33
Total	**23,252**	**100**

PRODUCTS/OPERATIONS

2009 Sales

	$ mil.	% of total
Software	18,877	81
Services	4,375	19
Total	**23,252**	**100**

Selected Software Lines

Business applications
 Corporate performance management
 Customer relationship management
 Financial management
 Human capital management
 Procurement
 Project management
 Supply chain management
Databases
Enterprise application integration
Middleware

COMPETITORS

Accenture	i2 Technologies
ADP	IBM
BMC Software	Lawson Software
Borland Software	Microsoft
CA, Inc.	NCR
CDC Software	Progress Software
Ceridian	salesforce.com
Cognos	SAP
EDS	Sybase

HISTORICAL FINANCIALS

Company Type: Public

Income Statement

	REVENUE ($ mil.)	NET INCOME ($ mil.)	NET PROFIT MARGIN	EMPLOYEES
				FYE: May 31
5/09	23,252.0	5,593.0	24.1%	86,000
5/08	22,430.0	5,521.0	24.6%	84,233
5/07	17,996.0	4,274.0	23.7%	74,674
5/06	14,380.0	3,381.0	23.5%	56,133
5/05	11,799.0	2,886.0	24.5%	49,872
Annual Growth	**18.5%**	**18.0%**	**—**	**14.6%**

2009 Year-End Financials

Debt ratio: 46.5%
Return on equity: 23.2%
Cash ($ mil.): 8,995
Current ratio: 2.03
Long-term debt ($ mil.): 11,660

No. of shares (mil.): 5,007
Dividends
 Yield: 0.3%
 Payout: 4.6%
Market value ($ mil.): 98,092

Stock History

NASDAQ (GS): ORCL

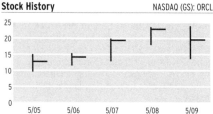

	STOCK PRICE ($) FY Close	P/E High/Low		PER SHARE ($) Earnings	Dividends	Book Value
5/09	19.59	22	13	1.09	0.05	5.01
5/08	22.84	22	17	1.06	0.00	4.60
5/07	19.38	24	16	0.81	0.00	3.38
5/06	14.22	24	18	0.64	0.00	3.00
5/05	12.80	27	18	0.55	0.00	2.16
Annual Growth	**11.2%**	**—**	**—**	**18.6%**	**—**	**23.4%**

Oshkosh Corporation

Whether you need to plow your way through Sahara sands or Buffalo snow, Oshkosh has your vehicle, by gosh. The company makes heavy-duty vehicles for commercial, fire and emergency, and military applications. Oshkosh's commercial and emergency/rescue vehicles include concrete carriers and refuse trucks (McNeilus brand), snow blowers, aircraft rescue and fire-fighting vehicles (Pierce brand), and towing equipment (Jerr-Dan). Oshkosh's vehicles are used in airport, institutional, and municipal markets. The company also makes heavy-payload tactical trucks for the US Department of Defense. Oshkosh gets 70% of its sales in the US.

In 2008 Oshkosh changed its name from Oshkosh Truck Corporation to simply Oshkosh Corporation in order to reflect its increasingly diverse lineup of product offerings. A series of acquisitions expanded the company's product portfolio and greatly increased its annual sales.

The following year Oshkosh sold its Dutch subsidiary, the Geesink Norba Group, to Platinum Equity. The company retained Geesink Norba's plant in Romania, which fabricates parts for both Geesink Norba and Oshkosh's JLG Industries subsidiary.

HISTORY

Bernhard Mosling and William Besserdich founded Oshkosh Truck in 1917, attracting investors with *Old Betsy*, a four-wheel-drive, 3,000-lb. truck. Over the next few decades, the company developed a range of heavy-duty vehicles. Sales took off when the US Army gave truck contracts to Oshkosh during WWII. Commercial sales increased after the war, the result of demand from mining and plantation companies. Oshkosh Truck went public in 1985.

Defense cutbacks prompted the company to diversify. It acquired Deere & Company's motorhome chassis business in 1989 and Miller Trailers the next year.

In 1995 Oshkosh formed a strategic alliance with Daimler-Benz's (now Daimler AG) Freightliner Corporation (now Daimler Trucks North America), although the transfer of its chassis business caused the company's sales to drop by more than $100 million in fiscal 1995. The following year Oshkosh bought fire truck maker Pierce Manufacturing for $158 million. Robert Bohn became CEO in 1997, succeeding R. Eugene Goodson, who quit in a disagreement with the board. Oshkosh also bought Quebec-based Nova Quintech's firefighting ladder technology that year.

The company acquired McNeilus Companies, a leading maker of concrete mixers and bodies for refuse trucks, for $250 million in 1998. It also won the initial contract for the US Marine Corps' Medium Tactical Truck Replacement program, potentially worth up to $1.2 billion. In 1999 Oshkosh bought Kewaunee Engineering, which made parts for aerial devices, for $6.3 million. The next year Oshkosh picked up Viking Truck and Equipment (concrete mixer sales and service). Later in 2000 Oshkosh diversified into ambulances with the purchase of Medtec Ambulance Corporation.

Oshkosh expanded its European presence in 2001 when it bought the Geesink Norba Group (refuse collection truck bodies, mobile and stationary compactors, and transfer stations) from Powell Duffryn Ltd. for $137 million. In 2004 Oshkosh acquired Jerr-Dan, a towing equipment manufacturer, from Littlejohn & Co. for about $80 million. Later that year the company acquired 75% of two Italy-based firefighting equipment manufacturers, BAI Brescia Antcendi International and BAI Tecnica.

The following year Oshkosh bought Canadian concrete mixer truck company London Machinery Inc.

Oshkosh acquired access equipment manufacturer JLG Industries in 2006.

2006 was a record year for Oshkosh's sales and profits, but thanks to its acquisition of JLG Industries, Oshkosh's 2007 sales and profits were lifted to even greater heights. The addition of JLG was largely responsible for Oshkosh increasing sales by 84% compared with the previous year, which was pretty good.

The acquisition of JLG marked Oshkosh's expansion into the aerial platform market, and JLG instantly became Oshkosh's largest product segment. The move also gave Oshkosh purchasing leverage, and gave the company exposure to complementary markets.

Not surprisingly, the company's defense products also enjoyed brisk sales of parts and services for the thousands of Oshkosh trucks currently in service in Iraq. Oshkosh also won market share for its line of emergency vehicles, including response vehicles used in homeland security applications.

Also in 2006 Oshkosh acquired AK Specialty Vehicles (since renamed Oshkosh Specialty Vehicles) from HealthTronics for about $140 million. Oshkosh Specialty Vehicles makes mobile medical, broadcast, and homeland security command and control vehicles — new specialty vehicle markets for Oshkosh. Buying AK Specialty Vehicles also increased Oshkosh's presence in Europe. Later in 2006 Oshkosh bought Iowa Mold Tooling, a maker of tire service, general mechanics, and lubrication trucks. The purchase boosted Oshkosh's market presence for trucks serving the construction, tire service, and mining industries.

EXECUTIVES

Chairman and CEO: Robert G. (Bob) Bohn, age 55
President, COO, and Director:
Charles L. (Charlie) Szews, age 52
EVP and CFO: David M. Sagehorn, age 46
EVP Technology: Donald H. Verhoff, age 62
EVP and Chief Administration Officer:
Matthew J. Zolnowski, age 55
SVP; President, JLG Industries: Craig E. Paylor, age 53
EVP; President, Defense Business:
William J. (John) Stoddart, age 63
EVP; EVP, Marketing, Sales, and Dealer Distribution; COO, Pierce Manufacturing: Mark A. Meaders
EVP; President, Commercial Segment:
Michael J. Wuest, age 49
EVP, General Counsel, and Secretary:
Bryan J. Blankfield, age 47
EVP Global Manufacturing Services: Thomas D. Fenner, age 53
EVP; President, Fire & Emergency and Pierce Manufacturing: Wilson N. Jones, age 48
EVP and President, Defense: R. Andy Hove
EVP Government Operations and Industry Relations:
Joseph H. Kimmitt, age 58

SVP Finance and Controller: Thomas J. Polnaszek
SVP and Chief Procurement Officer:
Gregory L. (Greg) Fredericksen
VP Investor Relations: Patrick N. Davidson
VP Human Resources: Michael K. Rohrkaste
VP Information Technology: Michael S. Guzowski
VP Marketing Communications: Ann Stawski
Auditors: Deloitte & Touche LLP

LOCATIONS

HQ: Oshkosh Corporation
2307 Oregon St., Oshkosh, WI 54902
Phone: 920-235-9151   **Fax:** 920-233-9268
Web: www.oshkoshcorporation.com

2008 Sales

	$ mil.	% of total
North America		
US	4,997.2	70
Other countries	180.6	2
Europe, Africa & Middle East	1,544.1	22
Other regions	416.4	6
Total	**7,138.3**	**100**

PRODUCTS/OPERATIONS

2008 Sales

	$ mil.	% of total
Access equipment	3,085.9	43
Defense	1,891.9	26
Fire & emergency	1,192.8	17
Commercial	1,037.0	14
Adjustments	(69.3)	—
Total	**7,138.3**	**100**

Selected Products

Access equipment
  Aerial work platforms
  Excavators
  Telehandlers
  Trailers

Defense
  Heavy equipment transporter (HET)
  Heavy expanded mobility tactical trucks (HEMTT)
  Load handling systems (LHS)
  Logistic vehicle system (LVS)
  Medium tactical vehicle replacements (MTVR)
  Palletized load system (PLS)

Commercial
  Portable concrete batch plants
  Rear- and front-discharge concrete mixers
  Refuse truck bodies

Fire and emergency
  Aircraft rescue vehicles
  Airport snow removal vehicles
  Custom ambulances
  Firefighting vehicles
  Rescue and homeland security vehicles
  Snow blowing and plow trucks
  Towing and recovery equipment

COMPETITORS

AM General	Leyland Trucks
American LaFrance	Mack Trucks
BAE Systems	MAN
Collins Industries	MANITOU BF
Daimler	Miller Industries
Daimler Trucks	Navistar
Dover Corp.	Navistar International
E-ONE	Nissan Diesel
Federal Signal	PACCAR
Force Protection	Pinguely-Haulotte
General Dynamics	Skyjack
Heil Environmental	Spartan Motors
Hyundai Motor	Terex
Iveco S.p.A.	Trinity Industries
J C Bamford Excavators	Volvo
L-3 Communications	

HISTORICAL FINANCIALS

Company Type: Public

Income Statement

FYE: September 30

	REVENUE ($ mil.)	NET INCOME ($ mil.)	NET PROFIT MARGIN	EMPLOYEES
9/08	7,138.3	79.3	1.1%	14,000
9/07	6,307.3	268.1	4.3%	14,200
9/06	3,427.4	205.5	6.0%	9,387
9/05	2,959.9	160.2	5.4%	7,960
9/04	2,262.3	112.8	5.0%	6,820
Annual Growth	33.3%	(8.4%)	—	19.7%

2008 Year-End Financials

Debt ratio: 193.0%
Return on equity: 5.7%
Cash ($ mil.): 88
Current ratio: 1.47
Long-term debt ($ mil.): 2,681

No. of shares (mil.): 74
Dividends
Yield: 3.0%
Payout: 37.7%
Market value ($ mil.): 980

Stock History

NYSE: OSK

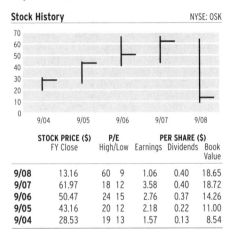

	STOCK PRICE ($) FY Close	P/E High/Low		PER SHARE ($) Earnings	Dividends	Book Value
9/08	13.16	60	9	1.06	0.40	18.65
9/07	61.97	18	12	3.58	0.40	18.72
9/06	50.47	24	15	2.76	0.37	14.26
9/05	43.16	20	12	2.18	0.22	11.00
9/04	28.53	19	13	1.57	0.13	8.54
Annual Growth	(17.6%)	—	—	(9.4%)	32.4%	21.6%

Owens & Minor

Owens & Minor makes sure hospitals are prepared for major surgeries. A leading distributor of medical and surgical supplies, Owens & Minor carries some 220,000 products from about 1,600 manufacturers. Products distributed by the company include surgical dressings, endoscopic and intravenous products, needles, syringes, sterile procedure trays, gowns, gloves, and sutures. The firm also offers software, consulting, and other services to help customers manage their supplies. Owens & Minor's customers are primarily hospitals and health systems and the purchasing organizations that serve them. It delivers products to roughly 4,500 health care providers from 55 distribution centers across the US.

The company's major suppliers include Covidien and Johnson & Johnson, whose products each account for more than 10% of O&M's revenues. The distributor sells some 1,800 value products under its own MediChoice label.

Most of Owens & Minor's sales come from acute-care hospitals, which are often represented by group purchasing organizations (GPOs) or integrated health care networks (IHNs). GPO Novation accounts for around 40% of the company's earnings, and GPOs Premier and Broadlane account for about 20% and 10%, respectively. The

company also has an ongoing exclusive supplier agreement with the US Department of Defense.

As the health care industry has consolidated, so have the industries that serve it, and Owens & Minor has tried to remain competitive by providing supply chain management tools and services in addition to supplies to help its customers control costs. Its OMSolutions business unit provides outsourcing and resource management services, including one-on-one consultations and physical inventory reviews. Its technology offerings include WISDOM, which allows customers to track inventory, usage, and other information to keep costs down, and PANDAC, which helps operating rooms track and control their inventory.

O&M doesn't shy away from acquisitions as another way to help boost sales. To help bolster its core distribution business, in 2008 O&M acquired private Midwest distributor The Burrows Company for $30 million plus debt assumptions.

In 2009, in a move designed to increase focus on its core acute care distribution operations, the company sold its direct-to-consumer diabetes supply business, Access Diabetic Supply, to Liberty Medical (a division of Medco Health Solutions) for $63 million.

HISTORY

George Gilmer Minor Jr.'s great-grandfather was an apothecary and surgeon in colonial Williamsburg, Virginia. His grandfather was Thomas Jefferson's personal physician. Minor himself worked as a wholesale drug salesman in Richmond after the Civil War. In 1882 he and rival wholesaler Otho Owens partnered to form the Owens & Minor Drug Company. The company was both a retail and wholesale business, with a storefront that filled prescriptions and sold sundries, paints, oils, and window glass. When Owens died in 1906, Minor became the company's president.

During the 1920s, the Owens family sold their stake in the firm. George Gilmer Minor III served briefly as the company's president in the early 1940s; his son, George Gilmer Minor IV (called Mr. Minor Jr. to differentiate him from his father), became president in 1947.

In 1954 Owens & Minor installed its first computerized order fulfillment system. The following year the firm became Owens, Minor & Bodeker when it bought the Bodeker Drug Company, which was both older and larger than Owens & Minor.

After 84 years in the drug wholesale business, the company entered the medical and surgical distribution business after buying A&J Hospital Supply in 1966 and Powers & Anderson in 1968. In 1971 Owens, Minor & Bodeker went public. By the end of the decade, the company had operations in 10 states.

The fourth Minor to run the firm, G. Gilmer Minor III (Mr. Minor Jr.'s son), was named president in 1981 (he became CEO in 1984). Under his direction Owens, Minor & Bodeker would complete the transition from a drug wholesaler to a medical supplies distributor. In 1981 it purchased the Will Ross subsidiary of G.D. Searle (then the country's #2 medical and surgical supplies distributor).

The company reverted to its original name on its 100th anniversary in 1982. By 1984 medical supplies supplanted wholesale drugs as its primary source of income. In 1988 Owens & Minor listed on the NYSE.

The company passed the $1 billion revenue mark in 1990 and later sold its wholesale drug business. It extended its reach with the purchase of Lyons Physician Supply in 1993 and Stuart Medical (the #3 national distributor) in 1994.

The company consolidated its warehouse operations and upgraded its computer system in 1995. To make up for losses attributed to restructuring costs and discounting prices for large accounts, Owens & Minor eliminated or reassigned jobs at several distribution centers.

In 1998 it lost its biggest customer when embattled Columbia/HCA (now HCA) canceled its contract. Owens & Minor replaced this business by contracting with such providers as Sutter Health.

In 1999 the company formed an alliance with drug distributor AmeriSource Health (now AmerisourceBergen) to streamline transactions with Sutter Health. In 2002 Owens & Minor launched an initiative to offer automated supply chain management services to its clients.

Chairman and CEO G. Gilmer Minor III stepped down from the CEO post after 21 years in July 2005 but remained the company's chairman; Craig R. Smith, the company's former COO, was named CEO.

Also in 2005, the company expanded into the diabetic direct-to-consumer supply business by acquiring Access Diabetic Supply. (That division was later divested, however.)

The company in 2006 acquired the acute care medical and surgical supply business of McKesson Medical-Surgical, a subsidiary of McKesson Corporation, for $165 million.

EXECUTIVES

Chairman: G. Gilmer Minor III, age 68
President, CEO, and Director: Craig R. Smith, age 57, $3,595,104 total compensation
CFO and SVP: James L. (Jim) Bierman, age 57, $1,126,578 total compensation
SVP and CIO: Richard W. Mears, age 48
EVP Administration: Charles C. Colpo, age 51, $1,125,578 total compensation
EVP Distribution: E. V. Clarke, age 48
SVP Human Resources: Erika T. Davis, age 45
SVP, General Counsel, and Corporate Secretary: Grace R. den Hartog, age 57, $1,017,680 total compensation
SVP Strategic Planning and Business Development: Mark A. Van Sumeren, age 51, $1,142,057 total compensation
SVP Sales and Marketing: W. Marshall Simpson, age 40
VP Quality and Communications: Hugh F. Gouldthorpe Jr., age 70
VP and Treasurer: Richard F. (Dick) Bozard, age 61
Director Finance: Chuck Graves
Director Investor Communications and Media Relations: Truitt (Trudi) Allcott
Auditors: KPMG LLP

LOCATIONS

HQ: Owens & Minor, Inc.
9120 Lockwood Blvd., Mechanicsville, VA 23116
Phone: 804-723-7000 **Fax:** 804-723-7100
Web: www.owens-minor.com

PRODUCTS/OPERATIONS

Selected Subsidiaries

Medical Supply Group, Inc.
O&M Canada, Inc.
O&M Funding Corp.
OM Solutions International, Inc.
OMI International, Ltd. (British Virgin Islands)
Owens & Minor Distribution, Inc.
Owens & Minor Healthcare Supply, Inc.
Owens & Minor Medical, Inc.

COMPETITORS

AmerisourceBergen	Nyer Medical
Buffalo Supply	Patterson Companies
Cardinal Health	PSS World Medical
CVS Caremark	Rite Aid
Henry Schein	Surgical Express
Invacare Supply Group	Tri-anim
McKesson	Walgreen
Medline Industries	

HISTORICAL FINANCIALS

Company Type: Public

Income Statement

FYE: December 31

	REVENUE ($ mil.)	NET INCOME ($ mil.)	NET PROFIT MARGIN	EMPLOYEES
12/08	7,243.2	93.3	1.3%	5,300
12/07	6,800.5	72.7	1.1%	4,800
12/06	5,533.7	48.8	0.9%	4,600
12/05	4,822.4	64.4	1.3%	3,700
12/04	4,525.1	60.5	1.3%	3,392
Annual Growth	12.5%	11.4%	—	11.8%

2008 Year-End Financials

Debt ratio: 52.1%	No. of shares (mil.): 42
Return on equity: 14.3%	Dividends
Cash ($ mil.): 8	Yield: 2.1%
Current ratio: 1.97	Payout: 35.6%
Long-term debt ($ mil.): 359	Market value ($ mil.): 1,573

Stock History

NYSE: OMI

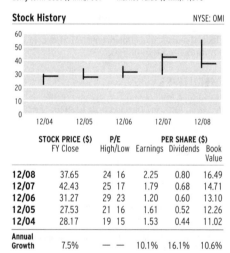

	STOCK PRICE ($) FY Close	P/E High/Low		PER SHARE ($) Earnings	Dividends	Book Value
12/08	37.65	24	16	2.25	0.80	16.49
12/07	42.43	25	17	1.79	0.68	14.71
12/06	31.27	29	23	1.20	0.60	13.10
12/05	27.53	21	16	1.61	0.52	12.26
12/04	28.17	19	15	1.53	0.44	11.02
Annual Growth	7.5%	—	—	10.1%	16.1%	10.6%

Owens-Illinois

Owens-Illinois (O-I) is involved in more toasts than Dick Clark and all Irish writers combined. The world's largest maker of glass containers, it has market-leading positions in the Americas, Europe, and the Asia/Pacific region. O-I's glass containers include bottles in a wide range of shapes and sizes used to hold beer, soft drinks, liquor, wine, juice, and other beverages. It also makes glass containers for food products, such as soups, salad dressings, and dairy products. Major customers include Anheuser-Busch, H.J. Heinz, and SABMiller. Europe and the Americas are O-I's leading geographic markets.

Since 1990 O-I has acquired more than 20 glass container businesses, expanding its presence in Asia, Europe, and the Americas to 80 manufacturing facilities in 22 countries. It also operates machine shops and mold-making shops that provide its glass-making equipment and industrial molds.

O-I's glass operations however are being chipped away by the economic downturn. Aligning supply with demand in 2009, the company shuttered a plant in Finland, laying off 100 workers. The contraction, aimed at also trimming energy consumption and manufacturing costs, will force a second European plant to close, too. In 2008 the company closed a glass container plant in New Brunswick, transferring production to other facilities in Canada. The shutdown was a response to decreased demand in the region. Meanwhile, down in South America, the company is expanding operations at its plant in Lurin, Peru. It is adding a second furnace that will double the plant's capacity. O-I also plans to transfer its engineering resources from the US to a newly built facility near its Peruvian plant, where the company believes it can better support its global operations.

Back in the US, the company launched an investigation into why select bottles manufactured for The Boston Beer Company contained bits of glass. The company acknowledged making the bottles, but concluded they were made to their normal specifications. The discovery led to a recall of the bottles in question.

In 2007 the company sold its plastics packaging business, which manufactured prescription bottles, tamper-proof closures, and injection-molded containers. Early that year the company began reviewing strategic options for its plastics operations (O-I Plastics), including a possible sale of the business. Several months later, O-I sold its plastics division to Rexam for $1.8 billion. The sale included nearly 20 plants in the Americas, Asia, and Europe, including its interests in two Mexican joint ventures the company formed in 2007. Owens-Illinois was already boosting its glass operations and whittling down its plastics business, which accounted for a little more than 10% of sales before it was divested.

HISTORY

The Owens Bottle Machine Corp. was incorporated in Toledo, Ohio, in 1907 as the successor to a four-year-old New Jersey company of the same name. It initially grew by acquiring small glass companies. In 1929 Owens bought the Illinois Glass Co. (medical and pharmaceutical glass) and became Owens-Illinois Glass.

The company bought Libbey Glass (tableware) in 1935. Three years later Owens-Illinois and Corning Glass, which were both studying uses for glass fiber, began Owens-Corning Fiberglass, a joint venture with a virtual industry monopoly.

After WWII Owens-Illinois (O-I) started to diversify beyond glass. The company went public in 1952. In 1956 it bought National Container (cardboard boxes). It also created a semi-rigid plastic container that was adopted by bleach and detergent companies.

The introduction of the non-returnable bottle in the 1960s gave new life to the glass industry. During the late 1960s the company bought Lily Tulip Cups (sold in 1981). In the 1970s the company started producing specialty optical and TV glass.

With the glass industry foundering at the beginning of the 1980s, O-I invested over $600 million in its glass operations. In 1986 O-I refused an initial purchase offer by Kohlberg Kravis Roberts & Co. (KKR), but KKR raised the offer and O-I was sold and went private. Total debt after the LBO was $4.4 billion.

In the years following the LBO, the company sold its forest products, mortgage banking, and health care businesses. O-I went public again in 1991 and expanded its plastics business with the purchase of Specialty Packaging Products in 1992, which added trigger sprayers and finger pumps to its line. The next year the company expanded its South American operations. O-I spun off Libbey Glass as a separate public firm and sold 51% of its interest in Kimble Glass (specialty packaging and laboratory ware; the rest was sold in 1997). The company acquired a majority stake in Ballarpur Industries, one of India's largest makers of glass containers.

In 1997 O-I acquired assets of a bankrupt competitor, Anchor Glass, which gave it more than a 40% share of the US glass container market. In 1999 the company sold its UK-based glass container maker, Rockware Group, to Ireland-based container maker Ardagh, and its Chicago Heights pharmaceutical glass business to Germany-based glassmaker Gerresheimer Glas.

In 2000, following a short-lived victory for the company in asbestos-related litigation, a US district judge in Texas overturned a $1.6 billion default judgment to be awarded the company by former asbestos maker T&N Ltd. Charges related to asbestos litigation and restructuring fees cost the company dearly in 2000 as it posted a $270 million loss for the year.

In 2001 O-I sold its Harbor Capital Advisors business to the Netherlands-based Robeco Groep for an estimated $490 million.

In 2003 Joseph Lemieux stepped down as CEO of the company. Steven McCracken was named president and CEO. McCracken replaced Lemieux as chairman in 2004.

O-I completed its acquisition of BSN Glasspack, Europe's #2 glass container maker, for about $1.3 billion the same year. The deal made O-I Europe's largest container company. Late in 2004 O-I sold its American and European blow-molded plastics operations to Graham Packaging Company. The company's asbestos-related cash payments in 2005 were $171 million (down from $190 million in 2004). The company announced in 2005 that it would begin doing business as O-I.

Late in 2006, Steven McCracken resigned as chairman and CEO. Company board member Albert Stroucken, who held similar leadership roles at H.B. Fuller, succeeded McCracken. That same year O-I shuttered a factory that made machine parts, and it closed a small recycling facility as part of its effort to focus on its core glass business and reduce costs.

EXECUTIVES

Chairman and CEO: Albert P. L. (Al) Stroucken, age 61, $5,866,438 total compensation
SVP and CFO: Edward C. White, age 61, $1,293,435 total compensation
VP and CIO: Ron White
VP and Chief Strategy Officer: Gregory T. (Greg) Sipla, age 42
SVP Strategic Planning and General Counsel: James W. Baehren, age 58, $1,315,825 total compensation
SVP and Chief Human Resources Officer: Stephen P. Malia
VP, General Counsel: Philip McWeeny
VP Global Accounts Management: John W. Bachey
VP and Chief Procurement Officer: Raymond C. Schlaff
VP Glass Container Research and Development: Robert E. Lachmiller

VP Finance: Stephen P. Bramlage Jr.
VP Investor Relations: John Haudrich
VP Distribution, Drug and Chemicals: Paul F. Butts
President, Global Glass Operations:
 L. Richard (Rich) Crawford, age 48,
 $1,436,229 total compensation
President, OI Asia Pacific: Greg W. J. Ridder,
 $1,165,691 total compensation
President, Europe: Jose A. Lorente
President, O-I North America: Miguel Escobar
President, O-I Latin America: Andres Lopez
Managing Director, China: Paul Wang
Chief Communications Officer: Carol R. Gee
Auditors: Ernst & Young LLP

LOCATIONS

HQ: Owens-Illinois, Inc.
 1 Michael Owens Way, Perrysburg, OH 43551
Phone: 567-336-5000 **Fax:** 419-247-7107
Web: www.o-i.com

2008 Sales

	$ mil.	% of total
Europe	3,497.8	44
North America	2,209.7	28
South America	1,135.9	15
Asia/Pacific	964.1	12
Other regions	77.2	1
Total	**7,884.7**	**100**

COMPETITORS

Alcoa
Amcor
Anchor Glass
AptarGroup
Ball Corp.
Bemis
Berry Plastics
BWAY
Canal Corp.
Consolidated Container
Constar International
Crown Holdings
Graham Packaging
Jarden
Newell Rubbermaid
Plastipak Holdings
Rexam
Saint-Gobain
Saint-Gobain Containers
Sealed Air Corp.
Silgan
Sonoco Products
Tetra Pak
Tupperware Brands
Vitro

HISTORICAL FINANCIALS

Company Type: Public

Income Statement

FYE: December 31

	REVENUE ($ mil.)	NET INCOME ($ mil.)	NET PROFIT MARGIN	EMPLOYEES
12/08	7,884.7	258.3	3.3%	23,000
12/07	7,679.2	1,340.6	17.5%	24,000
12/06	7,523.5	(27.5)	—	28,000
12/05	7,189.7	(558.6)	—	28,200
12/04	6,263.4	235.5	3.8%	28,700
Annual Growth	**5.9%**	**2.3%**	**—**	**(5.4%)**

2008 Year-End Financials

Debt ratio: 282.6%
Return on equity: 18.6%
Cash ($ mil.): 380
Current ratio: 1.22
Long-term debt ($ mil.): 2,940

No. of shares (mil.): 168
Dividends
 Yield: 0.0%
 Payout: —
Market value ($ mil.): 4,602

NYSE: OI

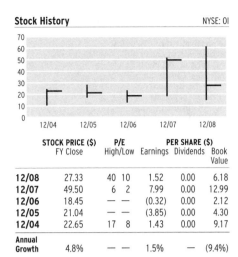

	STOCK PRICE ($) FY Close	P/E High/Low		PER SHARE ($) Earnings	Dividends	Book Value
12/08	27.33	40	10	1.52	0.00	6.18
12/07	49.50	6	2	7.99	0.00	12.99
12/06	18.45	—	—	(0.32)	0.00	2.12
12/05	21.04	—	—	(3.85)	0.00	4.30
12/04	22.65	17	8	1.43	0.00	9.17
Annual Growth	**4.8%**	**—**	**—**	**1.5%**	**—**	**(9.4%)**

PACCAR Inc

Old PACCARs never die, they just get a new Peterbilt. PACCAR is one of the world's largest designers and manufacturers of big rig trucks. Its lineup of light-, medium-, and heavy-duty trucks include the Kenworth, Peterbilt, and DAF nameplates. The company also manufactures and distributes aftermarket truck parts for these brands. PACCAR's other products include Braden, Carco, and Gearmatic industrial winches. With the exception of a few company-owned branches, PACCAR's trucks and parts sold through independent dealers. The company's PACCAR Financial Corporation and PacLease subsidiaries offer financing and truck leasing, respectively.

Truck sales declined in 2008, and PACCAR expects the number of units to drop by approximately 40,000 in 2009. The company reduced its headcount by about 14% in 2008 as a result. Concomitantly, PACCAR plans to increase its capital investments and related research and development spending in order to design and launch a new range of vehicles, increase global production capacity, and develop a new line of engines. The company views the implementation of updated North American engine emission standards in 2010 as positive; some operators may be encouraged to pull forward their truck purchases. The opening of a new engine assembly plant in Mississippi was delayed, pushed back by a year to late 2010. PACCAR continues to examine business opportunities in Asia, with a primary focus on China and India.

In 2008 the company unveiled an enhanced engine research and development center in PACCAR's Technical Center, opened a new parts distribution center in Budapest, and achieved a 20% capacity improvement at the Leyland (a PACCAR subsidiary) manufacturing facility in the UK.

Commercial trucks and related replacement parts comprise the largest segment of the Company's business. PACCAR's trucks are used worldwide for hauling freight, petroleum, wood products, construction, and other materials. The truck segment manufactures from four plants in the US, three in Europe, and one each in Australia,

Canada, and Mexico. It delivers products and services to customers in more than 100 countries through a dealer network of about 1,800 locations. The company competes in the European light/medium market with DAF cab-over-engine trucks assembled in the UK by Leyland.

The Pigott family, descendants of PACCAR's founder, owns about 7% of the company.

HISTORY

William Pigott founded the Seattle Car Manufacturing Company in 1905 to produce railroad cars for timber transport. Finding immediate success, Pigott began to make other kinds of railcars in 1906. When the Seattle plant burned the next year, the company moved near Renton, Washington. In 1911 Pigott renamed the company Seattle Car & Foundry.

In 1917 Seattle Car merged with the Twohy Brothers of Portland. The new company, Pacific Car & Foundry, was sold to American Car & Foundry in 1924. Pacific Car then diversified into bus manufacturing, structural steel fabrications, and metal technology.

Pacific Car was in decline by 1934 when William's son Paul bought it; since then the company has remained under family management. Paul Pigott added Hofius Steel and Equipment and Tricoach, a bus manufacturer, in 1936. The company entered the truck-making business with the 1945 purchase of Seattle-based Kenworth.

In the 1950s Pacific Car became the industry leader in mechanical refrigerator car production. It began producing off-road, heavy trucks and acquired Peterbilt Trucks of Oakland (1958). To augment its winch business, Pacific Car bought Canada's Gearmatic in 1963.

The company moved its headquarters to Bellevue, Washington, in 1969 and changed its name to PACCAR in 1971. Acquisitions in the 1970s included Wagner Mining Equipment (1973); International Car, the largest US caboose producer (1975); and Braden Winch (1977). In 1980 PACCAR acquired UK-based Foden Trucks.

Demand for smaller trucks caused heavy-truck sales to drop 35% between 1979 and 1986, leading PACCAR to close two factories, its first closures in 41 years. In 1987 PACCAR bought Trico Industries (oil-drilling equipment). Also that year PACCAR entered the auto parts sales market, buying Al's Auto Supply; in 1988, it bought Grand Auto.

Truck demand hit a nine-year low in 1990. PACCAR responded by cutting its workforce by 11% that year and withdrawing from the auto parts wholesale market in 1991. The following year PACCAR acquired an interest in Wood Group ESP, a maker and servicer of oil-field equipment. In 1993 PACCAR bought Caterpillar's line of winches.

In 1995 PACCAR opened a truck assembly plant in South Africa and bought the rest of VILPAC, its truck-making joint venture in Mexico. When workers in Quebec went on strike, the company closed the plant after eight months and shifted production to Mexico.

PACCAR expanded in Europe in 1996 by acquiring medium- and heavy-duty truck maker DAF Trucks (the Netherlands). Charles Pigott retired in 1996, and his son Mark became chairman and CEO. In 1997 PACCAR sold Trico Industries to EVI. The next year PACCAR bought light- and medium-duty truck maker Leyland Trucks (UK).

Slow sales of large trucks prompted the company to lay off about one-third of its hourly — and almost one-fifth of its salaried — Peterbilt workers in 2000. In 2001 PACCAR entered a long-term contract with Cummins for the supply of heavy-duty engines. Later that year, in order to bring production in line with worldwide demand, PACCAR closed two truck manufacturing facilities — the Seattle Kenworth plant and a Foden plant in the UK (the entire Foden line would be retired in 2006). The Peterbilt Motors Company plant in Nashville signed a five-year labor agreement with the UAW labor union in 2003.

Although the demand for PACCAR trucks in the US and Canada (primarily the Kenworth and Peterbilt brands) dipped in 2007, it was offset to a degree by a rise in both European truck sales and aftermarket products. In 2007 truck deliveries in Europe were up 8% over 2006 figures. In an effort to dedicate production efforts of its DAF branded trucks, PACCAR retired the Foden Trucks line of trucks in 2006. Unit deliveries to Australia, Mexico, and other areas not deemed primary regions were up 35%.

EXECUTIVES

Chairman and CEO: Mark C. Pigott, age 55, $5,819,514 total compensation
Vice Chairman: Thomas E. (Tom) Plimpton, age 59, $2,936,178 total compensation
President: James G. (Jim) Cardillo, age 60, $1,849,741 total compensation
VP and Controller: Michael T. Barkley, age 53
VP and CIO: Janice Skredsvig, age 48
EVP: Daniel D. (Dan) Sobic, age 55, $1,198,489 total compensation
SVP: Robert J. (Bob) Christensen, age 52
SVP: Ronald E. Armstrong, age 53
VP and General Counsel: David C. Anderson, age 55
VP Human Resources: Jack LeVier
VP: Richard E. Bangert II
VP: George E. West Jr.
VP: Helene N. Mawyer
VP: William D. Jackson
VP: Thomas A. Lundahl
VP: Timothy M. Henebry
VP: Aad L. Goudriaan
VP: Richard T. Gorman
VP: William R. Kozek
Secretary: Janice M. D'Amato
Treasurer: Robin E. Easton
Auditors: Ernst & Young LLP

LOCATIONS

HQ: PACCAR Inc
777 106th Ave. NE, Bellevue, WA 98004
Phone: 425-468-7400   **Fax:** 425-468-8216
Web: www.paccar.com

2008 Sales

	$ mil.	% of total
Europe	7,023.4	47
US	4,765.6	32
Other regions	3,183.5	21
Total	**14,972.5**	**100**

PRODUCTS/OPERATIONS

2008 Sales

	$ mil.	% of total
Trucks & other	13,709.6	92
Financial services	1,262.9	8
Total	**14,972.5**	**100**

Selected Divisions and Subsidiaries

DAF Trucks, N.V. (the Netherlands)
Kenworth Mexicana S.A. de C.V.
Leyland Trucks Limited (UK)
PACCAR Australia Pty. Ltd.
PACCAR of Canada Ltd.
　Canadian Kenworth Co.
　Peterbilt of Canada
PACCAR Financial Corp.
PACCAR Mexico, S.A. de C.V.

COMPETITORS

Daimler
Eaton
Fiat
Ford Motor
General Motors
Grupo Dina
Hino Motors
Isuzu
Iveco S.p.A.
Mack Trucks
Navistar International
Nissan Diesel
Oshkosh Truck
Scania
Volvo

HISTORICAL FINANCIALS

Company Type: Public

Income Statement

FYE: December 31

	REVENUE ($ mil.)	NET INCOME ($ mil.)	NET PROFIT MARGIN	EMPLOYEES
12/08	14,972.5	1,017.9	6.8%	18,700
12/07	15,221.7	1,227.3	8.1%	21,800
12/06	16,454.1	1,496.0	9.1%	21,000
12/05	14,057.4	1,133.2	8.1%	21,900
12/04	11,396.3	906.8	8.0%	20,500
Annual Growth	**7.1%**	**2.9%**	**—**	**(2.3%)**

2008 Year-End Financials

Debt ratio: 80.6%
Return on equity: 20.6%
Cash ($ mil.): 1,955
Current ratio: 2.08
Long-term debt ($ mil.): 3,909
No. of shares (mil.): 363
Dividends
Yield: 2.5%
Payout: 25.9%
Market value ($ mil.): 10,391

Stock History

NASDAQ (GS): PCAR

	STOCK PRICE ($) FY Close	P/E High/Low		PER SHARE ($) Earnings	Dividends	Book Value
12/08	28.60	19	8	2.78	0.72	13.34
12/07	54.48	20	13	3.29	0.65	13.80
12/06	43.27	12	8	3.97	0.51	12.27
12/05	30.77	12	10	2.92	0.39	10.74
12/04	35.77	16	10	2.29	0.33	10.36
Annual Growth	**(5.4%)**	**—**	**—**	**5.0%**	**21.5%**	**6.5%**

Pall Corporation

Pall takes liquids and gases to the cleaners. The company makes filtration and separation systems designed to remove solid, liquid, and gaseous contaminants from a variety of materials. Pall's industrial business segment makes filtration products for general industrial applications, including water purification, as well as for use in the aerospace and microelectronics industries. The company's industrial business units include Pall Aeropower. Products of Pall's life-sciences segment are used to help develop and manufacture drugs and for medical functions such as removing white blood cells from blood. Most of Pall's sales are made outside the US.

The company makes filter media from chemical film, metals, paper, and plastics; it also makes metal and plastic housings for its filters. It hopes to grow by selling more specially engineered filtration systems, which offer long-term revenue potential.

Pall reported in 2007 that some of its financial statements dating back to 1999 would need to be restated because it had understated US income tax payments during the time period.

In 2008 Pall acquired GeneSystems, a France-based biotechnology company that has developed an easy-to-use and cost-effective molecular diagnostics platform.

HISTORY

Canadian-born chemist David Pall worked on the Manhattan Project, helping develop systems to refine uranium for the first atomic bomb. In 1946 he founded Micro Metallic to develop filters for commercial applications. Pall added Abraham Krasnoff, a CPA, in 1950. The company went public in 1957 and was renamed Pall Corporation. During the 1960s it specialized in aircraft hydraulics and fuel systems for the defense industry. In 1969 Krasnoff became CEO.

In the late 1970s and during the 1980s, the company moved into the growing semiconductor and biotechnology industries. This process accelerated after the defense industry was hit by budget cuts late in the 1980s.

Pall researchers announced in 1995 the development of a filter that reduces the levels of HIV in blood serum to below detectable levels. In 1997 the company bought Gelman Sciences, maker of polymeric membranes and specialized medical disposable filters.

In 1998 Pall acquired Germany-based Rochem, an osmosis filtration system manufacturer, and entered a technology partnership with VI Technologies (Vitex) for exclusive marketing rights to Vitex's viral and bacterial inactivation chemistry. The following year Pall signed a $6 million water-purification deal with the Pittsburgh Water and Sewer Authority. Also in 1999 Pall announced a restructuring plan calling for job cuts and other spending reductions. The company sold its Well Technology division (filtration equipment and drilling services to oil and gas companies) to Oiltools International in 1999.

The German Red Cross Transfusion Center awarded Pall a $6 million contract for blood filtration equipment in 2000 after the German government mandated that all transfused blood must be filtered. Highlights in 2001 included alliances with biopharmaceutical companies QIAGEN N.V. and Stedim SA. In early 2002 Pall completed the acquisition of the Filtration and Separations Group from US Filter (now Siemens Water Technologies) for about $360 million. In 2003 Pall purchased Whatman HemaSure, the blood filtration business of Whatman plc.

Pall expanded in 2004 by buying BioSepra, a provider of chromatography technologies (used for protein purification and optimization), from Ciphergen Biosystems for about $32 million.

EXECUTIVES

Chairman and CEO: Eric Krasnoff, age 57
President: Donald B. (Don) Stevens, age 64
CFO and Treasurer: Lisa McDermott, age 43
SVP; President, Microelectronics Group:
Steven Chisolm
SVP; President, Machinery and Equipment Group:
Reed Sarver
SVP; President, Life Sciences Group: Roberto Perez, age 59
SVP; President, Aerospace Group:
James R. (Jim) Western Jr., age 53
SVP Pall Industrial: Michael J. Ywaniw
SVP and General Counsel: Sandra Marino, age 38
Group VP; President, European Operations:
Heinz Ulrich Hensgen
Group VP; President, BioPharmaceuticals Group:
Neil MacDonald
VP Investor Relations & Communications:
Patricia Iannucci
VP Executive Management: Glen Petaja
VP, Corporate Controller: Frank Moschella
Auditors: KPMG LLP

LOCATIONS

HQ: Pall Corporation
2200 Northern Blvd., East Hills, NY 11548
Phone: 516-484-5400   **Fax:** 516-484-5228
Web: www.pall.com

2008 Sales

	$ mil.	% of total
Europe	1,107.0	43
Western Hemisphere	810.6	32
Asia	654.0	25
Total	**2,571.6**	**100**

PRODUCTS/OPERATIONS

2008 Sales

	$ mil.	% of total
Industrial		
Energy, Water & Process Technologies	981.3	38
Microelectronics	308.5	12
Aerospace & Transportation	306.6	12
Life Sciences		
Medical	491.8	19
BioPharmaceuticals	483.4	19
Total	**2,571.6**	**100**

COMPETITORS

CLARCOR
CUNO
Donaldson Company
Entegris
ESCO Technologies
GE Healthcare
Millipore
Parker Hannifin
Sartorius
Siemens Water Technologies

HISTORICAL FINANCIALS

Company Type: Public

Income Statement

FYE: July 31

	REVENUE ($ mil.)	NET INCOME ($ mil.)	NET PROFIT MARGIN	EMPLOYEES
7/08	2,571.6	217.3	8.4%	10,600
7/07	2,249.9	127.5	5.7%	10,700
7/06	2,016.8	145.5	7.2%	10,828
7/05	1,902.3	140.8	7.4%	10,400
7/04	1,770.7	151.6	8.6%	10,300
Annual Growth	**9.8%**	**9.4%**	**—**	**0.7%**

2008 Year-End Financials

Debt ratio: 86.1%
Return on equity: 19.8%
Cash ($ mil.): 454
Current ratio: 2.89
Long-term debt ($ mil.): 980
No. of shares (mil.): 118
Dividends
  Yield: 1.5%
  Payout: 35.2%
Market value ($ mil.): 4,767

Stock History

NYSE: PLL

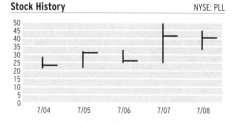

	STOCK PRICE ($) FY Close	P/E High/Low		PER SHARE ($) Earnings	Dividends	Book Value
7/08	40.42	25	19	1.76	0.62	9.66
7/07	41.52	48	25	1.02	0.35	8.99
7/06	26.08	28	22	1.16	0.43	9.99
7/05	30.97	28	20	1.12	0.39	9.67
7/04	23.17	23	18	1.20	0.36	8.94
Annual Growth	**14.9%**	**—**	**—**	**10.0%**	**14.6%**	**2.0%**

Palm, Inc.

Palm is trying hard to reverse its loosening grip on the mobile communications market. Historically the leading provider of handheld computers, the company now primarily markets Internet-enabled mobile phones (also known as smart phones). Its phone line includes the entry-level Centro and more advanced Treo and Pre lines. The company sells its products directly and through distributors, wireless service carriers, retailers, and resellers. Its carrier partners include AT&T, Sprint Nextel, and Verizon Wireless. The company markets its products globally; however, the majority of its revenue comes from sales in the US.

The company's move from its comfortable position in the handheld computer market to the phone provider market has, at times, proved challenging. During its 2009 fiscal year, Palm suffered heavy losses in operating cash and revenue (down 44% from the previous year). The company had trouble generating revenue from the sales of its phones products. Other reasons include competition from established companies like Apple, Sony, Nokia, Research in Motion (RIM), and others in the handset and smart phone business. In part, Palm found it difficult to attract consumers who were flocking to

Apple's iPhone and other phones that use touch-screen technologies (a feature that was not available in its own products at the time).

In an effort to make its product line more attractive to consumers, Palm unveiled a new smart phone in 2009 designed to compete with the iPhone and RIM's Blackberry line. The Palm Pre features a touch screen and runs on a new operating system called Palm webOS. The device is offered exclusively through Sprint Nextel (at least initially) and it features the ability to download music directly from Apple's iTunes store.

While the company is making changes to its products, it is also experiencing changes in management. In 2009 Palm announced that longtime Palm executive Ed Colligan would step down as CEO. Executive chairman Jon Rubenstein was named to replace him. A former Apple executive, Rubenstein was instrumental in the development of Apple's iMac, iBook, and iPod products.

Elevation Partners (of which directors Fred Anderson and Roger McNamee are principals) owns about 33% of Palm.

HISTORY

Jeff Hawkins and Donna Dubinsky joined forces in 1992 to form Palm Computing. Ed Colligan joined the following year. Hawkings had worked at Intel and GRiD Systems (which brought the first pen-based computer to the market); Dubinsky at Apple and Claris; and Colligan at Radius Corp. (a maker of Macintosh clones). The company's initial product was Graffiti input software for handheld devices.

U.S. Robotics, a leading maker of computer modems, bought Palm for $44 million in 1995. The following year Palm unveiled its PalmPilot connected organizer. More than a million Pilots were sold within 18 months.

When U.S. Robotics was bought by 3Com in 1997, Palm became a subsidiary of the networking giant. 3Com sold 1.2 million Palms in 1998. That year Hawkins, Dubinsky, and Colligan left to form rival Handspring, which launched its Visor product in 1999.

In 1999, 3Com released the Internet-ready Palm VII and launched its Palm.net Internet service (now MyPalm) for handheld devices. The following year it named former Sony president Carl Yankowski to Palm's CEO post. In 2000, 3Com sold a minority stake in Palm (by then its fastest-growing unit) to the public in an offering worth about $875 million. Palm's separation from 3Com was completed later that year when 3Com distributed to its shareholders its remaining shares of Palm.

With an eye toward strengthening its dominant position in the corporate market, Palm in early 2001 agreed to acquire infrastructure software maker Extended Systems. Faced with slowing sales during an industrywide downturn, Palm announced soon after that it would cut as much as 15% of its workforce. The company then terminated its plan to buy Extended Systems, agreeing later to sell Extended software, which allows access to databases through Palm products.

Palm also created a separate unit for its operating systems (OS) software, and acquired the software and intellectual property assets of OS specialist Be. In the wake of Palm's restructuring efforts, Yankowski resigned as CEO in late 2001; Benhamou was named CEO.

The company's product line received a makeover in 2002, when Palm unveiled two new offerings: Tungsten for enterprise applications at the high end, and the low-priced Zire for the consumer market.

Palm spun off its operating system licensing business as PalmSource (later renamed ACESS Systems Americas) in 2003 and changed its name to palmOne. Todd Bradley became CEO of palmOne. After it completed the spinoff, palmOne acquired Handspring in a stock swap valued at about $169 million. The acquisition brought Handspring's line of Treo smart phones to the Palm lineup.

Early in 2005 Bradley stepped down as CEO and Colligan replaced him. Later that year it agreed to pay PalmSource $30 million for full rights to the Palm brand. Palm missed a chance to acquire PalmSource when it was outbid by Japan's ACCESS. palmOne changed its name back to Palm in mid-2005.

In 2006 Palm agreed to pay $22.5 million to settle a long-running patent dispute with Xerox over handwriting recognition technology.

Looking to augment its Treo line, the company introduced a portable computer called Foleo in 2007; it canceled the product before its release, however, citing a need to focus on its operating system and Treo development.

Also in 2007, Palm underwent a recapitalization that saw private equity firm Elevation Partners purchase a 25% stake in the company for $325 million. Concurrent with the closing of the transaction, two Palm board members, including chairman Eric Benhamou, resigned; they were replaced by three new directors, including two former Apple executives. The deal included a payout of $940 million ($325 million from Elevation, $400 million in debt, plus existing cash) to Palm shareholders. Elevation agreed to invest an additional $100 million in Palm late in 2008.

Early in 2009 Palm unveiled the Pre, a smart phone featuring a touch screen and a new operating system called Palm webOS. In mid-2009 Colligan stepped down as CEO and Palm executive chairman Jon Rubinstein, a veteran of Apple, was named chairman and CEO.

EXECUTIVES

Chairman and CEO: Jonathan (Jon) Rubinstein, age 53, $4,180,846 total compensation
SVP and CFO: Douglas C. (Doug) Jeffries, age 53, $238,274 total compensation
SVP, General Counsel, and Secretary: Mary E. Doyle, age 57
SVP Business Development: Mark S. Bercow, age 48
SVP Product Marketing: Kathleen C. (Katie) Mitic
SVP Human Resources: Renata A. (Rena) Lane, age 54
SVP Applications Software and Services: Michael Abbott, $1,413,282 total compensation
SVP Product Development: Mike Bell
SVP System Software: Way Ting
SVP Brand Design: Jeffrey S. (Jeff) Zwerner
SVP Worldwide Sales: David (Dave) Whalen, age 48
Media Relations: Derick Mains
Corporate Public Relations Manager: Dianne Rambke
Auditors: Deloitte & Touche LLP

LOCATIONS

HQ: Palm, Inc.
950 W. Maude Ave., Sunnyvale, CA 94085
Phone: 408-617-7000 **Fax:** 408-617-0100
Web: www.palm.com

2009 Sales

	$ mil.	% of total
US	614.0	83
Other countries	121.9	17
Total	**735.9**	**100**

PRODUCTS/OPERATIONS

2009 Sales

	$ mil.	% of total
Smartphones	666.4	91
Handheld computers	69.5	9
Total	**735.9**	**100**

Selected Products

Smart phones (Centro, Pre, Treo)
Handhelds (Palm, Tungsten)

COMPETITORS

Acer
Apple Inc.
BenQ
CASIO COMPUTER
Dell
Fujitsu
Fujitsu Technology Solutions
Garmin
Hewlett-Packard
High Tech Computer
Kyocera
MiTAC
Motorola, Inc.
NEC
Nokia
OQO
Psion
Research In Motion
Samsung Electronics
SANYO
Sharp Corp.
Sharp Electronics
Sony
Sony Ericsson Mobile
Toshiba

HISTORICAL FINANCIALS

Company Type: Public

Income Statement

FYE: Friday nearest May 31

	REVENUE ($ mil.)	NET INCOME ($ mil.)	NET PROFIT MARGIN	EMPLOYEES
5/09	735.9	(732.2)	—	939
5/08	1,318.7	(105.4)	—	1,050
5/07	1,560.5	56.4	3.6%	1,247
5/06	1,578.5	336.2	21.3%	1,103
5/05	1,270.4	66.4	5.2%	907
Annual Growth	(12.8%)	—	—	0.9%

2009 Year-End Financials

Debt ratio: —
Return on equity: —
Cash ($ mil.): 152
Current ratio: 1.03
Long-term debt ($ mil.): 396

No. of shares (mil.): 140
Dividends
  Yield: 0.0%
  Payout: —
Market value ($ mil.): 1,709

Stock History

NASDAQ (GS): PALM

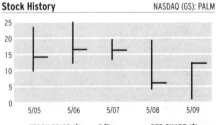

	STOCK PRICE ($) FY Close	P/E High/Low		PER SHARE ($) Earnings	Dividends	Book Value
5/09	12.19	—	—	(6.51)	0.00	(2.95)
5/08	6.06	—	—	(1.05)	0.00	0.79
5/07	16.27	36	25	0.54	0.00	7.58
5/06	16.48	8	4	3.19	0.00	7.02
5/05	14.21	36	15	0.64	0.00	4.14
Annual Growth	(3.8%)	—	—	—	—	—

The Pantry

If you've ever passed through the Carolinas on business, or made the drive to Disney World, chances are The Pantry has provided fuel for your car and body. The company is the leading convenience store operator in the southeastern US with about 1,680 shops in about a dozen states. (Florida accounts for more than a quarter of the company's sales.) Most of the company's stores do business under the Kangaroo Express banner. Other store names include Golden Gallon, Lil' Champ, The Pantry (naturally), and Petro Express. The stores sell beverages, candy, gasoline, magazines, and tobacco products, among other items. Fuel accounts for about 80% of the company's sales.

About a third of the company's outlets, which are conventional in size (about 2,700 sq. ft.), are located near such tourist destinations as Myrtle Beach and Hilton Head, South Carolina, and Orlando, Florida, and another 25% along major interstates and highways.

Over the past few years the convenience store operator has been busy converting stores to the Kangaroo Express name in an effort to establish a consistent identity in the Southeast, much like its rivals 7-Eleven and Couche-Tard (Circle K) have developed consistent national brands. Currently, more than 1,500 of its locations are branded Kangaroo or Kangaroo Express.

The fast-growing firm has used a roll-up strategy of acquiring other businesses within its industry in order to grow in the Southeast. After a brief hiatus in 2008 due to tough retail environment and record gas prices, in mid-2009 The Pantry acquired 38 convenience stores from Herndon Oil. The purchase included about 30 shops in Mobile, Alabama, as well as locations in Florida, Louisiana, and Mississippi. Previously, the company purchased about 150 stores, including 66 Petro Express convenience stores in North and South Carolina, in 2007.

The Pantry is working to increase merchandise sales, including food service and private label products, which carry substantially higher margins than gasoline sales. About 255 stores have fast-food outlets, including Subway, Church's, and Hardee's.

The company currently receives about two-thirds of its gasoline supply from CITGO (who also supplies the company's private label Kangaroo brand), Chevron, BP, and ExxonMobil.

The firm plans to move its corporate headquarters from Sanford to Cary, North Carolina. Also, CEO Peter Sondini retired in September 2009, he was succeeded by Terry Marks, a former EVP at Coca-Cola Enterprises.

HISTORY

North Carolina businessmen Sam Wornom and Truby Proctor (president of Lee Moore Oil Co.) founded The Pantry in 1967 in Sanford, North Carolina. The chain added new stores by borrowing against its existing stores, paying the debt with new sales.

The Pantry had grown to about 480 outlets in 1987 when investment firm Montrose Capital bought Wornom's stake. Founded by former Duke University business professor Clay Hamner, Montrose's shareholders included J. B. Fuqua (after whom the Duke business school is named), the late Dave Thomas (the Wendy's fast-food chain founder), and Wayne Rogers (Trapper John in the TV series M*A*S*H). Montrose gained control of The Pantry when it acquired half of Proctor's shares in 1990. Proctor remained as CEO.

With poor sales, the company restructured during the early 1990s, closing unprofitable stores and cutting costs. After struggling in 1991 and 1992, The Pantry made a slim profit in 1993. However, burdened by debt, the company was without the cash to make further substantive acquisitions, and it resumed its annual losses the following year.

In 1995 Proctor sold his remaining shares to Freeman Spogli & Co., a California-based investment firm specializing in management-led buyouts, and Chase Manhattan Capital. The next year Freeman Spogli and Chase Manhattan acquired the rest of the company from Montrose. Freeman Spogli owned 76% of The Pantry and Chase Manhattan owned 23% until more shares were issued to management and directors. Peter Sodini, a former CEO with supermarket chain Purity Supreme (acquired by Stop & Shop), became CEO that year.

After a string of small acquisitions in early 1997, The Pantry more than doubled in size by paying about $135 million to Docks U.S.A. for the Lil' Champ Food Stores convenience store chain. Lil' Champ — named after founder Julian Jackson, a bantamweight boxing champion in the 1930s — had 489 outlets, including 150 outlets in Jacksonville, Florida.

The Pantry continued to bulk up in 1998, acquiring nearly 155 stores through seven separate purchases of small chains. The biggest purchases among them included Quick Stop, a 75-store chain in the Carolinas, and 41 Zip Mart stores in North Carolina and eastern Virginia. The company exited the Georgia market that year.

In early 1999 The Pantry acquired 121 Handy Way stores in central Florida, many of which operated fast-food outlets such as Hardee's and Subway. The Pantry went public that year to raise money to pay nearly $450 million in debt stemming from its acquisitions. Shortly thereafter, the company bought 53 Depot Food Store outlets in Georgia and South Carolina from R & H Maxxon.

In late 1999 The Pantry added the 49-store Kangaroo chain in Georgia, and in early 2000 it purchased the On-The-Way Foods Stores chain of 12 stores in Virginia and North Carolina. Other purchases in 2000 furthering the company's southeastern US expansion included 33 MiniMart and Big K chain stores, and 26 Fast Lane convenience stores in Louisiana and Mississippi from R.R. Morrison and Son.

In 2003 The Pantry reached agreements with BP Products and Citgo Petroleum to brand and supply most of its gasoline for the next five years. In October, the company completed the acquisition of the 138-store Golden Gallon chain from Ahold USA. The Pantry acquired D & D Oil Co. (operator of 53 convenience stores under the Cowboys banner in Alabama, Georgia, and Mississippi) in 2005.

In 2006 the company acquired the 38-store Shop-A-Snak Food Mart convenience store chain in Alabama, doubling its store count in the state. It closed on 66 Petro Express convenience stores in North and South Carolina and its affiliated wholesale fuels business Carolina Petroleum Distributors in 2007.

In June 2009 the company acquired 38 convenience stores from Herndon Oil Co. The terms of the cash purchase were not disclosed.

EXECUTIVES

President, CEO, and Director:
Terrance M. (Terry) Marks, age 49
EVP Business Operations, CFO, and Secretary:
Frank G. Paci, age 51
VP Information Services: Ed Collupy
SVP Human Resources: Melissa H. Anderson, age 44
SVP Fuels: Keith S. Bell, age 45
SVP Field Operations: R. Brad Williams, age 38
VP Food Service: Brandon Frampton
Corporate Controller: Berry Epley
Director, Total Rewards: Diana King
Auditors: Deloitte & Touche LLP

LOCATIONS

HQ: The Pantry, Inc.
1801 Douglas Dr., Sanford, NC 27330
Phone: 919-774-6700   **Fax:** 919-774-3329
Web: www.thepantry.com

2008 Stores

	No.
Florida	453
North Carolina	385
South Carolina	283
Georgia	133
Tennessee	104
Mississippi	99
Alabama	81
Virginia	50
Kentucky	30
Louisiana	26
Indiana	9
Total	**1,653**

PRODUCTS/OPERATIONS

2008 Merchandise Sales

	% of total
Tobacco products	32
Packaged beverages	19
Beer & wine	16
General merchandise, health & beauty care	5
Self-service fast foods & beverages	6
Salty snacks	4
Candy	4
Fast food service	4
Dairy products	3
Services	4
Bread & cakes	2
Newspapers & magazines	1
Total	**100**

2008 Sales

	$ mil.	% of total
Gasoline	7,358.9	82
Merchandise	1,636.7	18
Total	**8,995.6**	**100**

Selected Banners and Trademarks

Aunt M's	Market Express
Bean Street Coffee	Mini Mart
Big Chill	The Chill Zone
Celeste	The Pantry
Cowboys	Petro Express
Golden Gallon	Quickstop
Kangaroo	Sprint
Kangaroo Express	Worth

COMPETITORS

7-Eleven	Gate Petroleum
BI-LO	Publix
Couche-Tard	Racetrac Petroleum
Crown Central	SPINX Company
Cumberland Farms	Winn-Dixie
Delhaize America	Worsley
Exxon	

HISTORICAL FINANCIALS

Company Type: Public

Income Statement

FYE: Last Thursday in September

	REVENUE ($ mil.)	NET INCOME ($ mil.)	NET PROFIT MARGIN	EMPLOYEES
9/08	8,995.6	31.8	0.4%	14,221
9/07	6,911.2	26.7	0.4%	13,232
9/06	5,961.7	89.2	1.5%	12,005
9/05	4,429.2	57.8	1.3%	10,803
9/04	3,493.1	17.6	0.5%	9,751
Annual Growth	**26.7%**	**15.9%**	**—**	**9.9%**

2008 Year-End Financials

Debt ratio: 328.0%
Return on equity: 8.6%
Cash ($ mil.): 217
Current ratio: 1.50
Long-term debt ($ mil.): 1,279
No. of shares (mil.): 22
Dividends
  Yield: 0.0%
  Payout: —
Market value ($ mil.): 477

Stock History

NASDAQ (GS): PTRY

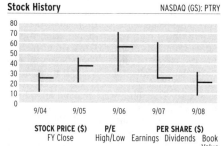

	STOCK PRICE ($) FY Close	P/E High/Low		PER SHARE ($) Earnings	Dividends	Book Value
9/08	21.19	22	6	1.43	0.00	17.33
9/07	25.63	52	22	1.17	0.00	15.73
9/06	56.37	18	8	3.88	0.00	14.98
9/05	37.37	17	8	2.64	0.00	11.20
9/04	25.17	35	14	0.85	0.00	6.77
Annual Growth	**(4.2%)**	**—**	**—**	**13.9%**	**—**	**26.5%**

Parker Hannifin

Motion-control equipment made by Parker Hannifin helped sink the replicated *Titanic* in the Academy Award-winning film. Parker Hannifin's motion-control products use hydraulic (liquid) or pneumatic (gas or air) systems to move and position materials or to control equipment. Its industrial products include fluid connectors, hydraulic and automation systems, electromechanical devices, seals and filters, and process instrumentation. These are sold to customers in manufacturing, transportation, and food processing industries. The company also makes climate and industrial controls (refrigeration and air conditioning components) and aerospace components such as fuel systems.

Of the three business segments, Industrial is the largest; it is made up of the Automation, Filtration, Fluid Connectors, Hydraulics, Instrumentation, and Seal groups. Customers for industrial products are generally in the manufacturing, transportation, and food processing industries. The Aerospace segment designs and manufactures aircraft wheels and brakes for military and general aviation markets. In addition to refrigeration, Climate & Industrial Controls produces systems and components for use in fluid control applications, such as fuel dispensing, beverage dispensing, and mobile emissions. Centers throughout the world distribute the company's original and replacement equipment.

The negative worldwide economic conditions and the credit market crunch have impacted the company, along with its distributors, customers, and suppliers. Net sales for 2009 were about 15% lower than 2008. Parker Hannifin expects the recessionary tone to continue throughout 2010, and it has taken steps to reduce its workforce, freeze salaries, and implement shorter work weeks.

Still, the company seeks international expansion — customers outside of North America constitute over 40% of net sales. In October 2008 the company acquired the Legris SA division from Groupe Legris Industries. Legris SA complements Parker Hannifin with its strong brand recognition in pneumatic, hydraulic, and chemical processing applications, as well as its fluid command and control systems technology. Legris SA has a well-established distribution network and presence in the European market.

Continuing with international acquisitions, Parker Hannifin purchased Origa Group (actuators, cylinders, and valves), which has operations in Germany and Austria. The company acquired the 51% in Parker Seal de México it did not already own. The unit brings in about $8 million per year, and the acquisition was meant to strengthen Parker Hannifin's foothold in Mexico.

Another 2008 purchase was that of Malaysian firm EmiTherm, which makes shielding materials used by electronics manufacturers. The company will join Parker Hannifin's Seal Group and improve the company's Asian offerings.

Additional activity in 2008 saw Vansco Electronics give the company additional global distribution capacity, as well as expand the company's electronic controls and sensors product lines. Parker Hannifin also bought Titan Industries, which makes rubber products and custom-made and composite hoses. These hose products give the company entry into the marine and aircraft refueling markets. Titan will be rolled into Parker Hannifin's Industrial Hose Products division. In late 2008 the Fluid Connector Group also picked up a new addition, Canada-based Nexgen Hose, a hose and tubing maker.

Separate from its acquisition activity, 2008 proved to be a lucrative year. The company inked a major deal with French aircraft maker Airbus. The deal, which is worth more than $2 billion, calls for Parker Hannifin to provide the fuel system equipment and hydraulic systems for Airbus' A350 aircraft. That deal alone should help Parker Hannifin brace for anticipated slowdowns in some of its major industries, including automotive and construction.

HISTORY

Entrepreneurial engineer Arthur Parker founded the Parker Appliance Company in 1918 to make pneumatic brake boosters. Its products were designed to help trucks and buses stop more easily. Unfortunately, Parker's own truck slid off an icy road and over a cliff in 1919, destroying the company's inventory and ending that line of business.

Undeterred, Parker started a hydraulics and pneumatic components business in 1924 to serve automotive and industrial clients. In 1927 the fuel-linkage system the company developed

for the *Spirit of St. Louis* helped Lindbergh cross the Atlantic. The company prospered during the Depression; sales reached $2 million in 1934. Two of Parker's long-term clients were Douglas Aircraft and Lockheed.

The company went public in 1938. It employed 5,000 defense workers during WWII. After Parker died in 1945, his wife Helen hired new management to focus on the automation market. The firm bought cylinder maker Hannifin in 1957 and became Parker Hannifin.

In 1960 Parker Hannifin formed an international unit in Amsterdam, and it set up a German subsidiary in 1962. Overseas acquisitions and increased demand from the space program and the aviation market spurred growth in the 1960s. Patrick Parker, the founder's son, became president in 1968 and chairman in 1977. Parker Hannifin expanded its aerospace business in 1978 with the purchase of Bertea (electrohydraulic flight controls). Patrick Parker continued as CEO until 1983 and as chairman until 1999.

During the 1980s Parker Hannifin bought several smaller companies in niche markets, including Schrader Bellows (pneumatics, 1985), Compumotor (electromechanical applications, 1986), and Stratoflex and Gull Corp. (hoses and fittings and aerospace electronics, respectively, 1988).

The company again pushed into Europe during the 1990s, buying Sweden-based Trelleborg (hydraulic hoses) in 1992 and Atlas Automation (pneumatic components for automation equipment) in 1993.

Parker Hannifin expanded into the medical, petrochemical, and semiconductor markets in 1988 by purchasing Veriflo (high-purity valves and regulators) and into mobile equipment makers with Fluid Power Systems (hydraulic valves and electrohydraulic systems).

Overseas expansion included the 1998 purchase of Sempress Pneumatics (pneumatic cylinders, the Netherlands).

In 2000 Parker Hannifin acquired motion-control maker Commercial Intertech in a deal worth around $473 million. It also bought Whatman's industrial business (purification products and gas generators) and Wynn's International (industrial sealing products, in a $498 million deal).

President and COO Donald Washkewicz succeeded Duane Collins as CEO in 2001. (Collins remained chairman until his retirement in 2004, when Washkewicz replaced him in that role, too.) Parker Hannifin acquired Eaton's air conditioning unit, Aeroquip, the same year.

Parker Hannifin completed the acquisition of Denison International early in 2004 for about $2.4 billion.

Early in 2005 Parker Hannifin sold Wynn Oil (chemical car care products) to Illinois Tool Works for an undisclosed sum. It continued to grow internationally through acquisitions such as India's Markwel Hose Products, which it bought in early 2005, a move that expanded its operations in the Asian motion and control markets. Wanting to secure its foothold in the water filtration market, Parker Hannifin acquired UK-based domnick hunter group after winning a bidding war with Eaton Corporation. domnick hunter drew such avid interest in part because it had developed products designed to protect against nuclear, biological, and chemical weapons.

EXECUTIVES

Chairman, President, and CEO:
Donald E. (Don) Washkewicz, age 58
EVP Finance and Administration and CFO:
Timothy K. Pistell, age 61,
$6,316,034 total compensation
VP and CIO: William G. Eline, age 52
EVP Sales, Marketing, and Operations Support:
Marwan M. Kashkoush, age 54
EVP and Operating Officer: Lee C. Banks, age 45
EVP and Operating Officer; President, Aerospace Group: Robert P. (Bob) Barker, age 58
EVP and Operating Officer: Thomas L. (Tom) Williams, age 50
SVP Finance: Dana A. Dennis, age 60
VP, General Counsel, and Secretary:
Thomas A. Piraino Jr., age 59
VP Corporate Communications: Christopher M. Farage
VP Technology and Innovation: M. Craig Maxwell, age 50
VP Human Resources: Daniel S. (Dan) Serbin, age 54
VP Global Supply Chain and Procurement:
John G Dedinsky, age 51
VP; President, Automation Group: Roger S. Sherrard, age 42
VP; President, Fluid Connectors Group:
Robert W. (Bob) Bond, age 50
VP; President, Instrumentation Group: John R. Greco, age 54
VP; President, Climate and Industrial Controls Group:
Thomas F. Healy, age 48
VP; President, Hydraulics Group: Jeffrey A. Cullman, age 53
VP; President, Filtration Group: Peter Popoff, age 56
VP; President, Seal Group: Kurt Keller, age 51
Auditors: PricewaterhouseCoopers LLP

LOCATIONS

HQ: Parker Hannifin Corporation
6035 Parkland Blvd., Cleveland, OH 44124
Phone: 216-896-3000   **Fax:** 216-896-4000
Web: www.parker.com

2009 Sales

	$ mil.	% of total
North America	6,090.2	59
Other regions	4,218.8	41
Total	**10,309.0**	**100**

PRODUCTS/OPERATIONS

2009 Sales

	$ mil.	% of total
Industrial		
International	3,895.9	38
North America	3,734.6	36
Aerospace	1,883.3	18
Climate & industrial controls	795.2	8
Total	**10,309.0**	**100**

Operating Groups and Selected Products

Aerospace
  Aircraft wheels and brakes
  Flight control components
  Fuel systems
  Pneumatic pumps and valves
Automation
  Human/machine interface hardware and software
  Indexers
  Multi-axis positioning tables
  Pneumatic valves
  Stepper and servo drives
  Structural extrusions
  Vacuum products

William Leonard first stepped in as interim CEO. Then in early 2007 Jeffrey Rachor was named CEO and president. Rachor had previously served as president and COO of top auto retailer Sonic Automotive. Rachor left the company in spring 2008 to head an auto dealership venture and Pep Boys' COO Mike Odell stepped up to serve as interim CEO. He was named to the post permanently in September 2008.

HISTORY

Philadelphians Emanuel (Manny) Rosenfeld, Maurice (Moe) Strauss, Graham (Jack) Jackson, and Moe Radavitz founded Pep Auto Supplies in 1921, named in part from a product, Pep Valve Grinding Compound. (Radavitz pulled out after a few years.) Two years later the men renamed the store The Pep Boys — Manny, Moe & Jack. A friend created the corporate caricature of the three, though the version that became famous is actually of Manny, Moe, and Izzy (Moe's brother); it was drawn after Jack left.

By 1928 there were 12 Pep Boys stores in the Philadelphia area. In 1932 the car-friendly West Coast beckoned, and the boys dispatched Murray Rosenfeld to launch Pep Boys West. Intense competition in California spurred Pep Boys West to increase parts selection, while the Philadelphia stores focused more on service. The company went public in 1946 with Manny as president and Moe as chairman, but its growth was hindered by overly conservative management; Pep Boys would not lease stores and avoided debt like a crowded freeway. Moe became president after Manny's death in 1959, and as the fiscal caution continued, the company grew by only two stores between 1964 and 1984.

Moe held both posts until 1973, when his son Ben became president. In 1977 Moe stepped down as chairman but remained on the board until his death in 1982. That year Ben became chairman and CEO, and Moe's son-in-law Morton Krause became president. In 1984 Krause retired, and two years later Ben tapped Mitchell Leibovitz as president — the first from outside the founding families. As head of eastern operations, Leibovitz had closed 32 small stores between 1979 and 1984. Between 1984 and 1986 he opened 60 bond-financed stores.

In 1986 Pep Boys was the #2 parts retailer in the US, behind Western Auto, and Leibovitz set up a plan to modernize and overhaul the entire business. Between 1986 and 1991 Pep Boys spent $477 million improving distribution, merchandising, and marketing: The number of stores doubled to 337, and the number of items offered went from about 9,000 to 24,000. The company adopted an everyday-low-price strategy, and many locations were expanded into 23,000-sq.-ft. superstores with more service bays and related services.

Leibovitz was named CEO in 1990. Pep Boys topped $1 billion in annual sales the following year. The recession of the early 1990s hurt profits; however, cash flow picked up, and the company was able to retire some debt and to open 30 stores in 1992. In 1993 Leibovitz put mechanics on commission, with safeguards to prevent overcharging.

Store count doubled during the next five years. In 1994 Leibovitz became chairman. Also that year the company began opening Parts USA stores (renamed Pep Boys Express in 1997), which had no service bays or tires. The conversion, along with tightening margins, adversely impacted profits in fiscal 1998, and Pep Boys decided in 1998 to sell 100 of its Pep Boys Express stores to AutoZone. Also in 1998 the company rolled out APD, a parts delivery service aimed at professional installers.

In 2000 Pep Boys closed 38 unprofitable stores and two distribution centers, citing stagnant sales. It also cut about 5% of its workforce (1,500 jobs). Pep Boys settled a lawsuit in 2002 alleging that it received discriminatory prices from auto parts manufacturers.

Leibovitz retired in 2003. Lawrence Stevenson, formerly the CEO of Chapters, a Canadian book retailer, became CEO. In 2004 Stevenson also assumed the company chairmanship.

Under pressure from dissatisfied investors, in February 2006 Stevenson relinquished the chairman's title, which was bestowed on director William Leonard. In mid-July Leonard was named interim CEO when Stevenson resigned from that position as well. (Leonard left the company in 2008 and James Mitarotonda took over as chairman.)

EXECUTIVES

Chairman: Max L. Lukens, age 60
CEO and Director: Michael R. (Mike) Odell, age 45, $1,039,379 total compensation
EVP and CFO: Raymond L. (Ray) Arthur, age 50
SVP Business Development: Joseph A. (Joe) Cirelli, age 50, $1,873,422 total compensation
SVP, General Counsel, and Secretary: Brian D. Zuckerman, age 39
SVP Merchandising and Marketing: Scott A. Webb, age 45, $704,008 total compensation
SVP Human Resources: Troy E. Fee, age 40, $454,737 total compensation
SVP Stores: William (Bill) Shull, age 50
VP Marketing: Ronald J. Stoupa
Auditors: Deloitte & Touche LLP

LOCATIONS

HQ: The Pep Boys – Manny, Moe & Jack
3111 W. Allegheny Ave., Philadelphia, PA 19132
Phone: 215-430-9000   **Fax:** 215-227-7513
Web: www.pepboys.com

2009 Stores

	No.
California	118
Texas	47
Florida	43
Pennsylvania	42
New York	29
New Jersey	29
Georgia	22
Illinois	22
Arizona	22
Maryland	18
Virginia	16
Nevada	12
Ohio	10
North Carolina	8
Louisiana	8
Indiana	7
Colorado	7
Connecticut	7
New Mexico	8
Massachusetts	6
Michigan	5
Tennessee	7
Delaware	6
Oklahoma	5
South Carolina	6
Utah	6
Kentucky	4
New Hampshire	4
Other states	11
Puerto Rico	27
Total	**562**

PRODUCTS/OPERATIONS

2009 Sales

	$ mil.	% of total
Parts & accessories	1,256.0	65
Service	358.1	19
Tires	313.7	16
Total	**1,927.8**	**100**

Selected Products

Additives
Air-conditioning parts
Air filters
Alarms
Antifreeze
Batteries
Belts
Brake parts
Engines and engine parts
Floor mats
Gauges
Hand tools
Hoses
Ignition parts
Mobile electronics
Motor oil
Mufflers
Oil filters
Paints
Polishes
Seat covers
Sound systems
Suspension parts
Truck and van accessories

Selected Private-Label Brands

CORNELL
FUTURA
Pep Boys
PROCOOL
PROLINE
PROSTART
PROSTOP
PROSTEER
VARSITY

COMPETITORS

Advance Auto Parts	Les Schwab Tire Centers
AutoZone	Meineke
Bridgestone	Midas
CARQUEST	Monro Muffler Brake
Commercial Tire	O'Reilly Automotive
Cottman Transmission	Precision Auto
Discount Tire	Sears
General Parts	Snap-on
Goodyear Tire & Rubber	TBC
Jeg's	VIP
Jiffy Lube	Wal-Mart

HISTORICAL FINANCIALS

Company Type: Public

Income Statement			FYE: Saturday nearest January 31	
	REVENUE ($ mil.)	NET INCOME ($ mil.)	NET PROFIT MARGIN	EMPLOYEES
1/09	1,927.8	(30.4)	—	18,458
1/08	2,138.1	(41.0)	—	18,564
1/07	2,272.2	(2.7)	—	18,794
1/06	2,235.2	(35.5)	—	19,980
1/05	2,272.9	23.6	1.0%	21,331
Annual Growth	**(4.0%)**	**—**	**—**	**(3.6%)**

2009 Year-End Financials

Debt ratio: 83.3%
Return on equity: —
Cash ($ mil.): 21
Current ratio: 1.33
Long-term debt ($ mil.): 352
No. of shares (mil.): 52
Dividends
  Yield: 9.3%
  Payout: —
Market value ($ mil.): 151

Stock History

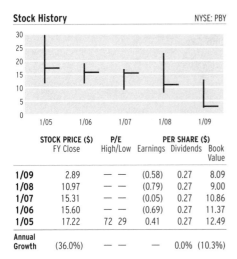

NYSE: PBY

	STOCK PRICE ($) FY Close	P/E High/Low	PER SHARE ($) Earnings	Dividends	Book Value
1/09	2.89	— —	(0.58)	0.27	8.09
1/08	10.97	— —	(0.79)	0.27	9.00
1/07	15.31	— —	(0.05)	0.27	10.86
1/06	15.60	— —	(0.69)	0.27	11.37
1/05	17.22	72 29	0.41	0.27	12.49
Annual Growth	(36.0%)	— —	—	0.0%	(10.3%)

Pepco Holdings

Pepco Holdings has more power than any politician in the populace of the US capital. The holding company distributes electricity and natural gas through its Potomac Electric Power (Pepco), Delmarva Power & Light, and Atlantic City Electric utilities to more than 1.9 million customers in Delaware, Maryland, New Jersey, and Washington, DC. Nonregulated operations include independent power production (4,600 MW of generating capacity), wholesale and retail energy marketing, and energy management services, through the company's Conectiv Energy and Pepco Energy Services units.

Pepco Holdings' flexible business strategy allows it to develop opportunities for growth or operational streamlining in both its regulated and unregulated segments.

In 2008 Delmarva Power transferred control of its Virginia operations to A&N Electric Cooperative and Old Dominion Electric Cooperative to raise cash.

In 2009 company veteran Joseph Rigby succeeded the retiring Dennis Wraase as president and CEO.

Pepco Holdings, formerly named Potomac Electric Power, changed its name by forming a holding company in 2002; the name change took effect upon the completion of Pepco's acquisition of rival utility Conectiv (now Delmarva Power & Light).

EXECUTIVES

Chairman, President, and CEO: Joseph M. (Joe) Rigby, age 51, $2,115,469 total compensation
Vice Chairman and Chief Legal Officer:
William T. Torgerson, age 64,
$3,509,504 total compensation
SVP and CFO: Anthony J. (Tony) Kamerick, age 57
VP and CIO: Kenneth P. Cohn, age 55
Director Risk Management and Chief Risk Officer:
Mark W. Finfrock
EVP Power Delivery: David M. (Dave) Velazquez, age 49, $985,005 total compensation

SVP and General Counsel: Kirk J. Emge, age 59
SVP Government Affairs and Public Policy:
Beverly L. Perry, age 61
SVP Asset Management and Planning, Pepco, Delmarva Power, and Atlantic City Electric: William M. Gausman
SVP Operations, Pepco, Delmarva Power, and Atlantic City Electric: Michael J. Sullivan
VP and Corporate Secretary: Ellen Sheriff Rogers
VP Human Resources: Ernest L. Jenkins
VP Communications: Debbi Jarvis
President and CEO, Connective Energy:
Gary J. Morsches, age 49
President and CEO, Pepco Energy Services:
John U. Huffman, age 49
Director Investor Relations: Donna J. Kinzel
Auditors: PricewaterhouseCoopers LLP

LOCATIONS

HQ: Pepco Holdings, Inc.
701 9th St. NW, Washington, DC 20068
Phone: 202-872-2000 **Fax:** 202-331-6750
Web: www.pepcoholdings.com

Pepco Holdings has regulated utility operations in Delaware, Maryland, New Jersey, Virginia, and Washington, DC. The company generates power, markets energy, and provides energy-related services in the Northeast and mid-Atlantic regions; it also has utility and power plant operations in Australia, Austria, and the Netherlands.

PRODUCTS/OPERATIONS

2008 Sales

	$ mil.	% of total
Power delivery	5,487	49
Conectiv Energy	3,047	27
Pepco Energy Services	2,648	24
Adjustments	(482)	—
Total	**10,700**	**100**

Selected Subsidiaries

Conectiv
Atlantic City Electric Company (operates as Conectiv Power Delivery, electric utility)
Conectiv Energy Holdings (nonregulated operations)
Conectiv Energy Supply (power generation; energy trading, marketing, and management services)
Delmarva Power & Light Company (operates as Conectiv Power Delivery, electric and gas utility)
Pepco Energy Services, Inc. (power generation, retail and wholesale energy marketing, and management services)
PHI Service Company (support services)
Potomac Capital Investment Corporation (investments)
Potomac Electric Power Company (Pepco, electric utility)

COMPETITORS

AEP
Allegheny Energy
Appalachian Power
Baltimore Gas and Electric
Chesapeake Utilities
Con Edison
Constellation Energy Group
Dominion Resources
Exelon
FirstEnergy
New Jersey Resources
Northern Virginia Electric Cooperative
PPL Corporation
Public Service Enterprise Group
Virginia Electric and Power
WGL Holdings

HISTORICAL FINANCIALS

Company Type: Public

Income Statement

FYE: December 31

	REVENUE ($ mil.)	NET INCOME ($ mil.)	NET PROFIT MARGIN	EMPLOYEES
12/08	10,700.0	300.0	2.8%	5,474
12/07	9,366.4	334.2	3.6%	5,131
12/06	8,362.9	248.3	3.0%	5,156
12/05	8,065.5	362.2	4.5%	5,481
12/04	7,221.8	258.7	3.6%	5,592
Annual Growth	10.3%	3.8%	—	(0.5%)

2008 Year-End Financials

Debt ratio: 128.4%
Return on equity: 7.3%
Cash ($ mil.): 384
Current ratio: 1.29
Long-term debt ($ mil.): 5,378
No. of shares (mil.): 229
Dividends
Yield: 6.1%
Payout: 73.5%
Market value ($ mil.): 4,074

Stock History

NYSE: POM

	STOCK PRICE ($) FY Close	P/E High/Low	PER SHARE ($) Earnings	Dividends	Book Value
12/08	17.76	20 10	1.47	1.08	18.27
12/07	29.33	18 14	1.72	1.04	17.52
12/06	26.01	21 17	1.30	1.04	15.75
12/05	22.37	12 10	1.96	1.00	15.72
12/04	21.32	15 12	1.47	1.00	14.79
Annual Growth	(4.5%)	— —	0.0%	1.9%	5.4%

Pepsi Bottling Group

Psychotherapists might disagree, but keeping things bottled up can be beneficial — if you're The Pepsi Bottling Group. As the world's #1 manufacturer and distributor of Pepsi-Cola beverages, The Pepsi Bottling Group (PBG) has a US market share for Pepsi brands that is close to 40%. PBG operates manufacturing and distribution facilities and delivers its drinks (including Aquafina water, Lipton's Iced Tea, Mountain Dew, Slice, and the world's #2 soft drink, Pepsi-Cola) directly to stores as well as through third-party distributors. In 2009 the company, along with fellow bottler PepsiAmericas, agreed to be taken over by PepsiCo.

PepsiCo, which owns 33% of PBG and 43% of PepsiAmericas (its #2 bottler), initially offered some $6 billion to acquire 100% of both companies. PBG rejected PepsiCo's takeover offer as being "grossly inadequate." (PepsiAmericas' reaction was much the same.) However, Pepsi retooled its cash and stock offer a few months later, upping the value of the deal to $7.8 billion, at which point both bottlers agreed to be taken over.

The deal will give PepsiCo ownership of some 80% of its North American beverage distribution and create one of the largest food and beverage companies in the world. It will be able to cut costs, manage its supply-chain more profitably, and bring new products to market faster. The deal is contingent upon regulatory and shareholder approvals. (PBG had originally been spun off from PepsiCo in 1999 in order to allow the beverage maker to better compete with chief rival Coca-Cola, which had spun off its bottling operations in 1986.)

PBG has been expanding through a series of acquisitions, including its 2008 purchase of #1 Russian juice maker JSC Lebedyansky in partnership with PepsiCo. The $1.4 billion buyout gave PBG a 25% stake in the international business, while PepsiCo owns the rest. (Lebedyansky's baby food and bottled water businesses were not included in the deal.) The following year, PBG acquired Better Beverages, a Pepsi and Dr Pepper bottler serving parts of Texas. Later that year, it acquired another Texas bottler, Ab-Tex Beverage.

PBG has exclusive rights to sell Pepsi beverages in 42 states and the District of Columbia, and in nine Canadian provinces, Spain, Greece, Russia, and Turkey. The company also owns Mexican bottler Pepsi-Gemex, which includes Electropura, that country's largest purified water company. Mexico accounts for about 10% of PBG's sales. PBG also distributes Dr Pepper for Dr Pepper Snapple Group in some parts of the US. The company operates nearly 600 manufacturing and distribution facilities and operates a fleet of more than 38,000 vehicles.

HISTORY

Pepsi-Cola inventor Caleb Bradham started bottling his drink in 1904. He quickly set about developing a system of bottling franchises for the drink, named for the claim that it cured dyspepsia, or indigestion. (The Coca-Cola Company had set up a similar franchise system a few years before.) By the end of 1910, there were nearly 300 Pepsi bottlers in Virginia and North and South Carolina.

Bradham went bankrupt in 1923 after unsuccessful speculation in sugar prices. Pepsi went through several owners until Charles Guth's Loft Candy Company bought it in 1931. Guth doubled Pepsi's bottle size to 12 ounces (for the same nickel price) two years later. By the end of 1934, profits were pouring in and Guth looked for new bottlers to join the Pepsi franchise. Loft Candy merged with its Pepsi subsidiary in 1941 to become the Pepsi-Cola Company (the company would become PepsiCo with the 1965 purchase of Frito-Lay).

Between 1951 and 1957 new equipment (such as carton openers and electronic inspection units) helped increase bottling plants' maximum speed from 260 to 500 bottles per minute. About 140 new plants opened or began construction during this time. At the end of the decade, there were nearly 550 US Pepsi bottling plants. The 1960s brought faster speeds and canning operations to the facilities, and innovations in the 1970s such as lighter weight plastic (PET) bottles also increased productivity.

By the early 1980s PepsiCo subsidiary Pepsi-Cola Bottling brought in about one-fifth of its parent's US bottling volume. Pepsi decided to focus on building its company-owned bottling group, buying up some franchises. In 1986 Pepsi-Cola Bottling acquired the San Francisco-area Pepsi bottling operation along with two smaller franchises and a 50% stake in another; this raised its volume to about one-third of domestic Pepsi product.

Acquisitions in the late 1980s totaled more than 80 franchises, including the bottling operations of General Cinema and Grand Metropolitan (then the #3 independent US Pepsi bottler).

Parent PepsiCo, through its Pepsi-Cola International unit, focused on expanding its overseas bottling operations (including Brazil, Egypt, and Mexico) during the early and mid-1990s. Still, by 1996 Pepsi's overseas sales only brought in 6% of its profits — compared to 70% of Coke's profits.

Separating its North American beverage business into bottling and marketing divisions, PepsiCo officially created The Pepsi Bottling Group (PBG) in 1998 to help the firm acquire other bottlers. Craig Weatherup, who ran Pepsi's global beverage business, was named CEO.

In 1999 PepsiCo sold about 65% of PBG in a tepidly received IPO. PepsiCo also agreed to sell several US and European territories to Whitman Corp., the second-largest Pepsi-Cola bottler. The deal gave PepsiCo a 38% stake in Whitman.

In 2001 Weatherup stepped down as CEO, but retained his title as chairman. PBG president and COO John Cahill took Weatherup's place as CEO. Also that year PBG purchased an interest in Pepsi-Cola Bottling of Northern California, which serves 13 counties in its part of the state.

In 2002 PBG acquired the right to sell, manufacture, and distribute Pepsi's international beverages in Turkey for about $100 million. Its bid to buy Pepsi-Gemex also was completed in 2002, and in early 2003 it purchased Pepsi-Cola Buffalo Bottling Corp. Cahill assumed the chairmanship while continuing as CEO after Weatherup retired in 2003.

Cahill resigned as top of pop in 2006, and COO Eric Foss was named president and CEO.

EXECUTIVES

Chairman and CEO: Eric J. Foss, age 50,
 $7,500,818 total compensation
SVP Worldwide Operations: Victor L. Crawford, age 47,
 $2,473,579 total compensation
SVP and CFO: Alfred H. (Al) Drewes, age 53,
 $2,521,948 total compensation
SVP and CIO: Neal A. Bronzo
SVP and Chief Strategy Officer: Eric Llopis
EVP and President, PBG North America:
 Robert C. King, age 50, $2,259,186 total compensation
SVP, General Counsel, and Secretary: Steven M. Rapp,
 age 55
SVP Human Resources: John L. Berisford
VP Investor Relations and Public Relations:
 Mary Winn Settino
VP Strategy: Kathleen M. Dwyer
VP and Controller: Thomas M. Lardieri, age 48,
 $840,960 total compensation
VP Finance, North America: Nick D'Alessando
President, PBG Europe: Yiannis Petrides, age 50,
 $3,734,309 total compensation
President and General Manager, PBG Mexico:
 Pablo Lagos, age 53
President, PBG Mexico: Brent J. Franks
Auditors: Deloitte & Touche LLP

LOCATIONS

HQ: The Pepsi Bottling Group, Inc.
 1 Pepsi Way, Somers, NY 10589
Phone: 914-767-6000 **Fax:** 914-767-7761
Web: www.pbg.com

2008 Sales

	$ mil.	% of total
US & Canada	10,300	75
Europe	2,115	15
Mexico	1,381	10
Total	**13,796**	**100**

PRODUCTS/OPERATIONS

Selected Brands

Canada and US
AMP
Aquafina
Aquafina Alive
Aquafina FlavorSplash
Diet Mountain Dew
Diet Pepsi
Diet Pepsi Max
Dole (licensed)
Dr Pepper (licensed)
G2
Lipton (licensed)
Mountain Dew
Mountain Dew Code Red
Mug Root Beer
Muscle Milk (licensed)
Pepsi
Pepsi Lime
Pepsi ONE
Propel
Sierra Mist
Sierra Mist Free
SoBe
SoBe Life Water
SoBe No Fear
Starbucks Frappuccino (licensed)
Tropicana
Tropicana Twister
Wild Cherry Pepsi

Europe
7UP
Aqua Minerale
Fiesta
Fruko
IVI
KAS
Lipton (licensed)
Mirinda
Pepsi
Pepsi Light
Pepsi Max
Tamek
Tropicana
Yedigun

Mexico
7UP
Aguas Frescas
Belight
Electropura
e-pura
Garci Crespo
Jarritos
KAS
Manzanita Sol
Mirinda
Pepsi
Pepsi Light
Squirt (licensed)

COMPETITORS

AMCON Distributing
Aquaterra Corporation
Britvic Plc
Clearly Canadian
Coca-Cola Bottling Consolidated
Coca-Cola Enterprises
Coca-Cola FEMSA
Coca-Cola HBC
Coca-Cola North America
Coke United
Cott
Danone Water
Embotelladoras Arca
Energy Brands
Ferolito, Vultaggio
Hansen Natural
Impulse Energy USA
Jones Soda
Leading Brands
Naked Juice
National Beverage
Nestlé
Nestlé Waters
Odwalla
Pepsi Bottling of Knoxville
Pepsi-Cola Bottling Company of NY
Philadelphia Coca-Cola
Red Bull
Reed's
Suntory Holdings
Wet Planet Beverages

HISTORICAL FINANCIALS

Company Type: Public

Income Statement

FYE: Last Saturday in December

	REVENUE ($ mil.)	NET INCOME ($ mil.)	NET PROFIT MARGIN	EMPLOYEES
12/08	13,796.0	162.0	1.2%	66,800
12/07	13,591.0	532.0	3.9%	69,100
12/06	12,730.0	522.0	4.1%	70,400
12/05	11,885.0	466.0	3.9%	66,900
12/04	10,906.0	457.0	4.2%	64,700
Annual Growth	6.1%	(22.8%)	—	0.8%

2008 Year-End Financials

Debt ratio: 356.2%
Return on equity: 8.2%
Cash ($ mil.): 966
Current ratio: 1.02
Long-term debt ($ mil.): 4,784
No. of shares (mil.): 215
Dividends
  Yield: 2.9%
  Payout: 87.8%
Market value ($ mil.): 4,850

Stock History

NYSE: PBG

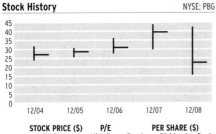

	STOCK PRICE ($) FY Close	P/E High/Low	Earnings	PER SHARE ($) Dividends	Book Value
12/08	22.51	57 21	0.74	0.65	6.23
12/07	39.46	19 13	2.29	0.53	12.14
12/06	30.91	17 13	2.16	0.41	9.67
12/05	28.61	16 14	1.86	0.29	9.48
12/04	27.04	18 14	1.73	0.16	9.05
Annual Growth	(4.5%)	— —	(19.1%)	42.0%	(8.9%)

PepsiAmericas, Inc.

PepsiAmericas holds more than a bubbling interest in the Pepsi Generation. The world's #2 Pepsi bottler (behind Pepsi Bottling Group) distributes all the familiar Pepsi brands, along with Lipton Iced Teas, Dr Pepper, 7UP, and Crush from the Dr Pepper Snapple Group, Starbucks Frappuccino, and Aquafina bottled water. PepsiAmericas operates in 19 US states (mostly in the Midwest) and holds nearly 20% of the US market for Pepsi products. It also distributes drinks in nearly a dozen European countries and in several Caribbean nations. In 2009 PepsiAmericas, along with The Pepsi Bottling Group (PBG), agreed to be acquired by PepsiCo.

PepsiCo, which owns 43% of PepsiAmericas and 33% of PBG (its #1 bottler), initially offered some $6 billion in a cash and stock deal to acquire 100% of both companies. But the companies rejected the price as being too low. However, Pepsi bid again some months later, upping the value of the deal to $7.8 billion, and this time PepsiAmericas and PBG agreed to be taken over.

The deal will give PepsiCo ownership of about 80% of its North American beverage distribution and create one of the largest food and beverage companies in the world. It will be able to cut costs, manage its supply-chain more profitably, and bring new products to market faster. The deal is contingent upon regulatory and shareholder approvals.

PepsiAmericas has been focused on boosting sales of bottled water such as Aquafina and other noncarbonated beverages in an effort to make up for slumping cola sales. Expanding its international business, the company formed a joint venture with PepsiCo to acquire Ukrainian juice maker Sandora. PepsiAmericas owns 60% of the venture and PepsiCo owns the rest.

In addition to beverages, the company distributes food products from PepsiCo's Frito-Lay unit in a small number of countries. Retail giant Wal-Mart and its SAM'S CLUB supercenters account for about 15% of sales.

HISTORY

PepsiAmericas is a very different business from its predecessor, the Illinois Central Railroad. Started in 1851 with a 3.6-million-acre land grant, Illinois Central became one of the nation's 10 largest rail systems, boasting 4,200 rail miles in 13 states by 1901, including the City of New Orleans line. It was renamed Illinois Central Industries in 1962.

William Johnson, former president of Railway Express Agency, became president in 1966. Johnson reduced the focus on railroads and helped transform the company into a multinational conglomerate (renamed IC Industries in 1975) that bought numerous companies, including Pepsi-Cola General Bottlers (1970), Midas International auto muffler shops (1972), Pet Inc., and refrigeration equipment maker, Hussmann (1978).

Pepsi-Cola General Bottlers was founded in 1935 as Pepsi-Cola Bottling Company of Chicago, a Pepsi franchise. To fund growth, it went public in 1938 and was renamed Pepsi-Cola General Bottlers in 1954. Pet began in 1885 as an evaporated milk company and later added Downyflake Foods, Stuckey roadside candy stores, and chocolate company, Stuart F. Whitman and Son. Because of the growth of its varied subsidiaries, the railroad provided only 1% of IC's pretax profits by

the late 1970s. One month after its spinoff in 1989, the company's rail business was bought by a private concern, Prospect Group.

The company changed its name in 1988 to Whitman (after its chocolate unit) to reflect its concentration on consumer goods and services. During the 1980s Whitman sold 65 companies (including its Pneumo Abex aerospace operations, 1988) and bought 98 companies (including Van de Kamp's frozen seafood, 1989).

Facing heavy debt, the company restructured. It spun off its Pet food unit (and all food brands) to shareholders. Whitman purchased 39 European muffler shops and three Pepsi franchises in the early 1990s. Bruce Chelberg became chairman and CEO in 1992. The firm sold Whitman Chocolates to Russell Stover Candies in 1993.

Its original Pepsi subsidiary, Pepsi General, sparked increased sales with new products in 1995, such as All Sport, Caffeine Free Mountain Dew, Slice, and Wild Cherry Pepsi. The next year it added new All Sport flavors, bottled water, and Ocean Spray juices, and replaced its root beer lines with Mug Root Beer. It also acquired some Russian assets from PepsiCo so that it could distribute Pepsi products in Russia and Belarus, as well as Estonia, Latvia, and Lithuania. In 1998 the company spun off two businesses — Midas and Hussmann International — into separately traded companies.

In early 1999 Whitman bought additional bottling operations in the Midwest and in Eastern Europe from PepsiCo. As part of the complex deal, it sold operations in three states and Russia, while giving PepsiCo a 38% stake in Whitman. In return, Whitman gained exclusive bottling rights in some of its territories. PepsiCo then named Whitman an anchor bottler in its reorganized system. Later that year Whitman bought Toma (Czech Republic) and began distributing Hortex and Rauch juice drinks in Poland and Hungary, respectively.

Whitman sold its Baltic operations in 2000. The company bought the #3 Pepsi bottler, PepsiAmericas, in 2000 in a deal worth about $660 million. Robert Pohlad subsequently became CEO of the new, combined company, which dropped the Whitman name in 2001 in favor of PepsiAmericas.

Also that year, PepsiAmericas purchased 90% of Pepsi-Cola Trinidad Bottling Company to expand in the Caribbean. In 2003 and 2004 the ongoing beverage war between Coca-Cola and PepsiCo produced new flavors and colors. While Coca-Cola freshened its product mix with Vanilla Coke, PepsiAmericas slapped back with Dr Pepper's Red Fusion, Pepsi Blue, and Mountain Dew LiveWire. The company also rolled out 8-ounce cans and Fridge-Mate, a 12-pack, 12-ounce-can package.

In 2005 the company bought the seventh-largest Pepsi bottler, Central Investment Corporation, for $352 million, and in 2006 it acquired Nutrisoda bottler Ardea Beverage. Also that year it acquired distribution rights in Romania.

EXECUTIVES

Chairman and CEO: Robert C. Pohlad, age 54, $4,368,028 total compensation
President and COO: Kenneth E. (Ken) Keiser, age 57, $4,238,831 total compensation
EVP and CFO: Alexander H. (Alex) Ware, age 46, $2,270,377 total compensation
SVP and CIO: Kenneth L. (Ken) Johnsen, age 47

EVP US: G. Michael Durkin Jr., age 49, $2,085,027 total compensation
EVP Worldwide Supply Chain: Jay S. Hulbert, age 55
EVP Human Resources: Anne D. Sample, age 45
EVP International: James R. Rogers, age 54, $1,349,392 total compensation
SVP Corporate Development: Matthew E. (Matt) Carter
SVP and Controller: Timothy W. Gorman, age 48
VP and Treasurer: Andrew R. Stark, age 45
VP US Finance and CFO Domestic: Sandy Mathias
VP Investor Relations: Sara Zawoyski
VP Compensation and Wellness: Barbara Kallay
Corporate Secretary: Brian D. Wenger
Auditors: KPMG LLP

LOCATIONS

HQ: PepsiAmericas, Inc.
60 S. 6th St., Minneapolis, MN 55402
Phone: 612-661-4000   **Fax:** 612-661-3737
Web: www.pepsiamericas.com

2008 Sales

	$ mil.	% of total
US	3,429.9	69
Central Europe	1,260.9	26
Caribbean	246.4	5
Total	**4,937.2**	**100**

PRODUCTS/OPERATIONS

Selected Beverages

Caribbean
7UP
Desnoes
Diet Pepsi
Geddes
Pepsi
Tropicana

Central Europe
Lipton Iced Tea
Pepsi
Aadochok
Sandora
Toma

US
Aquafina
Diet Mountain Dew
Diet Pepsi
Mountain Dew
Pepsi

Selected Subsidiaries

Ardea Beverage Company
Beverage Plastics, LLC
Caribbean Flavors, Ltd.
Caribbean Juices Limited (UK)
DakBev, LLC
Delta Beverage Group, Inc.
Marquette Bottling Works, Inc.
Pepsi-Cola Bottling Company of Ft. Lauderdale-Palm Beach, Inc.
Pepsi-Cola General Bottlers IL, LLC
Pepsi-Cola General Bottlers of Indiana, Inc.
Pepsi-Cola General Bottlers of Iowa, Inc.
Pepsi-Cola General Bottlers of Mansfield, Inc.
Pepsi-Cola General Bottlers of Ohio, Inc.
Pepsi-Cola General Bottlers Poland Sp.z.o.o.
Pepsi-Cola General Bottlers, Inc.
Pepsi-Cola General Bottlers, KY, LLC
Pepsi-Cola General Bottlers, LLC
Pepsi-Cola Jamaica Bottling Company Limited
Pepsi-Cola Puerto Rico Distributing, LLC (US)
Pepsi-Cola Puerto Rico Manufacturing, LLC (US)
Pepsi-Cola SR s.r.o. (Republic of Slovakia)
Pepsi-Cola Trinidad Bottling Company Limited Trinidad and Tobago
Quadrant-Amroq Beverages Moldova S.A.
Quadrant-Amroq Beverages, S.R.L. (Romania)

COMPETITORS

Clearly Canadian	Jones Soda
Coca-Cola Bottling	National Beverage
Coca-Cola Enterprises	Pepsi Bottling
Coca-Cola HBC	Red Bull
Cott	Snapple
Ferolito, Vultaggio	South Beach Beverage
Hansen Natural	Suntory Holdings
Impulse Energy USA	

HISTORICAL FINANCIALS

Company Type: Public

Income Statement

FYE: Saturday nearest December 31

	REVENUE ($ mil.)	NET INCOME ($ mil.)	NET PROFIT MARGIN	EMPLOYEES
12/08	4,937.2	226.4	4.6%	20,800
12/07	4,479.5	212.1	4.7%	20,700
12/06	3,972.4	158.3	4.0%	17,100
12/05	3,726.0	194.7	5.2%	16,000
12/04	3,344.7	181.9	5.4%	15,100
Annual Growth	**10.2%**	**5.6%**	**—**	**8.3%**

2008 Year-End Financials

Debt ratio: 107.8%
Return on equity: 13.4%
Cash ($ mil.): 242
Current ratio: 0.86
Long-term debt ($ mil.): 1,642
No. of shares (mil.): 125
Dividends
  Yield: 2.0%
  Payout: 23.0%
Market value ($ mil.): 2,535

Stock History

NYSE: PAS

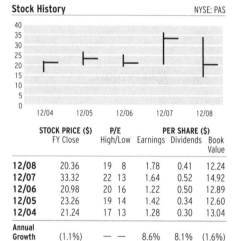

	STOCK PRICE ($) FY Close	P/E High/Low		PER SHARE ($) Earnings	Dividends	Book Value
12/08	20.36	19	8	1.78	0.41	12.24
12/07	33.32	22	13	1.64	0.52	14.92
12/06	20.98	20	16	1.22	0.50	12.89
12/05	23.26	19	14	1.42	0.34	12.60
12/04	21.24	17	13	1.28	0.30	13.04
Annual Growth	**(1.1%)**	**—**	**—**	**8.6%**	**8.1%**	**(1.6%)**

PepsiCo, Inc.

The PepsiCo challenge (to keep up with archrival The Coca-Cola Company) never ends for the world's #2 carbonated soft-drink maker. Its soft drinks include Pepsi, Mountain Dew, and Slice. Cola is not the company's only beverage: Pepsi sells Tropicana orange juice brands, Gatorade sports drink, and Aquafina water. The company also owns Frito-Lay, the world's #1 snack maker with offerings such as corn chips (Doritos, Fritos) and potato chips (Lay's, Ruffles). Its Quaker Foods division offers breakfast cereals (Life), pasta (Pasta Roni), rice (Rice-A-Roni), and side dishes (Near East). Pepsi's products are available in some 200 countries.

PepsiCo announced plans to consolidate its bottling and distribution operations in 2009, offering to acquire 100% of both The Pepsi Bottling Group (PBG) and PepsiAmericas (its two largest bottlers) in a deal worth $6 billion. PepsiCo already owns 33% of PBG and 43% of PepsiAmericas. However, PBG rejected the offer as being "grossly inadequate." PepsiAmericas also rejected PepsiCo's offer on the same grounds.

Not content with a "no," PepsiCo made the offer again some months later, this time upping its cash and stock proposal to a deal valued at $7.8 billion. This time the offer was accepted by both companies. The takeover will give PepsiCo control over some 80% of its North American bottling and distribution volume. It will allow the company to cut significant costs and allow it to make any desired changes to the supply-chain more rapidly. In addition, the takeover will also create one of the largest food and beverages businesses in the world. The deal is contingent upon regulatory and shareholder approvals.

International Dairy and Juice Limited (IDJ), the joint venture it has with Saudi dairy company Almarai, purchased a 75% stake in top Jordanian dairy and juice company, Teeba Investment for Developed Food Processing Company (or Teeba) in 2009. Pepsi owns 52% of IDJ, and Almarai owns 48%. The Teeba purchase furthers Pepsi's strategy of building a diversified global portfolio of foods and beverages.

Looking to expand its business internationally, PepsiCo and its largest bottler Pepsi Bottling Group (PBG) acquired #1 Russian juice maker JSC Lebedyansky for about $1.4 billion in 2008. PepsiCo controls a 75% stake, while PBG owns the rest.

Product development plays a major role in PepsiCo's battle for the hearts and minds of beverage drinkers. The company introduced SoBe Lifewater (through subsidiary South Beach Beverage Company) and Trop50 (from its Tropicana unit), two new brands using zero-calorie sweetener PureVia. PepsiCo jumped into the vitaminwater market in 2007 with Aquafina Alive. The company also has licensing agreements to produce Ben & Jerry's branded milkshakes, Dole juices, and Lipton ready-to-drink tea.

HISTORY

Pharmacist Caleb Bradham invented Pepsi in 1898 in New Bern, North Carolina. He named his new drink Pepsi-Cola (claiming it cured dyspepsia, or indigestion) and registered the trademark in 1903. Following The Coca-Cola Company's example, Bradham developed a bottling franchise system. By WWI, 300 bottlers had signed up. After the war, Bradham stockpiled sugar to safeguard against rising costs, but in 1920 sugar prices plunged, forcing him into bankruptcy in 1923.

Pepsi existed on the brink of ruin under various owners until Loft Candy bought it in 1931. Its fortunes improved in 1933 when, in the midst of the Depression, it doubled the size of its bottles to 12 ounces without raising the five-cent price. In 1939 Pepsi introduced the world's first radio jingle. Two years later Loft Candy merged with its Pepsi subsidiary and became The Pepsi-Cola Company.

Donald Kendall, who became Pepsi-Cola's president in 1963, turned the firm's attention to young people ("The Pepsi Generation"). It acquired Mountain Dew in 1964 and became PepsiCo in 1965, when it acquired Frito-Lay.

In 1972 PepsiCo agreed to distribute Stolichnaya vodka in the US in exchange for being the only Western firm allowed to bottle soft drinks in the USSR. With the purchases of Pizza Hut (1977), Taco Bell (1978), and Kentucky Fried Chicken (1986), it became a major force in the fast-food industry.

When Coca-Cola changed its formula in 1985, Pepsi had a short-lived victory in the cola wars (until the splashy return of Coca-Cola classic). The rivalry was extended to ready-to-drink tea in 1991 when, in response to Coca-Cola's Nestea venture with Nestlé, PepsiCo teamed up with Lipton. Between 1991 and 1996 PepsiCo aggressively expanded its overseas bottling operations. Roger Enrico became CEO in 1996. A year later PepsiCo spun off its $10 billion fast-food unit as TRICON Global Restaurants (now known as YUM! Brands, Inc.), putting itself in a better position to sell its soft drinks at other restaurants.

In 1998 the company bought Seagram's market-leading Tropicana juices (rival of Coca-Cola's Minute Maid) for $3.3 billion. The firm sold a 65% stake in its new Pepsi Bottling Group to the public in 1999.

Its more than $13 billion purchase of The Quaker Oats Company in 2001 added the dominant Gatorade sports drink brand to its lineup. Later that year the company named president and COO Steve Reinemund as chairman and CEO; Enrico stayed as vice chairman (where he remained through 2002).

PepsiCo also found opportunities for growth overseas in 2003. However, claims surfaced that year that both Coke and Pepsi products bottled in India contained traces of DDT, malathion, and other pesticides that exceeded government limits. Coke and Pepsi denied the reports in a rare joint press conference. Government labs cleared the colas, saying the drinks were safe, but not before both soft-drink companies saw sales dip by as much as 50% in a two-week period.

PepsiCo bought General Mills' stake of their joint venture, Snack Ventures Europe (SVE), in 2005 for $750 million. The deal gave Pepsi control of Europe's largest snack food company.

Later that year the company revealed it was subject to an SEC investigation involving transactions it had with Kmart. Allegedly, lower-level employees within its cola and snack divisions signed documents that Kmart used to improperly record nearly $6 million in revenue. PepsiCo cooperated with the investigation, which led to the resignations of a PepsiCo national account manager and a sales director.

CEO Steve Reinemund stepped down as CEO in 2006 in order to spend more time with his family. His replacement, Indra Nooyi, had served as the company's president and CFO.

EXECUTIVES

Chairman and CEO: Indra K. Nooyi, age 53, $13,382,035 total compensation
Vice Chairman; Chairman and CEO, PepsiCo International: Michael D. (Mike) White, age 57, $10,060,437 total compensation
CFO: Richard A. Goodman, age 60, $3,655,457 total compensation
CIO: Robert Dixon
SVP Chief Global Diversity and Inclusion Officer: Ronald C. (Ron) Parker
Chief Scientific Officer: Mehmood Khan

SVP and Chief Procurement Officer: Mitch Adamek
SVP and Controller: Peter A. Bridgman, age 56
SVP PepsiCo Human Resources: Cynthia M. Trudell, age 55
SVP Investor Relations: Lynn A. Tyson
SVP and General Counsel, PepsiCo Americas Foods: Clay G. Small
SVP Finance and Treasurer: Tessa Hilado
SVP Government Affairs, General Counsel, and Secretary: Larry D. Thompson, age 63
SVP Corporate Strategy: Wahid Hamid, age 50
SVP Communications: Julie A. Hamp
SVP Tax: Sarah McGill
SVP R&D Global Beverages: Jonathan (Jon) McIntyre
VP Investor Relations: Jane Nielsen
VP Sales and Chief Marketing Officer: Annie Young-Scrivner
President and CEO, Frito-Lay North America: Albert P. (Al) Carey, age 57, $5,232,826 total compensation
CEO, PepsiCo Americas Foods: John C. Compton, age 47, $5,929,562 total compensation
Auditors: KPMG LLP

LOCATIONS

HQ: PepsiCo, Inc.
    700 Anderson Hill Rd., Purchase, NY 10577
Phone: 914-253-2000   **Fax:** 914-253-2070
Web: www.pepsico.com

2008 Sales

	$ mil.	% of total
US	22,525	52
Mexico	3,714	8
Canada	2,107	5
UK	2,099	5
Other countries	12,806	30
Total	**43,251**	**100**

PRODUCTS/OPERATIONS

Selected Brands

7UP	Pepsi
Alegro	Pepsi Max
Amp Energy	Pepsi One
Aquafina	Propel
Aunt Jemima	Quaker
Cap'n Crunch	Quaker Chewy
Cheetos	Quakes
Cracker Jack	Rice-A-Roni
Diet 7UP (outside the US)	Rold Gold
Diet Pepsi	Ruffles
Dole (licensed)	Sabritas
Doritos	Sakata
Duyvis	Sierra Mist
Frito-Lay	Simba
Fritos	Smith's
Fruktovy Sad	Snack a Jacks
Frustyle	SoBe
Gamesa	SoBe Lifewater
Gatorade	Sonric's
Grandma's	Stacy's
Izze	Starbucks (licensed)
Lay's	SunChips
Life	Tonus
Lipton (licensed)	Tostitos
Matutano	Tropicana
Mirinda	Tropicana Pure Premium
Mountain Dew	Tropicana Twister
Naked	TrueNorth
Near East	V Water
Ocean Spray (licensed)	Walkers
Pasta Roni	Ya

COMPETITORS

American Beverage
Avani International Group
Beer Nuts
Big Red
Campbell Soup
Carolina Beverage
Celestial Seasonings
Chiquita Brands
Clearly Canadian
Coca-Cola
Coca-Cola North America
ConAgra
Cool Mountain Beverages
Cott
Cranberries Limited
Danone Water
Dr Pepper Snapple Group
DS Waters
Energy Brands
Evans Food Products Company
Faygo
Ferolito, Vultaggio
Florida's Natural
Fuze Beverage
General Mills
Golden Enterprises
Grupo Bimbo
Hansen Natural
Hawaiian Springs
Impulse Energy USA
Inventure
IZZE
Jones Soda
Kellogg U.S. Snacks
Kettle Foods
Kraft Foods
Kraft North America
Lance Snacks
Mountain Valley
Naked Juice
National Beverage
National Grape Cooperative
Nestlé
Nestlé Waters
New Attitude Beverage Corporation
Ocean Spray
Odwalla
Pinahs Company
Polar Beverages
Procter & Gamble
Ralcorp
R.C. Bigelow
Red Bull
Reed's
Republic of Tea
Snyder's of Hanover
Stash Tea
Sunny Delight
Suntory Holdings
Sweet Leaf Tea
Tata Group
Tree Top
Unilever NV
Weaver Popcorn Company
Wet Planet Beverages
XELR8

HISTORICAL FINANCIALS

Company Type: Public

Income Statement

	REVENUE ($ mil.)	NET INCOME ($ mil.)	NET PROFIT MARGIN	EMPLOYEES
12/08	43,251.0	5,142.0	11.9%	198,000
12/07	39,474.0	5,658.0	14.3%	185,000
12/06	35,137.0	5,642.0	16.1%	168,000
12/05	32,562.0	4,078.0	12.5%	157,000
12/04	29,261.0	4,212.0	14.4%	153,000
Annual Growth	10.3%	5.1%	—	6.7%

FYE: Last Saturday in December

2008 Year-End Financials

Debt ratio: 64.4%
Return on equity: 34.8%
Cash ($ mil.): 2,064
Current ratio: 1.23
Long-term debt ($ mil.): 7,858
No. of shares (mil.): 1,558
Dividends
Yield: 3.0%
Payout: 51.4%
Market value ($ mil.): 85,324

Stock History

NYSE: PEP

	STOCK PRICE ($) FY Close	P/E High/Low		PER SHARE ($) Earnings	Dividends	Book Value
12/08	54.77	25	15	3.21	1.65	7.86
12/07	75.90	23	18	3.41	1.42	11.15
12/06	62.55	20	17	3.34	1.16	9.86
12/05	59.08	25	21	2.39	1.01	9.15
12/04	52.20	23	19	2.44	0.85	8.68
Annual Growth	1.2%	—	—	7.1%	18.0%	(2.5%)

PerkinElmer, Inc.

If you know the difference between covalent and ionic bonds, you can probably appreciate the products from PerkinElmer. The company makes a wide range of analytical instruments used for chemical and thermal analysis, including calorimeters, chromatographs, and spectrometers. PerkinElmer Optoelectronics makes fiber-optic test systems and lithography systems used in medical, industrial, and telecommunications applications. PerkinElmer Life and Analytical Sciences makes products used for drug discovery and genetic disease screening, including labeling reagents and cell imaging systems; it accounts for about three-quarters of sales.

The ongoing recession and continuing credit crisis are among the company's challenges in 2009. The global recession means there are no safe havens in PerkinElmer's international markets. The company is also carefully monitoring its supply of raw materials and key components, especially from single-source suppliers.

In 2009 the company acquired Analytica of Branford, Inc. The deal increases PerkinElmer's human health and environmental health portfolio with know-how in mass spectrometry and ion source technology. The advance caters to markets in drug discovery and molecular diagnostics, as well as environmental detection and analysis and industrial monitoring.

Looking to improve its international reach, particularly in the Asia/Pacific region, PerkinElmer opened an R&D center in Singapore in 2008. Also that year the company opened an application and technical center in Mumbai, India.

In late 2007 the company acquired ViaCell (now ViaCord) for about $300 million in cash. PerkinElmer sees the acquisition expanding its offerings in neonatal and prenatal markets.

HISTORY

PerkinElmer traces its roots back to the invention of the strobe light in 1931. MIT professor Harold Edgerton, who invented the strobe light while doing research on electric motors, formed a consulting business with former student Kenneth Germeshausen that used strobe lights and high-speed photography to solve manufacturing problems. As business picked up, they brought in another former student, Herbert Grier, and in 1947 formed Edgerton, Germeshausen and Grier. Their first contract job was to photograph nuclear weapons tests for the US government. The company went public in 1959 and changed its name to EG&G in 1966.

Over the next 30 years, EG&G bought scores of companies involved in electronic instruments and components, biomedical services, energy and nuclear weapons R&D, seal and gasket manufacturing, automotive testing, and the aerospace industry. Key acquisitions included Reynolds Electrical & Engineering (1967), which provided support services for the Department of Defense (including the nuclear weapons testing program); Sealol (1968), a maker of seals for industrial applications; and Automotive Research Associates (1973).

Company veteran John Kucharski became CEO in 1987 and chairman in 1988. The company took over operation of Department of Energy (DOE) facilities in Miamisburg, Ohio (1988) and Rocky Flats, Colorado (1990). The company bought the optoelectronics businesses of General Electric Canada in 1990, and the next year it purchased Heimann, a German maker of optoelectronic devices, from Siemens. EG&G acquired Finland's Wallac Group (analytical and diagnostic systems) from Procordia AB in 1993. The following year it bought IC Sensors (sold in 1999).

The close of the Cold War put an end to DOE-sponsored nuclear weapons programs, while activists' questions about worker safety and environmental protection measures led to lawsuits against the company. In 1994 EG&G announced that it would discontinue its nuclear business (which had accounted for about 50% of sales) as its contracts ran out.

In 1998 the company sold its mechanical components businesses (Sealol, Rotron) and created a separate life sciences unit. Kucharski retired that year and president Gregory Summe, a former AlliedSignal (now Honeywell International) and General Electric executive, was named CEO.

In 1999 the company bought Lumen Technologies, a maker of specialty light sources, and paid $425 million for the analytical instruments division of PE Corporation (formerly PerkinElmer, now Applied Biosystems). EG&G later changed its name to PerkinElmer. That same year the company sold its technical services business to The Carlyle Group in a $250 million deal. Acquisitions such as Vivid Technologies (explosives detection systems) and NEN Life Sciences (drug discovery products and services) continued in 2000.

In 2001 the company acquired Packard BioScience, a maker of drug discovery products, for $650 million. Late that year PerkinElmer sold two units, Voltarc Technologies (specialty lighting products) and Instruments for Research and Applied Science (scientific instrumentation).

In 2002 the company sold its Detection Systems business to defense contractor L-3 Communications for about $100 million.

In 2004 PerkinElmer announced a multiyear, $250 million agreement to supply digital X-ray detectors to GE Medical Systems. The following year PerkinElmer acquired Elcos, a maker of light-emitting diode (LED) products for biomedical and industrial applications.

In 2005 PerkinElmer divested the operations that comprised its fluid sciences business segment to focus on products related to health sciences and photonics. It sold the Automotive Research Laboratory segment of its fluid sciences division to Intertek Caleb Brett, a division of Intertek Group, in 2005. The company also sold its aerospace business to Eaton for approximately $333 million. The following year it sold the semiconductor components portion of the business to Tara Capital for roughly $27 million. The fluid sciences segment accounted for less than 15% of its total sales in 2004.

In 2006 PerkinElmer acquired the assets of Spectral Genomics, a supplier of molecular karyotyping technology, for about $12 million in cash. Spectral Genomics' array products and analysis software help pharmaceutical, biotechnology, cytogenetic, and clinical researchers identify chromosomal abnormalities related to the study of cancer and pre- and postnatal genetic disorders. The acquisition complemented PerkinElmer's portfolio in molecular medicine and genetic screening.

President/COO Robert Friel was promoted to CEO in early 2008, succeeding Gregory Summe, who remained executive chairman. Friel joined the company in 1999 as CFO.

EXECUTIVES

Chairman, President, and CEO: Robert F. (Rob) Friel, age 53, $6,935,416 total compensation
SVP, CFO, and Chief Accounting Officer: Frank A. (Andy) Wilson
CIO: Aaron Lindberg
SVP and Chief Admistrative Officer: Richard F. Walsh, age 56, $2,295,414 total compensation
SVP and Chief Scientific Officer; President, Greater China: Daniel R. (Dan) Marshak, age 51, $1,069,483 total compensation
SVP and Chief Marketing Officer: Lapo Paladini
SVP; President, Environmental Health: John A. Roush, age 43, $2,382,943 total compensation
SVP, General Counsel, and Secretary: Joel S Goldberg, age 40
VP Business Development: Aaron Geist
VP and Controller: Michael L. Battles, age 40, $789,287 total compensation
VP Automation and Detection Solutions: Nance Hall
VP Cellular Imaging and Analysis: Achim von Leoprechting
VP Corporate Communications: Stephanie R. Wasco
President, Molecular Medicine, PerkinElmer Life and Analytical Sciences: Richard Eglen
President, Illumination and Detection Solutions: David Nislick
President, PerkinElmer India: Fedja Bobanovic
Director Marketing, Optoelectronics/Medical Imaging: Francine S. Bernitz
Director Laboratory Operations, Genetic Screening Business: John E. Sherwin
VP Business Development, Life and Analytical Sciences: Alan Fletcher
Auditors: Deloitte & Touche LLP

LOCATIONS

HQ: PerkinElmer, Inc.
940 Winter St., Waltham, MA 02451
Phone: 781-663-6900   **Fax:** 203-944-4904
Web: www.perkinelmer.com

2008 Sales

	$ mil.	% of total
US	752.4	39
Europe		
Germany	175.0	9
UK	127.9	7
France	86.1	4
Italy	85.9	4
China	91.4	5
Japan	79.2	4
Other countries	539.6	28
Total	**1,937.5**	**100**

PRODUCTS/OPERATIONS

2008 Sales

	$ mil.	% of total
Life & Analytical Sciences	1,512.6	78
Optoelectronics	424.9	22
Total	**1,937.5**	**100**

Selected Products

Analytical Instruments
 Chromatography
  Gas chromatographs
  Hybrid gas chromatography/mass spectrometers
  Liquid chromatographs
 Consumables and accessories
 Informatics
  Chromatography Data Systems software
   (TotalChrom)
  Laboratory information management systems
   (LABWORKS)
  Web-based instrument and data management
   systems (Sombrilla)
 Inorganic analysis
  Atomic absorption spectrometers
  Inductively coupled plasma (ICP) mass
   spectrometers
  ICP optical emission spectrometers
  Sample preparation equipment
 Molecular spectroscopy
  Fourier transform-infrared (FT-IR) spectroscopes
  Luminescence spectrometers
  Polarimeters
  Ultraviolet-visible spectroscopes
 Thermal and elemental analysis
  Elemental
   Carbon, hydrogen, nitrogen, sulfur, and oxygen
    (CHNS/O) analyzers
   Nitrogen analyzers
  Thermal
   Differential scanning calorimeters
   Dynamic mechanical analyzers
   Thermogravimetric analyzers
   Thermomechanical analyzers
Life Sciences
 Automated liquid handling high-throughput screening
  (HTS) systems
 Chemical reagents for heterogenous and homogenous
  assays
 Live cell imaging systems for proteomics research
 Multilabel counters and plate readers
 Parallel plate processing systems
Optoelectronics
 Health sciences
  Endoscopic surgical lamps
  Gas sensors for patient monitoring equipment
  Single photon counting modules (SPCMs)
  Thermopiles
 Industrial
  Charge-coupled display cameras
  Mercury ultraviolet lamps
  Ultraviolet laser-based direct imaging systems for
   newspaper printing

COMPETITORS

Agilent Technologies
Beckman Coulter
Bio-Rad Labs
Bruker
Danaher
Dionex
Harvard Bioscience
Honeywell International
IDEXX Labs
Kaydon
MDS
Mettler-Toledo
MTS Systems
Nanosphere
OSI Systems
Roper Industries
Shimadzu Scientific Instruments
Siemens AG
Thermo Fisher Scientific
Tyco
Varian
Varian Medical Systems
Waters Corp.

HISTORICAL FINANCIALS

Company Type: Public

Income Statement

FYE: Sunday nearest December 31

	REVENUE ($ mil.)	NET INCOME ($ mil.)	NET PROFIT MARGIN	EMPLOYEES
12/08	1,937.5	126.4	6.5%	7,900
12/07	1,787.3	131.7	7.4%	8,700
12/06	1,546.4	119.6	7.7%	8,500
12/05	1,473.8	268.1	18.2%	8,000
12/04	1,687.2	96.0	5.7%	10,000
Annual Growth	**3.5%**	**7.1%**	**—**	**(5.7%)**

2008 Year-End Financials

Debt ratio: 32.5%
Return on equity: 8.0%
Cash ($ mil.): 179
Current ratio: 1.61
Long-term debt ($ mil.): 509
No. of shares (mil.): 117
Dividends
 Yield: 2.0%
 Payout: 26.2%
Market value ($ mil.): 1,623

Stock History

NYSE: PKI

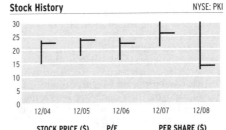

	STOCK PRICE ($) FY Close	P/E High/Low		Earnings	PER SHARE ($) Dividends	Book Value
12/08	13.91	28	12	1.07	0.28	13.44
12/07	26.02	28	20	1.09	0.28	13.50
12/06	22.23	25	17	0.95	0.28	13.52
12/05	23.56	12	9	2.04	0.28	14.14
12/04	22.49	31	20	0.74	0.28	12.51
Annual Growth	**(11.3%)**	**—**	**—**	**9.7%**	**0.0%**	**1.8%**

Perot Systems

It doesn't take many charts and graphs to see that Perot Systems is one of the leading providers of technology services and outsourcing. The company, founded by one-time presidential candidate Ross Perot Sr., offers applications development, systems integration, and strategic consulting services through its operations in the US and 10 other countries. In addition, it provides a variety of business process outsourcing (BPO) services, including claims processing and call center operations. Perot Systems serves commercial customers in a number of industries, including financial services, health care, and transportation; it also serves government agencies. In 2009 Dell agreed to buy Perot for about $3.9 billion in cash.

Adding Perot Systems to the Dell Global Services organization will create an IT services group with some $8 billion in annual revenues. The company will become Dell's services unit and the combined organization will be led by Perot CEO Peter Altabef. Dell/Perot will be able to offer a broader range of IT services to clients, and to sell more Dell computers to Perot clients. The combination should widen the geographic reach of Perot, which is concentrated in the US. Dell gets nearly half of its sales outside the US.

Work for the health care sector has historically been one of the company's major business segments, accounting for 47% of sales. Perot Systems works with clients such as hospitals and health care organizations that are moving toward electronic records and technologically complex environments, as well as with customers looking to outsource tasks such as claims processing and records management.

Another key business area is its commercial business (30% of sales), which serves the manufacturing, consumer products and services, and engineering and construction industries. It also focuses on the insurance industry, offering services such as consulting and application development and integration.

Perot Systems established its government services sector in 2002 and has quickly built it into a major source of sales, accounting for about 23% of revenue. Key government clients include the Department of Defense, the Department of Homeland Security, and NASA.

Ross Perot and his family own about 28% of the company.

HISTORY

Ross Perot sold Electronic Data Systems (EDS), the data and computer services firm he founded in 1962, to General Motors for $2.5 billion in 1984. It wasn't long before he became irritated with GM; the feeling was mutual. By 1986 neither party could stand the other, and the company paid Perot $700 million for his GM stock on the condition that he go away and not hire any EDS workers for a year and a half.

In June 1988 Perot founded Perot Systems and hired eight EDS veterans. The new firm quickly scored a 10-year contract to cut costs at the US Postal Service. Perot's separation agreement with GM, however, prohibited him from competing with EDS for profit until December 1989, so Perot Systems worked for free until then. Pressure from GM eventually killed the

Postal Service contract, but the publicity generated for Perot Systems led to a long list of customers who saw the nonprofit clause as a chance to undertake massive service and support efforts without paying high prices.

The company, however, soon began to founder — in part, some said, because it had promised more than it could deliver. Perot also alienated Hispanics with anti-NAFTA political rhetoric just as his company was working on deals with Volkswagen de México and Multibanco Mercantil Probursa. In 1992 Perot stepped down to concentrate on his bid for the US presidency. Former Perot aide and EDS executive Morton Meyerson became CEO and began leading the company away from computer outsourcing and toward higher-margin consulting services.

Perot Systems bought a division of financial software company Platinum Software (now Epicor Software) in 1994. In 1995 James Cannavino, who shared a past at IBM with Perot, became president (Perot had been a top Big Blue salesman; Cannavino was a strategist who left after he was denied the IBM chairmanship). A seven-year deal with Tenet Healthcare marked one of the first times that computer operations for the health care industry were outsourced.

An aggressive emphasis on risk-sharing alliances, in which the company is compensated based on its customers' results instead of through consultants' fees, spurred Perot Systems' growth. Perot Systems bought four firms in 1996, including Technical Resource Connection (object-oriented programming) and CommSys (telecommunications billing).

Rising costs and falling earnings that year preceded the resignation of Cannavino. In 1998 Meyerson resigned as chairman and Perot retook the helm, waiving his own pay, pushing recruitment from the military, and making other changes to control costs.

Perot Systems went public in 1999. That year it signed a pact with French technology services specialist Atos (now Atos Origin) to jointly provide services to multinational clients.

Ross Perot Jr., company director and son of the founder, was named CEO in 2000. In 2001 Perot Systems expanded with acquisitions, including the purchases of Covation, an application service provider serving the health care industry, and Advanced Receivables Strategy, a provider of IT services for the same industry.

Perot Systems expanded into providing government services with its acquisition of ADI Technology for $47 million in 2002. The company acquired IT services provider Soza & Co. for up to $107 million in early 2003, adding several federal agencies to its client base.

Perot built his company into a technology powerhouse in large part though his personality and deal-making abilities. Those same qualities, however, gave Perot Systems a very loose organizational structure. Ross Jr. helped align the operations and organization of Perot Systems following his appointment as CEO in 2000.

By 2004, the Perots were ready pull back from overseeing the day-to-day operations of their company and they surprised the business community by handing the reins over to longtime general counsel Peter Altabef that year. Concurrently, Ross Perot Sr., became chairman emeritus and Ross Jr. gave up the titles of president and CEO to become chairman.

The company was dealt a blow in 2005 when Harvard Pilgrim Health Care terminated its 10-year, $700 million services deal with four years left on the contract.

Perot Systems used acquisitions from 2007-2008 to fill in gaps in its product lines as well as to gain ground in overseas markets. Early in 2007 the company acquired IT company QSS Group for approximately $250 million and integrated it into the Perot Systems government services unit. Later that year the company bought JJWild (later renamed MEDITECH Solutions Group), an IT services provider serving the health care sector, for $89 million. In 2008 the company purchased HighQ-IT, a German IT services provider specializing in SAP products, in a bid to expand its European footprint.

EXECUTIVES

Chairman Emeritus: Ross Perot Sr., age 78
Chairman: Ross Perot Jr., age 50,
$1,630,562 total compensation
President, CEO, and Director: Peter A. Altabef, age 49,
$3,302,525 total compensation
VP and COO: Russell (Russ) Freeman, age 45,
$1,870,542 total compensation
VP and CFO: John E. Harper, age 47,
$988,365 total compensation
CIO: Susan Nolan
Chief Strategy Officer: Raj G. Asava
Chief Marketing Officer: Atul Vohra
EVP Global Sales and Marketing: Jeffrey (Jeff) Renzi,
age 48
EVP International Healthcare: Kevin M. Fickenscher
EVP Sales: Elizabeth Smith
SVP Sales, Civilian Services: Doug Sickler
VP: John E. King
VP Healthcare Group: Charles A. (Chuck) Lyles, age 42
VP Corporate Support and Chief People Officer:
Darcy G. Anderson, age 52
VP, General Counsel, and Secretary:
Thomas D. (Del) Williams, age 48,
$1,173,735 total compensation
VP Infrastructure Solutions: Scott Barnes
Global VP Human Resources: Maureen McDonald
Chairman Consulting Practice and Head Strategy:
James A. (Jim) Champy, age 66
President Commercial Solutions: Steve Curts
Director Corporate Communications: Joe McNamara
Auditors: PricewaterhouseCoopers LLP

LOCATIONS

HQ: Perot Systems Corporation
2300 W. Plano Pkwy., Plano, TX 75075
Phone: 972-577-0000
Web: www.perotsystems.com

2008 Sales

	$ mil.	% of total
US	2,423	87
UK	123	4
India	107	4
Other countries	126	5
Total	**2,779**	**100**

PRODUCTS/OPERATIONS

2008 Sales

	$ mil.	% of total
Industry solutions	2,128	77
Government services	654	23
Adjustments	(3)	—
Total	**2,779**	**100**

Selected Services and Operations

Business process outsourcing
  Call center management
  Claims processing
  Payment processing
  Receivables collection
Management consulting
Project management
Systems and technology services
  Application development
  Business intelligence
  Data center management
  Hardware maintenance
  Help desk
  Messaging services
  Network management and security
  Process and change management
  Risk management
  Systems integration and testing
  Technology assessment
  Video, voice, and data services
  Web hosting

COMPETITORS

Accenture
Affiliated Computer Services
Atos Origin
Bain & Company
BearingPoint
Booz Allen
Boston Consulting
Bull
CACI International
Capgemini
Cerner
CGI Group
CIBER
Cognizant Tech Solutions
Computer Sciences Corp.
Deloitte Consulting
EDS
Fujitsu Services
General Dynamics
Getronics
HCL Technologies
HP Technology Solutions Group
IBM Global Services
Infosys
Keane
Lockheed Martin Information Systems
Logica
McKesson
McKinsey & Company
PA Consulting
Patni Computer Systems
Pegasus Solutions
Sapient
Siemens IT Solutions and Services
SRA International
Tech Mahindra Limited
Unisys
Wipro Technologies

HISTORICAL FINANCIALS

Company Type: Public

Income Statement				FYE: December 31
	REVENUE ($ mil.)	NET INCOME ($ mil.)	NET PROFIT MARGIN	EMPLOYEES
12/08	2,779.0	117.0	4.2%	23,100
12/07	2,612.0	115.0	4.4%	23,100
12/06	2,298.0	81.0	3.5%	21,200
12/05	1,998.3	111.1	5.6%	18,100
12/04	1,773.5	94.3	5.3%	15,900
Annual Growth	11.9%	5.5%	—	9.8%

2008 Year-End Financials

Debt ratio: 13.9%
Return on equity: 9.2%
Cash ($ mil.): 234
Current ratio: 2.23
Long-term debt ($ mil.): 181

No. of shares (mil.): 121
Dividends
Yield: 0.0%
Payout: —
Market value ($ mil.): 1,653

Stock History

NYSE: PER

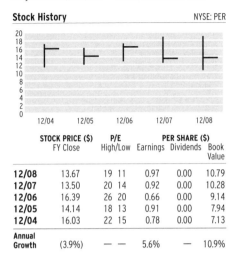

	STOCK PRICE ($) FY Close	P/E High/Low	PER SHARE ($) Earnings	Dividends	Book Value
12/08	13.67	19 11	0.97	0.00	10.79
12/07	13.50	20 14	0.92	0.00	10.28
12/06	16.39	26 20	0.66	0.00	9.14
12/05	14.14	18 13	0.91	0.00	7.94
12/04	16.03	22 15	0.78	0.00	7.13
Annual Growth	(3.9%)	— —	5.6%	—	10.9%

Perrigo Company

Perrigo makes its name by making sure you never see it. One of the US's largest manufacturers of generic and private-label over-the-counter pharmaceuticals and supplements, Perrigo makes products that use similar packaging and discount pricing to compete with leading national brands. The company makes some 1,100 products, including pain relievers, cough and cold remedies, and nutritional supplements — some of which are sold under its own Good Sense brand. It also makes more than 250 generic prescription products for other companies. Its Active Pharmaceutical Ingredients (API) division manufactures the raw materials used by generic and branded pharmaceutical companies worldwide.

Perrigo's international consumer health care product subsidiaries Quimica y Farmacia (Mexico) and Wrafton (UK) offer over-the-counter and store-brand pharmaceutical products. Perrigo manufactures generic prescription drugs at facilities in the US and Israel, and subsidiary Chemagis makes APIs in Israel, Germany, and China.

To offset sales losses related to the limit on the production and sale of products containing pseudoephedrine, in 2007 Perrigo purchased Qualis Inc., manufacturer primarily of head lice treatment products. It also acquired nine generic dermatological products and four pipeline products from Stiefel Laboratories subsidiary Glades Pharmaceuticals. It added several smoking cessation products, including a nicotine gum meant to compete as a store brand with Glaxo-SmithKline's Nicorette.

In 2008 it bought UK company Galpharm Healthcare Ltd., a manufacturer of store brand products, broadening its UK presence. It also acquired US contract manufacturer JB Laboratories for $44 million and Mexican drugmaker Laboratorios Diba for $25 million to expand its manufacturing capacity. Later that year Perrigo snapped up Unico Holdings, a US maker of nutrition and hygiene products, for $49 million.

Perrigo's ongoing efforts to introduce a generic version of Mucinex (guaifenesin) have been stymied by Mucinex maker Adams Respiratory, which has filed a blizzard of patent infringement lawsuits seeking to protect its lucrative market niche.

Perrigo's clients include such retailers as Wal-Mart, CVS, and Walgreen and such wholesalers as SUPERVALU and McKesson. Wal-Mart is its largest customer, however, and accounts for more than 20% of sales. The company's consumer health care segment has its own sales force to work with its largest customers.

Vice Chairman Moshe Arkin owns about 10% of Perrigo, and director Michael Jandernoa holds a 3% stake.

HISTORY

Brothers Luther and Charles Perrigo moved from New York to Michigan in 1887 and opened a general store. Soon they began packaging home remedies. Charles left the company, but Luther continued, incorporating in 1892. Their family ran the business for most of the next century.

After WWII Perrigo began making drugs and personal products. In 1979 Michael Jandernoa became VP of finance for the firm, which by the next year led the store-brand products industry. In 1984 it bought Bell Pharmacal Labs.

Perrigo went public in 1986 as part of manufacturing conglomerate the Grow Group, then was bought by management in 1988 and taken public again in 1991. Perrigo built its own packaging and labeling plant in 1992.

After several years of growth, Perrigo slipped in 1995 and 1996, in part because of restructuring, ongoing lawsuits, and costs associated with its 1994 purchase of product lines and facilities from rival Vi-Jon Laboratories. But sales picked up with the launches of off-patent versions of popular brand-name drugs (such as Aleve and Rogaine).

In 1997, Perrigo bought 88% of Mexican drugmaker Quimica y Farmacia and took a stake in the largest drug distributor in Russia and Ukraine. The latter's failure (spurred by Russia's economic crisis) and slumping OTC drug sales walloped the company in 1998. Perrigo responded by restructuring and closing facilities to cut costs. It sold its personal care products line in 1999. The next year the company hired CEO David Gibbons, a 3M and Rubbermaid veteran known as a turnaround specialist.

Perrigo acquired Israeli pharmaceutical company Agis in 2005. The move expanded its reach into Israel and gave Perrigo a large foothold in the active pharmaceutical ingredients (APIs) market.

Perrigo took a big hit in late 2006, when more than 10 million packages of the company's acetaminophen were recalled from drug retailers across the US because the pills were found to contain metal fragments. Some of the packaged containers of 500-milligram tablets were distributed more than three years prior; more than 120 retail chains were affected.

That same year, prompted by concerns of misuse, Congress mandated a limit on the production and distribution of products containing the decongestant pseudoephedrine. Perrigo's sales of pseudoephedrine dropped more than two thirds in a two-year period, and the company scrambled (along with the entire industry) to reformulate its products with an alternative decongestant.

The company named Joseph Papa CEO in 2006; Gibbons remained as chairman until late 2007, when Papa became chairman as well.

EXECUTIVES

Chairman, President, and CEO: Joseph C. Papa, age 53
EVP and CFO: Judy L. Brown, age 40
SVP and CIO: Thomas M. (Tom) Farrington, age 51
EVP Global Operations and Supply Chain: John T. Hendrickson, age 45
EVP; President, Perrigo Israel: Refael Lebel, age 50
EVP U.S. Generics: Sharon Kochan, age 40
SVP Commercial Business Development: Jeffrey R. Needham, age 52
SVP Global Human Resources: Michael R. Stewart, age 56
SVP Consumer Healthcare Sales: James C. Tomshack, age 57
SVP Global Quality and Compliance: Louis W. Yu, age 58
VP Investor Relations and Communication: Arthur J. Shannon
EVP General Counsel and Secretary: Todd W. Kingma, age 48
Auditors: BDO Seidman, LLP

LOCATIONS

HQ: Perrigo Company
515 Eastern Ave., Allegan, MI 49010
Phone: 269-673-8451   **Fax:** 269-673-9128
Web: www.perrigo.com

2009 Sales

	$ mil.	% of total
US	1,607.3	80
Israel, UK & Mexico	399.6	20
Total	**2,006.9**	**100**

PRODUCTS/OPERATIONS

2009 Sales

	$ mil.	% of total
Consumer healthcare	1,638.8	82
Prescription pharmaceuticals	164.2	8
Pharmaceutical ingredients	136.0	7
Other	67.9	3
Total	**2,006.9**	**100**

Selected Products

Analgesics
Antacids
Cough/cold remedies
Diagnostic test kits
Feminine hygiene products
First aid
Laxatives
Nutritional drinks
Nutritional supplements
Sleep aids
Smoking cessation
Vitamins

COMPETITORS

Abbott Labs
AccuMed
Actavis
Apotex
Barr Pharmaceuticals
Bayer AG
Bristol-Myers Squibb
Caraco Pharmaceutical
Chattem
Dr. Reddy's
GlaxoSmithKline
Hi-Tech Pharmacal
Mylan
NBTY
Novartis
Nycomed US
Paddock Laboratories
Par Pharmaceutical Companies
Pfizer
Roxane Laboratories
Sandoz International GmbH
Schering-Plough
Stiefel Laboratories
Taro
Teva Pharmaceuticals
Watson Pharmaceuticals
Wyeth

HISTORICAL FINANCIALS

Company Type: Public

Income Statement

FYE: June 30

	REVENUE ($ mil.)	NET INCOME ($ mil.)	NET PROFIT MARGIN	EMPLOYEES
6/09	2,006.9	144.0	7.2%	7,250
6/08	1,822.1	135.8	7.5%	6,200
6/07	1,447.4	73.8	5.1%	6,200
6/06	1,366.8	71.4	5.2%	5,969
6/05	1,024.1	(353.0)	—	5,848
Annual Growth	18.3%	—	—	5.5%

2009 Year-End Financials

Debt ratio: 94.9%
Return on equity: 15.5%
Cash ($ mil.): 316
Current ratio: 2.30
Long-term debt ($ mil.): 875
No. of shares (mil.): 92
Dividends
  Yield: 0.8%
  Payout: 14.3%
Market value ($ mil.): 2,562

Stock History

NASDAQ (GS): PRGO

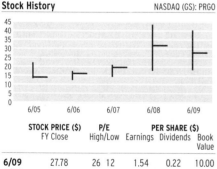

	STOCK PRICE ($) FY Close	P/E High/Low		PER SHARE ($) Earnings	Dividends	Book Value
6/09	27.78	26	12	1.54	0.22	10.00
6/08	31.77	30	13	1.43	0.19	10.12
6/07	19.58	26	19	0.79	0.18	8.18
6/06	16.10	23	17	0.76	0.17	6.95
6/05	13.94	—	—	(4.57)	0.16	6.41
Annual Growth	18.8%	—	—	—	8.3%	11.8%

Peter Kiewit Sons'

Peter Kiewit Sons' is a heavyweight in the heavy construction industry. The general contractor and its subsidiaries has a breadth of expertise, building everything from roads and dams to high-rise office towers and power plants throughout the US and Canada. Its transportation projects, which include bridges, rail lines, airport runways, and mass transit systems, account for a majority of its sales. Kiewit also serves the oil and gas, electrical, power, and waterworks industries. Public contracts, most of which are awarded by government agencies, are handled by its Kiewit Federal Group. The company, also an owner of coal mines, is owned by current and former employees and Kiewit family members.

As a leader in construction in the transportation sector, Kiewit is responsible for several notable highway and bridge projects, from replacing a segment of the San Francisco-Oakland Bay Bridge Skyway to upgrading the Sea-to-Sky Highway between Vancouver and Whistler, British Columbia. Water supply and dam projects include the Olivenhain and East dams in California, underground storage tanks for the Hollywood Hills Quality Improvement Project, and an intake valve at Lake Mead in Nevada.

Peter Kiewit Sons' also has steadily built its expertise working on environmentally sensitive projects in the power sector. Through its Kiewit Power Engineers Co., the company has been contracted by Plutonic Energy Corporation and GE Energy Financial Services to work on one of British Columbia's largest renewable energy projects, building six hydroelectric projects with intakes, penstocks, and a transmission line that will reduce dependence on non-renewable imported energy. The firm is working with the local Native American community, First Nations, creating jobs to help complete the project. Kiewit also has experience working on wind energy farms in Canada.

The company's mining operations (Kiewit Mining Group) include ownership of coal mines in Texas, Montana, and Wyoming and management of two additional mines, all of which are surface mines.

Subsidiary Kiewit Offshore Services fabricates complex offshore oil production platforms at a facility in Texas. Another subsidiary, Kiewit Energy Group, focuses on the petroleum refining business.

In 2008 the group acquired TIC Holdings, a heavy industrial construction and engineering firm based in Colorado. TIC, which operates through divisions including TIC Industrial and Western Summit Constructors, continues to operate as a standalone subsidiary. The deal put two of the largest North American construction companies under the same ownership.

HISTORY

Born to Dutch immigrants, Peter Kiewit and brother Andrew founded Kiewit Brothers, a brickyard, in 1884 in Omaha, Nebraska. By 1912 two of Peter's sons worked at the yard, which was named Peter Kiewit & Sons. When Peter Kiewit died in 1914, his son Ralph took over, and the firm took the name Peter Kiewit Sons'. Another son, Peter, joined Ralph at the helm in 1924 after dropping out of Dartmouth, and later took over.

During the Depression, Kiewit managed huge federal public works projects, and in the 1940s it focused on war-related emergency construction projects.

One of the company's most difficult projects was top-secret Thule Air Force Base in Greenland, above the Arctic Circle. For more than two years 5,000 men worked around the clock, beginning in 1951; the site was in development for 15 years. In 1952 the company won a contract to build a $1.2 billion gas diffusion plant in Portsmouth, Ohio. It also became a contractor for the US interstate highway system (begun in 1956).

Peter Kiewit died in 1979, after stipulating that the largely employee-owned company should remain under employee control and that no one employee could own more than 10%. His 40% stake, when returned to the company, transformed many employees into millionaires. Walter Scott Jr., whose father had been the first graduate engineer to work for Kiewit, took charge. Scott made his mark by parlaying money from construction into successful investments.

When the construction industry slumped, Kiewit began looking for other investment opportunities, and in 1984 it acquired packaging company Continental Can Co. (selling off noncore insurance, energy, and timber assets). Continental was saddled with a 1983 class action lawsuit alleging that it had plotted to close plants and lay off workers before they were qualified for pensions. In 1991 Kiewit agreed to pay $415 million to settle the lawsuit. In the face of a consolidating packaging industry, the company sold Continental in the early 1990s.

In 1986 Kiewit loaned money to a business group to build a fiber-optic loop in Chicago; by 1987 it had launched MFS Communications to build local fiber loops in downtown districts. In 1992 Kiewit split its business into two pieces: the construction group, which was strictly employee-owned; and a diversified group, to which it added a controlling stake in phone and cable TV company C-TEC in 1993. That year Kiewit took MFS public; by 1995 it had sold all its shares, and the next year MFS was bought by telecom giant WorldCom.

In 1996 Kiewit assisted CalEnergy (now MidAmerican Energy) in a hostile $1.3 billion takeover of the UK's Northern Electric. Kiewit got stock in CalEnergy and a 30% stake in the UK electric company, all of which it sold to CalEnergy in 1998.

That year Kiewit spun off its telecom and computer services holdings into Level 3 Communications. Scott, who had been hospitalized the year before for a blood clot in his lung, stepped down as CEO, and Ken Stinson, CEO of Kiewit Construction Group, took over Peter Kiewit Sons'.

Kiewit spun off its asphalt, concrete, and aggregates operations in 2000 as Kiewit Materials. Also that year it created Kiewit Offshore Services to focus on construction for the offshore drilling industry. Kiewit made history in 2002 for the fastest completion of a project of its type when it completed the rebuilding of Webbers Falls I-40 Bridge in Oklahoma at the end of July. (The bridge had collapsed in May after being hit by a pair of barges, resulting in 14 fatalities.)

In 2004 Kiewit greatly increased its coal sales and reserves with the acquisition of the Buckskin Mine in Wyoming from Arch Coal.

Also that year 22-year veteran Bruce Grewcock took the reins as the company's fourth CEO since its founding. Stinson stayed on as the company's chairman.

EXECUTIVES

Chairman: Kenneth E. (Ken) Stinson, age 66
Chairman Emeritus: J. Walter (Walter) Scott Jr., age 77
President and CEO: Bruce E. Grewcock, age 54
SVP and CFO: Michael J. Piechoski, age 53
EVP; EVP, Kiewit Corporation and Kiewit Pacific Co.:
Richard W. Colf, age 64
EVP: Douglas E. Patterson, age 56
EVP and Division Manager; EVP, Kiewit Corporation and Kiewit Construction; President, Gilbert Industrial Corp.: Scott L. Cassels, age 49
EVP and Division Manager and Director; EVP, Kiewit Corporation, Kiewit Construction, Kiewit Pacific Co., and Kiewit Western Co.: R. Michael Phelps, age 54
SVP, General Counsel, and Secretary: Tobin A. Schropp, age 45
SVP and Hawaii Area Manager, Kiewit Building Group; VP Kiewit Pacific: Lance K. Wilhelm
VP and Treasurer: Ben E. Muraskin, age 43
Division Manager, VP, and Director; SVP, Kiewit Corporation; President, Kiewit Mining Group:
Christopher J. Murphy, age 53
VP Human Resources and Administration:
Michael Gary
Division Manager and Director; SVP, Kiewit Corporation and Kiewit Construction; President, Kiewit Energy Group: Thomas S. Shelby, age 49
CEO, Kiewit Federal Group: Kirk R. Samuelson, age 50
President, Kiewit Engineering Co. (KECo):
Gary Pietrok
Controller and Assistant Secretary; VP and Controller, Kiewit Corporation: Michael J. Whetstine, age 41
Auditors: KPMG LLP

LOCATIONS

HQ: Peter Kiewit Sons', Inc.
Kiewit Plaza, 3555 Farnam St., Omaha, NE 68131
Phone: 402-342-2052   **Fax:** 402-271-2939
Web: www.kiewit.com

PRODUCTS/OPERATIONS

Selected Subsidiaries and Affiliates

Ben Holt Company
Bighorn Walnut, LLC
Buckskin Mining Company
CMF Leasing Co.
Continental Alarm & Detection Company
Continental Fire Sprinkler Company
General Construction Company
Gilbert Central Corp.
Gilbert Industrial Corporation
Gilbert Network Services, L.P.
Gilbert/Healy, L.P.
Global Surety & Insurance Co.
GSC Atlanta, Inc.
GSC Contracting, Inc.
Guernsey Construction Company
KES Inc.
KiEnergy, Inc.
Kiewit Power Engineers (formerly Bibb and Associates)
KT Developers, LLC
KT Mining Inc.
Lac De Gras Excavation Inc.
Mass. Electric Construction Canada Co.
Mass. Electric Construction Co.
Mass. Electric Construction Venezuela, S.A.
Mass. Electric International, Inc.
MECC Rail Mexicana, S.A. de C.V.
Midwest Agencies, Inc.
Mission Materials Company
Seaworks, Inc.
Servitec de Sonora, S.A. de C.V.
TIC Holdings, Inc.
Twin Mountain Construction II Company
V. K. Mason Construction Co.
Walnut Creek Mining Company

COMPETITORS

ABB
Ames Construction
Balfour Beatty Infrastructure
Bechtel
Black & Veatch
Bovis Lend Lease
CH2M HILL
Fluor
Foster Wheeler
Granite Construction
Halliburton
Hubbard Group
Jacobs Engineering

KBR
Lane Construction
Parsons Corporation
Raytheon
Rio Tinto plc
Skanska USA Civil
Turner Corporation
Tutor Perini
Tutor-Saliba
Walsh Group
Washington Division
Whiting-Turner
Williams Companies

HISTORICAL FINANCIALS

Company Type: Private

Income Statement

FYE: Last Saturday in December

	REVENUE ($ mil.)	NET INCOME ($ mil.)	NET PROFIT MARGIN	EMPLOYEES
12/08	8,000.0	—	—	15,000
12/07	6,200.0	—	—	15,000
12/06	5,049.0	—	—	14,700
12/05	4,145.0	—	—	14,500
12/04	3,352.0	—	—	14,000
Annual Growth	24.3%	—	—	1.7%

Revenue History

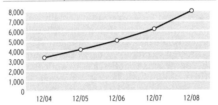

PetSmart, Inc.

PetSmart is the top dog and the cat's meow in its industry. The #1 US specialty retailer of pet food and supplies has more than 1,100 stores in the US and Canada. Both pets and their masters may lay paws, claws, or hands on its 10,000 products, which range from scratching posts to iguana harnesses, and are sold under national brands and PetSmart's own private labels. The retailer offers products through its PetSmart Web site. PetSmart stores also provide in-store boarding facilities, grooming services, and obedience training. Veterinary services are available in some 700 shops through pet hospital operator Medical Management International (known as Banfield).

PetSmart owns about 40% of Banfield's parent company, MMI Holdings, Inc.

While most of PetSmart's sales come from pet food and supplies, the service side (grooming, pet training, boarding, and day camp) of its business has been growing. The company operates about 140 in-store PetsHotel boarding facilities and Doggie Day Camps. The company plans to build out more than 400 PetsHotels.

As the pet products firm chases after the more profitable services business, PetSmart sold its State Line Tack subsidiary — exiting the equine niche altogether — to Web-based retailer PetsUnited. State Line Tack joins existing PetsUnited entities dog.com, fish.com, and horse.com. As part of the 2007 agreement, PetsUnited moved State Line Tack's Brockport, New York-based business, which consists of an online and catalog component, to its Hazleton, Pennsylvania, facility.

In 2008 PetSmart suspended sales of birds in its stores nationwide after discovering that birds with the bacterial infection psittacosis could spread the disease to humans. The company still sells fish, reptiles, and other small animals. To encourage adoption of dogs and cats, PetSmart sponsors in-store adoption programs with local humane organizations.

Ultimately the company thinks there is room for at least 1,400 of its stores throughout North America. Robert Moran, formerly president and COO of the company, was promoted to CEO in mid-2009. He retained the title of president. Phil Francis, who led the company for more than a decade, was named executive chairman.

The company was affected in 2007 by a recall of pet foods made by Menu Foods, a manufacturer whose products contained a wheat gluten that had been contaminated with the chemical melamine. The affected foods were linked to pet illnesses and deaths across the country. PetSmart has been named in several lawsuits for distributing the tainted product.

HISTORY

In the mid-1980s the owner of a California pet supply wholesaler had an idea: If the company opened its own retail stores, it could make a bundle supplying itself. Not wanting to compete with its own retail customers in California, the company hired Jim and Janice Dougherty to run the first store in Las Vegas, called Pet Food Supermarket. In response to customer requests, the store began offering a broader range of products and soon business was booming. The store moved to a larger location, and four more stores were eventually opened in Phoenix.

While managing the Pet Food Supermarkets, the Doughertys met Ford Smith, a retailer who had developed a plan for giant pet-supply stores while in business school. Together they agreed to give the Toys "R" Us superstore format a try for pet supplies. They opened two PetFood Warehouse stores in Arizona in 1987. The next year there were seven stores in Arizona, Colorado, and Texas.

In 1989 PetFood Warehouse officially became PETsMART, Jim left the company due to health reasons (Janice followed shortly thereafter), and supermarket executive Sam Parker came on as CEO. His management team recrafted the PETsMART business strategy and gave the store a new look: brightly lit, low shelves with various pet supplies in the front of the store, and high warehouse-style shelves with bulk pet food in the back.

The 1990s saw PETsMART adding services such as in-store grooming, obedience training, veterinary exams, and adoption programs; it also began selling birds and fish. In 1991 the company added 15 new stores. The following year 32 stores were opened.

PETsMART went public in 1993. The company added more than 40 stores that year. In 1994 PETsMART bought the Weisheimer Companies, which operated about 30 pet superstores in the Midwest under the name Petzazz.

A year later the company went on an acquisition spree, buying two pet superstore operators (56-store, Georgia-based Petstuff and 10-store, New Jersey-based Pet Food Giant) and two specialty-catalog retailers of pet and animal supplies. Some 80 stores were added in 1995, and Mark Hansen replaced Parker as CEO; Parker remained chairman.

Hansen took PETsMART overseas in 1996 through the acquisition of Pet City Holdings, which operated more than 50 stores in the UK. The company also entered Canada that year. But the aggressive expansion campaign diverted the company's attention from daily operations and inventory management, eroding PETsMART's earnings in fiscal year 1998. In response, the company instituted a back-to-basics strategy of improved customer service and lower prices. Phil Francis, formerly with Shaw's Supermarkets, became CEO in 1998.

In 1999 PETsMART launched PETsMART.com in conjunction with PetJungle.com, an online pet retailer backed by Internet incubator idealab!. The move intensified a catfight with several lavishly funded online pet supply stores, including now-defunct Pets.com, which was backed by dominant e-tailer Amazon.com. Soon thereafter, the company bought AcmePet.com, an online community oriented to pets.

The company sold its 92 UK stores to Pets At Home in late 1999. The company acquired PETsMART.com's remaining shares in 2002. Carrefour sold its 9.9% stake in PETsMART for $194 million through a public offering that year.

In 2003 PETsMART finished remodeling its stores; the company replaced the traditional warehouse feel with a specialty-store shopping atmosphere. The company added 100 new stores in 2005. In line with those changes, in 2006, PETsMART changed how its name is styled to PetSmart, with the emphasis on "smart" rather than "mart."

In 2007 PetSmart boosted its Canadian presence with the acquisition of 19 stores from the Super Pet chain. It exited the equine products business in May 2007 when it sold State Line Tack to PetsUnited.

EXECUTIVES

Chairman: Philip L. (Phil) Francis, age 61, $3,569,635 total compensation
President and CEO: Robert F. (Bob) Moran, age 58, $2,513,585 total compensation
SVP and CFO: Lawrence (Chip) Molloy, age 47, $909,058 total compensation
SVP and CIO: Donald E. (Don) Beaver, age 50
SVP and Chief Marketing Officer: Mary L. Miller, age 48
SVP People: Francesca M. Spinelli, age 55
SVP Store Operations and Human Resources: David K. Lenhardt, age 39, $1,283,504 total compensation
SVP Merchandising and Supply Chain: Joseph D. (Joe) O'Leary, age 50, $1,311,682 total compensation
SVP: Kenneth T. (Ken) Hall, age 40
SVP, General Counsel, and Secretary: Emily D. Dickinson
SVP Real Estate and Development: Jaye D. Perricone, age 50
SVP Human Resources: Neil H. Stacey
Director External Communications: Bruce Richardson
Director Corporate Planning: Christina Vance
Auditors: Deloitte & Touche LLP

LOCATIONS

HQ: PetSmart, Inc.
19601 N. 27th Ave., Phoenix, AZ 85027
Phone: 623-580-6100   **Fax:** 623-580-6183
Web: www.petsmart.com

2009 Stores

	No.
US	1,051
Canada	61
Total	**1,112**

PRODUCTS/OPERATIONS

2009 Sales

	$ mil.	% of total
Merchandise	4,538.6	90
Pet services	526.7	10
Total	**5,065.3**	**100**

Selected Merchandise

Animal carriers	Health aids
Aquariums	Leashes
Bedding	Litter
Bird cages	Magazines
Books	Medications
Cat furniture	Pet food
Collars	Reptiles
Dog houses	Shampoos
Freshwater tropical fish	Toys
Greeting cards	Treats

Selected Services

Boarding
Doggie day camp
Grooming
Obedience training
Veterinary services

Private Labels

Pet Food
  Authority (cat and dog food, treats)
  Grreat Choice (dog treats)
  SophistaCat (cat food)
Pet Supplies
  Top Fin
  Top Paw
  Top Wing

COMPETITORS

Ahold USA	PETCO
Albertsons	Petland
Costco Wholesale	PetMed
Drs. Foster & Smith	Sears Holdings
Fat Cat	Target
J and J Dog Supplies	United Pharmacal
Pet Supermarket	VCA Antech
Pet Valu	Wal-Mart
PetCareRx	Weis Markets

HISTORICAL FINANCIALS

Company Type: Public

Income Statement				FYE: Sunday nearest January 31
	REVENUE ($ mil.)	NET INCOME ($ mil.)	NET PROFIT MARGIN	EMPLOYEES
1/09	5,065.3	192.7	3.8%	46,000
1/08	4,672.7	258.7	5.5%	43,000
1/07	4,233.9	185.1	4.4%	38,400
1/06	3,760.5	182.5	4.9%	34,600
1/05	3,363.5	171.2	5.1%	30,300
Annual Growth	**10.8%**	**3.0%**	**—**	**11.0%**

2009 Year-End Financials

Debt ratio: 48.4%
Return on equity: 18.1%
Cash ($ mil.): 126
Current ratio: 1.83
Long-term debt ($ mil.): 554
No. of shares (mil.): 125
Dividends
  Yield: 0.6%
  Payout: 7.9%
Market value ($ mil.): 2,347

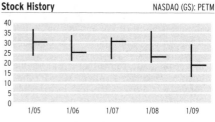

Stock History   NASDAQ (GS): PETM

	STOCK PRICE ($) FY Close	P/E High/Low		PER SHARE ($) Earnings	Dividends	Book Value
1/09	18.77	19	9	1.52	0.12	9.15
1/08	22.87	18	10	1.95	0.12	7.89
1/07	30.54	24	17	1.33	0.12	8.01
1/06	25.06	27	17	1.25	0.12	7.52
1/05	30.23	32	21	1.14	0.12	7.61
Annual Growth	**(11.2%)**	**—**	**—**	**7.5%**	**0.0%**	**4.7%**

Pfizer Inc.

Pfizer pfabricates pfarmaceuticals pfor quite a pfew inpfirmities. The company is the world's largest research-based pharmaceuticals firm. Its best-known products include erectile dysfunction therapy Viagra, pain management drug Celebrex, high-blood-pressure therapy Norvasc, and cholesterol-lowering Lipitor. Pfizer also keeps Fluffy and Fido in mind with its animal health products, including Revolution (antiparasitic). In 2009 Pfizer agreed to acquire pharma rival Wyeth in a $68 billion deal.

The agreement is designed to help both companies deal with upcoming patent losses on top-selling drugs and will broaden Pfizer's traditional and biological product offerings in areas including vaccines, antibiotics, women's health, inflammatory and cardiovascular conditions, and gastroenterology. The combined company will also have an expanded development pipeline for targets including Alzheimer's disease, cancer, pain, and psychosis.

The company launched a 10% workforce reduction to prepare for the transaction, and it estimates that the Wyeth merger will result in an overall 15% reduction of the combined workforce. The acquisition of Wyeth will also expand Pfizer's animal health business, and it will bring Pfizer back into the consumer health arena, adding products such as Advil and Robitussin. Pfizer sold its consumer unit — which made such sniffle-and-sneeze treatments as Benadryl and Sudafed — to Johnson & Johnson in 2006.

Pfizer had four drugs topping $2 billion in sales in 2008: Lipitor, Norvasc, Celebrex, and pain medication Lyrica. Five more drugs pulled in over $1 billion, including Viagra. However, Pfizer's revenues from these established blockbusters continue to slide due to one of the pitfalls of the drug game: patent expiration. Bestsellers Norvasc and antidepressant Zoloft lost patent protection in 2007, and former best-selling allergy medication Zyrtec (which the company has since divested) faced generic competition starting in 2008.

The company's largest patent threat has been over cash cow Lipitor, the world's top-selling drug, which has over $12 billion in annual sales. Pfizer reached a settlement agreement with the generics maker Ranbaxy in 2008 allowing it to sell a generic Lipitor version in the US after November 30, 2011.

The drug giant claims that it will be able to launch new blockbusters to make up for the off-patent losses. Pfizer's pipeline includes about 100 projects in development, including drugs for diabetes, breast cancer, epilepsy, pain, and anxiety disorders. Products launched in 2007 and 2008 include AIDS drug Selzentry, smoking-cessation aid Chantix, and overactive-bladder treatment Toviaz.

Pfizer purchased Coley Pharmaceutical in 2008 to gain access to Coley's vaccine-facilitating technology. Pfizer also expanded through acquisitions in key growth areas including oncology (Serenex), cardiovascular therapies (Encysive Pharmaceuticals), and animal health (Embrex and several of Schering-Plough's European products).

CEO Jeffrey Kindler took the reins in 2006 and began a major program to tighten the company financially and operationally. It was launched in early 2007; about 12% of the company's workforce was eliminated that year.

During 2008 Kindler outlined a strategy to increase the number of drug candidates in late-stage trials in select targeted areas such as oncology, pain, and biotechnology. As a result, the company cut some early-stage development projects and reduced the overall number of drug candidates by nearly half. Kindler also stated that the company would continue to consolidate manufacturing facilities and expand its Asian operations. Pfizer aims to reduce costs by another $3 billion by the end of 2010.

Pfizer took a financial hit, however, in 2009 when it agreed to pay $2.3 billion to settle allegations that it improperly marketed several drugs, including discontinued painkiller Bextra. In a recent crackdown effort against pharmaceutical marketing fraud (promoting drugs for unapproved uses), the federal government has reached several settlement agreements with large pharmaceutical companies (including smaller deals with Pfizer); however, Pfizer's 2009 settlement was the largest to date.

HISTORY

Charles Pfizer and his cousin, confectioner Charles Erhart, began making chemicals in Brooklyn in 1849. Products included camphor, citric acid, and santonin (an early antiparasitic). The company, incorporated in 1900 as Chas. Pfizer & Co., was propelled into the modern drug business when it was asked to mass-produce penicillin for the war effort in 1941.

Pfizer discovered Terramycin and introduced it in 1950. Three years later it bought drugmaker Roerig, its first major acquisition. In the 1950s the company opened branches in Belgium, Canada, Cuba, Mexico, and the UK and began manufacturing in Asia, Europe, and South America. By the mid-1960s Pfizer had worldwide sales of more than $200 million.

Beginning in the late 1950s, Pfizer made Salk and Sabin polio vaccines and added new drugs, such as Diabinese (antidiabetic, 1958) and Vibramycin (antibiotic, 1967). It moved into consumer products in the early 1960s, buying

BenGay, Desitin, and cosmetics maker Coty (sold 1992). It bought hospital products company Howmedica in 1972 (sold 1998) and heart-valve maker Shiley in 1979.

When growth slowed in the 1970s, new chairman Edmund Pratt increased R&D expenditures, resulting in Minipress (antihypertensive, 1975), Feldene (arthritis pain reliever, 1980), and Glucotrol (antidiabetic, 1984). Licensing agreements with foreign companies let Pfizer sell antihypertensive Procardia XL and antibiotic Cefobid. In the 1980s Pfizer expanded its hospital products division, buying 18 product lines and companies.

Lawsuits over the failure of about 500 heart valves and the alleged falsification of records led Pfizer to divest most of Shiley's operations in 1992. Drugs released that year included antidepressant Zoloft, antibiotic Zithromax, and cardiovascular agent Norvasc.

In 1997 Pfizer began promoting Lipitor, the cholesterol-lowering drug discovered by Warner-Lambert; it grabbed nearly 13% of the market in its first four months. Pfizer made headlines (and lots of happy men) when the company won FDA approval for Viagra in 1998. The little blue pill became a pop icon, and made the company a household name.

When Warner-Lambert said in 1999 that it would merge with American Home Products (now Wyeth), Pfizer sued to prevent the union and eventually succeeded with its own hostile bid. The merger with Warner-Lambert was completed, and CEO William Steere retired.

In 2003 Pfizer purchased rival Pharmacia for $54 billion, making it the world's largest research-based pharmaceutical company. Following its two giant acquisitions, the company trimmed some 20,000 people.

While acquiring new holdings on the pharmaceutical front, the company trimmed its non-pharmaceutical businesses between 2003 and 2005, including operations it acquired with Pharmacia and its European generics portfolio.

Pfizer sold its consumer unit to Johnson & Johnson in 2006, including such brands as Benadryl, Listerine, Nicorette, Rolaids, and Sudafed, for $16.6 billion.

As part of its ongoing acquisition strategy, Pfizer bought biotech firm Rinat Neuroscience, which was developing drugs for pain, Alzheimer's disease, and other neurological disorders, in 2006.

Pfizer's board dismissed Hank McKinnell as its CEO in 2006, replacing him with company general counsel, Jeffrey Kindler.

EXECUTIVES

Chairman and CEO: Jeffrey B. (Jeff) Kindler, age 53, $13,102,886 total compensation
Chairman Emeritus: William C. Steere Jr., age 72
Chairman Emeritus: M. Anthony Burns, age 66
CFO: Frank A. D'Amelio, age 51, $5,978,830 total compensation
SVP Worldwide Communications and Chief Communications Officer: Sally Susman, age 47
SVP and Chief Medical Officer: Joseph M. (Joe) Feczko, age 59
VP and Chief Talent Officer: Tanya Clemons
Chief Scientific Officer, Vaccine Research: Emilio A. Emini, age 55
SVP and Chief Medical Officer: Freda C. Lewis-Hall, age 53
Chief Scientific Officer, Neuroscience Research: Menelas Pangalos

SVP Global Research and Development; Site Director, La Jolla and Leader, External Research Network, Western US: Catherine J. (Kitty) Mackey
SVP, Philanthropy/Stakeholder Advocacy: Robert L. Mallett
SVP Strategy and Business Development: William R. (Bill) Ringo Jr., age 63
SVP; President, Pfizer Global Manufacturing: Natale S. (Nat) Ricciardi, age 60
SVP Human Resources: Mary S. McLeod, age 52
SVP; President, Worldwide Pharmaceutical Operations: Ian C. Read, age 55, $6,046,820 total compensation
SVP Worldwide Business Development: Edmund P. (Ed) Harrigan
SVP; Head of Worldwide Public Affairs and Policy: Richard H. (Rich) Bagger, age 48
SVP Investor Relations: Charles E. (Chuck) Triano
SVP; President, Global Research and Development: Martin Mackay, age 53, $5,173,091 total compensation
SVP, Marketing: Marie-Caroline Sainpy
SVP and General Counsel: Amy Schulman, age 48
Auditors: KPMG LLP

LOCATIONS

HQ: Pfizer Inc.
235 E. 42nd St., New York, NY 10017
Phone: 212-733-2323
Web: www.pfizer.com

2008 Sales

	$ mil.	% of total
US	20,435	42
Europe	14,980	31
Japan & Asia	7,166	15
Canada, Latin America, Africa & Middle East	5,715	12
Total	**48,296**	**100**

PRODUCTS/OPERATIONS

2008 Sales

	$ mil.	% of total
Pharmaceuticals		
Cardiovascular & metabolic		
Lipitor	12,401	26
Norvasc	2,244	4
Chantix/Champix	846	2
Caduet	589	1
Cardura	499	1
Other	1,343	3
CNS		
Lyrica	2,573	5
Geodon/Zeldox	1,007	2
Zoloft	539	1
Aricept	482	1
Neurontin	387	1
Xanax/Xanax XR	350	1
Other	667	1
Infectious & respiratory		
Zyvox	1,115	2
Vfend	743	1
Zithromax/Zmax	429	1
Diflucan	373	1
Other	1,271	3
Urology		
Viagra	1,934	4
Detrol/Detrol LA	1,214	3
Other	56	—
Arthritis & pain		
Celebrex	2,489	5
Other	607	1
Other pharmaceuticals	7.765	15
Alliance revenues	2,251	5
Animal health	2,825	6
Corporate & other	1,297	3
Total	**48,296**	**100**

Selected Products

Pharmaceuticals
- Aricept (Alzheimer's disease)
- Aromasin (breast cancer)
- Caduet (high cholesterol and blood pressure dual therapy)
- Camptosar (colorectal cancer)
- Cardura (hypertension and enlarged prostate disease)
- Celebrex (arthritis pain)
- Chantix/Champix (smoking cessation)
- Detrol (overactive bladder)
- Diflucan (antifungal)
- Genotropin (growth hormone deficiency)
- Geodon (sciczophrenia, Zeldox outside of the US)
- Lipitor (cholesterol)
- Lyrica (nerve pain)
- Neurontin (epilepsy)
- Norvasc (hypertension)
- Rebif (multiple sclerosis)
- Relpax (migraines)
- Selzentry (HIV)
- Spiriva (chronic obstructive pulmonary disease)
- Sutent (carcinoma and tumors)
- Vfend (fungal infections)
- Viagra (impotence)
- Xalatan/Xalacom (glaucoma)
- Xanax (anti-anxiety treatment)
- Zithromax/Zmax (antibiotic)
- Zoloft (depression)
- Zyvox (antibiotic)

Animal Health
- BoviShield (vaccine for cattle respiratory disease)
- Clavamox/Synulox (canine and feline antibiotics)
- Dectomax (livestock anti-infective)
- Gletvax (swine E. coli vaccines)
- Naxcel/Excenel (antibiotic)
- Rabdomun (Rabies vaccine)
- Revolution (antiparasitic for dogs and cats)
- Rimadyl (canine osteoarthritis treatment)

COMPETITORS

Abbott Labs	Meda Pharmaceuticals
Amgen	Merck
Apotex	Novartis
AstraZeneca	Novo Nordisk
Bayer AG	Procter & Gamble
Biogen Idec	Ranbaxy Laboratories
Bristol-Myers Squibb	Repros Therapeutics
Eli Lilly	Roche Holding
Forest Labs	Sanofi-Aventis
Genentech	Schering-Plough
Genzyme	Sun Pharmaceutical
GlaxoSmithKline	Teva Pharmaceuticals
Johnson & Johnson	

HISTORICAL FINANCIALS

Company Type: Public

Income Statement

FYE: December 31

	REVENUE ($ mil.)	NET INCOME ($ mil.)	NET PROFIT MARGIN	EMPLOYEES
12/08	48,296.0	8,104.0	16.8%	81,800
12/07	48,418.0	8,144.0	16.8%	86,600
12/06	48,371.0	19,337.0	40.0%	98,000
12/05	51,298.0	8,110.0	15.8%	106,000
12/04	52,516.0	11,361.0	21.6%	115,000
Annual Growth	(2.1%)	(8.1%)	—	(8.2%)

2008 Year-End Financials

Debt ratio: 25.3%	No. of shares (mil.): 6,749
Return on equity: 13.2%	Dividends
Cash ($ mil.): 2,122	Yield: 7.2%
Current ratio: 1.59	Payout: 106.7%
Long-term debt ($ mil.): 14,531	Market value ($ mil.): 119,527

Stock History

NYSE: PFE

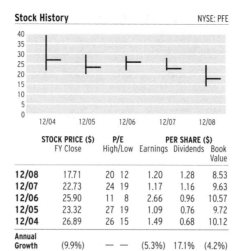

	STOCK PRICE ($) FY Close	P/E High/Low		PER SHARE ($) Earnings	Dividends	Book Value
12/08	17.71	20	12	1.20	1.28	8.53
12/07	22.73	24	19	1.17	1.16	9.63
12/06	25.90	11	8	2.66	0.96	10.57
12/05	23.32	27	19	1.09	0.76	9.72
12/04	26.89	26	15	1.49	0.68	10.12
Annual Growth	(9.9%)	—	—	(5.3%)	17.1%	(4.2%)

PG&E Corporation

Utility holding company PG&E Corporation is still recharging its batteries after losing power and declaring bankruptcy following California's energy crisis and the ensuing collapse of the wholesale energy trading industry. Its Pacific Gas and Electric utility serves approximately 5.1 million electric customers and 4.3 million natural gas customers in California. The utility (which was founded in 1905) is also engaged in electricity generation; procurement and transmission; and natural gas procurement, transportation and storage.

To help comply with the State of California's long term carbon emission requirements, PG&E is pushing energy efficiency (both at its plants and its customers' facilities), but it is also breaking new ground. In 2008 it announced a 15-year purchase agreement with Canada's Finavera Renewables to use wave power captured off the Northern California coastline. PG&E is the first US utility company that has committed to purchasing wave-generated power. It is expected to be attached to the power grid by 2010.

PG&E emerged from Chapter 11 in 2004 after reaching agreement with the California Public Utilities Commission (CPUC) in a dispute over the two entities' opposing reorganization plans. PG&E's original plan would have split the utility into several companies. The agreed-upon plan, which won bankruptcy court approval, left the utility intact under the CPUC's jurisdiction.

HISTORY

Peter Donahue founded the first gas company in the western US, San Francisco Gas, in 1852, which merged with Edison Light & Power to become San Francisco Gas & Electric (SFG&E) in 1896. Meanwhile, also in San Francisco, money broker George Roe and other investors founded California Electric Light (1879). The first electric utility in the US, it predated Edison's New York Pearl Street Station by three years. California Electric and SFG&E consolidated in 1905 to form Pacific Gas and Electric (PG&E).

In 1928 PG&E discovered natural gas in California, and in 1930 it began converting more

than 2.5 million appliances to burn this fuel. The company started exploring for out-of-state gas supplies in the 1950s, first in Texas and New Mexico and then in western Canada.

The utility opened the world's first private atomic power plant (Vallecitos) in 1957, and in 1960 it developed the first geothermal plant (The Geysers) in North America. Its Humboldt Bay facility (completed 1963) was one of the first nukes to produce electricity at a cost comparable to that of conventional plants. Stanley Skinner began his 33-year career at PG&E in 1964 (he became CEO in 1995).

By the late 1970s PG&E had acquired some 500 electric, gas, and water utilities, but it left the water business in the 1980s. That year Unit 1 of the Diablo Canyon nuclear facility went on line, despite protests over its earthquake-fault location. Unit 2 was operating by 1986. PG&E fell on hard times in the mid-1980s as industrial customers began to generate their own electricity or buy gas directly from suppliers. In response, PG&E cut 2,500 jobs in 1987 and formed an independent power producer, which became U.S. Generating, with construction giant Bechtel. In 1995, as deregulation accelerated in California, the company formed an energy services division to serve large customers.

In 1996 PG&E was hit by an outage originating in the Pacific Northwest that affected nine western states and raised doubts over the power grid's stability. That year PG&E's gas unit bought a pipeline in Australia.

PG&E Corporation was formed as a holding company in 1997, and utility Pacific Gas and Electric became a subsidiary. The company also bought Bechtel's 50% stake in U.S. Generating. That year Skinner retired and president Robert Glynn became CEO. PG&E also settled a lawsuit filed in 1993 that claimed it had polluted groundwater by discharging toxic wastewater. (The case was the subject of a movie, *Erin Brockovich*, released in 2000.)

As its home state deregulated in 1998, PG&E was required to sell off most of its California power plants. The company auctioned off some of its hydro plants, and Duke Energy picked up three of the utility's fossil-fuel plants in California and its Australian pipeline. (The divestiture requirement was reversed by regulatory agencies in 2000.) PG&E also bought 18 power plants (4,800 MW) from New England Electric System.

In 1999 the company sold its Texas gas operations to El Paso Corporation, agreed to sell most of its retail marketing arm (PG&E Services) to Enron, and moved the headquarters of its nonregulated operations (PG&E National Energy Group) to Bethesda, Maryland. PG&E suffered a loss that fiscal year.

A price squeeze brought on in part by deregulation battered Pacific Gas and Electric in 2000. Prices on the wholesale power market soared, but a California rate freeze prevented the utility from passing along increasing costs to customers. In 2001 it suspended payments to creditors and suppliers to conserve cash, but gained some prospect of relief when California's governor signed legislation to allow a state agency to buy power from wholesalers under long-term contracts. Also that year PG&E sold its nonregulated energy services unit and its natural gas liquids businesses.

Later in 2001 the California Public Utilities Commission (CPUC) approved a significant increase in retail electricity rates, and the Federal Energy Regulatory Commission (FERC) approved a plan to limit wholesale energy prices during periods of severe shortage in 11 western states. The moves didn't come quickly enough for Pacific Gas and Electric, which filed for bankruptcy protection. The unit completed its reorganization in 2004.

Poor conditions in the wholesale power market drove PG&E National Energy Group into bankruptcy in 2003; the unit changed its name to National Energy & Gas Transmission shortly after to signify separation from PG&E following its emergence from bankruptcy.

EXECUTIVES

Chairman, President, and CEO: Peter A. Darbee, age 56, $13,371,479 total compensation
SVP, CFO, and Chief Risk and Audit Officer: Kent M. Harvey, age 51
SVP and CIO: Patricia M. (Pat) Lawicki, age 48
SVP Corporate Relations: Greg S. Pruett, age 51
SVP and General Counsel: Hyun Park, age 47, $2,437,158 total compensation
SVP and COO, Pacific Gas and Electric Company: John S. (Jack) Keenan, age 60, $1,911,443 total compensation
SVP Energy Procurement: Fong Wan, age 47
SVP Public Affairs and SVP Public Affairs, Pacific Gas and Electric Company: Nancy E. McFadden, age 50
SVP Corporate Strategy and Development: Rand L. Rosenberg, age 55, $2,158,908 total compensation
SVP Human Resources; SVP Human Resources, Pacific Gas and Electric Company: John R. Simon, age 44
VP Corporate Environmental and Federal Affairs: Steven L. Kline, age 54
VP Investor Relations: Gabriel B. Togneri, age 53
VP Corporate Governance and Corporate Secretary: Linda Y. H. Cheng, age 49
President, Pacific Gas and Electric Company: Christopher P. (Chris) Johns, age 48, $2,353,076 total compensation
Treasurer: Nicholas Bijur
Auditors: Deloitte & Touche LLP

LOCATIONS

HQ: PG&E Corporation
1 Market Spear Tower, Ste. 2400
San Francisco, CA 94105
Phone: 415-267-7000   **Fax:** 415-267-7268
Web: www.pgecorp.com

PRODUCTS/OPERATIONS

2008 Sales

	$ mil.	% of total
Electric	10,738	73
Natural gas	3,890	27
Total	**14,628**	**100**

COMPETITORS

AEP	Northern California Power
AES	NV Energy
Avista	PacifiCorp
Calpine	RRI Energy
Constellation Energy	Sacramento Municipal
Duke Energy	Utility
Edison International	Sempra Energy
Entergy	Southern Company
Exelon	SUEZ-TRACTEBEL
FirstEnergy	Turlock Irrigation District
Mirant	Western Area Power
Modesto Irrigation District	Administration
North Baja Pipeline	

HISTORICAL FINANCIALS

Company Type: Public

Income Statement

FYE: December 31

	REVENUE ($ mil.)	NET INCOME ($ mil.)	NET PROFIT MARGIN	EMPLOYEES
12/08	14,628.0	1,338.0	9.1%	14,649
12/07	13,237.0	1,006.0	7.6%	20,050
12/06	12,539.0	991.0	7.9%	20,400
12/05	11,703.0	917.0	7.8%	19,800
12/04	11,080.0	4,504.0	40.6%	20,200
Annual Growth	**7.2%**	**(26.2%)**	**—**	**(7.7%)**

2008 Year-End Financials

Debt ratio: 112.3%
Return on equity: 14.9%
Cash ($ mil.): 219
Current ratio: 0.84
Long-term debt ($ mil.): 10,534

No. of shares (mil.): 371
Dividends
Yield: 4.0%
Payout: 43.0%
Market value ($ mil.): 14,349

Stock History

NYSE: PCG

	STOCK PRICE ($) FY Close	P/E High/Low		PER SHARE ($) Earnings	Dividends	Book Value
12/08	38.71	13	7	3.63	1.56	25.30
12/07	43.09	19	15	2.78	1.44	23.07
12/06	47.33	17	13	2.76	1.32	21.07
12/05	37.12	17	13	2.37	1.23	19.47
12/04	33.28	3	2	10.57	0.00	24.06
Annual Growth	**3.9%**	**—**	**—**	**(23.4%)**	**—**	**1.3%**

Phillips-Van Heusen

Phillips-Van Heusen (PVH) has the buttoned-down look all sewn up. The top US dress shirt maker sells clothes, sunglasses, and shoes for men, women, and children under its own brands, such as Calvin Klein, Van Heusen, IZOD, Bass, and ARROW, as well as under licensed names the likes of Geoffrey Beene, BCBG Max Azria, CHAPS, Sean John, DKNY, Nautica, and Tommy Hilfiger, and under private labels. PVH distributes its products to department stores, including Macy's, Kohl's, JCPenney, Stage Stores, Wal-Mart, and other wholesale clients. The company also peddles its products through some 650 outlet stores located mostly in US open-air malls and operated under brand-name banners.

PVH's primary strategy is to grow its Calvin Klein brands globally. To give it greater control, PVH in 2008 acquired CMI, the licensee of the high-end collection of apparel and accessories for men and women. The company's also opening stores in China, Southeast Asia, Japan, Europe, and the Middle East under the ck Calvin Klein banner. It operates more than 60 free-standing stores in those regions, with some 30 more expected to be opened by licensees by 2010.

To extend its reach into niche markets, PVH bought privately held necktie maker Superba for more than $110 million in 2007 to market Calvin Klein and IZOD neckwear. The company also entered a licensing deal with B Robinson Optical in mid-2006 to make and market men's and women's IZOD-branded sunglasses. Other IZOD licensing deals include watches, footwear, and handbags.

Looking to keep ahead of the US economic downturn and lower its operating expenses, PVH in January 2009 announced plans to shutter some 175 stores and shed about 400 employees, comprising 250 salaried positions and 150 people from its neckwear unit.

While PVH is entering new markets, the company has been fine-tuning its licensing and international strategies. In 2008 PVH partnered with Timberland in a licensing agreement to make men's apparel (in 2008) and women's apparel (in 2009). PVH also partnered with G-III Apparel Group in December 2007 to manufacture and distribute Calvin Klein Performance-branded clothing for women.

PVH extended the reach for IZOD's European unit by partnering with Rousseau SAS in mid-2006. Rousseau markets and distributes an IZOD-branded men's sportswear line sold in France, Belgium, Andorra, Luxembourg, and Monaco.

FMR owns about 10% of the company, while Earnest Partners holds a more than 7% stake in PVH. In mid-2005 chairman Bruce Klatsky passed his CEO title to Mark Weber. Weber left within a year and was replaced by president and COO Emanuel Chirico. Klatsky retired in 2007 after nearly 36 years with the firm. Chirico, who assumed the title of chairman, and Klatsky had worked together for about two decades.

HISTORY

In 1881 Moses Phillips came to America from Poland. While living in a one-room apartment in Pottsville, Pennsylvania, he sold flannel shirts (which his wife sewed) to coal miners from a pushcart. He soon brought the rest of his family to the US and upgraded the pushcart to a horse and buggy. Business continued to grow, and the Phillips-Jones Corporation was formed in 1907.

The company moved to New York in 1914, and control passed from father to son for four generations. Isaac followed Moses, then Seymour took over in 1941 until he handed the reins to Lawrence, who joined the company in 1948 and became president and CEO in 1969. Ads in the 1950s featured such actors as Anthony Quinn, Burt Lancaster, and Ronald Reagan in Van Heusen shirts. In 1957 the company received its present name. Phillips-Van Heusen (PVH) grew via acquisitions throughout the 1970s and began selling its merchandise at its own outlet stores in 1979, but it didn't want its products sold at the off-price outlets that became popular in the early 1980s. The company stopped doing business with stores and distributors that allowed PVH merchandise to reach cut-price vendors.

In 1987 PVH acquired G. H. Bass & Co., maker of Bass and Weejun shoes, for $79 million. It also bought back over 5 million shares of stock in order to fend off an acquisition bid by the Hunt family of Texas. Lawrence stepped down in 1993, ending the unbroken chain of Phillipses at the helm. Bruce Klatsky, a human rights supporter who had started work at the company 22 years earlier as a merchandising trainee, took over as CEO. In 1995 the Phillips family sold its stake in the business. PVH acquired the Gant

Plains All American Pipeline

The term "All American" includes Canada for Plains All American Pipeline, which has expanded its pipeline operations north of the border. The limited partnership is engaged in the transportation, storage, terminalling and marketing of crude oil, refined products and LPG, and owns extensive gathering, terminal, and storage facilities in California, Louisiana, Oklahoma, Texas, and in Alberta and Saskatchewan. Plains All American Pipeline owns about 17,000 miles of gathering and mainline crude oil pipelines throughout the US and Canada, operates a large fleet of trucks and barges, and owns storage capacity of 24 million barrels. Paul Allen's Vulcan Energy holds just more than 50% of its general partner.

Plains All American Pipeline handles more than 3 million barrels of crude oil, refined products and LPG per day through its extensive network based in key North American producing basins and transportation gateways. It has steadily built its network through acquisitions, and has also expanded into refining and marketing.

In 2006 the company acquired Andrews Petroleum and Lone Star Trucking for $205 million. It also acquired stakes in a number of Gulf Coast crude oil pipeline systems from BP Oil Pipeline Company for $133.5 million. That year, in a major deal, the company acquired Pacific Energy Partners for $2.4 billion, moving the company beyond crude oil and into the refined products and barging businesses.

In 2007 Plains All American Pipeline acquired LPG storage facilities in Arizona and South Carolina. The next year Occidental Petroleum acquired 10% of the company's general partner, boosting the amount of new capital available for Plains All American Pipeline to pay down debt and make further acquisitions.

HISTORY

Goodyear Tire & Rubber subsidiary Celeron began designing the All American Pipeline in 1983 to bring heavy crude from California to the less-regulated refineries of Texas. It was completed in 1987 at a cost of $1.6 billion, but by 1991 only a trickle of oil was dribbling through. The pipeline did not post a profit until 1994.

Prospects began to look up in the mid-1990s when Chevron, Texaco, and Exxon signed contracts to use the pipeline, beginning in 1996. Plains Resources bought the pipeline in 1998 for $400 million; the company created Plains All American Pipeline to acquire and operate the pipeline, then sold off a 43% stake in an IPO that raised $260 million. The next year Plains All American bought Scurlock Permian (2,300 miles of pipeline) from Marathon Ashland Petroleum for $141 million and the West Texas Gathering System from Chevron (450 miles) for $36 million.

Shareholders sued Plains All American in 1999 after it reported that an employee's unauthorized crude-oil trading would cost the company about $160 million. (In 2000 the company agreed to pay $29.5 million, plus interest, to settle the cases.)

Plains All American announced plans to mothball all but the California section of the All American Pipeline in 1999. The next year El Paso Energy bought the 1,088-mile section of the pipeline that was to be deactivated, plus the right to run fiber-optic cable over the entire pipeline, for $129 million.

Targeting Canada as part of its expansion strategy, in 2001 Plains All American bought about 450 miles of oil pipeline and other midstream assets from Murphy Oil and acquired crude oil and LPG marketing firm CANPET Energy. Also that year Plains Resources reduced its stake in Plains All American from 44% to 29%.

In 2002 the company acquired the Wapella Pipeline System, located in southeastern Saskatchewan and southwestern Manitoba. It also bought Shell Pipeline's West Texas crude oil pipeline assets for $315 million. Plains All American Pipeline continued its acquisition streak in 2003 with the acquisitions of the South Saskatchewan pipeline system in Canada and the ArkLaTex pipeline system originating in Sabine, Texas.

In 2004 Plains All American continued its expansion with the acquisition of interests in the Capline and Capwood pipeline systems from Shell Pipeline Company for about $158 million. It also acquired the crude oil and pipeline operations of Link Energy for about $330 million and the Cal Ven pipeline system from Unocal Canada for about $19 million. Later that year, the company continued its system expansion by acquiring the Schaefferstown propane storage facility from Koch Hydrocarbon for about $32 million.

EXECUTIVES

Chairman and CEO: Greg L. Armstrong, age 50
President, COO, and Director: Harry N. Pefanis, age 51
SVP and CFO: Al Swanson, age 45
SVP Technology, Process, and Risk Management: Alfred A. (Al) Lindseth, age 39
VP Accounting and Chief Accounting Officer: Tina L. Val, age 39
EVP: Phillip D. (Phil) Kramer, age 52
SVP Operations and Business Development: Mark J. Gorman, age 54
SVP Commercial Activities: John P. vonBerg, age 54
VP, Secretary, and General Counsel: Tim Moore, age 51
VP, General Counsel Commercial & Litigation, and Assistant Secretary: Lawrence J. (Larry) Dreyfuss, age 54
VP Strategic Planning: A. Patrick (Pat) Diamond, age 36
VP Environmental, Health, and Safety: Troy E. Valenzuela, age 47
VP Refinery Supply: James B. (Jim) Fryfogle, age 57
VP Engineering: Daniel J. Nerbonne, age 51
VP Human Resources: Roger D. Everett, age 63
VP Terminals: John R. Keffer, age 49
VP and Treasurer: Charles Kingswell-Smith, age 57
President, Natural Gas Storage, LLC: Constantine S. (Dean) Liollio, age 50
President, PMC (Nova Scotia): W. David (Dave) Duckett, age 53
Manager Investor Relations: Roy I. Lamoreaux
Auditors: PricewaterhouseCoopers LLP

LOCATIONS

HQ: Plains All American Pipeline, L.P.
333 Clay St., Ste. 1600, Houston, TX 77002
Phone: 713-646-4100   **Fax:** 713-646-4572
Web: www.plainsallamerican.com

2008 Sales

	$ mil.	% of total
US	25,183	84
Canada	4,878	16
Total	**30,061**	**100**

PRODUCTS/OPERATIONS

2008 Sales

	$ mil.	% of total
Marketing	29,348	98
Transportation	556	2
Storage & other	157	—
Total	**30,061**	**100**

COMPETITORS

Buckeye Partners
Enbridge
Kinder Morgan
Sunoco Logistics
TEPPCO Partners
TransMontaigne

HISTORICAL FINANCIALS

Company Type: Public

Income Statement

FYE: December 31

	REVENUE ($ mil.)	NET INCOME ($ mil.)	NET PROFIT MARGIN	EMPLOYEES
12/08	30,061.0	437.0	1.5%	3,302
12/07	20,394.0	365.0	1.8%	3,100
12/06	22,444.4	278.8	1.2%	2,900
12/05	31,177.3	217.8	0.7%	2,000
12/04	20,975.5	133.1	0.6%	1,950
Annual Growth	**9.4%**	**34.6%**	**—**	**14.1%**

2008 Year-End Financials

Debt ratio: —
Return on equity: —
Cash ($ mil.): 11
Current ratio: 0.88
Long-term debt ($ mil.): 3,259

No. of shares (mil.): 129
Dividends
  Yield: 10.1%
  Payout: 130.7%
Market value ($ mil.): 4,473

Stock History

NYSE: PAA

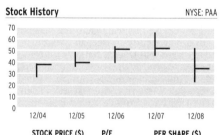

	STOCK PRICE ($) FY Close	P/E High/Low		PER SHARE ($) Earnings	Dividends	Book Value
12/08	34.69	19	9	2.67	3.49	—
12/07	52.00	26	18	2.52	3.28	—
12/06	51.20	18	14	2.88	2.87	—
12/05	39.57	18	13	2.72	2.58	—
12/04	37.74	20	14	1.89	2.30	—
Annual Growth	**(2.1%)**	**—**	**—**	**9.0%**	**11.0%**	**—**

Plexus Corp.

Plexus isn't perplexed by even complex contract electronics manufacturing. The company develops and manufactures electronic products for companies in the telecommunications, medical, industrial, and computer markets. Plexus provides product design and engineering and assembles printed circuit boards (PCBs), test equipment, and other electronic components. The company also offers prototyping, materials procurement, warehousing and distribution, and other support services. Its customers include networking equipment maker Juniper Networks (20% of sales), Siemens Healthcare, and General Electric. Customers located in the US account for nearly two-thirds of Plexus' sales.

While the majority of its sales comes from within the US, the acquisitive company has expanded internationally with the purchases of manufacturing facilities in China, Malaysia, Mexico, and the UK.

In 2008 Plexus completed the implementation of an enterprise resource planning (ERP) system covering all manufacturing sites around the world. The ERP installation augments other management information systems the company uses and includes software from Oracle and other vendors.

HISTORY

In the 1970s Peter Strandwitz needed a contract electronics manufacturer when his small electronics business suffered from a lack of engineering expertise. He founded Plexus in 1979 and marketed its services to electronics companies that could not efficiently operate their own manufacturing facilities. The company went public in 1986. Three years later it discontinued its faltering International Communications subsidiary, which made pay phones, to concentrate on its core business.

Plexus grew throughout the early 1990s, and in 1994 doubled its manufacturing capabilities with a new facility in Neenah, Wisconsin. In 1996 Plexus and Oneida Nation Electronics, a company owned by the Native American Oneida tribe, built an electronics fabrication plant in Green Bay, Wisconsin. The next year, Plexus acquired NEI Electronics and computer parts maker Tertronics.

In 1998 Plexus began building components for General Motors' test electric vehicles. The following year the company boosted its reach into the Pacific Northwest when it bought SeaMED, a Seattle-area designer and manufacturer of electronic equipment for the medical industry.

In 2000 the company continued its acquisition binge, purchasing manufacturing facilities in Mexico and the UK, as well as US-based electronic manufacturing services providers Agility and e2E.

In 2001 COO John Nussbaum succeeded Strandwitz as CEO (Strandwitz remained chairman until the next year). Also in 2001 Plexus agreed to acquire most of the assets of contract manufacturer MCMS; the deal, which closed early in 2002, expanded Plexus' reach into Asia thanks to MCMS's plants in Malaysia and China.

In 2002 COO Dean Foate succeeded Nussbaum as CEO (Nussbaum remained chairman).

Plexus lined up AuthenTec, the developer of biometric chips, as a customer in 2003, providing design, engineering, and integration services to the supplier of fingerprint sensors.

The company went through a corporate restructuring in 2004, closing a plant in the Seattle area. Plexus also mothballed facilities in New Hampshire and Oregon.

In 2006 Plexus expanded its manufacturing capacity in China and Malaysia.

Plexus decided in 2008 to close its facility in Ayer, Massachusetts, primarily transferring production to Neenah, Wisconsin. The company expanded plants in Buffalo Grove, Illinois, and Fremont, California, during the year, and leased about 106,000 square feet at an industrial park in Hangzhou, China.

EXECUTIVES

Chairman: John L. Nussbaum, age 66
President, CEO, and Director: Dean A. Foate, age 50
VP and CFO: Ginger M. Jones, age 44
VP and CIO: Thomas J. Czajkowski, age 44
Corporate Treasurer and Chief Treasury Officer:
George W. F. Setton, age 62
SVP Global Market Development: Michael T. Verstegen, age 50
SVP Global Manufacturing Operations: Mike Buseman, age 47
SVP Global Engineering Services: Steve Frisch, age 42
SVP Global Customer Services: Todd Kelsey, age 43
VP, General Counsel, and Secretary:
Angelo M. Ninivaggi Jr., age 41
VP Global Human Resources: Joseph E. (Joe) Mauthe, age 46
Regional President, Asia Pacific: Yong Jin (YJ) Lim, age 48
Corporate Investor Relations: Dianne Boydstun
Sales and New Business Development, North America:
Mark Wolfgram
Sales and New Business Development, Asia: Mandy Lin
Sales and New Business Development, Europe:
Anthony Green
Auditors: PricewaterhouseCoopers LLP

LOCATIONS

HQ: Plexus Corp.
55 Jewelers Park Dr., Neenah, WI 54957
Phone: 920-722-3451   **Fax:** 920-751-5395
Web: www.plexus.com

Plexus has operations in California, Colorado, Idaho, Illinois, North Carolina, and Wisconsin, and also in China, Malaysia, Mexico, and the UK.

2008 Sales

	$ mil.	% of total
Americas		
US	1,267.9	64
Mexico	78.3	4
Asia		
Malaysia	486.8	25
China	87.3	4
UK	68.8	3
Adjustments	(147.5)	—
Total	**1,841.6**	**100**

PRODUCTS/OPERATIONS

2008 Sales

	% of total
Wireline & networking	44
Medical	21
Industrial & commercial	16
Defense, security & aerospace	10
Wireless infrastructure	9
Total	**100**

Selected Services

Assembly
Design (printed circuit boards, product housings)
Distribution
Materials procurement
New product introduction
Product development and testing
Product manufacture and assembly
Prototyping
Support
Warehousing

COMPETITORS

Avnet
Benchmark Electronics
Celestica
Cofidur
CTS Corp.
Flextronics
Hon Hai
Jabil
Key Tronic
Kimball International
LaBarge
Merix
Nam Tai
Quanta Computer
Sanmina-SCI
Saturn Electronics
Silicon Forest Electronics
SMTC Corp.
Sparton
Suntron
SYNNEX
TTM Technologies
Viasystems

HISTORICAL FINANCIALS

Company Type: Public

Income Statement

FYE: September 30

	REVENUE ($ mil.)	NET INCOME ($ mil.)	NET PROFIT MARGIN	EMPLOYEES
9/08	1,841.6	84.1	4.6%	7,900
9/07	1,546.3	65.7	4.2%	7,500
9/06	1,460.6	100.5	6.9%	7,800
9/05	1,228.9	(12.4)	—	6,800
9/04	1,040.9	(31.6)	—	6,000
Annual Growth	**15.3%**	**—**	**—**	**7.1%**

2008 Year-End Financials

Debt ratio: 32.6%   No. of shares (mil.): 39
Return on equity: 16.1%   Dividends
Cash ($ mil.): 166   Yield: 0.0%
Current ratio: 2.26   Payout: —
Long-term debt ($ mil.): 155   Market value ($ mil.): 817

Stock History

NASDAQ (GS): PLXS

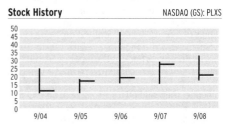

	STOCK PRICE ($) FY Close	P/E High/Low		PER SHARE ($) Earnings	Dividends	Book Value
9/08	20.70	17	9	1.92	0.00	12.01
9/07	27.40	20	11	1.41	0.00	14.52
9/06	19.20	22	7	2.15	0.00	12.20
9/05	17.09	—	—	(0.29)	0.00	8.61
9/04	11.04	—	—	(0.74)	0.00	8.90
Annual Growth	**17.0%**	**—**	**—**	**—**	**—**	**7.8%**

PNC Financial Services

PNC Financial Services has returned to its traditional banking roots. Its PNC Bank and National City Bank subsidiaries operate about 2,600 branches in the mid-Atlantic region and the Midwest. In addition to retail banking, the company offers asset management, insurance, investments, and capital markets products and services. It provides fund administration services through PNC Global Investment Servicing. PNC also owns boutique investment bank Harris Williams and about a third of money management giant BlackRock. One of the first banks to take advantage of the US Treasury's $250 billion plan to bolster the banking industry, PNC used some of the funds to acquire troubled rival National City in 2008.

In order to acquire National City, PNC parlayed a $7.6 billion investment in its preferred shares by the government into the $6.1 billion of cash and stock deal, which came after months of speculation that the two companies would join. The purchase doubled PNC's branch network and extended it westward to Chicago and Milwaukee. PNC chairman and CEO Jim Rohr leads the merged bank.

As part of the National City deal, PNC was required to divest 61 of National City's 170 branches. PNS sold some 57 branches to First Niagra Financial of Buffalo, New York, and announced that it was closing another 12 branches in Pittsburgh in 2009.

Increasingly focusing its brokerage business on input print activities, PNC sold brokerage firm Hilliard Lyons to Houchens Industries in 2008. The company reported fourth-quarter losses for 2008, primarily related to the National City acquisition and increased credit provisions, and has announced plans to cut about 20% of its workforce. PNC also sold nearly 60 National City branches in Western Pennsylvania to First Niagara Financial in order to settle antitrust concerns stemming from the National City deal.

Prior to buying National City, PNC in 2007 acquired Yardville National Bancorp and its 35 branches in central New Jersey and eastern Pennsylvania, and Mercantile Bankshares, which added some 240 branches in the mid-Atlantic region. Also that year PNC expanded its commercial mortgage operations with the acquisition of multifamily housing lender ARC Commercial Mortgage (now PNC ARCS).

The following year PNC finalized its acquisition of multibank holding company Sterling Financial, which provided banking, leasing, trust, investment, and brokerage services to individuals and businesses through nearly 70 branches in Delaware, Maryland, and Pennsylvania.

The company beefed up PNC Global Investment Servicing (formerly PFPC), which provides processing, technology, and business products and services to the global investment industry, through the 2007 acquisitions of Albridge Solutions, a provider of enterprise wealth management services, and Coates Analytics, which provides Web-based tools for asset managers.

HISTORY

First National Bank of Pittsburgh opened in 1863. In 1913 the bank consolidated with Second National Bank of Pittsburgh, and in 1921 it bought Peoples National.

The company changed its name to Pittsburgh National after expansion following the Depression and WWII. The bank entered the credit card business in 1965 and joined the BankAmericard program (Visa's forerunner) four years later. In the inflationary 1970s Pittsburgh National diversified, moving into commercial paper financing (1972); lease financing (1979); and credit life, health, and accident reinsurance (1979).

In 1983 Pittsburgh National merged with Provident National of Philadelphia (founded by Quakers in 1865) to form PNC Corp. The union combined Pittsburgh National's corporate lending strength with Provident's money management and trust operations. PNC expanded through the 1980s by buying more Pennsylvania banks and then moved into Kentucky in 1987. That year PNC, with $37 billion in assets, passed Mellon Bank as Pennsylvania's largest bank.

This growth was accompanied by investment in risky commercial mortgages, so when the real estate market unraveled in 1989-90, PNC was stuck with millions of dollars in problem loans. It soon began selling its bad loans and property and tightening underwriting standards.

PNC reorganized in 1991, operating its several state-chartered banks as if they were a single entity. Acquisitions continued, including BlackRock Financial Management, Sears Mortgage, 84 banking branches orphaned by the Chase Manhattan/Chemical Bank merger, and New Jersey-based Midlantic Corp (founded in 1804 as Newark Banking and Insurance).

PNC's acquisitions focused more sharply on mortgages in 1997 and 1998; it bought Midland Loan Services, as well as the mortgage origination offices of what became FleetBoston. The former purchase moved the company strongly into servicing and securitization to become a major buyer in the secondary commercial-mortgage market.

In addition to consolidating its asset management operations under the BlackRock subsidiary in 1998 (spun off the next year), PNC bought BTM Capital, an asset-based lender headquartered in Boston. After rules separating banking from securities activities were relaxed in 1998, the firm bought Louisville, Kentucky-based securities brokerage Hilliard Lyons. Also that year the company paid $30 million to attach its name to the Pittsburgh Pirates' baseball stadium for 20 years. Christened PNC Park, it opened in 2001.

In 1999 PNC bought credit card processor First Data's Investor Services Group, which it merged into PFPC. That year PNC agreed to pay $375,000 to 31 women employees in response to a Labor Department charge that PNC had a "glass ceiling." Later in 1999 the company signed on as the exclusive banking services provider for iVillage.com, an Internet site for women.

PNC exited the vehicle leasing and residential mortgage businesses in 2001.

Belying speculation that it was a takeover target itself, PNC bought United National Bancorp in 2004 and, after much drama, acquired Riggs National the following year.

PNC had originally agreed to buy Riggs in 2004, but lowered its bid after Riggs pleaded guilty to Bank Secrecy Act violations in early 2005. (Riggs also paid millions in fines and technology upgrades to comply with the anti-terrorism measure.) Riggs sued PNC for damages for backing out on the deal, but dropped the charges after agreeing on a renegotiated sale price.

After the dust settled, PNC wasted no time making its presence known in the coveted Washington, DC, market where Riggs had been the #1 bank. It quickly obliterated the vestiges of troubled Riggs, removing that institution's signs and replacing them with its own during the weekend after the deal was finalized.

In 2005 the company bought boutique investment bank Harris Williams, which specializes in mergers and acquisitions advisory services.

PNC sold part of its 70% share in BlackRock to Merrill Lynch in 2006, retaining 34%. PNC netted some $1.6 billion from the transaction.

EXECUTIVES

Chairman and CEO: James E. (Jim) Rohr, age 60, $14,618,789 total compensation
Senior Vice Chairman: William S. (Bill) Demchak, age 46, $6,104,992 total compensation
Vice Chairman: Thomas K. (Tom) Whitford, age 52
Vice Chairman: Timothy G. (Tim) Shack, age 57, $4,577,332 total compensation
President: Joseph C. (Joe) Guyaux, age 58, $5,400,199 total compensation
EVP and CFO: Richard J. Johnson, age 52, $2,446,325 total compensation
CIO: Anuj Dhanda
EVP and Chief Risk Officer: Michael J. Hannon, age 52
EVP and General Counsel: Helen P. Pudlin, age 59
EVP Human Resources: Joan L. Gulley, age 61
EVP and Deputy Manager, Corporate Banking: James Graham
SVP and Controller: Samuel R. Patterson, age 50
SVP and Director of Investor Relations: William H. Callihan
SVP and Chief Regulatory Officer: John J. (Jack) Wixted Jr., age 57
SVP and Chief Economist: Stuart G. Hoffman
Chairman and CEO, BlackRock: Laurence D. Fink, age 55, $26,421,106 total compensation
Head Retail Distribution, PNC Bank: Neil F. Hall
Managing Director and Co-Founder, Harris Williams: H. Hiter Harris III
Managing Director and Co-Founder, Harris Williams: Christopher H. (Chris) Williams
Managing Director, PNC Wealth Management: Stephen C. Thormahlen
Director of External Communications: Brian Goerke
Corporate Secretary: George P. Long III
Auditors: Deloitte & Touche LLP

LOCATIONS

HQ: The PNC Financial Services Group, Inc.
1 PNC Plaza, 249 5th Ave., Pittsburgh, PA 15222
Phone: 412-762-2000   **Fax:** 412-762-7829
Web: www.pnc.com

PRODUCTS/OPERATIONS

2008 Gross Revenue

	$ mil.	% of total
Interest		
Loans	4,138	42
Investment securities	1,746	18
Other	429	4
Noninterest		
Fund servicing	904	9
Corporate services	704	7
Asset management	686	7
Consumer services	623	6
Service charges on deposits	372	4
Other	284	3
Total	**9,886**	**100**

HISTORICAL FINANCIALS

Company Type: Public

Income Statement

FYE: December 31

	ASSETS ($ mil.)	NET INCOME ($ mil.)	INCOME AS % OF ASSETS	EMPLOYEES
12/08	291,081.0	882.0	0.3%	59,595
12/07	138,920.0	1,467.0	1.1%	28,320
12/06	101,820.0	2,595.0	2.5%	23,783
12/05	91,954.0	1,325.0	1.4%	25,348
12/04	79,723.0	1,197.0	1.5%	23,700
Annual Growth	38.2%	(7.4%)	—	25.9%

2008 Year-End Financials

Equity as % of assets: 8.7%
Return on assets: 0.4%
Return on equity: 4.4%
Long-term debt ($ mil.): 42,998
No. of shares (mil.): 461

Dividends
  Yield: 5.3%
  Payout: 106.1%
Market value ($ mil.): 22,609
Sales ($ mil.): 7,190

Stock History

NYSE: PNC

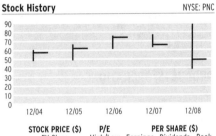

	STOCK PRICE ($) FY Close	P/E High/Low		PER SHARE ($) Earnings	Dividends	Book Value
12/08	49.00	36	16	2.46	2.61	55.10
12/07	65.65	18	15	4.35	2.44	32.19
12/06	74.04	9	7	8.73	2.15	23.38
12/05	61.83	14	11	4.55	2.00	18.56
12/04	57.44	14	12	4.21	2.00	16.20
Annual Growth	(3.9%)	—	—	(12.6%)	6.9%	35.8%

Polaris Industries

Polaris Industries is one of the world's top makers of snowmobiles and off-road vehicles, which include all-terrain vehicles (ATVs) and side-by-side recreational and utility RANGER vehicles. The company is also known for its Victory cruiser and touring motorcycles. Other products include replacement parts, accessories (covers, tow hitches, cargo racks), and recreational clothing and gear (boots and helmets). Polaris has a joint venture with Fuji Heavy Industries to build engines for its products and for companies in non-competitive industries, as well as agreements with manufacturers in Taiwan and Germany to produce youth ATVs and engines for snowmobiles.

Polaris sees sales declining by 15-23% in 2009, due to the continuing recession. Early in the year the company laid off about 460 contractors and employees, a workforce reduction of about 14%. To shore up the bleak economic forecast Polaris is focused on developing new products, including its first luxury touring motorcycle models and a variety of replacement parts and accessories for its vehicles.

Also in 2009 Polaris formed an On-Road Vehicle Division to help drive cohesive and strategic growth for the Victory Motorcycles brand and its other on-road brands and products. The company gets about two-thirds of its sales from off-road vehicles.

The company sells its products through dealers and distributors located primarily in the US, Canada, and Europe. The majority of its sales are made in the US. Subsidiaries are located in North America, Europe, and Australia.

Fuji Heavy Industries owns about 6% of Polaris Industries. Former CEO Thomas Tiller holds around 5% of the company.

HISTORY

Originally called Hetteen Hoist & Derrick, Polaris Industries was founded in Roseau, Minnesota, in 1945 by Edgar Hetteen and David Johnson. The friends did welding and repair work and made custom machinery for local farmers.

In the early 1950s Johnson invented a gas-powered sled to ride to his winter hunting ground. The contraption attracted the attention of a neighbor, who bought the machine. In 1954 the company began making snowmobiles under the Polaris brand. It built five machines in the winter of 1954-55 and was up to 300 per year within three years. Hetteen's younger brother Allen also joined the firm during the 1950s.

Snowmobiles made inroads as utility vehicles, but didn't catch on as recreational vehicles. To spur interest, in 1960 Edgar Hetteen led a snowmobile team on a thousand-mile trip across Alaska. When the company's backers complained about the expense of the trip, Hetteen left Polaris. He later founded Arctic Enterprises, which produced the Arctic Cat snowmobile and was, for a time, the top US snowmobile maker.

With Edgar's departure, Allen Hetteen became president of Polaris. The firm's fortunes rose as the snowmobile gained popularity, and in 1968 diversified manufacturer Textron (Bell helicopters, Schaefer pens, Talon zippers) acquired Polaris.

The snowmobile industry peaked in 1971, with sales topping 495,000 units; the industry declined through the rest of the 1970s. Polaris continued to introduce new models and to sponsor snowmobile racing teams. In 1981 Textron refocused on its defense segments and planned to shut Polaris down. Company president Hall Wendel, an outdoorsman who would later climb Mt. Everest, led a management buyout.

In 1982 Polaris tried to buy Arctic Cat; Arctic Enterprises temporarily closed soon after, leaving Polaris as the US's sole snowmobile maker for a time.

Under Wendel, Polaris began looking for another product to fill production during snowmobiling's off-season. In 1985 it entered the ATV market, going up against several established Japanese manufacturers, including Honda and Suzuki. The company positioned its ATVs not as recreational vehicles, but as utility vehicles, and soon Polaris slipped into the #2 spot behind Honda. It became the world's #1 snowmobile maker in 1991. The next year Polaris began marketing personal watercraft, which made up about 10% of sales in 1993 (dropped to 4% in 1998). The company went public in 1994.

Polaris and Fuji Heavy Industries formed a joint venture — Robin Manufacturing, USA — in 1995 to build engines for its products and noncompeting companies. In 1997 Polaris announced its plans for the Victory motorcycle. In 1998 the company was slapped with a nearly $45 million judgment in a trade-secret lawsuit brought by the inventor of an engine fuel-injection system. Partner Fuji Heavy Industries was ordered to pay $11.6 million.

Polaris became the first American manufacturer in 50 years to enter the motorcycle market when it unveiled the Victory, a cruiser-style cycle, in 1998. *Cycle World* magazine named Victory the cruiser of the year. Thomas Tiller, a 15-year veteran of General Electric, succeeded Wendel as CEO that year.

The following year Victory sales tripled and a second model was introduced. In 2000 company founders and septuagenarians Hetteen and Johnson, along with Tiller, trekked across Alaska in snowmobiles, hoping the publicity would increase snowmobile sales (similar to the trip Hetteen made to boost sales 40 years earlier). Polaris launched the All Surface Loader, a new landscaping product, in 2001.

The following year Polaris introduced its first true sport ATV, the Predator. The first Arlen Ness limited-edition cruiser motorcycle (named after motorcycle designers Arlen and Corey Ness) rolled off the assembly line in 2003.

Citing increasing costs and competitive pressures, Polaris decided to liquidate its unprofitable watercraft unit in 2004. In 2005 Polaris purchased a 25% stake in Austrian motorcycle maker KTM Power Sports AG. The move was to give Polaris a better foothold in Europe through KTM's extensive dealer network. Polaris sold most of that stake two years later in an effort to pay down debt.

Tiller stepped down as CEO in 2008 and resigned from the board in 2009. He was succeeded as CEO by Scott Wine, a former executive of Danaher and United Technologies.

In the early 1950s a group of Oregon Saw's casting employees developed a process for producing parts as large as 60 inches by use of investment casting, making products that rivaled the strength of forged and machined parts at a fraction of the cost. After a two-year search, they landed their first aerospace customer — Air Research Corp. — with many to follow. The higher operating temperatures generated by aircraft engines led the company to buy a vacuum furnace in 1959 to fabricate parts that could tolerate greater heat; two more vacuum furnaces were added and sales vaulted toward $10 million by 1967. PCC went public in 1968 and continued to grow. In 1976 the company acquired Centaur Cast Alloys (small investment castings, UK) to make parts for the European aerospace industry. By that time General Electric (GE) and Pratt & Whitney accounted for most of PCC's business. Edward Cooley, who had masterminded the company's growth since incorporation, forged ahead with plans to double production capacity.

In 1980 the airline industry crashed, but PCC's sales held at about $90 million. Structural airplane products soon picked up, and in 1984 the company bought two titanium foundries in France. To diversify, it added TRW's cast airfoils (used in aircraft engines and industrial gas turbines) division in 1986. That acquisition, renamed PCC Airfoils, increased PCC's annual sales by about 80%.

The company broadened its offerings again in 1991 when it acquired Advanced Forming Technology, which made small, complex, metal-injection molded parts used in everything from adding machines to military ordnance. The early 1990s recession hit the airline industry and sales dropped. Cooley retired as chairman in 1994 and GE veteran William McCormick replaced him. The next year PCC acquired Quamco, Inc. (industrial tools and machines). In 1996 PCC flowed into the fluid management market with the acquisition of NEWFLO for about $300 million.

In 1997 PCC spent $437 million to acquire seven more companies that helped boost sales 75% from 1996 levels. The next year it purchased four metalworking companies that served industries other than aerospace. Having reduced dependence on sales to the aerospace industry to just over 50%, PCC began consolidating operations and closing plants to reduce costs.

The company continued to diversify through acquisitions in 1999, but it also expanded its aerospace operations with the purchase of Wyman-Gordon, a leading maker of advanced metal forgings for the aerospace market. PCC's 2000 acquisitions included the aerospace division of United Engineering Forgings and Germany-based Convey Engineering (heavy-duty valves).

In 2003 Precision Castparts' PCC Structurals unit reached a $400 million agreement with Rolls-Royce to supply large titanium and steel castings. That year the company acquired SPS Technologies, a producer of fasteners and other metal components for the aerospace, automotive, and industrial markets.

PCC acquired Air Industries Corporation in early 2005. In 2006 PCC bought Special Metals Corporation (SMC), a maker of nickel alloys and super alloys. Later that year PCC bought Shur-Lok Corporation, a manufacturer of aerospace fasteners.

Early in 2007 PCC completed the purchase of GSC, a leading maker of aluminum and steel structural investment casting for the aerospace, energy, and medical markets.

EXECUTIVES

Chairman and CEO: Mark Donegan, age 52, $7,417,002 total compensation
SVP, CFO, and Assistant Secretary: Shawn R. Hagel, age 43, $1,476,045 total compensation
VP and CIO: Byron J. Gaddis, age 52
EVP: Steven G. (Steve) Hackett, age 52, $2,615,104 total compensation
EVP; President, PCC Airfoils and Wyman-Gordon: Kenneth D. (Ken) Buck, age 49, $2,069,543 total compensation
EVP and President, Fastener Products: Kevin M. Stein, age 43
SVP, General Counsel, and Secretary: Roger A. Cooke, age 60, $1,913,996 total compensation
SVP Corporate Training and Organizational Development: John W. Ericksen, age 47
SVP; President, Structurals Casting Operations: Ross M. Lienhart, age 56
SVP; President, Special Metals: Joseph I. Snowden, age 52
VP Strategic Planning and Corporate Development: Kirk G. Pulley, age 40
VP, Corporate Controller, and Assistant Secretary: Russell S. Pattee, age 45
VP, Treasurer, and Assistant Secretary: Steven C. Blackmore, age 47
VP Corporate Taxes and Assistant Secretary: Roger P. Becker, age 55
Director Communications: Dwight E. Weber
Auditors: Deloitte & Touche LLP

LOCATIONS

HQ: Precision Castparts Corp.
4650 SW Macadam Ave., Ste. 440
Portland, OR 97239
Phone: 503-417-4800   **Fax:** 503-417-4817
Web: www.precast.com

2009 Sales

	$ mil.	% of total
US	5,535.1	81
UK	866.3	13
Other countries	426.5	6
Total	**6,827.9**	**100**

PRODUCTS/OPERATIONS

2009 Sales

	$ mil.	% of total
Forged products	2,978.4	44
Investment cast products	2,291.3	33
Fastener products	1,558.2	23
Total	**6,827.9**	**100**

2009 Sales by Industry

	$ mil.	% of total
Aerospace	3,611.2	53
Power Generation	1,703.3	25
General Industrial	1,513.4	22
Total	**6,827.9**	**100**

Selected Products

Fastener Products
  Bolts
  Nuts
  Refiner plates
  Screen cylinders
  Socket screws
Forged Products
  Nickel and cobalt alloy product forms
  Seamless and extruded pipe
Investment Cast Products
  PCC airfoils
  PCC structurals
  Specialty materials and alloy

COMPETITORS

Alcoa
Allegheny Technologies
BAE Systems Steel Products
Carpenter Technology
Chicago Rivet
Citation Corp.
Crane Co.
Curtiss-Wright
ESCO
Farwest Steel Corporation
Federal Screw Works
Georg Fischer
Goodrich Corp.
Hawk Corp.
Haynes International
Hitachi Metals
Kennametal
Ladish Co.
LISI
Metalico
Mettis Aerospace
Nucor
Pacific Aerospace
Sumitomo
Sumitomo Metal Industries
Swagelok
Teleflex
ThyssenKrupp
United Technologies
Universal Stainless
V & M Tubes (USA)
Volvo Aero
Worthington Industries

HISTORICAL FINANCIALS

Company Type: Public

Income Statement

FYE: Sunday nearest March 31

	REVENUE ($ mil.)	NET INCOME ($ mil.)	NET PROFIT MARGIN	EMPLOYEES
3/09	6,827.9	1,044.5	15.3%	20,300
3/08	6,852.1	987.3	14.4%	21,600
3/07	5,361.2	633.1	11.8%	19,800
3/06	3,546.4	350.6	9.9%	16,000
3/05	2,919.0	(1.7)	—	15,800
Annual Growth	23.7%	—	—	6.5%

2009 Year-End Financials

Debt ratio: 5.2%	No. of shares (mil.): 140
Return on equity: 23.5%	Dividends
Cash ($ mil.): 555	Yield: 0.2%
Current ratio: 2.63	Payout: 1.6%
Long-term debt ($ mil.): 251	Market value ($ mil.): 8,399

Stock History

NYSE: PCP

	STOCK PRICE ($) FY Close	P/E High/Low		PER SHARE ($) Earnings	Dividends	Book Value
3/09	59.90	18	6	7.43	0.12	34.66
3/08	102.08	23	13	7.04	0.12	28.85
3/07	104.05	23	11	4.59	0.12	20.23
3/06	59.40	24	14	2.58	0.10	15.27
3/05	38.51	—	—	(0.01)	0.06	12.70
Annual Growth	11.7%	—	—	—	18.9%	28.5%

priceline.com

priceline.com would like to name itself the king of online travel. At priceline.com's Web site, buyers can "name their own price" for airline tickets, home financing, hotel rooms, rental cars, cruises, and vacation packages. With its patented business model, priceline.com generates virtually all of its revenue from travel-related services. In the case of airline tickets and hotel reservations, priceline.com generates revenue on the margin, keeping the difference between the price paid by the individual and what priceline.com paid for the ticket or hotel room (the company also charges airline ticket buyers a handling fee). The company was founded in 1997.

Not everyone who hooks up with priceline.com gets his ticket to ride, however. The company considers an individual's named price for a plane ticket "reasonable" if it's no more than 30% lower than the lowest fare for the route.

The travel services company is setting its sights on international expansion. As a result, in 2006 the US accounted for 84% of its revenue; two years later, that percentage dropped to 67%. Revenue deriving from The Netherlands spiked to 22% in 2008 (it represented only 10% in 2006). Overall, international revenue mainly derives from its hotel reservation services.

HISTORY

priceline.com founder Jay Walker launched a string of ventures before making the leap into e-commerce. In 1994 he founded Walker Digital, an entrepreneurial think tank formed to develop business models that could germinate into new companies.

In 1996 Walker Digital found the impetus that would drive priceline.com: Each day major airlines have more than 500,000 empty seats. Walker's team reasoned that if the airlines were offered even a discounted price for these empty seats, they'd jump at the chance to cut their losses. Based on that premise, Walker Digital developed a "name your price" system and founded priceline.com in 1997.

The company launched its airfare service in 1998 and obtained financing from General Atlantic Partners and Paul Allen's Vulcan Ventures (now called Vulcan Northwest). That year it expanded into hotel reservations and added a car-buying service. Richard Braddock became chairman and CEO in 1998.

priceline.com added home financing services to its offerings in 1999. The company went public with a chart-busting IPO later that year. priceline.com also launched a rental car service. Branching into the retail arena, it licensed its technology to WebHouse Club for use in selling grocery products. The company sued Microsoft in 1999, claiming that company's Expedia unit's name-your-own-price hotel reservation service violates priceline.com's patent.

In 2000 the company licensed its business model to several international ventures including General Atlantic Partners' Priceline.com Europe (headed by former Burger King CEO Dennis Malamatinas), SOFTBANK's Priceline.com Japan (a deal that was later cancelled), MyPrice in Australia and New Zealand (also cancelled), and Asian conglomerate Hutchinson Whampoa. In collaboration with Alliance Capital (now Alliance-Bernstein), priceline.com created subsidiary pricelinemortgage to act as a mortgage broker.

Daniel Schulman became CEO later that year. Jay Walker resigned as vice chairman at the end of 2000, after taking on the role of CEO at Walker Digital. After deciding it would probably never be profitable, WebHouse Club shut down, ending priceline.com's foray into grocery sales. Known for its splashy ads, priceline.com dumped pop icon William Shatner as its TV spokesperson in favor of *Sex and the City* star Sarah Jessica Parker. (Shatner returned in 2002.) Later that year the company fired Schulman and reappointed Braddock as CEO.

In 2002 the company joined with National Leisure Group to offer cruises from its Web site. Later that year priceline.com purchased the assets of discount travel site Lowestfare.com. It also announced plans to sell cars under a marketing agreement with Autobytel. In late 2002 Braddock passed his CEO responsibilities to president Jeffery H. Boyd. (Braddock remained as chairman.)

In 2002 the company purchased the assets of discount travel site Lowestfare.com. In August 2003 a handful of new international destinations (Australia, Japan, Indonesia, Malaysia, South Korea, Taiwan) were added to priceline.com's hotel reservation service. In April 2004 chairman Richard Braddock (former president of Citicorp and one of the last remaining high-profile board members) resigned from the company. Director Ralph Bahna was then named chairman. The following month priceline.com acquired most of Travelweb.com. In September 2004 it bought Active Hotels of Britain for about $161 million. Later that year priceline.com acquired the remaining stake in Travelweb for about $4 million.

EXECUTIVES

Chairman: Ralph M. Bahna, age 66
Vice Chairman; Head Worldwide Strategy and Planning: Robert J. (Bob) Mylod Jr., age 42, $3,744,657 total compensation
President, CEO, and Director: Jeffery H. (Jeff) Boyd, age 52, $6,024,326 total compensation
SVP Customer Service and Operations: Lisa Gillingham
SVP, CFO, and Chief Accounting Officer: Daniel J. Finnegan, age 47
CIO: Ronald V. (Ron) Rose, age 58
Chief Marketing Officer: Brett Keller, age 41
Chief Distribution Officer: Paul J. Hennessy
EVP, General Counsel, and Corporate Secretary: Peter J. Millones Jr., age 39, $1,904,450 total compensation
SVP International; Senior Manager, Priceline.co.uk: Glenn D. Fogel
SVP Hotels: Tim Gordon
SVP Air: Mark Koehler
SVP Vacation Packages: Thomas L. (Tom) Trotta, age 46
SVP Rental Cars: Patricia (Patti) D'Angelo
SVP Finance and Investor Relations: Matthew N. Tynan, age 32
President, North American Travel: Christopher L. (Chris) Soder, age 49, $1,877,802 total compensation
CEO, Booking.com B.V.: Kees Koolen, age 43, $4,981,619 total compensation
Media Relations: Brian Ek
Auditors: Deloitte & Touche LLP

LOCATIONS

HQ: priceline.com Incorporated
 800 Connecticut Ave., Norwalk, CT 06854
Phone: 203-299-8000   **Fax:** 203-299-8948
Web: www.priceline.com

2008 Sales

	$ mil.	% of total
US	1,265.0	67
The Netherlands	406.2	22
UK & other	213.6	11
Total	**1,884.8**	**100**

PRODUCTS/OPERATIONS

2008 Sales

	$ mil.	% of total
Merchant	1,218.2	65
Agency	648.8	34
Other	17.8	1
Total	**1,884.8**	**100**

Selected Products

Airline tickets
Cruises
Home financing (home equity loans, mortgages, refinancing)
Hotel rooms
Rental cars
Vacation packages

Selected Participating Airlines

America West Airlines
American Airlines
Continental Airlines
Delta Air Lines
Northwest Airlines
United Airlines
US Airways

Selected Participating Hotels

Hilton
Hyatt
Marriott
Starwood Hotels & Resorts

Selected Participating Rental Car Services

Avis
Budget
Hertz
National

COMPETITORS

Amadeus	Hotwire, Inc.
American Express	Internet Brands
Autobytel	Intuit
AutoNation	Kayak.com
AutoTrader	lastminute.com
BCD Travel	Orbitz Worldwide
Carlson Wagonlit	Prestige Travel
E-LOAN	Sabre Holdings
Expedia	Travelocity
GetThere	Travelzoo
Hotels.com	TripAdvisor

HISTORICAL FINANCIALS

Company Type: Public

Income Statement

FYE: December 31

	REVENUE ($ mil.)	NET INCOME ($ mil.)	NET PROFIT MARGIN	EMPLOYEES
12/08	1,884.8	193.5	10.3%	1,780
12/07	1,409.4	157.1	11.1%	1,324
12/06	1,123.1	74.5	6.6%	696
12/05	962.7	192.7	20.0%	532
12/04	914.4	31.5	3.4%	438
Annual Growth	**19.8%**	**57.4%**	**—**	**42.0%**

2008 Year-End Financials

Debt ratio: —
Return on equity: 29.6%
Cash ($ mil.): 365
Current ratio: 1.14
Long-term debt ($ mil.): —
No. of shares (mil.): 42
Dividends
 Yield: 0.0%
 Payout: —
Market value ($ mil.): 3,113

	STOCK PRICE ($) FY Close	P/E High/Low		PER SHARE ($) Earnings	Dividends	Book Value
12/08	73.65	36	11	3.98	0.00	17.28
12/07	114.86	35	12	3.42	0.00	13.70
12/06	43.61	26	13	1.68	0.00	8.25
12/05	22.32	6	4	4.21	0.00	8.73
12/04	23.59	39	23	0.76	0.00	4.71
Annual Growth	32.9%	—	—	51.3%	—	38.4%

Pricewaterhouse-Coopers International

Not merely the firm with the longest one-word name, PricewaterhouseCoopers (PwC) is also one of the world's largest accounting firms. PwC was formed when Price Waterhouse merged with Coopers & Lybrand in 1998, bypassing then-leader Andersen. With some 770 offices in more than 150 countries, the accountancy provides clients with services in three business lines: assurance (including financial and regulatory reporting), tax, and advisory. The umbrella entity for the PwC worldwide network of member firms is one of accounting's Big Four, along with Deloitte Touche Tohmatsu, Ernst & Young, and KPMG. PwC provides services in some capacity for most of the world's largest companies as well as smaller businesses.

PwC puts its heft to good use: Non-North American clients make up nearly two-thirds of the firm's sales. The company has expanded in developing economies, including Brazil, China, India, and Russia

The accounting business as a whole got a boost from the implementation of such regulatory and financial reporting rules as the International Financial Reporting Standards (IFRS) and the Sarbanes-Oxley Act. The industry has faced criticism for the practice of mark-to-market accounting, which many say contributed to the global economic crisis in 2008. PwC stands behind the practice as the best accounting method of complex financial instruments.

In 2007 US arm PricewaterhouseCoopers agreed to pay a whopping $225 million to settle a class-action lawsuit related to the Tyco International financial scandal. The suit asserted that the auditors should have uncovered a $5.8 billion overstatement of earnings during the four years ending in 2002. The fraud sent Tyco top executives to prison.

In 2009 PwC acquired the North American commercial services business of the bankrupt firm BearingPoint. PwC Advisory, its Japanese subsidiary, acquired BearingPoint's consulting practice in that country.

HISTORY

In 1850 Samuel Price founded an accounting firm in London and in 1865 took on partner Edwin Waterhouse. The firm and the industry grew rapidly, thanks to the growth of stock exchanges that required uniform financial statements from listees. By the late 1800s Price Waterhouse (PW) had become the world's best-known accounting firm.

US offices were opened in the 1890s, and in 1902 United States Steel chose the firm as its auditor. PW benefited from tough audit requirements instituted after the 1929 stock market crash. In 1935 the firm was given the prestigious job of handling Academy Awards balloting. It started a management consulting service in 1946. But PW's dominance slipped in the 1960s, as it gained a reputation as the most traditional and formal of the major firms.

Coopers & Lybrand, the product of a 1957 transatlantic merger, wrote the book on auditing. Lybrand, Ross Bros. & Montgomery was formed in 1898 by William Lybrand, Edward Ross, Adam Ross, and Robert Montgomery. In 1912 Montgomery wrote *Montgomery's Auditing,* which became the bible of accounting.

Cooper Brothers was founded in 1854 in London by William Cooper, eldest son of a Quaker banker. In 1957 Lybrand joined up to form Coopers & Lybrand. During the 1960s the firm expanded into employee benefits and internal control consulting, building its technology capabilities in the 1970s as it studied ways to automate the audit process.

Coopers & Lybrand lost market share as mergers reduced the Big Eight accounting firms to the Big Six. After the savings and loan debacle of the 1980s, investors and the government wanted accounting firms held liable not only for the form of audited financial statements but for their veracity. In 1992 the firm paid $95 million to settle claims of defrauded investors in MiniScribe, a failed disk-drive maker. Other hefty payments followed, including a $108 million settlement relating to the late Robert Maxwell's defunct media empire.

In 1998 Price Waterhouse and Coopers & Lybrand combined PW's strength in the media, entertainment, and utility industries, and Coopers & Lybrand's focus on telecommunications and mining. But the merger brought some expensive legal baggage involving Coopers & Lybrand's performance of audits related to a bid-rigging scheme involving former Arizona governor Fife Symington.

Further growth plans fell through in 1999 when merger talks between PwC and Grant Thornton International failed. The year 2000 began on a sour note: An SEC conflict-of-interest probe turned up more than 8,000 alleged violations, most involving PwC partners owning stock in their firm's audit clients.

As the SEC grew ever more shrill in its denunciation of the potential conflicts of interest arising from auditing companies that the firm hoped to recruit or retain as consulting clients, PwC saw the writing on the wall and in 2000 began making plans to split the two operations. As part of this move, the company downsized and reorganized many of its operations.

The following year PwC paid $55 million to shareholders of MicroStrategy Inc., who charged that the audit firm defrauded them by approving the client firm's inflated earnings and revenues figures.

The separation of PwC's auditing and consulting functions finally became a reality in 2002,

when IBM bought the consulting business. (The acquisition took the place of a planned spinoff.)

Like the other members of the Big Four, PwC picked up business and talent as scandal-felled Andersen was winding down its operations in 2002. The former Andersen organization in China and Hong Kong joined PwC, accounting for about 70% of the approximately 3,500 Andersen alumni that came aboard.

In 2003 former client AMERCO (parent of U-Haul) sued PwC for $2.5 billion, claiming negligence and fraud in relation to a series of events that led to AMERCO restating its results. The suit was settled for more than $50 million the following year. In 2005 PwC was ranked among the Top 10 companies in the US for working mothers by *Working Mother* magazine; it was given that honor again two years later.

PwC endured a two-month suspension in Japan in 2006 after three partners of its firm there were implicated in a fraud investigation involving a PwC client, Kanebo. To distance itself from the scandal, PwC's existing Japanese firm was renamed and a second firm was launched.

EXECUTIVES

Chairman: Dennis M. Nally, age 56
Chairman, International Network: Paul V. Brasher
Global Leader, Operations: Paul Boorman
Chairman and Senior Partner, UK: Kieran C. Poynter
Global Assurance Leader: Donald A. McGovern
Chairman, Regional Asia Board: Silas S.S. Yang
Global Leader, Tax; Managing Partner, PricewaterhouseCoopers, UK: Richard Collier-Keywood
Chairman and Senior Partner, PricewaterhouseCoopers, London: Ian Powell
Global Leader, Advisory Services: Juan Pujadas
Chairman and Senior Partner US: Robert E. Moritz
Global Leader, Strategy: Anthony P.D. Harrington
Global Leader, People and Culture, Brand and Communications: Moira Elms
Global Leader, Global Strategic Sourcing: Edgardo Pappacena
Global Leader, Clients and Markets: Donald V. Almeida
Director Communications: Mike Davies
Global General Counsel: Javier H. Rubinstein
Global Board Member, Hong Kong: Carrie Yu
Global Leader, Public Policy and Regulation: Peter L. Wyman
Global Leader for Risk and Quality: Pierre Coll

LOCATIONS

HQ: PricewaterhouseCoopers International Limited
300 Madison Ave., New York, NY 10017
Phone: 646-471-4000   **Fax:** 813-286-6000
Web: www.pwcglobal.com

PricewaterhouseCoopers has more than 770 offices in 150 countries.

2008 Sales

	% of total
Europe	
Western Europe	45
Central & Eastern Europe	3
North America & the Caribbean	33
Asia	9
Australasia & Pacific Islands	5
Middle East & Africa	3
South & Central America	2
Total	**100**

PRODUCTS/OPERATIONS

2008 Sales

	% of total
Assurance	49
Tax	27
Advisory	24
Total	**100**

2008 Sales by Industry

	% of total
Industrial products	22
Investment management	12
Banking & capital markets	11
Retail & consumer	10
Energy, utilities & mining	8
Technology	7
Insurance	5
Entertainment & media	5
Professional services	4
Pharmaceuticals	4
Government & public service	4
Automotive	3
Information & communications	3
Health care	2
Total	**100**

Selected Products and Services

Audit and assurance
  Actuarial services
  Assistance on capital market transactions
  Corporate reporting improvement
  Financial accounting
  Financial statement audit
  IFRS reporting
  Independent controls and systems process assurance
  Internal audit
  Regulatory compliance and reporting
  Sarbanes-Oxley compliance
  Sustainability reporting

Crisis management
  Business recovery services
  Dispute analysis and investigations

Human resources
  Change and program effectiveness
  HR management
  International assignments
  Reward

Performance improvement
  Financial effectiveness
  Governance, risk, and compliance
  IT effectiveness

Tax
  Compliance
  EU direct tax
  International assignments
  International tax structuring
  Mergers and acquisitions
  Transfer pricing

Transactions
  Accounting valuations
  Advice on fundraising
  Bid support and bid defense services
  Commercial and market due diligence
  Economics
  Financial due diligence
  Independent expert opinions
  Mergers and acquisitions advisory
  Modeling and business planning
  Post deal services
  Private equity advisory
  Privatization advice
  Project finance
  Public company advisory
  Structuring services
  Tax valuations
  Valuation consulting

COMPETITORS

Bain & Company	H&R Block
Baker Tilly International	Hewitt Associates
BDO International	KPMG
Booz Allen	Marsh & McLennan
Boston Consulting	McKinsey & Company
Deloitte	Towers Perrin
Ernst & Young Global	Watson Wyatt
Grant Thornton	

HISTORICAL FINANCIALS
Company Type: Partnership

Income Statement

FYE: June 30

	REVENUE ($ mil.)	NET INCOME ($ mil.)	NET PROFIT MARGIN	EMPLOYEES
6/08	28,185.0	—	—	155,693
6/07	25,150.0	—	—	146,767
6/06	21,986.0	—	—	142,162
6/05	18,998.0	—	—	130,203
6/04	16,283.0	—	—	122,471
Annual Growth	**14.7%**	**—**	**—**	**6.2%**

Revenue History

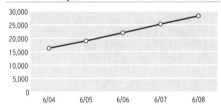

Principal Financial

Ah, the circle of life. For a child in elementary school, avoiding the principal is paramount. However, folks looking toward retirement may actually seek out The Principal. Principal Financial Group (or The Principal) offers pension products and services (the company is a top administrator of employer-sponsored retirement plans), mutual funds, annuities, asset management, trust services, and investment advice. Its insurance segment provides group and individual life, health, disability, dental, and vision coverage. To compete with banks encroaching on the company's territory and to maximize customer asset retention, subsidiary Principal Bank offers online banking.

The Principal has about 19 million customers and some $250 billion of assets under management. Its products are offered through a network of more than 8,000 independent brokers and agents, as well as through its own sales force at more than 40 offices nationwide.

With operations in about a dozen countries, The Principal aims to become a global player in retirement services, targeting countries in Asia and Latin America that rely on private-sector defined-contribution pension plans to accommodate their growing number of retirees. It also does business in Australia and Europe.

In the US, the company courts firms with fewer than 1,000 employees for its insurance and pension products and large institutional clients for its asset management operations, which include Principal Global Investors.

HISTORY

Principal Financial was founded as the Bankers Life Association in 1879 by Edward Temple, a Civil War veteran and banker. Life insurance became popular after the war, but some dishonest insurers canceled customers' policies before they had to pay out benefits. Bankers Life, an assessable association (members shared the cost of death benefits as the claims arose), was intended to provide low-cost protection to bankers and their families. The company soon began offering life insurance to nonbankers, but it refused to insure women because of the high mortality rate among mothers during childbirth.

Bankers Life relied on volunteer workers until 1893. By 1900 it was operating in 21 states. Temple died in 1909, and two years later the company converted to a legal reserve mutual life insurance company with a new name: the Bankers Life Company. The conversion scared many customers away, however. About 50,000 policies were lost over the next three years. In 1915 Bankers Life began insuring women.

WWI slowed growth, and the 1918-1919 influenza epidemic, which killed many policyholders, hit the company hard. The Depression also stunted growth. In 1941 the firm started offering group life insurance, and during WWII it became a major force in that area.

Bankers Life grew through the 1950s and 1960s, adding individual accident and health insurance (1952) and other products. In 1968 it began offering variable annuities for profit-sharing plans and mutual funds, forming what are now Princor Financial Services and Principal Management. In 1977 Bankers Life introduced an adjustable life insurance product that allowed policyholders to change both premium costs and coverage.

In 1986 the company made a few name changes, becoming The Principal Financial Group and renaming its largest unit Principal Mutual Life Insurance (now Principal Life Insurance). That year Principal Financial acquired Eppler, Guerin & Turner, the largest independent stock brokerage firm in the Southwest.

In 1993 Principal Financial was issued Mexico's first new insurance license in 50 years; subsequent expansion included Argentina, China, and Spain.

In 1996 Principal Financial expanded its health care operations, purchasing third-party administrator The Admar Group. The next year the company bought the 76,000-member FHP of Illinois health plan. Despite this fast buildup, Principal Financial decided to exit the direct provision of health care; in 1997 it sold these operations to what is now Coventry Health Care for a 40% stake in the firm, which it also later sold.

Continuing to refocus, the company in 1998 sold its Principal Financial Securities brokerage and bought ReliaStar Mortgage to build a mortgage banking franchise. The company also launched online banking services. Also that year Principal Financial converted to a mutual holding structure. It formed joint ventures in such countries as Chile, Mexico, and India as part of its move into asset management overseas. The company went public in 2001.

As with its health care operations, Principal Financial made a hasty exit from the mortgage business after building that part of its business through acquisitions. Amid rising interest rates and an industry-wide decrease in loan volume, the company sold its retail mortgage branches to American Home Mortgage in 2003, then sold its remaining mortgage banking business to Citigroup the following year. Also in 2004 the company bolstered its core operations by purchasing health care claims processor J.F. Molloy & Associates and the US trust operations of Dutch banking giant ABN AMRO.

At the end of 2006 The Principal finalized its purchase of WM Advisors, the former mutual fund operations of Washington Mutual.

EXECUTIVES

Chairman, President, and CEO; President and CEO, Principal Life: Larry D. Zimpleman, age 57, $4,163,906 total compensation
SVP and CFO: Terry J. Lillis, age 56, $772,476 total compensation
SVP and CIO, Principal Financial and Principal Life: Gary P. Scholten, age 51
VP and Chief Medical Officer: Naim Munir
EVP, International Asset Accumulation, Principal Financial and Principal Life; President, Principal International: Norman R. Sorensen, age 63, $1,187,476 total compensation
EVP and General Counsel, Principal Financial Group and Principal Life: Karen E. Shaff, age 54
SVP, Investor Relations: Thomas J. (Tom) Graf
SVP and Chief Marketing Officer, Principal Financial and Principal Life: Mary A. O'Keefe, age 52
SVP and Chief Risk Officer, Principal Financial Group and Principal Life: Ellen Z. Lamale, age 55
SVP and Chief Investment Officer, Principal Financial Group and Principal Life: Julia M. Lawler, age 49
SVP and Corporate Secretary: Joyce Nixson Hoffman
SVP, Individual Life and Specialty Benefits: Deanna D. Strable
SVP, Health Division: G. David Shafer
SVP and Controller: Greg Elming
President, Insurance and Financial Services, Principal Financial Group and Principal Life: John E. Aschenbrenner, age 59
President, Retirement and Investor Services: Daniel J. (Dan) Houston, age 47, $1,097,417 total compensation
President, Global Asset Management, Principal Financial and Principal Life: James P. (Jim) McCaughan, age 55, $2,029,614 total compensation
Auditors: Ernst & Young LLP

LOCATIONS

HQ: Principal Financial Group, Inc.
711 High St., Des Moines, IA 50392
Phone: 515-247-5111 **Fax:** 515-246-5475
Web: www.principal.com

PRODUCTS/OPERATIONS

2008 Sales

	$ mil.	% of total
Premiums & other considerations	4,209	40
Net investment income	3,994	38
Fees & other revenues	2,427	22
Net capital losses	(694)	—
Total	**9,936**	**100**

COMPETITORS

Aetna	MassMutual
AIG	MetLife
Allianz	Morgan Stanley
Allstate	Nationwide
AXA	Nationwide Financial
Blue Cross	New York Life
CIGNA	Northwestern Mutual
Citigroup	Pacific Mutual
CNA Financial	Prudential
FMR	State Farm
Guardian Life	State Street
The Hartford	T. Rowe Price
ING	Travelers Companies
John Hancock Financial	UBS Financial Services
JPMorgan Chase	UnitedHealth Group
Liberty Mutual	Unum Group
Manulife Financial	The Vanguard Group

HISTORICAL FINANCIALS

Company Type: Public

Income Statement

FYE: December 31

	ASSETS ($ mil.)	NET INCOME ($ mil.)	INCOME AS % OF ASSETS	EMPLOYEES
12/08	128,182.4	458.1	0.4%	16,234
12/07	154,520.2	860.3	0.6%	16,585
12/06	143,658.1	1,064.3	0.7%	15,289
12/05	127,035.4	919.0	0.7%	14,507
12/04	113,798.1	960.1	0.8%	13,976
Annual Growth	**3.0%**	**(16.9%)**	**—**	**3.8%**

2008 Year-End Financials

Equity as % of assets: 1.9%	Dividends
Return on assets: 0.3%	Yield: 2.0%
Return on equity: 9.3%	Payout: 27.6%
Long-term debt ($ mil.): 1,291	Market value ($ mil.): 7,198
No. of shares (mil.): 319	Sales ($ mil.): 9,936

Stock History

NYSE: PFG

	STOCK PRICE ($) FY Close	P/E High/Low		PER SHARE ($) Earnings	Dividends	Book Value
12/08	22.57	41	5	1.63	0.45	7.75
12/07	68.84	23	17	3.09	0.90	23.27
12/06	58.70	16	12	3.74	0.80	24.65
12/05	47.43	17	12	3.11	0.65	24.48
12/04	40.94	16	12	2.62	0.55	23.65
Annual Growth	**(13.8%)**	**—**	**—**	**(11.2%)**	**(4.9%)**	**(24.3%)**

Procter & Gamble

The Procter & Gamble Company (P&G) boasts boatloads of brands. The world's #1 maker of household products courts market share and billion-dollar names. It's divided into three global units: health and well being, beauty, and household care. The company also makes pet food and water filters and produces soap operas. Some 25 of P&G's brands are billion-dollar sellers, including Fusion, Always/Whisper, Braun, Bounty, Charmin, Crest, Downy/Lenor, Gillette, Iams, Olay, Pampers, Pantene, Pringles, Tide, and Wella, among others. P&G shed its coffee brands in late 2008. Being the acquisitive type, with Clairol and Wella as notable conquests, P&G's biggest buy in company history was Gillette in late 2005.

The company's hundreds of brands are available in more than 180 countries.

As the recession was gaining momentum in 2008, P&G initiated several changes. In a push to increase productivity, P&G shed about 15% of its management staff. Also, the consumer products giant began to focus greater resources on its best-selling brands. It sold its Folgers business to The J. M. Smucker Company for more than $3 billion in 2008.

P&G also is looking to fast-growing markets, such as Brazil, Russia, India, and China, to help it offset an economic slowdown in the US.

P&G's purchase of Gillette, for $57 billion in 2005, added well-known complementary brands to its already vast portfolio, such as Gillette razors and blades, Duracell batteries, Oral-B oral care items, and Braun appliances. Because some of the two companies' brands competed (such as P&G's Old Spice and Crest vs. Gillette's Right Guard and Oral-B) and to satisfy antitrust regulators, P&G divested certain assets.

Alan G. Lafley resigned from his position as CEO in July 2009 but remained with the company as chairman. The company named COO Robert McDonald to take over the roles of president and chief executive.

In August 2009 P&G announced that it has agreed to sell its prescription-drug unit (about $2 billion in sales) to drug maker Warner Chilcott for about $3 billion. P&G, which has struggled for years to gain traction in pharmaceuticals, will instead focus on consumer health care.

The company has logged some less-than-successful business adventures over the years. As such, P&G lost its patience with olestra ("fake fat") branded as Olean when it repeatedly failed to deliver profits. It sold its olestra production plant in 2002, but P&G retains the rights to the Olean brand and technology.

P&G also continues to contribute to the broadcast television industry. The consumer products giant boasts a long-standing relationship with CBS for *Guiding Light* (which began as a radio program in 1937) and *As the World Turns* (which had been on the air for 50 years in 2006). To reach younger consumers, P&G has launched an online soap opera called "Crescent Heights," which viewers can watch on their PCs and cell phones.

Despite its alliance with CBS, it's lights out for *Guiding Light* as of September 18, 2009, when the show aired its last episode.

HISTORY

Candle maker William Procter and soap maker James Gamble merged their small Cincinnati businesses in 1837, creating The Procter & Gamble Company (P&G), which incorporated in 1905. By 1859 P&G had become one of the largest companies in Cincinnati, with sales of $1 million. It introduced Ivory, a floating soap, in 1879, and Crisco shortening in 1911.

The Ivory campaign was one of the first to advertise directly to the consumer. Other advertising innovations included sponsorship of daytime radio dramas in 1932. P&G's first TV commercial, for Ivory, aired in 1939.

Family members headed the company until 1930, when William Deupree became president. In the 29 years that he served as president and then chairman, P&G became the largest US seller of packaged goods.

After years of researching cleansers for use in hard water, in 1947 P&G introduced Tide detergent. It began a string of acquisitions when it picked up Spic and Span (1945; sold 2001), Duncan Hines (1956; sold 1998), Charmin Paper Mills (1957), and Folgers Coffee (1963). P&G launched Crest toothpaste in 1955 and Head & Shoulders shampoo and Pampers disposable diapers in 1961.

Rely tampons were pulled from shelves in 1980 when investigators linked them to toxic shock syndrome. In 1985 P&G moved into health care when it purchased Richardson-Vicks

(NyQuil, Vicks) and G.D. Searle's nonprescription drug division (Metamucil). The acquisitions of Noxell (1989; CoverGirl, Noxzema) and Max Factor (1991) made it a top cosmetics company in the US.

P&G began a major restructuring in 1993, cutting 13,000 jobs and closing 30 plants. The firm in 1996 sued rival Amway over rumors connecting P&G and its moon-and-stars logo to Satanism. (The suit was dismissed in 1999.) Also in 1996 the FDA approved the use of olestra, a controversial fat substitute developed by P&G.

In 1997 it acquired Tambrands (Tampax tampons), making P&G #1 in feminine sanitary protection. Chairman John Pepper handed over his chairman and CEO title in 1999 to president Durk Jager, who promised five new products a year and a shakeup of the corporate culture.

In 1999 the company announced further reorganization plans, including 15,000 job cuts worldwide by 2005. That same year P&G bought The Iams Company (maker of Eukanuba- and Iams-brand dog and cat foods).

With earnings flat, Jager resigned in 2000. P&G insider Alan G. Lafley immediately assumed the president and CEO duties, and Pepper returned to succeed Jager as chairman.

In 2001 P&G announced job cuts for 9,600 employees to further reduce costs. It also sold its Comet cleaner business. That year P&G completed its purchase of the Clairol hair care unit from Bristol-Myers Squibb for nearly $5 billion.

In 2003 P&G entered the premium pet food market with its purchase of The Iams Company for $2.3 billion. And to secure its foothold in China, it bought the remaining 20% stake in its joint venture with Hutchison Whampoa China Ltd. in 2004 for $1.8 billion.

Further expanding its luxury hair-care portfolio, in May 2008 P&G purchased Frédéric Fekkai & Co. from Chrysallis. The acquisition gives P&G a foothold in department store hair care. Fekkai caters to prestige stores located in the US, such as Neiman Marcus, Nordstrom, and Sephora.

EXECUTIVES

Chairman: Alan G. (A.G.) Lafley, age 62
President, CEO, and Director:
 Robert A. (Bob) McDonald, age 56
CFO: Jon R. Moeller, age 45
President, Global Business Services and CIO:
 Filippo Passerini, age 52
CTO: Bruce Brown, age 51
Chief Legal Officer and Secretary: Steven W. Jemison, age 57
SVP Research and Development, Global Fabric Care:
 Sharon J. Mitchell
SVP and Treasurer: Teri L. List, age 46
VP and General Manager, P&G Professional, North America: Norb Mayrhofer
VP, Global Licensing and External Business Development: Jeff Weedman
VP and General Manager, Multicultural Development:
 Graciela Eleta
VP and General Counsel: Deborah Platt Majoras
Global Marketing and Brand-Building Officer:
 Marc S. Pritchard, age 49
Global Human Resources Officer: Moheet Nagrath, age 50
Global Design Officer: Philip J Duncan, age 44
Vice Chairman Global Operations: Werner Geissler, age 56
Vice Chairman Global Household Care:
 E. Dimitri Panayotopoulos, age 57
Vice Chairman Global Health and Well-Being:
 Robert A. (Rob) Steele, age 53
Vice Chairman Global Beauty and Grooming:
 Edward D. (Ed) Shirley, age 52
Investor Relations: Mark Erceg
Auditors: Deloitte & Touche LLP

LOCATIONS

HQ: The Procter & Gamble Company
 1 Procter & Gamble Plaza, Cincinnati, OH 45202
Phone: 513-983-1100   **Fax:** 513-983-9369
Web: www.pg.com

2009 Sales

	$ mil.	% of total
International	47,949	61
US	31,080	39
Total	**79,029**	**100**

2009 Sales

	% of total
North America	43
Developing markets	32
Western Europe	21
Northeast Asia	4
Total	**100**

PRODUCTS/OPERATIONS

2009 Sales

	$ mil.	% of total
Beauty		
Beauty	18,789	24
Grooming	7,543	10
Health & Well Being		
Health Care	13,623	17
Snacks & Pet Care	3,114	4
Household Care		
Fabric Care & Home Care	23,186	29
Baby Care & Family Care	14,103	18
Corporate	(1,329)	(2)
Total	**79,029**	**100**

Global Business Units and Reportable Segments

Beauty Care
 Beauty
 Grooming
Health & Well Being
 Health Care
 Snacks & Pet Care
Household Care
 Fabric Care & Home Care
 Baby Care & Family Care

Selected Brand Names by Global Business Unit

Beauty Care
 Braun
 Clairol
 CoverGirl
 Frédéric Fekkai & Co.
 Fusion
 Gillette
 Head & Shoulders
 Herbal Essence
 I-Iman
 Ivory
 Mach3
 Max Factor
 Nice 'n Easy
 Olay
 Old Spice
 Pantene
 Safeguard
 Secret
 Ultresse
 Wella
 Zest
Health & Well Being
 Actonel
 Always
 Crest
 Iams
 Oral-B
 Prilosec
 Pringles

Household Care
 Ariel
 Bounty
 Charmin
 Dawn
 Downy
 Duracell
 Gain
 Pampers
 P&G Pro Line (commercial cleaning)
 Swiffer
 Tide

Soap Operas

As The World Turns
Guiding Light

COMPETITORS

Alberto-Culver
Alticor
American Safety Razor
Amway
Avon
Bath & Body Works
Baxter of California
BIC
Body Shop
Bristol-Myers Squibb
Church & Dwight
Clorox
Colgate-Palmolive
Discus Dental
Dr. Bronner's
Energizer Holdings
Estée Lauder
Frito-Lay
Hain Celestial
Heinz
Henkel
Johnson & Johnson
Kimberly-Clark
Kraft Foods
L'Oréal
Mary Kay
Meda Pharmaceuticals
Nestlé
PepsiCo
Pfizer
Philips Electronics
Revlon
Salton
Sanofi-Aventis
SANYO
Sara Lee Household and Body Care
S.C. Johnson
Scott's Liquid Gold
SEB
Shiseido
Spectrum Brands
Tom's of Maine
Turtle Wax
Unilever
VIVUS
Wyeth

HISTORICAL FINANCIALS

Company Type: Public

Income Statement

	REVENUE ($ mil.)	NET INCOME ($ mil.)	NET PROFIT MARGIN	EMPLOYEES
6/09	79,029.0	13,436.0	17.0%	135,000
6/08	83,503.0	12,075.0	14.5%	138,000
6/07	76,476.0	10,340.0	13.5%	138,000
6/06	68,222.0	8,684.0	12.7%	138,000
6/05	56,741.0	7,257.0	12.8%	110,000
Annual Growth	8.6%	16.6%	—	5.3%

FYE: June 30

2009 Year-End Financials

Debt ratio: 33.4%
Return on equity: 20.7%
Cash ($ mil.): 4,781
Current ratio: 0.71
Long-term debt ($ mil.): 20,652

No. of shares (mil.): 2,919
Dividends
Yield: 3.2%
Payout: 38.5%
Market value ($ mil.): 149,155

Stock History

NYSE: PG

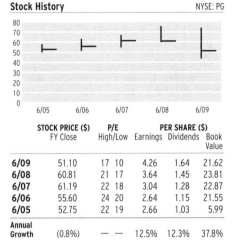

	STOCK PRICE ($)	P/E		PER SHARE ($)		
	FY Close	High/Low		Earnings	Dividends	Book Value
6/09	51.10	17	10	4.26	1.64	21.62
6/08	60.81	21	17	3.64	1.45	23.81
6/07	61.19	22	18	3.04	1.28	22.87
6/06	55.60	24	20	2.64	1.15	21.55
6/05	52.75	22	19	2.66	1.03	5.99
Annual Growth	(0.8%)	—	—	12.5%	12.3%	37.8%

Progress Energy

Without progress, millions of people would be without energy. Progress Energy provides electricity to 3.1 million customers. It serves customers in North and South Carolina, through utility Carolina Power & Light (dba Progress Energy Carolinas), and in Florida, through Florida Power (or Progress Energy Florida). The company generates most of its energy from nuclear and fossil-fueled plants and has a total capacity of more than 21,000 MW. In a move to refocus on its core retail and wholesale power businesses, in 2007 the company shut down its Competitive Commercial Operations unit and exited its synthetic fuels business, and in 2008 it sold its remaining coal mine and coal terminal services.

Due to a weak wholesale market, Progress Energy scaled back plans to enlarge its power generation portfolio; it is also reducing its power marketing and trading activities.

In 2007 it sold its nonregulated power plants, hedges, and contracts for $480 million. In 2008 the company sold its Powell Mountain Coal Company, Dulcimer Land Company, and Kanawha River Terminals to an investor group for $94 million.

HISTORY

Central Carolina Power was incorporated in 1908. Later that year, under the aegis of the Electric Bond and Share Co. (EBS, a subsidiary of General Electric), Central Carolina Power crossed lines with Raleigh Electric and Consumers Light & Power to form Carolina Power & Light (CP&L).

EBS president S. Z. Mitchell was a leader in the young industry, espousing economies of scale through mergers and promoting lower rates to encourage sales. CP&L had three hydroelectric plants by 1911, and by 1912 it had acquired three neighboring utilities, including Asheville Power & Light. The company began selling power wholesale to municipal utilities, in addition to its retail sales.

Demand soared after WWI as textile mills switched from steam engines to electricity and residential customers became enamored of modern appliances sold by CP&L. The company merged with four other utilities and reincorporated in 1926. The next year it became part of National Power & Light, a huge utility holding company created by EBS.

CP&L struggled during the Depression as demand slackened. To add legislative insult to financial injury, Congress passed the Public Utility Holding Company Act of 1935 (repealed in 2005) to break up vast utility trusts. The act inaugurated 60 years of regional monopolies regulated by state and federal authorities. In 1948 CP&L was divested from EBS and went public.

The postwar boom increased the demand for power, and to keep up CP&L built several large coal-fired plants. By the early 1960s the company had begun building its first nuclear facility, the Robinson plant, which was completed in 1971. CP&L also continued to build huge, coal-fired plants.

The company completed its second nuke (Brunswick) in 1977. But two years later the accident at Pennsylvania's Three Mile Island cast a pall on the industry. After numerous delays CP&L decided to complete just one more nuke (Harris). The plant went on line in 1987, and CP&L requested a 13% rate increase to help cover its $3.8 billion cost. In contrast to its brothers, Harris ran quite well. But problems continued to plague CP&L's nuclear program into the early 1990s.

The Federal Energy Policy Act of 1992 dramatically changed the utility industry by allowing wholesale power competition. The following year CP&L hired new nuke management to turn around its troubled Brunswick plant.

In 1996 the utility lost $100 million to damages from Hurricane Fran. The next year the company unveiled Strategic Resource Solutions, a nonregulated energy services company created out of the former Knowledge Builders. In 1998 CP&L began marketing wholesale power.

To expand into natural gas distribution, CP&L bought North Carolina Natural Gas (NCNG) in 1999 for about $354 million in stock. The company also agreed to buy utility holding company Florida Progress for $5.4 billion in cash and stock and $2.7 billion in assumed debt. In preparation for its Florida Progress purchase, CP&L adopted a holding company structure in 2000 and was renamed CP&L Energy Inc. The Florida Progress deal was completed later that year, and CP&L Energy became Progress Energy. In 2000 it also formed a new unregulated energy marketing subsidiary, Progress Energy Ventures.

As a condition of the merger, Progress Energy agreed to divest some noncore assets; in 2001 it sold its MEMCO Barge Line unit to American Electric Power for $270 million.

In 2002 Progress Energy Ventures purchased two Georgia power plants (one operational and one under construction) for $345 million from LG&E Energy.

Progress Energy exited the natural gas distribution business in 2003 with the sale of its North Carolina Natural Gas utility to Piedmont Natural Gas for about $425 million. The company has also sold its transportation assets, and a portion of its oil and gas production operations.

In 2004 Progress Energy sold its Progress Rail Services to One Equity Partners for $405 million. (One Equity turned around 18 months later and sold the railroad maintenance and repair service company to Caterpillar for a cool $1 billion.)

Progress Energy sold its Winchester Energy natural gas exploration and production business in 2006 to EXCO Resources for $1.2 billion.

EXECUTIVES

Chairman, President, and CEO:
William D. (Bill) Johnson, age 55,
$6,389,426 total compensation
SVP and CFO: Mark F. Mulhern, age 49,
$2,280,661 total compensation
VP Information Technology and Telecommunications and CIO: Dede F. Ramoneda
SVP and Chief Nuclear Officer PEC and PEF:
James (Jim) Scarola, age 53
Chief Accounting Officer and Controller, Progress Energy and Florida Progress: Jeffrey M. (Jeff) Stone, age 48
EVP and Secretary: John R. McArthur, age 53,
$1,797,802 total compensation
EVP Corporate Development: Jeffrey J. (Jeff) Lyash, age 47, $2,027,619 total compensation
SVP Energy Delivery, Progress Energy Carolinas:
Jeffrey A. (Jeff) Corbett, age 49
SVP Compliance and General Counsel, Progress Energy: Frank A. Schiller, age 47
SVP Power Operations, PEC and PEF: Paula J. Sims, age 47
SVP Energy Delivery, PEF: Michael A. Lewis, age 46
VP Regulated Fuels and Capital Planning:
Robert H. (Bob) Bazemore Jr., age 55
VP Human Resources: Anne M. Huffman
VP Investor Relations: Robert F. (Bob) Drennan Jr.
VP Plant Construction and Technical Services:
Joel Y. Kamya
VP Customer and Market Services: R. Tucker Mann
VP Chief Risk Officer, and Treasurer:
Thomas R. (Tom) Sullivan
VP Corporate Communications: Nancy H. Temple
President and CEO, Progress Energy Florida:
Vincent M. (Vinny) Dolan, age 54
President and CEO, Progress Energy Carolinas:
Lloyd M. Yates, age 48, $2,488,057 total compensation
Auditors: Deloitte & Touche LLP

LOCATIONS

HQ: Progress Energy, Inc.
410 S. Wilmington St., Raleigh, NC 27601
Phone: 919-546-6111   **Fax:** 919-546-2920
Web: www.progress-energy.com

Progress Energy distributes electricity in North Carolina, northeastern South Carolina, and west central Florida.

PRODUCTS/OPERATIONS

2008 Sales

	% of total
Residential	35
Commercial	25
Wholesale	20
Industrial	15
Other	5
Total	**100**

2008 Sales

	$ mil.	% of total
PEF	4,730	52
PEC	4,429	48
Corporate & other	8	—
Total	**9,167**	**100**

Selected Subsidiaries

Carolina Power & Light Company (operates as Progress Energy Carolinas, electric utility; PEC)
Florida Power Corporation (operates as Progress Energy Florida, electric utility; PEF)

COMPETITORS

ACES Power Marketing
AEP
ALLETE
CenterPoint Energy
Dominion Resources
Duke Energy
Entergy
FPL Group
JEA
Mississippi Power
North Carolina Electric Membership
Oglethorpe Power
Piedmont Natural Gas
Santee Cooper
SCANA
Seminole Electric
Southern Company
TECO Energy
TVA

HISTORICAL FINANCIALS

Company Type: Public

Income Statement

FYE: December 31

	REVENUE ($ mil.)	NET INCOME ($ mil.)	NET PROFIT MARGIN	EMPLOYEES
12/08	9,167.0	830.0	9.1%	11,000
12/07	9,153.0	504.0	5.5%	11,000
12/06	9,570.0	571.0	6.0%	11,000
12/05	10,108.0	696.0	6.9%	11,600
12/04	9,772.0	759.0	7.8%	15,700
Annual Growth	(1.6%)	2.3%	—	(8.5%)

2008 Year-End Financials

Debt ratio: 124.0%
Return on equity: 9.7%
Cash ($ mil.): 180
Current ratio: 1.01
Long-term debt ($ mil.): 10,890

No. of shares (mil.): 279
Dividends
  Yield: 6.2%
  Payout: 77.4%
Market value ($ mil.): 11,118

Stock History

NYSE: PGN

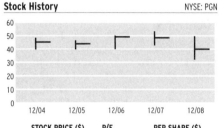

	STOCK PRICE ($) FY Close	P/E High/Low	PER SHARE ($) Earnings	PER SHARE ($) Dividends	PER SHARE ($) Book Value
12/08	39.85	15 10	3.18	2.46	31.47
12/07	48.43	27 22	1.96	2.44	30.19
12/06	49.08	22 18	2.28	1.82	29.70
12/05	43.92	16 14	2.82	2.38	29.14
12/04	45.24	15 13	3.12	2.89	27.69
Annual Growth	(3.1%)	— —	0.5%	(3.9%)	3.2%

Progressive Corporation

It's risky business, and Progressive loves it. Long a leader in nonstandard, high-risk personal auto insurance, The Progressive Corporation has motored beyond its traditional business into standard-risk and preferred auto insurance, as well as other personal-use vehicle coverage (motorcycles, recreational vehicles, and snowmobiles). Progressive also offers commercial policies for heavy trucks, vans, and lighter trucks. It writes a bit of professional liability insurance for directors' and officers' insurance of community banks. The company markets directly to consumers online and by phone, and through 30,000 independent agents which account for 60% of the company's business.

Focusing on its core auto business, Progressive stopped writing homeowners insurance years ago, but continues to offer coverage to its auto insurance customers, underwritten by third party Homesite Insurance. Progressive also offers personal umbrella insurance that provides coverage for the extras in life, such as personal injury and legal defense.

Unlike some insurers who, in fat markets, earn more from their investments than their premiums, more than 90% of Progressive's revenues have historically come from policy premiums. This quirk allowed the company to maintain a bit more serenity than its competitors during most market fluctuations. However, it loaded up on subprime investments in 2007, which proved a regrettable strategy. Subsequently, in 2008 Progressive experienced its first loss in 26 years.

Despite that loss, the company's actual insurance operations have remained profitable and grown as it has entered into new geographic markets and expanded distribution of its personal auto products online. Already among the leading US auto insurers based on volume (behind State Farm and Allstate), Progressive is aiming to be on top.

Colorful chairman Peter Lewis (who supports legalizing marijuana and holds that contemporary art in the company's hallways stimulates innovation) is the son of one of the insurer's founders. He built Progressive up from a regional operation to a national player and controls more than 5% of the company.

HISTORY

Attorneys Jack Green and Joseph Lewis founded Progressive Mutual Insurance in Cleveland in 1937. Initially offering standard auto insurance, the company attracted customers through such innovations as installment plans for premiums (a payment method popularized during the Depression) and drive-in claims services (the company was headquartered in a garage). Progressive's early years were uncertain — at one point the founders were even advised to go out of business — but the advent of WWII bolstered business: Car and insurance purchases were up, but accidents were down as gas rationing limited driving.

Then came the suburbs and cars of the 1950s. While most competitors sought low-risk drivers, Progressive exploited the high-risk niche

through careful underwriting and statistical analysis. Subsidiary Progressive Casualty was founded in 1956 (the year after Joseph Lewis died) to insure the best of the worst. Lewis' son Peter joined the company in 1955 and helped engineer its early-1960s expansion outside Ohio. After Green retired in 1965, Peter gained control of the company through a leveraged buyout and renamed it The Progressive Corporation. Six years later, Lewis took it public and formed subsidiary Progressive American in Florida.

In the mid-1970s the industry went into a funk as it was hit by a wave of consolidations and rising interest rates. Lewis set a goal for the company to always earn an underwriting profit instead of depending on investments to make a profit. Progressive achieved stellar results during the 1970s, especially after states began requiring drivers to be insured and other insurers began weeding out higher risks.

Competition in nonstandard insurance grew in the 1980s, as major insurers such as Allstate and State Farm joined the fray with their larger sales forces and deeper pockets. In 1988 California's Proposition 103 retroactively reduced rates; Progressive fought California's demand for refunds but set aside reserves to pay them.

That year Lewis hired Cleveland financier Alfred Lerner to guide company investments. Lerner invested $75 million in Progressive via a convertible debenture; five years later he converted it to stock, half of which he sold for $122 million. Soon after, he was asked to resign. In 1993 Progressive settled with California for $51 million and applied to earnings the remaining $100 million in refund reserves. (Company soul-searching related to Proposition 103 led to the launch of Progressive's now-famous "Immediate Response" vehicles, which provide 24-hour claims service at accident sites.)

In 1995 Progressive's practice of using consumer credit information to make underwriting decisions drew the attention of Arkansas and Vermont insurance regulators, who said the company might be discriminating against people who didn't have the credit cards Progressive used to evaluate creditworthiness. In 1996 insurance regulators in Alaska, Maryland, and Texas also began probing Progressive's credit information practices.

In 1997 Progressive bought nonstandard auto insurer Midland Financial Group. As competition grew in 1999, the company cut rates and said it would write no new policies in Canada. In 2000 — with underwriting margins dropping industrywide — the company continued advertising aggressively. Progressive stopped writing new homeowners insurance in 2002, instead concentrating on its core operations. In 2006 the company began offering personal umbrella coverage.

EXECUTIVES

Chairman: Peter B. Lewis, age 75
President, CEO, and Director: Glenn M. Renwick, age 53, $5,854,408 total compensation
VP and CFO: Brian C. Domeck, age 49, $1,065,951 total compensation
CIO: Raymond M. Voelker, age 45, $1,170,457 total compensation
VP and Chief Accounting Officer: Jeffrey W. Basch, age 50
VP, Chief Legal Officer, and Secretary: Charles E. Jarrett, age 51, $1,257,148 total compensation
Chief Investment Officer: William M. Cody, age 46, $855,059 total compensation

Chief Marketing Officer: Larry Bloomenkranz, age 51
Chief Human Resource Officer: Valerie Krasowski, age 43
VP and Treasurer: Thomas A. King, age 49
Group President, Sales and Service: Richard H. Watts, age 54
Claims Group President: Susan P. Griffith, age 44, $1,195,628 total compensation
President, Group Lines: John A. Barbagello, age 49
Group President, Commercial Auto: Brian A. Silva, age 55
Group President, Personal Lines: John P. Sauerland, age 44, $1,074,153 total compensation
President, Progressive Casualty Insurance Co.: David J. Skove
Snow Mobile Product Manager: Rick Stern
Investor Relations: Patrick Brennan
Auditors: PricewaterhouseCoopers LLP

LOCATIONS

HQ: The Progressive Corporation
6300 Wilson Mills Rd., Mayfield Village, OH 44143
Phone: 440-461-5000   **Fax:** 800-456-6590
Web: www.progressive.com

PRODUCTS/OPERATIONS

2008 Revenues

	$ mil.	% of total
Premiums		
Personal lines	11,847.8	87
Commercial auto	1,762.2	13
Other	21.4	—
Service businesses	16.1	—
Investment losses	(807.4)	—
Total	**12,840.1**	**100**

COMPETITORS

21st Century Insurance
Allstate
American Family Insurance
Cincinnati Financial
GEICO
Liberty Mutual
Nationwide
Ohio Casualty
Old Republic
State Auto Financial
State Farm
Travelers Companies
USAA
White Mountains Insurance Group

HISTORICAL FINANCIALS

Company Type: Public

Income Statement

FYE: December 31

	ASSETS ($ mil.)	NET INCOME ($ mil.)	INCOME AS % OF ASSETS	EMPLOYEES
12/08	18,250.5	(70.0)	—	25,929
12/07	18,843.1	1,182.5	6.3%	26,851
12/06	19,482.1	1,647.5	8.5%	27,778
12/05	18,898.6	1,393.9	7.4%	28,336
12/04	17,184.3	1,648.7	9.6%	27,085
Annual Growth	**1.5%**	**—**	**—**	**(1.1%)**

2008 Year-End Financials

Equity as % of assets: 23.1%
Return on assets: —
Return on equity: —
Long-term debt ($ mil.): 2,176
No. of shares (mil.): 679
Dividends
  Yield: 1.0%
  Payout: —
Market value ($ mil.): 10,050
Sales ($ mil.): 12,840

Stock History

NYSE: PGR

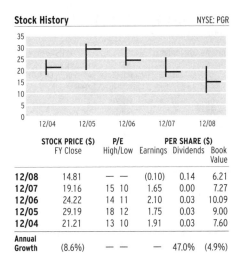

	STOCK PRICE ($) FY Close	P/E High/Low		PER SHARE ($) Earnings	Dividends	Book Value
12/08	14.81	—	—	(0.10)	0.14	6.21
12/07	19.16	15	10	1.65	0.00	7.27
12/06	24.22	14	11	2.10	0.03	10.09
12/05	29.19	18	12	1.75	0.03	9.00
12/04	21.21	13	10	1.91	0.03	7.60
Annual Growth	**(8.6%)**	**—**	**—**	**—**	**47.0%**	**(4.9%)**

Protective Life

Protective Life wants to cushion its customers from the nasty blows of life and death. The company focuses on life insurance products sold through its Life Marketing business segment (via its own agents, independent agents, worksite plans, and financial institutions). Its Acquisitions segment brings in blocks of life insurance policies sold elsewhere. The company's Asset Protection segment sells extended service contracts and credit life insurance through auto and marine dealers nationwide. Other products include annuities and guaranteed investment contracts (GICs) for 401(k) plans. The company operates through subsidiaries Protective Life Insurance and West Coast Life Insurance.

Along with the GICs, the company's Stable Value Products segment markets funding agreements for financial instruments, such as municipal bonds and money market funds.

Protective Life's combined life insurance operations (Marketing and Acquisitions) account for nearly 70% of the company's revenue. Protective Life has aggressively capitalized on the industry trend of consolidation, carefully selecting small and midsized firms that complement its existing operations. It has acquired more than 40 insurance companies or blocks of policies in the past three decades, allowing the company to gain premiums without expensive commissions.

Protective briefly considered acquiring The Bank of Bonifay, a small Florida bank in early 2009. The purchase would have helped it obtain status as a bank holding company, potentially allowing it to tap into the US Treasury's Troubled Asset Relief Program (TARP). However, after observing the glacial speed with which the Treasury was considering such applications, Protective scrapped the plan and stuck with insurance.

Prior to the implosions in the lending and credit markets, the company invested a significant portion of its assets into mortgage-backed securities, preferring to invest in pools of prime residential mortgages and non-speculative commercial properties such as strip-center retailers.

HISTORY

In 1907 — when former Alabama governor William Jelks founded Protective Life in Birmingham — the South had not yet risen again, and most insurance business was controlled by northern companies. Protective Life survived the financial panic that year and grew steadily, paying its first dividends in 1916. It was sorely tested in 1918, as were most insurance companies, when the influenza pandemic took thousands of lives, particularly in large cities.

In 1927 Protective Life merged with another Birmingham-based insurance company, Alabama National Insurance, founded in 1908 as Great Southern Life Insurance. Alabama National's Samuel Clabaugh, a former banker, was appointed president, and under his guidance the company passed through the Depression intact, having cautiously conserved its capital. Another Alabama National alumnus, William Rushton, whose family name would become synonymous with Protective Life in Birmingham, took over as CEO in 1937. Colonel Rushton, as he became known after his stint in WWII, continued to lead the company for the next 20 years, investing in southern economic development.

In 1963 Protective Life formulated a new strategy, concentrating on the upper-income market, advanced underwriting, business insurance, and estate planning. The company planned to expand geographically, with hopes of going nationwide. Protective Life was operating in 14 states by 1969, the year that Rushton's son, William Rushton III, assumed command from the colonel.

Under the younger Rushton, Protective expanded its operations to all 50 states. The firm purchased 39 companies and numerous blocks of policies between 1970 and 1997.

In 1992 Rushton was named chairman and Drayton Nabers was appointed CEO. In 1994 Protective teamed with Indonesia's Lippo Group (which has interests in securities, banking, and insurance) to form Hong Kong-based Lippo Protective Life Insurance, now CRC Protective Life Insurance. The joint venture introduced US-style universal life insurance to Hong Kong. Denomination of policies in US dollars attracted clients wary of unstable Asian currencies.

In the early 1990s Protective pioneered the concept of selling indemnity dental insurance on a voluntary payroll-deduction basis. In 1995 the company purchased National Health Care Systems of Florida, operating under the trade name DentiCare, and entered the managed dental care business.

In 1997 Protective acquired West Coast Life Insurance and Western Diversified Group. It also continued to build its dental care operations through the 1997 acquisitions of three more small, managed dental care companies and its 1998 purchase of United Dental Care, making it the third-largest managed dental care company in the US. In 1999 Nabers took on the additional role of chairman, taking over after William Rushton resigned. That year the company began distributing term life insurance over the Internet through agreements with HomeCom Communications and Matrix Direct Insurance Services. (Matrix was sold to American International Group in 2007.)

In 2000 Protective bought specialty insurer Lyndon Insurance Group from Frontier Insurance Group. Then Protective's subsidiary Protective Life Insurance acquired 70,000 life insurance policies from Standard Insurance. Nabers stepped down as CEO at the end of 2001.

The company sold its dental benefits division to Fortis Inc. in 2002. The following year Nabers resigned as chairman to become Alabama's finance director and Protective CEO John Johns was named chairman.

EXECUTIVES

Chairman, President, and CEO: John D. Johns, age 57, $2,561,186 total compensation
Vice Chairman and CFO: Richard J. (Rich) Bielen, age 48
EVP and COO: Carolyn M. Johnson, age 48, $747,946 total compensation
SVP and CIO: David Gutierrez
EVP and Chief Investment Officer: Carl S. Thigpen, age 52, $900,340 total compensation
SVP, Controller, and Chief Accounting Officer: Steven G. Walker, age 49
SVP and Chief Distribution Officer: John B. Deremo
SVP and Chief Human Resources Officer: D. Scott Adams, age 44
EVP and Chief Risk Officer: Edward M. Berko
EVP, General Counsel, and Secretary: Deborah J. Long, age 55, $681,480 total compensation
EVP and COO, West Coast Life: Bernard L. (Bernie) Robins, age 70
SVP Information Services: Thomas D. Keyes, age 56
SVP Stable Value Products: Judy Wilson, age 50
SVP and Chief Actuary: Wayne E. Stuenkel, age 55
SVP Acquisitions: Carolyn King, age 59
SVP Asset Protection: Brent E. Griggs, age 53
SVP Sales, West Coast Life Insurance: Mark S. Rush
VP Corporate Finance and Investor Relations: Chip Wann
VP Investor Relations: Eva Robertson
President, First Protective: Andrew Martin
Auditors: PricewaterhouseCoopers LLP

LOCATIONS

HQ: Protective Life Corporation
2801 Hwy. 280 South, Birmingham, AL 35223
Phone: 205-268-1000   **Fax:** 205-268-3196
Web: www.protective.com

PRODUCTS/OPERATIONS

2008 Sales

	$ mil.	% of total
Premiums & policy fees	2,692.6	58
Net investment income	1,675.2	36
Realized investment gains		
Derivative financial instruments	116.6	2
All other investments (losses)	(584.5)	—
Other	188.5	4
Reinsurance ceded	(1,582.8)	—
Total	**2,505.6**	**100**

Selected Subsidiaries

Lyndon Insurance Group (in Massachusetts)
Protective Life Insurance Company
West Coast Life Insurance Company

COMPETITORS

AEGON USA	MassMutual
AIG	MetLife
APCO	Nationwide
C.A.R.S. Protection Plus	New York Life
CIGNA	Northwestern Mutual
Conseco	Pacific Mutual
Hartford Life	Principal Financial
ING Americas	Prudential
Interstate National Dealer	UNIFI Companies
Services	Warrantech

HISTORICAL FINANCIALS

Company Type: Public

Income Statement

FYE: December 31

	ASSETS ($ mil.)	NET INCOME ($ mil.)	INCOME AS % OF ASSETS	EMPLOYEES
12/08	39,572.4	(41.9)	—	2,372
12/07	41,786.0	289.6	0.7%	2,406
12/06	39,795.3	281.6	0.7%	2,743
12/05	28,967.0	246.6	0.9%	2,192
12/04	27,211.4	250.4	0.9%	2,272
Annual Growth	**9.8%**	**—**	**—**	**1.1%**

2008 Year-End Financials

Equity as % of assets: 1.8%
Return on assets: —
Return on equity: —
Long-term debt ($ mil.): 1,240
No. of shares (mil.): 86
Dividends
  Yield: 5.7%
  Payout: —
Market value ($ mil.): 1,228
Sales ($ mil.): 2,506

Stock History

NYSE: PL

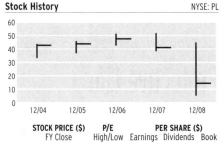

	STOCK PRICE ($) FY Close	P/E High/Low		PER SHARE ($) Earnings	Dividends	Book Value
12/08	14.35	— —		(0.59)	0.81	8.89
12/07	41.02	13 10		4.05	0.89	28.71
12/06	47.50	13 11		3.94	0.84	27.03
12/05	43.77	13 11		3.46	0.76	25.52
12/04	42.69	13 10		3.30	0.69	25.31
Annual Growth	**(23.9%)**	**— —**		**—**	**4.1%**	**(23.0%)**

Prudential Financial

Prudential Financial wants to make sure its position near the top of the life insurance summit is set in stone. Prudential, known for its Rock of Gibraltar logo, is the second largest US life insurer (behind MetLife) and one of the largest insurers worldwide. The firm is perhaps best known for its individual life insurance, though it also sells group life, long-term care, and disability insurance. Prudential also offers investment products and services, including asset management services, mutual funds, and retirement services. Other lines include a national real estate brokerage franchise and relocation services.

Additionally, the company sells annuities through its aptly-named Prudential Annuities Life Assurance subsidiary. Prudential's 38% ownership of Wachovia Securities had allowed its customers access to securities brokerage and financial advice; however, the company sold off its holdings in Wachovia Securities to Wells Fargo for some $5 billion when that company acquired Wachovia in late 2008.

Prudential's international insurance business offers individual life insurance policies through its Life Planners, Life Advisors, and Gibraltar Life

units to affluent and middle income customers, primarily in Japan and South Korea, but also in other Asian, European, and Latin American countries. Its international investment unit provides asset management and investment advice in non-US markets.

Since its 2001 demutualization, Prudential has shed non-life insurance operations, picked up some annuities businesses, and struck joint ventures near and far. It acquired specialty commercial insurer MullinTBG in 2008 to pad its Prudential Retirement business.

HISTORY

In 1873 John Dryden founded the Widows and Orphans Friendly Society in New Jersey to sell workers industrial insurance (low-face-value weekly premium life insurance). In 1875 it became The Prudential Friendly Society, taking the name from England's Prudential Assurance Co. The next year Dryden visited the English company and copied some of its methods, such as recruiting agents from its targeted neighborhoods.

Prudential added ordinary whole life insurance in 1886. By 1900 the firm was selling more than 2,000 such policies annually and had 3,000 agents in eight states. In 1896 the J. Walter Thompson advertising agency (now the WPP Group) designed Prudential's Rock of Gibraltar logo.

The firm issued its first group life policy in 1916 (Prudential became a major group life insurer in the 1940s). In 1928 it introduced an Accidental Death Benefit, which cost it an extra $3 million in benefits the next year alone (death claims rose drastically early in the Depression).

In 1943 Prudential mutualized. The company began decentralizing operations in the 1940s. Later it introduced a Property Investment Separate Account (PRISA), which gave pension plans a real estate investment option. By 1974 the firm was the US's group pension leader.

The insurer bought securities brokerage The Bache Group to form Pru Bache (now Prudential Securities) in 1981. Bache's forte was retail investments, an area expected to blend well with Prudential's insurance business. Under George Ball, Pru Bache tried to become a major investment banker — but failed. In 1991 Ball resigned, leaving losses of almost $260 million and numerous lawsuits involving real estate limited partnerships.

Despite the 1992 settlement of the real estate partnership suits, Prudential remained under scrutiny by several states because of "churning," a process by which agents generated commissions by inducing policyholders to trade up to more expensive policies. In 1995 new management, led by former Chase Manhattanite Arthur Ryan, brought sales under control, sold such units as reinsurance and mortgage servicing, and put its $6 billion real estate portfolio on the block. (In 1997 it sold its property management unit and Canadian commercial real estate unit; in 1998 it sold its landmark Prudential Center complex in Boston.)

In 1996 regulators from 30 states found that Prudential knew about the churning earlier than it had admitted, had not stopped them, and had even promoted wrongdoers. A 1997 settlement called for the company to pay restitution, but the more than $2 billion estimated cost was thought to be less than the losses customers had suffered.

As the financial services industry continued to restructure, Prudential in 1998 announced plans to demutualize. To focus on life insurance, the company sold its health care unit to Aetna in

1999. The same year, Prudential paid $62 million to resolve more churning claims, revamped itself into international, institutional, and retail divisions, and trimmed jobs.

Prudential Financial's 2001 IPO — one of the largest ever in the insurance industry — raised more than $3 billion. Prudential Financial became the holding company name for all operations, making Prudential Insurance (the company's former name) a subsidiary and pure life insurer.

Following the IPO, Prudential got busy at rearranging its portfolio. It sold off its property/casualty insurance businesses to Liberty Mutual in 2003. Prudential also sold its brokerage division to banking powerhouse Wachovia in 2003, turning Wachovia Securities (38% owned by Prudential) into the third-largest brokerage firm in the US.

Variable annuities held a special allure for the company. It bought Swedish insurer Skandia's US operations in 2003 and then Allstate's variable annuity business in 2006. During 2004 it bought CIGNA's retirement business.

Prudential agreed to pay NASD a $2 million fine and to reimburse customers nearly $10 million in 2004 because of alleged rules violations regarding the sale of annuities. In late 2006 the company agreed to pay $19 million ($16.5 million in restitution and $2.5 million as penalty) after the New York Attorney General determined that certain payments to insurance brokers amounted to collusion.

The company added to its substantial Japanese operations (which include subsidiary Gibraltar Life) by acquiring Aoba Life Insurance Company in 2004. Its acquired South Korean asset management firm Hyundai Investment and Securities in 2004 and renamed it Prudential Investment Securities. To keep all things in balance, the company shuttered its Philippine insurance operations in 2006 and its Dryden Wealth Management business, which operated in Europe and Asia, in 2005.

EXECUTIVES

Chairman, President, and CEO: John R. Strangfeld Jr., age 55, $14,018,355 total compensation
Vice Chairman: Mark B. Grier, age 56, $5,254,019 total compensation
EVP Operations and Systems: Robert C. Golden, age 62
EVP and CFO: Richard J. Carbone, age 61, $2,837,158 total compensation
SVP, Company Actuary, and Chief Risk Officer: Helen M. Galt, age 61
Chief Market Strategist, Annuities: Quincy Krosby
Chief Investment Officer: Michael Lillard
Chief Security Officer: Lori Hennon-Bell
VP Human Resources and Chief Diversity Officer: Emilio Egea
Chief Medical Officer: K. Andrew Crighton
Chief Communications Officer: Bob DeFillippo
Chief Domestic Investment Officer: Scott Sleyster
EVP, US Businesses: Bernard B. Winograd, age 59, $5,646,887 total compensation
EVP, International Businesses: Edward P. (Ed) Baird, age 60, $5,254,019 total compensation
EVP and Head of Life Insurance, Japan: Kazuo Maeda
SVP Corporate Human Resources: Sharon C. Taylor, age 54
SVP and General Counsel: Susan L. Blount, age 51
SVP Sales, Wachovia, AG Edwards, and Raymond James: Richard Jimenez
SVP Sales, Merrill Lynch, Morgan Stanley, Smith Barney, and UBS: Jonathan Cressman
Managing Director: Eileen Power
Auditors: PricewaterhouseCoopers LLP

LOCATIONS

HQ: Prudential Financial, Inc.
751 Broad St., Newark, NJ 07102
Phone: 973-802-6000   **Fax:** 973-802-4479
Web: www.prudential.com

PRODUCTS/OPERATIONS

2008 Sales

	$ mil.	% of total
Premiums	15,468	49
Net investment income	11,883	37
Policy charges & fees	3,138	10
Realized investment gains (losses)	(2,375)	—
Asset management fees & other income	1,161	4
Total	**29,275**	**100**

2008 Sales

	$ mil.	% of total
Financial Services		
International		
Insurance	9,185	28
Investment	285	1
US Retirement Solutions		
Retirement	4,844	15
Individual annuities	1,999	6
Asset management	1,686	5
US Individual Life & Group Insurance		
Group	4,960	15
Individual life	2,754	8
Real Estate & Relocation Services	212	1
Corporate operations	119	—
Realized investment gains (losses)	(2,267)	—
Adjustments	(1,561)	—
Closed Block Business	7,059	21
Total	**29,275**	**100**

COMPETITORS

AEGON
Aetna
AIG
Allianz
American Financial Group
Aviva
AXA
Berkshire Hathaway
Charles Schwab
Citigroup
COUNTRY Financial
Dai-ichi Mutual Life
FMR
The Hartford
HomeServices
ING
John Hancock Financial Services
Legal & General Group
MassMutual
Merrill Lynch
MetLife
Nationwide Life Insurance
Nippon Life Insurance
Northwestern Mutual
Principal Financial
Prudential plc
The Vanguard Group
Zurich Financial Services

HISTORICAL FINANCIALS

Company Type: Public

Income Statement

FYE: December 31

	ASSETS ($ mil.)	NET INCOME ($ mil.)	INCOME AS % OF ASSETS	EMPLOYEES
12/08	445,011.0	(1,073.0)	—	41,844
12/07	485,814.0	3,704.0	0.8%	40,703
12/06	454,266.0	3,428.0	0.8%	39,814
12/05	417,776.0	3,540.0	0.8%	38,853
12/04	401,058.0	2,314.0	0.6%	39,418
Annual Growth	**2.6%**	**—**	**—**	**1.5%**

2008 Year-End Financials

Equity as % of assets: 3.0%	Dividends
Return on assets: —	Yield: 1.9%
Return on equity: —	Payout: —
Long-term debt ($ mil.): 20,290	Market value ($ mil.): 13,950
No. of shares (mil.): 461	Sales ($ mil.): 29,275

Stock History

NYSE: PRU

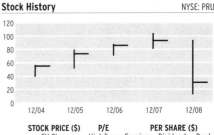

	STOCK PRICE ($) FY Close	P/E High/Low		PER SHARE ($) Earnings	PER SHARE ($) Dividends	PER SHARE ($) Book Value
12/08	30.26	—	—	(2.42)	0.58	29.11
12/07	93.04	14	11	7.61	1.15	50.88
12/06	85.86	13	11	6.50	0.95	49.66
12/05	73.19	12	8	6.34	0.78	49.38
12/04	54.96	17	12	3.31	0.63	48.47
Annual Growth	**(13.9%)**	**—**	**—**	**—**	**(2.0%)**	**(12.0%)**

PSS World Medical

From basic supplies to sophisticated equipment, PSS World Medical keeps doctors and nursing homes fully stocked. The company distributes medical supplies, equipment, and pharmaceuticals to doctors' offices, long-term care facilities, and home health care providers nationwide through a network of about 40 distribution centers. The company operates in two business segments. Its Physician Sales & Service unit distributes products to primary care doctors, while its Elder Care segment (represented by subsidiary Gulf South Medical Supply) sells medical supplies to nursing homes and home health care providers. PSS reaches its customers through its team of more than 830 sales representatives.

PSS World Medical has supplier agreements with some 80 manufacturers in nine countries to distribute both branded and private-label products. The company's Physician segment offers more than 155,000 different products, including pharmaceuticals that are administered in the doctor's office; Gulf Coast Medical Supply sells about 45,000 items. Expanding its private label Select Medical Products brand is part of the company's growth strategy. Cheaper non-US manufacturers, particularly those based in Asia, are key to this plan.

The company has also placed an emphasis on its technology infrastructure and services. It distributes information technology solutions through its Physician segment, and offers Medicare Part B billing services through its Elder Care unit's ProClaim subsidiary.

Acquisitions have historically been part of PSS World Medical's growth strategy, but the company has become more selective after a spree in the late 1990s that eventually hurt earnings. Still, the company continues to snap up small firms that complement its product offering. In 2008 it purchased Washington-based Cascade Medical Supply, a distributor of nursing home supplies.

HISTORY

Like an inner tube hooked to an air compressor, PSS expanded from a shoestring-budget medical supply company into a major player in just five years. Former chairman Patrick Kelly and two others founded Physician Sales & Service (PSS) in 1983 to supply physicians; the company made deliveries by U-Haul in the early days. By 1988 the company was the largest supplier of its type in Florida, with $13 million in revenues. The company expanded into other states by acquisition. PSS went public in May 1994.

Improved medical technology and cost-saving efforts by insurance companies led PSS to ink an exclusive agreement with US pharmaceutical and diagnostics powerhouse Abbott Laboratories in 1995. PSS began to sell Abbott's diagnostic equipment to offices of up to 25 doctors; Abbott bought 4% of PSS. That year Taylor Medical, the #4 medical supplies distributor in the US, merged with PSS, forming the first national physician supply company.

In 1996 PSS formed its WorldMed subsidiary to assimilate acquisitions. PSS also expanded its radiology and imaging equipment operations by purchasing distributor Diagnostic Imaging; in 1997 and 1998 acquisitions moved the imaging unit into Arizona, California, Florida, Minnesota, New Mexico, New York, and Wisconsin.

PSS changed its name to PSS World Medical in 1998 and bought nursing home supplier Gulf South Medical Supply. However, unforeseen expenses related to the purchase and reorganization (as well as SEC-mandated accounting adjustments) led to a drop in the company's overall earnings; this prompted shareholder lawsuits in 1999. To reverse the tide, PSS streamlined its distribution centers and back-office functions. Nonetheless, the company continued to acquire, buying Salt Lake City-based Physician Supply Co. in 1999.

The following year Fisher Scientific International made plans to buy PSS, but the acquisition fell through. About a month later, PSS founder Patrick Kelly resigned as chairman and CEO, along with COO Frederick "Gene" Dell.

Disappointments in sales prompted the company to sell its European operations in 2001. Also that year PSS was charged with securities fraud in a class action suit on behalf of shareholders. The company sold its Diagnostic Imaging business in 2002. In 2003 PSS acquired ProClaim, a provider of billing services to the long-term care industry, and Highpoint Healthcare, a marketing and distribution organization for assisted living, long-term health, and home care businesses.

EXECUTIVES

Chairman and CEO: David A. Smith, age 49, $2,639,764 total compensation
EVP and COO: Gary A. Corless, age 44, $1,230,237 total compensation
EVP and CFO: David M. Bronson, age 56, $1,024,682 total compensation
VP and CIO: Carl A. Duhnoski, age 39
EVP and Chief Marketing Officer: John F. Sasen Sr., age 67, $895,699 total compensation

SVP Corporate Development: Jeffrey H. Anthony, age 48
SVP Supplier Operations: Kevin P. English, age 40
SVP Operations: Bradley J. Hilton, age 38, $726,152 total compensation
SVP Sales, Physician Sales and Service: Edward D. (Eddie) Dienes
VP Investor Relations: Robert C. Weiner, age 46
VP and Treasurer: David D. Klarner, age 39
VP Global Sourcing: Thomas D'Innocenzi
VP Internal Audit: John G. Kammlade
VP Sales, Gulf South Medical Supply: Billy Ray Clemons Jr.
VP Operational Compliance: Andrew S. Woods
VP Legal Affairs and Secretary: Joshua H. DeRienzis, age 40
Senior Associate Public Relations: Brian C. Kosoy
Auditors: KPMG LLP

LOCATIONS

HQ: PSS World Medical, Inc.
4345 Southpoint Blvd., Jacksonville, FL 32216
Phone: 904-332-3000   **Fax:** 904-332-3213
Web: www.pssworldmedical.com

PRODUCTS/OPERATIONS

2009 Sales

	$ mil.	% of total
Physician business	1,357.4	70
Elder care business	594.5	30
Corporate shared services	0.8	—
Total	**1,952.7**	**100**

COMPETITORS

Cardinal Supply Chain Medical
McKesson Medical-Surgical
Medline Industries
Metro Medical Supply
Moore Medical
Nyer Medical
Owens & Minor
SourceOne
Surgical Express
Tri-anim
Universal Hospital

HISTORICAL FINANCIALS

Company Type: Public

Income Statement

FYE: Friday nearest March 31

	REVENUE ($ mil.)	NET INCOME ($ mil.)	NET PROFIT MARGIN	EMPLOYEES
3/09	1,952.7	58.0	3.0%	3,680
3/08	1,855.8	56.8	3.1%	3,593
3/07	1,741.6	50.5	2.9%	3,349
3/06	1,619.4	44.3	2.7%	3,269
3/05	1,473.8	39.0	2.6%	3,169
Annual Growth	**7.3%**	**10.4%**	**—**	**3.8%**

2009 Year-End Financials

Debt ratio: 66.9%
Return on equity: 17.0%
Cash ($ mil.): 82
Current ratio: 2.35
Long-term debt ($ mil.): 232
No. of shares (mil.): 59
Dividends
   Yield: 0.0%
   Payout: —
Market value ($ mil.): 854

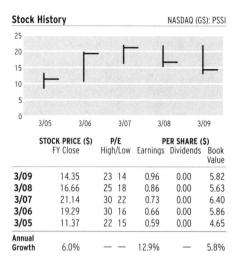

Stock History

NASDAQ (GS): PSSI

	STOCK PRICE ($) FY Close	P/E High/Low	PER SHARE ($) Earnings	Dividends	Book Value
3/09	14.35	23 14	0.96	0.00	5.82
3/08	16.66	25 18	0.86	0.00	5.63
3/07	21.14	30 22	0.73	0.00	6.40
3/06	19.29	30 16	0.66	0.00	5.86
3/05	11.37	22 15	0.59	0.00	4.65
Annual Growth	**6.0%**	**— —**	**12.9%**	**—**	**5.8%**

Psychiatric Solutions

Sufferers of mental illness may find an answer to their problems with Psychiatric Solutions. The company owns or leases some 90 psychiatric hospitals and residential treatment facilities housing more than 10,000 beds. Its hospitals provide acute behavioral health care, including round-the-clock nursing and psychiatric observation and treatment; while its residential treatment centers offer longer-term treatment for troubled teens and kids. Its facilities are located across the US and in Puerto Rico and the US Virgin Islands. In addition to its inpatient services, the company manages psychiatric units within medical-surgical hospitals.

Psychiatric Solutions focuses on growing its main line of business — inpatient behavioral health care services — primarily through acquisitions and by expanding its existing facilities. Between 2007 and 2009 the company added 20 mental health hospitals to its portfolio with the purchases of Horizon Health and United Medical. Psychiatric Solutions uses the Horizon Health name as the brand under which it offers contract management services.

Along with acquisitions, Psychiatric Solutions has branched out by opening new facilities, adding new services, and increasing referrals by developing a reputation for providing high-quality care. The company opened Lincoln Prairie Behavioral Health Center, a 120-bed inpatient hospital, at the end of 2008 and the 80-bed Rolling Hills Hospital in early 2009.

To better focus on its other programs, Psychiatric Solutions has announced that it intends to sell off its employee assistance program business to Aetna. The business, Horizon Behavioral Services, LLC, will be sold for $70 million.

Psychiatric Solutions boasts a fairly diverse payor mix. Medicaid and Medicare account for the bulk of the company's revenue (about 42%), followed by payments from HMO/PPO, commercial and private payors (30%). State agencies and other payors make up the rest.

HISTORY

Psychiatric Solutions may never have made it without the path laid before it by its predecessor, Psychiatric Management Resources (PMR). That company's story goes back to the 1980s, when certain trends in mental health care presented a perfect environment for its creation: the growth of outpatient services, advances in drugs to treat mental illness, and the industry's need to regain credibility. Psychiatric Management Resources was founded and went public in 1988. The next year Zaron Capital acquired the company and renamed it PMR Corporation.

PMR grew quickly in the early 1990s. In 1994 government probes of partial hospitalization programs such as those administered by PMR led to changes in how program operators could bill payors. Hit by retroactive changes, delayed or lost claims caused PMR to lose money in 1995.

In 1997 the company retooled to support its growth in existing and developing markets. In early 1998 ScrippsHealth, PMR's largest customer, lost its "provider-based" status, meaning Medicare would no longer reimburse PMR for its services. A poor market ended the company's plans to acquire psychiatric hospital operator Behavioral Healthcare Corporation (BHC); the two companies did agree to operate outpatient programs jointly at 10 BHC facilities. That year PMR formed a specialty pharmacy joint venture with what is now Stadt Holdings, a subsidiary of Bergen Brunswig (now AmerisourceBergen).

The company's proposed acquisition of some American Psych Systems divisions fell through in 1998. In 1999 PMR suffered a loss after a change in accounting methods.

PMR opened 2000 by selling its stake in Stadt Solutions, and it ended its pilot managed care project with two California-based HMOs. That year the company changed its strategy again to focus on its health information operation InfoScriber after Medicare and Medicaid cutbacks caused the firm to pare its outpatient programs.

InfoScriber failed to yield anything more than losses, and PMR shifted its attention back to its management services in 2001. The company also shut down InfoScriber and was acquired by Psychiatric Solutions in August 2002.

Psychiatric Solutions combined PMR's operations with its own and changed the name of the combined company to Psychiatric Solutions. The newly merged firm also changed its strategy to one of growth by acquisition, particularly of inpatient facilities.

To that end, the company acquired The Brown Schools and Alliance Health Center in 2003; and two inpatient facilities from Brentwood Behavioral Health and four inpatient behavioral health care facilities from Heartland Health in 2004.

The following year the firm bought 20 inpatient psychiatric facilities from Ardent Health Services and acquired 19 inpatient facilities throughout 2006. The 2006 acquisitions included Alternative Behavioral Services, which operates inpatient facilities, from FHC Health Systems.

EXECUTIVES

Chairman, President, and CEO: Joey A. Jacobs, age 55, $5,209,681 total compensation
Co-COO: Ronald M. Fincher, age 55
Co-COO: Terrance R. (Terry) Bridges, age 56, $1,722,622 total compensation
EVP Finance and Administration: Brent Turner, age 43, $1,701,316 total compensation
Chief Development Officer: Steven T. Davidson, age 51
EVP and Chief Accounting Officer: Jack E. Polson, age 42, $1,701,360 total compensation
EVP, General Counsel, and Secretary: Christopher L. (Chris) Howard, age 42, $1,690,510 total compensation
Director Human Resources: Cindy Dill
Auditors: Ernst & Young LLP

LOCATIONS

HQ: Psychiatric Solutions, Inc.
6640 Carothers Pkwy., Ste. 500, Franklin, TN 37067
Phone: 615-312-5700 **Fax:** 615-312-5711
Web: www.psysolutions.com

PRODUCTS/OPERATIONS

2008 Sales

	% of total
Inpatient behavioral health care facilities	90
Other behavioral health care services	10
Total	**100**

2008 Payor Mix

	% of total
Managed care, commercial & private payors	30
Medicaid	29
Medicare	13
State agencies excluding Medicaid	15
Other	13
Total	**100**

COMPETITORS

Comprehensive Care	Magellan Health
HCA	Mental Health Network
Health Management Associates	OptimumCare Corporation
Horizon Health	PHC
	Universal Health Services

HISTORICAL FINANCIALS

Company Type: Public

Income Statement

FYE: December 31

	REVENUE ($ mil.)	NET INCOME ($ mil.)	NET PROFIT MARGIN	EMPLOYEES
12/08	1,766.0	105.0	5.9%	23,000
12/07	1,482.0	76.2	5.1%	21,800
12/06	1,026.5	60.6	5.9%	18,700
12/05	727.8	27.2	3.7%	13,300
12/04	487.2	16.8	3.4%	12,100
Annual Growth	38.0%	58.1%	—	17.4%

2008 Year-End Financials

Debt ratio: 143.8%	No. of shares (mil.): 56
Return on equity: 12.8%	Dividends
Cash ($ mil.): 51	Yield: 0.0%
Current ratio: 1.73	Payout: —
Long-term debt ($ mil.): 1,280	Market value ($ mil.): 1,567

Stock History

NASDAQ (GS): PSYS

	STOCK PRICE ($) FY Close	P/E High/Low		PER SHARE ($) Earnings	Dividends	Book Value
12/08	27.85	22	12	1.87	0.00	15.82
12/07	32.50	31	23	1.37	0.00	13.42
12/06	37.52	35	23	1.12	0.00	11.16
12/05	29.37	51	29	0.59	0.00	9.59
12/04	18.28	39	18	0.48	0.00	4.35
Annual Growth	11.1%	—	—	40.5%	—	38.1%

Public Service Enterprise Group

In the Garden State, Public Service Enterprise Group's (PSEG) diversified business model has it smelling like a rose. Regulated subsidiary Public Service Electric and Gas (PSE&G) transmits and distributes electricity to 2.1 million customers and natural gas to 1.7 million customers in New Jersey. Nonregulated subsidiary PSEG Power operates PSEG's generating plants. PSEG Power's 13,600-MW generating capacity comes mostly from nuclear and fossil-fueled plants in the US Northeast. Other operations (under PSEG Energy Holdings) include energy infrastructure investments and wholesale energy marketing. The company also invests in overseas independent power plants and distribution systems.

PSEG Global (a unit of PSEG Energy Holdings) owns stakes in power plants (2,500 MW of capacity) primarily in Texas and California, but also in India and Venezuela.

In order to focus on its core North American power businesses PSEG has sold most of its overseas independent power plant interests, and it has scaled down plans to expand its energy generation and marketing businesses. In 2006 PSEG Global sold its 32% stake in RGE, a Brazilian electric distribution company with approximately 1.1 million customers, to Companhia Paulista de Forcae Luz. In 2008 it sold the SAESA Group of Companies (a power distribution group) in southern Chile to a consortium formed by Morgan Stanley Infrastructure and the Ontario Teachers' Pension Plan for $887 million. It also sold its 85% stake in Bioenergie in Italy

In 2009 PSEG announced plans to invest in solar and wind power initiatives to meet its commitment to reduce greenhouse gas emissions.

HISTORY

Tragedy struck Newark, New Jersey, in 1903 when a trolley slid down an icy hill and collided with a train, killing more than 30 people. While investigating the accident, state attorney general Thomas McCarter discovered the mismanagement of the trolley company and many of New Jersey's other transportation, gas, and electric companies. Planning to buy and consolidate these companies, McCarter resigned and established the Public Service Corporation in 1903 with several colleagues.

The company formed divisions for gas utilities, electric utilities, and transportation companies. The trolley company generated almost half of Public Service's sales during its first year.

In 1924 the gas and electric companies consolidated as Public Service Electric and Gas (PSE&G). A new company was formed that year to operate buses, and in 1928 it merged with the trolley company to form Public Service Coordinated Transport (later Transport of New Jersey). PSE&G signed interconnection agreements with two Pennsylvania electric companies in 1928 to form the first integrated power pool — later known as the Pennsylvania-New Jersey-Maryland Interconnection. The Public Utility Holding Company Act of 1935 ushered in the era of regulated regional monopolies, ensuring PSE&G a captive market.

During the 1960s PSE&G joined Philadelphia Electric to build its first nuclear plant, at Peach Bottom, Pennsylvania. The company completed a second nuke in 1977, at Salem, New Jersey. Its third one went on line at Hope Creek, New Jersey. However, plant mismanagement earned PSE&G a slew of fines in the 1980s and 1990s.

The company sold its transportation system to the State of New Jersey in 1980. Five years later PSE&G formed holding company Public Service Enterprise Group (PSEG) to move into nonutility enterprises and created Community Energy Alternatives (CEA, now PSEG Global) to invest in independent power projects. In 1989 Enterprise Diversified Holdings (now PSEG Energy Holdings) was formed to handle activities ranging from real estate to oil and gas production.

CEA and three partners acquired a Buenos Aires power plant in 1993. Taking advantage of overseas privatization in the late 1990s, it expanded into Asia and, with AES, purchased two Argentine electric companies.

PSE&G's nuclear problems resurfaced when the Salem plant was shut down in 1995 to rectify equipment breakdowns. In 1997 PSEG paid Salem partners Delmarva Power & Light and PECO Energy $82 million to settle their lawsuits charging mismanagement of Salem; both units were back on line by 1998.

Continuing to diversify in the late 1990s, PSEG formed PSEG Energy Technologies in 1997 to market power and acquired five mechanical services companies in 1998 and 1999.

In 1999 PSEG Global teamed up with Panda Energy International to build three merchant plants in Texas (to be completed by 2001). It also planned plants in India and Venezuela and joined Sempra Energy to buy 90% of Chilquinta Energía, an energy distributor in Chile and Peru. In 2000 it bought 90% of a distributor serving Argentina and Brazil.

New Jersey's electricity markets were deregulated in 1999; a year later the company transferred PSE&G's generation assets to nonregulated unit PSEG Power. PSEG Power also took charge of PSEG Global's plants under development in Illinois, Indiana, and Ohio; announced plans for new plants in New Jersey; and acquired an Albany, New York, plant from Niagara Mohawk.

In 2001 PSEG Global completed a power plant in Texas. It also bought 94% of generator and distributor Saesa from Chile's largest conglomerate, Copec, for $460 million; it later acquired the rest of Saesa through a tender offer. It also purchased a Peruvian generation firm, ElectroAndes, for $227 million.

In 2002 PSEG Power acquired two Connecticut plants from Wisconsin Energy for approximately $270 million.

PSEG had agreed to be acquired by Exelon, but both New Jersey and Pennsylvania opposed the merger, and the deal fell through in 2006.

EXECUTIVES

Chairman, President, and CEO: Ralph Izzo, age 51, $6,000,747 total compensation
EVP and CFO: Caroline Dorsa, age 49
VP IT and CIO, PSEG Services: Manoj S. Chouthai
VP Risk Management and Chief Risk Officer: Laura L. Langer Brooks
SVP Human Resources and Chief Human Resources Officer, PSEG Services: Margaret M. Pego
President and COO, PSE&G: Ralph A. LaRossa, age 45, $1,508,747 total compensation
President and COO, PSEG Power, and Director: William (Bill) Levis, age 52, $2,748,695 total compensation
President and Chief Nuclear Officer, PSEG Power: Thomas P. Joyce, age 56
EVP, General Counsel, and Director; EVP and General Counsel, PSE&G, and PSEG Power: R. Edwin (Ed) Selover, age 63, $1,770,852 total compensation
SVP Fossil Operations, PSEG Power: Richard D. Machon
VP Construction, PSEG Power: Frederick Pastor Jr.
VP and Treasurer; VP and Treasurer, PSE&G: Morton A. Plawner
VP and Controller; VP and Controller, PSE&G, PSEG Services, PSEG Energy Holdings, and PSEG Power: Derek M. Di Risio, age 44
VP Corporate Planning: Kevin J. Quinn, age 52
VP Investor Relations: Kathleen A. Lally
VP Human Resources Client Services, PSEG Services: Cora Brina
Auditors: Deloitte & Touche LLP

LOCATIONS

HQ: Public Service Enterprise Group Incorporated 80 Park Plaza, Newark, NJ 07102
Phone: 973-430-7000   **Fax:** 973-824-7056
Web: www.pseg.com

PRODUCTS/OPERATIONS

2008 Sales

	$ mil.	% of total
PSE&G	9,038	53
Power	7,770	45
Energy Holdings	345	2
Adjustments	(3,831)	—
Total	**13,322**	**100**

Selected Subsidiaries

PSEG Energy Holdings Inc. (nonutility companies)
   PSEG Global Inc. (international development of independent power plants and distribution operations)
   PSEG Resources Inc. (energy infrastructure investments)

PSEG Power LLC
   PSEG Fossil LLC (operator of PSEG's fossil fuel plants)
   PSEG Nuclear LLC (operator of PSEG's nuclear plants)
   PSEG Energy Resources and Trade LLC (energy marketing)
PSEG Services Corporation (management and administrative services for PSEG)
Public Service Electric and Gas Company (PSE&G, distribution of electricity and gas)

COMPETITORS

AES
CenterPoint Energy
Con Edison
Constellation Energy Group
Delmarva Power
Exelon
FirstEnergy
FPL Group
Mirant
National Grid USA
New Jersey Resources
Northeast Utilities
NRG Energy
PPL Corporation
Sempra Energy
Sempra Energy Trading
South Jersey Industries
SUEZ-TRACTEBEL

HISTORICAL FINANCIALS

Company Type: Public

Income Statement

FYE: December 31

	REVENUE ($ mil.)	NET INCOME ($ mil.)	NET PROFIT MARGIN	EMPLOYEES
12/08	13,322.0	1,188.0	8.9%	6,069
12/07	12,853.0	1,335.0	10.4%	2,538
12/06	12,164.0	739.0	6.1%	6,154
12/05	12,430.0	678.0	5.5%	6,335
12/04	10,996.0	726.0	6.6%	6,327
Annual Growth	**4.9%**	**13.1%**	**—**	**(1.0%)**

2008 Year-End Financials

Debt ratio: 102.0%
Return on equity: 15.7%
Cash ($ mil.): 321
Current ratio: 1.17
Long-term debt ($ mil.): 8,005

No. of shares (mil.): 506
Dividends
   Yield: 4.4%
   Payout: 55.1%
Market value ($ mil.): 14,759

Stock History

NYSE: PEG

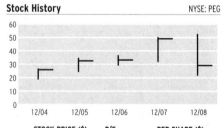

	STOCK PRICE ($) FY Close	P/E High/Low		PER SHARE ($) Earnings	Dividends	Book Value
12/08	29.17	22	9	2.34	1.29	15.52
12/07	49.12	19	12	2.62	1.17	14.43
12/06	33.19	25	20	1.47	1.14	13.33
12/05	32.49	25	18	1.36	1.12	11.90
12/04	25.89	17	12	1.52	1.10	11.34
Annual Growth	**3.0%**	**—**	**—**	**11.4%**	**4.1%**	**8.1%**

Publix Super Markets

Publix Super Markets tops the list of privately owned supermarket operators in the US. By emphasizing service and a family-friendly image over price, Publix has grown faster and been more profitable than Winn-Dixie Stores and other rivals. More than two-thirds of its 1,000 stores are in Florida, but it also operates in Alabama, Georgia, South Carolina, and Tennessee. Publix makes some of its own bakery, deli, and dairy goods, and many stores house pharmacies, and banks. The firm also operates liquor stores, convenience stores, and Crispers restaurants in Florida. Founder George Jenkins began offering stock to Publix employees in 1930. Employees own about 30% of Publix, which is still run by the Jenkins family.

The fast-growing grocer opened its 1,000th supermarket in early 2009 and plans to open approximately 40 more stores this year, including about a dozen locations acquired from Albertsons. While the purchase of Albertsons' Florida stores eliminated one rival, Publix is facing increased competition from Winn-Dixie, following its stint in bankruptcy; Sweetbay; and supercenter operator Wal-Mart. (Low cost ALDI is also expanding in Florida.) Aggressive price cutting by Publix and its rivals in response to the downturn in the Florida economy, is putting a squeeze on profits. In the Atlanta market, Publix is facing increased heat from Kroger.

To stay on top of the competitive Florida grocery market, Publix keeps up with national trends in grocery retailing. In 2007 it began offering free antibiotics at its 680-plus in-store pharmacies. The grocery chain also fills other generic prescriptions for $4, thereby matching Wal-Mart's low-cost generic drug program. To better serve its Latino customers, Publix has launched its own line of pre-packaged Hispanic foods, including frozen plantains and ready-to-eat black beans. It also launched a Hispanic-themed format called Publix Sabor in 2005, which operates two stores in Miami.

In 2007 the company launched a new store format called GreenWise Market (the name Publix has already given to its store-within-a-store natural/organic sections and private-label line of specialty foods) to court more health-conscious consumers and compete with national organic chains, such as Whole Foods.

In addition to grocery stores, Publix also operates liquor stores next to about 75 of its supermarkets in Florida. Other ventures include its majority-owned restaurant chain Crispers in Florida. Currently, the soup-salad-and-sandwich chain operates about 40 locations.

HISTORY

George Jenkins, age 22, resigned as manager of the Piggly Wiggly grocery in Winter Haven, Florida, in 1930. With money he had saved to buy a car, he opened his own grocery store, Publix, next door to his old employer. The small store (named after a chain of movie theaters) prospered despite the Depression, and in 1935 Jenkins opened another Publix in the same town.

Five years later, after the supermarket format had become popular, Jenkins closed his two smaller locations and opened a new, more modern Publix Market. With pastel colors and electric-eye doors, it was also the first US store to feature air conditioning.

Publix Super Markets bought the All-American chain of Lakeland, Florida (19 stores), in 1944 and moved its corporate headquarters to that city. The company began offering S&H Green Stamps in 1953, and in 1956 it replaced its original supermarket with a mall featuring an enlarged Publix and a Green Stamp redemption center. Publix expanded into South Florida in the late 1950s.

As Florida's population grew, Publix continued to expand, opening its 100th store in 1964. Publix was the first grocery chain in the state to use bar-code scanners — all its stores had the technology by 1981. The company beat Florida banks in providing ATMs and during the 1980s opened debit card stations.

Publix continued to grow in the 1980s, safe from takeover attempts because of its employee ownership. In 1988 it installed the first automated checkout systems in South Florida, giving patrons an always-open checkout lane.

The chain stopped offering Green Stamps in 1989, and most of the $19 million decrease in Publix advertising expenditures was attributed to the end of the 36-year promotion. That year, after almost six decades, "Mr. George" — as founder Jenkins was known — stepped down as chairman in favor of his son Howard. (George died in 1996.)

In 1991 Publix opened its first store outside Florida, in Georgia, as part of its plan to become a major player in the Southeast. Publix entered South Carolina in 1993 with one supermarket; it also tripled its presence in Georgia to 15 stores.

The United Food and Commercial Workers Union began a campaign in 1994 against alleged gender and racial discrimination in Publix's hiring, promotion, and compensation policies.

Publix opened its first store in Alabama in 1996. That year a federal judge allowed about 150,000 women to join a class-action suit filed in 1995 by 12 women who had sued Publix, charging that the company consistently channeled female employees into low-paying jobs with little chance for good promotions. The case, which at the time was said to be the biggest sex discrimination lawsuit ever, was set to go to trial, but in 1997 the company paid $82.5 million to settle and another $3.5 million to settle a complaint of discrimination against black applicants and employees.

Publix promised to change its promotion policies, but two more lawsuits alleging discrimination against women and blacks were filed in 1997 and 1998. The suit filed on behalf of the women was denied class-action status in 2000. Later that year the company settled the racial discrimination lawsuit for $10.5 million. Howard Jenkins stepped down as CEO in mid-2001; his cousin Charlie Jenkins took the helm.

In 2002 Publix entered the Nashville, Tennessee, market with the purchase of seven Albertsons supermarkets, a convenience store, and a fuel center. In mid-2003 Publix pulled the plug on its online store PublixDirect, which offered delivery service in parts of Florida, citing disappointing sales.

In 2007 the chain began offering seven popular antibiotics free at some 685 Publix Pharmacies. The drugs account for almost 50% of the generic, pediatric prescriptions filled at Publix.

CEO Charlie Jenkins Jr. retired at the end of March 2008. Jenkins was succeeded by his cousin and Publix president Ed Crenshaw. In September Publix completed the acquisition of 49 Albertsons stores in Florida.

EXECUTIVES

Chairman: Charles H. (Charlie) Jenkins Jr., age 65
Vice Chairman: Hoyt R. (Barney) Barnett, age 65
CEO and Director: William E. (Ed) Crenshaw, age 58
President: Randall T. (Todd) Jones Sr., age 46
CFO and Treasurer: David P. Phillips, age 49
SVP and CIO: Laurie Z. Douglas, age 45
SVP, General Counsel, and Secretary:
 John A. Attaway Jr., age 50
SVP: R. Scott Charlton, age 50
SVP: John T. Hrabusa, age 54
VP and Controller: G. Gino DiGrazia, age 46
VP Manufacturing: Michael R. (Mike) Smith, age 49
VP, Real Estate, Crispers: Cliff Wiley
VP Risk Management: Marc Salm, age 48
VP and Controller: Sandra J. Estep, age 49
Chairman and CEO, Crispers Restaurants: Ron Fuller
Assistant Secretary and Executive Director Publix
 Super Markets Charities: Sharon A. Miller, age 65
Director, Media and Community Relations: Maria Brous
Director Marketing and Research: Mark Lang
Director Marketing and Advertising: Kevin Lang
Auditors: KPMG LLP

LOCATIONS

HQ: Publix Super Markets, Inc.
 3300 Publix Corporate Pkwy., Lakeland, FL 33811
Phone: 863-688-1188   **Fax:** 863-284-5532
Web: www.publix.com

2008 Supermarkets

	No.
Florida	713
Georgia	176
South Carolina	42
Alabama	37
Tennessee	25
Total	**993**

PRODUCTS/OPERATIONS

2008 Stores

	No.
Supermarkets	993
Liquor stores	73
Crispers restaurants	41
Pix convenience stores	10
Total	**1,117**

Selected Supermarket Departments

Bakery
Banking
Dairy
Deli
Ethnic foods
Floral
Groceries
Health and beauty care
Housewares
Meat
Pharmacy
Photo processing
Produce
Seafood

Foods Processed

Baked goods
Dairy products
Deli items

COMPETITORS

ALDI	The Pantry
BI-LO	Rite Aid
Costco Wholesale	Ruddick
CVS Caremark	Sedano's
IGA	Sweetbay
Ingles Markets	Walgreen
Kerr Drug	Wal-Mart
Kmart	Whole Foods
Kroger	Winn-Dixie
Nash-Finch	

HISTORICAL FINANCIALS

Company Type: Private

Income Statement				FYE: Last Saturday in December
	REVENUE ($ mil.)	NET INCOME ($ mil.)	NET PROFIT MARGIN	EMPLOYEES
12/08	24,109.6	1,089.8	4.5%	144,000
12/07	23,193.6	1,183.9	5.1%	144,000
12/06	21,819.7	1,097.2	5.0%	140,000
12/05	20,744.8	989.2	4.8%	134,000
12/04	18,686.4	819.4	4.4%	128,000
Annual Growth	6.6%	7.4%	—	3.0%

Net Income History

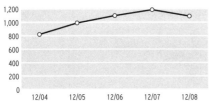

Pulte Homes

Pulte Homes pulls its weight in providing homes for the Great American Family. The company, which buys land to build single-family houses, duplexes, townhouses, and condominiums became the top homebuilder in the US when it acquired rival Centex in 2009. The company now targets a cross-section of homebuyers around the country. The Centex brand is focused on entry-level buyers, while the Pulte name is used for customers looking to trade-up. Pulte also builds Del Webb retiree communities, mostly in Sunbelt locales, for the growing number of buyers in the 55-plus age range. The company sells its homes in 900 communities across some 30 states.

The $1.5 billion in stock deal to buy Centex helped Pulte strengthen its focus on first-time homebuyers — a market that has some of the most promise for growth. The combination also gave Pulte access to the Fox & Jacobs brand and the Centex Homes label. The merger occurred during one of the worst economic downturns in history when home construction was at extremely low levels. Pulte is hoping that the combination of its expertise in retirement housing and Centex's focus on new homebuyers will help it weather the bad housing market. Upon the merger CEO Richard Dugas became chairman and chief executive of the combined company. As part of the transition Pulte plans to streamline

operations by cutting jobs and discontinuing or moving Centex operations to other Pulte offices.

The downturn in the US housing market — due to a toxic cocktail of higher home prices, increased foreclosures, and constraints on mortgage lending — has led to weakened demand for new homes and higher cancellation rates. For Pulte, this trend has meant decreased profitability and a decrease in homebuilding activity. In 2007 the company chose to restructure, cutting about 16% of its workforce (nearly 2,000 jobs) and shuttering its Virginia plant, which made prefabricated home components. It has also been named in lawsuits by subcontractors alleging breach of overtime payment and homebuyers alleging shoddy construction of homes.

Within its competitive industry, Pulte has maintained a diverse land portfolio. However, in light of the current economic conditions, Pulte has scaled back its land acquisitions and land and development practices (through the Centex acquisition added tracts in Texas and the Carolinas). Some planned development have been delayed and construction has slowed.

Over its history, Pulte has constructed nearly 500,000 homes. Like most big homebuilders, the company also runs a subsidiary, Pulte Mortgage, that provides mortgage financing for its homes.

Pulte shareholders (including founder William Pulte) own about 68% of the company, while Centex shareholders own another 32%.

HISTORY

William Pulte built his first home in Detroit in 1950 and incorporated his business in 1956 as William J. Pulte, Inc. In 1961 the company built its first subdivision, in Detroit. During that decade Pulte moved into Washington, DC (1964), Chicago (1966), and Atlanta (1968). In 1969 Pulte merged with Colorado's American Builders to form the Pulte Home Corporation, a publicly traded company.

Originally a builder of high-priced, single-family homes, Pulte began expanding into affordable and midranged housing markets. To lower costs, it pioneered modular designs and prebuilt components. Pulte architects designed the Quadrominium, a large structure with four separate two-bedroom units, each with its own entrance and garage (priced at a mere $20,000 per unit in the 1970s).

Pulte formed Intercontinental Mortgage (later renamed ICM Mortgage) and began making home loans in 1972. The company ran into trouble in 1988 when it was accused of forcing Pulte homebuyers in Baltimore to use ICM financing instead of cheaper loans from the county. Pulte settled by repaying the difference in loan costs.

By the mid-1980s Pulte was one of the US's largest on-site homebuilders. PHM Corporation was created in 1987 as a holding company for the Pulte group of companies. That year PHM entered the thrift business by assisting the Federal Savings and Loan Insurance Corp.'s S&L bailout. It acquired five Texas S&Ls (with assets of $1.3 billion) for $45 million and eventually combined them to form First Heights (finally discontinuing the business in 1994).

Renamed Pulte Corporation in 1993, the company soon faced rising interest rates, which dampened the US housing market and affected the Mexican peso. Nonetheless, it began a second joint venture in that country in 1995 and helped form mortgage bank Su Casita with nine Mexican homebuilders to finance home construction on its border.

In 1996 its Mexican joint venture Condake-Pulte began building thousands of affordable homes for General Motors and Sony employees in maquiladora residential areas near the US-Mexico border. Pulte in 1998 acquired DiVosta, one of Florida's largest homebuilders, and Tennessee-based Radnor Homes.

Pulte's 1988 foray into S&Ls came back to haunt it in 1998: the Federal Deposit Insurance Corp. won a lawsuit that accused the builder of abusing tax benefits associated with the S&Ls. (Pulte settled in 2001, paying $41.5 million.)

The company changed its name to Pulte Homes in 2001. That year Mark O'Brien became the company's CEO. He directed Pulte through the major acquisition of retirement community developer Del Webb for about $800 million in stock and $950 million in assumed debt. The combined company became the largest US homebuilder.

Pulte expanded its operations in the fast-growing San Diego area in 2003 by purchasing assets of ColRich Communities. It boosted its presence in the Albuquerque, Phoenix, and Tucson markets by acquiring Sivage-Thomas Homes (Albuquerque), with about 7,000 lots in the region, and Del Webb entered the Reno market with its Sierra Canyon active adult community. O'Brien left the company in June 2003. EVP and COO Richard Dugas stepped up to become the company's president and CEO at that time.

In September 2003 the US Court of Federal Claims awarded Pulte and related parties $48.7 million as a result of a breach of contract by the US government related to Pulte's acquisition of five savings and loans in 1988.

At the close of 2004, Pulte sold some operations in Argentina to real estate developer Grupo Farallon. The next year it sold its Mexican and remaining Argentine homebuilding enterprises to focus exclusively on US operations.

EXECUTIVES

Chairman, President, and CEO: Richard J. Dugas Jr., age 43, $8,505,595 total compensation
EVP and COO: Steven C. (Steve) Petruska, age 50, $5,632,032 total compensation
EVP and CFO: Roger A. Cregg, age 52, $4,549,322 total compensation
VP and CIO: Jerry R. Batt, age 57
EVP Human Resources: James R. Ellinghausen, age 50
SVP Operations: Peter J. Keane, age 43, $2,753,597 total compensation
SVP, General Counsel, and Secretary: Steven M. Cook, age 50
VP and Treasurer: Bruce E. Robinson, age 47
VP and Assistant Secretary: Gregory M. Nelson, age 53
VP Strategic Marketing: Steven A. Burch
VP Merchandising: Janice M. Jones
VP Investor and Corporate Communications: Calvin R. Boyd
VP Finance and Homebuilding Operations: Timothy M. Stewart
VP Supply Chain: Anthony C. Koblinski
VP, Controller, and Principal Accounting Officer: Michael J. Schweninger, age 40
President and CEO, Pulte Mortgage: Debra W. (Deb) Still
Director Corporate Communications: Mark Marymee
Auditors: Ernst & Young LLP

LOCATIONS

HQ: Pulte Homes, Inc.
100 Bloomfield Hills Pkwy., Ste. 300,
Bloomfield Hills, MI 48304
Phone: 248-647-2750   **Fax:** 248-433-4598
Web: www.pulte.com

2008 Sales

	$ mil.	% of total
Atlantic Coast	1,840.0	29
Southwest	1,486.0	24
Gulf Coast	1,225.9	19
California	827.7	13
Midwest	732.5	12
Financial services	151.0	3
Other	26.4	—
Total	**6,289.5**	**100**

US Homebuilding Regions

Atlantic (Connecticut, Delaware, Maryland, Massachusetts, New Jersey, New York, North Carolina, Pennsylvania, Rhode Island, South Carolina, Tennessee, Virginia)
Gulf Coast (Florida, Texas)
Midwest (Colorado, Illinois, Indiana, Michigan, Minnesota, Missouri, Ohio)
Southwest (Arizona, Nevada, New Mexico)
California

PRODUCTS/OPERATIONS

2008 Sales

	$ mil.	% of total
Homebuilding	6,112.1	97
Financial Services	151.0	3
Other	26.4	—
Total	**6,289.5**	**100**

Selected Brands

Centex
Del Webb
DiVosta Homes
Pulte Homes

COMPETITORS

Ball Homes
Banamex
Beazer Homes
Capital Pacific
Corporación GEO
D.R. Horton
Hovnanian Enterprises
J.F. Shea
KB Home
Lennar
M.D.C.
Meritage Homes
MGIC Investment
M/I Homes
NVR
Pardee Homes
PMI Group
The Ryland Group
Standard Pacific
Toll Brothers
Weyerhaeuser Real Estate
Woodbridge Holdings

HISTORICAL FINANCIALS

Company Type: Public

Income Statement

FYE: December 31

	REVENUE ($ mil.)	NET INCOME ($ mil.)	NET PROFIT MARGIN	EMPLOYEES
12/08	6,289.5	(1,473.1)	—	5,300
12/07	9,263.1	(2,255.8)	—	8,500
12/06	14,274.4	687.5	4.8%	12,400
12/05	14,694.5	1,491.9	10.2%	13,400
12/04	11,711.2	986.5	8.4%	13,000
Annual Growth	(14.4%)	—	—	(20.1%)

2008 Year-End Financials

Debt ratio: 111.7%
Return on equity: —
Cash ($ mil.): 1,655
Current ratio: 3.52
Long-term debt ($ mil.): 3,166
No. of shares (mil.): 259
Dividends
  Yield: 1.5%
  Payout: —
Market value ($ mil.): 2,827

Stock History

NYSE: PHM

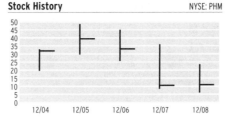

	STOCK PRICE ($) FY Close	P/E High/Low		PER SHARE ($) Earnings	Dividends	Book Value
12/08	10.93	—	—	(5.81)	0.16	10.96
12/07	10.54	—	—	(8.94)	0.16	16.70
12/06	33.12	17	10	2.66	0.16	25.43
12/05	39.36	8	5	5.68	0.13	23.03
12/04	31.90	9	5	3.79	0.10	17.49
Annual Growth	(23.5%)	—	—	—	12.5%	(11.0%)

QUALCOMM

Cell phone makers, wireless carriers, and governments worldwide call on QUALCOMM to engineer a quality conversation. The company pioneered the commercialization of the code-division multiple access (CDMA) technology used in wireless communications equipment and satellite ground stations mainly in North America. It licenses CDMA semiconductor technology and system software to more than 150 equipment and cell phone makers. QUALCOMM's OmniTRACS satellite vehicle tracking system is used by the trucking industry to manage vehicle fleets. QUALCOMM Ventures invests in wireless communications and Internet startups. Customers in the Asia/Pacific region account for more than two-thirds of sales.

In early 2009 QUALCOMM acquired graphics and multimedia assets from AMD for $65 million in cash. The company previously licensed graphics cores from AMD's handheld business.

QUALCOMM is fighting legal battles over patents with rival Broadcom on several fronts. The most crucial case involves a ruling from the International Trade Commission, which held in mid-2007 that new mobile phones being imported into the US with certain QUALCOMM chipsets may be barred from sale. The QUALCOMM chipsets infringe on a Broadcom patent, the commission decided in a 4-2 vote. QUALCOMM appealed the ITC ruling to both the federal courts and the White House, but the Bush Administration decided to let the ITC decision stand.

The advanced handsets in question, made principally by LG Electronics and Samsung Electronics, were designed for use on the networks of AT&T Mobility, Sprint Nextel, and Verizon Wireless. Three months after the ITC ruling, a federal appeals judge stayed the import ban, allowing handset manufacturers to bring affected phones into the US and wireless carriers to offer the handsets to the public.

Although the US was long QUALCOMM's (and CDMA's) main market, the company has sown the seeds of expansion in Asia — particularly China and South Korea — and South America by partnering with such wireless service providers as China Unicom and Brazil-based Vésper. (South Korea now represents the company's largest national market.)

Kyocera, Samsung, and SANYO are all building phones designed around QUALCOMM's next-generation WCDMA chips, which are designed to ease the transmission of multimedia content.

Perhaps piling on in the wake of the International Trade Commission ruling against QUALCOMM, Nokia filed a patent infringement claim against the company with the ITC. Nokia and QUALCOMM also filed patent claims against each other in courts around the world. According to analysts' estimates, Nokia was paying about $500 million a year in licensing fees to QUALCOMM under their previous cross-licensing agreement, which expired in April 2007.

Nokia and QUALCOMM reached a legal settlement on patents in July 2008, agreeing to dismiss all litigation.

HISTORY

Professors Irwin Mark Jacobs and Andrew Viterbi founded digital signal processing equipment company Linkabit in 1968. M/A-COM acquired the company in 1980. Led by Jacobs, Viterbi and five other executives left M/A-COM Linkabit in 1985 to start engineer-focused QUALCOMM (for "quality communications") to provide contract R&D services. The company's first home was located above a strip mall pizza parlor in San Diego. CEO Jacobs dreamed of modifying code-division multiple access (CDMA) — a secure wireless transmission system developed during WWII — for commercial use.

In 1988 QUALCOMM introduced OmniTRACS, a satellite-based system that tracks the location of long-haul truckers. By 1989, when QUALCOMM unveiled its version of CDMA, the company was working on military contracts worth $15 million.

In 1990 the company interrupted the Cellular Telecommunications Industry Association's (CTIA) plans to adopt a rival technology called time-division multiple access when communications service providers NYNEX (now part of Verizon) and Ameritech (later part of SBC Communications and now part of AT&T) adopted QUALCOMM's maverick technology. QUALCOMM initiated a public relations blitz and by 1991 Motorola, AT&T, Clarion, and Nokia had signed product development and testing agreements.

The company went public in 1991 and introduced the Eudora e-mail software program (named for "Why I Live at the P.O." author Eudora Welty), which it licensed from the University of Illinois. That year QUALCOMM and Loral Corporation unveiled plans for Globalstar, a satellite telecommunications system similar to the Iridium system. The CTIA adopted CDMA as a North American standard for wireless communications in 1993.

In 1996 most of the major US cellular carriers upgraded to CDMA. In 1997 Russia charged a QUALCOMM technician with espionage but allowed him to return to the US. The company spun off its wireless phone service operations in 1998 as Leap Wireless International.

In 1999 QUALCOMM and rival Ericsson settled a bitter dispute over the use of CDMA as an industry standard when they signed a cross-licensing deal. QUALCOMM sold its cell phone operations to Kyocera in 2000. The company also signed a potentially huge deal with China Unicom. In 2001 the Chinese government, after years of balking at CDMA in favor of 3G, granted

QUALCOMM and China Unicom permission to install a CDMA-based network.

EVP Paul Jacobs, son of co-founder Irwin Mark Jacobs, took over as CEO in mid-2005; his father remained chairman of the company. In 2006 it acquired Flarion Technologies, a developer of a proprietary version of OFDM (orthogonal frequency-division multiplexing) technology called FLASH-OFDM. An alternative to WiMAX, FLASH-OFDM is a cellular broadband technology used to connect mobile devices to networks.

In 2006 QUALCOMM paid a $1.8 million fine to the federal government for exercising operational control over Flarion before actually closing the transaction to acquire the chipset company. The fine was part of an agreement with the US Department of Justice; QUALCOMM officially denied any wrongdoing, saying it disagreed with the Justice Department that its acquisition agreement with Flarion violated any federal laws or regulations.

The Eudora e-mail program became an open-source product in May 2007, with QUALCOMM ceasing commercial sales of the product.

EXECUTIVES

Chairman and CEO: Paul E. Jacobs, age 46
President: Steven R. (Steve) Altman, age 47
EVP and COO: Len J. Lauer, age 43
EVP and CFO: William E. Keitel, age 56
SVP and CIO: Norm Fjeldheim
EVP and CTO: Roberto Padovani, age 55
EVP and Chief Marketing Officer:
Jeffrey A. (Jeff) Jacobs, age 43
EVP Human Resources: Daniel L. Sullivan
EVP Americas and India: Margaret L. (Peggy) Johnson, age 47
EVP Asia/Pacific and Middle East and Africa: Jing Wang
EVP, General Counsel, and Corporate Secretary:
Donald J. Rosenberg
EVP; President, Qualcomm Internet Services (QIS), MediaFLO Technologies (MFT), and Qualcomm Europe: Andrew Gilbert
EVP; President, CDMA Technologies: Steve Mollenkopf
EVP; President, Qualcomm Technology Licensing: Derek Aberle
EVP, Qualcomm CDMA Technologies Strategic Planning and Finance: James Lederer
SVP; President, QUALCOMM Government Technologies: Kimberly M. Koro
SVP Strategy and Market Development: Jeffrey K. Belk
SVP Global Marketing and Investor Relations:
William F. (Bill) Davidson Jr.
President, QUALCOMM India and SAARC:
Kanwalinder Singh
President, QUALCOMM Europe: Pertti Johansson
Corporate Communications: Emily Kilpatrick
Auditors: PricewaterhouseCoopers LLP

LOCATIONS

HQ: QUALCOMM Incorporated
5775 Morehouse Dr., San Diego, CA 92121
Phone: 858-587-1121   **Fax:** 858-658-2100
Web: www.qualcomm.com

QUALCOMM has facilities in Brazil, China, France, Germany, India, Israel, Italy, Japan, Mexico, South Korea, Taiwan, the UK, and the US.

2008 Sales

	$ mil.	% of total
Asia/Pacific		
South Korea	3,872	35
China	2,309	21
Japan	1,598	14
US	970	9
Other countries	2,393	21
Total	**11,142**	**100**

PRODUCTS/OPERATIONS

2008 Sales

	$ mil.	% of total
QUALCOMM CDMA Technologies (QCT)	6,717	60
QUALCOMM Technology Licensing (QTL)	3,622	33
QUALCOMM Wireless & Internet (QWI)	785	7
QUALCOMM Strategic Initiatives (QSI)	12	—
Other	6	—
Total	**11,142**	**100**

Selected Operations and Products

Code-Division Multiple Access (CDMA) Technologies Group
  Integrated circuits
    Baseband
    Intermediate-frequency
    Power management
    Radio-frequency
  Systems software
Technology Licensing Group
  CDMA technologies and patents (cdmaOne, CDMA2000, WCDMA, TD-SCDMA)
  Royalties from products incorporating CDMA technology
Wireless and Internet Group
  Digital Media
    Digital motion picture delivery systems (under development)
    Government systems (development and analysis services; wireless base stations and phones)
  Internet Services
    Applications development software for wireless devices (BREW)
  Wireless Systems
    Low-Earth-orbit satellite-based telecommunications system (Globalstar)
    Satellite and terrestrial two-way data messaging and position reporting systems and services (OmniTRACS, OmniExpress, TruckMAIL)

COMPETITORS

Andrew Corporation	NAVTEQ
Atheros	NEC Electronics
Broadcom	Nokia
Ericsson	Nortel Networks
Freescale Semiconductor	NXP
IBM Microelectronics	Panasonic Corp
Infineon Technologies	Remote Dynamics
Intel Corp.	Samsung Electronics
InterDigital	SiRF Technology
LG Group	ST-Ericsson
Marvell Technology	STMicroelectronics
Maxim Integrated Products	Texas Instruments
MediaTek	Trimble Navigation
Motorola, Inc.	

HISTORICAL FINANCIALS

Company Type: Public

Income Statement

FYE: Last Sunday in September

	REVENUE ($ mil.)	NET INCOME ($ mil.)	NET PROFIT MARGIN	EMPLOYEES
9/08	11,142.0	3,160.0	28.4%	15,400
9/07	8,871.0	3,303.0	37.2%	12,800
9/06	7,526.0	2,470.0	32.8%	11,200
9/05	5,673.0	2,143.0	37.8%	9,300
9/04	4,880.0	1,720.0	35.2%	7,600
Annual Growth	**22.9%**	**16.4%**	**—**	**19.3%**

2008 Year-End Financials

Debt ratio: —
Return on equity: 18.7%
Cash ($ mil.): 1,840
Current ratio: 5.12
Long-term debt ($ mil.): —
No. of shares (mil.): 1,662
Dividends
  Yield: 1.4%
  Payout: 31.6%
Market value ($ mil.): 71,429

Stock History

NASDAQ (GS): QCOM

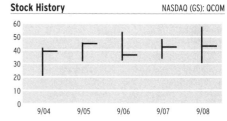

	STOCK PRICE ($) FY Close	P/E High/Low		PER SHARE ($) Earnings	Dividends	Book Value
9/08	42.97	30	16	1.90	0.60	10.79
9/07	42.26	24	17	1.95	0.52	9.53
9/06	36.35	37	23	1.44	0.42	8.06
9/05	44.75	36	25	1.26	0.32	6.69
9/04	39.04	40	21	1.03	0.19	5.81
Annual Growth	**2.4%**	**—**	**—**	**16.5%**	**33.3%**	**16.7%**

Quest Diagnostics

Quest Diagnostics is testing its ability to be the world's leading clinical lab. The company performs tests on about 150 million specimens each year, including routine tests such as cholesterol checks, Pap smears, HIV screenings, and drug tests. Quest Diagnostics also performs esoteric testing (such as genetic screening) and anatomic pathology testing (such as tissue biopsies for cancer testing). The company directly serves doctors and hospitals, as well as corporations, government agencies, and other clinical labs. It has more than 2,000 patient service centers where samples are collected, along with about 30 primary labs and 150 rapid response labs throughout the US, as well as internationally.

While more than 90% of Quest's revenue comes from routine and esoteric testing services, mostly in the US market, the company offers a number of other products, including online data management system Care360 Physician Portal, which lets doctors order diagnostic tests, review results, prescribe medication, and manage patient files. Quest's MedPlus subsidiary developed the tool.

A small portion of sales comes from providing testing services to international drug companies for their clinical trials; GlaxoSmithKline, which owns nearly 20% of Quest, accounts for about 40% of such revenue. Additionally, Quest provides global testing and risk assessment services for the life insurance industry, as well as drug-of-abuse screening for employers.

Quest strives to make itself ubiquitous, with a comprehensive menu of tests (more than 3,000) and a network of labs and collection sites that blanket the country. It keeps looking to grow its service offering, however, by acquiring firms with complementary testing capabilities and through developing its own novel tests. It introduced a number of new tests in 2008, including diagnostics for oncology and urology ailments, as well as genetic tests.

In 2007 the company acquired laboratory services firm AmeriPath in a deal worth about $2 billion. The purchase strengthened Quest's operations in a number of areas, including anatomic pathology (especially cancer testing) and molecular diagnostics.

The company has also made a number of smaller acquisitions that have increased its presence internationally and in specific testing categories, including the 2007 purchase of Sweden-based HemoCue, which makes point-of-care blood testing systems that are performed at the bedside or in the doctor's office and produce results more quickly.

Key markets outside the US include Canada, Mexico, Brazil, and the UK. One international target for Quest is the developing world, where the diagnostic testing market is more fragmented. It began providing testing services in India in 2008, including esoteric testing for hospitals, tests for the life insurance industry, and diagnostics for global clinical trials.

HISTORY

Quest Diagnostics began as one man's quest to make clinical tests more affordable. Pathologist Paul Brown started Metropolitan Pathological Laboratory (MetPath) in his Manhattan apartment in 1967. To help his business take off, in 1969 he bought two $55,000 blood analyzers that could automatically perform a dozen common tests; the machines allowed him to charge patients $5.50 while hospitals and other labs were charging upwards of $40. Investments in emerging lab technology helped MetPath continue to beat competitors' prices and grow its business. It made its first profit in 1971 and eventually attracted the attention of Corning Glass Works, which bought 10% of the company in 1973.

MetPath's growth was due in part to investments in technology. The company built a state-of-the-art central lab in New Jersey in 1978 that could process some 30,000 specimens daily; it also went on an acquisition spree to expand across the US. These investments left the firm swamped with debt, and Corning bought the company in 1982.

An autonomous unit of Corning, MetPath continued to grow as Medicare reimbursement for lab tests went up and more doctors ordered more tests to catch and prevent disease before it happened. To cut costs in the mid-1980s, the company reorganized its facilities to create a regional lab network. A reorganization in 1990 at its parent placed MetPath in the Corning Lab Services subsidiary.

Corning Lab Services strengthened its operations in the early 1990s by buying labs from regional operators. In 1994 MetPath became Corning Clinical Laboratories. Around the same time, the company was besieged with demands from HMOs and other managed care providers to lower its costs. Also during this time, the company settled a handful of federal suits accusing it of fraudulent Medicare billing. In the face of increasing pressure, parent Corning spun off its lab testing business to the public as Quest Diagnostics in 1996.

On its own, Quest aimed to grow through acquisitions. In 1999 it bought rival SmithKline Beecham Clinical Laboratories and has continued its growth strategy in the 21st century. It bought American Medical Laboratories to expand its esoteric testing operations in 2002. The company was finally able to close its acquisition of Unilab in early 2003 after the deal ran into delays with the FTC. Quest sold some labs and service contracts in northern California to LabCorp to appease FTC regulators.

Quest Diagnostics acquired LabOne, a provider of risk assessment services for life insurance companies, in 2005. The following year it purchased point-of-care test makers Enterix (colorectal cancer screens) and Focus Diagnostics (infectious disease and esoteric testing).

EXECUTIVES

Chairman, President, and CEO: Surya N. Mohapatra, age 59, $11,964,632 total compensation
VP Operations: Wayne R. Simmons, age 53, $2,135,960 total compensation
SVP and CFO: Robert A. Hagemann, age 52, $4,124,174 total compensation
SVP and Chief Medical Officer: Jon R. Cohen
VP and Chief Laboratory Officer: Joyce G. Schwartz
SVP and General Counsel: Michael E. Prevoznik, age 47, $2,360,802 total compensation
SVP Pathology and Hospital Services: Joan E. Miller, age 54, $2,353,500 total compensation
VP Communications and Investor Relations: Laure E. Park
VP Compliance: Timothy Sharpe
Director Purchasing Controls and Governance and Supplier Diversity: Gladys Daniel
Director Media Relations: Nancy Fitzsimmons
Auditors: PricewaterhouseCoopers LLP

LOCATIONS

HQ: Quest Diagnostics Incorporated
   3 Giralda Farms, Madison, NJ 07940
Phone: 201-393-5000   **Fax:** 201-729-8920
Web: www.questdiagnostics.com

2008 Sales

	% of total
US	97
Other countries	3
Total	**100**

PRODUCTS/OPERATIONS

2008 Sales

	$ mil.	% of total
Clinical laboratory testing	6,617.0	91
Other	632.4	9
Total	**7,249.4**	**100**

Selected Products and Services

Clinical laboratory testing
  Anatomic pathology testing
  Esoteric testing
    Endocrinology
    Genetics
    Immunology
    Microbiology
    Oncology
    Serology
    Toxicology
  Routine testing
    Alcohol and other substance-abuse tests
    Blood cholesterol
    Complete blood counts
    Pap smears
    Pregnancy testing
    Urinalyses
Other products and services
  Clinical trials testing
  Medical data management systems
  Life insurance risk assessment services

COMPETITORS

AcuNetx
Associated Regional and University Pathologists
Bio-Reference Labs
Celera
Covance
Genomic Health
Genzyme
Kroll Background Screening
LabCorp
Medtox Scientific
Mid America Clinical Laboratories
Oncolab
Orchid Cellmark
PA Labs
PAREXEL
Pathology Associates Medical Laboratories
Pharmaceutical Product Development
Psychemedics
Quintiles Transnational
Spectrum Laboratory Network

HISTORICAL FINANCIALS

Company Type: Public

Income Statement

FYE: December 31

	REVENUE ($ mil.)	NET INCOME ($ mil.)	NET PROFIT MARGIN	EMPLOYEES
12/08	7,249.4	581.5	8.0%	42,800
12/07	6,704.9	339.9	5.1%	43,500
12/06	6,268.7	586.4	9.4%	41,000
12/05	5,503.7	546.3	9.9%	41,500
12/04	5,126.6	499.2	9.7%	38,600
Annual Growth	**9.0%**	**3.9%**	**—**	**2.6%**

2008 Year-End Financials

Debt ratio: 85.4%
Return on equity: 16.8%
Cash ($ mil.): 254
Current ratio: 1.22
Long-term debt ($ mil.): 3,078

No. of shares (mil.): 186
Dividends
  Yield: 0.8%
  Payout: 13.5%
Market value ($ mil.): 9,642

Stock History

NYSE: DGX

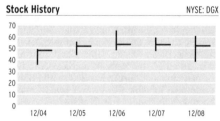

	STOCK PRICE ($) FY Close	P/E High/Low		PER SHARE ($) Earnings	Dividends	Book Value
12/08	51.91	20	13	2.97	0.40	19.41
12/07	52.90	34	28	1.74	0.50	17.90
12/06	53.00	22	17	2.94	0.39	16.25
12/05	51.48	21	17	2.66	0.27	14.87
12/04	47.78	21	15	2.35	0.30	12.32
Annual Growth	**2.1%**	**—**	**—**	**6.0%**	**7.5%**	**12.0%**

Quiksilver, Inc.

Quiksilver rides the wave of youth appeal. It caters to the young and athletic with surfwear, snowboardwear, and sportswear sold under such brands as Quiksilver, Roxy, Raisins, Hawk, Radio Fiji, and Gnu. The company also peddles DC-branded skateboard shoes, snowboard boots, sandals, and apparel for young men and juniors. Quiksilver sells its products in surf, specialty, and department stores worldwide. It also owns about 470 of its own stores, including Boardriders Clubs (board sports), Roxy (junior apparel), and Quicksilver Youth. Quiksilver has expanded its stable of products to include eyewear, watches, and personal care products, while shedding its Rossignol wintersports equipment business.

During 2009, the company has cut 200 jobs and taken other steps to reduce expenses in its Americas division in response to the dismal retail climate in the US. It relies on California, Florida, and Hawaii — some of its biggest markets — for its sales, but the states have been hit with a noteworthy housing collapse.

Until November 2008, Quiksilver also sold snow skis, boots, and bindings through its Rossignol business under the Rossignol, Dynastar, Lange, and Look brands. Since acquiring Rossignol in 2005, however, the company grew to dislike its exposure to the hardgoods manufacturing side of business and longed to return to its roots as an apparel and footwear maker. The company eventually sold the underperforming business to Chartreuse & Mont Blanc, a company headed by Rossignol's former CEO Bruno Cercley. Quiksilver sold its golf equipment unit (Roger Cleveland Golf), which was part of the Rossignol buy, to SRI Sports Limited in 2007.

In recent years, Quiksilver has been busy extending its reach into many new, potentially lucrative markets. The company in 2005 acquired Australia's top boardriding retailer, Surfection, to pave the way for its expansion into Asia/Pacific, specifically Japan, China, and Southeast Asia. To enter the Mexican market, Quiksilver formed a joint venture in late 2006 with PBM International (of which Quiksilver owns a majority stake) to peddle the Quiksilver and Roxy brands in Mexico. (PBM distributes Le Coq Sportif, Arena, and FIFA branded footwear, apparel, and accessories.) Quiksilver entered the Russian wholesale and retail markets in mid-2006 through its joint venture with Sprandi International, a top sports and outdoor products manufacturer in Russia and Eastern Europe that specializes in footwear, apparel, and accessories.

Like many surf/skate/snowboarding companies, Quiksilver promotes its brands not so much through advertising as much as through sponsorship of events featuring its products, e.g., major surf and skateboard competitions. It forms associations with well-known athletes in the field, such as skateboarder Tony Hawk, to promote its products. Another division, Quiksilver Entertainment, produces programming that covers these events while also promoting the boardriding (and hence Quiksilver) lifestyle.

Quiksilver also has ventured into personal care products for its namesake and Roxy lines.

Through an exclusive worldwide licensing agreement, Inter Parfums develops and distributes (Roxy) fragrance, sun care, skin care, and related items, as well as (Quiksilver) sun care and other products through 2017.

HISTORY

Australian surfers Alan Green and John Law started Quiksilver in 1969 to make "boardshorts" for surfers. In 1976 surfers Jeff Hakman and Bob McKnight bought the US rights to the Quiksilver name — Hakman displayed his enthusiasm for the line by eating a doily at a dinner with Green — and established Quiksilver, USA. The firm went public in 1986.

The recession of the early 1990s and the dominance of grunge as the fashion du jour hurt Quiksilver and prompted it to restructure. It acquired French affiliate Na Pali in 1991 and began building its European operations.

To gain surer footing in the fickle teen fashion market, Quiksilver broadened its product offerings. It added the Roxy women's swimwear line in 1991, expanding it to clothing in 1993. It also launched the Boardriders Club concept — stores featuring Quiksilver merchandise but owned by independent retailers.

In 1994 the company acquired swimwear maker The Raisin Company. In 1997 Quiksilver began advertising nationally and entered the snowboard market, buying Mervin Manufacturing, maker of Lib Technologies, Gnu, and Bent Metal snowboard products.

With its women's lines making waves and a strong current from European sales, Quiksilver began opening its own Boardriders Club stores in 1998. In 1999 it launched the Quik Jeans and Roxy Jeans denim lines, and the next year it added the Alex Goes line for women 25 to 40. Riding a tide of rising profits, in 2000 the company acquired Fidra men's golf apparel; Freestyle, the European licensee of rival youth wear label Gotcha; and pro-skateboarder Tony Hawk's apparel and accessories business. In a tail-that-wags-the-dog move, the company bought its progenitor, Quiksilver International, the same year; in doing so, Quiksilver gained sole possession of the Quiksilver name worldwide.

In June 2002 Quiksilver launched Quiksilver Entertainment, a production company that creates actionsport-based programming for the entertainment industry. Later that year Quiksilver acquired Ug Manufacturing in Australia and Quiksilver Japan, in an effort to gain control over nearly all its global business, with the exception of a few licenses in small niche markets.

The company formed a 50/50 joint venture in 2003 with Glorious Sun Enterprises to expand into China.

In 2004 Quiksilver's entertainment unit launched an actionsport film distribution company, Union, which is a supplier to more than 1,000 retail locations in Australia, China, Europe, Japan, and the US. In 2004 Quiksilver completed its purchase of DC Shoes and bought the footwear firm's Canadian distributor, Centre Skateboard Distribution, Ltd., in 2005.

In 2005 Quiksilver flipped its board in a new direction, however, and broadened its reach into the mainstream. The company announced it has signed an exclusive licensing deal with Kohl's

and Tony Hawk to give traction to its apparel, outerwear, and accessories. As part of the agreement, Quiksilver will continue to design the Tony Hawk clothing brand and Kohl's will do the rest, including sourcing, distributing, marketing, and other functions.

In November 2008 Quiksilver exited the sports equipment manufacturing business when it sold its Rossignol unit.

EXECUTIVES

Chairman, President, and CEO:
Robert B. (Bob) McKnight Jr., age 55,
$1,878,000 total compensation
EVP and COO: David H. Morgan, age 49,
$2,811,600 total compensation
EVP and CFO: Joseph (Joe) Scirocco, age 52,
$1,237,100 total compensation
Chief Administrative Officer, General Counsel and Director: Charles S. Exon, age 59,
$910,300 total compensation
EVP, Quiksilver Sales: Tom Holbrook
SVP Sales, Roxy Girl: Deanna Jackson
SVP, Global Marketing, Roxy: Randy Hild
SVP Sales, Quiksilver Brands and Quiksilver Americas:
John Mills
VP Sales for Roxy Girl and Roxy Footwear:
Susan Branch
VP, Human Resources: Carol Sherman
VP, Quiksilver Entertainment: Rob Colby
VP Accounting and Financial Reporting:
Brad L. Holman, age 33
President, Women's Division: Steve Tully
President of Retail, Americas: Carol Christopherson
President, Quiksilver Asia Pacific: Clive Fitts
President, Quiksilver Europe: Pierre Agnes, age 44,
$1,670,400 total compensation
Executive Advisor: Harry Hodge
Auditors: Deloitte & Touche LLP

LOCATIONS

HQ: Quiksilver, Inc.
15202 Graham St., Huntington Beach, CA 92649
Phone: 714-889-2200   **Fax:** 714-889-2315
Web: www.quiksilver.com

2008 Sales

	% of total
Americas	47
Europe	41
Asia/Pacific	12
Total	**100**

PRODUCTS/OPERATIONS

2008 Sales

	% of total
Apparel	65
Footwear	20
Accessories	15
Total	**100**

Selected Brands

DC Shoes (men's and women's extreme sportswear and footwear)
Hawk Clothing (men's and boys' skateboard apparel and accessories)
Leilani (women's swimwear)
Quiksilver (sportswear, beachwear, activewear, and outerwear)
Quiksilver Boys (boys' sportswear)
Quiksilver Roxy (junior sportswear, footwear, accessories, and swimwear)
Quiksilver Silver Edition (men's sportswear, beachwear, activewear, and outerwear)
Quiksilver Toddler (children's sportswear)
Radio Fiji (junior swimwear)
Raisins (junior swimwear)

COMPETITORS

Abercrombie & Fitch
adidas
Amer Sports
Amerex
Ashworth, Inc.
Bauer Nike Hockey
Billabong
Body Glove
Burton Snowboards
Calvin Klein
Columbia Sportswear
Fat Face
FUBU
Head N.V.
Levi Strauss
Life is good
Nautica Apparel
NIKE
Oakley
Orange 21
Pacific Sunwear
Sole Technology
Stüssy
Tecnica
Tommy Hilfiger
Volcom
Warnaco Swimwear

HISTORICAL FINANCIALS

Company Type: Public

Income Statement				FYE: October 31
	REVENUE ($ mil.)	NET INCOME ($ mil.)	NET PROFIT MARGIN	EMPLOYEES
10/08	2,264.6	(226.3)	—	8,400
10/07	2,426.0	(121.1)	—	9,600
10/06	2,362.3	93.0	3.9%	9,200
10/05	1,780.9	107.1	6.0%	7,875
10/04	1,266.9	81.4	6.4%	4,350
Annual Growth	15.6%	—	—	17.9%

2008 Year-End Financials

Debt ratio: 131.7%
Return on equity: —
Cash ($ mil.): 53
Current ratio: 1.86
Long-term debt ($ mil.): 790

No. of shares (mil.): 128
Dividends
Yield: 0.0%
Payout: —
Market value ($ mil.): 332

Stock History

NYSE: ZQK

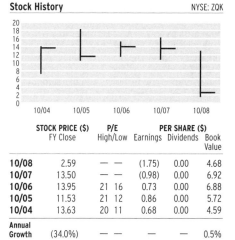

	STOCK PRICE ($) FY Close	P/E High/Low		PER SHARE ($) Earnings	Dividends	Book Value
10/08	2.59	—	—	(1.75)	0.00	4.68
10/07	13.50	—	—	(0.98)	0.00	6.92
10/06	13.95	21	16	0.73	0.00	6.88
10/05	11.53	21	12	0.86	0.00	5.72
10/04	13.63	20	11	0.68	0.00	4.59
Annual Growth	(34.0%)	—	—	—	—	0.5%

Qwest Communications

A journey at the speed of light: Qwest Communications spans the globe with its high-capacity broadband fiber-optic network. The company is among the leading US local phone providers and serves nearly 12 million access lines in a 14-state region stretching from Arizona north to Wyoming and east to Minnesota. Qwest also provides long-distance and international calling, as well as broadband data, voice, and video services to business customers. The company's wholesale network extends outside of its local service area, linking major global metropolitan areas and providing high-volume transmission capacity and other wholesale services to other carriers and resellers.

Qwest also offers consumer wireless services through an agreement with Verizon Wireless while satellite television services are made possible through a marketing partnership with DIRECTV. Qwest in 2008 expanded its wireless services by making mobile broadband Internet access available to mobile customers.

The company has said that its fastest growing areas are data, Internet, and video services; its marketing efforts include packaging services together in order to encourage subscribers to add functionality. Citing dwindling numbers of traditional phone customers, the company in 2008 cut more than 10% of its workforce (mainly from its operations in the Western US) in order to bring down costs.

In addition to consumer and commercial clients, Qwest is increasingly signing up public sector agencies. Notable clients added in 2008 include NASA, the US General Services Administration, and the US Department of Veterans Affairs.

HISTORY

Philip Anschutz bought Southern Pacific Rail in 1988 and established subsidiary Southern Pacific Telecommunications Company (SPT) to lay fiber-optic cable for long-distance carriers beside its parent's rails. By 1993 it was offering long-distance services to companies in the southwestern US and selling switched phone services to businesses.

In 1995 SPT acquired Qwest Communications, which owned a digital microwave system that covered areas SPT's fiber-optic network didn't reach. The combined company took the Qwest moniker and announced it was building a nationwide state-of-the-art fiber-optic network the next year. Frontier, WorldCom (later merged with MCI), and GTE all agreed to buy fiber installed by Qwest along its network, which helped defray construction costs.

Opportunities increased with the passage of the Telecommunications Act of 1996, which began opening up US telecom markets. Anschutz sold Southern Pacific to Union Pacific that year but held on to the telecom operation. In 1997 Qwest hired Joseph Nacchio, a former AT&T Corp. executive, to run the company. It went public that year.

Nacchio charged into long-distance services, launching Internet protocol (IP) telephony and a 7.5-cents-a-minute rate. In 1998 Qwest paid $27 million for long-distance reseller Phoenix Network and another $4.4 billion for long-

distance provider LCI International, which more than doubled Qwest's size.

Qwest also acquired Amsterdam-based EUnet International, a European ISP, for about $155 million and later contributed it to KPNQwest, Qwest's venture with Dutch phone company KPN. The joint venture was created in 1998 to build a fiber-optic network in Europe. But after rapid expansion that created a capacity exceeding demand for services, the venture was forced into bankruptcy (in 2002) and subsequently folded.

In 1999 Qwest bought Icon CMT, which offered Web-based applications for businesses, and acquired a 19% stake in fixed wireless carrier Advanced Radio Telecom. The company joined Hewlett-Packard and SAP America to deliver SAP's business software over the Qwest network.

Nacchio became executive chairman in 1999, and Anschutz was named chairman of the board. Qwest more than doubled in size and gained 25 million local phone service customers in 14 states in the US with the acquisition in 2000 of Baby Bell U S WEST. The stock deal was valued at $43.5 billion. To gain regulatory approval for the U S WEST deal, Qwest had to sell its long-distance business in the Baby Bell's 14-state territory. Following the acquisition of U S WEST, the expanded company cut 11,000 jobs, or 16% of its workforce.

Amid the recession that dramatically slowed expansion in the telecom industry, Qwest was forced to halt some network expansion plans and reduce its workforce by more than 25%. In 2002 the SEC began a review of the company's accounting practices. Amid the controversies, Nacchio resigned at the request of the company's board of directors (he was convicted in 2007 of 19 counts of insider trading). Anschutz also resigned his position as non-executive chairman but remained on the board of directors. Richard Notebaert, previously the CEO of Tellabs, was named CEO of Qwest in 2002.

Strapped for cash, Qwest sold billions of dollars in assets, including its phone directory business, which was acquired by the Carlyle Group and Welsh, Carson, Anderson & Stowe for more than $7 billion.

In 2003 Qwest gained approval from the FCC to offer long-distance service in Arizona, the final step in its effort to reenter the long-distance business after its purchase of U S WEST. Meanwhile the SEC and Justice Department began investigations of questionable accounting practices at the company. Later in 2003 the company acquired network assets, mostly outside the Qwest local service area, from bankrupt Allegiance Telecom. The next year the company sold its wireless assets to Verizon Wireless in a cash deal valued at about $418 million, then reached an agreement with Sprint (now Sprint Nextel) to resell wireless services.

Perhaps feeling left out of the telecom industry consolidation movement, Qwest in 2005 made an offer to acquire MCI, but the MCI board consistently favored Verizon Communications as a suitor. After the MCI board accepted as superior a bid from Verizon valued at $8.4 billion, Qwest dropped out of the bidding.

In 2007 Notebaert announced his retirement. Edward Mueller, a veteran CEO who led companies ranging from Ameritech to Williams-Sonoma, was named chairman and CEO of Qwest.

EXECUTIVES

Chairman and CEO: Edward A. (Ed) Mueller, age 62, $10,432,615 total compensation
COO: Teresa A. Taylor, age 45
EVP and CFO: Joseph J. (Joe) Euteneuer, age 53, $1,000,416 total compensation
VP and CIO: Girish K. Varma
VP and CTO: Pieter Poll
EVP, General Counsel, and Chief Administrative Officer: Richard N. (Rich) Baer, age 52, $3,726,027 total compensation
VP Risk Management and Chief Ethics and Compliance Officer: David (Dave) Heller
VP Real Estate and Chief Procurement Officer: John McGuire
EVP Mass Markets Organization: C. Daniel (Dan) Yost, age 60
EVP Product and IT: Neil E. Cox, age 59
EVP Corporate Strategy: Stephanie G. Comfort
EVP Wholesale Markets: Roland R. Thornton, age 55
EVP Network Operations: Robert D. (Bob) Tregemba, age 61
EVP Business Markets Group: Christopher (Chris) Ancell, age 47
SVP and Treasurer: Rahn K. Porter, age 54
SVP Investor Relations: Kurt Fawkes
SVP Public Policy: R. Steven (Steve) Davis
SVP, Controller, and Chief Accounting Officer: R. William Johnston, age 53
VP Corporate Communications: Nicholas (Nick) Sweers
VP Human Resource: Felicity O'Herron
Auditors: KPMG LLP

LOCATIONS

HQ: Qwest Communications International Inc.
1801 California St., Denver, CO 80202
Phone: 800-899-7780   **Fax:** 303-992-1724
Web: www.qwest.com

PRODUCTS/OPERATIONS

2008 Sales by Service

	$ mil.	% of total
Voice	7,246	54
Data, Internet, & video	5,405	40
Wireless	459	3
Other	365	3
Total	**13,475**	**100**

2008 Sales by Market

	$ mil.	% of total
Mass (consumer & small business)	5,740	43
Business	4,099	30
Wholesale	3,271	24
Other	365	3
Total	**13,475**	**100**

Selected Services

Wireline
  Asynchronous transfer mode (ATM)
  Colocation
  Custom calling features (caller ID, call waiting, call return, and 3-way calling)
  Customer premises equipment (CPE)
  Directory assistance
  Frame relay
  Internet access (dedicated, dial-up, and digital subscriber lines [DSL])
  Internet protocol (IP)
  Local-exchange access
  Long-distance (intraLATA, interLATA, and international)
  Network management
  Private lines
  Switching
  Virtual private network (VPN)
  Voice mail
  Web hosting
Wireless
  Personal communication services (PCS) resale

COMPETITORS

360networks	New Ulm Telecom
AT&T	Sprint Nextel
Global Crossing	tw telecom
Iowa Telecommunications	Verizon
Level 3 Communications	XO Holdings

HISTORICAL FINANCIALS

Company Type: Public

Income Statement

FYE: December 31

	REVENUE ($ mil.)	NET INCOME ($ mil.)	NET PROFIT MARGIN	EMPLOYEES
12/08	13,475.0	681.0	5.1%	32,937
12/07	13,778.0	2,917.0	21.2%	37,000
12/06	13,923.0	593.0	4.3%	38,000
12/05	13,903.0	(757.0)	—	39,000
12/04	13,809.0	(1,794.0)	—	41,000
Annual Growth	(0.6%)	—	—	(5.3%)

2008 Year-End Financials

Debt ratio: —
Return on equity: —
Cash ($ mil.): 565
Current ratio: 0.77
Long-term debt ($ mil.): 12,839

No. of shares (mil.): 1,724
Dividends
  Yield: 8.8%
  Payout: 82.1%
Market value ($ mil.): 6,275

Stock History

NYSE: Q

	STOCK PRICE ($) FY Close	P/E High/Low	PER SHARE ($) Earnings	Dividends	Book Value
12/08	3.64	17 5	0.39	0.32	(0.84)
12/07	7.01	7 4	1.52	0.00	0.33
12/06	8.37	31 17	0.30	0.00	(0.84)
12/05	5.65	— —	(0.42)	0.00	(1.87)
12/04	4.44	— —	(1.00)	0.00	(1.52)
Annual Growth	(4.8%)	— —	—	—	—

RadioShack Corporation

These stores are tuned in to your electronics needs and desires. RadioShack is one of the leading consumer electronics retail chains with some 4,450 outlets in the US, Puerto Rico, and the Virgin Islands. Its stores and Web site offer a variety of products, including wireless and residential telephones, computers, DVD players, electronic toys, and, of course, radios. The stores also sell third-party services such as wireless calling plans and direct satellite service. In addition, RadioShack sells a wide range of electronics parts and components. The chain includes about 1,400 dealer outlets and some 600 wireless phone kiosks located primarily in malls and SAM'S CLUB stores (kiosks are not RadioShack-branded).

Unlike its big-box competitors, RadioShack has built its chain with smaller but more numerous locations. (Its stores are about 2,500 sq. ft. on average.) Following that philosophy, the company took over operation of kiosks located in SAM'S CLUB stores and has significantly expanded that business through partnerships with such companies as Sprint Nextel and AT&T Mobility (formerly Cingular Wireless).

RadioShack has been closing locations and cutting jobs since it launched a turnaround plan in 2005. However, the worsening economy in the US isn't helping efforts to revive the business. The company does hope to profit from its new partnership with seven-time Tour de France winner Lance Armstrong as the sponsor of a new cycling team in 2010.

Maintaining consistency in the executive suite has proven to be difficult in recent years. Long-time CEO Len Roberts retired in 2005 and turned the reigns over to David Edmondson, who resigned after a year. RadioShack hired Julian Day, a turnaround specialist with experience at Safeway and Kmart, as chairman and CEO. Soon after Day's appointment Hall Financial Group, a Texas-based private investment firm, took a nearly 6% stake in the company. About a year later, Goldman Sachs bought a 13% stake in the firm, making it RadioShack's largest investor.

HISTORY

During the 1950s Charles Tandy expanded his family's small Fort Worth, Texas, leather business (founded 1919) into a nationwide chain of leather craft and hobby stores. By 1960 Tandy stock was being traded on the NYSE. In the early 1960s Tandy began to expand into other retail areas, buying Leonard's, a Fort Worth department store.

In 1963 Tandy purchased RadioShack, a nearly bankrupt electronics parts supplier with a mail-order business and nine retail stores in the Boston area. Tandy collected part of the $800,000 owed the company and started expanding. Between 1961 and 1969 Tandy's sales grew from $16 million to $180 million; the bulk of the growth was due to the expansion of RadioShack. Between 1968 and 1973 Tandy ballooned from 172 to 2,294 stores; RadioShack provided over 50% of sales and 80% of earnings in 1973.

Tandy sold its department store operations to Dillard's in 1974. The next year Tandy spun off its leather products business to its shareholders as Tandy Brands and its hobby and handicraft business as Tandycrafts, focusing Tandy on the consumer electronics business. During 1976 the boom in CB radio sales pushed income up 125% as Tandy opened 1,200 stores. The following year it introduced the first mass-marketed PC.

In 1984 the company introduced the Tandy 1000, the first IBM-compatible PC priced under $1,000. Then came acquisitions — electronics equipment chain stores Scott/McDuff and VideoConcepts (1985), laptop specialist GRiD Systems (1988), and microcomputer makers Victor Microcomputer and Micronic (1989, later merged as Victor Technologies).

In 1987 Tandy spun off its foreign retail operations as InterTAN. Realizing that RadioShack had nearly exhausted its expansion possibilities, the company focused on alternate retail formats such as GRiD Systems Centers and in 1991 opened Computer City and the Edge in Electronics. Also that year it introduced name-brand products into RadioShack stores.

Tandy sold Memtek Products (magnetic tape), LIKA (printed circuit boards), and its computer manufacturing and marketing operations in 1993 and spun off O'Sullivan Industries (ready-to-assemble furniture) to the public in 1994. As part of the restructuring, Tandy began to scale back VideoConcepts and McDuff Electronics.

A year later the company announced that it would close all of its VideoConcepts mall stores and half its McDuff electronics stores. Also in 1995 it sold its credit card business.

In 1996 and 1997 Tandy closed down its 19-store Incredible Universe "gigastores" chain, shuttered the 53-store McDuff chain, and closed about 20 of its Computer City stores and sold others in Europe.

Longtime CEO John Roach stepped down in 1998, and president Leonard Roberts replaced him. Tandy then sold the Computer City chain to CompUSA for $211 million.

The company changed its name to RadioShack in 2000. In 2001 RadioShack announced plans to sell products in about 5,000 Blockbuster video stores; the plan included kiosks and store-within-a-store shops. In December the company announced that it would incur a $124 million charge, reflecting the sale of its headquarters building (the Charles D. Tandy Center), its exit from the commercial installation business, and the closure of 35 stores. (RadioShack completed construction of a new headquarters in down-town Fort Worth in 2004.)

After a six-month trial, RadioShack halted plans to install boutiques in Blockbuster video stores in January 2002.

Roberts retired as CEO in 2005 and turned the reigns of the company over to David Edmondson, who had joined RadioShack from direct marketer ADVO in 1994. However, Edmondson was forced to resign the following year after it was revealed he may have misrepresented his academic record on his resume. The company in July 2006 named former Sears executive Julian Day as Edmonson's replacement. Later that month CFO David Barnes announced he would leave the electronics retailer to take a job with The Western Union Company.

In 2006 the company closed 500 of its traditional retail outlets and cut some 1,500 jobs.

In December 2008, the company acquired 100% ownership of its joint venture in Mexico with Grupo Gigante, S.A.B.

EXECUTIVES

Chairman and CEO: Julian C. Day, age 56,
$9,847,196 total compensation
EVP Store Operations: Bryan Bevin, age 46,
$2,908,485 total compensation
EVP and CFO: James F. (Jim) Gooch, age 41,
$2,908,485 total compensation
SVP and CIO: Sharon S. Stufflebeme
EVP and Chief Marketing Officer: Lee Applbaum, age 38
EVP and Chief Merchandise Officer: Peter J. Whitsett,
age 43, $1,781,102 total compensation
SVP Human Resources: Kim Warmbier
VP Learning and Development: Rich Pendergast
VP Dealer/Franchise Operations: Paul Rickels
VP Investor Relations: Phyllis J. Proffer
VP, General Counsel, and Secretary:
Robert C. (Bob) Donohoo, age 47
VP and Corporate Controller: Martin O. Moad, age 52
VP Northeast: Bill Nebes
VP Southeast: Steve Schmidt
VP Great Lakes Area: Sal Todaro
VP Southwest: Gregory Pattakos
VP West: Tom Schultz
VP Caribbean: John Wissinger
VP Central Operations: Debi Gladu
VP Finance: Kathy Buckley
Media Relations: Mary De La Garza
Auditors: PricewaterhouseCoopers LLP

LOCATIONS

HQ: RadioShack Corporation
300 RadioShack Cir., Fort Worth, TX 76102
Phone: 817-415-3011   **Fax:** 817-415-2647
Web: www.radioshack.com

PRODUCTS/OPERATIONS

2008 Locations

	No.
Company-operated	
Stores	4,453
Kiosks	688
Dealers & other	1,361
Total	**6,502**

2008 Sales

	$ mil.	% of total
Company-operated		
US Stores	3,611.1	85
Kiosks	283.5	7
Other sales	329.9	8
Total	**4,224.5**	**100**

2008 Sales

	$ mil.	% of total
Wireless	1,393.8	33
Accessory	1,183.9	28
Personal electronics	545.7	13
Modern home	527.1	13
Power	242.4	6
Technical	183.7	4
Service	95.8	2
Service centers & other	52.1	1
Total	**4,224.5**	**100**

COMPETITORS

Amazon.com
Apple Inc.
Best Buy
Brookstone
Costco Wholesale
Dell
Fry's Electronics
GameStop
Gateway, Inc.
Home Depot
Office Depot
PC Mall
Sears
Sprint Nextel
Staples
Systemax
Target
TSIC
Verizon
Wal-Mart

HISTORICAL FINANCIALS

Company Type: Public

Income Statement

				FYE: December 31
	REVENUE ($ mil.)	NET INCOME ($ mil.)	NET PROFIT MARGIN	EMPLOYEES
12/08	4,224.5	192.4	4.6%	36,800
12/07	4,251.7	236.8	5.6%	35,800
12/06	4,777.5	73.4	1.5%	40,000
12/05	5,081.7	269.9	5.3%	47,000
12/04	4,841.2	337.2	7.0%	42,000
Annual Growth	(3.3%)	(13.1%)	—	(3.3%)

2008 Year-End Financials

Debt ratio: 89.6%
Return on equity: 24.2%
Cash ($ mil.): 815
Current ratio: 2.81
Long-term debt ($ mil.): 733
No. of shares (mil.): 125
Dividends
Yield: 2.1%
Payout: 16.8%
Market value ($ mil.): 1,495

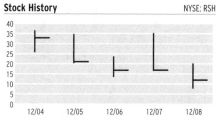

Stock History					NYSE: RSH

	STOCK PRICE ($) FY Close	P/E High/Low		PER SHARE ($) Earnings	Dividends	Book Value
12/08	11.94	13	5	1.49	0.25	6.53
12/07	16.86	20	10	1.74	0.25	6.15
12/06	16.78	43	25	0.54	0.25	5.22
12/05	21.03	19	11	1.79	0.25	4.70
12/04	32.88	17	13	2.08	0.25	7.37
Annual Growth	(22.4%)	—	—	(8.0%)	0.0%	(3.0%)

Ralcorp Holdings

Ralcorp Holdings reminds us that you can't judge food by its cover. The company is the top US maker of private-label or "store-brand" ready-to-eat and hot breakfast cereals. Ralcorp has stocked its pantry with a widening variety of private-label cookies, crackers, peanut butter, ketchup, snack nuts, and candy. The company also makes branded products: Ralston Hot Cereal, Ry Krisp crackers, 3 Minute Brand Oats oatmeal, and Rippin' Good cookies. Its Carriage House unit produces private-label dressings, syrups, jellies, and sauces, and its Lofthouse and Cascade Cookie businesses provide frozen cookies to in-store bakeries. In 2008 Ralcorp acquired the Post breakfast cereals business from Kraft Foods.

The company's strategy is to round out its larder through acquisitions. It kept to that strategy when, in 2009, it acquired Harvest Manor Farms, a Cedar Rapids, Iowa-based maker of private-label and Hoody's branded snack nuts.

Its acquisition of Post cereals will hopefully be a shot in the arm for Ralcorp. The brand is the #3 US breakfast cereal (behind Kellogg and General Mills). It brought in more than $1 billion in 2006 for former owner Kraft. Post makes such well-known brands as Honey Bunches of Oats, Pebbles, Shredded Wheat, Grape-Nuts, and Honeycomb. The all-stock transaction was worth some $2.6 billion.

Its 2007 purchase of Bakery Chef (frozen food-service pancakes and waffles) allows Ralcorp to reach people eating breakfast at restaurants. The addition of snack-food maker Medallion Foods (corn and tortilla chips) indicates another move in diversifying beyond breakfast food. It bought Bloomfield Bakers for about $140 million that year as well. The deal included Bloomfield affiliate, Lovin Oven. Bloomfield makes nutritional and cereal bars.

The company's operating divisions include Ralston Foods (cereals), Bremner Foods (cookies, crackers), Nutcracker (snack nuts), Ralcorp

Frozen Bakery Products (pancakes, waffles), and Carriage House (syrups, jellies).

Wal-Mart accounted for approximately 17% of the company's 2008 sales.

The mutual fund investment firm, FMR, owns about 10% of Ralcorp.

HISTORY

Ralston Purina spun off Ralcorp Holdings, then a maker of name-brand and private-label foods, in 1994 under co-CEOs Richard Pearce and Joe Micheletto. Ralston was concerned that its huge pet food and Eveready battery interests had overshadowed its smaller consumer foods and ski resort businesses.

A cereal price war in 1996 ate at Ralcorp's price advantage and devoured margins. To focus on its core private-label business, the firm in 1997 sold its branded snack and cereal businesses (which included Cookie Crisp and Chex) to General Mills for about $570 million and its ski resort holdings to Vail Resorts for $310 million (it received a 22% stake in Vail; shares were gradually reduced until by 2009 Ralcorp owned less than 5%). Pearce resigned while the sales were in progress; Micheletto stayed on as CEO.

The company expanded its cookie and cracker division by adding the Wortz Company (the #2 US private-label cracker and cookie maker) for about $46 million in 1997 and Sugar Kake Cookie the following year. In 1998 Ralcorp entered a new private-label category, snack nuts, by purchasing nut makers Flavor House and Nutcracker Brands. Faced with price competition and decreasing demand, it sold its Beech-Nut baby food business that year for $68 million to the Milnot company.

To broaden its private-label portfolio further, in early 1999 Ralcorp bought Martin Gillet (mayonnaise and salad dressings) and Southern Roasted Nuts of Georgia. In late 1999 the company bought Ripon Foods (cookies, sugar wafers, breakfast bars). And, seeing breakfast cereal sales shrinking, Ralcorp purchased Ripon Foods in 1999, in part, for its ability to make private-label breakfast bars.

In 2000 Ralcorp purchased private-label chocolate candy maker James P. Linette and the Cascade Cookie Company. That same year it bought Red Wing (syrups, peanut butter, jelly, barbecue sauce) from Tomkins for about $132 million. Also in 2000 Ralcorp said it would merge with animal feed company Agribrands International, but the agreement fell through. Additionally that year the company said it would buy Genesee Corporation's Ontario Foods business (powdered drinks, soups, prepared meals) for $50 million, but called off that deal too.

During 2002 Ralcorp purchased cookie-maker Lofthouse Foods. Early in 2003 the company sold off its industrial tomato paste facility. Later that same year, Ralcorp purchased frozen breakfast foods company Bakery Chef for $287.5 million.

In 2004 the company acquired Concept 2 Bakers (C2B), a frozen, par-baked artisan bread maker, from McGlynn Bakeries. The next year it purchased private-label corn-snack (tortillas) manufacturer Medallion Foods and Canadian private-label griddle-product maker Western Waffles. It purchased Parco Foods, a Chicago-based cookie maker for in-store bakeries, and Cottage Bakeries, a frozen bread dough maker in 2006.

EXECUTIVES

Chairman: William P. (Bill) Stiritz, age 74
Co-CEO, President, and Director; President and CEO, Ralcorp Frozen Bakery Products: Kevin J. Hunt, age 57
Co-CEO, President, and Director: David P. Skarie, age 62
Corporate VP and Controller: Thomas G. Granneman, age 59
Coporate VP; President, Ralston Foods: Ronald D. (Ron) Wilkinson, age 58
VP and Director Human Resources: Jack Owczarczak
Corporate VP and Treasurer: Scott Monette, age 47
VP, General Counsel, and Secretary: Charles G. (Chuck) Huber Jr., age 44
Corporate VP; President, Carriage House, Bremner Food Group, and Nutcracker Brands: Richard R. Koulouris, age 52
Corporate VP; President, Post Foods: Stephen Van Tassel
Auditors: PricewaterhouseCoopers LLP

LOCATIONS

HQ: Ralcorp Holdings, Inc.
800 Market St., St. Louis, MO 63101
Phone: 314-877-7000   **Fax:** 314-877-7900
Web: www.ralcorp.com

PRODUCTS/OPERATIONS

2008 Sales

	$ mil.	% of total
Cereals, crackers & cookies		
Ralston Foods	819.9	29
Bremner	349.4	12
Post Foods	180.5	7
Frozen bakery products	711.8	25
Dressings, syrups, jellies & sauces	489.1	17
Snack nuts & candy	273.7	10
Total	**2,824.4**	**100**

Selected Branded Products

3 Minute Brand (instant breakfast cereal)
Cascade (cookies)
Champagne (cookies)
Flavor House (snack nuts)
Hoody's (snack nuts)
JERO (bottled cocktail mixes)
Lofthouse (cookies)
Krusteaz (frozen breakfast foods)
Major Peters' (condiments)
Medallion (corn and tortilla chips)
Nutcracker (snack nuts)
Parco (cookies)
Post (bready-to-eat breakfast cereal)
  Grape-Nuts
  Honey Bunches of Oats
  Honeycomb
  Pebbles
  Raisin Bran
  Shredded Wheat
  Spoon Size Shredded Wheat
  Trail Mix Crunch
Ralson (instant breakfast cereal)
Rippin' Good (cookies)
Ry Krisp (crackers)

COMPETITORS

ak-mak Bakeries	McKee Foods
Campbell Soup	National Grape Cooperative
Fehr Foods	Otis Spunkmeyer
Frito-Lay	Pepperidge Farm
General Mills	PepsiCo
Gilster-Mary Lee	Renée's Gourmet Foods
Heinz	Sara Lee Food and
Interbake Foods	Beverage
John Sanfilippo & Son	Silver Lake
Kellogg	Smucker
Kellogg U.S. Snacks	Unilever PLC
Kraft Foods	Voortman Cookies
Lance Snacks	Welch's
Malt-O-Meal	Weston Foods

HISTORICAL FINANCIALS

Company Type: Public

Income Statement

FYE: September 30

	REVENUE ($ mil.)	NET INCOME ($ mil.)	NET PROFIT MARGIN	EMPLOYEES
9/08	2,824.4	167.8	5.9%	9,000
9/07	2,233.4	31.9	1.4%	7,800
9/06	1,850.2	68.3	3.7%	6,500
9/05	1,675.1	71.4	4.3%	6,370
9/04	1,558.4	65.1	4.2%	6,000
Annual Growth	**16.0%**	**26.7%**	**—**	**10.7%**

2008 Year-End Financials

Debt ratio: 69.2%
Return on equity: 11.6%
Cash ($ mil.): 14
Current ratio: 1.65
Long-term debt ($ mil.): 1,669

No. of shares (mil.): 57
Dividends
  Yield: 0.0%
  Payout: —
Market value ($ mil.): 3,816

Stock History

NYSE: RAH

	STOCK PRICE ($) FY Close	P/E High/Low	PER SHARE ($) Earnings	Dividends	Book Value
9/08	67.41	14 9	5.38	0.00	42.60
9/07	55.82	59 40	1.17	0.00	8.54
9/06	48.23	22 14	2.41	0.00	8.42
9/05	41.92	20 15	2.34	0.00	9.16
9/04	36.10	17 12	2.17	0.00	7.85
Annual Growth	**16.9%**	**— —**	**25.5%**	**—**	**52.6%**

Raymond James Financial

You could call it Ray. You could call it Ray Jay. But Raymond James Financial will do just fine. The company offers investment and financial planning services primarily through subsidiary Raymond James & Associates (RJA), which provides securities brokerage, investment banking, and financial advisory services throughout the US; and Raymond James Financial Services, which offers financial planning and brokerage services through independent contractors, as well as through alliances with community banks. Other divisions provide asset management, trust, and retail banking services. Raymond James Financial has approximately 2,300 offices worldwide.

The company's business is divided into seven primary segments. The Private Client Group is the largest, accounting for more than half of the company's sales; it provides retail brokerage and financial planning services to some 1.8 million customers in the US, Canada, and the UK. Capital Markets performs investment banking and equity research services. The Asset Management segment includes Eagle Asset Management, Eagle Fund Management (formerly Heritage Asset Management), and Eagle Boston Investment Management.

Raymond James Bank (RJBank), securities lending, propriety investments, and the Emerging Markets segment, which is involved in joint ventures in Latin America and Turkey, round out the company's operations.

In response to turmoil in the financial markets Raymond James Financial in 2008 announced that it would switch to a bank holding company structure. Larger rivals Morgan Stanley and Goldman Sachs have done the same, but their conversions were mandated by the US government. Raymond James said it had been mulling the move for a while, and that economic conditions hastened its decision. It should help the company continue to build its burgeoning portfolio of usually more-profitable commercial loans.

In 2009, the firm acquired Boston-based boutique bank Lane, Berry & Co. Terms of the deal with not disclosed. Lane, Berry's 21 professionals will be folded into Raymond James' investment banking group.

In 2006 Raymond James extended its deal to attach its name to the home stadium of the NFL's Tampa Bay Buccaneers through 2015.

Chairman and CEO Thomas James owns about 12% of Raymond James Financial.

HISTORY

Robert James, often called the "founder of financial planning," first started a construction business in Ohio after his WWII service in the US Navy and then began a Florida home-building company. He got into the financial services business in 1954 with Florida Mutual Fund, a company he and Gerard Jobin formed that eventually became American National Growth Fund. But when most companies were selling just stocks or mutual funds, James saw a need for a more comprehensive approach to investing. He decided to focus on helping individual clients, learning about their financial needs and goals and then working with them on everything from investments to taxes. To that end, he began offering seminars for retirees.

In 1960 those seminars had turned into a new company, James and Associates, which two years later became Robert A. James Investments. In 1964 James acquired Raymond and Associates, a firm started by Edward Raymond in 1962; the newly merged firm was renamed Raymond James & Associates (RJA).

James' son Thomas joined the firm in 1966, the year the company's revenues first surpassed $1 million. Over the next several years, the company expanded its investment offerings and set up new divisions. It added Investment Management & Research as an affiliate broker/dealer in 1967 and Planning Corporation of America as a general insurance agency in 1968.

Raymond James Financial (RJF) incorporated as a holding company in 1969, and Thomas James was named CEO the following year. RJA formed Eagle Asset Management in 1975, RJ Oil & Gas (a subsidiary for oil and gas limited partnerships) in 1977, Robert Thomas Securities and RJ Properties (securities and real estate subsidiaries, respectively) in 1980, and an equipment leasing subsidiary (RJ Leasing) in 1982.

RJF went public in 1983, the year Robert James died. Two years later the company organized its Heritage Family of Funds. RJA became an international company in the late 1980s,

opening an office in Paris in 1987 and in Geneva the next year. It also began offering a cash management program in 1988 and began its Stock Loan Department. Trust and banking subsidiaries were begun in 1992 and 1994, respectively, followed by the creation of Equity Capital Markets Group in 1996.

In 2000 RJF crossed the billion-dollar-mark, hitting $1.7 billion in sales. That year it acquired Canadian investment firm Goepel McDermid Inc., (renamed Raymond James Ltd.) to offer individual and institutional investment services to the Canadian market, and it launched Raymond James Killik (a UK joint venture that became Raymond James Investment Services in 2002). In 2006 RJF reduced front-end commissions with variations of variable annuity products; the next year it kicked off its Wealth Solutions department, a unit designed to help high-net-worth clients and their advisors.

EXECUTIVES

Chairman and CEO: Thomas A. (Tom) James, age 66
Vice Chairman: Francis S. (Bo) Godbold, age 65
President and Director: Paul C. Reilly, age 53
President, COO, and Director: Chester B. (Chet) Helck, age 56
SVP Finance and CFO: Jeffrey P. (Jeff) Julien, age 52
CIO, Raymond James & Associates: J. Timothy (Tim) Eitel, age 59
Chief Administrative Officer: Angela M. Biever, age 55
Controller and Chief Accounting Officer: Jennifer C. Ackart, age 44
EVP, Equity Capital Markets, Raymond James & Associates: Jeffrey E. Trocin, age 49
EVP; CEO, Eagle and Heritage: Richard K. Riess, age 59
EVP Operations and Administration, Raymond James & Associates: Thomas R. (Thom) Tremaine, age 52
EVP and Managing Director, Independent Contractor Division Sale: James A. (Jim) Fulp
SVP Fixed Income, Raymond James & Associates: Van C. Sayler, age 53
SVP, General Counsel, and Director Compliance: Paul L. Matecki, age 52
SVP and Chief Risk Officer: George Catanese, age 49
VP and Director of Human Resources: Courtland W. (Court) James, age 31
President, Raymond James & Associates: Dennis W. Zank, age 54
President, Raymond James Trust Companies: David Ness
Chairman, Raymond James Ltd.; Director: Kenneth A. Shields, age 60
Chairman and CEO, Raymond James Financial Services: Richard G. (Dick) Averitt III, age 63
Auditors: KPMG LLP

LOCATIONS

HQ: Raymond James Financial, Inc.
880 Carillon Pkwy., St. Petersburg, FL 33716
Phone: 727-567-1000   **Fax:** 727-567-8915
Web: www.rjf.com

Raymond James Financial has offices in Argentina, Belgium, Canada, France, Germany, Luxembourg, Switzerland, Turkey, and Uruguay, as well as in the US and the UK.

2008 Gross Revenues

	$ mil.	% of total
US	2,852.6	89
Canada	254.5	8
Europe	60.0	2
Other	37.8	1
Total	**3,204.9**	**100**

PRODUCTS/OPERATIONS

2008 Gross Revenues

	$ mil.	% of total
Securities commissions & fees	1,888.7	59
Interest	724.1	22
Investment advisory fees	212.5	7
Financial service fees	130.6	4
Interest banking	124.0	4
Other	126.7	4
Adjustments	(1.7)	—
Total	**3,204.9**	**100**

2008 Gross Revenues by Segment

	$ mil.	% of total
Private Client Group	1,950.3	61
Capital Markets	506.0	16
RJBank	405.3	13
Asset Management	236.9	7
Emerging Markets	41.3	1
Stock Loan/Borrow	36.8	1
Proprietary Capital	22.8	1
Other	5.5	—
Total	**3,204.9**	**100**

COMPETITORS

Charles Schwab	Merrill Lynch
Citigroup	Morgan Keegan
Deutsche Bank Alex.	Morgan Stanley
Brown	Piper Jaffray
E*TRADE Financial	Principal Financial
Edward Jones	TD Ameritrade
FMR	UBS Financial Services
Legg Mason	Wells Fargo Advisors
LPL Financial	

HISTORICAL FINANCIALS

Company Type: Public

Income Statement

FYE: September 30

	REVENUE ($ mil.)	NET INCOME ($ mil.)	NET PROFIT MARGIN	EMPLOYEES
9/08	2,812.7	235.1	8.4%	6,900
9/07	2,609.9	250.4	9.6%	5,788
9/06	2,336.1	214.3	9.2%	6,616
9/05	2,039.2	151.0	7.4%	6,790
9/04	1,781.3	127.6	7.2%	7,017
Annual Growth	12.1%	16.5%	—	(0.4%)

2008 Year-End Financials

Debt ratio: —
Return on equity: 12.9%
Cash ($ mil.): 3,207
Current ratio: —
Long-term debt ($ mil.): —
No. of shares (mil.): 123
Dividends
Yield: 1.3%
Payout: 22.3%
Market value ($ mil.): 4,064

Stock History

NYSE: RJF

	STOCK PRICE ($) FY Close	P/E High/Low	Earnings	Dividends	Book Value
9/08	32.98	19 10	1.97	0.44	15.29
9/07	32.85	17 13	2.11	0.40	14.26
9/06	29.24	17 11	1.85	0.32	11.88
9/05	21.41	17 12	1.33	0.21	10.08
9/04	16.08	16 13	1.15	0.18	8.64
Annual Growth	19.7%	— —	14.4%	25.0%	15.3%

Raytheon Company

Raytheon ("light of the gods") took a shine to its place in the upper pantheon of US military contractors; the company regularly places among the Pentagon's top 10 prime contractors. The company's defense offerings include reconnaissance, targeting, and navigation systems, as well as missile systems (Patriot, Sidewinder, and Tomahawk), and radars. Raytheon also makes radios, air traffic control systems and radars, and satellite communications systems. Raytheon also offers commercial electronics products and services, but the US government accounts for more than 85% of sales.

US defense spending is shifting toward supporting ongoing operations (Afghanistan and Iraq) and increasing the military's speed, flexibility, and precision. With that in mind, Raytheon is focusing on four business areas: missile defense; precision engagement; intelligence, surveillance, and reconnaissance; and homeland security.

As the world's #1 missile maker, Raytheon is a key player in US efforts to construct a comprehensive missile defense system. Such systems need intercept vehicles, sensors, command and control systems, and systems integration expertise, and Raytheon is a leader in all those areas. Raytheon's precision engagement offerings include the company's missiles as well as radars, data links, targeting and warning systems, and lasers.

Intelligence, surveillance, and reconnaissance systems use sensing, processing, and dissemination technologies to obtain actionable information and get it from one place to another quickly. Raytheon's products in this area include sensor suites for UAVs, space-based radars, satellite systems, and communications systems. As for homeland security, the systems Raytheon makes for traditional defense applications are readily transferable to homeland security applications.

Multiple acquisitions reflect Raytheon's focus on building up its security and intelligence services portfolio. Raytheon moved to acquire BBN Technologies in 2009. The deal scores BBN's array of advanced networking, and technologies for speech and language and information, as well as sensor systems, and cyber security. The acquisition fell on the heels of picking up Telemus Solutions in 2008. Telemus provides information security and intelligence services and support for military customers.

HISTORY

In 1922 Laurence Marshall and several others founded American Appliance Company to produce home refrigerators. When their invention failed, Marshall began making Raytheon (meaning "light of/from the gods") radio tubes. Raytheon was adopted as the company's name in 1925. It bought the radio division of Chicago's Q. R. S. Company in 1928 and formed Raytheon Production Company with National Carbon Company (makers of the Eveready battery) to market Eveready Raytheon tubes in 1929.

Growing rapidly in WWII, Raytheon became the first producer of magnetrons (tubes used in radar and later in microwave ovens). Wartime sales peaked at $173 million but dwindled by 1947. Amid rumors of bankruptcy, Charles Adams became Raytheon's president. He sold Raytheon's unprofitable radio and TV business in 1956.

In 1964 Adams (then chairman) named missile engineer Thomas Phillips president. Phillips oversaw several purchases designed to balance Raytheon's commercial and military earnings, beginning with Amana Refrigeration (1965), D.C. Heath (textbooks, 1966), Caloric (stoves, 1967), and three petrochemical firms (1966-69).

Raytheon began making computer terminals in 1971 (exited 1984). In 1980 it bought Grumman's Beech Aircraft division. Despite efforts to diversify, Raytheon still relied on missiles, radar, and communications systems for most of its sales in 1987. In 1991 it won an $800 million US Army contract to upgrade Patriot missiles used in the Persian Gulf War. After 43 years with Raytheon, Phillips retired that year, and president Dennis Picard became chairman.

Raytheon expanded as it bought the business jet division of British Aerospace (1993), E-Systems (advanced electronics and surveillance equipment, 1995), and most of Chrysler's aerospace and defense holdings (1996).

By 1997 Raytheon had doubled in size and had become the #1 US missile maker, after buying Texas Instruments' missile and defense electronics holdings for about $3 billion and Hughes Electronics' (now The DIRECTV Group) defense business for $9.5 billion. It consolidated those and other electronics units into Raytheon Systems (dismantled in 2000). Raytheon sold its analog chip-making business to Fairchild Semiconductor (1997); its home appliance, heating and air-conditioning, and commercial cooking units to Goodman Holding (1997); and its flight controls business to Moog (1998).

Weak sales in Asia hurt Raytheon in 1998, and it announced cuts of some 14,000 defense jobs (16% of the unit's workforce) and the closure of 28 plants over two years. Former AlliedSignal VC Daniel Burnham became CEO in 1998, succeeding Picard. Raytheon also began a legal battle with Hughes, claiming it had been overcharged $1 billion in 1997 for Hughes' defense unit (the suit was settled for about $650 million in 2001).

In 1999 Raytheon cut more jobs and made plans to close or combine 10 facilities and take a $668 million charge to correct financial problems in its defense electronics business.

Raytheon sold its flight simulation and training business to L-3 Communications for $160 million in 2000 and its engineering and construction unit to Washington Group International (formerly Morrison Knudsen) for about $500 million. That year Raytheon sold $800 million in aircraft loans and leases to debis Capital Services.

In 2002 Raytheon sold its aircraft integration unit to L-3 Communications for about $1.13 billion in cash and made a bid for TRW's satellite and missile defense operations. It continued to sell non-core units, including its commercial infrared unit (to L-3 Communications) in 2004.

In 2005 Raytheon agreed to team up with EADS North America to bid on the Army's $1 billion Future Cargo Aircraft program. Under the agreement, Raytheon will be prime contractor; EADS will assemble and deliver the medium cargo transport planes.

As 2006 wound to a close, Raytheon announced it would sell Raytheon Aircraft to a new company, Hawker Beechcraft, formed by Goldman Sachs and Onex Corporation, for $3.3 billion. The deal was completed in 2007. In late 2007 Raytheon sold Flight Options, which provided fractional jet ownership services, to H.I.G. Capital.

EXECUTIVES

Chairman and CEO: William H. Swanson, age 60, $15,056,151 total compensation
Lead Director: Michael C. (Mike) Ruettgers, age 66
SVP and CFO: David C. Wajsgras, age 49, $3,948,952 total compensation
VP and CIO: Rebecca B. Rhoads
VP and Chief Accounting Officer: Michael J. Wood, age 40
EVP Business Development; CEO, Raytheon International: Thomas M. Culligan
SVP Human Resources: Keith J. Peden, age 58
SVP, General Counsel, and Secretary: Jay B. Stephens, age 62, $3,702,428 total compensation
VP Corporate Development and Treasurer: Richard A. Goglia, age 57
VP Corporate Affairs and Communications: Pamela A. (Pam) Wickham
Acting VP Homeland Security: Timothy W. Josiah
VP; President, Network Centric Systems: Colin J.R. Schottlaender, age 53
VP; President, Integrated Defense Systems: Daniel L. (Dan) Smith, age 56, $3,018,636 total compensation
VP Corporate Public Affairs: Kristin Hilf
VP; President, Space and Airborne Systems: Jon C. Jones, age 54
VP; President, Raytheon Technical Services Company: Richard R. (Rick) Yuse, age 57
VP; President, Raytheon Missile Systems: Taylor W. Lawrence, age 45, $3,221,794 total compensation
VP; President, Intelligence and Information Systems: Lynn A. Dugle, age 49
VP Investor Relations: Marc Kaplan
Director Investor Relations: Jim Singer
Auditors: PricewaterhouseCoopers LLP

LOCATIONS

HQ: Raytheon Company
870 Winter St., Waltham, MA 02451
Phone: 781-522-3000 **Fax:** 781-522-3001
Web: www.raytheon.com

2008 Sales

	$ mil.	% of total
US	18,596	80
Asia/Pacific	2,086	9
Europe & other regions	2,492	11
Total	**23,174**	**100**

PRODUCTS/OPERATIONS

2008 Sales

	$ mil.	% of total
Missile Systems	5,377	21
Integrated Defense Systems	5,148	21
Network Centric Systems	4,510	18
Space & Airborne Systems	4,372	17
Intelligence & Information Systems	3,132	13
Technical Services	2,601	10
Adjustments	(1,966)	—
Total	**23,174**	**100**

Selected Products

Missile Systems
Advanced Medium-Range Air-to-Air missile (AMRAAM)
AIM-9X Sidewinder
Evolved SeaSparrow (ESSM)
Excalibur long-range artillery system
Exoatmospheric Kill Vehicle
Extended Range Guided Munition (ERGM)
High-Speed Anti-Radiation Missile Targeting System
Paveway laser guided bombs
Maverick AGM-65 missiles
Tomahawk and Tactical Tomahawk cruise missiles
TOW, Javelin, Phalanx, Standard, and SeaRAM missiles

Integrated Defense Systems
Aegis Weapon Systems radar equipment
AN/AQS Minehunting Sonar System
Joint Land Attack Cruise Missile Defense Elevated
Netted Sensor (JLENS)
Landing Platform Dock Amphibious Ship LPD-17
Patriot Air and Missile Defense System
Sea-Based X-Band Radar (SBX)
Ship Self-Defense System (SSDS)
Surface-Launched AMRAAM (SLAMRAAM)
Terminal High Altitude Area Defense (THAAD) Radar
Network Centric Systems
Airspace Management and Homeland Security
Command and Control Systems
Combat Systems
Integrated Communications Systems
JPS Communications, Inc.
Precision Technologies and Components
Space and Airborne Systems
Active electronically scanned array radars
Airborne radars and processors
Electronic warfare systems
Electro-optic/infrared sensors
Intelligence, surveillance, and reconnaissance systems
Space and missile defense technology
Intelligence and Information Systems
Army Research Lab
Communications systems
Department of Education programs
Distributed Common Ground System
Emergency Patient Tracking System
Global Broadcast Service
Global Hawk Ground Segment
Information solutions programs
Managed data storage solutions
Mobile Very Small Aperture Satellite Terminal
National Polar-orbiting Operational Environmental
Satellite System Program
RedWolf telecommunications surveillance
Signal and Imagery Intelligence Programs
Supercomputing
U-2
UAV systems and Ground Stations
Technical Services
Base operations
Logistics support
Maintenance support
Professional services
Treaty compliance monitoring
Weapons security and destruction

COMPETITORS

BAE Systems Inc.
Boeing
Crane Aerospace & Electronics
Daimler
Emerson Electric
Fluor
GE
Harris Corp.
Herley Industries
Honeywell Aerospace
Interstate Electronics
ITT Defense
L-3 Avionics
Lockheed Martin
MBDA
McDermott
Meggitt USA
Northrop Grumman
Olin
Rockwell Collins
Saab AB
Sierra Nevada Corp
Sperry Marine

HISTORICAL FINANCIALS
Company Type: Public

Income Statement

FYE: December 31

	REVENUE ($ mil.)	NET INCOME ($ mil.)	NET PROFIT MARGIN	EMPLOYEES
12/08	23,174.0	1,672.0	7.2%	73,000
12/07	21,301.0	2,578.0	12.1%	72,100
12/06	20,291.0	1,283.0	6.3%	80,000
12/05	21,894.0	871.0	4.0%	80,000
12/04	20,245.0	376.0	1.9%	79,000
Annual Growth	3.4%	45.2%	—	(2.0%)

2008 Year-End Financials

Debt ratio: 25.4%
Return on equity: 15.5%
Cash ($ mil.): 2,259
Current ratio: 1.44
Long-term debt ($ mil.): 2,309
No. of shares (mil.): 389
Dividends
  Yield: 2.2%
  Payout: 28.4%
Market value ($ mil.): 19,874

Stock History

NYSE: RTN

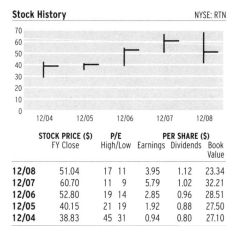

	STOCK PRICE ($) FY Close	P/E High/Low		PER SHARE ($) Earnings	Dividends	Book Value
12/08	51.04	17	11	3.95	1.12	23.34
12/07	60.70	11	9	5.79	1.02	32.21
12/06	52.80	19	14	2.85	0.96	28.51
12/05	40.15	21	19	1.92	0.88	27.50
12/04	38.83	45	31	0.94	0.80	27.10
Annual Growth	7.1%	—	—	43.2%	8.8%	(3.7%)

Regions Financial

Regions Financial ain't just whistling Dixie anymore. The holding company for Regions Bank, which sprouted in the South, has grown by acquiring other financial services firms over the years. Regions has some 1,900 branches in 16 states, roughly stretching from the Mississippi River Valley in the US heartland to the Southeast and Texas. It also owns Memphis-based investment bank and brokerage Morgan Keegan, which has more than 300 offices on its parent's turf, plus New York and Massachusetts. In addition to traditional banking, Regions offers a variety of other services, including mortgage banking (Regions Mortgage), equipment financing, and life, health, and property/casualty insurance (Regions Insurance).

Another unit, Regions Interstate Billing Service, factors accounts receivable and performs billing and collection services, primarily for the automotive service industry. Regions is also building its private banking business.

Since its inception in 1971 Regions has looked for acquisitions in order grow geographically and diversify its product and services mix. It fortified its foothold in the South and expanded into the Midwest with its blockbuster merger with

Union Planters in 2004. Regions later acquired fellow Birmingham-based bank AmSouth for nearly $10 billion in stock.

The AmSouth deal created one of the 10 largest banks in the US and helped the company keep pace with other megabanks in its markets, such as Bank of America and SunTrust.

However, economic conditions have forced Regions to shed some of its weight. After the mortgage sector got battered by the housing bust and rising interest rates in 2006, the company in 2007 sold its subprime mortgage origination unit EquiFirst to Barclays Bank (the flagship subsidiary of UK-based Barclays).

The market turmoil also has provided opportunities. In 2008 Regions Financial assumed control of the branches and deposits of failed Atlanta-area financial institution Integrity Bank in an FDIC-assisted transaction; it did the same with another failed Georgia bank, FirstBank Financial Services, in 2009.

HISTORY

Regions Financial was created out of three venerable Alabama banks. The oldest, First National Bank of Huntsville, was founded in 1855. When, 10 years later, the bank was besieged by Union troops, a loyal cashier hid securities in the chimney and refused to tell the soldiers where they were. A few years later it was robbed by Jesse James (for years the bank kept in its vaults a gun purported to belong to a James gang member). First National Bank of Montgomery was founded in 1871, and Exchange Security Bank in 1928.

Banking veteran Frank Plummer consolidated the three banks to form Alabama's first multi-bank holding company, First Alabama Bancshares, in 1971. The combined firm then became the bank that ate Alabama. But even as it gobbled up other banks, its diet remained bland: Its lending programs were modest and focused on a narrow range of business.

The bank's growth in the 1980s was solid, if unexciting, as it picked up community banks in Alabama (Anniston National Bank and South Baldwin Bank, among others) and Georgia (Georgia Co., a mortgage subsidiary of Columbus Bank and Trust). Before he died in 1987, Plummer brought in Willard Hurley as chairman. Hurley put the brakes on acquisitions when they overloaded the bank's data-processing systems. He also put the company up for sale, igniting its stock price for a while, but there were no serious suitors.

When Hurley passed the baton to Stanley Mackin in 1990 the bank was still rumored to be for sale. But Mackin had other ideas. He put the bank back on its acquisition track and raised the bar on profitability expectations for each department. In 1993 Mackin orchestrated First Alabama's purchase of Secor, a failed New Orleans thrift, outbidding rival AmSouth Bancorporation. The Secor purchase raised eyebrows, but First Alabama sold some branches and folded other operations into its organization.

In 1994 First Alabama changed its name to Regions Financial in order to reflect its out-of-state operations. The next year Regions rolled into Georgia in a big way, leaping from a few banks to holdings with approximately $4 billion in assets. Rumors of a merger with either Wachovia or SunTrust Banks popped up in 1996, but the bank continued on its independent course. The next year the company's tanklike progress was halted when it was outbid for Mississippi's Deposit Guaranty Corp. by First American.

By way of consolation, Regions in 1998 bought First Commercial Corp. of Little Rock, paying a premium price for its 26 banks, mortgage company, and investment company. Regions also acquired 13 other companies that year and began a major overhaul of its systems concurrently with the assimilation of these operations. This effort included the consolidation of the back-office aspects of its retail and indirect lending operations.

Mackin retired in 1998, and banking veteran Carl Jones Jr. became CEO. Under his direction the bank continued its geographic infill strategy with acquisitions of banks and branches in Arkansas, Florida, Louisiana, Tennessee, and Texas in 1999 and 2000. The company also sold its credit card portfolio to MBNA (since acquired by Bank of America) and in 2001 acquired Memphis-based investment bank Morgan Keegan.

Jones helped mastermind the $6 billion acquisition of Union Planters in 2004; he stepped down as CEO after the merger, but remained Regions' chairman until 2006. Jackson Moore, chairman and CEO of Union Planters, took over the reins of Regions as president and CEO. The company's acquisition of AmSouth for $10 billion in 2006 saw yet another change in leadership, with Moore becoming executive chairman and AmSouth's top executive, C. Dowd Ritter, becoming chairman, president, and CEO.

EXECUTIVES

Chairman, President, and CEO: C. Dowd Ritter, age 61, $9,261,865 total compensation
Vice Chairman, SEVP, and Head of General Banking Group, Operations, Technology and Properties: O. B. Grayson Hall Jr., age 51, $4,538,742 total compensation
SEVP and CFO: Irene M. Esteves, age 50, $2,441,057 total compensation
CIO: John B. Owen, age 47
Interim Chief Credit Officer: G. Timothy (Tim) Laney, age 48
Controller and Chief Accounting Officer: Brad Kimbrough, age 45
Chief Marketing Officer: Scott Peters
SEVP and Head of Human Resources: David B. Edmonds, age 55, $2,785,601 total compensation
SEVP, Chief Risk Officer,and Head of Risk Management Group: William C. (Bill) Wells II, age 50, $1,841,575 total compensation
SEVP, Corporate Secretary, and General Counsel: John D. Buchanan
SEVP Consumer Services: David H. Rupp, age 45
EVP Service Quality: William E. (Bill) Askew, age 58
EVP, Regions Mortgage: E. Todd Chamberlain
EVP Community Banking: Mike Hart
EVP Private Banking: James B. (Jim) Nonnengard
EVP Business Banking: John C. Asbury
EVP Commercial Real Estate: Rex Bradley
EVP Sales and Performance: Steve Nivet
EVP HR Systems and Administration: Christine Germanson
CEO Morgan Keegan: John C. Carson Jr., age 52
Investor Relations: M. List Underwood Jr.
Auditors: Ernst & Young LLP

LOCATIONS

HQ: Regions Financial Corporation
1900 5th Ave. North, Birmingham, AL 35203
Phone: 205-944-1300 **Fax:** 901-580-3915
Web: www.regions.com

2008 Branches

	No.	% of total
Florida	427	22
Tennessee	314	17
Alabama	255	13
Mississippi	165	9
Georgia	155	8
Louisiana	129	7
Arkansas	114	6
Texas	84	4
Illinois	72	4
Missouri	68	3
Indiana	66	3
South Carolina	37	2
Kentucky	19	1
Iowa	18	1
North Carolina	9	—
Virginia	3	—
Total	**1,900**	**100**

PRODUCTS/OPERATIONS

2008 Gross Revenues

	$ mil.	% of total
Interest		
Loans, including fees	5,549.9	63
Securities	867.7	8
Loans held for sale	35.7	1
Other	110.0	1
Noninterest		
Service charges on deposit accounts	1,148.0	11
Brokerage & investment banking	1,027.5	8
Trust department income	233.5	2
Mortgage income	137.7	1
Other	526.6	5
Total	**9,636.6**	**100**

COMPETITORS

BancorpSouth
Bank of America
BB&T
Capital One
Citigroup
Compass Bancshares
First Citizens BancShares
First Horizon
RBC Bank
SunTrust
Synovus Financial
Trustmark
Wells Fargo

HISTORICAL FINANCIALS

Company Type: Public

Income Statement

FYE: December 31

	ASSETS ($ mil.)	NET INCOME ($ mil.)	INCOME AS % OF ASSETS	EMPLOYEES
12/08	146,247.8	(5,595.8)	—	30,784
12/07	141,041.7	1,251.1	0.9%	33,161
12/06	143,369.0	1,353.1	0.9%	35,900
12/05	84,785.6	1,000.5	1.2%	25,000
12/04	84,106.4	817.7	1.0%	26,000
Annual Growth	**14.8%**	**—**	**—**	**4.3%**

2008 Year-End Financials

Equity as % of assets: 9.2%
Return on assets: —
Return on equity: —
Long-term debt ($ mil.): 19,231
No. of shares (mil.): 1,188

Dividends
Yield: 12.1%
Payout: —
Market value ($ mil.): 9,458
Sales ($ mil.): 6,916

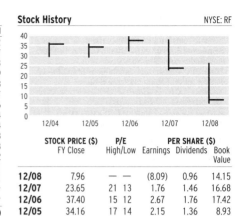

Stock History NYSE: RF

	STOCK PRICE ($) FY Close	P/E High/Low		Earnings	Dividends	Book Value
12/08	7.96	—	—	(8.09)	0.96	14.15
12/07	23.65	21	13	1.76	1.46	16.68
12/06	37.40	15	12	2.67	1.76	17.42
12/05	34.16	17	14	2.15	1.36	8.93
12/04	35.59	16	13	2.19	0.67	9.05
Annual Growth	**(31.2%)**	**—**	**—**	**—**	**9.4%**	**11.8%**

Regis Corporation

Regis is hair, there, and everywhere. It is the world's largest operator of hair salons, with more than 12,900 company-owned or franchised salons (primarily in the US) and about 95 Hairclub for Men and Women hair restoration centers. Formats range from mall-based to Wal-Mart-based (2,300 SmartStyle and Cost Cutters), with its salons selling hair care products branded under the Regis, MasterCuts, and Cost Cutters names. Regis also runs a variety of store formats in strip malls, including more than 5,400 franchised and company-owned shops. The company has more than 440 locations in the UK and Germany.

The company's North American salons account for more than 85% of revenues. Most of those sales are to women, but the company is testing a new concept, Raze, aimed at men looking for a more sophisticated experience than typical sport-related hair cutters and barbershops.

Despite its size, Regis still commands only a small percentage of the highly fractured US market. It has been sweeping up market share through the construction of new salons and acquisitions both internationally and at home. Since 1995 Regis has acquired more than 8,000 salons. However, competition within the personal hair care industry is prompting Regis to evaluate its 10,000 company-owned salons; it closed more than 300 in fiscal 2009 to help enhance profitability. It laid off 150 people from corporate HQ about the same time.

The salon closures came on the heels of the company's efforts to boost its stake in the European hair care market. It completed a merger of its continental European franchise salon operations with the Franck Provost Salon Group in early 2008. As part of the deal, Regis owns a 30% minority interest in the newly formed Provalliance Group, now the largest hair salon company in Europe. Regis retained sole ownership of its salons in the UK and Germany.

To keep its shops stocked with trained professionals, the company owns a majority stake in Empire Education Group, which runs nearly 100 cosmetology training centers.

HISTORY

Russian-born immigrant Paul Kunin started with one local barbershop in Minneapolis in 1922. Within the next three decades he owned 60 salons, which were mainly leased departments in stores. Paul sold the business in 1954 to his son Myron and daughter Diana. Myron bought Diana's share some years later.

Once at the helm, Myron shifted stores into the enclosed malls that sprouted during the 1960s. Eschewing franchising, Regis benefited from the complete control of its stores, maintaining an upscale image that fared well against small-time salons. By 1975 the company had 161 salons and it grew during the late 1970s and early 1980s. Regis went public in 1983.

The next year it attempted to diversify from its largely female clientele with the purchase of Your Father's Mustache, a chain of 60 barbershops. However, the unsuccessful attempt caused earnings to suffer for two years while Regis converted the shops into other formats.

Wanting to reward its managers with company ownership, Regis went private again in 1988, taking on a heavy load of debt. This hindered Myron's efforts to expand in the department store niche. In response, in 1990 he joined MEI Diversified, a cash-rich investment company, to form MEI-Regis Salon (of which MEI owned 80%) in order to buy Essanelle (department store salons).

However, the deal quickly gave all parties a bad hair day: Lawsuits, claims of mismanagement and misrepresentation, and poor earnings conspired to destroy the partnership. MEI-Regis went public again in 1991, but the offering did not make enough to pay bank debt, and it posted a loss. MEI and Regis sued each other in 1992, and Regis called for unpaid expenses related to management while MEI accused Regis of fraud and racketeering.

While all this was going on, Regis continued to expand. Acquisitions such as Trade Secret (1993) moved Regis into higher-margin beauty products. MEI went into Chapter 11 in 1993 and the dispute between the companies was finally settled in bankruptcy court, costing Regis $15 million.

Over the next two years, Regis expanded both in the US and abroad. Overseas, the company bought some 170 UK salons in 1995 and 1996. It moved away from its mall stronghold with the purchase of competitor Supercuts in 1996, adding more than 1,100 stores, mainly in strip malls. Then #2, Supercuts was struggling; ousted CEO David Lipson sued and won a $6.7 million settlement from Regis in 1997. Also in 1996 Regis bought 154 salons operating inside Wal-Mart stores from National Hair Centers. That year COO Paul Finkelstein was promoted to CEO.

The firm took another giant step forward in 1999 when it bought The Barbers, Hairstyling for Men & Women, an operator of about 980 salons, including the Cost Cutters and We Care Hair chains. The deal made Regis the only provider of salon services in Wal-Mart stores.

Regis continued making acquisitions, including Haircrafters, about 550 salons mostly in Canada, and 523 franchised salons in France.

International expansion continued in 2002 with its acquisition of Jean Louis David, Europe's #1 salon chain (nearly 1,200 salons). Also that year Regis acquired BoRics (328 strip-center salons mostly located in Illinois, Michigan, Ohio, and Pennsylvania).

In May 2004 Myron Kunin stepped down as chairman, passing his title to longtime president and CEO Finkelstein. Kunin assumed the role of vice chairman.

In December 2004 Regis added significantly to its hair restoration operations when it inked a deal to make Hair Club for Men and Women a wholly owned subsidiary.

In January 2006, Regis agreed to be acquired by personal care products maker Alberto-Culver in a complex $2.6 billion deal; however, in April, the negotiations hit an abrupt snag after Regis' projected forecast for subsequent quarters was lower than originally expected. Regis ended up having to pay a termination fee to Alberto-Culver.

In August 2007 Regis combined its beauty school business with that of a rival school operator, Empire Education Group. Regis took a 49% stake in the expanded Empire Education Group, which following the transaction owns nearly 90 schools and has an estimated annual revenue of about $130 million.

In 2009 Regis sold its Trade Secret beauty products retail division to Premier Salons Beauty. Regis did not receive any proceeds from the sale of the 655 company-owned salons and 57 franchised locations, but recorded an impairment charge of about $183 million for the fiscal year ended June 2009. The Trade Secret sale included PureBeauty and BeautyFirst (acquired in early 2008).

EXECUTIVES

Chairman, President, and CEO: Paul D. Finkelstein, age 66
COO, Supercuts: Diane Calta, age 39
Senior EVP, Chief Administrative Officer, and CFO: Randy L. Pearce, age 53
EVP Fashion, Education, and Marketing: Gordon B. Nelson, age 57
EVP Design and Construction: Bruce D. Johnson, age 54
EVP Fashion, Education, and Marketing: Mark Kartarik, age 52
EVP Merchandising and COO, Trade Secret Division: Norma Knudsen, age 50
SVP and International Managing Director, UK: Raymond Duke, age 57
SVP and President, SmartStyle Family Hair Salons: C. John Briggs, age 64
SVP Law, General Counsel, and Secretary: Eric A. Bakken, age 41
VP, The Regis Foundation, and Director: David B. Kunin, age 49
President, International Division: Andrew Cohen, age 45
President and CEO, Hair Club for Men and Women: Darryll Porter, age 45
Public Relations: Leann Dake
COO, MasterCuts: David Bortnem, age 41
COO, Promenade Salon Concepts: Amy Edwards, age 39
COO, SmartStyle Family Hair Care: John Exline, age 45
Auditors: PricewaterhouseCoopers LLP

LOCATIONS

HQ: Regis Corporation
7201 Metro Blvd., Minneapolis, MN 55439
Phone: 952-947-7777 **Fax:** 952-947-7600
Web: www.regiscorp.com

2009 Salons

	No.
North America	
Company-owned	7,537
Franchised	2,045
International (company-owned)	444
Total	**10,026**

2009 Sales

	$ mil.	% of total
North America (includes Hair Club)	2,258.2	93
International	171.6	7
Total	**2,429.8**	**100**

PRODUCTS/OPERATIONS

2009 Company-Owned Salons

	No.
romenade	3,351
SmartStyle/Cost Cutters	2,422
Supercuts	2,136
Regis	1,071
International	444
Mastercuts	602
Total	**10,026**

2009 Sales

	$ mil.	% of total
Salons		
North America	2,117.7	87
International	171.6	7
Hair restoration centers	140.5	6
Total	**2,429.8**	**100**

2008 Sales

	% of total
Service	75
Product	23
Royalties & fees	2
Total	**100**

Selected Stores

Affilie (Jean Louis David, international salons)
BoRics (regional strip-center salons)
Cost Cutters (national strip-center salons and Wal-Mart store salons)
First Choice Haircutters (national strip-center salons)
Hair Masters (regional strip-center salons)
Magicuts (national strip-center salons)
MasterCuts Family Haircutters (regional-mall salons)
Mia & Maxx Hair Salons (regional-mall salons)
Regis Hairstylists (international salons)
Regis Salons (regional-mall salons)
Saint Algue (international salons)
SmartStyle (Wal-Mart store salons)
Supercuts (national strip-center salons in the US and international salons)
Trade Secret (regional-mall salons in the US and international salons)
We Care Hair (national strip-center salons)

COMPETITORS

Alberto-Culver	Premier Salons
Bath & Body Works	Procter & Gamble
Body Shop	Ratner Companies
Cool Cuts	Shiseido
Great Clips	Sport Clips
L'Oréal	Ulta
Mascolo	Wella AG

Income Statement

FYE: June 30

	REVENUE ($ mil.)	NET INCOME ($ mil.)	NET PROFIT MARGIN	EMPLOYEES
6/09	2,429.8	(124.5)	—	59,000
6/08	2,738.9	85.2	3.1%	65,000
6/07	2,626.6	83.2	3.2%	62,000
6/06	2,430.9	109.6	4.5%	59,000
6/05	2,194.3	64.6	2.9%	55,000
Annual Growth	2.6%	—	—	1.8%

2009 Year-End Financials

Debt ratio: 72.1%
Return on equity: —
Cash ($ mil.): 43
Current ratio: 1.29
Long-term debt ($ mil.): 579

No. of shares (mil.): 57
Dividends
  Yield: 0.9%
  Payout: —
Market value ($ mil.): 994

Stock History

NYSE: RGS

	STOCK PRICE ($) FY Close	P/E High/Low		PER SHARE ($) Earnings	Dividends	Book Value
6/09	17.41	—	—	(2.89)	0.16	14.06
6/08	26.35	20	11	1.95	0.16	17.09
6/07	38.25	24	18	1.82	0.16	15.99
6/06	35.61	18	14	2.36	0.16	15.26
6/05	39.08	34	24	1.39	0.16	13.22
Annual Growth	(18.3%)	—	—	—	0.0%	1.6%

Rent-A-Center

Rent-A-Center (RAC) wants its customers to rent while it buys. The firm became the #1 rent-to-own chain nationwide through a string of acquisitions. It owns and operates more than 3,000 stores in North America and Puerto Rico under the Rent-A-Center, Get It Now, and Home Choice names, and franchises some 220 through subsidiary ColorTyme. The stores rent name-brand home electronics, furniture, accessories, appliances, and computers. While customers have the option to eventually own their rented items, only about 25% ever do. RAC also offers financial services, including loans, check cashing and money transfer services, and tax preparation, to its customers in some 350 stores. Lately, it's been closing stores.

The store closings represent a retreat for RAC, which has climbed to the top of the US rent-to-own industry through no fewer than 60 acquisitions during the last two decades. Its purchase of rival Rent-Way in 2006 eliminated one of the firm's primary competitors.

Employing its buy-and-purge strategy as it acquires additional banners, in late 2007 RAC closed or merged with existing RAC locations about 275 stores to boost its operating income. Another dozen or so locations met with the same fate in early 2008. Those closings and mergers represented about 8% of the company's total units. (In late 2005 the company undertook a similar purge, shuttering about 150 stores due to "overpenetration" in some markets as a result of a prior bout of acquisitiveness.)

RAC operates about 30 stores under the Get It Now and Home Choice banners in the Midwest that sell merchandise on an installment plan.

To attract new customers, the rent-to-own chain has been expanding its offerings of upscale brands (Sony Electronics, Ashley Furniture) and rolling out a line of financial services products (introduced in 2005) to more of its stores. The products include loans, bill paying, debit cards, check cashing, and money transfer services. By 2007's end, about 275 of the company's stores in 15 states were offering the new products.

HISTORY

Ernest Talley is a pioneer in the rent-to-own industry, having founded one of the first rent-to-own chains in 1963. He sold that business in 1974 and went into commercial real estate in Dallas. In 1987, after the Texas real estate crash, Talley and his son Michael started Talley Leasing, which rented appliances to apartment complex owners.

Talley bought Vista Rent To Own, a chain of 22 stores in New Jersey and Puerto Rico, in 1989. He upgraded merchandise, increased selection, updated information and data systems, and improved store management. In 1993 the company acquired DEF, an 84-store chain, and repeated the upgrading process. That year the company changed its name to Renters Choice. It went public in 1995 and used the proceeds to make more acquisitions.

The purchases of Crown Leasing and Pro Rental (parent of Magic Rent-to-Own) moved Renters Choice into the southern US and increased its store count from just more than 100 to 322. In 1996 the company acquired Texas-based competitor ColorTyme, adding another 320 stores (most of them franchises). Renters Choice acquired Trans Texas Capital, another rental purchase enterprise, the following year.

In 1998 the company bought Central Rents, owner of about 180 stores, for $103 million and paid $900 million (most of it borrowed) for rival Thorn Americas, which operated some 1,400 stores under the Rent-A-Center, Remco, and U-Can-Rent brands. Renters Choice then changed its name to Rent-A-Center. Also that year it settled a class-action lawsuit with 20,000 customers for $12 million; the suit alleged that the company had misled consumers about actual finance costs.

Rent-A-Center lost an appeal of another lawsuit in 1999 and was ordered to pay $30 million to 30,000 consumers for charging interest rates as high as 750%.

After making no acquisitions in 1999, Rent-A-Center announced in 2000 that it would be adding 100-plus stores annually. The company also began offering Internet service (originally for $5.95 per week through BellSouth and then, in 2001, offering free service through NetZero).

In October 2001 Ernest Talley retired and Mark Speese was named chairman and CEO. In February 2003 Rent-A-Center bought 295 stores (located in 38 states) from rival Rent-Way for just more than $100 million. In 2004 the company acquired Rent Rite (90 stores in 11 states) and Rainbow Rentals (124 stores in 15 states). Also that year Rent-A-Center broke into the Canadian market with the purchase of five stores in Alberta for $2.4 million.

In April 2005 the company settled a lawsuit related to its business practices in California — *Benjamin Griego, et al. v. Rent-A-Center, Inc.* — by agreeing to pay the plaintiff's attorneys' fees as well as about $37.5 million cash to eligible customers who entered into rental-purchase agreements with the company between early 1999 and late 2004.

In December 2005 the company sold the rental contracts and merchandise of 19 stores to Aaron's for about $4.4 million.

In 2006 Rent-A-Center acquired Rent-Way for about $600 million. As a result, Rent-Way became a wholly owned indirect subsidiary.

In December 2007 Rent-A-Center closed or merged about 275 stores. Another dozen or so locations met with a similar fate in early 2008. The closings were designed to relieve oversaturation in some of the company's markets.

EXECUTIVES

Chairman and CEO: Mark E. Speese, age 51, $1,221,732 total compensation
President, COO, and Director: Mitchell E. Fadel, age 51, $730,721 total compensation
EVP Finance, CFO, and Treasurer: Robert D. Davis, age 37, $495,792 total compensation
SVP Information Technology and CIO: Tony F. Fuller
SVP Marketing and Advertising and Chief Marketing Officer: Ann L. Davids
EVP Operations: Christopher A. Korst, age 49, $428,108 total compensation
EVP Operational Services: David E. West, age 58
EVP, General Counsel, and Secretary: Ronald D. DeMoss, age 58
SVP Government Affairs: Dwight D. Dumler
VP Risk Management: David M. Glasgow
VP Business Intelligence: John H. Whitehead
VP Investor Relations: David E. (Dave) Carpenter
VP Development: Kent W. Brown
VP Sales: Joe T. Arnette
VP Internal Audit: Fred E. Herman
VP Finance and Controller: Ned W. Villemarette
VP Strategic Planning: Joel M. Mussat
VP Business Development: Daniel R. Eichelberger
VP Training: John D. Gray
VP Field Human Resources: Rebecca O. Crawford
President and CEO, ColorTyme: Robert F. (Bob) Bloom, age 55
Director Corporate Communications: Mary Gazioglu
Auditors: Grant Thornton LLP

LOCATIONS

HQ: Rent-A-Center, Inc.
  5501 Headquarters Dr., Plano, TX 75024
Phone: 972-801-1100   **Fax:** 866-260-1424
Web: www.rentacenter.com

2008 Stores

	Company-Owned	Franchised	Stores with Financial Services
Texas	292	35	113
Florida	188	20	—
Ohio	183	4	51
New York	178	3	—
Pennsylvania	152	3	—
California	139	5	—
North Carolina	133	15	—
Illinois	110	8	—
Michigan	104	9	—
Indiana	101	4	—
Tennessee	91	4	37
Georgia	88	12	—
Virginia	70	11	—
Massachusetts	69	1	—
South Carolina	67	6	—
Kentucky	67	3	20
Maryland	65	11	—
Missouri	65	—	16
Alabama	60	5	—
Arizona	58	—	6
Louisiana	45	5	—
Oklahoma	44	6	—
Washington	44	3	25
Colorado	44	1	13
New Jersey	44	—	—
Puerto Rico	43	—	—
Connecticut	40	1	—
Arkansas	39	1	—
Mississippi	35	1	—
Kansas	34	8	13
West Virginia	33	—	—
Maine	28	9	—
Oregon	27	4	—
Iowa	27	—	11
New Mexico	26	9	10
Nevada	23	—	4
Wisconsin	21	—	—
New Hampshire	20	1	—
Delaware	20	—	—
Rhode Island	16	2	—
Utah	16	—	8
Nebraska	14	—	1
Hawaii	11	5	7
Idaho	11	3	6
Other states	52	4	10
Total	**3,037**	**222**	**351**

PRODUCTS/OPERATIONS

2008 Sales

	$ mil.	% of total
Store		
Rentals & fees	2,505.3	87
Merchandise sales	256.7	9
Installment sales	41.2	1
Other	42.8	2
Franchise		
Merchandise sales	33.3	1
Royalty income & fees	4.9	—
Total	**2,884.2**	**100**

2008 Sales

	% of total
Consumer electronics	35
Furniture & accessories	33
Appliances	16
Computers	16
Total	**100**

Store Names

ColorTyme
Get It Now
Home Choice
Rent-A-Center

Selected Merchandise

Appliances
Computers
Furniture
Home accessories
Home electronics

Selected Brand Names

Ashley
Berkline
Compaq
Dell
England-Corsair
Hewlett-Packard
IBM
JVC
Mitsubishi
Philips
Sealy
Sony
Standard
Toshiba
Whirlpool

COMPETITORS

Aaron's, Inc.
Advance America
Best Buy
Bestway
Brook Furniture
Cash America
Dollar Financial
EZCORP
Family Dollar Stores
First Cash Financial Services
Sears
Wal-Mart

HISTORICAL FINANCIALS

Company Type: Public

Income Statement

FYE: December 31

	REVENUE ($ mil.)	NET INCOME ($ mil.)	NET PROFIT MARGIN	EMPLOYEES
12/08	2,884.2	139.6	4.8%	17,900
12/07	2,906.1	76.3	2.6%	18,600
12/06	2,433.9	103.1	4.2%	19,740
12/05	2,339.1	135.7	5.8%	15,480
12/04	2,313.3	155.9	6.7%	16,431
Annual Growth	**5.7%**	**(2.7%)**	**—**	**2.2%**

2008 Year-End Financials

Debt ratio: 87.8%
Return on equity: 13.8%
Cash ($ mil.): 87
Current ratio: 10.92
Long-term debt ($ mil.): 947

No. of shares (mil.): 66
Dividends
  Yield: 0.0%
  Payout: —
Market value ($ mil.): 1,166

Stock History

NASDAQ (GS): RCII

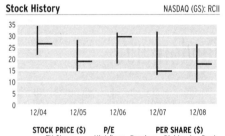

	STOCK PRICE ($) FY Close	P/E High/Low		PER SHARE ($) Earnings	Dividends	Book Value
12/08	17.65	13	5	2.08	0.00	16.34
12/07	14.52	29	12	1.10	0.00	14.34
12/06	29.51	21	12	1.46	0.00	14.28
12/05	18.86	15	8	1.83	0.00	12.47
12/04	26.50	17	11	1.94	0.00	12.03
Annual Growth	**(9.7%)**	**—**	**—**	**1.8%**	**—**	**8.0%**

Republic Services

Homeowners and businesses in 40 states pledge allegiance to Republic Services and the trash collection for which it stands. In 2008, the once #3 industry player acquired #2 company Allied Waste for $6 billion to place it closer to industry leader Waste Management in terms of revenues and geographic coverage. The enlarged company provides waste disposal services for commercial, industrial, municipal, and residential customers through its network of 427 collection companies. Republic Services owns or operates some 219 solid waste landfills, 255 transfer stations, and 86 recycling centers. In 2008 Republic Services rebuffed a Waste Management takeover bid.

Republic Services organizes its operations into five regions: eastern, central, southern, southwestern, and western. Each region is further divided into several operating areas, each of which provides collection, transfer, disposal, and recycling services. Regional and area managers are given considerable authority under the company's decentralized management structure.

Republic Services has grown by buying smaller waste management operations, and the company is looking to make more acquisitions in its existing service areas and in new regions. Likely candidates include assets of municipalities that are privatizing their waste management services.

In 2007 the company sold Living Earth Technology Company (a non-core, stand-alone business in Texas) for about $37 million.

Prior to the Allied Waste acquisition the company's largest shareholder was Microsoft chairman Bill Gates, who owned about 14% of Republic Services through Cascade Investment LLC.

HISTORY

Republic Services began in 1980 as Republic Resources, an oil exploration and production company. In 1989, after a stockholder group tried to force Republic into liquidation, Browning-Ferris (BFI) founder Thomas Fatjo stepped in, gained control of Republic Resources, and refocused it on a field he knew well — solid waste. Renamed Republic Waste, the company began making acquisitions.

In 1990 Michael DeGroote, founder of BFI competitor Laidlaw, bought into Republic Waste. In 1995 Wayne Huizenga — who co-founded Waste Management in 1971 and was beginning to develop a national auto sales organization in the mid-1990s after his tenure as chairman and CEO of Blockbuster Entertainment — approached DeGroote about a deal. They rejected an immediate merger of the waste and auto businesses because the latter was not well-enough developed and would drag down Republic's numbers. Instead, they agreed to merge Republic and the Hudson Companies (a trash business owned by Huizenga's brother-in-law, Harris Hudson), to sell Huizenga a large interest in Republic through a private offering, and to give him control of the board (in 1995). The company became Republic Industries.

Huizenga's investment brought a flood of new investors. With new resources, Republic Industries became a driving force in the garbage industry's consolidation binge, and the company bought more than 100 smaller waste haulers between 1995 and 1998. Republic Industries spun off about 30% of its waste business as Republic

Services in 1998; the IPO raised $1.3 billion. Republic's acquisition trend continued, as it agreed to buy 16 landfills, 136 commercial collection routes, and 11 transfer stations from Waste Management for $500 million. Later that year Waste Management veteran James O'Connor succeeded Huizenga as CEO, although Huizenga continued as chairman.

Investors filed class action lawsuits against Republic in 1999, claiming the Waste Management purchases held far more integration problems than the company admitted. In 2000 the company swapped nine of its solid waste operations for eight Allied Waste businesses, which Allied needed to divest in order to gain federal approval for its merger with BFI.

While many firms in the industry were selling off assets in 2001, Republic was expanding its operations in the northern California market by acquiring Richmond Sanitary Services. Huizenga retired as chairman at the end of 2002 and was once again succeeded by O'Connor. Huizenga stayed on the board as a director until May 2004.

EXECUTIVES

Chairman and CEO: James E. (Jim) O'Connor, age 59, $8,394,237 total compensation
President and COO: Donald W. (Don) Slager, age 47, $100,653 total compensation
EVP and CFO: Tod C. Holmes, age 60, $3,866,253 total compensation
VP and CIO: Bill Halnon
SVP and Chief Accounting Officer: Charles F. Serianni
EVP Business Development: Brian A. Bales
EVP Communications: William C. (Will) Flower
EVP Sales and Marketing: Gary L. Sova
EVP Human Resources: Jeff Hughes
SVP Finance and Treasurer: Edward A. Lang III
SVP Midwestern Operations: Kevin C. Walbridge
SVP Eastern Operations: Ronald R. (Ron) Krall
SVP Western Operations: Jeff Andrews
SVP Southern Operations: Chris Synek
VP and Controller: Jerry S. Clark
VP and Acting General Counsel: Michael Rissman
Manager Internal Communications: Nancy Bretas
Auditors: Ernst & Young LLP

LOCATIONS

HQ: Republic Services, Inc.
    18500 N. Allied Way, Phoenix, AZ 82054
Phone: 954-769-2400   **Fax:** 954-769-2664
Web: www.republicservices.com

2008 Sales

	$ mil.	% of total
Western	1,130.6	31
Southern	840.2	23
Central	674.4	18
Eastern	576.1	16
Allied	463.7	12
Corporate	0.1	—
Total	**3,685.1**	**100**

PRODUCTS/OPERATIONS

2008 Sales

	$ mil.	% of total
Collection		
Commercial	1,161.4	32
Residential	966.0	26
Industrial	711.4	19
Other	23.2	1
Transfer & disposal	659.9	18
Other	163.2	4
Total	**3,685.1**	**100**

COMPETITORS

Casella Waste Systems	Veolia ES Solid Waste
IESI-BFC	Waste Connections
Recology	Waste Industries USA
Rumpke	Waste Management

HISTORICAL FINANCIALS
Company Type: Public

Income Statement

FYE: December 31

	REVENUE ($ mil.)	NET INCOME ($ mil.)	NET PROFIT MARGIN	EMPLOYEES
12/08	3,685.1	73.8	2.0%	35,000
12/07	3,176.2	290.2	9.1%	13,000
12/06	3,070.6	279.6	9.1%	13,000
12/05	2,863.9	253.7	8.9%	13,000
12/04	2,708.1	237.9	8.8%	13,400
Annual Growth	8.0%	(25.4%)	—	27.1%

2008 Year-End Financials

Debt ratio: 98.9%	No. of shares (mil.): 379
Return on equity: 1.7%	Dividends
Cash ($ mil.): 69	Yield: 2.9%
Current ratio: 0.52	Payout: 194.6%
Long-term debt ($ mil.): 7,199	Market value ($ mil.): 9,400

Stock History

NYSE: RSG

	STOCK PRICE ($) FY Close	P/E High/Low	PER SHARE ($) Earnings	Dividends	Book Value
12/08	24.79	99 49	0.37	0.72	19.20
12/07	31.35	23 17	1.51	0.55	3.44
12/06	27.11	21 18	1.38	0.40	3.75
12/05	25.03	22 17	1.17	0.35	4.23
12/04	22.36	22 16	1.02	0.24	4.94
Annual Growth	2.6%	— —	(22.4%)	31.6%	40.4%

Revlon, Inc.

Revlon has the look of a leader in the US mass-market cosmetics business, alongside L'Oréal's Maybelline and Procter & Gamble's Cover Girl. In addition to Revlon's makeup and skin care products (Revlon, Almay, and Ultima II), the firm makes fragrances (Charlie, Jean Naté) and other personal care products (Revlon ColorSilk, Mitchum). New York socialite Ron Perelman owns about 60% of Revlon — and controls about 75% of its voting power — through holding companies, including MacAndrews & Forbes Holdings. FMR owns about 15% of Revlon. While Perelman's involvement with Revlon has fueled his celebrity, the cosmetics maker has seen stalled revenue in recent years. Regardless, Perelman continues to fund the firm.

Revlon sells its products in more than 100 countries, primarily through mass merchandisers, drugstores, and supermarkets. It typically refreshes its lines with new brands. Über retailer Wal-Mart is Revlon's largest customer, accounting for about 25% of the company's annual sales.

What started as a company that developed and sold nail polish has become nails on a chalkboard to some investors, but Revlon is trying to make up for lost time by turning its future toward profits. The company's strategy focuses on developing its core brands, Revlon and Almay, while boosting growth in its personal care products segment with women's hair color, beauty tools, deodorants, and skin care items.

With international business representing about 40% of Revlon's revenue, the company is concentrating on growing its market share abroad through improved business operations, including increased promotions and higher shipments. The company holds leading market positions for its products in Australia, Canada, and South Africa.

The company established an "office of the vice chairman" executive structure in May 2009 to oversee and steer the company's strategy. The structure comprises three executives. CEO David Kennedy was promoted to vice chairman and tapped as EVP at MacAndrews & Forbes. Alan Ennis took the CEO title, and Chris Elshaw, the US region's EVP and general manager, was elected EVP and COO.

In 2008 the company sold its non-core brands in Brazil, including its men's skin care brand Bozzano, for nearly $110 million to Hypermarcas. Revlon consolidated facilities in 2007 to cut costs, after announcing it would cut about 10% of its workforce and cancel its newly developed Vital Radiance line of cosmetics. A couple of years earlier, a debt-for-equity swap deal with Fidelity Management & Research Co. and Mafco Holdings was necessary to help reduce some $780 million of the company's debt.

HISTORY

Legend has it that, jobless in New York City in the depths of the Depression, Charles Revson became a cosmetics salesman by the toss of a coin — tails, he'd apply for a job selling household appliances; heads, he'd answer an ad for a cosmetics salesman. It was heads, and in 1931 Revson began selling Elka nail polish to beauty salons. He painted his own nails with different colors so he wouldn't need a color chart.

Revson and his brother Joseph decided to start their own nail polish company. They scraped together $300, hooked up with nail polish supplier Charles Lachman, and in 1932 began Revlon (the "L" in the name came from Lachman). The nail polish, emulating Elka's, was opaque rather than transparent, available in many colors, and an immediate hit with beauty salons. Revlon grew rapidly, and by 1937 Revson was selling his nail polish in upscale department stores.

Seeing nail polish as a fashion accessory, Revson introduced new colors twice a year, giving them — and the matching lipsticks introduced in 1940 — names like Kissing Pink and Fifth Avenue Red. More opportunist than innovator, he let his competitors do the research and make the mistakes, and then he would make a better version of the product, outpackaging and outadvertising his rivals.

Revlon introduced Fire & Ice in 1952, one of its most successful launches ever. Its sole sponsorship of *The $64,000 Question* quiz show in

1955 boosted sales of some products by 500%. Later that year Revlon went public. To diversify and expand its markets, it began making acquisitions (although many were soon dumped) and selling its products overseas.

The company bought deodorant maker Mitchum in 1970, and three years later it introduced Charlie, its wildly popular fragrance. In 1974 a dying Revson handpicked his successor, Michel Bergerac, president of European operations for IT&T. Revson died the next year. Bergerac began a new push for diversification and lower costs. Acquisitions included ophthalmic and pharmaceuticals companies. However, while Revlon's health care operations were rising, its cosmetics star was losing market share and profits were falling.

Social-climbing conglomateur Ron Perelman bought Revlon in an LBO in 1985 with funds raised by friend Michael Milken. Hoping to restore the firm as a beauty business, Perelman began selling off the profitable health care businesses and buying beauty companies.

In 1994 Revlon introduced ColorStay lipstick, which quickly became the top-selling brand. Revlon went public in 1996. George Fellows was promoted to CEO the next year. The company merged its Prestige Fragrance & Cosmetics chain into Perelman's Cosmetic Center chain in 1997; Revlon sold its 85% stake in the combination at a loss in 1998.

Still deep in debt and suffering from domestic competition, too much inventory, and troubles in Russia and Brazil, Revlon closed three plants and cut 3,000 jobs in 1998. Fellows resigned in 1999 and was replaced by Jeff Nugent, the former president of Neutrogena (and brother of rocker Ted Nugent). Sales fell as retailers cut inventory.

Revlon sold its professional products business in 2000 to an investment group led by the unit's chairman, Carlos Colomer (now chairman of Colomer USA). Also in 2000 Revlon sold its Plusbelle line (Argentina) to consumer products company Dial. In 2001 it sold its Colorama brand of cosmetics and hair care products to rival L'Oréal.

In February 2002 CEO Nugent abruptly resigned after it was reported that chairman Ron Perelman planned to replace him with Jack Stahl, former president and COO at The Coca-Cola Company; Stahl took office that month. The same year Perelman offered a cash infusion of $150 million to the struggling company. Revlon's board accepted the proposal in 2003.

Stahl left the troubled company in September 2006 to pursue other interests and was succeeded as president and CEO of Revlon by David Kennedy, the firm's CFO.

EXECUTIVES

Chairman: Ronald O. (Ron) Perelman, age 65
Vice Chairman: David L. Kennedy, age 62, $2,990,891 total compensation
President, CEO, and Director: Alan T. Ennis, age 39, $1,009,976 total compensation
EVP and COO: Chris Elshaw, age 48
EVP, CFO, and Treasurer: Steven Berns, age 44
EVP Human Resources, Chief Legal Officer, General Counsel, and Secretary: Robert K. Kretzman III, age 57, $1,816,995 total compensation
EVP and Chief Science Officer: Alan J. Meyers, age 51
SVP, Corporate Controller, and Chief Accounting Officer: Gina Mastantuono
EVP Technical Affairs and Worldwide Operations: Carl K. Kooyoomjian, age 58
EVP North American Sales: Karl Obrecht

SVP and Managing Director, Asia/Pacific: Graeme Howard
SVP Worldwide Manufacturing: Arthur Franson
SVP and Managing Director, Europe: Simon Worraker
SVP, Deputy General Counsel, and Assistant Secretary: Michael Sheehan
SVP and General Tax Counsel: Mark M. Sexton
SVP and Managing Director, Latin America: Manuel Blanco
SVP Investor Relations and Corporate Communications: Abbe F. Goldstein
VP Public Relations: Jennine Hannaway
Auditors: KPMG LLP

LOCATIONS

HQ: Revlon, Inc.
237 Park Ave., New York, NY 10017
Phone: 212-527-4000   **Fax:** 212-527-4995
Web: www.revloninc.com

2008 Sales

	$ mil.	% of total
US	782.6	58
International	564.2	42
Total	**1,346.8**	**100**

PRODUCTS/OPERATIONS

2008 Sales

	$ mil.	% of total
Color cosmetics	831.0	62
Beauty care & fragrance	515.8	38
Total	**1,346.8**	**100**

Selected Products and Brands

Cosmetics
  Almay
  Age Defying
  Beyond Natural
  Botafirm
  ColorStay
  Cutex (in South America and Africa)
  Fabulash
  Gatineau
  LiquiSilk
  Revlon
  Super Lustrous
  Ultima II
Beauty tools
  Revlon
Deodorants
  Mitchum
Fragrance
  Charlie
  Jean Naté
Hair
  Revlon ColorSilk
Skin Care
  Gatineau
  Ultima II

COMPETITORS

Alberto-Culver	Joh. A. Benckiser
Alticor	John Paul Mitchell
Avlon	Johnson & Johnson
Avon	L'Oréal
Bath & Body Works	LVMH
Beiersdorf	Mary Kay
Body Shop	Nu Skin
Bristol-Myers Squibb	Orly International
Clarins	Procter & Gamble
Colgate-Palmolive	Puig Beauty & Fashion
Colomer USA	Shiseido
Combe	SoftSheen/Carson
Coty Inc.	Unilever NV
Estée Lauder	

HISTORICAL FINANCIALS

Company Type: Public

Income Statement

	REVENUE ($ mil.)	NET INCOME ($ mil.)	NET PROFIT MARGIN	EMPLOYEES
12/08	1,346.8	57.9	4.3%	5,600
12/07	1,400.1	(16.1)	—	5,600
12/06	1,331.4	(251.3)	—	6,000
12/05	1,332.3	(83.7)	—	6,800
12/04	1,297.2	(51.8)	—	6,300
Annual Growth	**0.9%**	**—**	**—**	**(2.9%)**

FYE: December 31

2008 Year-End Financials

Debt ratio: —
Return on equity: —
Cash ($ mil.): 53
Current ratio: 1.32
Long-term debt ($ mil.): 1,310

No. of shares (mil.): 52
Dividends
  Yield: 0.0%
  Payout: —
Market value ($ mil.): 344

Stock History

NYSE: REV

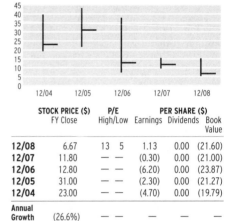

	STOCK PRICE ($) FY Close	P/E High/Low		PER SHARE ($) Earnings	PER SHARE ($) Dividends	PER SHARE ($) Book Value
12/08	6.67	13	5	1.13	0.00	(21.60)
12/07	11.80	—	—	(0.30)	0.00	(21.00)
12/06	12.80	—	—	(6.20)	0.00	(23.87)
12/05	31.00	—	—	(2.30)	0.00	(21.27)
12/04	23.00	—	—	(4.70)	0.00	(19.79)
Annual Growth	**(26.6%)**	**—**	**—**	**—**	**—**	**—**

Reynolds American

Together, no one can stop us. No doubt that is what R.J. Reynolds Tobacco Holdings and Brown & Williamson were thinking when the two merged to create Reynolds American (RAI). R.J. Reynolds has been smoking for more than 120 years, but increasing competition and the need to cut costs convinced the #2 US tobacco company to merge with #3 Brown & Williamson. However, RAI still trails the Altria Group (owner of Philip Morris), which steers about half of the US tobacco market. Still, RAI's RJR Tobacco unit boasts five of the 10 best-selling brands of cigarettes in the US: Camel, Kool, Pall Mall, Doral, and Winston. Brown & Williamson's former parent British American Tobacco owns about 42% of RAI.

While RJR Tobacco contributes more than 85% of its parent company's sales, the balance comes from smokeless tobacco producer Conwood Company (acquired in 2006), maker of the top-selling Grizzly and Kodiak brands of moist snuff. Conwood also distributes tobacco products manufactured by Lane, Limited, including cigars and roll-your-own tobacco. (Lane was acquired along with Brown & Williamson.)

Unlike the market for cigarettes in the US, which is mature and declining, the market for moist snuff and other smokeless tobacco products is growing (up more than 7% in 2008). Within the smokeless products category, value-priced brands, such as Grizzly, are outperforming more expensive premium brands.

RAI's archrival Altria (the parent company of Philip Morris USA) acquired Conwood's largest competitor UST in January 2009, bumping RAI from the #1 spot to the #2 spot in the smokeless tobacco market. After Altria combined Copenhagen and Skoal snuff with its Marlboro cigarettes business, RAI announced restructuring changes and the elimination of some 570 jobs at its headquarters and its R.J. Reynolds' tobacco subsidiary in Winston-Salem.

The Altria/UST merger and the passage six months later of landmark legislation giving the U.S. Food and Drug Administration unprecedented authority to regulate tobacco products is reshaping the tobacco industry and RAI's future. Balking at "unprecedented restrictions" on First Amendment rights, RAI and rival Lorillard filed a lawsuit against the FDA in August 2009. RAI's position in that it isn't against the decision to give FDA authority to regulate tobacco, but it is protesting several provisions in the legislation.

HISTORY

R. J. Reynolds formed the R.J. Reynolds Tobacco Company in 1875 in Winston, North Carolina, to produce chewing tobacco. In the late 1890s, Reynolds lost two-thirds of the company to the American Tobacco Trust, but he regained control in 1911 after the trust was dismantled by the government. Two years later the company introduced Camel.

After Reynolds died in 1918, leadership passed to Bowman Gray, whose family ran the company for the next 50 years. Camel held the #1 or #2 cigarette position throughout the 1930s and 1940s, and Reynolds became the largest domestic cigarette company. In response to growing health concerns in the 1950s, the company introduced its filtered Winston (1954) and Salem (1956) brands.

In response to growing anti-smoking sentiment, Reynolds Tobacco began diversifying into foods and other nontobacco businesses beginning in the 1960s. Acquisitions included Chun King, Patio Foods, American Independent Oil, Del Monte, Inglenook wines, Smirnoff vodka, Kentucky Fried Chicken, Sunkist beverages, and Canada Dry, all of which it had sold by 1991. In September 1985 Reynolds acquired Nabisco Brands (Newtons, Oreo, Planters nuts) for $4.9 billion. In 1986 the parent company was renamed RJR Nabisco Inc.

In November 1988 RJR Nabisco agreed to be acquired by Kohlberg Kravis Roberts (KKR). The deal, valued in excess of $25 billion, closed in April 1989. After being privately held for a period, KKR took RJR Nabisco Holdings public in 1991. In early 1995 KKR divested its remaining holdings in RJR Nabisco. Also that year Andrew Schindler was promoted to CEO of the firm.

The tobacco unit ended the much-criticized Joe Camel campaign in the US in 1997 and cut its tobacco workforce by 10%. The big US tobacco companies reached a $206 billion settlement in 1998 covering 46 states (four states had already settled for $40 billion) and began hiking cigarette prices by 45 cents a pack.

Prior to 1999, RJR was a subsidiary of RJR Nabisco Holdings Corp. (RJRN). In 1999, following the sale of the company's international tobacco business to Japan Tobacco for $8 billion, the remaining tobacco and food businesses were separated and RJRN was renamed Nabisco Group Holdings Corp. (NGH). In June the former parent company, RJRN, was renamed RJ Reynolds Tobacco Holdings, Inc., and became an independent, publicly traded company again, with RJ Reynolds Tobacco Company as its wholly owned subsidiary. (The separation was accomplished through a spinoff of the domestic tobacco business to RJR Nabisco stockholders.)

A Florida jury rendered a $35 billion punitive damages verdict against RJRT in 2000. The company filed an appeal, as it and four other Big Tobacco firms claimed the verdict, totaling $145 billion, would put them out of business (which violates Florida tort law). A state appeals court later threw out the verdict saying the thousands of Florida smokers named in the case could not lump their complaints into one lawsuit. That decision is now under review by the Florida Supreme Court.

RJRT spun off its Targacept subsidiary (created in 1999) in August 2000, retaining a 43% stake. In December, RJRT acquired its former parent company, Nabisco Group Holdings Corp., for $9.8 billion.

In January 2002 RJRT acquired the Santa Fe Natural Tobacco Company, maker of the Natural American Spirit additive-free cigarette brand, for $340 million in cash. That year RJR also formed a joint venture with UK-based Gallaher to sell American blend cigarettes in Europe, particularly in France, Spain, Italy, and the Canary Islands. In early 2008 RJR terminated its Gallaher joint venture.

While pursuing new markets overseas, RJRT scaled back marketing efforts at home — in part because of the agreement it signed with US states in 1998. In June 2003 NASCAR and RJRT parted ways, signaling the end to NASCAR's Winston Cup series. The race circuit is now called the Sprint Cup.

In September 2003 the company said it would focus marketing activities on its Camel and Salem brands. It also launched a two-year plan to cut costs by $1 billion, which included cutting jobs by 40%. By the end of 2003, RJRT had cut 1,400 jobs. Shortly thereafter, the company announced merger plans with Brown & Williamson.

Before combining with RJRT to create Reynolds American in July 2004, Brown & Williamson had been ordered to cut back on promoting its Kool brand, which was associated with hip-hop music. The issue carried over to Reynolds American, which agreed in October 2004 to settle several related lawsuits in New York, Illinois, and Maryland by paying $1.5 million toward antismoking campaigns and severely restricting Kool promotions that critics said targeted black youths.

In 2006 Lane Limited sold its Dr. Grabow line of pipes and filters, Dill's pipe cleaners, and Sparta, North Carolina, manufacturing facility to International Pipes & Accessories LLC for about $4.3 million. Lane Limited sold the brands and plant to focus on making and marketing its premium tobacco products.

In June 2009 the passage of the Family Smoking and Tobacco Control Act by the US Congress gave the FDA unprecedented authority to regulate tobacco products, including the authority to regulate marketing, ban candy flavorings, and reduce nicotine in tobacco products.

EXECUTIVES

Chairman, President, and CEO; Chairman, R.J. Reynolds Tobacco Company: Susan M. Ivey, age 50, $8,901,101 total compensation
EVP and CFO: Thomas R. (Tom) Adams, age 58, $2,225,912 total compensation
EVP and CIO, Reynolds American and R.J. Reynolds Tobacco Company: Donald I. Lamonds
SVP and Chief Accounting Officer: Michael S. Desmond
SVP and Chief Accounting Officer: Frederick W. Smothers, age 45
EVP Public Affairs: Tommy J. Payne, age 51, $1,570,631 total compensation
EVP and General Counsel: E. Julia (Judy) Lambeth, age 57, $2,082,696 total compensation
EVP Operations, R.J. Reynolds Tobacco Company: Daniel D. Snyder
Group EVP: Jeffery S. (Jeff) Gentry, age 51
EVP Consumer and Trade Marketing, R.J. Reynolds Tobacco Company: Gavin D. Little
EVP Human Resources, Reynolds American and R.J. Reynolds Tobacco Company: Lisa J. Caldwell, age 48
SVP, Deputy General Counsel, and Secretary; SVP, Secretary, and Director, R.J. Reynolds Tobacco Company: McDara P. Folan III, age 50
SVP Strategy and Business Development: E. Kenan (Ken) Whitehurst, age 52
SVP and Treasurer: Daniel A. Fawley, age 51
President and CEO, R.J. Reynolds Tobacco Company: Daniel M. (Daan) Delen, age 43
President and CEO, Conwood Company, LLC: Bryan K. Stockdale, age 50
President and CEO, Santa Fe Natural Tobacco: Nicholas A. (Nick) Bumbacco, age 44
Auditors: KPMG LLP

LOCATIONS

HQ: Reynolds American Inc.
401 N. Main St., Winston-Salem, NC 27101
Phone: 336-741-2000   **Fax:** 336-741-4238
Web: www.reynoldsamerican.com

PRODUCTS/OPERATIONS

2008 Sales

	$ mil.	% of total
RJR Tobacco	7,678	87
Conwood	723	8
Other	444	5
Total	**8,845**	**100**

Selected Brands

Cigarettes
  Camel
  Capri
  Doral
  Kool
  Misty
  Pall Mall
  Salem
  Winston

Smokeless tobacco
  Grizzly
  Kodiak

COMPETITORS

British American Tobacco
Commonwealth Brands
JT International
Lorillard
Nat Sherman
Philip Morris USA
Smokin Joes
Star Scientific
Swisher International
UST llc
Vector Group
Wellstone Filters

HISTORICAL FINANCIALS
Company Type: Public

Income Statement
FYE: December 31

	REVENUE ($ mil.)	NET INCOME ($ mil.)	NET PROFIT MARGIN	EMPLOYEES
12/08	8,845.0	1,338.0	15.1%	6,600
12/07	9,023.0	1,307.0	14.5%	7,300
12/06	8,510.0	1,136.0	13.3%	7,800
12/05	8,256.0	987.0	12.0%	8,200
12/04	6,437.0	639.0	9.9%	9,300
Annual Growth	8.3%	20.3%	—	(8.2%)

2008 Year-End Financials
Debt ratio: 71.9%
Return on equity: 19.5%
Cash ($ mil.): 2,578
Current ratio: 1.28
Long-term debt ($ mil.): 4,486
No. of shares (mil.): 291
Dividends
  Yield: 8.4%
  Payout: 74.4%
Market value ($ mil.): 11,745

Stock History
NYSE: RAI

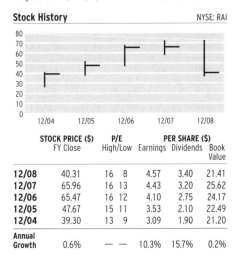

	STOCK PRICE ($) FY Close	P/E High/Low		PER SHARE ($) Earnings	Dividends	Book Value
12/08	40.31	16	8	4.57	3.40	21.41
12/07	65.96	16	13	4.43	3.20	25.62
12/06	65.47	16	12	4.10	2.75	24.17
12/05	47.67	15	11	3.53	2.10	22.49
12/04	39.30	13	9	3.09	1.90	21.20
Annual Growth	0.6%	—	—	10.3%	15.7%	0.2%

Rite Aid

Rite Aid may have found the right aid for its ills: growth. The nation's #3 drugstore chain (behind CVS and Walgreen), the company runs more than 4,800 drugstores in 30-plus states and the District of Columbia. Rite Aid stores fill prescriptions (two-thirds of sales) and sell health and beauty aids, convenience foods, greeting cards, and other items, including some 3,300 private-label products. No longer a distant third behind Walgreen and CVS, Rite Aid acquired more than 1,850 Brooks and Eckerd drugstores from Canada's Jean Coutu Group for about $4 billion in 2007.

The company's heavy debt load and the downturn in the economy have put it in a vulnerable position. Rite Aid has been closing underperforming drugstores and reducing inventory, and has cut its budget for capital expenditures.

The deal for Jean Coutu's US subsidiary created the largest drugstore chain on the East Coast and added key new markets, such as the Carolinas. All the stores were renamed Rite Aid and their integration was completed in mid-2008.

Mounting losses due to the recession and a weak cold-and-flu season pushed the retailer to announce that it would be shuttering about 120 stores across the US and distribution centers in New York and Georgia in 2009.

The company struck a deal with FUJIFILM USA in 2008 that will bring photo services such as online and in-store photo finishing to all of Rite Aid's stores. Partnering with General Nutrition Companies (GNC), more than a third of Rite Aid stores have GNC concessions inside, and the two firms jointly market a line of vitamins and supplements (PharmAssure). It plans to open an additional 625 GNC LiveWell stores-within-a-store inside Rite Aid locations by the end of 2014.

In 2009 Rite Aid agreed to pay $500,000 in consumer refunds to settle charges by the FTC that the company falsely advertised its Germ Defense line of cold-and-flu remedies as preventing illness or reducing the severity and duration of symptoms.

Jean Coutu, which received a 32% stake in Rite Aid in the Brooks/Eckerd deal, currently owns about 28% of of the company.

HISTORY

Wholesale grocer Alex Grass founded Rack Rite Distributors in Harrisburg, Pennsylvania, in 1958 to provide health and beauty aids and other sundries to grocery stores. He offered the same products at his first discount drugstore, Thrif D Discount Center, opened in 1962 in Scranton, Pennsylvania. Four years later the company began placing pharmacies in its 36 stores. Rite Aid went public and adopted its current name in 1968, and the next year it made the first of many diverse acquisitions: Daw Drug, Blue Ridge Nursing Homes, and plasma suppliers Immuno Serums and Sero Genics.

Purchases in the 1970s included Sera-Tec Biologicals of New Jersey (blood plasma) and nearly 300 stores. By 1981 Rite Aid was the #3 drugstore chain, and sales exceeded $1 billion. In 1984 it bought the American Discount Auto Parts chain and Encore Books discount chain and spun off its wholesale grocery operation in 1984 as Super Rite, retaining a 47% stake (sold 1989).

Acquisitions added almost 900 stores during the 1980s. Expansion costs eroded Rite Aid's profit margins, and the company focused on integrating its buys in 1990.

Martin Grass took Rite Aid's reins from his dad in 1995. That year the company agreed to buy Revco, at the time the #2 drugstore operator, but the deal was derailed by FTC and Department of Justice objections in 1996. Rite Aid bounced back and acquired Thrifty PayLess (with more than 1,000 stores) for about $2.3 billion in 1996. The deal gave the company more than 3,600 stores and a presence in the western US. In 1998 it closed many smaller stores and bought PCS Health Systems (the #1 US pharmacy benefits manager) from drug maker Eli Lilly.

In 1999, after a *Wall Street Journal* investigation, Rite Aid revealed that Martin Grass, Alex Grass, and other family members held stakes in several suppliers and real estate interests doing business with the company. That year Rite Aid partnered with General Nutrition Companies, Inc. (GNC) and took a 25% stake in the Internet retailer drugstore.com. Later in 1999 Rite Aid began slashing its $5.1 billion debt by cutting corporate staff and selling off some stores in California and the Pacific Northwest. CEO Martin Grass resigned, and a team of former Fred Meyer officers — led by Robert Miller — took over.

In July 2000 the company announced it would restate profits that, over the past two years, had been inflated in excess of $1 billion. Later that year Rite Aid sold PCS Health Systems to pharmacy benefits manager Advance Paradigm for more than $1 billion (about $500 million less than what Rite Aid originally paid for it).

To raise cash Rite Aid sold large blocks of its drugstore.com stock, trimming its original 25% stake to less than 10% by April 2002. Former chairman and CEO Martin Grass, former general counsel and vice chairman Franklin Brown, and former CFO Frank Bergonzi, among others, were indicted on June 21, 2002, for allegedly falsifying Rite Aid's books.

In April 2003 former chairman and CEO Martin Grass agreed to pay nearly $1.5 million to settle a lawsuit in which shareholders alleged that Rite Aid's books were falsified, inflating the stock's value. In June Grass and former CFO Bergonzi both pleaded guilty to conspiracy to defraud shareholders. Eric Sorkin, Rite Aid's former VP of Pharmacy Services, pleaded guilty to conspiring to obstruct justice. The following month Rite Aid began mailing checks totaling nearly $140 million to thousands of its current and former shareholders damaged by the accounting scandal at the company. In October, former chief counsel Brown was convicted of conspiracy and lying to the Securities and Exchange Commission, among other charges.

In May 2004 Grass, whose father founded Rite Aid, struck a plea deal with prosecutors under which he was sentenced to eight years in prison. Also in May, several other former company executives, including ex-CFO Bergonzi and vice president Sorkin, were sentenced in the accounting scandal. In June, Rite Aid agreed to pay the US government $5.6 million (plus another $1.4 million to more than 20 states) to settle a federal lawsuit alleging the drugstore chain submitted false prescription claims to government insurance programs. In October, former vice chairman Brown was sentenced to 10 years in prison, the longest sentence of six Rite Aid officials charged in the accounting scandal.

Rite Aid founder Alex Grass died in August 2009 at the age of 82.

EXECUTIVES

Chairman and CEO: Mary F. Sammons, age 62, $2,536,396 total compensation
President and COO: John T. Standley, age 45, $755,490 total compensation
SEVP, CFO, and Chief Administrative Officer: Frank G. Vitrano, age 53, $515,483 total compensation
SVP and CIO: Don P. Davis
SVP and Chief Accounting Officer: Douglas (Doug) Donley, age 46
SVP and Chief Compliance Officer: Anthony J. (Tony) Bellezza, age 42
SEVP Merchandising, Marketing, and Logistics: Kenneth A. (Ken) Martindale, age 48
EVP, General Counsel, and Secretary: Marc A. Strassler, age 58
EVP Store Operations: Brian Fiala, age 48, $913,636 total compensation
SVP Strategic Business Development: Christopher S. (Chris) Hall, age 38
SVP Supply Chain: Wilson A. Lester Jr., age 50
SVP Pharmacy Operations: Philip J. Keough IV, age 38
SVP Marketing: John Learish, age 43
SVP Corporate Communications: Karen Rugen
SVP Indirect Procurement: Gerald P. (Jerry) Cardinale
SVP Human Resources: Steve Parsons, age 44
Auditors: Deloitte & Touche LLP

LOCATIONS

HQ: Rite Aid Corporation
  30 Hunter Ln., Camp Hill, PA 17011
Phone: 717-761-2633   **Fax:** 717-975-5871
Web: www.riteaid.com

2009 Stores

	No.
New York	674
California	605
Pennsylvania	583
Michigan	296
New Jersey	277
North Carolina	248
Ohio	239
Georgia	213
Virginia	201
Massachusetts	165
Maryland	147
Washington	138
Kentucky	117
South Carolina	105
West Virginia	104
Alabama	97
Tennessee	88
Connecticut	80
Maine	81
Louisiana	68
Oregon	71
New Hampshire	69
Rhode Island	46
Delaware	43
Vermont	38
Mississippi	27
Utah	23
Colorado	21
Idaho	19
Indiana	10
District of Columbia	7
Nevada	1
Total	**4,901**

PRODUCTS/OPERATIONS

2009 Sales

	% of total
Prescription drugs	67
General merchandise & other	19
Over-the-counter medications & personal care	9
Health & beauty aids	5
Total	**100**

2009 Sales

	$ mil.	% of total
Pharmacy	17,604.3	67
Front-end	8,581.1	33
Other	103.9	—
Total	**26,289.3**	**100**

Selected Merchandise and Services

Beverages
Convenience foods
Cosmetics
Designer fragrances
Greeting cards
Health and personal care products
Household items
Over-the-counter drugs
Photo processing
Prescription drugs
Private-label products
Seasonal merchandise
Vitamins and minerals

COMPETITORS

A&P	Kroger
Ahold USA	Marc Glassman
Costco Wholesale	Medicine Shoppe
CVS Caremark	Penn Traffic
Discount Drug	Publix
Dollar General	Safeway
Duane Reade	Target
Family Dollar Stores	Walgreen
Kmart	Wal-Mart

HISTORICAL FINANCIALS

Company Type: Public

Income Statement

FYE: Saturday nearest last day of Feb.

	REVENUE ($ mil.)	NET INCOME ($ mil.)	NET PROFIT MARGIN	EMPLOYEES
2/09	26,289.3	(2,915.4)	—	103,000
2/08	24,326.8	(1,076.2)	—	112,800
2/07	17,507.7	(4.7)	—	69,700
2/06	17,271.0	1,240.2	7.2%	70,200
2/05	16,816.4	267.1	1.6%	71,200
Annual Growth	**11.8%**	**—**	**—**	**9.7%**

2009 Year-End Financials

Debt ratio: —
Return on equity: —
Cash ($ mil.): 152
Current ratio: 1.90
Long-term debt ($ mil.): 5,971

No. of shares (mil.): 885
Dividends
  Yield: 0.0%
  Payout: —
Market value ($ mil.): 248

Stock History

NYSE: RAD

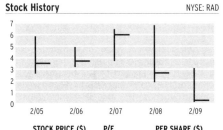

	STOCK PRICE ($) FY Close	P/E High/Low		PER SHARE ($) Earnings	Dividends	Book Value
2/09	0.28	—	—	(3.49)	0.00	(1.36)
2/08	2.67	—	—	(1.54)	0.00	1.93
2/07	5.97	—	—	(0.01)	0.00	1.88
2/06	3.69	3	2	1.89	0.00	1.82
2/05	3.50	12	6	0.47	0.00	0.36
Annual Growth	**(46.8%)**	**—**	**—**	**—**	**—**	**—**

Robert Half

Robert Half International carries a full load of personnel services. The company places temporary and permanent staff through seven divisions: Accountemps, Robert Half Finance and Accounting, Robert Half Legal, OfficeTeam (general administrative), Robert Half Technology (information technology), Robert Half Management Resources (senior level professionals), and The Creative Group (advertising, marketing, and Web design). The firm has also established internal audit and risk consulting subsidiary Protiviti. Robert Half operates from more than 370 offices in some 40 states and 20 countries.

The firm places about 220,000 employees in temporary assignments each year, recruiting them through direct marketing and print, radio, and Internet advertising. It also has joint marketing agreements with many tech-related companies to coordinate joint mailings, cooperative advertising, and other promotions.

CEO Harold "Max" Messmer moonlights as an author and has published several popular employment books, including *Human Resources Kit For Dummies*. The company also publishes job reports and surveys on the latest employment trends and annual salary guides to track pay trends.

HISTORY

Robert Half founded Robert Half Inc. in 1948 as an employment agency for accountants. He developed Accountemps on the side to supply firms with accountants and other finance professionals on a temporary basis. His concept was a hit, and Half became known as a pioneer in the specialized employment services industry. He started franchising his business nationwide. The temp industry grew slowly in the 1960s and 1970s, until the 1980s brought a rapid expansion. By 1985 there were 150 independent Accountemps and Robert Half franchises.

Harold "Max" Messmer joined the company in 1985 for what would prove to be a tumultuous first couple of years. In 1986 Boothe Financial Corporation bought all of Robert Half's outstanding stock, and Messmer launched a program to buy all the Robert Half franchises. A year later Boothe sold Robert Half, which then went public as Robert Half International, placing Messmer at the helm as CEO and president.

Robert Half's focus on the accounting and financial services niche helped the company avoid the industry's price war of the early 1990s. The company's permanent placement operations accounted for nearly 20% of Robert Half's business in 1990. As corporate downsizing lessened the demand for permanent employees, the company's business slumped. The slow economy brought on some changes (reduced overhead and advertising cuts) and facilitated buybacks of Robert Half and Accountemps franchises.

In 1991 Robert Half started its OfficeTeam division to place temporary administrative office personnel. The division got off to a fast start in its initial year, earning some $2 million. Its success continued the following year, with sales rising to about $12 million. The permanent placement business, however, wasn't faring as well, and the company attempted to streamline those operations by combining its Robert Half and Accountemps facilities.

Robert Half bought The Affiliates, a firm specializing in temporary legal support staff, in 1992. The company then expanded in the eastern US and Europe (through new offices in France, Belgium, and the UK) the next year. In 1994 Robert Half founded RHI Consulting, which provided information technology workers. By then the company had bought all but four of the original 150 Robert Half and Accountemps franchises. Messmer, meanwhile, had *Job Hunting For Dummies* published in 1995 (other books followed).

Robert Half announced a new division in 1997: RHI Management Resources, an operation that targets start-up companies in need of executive-level financial personnel. In 1999 the company added The Creative Group division, which provides advertising, marketing, and Web design staff, to its collection of services. Robert Half made its first foray into Eastern Europe in 2000 when it bought a Czech recruitment agency. The following year it began offering free online courses to finance and accounting professionals through an affiliation with SmartForce, which has been acquired by SkillSoft.

In 2002 Robert Half created Protiviti, an internal audit and risk consulting subsidiary, by hiring more than 750 former employees of Arthur Andersen's internal audit and risk consulting practice. The company bought the two remaining independent Robert Half franchises in 2003.

EXECUTIVES

Chairman and CEO: Harold M. (Max) Messmer Jr., age 63, $15,399,592 total compensation
Vice Chairman, President, and CFO: M. Keith Waddell, age 51, $9,425,403 total compensation
President and COO, Staffing Services: Paul F. Gentzkow, age 53, $7,527,176 total compensation
EVP, Chief Administrative Officer, and Treasurer: Michael C. Buckley, age 42, $2,175,925 total compensation
EVP Corporate Development: Robert W. Glass, age 50, $2,506,231 total compensation
SVP, Secretary, and General Counsel: Steven Karel, age 59
SVP Corporate Communications: Reesa M. Staten
SVP Operational Finance and Accounting: Paula Streit
SVP Marketing: Elena West
Executive Director, Accountemps: Andrew G. Denka
Managing Director, Robert Half Finance and Accounting: Phil Sheridan
President and CEO, Protiviti: Joseph A. Tarantino
Executive Director, Robert Half Legal: Charles Volkert
Executive Director, OfficeTeam: Robert Hosking
Executive Director, The Creative Group: Megan Slabinski
Executive Director, Robert Half Technology: Dave Wilmer
Auditors: PricewaterhouseCoopers LLP

LOCATIONS

HQ: Robert Half International Inc.
2884 Sand Hill Rd., Menlo Park, CA 94025
Phone: 650-234-6000 **Fax:** 650-234-6999
Web: www.rhii.com

2008 Sales

	$ mil.	% of total
Domestic	3,278.6	71
Foreign	1,322.0	29
Total	**4,600.6**	**100**

PRODUCTS/OPERATIONS

2008 Sales

	$ mil.	% of total
Temporary & consultant staffing	3,626.2	79
Risk consulting & internal audit services	546.9	12
Permanent placement staffing	427.5	9
Total	**4,600.6**	**100**

Selected Operating Units

Accountemps (temporary accounting and finance personnel)
The Creative Group (advertising, marketing, and Web design)
OfficeTeam (temporary administrative and office personnel)
Protiviti (internal audit and risk consulting)
Robert Half Finance and Accounting (temporary accounting and finance personnel)
Robert Half Legal (temporary and full-time legal support personnel)
Robert Half Management Resources (senior-level accounting and finance personnel)
Robert Half Technology (temporary and contract IT personnel)

COMPETITORS

Adecco	Kforce
COMSYS IT Partners	KPMG
Deloitte Consulting	Manpower
Ernst & Young Global	MPS
General Employment	PricewaterhouseCoopers
Enterprises	Randstad Holding
Headway Corporate	Solomon Page
Resources	Spherion
Kelly Services	Winston Resources

HISTORICAL FINANCIALS

Company Type: Public

Income Statement

FYE: December 31

	REVENUE ($ mil.)	NET INCOME ($ mil.)	NET PROFIT MARGIN	EMPLOYEES
12/08	4,600.6	250.2	5.4%	13,300
12/07	4,645.7	296.2	6.4%	272,300
12/06	4,013.5	283.2	7.1%	255,400
12/05	3,338.4	237.9	7.1%	230,000
12/04	2,675.7	140.6	5.3%	9,200
Annual Growth	**14.5%**	**15.5%**	—	**9.7%**

2008 Year-End Financials

Debt ratio: 0.2%
Return on equity: 25.4%
Cash ($ mil.): 355
Current ratio: 2.50
Long-term debt ($ mil.): 2
No. of shares (mil.): 152
Dividends
Yield: 2.1%
Payout: 27.0%
Market value ($ mil.): 3,162

Stock History

NYSE: RHI

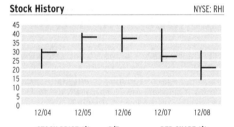

	STOCK PRICE ($) FY Close	P/E High/Low		PER SHARE ($) Earnings	Dividends	Book Value
12/08	20.82	18	9	1.63	0.44	6.48
12/07	27.04	23	13	1.81	0.40	6.48
12/06	37.12	27	18	1.65	0.32	6.87
12/05	37.89	29	18	1.36	0.28	6.39
12/04	29.43	39	26	0.79	0.18	6.00
Annual Growth	**(8.3%)**	—	—	**19.9%**	**25.0%**	**1.9%**

Rock-Tenn Company

A rock-solid reputation? Ten out of ten for effort? You betcha. Show Rock-Tenn a product, and it will provide the packaging for it. The company, one of North America's leading folding carton makers, produces packaging for food, paper goods, hardware, apparel, and other consumer goods. It uses recycled and virgin paperboard to make these products and also converts paperboard for use in book covers, furniture, and automotive components. Other products include specialty corrugated packaging and point-of-purchase displays. Rock-Tenn also sells recycled paperboard to other American firms. The company makes most of its sales in the US.

The company is pursuing a mixture of cost-cutting efforts and strategic acquisitions to build upon its core packaging products.

Like other paper manufacturers, Rock-Tenn was faced with increased raw material costs in mid-2007 that led the company to increase its per-ton prices on all of its paperboard products. The decision appeared to pay off, as Rock-Tenn reported record earnings in fiscal 2007 largely due to the higher pricing. Profits remained high into fiscal 2008, despite the economic downturn that took hold during the year.

The increase in raw material costs continued into 2008 and so did the company's price increases. However, it did not stop Rock-Tenn from dropping $851 million in cash to acquire Southern Container Corp., a New York-based private containerboard and corrugated packaging manufacturer. Southern Container operates a mill in Syracuse, New York, that has an annual capacity of 770,000 tons of recycled containerboard.

HISTORY

Former preacher Arthur Morris founded Rock-Tenn in 1936 as Southern Box Co., a folding carton maker. Acquisitions fueled the company's growth in the following years. During WWII it became Rock City Box Co. Morris' son-in-law, A. Worley Brown, was appointed CEO in 1967.

The company adopted its current name in 1973, after merging with Tennessee Paper Mills. Rock-Tenn bought Mead's recycled products unit in 1988 and began book cover production. Brad Currey, a banker who was recruited by Brown in 1976, became CEO in 1989.

Rock-Tenn bought a folding carton plant in Canada in 1993, and in 1994 the company went public. It acquired Olympic Packaging (folding cartons) and Alliance Display & Packaging (corrugated displays) in 1995. The company boosted its position as a leading maker of folding cartons in 1997 with its $414 million purchase of Waldorf Corporation, its largest acquisition to date. That year Rock-Tenn also bought two paperboard companies and formed RTS Packaging, its 65%-owned joint venture with Sonoco Products.

To cut costs and compensate for stagnant demand, Rock-Tenn closed several US plants in 1999. The following year CEO Brad Currey retired and was replaced by Jim Rubright, formerly an EVP at energy firm Sonat (El Paso Energy). Also in 2000 Rock-Tenn entered the gypsum paperboard liner business through a joint venture with Lafarge. In 2001 the company announced additional plant closings as demand for its products bottomed out.

In 2002 in a rebounding market Rock-Tenn bought point-of-purchase display and fixture maker Athena Industries, increasing annual sales by an estimated $12 million.

In 2003 Pactiv purchased Rock-Tenn's packaging business for about $60 million.

The next year Rock-Tenn acquired a corrugated sheet facility located in Athens, Alabama, from Menasha Packaging Company. That move was part of an effort to expand its geographic reach. In 2005 the company acquired pulp and packaging assets from Gulf States Paper (now The Westervelt Company).

EXECUTIVES

Chairman and CEO: James A. (Jim) Rubright, age 62
EVP, CFO, and Chief Administrative Officer:
 Steven C. Voorhees, age 54
VP and CIO: Paul W. Stecher
Chief Accounting Officer: A. Stephen Meadows, age 58
EVP Containerboard and Corrugated Packaging:
 Jim Porter Jr.
EVP: President and CEO, RTS: Richard E. (Dick) Steed
EVP and General Manager, Alliance Division:
 James L. Einstein, age 63
**EVP and General Manager, Corrugated Packaging
 Division, and Director:** Russell M. Currey, age 47
EVP and General Manager, Folding Carton Division:
 Michael E. (Mike) Kiepura, age 52
EVP and General Manager, Recycled Fiber Division:
 Erik Deadwyler
**EVP and General Manager, Mill Operations, Paperboard
 Division:** Thomas J. Garland
SVP, General Counsel, and Secretary:
 Robert B. McIntosh, age 51
SVP Health and Beauty: Pierre Beaudoin
SVP Integration: Mike Sheffield
VP and Treasurer: John Stakel
Auditors: Ernst & Young LLP

LOCATIONS

HQ: Rock-Tenn Company
 504 Thrasher St., Norcross, GA 30071
Phone: 770-448-2193   **Fax:** 678-291-7666
Web: www.rocktenn.com

PRODUCTS/OPERATIONS

2008 Sales

	$ mil.	% of total
Consumer packaging	1,533.3	54
Corrugated packaging	576.4	20
Specialty paperboard products	378.8	13
Merchandising displays	350.4	13
Total	**2,838.9**	**100**

Selected Products

Packaging products
 Folding cartons (for food items, hardware products,
  paper goods, and other items)
 Protective packaging (solid fiber partitions)

Paperboard
 100% recycled coated and uncoated grades
 Laminated paperboard (for book covers, book binders,
  and furniture products)

Specialty corrugated packaging and displays
 Corrugated packaging and sheet
 Point-of-purchase displays

COMPETITORS

Caraustar	Shorewood Packaging
Georgia-Pacific	Smurfit-Stone Container
Graphic Packaging	Sonoco Products
Green Bay Packaging	Temple-Inland
International Paper	

HISTORICAL FINANCIALS

Company Type: Public

Income Statement

FYE: September 30

	REVENUE ($ mil.)	NET INCOME ($ mil.)	NET PROFIT MARGIN	EMPLOYEES
9/08	2,838.9	81.8	2.9%	10,700
9/07	2,315.8	81.7	3.5%	9,300
9/06	2,138.1	28.7	1.3%	9,500
9/05	1,733.5	17.6	1.0%	9,600
9/04	1,581.3	17.6	1.1%	8,266
Annual Growth	**15.8%**	**46.8%**	**—**	**6.7%**

2008 Year-End Financials

Debt ratio: 225.9%   No. of shares (mil.): 39
Return on equity: 13.3%   Dividends
Cash ($ mil.): 53   Yield: 1.0%
Current ratio: 1.09   Payout: 18.7%
Long-term debt ($ mil.): 1,447   Market value ($ mil.): 1,543

Stock History   NYSE: RKT

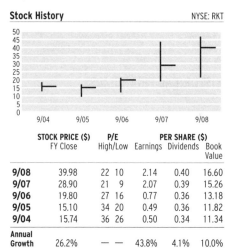

	STOCK PRICE ($) FY Close	P/E High/Low		PER SHARE ($) Earnings	Dividends	Book Value
9/08	39.98	22	10	2.14	0.40	16.60
9/07	28.90	21	9	2.07	0.39	15.26
9/06	19.80	27	16	0.77	0.36	13.18
9/05	15.10	34	20	0.49	0.36	11.82
9/04	15.74	36	26	0.50	0.34	11.34
Annual Growth	**26.2%**	**—**	**—**	**43.8%**	**4.1%**	**10.0%**

Rockwell Automation

Formerly a giant military contractor, Rockwell Automation is now rocking along as one of the world's largest industrial automation companies. The company's Control Products & Solutions unit makes industrial automation products, such as motor starters and contactors, relays, timers, signaling devices, and variable-speed drives. To complement its automation product offerings, Rockwell also offers factory management software. In 2007 the company sold most of the operations of its former power systems unit, which offered motors and motor repair services, as well as bearings, bushings, clutches, and brakes. Rockwell Automation makes half of its sales in the US.

Early in 2007 Rockwell sold its Dodge mechanical power transmission division, as well as the industrial motors unit of its Reliance Electric subsidiary to Baldor Electric for $1.8 billion. (Rockwell retained the rest of Reliance, which makes electrical drives.) These units made up most of the company's power systems unit, which previously accounted for about a fifth of Rockwell's revenue — that is, about a billion dollars.

Acquisitions are a key link to the company's growth. It acquired software makers Pavilion Technologies and Incuity Software in 2007 and 2008, respectively. Both deals helped strengthen its product portfolio in automation and enterprise intelligence software. Internationally, Rockwell Automation bought UK firm Industrial Control Services (ICS Triplex) in 2007 and Chinese engineering firm Xi'An Hengsheng Science & Technology Company in 2008 to help expand its Control Products & Solutions unit.

In 2009 the company announced an agreement to buy a majority of Canadian engineering firm Rutter Hinz Inc.'s North American assets for

an undisclosed price. The deal will add engineering expertise in industrial automation, process control, and power distribution, specifically for the oil and gas industry. Rutter Hinz is a subsidiary of Rutter Inc.

HISTORY

Rockwell Automation is the legacy of two early-20th-century entrepreneurs: Willard Rockwell and Clement Melville Keys. Rockwell gained control of Wisconsin Parts Company, an Oshkosh, Wisconsin, maker of automotive axles, in 1919. He went on to buy a number of industrial manufacturers, merging them in 1953 to create Rockwell Spring & Axle. Renamed Rockwell-Standard in 1958, it led the world in the production of mechanical automotive parts by 1967.

In 1928 Keys founded North American Aviation (NAA) as a holding company for his aviation interests. General Motors bought NAA in 1934 and named James Kindelberger as its president. The company moved in 1935 from Maryland to Inglewood, California, where it built military training planes.

NAA made more than 15,000 AT-6 trainers during WWII, and it produced the B-25 bomber and the P-51 fighter planes. By the end of the war, NAA had built nearly 43,000 aircraft, more than any other US manufacturer. NAA's sales plunged at the end of WWII. In 1948 GM took its subsidiary public; Kindelberger revitalized the company with new factories in California and Ohio. Major products included the F-86 (1948) and its successor, the F-100 (1953). NAA also produced the X-15 rocket plane (1959).

In the 1960s NAA built rocket engines and spacecraft for the Apollo program. NAA merged with Rockwell-Standard, creating North American Rockwell in 1967. The company adopted the Rockwell International name in 1973.

Rockwell won the contract for the B-1 bomber in 1970 and the space shuttle orbiter in 1972. The following year it bought Collins Radio, the backbone of its avionics segment. Rockwell briefly ventured into consumer goods, buying Admiral (appliances) in 1974 and selling it in 1979.

The company bought Allen-Bradley (industrial electronics) in 1985. Facing declining military-related revenues as B-1 production ended, Don Beall, who became CEO in 1988, spent billions on modernizing plants and research and development for Rockwell's electronics and graphics units. In 1989 Rockwell sold its Measurement & Flow Control Division and bought the Baker Perkins printing machinery business in the UK.

Rockwell sold its fiber-optic transmission equipment unit to Alcatel (now Alcatel-Lucent) in 1991. It acquired industrial automation supplier Sprecher + Schuh in 1993 and Reliance Electric (which was merged with Allen-Bradley) in 1995. The next year Rockwell sold its aerospace and defense divisions to Boeing for $3.2 billion and its Graphic Systems business to investment firm Stonington Partners. It also acquired integrated circuit maker Brooktree Corp. in 1996.

A 1997 federal court order forced Rockwell to pay Celeritas Technologies nearly $58 million for breaching patent protections and misappropriating trade secrets related to computer and cell phone communication technology. That year Rockwell acquired Hughes Electronics' airline passenger communications and entertainment systems unit (now The DIRECTV Group), and it spun off its automotive unit as Meritor Automotive (now ArvinMeritor). President Don Davis also became CEO in 1997.

Rockwell spun off its sluggish semiconductor business to shareholders (as Conexant Systems) in 1998 in a move to cut losses and focus on its faster-growing industrial automation operations.

In 1999 Rockwell moved its headquarters from California to Milwaukee, the base of its automation division. That year the company's Rockwell Collins unit bought out Kaiser Aerospace and Electronics' interest in their avionics joint venture, Flight Dynamics.

In 2000 the company announced plans to spin off its Rockwell Collins avionics and communications unit to its shareholders. The spinoff was completed in July 2001. Concurrently, Rockwell International changed its name to Rockwell Automation to reflect its new focus.

Between 1997 and 2001, the old Rockwell parted company with its aerospace and defense units (sold to Boeing), its automotive unit (spun off as Meritor Automotive, now ArvinMeritor), its semiconductor unit (spun off as Conexant Systems), its computer telephony (FirstPoint), and its large power transformer operations.

In 2004 Davis stepped down as CEO and was replaced by Keith Nosbusch, who also took on the chairman's role the following February. Nosbusch was in charge of Control Systems from 1998 until he was named president and CEO in February 2004.

EXECUTIVES

Chairman, President, and CEO: Keith D. Nosbusch, age 58
SVP and CFO: Theodore D. Crandall, age 53, $2,558,148 total compensation
SVP, Strategic Development and Communications: John D. Cohn, age 54
SVP, General Counsel, and Secretary: Douglas M. Hagerman
SVP Global Sales and Solutions: John P. McDermott
SVP Architecture and Software: Steven A. Eisenbrown
SVP Human Resources: Susan Schmitt
VP and General Tax Counsel: Kent G. Coppins
VP and Controller: David M. Dorgan
VP and Chief Intellectual Property Counsel: John M. Miller
VP and General Auditor: A. Lawrence Stuever
VP Customer Support and Maintenance: Mike Laszkiewicz
VP and General Manager, Manufacturing and Process Solutions Business: Terry Gebert
President, Europe, Middle East, and Africa: Jordi Andreu
Head, Control Products and Solutions: Robert A. Ruff
President, Asia-Pacific: Keiran Coulton
Investor Relations: Rondi Rohr-Dralle
Media Relations: John Bernaden
Auditors: Deloitte & Touche LLP

LOCATIONS

HQ: Rockwell Automation, Inc.
1201 S. 2nd St., Milwaukee, WI 53204
Phone: 414-382-2000   **Fax:** 414-382-4444
Web: www.rockwellautomation.com

2008 Sales

	$ mil.	% of total
Americas		
US	2,850.8	50
Latin America	414.4	7
Canada	396.4	7
Europe, Middle East & Africa	1,319.0	23
Asia/Pacific	717.2	13
Total	**5,697.8**	**100**

PRODUCTS/OPERATIONS

2008 Sales

	$ mil.	% of total
Control Products & Solutions	3,278.1	58
Architecture & Software	2,419.7	42
Total	**5,697.8**	**100**

Selected Products and Services

Condition sensors
Drive systems
Motion control systems
Motor control centers
Motor starters and contactors
Pushbuttons
Relays and timers
Signaling devices
Software
Termination and protection devices
Variable-speed drives

COMPETITORS

ABB	Metso
Baldor Electric	Mitsubishi Corp.
Danaher	OMRON
Dematic GmbH	RBS Global
Eaton	Samsung Group
Emerson Electric	Schneider Electric
GE Fanuc Automation	Siemens AG
Hitachi	Toshiba
Honeywell ACS	Weiss Instrument
Invensys	

HISTORICAL FINANCIALS

Company Type: Public

Income Statement

FYE: September 30

	REVENUE ($ mil.)	NET INCOME ($ mil.)	NET PROFIT MARGIN	EMPLOYEES
9/08	5,697.8	577.6	10.1%	21,000
9/07	5,003.9	1,487.8	29.7%	20,000
9/06	5,561.4	625.1	11.2%	23,000
9/05	5,003.2	540.0	10.8%	21,000
9/04	4,411.1	414.9	9.4%	21,000
Annual Growth	**6.6%**	**8.6%**	**—**	**0.0%**

2008 Year-End Financials

Debt ratio: 53.6%
Return on equity: 33.7%
Cash ($ mil.): 582
Current ratio: 1.87
Long-term debt ($ mil.): 904
No. of shares (mil.): 142
Dividends
  Yield: 3.1%
  Payout: 29.7%
Market value ($ mil.): 5,301

Stock History

NYSE: ROK

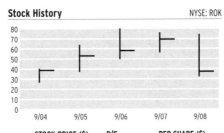

	STOCK PRICE ($) FY Close	P/E High/Low		PER SHARE ($) Earnings	Dividends	Book Value
9/08	37.34	19	8	3.90	1.16	11.90
9/07	69.51	8	6	9.23	1.16	12.28
9/06	58.10	24	15	3.37	0.90	13.51
9/05	52.90	22	13	2.88	0.78	11.62
9/04	38.70	18	13	2.17	0.66	13.11
Annual Growth	**(0.9%)**	**—**	**—**	**15.8%**	**15.1%**	**(2.4%)**

Roper Industries

"Control, pump, scan, authorize, and analyze" could be Roper Industries' motto. The company designs, manufactures, and distributes high-tech industrial equipment and analytical instruments for niche markets involving radio frequency (RF) applications, water, energy, research and medical, education, and security. Roper divides its products into four business segments: Energy Systems and Controls, Scientific and Industrial Imaging Products and Software, Industrial Technology Products, and RF Products and Services. The company carefully selects global end markets needing value-added, engineered products. It is typically a market leader, or a competitive alternative to the leader.

Roper's strategy focuses on accelerating its growth by funding new product introductions through acquisitions that promise increased end-market exposure. Internal operating performance is raised simultaneously through new product research and development, and development of new product applications for existing customers. Roper's customer base is expanded by aggressive distribution, selling other products through existing channels, and entering adjacent markets.

In 2008 the company acquired The CBORD Group for $375 million. CBORD makes electronic ID and debit cards for colleges and universities, hospitals, supermarkets, and other businesses and institutions. The acquisition extends the company's RF Technology interests beyond transportation and water utilities to health care and education end-markets.

The purchase total of all other acquisitions in 2008 ran $331 million, with the RF Technology segment receiving the biggest boost with Getloaded.com, Technolog, and Horizon Software. Horizon Software builds upon the capabilities already brought in by CBORD. A provider of software, Horizon captures corporate dining, health care, K-12 education, military, and senior living markets. The two other deals (Tech-Pro and Chalwyn) grow the company's Energy Systems and Controls segment by providing industrial test instruments and software and air shut-off valves.

T. Rowe Price owns about 11% of Roper Industries. Capital World Investors holds around 6% of the company. Franklin Resources has an equity stake of approximately 5%.

HISTORY

George Roper founded the company in 1919 in Rockford, Illinois, to make gas stoves and gear pumps. In the late 1950s the stove works were spun off to Sears as the Roper Corporation, and the pump-making operations were moved to Georgia. Roper was a public company until a 1981 LBO. UK-born Derrick Key, who joined Roper in 1982, became CEO in 1991. The company went public again the next year as Roper Industries.

During the 1990s Roper grew by acquisitions both at home and abroad. However, it gained entry into Eastern Europe in 1993 by winning a seven-year contract worth $350 million with Russian gas czar OAO Gazprom to install advanced control systems across Russia's vast pipeline system.

The company added digital-imaging and analytical systems for electron microscopes in

1996 by purchasing Gatan International, a California company with branches in Germany and the UK. Roper's 1997 purchases included Industrial Data Systems (leak-testing equipment, Utah); Petrotech (systems integration for fluid-control products; Louisiana, with an Indonesian unit); and Princeton Instruments (spectral and imaging cameras; New Jersey, with locations in France and the UK).

Roper expanded its digital-imaging line in 1998 by acquiring Photometrics, Ltd. (digital cameras and detectors) and PMC/Beta Limited (vibration sensing and control equipment). Roper's bid to buy Leach Holding fell through impeding its effort to boost its industrial components offerings. In 1999 it bought Varlen's petroleum analysis instrumentation unit and Eastman Kodak's motion analysis operations (digital video equipment).

Roper's focus on providing high-margin products to niche markets spurred growth through acquisitions that included Eastman Kodak's high-speed and high-resolution digital video equipment unit, as well as makers of testing equipment for the petroleum industry. And, in its largest acquisition to date, the company bought Struers Holdings' two operating units, which provided preparation equipment used in quality inspection (Struers A/S), and material shaping equipment used to make semiconductors and optoelectronics (Logitech).

Roper didn't rest after acquiring Hansen Technologies and adding Streurs' operating units in 2001; in 2002 it spent about $83 million on Zetec (industrial testing equipment), Duncan Technologies (industrial digital cameras), AiCambridge/"Qualitek" (leak detection equipment), Quantitative Imaging (industrial and scientific digital cameras), and Definitive Imaging (image analysis software). At the same time, however, Roper exited some of its Petrotech businesses and was hit by the downturn in the semiconductor industry, the oil and gas exploration markets, and the generally weak economy.

At the end of 2003 Roper acquired Neptune Technology Group Holdings (meter-reading technology) for $475 million. Expanding beyond its core controls, pumps, and analytical tools businesses, Roper acquired radio-frequency identification technology and related services provider TransCore Holdings for $597 million in 2004.

In 2005 the company purchased Louisville, Colorado-based security applications technologies provider Inovonics Wireless Corporation for $45 million. Roper strengthened its presence in the medical imaging market in 2005 by acquiring Kalona, Iowa-based CIVCO Medical Instruments Co., Inc., a supplier of specialized medical products, from KRG Capital Partners, LLC. It also bought Orange City, Iowa-based MEDTEC, Inc., a maker of technology used in diagnosing and treating cancer, for about $150 million, to fold into its CIVCO operations.

In late 2006 the company acquired Dynisco LLC for $243 million from the Audax Group, a private equity investment firm. Also known as Dynisco Instruments, the business made pressure and temperature measurement and control instruments, primarily for the plastics industry, with applications in life sciences. In recent years Dynisco had acquired Alpha Technologies and Viatran Corp., suppliers of analytical instruments and sensors for various applications. Dynisco became part of Roper's Energy Systems and Controls segment.

EXECUTIVES

Chairman, President, and CEO: Brian D. Jellison, age 63, $17,212,476 total compensation
VP and CFO: John Humphrey, age 43, $3,124,778 total compensation
VP Instrumentation: Nigel W. (Will) Crocker, age 54
VP, Energy Systems and Controls: Timothy J. Winfrey, age 48, $1,619,327 total compensation
VP, Scientific and Industrial Imaging: Benjamin W. (Ben) Wood, age 48, $1,394,336 total compensation
VP, General Counsel and Secretary: David B. Liner, age 53, $1,372,649 total compensation
VP and Controller: Paul J. Soni
Auditors: PricewaterhouseCoopers LLP

LOCATIONS

HQ: Roper Industries, Inc.
6901 Professional Pkwy. E., Ste. 200, Sarasota, FL 34240
Phone: 941-556-2601 **Fax:** 941-556-2670
Web: www.roperind.com

2008 Sales

	$ mil.	% of total
US	1,709.9	75
Other countries	596.5	25
Total	**2,306.4**	**100**

PRODUCTS/OPERATIONS

2008 Sales

	$ mil.	% of total
Industrial Technology	687.6	30
RF Technology	695.0	30
Energy Systems & Controls	548.2	24
Scientific & Industrial Imaging	375.6	16
Total	**2,306.4**	**100**

COMPETITORS

ABB
Agilent Technologies
Ampco-Pittsburgh
Cameron International
CEM
CIRCOR International
Coherent, Inc.
Colfax
Curtiss-Wright
DXP Enterprises
Emerson Electric
Entegris
Flowserve
Gorman-Rupp
Halliburton
Hamilton Sundstrand
Haskel
Honeywell International
IBM Software
IDEX
IMI plc
Itron
ITT Corp.
Microsoft
Newport Corp.
Oracle
Parker Hannifin
PerkinElmer
Precision Castparts
Robbins & Myers
Rotork
Schneider Electric
SpiraxSarco
SPX
Sumitomo Electric
Thermo Fisher Scientific
Transcat
Tuthill
Tyco
Varian

HISTORICAL FINANCIALS

Company Type: Public

Income Statement

FYE: December 31

	REVENUE ($ mil.)	NET INCOME ($ mil.)	NET PROFIT MARGIN	EMPLOYEES
12/08	2,306.4	286.5	12.4%	7,900
12/07	2,102.0	250.0	11.9%	7,100
12/06	1,700.7	193.3	11.4%	6,900
12/05	1,453.7	153.2	10.5%	6,000
12/04	969.8	93.9	9.7%	5,600
Annual Growth	**24.2%**	**32.2%**	**—**	**9.0%**

2008 Year-End Financials

Debt ratio: 51.6%
Return on equity: 15.1%
Cash ($ mil.): 178
Current ratio: 1.39
Long-term debt ($ mil.): 1,034

No. of shares (mil.): 91
Dividends
Yield: 0.9%
Payout: 12.1%
Market value ($ mil.): 3,943

Stock History

NYSE: ROP

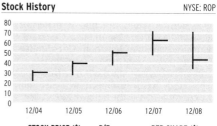

	STOCK PRICE ($) FY Close	P/E High/Low	Earnings	Dividends	Book Value
12/08	43.41	23 11	3.06	0.37	22.06
12/07	62.54	26 18	2.68	0.26	19.71
12/06	50.24	24 18	2.13	0.24	16.37
12/05	39.51	24 16	1.74	0.21	13.76
12/04	30.39	26 18	1.24	0.19	12.27
Annual Growth	**9.3%**	**— —**	**25.3%**	**18.1%**	**15.8%**

Ross Stores

Ross wants to let you dress (and lots more) for less. The #2 off-price apparel retailer (behind TJX Cos.) operates more than 950 Ross Dress for Less and dd's DISCOUNTS stores that sell mostly close-out merchandise, including men's, women's, and children's clothing, at prices well below those of department and specialty stores. While apparel accounts for more than 50% of sales, the stores also sell small furnishings, toys and games, luggage, and gourmet foods in select stores. Featuring the Ross "Dress for Less" trademark, the chain targets 18- to 54-year-old white-collar shoppers from primarily middle-income households. Ross stores are located in strip malls in 27 states, mostly in the western US, and Guam.

About a quarter of Ross Stores are in California, where discount department store operator Kohl's is expanding rapidly and the chain is poised to benefit from the demise of discounter Mervyn's.

The fast-growing retailer added about 160 stores in 2008 and 2007, and doubled the number of dd's DISCOUNTS locations it operates. Going forward, it plans to continue to open both new Ross and dd's DISCOUNTS stores, although the company has reduced its 2009 budget for capital expenditures somewhat.

Ross Stores' off-price business model has served the company well as the US economy entered a deep recession and consumers searched for bargains.

To boost its relationships with suppliers, Ross does not require them to provide markdown/promotional allowances or return privileges. This, combined with opportunistic purchases (closeouts such as manufacturer overruns and canceled orders), allows the company to obtain large discounts on merchandise. As a result, Ross Stores' customers typically pay 20% to 60% less than department and specialty store prices. Ross holds down costs by offering minimal service and few frills inside its stores. Other items Ross sells at a discount include accessories, footwear, fragrances, and bed and bath items.

Digging deeper into the discount apparel market, Ross Stores launched dd's DISCOUNTS in California in 2004. The ultra-low-price spinoff, which offers brand-name apparel at a 20%-70% discount, has since grown to number more than 50 locations in four states. The 25,000-sq.-ft. stores are located in strip shopping centers in urban and suburban neighborhoods.

HISTORY

In 1957 the Ross family founded Ross Stores and opened its first junior department store; by 1982 there were six of the stores in the San Francisco area. That year two retailing veterans, Stuart Moldaw (founder of Country Casuals and The Athletic Shoe Factory) and Donald Rowlett (creator of Woolworth's off-price subsidiary, J. Brannam), led the acquisition of the company. Moldaw (chairman) and Rowlett (president) wanted to create an off-price chain in California, where — despite the success such endeavors were having in the rest of the country — such stores were largely absent. The duo intended to establish a foothold by saturating California markets before competitors muddied the waters.

They restocked the stores with brand-name men's, women's, and children's apparel, shoes, accessories, and domestics merchandise at reduced prices. Before the end of 1982, they opened two more Ross "Dress for Less" stores; the next year 18 more were added, including the chain's first non-California store, in Reno, Nevada (much of the chain's expansion came through the acquisition of existing strip mall stores). Another 40 stores were added in 1984.

The company went public in 1985 to help fund its expansion and extended its reach to include Colorado, Florida, Georgia, New Mexico, and Oregon; that year it opened 41 stores. In 1986, 39 new stores were opened, including locations in Maryland, North Carolina, and Virginia, though the company was forced to close 25 unprofitable stores, primarily in recession-hammered Texas and Oklahoma. Ross lost more than $41 million for the year, and the honeymoon was over.

Rowlett resigned in 1987, and company veteran Norman Ferber was soon named CEO. Ross opened only 11 stores that year, all of which were located in markets the company had already broached. It also decided to focus its expansion efforts in three markets: the West Coast; the Washington, DC, area; and Florida. On the merchandise side, housewares were dropped and cosmetics, fragrances, and high-end clothing were

added. Ross returned to the black in 1987, posting an $11 million profit. The company continued refining its merchandising strategy, and by 1989 it had more than 150 stores, making it one of the largest off-price retailers.

Ross opened 72 stores between 1990 and 1992, bringing its total to more than 220 stores as sales passed the $1 billion mark. Ferber became chairman in 1993 and continued to focus the company on existing markets. The chain grew to more than 290 stores by the end of 1995. VP Michael Balmuth was named CEO the next year.

By 1998 the company's buying department had more than tripled in size, allowing it to have buyers in the right place at the right time to take advantage of buying opportunities. The non-apparel business tripled during the same time, both keys to the retailer's success. In 1998 Ross added fine jewelry, maternity wear, sporting goods, small furnishings, and educational toys to its list of product offerings. Ross opened 30 stores in 1999; its 34 openings in 2000 included its first non-US store in Guam.

In 2001 the company entered new markets in Georgia, Montana, North Carolina, South Carolina, and Wyoming, and opened new stores in existing markets, for a total of 45 new stores.

In 2002 Ross opened 60 new stores and closed five others, followed in 2003 by 61 new stores, some of which were in new markets such as Louisiana and Tennessee.

In August 2004 Ross opened its first three dd's DISCOUNTS stores in Vallejo, San Leandro, and Fresno, California. The retailer moved its headquarters from Newark, California, to Pleasanton in mid-2004 and then sold the Newark property for about $17 million.

In 2005 the company opened 10 dd's DISCOUNTS stores and about 75 Ross stores. Ross Stores also purchased a 685,000-sq. ft. warehouse in Moreno Valley, California, that year.

The retailer's deal with supermarket operator Albertsons, inked in late 2006, fueled its 2007 expansion plans and secured 46 Albertsons stores located in Arizona, California, Colorado, Florida, Oklahoma, and Texas. dd's DISCOUNTS expanded beyond California in 2007, with its first stores in Arizona, Florida, and Texas.

EXECUTIVES

Chairman: Norman A. Ferber, age 60
Vice Chairman, President, and CEO:
 Michael A. Balmuth, age 58,
 $8,208,732 total compensation
EVP and COO: Gary L. Cribb, age 44
SVP and CFO: John G. Call, age 50,
 $1,236,418 total compensation
Group SVP Supply Chain and CIO:
 Michael K. (Mike) Kobayashi
EVP and Chief Administrative Officer:
 Michael B. O'Sullivan, age 45,
 $2,271,034 total compensation
EVP Property Development, Construction, and Store Design: James S. Fassio, age 54
EVP Merchandising: Barbara Rentler, age 51,
 $2,956,088 total compensation
EVP Merchandising: Lisa Panattoni, age 46,
 $2,677,400 total compensation
SVP Supply Chain: Michael L. Wilson
SVP Human Resources: D. Jane Marvin
SVP and General Counsel: Mark LeHocky
SVP Merchandise Control: Art Roth
SVP Strategy, Marketing, Store Planning, and Allocations: Ken Caruana
SVP Planning: Lisa Albani
Senior Director Investor Relations: Bobbi Chaville
Auditors: Deloitte & Touche LLP

LOCATIONS

HQ: Ross Stores, Inc.
 4440 Rosewood Dr., Pleasanton, CA 94588
Phone: 925-965-4400
Web: www.rossstores.com

2009 Stores

	No.
US	
California	247
Texas	143
Florida	114
Arizona	52
Georgia	44
North Carolina	32
Virginia	30
Pennsylvania	29
Washington	29
Colorado	27
Oregon	25
Tennessee	24
South Carolina	20
Nevada	19
Alabama	17
Maryland	17
Oklahoma	16
Utah	12
Hawaii	11
Louisiana	10
Idaho	9
New Jersey	9
Montana	6
Mississippi	5
New Mexico	5
Wyoming	2
Delaware	1
Guam	1
Total	**956**

PRODUCTS/OPERATIONS

2009 Stores

	No.
Ross Dress for Less	904
dd's DISCOUNTS	52
Total	**956**

2009 Sales

	% of total
Women's apparel	32
Home accents, bed & bath	23
Men's apparel	14
Fine jewelry, accessories, lingerie & fragrances	12
Shoes	10
Children's apparel	9
Total	**100**

Selected Merchandise

Bed and bath
Children's apparel
Cookware
Educational toys
Fine jewelry
Fragrances
Gourmet foods
Home accents
Ladies' apparel
 Accessories
 Dresses
 Junior
 Lingerie
 Maternity
 Misses sportswear
 Petites
 Women's World
Luggage
Men's apparel
 Traditional men's
 Young men's
Shoes
Small electronics
Small furnishings
Sporting goods and exercise equipment

COMPETITORS

Big Lots	J. C. Penney
Burlington Coat Factory	Kmart
Cato	Kohl's
Charming Shoppes	Men's Wearhouse
Dress Barn	Sears
Family Dollar Stores	Target
Filene's Basement	TJX Companies
Fred's	Wal-Mart

HISTORICAL FINANCIALS

Company Type: Public

Income Statement

FYE: Saturday nearest January 31

	REVENUE ($ mil.)	NET INCOME ($ mil.)	NET PROFIT MARGIN	EMPLOYEES
1/09	6,486.1	305.4	4.7%	40,000
1/08	5,975.2	261.1	4.4%	39,100
1/07	5,570.2	241.6	4.3%	35,800
1/06	4,944.2	199.6	4.0%	33,200
1/05	4,240.0	169.9	4.0%	30,100
Annual Growth	11.2%	15.8%	—	7.4%

2009 Year-End Financials

Debt ratio: 15.1%	No. of shares (mil.): 127
Return on equity: 31.1%	Dividends
Cash ($ mil.): 321	Yield: 1.3%
Current ratio: 1.38	Payout: 16.3%
Long-term debt ($ mil.): 150	Market value ($ mil.): 3,726

Stock History

NASDAQ (GS): ROST

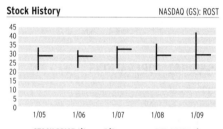

	45 40 35 30 25 20 15 10 5 0
	1/05 1/06 1/07 1/08 1/09

	STOCK PRICE ($) FY Close	P/E High/Low	PER SHARE ($) Earnings	Dividends	Book Value
1/09	29.42	18 9	2.33	0.38	7.87
1/08	29.15	19 11	1.90	0.30	7.66
1/07	32.39	20 13	1.70	0.24	7.18
1/06	28.50	23 16	1.36	0.21	6.60
1/05	28.62	29 19	1.13	0.17	6.04
Annual Growth	0.7%	— —	19.8%	22.3%	6.8%

Rowan Companies

Where does a gorilla drill for oil? Anywhere it wants if it is one of Rowan Companies' *Gorilla*-class heavy-duty offshore drilling rigs. Rowan performs contract drilling of oil and gas wells. Its fleet consists of 22 jack-up rigs and 32 land drilling rigs. The company performs contract drilling primarily in the Middle East, Texas, the Gulf of Mexico, and in the North Sea. Rowan plans to maintain its competitive edge by beefing up its current fleet of equipment. Subsidiary LeTourneau Technologies operates a mini-steel mill and manufactures heavy equipment including front-end loaders, log stackers, and gantry cranes. LeTourneau's marine group builds offshore jack-up drilling rigs.

Rowan Companies' combination of contract drilling and an in-house manufacturing company that supplies rigs, gives the company a distinct edge over its drilling rivals, most of which have to engage third-party manufacturers to supply its rigs.

To diversify its fleet, the company has added *Tarzan*-class jack-up rigs designed for deep drilling in shallow water on the outer continental shelf of the Gulf of Mexico. Its fourth *Tarzan*-class rig was completed in 2008.

In 2008 the company secured a term drilling contract for offshore Saudi Arabia. That year Saudi Aramco accounted for 15% of revenues.

HISTORY

Rowan Drilling Company was founded in 1923 as a contract drilling business. In 1947 it incorporated as Rowan Companies. Twenty years later Rowan acquired Era Aviation, a small, Alaska-based helicopter company. Rowan began to concentrate on jack-up rigs in 1970. Two years later Bob Palmer, who had started with the company in 1953 as a roughneck, became president.

The boom times for the oil industry went bust in the mid-1980s, and so did Rowan's net income. In 1991 Era acquired 49% of KLM Helikopters, a subsidiary of KLM Airlines. The company bought Marathon LeTourneau from General Cable Corp. in 1994 and rechristened it LeTourneau. In 1996 Rowan sold its Argentine drilling subsidiary. Two years later Era dumped its 49% stake in KLM ERA Helicopters to facilitate KLM's exit from the helicopter business.

With oil prices rebounding from a slump, the company had most of its 15 Gulf of Mexico rigs hired out by the end of 1999, up from only one-third in action earlier in the year. In 2000 the company relocated its rigs remaining in the North Sea to the Gulf of Mexico and added a new rig, the *Gorilla VI* super-jack-up, to its drilling fleet.

The company reached 97% utilization of its total offshore fleet in 2001.

In 2002 Rowan expanded its manufacturing capacity with the acquisition of assets from Oilfield-Electric-Marine, and Industrial Logic Systems. That year it also won a $175 million settlement from BP as part of resolving a 3-year dispute over a Rowan *Gorilla*-class drilling rig contract.

Refocusing on its core businesses, in 2005 Rowan sold its Era Aviation aircraft services subsidiary to Seacor Holdings for $118 million.

EXECUTIVES

Chairman: Henry E. (Jack) Lentz Jr., age 64
President, CEO, and Director: W. Matthew (Matt) Ralls, age 59
VP Finance and CFO: William H. Wells, age 46, $1,661,779 total compensation
EVP Business Development: Mark A. Keller, age 56, $2,595,445 total compensation
EVP Legal: John L. Buvens, age 53, $1,801,573 total compensation
EVP Drilling Operations: David P. Russell, age 47, $3,185,821 total compensation
VP Manufacturing; President and CEO, LeTourneau Technologies: Dan C. Eckerman, age 61
VP Health, Safety, and Environmental Affairs: Barbara Carroll, age 54
VP Engineering: Michael J. (Mike) Dowdy, age 49
VP Human Resources: Terry D. Woodall, age 60
VP Strategic Planning: Kevin Bartol, age 49
Director Investor Relations: Suzanne M. McLeod
Corporate Secretary and Special Assistant to the CEO: Melanie M. Trent, age 44
Controller: Gregory M. (Greg) Hatfield, age 39
Compliance Officer: George C. Jones, age 43
Auditors: Deloitte & Touche LLP

LOCATIONS

HQ: Rowan Companies, Inc.
2800 Post Oak Blvd., Ste. 5450, Houston, TX 77056
Phone: 713-621-7800   **Fax:** 713-960-7660
Web: www.rowancompanies.com

2008 Sales

	$ mil.	% of total
US	1,331.1	60
Middle East	486.3	22
Europe	166.5	8
West Africa	117.5	5
Australia	69.1	3
Other regions	42.2	2
Total	**2,212.7**	**100**

PRODUCTS/OPERATIONS

2008 Sales

	$ mil.	% of total
Drilling services	1,451.6	66
Manufacturing sales & services	761.1	34
Total	**2,212.7**	**100**

Major Subsidiary

LeTourneau Technologies, Inc.

COMPETITORS

Acergy	Nucor
Diamond Offshore	Oshkosh Truck
ENSCO	Precision Drilling
Helmerich & Payne	Pride International
Nabors Industries	Terex
Noble	Transocean Inc.

HISTORICAL FINANCIALS

Company Type: Public

Income Statement

FYE: December 31

	REVENUE ($ mil.)	NET INCOME ($ mil.)	NET PROFIT MARGIN	EMPLOYEES
12/08	2,212.7	427.6	19.3%	6,023
12/07	2,095.0	483.8	23.1%	5,704
12/06	1,510.7	320.9	21.2%	5,160
12/05	1,068.8	229.8	21.5%	4,577
12/04	708.5	(43.6)	—	4,386
Annual Growth	32.9%	—	—	8.3%

2008 Year-End Financials

Debt ratio: 13.4%	No. of shares (mil.): 114
Return on equity: 17.1%	Dividends
Cash ($ mil.): 222	Yield: 2.5%
Current ratio: 1.84	Payout: 10.6%
Long-term debt ($ mil.): 356	Market value ($ mil.): 1,809

Stock History

NYSE: RDC

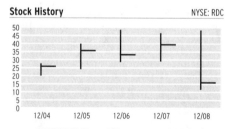

	50 45 40 35 30 25 20 15 10 5 0
	12/04 12/05 12/06 12/07 12/08

	STOCK PRICE ($) FY Close	P/E High/Low	PER SHARE ($) Earnings	Dividends	Book Value
12/08	15.90	13 3	3.77	0.40	23.38
12/07	39.46	11 7	4.31	0.40	20.65
12/06	33.20	17 10	2.85	0.30	16.48
12/05	35.64	19 12	2.08	0.00	14.24
12/04	25.90	— —	(0.01)	0.00	12.39
Annual Growth	(11.5%)	— —	—	—	17.2%

Royal Caribbean Cruises

Royal Caribbean Cruises does not practice berth control. The world's second-largest cruise line (behind the combined Carnival and Carnival plc behemoth), the company operates about 35 ships with more than 78,000 berths overall. Its three main cruise brands, Royal Caribbean International, Celebrity Cruises, and Pullmantur Cruises, carry about 4 million passengers a year to about 425 ports, including ones in Alaska, Asia, Australia, Canada, the Caribbean, Latin America, and Europe. Other brands include Azamara Cruises and CDF Croisières de France. In addition, Royal Caribbean operates land-based tours and expeditions through Royal Celebrity Tours.

Battered in 2008 by the recession and high fuel prices, Royal Caribbean is seeking to stem losses by diversifying its customer base in international markets.

In 2008 the company expanded in the Asian, European, Latin American, and Caribbean markets with additional cruises from the UK, Spain, and Italy as well as new routes from Australia, New Zealand, the South Pacific, Panama, Singapore, and Shanghai. Royal Caribbean entered a joint venture with TUI AG in 2008 to form TUI Cruises, which will serve the growing German cruise market. Operations began in mid-2009.

Despite tough financial times, Royal Caribbean International is going full steam ahead in adding two massive new ships to its line, *Oasis of the Seas* and *Allure of the Seas*. Touted as the world's largest cruise ships, the gigantic vessels will be 220,000 gross tons, have 5,400 berths, span 16 decks, and include themed "neighborhood" areas and amphitheaters. *Oasis of the Seas* will start service to the eastern Caribbean in late 2009. The company hasn't announced where *Allure of the Seas* will sail when it begins service in late 2010.

In 2008 Royal Caribbean sold its stake in Island Cruises, a joint venture with UK-based tour operator TUI Travel, to First Choice Holidays Ltd., a subsidiary of TUI. Island Cruises operates two vessels, one of which belongs to Royal Caribbean. That vessel, *Island Star*, will be redeployed to Pullmantur, renamed *Pacific Dream*, and will serve the expanding Latin American market.

Co-founder Arne Wilhelmsen owns about 20% of Royal Caribbean and the Pritzker family owns about 16%.

HISTORY

When Arne Wilhelmsen (director) and Edwin Stephan (former vice chairman) helped found Royal Caribbean Cruise Lines in 1969, they created an entire industry. Royal Caribbean's first vessel, *Song of Norway*, (1970) touted endless sun decks and glass-walled dining rooms, initiating the concept of year-round cruising. Stephan, inspired by Seattle's Space Needle and its revolving restaurant, designed a cocktail lounge cantilevered from the ship's smokestack. The panoramic observation point became the signature of Royal Caribbean vessels. The company operated three ships during the 1970s; by 1972 it was the largest Caribbean cruise line.

Through the 1970s and early 1980s, it launched larger and more modern cruise ships and introduced air/sea inclusive vacations, fitness programs, and other industry firsts. Royal Caribbean moved out of the Caribbean for the first time in 1985 with Bermuda cruises from New York. The company bought Admiral Cruises in 1988 (sold in 1992, though it retained rights to the name) and Richard Fain, Admiral's chairman, became chairman and CEO of Royal Caribbean. With the goal of turning the company from a regional party fleet into an international vacation powerhouse, he expanded the company's fleet by four vessels in four years, including the world's first megaship, *Sovereign of the Seas*, with 2,250 berths.

In 1990 Royal Caribbean broadened its destination list to include Mexico, Alaska, and Europe. To enhance its relationship with the travel agents who booked its cruises, Royal Caribbean developed the industry's first computerized booking system. However, a fire that year severely damaged one of its under-construction vessels. Unstable earnings and ship construction and refurbishing costs left Royal Caribbean with almost $1 billion in long-term debt by 1992; the company went public in 1993 to ease its burden.

Royal Caribbean's next class of vessels, introduced in 1995, included high-tech movie theaters, shopping malls, and other accoutrements. In 1996 the company changed its name from Royal Caribbean Cruise Lines to Royal Caribbean Cruises Ltd., in order to reflect its growing breadth.

In 1997 the company acquired Celebrity Cruise Lines and its four working ships at a cost of $1.3 billion. (Rival Carnival had earlier bid $525 million for Celebrity.) In 1998 Royal Caribbean pleaded guilty to obstruction of justice in federal court for covering up its illegal dumping of oil off the coasts of Florida and Puerto Rico between 1990 and 1994. The company agreed to pay a $9 million fine and was put on probation for five years.

In 1999 the company was again indicted on oil-dumping charges and eventually pleaded guilty to 21 felony counts. It was slapped with a record $18 million fine. The following year it agreed to pay the State of Alaska another $3.3 million to settle similar charges. In 2001 it began offering land-based tours in Alaska through Royal Celebrity Tours.

In an effort to trim costs and better compete with airlines, Royal Caribbean announced that year that it would halve the commissions paid to travel agents for the air-travel part of cruise bookings. In 2002 the company launched Island Cruises, a joint venture with First Choice Holidays. (First Choice Holidays became TUI Travel after it was acquired by TUI in 2007.)

Royal Caribbean hoped to reduce administrative costs and increase buying power by merging with P&O Princess Cruises, but P&O dropped the deal in favor of an acquisition by Carnival in 2003.

Celebrity Xpeditions (Celebrity Cruises' limited-capacity cruise line) debuted in 2004, offering service to the Galapagos Islands.

One of the largest cruise ships in the world, *Freedom of the Seas*, set sail from England in mid-2006. The Royal Caribbean ship holds more than 3,600 guests. Also that year, Royal Caribbean expanded its tour operations in Spain with the $900 million purchase of the Pullmantur line.

EXECUTIVES

Chairman and CEO: Richard D. Fain, age 61, $5,781,241 total compensation
EVP and CFO: Brian J. Rice, age 50, $1,799,079 total compensation
CIO: Mike Sutten
EVP Maritime: Harri U. Kulovaara, age 56, $1,490,009 total compensation
SVP Marketing, Celebrity and Azamara Cruises: Wayne W. Wielgus
SVP Marine Operations, Royal Caribbean International: William S. Wright
SVP Hotel Operations, Royal Caribbean International: Lisa Bauer, age 35
SVP International, Royal Caribbean International: Michael Bayley
SVP Sales, Royal Caribbean International: Vicki Freed
VP Human Resources: Maria Del Busto
VP, General Counsel, and Corporate Secretary: Bradley Stein
VP and Corporate Controller: Henry J. Pujol, age 41
VP Investor Relations: Ian Bailey
President and CEO, Celebrity Cruises: Daniel J. (Dan) Hanrahan, age 51, $1,837,924 total compensation
President, Royal Celebrity Tours: Craig S. Milan
President and CEO, Royal Caribbean International: Adam M. Goldstein, age 49, $3,004,541 total compensation
President and CEO, Pullmantur: Gonzalo Chico Barbier, age 48
President, ABREMAR: Ricardo Amaral
President and CEO, Azamara Cruises: Larry Pimentel
Auditors: PricewaterhouseCoopers LLP

LOCATIONS

HQ: Royal Caribbean Cruises Ltd.
   1050 Caribbean Way, Miami, FL 33132
Phone: 305-539-6000   **Fax:** 305-539-0562
Web: www.royalcaribbean.com

2008 Passenger Ticket Sales

	% of total
US	60
Other countries	40
Total	**100**

PRODUCTS/OPERATIONS

2008 Sales

	$ mil.	% of total
Passenger tickets	4,730.3	72
Onboard & other	1,802.2	28
Total	**6,532.5**	**100**

Selected Cruise Ships

Azamara Cruises
  Journey (2004; Europe and South America; 700 berths)
  Quest (2006; Asia, Caribbean, Europe, and Panama Canal; 700 berths)
CDF Croisières de France
  Bleu de France (2005; Caribbean and Mediterranean; 750 berths)
Celebrity Cruises
  Century (1995; Caribbean and Europe; 1,800 berths)
  Constellation (2002; Caribbean, Europe, and Canada/New England; 2,050 berths)
  Galaxy (1996; Southern Caribbean and Europe; 1,850 berths)
  Infinity (2001; Hawaii, Alaska, Panama Canal, and South America; 2,050 berths)
  Mercury (1997; Alaska, Pacific Coastal, California, and Mexican Riviera; 1,850 berths)
  Millennium (2000; Eastern Caribbean and Europe; 2,050 berths)
  Solstice (2008; Eastern Caribbean; 2,850 berths)
  Summit (2001; Caribbean, Alaska, Panama Canal, and Pacific Coastal; 2,050 berths)
  Xpedition (2004; Galapagos Islands; 100 berths)

Pullmantur Cruises
Empress (1990; Caribbean and Bermuda; 1,600 berths)
Oceanic (2001; Western Mediterranean; 1,150 berths)
Ocean Dream (2008; Western Mediterranean; 1,000 berths)
Sky Wonder (2006; Eastern Mediterranean; 1,200 berths)
Sovereign (1988; Bahamas; 2,300 berths)
Zenith (1992; Caribbean, Bahamas, and Bermuda; 1,400 berths)
Royal Caribbean
Adventure of the Seas (2001; Caribbean; 3,100 berths)
Brilliance of the Seas (2002; Caribbean, Europe, and Panama Canal; 2,100 berths)
Enchantment of the Seas (1997; Caribbean; 2,250 berths)
Explorer of the Seas (2000; Caribbean; 3,100 berths)
Freedom of the Seas (2006; Caribbean; 3,600 berths)
Grandeur of the Seas (1996; Caribbean, Bahamas, and Canada/New England; 1,950 berths)
Independence of the Seas (2008; Caribbean and Europe; 3,600 berths)
Jewel of the Seas (2004; Caribbean, Canada/New England, and Europe; 2,100 berths)
Legend of the Seas (1995; Hawaii, Mexican Riviera, and Panama Canal; 1,800 berths)
Liberty of the Seas (2007; Caribbean; 3,600 berths)
Majesty of the Seas (1992; Bahamas; 2,350 berths)
Mariner of the Seas (2003; Caribbean; 3,100 berths)
Monarch of the Seas (1991; Baja, Mexico; 2,350 berths)
Navigator of the Seas (2002; Caribbean; 3,100 berths)
Radiance of the Seas (2001; Caribbean, Pacific Northwest, Alaska, Hawaii, and Panama Canal; 2,100 berths)
Rhapsody of the Seas (1997; Caribbean; 2,000 berths)
Serenade of the Seas (2003; Alaska, Caribbean, Panama Canal, and Hawaii; 2,100 berths)
Splendour of the Seas (1996; Caribbean, Panama Canal, and Europe; 1,800 berths)
Vision of the Seas (1998; Hawaii, Alaska, Mexican Riviera, and Pacific Northwest; 2,000 berths)
Voyager of the Seas (1999; Caribbean and Canada; 3,100 berths)

COMPETITORS

Carnival Corporation & plc
Carnival plc
Club Med
Disney Parks & Resorts
Holland America
NCL
Princess Cruise Lines
Siem Industries
Star Cruises
Vard

HISTORICAL FINANCIALS

Company Type: Public

Income Statement

FYE: December 31

	REVENUE ($ mil.)	NET INCOME ($ mil.)	NET PROFIT MARGIN	EMPLOYEES
12/08	6,532.5	573.7	8.8%	5,050
12/07	6,149.1	603.4	9.8%	5,068
12/06	5,229.6	633.9	12.1%	42,958
12/05	4,903.2	663.5	13.5%	39,400
12/04	4,555.4	474.7	10.4%	3,670
Annual Growth	9.4%	4.8%	—	8.3%

2008 Year-End Financials

Debt ratio: 96.1%
Return on equity: 8.5%
Cash ($ mil.): 403
Current ratio: 0.37
Long-term debt ($ mil.): 6,540

No. of shares (mil.): 214
Dividends
  Yield: 3.3%
  Payout: 16.8%
Market value ($ mil.): 2,940

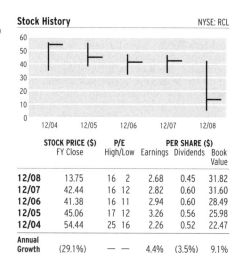

Stock History

NYSE: RCL

	STOCK PRICE ($) FY Close	P/E High/Low		PER SHARE ($) Earnings	Dividends	Book Value
12/08	13.75	16	2	2.68	0.45	31.82
12/07	42.44	16	12	2.82	0.60	31.60
12/06	41.38	16	11	2.94	0.60	28.49
12/05	45.06	17	12	3.26	0.56	25.98
12/04	54.44	25	16	2.26	0.52	22.47
Annual Growth	(29.1%)	—	—	4.4%	(3.5%)	9.1%

RPM International

If you've ever done any sort of home improvement, there's a good chance you've used RPM International's products. Maker of home repair favorites like Rust-Oleum, Zinsser, and DAP, RPM is divided into two units: industrial and consumer products. Industrial offerings, which account for about two-thirds of sales, include products for waterproofing, corrosion resistance, floor maintenance, and wall finishing. RPM's do-it-yourself items include caulks and sealants, rust-preventatives and general-purpose paints, repair products, and hobby paints. The company operates 90 manufacturing facilities worldwide and does more than a third of its business outside the US.

RPM's industrial products include roofing systems (Tremco, Republic, Vulkem, and Dymeric), corrosion control coatings (Carboline, Nullifire, and Plasite), flooring systems (Stonhard and Fibergrate), concrete and masonry additives (Euco), fluorescent pigments (Day-Glo), exterior insulation finishing systems (Dryvit), commercial carpet cleaning products (Chemspec), wood treatments (Kop-Coat), and marine coatings (Pettit, Woolsey, and Z-Spar). The industrial segment accounts for a vast majority of RPM's international sales.

For the do-it-yourselfer, RPM offers rust-preventatives and paints (Rust-Oleum), caulks and sealants (DAP), primer-sealers and wall-covering preparation and removal products (Zinsser), interior stains and finishes (Varathane), patch and repair products (Plastic Wood), deck coatings (Wolman), wall coverings and fabrics (Thibaut), and hobby products (Testors).

The company tendency is to grow its operations through acquisitions, keeping the acquired name brands intact. In 2008 the company acquired UK-based Flowcrete Group, which makes flooring products for industrial and commercial applications. The next year saw the acquisition of a just-less-than-half stake in Chinese licensee Carboline Dalian Paint Production Co. by subsidiary Carboline Company. RPM also made smaller deals for a Swiss sealants maker and a US weatherproofing agents manufacturer.

As can be expected, consumer home centers account for much of the company's business; retailers like Home Depot, Lowe's, Wal-Mart, and Ace Hardware represent about 65% of the Consumer segment's sales.

HISTORY

In 1947 Frank Sullivan founded Republic Powdered Metals to make an industrial aluminum paint. The company went public in 1963, and three years later it bought Reardon Co. (household coatings), its first of more than 50 acquisitions. After his father's death in 1971, Thomas Sullivan took over and reorganized RPM as a holding company.

By 1979 RPM, though successful, was taken to task by its board for lack of formal planning. In 1985 it bought Sun Oil's Carboline coating and tank-lining subsidiary. This purchase forced RPM to lay off employees for the first time.

RPM bought Rust-Oleum in 1994. In its largest acquisition at that time, the company bought roofing-product expert Tremco in 1996 for $236 million. The purchase amassed debt, and to compensate, RPM sold its Craft House hobby activity subsidiary and Swiggle Insulating Glass in 1997.

RPM resumed acquisitions and overseas expansion in 1998 by purchasing Flecto (wood finish), the UK's Nullifire (fireproof coatings), and Germany's Alteco Technik (floors); it also established joint ventures in Russia and China. In 1999 RPM paid $290 million for UK-based Wassall's DAP adhesives division. Softer sales in the Americas and Asia, plus increased distribution expenses that fiscal year, prompted the company to begin restructuring its operations.

RPM sold its Alox metalworking additive business to Lubrizol in 2000. The next year the company finished its restructuring — which had resulted in 17 plant closures and a 10% workforce reduction — and set its sights on reducing debt.

Thomas C. Sullivan's son — and grandson of RPM's founder — Frank Sullivan took the chief executive reins in 2002; Thomas Sullivan remained with the company as chairman.

The company went through a spate of acquisitions in the middle of the decade. Its flooring services division has acquired National Building Facilities Services and Harsco's fiberglass-reinforced plastics business, and its corrosion control division has acquired AD Fire Protection Systems. Tremco has acquired German sealant manufacturer Illbruck Sealant Systems. In early 2007 Rust-Oleum acquired the UK's Tor Coatings in an effort to grow the unit's European coatings operations. Later that year the company sold its auto restoration products subsidiary, Bondo, to 3M.

EXECUTIVES

Chairman and CEO: Frank C. Sullivan, age 48, $2,672,473 total compensation
President and COO: Ronald A. Rice, age 46, $1,285,622 total compensation
EVP Administration and CFO: P. Kelly Tompkins, age 52, $1,064,113 total compensation
SVP Manufacturing and Operations and CIO: Paul G. P. Hoogenboom, age 49, $727,055 total compensation
VP Information Technology: Lonny R. DiRusso
SVP Corporate Development: Stephen J. (Steve) Knoop, age 44, $695,240 total compensation

VP, Treasurer, and Assistant Secretary: Keith R. Smiley, age 45
VP Corporate Development: Thomas C. Sullivan Jr.
VP Global Taxes: Matthew T. (Matt) Ratajczak, age 41
VP, General Counsel, and Secretary: Edward W. Moore
VP Corporate Planning: Russell L. Gordon
VP Corporate Benefits and Risk Management:
 Janeen B. Kastner
VP Public Affairs: Randell McShepard
VP Corporate Development: John F. Kramer
VP and Controller: Barry M. Slifstein
Manager Investor Relations: Kathie M. Rogers
Auditors: Ernst & Young LLP

LOCATIONS

HQ: RPM International Inc.
 2628 Pearl Rd., Medina, OH 44258
Phone: 330-273-5090   Fax: 330-225-8743
Web: www.rpminc.com

2009 Sales

	$ mil.	% of total
US	2,161.5	64
Europe	734.9	22
Canada	260.9	8
Other regions	210.9	6
Total	**3,368.2**	**100**

PRODUCTS/OPERATIONS

2009 Sales

	$ mil.	% of total
Industrial	2,266.0	67
Consumer	1,102.2	33
Total	**3,368.2**	**100**

Selected Products

Industrial
 Carboline (industrial coatings)
 Chemspec (commercial carpet cleaning chemicals)
 Day-Glo (fluorescent colorants and pigments)
 Dryvit (exterior finishing systems)
 Dymeric (sealants)
 Fibergrate (reinforced plastic grating)
 Kop-Coat (wood and lumber treatments)
 Nullifire (fireproofing coatings)
 Republic (roofing products)
 Stonhard (flooring products)
 TCI (powder coatings)
 Tremco (industrial and commercial sealants)
 Vulkem (sealants)
 Woolsey/Z-Spar (marine coatings)

Consumer
 American Accents (decorative finishes)
 Chemical Coatings (industrial coatings)
 DAP (sealants, caulks, and patch and repair products)
 OKON (sealants and stains)
 Painter's Touch (general purpose coatings)
 Rust-Oleum (rust preventative coatings)
 Testors (hobby and leisure products)
 Tremclad (coatings)
 Varathane (wood finishes)
 Watco (wood finishes)
 Zinsser (primer-sealers and wallcovering removers)

COMPETITORS

3M
Akzo Nobel
Ameron
Benjamin Moore
DuPont Coatings & Color Technologies
Ferro
H.B. Fuller
Henkel
Masterchem Industries
PPG Industries
Rohm and Haas
Sherwin-Williams
Tennant
Valspar
Zep Inc.

HISTORICAL FINANCIALS
Company Type: Public

Income Statement

	REVENUE ($ mil.)	NET INCOME ($ mil.)	NET PROFIT MARGIN	EMPLOYEES
5/09	3,368.2	119.6	3.6%	9,674
5/08	3,643.8	47.7	1.3%	10,360
5/07	3,338.8	208.3	6.2%	9,424
5/06	3,008.3	(76.2)	—	9,213
5/05	2,555.7	105.0	4.1%	8,213
Annual Growth	**7.1%**	**3.3%**	**—**	**4.2%**

FYE: May 31

2009 Year-End Financials

Debt ratio: 66.7%
Return on equity: 10.5%
Cash ($ mil.): 253
Current ratio: 1.83
Long-term debt ($ mil.): 762
No. of shares (mil.): 129
Dividends
 Yield: 5.2%
 Payout: 84.9%
Market value ($ mil.): 1,975

Stock History

NYSE: RPM

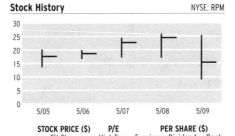

	STOCK PRICE ($) FY Close	P/E High/Low		PER SHARE ($) Earnings	Dividends	Book Value
5/09	15.32	27	10	0.93	0.79	8.87
5/08	24.53	66	44	0.39	0.75	8.82
5/07	22.72	15	11	1.64	0.69	8.43
5/06	18.63	—	—	(0.65)	0.63	7.18
5/05	17.60	23	16	0.86	0.59	8.12
Annual Growth	**(3.4%)**	**—**	**—**	**2.0%**	**7.6%**	**2.2%**

R.R. Donnelley

If you can read it, R.R. Donnelley & Sons can print it. A leading full-service printing company, R.R. Donnelley produces magazines, catalogs, and books, as well as advertising material, business forms, financial reports, and telephone directories. The company offers graphics and prepress services in conjunction with printing. In addition, it provides logistics, distribution, and business process outsourcing services related to getting printed material to its audience. Along with publishers, R.R. Donnelley's customers include companies in the advertising, financial services, health care, retail, and technology industries. The company does business mainly in the US, but also in Europe, Asia, and Latin America.

The global economic slowdown and technological changes (such as the migration of print from paper to the digital realm) have impacted R.R. Donnelley and other printing companies as they scramble to adjust to a fast-changing and challenging business environment.

Despite the gloomy economic backdrop, the company has been and plans to continue bolstering its operations at home and abroad through acquisitions. R.R. Donnelley in 2009 acquired Prospectus Central, which provides

electronic delivery of investment prospectuses. Also that year the company purchased the assets of Santiago, Chile-based PROSA, a Web-based printing company. In 2008 it bought newspaper inserts printer Pro Line Printing in Irving, Texas, for about $120 million. Its 2007 purchases included: business forms company Cardinal Brands for $130 million; rival Banta for $1.3 billion; Perry Judd's Holdings, a magazine and catalog printer, for $176 million; and textbook printer Von Hoffman for $413 million. It also hopes to grow by having its various business units cross-sell their services.

Not all of R.R. Donnelley's acquisition attempts have been successful, however. In 2009 the company offered about $1.5 billion to take over the operations of rival printer Quebecor World, which had filed for bankruptcy in 2008. Quebecor World rejected the bid, however, saying it was on track to emerge from bankruptcy protection by late summer.

In the midst of its buying spree, R.R. Donnelley has been streamlining operations and selling noncore holdings to focus on commercial printing and business process outsourcing.

HISTORY

In 1864 Canadian Richard Robert Donnelley joined Chicago publishers Edward Goodman and Leroy Church to form what eventually would become Lakeside Publishing and Printing. The company's building and presses were destroyed in the 1871 Chicago fire but soon were rebuilt.

By 1890 Richard Donnelley's son Thomas was leading the company, which was incorporated as R.R. Donnelley & Sons. The company spun off its phone directory publishing subsidiary, the Chicago Directory Company, in 1916. (Renamed the Reuben H. Donnelley Corporation after another of Richard Donnelley's sons, the business was acquired by Dun & Bradstreet — now D&B — in 1961, which spun it off as R. H. Donnelley in 1998.)

R.R. Donnelley began printing *Time* in 1928 and *LIFE* in 1936. The company endured limits on commercial printing and paper shortages during WWII. It went public in 1956. Thomas Donnelley's son Gaylord steered the company from 1964 until 1975, when Charles Lake, the first CEO who was not a member of the Donnelley family, replaced him.

During the 1980s R.R. Donnelley developed the Selectronic process, which allowed magazine publishers to tailor content and ads to different geographic audiences. The company acquired Metromail, the largest US mailing list business, in 1987. John Walter became CEO in 1988. R.R. Donnelley's South Side Chicago plant, its oldest, was shuttered in 1993 when Sears stopped publishing its catalogs.

R.R. Donnelley merged its software operations with Corporate Software to form Stream International (technical support, software licensing, and fulfillment) in 1995. That year Donnelley expanded internationally into Chile, China, India, and Poland.

In 1996 Donnelley took both its Donnelley Enterprise Solutions subsidiary (IT services) and its Metromail subsidiary public, retaining about 43% and 38% of each company, respectively. Controversy erupted that year when it was revealed that Metromail had sold personal information in its customer database and, through contracting, had given prison inmates access to its database. In the wake of these revelations,

Walter resigned in 1996. Former Emerson Electric executive William Davis was appointed CEO in 1997.

Davis restructured the company, reorganized Stream's operations, and integrated digital printing into R.R. Donnelley's other operations. He also pushed the company to jettison underperforming units. In 1998 the company sold its interests in Metromail and Donnelley Enterprise Solutions.

Sharpening its focus in commercial printing, R.R. Donnelley continued divesting in 1999, selling most of its stake in Stream International (which was later acquired by Solectron), and its stakes in software distributor Corporate Software & Technology and manufacturing and fulfillment firm Modus Media International. The company's Internet unit also unveiled ePublish, a turnkey system enabling magazine publishers to publish on the Web.

In early 2000 the company doubled the size of its logistics unit when it bought business-to-home parcel mailer CTC Distribution Direct. In 2001 the company announced closures of a handful of plants as part of a streamlining effort. It also cut about 1,700 jobs.

The company acquired distribution service provider Momentum Logistics in 2003, and in 2004 it bought business forms and label printer Moore Wallace for about $2.8 billion. Moore Wallace CEO Mark Angelson took over leadership of the combined company.

In its continuing efforts to divest itself of noncore assets, R.R. Donnelley sold off its package logistics business, including CTC Distribution Direct, in 2004; it retained its print logistics and distribution businesses.

In 2005 R.R. Donnelley sold Peak Technologies, a former Moore Wallace company that integrated and resold automated data capture and identification systems, to Platinum Equity. R.R. Donnelley also acquired a number of regional printers in the US in 2005.

Angelson retired in early 2007 and CFO Thomas Quinlan replaced him as president and CEO in April of that year.

EXECUTIVES

Chairman: Stephen M. Wolf, age 67
President, CEO, and Director:
 Thomas J. (Tom) Quinlan III, age 46,
 $2,017,406 total compensation
COO: John R. Paloian, age 50,
 $1,515,499 total compensation
EVP and CFO: Miles W. McHugh, age 44,
 $936,091 total compensation
EVP, General Counsel, Corporate Secretary, and Chief Compliance Officer: Suzanne S. (Sue) Bettman, age 44,
 $867,566 total compensation
SVP, Controller, and Chief Accounting Officer:
 Andrew B. Coxhead, age 40
EVP and Chief Human Resources Officer:
 Thomas M. Carroll
EVP Communications: Douglas W. (Doug) Fitzgerald,
 age 50
EVP Strategy: Michael S. Kraus, age 36
Group EVP, Forms, Labels, and Office Products:
 Richard D. McMichael, age 41
Group EVP Marketing, Publishing and Retail Services:
 Ann Marie Bushell
Group EVP Manufacturing, Publishing and Retail Services: James R. Riffe
Group EVP, Forms, Labels, and Office Products:
 Gary M. Hubbard, age 49
Group EVP Finance, Short-Run and Variable Print Solutions: Christopher M. Savine, age 46

SVP Human Resources: Andrew B. Panega, age 51
SVP and Treasurer: Daniel N. (Dan) Leib, age 38
Group President, Forms, Labels, and Office Products:
 Thomas G. (Tom) Brooker, age 50,
 $623,201 total compensation
Group President, R.R. Donnelley Brand:
 Daniel L. (Dan) Knotts, age 44
Chief Administrative Officer and Secretary:
 Theodore J. Theophilos, age 55
SVP Public Affairs: Gian-Carlo Peressutti
Auditors: Deloitte & Touche LLP

LOCATIONS

HQ: R.R. Donnelley & Sons Company
 111 S. Wacker Dr., Chicago, IL 60606
Phone: 312-326-8000   **Fax:** 312-326-7156
Web: www.rrdonnelley.com

2008 Sales

	$ mil.	% of total
US	8,938.4	77
Europe	1,409.6	12
Asia	509.7	5
Other regions	723.9	6
Total	**11,581.6**	**100**

PRODUCTS/OPERATIONS

2008 Sales

	$ mil.	% of total
US print & related services	8,704.2	75
International	2,877.4	25
Total	**11,581.6**	**100**

Selected Operations

US Print and Related Services
 Book (consumer, religious, educational and specialty, and telecommunications)
 Direct mail (content creation, database management, printing, personalization, finishing, and distribution in North America)
 Directories (yellow and white pages)
 Logistics (consolidation and delivery of printed products; expedited distribution of time-sensitive and secure material; print-on-demand, warehousing, and fulfillment services)
 Magazine, catalog, and retail inserts
 Short-run commercial print (annual reports, marketing brochures, catalog and marketing inserts, pharmaceutical inserts and other marketing, retail point-of-sale and promotional materials and technical publications)
International
 Business process outsourcing
 Digital solutions (conventional and digital photography, creative, color matching, page production, and content management services)
 Financial print (information management, content assembly, and printing service)
 Forms, labels, and statement printing
 RR Donnelley Global Document Solutions (UK; business process outsourcing, transactional print and mail services, data and print management, and document production; direct mail and marketing support services in Europe)

COMPETITORS

Accenture	Merrill
Arandell	Penn Lithographics
Bowne	Polestar Group
Capgemini	Quad/Graphics
Cenveo	Quebecor World
Consolidated Graphics	St Ives
Courier Corporation	St. Joseph
Dai Nippon Printing	Communications
Deluxe Corporation	Taylor Corporation
EBSCO	Toppan Printing
Harte-Hanks	Transcontinental Inc.
IBM Global Services	Valassis
Infosys	Vertis Inc
M & F Worldwide	

Income Statement

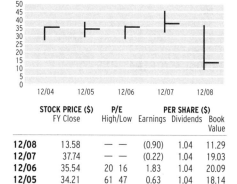

	REVENUE ($ mil.)	NET INCOME ($ mil.)	NET PROFIT MARGIN	EMPLOYEES
12/08	11,581.6	(189.9)	—	62,000
12/07	11,587.1	(48.9)	—	65,000
12/06	9,316.6	400.6	4.3%	53,000
12/05	8,430.2	137.1	1.6%	50,000
12/04	7,156.4	184.9	2.6%	43,000
Annual Growth	12.8%	—	—	9.6%

FYE: December 31

2008 Year-End Financials
Debt ratio: 138.2%   No. of shares (mil.): 205
Return on equity: —   Dividends
Cash ($ mil.): 324   Yield: 7.7%
Current ratio: 1.32   Payout: —
Long-term debt ($ mil.): 3,203   Market value ($ mil.): 2,788

Stock History
NYSE: RRD

	STOCK PRICE ($) FY Close	P/E High/Low		PER SHARE ($) Earnings	Dividends	Book Value
12/08	13.58	—	—	(0.90)	1.04	11.29
12/07	37.74	—	—	(0.22)	1.04	19.03
12/06	35.54	20	16	1.83	1.04	20.09
12/05	34.21	61	47	0.63	1.04	18.14
12/04	35.29	40	31	0.88	1.04	19.42
Annual Growth	(21.2%)	—	—	—	0.0%	(12.7%)

Ryder System

When it comes to commercial vehicles and distribution, Ryder System wants to be the designated driver. The company's Fleet Management Solutions (FMS) segment acquires, manages, maintains, and disposes of fleet vehicles for commercial customers. Similarly, the Supply Chain Solutions (SCS) segment provides logistics and supply chain services from industrial start (raw material supply) to finish (product distribution). Ryder also offers Dedicated Contract Carriage (DCC) services in which the company supplies trucks, drivers, and management and administrative services to customers on a contract basis. Ryder's worldwide fleet of more than 160,000 vehicles ranges from tractor-trailers to light-duty trucks.

Ryder's FMS business provides full service leasing, contract maintenance and commercial rental to customers from small businesses to large national enterprises.

Ryder maintains 677 FMS locations in the US, Puerto Rico, and Canada, along with 222 on-site maintenance facilities. It also maintains 140 international locations in the UK, Ireland, Germany, Mexico, Argentina, Brazil, Chile, China, Thailand, and Singapore.

of Energy's civilian radioactive waste management program.

The omnipresent and self-described workaholic Beyster retired as CEO in 2003, turning the position over to Kenneth Dahlberg, a former executive of General Dynamics. (Dahlberg became chairman of SAIC the following year.) In 2005 the company sold its Telcordia subsidiary to investment firms Warburg Pincus and Providence Equity Partners for $1.3 billion.

SAIC's IPO in late 2006 ended the company's reign as the largest employee-owned research and engineering firm.

SAIC acquired Applied Marine Technology — a company with expertise in special operations, special mission units, and other areas of special warfare operations, as well as in homeland security and terrorism — in 2006. Other 2006 acquisitions included AETC, a San Diego-based provider of remote sensing systems for the Department of Defense; Varec, a provider of measurement, control, and automation systems; aerospace engineering and IT services firm bd Systems; and Applied Ordnance Technology, a provider of technical products and services catering to weapons systems.

In 2007 SAIC acquired Benham Investment Holdings, a provider of consulting, engineering, architecture, design/build, and other related services, as well as Scicom Technologies. It also split its joint venture, Amsec, with Northrop Grumman in 2007. SAIC inherited the aviation, combat systems, and strike force integration businesses, while Northrop Grumman received the ship engineering, logistics, and technical services components of the venture.

EXECUTIVES

Chairman and CEO: Kenneth C. (Ken) Dahlberg, age 64, $8,695,878 total compensation
CEO and Director: Walter P. (Walt) Havenstein
EVP and CFO: Mark W. Sopp, age 43, $1,867,448 total compensation
SVP and CTO: Amy E. Alving, age 46
EVP Special International Assignment: Donald H. (Don) Foley, age 63
EVP Human Resources: Brian F. Keenan, age 52
EVP Strategic Initiatives: Joseph P. (Joe) Walkush, age 57
EVP, General Counsel, and Secretary: Douglas E. Scott, age 52
EVP Government Affairs, Communications, and Support Operations: Arnold L. Punaro, age 62, $2,735,249 total compensation
SVP Investor Relations: Stuart Davis
SVP and Treasurer: Steven P. Fisher, age 48
SVP and Corporate Controller: John R. Hartley, age 48
President, IT and Network Solutions Group: Charles F. Koontz, age 47
President, Defense Solutions Group: Deborah H. (Deb) Alderson, age 52, $1,739,551 total compensation
President, Infrastructure, Logistics, and Product Solutions: Joseph W. (Joe) Craver III, age 50
Auditors: Deloitte & Touche LLP

LOCATIONS

HQ: SAIC, Inc.
10260 Campus Point Dr., San Diego, CA 92121
Phone: 858-826-6000 **Fax:** 858-826-6800
Web: www.saic.com

2009 Sales

	$ mil.	% of total
US	9,892	98
Other countries	178	2
Total	**10,070**	**100**

PRODUCTS/OPERATIONS

2009 Sales

	$ mil.	% of total
Government	9,597	95
Commercial	476	5
Adjustments	(3)	—
Total	**10,070**	**100**

COMPETITORS

Accenture
American Science and Engineering
BAE Systems Inc.
Battelle Memorial
BearingPoint
Boeing
Booz Allen
CACI International
CH2M HILL
Computer Sciences Corp.
EDS
General Dynamics
IBM Global Services
L-3 Titan
Lockheed Martin
ManTech
Northrop Grumman
OSI Systems
Raytheon
Serco Group
SRA International
Unisys

HISTORICAL FINANCIALS

Company Type: Public

Income Statement

FYE: January 31

	REVENUE ($ mil.)	NET INCOME ($ mil.)	NET PROFIT MARGIN	EMPLOYEES
1/09	10,070.0	452.0	4.5%	45,400
1/08	8,935.0	415.0	4.6%	43,800
1/07	8,294.0	391.0	4.7%	44,100
1/06	7,792.0	927.0	11.9%	43,100
1/05	7,172.0	409.0	5.7%	—
Annual Growth	**8.9%**	**2.5%**	**—**	**1.7%**

2009 Year-End Financials

Debt ratio: 52.7%
Return on equity: —
Cash ($ mil.): 936
Current ratio: 1.91
Long-term debt ($ mil.): 1,099
No. of shares (mil.): 204
Dividends
 Yield: 0.0%
 Payout: —
Market value ($ mil.): 4,024

Stock History

NYSE: SAI

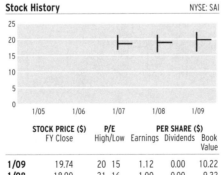

	STOCK PRICE ($) FY Close	P/E High/Low		PER SHARE ($) Earnings	Dividends	Book Value
1/09	19.74	20	15	1.12	0.00	10.22
1/08	18.90	21	16	1.00	0.00	9.32
1/07	18.55	20	16	1.07	0.00	7.53
Annual Growth	**3.2%**	**—**	**—**	**2.3%**	**—**	**16.5%**

St. Jude Medical

If your heart has trouble catching the beat, St. Jude Medical's got rhythm to spare. The company's main products are pacemakers and implantable cardioverter defibrillators (ICDs), both of which use electrical impulses to shock irregularly beating hearts back into rhythm. St. Jude also makes mechanical and tissue heart valves; items used in interventional cardiology procedures, such as catheters and guidewires; and ablation systems used to treat atrial fibrillation. Its neuromodulation business makes implantable devices (similar to pacemakers) that treat chronic pain using electrical stimulation. The company markets its products worldwide through its own sales force and distributors.

St. Jude started out in life making mechanical heart valves, but most of its revenue these days comes from its Cardiac Rhythm Management division, which makes pacemakers and ICDs. ICDs correct for tachycardia, or overly fast heartbeats, and the company has been aggressively introducing new ICD products and taking market share from its larger competitors in the field, Medtronic and Boston Scientific. Pacemakers, in contrast, are used to treat patients whose hearts beat too slowly. The company also offers external devices and software that allow physicians to monitor patients with implanted devices.

St. Jude merged its former Cardiology and Cardiac Surgery divisions at the beginning of 2007 into a new Cardiovascular division. The unit makes mechanical and tissue heart valves, annuloplasty rings that repair damaged valves, and products used in interventional cardiology procedures. The unit acquired Radi Medical Systems in 2008 to gain that company's closure products used to help arrest arterial bleeding.

The company's Atrial Fibrillation division makes diagnostic products and ablation systems, as well as cardiac mapping technology, used to treat irregular rhythms in the heart's upper chambers. The ablation systems use catheters and radiofrequency energy to zap away heart tissue that is causing arrhythmias.

In a move to expand its Atrial Fibrillation business, in 2008 St. Jude acquired EP Medsystems for about $92 million and MediGuide for $283 million. EP Medsystems makes the EP WorkMate, an electrophysiology recording system, as well as cardiac stimulators, and an intracardiac ultrasound system called ViewMate. The acquisition of this last product marked St. Jude's entry into the intracardiac ultrasound echocardiography market.

St. Jude's neuromodulation business got a boost when the company acquired the intellectual property and non-cash assets of Northstar Neuroscience in 2009. While Northstar's implanted neurostimulator device had fizzled in clinical trials, St. Jude saw potential promise in the technology and paid $2 million for the portfolio.

HISTORY

Manuel Villafana, who started Cardiac Pacemakers in 1972, founded St. Jude Medical four years later to develop the bileaflet heart valve. In 1977 patient Helen Heikkinen received the first St. Jude heart valve. The firm also went public that year.

Villafana left in 1981, and established competitor Helix Biocore. St. Jude expanded into tissue valves with its purchase of BioImplant in 1986.

In the mid-1980s St. Jude gained market share when devices from Pfizer and Baxter International had problems. Concerns that the company hadn't diversified led to a joint venture in 1992 with Hancock Jaffe Laboratories to develop a bioprosthetic (constructed of animal tissue) heart valve. In 1994 it bought Siemens' pacemaker unit, doubling revenues and tripling its sales force.

The firm continued diversifying, buying Daig (cardiac catheters) in 1996 and Ventritex (cardiac defibrillators) in 1997. In 1997 the FDA approved St. Jude's Toronto SPV tissue valve, marking its entry into that market. In 1999 St. Jude landed on CalPERS' list of worst-performing companies as it lagged behind rivals Guidant and Medtronic. A management shake-up followed, and the firm strengthened its product lines, buying Tyco International's Angio-Seal subsidiary (cardiac sealant) and Vascular Science (artery connectors). The next year the FDA stepped up its regulatory oversight after the company and its competitors recalled or issued warnings regarding defective or potentially defective devices.

In 2002 St. Jude bought Getz Bros., its largest distributor in Japan. The firm scooped up two other firms, Irvine Biomedical and Epicor Medical, in 2004.

The company acquired both Endocardial Solutions, which makes diagnostic and therapeutic catheters marketed under the EnSite System brand, and Velocimed, a privately owned maker of interventional cardiology devices, in early 2005. Velocimed's products included the Venture catheter and the Premere system, used to seal a tiny hole between the left and right upper chambers of the heart that fails to close in some babies.

Also in 2005 St. Jude spent more than $1.3 billion to acquire Advanced Neuromodulation Systems, establishing its presence in the neurostimulation market.

EXECUTIVES

Chairman, President, and CEO: Daniel J. Starks, age 54, $4,291,232 total compensation
EVP and CFO: John C. Heinmiller, age 54, $2,928,143 total compensation
VP Information Technology and CIO:
 Thomas R. Northenscold, age 51
SVP Clinical Affairs, Cardiac Rhythm Management Division and Chief Medical Officer: Mark D. Carlson
VP Corporate Relations: Angela D. Craig, age 37
VP, General Counsel, and Secretary: Pamela S. Krop, age 50
VP Human Resources: I. Paul Bae, age 44
VP and Corporate Controller: Donald J. Zurbay, age 41
President, Neuromodulation:
 Christopher G. (Chris) Chavez, age 53
Group President, Cardiac Rhythm Management, Atrial Fibrillation, Cardiovascular and Neuromodulation Divisions: Michael T. Rousseau, age 53, $2,603,811 total compensation
Interim President, US: Joseph H. McCullough, age 59, $2,361,086 total compensation
President, Atrial Fibrillation: Jane J. Song, age 46
President, Cardiac Rhythm Management: Eric S. Fain, age 48
President, International: Denis M. Gestin, age 45, $1,715,640 total compensation
President, Cardiovascular Division: Frank J. Callaghan, age 55
Auditors: Ernst & Young LLP

LOCATIONS

HQ: St. Jude Medical, Inc.
 1 Lillehei Plaza, St. Paul, MN 55117
Phone: 651-483-2000
Web: www.sjm.com

2008 Sales

	$ mil.	% of total
US	2,319.6	53
Europe	1,152.6	27
Japan	387.7	9
Asia/Pacific	234.1	5
Other regions	269.3	6
Total	**4,363.3**	**100**

PRODUCTS/OPERATIONS

2008 Sales

	$ mil.	% of total
Cardiac rhythm management	2,701.5	62
Cardiovascular	862.1	20
Atrial fibrillation	545.5	12
Neuromodulation	254.2	6
Total	**4,363.3**	**100**

COMPETITORS

Abbott Labs
ATS Medical
Bard
Biosense Webster
Boston Scientific
Cyberonics
Datascope
Edwards Lifesciences
Empi
Johnson & Johnson
Medtronic
Sorin

HISTORICAL FINANCIALS

Company Type: Public

Income Statement			FYE: Saturday nearest December 31	
	REVENUE ($ mil.)	NET INCOME ($ mil.)	NET PROFIT MARGIN	EMPLOYEES
12/08	4,363.3	384.3	8.8%	14,000
12/07	3,779.3	559.0	14.8%	12,000
12/06	3,302.4	548.3	16.6%	11,000
12/05	2,915.3	393.5	13.5%	10,000
12/04	2,294.2	409.9	17.9%	7,900
Annual Growth	17.4%	(1.6%)	—	15.4%

2008 Year-End Financials

Debt ratio: 34.8%
Return on equity: 12.5%
Cash ($ mil.): 136
Current ratio: 2.02
Long-term debt ($ mil.): 1,126
No. of shares (mil.): 348
Dividends
Yield: 0.0%
Payout: —
Market value ($ mil.): 11,469

Stock History NYSE: STJ

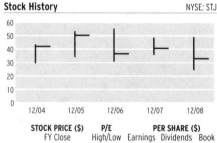

	STOCK PRICE ($) FY Close	P/E High/Low		PER SHARE ($) Earnings	Dividends	Book Value
12/08	32.96	44	23	1.10	0.00	9.30
12/07	40.64	30	23	1.59	0.00	8.41
12/06	36.56	37	21	1.47	0.00	8.53
12/05	50.20	51	33	1.04	0.00	8.29
12/04	41.93	39	27	1.10	0.00	6.71
Annual Growth	(5.8%)	—	—	0.0%	—	8.5%

Sanderson Farms

Sanderson Farms has steadily scratched its way up the pecking order of poultry processors. The company sells fresh, chill-pack, and frozen chicken in whole, cut-up, and boneless forms under the Sanderson Farms label. Its customers include food retailers, distributors, restaurants, and other foodservice operators located mainly in the southeastern, southwestern, northeastern, and western US. In addition to buying chicks from about 180 breeders, the company maintains its own breeder flocks and contracts with about 550 independent chicken farmers, who raise the chicks for Sanderson. Its preparedfoods division sells value-added processed and prepared food items, including frozen entrées.

Vertically integrated Sanderson Farms operates seven hatcheries, six feed mills, and eight processing facilities — four in Mississippi and one each in Louisiana, Georgia, and Texas. In 2008 the company processed some 390 million chickens and produced more than 2.4 billion pounds of chicken products.

While most of its sales are generated in the US, the company's major foreign markets include Russia, Eastern Europe, Asia, Mexico, and the Caribbean.

Investment firm Royce & Associates owns about 14% of the company; an employee trust owns about 8%.

HISTORY

Sanderson Farms began in 1947 when Dewey Sanderson started a Mississippi farm supply business to sell seed, feed, fertilizer, and other supplies. Brothers Dewey Jr. and Joe Frank Sanderson joined the company in 1951, and it then became Sanderson Brothers. It began breeding poultry and was incorporated four years later as Sanderson Brothers Farms. The company became vertically integrated with its 1961 purchase of broiler processor Miss Goldy.

Throughout the 1960s and 1970s, the company expanded, constructing new plants in Mississippi and acquiring facilities in Louisiana. Sanderson Farms expanded into the processed and prepared foods business with the 1986 acquisition of National Prepared Foods. It went public the following year.

From 1987 to 1992 the company expanded existing facilities, constructed new sites, and added shifts at processing facilities. Joe Jr. was named president and CEO in 1989. In 1993 Sanderson Farms built its second complete poultry-processing complex.

Sanderson Farms completed a $68 million poultry complex in 1997 in Texas' Brazos and Robertson Counties (eking out only a small profit as a result of the expense). Co-founder Joe died in 1998, and his son took the additional role of chairman. Dewey Jr. died in 1999.

A 2002 Russian embargo on US poultry hit the Sanderson Farms' export business hard.

EXECUTIVES

Chairman and CEO: Joe F. Sanderson Jr., age 61
President, COO, and Director: Lampkin Butts, age 57
CFO, Treasurer, and Director:
 D. Michael (Mike) Cockrell, age 51
Director Technical Services: John Rice

Secretary and Chief Accounting Officer:
James A. (Jimmy) Grimes, age 60
Chief Financial Analyst: Bob Rosa
Director Sales: Neil Morgan
Processing Director: Doug Lee
Administration Director: Brian Romano
Director Development and Engineering: Bob Billingsley
Organizational Development and Corporate
 Communication Director: Robin Robinson
Director Production: Randy Pettus
Auditors: Ernst & Young LLP

LOCATIONS

HQ: Sanderson Farms, Inc.
 127 Flynt Rd., Laurel, MS 39440
Phone: 601-649-4030   **Fax:** 601-426-1461
Web: www.sandersonfarms.com

2008 Sales

	% of total
US	99
Other countries	1
Total	**100**

PRODUCTS/OPERATIONS

2008 Sales

	% of total
Value-added chicken	
Fresh bulk pack	46
Chill pack	31
Frozen	14
Prepared chicken	8
Non-value-added chicken	1
Total	**100**

COMPETITORS

Allen Family Foods
Cagle's
Coleman Natural Foods
Cooper Farms
Fieldale Farms
Lincoln Poultry
MBA Poultry
New Market Poultry
On-Cor Frozen Foods
Perdue Incorporated
Pilgrim's Pride
Raeford Farms
Townsends
Tyson Foods
Wayne Farms LLC

HISTORICAL FINANCIALS

Company Type: Public

Income Statement

FYE: October 31

	REVENUE ($ mil.)	NET INCOME ($ mil.)	NET PROFIT MARGIN	EMPLOYEES
10/08	1,723.6	(43.1)	—	10,739
10/07	1,474.8	78.8	5.3%	9,705
10/06	1,047.9	(11.5)	—	8,711
10/05	1,006.2	70.6	7.0%	8,645
10/04	1,052.3	91.4	8.7%	8,300
Annual Growth	**13.1%**	**—**	**—**	**6.7%**

2008 Year-End Financials

Debt ratio: 64.5%
Return on equity: —
Cash ($ mil.): 4
Current ratio: 3.40
Long-term debt ($ mil.): 228

No. of shares (mil.): 20
Dividends
 Yield: 1.8%
 Payout: —
Market value ($ mil.): 635

SanDisk Corporation

If forgetting things drives you crazy, SanDisk's products might help preserve your sanity. The company is a top producer of data storage products based on flash memory, which retains data even when power is interrupted. SanDisk's products include removable and embedded memory cards used in digital still cameras, medical devices, networking equipment, notebook computers, and other electronics. The company sells to such manufacturers as Canon, Eastman Kodak, Ericsson, Panasonic, and Siemens, as well as through retailers, including Best Buy and Office Depot. It also licenses its technology to customers such as Intel, Sharp, Sony, and Toshiba.

In 2008 Samsung Electronics made a hostile takeover bid, valued at $5.85 billion in cash. SanDisk quickly rejected the bid, saying it undervalued the company and was not in the best interests of its shareholders. The company also charged that the takeover offer might be an attempt to take advantage in the patent licensing negotiations between Samsung and SanDisk.

SanDisk has become a leading competitor in the market for music/video players with its Sansa brand. To strengthen the Sansa product line, the company in 2008 bought MusicGremlin, a developer of digital content distribution technologies.

The company further delved into the digital music market in 2008 with the unveiling of its slotMusic microSD cards. Best Buy and Wal-Mart sell the fingernail-sized memory cards, which can plug into mobile phones and MP3 players, loaded with full albums. SanDisk signed licensing deals with the four biggest recording companies — EMI Music, Sony Music, Universal Music, and Warner Music — to put out albums by top artists.

In 2007 the company received subpoenas from a federal grand jury in northern California investigating possible monopolistic practices in the NAND flash memory market. (CEO Eli Harari was specifically subpoenaed to testify.) SanDisk also reported that Canada's Competition Bureau is investigating alleged anti-competitive activity in selling NAND flash memory parts to Canadian customers.

The US Department of Justice has a long-running investigation into antitrust violations in the DRAM industry and has reached legal settlements with the four biggest suppliers in that market; several executives have pleaded guilty to federal price-fixing charges.

The company has formed several joint ventures with Toshiba — Flash Alliance, Flash Partners, and FlashVision — which manufacture flash storage cards for cell phones and digital audio players and cameras.

In early 2008 SanDisk and Toshiba agreed on building their fifth JV fab in Japan. Construction began in 2009, with production starting up in 2010.

The companies signed a definitive agreement in early 2009, transferring more than 20% of the JVs' capacity to Toshiba, with SanDisk receiving about $890 million in cash and reduced equipment lease obligations.

HISTORY

SanDisk was founded as SunDisk in 1988 by Eli Harari (now CEO), an expert on non-volatile memory technology. SunDisk's first product, based on a four-megabit flash chip, was developed with AT&T Bell Labs and released in 1991. In 1992 the company formed a development partnership with disk drive maker Seagate Technology; as part of the pact, Seagate acquired 25% of SunDisk.

Because SunDisk was being confused with Sun Microsystems, in 1995 the company changed its name to SanDisk. It went public that year and introduced the industry's smallest Type II (a PC card slot size designation) flash storage card — the CompactFlash. Sales increased by nearly 80% in 1995, SanDisk's first profitable year. The next year SanDisk and Matsushita (now Panasonic) developed double-density flash, a breakthrough technology that doubled the capacity of flash storage products.

In 1997 SanDisk started production of its double-density flash series, investing $40 million in a semiconductor plant in Taiwan with United Microelectronics. In 1999 SanDisk said it would move about 75% of its production to China, partly through a partnership with Celestica.

In 2000 Seagate divested the last of its ownership stake in SanDisk. Also that year, SanDisk and Toshiba formed a joint venture, FlashVision, to produce advanced flash memory at a Toshiba semiconductor plant in Virginia. FlashVision commenced production the following year. (The joint venture's operations were moved to one of Toshiba's Japanese plants after Toshiba announced the sale of the Virginia factory — which had primarily made DRAM chips — to Micron Technology at the end of 2001.)

SanDisk and Toshiba consolidated manufacturing at Toshiba's Yokkaichi memory fab in 2002.

In 2004 SanDisk opened a retail distribution center in China and formed a new joint venture with Toshiba, Flash Partners, for the purpose of adding manufacturing capacity.

The following year, Toshiba began operation of a new fab in Yokkaichi for making NAND flash memory devices. The semiconductors will be produced on silicon wafers measuring 300mm (12 inches) across.

In 2006 SanDisk acquired Matrix Semiconductor, a developer of 3-D, one-time programmable (OTP) chip technology, for about $300 million in stock and cash. The companies began working together on integrating the Matrix technology into SanDisk's product line.

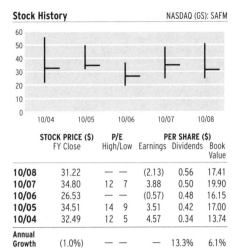

Stock History   NASDAQ (GS): SAFM

	STOCK PRICE ($) FY Close	P/E High/Low		PER SHARE ($) Earnings	Dividends	Book Value
10/08	31.22	—	—	(2.13)	0.56	17.41
10/07	34.80	12	7	3.88	0.50	19.90
10/06	26.53	—	—	(0.57)	0.48	16.15
10/05	34.51	14	9	3.51	0.42	17.00
10/04	32.49	12	5	4.57	0.34	13.74
Annual Growth	**(1.0%)**	**—**	**—**	**—**	**13.3%**	**6.1%**

After passing on an opportunity to acquire competitor Lexar Media (which went to chip maker Micron Technology earlier in 2006), SanDisk pursued msystems instead, widening its portfolio of flash memory-based data storage products. In late 2006 SanDisk purchased rival msystems for about $1.5 billion in stock.

Responding to the dramatic collapse of prices in the NAND flash memory market, SanDisk set a number of cost-cutting measures in early 2007. These included the layoff of up to 10% of the worldwide staff (approximately 250 employees), salary cuts for senior executives, salary freezes for all other employees, and a hiring freeze for most areas.

EXECUTIVES

Chairman and CEO: Eli Harari, age 63,
$6,831,336 total compensation
Vice Chairman: Irwin Federman, age 73
President and COO: Sanjay Mehrotra, age 50,
$4,976,143 total compensation
EVP Administration and CFO: Judy Bruner, age 50,
$3,620,085 total compensation
Chief Intellectual Property Counsel:
E. Earle Thompson, age 52
EVP Mobile Business Unit and Corporate Engineering:
Yoram Cedar, age 56, $2,458,238 total compensation
SVP, General Counsel, and Corporate Secretary:
James (Jim) Brelsford
SVP Memory Technology and Product Development:
Khandker Nazrul Quader
SVP Human Resources: Tom Baker
VP Business Development:
Richard S. O. (Rich) Chernicoff
President, SanDisk Limited: Atsuyoshi Koike, age 56
Director Public Relations: Mike Wong
Director Investor Relations: Jay Iyer
Auditors: Ernst & Young LLP

LOCATIONS

HQ: SanDisk Corporation
601 McCarthy Blvd., Milpitas, CA 95035
Phone: 408-801-1000   **Fax:** 408-801-8657
Web: www.sandisk.com

SanDisk has facilities in China, Germany, Hong Kong, India, Ireland, Israel, Japan, the Netherlands, South Korea, Spain, Taiwan, the UK, and the US.

2008 Sales

	$ mil.	% of total
Asia/Pacific		
Japan	215.4	6
Other countries	1,265.3	38
US	1,047.0	31
Europe, Middle East & Africa	752.9	23
Other regions	70.8	2
Total	**3,351.4**	**100**

PRODUCTS/OPERATIONS

2008 Sales

	$ mil.	% of total
Products	2,843.3	85
Licenses & royalties	508.1	15
Total	**3,351.4**	**100**

2008 Product Sales by Channel

	% of total
Retail	64
OEM	36
Total	**100**

Selected Products

Embedded data storage devices (FlashDrive)
MP3 music players (Sansa)
Portable storage devices (Cruzer)
Removable storage cards (used in cellular phones, digital cameras, digital music players, digital voice recorders, and personal digital assistants)
  CompactFlash
  Memory Stick
  MultiMedia
  Secure Digital
  SmartMedia

COMPETITORS

Apple Inc.	Panasonic Corp
Atmel	PNY Technologies
Buffalo Technology	Qimonda
Creative Technology	Renesas Technology
Eastman Kodak	Saifun
FUJIFILM	Samsung Electronics
Hynix	Seagate Technology
IM Flash Technologies	Sharp Corp.
Intel Corp.	Silicon Storage
Iomega	SMART Modular
Iriver	Technologies
Kingston Technology	SMDK
Lexar	Sony
Macronix International	STEC
Memorex	STMicroelectronics
Micron Technology	TDK
Microsoft	Toshiba Semiconductor
Netlist	Verbatim Corp.
Numonyx	Viking InterWorks

HISTORICAL FINANCIALS

Company Type: Public

Income Statement

FYE: December 31

	REVENUE ($ mil.)	NET INCOME ($ mil.)	NET PROFIT MARGIN	EMPLOYEES
12/08	3,351.4	(2,056.8)	—	3,565
12/07	3,896.4	218.4	5.6%	3,172
12/06	3,257.5	198.9	6.1%	2,586
12/05	2,306.1	386.4	16.8%	1,083
12/04	1,777.1	266.6	15.0%	876
Annual Growth	**17.2%**	**—**	**—**	**42.0%**

2008 Year-End Financials

Debt ratio: 38.6%
Return on equity: —
Cash ($ mil.): 962
Current ratio: 2.14
Long-term debt ($ mil.): 1,225

No. of shares (mil.): 227
Dividends
  Yield: 0.0%
  Payout: —
Market value ($ mil.): 2,180

Stock History

NASDAQ (GS): SNDK

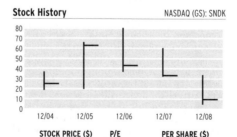

	STOCK PRICE ($) FY Close	P/E High/Low	PER SHARE ($) Earnings	Dividends	Book Value
12/08	9.60	— —	(9.13)	0.00	13.98
12/07	33.17	64 35	0.93	0.00	21.84
12/06	43.03	83 39	0.96	0.00	21.00
12/05	62.82	33 10	2.00	0.00	11.12
12/04	24.97	25 13	1.44	0.00	8.54
Annual Growth	**(21.3%)**	**— —**	**—**	**—**	**13.1%**

Sanmina-SCI

Sanmina-SCI's services help keep electronics makers sane. The company is a top contract manufacturer of sophisticated electronic components, including printed circuit boards and backplane assemblies (circuit boards with slots and sockets for plugging in other boards and cables). Other products include cable and wiring harness assemblies, custom enclosures, and memory modules. In addition, the company provides services such as design and engineering, materials management, order fulfillment, and in-circuit testing. The US accounts for about 30% of Sanmina-SCI's sales.

Sanmina-SCI's customers include companies in the automotive, communications, computing, medical, military/aerospace, and multimedia markets.

Having lost money for seven straight years, Sanmina-SCI is restructuring its worldwide operations to cut costs. Among the moves made by the company was the closing of its Phoenix plant in mid-2007, resulting in the layoff of some 600 employees.

In early 2008 Sanmina-SCI set plans to stop manufacturing PCs, saying the barely profitable business was no longer integral to the company's long-term strategy. The company transferred its PC plant in Monterrey, Mexico, to Lenovo Group and sold certain assets to the giant Chinese PC maker. Other assets of the PC business in Hungary, Mexico, and the US were sold to Foxteq Holdings, a unit of Foxconn Technology Group, which is part of Hon Hai Precision Industry, the world's largest contract electronics manufacturer. The PC business previously represented nearly one-third of Sanmina-SCI's revenues.

Sanmina-SCI is building a manufacturing complex near Chennai, its first plant in India. The company selected a site of approximately 100 acres in Oragadam. The facilities also will house Sanmina-SCI's operations in engineering, IT services, and supply chain management, presently located in Chennai.

The company's $6 billion acquisition of rival SCI Systems in 2001 vaulted Sanmina-SCI into the top ranks with contract manufacturers such as Flextronics and Celestica. The deal also crowned a buying spree that expanded the company into Europe and Asia, and into a growing number of markets. In several cases Sanmina-SCI acquired manufacturing facilities from major customers, such as IBM and Elscint, in deals that included long-term contracts for Sanmina-SCI to supply products back to those same customers.

HISTORY

Bosnian immigrants Jure Sola (chairman and CEO) and Milan Mandaric founded Sanmina in 1980 to provide just-in-time manufacturing of printed circuit boards (PCBs). The name Sanmina comes from the names of Mandaric's children.

During the late 1980s and early 1990s Sanmina shifted production to higher-margin components, such as backplane assemblies and subassemblies. Mandaric, an entrepreneur with other interests, left in 1989. The company went public in 1993.

Like other contract manufacturers, Sanmina began bolstering its operations through acquisitions. The company bought manufacturing plants from Comptronix (1994), Assembly Solutions (1995), Golden Eagle Systems (1996), and Lucent Technologies (1996). In 1997 the company bought contract electronics maker Elexsys International, which was headed by Milan Mandaric. Sanmina also opened a plant in Ireland.

Sanmina's 1998 acquisitions included Massachusetts-based Altron, its #1 competitor in backplane manufacturing. In 1999 the company acquired assets from Nortel Networks and Devtek Electronics Enclosure, a designer of enclosure systems for the telecommunications and networking industries.

In 2000 Sanmina acquired PCB maker Hadco in a $1.3 billion deal, expanding its global presence. That year the company also purchased Swedish contract manufacturer Essex AB, entered into a joint venture with Siemens to manufacture complex PCBs, and acquired some plants from Nortel and Lucent.

In mid-2001 Sanmina agreed to buy rival SCI Systems, one of the world's largest contract manufacturers, for about $4.5 billion. (Sanmina also assumed $1.5 billion of SCI's debt.) Later that year it also acquired a facility in Texas from (and signed a multiyear supplier agreement with) French telecom titan Alcatel (now Alcatel-Lucent). When its acquisition of SCI Systems closed late in the year, Sanmina changed its name to Sanmina-SCI. (Sola and SCI Systems chairman and CEO Eugene Sapp became co-chairmen; Sola remained CEO of the combined company.)

Sanmina-SCI forged several deals in early 2002. The company announced a three-year, $5 billion agreement with IBM to produce desktop PCs. As part of the deal, Sanmina-SCI acquired two US plants from IBM. In addition, Sanmina-SCI and HP penned a deal whereby the company produces some HP products and acquired HP's manufacturing operations in France for $65.8 million. Also that year Sanmina-SCI acquired plants in France, Germany, and Spain from Alcatel for $129.9 million as part of a multiyear supply agreement. All three deals were completed by mid-year.

After a year as co-chairman, Eugene Sapp stepped down from that post in late 2002, while remaining a director of the company.

In 2003 Sanmina-SCI acquired privately held Newisys, a developer of enterprise-class servers.

In mid-2006 the company opened a new enclosures manufacturing facility, measuring 347,000 sq. ft., in Guadalajara, Mexico.

Like dozens of other tech companies, Sanmina-SCI found problems in 2006 with its past practices in granting stock options to executives and other employees. An internal investigation by a special board committee, going back to the beginning of 1997, found that most grants in the prior decade were not correctly dated or accounted for, requiring the company to restate financial results and record non-cash compensation charges.

Among other changes recommended by the special committee, the board adopted a policy of establishing fixed dates for granting equity-based awards, reducing or eliminating the possibility of backdating or springloading options.

The company stated that an executive had resigned as a result of the options investigation. Carmine Renzulli, the EVP for global human resources, left Sanmina-SCI about that time.

Sanmina-SCI shuttered Newisys in 2007, laying off 87 employees.

EXECUTIVES

Chairman and CEO: Jure Sola, age 57
President and COO: Hari Pillai, age 49
VP Enterprise Services: Manesh Patel
EVP Memory Modules: Ralph Kaplan
EVP Worldwide Sales and Marketing: Dennis Young, age 56
EVP, General Counsel, and Secretary:
  Michael R. (Mike) Tyler, age 53
President and General Manager, PCB Fabrication Division: Stephen F. (Steve) Bruton
President, Technology Components Group:
  Walt Hussey, age 56
Investor Relations: Paige Bombino
Director Worldwide Marketing and Public Relations:
  Michael Kovacs
Director Marketing and Strategic Business Development, Europe: Ulrike Winter
Assistant Corporate Secretary:
  Christopher K. Sadeghian
Auditors: KPMG LLP

LOCATIONS

HQ: Sanmina-SCI Corporation
  2700 N. 1st St., San Jose, CA 95134
Phone: 408-964-3555   **Fax:** 408-964-3636
Web: www.sanmina-sci.com

Sanmina-SCI has manufacturing facilities in Brazil, Canada, China, Finland, Germany, Hong Kong, Hungary, India, Indonesia, Ireland, Israel, Japan, Malaysia, Mexico, Singapore, Sweden, Thailand, the UK, and the US.

2008 Sales

	$ mil.	% of total
US	2,180.1	30
Other countries	5,022.3	70
Total	**7,202.4**	**100**

PRODUCTS/OPERATIONS

Selected Services

Backplane assembly
Cable assembly
Circuit assembly
Circuit fabrication
Configuration
Distribution
Enclosures
Engineering
In-circuit testing
Materials management
Order fulfillment
Printed circuit board design
System assembly and testing

COMPETITORS

Benchmark Electronics
BenQ
Cal-Comp Electronics
Celestica
CTS Corp.
Elcoteq
Flextronics
Hon Hai
IBM Canada
Inventec
Jabil
Jurong Technologies
Merix
Nam Tai
Plexus
SMTC Corp.
Suntron
SYNNEX
TTM Technologies
Universal Scientific
Venture Corp.
Viasystems
Wistron

HISTORICAL FINANCIALS

Company Type: Public

Income Statement

FYE: September 30

	REVENUE ($ mil.)	NET INCOME ($ mil.)	NET PROFIT MARGIN	EMPLOYEES
9/08	7,202.4	(486.3)	—	45,610
9/07	10,384.3	(1,134.7)	—	52,607
9/06	10,955.4	(144.4)	—	54,397
9/05	11,734.7	(1,006.0)	—	48,621
9/04	12,204.6	(15.0)	—	48,721
Annual Growth	**(12.4%)**	**—**	**—**	**(1.6%)**

2008 Year-End Financials

Debt ratio: 212.9%
Return on equity: —
Cash ($ mil.): 870
Current ratio: 2.29
Long-term debt ($ mil.): 1,482

No. of shares (mil.): 79
Dividends
  Yield: 0.0%
  Payout: —
Market value ($ mil.): 660

Stock History

NASDAQ (GS): SANM

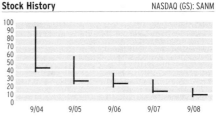

	STOCK PRICE ($) FY Close	P/E High/Low	PER SHARE ($) Earnings	Dividends	Book Value
9/08	8.40	— —	(5.52)	0.00	8.85
9/07	12.72	— —	(12.90)	0.00	14.92
9/06	22.44	— —	(1.62)	0.00	28.88
9/05	25.74	— —	(11.58)	0.00	30.26
9/04	42.30	— —	(0.12)	0.00	42.67
Annual Growth	**(33.2%)**	**— —**	**—**	**—**	**(32.5%)**

Sara Lee

Sara Lee chose cheesecake over clothing. Jettisoning its apparel business, Sara Lee now peddles mostly food and drink, along with some household goods. The Sara Lee Food & Beverage group is a major packaged-meat maker (Ball Park, Jimmy Dean), and a leading manufacturer of packaged sliced bread, as well as Ms. Lee's famous raid-the-refrigerator-at-midnight frozen cheesecakes. Sara Lee International oversees coffee, tea, and bakery operations in Europe, Australia, and Brazil. The Household and Body Care unit markets non-food products such as Kiwi shoe polish, Ambi Pur air fresheners, and Ridsect insecticides overseas. Its Foodservice group supplies coffee, meat, and bakery to North American foodservice operators.

Chairman and CEO Brenda Barnes was given the keys to the Sara Lee kingdom in 2005 and, facing flat sales, began a major overhaul of the company and she's still at it.

To streamline Sara Lee's operations into cohesive units, Barnes first oversaw the spinoff of its $4.5 billion Americas/Asia Branded Apparel group (consisting of Hanes, Champion, Playtex, and other brands) to form an independent, publicly traded company called Hanesbrands Inc., which began trading in 2006. This move dictated cutting some 775 positions. Also in 2006 Sara Lee, after months of negotiations, sold its European meats unit to a 50-50 joint venture of Smithfield Foods and Oaktree Capital Management. (Its European meats business generated sales of some $1.1 billion in 2005.)

All the units sold or spun off represented some $8.2 billion in sales, or about 40% of the firm's annual revenue. This was a significant change to Sara Lee's portfolio, particularly since it had been growing more diverse.

In order to fund its growth businesses as it moved forward, the firm sold numerous operations. Its European packaged meats business (Aoste and Imperial) was sold in 2006. The company brewed up a deal with Segafredo Zanetti to buy its US retail coffee brands (Chock full o'Nuts, Hills Bros, MJB, Chase & Sanborn). It secured a buyer for its international direct-selling operation, which peddles beauty and personal-care products through 950,000 independent consultants primarily located in Asia/Pacific and Latin America. Tupperware Brands bought the business for $557 million.

Sara Lee sold the $1.2 billion European apparel business to Florida's Sun Capital Partners. The deal — which included the Dim, Playtex, Wonderbra, Abanderado, Nur Die, and Unno brands, but excluded the company's UK-based Sara Lee Courtaulds division — became final in 2006.

In 2007 Sara Lee began building new R&D facilities and upping its research staff by 50% in order to develop new retail-food and foodservice products. The company laid off about 1,700 workers at its Mississippi pork plant that year. It also announced plans to cut some 500 other jobs. Both employee-reductions are part of its overall restructuring plan.

The company sold its foodservice sauce and salad dressing business to Richelieu Foods in 2008; it also disposed of its Mexican meat operations that year.

Wal-Mart is the company's largest customer and accounted for 10% of its sales in 2008.

HISTORY

Businessman Nathan Cummings bought the C. D. Kenny Co., a Baltimore coffee, tea, and sugar wholesaler, in 1939. Cummings soon purchased several grocery firms and later changed the company's name to Consolidated Grocers (1945). The operation went public in 1946 and was renamed Consolidated Foods Corp. (CFC) in 1954.

Two years later CFC bought the Kitchens of Sara Lee, a Chicago bakery founded by Charles Lubin in 1951. Introduced in 1949 and named after Lubin's daughter, Sara Lee cheesecake had become the bakery's most popular product.

In 1968 CFC sold its Eagle Complex, which included Piggly Wiggly Midwest supermarkets and Eagle Food Centers, and it bought Bryan Foods. The firm continued to buy and sell businesses in the US, including beverage, appliance, and chemical companies. Some major US purchases were Hanes Corp. (1979), Jimmy Dean Meat Co. (1984), Coach Leatherware International (1985), and Champion Products (athletic knitwear, 1989). Cummings served as president until 1970.

CFC began building its international markets with its first European acquisition in 1962. Following that purchase, it expanded its global presence with the purchases of Douwe Egberts (coffee, tea, and tobacco; the Netherlands; 1978), Nicholas Kiwi (shoe care and pharmaceuticals,

Australia, 1984), and Dim (hosiery and underwear, France, 1989).

Using one of its most respected brand names to enhance the public's awareness of the company, CFC changed its name to Sara Lee in 1985. It continued making acquisitions in the 1990s, including Playtex Apparel. In 1997 Sara Lee began a restructuring that included selling noncore businesses and increasing its use of outsourcing, closed more than 90 manufacturing and distribution facilities, and laid off 9,400 employees (about 7% of its workforce).

Sara Lee sold its loose tobacco business (Amphora, Drum, Van Nelle) in 1998 to the UK's Imperial Tobacco for $1.1 billion and purchased Quaker Oats' coffee marketer, Continental Coffee Products. Also that year Sara Lee recalled hot dogs and packaged meats produced by its Bil Mar Foods unit after the items were linked to nearly two dozen fatal food-poisoning cases. (The company settled class-action suits over the incident in 2000.)

While closing more than 100 facilities, during 1999 Sara Lee continued acquiring, including coffee company Chock full o'Nuts, and the Hills Bros., MJB, and Chase & Sanborn coffee operations from Nestlé.

During 2000 Sara Lee spun off its Coach (leather goods) business and sold off its foodservice operation, PYA/Monarch, to a Royal Ahold subsidiary as the first move to refocus on its core brands. In 2000 president Steven McMillan added the CEO title to his duties; he was named chairman that October.

In 2001 Sara Lee continued to dispose of noncore operations. However, in August that year it acquired The Earthgrains Company, the second-largest fresh-bread company in the US.

The Sara Lee Bakery Group was slapped with a $5.25 million fine in 2003 when the EPA determined that ozone-depleting chemicals were leaking from refrigeration systems in many of its plants. The company agreed to pay the fine and spend an additional $5 million on repairs.

In 2005 McMillan retired and handed over the titles of president, CEO, and chairman to Brenda Barnes.

EXECUTIVES

Chairman and CEO: Brenda C. Barnes, age 54
VP, Interim CFO, and Principal Financial Officer: Mark Garvey, age 44
EVP Human Resources: Stephen J. Cerrone, age 49
EVP; CEO, Household and Body Care Division, Sara Lee International: Vincent H. A. M. Janssen, age 55
EVP; CEO, Sara Lee Fresh Bakery: James W. Nolan, age 52
EVP; CEO, North American Retail and Foodservice: Christopher J. (CJ) Fraleigh, age 45
EVP; CEO, Coffee and Tea Division, Sara Lee International: Frank van Oers, age 49
EVP and General Counsel: Brett J. Hart, age 40
SVP, Taxes: Donald L. Meier, age 61
SVP and Chief Supply Chain Officer, North America: George Chappelle, age 47
SVP and Chief People Officer: Lois M. Huggins, age 45
SVP, Research & Development Sara Lee Foodservice: Paul Bernthal
SVP, Corporate Affairs: J. Randall White
SVP Global Communications: Jon Harris
SVP Strategic Planning and Corporate Development: B. Thomas Hansson, age 48
SVP and Controller: Thomas S. Shilen Jr., age 49
VP; President, Sara Lee Foods Retail, Sara Lee Food & Beverage: Ellen L. Turner, age 43
Executive Director, Investor Relations: Aaron Hoffman
Auditors: PricewaterhouseCoopers LLP

LOCATIONS

HQ: Sara Lee Corporation
3500 Lacey Rd., Downers Grove, IL 60515
Phone: 630-598-8100   **Fax:** 630-598-8482
Web: www.saralee.com

2009 Sales

	$ mil.	% of total
North America	7,059	55
Other regions	5,856	45
Adjustments	(34)	—
Total	**12,881**	**100**

PRODUCTS/OPERATIONS

2009 Sales

	$ mil.	% of total
International beverage	3,041	24
North American retail	2,767	21
North American fresh bakery	2,200	17
North American foodservice	2,092	16
International household & body care	2,025	16
International bakery	790	6
Adjustments	(34)	—
Total	**12,881**	**100**

Selected Brands and Products

Foodservice
Bakery
Bagels
Bread
Buns
Frozen pies, cakes, and cheesecakes
Muffins
Refrigerated dough
Rolls
Specialty breads
Beverages
Roast, ground and liquid coffee, cappuccinos, lattes, and teas
Condiments
Sauces and dressings
Meats
Bacon
Breakfast sausages and sandwiches
Cooked and dry hams
Corn dogs
Deli and luncheon meats
Hot dogs
Meat snacks
Smoked and dinner sausages

Household and Body Care
Ambi Pur
Bloom
Catch
Duschdas
GoodKnight
Kiwi
Monsavon
Radox
Ridsect
Sanex
Vapona
Zendium

International Bakery
Bimbo
BonGateaux
CroustiPate
Ortiz
Sara Lee

North American Retail Bakery
Colonial
Earth Grains
Healthy Choice
Heiner's
Holsum
IronKids
Mother's
Rainbo
Roman Meal
Sara Lee
Sunbeam
Sun-Maid

North American Retail Meats
  Ball Park
  Bryan
  Hillshire Farm
  Jimmy Dean
  Kahn's
  Sara Lee
  State Fair

COMPETITORS

Canada Bread Company	King's Hawaiian
Cheesecake Factory	Kraft Foods
Church & Dwight	Maple Leaf Foods
Clorox	Millstone
Colgate-Palmolive	Nestlé
ConAgra	Pepperidge Farm
Farmland Foods	Plumrose USA
Flowers Foods	Procter & Gamble
Folger	Procter & Gamble ltd
George Weston Bakeries	Reckitt Benckiser
Heinemann's Bakeries	S.C. Johnson
Hormel	Smucker
Interstate Bakeries	Starbucks
Johnsonville Sausage	SYSCO
Jones Dairy Farm	Tyson Foods
Karl Ehmer	Unilever
Kellogg USA	Usinger's

HISTORICAL FINANCIALS

Company Type: Public

Income Statement				FYE: Saturday nearest June 30
	REVENUE ($ mil.)	NET INCOME ($ mil.)	NET PROFIT MARGIN	EMPLOYEES
6/09	12,881.0	364.0	2.8%	41,000
6/08	13,212.0	(55.0)	—	44,000
6/07	12,278.0	504.0	4.1%	52,400
6/06	15,944.0	555.0	3.5%	109,000
6/05	19,254.0	719.0	3.7%	137,000
Annual Growth	**(9.6%)**	**(15.6%)**	**—**	**(26.0%)**

2009 Year-End Financials

Debt ratio: 134.8%	No. of shares (mil.): 696
Return on equity: 15.0%	Dividends
Cash ($ mil.): 959	Yield: 4.5%
Current ratio: 1.35	Payout: 84.6%
Long-term debt ($ mil.): 2,745	Market value ($ mil.): 6,790

Stock History   NYSE: SLE

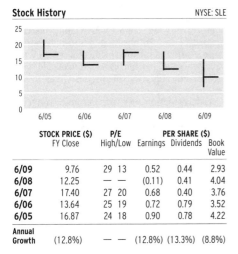

	STOCK PRICE ($) FY Close	P/E High/Low	PER SHARE ($) Earnings	Dividends	Book Value
6/09	9.76	29 13	0.52	0.44	2.93
6/08	12.25	— —	(0.11)	0.41	4.04
6/07	17.40	27 20	0.68	0.40	3.76
6/06	13.64	25 19	0.72	0.79	3.52
6/05	16.87	24 18	0.90	0.78	4.22
Annual Growth	**(12.8%)**	**— —**	**(12.8%)**	**(13.3%)**	**(8.8%)**

S.C. Johnson

S.C. Johnson & Son helped to replace the fly-swatter with the spray can. The company is one of the world's largest makers of consumer chemical products, including Glade, Mr. Muscle, Raid, Pledge, Brise, Drano, Fantastik, Kabbikiller, OFF!, Scrubbing Bubbles, Saran, Shout, Vanish, Windex, and Ziploc. S.C. Johnson peddles its products in more than 110 countries. The founder's great-grandson and once one of the richest men in the US, Samuel Johnson, died in 2004. His immediate family owns about 60% of S.C. Johnson; descendants of the founder's daughter own about 40%. Chairman Dr. Fisk Johnson assumed the title of CEO when president, CEO, and director Bill Perez left for Nike in late 2004.

Many of S.C. Johnson's products have been and remain top sellers in their markets. However, after seeing its Edge and Skintimate shave preparation brands lose market share to rival P&G's Gillette, the company in June 2009 sold the two brands to Energizer, which already competes with P&G in the razors business with its Schick-Wilkinson Sword unit.

The company's commercial products division (Johnson Wax Professional and Johnson Polymer) was spun off as a private company owned by the Johnson family.

In recent years, consumers have avoided use of some plastic storage containers for fear that they contain biphenyl A (BPA). S.C. Johnson in September 2008 attempted to head off speculation and possible reduced sales of its plastic wraps by announcing that its Ziploc and Saran products do not contain BPA.

The company boasts operations in more than 70 countries, including Canada, Australia, Costa Rica, Mexico, and Puerto Rico. For three years since 2006 *Working Mother* magazine has recognized S.C. Johnson as one of the 100 best companies for working mothers.

HISTORY

Samuel C. Johnson, a carpenter whose customers were as interested in his floor wax as in his parquet floors, founded S.C. Johnson in Racine, Wisconsin, in 1886. Forsaking carpentry, Johnson began to manufacture floor care products. The company, named S.C. Johnson & Son in 1906, began establishing subsidiaries worldwide in 1914. By the time Johnson's son and successor, Herbert Johnson, died in 1928, annual sales were $5 million. Herbert Jr. and his sister, Henrietta Lewis, received 60% and 40% of the firm, respectively. The original section of S.C. Johnson's headquarters, designed by Frank Lloyd Wright and called "the greatest piece of 20th-century architecture" in the US, was finished in 1939.

In 1954, with $45 million in annual sales, Herbert Jr.'s son Samuel Curtis Johnson joined the company as new products director. Two years later it introduced Raid, the first water-based insecticide, and soon thereafter, OFF! insect repellent. Each became a market leader. The company unsuccessfully attempted to diversify into paint, chemicals, and lawn care during the 1950s and 1960s. The home care products segment prospered, however, with the introduction of Pledge aerosol furniture polish and Glade aerosol air freshener.

After Herbert Jr. suffered a stroke in 1965, Samuel became president. In 1975 the firm banned the use of the chlorofluorocarbons (CFCs) in its products, three years before the US government banned CFCs. Samuel started a recreational products division that was bought by the Johnson family in 1986. That company went public in 1987 as Johnson Worldwide Associates, with the family retaining control.

The company launched Edge shaving gel and Agree hair products in the 1970s but had few products as successful in the 1980s. It moved into real estate with Johnson Wax Development (JWD) in the 1970s, but sold JWD's assets in the late 1980s.

S. Curtis Johnson, Samuel's son, joined the company in 1983. In 1986 S.C. Johnson bought Bugs Burger Bug Killers, moving into commercial pest control; in 1990 it entered into an agreement with Mycogen to develop biological pesticides for household use.

In 1993 it bought Drackett, bringing Drano and Windex to its product roster along with increased competition from heavyweights such as Procter & Gamble and Clorox. That year S.C. Johnson sold the Agree and Halsa lines to DEP. In 1996 it launched a line of water-soluble pouches for cleaning products that allow work to be done without touching hazardous chemicals. President William Perez became CEO the next year (and left in late 2004 to become president, CEO, and director of Nike, Inc.).

S.C. Johnson bought Dow Chemical's DowBrands unit, maker of bathroom cleaner (Dow), plastic bags (Ziploc), and plastic wrap (Saran Wrap), for $1.2 billion in 1998. It then sold off other Dow brands (cleaners Spray 'N Wash, Glass Plus, Yes, and Vivid) to the UK's Reckitt & Colman to settle antitrust issues.

A year later S.C. Johnson sold its skin care line, including Aveeno, to health care products maker Johnson & Johnson, and spun off its commercial products unit as a private firm owned by the Johnson family. Boosting its home cleaning line, in 1999 it introduced two new products: AllerCare (for dust mite control) and Pledge Grab-It (electrostatically charged cleaning sheets).

In 2000 S.C. Johnson pulled its AllerCare carpet powder and allergen spray from store shelves after some consumers had negative reactions to the fragrance additive in the products. That year H. Fisk Johnson succeeded his father (who became chairman emeritus) as chairman.

In 2001 the company was fined $950,000 for selling banned Raid Max Roach Bait traps in New York after agreeing to pull them from store shelves. Also that year S.C. Johnson's Japanese subsidiary agreed to buy that country's leading drain cleaner brand, Pipe Unish, from Unicharm.

In October 2002 the company acquired the household insecticides unit of German drug giant Bayer Group for $734 million. The following year S.C. Johnson invested in Karamchand Appliances Private Limited, which owns India's second-leading insect control brand *AllOut*.

Chairman emeritus Samuel C. Johnson died in May 2004 at the age of 76. Chairman Dr. Fisk Johnson became CEO of the company again in late 2004.

In June 2009 S. C. Johnson sold its Edge and Skintimate pre-shave brands to Energizer Holdings for an aggregate purchase price of $275 million.

EXECUTIVES

Chairman and CEO: H. Fisk Johnson
EVP and CFO: W. Lee McCollum, age 59
VP and CIO: Mark H. Eckhardt
EVP, Worldwide Corporate and Environmental Affairs:
Jane M. Hutterly
EVP, Worldwide Human Resources: Gayle P. Kosterman
SVP, General Counsel, and Secretary: David Hecker
SVP, Worldwide Manufacturing and Procurement:
Darcy D. Massey
SVP, New Products: Gregory J. (Greg) Barron
VP, Human Resources Asia Pacific:
Jeffrey M. (Jeff) Waller
VP and Corporate Treasurer: William H. Van Lopik
VP and Group Managing Director, Europe:
Filippo Meroni
VP, North American Sales: Darwin Lewis
VP Global Environmental and Safety Actions:
Scott Johnson
VP Global Public Affairs and Communications:
Kelly M. Semrau

LOCATIONS

HQ: S.C. Johnson & Son, Inc.
1525 Howe St., Racine, WI 53403
Phone: 262-260-2000   **Fax:** 262-260-6004
Web: www.scjohnson.com

PRODUCTS/OPERATIONS

Selected Products and Brands

Air Care
Air freshener (Glade, Glade Duet)
Home Cleaning
Bathroom/drain (Drano, Scrubbing Bubbles, Vanish)
Cleaners (Fantastik, Windex, Windex Multi-Surface
Cleaner with Vinegar)
Floor care (Pledge, Johnson)
Furniture care (Pledge, Pledge Wipes, Pledge Grab-it
Dry Dusting Mitts)
Laundry/carpet care (Shout)
Home Storage
Plastic bags (Ziploc)
Plastic wrap (Handi-Wrap, Saran Wrap)
Insect Control
Insecticides (Raid, Raid Max)
Repellents (Deep Woods OFF!, OFF!, OFF! Mosquito
Lamp, OFF! Skintastic)

COMPETITORS

3M
Alticor
Blyth
Church & Dwight
Clorox
Colgate-Palmolive
Dow Chemical
DuPont
Henkel Corp.
IWP International
Procter & Gamble
Reckitt Benckiser
Shaklee
Unilever
Yankee Candle

HISTORICAL FINANCIALS

Company Type: Private

Income Statement

FYE: Friday nearest June 30

	REVENUE ($ mil.)	NET INCOME ($ mil.)	NET PROFIT MARGIN	EMPLOYEES
6/08	8,000.0	—	—	12,000
6/07	8,750.0	—	—	12,000
6/06	7,000.0	—	—	12,000
6/05	6,500.0	—	—	12,000
6/04	6,500.0	—	—	12,000
Annual Growth	5.3%	—	—	0.0%

Revenue History

SCANA Corporation

SCANA is cooking with (natural) gas and electricity all over South and North Carolina. The holding company serves 649,600 electricity customers and 307,200 gas customers in the neighboring states through utilities South Carolina Electric & Gas (SCE&G) and Public Service Company of North Carolina (operating as PSNC Energy). SCANA has an electric generating capacity of about 4,900 MW, which is derived mainly from fossil-fueled power plants; it also operates hydroelectric and nuclear generation facilities. Other operations include retail and wholesale energy marketing and trading, gas transportation, power plant management, fiber-optic telecommunications services, and appliance and HVAC maintenance.

With utility deregulation, SCANA has been seeking out customers in new territories. The company operates in Georgia's deregulated gas market, where it has emerged as a leader with 460,000 retail supply customers. In 2009 SCANA won a competitive bid to continue serving as Georgia's sole regulated provider of natural gas, a role the company has had since the Georgia Public Service Commission launched the regulated provider program in 2002.

SCANA in 2006 merged its two gas transportation units (SCG Pipeline and South Carolina Pipeline) as Carolina Gas Transmission.

SCANA has sold some assets to focus on its core energy businesses. The company has sold its metro-bus transit system to the City of Columbia (South Carolina) in 2002 ; it has also sold some telecom interests.

HISTORY

SCANA's earliest ancestors include Charleston Gas Light Company (1846) and Columbia Gas Light Company (1852), formed to light those cities' streets. After barely surviving the Civil War, the companies rebuilt, only to face the greater challenge posed by Thomas Edison's lightbulb in 1879.

Electric utilities such as Charleston Electric Light Company (1886) began to emerge, and they also introduced electric trolleys, which were commonly operated by electric utilities to boost power consumption. After a series of mergers among utilities in South Carolina, the Columbia Electric Street Railway, Light and Power Company (1892) and Charleston Consolidated Railway, Gas and Electric Company (1897) were formed to handle energy and transit needs in their respective cities.

The 1920s brought another wave of utility mergers and consolidation in South Carolina. Columbia Electric Street Railway became part of the Broad River Power Company in 1925, and Charleston Consolidated Railway became a part of South Carolina Power Company the next year. In 1937 Broad River was renamed South Carolina Electric & Gas (SCE&G).

SCE&G went public in 1948. After a two-year fight with the South Carolina Public Service Authority, SCE&G finally gained approval to purchase South Carolina Power Company in 1950. During the 1950s it built several power plants and natural gas distribution lines and joined other utilities to build the Southeast's first nuclear plant prototype in 1959.

A dozen years later SCE&G and the South Carolina Public Service Authority began building a nuke near the pilot plant. Because of delays related to the Three Mile Island accident and stricter regulations, the plant cost $1.3 billion by the time it was completed in 1984.

SCE&G and Carolina Energies merged in 1982 under the SCE&G name. SCANA Corporation was formed two years later to allow the company to separate its utility business from nonregulated activities. The company formed an energy marketing subsidiary in 1988.

In 1989 Hurricane Hugo wiped out power to 300,000 customers. SCE&G's efforts to quickly restore power in its storm-ravaged territory won it industry praise.

Moving into telecommunications, SCANA in 1994 joined ITC Holding (now ITC^DeltaCom) to build a fiber-optic network in the Southeast. In 1996 SCANA invested in Powertel, which launched PCS wireless phone service in the Southeast later that year.

Meanwhile, in 1995 SCANA and Westvaco formed a joint venture, Cogen South, to build a cogeneration plant to provide power to a Westvaco paper mill in Charleston. SCANA sold its oil and gas subsidiary, Petroleum Resources, to Kelley Oil in 1997.

As deregulation overtures became stronger in 1998, SCANA expanded its natural gas business by entering Georgia's deregulated market, where it quickly became a leader. In 1999 it began planning to extend its gas pipeline into North Carolina, sold its propane assets to Suburban Propane to reduce debt, and agreed to buy natural gas distributor Public Service Company of North Carolina in a $900 million deal, which closed in 2000.

Also in 2000 SCANA sold its home security business and swapped its 27% stake in Powertel for stock in Deutsche Telekom, which took control of the PCS provider. The following year SCANA agreed to sell its 800 MHz emergency radio network to Motorola; the deal was completed in 2002. Also that year SCANA sold its Deutsche Telekom interest.

SCANA purchased 50,000 retail customer accounts in Georgia from Energy America, a unit of UK utility Centrica, in 2004.

EXECUTIVES

Chairman, President, and CEO; Chairman and CEO, South Carolina Electric & Gas:
William B. Timmerman, age 62, $6,821,202 total compensation
SVP and CFO; SVP and CFO, South Carolina Electric & Gas: James E. (Jimmy) Addison, age 48, $1,365,318 total compensation
CIO: Randal M. (Randy) Senn
SVP Human Resources: Joseph C. Bouknight, age 56
SVP Generation, Nuclear, and Fossil Hydro, South Carolina Electric & Gas: Stephen A. Byrne, age 49, $1,752,564 total compensation
SVP Fuel Procurement and Asset Management, SCANA Services: Sarena D. Burch, age 51
SVP Governmental Affairs and Economic Development: Charles B. McFadden, age 64
SVP, General Counsel, and Assistant Secretary; SVP, General Counsel, and Assistant Secretary, South Carolina Electric & Gas: Francis P. (Frank) Mood Jr., age 71
President and COO, SCANA Energy Marketing, SCANA Energy-Georgia, SCANA Communications, and ServiceCare: George J. Bullwinkel Jr., age 58, $1,945,421 total compensation
President and COO, South Carolina Electric & Gas: Kevin B. Marsh, age 53, $2,627,308 total compensation
President and COO, Carolina Gas Transmission: Paul V. Fant, age 55
President and COO, PSNC Energy: D. Russell (Rusty) Harris
Corporate Secretary, Associate General Counsel, and Director Corporate Governance: Gina S. Champion
Director Financial Planning and Investor Relations: Elizabeth (Betty) Best
Auditors: Deloitte & Touche LLP

LOCATIONS

HQ: SCANA Corporation
1426 Main St., Columbia, SC 29201
Phone: 803-217-9000   **Fax:** 803-217-8119
Web: www.scana.com

PRODUCTS/OPERATIONS

2008 Sales

	$ mil.	% of total
Electric operations	2,236	42
Gas (nonregulated)	1,836	35
Gas (regulated)	1,247	23
Total	**5,319**	**100**

Selected Operations

Carolina Gas Transmission Corp. (gas transportation and natural gas purchase, transmission, and sale; LNG liquefaction, storage, and regasification plants)
Public Service Company of North Carolina, Incorporated (dba PSNC Energy, natural gas distribution)
SCANA Communications, Inc. (fiber-optic telecommunications, tower construction, and investments)
SCANA Energy Marketing, Inc. (electricity and natural gas marketing)
SCANA Energy (retail natural gas marketing)
SCANA Services, Inc. (support services)
ServiceCare, Inc. (maintenance for home appliances)
South Carolina Electric & Gas Company (SCE&G, electric and gas utility)
South Carolina Fuel Company, Inc. (financing for SCE&G's nuclear fuel, fossil fuel, and sulfur dioxide emission allowances)
South Carolina Generating Company, Inc. (GENCO, owns and operates Williams power plant and sells electricity to SCE&G)

COMPETITORS

AEP
AGL Resources
CenterPoint Energy
Dominion Resources
Duke Energy
Dynegy
El Paso
Entergy
FPL Group
Green Mountain Energy
Laclede Group
North Carolina Electric Membership
Piedmont Natural Gas
Progress Energy
PS Energy
Santee Cooper
Sempra Energy
Southern Company
TVA

HISTORICAL FINANCIALS

Company Type: Public

Income Statement

FYE: December 31

	REVENUE ($ mil.)	NET INCOME ($ mil.)	NET PROFIT MARGIN	EMPLOYEES
12/08	5,319.0	338.0	6.4%	5,786
12/07	4,621.0	333.0	7.2%	5,703
12/06	4,563.0	320.0	7.0%	5,683
12/05	4,777.0	327.0	6.8%	5,628
12/04	3,885.0	257.0	6.6%	5,549
Annual Growth	**8.2%**	**7.1%**	**—**	**1.1%**

2008 Year-End Financials

Debt ratio: 143.2%
Return on equity: 7.6%
Cash ($ mil.): 272
Current ratio: 1.59
Long-term debt ($ mil.): 4,361
No. of shares (mil.): 163
Dividends
  Yield: 5.2%
  Payout: 62.4%
Market value ($ mil.): 5,796

Stock History

NYSE: SCG

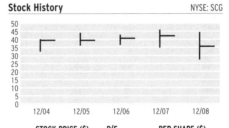

	STOCK PRICE ($) FY Close	P/E High/Low	Earnings	Dividends	Book Value
12/08	35.60	15 9	2.95	1.84	19.35
12/07	42.15	17 13	2.74	1.76	36.56
12/06	40.62	16 14	2.68	1.68	37.02
12/05	39.38	16 13	2.81	1.56	17.14
12/04	39.40	17 14	2.30	1.46	15.71
Annual Growth	**(2.5%)**	**— —**	**6.4%**	**6.0%**	**5.4%**

ScanSource, Inc.

There are more than a few fine lines between ScanSource and its competitors. The company is a leading distributor of automatic identification and data capture (AIDC) products, such as bar code scanners, label printers, and portable data collection terminals. It also provides point-of-sale (POS) products, including PC-based alternatives to cash registers. In addition, ScanSource distributes voice and data communications products and electronic security equipment. The company sells products from vendors such as Avaya, IBM, NCR, and Zebra Technologies to resellers and systems integrators.

ScanSource has used acquisitions to build its international business, which primarily serves Europe and Latin America. The company generated 18% of its revenues outside of the US and Canada in fiscal 2008. It acquired UK-based MTV Telecom, a distributor of voice and data products, in 2008.

The company sells communications through two sales units: Catalyst Telecom and ScanSource Communications. Communications products accounted for almost 40% of the company's fiscal 2008 revenues.

HISTORY

In 1992 — as bar codes were evolving from checkout counter aids into tools used for managing distribution and inventory — Steven Owings and Mike Baur started ScanSource as a joint venture with a PC products distributor. The next year the company bought point-of-sale (POS) distributor Alpha Data Systems. ScanSource went public in 1994 and acquired the hardware distribution business of Micro-Biz. ScanSource was named the first US distributor for IBM's POS division.

The company unveiled its own warehousing and management information services operation in 1995 (previously handled by computer distributor MicroAge). That year it became one of two distributors of Epson's Intelligent Terminals and added Zebra Technologies (bar code equipment), among others, to its supplier roster. In 1996 ScanSource bought out its joint venture partner. The following year it entered into an agreement with Lucent to distribute telephony products.

ScanSource bought distributor POS ProVisions in 1998 and broadened its distribution of computer telephony integration (CTI) products with the purchase of CTI Authority. The next year the company opened a distribution center in Tennessee, tripling capacity. In 2000 ScanSource named president Michael Baur to the additional post of CEO, replacing Owings, who remained chairman. The company also that year reorganized its logistics and fulfillment services and Web-based development organizations into subsidiary ChannelMax.

In 2001 ScanSource acquired the Pinacor CTI sales unit from ailing MicroAge for about $21 million. Also that year the company acquired Miami-based distributor Netpoint International, and began exporting into the Latin American market.

Early in 2002 the company further expanded its operations by opening its ScanSource Europe division with a headquarters office and distribution center in Belgium. Later that year the company acquired UK-based ABC Technology Distribution. Founder Owings resigned as chairman in 2005.

EXECUTIVES

Chairman: James G. Foody, age 78
President, CEO, and Director: Michael L. (Mike) Baur, age 51
President, Worldwide Operations: R. Scott Benbenek, age 53
VP and CFO: Richard P. (Rich) Cleys, age 57
VP and CTO: Gregory B. (Greg) Dixon
EVP Operations and Corporate Development: Andrea D. Meade, age 38, $239,423 pay

VP Marketing: Robert S. (Bobby) McLain Jr., age 48
VP, General Counsel, and Secretary: John J. Ellsworth
VP and Treasurer: Linda B. Davis
VP Human Resources: Marsha M. Madore
President, Catalyst Telecom: John K. Black
President, ScanSource Communications:
  Glen D. (Buck) Baker
President, ScanSource POS and Barcoding:
  Jeffrey E. (Jeff) Yelton, age 47
President, ScanSource Latin America: Elias Botbol
Auditors: Ernst & Young LLP

LOCATIONS

HQ: ScanSource, Inc.
  6 Logue Ct., Greenville, SC 29615
Phone: 864-288-2432   **Fax:** 864-288-1165
Web: www.scansource.com

2009 Sales

	$ mil.	% of total
North America	1,500.2	81
Other regions	347.8	19
Total	**1,848.0**	**100**

PRODUCTS/OPERATIONS

2009 Sales

	$ mil.	% of total
AIDC, POS & security	1,162.0	63
Communications products	686.0	37
Total	**1,848.0**	**100**

Selected Products

Automatic identification and data capture (AIDC)
  Bar code printers and labeling devices
  Contact wands
  Light pens
  Handheld and fixed-mount laser scanners
  Keyboard wedges
  Magnetic stripe readers
  Portable data collection devices

Point-of-sale (POS)
  Cash drawers
  Computer-based terminals
  Keyboards
  Monitors
  Peripheral equipment
  Pole displays
  Receipt printers
  Retail application-based processing units

Converged communications
  Business telephone systems (PBXs, key systems, handsets, cabling)
  Components used in voice, fax, data, voice recognition, other applications
  Electronic security equipment

COMPETITORS

CAM Commerce Solutions
Datalogic Scanning
Hypercom
Ingenico Corp.
Ingram Micro
Intermec
International Imaging Materials
McRae Industries
MICROS Systems
Motorola, Inc.
PAR Technology
PEAK Technologies
Retalix
Tech Data
VeriFone
Westcon

HISTORICAL FINANCIALS

Company Type: Public

Income Statement

FYE: June 30

	REVENUE ($ mil.)	NET INCOME ($ mil.)	NET PROFIT MARGIN	EMPLOYEES
6/09	1,848.0	47.7	2.6%	1,017
6/08	2,175.5	55.6	2.6%	1,059
6/07	1,986.9	42.6	2.1%	992
6/06	1,665.6	40.1	2.4%	916
6/05	1,469.1	35.7	2.4%	887
Annual Growth	**5.9%**	**7.5%**	**—**	**3.5%**

2009 Year-End Financials

Debt ratio: 6.8%
Return on equity: 11.3%
Cash ($ mil.): 128
Current ratio: 2.52
Long-term debt ($ mil.): 30

No. of shares (mil.): 27
Dividends
  Yield: 0.0%
  Payout: —
Market value ($ mil.): 650

Stock History

NASDAQ (GS): SCSC

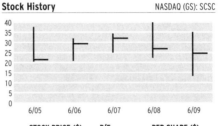

	STOCK PRICE ($) FY Close	P/E High/Low		PER SHARE ($) Earnings	Dividends	Book Value
6/09	24.52	19	8	1.79	0.00	16.79
6/08	26.76	19	11	2.10	0.00	14.92
6/07	31.99	21	15	1.63	0.00	12.24
6/06	29.32	21	14	1.53	0.00	10.35
6/05	21.47	27	15	1.38	0.00	8.52
Annual Growth	**3.4%**	**—**	**—**	**6.7%**	**—**	**18.5%**

Schlumberger Limited

No sleeper, Schlumberger is one of the world's largest oil field services companies, along with Halliburton. The company — whose name is more or less pronounced SHLUM-ber-ZHAY — provides a full range of oil and gas services, including seismic surveys, drilling, wireline logging, well construction and completion, and project management. Organized into 31 geographic teams, Schlumberger's Oilfield Services unit provides reservoir evaluation, reservoir development, and reservoir management services. Schlumberger is also working to develop new technologies for reservoir optimization. Through its WesternGeco business, the company provides seismic services to customers worldwide.

The company, which has grown through a series of acquisitions, bought Baker Hughes' 30% stake in WesternGeco in 2006 for $2.4 billion, giving it full control of the company. In 2007 Schlumberger acquired seismic surveying firm Eastern Echo Holdings for $679 million.

National Oilwell Varco and Schlumberger teamed up in 2008 to form a joint venture that combines their expertise in the manufacturing and technology development of advanced wired drillpipe systems. Another joint venture is drilling

and completion fluids producer M-I SWACO, of which Smith International owns 60%.

In 2009 Schlumberger acquired Techsia SA, a supplier of petrophysical software based in France.

HISTORY

In a Paris basement in 1912, physicist Conrad Schlumberger experimented with wire and a sand-filled bathtub, eventually hoping to use electric current to find ore deposits. With his father's money, Conrad and his brother Marcel began "electrical prospecting" in 1919. Société de Prospection Électrique (SPE) began using the methods for oil exploration in 1923. In 1927 Conrad asked son-in-law Henri Doll to design a tool to chart where oil lay in a well, and wireline logging was born.

To survive the Depression, SPE teamed with rival SGRM in 1931. SPE handled logging, and the two firms formed Compagnie Générale de Géophysique (CGG) for subsurface operations. After entering the US in 1932, the Schlumbergers formed a company in Houston in 1934 and moved headquarters there in 1940.

Also in the 1930s SPE and CGG moved into the Soviet Union, which was desperate for industry. While developing the nation's oil fields, SPE began its policy of adapting to other cultures. Stalin banished the firms in 1936. Conrad died that year, and Marcel followed in 1953.

Led by chairman Doll and Marcel's son Pierre (CEO), the company went public as Schlumberger Limited in 1956. It also bought 50% of Forex, a drilling rig firm, in 1959. The next year Schlumberger sold its stake in CGG and formed an oil services venture with Dow Chemical.

Schlumberger nearly doubled in size with the 1962 acquisition of electronics maker Daystrom. In 1964 the firm combined its 50% stakes in Forex and Languedocienne to create drilling company Neptune. After Jean Riboud became CEO in 1966, the company moved to New York. Doll retired the next year; by then some 40% of the firm's sales stemmed from his inventions. Schlumberger bought a utility meter manufacturer in 1970.

Continuing to build its drilling operations, it bought the rest of Forex in 1972 and SEDCO in 1984 (to form Sedco Forex Drilling in 1985). Also in 1984 Schlumberger combined its 1977 purchase, The Analysts (computerized mud logging), with Dowell's drilling unit to form directional driller Anadrill. (Schlumberger took over Anadrill in 1993.) When oil prices crashed, Schlumberger merged its wireline logging businesses with Flopetrol (acquired 1971) in 1986. It also began seismic analysis, buying GECO (50% in 1984, the rest in 1988) and PRAKLA-SEISMOS (1991, folded into GECO).

Meanwhile, the firm introduced smart cards in 1982. Schlumberger bought GeoQuest (well data management software) in 1992 and formed the Omnes communications venture with Cable & Wireless in 1995. (Schlumberger took over Omnes in 1999.)

In 1998 Schlumberger bought Camco International (drilling services and equipment). Facing the 1999 oil slump, the firm cut staff and combined four engineering and consulting units into Holditch-Reservoir Technologies. It also created a drilling fluids joint venture with Smith International's M-I. Schlumberger finished the year by spinning off Sedco Forex, which then merged with Transocean.

Schlumberger boosted its utility meter business in 2000 by buying CellNet, a UK telemetry services firm, and it acquired control of information technology company Convergent Group. It also created a surface seismic joint venture (WesternGeco) between its Geco-Prakla unit and Baker Hughes' Western Geophysical.

In 2001 SchlumbergerSema was formed when Schlumberger bought Sema, a software and support provider for electronic payment systems, for about $5 billion. It also acquired UK-based Phoenix Petroleum Services, a leading player in optimizing production in artificially lifted wells.

Schlumberger began expanding its IT assets and reorganizing its SchlumbergerSema operations in 2002 in an effort to expand its IT offerings to its Oilfield Service customers. The company acquired Norway-based Inside Reality, an oil services virtual reality technology development company.

In 2003 Andrew Gould was promoted to the position of chairman and CEO following the resignation of Euan Baird. The company began its exit from the chip-testing business by selling off its Schlumberger Verification Systems business unit to Soluris. It also sold its NPTest subsidiary to investment group Francisco Partners and Shah Management. Schlumberger decreased its ownership of SchlumbergerSema from 29% to 14% after selling part of the unit to Atos Origin.

In 2004 Schlumberger completed the sale of its telecom software business for $104 million. Later that year, the company sold its Infodata unit for $37 million. It also sold its electricity meter business to Itron for $248 million, and its business continuity services business to IBM for about $233 million. In an effort to expand its Information Solutions units, the company acquired Austria-based Decision Team, a provider of oil and gas software and consulting services. It expanded its oil and gas services division by acquiring a 26% stake (increased to 100% in 2006) in PetroAlliance Services, Russia's largest oilfield services company. In 2005 Schlumberger sold a manufacturing facility in Montrouge, France, for $227 million.

EXECUTIVES

Chairman and CEO: Andrew Gould, age 62, $14,148,907 total compensation
EVP and CFO: Simon Ayat, age 54, $2,834,340 total compensation
VP and CTO: Ashok Belani, age 50
CIO: Sophie Zurquiyah-Rousset, age 42
Chief Accounting Officer and Director: Howard Guild, age 37
EVP, Schlumberger Oilfield Services: Chakib Sbiti, age 54, $5,410,031 total compensation
EVP Industry Affairs: Dalton Boutte, age 54, $3,162,686 total compensation
VP and Director Taxes: Mark Danton, age 52
VP Operations, Oilfield Services: Satish Pai, age 47, $2,359,599 total compensation
VP Engineering, Manufacturing, and Sustaining: Paal Kibsgaard, age 41
VP Investor Relations: Malcolm Theobald, age 47
VP and Treasurer: H. Sola Oyinlola, age 53
VP Communications: Rodney Nelson, age 50
VP Personnel: Catherine MacGregor, age 36
President, Oilfield Services, Europe and Africa: Mark Corrigan, age 50
Secretary and General Counsel: Ellen Summer, age 62
Investor Relations Manager: Debashis Gupta
Auditors: PricewaterhouseCoopers LLP

LOCATIONS

HQ: Schlumberger Limited
5599 San Felipe, 17th Fl., Houston, TX 77056
Phone: 713-513-2000
Web: www.slb.com

2008 Sales

	% of total
Oilfield Services	
Europe/CIS/West Africa	29
North America	22
Middle East & Asia	21
Latin America	16
Other regions	1
WesternGeco	11
Total	**100**

PRODUCTS/OPERATIONS

2008 Sales

	% of total
Oilfield services	89
WesternGeco	11
Total	**100**

Selected Subsidiaries and Affiliates

Schlumberger Antilles N.V. (Netherlands Antilles)
Schlumberger Offshore Services N.V. (Limited) (Netherlands Antilles)
Schlumberger B.V. (The Netherlands)
Schlumberger Canada Limited
Schlumberger SA (France)
Services Petroliers Schlumberger (France)
WesternGeco B.V. (The Netherlands)
WesternGeco A.S. (Norway)
Schlumberger Oilfield Holdings Limited (British Virgin Islands)
Dowell Schlumberger Corporation (British Virgin Islands)
Schlumberger Holdings Limited (British Virgin Islands)
Schlumberger Middle East S.A. (Panama)
Schlumberger Overseas, S.A (Panama)
Schlumberger Seaco, Inc. (Panama)
Schlumberger Surenco, S.A. (Panama)
WesternGeco Seismic Holdings Limited (British Virgin Islands)
Schlumberger Technology Corporation
WesternGeco L.L.C.

COMPETITORS

Baker Hughes
BJ Services
Core Laboratories
Fortum
Halliburton
Petroleum Geo-Services
Stolt-Nielsen
Technip

HISTORICAL FINANCIALS

Company Type: Public

Income Statement

FYE: December 31

	REVENUE ($ mil.)	NET INCOME ($ mil.)	NET PROFIT MARGIN	EMPLOYEES
12/08	27,162.9	5,434.8	20.0%	87,000
12/07	23,276.5	5,176.5	22.2%	80,000
12/06	19,230.5	3,709.9	19.3%	70,000
12/05	14,309.2	2,207.0	15.4%	60,000
12/04	11,480.2	1,223.9	10.7%	52,500
Annual Growth	24.0%	45.2%	—	13.5%

2008 Year-End Financials

Debt ratio: 21.9%
Return on equity: 34.2%
Cash ($ mil.): 189
Current ratio: 1.59
Long-term debt ($ mil.): 3,694
No. of shares (mil.): 1,198
Dividends
Yield: 2.0%
Payout: 18.9%
Market value ($ mil.): 50,704

Stock History

NYSE: SLB

	STOCK PRICE ($) FY Close	P/E High/Low		PER SHARE ($) Earnings	Dividends	Book Value
12/08	42.33	25	8	4.45	0.84	14.08
12/07	98.37	27	13	4.20	0.70	12.42
12/06	63.16	25	16	3.01	0.50	8.70
12/05	48.58	28	17	1.82	0.42	6.34
12/04	33.47	34	26	1.02	0.38	5.11
Annual Growth	6.0%	—	—	44.5%	21.9%	28.9%

Schnitzer Steel Industries

Your old car could end up in a Malaysian office building if Schnitzer Steel Industries gets its steel jaws on it. The company processes scrap steel and iron, which it obtains from sources such as auto salvage yards, industrial manufacturers, and metals brokers. The company sells more of that scrap to steelmakers in Asia than anywhere else; much of the rest goes to Schnitzer Steel's own steelmaking business, Cascade Steel Rolling Mills, which produces merchant bar, steel reinforcing bar, and other products at its minimill in Oregon. Schnitzer Steel's Pick-N-Pull Auto Dismantlers unit operates auto salvage yards. The family of founder Sam Schnitzer controls the company through a voting trust.

Considering itself primarily a ferrous metals recycling business, Schnitzer Steel plans to continue to expand this business segment through acquisitions in North America. It has regularly made acquisitions throughout the US, primarily focusing on buying small, regional operations. In addition to growing through acquisitions, Schnitzer Steel hopes to improve the efficiency of its recycling operations by investing in new processing technology.

Toward the end of 2008 president and CEO John Carter was named chairman of Schnitzer, and executive Tamara Lundgren moved up the ladder and took over as president and CEO. Lundgren joined Schnitzer in 2005 after a career spent primarily in investment banking.

HISTORY

Sam Schnitzer, a draftee into the Russian army, found his way to Austria, then to the US in 1904. The next year he moved to Portland, where he and partner Henry Wolf formed Alaska Junk in 1908. The enterprise grew, buying sawmills, logging camps, and shipyards. Sam's son, Morris, formed Schnitzer Steel Products on his own in 1936. After WWII the patriarch turned

Alaska Junk over to sons Gilbert, Leonard, Manuel, and Morris.

The brothers changed the company's name to Alaska Steel and acquired Woodbury, a local steel distributor, in 1956. The Schnitzers formed Lasco Shipping in 1963. Morris' Schnitzer Steel Products returned to family control, and in 1978 Alaska Steel and Woodbury combined to make Metra Steel. The company boosted its vertical integration by acquiring the Cascade Steel minimill in 1984.

Leonard Schnitzer's son-in-law Robert Philip became president in 1991. Two years later the family's steel businesses went public as Schnitzer Steel Industries. In 1994 the company launched a $42 million expansion program. It bought Manufacturing Management (then Washington's #1 scrap processor, 1995) and Proler International (scrap-related environmental services, 1996), adding 17 scrap-collecting and -processing facilities, primarily on the East Coast.

Schnitzer Steel Industries began producing wire rod and coiled rebar at its Oregon facility in 1997. The next year Schnitzer Steel Industries and joint venture partner Hugo Neu added facilities in Maine, Massachusetts, and New Hampshire. Also in 1998 a marked drop in scrap export prices due to an economic downturn in Asia hurt the company's earnings. Its Asian exports declined some 20% in 1999.

To maximize its potential and reduce costs, Schnitzer Steel Industries installed an automobile shredder capable of processing 2,000 tons per day at its Tacoma, Washington, facility in 2000. In 2001 the company experienced improvements in its metal recycling business, the result of a temporary backlog that helped boost sales. However, the slowdown in the economy hurt sales at its steel manufacturing segment.

In 2002 the company's Portland, Oregon, metals recycling facility went through a $4.4 million renovation to increase efficiency in loading recycled metal cargoes. The next year, Schnitzer Steel Industries purchased Pick-N-Pull, a major operator of auto salvage yards, for about $71 million.

Schnitzer Steel Industries unwound its joint ventures with Hugo Neu in 2005. That same year the company named John Carter as its new president and CEO.

EXECUTIVES

Chairman: John D. Carter, age 63
President, CEO, and Director: Tamara L. Lundgren, age 51
SVP and CFO: Richard D. Peach, age 45
EVP Business Development: Gary A. Schnitzer, age 66
SVP and President, Steel Manufacturing Business: Jeffrey Dyck, age 45
SVP and President, Metals Recycling Business: Donald W. Hamaker, age 56
SVP and President, Auto Parts Business: Thomas D. Klauer Jr., age 55
SVP, General Counsel, and Secretary: Richard C. (Rich) Josephson, age 60
VP Human Resources: Andrew (Drew) Lipay
VP, Corporate Controller, and Principle Accounting Officer: Jeff P. Poeschl, age 44
VP Environmental and Public Affairs: Thomas (Tom) Zelenka, age 59
Executive Director, Schnitzer Southeast: Byron Kopman
Executive Director, Schnitzer Southeast: David Romanoff
Investor Relations: Rob Stone
Health and Safety: Doug Dunaway
Compliance: Callie Pappas
Auditors: PricewaterhouseCoopers LLP

LOCATIONS

HQ: Schnitzer Steel Industries, Inc.
3200 NW Yeon Ave., Portland, OR 97210
Phone: 503-224-9900
Web: www.schnitzersteel.com

2008 Sales

	$ mil.	% of total
North America	1,859.5	46
Asia	1,451.8	36
Europe	446.0	11
Africa	261.5	7
Adjustments	(377.2)	—
Total	**3,641.6**	**100**

PRODUCTS/OPERATIONS

2008 Sales

	$ mil.	% of total
Metals Recycling	3,062.9	76
Steel Manufacturing	603.2	15
Auto Parts	352.7	9
Adjustments	(377.2)	—
Total	**3,641.6**	**100**

COMPETITORS

AK Steel Holding Corporation
Aleris International
CFF Recycling
Commercial Metals
Nippon Steel
Nucor
SHV Holdings
Sims Metal Management
Steel Dynamics
United States Steel

HISTORICAL FINANCIALS

Company Type: Public

Income Statement

FYE: August 31

	REVENUE ($ mil.)	NET INCOME ($ mil.)	NET PROFIT MARGIN	EMPLOYEES
8/08	3,641.6	248.7	6.8%	3,669
8/07	2,572.3	131.3	5.1%	3,499
8/06	1,854.7	143.1	7.7%	3,252
8/05	853.1	146.9	17.2%	1,799
8/04	688.2	111.2	16.2%	1,624
Annual Growth	**51.7%**	**22.3%**	**—**	**22.6%**

2008 Year-End Financials

Debt ratio: 16.2%
Return on equity: 28.5%
Cash ($ mil.): 15
Current ratio: 2.26
Long-term debt ($ mil.): 159
No. of shares (mil.): 28
Dividends
Yield: 0.1%
Payout: 0.8%
Market value ($ mil.): 1,933

Stock History

NASDAQ (GS): SCHN

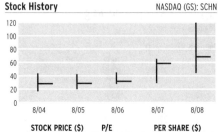

	STOCK PRICE ($) FY Close	P/E High/Low		PER SHARE ($) Earnings	Dividends	Book Value
8/08	68.41	14	5	8.61	0.07	34.62
8/07	58.43	15	7	4.32	0.07	27.08
8/06	31.75	9	6	4.65	0.07	25.98
8/05	28.60	9	4	4.72	0.07	20.51
8/04	28.10	12	5	3.58	0.07	14.83
Annual Growth	**24.9%**	**—**	**—**	**24.5%**	**0.0%**	**23.6%**

Scholastic Corporation

Once upon a time, a company grew up to become one of the world's leading children's book publishers. Scholastic Corporation sells more than 320 million books (including the *Harry Potter* series) annually to children in the US. It also sells products in more than 140 countries. It operates through four divisions: Children's Book Publishing and Distribution; Educational Publishing; Media, Licensing and Advertising; and International. Known for its school book clubs and fairs, Scholastic also publishes magazines, textbooks, and software for students and teachers; and produces children's TV programming, videos, and films. The company additionally owns *Encyclopedia Americana* publisher Scholastic Library Publishing.

The recession has caused a decrease in spending among families and school districts. As a result, Scholastic has cut costs by reducing salaries and exiting noncore businesses (such as its direct-to-home continuities businesses). The company is also increasing the price of children's books in select categories, and expects sales to be boosted by federal stimulus money alloted to school districts in 2009 and 2010.

Scholastic created some sales magic when it agreed to be the US distributor of the J.K. Rowling *Harry Potter* series about a boy wizard, which has broken sales records and become the best-selling children's series of all time. Scholastic also paid close to $10 million for the rights to the popular spooky kids' series *Goosebumps* by R.L. Stine. Other popular brands include *Clifford the Big Red Dog*, *I Spy*, and *The Baby-sitters Club*.

The company had been busy growing the business through deals and acquisitions. The company struck a deal to license publications based on five future animated movies from DreamWorks SKG. On the horizon is the big screen version of Scholastic's *The 39 Clues*. The company partnered with LEGO Group to publish books and other products using LEGO brands, such as *Lego Reader: Space Adventures: Mars Alien Attack!*. In addition, Scholastic partnered up with NBC and Telemundo (along with other content and broadcasting companies) to create a new television network for children called Qubo. The network airs on NBC, i network, and Telemundo in English and Spanish. Spots reinforce the importance of books and reading.

Chairman and CEO Richard Robinson (a descendant of founder Maurice Robinson) owns about 20% of the company.

HISTORY

Fresh from a stint on his college newspaper, Maurice Robinson returned to his hometown of Wilkinson, Pennsylvania, in 1920 and launched *The Western Pennsylvania Scholastic*, a newspaper geared toward high school students. By 1922 its circulation had grown to 4,000 — prompting Robinson to incorporate his business as Scholastic Publishing Company and launch *Scholastic*, a national version of the newspaper.

The Depression found the unprofitable Scholastic struggling to improve its financial picture. In 1932 the company changed its name to Scholastic Corporation. A cost-cutting program helped it achieve a profit for the first time four years later. Profitability, however, would be fleeting: Accusations that Scholastic's publications promoted Communism prompted some schools to ban them.

During WWII, paper rationing compelled Scholastic to print slimmer publications and turn away subscribers. Following the war the company introduced a string of publications and initiated a sales push that permitted it to pay its first dividend in 1951. In the 1950s, while weathering another spate of accusations that the company had Communist leanings, Scholastic continued to expand its list of publications. The company also created two book clubs that decade, launching what would become one of its most successful endeavors.

During the 1960s Scholastic broadened its interests to include instructional materials and hardcover books. The company went public in 1969 and continued its expansion during the 1970s with ventures into record production and filmstrips. In 1974 Maurice's son, Richard, was appointed president.

Scholastic began producing educational software and TV programming during the 1980s. In 1987 Richard took the company private again in order to help it regain financial stability. His timing was fortuitous — the children's book market was on an upswing, and by the time he took Scholastic public again in 1992, the company's book sales had doubled.

The 1992 launch of its *Goosebumps* books initially met with great success. But by 1996, when kids had grown weary of *Goosebumps,* book returns caused profits to take a nosedive. Robinson responded by instituting cost-cutting and layoffs, and Scholastic divested itself of products not associated with its core business. The company continued to expand its TV and film interests during the 1990s, producing TV shows such as *Scholastic's The Magic School Bus* and feature films such as *The Indian in the Cupboard* for worldwide audiences.

In 1998 Scholastic created a new publishing unit to issue professional and parenting magazines. Also that year it published the first *Harry Potter* book by then-unknown British author J.K. Rowling. In addition, the company inked a deal with Warner Brothers Worldwide Publishing to create children's books based on Warner Brothers' movie and TV properties. The following year it relaunched its six-year-old subscription-based Internet site as a free site for teachers, kids, and parents.

In 2000 Scholastic published the fourth book in the *Harry Potter* series, *Harry Potter and the Goblet of Fire*, which had the largest first printing in history (later bested by other books in the series). Later that year it purchased children's book and reference publisher Grolier from Lagardère for $400 million. The following year Scholastic announced that it would establish shops in Toys "R" Us stores to sell toys and games. In 2001 the company bought educational software maker Tom Snyder Productions and animated TV producer Soup2Nuts; both are units of Torstar.

In 2002 the company acquired Klutz, a maker of children's products and books, from Corus Entertainment and bought a 15% interest in The Book People, a UK book distributor. Citing poor industry conditions, Scholastic cut about 400 employees (about 4% of the workforce) in 2003.

In 2007 the last book in the *Harry Potter* series, *Harry Potter and the Deathly Hallows*, set sales records after 8.3 million copies vanished from shelves in 24 hours, ousting the previous record set in 2005 by *Harry Potter and the Half-Blood Prince.*

EXECUTIVES

Chairman, President, and CEO:
Richard (Dick) Robinson, age 72,
$3,595,707 total compensation
SVP Operations: Thomas K. Hoekzema
EVP, CFO, and Chief Administrative Officer:
Maureen E. O'Connell, age 47,
$1,796,215 total compensation
EVP; President, International Group: Hugh Roome, age 57
EVP; President, Scholastic Entertainment and Scholastic Media: Deborah A. Forte, age 55
EVP; President, Scholastic Education:
Margery W. Mayer, age 57,
$1,086,710 total compensation
EVP Marketing: Linda B. Keene
EVP; President, Book Clubs: Judith A. (Judy) Newman, age 51, $1,209,045 total compensation
EVP; President, e-Scholastic and Scholastic at Home:
Seth D. Radwell, age 46
EVP; President, Scholastic Book Fairs and International: Michael Hansen
SVP Human Resources and Employee Services:
Cynthia H. Augustine, age 51,
$607,248 total compensation
SVP Education and Corporate Relations:
Ernest B. (Ernie) Fleishman, age 72
SVP and Chief Accounting Officer: Robert J. Jackson, age 54
SVP and CIO: Reg Maton
SVP Finance and Operations: Ed Monagle
SVP, General Counsel, and Secretary:
Devereux Chatillon, age 55
VP Corporate Communications and Media Relations:
Kyle Good
Auditors: Ernst & Young LLP

LOCATIONS

HQ: Scholastic Corporation
557 Broadway, New York, NY 10012
Phone: 212-343-6100   **Fax:** 212-343-6934
Web: www2.scholastic.com

PRODUCTS/OPERATIONS

2009 Sales

	$ mil.	% of total
Children's book publishing & distributing	913	49
International	399	22
Educational publishing	384	21
Media, licensing, & advertising	153	8
Total	**1,849**	**100**

Selected Products and Services

Audiovisual children's books
  Make Way for Ducklings
  Where the Wild Things Are
Book Fairs
  Scholastic Book Fairs
Educational software and programs
  I Spy
  Literacy Place
  Read 180
  Solares
  Success with Writing
  WiggleWorks
Feature films
  The Baby-Sitters Club
  Clifford's Really Big Movie
  Indian in the Cupboard
Products
  Klutz (book and toy packages)
School-based book clubs
  Arrow
  Firefly
  Honeybee
  Lucky
  SeeSaw
  TAB

Television properties
  Animorphs
  Clifford the Big Red Dog
  Dear America
  Goosebumps
  I Spy
  Maya & Miguel
  Scholastic's The Magic School Bus

Selected Book Titles

Animorphs
The Baby-Sitters Club
Captain Underpants
Clifford the Big Red Dog
Dear America
Goosebumps
Harry Potter
The Magic School Bus
Miss Spider
The Scholastic Encyclopedia of Presidents
The Scholastic Encyclopedia of Women

Scholastic Library Publishing

Kids Clubs
  Barbie book club
  Beginning Reader's Program (featuring Dr. Seuss books)
  Disney book club
Publishing
  Cumbre (Spanish-language encyclopedia)
  Encyclopedia Americana
  New Book of Knowledge

COMPETITORS

Addison-Wesley
American Girl
The Aristotle Corporation
Cengage Learning
Channel One Network
Cookie Jar Group
Disney Publishing
Educational Development
HarperCollins
Highlights for Children
HIT Entertainment
Houghton Mifflin Holding Company
John Wiley
LeapFrog
Little, Brown Book Group
McGraw-Hill
Pearson plc
Random House
RD School & Educational Services
Simon & Schuster

HISTORICAL FINANCIALS

Company Type: Public

Income Statement

FYE: May 31

	REVENUE ($ mil.)	NET INCOME ($ mil.)	NET PROFIT MARGIN	EMPLOYEES
5/09	1,849.3	(14.3)	—	9,100
5/08	2,205.6	(17.2)	—	10,200
5/07	2,179.1	60.9	2.8%	10,200
5/06	2,283.8	68.6	3.0%	10,400
5/05	2,079.9	64.3	3.1%	10,800
Annual Growth	(2.9%)	—	—	(4.2%)

2009 Year-End Financials

Debt ratio: 38.8%
Return on equity: —
Cash ($ mil.): 144
Current ratio: 2.01
Long-term debt ($ mil.): 305

No. of shares (mil.): 36
Dividends
  Yield: 1.5%
  Payout: —
Market value ($ mil.): 713

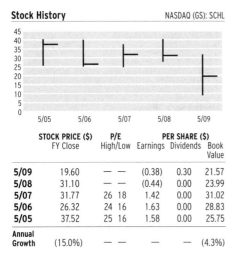

	STOCK PRICE ($) FY Close	P/E High/Low		PER SHARE ($) Earnings	Dividends	Book Value
5/09	19.60	—	—	(0.38)	0.30	21.57
5/08	31.10	—	—	(0.44)	0.00	23.99
5/07	31.77	26	18	1.42	0.00	31.02
5/06	26.32	24	16	1.63	0.00	28.83
5/05	37.52	25	16	1.58	0.00	25.75
Annual Growth	(15.0%)	—	—	—	—	(4.3%)

Scotts Miracle-Gro

The grass sure seems greener over at Scotts Miracle-Gro (SMG), the world's largest maker and marketer of horticultural and turf products. Its garden and indoor plant care items include grass seeds, fertilizers, herbicides, potting soils, and related tools. Brand names include Ortho, Miracle-Gro, Hyponex, and Turf Builder. SMG markets Monsanto's Roundup herbicide products for the consumer market and has a lawn and shrub care service. It also owns upscale garden retailer Smith & Hawken. Siblings James Hagedorn (chairman and CEO) and Katherine Littlefield (a director) own a third of SMG. Hagedorn and Littlefield are the children of Horace Hagedorn, the creator of Miracle-Gro plant food.

Scotts also sells directly to professionals (i.e., nurseries, greenhouses, and specialty crop growers). To make its balance sheet even greener, Scotts has a business development group that focuses on three main areas: improving sales and profits in businesses such as hardware and independent garden centers, expanding the company's presence into grocery and drug stores, and expanding into ancillary products such as tools, pottery, and watering equipment. Smith & Hawken itself has about 60 retail stores around the country and also does business through catalog and online sales. In 2009 Scotts Miracle-Gro announced it would shutter the Smith & Hawken business, another casualty of the troubled economy.

While the company has international operations, the North American market accounts for more than 80% of sales. As well, while the company does target professional landscapers, its consumer business accounts for three-quarters of its sales. Within that market, Scotts' largest customers are The Home Depot (about 30% of sales), Wal-Mart (about 15%), and Lowe's (about 15%). Because of this reliance on such a small number of businesses, the company has focused on enhancing its relationships with the retailers of late.

The Scotts LawnService unit has grown — through both acquisitions and internal growth — from $42 million in sales in 2001 to well more than $200 million in 2008. It is the #2 lawn care services company in the US, after TruGreen.

Following the 2008 announcement by Spectrum Brands that that company would stop providing private label lawn fertilizer and growing products to retailers, SMG said that it would hold talks with its retail partners to gauge their interest in Scotts Miracle-Gro stepping into that vacancy.

HISTORY

Founded by Orlando Scott in Marysville, Ohio, in 1868 as O.M. Scott & Sons, the firm originally cleaned crop seed. It later began selling grass seed, and in 1928 debuted the US's first lawn fertilizer, Turf Builder. The family-owned business became a subsidiary of conglomerate ITT in 1971; it broke away in a 1986 management-led LBO. It went public as The Scotts Company in 1992.

Acquisitions include Hyponex (1988), lawn and garden equipment maker Republic Tool and Manufacturing (1992), and specialty fertilizer maker Grace-Sierra Horticultural Products (1993). In 1995 Scotts merged with Stern's Miracle-Gro, a company that Horace Hagedorn had started in 1951; the deal married the #1 lawn care company with the #1 garden plant food firm. The company simplified its product line by cutting more than 300 products in 1996.

Scotts launched an acquisition program in 1997 to increase sales in Europe. That year Scotts acquired the UK's Levington Horticulture (fertilizers and pesticides) and 80% of Sanford Scientific (genetically engineered grasses and plants). The next year Scotts landed a deal to market Monsanto's Roundup herbicide products internationally and bought two European lawn and garden product firms — ASEF and Rhone-Poulenc Jardin (#1 in Europe). International sales jumped almost 75% for the year. In 1999 Scotts bought Monsanto's lawn and garden businesses (including its Ortho line) for $300 million.

In 2000 Scotts bought the distribution rights for peat products manufactured by Bord na Mona, one of Europe's largest peat producers. It also sold its US and Canadian professional turf operations to The Andersons, Inc. The same year Scotts acquired Henkel's European fertilizer and plant care brand, Substral. Due to sluggish growth Scotts reorganized its European operations in 2002, pledging an investment of about $50 million by 2005. The company took a $9 million charge as a result in 2003.

President and COO James Hagedorn was named CEO in 2001; James, Horace's son, retained the title of president. He assumed the additional role of chairman in 2003. The following year Scott's ventured into the gardening retail market with the acquisition of Smith & Hawken. In the fall of 2004 Scotts paid $72 million for the high-end gardening retail chain.

Horace Hagedorn died in early 2005. The Scotts Company changed its name to The Scotts Miracle-Gro Company that same year.

EXECUTIVES

Chairman and CEO: James (Jim) Hagedorn, age 53
EVP: Michael P. (Mike) Kelty, age 59
President, COO, and Director; President and COO, The Scotts Company LLC: Mark R. Baker, age 52
EVP and CFO: David C. (Dave) Evans, age 46
Chief Environmental Officer: Rich Martinez
EVP International and Chief Marketing Officer: Claude Lopez, age 48
EVP Global Human Resources: Denise S. Stump, age 55
EVP North American Businesses: Barry W. Sanders, age 44
EVP Global Technologies and Operations: Mike Lukemire, age 51
EVP, General Counsel, and Secretary: Vincent C. Brockman, age 46
SVP North America Growth and Innovation: Dan Paradiso
SVP North America Sales, Scotts Company: Brian Kura
SVP Scotts LawnService: Peter Korda
SVP Global Supply Chain: Dave Swihart
SVP Global Professional Seed, Asia/Pacific and Emerging Markets: Korbin Riley
SVP Global Research and Development: Jeff Garascia
VP Corporate Communications and Investor Relations: James D. (Jim) King
Auditors: Deloitte & Touche LLP

LOCATIONS

HQ: The Scotts Miracle-Gro Company
14111 Scottslawn Rd., Marysville, OH 43041
Phone: 937-644-0011   **Fax:** 937-644-7614
Web: www.scotts.com

2008 Sales

	$ mil.	% of total
North America	2,435.7	82
Other regions	546.1	18
Total	**2,981.8**	**100**

PRODUCTS/OPERATIONS

2008 Sales

	$ mil.	% of total
Global Consumer	2,250.1	75
Global Professional	348.8	12
Scotts Lawn Service	247.4	8
Corporate & other	158.6	5
Adjustments	(23.1)	—
Total	**2,981.8**	**100**

Selected Products

Garden and indoor plant care items
Garden tools
Grass seed
Herbicides
Insecticides
Lawn fertilizers
Lawn spreaders and other application devices
Pesticides
Plant foods
Potting soils
Wild bird seed

Selected Brands

ASEF (Benelux countries)
Bug-B-Gon
Celaflor (Germany and Austria)
Earthgro (growing media such as potting mix)
Evergreen (lawn fertilizer, UK)
Fertiligene (France)
Hyponex (growing media such as potting mix)
KB (France and Benelux countries)
Levington (growing media, UK)
Miracle-Gro (plant food)
Morning Song (bird seed)
Nature Scapes (growing media such as potting mix)
Nexa-Lotte (Germany and Austria)
Ortho (weed, insect, and disease control)
Osmocote
Pathclear (herbicide, UK)
Peters Professional
Roundup (licensed by Monsanto, herbicide)

Scotts
Shamrock (Europe)
Smith & Hawken
Substral (Europe)
Turf Builder (lawn fertilizer and weed control)
Weed-B-Gon
Weedol (herbicide, UK)

COMPETITORS

Acuity Brands
Applied Energetics
BASF SE
Bayer CropScience
Brookstone
Central Garden & Pet
Dow AgroSciences
Home Depot
K+S
LESCO
Restoration Hardware
Spectrum Brands
Trans-Resources
TruGreen Landcare
Williams-Sonoma

HISTORICAL FINANCIALS

Company Type: Public

Income Statement

FYE: September 30

	REVENUE ($ mil.)	NET INCOME ($ mil.)	NET PROFIT MARGIN	EMPLOYEES
9/08	2,981.8	(10.9)	—	6,378
9/07	2,871.8	113.4	3.9%	6,120
9/06	2,697.1	132.7	4.9%	5,720
9/05	2,369.3	100.6	4.2%	5,291
9/04	2,037.9	100.9	5.0%	4,985
Annual Growth	10.0%	—	—	6.4%

2008 Year-End Financials

Debt ratio: 194.5%
Return on equity: —
Cash ($ mil.): 85
Current ratio: 1.54
Long-term debt ($ mil.): 850

No. of shares (mil.): 66
Dividends
  Yield: 2.1%
  Payout: —
Market value ($ mil.): 1,554

Stock History

NYSE: SMG

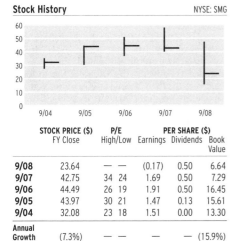

	STOCK PRICE ($) FY Close	P/E High/Low	PER SHARE ($) Earnings	Dividends	Book Value
9/08	23.64	— —	(0.17)	0.50	6.64
9/07	42.75	34 24	1.69	0.50	7.29
9/06	44.49	26 19	1.91	0.50	16.45
9/05	43.97	30 21	1.47	0.13	15.61
9/04	32.08	23 18	1.51	0.00	13.30
Annual Growth	(7.3%)	— —	—	—	(15.9%)

Seaboard Corporation

With pork from Oklahoma, flour from Haiti, and sugar from Argentina, Seaboard has a lot on its plate. The diversified agribusiness and transportation company has operations in some 30 countries in the Americas, the Caribbean, and Africa. Seaboard sells pork in the US and foreign markets. Overseas it trades grain (wheat, soya); operates power plants and feed and flour mills; and grows and refines sugar cane. Seaboard operates a shipping service for containerized cargo between the US, the Caribbean, and South America; it owns shipping terminals in Miami and Houston and a fleet of 40 vessels (12 owned, the rest chartered) that ship worldwide to some 40 ports. The descendants of founder Otto Bresky own 72% of the company.

In the US, Seaboard is primarily engaged in pork production and processing and ocean transportation. Overseas, the company operates mainly commodity merchandising, grain processing, sugar production, and electric power generation.

In addition to shipping and the trading of sugar, pork and commodities, Seaboard grows and processes citrus and sugar and has distillery opertions in Argentina; in the US it manufactures ethanol and has trucking transportation operations. It also owns jalapeño farms in Texas and Honduras.

Despite what some consider to be an industry oversupply of pork, Seaboard has significantly expanded its pork business with an emphasis on private-label preseasoned pork products. It markets some of its pork products under the Prairie Fresh (in the US), Seaboard Farms (international), and Daily's brands. Seaboard has an agreement with Missouri-Based Triumph Foods to process and market all of Triumph's pork products.

In order to increase sales in its sugar and citrus segment, Seaboard planted an additional 15,000 acres of sugar cane in 2007.

HISTORY

Otto Bresky founded his company as a flour broker in 1916. He acquired his first flour mill in Atchison, Kansas, in 1918 and the following year purchased the Imperial Brewery Co. in Kansas City and converted it to a flour mill. Over the next four decades, Bresky ground out a series of acquisitions of milling companies. In 1928 he purchased Rodney Milling Co. and retained the name as the identity for the family business. The company then purchased Ismert-Hincke Milling Co. (1938) and the Consolidated Flour Mills Co. (1950). In 1959 Rodney Milling merged with publicly traded Hathaway Industries and changed its name to Seaboard Allied Milling Corp.

In the 1960s Seaboard Allied became one of the first millers to shift flour milling from the source of the raw materials (the wheat fields of the Great Plains) to the population centers in the Southeast and on the East Coast. In 1962 Seaboard Allied built a flour mill in Chattanooga, Tennessee. It then purchased George Urban Milling Company in Buffalo, New York (1965), and built a flour mill in Jacksonville, Florida (1966). But Bresky's expansionist strategy did not stop at the Atlantic Seaboard. The company acquired a flour mill in Guayaquil, Ecuador, in 1966

(a joint venture with Continental Grain Co.), then constructed flour mills in Freetown, Sierra Leone (1968), and Georgetown, Guyana (1969).

Bresky retired in 1973 and was succeeded by his son Harry. A chip off the old block, Harry acquired a flour mill in Cleveland, Tennessee, and built flour mills in Buchanan, Liberia, and in Sapele, Nigeria, that year. In 1978 Seaboard Allied acquired Mochasa, Ecuador's leading producer of animal feed, and launched Top Feeds, a mixed-feed plant in Sapele.

Facing stiff competition in the mill business from agribusiness giants, in 1982 Seaboard Allied sold all its US flour mills to Cargill. The company changed its name to Seaboard that year and began expanding outside the US. In 1983 the company formed Seaboard Marine, a shipping business in Florida, to serve its increasingly far-flung enterprises.

In addition to geographic diversification, the company expanded into new agribusiness areas. Seaboard acquired Central Soya's poultry unit in 1984, and it bought the Elberton Poultry Company the next year. Seaboard commenced shrimp farming operations in Ecuador in 1986 and in Honduras in 1987. Two years later Transcontinental Capital Corporation (Bermuda), a subsidiary, began supplying power from a floating power barge to the Dominican Republic.

Seaboard entered the hog business in 1990 by acquiring a pork-processing plant in Albert Lea, Minnesota. It opened a hog-processing facility in Guymon, Oklahoma, in 1996 and closed the Minnesota plant. That year the company bought a stake in Ingenio y Refinerio San Martin del Tabacal, an Argentina-based sugar cane and citrus company. It then acquired flour-mill, pasta-plant, and cookie operations in Beira, Mozambique.

During 1998 Seaboard bought a controlling interest in the Argentine sugar business, purchased a Bulgarian winery, and acquired a flour and feed milling business in Zambia.

In 2000 Seaboard sold its poultry division to ConAgra for $375 million. Also that year the company acquired a 35% stake in Unga Group, (feed milling, Kenya) and the JacintoPort marine terminal in Houston.

During 2001 the company traded its non-controlling interest in a joint-venture salmon processor (ContiSea LLC) to Norway's Fjord Seafood ASA for stock, and swapped its majority ownership of one Bulgarian winery for minority ownership in a larger one. That same year it ceased production at its Honduran shrimp farms and jalapeño pickling operations.

Seaboard purchased more of Fjord Seafood in 2002; with 20% of the company, it became the largest shareholder. However, by the end of 2003 Seaboard sold off its entire investment in Fjord Seafood for $37 million. That same year the company sold its closed shrimp businesses. In 2004 the company acquired a controlling stake in a Mozambique grain milling business.

Seaboard acquired Daily's Foods for $45 million in 2005; the bacon processor and foodservice supplier has been added to the company's Seaboard Foods (formerly Seaboard Farms) unit.

After serving as CEO for more than 30 years, in 2006 Harry Bresky stepped down as CEO (but remained as chairman) and turned over the company's reins to his son, Steven. Harry Bresky died in 2007.

EXECUTIVES

President, CEO, and Director: Steven J. Bresky, age 55, $3,727,563 total compensation
SVP and CFO: Robert L. Steer, age 49, $2,618,257 total compensation
VP, Corporate Controller, and Chief Accounting Officer: John A. Virgo, age 48
VP Engineering: James L. (Jim) Gutsch, age 55
VP, General Counsel, and Secretary: David M. Becker, age 47
VP Finance and Treasurer: Barry E. Gum, age 42
VP Governmental Affairs: Ralph L. Moss, age 63
VP Taxation and Business Development: David S. Oswalt, age 41
President, Seaboard Foods: Rodney K. (Rod) Brenneman, age 44, $1,997,545 total compensation
President, Seaboard Marine: Edward A. (Eddie) Gonzalez, age 43, $1,429,670 total compensation
President, Seaboard Overseas Trading Group: David M. Dannov, age 47, $1,483,776 total compensation
Assistant Secretary and Senior Attorney: William H. Croutch
Auditors: KPMG LLP

LOCATIONS

HQ: Seaboard Corporation
9000 W. 67th St., Shawnee Mission, KS 66202
Phone: 913-676-8800   **Fax:** 913-676-8872
Web: www.seaboardcorp.com

2008 Sales

	$ mil.	% of total
Caribbean, Central & South America	1,726.8	40
Africa	1,269.5	30
North America		
US	924.5	22
Canada & Mexico	143.7	3
Pacific Basin & Far East	162.1	4
Eastern Mediterranean	23.7	1
Europe	17.5	—
Total	**4,267.8**	**100**

PRODUCTS/OPERATIONS

2008 Sales

	$ mil.	% of total
Commodity trading & milling	1,897.4	45
Pork	1,126.0	26
Marine	958.0	23
Sugar & citrus	142.1	3
Other	144.3	3
Total	**4,267.8**	**100**

Selected Operations

Cargo shipping
Citrus production and processing
Commodity merchandising (wheat, corn, and soybean meal)
Domestic trucking transportation
Electric power generation
Flour, maize, and feed milling
Jalapeño-pepper processing
Pork production and processing
Sugar production and refining

Selected Subsidiaries

Cape Fear Railways, Inc.
Cayman Freight Shipping Services, Ltd.
Chestnut Hill Farms Honduras, S. de R.L. de C.V.
Eureka Chickens Limited (Zambia)
Fairfield Rice Incorporated (Guyana)
Gloridge Bakery (PTY) Limited (South Africa)
Granjas Porcinas del Ecuador, S.A.
Green Island Maritime, Inc.
High Plains Bioenergy, LLC
Hybrid Poultry (Mauritius) Limited
H&H Shipping Limited (Liberia)
JacintoPort International LLC
Lesotho Flour Mills Limited

Life Flour Mill Ltd. (Nigeria)
Mount Dora Farms de Honduras, S.R.L.
Mount Dora Farms Inc.
National Milling Company of Guyana, Inc.
National Milling Corporation Limited (Zambia)
Sea Cargo, S.A. (Panama)
SSI Ocean Services, Inc.
Top Feeds Limited (Nigeria)
Unga Farmcare (East Africa) Limited (Kenya)

COMPETITORS

ADM	Kraft Foods
American Crystal Sugar	Louis Dreyfus Group
APL	M A Patout
Bay State Milling	Makino
Bunge Limited	Neptune Orient
Cargill	Nicor
Carr's Milling	Nitto Flour
Chelsea Milling	Nutreco
Chiquita Brands	NYK Line
CHS	Organic Milling
Colonial Group	Overseas Shipholding
ContiGroup	Group
Crowley Maritime	Südzucker
CSX	Sara Lee Food and
Della Natura Commodities	Beverage
Dole Food	Sempra Energy Trading
Evergreen Marine	Smithfield Foods
Evergreen Mills	Southern States
Farmers Rice Milling	Star of the West
Fresh Del Monte Produce	Sunkist
Genco Shipping and	Tate & Lyle
Trading	Tyson Foods
Horizon Milling	U.S. Sugar
Hormel	Viterra Inc.
Imperial Sugar	Western Sugar Cooperative
Johnsonville Sausage	

HISTORICAL FINANCIALS

Company Type: Public

Income Statement

FYE: December 31

	REVENUE ($ mil.)	NET INCOME ($ mil.)	NET PROFIT MARGIN	EMPLOYEES
12/08	4,267.8	146.9	3.4%	10,734
12/07	3,213.3	181.3	5.6%	10,663
12/06	2,707.4	258.7	9.6%	10,363
12/05	2,688.9	266.7	9.9%	10,357
12/04	2,684.0	168.1	6.3%	9,532
Annual Growth	**12.3%**	**(3.3%)**	**—**	**3.0%**

2008 Year-End Financials

Debt ratio: 5.4%
Return on equity: 10.4%
Cash ($ mil.): 61
Current ratio: 2.32
Long-term debt ($ mil.): 79
No. of shares (mil.): 1
Dividends
  Yield: 0.3%
  Payout: 2.5%
Market value ($ mil.): 1,477

Stock History

NYSE Alternext: SEB

	STOCK PRICE ($) FY Close	P/E High/Low		Earnings	PER SHARE ($) Dividends	Book Value
12/08	1,194.00	16	6	118.19	3.00	1,179.98
12/07	1,470.00	19	9	144.15	3.00	1,094.98
12/06	1,765.00	9	6	205.09	3.00	972.95
12/05	1,511.00	9	4	211.94	3.00	790.67
12/04	998.00	8	2	133.94	3.00	560.08
Annual Growth	**4.6%**	**—**	**—**	**(3.1%)**	**0.0%**	**20.5%**

SEACOR Holdings

SEACOR's core business is anchored in the sea. With nearly 200 vessels, the marine services company delivers cargo and personnel, anchors drilling rigs, and provides construction and maintenance work to oil and gas companies operating offshore. Its fleet includes about 75 crew boats and 40 supply and towing supply vessels. SEACOR also provides standby safety support, logistics services, training and consulting, and environmental services such as oil spill response. In addition, the company has inland river barges that transport grain and other bulk commodities and it operates helicopter services through its fleet of more than 185 helicopters.

SEACOR does business primarily in the Gulf of Mexico, where more than half its vessels are stationed, but it also provides its services in oil-rich regions such as Latin America, the North Sea, and offshore Asia and West Africa.

HISTORY

With only two vessels, SEACOR was founded in 1989 to service offshore oil rigs in the Gulf of Mexico. It quickly expanded its fleet by buying 36 vessels from Midwest utility holding company Nicor, which had diversified into oil services in the late 1970s.

When the *Exxon Valdez* oil spill prompted a 1990 federal law requiring energy companies to have cleanup plans, SEACOR was among the first to enter the safety business. In 1991 the company joined a joint venture that operated safety standby vessels in the North Sea. By the time SEACOR went public in 1992, it had formed a similar joint venture in the US.

SEACOR expanded its Gulf operations throughout the 1990s. In 1994 it formed a joint venture with Transportacion Maritima Mexicana to operate off the coast of Mexico. The company also gained some 165 ships by acquiring John E. Graham & Sons (1995) and McCall Enterprises (1996).

Also in 1996 SEACOR bought 45 offshore support vessels from the Netherlands' SMIT Internationale. As a result of the deal, the company changed its name to SEACOR SMIT Inc. in 1997. That year the firm created another joint venture to operate offshore Argentina, and SEACOR grabbed a 55% stake in Chiles Offshore, which began building two jack-up offshore drilling rigs.

In 1998 SEACOR paid $37 million for SMIT Internationale's 5% stake in the company. It also sold 34 vessels for $144 million (11 of these were chartered back to SEACOR) and accepted delivery of 10 new vessels. Also that year SEACOR invested in Globe Wireless, a marine telecommunications company concentrating on e-mail and data transfer. In 1999 SEACOR bought Kvaerner's Marinet Systems, which provides communications services to the shipping industry, with the intent of integrating its operations into Globe Wireless.

Chiles Offshore went public in 2000; SEACOR retained a 27% stake. In 2001 SEACOR acquired UK shipping firm Stirling Shipping. The next year SEACOR sold its stake in Chiles Offshore to ENSCO International and acquired the remaining 80% of Tex-Air Helicopters, expanding its air support operations.

In 2004 SEACOR SMIT changed its name to SEACOR Holdings. That year SEACOR acquired Era Aviation, including its fleet of 128 helicopters, 16 aircraft, and 14 operating bases, from Rowan Companies for about $118 million.

In 2005 the company acquired former rival Seabulk International for $1 billion, including assumed debt. It sold its Globe Wireless unit two years later, exiting the maritime telecommunications business.

EXECUTIVES

Chairman, President, and CEO: Charles L. Fabrikant, age 64, $7,096,537 total compensation
SVP and CFO: Richard Ryan, age 54, $982,359 total compensation
VP and Chief Accounting Officer: Matthew Cenac, age 43
SVP Legal Affairs and Risk Management: Alice N. Gran, age 59
SVP; Chairman, President, and CEO, Environmental Services: Randall Blank, age 58, $2,108,758 total compensation
SVP Corporate Development and Treasurer: Dick Fagerstal, age 48, $998,164 total compensation
SVP Strategy and Corporate Development: James A. F. Cowderoy, age 49
SVP International: John Gellert, age 38, $2,860,226 total compensation
SVP, General Counsel, and Corporate Secretary: Paul L. Robinson, age 41
Auditors: Ernst & Young LLP

LOCATIONS

HQ: SEACOR Holdings Inc.
2200 Eller Dr., Fort Lauderdale, FL 33316
Phone: 954-523-2200   **Fax:** 954-524-9185
Web: www.seacorholdings.com

2008 Sales

	$ mil.	% of total
North America	1,130.9	68
Africa	163.0	10
Latin America	118.4	7
Middle East	88.4	5
UK	80.0	5
Asia	45.2	3
Other regions	30.1	2
Total	**1,656.0**	**100**

PRODUCTS/OPERATIONS

2008 Sales

	$ mil.	% of total
Offshore marine services	706.0	43
Aviation services	248.6	15
Commodity trading	208.3	13
Environmental services	167.9	10
Inland river services	138.7	8
Marine transportation services	114.0	7
Other	72.5	4
Total	**1,656.0**	**100**

Selected Services

Cargo delivery
Crew transportation
Environmental services
Helicopter services
Inland barge transportation
Line handling (assist tankers while loading)
Logistics services
Offshore construction support
Offshore drilling
Offshore maintenance work support
Oil spill response services
Salvage
Seismic data gathering support
Telecommunications
Towing and anchor handling (drill rigs and other equipment)
Well stimulation support

COMPETITORS

Baker Hughes
BJ Services
Bristow Group Inc
Cameron International
CHC Helicopter
Crowley Maritime
ENSCO
Global Industries
GulfMark Offshore
Halliburton
Helix Energy Solutions
Martin Resource Management
Oceaneering International
PHI, Inc.
Schlumberger
Tidewater Inc.
Trico Marine
Weatherford International

HISTORICAL FINANCIALS
Company Type: Public

Income Statement

	REVENUE ($ mil.)	NET INCOME ($ mil.)	NET PROFIT MARGIN	FYE: December 31 EMPLOYEES
12/08	1,656.0	223.7	13.5%	5,316
12/07	1,359.2	241.6	17.8%	5,268
12/06	1,323.4	234.4	17.7%	4,994
12/05	972.0	170.7	17.6%	5,035
12/04	491.9	19.9	4.0%	3,900
Annual Growth	**35.5%**	**83.1%**	**—**	**8.1%**

2008 Year-End Financials

Debt ratio: 57.5%	No. of shares (mil.): 20
Return on equity: 13.8%	Dividends
Cash ($ mil.): 275	Yield: 0.0%
Current ratio: 2.71	Payout: —
Long-term debt ($ mil.): 929	Market value ($ mil.): 1,347

Stock History

NYSE: CKH

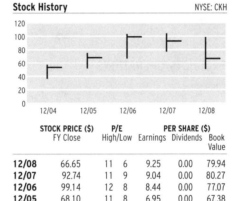

	STOCK PRICE ($) FY Close	P/E High/Low		PER SHARE ($) Earnings	Dividends	Book Value
12/08	66.65	11	6	9.25	0.00	79.94
12/07	92.74	11	9	9.04	0.00	80.27
12/06	99.14	12	8	8.44	0.00	77.07
12/05	68.10	11	8	6.95	0.00	67.38
12/04	53.40	52	35	1.08	0.00	39.29
Annual Growth	**5.7%**	**—**	**—**	**71.1%**	**—**	**19.4%**

Seagate Technology

Seagate Technology knows that if you want to survive in the storage market, you'd better have drive. The company is a leading independent maker of rigid disk drives (or hard drives) used to store data in computers. Its drives are used in systems ranging from personal computers and consumer electronics to high-end servers and mainframes. Seagate sells directly to computer manufacturers and through distributors. About two-thirds of Seagate's sales are to computer hardware manufacturers, which include Hewlett-Packard, Dell, EMC, IBM, and Sun Microsystems; distributors and retailers account for the rest.

The global recession impacted Seagate's operations; sales were down by about 23% in fiscal 2009 and the company went into the red for the first time in eight years. The accompanying credit crisis has several effects. Key suppliers have become insolvent, resulting in product delays, and some customers are unable to finance purchases of Seagate products.

Intense competition in the disk drive industry helps lower prices. Pricing erosion moderated in mid-2009, returning to historical rates after a period of intense price slashing to survive in the recessionary climate; that helped reduce sales. Seagate also experiences seasonality in sales, with the second half of the fiscal year (the first half of the calendar year) seeing lower sales after back-to-school and holiday purchases buoy revenues earlier in the fiscal year.

In an industry that sees constantly falling PC prices, Seagate managed to stay at the front of the disk drive market by significantly undercutting competitors' prices, instituting global layoffs, and consolidating facilities.

Investment firms Silver Lake Partners and Texas Pacific Group took Seagate private in 2000. Prior to being taken private — a transaction that allowed Seagate to realize the value of its large holding in VERITAS Software while avoiding certain tax liabilities — the company had operations that included a business intelligence software developer (Crystal Decisions), a subsidiary that develops storage networking products (Biotech), and a unit devoted to tape storage products. The reorganized Seagate generates virtually all of its sales from its core hard-drive business. It went public again in 2002.

HISTORY

Seagate Technology was founded in 1979 by Alan Shugart, an 18-year veteran of IBM who made floppy disks standard on microcomputers; manufacturing expert and longtime technology industry veteran Tom Mitchell; design engineer Douglas Mahon; and Finis Conner. Seagate pioneered the miniaturizing of larger mainframe hard disk drives for PCs.

Seagate's first product, a 5.25-in. hard disk, sold briskly. With IBM as a customer, the company had grabbed half of the market for small disk drives by 1982; sales reached $344 million by 1984. But Seagate's heavy dependence on IBM showed its double edge as dwindling PC demand prompted IBM to cut orders. Sales in 1985 dropped to $215 million, and profits to $1 million (from $42 million). Seagate transferred its manufacturing to Singapore and cut its California workforce in half. That year Conner, after a quarrel with Shugart, left Seagate to start his own disk drive company, Conner Peripherals. (Mitchell later joined him.)

Using acquisitions to grow, the company purchased Grenex (thin-film magnetic media, 1984), Aeon (aluminum substrates, 1987), and Integrated Power Systems (custom semiconductors, 1987). Seagate also lured back IBM, which turned to an alternate supplier in the interim.

With sales more than doubling in 1986 and again in 1987, Seagate continued to invest in 5.25-in. production, ignoring signs of a coming 3.5-in. drive standard. The strong market in 1988 for the smaller drives prompted Seagate's quick shift to 3.5-in. production. Seagate's purchase of Imprimis in 1989 made it the world's premier independent drive maker and a leader in high-capacity drives.

In 1993 the company acquired a stake in flash memory storage specialist SunDisk (now San-Disk). That year, when Sun Microsystems accounted for 11% of sales, Seagate was the only profitable independent disk drive company. In 1994 it began pursuing its software initiative, acquiring companies including Palindrome and Crystal Computer Services.

Shugart, an iconoclast who once ran his dog for Congress, had a small comeuppance in 1996 when Seagate paid just over $1 billion for Conner Peripherals, which banked on 3.5-in. disk drives from the start and went public in 1988. By the time of the acquisition, Conner was a leading maker of disk and tape drives, storage systems, and software.

Seagate merged Conner's software subsidiary with its own holdings to form Seagate Storage Management Group and continued to expand by buying management software companies. In 1997 the company bought disk drive developer Quinta. Seagate took a charge that year following a ruling that it had sold faulty drives to Arm-strad PLC.

An industry slump, production problems, and lowered PC demand prompted Seagate to cut 20% of its workforce, streamline development, fire Shugart, and replace him with president and COO — and former investment banker — Stephen Luczo. The downturn took its toll when the company suffered a $530 million loss for fiscal 1998. The next year Seagate gained a stake of about 33% in VERITAS Software when it sold its network and storage management software operations to that company for $3.1 billion. Seagate also laid off another 10% of its workforce of nearly 80,000.

In 2000 the company acquired XIOtech, a maker of virtual storage and storage area network systems, for about $360 million. Later that year Seagate entered into an intricate deal with VERITAS, whereby the software maker bought back the stake owned by Seagate. As part of the deal, Seagate was taken private in a buyout led by Silver Lake Partners and Texas Pacific Group.

Also in 2000 COO William Watkins, who joined Seagate when it bought Conner Peripherals, replaced Luczo as president; Luczo remained CEO. The company went public again in 2002. In 2004 Luczo passed the CEO reins to Watkins, but retained his chairmanship. (At the beginning of 2009, however, Watkins stepped down as CEO and Luczo reprised his role as head of the company.)

In a major step to expand its operations, the company agreed in 2005 to acquire rival storage device maker Maxtor for about $1.9 billion in stock; the deal closed in mid-2006. Seagate retained the Maxtor brand.

Co-founder Alan Shugart died in 2006.

EXECUTIVES

Chairman, President, and CEO:
Stephen J. (Steve) Luczo, age 51,
$1,178,553 total compensation
EVP and CFO: Patrick J. O'Malley, age 47,
$1,130,070 total compensation
EVP Product and Process Development and CTO:
Robert (Bob) Whitmore, age 46,
$2,265,132 total compensation
SVP and CIO: Mark Brewer
EVP and General Manager Personal Compute Products:
Michael J. (Mike) Wingert, age 47
EVP Sales, Marketing, and Product Line Management:
Dave Mosley, $1,990,503 total compensation
EVP, General Counsel, and Corporate Secretary:
William L. Hudson, age 56

EVP Sales and Customer Service Operations:
Kurt Richarz, age 48, $1,209,571 total compensation
SVP and General Manager, New Business Initiatives:
Philip (Phil) Pollok, age 52
SVP Recording Heads and Media:
Jaroslaw S. Glembocki, age 51
SVP and General Manager Consumer Electronics:
Patrick D. (Pat) King, age 43
SVP Consumer Solutions Division and i365:
Terry R. Cunningham, age 49
SVP and General Manager, Branded Solutions:
James Druckrey
SVP and General Manager, Seagate Services Group:
Mark Grace
SVP Worldwide Finance: Glen A. Peterson, age 47
SVP, General Counsel, and Corporate Secretary:
Kenneth M. (Ken) Massaroni, age 48
SVP Global Human Resources: Karen Hanlon
SVP Quality: John Scaramuzzo
VP Investor Relations: Rod Cooper
Business Development Officer, Strategic Planning and Corporate Development: Charles C. Pope, age 54,
$2,469,841 total compensation
Chief Technologist: Robert Thibadeau
Auditors: Ernst & Young LLP

LOCATIONS

HQ: Seagate Technology LLC
920 Disc Dr., Scotts Valley, CA 95066
Phone: 831-438-6550 **Fax:** 831-429-6356
Web: www.seagate.com

2009 Sales

	$ mil.	% of total
Singapore	4,186	43
Netherlands	2,849	29
US	2,695	27
Other countries	75	1
Total	**9,805**	**100**

PRODUCTS/OPERATIONS

2009 Sales

	% of total
OEM	64
Distributors	27
Retailers	9
Total	**100**

Selected Products

Personal computing disk drives
 Desktop (Barracuda, DiamondMax)
 Notebook (Momentus)
Enterprise computing disk drives (Barracuda, Cheetah, Savvio)
Online backup, data protection, and recovery services (EVault)

COMPETITORS

Fujitsu	Micron Technology
Hitachi Global Storage	Samsung Electronics
Imation	SanDisk
Intel Corp.	STEC
Iomega	Toshiba
LaCie	Western Digital

HISTORICAL FINANCIALS

Company Type: Public

Income Statement

FYE: Friday nearest June 30

	REVENUE ($ mil.)	NET INCOME ($ mil.)	NET PROFIT MARGIN	EMPLOYEES
6/09	9,805.0	(3,086.0)	—	9,805
6/08	12,708.0	1,262.0	9.9%	54,000
6/07	11,360.0	913.0	8.0%	54,000
6/06	9,206.0	840.0	9.1%	60,000
6/05	7,553.0	707.0	9.4%	44,000
Annual Growth	**6.7%**	**—**	**—**	**(31.3%)**

2009 Year-End Financials

Debt ratio: 128.3%	No. of shares (mil.): 495
Return on equity: —	Dividends
Cash ($ mil.): 1,427	Yield: 2.6%
Current ratio: 1.34	Payout: —
Long-term debt ($ mil.): 1,956	Market value ($ mil.): 5,182

Stock History

NASDAQ (GS): STX

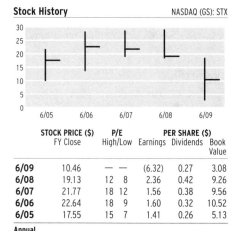

	STOCK PRICE ($) FY Close	P/E High/Low		PER SHARE ($) Earnings	Dividends	Book Value
6/09	10.46	—	—	(6.32)	0.27	3.08
6/08	19.13	12	8	2.36	0.42	9.26
6/07	21.77	18	12	1.56	0.38	9.56
6/06	22.64	18	9	1.60	0.32	10.52
6/05	17.55	15	7	1.41	0.26	5.13
Annual Growth	**(12.1%)**	**—**	**—**	**—**	**0.9%**	**(12.0%)**

Sealed Air Corp.

It's no secret — Sealed Air keeps its customers' products under wraps. The company's largest segment, Food Packaging, produces Cryovac bags, absorbent pads, and foam trays used by food processors and supermarkets to protect meat and poultry. Its Protective Packaging segment produces Bubble Wrap, Instapak foam, Jiffy Mailer envelopes, and Fill-Air inflatable packaging systems. Other products include shrink packaging for consumer goods, such as toys and CDs; medical packaging that holds everything from pacemakers to IV fluid; and specialty packaging for the construction and transportation industries. Sealed Air has more than 100 manufacturing facilities worldwide.

The US accounts for almost half of its sales. The company has embarked on a manufacturing strategy in which it plans to expand its capacity in emerging markets and improve efficiencies at existing facilities.

In 2007 the company bought selected assets of The Dow Chemical Company's Ethafoam product line. The acquisition gave Sealed Air all the rights to technologies, customer contracts, and trademarks, as well as production equipment for Ethafoam, Synergy, Equifoam, and Envision branded foam products. Dow will make the products until 2009, at which time Sealed Air will take over the manufacturing. Sealed Air also announced plans to build a new manufacturing facility in Louisville, Kentucky. It anticipates the plan will be fully operational early in 2009.

Davis Selected Advisers holds a 36% stake in the company.

HISTORY

In the late 1950s, after US engineer Al Fielding and Swiss inventor Marc Chavannes found no takers for their plastic air-bubble-embossed wallpaper, they looked for another use for the material.

They came up with Bubble Wrap, the first product of Sealed Air, which they founded in 1960 and took public soon after. AirCap, as the material was first known, didn't just protect products from damage; it also reduced storage and shipping costs.

Sealed Air expanded in the early 1970s into bubble-lined mailers and adhesive products with subsidiary PolyMask. With the $5 million company in the doldrums, Dublin-born packaging veteran Dermot Dunphy was brought in as CEO in 1971. New products followed Dunphy's entrance, including the Bubble Wrap-based Solar Pool Blanket. Sealed Air's sales moved beyond the US in the 1970s into Canada, Japan, and Western Europe. The company bought Instapak in 1977.

The purchase in 1983 of the Dri-Loc product line moved Sealed Air into food packaging. The company began selling static-control packaging in 1984, and in 1987 it bought padded-mailer maker Jiffy Packaging. Fielding and Chavannes both retired in 1987. Sealed Air pleaded guilty in 1989 to making illegal chemical shipments to Libya (made by a division the company had since sold).

By 1989 Sealed Air had plenty of cash on hand, but with no appealing acquisitions to spend it on, the company was a potential takeover target. It had also grown complacent. To provide greater incentive to the company's rank and file while warding off any buyout overtures, Dunphy and CFO Bill Hickey took Sealed Air through a risky recapitalization. This plunged the company into debt but more than doubled its employees' ownership stake. The newly inspired packaging maker became more efficient, the cost of Sealed Air's raw materials dropped, and the company brought its debt back down over the next several years.

The acquisition of Korrvu in 1991 gave Sealed Air a gateway to innovative packaging for electronics manufacturers. The company made a host of mostly small purchases in Asia, Australia, Europe, and North America between 1993 and 1996. When Sealed Air bought New Zealand-based Trigon Industries in 1995, its food-packaging business nearly doubled in size, along with sales outside the US.

In 1998 Sealed Air made an Instapak-like expansion when it combined with W. R. Grace's packaging business (including the Cryovac, Formpac, and Omicron lines). Grace structured a deal with Sealed Air that gave Grace's shareholders about two-thirds of the resulting packaging-only company. Sealed Air tripled its sales and number of employees with the purchase.

The company restructured its operations in 1999 to integrate its newly acquired businesses. It closed facilities with overlapping operations and eliminated 750 jobs (5% of its workforce). Dunphy retired in 2000 (although he remains a director) and president William Hickey became CEO. That year Sealed Air acquired Dolphin Packaging (plastic packaging products) and Shanklin (high-performance shrink-film packaging equipment) to complement its shrink films.

In 2001, more than three years after the company combined its operations with W. R. Grace's packaging business, Sealed Air continued to defend itself against asbestos lawsuits related to Grace's past operations. (In 2005 the company's definitive settlement agreement was accepted by the bankruptcy court.)

Another lawsuit was prompted by a 2003 fire in a New Jersey nightclub that killed 100 people. The fire occured during a concert by the rock band Great White. Their pyrotechnics set fire to soundproofing material on the walls inside the club. The material was allegedly supplied by Sealed Air, which did not admit to any wrongdoing. However, the company agreed to pay $25 million to the victim's families in 2008.

Sealed Air restructured its reporting system in 2004, bringing its medical films, connectors, and tubing under its Food Packaging segment. It also cut nearly 400 employees and consolidated some of its operations.

Early in 2006 Sealed Air acquired Nelipak Holdings, a Netherlands-based rigid packaging company. The company sold its security bag business (Trigon) to Ampac in 2007, and it sold its interest in joint venture PolyMask (surface protection films) to partner 3M.

EXECUTIVES

President, CEO, and Director: William V. Hickey, age 64, $2,490,424 total compensation
SVP and CFO: David H. Kelsey, age 58, $1,037,125 total compensation
VP Technology and Innovation: Ann Savoca
SVP: Robert A. Pesci, age 63, $829,648 total compensation
SVP: David B. Crosier, age 59, $853,025 total compensation
VP, General Counsel, and Secretary: H. Katherine White, age 63
VP: Manuel Mondragón, age 59
VP: Jonathan B. Baker, age 55
Controller: Jeffrey S. Warren, age 55
Treasurer: Tod S. Christie, age 50
Investor and Media Relations: Eric D. Burrell
Director Corporate Communications: Ken Aurichio
Director Investor Relations: Amanda Butler
Auditors: KPMG LLP

LOCATIONS

HQ: Sealed Air Corporation
200 Riverfront Blvd., Elmwood Park, NJ 07407
Phone: 201-791-7600 **Fax:** 201-703-4205
Web: www.sealedair.com

2008 Sales

	$ mil.	% of total
US	2,185.2	45
International	2,658.3	55
Total	**4,843.5**	**100**

PRODUCTS/OPERATIONS

2008 Sales

	$ mil.	% of total
Food packaging	1,969.4	41
Food solutions	988.3	20
Protective packaging	1,480.3	31
Other	405.5	8
Total	**4,843.5**	**100**

Selected Products

Food Packaging
  Absorbent pads & case liners
  Bulk packaging
  Foam trays
  Laminates
  Lidstock
  Pouches
  Rollstock
  Vacuum bags
Medical Packaging
  Cleanroom blisters
  Films
  Lidding material
  Medical device packaging
  Sealing machines

Protective Packaging
  Air cushioning (Bubble Wrap)
  Cushioned mailing bags (Jiffy Mailer)
  Foam packaging (Instapak)
  Inflatable packaging and cushioning (Fill-Air and FillTeck)
  Paper cushioning (PackTiger)
  Paper packaging (Kushion Kraft and Custom Wrap)
  Polyethylene fabrication foam (Cellu-Cushion, CelluPlank, Stratocell)
  Polyethylene foam (Cell-Aire)
  Suspension and retention packaging (Korrvu)
Shrink Packaging
  Equipment
  Films
Specialty Materials
  Foams
  Solar pool heating

COMPETITORS

3M
AEP Industries
Bemis
Curwood
Huhtamäki
Intertape Polymer
Packaging Dynamics
Pactiv
Pliant Corporation
Polyair Inter Pack
Printpack
Reynolds Food Packaging
Sonoco Products
Tekni-Plex
Winpak

HISTORICAL FINANCIALS

Company Type: Public

Income Statement

FYE: December 31

	REVENUE ($ mil.)	NET INCOME ($ mil.)	NET PROFIT MARGIN	EMPLOYEES
12/08	4,843.5	179.9	3.7%	17,000
12/07	4,651.2	353.0	7.6%	17,700
12/06	4,327.9	274.1	6.3%	17,400
12/05	4,085.1	255.8	6.3%	17,000
12/04	3,798.1	215.6	5.7%	17,600
Annual Growth	6.3%	(4.4%)	—	(0.9%)

2008 Year-End Financials

Debt ratio: 67.0%
Return on equity: 9.1%
Cash ($ mil.): 129
Current ratio: 1.03
Long-term debt ($ mil.): 1,290
No. of shares (mil.): 159
Dividends
  Yield: 3.2%
  Payout: 48.5%
Market value ($ mil.): 2,372

Stock History

NYSE: SEE

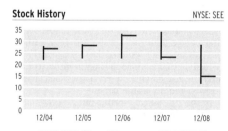

	STOCK PRICE ($) FY Close	P/E High/Low		PER SHARE ($) Earnings	Dividends	Book Value
12/08	14.94	29	12	0.99	0.48	12.12
12/07	23.14	18	12	1.89	0.40	12.72
12/06	32.46	22	16	1.47	0.30	10.42
12/05	28.08	21	17	1.35	0.00	8.77
12/04	26.64	24	20	1.13	0.00	8.40
Annual Growth	(13.5%)		— —	(3.3%)	—	9.6%

Sealy Corporation

Sealy is a slumbering giant. It's the world's largest maker of bedding products and a leading US manufacturer, with a 20% market share. Sealy makes mattresses and box springs under the Sealy, Bassett, and Stearns & Foster names and sells them in more than 7,000 stores. Its customers include sleep shops, furniture and department stores, warehouse clubs, and mass merchandisers, as well as the hospitality industry. Sealy also licenses its name to makers of other bedding products and home furnishings. Sealy, formerly owned by Bain Capital, was bought by Kohlberg Kravis Roberts (KKR) in 2004. KKR owns some 51% of Sealy, which filed an IPO in 2005 and began trading in March 2006.

Since its initial public offering, the mattress maker has been working to expand its US operations. In 2007 Sealy created a North American division as it realigned its business to ensure continued sales gains. Amid the worsening US economy, Sealy reorganized its US operations in 2008 by reducing the number of regional divisions from three to two (East and West) and by eliminating an unspecified number of jobs. The regional reorganization was designed to cut costs and keep the company competitive.

While the majority of Sealy's sales come from the US, the company also has licensees and sales operations worldwide. Sealy is making acquisitions and building plants to expand its business in the Latin American region. Sealy operates a network of some 30 factories worldwide.

In early 2008 David McIlquham, a 20-year Sealy veteran, resigned as chairman and CEO. He was replaced on an interim basis by Larry Rogers, another Sealy long-timer who had been president of the company's North American operations. Rogers became the company's permanent president and CEO in July 2008.

HISTORY

Daniel Haynes, a cotton gin builder, first made a new, more resilient type of cotton-filled mattress in 1881 in Sealy, Texas. In 1889 he patented a machine to mass-produce his increasingly popular product. Haynes sold manufacturing rights to firms in other cities, and in 1906 he sold his patents to a Texas firm that renamed itself Sealy.

Sealy expanded by advertising in national magazines and finding licensees to open mattress factories. By 1920 the company had 28 licensed plants. When doctors in the 1940s advised that people with back problems sleep on firm mattresses, Sealy designed the Orthopedic Firm-O-Rest; it was renamed the Posturepedic in 1950 after the FTC banned the use of the medical term "orthopedic" in brand names.

In the 1950s Sealy sprung out geographically (it added Canadian licensees in 1954) and financially (sales quintupled to $48 million during the decade). During the 1960s it became the first mattress firm to advertise on prime-time TV.

The princess had her uncomfortable pea; Sealy had The Ohio Mattress Company, one of its independent licensees. In the 1950s Ohio Mattress began entering other licensees' territories (despite exclusive territory agreements) and lowering its prices to force its new rivals to sell out. In 1963 Ernest Wuliger succeeded his father as president of Ohio Mattress and began an aggressive expansion campaign. He acquired a Sealy licensee in Texas and Oklahoma in 1967, but Sealy bought some of the licensees that Wuliger wanted. The Supreme Court found Sealy guilty that year of antitrust violations regarding price-fixing and exclusive territories. Still, by the end of the 1960s, Sealy had sales of $113 million and additional international licensees.

Wuliger took Ohio Mattress public in 1970. The next year Wuliger began a series of antitrust lawsuits against Sealy that lasted fifteen years. Ohio Mattress acquired bedding maker Stearns & Foster (1983) and Woodstuff Manufacturing (1985). In 1986 the legal bedding battle ended, and Ohio Mattress was awarded $77 million. In 1987 Ohio Mattress opted to buy Sealy and all but one of Sealy's nine US licensees. It acquired the holdout licensee's Sealy license later in 1987 and became the leading mattress manufacturer.

Investment firm Gibbons Goodwin van Amerongen led a $965 million, junk-bond-financed LBO of Ohio Mattress in 1989; it renamed the company Sealy in 1990. Amid a downturn in the junk-bond market, from 1991 to 1993 Sealy changed owners twice, ending up with investment fund Zell/Chilmark. It also found itself in bed with a variety of new CEOs. Right after the LBO, Wuliger resigned due to conflicts with the new owners. COO Malcolm Candlish was promoted to CEO. In 1992 Candlish resigned and was replaced by Lyman Beggs, who lasted until 1995, when he was replaced by Ronald Jones, former head of Masco Home Furnishings.

In 1997 investment firm Bain Capital bought a majority stake in Sealy. Sealy also sold its Samuel Lawrence bedroom furniture unit (formerly Woodstuff Manufacturing) that year. The company relocated from Ohio to North Carolina in 1998. Sealy lost $34 million that fiscal year, in part due to early debt repayment related to the Bain Capital buyout.

In 2000 Sealy acquired the Bassett bedding license and Carrington-Chase brand from Premier Bedding; the deal included the corresponding factory. Sealy also bought control of Argentina-based bedding maker Rosen and built a factory in Brazil. In 2001 Sealy announced it would close its Tennessee bedding plant because it wasn't profitable. Marking its entrance into Europe, Sealy acquired Paris-based Sapsa Bedding the same year. In April 2002 David McIlquham replaced Jones as CEO; Jones remained as chairman until 2004.

In April 2004 Sealy was bought by Kohlberg Kravis Roberts (KKR) for about $1.5 billion. It went public in 2006.

In 2008 McIlquham resigned his posts and was replaced by company executive Larry Rogers as president and CEO.

EXECUTIVES

Chairman: Paul J. Norris, age 61
President and CEO: Lawrence J. (Larry) Rogers, age 60, $1,188,027 total compensation
EVP Operations, North America: G. Michael Hofmann, age 50, $390,378 total compensation
EVP and CFO: Jeffrey C. (Jeff) Ackerman, age 45, $810,022 total compensation
VP IT and CIO: David Twine
SVP Research and Engineering and Chief Science Officer: Alan Letton
EVP Sales: Louis R. Bachicha, age 53
SVP National Accounts: Steve Rusing
VP and Treasurer: Mark D. Boehmer
VP Marketing: Mark Delahanty
VP and COO, Sealy Canada: Kevin Sisson
Auditors: Deloitte & Touche LLP

LOCATIONS

HQ: Sealy Corporation
1 Office Pkwy. at Sealy Dr., Trinity, NC 27370
Phone: 336-861-3500   **Fax:** 336-861-3501
Web: www.sealy.com

2008 Sales

	$ mil.	% of total
Americas		
US	1,055.7	70
Canada	187.7	13
Other International	105.9	7
Europe	148.7	10
Total	**1,498.0**	**100**

PRODUCTS/OPERATIONS

Brand Names

Advanced Generation Sealy Posturepedic
Bassett
Bed Time
Carrington-Chase
Meyer
Sealy
Sealy Back Saver
Sealy Correct Comfort
Sealy Kids
Sealy Posture Premier
Sealy Posturematic
Sealy Posturepedic
Sealy Posturepedic Crown Jewel
Stearns & Foster

COMPETITORS

Mattress Giant	Simmons Bedding
Mattress Holding	Spring Air
Select Comfort	Tempur-Pedic
Serta	W. S. Badcock

HISTORICAL FINANCIALS

Company Type: Public

Income Statement

FYE: Sunday nearest November 30

	REVENUE ($ mil.)	NET INCOME ($ mil.)	NET PROFIT MARGIN	EMPLOYEES
11/08	1,498.0	(2.9)	—	4,817
11/07	1,702.1	79.4	4.7%	6,099
11/06	1,582.8	74.0	4.7%	6,233
11/05	1,469.6	68.5	4.7%	6,208
11/04	1,314.0	(47.9)	—	6,399
Annual Growth	**3.3%**	**—**	**—**	**(6.9%)**

2008 Year-End Financials

Debt ratio: —
Return on equity: —
Cash ($ mil.): 27
Current ratio: 1.24
Long-term debt ($ mil.): 762

No. of shares (mil.): 92
Dividends
  Yield: 2.5%
  Payout: —
Market value ($ mil.): 277

Stock History

NYSE: ZZ

	STOCK PRICE ($) FY Close	P/E High/Low	PER SHARE ($) Earnings	PER SHARE ($) Dividends	PER SHARE ($) Book Value
11/08	3.01	— —	(0.03)	0.08	(1.79)
11/07	13.04	22 14	0.82	0.30	(1.40)
11/06	14.88	21 14	0.83	0.15	(1.88)
Annual Growth	**(55.0%)**	**— —**	**—**	**(27.0%)**	**—**

Sears, Roebuck

Sears, Roebuck and Co. hasn't outgrown the mall scene, but it's spending more time in other places. Beyond its 855 US mall-based stores, Sears has more than 1,230 other locations nationwide. The company operates more than 870 independently-owned Sears Hometown Stores (formerly known as dealer stores) in small towns and about 110 Sears hardware stores and some 85 Orchard Supply Hardware shops. Sears' stores sell apparel, tools, and appliances, and provide home services (remodeling, appliance repairs) under the Sears Parts & Repair Services and A&E Factory brands. It also sells appliances and tools online. Sears was acquired by Kmart Holding Corp. in 2005. The deal formed Sears Holdings, which owns both chains.

Sears Holdings is among the nation's largest and most troubled retailers, with about 3,000 stores and about $46 billion in annual sales which is down from more than $50 billion the previous year. (Since the megamerger, several hundred Kmart locations — mainly in urban and dense suburban markets — have been converted to Sears stores.)

To date, the merger has failed to improve the retail performance of either Sears or Kmart. Indeed, Sears Holdings has announced that it will shutter about two dozen underperforming stores (including Sears, Roebuck locations) in 2009, following a dismal 2008 holiday season for retailers. The company closed 28 stores in 2008.

Sales at both chains have declined. Aylwin Lewis, who served since 2005 as president and CEO of the company, stepped down. Lewis was replaced on an interim basis by EVP W. Bruce Johnson while the company searches for a permanent replacement — who will face the tough job of reviving the sagging retail operations at both chains.

The combination of Sears and Kmart was a response to the pounding both companies endured at the hands of Wal-Mart and other discount and mass merchandisers. Sears' previous responses include pushing its private brands of apparel, tools, and appliances (Crossroads, Craftsman, Kenmore, respectively). It has also cut prices on some appliances to fend off rival chains, such as Home Depot and Lowe's. The retailer is also working to improve its online operations to drive Web customers to its stores and store customers to the Web.

The company's freestanding off-the-mall format — 70-plus Sears Essentials/Grand stores — is designed to compete directly with supercenters by selling consumables, health and beauty aids, housewares, and toys, among other offerings, all under one very large roof.

In search of an identity to boost flat sales, the company is consolidating eight of its private-label clothing lines under one name: Covington. Sears also purchased catalog retailer Lands' End, which brought the Lands' End apparel brand as well as the company's strong direct marketing and online sales to the Sears fold. There are about 220 Lands' End departments inside Sears stores, and more are planned.

To breathe new life into what some see as a stale image, Sears is ramping up efforts to tap into the youth market. With a focus on hip and urban youth consumers, the company began stocking teen footwear line Skechers and is adding a line of street clothes and accessories designed by hip hop artist LL Cool J. Sears is also teaming up with MTV to produce a back-to-school movie.

Sears also hopes to make an impression on younger customers by bringing toys back to its lineup. In 2009 about 20 stores made way for toy departments that will carry playthings from makers such as Hasbro, Mattel, and LeapFrog. The company hopes to attract shoppers who frequented KB Toys and other specialty outlets that have since shut down.

Chairman Edward Lampert owns about 50% of Sears Holdings through ESL Investments.

HISTORY

Richard Sears, a Minnesota railway agent, bought a load of watches in 1886 that were being returned to the maker. He started the R. W. Sears Watch Company six months later, moved to Chicago, and in 1887 hired watchmaker Alvah Roebuck. Sears sold the watch business in 1889 and two years later formed the mail-order business that in 1893 became Sears, Roebuck and Co. It issued its first general catalog in 1896, targeting mainly farmers.

Roebuck left the company in 1895, and Sears found two new partners: Aaron Nussbaum (who left in 1901) and Julius Rosenwald. In 1906 the company went public to finance expansion. Differences soon arose between Sears and Rosenwald; Sears departed in 1908, and Rosenwald became president.

In 1925 the firm brought out a line of tires under the name Allstate. That year it opened its first retail store, and by 1931 the company's catalog sales trailed its retail sales. The rapid growth of Sears' retail operations was instrumental in the development of its prominent lines of store-brand merchandise. Sears began offering Allstate auto insurance in 1931.

Sales shot up after WWII, passing the $1 billion mark in 1945 and doubling just a year later. Sears targeted the fast-growing Sun Belt and nascent suburbs for expansion. By the early 1950s, sales of durable goods had fallen off, and the company began stocking more clothing.

After struggling through the late 1970s, Sears diversified. It acquired Coldwell Banker (real estate sales) and Dean Witter Reynolds (stock brokerage) in 1981 and launched the Discover credit card in 1985.

In reaction to falling market share in the 1980s, Sears lurched from one retail strategy to another and diversified into auto supplies and repairs. In 1993 the company sold its remaining stake in Coldwell Banker and spun off Dean Witter and Discover.

In 2005 the firm spun off insurer Allstate. Sears' top merchandiser, Arthur Martinez, became CEO that year. He gave Sears a makeover, catering especially to its mainly female clientele.

In 1996 and 1997 Sears abandoned a pair of ventures with IBM, including Prodigy (an online service that the two companies sold at a huge loss).

Again revamping its retail strategy, in 1998 the company sold its Western Auto wholesale business (which also operated about 600 Parts America stores) to Advance Holding. In 1998 a stream of high-ranking officers left the company. The executive departures continued in 1999 as Sears reorganized its automotive and direct-marketing units and eventually cut some 1,400 jobs at headquarters.

In 2000 Martinez stepped down as CEO; president of services Alan Lacy assumed the role in October 2000. In 2002 the company laid off about 22% of its workforce. In June of the same year Sears bought catalog retailer Lands' End for almost $2 billion.

In September 2003 Sears sold its giant credit-card business to Citigroup for about $6 billion in pretax cash. (It was the nation's eighth-largest credit card portfolio, with about 25 million active accounts.) The business contributed about 55% to Sears' annual profits. To better focus on core operations, Sears sold its National Tire & Battery (NTB) chain to TBC Corporation for $225 million in December 2003.

In 2005 Kmart Holding Corp acquired Sears, Roebuck. The deal formed a new company, Sears Holdings, which is now the parent company of both chains.

EXECUTIVES

Interim President and Interim CEO: W. Bruce Johnson, age 57, $1,166,293 total compensation
SVP Supply Chain and Operations: James P. (Jim) Mixon, age 64
CFO: Michael D. (Mike) Collins, $618,593 total compensation
SVP, Controller, and Chief Accounting Officer: William K. Phelan, age 46
VP and Chief Marketing Officer: Don Hamblen
EVP and Chief Administrative Officer; Chairman, Sears Canada: William C. Crowley, age 51
EVP Store Operations: Kevin R. Holt, age 50, $2,248,833 total compensation
SVP; President, Apparel: Craig M. Israel
SVP; President, Tools, Lawn, and Garden: John W. Froman, age 54
SVP; President, Appliances: Douglas T. (Doug) Moore, age 52
SVP Human Resources, General Counsel, and Corporate Secretary: William R. Harker, age 36
VP and General Manager, Kenmore: Betsy Owens
VP and General Merchandise Manager: Steven Light
VP Tools, Hardware, and Paint: Dave Figler
President, Home Electronics: Karen A. Austin, age 47
Auditors: Deloitte & Touche LLP

LOCATIONS

HQ: Sears, Roebuck and Co.
3333 Beverly Rd., Hoffman Estates, IL 60179
Phone: 847-286-2500 **Fax:** 800-326-0485
Web: www.sears.com

PRODUCTS/OPERATIONS

2009 Stores

	No.
Specialty	1,233
Full-line mall	856
Sears Grand/Essentials	73
Total	**2,162**

Selected Brands

Hard Goods
 Craftsman
 DieHard
 Kenmore
 WeatherBeater

Soft Goods
 Apostrophe
 Canyon River Blues
 Covington
 Lands' End
 TKS Basics

Selected Specialty Stores

Lands' End (casual apparel and accessories)
Orchard Supply Hardware (neighborhood hardware stores)
Sears Auto Centers
Sears Hometown Stores (independently owned)
Sears Hardware
The Great Indoors (home decorating and remodeling superstores)

COMPETITORS

Ace Hardware	J. C. Penney
Army and Air Force Exchange	Kohl's
	L.L. Bean
AutoZone	Lowe's
Bed Bath & Beyond	Men's Wearhouse
Belk	Pep Boys
Best Buy	RadioShack
Big 5	Ross Stores
Big Lots	ShopKo Stores
Brown Shoe	Snap-on
Burlington Coat Factory	Target
Collective Brands	TJX Companies
Family Dollar Stores	Toys "R" Us
Foot Locker	True Value
Home Depot	Wal-Mart

Sempra Energy

Sempra Energy isn't joining the Marines, but it is faithful to making money in utility markets in the US and around the world. In the US Sempra distributes natural gas to some 5.7 million customers and electricity to 1.4 million customers through Southern California Gas (SoCalGas) and San Diego Gas & Electric (SDG&E), its subsidiary utilities. Unregulated subsidiaries include Sempra Pipelines & Storage, Sempra Generation, and Sempra LNG, which have global energy projects and serve power and gas customers (mainly in Latin America). Sempra Energy companies serve more that 29 million customers worldwide.

The company develops and acquires merchant power plants (Sempra Generation, formerly Sempra Energy Resources), liquefied natural gas (LNG) regasification facilities (Sempra LNG), and affordable housing properties.

To expand its commodities trading business, in 2008 Sempra formed a partnership with The Royal Bank of Scotland to operate RBS Sempra Commodities, including Sempra Energy Trading, which trades and markets wholesale energy commodities in Asia, Europe, and North America.

In a move to expand its midstream and distribution assets in the Southeastern US, that year the company acquired EnergySouth for $510 million.

HISTORY

Sempra Energy is the latest incarnation of some of California's leading lights. Formed by the $6.2 billion merger between Enova and Pacific Enterprises, the company traces its roots back to the 1880s.

Enova began as San Diego Gas, which lit its first gaslights in 1881 and added electricity in 1887 (when it became San Diego Gas & Electric Light). Massive utility holding company Standard Gas & Electric bought the company in 1905 and renamed it San Diego Consolidated Gas & Electric. Over the next few decades, San Diego Consolidated expanded through acquisitions and even stayed profitable during the Depression. But the 1935 Public Utilities Holding Company Act forced Standard to divest many of its widespread utilities, and in 1940 San Diego Consolidated went public as San Diego Gas & Electric (SDG&E).

SDG&E grew quickly until the 1970s, when new environmental laws slowed plans to build more power plants, and rates soared because the company had to purchase power. The company finally added more generating capacity in the 1980s, and the state of California allowed SDG&E to diversify into real estate, software, and oil and gas distribution. In 1995 it created Enova to serve as its holding company.

Meanwhile, up the coast in San Francisco, Pacific Enterprises began as gas lamp rental firm Pacific Lighting in 1886; it quickly moved into gas distribution to defend its market against electricity. The firm bought three Los Angeles gas and electric utilities in 1889 and continued to grow through acquisitions; it consolidated all of its utilities in the 1920s. Pacific Lighting sold its electric properties to the city of Los Angeles in 1937 in exchange for a long-term gas franchise.

The company entered oil and gas exploration in 1960. A decade later it merged its gas utility operations into Southern California Gas (SoCalGas). Pacific Lighting continued to diversify in the 1980s, buying two oil and gas companies and three drugstore chains. Renamed Pacific Enterprises in 1988, the company launched an unsuccessful diversification effort that cost $88 million in 1991. Over the next two years it sold off noncore businesses to focus on SoCalGas, and in the mid-1990s it began moving into South and Central America. This included a joint venture with Enova and Mexico's Proxima SA to build and operate Mexico's first private utility.

Pacific Enterprises and Enova agreed in 1997 to a $6.2 billion merger; Sempra Energy was born in 1998. That year California began deregulating its retail power market. In response, Sempra sold SDG&E's non-nuclear power plants (1,900 MW) in 1999. It used the proceeds to eliminate its competitive transition charge and, in turn, lowered its electric rates.

But under deregulation, rates tripled by mid-2000; that summer the California Public Utilities Commission (CPUC) implemented a rate freeze for electric customers. Wholesale power prices soared, and rolling blackouts occurred in 2000 and 2001 as a result of the state's inadequate energy supply. In 2001 the CPUC began allowing utilities to increase their rates, and SDG&E agreed to sell its transmission assets to the state for about $1 billion.

Sempra sold its 72.5% share in power marketing firm Energy America to British energy company Centrica in 2001. In 2002 the company purchased bankrupt utility Enron's London-based metals trading unit for about $145 million; later that year it purchased Enron's metals concentrates and metals warehousing businesses.

The company restructured its competitive energy business units in 2005, renaming several divisions and dividing the former Sempra Energy Solutions operations (retail energy marketing and services for commercial and industrial customers) under the Commodities and Generation divisions. That year Sempra sold one of its gas storage units to Vulcan Capital, an investment company headed up by Microsoft co-founder Paul Allen, for a reported $250 million.

In 2006 the company settled class action litigation that claimed that two of its subsidiaries, Southern California Gas and San Diego Gas & Electric, helped to create the 2000-2001 energy crises in California by restricting the supply of natural gas to the state.

In 2007 Sempra was awarded a $172 million settlement arising from a 2002 dispute over the company's minority stakes in two Argentine natural gas holding companies.

EXECUTIVES

Chairman and CEO: Donald E. Felsinger, age 61, $11,979,186 total compensation
President, COO, and Director: Neal E. Schmale, age 62, $7,205,487 total compensation
EVP and CFO: Mark A. Snell, age 52, $3,760,448 total compensation
VP and Chief Compliance Officer: Randall B. Peterson, age 51
EVP Corporate Development: Edwin A. Guiles, age 59, $5,505,556 total compensation
EVP External Affairs: Jessie J. Knight Jr., age 58
EVP and General Counsel: M. Javade Chaudhri, age 56, $4,523,237 total compensation
SVP Human Resources and Chief Ethics Officer: G. Joyce Rowland, age 53
SVP and Treasurer: Charles A. McMonagle, age 58
SVP, Controller, and Chief Accounting Officer: Joseph A. (Joe) Householder, age 53
SVP and Chief Ethics Officer, Human Resources: G. Joyce Rowland
VP Tax and Chief Tax Counsel: Paul Yong
VP Mergers and Acquisitions: Richard A. Vaccari
VP Government Relations: J. William (Bill) Ichord, age 53
VP Investor Relations: Jeffery W. Martin, age 47
VP, Audit Services: Amy Chiu
Corporate Secretary and Assistant General Counsel: Randall L. Clark
Auditors: Deloitte & Touche LLP

LOCATIONS

HQ: Sempra Energy
101 Ash St., San Diego, CA 92101
Phone: 619-696-2000　　**Fax:** 619-696-2374
Web: www.sempra.com

2008 Sales

	$ mil.	% of total
North America		
US	9,743	91
Canada	(12)	—
Latin America	918	8
Europe	93	1
Asia	16	—
Total	**10,758**	**100**

PRODUCTS/OPERATIONS

2008 Sales

	$ mil.	% of total
Southern California Gas Company	4,768	44
San Diego Gas & Electric	3,251	30
Sempra Generation	1,784	16
RBS Sempra Commodities	500	6
Sempra Pipelines & Storage	457	4
Adjustments	(2)	—
Total	**10,758**	**100**

Selected Subsidiaries

Sempra Energy Utilities
　San Diego Gas & Electric (SDG&E, regulated gas and electric utility)
　Southern California Gas Company (SoCalGas, regulated gas utility)
Sempra Global (formerly Sempra Energy Global Enterprises)
　RBS Sempra Commodities (50%; wholesale and retail energy trading and marketing, metals trading; Sempra Energy Trading)
　Sempra Generation (formerly Sempra Energy Resources, independent power production)
　Sempra LNG (formerly Sempra Energy LNG, acquisition and development of liquefied natural gas facilities)
　Sempra Pipelines & Storage (formerly Sempra Energy International, power generation and distribution and gas distribution, transportation, and compression)
Other operations
　Sempra Energy Financial (affordable housing properties and alternative fuel projects)

HISTORICAL FINANCIALS

Company Type: Public

Income Statement

FYE: December 31

	REVENUE ($ mil.)	NET INCOME ($ mil.)	NET PROFIT MARGIN	EMPLOYEES
12/08	10,758.0	1,113.0	10.3%	13,673
12/07	11,438.0	1,099.0	9.6%	14,314
12/06	11,761.0	1,406.0	12.0%	14,061
12/05	11,737.0	920.0	7.8%	13,420
12/04	9,410.0	895.0	9.5%	13,381
Annual Growth	3.4%	5.6%	—	0.5%

2008 Year-End Financials

Debt ratio: 82.1%	No. of shares (mil.): 245
Return on equity: 13.6%	Dividends
Cash ($ mil.): 331	Yield: 3.2%
Current ratio: 0.69	Payout: 30.9%
Long-term debt ($ mil.): 6,544	Market value ($ mil.): 10,459

Stock History

NYSE: SRE

	STOCK PRICE ($) FY Close	P/E High/Low		PER SHARE ($) Earnings	Dividends	Book Value
12/08	42.63	14	8	4.43	1.37	32.48
12/07	61.88	16	12	4.16	1.24	33.99
12/06	56.04	11	8	5.38	1.20	30.61
12/05	44.84	13	10	3.65	1.16	25.11
12/04	36.68	10	8	3.83	1.00	19.83
Annual Growth	3.8%	—	—	3.7%	8.2%	13.1%

Service Corporation

Service Corporation International (SCI) is to death what H&R Block is to taxes. SCI, the largest funeral and cemetery services company in North America, operates some 1,300 funeral homes and about 370 cemeteries in 40-plus US states, the District of Columbia, Puerto Rico, Canada, and Germany. The company's primary services include embalming, burial, and cremation. As part of its business, SCI also sells traditional funeral necessities, including prearranged funeral services, caskets, burial vaults, cremation receptacles, flowers, and burial garments. The company expanded significantly in late 2006 by acquiring its chief rival, Alderwoods Group.

The Alderwoods deal has been the latest — and biggest — in a series of acquisitions that have fueled SCI's growth. The purchases have enabled the company to operate clusters of funeral homes in the same geographic region, allowing them to share personnel, vehicles, and preparation services, thereby lowering their operating costs. SCI maintains the local identity of each home, allowing it to handle services for different religious and ethnic groups. In Manhattan, for example, SCI owns the top Christian funeral home (Campbell) and the leading Jewish funeral home (Riverside).

Its aggressive acquisition program, however, led to daunting debt. SCI, in turn, spent 2007 selling off certain assets. In December 2007, the firm sold 46 cemeteries and 30 funeral homes to competitor StoneMor Partners for $71 million. It sold its Mayflower National Life Insurance Company, acquired alongside Alderwoods, in July 2007 to Assurant for more than $67 million.

During the past few years, SCI has been reducing its international holdings to focus on its core business: North American funeral service locations and cemeteries. To that end, it has sold its minority interest in its UK operation and its funeral homes in Argentina, Chile, Singapore, and Uruguay. SCI also is looking to sell about a dozen funeral homes in Germany, which represents its only remaining international holding.

As the popularity of lower-cost cremation in North America has increased to about 42% of SCI's business (up from about a third 10 years ago), the company has been focused on adding new products and services, including online memorials and themed ceremonies, in an attempt to boost revenue. Other parties cutting into SCI's profits include competition from casket wholesalers, online retailers, and independently owned funeral homes.

Call it unburied treasure: SCI has more than $6 billion worth of backlogged unfulfilled funeral contracts.

HISTORY

When Robert Waltrip was just 20, in the early 1950s, he inherited Houston's Heights Funeral Home, which his father and aunt had founded in 1926. Waltrip acquired several other funeral homes, modeling his operations on other popular service chains, such as Holiday Inn and McDonald's. In 1962 he incorporated Service Corporation International (SCI) and began expanding across the country.

SCI went public in 1969, and by 1975 it was the largest provider of funeral services in the US. However, that year the FTC accused the company of overcharging customers for flowers, cremation, and other services. SCI was ordered to refund overcharges it had made to cremation customers (it had charged them for caskets), and the FTC issued industry guidelines to prevent deceptive practices.

Two years later SCI began offering advance sales of funeral services so that clients could avoid the effects of inflation by reserving future services and caskets at current prices. While it was barred from using the prepaid funds until funerals were performed, some states allowed the use of investment profits from those funds.

The company moved into flower shops in 1982, and two years later SCI bought Amedco, a top casket maker and a major supplier of embalming fluid, burial clothing, and mortuary furniture. (Amedco was later sold.)

SCI spun off 71 rural funeral homes as Equity Corporation International (ECI) in 1991 (it sold its remaining 40% stake in 1996). The company continued its rapid pace of acquisitions, buying 342 homes and 57 cemeteries from 1991 to 1993. It made its first acquisition outside North America in 1993 with the purchase of Pine Grove Funeral Group, the largest funeral and cremations provider in Australia. SCI entered the European market by acquiring Great Southern Group and Plantsbrook of the UK in 1994, as well as the funeral operations of Lyonnaise des Eaux of France a year later.

In 1997 and 1998 it swallowed up 602 funeral homes, 98 cemeteries, and 37 crematoria. SCI bought American Annuity Group's prearranged funeral services unit in 1998. In 1999 it bought back all of Equity Corporation International (about 440 US funeral homes and cemeteries).

With SCI's earnings slumping — which the company attributed in part to declining mortality rates — president and COO William Heiligbrodt resigned in 1999. Also in 1999 SCI deep-sixed about 2,000 jobs and consolidated its funeral home and cemetery groups in the US down to 87 (from 200).

To help pay down its debt, SCI sold its French insurance subsidiary and its Northern Ireland funeral operations in 2000 and sold more than 500 funeral locations and cemeteries the next year.

A class-action lawsuit filed in December 2001 claimed the company broke open burial vaults and dumped the contents, crushed vaults to make room for others, and mixed body parts from different individuals; the company denied the charges. In May 2003 SCI agreed to pay penalties of approximately $10 million stemming from the lawsuit and faced felony charges filed against the company and two of its Florida cemetery executives. SCI agreed in December 2003 to pay $100 million to settle the class-action lawsuit and individual lawsuits pending regarding its Florida cemetery operations.

In early 2004 SCI sold its French funeral operation, OGF Group, to Vestar Capital Partners in a management buyout transaction. Vestar and SCI reinvested in the operation and took about a 25% ownership.

In November 2006 SCI acquired its chief rival, Alderwoods Group, for about $856 million and assumed some $374 million in debt. To gain regulatory approval for the transaction, SCI agreed to sell some 40 funeral homes and 15 cemeteries in areas where the combined company's market share would have been too large.

EXECUTIVES

Chairman: Robert L. (Bob) Waltrip, age 78, $2,720,916 total compensation
President, CEO, and Director: Thomas L. Ryan, age 43, $4,012,807 total compensation
EVP and COO: Michael R. Webb, age 50, $2,295,332 total compensation
SVP, CFO, and Treasurer: Eric D. Tanzberger, age 40, $1,090,015 total compensation
VP Process and Technology: Elisabeth G. Nash, age 47
SVP and Chief Marketing Officer: Philip C. (Phil) Jacobs, age 54
SVP Middle Market Operations: Stephen M. Mack, age 57
SVP Operations Support: J. Daniel Garrison, age 57
SVP Major Market Operations: Sumner J. Waring III, age 40, $1,095,215 total compensation
SVP, General Counsel, and Secretary: Gregory T. Sangalis, age 53
VP Human Resources: Jane D. Jones, age 53
VP Business Development: Christopher H. Cruger, age 34
VP and Treasurer: Harris E. Loring III
Managing Director, Marketing: George J. Owens
Corporate Controller: Tammy R. Moore, age 42
Auditors: PricewaterhouseCoopers LLP

LOCATIONS

HQ: Service Corporation International
1929 Allen Pkwy., Houston, TX 77019
Phone: 713-522-5141   **Fax:** 713-525-5586
Web: www.sci-corp.com

2008 Sales

	$ mil.	% of total
North America	2,148.6	99
Germany	7.0	1
Total	**2,155.6**	**100**

PRODUCTS/OPERATIONS

Selected Products

Burial garments
Burial vaults
Caskets
Coffins
Cremation receptacles
Flowers
Lawn crypts
Mausoleum spaces
Stone and bronze memorials

Selected Services

Bereavement travel
Cremation
Development loans
Floral arrangements
Grief counseling
Grounds management and maintenance
Interment
Perpetual care
Prearranged funeral services
Transportation

COMPETITORS

Alcor
Arbor Memorial Services
Aurora Casket
Batesville Casket
Carriage Services, Inc.
Eternal Reefs
Forever Enterprises
Matthews International
Rock of Ages
Security National Financial
Stewart Enterprises
StoneMor
Wilbert
York Group

HISTORICAL FINANCIALS

Company Type: Public

Income Statement

FYE: December 31

	REVENUE ($ mil.)	NET INCOME ($ mil.)	NET PROFIT MARGIN	EMPLOYEES
12/08	2,155.6	97.1	4.5%	20,771
12/07	2,285.3	247.7	10.8%	20,591
12/06	1,747.3	56.5	3.2%	22,623
12/05	1,715.6	60.8	3.5%	16,722
12/04	1,859.3	160.8	8.6%	20,598
Annual Growth	**3.8%**	**(11.8%)**	**—**	**0.2%**

2008 Year-End Financials

Debt ratio: 140.8%
Return on equity: 7.0%
Cash ($ mil.): 34
Current ratio: 1.09
Long-term debt ($ mil.): 1,821
No. of shares (mil.): 251
Dividends
Yield: 3.2%
Payout: 43.2%
Market value ($ mil.): 1,247

Stock History

NYSE: SCI

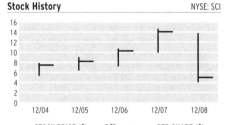

	STOCK PRICE ($) FY Close	P/E High/Low		PER SHARE ($) Earnings	Dividends	Book Value
12/08	4.97	37	11	0.37	0.16	5.15
12/07	14.05	17	12	0.85	0.12	5.94
12/06	10.25	56	39	0.19	0.10	6.35
12/05	8.18	—	—	(0.41)	0.08	6.33
12/04	7.45	22	16	0.35	0.00	7.38
Annual Growth	**(9.6%)**	**—**	**—**	**1.4%**	**—**	**(8.6%)**

The Shaw Group

The Shaw Group is one of the largest engineering and construction contractors for the power generation market and one of the top environmental services firms. Shaw designs, builds, and maintains fossil fuel and nuclear power plants; provides consulting services to the chemical industry; performs environmental rehabilitations services; manages US government facilities; and manufactures pipe fittings. The group's largest segment is its global fossil and nuclear power arm. Clients include multinational oil companies, industrial corporations and manufacturers, utilities, and government agencies. The Shaw Group serves clients across the Americas, Middle East, Europe, and Pacific Rim through more than 150 offices.

Shaw is placing some of its eggs in the nuclear energy basket (the company claims to have worked on 95% of the nuclear power facilities in the US). With rising oil prices and a growing focus on alternative energy sources, the nuclear industry has seen a serious boost in interest. The Shaw Group has scaled up its operations to meet demand by Duke Energy and other companies that may be restarting their nuclear construction programs. The company also owns a 20%

stake in nuclear reactor designer Westinghouse Electric.

In 2008, the company sold its Energy Delivery Services (powerline services) business to Pike Electric for some $24 million. The transmission and distribution market had become a noncore operation for Shaw as it continues to focus on facilities engineering, construction, and maintenance.

Shaw operates in the Americas, the Middle East, Europe, and the Pacific Rim.

HISTORY

James Bernhard formed National Fabricators in 1986. After visiting the Benjamin F. Shaw Company's plant in South Carolina to bid on its inventory, he established The Shaw Group in 1987 and bought the 100-year-old maker of power-station piping systems. From 1988 to 1990 Shaw expanded its business by leasing three plants in Louisiana and Texas. The company bought a plant in 1992.

Shaw formed a joint venture with Venezuela-based Formiconi in 1993 to open a plant there. The company began making pipes for chemicals and oil refining with its purchase of Sunland Fabricators. Shaw also went public that year.

In 1994 Shaw acquired Fronek Company (pipe engineering and design services), bought out its Venezuelan partner, and watched its domestic fiscal earnings bend south when its South Carolina plant had to repair a botched fabrication job.

Shaw expanded plant capacity and added more induction bending machines to its inventory in 1996 and 1997. It purchased NAPTech (industrial piping systems) in 1997. Company spending continued with the 1998 acquisitions of Lancas (construction, Venezuela), Cojafex BV (induction bending equipment, the Netherlands), and Bagwell Brothers (offshore platforms, heliports, and vessels for the petroleum industry). The Cojafex buy proved to be one of the company's best acquisitions, because its pipe-bending machines eliminated much of the cost of welding. Also in 1998 Shaw sold its NAPTech Pressure Systems (pressure vessels) subsidiary and others that provided welding supplies, boiler steam leak-detection devices, and corrosion-resistant pipe systems.

In 1999 Shaw won a five-year contract to supply 90% of the piping for GE's gas turbines for power plants. In 2000 Shaw signed a letter of intent with a US power developer to build a $380 million power plant in central Texas. It also created EntergyShaw, a joint venture with Entergy Corporation, to build cookie-cutter power plants in North America and Europe in hopes of driving down costs and speeding construction time. That year the company purchased Stone & Webster, Inc., for about $38 million and around 2.5 million shares of stock.

In 2002 Shaw acquired the assets of The IT Group (which was in bankruptcy) for about $105 million in cash and up to $95 million in assumed debt and made the environmental services firm a subsidiary, Shaw Environmental & Infrastructure. It also entered into an agreement to buy industrial construction group Turner Industries, but quickly terminated discussions with its hometown rival.

Despite a downturn in the domestic power generation market, Shaw made a strong showing in 2002, which it attributed to its diversified portfolio. However, the group lowered its earnings

LOCATIONS

HQ: Simon Property Group, Inc.
225 W. Washington St., Indianapolis, IN 46204
Phone: 317-636-1600 **Fax:** 317-263-2318
Web: www.simon.com

PRODUCTS/OPERATIONS

2008 Sales

	$ mil.	% of total
Minimum rent	2,291.9	61
Tenant reimbursements	1,066.0	28
Overage rent	100.2	3
Management fees & other	132.5	3
Other	192.6	5
Total	**3,783.2**	**100**

COMPETITORS

Belz
Cadillac Fairview
CBL & Associates Properties
General Growth Properties
Glimcher Realty
Horizon Group Properties
Kimco Realty
Lincoln Property
Macerich
Taubman Centers
Vornado Realty
Weingarten Realty

HISTORICAL FINANCIALS

Company Type: Public

Income Statement

FYE: December 31

	REVENUE ($ mil.)	NET INCOME ($ mil.)	NET PROFIT MARGIN	EMPLOYEES
12/08	3,783.2	463.6	12.3%	5,300
12/07	3,650.8	519.2	14.2%	5,100
12/06	3,332.2	563.8	16.9%	4,300
12/05	3,166.9	612.5	19.3%	4,700
12/04	2,641.8	449.9	17.0%	4,610
Annual Growth	9.4%	0.8%	—	3.5%

2008 Year-End Financials

Debt ratio: 690.1%	No. of shares (mil.): 283
Return on equity: 17.1%	Dividends
Cash ($ mil.): 774	Yield: 6.8%
Current ratio: —	Payout: 191.9%
Long-term debt ($ mil.): 18,043	Market value ($ mil.): 14,933

Stock History

NYSE: SPG

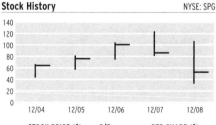

	STOCK PRICE ($) FY Close	P/E High/Low	PER SHARE ($) Earnings	Dividends	Book Value
12/08	52.73	57 18	1.86	3.57	10.73
12/07	86.20	64 42	1.94	3.33	12.58
12/06	100.53	48 35	2.17	3.02	14.05
12/05	76.05	44 32	1.81	2.78	15.21
12/04	64.18	46 31	1.43	2.58	16.39
Annual Growth	(4.8%)	— —	6.8%	8.5%	(10.0%)

Skadden, Arps

Have you heard about the law firm that sued the business information publisher for a profile that opened with a wickedly clever lawyer joke? Neither have we, and we would like to keep it that way. Skadden, Arps, Slate, Meagher & Flom, a leading US law firm and one of the largest in the world, has some 2,000 attorneys in some 25 offices around the globe, from Boston to Beijing and from London to Los Angeles. The firm is best known for its work in mergers and acquisitions, corporate restructuring, and corporate finance, but it represents businesses in a wide variety of practice areas, including intellectual property and litigation. Skadden was founded in 1948.

Skadden has worked for a number of *FORTUNE* 500 companies. High-profile clients have included JPMorgan Chase and State Farm, as well as Arcelor, Merrill Lynch, and Toshiba.

Over the years Skadden has grown organically rather than by merging with other firms. The New York office is the firm's largest, but offices outside the US have been growing faster. As part of its plan to expand outside the US, Skadden opened offices in Shanghai and São Paulo in 2008 — giving the firm greater access to growing markets less affected by the economic downturn.

HISTORY

Marshall Skadden, Leslie Arps, and John Slate hung out their shingle in New York City on April Fool's Day, 1948. Skadden and Arps came from a Wall Street law firm, and Slate had been counsel to Pan American World Airways. Without the reputation and connections of the established New York law firms, the firm found work one case at a time from referrals, handling mainly commercial, corporate, and litigations work. Marshall Skadden died in 1958.

Denied the luxury of steady clients, the firm was forced to be innovative and, at times, unorthodox. Joe Flom, who had joined as the firm's first associate, specialized in corporate law and proxy fights. During the 1960s, when tender offers and hostile takeovers increased, many of the more venerable firms referred clients engaged in the undignified corporate raids to Flom to preserve their gentlemanly reputations. With "white shoe" lawyers on Wall Street hesitant to tread into the uncivilized region of corporate takeovers, Skadden, Arps went for it, and the firm virtually pioneered the business of mergers and acquisitions (M&A) under Flom.

When Congress passed the Williams Act in 1968, which "legitimized" tender offers by providing regulation, other law firms started to get in on the act. Skadden, Arps was way ahead of the game, however, and as corporations and lawyers realized that aggressive legal tactics helped win corporate takeover battles, it also became apparent that Joe Flom was the expert. As takeover fights became more frequent in the early 1970s, the firm earned more than just respect. Earnings came not just from some of the highest hourly rates in the industry, but from hefty retainers (now a common practice at many firms) on the theory that association with Flom would scare raiders off. The only other name that could strike such fear in people's hearts was Marty Lipton of rival takeover specialists Wachtell, Lipton, Rosen & Katz. From the late 1970s through the 1980s, Skadden, Arps was involved in almost every important M&A case in the US.

The firm used its success in mergers and acquisitions to build its practice in other areas. In the early 1980s it branched into bankruptcy, product liability, and real estate law. By then it had opened offices in Boston; Chicago; Los Angeles; Washington, DC; and Wilmington, Delaware. Les Arps died in 1987.

With the boom in mergers and acquisitions activity and bankruptcies in the late 1980s, the firm grew to almost 2,000 lawyers by 1989. Then came the recession, and M&A work virtually dried up. Skadden, Arps responded by shedding more than 500 lawyers between 1989 and 1990. It also scrambled to diversify and expand internationally. As takeover activity rebounded in the mid-1990s, the diversification strategy actually began to work against Skadden, Arps because profits didn't skyrocket like those of M&A specialist firms.

The firm opened an office in Singapore in 1995 to coordinate its Asian business, signaling that city's growing importance as a financial center. Two years later two-thirds of the firm's Beijing team defected to a rival firm. Headquarters shrugged it off and flew in replacements. Representing President Bill Clinton, Skadden, Arps won one of its highest-profile cases in 1998 when the sexual harassment suit brought by Paula Jones was thrown out.

With its M&A practice in full swing again, Skadden, Arps was involved in 70 announced M&A deals in 1999, including the $75 billion merger of oil companies Exxon and Mobil. It also became the first US law firm to reach $1 billion in revenue in 2000. The company announced an alliance with Italian law firm Studio Chiomenti the following year and took part in three of the top 10 M&A deals of 2002. Skadden, Arps helped struggling discount retailer Kmart emerge from its titanic bankruptcy the next year.

EXECUTIVES

Executive Partner: Eric J. Friedman, age 44
Managing Director: Earle Yaffa
CFO: Noah J. Puntus
CTO: Harris Z. Tilevitz
Chief Administrative Officer: Laurel E. Henschel
Senior Director: Carol A. Sawdye
Managing Attorney: Robert Abrams
Corporate Deputy Legal Practice Partner:
Thomas H. Kennedy
Senior Partner, Corporate Practice: Roger S. Aaron
International Litigation Legal Practice Leader:
William P. Frank
**Global Head, Real Estate Investment Trust Practice
Group:** Barnet Phillips IV
Head of Washington, D.C., Office: Michael P. Rogan
**Head of New York Office and International Real Estate
Group:** Wallace L. Schwartz
Head of European Offices: Bruce M. Buck
Head of Palo Alto and San Francisco Offices:
Kenton J. King
Head of Asia Energy and Project Finance Group:
Alan G. Schiffman
Director Marketing and Business Development:
Sally J. Feldman
Director Human Resources: Vaughn Burke
Corporate Partner: Joseph H. Flom

LOCATIONS

HQ: Skadden, Arps, Slate, Meagher & Flom LLP
4 Times Sq., New York, NY 10036
Phone: 212-735-3000 **Fax:** 212-735-2000
Web: www.skadden.com

PRODUCTS/OPERATIONS

Selected Practice Areas

Alternative dispute resolution
Antitrust
Appellate litigation and legal issues
Asia
Australia and New Zealand
Banking and institutional investing
Biological and chemical technology diligence and
  transactions
Brazil
Canada
CFIUS
China
Class action litigation
Climate change
Communications
Consumer financial services enforcement and litigation
Corporate
Corporate compliance programs
Corporate finance
Corporate governance
Corporate restructuring
Crisis management
Derivative financial products, commodities, and futures
Energy and infrastructure projects
Energy regulation and litigation
Environmental
Environmental litigation
Europe
European Union/international competition
Executive compensation and benefits
Exempt and nonprofit organizations
False Claims Act defense
Financial institutions
Financial institutions regulation and enforcement
Foreign Corrupt Practices Act defense
Franchise law
Gaming
Government contract disputes
Government enforcement and white collar crime
Health care
Health care and life sciences
Hong Kong
India
Information technology and e-commerce
Insurance
Intellectual property and technology
International law and policy
International litigation and arbitration
International tax
International trade
Investment management
Israel
Italy
Japan
Labor and employment law
Latin America
Lease financing
Litigation
Mass torts and insurance litigation
Media and entertainment
Mergers and acquisitions
Outsourcing
Patent and technology litigation and counseling
Pharmaceutical, biotechnology, and medical device
  licensing
Political law
Private equity
Private equity funds
Pro bono
Public policy
Real estate
Real estate investment trusts
Russia and CIS
Securities enforcement and compliance
Securities litigation
Sports
Structured finance
Tax
Tax controversy and litigation
Trademark, copyright, and advertising litigation and
  counseling
Trusts and estates
UCC and secured transactions
Utilities mergers and acquisitions

COMPETITORS

Baker & McKenzie	O'Melveny & Myers
Clifford Chance	Shearman & Sterling
Davis Polk	Sidley Austin
Gibson, Dunn & Crutcher	Sullivan & Cromwell
Jones Day	Wachtell, Lipton
Kirkland & Ellis	Weil, Gotshal & Manges
Latham & Watkins	White & Case
Mayer Brown	WilmerHale
McDermott Will & Emery	

HISTORICAL FINANCIALS

Company Type: Partnership

Income Statement

FYE: December 31

	REVENUE ($ mil.)	NET INCOME ($ mil.)	NET PROFIT MARGIN	EMPLOYEES
12/08	2,200.0	—	—	4,500
12/07	2,170.0	—	—	4,721
12/06	1,850.0	—	—	4,520
12/05	1,610.0	—	—	4,400
Annual Growth	11.0%	—	—	0.8%

Revenue History

SkyWest, Inc.

SkyWest flies in every direction. The company's main subsidiaries, regional carriers SkyWest Airlines and Atlantic Southeast Airlines (ASA), serve about 220 destinations in the US, Canada, Mexico and the Caribbean, mainly for Delta Air Lines and UAL's United Airlines. SkyWest Airlines flies as Delta Connection from Atlanta and Salt Lake City and as United Express from hubs in Chicago, Denver, Los Angeles, and San Francisco. ASA flies for Delta, mainly from Atlanta and Cincinnati. Combined, the carriers operate a fleet of about 440 aircraft, consisting of more than 370 Canadair regional jets (CRJs), made by Bombardier) and about 70 turboprops.

In June 2009 SkyWest announced it was pulling the plug on its contract to provide regional service for Midwest Airlines. SkyWest became a Midwest Connect carrier in in 2007, but the relationship began to falter in 2008, as Midwest (along with the rest of the airline industry) ran into trouble with high fuel prices followed by the economic downturn. By mid-2008 Midwest needed to pull back the number of jets in its contract with SkyWest. The companies agreed to reduce number of aircraft from 21 to 12, and SkyWest deferred weekly payments for a handful of months. The change wasn't enough to convince SkyWest to continue. The carrier agreed to cancel a $9.3 million unsecured note from Midwest in exchange for a $4 million payment. SkyWest started removing its jets from Midwest's routes in June 2009.

Owning both SkyWest Airlines and ASA makes SkyWest a strong competitor for more business from Delta and United, or for contracts from other carriers. To grow, SkyWest has ordered more than 25 additional CRJs for delivery by 2010, all of which are to be incorporated into service under the company's existing contracts.

SkyWest attempted to further diversify its operations when it made an unsolicited bid to buy rival regional carrier ExpressJet in April 2008. ExpressJet rejected the offer of about $182 million as too low, but left the door open for negotiations; SkyWest withdrew its bid in June 2008, however, after ExpressJet signed a new agreement to provide feeder service for Continental.

Along with regional passenger transportation, which accounts for nearly all of its sales, SkyWest provides ground handling services — loading and unloading of aircraft — for other airlines at several of the airports where it operates.

HISTORY

In 1972 Ralph Atkin founded SkyWest with one airplane that served three points in Utah. The company doubled in size in 1984 when it bought California-based Sun Aire Lines; two years later it went public. Growth also was fueled by the trend toward code-sharing agreements between major airlines and regional airlines serving rural markets. SkyWest jumped on board with Delta in 1987 to become one of four Delta Connection carriers.

Atkin stepped down as chairman in 1991 and was replaced by his nephew, CEO Jerry Atkin. By 1993 SkyWest had assembled a fleet of about 50 turboprop aircraft; that year it placed an order for 10 Canadair Regional Jets (CRJs) from Bombardier. The jets would prove to be popular among travelers.

SkyWest became a United affiliate in 1997 with 120 daily United Express departures from Los Angeles. The next year SkyWest expanded its United Express service into additional markets in California, Oregon, and Washington. Meanwhile, the company sold most of its air tours business, Scenic Airlines, to Eagle Canyon Airlines in 1998; it sold the rest in 1999.

With business booming, SkyWest placed orders for 55 more CRJs in 1999. Amid unusually cordial labor relations for an airline, SkyWest fliers voted down a chance to join the pilots' union. Also in 1999 SkyWest and Delta terminated their Los Angeles code-sharing agreement because of SkyWest's close ties to United in the city. The following year SkyWest agreed to sell the outstanding shares of subsidiary National Parks Transportation, a provider of rental car services at six airports served by the airline.

SkyWest began providing regional service for Continental Airlines in 2003, but the companies ended the deal in 2005.

In a major expansion, SkyWest in 2005 bought fellow regional carrier Atlantic Southeast Airlines (ASA) from Delta for about $425 million and some $1.25 billion in debt. The purchase was completed just before Delta filed for Chapter 11 bankruptcy protection. The acquisition diversified SkyWest's operations geographically and added Delta business to a revenue mix that had leaned heavily toward United. In conjunction with the acquisition, SkyWest negotiated new, 15-year Delta Connection contracts for both SkyWest Airlines and ASA.

EXECUTIVES

Chairman, President, and CEO; Chairman and CEO, SkyWest Airlines: Jerry C. Atkin, age 60, $1,268,826 total compensation
EVP, CFO, and Treasurer, SkyWest, Inc. and SkyWest Airlines: Bradford R. Rich, age 47, $890,770 total compensation
VP Information Technology, SkyWest, Inc., SkyWest Airlines, and Atlantic Southeast Airlines: James B. Jensen
VP Planning, SkyWest, Inc., SkyWest Airlines, and Atlantic Southeast Airlines: Eric D. Christensen
VP Finance and Treasurer, SkyWest, Inc., SkyWest Airlines, and Atlantic Southeast Airlines: Michael J. (Mike) Kraupp
VP and Controller: Eric Woodward
President and COO, Atlantic Southeast Airlines: Bradford R. (Brad) Holt, $613,411 total compensation
President and COO, SkyWest Airlines: Russell A. (Chip) Childs, age 41, $718,930 total compensation
General Counsel, SkyWest Airlines: Todd Emerson
Director Benefits: Bryce Higgins
Director Communications and Development: Amber Hunter
Manager Corporate Communications: Marissa Snow
Auditors: Ernst & Young LLP

LOCATIONS

HQ: SkyWest, Inc.
444 S. River Rd., St. George, UT 84790
Phone: 435-634-3000   **Fax:** 435-634-3105
Web: www.skywest.com

PRODUCTS/OPERATIONS

2008 Sales

	$ mil.	% of total
Passenger	3,466.3	99
Ground handling & other	29.9	1
Total	**3,496.2**	**100**

COMPETITORS

Air Wisconsin Airlines
American Eagle
Comair
ExpressJet
Horizon Air
Mesa Air
Pinnacle Airlines
Republic Airways
Trans States

HISTORICAL FINANCIALS

Company Type: Public

Income Statement   FYE: December 31

	REVENUE ($ mil.)	NET INCOME ($ mil.)	NET PROFIT MARGIN	EMPLOYEES
12/08	3,496.2	112.9	3.2%	13,335
12/07	3,374.3	159.2	4.7%	10,249
12/06	3,114.7	145.8	4.7%	8,792
12/05	1,964.0	112.3	5.7%	13,647
12/04	1,156.0	82.0	7.1%	6,747
Annual Growth	**31.9%**	**8.3%**	**—**	**18.6%**

2008 Year-End Financials

Debt ratio: 131.8%	No. of shares (mil.): 56
Return on equity: 9.0%	Dividends
Cash ($ mil.): 126	Yield: 0.7%
Current ratio: 3.16	Payout: 6.7%
Long-term debt ($ mil.): 1,682	Market value ($ mil.): 1,034

Stock History   NASDAQ (GS): SKYW

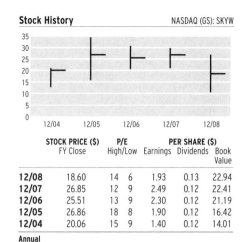

	STOCK PRICE ($) FY Close	P/E High/Low		PER SHARE ($) Earnings	Dividends	Book Value
12/08	18.60	14	6	1.93	0.13	22.94
12/07	26.85	12	9	2.49	0.12	22.41
12/06	25.51	13	9	2.30	0.12	21.19
12/05	26.86	18	8	1.90	0.12	16.42
12/04	20.06	15	9	1.40	0.12	14.01
Annual Growth	**(1.9%)**	**—**	**—**	**8.4%**	**2.0%**	**13.1%**

Smithfield Foods

When Smithfield Foods waddles up to the trough, the other porkers stand back. Fat from acquisitions, the company is the world's largest hog producer and pork processor. Its products include fresh pork and processed, value-added pork products sold under the Armour, Cook's, John Morrell, Lykes, Patrick Cudahy, and Smithfield Premium names. Smithfield distributes its meats in the US and internationally, mainly in Mexico, Western Europe, the UK, Poland, Romania, and China. In addition to pork, the company produces turkey and turkey products through its Armour-Eckrich operations and its minority holding in Butterball.

Beef was an important part of Smithfield's diet, and the company was one of the largest beef processors in the US. However, in October 2008 it sold its beef operations, Smithfield Beef Group (now JBS Packerland), and its feedlot joint venture, Five Rivers Ranch Cattle Feeding, to Brazilian meat giant, JBS. Smithfield used the proceeds ($565 million in cash) from the sale to pay down debt. In order to sell the feedlot joint venture, Smithfield bought out the 50% interest that was owned by ContiGroup for some 2 million shares of its stock.

In order to stay competitive, the company has streamlined its operations. In 2008 the company merged its Groupe Smithfield Holdings with Spanish meat processor Campofrio Alimentacion. The all-stock transaction created a leading European meat processor. Smithfield owns 37% of the combined companies, which operates under the Campofrio Food Group name.

Streamlining continued in 2009 with the restructuring of Smithfield's pork segment, and included making Patrick Cudahy and Carando Foods part of the John Morrell group, making North Side Foods part of Farmland Foods, and moving Cumberland Gap Provision to the Smithfield Packing Company operations. The company also closed six plants (in Florida, Kansas, Nebraska, North Carolina, Ohio, and Virginia) and moved their operations to other facilities. Some 1,800 jobs were eliminated.

Its biggest deal recently was the acquisition of Premium Standard Farms. The company paid

some $800 million (including $125 million in debt) for it in 2007. As the US's #1 pork processor and marketer, Smithfield's takeover of Premium Standard (the nation's #2 pork producer) created a pig-production powerhouse. Premium Standard brought brands such as All Natural, Fresh & Tender, Lundy's, Natural Excellence, and Premium Farms to the Smithfield roster.

Smithfield has tried to increase sales by placing more emphasis on the production of higher-margin pre-cooked meats and entrees. However, it is still in a commodity business, and low hog prices can affect earnings.

HISTORY

Joseph Luter's father and grandfather set up Smithfield Foods in 1936 and built it into a regional pork producer. Luter began to manage the business in 1962 after his father died. In 1969 he sold the company to conglomerate Liberty Equities for $20 million and was retained as its manager, but he was soon dismissed.

Smithfield Foods floundered in his absence and grew weak from overexpansion and non-pork diversifications. Luter bought the business back in 1975, paying a fraction of what he had sold it for. At that time the company was a wholesaler of pork and fish products and was operating 27 seafood restaurants. Luter trimmed the fat to pay down debt, leaving only the pork operations. He then began to expand in the pork business through acquisitions, including Gwaltney Packing in 1982, thereby doubling its size. Other purchases included pork processors Patrick Cudahy (1985) and Esskay (1986).

The company formed a joint venture with pork producer Carroll's Foods in 1987 to help lessen its dependence on Midwestern hog farmers. To move toward higher-quality pork, the joint venture acquired North American rights from National Pig Development (a UK-based, family-owned firm) for a long and lean English breed — the NPD hog, which became the basis for the company's flagship brand, Smithfield Lean Generation Pork.

The company co-founded Circle Four Farms, a giant hog farm in Utah, in 1994 with partners Murphy's Family Farms, Carroll's, and Prestage Farms. (Two years later it bought out the other partners.) Smithfield Foods also bought regional processors Valleydale Foods (1993) and John Morrell (1995) and struggling Lykes Meat Group (1996), thereby transforming it into a national concern. In 1997 the company was ticketed with $12.6 million in fines by the EPA for water violations. The fine was later lowered by $6 million by an appellate court.

Beginning in 1998, Smithfield Foods went shopping abroad, starting with Canadian meat processor Canada's Schneider Corporation and Société Bretonne de Salaisons, France's largest private-label maker of hams and bacon.

In 2000 the company acquired Murphy Family Farms for about $460 million, doubling its pig production. Now with a taste for beef, in 2001 Smithfield acquired midsized beef processors Moyer Packing Company (MOPAC) and Packerland Holdings. Smithfield began a joint venture in late 2001 with Artal Holland to distribute processed meat products in China.

Despite cries of antitrust, in late 2003 Smithfield spent $367 million to purchase the Farmland Foods pork production and processing businesses from ailing cooperative Farmland Industries. The purchase gave Smithfield control of 27% of the US pork industry.

In 2005 Smithfield acquired MF Cattle Feeding, which has operations in Colorado and Idaho. Later that year MF and ContiGroup subsidiary ContiBeef formed a 50/50 joint venture cattle-feeding business named Five Rivers Ranch Cattle Feeding.

Extending its reach into Europe, in 2005 Smithfield purchased French meat processor Jean Caby. In 2006 it purchased Sara Lee's European meats business. Smithfield financed the purchase through a 50-50 joint venture with Oaktree Capital Management. The company purchased Cook's Ham from ConAgra in 2006. Later that year, it purchased the bulk of ConAgra's refrigerated meats business.

The deal included the Eckrich, Armor, Longmont, LunchMakers, and Margherita brands. The Butterball brand was sold to Carolina Turkeys (now Butterball, LLC), of which Smithfield owns 49%.

After 31 years as Smithfield's CEO and chairman, Joseph Luter stepped down as CEO in 2006. However, he remained as non-executive chairman of the company. President and COO C. Larry Pope, a 25-year veteran of Smithfield, succeeded Luter as CEO.

EXECUTIVES

Chairman: Joseph W. Luter III, age 70
President, CEO, and Director: C. Larry Pope, age 54
EVP International Operations and CFO:
  Robert W. (Bo) Manly IV, age 56
CIO: Mansour T. Zadeh, age 54
President and COO, Pork Group: George H. Richter, age 64
VP and Chief Accounting Officer: Kenneth M. Sullivan, age 45
VP and Chief Internal Auditor: Craig R. Harlow
EVP: Richard J. M. Poulson, age 70
EVP Sales and Marketing: Joseph W. (Joe) Luter IV, age 44
Senior Corporate VP Operations and Engineering:
  Henry L. Morris, age 66
VP Investor Relations and Corporate Communications:
  Jerry Hostetter, age 64
VP, Chief Legal Officer, and Secretary: Michael H. Cole, age 49
VP and Corporate Controller: Jeffrey A. Deel, age 51
VP Sales and Marketing: James D. Schloss, age 63
VP Finance: Carey J. Dubois, age 49
CEO, Smithfield S.L.: Robert A. Sharpe II
President, John Morrell: Joseph B. Sebring, age 61
President, Smithfield Beef Group: Richard V. Vesta, age 62
President, Murphy-Brown: Jerry H. Godwin, age 62
Corporate Treasurer: Houghton Lewis
Manager, Investor Relations: Keira Ullrich
Auditors: Ernst & Young LLP

LOCATIONS

HQ: Smithfield Foods, Inc.
  200 Commerce St., Smithfield, VA 23430
Phone: 757-365-3000   **Fax:** 757-365-3017
Web: www.smithfieldfoods.com

2009 Sales

	$ mil.	% of total
US	11,149.2	89
International	1,338.5	11
Total	**12,487.7**	**100**

PRODUCTS/OPERATIONS

2009 Pork Sales

	% of total
Packaged	59
Fresh	40
By-products, rendering & other	1
Total	**100**

Selected Brands

Aoste	Krakus
Armour	Kretschmar Deli
Basse's Choice	Krey
Big 8's	La Abuelita
Bistro	Lunchmakers
Butterball	Lundy's
Campofrío	Lykes
Carando	Marcassou
Carolina Turkey	Margherita
Casa Taraneasca	Maverick
Cochonou	Mayrose
Comtim	Mazury
Cook's	Milano's Italian Grille
Cumberland Gap	Morliny
Curly's Foods	Mosey's Corned Beef
Del Mare	Nobre
Dinner Bell	Norson
Eckrich	Olde Kentucky
El Miño	Party Dipper
Ember Farms	Patrick Cudahy
Esskay	Paula Deen Collection
E-Z-Cut Hams	Pavone
Farmland	Peyton's
Farmstead	Premium Standard Farms
Flavoré	Pure Farms
Genuine Smithfield Ham	Quick-N-Easy
Great	Rath Black Hawk
Gwaltney	Ready Crisp
Healthy Ones	Realean
Higüeral	Riojano
Hunter	Rip-n-Dip
Jean Caby	Rodeo
John Morrell	Simply Natural
John Morrell Off the Bone	Sizzle & Serve
Justin Bridou	

COMPETITORS

Boar's Head
Cargill Meat Solutions
Coleman Natural Foods
ConAgra
ContiGroup
Cooper Farms
Eberly Poultry
Empire Kosher Poultry
Hormel
JBS
JBS USA
Jennie-O
Johnsonville Sausage
Kraft Foods
Northern Pride
Oberto Sausage Company
Pederson's
Perdue Incorporated
Pilgrim's Pride
Plainville Farms
Raeford Farms
Sadia
Sara Lee Food and Beverage
Shelton's
Texacan Beef & Pork Co.
Tyson Foods
Usinger's
Zacky Farms

HISTORICAL FINANCIALS

Company Type: Public

Income Statement

FYE: Sunday nearest April 30

	REVENUE ($ mil.)	NET INCOME ($ mil.)	NET PROFIT MARGIN	EMPLOYEES
4/09	12,487.7	(190.3)	—	52,400
4/08	11,351.2	128.9	1.1%	58,100
4/07	11,911.1	178.9	1.5%	53,100
4/06	11,403.6	172.7	1.5%	52,500
4/05	11,354.2	296.2	2.6%	51,290
Annual Growth	**2.4%**	**—**	**—**	**0.5%**

2009 Year-End Financials

Debt ratio: 103.5%
Return on equity: —
Cash ($ mil.): 119
Current ratio: 2.16
Long-term debt ($ mil.): 2,650

No. of shares (mil.): 144
Dividends
  Yield: 0.0%
  Payout: —
Market value ($ mil.): 1,241

Stock History

NYSE: SFD

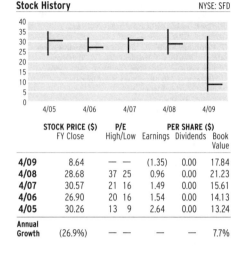

	STOCK PRICE ($) FY Close	P/E High/Low	PER SHARE ($) Earnings	Dividends	Book Value
4/09	8.64	— —	(1.35)	0.00	17.84
4/08	28.68	37 25	0.96	0.00	21.23
4/07	30.57	21 16	1.49	0.00	15.61
4/06	26.90	20 16	1.54	0.00	14.13
4/05	30.26	13 9	2.64	0.00	13.24
Annual Growth	**(26.9%)**	**— —**	**—**	**—**	**7.7%**

Snap-on Incorporated

Snap-on understands the mechanics of the automotive repair business. It's a leading maker and distributor of high-quality hand tools, as well as auto diagnostic equipment and "under-car" shop implements, such as hydraulic lifts and tire changers. The firm serves mechanics, car manufacturers, and government and industrial organizations. Its products — with brand names Snap-on, Blackhawk, Mitchell, ShopKey, Sun, and others — include collision repair equipment, management software, roll cabinets, tool chests, wheel balancers, and wrenches. Snap-on operates finance subsidiaries in international markets where it has franchises. Its Snap-on Credit is a 50%-owned joint venture between Snap-on and The CIT Group.

Snap-on points to its financial services business as a primary segment that is keeping the company firing on all pistons during the US economic downturn. In 2008 the segment's revenue rose more than 29%. Those increases helped to offset declines in Snap-on's tools group.

Snap-on worked to balance its desire to invest in growth opportunities with its need to reduce costs as the global recession took root in 2008 and 2009. Its last investment was in China. To boost its commercial and industrial group and expand its manufacturing to low-cost regions, Snap-on in March 2008 acquired a 60% stake in Zhejiang Wanda Tools Co. for more than $15 million. In one of its larger acquisitions, Snap-on bought the automotive parts and services information systems business of Voyager Learning Center (then ProQuest) for about $527 million in late 2006. The purchase expanded Snap-on's diagnostics and information business unit.

Acquisitions (more than 20 since 1992) have moved Snap-on beyond its US-based network that serves mechanics. It now sells through a variety of channels (including to body shops) in about 130 countries. Snap-on generates more than half of its sales in the US, with Europe and other regions representing the balance.

Snap-on originated the mobile van tool distribution channel in the automotive repair market. Snap-on's US van salespeople are primarily franchisees who buy tools at a discount, then sell them to mechanics at a price they determine.

Snap-on made changes to its executive suite in December 2007. Chairman, president, and CEO Jack Michaels handed his titles of president and CEO to Nicholas Pinchuk; Michaels remained chairman.

Lord, Abbett & Co. owns a more than 8% stake in Snap-on, as well as Harris Associates with more than 7% and Earnest Partners with about 6%.

HISTORY

Joe Johnson's boss at American Grinder Manufacturing rejected his idea for interchangeable wrench handles and sockets in 1919, and Snap-on Tools was born. With practically no capital, Joe and co-worker William Seidemann made a set of five handles and 10 sockets, and two Wisconsin salesmen sold over 500 orders. Snap-on Wrench Company was incorporated in 1920. Stanton Palmer and Newton Tarble, both salesmen, developed a distribution business based on demonstrations at customer sites and formed Motor Tool Specialty Company in 1920. The next year they bought out Johnson's original supporters, and Palmer became president, holding the office until his death in 1931.

By 1925 Snap-on had salesmen working out of 17 branches; by 1929 it had about 300 salesmen and 26 branches. Overextended when the Depression hit, Snap-on was rescued by Forged Steel Products. Later, during WWII, tool shortages forced salesmen to carry excess stock in their vehicles. By 1945 walk-in vans loaded with tools were commonplace. Salesmen retailing to mechanics became independent dealers with their own regions.

In the 1960s Snap-on started buying branch outlets, giving it complete control over distribution and marketing. Research and development during the 1960s produced pneumatic, hydraulic, and electric tools, as well as the patented Flank Drive wrench with superior gripping. The company went public in 1978.

During the 1980s Snap-on became the sole supplier of tools to NASA for the space shuttles. In 1985 it had 4,000 dealers, and by 1990 over 5,000.

Robert Cornog became CEO in 1991, the same year Snap-on began signing new dealers as franchisees and offering existing dealers the option to convert. The changeover was prompted by several lawsuits from dealers claiming the company misrepresented their earnings potential. Snap-on purchased all of its minority-owned affiliate, Balco (engine diagnostic and wheel service equipment), in 1991 and acquired Sun Electric (automotive diagnostic, test, and service equipment) in 1992. The following year it acquired J. H. Williams Industrial Products (hand tools).

The company changed its name to Snap-on Incorporated in 1994. It also launched its first national advertising campaign. The next year Snap-on increased its stake in Edge Diagnostic Systems (automobile diagnostic software) to 90%. The company also acquired Consolidated Devices (torque application and measuring equipment) in 1995 and Spain-based Herramientas Eurotools SA (hand tools), doubling its European sales.

In 1996 Snap-on purchased the automotive service equipment division of FMC Corp. The following year it moved head-on into the collision repair industry by purchasing Breco Collision Repair System and acquiring a 50% stake in Mitchell Repair Information (upped to 99% in 1998).

Snap-on in 1998 bought Hein-Werner (collision repair equipment) and formed Snap-on Credit LLC, a joint venture with Newport Credit Group, to offer customer financing services. After difficulty integrating new acquisitions and the company-wide computer system, Snap-on announced in 1998 that it would "simplify" its operations by cutting 8% of its workers and 10% of its product line.

In 1999 Snap-on bought Sandvik Saws and Tools, a division of Sweden's Sandvik AB, for $400 million; the deal helped Snap-on expand in Asia and South America. In mid-2001 executive Dale Elliott was promoted to president and CEO; Cornog remained as chairman until 2002, when Elliott took that position. In late 2001 Snap-on lost a $44 million arbitrator's decision to industrial products and services company SPX Corp. in a case involving alleged patent infringement.

In November 2004 Elliott resigned and director Jack Michaels was named as his replacement. Michaels became chairman in late 2007, when Nicholas Pinchuk was named CEO.

EXECUTIVES

Chairman, President, and CEO:
Nicholas T. (Nick) Pinchuk, age 62, $3,957,423 total compensation
SVP Finance and CFO: Martin M. (Marty) Ellen, age 55, $2,596,972 total compensation
VP and CIO: Jeanne M. Moreno, age 54, $1,177,949 total compensation
SVP, Finance and Accounting, Snap-on Tools Company, LLC: Blaine A. Metzger, age 50
SVP; President, Commercial Group: Thomas L. Kassouf, age 56, $1,028,270 total compensation
VP, Operations Development: Gary S. Henning, age 56
VP and General Manager, Worldwide Industrial Sales: Donald E. Broman, age 59
VP, North American Technical Sales: David E. Cox, age 63
SVP; President, Snap-on Tools: Thomas J. Ward, age 56, $2,445,525 total compensation
VP and Controller: Constance R. Johnsen, age 51
VP, Worldwide Business Development and Corporate Planning: Bradley R. Lewis, age 45
VP, Operations and Information Technology, Snap-on Credit: John Watters
VP and Chief Marketing Officer: Andrew R. (Andy) Ginger
VP Innovation: Ben Brenton
VP Human Resources: Iain Boyd, age 46
VP Operations Processes: Anup Banerjee
Investor Relations Assistant: Christine Doss
Manager, Corporate Communications: Richard Secor
Auditors: Deloitte & Touche LLP

LOCATIONS

HQ: Snap-on Incorporated
2801 80th St., Kenosha, WI 53143
Phone: 262-656-5200   **Fax:** 262-656-5577
Web: www.snapon.com

PRODUCTS/OPERATIONS

2008 Sales

	$ mil.	% of total
Commercial & Industrial Group	1,409.3	49
Snap-on Tools Group	1,104.0	39
Diagnostics & Information Group	627.8	22
Adjustments	(287.8)	(10)
Total	**2,853.3**	**100**

2008 Sales

	$ mil.	% of total
Tools	1,694.9	59
Diagnostic & repair information	589.8	21
Equipment	568.6	20
Total	**2,853.3**	**100**

Selected Products and Services

Diagnostic and shop equipment
  Air-conditioning service equipment
  Brake testers
  Collision repair equipment
  Engine and emissions analyzers
  Lifts and hoists
  Wheel-balancing and alignment equipment
Hand tools
  Cutting tools
  Pliers
  Ratchets
  Screwdrivers
  Sockets
  Wrenches
Information services
  Management software
  Vehicle service information
Power tools
  Battery-powered tools
  Electric tools
  Pneumatic tools
Tool storage products
  Roll cabinets
  Tool chests

COMPETITORS

Ace Hardware	IRWIN Industrial Tool
Atlas Copco	Klein Tools
Atlas Copco North America	L. S. Starrett
AutoZone	Lowe's
Black & Decker	Makita
Cooper Industries	MSC Industrial Direct
Cornwell Parker	Myers Industries
Danaher	Newell Rubbermaid
Dover Corp.	Pep Boys
Emerson Electric	Robert Bosch Tool
Fluke Corporation	Rotary Lift
Home Depot	Sears
Hunter Engineering	SPX
Illinois Tool Works	Stanley Works
Industrial Distribution	Techtronic
Group	W.W. Grainger
Ingersoll-Rand	

HISTORICAL FINANCIALS

Company Type: Public

Income Statement			FYE: Saturday nearest December 31	
	REVENUE ($ mil.)	NET INCOME ($ mil.)	NET PROFIT MARGIN	EMPLOYEES
12/08	2,853.3	236.7	8.3%	11,500
12/07	2,904.2	181.2	6.2%	11,600
12/06	2,522.4	100.1	4.0%	12,400
12/05	2,362.2	92.9	3.9%	11,400
12/04	2,407.2	81.7	3.4%	11,500
Annual Growth	**4.3%**	**30.5%**	**—**	**0.0%**

2008 Year-End Financials

Debt ratio: 42.4%
Return on equity: 19.2%
Cash ($ mil.): 116
Current ratio: 2.08
Long-term debt ($ mil.): 503
No. of shares (mil.): 58
Dividends
  Yield: 3.0%
  Payout: 29.5%
Market value ($ mil.): 2,273

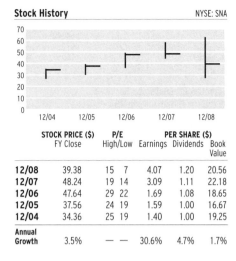
Solutia Inc.

Solutia manufactures plastics, films, and chemicals for the construction, automotive, and rubber manufacturing industries. The company operates through three segments. The company's technical specialties unit manufactures chemicals for rubber manufacturers. Its Saflex unit produces polyvinyl butyral (PVB) sheet, which is used as an interlayer in the manufacture of glass. CPFilms makes various plastic films for use in glass, tapes, and packaging products. Solutia entered Chapter 11 bankruptcy protection in late 2003, after years of litigation and a load of debt remaining from its spinoff from the former Monsanto. It emerged from bankruptcy finally in early 2008.

Not long after that, the company announced a new strategic direction, which included the divestment of its nylon business. Solutia had decided it preferred the relatively high margins of its performance materials and specialty chemicals business and so chose to sell the larger nylon segment. That business made fibers for carpets, space shuttle tires, upholstery, and dental floss, accounting for more than half of Solutia's annual sales. In 2009 the company sold the business to private equity group SK Capital Partners for about $50 million. Solutia also received a small stake in the company SK Capital set up to operate the business. The company used the $50 million to pay down debt.

Spun off by the old Monsanto (which became Pharmacia before being bought by Pfizer) in 1997, Solutia started out saddled with more than $1 billion in debt (a parting gift from Monsanto). Since then it has sold businesses, trimmed its workforce, and narrowed its focus.

All of these moves, though, were unable to keep the company's head completely above water. Solutia filed for Chapter 11 at the end of 2003 as a result of legacy costs associated with its spin-off from Monsanto, including Monsanto retiree health care obligations.

HISTORY

Before going solo, Solutia was the chemical side of the former Monsanto (which in 2000 had merged with Pharmacia & Upjohn and changed its name to Pharmacia; the new entity spun off its seeds and crop protection business as the new Monsanto before Pharmacia itself was acquired by Pfizer in 2003). John Queeny, dubbing the company with his wife's maiden name, started Monsanto in St. Louis after seeing an opening in the artificial-sweetener market. Saccharin was its first product (1902), followed by caffeine (1904), vanillin (1904), and aspirin (1917).

The company acquired R. A. Graesser Chemical Works, the UK's leading producer of phenol (an ingredient in nylon), in 1919. It went public in 1927. A year later Queeny's son, Edgar, became president and expanded the company through aggressive licensing and acquisitions.

In 1938 the company entered the plastics and resins market. It bought Fiberloid (producer of celluloid, the first man-made plastic) and 50% of Shawinigan Resins (it bought the rest in 1963). In 1943 Monsanto produced styrene monomer, a key material for synthetic rubber needed by the US in WWII.

Seven years later Monsanto and American Viscose formed Chemstrand to make Acrilan acrylic fiber and nylon. An agricultural division was created in 1960.

Monsanto created AstroTurf (based on Monsanto's carpet-fiber technology) in 1966 to surface Houston's Astrodome field. In 1976 it produced the first plastic pop bottles, which were promptly taken off the market for possible cancer risks. A reformulated bottle gained approval in 1983, but the market had already been lost to other bottle makers.

The company restructured in the 1980s and early 1990s. It sold its largest chemical business and purchased G.D. Searle (producer of Nutrasweet, 1985). Monsanto cut its workforce and divided its business into three life-sciences units and one chemical group. Monsanto used the chemical unit's strong cash flow to fund high-risk ventures in life sciences. Recognizing that investments in the chemical side of the company would take funds away from the agricultural aspect, Monsanto spun off the chemicals division in 1997. As part of the breakup, Solutia took $1 billion of Monsanto's corporate debt and $1 billion in retirement medical benefit payments.

Solutia's then-CEO, Robert Potter, eliminated some excess administrative levels, cut 800 jobs, and linked executive pay to financial performance. He also started overhauling Solutia's entire supply chain and business processes.

In 1998 Solutia teamed with Bayer, Novus, and a Japanese company to double the size of its acrylonitrile (used in nylon carpet fibers, acrylic fibers, and other products) plant in Alvin, Texas. It also introduced an ingredient that prevents animal feed from becoming rancid.

In 1999 the company bought the window films business of chemical firm Akzo Nobel for $200 million and purchased Germany-based Vianova Resins for $640 million from Morgan Grenfell Private Equity Ltd. Potter retired that year, and John Hunter, a Monsanto veteran since 1969, was named CEO.

By mid-1999, using the strong cash flow from its established businesses and cost reductions, Solutia managed to retire nearly half the debt it inherited at the time of the spinoff. Meanwhile, the company continued to make acquisitions.

Solutia bought Switzerland-based pharmaceutical R&D companies CarboGen Laboratories

and AMCIS in 2000. It also combined its phosphorus operations with FMC to form joint venture Astaris. (The company divested its stake in Astaris in 2005; Astaris' name was subsequently changed to ICL Performance Products.) On the divestiture side, Solutia sold its polymer modifiers business to Ferro Corporation and its light denier industrial nylon fibers business to South African Nylon Spinners (SANS).

In 2002 Solutia sold its 50% stake in an elastomer joint venture with ExxonMobil Chemical for about $100 million. In early 2003 the company sold several specialty products businesses to UCB.

Solutia filed for Chapter 11 at the end of 2003 as a result of legacy costs associated with its spin-off from Monsanto, including Monsanto retiree health care obligations. In the middle of 2005 the company reached an agreement-in-principal with unsecured creditors and the new Monsanto to resolve historical liabilities. (The present-day Monsanto agreed to take over certain liabilities from Pharmacia when it was spun off in 2000.) One step toward solvency was the company's sale of ICL Performance Products (formerly Astaris), its joint venture with FMC Corporation, to Israel Chemicals Limited for $255 million.

EXECUTIVES

Chairman, President, and CEO: Jeffry N. (Jeff) Quinn, age 50, $5,897,482 total compensation
EVP, CFO, and Treasurer: James M. Sullivan, age 48, $2,269,309 total compensation
CIO: Rahul Goturi
SVP, General Counsel, and Chief Administrative Officer: Paul J. Berra III, age 40
EVP Global Operations: James R. Voss, age 42, $1,757,253 total compensation
SVP Human Resources: Hal Wallach, age 46
SVP Business Operations: Robert T. DeBolt, age 49
VP Commercial Services, Flexsys: Ray Kollar
VP Environment, Safety, and Health: Max W. McCombs
Director Media Relations: Dan Jenkins
Investor Relations: Susannah Livingston
Auditors: Deloitte & Touche LLP

LOCATIONS

HQ: Solutia Inc.
575 Maryville Centre Dr., St. Louis, MO 63141
Phone: 314-674-1000   **Fax:** 314-674-1585
Web: www.solutia.com

2008 Sales

	% of total
Europe	36
US	25
Asia/Pacific	24
Other regions	15
Total	**100**

PRODUCTS/OPERATIONS

2008 Sales

	% of total
Technical Specialties	49
Saflex	40
CPFilms	11
Total	**100**

COMPETITORS

3M
Bekaert Corp.
Chemtura
DuPont
ExxonMobil Chemical
Mitsubishi Chemical
Nitto Denko
Sekisui Chemical

Company Type: Public

Income Statement
FYE: December 31

	REVENUE ($ mil.)	NET INCOME ($ mil.)	NET PROFIT MARGIN	EMPLOYEES
12/08	2,110.0	786.0	37.3%	3,700
12/07	3,535.0	(208.0)	—	6,000
12/06	2,905.0	11.0	0.4%	5,100
12/05	2,825.0	11.0	0.4%	5,400
12/04	2,697.0	(316.0)	—	5,700
Annual Growth	(6.0%)	—	—	(10.2%)

2008 Year-End Financials

Debt ratio: 260.8%
Return on equity: —
Cash ($ mil.): 32
Current ratio: 1.87
Long-term debt ($ mil.): 1,359

No. of shares (mil.): 119
Dividends
　Yield: 0.0%
　Payout: —
Market value ($ mil.): 537

Stock History
NYSE: SOA

	STOCK PRICE ($) FY Close	P/E High/Low	PER SHARE ($) Earnings	Dividends	Book Value
12/08	4.50	2　0	9.80	0.00	4.36

Sonoco Products

Sonoco Products is a package deal. The company is one of the world's largest makers of industrial and consumer packaging used by customers in the food, consumer products, construction, and automotive industries. Sonoco's largest unit specializes in paperboard tubes and cores. Its consumer packaging segment makes round and shaped composite cans for snack foods, powdered beverages, and pet food, as well as flexible and rigid packaging made from both paper and plastic for food, chemicals, and personal care items. Sonoco also offers a comprehensive set of packaging services, including brand artwork management, supply chain management, and point-of-purchase display design and assembly.

Other operations include the making of reels for wire and cable manufacturers and specialty protective packaging for household appliances, fitness equipment, lawn and garden products, and office furnishings. Sonoco Products has operations on five continents; the US accounts for a majority of its sales.

In 2007 the company outlined an aggressive growth plan to take shape over the next five years. With the aim of being a low-cost global leader in the packaging industry, Sonoco intends to grow its consumer-related business faster than its industrial-related business, with a 60% to 40% mix by 2012. Over that time period, revenue is expected to be split equally between organic growth (new products and geographic expansion) and acquisitions. The company also plans to maintain productivity by monitoring and, in some cases, cutting underperforming operations.

Barclays Global Investors holds about a 12% stake in Sonoco Products.

HISTORY

Sonoco Products originated during the South's industrial renewal after the Civil War. Major James Coker and son James Jr. (who had been badly wounded at the Battle of Chickamauga) founded the Carolina Fiber company in Hartsville, South Carolina, to make pulp and paper from pine trees. The business was based on a thesis James Jr. wrote in 1884 at Stevens Institute of Technology in Hoboken, New Jersey. The essay explained how to make paper pulp using the sulfite process.

After failing to sell the pulp commercially, the Cokers decided to use it to make paper cones for the textile industry, which was seeing rapid growth in the southern US. In 1899 Major Coker and investor W. F. Smith formed the Southern Novelty Company. Major Coker's son Charles became president in 1918. As sales neared $1 million in 1923, the company changed its name to Sonoco.

In the 1920s Sonoco formed a joint venture in the UK to make Sonoco-style textile carriers. The venture became the Textile Paper Tube Company, which later set up plants in Germany, India, Ireland, the Netherlands, and South Africa.

When Charles died in 1931, his 27-year-old son James became president. James eventually set up eight plants in the US and established a Canadian subsidiary. With the introduction of manmade fibers, the textile industry expanded dramatically, and Sonoco kept pace with the technological changes. By the late 1940s it had eight paper machines in operation at its Hartsville mill.

In the 1950s Sonoco formed a Mexican subsidiary; began tube operations in California, Indiana, and Texas; and diversified into corrugated materials. The company forged a business relationship in 1964 with Showa Products Company of Japan.

Charles Coker, great-grandson of the founder, became president in 1970. The company entered the wastepaper-packing business in 1972 and the folding-carton and fiber-partitions businesses in 1973. It expanded rapidly, and by 1986 Sonoco had 150 plants. The next year it acquired the consumer packaging division of Boise Cascade, which was then the country's #1 producer of composite cans. By 1989 Sonoco was the world's top maker of uncoated, recycled cylinder paperboard.

Charles became CEO in 1990. The company set up a Singapore office and a tube and core plant in Malaysia in 1992 and acquired specialty packager Engraph the following year. In 1995 Sonoco formed a joint venture to produce paperboard in China and bought a paper mill and a tube-making plant in France. The company acquired paper-mill assets in Brazil in 1996 and entered a joint venture in Indonesia to make composite cans.

The next year saw further expansion as Sonoco entered a joint venture in Chile and a second joint venture in Brazil. In 1997 packaging maker Greif Bros. bought most of Sonoco's industrial-related business, with a 60% to 40% container division, and in 1998 Sonoco sold its North American pressure-sensitive-labels business to CCL Industries. President Peter Browning also replaced Charles as CEO (Charles remained chairman). Also in 1998, the company cut about 13% of its workforce and closed five plants to trim costs and consolidate operations.

In 1999 Sonoco bought the composite can assets of Crown Cork & Seal (now Crown Holdings) and doubled its flexible packaging business with the purchase of Graphic Packaging International's flexible packaging unit. CEO Peter Browning retired in 2000 and was replaced by company veteran Harris DeLoach. Sonoco announced several plant closures in 2001. It also acquired four packaging companies — U.S. Paper Mills Corp., Plywood Reel Co., Phoenix Packaging, and Hayes Manufacturing Group — as well as the assets of Pac One Corporation's flexible packaging business.

In 2003 Sonoco purchased Australian Tube Company (ATC), a maker of paper-based tubes and cores. In 2004 the company acquired CorrFlex Graphics, which offers point-of-purchase displays and related products, for about $250 million.

In 2006 Sonoco bought The Cin-Made Packaging Group, which makes rigid composite containers. At the end of that year Sonoco bought privately held Clear Pack Company, which makes rigid plastic containers.

In 2007 the company acquired private Canadian rigid plastic container maker Matrix Packaging for $210 million. It also acquired six manufacturing facilities from Caraustar Industries. The purchase included Caraustar's fiber container operations that make recycled paperboard containers and its plastics operations that make injection molding, film packaging, and adhesive products.

The company announced in 2008 its intention to acquire Canada-based VoidForm International, which makes fiber-based concrete forms.

EXECUTIVES

Chairman, President, and CEO: Harris E. DeLoach Jr., age 64, $5,959,193 total compensation
SVP, CFO, and Corporate Secretary: Charles J. Hupfer, age 62, $1,552,538 total compensation
VP and CIO: Bernard W. (Bernie) Campbell
VP, Corporate Controller, and Chief Accounting Officer: Barry L. Saunders
EVP Industrial: M. Jack Sanders, age 55, $1,519,760 total compensation
EVP Global Consumer: Charles L. Sullivan Jr., age 65, $3,359,377 total compensation
SVP Human Resources: Cynthia A. (Cindy) Hartley, age 60
SVP Global Paper Operations: Jim C. Bowen, age 58, $1,177,264 total compensation
Staff VP; Global Controller, Consumer Products: Michael W. Bullington
Staff VP Operating Excellence: John M. Grups
VP Customer and Business Development: Charles W. Coker Jr.
VP Corporate Planning: Kevin P. Mahoney
VP Global Rigid Paper and Closures: Rodger D. Fuller
VP Global Manufacturing, Industrial: Marty F. Pignone
VP Investor Relations and Corporate Affairs: Roger P. Schrum
VP and Treasurer: Ritchie L. Bond
Auditors: PricewaterhouseCoopers LLP

LOCATIONS

HQ: Sonoco Products Company
　1 N. 2nd St., Hartsville, SC 29550
Phone: 843-383-7000　　**Fax:** 843-383-7008
Web: www.sonoco.com

2008 Sales

	$ mil.	% of total
US	2,596.6	64
Europe	762.2	18
Canada	374.1	9
All other	389.5	9
Total	**4,122.4**	**100**

PRODUCTS/OPERATIONS

2008 Sales

	$ mil.	% of total
Consumer packaging	1,570.3	38
Tubes & cores/paper	1,674.7	41
Packaging services	517.5	12
All other	359.9	9
Total	**4,122.4**	**100**

Selected Products and Services

Consumer packaging
  Rigid packaging — paper
    Paperboard cans
    Paperboard pails
    Fiber cartridges
  Rigid packaging — blow molded plastics
    Monolayer and multilayer bottles, jars, tub, and
      squeeze tubes
  Rigid packaging — thermoformed plastic
    Laminated tubs, cups, and consumer and
      institutional trays
  Ends and closures
    Aluminum, steel, and peelable membrane closures
      for composite, metal, and plastic containers
  Printed flexible packaging

Tubes and cores/paper
  Boxboard
  Chipboard
  Concrete forms
  Linerboard
  Lightweight corestock
  Molded plugs
  Pallet components
  Paperboard tubes and cores
  Recycled paperboard
  Roll packaging
  Rotary die boards
  Tubeboard

Packaging services
  Point-of-purchase displays
  Supply chain management

All other
  Coasters and glass covers
  Molded and extruded plastics
  Protective packaging
  Wire and cable reels

COMPETITORS

Amcor
AptarGroup
Avery Dennison
Ball Corp.
Bemis
Canal Corp.
Caraustar
Crown Holdings
Graphic Packaging Holding
Greif
International Paper
MeadWestvaco
The Newark Group
Owens-Illinois
Pactiv
Rock-Tenn
Sealed Air Corp.
Silgan
Smurfit-Stone Container
Temple-Inland

HISTORICAL FINANCIALS

Company Type: Public

Income Statement   FYE: December 31

	REVENUE ($ mil.)	NET INCOME ($ mil.)	NET PROFIT MARGIN	EMPLOYEES
12/08	4,122.4	164.6	4.0%	17,500
12/07	4,040.0	214.2	5.3%	18,600
12/06	3,656.8	195.1	5.3%	17,700
12/05	3,528.6	161.9	4.6%	17,600
12/04	3,155.4	151.2	4.8%	17,100
Annual Growth	**6.9%**	**2.1%**	**—**	**0.6%**

2008 Year-End Financials

Debt ratio: 56.5%
Return on equity: 12.6%
Cash ($ mil.): 102
Current ratio: 1.33
Long-term debt ($ mil.): 657

No. of shares (mil.): 100
Dividends
  Yield: 4.6%
  Payout: 65.6%
Market value ($ mil.): 2,314

Stock History   NYSE: SON

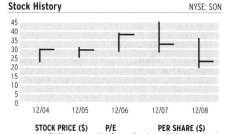

	STOCK PRICE ($) FY Close	P/E High/Low	Earnings	Dividends	Book Value
12/08	23.16	22 12	1.63	1.07	11.64
12/07	32.68	21 14	2.10	1.02	14.43
12/06	38.06	20 15	1.92	0.95	12.20
12/05	29.40	19 16	1.61	0.91	12.65
12/04	29.65	19 15	1.53	0.87	11.54
Annual Growth	**(6.0%)**	**— —**	**1.6%**	**5.3%**	**0.2%**

Sotheby's

Sotheby's believes that every man's trash (or treasure) is another man's treasure — especially when that trash just so happens to be a pricey antique, a rare collectible, or anyone's idea of art. The company (along with rival Christie's International) dominates the world's auction house market. Sotheby's orchestrates hundreds of sales each year at its auction centers around the world dealing mainly in fine art, antiques, and collectibles. The company collects commissions and fees from both the buyer and the seller on each sale. Sotheby's also provides loans (secured against works of art) to clients as part of its finance services and acts as an art dealer through its Noortman Master Paintings business.

The past decade has been a bit of a wild ride for Sotheby's, which while recovering from the dot-com bust of the early 2000s was hit by an alleged commission fixing scandal involving its former CEO and chairman. Having put its tarnished past behind it and riding high on the booming market for Impressionist and Contemporary art, Sotheby's then fell victim to the global economic downturn.

The company is scrambling to respond to the marked decline in its fortunes (and those of its wealthy clients). In response, the art and antiques

auctioneer has announced a restructuring plan, which includes salary cuts and layoffs, designed to cut costs by $7 million in 2009 vs. 2008. The firm is also looking to emerging markets, such as Turkey and Qatar, for growth. The auction house will be conducting its first ever sales in Qatar in 2009.

Live auctions account for the bulk of Sotheby's revenues. The company has overseen the sales of such items as Picasso's *Femme Assise dans un Jardin*, Degas' *Petite Danseuse de Quatorze Ans*, and the last baseball glove used by Lou Gehrig. Sotheby's has leveraged its expertise and profile in art circles to offer such services as secured financing and insurance, as well as serving as a broker for private sales. Additionally, the company offers restoration and appraisal services and operates two art institutes in New York City and London. In 2006 Sotheby's expanded when it acquired Noortman Master Paintings (NMP), an art dealer specializing in Dutch, Flemish, and French paintings.

HISTORY

Sotheby's Holdings traces its roots to Samuel Baker, a London bookseller, who held his first auction in 1744 to dispose of an English nobleman's library. After Baker died in 1778, his nephew John Sotheby took over, placing his name over the door of the business. During the 19th century Sotheby's expanded into antiquities, paintings, jewelry, and furniture. Business boomed as newly wealthy Americans swarmed across the Atlantic seeking the status symbols of the Old World.

By the end of WWI, Sotheby's had become fully entrenched in the art market, and in 1917 the company moved to New Bond Street (where its London office still stands). Following WWII, Sotheby's expanded into the US, opening its first office in New York City in 1955. It later acquired Parke-Bernet, a leading US art auction house, in 1964. The company prospered and expanded during the 1970s as rising interest rates and inflation fueled an art market boom, and in 1977 Sotheby's went public.

A collapse of the art market left Sotheby's a target for corporate raiders in the early 1980s. The company's board asked US shopping center magnate Alfred Taubman to lead a buyout group in 1983. After weathering the storm, the company was well positioned when the art market rebounded, a turnaround driven in part by the desire of newly wealthy Japanese to confirm their status — just as Americans had done a century before. In 1988 the company went public again, with Taubman as chairman.

After the boom peaked in 1990 (Christie's International sold van Gogh's *Portrait of Dr. Gachet* that year for a record $82.5 million), Sotheby's earnings plummeted, and its share price tanked. In 1994 Diana Brooks became president and CEO. The company posted solid results in 1995, but the company slipped to the #2 auctioneer in the world for the first time in more than 20 years.

In 1997 Sotheby's acquired Chicago-based Leslie Hindman Auctioneers and Chicago wine auctioneers Davis & Co. in 1998. The next year Sotheby's created a co-branded auction Web site with Amazon.com. The site never turned a profit and was scaled back in 2000 and the partnership terminated in 2001. In 2002 Sotheby's partnered with eBay to sell high-end merchandise online within the eBay Web site.

In 2000 the US Justice Department reopened a 1997 investigation of an alleged price fixing scheme involving Sotheby's and Christie's. After the allegations became public, Taubman and Brooks resigned, replaced by Michael Sovern (chairman) and William Ruprecht (CEO). The probe sparked additional lawsuits and investigations. Both companies agreed to pay $256 million each to settle the civil claims. Brooks pleaded guilty to violating antitrust laws but testified against Taubman in exchange for leniency. Taubman pleaded innocent and was convicted and sentenced to one year in prison after a vicious trial.

In 2001 Sotheby's laid off about 8% of its staff and raised fees in 2002 in its efforts to offset losses. The bleeding continued into 2002 as the company sold its Upper East Side headquarters in New York for $175 million and laid off 7% of its staff. In 2004 Sotheby's sold its International Realty operations to Cendant for about $100 million. (Cendant spun off its real estate businesses as Realogy in 2006.)

Sotheby's dropped "Holdings" from its official name in mid-2006.

The auction house's legal woes continued in August 2007 when a Canadian antitrust entity obtained a restrictive order against Sotheby's, claiming that the company had agreed with competitors to fix the prices it charged to customers (between the years of 1993 to 2000).

EXECUTIVES

Chairman: Michael I. Sovern, age 77
Deputy Chairman: The Duke of Devonshire, age 64
President, CEO, and Director:
  William F. (Bill) Ruprecht, age 53,
  $6,424,262 total compensation
EVP and COO: Bruno Vinciguerra, age 46,
  $1,219,957 total compensation
EVP and CFO: William S. Sheridan, age 55,
  $2,110,006 total compensation
SVP and Chief Technology and Strategy Officer:
  David Ulmer, age 52
SVP, Controller, and Chief Accounting Officer:
  Kevin M. Delaney
EVP and Director; Chief Executive, Sotheby's International: Robin G. Woodhead, age 57,
  $1,897,412 total compensation
EVP and Worldwide Director, Press and Corporate Affairs: Diana Phillips, age 62
EVP, Worldwide General Counsel, and Secretary:
  Gilbert L. Klemann II, age 58
EVP and Worldwide Head of Human Resources:
  Susan Alexander, age 55
EVP and Director, Boston: William Cottingham
SVP, Controller, and Chief Accounting Officer:
  Michael L. Gillis
Chairman, Sotheby's Financial Services and President, Sotheby's Venture, LLC: Mitchell Zuckerman, age 62,
  $1,217,435 total compensation
Managing Director, Sotheby's Europe: George Bailey, age 55
EVP Global Client Development: Richard C. Buckley, age 46
Managing Director, Sotheby's CIS: Mikhail Kamensky
Chairman, North and South America:
  Donaldson C. Pillsbury, age 66
Client Development: Anne Dignath
Auditors: Deloitte & Touche LLP

LOCATIONS

HQ: Sotheby's
  1334 York Ave., New York, NY 10021
Phone: 212-606-7000   **Fax:** 212-606-7107
Web: www.sothebys.com

2008 Sales

	$ mil.	% of total
UK	296.7	43
US	227.6	33
China	52.3	7
France	41.6	6
Other countries	76.7	11
Adjustments	(3.3)	—
Total	**691.6**	**100**

PRODUCTS/OPERATIONS

2008 Sales

	$ mil.	% of total
Auction	616.6	89
Dealer segment	55.6	8
Finance segment	17.5	2
Other	5.2	1
Adjustments	(3.3)	—
Total	**691.6**	**100**

Selected Operations

Acquavella Modern Art (50%, art sale brokerage)
Noortman Master Paintings B.V. (art dealer, The Netherlands)
Sotheby's (live auctions)
Sotheby's Financial Services (art financing)
Sotheby's Insurance Brokerage Services

COMPETITORS

Ableauctions.com	GoIndustry-DoveBid
Bonhams	Phillips, de Pury
Christie's	Spectrum Group
eBay	Tiffany & Co.
Finarte-Semenzato	

HISTORICAL FINANCIALS

Company Type: Public

Income Statement

FYE: December 31

	REVENUE ($ mil.)	NET INCOME ($ mil.)	NET PROFIT MARGIN	EMPLOYEES
12/08	691.6	28.3	4.1%	1,638
12/07	917.7	213.1	23.2%	1,555
12/06	664.8	107.0	16.1%	1,497
12/05	513.5	62.7	12.2%	1,443
12/04	496.7	86.7	17.5%	1,411
Annual Growth	**8.6%**	**(24.4%)**	**—**	**3.8%**

2008 Year-End Financials

Debt ratio: 89.1%
Return on equity: 4.9%
Cash ($ mil.): 253
Current ratio: 2.18
Long-term debt ($ mil.): 493
No. of shares (mil.): 67
Dividends
  Yield: 6.7%
  Payout: 139.5%
Market value ($ mil.): 595

Stock History

NYSE: BID

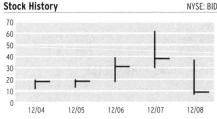

	STOCK PRICE ($) FY Close	P/E High/Low		PER SHARE ($) Earnings	Dividends	Book Value
12/08	8.89	85	17	0.43	0.60	8.28
12/07	38.10	19	9	3.25	0.50	9.03
12/06	31.02	22	11	1.72	0.20	4.51
12/05	18.36	19	13	1.00	0.00	1.89
12/04	18.16	14	9	1.38	0.00	3.53
Annual Growth	**(16.4%)**	**—**	**—**	**(25.3%)**	**—**	**23.8%**

Southern Company

Southern Company isn't just whistling Dixie. The holding company is one of the largest electricity distributors in the US. It operates regulated utilities Alabama Power, Georgia Power, Gulf Power, and Mississippi Power, which combined have a generating capacity of more than 42,600 MW and serve more than 4.4 million electricity customers in the southeastern US. The good ol' power company also has energy marketing operations, and it provides energy consulting and management services for businesses and institutions. Through its Southern LINC Wireless unit, it provides wireless communications services in its US utility territory; its Southern Telecom unit offers wholesale fiber-optic services.

Southern Company also participates in the nonregulated energy sector: It markets excess energy from its retail plants and is building competitive plants across the southeastern US through subsidiary Southern Power. To improve operating efficiencies, in 2006 the company merged its Savannah Electric unit into another subsidiary, Georgia Power.

In keeping with the federal regulatory framework, which demands that utilities cut back on carbon emissions, in 2009 Southern Company's Mississippi Power filed plans to build a 582-MW integrated gasification combined cycle power plant near Orlando, Florida. This is one of first advanced gasification generating facilities with carbon capture capabilities in the US.

HISTORY

Steamboat captain W. P. Lay founded the Alabama Power Company in 1906 to develop electric power on the Coosa River. James Mitchell took over in 1912, moved headquarters from Montgomery to Birmingham, and bought a number of Alabama's utilities, consolidating them with Alabama Power under his Canadian holding company, Alabama Traction Light & Power (ATL&P).

In 1920 ATL&P became Southeastern Power & Light, forming Mississippi Power (1924) and Georgia Power (1927) to take over electric utilities in those states, and Gulf Power to do the same in northern Florida (1925).

Southeastern merged with Penn-Ohio Edison to form Commonwealth & Southern in 1929. But by 1942 Commonwealth & Southern was dissolved under the Public Utilities Holding Company Act of 1935 since it owned 11 unrelated, unconnected utilities. Alabama Power, Georgia Power, Gulf Power, and Mississippi Power were placed under a new holding company, Southern Company, which began full operations in 1949.

In 1975, amid an anti-utility political environment created by energy shortages, Georgia Power was near bankruptcy; Alabama Power stopped work on new construction and laid off 4,000 employees in 1978. That year, when Alabama governor and utility critic George Wallace left office, state regulators granted Southern long-sought rate relief.

The SEC allowed Southern to diversify into unregulated operations — a first in the US — with the 1981 formation of Southern Energy, which began investing in independent power projects and companies. In 1988 Southern bought Savannah Electric and Power.

Meanwhile, the industry was undergoing major changes, and utilities were venturing outside their territories. Southern sold a Georgia power plant to two Florida utilities in 1990. Two years later it bought 50% of Bahamian utility Freeport Power, and by 1994 Southern had a 49% stake in three power plants in Trinidad and Tobago. At home the company formed Southern LINC in 1995 to offer wireless telecom services in the southeastern US via specialized mobile radio (SMR) technology.

Also that year the company joined other US electric companies in raiding Britain's deregulated electricity larder. It bought UK utility South Western Electricity (SWEB) in 1995, though it later turned over a 51% stake to partner PP&L Resources. In 1996 it acquired 80% of Hong Kong's Consolidated Electric Power Asia, buying the rest the next year.

The first US company to enter Germany's electric utility market, Southern bought a 25% stake in Berlin's electric utility, Bewag, in 1997. That year and the next Southern expanded into the northeastern US and California, buying power plants from Commonwealth Energy, Eastern Utilities, ConEd, PG&E, and Orange and Rockland Utilities.

Focusing on power transmission in the UK, Southern and PP&L Resources (which became PPL in 2000) sold SWEB's power supply business and the SWEB brand name to London Electricity, an Electricité de France unit, in 1999. The former SWEB's distribution network was renamed Western Power Distribution.

In 2000 Southern sold a 20% stake in Southern Energy, which included the company's merchant energy operations (excluding those in the southeastern US) and its overseas investments, to the public. Southern Energy changed its name to Mirant in 2001, and that year Southern spun off its remaining stake in the unit to its shareholders.

EXECUTIVES

Chairman, President, and CEO: David M. Ratcliffe, age 60, $9,613,337 total compensation
EVP and COO: Thomas A. (Tom) Fanning, age 52, $2,529,606 total compensation
EVP and CFO: W. Paul Bowers, age 52, $2,773,277 total compensation
SVP Human Resources and Chief Diversity Officer: Marsha S. Johnson
EVP; President and CEO, Alabama Power: Charles D. McCrary, age 57, $2,877,268 total compensation
EVP; President, External Affairs: Christopher C. (Chris) Womack, age 50
EVP; President and CEO, Georgia Power: Michael D. (Mike) Garrett, age 59, $2,926,582 total compensation
EVP, General Counsel, and Corporate Secretary: G. Edison Holland Jr., age 56
VP Internal Auditing: Ronnie R. Labrato, age 53
VP Investor Relations: Glen A. Kundert
VP, Fuel Services: Jeff L. Wallace
President and CEO, SCS: C. Alan Martin, age 61
President and CEO of Southern Power: Ronnie L. Bates, age 49
President and CEO, Gulf Power: Susan N. Story, age 48
President and CEO, Mississippi Power: Anthony J. Topazi, age 58
President and CEO, SouthernLINC Wireless and Southern Telecom: Robert G. Dawson
President and CEO, Southern Nuclear: James H. (Jim) Miller III, age 59
SVP Sales, SouthernLINC Wireless: Rodney Johnson
Auditors: Deloitte & Touche LLP

LOCATIONS

HQ: Southern Company
   30 Ivan Allen Jr. Blvd. NW, Atlanta, GA 30308
Phone: 404-506-5000   **Fax:** 404-506-0455
Web: www.southernco.com

PRODUCTS/OPERATIONS

2008 Sales

	$ mil.	% of total
Electric		
Retail	14,055	82
Wholesale	2,400	14
Other	545	3
Other revenues	127	1
Total	**17,127**	**100**

Selected Subsidiaries and Affiliates

Alabama Power Company (electric utility)
Georgia Power Company (electric utility)
Gulf Power Company (electric utility)
Mississippi Power Company (electric utility)
Southern Communications Services, Inc. (Southern LINC Wireless, digital wireless communications)
Southern Company Gas, LLC (retail gas marketing)
Southern Company Generation and Energy Marketing (power generation and wholesale marketing)
   Southern Power Company (independent power production)
Southern Company Holdings, Inc. (interests in leveraged leases, synthetic fuel products, and energy services)
   Southern Company Energy Solutions LLC (energy services)
Southern Company Services, Inc. (administrative services, limited energy trading)
Southern Electric Generating Company (SEGCO, power generation, jointly owned by Alabama Power and Georgia Power)
SouthernLINC Wireless (wireless services)
Southern Nuclear Operating Company, Inc. (operates and maintains Alabama Power's and Georgia Power's nuclear plants)

COMPETITORS

AEP
AGL Resources
CenterPoint Energy
Cleco
Constellation Energy Group
Duke Energy
Energen
Entergy
FirstEnergy
Florida Public Utilities
FPL Group
JEA
MEAG Power
Oglethorpe Power
PacifiCorp
Progress Energy
SCANA
TECO Energy
TVA
Xcel Energy

HISTORICAL FINANCIALS

Company Type: Public

Income Statement

FYE: December 31

	REVENUE ($ mil.)	NET INCOME ($ mil.)	NET PROFIT MARGIN	EMPLOYEES
12/08	17,127.0	1,742.0	10.2%	27,276
12/07	15,353.0	1,686.0	11.0%	26,742
12/06	14,356.0	1,573.0	11.0%	26,091
12/05	13,554.0	1,591.0	11.7%	25,554
12/04	11,902.0	1,559.0	13.1%	25,648
Annual Growth	**9.5%**	**2.8%**	**—**	**1.6%**

2008 Year-End Financials

Debt ratio: 126.7%   No. of shares (mil.): 835
Return on equity: 13.6%   Dividends
Cash ($ mil.): 417   Yield: 4.5%
Current ratio: 1.03   Payout: 73.8%
Long-term debt ($ mil.): 16,816 Market value ($ mil.): 30,897

Stock History

NYSE: SO

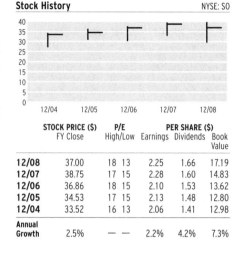

	STOCK PRICE ($) FY Close	P/E High/Low		PER SHARE ($) Earnings	Dividends	Book Value
12/08	37.00	18	13	2.25	1.66	17.19
12/07	38.75	17	15	2.28	1.60	14.83
12/06	36.86	18	15	2.10	1.53	13.62
12/05	34.53	17	15	2.13	1.48	12.80
12/04	33.52	16	13	2.06	1.41	12.98
Annual Growth	**2.5%**	**—**	**—**	**2.2%**	**4.2%**	**7.3%**

Southern Union

One of the largest diversified natural gas operations in the US, Southern Union is looking to form a more perfect union of natural gas transportation, storage, gathering, processing, and distribution assets. The company's major utility, Missouri Gas Energy, distributes natural gas to customers in four states. Southern Union has interests in gas storage facilities and more than 20,000 miles of pipeline throughout the US (primarily through Panhandle Energy and its 50% ownership of Florida Gas). Subsidiary Southern Union Gas Services is a transmission and gathering unit that operates in Texas and New Mexico.

It was able to ward off a proxy fight by institutional investor Sandell Asset Management, which owns about 9% of Southern Union, in 2009 by giving Sandell the right to nominate two candidates to stand for election to Southern Union's Board in 2009 and 2010.

HISTORY

Southern Union's earliest predecessor was the Wink Gas Co., formed in 1929 in Wink, Texas, during the West Texas oil boom. Although its first customer had to lay his own pipeline, the company grew, and in 1932 it became the Southern Union Company. In 1949 Southern Union won the Austin, Texas, gas franchise by merging with Texas Public Service Co.

The energy crisis of the 1970s led Southern Union to diversify into unrelated areas (such as real estate) that turned sour by the 1980s. Shortly after the natural gas industry was deregulated in the 1980s, the company formed Mercado Gas Services in 1986 to market gas to commercial and industrial customers.

Four years later, New York entrepreneur George Lindemann acquired Southern Union and installed Peter Kelley as president. Kelley wasted no time in shifting the corporate culture from a lethargic, top-heavy bureaucracy to an efficient sales organization.

Southern Union bought several Texas natural gas companies in 1993 and nearly doubled its customer base in 1994 with the purchase of Gas Service of Kansas City (now Missouri Gas Energy, or MGE). Moving into Florida in 1997, Southern Union acquired gas distributor Atlantic Utilities.

Continuing to look for acquisitions, Southern Union in 1999 submitted a bid to buy Las Vegas-based Southwest Gas, which instead accepted a lower offer from ONEOK. Southern Union sued Southwest Gas to block the ONEOK deal, and ONEOK terminated the agreement in 2000. Southern Union also filed fraud claims against ONEOK and Southwest Gas. (Southwest Gas paid Southern Union $17.5 million in 2002 to settle the suits.)

Southern Union decided to move north in 1999, when it bought natural gas distributor Pennsylvania Enterprises (150,000 customers). The next year Southern Union gained nearly 300,000 customers in New England by buying two Rhode Island gas utilities, Valley Resources and Providence Energy, and Massachusetts-based Fall River Gas. In 2001 the three utilities began operating as New England Gas.

Kelley resigned for health reasons in 2001, and Thomas Karam moved from the company's Pennsylvania operations to replace him. In a cost-cutting effort, Southern Union that year offered early retirement programs to 400 employees and laid off 48 workers in a reorganization of corporate management functions.

The company also began selling noncore assets, including the gas marketing business of PG Energy Services, its Keystone Pipeline Services unit, two small propane/heating oil distribution units, and a plumbing and heating services unit (Morris Merchants).

The company sold its Texas gas distribution utility (Southern Union Gas), as well as SUPro Energy (propane distribution in Texas and New Mexico), Mercado Gas Services (natural gas marketing), its Mexican gas utility interest, and some gas pipeline interests, to ONEOK for about $420 million. Southern Union has also sold its Florida gas distribution businesses, its propane distribution operations in Florida and Pennsylvania, and its outsourced energy management unit, ProvEnergy. New England Gas was sold to National Grid USA for a reported $575 million (and $77 million of assumed debt).

Proceeds from the asset sales were applied to the 2003 purchase from CMS Energy of the Panhandle Energy companies, which together operated a 10,000-mile gas pipeline system. The $1.8 billion deal included the assumption of nearly $1.2 billion in debt.

In 2004 Southern Union subsidiary CCE Holdings purchased Enron's CrossCountry Energy unit for $2.45 billion (including debt assumption). CrossCountry Energy owned the Transwestern Pipeline (sold in 2006) and a holds a 50% stake in Citrus Corp. (the owner of Florida Gas Transmission). Following this transaction, CCE Holdings sold CrossCountry subsidiary Northern Plains Natural Gas, a general partner

of Northern Border Partners (now ONEOK Partners), to ONEOK for $175 million.

In 2006 Southern Union sold its PG Energy operating division and its interests in PG Energy Services to UGI Corporation for a reported $580 million. It also went in the other direction that year with the acquisition of natural gas gathering and processing firm Sid Richardson Energy Services for $1.6 billion.

EXECUTIVES

Chairman Emeritus: Franklin W. (Frank) Denius, age 84
Chairman and CEO: George L. Lindemann, age 73
Vice Chairman, President, and COO:
Eric D. Herschmann, age 45
SVP and CFO: Richard N. (Rick) Marshall, age 50
VP, Controller, and Chief Accounting Officer:
George E. Aldrich, age 59
SVP Pipeline Operations; President and COO, Panhandle Energy and CrossCounrty Energy:
Robert O. (Rob) Bond, age 49
SVP Associate General Counsel: Monica M. Gaudiosi, age 46
VP, Assistant General Counsel, and Secretary:
Robert M. Kerrigan III
VP Investor Relations: John F. (Jack) Walsh
President, Gathering and Processing Business:
Roger A. Farrell, age 50
Director External Affairs: John P. Barnett
Auditors: PricewaterhouseCoopers LLP

LOCATIONS

HQ: Southern Union Company
5444 Westheimer Rd., Houston, TX 77056
Phone: 713-989-2000   **Fax:** 713-989-1121
Web: www.southernunionco.com

PRODUCTS/OPERATIONS

2008 Sales

	$ mil.	% of total
Gas gathering & processing	1,521.0	49
Gas distribution	821.7	27
Gas transportation & storage	721.6	24
Other	5.9	—
Total	**3,070.2**	**100**

Selected Subsidiaries

CCE Holdings, LLC (natural gas transportation)
  Citrus Corp. (50%)
    Florida Gas Transmission Company (50%)
Missouri Gas Energy (natural gas utility)
New England Gas Company (natural gas utility)
Panhandle Energy (natural gas transportation)
  Panhandle Eastern Pipe Line Company
  Sea Robin Pipeline Company
  Pan Gas Storage (dba Southwest Gas Storage)
  Trunkline Gas Company
  Trunkline LNG Company
PEI Power Corporation (independent power production)

COMPETITORS

Ameren
Atmos Energy
Dominion Peoples
Dominion Resources
Dominion Transmission
Duke Energy
El Paso
Empire District Electric
Exelon
Great Plains Energy
Laclede Group
National Fuel Gas
NiSource
ONEOK
Transcontinental Gas Pipe Line

HISTORICAL FINANCIALS

Company Type: Public

Income Statement

FYE: December 31

	REVENUE ($ mil.)	NET INCOME ($ mil.)	NET PROFIT MARGIN	EMPLOYEES
12/08	3,070.2	295.2	9.6%	2,413
12/07	2,616.7	228.7	8.7%	2,337
12/06	2,340.1	64.1	2.7%	2,312
12/05*	2,019.4	20.7	1.0%	2,888
6/04	1,800.0	114.0	6.3%	3,012
Annual Growth	**14.3%**	**26.9%**	**—**	**(5.4%)**

*Fiscal year change

2008 Year-End Financials

Debt ratio: 144.6%
Return on equity: 14.0%
Cash ($ mil.): 4
Current ratio: 0.76
Long-term debt ($ mil.): 3,257
No. of shares (mil.): 124
Dividends
  Yield: 4.6%
  Payout: 26.5%
Market value ($ mil.): 1,618

Stock History

NYSE: SUG

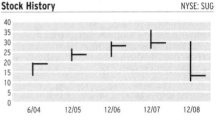

	STOCK PRICE ($) FY Close	P/E High/Low	PER SHARE ($) Earnings	Dividends	Book Value
12/08	13.04	13 5	2.26	0.60	19.09
12/07	29.36	20 15	1.75	0.45	17.78
12/06	27.95	74 57	0.40	0.40	16.53
12/05*	23.63	876 692	0.03	0.00	14.95
6/04	19.12	16 11	1.18	0.00	10.17
Annual Growth	**(9.1%)**	**— —**	**17.6%**	**—**	**17.0%**

*Fiscal year change

Southwest Airlines

Southwest Airlines will fly any plane, as long as it's a Boeing 737, and let passengers sit anywhere they like, as long as they get there first. Sticking with what has worked, Southwest has expanded its low-cost, no-frills, no-reserved-seats approach to air travel throughout the US to serve about 65 cities in more than 30 states. Now among the leading US airlines, Southwest nevertheless stands as an inspiration for scrappy low-fare upstarts the world over. The carrier has enjoyed 35 straight profitable years amid the airline industry's ups and downs.

In August 2009 Southwest made a move to expand westward when it placed a $170 million bid to buy troubled airline Frontier, but the bid was rejected. Southwest's bid was rebuffed in favor of another bid placed by Republic Airways.

In the meantime, Southwest has an airline to run, and simplicity has been a key to its success. Most Southwest flights are less than two hours, and the airline usually lands at small airports to avoid congestion at competitors' larger hubs; in Dallas it's the big dog at little Love Field, its birthplace, and in Chicago it accounts for most of the traffic at Midway Airport. Southwest's fleet of more than 500 aircraft consists only of one type — the Boeing 737 — to minimize training and maintenance costs.

Over the years Southwest has grown well beyond its home region, but economic woes in 2008 caused the carrier to scale back its expansion plans in destinations as well as with its fleet.

In the wake of the global economic recession, airlines are searching for new revenue streams. Many have piled on charges for everything from checking extra bags to pillow-and-blanket sets to choosing a seat. In May 2009 Southwest saw the value in fees and rolled out various measures that are expected to add tens of millions of dollars to its annual revenues (although it retains its policy of no charge for the first two bags).

Southwest sees code-sharing, in which airlines sell tickets on one another's flights and thus offer potential passengers more destinations, as a way to grow without expanding its own network. At the end of 2008 it inked an agreement for an alliance with Canada-based WestJet to begin a joint code-sharing program and with Mexican carrier Volaris.

After a year of tense meetings with FAA officials, Southwest agreed in early 2009 to pay a $7.5 million fine over missed required structural inspections in 2008 on 46 planes. The carrier removed the planes from service for inspection, causing some canceled flights, but went back to business as usual within a few days.

HISTORY

Texas businessman Rollin King and lawyer Herb Kelleher founded Air Southwest in 1967 as an intrastate airline linking Dallas, Houston, and San Antonio. The now-defunct Braniff and Texas International sued, questioning whether the region needed another airline, but the Texas Supreme Court ruled in Southwest's favor. In 1971 the company, renamed Southwest Airlines, made its first scheduled flight.

Operating from Love Field in Dallas, Southwest adopted "love" as the theme of its early ad campaigns, serving love potions (drinks) and love bites (peanuts). When other airlines moved to the new Dallas/Fort Worth Airport (DFW) in 1974, Kelleher insisted on staying at Love Field, gaining a virtual monopoly there.

When Kelleher decided to fly outside Texas, Congress passed the Wright Amendment in 1979. Designed to protect DFW, the law restricted the states served directly from Love Field. (Arkansas, Louisiana, New Mexico, and Oklahoma were on the original list; a 1997 amendment added Alabama, Kansas, and Mississippi. In 2000 a federal court removed the restrictions for planes with 56 or fewer seats. Later Missouri was added to the list of states eligible for direct service from Love Field.)

When Lamar Muse, Southwest's president, resigned in 1978 because of differences with King, Kelleher assumed control. (Muse later took over his son Michael's nearly bankrupt airline, Muse Air, which was sold in 1985 to Southwest. The airline was liquidated in 1987.)

An industry maverick, Kelleher introduced advance-purchase Fun Fares in 1986 and a frequent-flier program in 1987 based on the number of flights taken instead of mileage. He gained attention in 1992 for starring in Southwest's TV commercials and for arm wrestling Stevens Aviation chairman Kurt Herwald for the rights to the "Just Plane Smart" slogan. When Southwest became the official airline of Sea World in Texas, Kelleher had a 737 painted as a killer whale.

Southwest took on the East Coast with service to Baltimore in 1993 and bought Salt Lake City-based Morris Air in 1994. That year it launched a ticketless system and adopted its own passenger reservation system to cut costs. Agreements with Icelandair in 1996 and 1997 allowed Southwest passengers to connect from four US cities to Europe through Icelandair's Baltimore hub.

In 2001 Southwest experienced a rare labor dispute when stalled contract negotiations led to picketing by the airline's ground crew union.

Kelleher stepped down as president and CEO in 2001. General counsel Jim Parker took over as CEO, and EVP Colleen Barrett — who first worked for Kelleher as his secretary and is given much of the credit for maintaining Southwest's corporate spirit — was named COO.

Parker would reign over the airline during one of the most tumultuous times in its history. Despite an industrywide downturn resulting from the lagging US economy and exacerbated by the September 11 terrorist attacks, Southwest managed to post a profit for 2001 as well as 2002, but it did not come easily.

Increased Internet sales led the airline to close its call centers in Dallas, Little Rock, and Salt Lake City in 2003. Nearly 2,000 workers were given the choice of relocating to another call center or accepting a severance package.

Union negotiations with flight attendants began in 2002 and lasted for two years, during which time Parker was publicly chastised for being uncooperative. A resolution was not reached until Kelleher and Barrett were asked to step in by Parker, who resigned in 2004, after negotiations ended. He was replaced by former CFO Gary Kelly.

After intense lobbying from both Southwest and American Airlines, Congress revisited the Wright Amendment in 2006. A compromise measure signed into law that year allowed Southwest to offer direct, one-stop service from Love Field to states not covered by the original Wright law or its revisions.

Marking a milestone for Southwest, Kelleher and Barrett stepped down from the board in 2008, and Kelly replaced Kelleher as chairman.

EXECUTIVES

Chairman, President, and CEO: Gary C. Kelly, age 53, $1,680,272 total compensation
EVP and COO: Michael G. (Mike) Van de Ven, age 47, $865,758 total compensation
SVP Finance and CFO: Laura H. Wright, age 48, $689,106 total compensation
VP Technology and CIO: Jan Marshall
SVP Administration and Chief People Officer: A. Jeff Lamb III
EVP Strategy and Planning: Robert E. (Bob) Jordan, age 48, $722,044 total compensation
EVP Corporate Services and Corporate Secretary: Ron Ricks, age 57, $881,341 total compensation
SVP Marketing and Revenue Management: Davis S. (Dave) Ridley, age 55
SVP Corporate Communications: Ginger C. Hardage
SVP Operations: Greg Wells
SVP Customer Services: Daryl Krause
VP and Director Operations: Gregory N. (Greg) Crum
VP Customer Relations and Rapid Rewards: James A. (Jim) Ruppel
VP Marketing, Sales, and Distribution: Kevin M. Krone
VP and General Counsel: Madeleine Johnson
VP and Treasurer: Scott E. Topping
Auditors: Ernst & Young LLP

LOCATIONS

HQ: Southwest Airlines Co.
2702 Love Field Dr., Dallas, TX 75235
Phone: 214-792-4000   **Fax:** 214-792-5015
Web: www.southwest.com

PRODUCTS/OPERATIONS

2008 Revenues

	$ mil.	% of total
Passenger	10,549	96
Freight	145	1
Other	329	3
Total	**11,023**	**100**

COMPETITORS

AirTran Holdings
Alaska Air
AMR Corp.
Continental Airlines
Delta Air Lines
Frontier Airlines
JetBlue
Northwest Airlines
UAL
US Airways

HISTORICAL FINANCIALS

Company Type: Public

Income Statement				FYE: December 31
	REVENUE ($ mil.)	NET INCOME ($ mil.)	NET PROFIT MARGIN	EMPLOYEES
12/08	11,023.0	178.0	1.6%	35,499
12/07	9,861.0	645.0	6.5%	34,378
12/06	9,086.0	499.0	5.5%	32,664
12/05	7,584.0	548.0	7.2%	31,729
12/04	6,530.0	313.0	4.8%	31,011
Annual Growth	14.0%	(13.2%)	—	3.4%

2008 Year-End Financials

Debt ratio: 70.6%
Return on equity: 3.0%
Cash ($ mil.): 1,368
Current ratio: 1.03
Long-term debt ($ mil.): 3,498

No. of shares (mil.): 741
Dividends
  Yield: 0.2%
  Payout: 8.3%
Market value ($ mil.): 6,391

Stock History

NYSE: LUV

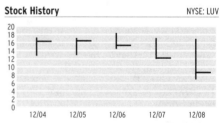

	STOCK PRICE ($) FY Close	P/E High/Low		PER SHARE ($) Earnings	Dividends	Book Value
12/08	8.62	70	29	0.24	0.02	6.68
12/07	12.20	20	14	0.84	0.02	9.36
12/06	15.32	30	24	0.61	0.02	8.70
12/05	16.43	25	19	0.67	0.02	9.00
12/04	16.28	45	34	0.38	0.02	7.45
Annual Growth	(14.7%)	—	—	(10.9%)	0.0%	(2.7%)

Southwest Gas

The sunny southwestern US is smiling on Southwest Gas. The largest gas supplier in Arizona and Nevada, it provides natural gas to more than 1.8 million customers in the two states, as well as in portions of California. Southwest Gas acquires its natural gas from 46 suppliers and pumps it through distribution mains. It also owns a transmission pipeline that supplies the Las Vegas area, and subsidiary Paiute Pipeline transports gas from the Idaho-Nevada border to Reno and Lake Tahoe. Another Southwest Gas subsidiary, Northern Pipeline Construction, is an underground piping contractor that serves gas distributors. During 2008 this unit served 63 customers.

The company secures natural gas supplies for its southern system (Arizona, southern Nevada, and southern California properties) from producing regions in Colorado and New Mexico (San Juan basin), Texas (Permian basin), and Rocky Mountain areas. The northern system (northern Nevada and northern California properties) is supplied from Rocky Mountain gas producing areas and from Canada.

Southwest Gas added 29,000 net new customers in 2007. In 2008 some 33,000 new customers (gross) were added. However, the downturn in the real estate market resulted in a plethora of vacated homes, and meant that only 6,000 net new customers were added that year.

EXECUTIVES

Chairman: James J. Kropid, age 71
CEO and Director: Jeffrey W. Shaw, age 50, $1,903,840 total compensation
President: James P. Kane, age 62, $1,070,491 total compensation
EVP, CFO, Corporate Secretary, and Director: George C. Biehl, age 61, $919,617 total compensation
SVP and Chief Knowledge and Technology Officer: Dudley J. Sondeno, age 56, $792,009 total compensation
VP, Controller, and Chief Accounting Officer: Roy R. Centrella, age 51
SVP Finance: Edward A. Janov, age 54
SVP Regulatory Affairs and Energy Resources: John P. Hester, age 46, $583,844 total compensation
VP Pricing: Roger C. Montgomery
VP Information Services: Robert J. Weaver
VP Engineering: James F. Wunderlin
VP and Treasurer: Kenneth J. Kenny, age 46
VP Gas Resources: William N. Moody
VP, General Counsel, and Compliance Officer: Karen S. Haller
VP Human Resources: Laura Lopez Hobbs
VP External Affairs: Donald L. Soderberg
Auditors: PricewaterhouseCoopers LLP

LOCATIONS

HQ: Southwest Gas Corporation
5241 Spring Mountain Rd., Las Vegas, NV 89193
Phone: 702-876-7011   **Fax:** 702-364-3180
Web: www.swgas.com

PRODUCTS/OPERATIONS

2008 Sales

	$ mil.	% of total
Gas	1,791.4	84
Construction	353.3	16
Total	**2,144.7**	**100**

Selected Subsidiaries

Northern Pipeline Construction Co. (pipeline construction)
Paiute Pipeline Company (pipeline transmission systems)

Major Natural Gas Suppliers and Transporters

El Paso Corporation
Kern River Gas Transmission Company
Northwest Pipeline Corporation
Southern California Gas Company
Transwestern Pipeline Company

COMPETITORS

Edison International
El Paso
Energy West
Holloman
IDACORP
Impax Group
NV Energy
ONEOK
PG&E Corporation
Pinnacle West
SEMCO Energy
Sempra Energy
SRP
TransCanada
UniSource Energy

HISTORICAL FINANCIALS

Company Type: Public

Income Statement

FYE: December 31

	REVENUE ($ mil.)	NET INCOME ($ mil.)	NET PROFIT MARGIN	EMPLOYEES
12/08	2,144.7	61.0	2.8%	2,447
12/07	2,152.1	83.2	3.9%	2,538
12/06	2,024.8	83.9	4.1%	2,525
12/05	1,714.3	43.8	2.6%	2,590
12/04	1,477.1	56.8	3.8%	2,548
Annual Growth	**9.8%**	**1.8%**	**—**	**(1.0%)**

2008 Year-End Financials

Debt ratio: 123.9%
Return on equity: 6.0%
Cash ($ mil.): 26
Current ratio: 0.86
Long-term debt ($ mil.): 1,285
No. of shares (mil.): 45
Dividends
  Yield: 3.5%
  Payout: 64.0%
Market value ($ mil.): 1,130

Stock History

NYSE: SWX

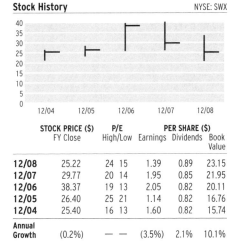

	STOCK PRICE ($) FY Close	P/E High/Low		PER SHARE ($) Earnings	Dividends	Book Value
12/08	25.22	24	15	1.39	0.89	23.15
12/07	29.77	20	14	1.95	0.85	21.95
12/06	38.37	19	13	2.05	0.82	20.11
12/05	26.40	25	21	1.14	0.82	16.76
12/04	25.40	16	13	1.60	0.82	15.74
Annual Growth	**(0.2%)**	**—**	**—**	**(3.5%)**	**2.1%**	**10.1%**

Spartan Stores

This company fights to win on the battlefield of grocery distribution. Spartan Stores is a leading grocery wholesaler in the Midwest, distributing about 43,000 food and general merchandise items to about 350 independent grocery stores, primarily in Indiana, Michigan, and Ohio. From its two distribution centers, the company supplies mostly national brands, as well as items sold under such private labels as Full Circle and Valu Time, as well as its own Spartan banner. Spartan Stores also operates about 100 retail supermarkets in Michigan and Ohio under such names as D&W Fresh Markets, Family Fare Supermarkets, Felpausch Food Centers, Glen's Markets, and VG's Food and Pharmacy.

Spartan Stores has been focused on boosting its retail grocery business through a series of acquisitions. It purchased more than 15 properties from V.G.'s Food Center late in 2008 after acquiring G&R Felpausch and its chain of 20 Felpausch Food Centers the previous year. At the same time, Spartan Stores has divested some non-core properties, including its chain of drug stores (operating under the name The Pharm), which were sold to Rite Aid in 2008. Retail supermarkets now account for more than 50% of sales.

Meanwhile, the company has been investing in efforts to lower costs within its wholesale supply business, including new software systems and other improvements at its distribution facilities. Other initiatives have included wage controls and hiring freezes.

Dennis Eidson was promoted to CEO in 2008 replacing Craig Sturken who stepped down. After joining the company in 2003 as head of marketing, Eidson rose to the position of COO in 2007. He previously served as Midwest regional chief for The Great Atlantic & Pacific Tea Company (A&P). Sturken, who had also joined the company from A&P, remained with Spartan Stores as chairman.

HISTORY

Making dinner in the early 1900s often required several shopping stops: the grocer for canned goods, a butcher for meat, and yet another place for produce. Eventually the big grocery chains began offering one-stop shopping, not to mention better prices due to greater buying power. Worrying about how to compete, in 1917 approximately 100 small grocers met in Grand Rapids, Michigan, to discuss organizing a cooperative; almost half of those formed the Grand Rapids Wholesale Grocery Co. The stores remained independent, operating under different names but achieving economies of scale and volume buying through the co-op. They also began developing a variety of services for member stores. Sales topped $1 million in 1934.

Over the years the company expanded beyond its Grand Rapids origins. In 1950 it formed subsidiary United Wholesale, which served independent grocers on a cash-and-carry basis. It acquired the Grand Rapids Coffee Company in 1953. The next year the co-op launched its first private-label item, Spartan Coffee, with a green Spartan logo reminiscent of the Michigan State University mascot. The company changed its name to Spartan Stores in 1957.

Spartan Stores entered retailing in the early 1970s when it bought 19 Harding's stores. It became a for-profit company in 1973, but continued to provide rebates to customers based on their purchases. Spartan Stores began offering insurance to its customers in 1979.

Concerned about the direction of the company, customers named Patrick Quinn, formerly a VP at a small chain of grocery stores, as president and CEO in 1985. To focus on the wholesale business, and to avoid any appearance of conflict of interest in both supplying member stores and operating competing stores, Spartan Stores sold its 23 retail stores between 1987 and 1994, giving customer stores the first option on them. It entered the convenience store wholesale business with its 1987 acquisition of L&L/Jiroch. Two years later the co-op acquired Associated Grocers of Michigan (later known as Capistar, closed in 1996).

Sales topped $2 billion in 1991. Spartan Stores expanded its convenience store operations in 1993 by buying wholesaler J.F. Walker. Despite record sales in 1996, a $46 million restructuring charge that included extensive technological improvements led to a $21.7 million loss, the largest in the company's history. The following year Jim Meyer, who had joined Spartan Stores in 1973, replaced the retiring Quinn as president and CEO. Also in 1997 the company stopped giving its customers rebates, finally doing away with the last remnants of its co-op years.

To keep Michigan customers out of the clutches of its wholesaling rivals, Spartan Stores re-entered retailing in 1999 by acquiring eight Ashcraft's Markets. It bought 13 Family Fare stores and 23 Glen's grocery stores that year. In early 2000 the company sold off its insurance business. Later that year Spartan Stores acquired food and drug chain Seaway Food Town (Michigan and Ohio) for about $180 million and began publicly trading.

In 2001 the company purchased longtime customer Prevo's Family Markets, a supermarket chain with 10 stores in western Michigan. In an effort to reduce debt and improve profitability in mid-2002 the company announced plans to close its Food Town stores, which suffered from competitors such as Meier, Kroger, and Farmer Jack's. (By mid-2003, Spartan had sold the last of its 26 Food Town stores. Spartan Store's retail operations had accounted for about 40% of the company's sales.)

In 2003 Spartan Stores sold seven shopping centers in Michigan for $46 million as part of its strategy to sell non-core properties and focus on its retail and distributions businesses. That year James Meyer retired as president and CEO of Spartan Stores and was succeeded by Craig Sturken, a former executive of the Great Atlantic & Pacific Tea Company. Later the company sold convenience store suppliers L&L/Jiroch and J.F. Walker to Knoxville, Tennessee-based distributor H.T. Hackney Co.

Spartan Stores sold the assets of United Wholesale Grocery Co., a privately held firm in Michigan, for about $10 million in 2004. The sale marked Spartan's exit from the convenience store distribution business.

In 2005 the company opened three fuel centers in Michigan under the Family Fare Quick Stops and Glen's Quick Stop banners. The company acquired D&W Food Centers the following year and purchased about 20 stores from G&R Felpausch in 2007. Spartan Stores' retail expansion continued in 2008 when it acquired more than 15 stores from V.G.'s Food Center. Sturken stepped down as CEO that year and was replaced by Dennis Eidson.

EXECUTIVES

Chairman: Craig C. Sturken, age 65, $2,885,199 total compensation
President, CEO, and Director: Dennis Eidson, age 54, $1,512,627 total compensation
EVP and CFO: David M. (Dave) Staples, age 45, $914,414 total compensation
VP Information Technology: David deS. (Dave) Couch, age 58
EVP, General Counsel, and Corporate Secretary: Alex J. DeYonker, age 59, $688,145 total compensation
EVP Merchandising: Alan Hartline
EVP Retail Operations: Theodore C. (Ted) Adornato, age 54, $672,511 total compensation
EVP Supply Chain: Derek Jones, age 40
VP Fresh Merchandising: Scott R. Ruth
VP Finance: Thomas A. (Tom) Van Hall, age 52
VP Corporate Affairs: Jeanne Norcross
VP Center Store Merchandising: Brian Haaraoja
VP Human Resources: Linda Esparza
VP Operations and Finance: Francis Wong
VP Marketing: Ken Thewes
VP Center Store Merchandising: Larry Pierce
Manager, Retail Services: Tom Montgomery
Auditors: Deloitte & Touche LLP

LOCATIONS

HQ: Spartan Stores, Inc.
850 76th St. SW, Grand Rapids, MI 49518
Phone: 616-878-2000   **Fax:** 616-878-8561
Web: www.spartanstores.com

PRODUCTS/OPERATIONS

2009 Sales

	$ mil.	% of total
Retail	1,328.1	52
Distribution	1,248.6	48
Total	**2,576.7**	**100**

Selected Retail Brands

Full Circle
Spartan
Top Care
Valu Time

Selected Retail Stores

D&W Fresh Markets
Family Fare Supermarkets
Felpausch Food Centers
Glen's Markets
VG's Food and Pharmacy

COMPETITORS

Associated Wholesale Grocers	McLane
C & S Wholesale	Meijer
Certified Grocers Midwest	Miner's
Costco Wholesale	Nash-Finch
IGA	S. Abraham & Sons
Kroger	SUPERVALU
Laurel Grocery	Wal-Mart

HISTORICAL FINANCIALS

Company Type: Public

Income Statement

FYE: Last Saturday in March

	REVENUE ($ mil.)	NET INCOME ($ mil.)	NET PROFIT MARGIN	EMPLOYEES
3/09	2,576.7	38.8	1.5%	9,700
3/08	2,476.8	34.3	1.4%	8,100
3/07	2,370.4	25.2	1.1%	7,300
3/06	2,039.9	18.2	0.9%	7,500
3/05	2,043.2	18.8	0.9%	6,300
Annual Growth	**6.0%**	**19.9%**	**—**	**11.4%**

2009 Year-End Financials

Debt ratio: 92.0%	No. of shares (mil.): 22
Return on equity: 17.6%	Dividends
Cash ($ mil.): 7	Yield: 1.3%
Current ratio: 1.13	Payout: 11.2%
Long-term debt ($ mil.): 216	Market value ($ mil.): 346

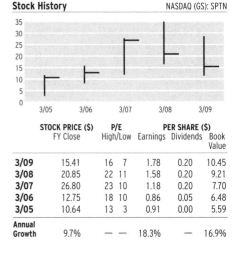

Stock History

NASDAQ (GS): SPTN

	STOCK PRICE ($) FY Close	P/E High/Low		PER SHARE ($) Earnings	Dividends	Book Value
3/09	15.41	16	7	1.78	0.20	10.45
3/08	20.85	22	11	1.58	0.20	9.21
3/07	26.80	23	10	1.18	0.20	7.70
3/06	12.75	18	10	0.86	0.05	6.48
3/05	10.64	13	3	0.91	0.00	5.59
Annual Growth	**9.7%**	**—**	**—**	**18.3%**	**—**	**16.9%**

Spherion Corporation

Spherion seeks to circumvent your personnel problems. The company provides traditional temporary staffing along with services such as professional and executive recruitment and employee consulting and assessment. In addition, Spherion provides staffing and technology services in such areas as project management, quality assurance, and data center and network operations. The company also offers customer care and administrative and support services. Spherion operates through a network of more than 650 locations in the US and Canada, serving more than 8,000 clients ranging from small businesses to *FORTUNE* 500 companies. Spherion was founded in 1946.

Through its Mergis Group division, Spherion formed a Troubled Assets Relief Program and government bailout team in early 2009 to supply recruiting and staffing for the federal government's efforts to stimulate the weak US economy. The team aims to provide services including executive recruitment, project management, staffing in accounting and finance, information technology, and other professional-office management roles.

Over the years, Spherion has discontinued its staffing operations in Australia, the Netherlands, and the UK in order to focus on its business in North America. The company also cut some operations in the US, including its call center outsourcing division and court reporting business. In mid-2007, Spherion sold its HR consulting business to IMPACT Group, a career-transition services firm.

In 2007 the company bought Resulté Universal to tap into Texas' growing demand for specialty staffing in IT, accounting, and finance. That year, Spherion boosted its administrative, legal, and financial personnel offerings with the acquisition of Todays Office Professionals (formerly Todays Staffing) from rival CDI. Also in

2007, Spherion enhanced its IT staffing and consulting operations by acquiring Technisource. Spherion combined Technisource's operations with its own IT staffing unit under the Technisource brand.

HISTORY

LeRoy Dettman founded City Car Unloaders in 1946 to provide railroad car workers in Chicago. As it grew, the company added industrial and clerical workers; it moved into health care staffing in 1966. H&R Block acquired the company (then named Personnel Pool) in 1978, bought personnel placement firm Interim Systems in 1991, and combined the two under the Interim name. Also that year Raymond Marcy became CEO of the company. In 1994 Interim went public.

Interim used the proceeds of its IPO to fund more acquisitions, particularly in the higher-margin professional staffing fields such as medicine and law. In 1995 it began targeting information technology by acquiring Computer Power Group and a year later, computer staffing firm Brandon Systems. Also in 1996 the company acquired Netherlands-based staffing firms Allround and Interplan.

In a move to expand internationally, Interim acquired London-based Michael Page Group for about $574 million in 1997. Also that year Interim bought AimExecutive Holdings, adding outplacement services to its business. In 1998 the company acquired London-based staffing company Crone Corkill Group. The following year it bought rival Norrell in a $550 million deal, adding nearly 400 offices to its operations.

To broaden its e-business services, Interim bought Applied Internet Consultancy in 2000 and soon changed its name to Spherion. It also expanded its online recruiting services with its launch of CareerZone.com, a Web site for job seekers, and its acquisition of an 80% stake in JobOptions.com.

In 2001 Spherion spun off Michael Page as a public company. Later that year the company announced a broad reorganization plan, including office closures, job cuts, and the divestiture of noncore or underperforming units. In 2002 Spherion sold consulting businesses in the UK and the Netherlands. In 2003 the company reorganized its operations into two divisions, Staffing Services and Professional Services. Spherion sold its noncore businesses in Australia, the Netherlands, and the UK in 2004.

In 2007, the company made some big moves to expand; it bought administrative, legal, and financial staffing firm Todays Staffing, Resulté Universal, and Technisource, which added to its IT consulting operations.

EXECUTIVES

President, CEO, and Director: Roy G. Krause, age 62, $2,295,404 total compensation
EVP and COO: William J. (Bill) Grubbs, age 51, $919,034 total compensation
EVP and CFO: Mark W. Smith, age 46, $718,835 total compensation
VP and CIO: Richard Harris, age 49
SVP and Chief Human Resources Officer: John D. Heins, age 49, $497,529 total compensation
SVP; President Staffing Services: Loretta A. Penn, age 59, $298,735 total compensation
SVP Recruitment Process Outsourcing (RPO): Rebecca Callahan
VP and Treasurer: Teri Miller
Director Public Relations and Corporate Marketing: Kip Havel

Interim General Counsel and Assistant Secretary: Thad Florence
VP Operations, Recruitment Process Outsourcing: Greg Eierman
VP Strategy Management Office, Recruitment Process Outsourcing: Jennifer Beck
VP New Business Client Partnerships, Recruitment Process Outsourcing: Sue Marcus
Auditors: Deloitte & Touche LLP

LOCATIONS

HQ: Spherion Corporation
2050 Spectrum Blvd., Fort Lauderdale, FL 33309
Phone: 954-308-7600   **Fax:** 954-308-7666
Web: www.spherion.com

PRODUCTS/OPERATIONS

2008 Revenues

	$ mil.	% of total
Staffing services		
Temporary staffing	1,283.5	58
Managed services	141.7	7
Permanent placement	15.5	1
Professional services		
Temporary staffing	701.7	32
Permanent placement	46.8	2
Total	**2,189.2**	**100**

Selected Staffing Areas

Staffing services
Administrative
Clerical
Light industrial
Professional services
Administrative
Engineering
Finance and accounting
Human resources
Information technology
Legal
Sales and marketing

COMPETITORS

Accenture	Keane
Adecco	Kelly Services
ADP	Kforce
Allegis Group	Manpower
Butler International	MPS
COMFORCE	Randstad Holding
Diversified Search	Robert Half
EDS	TAC Worldwide
Express Employment	Volt Information
Hudson Highland Group	WJM Associates
IBM Global Services	

HISTORICAL FINANCIALS

Company Type: Public

Income Statement

FYE: Last Friday in December

	REVENUE ($ mil.)	NET INCOME ($ mil.)	NET PROFIT MARGIN	EMPLOYEES
12/08	2,189.2	(118.5)	—	215,000
12/07	2,017.1	25.3	1.3%	258,000
12/06	1,933.1	54.7	2.8%	273,000
12/05	1,971.7	12.0	0.6%	302,000
12/04	2,032.7	56.5	2.8%	285,000
Annual Growth	1.9%	—	—	(6.8%)

2008 Year-End Financials

Debt ratio: 0.5%
Return on equity: —
Cash ($ mil.): 8
Current ratio: 1.59
Long-term debt ($ mil.): 2

No. of shares (mil.): 51
Dividends
Yield: 0.0%
Payout: —
Market value ($ mil.): 114

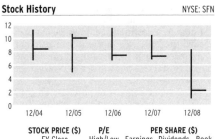
Sprint Nextel

Running to keep up in the US telecom race, Sprint Nextel is the #3 wireless carrier behind Verizon Wireless and AT&T Mobility in terms of subscribers. Sprint Nextel serves nearly 40 million customers with mobile voice, data, and Web services over its nationwide network. While the namesake brand is reserved for postpaid accounts, the company also offers prepaid mobile access (mainly to the youth market) through its Boost Mobile subsidiary. Sprint Nextel also provides cellular access to other carriers on a wholesale basis. The company's smaller legacy wireline business provides long-distance voice, Internet, and data network services primarily to corporate customers and other carriers.

Sprint Nextel is partnering with other telecommunications companies and shedding physical assets in order to cut operational costs and increase liquidity. The company in 2009 announced an agreement with Sweden-based wireless networking equipment and services stalwart Ericsson in which the daily operation, resource provisioning, and maintenance of Sprint Nextel's core wireless and wireline networks will be outsourced to Ericsson.

The previous year, the company formed a joint venture with wireless ISP Clearwire that combined the infrastructure of Sprint Nextel's next-generation, wireless broadband network (based on the emerging WiMAX transmission protocol) with Clearwire's network. In return for contributing its WiMAX network, Sprint Nextel received a 51% stake in the venture, which operates under the Clearwire name. Other Clearwire investors include Google, Comcast, Time Warner Cable, and Bright House Networks.

The increased data capacity of the emerging WiMAX protocol has been long-championed by Intel, but the technology is seen as something of a gamble for Sprint Nextel due to its largely unproven efficacy for large scale deployment. Sprint Nextel is betting on strong demand for its wireless Internet services to justify the expense of the new network, which is intended not only to deliver video and other advanced services to cell phones, but to enable wireless broadband service for residential and business users as an alternative to cable or DSL.

Further divestment of physical assets included the 2008 sale of more than 3,000 of its cell towers to private equity firm TowerCo. Sprint Nextel retained use of the towers through a lease agreement.

The company agreed to purchase Virgin Mobile USA for about $700 million in 2009. The acquisition is intended to give Sprint Nextel's prepaid business, Boost, a bump.

As part of a joint venture with cable titans including Advance/Newhouse Communications, Comcast, Cox Communications, and Time Warner, the company is testing a program to provide cable television, home phone, and wireless phone services in a single package.

HISTORY

In 1899 Jacob Brown and son Cleyson began operating the Brown Telephone Company, one of the first non-Bell phone companies in the western US, in Abilene, Kansas. Cleyson later formed Union Electric (phone equipment, 1905) and Home Telephone and Telegraph (long-distance, 1910). In 1911 he consolidated his company with other Kansas independents as United Telephone, then obtained capital from rival Missouri and Kansas Telephone (later Southwestern Bell), which bought 60% of United's stock.

Cleyson sold his electric utility to finance expansions in telephone services, and in 1925 he incorporated United Telephone and Electric. Reorganized as United Utilities after the Depression, United continued to buy local exchanges. A post-WWII order backlog halted United's acquisition activity until 1952, but the company soon began further expansion, becoming the second largest non-Bell phone company in the US before 1960.

During the 1960s United focused on satellites, nuclear power plants, and cable TV, and it bought North Electric (1965), the US's oldest independent phone equipment maker. The company was renamed United Telecommunications in 1972. Meanwhile, Southern Pacific had developed the telegraph system along its railroad tracks into a microwave long-distance network called Southern Pacific Communications (1970) and known as SPRINT (for Southern Pacific Railroad Internal Telecommunications). In 1983 GTE acquired the network and renamed it GTE Sprint Communications. The next year United acquired U.S. Telephone, the Dallas-based reseller of long-distance services and the eighth-largest US long-distance company.

A year after the 1984 AT&T Corp. breakup, United bought 50% of GTE Sprint (United bought another 30% in 1989 and the balance in 1992). United and GTE teamed up to combine their long-distance systems — GTE Sprint and US Telecom — to form US Sprint. The new unit began offering long-distance in 1986 and completed a nationwide fiber-optic network the next year (The US was later dropped from the partnership's name, leaving Sprint). It was renamed Sprint Corporation in 1992.

In 1998 Sprint Spectrum, a wireless partnership with several cable firms, was combined with PhillieCo (another cable partnership) and SprintCom (its PCS subsidiary) to form Sprint PCS Group.

Selling a 10% stake in PCS Group to the public, Sprint split its stock into the FON Group (non-wireless operations) and the PCS Group. In

2003 Sprint named BellSouth vice chairman Gary Forsee as its CEO.

Sprint has not been immune to the economic despair that has plagued the telecom industry. Its reorganization plans, designed to cut expenses, included deep job cuts — it eliminated more than 20,000 jobs in two years. Sprint FON in early 2003 completed the sale of its directory-publishing unit to R. H. Donnelley for $2.1 billion in a move to pay down its $21 billion debt.

Sprint Nextel in 2005 began leasing its cell phone tower business to Global Signal in a deal valued at $1.2 billion.

Chairman William Kennard resigned in early 2007. Forsee added chairman to his title, but resigned from the company later that year. Board member James Hance Jr. was named non-executive chairman, and Terabeam chairman and CEO Daniel Hesse was hired as the new chief executive.

As it struggled under its own weight to keep pace with rivals, the company used layoffs during 2007 and 2008 to cut costs. Additionally, it closed about 10% of its 1,400 retail shops and 20% of its 20,000 distribution points to bring down expenses. Sprint Nextel spun off its local consumer wireline voice operations to focus on its wireless broadband services in 2008.

EXECUTIVES

Chairman: James H. (Jim) Hance Jr., age 64
CEO, President, and Director: Daniel R. (Dan) Hesse, age 55, $19,201,372 total compensation
CFO: Robert H. (Bob) Brust, age 65, $4,949,376 total compensation
Chief Service Officer: Robert L. Johnson, age 50, $3,608,038 total compensation
SVP and Controller: Charles L. (Charlie) Hall
SVP Corporate Communications: Bill White
SVP Human Resources: Sandra J. (Sandy) Price
VP Enterprise and Federal Sales: John Dupree
President, Strategy and Corporate Development: Keith O. Cowan, age 53, $8,319,481 total compensation
President, CDMA Business Unit: Robert H. (Bob) Johnson, age 55
President, Business Markets Group: Paget A. Alves, age 54
President, Wholesale Services: James (Jim) Patterson
President, Sprint Nextel iDEN: Danny Bowman
President, Network Operations and Wholesale: Steven L. (Steve) Elfman, age 54, $4,317,384 total compensation
Communications Director, National/Business Media and Financial Communications: James Fisher
Director, Industry Analyst Relations and Strategic Communications: Joseph M. (Joe) Mandacina
General Counsel and Corporate Secretary: Charles Wunsch, age 52
Auditors: KPMG LLP

LOCATIONS

HQ: Sprint Nextel Corporation
6200 Sprint Pkwy., Overland Park, KS 66251
Phone: 703-433-4000
Web: www.sprint.com

PRODUCTS/OPERATIONS

2008 Sales

	$ mil.	% of total
Wireless	30,427	85
Wireline	5,208	15
Total	**35,635**	**100**

COMPETITORS

Alltel	MetroPCS
AT&T Mobility	Qwest Communications
Cellco	T-Mobile USA
CenturyTel	U.S. Cellular
Cincinnati Bell	Verizon
Level 3 Communications	

HISTORICAL FINANCIALS
Company Type: Public

Income Statement
FYE: December 31

	REVENUE ($ mil.)	NET INCOME ($ mil.)	NET PROFIT MARGIN	EMPLOYEES
12/08	35,635.0	(2,796.0)	—	56,000
12/07	40,146.0	(29,580.0)	—	60,000
12/06	41,028.0	1,329.0	3.2%	103,483
12/05	34,680.0	1,801.0	5.2%	79,900
12/04	27,428.0	(1,012.0)	—	59,900
Annual Growth	**6.8%**	**—**		**(1.7%)**

2008 Year-End Financials

Debt ratio: 107.1%	No. of shares (mil.): 2,876
Return on equity: —	Dividends
Cash ($ mil.): 3,691	Yield: 0.0%
Current ratio: 1.33	Payout: —
Long-term debt ($ mil.): 20,992	Market value ($ mil.): 5,263

Stock History
NYSE: S

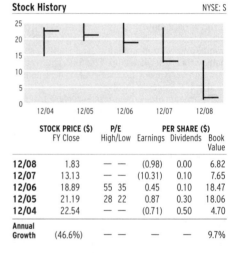

	STOCK PRICE ($) FY Close	P/E High/Low		PER SHARE ($) Earnings	Dividends	Book Value
12/08	1.83	—	—	(0.98)	0.00	6.82
12/07	13.13	—	—	(10.31)	0.10	7.65
12/06	18.89	55	35	0.45	0.10	18.47
12/05	21.19	28	22	0.87	0.30	18.06
12/04	22.54	—	—	(0.71)	0.50	4.70
Annual Growth	**(46.6%)**			**—**	**—**	**9.7%**

SPX Corporation

SPX likes to mix things up. The company's segments include industrial products (compactors, power systems, broadcast antenna systems, and aerospace components), flow technology (pumps, valves, and other fluid handling devices), service systems (automotive diagnostic gear), and cooling technologies (cooling towers and services). Its portfolio also includes large power transformers and test instrumentation. SPX makes electrical fittings and industrial lighting products through a joint venture with Emerson Electric called EGS Electrical Group, of which it owns 44.5%. SPX gets more than half of its sales in the US.

Challenges for 2009 include dealing with the worldwide economic downturn and the continuing credit crisis, which are affecting many industries and SPX customers. The company is looking to grow its sales in emerging and developing markets.

SPX typically looks to buy what it terms "bolt-on" businesses that easily mesh into existing operations. the company's also divested a number of its holdings.

In 2008 the company sold its LDS Test and Measurement business unit to Spectris for about $86 million. LDS makes vibration testing and data acquisition equipment.

HISTORY

Paul Beardsley and Charles Johnson founded SPX in 1911 as The Piston Ring Company. The company, which had its start making piston rings for major automakers, expanded through a series of acquisitions. In 1931 it changed its name to Sealed Power to reflect the increasing diversity of its products. Expansion continued after WWII, and the company went public in 1955. By 1959 Sealed Power made half of its sales from replacement parts.

Following further diversification and international growth in the 1960s and 1970s, the company moved its stock listing to the New York Stock Exchange in 1972 and changed its name to SPX Corporation in 1988.

SPX ran into trouble in the early 1990s when a US recession resulted in losses. The company restructured, however, and by the time the auto industry rebounded in 1994, it was focused on specialty service tools and components.

Flat sales and losses in 1995-96 prompted the ouster of Dale Johnson (CEO from 1991 to 1995). He was replaced by GE veteran John Blystone, who set about streamlining the business, selling inefficient units and beefing up profitable lines. In 1997 SPX sold the Sealed Power division (its original business) for $223 million and acquired A. R. Brasch Marketing (owner's manuals and technical service and training materials).

SPX made a bold hostile takeover bid for much-larger auto parts maker Echlin in 1998, prompting rival Dana to step in and buy Echlin. Also that year the company paid $2.3 billion for General Signal, a company nearly twice its size that provided SPX the opportunity to lower its exposure to the auto parts industry and to expand its offerings. SPX later announced it would cut 1,000 jobs and close about two dozen factories and warehouses it had picked up in the deal. Other buys that year included Tecnotest, Toledo Trans-Kit, and Valley Forge Group.

In 2000 SPX acquired Fenner Fluid Power, a division of Fenner plc; SPX's Inrange Technologies subsidiary picked up Varcom Corporation (network management hardware, software, and services) and Computerm Corporation (channel extension products); and the DeZurik unit acquired Copes-Vulcan's US and UK assets (control valves and turbine bypass systems).

In 2001 SPX acquired United Dominion Industries Limited (flow technology, machinery, specialty engineered products, and test instrumentation) in a deal valued at $1.83 billion, including the assumption of $876 million in United Dominion debt. In August of that year, SPX announced plans to close 49 facilities and cut 2,000 jobs (about 7% of its workforce) by 2003. SPX acquired Daniel Valve Company from Emerson Electric in early 2002.

Following the security trend, SPX acquired the US-based IDenticard Systems in early 2003. SPX sold Inrange Technologies to Computer Network Technology (CNT) in 2003 for $190 million. The following year SPX acquired the Kline Towers division (broadcast tower design, engineering, and construction) of Kline Iron & Steel.

In 2004 SPX acquired Bill-Jay Machine Tool (rotor head components for helicopters) to augment its Fenn Technologies aerospace components business. It also acquired the assets of Actron Manufacturing, a maker of automotive test equipment and instruments under the Actron, KAL-EQUIP, and Faze brand names, among others. Late in 2004 SPX announced its Service Solutions business had acquired automotive diagnostic test equipment maker AutoXray.

Also in late 2004 chairman and CEO Blystone abruptly resigned. The company separated the board and officer positions, naming director Charles Johnson as chairman, and VP Christopher Kearney as president and CEO.

In late 2006 the company acquired AB Custos, a Swedish manufacturer of pumps for industrial and marine markets, and aerator filters and regulators for the HVAC heating and plumbing market. It paid about $184 million.

Johnson retired from the board at the annual meeting in 2007. The board designated Kearney to succeed him as chairman, reuniting the top board and management posts. The board named J. Kermit Campbell, an SPX director since 1993, as lead director for a two-year term. Campbell was CEO of Herman Miller.

In 2007 the company made two European acquisitions to expand its service solutions segment: It purchased the regional diagnostics division of Johnson Controls and it acquired Matra-Werke, the German vehicle-repair division of KION Group.

In late 2007 SPX acquired the APV division of Invensys for nearly $516 million (about £250 million) in cash. APV made pumps, valves, heat exchangers, and homogenizers for the beverage, dairy, food, and pharmaceutical industries. APV became part of SPX's Flow Technology segment.

In 2007 the company sold its Contech automotive components business to Marathon Automotive Group for about $146 million in cash. SPX saw the business as no longer strategic to its long-term interests. Marathon Automotive Group was an entity formed by a private equity firm, Marathon Asset Management. SPX used most of the proceeds from the sale to buy back its own stock.

Also in 2007 SPX put its Air Filtration business unit on the auction block. It sold the business to The Riverside Company in 2008.

EXECUTIVES

Chairman, President, and CEO:
Christopher J. (Chris) Kearney, age 54, $16,279,979 total compensation
EVP, CFO, and Treasurer: Patrick J. O'Leary, age 51, $6,161,950 total compensation
VP, Corporate Controller, and Chief Accounting Officer: Michael A. Reilly
EVP Global Business Systems and Services; President, Asia/Pacific: Robert B. Foreman, age 52, $6,865,416 total compensation
SVP, Secretary, and General Counsel: Kevin L. Lilly, age 56, $2,980,636 total compensation
VP and Chief Marketing Officer: Sharon K. Jenkins
VP Finance: Jeremy W. Smeltser, age 34
VP Business Development: J. Michael Whitted, age 37

President, Industrial Products and Services:
Lee Powell, age 51
President, Test and Measurement Segment:
David A. (Dave) Kowalski, age 51
President, Flow Technology Segment: Don L. Canterna, age 58, $3,252,282 total compensation
President, Thermal Equipment and Services Segment:
Drew T. Ladau, age 49
Director, Corporate Communications: Tina Betlejewski
Auditors: Deloitte & Touche LLP

LOCATIONS

HQ: SPX Corporation
13515 Ballantyne Corporate Place
Charlotte, NC 28277
Phone: 704-752-4400   **Fax:** 704-752-4505
Web: www.spx.com

SPX has operations in more than 40 countries in Asia, Europe, and the Americas, with sales in more than 150 countries around the world.

2008 Sales

	$ mil.	% of total
US	3,055.5	52
Germany	864.9	15
China	301.2	5
UK	278.0	5
Other countries	1,356.1	23
Total	**5,855.7**	**100**

PRODUCTS/OPERATIONS

2008 Sales

	$ mil.	% of total
Flow technology	1,998.7	34
Thermal equipment & services	1,690.1	29
Test & measurement	1,100.3	19
Industrial products & services	1,066.6	18
Total	**5,855.7**	**100**

COMPETITORS

ABB
Alfa Laval
AMETEK
Andrew Corporation
Baltimore Aircoil
BBT Thermotechnik
BorgWarner
Converteam
Cubic Transportation Systems
Dana Holding
Danaher
Dresser, Inc.
Eaton
Emerson Electric
Endress + Hauser
Evapco
Federal-Mogul
Franklin Electric
GE Infrastructure
GEA Group
Glen Dimplex
Harris Corp.
Harsco
Hickok
Honeywell International
Ingersoll-Rand
Interpump
ITT Corp.
Johnson Controls
Leybold
Parker Hannifin
Robbins & Myers
Robert Bosch LLC
Roper Industries
SANYO
Snap-on
Telvent
Trippe Manufacturing
United Technologies

HISTORICAL FINANCIALS

Company Type: Public

Income Statement

FYE: December 31

	REVENUE ($ mil.)	NET INCOME ($ mil.)	NET PROFIT MARGIN	EMPLOYEES
12/08	5,855.7	247.9	4.2%	17,800
12/07	4,822.3	294.2	6.1%	17,800
12/06	4,313.3	170.7	4.0%	14,300
12/05	4,292.2	1,090.0	25.4%	18,300
12/04	4,372.0	(17.1)	—	23,800
Annual Growth	7.6%	—	—	(7.0%)

2008 Year-End Financials

Debt ratio: 57.5%
Return on equity: 12.3%
Cash ($ mil.): 476
Current ratio: 1.39
Long-term debt ($ mil.): 1,155

No. of shares (mil.): 49
Dividends
 Yield: 2.5%
 Payout: 21.8%
Market value ($ mil.): 1,990

Stock History

NYSE: SPW

	STOCK PRICE ($) FY Close	P/E High/Low	PER SHARE ($) Earnings	Dividends	Book Value
12/08	40.55	31 6	4.59	1.00	40.97
12/07	102.85	21 12	5.22	1.00	40.87
12/06	61.16	22 16	2.83	1.00	42.98
12/05	45.77	3 2	15.33	1.00	43.01
12/04	40.06	— —	(0.23)	1.00	43.35
Annual Growth	0.3%	— —	—	0.0%	(1.4%)

Staples, Inc.

Staples is clipping along as the #1 office supply superstore operator in the US. It sells office products, furniture, computers, and other supplies through its chain of 2,200-plus Staples and Staples Express stores in the US, Canada, the UK, and a dozen other countries. (More than 1,800 of its superstores are located in North America.) In addition to its retail outlets, Staples sells office products via the Internet and through its catalog and direct sales operations, including subsidiary Quill Corporation. Staples also provides document management and copying services through its retail chain, as well as promotional products. It targets customers worldwide through its newly acquired Corporate Express business.

In a move that enlarged its footprint in Europe significantly, Staples acquired Netherlands-based business supply wholesaler Corporate Express NV in July 2008 in a deal valued at about $2.7 billion. Corporate Express is a major office products wholesaler, with more than half of its sales in the US through Corporate Express US. The Dutch office supplies distributor finally accepted Staples sweetened buyout offer — first proffered in early 2008 — after Staples raised its bid three times.

International expansion is a priority for the office products retailer as sales in North America slow as a result of the deep recession here. To that end, Staples is focused on further expanding its operations in Europe, where it already has about 335 retail locations, and entering emerging markets, such as India, China, and Brazil. In early 2007 the American office supply chain formed a 50:50 joint venture with India's largest retailer Pantaloon to bring office supply warehouse stores to India. In China, where the company has about 25 stores, Staples has partnered with United Parcel Service to launch co-branded stores there.

Staples' North American retail operation had been expanding at a rapid pace but now is slowing. About 90 new stores opened in 2008, compared to 120 in 2007. Some of those stores were smaller in size than Staples' traditional warehouse locations and designed to target urban and other niche markets. The company is also expanding the number of Staples-branded products sold in its stores.

A large part of the company's growth, though, has come from its catalog and direct sales business, which now accounts for almost a third of its revenue. It plans to continue its investments in infrastructure upgrades to help its delivery business become more efficient.

HISTORY

A veteran of the supermarket industry (and the man who developed the idea for generic food), Thomas Stemberg was fired from his executive position with Connecticut supermarket Edwards-Finast in 1985. Stemberg began searching for a niche retail market — he found one in office supplies, which he estimated at $100 billion.

While large companies could buy in bulk from dealers, smaller businesses were served by mom-and-pop office supply stores that charged much higher prices. Applying the supermarket model to office supply, Stemberg founded Staples in late 1985 with Leo Kahn, a former competitor in the supermarket business. With money from Kahn and venture capital firms, Staples opened its first store in a Boston suburb the next year.

In 1987 the retailer moved into the New York City area and continued to expand throughout the Northeast. By early 1989 — the year it went public — it had 23 stores. The company introduced a line of low-priced private-label products in 1989.

Aggressive expansion began the following year when Staples opened three stores in Southern California and introduced two new concepts: Staples Direct (delivery operations for midsized businesses) and Staples Express (downtown stores offering smaller merchandise selections). International growth included buying a stake in Canada's Business Depot (1991) and 48% of MAXI-Papier, a European office supply store chain (1992). It also paired up with Kingfisher to establish stores in the UK (Kingfisher sold its interest to Staples in 1996).

Additional acquisitions gave Staples more than 200 stores by the end of 1993. The next year Staples entered Arizona, Virginia, and Kentucky (by acquiring selected Office America stores); acquired the rest of Canada's Business Depot; and began expanding into the contract stationer business. It started Staples Business Advantage, a regional stationer, in 1995. The company agreed to buy Office Depot, its biggest rival, in 1996, but the FTC rejected the $4.3 billion deal on antitrust grounds.

Staples continued opening new stores and adding operations. Acquisitions included the privately held Quill (to expand its direct-sales business, 1998) and Claricom Holdings (telecommunications services to small businesses, renamed Staples Communications, 1999; sold, 2001). In addition, the company continued its international expansion that year, introducing its Quill catalog business in the UK and buying three European office supply companies (which added about 40 stores, extending the company's presence in Germany and moving it into the Netherlands and Portugal).

During 2002 Staples acquired Medical Arts Press (specialized medical software and forms to medical providers) and the mail-order business of Guilbert, a subsidiary of French retailer PPR (formerly Pinault-Printemps-Redoute); the $815 million Guilbert deal provided entrée for Staples in France, Italy, Spain, and Belgium. Company veteran Ron Sargent took over as CEO that same year.

The company continued to expand its international operations through acquisitions in 2004, buying Globus Office World (UK), Pressel Versand International (Austria), and Malling Beck (Denmark). CEO Sargent took on the added title of chairman when Stemberg resigned in 2005.

A 2006 joint venture with UB Office Systems brought the company into the Taiwan market.

In 2007 Staples entered China and India through partnerships in both countries. In late 2007 the company reached a settlement in a California class-action lawsuit brought by store managers seeking overtime pay dating back to 1995. Staples has agreed to pay $38 million, subject to court approval. Again, in early 2009, the firm was ordered to pay almost $2.5 million to 343 plaintiffs in a case brought under the Fair Labor Standards Act. A federal court jury ruled that Staples violated the law by classifying employees as exempt and failing to pay them overtime.

EXECUTIVES

Chairman and CEO: Ronald L. (Ron) Sargent, age 53,
 $8,377,420 total compensation
Vice Chairman and CFO: John J. Mahoney, age 57,
 $4,363,376 total compensation
Named President and COO; President, Staples International: Michael A. (Mike) Miles Jr., age 47,
 $2,967,014 total compensation
EVP and CIO: Brian T. Light, age 45
EVP Human Resources: Shira D. Goodman, age 48
SVP and Controller: Christine T. Komola, age 41
SVP Business Services: John F. Burke
SVP, General Counsel, and Secretary:
 Kristin A. Campbell, age 47
SVP Strategy: Amee Chande
SVP Supply Chain and Logistics: Don Ralph
President, Staples North American Delivery:
 Joseph G. (Joe) Doody, age 56,
 $3,403,470 total compensation
President, US Retail: Demos Parneros, age 46,
 $1,830,384 total compensation
President, Staples Europe: Rob Vale
President, Staples Business Depot — Canada:
 Steven E. Matyas
SVP Finance, North American Delivery:
 Steven (Steve) Bussberg
SVP Finance, US Stores: Luis Borgen
Auditors: Ernst & Young LLP

LOCATIONS

HQ: Staples, Inc.
 500 Staples Dr., Framingham, MA 01702
Phone: 508-253-5000 **Fax:** 508-253-8989
Web: www.staples.com

2009 Sales

	$ mil.	% of total
US	15,787.3	68
Canada	2,632.1	12
Other countries	4,664.4	20
Total	**23,083.8**	**100**

2009 Locations

	No.
US	
California	209
New York	136
Pennsylvania	93
New Jersey	88
Massachusetts	78
Florida	91
Ohio	60
Illinois	54
North Carolina	52
Maryland	45
Michigan	43
Connecticut	39
Virginia	42
Texas	50
Georgia	40
Arizona	40
Indiana	32
Washington	30
New Hampshire	23
Tennessee	22
Oregon	20
Colorado	21
South Carolina	18
Oklahoma	17
Iowa	14
Alabama	12
Maine	13
Kentucky	17
Rhode Island	10
Utah	13
Wisconsin	11
Missouri	11
New Mexico	10
Other states	69
Other countries	695
Total	**2,218**

PRODUCTS/OPERATIONS

2009 Sales

	% of total
Office supplies & services	47
Business machines & related products	28
Computers & related products	18
Office furniture	7
Total	**100**

2009 Sales

	$ mil.	% of total
North American retail	9,489.5	41
North American delivery	8,929.9	39
International	4,664.4	20
Total	**23,083.8**	**100**

COMPETITORS

Best Buy	Norwood Promotional
BJ's Wholesale Club	Products
CDW	Office Depot
Corvest	OfficeMax
Costco Wholesale	RadioShack
Dell	Shumsky Enterprises
FedEx Office	Signature Marketing
Fry's Electronics	S.P. Richards
HALO Holding	Systemax
Hewlett-Packard	Unisource
IKON	United Stationers
Insight Enterprises	Wal-Mart
Mail Boxes Etc.	

HISTORICAL FINANCIALS

Company Type: Public

Income Statement

FYE: Saturday nearest January 31

	REVENUE ($ mil.)	NET INCOME ($ mil.)	NET PROFIT MARGIN	EMPLOYEES
1/09	23,083.8	805.3	3.5%	91,125
1/08	19,372.7	995.7	5.1%	75,588
1/07	18,160.8	973.7	5.4%	73,646
1/06	16,078.9	834.4	5.2%	68,533
1/05	14,448.4	708.4	4.9%	65,078
Annual Growth	**12.4%**	**3.3%**	**—**	**8.8%**

2009 Year-End Financials

Debt ratio: 35.4%
Return on equity: 14.3%
Cash ($ mil.): 634
Current ratio: 1.20
Long-term debt ($ mil.): 1,969

No. of shares (mil.): 722
Dividends
  Yield: 2.1%
  Payout: 29.2%
Market value ($ mil.): 11,514

Stock History

NASDAQ (GS): SPLS

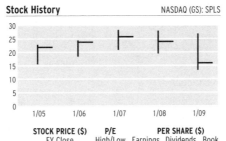

	STOCK PRICE ($) FY Close	P/E High/Low		PER SHARE ($) Earnings	Dividends	Book Value
1/09	15.94	24	12	1.13	0.33	7.70
1/08	23.94	20	14	1.38	0.29	7.92
1/07	25.72	21	16	1.32	0.22	6.95
1/06	23.71	22	17	1.12	0.17	6.13
1/05	21.83	24	17	0.93	0.13	5.70
Annual Growth	**(7.6%)**	**—**	**—**	**5.0%**	**26.2%**	**7.8%**

Starbucks Corporation

Wake up and smell the coffee — Starbucks is everywhere. The world's #1 specialty coffee retailer, Starbucks has more than 16,000 coffee shops in more than 35 countries. The outlets offer coffee drinks and food items, as well as roasted beans, coffee accessories, and teas. Starbucks owns more than 9,000 of its shops, which are located in about 10 countries (mostly in the US), while licensees and franchisees operate more than 7,400 units worldwide (primarily in shopping centers and airports). The company also owns the Seattle's Best Coffee and Torrefazione Italia coffee brands. In addition, Starbucks markets its coffee through grocery stores and licenses its brand for other food and beverage products.

What was once a simple chain of coffeehouses has become a force of nature in the retail business. With so many outlets throughout the world, Starbucks has used its chain to branch out into other retail segments, including CDs, books, and similar lifestyle products. Through partnerships with food manufacturers, it also licenses the Starbucks brand for such products as ice cream (made by Nestlé's Dreyer's Grand Ice Cream subsidiary), coffee flavored liqueur (Beam Global Spirits), and bottled Frappuccino (PepsiCo).

Sales at its US locations, however, have been slowing in part due to consumer concerns over the economy, as well as competitors such as Dunkin' Donuts and McDonald's cutting in on the gourmet coffee market. Chairman Howard Schultz, who owns nearly 5% of the company, returned as CEO in 2008 (replacing Jim Donald) and implemented a restructuring plan to turn the business around. Among other initiatives, Schultz has shuttered hundreds of underperforming US locations and reduced headcount to cut costs. The company has also cut back on plans for new locations, putting an emphasis on growth of licensed units in international markets.

At its coffeehouses, the company has been rolling out an expanded menu of breakfast items and other hot foods, as well as a new menu of cold drink options. Other enhancements include expanded free wi-fi service through a partnership with AT&T and a customer-loyalty card program. Starbucks also continues to expand the number of locations offering drive-thru service.

HISTORY

Starbucks was founded in 1971 in Seattle by coffee aficionados Gordon Bowker, Jerry Baldwin, and Ziv Siegl, who named the company for the coffee-loving first mate in *Moby Dick* and created its famous two-tailed siren logo. They aimed to sell the finest-quality whole bean and ground coffees. By 1982 Starbucks had five retail stores and was selling coffee to restaurants and espresso stands in Seattle. That year Howard Schultz joined Starbucks to manage retail sales and marketing. In 1983 Schultz traveled to Italy and was struck by the popularity of coffee bars. He convinced Starbucks' owners to open a downtown Seattle coffee bar in 1984. It was a success; Schultz left the company the following year to open his own coffee bar, Il Giornale, which served Starbucks coffee.

Frustrated by its inability to control quality, Starbucks sold off its wholesale business in 1987. Later that year Il Giornale acquired its retail operations for $4 million. (Starbucks' founders held on to their other coffee business, Peet's Coffee & Tea.) Il Giornale changed its name to Starbucks Corporation, prepared to expand nationally, and opened locations in Chicago and Vancouver. In 1988 the company published its first mail-order catalog.

Starbucks lost money in the late 1980s as it focused on expansion (it tripled its number of stores to 55 between 1987 and 1989). Schultz brought in experienced managers to run Starbucks' stores. In 1991 it became the nation's first privately owned company to offer stock options to all employees.

In 1992 Starbucks went public and set up shops in Nordstrom's department stores. The following year it began operating cafes in Barnes & Noble bookstores. The company had nearly 275 locations by the end of 1993. Starbucks inked a deal in 1994 to provide coffee to ITT/Sheraton hotels (later acquired by Starwood Hotels & Resorts). The next year it capitalized on its popular in-house music selections by selling compact discs. Also in 1995 Starbucks joined with PepsiCo to develop a bottled coffee drink and agreed to produce a line of premium coffee ice cream with Dreyer's.

Starbucks expanded into Japan and Singapore in 1996. Also that year the company created Caffe Starbucks, an online store located on AOL's marketplace. In 1998 Starbucks expanded into the

UK when it acquired that country's Seattle Coffee Company chain (founded in 1995) for about $86 million and converted its stores into Starbucks locations. It also announced plans to sell coffee in supermarkets nationwide through an agreement with Kraft Foods. In 1999 Starbucks bought Tazo, an Oregon-based tea company, as well as music retailer Hear Music, and opened its first store in China.

In 2000 Schultz ceded the CEO post to president Orin Smith, remaining chairman but focusing primarily on the company's global strategy. Starbucks jumpstarted its worldwide expansion the next year, opening about 1,100 stores worldwide, including locations in a handful of new European countries such as Austria and Switzerland. It also spun off its Japanese operations as a public company. In 2002 it announced large-scale expansion plans in Mexico and Latin America.

The next year Starbucks acquired Seattle Coffee Company from AFC Enterprises. The deal gave Starbucks an additional 150 coffee shops (as if it needed them), but more importantly it gave the coffee giant the Seattle's Best Coffee brand and wholesale coffee business. It also got something new out of the deal: franchised locations.

Starbucks was one of the first national retailers to jump on the Wi-Fi bandwagon, teaming with Hewlett-Packard and Deutsche Telekom's T-Mobile unit to offer high-speed wireless Internet access at 1,200 of its locations in the US, London, and Berlin.

In 2005 in conjunction with Jim Beam Brands (now Beam Global Spirits & Wine) it introduced Starbucks Coffee Liqueur and Starbucks Cream Liqueur. That year Starbucks signed agreements with Suntory in Japan and Uni-President in Taiwan to sell its ready-to-drink coffees in those countries. Additionally, Smith retired as president and CEO in 2005; he was replaced by Starbucks' North American president Jim Donald.

While Starbucks continued to dominate the coffee business, traffic at its stores began to decline in 2007. The company brought Schultz back as CEO in 2008, replacing Donald.

EXECUTIVES

Chairman, President, and CEO: Howard D. Schultz, age 55
EVP and CFO: Troy Alstead, age 45
SVP and CIO: Stephen Gillett
SVP, Deputy General Counsel, and Chief Compliance Officer: David Landau
EVP Law and Corporate Affairs, General Counsel, and Secretary: Paula E. Boggs, age 49
Interim EVP Partner Resources and Director: Olden Lee, age 67
EVP Global Strategy, Office of the CEO: Dorothy J. Kim, age 46
EVP Global Supply Chain Operations: Peter D. Gibbons, age 47
EVP Marketing and Category: Michelle Gass, age 41
EVP; President, Global Consumer Products, Foodservice, and Seattle's Best Coffee: John Culver
SVP Marketing: Terry Davenport, age 52
SVP Culture and Leadership Development: Dave Olsen
SVP Coffee and Global Procurement: Willard (Dub) Hay
SVP; President, Starbucks Coffee EMEA: Buck Hendrix
SVP; President, Starbucks Coffee Americas: Colin Moore
SVP Global Logistics: Juan Guerrero
SVP Public Affairs: Vivek Varma
President, Starbucks Coffee International: Martin Coles, age 53
President, Starbucks Coffee US: Clifford Burrows, age 44
President, Global Development: Arthur Rubinfeld, age 55
Auditors: Deloitte & Touche LLP

LOCATIONS

HQ: Starbucks Corporation
2401 Utah Ave. South, Seattle, WA 98134
Phone: 206-447-1575   **Fax:** 206-447-0828
Web: www.starbucks.com

2008 Company-Owned Locations

	No.
US	7,238
Canada	731
UK	664
China	178
Germany	131
Thailand	127
Singapore	57
Australia	23
Other countries	68
Total	**9,217**

PRODUCTS/OPERATIONS

2008 Sales

	$ mil.	% of total
Company-operated retail	8,771.9	85
Licensing	1,171.6	11
Foodservice & other	439.5	4
Total	**10,383.0**	**100**

2008 Locations

	No.
Company-owned	9,217
Licensed	
US	4,329
International	3,134
Total	**16,680**

COMPETITORS

Caffè Nero
Caribou Coffee
Cinnabon
The Coffee Bean
Community Coffee
Dunkin
Einstein Noah Restaurant Group
Farmer Bros.
Folger
Green Mountain Coffee
Greggs
illy
Lavazza
McDonald's
Nestlé
Panera Bread
Tim Hortons
Van Houtte
Whitbread

HISTORICAL FINANCIALS

Company Type: Public

Income Statement

FYE: Sunday nearest September 30

	REVENUE ($ mil.)	NET INCOME ($ mil.)	NET PROFIT MARGIN	EMPLOYEES
9/08	10,383.0	315.5	3.0%	176,000
9/07	9,411.5	672.6	7.1%	172,000
9/06	7,786.9	581.5	7.5%	145,800
9/05	6,369.3	494.5	7.8%	115,000
9/04	5,294.2	391.8	7.4%	96,700
Annual Growth	**18.3%**	**(5.3%)**	**—**	**16.2%**

2008 Year-End Financials

Debt ratio: 22.1%
Return on equity: 13.2%
Cash ($ mil.): 270
Current ratio: 0.80
Long-term debt ($ mil.): 550
No. of shares (mil.): 737
Dividends
  Yield: 0.0%
  Payout: —
Market value ($ mil.): 10,961

Stock History   NASDAQ (GS): SBUX

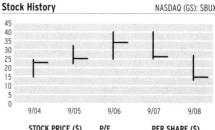

	STOCK PRICE ($) FY Close	P/E High/Low		PER SHARE ($) Earnings	Dividends	Book Value
9/08	14.87	62	31	0.43	0.00	3.38
9/07	26.20	46	29	0.87	0.00	3.10
9/06	34.05	56	35	0.71	0.00	3.02
9/05	25.05	53	37	0.61	0.00	2.84
9/04	22.73	51	31	0.47	0.00	3.37
Annual Growth	**(10.1%)**	**—**	**—**	**(2.2%)**	**—**	**0.0%**

Starwood Hotels & Resorts

Starwood Hotels & Resorts Worldwide knows how to shine a light on hospitality. The company is one of the world's largest hotel and leisure companies, with about 950 properties in some 100 countries. Its hotel empire consists of luxury and upscale brands such as Four Points, Sheraton, and Westin. Starwood operates 70 high-end resorts and hotels through its St. Regis and Luxury Collection, while its chain of about 20 W Hotels offers ultra-modern style for sophisticated business travelers. Other brands include Le Méridien, Aloft, and Element. In addition, the company's Starwood Vacation Ownership subsidiary operates nearly 30 time-share resorts.

Notable Starwood hotels include the St. Regis in New York, New York; The Phoenician in Scottsdale, Arizona; the Hotel Gritti Palace in Venice, Italy; and the St. Regis in Beijing, China. Starwood expanded its portfolio in 2008 with the introduction of new brands Aloft (select-service hotels) and Element (extended stay hotels).

Some 440 of Starwood's hotels are owned and operated by franchisees; the company owns or leases about 70 locations, and manages another 440 hotels on behalf of third parties. The company's strategy involves a continued reduction of its investment in owned real estate and an increased focus on the management and franchise business.

Steven Heyer, who took over as CEO from founder Barry Sternlicht in 2004, left the company in 2007. Chairman Bruce Duncan served as interim chief until Frits van Paasschen, formerly an executive at Molson Coors Brewing Company, was brought in as his replacement.

HISTORY

Barry Sternlicht earned his MBA from Harvard in 1986 and joined the fast track at JMB Realty, bringing the company a UK real estate deal involving Randsworth Trust in 1989. He left two years later to start Starwood Capital Group, with backers including the wealthy Burden and Ziff families. (JMB and its pension fund partners, meanwhile, lost their shirts when Randsworth went belly-up during the recession of the early 1990s.) In 1995 Starwood Capital joined Goldman Sachs and Nomura Securities to buy Westin Hotel (renamed Westin Hotels & Resorts) from Japanese construction firm Aoki. Founded in Washington State in 1930, Westin was acquired by UAL in 1970, then Aoki bought it in 1988 during a boom in Japanese investments in US real estate.

Also in 1995 Sternlicht bought Hotel Investors Trust (a hotel REIT) and Hotel Investors Corp. (hotel management), two struggling firms whose chief attraction was their rare paired-share status, allowing management company profits to flow through the REIT to investors exempt from corporate income tax. (The structure was banned in 1984, but four such entities were grandfathered in under the law.) The companies were renamed Starwood Lodging Trust and Starwood Lodging Corp. (together, Starwood Lodging). Through more acquisitions, Starwood had amassed a collection of about 110 hotels by 1997.

Starwood's industry standing took a quantum leap in early 1998 when it acquired the 50% of the Westin hotel chain that Starwood Capital didn't already own and bought lodging giant ITT, the former telephone industry conglomerate and owner of the Sheraton hotel chain. ITT — with more than 400 hotels and gaming properties (Desert Inn, Caesars) — fought off a hostile takeover bid from Hilton Hotels and accepted Starwood Lodging's $14.6 billion offer. (Starwood Capital made $22 million in advising fees on the deal.) Later that year the firm changed its name to Starwood Hotels & Resorts, bought four former Ritz-Carlton hotels, and sold eight all-suite hotels to FelCor Suite Hotels (now FelCor Lodging Trust). Sternlicht then chose Walt Disney executive and Harvard classmate Richard Nanula to take the reins of Starwood's operating company. In late 1998 it launched W Hotels.

Before Congress closed the paired-share loophole for new acquisitions, Starwood Hotels went on a shopping spree, becoming a standard corporation in 1999. Nanula resigned that year, apparently after repeated clashes with Sternlicht. The company bought time-share resort company Vistana — renamed Starwood Vacation Ownership (SVO) — and purchased the portion of European hotel operator Ciga (part of which Sheraton had acquired in 1994) that it didn't already own.

Gaming profits had begun to fall off in 1999, however, as the Asian economic crisis stymied the flow of gambling-hungry tourists. The following year Starwood sold its Caesars unit to Park Place Entertainment (later Caesars Entertainment, now owned by Harrah's) for $3 billion and its Desert Inn hotel and casino to Mirage Resorts founder Steve Wynn for about $270 million. Tight economic conditions forced Starwood to cut costs and curtail discretionary spending. That year SVO began building new resorts in Arizona, Colorado, and Hawaii. Starwood saw its business begin to suffer following the September 11, 2001, terrorist attacks, which kept many potential travelers at home. As a result, Starwood cut about 12,000 jobs, roughly 25% of its workforce.

To pay down its debt, Starwood raised about $1.5 billion in capital by selling bonds (2002),

and sold its Italian Ciga assets — including luxury hotels, a golf club, and other real estate interests — to Colony Capital (2003).

In 2004 Steven Heyer, former president and COO of Coca-Cola, was named CEO as Sternlicht began setting the stage for his retirement from the company. He stayed on for nearly another year as executive chairman, however, before leaving the company altogether.

The company's expansion efforts in 2005 included the acquisition of the Le Meridien brand for $225 million. (In a separate agreement, Lehman Brothers and Starwood Capital Group, an unaffiliated private equity fund managed by former Starwood CEO Barry Sternlicht, jointly acquired the real estate properties.) In 2006 Starwood sold some 30 properties to Host Hotels & Resorts for about $4 billion. New hotels added in 2006 included The Westin Chicago North Shore (Wheeling, Illinois), The U.S. Grant (San Diego, California), and The Westin St. Maarten, Dawn Beach Resort & Spa (St. Maarten, Netherland Antilles).

Heyer resigned from the company in 2007; chairman Bruce Duncan was tapped to serve as interim CEO. Later that year Frits van Paasschen was named CEO.

EXECUTIVES

Chairman: Bruce W. Duncan, age 57
CEO and Director: Frits D. van Paasschen, age 48, $5,722,876 total compensation
EVP and CFO: Vasant M. Prabhu, age 49, $3,492,163 total compensation
CIO: Todd Thompson
Chief Administrative Officer, Secretary, and General Counsel: Kenneth S. (Ken) Siegel, age 53, $3,488,695 total compensation
EVP and Chief Brand Officer: Phil P. McAveety, age 42, $1,690,598 total compensation
EVP and Chief Human Resources Officer: Jeffrey M. (Jeff) Cava, age 57
SVP and Corporate Controller: Alan M. Schnaid
SVP Human Resources: Michelle Crosby
SVP Global Sales: Christie Hicks
SVP Owner Relations and Franchise: Lynne Dougherty
SVP Brand Design and Innovation: Mike Tiedy, age 48
President, Latin America: Osvaldo V. Librizzi
President, Starwood Vacation Ownership: Sergio D. Rivera, age 46
President, Europe, Africa, and Middle East Division: Roeland Vos
President, Asia/Pacific: Miguel Ko
President, Global Development: Simon M. Turner, age 47, $1,656,623 total compensation
SVP, Westin Hotels & Resorts: Sue A. Brush
President, Hotel Group: Matthew E. (Matt) Avril, age 48, $3,067,154 total compensation
President, North America Division: Denise M. Coll
Auditors: Ernst & Young LLP

LOCATIONS

HQ: Starwood Hotels & Resorts Worldwide, Inc.
1111 Westchester Ave., White Plains, NY 10604
Phone: 914-640-8100　　**Fax:** 914-640-8310
Web: www.starwoodhotels.com

2008 Sales

	$ mil.	% of total
US	4,211	71
Italy	370	6
Other countries	1,326	23
Total	**5,907**	**100**

PRODUCTS/OPERATIONS

2008 Sales

	$ mil.	% of total
Owned, leased & consolidated joint venture hotels	2,259	38
Management fees, franchise fees & other income	857	14
Vacation ownership & residential	749	13
Other revenues from managed & franchise properties	2,042	35
Total	**5,907**	**100**

2008 Sales

	$ mil.	% of total
Hotel	5,013	85
Vacation ownership & residential	894	15
Total	**5,907**	**100**

Selected Brands

Aloft
Element
Four Points by Sheraton
Luxury Collection
Le Méridien
Sheraton
Westin

COMPETITORS

Accor	InterContinental Hotels
Bluegreen	Loews Hotels
Carlson Hotels	LXR Luxury Resorts
Diamond Resorts	Marriott
Fairmont Raffles	Millennium & Copthorne
Four Seasons Hotels	Omni Hotels
Hilton Hotels	Silverleaf Resorts
Hyatt	Wyndham Worldwide

HISTORICAL FINANCIALS

Company Type: Public

Income Statement

FYE: December 31

	REVENUE ($ mil.)	NET INCOME ($ mil.)	NET PROFIT MARGIN	EMPLOYEES
12/08	5,907.0	329.0	5.6%	145,000
12/07	6,153.0	542.0	8.8%	155,000
12/06	5,979.0	1,113.0	18.6%	145,000
12/05	5,977.0	422.0	7.1%	145,000
12/04	5,368.0	395.0	7.4%	120,000
Annual Growth	**2.4%**	**(4.5%)**	**—**	**4.8%**

2008 Year-End Financials

Debt ratio: 216.0%　　No. of shares (mil.): 187
Return on equity: 17.8%　Dividends
Cash ($ mil.): 389　　　Yield: 5.0%
Current ratio: 0.81　　　Payout: 50.8%
Long-term debt ($ mil.): 3,502　Market value ($ mil.): 3,344

Stock History

NYSE: HOT

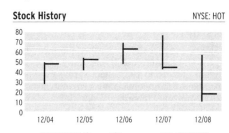

	STOCK PRICE ($) FY Close	P/E High/Low		PER SHARE ($) Earnings	Dividends	Book Value
12/08	17.90	32	6	1.77	0.90	8.68
12/07	44.03	29	17	2.57	0.90	11.11
12/06	62.50	14	10	4.69	0.84	16.10
12/05	52.07	28	22	1.88	0.84	27.89
12/04	47.62	26	15	1.84	0.84	25.63
Annual Growth	**(21.7%)**	**—**	**—**	**(1.0%)**	**1.7%**	**(23.7%)**

State Farm Mutual Automobile Insurance

Like an enormous corporation, State Farm is everywhere. The leading US personal lines property/casualty company (by premiums), State Farm Mutual Automobile Insurance Company is the #1 provider of auto insurance. It also is the leading home insurer and offers nonmedical health and life insurance through its subsidiary companies. Its products are marketed via some 17,000 agents in the US and Canada. Competition has increased with the fall of barriers between the banking, securities, and insurance industries. State Farm's efforts to diversify include a federal savings bank charter (State Farm Bank) that offers consumer and business loans through its agents and by phone, mail, and the Internet.

The company also established itself as a financial services provider in 1999, and its mutual funds have since built up $4.6 billion in assets. However, insurance is still its main source of income. And, while State Farm already insures 15% of the automobiles on US roads, it is scrambling to hang on to that much while attempting to grab an even larger portion of the pie.

Meanwhile, homeowners insurance has been a thornier issue. State Farm still insures more than 20% of the single-family homes in the US, but the insurer stopped writing new homeowners policies in some 15 states in an effort to improve profitability. Citing that it spends $1.20 for every dollar it earns in Florida, in 2008 it filed for permission to raise its homeowners rates. When Florida insurance regulators denied the request in 2009, State Farm announced that it would discontinue writing new homeowners and other property policies in the state.

Hurricanes Katrina, Wilma, and Rita brought State Farm customer claims totaling $6.3 billion in property and casualty losses. For residents along the Gulf Coast, at first it seemed like State Farm would stay put. However, as the claims keep rolling in, the company has rewritten its underwriting guidelines to limit its risk. New homeowner policies in places such as New Orleans now have steeper deductibles and less coverage, and the company has completely stopped offering new homeowners and commercial property policies in the state of Mississippi.

Since its founding, the group's companies have been run by only two families, the Mecherles (1922-54) and the Rusts (1954-present).

HISTORY

Retired farmer George Mecherle formed State Farm Mutual Automobile Insurance in Bloomington, Illinois, in 1922. State Farm served only members of farm bureaus and farm mutual insurance companies, charging a one-time membership fee and a premium to protect an automobile against loss or damage.

Unlike most competitors, State Farm offered six-month premium payments. The insurer billed and collected renewal premiums from its home office, relieving the agent of the task. In addition, State Farm determined auto rates by a simple seven-class system, while competitors varied rates for each model.

State Farm in 1926 started City and Village Mutual Automobile Insurance to insure nonfarmers' autos; it became part of the company in 1927. Between 1927 and 1931 it introduced borrowed-car protection, wind coverage, and insurance for vehicles used to transport schoolchildren.

State Farm expanded to California in 1928 and formed State Farm Life Insurance the next year. In 1935 it established State Farm Fire Insurance. George Mecherle became chairman in 1937, and his son Ramond became president. In 1939 George challenged agents to write "A Million or More (auto policies) by '44." State Farm saw a 110% increase in policies.

During the 1940s State Farm focused on urban areas after most of the farm bureaus formed their own insurance companies. In the late 1940s and 1950s, it moved to a full-time agency force.

Homeowners coverage was added to the insurer's offerings under the leadership of Adlai Rust, who led State Farm from 1954 until 1958, when Edward Rust took over. He died in 1985 and his son, Edward Jr., currently holds the top spot.

Between 1974 and 1987 the insurer was hit by several gender-discrimination suits (a 1992 settlement awarded $157 million to 814 women). State Farm has since tried to hire more women and minorities.

Serial disasters in the early 1990s, including Hurricane Andrew and the Los Angeles riots, proved costly. The 1994 Northridge earthquake alone generated more than $2.5 billion in claims and contributed to a 72% decline in earnings.

State Farm — the top US home insurer since the mid-1960s — canceled 62,500 residential policies in South Florida in 1996 to cut potential hurricane loss an estimated 11%. In response, Florida's insurance regulators rescinded a previously approved rate hike. That year the company agreed to open more urban neighborhood offices to settle a discrimination suit brought by the Department of Housing and Urban Development, which accused State Farm of discriminating against potential customers in minority-populated areas.

Legal trouble continued. In 1997 State Farm settled with a California couple who alleged the company forged policyholders' signatures on forms declining coverage and concealed evidence to avoid paying earthquake damage claims. That year a policyholder sued to keep State Farm from "wasting company assets" on President Clinton's legal defense against Paula Jones' sexual harassment charges (Clinton held a State Farm personal liability policy).

Relations with its sales force already rocky, State Farm in 1998 proposed to reduce up-front commissions and cut base pay in favor of incentives for customer retention and cross-selling. Reduced auto premiums and increased catastrophe claims from across the US eroded State Farm's bottom line that year. A federal thrift charter obtained in 1998 let the company launch banking operations the next year.

In 2000 the company was hit with a class-action lawsuit about its denial of personal-injury claims; previous suits had been individual cases.

In 2002 State Farm Indemnity, the company's auto-only New Jersey subsidiary, withdrew from the Garden State's auto insurance market but began phasing back into the market in 2005.

Like all reinsurers, State Farm's reinsurance business was tested by the 2005 hurricane season. It underwrote losses of $2.8 billion.

EXECUTIVES

Chairman and CEO: Edward B. (Ed) Rust Jr., age 58
Vice Chairman and Chief Administrative Officer: James E. (Jim) Rutrough
Vice Chairman, CFO, and Treasurer: Michael L. Tipsord
Vice Chairman and Chief Agency and Marketing Officer: Michael C. Davidson
EVP: Barbara Cowden
EVP, General Counsel, and Secretary: Kim M. Brunner
EVP: William K. (Bill) King
EVP: Brian V. Boyden
EVP: Willie G. Brown
EVP: Deborah Traskell
SVP, State Farm Mutual; President and CEO, State Farm General: Gregory (Greg) Jones
President, State Farm Bank: Mike Smith
Auditors: PricewaterhouseCoopers LLP

LOCATIONS

HQ: State Farm Mutual Automobile Insurance Company
1 State Farm Plaza, Bloomington, IL 61710
Phone: 309-766-2311 **Fax:** 309-766-3621
Web: www.statefarm.com

PRODUCTS/OPERATIONS

Selected Subsidiaries

State Farm Bank, FSB
State Farm Fire and Casualty Company (homeowners, boat owners, and commercial insurance)
State Farm Florida Insurance Company (homeowners and renters insurance)
State Farm General Insurance Company (property insurance)
State Farm Indemnity Company (auto insurance in New Jersey)
State Farm Investment Management Corp
State Farm Life and Accident Assurance Company
State Farm Life Insurance Company
State Farm Lloyds, Inc.
State Farm VP Management Corp

COMPETITORS

Allstate	Liberty Mutual
American Family Insurance	MetLife
Berkshire Hathaway	Nationwide
CNA Financial	Philadelphia Insurance
COUNTRY Financial	Progressive Corporation
GEICO	Prudential
GMAC Insurance	Torchmark
The Hartford	USAA
	W. R. Berkley

HISTORICAL FINANCIALS

Company Type: Mutual company

Income Statement

FYE: December 31

	REVENUE ($ mil.)	NET INCOME ($ mil.)	NET PROFIT MARGIN	EMPLOYEES
12/08	61,300.0	(542.0)	—	68,600
12/07	61,600.0	5,460.0	8.9%	68,000
12/06	60,500.0	5,320.0	8.8%	68,000
12/05	59,200.0	3,240.0	5.5%	79,200
12/04	58,800.0	5,300.0	9.0%	79,200
Annual Growth	1.0%	—	—	(3.5%)

Net Income History

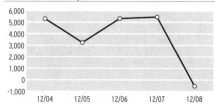

State Street Corporation

Ol' Blue Eyes sang about the State Street (that great street) in Chicago, but investors may find Boston's State Street more melodious. Through State Street Bank, the company is among the top providers of mutual fund and pension processing and custody services; institutional and corporate clients choose from services including accounting, foreign exchange, cash management, securities lending, and more. Unit State Street Global Advisors (SSgA) performs asset management services; Street Alternative Investment Solutions combines hedge funds, private equity, and alternative risk products. Boston Financial Data Services, a partnership with DST Systems, provides shareholder services to clients.

At the vanguard of financial services technology, State Street banks on its computerized analytical and organizational tools to woo and retain clients. Offerings include foreign exchange trading platform FX Connect and Global Link, which provides market research and portfolio analysis. The company boosted its foreign exchange offerings with the acquisition of Currenex in 2007.

One of the world's largest managers of institutional accounts, the company is also at the top of the custody-services heap (particularly in the US and key European markets), with assets under custody of more than $12 trillion. The company added bulk by acquiring another Boston-based fund accounting and servicing provider, Investors Financial Services, in 2007. The following year State Street sold CitiStreet, a retirement and pension plan management joint venture with Citigroup, to ING Groep.

Also in 2008 the company's asset management division took a hit due to overall declines in the equity markets; on the flipside, the bank's servicing division benefited from the volatile trading market. The US Treasury invested $2 billion in State Street as part of a broader injection of cash into the nation's financial system to restore confidence in the ailing economy. State Street was among eight other top banks that received a combined $250 billion bailout. State Street repaid the full amount by mid-2009.

HISTORY

The US's chaotic postrevolutionary era gave birth to the first ancestor of State Street Corporation. Union Bank was founded in 1792 by Boston businessmen, breaking the eight-year monopoly held on Boston banking by Massachusetts Bank (a forerunner of FleetBoston, which was acquired by Bank of America in 2004). Governor John Hancock's distinctive signature graced Union's charter; the bank set up shop at 40 State Street near the port and enjoyed the glory days of New England's shipping trade.

In the mid-19th century, Boston's financial eminence faded as New York flexed its economic muscle. In 1865 the bank was nationally chartered and changed its name to National Union Bank of Boston. It got a new neighbor in 1891: Directors of Third National Bank set up State Street Deposit & Trust to engage in the newfangled business of trusts.

In 1925 National Union Bank merged with State Street and inherited its custodial business.

The bank grew through the 1950s; acquisitions included the Second National Bank and the Rockland-Atlas National Bank.

In 1970 State Street converted to a holding company — the State Street Boston Financial Corp. (State Street Boston Corp. as of 1977). The company also went international that decade, opening an office in Munich, Germany.

Soaring inflation and the recession of the 1970s forced the company to radically rethink its mission. The 1974 passage of the Employee Retirement Income Security Act changed the laws governing the management of pension funds and created an opportunity. State Street was one of the first banks to move aggressively into high-tech information processing, and affiliate Boston Financial Data Services began servicing pension assets in 1974.

Encouraged by that success, in 1975 new CEO William Edgerly (who served until 1992) steered State Street away from branch banking and into investments, trusts, and securities processing. An early achievement was designing PepsiCo's retirement plan. Fee-based sales approached 50% of revenues; the company could now quit focusing on lending. In the 1980s and 1990s the company built its administration and investment management businesses overseas and moved into software.

Evolving in the late 1990s, State Street left noncore businesses but expanded globally. In 1997 it formed European Direct Capital Management to invest in eastern and central Europe. State Street Global Advisors opened a London office to serve wealthy individuals outside the US in 1998.

The company sold its commercial banking business to Royal Bank of Scotland in 1999, signaling an exit from that business and narrowing State Street's scope to the asset and investment management businesses. The company also bought Wachovia's custody and institutional trust business and teamed with Citigroup to sell 401(k) retirement products.

In 2000 State Street created FX Connect, an electronic foreign exchange trading system. Also that year David Spina took over as CEO from the retiring Marshall Carter.

The firm bought Bel Air Investment Advisors and its broker/dealer affiliate Bel Air Securities in 2001 to cater to the ultrawealthy. In 2003 State Street sold its corporate trust business to U.S. Bancorp and its private asset management business to Charles Schwab's U.S. Trust. Spina retired in 2004; his protégé, Ron Logue, stepped in as chairman and CEO.

The company was reappointed as the financial advisor for the $2.4 billion Suffolk County (New York) Council Pension Fund in 2007.

EXECUTIVES

Chairman and CEO: Ronald E. (Ron) Logue, age 63, $28,712,476 total compensation
Vice Chairman; Head, North American Investor Services and Global Investment Manager Outsourcing Services: Joseph C. Antonellis, age 54, $11,401,905 total compensation
President and COO: Joseph L. (Jay) Hooley, age 52, $11,598,353 total compensation
EVP and CFO: Edward J. Resch, age 56, $11,448,094 total compensation
EVP and CIO: Christopher Perretta
EVP and CTO: Albert J. (Jerry) Cristoforo
EVP, Chief Legal Officer, and Secretary: Jeffrey N. (Jeff) Carp, age 52
EVP and Chief Risk Officer: Maureen J. Miskovic, age 51

EVP and Chief Administrative Officer, State Street Global Advisors: Marc P. Brown
EVP and Chief Compliance Officer: Tracy Atkinson
EVP and Chief Investment Officer: Paul J. Selian
EVP and Chief Risk Officer, State Street Global Advisors: Jacques M. Longerstaey
EVP Global Human Resources: David C. O'Leary, age 62
EVP; Head Global Infrastructure Services: Madge M. Meyer
EVP: James S. Phalen, age 58, $10,304,344 total compensation
EVP Investment Services: Gunjan Kedia
EVP Corporate Finance: Maureen P. Corcoran
EVP; President, State Street Bank Realty: Donald E. Conover
EVP, General Counsel, and Assistant Secretary: David C. Phelan, age 51
EVP and Head Global Marketing: Hannah Grove
Auditors: Ernst & Young LLP

LOCATIONS

HQ: State Street Corporation
1 Lincoln St., Boston, MA 02111
Phone: 617-786-3000   **Fax:** 617-664-4299
Web: www.statestreet.com

PRODUCTS/OPERATIONS

2008 Sales

	$ mil.	% of total
Servicing Fees	3,745	35
Interest	2,650	25
Trading services	1,467	14
Securities finance	1,230	11
Management fees	1,028	10
Processing fees & other	573	5
Total	**10,693**	**100**

COMPETITORS

Ameriprise
Bank of New York Mellon
Barclays
BBVA Provida
Citigroup
Credit Suisse (USA)
Deutsche Bank
DST
First Data
Fiserv
Franklin Resources
GAMCO Investors
Morgan Stanley
National Financial Partners
Northern Trust
Principal Financial
SEI Investments
UBS Financial Services

HISTORICAL FINANCIALS

Company Type: Public

Income Statement

	ASSETS ($ mil.)	NET INCOME ($ mil.)	INCOME AS % OF ASSETS	EMPLOYEES
12/08	173,631.0	1,811.0	1.0%	28,475
12/07	142,543.0	1,261.0	0.9%	27,110
12/06	107,353.0	1,106.0	1.0%	21,700
12/05	97,968.0	838.0	0.9%	20,965
12/04	94,040.0	798.0	0.8%	19,668
Annual Growth	16.6%	22.7%	—	9.7%

FYE: December 31

2008 Year-End Financials

Equity as % of assets: 6.3%
Return on assets: 1.1%
Return on equity: 16.3%
Long-term debt ($ mil.): 4,419
No. of shares (mil.): 494
Dividends
 Yield: 2.4%
 Payout: 22.1%
Market value ($ mil.): 19,448
Sales ($ mil.): 10,693

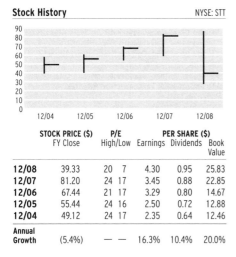

	STOCK PRICE ($) FY Close	P/E High/Low		PER SHARE ($) Earnings	Dividends	Book Value
12/08	39.33	20	7	4.30	0.95	25.83
12/07	81.20	24	17	3.45	0.88	22.85
12/06	67.44	21	17	3.29	0.80	14.67
12/05	55.44	24	16	2.50	0.72	12.88
12/04	49.12	24	17	2.35	0.64	12.46
Annual Growth	(5.4%)	—	—	16.3%	10.4%	20.0%

Steelcase Inc.

For those really tough office meetings, there's Steelcase, a top office furniture maker worldwide. The company manufactures a wide variety of products, from file cabinets that come with a lifetime warranty to premium Coalesse-branded contemporary furnishings. Steelcase also sells staples, such as tables, desks, and lighting. Its brands include Brayton, Designtex, Details, Metro, PolyVision, Steelcase, Turnstone, and Vecta, among others. Steelcase offers a variety of services, including workspace planning, interior construction, and project management. In addition the company focuses on high-end furniture and specialty markets through various subsidiaries and affiliates.

In 2009 the company extended its reach into premium furniture with its launch of the Coalesse brand. The collection is targeted to corporate, hospitality, and residential clients. It's a blend of Steelcase's Metro Furniture, Brayton International, and Vecta product lines.

Steelcase in 2008 entered an agreement with IDEO, a Steelcase subsidiary that specializes in innovation and "human-centered" design. As part of the agreement, IDEO management is able to purchase a controlling equity interest in IDEO in two phases ending in 2013. In February 2009, IDEO management acquired a 20% stake in IDEO. The next phase is slated for 2010 and would give management another 60% interest.

During the past few years, Steelcase has expanded its operations globally through acquisitions. The company acquired the office furniture business of China-based Ultra Group Holdings for more than $13 million in 2007 to expand its business in Asia. The purchase added about 1,000 employees to Steelcase's operations in China and stands to beef up the company's international sales, which accounted for 29% of 2009 revenue. About 70% of its international business was generated in Western Europe, with the balance coming from Central and Eastern Europe, Latin America, and Asia. Its global efforts are helping to offset declines in the US due to an economic downturn, as well. From 2008 to 2009, Steelcase's sales in the US dropped from 67% of revenue to 63%. Indeed, as US joblessness mounts the demand for office furniture falls. In response, the firm has cut costs through layoffs, salary cuts, and the consolidation of facilities.

It's also reaching into new niches to diversify its business. Steelcase's purchase of whiteboard maker PolyVision expanded the company's business in the corporate learning and higher education markets. It also made inroads into the automotive sector with its agreement with Johnson Controls to improve vehicle seats with Steelcase technology. In 2006 the company acquired hospital furniture maker Softcare Innovations and its sister company DJRT Manufacturing.

Descendants of Steelcase's founders control the company.

HISTORY

In the early 1900s, when wooden office furniture was the rule, sheet-metal designer Peter Wege began espousing the benefits of fireproof steel furniture. In 1912 Wege persuaded a group of investors, led by Grand Rapids, Michigan, banker Walter Idema, to create the Metal Office Furniture Company. Salesman David Dyer Hunting — a onetime vaudeville press agent who is considered the company's third founder — joined in 1914. Metal Office Furniture's first big hit was a metal wastepaper basket.

Businesses were slow to switch from wood to the more expensive metal furniture, but US government architects, concerned with fire safety, began specifying metal furniture in their designs. Metal Office Furniture won its first government contract in 1915.

Wege hired media consultant Jim Turner in 1921 to tout the benefits of metal furniture. Turner came up with a trademark to describe the indestructible nature of the company's products — Steelcase. The company patented the suspension cabinet in 1934 and teamed with Frank Lloyd Wright in 1937 to create office furniture for the Johnson Wax headquarters building.

Metal Office Furniture provided the US Navy with shipboard furniture during WWII and sold Navy-inspired modular furniture after the war. In 1954 the company changed its name to Steelcase. Five years later it introduced Convertibles and Convertiwalls, a system of frames, cabinets, and panels that could tailor a work area to an individual worker's needs. By 1968 Steelcase had become the world's #1 maker of metal office furniture.

To boost its presence overseas, the company signed deals with firms such as Strafor Facom (1974, France). Steelcase began a series of acquisitions in 1978, fueling growth that helped triple its sales during the 1980s.

In 1987 Steelcase positioned itself as a more design-oriented company by creating the Steelcase Design Partnership. The partnership, which was made up of seven companies, provided products for special market niches such as fabrics (DesignTex).

The firm was hit hard by the recession of the early 1990s as many businesses postponed buying new furniture. Steelcase was forced to lay off hourly workers, but by 1992 it was able to recall them all. In 1993 Steelcase launched Turnstone, serving small businesses and home office workers. Turnstone president James Hackett was named CEO of Steelcase the next year.

In 1996 Steelcase joined with computer mouse pioneer IDEO to co-design furniture for computers. Steelcase went public in 1998 at the urging of the Wege and Hunting families; Peter Wege, son of one of the company's founders, gave nearly $140 million (of the $214 million he gained from the IPO) to his charity, the Wege Foundation.

Acquisitions in the late 1990s included Germany's wood office furniture maker Werndl BuroMobel;, US company J.M. Lynne (wall coverings); and the remaining 50% stake of its French joint venture, Steelcase Strafor, from Strafor Facom.

In the face of declining office furniture sales, however, Steelcase was also laying off workers. More than 6,600 hourly, temporary, and salaried positions were eliminated between December 2000 and March 2002, or 27% of the workforce. After losing more than $15 million in 2002, the company temporarily closed its North American operations for one week in April 2003. The shutdown was the company's first in its 90-year history.

In September 2003 Steelcase sold Attwood Corporation, a marine parts manufacturing subsidiary, to leisure products industry leader Brunswick Corporation.

EXECUTIVES

Chairman: Robert C. (Rob) Pew III, age 58
President, CEO, and Director: James P. Hackett, age 54, $1,756,593 total compensation
SVP and Global Operations Officer: Mark A. Baker, age 48, $916,278 total compensation
VP and CFO: David C. Sylvester, age 44, $807,137 total compensation
SVP, Chief Administrative Officer, and Secretary: Nancy W. Hickey, age 57
VP, Chief Legal Officer, and Secretary: Lizbeth S. O'Shaughnessy, age 47
Corporate Controller and Chief Accounting Officer: Mark T. Mossing, age 51
SVP WorkSpace Futures and E X P: Mark T. Greiner, age 57
VP Global Corporate Community Relations: Brian Cloyd
VP Growth Initiatives: John S. Malnor, age 47
VP Global Design: James Ludwig
President, Steelcase Group: James P. (Jim) Keane, age 49, $1,029,211 total compensation
President, Nurture by Steelcase: Michael I. (Mike) Love, age 60
President, Coalesse: Frank H. Merlotti Jr., age 58, $918,979 total compensation
President, Steelcase International: James G. (Jim) Mitchell, age 59
Director Corporate Strategy and Development: Raj Mehan
Director UK Sales: Nikos Liapis
Director Global Environmental Strategy: Angela Nahikian
Corporate Communications: Jeanine Holquist
Auditors: BDO Seidman, LLP

LOCATIONS

HQ: Steelcase Inc.
901 44th St. SE, Grand Rapids, MI 49508
Phone: 616-247-2710   **Fax:** 616-475-2270
Web: www.steelcase.com

2009 Sales

	$ mil.	% of total
US	2,000.6	63
Other countries	1,183.1	37
Total	**3,183.7**	**100**

2009 Sales

	$ mil.	% of total
North America	1,740.0	55
International	922.2	29
Other countries	521.5	16
Total	**3,183.7**	**100**

PRODUCTS/OPERATIONS

2009 Sales

	$ mil.	% of total
Systems & storage	1,454.2	46
Seating	740.5	23
Other	989.0	31
Total	**3,183.7**	**100**

Selected Products

Desks and suites (standard, executive)
Interior architecture (flooring, space dividers)
Lighting (task, ambient, accent)
Seating (general, executive, guest, lounge)
Storage (shelves, cabinets, files)
Systems (workstation, panel systems)
Tables (meeting, personal, cafe)
Technology (appliances)
Textiles (seating upholstery, panel fabric)
Worktools (organizers, boards and easels)

Selected Brand Names

Brayton International	PolyVision
Braytonspaces	Steelcase
Designtex	Turnstone
Details	Vecta
Metro	

COMPETITORS

ABCO Office Furniture	Inscape corp
CFGroup	KI
Design Within Reach	Kimball International
Haworth, Inc.	Knoll, Inc.
Herman Miller	Shelby Williams
HNI	Teknion
The HON Company	

HISTORICAL FINANCIALS

Company Type: Public

Income Statement

FYE: Last Friday in February

	REVENUE ($ mil.)	NET INCOME ($ mil.)	NET PROFIT MARGIN	EMPLOYEES
2/09	3,183.7	(11.7)	—	13,000
2/08	3,420.8	133.2	3.9%	13,500
2/07	3,097.4	106.9	3.5%	13,000
2/06	2,868.9	48.9	1.7%	13,000
2/05	2,613.8	12.7	0.5%	14,500
Annual Growth	**5.1%**	**—**	**—**	**(2.7%)**

2009 Year-End Financials

Debt ratio: 34.2%	No. of shares (mil.): 133
Return on equity: —	Dividends
Cash ($ mil.): 118	Yield: 13.2%
Current ratio: 1.45	Payout: —
Long-term debt ($ mil.): 251	Market value ($ mil.): 535

Stock History

NYSE: SCS

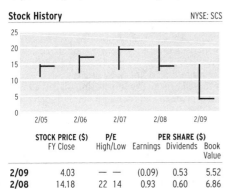

	STOCK PRICE ($) FY Close	P/E High/Low		PER SHARE ($) Earnings	Dividends	Book Value
2/09	4.03	—	—	(0.09)	0.53	5.52
2/08	14.18	22	14	0.93	0.60	6.86
2/07	19.42	28	19	0.71	0.45	9.32
2/06	17.00	53	37	0.33	0.33	9.07
2/05	14.28	163	123	0.09	0.24	9.01
Annual Growth	**(27.1%)**	**—**	**—**	**—**	**21.9%**	**(11.5%)**

Sun Healthcare

Sun Healthcare Group shines its rays on nursing homes across the US. The company provides long-term, subacute, and related health care services at more than 200 inpatient facilities in 25 states (totaling some 23,000 beds) through its SunBridge Healthcare subsidiary. SunBridge's facilities are primarily skilled nursing centers for seniors; it also offers assisted and independent living arrangements and behavioral health services. The firm's SunDance Rehabilitation unit offers physical, occupational, and speech therapy, and its SolAmor division provides hospice services. Sun Healthcare also provides temporary medical staffing through its CareerStaff Unlimited unit.

Sun Healthcare gets more than 85% of its revenues from inpatient facility operations, and most of that revenue comes from Medicaid and Medicare. The company is focused on growing its inpatient business (primarily within the Medicare and high-need market) in select geographic areas in order to reduce overhead and maximize synergies in its operating markets.

To this end, Sun Healthcare acquired Harborside Healthcare in early 2007 from majority shareholder Investcorp and other investors for $350 million, plus the assumption of $275 million in debt. Harborside added some 75 skilled nursing and assisted living facilities (9,000 beds) in nine eastern US states to SunBridge Healthcare's operations.

The company also intends to further grow its hospice and rehabilitation businesses through acquisitions and internal efforts, as it feels that the two units compliment its focus on providing integrated, full-time inpatient care. For example, SolAmor Hospice acquired New Jersey-based Holisticare Hospice in 2008. Sun Healthcare is also adding Rehab Recovery Suites (for Medicare and managed care patients) and Alzheimer's care wings to several of its skilled nursing homes.

After surviving a bankruptcy filing and emergence early in the century, the company sold off numerous unprofitable operations to improve its bottom line. Since then the industry outlook has improved, partially because the US population is growing older and living longer. The company continues to evaluate its operations and pare off some less-profitable assets.

HISTORY

In 1987 Andrew Turner left long-term care chain Hillhaven Corp. to form a smaller, similar operation named Horizon Healthcare. Two years later he formed another health care business, Sunrise Healthcare, by buying and turning around seven unprofitable facilities in Washington and Connecticut. Sunrise Healthcare was based in Albuquerque, New Mexico.

Acquisitive Sunrise Healthcare bought some 20 facilities between 1990 and 1992 and added a therapy services division, SunDance Rehabilitation (1991). But the company went supernova in 1993, when Turner added SunScript Pharmacy and bundled Sunrise, SunDance, and SunScript into Sun Healthcare Group, taking the holding company public. Sun Healthcare used the proceeds to acquire 42 nursing homes, including Honorcare, which had 14 facilities in four states. That year the group added subacute care, a lucrative market with higher reimbursement rates, to its services.

The growth continued throughout the mid-1990s. Sun added 60 more facilities to its network in 1994, including 36 nursing homes from its merger with The Mediplex Group. By combining the two companies' subacute care facilities, Sun became one of the US's largest subacute care providers. Recognizing the potential in less-developed markets outside the US, the company ventured overseas. Sun acquired Exceler, which had 20 nursing homes in the UK.

As the long-term-care industry continued to consolidate, Sun realigned its operations in 1995, selling off the mental health and substance abuse facilities it had acquired with Mediplex. That year the group also acquired CareerStaff Unlimited, broadening SunDance's ability to provide a continuum of care to affiliated and nonaffiliated facilities. Sun continued to expand overseas, acquiring UK long-term-care providers Ashbourne and Hesslewood Nursing & Residential Care Home.

The company reorganized its management in 1996 to better control its diverse health care services. Sun strengthened its pharmacy unit by adding a medical/surgical supply business and buying 10% of OmniCell, which makes medical supply distribution software.

In the late 1990s Sun continued its bigger-is-better strategy, acquiring US nursing home operators Regency (1997) and Retirement Care Associates and Contour Medical (1998), Australia's Alpha Healthcare Ltd. (38%, 1997) and Moran Health Care Group (1997), Spain's Eurosar (1997), and Germany's Heim Plan-Uternehmensgruppe (1997). Shadows loomed in 1998, however, when the company was accused in a California lawsuit of giving substandard care; a comatose patient in a Massachusetts facility was raped and impregnated; and Sun Healthcare employees in New England went on strike.

But Sun faced its darkest hours in 1999, when major losses due to changes in Medicare reimbursement led to a reorganization and prompted the company to file for Chapter 11 protection. Shareholders also filed suit over these losses. That year and into 2000 the company cut its workforce, sold nonperforming homes, and sold its operations in Spain to shore up its bottom line.

The selling spree continued in 2001 when the company shed its remaining overseas operations and its medical supplies unit. In early 2002, Sun Healthcare emerged from Chapter 11 bankruptcy after securing a $150 million senior credit line with lenders, led by Heller Healthcare Finance, a GE Capital company.

Sun Healthcare divested more than 130 underperforming facilities in 2003 and 2004. The company also sold its SunScript Pharmacy unit and its software development operations.

In 2005, as finances improved, the company beefed up its health care staffing business. Its CareerStaff Unlimited subsidiary acquired SingleSource Staffing and Goddard Healthcare Consulting, both based in Texas.

Sun Healthcare also acquired Peak Medical Corporation in 2005. Spanning some seven states, Peak's operations (55 inpatient facilities with 5,000 beds) were folded into SunBridge Healthcare's western division.

The company acquired hospice operator SolAmor Hospice in 2006. Sun Healthcare also sold its home health division that year, as well as its remaining laboratory and radiology businesses.

EXECUTIVES

Chairman and CEO: Richard K. Matros, age 55,
$2,400,574 total compensation
EVP and CFO: L. Bryan Shaul, age 64,
$1,186,703 total compensation
Chief Risk Officer and Chief Compliance Officer:
Chauncey J. Hunker, age 58
EVP and General Counsel: Michael Newman, age 60,
$826,818 total compensation
SVP Clinical Operations: Sue Coppola
SVP Human Resources: Cindy Chrispell, age 48
VP and Treasurer: Michael A. Montevideo
VP and Corporate Controller: Jeffrey M. Kreger
President and COO, SunBridge HealthCare:
William A. (Bill) Mathies, age 49,
$1,401,993 total compensation
President, SunDance Rehabilitation:
Susan E. (Sue) Gwyn, age 57
President, CareerStaff Unlimited: Richard L. Peranton,
age 60, $687,289 total compensation
President, SolAmor Hospice: Glen R. Cavallo
Investor Relations: Bernadette Bell
Auditors: Ernst & Young LLP

LOCATIONS

HQ: Sun Healthcare Group, Inc.
18831 Von Karman, Ste. 400, Irvine, CA 92612
Phone: 949-255-7100   **Fax:** 949-255-7054
Web: www.sunh.com

2008 Inpatient Facilities

	No.
Kentucky	20
Massachusetts	19
Ohio	17
California	15
New Hampshire	15
New Mexico	12
Connecticut	10
Idaho	10
Colorado	9
Florida	9
Georgia	9
Oklahoma	9
North Carolina	8
Tennessee	8
Alabama	7
West Virginia	7
Washington	6
Montana	5
Maryland	3
Indiana	2
Rhode Island	2
Utah	2
Arizona	1
New Jersey	1
Wyoming	1
Total	**207**

PRODUCTS/OPERATIONS

2008 Sales

	$ mil.	% of total
Inpatient	1,616.8	86
Rehabilitation therapy	150.5	8
Medical staffing	120.4	6
Adjustments	(63.5)	—
Total	**1,824.2**	**100**

2008 Sales

	$ mil.	% of total
Medicaid	729.0	40
Medicare	522.6	29
Managed care & commercial insurance	91.7	5
Private pay & other	480.9	26
Total	**1,824.2**	**100**

COMPETITORS

Advocat
AMN Healthcare
Assisted Living Concepts
ATC Healthcare
Consulate Health Care
Covenant Care
Cross Country Healthcare
Emeritus Corporation
Ensign Group
Extendicare REIT
Five Star Quality Care
Golden Horizons
InteliStaf Healthcare
Kelly Services
Kindred Healthcare
Life Care Centers
Manor Care
Medical Staffing Network
Odyssey HealthCare
RehabCare
SavaSeniorCare
Skilled Healthcare Group
Sunrise Senior Living
Tenet Healthcare
Ventas
VITAS Healthcare

HISTORICAL FINANCIALS

Company Type: Public

Income Statement

FYE: December 31

	REVENUE ($ mil.)	NET INCOME ($ mil.)	NET PROFIT MARGIN	EMPLOYEES
12/08	1,824.2	109.3	6.0%	29,845
12/07	1,587.3	57.5	3.6%	36,850
12/06	1,045.6	27.1	2.6%	19,350
12/05	882.1	24.8	2.8%	22,000
12/04	820.1	(18.6)	—	15,800
Annual Growth	**22.1%**	**—**	**—**	**17.2%**

2008 Year-End Financials

Debt ratio: 179.2%
Return on equity: 33.6%
Cash ($ mil.): 92
Current ratio: 1.72
Long-term debt ($ mil.): 723
No. of shares (mil.): 44
Dividends
  Yield: 0.0%
  Payout: —
Market value ($ mil.): 387

Stock History

NASDAQ (GS): SUNH

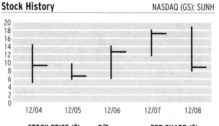

	STOCK PRICE ($) FY Close	P/E High/Low		PER SHARE ($) Earnings	Dividends	Book Value
12/08	8.85	8	3	2.49	0.00	9.23
12/07	17.17	14	9	1.33	0.00	5.63
12/06	12.63	16	7	0.85	0.00	3.30
12/05	6.61	6	4	1.55	0.00	(0.07)
12/04	9.21	—	—	(1.28)	0.00	(2.82)
Annual Growth	**(1.0%)**	**—**	**—**	**—**	**—**	**—**

Sunoco, Inc.

A leading independent oil refiner and marketer, Sunoco has screened its operations, shed nonperforming ones, and buffed the others in hopes that the sun will shine on future profits. The company operates five refineries, which have a combined processing capacity of 910,000 barrels of crude oil a day, and it has about 6,000 miles of oil and refined products pipelines and 45 product terminals. More than half of its crude oil is sourced from West Africa. It markets its Sunoco gasoline through more than 4,700 retail outlets (including Ultra Service Centers and APlus convenience stores). Sunoco also produces lubricants, mines coal for coke processing, and operates a chemicals business.

In the latter half of this decade Sunoco has implemented its Retail Portfolio Management (RPM) program, which was created to decrease investment in outlets leased or owned by the company while retaining fuel sales to those locations through long-term contracts. Some of Sunoco's pipeline, terminal, and storage assets are held through publicly traded Sunoco Logistics Partners, which is 43% controlled by Sunoco unit Sunoco Partners.

The company's Sunoco Chemicals unit produces polypropylene, phenol, and plasticizers. At the end of 2008 Sunoco announced that it would explore the sale of the chemicals business.

Veteran oil industry executive Lynn Laverty Elsenhans was elected CEO in 2008.

In 2009, as part of rationalizing and streamlining its business, the company sold its 85,000-barrels-per-day Tulsa, Oklahoma, refinery to regional player Holly Coproration. That year it also acquired the largest ethanol plant in the Northeast, which is targeted to provide a quarter of the company's ethanol production.

HISTORY

Joseph Newton Pew began his energy career in 1876 when he helped form a Pennsylvania gas pipeline partnership that became Pittsburgh's first natural gas system. When oil discoveries in northwestern Ohio sparked an 1886 boom, Pew began buying oil leases and pipelines and organized the assets into The Sun Oil Company of Ohio in 1890. Four years later the company bought Diamond Oil and its refinery in Toledo, Ohio. The firm traces its trademark diamond pierced by an arrow to the short-lived Diamond subsidiary.

After the 1901 Spindletop gusher, Pew dispatched nephew Edgar Pew to Texas, where he bought the oil-rich properties of a bankrupt firm. Back East, the elder Pew bought Delaware River acreage in Pennsylvania for a shipping terminal and refinery to process Texas crude into Red Stock. The lubricating oil carved Sun Oil a place in the Standard Oil-dominated petroleum industry.

Joseph Pew died in 1912 and was succeeded by sons Howard and Joseph Newton Jr. The company moved into shipbuilding (1916) and gasoline stations (1920). Sun Oil's gasoline was dyed blue (legend says it matched a Chinese tile chip Joseph Jr. and his wife had received on their honeymoon) and sold as Blue Sunoco. The firm went public as Sun Oil in 1925.

When Howard retired in 1947, Joseph Jr. became chairman, and Robert Dunlop became the first non-Pew president of Sun Oil. The company had its first major foreign oil strike in Venezuela in 1957.

In 1967 Dunlop's chance meeting with a Sunray DX Oil executive led to Sun Oil's acquisition of that company the next year. The Sunray DX addition diluted the Pew family's stake in the company. Sun Oil's Venezuelan holdings were nationalized in 1975. The next year the company dropped "Oil" from its name.

In the early 1980s the company sold its shipbuilding arm (1982) and began building its oil holdings, gaining interests in the North Sea and offshore China. In the US Sun purchased Seagram's Texas Pacific Oil for $2.3 billion (1980) and acquired Exeter Oil, Victory Oil, and the interests of Petro-Lewis (1984).

Sun began to shed exploration and production assets in 1988 to focus on refining and marketing. That year it spun off its domestic oil and gas properties into what became Oryx Energy (acquired by Kerr-McGee in 1999). Sun also acquired Atlantic Petroleum and gained more than 1,000 service stations in the process.

In 1993 Sun sold Cordero Mining to Kennecott and cut its stake in Canadian petroleum company Suncor from 68% to 55%. The next year Sun bought a refinery in Philadelphia from Chevron and a stake in a pipeline connecting that refinery to New York Harbor.

In 1995 Sun sold its 55% interest in Suncor, and the following year sold its international oil and gas production business. It also bought the Kendall/Amalie motor oils and lubricants unit of Witco Corporation. In 1998 the company changed its name to Sunoco. Sunoco acquired a Philadelphia phenol plant from AlliedSignal that year.

The company experienced a strike (settled after five months) at its Yabucoa, Puerto Rico, lubricants refinery in 1999. (In 2001 it decided to close the plant.) CEO Robert Campbell retired in 2000 and was replaced by COO John Drosdick.

In 2001 Sunoco bought Mitsubishi subsidiary Aristech Chemical, which operated five chemical plants in the US. It also beefed up its retail operations that year, acquiring more than 230 outlets in 12 eastern states from Coastal Corp.

That year the company formed Sunoco Logistics Partners to acquire, own, and operate a major portion of its midstream and downstream assets.

The company acquired 193 gas stations in the southeastern US in 2003 from Marathon Ashland Petroleum's (now Marathon Petroleum) Speedway SuperAmerica unit. That year Sunoco also bought the Eagle Point refinery (adjacent to its own Philadelphia refining complex) from El Paso Corp. for $111 million and related assets for $135 million.

In 2004 the company acquired 340 gas stations in Delaware; Maryland; Washington, DC; and Virginia from ConocoPhillips.

EXECUTIVES

Chairman, President, and CEO: Lynn L. Elsenhans, age 52, $1,940,730 total compensation
SVP and CFO: Brian P. MacDonald, age 43
Chief Governance Officer, Corporate Secretary, and Assistant General Counsel: Ann C. Mulé
SVP and Chief Human Resources Officer: Dennis Zeleny, age 53
SVP; President, SunCoke Energy: Michael J. (Mike) Thomson, age 50, $1,981,898 total compensation
SVP Strategy and Portfolio: Bruce G. Fischer, age 53

SVP Marketing: Robert W. Owens, age 55, $2,180,908 total compensation
SVP and General Counsel: Michael S. Kuritzkes, age 48
SVP Refining and Supply: Vincent J. (Vince) Kelley, age 49, $1,662,890 total compensation
VP Chemicals: Bruce D. Rubin, age 51
President and CEO, Logistics: Deborah M. Fretz, age 60, $4,749,990 total compensation
Comptroller: Joseph P. Krott, age 45
Manager Marketing Services: Charles Valis
Management Attorney: Wanda E. Flowers
Treasurer: Michael Colavita
Auditors: Ernst & Young LLP

LOCATIONS

HQ: Sunoco, Inc.
1735 Market St., Ste. LL, Philadelphia, PA 19103
Phone: 215-977-3000   **Fax:** 215-977-3409
Web: www.sunocoinc.com

PRODUCTS/OPERATIONS

2008 Sales

	$ mil.	% of total
Refining & supply	26,663	49
Retail marketing	16,097	30
Logistics	7,540	14
Chemicals	2,925	5
Coke	827	2
Other income	94	—
Total	**54,146**	**100**

COMPETITORS

BP
CITGO Refining and Chemicals
ConocoPhillips
Eni
Exxon
Hess Corporation
HOVENSA
Imperial Oil
Koch Industries, Inc.
Marathon Oil
Motiva Enterprises
Shell Oil Products
United Refining
U.S. Oil
Valero Energy

HISTORICAL FINANCIALS

Company Type: Public

Income Statement

FYE: December 31

	REVENUE ($ mil.)	NET INCOME ($ mil.)	NET PROFIT MARGIN	EMPLOYEES
12/08	54,146.0	776.0	1.4%	13,700
12/07	44,728.0	891.0	2.0%	14,200
12/06	38,715.0	979.0	2.5%	14,000
12/05	33,764.0	974.0	2.9%	13,800
12/04	25,508.0	605.0	2.4%	14,200
Annual Growth	**20.7%**	**6.4%**	**—**	**(0.9%)**

2008 Year-End Financials

Debt ratio: 60.0%
Return on equity: 28.9%
Cash ($ mil.): 240
Current ratio: 0.72
Long-term debt ($ mil.): 1,705

No. of shares (mil.): 117
Dividends
  Yield: 2.7%
  Payout: 17.6%
Market value ($ mil.): 5,080

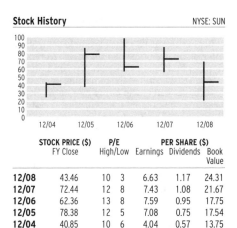

Stock History

NYSE: SUN

	STOCK PRICE ($) FY Close	P/E High/Low		PER SHARE ($) Earnings	Dividends	Book Value
12/08	43.46	10	3	6.63	1.17	24.31
12/07	72.44	12	8	7.43	1.08	21.67
12/06	62.36	13	8	7.59	0.95	17.75
12/05	78.38	12	5	7.08	0.75	17.54
12/04	40.85	10	6	4.04	0.57	13.75
Annual Growth	**1.6%**	**—**	**—**	**13.2%**	**19.7%**	**15.3%**

SunTrust Banks

Coca-Cola, fast cars, and SunTrust Banks — this Sun Belt financial holding company is southern to its core. Its eponymous flagship subsidiary SunTrust Bank operates more than 1,690 bank branches across an arc of about a dozen southeastern states, including Alabama, the Carolinas, Florida, Georgia, Maryland, Tennessee, and Virginia, plus Washington, DC. The bank's offerings include retail and commercial banking, as well as trust services, credit cards, mortgage banking, mutual funds, insurance, lease financing, asset management, and securities underwriting and dealing. SunTrust bought Atlanta-area bank holding company GB&T Bancshares in 2008.

The GB&T Bancshares acquisition added 17 banking offices to SunTrust's presence in north and central Georgia. To augment capital, the company sold its interests in Lighthouse Investment Partners, an investment brokerage; First Mercantile Trust Company, a retirement plan services firm; and TransPlatinum, a fuel card services firm. Like many other bank holding companies, in 2008 SunTrust took part in the Federal Reserve's bailout. It sold the government about $4.9 billion in preferred shares.

Legend has it that the only written copy of the Coke formula lies in a SunTrust vault. The company is the second-largest shareholder of fellow Atlanta icon Coca-Cola (after Warren Buffett's Berkshire Hathaway), but is slowly selling off more than half of its shares. SunTrust also has a marketing pact to be the official bank of Grand American Road Racing, and it helped fund the construction of the home of the Daytona 500, Daytona International Speedway in Florida. It has a private banking unit that caters to folks in the sports and entertainment industries, particularly motor sports and country music.

HISTORY

SunTrust was born from the union of old-money Georgia and new-money Florida. Founded in 1891, the Trust Company of Georgia (originally Commercial Traveler's Savings Bank) served Atlanta's oldest and richest institutions. It helped underwrite Coca-Cola's IPO in 1919; the bank's ownership stake in Coke stemmed from its early involvement with the beverage maker.

Beginning in 1933 Trust acquired controlling interests in five other Georgia banks. As regulation of multibank ownership relaxed in the 1970s, Trust acquired the remaining interests in its original banks and bought 25 more. At the height of the Sunbelt boom in 1984, Trust was the most profitable bank in the nation. The next year it united with Sun Banks.

Sun Banks was formed in 1934 as the First National Bank at Orlando. It grew into a holding company in 1967 and in the early 1970s helped assemble the land for Walt Disney World. The Sun name was adopted in 1973.

Under president and CEO Joel Wells, Sun Banks began an acquisition-fueled expansion within Florida. Between 1976 and 1984, Sun Banks' approximate asset growth was an astronomical 500%, and branch count grew fivefold (51 to 274).

After a lingering courtship, Sun and Trust formed a super holding company over the two organizations. When the marriage was consummated in 1985, Sun brought a dowry of $9.4 billion in assets, and Trust contributed $6.2 billion. Trust's chairman, Bob Strickland, became chairman and CEO for the new Atlanta-based SunTrust, and Wells became president.

In 1986 SunTrust bought Nashville, Tennessee-based Third National Bank, the #2 banking company in the Volunteer State. But problems with Tennessee real estate loans plagued SunTrust. In 1990 it increased the amount of loans it wrote off; the bank's ratings suffered because of nonperforming loans on properties in overbuilt Florida. While nonperforming assets decreased in Tennessee in 1991, they climbed in Florida and Georgia.

Strickland stepped down as chairman and CEO in 1990. Wells died in 1991, and James Williams, a conservative banker who instilled strict fiscal management in the Trust banks, became chairman and CEO. Under his direction the company reduced its nonperforming assets and began diversifying its business lines.

In 1993 the bank adopted accounting rules that caused it to revalue its Coca-Cola stock from its historic value of $110,000 to almost $1.1 billion. The dividends from these holdings contributed substantially to revenues.

SunTrust continued developing its nonbanking financial services: It expanded its investment services outside its traditional southern US market and bought Equitable Securities (now SunTrust Equitable Securities) in 1998. That year president Phillip Humann succeeded Williams as chairman and CEO. SunTrust also nearly doubled its branch count when it bought Crestar Financial, a banking powerhouse in the mid-Atlantic and Southeast.

In 1999 the company created a new trust business to serve high-net-worth clients, and it consolidated its 27 banking charters in six states into one based in Georgia the following year. In 2001 SunTrust made an unsolicited offer for Wachovia, which was on track to be acquired by First Union. After a heated proxy campaign, Wachovia's board of directors and shareholders voted down SunTrust's bid.

SunTrust bought National Commerce Financial in 2004 for some $7 billion. The deal helped the bank expand in existing territories, as well as provide entry into the growing North Carolina market, where SunTrust had been conspicuously absent. The company divested its 49% stake in First Market Bank (Ukrop's Super Markets owns the rest), which it acquired in the National Commerce deal. SunTrust unloaded the unit in part because it has branches in Kroger, Publix, Safeway, and Wal-Mart stores.

The company placed on administrative leave or dismissed several financial officers after it had to restate its earnings for the first two quarters of 2004 due to miscalculations of its loan loss reserves. (The SEC concluded an investigation into the matter in 2006 without recommending penalties.)

Former president and COO Jim Wells became CEO in 2007; Humann remained as chairman but stepped down the following year.

EXECUTIVES

Chairman and CEO: James M. (Jim) Wells III, age 62, $5,450,214 total compensation
President: William H. (Bill) Rogers Jr., age 51, $1,862,076 total compensation
Corporate EVP and CFO: Mark A. Chancy, age 44, $2,485,836 total compensation
Corporate EVP and CIO: Timothy E. Sullivan, age 58, $1,698,634 total compensation
Corporate EVP and Chief Administrative Officer: David F. Dierker, age 51
Corporate EVP, Chief Credit Officer, and Chief Risk Officer: Thomas E. (Tom) Freeman, age 57
Chief Marketing Officer: Rilla Delorier, age 42
Corporate EVP, Corporate Sales Administration: Dennis M. Patterson
Corporate EVP, General Counsel, and Corporate Secretary: Raymond D. Fortin, age 56
Corporate EVP: E. Jenner Wood III, age 57
Corporate EVP, Commercial Line of Business: Gay O. Abbott
Corporate EVP and Director Human Resources: Frances L. Breeden, age 58
Director Investor Relations: Steven P. Shriner
Chairman, SunTrust Investment Services: John T. Rhett III
Auditors: Ernst & Young LLP

LOCATIONS

HQ: SunTrust Banks Inc.
303 Peachtree St. NE, Atlanta, GA 30308
Phone: 404-588-7711   **Fax:** 404-332-3875
Web: www.suntrust.com

PRODUCTS/OPERATIONS

2008 Gross Revenues

	$ mil.	% of total
Interest		
Loans, including fees	6,933.7	53
Securities available for sale, including dividends	775.1	6
Trading accounts	302.8	2
Loans held for sale	289.9	2
Other	25.9	—
Noninterest		
Net securities gains	1,073.3	8
Service charges on deposit accounts	904.1	7
Trust & investment management	592.3	5
Card fees	308.4	2
Retail investment services	289.1	2
Investment banking	236.5	2
Net gain on sale of businesses	198.2	2
Other charges & fees	510.8	4
Other	572.6	5
Total	**13,012.7**	**100**

2008 Assets

	$ mil.	% of total
Cash & equivalents	6,637	3
Trading assets	10,396	6
Securities available for sale	19,697	10
Loans held for sale	4,032	2
Net loans	124,648	66
Other	23,728	13
Total	**189,138**	**100**

Selected Subsidiaries and Affiliates

Asset Management Advisors, L.L.C. (investment advisory and wealth management)
Premium Assignment Corporation (insurance premium financing for small businesses)
SunTrust Capital Markets, Inc. (investment banking)
SunTrust Community Development Corporation (affordable housing)
SunTrust Delaware Trust Company
SunTrust Insurance Company (credit life, accident, and health reinsurance)
SunTrust Leasing Corporation (equipment lease financing)
SunTrust Mortgage, Inc. (origination, purchase, and sale of mortgages)
SunTrust Securities, Inc. (brokerage and investment advisory for retail clients)
RidgeWorth Capital Management, Inc. (asset management for institutional clients and mutual fund management)

COMPETITORS

BancorpSouth	Regions Financial
Bank of America	South Financial Group
BB&T	Southeastern Bank
Citigroup	Financial
Compass Bancshares	StellarOne
First Citizens BancShares	Synovus Financial
First Horizon	Wachovia Corp
RBC Bank	

HISTORICAL FINANCIALS

Company Type: Public

Income Statement

FYE: December 31

	ASSETS ($ mil.)	NET INCOME ($ mil.)	INCOME AS % OF ASSETS	EMPLOYEES
12/08	189,138.0	795.8	0.4%	29,333
12/07	179,573.9	1,603.7	0.9%	32,323
12/06	182,161.6	2,109.7	1.2%	33,599
12/05	179,712.8	1,987.2	1.1%	33,406
12/04	158,869.8	1,572.9	1.0%	33,156
Annual Growth	**4.5%**	**(15.7%)**	**—**	**(3.0%)**

2008 Year-End Financials

Equity as % of assets: 9.1%
Return on assets: 0.4%
Return on equity: 4.6%
Long-term debt ($ mil.): 26,812
No. of shares (mil.): 499
Dividends
Yield: 9.6%
Payout: 133.8%
Market value ($ mil.): 14,735
Sales ($ mil.): 9,093

Stock History

NYSE: STI

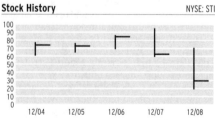

	STOCK PRICE ($) FY Close	P/E High/Low	PER SHARE ($)		
			Earnings	Dividends	Book Value
12/08	29.54	33 9	2.13	2.85	44.88
12/07	62.49	21 13	4.55	2.92	36.19
12/06	84.45	15 12	5.82	2.44	35.71
12/05	72.76	14 12	5.47	2.20	33.85
12/04	73.88	15 12	5.19	2.00	32.05
Annual Growth	**(20.5%)**	**— —**	**(20.0%)**	**9.3%**	**8.8%**

SUPERVALU INC.

SUPERVALU is feeling pretty super following the acquisition of more than 1,100 supermarkets from fallen grocery giant Albertsons. Its 2006 purchase of the Albertsons's stores catapulted the chain to second place in the traditional grocery retail market (behind Kroger) with about 2,420 stores in some 40 US states. The deal added half a dozen new banners, including Albertsons, Acme Markets, and Shaw's, to SUPERVALU's store roster (which includes Shoppers Food & Pharmacy, Cub Foods, Shop 'n Save). SUPERVALU also bought Albertsons' in-store pharmacy operations. The company is also one of the nation's largest food wholesalers, supplying some 2,000 grocery stores nationwide with brand-name and private-label goods.

Leading the charge is SUPERVALU's new president and CEO Craig Herkert, who joined the company from Wal-Mart, where he served as president and CEO of The Americas.

SUPERVALU cherry-picked Albertsons' most attractive supermarket assets including Acme, the upscale Bristol Farms chain in California, Jewel-Osco in the Chicago area, Star Markets in New England, and the Osco Drug and Sav-on banners, among others. SUPERVALU was part of a consortium of investors, which included drugstore operator CVS, that bought Albertsons, previously the nation's #2 grocery chain, in 2006.

In early 2009 SUPERVALU announced it would close about 50 stores nationwide, including Albertsons stores in Utah, Nevada, and California. The closings are part of an effort by the company to scale back spending, in addition to opening fewer stores and delaying remodeling. The company also agreed to sell about 40 Albertsons stores in Utah to grocery wholesaler Associated Food Stores that year.

Other banners operated by the company include bigg's, the extreme-value format Save-A-Lot stores, Farm Fresh, and Hornbacher's. The grocery chain also operates about 130 fuel centers at its stores.

The company also operates some 900 in-store pharmacies, primarily under the Osco, Sav-on, and local banner names, that account for about 6% of the company's sales.

SUPERVALU is under increasing pressure from expanding supercenters and warehouse clubs, such as Wal-Mart and Costco, which have stolen sales from conventional grocery retailers. To better compete with big discounters, it's expanding its extreme-value Save-A-Lot format, which already holds the #1 spot (based on revenues) in the extreme-value grocery market. The 1,175 Save-A-Lot limited assortment stores (about 310 are company owned) sell mostly private-label goods. SUPERVALU has big plans for Save-A-Lot, including more than doubling the number of outlets in a nationwide expansion.

SUPERVALU's wholesale customers include conventional and upscale supermarkets, combination food and drugstores, supercenters, convenience stores, limited assortment stores, and e-tailers. SUPERVALU offers its retailers private labels in every price range and in virtually every store category, from the value-priced Shoppers Value brand to the premium Preferred Selection line. It added a private label organic food line, called Wild Harvest, in 2008. SUPERVALU also offers retailers support services, such as store design and construction.

HISTORY

SUPERVALU's predecessor was formed in Minneapolis in the 1870s — and again in 1926. In 1871 wholesalers Hugh Harrison, George Newell, and W. D. Washburn joined forces to create Newell and Harrison. Newell bought out his partners in 1874 and renamed the firm George R. Newell Co. Five years later Harrison formed his own operation, H. G. Harrison Co. In 1926 the companies merged, creating Winston & Newell Co., the largest grocery distributor to independent grocers in the Midwest.

The company was part of the Independent Grocers Alliance from 1928-1942 before adopting the name Super Valu Stores in 1954. It expanded by acquiring chains such as Piggly-Wiggly Midland (1958, Wisconsin) and a number of wholesale operations across the US.

Super Valu entered nonfood retailing in 1971 by acquiring ShopKo, a discount department store chain. Two years later it founded clothing chain County Seat (sold 1983). Super Valu added a new format to its food operations by purchasing Cub Stores (warehouse-style groceries) in 1980; it later combined its Cub Stores and ShopKo formats. More acquisitions followed, including Atlanta's Food Giant chain. Super Valu named Michael Wright CEO in 1981 and chairman in 1982.

Super Valu acquired Scott's, an Indiana food store chain, in 1991 and sold a 54% interest in ShopKo to the public. The company changed its name to SUPERVALU in 1992 and bought food wholesaler Wetterau, making it the #1 independent food distributor in the US and giving it the Save-A-Lot franchise (launched in 1978).

Experiencing sluggish distribution growth, SUPERVALU continued to expand its retail holdings. Acquisitions in 1994 included Sweet Life Foods (280 stores) and 30 Texas T Stores. In 1996 it acquired Fleming's Sav-U-Foods, converting the 21 stores to Save-A-Lots and establishing a presence in California. SUPERVALU sold its remaining 46% stake in ShopKo the next year.

SUPERVALU later announced plans to cut 7% of its workforce and close some of its distribution centers and stores, including its Laneco stores in Pennsylvania and New Jersey, and its central Indiana Cub stores. Wright retired as CEO in mid-2001 and remained as chairman; president and CFO Jeff Noddle became CEO.

Later in the month, Wright retired as chairman and was succeeded by Noddle. In June the company announced it would take a charge of up to $21 million because of accounting irregularities in its pharmacy division.

SUPERVALU expanded its agreement in 2003 with Target Corporation to supply all Super Target stores. In 2004 it sold off its minority interest in the regional grocery chain, WinCo Foods.

In February 2005 SUPERVALU acquired Total Logistics, a provider of third-party logistics services and maker of refrigeration systems.

The company completed its acquisition of 1,124 stores from Albertson's in June 2006. Looking to take back sales lost to natural and organic grocery chains, SUPERVALU launched its own natural foods division, called Sunflower Market, in 2006; but in early 2008 the company announced it would close its five Sunflower Markets as they did not deliver expected results.

In 2007 SUPERVALU sold its 18 Scott's Food & Pharmacy stores in Indiana to rival Kroger.

In 2009 the company named Craig Herkert, a former Wal-Mart executive, as its new president and CEO, succeeding Jeff Noddle, who stayed on as the firm's executive chairman.

EXECUTIVES

Chairman: Jeffrey (Jeff) Noddle, age 62, $7,450,438 total compensation
President, CEO, and Director: Craig R. Herkert, age 49
EVP and CFO: Pamela K. (Pam) Knous, age 55, $1,785,802 total compensation
VP, Corporate Secretary, and Chief Securities Counsel: Burt M. Fealing
EVP: David L. (Dave) Boehnen, age 62
EVP Retail Operations: Pete Van Helden, age 48
EVP Merchandising and Marketing; Head Health and Wellness: Duncan C. MacNaughton, age 46
EVP Human Resources: David E. (Dave) Pylipow, age 51
EVP; President and COO, Supply Chain Services: Janel S. Haugarth, age 54
SVP Finance and Principal Accounting Officer: Sherry M. Smith, age 47
SVP Specialty Retail: Brian Huff, age 50
VP Investor Relations: David M. Oliver
Group VP, Fresh Food Merchandising: Jim Smits
Group VP and Controller: Adrian J. Downes, age 45
President, Shaw's Supermarkets: Mike Witynski, age 46
National Media Manager: Haley Meyer
Auditors: KPMG LLP

LOCATIONS

HQ: SUPERVALU INC.
11840 Valley View Rd., Eden Prairie, MN 55344
Phone: 952-828-4000 **Fax:** 952-828-8998
Web: www.supervalu.com

2009 Company-Owned Food Stores

	No.
California	262
Connecticut	27
Delaware	15
Florida	82
Georgia	11
Idaho	33
Illinois	209
Louisiana	11
Maine	22
Maryland	61
Massachusetts	96
Minnesota	44
Missouri	47
Montana	30
Nevada	35
New Hampshire	34
New Jersey	67
Ohio	47
Oregon	53
Pennsylvania	76
Rhode Island	17
Texas	19
Utah	43
Vermont	19
Virginia	75
Washington	77
Wyoming	10
Other states	37
Total	**1,559**

PRODUCTS/OPERATIONS

2009 Company-Owned Stores

	No.
Combination food & drug stores	874
Food stores	369
Limited assortment food stores	316
Total	**1,559**

2009 Stores

	No.
Company-owned	1,559
Licensed	862
Total	**2,421**

2009 Sales

	$ mil.	% of total
Retail food	34,664	78
Supply chain service	9,900	22
Total	**44,564**	**100**

Selected Retail Food Stores and Formats

Extreme Value Stores
Save-A-Lot

Price Superstore
bigg's
Cub Foods
Shop 'n Save
Shoppers Food & Pharmacy

Supermarkets
Acme Markets
Albertsons
Bristol Farms
Farm Fresh
Hornbacher's
Jewel-Osco
Lucky
Shaw's Supermarkets
Star Markets

Selected Services

Accounting
Category management
Consumer and market research
Financial assistance
Insurance
Merchandising assistance
Personnel training
Private-label program
Retail operations counseling
Site selection and purchasing or leasing assistance
Store design and construction
Store equipment
Store management assistance
Store planning
Strategic and business planning

COMPETITORS

A&P
Ahold USA
ALDI
Alex Lee
Arden Group
Associated Wholesale Grocers
Associated Wholesalers
Big Y Foods
Bozzuto's
C & S Wholesale
Costco Wholesale
CVS Caremark
Delhaize America
Di Giorgio
Dierbergs Markets
Giant Eagle
Hannaford Bros.
Jetro Cash & Carry
Krasdale Foods
Kroger
Marsh Supermarkets
McLane
Meijer
Nash-Finch
Piggly Wiggly Midwest
Ralphs Grocery
Rite Aid
Roundy's Supermarkets
Safeway
Schnuck Markets
Sherwood Food
Spartan Stores
Stop & Shop
Vons
Wakefern Food
Walgreen
Wal-Mart
Whole Foods
Winn-Dixie

HISTORICAL FINANCIALS

Company Type: Public

Income Statement

FYE: Last Saturday in February

	REVENUE ($ mil.)	NET INCOME ($ mil.)	NET PROFIT MARGIN	EMPLOYEES
2/09	44,564.0	(2,855.0)	—	178,000
2/08	44,048.0	593.0	1.3%	192,000
2/07	37,406.0	452.0	1.2%	191,400
2/06	19,863.6	206.2	1.0%	52,400
2/05	19,543.2	385.8	2.0%	56,000
Annual Growth	22.9%	—	—	33.5%

2009 Year-End Financials

Debt ratio: 308.7%
Return on equity: —
Cash ($ mil.): 240
Current ratio: 0.92
Long-term debt ($ mil.): 7,968

No. of shares (mil.): 212
Dividends
Yield: 4.4%
Payout: —
Market value ($ mil.): 3,309

Stock History

NYSE: SVU

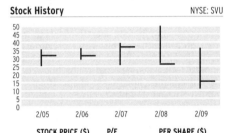

	STOCK PRICE ($) FY Close	P/E High/Low		PER SHARE ($) Earnings	Dividends	Book Value
2/09	15.61	—	—	(13.51)	0.69	12.18
2/08	26.25	18	10	2.76	0.68	28.08
2/07	36.96	17	11	2.32	0.66	25.03
2/06	31.60	25	20	1.46	0.64	12.36
2/05	31.77	13	9	2.71	0.60	11.84
Annual Growth	(16.3%)	—	—	—	3.6%	0.7%

Symantec Corporation

Symantec has never had a problem with insecurity. The company provides security, storage, and systems management software for consumers and businesses. Its applications handle such functions as virus protection, PC maintenance, data backup and recovery, intrusion detection, data loss prevention, spam control, content filtering, and remote server management. Symantec sells its products through a direct sales force, as well as through distributors, resellers, original equipment manufacturers, and systems integrators. The company also provides consulting, managed services, and training. Customers outside the Americas account for about half of sales.

Symantec may be best known for its popular Norton family of consumer security software, but the company generates more of its revenues from enterprise infrastructure management, security and compliance applications, and services.

Symantec has pursued an aggressive acquisition strategy to grow its enterprise business. The company expanded its enterprise security and compliance line when it purchased longtime partner AppStream in 2008. AppStream developed application streaming technology that allows for remote program deployment and

management. The purchase bolstered the company's software-as-a-service offerings, a segment Symantec is targeting for growth.

The company also grew its professional services portfolio with the acquisition of MessageLabs for $695 million in 2008. MessageLabs provided Symantec with a managed service for protecting e-mail and other electronic communications. Symantec also holds a 49% stake in a joint venture with Huawei Technologies that develops security and storage products for telecom service providers.

Consumer products still account for about 30% of Symantec's revenues, and the company continues to develop technologies and make acquisitions that supplement that segment of its business. Symantec augmented its consumer product line with the purchases of PC Tools and SwapDrive in 2008. PC Tools provides privacy and security software for Windows-based PCs. SwapDrive developed file sharing and data backup services.

The company saw its top leadership change in 2009. Chairman John Thompson stepped down as CEO after a ten year stint; Symantec veteran (and former COO) Enrique Salem took over as chief executive.

HISTORY

Artificial intelligence expert Gary Hendrix founded Symantec in 1982. Gordon Eubanks, a former student of the late industry pioneer Gary Kildall and founder of C&E Software, was appointed CEO in 1983 and bought the company in 1984. Realizing that Symantec could not compete against Microsoft and Lotus, Eubanks began buying niche-market software firms. In 1990, a year after going public, Symantec merged with DOS utilities market leader Peter Norton Computing. It bought 13 companies between 1990 and 1994.

Symantec bought Delrina (maker of WinFax) in 1995. Symantec slowed its acquisition pace and concentrated on the growing Internet market. In 1996 it sold Delrina's electronic forms business to JetForm.

Symantec in 1997 filed copyright-infringement charges against Network Associates. The next year a suit was filed against Symantec on behalf of antivirus product users, alleging that it ignored its warranty by charging to fix a year-2000 software glitch.

The company went on another acquisition binge, buying the antivirus operations of both IBM and Intel in 1998 and acquiring rival Quarterdeck in 1999. When Eubanks left that year, IBM exec John Thompson stepped in and became the first African-American CEO of a major software company.

In 2000 Symantec sold its Internet tools division to software developer BEA Systems in a deal valued at about $75 million. It also acquired L-3 Communications' network security operations. Late that year it bought rival network security software maker AXENT Technologies in a $975 million deal.

The company divested its Web access management product line in 2001. Later that year the company acquired Foster-Melliar's enterprise security management division.

In 2002 the company continued its acquisitive ways, purchasing Recourse Technologies, Riptech, and SecurityFocus. The following year the company acquired Nexland, PowerQuest, and SafeWeb. The company purchased infrastructure management software provider ON Technology for about $100 million early in 2004. Later that year Symantec also purchased antispam software provider Brightmail for $370 million.

Symantec announced plans to purchase VERITAS in December 2004. The deal was completed in July of the following year.

It purchased WholeSecurity, Inc. (a maker of security software used to thwart viruses, worms, and other malicious code) and Sygate Technologies (network access control solutions) in 2005. Also in 2005 Symantec acquired VERITAS for about $11 billion. The following year it bought BindView Development Corporation (computer network management and security), IMlogic (enterprise instant messaging), and Relicore (data center change and configuration management). It also acquired UK-based Company-i, a data center services firm focused on the finance sector, as well as data protection software developer Revivio.

In 2007 Symantec acquired IT asset management software maker Altiris for approximately $830 million, and data loss prevention specialist Vontu for $350 million. The company also formed a joint venture with China-based Huawei Technologies in 2007.

Early in 2008 Symantec sold its Application Performance Management (APM) division to Vector Capital.

Thompson stepped down as CEO in 2009; he remained chairman. COO Enrique Salem was promoted to chief executive.

EXECUTIVES

Chairman: John W. Thompson, age 59
President and CEO: Enrique T. Salem, age 43
EVP and CFO: James A. Beer, age 47
EVP and CTO: Mark Bregman
EVP and Chief Human Resources Officer:
Rebecca A. Ranninger, age 50
SVP Finance and Chief Accounting Officer:
George W. Harrington, age 56
EVP, General Counsel, and Secretary: Scott C. Taylor, age 44
EVP Worldwide Sales: William T. (Bill) Robbins
EVP, General Counsel, and Secretary:
Arthur F. Courville
SVP Marketing: Carine Clark
SVP New Business Investments: Arthur W. Wong
SVP Consumer Business: Rowan M. Trollope
President, Symantec Japan and VP Japan Region, Symantec: Susumu Kagayama
Group President, Information Technology and Services:
J. David Thompson
Group President, Consumer Business Unit:
Janice D. Chaffin, age 54
Group President, Enterprise Product Group:
Gregory W. (Greg) Hughes, age 44
Director Corporate Communications:
Genevieve Haldeman
Investor Relations: Helyn Corcos
Auditors: KPMG LLP

LOCATIONS

HQ: Symantec Corporation
20330 Stevens Creek Blvd., Cupertino, CA 95014
Phone: 408-517-8000   **Fax:** 408-517-8186
Web: www.symantec.com

2009 Sales

	$ mil.	% of total
Americas	3,316	54
Europe, Middle East & Africa	1,958	32
Asia/Pacific	876	14
Total	**6,150**	**100**

PRODUCTS/OPERATIONS

2009 Sales

	$ mil.	% of total
Content, subscriptions & maintenance	4,862	79
Licenses	1,288	21
Total	**6,150**	**100**

2009 Sales

	$ mil.	% of total
Storage & server management	2,295	37
Consumer products	1,773	29
Security & compliance	1,611	26
Services	470	8
Other	1	—
Total	**6,150**	**100**

Selected Products

Storage and server management
  Data protection
  Endpoint security
  Storage and server management
Consumer products
  Backup
  Internet security
  PC tuneup
Security and compliance
  Compliance and security management
  Messaging management
Services
  Consulting
  Maintenance and support
  Training

COMPETITORS

Avocent
CA, Inc.
Check Point Software
Cisco Systems
CommVault
Courion
DataCore
EMC
F5 Networks
FalconStor
F-Secure
Hewlett-Packard
IBM
Kaspersky Lab
McAfee
Microsoft
Novell
NTRU
Oracle
Postini
Quest Software
SecureWorks
Smith Micro
Sophos
Sun Microsystems
Trend Micro
VeriSign
VMware
Zone Labs

HISTORICAL FINANCIALS

Company Type: Public

Income Statement

FYE: Friday closest to Mar. 31

	REVENUE ($ mil.)	NET INCOME ($ mil.)	NET PROFIT MARGIN	EMPLOYEES
3/09	6,149.9	(6,728.9)	—	17,400
3/08	5,874.4	463.9	7.9%	17,600
3/07	5,199.4	404.4	7.8%	17,100
3/06	4,143.4	156.9	3.8%	16,000
3/05	2,582.8	536.2	20.8%	6,500
Annual Growth	**24.2%**	**—**	**—**	**27.9%**

2009 Year-End Financials

Debt ratio: 53.2%
Return on equity: —
Cash ($ mil.): 1,793
Current ratio: 0.94
Long-term debt ($ mil.): 2,100
No. of shares (mil.): 815
Dividends
  Yield: 0.0%
  Payout: —
Market value ($ mil.): 12,169

Stock History

NASDAQ (GS): SYMC

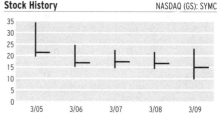

	STOCK PRICE ($) FY Close	P/E High/Low		PER SHARE ($) Earnings	Dividends	Book Value
3/09	14.94	—	—	(8.10)	0.00	4.85
3/08	16.62	41	28	0.52	0.00	13.47
3/07	17.30	54	36	0.41	0.00	14.24
3/06	16.83	163	102	0.15	0.00	16.78
3/05	21.33	46	27	0.74	0.00	4.55
Annual Growth	**(8.5%)**	**—**	**—**	**—**	**—**	**1.6%**

SYSCO Corporation

This company has the menu that restaurants depend on. SYSCO is the #1 foodservice supplier in North America, serving more than 400,000 customers through 180 distribution centers in the US and Canada. Its core broadline distribution business supplies both food and non-food products to restaurants, schools, hotels, health care institutions, and other foodservice customers; its SYGMA Network operation focuses on supplying chain restaurants. SYSCO distributes nationally branded products, as well as its own private-label goods. In addition, SYSCO supplies customers with specialty produce and meat products, and it distributes kitchen equipment and supplies for the hospitality industry.

The wholesale foodservices distribution business is highly fragmented with a patchwork of regional and local suppliers to compete against. On a national scale, meanwhile, SYSCO competes for customers with rivals U.S. Foodservice and Performance Food Group. The company claims to have more than 15% of the market. Customers in the restaurant industry account for more than 60% of sales, with hamburger chain Wendy's accounting for 5% of SYSCO's business.

With the downturn in the economy hurting many dining operators, SYSCO and other suppliers have been forced to cut costs to help offset sales declines. The company has consolidated some of its regional operations and reduced headcount as part of that effort.

Poor economic conditions have also slowed the company's expansion activities, which have traditionally focused on acquiring local distributors that specialize in items such as premium steaks and hotel supplies. Meanwhile, SYSCO made its first bold move towards expansion outside North America in 2009 when it acquired Pallas Foods, a leading broadline supplier serving the foodservice industry in Ireland.

Bill DeLaney was promoted to CEO in 2009, replacing Richard Schnieders who retired from the company. A company veteran, DeLaney had served as CFO at SYSCO since 2007.

HISTORY

SYSCO was founded in 1969 when John Baugh, a Houston wholesale food distributor, formed a national distribution company with the owners of eight other US wholesalers. Joining Baugh's Zero Foods of Houston to form SYSCO were Frost-Pack Distributing (Grand Rapids, Michigan), Louisville Grocery (Louisville, Kentucky), Plantation Foods (Miami), Thomas Foods and its Justrite subsidiary (Cincinnati), Wicker (Dallas), Food Service Company (Houston), Global Frozen Foods (New York), and Texas Wholesale Grocery (Dallas). The company went public in 1970. SYSCO, which derives its name from Systems and Services Company, benefited from Baugh's recognition of the trend toward dining out. Until SYSCO was formed, small, independent operators almost exclusively provided food distribution to restaurants, hotels, and other non-grocers.

The company expanded through internal growth and the acquisition of strong local distributors, benefiting through buyout agreements requiring the seller to continue managing its own operation while earning a portion of the sale price with future profits.

In 1988, when SYSCO was already the largest North American foodservice distributor, it acquired CFS Continental, the third-largest North American food distributor. The CFS acquisition added a large truck fleet and increased the company's penetration along the West Coast of the US and into Canada. Also that year SYSCO purchased Olewine's, a Pennsylvania-based distributor. In 1990 the company bought Oklahoma City-based Scrivner, later renamed SYSCO Food Services of Oklahoma.

In 1992 SYSCO acquired Collins Foodservice (serving the Northwest) and Benjamin Polakoff & Son and Perloff Brothers (both serving the Northeast). In 1994 it bought Woodhaven Foods, a distributor owned by ARA (now ARAMARK), one of the nation's largest cafeteria and concession operators.

In 1997 the company formed an alliance with National Healthcare Logistics to improve distribution to hospitals and integrated health care systems. Baugh, at age 81, retired from his senior chairman post later that year.

The company completed a number of large acquisitions in 1999, including Atlanta-based Buckhead Beef Company, Newport Meat Company of Southern California, and Virginia-based Doughtie's Foods (renamed SYSCO Food Services of Hampton Roads).

SYSCO president Charles Cotros succeeded Bill Lindig as CEO in 2000. That year SYSCO bought Dallas-based produce distributor FreshPoint. It also purchased Canadian foodservice distributor North Douglas Distributors. In 2001 SYSCO acquired specialty meat supplier The Freedman Companies and Guest Supply, which distributes personal care amenities and housekeeping supplies to the lodging industry.

In 2002 SYSCO acquired SERCA Foodservice, which distributes to 80,000 customers in Canada, from Canada's Sobeys. It also completed the acquisition of privately held Abbott Foods, a broadline foodservice distributor located in Columbus, Ohio.

SYSCO's chairman and CEO Charles Cotros retired at the end of 2002, passing the torch to then president and COO Richard Schnieders. In 2003 SYSCO acquired Maine-based Reed Distributors and the specialty meat-cutting division of the Colorado Boxed Beef Company and its Florida broadline foodservice operation, J&B Foodservice.

SYSCO unit SYSCO Food Services of Central Alabama announced in 2004 that it planned to expand its foodservice agreement with Cuba and had signed a letter of intent with the Cuban food import agency Alimport. The unit had generated $500,000 in sales in Cuba since the previous year. Within the same month, though, the SYSCO subsidiary retracted its offer, reporting that the agreement asked for SYSCO to assist "in normalizing trade relations" between the US and Cuba. Subsidiaries of SYSCO Corporation are not permitted to make political or government policy statements.

SYSCO acquired International Food Group, a foodservice distributor to chain restaurants in international markets, in mid-2004. The company added to its specialty meat offerings with the 2005 acquisitions of California-based Facciola Meat Company and Florida-based Royalty Foods. That year it also acquired specialty-food importer Walker Foods, and fresh fruit and vegetable distributor Piranha Produce.

In 2006 SYSCO acquired the foodservice assets of Bunn Capitol, a supplier to restaurants and other customers in Illinois. Founder Baugh died in 2007. Two years later, CEO Schnieders retired and was replaced by Bill DeLaney, a company veteran who had previously served as CFO.

EXECUTIVES

Chairman: Manuel A. (Manny) Fernandez, age 62
Vice Chairman, President, and COO: Kenneth F. Spitler, age 59
CEO, CFO, and Director: William J. (Bill) DeLaney III, age 53
VP and CIO: Twila M. Day, age 43
VP Controller and Chief Accounting Officer: G. Mitchell Elmer, age 49
EVP; EVP Global Sourcing and Supply Chain: Larry G. Pulliam, age 52
EVP Northeast and North Central U.S. Foodservice Operations: Michael W. Green, age 49
EVP South and West U.S. Foodservice Operations: Stephen F. Smith, age 58
SVP Finance and Treasurer: Kirk G. Drummond, age 53
SVP, General Counsel, and Corporate Secretary: Michael C. Nichols, age 56
SVP Supply Chain: William B. Day, age 50
SVP Foodservice Operations (South Region): James E. Lankford
SVP Sourcing: Joseph R. Barton, age 48
SVP Canadian Foodservice Operations: G. Kent Humphries
SVP Sales and Marketing: James D. Hope, age 48
SVP Foodservice Operations (West Region): Scott A. Sonnemaker
SVP Marketing Development: Robert J. Davis, age 50
SVP Foodservice Operations (North Central Region): Charles W. Staes, age 53
SVP Foodservice Operations (Northeast Region): James M. Danahy
VP Corporate Communications: Mark A. Palmer, age 45
VP Investor Relations: Neil A. Russell, age 38
VP Human Resources: Evelyn J. Pulliam, age 46
Auditors: Ernst & Young LLP

LOCATIONS

HQ: SYSCO Corporation
1390 Enclave Pkwy., Houston, TX 77077
Phone: 281-584-1390   **Fax:** 281-584-2721
Web: www.sysco.com

2009 Sales

	$ mil.	% of total
US	33,378.5	91
Canada	3,135.0	8
Other countries	339.8	1
Total	**36,853.3**	**100**

PRODUCTS/OPERATIONS

2009 Sales

	$ mil.	% of total
Broadline	29,234.2	78
SYGMA	4,839.0	13
Other	3,242.1	9
Adjustments	(462.0)	—
Total	**36,853.3**	**100**

2009 Sales

	$ mil.	% of total
Canned & dry products	7,091.4	19
Fresh & frozen meats	6,394.4	17
Frozen fruits, vegetables, bakery & other	5,122.4	14
Dairy products	3,750.7	10
Poultry	3,709.6	10
Fresh produce	3,017.6	8
Paper & disposables	2,911.0	8
Seafood	1,740.3	5
Beverage products	1,322.3	4
Janitorial products	940.1	3
Equipment & smallwares	661.3	2
Medical supplies	192.8	—
Total	**36,853.3**	**100**

2009 Sales

	% of total
Restaurants	62
Hospitals & nursing homes	11
Hotels & motels	6
Schools & colleges	5
Other	16
Total	**100**

Selected Operations

Broadline foodservice distribution
SYGMA (chain restaurant supply)
Other
    Custom meats
    Lodging industry products
    Specialty produce

COMPETITORS

Edward Don	McLane Foodservice
Foodbuy	Meadowbrook Meat
Golden State Foods	Performance Food
Gordon Food Service	Services Group of America
Keystone Foods	UniPro Foodservice
MAINES	U.S. Foodservice

HISTORICAL FINANCIALS

Company Type: Public

Income Statement   FYE: Saturday nearest June 30

	REVENUE ($ mil.)	NET INCOME ($ mil.)	NET PROFIT MARGIN	EMPLOYEES
6/09	36,853.3	1,055.9	2.9%	47,000
6/08	37,522.1	1,106.2	2.9%	50,000
6/07	35,042.1	1,001.1	2.9%	50,900
6/06	32,628.4	846.0	2.6%	49,600
6/05	30,281.9	961.5	3.2%	47,500
Annual Growth	**5.0%**	**2.4%**	**—**	**(0.3%)**

2009 Year-End Financials

Debt ratio: 71.5%   No. of shares (mil.): 591
Return on equity: 30.8%   Dividends
Cash ($ mil.): 1,087   Yield: 4.2%
Current ratio: 1.67   Payout: 53.1%
Long-term debt ($ mil.): 2,467   Market value ($ mil.): 13,286

Stock History

NYSE: SYY

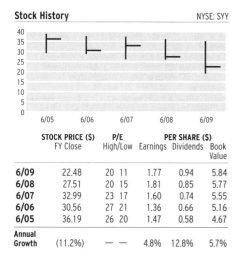

6/05	6/06	6/07	6/08	6/09

	STOCK PRICE ($) FY Close	P/E High/Low		PER SHARE ($) Earnings	Dividends	Book Value
6/09	22.48	20	11	1.77	0.94	5.84
6/08	27.51	20	15	1.81	0.85	5.77
6/07	32.99	23	17	1.60	0.74	5.55
6/06	30.56	27	21	1.36	0.66	5.16
6/05	36.19	26	20	1.47	0.58	4.67
Annual Growth	(11.2%)	—	—	4.8%	12.8%	5.7%

T. Rowe Price Group

T. Rowe Price Group administers an eponymous family of mutual funds, offering a variety of investment styles, as well as asset management advisory services (including retirement plan advice for individuals) and discount brokerage. Other services include corporate retirement plan management and transfer agency and shareholder services. T. Rowe Price manages more than 90 funds in all. Traditionally oriented toward growth investing, the funds offer products in many risk and taxation profiles, including small-, mid-, and large-cap stock funds; money market funds; and bond funds, both taxable and nontaxable.

Almost two-thirds of the company's approximately $400 billion of assets under management are held in retirement plans and variable annuities. Most of the firm's clients — individual and institutional investors, retirement plans, third-party distributors — are in the US, but T. Rowe Price Group also has offices in Asia, Europe, and South America and serves clients in some 30 countries. It is pursuing growth in India and China by introducing new products and services there.

HISTORY

Thomas Rowe Price Jr. left a brokerage job at Mackubin, Goodrich & Co. to found his own investment advisory firm in 1937. He pushed investing for the long haul, choosing stocks of promising young companies (the firm invested in IBM in 1950). Price's company was incorporated in 1947 and was employee-owned until it went public in 1986.

The firm moved into international investments in 1979. T. Rowe Price was primarily an institutional pension fund manager until the 1980s. Creativity lagged as fund managers made investments from a list selected by the research department, and the Growth Stock Fund underperformed the S&P 500. In 1987 the firm opened its funds to individual investors.

Thereafter it introduced a slew of new funds, slicing and dicing the market to appeal to the broadest possible industry and risk investment profiles, including offerings in emerging market stocks and health and science stocks. In 1996 longtime president and CEO George Collins retired, and was succeeded by then-CFO George Roche, who is now also the company's chairman.

In the late 1990s, however, the company's value investing strategy brought lagging fund results, and a stagnant corporate stock price. Nevertheless, cash continued to pour into the company's funds until the collapse of Russian and Asian markets in 1998. US investors got the willies, slowing asset flows to T. Rowe Price and other mutual fund managers.

In response, Roche began moving the company into overseas asset management markets. In 1999 the firm joined with Sumitomo Bank (now part of Sumitomo Mitsui Financial Group) and Daiwa Securities to form asset manager Daiwa SB Investments in Japan. It also targeted Europe, where the growth of private retirement plans opened up new opportunities. Nevertheless, the company missed out on many of the explosive returns of the high-tech boom.

In 2000, however, the high-tech bubble burst, seeming to vindicate T. Rowe Price's conservative approach. That year the company bought out the remaining 50% of its Rowe Price-Fleming International asset management joint venture with Robert Fleming (which is now part of JPMorgan Chase). Also that year the company reorganized itself into holding company T. Rowe Price Group. The company's UK subsidiary received regulatory approval to expand to the European continent in 2001.

EXECUTIVES

Chairman and Chief Investment Officer:
Brian C. Rogers, age 53, $6,529,027 total compensation
Vice Chairman and President, T. Rowe Price Investment Services: Edward C. Bernard, age 53, $5,475,120 total compensation
President, CEO, and Director: James A. C. Kennedy, age 55, $5,568,688 total compensation
VP and CFO: Kenneth V. Moreland, age 52, $1,499,396 total compensation
VP and Director of Fixed Income: Mary J. Miller, age 53
VP Legal Division: Henry H. Hopkins, age 66
VP and Treasurer: Joseph P. Croteau, age 54
VP and Director of Equities and Global Equity Research: William J. Stromberg, age 48, $5,188,803 total compensation
VP; Manager, Growth Stock Fund:
P. Robert (Rob) Bartolo
President, T. Rowe Price International:
Christopher D. Alderson, age 46
President, T. Rowe Price Retirement Plan Services:
Cynthia L. Egan
Senior Portfolio Specialist, Fixed Income Division:
Steven C. Huber, age 50
Secretary: Barbara A. Van Horn
Auditors: KPMG LLP

LOCATIONS

HQ: T. Rowe Price Group, Inc.
100 E. Pratt St., Baltimore, MD 21202
Phone: 410-345-2000   **Fax:** 410-345-2394
Web: www.troweprice.com

PRODUCTS/OPERATIONS

2008 Sales

	$ mil.	% of total
Investment advisory fees	1,761.0	83
Administrative fees	353.9	17
Savings bank subsidiary	6.4	—
Adjustments	(5.0)	—
Total	**2,116.3**	**100**

COMPETITORS

AllianceBernstein
American Century
AXA Financial
BlackRock
Capital Group
Charles Schwab
FAF Advisors
FMR
Franklin Resources
Invesco
Janus Capital
Legg Mason
MFS
Morgan Stanley
Northwestern Mutual
Old Mutual (US)
Prudential
Putnam
Raymond James Financial
UBS Financial Services
USAA
Van Kampen Investments
The Vanguard Group

HISTORICAL FINANCIALS

Company Type: Public

Income Statement

FYE: December 31

	ASSETS ($ mil.)	NET INCOME ($ mil.)	INCOME AS % OF ASSETS	EMPLOYEES
12/08	2,819.4	490.8	17.4%	5,385
12/07	3,177.3	670.6	21.1%	5,081
12/06	2,765.3	529.6	19.2%	4,605
12/05	2,310.5	430.9	18.6%	4,372
12/04	1,928.8	337.3	17.5%	4,139
Annual Growth	10.0%	9.8%	—	6.8%

2008 Year-End Financials

Equity as % of assets: 88.3%
Return on assets: 16.4%
Return on equity: 18.6%
Long-term debt ($ mil.): —
No. of shares (mil.): 256
Dividends
  Yield: 2.7%
  Payout: 52.7%
Market value ($ mil.): 9,077
Sales ($ mil.): 2,116

Stock History

NASDAQ (GS): TROW

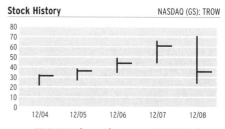

12/04	12/05	12/06	12/07	12/08

	STOCK PRICE ($) FY Close	P/E High/Low		PER SHARE ($) Earnings	Dividends	Book Value
12/08	35.44	39	13	1.82	0.96	9.72
12/07	60.88	27	19	2.40	0.75	10.84
12/06	43.77	26	18	1.90	0.59	9.48
12/05	36.01	24	17	1.58	0.49	7.95
12/04	31.10	25	17	1.25	0.40	6.63
Annual Growth	3.3%	—	—	9.8%	24.5%	10.0%

Target Corporation

Purveyor of all that is cheap, yet chic, fast-growing Target Corporation has bulked up by slimming down. The nation's #2 discount chain (behind Wal-Mart) now operates about 1,700 Target and SuperTarget stores in 48 states, as well as an online business called Target.com. Target and its larger grocery-carrying incarnation, SuperTarget, have carved out a niche by offering more upscale, fashion-forward merchandise than rivals Wal-Mart and Kmart. After years of struggling to turn around its Marshall Field's and Mervyns department stores divisions, the discounter sold them both in 2004.

Historically a stellar performer in the retail arena, Target has missed the bulls eye of late, posting slower sales and earnings growth than investors have come to expect. Indeed, sales of apparel and home furnishings and decor (historically strong suits for Target) are down, while electronics, entertainment, sporting goods and toys are flat. To capitalize on the new frugality, Target is taking a page from archrival Wal-Mart's playbook and opening new formats that devote more space to food, especially its house brands Archer Farms and Market Pantry, and other household basics.

Until its recent reversal, Target had successfully distinguished itself from other discounters by employing a strategy that relied on exclusive private-label offerings from big name designers. Target's most high-profile partnership was with fashion designer Isaac Mizrahi, who joined the discounter's stable of in-house talent in mid-2003. Mizrahi rang up as much as $300 million each year for Target and helped the chain become a destination for cheap-chic apparel. The partnership ended at the end of 2008 when Mizrahi moved to Liz Claiborne. Other designers with exclusive lines at Target include Amy Coe (children's bedding and accessories), Liz Lange (maternity), Mossimo (junior fashions), and architect Michael Graves (housewares).

Despite its sagging fortunes, the company plans to continue opening stores over the next several years, bringing Target's store count to about 2,000 stores by 2011. Target is testing two new store prototypes designed to be larger and "greener" than existing Target stores. Both formats devote more space to food and electronics. The company plans to roll out more than 100 of the newly-designed stores beginning in 2009.

In May 2008 Bob Ulrich, who had been chairman and CEO since 1994, handed his CEO title to president Gregg Steinhafel. Steinhafel, who joined the retailer in 1979 and worked his way up the ranks, added the chairman's title in early 2009 following Ulrich's retirement from Target's board of directors. Soon after ascending to the chairman's seat, Steinhafel successfully fended off a vigorous and expensive proxy contest waged by the activist investor William Ackman of Pershing Square Capital Management. Ackman, whose hedge fund — at the time — owned more than $1 billion in Target stock, was seeking representation on the company's board, including a spot for himself and several other directors. However, shareholders elected Target's slate of incumbent directors at the annual meeting in May 2009. In August Pershing Square reduced its stake in Target to just about 4% from nearly 8%.

HISTORY

The panic of 1873 left Joseph Hudson bankrupt. After he paid his debts at 60 cents on the dollar, he saved enough to open a men's clothing store in Detroit in 1881. Among his innovations were merchandise-return privileges and price marking in place of bargaining. By 1891 Hudson's was the largest retailer of men's clothing in the US. Hudson repaid his creditors from 1873 in full, with interest. When Hudson died in 1912, four nephews expanded the business.

Former banker George Dayton established a dry-goods store in 1902 in Minneapolis. Like Hudson, he offered return privileges and liberal credit. His store grew to a 12-story, full-line department store.

After WWII both companies saw that the future lay in the suburbs. In 1954 Hudson's built Northland in Detroit, then the largest US shopping center. Dayton's built the world's first fully enclosed shopping mall in Edina, a Minneapolis suburb, in 1956. In 1962 Dayton's opened its first discount store in Roseville (naming the store Target to distinguish the discounter from its higher-end department stores).

Dayton's went public in 1966, the same year it began the B. Dalton bookstore chain. Three years later it merged with the family-owned Hudson's, forming Dayton Hudson. Dayton Hudson purchased more malls and invested in such specialty areas as consumer electronics and hard goods. Target had 24 stores by 1970.

The Target chain became the company's top moneymaker in 1977. The next year Dayton Hudson bought California-based Mervyn's (now Mervyns). In the late 1970s and 1980s, it sold nine regional malls and several other businesses, including the 800-store B. Dalton chain to Barnes & Noble. The Target stores division purchased Indianapolis-based Ayr-Way (1980) and Southern California-based Fedmart stores (1983). In the late 1980s Dayton Hudson took Target to Los Angeles and the Northwest. Robert Ulrich, who began with the company as a merchandise trainee in 1967, became president and CEO of the Target stores division in 1987 and chairman and CEO of Dayton Hudson in 1994.

Dayton Hudson opened the first Target Greatland store in 1990. By this time it had 420 Target stores. Also that year Dayton Hudson bought the Marshall Field's chain of 24 department stores from B.A.T Industries. Marshall Field's began as a dry-goods business that Marshall Field bought in 1865 and subsequently built into Chicago's premier upscale retailer.

In 2000 Dayton Hudson renamed itself Target Corporation. The year 2004 was a time of divestments for Target. In January the discounter announced it was exiting the catalog business. In July Target sold its Marshall Field's business to The May Department Stores Co. for about $3.2 billion in cash. In September Target completed the sale of 257 Mervyns stores in 13 states to an investment group that includes Cerberus Capital Management, Lubert-Adler/Klaff and Partners, and Sun Capital Partners, as well as its Mervyns credit card receivables to GE Consumer Finance for a combined sum of approximately $1.65 billion in cash.

In the largest mass opening in Target's history, the retailer opened 60 new stores on October 9.

In May 2008 Target closed on the sale of a 47% stake in its credit-card receivable to JPMorgan Chase for $3.6 billion.

EXECUTIVES

Chairman, President, and CEO: Gregg W. Steinhafel, age 53
EVP and CFO: Douglas A. Scovanner, age 53
SVP Technology Services and CIO: Beth M Jacob
EVP and Chief Marketing Officer: Michael R. Francis, age 46
EVP Property Development: John D. Griffith, age 47
EVP Merchandising: Kathryn A. (Kathee) Tesija, age 46
EVP Human Resources: Jodeen A. Kozlak, age 45
EVP Stores: Troy H. Risch, age 41
EVP Target Sourcing Services, Global Operations: Ellen Tansey
SVP Communications: Susan D. Kahn
EVP, General Counsel, and Corporate Secretary: Timothy R. Baer, age 48
SVP Finance: Jane P. Windmeier
SVP Distribution: Mitchell L. (Mitch) Stover
SVP Marketing: Karen Gershman
President, Community Relations and Target Foundation: Laysha Ward, age 41
President, Target Financial Services: Terrence J. Scully, age 56
President, Target Sourcing Services: Stacia J. Anderson
President and Managing Director, Target India: Lalit Ahuja
President, Target.com: Steve Eastman
Auditors: Ernst & Young LLP

LOCATIONS

HQ: Target Corporation
1000 Nicollet Mall, Minneapolis, MN 55403
Phone: 612-304-6073   **Fax:** 612-696-5400
Web: www.target.com

2009 Locations

	No.
California	236
Texas	143
Florida	122
Illinois	85
Minnesota	73
Ohio	63
New York	62
Michigan	60
Virginia	55
Georgia	54
Pennsylvania	51
North Carolina	47
Arizona	48
Colorado	41
New Jersey	42
Washington	35
Wisconsin	35
Missouri	35
Indiana	33
Maryland	36
Massachusetts	31
Tennessee	31
Iowa	21
Alabama	19
Kansas	19
Oregon	18
South Carolina	18
Connecticut	19
Nevada	16
Nebraska	14
Louisiana	14
Kentucky	12
Oklahoma	12
Utah	11
New Mexico	9
New Hampshire	8
Montana	7
Arkansas	7
Other states	36
Total	**1,682**

PRODUCTS/OPERATIONS

2009 Sales

	% of total
Consumables & commodities	37
Electronics, entertainment, sporting goods & toys	22
Home furnishings & décor	21
Apparel & accessories	20
Total	**100**

2009 Stores

	No.
Target	1,443
SuperTarget	239
Total	**1,682**

Selected Designer Private Labels

Amy Coe (children's bedding and accessories)
Liz Lange (maternity)
Michael Graves Design (housewares)
Mossimo (junior fashions)
Sonia Kashuk (cosmetics and fragrances)
Todd Oldham (bedding and furniture)

Selected Private Labels

Archer Farms (food)
Cherokee (apparel)
Choxie (candy)
Furio (housewares)
Honors (apparel)
In Due Time (maternity wear)
Market Pantry
Merona (apparel)
Nick & Nora (apparel)
Playwonder (toys)
Utility (apparel)
Xhilaration (apparel)

Store Formats

SuperTarget (groceries and general merchandise)
Target (upscale discount stores)

COMPETITORS

Bed Bath & Beyond
Best Buy
Burnes Home Accents
Container Store
Costco Wholesale
CVS Caremark
Dillard's
Dollar General
eBay
Euromarket Designs
Foot Locker
The Gap
Home Depot
J. C. Penney Company
Kmart
Kohl's
Kroger
Limited Brands
Macy's
PETCO
Ross Stores
Sears
SUPERVALU
TJX Companies
Toys "R" Us
Walgreen
Wal-Mart
Williams-Sonoma

HISTORICAL FINANCIALS

Company Type: Public

Income Statement

FYE: Saturday nearest January 31

	REVENUE ($ mil.)	NET INCOME ($ mil.)	NET PROFIT MARGIN	EMPLOYEES
1/09	64,948.0	2,214.0	3.4%	351,000
1/08	63,367.0	2,849.0	4.5%	366,000
1/07	59,490.0	2,787.0	4.7%	352,000
1/06	52,620.0	2,408.0	4.6%	338,000
1/05	46,839.0	3,198.0	6.8%	292,000
Annual Growth	**8.5%**	**(8.8%)**	**—**	**4.7%**

2009 Year-End Financials

Debt ratio: 127.6%
Return on equity: 15.3%
Cash ($ mil.): 864
Current ratio: 1.66
Long-term debt ($ mil.): 17,490
No. of shares (mil.): 752
Dividends
  Yield: 1.4%
  Payout: 15.4%
Market value ($ mil.): 23,458

Stock History

NYSE: TGT

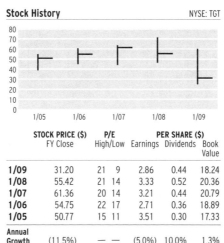

	STOCK PRICE ($) FY Close	P/E High/Low	PER SHARE ($) Earnings	Dividends	Book Value
1/09	31.20	21 9	2.86	0.44	18.24
1/08	55.42	21 14	3.33	0.52	20.36
1/07	61.36	20 14	3.21	0.44	20.79
1/06	54.75	22 17	2.71	0.36	18.89
1/05	50.77	15 11	3.51	0.30	17.33
Annual Growth	**(11.5%)**	**— —**	**(5.0%)**	**10.0%**	**1.3%**

TD Ameritrade

If your stock makes a big move while you're stuck in traffic, don't worry — TD AMERITRADE lets you buy and sell by phone, fax, and the Internet. Through subsidiaries, the firm serves active traders, investment advisors, and long-term investors by providing a variety of brokerage services, ranging from traditional discount trading to advanced products for the more sophisticated trader. Subsidiary TD AMERITRADE Clearing provides clearing and execution services. Products available on TD AMERITRADE's trading platform include common and preferred US stock, fixed income assets, ETFs, mutual funds, and option trades. The company also operates a retail network of approximately 100 branches.

In 2009 TD AMERITRADE acquired online brokerage thinkorswim Group, which specializes in options trading and investor education, for some $600 million in cash and stock.

The company acquired most of the business and assets of Fiserv ISS, a trustee of nearly 300,000 retirement and custodial accounts, in 2008. The $225 million transaction added some $25 billion in client assets and $10 billion in

plans administered by third-party administrators. It also bulked up its TD AMERITRADE Institutional business, which has more than $100 billion in assets under management.

TD AMERITRADE's expanded account base has helped it keep the pressure on competitors E*TRADE and Charles Schwab. The company has remained focused on its core business of online trading, supplementing its growth with products such as mutual funds and money market accounts, as well as multimillion-dollar brand-building advertising campaigns.

E*TRADE offered to buy the company, then named Ameritrade, for more than $6 billion in mid-2005, but the company said that it wasn't for sale. In 2006, Ameritrade bought the US operations of TD Waterhouse and added the "TD" to its name, as well as some 100 branch locations.

As part of Ameritrade's deal to acquire TD Waterhouse's US business, Canada-based TD Bank assumed a 40% stake in the firm. Money market sweep arrangements with TD Bank account for about one-third of TD AMERITRADE's sales.

In 2009 TD Bank increased its ownership stake to 45% by buying shares from Ameritrade founder Joe Ricketts (who retired in 2008) and his family, who now own 17% of the company. Ricketts' son Tom will use proceeds of the sale to help fund his planned acquisition of the Chicago Cubs from the Tribune Company.

Joe Moglia took over as chairman upon Ricketts' retirement; Fred Tomczyk became CEO.

HISTORY

Ameritrade began in 1971 as investment bank TransTerra. Dean Witter veteran Joe Ricketts transformed the firm into a discount broker in 1975. TransTerra formed Televest/Bancvest (now AmeriVest) in 1982 and Ameritrade Clearing (now Advanced Clearing) in 1983.

In 1988 the company became the first to offer Touch-Tone telephone trading, and added Internet trading in 1994. TransTerra formed Ceres Securities, a deep-discount brokerage service that added research to its services when it bought brokerage firms K. Aufhauser and All American in 1995. The company formed its eBroker all-Internet brokerage service in 1996, and became Ameritrade late that year.

In 1997 the company went public and combined its service-oriented subsidiaries. It also formed an alliance that directed users of America Online's investor site to Ameritrade's Web sites. The company grew rapidly in the late 1990s, but like most technology-based companies, suffered the impact of the subsequent tech wreck and the struggling economy.

Later, TD AMERITRADE led a wave of consolidation within the electronic brokerage industry. It purchased rivals National Discount Brokers and Datek in 2001 and 2002, but didn't stop there. In 2003 the company acquired the accounts of Mydiscountbroker.com from SWS Group, and the retail accounts of BrokerageAmerica, which together helped push the company's account base past the 3 million mark. It gained another 145,000 accounts from brokerage firms Bidwell & Company and JB Oxford Holdings in 2004 and 2005.

EXECUTIVES

Chairman: Joseph H. (Joe) Moglia, age 59
Vice Chairman: W. Edmund (Ed) Clark, age 61
President, CEO, and Director:
Fredric J. (Fred) Tomczyk, age 53
EVP and COO: David M. Kelley, age 49
EVP and CFO: William J. (Bill) Gerber, age 51
Chief Human Resources Officer: Karen Ganzlin
SVP and Chief Marketing Officer: Laurine M. Garrity, age 47
EVP, General Counsel, and Secretary:
Ellen L.S. Koplow, age 49
EVP Product and Marketing: Peter Sidebottom
VP Business Development: Wayne Ferbert
President, Retail Distribution: John B. Bunch
President, TD AMERITRADE Institutional:
Tom Bradley
Managing Director, Finance and Treasurer:
Michael D. Chochon, age 40
Manager Corporate Communications: Kim Hillyer
Auditors: Ernst & Young LLP

LOCATIONS

HQ: TD AMERITRADE Holding Corporation
4211 S. 102nd St., Omaha, NE 68127
Phone: 402-331-7856   **Fax:** 402-597-7789
Web: www.amtd.com

PRODUCTS/OPERATIONS

2008 Gross Revenues

	$ mil.	% of total
Commissions & transaction fees	1,017.5	36
Interest	799.2	29
Money market deposit account fees	628.7	23
Investment product fees	309.4	11
Other	32.2	1
Total	**2,787.0**	**100**

Selected Subsidiaries

Ameritrade Advisory Services, LLC
Ameritrade International Company, Inc. (Cayman Islands)
Amerivest Investment Management, LLC
Financial Passport, Inc.
National Investors Service Corp.
Nebraska Hudson Company, Inc.
TD AMERITRADE Clearing, Inc.
TD AMERITRADE, Inc.
TD AMERITRADE IP Company, Inc.
TD AMERITRADE Online Holdings Corp.
TD AMERITRADE Services Company, Inc. (aka Ameritrade Support Services Corporation)
TD Waterhouse Canadian Call Center, Inc.
TD Waterhouse Capital Markets, Inc.
TenBagger, Inc.
ThinkTech, Inc. (aka T2 Technology Support, Inc.)
TradeBridge, Inc.

COMPETITORS

Bank of America
Charles Schwab
Citigroup Global Markets
E*TRADE Financial
Edward Jones
FMR
JPMorgan Chase
Morgan Stanley
Scottrade
ShareBuilder
The Vanguard Group

HISTORICAL FINANCIALS

Company Type: Public

Income Statement

FYE: Friday nearest September 30

	REVENUE ($ mil.)	NET INCOME ($ mil.)	NET PROFIT MARGIN	EMPLOYEES
9/08	550.5	803.9	146.0%	4,660
9/07	2,176.9	645.9	29.7%	3,882
9/06	1,803.5	526.8	29.2%	3,947
9/05	1,003.2	339.8	33.9%	2,052
9/04	880.1	272.3	30.9%	1,961
Annual Growth	**(11.1%)**	**31.1%**	**—**	**24.2%**

2008 Year-End Financials

Debt ratio: 49.4%
Return on equity: 31.6%
Cash ($ mil.): 934
Current ratio: —
Long-term debt ($ mil.): 1,445
No. of shares (mil.): 586
Dividends
Yield: 0.0%
Payout: —
Market value ($ mil.): 9,774

Stock History

NASDAQ (GS): AMTD

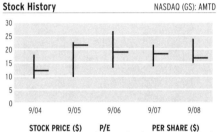

	STOCK PRICE ($) FY Close	P/E High/Low		PER SHARE ($) Earnings	Dividends	Book Value
9/08	16.67	18	11	1.33	0.00	4.99
9/07	18.22	20	13	1.06	0.00	3.68
9/06	18.85	28	14	0.95	0.00	2.95
9/05	21.47	27	12	0.82	0.00	2.59
9/04	12.01	28	15	0.64	0.00	2.07
Annual Growth	**8.5%**	**—**	**—**	**20.1%**	**—**	**24.7%**

Tech Data Corporation

Tech Data is 100% committed to IT products distribution. The world's #2 distributor of computer products (behind Ingram Micro), Tech Data provides more than 100,000 different items to more than 100,000 resellers in 100 countries. Its catalog of products includes computer components (disk drives, keyboards, and video cards), networking equipment (routers and bridges), peripherals (printers, modems, and monitors), systems (PCs and servers), and software. Tech Data also provides technical support, configuration, integration, financing, electronic data interchange (EDI), and other logistic and product fulfillment services.

Tech Data distributes products from such vendors as Hewlett-Packard (which accounts for nearly 30% of sales), Apple, Cisco Systems, IBM, Microsoft, and Sony.

As manufacturers have promoted more direct relationships with their customers, the need for middlemen in the industry has dwindled and many tech product distributors have gone under. Tech Data has been spared this fate due to its size and scope, but it continually looks to cut costs in order to survive in a business characterized by thin margins. The company has also expanded its service offerings, which range

from pre- and post-sale technical support to customized shipping documents and electronic commerce integration.

More than half of Tech Data's revenues are generated in Europe. The company increased its presence in Northern Europe with the purchase of Swedish technology distributor Scribona Nordic for $78 million in 2008.

HISTORY

Tech Data grew out of an electronics distribution business founded by Edward Raymund, a University of Southern California graduate who started out as a representative for electronics manufacturers. By the early 1960s he had established an industrial electronics distribution business in Florida. In 1974 he incorporated that business as Tech Data.

In 1981 Raymund's 25-year-old son, Steven, who had earned master's degrees in economics and international politics from Georgetown University's School of Foreign Service, joined Tech Data on a temporary basis to work on the company's catalog. At that time Tech Data sold diskettes and other computer supplies to local companies and had about $2 million in sales.

Steven Raymund's favored status at the company angered a group of managers. Shortly after he arrived at Tech Data, they copied the company's client list and walked out. The defection nearly sank Tech Data, but Steven Raymund stayed on when his father handed him two-thirds of the company.

With the PC industry beginning to take off, Steven Raymund positioned Tech Data as a middleman between computer and peripheral manufacturers and resellers. Steven was named COO in 1984. He became CEO in 1986, the year the company went public.

In 1990 fast growth strained Tech Data's resources, and earnings slumped. The company cut inventory and management costs. The following year Steven Raymund became chairman when his father retired.

Tech Data began to distribute software in 1992, and a year later the company signed up Microsoft and inked a distribution deal for IBM computer systems.

In 1994 Tech Data purchased U.S. Software Resource, a California-based distributor of more than 500 business and entertainment software titles, thereby increasing its software list and gaining high-profile publishers such as Borland and Corel as suppliers. Also that year Tech Data began a global expansion when it bought France's largest distributor of wholesale computer products, Softmart International.

Tech Data won US distribution rights for Apple subsidiary Claris' (now named FileMaker) software line in 1995. The company one-upped its rivals that year when, through a deal with MCI (now part of WorldCom), it became the first distributor to resell telephone line service employing advanced data transmission technologies. Tech Data resellers packaged line services with their computer networks; the resellers and Tech Data earned monthly usage fees on the services.

Tech Data in 1998 bought VIAG AG's majority stake in European distributor Computer 2000 for about $390 million. (To avoid geographic overlap, the company sold its controlling stake in Germany-based Macrotron, acquired in 1997, to rival Ingram Micro for $100 million.) Also in 1998 Tech Data began direct assembly and shipping at its distribution centers. In 1999 the company inked an estimated $2 billion outsourcing deal

In 2000, amid poor results, Tenneco Automotive announced that it would cut 700 jobs (about 16% of its workforce). In 2001 the company announced that more than 400 more jobs would be eliminated. Also in 2001 Tenneco Automotive acquired a Polish maker of shock absorbers.

To further cut costs and pay down debt incurred by the spin-off of Pactiv, in 2002 Tenneco Automotive announced 900 more job cuts as well as the closure of eight plants in North America and Europe.

In keeping with its strategy to transfer some manufacturing operations to low-labor-cost regions, Tenneco Automotive opened a new plant in Togliatti, Russia, in 2003. The plant was intended to provide exhaust components for the Chevrolet Niva, a car built by a joint venture between GM and Russian carmaker AvtoVAZ.

Tenneco Automotive in 2004 said it would spend several million dollars to build an engineering center to provide support for the company's five joint ventures in China.

EXECUTIVES

Chairman and CEO: Gregg M. Sherrill, age 55, $3,986,838 total compensation
EVP and CFO: Kenneth R. Trammell, age 48, $1,199,349 total compensation
SVP and CTO: Timothy E. (Tim) Jackson, age 51, $1,005,924 total compensation
VP and CIO: H. William Haser, age 47
EVP and Director; President, International: Hari N. Nair, age 48, $1,553,431 total compensation
EVP North America: Neal A. Yanos, age 47, $859,564 total compensation
EVP, General Counsel, and Corporate Secretary: David A. Wardell, age 54
SVP Global Administration: Richard P. Schneider, age 61
SVP and General Manager, North American Original Equipment Emission Control Group: Brett J. Bauer, age 53
VP and Controller: Paul D. Novas, age 50
VP Global Communications: James K. Spangler
VP Global Emissions Control Engineering: Herman Weltens
VP Tax and Treasurer: John E. Kunz
VP Global Supply Chain Management and Manufacturing: Michael J. (Mike) Charlton, age 50
Director Human Resources: Barbara Kluth
Director Corporate Communications: Jane Ostrander
Director Business Development: Gregg J. DeSilvio
Managing Director China: Patrick Guo
Auditors: Deloitte & Touche LLP

LOCATIONS

HQ: Tenneco Inc.
500 North Field Dr., Lake Forest, IL 60045
Phone: 847-482-5000   **Fax:** 847-482-5940
Web: www.tenneco.com

2008 Sales

	$ mil.	% of total
North America	2,641	43
Europe, South America & India	2,983	48
Asia/Pacific	543	9
Adjustments	(251)	—
Total	**5,916**	**100**

PRODUCTS/OPERATIONS

2008 Sales

	$ mil.	% of total
Emission-control systems & products		
OEM	3,620	61
Aftermarket	358	6
Ride-control systems & products		
OEM	1,177	20
Aftermarket	761	13
Total	**5,916**	**100**

Selected Brands and Products

Elastomers (Clevite)
  Engine and body mounts
  Exhaust isolators
  Leaf and coil springs
  Spring seats
  Suspension, control arm, link and stabilizer bar bushings
Emission-control systems (DNX, DynoMax, Fonos, Gillet, Thrush, and Walker)
  Catalytic converters
  Center and rear mufflers
  Diesel particulate filters
  Downpipes and tailpipes
  Fabricated manifolds
  Heat exchangers
  Mufflers
Ride-control systems (DNX, Fric-Rot, Kinetic, Monroe, and Rancho)
  Shock absorbers
  Struts
  Suspensions

COMPETITORS

Arvin Sango
ArvinMeritor
Benteler Automotive
Cooper-Standard Automotive
Edelbrock
Faurecia
Faurecia Exhaust Systems
Kolbenschmidt Pierburg
Letts Industries
Metaldyne
Wescast Industries
ZF Group NAO

HISTORICAL FINANCIALS

Company Type: Public

Income Statement

FYE: December 31

	REVENUE ($ mil.)	NET INCOME ($ mil.)	NET PROFIT MARGIN	EMPLOYEES
12/08	5,916.0	(415.0)	—	21,000
12/07	6,184.0	(5.0)	—	21,000
12/06	4,685.0	51.0	1.1%	19,000
12/05	4,441.0	58.0	1.3%	19,000
12/04	4,213.0	13.0	0.3%	18,400
Annual Growth	**8.9%**	**—**	**—**	**3.4%**

2008 Year-End Financials

Debt ratio: —
Return on equity: —
Cash ($ mil.): 126
Current ratio: 1.16
Long-term debt ($ mil.): 1,402

No. of shares (mil.): 47
Dividends
  Yield: 0.0%
  Payout: —
Market value ($ mil.): 139

Stock History

NYSE: TEN

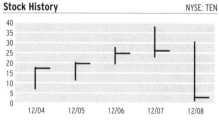

	STOCK PRICE ($) FY Close	P/E High/Low		PER SHARE ($) Earnings	Dividends	Book Value
12/08	2.95	—	—	(8.95)	0.00	(5.31)
12/07	26.07	—	—	(0.11)	0.00	8.46
12/06	24.72	25	18	1.10	0.00	4.67
12/05	19.61	16	9	1.29	0.00	2.73
12/04	17.24	56	23	0.31	0.00	3.17
Annual Growth	**(35.7%)**	—	—	—	—	—

Tennessee Valley Authority

The Tennessee Valley Authority (TVA) may not be an expert on Tennessee attractions like Dollywood and the Grand Ole Opry, but it is an authority on power generation. TVA is the largest publicly owned power producer in the US, with more than 35,000 MW of generating capacity. Its facilities include 11 fossil-powered plants, 29 hydroelectric dams, three nuclear plants, and six combustion turbine plants. The federal corporation transmits electricity to about 160 local distribution utilities, which in turn serve some nine million consumers, as well as industrial facilities and government agencies, in most of Tennessee and neighboring parts of Alabama, Georgia, Kentucky, Mississippi, North Carolina, and Virginia.

The TVA also manages the Tennessee River system for flood control and navigation.

Most of TVA's power comes from traditional generation sources, but the company is also exploring alternative energy technologies. It has developed nearly 20 solar, wind, and methane gas facilities. Government appropriations for the authority ceased in 1999; since that time the company has funded its activities almost entirely from the sale of electricity. The TVA is, however, exempt from federal and state income taxes. Nonetheless, it is working on reducing a $20 billion-plus debt load.

In 2008 a holding pond at TVA's coal-burning Kingston Fossil Plant failed and dumped some 5.4 million cu. yd. of fly ash over 400 acres in eastern Tennessee's Roane County. The slide knocked down utility poles and trees and damaged at least a dozen homes (some beyond repair). Although nobody was hurt, some residents were cut off by the spill, prompting officials to build a new road. The flooding was the pond's third reported incident in six years.

TVA has an agreement to produce tritium, a radioactive gas that boosts the power of nuclear weapons, for the US Department of Energy at its Watts Bar nuclear plant. The company also plans to add three more nuclear plants by 2020 and is working with the DOE to reprocess waste from its existing plants.

HISTORY

In 1924 the Army Corps of Engineers finished building the Wilson Dam on the Tennessee River in Alabama to provide power for two WWI-era nitrate plants. With the war over, the question of what to do with the plants became a political football.

An act of Congress created the Tennessee Valley Authority (TVA) in 1933 to manage the plants and Tennessee Valley waterways. New Dealers saw TVA as a way to revitalize the local economy through improved navigation and power generation. Power companies claimed the agency was unconstitutional, but by 1939, when a federal court ruled against them, TVA had five operating hydroelectric plants and five under construction.

During the 1940s TVA supplied power for the war effort, including the Manhattan Project in Tennessee. During the postwar boom between 1945 and 1950, power usage in the Tennessee Valley nearly doubled. Despite adding dams, TVA couldn't keep up with demand, so in 1949 it began building a coal-fired unit. Because coal-fired plants weren't part of TVA's original mission, in 1955 a Congressional panel recommended the authority be dissolved.

Though TVA survived, its funding was cut. In 1959 it was allowed to sell bonds, but it no longer received direct government appropriations for power operations. In addition, it had to pay back the government for past appropriations.

TVA began to build the first unit of an ambitious 17-plant nuclear power program in Alabama in 1967. However, skyrocketing costs forced it to raise rates and cut maintenance on its coal-fired plants, which led to breakdowns. In 1985 five reactors had to be shut down because of safety concerns.

In 1988 former auto industry executive Marvin Runyon was appointed chairman of the agency. "Carvin' Marvin" cut management, sold three airplanes, and got rid of peripheral businesses, saving $400 million a year. In 1992 Runyon left to go to the postal service and was replaced by Craven Crowell, who began preparing TVA for competition in the retail power market.

TVA ended its nuclear construction program in 1996 after bringing two nuclear units on line within three months, a first for a US utility. The next year it raised rates for the first time in 10 years, planning to reduce its debt. In response to a lawsuit filed by neighboring utilities, it agreed to stop "laundering" power by using third parties to sell outside the agency's legally authorized area.

In 1999 the authority finished installing almost $2 billion in scrubbers and other equipment at its coal-fired plants so that it could buy Kentucky coal along with cleaner Wyoming coal. That year, however, the EPA charged TVA with violating the Clean Air Act by making major overhauls on some of its older coal-fired plants without getting permits or installing updated pollution-control equipment. It ordered TVA to bring most of its coal-fired plants into compliance with more current pollution standards. The next year TVA contested the order in court, stating compliance would jack up electricity rates.

TVA was fined by the US Nuclear Regulatory Commission in 2000 for laying off a nuclear plant whistleblower. Crowell resigned in 2001, and Glenn McCullough Jr. was named chairman; he served in that role until May 2005. He was replaced by Bill Baxter (who served until March 2006) and then by William Sansom.

EXECUTIVES

President and CEO: Tom D. Kilgore, age 60
COO: William R. (Bill) McCollum Jr., age 57
EVP Financial Services, CFO, and Chief Risk Officer: Kimberly (Kim) Scheibe-Greene, age 42
EVP Administrative Services and Chief Administrative Officer: John E. Long Jr., age 56
EVP, General Counsel, and Secretary: Maureen H. Dunn, age 59
EVP Fossil Power Group: Preston D. Swafford, age 48
EVP Customer Resources: Kenneth R. Breeden, age 60
EVP TVA Nuclear and Chief Nuclear Officer: William R. (Bill) Campbell Jr., age 57
EVP PowerSystem Operations: Robin E. Manning, age 52
EVP Power Supply and Fuels: Van M. Wardlaw, age 48

SVP Pricing and Strategic Planning: Theresa A. Flaim
SVP Economic Development: John J. Bradley
SVP Office of Environment and Research: Anda A. Ray, age 52
SVP and Treasurer: John M. Hoskins, age 53
SVP Corporate Responsibility and Diversity, Chief Ethics and Compliance Officer, and External Ombudsman: Peyton T. Hairston Jr., age 53
SVP Communications, Government, and Valley Relations: Emily J. Reynolds, age 52
SVP Fossil Engineering and Technical Services; Acting Manager, Resource Planning and System Forecasting: Marcia Cooper
Interim SVP, Treasurer, and Investor Relations: Tammy Wilson
SVP Nuclear Generation Development and Construction: Ashok S. Bhatnagar, age 52
VP, Controller, and Chief Accounting Officer: John M. Thomas III, age 45
Auditors: Ernst & Young LLP

LOCATIONS

HQ: Tennessee Valley Authority
  400 W. Summit Hill Dr., Knoxville, TN 37902
Phone: 865-632-2101   **Fax:** 888-633-0372
Web: www.tva.gov

2008 Sales

	$ mil.	% of total
Electricity sales		
Tennessee	6,389	62
Alabama	1,410	14
Kentucky	1,192	12
Mississippi	923	9
Georgia	238	2
North Carolina	50	—
Virginia	37	—
Other revenues	143	1
Total	**10,382**	**100**

PRODUCTS/OPERATIONS

2008 Sales

	$ mil.	% of total
Electricity sales		
Municipalities & cooperatives	8,659	84
Industries directly served	1,472	14
Federal agencies & other	121	1
Other revenues	130	1
Total	**10,382**	**100**

HISTORICAL FINANCIALS

Company Type: Government-owned

Income Statement				FYE: September 30
	REVENUE ($ mil.)	NET INCOME ($ mil.)	NET PROFIT MARGIN	EMPLOYEES
9/08	10,382.0	817.0	7.9%	11,584
9/07	9,244.0	383.0	4.1%	12,013
9/06	9,175.0	329.0	3.6%	12,600
9/05	7,794.0	85.0	1.1%	12,703
9/04	7,533.0	386.0	5.1%	12,742
Annual Growth	**8.3%**	**20.6%**	**—**	**(2.4%)**

Net Income History

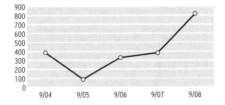

Terex Corporation

Terex lifts and digs for pay dirt. The company has four business segments that make cranes, construction equipment, aerial platforms, and mining equipment. Terex sells its products under such brands as Genie, Powerscreen, and Bid-Well. The company's construction division makes off-highway trucks, excavators, backhoes, large wheel loaders, and road building equipment. Aerial work platforms, material lifts, portable generators, and telescopic booms are used in industrial and construction applications for overhead work. The mining equipment division includes crushing and screening equipment, surface mining trucks, drills, and excavators. Terex also offers financing services for equipment purchases.

Terex's equipment is marketed worldwide to the construction, forestry, quarrying, government, recycling, shipping, and utility industries, among others. The company is acquisition-driven in its efforts to expand its product offerings and geographic market reach. It targets expansion in developing markets such as China, India, Russia, the Middle East, and Latin America, which accounts for nearly 25% of sales.

It is focusing on integrating acquisitions, executing cost-saving initiatives, and penetrating into new markets for certain product categories. Its strategy is to build its own eponymous brand name in an effort to get all of its products labeled as a Terex product.

Early in 2008 Terex acquired rubber track loader manufacturer ASV Inc. for about $488 million.

In 2009 Terex consolidated its roadbuilding operations with its construction division. Both divisions were impacted by the economic downturn and Terex was forced to reduce its workforce and slow production at some of its plants in order to meet declining global demand. The company also has considered selling the roadbuilding division, which produces pavers and mixers, as well as landfill compactors, and utility equipment. Spying longer term opportunities in manufacturing and servicing port equipment, Terex acquired diversified crane makers Fantuzzi Industries S.a.r.l and Noell Crane. The addition expands Terex's existing lineup of reach stackers.

Under investigation by the SEC for the circumstances of restating its financial statements for 2000-2004, and for transactions between the company and United Rentals in 2000-2001, Terex agreed with the SEC staff to settle the case, paying a civil penalty of $8 million. The proposed settlement does not address the roles of any current or former employees of the company, including chairman and CEO Ronald DeFeo.

HISTORY

Real estate entrepreneur Randolph Lenz moved into heavy equipment manufacturing with the purchase of bankrupt snowplow maker FWD Corporation in 1981. That was followed the same year with the acquisition of Northwest Engineering, a maker of construction equipment started in the 1920s.

In 1986 the company acquired Terex USA, the North American distributor of parts for off-highway Terex trucks, from General Motors, and later Terex Equipment, the UK-based truck maker. The company changed its corporate name to Terex Corporation in 1987. That year Terex entered the mobile-crane market with the purchase of Koehring Cranes. Terex acquired mining-truck maker Unit Rig in 1988 and trailer maker Fruehauf in 1989. It moved into aerial work platforms in 1991 with the acquisition of Mark Industries and picked up the forklift business of Clark Equipment the following year. (Clark invented the forklift truck in 1928.)

Overexpansion and heavy debt led to losses as the US slipped into recession in the early 1990s, and Terex teetered on the brink of bankruptcy. The losses prompted the 1993 installation of new management led by former Case executive Ron DeFeo, who refocused Terex on its core earthmoving and lifting businesses. In 1995 the company sold its stake in Fruehauf. It sold Clark Material Handling in 1996.

Terex added to its lifting-product business with the acquisition of PPM Cranes in 1995 and Simon Access and Baraga Products in 1997. It strengthened its earthmoving product line with the 1998 purchases of O&K Mining, a maker of hydraulic mining excavators, and Gru Comedil, a maker of tower cranes. That year Lenz stepped down as chairman and DeFeo replaced him.

The company settled long-lived SEC and IRS investigations in 1999, which had negatively affected the company's stock price. (The IRS had audited the company; the SEC was probing its accounting methods.)

Terex began piling on new earthmoving businesses in 1999, including Amida Industries, a maker of front-end dumpers and mobile floodlight towers. Also in 1999 Terex paid $294 million for UK-based Powerscreen International, a maker of screening and crushing equipment for quarries, and $170 million for Cedarapids, Raytheon's road construction-equipment business. Terex then boosted its lifting business by acquiring Allegheny Teledyne's lift truck unit and Australian crane maker Franna Cranes.

Early in 2001 Terex acquired Fermec Holdings Limited, a UK-based maker of loader backhoes, from CNH Global. Later the same year, it added CMI Corporation, a maker of large-scale construction equipment, and cut operating costs (about 30% of its workforce). The company also entered the power generation business, selling diesel generators under the name Terex Power. In addition, Terex expanded its reach into Europe by acquiring Atlas Weyhausen (cranes and excavators, Germany) in 2001, and The Schaeff Group (construction equipment; Germany) in early 2002.

Also in 2002 Terex initiated investments in Tatra a.s. (heavy-duty trucks with commercial and military applications, Czech Republic), increasing its share to 71% in 2003. Other 2002 acquisitions included distributors Utility Equipment (Oregon) and EPAC Holdings (which operated as Telelect East and Eusco, or Telelect Southeast), Advance Mixer (cement mixer trucks), Demag Mobile Cranes (Germany) from Siemens AG, and Genie Holdings (aerial work platforms) for $75 million.

The company continued to buy in 2003, adding utility equipment distributors Commercial Body and Combatel. The distributors perform final assembly and provide equipment rental and after-market services for the utility and telecom industries in the southern US. A deal that would have sent Terex's mining truck to Caterpillar and Caterpillar's mining shovel business to Terex was terminated in late 2003.

In late 2006 Terex sold its interest in Czech truck maker Tatra a.s. to Blue River s.r.o. a Czech-based private investment concern.

EXECUTIVES

Chairman and CEO: Ronald M. (Ron) DeFeo, age 56, $11,794,758 total compensation
President and COO: Thomas J. (Tom) Riordan, age 52, $3,714,833 total compensation
SVP and CFO: Phillip C. Widman, age 54, $2,975,203 total compensation
Chief Information Officer: Greg Fell
SVP and Chief Marketing Officer: Katia A. Facchetti
SVP Finance and Business Development: Brian J. Henry, age 50
SVP, General Counsel, and Secretary: Eric I. Cohen, age 50
SVP Human Resources: Kevin A. Barr, age 49
SVP, Terex Business Systems: Colin Fox
VP Business Development: Tom Gelston
VP, Controller, and Chief Accounting Officer: Jonathan D. (Jon) Carter
VP Manufacturing Services; Head of Terex Utilities: George Ellis
President, Terex Aerial Work Platforms: Timothy A. Ford, age 47, $2,226,986 total compensation
President, Terex Cranes: Richard (Rick) Nichols, age 47, $2,166,567 total compensation
President, Developing Markets and Strategic Accounts: Steve (Steve) Filipov, age 40
President, Terex Asia: Hyeryun Lee Park
President, Terex Construction: Robert G. Isaman, age 47
President, Terex Materials Processing and Mining: Eric A. Nielsen, age 49
Director Investor Relations: Laura Kiernan
Auditors: PricewaterhouseCoopers LLP

LOCATIONS

HQ: Terex Corporation
200 Nyala Farms Rd., Westport, CT 06880
Phone: 203-222-7170 **Fax:** 203-222-7976
Web: www.terex.com

2008 Sales

	$ mil.	% of total
US	2,972	30
Europe		
UK	622	6
Germany	724	7
Other countries	2,270	23
Other regions	3,302	34
Total	**9,890**	**100**

PRODUCTS/OPERATIONS

2008 Sales

	$ mil.	% of total
Cranes	2,889	29
Materials processing & mining	2,457	24
Aerial work platforms	2,074	21
Construction	1,888	19
Roadbuilding	718	7
Adjustments	(136)	—
Total	**9,890**	**100**

Selected Products

Cranes
  All terrain cranes
  Boom trucks
  Container stackers
  Lattice boom cranes
  Lift and carry cranes
  Rough terrain cranes
  Telescopic truck cranes
  Tower cranes
  Truck-mounted cranes
Materials processing and mining
  All-wheel-drive rigid off-highway trucks
  Electric rear/bottom dump haulers
  Large hydraulic excavators
Aerial work platforms
  Aerial devices
  Portable material lifts

Construction
  Compaction rollers
  Crushers
  Excavators
  Generators
  Loader backhoes
  Off-highway trucks
  Scrapers
  Screens
  Telehandlers
  Trailers
  Wheel loaders
Roadbuilding, utility products, and other
  Asphalt pavers
  Asphalt plants
  Concrete trucks
  Generators
  Grinders
  Light towers
  Portable floodlights and traffic control
  Reclaimers
  Stabilizers
  Trailers
  Tree trimmers
  Truck mounted aerial devices
  Vibratory plate compactors

COMPETITORS

Altec Industries
Astec Industries
Atlas Copco
Blount International
Caterpillar
Charles Machine Works
CNH Global
Deere
Doosan Heavy Industries
Dynapac
Fontaine Trailer
Furukawa
Gehl
Hitachi Construction Machinery
Hyundai Heavy Industries
Instant UpRight
J C Bamford Excavators
JLG Industries
Kobelco Construction Machinery America
Komatsu
Legris Industries Group
Liebherr International
MANITOU BF
Manitowoc
Marmon Group
Metso
Multiquip
Oshkosh Truck
Pinguely-Haulotte
Sandvik
Skyjack
Sumitomo
Textron
Trail King Industries
Volvo
Wacker Neuson

HISTORICAL FINANCIALS

Company Type: Public

Income Statement

FYE: December 31

	REVENUE ($ mil.)	NET INCOME ($ mil.)	NET PROFIT MARGIN	EMPLOYEES
12/08	9,889.6	71.9	0.7%	20,000
12/07	9,137.7	613.9	6.7%	21,000
12/06	7,647.6	407.6	5.3%	18,000
12/05	6,380.4	188.5	3.0%	17,600
12/04	5,019.8	324.1	6.5%	18,000
Annual Growth	**18.5%**	**(31.4%)**	**—**	**2.7%**

2008 Year-End Financials

Debt ratio: 81.1%
Return on equity: 3.5%
Cash ($ mil.): 484
Current ratio: 2.21
Long-term debt ($ mil.): 1,396

No. of shares (mil.): 108
Dividends
  Yield: 0.0%
  Payout: —
Market value ($ mil.): 1,871

Stock History

NYSE: TEX

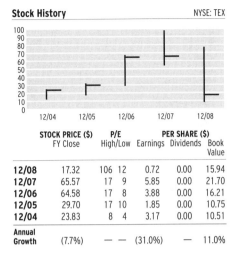

	STOCK PRICE ($) FY Close	P/E High/Low		PER SHARE ($) Earnings	Dividends	Book Value
12/08	17.32	106	12	0.72	0.00	15.94
12/07	65.57	17	9	5.85	0.00	21.70
12/06	64.58	17	8	3.88	0.00	16.21
12/05	29.70	17	10	1.85	0.00	10.75
12/04	23.83	8	4	3.17	0.00	10.51
Annual Growth	(7.7%)	—	—	(31.0%)	—	11.0%

Terra Industries

Terra would be happier if fertilizer prices were a little firma. The company ranks among the leading North American producers of nitrogen fertilizers. Through its North American nitrogen plants, it produces ammonia, urea, urea ammonium nitrate solution (UAN), and ammonium nitrate (AN). Terra operates plants in the US, Canada, and the UK through subsidiaries, joint ventures, and limited partnerships, including Terra Nitrogen, of which Terra Industries owns 75%. The company sells its products to dealers, retailers, cooperatives, and chemical companies. In 2009 CF Industries offered to buy Terra for about $2.1 billion, but Terra's Board turned down the offer.

UAN accounts for about one-third of the company's sales. Terra Industries operates its UK operations through a joint venture with Kemira GrowHow called GrowHow UK.

The company mothballed an ammonia plant in Louisiana in 2005 and had been using it as a storage and distribution terminal since then. But toward the end of 2008 the company restarted production there, a sign of Terra's good health. It had also produced methanol, which is used to make oxygenated fuels or as a feedstock in other chemical processes, but sold that facility in 2008.

HISTORY

Terra Chemicals International was founded in 1964 with a nitrogen fertilizer plant in Iowa. The next year it acquired Grand Forks Seed Co., operator of 12 farm service centers. The company began producing nitrogen-based fertilizer in 1967 and went public in 1974. Terra Chemicals bought Memphis-based Riverside Chemical Co. in 1977 and became one of the US's largest independent producers and distributors of fertilizer, seed, and agricultural chemicals.

South African natural resources company Minorco acquired the company in 1981. In 1985 Terra Chemicals extended its marketing reach into Illinois, Indiana, Ohio, and Michigan by buying ADI Distributors.

The company changed its name to Terra Industries in 1992 and expanded into Canada in 1993. Terra Industries moved beyond North America in 1997 with the purchase of two nitrogen fertilizer plants in the UK. In 1999 Terra Industries sold its 400-location distribution business (now called Agro Distribution) to Cenex/Land O' Lakes for $390 million. Also that year Minorco was absorbed by its parent, Anglo American, which assumed majority control of Terra Industries (which was then reduced to just under 50% and then sold entirely in 2004).

High natural gas prices forced the company to idle several plants in late 2000. All but the Blytheville, Arkansas, plant were restarted by March 2001. The company also agreed to pay Mississippi Chemical $18 million that year to settle a defamation countersuit related to a 1994 explosion at a Terra fertilizer plant. In 2002 Terra Industries recorded a financial charge of about $11 million for discontinued operations.

Like most fertilizer companies, Terra had been hurt by depressed prices for nitrogen fertilizers, high raw materials costs, and cheap imports. After a couple of years of ramping up production only to idle the plant again, Terra announced in 2004 that the Blytheville plant would end production in May and close down permanently. Terra bought Mississippi Chemical in 2004, pulling it out of Chapter 11 and making it a wholly owned subsidiary of Terra.

Anglo American, the UK company that controls the De Beers empire, had owned as much as 49% of Terra but sold its remaining shares in 2004.

EXECUTIVES

Chairman: Henry R. Slack, age 59
President, CEO, and Director:
  Michael L. (Mike) Bennett, age 55,
  $5,390,994 total compensation
SVP and CFO: Daniel D. (Dan) Greenwell, age 46,
  $1,331,403 total compensation
VP Information Technology: Geoffrey J. (Geoff) Obeney,
  age 51
SVP Commercial Operations: Joseph D. (Joe) Giesler,
  age 50, $1,048,241 total compensation
SVP Sales and Marketing: Douglas M. (Doug) Stone,
  age 43
VP, General Counsel, and Corporate Secretary:
  John W. Huey, age 61, $987,476 total compensation
VP Investor Relations and Human Resources:
  Joe A. Ewing, age 58
VP Manufacturing: Richard S. Sanders Jr., age 51,
  $1,030,053 total compensation
VP and Controller: Edward J. Dillon, age 41
VP Business Development: Earl B. Smith, age 48
Director, Risk Management: Tim Sterling
Auditors: Deloitte & Touche LLP

LOCATIONS

HQ: Terra Industries Inc.
  600 4th St., Sioux City, IA 51101
Phone: 712-277-1340   **Fax:** 712-277-7364
Web: www.terraindustries.com

2008 Sales

	$ mil.	% of total
US	2,785.3	96
Canada	106.2	4
Total	**2,891.5**	**100**

PRODUCTS/OPERATIONS

Selected Products

Ammonium nitrate (AN)
Urea
Urea ammonium nitrate solution (UAN)

COMPETITORS

Agrium
Bunge Limited
Cargill
CF Industries
Mosaic Company
PotashCorp
Sumitomo Chemical
Yara

HISTORICAL FINANCIALS

Company Type: Public

Income Statement				FYE: December 31
	REVENUE ($ mil.)	NET INCOME ($ mil.)	NET PROFIT MARGIN	EMPLOYEES
12/08	2,891.5	641.0	22.2%	938
12/07	2,360.1	196.8	8.3%	871
12/06	1,836.7	(0.9)	—	1,238
12/05	1,939.1	17.0	0.9%	1,209
12/04	1,509.1	67.6	4.5%	1,323
Annual Growth	17.7%	75.5%	—	(8.2%)

2008 Year-End Financials

Debt ratio: 31.2%
Return on equity: 76.3%
Cash ($ mil.): 967
Current ratio: 2.99
Long-term debt ($ mil.): 330

No. of shares (mil.): 100
Dividends
  Yield: 1.8%
  Payout: 4.8%
Market value ($ mil.): 1,663

Stock History

NYSE: TRA

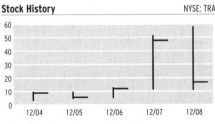

	STOCK PRICE ($) FY Close	P/E High/Low		PER SHARE ($) Earnings	Dividends	Book Value
12/08	16.67	9	2	6.20	0.30	10.62
12/07	47.76	27	6	1.90	0.00	6.22
12/06	11.98	—	—	(0.01)	0.00	4.84
12/05	5.60	52	27	0.18	0.00	6.10
12/04	8.88	11	4	0.85	0.00	4.60
Annual Growth	17.1%	—	—	64.3%	—	23.2%

Tesoro Corporation

Once a player in the exploration and production field, Tesoro Corporation (formerly Tesoro Petroleum) has been enjoying a more refined existence in recent years. The independent oil refiner and marketer operates seven US refineries — in Alaska, California (two), Hawaii, North Dakota, Utah, and Washington — with a combined capacity of 658,000 barrels per day. It produces gasoline, jet fuel, diesel fuel, fuel oil, liquid asphalt, and other fuel products. Tesoro markets fuel to 880 branded retail gas stations (including 290 company-owned stations under the Tesoro, Shell, Mirastar, and USA Gasoline brands), in Alaska, Hawaii, and 15 western states.

As part of a strategy to step up its marketing efforts on the US West Coast, Tesoro has an agreement with Wal-Mart to build and operate up to 200 Mirastar-branded gas stations at Wal-Mart locations in 13 states.

Tesoro acquired a Los Angeles refinery and some 276 gas stations from Shell Oil Products US for about $1.6 billion in 2007. It then acquired more than 130 USA Petroleum gas stations, primarily in California; these acquisitions nearly doubled Tesoro's retail presence.

In a significant supply agreement, in 2008 the company entered into a throughput deal that will allow it (beginning in 2009) to transport crude oil in a pipeline owned by Petroterminal de Panamá (PTP). PTP will reverse the flow of its 81-mile trans-Panamanian pipeline to more economically transport crude oils produced in Africa, the Atlantic coast of South America and the North Sea to Tesoros's five refineries on the Pacific Rim.

HISTORY

Founded by Robert West in 1964 as a spinoff of petroleum producer Texstar, Tesoro Petroleum was hamstrung by debt from the get-go. In 1968 West merged Tesoro with Intex Oil and Sioux Oil to invigorate its financial standing.

Reborn, the company constructed an Alaska refinery and began a 10-year stretch of petroleum-related acquisitions, usually at bargain prices, including almost half of the oil operations of British Petroleum (BP) in Trinidad, which became Trinidad-Tesoro Petroleum. By 1973 earnings had quintupled.

In 1975 Tesoro paid $83 million for about a third of Commonwealth Oil Refining Company (Corco), a troubled Puerto Rican oil refiner one-and-a-half times its size. Debt soon was troubling Tesoro again, and the company divested many of its holdings, including refineries in Montana and Wyoming. Corco declared bankruptcy in 1978. That year Tesoro was hit with tax penalties and revealed it had bribed officials in foreign countries.

The company fought takeover attempts and bankruptcy in the 1980s and sold its half of Trinidad-Tesoro in 1985. In the 1990s it expanded its natural gas operations and returned to profitability.

In 1998 Tesoro bought a refinery and 32 retail outlets in Hawaii from an affiliate of BHP, and a refinery in Washington from an affiliate of Shell. To concentrate on its downstream businesses, the company in 1999 sold its exploration and production operations in the US (to EEX for $215 million) and in Bolivia (to BG for about $100 million).

Tesoro West Coast Co., a Tesoro subsidiary, entered into a lease agreement with Wal-Mart in 2000 to build and operate retail fueling facilities at Wal-Mart locations in 11 western states (subsequently expanded to 13 states). That year the company reviewed the possibility of closing part or all of its Alaska properties, including its under-performing refinery. But boosted by higher crude prices and its new deal with Wal-Mart, Tesoro decided to leave its Alaska operations untouched.

In 2001 Tesoro bought refineries in North Dakota and Utah, plus 45 gas stations and contracts to supply 300 others, from BP for about $675 million. Tesoro bought the Golden Eagle (San Francisco-area) refinery and 70 retail service stations in Northern California from Valero Energy for $945 million in 2002. At the end of the year Tesoro sold 47 of those gas stations to help pay down debt. It also sold its Northern Great Plains Products System to Kaneb Pipe Line Partners L.P. for $100 million.

The 2003 sale of its marine services unit for $32 million was also part of the company's plan to focus on its refining and marketing operations and pay down debt. It achieved its goal of shedding some $500 million of debt by the end of 2003 through asset sales and cost reductions.

EXECUTIVES

Chairman, President, and CEO: Bruce A. Smith, age 65, $14,661,294 total compensation
EVP and COO: Everett D. Lewis, age 61, $3,396,268 total compensation
EVP and CFO: Gregory A. (Greg) Wright, $2,356,036 total compensation
SVP External Affairs and Chief Economist: Lynn D. Westfall, age 56
EVP Strategy and Corporate Development: William J. (Bill) Finnerty, age 60, $4,127,888 total compensation
EVP, General Counsel, and Secretary: Charles S. (Chuck) Parrish, age 51, $1,614,798 total compensation
SVP Risk Management: G. Scott Spendlove, age 45
SVP Refining: Daniel J. (Dan) Porter, age 53
SVP Administration: Susan A. Lerette, age 50
SVP Business Development and Logistics: Joseph M. (Joe) Monroe, age 54
SVP System Optimization: Claude A. (Chuck) Flagg, age 55
SVP Marketing: Claude P. Moreau, age 54
SVP Supply and Optimization: Joe McCoy, age 60
VP, Kenai Refinery: Stephen W. Hansen, age 63
VP Wholesale Marketing: Mark Wilson
VP and Controller: Arlen O. Glenewinkel Jr., age 52
Manager Investor Relations: Scott Phipps
Auditors: Deloitte & Touche LLP

LOCATIONS

HQ: Tesoro Corporation
19100 Ridgewood Pkwy, San Antonio, TX 78259
Phone: 210-626-6000   **Fax:** 210-579-4574
Web: www.tsocorp.com

PRODUCTS/OPERATIONS

2008 Sales

	$ mil.	% of total
Refining		
Refined products	26,759	83
Crude oil resales & other	1,019	3
Retail		
Fuel	4,184	13
Merchandise & other	248	1
Adjustments	(3,901)	—
Total	**28,309**	**100**

Major Subsidiaries

Tesoro Alaska Company
Tesoro Hawaii Corporation
Tesoro Refining and Marketing Company

COMPETITORS

Arctic Slope
BP
Branch & Associates
Chevron
ConocoPhillips
Exxon Mobil
Shell Oil Products
Valero Energy

HISTORICAL FINANCIALS

Company Type: Public

Income Statement

FYE: December 31

	REVENUE ($ mil.)	NET INCOME ($ mil.)	NET PROFIT MARGIN	EMPLOYEES
12/08	28,309.0	278.0	1.0%	5,620
12/07	21,915.0	566.0	2.6%	5,500
12/06	18,104.0	801.0	4.4%	3,950
12/05	16,581.0	507.0	3.1%	3,928
12/04	12,262.2	327.9	2.7%	3,640
Annual Growth	**23.3%**	**(4.0%)**	**—**	**11.5%**

2008 Year-End Financials

Debt ratio: 50.0%
Return on equity: 8.9%
Cash ($ mil.): 20
Current ratio: 1.14
Long-term debt ($ mil.): 1,609
No. of shares (mil.): 140
Dividends
  Yield: 3.0%
  Payout: 20.0%
Market value ($ mil.): 1,838

Stock History

NYSE: TSO

	STOCK PRICE ($) FY Close	P/E High/Low		PER SHARE ($) Earnings	Dividends	Book Value
12/08	13.17	22	3	2.00	0.40	23.06
12/07	47.70	16	8	4.06	0.35	21.87
12/06	32.88	7	5	5.73	0.20	17.93
12/05	30.77	10	4	3.60	0.10	13.52
12/04	15.93	7	3	2.38	0.00	9.51
Annual Growth	**(4.6%)**	**—**	**—**	**(4.3%)**	**—**	**24.8%**

Tetra Tech

Tetra Tech puts technical know-how to work. The environmental management, consulting, and technical services group focuses on resource management, infrastructure, and communications. Services include environmental engineering, restoration, groundwater cleanup, watershed management, and operations and maintenance support. For major network services providers, the group offers broadband network planning, development, and deployment assistance. Tetra Tech provides engineering and construction services for public and private facilities and designs and builds water supply systems. US federal contracts account for almost half of its annual revenues.

In addition to sales it earns from federal contracts, Tetra Tech brings in another almost 20% from state and local clients. Earning almost two-thirds of its revenues from government contracts has helped position the company among the top environmental firms worldwide. Tetra Tech's strategy has been to establish its consulting practice in a new business area and then offer additional technical services.

It has also expanded geographically through acquisitions — such as the 2008 acquisition of international services firm ARD and of nuclear services provider Haselwood Enterprises the next year — and it continues to market to public-sector clients for more predictable revenues. In 2009 it also acquired construction management firm Tesoro Corporation, environmental consulting firm Mussetter Engineering of Fort Collins, Canadian power engineering specialists ACI Engineering, and the Californian consulting and engineering firm Bryan A. Stirrat.

The company offers services such as environmental restoration, conservation, planning, compliance, and pollution prevention. It also provides engineering and construction of military facilities and homeland security projects. In Iraq it is providing services to clean up unexploded ordnance. Commercial customers include companies in the chemical, energy, mining, and pharmaceutical industries.

HISTORY

Tetra Tech was founded in 1966 by Nicholas Boratynski as a coastal and marine engineering firm. One of its first jobs was measuring water waves to determine the damage an offshore nuclear bomb could do to the coastline. The company developed expertise in water management in the 1970s. Honeywell bought the company in 1982, and Tetra Tech management in turn bought out Honeywell in 1988. Tetra Tech went public in 1991.

Since 1993 Tetra Tech has grown largely through acquisitions. In 1997 the company expanded into infrastructure and telecommunications. Tetra Tech acquired two site development firms — CommSite Development Corp. and Whalen & Company — to capitalize on the growing telecom market. It also enlarged its environmental business with the purchase of Halliburton's Brown & Root and Halliburton NUS environmental service units.

Continuing to build up its telecom business in 1998, it bought Sentrex Cen-Comm Communications Systems, an engineering firm serving the cable TV, telephone, and data networking industries.

A year later the company won a $105 million contract from the US Department of Energy to help monitor the nation's nuclear weapons stockpile. In 2000 Tetra Tech won a $375 million contract from WideOpenWest, a leading broadband wired access provider in the Denver area. It also snapped up nine companies that fiscal year.

In 2001 Tetra Tech expanded its energy services to include power plant relicensing projects in the US. The company also expanded its consulting services to the energy and mining industries through acquisitions. In 2002 the company acquired The Thomas Group, a leading designer of educational and health care facilities. It also picked up Florida-based consulting engineering firm Ardaman & Associates, adding to its water resources management operations.

The next year the group expanded even more by acquiring nearly all the assets of environmental services management firm Foster Wheeler Environmental Corp., a unit of Foster Wheeler. Tetra Tech renamed the group, which provides hazardous and nuclear waste management primarily to the federal government, Tetra Tech FW. In 2003 it strengthened its position in the federal market even more by acquiring California-based engineering firm Engineering Management Concepts (EMC), which provides weapons test range services and systems logistics support to the Department of Defense.

The group was buying again in 2004 with its purchase of Advanced Management Technology Inc., which enhanced its position in the security and defense market. In 2005, however, Tetra Tech exited the wireless communications arena and began consolidating its infrastructure operations.

EXECUTIVES

Chairman, CEO, and President: Dan L. Batrack, age 50
EVP, CFO, and Treasurer: David W. King, age 52
VP and CIO: Craig L. Christensen, age 55
SVP Corporate Administration: Richard A. Lemmon, age 49
SVP and Corporate Controller: Steven M. Burdick, age 44
SVP; President, Infrastructure Business Group: Douglas G. (Doug) Smith, age 59
SVP; President, Environmental Engineering and Consulting Group: William R. Brownlie, age 55
SVP; President, Remediation and Construction Group: Donald I. Rogers Jr., age 64
SVP; President, Systems Support and Security Group: Patrick D. Haun, age 48
SVP and President, Technical Support Services: Ronald J. Chu, age 51
SVP Strategic Initiatives: Leslie L. Shoemaker, age 51
VP Business and Corporate Development: Michael A. (Mike) Bieber, age 40
VP, General Counsel, and Secretary: Janis B. Salin, age 55
VP Project Risk Management: Sam W. Box, age 63
VP Investor Relations: Jorge Casado
Director, Corporate Communications: Talia Starkey
Auditors: PricewaterhouseCoopers LLP

LOCATIONS

HQ: Tetra Tech, Inc.
3475 E. Foothill Blvd., Pasadena, CA 91107
Phone: 626-351-4664 **Fax:** 626-351-5291
Web: www.tetratech.com

PRODUCTS/OPERATIONS

2008 Sales

	% of total
Resource management	68
Infrastructure	27
Communications	5
Total	**100**

2008 Sales

	% of total
Federal government	43
Commercial	38
State & local government	18
International	1
Total	**100**

Selected Subsidiaries

Advanced Management Technology, Inc.
Ardaman & Associates, Inc.
Cosentini Associates, Inc.
Engineering Management Concepts, Inc. (EMC)
Evergreen Utility Contractors, Inc.
FHC, Inc.
Hartman & Associates, Inc.
MFG, Inc.
Rizzo Associates, Inc.
Sciences International, Inc.
SCM Consultants, Inc.

Tetra Tech EM Inc.
Tetra Tech NUS, Inc
The Thomas Group of Commpanies, Inc.
Vector Colorado, LLC.
Western Utility Cable, Inc.
Western Utility Contractors, Inc.
Whalen & Company, Inc.
Whalen/Sentrex LLC

COMPETITORS

AECOM
ARCADIS
Baran Telecom
Black & Veatch
Brown and Caldwell
Camp Dresser McKee
CH2M HILL
EA Engineering
Earth Tech
Ecology and Environment
ERM
Foster Wheeler
Geocon Group
Jacobs Engineering
Kratos Defense & Security Solutions
MasTec
MWH Global
Quanta Services
RECON Environmental
Shaw Group
Stantec
Tracer Environmental Sciences
TRC Companies
URS
Weston

HISTORICAL FINANCIALS

Company Type: Public

Income Statement			FYE: Sunday nearest September 30	
	REVENUE ($ mil.)	NET INCOME ($ mil.)	NET PROFIT MARGIN	EMPLOYEES
9/08	2,145.3	60.9	2.8%	9,200
9/07	1,553.9	46.4	3.0%	7,800
9/06	1,414.7	36.6	2.6%	7,300
9/05	1,286.0	(99.5)	—	7,200
9/04	1,437.6	23.7	1.6%	8,600
Annual Growth	**10.5%**	**26.6%**	**—**	**1.7%**

2008 Year-End Financials

Debt ratio: 10.4%
Return on equity: 13.1%
Cash ($ mil.): 51
Current ratio: 1.48
Long-term debt ($ mil.): 53

No. of shares (mil.): 61
Dividends
　Yield: 0.0%
　Payout: —
Market value ($ mil.): 1,457

Stock History

NASDAQ (GS): TTEK

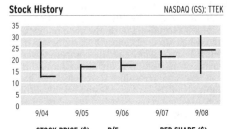

	STOCK PRICE ($) FY Close	P/E High/Low		PER SHARE ($)		
				Earnings	Dividends	Book Value
9/08	24.06	30	14	1.02	0.00	8.45
9/07	21.12	30	21	0.79	0.00	6.86
9/06	17.42	32	23	0.63	0.00	5.86
9/05	16.82	—	—	(1.75)	0.00	5.03
9/04	12.67	67	30	0.41	0.00	6.56
Annual Growth	**17.4%**	**—**	**—**	**25.6%**	**—**	**6.5%**

Texas Instruments

Say hello to the big Texan. One of the world's oldest and largest semiconductor makers, Texas Instruments (TI) is the market leader in digital signal processors (DSPs). Many of the wireless phones sold worldwide contain TI's DSPs, which are also found in other products, such as DVD players, automotive systems, and computer modems. TI jockeys back and forth with European chip giant STMicroelectronics to be the world's top maker of analog chips; both companies far outpace other analog rivals. Additional TI semiconductor offerings include logic chips, microprocessors, microcontrollers, and display components. The company also makes calculators. Nokia accounts for about 20% of sales; two-thirds of sales are in Asia.

In 2009 TI announced plans to cut its workforce by about 3,400 positions, a 12% reduction in force. The chip maker will lay off around 1,800 workers and anticipates approximately 1,600 positions will see voluntary retirements and departures. In 2009, the company announced that it had agreed to purchase certain assets of bankrupt Germany chipmaker Qimonda for over $170 million. Texas Instruments is purchasing the manufacturing equipment only, not the US unit itself, and will use the equipment to make analog and embedded semiconductors.

While TI signaled that it will be spending less money on R&D for semiconductor process development in the future, the giant chip maker is flexing its financial muscle in other ways. In mid-2009 it scored the microcontroller (MCU) portfolio of Luminary Micro, a power player in supplying ARM Cortex-M3-based 32-bit MCUs.

The company expanded its analog chip capabilities in 2008 when it acquired Innovative Design Solutions, which specializes in making analog chips.

During the late 1990s and the early 21st century, the company sold off non-core businesses and made a series of acquisitions to focus on its analog and DSP lines. TI touts its combination of expertise in analog and DSP technologies as a key advantage in allowing it to deliver more highly integrated components for customers in areas such as wireless and broadband communications. The company is also banking on even larger markets for its DSPs in the future, as their use becomes more widespread in areas such as wireline communications and medical equipment.

TI began shipping its Digital Light Processing (DLP) device in 1996. The part is a microelectromechanical system (MEMS) device, also known as a digital micromirror device. It contains more than 2 million microscopic mirrors on the surface of the device, mirrors that can individually move to create a sharper image. For years, the DLP seemed to be a product in search of an application, but it eventually found its way into HDTV sets, digital projectors, and digital cinema equipment. TI has shipped more than 20 million DLP subsystems to manufacturers.

HISTORY

Clarence "Doc" Karcher and Eugene McDermott founded Geophysical Service, Inc. (GSI) in Newark, New Jersey, in 1930 to develop reflective seismology, a new technology for oil and gas exploration. In 1934 GSI moved to Dallas. The company produced military electronics during WWII, including submarine detectors for the US Navy. GSI changed its name to Texas Instruments (TI) in 1951.

TI began making transistors in 1952 after buying a license from Western Electric. The company went public on the New York Stock Exchange in 1953. In 1954 it introduced the Regency Radio, the first pocket-sized transistor radio. (That year TI also produced the first commercial silicon transistor.) Impressed by the radio, IBM president Thomas Watson made TI a major supplier to IBM in 1957. That year the company opened a plant in the UK — its first foreign operation.

TI engineer Jack Kilby invented the integrated circuit (IC) in 1958. (Working independently, Intel co-founder Robert Noyce developed an IC at the same time, while working at Fairchild Semiconductor; the two men are credited as co-inventors. In 2000 Kilby was awarded the Nobel Prize in Physics for his work; Noyce could not be awarded the prize, since he had died 10 years earlier.)

Other breakthroughs for the company included terrain-following airborne radar (1958), handheld calculators (1967), and single-chip microcomputers (1971). During the 1970s TI introduced innovative calculators, digital watches, home computers, and educational toys such as the popular Speak & Spell — the first TI product to use digital signal processors (DSPs), which decades later would become a major driver of TI's growth.

Low-cost foreign competition led TI to abandon its digital watch and PC businesses. Price competition in the chip market contributed to the company's first loss in 1983. In 1988 the company sold most of its remaining oil and gas operations to Halliburton.

As the chip market toughened, TI leveraged its DRAM device know-how through strategic alliances, including a 1993 agreement with Hitachi (the venture ended in 1998). TI sold its line of educational toys to Tiger Electronics in 1995.

When company head Jerry Junkins, who built TI into a semiconductor force, died unexpectedly in 1996, he was replaced by company veteran Thomas Engibous as president and CEO. (Engibous became chairman in 1998.)

Engibous refocused TI, which in 1996 sold its custom manufacturing business to Solectron and acquired Silicon Systems (chips for mass storage devices). In 1997 TI sold its notebook computer business to Acer, its defense electronics operation to Raytheon, and its enterprise applications software unit to Sterling Software (now part of CA).

A global chip slump and the loss of the memory chip business lowered TI's results in 1998 and led to the layoff of 3,500 employees.

TI paid $7.6 billion in 2000 to acquire Burr-Brown, an Arizona-based maker of analog and mixed-signal chips. In 2001 TI began to lay off about 2,500 workers in reaction to a softening market for its chips. In 2004 COO Richard Templeton succeeded Engibous as president and CEO; Engibous remained chairman.

In 2006 TI sold its Sensors and Controls business to Bain Capital for $3 billion in cash. The business was rechristened Sensata Technologies. In selling the sensors and controls business, TI held on to its radio-frequency identification (RFID) tags business, making chips used in contactless payment systems, health care, manufacturing, retail supply chain management, and other applications.

In 2008 Tom Engibous retired as chairman and was succeeded by Rich Templeton.

EXECUTIVES

Chairman, President, and CEO:
Richard K. (Rich) Templeton, age 50,
$9,394,073 total compensation
SVP and CFO: Kevin P. March, age 51,
$2,718,669 total compensation
CIO: Brian Bonner
SVP and Manager, Communications and Investor Relations: Teresa L. (Terri) West, age 48
SVP, General Counsel, and Secretary:
Joseph F. (Joe) Hubach, age 51
SVP and General Manager, Application Specific Products: Michael J. (Mike) Hames, age 50,
$2,991,260 total compensation
SVP, Analog Business Unit: Gregg A. Lowe, age 46,
$3,976,365 total compensation
SVP, Technology and Manufacturing Group:
Kevin J. Ritchie, age 52, $3,375,752 total compensation
SVP and General Manager, DLP Products:
John C. Van Scoter, age 47
SVP, High-Volume Analog and Logic:
David K. (Dave) Heacock, age 48
SVP; President, Education Technology: Melendy Lovett, age 51
SVP, Worldwide Wireless Terminals Business Unit:
Gregory Delagi, age 46
SVP and General Manager, High Performance Analog Business Unit: Arthur L. (Art) George, age 47
SVP and Director, Worldwide Human Resources:
Darla Whitaker, age 43
VP and Tax Director: Katrina Welch
President, Texas Instruments Europe:
Jean-Francois Fau
President, Asia Operations: Larry Tan, age 51
Auditors: Ernst & Young LLP

LOCATIONS

HQ: Texas Instruments Incorporated
12500 TI Blvd., Dallas, TX 75266
Phone: 972-995-2011   **Fax:** 972-927-6377
Web: www.ti.com

2008 Sales

	$ mil.	% of total
Asia/Pacific		
Japan	1,268	10
Other countries	7,387	59
Europe	1,875	15
US	1,551	13
Other regions	420	3
Total	**12,501**	**100**

PRODUCTS/OPERATIONS

2008 Sales

	$ mil.	% of total
Analog	4,857	39
Wireless	3,383	27
Embedded Processing	1,631	13
Other	2,630	21
Total	**12,501**	**100**

Selected Products

Semiconductors
  Analog and mixed-signal
    Amplifiers and comparators
    Clocks and timers
    Data converters
    Power management chips
    Radio-frequency (RF) chips
  Application-specific integrated circuits (ASICs)
  Digital light processors (DLPs, micro-mirror-based devices for video displays)
  Digital signal processors (DSPs)
  Microcontrollers
  Reduced instruction set computer (RISC) microprocessors
  Standard logic
Educational Technology
  Calculators (including graphing, handheld, and printing models)

Selected Acquisitions

Radia Communications (July 2003, terms undisclosed, radio-frequency chips and subsystems for 802.11 wireless LAN radios)

Alantro Communications (September 2000, $300 million, wireless broadband integrated circuits)

Dot Wireless, Inc. (September 2000, $475 million, wireless communications chips)

Burr-Brown Corp. (August 2000, $7.6 billion, analog and mixed-signal chips)

Toccata Technology (March 2000, digital audio amplifier technology, Denmark)

ATL Research (1999, radio-frequency technology, Denmark)

Power Trends (1999, $145 million, point-of-use power products)

Unitrode (October 1999; about $1.25 billion; power supply, interface, and battery management components)

Integrated Sensor Solutions (August 1999, $67 million, high-performance sensors)

Telogy Networks (August 1999, $435 million, voice-over Internet Protocol software)

Libit Signal Processing (June 1999, $365 million, cable modem chipsets, Israel)

Butterfly VLSI (February 1999, $52 million, chipsets for short-distance wireless communications applications)

GO DSP (1998, DSP software tools)

Spectron Microsystem (1998, $25 million, DSP software and development tools, Canada)

Amati Communications (February 1998, $514 million, digital subscriber line products)

COMPETITORS

Analog Devices	Marvell Technology
Atmel	Maxim Integrated Products
Avago Technologies	MediaTek
Broadcom	National Semiconductor
Canon	NEC Electronics
CASIO COMPUTER	NVIDIA
Conexant Systems	NXP
Cypress Semiconductor	Oki Semiconductor
Fairchild Semiconductor	ON Semiconductor
Freescale Semiconductor	QUALCOMM
Fujitsu Microelectronics	Renesas Technology
Hewlett-Packard	SANYO Semiconductor
Hitachi	ST-Ericsson
IBM Microelectronics	STMicroelectronics
Infineon Technologies	Sun Microsystems
Intel Corp.	Toshiba Semiconductor
International Rectifier	Vishay Intertechnology
Linear Technology	Xilinx
LSI Corp.	

HISTORICAL FINANCIALS

Company Type: Public

Income Statement

FYE: December 31

	REVENUE ($ mil.)	NET INCOME ($ mil.)	NET PROFIT MARGIN	EMPLOYEES
12/08	12,501.0	1,920.0	15.4%	29,537
12/07	13,835.0	2,657.0	19.2%	30,175
12/06	14,255.0	4,341.0	30.5%	30,986
12/05	13,392.0	2,324.0	17.4%	32,507
12/04	12,580.0	1,861.0	14.8%	35,472
Annual Growth	(0.2%)	0.8%	—	(4.5%)

2008 Year-End Financials

Debt ratio: —	No. of shares (mil.): 1,261
Return on equity: 19.9%	Dividends
Cash ($ mil.): 1,046	Yield: 2.6%
Current ratio: 3.78	Payout: 28.3%
Long-term debt ($ mil.): —	Market value ($ mil.): 19,577

Stock History

NYSE: TXN

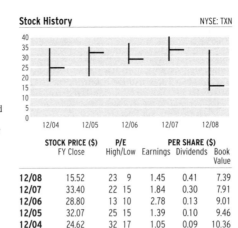

	STOCK PRICE ($) FY Close	P/E High/Low		PER SHARE ($) Earnings	Dividends	Book Value
12/08	15.52	23	9	1.45	0.41	7.39
12/07	33.40	22	15	1.84	0.30	7.91
12/06	28.80	13	10	2.78	0.13	9.01
12/05	32.07	25	15	1.39	0.10	9.46
12/04	24.62	32	17	1.05	0.09	10.36
Annual Growth	(10.9%)	—	—	8.4%	46.1%	(8.1%)

Textron Inc.

Executives should like Textron: The company's golf carts enrich their golfing jaunts; its Cessna airplanes and Bell helicopters whisk them around; its auto parts keep their cars running; and its financial subsidiary provides loans. Cessna and Bell are bright spots in Textron's financial results. Cessna accounts for more than half of profits; Bell about 20%. While Textron enjoyed healthy sales growth and good profit margins for several years, changes in the Pentagon budget and the global recession may dampen business in several segments. The US government accounts for about one-quarter of Textron's sales; geographically, customers in the US represent nearly two-thirds of sales.

The global recession affecting its sales and profitability, Textron laid off 8,300 employees in 2009, a reduction in force of about 20%.

Textron has four operating segments: Industrial, which makes golf carts, turf equipment, tools, fuel systems, and transmissions; Bell Helicopter; Textron Systems (smart weapons, surveillance systems, actuators); and Cessna Aircraft, which makes business jets and single-engine turboprops and piston planes. Finance offers commercial loans for clients purchasing the company's products.

In late 2008 the financial arm of the company, Textron Financial, exited its non-captive finance business (offering miscellaneous financial products through third-party companies) to focus on providing commercial loans that facilitate the purchase of Textron-manufactured products.

In 2007 Textron paid $1.1 billion for United Industrial Corporation, a maker of avionics testing equipment, combat systems training simulators, and perhaps most important — unmanned aerial vehicles (UAVs). The US military is expected to spend plenty on UAVs in the future as they have proven themselves on the battlefields of Iraq and Afghanistan. Textron, which did not previously have any UAV operations, is anxious to get in on the growing market for UAVs.

In 2009 Textron sold its HR Textron unit to Woodward Governor for $365 million in cash. HR Textron makes actuators and other products

for aircraft, armored vehicles, guided weapons, and turbine engines.

Early in 2008 Bell Helicopter acquired SkyBOOKS, a company that provides necessary information resources for regulatory compliance with the FAA. SkyBOOKS' online service tracks maintenance, flight operations, expenses, and document archiving. The move broadens Bell's offering of integrated services for its customers.

The company's Greenlee unit was also busy with acquisitions in 2008 with the additions of the UK-based Utilux (cable connectors and assemblies) and Telefonix, a cable testing equipment maker headquartered in California.

That same year Textron sold its Fluid & Power business unit to the UK-based Clyde Blowers Ltd.

HISTORY

Pioneer conglomerate builder Royal Little founded Special Yarns Corporation, a Boston textile business, in 1923 and merged it with the Franklin Rayon Dyeing Company in 1928. The result, Franklin Rayon Corporation, moved its headquarters to Providence, Rhode Island, in 1930 and changed its name to Atlantic Rayon in 1938.

The company expanded during WWII to make parachutes, and in 1944 adopted the name Textron to reflect the use of synthetics in its textiles. Between 1953 and 1960 Textron bought more than 40 businesses, including Bell Helicopter, before banker Rupe Thompson took over in 1960.

Thompson sold weak businesses such as Amerotron, Textron's last textile business (1963), but also bought 20 companies between 1960 and 1965. By 1968, when former Wall Street attorney William Miller replaced Thompson as CEO, Textron made products ranging from chain saws to watchbands. Miller sold several companies and bought Jacobsen Manufacturers (lawn-care equipment, 1978) before leaving Textron in 1978 to head the Federal Reserve and become treasury secretary under President Jimmy Carter.

B. F. Dolan, who became president in 1980, sold Textron's least-profitable businesses. The company bought Avco Corporation (aerospace and financial services, 1985) and UK-based Avdel (metal fastening systems, 1989).

In 1992 Textron bought Cessna Aircraft. The company sold its Lycoming Turbine Engine division in 1994 and acquired Orag Inter AG of Switzerland, Europe's #1 distributor of golf and turf-care equipment. In 1995-96 Textron bought Household Finance of Australia and three fastening systems companies. Also in 1996 Textron acquired Kautex Werke Reinold Hagen AG (plastic fuel tanks) and sold most of its aircraft wing division to The Carlyle Group.

In 1997 Provident (now UNUMProvident) bought Textron's 83% stake in Paul Revere Corp. (insurance). The following year Textron bought UK-based Ransomes plc (turf-care machinery and Cushman-brand transports) and David Brown Group plc (industrial gears and hydraulic systems). Lewis Campbell, Textron's president and COO, became CEO in 1998 and added chairman to his duties in 1999.

In 1999 the company bought 18 companies for about $2.5 billion; the largest of these included Flexalloy (vendor-managed inventory services), Omniquip International (telescopic material-handling equipment), and the industry and aircraft finance divisions of Green Tree Financial Servicing.

In 2000 Textron acquired Karl Oelschlager GmbH & Co., a German maker of stamped metal parts, and in early 2001 it acquired telecommunications test equipment maker Tempo Research. Around the same time, Textron said it would close or consolidate operations at about 20 manufacturing sites and cut more than 3,600 jobs.

Late in 2001 Textron closed more plants and cut more jobs, running the total announced layoffs for the year to around 7,500 (the cutbacks were spread through the end of 2002). In December 2001 the company sold its TAC-Trim automotive trim unit to Collins & Aikman in a deal worth about $1.34 billion.

Restructuring continued in 2003 and 2004 and the cost savings goal grew to a reduction of 10,000 jobs and 99 facilities. In 2006 Textron sold its Fastening Systems business.

Later in 2006 Textron sold its Jacobsen commercial grounds care products unit in order to focus more on its golf and professional turf operations. Near the end of 2006 Textron agreed to purchase Overwatch Systems for about $325 million. Overwatch is a maker of communications products and intelligence analysis tools for the US Department of Defense, Homeland Security, and certain friendly foreign militaries.

EXECUTIVES

Chairman and CEO: Lewis B. Campbell, age 62, $11,352,363 total compensation
President and COO: Scott C. Donnelly, age 47, $12,118,588 total compensation
EVP and CFO: Frank T. Connor, age 49
VP and CIO: Gary Cantrell
EVP Administration and Chief Human Resources Officer: John D. Butler, age 61
EVP and Chief Innovation Officer: Kenneth C. (Ken) Bohlen, age 56
EVP Government Affairs, Strategy and Business Development, International, Communications, and Investor Relations: Mary L. Howell, age 56, $3,967,550 total compensation
EVP and General Counsel: Terrence (Terry) O'Donnell, age 65, $4,885,237 total compensation
SVP International: R. Siisi Adu-Gyamfi
SVP, Textron Six Sigma, Integrated Supply Chain and Transformation: Peter N. Riley
SVP and Corporate Controller: Richard L. (Dick) Yates, age 58
SVP Strategy and Business Integration: Stuart Grief
VP and Treasurer: Mary F. Lovejoy
VP Business Ethics and Corporate Secretary: Frederick K. Butler
VP Government Affairs: Robert O. Rowland
VP Investor Relations: Douglas R. Wilburne
VP, Communications: Susan M. Tardanico
VP Strategy and Business Development: Peter (Pete) Durette
Auditors: Ernst & Young LLP

LOCATIONS

HQ: Textron Inc.
40 Westminster St., Providence, RI 02903
Phone: 401-421-2800   **Fax:** 401-457-2220
Web: www.textron.com

2008 Sales

	$ mil.	% of total
Americas		
US	8,821	62
Latin America & Mexico	1,131	8
Canada	442	3
Europe	2,613	18
Asia & Australia	754	5
Middle East & Africa	485	4
Total	**14,246**	**100**

PRODUCTS/OPERATIONS

2008 Sales

	$ mil.	% of total
Cessna	5,662	40
Industrial	2,918	20
Bell	2,827	20
Textron Systems	2,116	15
Financial	723	5
Total	**14,246**	**100**

Selected Products

Cessna
  Business jets
  Overnight express package carrier aircraft
  Piston planes
  Turboprop planes
Bell
  Commercial helicopters
  Military helicopters
Industrial
  Automatic clear vision systems
  Blow-molded functional components
  Compact construction equipment
  Electrical connectors
  Electrical test instruments
  Golf and turf care products
  Hand and hydraulic tools
  Iron castings
  Plastic fuel tank systems
  Utility vehicles
Textron Systems
  Geospatial systems
  Light armored combat vehicles
  Marine craft
  Multi-source intelligence framework systems
  Piston engines
  Unmanned aircraft systems
Finance
  Commercial loans and leases

Selected Industrial Brands

Electrical measurement instruments, tools, and fiber-optic connectors
  Fairmont
  Greenlee
  Klauke
  Progressive
  Tempo
Golf and turf care
  Cushman
  E-Z-GO
  Ransomes

COMPETITORS

AgustaWestland	Johnson Controls
Black & Decker	Kaman
Boeing	Lockheed Martin
Bombardier	Magna International
Cirrus Design	Moog
Claverham	Northrop Grumman
Deere	Northstar Aerospace
EADS	Piper Aircraft
Eaton	Raytheon
Electrolux	Rolls-Royce
Embraer	Spirit AeroSystems
GE	Sun Hydraulics
General Dynamics	Terex
Honda	Toro
Honeywell International	TRW Automotive
Illinois Tool Works	United Technologies
Ingersoll-Rand	

HISTORICAL FINANCIALS

Company Type: Public

Income Statement

FYE: Saturday nearest December 31

	REVENUE ($ mil.)	NET INCOME ($ mil.)	NET PROFIT MARGIN	EMPLOYEES
12/08	14,246.0	486.0	3.4%	43,000
12/07	13,225.0	917.0	6.9%	44,000
12/06	11,490.0	601.0	5.2%	40,000
12/05	10,043.0	203.0	2.0%	37,000
12/04	10,242.0	365.0	3.6%	44,000
Annual Growth	**8.6%**	**7.4%**	**—**	**(0.6%)**

2008 Year-End Financials

Debt ratio: 384.1%
Return on equity: 16.6%
Cash ($ mil.): 547
Current ratio: 1.10
Long-term debt ($ mil.): 9,081
No. of shares (mil.): 270
Dividends
  Yield: 6.6%
  Payout: 47.2%
Market value ($ mil.): 3,748

Stock History

NYSE: TXT

	STOCK PRICE ($) FY Close	P/E High/Low		PER SHARE ($) Earnings	Dividends	Book Value
12/08	13.87	34	5	1.95	0.92	8.76
12/07	71.30	21	12	3.60	0.85	12.98
12/06	46.88	21	16	2.31	0.78	9.80
12/05	38.49	54	44	0.75	0.70	12.12
12/04	36.90	29	19	1.30	0.66	13.51
Annual Growth	**(21.7%)**	**—**	**—**	**10.7%**	**8.7%**	**(10.3%)**

Thermo Fisher Scientific

Whether for research, analysis, discovery, or diagnostics, Thermo Fisher gets the laboratory ready to assist mankind with solutions big and small. The company makes and distributes analytical instruments, equipment, and laboratory supplies — from chromatographs to Erlenmeyer flasks. Thermo Fisher serves more than 350,000 customers worldwide in biotech and pharmaceutical companies, clinical diagnostic labs and hospitals, government agencies, research organizations, and universities, as well as environmental and industrial quality control settings. The company was formed in 2006 by merging Thermo Electron with Fisher Scientific International in a stock-swap valued at nearly $11 billion.

As separate entities, Thermo and Fisher were among the biggest companies in the scientific and technical instruments field. Fisher was twice the size of Thermo, in terms of sales, but combining the two created more muscle to compete against big names such as Agilent Technologies and Becton Dickinson. The merger worked because Thermo Electron was, for the most part, a manufacturer of scientific instruments, while

Fisher Scientific was largely a distributor of laboratory equipment and supplies. There was little overlap between their respective product lines. Their sales forces were familiar with each other and with many of the same customers.

Together as Thermo Fisher Scientific, the company pushes a one-stop catalog of products and services that captures a large list of drug companies and laboratories. Product lines are marketed under two names, Fisher Scientific (technology brands) and Thermo Scientific (convenience brands, or products and services available through a direct sales network).

Strategically, the cash from making bread-and-butter medical equipment (beakers and microscope slides) is used to buy small, innovative companies that benefit from the company's resources and that can drive Thermo Fisher's double-digit growth and ongoing expansion plans. (It is one of the top-10 fast growth companies in China.) The company scored the scientific and medical division (Biolab) of Australian distributor Alesco Corporation in 2009. It also strengthened its position in the ribonucleic acid (RNA) product market through its 2008 acquisition of Open Biosystems, a provider of RNA interference and protein detection products. In addition, the company tied up carbon fiber centrifuge rotor manufacturer FIBERLite Centrifuge, and histology and anatomical pathology product manufacturer Raymond A. Lamb.

HISTORY

In 1902, 20-year-old Chester Fisher bought the stockroom of Pittsburgh Testing Laboratories (established 1884) and formed Scientific Materials Co. The company's earliest products, supplied from Europe, included simple tools such as microscopes, balances, and calorimeters. It published its first catalog in 1904.

When the outbreak of WWI disrupted supplies from Europe, Scientific Materials established its own R&D and manufacturing facilities. It acquired Montreal-based Scientific Supplies in 1925 and the following year changed its name to Fisher Scientific Company. By 1935 Fisher had doubled its size, adding glass-blowing operations and an instrument shop.

During the German occupation of Greece in WWII, George Hatsopoulos, part of a well-to-do family packed with politicians and engineering professors, made radios for the Greek resistance. After the war he came to the US and became a professor of mechanical engineering at MIT. With a $50,000 loan, Hatsopoulos founded Thermo Electron in 1956 to identify emerging technology needs and create solutions for them.

That year he built a machine that would turn heat directly into electrons. This thermionic converter, though itself never commercialized, formed the basis of many of the company's successful products, including a battery-operated heart pump and a process for incinerating toxic material in polluted soils.

Thermo Electron went public in 1967 and in the early 1970s introduced efficient industrial furnaces for the paper and metals markets.

Chester Fisher died in 1965 — the same year Fisher Scientific went public — leaving Fisher to sons Aiken, Benjamin, and James.

Aiken retired as chairman in 1975 and was replaced by Benjamin. That year former Pfeiffer Glass president Edward Perkins was appointed president and CEO — the first non-family member to hold this position.

Besides developing its own business lines, Thermo Electron expanded through several acquisitions in the 1990s. The company bought the analytical instrument and process-control businesses of Baker Hughes (1994), the scientific-instruments division of Fisons (now part of Sanofi-Aventis, 1995), and respiratory-care equipment maker Sensormedics (1996).

In 1992 Fisher bought Hamilton Scientific, the top US maker of laboratory workstations, as well as a majority interest in Kuhn + Bayer, a German supplier of scientific equipment.

Former American Stock Exchange CEO Richard Syron replaced Hatsopoulos as CEO of Thermo Electron in 1999. The next year Syron announced a reorganization in which the Thermo Electron family would be reduced to three companies: Thermo Electron would concentrate on measurement and detection instruments, while Thermo Fibertek (renamed Kadant in 2001) and a medical products company (later dubbed Viasys Healthcare) would be spun off to shareholders.

Late in 2002 Syron was named executive chairman, and replaced as CEO by president and COO Marijn Dekkers. The next year Syron resigned as chairman and was replaced by board member Jim Manzi.

In 2003 Fisher acquired Sweden-based Perbio Science (consumable tools for protein-related research) for about $700 million. The following year Fisher continued its push into the life sciences market with two acquisitions: UK-based Oxoid (tools used to test for bacterial contamination) for $330 million and privately held Dharmacon (synthesized RNA used in genetic research) for $80 million.

Also in 2004, Fisher acquired Apogent Technologies, a maker of laboratory and life sciences equipment for health care and scientific research applications, for nearly $4 billion.

In 2005 Thermo Electron acquired SPX's Kendro Laboratory Products business for approximately $834 million.

In late 2006 Thermo Electron merged with Fisher Scientific International in a stock-swap transaction valued at nearly $11 billion.

EXECUTIVES

Chairman: Jim P. Manzi, age 57
President, CEO, and Director: Marijn E. Dekkers, age 51, $9,613,905 total compensation
EVP and COO: Marc N. Casper, age 41, $3,825,593 total compensation
SVP and CFO: Peter M. Wilver, age 49, $2,089,755 total compensation
VP and Chief Accounting Officer: Peter E. Hornstra, age 49
SVP, General Counsel, and Secretary: Seth H. Hoogasian, age 54, $2,071,310 total compensation
SVP: Guy Broadbent, age 45
SVP Human Resources: Stephen G. Sheehan, age 53
SVP and President, Analytical and Scientific Instruments: Gregory J. (Greg) Herrema, age 43
SVP; President, Laboratory Products: Alan J. Malus, age 49, $2,413,867 total compensation
SVP Customer Excellence: Fredric T. Walder, age 51
SVP Global Business Services: Alexander G. Stachtiaris, age 45
SVP; President, Specialty Diagnostics: Yuh-Geng Tsay, age 60
SVP; President, Customer Channels: Edward A. Pesicka
SVP Corporate Strategy and Development: Elizabeth A. Mily
VP Investor Relations: Kenneth J. Apicerno
VP Global Research and Development: Ian D. Jardine
VP Corporate Communications: Karen A. Kirkwood
VP Tax and Treasury: Anthony H. Smith
Auditors: PricewaterhouseCoopers LLP

LOCATIONS

HQ: Thermo Fisher Scientific Inc.
81 Wyman St., Waltham, MA 02454
Phone: 781-622-1000   **Fax:** 781-622-1207
Web: www.thermofisher.com

2008 Sales

	$ mil.	% of total
US	7,165.0	59
UK	978.2	8
Germany	1,134.6	9
Other countries	2,934.3	24
Adjustments	(1,714.1)	—
Total	**10,498.0**	**100**

PRODUCTS/OPERATIONS

2008 Sales

	$ mil.	% of total
Laboratory Products & Services	6,453.3	59
Analytical Technologies	4,471.2	41
Adjustments	(426.5)	—
Total	**10,498.0**	**100**

Selected Products

Analytical Instrumentation
  Analysis instruments
  Electron backscattered diffraction systems
  Gas chromatography equipment
  High-performance liquid chromatography/ion chromatography (HPLC/IC) systems
  Ion energy analyzers
  Mass spectrometers (hybrid, ion trap, quadrupole)
  Microscopes
Laboratory Equipment
  Clinical diagnostics
    Anatomical pathology equipment
    Chemistry reagents
    Ion-selective electrolyte (ISE) consumables
  Lab furnishings
  Laboratory consumables
  Laboratory information management systems
  Laboratory instrument services
    Certification
    Consulting
    Instrument and computer systems validation
    Metrology
    Regulatory compliance
  Liquid handling equipment
    Automated liquid handling
    Microplates
    Pipettes and tips
    Pumps
  Meters, monitors, and electrochemical equipment
    Biosensors
    Colorimeters
    Detectors
    Electrodes, probes, and cells
    Meters
    Microplate instruments
    Monitors and analyzers
    Titrators
  Sample preparation equipment
    Baths
    Centrifuges
    Concentrators
    Extraction equipment
    Freeze dryers
    Incubators
    Luminometric systems
    Ovens
  Vacuum equipment

Process Equipment
  Analysis instruments
    Chromatographs
    Elemental analyzers
    Fourier transform infrared analyzers
    Gas measurement
    Guided microwave spectrometry
    Mass spectrometers
    Moisture analyzers
    Near infrared analyzers
    Particle analyzers
    Surface analyzers
    X-ray spectrometers
  Coding and marking systems
  Foreign object detection equipment
  Nuclear radiation
    Neutron flux monitoring systems
    Neutron sources
    Reactor protection systems
  Nuclear reactor instrumentation systems
  Physical measurement and control systems
  Polymer testing equipment
  Process monitoring and control equipment
Security and Detection Devices
  Chemical and biological detection
    Aerosol monitors
    Ambient air analyzers
    Particle sizing impactors
    Unknown material identification instruments
  Explosives trace detection systems
  Radiological and nuclear detection
    Contamination survey meters
    Isotope identifiers
    Mobile gamma radiation monitors
    Neutron generators
    Nuclear incident emergency response kit
    Personal dosimeters
    Radioactivity monitors
    Rapid response vans

COMPETITORS

Abbott Labs	Mettler-Toledo
Agilent Technologies	Newport Corp.
Beckman Coulter	PerkinElmer
Becton, Dickinson	QIAGEN
Bio-Rad Labs	Roche Diagnostics
Bruker	Roper Industries
Corning	Shimadzu
Danaher	Sigma-Aldrich
Emerson Electric	Tektronix
Harvard Bioscience	Varian
Hitachi	VWR International
Johnson & Johnson	Waters Corp.
Life Technologies	Yokogawa Electric
MDS	

HISTORICAL FINANCIALS

Company Type: Public

Income Statement				FYE: Saturday nearest December 31
	REVENUE ($ mil.)	NET INCOME ($ mil.)	NET PROFIT MARGIN	EMPLOYEES
12/08	10,498.0	994.2	9.5%	34,500
12/07	9,746.4	761.1	7.8%	33,000
12/06	3,791.6	168.9	4.5%	30,500
12/05	2,633.0	223.2	8.5%	11,500
12/04	2,206.0	361.8	16.4%	9,900
Annual Growth	47.7%	28.8%	—	36.6%

2008 Year-End Financials

Debt ratio: 13.7%
Return on equity: 6.8%
Cash ($ mil.): 1,281
Current ratio: 2.82
Long-term debt ($ mil.): 2,044
No. of shares (mil.): 408
Dividends
  Yield: 0.0%
  Payout: —
Market value ($ mil.): 13,906

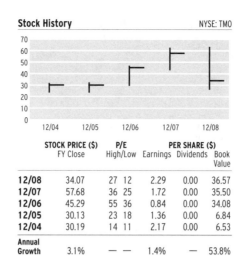

Stock History — NYSE: TMO

	STOCK PRICE ($) FY Close	P/E High/Low		PER SHARE ($) Earnings	Dividends	Book Value
12/08	34.07	27	12	2.29	0.00	36.57
12/07	57.68	36	25	1.72	0.00	35.50
12/06	45.29	55	36	0.84	0.00	34.08
12/05	30.13	23	18	1.36	0.00	6.84
12/04	30.19	14	11	2.17	0.00	6.53
Annual Growth	3.1%	—	—	1.4%	—	53.8%

Thomas & Betts

Thomas & Betts (T&B) is betting on its connections. The company provides electrical connectors, HVAC equipment, and transmission towers to the commercial, communications, industrial, and utility markets. It has three business segments: electrical (electrical connectors, enclosures, raceways, installation tools); HVAC (heaters, gas-fired duct furnaces, and evaporative cooling products); and steel structures (poles and transmission towers for power and telecommunications companies). T&B's many brands include Color-Keyed, Elastimold, Kindorf, Red Dot, Reznor, Sta-Kon, Snap-N-Seal, and Steel City. Sales outside the US account for about one-third of its revenues.

T&B's challenges in 2009 include its dependence on the US market, where the economy is struggling through an extended recession. Volatile costs for commodity raw materials (aluminum, copper, rubber compounds, steel, and zinc among them) and for energy are another challenge. The credit crisis is forcing the company to keep a close eye on the creditworthiness of leading customers, although T&B doesn't have any customers with a large amount of trade receivables owed.

The company streamlined its operations, consolidating production and distribution facilities and divesting stakes in joint ventures in Belgium and Japan. T&B also made sizable strategic acquisitions to supplement its product portfolio. T&B's largest segment, electrical, accounts for more than 80% of its sales.

HISTORY

In 1898 in New York City, Princeton engineering graduates Hobart D. Betts and Robert Mc-Kean Thomas founded a distribution company for the infant electrical industry; they quickly moved into designing conduits and fittings. In 1905 the company incorporated as Thomas and Betts Company, and in 1912 it began manufacturing with the purchase of Standard Electric Fittings. In 1917 the two merged to form The Thomas & Betts Company, consolidating operations in Elizabeth, New Jersey.

Thomas & Betts was one of the first manufacturers of electrical products to embrace electrical distributors as marketing and sales partners, not competitors. In the early 1930s the company adopted its first marketing slogan: "Wherever Electricity Goes, So Do We."

The company made products that were used to wire the Hoover Dam and the New York City subway system, and by the US military during WWII. During this period Thomas & Betts grew internally and through acquisitions. In 1959 the company went public. It changed its name to Thomas & Betts Corporation (T&B) in 1968.

In 1992 T&B acquired American Electric, an electrical products manufacturer, and relocated its corporate offices to American Electric's headquarters in Memphis. The company acquired Augat, a maker of electronic connectors, in 1996; consolidation expenses brought a severe drop in profits for the year.

President Clyde Moore was named CEO in 1997. T&B made another 15 acquisitions in 1997 and 1998, continuing to expand upon its product offerings for fiber-optic and telecommunications companies. Among the acquisitions were Pride Product Services, a maker of fiber-optic sleeves; and Kaufel Group, a Canadian manufacturer of industrial and emergency lighting products. The latter more than doubled the extent of T&B's lighting product line. Also in 1998 T&B entered a new market with its $74 million acquisition of Telecommunications Devices, a maker of batteries for cell phones and laptops.

The company's 1999 acquisitions included Ocal, which makes plastic-coated conduits and components, and L.E. Mason, a manufacturer of electrical boxes and related products. But its bid to acquire cable maker AFC Cable was topped by rival Tyco International. That year losses caused T&B to exit the active-components portion of its cable TV business; the company sold its Megaflex, Photon, and broadband radio-frequency amplifier product lines.

In 2000 T&B sold its electronics manufacturing operations to Tyco for $750 million, and Moore was elected chairman. He later resigned his post, and director T. Kevin Dunnigan (who had previously served as both chairman and CEO of T&B), assumed Moore's position.

In early 2001 T&B announced that the SEC was investigating its accounting practices; the company also announced it was restating earnings for 2000. Later in the year T&B sold its American Electric and Dark-To-Light product lines to US-based rival National Service Industries. It also divested its ground rod business as the company began to exit the low-voltage circuit protection market.

Five class-action lawsuits over the accounting issues were filed in 2000, and they were consolidated into one action late in the year. A US District Court ordered formal mediation in the litigation in mid-2002, which resulted in a settlement agreement later that year. Without T&B admitting any liability or wrongdoing, the parties agreed to dismiss the lawsuit and the company paid $46.5 million to the plaintiffs.

Dominic Pileggi, president of T&B's main electrical business, was promoted to president and COO of the company at the beginning of 2003. Later in 2003 the company reached a settlement with the SEC, basically agreeing to more closely follow accounting and financial reporting regulations, while the commission brought no charges against the company.

In late 2003 Pileggi was named to succeed Dunnigan as CEO in early 2004. Dunnigan became non-executive chairman of the board, while Pileggi was also elected as a director.

In 2005 T&B acquired the assets of Southern Monopole and Utilities, a subsidiary of Qualico Steel Company. Pileggi succeeded Dunnigan as chairman at the end of 2005, as Dunnigan retired as chairman and a member of the board.

In 2007 the company acquired competitor Lamson & Sessions for around $450 million in cash. In the biggest acquisition in its history, T&B saw a strategic fit with the Lamson & Sessions product portfolio of non-metallic electrical boxes, fittings, flexible conduit, and industrial PVC pipe.

Following the L&S acquisition, T&B decided to divest its portfolio of PVC and high-density polyethylene (HDPE) conduits, ducts, and pressure pipes used in the construction, industrial, municipal, utility, and telecommunications markets. Also in 2007 T&B acquired the power quality business of Danaher for $280 million in cash..

That same year T&B also bought Drilling Technical Supply SA (DTS), a privately held French manufacturer of hazardous lighting and electrical controls.

EXECUTIVES

Chairman, President, and CEO: Dominic J. Pileggi, age 57, $9,230,928 total compensation
SVP and CFO: Kenneth W. (Ken) Fluke, age 49
VP and Controller: William E. Weaver Jr.
VP Information Technologies: Joseph (Joe) DiCianni
Chief Compliance Officer, Assistant General Counsel, and Assistant Secretary: W. David Smith Jr.
SVP Global Operations: Imad Hajj, age 48, $1,295,620 total compensation
SVP; President Electrical: Charles L. (Chuck) Treadway
VP, General Counsel, and Secretary: James N. (Jim) Raines, age 65
VP Investor and Corporate Relations: Patricia A. (Tricia) Bergeron
VP Business Development and Strategic Planning: Stanley P. (Stan) Locke, age 49, $769,054 total compensation
VP Business Development: Dennis I. Smith
VP Tax: Joseph F. Warren
President, Canada, Australia, and EMEA/Asia: Michael B. (Mike) Kenney
President, Steel Structures and Communications: James R. (Jim) Wiederholt
President, U.S. Electrical: E. F. (Ned) Camuti
President, HVAC: Hugh Windsor
President, Canada: Nathalie Pilon
Auditors: KPMG LLP

LOCATIONS

HQ: Thomas & Betts Corporation
8155 T&B Blvd., Memphis, TN 38125
Phone: 901-252-8000   **Fax:** 901-252-1354
Web: www.tnb.com

Thomas & Betts has manufacturing facilities in Australia, Belgium, Canada, France, Germany, Hungary, Japan, Mexico, the Netherlands, the UK, and the US.

2008 Sales

	$ mil.	% of total
US	1,622.8	66
Canada	433.5	17
Europe	268.6	11
Other regions	148.9	6
Total	**2,473.8**	**100**

PRODUCTS/OPERATIONS

2008 Sales

	$ mil.	% of total
Electrical	2,103.1	85
Steel structures	231.6	9
HVAC	139.1	6
Total	**2,473.8**	**100**

Selected Segments and Brands

Electrical
Boxes and covers (Bowers, Commander, Steel City)
Cable ties (Catamount, Ty-Fast, Ty-Rap)
Cable tray systems (Canstrut, Cen-Tray, Electrotray, Pilgrim, T&B)
Communications connectors, grounding products, meter sockets (Anchor, Blackburn)
Connectors (Blackburn, Color-Keyed)
Electrical maintenance products (Valon)
Electricians' supplies (Thomas & Betts)
Fittings and grounding systems (Thomas & Betts)
Industrial connectors (Russellstoll)
Metal framing (Kindorf, Superstrut)
Outlet boxes (Bowers, Union)
Terminals and connectors (STA-KON)
Timers and relays (Agastat)
Wiring ducts (Taylor)

Steel Structures
Power connectors and accessories (Elastimold)
Steel poles (Meyer)
Transmission towers (Lehigh)

HVAC
Evaporative cooling and energy recovery equipment (International Energy Saver)
Heaters (EK Campbell, Reznor)
Heating, mechanical, and refrigeration supplies (Thomas & Betts)

COMPETITORS

3M
Amphenol
Andrew Corporation
Beghelli
Cembre
Cooper Industries
Corning
Eaton
Encore Wire
Fujikura Ltd.
GE Consumer & Industrial
Gewiss
Hubbell
ITT Corp.
Legrand
Methode Electronics
Molex
Panasonic Corp
POWERTRUSION
Siemens AG
Smiths Group
Spirent
Sumitomo Electric
Tyco
Valmont Industries

HISTORICAL FINANCIALS

Company Type: Public

Income Statement

	REVENUE ($ mil.)	NET INCOME ($ mil.)	NET PROFIT MARGIN	EMPLOYEES
				FYE: Sunday nearest December 31
12/08	2,473.8	265.3	10.7%	10,000
12/07	2,136.9	183.2	8.6%	11,000
12/06	1,868.7	175.1	9.4%	9,000
12/05	1,695.4	113.4	6.7%	9,000
12/04	1,516.3	93.3	6.2%	9,000
Annual Growth	13.0%	29.9%	—	2.7%

2008 Year-End Financials

Debt ratio: 44.7%
Return on equity: 22.4%
Cash ($ mil.): 292
Current ratio: 1.82
Long-term debt ($ mil.): 512
No. of shares (mil.): 53
Dividends
  Yield: 0.0%
  Payout: —
Market value ($ mil.): 1,270

Stock History

NYSE: TNB

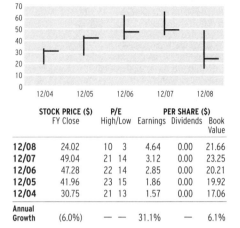

	STOCK PRICE ($) FY Close	P/E High/Low		PER SHARE ($) Earnings	Dividends	Book Value
12/08	24.02	10	3	4.64	0.00	21.66
12/07	49.04	21	14	3.12	0.00	23.25
12/06	47.28	22	14	2.85	0.00	20.21
12/05	41.96	23	15	1.86	0.00	19.92
12/04	30.75	21	13	1.57	0.00	17.06
Annual Growth	(6.0%)	—	—	31.1%	—	6.1%

Thor Industries

The Vikings and their Norse gods might have laughed at the idea of bathrooms on wheels, but that doesn't slow down RV maker Thor Industries. The company makes a range of RVs, including motor homes and travel trailers. Brands include the well-known Airstream and Dutchmen lines. It is also a leading US producer of small and midsize buses. Thor has bus and RV plants, as well as distributors, throughout the US and Canada. It also operates a joint venture with Cruise America that rents RVs to the public. The company was formed in 1980 when co-founder and CEO Wade Thompson and co-founder and vice chairman Peter Orthwein purchased the ailing Airstream business.

Skyrocketing fuel prices in 2008 helped torpedo sales of RVs, with sales of motorized RVs down about 18% by dollar volume and down around 23% by unit volume in fiscal 2008, compared with the previous year. Motorized RVs were unprofitable for 2008, with the other lines of business showing respectable profit margins.

In light of the plunging RV sales, along with GE Consumer Finance ending its relationship with Thor Industries, the company revived its Thor Credit retail financing business in late 2008. The unit will help customers at Thor dealers finance purchases of new and used RVs.

RVs continue to be Thor's thoroughbred in terms of revenue, with bus sales coming in a distant second. Although its 2000 bid for rival RV maker Coachmen Industries fell through, Thor managed to pick up Keystone RV Company for $145 million the following year, making it the US's largest manufacturer of travel trailers, with 20% of the market. Thor later bought class A motor home maker Damon Corporation. The Damon purchase also gave Thor a new product line, the Breckenridge brand of park models. Park models are factory-built second homes that usually are towed to a location, such as a lakeshore or wooded area, and are used as a country cottage.

Thor strengthened its bus operations with the purchase of the bankrupt Goshen Coach for $9.5 million in mid-2005. The deal gave Thor about a 37% share of the small to midsize bus market in the US.

Founders Thompson and Orthwein together own about 34% of the company.

HISTORY

Mergers and acquisitions specialist Wade Thompson and investment banker Peter Orthwein saw the potential of the RV market after buying Hi-Lo Trailer in 1977. Thor Industries was formed when they bought the troubled Airstream Trailers unit (founded in 1931) from Beatrice Foods in 1980. Named after the mythical Norse god of thunder and containing the first two letters of the founders' last names, Thor Industries formed Citair in 1982 to buy the RV division of Commodore Corp. (founded 1948). The company went public in 1984, and it entered the bus business with the acquisitions of ElDorado Bus company in 1988 and National Coach in 1991. Thor expanded its RV line with the purchases of Dutchmen Manufacturing in 1991 and Four Winds International in 1992.

The company continued acquisitions in 1995, buying Skamper Corp. (folding trailers) and Komfort Trailers. In 1996 its bus operations received significant orders from National Car Rental and the suburban Chicago transit company, PACE.

Bus sales did well in 1997, but RV sales were flat. That year Thor sold its Henschen Axle manufacturing operation. In response to weak sales, the company opened new channels, such as its RV rental joint venture. In 1998 it bought Champion Motor Coach (small and midsize buses) from manufactured-home company Champion Enterprises for about $10 million. It also sold its unprofitable motor homes unit, Thor West, to the division's managers.

In 1999 Thor won a $45 million contract to build 1,135 buses for the state of California. The following year the company made a bid to buy rival RV company Coachmen Industries; that bid was later rejected and withdrawn.

Thor regained its thunder in 2001 with the $145 million purchase of Keystone RV Company. The deal made the company the US's leading manufacturer of travel trailers and third wheels (with 25% of the market), as well as the largest builder of small and midsize buses (with 37% of the market).

In 2003 Thor paid nearly $30 million for Damon Corporation, a maker of class A motor homes and park models. Thor paid $27 million for fifth wheel and travel trailer manufacturer CrossRoads RV in 2004.

EXECUTIVES

Chairman, President, and CEO: Wade F. B. Thompson, age 68
Vice Chairman and Treasurer: Peter B. Orthwein, age 63
SVP and CFO: Christian G. (Chris) Farman, age 49
EVP, Chief Administrative Officer, and Secretary: Walter L. Bennett, age 63
President General Coach Ontario: Roger Faulkner
President Dutchmen: Richard W. Florea
President Four Winds: Jeffery L. Kime
President Thor Commercial Bus: Andrew Imanse
President Keystone: Ronald J. (Ron) Fenech
President Damon Corporation: William C. (Bill) Fenech
President Breckenridge: Tim J. Howard

President and CEO, Airstream: Robert Wheeler
President Crossroads: Mark R. Lucas
President Champion Bus: John Resnik
President Goshen Coach: Troy Snyder
President Komfort: John P. Attila
President General Couch British Columbia: George W. Bruneau
Auditors: Deloitte & Touche LLP

LOCATIONS

HQ: Thor Industries, Inc.
419 W. Pike St., Jackson Center, OH 45334
Phone: 937-596-6849   **Fax:** 937-596-6539
Web: www.thorindustries.com

PRODUCTS/OPERATIONS

2008 Sales

	$ mil.	% of total
Recreation vehicles		
Towables	1,763.1	67
Motorized	461.9	17
Buses	415.7	16
Total	**2,640.7**	**100**

Selected Products

Recreational Vehicles
 Airstream (premium and medium-high-priced travel trailers and motor homes)
 Breckenridge (factory built cottage homes)
 Citair (travel trailers, fifth wheels, class C motorhomes, and truck campers)
 Damon Motor Coach (gasoline and diesel class A motor homes)
 Dutchmen (travel trailers and fifth wheels)
 Four Winds (motor homes)
 Keystone (travel trailers and fifth wheels)
 Komfort (travel trailers and fifth wheels for sale in the western US and Canada)
 Thor California (travel trailers and fifth wheels)
Buses
 Champion Bus (small and midsize buses)
 ElDorado National (small and midsize buses for airport, car rental, and hotel and motel shuttles, tour and charter operations, community transit systems, and other uses)
 Goshen Coach (small and midsize buses)

COMPETITORS

Blue Bird	Jayco, Inc.
Champion Enterprises	Kingsley Coach
Clayton Homes	Monaco RV
Coachmen	Motor Coach Industries
Collins Industries	Prevost Car
Daimler Buses	Rexhall Industries
Elixir Industries	Skyline
Fairmont Homes	Supreme Industries
Featherlite	TRIGANO
Fleetwood Enterprises	Volvo
Fleetwood Folding Trailers	Wells Cargo
Forest River	Winnebago
Hino Motors	

HISTORICAL FINANCIALS

Company Type: Public

Income Statement

FYE: July 31

	REVENUE ($ mil.)	NET INCOME ($ mil.)	NET PROFIT MARGIN	EMPLOYEES
7/08	2,640.7	92.7	3.5%	7,064
7/07	2,856.3	134.7	4.7%	8,689
7/06	3,066.3	172.5	5.6%	9,363
7/05	2,558.4	121.8	4.8%	8,473
7/04	2,187.7	106.1	4.8%	7,471
Annual Growth	**4.8%**	**(3.3%)**	**—**	**(1.4%)**

2008 Year-End Financials

Debt ratio: —	No. of shares (mil.): 55
Return on equity: 12.6%	Dividends
Cash ($ mil.): 190	Yield: 1.4%
Current ratio: 2.13	Payout: 16.9%
Long-term debt ($ mil.): —	Market value ($ mil.): 1,088

Stock History

NYSE: THO

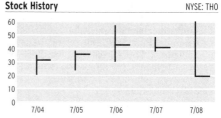

	STOCK PRICE ($) FY Close	P/E High/Low		PER SHARE ($) Earnings	Dividends	Book Value
7/08	19.62	36	12	1.66	0.28	12.62
7/07	41.02	20	16	2.41	0.28	13.82
7/06	42.84	19	10	3.03	0.24	12.86
7/05	35.80	18	11	2.13	0.12	10.65
7/04	31.31	19	11	1.84	0.09	9.23
Annual Growth	**(11.0%)**	**—**	**—**	**(2.5%)**	**32.8%**	**8.1%**

TIAA-CREF

It's punishment enough to write the name once on a blackboard. Teachers Insurance and Annuity Association — College Retirement Equities Fund (TIAA-CREF) is one of the largest, if not longest-named, private retirement systems in the US, providing for more than 3 million members of the academic community and for investors outside academia's ivied confines. It also serves institutional investors. TIAA-CREF's core offerings include financial advice, investment information, retirement accounts, pensions, annuities, individual life and disability insurance, tuition financing, and trust services (through TIAA-CREF Trust). The system, a not-for-profit organization, also manages a line of mutual funds.

TIAA-CREF is one of the nation's heftiest institutional investors, with more than $435 billion in assets under management, and it has not been afraid to throw its weight around corporate boardrooms. The organization is known for active and choosy investing and is a vocal critic of extravagant executive compensation packages.

In 2006 TIAA-CREF bought Kapsick & Company, which manages planned giving assets for colleges, universities, and other not-for-profits. The acquisition makes the system the largest provider of such services in the US. TIAA-CREF also owns one of the nation's largest portfolios of real estate investments.

HISTORY

With $15 million, the Carnegie Foundation for the Advancement of Teaching in 1905 founded the Teachers Insurance and Annuity Association (TIAA) in New York City to provide retirement benefits and other forms of financial security to educators. When Carnegie's original endowment was found to be insufficient, another

$1 million reorganized the fund into a defined-contribution plan in 1918. TIAA was the first portable pension plan, letting participants change employers without losing benefits and offering a fixed annuity. The fund required infusions of Carnegie cash until 1947.

In 1952 TIAA CEO William Greenough pioneered the variable annuity, based on common stock investments, and created the College Retirement Equities Fund (CREF) to offer it. Designed to supplement TIAA's fixed annuity, CREF invested participants' premiums in stocks. CREF and TIAA were subject to New York insurance (but not SEC) regulation.

During the 1950s, TIAA led the fight for Social Security benefits for university employees and began offering group total disability coverage (1957) and group life insurance (1958).

In 1971 TIAA-CREF began helping colleges boost investment returns from endowments, then moved into endowment management. It helped found a research center to provide objective investment information in 1972.

For 70 years retirement was the only way members could exit TIAA-CREF. Their only investment choices were stocks through CREF or a one-way transfer into TIAA's annuity accounts based on long-term bond, real estate, and mortgage investments. In the 1980s CREF indexed its funds to the S&P average.

By 1987's stock crash, TIAA-CREF had a million members, many of whom wanted more protection from stock market fluctuations. After the crash, Clifton Wharton (the first African-American to head a major US financial organization) became CEO; the next year CREF added a money market fund, for which the SEC required complete transferability, even outside TIAA-CREF. Now open to competition, TIAA-CREF became more flexible, adding investment options and long-term-care plans.

John Biggs became CEO in 1993. After the 1994 bond crash, TIAA-CREF began educating members on the ABCs of retirement investing, hoping to persuade them not to switch to flashy short-term investments and not to panic during such cyclical events as the crash.

In 1996 it went international, buying interests in UK commercial and mixed-use property. TIAA-CREF filed for SEC approval of more mutual funds in 1997. Although federal tax legislation took away TIAA-CREF's tax-exempt status in 1997, the change was made without decreasing annuity incomes for the year.

The status change let TIAA-CREF offer no-load mutual funds to the public in 1998. A trust company and financial planning services were added; all new products were sold at cost, with TIAA-CREF waiving fees. TIAA-CREF in 1998 became the first pension fund to force out an entire board of directors (that of sputtering cafeteria firm Furr's/Bishop's). Also that year TIAA-CREF's crusade to curb "dead hand" poison pills (an antitakeover defense measure) found favor with the shareholders of Bergen Brunswig (now AmerisourceBergen), Lubrizol, and Mylan Laboratories.

Biggs retired in 2002 and was succeeded by Herbert Allison.

EXECUTIVES

Chairman: Ronald L. Thompson, age 58
President, CEO, and Director: Roger W. Ferguson Jr., age 58
EVP and CFO: Georganne C. Proctor, age 52
EVP and CTO: Susan S. Kozik
EVP and Chief Institutional Development and Sales Officer: Bertram L. Scott, age 57
Senior Managing Director and Chief Strategy Officer: Keith Stock, age 56
SVP and Chief Compliance Officer: Janice Innis-Thompson
Chief Information Security Officer: Peter F. Murphy III
EVP and Chief Legal Officer: Brandon Becker
EVP and Head of Fixed Income and Real Estate: John A. Somers
EVP Asset Management; CEO Teachers Advisors and TIAA-CREF Investment Management: Scott C. Evans
EVP Individual Client Services; President, TIAA-CREF Individual & Institutional Services: Maliz E. Beams, age 53
EVP Public Affairs: I. Steven (Steve) Goldstein
EVP Human Resources and Corporate Services: Dermot J. O'Brien
EVP Risk Management: Erwin W. Martens
EVP Technology and Operations: Cara L. Schnaper
SVP Marketing and Advertising: Jamie DePeau
SVP and General Counsel: Jonathan Feigelson
Chairman, President, and CEO, TIAA-CREF Life Insurance: Bret L. Benham
Director, Corporate Governance: Linda E. Scott
Senior Managing Director and Chief Investment Officer: Edward J. Grzybowski
Senior Managing Director and Head of Strategy: Sheila Hooda

LOCATIONS

HQ: Teachers Insurance and Annuity Association — College Retirement Equities Fund
730 3rd Ave., New York, NY 10017
Phone: 212-490-9000   **Fax:** 212-916-4840
Web: www.tiaa-cref.org

PRODUCTS/OPERATIONS

Selected Subsidiaries and Units

Kapsick & Company
Teachers Personal Investors Services, Inc. (mutual fund management)
TIAA-CREF Individual & Institutional Services, Inc. (broker-dealer)
TIAA-CREF Life Insurance Company (insurance and annuities)
TIAA-CREF Trust Company, FSB (trust services)
TIAA-CREF Tuition Financing, Inc. (state tuition savings program management)

Selected Mutual Funds

Bond
Bond Plus II
Equity Index
Growth & Income
High-Yield II
Inflation-Linked Bond
International Equity
Large-Cap Growth
Large-Cap Value
Managed Allocation II
Mid-Cap Growth
Mid-Cap Value
Money Market
Real Estate Securities
Short-Term Bond II
Small-Cap Equity
Social Choice Equity
Tax-Exempt Bond II

COMPETITORS

Aetna	JPMorgan Chase
AIG	MassMutual
AIG Retirement	Merrill Lynch
Ameriprise	MetLife
AXA Financial	New York Life
Bank of New York Mellon	Northwestern Mutual
Berkshire Hathaway	Principal Financial
CalPERS	Prudential
Charles Schwab	T. Rowe Price
CIGNA	US Global Investors
Citigroup	USAA
FMR	The Vanguard Group
John Hancock Financial	

HISTORICAL FINANCIALS

Company Type: Private

Income Statement

FYE: December 31

	REVENUE ($ mil.)	NET INCOME ($ mil.)	NET PROFIT MARGIN	EMPLOYEES
12/07	13,187.0	1,465.0	11.1%	7,500
12/06	12,378.0	3,453.0	27.9%	5,500
12/05	11,703.0	1,878.0	16.0%	5,500
12/04	10,864.0	540.0	5.0%	6,000
12/03	12,814.9	504.0	3.9%	6,000
Annual Growth	0.7%	30.6%	—	5.7%

Net Income History

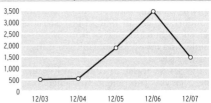

Tiffany & Co.

Breakfast at Tiffany & Co. has turned into a bountiful buffet, complete with the finest crystal and flatware, as well as more ubiquitous fare. Its specialty is fine jewelry, but the company also puts its name on timepieces, silverware, china, stationery, and other luxury items. Many products are packaged in the company's trademarked Tiffany Blue Box. To entice budget-minded Buffys to do more than window shop, Tiffany has broadened its merchandise mix to include key chains and other items that sell for much less than the typical Tiffany price tag. The firm sells its goods exclusively through more than 180 Tiffany & Co. stores and boutiques worldwide, It also markets through its Selections and Collections catalogs, through its Web site, and through its iconic annual Blue Book catalog.

Tiffany generates about 88% of sales from jewelry, including exclusive designs by Frank Gehry, Elsa Peretti, and Paloma Picasso. Within that segment of its business, gemstone jewelry and sterling silver items lead sales in the US.

Tiffany has been expanding its retail presence while diversifying its customer reach through other retail venues. About 85 stores are located in the US and the company plans to continue adding a few stores each year. Its famed flagship location on Manhattan's Fifth Avenue accounts for 10% of sales.

Tiffany had extended its reach into other specialty retailing, such as through Little Switzerland (some 25 duty-free cruise-ship destinations in the Caribbean and Florida). However, Tiffany grew tired of Little Switzerland's losses and sold the specialty retailer to NXP, which operates stores under the Jewels and Azura by Jewels banners in the Caribbean.

Pointing to the mounting recession in the US, the company announced plans to shutter its nearly 20-store Iridesse chain, which focused exclusively on high-end pearl jewelry, in 2009.

Aiming to broaden its accessories collections, Tiffany acquired luxury handbag and footwear brand Lambertson Truex from Samsonite in 2009. The upscale design firm had filed for Chapter 11 bankruptcy protection earlier in the year. The jewelry maker follows others in its industry making a push into the leather goods and handbag market.

These days the famous surname is showing up next to more middle-class monikers, such as Barnes & Noble and California Pizza Kitchen, as Tiffany's expansion plans include new locations in such venues as malls and upscale shopping centers. Although previous Tiffany stores have ranged in size from 1,500 sq. ft. to 16,000 sq. ft., new stores are generally kept between 4,000 sq. ft. and 7,000 sq. ft., with a greater portion of floor space dedicated to retail sales.

Peter May and his Trian Fund Management own about an 17% stake in Tiffany.

HISTORY

Charles Lewis Tiffany and John Young founded Tiffany & Young in New York City in 1837. The store sold stationery and costume jewelry and offered a unique, no-haggling approach (prices were clearly marked). In 1845 the company began selling real jewelry and also published its first mail-order catalog. During the late 1840s it added silverware, timepieces, perfumes, and other luxury offerings.

In 1851 Tiffany & Young bought the operations of silversmith John Moore, adding the design and manufacture of silver to its business (its standard for sterling silver was later adopted as the US standard). Tiffany bought out his partners (including a third partner, J. L. Ellis) two years later, renaming the company Tiffany & Co.

Although it served European royalty, Tiffany found its primary clientele in the growing number of wealthy Americans. In 1878 it acquired the Tiffany Diamond, one of the largest yellow diamonds in the world, weighing 128.5 carats (on display in its flagship New York City store). By 1887 the company had more than $40 million in precious stones in its vaults.

Tiffany died in 1902, and his son Louis Comfort Tiffany joined the firm that year as artistic director. Louis designed jewelry and stained glass patterned after nature and art, and remains one of the most celebrated glass designers (Tiffany lamps are very popular with collectors). Tiffany's sales hit nearly $18 million in 1919, then stalled during the 1920s. Because of the Depression, sales dropped to less than $3 million in 1932, forcing the company to lay off employees and dip into its cash reserves to pay dividends. Louis died in 1933.

The company moved in 1940 to its present Fifth Avenue location, which was showcased in Truman Capote's 1958 novella *Breakfast at Tiffany's* (the story became an Audrey Hepburn

movie in 1961). To keep Bulova Watch Co., which owned a 30% stake, from controlling Tiffany, in 1955 the Tiffany heirs sold their share of the company to Hoving Corp., which owned retailer Bonwit Teller. Walter Hoving, Tiffany's new chairman and CEO, and other investors bought the chain from Hoving's parent, Genesco, and Bulova in 1961. The company opened its first store outside of New York City, in San Francisco, two years later, and it added locations in Beverly Hills, California, and Houston in 1964.

Sales grew through the 1970s. Tiffany was sold to cosmetics seller Avon Products in 1979, and Hoving retired as chairman and CEO the next year. Avon increased the stores' selection of less expensive items, a decision some felt hurt Tiffany. In 1984 Avon sold Tiffany to a group of investors led by Tiffany's then chairman William Chaney and backed by Bahrain-based Investcorp. Chaney set about improving Tiffany's tarnished image with affluent shoppers. In 1986 the company expanded into Europe, opening a store in London. To retire debt, it went public the next year with about 30 retail locations worldwide.

Japanese retailer Mitsukoshi, a seller of Tiffany's items in department stores and Tiffany & Co. boutiques in Japan, increased its stake in the company to 10% in 1989. The company expanded dramatically in the US during the 1990s, opening stores in more than 20 cities.

President and COO Michael Kowalski became CEO in 1999 and Mitsukoshi sold its stake in the company. Tiffany then paid $72 million for a 15% stake in diamond supplier Aber Resources. Tiffany also opened an online store in 1999. In an attempt to gain greater control of its brand, Tiffany discontinued sales to retailers in the US and Europe in 2000. In May 2001 Tiffany purchased 45% of duty-free store operator Little Switzerland through its Tiffany & Co. International affiliate; in 2002 it brought its Little Switzerland holdings to about 98%. In 2003 Chaney retired and Kowalski added the title of chairman. In 2007 Tiffany sold its Little Switzerland unit.

EXECUTIVES

Chairman and CEO: Michael J. Kowalski, age 57, $2,449,671 total compensation
President: James E. Quinn, age 57, $1,508,548 total compensation
SVP Operations: John S. Petterson, age 50
EVP and CFO: James N. Fernandez, age 53, $1,505,555 total compensation
SVP and Chief Marketing Officer: Caroline D. Naggiar, age 51
EVP: Beth O. Canavan, age 54, $1,274,942 total compensation
EVP: Jon M. King, age 52, $1,215,292 total compensation
SVP, General Counsel, and Secretary: Patrick B. Dorsey, age 58
SVP Global Human Resources: Victoria Berger-Gross, age 53
SVP Finance: Patrick F. McGuiness, age 43
SVP Merchandising: Pamela Cloud, age 39
VP Investor Relations: Mark L. Aaron
Group VP; Managing Director, United Kingdom: Melvyn Kirtley
VP and Managing Director, Europe: Cesare Settepassi
President, The Tiffany & Co, Foundation: Fernanda M. Kellogg, age 62
President, Tiffany & Co. Japan: Michael C. (Mike) Christ
Design Director Emeritus: John Loring
Chief Gemologist: Peter C. Schneirla
Auditors: PricewaterhouseCoopers LLP

LOCATIONS

HQ: Tiffany & Co.
727 5th Ave., New York, NY 10022
Phone: 212-755-8000 **Fax:** 212-605-4465
Web: www.tiffany.com

2009 Sales

	$ mil.	% of total
Americas	1,586.6	56
Asia/Pacific	922.0	32
Europe	284.6	10
Other regions	66.8	2
Total	**2,860.0**	**100**

PRODUCTS/OPERATIONS

2009 Sales

	$ mil.	% of total
Non-gemstone sterling silver jewelry	843.8	29
Gemstone jewelry & band rings	764.2	27
Diamond rings & wedding bands	568.1	20
Non-gemstone gold or platinum jewelry	302.2	11
Other	381.7	13
Total	**2,860.0**	**100**

Selected Merchandise and Brands

China and other tableware
Crystal
Fashion and personal accessories
Fine jewelry (Faraone)
Fragrances (Tiffany, Tiffany for Men)
Glassware (Judel)
Stationery
Sterling silver (desk accessories, flatware, hollowware, key holders, picture frames, trophies)
Watches and clocks
Writing instruments

COMPETITORS

ARC International	Neiman Marcus
Armani	Nordstrom
Asprey	Parlux Fragrances
Blue Nile, Inc.	Richard-Ginori 1735
Bulgari	Richemont
Cartier	Rolex
Chanel	Royal Doulton
Christie's	Saks Fifth Avenue
Citizen	Shiseido
Elizabeth Arden Inc	Signet
Gucci	Société du Louvre
H. Stern	Union Diamond
Hermès	Van Cleef & Arpels
Inter Parfums	Waterford Wedgwood
LVMH	Yves Saint-Laurent Groupe
Movado Group	Zale

HISTORICAL FINANCIALS

Company Type: Public

Income Statement

FYE: January 31

	REVENUE ($ mil.)	NET INCOME ($ mil.)	NET PROFIT MARGIN	EMPLOYEES
1/09	2,860.0	220.0	7.7%	9,000
1/08	2,938.8	303.8	10.3%	8,800
1/07	2,648.3	253.9	9.6%	8,800
1/06	2,395.2	254.7	10.6%	8,120
1/05	2,204.8	304.3	13.8%	7,341
Annual Growth	**6.7%**	**(7.8%)**	**—**	**5.2%**

2009 Year-End Financials

Debt ratio: 26.8%
Return on equity: 13.6%
Cash ($ mil.): 160
Current ratio: 3.40
Long-term debt ($ mil.): 425
No. of shares (mil.): 124
Dividends
  Yield: 3.2%
  Payout: 37.9%
Market value ($ mil.): 2,575

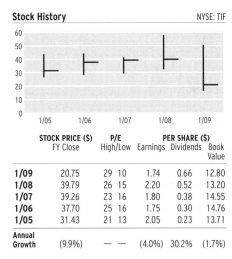

	STOCK PRICE ($)	P/E		PER SHARE ($)		
	FY Close	High/Low		Earnings	Dividends	Book Value
1/09	20.75	29	10	1.74	0.66	12.80
1/08	39.79	26	15	2.20	0.52	13.20
1/07	39.26	23	16	1.80	0.38	14.55
1/06	37.70	25	16	1.75	0.30	14.76
1/05	31.43	21	13	2.05	0.23	13.71
Annual Growth	(9.9%)	—	—	(4.0%)	30.2%	(1.7%)

The Timberland Company

Even non-hikers can get a kick out of Timberlands. The Timberland Company is best known for making men's, women's, and kids' footwear. Its footwear includes yellow hiking boots, boat shoes, dress and outdoor casual footwear, and sandals. Timberland also makes apparel (outerwear, shirts, pants, socks) and accessories, such as sunglasses, watches, and belts. Its brands include SmartWool, howies, IPATH, and Timberland. The firm sells its products through about 215 company-owned stores and through department and athletic shops in Asia, Canada, Europe, Latin America, the Middle East, and the US. The founding Swartz family, including CEO Jeffrey Swartz, controls about 73% of its voting power.

Footwear, Timberland's top product segment, accounted for some 71% of its 2008 sales. The company's acquisitions of howies (2006) and IPATH (2007), along with a boost in sales of casual and outdoor performance footwear in 2008, have collectively helped to raise the segment's revenue and offset a decline in sales of boots and kids' footwear.

About 45% of the company's sales come from North America; however, Timberland is pushing into global markets, such as Europe and Asia, to diversify its revenue streams. Growth in European distribution operation and gains in Scandinavia were key to balancing stalled sales across Europe in 2008. In Asia, Timberland saw its distributor business gain a foothold, showing some traction in China. Additional growth in Malaysia, Japan, and Singapore helped make up for declines in Taiwan.

Licensing deals and a debt-free balance sheet have helped to keep Timberland's head above water during the global economic downturn. Indeed, sales in both North America and abroad are down by double digits. Licensing revenue rose in 2008 due, in part, to the company's licensed Timberland PRO apparel and licensed kids' apparel. Getting into the bling of things, Timberland's agreement with Endura brought a collection of performance and casual watches. The company's

licensing agreement with Phillips-Van Heusen in 2007 added Timberland-branded apparel.

Not only was Timberland's purchase of SmartWool a strategic acquisition for a footwear manufacturer, but the sock maker allowed Timberland to expand into international outlets. Timberland bought the Colorado-based maker of wool socks, apparel, and accessories from RAF Industries and the Stripes Group for about $82 million. SmartWool items are sold in more than 2,000 outdoor specialty stores in the US and through independent distributors in Canada, Europe, and Asia.

In 2008 Timberland pared down its retail locations, opting for a smaller, more footwear-focused concept. The company shuttered about 40 of its larger specialty stores in the US, Europe, and Asia and planned to close several underperforming US factory outlet stores.

HISTORY

After buying a 50% interest in the Abington Shoe Company in 1952, Nathan Swartz purchased the rest three years later and brought his 19-year-old son Sidney on board. Abington Shoe made handmade private-label footwear during the 1950s and 1960s.

In 1968 Nathan retired, leaving sons Sidney and Herman in charge. The brothers persuaded Goodyear to make a synthetic rubber sole, which the Swartzes then bonded to blond leather, creating the first waterproof Timberland boot in 1973. Because of the boot's popularity, the company changed its name to The Timberland Company five years later.

The boots were a cult hit on US college campuses, but they really kicked up a following when they reached Italy in 1980. Spurred by the success overseas, US retailers gave the boots an increased focus, and by the late 1980s Timberland was riding the crest of the outdoors craze. The company opened its first store in 1986 and went public a year later.

Timberland's success brought competition from NIKE and Reebok. As the "brown shoes" market became saturated, the company closed its US plants and started outsourcing production in 1994. Timberland streamlined its product lines and announced plans to revamp retail stores in 1997. The next year it introduced the "beige shoe," a boot and sneaker hybrid under the Gorge MPO brand. Also in 1998 Jeffrey Swartz stepped into his father's Timberlands as CEO.

In 1999 Timberland unveiled the Mountain Athletics product line aimed at the 18- to 25-year-old outdoor athlete market, and Timberland Pro — footwear for the tradesperson (construction workers, factory foremen). Timberland reacquired the Asian distribution of its products from Inchcape in February 2000. In 2001 the company launched its "Around the World" ad campaign, the company's most ambitious ever.

In 2003 Timberland penned a licensing agreement with Italy's Marcolin, S.p.A to make and distribute Timberland-brand eyewear.

EXECUTIVES

Chairman: Sidney W. Swartz, age 73
President, CEO, and Director: Jeffrey B. Swartz, age 49, $3,706,328 total compensation
VP Finance and CFO: John D. Crimmins III, age 52, $730,500 total compensation
SVP, Chief Administrative Officer, and Director:
Carden N. Welsh, age 55, $741,178 total compensation

VP, Corporate Controller, and Chief Accounting Officer: John J. Fitzgerald Jr., age 46
VP, General Counsel, and Secretary: Danette Wineberg, age 62
VP and Corporate Culture Officer: John Pazzani, age 45
Co-President, Timberland brand:
Michael J. (Mike) Harrison, age 48, $1,245,799 total compensation
Co-President, Timberland brand:
Eugene R. (Gene) McCarthy, age 52, $924,009 total compensation
Senior Manager, Investor Relations: Karen Blomquist
Auditors: Deloitte & Touche LLP

LOCATIONS

HQ: The Timberland Company
200 Domain Dr., Stratham, NH 03885
Phone: 603-772-9500   **Fax:** 603-773-1640
Web: www.timberland.com

2008 Sales

	% of total
US	45
Europe	39
Asia	12
Other regions	4
Total	**100**

PRODUCTS/OPERATIONS

2008 Sales

	$ mil.	% of total
Footwear	974.3	71
Apparel & accessories	367.1	27
Royalties & other	23.2	2
Total	**1,364.6**	**100**

COMPETITORS

Billabong
Birkenstock Distribution USA
Columbia Sportswear
Deckers Outdoor
Eddie Bauer Holdings
Fossil, Inc.
L.L. Bean
NIKE
Norm Thompson
North Face
Patagonia, Inc.
Phillips-Van Heusen
Polo Ralph Lauren
R. Griggs
Reebok
Rocky Brands
Skechers U.S.A.
Wolverine World Wide

HISTORICAL FINANCIALS

Company Type: Public

Income Statement

				FYE: December 31
	REVENUE ($ mil.)	NET INCOME ($ mil.)	NET PROFIT MARGIN	EMPLOYEES
12/08	1,364.6	42.9	3.1%	6,000
12/07	1,436.5	40.0	2.8%	6,300
12/06	1,567.6	106.4	6.8%	6,300
12/05	1,565.7	164.6	10.5%	5,300
12/04	1,500.6	152.7	10.2%	5,600
Annual Growth	(2.3%)	(27.2%)	—	1.7%

2008 Year-End Financials

Debt ratio: —
Return on equity: 7.4%
Cash ($ mil.): 217
Current ratio: 2.80
Long-term debt ($ mil.): —
No. of shares (mil.): 56
Dividends
  Yield: 0.0%
  Payout: —
Market value ($ mil.): 648

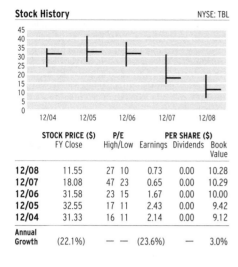

Stock History   NYSE: TBL

	STOCK PRICE ($) FY Close	P/E High/Low		PER SHARE ($) Earnings	Dividends	Book Value
12/08	11.55	27	10	0.73	0.00	10.28
12/07	18.08	47	23	0.65	0.00	10.29
12/06	31.58	23	15	1.67	0.00	10.00
12/05	32.55	17	11	2.43	0.00	9.42
12/04	31.33	16	11	2.14	0.00	9.12
Annual Growth	(22.1%)	—	—	(23.6%)	—	3.0%

Time Warner

Even among media titans, this company is a giant. Time Warner is the world's largest media conglomerate, with operations spanning film, television, cable TV, publishing, and online content and services. Its film and TV production division Warner Bros. Entertainment includes Warner Bros. Pictures and New Line Cinema. Its Turner Broadcasting unit oversees such cable channels as TBS, TNT, and Cartoon Network. Time Warner also operates pay-TV channels HBO and Cinemax. Online, its AOL unit attracts more than 100 million Internet users to its online content portal. Venerable Time Inc. is the top consumer magazine publisher with such titles as *FORTUNE, People,* and *Time.*

Like other diversified media conglomerates, Time Warner is focused on maximizing the profit potential of its content (movies and TV shows) by distributing that material through multiple channels. Those distribution outlets include most notably its own cable TV networks, as well as home video sales and Internet distribution. The company also uses its vast array of media outlets to cross-promote movies, TV shows, and magazines.

Cable television continues to be a leading source of revenue for Time Warner, accounting for more than 20% of sales. Its TBS Superstation and TNT channels rank among the most watched ad-supported channels. While advertising has been weak due to the recession, the cable networks have been able to make up the difference in higher carriage fees charged to cable systems. Its flagship HBO pay-TV service has managed to hold the interest of cable subscribers despite the loss of hit series *The Sopranos,* thanks to such shows as *Entourage.*

Time Warner's filmed entertainment division, meanwhile, has been delivering at the box office with such hits as *Watchmen, The Hangover,* and *Harry Potter and the Half-Blood Prince* in 2009, following on the heels of 2008's *The Dark Knight.* The global economic slowdown, however, forced Warner Bros. to focus on cost cutting measures early in 2009 when it cut about 10% of its workforce, outsourcing many positions to consulting firm Capgemini.

Time Warner's publishing unit has not fared well, however, struggling against a downturn in print advertising and readership. In response, Time Inc. has restructured its US operations.

The company's biggest challenge has been revitalizing its AOL subsidiary. Once the leading provider of online access services, AOL has all but abandoned that model in favor of being an ad-supported content portal and a provider of online marketing services. That transformation has not yet produced profitable results, however, and in 2009 Time Warner announced plans to spin off the Internet business to shareholders as a separate, publicly traded company. The spinoff will close a long and sometimes torturous chapter of Time Warner's history that began when it merged with AOL in 2001.

Time Warner got out of the cable TV system business in 2009 when the company spun off its 84% stake in Time Warner Cable, which had accounted for about a third of sales. The spinoff also had some economic benefits: Time Warner reaped a $9.25 billion dividend and was able to cut its debt in half.

HISTORY

Though formed in 2001, AOL Time Warner was the product of decades of media history. An elder statesman compared to relative newcomer America Online, Time Warner's roots extend back to 1922 — the year that Henry Luce and Briton Hadden founded Time Inc. to publish *Time* magazine, and brothers Harry, Abe, Jack, and Sam Warner established the origins of Warner Bros., which later became Warner Communications.

America Online's ancestry stretches back to the early 1980s when Stephen Case joined the management of a company called Control Video. Later renamed Quantum Computer Services, the company created the online service that would become America Online in 1985. Quantum Computer Services changed its name to America Online in 1991. It went public the next year.

As America Online was germinating, Time Inc. and Warner Communications were eyeing each other. The two companies merged in 1990 to form Time Warner. Gerald Levin was appointed CEO in 1992. To shave off debt, Time Warner grouped several of its properties into Time Warner Entertainment in 1992, in which U S West (which later became MediaOne Group) bought a 25% interest.

Time Warner's 1996 acquisition of Ted Turner's Turner Broadcasting System further elevated Time Warner's profile on the media stage. After AT&T's announcement that it would acquire MediaOne, MediaOne gave up its 50% management control of Time Warner Entertainment but retained its 25% ownership interest. AT&T's acquisition of MediaOne was completed in 2000, thus giving AT&T 25% of Time Warner Entertainment. (AT&T later boosted its stake to 27%.)

America Online announced that it would acquire Time Warner in early 2000. After a lengthy review by regulatory bodies, America Online acquired Time Warner for $106 billion and formed AOL Time Warner in 2001. Case became chairman, and Levin was appointed CEO. The newly formed company soon began streamlining, cutting more than 2,400 jobs in the process. (It cut another 1,700 jobs at America Online later that year.)

Levin retired from the company in 2002 and was replaced by co-COO Richard Parsons. The following year AOL Time Warner finally succeeded in buying Comcast's stake in Time

Warner Entertainment (Comcast gained its share of TWE when it bought the cable assets of AT&T in 2002). The following year Case and Turner both resigned their executive positions with the company. And in a move to distance itself from the struggling online unit, the company dropped AOL from its moniker and returned to being known as Time Warner Inc.

Time Warner started off 2004 by ridding itself of Warner Music Group, which it sold for $2.6 billion to a group led by former Seagram executive Edgar Bronfman Jr. and investment firm Thomas H. Lee Partners.

In 2006 Time Warner sold its book publishing unit, Time Warner Book Group, to French media firm Lagardère. Time Warner Cable joined with Comcast to acquire Adelphia Communications for $17.6 billion in cash and stock; as part of the deal, Adelphia shareholders sold part of their newly acquired stake in TWC through an IPO in 2007.

Parsons retired as CEO at the beginning of 2008 and was replaced by Jeffery Bewkes.

Time Warner spun off its remaining stake in Time Warner Cable in 2009.

EXECUTIVES

Chairman and CEO: Jeffrey L. (Jeff) Bewkes, age 56, $19,850,350 total compensation
EVP and CFO: John K. Martin Jr., age 41, $4,440,380 total compensation
EVP Global Public Policy: Carol A. Melton, age 54
EVP Administration: Patricia (Pat) Fili-Krushel, age 55, $4,730,545 total compensation
EVP and General Counsel: Paul T. Cappuccio, age 47, $5,712,375 total compensation
EVP Corporate Communications: Edward I. (Ed) Adler, age 55
SVP Corporate Responsibility: Lisa M. Quiroz
SVP and Treasurer: Edward B. (Ed) Ruggiero, age 56
SVP Global Public Policy: Steve Vest, age 44
SVP and Controller: Pascal Desroches, age 44
VP Corporate Communications: Keith Cocozza
VP Investor Relations: Douglas (Doug) Shapiro
Chairman and CEO, Time Inc.: Ann S. Moore
Chairman and CEO, Warner Bros. Entertainment: Barry M. Meyer
President, Warner Bros. Television Group: Bruce Rosenblum, age 50
President, Warner Bros. Home Entertainment Group: Kevin Tsujihara
Chairman and CEO, AOL: Tim Armstrong
Chairman and CEO, Home Box Office: Bill Nelson, age 60
President, CNN Worldwide: Jim Walton, age 50
Chairman and CEO, Turner Broadcasting System: Philip I. (Phil) Kent, age 54
President and Chief Creative Officer, Global Media Group: Mark D'Arcy
Secretary: Paul F. Washington
Auditors: Ernst & Young LLP

LOCATIONS

HQ: Time Warner Inc.
   1 Time Warner Center, New York, NY 10019
Phone: 212-484-8000
Web: www.timewarner.com

2008 Sales

	$ mil.	% of total
US	38,808	83
UK	2,067	5
Germany	646	1
Canada	645	1
France	622	1
Japan	445	1
Other countries	3,751	8
Total	**46,984**	**100**

PRODUCTS/OPERATIONS

2008 Sales

	$ mil.	% of total
Subscriptions	25,786	55
Content	11,432	24
Advertising	8,742	19
Other	1,024	2
Total	**46,984**	**100**

2008 Sales

	$ mil.	% of total
Cable	17,200	35
Filmed entertainment	11,398	23
Networks	11,154	23
Publishing	4,608	10
AOL	4,165	9
Adjustments	(1,541)	—
Total	**46,984**	**100**

Selected Operations

AOL LLC (online content and services)
  Platform-A (online advertising distribution)
  AOL.com (information portal)
  Bebo (social networking)
  ICQ (online chat client)
  MapQuest
  Truveo (video search engine)
Cinemax (pay-television service)
Home Box Office (HBO, pay-television service)
Time Inc. (magazine publishing)
  Entertainment Weekly
  Fortune
  InStyle
  People
  Real Simple
  Southern Living
  Sports Illustrated
  Time
Turner Broadcasting System (cable television networks)
  Boomerang (classic cartoons)
  Cartoon Network
  Cable News Network (CNN)
  TBS
  truTV
  Turner Classic Movies (TCM)
  Turner Network Television (TNT)
Warner Bros. Entertainment (filmed entertainment)
  The CW Network (50%, broadcast television network)
  DC Comics
  New Line Cinema
  Warner Bros.
    Castle Rock Entertainment
    Warner Bros. Pictures
  Warner Bros. Consumer Products (product licensing)
  Warner Bros. Home Entertainment
    Warner Bros. Digital Distribution
    Warner Bros. Interactive Entertainment
    Warner Home Video
  Warner Bros. Television Group
    Telepictures Productions
    Warner Bros. Animation
    Warner Bros. Television
    Warner Horizon Television

COMPETITORS

CBS Corp
Condé Nast
Disney
Google
Hearst Corporation
Lagardère Active
MSN
NBC Universal
News Corp.
Sony Pictures Entertainment
Viacom
Yahoo!

HISTORICAL FINANCIALS

Company Type: Public

Income Statement

FYE: December 31

	REVENUE ($ mil.)	NET INCOME ($ mil.)	NET PROFIT MARGIN	EMPLOYEES
12/08	46,984.0	(13,402.0)	—	87,000
12/07	46,482.0	4,387.0	9.4%	86,400
12/06	44,224.0	6,527.0	14.8%	92,700
12/05	43,652.0	2,905.0	6.7%	87,850
12/04	42,089.0	3,330.0	7.9%	84,900
Annual Growth	**2.8%**	**—**	**—**	**0.6%**

2008 Year-End Financials

Debt ratio: 89.0%
Return on equity: —
Cash ($ mil.): 6,682
Current ratio: 1.19
Long-term debt ($ mil.): 37,616

No. of shares (mil.): 1,186
Dividends
  Yield: 3.4%
  Payout: —
Market value ($ mil.): 26,434

Stock History

NYSE: TWX

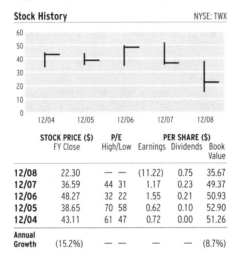

	STOCK PRICE ($) FY Close	P/E High/Low		PER SHARE ($) Earnings	Dividends	Book Value
12/08	22.30	—	—	(11.22)	0.75	35.67
12/07	36.59	44	31	1.17	0.23	49.37
12/06	48.27	32	22	1.55	0.21	50.93
12/05	38.65	70	58	0.62	0.10	52.90
12/04	43.11	61	47	0.72	0.00	51.26
Annual Growth	**(15.2%)**	**—**	**—**	**—**	**—**	**(8.7%)**

The Timken Company

The Timken Company tries to keep its bearings straight. The company makes bearings that range in weight from a mere half ounce to nine tons. Timken bearings find their way into products from computers to railroad cars. Timken and its subsidiaries also manufacture alloy and specialty steels, such as steel tubing, high-strength alloy steels, and die layout-ready ground blocks; the products are used primarily by industrial and automotive customers. The company derives about two-thirds of its sales from the US. Five generations of the Timken family have served the company since its founding by one-time carriage maker Henry Timken in 1899.

As the worldwide recession took hold, Timken trimmed its headcount by more than 10% and cut production by shortening work weeks and operating hours.

During 2009 Timken began expanding production capacity at its Tyger River plant in South Carolina to make more large-bore bearings used in the main-rotor shafts and gear drives of wind turbines. Wind power is seeing increased usage around the world as an alternative to fossil-fuel-based power generation, driving higher sales of wind turbines from such manufacturers as

Gamesa, GE Energy, and Vestas Wind Systems. Timken expects to bring the new capacity at Tyger River on line in 2010. Simultaneously, the company prepared to exit its needle bearing operations. JTEKT, an auto parts maker tied to Toyota Motor Corp., agreed to acquire the assets of the operations for about $330 million in cash, relieving Timken of a less than promising earnings business segment.

Timken is fortifying its presence in China. Acquisitions and joint ventures there, coupled with Timken's businesses in India, are part of a plan to grow its Asian business fivefold, to $1 billion, by 2010. The company also built a new plant in Chennai, India, and is expanding its factory in Altavista, Virginia.

The Timken family, through individual holdings and its foundation, controls 11% of the company. In 2005 President Bush nominated William Timken Jr. to become US ambassador to Germany. When he took office, William resigned as chairman and was replaced by his nephew Tim.

The company's pension plan owns about 7% of Timken.

HISTORY

Veteran St. Louis carriage maker Henry Timken patented a design in 1898 for tapered roller bearings (enclosed bearings between a pair of concentric rings). The following year Timken and his sons, William and Henry (H. H.) Timken, founded the Timken Roller Bearing Axle Company to make bearings for carriage axles.

In 1902 the company moved to Canton, Ohio, to be near the growing steelworks of Pittsburgh and the new auto industries of Buffalo, New York; Cleveland; and Detroit. With the debut of the Ford Motor Model T in 1908, the Timkens' business soared. In 1909 Henry Timken died. That year a separate company, the Timken-Detroit Axle Company, was formed in Detroit to serve the auto industry. The original company changed its name to the Timken Roller Bearing Company and continued to produce bearings. Also in 1909 Vickers began making bearings and axles under license from Timken (Timken acquired that operation in 1959).

Suffering steel shortages during WWI, in 1916 the company began making its own steel. By the 1920s the rail industry had adopted Timken bearings to increase the speed of trains. Timken stock was sold to the public for the first time in 1922.

WWII created increased demand for Timken's products, and the company opened several new plants. The AP bearing — a revolutionary prelubricated, self-contained railroad bearing unveiled by Timken in 1954 — boosted the company's railroad segment, and a new plant, the Columbus Railroad Bearing Plant, opened in 1958.

H. H. Timken's son, W. Robert Timken, became president in 1960 and chairman in 1968. The company continued to grow during the 1960s by opening plants in Brazil and France. It adopted its current name in 1970. W. R. Timken Jr., grandson of the founder, became chairman in 1975. That year the company bought specialty alloy maker Latrobe Steel.

In 1982, with increasing competition from Europe and Japan, the company suffered its first loss since the Depression. Five years later it established Indian joint venture Tata Timken to make bearings for agricultural equipment, heavy machinery, and railcars.

Timken bought precision-bearing maker MPB Corporation in 1990. The company opened its first European steel operations in 1993 and the following year introduced its environmentally progressive Dynametal steel products. It bought the Rail Bearing Service Corporation in 1995.

Timken formed joint venture Yantai Timken in 1996 to make bearings in China. In 1997 Timken purchased Gnutti Carlo SpA (bearings, Italy) and the aerospace bearing operations of UK-based Torrington.

In 1999 Timken cut production capacity to 80% and continued to consolidate operations and restructure into global business units. The company closed plants in Australia, restructured operations in South Africa (cutting about 1,700 jobs), and transferred its European distribution to an outside company in France.

In early 2001 the company announced that it would lay off more than 7% of its workforce. Timken's 2003 acquistion of Ingersoll-Rand unit, The Torrington Co., for $840 million, made Timken the third-largest bearing company in the world.

Blaming the woes of the North American automotive industry, Timken laid off approximately 700 employees, or about 5% of its Automotive Group, in the fall of 2006. Soon after, the company said it would close the group's factory in São Paulo, Brazil, by the end of 2007, eliminating manufacturing redundancies. The company then closed down its unprofitable plant in Desford, UK, which made seamless steel tubes. Four hundred employees lost their jobs as a result.

In 2006 Timken sold its Latrobe Steel subsidiary to an investors group led by the Watermill Group, Hicks Holdings, and Sankaty Advisors (part of Bain Capital).

Timken supplemented its aerospace business in 2007 by acquiring the assets of The Purdy Corp, a maker of transmissions, gears, rotorhead systems, and other components for helicopters and fixed-wing aircraft.

In 2007 Timken formed a joint venture with Xiangtan Electric Manufacturing Co., Ltd. to manufacture ultra-large-bore bearings for the main rotor shafts of multi-megawatt wind turbines for the Chinese wind energy market.

EXECUTIVES

Chairman: Ward J. (Tim) Timken Jr., age 41, $4,153,718 total compensation
President, CEO, and Director: James W. Griffith, age 55, $5,740,669 total compensation
EVP, Finance and Administration: Glenn A. Eisenberg, age 47, $2,332,689 total compensation
SVP, Strategy and CIO: Daniel E. Muller
EVP; President, Bearings and Power Transmission Group: Michael C. Arnold, age 52, $2,518,674 total compensation
SVP, Quality and Six Sigma: Donna J. Demerling
SVP and General Counsel: William R. Burkhart, age 43
SVP, Asia Pacific: Roger W. Lindsay
SVP, Human Resources and Organizational Advancement: Donald L. Walker
SVP, Tax and Treasury: Philip D. (Phil) Fracassa, age 39
SVP and Controller: J. Ted Mihaila, age 54
SVP, Technology: Douglas H. Smith
President, Steel Group: Salvatore J. Miraglia Jr., age 58, $1,972,475 total compensation
President, Specialty Steel: Hans J. Sack
President, Aerospace and Defense, Bearings, and Power Transmission Group: James R. (Ron) Menning
President, Process Industries: Christopher A. Coughlin
President, Precision Steel Components: Cengiz Kurkcu
President, Mobile Industries: Richard G. Kyle
Corporate Secretary and Assistant General Counsel: Scott A. Scherff, age 51
Manager, Investor Relations: Steve D. Tschiegg
Auditors: Ernst & Young LLP

LOCATIONS

HQ: The Timken Company
   1835 Dueber Ave. SW, Canton, OH 44706
Phone: 330-438-3000   **Fax:** 330-471-3452
Web: www.timken.com

2008 Sales

	$ mil.	% of total
US	3,625.5	64
Europe	1,098.1	19
Other regions	940.1	17
Total	**5,663.7**	**100**

PRODUCTS/OPERATIONS

2008 Sales

	$ mil.	% of total
Bearings & Power Transmission Group		
Mobile Industries	2,264.2	40
Process Industries	1,274.4	22
Aerospace & Defense	431.1	8
Steel group	1,694.0	30
Total	**5,663.7**	**100**

Selected Products

Bearings
   Cylindrical bearings
   Spherical bearings
   Straight ball bearings
   Super-precision ball and roller bearings
   Tapered bearings
Steel
   Mechanical seamless steel tubing
   Specialty steels and alloys
   Tool steel

COMPETITORS

Allegheny Technologies	NSK
Amatsuji Steel Ball	NTN
ArcelorMittal	Nucor
BÖHLER-UDDEHOLM	PAV Republic
Corus Group	Plymouth Tube
Crucible Materials	Quanex Building Products
Delphi Corp.	RBC Bearings
Dofasco	RBS Global
General Bearing	Schaeffler
JTEKT	SKF
Kaydon	Steel Dynamics
Linamar Corp.	Tenaris
Macsteel Service Centres	United States Steel
Metaldyne	Universal Stainless
MINEBEA	V & M Tubes (USA)
Nippon Bearing	

HISTORICAL FINANCIALS

Company Type: Public

Income Statement

FYE: December 31

	REVENUE ($ mil.)	NET INCOME ($ mil.)	NET PROFIT MARGIN	EMPLOYEES
12/08	5,663.7	267.7	4.7%	25,662
12/07	5,236.0	220.1	4.2%	25,175
12/06	4,973.4	222.5	4.5%	25,418
12/05	5,168.4	260.3	5.0%	27,000
12/04	4,513.7	135.7	3.0%	26,000
Annual Growth	**5.8%**	**18.5%**	**—**	**(0.3%)**

2008 Year-End Financials

Debt ratio: 31.4%
Return on equity: 14.9%
Cash ($ mil.): 116
Current ratio: 2.55
Long-term debt ($ mil.): 515
No. of shares (mil.): 97
Dividends
   Yield: 3.6%
   Payout: 25.2%
Market value ($ mil.): 1,901

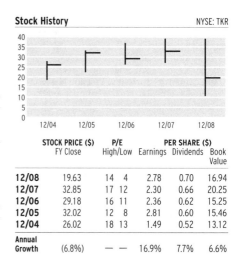

Stock History   NYSE: TKR

	STOCK PRICE ($) FY Close	P/E High/Low		PER SHARE ($) Earnings	Dividends	Book Value
12/08	19.63	14	4	2.78	0.70	16.94
12/07	32.85	17	12	2.30	0.66	20.25
12/06	29.18	16	11	2.36	0.62	15.25
12/05	32.02	12	8	2.81	0.60	15.46
12/04	26.02	18	13	1.49	0.52	13.12
Annual Growth	**(6.8%)**	**—**	**—**	**16.9%**	**7.7%**	**6.6%**

TJX Companies

Rifling through the racks is an art at TJX stores. The TJX Companies operates eight retail chains, including the two largest off-price clothing retailers in the US, T.J. Maxx and Marshalls. T.J. Maxx sells brand-name family apparel, accessories, women's shoes, domestics, giftware, and jewelry at discount prices at some 875 stores nationwide. Marshalls offers a full line of shoes and a broader selection of menswear through 800-plus stores. Its HomeGoods chain of about 320 stores nationwide focuses entirely on home furnishings, while 135 A.J. Wright clothing stores aim for lower-income shoppers. T.K. Maxx is the company's European retail arm with about 235 stores in the UK, Ireland, and Germany.

The retailer targets middle-to-upper income, fashion-conscious females between the ages of 25 and 54 who tend to shop at high-end department and specialty stores.

Despite the economic downturn in Europe and North America, the company's retail chains have shown sales growth. But TJX isn't letting success go to its head. The company's focus on value across its many chains is well suited to appeal to shoppers' new-found frugality.

T.J. Maxx and Marshalls, which together contributed about two-thirds of TJX's total sales, share similar concepts, selling items generally priced 20% to 60% below similar items at department stores. However, Marshalls offers a bigger men's department than T.J. Maxx, a larger shoe department, and costume jewelry. Marshalls has stores in more than 40 states and about a dozen locations in Puerto Rico.

Its HomeGoods stores are both stand-alone outlets and located within superstores such as T.J. Maxx 'N More and Marshalls Mega-Stores. North of the border, TJX also operates HomeSense in Canada, with about 75 stores, and a chain of family clothing stores called Winners Apparel (200 stores).

In one of the more serious security breaches reported by a major retailer to date, banks allege that data from more than 100 million credit card accounts may have been stolen from TJX's computer systems. The security breach, about twice what the company initially estimated in early

2007, led to the filing of a class action suit. In March 2008 under a settlement agreement reached with the FTC, TJX agreed to have its data-security systems audited every other year for the next 20 years. Also, under an agreement with credit card firms, including Visa and MasterCard, the retailer agreed to conduct annual audits of its security systems. The company still faces investigations by the attorneys general of 39 states, including its home state of Massachusetts.

HISTORY

Cousins Stanley and Sumner Feldberg opened the first Zayre (Yiddish for "very good") store in Hyannis, Massachusetts, in 1956. During the next 15 years the number of stores grew to nearly 200.

Zayre purchased the Hit or Miss chain, which sold upscale women's clothing at discounted prices, in 1969. When the recession of the early 1970s hit, superb results at Hit or Miss prompted Zayre to look for further opportunities in the off-price apparel marketplace. Zayre hired Ben Cammarata to create a new store concept, and in March 1977 he opened the first T.J. Maxx, in Auburn, Massachusetts, to market discounted upscale family clothing. Six years later Zayre formed the catalog retailer Chadwick's of Boston to sell Hit or Miss apparel by mail.

The company came to rely increasingly on its specialty operations to provide consistent sales and income as its flagship general merchandise stores often struggled. By 1983 the specialty chains were producing almost half of Zayre's sales.

In the second half of the 1980s, Zayre's upscale (yet still off-priced) retailers' sales rose, while its general merchandise stores (targeting lower-income customers) dropped. To keep its specialty stores unhindered by its flagging Zayre stores, it established The TJX Companies as a public company in 1987. Zayre sold about 17% of its new subsidiary to the public, with Cammarata as CEO. Zayre sold its 400 general merchandise stores in 1988 to Ames for about $430 million in cash, $140 million in Ames stock, and a receivable note. The next year the company merged with its subsidiary, The TJX Companies, taking that name.

TJX acquired Winners Apparel, a Toronto-based five-store apparel chain, in 1990. That year, in the same month that Ames declared bankruptcy, TJX established a $185 million reserve against losses it might suffer through its ownership of Ames' stock. Ames emerged from bankruptcy two years later, and TJX was left with 4% of Ames' voting shares and over 100 empty Ames stores. TJX sold or leased most of them.

Also in 1992 TJX opened HomeGoods gift and houseware outlets in three of its remaining Ames stores and closed about 70 Hit or Miss stores. Encouraged by the success of its off-price operations in Canada, in 1994 TJX opened five T.K. Maxx stores (similar to T.J. Maxx and Winners Apparel) in the UK.

A year later TJX paid $550 million for Melville's ailing chain of 450 Marshalls clothing stores. In addition, the company sold its Hit or Miss apparel chain. To help pay for Marshalls, TJX sold the Chadwick's of Boston catalog in 1996 to retailer Brylane. It debuted the A.J. Wright discount chain in New England in 1998.

In 1999 TJX elected Cammarata to the additional post of chairman and elevated Ted English to president and COO. In 2000 Cammarata relinquished his CEO post to English but remained chairman. Citing the successes of its new stores,

the company announced in early 2001 it expected to increase its total number of stores 12% annually for the next several years. Seven TJX employees perished on September 11, 2001, when their flight, bound for Los Angeles, crashed into the World Trade Center during the worst terrorist attack in US history.

In 2002 the company opened HomeSense, a new Canadian home furnishings chain fashioned after its US counterpart HomeGoods.

In September 2005 English resigned abruptly after five years as the company's CEO. TJX named company president Carol Meyrowitz to the post. In March 2006 TJX cut about 250 jobs in its corporate and divisional offices and reduced the salaries of a dozen senior executives, including its chairman and acting CEO and its president, by 10%.

In 2007 TJX reached a settlement with Visa and Fifth Third Bancorp stemming from a breach of its computer systems in which customer data was stolen. Under the terms of the agreement, TJX will fund up to $40.9 million for recovery payments for US Visa issuers. Also in 2007 the retailer's European arm, T.K. Maxx, entered the German market with five stores there.

EXECUTIVES

Chairman: Bernard (Ben) Cammarata, age 69
President, CEO, and Director: Carol M. Meyrowitz, age 55, $8,719,072 total compensation
SEVP, CFO, and Chief Administrative Officer: Jeffrey G. (Jeff) Naylor, age 50, $2,860,826 total compensation
EVP and CIO: Paul Butka
SEVP; President, The Marmaxx Group: Ernie Herrman, age 48, $3,184,744 total compensation
SEVP; Group President, Europe: Paul Sweetenham, age 44
SEVP and Group President: Jerome Rossi, age 65
SEVP and COO, The Marmaxx Group: Richard Sherr, age 51
EVP and Chief Human Resources Officer: Greg Flores III
EVP, Real Estate and New Business Development: Michael Skirvin
EVP, General Counsel, and Secretary: Ann McCauley, age 58
EVP and Chief Logistics Officer: Peter Lindenmeyer
SVP Investor and Public Relations: Sherry Lang
SVP Corporate Controller: Ken Canestrari
President, A.J. Wright: Celia Clancy, age 52
President, HomeGoods: Nan Stutz, age 51
President, Winners/HomeSense: Robert Cataldo, age 50
Auditors: PricewaterhouseCoopers LLP

LOCATIONS

HQ: The TJX Companies, Inc.
770 Cochituate Rd., Framingham, MA 01701
Phone: 508-390-1000   **Fax:** 508-390-2828
Web: www.tjx.com

2009 Sales

	$ mil.	% of total
US		
Marmaxx	12,362.1	65
HomeGoods	1,578.3	8
A.J. Wright	677.6	4
UK		
T.K. Maxx/HomeSense	2,242.1	12
Canada		
Winners/HomeSense/StyleSense	2,139.4	11
Total	**18,999.5**	**100**

2009 Stores

	No.
US	2,133
Canada	277
Europe	242
Total	**2,652**

PRODUCTS/OPERATIONS

2009 Stores

	No.
T.J. Maxx	874
Marshalls	806
HomeGoods	318
T.K. Maxx	235
Winners	200
A.J. Wright	135
HomeSense	82
StyleSense	2
Total	**2,652**

Selected Stores

A.J. Wright (US, discount chain aimed at moderate-income shoppers)
HomeGoods (US, off-price home fashion chain)
HomeSense (Canada and Europe, off-price home fashion chain)
Marshalls (US, off-price retailer of apparel, shoes, home fashions)
Marshalls Mega-Stores (US, combination Marshalls and HomeGoods stores)
StyleSense (Canada, shoes and accessories)
T.J. Maxx (US, off-price retailer of apparel, shoes, home fashions)
T.J. Maxx 'N More (combination T.J. Maxx and HomeGoods stores)
T.K. Maxx (Europe, off-price retailer of apparel, shoes, home fashions)
Winners Apparel (Canada, off-price family apparel chain)

COMPETITORS

Bed Bath & Beyond	J. C. Penney
Belk	Kmart
Big Lots	Kohl's
Brown Shoe	Loehmann's
Burlington Coat Factory	Macy's
Cato	Men's Wearhouse
Charming Shoppes	Ross Stores
The Children's Place	Sears
Claire's Stores	ShopKo Stores
Collective Brands	Stage Stores
Dillard's	Stein Mart
Dollar General	Target
Eddie Bauer llc	Wal-Mart
Foot Locker	Zellers
The Gap	

HISTORICAL FINANCIALS

Company Type: Public

Income Statement				FYE: Last Saturday in January
	REVENUE ($ mil.)	NET INCOME ($ mil.)	NET PROFIT MARGIN	EMPLOYEES
1/09	18,999.5	880.6	4.6%	133,000
1/08	18,647.1	771.8	4.1%	129,000
1/07	17,404.6	738.0	4.2%	125,000
1/06	16,057.9	690.4	4.3%	119,000
1/05	14,913.5	664.1	4.5%	113,000
Annual Growth	**6.2%**	**7.3%**	**—**	**4.2%**

2009 Year-End Financials

Debt ratio: 18.0%
Return on equity: 41.3%
Cash ($ mil.): 454
Current ratio: 1.31
Long-term debt ($ mil.): 384
No. of shares (mil.): 424
Dividends
  Yield: 1.7%
  Payout: 16.5%
Market value ($ mil.): 8,231

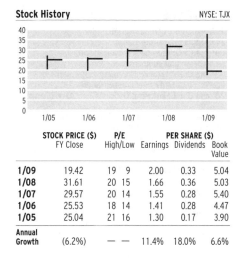
	STOCK PRICE ($) FY Close	P/E High/Low		PER SHARE ($) Earnings	Dividends	Book Value
1/09	19.42	19	9	2.00	0.33	5.04
1/08	31.61	20	15	1.66	0.36	5.03
1/07	29.57	20	14	1.55	0.28	5.40
1/06	25.53	18	14	1.41	0.28	4.47
1/05	25.04	21	16	1.30	0.17	3.90
Annual Growth	(6.2%)	—	—	11.4%	18.0%	6.6%

Toll Brothers

Ask not for whom the Tolls build, because if you have to ask you can't afford it. Toll Brothers, a top US builder of luxury homes, builds for move-up, empty-nester, active-adult, and second-home buyer markets in more than 300 suburban communities in some two dozen states. Its single-family detached homes and apartments range from $229,000 to about $2.16 million. Toll Brothers develops active-adult communities (some with golf courses) and operates country club communities. Through subsidiaries, it offers insurance, landscaping, and title and mortgage services. Toll delivered nearly 8,600 homes in 2006 but that figure dropped precipitously to about 6,700 in 2007 and just over 4,800 in 2008.

Those years were somber ones for the housing industry as a whole, as builders overbuilt and were left holding large inventories. Compounding the issue, the subprime mortgage crisis left many borrowers in default and homes in foreclosure. Toll finished up 2007 with a backlog of around 3,950 homes for sale but managed to reduce that figure by about half in 2008.

Toll Brothers sold its subsidiary Advanced Broadband, which provided fiber-optic networks in its communities, to Comcast in 2007. It also sold its security monitoring operations that year.

Brothers Robert (chairman) and Bruce Toll (vice chairman) own 17% and 4% of the company, respectively.

HISTORY

Homebuilder Albert Toll's two sons, Robert and Bruce Toll, founded their own business in 1967. The duo began by building starter homes in the Philadelphia suburbs of Elkins Park and Yardley. As Philadelphia's population began to sprawl beyond these older suburban areas, the company grew, and in 1982 it moved beyond Pennsylvania to build houses in New Jersey. The young firm also began to distinguish itself by catering to upmarket customers.

Toll Brothers, Inc., went public in 1986 and later expanded around New York City, north to the Boston area, and south to the suburbs of Washington, DC. The firm survived the late 1980s real estate recession in the Northeast because, unlike many builders, it did not overextend itself.

Until the 1990s Toll Brothers operated primarily in the northeastern US, but it expanded as the housing market began an upward cycle. It entered California and North Carolina in 1994, and Arizona, Florida, and Texas in 1995. In 1997 Toll Brothers began work in Nashville, Tennessee, and Las Vegas. The next year the company entered the active adult market, building its first two age-qualified communities in New Jersey. Also in 1998 the company joined other investors, including the Pennsylvania State Employees Retirement System, and formed the Toll Brothers Realty Trust to acquire and develop commercial property.

In 1999 Toll Brothers acquired Silverman Companies, a leading homebuilder and developer of luxury apartments with more than 80 years of experience in Detroit. The company also began building homes in the Chicago, San Diego, and San Francisco markets that year, and it teamed with Marriott International to begin developing an assisted-living community in Reston, Virginia.

It set up its cable and broadband subsidiary, Advanced Broadband, that year, to serve its communities with Internet connectivity. Toll sold those operations to Comcast in 2007.

The company began operating in Rhode Island and New Hampshire in 2000, and the next year entered Colorado. In 2002 the company entered South Carolina in the Hilton Head area to develop Hampton Hall, a luxury country club community with a master-planned golf course.

In 2003 Toll Brothers acquired Jacksonville, Florida-based homebuilder Richard R. Dostie, Inc., and affiliates of the company for an undisclosed cash amount. The company also expanded its luxury urban in-fill market operations by acquiring The Manhattan Building Company, which develops luxury mid- and high-rise condos on northern New Jersey's waterfront. The next year Toll Brothers and Pinnacle Ltd. jointly began development of an 832-home luxury condominium community (Maxwell Place on the Hudson) on the waterfront of Hoboken, New Jersey, overlooking Manhattan.

For its 12th consecutive year, Toll Brothers produced record fiscal-year-end results for earnings, revenues, contracts, and backlog in 2004. The company's net income grew 57% over the previous year's earnings, and it operated in more communities and offered more product lines than it had in previous years. 2005 was another record year; revenue from home sales increased 50% and net income increased 97%. In 2005 Toll Brothers began operations in West Virginia but stopped selling homes in Ohio.

Toll correctly predicted an industry slowdown in 2006, and for both 2006 and 2007 the number of homes it built dropped from 8,600 to around 6,700. Also in 2006 the company sold its cable and Internet operations and its home security business.

EXECUTIVES

Chairman and CEO: Robert I. Toll, age 68
Vice Chairman: Bruce E. Toll, age 65
President, COO, and Director: Zvi Barzilay, age 62
EVP, CFO, Treasurer, and Director: Joel H. Rassman, age 63
SVP and CIO: George W. Nelson
SVP, Secretary, and Chief Planning Officer:
  Michael I. Snyder
SVP Acquisitions: Werner Thiessen
SVP and Chief Accounting Officer: Joseph R. Sicree
SVP and Controller: Kevin J. McMaster
SVP and Chief Marketing Officer: Kira McCarron
SVP Human Resources: Jonathan C. Downs
SVP Finance and Investor Relations:
  Frederick N. Cooper
SVP, General Counsel, and Chief Compliance Officer:
  Mark K. Kessler
SVP Toll Brothers Realty Trust: James M. Steuterman
President, TBI Mortgage Company: Donald L. Salmon
President, Toll Architecture, Inc.: Jed Gibson
President, Westminster Title Company, Inc.:
  William T. Unkel
Auditors: Ernst & Young LLP

LOCATIONS

HQ: Toll Brothers, Inc.
  250 Gibraltar Rd., Horsham, PA 19044
Phone: 215-938-8000   **Fax:** 215-938-8010
Web: www.tollbrothers.com

Toll Brothers operates in Arizona, California, Colorado, Connecticut, Delaware, Florida, Georgia, Illinois, Maryland, Massachusetts, Michigan, Minnesota, Nevada, New Jersey, New York, North Carolina, Pennsylvania, Rhode Island, South Carolina, Texas, Virginia, and West Virginia.

2008 Sales

	$ mil.	% of total
North	932.9	29
Mid-Atlantic	881.0	28
West	782.2	25
South	562.1	18
Total	**3,158.2**	**100**

2008 Homes Closed

	No. units	% of total
Mid-Atlantic	1,443	31
North	1,300	27
South	1,095	23
West	905	19
Total	**4,743**	**100**

PRODUCTS/OPERATIONS

2008 Sales

	$ mil.	% of total
Housing		
Completed contract	3,106.3	99
Percentage of completion	41.9	1
Land sales	10.0	—
Total	**3,158.2**	**100**

Selected Operations

Architectural design services
Golf course development and operation
Engineering services
House component assembly
Land development
Landscape services
Lumber distribution
Mortgage lending
Title insurance

COMPETITORS

Centex
David Weekley Homes
D.R. Horton
Hovnanian Enterprises
John Wieland Homes
KB Home
Larwin Company
Lennar
Orleans Homebuilders
Pulte Homes
The Ryland Group
Shapell Industries
Standard Pacific
William Lyon Homes

HISTORICAL FINANCIALS

Company Type: Public

Income Statement

FYE: October 31

	REVENUE ($ mil.)	NET INCOME ($ mil.)	NET PROFIT MARGIN	EMPLOYEES
10/08	3,158.2	(297.8)	—	3,160
10/07	4,647.0	35.7	0.8%	4,329
10/06	6,123.5	687.2	11.2%	5,542
10/05	5,793.4	806.1	13.9%	5,581
10/04	3,893.1	409.1	10.5%	4,655
Annual Growth	(5.1%)	—	—	(9.2%)

2008 Year-End Financials

Debt ratio: 66.0%
Return on equity: —
Cash ($ mil.): 1,633
Current ratio: 5.46
Long-term debt ($ mil.): 2,138

No. of shares (mil.): 161
Dividends
  Yield: 0.0%
  Payout: —
Market value ($ mil.): 3,727

Stock History

NYSE: TOL

	STOCK PRICE ($) FY Close	P/E High/Low	PER SHARE ($) Earnings	Dividends	Book Value
10/08	23.12	— —	(1.88)	0.00	20.09
10/07	22.91	162 86	0.22	0.00	21.88
10/06	28.91	10 5	4.17	0.00	21.19
10/05	36.91	12 5	4.78	0.00	17.14
10/04	23.17	10 7	2.52	0.00	11.91
Annual Growth	(0.1%)	— —	—	—	14.0%

Torchmark Corporation

Torchmark aims to be a beacon in the world of insurance. It is the holding company for a family of firms; its member companies specialize in lower-end individual life insurance, supplemental health insurance, and annuities. Torchmark subsidiaries, which include flagship Liberty National Life, offer annuities, whole and term life insurance, health insurance, accidental death insurance, Medicare supplements, and long-term care health policies for the elderly. Its American Income Life sells life insurance policies to labor union members. Torchmark sells its products through direct marketing, as well as a network of exclusive and independent agents.

Targeting middle-income citizens, Liberty National Life operates primarily in the Southeast. A smaller subsidiary, Globe Life and Accident, (along with part of Liberty National Life) offers life insurance to active and retired military officers.

In 2008 Torchmark said it would move many of its subsidiaries to Nebraska, where it said the tax rate and available labor pool were better than other states. United American Life Insurance and Globe Life And Accident Insurance made the move with more to follow.

HISTORY

It began as a scam, plain and simple. In 1900 the Heralds of Liberty was founded as a fraternal organization — but its real reason for existence was to funnel money to its founders, according to Frank Samford, Torchmark's CEO from 1967 until 1985; Samford was also the great-grandson of the governor who signed the group's charter, and the son of the state insurance commissioner who oversaw the Heralds of Liberty's rehabilitation into a real insurance company.

The Heralds offered a joint life distribution plan, under which policyholders were divided by age; when a person died, his or her beneficiary was paid along with the holder of the lowest-numbered insurance certificate in the class (if they were paid at all; the Heralds were not scrupulous about that). Postal authorities called this plan a lottery, and it was illegal in many states. But the Heralds' fraternal order status allowed it to circumvent Alabama insurance laws until 1921, when its infractions could no longer be ignored.

The organization operated under state supervision until 1929, when it was recapitalized as stock company Liberty National. By 1934, despite the Depression, the company was financially sound.

In 1944 Liberty National merged with funeral insurance company Brown-Service, whose large sales force began selling Liberty National's policies. The added sales helped the company grow and make acquisitions from the 1950s through the 1970s. Even after it discontinued funeral insurance, the company still paid out benefits. (As late as 1985, half of all Alabamans who died had the policies.)

Liberty National reorganized itself as a holding company in 1980 to accommodate the purchase of Globe Life And Accident. In 1981 it acquired Continental Investment Corp., which owned United Investors Life Insurance, Waddell & Reed (financial services), and United American Insurance. In 1982 the holding company became Torchmark. Throughout its growth spurt it refrained from offering high-yield financial products and thus escaped the worst effects of the economic disruptions of the late 1980s. Its 1990 acquisition of Family Service Life Insurance put it back in the funeral insurance business (it exited again in 1995 and sold the unit in 1998).

Sales in the 1990s were affected by a decline in cash-value life insurance and Medicare supplements. Slack sales forced the company to stop having agents collect premiums personally, and by 1996 all accounts were handled by mail.

In 1998 the company sought to sell its 28% stake in property insurer Vesta Insurance Group after that company became the target of numerous lawsuits. Torchmark was only able to reduce its stake to 24% on the open market, but in 2000 Vesta bought out Torchmark's holdings.

Torchmark was haunted in 2000 by its own version of the undead — burial policies. An investigation by Alabama regulators was sparked by a Florida court order forcing the company to stop collecting premiums on old burial policies for which African-Americans had been charged higher premiums. In 2001 and 2002, Torchmark was hit by another dozen lawsuits, including allegations of overcharging.

EXECUTIVES

Chairman and CEO: Mark S. McAndrew, age 55, $4,017,933 total compensation
EVP and CFO: Gary L. Coleman, age 56, $2,003,146 total compensation
EVP and Chief Actuary: Rosemary J. Montgomery, age 59, $2,211,707 total compensation
EVP and Chief Marketing Officer: Glenn D. Williams, age 49
EVP and Chief Administrative Officer; CEO, United American: Vern D. Herbel, age 51, $1,519,092 total compensation
VP and Chief Accounting Officer: Danny H. Almond, age 57
VP and Chief Investment Officer: W. Michael Pressley, age 57
EVP and General Counsel: Larry M. Hutchison, age 55, $1,883,559 total compensation
VP, Associate Counsel, and Secretary: Carol A. McCoy
VP and Director Tax: Frank M. Svoboda
VP and Director Human Resources: Arvelia Bowie
VP and Actuary: Ben W. Lutek
VP Investor Relations: Mike Majors
CEO, Liberty National Life; President and CEO, United Investors Life: Anthony L. McWhorter, age 59
President and CEO, American Income Life: Roger C. Smith, age 56
President and Chief Marketing Officer, Liberty National Life and United American: Andrew W. King, age 51
President and CEO, Globe Life: Charles F. Hudson, age 52
Auditors: Deloitte & Touche LLP

LOCATIONS

HQ: Torchmark Corporation
3700 S. Stonebridge Dr., McKinney, TX 75070
Phone: 972-569-4000
Web: www.torchmarkcorp.com

PRODUCTS/OPERATIONS

2008 Sales

	$ mil.	% of total
Premiums		
Life	1,616.8	47
Health	1,127.1	33
Other	14.4	—
Net investment income	671.5	20
Realized investment loss	(107.5)	—
Other income	4.6	—
Total	**3,326.9**	**100**

Selected Subsidiaries

American Income Life Insurance Company
First United American Life Insurance Company
Globe Life And Accident Insurance Company
Liberty National Life Insurance Company
United American Insurance Company
United Investors Life Insurance Company

COMPETITORS

Aflac
Allstate
Aon
Citigroup
CNA Financial
Gerber Life
Guardian Life
Lincoln Financial Group
MassMutual
MetLife
Monumental Life
Northwestern Mutual
Pacific Mutual
Penn Treaty
Prudential
State Farm
T. Rowe Price
Travelers Companies
Unum Group
USAA

In 1926 St. Paul Fire and Marine organized its first subsidiary, St. Paul Mercury Indemnity, to write liability insurance policies. Other additions included coverage for automobiles, aircraft, burglary and robbery, and, in 1940, turkey farming.

During WWII, St. Paul Fire and Marine joined the War Damage Corp., a government-financed consortium that paid claims for war damage. The St. Paul Companies was formed in 1968 as an umbrella organization for the various subsidiaries, and the firm grew through purchases.

Lines of business blossomed during the 1970s, including life and title insurance, leasing, a mail-order consumer finance company, oil and gas, and real estate. Many of these were sold during the 1980s, but one, The John Nuveen Co. (1974), became the nucleus of St. Paul's financial services operations.

St. Paul posted a loss in 1992 after paying out huge claims related to Hurricane Andrew. In 1995 the company expanded its malpractice line when it bought NML Insurance. The Minet unit (a brokerage business) started Global Media Services that year to focus on insurance for the telecommunications industry. The division also bought London-based Special Risk Service, a top insurance broker, and Boston-based William Gallagher Associates, a high-tech and biotechnology insurer.

In 1997 St. Paul sold its unprofitable Minet division. That year and the next the company was struck by catastrophe losses, more than $150 million total.

St. Paul acquired USF&G in 1998. The purchase triggered a round of job cuts as the company assimilated its new operations; the deal also slammed the insurer's earnings. To focus on its more profitable commercial business, the firm sold its personal insurance business (1999) and jettisoned its nonstandard auto insurance business (2000). In 2000 it bought MMI Companies to build its health care risk operations and decided later that year to close Unionamerica Holdings, an unprofitable subsidiary of MMI. In 2001 St. Paul sold F&G Life, a subsidiary of USF&G, to UK-based insurer Old Mutual.

The World Trade Center attacks (in which the company paid out almost $1 billion in claims) and other disasters combined to make reinsurance a costlier game of dice. The company spun off its reinsurance business, St. Paul Re, into Bermuda-based Platinum Underwriters in 2002.

In a $16 billion blockbuster deal, The St. Paul Companies acquired Travelers Property Casualty in 2004. (Travelers had been a subsidiary of Citigroup until its IPO in early 2002.) Reflecting the acquisition, the company then changed its name to The St. Paul Travelers Companies. Then, in early 2007 the company changed its name to The Travelers Companies, Inc. and reclaimed the trademarked red umbrella logo used in previous Travelers incarnations.

EXECUTIVES

Chairman and CEO: Jay S. Fishman, age 56, $14,653,065 total compensation
Vice Chairman and CFO: Jay S. Benet, age 56, $5,422,060 total compensation
Vice Chairman and Chief Investment Officer: William H. Heyman, age 60, $6,212,684 total compensation
Vice Chairman and Chief Legal Officer: Alan D. Schnitzer, age 43, $6,314,143 total compensation
Vice Chairman: Charles J. Clarke, age 73
Vice Chairman: Irwin R. Ettinger, age 70
President and COO: Brian W. MacLean, age 55, $7,857,814 total compensation

EVP Insurance Operations and CIO: William A. Bloom, age 45
EVP and Chief Administrative Officer: Andy F. Bessette, age 55
EVP and Chief Marketing Officer: Anne MacDonald, age 52
EVP Human Resources: John P. Clifford Jr.
EVP Market Development: Maria Olivo
EVP Strategic Development: Samuel G. Liss, age 52
EVP Enterprise Development: Kathleen L. Preston, age 46
EVP and General Counsel: Kenneth F. (Ken) Spence III, age 53
EVP Business Insurance: John J. Albano, age 59
EVP; President Personal Insurance: Greg Toczydlowski
SVP Investor Relations: Gabriella Nawi
SVP and Secretary: Matthew Furman
Auditors: KPMG LLP

LOCATIONS

HQ: The Travelers Companies, Inc.
385 Washington St., St. Paul, MN 55102
Phone: 651-310-7911 **Fax:** 651-310-3386
Web: www.travelers.com

2008 Sales

	$ mil.	% of total
US	22,809	93
Non-US	1,668	7
Total	**24,477**	**100**

PRODUCTS/OPERATIONS

2008 Sales

	$ mil.	% of total
Premiums		
Business insurance	11,180	45
Personal insurance	6,970	28
Financial, professional & international insurance	3,429	14
Net investment income	2,792	11
Fee income	390	2
Other revenues	131	—
Net realized investment losses	(415)	—
Total	**24,477**	**100**

Selected Subsidiaries

St. Paul Fire and Marine Insurance Company
Travelers Property Casualty Corp.
  The Standard Fire Insurance Company
  Travelers Casualty and Surety Company
    Travelers Casualty and Surety Company of America
  The Travelers Indemnity Company
    First Floridian Auto and Home Insurance Company
    First Trenton Indemnity Company (Travelers of New Jersey)
    The Premier Insurance Co. of Massachusetts
Travelers Insurance Company Ltd. (UK)

COMPETITORS

ACE Limited
AIG
Allianz
Allstate
American Financial Group
AXA
Chubb Corp
CNA Financial
The Hartford
Markel
Nationwide
W. R. Berkley
Zurich Financial Services

HISTORICAL FINANCIALS

Company Type: Public

Income Statement

FYE: December 31

	ASSETS ($ mil.)	NET INCOME ($ mil.)	INCOME AS % OF ASSETS	EMPLOYEES
12/08	109,751.0	2,924.0	2.7%	33,000
12/07	115,224.0	4,601.0	4.0%	33,300
12/06	113,761.0	4,208.0	3.7%	32,800
12/05	113,187.0	1,622.0	1.4%	31,900
12/04	111,815.0	955.0	0.9%	29,200
Annual Growth	**(0.5%)**	**32.3%**	**—**	**3.1%**

2008 Year-End Financials

Equity as % of assets: 23.0%
Return on assets: 2.6%
Return on equity: 11.3%
Long-term debt ($ mil.): 6,181
No. of shares (mil.): 568
Dividends
  Yield: 2.6%
  Payout: 24.7%
Market value ($ mil.): 25,654
Sales ($ mil.): 24,477

Stock History

NYSE: TRV

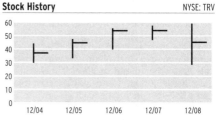

	STOCK PRICE ($) FY Close	P/E High/Low		PER SHARE ($) Earnings	Dividends	Book Value
12/08	45.20	12	6	4.82	1.19	44.61
12/07	53.80	8	7	6.86	1.13	46.90
12/06	53.69	9	7	5.91	1.01	44.29
12/05	44.67	20	14	2.33	0.91	39.30
12/04	37.07	29	20	1.53	0.95	37.35
Annual Growth	**5.1%**	**—**	**—**	**33.2%**	**5.8%**	**4.5%**

Trinity Industries

If Trinity Industries had a theme song, it would be sung by Boxcar Willie. The company manufactures auto carriers, box cars, gondola cars, hopper cars, intermodal cars, and tank cars — in short, railcars for hauling everything from coal to corn syrup. Trinity also leases and manages railcar fleets. The company's inland barge unit builds barges used to transport coal, grain, and other commodities. In addition to transportation, other Trinity businesses provide products and services to the industrial, energy (structural towers for wind turbines, metal containers for liquefied petroleum gas and fertilizer), and construction (concrete, aggregates, and highway guardrails) sectors.

Railcar loadings of bulk materials and large products dropped over 14% from 2007 to 2008. Falling demand for railcars and wind farms in 2008 prompted reductions or closures of several of Trinity's manufacturing facilities in Georgia, Missouri, Oklahoma, Texas, and Mexico. Trinity has reduced its workforce in the railcar and energy groups, which includes a 15% cut at the wind turbine plant in Oklahoma in early 2009.

Trinity Rail Group manufacturers freight railcars that transport liquids, gases, and dry cargo.

Auto carriers transport vehicles; box cars transport food and wood products, auto parts, and paper; gondola cars are used for hauling coal; hopper cars carry cargos such as grain, plastic pellets, and cement; intermodal cars are interchangeable among railcar, truck, and ship; specialty cars handle waste-hauling, starch, and flour; tank cars transport liquefied and pressurized commodities.

Trinity's Railcar and Leasing Management Services Group operates primarily through Trinity Industries Leasing Company (TILC), as well as other subsidiaries. It provides leasing options to companies involved in petroleum, chemical, agricultural, and energy industries.

Constructions Products Group produces concrete, aggregates, and asphalt; and it manufactures highway products, which include beams and girders used in highway bridge construction. Other highway products include guardrails, cable barrier systems, and crash cushions, which are sold in the US and 36 countries worldwide.

Inland Barge Group manufactures dry cargo barges (flat-deck and hopper), which transport products such as grain, coal, and aggregates. Tank barges carry petroleum, fertilizer, chemicals, and other liquid cargoes. It makes fiberglass barge covers, and deck hardware (brand name Nabrico), including hatches, castings, and winches for other watercraft and dock facilities. Primary customers are commercial marine transportation companies.

Energy Equipment Group makes tank containers and tank heads for pressure vessels, propane tanks, and structural wind towers. Trinity Industries de Mexico, under the brand name TATSA, manufactures containers for liquefied petroleum gas. It also manufactures containers for fertilizers, comestibles, and ammonia.

HISTORY

Trinity Industries resulted from the 1958 merger of Trinity Steel, a maker of metal products for the petroleum industry, and Dallas Tank Co. The enterprise was headed by Ray Wallace, a Trinity Steel veteran since the 1940s.

The company, which took the name Trinity Industries in 1966, acquired related tank, welding, and steel companies in the 1960s and quickly became the leading manufacturer of metal storage containers for liquefied petroleum gas. During this period it also applied its expertise to containers for another rapidly growing industry — fertilizer — and made custom products for the oil and chemical industries. Other products included hopper bodies and tanks for use on railcars.

During the 1970s Trinity diversified into building seagoing vessels by purchasing Equitable Equipment and its Louisiana shipyards in 1972. The next year the company bought Mosher Steel (steel beams and framing products). By the mid-1970s it was producing highway guardrails and other road construction products. Trinity expanded its railcar parts manufacturing in 1977 to building complete cars and created a railcar-leasing subsidiary.

The company was a leading producer of railcars by the early 1980s, but a change in federal tax laws and a glut of railcars caused demand to plummet; in 1985 Trinity suffered its first loss in 27 years.

Still, Trinity managed to snap up failing competitors, including Pullman Standard, once the US's top freight car maker. The company also bought Greenville Steel Car (1986), Ortner

Freight (1987), and Standard Forgings (locomotive axles, 1987). Through these purchases Trinity tripled its manufacturing capacity, so that it controlled more than half of the US freight car production capacity in the early 1990s.

The company also expanded its marine division with such acquisitions as Halter Marine (1983) and Bethlehem Steel's manufacturing plant and marine facilities in Beaumont, Texas (1989).

Trinity expanded its construction products line in 1992 with the purchase of Syro Steel (fabricated steel products) and added the Texas and Louisiana operations of Lafarge (concrete) in 1994. The company expanded into Mexico in 1995 by acquiring Grupo TATSA (fabricated steel products).

To fund expansion in other segments, Trinity spun off its Halter Marine Group in 1996. In 1997 Trinity acquired two manufacturing facilities from pipe fitting, flange, and valve industry specialist Ladish.

Ray Wallace retired as chairman and CEO in 1999 and was replaced by his son, Timothy Wallace. That year Trinity bought McConway and Torley (railcar couplers) and Excell Materials (ready-mix concrete). It also set up a railcar joint venture in Brazil.

Early in 2000 Trinity expanded its equipment manufacturing unit with the purchases of T.L. Smith Machine and Highlands Parts Manufacturer, makers of concrete mixers and parts. But less than two years after entering the concrete mixer market, Trinity got out of the struggling business. In the summer of 2001 Trinity agreed to acquire privately held railcar maker Thrall Car Manufacturing.

In 2006 the company focused on its core businesses and sold its Trinity Fittings Group to the division's management and investment firm Levine Leichtman Capital Partners.

In 2007 Trinity strengthened its construction products business with the acquisition of a number of holdings operating under the name Armor Materials. The operations included asphalt, ready mix concrete, and aggregates businesses.

EXECUTIVES

Chairman, President, and CEO: Timothy R. Wallace, age 55, $8,537,864 total compensation
SVP and CFO: William A. (Bill) McWhirter II, age 44, $2,021,995 total compensation
VP Information Technology: Madhuri A. Andrews, age 42
VP and Chief Legal Officer: S. Theis Rice, age 58, $1,233,809 total compensation
VP and Chief Audit Executive: Donald G. Collum, age 60
SVP and Group President: Mark W. Stiles, age 60, $2,452,777 total compensation
SVP and Group President, TrinityRail: D. Stephen (Steve) Menzies, age 53, $2,350,446 total compensation
VP Business Development: John M. Lee, age 48
VP, Deputy General Counsel, and Corporate Secretary: Paul M. Jolas, age 45
VP Human Resources and Shared Services: Andrea F. Cowan, age 46
VP Finance and Treasurer: James E. Perry, age 37
VP Organizational Development: Virginia C. Gray, age 49
President, Parts and Components: Patrick Wallace
Corporate Controller: Mary E. Henderson, age 50
Auditors: Ernst & Young LLP

LOCATIONS

HQ: Trinity Industries, Inc.
    2525 Stemmons Fwy., Dallas, TX 75207
Phone: 214-631-4420   **Fax:** 214-589-8810
Web: www.trin.net

PRODUCTS/OPERATIONS

2008 Sales

	$ mil.	% of total
Rail	1,381.0	36
Construction Products	719.7	18
Inland Barge	625.2	16
Energy Equipment	605.7	16
Railcar Leasing & Management Services	535.9	14
Other	15.3	—
Total	**3,882.8**	**100**

Selected Products and Services

Rail
    Box cars
    Freight cars
    Gondola cars
    Hopper cars
    Intermodal cars
    Tank cars
Construction products
    Aggregates
    Beams
    Girders
    Highway guardrails
    Highway safety devices
    Ready-mix concrete
Inland barge
    Deck barges
    Fiberglass barge covers
    Hopper barges
    Tank barges
Energy equipment
    Container heads
    Fertilizer containers
    Liquefied petroleum gas containers
    Wind towers
Railcar leasing and management services
    Railcar leasing, repair, and management

COMPETITORS

ALSTOM
American Railcar Industries
Amsted
Blue Tee
CEMEX
Clipper Windpower
Conrad Industries
FreightCar America
GATX
Greenbrier Companies
Greenbrier Rail Services
Holcim
Lafarge North America
Nippon Sharyo
Siemens Transportation Systems
TTX
Vulcan Materials

HISTORICAL FINANCIALS

Company Type: Public

Income Statement

FYE: December 31

	REVENUE ($ mil.)	NET INCOME ($ mil.)	NET PROFIT MARGIN	EMPLOYEES
12/08	3,882.8	285.8	7.4%	13,070
12/07	3,832.8	293.1	7.6%	14,400
12/06	3,218.9	230.1	7.1%	13,800
12/05	2,902.0	83.1	2.9%	15,224
12/04	2,198.1	(12.4)	—	14,217
Annual Growth	**15.3%**	**—**	**—**	**(2.1%)**

2008 Year-End Financials

Debt ratio: 104.1%   No. of shares (mil.): 79
Return on equity: 16.1%   Dividends
Cash ($ mil.): 162   Yield: 1.9%
Current ratio: 1.61   Payout: 8.4%
Long-term debt ($ mil.): 1,906 Market value ($ mil.): 1,249

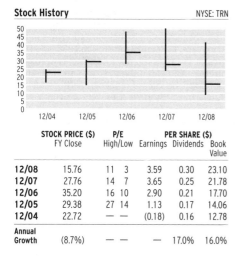

	STOCK PRICE ($)		P/E		PER SHARE ($)		
	FY Close		High/Low		Earnings	Dividends	Book Value
12/08	15.76		11	3	3.59	0.30	23.10
12/07	27.76		14	7	3.65	0.25	21.78
12/06	35.20		16	10	2.90	0.21	17.70
12/05	29.38		27	14	1.13	0.17	14.06
12/04	22.72		—	—	(0.18)	0.16	12.78
Annual Growth	(8.7%)		—	—	—	17.0%	16.0%

True Value

To survive against home improvement giants such as The Home Depot and Lowe's, True Value (formerly TruServ) is relying on the true value of service. Formed by the merger of Cotter & Company (which was the supplier to the True Value chain) and ServiStar Coast to Coast, the retailer-owned hardware cooperative serves some 5,400 retail outlets (down from nearly 7,200 in 2001), including its flagship True Value hardware stores. The co-op sells home improvement and garden supplies, as well as appliances, housewares, sporting goods, and toys. Members use the Taylor Rental, Grand Rental Station, Home & Garden Showplace, Induserve Supply, and other banners. True Value also manufactures its own brand of paints.

The merger of Cotter & Company and ServiStar Coast to Coast (operator of Coast to Coast and ServiStar hardware stores, most of which converted to the True Value banner) gave members — many of them mom-and-pop outlets — more buying clout to compete against the do-it-yourself mega-retailers, plus retail advice and advertising support. True Value has been growing its business in the rental and maintenance, repair, and operation (MRO) arenas, and has resumed supplying lumber and building materials. (The company sold its lumber and building materials business in 2000.) At the store level, True Value has been developing "lite" or smaller versions of its signature programs, such as Platinum Paint Shop, for the co-op's stores (more than half) that are less than 6,000 sq. ft.

True Value's smaller in-town locations have taken a beating at the hands of the big-box hardware chains, as is reflected in the steep decline in store count over the past decade. But rising gas prices, shoppers' ambivalence toward the big-box shopping experience, and improvements in True Value's retail operation may bode well for the co-op's future. Indeed, 2008 marked the first time in over a decade where revenue from new stores exceeded lost revenue from terminated stores. While the organization is focused on growing its retail presence, the weak housing market in the US has kept growth in check in 2009.

Outside the US the company serves about 700 stores in more than 50 countries.

HISTORY

Noting that hardware retailers had begun to form wholesale cooperatives to lower costs, John Cotter, a traveling hardware salesman, and associate Ed Lanctot started pitching the wholesale co-op idea in 1947 to small-town and suburban hardware retailers, and by early 1948 they had enrolled 25 merchants for $1,500 each. Cotter became chairman of the new firm, Cotter & Company.

The co-op created the Value & Service (V&S) store trademark in 1951 to emphasize the advantages of an independent hardware store. Acquisitions included the 1963 purchase of Chicago-based wholesaler Hibbard, Spencer, Bartlett, giving Cotter 400 new members and the well-known True Value trademark, which soon replaced V&S signs. Four years later Cotter broadened its focus by buying the General Paint & Chemical Company (Tru-Test paint). The V&S name was revived in 1972 for a five-and-dime store co-op, V&S Variety Stores.

In 1989 Cotter died and Lanctot retired. (Lanctot died in October 2003.) By 1989 there were almost 7,000 True Value Stores. Cotter moved into Canada in 1992 by acquiring hardware distributor and store operator Macleod-Stedman (275 outlets).

Juggling variety-store and hardware merchandise and delivering very small amounts of merchandise to a lukewarm co-op membership did not allow for economies of scale, so in 1995 the company quit its manufacturing operations and its US variety stores (though it still serves variety stores in Canada, operating as C&S Choices), tightened membership requirements, and introduced new services.

Two years later Cotter formed TruServ by merging with hardware wholesaler ServiStar Coast to Coast. ServiStar had its origins in the nation's first hardware co-op, American Hardware Supply, which was founded in Pittsburgh in 1910 by M. R. Porter, John Howe, and E. S. Corlett. By 1988, the year it changed its name to ServiStar, the co-op topped $1 billion in sales.

ServiStar expanded in the upper Midwest and on the West Coast in 1990 when it acquired the assets of the Coast to Coast chain (founded in 1928 as a franchise hardware store in Minneapolis); ServiStar brought Coast to Coast out of bankruptcy two years later, making it a co-op. Merging its 1992 acquisition of Taylor Rental Center with its Grand Rental Station stores in 1993 made ServiStar the #1 general rental chain. In 1996 it consolidated Coast to Coast's operations into its own and changed its name to ServiStar Coast to Coast.

President Don Hoye became CEO of the company in 1999. That year TruServ slashed 1,000 jobs and declared it would convert all its hardware store chains to the True Value banner. But TruServ lost $131 million in 1999 over bookkeeping gaffes, and co-op members received no dividends. Of 2,800 ServiStar dealers, only 1,900 raised the True Value flag. Others either declined to switch or were never offered the change because other True Value stores already shared their market area. In addition, stores began deserting the co-op because of inventory and other problems.

As competition continued to increase in 2001, the company was facing falling sales, lawsuits from shareholders, and accusations by retailers of unfair practices intended to pressure them into adopting the cooperative's flagship True Value banner. TruServ also had to confront a $200 million loan default. It made cuts in its corporate staff and divested its Canadian interests. In July 2001 Hoye resigned. The company's CFO and COO, Pamela Forbes Lieberman, was named the new CEO that November.

TruServ, under SEC investigation for alleged inventory, accounting, and other internal-control problems, was one of several companies that failed in 2002 to meet a government requirement to swear by their past financial results. TruServ settled the SEC's allegations in 2003, without admitting or denying them, and agreed to follow measures intended to ensure compliance with securities laws.

Lieberman resigned in November 2004. Director Thomas Hanemann was named interim CEO. TruServ changed its name to True Value in January 2005. In June 2005 Hanemann turned over the reins to Sears veteran Lyle G. Heidemann, who joined True Value as its new president and CEO.

In 2007 the company launched its new store format, called Destination TrueValue.

EXECUTIVES

Chairman; CEO, Krueger's True Value, Neenah, Wis.: Brian A. Webb
President, CEO, and Director: Lyle G. Heidemann, age 64
SVP and CFO: David A. (Dave) Shadduck
SVP and CIO: Leslie A. Weber
SVP and Chief Merchandising Officer: Michael Clark
SVP Human Resources, General Counsel, and Secretary: Cathy C. Anderson
SVP Logistics and Supply Chain Management: Stephen Poplawski
VP Retail and Specialty Businesses Development: Fred L. Kirst, age 55
VP Marketing: Carol Wentworth, age 49
VP and Corporate Treasurer: Barbara L. Wagner
VP Retail Finance: Jon Johnson
VP Retail Growth: Mark Flowers
VP and Controller: Donald J. (Don) Deegan
Auditors: PricewaterhouseCoopers LLP

LOCATIONS

HQ: True Value Company
8600 W. Bryn Mawr Ave., Chicago, IL 60631
Phone: 773-695-5000   **Fax:** 773-695-6516
Web: www.truevaluecompany.com

PRODUCTS/OPERATIONS

2008 Sales

	$ mil.	% of total
Hardware	1,932.2	96
Paint manufacturing & distribution	80.5	4
Total	**2,012.7**	**100**

Selected Operations

Grand Rental Station (general rental)
Home & Garden Showplace (nursery and giftware)
Induserve Supply (commercial and industrial)
Party Central (parties and corporate events)
Taylor Rental (general rental)
True Value (hardware)

COMPETITORS

84 Lumber
Ace Hardware
Akzo Nobel
Benjamin Moore
Do it Best
Fastenal
Home Depot
Kmart
Lowe's
McCoy Corp.
Menard
Northern Tool
Orgill
Reno-Depot
Sears
Sherwin-Williams
Stock Building Supply
Sutherland Lumber
United Rentals
Valspar
Wal-Mart

HISTORICAL FINANCIALS

Company Type: Cooperative

Income Statement

	REVENUE ($ mil.)	NET INCOME ($ mil.)	NET PROFIT MARGIN	EMPLOYEES
12/08	2,012.7	64.2	3.2%	3,000
12/07	2,040.6	63.8	3.1%	3,000
12/06	2,050.0	72.8	3.6%	3,000
12/05	2,043.0	47.6	2.3%	2,800
12/04	2,023.9	43.2	2.1%	2,800
Annual Growth	(0.1%)	10.4%	—	1.7%

FYE: December 31

Net Income History

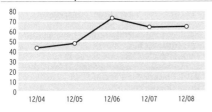

Tupperware Brands

Tupperware Brands Corporation (TBC) knows that there's more than one way to party. The company makes and sells household products and beauty items. Tupperware parties became synonymous with American suburban life in the 1950s, when independent salespeople organized gatherings to peddle their plasticware. TBC deploys a sales force of about 2.3 million people in about 100 countries. The company also sells its products online. Brands include Armand Dupree, Avroy Shlain, BeautiControl, Fuller, NaturCare, Nutrimetics, Nuvo, Swissgarde, and, of course, Tupperware. Its BeautiControl unit sells beauty and skin care products and fragrances in North America, Latin America, and the Asia/Pacific region.

TBC's direct sales force logged 15.5 million Tupperware parties worldwide in 2008. Though many consider the Tupperware brand to be something of an American institution, some 65% of the company's 2008 sales (up from 2007's 62%) were generated outside the US. TBC has pushed into new and developing markets (such as China, Eastern Europe, India, Japan, and Indonesia), offering region-specific products such as Kimono Keepers. The direct seller often targets areas where jobs are scarce and family ties are strong — the better for developing its sales network.

Its international growth and beauty segment have been gaining momentum, as well. The company's beauty segment accounted for about 35% of sales in 2008. TBC built its global beauty presence through one strategic acquisition. In 2005 it doubled its sales force of independent consultants who sell beauty and personal care products in the Asia/Pacific region and Latin America with the acquisition of Sara Lee Corporation's international direct selling unit. As part of the agreement, TBC paid $557 million and acquired the direct selling unit's staff of 884,000 consultants, as well. The company then changed its name from Tupperware Corporation to Tupperware Brands Corporation to reflect the firm's growing portfolio of brands. While the Tupperware brand accounted for 83% of 2005 sales, in 2008 it brought in about 65%, while its beauty segment blossomed.

State Street Bank and Trust Company and Barclays Global Investors each own 6% and 5%, respectively, of Tupperware.

HISTORY

Earl Tupper was a self-styled inventor with only a high school education when he went to work for DuPont in the 1930s. He left DuPont in 1938 to start his own company, taking with him an unwanted, smelly chunk of polyethylene, a by-product of the oil refining process. Tupper eventually developed his own refining process, and in 1942 he created a clear, lightweight, unbreakable, odorless, nontoxic plastic, which he called Poly-T.

Tupper continued to do contract work for DuPont during the war, making parts for gas masks and Navy signal lamps. He continued to work with Poly-T and founded Tupperware in 1946. The next year, inspired by a paint can lid, Tupper developed the Tupperware Seal, which creates an airtight, partial vacuum. The Tupperware food storage container was born and began to move onto retail shelves.

At the same time, a secretary in Detroit named Brownie Wise was selling Stanley Home Products' appliances through parties at her home to raise money for her son's medical bills. (The party system was actually developed in the 1920s to introduce communities to aluminum cookware.) Wise added a Tupperware set to her product mix, and sales took off. By the early 1950s Tupperware parties began to spread.

Wise, hired as VP and general manager, became Tupperware's inspirational leader. In 1951 all Tupperware products were removed from retail shelves, and subsidiary Tupperware Home Parties was officially founded. By 1954 sales multiplied 25 times and the company had about 9,000 independent sellers.

By 1958 Tupperware expanded into Canada. That year Wise left and Tupper sold the company to Rexall Drug. In 1969 Rexall became Dart Industries; by this time Tupperware had entered Western Europe, Latin America, and parts of Asia. In 1976 international sales pushed revenue past $500 million.

In 1980 Dart merged with Kraft to become Dart and Kraft, Inc. By 1984 sales began to slip due to the number of women entering the workforce. Tupperware introduced a catalog and revised the party plan to include gatherings in the workplace. Dart and Kraft split in 1986, and Dart became Premark International. Tupperware's national ad campaign the next year inadvertently increased the sales of retail competitors such as Rubbermaid. By 1990 sales were slowing across the US, Latin America, and Japan.

Tupperware restructured in 1992 and former Avon executive Rick Goings became president. Wall Street's belief that Tupperware was languishing as a subsidiary led to its spinoff from Premark as a public company in 1996. Tupperware established operations in China that year and began holding parties in Russia in 1997. The Asian economic crisis and domestic organizational problems led to slumping sales in 1997 and 1998.

The company experimented with new sales channels in 1998 and 1999, including infomercials, mall kiosks, a Web site, and catalogs. Tupperware made the best of Asia's troubled economy in 1998 by recruiting laid-off workers and launching "I Save With Tupperware" campaigns to help consumers stretch food budgets. German direct seller Vorwerk bought an 11% stake in Tupperware in 2000 (and sold it in early 2005). In October 2000 Tupperware purchased cosmetics company BeautiControl.

Tupperware's first foray into store retailing was short-lived. The company began selling some products in SuperTarget stores in October 2001, but the negative impact felt by Tupperware's direct sales channel quickly prompted the company to pull the items from Target stores' shelves in June 2003.

In December 2005 the company acquired Sara Lee Corporation's direct selling businesses — International Beauty — and at the same time changed its name from Tupperware Corp. to Tupperware Brands Corporation. The acquisition boosted the direct seller's sales force at the time to about 1.9 million independent consultants.

EXECUTIVES

Chairman and CEO: E.V. (Rick) Goings, age 63, $9,474,865 total compensation
President and COO: Simon C. Hemus, age 59, $2,776,825 total compensation
EVP and CFO: Michael S. (Mike) Poteshman, age 44, $1,185,466 total compensation
VP and CTO: Robert F. Wagner, age 47
EVP, Chief Legal Officer, and Secretary: Thomas M. Roehlk, age 57
EVP and Chief Human Resources Officer: Lillian D. Garcia, age 52
SVP Worldwide Operations: José R. Timmerman, age 59
SVP Tax and Governmental Affairs: Josef Hajek, age 50
SVP Worldwide Market Development: Christian E. Skröder, age 60
VP Internal Audit: V. Jane Garrard, age 45
VP and Treasurer: Edward R. Davis III, age 45
VP Investor Relations: Teresa Burchfield, age 45
VP Strategy and Business Development: Carl Benkovich, age 52
VP, Controller, and Principal Accounting Officer: Nicholas Poucher, age 46
VP Global Product Marketing: Rashit Ismail, age 46
Group President, Europe, Africa, and the Middle East: R. Glenn Drake, age 55, $1,533,103 total compensation
Group President, Asia/Pacific and North America: David T. Halversen, age 63, $1,706,789 total compensation
Auditors: PricewaterhouseCoopers LLP

LOCATIONS

HQ: Tupperware Brands Corporation
14901 S. Orange Blossom Trail, Orlando, FL 32837
Phone: 407-826-5050 **Fax:** 407-826-8268
Web: www.tupperwarebrands.com

2008 Sales

	$ mil.	% of total
Europe	769.6	36
North America	764.0	35
Asia/Pacific	336.1	16
Beauty other	292.1	13
Total	**2,161.8**	**100**

PRODUCTS/OPERATIONS

2008 Sales

	$ mil.	% of total
Tupperware	1409.0	65
Beauty	752.8	35
Total	**2,161.8**	**100**

Selected Product Lines

Children's educational toys
Cooking products
Cosmetics and skin care
Food storage containers
Serving and preparation products

Selected Trademarks

BeautiControl
Expressions
FridgeSmart
Modular Mates
One Touch
OvenWorks
Rock 'N Serve
Tupperware

COMPETITORS

Alticor
Avon
Body Shop
Clorox
Container Store
CPAC
Discovery Toys
The First Years
Hasbro
Home Products International
Kmart
Learning Curve International
Lifetime Brands
Mary Kay
Mattel
Newell Rubbermaid
Owens-Illinois
Pampered Chef
Sterilite
Target
Tastefully Simple
Wal-Mart
Williams-Sonoma
Wilton Products
WKI Holding
ZAG Industries

HISTORICAL FINANCIALS

Company Type: Public

Income Statement				FYE: Last Saturday in December
	REVENUE ($ mil.)	NET INCOME ($ mil.)	NET PROFIT MARGIN	EMPLOYEES
12/08	2,161.8	161.4	7.5%	14,740
12/07	1,981.4	116.9	5.9%	12,800
12/06	1,743.7	94.2	5.4%	12,300
12/05	1,279.3	86.2	6.7%	11,700
12/04	1,224.3	86.9	7.1%	5,900
Annual Growth	15.3%	16.7%	—	25.7%

2008 Year-End Financials

Debt ratio: 119.7%	No. of shares (mil.): 63
Return on equity: 32.4%	Dividends
Cash ($ mil.): 125	Yield: 3.9%
Current ratio: 1.56	Payout: 34.4%
Long-term debt ($ mil.): 567	Market value ($ mil.): 1,430

Stock History

NYSE: TUP

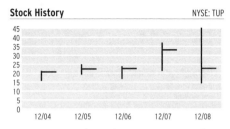

	STOCK PRICE ($) FY Close	P/E High/Low		PER SHARE ($) Earnings	Dividends	Book Value
12/08	22.70	18	6	2.56	0.88	7.53
12/07	33.03	20	12	1.87	0.88	8.30
12/06	22.61	15	11	1.54	0.88	6.36
12/05	22.40	18	14	1.41	0.88	5.33
12/04	20.72	14	11	1.48	0.88	4.62
Annual Growth	2.3%	—	—	14.7%	0.0%	13.0%

Tyco International

After its chief executive was sent to prison, Tyco International was all broken up. The company has disassociated itself from the free-spending ways of former CEO Dennis Kozlowski, who is serving jail time for taking millions of dollars from the company. In mid-2007 Tyco split into three publicly held companies: Tyco International, Covidien (formerly Tyco Healthcare Group), and Tyco Electronics. Tyco International is made up of five divisions: Fire Protection Services (fire detection and suppression systems), Electrical and Metal Products (steel tubing, pipes, and cables for commercial construction), ADT Worldwide (security systems), Safety Products (protective equipment), and Flow Control (valves).

Tyco's largest business, ADT Worldwide, which includes North American subsidiary ADT, provides security-system equipment, installation, and monitoring services. The company's Fire Protection Services segment includes its SimplexGrinnell subsidiary. Tyco offers fire suppression, breathing apparatus, and video and access control and intrusion security products through its Safety Products unit. Businesses such as Allied Tube and Conduit and AFC Cable Systems fall under the company's Electrical and Metal unit, while its Flow Control unit makes valves and related products for water, wastewater, and the oil and gas markets.

In 2008 ADT Worldwide acquired FirstService Security to strengthen its systems integration capabilities. Tyco divestitures that year included a subsidiary that makes and sells fire protection products in Japan, a European manufacturer of building products for the construction industry, a European manufacturer of public address and acoustic systems, and substantially all of its Infrastructure Services business. The divestitures gave Tyco a cash infusion of about $1 billion.

Tyco is legally domiciled in Switzerland but run primarily from Princeton, New Jersey.

HISTORY

Arthur Rosenberg founded Tyco, Inc., in 1960 to conduct experimental research for the government and commercial sectors. It successfully developed the Dynalux battery charger, the first blue-light laser, and the first laser with a nonstop beam. Under a new name, Tyco Laboratories (changed in 1965), the firm boosted sales through acquisitions in the mid-1960s to reach $41 million by 1969, up from $1 million in 1963. Rosenberg left Tyco Labs in 1970.

In 1974 Tyco Labs acquired venerable Simplex Wire & Cable, whose predecessor had developed water-resistant Anhydrex cables in the 1920s, made submarine cables during WWII, and began installing undersea cables in 1966. Tyco Labs almost tripled its sales in 1975 by acquiring ITT's Grinnell.

Tyco Labs bought polyethylene producer Armin in 1979 and packaging maker Ludlow two years later. It acquired Grinnell Flow Control, a valve distributor, from ITT in 1986 and Allied Pipe & Tube the next year. In 1988 Tyco Labs acquired Mueller, a water and gas pipe maker founded in 1885 by industry pioneer Hieronymous Mueller.

In 1993 Tyco replaced "Laboratories" with "International" in its name to reflect its multinational operations. The next year it bought Kendall International, which moved Tyco into the disposable health care products market.

Security giant ADT bought Tyco for $6.6 billion in a 1997 deal that left Tyco in control of the combined company. In 1999 it bought AMP, the world's largest supplier of electrical and electronic connectors, for $12.2 billion, and Raychem, a top electronic component maker.

Digesting its acquisitions, Tyco laid off more than 9,000 workers in 1998 and 1999. Also in 1999 Tyco's method of accounting for its acquisitions prompted an SEC inquiry, but no action was taken against the company.

In 2000 the company expanded its health care business with several purchases, including the $4.2 billion acquisition of Mallinckrodt, a leading maker of respiratory care equipment. At the end of 2000 Tyco bought Lucent's Power Systems division for $2.5 billion. In 2001 Tyco completed the $1.15 billion purchase of security products manufacturer Simplex Time Recorder and bought SecurityLink (security monitoring) from Cambridge Protection Industries for about $1 billion. Tyco also acquired Sensormatic, a manufacturer of electronic article surveillance systems, for about $2.3 billion.

Tyco moved into the financial services industry in 2001 by buying commercial lender CIT Group for $9.2 billion in stock and cash.

CEO Dennis Kozlowski resigned in 2002 after a newspaper reported that New York prosecutors suspected him of using family trusts to avoid paying state sales taxes. His predecessor, John Fort, stepped in as interim CEO. Later that year Kozlowski and two other former Tyco executives, including former CFO Mark Swartz, were indicted on charges that they took millions of dollars in unauthorized compensation. After about six months of testimony and intense jury deliberations, the New York State Supreme Court judge hearing the case declared a mistrial due to outside pressures that were placed upon a juror.

In 2005 Kozlowski and Swartz were retried and were both convicted of grand larceny and conspiracy, falsifying business records, and violating business law. They each were sentenced to serve from 100 months to 25 years in state prison and were ordered to repay $134 million to Tyco.

Kozlowski was also fined $70 million, and Swartz was fined $35 million.

Tyco spun off CIT Group in 2002. Also that year the company announced that former Motorola COO Edward Breen would take the helm at Tyco as the new chairman and CEO. In 2003 Tyco announced plans to reorganize its operations and cut costs by closing about 300 plants and by disposing of about 50 business units.

In 2006 the company settled with the SEC, agreeing to pay a fine of $50 million over accounting practices under the former management regime. Kozlowski settled his tax evasion charges with New York State by agreeing to pay $3.2 million in back sales taxes and $18 million in delinquent income taxes. Swartz paid $38 million in restitution to Tyco, and a New York court ordered the Manhattan district attorney's office to release $98 million from an escrow account in 2007 to satisfy Kozlowski's restitution.

In 2008 the company agreed to pay $250 million to settle a lawsuit from bondholders who claimed Tyco failed to get their approval when it spun off its electronics and health-care businesses. The bondholders alleged the breakup plan was merely a scheme to shield assets, and had filed a lawsuit aimed at stopping the plan after it was announced in 2006, claiming Tyco required their approval.

EXECUTIVES

Chairman and CEO: Edward D. (Ed) Breen Jr., age 52, $20,615,192 total compensation
EVP and CFO: Christopher J. Coughlin, age 57, $9,055,083 total compensation
SVP and Chief Tax Officer: John E. Evard Jr., age 62, $3,875,343 total compensation
SVP Operational Excellence and Chief Procurement Officer: Shelley Stewart Jr., age 55
SVP, Controller, and Chief Accounting Officer: Carol A. (John) Davidson, age 53
EVP and General Counsel: Judith A. Reinsdorf, age 45
SVP Strategy and Investor Relations: Edward C. (Ed) Arditte, age 53
SVP Human Resources and International Communications: Laurie A. Siegel, age 52
SVP and Treasurer: Arun Nayar
VP Corporate Communications: Paul Fitzhenry
VP Supply Chain Management: Jaime Bohnke
VP and Corporate Secretary: John S. Jenkins Jr.
President, Tyco Safety, Electrical, and Metal Products: George R. Oliver, age 48, $4,031,965 total compensation
President, ADT Worldwide: Naren K. Gursahaney, age 47, $3,657,460 total compensation
President, Tyco Flow Control: Patrick Decker, age 44
President, SimplexGrinnell: Jim Spicer
Auditors: Deloitte & Touche LLP

LOCATIONS

HQ: Tyco International Ltd.
9 Roszel Rd., Princeton, NJ 08540
Phone: 609-720-4200   **Fax:** 609-720-4208
Web: www.tyco.com

2008 Sales

	$ mil.	% of total
Americas		
US	9,661	48
Other	1,537	8
Europe, Middle East & Africa	5,749	28
Asia/Pacific	3,252	16
Total	**20,199**	**100**

PRODUCTS/OPERATIONS

2008 Sales

	$ mil.	% of total
ADT Worldwide	8,017	40
Flow Control	4,418	22
Fire Protection Services	3,553	18
Electrical & Metal Products	2,272	11
Safety Products	1,934	9
Corporate & other	5	—
Total	**20,199**	**100**

Selected Products and Operations

ADT Worldwide
  Senormatic
Electrical and Metal Products
  AFC Cable
  Allied Tube & Conduit
Fire Protection Services
  SimplexGrinnell
  Wormald
Flow Control
  Keystone
  Vanessa
Safety Products
  Ansul
  Scott

COMPETITORS

ADT Worldwide
Belden
Brink's
Cooper Industries
Crane Co.
Dresser, Inc.
Flowserve
G4S
GE
Honeywell International
Hubbell
Illinois Tool Works
Ingersoll-Rand
ITT Corp.
Johnson Controls
Parker Hannifin
Raytheon
Rentokil Initial
Roper Industries
Securitas
Siemens AG
Stryker
Sumitomo Electric
Thomas & Betts
United Technologies

HISTORICAL FINANCIALS

Company Type: Public

Income Statement

FYE: September 30

	REVENUE ($ mil.)	NET INCOME ($ mil.)	NET PROFIT MARGIN	EMPLOYEES
9/08	20,199.0	1,553.0	7.7%	113,000
9/07	18,781.0	(1,742.0)	—	118,000
9/06	40,960.0	3,727.0	9.1%	238,200
9/05	39,727.0	3,011.0	7.6%	247,900
9/04	40,153.0	2,879.0	7.2%	258,400
Annual Growth	**(15.8%)**	**(14.3%)**	**—**	**(18.7%)**

2008 Year-End Financials

Debt ratio: 23.9%
Return on equity: 10.0%
Cash ($ mil.): 1,519
Current ratio: 1.51
Long-term debt ($ mil.): 3,709
No. of shares (mil.): 474
Dividends
  Yield: 1.9%
  Payout: 20.4%
Market value ($ mil.): 16,603

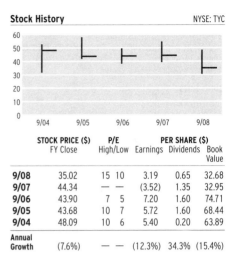
Tyson Foods

Think of Tyson Foods as an 800-pound chicken — with a bullish attitude. One of the largest US chicken producers, Tyson's purchase of beef and pork giant IBP Fresh Meats made it a giant in the worldwide meat-processing industry, serving retail, wholesale, and foodservice customers in the US and more than 90 countries overseas. In addition to fresh meats, Tyson produces processed and pre-cooked meats, refrigerated and frozen prepared foods, and animal feeds. Its chicken operations are vertically integrated — the company hatches the eggs and then supplies contracted growers with chicks and feed, and brings them back for processing when ready. Former chairman Don Tyson is the controlling owner of the company.

Saying that it no longer fit the company's long-term international strategy of focusing on Asia, Mexico, and South America, in 2009 Tyson sold its Canadian beef operations (Lakeside Farm Industries) to XL Foods. Due to what the company called challenging conditions in the pork market, in 2009 the company downsized its pork operations with the sale of five of its hog farms.

CEO Dick Bond resigned from the company in 2009. He was replaced on an interim basis by Leland Tollett, a former chairman and CEO of the company. Just one day after announcing Bond's departure, the company was fined $500,000 by a US District Court for safety violations that resulted in a Tyson worker's death at its animal-feed plant in Texarkana, Texas. The worker was killed as a result of exposure to hydrogen sulfide gas while he was repairing a piece of leaky equipment. Prosecutors, who charged the company with "willful violation of an OSHA standard resulting in the death of an employee," said an identical exposure injured a Tyson worker at the facility in 2002.

The company's fresh meat operations process chicken, beef, and pork. Tyson's pork operations offer processed pork products including sausage, ham, and bacon. Its prepared foods unit produces pizza toppings and entrées. Other activities include the production of livestock and pet feeds and rendering by-products. In 2009 the company acquired the Mississippi poultry rendering company, Central Industries.

Adding to its Asian operations, the company in 2008 purchased 60% of the Xinchang Group, the fifth largest poultry producer in China, with a processing capacity of 125 million birds a year. Also in 2008 Tyson bought three Brazilian poultry companies.

Recognizing the growing market for alternative and renewable fuels and recognizing its unending supply of meat by-products, Tyson decided to get into the alternative fuel market in 2007 with the formation of a 50-50 joint venture with fuel refiner, Syntroleum, to produce synthetic fuel for the diesel-, jet-, and military-fuel markets.

HISTORY

During the Great Depression, Arkansas poultry farmer John Tyson supported his family by selling vegetables and poultry. In 1935, after developing a method for transporting live poultry (he installed a food-and-water trough and nailed small feed cups on a trailer), he bought 500 chickens in Arkansas and sold them in Chicago.

For the next decade Tyson bought, sold, and transported chickens. By 1947, the year he incorporated the company as Tyson Feed & Hatchery, he was raising the chickens himself. He emphasized chicken production, opening his first processing plant in 1958, where he implemented an ice-packing system that allowed the company to send its products greater distances.

John's son Don took over as manager in 1960, and in 1963 it went public as Tyson Foods. Tyson Country Fresh Chicken (packaged chicken that would become the company's mainstay) was introduced in 1967.

Rapid expansion included a new egg processing building (1970), a new plant and computerized feed mill (1971), and the acquisitions of Prospect Farms (1969, precooked chicken) and the Ocoma Foods Division (1972, poultry), as well as hog operations.

Health-conscious consumers increasingly turned from red meats to poultry during the 1980s. Tyson became the industry leader with several key acquisitions of poultry operations, including the Tastybird division of Valmac (1985), Lane Processing (1986), and Heritage Valley (1986). Its 1989 purchase of Holly Farms added beef and pork processing.

Don Tyson relinquished the CEO position to Leland Tollett in 1991. In 1992 the firm plunged into seafood with the purchase of Arctic Alaska Fisheries and Louis Kemp Seafood.

In 1997 the company pleaded guilty to charges that it illegally gave former Agriculture Secretary Mike Espy thousands of dollars' worth of gifts; the settlement included $6 million in fines and fees. In 1998 John H. Tyson, grandson of the founder, was elected chairman. He became CEO in 2000.

As the winner in a bidding war with Smithfield Foods, in 2001 Tyson agreed to buy IBP, Inc., the #1 beef processor and #2 pork processor in the US, for nearly $3.2 billion.

In late 2001 Tyson Foods and six managers were indicted for conspiring to smuggle illegal immigrants from Mexico and Central America to work for lower than legal wages in 15 of its US poultry processing plants. Two managers made plea bargains and testified for the government; another manager committed suicide. Tyson and the remaining three managers were acquitted of the conspiracy charges in 2003.

In the wake of the discovery of a single case of BSE (mad cow disease) in the US, Tyson reduced production at its beef plants due to reduced demand for US beef overseas.

Following the discovery of bird flu on a Texas chicken farm in February 2004 and the resultant banning of the importation of US chicken products by other countries, Tyson consolidated and automated its poultry operations, resulting in hundreds of layoffs at the company.

In 2004 the SEC recommended civil action against the company for its failure to disclose $1.7 million in corporate perks given to Don Tyson without authorization from Tyson's compensation committee. Although Don Tyson had already reimbursed the company $1.53 million for then-unspecified benefits, the SEC also announced plans to recommend civil action be taken against him. With neither the company nor Tyson admitting any guilt, the case was settled in 2005 with Tyson paying the SEC $700,000 in fines and the company, $1.5 million.

In 2006 Don's son, John Tyson, stepped down as CEO; COO Richard L. Bond replaced him. Tyson remained as chairman.

EXECUTIVES

Interim President and Interim CEO: Leland E. Tollett, age 72
EVP and CFO: Dennis Leatherby, age 49
SVP and CIO: Gary Cooper
SVP, Controller, and Chief Accounting Officer: Craig J. Hart, age 53
Senior Group VP and Chief Development Officer: John S. Lea
SVP and Chief Environmental, Health, and Safety Officer: Kevin J. Igli
Chief Marketing Officer: Sue Quillin
EVP and General Counsel: David L. Van Bebber, age 53
EVP Corporate Affairs: Archie Schaffer III
Senior Group VP Poultry and Prepared Foods: Donnie Smith, age 50
Senior Group VP Fresh Meats and Margin Optimization: James V. (Jim) Lochner, age 56
SVP International: Mike Baker
SVP Human Resources: Kenneth J. Kimbro
SVP Sales: Randy Smith
SVP Food Quality Assurance: Rick Roop
SVP Tyson Renewable Products Group: Jeff Webster
SVP Ethics, Compliance, and Internal Audit: Karen Gilbert
SVP Corporate Research and Development: Craig Bacon
SVP External Relations: Sara Lilygren
Group VP Food Service: Bernard F. Leonard, age 56
VP, Associate General Counsel, and Secretary: R. Read Hudson
VP Sales: Lee Harrison
VP Investor Relations and Assistant Secretary: Ruth Ann Wisener
Auditors: Ernst & Young LLP

LOCATIONS

HQ: Tyson Foods, Inc.
2200 Don Tyson Pkwy., Springdale, AR 72762
Phone: 479-290-4000   **Fax:** 479-290-4061
Web: www.tysonfoodsinc.com

PRODUCTS/OPERATIONS

2008 Sales

	$ mil.	% of total
Beef	11,664	44
Chicken	8,900	33
Pork	3,587	13
Prepared foods	2,711	10
Total	**26,862**	**100**

Selected Products and Brands

Meats, fresh
   Bruss (beef, pork, lamb, veal)
   Chairman's Reserve (beef)
   Golden Trophy (beef)
   Nature's Farm (organic fresh chicken)
   Tyson (beef, chicken, pork)
   Tyson Holly Farms (chicken)
Meats, processed
   Corn King (bacon, ham, and lunchmeat)
   Thornapple Valley (bacon, hotdogs, lunchmeat, and ham)
   Weaver (chicken products)
   Wright (bacon and ham)
Prepared foods
   Doskocil (value-added meats for pizza industry)
   Lady Aster (entrees)
   Mexican Original (flour and corn tortilla products)

COMPETITORS

Buckhead Beef	Kraft North America
Butterball	Laura's Lean Beef Co.
Cargill	Maple Leaf Foods
Clougherty Packing	MBA Poultry
Coleman Natural Foods	National Beef
ConAgra	New Market Poultry
ContiGroup	Perdue Incorporated
Cooper Farms	Petaluma Poultry
Eberly Poultry	Pilgrim's Pride
Empire Kosher Poultry	Plainville Farms
Foster Farms	Raeford Farms
Freedman Meats	Sanderson Farms
Gusto Packing	Sara Lee
Hormel	Shelton's
JBS	Smithfield Foods
JBS USA	U.S. Premium Beef
Jennie-O	Wayne Farms LLC
Koch Foods	Zacky Farms

HISTORICAL FINANCIALS

Company Type: Public

Income Statement

FYE: Saturday nearest September 30

	REVENUE ($ mil.)	NET INCOME ($ mil.)	NET PROFIT MARGIN	EMPLOYEES
9/08	26,862.0	86.0	0.3%	107,000
9/07	26,900.0	268.0	1.0%	104,000
9/06	25,559.0	(191.0)	—	107,000
9/05	26,014.0	353.0	1.4%	114,000
9/04	26,441.0	403.0	1.5%	114,000
Annual Growth	0.4%	(32.0%)	—	(1.6%)

2008 Year-End Financials

Debt ratio: 57.6%	No. of shares (mil.): 377
Return on equity: 1.8%	Dividends
Cash ($ mil.): 250	Yield: 1.3%
Current ratio: 2.07	Payout: 66.7%
Long-term debt ($ mil.): 2,888	Market value ($ mil.): 4,501

Stock History

NYSE: TSN

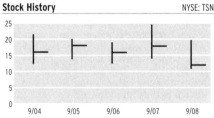

	STOCK PRICE ($) FY Close	P/E High/Low	PER SHARE ($) Earnings	Dividends	Book Value
9/08	11.94	81 46	0.24	0.16	13.30
9/07	17.85	32 19	0.75	0.16	12.55
9/06	15.88	— —	(0.58)	0.16	11.78
9/05	18.05	20 14	0.99	0.16	12.34
9/04	16.02	19 11	1.13	0.16	11.39
Annual Growth	(7.1%)	— —	(32.1%)	0.0%	4.0%

UAL Corporation

Airline operator UAL unites people and cities around the globe through its main subsidiary, United Airlines, one of the world's leading passenger and cargo carriers. United Airlines also provides regional feeder service in the US via United Express, which is operated by independent contractors. Overall, United serves more than 200 destinations in about 30 countries worldwide from hubs in Chicago, Denver, Los Angeles, San Francisco, and Washington, DC. Its mainline fleet includes about 460 jets; United Express partners operate about 280 aircraft.

United hopes to grow by focusing on the high end of the market. It offers multiple classes of service on many of its flights and believes it can continue to attract business travelers by taking advantage of its extensive global network — particularly between the US and the Asia/Pacific region — and the well-known United brand. The carrier extends its international coverage as part of the Star Alliance, a global airline marketing and code-sharing group that also includes Air Canada, Lufthansa, and Singapore Airlines.

The company continues to work on reducing its operating costs as it adapts to persistently high fuel prices. Hammered by more than $1 billion in losses at the end of 2008, UAL announced plans in January 2009 to cut as many as 2,000 jobs by year's end — bringing the total of job cuts since 2008 to about 9,000. In July 2009 about 2,100 flight attendants agreed to take voluntary furloughs from 10 to 30 months that will help the airline avoid some layoffs.

In late 2008 UAL reduced United's domestic mainline capacity by about 14% and its international capacity by 8%. The company also grounded 100 fuel-inefficient airplanes and is shutting down its one-class, low-fare carrier, Ted, and reconfiguring the unit's 55-plus aircraft to include first-class sections for mainline use.

In 2008 United and Continental unveiled plans for an extensive alliance — one that would go beyond code-sharing in terms of coordination of services but would not involve a merger or acquisition. Regulatory approval will be required for some aspects of the deal, and Continental will have to unwind agreements with its partners in the SkyTeam Alliance in order to join United in the Star group.

HISTORY

In 1929 aircraft designer Bill Boeing and engine designer Fred Rentschler of Pratt & Whitney joined forces to form United Aircraft and Transport. Renamed United Air Lines in 1931, the New York-based company offered one of the first coast-to-coast airline services. In 1934 United's manufacturing and transportation divisions split. Former banker Bill Patterson became president of the latter, United Air Lines, and moved it to the Chicago area.

Led by Patterson until 1963, United was slow to move and began offering jet service in 1959, after rival American. But in 1961 United bought Capital Airlines and became the US's #1 airline.

In 1969 UAL Corp. was formed as a holding company. In 1979, a year after airline deregulation, hotelier Richard Ferris became CEO. Dreaming of a travel conglomerate, he bought Hertz (1985) and Hilton International (1987). Angered by the diversification, the pilots struck

in 1985 and then tried to buy the airline in 1987. That year, after dropping $7.3 million to change United's name to Allegis, Ferris left when leading shareholder Coniston Partners threatened to oust the board and liquidate the firm. Assuming its old name and a new CEO, Stephen Wolf (former chief of cargo carrier Flying Tigers), UAL shed its hotels and car rental business and 50% of its computer reservation partnership, Covia.

A 1989 takeover bid by Los Angeles billionaire Marvin Davis and Coniston triggered an unsuccessful buyout effort by United pilots, management, and British Airways. Gerald Greenwald, a turnaround expert from Chrysler, headed the attempt. Coniston later sold most of its stake in exchange for two seats on the board.

United began expanding globally and added routes in the Asia/Pacific region (bought from Pan Am in 1986 and 1991). It also laid off thousands of employees and cut executive pay. Finally, the 1993 sale of United's kitchen operations (slashing 5,800 union jobs) brought the unions to the table with an employee stock ownership plan (ESOP). The ESOP, which ceded 55% of UAL to employees in exchange for $4.8 billion in wage concessions, was approved in 1994. The deal effectively ended Wolf's reign at UAL, since he had fallen out of favor with employees; Greenwald became CEO. United also launched its low-fare carrier that year.

In 1997 United formed the Star Alliance with Lufthansa, Scandinavian Airlines System, Air Canada, and Thai Airways. President James Goodwin, a 32-year United veteran, took over as CEO after Greenwald's 1999 retirement.

Also that year United Airlines lost two planes in the September 11 terrorist attacks on New York and Washington, DC. As demand for air travel slumped after the attacks, UAL eliminated flights and laid off more than 20% of its workforce. A month after the attacks, chairman and CEO James Goodwin resigned under pressure from employee unions; UAL director and former Weyerhaeuser chief John Creighton replaced him on an interim basis. The cutbacks, however, were not enough to prevent the airline from posting a $2.1 billion loss for 2001.

The following year UAL avoided a potentially disastrous strike by its mechanics when they approved a new contract giving them their first raise since 1994. The airline managed to convince its pilots and salaried managers to take a pay cut in 2002 to alleviate some of its debt. Also that year UAL applied for a $1.8 billion loan under the federal loan guarantee program created to help airlines in the aftermath of the September 11 attacks. Creighton retired and was replaced by Glenn Tilton, an oil industry executive. UAL's financial troubles continued to mount, however, and it filed for Chapter 11 bankruptcy protection in December 2002.

To assist with its emergence from bankruptcy, UAL petitioned for an additional loan from the US government in 2004, but it was denied. Instead, the government extended the repayment deadline. In the course of its reorganization, UAL launched low-fare carrier Ted, renegotiated labor agreements, and won court permission to terminate its four employee pension plans. Employees also lost their controlling stake in the company. The federal Pension Benefit Guaranty Corporation wound up with responsibility for the pension plans and a stake in UAL.

UAL emerged from bankruptcy protection in February 2006.

EXECUTIVES

Chairman, President, and CEO: Glenn F. Tilton, age 60, $6,471,062 total compensation
EVP and CFO: Kathryn A. Mikells, age 43, $1,017,746 total compensation
SVP and CIO, United Airlines: R. Keith Halbert
EVP and Chief Administrative Officer, UAL and United Airlines: Peter D. (Pete) McDonald, age 57, $4,193,340 total compensation
SVP and Chief Marketing and Customer Officer, United Airlines: Dennis M. Cary
SVP Corporate Communications and Chief Communications Officer: Antonio B. (Tony) Cervone
SVP Strategic Sourcing and Chief Procurement Officer, United Airlines: Grace M. Puma
EVP; President, United Airlines: John P. Tague, age 46, $3,165,827 total compensation
EVP; President, Mileage Plus: Graham W. Atkinson, age 57
SVP Human Resources: Marc C. Ugol, age 50
SVP Office of the Chairman, United Airlines: Sara A. Fields, age 65
SVP Planning, United Airlines: Kevin N. Knight
SVP Corporate and Government Affairs, UAL and United Airlines: Rosemary Moore, age 58
SVP Maintenance: James E. (Jim) Keenan
SVP, General Counsel, and Secretary, UAL and United Airlines: Paul R. Lovejoy, age 54, $1,762,008 total compensation
SVP Airport Operations and Cargo and United Express, United Airlines: Scott J. Dolan
SVP Onboard Service, United Airlines: Alexandria P. (Alex) Marren
SVP Operations, United Airlines: Joseph C. (Joe) Kolshak, age 50
SVP Worldwide Sales, United Airlines: Jeffrey T. (Jeff) Foland
Auditors: Deloitte & Touche LLP

LOCATIONS

HQ: UAL Corporation
77 W. Wacker Dr., Chicago, IL 60601
Phone: 312-997-8000
Web: www.united.com

2008 Sales

	$ mil.	% of total
Domestic (US & Canada)	12,819	64
Pacific	3,712	18
Atlantic	3,055	15
Latin America	608	3
Total	**20,194**	**100**

PRODUCTS/OPERATIONS

2008 Sales

	$ mil.	% of total
Passenger		
United Airlines	15,337	76
United Express (regional affiliates)	3,098	15
Cargo	854	4
Other	905	5
Total	**20,194**	**100**

COMPETITORS

Air France-KLM
Alaska Air
Alitalia
AMR Corp.
British Airways
Continental Airlines
Delta Air Lines
FedEx
Frontier Airlines
Japan Airlines
JetBlue
Northwest Airlines
Qantas
Southwest Airlines
UPS
US Airways
Virgin Atlantic Airways

HISTORICAL FINANCIALS

Company Type: Public

Income Statement

FYE: December 31

	REVENUE ($ mil.)	NET INCOME ($ mil.)	NET PROFIT MARGIN	EMPLOYEES
12/08	20,194.0	(5,348.0)	—	50,000
12/07	20,143.0	403.0	2.0%	55,000
12/06	19,340.0	22,876.0	118.3%	55,000
12/05	17,379.0	(21,176.0)	—	57,000
12/04	16,391.0	(1,721.0)	—	61,000
Annual Growth	5.4%	—	—	(4.8%)

2008 Year-End Financials

Debt ratio: —
Return on equity: —
Cash ($ mil.): 2,039
Current ratio: 0.67
Long-term debt ($ mil.): 7,199

No. of shares (mil.): 145
Dividends
  Yield: 0.0%
  Payout: —
Market value ($ mil.): 1,599

Stock History

NASDAQ (GS): UAUA

	STOCK PRICE ($) FY Close	P/E High/Low	PER SHARE ($) Earnings	Dividends	Book Value
12/08	11.02	— —	(42.21)	0.00	(16.99)
12/07	35.66	18 11	2.79	0.00	16.66
12/06	44.00	0 0	131.94	0.00	14.80
Annual Growth	(50.0%)	— —	—	—	—

UGI Corporation

UGI passes along gas and turns on power for the citizens of Pennsylvania. The company distributes propane and butane across the US and abroad. It also provides natural gas and electricity to customers in eastern Pennsylvania. UGI's 44%-owned propane distributor, AmeriGas Partners, makes up most of the holding company's sales and is one of the top two US propane marketers (along with Ferrellgas). Subsidiary UGI Utilities distributes electricity to more than 60,000 customers and gas to about 485,000 customers in Pennsylvania. Other UGI operations include energy marketing in the mid-Atlantic region, propane sales in Asia and Europe, electricity generation, and energy services.

Subsidiary AmeriGas sells propane to more than 1.3 million retail and wholesale customers a year from about 600 locations in 46 states. AmeriGas, which accounts for nearly half of the company's revenues, also offers propane-related products and services and provides propane storage services.

Subsidiary UGI Enterprises, which operates as the company's Energy Services division, markets natural gas and electricity to customers in the US mid-Atlantic region; has interests in propane distributors in Austria, China, the Czech Republic, France, and Slovakia; and offers HVAC (heating, ventilation, and air-conditioning) and

energy management services to more than 150,000 customers in the mid-Atlantic region of the US. Another subsidiary, UGI Development, is involved in a power generation venture with Allegheny Energy.

The company is focused on expanding its core natural gas, electric, and propane operations. It is also seeking complementary opportunities to continue its growth in the US and abroad. The company's AGZ Holding subsidiary is the parent company of French propane distributor Antargaz. It has also purchased BP's retail propane distribution business in the Czech Republic.

In 2006 the company acquired the natural gas utility assets of PG Energy for about $580 million. During the next year its Gas Utility unit purchased approximately 79 billion cu. ft. of natural gas for sale to retail core market and off-system sales customers.

To expand its base of gas customers in Pennsylvania, in 2008 UGI Utilities acquired PPL Gas Utilities for $32 million. It soon changed that company's name to UGI Central Penn Gas.

HISTORY

United Gas Improvement was set up in 1882 by Philadelphia industrialist Thomas Dolan and other investors to acquire a gasworks and a new coal-gas manufacturing process. The firm also bought electric utilities and street railways across the US and moved into construction. The 1935 Public Utility Holding Company Act led to United Gas Improvement's restructuring when the SEC ordered the divestiture of many of its operations in 1941. The company converted to natural gas in the 1950s and entered the liquefied petroleum gas (LPG) business in 1959. It became UGI Corporation in 1968.

UGI shifted its emphasis to propane in the late 1980s, buying Petrolane in 1995 and combining it with AmeriGas Propane to create AmeriGas Partners, which then went public. Overseas, UGI launched a joint venture in 1996 to build an LPG import project in Romania. The next year it signed a deal to distribute propane in China.

In 1999 UGI moved into consumer products by opening its first Hearth USA retail store in Rockville, Maryland, which offered hearth items, spas, grills, and patio accessories. It ventured into a growing European market by purchasing FLAGA GmbH, a leading gas distributor in Austria and the Czech Republic.

That year a 1997 Pennsylvania law kicked in, restructuring the state's electricity industry and enabling customers to choose their electricity provider. In response, UGI separated its distribution and power generation operations, and in 2000 contributed the bulk of its generation assets to a partnership with Allegheny Energy that sells power to UGI Utilities and other distributors.

In 2001 UGI Enterprises purchased a 20% interest in French propane distributor Antargaz. Also that year UGI closed its Hearth USA retail stores. Through its UGI Energy Services subsidiary, UGI completed the acquisition of TXU Energy, in 2003.

In 2004 UGI acquired the remaining 80% interest in Antargaz, expanding its operations in France. Later that year the company continued its European expansion through the acquisition of BP's retail propane distribution business in the Czech Republic.

EXECUTIVES

Chairman and CEO: Lon R. Greenberg, age 58
President, COO, and Director; Vice Chairman, President, and CEO UGI Utilities: John L. Walsh, age 53
VP Finance and CFO: Peter Kelly, age 52
VP Accounting and Financial Control, Chief Accounting Officer, and Chief Risk Officer: Davinder Athwal, age 41
VP New Business Development; President, UGI Enterprises: Bradley C. Hall, age 55
VP Human Resources: William D. Katz
VP, General Counsel, and Assistant Secretary: Robert H. Knauss, age 55
VP and Treasurer: Robert W. Krick
President and CEO, AmeriGas Propane: Eugene V. N. Bissell, age 55
Chairman and CEO, Antargaz: François Varagne, age 53
Director, Corporate Accounting and Reporting: Richard R. Eynon
Media and Investor Relations: Brenda Blake
Auditors: PricewaterhouseCoopers LLP

LOCATIONS

HQ: UGI Corporation
  460 N. Gulph Rd., King of Prussia, PA 19406
Phone: 610-337-1000   **Fax:** 610-992-3254
Web: www.ugicorp.com

PRODUCTS/OPERATIONS

2008 Sales

	$ mil.	% of total
AmeriGas propane	2,815.2	42
Energy services	1,619.5	23
Gas utility	1,138.3	16
International propane	1,124.8	16
Electric utility	139.2	2
Corporate & other	94.9	1
Adjustments	(283.7)	—
Total	**6,648.2**	**100**

Selected Subsidiaries and Affiliates

AmeriGas, Inc.
AmeriGas Propane, Inc.
  AmeriGas Partners, L.P. (44%)
  AmeriGas Propane L.P.
  AmeriGas Technology Group, Inc.
  Petrolane Incorporated
Four Flags Drilling Company, Inc.
Ashtola Production Company
  UGI Ethanol Development Corporation
Newbury Holding Company
UGI Enterprises, Inc. (energy marketing and services)
  CFN Enterprises, Inc.
  Eastfield International Holdings, Inc.
    FLAGA GmbH (propane distribution; Austria, the Czech Republic, and Slovakia)
  Eurogas Holdings, Inc.
  McHugh Service Company
  UGI Energy Services, Inc.
    GASMARK (gas marketing)
    POWERMARK (electricity marketing)
  UGI International Enterprises, Inc.
    UGI Europe, Inc.
      Antargaz (propane distribution, France)
UGI Properties, Inc.
UGI Utilities, Inc. (natural gas and electric utility)
United Valley Insurance Company

COMPETITORS

Chesapeake Utilities
Dominion Resources
Duquesne Light Holdings
Energy Transfer
Exelon
Ferrellgas Partners
National Fuel Gas
NorthWestern
PPL Corporation
Suburban Propane

HISTORICAL FINANCIALS

Company Type: Public

Income Statement

FYE: September 30

	REVENUE ($ mil.)	NET INCOME ($ mil.)	NET PROFIT MARGIN	EMPLOYEES
9/08	6,648.2	215.5	3.2%	5,900
9/07	5,476.9	204.3	3.7%	6,200
9/06	5,221.0	176.2	3.4%	5,900
9/05	4,888.7	187.5	3.8%	6,000
9/04	3,784.7	111.6	2.9%	6,100
Annual Growth	15.1%	17.9%	—	(0.8%)

2008 Year-End Financials

Debt ratio: 140.2%
Return on equity: 15.7%
Cash ($ mil.): 245
Current ratio: 1.13
Long-term debt ($ mil.): 1,987

No. of shares (mil.): 108
Dividends
　Yield: 2.9%
　Payout: 37.7%
Market value ($ mil.): 2,795

Stock History

NYSE: UGI

	STOCK PRICE ($) FY Close	P/E High/Low	PER SHARE ($) Earnings	Dividends	Book Value
9/08	25.78	15 12	1.99	0.75	13.08
9/07	25.98	16 12	1.89	0.72	12.19
9/06	24.45	17 12	1.65	0.69	10.14
9/05	28.15	17 10	1.77	0.65	9.20
9/04	18.63	16 13	1.15	0.60	7.69
Annual Growth	8.5%	— —	14.7%	5.7%	14.2%

Union Pacific

Venerable Union Pacific (UP) keeps on chugging down the track, just as it has since the 19th century. The company's Union Pacific Railroad is one of the US' leading rail freight carriers (along with rival Burlington Northern Santa Fe). Union Pacific Railroad transports coal, chemicals, industrial products, and other freight over a system of more than 32,000 route miles in 23 states in the western two-thirds of the US. The company owns more than 26,000 route miles of its rail network; leases and trackage rights, which allows UP to use other railroads' tracks, account for the rest. UP's biggest customers are container shipping company APL Limited followed by automaker General Motors.

To offset a drop in freight volumes brought on by the US economic downturn, UP will raise its rates by about 5-6 percent in 2009. The company also parked 400 locomotives and furloughed about 3,000 employees.

UP plans to continue to invest in upgrades to its infrastructure and its equipment fleet. A significant growth driver for UP is its intermodal business, which transports containerized freight that will travel by at least one additional mode of transportation, such as a truck or a ship.

UP expects growth along its Sunset Corridor, a 760-mile route between Los Angeles and El Paso, Texas. In 2008 the company added 45 miles of double track to the corridor, which carries about 20% of UP's traffic.

The company is well positioned to serve US power plants' growing demand for coal; its lines serve major coal production areas, particularly the Southern Powder River Basin of Wyoming. Rising demand for ethanol also has been a boon for UP in its shipping of agricultural products.

Besides its freight transportation operations, Union Pacific Railroad runs a commuter train operation in Chicago and provides logistics services through Union Pacific Distribution Services. UP's Transentric unit offers transportation and supply chain management software.

HISTORY

In 1862 the US Congress chartered the Union Pacific Railroad (UP) to build part of the first transcontinental railway. The driving of the Golden Spike at Promontory, Utah, in 1869 marked the linking of the East and West coasts, as UP's rails met those of Central Pacific Railroad (predecessor of Southern Pacific, or SP), which had been built east from Sacramento, California.

In 1872 the New York Sun revealed the Credit Mobilier scandal: UP officials had pocketed excess profits during the railroad's construction. Debt and lingering effects of the scandal forced UP into bankruptcy in 1893.

A syndicate headed by E. H. Harriman purchased UP in 1897. After reacquiring the Oregon branches it lost in the bankruptcy, UP gained control of SP (1901) and Chicago & Alton (1904). The Supreme Court ordered UP to sell its SP holdings in 1913 on antitrust grounds. In the 1930s UP diversified into trucking, and in the 1970s and 1980s it moved into oil and gas production.

UP bought trucking firm Overnite Transportation in 1986. During the 1980s UP also built up its rail operations, acquiring the Missouri Pacific and Western Pacific railroads in 1982 and the Missouri-Kansas-Texas Railroad in 1988. It joined Chicago and North Western (CNW) Railway managers in an investment group led by Blackstone Capital Partners that bought CNW in 1989.

CNW traced its roots to the Galena & Chicago Union Railroad, which was founded by Chicago's first mayor, W. B. Ogden, in 1836, and merged with CNW in 1864. By 1925 the North Western (as it was then known) had tracks throughout the Midwest. In 1995 UP completed its purchase of CNW and made a bid for SP.

SP was founded in 1865, but its history dates to 1861, when four Sacramento merchants founded Central Pacific. By building new track and buying other railroads (including SP, in 1868), Central Pacific had expanded throughout California, Texas, and Oregon by 1887. The two railroads merged in 1885 under the SP name. In 1983 SP was sold to a holding company controlled by Philip Anschutz, which in 1995 agreed to sell the company to UP.

UP completed its SP acquisition in 1996, but assimilation of the purchase led to widespread rail traffic jams. UP also sold its remaining interest in Union Pacific Resources, an oil company it had spun off the year before. In 1997 UP moved from Bethlehem, Pennsylvania, to Dallas and joined a consortium led by mining company Grupo Mexico that won a bid to run two major Mexican rail lines. In the US, however, UP's fatal collisions led to a federal review, which found a

breakdown in rail safety, such as overworked employees and widespread train defects. Meanwhile, regulators, seeking to resolve UP's massive freight backlog, ordered the railroad to open its Houston lines to competitors.

UP decentralized its management into three regions (north, south, and west) in 1998 to improve traffic flow. It also hired more workers, added new trains, and realigned routes, while selling Skyway Freight Systems, its logistics services unit.

In 1999 UP moved its headquarters from Dallas to Omaha, Nebraska, where Union Pacific Railroad offices already were located. In 2000 it formed Fenix, a holding company charged with developing and expanding the company's telecommunications and technology assets. (By 2003, however, UP had reabsorbed Fenix and scaled back its support for its remaining technology subsidiaries.)

UP expanded its less-than-truckload operations into the western US in 2001 by buying Motor Cargo Industries.

UP sold its trucking unit, Overnite Corporation (a holding company for Overnite Transportation and Motor Cargo Industries), in an IPO in 2003. (Overnite Corporation was acquired by United Parcel Service in 2005 and renamed UPS Freight the next year.) UP sold its Timera subsidiary (workforce management software) in 2004.

Traffic congestion in the UP system, brought on by a shortage of train crews, caused some freight from UPS and other customers to be rerouted onto trucks in 2004. The crew shortage was attributed in part to a greater-than-expected number of retirements in 2003. UP accelerated its hiring and training efforts, but the company still had to restrict freight volume in an effort to minimize bottlenecks.

In 2006 Union Pacific Railroad reorganized its operating structure, going from four regions to three: northern, southern, and western. Service units of the company's central region were reassigned to the northern and southern regions.

EXECUTIVES

Chairman, President, and CEO, Union Pacific Corporation and Union Pacific Railroad: James R. (Jim) Young, age 56, $17,428,212 total compensation
EVP Finance and CFO, Union Pacific Corporation and Union Pacific Railroad: Robert M. Knight Jr., age 51, $4,438,106 total compensation
SVP and CIO, Union Pacific Corporation and Union Pacific Railroad: Lynden L. Tennison
EVP Operations, Union Pacific Railroad: Dennis J. Duffy, age 58, $6,259,969 total compensation
EVP Marketing and Sales, Union Pacific Railroad: John J. (Jack) Koraleski, age 58, $5,260,096 total compensation
SVP Strategic Planning and Administration, Union Pacific Corporation and Union Pacific Railroad: Charles R. Eisele
SVP Human Resources and Secretary, Union Pacific Corporation and Union Pacific Railroad: Barbara W. Schaefer, age 55
SVP Corporate Relations, Union Pacific Corporation and Union Pacific Railroad: Robert W. Turner
SVP Law and General Counsel, Union Pacific Corporation and Union Pacific Railroad: J. Michael (Mike) Hemmer, age 59, $3,745,512 total compensation
VP and Treasurer; Treasurer, Union Pacific Railroad: Mary S. Jones
VP Taxes; VP and General Tax Counsel, Union Pacific Railroad: Bernard R. (Bernie) Gutschewski
Director Corporate Communications: Tom Lange
Auditors: Deloitte & Touche LLP

LOCATIONS

HQ: Union Pacific Corporation
1400 Douglas St., Omaha, NE 68179
Phone: 402-544-5000 **Fax:** 402-501-2133
Web: www.up.com

PRODUCTS/OPERATIONS

2008 Sales

	$ mil.	% of total
Commodity		
Energy	3,810	21
Industrial products	3,273	18
Agricultural	3,174	18
Intermodal	3,023	17
Chemicals	2,494	14
Automotive	1,344	7
Other	852	5
Total	**17,970**	**100**

COMPETITORS

American Commercial Lines
Burlington Northern Santa Fe
Canadian National Railway
Canadian Pacific Railway
CSX
Hub Group
Ingram Industries
J.B. Hunt
Kansas City Southern
Kirby Corporation
Landstar System
Norfolk Southern
Pacer International
Schneider National
Werner Enterprises

HISTORICAL FINANCIALS

Company Type: Public

Income Statement

FYE: December 31

	REVENUE ($ mil.)	NET INCOME ($ mil.)	NET PROFIT MARGIN	EMPLOYEES
12/08	17,970.0	2,338.0	13.0%	48,242
12/07	16,283.0	1,855.0	11.4%	50,089
12/06	15,578.0	1,606.0	10.3%	50,739
12/05	13,578.0	1,026.0	7.6%	49,747
12/04	12,215.0	604.0	4.9%	48,000
Annual Growth	**10.1%**	**40.3%**	**—**	**0.1%**

2008 Year-End Financials

Debt ratio: 55.7%
Return on equity: 15.1%
Cash ($ mil.): 1,249
Current ratio: 0.98
Long-term debt ($ mil.): 8,607
No. of shares (mil.): 504
Dividends
Yield: 2.1%
Payout: 21.6%
Market value ($ mil.): 24,106

Stock History

NYSE: UNP

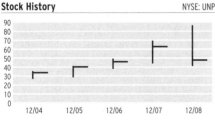

	STOCK PRICE ($) FY Close	P/E High/Low		PER SHARE ($) Earnings	Dividends	Book Value
12/08	47.80	19	9	4.54	0.98	30.63
12/07	62.81	20	13	3.45	0.75	30.90
12/06	46.01	16	13	2.95	0.60	30.36
12/05	40.26	21	15	1.92	0.60	27.18
12/04	33.63	30	24	1.15	0.60	25.09
Annual Growth	**9.2%**	**—**	**—**	**41.0%**	**13.0%**	**5.1%**

Unisys Corporation

Information systems of the world, unite. Unisys is a top player in the information technology (IT) consulting business. Its operations are split into two main segments: Services and Technology. The company's Services unit handles outsourcing, systems integration and consulting, infrastructure services, and core maintenance. Its technology division develops enterprise-class servers and specialized technologies such as check scanners. The company is among the largest government IT contractors, serving local, state, and federal agencies, as well as foreign governments. Other key sectors include communications, financial services, and transportation. Unisys markets its products worldwide. Customers include AIG, Air Canada, BT, and the US Department of Agriculture.

Unisys has seen its revenues slip in recent years as a weakening economy has slowed spending on services and servers, particularly in financial services. Since taking over as CEO in 2008, Edward Coleman has spearheaded a turnaround program designed to cut costs and improve Unisys' bottom line. In addition to the continuation of a multiyear workforce reduction trend, cost-cutting measures have included facility consolidation, reduction of benefits, and salary freezes.

The company's growth strategy includes focusing its investments in the areas of IT and physical security, data center transformation and outsourcing services, end-user outsourcing, and application modernization and outsourcing services. Unisys has been focused on securing more long-term outsourcing contracts for applications, data center, and network management as a way to offset cyclical downturns in the technology services sector. Outsourcing now accounts for about 40% of its sales.

The company's Technology division markets its own line of servers, as well as third-party systems. Unisys has key sales partnerships with such technology leaders as Cisco Systems, Dell, EMC, Oracle, and SAP.

HISTORY

Unisys was formed in 1986 when struggling mainframe computer giant Burroughs swallowed fellow mainframe maker Sperry Corporation. Burroughs traced its roots back to American Arithmometer (St. Louis, 1886), later Burroughs Adding Machine (Detroit, 1905), and then Burroughs Corporation (1953). It entered data processing by purchasing Electrodata (1956) and many other firms, including Memorex (1982).

Sperry was the product of the 1955 merger of Sperry Gyroscope (founded in 1910 by Elmer Sperry) and Remington Rand, an old-line typewriter manufacturer and maker of the first commercially viable computer, the UNIVAC. Sperry later bought RCA's faltering computer unit in 1971.

In 1986 Burroughs president Michael Blumenthal sought to achieve efficiency in parts and development by merging Burroughs' small-database managers with Sperry's defense-related number crunchers. The new company was called Unisys, a contraction of "United Information Systems."

As president of Unisys, Blumenthal quickly disposed of $1.8 billion in assets (Sperry Aerospace and Marine divisions and Memorex), closed plants, and cut jobs. He continued to support Sperry's flagship line of mainframes and nurtured Burroughs' prized "A" series of computers. The initial results were positive, with 1986's $43 million loss followed by 1987's $578 million profit.

Amid an industry trend toward stronger, smaller systems, Unisys in 1988 equipped its U line of servers with the open UNIX operating system and moved to smaller networked systems by acquiring Timeplex (voice/data networks) and Convergent (UNIX workstations). That year the US Department of Justice launched an investigation of illegal defense procurement practices committed by Sperry prior to its merger with Burroughs (Unisys settled the charges in 1991).

Plummeting mainframe demand in 1989 and 1990 led to heavy losses. Blumenthal left the company in 1990, and continuing losses prompted layoffs the following year (Unisys eventually laid off nearly two-thirds of its workforce). The company pared its product line and closed seven of its 15 plants.

In 1995 Unisys and Intel, from a joint venture begun two years earlier, unveiled a $700,000-plus parallel-processing computer that sped up computations. That year the company sold its defense unit to Loral for $862 million. Restructuring charges contributed to losses for the year. In 1996 shareholders rejected a proposal to split Unisys into three separate companies (computer manufacturing, consulting, and services).

Shareholders rejected another proposal to split the company in 1997. Former Andersen Worldwide CEO Larry Weinbach (who left the accounting giant long before it was brought down by scandal) took over as chairman, president, and CEO that year. He immediately began boosting employee morale — easing the company's travel policy, among other changes — and remaking Unisys in the image of his old consulting firm. Charges of more than $1 billion (largely to write off the value of the 1986 Sperry purchase, a move cheered by many analysts) led to a loss for 1997. Unisys hired about 7,000 workers in 1999 to install and maintain corporate computer networks.

In 2000 Unisys signed co-branding deals with Compaq and other manufacturers to market its high-end servers. The economy in general and technology spending in particular began to deteriorate in 2000, leading to smaller profits and eventually a loss in 2001. Unisys responded by placing more emphasis on long-term outsourcing contracts as a hedge against further economic decline. The company also took steps to reduce costs, including cutting staff.

Following the terrorist attacks of September 11, 2001, Unisys expanded its public sector business units as government agencies began focusing on homeland security issues.

In 2004 the company joined the widespread outsourcing trend, announcing its decision to relocate its technology development operations to India and to invest $180 million and hire 2,000 employees in that country by 2009. Weinbach stepped down as CEO in 2005, tapping Joe McGrath as his replacement, before retiring from the company altogether the following year.

Unisys sold its 28% stake in Japanese affiliate Nihon Unisys early in 2006. A year later it sold its media business to UK media software firm Atex Group.

McGrath was replaced as CEO by Edward Coleman, former CEO of Gateway, in 2008. Coleman was also named chairman of the board.

EXECUTIVES

Chairman and CEO: J. Edward (Ed) Coleman, age 56, $720,535 total compensation
SVP and CFO: Janet Haugen, age 50
SVP and CIO: Suresh V. Mathews
Chief Marketing Officer: Ellyn Raftery
SVP, General Counsel, and Secretary:
Nancy S. Sundheim, age 57,
$754,680 total compensation
SVP; President, Systems and Technology:
Richard C. (Rich) Marcello, age 51,
$1,149,980 total compensation
**SVP; President, Global Outsourcing and Infrastructure
Services:** Anthony P. (Tony) Doye, age 51,
$1,375,511 total compensation
SVP Worldwide Human Resources:
Patricia A. (Pat) Bradford, age 58
SVP Corporate Development: M. Lazane Smith, age 53
VP Investor Relations: Jack F. McHale, age 59
VP and Treasurer: Scott A. Battersby, age 50
**VP and Managing Partner, UKMEA, Global Public
Sector:** Holli I. Ploog
**SVP; President Global Industries and Worldwide
Strategic Services:** Dominick Cavuoto, age 55
VP and General Manager, North American Sales:
Jim Weynand
Auditors: KPMG LLP

LOCATIONS

HQ: Unisys Corporation
Unisys Way, Blue Bell, PA 19424
Phone: 215-986-4011   **Fax:** 215-986-2312
Web: www.unisys.com

2008 Sales

	$ mil.	% of total
US	2,243.0	43
UK	748.2	14
Other countries	2,242.0	43
Total	**5,233.2**	**100**

PRODUCTS/OPERATIONS

2008 Sales

	$ mil.	% of total
Services		
Outsourcing	2,006.6	38
Systems integration & consulting	1,490.5	29
Infrastructure	735.1	14
Core maintenance	371.4	7
Technology		
Enterprise-class servers	515.8	10
Specialized technologies	113.8	2
Total	**5,233.2**	**100**

Selected Products and Services

Services
 Application modernization and outsourcing
 Business process outsourcing
 Communication and collaboration
 End-user outsourcing
 Enterprise and asset modernization
 Enterprise content management
 Global commerce
 Infrastructure
 Security
 Supply chain management
 Systems integration
Technology
 Enterprise servers
 Mainframes
 Open Source
 Software
 Storage

COMPETITORS

Accenture
Affiliated Computer Services
Atos Origin
BearingPoint
Bull
Capgemini
Computer Sciences Corp.
Dell
Deloitte Consulting
EDS
Fujitsu
Hewlett-Packard
Hitachi
IBM
L-3 Titan
NEC
Perot Systems
SAIC
Siemens AG
Sun Microsystems
Toshiba

HISTORICAL FINANCIALS

Company Type: Public

Income Statement

FYE: December 31

	REVENUE ($ mil.)	NET INCOME ($ mil.)	NET PROFIT MARGIN	EMPLOYEES
12/08	5,233.2	(130.1)	—	29,000
12/07	5,652.5	(79.1)	—	30,000
12/06	5,757.2	(278.7)	—	31,500
12/05	5,758.7	(1,731.9)	—	36,100
12/04	5,820.7	38.6	0.7%	36,400
Annual Growth	**(2.6%)**	**—**	**—**	**(5.5%)**

2008 Year-End Financials

Debt ratio: —
Return on equity: —
Cash ($ mil.): 544
Current ratio: 1.15
Long-term debt ($ mil.): 1,059

No. of shares (mil.): 370
Dividends
Yield: 0.0%
Payout: —
Market value ($ mil.): 315

Stock History

NYSE: UIS

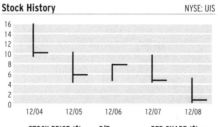

	STOCK PRICE ($) FY Close	P/E High/Low	Earnings	PER SHARE ($) Dividends	Book Value
12/08	0.85	— —	(0.36)	0.00	(3.93)
12/07	4.73	— —	(0.23)	0.00	0.99
12/06	7.84	— —	(0.81)	0.00	(0.17)
12/05	5.83	— —	(5.09)	0.00	(0.09)
12/04	10.18	144 86	0.11	0.00	4.07
Annual Growth	**(46.2%)**	**— —**	**—**	**—**	**—**

United Natural Foods

This distribution network comes together to serve healthy food fans. United Natural Foods is a leading wholesale distributor of natural and organic foods and other products in the US. It has 20 distribution centers supplying more than 60,000 items to 17,000 customers, including independently owned retail stores, supermarket chains, and buying clubs. The company offers natural groceries, personal care products, supplements, and frozen foods. In addition to its wholesale distribution business, United Natural Foods operates more than a dozen natural-products retail stores (mostly in Florida) and it produces roasted nuts, dried fruits, and other snack items through its Hershey Import Company subsidiary.

The bulk of the company's business comes from independently owned retail stores (more than 40%) and from supermarket chains that specialize in natural food products. Its broadline distribution business is anchored by subsidiary Albert's Organics, which supplies more than 5,000 customers with fruits, vegetables, and other perishable items. The company buys products from more than 5,000 suppliers, mostly in the United States; Hain Celestial Group accounts for more than 5% of its purchases.

United Natural Foods has in the past grown primarily through acquisitions of regional and niche market distributors. In 2007 it purchased specialty foods distributor Millbrook Distribution Services for about $85 million. The company is also focused on organic growth (no pun intended), opening additional distribution facilities in Florida, Texas, and the Northwest through 2008.

Two of the company's largest customers, Whole Foods and Wild Oats Markets, combined their operations during 2007. Whole Foods accounts for more than 30% of revenue. Other significant customers include supermarket chains Kroger, Publix, and Wegmans, along with mass market retailer Costco.

Company veteran Michael Funk stepped down as CEO in 2008 (he remained as chairman) and was replaced by former Performance Food Group chief Steven Spinner.

HISTORY

Rhode Island retailer Norman Cloutier founded Cornucopia Natural Foods in 1978 and soon focused on distribution. During the 1980s Cornucopia grew by acquiring other natural foods distributors. It bought suppliers Natural Food Systems (seafood) and BGS Distributing (vitamins) in 1987 and 1990, respectively. Cornucopia expanded into the Southeast in 1991 when it opened a distribution center in Georgia.

Reviving its interest in retailing, Cornucopia formed Natural Retail Group in 1993 to buy and run natural foods stores. During the next two years it acquired several retailers. It expanded its distribution operations in the West in 1995, adding Denver-based Rainbow Distributors.

In 1996 Cornucopia merged with the leading natural foods distributor in the western US, Sacramento-based Mountain People's, which Michael Funk had founded 20 years earlier. The combined company became United Natural Foods, with Cloutier as chairman and CEO and Funk as president and vice chairman; it went public later that year.

United Natural Foods became the largest natural foods distributor when it bought New Hampshire-based Stow Mills in 1997. The next year it added Hershey Imports, an importer and processor of nuts, seeds, and snacks, and Albert's, a distributor of organic produce. With the purchase of Mother Earth Markets in 1998, the company's retailing operations had grown to 16 stores, but by mid-1999 it had sold four stores. That year United Natural Foods' East Coast consolidation problems became so profound that top customer Whole Foods announced it was finding backup distribution sources.

Funk replaced Cloutier as CEO, and the company handed the chairman's post to board member Thomas Simone in 1999. In 2000, after the resignation of Cloutier from the board of directors, United Natural Foods adopted a poison-pill plan to block potential takeovers. The company leased a distribution center in the Los Angeles area in 2001 to increase market share in the Southwest. It also acquired Florida's Palm Harbor Natural Foods.

In mid-2002 United Natural Foods lost one of its two largest customers — Wild Oats Markets — when that company defected to rival specialty foods distributor Tree of Life. However, United Natural Foods soon won that business back. In October the company completed the acquisition of privately held Blooming Prairie Cooperative for approximately $31 million. In late 2002 the company merged with Northeast Cooperatives, a natural foods distributor in the Midwest and Northeast.

That year, United Natural Foods discontinued the management, sales, and support operations at its Hershey Imports subsidiary, but continued to manufacture and distribute products from the Edison, New Jersey, plant.

In 2004 the company renewed its distribution agreement with Wild Oats with a five-year pact. United Natural Foods later announced a new three-year distribution agreement with Whole Foods, which it renewed again in 2006. Whole Foods later acquired Wild Oats in 2007. That same year United Natural Foods acquired ethnic and specialty food distributor Millbrook Distribution Services for about $85 million.

CEO Funk stepped down in 2008 and was replaced by former Performance Food Group chief Steven Spinner.

EXECUTIVES

Chairman: Michael S. Funk, age 54
Vice Chairman: Thomas B. Simone, age 66
President, CEO, and Director:
Steven L. (Steve) Spinner, age 49
VP, CFO, and Treasurer: Mark E. Shamber, age 40
VP IT, Compliance, and Logistics, and CIO: John Stern, age 42
EVP, Chief Marketing Officer, and Corporate Secretary; President, Blue Marble Brands:
Daniel V. (Dan) Atwood, age 50
VP Sustainable Development: Thomas A. Dziki, age 47
VP Sales: Kate Tierney
VP Human Resources: Carl F. Koch III, age 41
President, Eastern Region: Michael D. Beaudry, age 44
President, Western Region: Randle E. Lindberg, age 57
President, Albert's Organics: Kurt Luttecke
President, Specialty Foods; President, Millbrook Distribution Services: Casey Van Rysdam
General Manager, Natural Retail Group: Mickey Jeffers
Auditors: KPMG LLP

LOCATIONS

HQ: United Natural Foods, Inc.
260 Lake Rd., Dayville, CT 06241
Phone: 860-779-2800 **Fax:** 860-779-2811
Web: www.unfi.com

Selected Distribution Centers

Atlanta
Auburn, WA
Aurora, CO
Bridgeport, NJ
Chesterfield, NH
Dayville, CT
East Brunswick, NJ
Fontana, CA
Greenwood, IN
Harrison, AR
Iowa City, IA
Leicester, MA
Moreno Valley, CA
Mounds View, MN
New Oxford, PA
Philadelphia
Ridgefield, WA
Rocklin, CA
Sarasota, FL
Vernon, CA

PRODUCTS/OPERATIONS

2008 Sales

	$ mil.	% of total
Wholesale	3,310.1	96
Other	140.0	4
Adjustments	(84.2)	—
Total	**3,365.9**	**100**

2008 Sales

	% of total
Independently owned retailers	42
Natural foods supermarkets	31
Conventional supermarkets	23
Other	4
Total	**100**

Selected Operations

Albert's Organics (fresh produce distribution)
Blue Marble Brands (marketing and branding services)
Hershey Import Company (dried fruit and nuts packaging and distribution)
Natural Retail Group (natural products retail stores)
Select Nutrition (health and beauty products distribution)
UNFI Specialty Distribution Services (wholesale ethnic and natural foods distribution)

COMPETITORS

Associated Wholesale Grocers
Associated Wholesalers
C & S Wholesale
Distribution Plus
Kehe Food
Nash-Finch
SUPERVALU
Tree of Life
Wal-Mart

HISTORICAL FINANCIALS

Company Type: Public

Income Statement

FYE: July 31

	REVENUE ($ mil.)	NET INCOME ($ mil.)	NET PROFIT MARGIN	EMPLOYEES
7/08	3,365.9	48.5	1.4%	6,300
7/07	2,754.3	50.2	1.8%	4,800
7/06	2,433.6	43.3	1.8%	4,500
7/05	2,059.6	41.6	2.0%	4,030
7/04	1,670.0	32.0	1.9%	3,900
Annual Growth	**19.2%**	**11.0%**	**—**	**12.7%**

2008 Year-End Financials

Debt ratio: 12.2%
Return on equity: 10.7%
Cash ($ mil.): 25
Current ratio: 1.21
Long-term debt ($ mil.): 58
No. of shares (mil.): 43
Dividends
Yield: 0.0%
Payout: —
Market value ($ mil.): 826

Stock History

NASDAQ (GS): UNFI

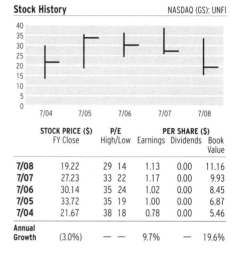

	STOCK PRICE ($) FY Close	P/E High/Low		PER SHARE ($) Earnings	Dividends	Book Value
7/08	19.22	29	14	1.13	0.00	11.16
7/07	27.23	33	22	1.17	0.00	9.93
7/06	30.14	35	24	1.02	0.00	8.45
7/05	33.72	35	19	1.00	0.00	6.87
7/04	21.67	38	18	0.78	0.00	5.46
Annual Growth	**(3.0%)**	**—**	**—**	**9.7%**	**—**	**19.6%**

United Parcel Service

It still relies on chocolate-colored trucks, but United Parcel Service (UPS) is more than a plain-vanilla ground delivery business. The world's largest package delivery company, UPS transports some 16 million packages and documents per business day throughout the US and to more than 200 countries and territories. Its delivery operations use a fleet of about 107,000 motor vehicles and about 570 aircraft. In addition to package delivery, the company offers services such as logistics and freight forwarding through UPS Supply Chain Solutions, and less-than-truckload (LTL) freight transportation through UPS Ground Freight. (LTL carriers combine freight from multiple shippers into a single truckload.)

Domestic package delivery remains the company's largest business segment, but growth in the segment has slowed along with the US economy. Archrival FedEx has expanded its US ground delivery business, but UPS doesn't intend to give up market share without a fight. The company is working to sell package delivery services to customers of its other units; at the same time, it is striving to control costs.

Package delivery revenue has grown faster in overseas markets, where UPS is continuing to expand. While Europe remains the company's largest market outside the US, it sees the Asia/Pacific region as particularly promising. UPS is adding facilities in China and offering direct air service from more Chinese markets. In addition, in 2008 it began construction on an intra-Asia hub in Shenzhen, located in southern China, which will replace its hub in the Philippines.

In June 2009 UPS announced plans to expand its reach into 21 countries in the Middle East and Central Asia by acquiring the small package operations of its shipping contractor in Turkey, Unsped Paket Servisi San ve Ticaret

UPS' extensive global reach is a selling point for its supply chain management offerings, which are tailored to customers in industries such as consumer goods and retail, health care, and technology. Freight forwarding and logistics customers are a potential source of small-package revenue; UPS also hopes to sell supply chain management services to more of its package delivery and freight transportation customers. Along with logistics and trucking, the company's supply chain and freight segment includes mail expediting (UPS Mail Innovations) and financial services (UPS Capital) businesses, as well as postal and business services store franchiser Mail Boxes Etc., which maintains UPS Store and Mail Boxes Etc. locations in the US and overseas.

HISTORY

Seattle teens Jim Casey and Claude Ryan started American Messenger Company, a delivery and errand service, in 1907. They were soon making small-parcel deliveries for local department stores, and in 1913 changed the company's name to Merchants Parcel Delivery. Casey, who led the company for 50 years, established a policy of manager ownership, best service, and lowest rates. In 1916 new employee Charlie Soderstrom chose the brown paint still used on the company's vehicles.

Service expanded outside Seattle in 1919 when Merchants Parcel bought Oakland, California-based Motor Parcel Delivery, later changing its name to United Parcel Service (UPS). By 1930 the company served residents in New York City (its headquarters from 1930 to 1975) and New Jersey, as well as all major cities along the Pacific Coast.

Offering small-package delivery within a 125-mile radius of certain cities, starting with Los Angeles in 1927, UPS grew in relative obscurity as it expanded westward from the East Coast and eastward from the West Coast. The company gained notice in 1952 when the U.S. Postal Service named UPS as a competitor. Noted for its employee-oriented culture, the company through the 1960s required all executives to start as drivers.

In 1975, after becoming the first package delivery company to serve every address in the 48 contiguous US states, UPS crossed the border to Canada, and Germany followed the next year. (UPS had been offering two-day air parcel delivery service to major cities on both coasts via cargo holds on regularly scheduled airline flights since 1953.) By 1977 UPS Blue Label Air (now UPS Next Day Air) guaranteed 48-hour delivery anywhere on the mainland.

Overnight service began in 1981 and was nationwide by 1985 (also serving six European countries). It started air express delivery from its hub in Louisville, Kentucky, in 1982. After purchasing its own jet cargo fleet and getting authorization from the FAA to operate its own aircraft, in 1988 UPS Airlines officially became an airline (and the fastest-growing one in FAA history). By 1990 UPS Airlines was delivering to more than 175 countries in North and South America, Africa, Europe, and Asia.

Moving to its headquarters in Atlanta in 1991, the company began to work on its customer service. As part of a technology revamp, UPS created the electronic clipboard still used by drivers to track packages and digitize signatures. In 1994 UPS went online, allowing customers to track packages in transit.

In 1994 Teamsters staged a one-day strike to protest UPS's new per-package weight limit (raised from 70 to 150 pounds). The next year the firm allowed rank-and-file employees to buy UPS stock. In 1997 UPS was hit by a 15-day Teamsters strike that cost the company hundreds of millions of dollars. UPS settled the strike by combining part-time jobs into 10,000 new full-time positions; in 1998 the company headed off another labor threat by giving its pilots a five-year contract with pay raises.

Chinese government-owned logistics giant Sinotrans proved more friendly than the IRS, teaming up with UPS in 1999 to expand UPS-branded service across China. To fund global expansion, UPS sold about 10% of its stock in 1999 in a public offering valued at more than $5 billion — then the largest IPO in US history.

In 2001 UPS bought Mail Boxes Etc., a franchiser of stores that offer mail, packing, and shipping services. It also acquired global logistics management provider Fritz Companies.

UPS in 2004 expanded its freight forwarding business by buying Menlo Worldwide Forwarding from Con-Way. The next year UPS bought trucking company Overnite for about $1.2 billion. The acquisition brought UPS into the less-than-truckload (LTL) freight transportation business and — not coincidentally — countered a move by FedEx, which formed nationwide LTL carrier FedEx Freight in 2001.

Vice chairman and CFO Scott Davis took over as chairman and CEO in 2008, succeeding Mike Eskew, who stepped down after five years of running the company.

EXECUTIVES

Chairman and CEO: D. Scott Davis, age 57, $5,603,239 total compensation
SVP and COO: David P. Abney, age 53, $1,945,941 total compensation
SVP, CFO, and Treasurer: Kurt P. Kuehn, age 54, $1,969,750 total compensation
SVP and CIO: David A. (Dave) Barnes, age 53
SVP Worldwide Sales and Marketing:
Alan Gershenhorn, age 50
SVP Engineering, Strategy, and Supply Chain Distribution: Robert E. (Bob) Stoffel, age 53, $1,658,726 total compensation
SVP; President, UPS International:
Daniel J. (Dan) Brutto, age 52
SVP Global Transportation Services and Labor Relations: John J. McDevitt, age 50
SVP Human Resources: Allen E. Hill, age 53
SVP Communications and Brand Management:
Christine M. Owens, age 53
SVP Legal, Compliance, and Public Affairs; General Counsel; and Corporate Secretary: Teri P. McClure, age 45
SVP US Operations: Myron A. Gray, age 51
VP Investor Relations: Andy Dolny, age 51
President, Mail Boxes Etc.: Stuart Mathis
President, UPS Capital: Robert J. (Bob) Bernabucci
President, UPS Global Freight Forwarding:
Kenneth A. (Ken) Torok, age 55
President, UPS Airlines: Robert L. (Bob) Lekites
President, UPS Freight: Jack A. Holmes, age 49
President, Corporate Transportation: Burt Wallace
President, The UPS Foundation: Ken Sternad
Director Customer Communications: Maureen Healy
Auditors: Deloitte & Touche LLP

LOCATIONS

HQ: United Parcel Service, Inc.
55 Glenlake Pkwy. NE, Atlanta, GA 30328
Phone: 404-828-6000 **Fax:** 404-828-6562
Web: www.ups.com

2008 Sales

	$ mil.	% of total
US	38,553	75
Other countries	12,933	25
Total	**51,486**	**100**

PRODUCTS/OPERATIONS

2008 Sales

	$ mil.	% of total
US domestic package		
Ground	21,394	42
Next-day air	6,559	13
Deferred	3,325	6
International package		
Export	8,294	16
Domestic	2,344	5
Cargo	655	1
Supply chain & freight		
Forwarding & logistics	6,293	12
Freight	2,191	4
Other	431	1
Total	**51,486**	**100**

COMPETITORS

Canada Post
Con-way Inc.
Deutsche Post
FedEx
Japan Post
La Poste
Lufthansa
Nippon Express
Northwest Airlines
Panalpina
Royal Mail
Ryder System
TNT
US Postal Service
YRC Worldwide

HISTORICAL FINANCIALS

Company Type: Public

Income Statement

FYE: December 31

	REVENUE ($ mil.)	NET INCOME ($ mil.)	NET PROFIT MARGIN	EMPLOYEES
12/08	51,486.0	3,003.0	5.8%	426,000
12/07	49,692.0	382.0	0.8%	425,300
12/06	47,547.0	4,202.0	8.8%	428,000
12/05	42,581.0	3,870.0	9.1%	407,000
12/04	36,582.0	3,333.0	9.1%	384,000
Annual Growth	**8.9%**	**(2.6%)**	**—**	**2.6%**

2008 Year-End Financials

Debt ratio: 115.0%
Return on equity: 31.7%
Cash ($ mil.): 507
Current ratio: 1.13
Long-term debt ($ mil.): 7,797
No. of shares (mil.): 994
Dividends
  Yield: 3.3%
  Payout: 61.2%
Market value ($ mil.): 54,854

Stock History

NYSE: UPS

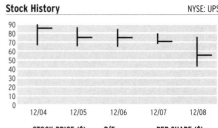

	STOCK PRICE ($) FY Close	P/E High/Low		PER SHARE ($) Earnings	Dividends	Book Value
12/08	55.16	26	15	2.94	1.80	6.82
12/07	70.72	219	191	0.36	1.68	12.25
12/06	74.98	22	17	3.86	1.52	15.57
12/05	75.15	25	19	3.47	1.32	16.98
12/04	85.46	30	23	2.93	1.12	16.48
Annual Growth	**(10.4%)**	**—**	**—**	**0.1%**	**12.6%**	**(19.8%)**

United Rentals

No cash to buy a bulldozer? No worries — just lease one from United Rentals. The company is the #1 commercial and construction equipment renter in the world, serving more than a million customers. From an integrated network of about 700 locations in Canada, Mexico, and 48 US states, the company rents thousands of equipment items — everything from heavy construction and industrial equipment to hand tools, special-event items such as light towers, and trench-safety equipment. It also sells new and used equipment, rental-related and contractor supplies, and parts. Although stung by an abandoned deal to be bought out by Cerberus Capital Management, United Rentals continues to seek future prospects.

United Rentals has become the champion equipment-rental company in North America by uniting with its mom-and-pop rivals; it has purchased more than 200 other leasing firms since the company's founding. It continues an aggressive strategy of consolidating the fragmented rental industry. In 2008 the company acquired U-Rent-It.

Because of its size, United Rentals flexes its muscle to rally more resources over smaller businesses. Competitive advantages include greater purchasing power, the ability to offer a broader range of equipment and services, and greater flexibility to transfer equipment among locations in response to, and in anticipation of, customer demand. The company acts additionally as a dealer of new equipment for many leading equipment makers like DeWalt, Honda USA, and Genie Industries. At most branches United Rentals sells various supplies and merchandise and offers repair and maintenance services.

Although United Rentals' customers range from *FORTUNE* 500 companies to small businesses and homeowners, it targets larger customers, which tend to rent for longer terms and are timely in payment.

Later in 2007, United Rentals announced that it had hired financial advisors UBS Investment Bank and Credit Suisse to help it explore strategic alternatives to maximize shareholder value, including the possible sale of the company. In July 2007 United Rentals announced its acquisition by Cerberus.

Buyout firms rarely abandon a deal unless there is a serious decline in the target company's business. The credit crisis hit and Cerberus' change of heart prompted United Rentals to take the would-be acquirer to court to force the acquisition. The judge concluded that while Cerberus suffered from "buyer's remorse," it did not have to complete the purchase. United Rentals then sought and received a $100 million termination fee. The Cerberus deal would have been worth $6.6 billion.

When the deal fell through, the company refocused on its core rental business, optimized its fleet, and trimmed operating costs. The effort effectively aimed to maximize resource usage by shifting fleet assets from low return locations to high return locations. Operations that failed to yield desired returns were closed, or downsized. United Rentals also reduced the scope of equipment sales tied to its contractor supplies business.

WEDGE Capital Management and Fairholme Capital Management collectively hold over a 25% stake in United Rentals.

HISTORY

Bradley Jacobs had made a fortune in the garbage business, having used United Waste Systems as a roll-up company to buy small trash-hauling firms in that fragmented industry. Flush with cash after he sold United Waste Systems in 1997 to USA Waste Services (now Waste Management), Jacobs launched the same roll-up strategy to consolidate the equipment-rental industry. He and his management team bought six leasing companies and started United Rentals. The company, which went public in 1997, had acquired 38 rental companies in 20 states by mid-1998.

United Rentals landed its biggest rival — U.S. Rentals — that year. U.S. Rentals had been founded in 1957, and by the 1960s it had become part of Leasing Enterprises, which was buying rental yards in western states. Richard Colburn bought a majority stake in 1975 and became the company's chairman. Leasing Enterprises and U.S. Rentals merged as U.S. Rentals; by 1984 Colburn owned the entire company. Between 1992 and 1995, U.S. Rentals bought 13 yards and opened 12 more. In 1997 U.S. Rentals went public and added 43 locations, expanding into the midwestern and southeastern US.

United Rentals bought U.S. Rentals for $1.1 billion in stock and assumed debt in 1998, forming the largest equipment-rental company in North America. Colburn quit, and Jacobs became chairman and CEO. In 1999 United Rentals continued its consolidation strategy, buying more than 60 competitors and moving into traffic-safety equipment rental. The next year it offered to buy a majority stake in lessor Neff Corp. for $37 million in stock and $277 million in debt, but the deal fell through in 2001. However, by 2001 the company had acquired more than 200 companies in four years.

In 2002 the company continued its growth-by-acquisition strategy, acquiring S&R Equipment, an equipment-rental unit of construction giant Fluor. It also acquired the trench shoring business (with 34 branches in 12 states) of rival NES Rentals for about $110 million. In 2003 chairman and CEO Bradley Jacobs stepped down from the position of CEO for the company. COO Wayland Hicks was his replacement.

The company was forced to delay its financial statements for 2004 due to an SEC investigation into accounting discrepancies. The problem reached a head in the summer of 2005 when the board of directors fired president and CFO John Milne, one of United Rentals' founding officers, after Milne declined to answer specific questions about the investigation.

Hicks retired as CEO in June 2007, and COO Michael Kneeland was named as his interim replacement. In August, Jacobs stepped down as chairman. In 2008 Kneeland was designated by the board as the company's president and CEO, and additionally was appointed to the board.

United Rentals reached a settlement with the SEC in 2008, agreeing to pay a civil penalty of $14 million, but without admitting or denying any wrongdoing.

EXECUTIVES

Chairman: Jenne K. Britell, age 66
President, CEO, and Director: Michael J. Kneeland, age 55, $696,122 total compensation
EVP and CFO: William B. Plummer, age 50, $44,477 total compensation
VP and CIO: Kenneth (Ken) DeWitt, age 59, $459,486 total compensation
CTO: Patrick A. Stephens
SVP Operations West: Steven E. Nadelman
SVP Operations East: Matthew J. Flannery
SVP Trench Pump and Power: Paul I. McDonnell
SVP, General Counsel, and Corporate Secretary: Jonathan M. Gottsegen, age 42
VP Customer Service Operations: Kenneth J. Perkins
VP and Treasurer: Irene Moshouris
VP, Controller, and Principal Accounting Officer: John J. Fahey, age 42, $699,522 total compensation
VP Sales: Joseph (Joe) Dixon, age 51
VP Service and Maintenance: Bruce W. Lafky
VP Marketing: C. Elise Arsenault
VP Corporate Communications and Investor Relations: Fred B. Bratman
VP Human Resources: Craig A. Pintoff
Auditors: Ernst & Young LLP

LOCATIONS

HQ: United Rentals, Inc.
5 Greenwich Office Park, Greenwich, CT 06831
Phone: 203-622-3131   **Fax:** 203-622-6080
Web: www.ur.com

2008 Sales

	$ mil.	% of total
US	2,837	87
Other countries (primarily Canada)	430	13
Total	**3,267**	**100**

PRODUCTS/OPERATIONS

2008 Sales

	$ mil.	% of total
General rentals	3,065	94
Trench safety, pump & power	202	6
Total	**3,267**	**100**

2008 Sales

	$ mil.	% of total
Equipment rental	2,469	76
Contractor supply sales	212	7
Rental equipment sales	264	8
New equipment sales	179	5
Service & other	143	4
Total	**3,267**	**100**

Selected Products

Aerial lifts
Backhoes
Barricades
Compressors
Cones
Contractor supplies
Ditching equipment
Earth-moving equipment
Forklifts
Generators
Hand tools
Heaters
Light towers
Material-handling equipment
Message boards
Pavement-marking systems
Portable power units
Power washers
Pumps
Skid-steer loaders
Trench shields
Warning lights
Water pumps

COMPETITORS

AMECO
Atlas Lift Truck Rentals
Hertz
Neff
NES Rentals
RDO Equipment
RSC Equipment Rental
Sunbelt Rentals
Western Power & Equipment
Ziegler inc

HISTORICAL FINANCIALS
Company Type: Public

Income Statement
FYE: December 31

	REVENUE ($ mil.)	NET INCOME ($ mil.)	NET PROFIT MARGIN	EMPLOYEES
12/08	3,267.0	(704.0)	—	9,900
12/07	3,731.0	362.0	9.7%	10,900
12/06	3,640.0	224.0	6.2%	12,000
12/05	3,563.0	187.0	5.2%	13,400
12/04	3,094.0	(84.0)	—	12,600
Annual Growth	1.4%	—	—	(5.9%)

2008 Year-End Financials

Debt ratio: —
Return on equity: —
Cash ($ mil.): 77
Current ratio: 1.65
Long-term debt ($ mil.): 3,332

No. of shares (mil.): 60
Dividends
Yield: 0.0%
Payout: —
Market value ($ mil.): 548

Stock History
NYSE: URI

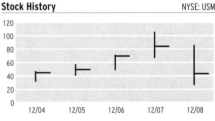

	STOCK PRICE ($) FY Close	P/E High/Low		PER SHARE ($) Earnings	Dividends	Book Value
12/08	9.12	—	—	(12.62)	0.00	(0.48)
12/07	18.36	11	5	3.25	0.00	33.56
12/06	25.43	18	10	2.06	0.00	25.58
12/05	23.39	14	9	1.80	0.00	20.44
12/04	18.90	—	—	(1.07)	0.00	17.06
Annual Growth	(16.7%)	—	—	—	—	—

United States Cellular

United States Cellular operates networks from sea to shining sea. Doing business as U.S. Cellular, the company provides wireless phone service to about 6.5 million customers in more than two dozen states in the US. Products and services — marketed through company stores, the Internet, and about 400 national chain stores — include mobile messaging, prepaid calling, international long-distance, roadside assistance, and directory assistance. U.S. Cellular also offers vehicle-mounted, transportable, and portable phones with features such as hands-free calling, caller ID, and short messaging services. Telephone and Data Systems owns 70% of U.S. Cellular (and a 96% voting interest).

The company operates some 6,900 cell sites, and makes its products available at over 400 company-operated retail locations as well as through other retailers at an additional 1,100 locations. While U.S. Celluar operates across the US, the bulk of its business is in the Midwest, where it has nearly 4 million customers.

HISTORY

LeRoy Carlson, a Chicago-based investor, formed Telephone and Data Systems (TDS) in 1969 by consolidating the rural phone companies he owned. In the early 1980s TDS began acquiring cellular licenses, including the rights to operate 5% of the Los Angeles market. Getting a jumpstart on the Bells, TDS created United States Cellular as a subsidiary in 1983.

In 1985 United States Cellular began operations in Knoxville, Tennessee, and Tulsa, Oklahoma. Three years later TDS took the company public and reduced its stake to 82%. Belgian cable TV operator Coditel was an initial investor.

Hefty startup and acquisition costs kept the company from making a profit until 1993. After moving into the black, it began selling its phones (purchased from suppliers) at kiosks in Wal-Mart stores in 1995. Meanwhile, it continued to add networks: In 1995 and 1996 United States Cellular added markets in Arizona, Florida, Iowa, Texas, and Virginia.

In 1997 United States Cellular traded its controlling interests in 10 markets, primarily in Indiana and Kentucky, for BellSouth's controlling interests in 12 markets in Illinois and Wisconsin (including Milwaukee). That year the firm also began converting its network to digital technologies (both TDMA, time division multiple access, and the newer CDMA, code division multiple access).

In 1998 United States Cellular acquired majority interests in six more markets. That year the firm also sold several minority interests in markets in which it did not operate to Vodafone. The following year the company introduced a new logo and began doing business as U.S. Cellular. Also in 1999 it began providing CDPD (cellular digital packet data) service, which allows for data transmission over cellular networks, to police departments and government agencies in Illinois.

The company agreed in 2001 to acquire PCS licenses in Illinois, Iowa, and Nebraska from McLeodUSA for $74 million to bolster its Midwest operations. It purchased PrimeCo Wireless Communications in a 2002 deal valued at $610 million, gaining entrance into the Chicagoland market, as well as Bloomington-Normal, Champaign-Urbana, Decatur, and Springfield, Illinois, with expanded service to Peoria and Rockford, Illinois. Additionally, U.S. Cellular provides service to South Bend and Fort Wayne, Indiana, and Benton Harbor, Michigan.

In a 2003 swap agreement with AT&T Wireless, the company acquired wireless licenses and properties in 13 states in the Midwest and northeastern US in exchange for assets in northern Florida and southern Georgia.

U.S. Cellular in 2008 exchanged surplus wireless spectrum licenses covering parts of Illinois for licenses held by Sprint Nextel for areas of Oklahoma, West Virginia, Maryland, and Iowa.

EXECUTIVES

Chairman: LeRoy T. (Ted) Carlson Jr., age 62, $3,913,510 total compensation
President, CEO, and Director: John E. (Jack) Rooney, age 66, $4,277,435 total compensation
EVP and COO: Jay M. Ellison, age 56, $2,267,361 total compensation
EVP Finance, CFO, and Treasurer: Steven T. Campbell, age 58, $1,187,786 total compensation
EVP Engineering and CTO: Michael S. (Mike) Irizarry, age 47, $1,705,692 total compensation
Chief Accounting Officer and Director; EVP and CFO, Telephone & Data Systems: Kenneth R. (Ken) Meyers, age 55, $1,724,904 total compensation

VP Sales Operations and Chief Marketing Officer: Alan D. Ferber, age 39
SVP Human Resources and Chief Human Resources Officer: Jeffrey J. (Jeff) Childs, age 52, $1,224,352 total compensation
VP Organizational Learning and Chief Teaching Officer: Thomas J. Griffin, age 51
VP Corporate Relations, TDS: Mark A. Steinkrauss, age 60
VP Business Support Services: George W. Irving
VP National Network Operations: Kevin R. Lowell
VP Financial Strategy: Thomas (Tom) Weber
VP Public Affairs and Communications: Karen C. Ehlers
VP Legal and Regulatory Affairs: John C. Gockley, age 53
VP Information Technology Delivery: John M. Cregier
VP Customer Service: R. Lynn Costlow
Auditors: PricewaterhouseCoopers LLP

LOCATIONS

HQ: United States Cellular Corporation
8410 W. Bryn Mawr, Ste. 700, Chicago, IL 60631
Phone: 773-399-8900 **Fax:** 773-399-8936
Web: www.uscellular.com

COMPETITORS

Alltel
AT&T Mobility
Cellco
CenturyTel
Leap Wireless
Sprint Nextel
T-Mobile USA

HISTORICAL FINANCIALS
Company Type: Public

Income Statement
FYE: December 31

	REVENUE ($ mil.)	NET INCOME ($ mil.)	NET PROFIT MARGIN	EMPLOYEES
12/08	4,243.2	33.0	0.8%	8,470
12/07	3,946.3	314.7	8.0%	8,400
12/06	3,473.2	179.5	5.2%	8,100
12/05	3,035.9	134.7	4.4%	7,700
12/04	2,837.6	109.0	3.8%	7,400
Annual Growth	10.6%	(25.8%)	—	3.4%

2008 Year-End Financials

Debt ratio: 31.1%
Return on equity: 1.0%
Cash ($ mil.): 171
Current ratio: 1.35
Long-term debt ($ mil.): 997

No. of shares (mil.): 87
Dividends
Yield: 0.0%
Payout: —
Market value ($ mil.): 3,756

Stock History
NYSE: USM

	STOCK PRICE ($) FY Close	P/E High/Low		PER SHARE ($) Earnings	Dividends	Book Value
12/08	43.24	224	72	0.38	0.00	36.91
12/07	84.10	29	19	3.56	0.00	36.79
12/06	69.59	35	24	2.04	0.00	34.46
12/05	49.40	37	27	1.54	0.00	31.66
12/04	44.76	37	26	1.26	0.00	29.79
Annual Growth	(0.9%)	—	—	(25.9%)	—	5.5%

United States Steel

Steel crazy after all these years, Pittsburgh-based United States Steel is the nation's #2 integrated steelmaker (behind Mittal Steel USA). The company operates mills throughout the Midwest in the US; in Ontario, Canada; and in Serbia and Slovakia. U.S. Steel makes sheet and semifinished steel, tubular and plate steel, and tin products; it produces about 25 million tons of raw steel annually. The company's customers are primarily in the automotive, construction, chemical, and steel service center industries. In addition, U.S. Steel offers services such as mineral resource management and engineering and consulting.

The company's European operations consist of two companies, U.S. Steel Serbia (which produces limestone, sheets, strip mill plate, and tin) and U.S. Steel Kosice in Slovakia (which manufactures sheet, strip mill plate, tin mill, tubular, and specialty steel products). They combine to form the company's second-largest segment, U.S. Steel Europe, and account for about a quarter of U.S. Steel's total sales.

U.S. Steel jumped into the industrywide consolidation game in 2007 when it spent a combined $3.3 billion to buy tubular goods maker Lone Star Technologies and the former Stelco in separate deals. Lone Star Technologies was among the nation's largest makers of welded steel tubes for use in the oilfield (called oil country tubular goods, or OCTG). The acquired business complemented U.S. Steel's own product line for the energy industry, which consisted largely of seamless tubes. The Stelco deal, on the other hand, added to U.S. Steel's core business. Focusing on slab products used in the flat-rolled market, Stelco raised U.S. Steel's production capacity to more than 30 million tons a year. (Though it's actual production rate is less than that.) It also broadened the company's geographic scope a bit. Upon closing of the deal, U.S. Steel changed Stelco's name to U.S. Steel Canada.

HISTORY

United States Steel Corporation was conceived through a 1901 merger of 10 steel companies that combined their furnaces, ore deposits, railroad companies, and shipping lines. The deal involved industrial pioneers Andrew Carnegie, Charles Schwab, Elbert Gary, and J. P. Morgan.

Morgan had helped organize the Federal Steel Company in 1898, and he then wanted to create a centralized trust to dominate the soaring steel market. Carnegie owned the largest US steel company at the time, Carnegie Steel, but wanted to retire.

In 1900 Schwab, Carnegie Steel's president, outlined the idea of the steel trust based on a merger of the Carnegie and Federal steel companies. Morgan asked Schwab to persuade Carnegie to sell his steel mills and name his price. Morgan didn't haggle when Carnegie responded that he would sell for almost half a billion dollars. The Carnegie-Morgan combination created the world's first billion-dollar company. It produced 67% of the country's steel in its first year (its steel complex and the Indiana town where it was located were named after Gary, who was CEO until 1927).

The company boomed during WWI and WWII. But its market share fell to about 30% by the 1950s, although it set new profit records in 1955. During the 1970s prospects for long-term growth in steel became dismal in light of rising costs, foreign competition, and competitive pricing.

In 1982 U.S. Steel doubled its size when it bought Marathon Oil, a major integrated energy company with huge oil and gas reserves in the US and abroad. It continued to cut back its steel-making capacity, laying off 100,000 employees, closing steel mills, and selling off assets.

The company bought Texas Oil & Gas in 1986 and renamed itself USX Corporation to reflect the decreasing role of steel in its business. Also that year corporate raider Carl Icahn, USX's largest single shareholder, unsuccessfully tried to get the company to sell its steel operations. In 1988 USX bought 49% of Transtar, a group of rail and water transport providers. (It purchased the remaining stake in 2001, making Transtar a wholly owned subsidiary.)

Stockholders in 1991 approved splitting the company into two separate units under the USX umbrella: U.S. Steel and Marathon. During the 1990s U.S. Steel continued to close steelmaking facilities. In 1992 USX joined five other leading US steel producers in a suit against subsidized foreign steelmakers.

The company agreed to pay $106 million in fines and improvements in 1996 to settle charges of air pollution violations involving its Indiana plant. U.S. Steel began upgrading several of its facilities in 1997 and 1998 and entered into a number of domestic and foreign joint ventures, including one in Slovakia and another in Mexico. Seeing prices drop in 1998 and 1999, the company cut production and joined other US steelmakers in charging rivals in Brazil, Japan, and Russia with unlawfully dumping low-priced steel in the US.

In early 2001 USX spun off its steel operations as United States Steel Corporation; the remaining energy businesses begain operating as Marathon Oil Corporation.

USX-U.S. Steel and Bethlehem Steel announced they were in talks about possibly merging the two companies in 2001. Subsequently, USX-U.S. Steel and National Steel (U.S. subsidiary of NKK) began talks of merging its businesses. In order for the deal to close, National Steel would have to restructure its debt and the Bush administration would have to implement its plan to curtail steel imports. That year USX-U.S. Steel split apart from its holding company, USX Corporation, and the steel operations unit went back to trading under its original name, United States Steel Corporation. The breakup left the company with over $1.3 billion in debt.

U.S. Steel, along with other US steelmakers, received concessions (40% import tariffs and assistance with its huge retiree health-care costs) from the Bush administration. In early March 2002 the Bush administration imposed tariffs between 8 to 30 percent providing temporary relief to U.S. Steel and the US steel industry. The Bush administration rejected any retiree bailout plan and in December 2003 ended the tariffs 16 months ahead of schedule.

In 2003 U.S. Steel made the monumental move to purchase National Steel for roughly $1.1 billion in cash. With the combined manufacturing capabilities of National Steel and U.S. Steel, the company's raw steel production came in at around 20 million tons of steel annually, both domestically and internationally, which made it the nation's largest steel producer until the formation of Mittal Steel USA in 2005.

2003 also saw the expansion of U.S. Steel's European businesses with the acquisition of Serbian steelmaker Sartid, which produces limestone, sheets, strip mill plate, and tin.

EXECUTIVES

Chairman and CEO: John P. Surma Jr., age 54, $13,033,876 total compensation
EVP and COO: John H. Goodish, age 60, $7,892,315 total compensation
EVP and CFO: Gretchen R. Haggerty, age 53, $4,374,058 total compensation
SVP Public Policy and Governmental Affairs: Terrence D. Straub, age 60
SVP Strategic Planning and Business Development: J. James Kutka Jr., age 60
SVP Labor Relations and Environmental Affairs and General Counsel: James D. Garraux, age 56, $3,689,123 total compensation
SVP Strategic Planning, Business Services, and Administration: David H. (Dave) Lohr, age 55, $4,225,044 total compensation
SVP Sales and Customer Service, North American Flat-Roll Operations: Joseph R. (Joe) Scherrbaum Jr., age 52
SVP North American Flat Roll Operations: Michael S. Williams, age 48
SVP European Operations; President, U. S. Steel Kosice: George F. Babcoke, age 53
VP Human Resources: Susan M. (Sue) Suver, age 49
VP Procurement, Raw Material, and Real Estate: Michael J. Hatcher, age 51
VP and Controller: Gregory A. Zovko, age 48
VP Supply Chain: John C. Price, age 61
VP Engineering and Technology: Anton Lukac, age 47
VP Operations, East: Anthony R. Bridge, age 55
VP Business Services: Eugene P. Trudell, age 57
VP and Treasurer: Larry T. Brockway, age 46
VP Tubular Operations; President, U.S. Steel Tubular Products: Douglas R. Matthews, age 43
President, U.S. Steel Canada: David J. Rintoul, age 52
Representative Public Affairs: Erin DiPietro
Auditors: PricewaterhouseCoopers LLP

LOCATIONS

HQ: United States Steel Corporation
600 Grant St., Pittsburgh, PA 15219
Phone: 412-433-1121   **Fax:** 412-433-5733
Web: www.ussteel.com

2008 Sales

	$ mil.	% of total
North America	18,269	77
Europe	5,487	23
Adjustments	(2)	—
Total	**23,754**	**100**

2008 Raw Steel Production

	Net tons (thou.)	% of total
North America		
Gary, Indiana	5,917	23
Great Lakes, Michigan	2,513	10
Mon Valley, Pennsylvania	2,461	10
Hamilton, Ontario	2,325	9
Granite City, Illinois	2,294	9
Fairfield, Alabama	2,082	8
Lake Erie, Ontario	1,598	6
Europe		
U.S. Steel Kosice	4,562	18
U.S. Steel Serbia	1,848	7
Total	**25,600**	**100**

PRODUCTS/OPERATIONS

2008 Sales

	$ mil.	% of total
Flat-rolled	13,789	58
US Steel Europe	5,487	23
Tubular Products	4,251	18
Other	227	1
Total	**23,754**	**100**

Selected Subsidiaries

Acero Prime S. R. L de CV (44%, steel processing and warehousing)
Delray Connecting Railroad Company (transportation)
Double Eagle Steel Coating Company (50%, steel processing, with Severstal)
PRO-TEC Coating Co. (50%, steel processing, with Kobe Steel, Ltd.)
Transtar, Inc. (transportation)
U. S. Steel Kosice sro (steelmaking, Slovakia)
USS-POSCO Industries (50%, steel processing, with Pohang Iron & Steel Co., Ltd.)
Worthington Specialty Processing (50%, steel processing, with Worthington Industries Inc.)

COMPETITORS

AK Steel Holding Corporation
Allegheny Technologies
ArcelorMittal
BÖHLER-UDDEHOLM
BHP Billiton
BlueScope Steel
Carpenter Technology
JFE Holdings
Kobe Steel
Nippon Steel
Nucor
POSCO
Salzgitter
Severstal North America
SSAB North America
Steel Dynamics
Ternium
ThyssenKrupp Steel

HISTORICAL FINANCIALS

Company Type: Public

Income Statement

	REVENUE ($ mil.)	NET INCOME ($ mil.)	NET PROFIT MARGIN	EMPLOYEES
12/08	23,754.0	2,112.0	8.9%	49,000
12/07	16,873.0	879.0	5.2%	28,000
12/06	15,715.0	1,374.0	8.7%	44,000
12/05	14,039.0	910.0	6.5%	46,000
12/04	14,108.0	1,077.0	7.6%	22,000
Annual Growth	13.9%	18.3%	—	22.2%

FYE: December 31

2008 Year-End Financials

Debt ratio: 62.6%
Return on equity: 40.5%
Cash ($ mil.): 724
Current ratio: 2.06
Long-term debt ($ mil.): 3,064

No. of shares (mil.): 143
Dividends
  Yield: 3.0%
  Payout: 6.1%
Market value ($ mil.): 5,332

Stock History

NYSE: X

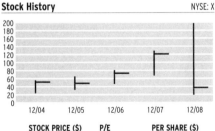

	STOCK PRICE ($) FY Close	P/E High/Low		PER SHARE ($) Earnings	Dividends	Book Value
12/08	37.20	11	1	17.96	1.10	34.15
12/07	120.91	17	9	7.40	0.80	38.59
12/06	73.14	7	4	11.18	0.60	30.46
12/05	48.07	9	5	7.00	0.38	23.19
12/04	51.25	6	3	8.48	0.20	27.70
Annual Growth	(7.7%)	—	—	20.6%	53.1%	5.4%

United Stationers

Don't think that United Stationers is just another paper pusher. The company is the leading wholesale distributor of office supplies and equipment in North America, offering more than 100,000 products to about 30,000 customers. Through operating units United Stationers Supply, Lagasse, and ORS Nasco, United Stationers supplies such items as business machines, computer products and peripherals, janitorial supplies, and office products and furniture. It also offers niche products for such markets as education and health care. United Stationers sells primarily to resellers through catalogs and over the Internet, as well as through its direct sales force.

Sales of technology products, including printers and print cartridges, data storage devices, and other computer peripherals, account for about one-third of the company's sales, making United Stationers one of the top computer products distributors in the country. Traditional office supplies make up about 30% of the company's business.

To strengthen its foothold in product distribution, United Stationers has acquired the assets of its rivals. In 2008 the company purchased Emco Distribution, a New Jersey-based business product distributor, for $15 million. It acquired ORS Nasco, a wholesale distributor of industrial supplies, for about $180 million in 2007.

Neuberger Berman owns about 10% of United Stationers.

HISTORY

Morris Wolf and Harry Hecktman, former office supply salesmen, and Israel Kriloff, a grocer, purchased Utility Supply Company (founded in 1906) and began selling office supplies in downtown Chicago in 1921. Weathering the Depression, Utility Supply's business grew steadily during the 1930s. In 1935 the company published its first catalog, and it opened its first retail store in downtown Chicago two years later. The partners bought out Kriloff in 1939.

WWII created a scarcity of raw materials, and Utility Supply had difficulty in obtaining merchandise. The company tried selling non-office products, unsuccessfully. Fortunately, the war's end brought an end to the inventory drought. During the postwar era, Utility Supply began mailing a series of catalogs to retailers nationwide. By 1948 mail-order business accounted for 40% of sales. A wholesale division to sell products to independent resellers was created in the 1950s.

In 1960 the company adopted the name United Stationers Supply, and the retail stores became the Utility Stationery Stores. Business increased as independent retailers began to appreciate the advantages of ordering through a wholesaler instead of a manufacturer — purchasing goods on an as-needed basis. Howard Wolf, the founder's son, became CEO in 1967 and began emphasizing computers and automation to track inventory and costs.

By 1970 wholesale trade accounted for about two-thirds of sales. United Stationers introduced a series of abridged catalogs targeting specific groups and marketing segments, such as furniture and electronics. The following year United Stationers developed regional redistribution centers that offered overnight delivery. The company sold its retail outlets in 1978.

Three years later United Stationers went public. During the 1980s the advent of warehouse clubs and office supply superstores threatened independent retailers. The company developed marketing concepts to help its independent resellers, even as it aggressively targeted mail-order houses and superstores. The downsizing trend in the late 1980s caused the corporate market to shrink, and United Stationers lowered prices; it instituted a decentralization plan in 1990.

The next year the company expanded into Canada, opening its first non-US subsidiary, and it acquired archrival Stationers Distributing and its distribution centers across the US in 1992. In 1994 it established its United Facility Supply unit to distribute maintenance supplies.

Investment firm Wingate Partners, which controlled rival Associated Stationers, bought United Stationers in 1995 and combined the operations of the two companies under the United Stationers name. United Stationers acquired janitorial supplies wholesaler Lagasse Bros. in 1996. In 1998 the company acquired the US and Mexican operations of Abitibi-Consolidated, including Azerty. (It acquired Azerty Canada in 2000.)

United Stationers launched a venture with E-Commerce Industries in 1999 to help customers sell products over the Internet. The next year the company started The Order People, a third-party call center fulfillment business aimed at online retailers; however, the dot-com bust and higher losses than planned led United Stationers to curtail operations in 2001. Also that year it bought Peerless Paper Mills (merging the wholesale distributor of janitorial and paper products into Lagasse).

The company sold its Canadian operations in 2006, following an accounting scandal. United Stationers discovered that its Canadian operation was incorrectly accounting for supplier allowances and other receivables.

EXECUTIVES

Chairman: Frederick B. (Fred) Hegi Jr., age 65
President, CEO, and Director: Richard W. Gochnauer, age 59, $2,351,597 total compensation
SVP Operations: Timothy P. Connolly, age 45
SVP and CFO: Victoria J. Reich, age 51, $1,122,057 total compensation
SVP and CIO: S. David Bent, age 48
SVP, General Counsel, and Secretary: Eric A. Blanchard, age 52
SVP Trade Development: Joseph R. Templet, age 61
SVP National Accounts and Channel Management: Jeffrey G. Howard, age 53
SVP Inventory Management: Ronald C. Berg, age 49
SVP Merchandising: James S. Fahey, age 58
SVP Sales and Marketing: Patrick T. (Pat) Collins, age 48, $656,279 total compensation
SVP Human Resources: Barbara Kennedy, age 42
VP and Treasurer: Robert J. Kelderhouse, age 53
VP, Controller, and Chief Accounting Officer: Kenneth M. Nickel, age 41
Group President, LagasseSweet and ORS Nasco: Stephen A. (Steve) Schultz, age 42, $806,731 total compensation
President, United Stationers Supply: P. Cody Phipps, age 47, $1,016,244 total compensation
President, LagasseSweet: Todd Shelton
Investor Relations Specialist: Mary Disclafani
Auditors: Cowan, Gunteski & Co., P.A.

LOCATIONS

HQ: United Stationers Inc.
  1 Parkway N. Blvd., Ste. 100, Deerfield, IL 60015
Phone: 847-627-7000   **Fax:** 847-627-7001
Web: www.unitedstationers.com/home

UnitedHealth Group

UnitedHealth Group wants to keep you connected with your health. A leading US health insurer, it offers a variety of health care plans and services to some 70 million customers in the US. Its health care services segment manages HMO, PPO, and POS (point-of-service) plans, as well as various Medicare and Medicaid options, through UnitedHealthcare, AmeriChoice (for public-sector programs), and Ovations (for members of AARP). Its OptumHealth division offers vision and dental care and other products and services. Ingenix provides health care information, while the Prescription Solutions unit provides pharmacy benefit management services.

The highly acquisitive company agreed to buy the northeastern US operations of rival Health Net to solidify its position in the region in 2009. The deal includes health plans in Connecticut, New Jersey, and New York.

UnitedHealth completed several large acquisitions in 2008. It bought Fiserv's health-related businesses, including Fiserv Health (benefits administration for 2 million members), Avidyn Health (care facilitation), and Innoviant Pharmacy Benefits Management). UnitedHealth also acquired Unison Health Plans.

UnitedHealth completed its controversial purchase of Nevada insurance provider Sierra Health Services for approximately $2.6 billion in early 2008, gaining some 600,000 health plan members in the state and boosting UnitedHealth's position in the growing Southwest market. The acquisition took nearly a year to receive approval from the Department of Justice due to political opposition in Nevada and extended antitrust reviews. The department's approval was contingent on UnitedHealth's divestiture of its Medicare Advantage program for individuals in the Las Vegas area to avoid an unfair advantage in the market; UnitedHealth sold its Las Vegas policies, representing some 27,000 customers, to Humana.

UnitedHealth is still weathering runoff from its $8.8 billion acquisition and subsequent integration of PacifiCare in 2005. The acquisition gave UnitedHealth a leading position in the West Coast market, but it also prompted a landslide of complaints from customers alleging mishandled claims. The California Insurance Commission and other state agencies are seeking fines of more than $1 billion.

After irregular stock option pricing caused inquiry and prompted a brisk housecleaning of the executive offices in 2006, the board made the position of Chief Ethics Officer a senior executive position, and equity awards were eliminated for the CEO and president. The shakeup was not enough, however, to prevent the SEC from opening a formal investigation into the company's stock-options practices in late 2006. The company resolved a couple of shareholder lawsuits over the scandal in 2008, agreeing to settlements totaling more than $900 million.

At the start of 2009 UnitedHealth found its Ingenix subsidiary at the root of several class-action lawsuits filed by state attorneys general in Connecticut, New York, and Texas. The suits allege that information Ingenix provided to health insurers resulted in underpayments of out-of-

network physicians, and placed undue financial burdens on customers. UnitedHealth reached a settlement in New York by agreeing to pay $50 million and stop using the Ingenix product.

HISTORY

Dr. Paul Ellwood became known as the Father of the HMO for his role as an early champion of the health care concept. As a neurology student in the 1950s, Ellwood recognized that applying business principles to medicine could minimize costs and make health care more affordable. Although the HMO was considered a radical approach to health care reform, Ellwood got Congress and the Nixon administration to approve his HMO model in 1970; the next year he hired Richard Burke to put the model into action. Burke established United HealthCare (UHC) in 1974 to manage the not-for-profit Physicians Health Plan of Minnesota (PHP). UHC incorporated in 1977.

The company bought HMOs and began managing others, operating 11 HMOs in 10 states by 1984, the year it went public. Its expansion continued with the purchases of HMOs Share Development (1985) and Peak Health Care (1986). Unfortunately, acquisitions and startups began to eat away at UHC's financial health. Meanwhile, Burke, CEO of both UHC and PHP, was accused by PHP doctors of having a conflict of interest after a change in the HMO's Medicare policy threatened to cut off patients from some member hospitals. Burke resigned in 1987 and was replaced by Kennett Simmons.

UHC lost nearly $16 million in 1987, largely from a restructuring that axed the company's Phoenix HMO, as well as startups in six other markets. In the late 1980s UHC adopted a new strategy of acquiring specialty companies that provided fee income. It also continued building its HMO network through acquisitions, hoping to gain critical mass in such varied markets as the Midwest and New England.

Physician William (Bill) McGuire was named UHC's chairman and CEO in 1991. The company's expansion accelerated in the 1990s with a string of purchases in the Midwest, but there were also divestitures. In 1994 UHC sold subsidiary Diversified Pharmaceutical Services, providing cash for still more purchases, including GenCare (St. Louis), Group Sales and Service of Puerto Rico, and MetraHealth.

The company in 1999 (now called United-Health Group) added UK-based contract research organization ClinPharm International to Ingenix. It also announced it would let doctors — not administrators — choose what treatment patients would get, partially because it was spending more on care scrutiny than the practice saved. Nevertheless, many doctors claimed the process was still restrictive.

In 2000 the American Medical Association sued the company, claiming it used faulty data to reduce payments to member doctors.

To expand its Medicaid services business, the firm bought AmeriChoice in 2002. Golden Rule was acquired in late 2003 so UnitedHealth could enter the individual health insurance market by providing medical savings accounts. To increase its market share in the northeastern US, the company bought Oxford Health Plans that year.

The company acquired PacifiCare Health Systems in 2005. The $8.8 billion acquisition brought UnitedHealth 3 million more customers, including a strong foothold in the California Medicare market.

Bill McGuire became the focus of inquiry in 2006 over a scandal involving the back-dating of stock options awarded to him and other company executives. Following a board inquiry, McGuire was replaced by Stephen Hemsley, formerly the company's COO.

EXECUTIVES

Chairman: Richard T. Burke Sr., age 65
President, CEO, and Director:
Stephen J. (Steve) Hemsley, age 56,
$3,241,042 total compensation
EVP and CFO: George L. (Mike) Mikan III, age 37,
$6,531,406 total compensation
EVP and Chief Medical Affairs: Reed V. Tuckson
SVP and Chief Communications Officer: Don Nathan
Chief Ethics Officer: Jack Radke
EVP; President Enterprise Services Group:
William A. Munsell, age 56
EVP: Jeannine M. Rivet
EVP; President, Public and Senior Markets Group:
Anthony Welters, age 53,
$5,635,177 total compensation
EVP; CEO, Ovations: Larry C. Renfro, age 55
EVP; President, Commercial Markets Group:
Gail K. Boudreaux, age 48
EVP; President, UnitedHealth Group Operations:
David S. Wichmann, age 46,
$4,638,870 total compensation
EVP; President, Global Health: Simon Stevens
EVP Human Capital: Lori K. Sweere, age 50
SVP and Chief Accounting Officer: Eric S. Rangen,
age 52
SVP, UnitedHealthcare: Jeff Lucht
CEO, UnitedHealthcare Central Region:
Kathryn M. Sullivan, age 52
CEO, UnitedHealthcare West Region:
Steven H. (Steve) Nelson, age 50
CEO, UnitedHealthcare Southeast Region:
Daniel Laurence (Dan) Ohman
CEO, UnitedHealthcare National Accounts:
Michael C. Matteo
CEO, UnitedHealthcare Northeast Region:
Jeffrey Donald Alter
Executive Assistant, Investor Relations: Frances Jacobs
Auditors: Deloitte & Touche LLP

LOCATIONS

HQ: UnitedHealth Group Incorporated
UnitedHealth Group Center, 9900 Bren Rd. East
Minnetonka, MN 55343
Phone: 952-936-1300   **Fax:** 952-936-1819
Web: www.unitedhealthgroup.com

PRODUCTS/OPERATIONS

2008 Sales

	$ mil.	% of total
Health care services	75,857	80
Prescription solutions	12,573	13
OptumHealth	5,225	5
Ingenix	1,552	2
Adjustments	(14,021)	—
Total	**81,186**	**100**

Selected Operations

Health care services
    AmeriChoice (plans for recipients of Medicaid and
        other state-sponsored programs)
    Ovations (plans for consumers over the age of 50)
    UnitedHealthcare National Accounts (corporate health
        care plan organization and administration)
    UnitedHealthcare (plans for multi-state, midsized, and
        small businesses and consumers)
Prescription Solutions (pharmacy benefits management,
    formerly included in the Ovations segment)

OptumHealth (formerly Specialized Care Services)
  OptumHealth Behavioral Solutions
    United Behavioral Health (mental health plans)
  OptumHealth Care Solutions
    ACN Group (benefit administration)
    LifeEra (employee assistance programs)
    Optum (disease management)
    United Resource Networks (critical disease
      manangement)
  OptumHealth Consumer Solutions (HealthAtoZ.com,
    online assessments)
  OptumHealth Bank (formerly Exante Bank)
  OptumHealth Financial Services (formerly Exante
    Financial Services)
  OptumHealth Specialty Benefits (formerly Dental and
    Vision)
    Dental Benefits Providers (dental benefits)
    National Benefit Resources (stop loss insurance)
    Spectera (vision benefits)
    Unimerica Workplace Benefits (life and other
      insurance products)
    UnitedHealthcare Dental (dental benefits)
INGENIX (information services)

COMPETITORS

Aetna
Blue Cross
CIGNA
Coventry Health Care
CVS Caremark
Delta Dental Plans
Express Scripts
Health Insurance of New York
Health Net
Humana
Kaiser Foundation Health Plan
Medco Health
WellPoint

HISTORICAL FINANCIALS

Company Type: Public

Income Statement

	REVENUE ($ mil.)	NET INCOME ($ mil.)	NET PROFIT MARGIN	EMPLOYEES
12/08	81,186.0	2,977.0	3.7%	75,000
12/07	75,431.0	4,654.0	6.2%	67,000
12/06	71,542.0	4,159.0	5.8%	58,000
12/05	45,365.0	3,300.0	7.3%	55,000
12/04	37,218.0	2,587.0	7.0%	40,000
Annual Growth	21.5%	3.6%	—	17.0%

FYE: December 31

2008 Year-End Financials

Debt ratio: 54.6%
Return on equity: 14.6%
Cash ($ mil.): 7,426
Current ratio: 0.76
Long-term debt ($ mil.): 11,338

No. of shares (mil.): 1,162
Dividends
  Yield: 0.1%
  Payout: 1.3%
Market value ($ mil.): 30,920

Stock History

NYSE: UNH

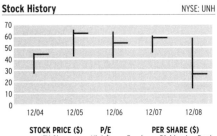

	STOCK PRICE ($) FY Close	P/E High/Low		PER SHARE ($) Earnings	Dividends	Book Value
12/08	26.60	24	6	2.40	0.03	17.88
12/07	58.20	17	13	3.42	0.03	17.26
12/06	53.73	21	14	2.97	0.03	17.90
12/05	62.14	26	17	2.48	0.01	15.26
12/04	44.01	23	14	1.97	0.01	9.22
Annual Growth	(11.8%)	—	—	5.1%	31.6%	18.0%

Universal Corporation

Smoking may be hazardous to your health, but providing the tobacco for the smokes has proven safe and profitable so far for Universal Corporation. The company selects, buys, processes, and ships leaf tobacco in the US and some 35 other nations, including Brazil, Canada, and Zimbabwe. The leaf is sold to cigarette makers. Universal also procures and processes dark tobacco used in cigars and smokeless products. A pure play in tobacco, the firm has sold its lumber and building products as well as its agricultural products businesses, which provided the food industry with such products as tea, dried fruit, and seeds. The firm's Universal Leaf subsidiaries are active in Africa, Europe, South America, and the US.

Acting as an intermediary between tobacco growers and cigarette and smokeless tobacco companies, Universal primarily deals in flue-cured (processed by artificial heat), burley (air-cured), and oriental (small-leafed) tobaccos, all of which are the major ingredients in American blend cigarettes. Philip Morris International and Japan Tobacco are among its biggest customers. However, Japan Tobacco's pending purchase of the UK's Triback Leaf and a pair of Brazilian firms will likely reduce the volume of tobacco it purchases from Universal. Also, the effects of the trend toward consolidation among tobacco product manufacturers, which involves some of Universal's customers, remains unclear. While consolidation increases the tobacco broker's reliance on a few key customers, it's unclear whether those customers will buy more or less tobacco from Universal.

In recent years Universal's sales have suffered as the number of US smokers has decreased and some US cigarette makers increasingly have bought tobacco abroad or directly from US farmers. In response, in 2009 the company announced the phase-out of its operations at its dark tobacco processing facility in Kenbridge, Virginia, and consolidation of all of its domestic dark tobacco processing at its plant in Lancaster, Pennsylvania.

In 2006 and 2007 Universal Corporation shed businesses unrelated to its tobacco operations and refocused its attention to the tobacco market. (The company's non-tobacco activities had brought in almost half of its revenues.)

HISTORY

Jaquelin Taylor founded Universal Leaf Tobacco Company in 1918 by combining six tobacco dealers, including his own J.P. Taylor Company of Virginia, and the company went public a few years later. The company launched subsidiaries in China in 1924 and in Canada the following year.

Philip Morris became a customer during the 1930s, and the cigarette maker's association with Universal became instrumental in its growth. By 1940 the company was the leading purchaser of leaf tobacco in the US. That year the US government filed antitrust charges against Universal and seven other tobacco companies. American, Liggett & Myers, and Reynolds stood trial for the whole group, and four years later each of the eight companies was fined $15,000.

Universal expanded into South America and Asia during the next several decades, and by the end of the 1960s it was operating in 15 countries outside the US. The company diversified under Gordon Crenshaw, who became president in 1965 and CEO soon thereafter. Universal made several

small acquisitions between 1966 and 1980, including fertilizer producer Royster in 1980 (sold in 1984). Its first significant venture outside agriculture came in 1984 when it bought both Lawyers Title and Continental Land Title for a total of $115 million. Two years later Universal bought Netherlands-based Deli-Maatschappij, which traded in tobacco and commodities such as tea, rubber, sunflower seeds, and timber.

In 1987 the company changed its name to Universal Corporation to reflect its diversifying interests. Henry Harrell replaced Crenshaw as CEO in 1988 (and as chairman in 1991). Also in 1988 Universal bought tobacco processor Thope and Ricks, and two years later it purchased Gebreder Kulenkampffag (tobacco, Germany), giving Universal a greater presence in the developing market in Eastern Europe.

The company acquired Kliemann (tobacco, Brazil) in 1991, ensuring access to Brazilian flue-cured tobacco. Also that year a depressed real estate market led the company to spin off its title insurance operation, Lawyers Title, to shareholders. Universal bought the Casalee Group, a UK tobacco processor with key operations in Brazil and Africa and trading operations in Europe and the Far East, for about $100 million in 1993. A global surplus in the tobacco markets hurt profits the following year.

In 1996 Universal formed a joint venture with COSUN, a Dutch sugar cooperative, creating the #1 spice enterprise in the Benelux market. As part of its plan to grow in emerging markets, the next year Universal acquired leaf-processing plants in Tanzania and Poland. Despite strong sales and profits, Universal's stock had flagged, and in 1998 the company bought back $100 million of its shares to improve their value. Universal formed Socotab, a joint venture with Socotab Leaf Company to combine both companies' oriental leaf businesses.

Sales fell in 1999 amid a worldwide glut of leaf tobacco. In 2000 Universal said it would close several US plants, eliminating about 175 full-time and 1,400 seasonal jobs. In 2001 the transition from the traditional auction market to direct contracting with farmers caused increases in the cost of doing business for Universal.

In January 2003 Harrell retired as chairman and CEO. He was succeeded by Allen King who had been with the company since 1969.

Universal sold its Dutch non-tobacco businesses, which included its lumber and building products distribution segment and most of its agri-products operations in September 2006. In December of that year George Freeman, III was named president and CEO of the company, while King remained chairman.

The remainder of Universal's ag-operations and assets were sold in 2007 and early 2008. The divestitures, which were effected to increase shareholder value and return to core competencies, involved selling a UK trading company, as well as trading companies in Virginia, Washington, and California. In its role as an agricultural products merchant, the company had provided the food industry with a number of products, including tea, dried fruit, and sunflower seeds. It also provided the tire manufacturing industry with rubber. Universal distributed building materials and lumber to wholesale/do-it-yourself chains and to the construction and prefabrication industries in the Netherlands and Belgium through regional outlets.

US Airways

US Airways Group takes wing with its US Airways unit, one of the nation's leading passenger carriers. Along with its regional affiliates, US Airways serves about 200 cities, mainly in the US and Canada but also in Latin America, the Caribbean, and Europe. It uses about 350 jets on mainline routes; regional service is provided by subsidiaries Piedmont Airlines, PSA, and several independent carriers with about 300 aircraft. US Airways extends its network via the Star Alliance, a marketing and code-sharing partnership led by United Airlines and Lufthansa.

After undergoing two bankruptcy reorganizations since 2002, US Airways Group has tried to catch a tailwind. The company emerged from Chapter 11 most recently in 2005 when it merged with America West. It returned to profitability in 2006 and 2007.

Along with bringing together two airlines, the company is trying to combine two approaches to the airline business: low-fare, low-cost (think Southwest Airlines and JetBlue); and international hub-and-spoke, with amenities (think American Airlines and United Airlines).

US Airways Group has unified its US Airways and America West businesses under the US Airways brand, but full integration of the carriers' operations has been delayed because pilots from the "old" US Airways and America West have been unable to unify their seniority lists. (Seniority is crucial for unionized pilots because it determines where, when, and what types of aircraft they fly.)

As it continues to integrate operations and keep a lid on costs, US Airways hopes to grow by adding international flights. The carrier won a coveted slot for a nonstop route between the US and China, and its Philadelphia-Beijing service is expected to begin in 2010. The carrier added its first flight to South America in 2009 with service from Philadelphia to Rio de Janeiro. US Airways hopes to add three or four international destinations a year between 2009 and 2011.

High fuel prices, however, have changed the trajectory for US Airways and the rest of the airline industry. In 2008 the carrier joined peers in cutting domestic capacity, reducing its workforce, and imposing new fees (including charges for checked bags, premium seats, and pillow-and-blanket sets). Those fees helped US Airways stem losses in 2008, and the company expects to generate $400 million annually from fees.

HISTORY

Richard du Pont (of the DuPont chemical dynasty) founded All American Aviation as an air-mail service in 1939 to serve Pennsylvania and the Ohio Valley. Pilots used a system of hooks and ropes to pick up and drop off mail "on the fly." Ten years later the company expanded its service, began carrying passengers, and changed its name to All American Airways.

The carrier became Allegheny Airlines in 1953. It bought smaller airlines in 1968 and 1972, expanding into the Midwest and up the East Coast. In 1978 the US airline industry was deregulated; Allegheny became USAir in 1979 and began flying across the South and to California.

In 1987 USAir bought two major regional carriers — Pacific Southwest Airlines and Piedmont Airlines. The USAir/Piedmont merger was at the time the largest in US airline history. It also gave USAir its hub in Charlotte, North Carolina; its first international route (Charlotte-London); and an East Coast commuter airline.

High fuel prices and fare wars in the early 1990s put USAir in the red for six years (and forced it to lay off 9,000 workers by 1996). Seth Schofield became CEO in 1991, and USAir acquired TWA's London routes in 1992. Taking a 40% stake in Trump Shuttle, USAir began a joint marketing effort under the name USAir Shuttle. (It bought the shuttle outright in 1997.) The next year USAir and British Airways (BA) began code-sharing, and BA took a stake in USAir, which gave up its London routes.

The year 1994 was not one of USAir's best: It took a beating as it lowered fares to compete with Continental Airlines, which by then challenged USAir in almost half its routes. The airline tried in vain to wring wage concessions from its unions. Then disaster struck: A jet carrying 132 passengers crashed at Pittsburgh — USAir's second fatal crash that year.

Though USAir returned to profitability in 1996, Schofield resigned. The new CEO Stephen Wolf, a UAL veteran, demanded labor concessions. USAir, which became US Airways in 1997, finally won a new contract with its pilots.

The company's relationship with BA soured after US Airways sued BA to gain access to London's Heathrow. The two canceled code-sharing in 1997, and by 1998 BA had sold its US Airways stock. The next year Wolf disciple Rakesh Gangwal became CEO; Wolf remained chairman. US Airways suffered a pilot shortage after more than 300 pilots took early retirement and others were called up by the US military to support the Kosovo conflict.

To remain aloft after the terrorist attacks in New York and Washington, DC, in 2001 the carrier announced that it would cut back on its flights and lay off about 20% of its workforce. Later that year Gangwal resigned, and Wolf stepped back in as CEO until March 2002, when Avis Rent A Car CEO David Siegel, a Continental Airlines veteran, replaced him.

The group filed for bankruptcy protection in 2002; in conjunction with its filing, the company received a bid from Texas Pacific Group, and it won a $900 million loan guarantee from the federal government. The Texas Pacific deal was replaced by The Retirement Systems of Alabama, which invested $240 million in exchange for a 36% ownership (and a 72% voting) stake in the company. It emerged from bankruptcy in 2003.

US Airways strengthened its European presence in 2003 when it began a code-sharing agreement with top German airline Lufthansa, which eventually led to its inclusion in the Star Alliance. Its new structure, however, didn't prove viable, and the carrier found itself overwhelmed by heavy costs, primarily record-high fuel prices. It was forced once again to seek the protection of bankruptcy courts in 2004. US Airways merged with America West and emerged from Chapter 11 the following year.

To accelerate its growth, US Airways offered to buy rival Delta in 2006. Delta failed to bite, however, spoiling US Airways' dreams of creating the world's largest airline.

In January 2009, US Airways Flight 1549 had just taken off from New York on its way to Charlotte, North Carolina, when it struck a flock of Canada geese, causing failure in both the plane's engines. Captain Chesley "Sully" Sullenberger made international news by skillfully "ditching" the plane in the Hudson River, saving the lives of all 155 people aboard.

EXECUTIVES

Chairman and CEO: W. Douglas (Doug) Parker, age 47, $5,426,702 total compensation
Vice Chairman: Bruce R. Lakefield, age 65
President: J. Scott Kirby, age 41, $3,638,463 total compensation
EVP and COO: Robert D. Isom Jr., age 45, $2,041,980 total compensation
EVP and CFO: Derek J. Kerr, age 44, $1,258,120 total compensation
SVP and CIO: Brad Jensen
EVP Corporate and General Counsel: Stephen L. (Steve) Johnson, age 52
SVP Public Affairs: C. A. Howlett, age 65
SVP People and Communications: Elise R. Eberwein, age 43, $1,213,718 total compensation
SVP East Coast, International, and Cargo Operations: Suzanne Boda
SVP Marketing and Planning: Andrew P. Nocella
SVP Technical Operations: David Seymour
SVP Flight Operations and Inflight: Edward W. (Ed) Bular
VP Financial Analysis; President, US Airways Express: Dion Flannery
VP Human Resources: Daniel (Dan) Pon, age 56
VP and Treasurer: Tom Weir
VP Corporate Communications: James (Jim) Olson, age 40
President and CEO, PSA Express: Keith D. Houk
President and CEO, Piedmont Airlines: Stephen R. (Steve) Farrow
Secretary: Caroline B. Ray
Director Investor Relations: Daniel E. Cravens
Auditors: KPMG LLP

LOCATIONS

HQ: US Airways Group, Inc.
111 W. Rio Salado Pkwy., Tempe, AZ 85281
Phone: 480-693-0800   **Fax:** 480-693-5546
Web: www.usairways.com

2008 Sales

	$ mil.	% of total
US	9,659	80
Other countries	2,459	20
Total	**12,118**	**100**

PRODUCTS/OPERATIONS

2008 Sales

	$ mil.	% of total
Mainline passenger	8,183	68
Express passenger	2,879	24
Cargo	144	1
Other	912	7
Total	**12,118**	**100**

COMPETITORS

Air France-KLM
AirTran Holdings
Alaska Air
AMR Corp.
British Airways
Continental Airlines
Delta Air Lines
Frontier Airlines
JetBlue
Northwest Airlines
Southwest Airlines
Virgin Atlantic Airways

HISTORICAL FINANCIALS

Company Type: Public

Income Statement

FYE: December 31

	REVENUE ($ mil.)	NET INCOME ($ mil.)	NET PROFIT MARGIN	EMPLOYEES
12/08	12,118.0	(2,210.0)	—	37,500
12/07	11,700.0	427.0	3.6%	39,600
12/06	11,557.0	303.0	2.6%	37,000
12/05	5,077.0	(335.0)	—	36,600
12/04	7,117.0	(611.0)	—	29,500
Annual Growth	14.2%	—	—	6.2%

2008 Year-End Financials

Debt ratio: —
Return on equity: —
Cash ($ mil.): 1,034
Current ratio: 0.79
Long-term debt ($ mil.): 3,634

No. of shares (mil.): 132
Dividends
Yield: 0.0%
Payout: —
Market value ($ mil.): 1,021

Stock History

NYSE: LCC

	STOCK PRICE ($) FY Close	P/E High/Low		PER SHARE ($) Earnings	Dividends	Book Value
12/08	7.73	—	—	(22.06)	0.00	(3.82)
12/07	14.71	14	3	4.52	0.00	10.90
12/06	53.85	19	8	3.33	0.00	7.35
12/05	37.14	—	—	(17.06)	0.00	3.18
Annual Growth	(40.7%)	—	—	—	—	—

U.S. Bancorp

Not quite a bank for the entire US, U.S. Bancorp has approximately 2,800 locations and 5,000 branded ATMs in two dozen midwestern and western states. The bank holding company, one of the 10 largest in the country, owns U.S. Bank and other subsidiaries that provide consumer and commercial banking, as well as credit card and ATM processing, mutual funds, mortgage banking, brokerage, wealth management, equipment leasing, trust services, corporate payments, and insurance. In late 2008 U.S. Bancorp acquired the banking operations of the failed California-based banks Downey Savings & Loan and PFF Bank & Trust in an FDIC-assisted transaction.

Also in 2008 U.S. Bancorp announced that it would receive $6.6 billion from the US government under the Treasury Department's program to invest some $250 billion in banks to help encourage more lending.

Earlier that year U.S. Bancorp bought Los Angeles-based Mellon 1st Business Bank from The Bank of New York Mellon. In 2007 the company acquired Montana-based bank United Financial and added about 20 branches in Colorado in 2006 with its purchase of holding company Vail Banks, which owned WestStar Bank.

U.S. Bancorp has one of the largest networks of branches inside grocery stores and continues to add locations. In 2008 it announced it would assume the leases of some 50 Zions Bank and Nevada State Bank in-store branches in Utah and Nevada. U.S. Bancorp has also been expanding its fee-based business services such as treasury management, corporate trust, institutional custody, merchant processing, and freight payment services. In 2009 U.S. Bank agreed to buy the corporate trust bond administration business of AmeriServ Financial, bringing the bank's corporate trust assets under administration to $2.1 trillion.

Its largest fee-gathering subsidiaries include Elavon (formerly NOVA Information Systems), a leading processor of merchant credit card transactions in the US, Canada, and Europe. Another unit, FAF Advisors (formerly U.S. Bancorp Asset Management), changed its name in 2006 to emphasize its relationship with the First American family of mutual funds that it manages.

Near the end of 2006 vice chairman Richard Davis succeeded CEO Jerry Grundhofer, who had been leading the company for more than a dozen years. Davis succeeded Grundhofer as chairman the following year.

HISTORY

When Farmers and Millers Bank was founded in 1853, it operated out of a strongbox in a rented storefront. After surviving a panic in the 1850s, the bank became part of the national banking system in 1863 as First National Bank of Milwaukee. The bank grew and in 1894 it merged with Merchants Exchange Bank (founded 1870).

In 1919 the bank merged again, with Wisconsin National Bank (founded 1892), to form First Wisconsin National Bank of Milwaukee, a leading financial institution in the area from the 1920s on.

First Wisconsin grew through purchases over the next decade, though the number of banks fell after the 1929 stock market crash; by the end of WWII it had 11 banks. State and federal legislation, particularly the 1956 Bank Holding Company Act (which proscribed acquisitions and branching), constrained postwar growth. In the 1970s Wisconsin eased restrictions on intrastate branching and the bank began to grow again.

Growth accelerated in the late 1980s after Wisconsin and surrounding states legalized interstate banking in adjoining states in 1987. That year First Wisconsin bought seven Minnesota banks and then moved into Illinois. The company focused on strong, well-run institutions. Also that year, it sold its headquarters and used the proceeds to fund more buys. In 1988, in its first foray outside the Midwest, the company bought Metro Bancorp in Phoenix, targeting midwestern retirees moving to Arizona.

In 1989 First Wisconsin changed its name to Firstar. The early 1990s saw the company move into Iowa (Banks of Iowa, 1990), buy in-state rivals (Federated Bank Geneva Capital Corporation, 1992), and then roll into Illinois (DSB Corporation, 1993). The next year it bought First Southeast Banking Corp. (Wisconsin) and merged it, along with Firstar Bank Racine and Firstar Bank Milwaukee, into one bank.

In 1994 the company was hit with a $13 million charge to cover losses from a check-kiting fraud.

To strengthen its position against larger competitors, Firstar continued its buying spree in 1995 (Chicago bank First Colonial Bankshares and Investors Bank Corp. of Minneapolis/St.

Paul) and 1996 (Jacob Schmidt Company). The acquisitions left the company bloated. In 1996 Firstar began a restructuring designed to cut costs and increase margins. The restructuring project ended in 1997, but by then its performance lagged behind other midwestern banks considerably. In an effort to diversify, it allied with EVEREN Securities to offer debt underwriting and sales, fixed income products, and public finance advisory services. But it was too little, too late; under pressure from major stockholders to seek a partner, Firstar began looking for a buyer.

It found Star Banc. Established in 1863 as The First National Bank of Cincinnati under a bank charter signed by Abraham Lincoln, Star Banc over the years added branches and bought other banks. The company renamed all of its subsidiary banks Star Bank in 1988 and took the name Star Banc in 1989.

In 1998 Star Banc chairman Jerry Grundhofer approached Firstar about a combination. Negotiations proceeded quickly, and a new Firstar was born. The next year Firstar bought Mercantile Bancorporation. The purchase enabled the bank to expand its international banking services into such markets as Kansas, Nebraska, and Missouri. In 2000 the company made arrangements to buy U.S. Bancorp, a Minneapolis-based bank with roots dating back to 1929. Under the terms of the acquisition, Firstar would shed its own name in favor of the more appropriate U.S. Bancorp moniker.

When the merger was completed in 2001, Firstar's Jerry Grundhofer became CEO of U.S. Bancorp, taking a seat next to his brother John, the company's chairman. Later that year the company bolstered its credit and debit card processing operations with the purchase of NOVA Corporation (now NOVA Information Systems). At the end of 2002, John Grundhofer retired from his chairman's post.

In late 2003 U.S. Bancorp unloaded its investment bank subsidiary Piper Jaffray in a spinoff to U.S. Bancorp shareholders.

EXECUTIVES

Chairman, President, and CEO: Richard K. Davis, age 51, $4,973,769 total compensation
Vice Chairman and CFO: Andrew Cecere, age 48, $2,559,818 total compensation
Vice Chairman: Joseph C Hoesley, age 54
Vice Chairman Technology and Operations Services: William L. Chenevich, age 65, $5,384,509 total compensation
Vice Chairman and Head Commercial Banking: Joseph M. Otting, age 51
Vice Chairman and Head Consumer Banking: Richard C. (Rick) Hartnack, age 63, $2,637,798 total compensation
Vice Chairman Payment Services: Pamela A. (Pam) Joseph, age 50
Vice Chairman and Head Corporate Banking: Richard B. Payne Jr., age 61
Vice Chairman and Head Wealth Management and Securities Services: Diane L. Thormodsgard, age 58
EVP and Chief Strategy Officer; Head Enterprise Revenue Office: Howell D. McCullough III, age 52
Chief Investment Officer: Timothy J. (Tim) Leach, age 53
EVP and Chief Risk Officer: Richard J. Hidy, age 46
EVP and Chief Credit Officer: P. W. (Bill) Parker, age 52
EVP National Corporate Banking: Leslie V. Godridge
EVP and Controller: Terrance R. (Terry) Dolan
EVP, General Counsel, and Secretary: Lee R. Mitau, age 60, $3,537,687 total compensation
EVP Human Resources: Jennie P. Carlson, age 48
EVP and Corporate Treasurer: Kenneth D. (Ken) Nelson, age 56
SVP Investor Relations: Judith T. (Judy) Murphy, age 51
Auditors: Ernst & Young LLP

LOCATIONS

HQ: U.S. Bancorp
800 Nicollet Mall, Minneapolis, MN 55402
Phone: 651-466-3000   **Fax:** 612-303-0782
Web: www.usbancorp.com

PRODUCTS/OPERATIONS

2008 Gross Revenues

	$ mil.	% of total
Interest		
Loans	10,278	51
Investment securities	1,984	10
Other	156	1
Noninterest		
Trust & investment management fees	1,314	6
Merchant processing services	1,151	6
Deposit service charges	1,081	5
Credit & debit card revenue	1,039	5
Corporate payment products	671	3
Treasury management fees	517	3
Commercial products	492	2
ATM processing services	366	2
Mortgage banking	270	1
Investment products fees & commissions	147	1
Securities loss	(978)	—
Other	741	4
Total	**19,229**	**100**

2008 Assets

	$ mil.	% of total
Cash & due from banks	6,859	3
Mortgage-backed securities	30,133	11
Other securities	9,388	4
Loans		
Loans held for sale	3,210	1
Commercial	56,618	21
Commercial real estate	33,213	12
Residential mortgages	23,580	9
Retail	60,368	22
Allowance for loan losses	(3,514)	—
Covered assets	11,450	4
Other	34,607	13
Total	**265,912**	**100**

Selected Subsidiaries

Elan Life Insurance Company
Elavon Financial Services Limited (Ireland)
FAF Advisors, Inc.
Miami Valley Insurance Company
Midwest Indemnity Inc.
Mississippi Valley Life Insurance Company
NOVA Canadian Holdings Company
NOVA European Holdings Company
Quasar Distributors, LLC
U.S. Bancorp Insurance and Investments, Inc.
U.S. Bancorp Insurance Company, Inc.
U.S. Bancorp Insurance Services, LLC
U.S. Bancorp Insurance Services of Montana, Inc.
U.S. Bancorp Investments, Inc.
U.S. Bank National Association
U.S. Bank National Association ND
U.S. Bank Trust Company, National Association
U.S. Bank Trust National Association
U.S. Bank Trust National Association SD

COMPETITORS

BancWest
Bank of America
Capital One
Citigroup
Citizens Financial Group
Fifth Third
First National of Nebraska
Huntington Bancshares
JPMorgan Chase
KeyCorp
Marshall & Ilsley
Old National Bancorp
TCF Financial
UnionBanCal
Washington Mutual
Wells Fargo
Zions Bancorporation

HISTORICAL FINANCIALS

Company Type: Public

Income Statement

FYE: December 31

	ASSETS ($ mil.)	NET INCOME ($ mil.)	INCOME AS % OF ASSETS	EMPLOYEES
12/08	265,912.0	2,946.0	1.1%	57,000
12/07	237,615.0	4,264.0	1.8%	54,000
12/06	219,232.0	4,703.0	2.1%	50,000
12/05	209,465.0	4,489.0	2.1%	49,684
12/04	195,104.0	4,166.8	2.1%	48,831
Annual Growth	**8.0%**	**(8.3%)**	**—**	**3.9%**

2008 Year-End Financials

Equity as % of assets: 6.9%
Return on assets: 1.2%
Return on equity: 15.3%
Long-term debt ($ mil.): 38,359
No. of shares (mil.): 1,912

Dividends
  Yield: 6.8%
  Payout: 105.6%
Market value ($ mil.): 47,818
Sales ($ mil.): 14,543

Stock History

NYSE: USB

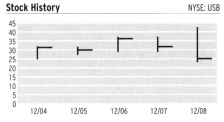

	STOCK PRICE ($) FY Close	P/E High/Low	Earnings	PER SHARE ($) Dividends	Book Value
12/08	25.01	26 15	1.61	1.70	13.76
12/07	31.74	15 12	2.43	1.63	11.01
12/06	36.19	14 11	2.61	1.39	11.09
12/05	29.89	13 11	2.42	1.23	10.51
12/04	31.32	15 12	2.18	1.02	10.22
Annual Growth	**(5.5%)**	**— —**	**(7.3%)**	**13.6%**	**7.7%**

US Postal Service

The United States Postal Service (USPS) handles cards, letters, and packages sent from sea to shining sea. The USPS delivers 203 billion pieces of mail a year to some 149 million addresses in the US and its territories. The independent government agency relies on postage and fees to fund operations. Though it has a monopoly on delivering the mail, the USPS faces competition for services such as package delivery. The US president appoints nine of the 11 members of the board that oversee the USPS. The presidential appointees select the postmaster general, and together they name the deputy postmaster general; the two also serve on the board.

A challenge for the agency is the growing use of the Internet, which has led to lower volume of some types of mail. To keep pace, the USPS has worked to gain delivery business generated by online shopping. The agency also is investing in the development of the Intelligent Mail Barcode, a mini-GPS system for tracking mail.

At the same time, the USPS is reducing its workforce through attrition and cutting hours of operation at some of its 36,000-plus post offices and other retail and delivery facilities. Trans-

portation is a major expense for the agency, however, and high fuel prices have pumped up costs for operating the agency's 219,000 vehicles.

With an eye on its bottom line, the USPS has accelerated the pace of its rate increases. Between January 2006 and May 2009 the price of a first-class stamp went from 37 cents to 44 cents.

To cater to customers who get stuck with some of the out-of-date stamps, USPS introduced a new concept in April 2007 — the Forever Stamp. The Liberty Bell-imaged stamp is sold at the same price as a first-class stamp but it can then be used, as the name says, forever, even as the price of first-class postage goes up.

The USPS was given some flexibility in setting rates, as well as some new restrictions, by the Postal Accountability and Enhancement Act of 2006, considered the farthest-reaching postal reform legislation since the agency became independent in 1970. The goal of the law was to enable the USPS adopt some private-sector management practices in order to ensure the agency's long-term financial health and to preserve universal mail service. Among the short-term effects of the legislation was a requirement that the agency pay into a new fund for retiree health benefits. The $5.4 billion payment caused the USPS to record a loss in 2007, the agency's first since 2002.

HISTORY

The second-oldest agency of the US government (after Indian Affairs), the Post Office was created by the Continental Congress in 1775 with Benjamin Franklin as postmaster general. The postal system came to play a vital role in the development of transportation in the US.

At that time, postal workers were riders on muddy paths delivering letters without stamps or envelopes. Letters were delivered only between post offices. Congress approved the first official postal policy in 1792: Rates ranged from six cents for less than 30 miles to 25 cents for more than 450. Letter carriers began delivering mail in cities in 1794.

First based in Philadelphia, in 1800 the Post Office moved to Washington, DC. In 1829 Andrew Jackson elevated the position of postmaster general to cabinet rank — it became a means of rewarding political cronies. Mail contracts subsidized the early development of US railroads. The first adhesive postage stamp appeared in the US in 1847.

Uniform postal rates (not varying with distance) were instituted in 1863, the year free city delivery began. The start of free rural delivery in 1896 spurred road construction in isolated US areas. Parcel post was launched in 1913, and new mail-order houses such as Montgomery Ward and Sears, Roebuck flourished.

The famous pledge beginning "Neither snow nor rain . . . " — not an official motto — was first inscribed at the main New York City post office in 1914. Scheduled airmail service between Washington, DC, and New York City began in 1918, stimulating the development of commercial air service. The ZIP code was introduced in 1963.

As mail volume grew, postal workers became increasingly militant under work stress. (Franklin's pigeonhole sorting method had barely changed.) A work stoppage in the New York City post office in 1970 spread within nine days to 670 post offices, and the US Army was deployed to handle the mail. Later that year the Postal Reorganization Act was passed. The new law established a board of governors to handle postal affairs and choose the postmaster general, who became CEO of an independent agency, the US Postal Service (USPS). The next year USPS negotiated the first US government collective-bargaining labor contract. Express mail service began in 1977, and USPS stepped up automation efforts.

In 1995 USPS launched Global Package Link, a program to expedite major customers' shipments to Canada, Japan, and the UK. The next year it overhauled rates, cutting prices for larger mailers who prepared their mail for automation and raising prices for small mailers who didn't.

Postmaster General Marvin Runyon — whose six-year tenure took the agency from the red into the black — retired in 1998 and was succeeded by USPS veteran William Henderson. The next year a one-cent hike in the price of first-class postage took effect. (Another one-cent increase took effect in 2001, and the rate rose once again the following year.) In a nod to the Internet, USPS in 1999 contracted with outside vendors to enable customers to buy and print stamps online.

In 2001 USPS formed a strategic alliance with rival FedEx through which FedEx agreed to provide air transportation for USPS mail, in return for the placement of FedEx drop boxes in post offices. Henderson stepped down at the end of May 2001, and EVP Jack Potter was named to replace him. That year several postal workers in a Washington, DC, branch office were exposed to anthrax-tainted letters.

Potter launched a series of cost-cutting programs, which together with rate increases enabled the USPS to post a profit in 2003 — the agency's first year in the black since 1999.

EXECUTIVES

Chairman: Alan C. Kessler
Vice Chairman: Carolyn Lewis Gallagher
Postmaster General, CEO, and Governor:
John E. (Jack) Potter
Deputy Postmaster, COO, and Governor:
Patrick R. Donahoe
EVP and CFO: Harold Glen Walker
EVP and CIO: Ross Philo
EVP and Chief Human Resources Officer:
Anthony J. (Tony) Vegliante
Acting Chief Postal Inspector: William R. Gilligan
SVP and Managing Director, Global Business:
Paul Vogel
SVP Intelligent Mail and Address Quality:
Thomas G. (Tom) Day
SVP and General Counsel: Mary Anne Gibbons
SVP Customer Service: Stephen M. (Steve) Kearney
SVP Operations: William P. (Bill) Galligan
SVP Strategy and Transition: Linda A. Kingsley
SVP Mailing Services: David B. Shoenfeld
VP and Treasurer: Robert J. Pedersen
VP Sales: Jerry W. Whalen
VP Corporate Communications: Mitzi R. Betman
President, Shipping and Mailing Services Division:
Robert F. Bernstock, age 58
Judicial Officer: William A. Campbell
Secretary: Julie S. Moore
Auditors: Ernst & Young LLP

LOCATIONS

HQ: United States Postal Service
475 L'Enfant Plaza SW, Washington, DC 20260
Phone: 202-268-2500   **Fax:** 202-268-4860
Web: www.usps.com

PRODUCTS/OPERATIONS

2008 Sales

	$ mil.	% of total
First-Class Mail	38,179	51
Standard Mail	20,586	27
Periodicals	2,295	3
Package Services	1,845	3
Shipping Services	8,382	11
Other Mailing Services	3,645	5
Total	**74,932**	**100**

HISTORICAL FINANCIALS

Company Type: Government agency

Income Statement				FYE: September 30
	REVENUE ($ mil.)	NET INCOME ($ mil.)	NET PROFIT MARGIN	EMPLOYEES
9/08	74,932.0	(2,806.0)	—	663,238
9/07	74,973.0	(5,142.0)	—	684,762
9/06	72,650.0	900.0	1.2%	696,138
9/05	69,907.0	1,445.0	2.1%	704,716
9/04	68,996.0	3,065.0	4.4%	707,485
Annual Growth	2.1%	—	—	(1.6%)

Net Income History

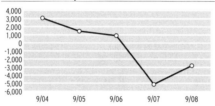

USAA

USAA has a decidedly military bearing. The mutual insurance company serves more than 6 million member customers, primarily military personnel, military retirees, and their families. It offers property/casualty (only to military personnel) and life insurance, banking, a discount brokerage, and investment management services. USAA relies largely on technology and direct marketing to sell its products, reaching clients via the telephone and Internet.

The company's USAA Alliance Services unit provides discount shopping (floral, jewelry, and home and auto safety items), and travel and delivery services to its members. Its USAA Real Estate division serves institutional and corporate customers with real estate development.

On average, members use five of the company's different products, and the company has begun tying its auto insurance rates to the number of products a member uses as well as how long they have held insurance with USAA.

The company is expecting its membership to continue growing, projecting it to nearly double by 2010. In an attempt to increase revenue, the company has entered new markets by making efforts to target people less affluent than military officers. At present, nearly 50% of its members are the grown children and grandchildren of people who have served in the military.

In recent years USAA has streamlined operations by reducing staff and closing down divisions (including mailing, printing, and information technology offices). Its efforts have rewarded members with lower prices.

HISTORY

In 1922 a group of 26 US Army officers gathered in a San Antonio hotel and formed their own automobile insurance association. The reason? As military officers who often moved, they had a hard time getting insurance because they were considered transient. So the officers decided to insure each other. Led by Major William Garrison, who became the company's first president, they formed the United States Army Automobile Insurance Association.

In 1924, when US Navy and Marine Corps officers were allowed to join, the company changed its name to United Services Automobile Association. By the mid-1950s the company had some 200,000 members. During the 1960s the company formed USAA Life Insurance Company (1963) and USAA Casualty Insurance Company (1968).

Robert McDermott, a retired US Air Force brigadier general, became president in 1969. He cut employment through attrition, established education and training seminars for employees, and invested in computers and telecommunications (drastically cutting claims-processing time). McDermott added new products and services, such as mutual funds, real estate investments, and banking. Under McDermott, USAA's membership grew from 653,000 in 1969 to more than 3 million in 1993.

During the 1970s, in an effort to go paperless, USAA became one of the insurance industry's first companies to switch from mail to toll-free (800) numbers. In the early 1980s the company introduced its discount purchasing program, USAA Buying Services. In 1985 it opened the USAA Federal Savings Bank. USAA began installing an optical storage system in the late 1980s to automate some customer service operations.

McDermott retired in 1993 and was succeeded by Robert Herres. The following year USAA Federal Savings Bank began developing a home banking system, offering members information and services over advanced screen telephones provided by IBM.

In the early 1990s USAA's real estate activities increased dramatically. In 1995 USAA restructured its interest in the Fiesta Texas theme park in San Antonio in order to focus on previously developed properties in geographically diverse areas. That year Six Flags Theme Parks (now Six Flags, Inc.) assumed operation and management of Fiesta Texas (which purchased it from USAA in 1998).

In 1997 USAA began including enlisted military personnel as members. It also started to experiment with a "plain English" mutual fund prospectus. In 1998 USAA also began offering Choice Ride in Orlando, Florida. For about $1,100 per quarter and a promise not to drive except in emergencies, the pilot program provided 36 round trips and a 90% discount on car insurance, in hopes of keeping older drivers from unnecessarily getting behind the wheel.

Also in 1998, as part of its new Financial Planning Network, USAA began offering retirement and estate planning assistance aimed at 25- to 55-year-olds for a yearly $250 fee. In 1999 claims doubled largely due to the impact of Hurricane

Floyd and spring hail storms hitting military communities in North Carolina and Virginia.

USAA also moved in 1999 to consolidate its customers' separate accounts (such as mutual fund holdings, stocks and bonds, and life insurance products) into one main account to strengthen customer relationships and reduce operational costs. The next year, after completing a number of technology projects, it laid off workers for the first time in its history.

In 2002, Robert Herres resigned as chairman and was succeeded by CEO Robert Davis. The next year the company saw increased sales and an improved net income thanks to a rebounding stock market and membership growth.

Robert Davis stepped down as chairman and CEO in 2007 and was replaced by John Moellering (chairman) and Joe Robles (CEO).

EXECUTIVES

Chairman: John H. Moellering
President and CEO: Josue (Joe) Robles Jr., age 63
CFO: Kristi A. Matus, age 40
SVP Information Technology and CIO: Greg Schwartz
EVP People Services: Elizabeth D. (Liz) Conklyn
EVP, General Counsel, and Corporate Secretary:
Steven A. Bennett
EVP Corporate Communications: Wendi E. Strong
EVP Enterprise Business Operations: S. Wayne Peacock
SVP Claims Service: Ken Rosen
President, USAA Financial Services Group:
Christopher W. Claus
**President, USAA Property & Casualty Insurance
Group:** Stuart Parker
President, USAA Federal Savings Bank: F. David Bohne
Auditors: Ernst & Young LLP

LOCATIONS

HQ: USAA
9800 Fredericksburg Rd., San Antonio, TX 78288
Phone: 210-498-2211
Web: www.usaa.com

USAA has major regional offices in Colorado Springs, Colorado; Las Vegas, Nevada; Norfolk, Virginia; Phoenix, Arizona; Sacramento, California; and Tampa, Florida. It operates international offices in London and Frankfurt, Germany.

PRODUCTS/OPERATIONS

2008 Revenues

	$ mil.	% of total
Insurance premiums	9,641	75
Fees, sales & loan income	2,008	15
Services & contractual income on securitizations	368	3
Investment return	254	2
Real estate investment income	171	1
Other revenue	470	4
Total	**12,912**	**100**

COMPETITORS

AIG	The Hartford
AIG American General	John Hancock Financial
Allstate	Liberty Mutual
American Financial Group	MetLife
AXA Financial	Mutual of Omaha
Berkshire Hathaway	Nationwide
Charles Schwab	New York Life
Chubb Corp	Northwestern Mutual
CIGNA	Pacific Mutual
Citigroup	Prudential
GEICO	State Farm
Guardian Life	T. Rowe Price

HISTORICAL FINANCIALS
Company Type: Mutual company

Income Statement
FYE: December 31

	ASSETS ($ mil.)	NET INCOME ($ mil.)	INCOME AS % OF ASSETS	EMPLOYEES
12/08	68,296.0	423.0	0.6%	21,900
12/07	67,177.0	1,855.0	2.8%	22,000
12/06	60,269.0	2,330.0	3.9%	22,000
12/05	51,038.0	1,388.0	2.7%	21,900
12/04	46,482.0	1,597.0	3.4%	21,000
Annual Growth	**10.1%**	**(28.3%)**	**—**	**1.1%**

2008 Year-End Financials

Equity as % of assets: —
Return on assets: 0.6%
Return on equity: —
Long-term debt ($ mil.): —
Sales ($ mil.): 12,912

Net Income History

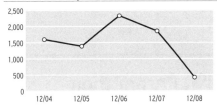

USEC Inc.

USEC beats radioactive swords into enriched uranium plowshares. The company processes used uranium — about half of which comes from old Russian atomic warheads — into enriched uranium, which it then supplies for commercial nuclear power plants. USEC is the radioactive recycler of choice for the "Megatons-to-Megawatts" program, a US-Russian agreement to convert uranium from warheads into nuclear fuel. USEC also processes uranium for the US Department of Energy. The company's NAC subsidiary provides consulting services to nuclear power plant operators and transportation of nuclear materials.

Contracts from the US government, Exelon, and Entergy each account for more than 10% of the company's sales. Fully three-quarters of USEC's business comes from the US; Japan is the company's other main country of business.

HISTORY

The US government's uranium enrichment program was born during WWII to produce material for the atomic bomb. Originally part of the Atomic Energy Commission, the program eventually came under the aegis of the Department of Energy (DOE). The Energy Policy Act of 1992 created the United States Enrichment Corporation (USEC) to encourage privatization. The act gave USEC four mandates: a consistent domestic supply of enriched uranium, competitive prices, support of US national security goals, and a transition into a fully privatized commercial business. USEC officially took over uranium enrichment operations in 1993.

In 1993 two of the USEC's mandates ran head-on into each other. As cash-poor, missile-laden

Russia struggled to revive its economy, President Clinton and Russian President Boris Yeltsin made a deal for the US to pay Russia for nuclear fuel derived from its atomic warheads. The 1994 contract locked USEC into a 20-year, $12 billion contract with the Russian Ministry for Atomic Energy to buy 500 metric tons of enriched uranium from nuclear warheads. Although this was good for national security, it was bad business because US material was cheaper. USEC balked, but the "Megatons-to-Megawatts" agreement went through, and by 1995 USEC had received six metric tons of the warhead uranium.

USEC's 1995 privatization plan faced a major production concern. Built in the 1950s, USEC's gaseous diffusion plants required vast amounts of electricity, while European competitors were using a much less expensive centrifuge process. To improve competitiveness, the US government transferred its Atomic Vapor Laser Isotope Separation (AVLIS) process to USEC, giving the firm a technology the government had spent $1.5 billion and 30 years in developing. (The company shelved the AVLIS project in 1999 because building such a plant would cost $2.5 billion.)

The USEC Privatization Act was ratified in 1996; its transition was approved a year later, and the company was put up for sale. The US government received only two bids for USEC; both were unacceptable, so the government sold stock to the public in 1998, and the sale raised $1.4 billion for the US Treasury.

The next year USEC took over management of its facilities from Lockheed Martin, marking the first time the program would not be run by contractors. The troubled company (facing high prices for raw material, low prices for finished products, and an in-depth government investigation into the company's long-term operations) eliminated 500 jobs and announced it would consider other job cuts.

In 2000 USEC signed a fuel supply contract with the Tennessee Valley Authority and invested heavily into laser-enrichment technology developed by Australian firm Silex Systems. Also that year a DOE report outlined many historically unsafe practices at the company's Paducah, Kentucky, plant, including experiments that intentionally exposed workers to radioactivity.

The next year USEC negotiated the rate at which it purchases commercial uranium from its Russian partner, Tenex; however, the Bush administration delayed approval of the deal. Also, the US Department of Commerce decided to work toward imposing duties on imported uranium from European companies (it ruled that the companies were selling uranium at unfairly low prices). Also in 2001 USEC repurchased 20% of its common stock.

In early 2004 USEC announced that it selected Piketon, Ohio as the site for its American Centrifuge plant. In late 2004 CEO William Timbers left the company, and chairman James Mellor took over as interim CEO.

General Dynamics veteran John Welch was named president and CEO of USEC in 2005.

EXECUTIVES

Chairman: James R. (Jim) Mellor, age 78
President and CEO: John K. Welch, age 58,
$4,273,161 total compensation
SVP and CFO: John C. Barpoulis, age 44,
$1,042,893 total compensation
Controller and Chief Accounting Officer: J. Tracy Mey, age 48

SVP, Uranium Enrichment: Robert Van Namen, age 47, $1,060,333 total compensation
SVP, American Centrifuge and Russian HEU: Philip G. Sewell, age 62, $1,656,076 total compensation
SVP, General Counsel, and Secretary: Peter B. Saba, age 47
SVP Human Resources and Administration: W. Lance Wright, age 61, $1,137,837 total compensation
SVP External Relations: Christine M. Ciccone
VP Finance and Treasurer: Stephen S. Greene, age 51
VP Government Relations: E. John Neumann, age 61
VP American Centrifuge: Russell B. (Russ) Starkey Jr., age 66
VP Marketing and Sales: John M. A. Donelson, age 44
VP American Centrifuge: Paul Sullivan, age 48
Director Corporate Communications: Elizabeth Stuckle
Director Investor Relations: Steven Wingfield
Auditors: PricewaterhouseCoopers LLP

LOCATIONS

HQ: USEC Inc.
2 Democracy Center, 6903 Rockledge Dr.
Bethesda, MD 20817
Phone: 301-564-3200   **Fax:** 301-564-3201
Web: www.usec.com

2008 Sales

	$ mil.	% of total
US	1,212.5	75
Japan	242.6	15
Other countries	159.5	10
Total	**1,614.6**	**100**

PRODUCTS/OPERATIONS

2008 Sales

	$ mil.	% of total
Separative work units	1,175.5	73
Uranium	217.1	13
US government contracts	222.0	14
Total	**1,614.6**	**100**

COMPETITORS

AREVA
Belgonucleaire
BNFL
Cameco
Japan Nuclear Fuel

HISTORICAL FINANCIALS

Company Type: Public

Income Statement

FYE: December 31

	REVENUE ($ mil.)	NET INCOME ($ mil.)	NET PROFIT MARGIN	EMPLOYEES
12/08	1,614.6	48.7	3.0%	2,978
12/07	1,928.0	96.6	5.0%	2,866
12/06	1,848.6	106.2	5.7%	2,677
12/05	1,559.3	22.3	1.4%	2,762
12/04	1,417.2	23.5	1.7%	2,871
Annual Growth	**3.3%**	**20.0%**	**—**	**0.9%**

2008 Year-End Financials

Debt ratio: 49.5%	No. of shares (mil.): 113
Return on equity: 3.9%	Dividends
Cash ($ mil.): 249	Yield: 0.0%
Current ratio: 2.64	Payout: —
Long-term debt ($ mil.): 575	Market value ($ mil.): 506

Stock History

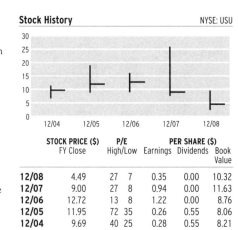

	STOCK PRICE ($) FY Close	P/E High/Low		PER SHARE ($) Earnings	Dividends	Book Value
12/08	4.49	27	7	0.35	0.00	10.32
12/07	9.00	27	8	0.94	0.00	11.63
12/06	12.72	13	8	1.22	0.00	8.76
12/05	11.95	72	35	0.26	0.55	8.06
12/04	9.69	40	25	0.28	0.55	8.21
Annual Growth	(17.5%)	—	—	5.7%	—	5.9%

USG Corporation

Where there's a wall, there's likely wallboard. USG, the maker of SHEETROCK, the world's #1 brand of wallboard, is one of the largest building products manufacturers and distributors in the US. The company operates in three divisions: North American Gypsum (more than half of USG's sales) manufactures wallboard, gypsum fiberboard, and other products for finishing interior walls, ceilings, and floors. The Worldwide Ceilings division makes interior ceiling grid systems and acoustic tile. USG's Building Products Distribution division distributes building products through L&W Supply. USG is the largest manufacturer of gypsum products in North America and the largest distributor of wallboard in the United States.

USG emerged from Chapter 11 bankruptcy protection in 2006 after establishing a $3.95 billion trust to pay asbestos claims. The company was one of several companies, including Owens Corning and W. R. Grace, that sought shelter from asbestos-related litigation in Chapter 11 to keep litigation from draining value from the company.

In a case of bad timing, the company emerged from bankruptcy a year before the construction industry suffered a severe downturn in 2007. USG's sales dropped 10% and its shipments of wallboard and other products fell. All was not lost, however: In 2007 L&W Supply purchased the inventory of California Wholesale Material Supply (CALPLY), which sells building products in seven western states and Mexico. The move is part of L&W's plan to grow its specialty dealer business.

To deal with the US downturn brought on by overbuilding and the subprime mortgage crisis, the company adjusted operations and programs and reduced its workforce by a third in 2008.

Currently, Warren Buffett's Berkshire Hathaway owns 17% of USG and German firm Gebr. Knauf Verwaltungsgesellschaft owns 15%.

However, in 2009, Buffet's Berkshire Hathaway, along with Fairfax Corp., purchased 26 million new convertible debt shares, injecting $400 million of much needed cash into the company. If Buffett chooses to convert his shares, he could increase his stake in USG to 32%.

HISTORY

In 1901 a group of 35 companies joined to form U.S.G., the largest gypsum producing and processing business in the industry. Sewell Avery became CEO in 1905 (he led U.S.G. until 1951).

U.S.G. began producing lime in 1915. It became United States Gypsum (U.S. Gypsum) in 1920 and began making paint in 1924. By 1931 it was producing insulating board and metal lath fields. It also added two lime businesses and two gypsum concerns.

Also in 1931 Avery became chairman of Montgomery Ward, managing both companies simultaneously. U.S. Gypsum entered asphalt roofing, mineral wool, hardboard, and asbestos-cement siding during the thirties. It made profits and paid dividends throughout the Depression.

Beginning in the late 1960s, U.S. Gypsum diversified into building materials and remodeling, buying such companies as Wallace Manufacturing (prefinished wood panels, 1970) and Kinkead Industries (steel doors and frames, 1972). U.S. Gypsum formed L&W Supply in 1971.

The company bought Masonite in 1984 and changed its name to USG the next year. It acquired Donn (remodeling materials) in 1986 and DAP (caulk and sealants) in 1987.

USG led a $776 million buyback of 20% of its stock to ward off a takeover that year. In 1988 Desert Partners of Midland, Texas, tried another takeover; the attempt was foiled nine months later when shareholders approved a management plan (including taking on $2.5 billion of new debt) to keep control of the company. By the end of 1989, USG had sold several assets and had shrunk by about 25%. Proceeds from the sale of Masonite (to International Paper Company), Kinkead, and Marlite netted $560 million, which was used to pay debt. USG defaulted on $40 million of scheduled payments to bondholders and banks in 1991, however, and sold its profitable DAP unit to the UK's Wassall for just $90 million.

The firm was among 20 manufacturers that agreed to a $1.3 billion class-action asbestos settlement in 1993. (The US Supreme Court voided the pact in 1997.) Also that year USG filed one of the largest prepackaged Chapter 11 bankruptcy cases on record. As a result of restructuring, USG cut its debt by $1.4 billion and its annual interest payments by $200 million. In 1994 USG sold 7.9 million new shares, raising $224 million to further reduce debt. Charges related to the sale or closure of certain operations contributed to another loss in 1995.

In 1997 USG announced a joint venture with Zhongbei Building Material Products Company; USG acquired 60% of the Chinese ceiling-grid manufacturer. In late 1999 the company acquired Sybex and The Synkoloid Company of Canada, both leading North American manufacturers of paper-faced metal corner bead (used to protect and strengthen the exposed edges of drywall).

In 2000 investor Warren Buffett revealed that he had built a 15% stake in USG. USG announced in 2001 that it would take an $850 million charge (for the fourth quarter of 2000) to cover against asbestos litigation. In June 2001 USG and 10 of its subsidiaries filed for bankruptcy protection.

The company closed a gypsum fiber panel plant in Nova Scotia, Canada, and a ceiling tile plant in Aubange, Belgium, in 2002. USG sold its UK-based access floor systems business in 2003. The next year subsidiary USG Interiors sold its relocatable walls business and ULTRAWALL System product line to California-based Ultrawall, LLC;

USG Interiors also agreed to supply the gypsum baseboard for use in the systems.

In 2005 USG took a $3.1 billion charge and outlined a plan to emerge from bankruptcy by settling outstanding claims; in 2006 it funded a trust with $900 million in cash and a $3.05 billion contingent note. That year it emerged from bankruptcy.

EXECUTIVES

Chairman and CEO: William C. Foote, age 58, $8,525,030 total compensation
President, COO and Director: James S. Metcalf, age 50, $3,787,538 total compensation
EVP and CFO: Richard H. (Rick) Fleming, age 61, $3,442,847 total compensation
VP and CTO: Dominic A. Dannessa, age 52
VP and CIO: Jennifer F. Scanlon, age 42
VP and Chief Innovation Officer: Donald S. Mueller, age 61
EVP and General Counsel: Stanley L. Ferguson, age 56, $1,793,276 total compensation
SVP Communications: Marcia S. (Marci) Kaminsky, age 50
SVP and Controller: D. Rick Lowes, age 54
SVP Human Resources: Brian J. Cook, age 51, $1,253,637 total compensation
VP and Treasurer: Karen L. Leets, age 52
VP; President and CEO, L&W Supply: Brendan J. Deely, age 43
VP; President, USG Building Systems: Fareed A, Khan, age 43
VP, Corporate Secretary, and Associate General Counsel: Ellis A. Regenbogen, age 62
VP; President, USG International; President, CGC Inc.: Christopher R. Griffin, age 47
Auditors: Deloitte & Touche LLP

LOCATIONS

HQ: USG Corporation
550 W. Adams St., Chicago, IL 60661
Phone: 312-436-4000   **Fax:** 312-436-4093
Web: www.usg.com

2008 Sales

	$ mil.	% of total
US	3,942	81
Other foreign	482	10
Canada	428	9
Adjustments	(244)	—
Total	**4,608**	**100**

PRODUCTS/OPERATIONS

2008 Sales

	$ mil.	% of total
North American Gypsum	2,358	46
Building Products Distribution	1,993	38
Worldwide Ceilings	846	16
Adjustments	(589)	—
Total	**4,608**	**100**

Selected Products

North American Gypsum
 DIAMOND (plaster products)
 DUROCK (cement board)
 FIBEROCK (fiber panels)
 LEVELROCK (poured gypsum underlayments)
 IMPERIAL (plaster products)
 RED TOP (plaster products)
 SHEETROCK (gypsum wallboard)
Worldwide Ceilings Products & Brands
 ACOUSTONE (ceiling tile)
 AURATONE (ceiling tile)
 CENTRICITEE (ceiling grid)
 COMPASSO (ceiling grid)
 CURVATURA (ceiling grid)
 DONN (ceiling grid)
 DX (ceiling grid)
 FINELINE (ceiling grid)

Selected Subsidiaries
CGC Inc. (Canada)
L&W Supply Corporation
United States Gypsum Company
USG Mexico SA (Mexico)

COMPETITORS

Allied Building Products
American Gypsum
Armstrong World Industries
BPB
CSR Limited
Eagle Materials
Georgia-Pacific
Gypsum Products
HeidelbergCement
Industrial Acoustics
James Hardie Industries
Knauf Gips KG
Lafarge
Lafarge North America
Louisiana-Pacific
New NGC
Pacific Coast Building Products
Rinker Materials
Saint-Gobain
Temple-Inland
Worthington Industries

HISTORICAL FINANCIALS
Company Type: Public

Income Statement

FYE: December 31

	REVENUE ($ mil.)	NET INCOME ($ mil.)	NET PROFIT MARGIN	EMPLOYEES
12/08	4,608.0	(463.0)	—	12,800
12/07	5,202.0	76.0	1.5%	14,800
12/06	5,810.0	288.0	5.0%	14,700
12/05	5,139.0	(1,425.0)	—	14,100
12/04	4,509.0	312.0	6.9%	13,800
Annual Growth	**0.5%**	**—**	**—**	**(1.9%)**

2008 Year-End Financials
Debt ratio: 105.9%
Return on equity: —
Cash ($ mil.): 471
Current ratio: 1.98
Long-term debt ($ mil.): 1,642
No. of shares (mil.): 99
Dividends
 Yield: 0.0%
 Payout: —
Market value ($ mil.): 798

Stock History

NYSE: USG

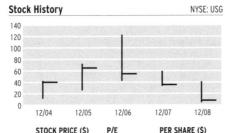

	STOCK PRICE ($) FY Close	P/E High/Low		PER SHARE ($) Earnings	Dividends	Book Value
12/08	8.04	—	—	(4.67)	0.00	15.62
12/07	35.79	75	44	0.78	0.00	22.10
12/06	54.80	28	10	4.33	0.00	15.46
12/05	65.00	—	—	(32.92)	0.00	(3.04)
12/04	40.27	6	2	7.26	0.00	10.32
Annual Growth	**(33.2%)**	**—**	**—**	**—**	**—**	**10.9%**

Valassis Communications

Valassis Communications offers door-to-door marketing without taking a toll on its shoes. A leading producer of newspaper inserts, Valassis sells space for advertising and coupons in its four-color booklets (accounting for about half of sales), which are distributed to some 60 million households through about 750 Sunday newspapers. Outside the US, Valassis produces the Shop & Save insert, which reaches about 5 million Canadian households. Valassis acquired direct mail marketing leader ADVO in 2007 for about $1.2 billion. The deal creates a giant in the marketing services industry, serving more than 15,000 advertisers worldwide with operations in more than 20 US states and nine other countries.

Before the transaction, ADVO reached about 114 million US households with its shared-mail distribution operations — that's 90% of the country's homes. The ADVO deal is an effort by Valassis to look for growth beyond the US newspaper insert business, which the company dominates. (News Corporation's News America is the industry's other major player.) In early 2008, the company changed the name of ADVO to Valassis Direct Mail and integrated its product portfolio into its own.

At the same time, Valassis launched its newest offering, RedPlum, a four-page advertisement booklet reaching 77 million households on a weekly basis.

HISTORY

George F. Valassis started commercial printing firm GFV Communications in 1969. Knowing that publishers had the technology to insert TV listings, Valassis joined with ad man Ted Isaacs in 1972 to pioneer freestanding newspaper inserts as a way to get full-color ads circulated at a lower cost. The idea was slow to catch on and Isaacs bailed out in the mid-1970s. By 1979, however, sales had reached $35 million.

That year Valassis turned the business over to son-in-law Larry Johnson, who recruited school chum David Brandon to help run the company. The industry exploded during the 1980s, leading to brutal price wars, but GFV remained the market leader. In 1986 Valassis sold the company for $400 million to Consolidated Press Holdings (CPH). Brandon was appointed president in 1989. Changing its name to Valassis Communications, the company went public in 1992 with CPH holding a 49% stake.

In 1993 Sullivan Marketing, backed by Morgan Stanley, tried muscling into the market, forcing prices down. Valassis cut prices to protect its market share, and Sullivan exited the business the next year. The company made several expansion efforts, including establishing Valassis of Canada through its 1995 acquisition of Canadian sale promoter McIntyre & Dodd. But in 1997 it ended its Mexican joint venture (begun in 1994) and French operations (acquired in 1994).

In 1997 Consolidated Press Holdings sold its stake in the company to the public, and Brandon added chairman to his title. Valassis put $13 million into capital improvements to gear up for future growth. The next year Alan Schultz replaced Brandon as chairman, president, and CEO.

Valassis acquired 50% of startup Save.com in 1999 to offer coupons over the Internet. It also bought a majority stake in Independent Delivery Services, which provides e-commerce software to grocery stores, and a 30% stake in Relationship Marketing Group. In 2000 Valassis expanded its online holdings with a minority investment in Coupons.com. Save.com shut down in 2001 amid the dot-com shake-out.

Keeping the acquisitions going, in 2002 the company bought the remaining stakes of Valassis Retail Marketing Systems. In 2003 Valassis acquired PreVision Marketing, LLC. The following year Catalina Marketing sold its direct mail division to Valassis, strengthening the company's own 1-to-1 loyalty-building direct mail business.

Valassis made huge waves in the marketing services industry in March 2007 when it acquired direct mail marketing leader ADVO for about $1.2 billion.

EXECUTIVES

Chairman, President, and CEO: Alan F. Schultz, age 50, $3,665,544 total compensation
EVP, CFO, and Director: Robert L. Recchia, age 52, $1,343,849 total compensation
SVP and Chief Information Officer: John Lieblang, age 51
Chief Sales Officer: Robert A. Mason, age 51
Chief Marketing Officer: Suzanne C. (Suzie) Brown, age 49
EVP Manufacturing and Client Services: William F. (Bill) Hogg Jr., age 62, $1,202,310 total compensation
EVP Sales and Marketing: Richard P. Herpich, age 56, $877,841 total compensation
SVP Strategic Sourcing: William (Bill) Blackmer
SVP Human Resources and Cultural Engagement: Carol Spann
SVP Administration, General Counsel, and Secretary: Todd Wisely
VP Consumer Engagement: Lisa Reynolds
President and CEO, NCH Marketing Services: Brian J. Husselbee, age 57, $709,662 total compensation
Director Investor Relations and Corporate Communications: Mary Broaddus
Director Talent Acquisition and Allocation: Christine Karaptian
Auditors: Deloitte & Touche LLP

LOCATIONS

HQ: Valassis Communications, Inc.
19975 Victor Pkwy., Livonia, MI 48152
Phone: 734-591-3000 **Fax:** 734-591-4994
Web: www.valassis.com

2008 Sales

	$ mil.	% of total
US	2,310.9	97
Other countries	71.0	3
Total	**2,381.9**	**100**

PRODUCTS/OPERATIONS

2008 Sales

	$ mil.	% of total
Shared mail (ADVO)	1,370.8	58
Neighborhood targeted products	469.2	20
Free-standing inserts	370.2	15
International, digital media & services	171.7	7
Total	**2,381.9**	**100**

Selected Products and Services

Household targeted
  Direct mail advertising and sampling
  Internet-delivered promotions
  Software and analytics

International and services
  Coupon clearing, promotion, and marketing
  Promotion security and consulting services
Market delivered products
  Cooperative free-standing inserts
  Run of Press
Neighborhood targeted products
  Door Hangers
  Preprinted inserts
  Newspaper delivered product sampling
  Newspaper Polybag advertising

COMPETITORS

Acxiom
Catalina Marketing
Grey Group
Harte-Hanks
HighQ BPO
MailSouth
News America Marketing
News Corp.
Norwood Promotional Products
Outlook Group
Penn Lithographics
Quebecor
R.R. Donnelley
SPAR Group
Sunflower Group
Valpak Direct Marketing Systems
Vertis Inc
yesmail

HISTORICAL FINANCIALS

Company Type: Public

Income Statement

FYE: December 31

	REVENUE ($ mil.)	NET INCOME ($ mil.)	NET PROFIT MARGIN	EMPLOYEES
12/08	2,381.9	(207.5)	—	7,200
12/07	2,242.2	58.0	2.6%	7,500
12/06	1,043.5	51.3	4.9%	3,600
12/05	1,131.0	95.4	8.4%	3,600
12/04	1,044.1	100.7	9.6%	4,100
Annual Growth	**22.9%**	**—**	**—**	**15.1%**

2008 Year-End Financials

Debt ratio: 10,000.0%
Return on equity: —
Cash ($ mil.): 127
Current ratio: 1.22
Long-term debt ($ mil.): 1,112
No. of shares (mil.): 48
Dividends
  Yield: 0.0%
  Payout: —
Market value ($ mil.): 63

Stock History

NYSE: VCI

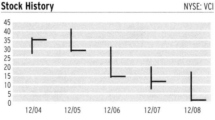

	STOCK PRICE ($) FY Close	P/E High/Low		Earnings	PER SHARE ($) Dividends	Book Value
12/08	1.32	—	—	(4.32)	0.00	0.11
12/07	11.69	16	6	1.21	0.00	4.57
12/06	14.50	29	13	1.07	0.00	3.48
12/05	29.07	21	15	1.90	0.00	2.15
12/04	35.01	19	14	1.93	0.00	2.92
Annual Growth	**(55.9%)**	**—**	**—**	**—**	**—**	**(55.7%)**

Valero Energy

Valero Energy is on a mission. Named after the Alamo (the Mission San Antonio de Valero), Valero is the largest independent oil refiner in the US. The company refines low-cost residual oil and heavy crude into cleaner-burning, higher-margin products, including low-sulfur diesels. It operates 16 refineries (with a total production capacity of about 3 million barrels per day) located in California, Delaware, Louisiana, New Jersey, Oklahoma, Tennessee, Texas, and in Aruba and Canada. It also has a network of some 5,800 retail gas stations and wholesale outlets bearing the Corner Store, Diamond Shamrock, Shamrock, Ultramar, Valero, Stop N Go, and Beacon names in 44 US states and in Canada.

In 2008 Valero announced that because of the US economic slowdown limiting fuel demand it was considering a long term strategy of selling about a third of its North American refineries, and exploring new projects in the Middle East and Asia. That year the company sold its Krotz Springs, Louisiana, refinery to Alon USA Energy for $333 million. It also announced in 2009 that it would close its Texas City refinery. The same year Valero agreed to acquire Dow Chemical's 45% interest in Dutch refinery Total Raffinaderij Nederland N.V.

Also that year the company successfully bid to buy seven ethanol production facilities from VeraSun Energy, which is operating under Chapter 11 bankruptcy protection. Valero paid about $475 million for the facilities.

The company became a retail giant overnight with its Ultramar Diamond Shamrock purchase in 2001. The 2005 acquisition of Premcor made Valero, the largest independent refiner on the Gulf Coast, a major national player.

HISTORY

Valero Energy was created as a result of the sins of its father, Houston-based Coastal States Gas Corporation. Led by flamboyant entrepreneur Oscar Wyatt, energy giant Coastal had established Lo-Vaca Gathering Company as a gas marketing subsidiary. Bound by long-term contracts to several Texas cities, Coastal was not able to meet its contractual obligations when gas prices rose in the early 1970s, and major litigation against the company resulted. The Texas Railroad Commission (the energy-regulating authority) ordered Coastal to refund customers $1.6 billion.

To meet the requirements, 55% of Lo-Vaca was spun off to disgruntled former customers as Valero Energy at the end of 1979. The new company was born fully grown — as the largest intrastate pipeline in Texas — with accountant-cum-CEO Bill Greehey, the court-appointed chief of Lo-Vaca, at its head. Greehey relocated the company to San Antonio, where it took its Valero name (from the Alamo, or Mission San Antonio de Valero) and put some distance between itself and its discredited former parent. Under Greehey's direction, Valero developed a squeaky-clean image by giving to charities, stressing a dress code, and keeping facilities clean.

Greehey diversified the company into refining unleaded gasoline. Valero bought residual fuel oil from Saudi Arabian refiners and in 1981 built a refinery in Corpus Christi, Texas, which went on line two years later. But in 1984 a glut of unleaded gasoline on the US market from European refiners undercut Valero's profits. To stay afloat, Valero sold pipeline assets, including 50% of its West Texas Pipeline in 1985 and 51% of its major pipeline operations in 1987. Refining margins finally began to improve in 1988. With one of the most modern refineries in the US, Valero did not have to spend a bundle to upgrade its refining processes to meet the tougher EPA requirements of the 1990s.

In 1992 Valero expanded its refinery's production capacity and acquired two gas processing plants and several hundred miles of gas pipelines from struggling oil firm Oryx Energy (acquired by Kerr-McGee in 1999). That year Valero became the first non-Mexican business engaged in Mexican gasoline production when it signed a deal with state oil company Petróleos Mexicanos S.A. to build a gasoline additive plant there.

To expand its natural gas business substantially, in 1994 Valero bought back the 51% of Valero Natural Gas Partners it didn't own. Valero also teamed up with regional oil company Swift Energy in a transportation, marketing, and processing agreement. As part of that arrangement, Valero agreed to build a pipeline linking Swift's Texas gas field with a Valero plant.

In 1997 the company sold Valero Natural Gas to California electric utility PG&E, gaining $1.5 billion for expansion. It then purchased Salomon's oil refining unit, Basis Petroleum (two refineries in Texas and one in Louisiana), and the next year picked up Mobil's refinery in Paulsboro, New Jersey.

With low crude oil prices hurting its bottom line in 1999, Valero explored partnerships with other refiners as a way to cut operating costs. In 2000 the company bought Exxon Mobil's 130,000 barrel-per-day Benicia, California, refinery, along with 340 retail outlets, for about $1 billion.

In 2001 Valero gained two small refineries when it bought Huntway Refining, a leading supplier of asphalt in California. Dwarfing that deal, Valero also bought Ultramar Diamond Shamrock for $4 billion in cash and stock (it assumed about $2.1 billion of debt in the deal). As part of the deal, and to comply with the demands of regulators, in 2002 Valero sold the Golden Eagle (San Francisco-area) refinery and 70 retail service stations in Northern California to Tesoro for $945 million.

In 2003 the company acquired Orion Refining's Louisiana refinery for about $530 million, and in 2004 it acquired an Aruba refinery from asset-shedding El Paso Corp. for $640 million. Suncor Energy bought a Colorado-based refinery from Valero for a reported $30 million in 2005.

Greehey turned over the leadership reins to another company veteran, Bill Klesse, in early 2006. The next year the company sold its Lima, Ohio, refinery to Husky Energy.

EXECUTIVES

Chairman, President, and CEO: William R. (Bill) Klesse, age 62, $10,471,795 total compensation
EVP and COO: Richard J. (Rich) Marcogliese, age 56, $5,990,158 total compensation
EVP and CFO: Michael S. (Mike) Ciskowski, age 51, $3,111,722 total compensation
SVP and CIO: Hal Zesch
EVP Corporate Development and Strategic Planning: S. Eugene (Gene) Edwards, age 52
EVP and General Counsel: Kimberly S. (Kim) Bowers, age 44, $1,278,998 total compensation
EVP Marketing and Supply: Joseph W. (Joe) Gorder, age 51, $1,637,542 total compensation
SVP Corporate Law and Secretary: Jay D. Browning
SVP Retail Marketing: Gary L. Arthur Jr.

SVP and Controller: Clayton E. (Clay) Killinger
SVP Human Resources: R. Michael (Mike) Crownover
VP Internal Audit: Lee Bailey
VP and Treasurer: Donna M. Titzman
VP Investor Relations and Corporate Communications: Eric Fisher
VP Wholesale Marketing: Eric Moeller
VP Regional Wholesale Marketing: Lee Rahmberg
VP Products Supply: Dave Parker
Auditors: KPMG LLP

LOCATIONS

HQ: Valero Energy Corporation
1 Valero Way, San Antonio, TX 78249
Phone: 210-345-2000 **Fax:** 210-345-2646
Web: www.valero.com

2008 Sales

	$ mil.	% of total
US	101,141	85
Canada	9,961	8
Other countries	8,012	7
Total	**119,114**	**100**

PRODUCTS/OPERATIONS

2008 Sales

	$ mil.	% of total
Refining	108,586	91
Retail	10,528	9
Total	**119,114**	**100**

2008 Sales

	$ mil.	% of total
Refining		
Gasolines & blendstocks	48,052	40
Distillates	45,672	38
Petrochemicals	4,221	4
Lubes & asphalts	2,770	2
Other	7,871	7
Retail		
Fuel sales (gasoline & diesel)	8,750	8
Merchandise sales & other	1,446	1
Home heating oil	332	—
Total	**119,114**	**100**

Selected Products

Asphalt
Bunker oils
CARB Phase II gasoline
Clean-burning oxygenates
Conventional gasoline
Crude mineral spirits
Customized clean-burning gasoline blends for export markets
Gasoline blendstocks
Home heating oil
Jet fuel
Kerosene
Low-sulfur diesel
Lube oils
Petrochemical feedstocks
Petroleum coke
Premium reformulated and conventional gasolines
Reformulated gasoline
Sulfur

COMPETITORS

BP	Motiva Enterprises
Chevron	National Cooperative
CITGO	Refinery Association
ConocoPhillips	Shell Oil Products
Exxon	Sinclair Oil
Frontier Oil	Sunoco
Hess Corporation	Tesoro
Holly Corporation	Texas Petrochemicals
Marathon Petroleum	TOTAL

HISTORICAL FINANCIALS

Company Type: Public

Income Statement

FYE: December 31

	REVENUE ($ mil.)	NET INCOME ($ mil.)	NET PROFIT MARGIN	EMPLOYEES
12/08	119,114.0	(1,131.0)	—	21,765
12/07	95,327.0	5,234.0	5.5%	21,651
12/06	91,833.0	5,461.0	5.9%	21,836
12/05	82,162.0	3,577.0	4.4%	22,068
12/04	54,618.6	1,791.3	3.3%	19,797
Annual Growth	**21.5%**	**—**	**—**	**2.4%**

2008 Year-End Financials

Debt ratio: 40.1%
Return on equity: —
Cash ($ mil.): —
Current ratio: 1.52
Long-term debt ($ mil.): 6,264
No. of shares (mil.): 563
Dividends
Yield: 2.6%
Payout: —
Market value ($ mil.): 12,178

Stock History

NYSE: VLO

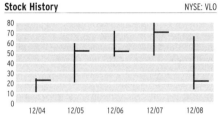

	STOCK PRICE ($) FY Close	P/E High/Low		PER SHARE ($) Earnings	Dividends	Book Value
12/08	21.64	—	—	(2.16)	0.57	27.76
12/07	70.03	9	5	8.88	0.48	32.89
12/06	51.16	8	5	8.64	0.30	33.06
12/05	51.60	10	3	6.10	0.19	26.74
12/04	22.70	7	4	3.27	0.14	13.86
Annual Growth	**(1.2%)**	**—**	**—**	**—**	**42.0%**	**19.0%**

The Valspar Corporation

Valspar wants you to put on a coat. The firm, which was founded in 1806, makes a variety of coatings and paints for manufacturing, automotive, and food-packaging companies, as well as for consumers. The company's industrial coatings — used by OEMs, including building product, appliance, and furniture makers — include coatings for metal, wood, plastic, and glass. Packaging products include coatings and inks for rigid containers, such as food and beverage cans. Its consumer paints include interior and exterior paints, primers, stains, and varnishes sold through mass merchandisers such as Wal-Mart and Lowe's. Valspar also makes auto paints, specialty polymers, colorants, and gelcoats.

Valspar has boosted its core business through acquisitions of coatings companies around the world; in the past decade it has made more than 20 acquisitions, including joint venture interests. That strategy has made Valspar one of the top global industrial coatings makers. Valspar acquired US stain and finish manufacturer Samuel Cabot in 2005. The next year the company reached into the Chinese market with the acquisition of an 80% stake in coatings manufacturer Huarun Paints, a maker of wood and furniture coatings. Huarun has annual sales of about $180 million. (In 2007 Valspar's sales in China reached 10% of total sales for the first time.) It also acquired the powder coatings business (for office furniture) of H.B. Fuller in late 2006 and coil coatings businesses in Brazil and Mexico in 2008.

Lowe's accounts for more than 10% of the company's sales, and the hardware and home repair giant has named Valspar paint supplier of the year eight times. In 2007 it began to use the Valspar brand, replacing three fairly generic-sounding store brands, at Lowe's in an effort to boost consumer recognition. Valspar has made a point to tailor its products to the needs of retail customers, to the point of placing in-store employees to answer paint questions.

HISTORY

Samuel Tuck began the company as Paint and Color in Boston in 1806. It was known as Valentine & Co. by 1866. Then-owner Lawson Valentine hired chemist Charles Homer (brother of artist Winslow Homer), who perfected finishing varnishes. In 1903 Valentine's grandson, L. Valentine Pulsifer, invented the first clear varnish — dubbed Valspar — which became the company's name in 1932. Valspar grew by mergers including Rockcote Paint (1960) and Minnesota Paints (1970). CEO Angus Wurtele became chairman in 1973. Valspar's sales tripled by the time it acquired Mobil Oil's packaging coatings business in 1984.

Valspar formed a joint venture with China Merchants in 1994 (packaging coatings) and then bought US-based Sunbelt Coatings (auto refinishing, 1995), Gordon Bartels (packaging coatings, 1996), and Sureguard (industrial coatings, 1997). Valspar swapped its maintenance coatings business in 1997 with Ameron International's product finishes unit and formed a joint venture in Brazil with Renner Herrmann SA.

President and CEO Richard Rompala replaced Wurtele as chairman in 1998. Acquisitions that year included Plasti-Kote (consumer aerosol and specialty paints), Australia-based Anzol (packaging and industrial coatings), and Dyflex Polymers (specialty water-based polymers).

The company began divesting noncore businesses, selling its functional powder coatings unit in 1998 and its marine and packaging coatings product lines in 1999. Also in 1999 it bought the packaging coatings business of Dexter Corporation (now a part of Life Technologies) and its subsidiary in France and the Netherlands-based resins maker Dyflex. The next year Valspar bought rival coatings maker Lilly Industries in a $975 million deal, which made Valspar a top global maker of coatings for wood, mirrors, and coils (used in doors and appliances).

From 1996 to 2001 in a four-phase deal, the company acquired packaging coatings firm Coates Coatings, which operated in North America, Europe, Australia, Africa, and Asia. This acquisition boosted Valspar into the top of the market for metal packaging coatings.

In 2004 the company acquired Dutch automotive coatings maker De Beer Lakfabrieken, as well as the Forest Products division of wood coatings firm Associated Chemists.

William Mansfield became CEO in February 2005, but Rompala stayed on as chairman until his retirement in mid-2005. Thomas McBurney assumed the chairmanship for two years before Mansfield was named chairman in 2007.

EXECUTIVES

Chairman, President, and CEO:
  William L. (Bill) Mansfield, age 61
President, COO, and Director: Gary E. Hendrickson, age 52
SVP and CFO: Lori A. Walker, age 51
VP Information Systems and Furniture Solutions:
  Kathleen J. (Kate) Bass
EVP: Steven L. Erdahl, age 56
EVP, General Counsel, and Secretary: Rolf Engh, age 55
EVP: Paul C. Reyelts, age 62
SVP Global Architectural: Howard C. Heckes, age 43
SVP Human Resources: Anthony L. Blaine, age 41
Group VP Architectural: Kenneth H. Arthur
Group VP General Industrial and Composites:
  Brian Falline
Group VP Global Packaging and President Europe, Middle east and Africa: Bern Ouimette
VP Corporate Purchasing: Thomas V. Kelliher
VP Research and Development: Larry B. Brandenburger
VP Coil and Extrusion Coatings: Alfred N. (Al) Dunlop
VP Sales and Marketing Architectural Group:
  Steve Person
VP and Controller: Tracy C. Jokinen
VP and Treasurer: Tyler N. Treat
President, Latin America: J.R. Benites
Auditors: Ernst & Young LLP

LOCATIONS

HQ: The Valspar Corporation
  1101 3rd St. South, Minneapolis, MN 55415
Phone: 612-332-7371   **Fax:** 612-375-7723
Web: www.valspar.com

2008 Sales

	$ mil.	% of total
US	2,067.4	59
Other countries	1,033.6	30
China	381.4	11
Total	**3,482.4**	**100**

PRODUCTS/OPERATIONS

2008 Sales

	$ mil.	% of total
Coatings	2,053.7	59
Paints	1,127.1	32
Other	301.6	9
Total	**3,482.4**	**100**

Selected Products

Industrial
  Fillers
  Mirror coatings
  Primers
  Stains
  Topcoats
Architectural, automotive, and specialty
  Aerosols
  Enamels
  Faux finishes
  Interior and exterior paints
  Primers
  Sealers
  Stains
  Varnishes
Packaging
  Coatings
  Inks
Other
  Colorants
  Composites
  Powder coatings for metal surfaces
  Specialty polymers

Selected Brands

Cabot
De Beer
Goof Off
House of Kolor
McCloskey
Mr. Spray
Plasti-Kote
Tempo
Valspar

COMPETITORS

Akzo Nobel
BASF Coatings AG
BEHR
Benjamin Moore
Detrex
Dunn-Edwards
DuPont
Ferro
H.B. Fuller
Kelly-Moore
NL Industries
PPG Industries
RPM International
Sherwin-Williams
Spraylat

HISTORICAL FINANCIALS

Company Type: Public

Income Statement

FYE: Last Friday in October

	REVENUE ($ mil.)	NET INCOME ($ mil.)	NET PROFIT MARGIN	EMPLOYEES
10/08	3,482.4	150.8	4.3%	9,400
10/07	3,249.3	153.5	4.7%	10,000
10/06	2,978.1	175.3	5.9%	9,556
10/05	2,713.9	147.6	5.4%	7,540
10/04	2,440.7	142.8	5.9%	7,500
Annual Growth	**9.3%**	**1.4%**	**—**	**5.8%**

2008 Year-End Financials

Debt ratio: 52.5%
Return on equity: 10.6%
Cash ($ mil.): 90
Current ratio: 1.19
Long-term debt ($ mil.): 763
No. of shares (mil.): 118
Dividends
  Yield: 2.7%
  Payout: 40.6%
Market value ($ mil.): 2,422

Stock History

NYSE: VAL

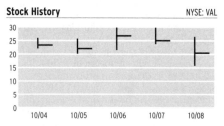

	STOCK PRICE ($) FY Close	P/E High/Low		PER SHARE ($) Earnings	Dividends	Book Value
10/08	20.45	19	12	1.38	0.56	12.27
10/07	25.03	20	16	1.50	0.52	11.66
10/06	26.79	17	13	1.71	0.44	10.47
10/05	22.05	18	14	1.42	0.40	8.96
10/04	23.33	19	16	1.36	0.36	8.45
Annual Growth	**(3.2%)**	**—**	**—**	**0.4%**	**11.7%**	**9.8%**

The Vanguard Group

If you buy low and sell high, invest for the long term, don't panic, and generally disapprove of those whippersnappers at Fidelity, then you may end up in the Vanguard of the financial market. The Vanguard Group offers individual and institutional investors a line of popular mutual funds and brokerage services. Claiming more than $1 trillion of assets under management, the firm is battling FMR (AKA Fidelity) for the title of largest retail mutual fund manager on the planet. Vanguard's fund options include more than 180 stock, bond, mixed, and international offerings, as well as variable annuity portfolios; its Vanguard 500 Index Fund is one of the largest in the US.

In 2008 Vanguard joined the government's money-market insurance plan, designed to keep nervous investors from emptying their funds by safeguarding deposits.

The company is known as much for its puritanical thriftiness and conservative investing as for its line of index funds, which track the performance of such groups of stock as the S&P 500. Retired company founder John Bogle is sometimes derisively called "St. Jack" for his zealous criticism of industry practices, but the company's reputation for being squeaky clean appears to have kept it unscathed by the mutual fund industry scandals of recent years.

Unlike other fund managers, Vanguard is set up like a mutual insurance company. The funds (and by extension, their more than 9 million investors) own the company, so fees are low to nonexistent; funds are operated on a tight budget so as not to eat into results. The company spends next to nothing on advertising, relying instead on strong returns and word-of-mouth.

And despite its no-broker, no-load background, Vanguard has developed cheap ways to dole out advice, especially through the use of toll-free numbers and the Internet and by quietly touting its online brokerage service.

HISTORY

A distant cousin of Daniel Boone, Walter Morgan knew a few things about pioneering. He was the first to offer a fund with a balance of stocks and bonds, serendipitously introduced early in 1929, months before the stock market collapsed. Morgan's balanced Wellington fund (named after Napoleon's vanquisher) emerged effectively unscathed.

John Bogle's senior thesis on mutual funds impressed fellow Princeton alum Morgan, who hired Bogle in 1951. Morgan retired in 1967 and picked Bogle to replace him. That year Bogle engineered a merger with old-school investment firm Thorndike, Doran, Paine and Lewis. After culture clashes and four years of shrinking assets, the Thorndike-dominated board fired Bogle, who appealed to the mutual funds and their separate board of directors. The fund directors decided to split up the funds and the advisory business.

Bogle named the fund company The Vanguard Group, after the flagship of Lord Nelson, another Napoleon foe. Vanguard worked like a co-operative; mutual fund shareholders owned the company, so all services were provided at cost. The Wellington Management Company remained Vanguard's distributor until 1977, when Bogle convinced Vanguard's board to drop the

affiliation. Without Wellington as the intermediary, Vanguard sold its funds directly to consumers as no-load funds (without service charges). In 1976 the company launched the Vanguard Index 500, the first index fund. These measures attracted new investors in droves.

Vanguard rode the 1980s boom. Its Windsor fund grew so large the company closed it, launching Windsor II in 1985. Vanguard weathered the 1987 crash and began the 1990s as the US's #4 mutual fund company. The actively managed funds of FMR (better known as Fidelity), most notably its Magellan fund, led the market then. The retirement of legendary Magellan manager Peter Lynch and the fund's consequential underperformance spurred a rush to index funds. Vanguard moved up to #2.

Vanguard played against type in 1995 when it introduced the Vanguard Horizon Capital Growth stock fund, an aggressively managed fund designed to vie directly with Fidelity's funds.

In 1997 Vanguard added brokerage services and began selling its own and other companies' funds on the Internet to allow clients to consolidate their financial activities. In 1998 Bogle passed the chairmanship to CEO John Brennan, a soft-spoken technology wonk. Morgan died that year at age 100.

Investors were ruffled when 70-year-old Bogle announced that corporate age limits would force him to leave the board of directors at the end of 1999. (Bogle retains an office at Vanguard headquarters and remains popular on the speaker circuit.)

Despite Vanguard's stated commitment to the little guy, by late 2002 the company was forced to mitigate realities of the economy and started courting investors with bigger bankrolls; it also raised fees for some customers with smaller accounts.

EXECUTIVES

Chairman: John J. (Jack) Brennan, age 54
President, CEO, and Director:
  F. William (Bill) McNabb III, age 51
Managing Director and CIO: Paul Heller
Chief Investment Officer: George U. (Gus) Sauter
Managing Director, Human Resources:
  Kathleen C. Gubanich
Managing Director, Institutional Investor Group:
  R. Gregory Barton
Managing Director, Planning and Development Group:
  Michael S. Miller
General Counsel: Heidi Stam
Managing Director, International Operations:
  James M. Norris
Managing Director, Strategy and Finance Group:
  Glenn Reed
Managing Director, Retail Investor Group:
  Mortimer J. (Tim) Buckley
Principal Education Markets Group: Alba Martinez

LOCATIONS

HQ: The Vanguard Group, Inc.
  100 Vanguard Blvd., Malvern, PA 19355
Phone: 610-648-6000   **Fax:** 610-669-6605
Web: www.vanguard.com

PRODUCTS/OPERATIONS

Selected Funds
500 Index Fund
Admiral Treasury Money Market Fund
Asset Allocation Fund
Balanced Index Fund
California Long-Term Tax-Exempt Fund
California Tax-Exempt Money Market Fund
Capital Opportunity Fund

Capital Value Fund
Convertible Securities Fund
Developed Markets Index Fund
Diversified Equity Fund
Dividend Appreciation Index Fund
Emerging Markets Stock Index Fund
Energy Fund
Equity Income Fund
European Stock Index Fund
Explorer Fund
Federal Money Market Fund
FTSE Social Index Fund
Global Equity Fund
GNMA Fund
Growth and Income Fund
Growth Equity Fund
Growth Index Fund
Health Care Fund
High-Yield Corporate Fund
Inflation-Protected Securities Fund
Insured Long-Term Tax-Exempt Fund
Intermediate-Term Bond Index Fund
International Explorer Fund
International Growth Fund
International Value Fund
Large-Cap Index Fund
LifeStrategy Growth Fund
LifeStrategy Income Fund
Limited-Term Tax-Exempt Fund
Long-Term Tax-Exempt Fund
Long-Term Treasury Fund
Mid-Cap Growth Fund
Mid-Cap Index Fund
Morgan Growth Fund
New Jersey Tax-Exempt Money Market Fund
New York Long-Term Tax-Exempt Fund
Ohio Long-Term Tax-Exempt Fund
Pacific Stock Index Fund
Pennsylvania Tax-Exempt Money Market Fund
Precious Metals and Mining Fund
Prime Money Market Fund
PRIMECAP Fund
REIT Index Fund
Selected Value Fund
Short-Term Federal Fund
STAR Fund
Strategic Equity Fund
Target Retirement 2010 Fund
Target Retirement 2015 Fund
Target Retirement 2020 Fund
Target Retirement 2025 Fund
Target Retirement 2030 Fund
Target Retirement 2035 Fund
Target Retirement 2040 Fund
Target Retirement 2045 Fund
Target Retirement 2050 Fund
Tax-Exempt Money Market Fund
Tax-Managed Growth and Income Fund
Tax-Managed International Fund
Total Bond Market Index Fund
Total International Stock Index Fund
Total Stock Market Index Fund
Treasury Money Market Fund
U.S. Growth Fund
U.S. Value Fund
Value Index Fund
Wellesley Income Fund

COMPETITORS

AIG	Invesco Aim
AllianceBernstein	Janus Capital
American Century	Legg Mason
AXA Financial	MFS
BlackRock	Principal Financial
Charles Schwab	Putnam
FMR	T. Rowe Price
Franklin Resources	TIAA-CREF
Invesco	USAA

VeriSign, Inc.

VeriSign has vowed to serve and protect Internet interactions. The company is a big part of what makes the Internet work. It operates two of the world's 13 root nameservers, which assign Internet protocol addresses to devices communicating across the Internet. VeriSign is also the only issuer of the .com and .net domain names that are sold to users by companies such as domain registrars Go Daddy and Register.com. In addition to its registry business, VeriSign provides digital certificate and SSL (secure socket layer) services for secure communications and transactions online. More than 90,000 domains in 145 countries use its digital certificates and 96 of the world's 100 largest banks use its SSL protection.

In support of its various Internet and communications offerings, VeriSign operates an enormous amount of Internet infrastructure, including secure data centers, routing and switching equipment, and servers. In 2007 it announced an initiative called Project Titan, aiming to grow the capacity of its infrastructure by 10 times by the year 2010.

VeriSign maintains its exclusive grip on Web site naming rights under agreements with ICANN and the US Department of Commerce. Originally granted that right in 2001, the company's contract was renewed in 2006, extending its rights to maintain the .com (and .net) registries until 2012. In 2008 VeriSign negotiated with ICANN for a fee increase for .com and .net domain registration, resulting in increases from $6.42 to $6.86 and from $3.85 to $4.23, respectively. These fees are paid by the domain name registrars. (VeriSign is not itself a registrar — it exited that business with the sale of Network Solutions in 2003.)

In 2007 VeriSign announced a major restructuring that included plans to divest all of its business lines in the Communications Services Group, encompassing connectivity and interoperability services, billing, and mobile commerce. The company agreed to sell the unit to Transaction Network Services for $230 million in 2009.

Continuing to hone its focus on Internet naming and authentication services, the company also divested other noncore assets in 2009, including its Managed Security Services business, sold to security services company SecureWorks, and its Real-Time Publisher Services (RTP) business, which provided content aggregation and business intelligence services. Later in the year, it agreed to sell its Messaging Business to network engineering services firm Syniverse Holdings for $175 million. It also sold its global security consulting business to ATT.

After the change in direction was mostly complete, the company named Mark McLaughlin, former EVP products and marketing, as president and COO in early 2009. Later in the year, he became CEO and a director.

HISTORY

VeriSign was founded by Stratton Sclavos and Jim Bidzos in 1995. Sclavos, a veteran of MIPS Computer Systems and two failed Silicon Valley startups, ran the company as RSA's digital certification division until it was spun off in 1995. Its early backers included Ameritech, Mitsubishi, and Visa. Apple and Netscape were among its first customers.

In 1996 VeriSign formed a Japanese subsidiary. The next year the company debuted its Financial Server ID, a digital certificate for use with the Open Financial Exchange, a home banking standard backed by Microsoft. VeriSign went public in early 1998 and added Sumitomo Bank and UPS as customers. Also in 1998 the company bought Secure It (Internet security consulting services).

In early 2000 the company stepped up expansion efforts, buying South Africa-based Thawte Consulting (digital certification products) and Signio (Internet payment services). Later that year VeriSign acquired Internet domain registrar Network Solutions for about $20 billion.

Looking to expand its communications service offerings, in 2001 the company acquired network service provider Illuminet Holdings for $1.3 billion. Also in 2001, VeriSign reached an agreement with ICANN to become the exclusive operator of the top level .com domain registry until 2007.

The company continued its acquisitive ways in 2002 and 2003, purchasing H.O. Systems ($350 million) and UNC-Embratel ($16 million). In late 2003 the company sold the portion of Network Solutions that sells domain names and provides Web hosting services to Pivotal Private Equity for about $100 million.

In 2004 the company acquired managed security services provider Guardent for about $140 million, and later that year purchased Germany-based wireless content service provider Jamba! for about $273 million.

The company moved beyond its legacy encryption and digital certificate products with a string of purchases in 2005. Verisign bought LightSurf, a provider of multimedia messaging and interoperability solutions for the wireless market, for $270 million. Later that year Verisign purchased Authorize.Net Holdings' PrePay INS business (wireless phone rate plan and calling plan tracking products) for about $17 million. Quick on the heels of the PrePay INS deal came VeriSign's purchase of iDEFENSE for $40 million in cash. Other 2005 purchases included Moreover Technologies (news aggregation), Weblogs.com (blog tracking), and Retail Solutions (point-of-sale tracking). The company sold its payment gateway business to Pay Pal, a subsidiary of eBay, for $370 million in 2005.

VeriSign's acquisition tear continued in 2006. It purchased Web-based billing and client management software company CallVision for $30 million in cash, as well as m-Qube, a developer of software for delivering content and connectivity services to wireless subscribers. It acquired Internet transaction security specialist GeoTrust for $125 million in cash.

Also in 2006, VeriSign renewed its contract with ICANN, extending its rights to the .com registry until 2012. It also bought Kontiki, a developer of technology for speeding up large downloads on the Internet, for $62 million.

In 2006 News Corporation acquired a majority stake in VeriSign's Jamba unit, which provides ring tones and other mobile phone content, for $188 million. (Jamba, also known as Jamster, operated as a joint venture between the two companies until 2008, when VeriSign sold its remaining stake to News Corp for $200 million.)

In 2007 Sclavos resigned and director William Roper was named president and CEO.

Formerly organized around its business units, VeriSign restructured its operations into functional groups in 2007; it formed a combined worldwide sales and services team as well as an integrated marketing and product development organization.

EXECUTIVES

Interim Chairman and Interim CEO: D. James (Jim) Bidzos, age 54, $2,349,654 total compensation
President and COO: Mark D. McLaughlin, age 43
SVP and Acting CFO: Brian G. Robins, age 39, $1,197,557 total compensation
SVP and CTO: Ken Silva
SVP and Chief Administrative Officer: Grant L. Clark, age 54
SVP, Chief Accounting Officer, and Corporate Controller: Robynne D. Sisco
SVP, Strategic Development: Russell S. (Rusty) Lewis, age 54, $1,564,589 total compensation
SVP, General Counsel, and Secretary: Richard H. (Rick) Goshorn, age 52, $1,416,238 total compensation
SVP, Corporate Development and Strategy: Kevin A. Werner, age 48, $1,429,159 total compensation
SVP, Global Human Resources: Anne-Marie Law, age 41
VP, VeriSign India: Shekhar Kirani
VP, Associate General Counsel: Paul B. Hudson
VP, Mobile Applications: Oliver Holle
VP, Security Services: Mike Denning
VP, Authentication Services: Fran Rosch
VP, Global Messaging Services: Charles Landry
VP, SSL: Chris Babel
President, VeriSign Messaging and Mobile Media: Charles Meyers, age 39
Investor Relations: Ken Bond
Auditors: KPMG LLP

LOCATIONS

HQ: VeriSign, Inc.
487 E. Middlefield Rd., Mountain View, CA 94043
Phone: 650-961-7500   **Fax:** 650-961-7300
Web: www.verisign.com

2008 Sales

	$ mil.	% of total
US	645.3	67
Switzerland	214.2	22
Japan	78.5	8
Other countries	23.7	3
Total	**961.7**	**100**

PRODUCTS/OPERATIONS

2008 Sales

	$ mil.	% of total
Internet infrastructure & identity services	936.3	97
Other	25.4	3
Total	**961.7**	**100**

Selected Products and Services

Commerce services
  Billing and payment
  Clearing and settlement
Content services
  Application and content delivery
  Messaging
Information services
  Content collection and distribution
  Digital brand management
  Domain name registry
  Supply chain information

Intelligent database services
Network connectivity and interoperability
Operations infrastructure
   Advanced telecommunications
   Distributed servers
   Network security
Security services
   Authentication
   Digital certificate
   Global security consulting
   iDefense
   Managed security services
      Firewall management
      Intrusion detection and prevention
      Vulnerability management
   Network and application security

COMPETITORS

Accenture
Alcatel-Lucent
Amdocs
AOL
Apple Inc.
arvato
AT&T
BT Managed Security Solutions Group
Comverse Technology
Convergys
Entrust
E-Plus
Go Daddy
Google
IBM Global Services
IdenTrust
InfoSpace
iTouch
Kansys
Microsoft
Monstermob
Motricity
NeuStar
Nokia
Orange
Register.com
RSA Security
Sprint Nextel
Symantec
Syniverse
Telcordia
Telefónica O2 Europe
T-Mobile International
Tucows
Verizon Business
Vodafone
Yahoo!

HISTORICAL FINANCIALS

Company Type: Public

Income Statement

FYE: December 31

	REVENUE ($ mil.)	NET INCOME ($ mil.)	NET PROFIT MARGIN	EMPLOYEES
12/08	961.7	(374.7)	—	3,297
12/07	1,496.3	(139.5)	—	4,251
12/06	1,575.2	379.0	24.1%	5,331
12/05	1,609.5	406.5	25.3%	4,076
12/04	1,166.5	186.2	16.0%	3,206
Annual Growth	(4.7%)	—	—	0.7%

2008 Year-End Financials

Debt ratio: 2,483.8%
Return on equity: —
Cash ($ mil.): 789
Current ratio: 1.66
Long-term debt ($ mil.): 1,262

No. of shares (mil.): 193
Dividends
  Yield: 0.0%
  Payout: —
Market value ($ mil.): 3,680

HOOVER'S HANDBOOK OF AMERICAN BUSINESS 2010

Stock History

NASDAQ (GS): VRSN

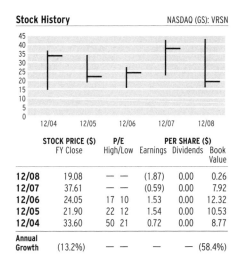

	STOCK PRICE ($) FY Close	P/E High/Low		PER SHARE ($) Earnings	Dividends	Book Value
12/08	19.08	—	—	(1.87)	0.00	0.26
12/07	37.61	—	—	(0.59)	0.00	7.92
12/06	24.05	17	10	1.53	0.00	12.32
12/05	21.90	22	12	1.54	0.00	10.53
12/04	33.60	50	21	0.72	0.00	8.77
Annual Growth	(13.2%)	—	—	—	—	(58.4%)

Verizon Communications

The second largest US telecommunications services provider (after AT&T) has taken the top spot in wireless services (ahead of AT&T Mobility). The company's wireline business provides local telephone, long-distance, and Internet access services to residential and business customers in 24 states and Washington, DC. It has about 40 million voice access lines in operation and serves about 8 million broadband Internet customers. Verizon Wireless (known legally as Cellco Partnership), the company's joint venture with Vodafone Group, serves more than 80 million customers. Verizon Business provides communications and information technology (IT) services to business and government clients in the US and abroad.

Verizon continues to use acquisitions of regional mobile phone companies as it transitions from its role as a wireline carrier into a primarily wireless business. The company bought smaller rival Rural Cellular Corporation in early 2009 for about $2.6 billion; the purchase increased Verizon's wireless subscriber base by more than 600,000.

The company made another, much larger investment later that year with the acquisition of Alltel for $28.1 billion. The deal added about 13 million subscribers to Verizon's books and created the largest cellular provider in the US. It also boosted the company's retail presence with the addition of 750 Alltel-branded distribution points. In order to meet regulatory approval for the acquisition, Verizon was compelled by the Federal Trade Commission to agree to sell assets in 22 states. Buyers included Frontier Communications, which agreed to pay $5.2 billion in stock for assets that included nearly 5 million subscriber lines in 14 states, and AT&T which agreed to pay $2.3 billion for assets that included 1.5 million in 18 states. Both transactions are expected to close in 2009.

Despite its efforts to build a wireless business, Verizon has not given up hope on its wireline op-

erations. With a competitive eye toward the continued convergence of wireline communications and broadcasting services, Verizon is building out its fiber-to-the-premises (FTTP) network at a cost of $18 billion in hopes of adding improved video transmission services and gaining a competitive edge on leading cable operators like Comcast and Time Warner.

The upgraded network infrastructure, which is slated for completion in 2010, will replace traditional copper network connections with fiber optics in order to increase broadband capacity. Verizon is exploiting the boost in bandwidth with a new digital video service. Known as FiOS TV, the service already reaches about 2 million customers in some service areas and includes digital music programming and high-definition TV.

Verizon has further retooled its structure with the divestiture of noncore subsidiaries. These include the 2009 sale of its Airfone business (which installed telephones in the back of US commercial airplane seats in the US) to JetBlue Airways, and the sale of its South African enterprise services operations (formerly overseen by Verizon Business) to MTN Group.

Also in 2009 Verizon announced it would combine the struggling landline businesses of its consumer and business units. The company has hopes that a single landline division will get better prices for equipment and contractor services by placing larger orders.

HISTORY

Verizon Communications (the name is a combination of *veritas*, the Latin word for truth, and horizon) was born in 2000 when Bell Atlantic bought GTE, but the company's roots are as old as the telephone. What is now Verizon began as one of the 1870s-era phone companies that evolved into AT&T Corp. and its Bell System of regional telephone operations.

AT&T lived happily as a regulated monopoly until a US government antitrust suit led to its breakup in 1984. Seven regional Bell operating companies (RBOCs, or Baby Bells) emerged in 1984, including Bell Atlantic. The new company, based in Philadelphia, received local phone service rights in six states and Washington, DC; cellular company Bell Atlantic Mobile Systems; and one-seventh of Bellcore, the R&D subsidiary (now Telcordia).

Bell Atlantic pursued unregulated businesses such as wireless, Internet, directory publishing, and catalog sales of computer parts and office supplies. It invested heavily in data-transport markets to supplement existing voice services, offering the first CO-LAN (central-office local area network) system in 1985. A year later it introduced a switched public data network and began testing integrating services digital network (ISDN) technology that combined voice and data transmissions over the same lines.

Bell Atlantic partnered with U S WEST to offer cellular services in the former Czechoslovakia in 1991, and in 1993 it bought a stake in Mexico's Grupo Iusacell (sold in 2003). Its 1992 acquisition of Metro Mobile gave it extensive East Coast cellular phone coverage.

In 1994 Bell Atlantic tried and failed to buy cable giant TCI (now part of AT&T), but succeeded in forming the PrimeCo partnership with NYNEX, U S WEST, and AirTouch, which began offering PCS. Enjoying freedom from wires, Bell Atlantic and NYNEX combined their cellular and paging operations in 1995. In 1996 Bell Atlantic and the six other RBOCs sold Bellcore to Science Applications International.

Bell Atlantic doubled in size with the $25.6 billion purchase of New York City-based NYNEX in 1997, moving from the Cradle of Liberty to the Big Apple. The deal created the second-largest US telecom services firm (after AT&T Corp.) but brought with it NYNEX's reputation for poor service.

In 1999 Bell Atlantic agreed to buy GTE, the giant non-Bell local phone company, in a $53 billion deal. To gain regulatory clearance to be acquired by Bell Atlantic, GTE sold off 90% of its Genuity Internet backbone operation (formerly GTE Internetworking). Later in 1999 the FCC granted Bell Atlantic permission to sell long-distance phone service in New York, making the company the first of the Baby Bells to be allowed to offer long-distance in its home territory.

Bell Atlantic and Vodafone AirTouch combined their US wireless operations, including PrimeCo, to form Verizon Wireless in 2000. Regulators later that year approved Bell Atlantic's acquisition of GTE, and Verizon Communications was formed. Tapped to run the new company were chairman and co-CEO Charles Lee, formerly of GTE, and president and co-CEO Ivan Seidenberg, formerly of Bell Atlantic (Lee later gave up the co-CEO position and announced he would step down as chairman in 2003).

In 2002 Verizon completed the sale of 675,000 access lines in Alabama and Missouri to CenturyTel, and it sold 600,000 access lines in Kentucky to ALLTEL, in deals valued at just over $4 billion.

The company sold its wireline business in Hawaii to The Carlyle Group in a 2005 deal valued at $1.65 billion. Verizon won a bidding war with Qwest Communications and paid nearly $8.5 billion for MCI in 2006. The deal enabled Verizon to expand its broadband data services, but led to about 7,000 job cuts at the combined company. Also that year, Verizon sold its Caribbean region and Latin American operations to companies controlled by Mexican entrepreneur Carlos Slim Helú in deals valued at a combined $3.7 billion.

EXECUTIVES

Chairman and CEO: Ivan G. Seidenberg, age 62
President and COO: Dennis F. (Denny) Strigl, age 62
EVP and CFO: John F. Killian, age 54
EVP and CTO: Richard J. (Dick) Lynch, age 60
EVP and CIO: Shaygan Kheradpir, age 48
EVP and Chief Marketing Officer: John G. Stratton, age 47
Chief Privacy Officer: Margo Hammar
Chief Security Officer: Michael A. Mason, age 51
EVP Public Affairs, Policy, and Communications: Thomas J. (Tom) Tauke, age 58
EVP; President and CEO, Verizon Wireless: Lowell C. McAdam, age 54
EVP Human Resources: Marc C. Reed, age 50
EVP Strategy, Development, and Planning: John W. Diercksen, age 59
EVP and COO, Verizon Telecom: Robert (Bob) Mudge
EVP and General Counsel: Randal S. (Randy) Milch
SVP, Deputy General Counsel, and Corporate Secretary: Marianne Drost
SVP Finance; CEO, Verizon Investment Management: William F. (Bill) Heitmann, age 60
SVP Investor Relations: Ronald H. (Ron) Lataille
President, Verizon Services: Daniel S. (Dan) Mead
President, Verizon Foundation: Patrick R. Gaston, age 51
President, Verizon Business: Francis J. (Fran) Shammo, age 48
Auditors: Ernst & Young LLP

LOCATIONS

HQ: Verizon Communications Inc.
140 West St., New York, NY 10007
Phone: 212-395-1000 **Fax:** 212-571-1897
Web: www.verizon.com

2008 Sales

	$ mil.	% of total
US	93,980	93
Other countries	3,374	7
Total	**97,354**	**100**

PRODUCTS/OPERATIONS

2008 Sales

	$ mil.	% of total
Domestic wireless	49,332	49
Wireline		
Verizon Telecom	29,912	30
Verizon Business	21,126	21
Adjustments	(3,016)	—
Total	**97,354**	**100**

Selected Services

Business
  Conferencing
  Customer premises equipment design and maintenance
  Data center outsourcing
  Hosted messaging
  Information technology (IT)
  Systems integration
  Voice and data networking
Telecom
  Billing and collections
  Directory assistance
  Internet access services
  Local exchange access
  Long-distance
  Public telephones
Wireless
  Equipment sales
  Paging
  Wireless voice and data services

COMPETITORS

360networks
AT&T
AT&T Mobility
Charter Communications
Comcast
Cox Communications
Global Crossing
Leap Wireless
Level 3 Communications
MetroPCS
Qwest Communications
Sprint Nextel
Time Warner Cable
T-Mobile USA
tw telecom
U.S. Cellular
XO Holdings
Yellow Book USA

HISTORICAL FINANCIALS

Company Type: Public

Income Statement

	REVENUE ($ mil.)	NET INCOME ($ mil.)	NET PROFIT MARGIN	EMPLOYEES
12/08	97,354.0	6,428.0	6.6%	223,900
12/07	93,469.0	5,652.0	6.0%	235,000
12/06	88,144.0	6,239.0	7.1%	242,000
12/05	75,112.0	7,397.0	9.8%	250,000
12/04	71,283.0	7,831.0	11.0%	210,000
Annual Growth	**8.1%**	**(4.8%)**	**—**	**1.6%**

FYE: December 31

2008 Year-End Financials

Debt ratio: 112.6%
Return on equity: 13.9%
Cash ($ mil.): 9,782
Current ratio: 1.01
Long-term debt ($ mil.): 46,959
No. of shares (mil.): 2,841
Dividends
  Yield: 6.5%
  Payout: 97.8%
Market value ($ mil.): 96,297

Stock History

NYSE: VZ

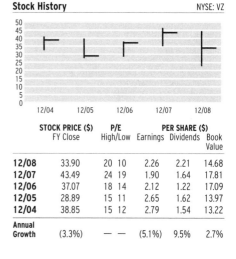

	STOCK PRICE ($) FY Close	P/E High/Low	PER SHARE ($) Earnings	Dividends	Book Value
12/08	33.90	20 10	2.26	2.21	14.68
12/07	43.49	24 19	1.90	1.64	17.81
12/06	37.07	18 14	2.12	1.22	17.09
12/05	28.89	15 11	2.65	1.62	13.97
12/04	38.85	15 12	2.79	1.54	13.22
Annual Growth	**(3.3%)**	**— —**	**(5.1%)**	**9.5%**	**2.7%**

V.F. Corporation

V.F. Corporation is the name behind the names. The #1 jeans maker worldwide boasts a bevy of brands, such as Lee, Riders, Rustler, and Wrangler jeans. Its other holdings include JanSport and Eastpak (backpacks); Lee (knitwear); The North Face and Eagle Creek (outdoor gear/apparel); Red Kap and Bulwark (industrial work clothes); Nautica and John Varvatos (men's and women's apparel); and Vans (hip footwear). V.F. operates about 700 retail stores under such banners as The North Face and Vans. It entered the premium-jeans niche in 2007 with 7 For All Mankind and Lucy jeans. V.F. makes NASCAR, MLB, NFL, and NBA apparel under license. Trusts established by founder John Barbey control about 20% of its shares.

The company is the top jeans maker in the US, holding about a quarter of the market. While the manufacturer maintains this momentum, V.F. has been disposing of unprofitable businesses to refocus on other areas for growth. It sold its lingerie business, consisting of US (Vanity Fair, Vassarette) and European brands (Gemma, Belcor) in 2007 to rival Fruit of the Loom. Its outdoor and action sports business — comprising some 36% of VF's sales — as well as its Imagewear and Sportswear segments, have seen growth. V.F.'s streamlining its operations by centralizing supply chain functions and reorganizing its global operations to prepare for growth in Japan and its outdoor business.

V.F.'s pursing an aggressive growth strategy just when many of its rivals in apparel manufacturing are pulling back in the face of the economic downturn. In its outdoor and action sports segment, V.F. is expanding into new product categories, opening more retail stores, expanding geographically, and looking to acquire lifestyle brands focused on the outdoors.

The company has been concentrating on expanding its portfolio of sports lifestyle brands. In

In 2001 Vishay made a bid to acquire General Semiconductor (electrical protection products that control power surges) for about $463 million, but was twice rejected — a decision that drew Zandman's public ire. Vishay upped the ante when Siliconix (a top rival of General and 80%-owned by Vishay) subsequently sued General for patent infringement. Vishay finally acquired General for about $540 million in stock and the assumption of $229 million in debt.

In 2002 Vishay plunged into the transducer market, acquiring Tedea-Huntleigh, Sensortronics, and two businesses from Thermo Electron (now Thermo Fisher Scientific) to form its Vishay Transducers Group. In 2004 it acquired the thin-film interconnects business of Aeroflex for about $9 million.

Late in 2004 Zandman announced that he would step down as CEO at the start of 2005, but he would remain an executive of the company. Vishay COO Gerald Paul succeeded Zandman as CEO.

In 2005 Vishay acquired the assets of CyOptics Israel and bought Alpha Electronics, a Japanese manufacturer of foil resistors. The company paid around $11 million for the two acquisitions and assumed some $8 million in debt.

Also in 2005 Vishay acquired SI Technologies for about $18 million in cash, plus the assumption of $12 million in debt. That same year the company acquired the 20% of Siliconix it didn't previously own, swapping Vishay common shares for those of Siliconix. Vishay's tender offer yielded enough shares to give the company ownership of more than 95% of Siliconix.

EXECUTIVES

Chairman, CTO, and Chief Business Development Officer: Felix Zandman, age 80, $5,122,804 total compensation
Vice Chairman and Chief Administration Officer; President, Vishay Israel Ltd: Marc Zandman, age 47, $907,163 total compensation
President, CEO, and Director: Gerald Paul, age 60, $3,098,039 total compensation
EVP, COO, and Director: Ziv Shoshani, age 43, $787,507 total compensation
EVP and CFO: Lior E. Yahalomi, $491,988 total compensation
EVP Finance and Chief Accounting Officer: Lori Lipcaman, age 51
SVP and Corporate Secretary: William M. Clancy
SVP Corporate Communications: Peter G. Henrici
VP and Treasurer: Steven Klausner
Public Relations Associate and Director: Ruta Zandman, age 71
Corporate Investor Relations: Brenda R. Tate
Auditors: Ernst & Young LLP

LOCATIONS

HQ: Vishay Intertechnology, Inc.
63 Lancaster Ave., Malvern, PA 19355
Phone: 610-644-1300   **Fax:** 610-889-9429
Web: www.vishay.com

Vishay Intertechnology has more than 60 manufacturing facilities located in Austria, Brazil, China, Costa Rica, the Czech Republic, France, Germany, Hungary, India, Israel, Italy, Japan, Malaysia, Mexico, the Netherlands, the Philippines, Portugal, Sweden, Taiwan, the UK, and the US.

2008 Sales

	$ mil.	% of total
Europe		
Germany	775.4	27
Other countries	313.3	11
Asia/Pacific	1,032.6	37
US	446.5	16
Israel	254.4	9
Total	**2,822.2**	**100**

PRODUCTS/OPERATIONS

2008 Sales

	$ mil.	% of total
Semiconductors	1,460.8	52
Passive components	1,361.4	48
Total	**2,822.2**	**100**

2008 Sales by Market

	% of total
Industrial	39
Computer	18
Automotive	16
Consumer products	12
Telecommunications	8
Military & aerospace	5
Medical	2
Total	**100**

Selected Products

Semiconductors (active components)
  Diodes
    Rectifiers
    Small-signal diodes
    Transient voltage suppressors
    Zener diodes
  Integrated circuits (ICs)
    Analog switches
    Infrared data communication (IrDC) transceivers
    Multiplexers
    Power ICs
  Optoelectronic components
    Displays
    Infrared emitters
    Light-emitting diodes (LEDs)
    Optocouplers
    Optosensors
    Photo detectors
  Transistors
    Bipolar power transistors
    Junction field-effect transistors (JFETs)
    Power MOSFETs (metal oxide semiconductor FETs)
    Radio-frequency transistors
    Small-signal FETs
Passive components
  Capacitors
    Aluminum
    Ceramic
    Film
    Tantalum
  Magnetics
    Custom magnetics
    Inductors
    Transformers
  Resistors
    Bulk metal foil resistors
    Fuse resistors
    Metal-film resistors and networks
    Panel controls
    Panel potentiometers
    Thermistors
    Thick-film resistors and networks
    Thin-film resistors and networks
    Trimming potentiometers
    Varistors

COMPETITORS

Allegro MicroSystems
Analogic Technologies
Avago Technologies
AVX
Bell Industries
Cogo Group
CTS Corp.
Diodes
EPCOS
Fairchild Semiconductor
Freescale Semiconductor
Infineon Technologies
International Rectifier
KEMET
Maxim Integrated Products
Microsemi
Murata Manufacturing
NEC Electronics
NXP
Ohmite
ON Semiconductor
Power Integrations
ROHM
Samsung Electronics
Sanken Electric
Sensata
Sharp Corp.
Shindengen Electric Manufacturing
STMicroelectronics
SunPower
Technitrol
Toshiba Semiconductor
Tyco Electronics
Yageo

HISTORICAL FINANCIALS

Company Type: Public

Income Statement

FYE: December 31

	REVENUE ($ mil.)	NET INCOME ($ mil.)	NET PROFIT MARGIN	EMPLOYEES
12/08	2,822.2	(1,731.4)	—	24,800
12/07	2,833.3	130.8	4.6%	27,900
12/06	2,581.5	139.7	5.4%	27,000
12/05	2,296.5	62.3	2.7%	26,100
12/04	2,413.6	44.7	1.9%	25,700
Annual Growth	**4.0%**	**—**	**—**	**(0.9%)**

2008 Year-End Financials

Debt ratio: 21.6%
Return on equity: —
Cash ($ mil.): 324
Current ratio: 2.87
Long-term debt ($ mil.): 334
No. of shares (mil.): 187
Dividends
  Yield: 0.0%
  Payout: —
Market value ($ mil.): 638

Stock History

NYSE: VSH

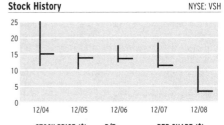

	STOCK PRICE ($) FY Close	P/E High/Low		PER SHARE ($) Earnings	Dividends	Book Value
12/08	3.42	—	—	(9.29)	0.00	8.28
12/07	11.41	26	16	0.69	0.00	17.99
12/06	13.54	24	17	0.73	0.00	16.51
12/05	13.76	45	31	0.34	0.00	15.30
12/04	15.02	93	43	0.27	0.00	14.86
Annual Growth	**(30.9%)**	**—**	**—**	**—**	**—**	**(13.6%)**

Volt Information Sciences

A jolt from Volt can discharge your personnel needs. Volt Information Sciences generates most of its sales by offering temporary and permanent employees to businesses through some 350 branch and on-site offices in Asia, Europe, and North and South America. Volt's staffing segment also includes businesses that provide project management and information technology services (VMC Consulting) and outsourced procurement services (ProcureStaff Technologies). In addition, the company provides telecommunications network engineering and construction services, as well as information systems, including directory assistance systems. The founding Shaw family owns a controlling stake in Volt.

Volt Information Sciences, Inc. Volt aims to grow by continuing to focus on large corporate customers that need staffing help at multiple locations. Because the company competes for that business with lower-cost providers based outside the US, Volt is moving to expand internationally. In 2008 several divisions of Microsoft accounted for 10% of Volt's total sales.

To reduce debt and to free capital for investment in core operations, Volt in September 2008 sold its telephone directory systems and services business and its US-based telephone directory publishing operations to Yellow Pages for about $180 million. Volt retained a directory publishing business based in Uruguay.

HISTORY

Brothers William and Jerome Shaw started their business in 1950 to provide freelance technical publication assistance; they chose the name Volt because it sounded technical. The company established a temporary technical staffing division in 1956 and went public in 1962.

Volt had expanded into clerical and administrative staffing, as well as telephone directory printing, by the late 1960s; it established a telecommunications services division in 1976. The company acquired Delta Resources (computerized directory assistance systems) in 1980 and began printing telephone directories in Uruguay and Australia several years later (the Australian operation was sold in 1997).

Volt's personnel segment grew in the 1990s as companies relied more on outside agencies to help staff their businesses, and increased telephone industry competition drove expansion in the telecommunications market. Electronic publishing was more problematic, however, and in 1996 the company merged its subsidiaries in that segment with Information International to form Autologic Information International (Volt took a 59% stake). In 1997 it expanded its breadth with the purchase of 11 US community telephone directories in North Carolina and West Virginia.

In 1999 Volt acquired UK-based Gatton Group. Also that year it bought the wired services business (installation of cable, wire, and small telecommunications systems) and professional staffing divisions of a Lucent Technologies unit. In 2000 the company created subsidiary ProcureStaff to provide supplemental staffing procurement services. In 2001 Agfa Corporation bought the company's 59%-owned subsidiary, Autologic Information International, for about

$24 million. Volt combined its telecommunications services units to form Volt Telecommunications Group in 2002. In 2003 the company's VMC Consulting subsidiary merged with IT consulting division Volt Integrated Solutions Group.

Volt acquired Volt Delta, the directory and operator services unit of Nortel, in 2004 to boost its computer systems segment. In 2007 the company merged one of its Volt Delta subsidiaries with LSSi Corp. The combined company was renamed LSSi Data.

William Shaw died in 2006.

EXECUTIVES

President, CEO, COO, and Director: Steven A. (Steve) Shaw, age 49, $581,970 total compensation
SVP and Principal Financial Officer: Jack Egan, age 59, $346,093 total compensation
EVP and Secretary: Jerome Shaw, age 82, $564,504 total compensation
SVP: Thomas (Tom) Daley, age 54, $494,520 total compensation
SVP and Treasurer: Ludwig M. Guarino, age 57
SVP and General Counsel: Howard B. Weinreich, age 66, $361,139 total compensation
VP Accounting Operations: Daniel G. Hallihan, age 60
VP Human Resources: Louise Ross, age 60
President, Volt Consulting - Managed Service Programs: Larry Kaylor
COO, VMC Consulting: Kristin Carrico
President, VoltDelta: Joe DiAngelo
Managing Director and SVP, Volt Europe: Stephanie Elliott
President, Volt Telecom Group: R.J. (Chip) Anderson
President, Maintech: Frank D'Alessio
President, ProcureStaff Technologies: Allen Rittscher
COO, Volt Telecom Group: Charles H. (Chuck) Scott
Auditors: Ernst & Young LLP

LOCATIONS

HQ: Volt Information Sciences, Inc.
560 Lexington Ave., New York, NY 10022
Phone: 212-704-2400   **Fax:** 212-704-2417
Web: www.volt.com

2008 Sales

	$ mil.	% of total
US	2,236.2	92
Europe	191.1	8
Total	**2,427.3**	**100**

PRODUCTS/OPERATIONS

2008 Sales

	$ mil.	% of total
Staffing	2,043.8	84
Computer systems	212.7	9
Telecommunications	171.7	7
Printing & other	16.9	—
Adjustments	(17.8)	—
Total	**2,427.3**	**100**

Selected Products and Services

Computer systems
 Directory assistance
 Information technology

Staffing
 Information technology services
 Professional placement
 Staffing procurement
 Temporary and contract staffing

Telecommunications
 Construction
 Design
 Engineering
 Installation
 Maintenance

COMPETITORS

Adecco	Kelly Services
Aquent	Manpower
Barrett Business Services	MPS
Butler International	Spherion
Edgewater Technology	TAC Worldwide
Express Employment	TeamStaff
Joulé	

HISTORICAL FINANCIALS

Company Type: Public

Income Statement

FYE: Sunday nearest October 31

	REVENUE ($ mil.)	NET INCOME ($ mil.)	NET PROFIT MARGIN	EMPLOYEES
10/08	2,427.3	64.2	2.6%	42,000
10/07	2,353.1	39.3	1.7%	43,000
10/06	2,338.5	30.6	1.3%	46,000
10/05	2,177.6	17.0	0.8%	48,000
10/04	1,924.8	33.7	1.8%	45,000
Annual Growth	**6.0%**	**17.5%**	**—**	**(1.7%)**

2008 Year-End Financials

Debt ratio: 3.1%
Return on equity: 17.3%
Cash ($ mil.): 121
Current ratio: 1.48
Long-term debt ($ mil.): 12
No. of shares (mil.): 21
Dividends
 Yield: 0.0%
 Payout: —
Market value ($ mil.): 159

Stock History

NYSE: VOL

	STOCK PRICE ($) FY Close	P/E High/Low	PER SHARE ($) Earnings	Dividends	Book Value
10/08	7.65	7 2	2.92	0.00	18.86
10/07	15.55	25 8	1.71	0.00	16.91
10/06	26.33	25 9	1.31	0.00	15.60
10/05	12.53	29 16	0.74	0.00	14.15
10/04	19.37	15 8	1.47	0.00	13.27
Annual Growth	**(20.7%)**	**— —**	**18.7%**	**—**	**9.2%**

Vulcan Materials

The road to just about everywhere is paved with Vulcan Materials' aggregates. The company is the largest producer of construction aggregates — crushed stone, gravel, and sand — in the US. Vulcan produces and distributes aggregates, asphalt mixes, ready-mixed concrete, and cement at more than 400 production plants in the US (primarily the Southeast and Mid-Atlantic) and Mexico. A majority of its aggregates are used to build and maintain highways, bridges, and other public works systems; they're also used in residential, commercial, and industrial building construction. Aggregates account for about 60% of Vulcan Materials' sales.

Increased spending by the federal government on infrastructure and highway projects is expected to sustain growth in Vulcan's aggregates sales. To stay ahead of rival Martin Marietta Materials, the acquisitive Vulcan plans to keep buying quarries. The company acquired Florida Rock Industries in late 2007 for some $4.6 billion. In addition to increasing the company's presence in Florida, the acquisition boosted its aggregates reserves by about 20%.

Vulcan Materials also expects that the multi-year nature of highway and infrastructure projects will continue to offset the downturn in the residential construction industry and drive recovery.

The company is in the process of expanding its Newberry, Florida-based cement plant, which produces portland and masonry cement. The expansion will double its capacity.

However, Vulcan has not been immune to the economic downturn. The housing crash in states such as Florida and California, coupled with decreased overall construction, has impacted sales volumes and earnings. As a result Vulcan has been focused on controlling costs.

In 2009 Vulcan realigned its business into two regions — the east and west. The new structure is aimed at business operations related to transportation and distribution.

Like many big corporations, the company has jumped on the corporate sustainability bandwagon, monitoring the amount of pollutants it generates. It has been commended in the state of California for tracking its greenhouse gas emissions and for building aggregates plants (such as its Corona, California, facility) that attempt to reduce and prevent those emissions by using a downhill conveyor that generates electricity as it carries rock to the processing plant below.

State Farm Mutual Automobile Insurance owns 11% of Vulcan Materials.

HISTORY

In 1916 the Ireland family purchased a 75% interest in Birmingham Slag, a small Alabama company established in 1909 to process slag from a Birmingham steel plant. For several decades the company prospered by selling its processed slag to the construction industry.

Third-generation Charles Ireland became president in 1951 and transformed Birmingham Slag from a regional operation into a national one. In 1956 the company bought Vulcan Detinning, renamed itself Vulcan Materials, and went public. By 1959 Vulcan was the largest producer of aggregates in the US, with sales over $100 million.

Vulcan owned 90 quarries by 1981 and claimed sales of some $780 million. It added about 50 operations and plants in the 1980s and in 1987 entered into a joint venture, the Crescent Market Project, with Mexico's Grupo ICA, largely to supply aggregates from a Yucatan quarry to US Gulf Coast markets.

In 1990 Vulcan bought Reed Crushed Stone and Reed Terminal, which included the largest US crushed-rock quarry (in Paducah, Kentucky). The Yucatan plant was fully operational in 1991 and was supported by two company-owned ships that moved materials to the US Gulf Coast. Also that year Vulcan entered a venture with Tetra Technologies to produce calcium chloride from hydrochloric acids; this new use for the acid eased Vulcan's status as a major polluter.

Vulcan built a sodium chlorite plant in Wichita in 1993 and plants in Port Edwards, Wisconsin, to produce potassium carbonate and sodium hydrosulfite. In 1994 the company bought Peroxidation Systems of Tucson (water-purification

technology, chemicals, and related equipment). That year Vulcan also acquired Callaway Chemical, boosting its specialty chemical line.

The company bought three food-processing chemical companies and Rio Linda Chemical (chlorine dioxide) in 1995. Acquisitions continued in 1996 as Vulcan purchased three chemical companies and several quarries. Also that year Vulcan sold its chlorine cylinder repackaging business and consolidated its paper and water-treatment businesses.

In 1997 the company sold its coal-handling business, added several quarries, and bought the textile chemical business of Laun-Dry Supply. Vulcan bought six aggregate operations in Georgia, Illinois, and Tennessee in 1998 and started three new aggregate operations in Alabama, Georgia, and Indiana. It also formed a joint venture with Mitsui to build a chlor-alkali plant.

In 1999 Vulcan paid about $890 million for rival aggregate producer CalMat. The company also bought 20 quarries throughout the US. Vulcan merged its specialty chemicals businesses into one unit — Vulcan Performance Chemicals — in 2000. The company also acquired Texas-based Garves W. Yates & Sons, adding six quarries. Also in 2000 Vulcan acquired the North American aggregates production and transportation assets that Anglo American's Titan Cement Company obtained from its purchase of Tarmac plc. In 2001 the company bought two aggregates facilities in Tennessee, two recycling facilities in Illinois, and its Mexico-based Crescent Markets joint venture.

In 2003 Vulcan divested its Performance Chemicals business unit, concluding with the sale of its industrial water treatment and pulp and paper operations. It did retain the sodium chlorite business and moved it under its Chloralkali operations. Vulcan expanded in central Tennessee with the purchase of Columbia Rock Products in 2004. In October 2004 the company agreed to sell the remainder of its chemical operations to Basic Chemical Company for an undisclosed sum; the deal was completed in 2005.

Vulcan spent $94 million on acquisitions in 2005, including 11 aggregate operations and five asphalt plants in Arizona, Georgia, Indiana, and Tennessee.

EXECUTIVES

Chairman and CEO: Donald M. (Don) James, age 60,
  $10,539,264 total compensation
SVP and CFO: Daniel F. Sansone, age 56,
  $1,940,235 total compensation
VP, Controller, and CIO: Ejaz A. Khan, age 51
SVP Construction Materials, West:
  Ronald G. (Ron) McAbee, age 61,
  $2,013,729 total compensation
SVP and General Counsel: Robert A. Wason IV, age 57
SVP Human Resources: J. Wayne Houston, age 56
SVP Construction Materials, East: Danny R. Shepherd,
  age 57, $1,662,254 total compensation
VP Safety, Health and Environment:
  Bradley C. (Brad) Rosenwald, age 55
VP Engineering Services: Randal C. Hall, age 53
VP Business Development: James P. Daniel, age 53
VP Tax and Assistant Treasurer: James W. O'Brien,
  age 51
VP Operations Support: Ronald L. Walker
VP Marketing Support Services: Sidney F. Mays, age 64
Director Community Relations: David A. Donaldson
Treasurer: J. Philip Alford, age 58
Investor Relations: Mark Warren
Secretary: Jerry F. Perkins Jr.
Manager Public Affairs: John English
Auditors: Deloitte & Touche LLP

LOCATIONS

HQ: Vulcan Materials Company
  1200 Urban Center Dr., Birmingham, AL 35242
Phone: 205-298-3000   **Fax:** 205-298-2960
Web: www.vulcanmaterials.com

PRODUCTS/OPERATIONS

2008 Sales

	$ mil.	% of total
Aggregates	2,406.8	62
Asphalt mix & concrete	1,201.2	30
Cement	106.5	3
Delivery revenues	198.4	5
Eliminations	(261.5)	—
Total	**3,651.4**	**100**

Selected Products

Construction materials
  Agricultural limestone
  Asphalt coating (Guardtop)
  Asphalt paving materials
  Chemical stone (high-calcium and -magnesium stone)
  Concrete
  Construction aggregates
    Crushed stone
    Gravel
    Sand
    Recrushed concrete
  Railroad ballast
  Ready-mix concrete (portland cement)
  Recycled materials

COMPETITORS

Aggregate Industries	Knife River
Ash Grove Cement	Lafarge North America
Buzzi Unicem USA	Lehigh Hanson
Cementos Portland	Martin Marietta Aggregates
Valderrivas	Martin Marietta Materials
CEMEX	MDU Resources
CEMEX Australia	New Enterprise Stone &
Continental Materials	Lime
CRH	Ready Mix Inc
Cytec	Ready Mix USA
Doan Companies	Rogers Group
Eagle Materials	St. Lawrence Cement
Edw. C. Levy	Superior Ready Mix
Giant Cement	Transit Mix Concrete
Hanson Limited	Trinity Industries
HeidelbergCement	TXI
Holcim Apasco	U.S. Lime & Minerals
Holcim (US)	

HISTORICAL FINANCIALS

Company Type: Public

Income Statement

FYE: December 31

	REVENUE ($ mil.)	NET INCOME ($ mil.)	NET PROFIT MARGIN	EMPLOYEES
12/08	3,651.4	(4.1)	—	9,320
12/07	3,327.8	450.9	13.5%	10,522
12/06	3,342.5	467.5	14.0%	7,983
12/05	2,895.3	388.8	13.4%	8,051
12/04	2,454.3	287.4	11.7%	7,238
Annual Growth	10.4%	—	—	6.5%

2008 Year-End Financials

Debt ratio: 61.1%   No. of shares (mil.): 125
Return on equity: —   Dividends
Cash ($ mil.): 10   Yield: 2.8%
Current ratio: 0.54   Payout: —
Long-term debt ($ mil.): 2,154   Market value ($ mil.): 8,697

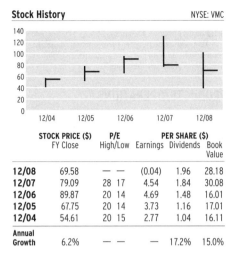

	STOCK PRICE ($) FY Close	P/E High/Low	PER SHARE ($) Earnings	Dividends	Book Value
12/08	69.58	— —	(0.04)	1.96	28.18
12/07	79.09	28 17	4.54	1.84	30.08
12/06	89.87	20 14	4.69	1.48	16.01
12/05	67.75	20 14	3.73	1.16	17.01
12/04	54.61	20 15	2.77	1.04	16.11
Annual Growth	6.2%	— —	—	17.2%	15.0%

Wakefern Food

Some might say you aren't shopping right if you don't get your groceries from stores supplied by this company. Wakefern Food is one of the leading wholesale distribution cooperatives in the US, supplying groceries and other merchandise to a chain of more than 200 ShopRite supermarkets in five eastern states. The company supplies national brand and private-label products (ShopRite, Chef's Express, Readington Farms) to its member stores; Wakefern also offers advertising, merchandising, insurance, and other business support services. The co-op, which boasts more than 40 members, was founded by seven grocers in 1946 and rebranded the individual stores with the ShopRite name five years later.

While the ShopRite chain boasts a loyal following in its core markets, the supermarkets have been feeling the pinch from rivals in the price-competitive grocery business. The company is especially feeling pressure from non-supermarket chains such as Wal-Mart, CVS/Caremark, and Wawa.

The cooperative added to its footprint in 2007 when it acquired about 10 underperforming retail locations from Stop & Shop. The stores, located mostly in South Jersey, were rebranded under the ShopRite banner.

HISTORY

Wakefern Food was founded in 1946 by seven New York- and New Jersey-based grocers: Louis Weiss, Sam and Al Aidekman, Abe Kesselman, Dave Fern, Sam Garb, and Albert Goldberg (the company's name is made up of the first letters of the last names of first five of those founders). Like many cooperatives, the association sought to lower costs by increasing its buying power as a group.

They each put in $1,000 and began operating a 5,000-sq.-ft. warehouse, often putting in double time to keep both their stores and the warehouse running. The shopkeepers' collective buying power proved valuable, enabling the grocers to stock many items at the same prices as their larger competitors.

In 1951 Wakefern members began pooling their resources to buy advertising space. A common store name — ShopRite — was chosen, and each week co-op members met to decide which items would be sale priced. Within a year, membership had grown to over 50. Expansion became a priority, and in the mid-1950s co-op members united in small groups to take over failed supermarkets. One such group, called the Supermarkets Operating Co. (SOC), was formed in 1956. Within 10 years it had acquired a number of failed stores, remodeled them, and given them the ShopRite name.

During the late 1950s sales at ShopRite stores slumped after Wakefern decided to buck the supermarket trend of offering trading stamps (which could then be exchanged for gifts), figuring that offering the stamps would ultimately lead to higher food prices. The move initially drove away customers, but Wakefern cut grocery prices across the board and sales returned. The company did embrace another supermarket trend: stocking stores with nonfood items.

The co-op was severely shaken in 1966 when SOC merged with General Supermarkets, a similar small group within Wakefern, becoming Supermarkets General Corp. (SGC). SGC was a powerful entity, with 71 supermarkets, 10 drugstores, six gas stations, a wholesale bakery, and a discount department store. Many Wakefern members opposed the merger and attempted to block the action with a court order. By 1968 SGC had beefed up its operations to include department store chains as well as its grocery stores. In a move that threatened to break Wakefern, SGC broke away from the co-op, and its stores were renamed Pathmark.

Wakefern not only weathered the storm, it grew under the direction of chairman and CEO Thomas Infusino, elected shortly after the split. The co-op focused on asserting its position as a seller of low-priced products. Wakefern developed private-label brands, including the ShopRite brand. In the 1980s members began operating larger stores and adding more nonfood items to the ShopRite product mix. With its number of superstores on the rise and facing increased competition from club stores in 1992, Wakefern opened a centralized, nonfood distribution center in New Jersey.

In 1995, 30-year Wakefern veteran Dean Janeway was elected president of the co-op. The company debuted its ShopRite MasterCard, co-branded with New Jersey's Valley National Bank, in 1996. The following year the co-op purchased two of its customers' stores in Pennsylvania, then threatened to close them when contract talks with the local union deteriorated. In 1998 Wakefern settled the dispute, then sold the stores.

The company partnered with Internet bidding site priceline.com in 1999, offering customers an opportunity to bid on groceries and then pick them up at ShopRite stores. Big V, Wakefern's biggest customer, filed for Chapter 11 bankruptcy protection in 2000 and said it was ending its distribution agreement with the co-op. In July 2002, however, Wakefern's ShopRite Supermarkets subsidiary acquired all of Big V's assets for approximately $185 million in cash and assumed liabilities.

Infusino retired in May 2005 after 35 years with Wakefern Food. He was succeeded by former vice chairman Joseph Colalillo.

EXECUTIVES

Chairman and CEO: Joseph S. (Joe) Colalillo, age 48
President and COO: Dean Janeway
CFO: Doug Wille
SVP and CIO: Natan Tabak
EVP: Joseph Sheridan
VP Corporate and Consumer Affairs: Karen Meleta
VP Merchandising and Advertising: Bill Crombie
VP Logistics: Pete Rolandelli
VP Information Services Division: Alan Aront
VP Human Resources: Ann Burke
Director Wholesale Division: Dave Baer
Director Advertising: Karen McAuvic
Director Consumer Affairs: Cheryl Macik
Director Private Label Branding: Loren Weinstein

LOCATIONS

HQ: Wakefern Food Corporation
600 York St., Elizabeth, NJ 07207
Phone: 908-527-3300   **Fax:** 908-527-3397
Web: www.shoprite.com

COMPETITORS

A&P	Krasdale Foods
Acme Markets	Stop & Shop
C & S Wholesale	SUPERVALU
CVS Caremark	Wal-Mart
IGA	Wawa, Inc.

HISTORICAL FINANCIALS

Company Type: Cooperative

Income Statement   FYE: September 30

	REVENUE ($ mil.)	NET INCOME ($ mil.)	NET PROFIT MARGIN	EMPLOYEES
9/08	10,600.0	—	—	50,000
9/07	9,900.0	—	—	50,000
9/06	7,500.0	—	—	50,000
9/05	7,239.0	—	—	50,000
9/04	7,116.0	—	—	50,000
Annual Growth	10.5%	—	—	0.0%

Revenue History

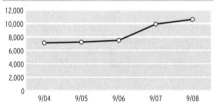

Walgreen Co.

Walgreen offers an old-fashioned tonic for fiscal fitness: quality over quantity and homespun growth rather than growth through acquisitions. It works. Walgreen operates 6,850-plus stores in 50 states, the District of Columbia, Guam, and Puerto Rico, as well as two mail-order facilities. Prescription drugs account for nearly two-thirds of sales; the rest comes from general merchandise, over-the-counter medications, cosmetics, and groceries. Walgreen usually builds rather than buys stores, so it can pick prime locations. For added convenience, most stores offer drive-through pharmacies, and almost all offer one-hour photo processing. Walgreen is slowing future store openings to focus on strengthening existing stores.

Walgreen's strategic shift coincides with a change in leadership, economic turmoil in the US, and follows its defeat by archrival CVS in a takeover battle for Longs Drug Stores in late 2008. (CVS's acquisition of Longs put it ahead of Walgreen with 6,800 retail pharmacies nationwide vs. 6,600 for Walgreen.) Walgreen proved more successful in its acquisition of the specialty pharmacy business of McKesson Corporation, completed in December 2008. It made the purchase to further strengthen the #4 position of its subsidiary, Walgreens Specialty Pharmacy LLC.

The drugstore chain has picked an insider to lead it as its next CEO: former president and COO Gregory Wasson, who joined Walgreen as a pharmacy intern nearly 30 years ago.

With more prescription drug business going to managed-care health plans, convenience has trumped price in the race to attract new customers. (Co-pays are the same at any chain, and sick folks are often short on patience.) Walgreen has led the movement in creating a "convenience drugstore" chain with freestanding stores. The strategy has several advantages. Walgreen's freestanding stores are more visible than those in strip malls and offer shoppers ample parking and easy in-and-out access. About a fifth of its stores are open 24 hours a day and the abundance of drive-through pharmacies adds to the chain's convenience offerings.

The worsening economic environment is causing Walgreen to curtail its break-neck pace of organic growth. The firm announced that it would cut costs, unclutter its stores, and change the way it fills prescriptions in response to increased competition and slowing drug sales. In 2009 the company trimmed its management ranks by about 1,000 positions (about 9% of its corporate management).

Walgreen also aims to play an increasingly important role in the solution to America's health care crisis through its operation of some 710 in-store clinics and worksite health centers. In a bid to diminish its reliance on retail stores for growth and expand its in-store network of health clinics, Walgreen has formed a new Health and Wellness division to operate clinics and pharmacies at large-company worksites. To that end, it has acquired two operators of worksite health centers, I-trax, Inc and Whole Health Management. The purchases gave Walgreen more than 600 worksite and retail health clinics in 40 states. Previously, Walgreen acquired in-store health clinic operator Take Care Health Systems, which managed about 145 clinics in about a dozen states.

HISTORY

In 1901 Chicago pharmacist Charles Walgreen borrowed $2,000 from his father for a down payment on his first drugstore. He sold a half interest in his first store in 1909 and bought a second, where he installed a large soda fountain and began serving lunch. In 1916 seven stores consolidated under the corporate name Walgreen Co. By 1920 there were 20 stores in Chicago, with sales of $1.55 million.

Walgreen popularized the milk shake in the early 1920s, and he promoted his chain with the first company-owned-and-operated airplane. The firm was first listed on the NYSE in 1927; two years later its 397 stores in 87 cities had sales of $47 million.

The company did comparatively well during the Great Depression. Although average sales per store dropped between 1931 and 1935, per-store earnings went up, thanks to a chainwide emphasis on efficiency. By 1940 Walgreen had 489 stores, but the chain shrank during WWII when unprofitable stores were closed.

The 1950s saw a major change in the way drugstores did business. Walgreen was an early leader in self-service merchandising, opening its first self-serve store in 1952; it had 22 by the end of 1953. Between 1950 and 1960, as small, older stores were replaced with larger, more efficient, self-service units, the total number of stores in the chain increased only about 10%, but sales grew by more than 90%.

By 1960 Walgreen had 451 stores, half of which were self-service. The company bought three Globe discount department stores in Houston in 1962 and expanded the chain to 13 stores by 1966, but Globe struggled in the early 1970s and was sold in 1975. During the 1960s Walgreen began phasing out its soda fountains, which had become unprofitable.

The 1970s and 1980s brought rapid growth and modernization to the chain. It opened its 1,000th store in 1984.

Walgreen began its Healthcare Plus subsidiary in 1992 to provide prescriptions by mail. Along with other independent drugstores, it helped set up Pharmacy Direct Network in 1994 to manage prescription drug programs for group health plans. In 1995 Walgreen launched a prescription benefits management company, WHP Health Initiatives, to target small to midsized employers and HMOs.

President (and pharmacist) L. Daniel Jorndt was promoted to CEO in early 1998 after the founder's grandson, Charles Walgreen III, stepped down; Jorndt became chairman in 1999.

Jorndt retired in January 2003. CEO David Bernauer added chairman to his job description. In 2006 Walgreens Home Care acquired Oklahoma City-based Canadian Valley Medical Solutions, a provider of home care services to patients in central and western Oklahoma.

In 2007 Bernauer was succeeded by Jeffrey Reins. Also, Charles R. Walgreen, Jr. — son of company founder, president of the company from 1939 to 1963, and chairman from 1963 until 1976 — died at the age of 100. Also that year the company agreed to pay $20 million to settle a class-action lawsuit filed by the US Equal Employment Opportunity Commission alleging that Walgreen discriminated against thousands of its black employees. Also, in 2007 Walgreen purchased Illinois-based Option Care, a specialty pharmacy and home infusion provider with more than 100 stores in 34 states, for about $850 million.

EXECUTIVES

Chairman: Alan G. McNally, age 63
President and CEO: Gregory D. (Greg) Wasson, age 50, $2,621,653 total compensation
EVP and CFO: Wade D. Miquelon, age 44, $499,715 total compensation
VP and CIO: Denise K. Wong, age 50
VP and Chief Marketing Officer: Kimberly L. Feil, age 49
VP New Product Development and Chief Innovation Officer: Colin Watts
VP and Chief Sales Officer: Jeffrey J. Zavada
EVP Store Operations: Mark A. Wagner, age 47

SVP, General Counsel, and Secretary: Dana I. Green, age 58
SVP; President, Walgreens Health and Wellness: Hal F. Rosenbluth, age 57
SVP Store Operations: R. Bruce Bryant, age 58
SVP Distribution and Logistics: J. Randolph (Randy) Lewis, age 59
SVP Pharmacy Innovation and Purchasing: George J. Riedl, age 49, $2,042,587 total compensation
SVP Human Resources: Kenneth R. (Ken) Weigand, age 51
SVP Pharmacy: Kermit R. Crawford, age 49
SVP Pharmacy Services: Donald C. (Don) Huonker Jr., age 47
SVP Store Operations: Debra M. (Debbie) Ferguson, age 51
SVP; President, Walgreen Health Services: Stanley B. Blaylock, age 45
SVP E-Commerce: Sona Chawla, age 41
Divisional VP and General Auditor: Chester G. Young, age 63
Divisional VP Marketing Development: Catherine Lindner, age 39
Auditors: Deloitte & Touche LLP

LOCATIONS

HQ: Walgreen Co.
200 Wilmot Rd., Deerfield, IL 60015
Phone: 847-914-2500   **Fax:** 847-914-2804
Web: www.walgreens.com

2008 Locations

	No.
Florida	781
Texas	631
Illinois	549
California	525
Ohio	259
Arizona	241
Tennessee	242
Wisconsin	221
Michigan	211
New York	208
Indiana	205
Missouri	180
Georgia	166
Colorado	150
Massachusetts	153
North Carolina	148
New Jersey	138
Minnesota	122
Louisiana	127
Washington	115
Connecticut	109
Pennsylvania	106
Oklahoma	105
Virginia	93
Alabama	90
Kentucky	89
South Carolina	83
Delaware	64
Nevada	76
Iowa	68
New Mexico	57
Kansas	61
Oregon	62
Nebraska	56
Mississippi	63
Arkansas	50
Maryland	48
Other states	197
Puerto Rico	95
Guam	1
Total	**6,934**

PRODUCTS/OPERATIONS

2008 Sales

	% of total
Prescription drugs	65
General merchandise	25
Nonprescription drugs	10
Total	**100**

2008 Locations

	No.
Drugstores	6,443
Worksite facilities	364
Home care facilities	115
Specialty pharmacies	10
Mail service facilities	2
Total	**6,934**

COMPETITORS

7-Eleven	Kmart
99 Cents Only	Kroger
A&P	Medicine Shoppe
Concentra	Meijer
Costco Wholesale	Nutritional Sourcing
CVS Caremark	Publix
Dollar General	Randall's
drugstore.com	Rite Aid
Duane Reade	Ritz Camera Centers
Express Scripts	Safeway
Family Dollar Stores	SHPS
Food Lion	Smith's Food & Drug
GNC	Snyder's Drug Stores
Health Fitness	SUPERVALU
Healthways, Inc.	Target
H-E-B	Wal-Mart
Kerr Drug	Winn-Dixie

HISTORICAL FINANCIALS

Company Type: Public

Income Statement

FYE: August 31

	REVENUE ($ mil.)	NET INCOME ($ mil.)	NET PROFIT MARGIN	EMPLOYEES
8/08	59,034.0	2,157.0	3.7%	237,000
8/07	53,762.0	2,041.3	3.8%	226,000
8/06	47,409.0	1,750.6	3.7%	195,000
8/05	42,201.6	1,559.5	3.7%	179,000
8/04	37,508.2	1,360.2	3.6%	163,000
Annual Growth	12.0%	12.2%	—	9.8%

2008 Year-End Financials

Debt ratio: 10.4%	No. of shares (mil.): 992
Return on equity: 18.0%	Dividends
Cash ($ mil.): 443	Yield: 1.1%
Current ratio: 1.57	Payout: 18.4%
Long-term debt ($ mil.): 1,337	Market value ($ mil.): 36,152

Stock History

NYSE: WAG

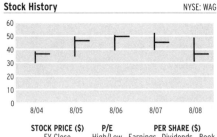

	STOCK PRICE ($) FY Close	P/E High/Low		PER SHARE ($)	
			Earnings	Dividends	Book Value
8/08	36.43	22 14	2.17	0.40	12.97
8/07	45.07	25 20	2.03	0.33	11.19
8/06	49.46	29 23	1.72	0.27	10.19
8/05	46.33	32 23	1.52	0.22	8.96
8/04	36.45	29 23	1.32	0.18	8.29
Annual Growth	(0.0%)	— —	13.2%	22.1%	11.8%

Wal-Mart Stores

Wal-Mart Stores is an irresistible (or at least unavoidable) retail force that has yet to meet any immovable objects. Bigger than Europe's Carrefour, Tesco, and Metro AG combined, it is the world's #1 retailer, with more than 7,870 stores, including about 890 discount stores, 2,970 combination discount and grocery stores (Wal-Mart Supercenters in the US and ASDA in the UK), and 600 warehouse stores (SAM'S CLUB). About 55% of its stores are in the US, but Wal-Mart continues expanding internationally; it is the #1 retailer in Canada and Mexico and it has operations in Asia (where it owns a 95% stake in Japanese retailer SEIYU), Europe, and South America. Founder Sam Walton's heirs own about 40% of Wal-Mart.

The company, which employs more than 2.1 million people worldwide, is famous for its low prices and breadth of merchandise. Another part of the retailing leviathan's appeal is its efforts to promote a small-town flavor, with friendly greeters and patriotic trappings.

Prescription drug sales at its more than 3,000 pharmacies make Wal-Mart the nation's third-largest drug retailer (behind Walgreen and CVS). It plans to branch out into the pharmacy-benefits field, in which it would help other employers manage their prescription plans.

Through joint ventures in China the company operates more than 240 stores. In a move that demonstrates how important the vast Chinese market is to the world's largest retailer, staunchly anti-union Wal-Mart has announced that it will work with officials there to establish labor unions in all Wal-Mart stores in China. Wal-Mart is poised to enter India's huge but fragmented market via a joint venture with the Bharti Enterprises Ltd.

The company is facing dozens of lawsuits alleging discrimination and violations of other labor and wage-and-hour laws. In December 2008 Wal-Mart agreed to pay up to $54.25 million in a class-action lawsuit brought by 100,000 current and former hourly Wal-Mart employees who worked at its Wal-Mart and Sam's Club stores in Minnesota between September 1998 and November 2008. It has also agreed to pay at least $352 million to settle 63 cases pending in federal and state courts in 42 states claiming that it forced employees to work off the clock.

Most notably, though, Wal-Mart has lost a bid to block a class action lawsuit (Betty Dukes v. Wal-Mart Stores, Inc.) filed in mid-2004 alleging discrimination against female employees. Covering 1.6 million current and former employees, Dukes v. Wal-Mart ranks as the largest workplace-bias lawsuit in US history.

Stung by criticism, Wal-Mart is taking a number of steps to polish its image as a benevolent employer and good corporate citizen, including raising starting salaries by about 6% at some stores and expanding health care coverage via the introduction of a new, cheaper health insurance plan with fewer restrictions.

Following the death of Helen Robson Walton in April 2007, the Walton family announced that much of the Wal-Mart stock held by Mrs. Walton through a family partnership will be donated to charity over several years. As a result, the Walton family's grip on the world's largest retailer will slip from 42% to about 33%, following the disposition of Mrs. Walton's 8.1% stake.

HISTORY

Sam Walton began his retail career as a J. C. Penney management trainee and later leased a Ben Franklin-franchised dime store in Newport, Arkansas, in 1945. In 1950 he relocated to Bentonville, Arkansas, and opened a Walton 5 & 10. By 1962 Walton owned 15 Ben Franklin stores under the Walton 5 & 10 name.

After Ben Franklin management rejected his suggestion to open discount stores in small towns, Walton, with his brother James "Bud" Walton, opened the first Wal-Mart Discount City in Rogers, Arkansas, in 1962. Wal-Mart Stores went public in 1970 with 18 stores and sales of $44 million. Avoiding regional retailers, Walton opened stores in small and midsized towns in the 1970s. The company sold its Ben Franklin stores in 1976. By 1980 Wal-Mart's 276 stores had sales of $1.2 billion.

In 1983 Wal-Mart opened SAM'S Wholesale Club, a concept based on the successful cash-and-carry, membership-only warehouse format pioneered by the Price Company of California (now Costco Wholesale Corp.). It started Hypermart*USA in 1987 as a joint venture with Dallas-based supermarket chain Cullum Companies. The discount store/supermarket hybrid was later retooled as Wal-Mart Supercenters. Sam stepped down as CEO in 1988 and president David Glass was appointed CEO. Wal-Mart bought out Cullum the next year.

Wal-Mart acquired wholesale distributor McLane Company in 1990. In 1992, the year Sam died, the company expanded into Mexico through a joint venture to open SAM'S CLUBS with Mexico's largest retailer Cifra (renamed Wal-Mart de México in 2000). Wal-Mart acquired 122 former Woolco stores in Canada in 1994. Co-founder Bud died a year later.

More international expansion included entering China in 1996; the acquisition of German hypermarket chain Wertkauf in 1997; the purchase of Brazilian retailer Lojas Americanas' 40% interest in a joint venture (1998); and the addition of four stores and other sites in South Korea. In 1999 Wal-Mart bought 74 German-based Interspar hypermarkets and acquired ASDA Group, the UK's third-largest supermarket chain.

COO Lee Scott succeeded Glass as CEO in 2000. In June 2001 a group of six current and former female Wal-Mart employees filed a sex-discrimination lawsuit (seeking to represent up to 500,000 current and former Wal-Mart workers) against the company.

In 2002 the company was crowned America's largest corporation by FORTUNE magazine. In 2003 Wal-Mart sold its McLane grocery distribution business to Berkshire Hathaway.

In 2005 the retailer settled a high-profile lawsuit by agreeing to pay $11 million to the US government to close an investigation into the use of illegal immigrants by Wal-Mart contractors to clean its stores.

Wal-Mart's former vice chairman Thomas Coughlin, who was accused of misusing more than $500,000 in company funds, pleaded guilty to fraud and tax charges in 2006. He was sentenced to 27 months of house arrest and ordered to pay $400,000 in restitution to his former employer. Wal-Mart itself was ordered by a Pennsylvania jury to pay more than $78 million in damages in a class action suit brought by employees alleging that it forced employees to work during breaks and off the clock.

CEO Lee Scott retired in early 2009. Mike Duke, who had run Wal-Mart's international operation, succeeded Scott.

EXECUTIVES

Chairman: S. Robson (Rob) Walton, age 64
Vice Chairman; President and CEO, Wal-Mart Stores Division U.S.: Eduardo Castro-Wright, age 54, $9,987,493 total compensation
President, CEO, and Director: Michael T. (Mike) Duke, age 59, $12,238,209 total compensation
EVP and COO: William S. (Bill) Simon
EVP and CFO: Thomas M. (Tom) Schoewe, age 56, $9,477,584 total compensation
EVP and CIO: Rollin Lee Ford, age 46
EVP and Chief Merchandising Officer: John E. Fleming
EVP and Chief Administrative Officer, Wal-Mart US: Thomas A. (Tom) Mars, age 51
EVP and Chief Marketing Officer: Stephen F. Quinn
Chief Diversity Officer: L. Mecole (Cole) Brown
EVP Legal, Compliance, Ethics and Corporate Secretary: Thomas D. (Tom) Hyde, age 60
EVP Corporate Affairs and Government Relations: Leslie A. Dach, age 54
EVP Merchandising and Replenishment, SAM'S CLUB: Gregory E. (Greg) Spragg
EVP; President and CEO, Wal-Mart International Division: C. Douglas (Doug) McMillon, age 42, $8,191,857 total compensation
EVP Finance and Treasurer: Charles M. Holley Jr.
EVP and General Counsel: Jeffrey J. (Jeff) Gearhart, age 44
President and CEO, Latin America: Vicente Trius
President and CEO, SAM'S CLUB: Brian C. Cornell, age 50
Director Investor Relations: Mike Beckstead
Auditors: Ernst & Young LLP

LOCATIONS

HQ: Wal-Mart Stores, Inc.
702 SW 8th St., Bentonville, AR 72716
Phone: 479-273-4000 **Fax:** 479-277-1830
Web: www.walmartstores.com

2009 Stores

	No.
US	4,258
International	
Argentina	28
Brazil	345
Canada	318
Chile	197
Costa Rica	164
El Salvador	77
Guatemala	160
Honduras	50
Japan	371
Mexico	1,197
Nicaragua	51
Puerto Rico	56
United Kingdom	358
China	243
Total	**7,873**

PRODUCTS/OPERATIONS

2009 Stores

	No.
US	
Supercenters	2,612
Discount stores	891
SAM'S CLUB	602
Neighborhood Markets	153
International stores	3,372
Chinese joint venture stores	243
Total	**7,873**

2009 Sales

	$ bil.	% of total
Wal-Mart US	255.7	63
International	98.6	24
SAM'S CLUB	46.9	12
Membership and other income	4.4	1
Total	**405.6**	**100**

2009 US Sales

	% of total
Grocery	49
Entertainment	13
Hardlines	12
Apparel	11
Health & wellness	10
Home	5
Total	**100**

Retail Divisions

ASDA (large, combination general merchandise and food stores)
Neighborhood Markets (traditional supermarkets)
SAM'S CLUB (members-only warehouse clubs)
Supercenters (large, combination general merchandise and food stores)
Wal-Mart International Division (foreign operations)
Wal-Mart Stores (general merchandise)

COMPETITORS

Ace Hardware	Kohl's
Albertsons	Kroger
ALDI	Lianhua Supermarket
Apple Inc.	Limited Brands
Army and Air Force Exchange	Loblaw
	Lowe's
Aurora Wholesalers	Maruetsu
AutoZone	Meijer
Bed Bath & Beyond	METRO AG
Best Buy	Microsoft
Big Lots	Office Depot
BJ's Wholesale Club	Pep Boys
Bridgestone Retail Operations	PETCO
	Publix
Carrefour	RadioShack
Costco Wholesale	Rite Aid
CVS Caremark	Royal Ahold
Dollar General	Safeway
Eby-Brown	Sears
Family Dollar Stores	Staples
The Gap	SUPERVALU
Home Depot	Target
Hudson's Bay	TJX Companies
J. C. Penney	Toys "R" Us
Katz Group	True Value
Kmart	Walgreen

HISTORICAL FINANCIALS

Company Type: Public

Income Statement

FYE: January 31

	REVENUE ($ mil.)	NET INCOME ($ mil.)	NET PROFIT MARGIN	EMPLOYEES
1/09	405,607.0	13,400.0	3.3%	2,100,000
1/08	378,799.0	12,731.0	3.4%	2,100,000
1/07	348,650.0	11,284.0	3.2%	1,900,000
1/06	312,427.0	11,231.0	3.6%	1,800,000
1/05	285,222.0	10,267.0	3.6%	1,700,000
Annual Growth	9.2%	6.9%	—	5.4%

2009 Year-End Financials

Debt ratio: 52.9%
Return on equity: 20.6%
Cash ($ mil.): 7,275
Current ratio: 0.88
Long-term debt ($ mil.): 34,549

No. of shares (mil.): 3,897
Dividends
 Yield: 2.0%
 Payout: 28.0%
Market value ($ mil.): 183,609

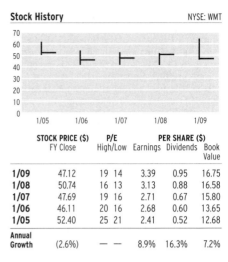

Stock History

NYSE: WMT

	STOCK PRICE ($) FY Close	P/E High/Low	PER SHARE ($) Earnings	Dividends	Book Value
1/09	47.12	19 14	3.39	0.95	16.75
1/08	50.74	16 13	3.13	0.88	16.58
1/07	47.69	19 16	2.71	0.67	15.80
1/06	46.11	20 16	2.68	0.60	13.65
1/05	52.40	25 21	2.41	0.52	12.68
Annual Growth	(2.6%)	— —	8.9%	16.3%	7.2%

The Walt Disney Company

The monarch of this magic kingdom is no man but a mouse — Mickey Mouse. The Walt Disney Company is the world's #2 media conglomerate (behind Time Warner) with assets encompassing movies, music, publishing, television, and theme parks. Its TV holdings include the ABC television network and 10 broadcast stations, as well as a portfolio of cable networks including ABC Family, Lifetime Entertainment (50%-owned), and ESPN (80%). Walt Disney Studios produces films through such imprints as Walt Disney Pictures, Touchstone, Pixar, and Miramax. Walt Disney Parks and Resorts is one of the top theme park operators in the world, anchored by its popular Walt Disney World and Disneyland resorts.

A substantial part of Disney's business comes from ancillary products mostly aimed at children created from its trove of characters and other intellectual property. To fuel that consumer products engine, Disney has traditionally relied on its creative units to continually produce new original properties. In 2009, however, the company announced plans to acquire comic book publisher Marvel Entertainment for about $4 billion in cash and stock. The deal will expand Disney's stable of intellectual property with the addition of such characters as Iron Man, Spider-Man, and the X-Men, which have all been turned into successful Hollywood blockbusters and licensed for other purposes.

Walt Disney's film units hit a rough patch during 2008 when such films as *The Chronicles of Narnia: Prince Caspian* under-performed at the box office. That trend continued into 2009 with such titles as *Bedtime Stories* and *Race to Witch Mountain*. Disney inked a distribution deal with Steven Spielberg's DreamWorks studio in 2009 in an effort to boost box office output. Disney's Pixar unit, meanwhile, continues to find ways to draw big audiences. In 2009 it released *Up* which took in nearly $70 million its first weekend, following up on the 2008 hit *WALL-E*.

Disney's theme parks and resorts continue to draw millions of visitors each year, but the recession has hurt the travel and tourism industry. In response the unit announced hundreds of job cuts early in 2009 as part of a cost-saving effort.

However, the company is in talks with the Chinese government about building another park in Shanghai as part of a broader expansion strategy targeting China.

The company's television segment has also been troubled by the recession and its effect on advertising. Disney's ABC network has foundered somewhat the past couple years despite such hit shows as *Grey's Anatomy* and *Desperate Housewives*. With advertising revenue declining, Disney-ABC Television announced significant job cuts early in 2009.

Disney continues to invest in digital and interactive media in an effort to stay ahead of rapid developments in technology. The company acquired a 30% stake in Hulu in 2009, joining fellow media giants News Corporation and NBCU as a partner in the online video venture.

Disney also distributes films and TV shows through Apple's iTunes store. (Apple CEO Steve Jobs is Disney's largest individual stockholder with a 7% holding he acquired when the company purchased Pixar.)

HISTORY

After getting started as an illustrator in Kansas City, Walt Disney and his brother Roy started Disney Brothers Studio in Hollywood, California, in 1923. Walt directed the first Mickey Mouse cartoon, *Plane Crazy,* in 1928 (the third, *Steamboat Willie,* was the first cartoon with a soundtrack). The studio produced its first animated feature film, *Snow White and the Seven Dwarfs,* in 1937. Walt Disney Productions went public in 1940 and later produced classics such as *Fantasia* and *Pinocchio.* The Disneyland theme park opened in 1955.

Roy Disney became chairman after Walt died of lung cancer in 1966. Disney World opened in Florida in 1971, the year Roy died. His son, Roy E., became the company's principal individual shareholder. Walt's son-in-law, Ron Miller, became president in 1980. Two years later Epcot Center opened in Florida. In 1984 the Bass family of Texas, in alliance with Roy E., bought a controlling interest in the company. New CEO Michael Eisner (from Paramount) and president Frank Wells (from Warner Bros.) ushered in an era of innovation, prosperity, and high executive salaries. The company later launched The Disney Channel and opened new theme parks, including Tokyo Disneyland (1984) and Disney-MGM Studios (1989; later renamed Hollywood Studios). In 1986 the company changed its name to The Walt Disney Company. Disneyland Paris (originally Euro Disney) opened in 1992.

Following Wells' death in a helicopter crash in 1994, boardroom infighting led to the acrimonious departure of studio head Jeffrey Katzenberg. (He was awarded $250 million in compensation in 1999.) The next year Eisner appointed Hollywood agent Michael Ovitz as president. (Ovitz left after 16 months with a severance package of more than $100 million.) Disney bought Capital Cities/ABC (now ABC, Inc.) for $19 billion in 1996, and two years later it bought Web services firm Starwave from Microsoft co-founder Paul Allen.

The company expanded its theme parks in Anaheim in 2001, opening Downtown Disney and Disney's California Adventure. Later Disney bought Fox Family Channel, which it renamed ABC Family, from News Corp. and Haim Saban for $2.9 billion in cash and assumption of $2.3 billion in debt. At Disney's annual shareholder meeting in 2004, about 45% of stock owners voted to not re-elect the embattled Eisner to the board. In response, Disney directors stripped Eisner of the chairman title and named director and former US senator George Mitchell to that position.

Disney boosted its children's entertainment properties in 2004 by purchasing the Muppet and *Bear in the Big Blue House* characters, along with their film and television libraries, from The Jim Henson Company.

In 2005 Eisner passed the CEO torch after more than 20 years to former COO Robert Iger. That same year Disney Parks opened Hong Kong Disneyland, its biggest foray into the world's most populated country. Also the Weinstein brothers left Miramax to form their own organization, The Weinstein Company, ending two of the most successful tenures of the independent film movement.

In mid-2006 Walt Disney completed a crucial acquisition — the $7.4 billion purchase of Pixar Animation. Disney almost lost Pixar as a production partner in the animation house's blockbuster films, but Iger successfully dodged the bullet.

In 2007 Disney spun off ABC's radio broadcasting operations to Citadel Broadcasting for $2.7 billion in cash and stock.

EXECUTIVES

Chairman: John E. Pepper Jr., age 70
President, CEO, and Director: Robert A. (Bob) Iger, age 57
SEVP and CFO: Thomas O. (Tom) Staggs, age 47
SVP and CIO: Susan O'Day
EVP Corporate Strategy, Business Development, and Technology: Kevin A. Mayer, age 46
EVP and Chief Human Resources Officer: Dennis W. Shuler, age 53
EVP and Chief Human Resources Officer: Jayne Parker
SEVP, General Counsel, and Secretary: Alan N. Braverman, age 60
EVP Corporate Communications: Zenia Mucha
EVP Corporate Finance, Real Estate, and Treasurer: Christine M. McCarthy, age 53
EVP Worldwide Government Relations: Preston Padden, age 60
EVP, Disney Media Advertising Sales and Marketing Group: Patricia (Tricia) Wilber
EVP Strategy and Research, Disney Media Networks: Peter Seymour, age 41
SVP Investor Relations: Lowell Singer
Chairman, Disney Consumer Products: Andrew P. (Andy) Mooney
Chairman, Walt Disney Parks and Resorts: James A. (Jay) Rasulo
Co-Chairman, Disney Media Networks; President, ESPN; President, ABC Sports: George W. Bodenheimer, age 50
Co-Chairman, Disney Media Networks; President, Disney-ABC Television: Anne M. Sweeney
Chairman, The Walt Disney Studios: Richard W. (Dick) Cook
Chairman, Disney Music Group: Robert (Bob) Cavallo
President, Walt Disney Animation Studios and Pixar Animation Studios: Edwin E. (Ed) Catmull, age 64
Auditors: PricewaterhouseCoopers LLP

LOCATIONS

HQ: The Walt Disney Company
500 S. Buena Vista St., Burbank, CA 91521
Phone: 818-560-1000   **Fax:** 818-560-1930
Web: disney.go.com

2008 Sales

	$ mil.	% of total
US & Canada	28,506	75
Europe	6,805	18
Asia/Pacific	1,811	5
Latin America & other regions	721	2
Total	**37,843**	**100**

PRODUCTS/OPERATIONS

2008 Sales

	$ mil.	% of total
Media networks	16,116	42
Parks & resorts	11,504	30
Studio entertainment	7,348	19
Consumer products	2,875	9
Total	**37,843**	**100**

Selected Operations

Consumer products
Buena Vista Worldwide Home Entertainment (video and DVD)
The Disney Catalog (direct marketing)
Disney Interactive Studios (children's software and video games)

Filmed entertainment
ABC Television Studio
Disney-ABC Domestic Television
Miramax Films
Pixar
Touchstone Pictures
Walt Disney Feature Animation
Walt Disney Pictures
Walt Disney Television

Internet
ABC.com
ABCNEWS.com
ABCSports.com
Disney.com
ESPN.com
FamilyFun.com
Hulu (30%)

Live entertainment (Disney Theatrical Group)
Disney Live Family Entertainment
Disney Theatrical Productions

Music
Buena Vista Records
Hollywood Records
Lyric Street
Walt Disney Records

Publishing
Discover (magazine)
Disney Adventures (magazine)
Disney Publishing Worldwide (children's books)
FamilyFun (magazine)
Hyperion (adult trade books)

Television networks
A&E Television Networks (37.5%)
A&E
The Biography Channel
The History Channel
ABC Family Channel
ABC Television Network
Disney Channel
ESPN (80%)
JETIX Europe
JETIX Latin America
Lifetime Entertainment Services (50%)
SOAPnet
Toon Disney

Television stations
KABC (Los Angeles)
KFSN (Fresno, CA)
KGO (San Francisco)
KTRK (Houston)
WABC (New York City)
WJRT (Flint, MI)
WLS (Chicago)
WPVI (Philadelphia)
WTVD (Raleigh-Durham, NC)
WTVG (Toledo, OH)

Theme parks and resorts
　Adventures by Disney (vacation packages)
　Disney Cruise Line
　Euro Disney (40%)
　Disneyland Resort (Anaheim, CA)
　ESPN Zone (theme restaurants)
　Hong Kong Disneyland (43%)
　Tokyo Disney Resort (owned and operated by Oriental
　　Land Co.; Disney earns royalties)
　Walt Disney Imagineering (planning and development)
　Walt Disney World Resort (Orlando, FL)

COMPETITORS

Busch Entertainment
CBS Corp
Discovery Communications
DreamWorks Animation
Liberty Media
Lucasfilm
MGM
NBC Universal
News Corp.
Six Flags
Sony Pictures Entertainment
Time Warner
Viacom
Yahoo!

HISTORICAL FINANCIALS

Company Type: Public

Income Statement

FYE: September 30

	REVENUE ($ mil.)	NET INCOME ($ mil.)	NET PROFIT MARGIN	EMPLOYEES
9/08	37,843.0	4,427.0	11.7%	150,000
9/07	35,510.0	4,687.0	13.2%	137,000
9/06	34,285.0	3,374.0	9.8%	133,000
9/05	31,944.0	2,569.0	8.0%	133,000
9/04	30,752.0	2,345.0	7.6%	129,000
Annual Growth	5.3%	17.2%	—	3.8%

2008 Year-End Financials

Debt ratio: 34.4%
Return on equity: 14.0%
Cash ($ mil.): 3,001
Current ratio: 1.01
Long-term debt ($ mil.): 11,110

No. of shares (mil.): 1,859
Dividends
　Yield: 1.1%
　Payout: 15.4%
Market value ($ mil.): 57,039

Stock History

NYSE: DIS

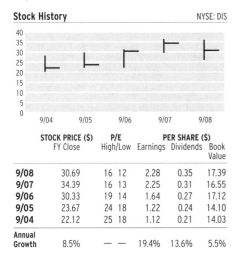

	STOCK PRICE ($) FY Close	P/E High/Low		PER SHARE ($) Earnings	Dividends	Book Value
9/08	30.69	16	12	2.28	0.35	17.39
9/07	34.39	16	13	2.25	0.31	16.55
9/06	30.33	19	14	1.64	0.27	17.12
9/05	23.67	24	18	1.22	0.24	14.10
9/04	22.12	25	18	1.12	0.21	14.03
Annual Growth	8.5%	—	—	19.4%	13.6%	5.5%

Warnaco Group

Underwear has long been The Warnaco Group's foundation. One of the leading marketers of bras, the firm boasts a diverse portfolio of its own and licensed brands, including Calvin Klein, Speedo, Chaps, Olga, and Warner's. Warnaco also makes menswear under the brands Calvin Klein and Chaps by Ralph Lauren. The manufacturer sells apparel to about 50,000 department, mass merchandise, and specialty stores in Asia, Europe, Mexico, and North America. The Warnaco Group also operates about 900 Calvin Klein retail stores worldwide and sells Calvin Klein and Speedo brand merchandise online. Warnaco sold its Lejaby business to Palmers Textil AG in early 2008 as part of its strategic realignment launched in late 2007.

Palmers Textil has picked up Lejaby for about $47 million in cash and $18 million in an interest-free note due December 31, 2013. As part of the deal, Lejaby will remain headquartered in Lyon. By selling Lejaby, Warnaco has effectively exited all owned manufacturing.

While it sheds manufacturing operations, Warnaco has been building its retail arm. In 2008 it acquired a business that operates about a dozen retail stores in China just in time for the Beijing Olympic Games, where the company's Speedo brand got plenty of exposure. Indeed, the company's Swimwear Group has placed its bet on Speedo and, with the exception of Calvin Klein swimwear, has exited the designer swimwear business. (In recent years it has sold its OP, Catalina, Anne Cole, and Cole of California lines.)

Warnaco has also increased its international business substantially, from about 42% of net revenues in 2006 to more than 54% in 2008. The company is looking to grow its business in Asia, Europe, and South America. Another growth area for the company is direct sales, which account for about a fifth of its net revenues. But sales of Calvin Klein brand merchandise remain the company's cash cow, contributing upwards of 70% of net revenues in 2008.

Dimensional Fund Advisors owns about 6% of the company.

HISTORY

The Warnaco Group was founded in 1874 by brothers DeVer and Lucien Warner. As doctors, they were concerned about the unhealthy effects of boned and tight-fitting women's corsets. After much research, DeVer came up with a new corset made only from cloth. Within a few weeks of selling their first goods from a one-room tailor shop in McGrawville, New York, the brothers had a flourishing business, which they called Warner Brother's or Warner's.

In a business largely dependent on the changing trends of fashion, Warner's tried to adapt to the corsetless era of the 1920s with wraparound undergarments and by making greater use of rubber and elastic, but sales soured. After WWII, however, Warner's surged ahead.

Warner's apparel division acquired shirtmaker Hathaway in 1960. The firm was renamed Warnaco in 1968. Despite expansion and diversification in the 1970s, it lost ground to cheaper imports. Warnaco succumbed to a $550 million hostile takeover in 1986 led by a group of investors, including Linda Wachner, who had worked for Warnaco in the mid-1970s.

As chairman and CEO, Wachner transformed Warnaco from a maker of a mishmash of apparel products to a highly focused branded-apparel producer. Wachner and a group of investors bought Warnaco's Speedo swimwear division in 1990 (taking it public as Authentic Fitness in 1992, only to purchase it again in 1999). In 1991 the firm held its own IPO. It bought Calvin Klein's underwear business in 1994.

In 1996 Warnaco acquired GJM Group (private-label sleepwear and lingerie), Bodyslimmers (shapeware), and French lingerie maker Lejaby Euralis. It also sold its prestigious but underperforming Hathaway men's dress shirt operations. Sales topped $1 billion in 1996, but costs associated with the Hathaway sale and restructuring led to an $8 million loss.

Warnaco bought Designer Holdings, a maker of Calvin Klein jeans and sportswear, in 1997. By 1999 Warnaco owned distribution rights for Calvin Klein jeans in Canada, giving the company control over Calvin Klein jeans production and distribution throughout the Americas.

In 1998 Warnaco took a $69 million charge to discontinue Valentino and other brands and close a dozen outlet stores and a warehouse. The following year it bought 70% of UK perfume retailer Penhaligon and in 1999 added ABS by Allen Schwartz, a lower-priced designer womenswear maker.

A lawsuit came between Wachner and her Calvins in 2000 when Calvin Klein sued both Warnaco and Wachner for trademark violation and breach of trust. Wachner returned fire, suing Klein and his company for trademark violations, defamation, and trade libel. The firms settled in the hours before their trial was set to begin in 2001.

After dismal 2000 year-end results, Warnaco announced in April 2001 its plans to end its licensed Fruit of the Loom bra operations. In 2001 Warnaco filed for Chapter 11 bankruptcy protection. The board of directors ousted Wachner and replaced her with Antonio ("Tony") Alvarez as CEO and Stuart Buchalter as chairman. Alvarez began a restructuring program, which led to the sale of noncore assets such as GJM's sleepwear division and the closure of Calvin Klein outlet stores in 2002.

Wachner sued Warnaco to get $25 million she says the company owed her. An agreement was reached in November 2002 in which Wachner received $3.5 million in stock in the reorganized company and $200,000 in cash. She remained on the board of directors until the company emerged from bankruptcy in early 2003.

The year 2002 also brought the first round of paring down retail outlets: the company closed 47 Speedo retail outlets, 64 domestic outlet stores, and almost half of its 26 Calvin Klein underwear stores. The next round came in late 2003, with closure of all remaining Speedo stores and sale of its White Stag line to Wal-Mart.

In April 2003 Alvarez left and Joe Gromek (former CEO of Brooks Brothers) took over as president and CEO.

The company acquired the license, wholesale, and retail units for Calvin Klein jeans and accessories in Europe and Asia in January 2006 for about €240 million ($292 million).

In 2007 Warnaco sold its OP women's and junior's swimwear brand (bought in 2004) to Iconix Brand Group for $54 million. (Previously, Warnaco had hoped to morph Op into a $1 billion brand.)

In early 2008 Warnaco acquired about a dozen retail stores in China for about $2.5 million.

EXECUTIVES

Chairman: Charles R. Perrin, age 63
President, CEO, and Director: Joseph R. (Joe) Gromek, age 62, $6,431,639 total compensation
EVP and CFO: Lawrence R. Rutkowski, age 51, $1,992,937 total compensation
Chief Creative Officer, Calvin Klein Underwear: Robert A. Mazzoli
EVP International Strategy and Business Development: Stanley P. Silverstein, age 56, $2,027,287 total compensation
SVP Retail: Robert F. (Bob) Dakin, age 50
SVP, General Counsel, and Secretary: Jay L. Dubiner, age 45
SVP Human Resources: Elizabeth Wood, age 47
VP Investor Relations: Deborah Abraham
President, Sportswear Group: Frank Tworecke, age 62, $2,806,243 total compensation
President, Intimate Apparel Group: Helen McCluskey, age 53, $2,670,298 total compensation
President, Global Sourcing, Distribution, and Logistics: Dwight F. Meyer, age 56
President, Calvin Klein Underwear: Kay LeGrange
President, Calvin Klein Jeans: David Cunningham
Managing Director Europe: Thomas Axmacher
Auditors: Deloitte & Touche LLP

LOCATIONS

HQ: The Warnaco Group, Inc.
501 7th Ave., New York, NY 10018
Phone: 212-287-8000   **Fax:** 212-287-8297
Web: www.warnaco.com

2008 Sales

	$ mil.	% of total
US	942.2	46
Europe	576.3	28
Asia	321.2	16
Canada	115.5	5
Mexico, Central & South America	109.8	5
Total	**2,065.0**	**100**

PRODUCTS/OPERATIONS

2008 Sales

	$ mil.	% of total
Sportswear group	1,102.8	53
Intimate apparel	702.2	34
Swimwear group	260.0	13
Total	**2,065.0**	**100**

Selected Brands

Intimate apparel
  Body Nancy Ganz/Bodyslimmers
  Calvin Klein
  Olga
  Warner's

Sportswear and accessories
  Calvin Klein (licensed)
  Chaps by Ralph Lauren (licensed)
  Lauren/Ralph Lauren
  Ralph/Ralph Lauren
  Polo Sport Ralph Lauren (licensed)
  Polo Sport-RLX (licensed)
  Ralph Lauren (licensed)
  Speedo/Fastskin (licensed)

COMPETITORS

adidas	Limited Brands
Benetton	Liz Claiborne
Delta Galil Industries Ltd.	Maidenform
Donna Karan	NIKE
Frederick's of Hollywood	Perry Ellis International
Group	Polo Ralph Lauren
Fruit of the Loom	Russell Corporation
Guess?	Tommy Hilfiger
Hanesbrands	Triumph Apparel
Jockey International	Under Armour
Kellwood	VF
Levi Strauss	

HISTORICAL FINANCIALS

Company Type: Public

Income Statement

FYE: Saturday nearest December 31

	REVENUE ($ mil.)	NET INCOME ($ mil.)	NET PROFIT MARGIN	EMPLOYEES
12/08	2,065.0	47.3	2.3%	5,200
12/07	1,860.1	79.1	4.3%	4,656
12/06	1,827.5	50.8	2.8%	10,287
12/05	1,504.4	52.1	3.5%	10,156
12/04	1,424.2	42.5	3.0%	10,662
Annual Growth	**9.7%**	**2.7%**	**—**	**(16.4%)**

2008 Year-End Financials

Debt ratio: 20.8%
Return on equity: 6.1%
Cash ($ mil.): 148
Current ratio: 2.15
Long-term debt ($ mil.): 164
No. of shares (mil.): 45
Dividends
  Yield: 0.0%
  Payout: —
Market value ($ mil.): 892

Stock History

NYSE: WRC

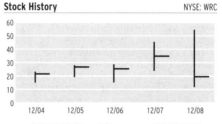

	STOCK PRICE ($) FY Close	P/E High/Low		PER SHARE ($) Earnings	Dividends	Book Value
12/08	19.63	53	12	1.01	0.00	17.34
12/07	34.80	26	14	1.70	0.00	17.02
12/06	25.38	26	15	1.08	0.00	15.03
12/05	26.72	25	18	1.11	0.00	13.91
12/04	21.60	24	17	0.93	0.00	12.70
Annual Growth	**(2.4%)**	**—**	**—**	**2.1%**	**—**	**8.1%**

Warner Music Group

These records were made to be listened to, not broken. Warner Music Group (WMG) is one of the largest recording companies in the world and ranks #3 in terms of US market share (behind Universal Music Group and Sony Music Entertainment). It operates through two businesses: Recorded Music and Music Publishing. The catalog of WMG's Recorded Music unit includes best-selling albums *The Eagles: Their Greatest Hits 1971-1975* and *Led Zeppelin IV*. Its Music Publishing business holds more than one million copyrights. The company's traditional A&R (artist and repertoire) work of finding and developing artists has helped WMG score hits from musicians such as Green Day and Faith Hill. Thomas H. Lee Partners owns more than 35% of WMG.

WMG's Recorded Music business produces, markets, and distributes recordings primarily through units Atlantic Records Group and Warner Bros. Records, and its Music Publishing business operates through Warner/Chappell Music.

Like all companies in the music business, WMG has struggled in the face of plummeting CD sales and slow growth in paid digital downloading. The company has responded through cost cutting and embracing new technologies.

Sales of digital music products, such as ringtones, videos, and downloaded songs and albums, now account for about 18% of the company's business. And while sales of physical albums and CDs continue to wither, WMG has committed to increasing its marketing and development efforts to expand into new digital media formats.

In late 2007 WMG began selling music online without copy protection (in the popular MP3 format) on Amazon.com's digital music store. WMG also embraced new video sharing mediums by striking a revenue-sharing deal with YouTube to distribute and license copyrighted songs, videos, and other materials. In addition, in 2008 WMG and the other major labels launched its MySpace Music joint venture with News Corp. to offer MySpace members a range of new music-listening and merchandising features.

In further efforts to beef up its music holdings, WMG acquired a nearly 75% stake in Roadrunner Music Group BV, which runs heavy metal label Roadrunner Records, in 2007. Later that year the company struck a deal with the family of Frank Sinatra to manage the exploitation of the singer's music, name, and likeness. The arrangement was completed through WMG's acquisition of a 50% stake in Frank Sinatra Enterprises for $50 million.

WMG approached its larger rival EMI Group with a $4.2 billion takeover bid in 2007, but the offer was rejected. On the flipside, WMB had rejected a $4.2 billion takeover bid from EMI in 2006. This follows a years-long battle of takeover attempts that stopped when EMI was eventually acquired by private equity firm Terra Firma in 2007. The companies had tried before to merge, only to be stopped by European regulators. If Warner Music and EMI were to combine, the deal would create a company worth an estimated $7 billion. The entity would control about 25% of the recorded music market, ranking second to Universal Music Group.

HISTORY

Warner Bros. co-founder Jack Warner expanded his film company's operations into music when he created Warner Bros. Records in 1958. Initially focused on sound tracks and comedy albums, the company soon expanded its scope by issuing recordings by the Everly Brothers and Peter, Paul & Mary. Warner bought Reprise Records in 1963, the label started by Frank Sinatra in 1961. Warner sold his entertainment empire in 1966 to Seven Arts Productions, which became Warner-Seven Arts. That year the company bought Atlantic Records, a label co-founded in 1947 by famed music producer Ahmet Ertegun. (Ertegun died in 2006.) Steven Ross' Kinney National Services purchased Warner-Seven Arts in 1969 and changed its name to Warner Communications.

Former Reprise Records chief Mo Ostin became CEO of Warner Bros. Records in the early 1970s and is credited with propelling the company into the forefront of the music industry. Reorganized as Warner Music, the company battled rival CBS Records (now part of Sony BMG Music Entertainment) for dominance in the music business by adding to its collection of labels, acquiring Elektra Records in 1970 and Asylum Records in 1974. The company later created a distribution arm, WEA (Warner-Electra-Atlantic), expanded internationally, and established a record pressing plant. Warner Music prospered in the 1980s, scoring hits with artists like R.E.M. and Madonna.

Parent Warner Communications was acquired by publisher Time Inc. in 1990, and Warner Music became part of media giant Time Warner. However, the company was losing market share and executive infighting was reaching a fevered pitch. Several top executives jumped ship. HBO chief Michael Fuchs took over in 1995 and cleaned house, but he himself was ousted later that year. Warner film studio chiefs Bob Daly and Terry Semel were later appointed co-CEOs.

While Daly and Semel helped restore order to the music group, they failed to revive sales. They announced their resignation in 1999, and Warner Music International executive Roger Ames was appointed chairman and CEO. To regain market share, Time Warner agreed to combine Warner Music with the UK's struggling EMI Group. Under the proposed deal, each would have held 50% of the resulting company. However, European regulators began to balk at the combination in light of America Online's offer to buy Time Warner. To save the larger deal, the combination with EMI was called off.

Following the merger of AOL and Time Warner in 2001, Ames began tightening the belt, cutting some 600 staff members and centralizing label operations.

In 2003 Warner sold the DVD and CD manufacturing businesses of WEA to Cinram for $1 billion. WEA's sales and marketing operations remained with Warner.

The following year Warner was taken private when a group of investors led by Edgar Bronfman, Jr., with backing from Thomas H. Lee Partners, Bain Capital, and Providence Equity Partners purchased the music company from Time Warner for $2.6 billion. The company went public in 2005.

Also that year the company signed a distribution deal with Sean "Diddy" Combs, taking a 50% stake in his Bad Boy Records (part of Bad Boy Worldwide Entertainment).

In 2006 Warner purchased Ryko Corporation and its Rykodisc label, one of the top independent record companies in the US.

EXECUTIVES

Chairman and CEO: Edgar M. Bronfman Jr., age 53
Vice Chairman Strategy and Operations:
Michael D. Fleisher, age 44
Vice Chairman Warner Music Group; Chairman and CEO, Recorded Music Americas and U.K.: Lyor Cohen, age 49
CFO: Steven Macri
SVP and CIO: Maggie Miller
EVP and Chief Communications Officer: Will Tanous, age 40
EVP Human Resources and Chief Compliance:
Mark Ansorge
EVP: Kevin Liles
EVP Global Human Resources: Caroline Stockdale, age 45
EVP Digital Strategy and Business Development:
Michael Nash, age 52
EVP and General Counsel: Paul M. Robinson, age 51
SVP New Media: Jeremy Welt
SVP Global Product Development: Nikke Slight
SVP Strategy and Product Development: George White
SVP Investor Relations and Corporate Development:
Jill S. Krutick
Chairman and CEO, Warner Bros. Records:
Tom Whalley
Chairman and CEO, Warner/Chappell Music:
David H. (Dave) Johnson, age 63

President, Atlantic Records Group: Julie Greenwald, age 39
Chairman and CEO, Atlantic Records Group:
Craig Kallman
President, Warner/Chappell Music and Chairman and CEO, Warner Chappell Music US: Scott Francis
President, WEA Corp.: John Esposito
Auditors: Ernst & Young LLP

LOCATIONS

HQ: Warner Music Group Corp.
75 Rockefeller Plaza, New York, NY 10019
Phone: 212-275-2000   **Fax:** 212-757-3985
Web: www.wmg.com

2008 Sales

	$ mil.	% of total
International	1,913	54
US	1,605	46
Adjustments	(27)	—
Total	**3,491**	**100**

PRODUCTS/OPERATIONS

2008 Sales

	$ mil.	% of total
Recorded Music		
Physical sales	2,040	58
Digital	599	17
Licensing	256	7
Music Publishing		
Performance	243	7
Mechanical	225	6
Synchronization	99	3
Digital and other	56	2
Adjustments	(27)	—
Total	**3,491**	**100**

Selected Operations

Recorded music
  Distribution
    Alternative Distribution Alliance
    Rhino Entertainment
  Recording labels
    Atlantic Records
    Elektra Records
    Lava Records
    Maverick Recording Company
    Nonesuch Records
    Roadrunner Records (75%)
    Reprise
    Rykodisc
    Sire
    Warner Bros. Nashville
    Warner Bros. Records
    Word Records
Music publishing
  Warner/Chappell Music

HISTORICAL FINANCIALS

Company Type: Public

Income Statement

FYE: September 30

	REVENUE ($ mil.)	NET INCOME ($ mil.)	NET PROFIT MARGIN	EMPLOYEES
9/08	3,491.0	(56.0)	—	3,800
9/07	3,385.0	(21.0)	—	3,800
9/06	3,516.0	60.0	1.7%	4,000
9/05	3,502.0	(169.0)	—	4,000
9/04	2,548.0	(270.0)	—	4,000
Annual Growth	**8.2%**	**—**	**—**	**(1.3%)**

2008 Year-End Financials

Debt ratio: —
Return on equity: —
Cash ($ mil.): 411
Current ratio: 0.67
Long-term debt ($ mil.): 2,242

No. of shares (mil.): 155
Dividends
  Yield: 1.7%
  Payout: —
Market value ($ mil.): 1,175

Stock History

NYSE: WMG

	STOCK PRICE ($) FY Close	P/E High/Low	PER SHARE ($) Earnings	Dividends	Book Value
9/08	7.60	— —	(0.38)	0.13	(0.56)
9/07	10.10	— —	(0.14)	0.52	(0.23)
9/06	25.95	77 38	0.40	0.52	0.38
9/05	18.51	— —	(1.40)	0.00	0.58
Annual Growth	**(25.7%)**	**— —**	**—**	**—**	**—**

Washington Post

It might be said this company can teach you something about newspapers. Best known as the publisher of *The Washington Post* newspaper, The Washington Post Company actually gets the lion's share of its revenue from Kaplan, the company's test preparation and education services division. Washington Post's other media operations include *Newsweek*, the #2 weekly news magazine (after Time Inc's *Time*), a portfolio of six TV stations, and the online publishing operations of Washingtonpost.Newsweek Interactive. Its Cable One subsidiary provides cable TV service to markets in about 20 states. *The Washington Post* boasts a circulation of nearly 640,000. The company is controlled by chairman Donald Graham and his family.

Washington Post has struggled along with its newspaper industry rivals as readership and advertising revenue have both been in decline. Its move to diversify into education services and cable television has paid off, though, as those units continue to make significant gains, helping to make up for the shortfall of its news publishing businesses.

With advertising accounting for nearly a quarter of revenue, Washington Post has been hurt in several quarters by the general recession. Its television and magazine operations have seen ad spending decline, along with the newspaper business. Looking to cut costs, the company announced a series of layoffs late in 2008, cutting staff at both *Newsweek* and *The Washington Post*. Marcus Brauchli, formerly head of the newsroom at the *Wall Street Journal* (published by News Corporation's Dow Jones unit), was named executive editor of the Post that same year. He replaced Leonard Downie Jr., who helmed the newspaper for 17 years.

In 2008 it formed The Slate Group, a new unit to oversee its flagship online magazine, Slate, along with sites TheRoot.com and The Big Money. Installing former Slate editor Jacob Weisberg as chairman of The Slate Group, Washington Post hopes to use the new division as an incubator for additional online businesses.

Chairman Donald Graham is the son of the late Katharine Graham, who had taken over the business after her husband died in the early 1960s and became a legend in the publishing business. She led the *Post* in its decisions to publish the Pentagon papers and pursue the Watergate story.

Investment icon Warren Buffett, through his Berkshire Hathaway organization, owns almost 20% of Washington Post.

HISTORY

The Washington Post was first published in 1877, focusing on society columns, color comics, and sensational headlines. Hard news coverage took a back page to crime and scandal — by 1916 the *Post* was filled with yellow journalism. Any credibility the paper had was ruined by owner Ned McLean's lying to a Senate committee in 1924 about his involvement in the Teapot Dome oil scandal.

Eugene Meyer bought the bankrupt *Post* for $825,000 in 1933 and built a first-class news staff. By 1946, when Meyer's son-in-law Philip Graham took over as publisher, the *Post* was in the black again. In 1948 Meyer transferred his stock to his daughter Katharine and to Philip, her husband. Graham bought radio and TV stations and established overseas bureaus. In 1961 he bought *Newsweek* magazine and started a news service with the *Los Angeles Times*. In 1963 Graham lost a struggle with manic depression and killed himself.

An editor since 1939, Katharine became publisher after her husband's death. The Washington Post Company began publishing the *International Herald Tribune* with The New York Times Company in 1967. In 1971 the company went public, though the Graham family retained control. The next year reporters Bob Woodward and Carl Bernstein broke the Watergate story, which led to President Richard Nixon's resignation and a Pulitzer Prize for the *Post*. In the 1970s and 1980s, under the tutelage of investor (and former *Post* paper boy) Warren Buffett, Katharine Graham bought TV and radio stations, cable TV firms, newspapers, newsprint mills, and Stanley H. Kaplan Educational Centers.

The guard changed at The Washington Post Company in 1991 when the Grahams' son Donald became CEO. In 1992 it invested in ACTV (interactive television) and bought 84% of Gaithersburg Gazette, Inc. (community newspapers, upped to 100% in 1993) and a sports cable TV system. Donald Graham became chairman when his mother stepped down in 1993.

In the search for a place in new media, The Washington Post Company made some mammoth errors. In 1995 the firm wrote off the $28 million it had invested in Mammoth Micro Products, a CD-ROM maker it had purchased in 1994. Also that year, blaming costs and delays, the company sold its 80% stake (acquired 1990) in American Personal Communications (wireless telephone systems).

In 1996 *Newsweek* columnist Joe Klein resigned after it was revealed that he was the anonymous author of *Primary Colors,* a thinly veiled satire of the 1992 Clinton campaign. Two years later the company completed the sale of its 28% interest in Cowles Media, publisher of the Minneapolis *Star Tribune,* and sought to bolster its coverage of information technology by buying two magazines and two Washington, DC-based conferences from Reed Elsevier.

The company sold key assets of its Legi-Slate service to Congressional Quarterly in 1999. Later that year it formed a partnership with TV network NBC in which the two firms agreed to share news content, technology, and promotional resources. The Washington Post Company branched out into travel information with its purchase of *Arthur Frommer's Budget Travel* near the end of 1999. In 2000 its Kaplan subsidiary created Kaplan Ventures to invest in education and career services companies and subsequently acquired postsecondary school operator Quest Education.

The Washington Post Company purchased 10 Maryland community papers from Chesapeake Publishing in 2001. The company's 2001 contract dispute with *Post* employees made headlines when reporters refused to allow their bylines to be used above their stories for several editions. Katharine Graham died later that year at age 84. In 2002 the company sold its stake in the *International Herald Tribune.*

Looking to expand its online publishing operations, Washington Post acquired Slate Magazine from Microsoft in 2005. The company shed its Post Newsweek Tech unit (trade publications and trade shows) in 2006.

EXECUTIVES

Chairman and CEO: Donald E. (Don) Graham, age 63, $811,960 total compensation
Vice Chairman; Chairman, Washington Post Newspaper: Boisfeuillet (Bo) Jones, age 62, $1,509,012 total compensation
SVP Finance and CFO: Hal S. Jones, age 56
VP Finance and Chief Accounting Officer: Wallace R. Cooney, age 46
SVP and Chief Digital Officer: Vijay Ravindran
SVP Finance: John B. (Jay) Morse Jr., age 62
SVP Planning and Development: Gerald M. Rosberg, age 62, $1,427,735 total compensation
SVP Planning and Development: Christopher Ma
SVP Human Resources: Ann L. McDaniel, $1,340,439 total compensation
SVP, General Counsel, and Secretary: Veronica Dillon, age 59
VP Communications and External Relations: Rima Calderon
VP Human Resources: Heather Hochberg
Chairman, Newsweek: Richard M. Smith, age 62
Chairman and CEO, Kaplan: Andrew S. (Andy) Rosen
President and CEO, Cable One: Thomas O. (Tom) Might
President and General Manager, The Washington Post: Stephen P. Hills
President and CEO, Post-Newsweek Stations: Alan Frank
CEO, Washington Post Media; Publisher, The Washington Post: Katharine Weymouth, age 42
VP At Large, The Washington Post: Benjamin C. Bradlee
Auditors: PricewaterhouseCoopers LLP

LOCATIONS

HQ: The Washington Post Company
1150 15th St. NW, Washington, DC 20071
Phone: 202-334-6000   **Fax:** 202-334-4536
Web: www.washpostco.com

PRODUCTS/OPERATIONS

2008 Sales

	$ mil.	% of total
Education	2,331.6	52
Advertising	1,083.1	25
Circulation & subscribers	901.9	20
Other	145.0	3
Total	**4,461.6**	**100**

2008 Sales

	$ mil.	% of total
Education	2,331.6	52
Newspapers	801.3	18
Cable television	719.1	16
TV broadcasting	325.1	7
Magazines	250.9	6
Other	39.4	1
Adjustments	(5.8)	—
Total	**4,461.6**	**100**

Selected Operations

Cable ONE (cable television systems)
Kaplan (education and training services)
Newspapers
  El Tiempo Latino (Spanish-language newspaper)
  Express (free daily tabloid)
  The Gazette Newspapers (Maryland newspapers)
  Greater Washington Publishing (advertising periodicals)
  The Herald (Everett, WA)
  Southern Maryland Newspapers
  The Washington Post
  Washingtonpost.Newsweek Interactive (online publishing)
  BudgetTravel.com
  Classified Ventures (17%, online classified advertising)
  newsweek.com
  The Slate Group
    The Big Money
    The Root
    Slate
  washingtonpost.com
Newsweek (weekly news magazine)
Televison broadcasting stations
  KPRC (NBC, Houston)
  KSAT (ABC, San Antonio)
  WDIV (NBC, Detroit)
  WJXT (Ind; Jacksonville, FL)
  WKMG (CBS; Orlando, FL)
  WPLG (ABC, Miami)
Other
  Bowater Mersey Paper Company (49%)
  CourseAdvisor.com (lead generation)

COMPETITORS

A. H. Belo
Advance Publications
Cengage Learning
DIRECTV
DISH Network Corporation
Gannett
Laureate Education
McClatchy Company
McGraw-Hill
New York Times
News Corp.
News World Communications
Pearson plc
Seattle Times
Time Inc.
Tribune Company
U.S. News & World Report

HISTORICAL FINANCIALS

Company Type: Public

Income Statement

	REVENUE ($ mil.)	NET INCOME ($ mil.)	NET PROFIT MARGIN	EMPLOYEES
			FYE: Sunday nearest December 31	
12/08	4,461.6	65.7	1.5%	20,000
12/07	4,180.4	288.6	6.9%	19,000
12/06	3,904.9	329.5	8.4%	17,100
12/05	3,553.9	313.4	8.8%	16,400
12/04	3,300.1	332.7	10.1%	14,800
Annual Growth	**7.8%**	**(33.3%)**	**—**	**7.8%**

1980s, building technologically up-to-date power plants, including the Wolf Creek nuclear plant.

KPL and KGE's 1992 merger was debated by those who feared major rate hikes, but the SEC approved it and KGE became a subsidiary of KPL. The company changed its name to Western Resources, but each utility operated under its own name. After the merger, Western Resources sold most of its natural gas operations and focused on electricity generation. In 1996 the firm set out to acquire another utility, Kansas City Power & Light. Western Resources transferred its natural gas holdings to ONEOK in 1996 for 45% of the Oklahoma gas company's stock.

In 1997 Western Resources diversified in preparation for utility deregulation that could hurt its energy business. In 2000 the company announced plans to spin off its nonregulated businesses to shareholders as a new company, Westar Industries, and its utility units to Public Service Company of New Mexico (now PNM Resources). In preparation for the spinoff, Western Resources sold its interests in marketing services company Paradigm Direct and oil and gas services company Hanover Compressor.

In 2001 PNM Resources filed suit to cancel its agreement to acquire KPL and KGE, and Western Resources filed a countersuit alleging a breach of the merger agreement. In 2002 PNM Resources terminated the agreement; however, both lawsuits were still pending. PNM Resources' termination of the agreement prompted Western Resources' decision to retain and focus on these assets. Later that year Western Resources changed its name to Westar Energy.

In 2003 the company filed a debt reduction plan with the Kansas Corporation Commission (KCC) to avoid a bankruptcy filing. The plan required the divestment of Westar Energy's nonutility assets and has replaced the company's earlier plans to spin off subsidiary Westar Industries, which held the company's ONEOK and Protection One stakes.

To begin reducing debt, the company in 2003 sold some of its ONEOK stock back to ONEOK. The deal netted Westar Energy $300 million and reduced its stake in the natural gas company from 45% to 27%. Westar Energy further reduced its ONEOK stake to about 15% later that year by selling additional shares to the public and to ONEOK, and it sold its remaining shares to Cantor Fitzgerald for $262 million in November 2003.

Former CEO David Wittig had been indicted in 2002 on fraud charges in connection with a real estate deal and a loan he received from Capital City Bank (the charges were not related to Westar Energy); shortly after the indictment, Wittig resigned from the company. He was later convicted for these charges.

In 2003 Wittig and former EVP Douglas Lake were indicted on conspiracy, fraud, and other criminal charges for allegedly looting more than $37 million in corporate funds for personal uses, including house renovations and travel expenses, and for attempting to cover up the scheme. The indictment also accused the executives of criminal activities related to the structuring of the Westar Industries spinoff. During the executives' tenure, Westar's debt rose to $3 billion and the company was pushed to the brink of bankruptcy. The executives' 2004 fraud trial was declared a mistrial due to a hung jury. In 2005 prosecutors announced that they would retry the case. At the retrial, both men were found guilty.

EXECUTIVES

Chairman: Charles Q. (Charlie) Chandler IV, age 55
President, CEO, and Director: William B. (Bill) Moore, age 56, $1,714,032 total compensation
EVP and COO: Douglas R. (Doug) Sterbenz, age 45, $1,134,311 total compensation
EVP and CFO: Mark A. Ruelle, age 47, $955,535 total compensation
EVP Public Affairs and Consumer Services: James J. (Jim) Ludwig, age 49, $474,067 total compensation
VP Operations Strategy and Support: Bruce A. Akin, age 44
VP, General Counsel, and Corporate Secretary: Larry D. Irick, age 52, $570,833 total compensation
VP Construction Services: Greg A. Greenwood
VP Transmission Operations and Environmental Services: Kelly B. Harrison
VP Customer Care: Peggy S. Loyd
VP and Controller: Leroy P. (Lee) Wages, age 60
VP Distribution Power Delivery: Caroline A. Williams
VP Generation: Ken Johnson
VP Regulatory Affairs: Michael Lennen, age 63
VP Corporate Compliance and Internal Audit: Jeffrey L. Beasley, age 51
Treasurer: Anthony D. (Tony) Somma
Director Investor Relations: Bruce Burns
Manager Corporate Communications: Karla Olsen
Auditors: Deloitte & Touche LLP

LOCATIONS

HQ: Westar Energy, Inc.
818 S. Kansas Ave., Topeka, KS 66612
Phone: 785-575-6300   **Fax:** 785-575-1796
Web: www.wr.com

Westar Energy distributes electricity in Kansas and markets power throughout the US.

PRODUCTS/OPERATIONS

2008 Sales

	$ mil.	% of total
Retail		
Residential	516.9	28
Commercial	485.0	26
Industrial	291.9	16
Wholesale marketing		
Tariff-based	239.7	13
Market-based	174.1	10
Transmission	98.6	5
Energy marketing	14.5	1
Other	24.4	1
Adjustments	(6.1)	—
Total	**1,839.0**	**100**

Selected Operations

Kansas Gas and Electric Company (KGE, operates as Westar Energy, electric utility and marketer)

COMPETITORS

AES
Ameren
Atmos Energy
Dynegy
Edison International
Empire District Electric
Great Plains Energy
MidAmerican Energy
OGE Energy
Southern Company
Xcel Energy

HISTORICAL FINANCIALS

Company Type: Public

Income Statement

FYE: December 31

	REVENUE ($ mil.)	NET INCOME ($ mil.)	NET PROFIT MARGIN	EMPLOYEES
12/08	1,839.0	178.1	9.7%	2,415
12/07	1,726.8	168.4	9.8%	2,323
12/06	1,605.7	165.3	10.3%	2,223
12/05	1,583.3	135.6	8.6%	2,191
12/04	1,464.5	178.9	12.2%	2,100
Annual Growth	5.9%	(0.1%)	—	3.6%

2008 Year-End Financials

Debt ratio: 105.7%
Return on equity: 8.9%
Cash ($ mil.): 23
Current ratio: 0.85
Long-term debt ($ mil.): 2,310
No. of shares (mil.): 109
Dividends
Yield: 5.7%
Payout: 68.2%
Market value ($ mil.): 2,233

Stock History

NYSE: WR

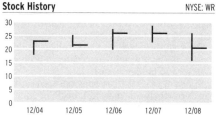

	STOCK PRICE ($) FY Close	P/E High/Low		PER SHARE ($) Earnings	Dividends	Book Value
12/08	20.51	15	9	1.70	1.16	20.28
12/07	25.94	16	12	1.83	1.08	16.98
12/06	25.96	15	11	1.87	1.00	14.34
12/05	21.50	16	14	1.54	0.92	13.20
12/04	22.87	11	8	2.13	0.80	12.95
Annual Growth	(2.7%)	—	—	(5.5%)	9.7%	11.9%

Western Digital

When it comes to data storage, Western Digital has drive. The company is one of the largest independent makers of hard-disk drives, which record, store, and recall volumes of data. Drives for PCs account for most of Western Digital's sales, although the company also makes devices for entry-level servers and home entertainment products, such as set-top boxes and video game consoles. The company sells to manufacturers and through retailers and distributors. About half of its sales are to OEMs. The company counts PC giant Dell among its customers. Western Digital gets around half of its sales in Asia.

Western Digital is one of a handful of manufacturers that dominate the hard-disk drive market — a sector characterized by harsh competition, short product life cycles, and aggressive price cuts.

The worldwide economic downturn and credit crisis are making it difficult for the company and its customers and suppliers to forecast market demand. There are signs that the recession is starting to lift, yet the economic recovery may take some time. The average selling prices of Western Digital products normally decline over time due to competition and product obsolescence, and it remains to be seen how global economic conditions will affect operations. The consumer market favors lower-priced computers during downturns, and Western Digital must remain competitive in supplying hard drives for low-cost PCs. Selling branded products through big retailers is an important market for the company in Europe and North America. Western Digital's top 10 customers account for nearly half of annual sales. The company relies on a limited number of qualified suppliers, such as LSI Corp., Nidec, and TDK.

Western Digital acquired disk component maker Komag for $1 billion in 2007. The purchase allowed Western Digital to manufacture the media and substrates used in its drives. In 2009 the company sold its media substrate manufacturing facility in Sarawak, Malaysia, which it acquired from Komag, to competitor Hitachi Global Storage Technologies. Western Digital, which is looking to cut costs, will continue to manufacture the majority of its magnetic media requirements at other Malaysian facilities.

The company moved into the solid-state drive market in 2009 when it purchased SiliconSystems for $65 million in cash.

In recent years the company has seen significant growth in its non-desktop PC segment, which includes devices used in notebook computers and consumer electronics such as DVRs.

HISTORY

Western Digital was founded in 1970 as a manufacturer of specialized semiconductors and electronic calculators. The company filed for Chapter 11 bankruptcy in 1976. However, it reorganized and emerged successfully in 1978. Roger Johnson, after a succession of executive positions at Memorex, Measurex, and Burroughs, came to Western Digital as EVP and COO in 1982. Sales were merely $34 million, hurt by the acquisition of several ill-fitting computer and electronics businesses. By 1984 Johnson became president and CEO; he sold off several companies to concentrate on storage control devices. A contract with IBM contributed to Western Digital's sales topping $460 million in 1987.

Anticipating a change in technology that would have disk drive makers building storage control into the drives themselves, Western Digital began to shift its efforts toward making disk drives in 1988. Ten-year company veteran Kathy Braun oversaw the purchase of Tandon's disk drive operations. Tandon was considered a second-rate manufacturer using aging technology, but its drives continued to sell well for a period following the acquisition. This created a false sense of security for Western Digital and delayed the development of more competitive drives. In 1990 the market for storage controller boards essentially disappeared. Losses prompted a restructuring that in turn violated Western Digital's credit agreements.

In 1991 the US economy slowed, and the disk drive industry began a price war. That year Western Digital, appearing close to bankruptcy, sold its profitable departmental network business to Standard Microsystems.

As the PC market improved in 1992, so did Western Digital's prospects. A big boost came when the cash-strapped company introduced a line of disk drives with a commonality of parts. In 1993 Western Digital's IPO and sale of its wafer factory to Motorola reduced its high debt. That year the Clinton administration appointed

CEO Johnson head of the General Services Administration. IBM veteran Charles Haggerty, who joined Western Digital in 1992, assumed the company's top post.

In 1994 Western Digital enjoyed its first profit in four years. The company sold off its Microcomputer Products Group, which made proprietary semiconductors, in 1996 and introduced its first hard drives aimed at the corporate network computing market.

In 1997 a number of Asian manufacturers jumped into the market at the same time that computer makers were taking on sales approaches to eliminate the need for large inventories of hard drives and other stock. Those factors, combined with stalled PC demand and Western Digital's slow transition to newer recording head technologies, caused a loss for fiscal 1998. To respond, Western Digital cut more than 20% of its workforce and slashed production. Braun, by then second in command at the company and one of the industry's highest-paid women, retired in 1998.

In 1999 Western Digital took a financial hit following its recall of 400,000 defective disk drives; it announced it would lay off another 2,500 employees, primarily in Singapore. In 2000 Haggerty retired from the CEO post; COO Matthew Massengill was tapped to replace him.

In 2001 Western Digital sold Connex to former rival Quantum after that company exited the hard drive market. Massengill was named chairman later that year. In 2003 it acquired most of the assets of bankrupt drive component maker Read-Rite for approximately $95 million in cash.

Massengill stepped down as CEO in 2005, while remaining executive chairman. Arif Shakeel, Western Digital's president and COO since 2002, succeeded Massengill as CEO.

Shakeel stepped down as CEO in 2007. John Coyne, a Western Digital employee since 1983, succeeded him in both posts. Also in 2007, Massengill stepped down as chairman, while remaining on the board, and was succeeded by Thomas Pardun, a veteran telecommunications executive who served as Western Digital's chairman for two years earlier in the decade.

EXECUTIVES

Chairman: Thomas E. Pardun, age 65
President, CEO, and Director: John F. Coyne, age 60
EVP and CFO: Timothy M. (Tim) Leyden, age 57
SVP Research and Development and CTO:
Hossein M. Moghadam, age 65
SVP Administration, General Counsel, and Secretary:
Raymond M. (Ray) Bukaty, age 52
SVP and General Manager Branded Products and Consumer Electronics Groups: Jim Welsh
VP, Controller, and Principal Accounting Officer:
Joseph R. Carrillo
VP and General Manager PC Components Group:
Richard E. Rutledge
VP and General Manager Enterprise Storage Solutions:
Tom McDorman
Sales Director, Middle East and Africa:
Khwaja Saifuddin
Public Relations: Steve Shattuck
Auditors: KPMG LLP

LOCATIONS

HQ: Western Digital Corporation
20511 Lake Forest Dr., Lake Forest, CA 92630
Phone: 949-672-7000   **Fax:** 949-672-5408
Web: www.westerndigital.com

2009 Sales

	$ mil.	% of total
Asia	3,639	49
Europe, Middle East & Africa	2,008	27
US	1,492	20
Other regions	314	4
Total	**7,453**	**100**

PRODUCTS/OPERATIONS

2009 Sales by Channel

	% of total
Manufacturers	54
Distributors	26
Retailers	20
Total	**100**

2009 Sales by Product

	% of total
Non-desktop	62
Desktop	38
Total	**100**

Selected Products

Internal Hard Drives
  Audio/Video hard drives (Performer)
  Desktop PCs and entry-level servers (Caviar, Protégé)
  Servers and storage systems (Raptor)
External Hard Drives
  FireWire for PCs and Macs
Accessories
  Desktop (FireWire adapter)
  Mobile (FireWire CardBus PC card)

COMPETITORS

EMC
Fujitsu
Hitachi Global Storage
IM Flash Technologies
Iomega
LaCie
Samsung Electronics
Seagate Technology
SMART Modular Technologies
STEC
TEAC
Toshiba

HISTORICAL FINANCIALS

Company Type: Public

Income Statement				FYE: Saturday nearest June 30
	REVENUE ($ mil.)	NET INCOME ($ mil.)	NET PROFIT MARGIN	EMPLOYEES
6/09	7,453.0	470.0	6.3%	45,991
6/08	8,074.0	867.0	10.7%	50,072
6/07	5,468.0	564.0	10.3%	29,572
6/06	4,341.3	394.6	9.1%	24,750
6/05	3,638.8	198.4	5.5%	23,161
Annual Growth	**19.6%**	**24.1%**	**—**	**18.7%**

2009 Year-End Financials

Debt ratio: 12.5%   No. of shares (mil.): 225
Return on equity: 16.0%   Dividends
Cash ($ mil.): 1,794   Yield: 0.0%
Current ratio: 2.12   Payout: —
Long-term debt ($ mil.): 400   Market value ($ mil.): 5,954

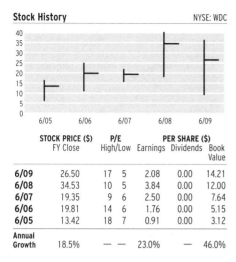

	STOCK PRICE ($)	P/E		PER SHARE ($)		
	FY Close	High	Low	Earnings	Dividends	Book Value
6/09	26.50	17	5	2.08	0.00	14.21
6/08	34.53	10	5	3.84	0.00	12.00
6/07	19.35	9	6	2.50	0.00	7.64
6/06	19.81	14	6	1.76	0.00	5.15
6/05	13.42	18	7	0.91	0.00	3.12
Annual Growth	18.5%	—	—	23.0%	—	46.0%

Weyerhaeuser Company

If a tree falls in a Weyerhaeuser forest, someone *is* there to hear it — and he has a chainsaw. Weyerhaeuser, one of the top US forest products companies, operates along several business lines, including Wood Products (lumber, plywood, and other building materials) and Pulp and Paper (pulp and coated and uncoated papers). Also, its Timberlands division manages some 6 million acres of company-owned US timberland and nearly 15 million acres of leased Canadian timberland. Its Real Estate unit develops housing and master-planned communities. Weyerhaeuser merged its fine paper business with Domtar.

According to the terms of the $3.3 billion deal, Weyerhaeuser shareholders got a 55% stake in the renamed company, Domtar Corporation (formerly Domtar Inc.) Weyerhaeuser controls the board, and several Weyerhaeuser executives manage the company. Transferred operations include about a dozen paper and pulp mills, 14 converting centers, a coated groundwood mill, and two softwood lumber mills.

Changing hemispheres, Weyerhaeuser has restructured its foreign timber business with a move from New Zealand to South America. Weyerhaeuser and Global Forest Partners (GFP), both previously involved through joint ventures around the globe, signed a deal that will relocate Weyerhaeuser's international timber operations from New Zealand to Uruguay. In exchange for the Los Piques plywood mill and some 41,000 hectares of Uruguay timberland, GFP will receive Weyerhaeuser New Zealand's operations, which includes a 67,000 hectare tract of forest and a sawmill.

In light of the downturn in the home building market, the company scaled back on its housing business, delayed land purchases and limited housing starts in 2007 and 2008.

As part of its ongoing efforts to streamline operations, Weyerhaeuser in 2007 sold its 16 Cana-

dian wholesale building materials distribution centers to Platinum Equity. It also sold 10 US distribution centers. Citing the housing slump as the contributing factor, Weyerhaeuser has decided to shutter its joist plant in Alberta, Canada.

The company continued to dispose of non-core assets in 2008 when it sold its container-board packaging and recycling operations to International Paper for $6 billion. Weyerhaeuser used much of the proceeds to pay down debt.

The following year, the company sold its Trus Joist commercial business, including four manufacturing plants, to Atlas Holdings.

HISTORY

Frederick Weyerhaeuser, a 24-year-old German immigrant, bought his first lumberyard in 1858 in Illinois. He also participated in joint logging ventures in Illinois, Minnesota, and Wisconsin. In 1900 he and 15 partners bought 900,000 timbered acres from the Northern Pacific Railway. The venture was named Weyerhaeuser Timber Company.

During the Depression the business recouped losses in the deflated lumber market by selling wood pulp. Frederick's grandson, J. P. "Phil" Weyerhaeuser Jr., took over as CEO in 1933.

Diversification into the production of containerboard (1949), particleboard (1955), paper (1956), and other products led the company to drop "Timber" from its name in 1959. In 1963 Weyerhaeuser went public and opened its first overseas office in Tokyo.

In the 1970s George Weyerhaeuser (Phil's son) diversified further to insulate the company from the forest-product industry's cyclical nature and ended up with a mishmash of businesses and products, from private-label disposable diapers to pet supplies.

The eruption of Mount St. Helens in 1980 destroyed 68,000 acres of Weyerhaeuser timber. That disaster and the soft US lumber market depressed the company's earnings through 1982. Weyerhaeuser reduced its workforce by 25% during this period.

Under John Creighton (president since 1988 and CEO from 1991 until 1998), Weyerhaeuser refocused on forest products and organized along product lines rather than by geographic region. Less-successful ventures were put up for sale, including milk carton, hardwood, and gypsum board plants. The company took a $497 million pretax charge in 1989 related to the decision to close unprofitable operations.

In 1992 the company outbid Georgia-Pacific, paying $600 million for two pulp mills, three sawmills, and more than 200,000 acres of forest land to boost its market-pulp capacity by 40%. The following year the company sold its disposable-diaper business through a public offering in a new company, Paragon Trade Brands.

The federal government in 1995 allowed the company to harvest trees in an area inhabited by the endangered northern spotted owl. The move angered environmental groups. In 1998 Steve Rogel, a veteran from competitor Willamette, succeeded Creighton as CEO and became the first outsider to head Weyerhaeuser.

In 1999 Weyerhaeuser paid $2.45 billion for Canada's MacMillan Bloedel, and early in 2000 it acquired TJ International, 51% owner of leading engineered lumber products company Trus Joist MacMillan (Weyerhaeuser already owned the other 49%).

After a protracted courtship, in March 2002 Weyerhaeuser acquired Oregon-based Willamette

Industries in a $6.1 billion cash deal. The company closed three North American plants (in Colorado, Louisiana, and Oregon) later that year. On the heels of the deals for MacMillan Bloedel, Trus Joist MacMillan, and Willamette, Weyerhaeuser moved to pay down debt. It sold more than 320,000 acres of the timberland (in the Carolinas and Tennessee) that it acquired with the Willamette purchase.

In 2003 Weyerhaeuser sold its Nipigon Multiply hardwood plywood underlayment operation in Ontario, Canada, to Columbia Forest Products. Late in the year the company closed its fine-paper operations in Longview, Washington (eliminating 119 jobs there). Altogether, Weyerhaeuser closed 12 facilities and sold about 444,000 acres of non-strategic timberlands in 2003.

In 2004 Weyerhaeuser sold roughly 270,000 acres of timberlands in central Georgia for about $400 million to investment and property firms in Georgia and South Carolina. Early in 2005 Weyerhaeuser agreed to sell five Canadian sawmills, two finishing plants, 635,000 acres of timber, and some government land cutting rights to Brascan for $970 million. Weyerhaeuser also closed a Saskatchewan pulp and paper mill in 2006, cutting 690 jobs.

EXECUTIVES

Chairman: Charles R. (Chuck) Williamson, age 60
President, CEO, and Director: Daniel S. (Dan) Fulton, age 60, $4,877,285 total compensation
EVP and CFO: Patricia M. (Patty) Bedient, age 55, $992,498 total compensation
SVP Research and Development and CTO: Miles P. Drake, age 59
VP Information Technology and CIO: Kevin Shearer, age 53
VP and Chief Accounting Officer: Jeanne M. Hillman, age 49
EVP Forest Products: Thomas F. (Tom) Gideon, age 57, $1,282,127 total compensation
SVP and General Counsel: Sandy D. McDade, age 57
SVP Timberlands: James M. (Mike) Branson, age 52
SVP Corporate Affairs: Ernesta Ballard, age 63
SVP Cellulose Fibers: Srinivasan (Shaker) Chandrasekaran, age 59, $1,282,127 total compensation
SVP Human Resources: John Hooper, age 54
VP Labor Relations: Gregory H. Yuckert
VP Federal and International Affairs: Heidi Biggs Brock
VP and Treasurer: Jeffrey W. Nitta
VP Investor Relations: Kathryn F. McAuley
VP, Secretary, and Assistant General Counsel: Claire S. Grace
VP Policy, Finance, and Strategic Planning: Scott R. Marshall
VP Environment, Health, and Safety: Sara S. Kendall
Auditors: KPMG LLP

LOCATIONS

HQ: Weyerhaeuser Company
33663 Weyerhaeuser Way South
Federal Way, WA 98003
Phone: 253-924-2345   **Fax:** 253-924-2685
Web: www.weyerhaeuser.com

2008 Sales

	% of total
US	78
Japan	6
Europe	4
Canada	3
China	2
Other countries	7
Total	**100**

PRODUCTS/OPERATIONS

2008 Sales

	% of total
Wood products	33
Containerboard, packaging & recycling	28
Cellulose fibers	15
Real estate & related assets	13
Timberlands	8
Corporate & other	3
Total	**100**

Selected Products and Services

Wood Products
  Engineered lumber products
  Lumber (softwood and hardwood)
  Oriented Strand Board
  Plywood
  Structural panels
  Veneer

Cellulose Fiber and White Paper
  Liquid packaging board
  Paper
  Pulp

Real Estate and Related Assets
  Master-planned communities
  Multifamily homes
  Residential lots
  Single-family homes

Timberlands

Other
  Recycling
  Transportation

Selected Subsidiaries

Columbia & Cowlitz Railway Company
DeQueen & Eastern Railroad Company
Golden Triangle Railroad
MacMillan Bloedel Pembroke Limited Partnership
  (Canada)
North Pacific Paper Corporation (50%, joint venture
  with Nippon Paper)
Westwood Shipping Lines, Inc.
Weyerhaeuser Real Estate Company

COMPETITORS

AbitibiBowater
Buckeye Technologies
Canfor
Cascades Boxboard
Champion Enterprises
ENCE
Georgia-Pacific
Indiana Veneers
International Paper
Louisiana-Pacific
MAXXAM
McFarland Cascade
MeadWestvaco
Myllykoski Paper
NewPage
Norbord
OfficeMax
Oji Paper
Packaging Corp. of America
Potlatch
Pratt Industries USA
Rayonier
Sierra Pacific Industries
Smurfit Kappa
Smurfit-Stone Container
Stora Enso
Tembec
Temple-Inland
Tenon
UPM-Kymmene
West Fraser Timber
White Birch Paper

HISTORICAL FINANCIALS

Company Type: Public

Income Statement

FYE: Last Sunday in December

	REVENUE ($ mil.)	NET INCOME ($ mil.)	NET PROFIT MARGIN	EMPLOYEES
12/08	8,018.0	(1,176.0)	—	19,850
12/07	16,308.0	790.0	4.8%	37,900
12/06	21,896.0	453.0	2.1%	46,700
12/05	22,629.0	733.0	3.2%	49,900
12/04	22,665.0	1,283.0	5.7%	53,600
Annual Growth	**(22.9%)**	**—**	**—**	**(22.0%)**

2008 Year-End Financials

Debt ratio: 116.5%
Return on equity: —
Cash ($ mil.): 2,294
Current ratio: 2.33
Long-term debt ($ mil.): 5,609
No. of shares (mil.): 211
Dividends
  Yield: 7.8%
  Payout: —
Market value ($ mil.): 6,470

Stock History

NYSE: WY

	STOCK PRICE ($) FY Close	P/E High/Low		Earnings	PER SHARE ($) Dividends	Book Value
12/08	30.61	—	—	(5.57)	2.40	22.78
12/07	73.74	24	17	3.59	2.40	37.76
12/06	70.65	41	29	1.84	2.20	42.98
12/05	66.34	24	20	2.98	1.90	46.37
12/04	67.22	13	10	5.43	1.60	43.79
Annual Growth	**(17.9%)**	**—**	**—**	**—**	**10.7%**	**(15.1%)**

Whirlpool Corporation

With brand names recognized by just about anyone who has ever separated dark colors from light, Whirlpool is one of the world's top home appliance makers. It makes washers, dryers, refrigerators, air conditioners, dishwashers, freezers, microwave ovens, ranges, trash compactors, air purifiers, and more. In addition to Whirlpool, the company sells its products under a bevy of brand names including KitchenAid, Bauknecht, Roper, Maytag, and Magic Chef. Whirlpool peddles its appliances in North America, Europe, Latin America, Africa, the Middle East, and Asia. Competition in the home appliances market has heated up in recent years, with Bosch Siemens, LG, Samsung, and Haier commanding equal attention.

Whirlpool has been investing more heavily in research and development to continue to pump out new products and improve existing ones. The company spent $436 million in 2008, $421 million in 2007, and $375 million in 2006.

Whirlpool acquired troubled competitor Maytag in early 2006. With the acquisition of Maytag for about $1.9 billion, Whirlpool added several top brands to its already bulging portfolio, including Admiral, Amana, Jenn-Air, Magic Chef, and of course, the eponymous Maytag. Once the

dust settled Whirlpool sold several businesses including Dixie-Narco, the Amana commercial business, its Hoover unit to Techtronic Industries, and its Jade unit to Middleby Corporation.

Buying Maytag has spurred Whirlpool to streamline operations and purge staff. In 2006 it laid off some 4,500 employees, consolidated duplicate functions related to administration and manufacturing, and shuttered some offices.

More recently, the deep recession in the US has Maytag looking for additional opportunities to reduce capacity as consumer spending on big-ticket items has slowed. To that end, in August 2009 the appliance maker announced that it plans to close a refrigerator factory in Evansville, Indiana and move production to Mexico. The move will result in the loss of some 1,100 jobs by mid-2010. Those job cuts follow previously announced reductions which will result in the loss of some 5,000 jobs (about 7% of its total workforce) including plant closures and salaried positions. Maytag will also shutter a washing machine manufacturing plant in Shanghai, as it consolidates its operations in China.

Facing a mature market in North America, Whirlpool has pursued a strategy of building market share in Europe and in emerging economies globally. To that end, in April 2008 the company formed a 50:50 joint venture with China's Hisense-Kelon Electrical Holdings to make and sell home appliances there. Despite such efforts, about 60% of Whirlpool's sales still come from North America, and the company is reinvesting in its US manufacturing operations. Also, the company is expanding appliance production in Mexico, reflecting growing sales in that country. In December 2007 Whirlpool acquired a minority stake in Elica Group in its effort to extend its reach into the global air ventilation market.

HISTORY

Brothers Fred and Lou Upton and their uncle, Emory Upton, founded the Upton Machine Company, manufacturer of electric motor-driven washing machines, in 1911 in St. Joseph, Michigan. Sears, Roebuck and Co. began buying their products five years later, and by 1925 the company was supplying all of Sears' washers. The Uptons combined their company with the Nineteen Hundred Washer Company in 1929 to form the Nineteen Hundred Corporation, the world's largest washing machine company.

Sears and Nineteen Hundred prospered during the Great Depression, and during WWII Nineteen Hundred's factories produced war materials. In 1948 it began selling its first automatic washing machine (introduced a year earlier) under the Whirlpool brand. In 1950 the company changed its name to Whirlpool following the success of the product, and introduced its first automatic dryer.

During the 1950s and 1960s Whirlpool became a full-line appliance manufacturer while continuing as Sears' principal Kenmore appliance supplier. In 1955 the company bought Seeger Refrigerator Company and the stove and air-conditioning interests of RCA. Three years later it made its first investment in Multibras Eletrodomésticos, an appliance maker in Brazil. (It has increased that investment over the years.) Other purchases included the gas refrigeration and ice-maker manufacturing facilities of Servel (1958); a majority interest in Heil-Quaker, makers of central heaters and space heaters (1964); Sears' major television set supplier, Warwick

LOCATIONS

HQ: Williams-Sonoma, Inc.
3250 Van Ness Ave., San Francisco, CA 94109
Phone: 415-421-7900 **Fax:** 415-616-8359
Web: www.williams-sonomainc.com

PRODUCTS/OPERATIONS

2009 Stores

	No.
Williams-Sonoma	264
Pottery Barn	204
Pottery Barn Kids	95
West Elm	36
Williams-Sonoma Home	10
Outlet stores	18
Total	**627**

2009 Sales

	$ mil.	% of total
Retail	1,962.5	58
Direct-to-consumer	1,399.0	42
Total	**3,361.5**	**100**

Retail

Design Studio (large-scale Pottery Barn)
Grande Cuisine (large-scale Williams-Sonoma)
PBteen (teen home furnishings)
Pottery Barn (home furnishings, flatware, and table accessories)
Pottery Barn Kids (children's home furnishings)
West Elm (home furnishings, decorative accessories, tabletop items, and textile collection)
Williams-Sonoma (cookware, cookbooks, cutlery, dinnerware, glassware, and table linens)
Williams-Sonoma Home (home furnishings and decorative accessories)

Selected Catalogs

PBteen (home furnishings for teenage market)
Pottery Barn (home furnishings and housewares)
Pottery Barn Bed + Bath (bed and bath products)
Pottery Barn Kids (children's linens and furniture)
West Elm (home furnishings and housewares)
Williams-Sonoma (kitchen products)
Williams-Sonoma Home (home furnishings)

COMPETITORS

Ashley Furniture
Bed Bath & Beyond
Brookstone
Container Store
Cornerstone Brands
Cost Plus
Dean & DeLuca
Decorize
Eddie Bauer Holdings
Ethan Allen
Euromarket Designs
Garden Ridge
Hammacher Schlemmer & Co.
Hanover Direct
IKEA
King Arthur Flour
Lands' End
Levenger
Lillian Vernon
Longaberger
Macy's
Neiman Marcus
Pampered Chef
Pier 1 Imports
Restoration Hardware
Room & Board
Smith & Hawken
Target
Tuesday Morning Corporation
Z Gallerie

HISTORICAL FINANCIALS

Company Type: Public

Income Statement

FYE: Sunday nearest January 31

	REVENUE ($ mil.)	NET INCOME ($ mil.)	NET PROFIT MARGIN	EMPLOYEES
1/09	3,361.5	30.0	0.9%	30,000
1/08	3,944.9	195.8	5.0%	39,000
1/07	3,727.5	208.9	5.6%	38,800
1/06	3,538.9	214.9	6.1%	37,200
1/05	3,136.9	191.2	6.1%	23,600
Annual Growth	**1.7%**	**(37.1%)**	**—**	**6.2%**

2009 Year-End Financials

Debt ratio: 0.9%
Return on equity: 2.6%
Cash ($ mil.): 149
Current ratio: 2.04
Long-term debt ($ mil.): 10
No. of shares (mil.): 106
Dividends
  Yield: 6.1%
  Payout: 171.4%
Market value ($ mil.): 837

Stock History

NYSE: WSM

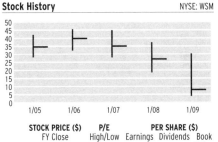

	STOCK PRICE ($) FY Close	P/E High/Low	PER SHARE ($) Earnings	Dividends	Book Value
1/09	7.92	106 16	0.28	0.48	10.86
1/08	26.88	21 11	1.76	0.46	11.03
1/07	35.00	25 16	1.79	0.40	10.89
1/06	39.78	25 18	1.81	0.00	10.64
1/05	34.60	26 18	1.60	0.00	9.06
Annual Growth	**(30.8%)**	**— —**	**(35.3%)**	**—**	**4.6%**

Winn-Dixie Stores

Winn-Dixie Stores has found — as Jefferson Davis did long ago — that winning Dixie ain't easy. The Deep South supermarket chain operates about 515 stores throughout Alabama, Florida, Georgia, Louisiana, and Mississippi. The company runs combination food and drug stores under the Winn-Dixie, Winn-Dixie Marketplace, and SaveRite (warehouse stores) banners. About 400 of Winn-Dixie's supermarkets have pharmacies, some 75 house liquor stores, and about a half a dozen sell gas. To fend off rivals (including Wal-Mart and Publix Super Markets) and stem red ink, Winn-Dixie has retrenched by exiting noncore markets and selling assets, including more than 500 supermarkets during a bankruptcy restructuring.

The regional grocery chain is going after a different customer in its post-bankruptcy incarnation. Instead of the blue-collar workers it had traditionally targeted, Winn-Dixie is moving up market by emphasizing better customer service, freshness, quality and cleanliness. It's a strategy that has worked well for archrival Publix. Whether Winn-Dixie can pull it off — given the sour economy in Florida — remains to be seen.

Since completing its reorganization, the grocery chain's focus has been on store renovations and improving customer service. Winn-Dixie says it's on track to finish remodels half of its 515 stores by June 2010 and substantially all of its locations by mid-2013. On the merchandising front, the chain is emphasizing "fresh and local" goods and expanding selection.

In a bid to rebuild the Winn-Dixie brand and improve profitability, the supermarket operator has redesigned and relaunched its corporate brands program, resulting in the addition of more than 2,500 new private-label products to its store shelves by mid-2009.

Winn-Dixie's turnaround plan appears to be meeting with some initial success. Despite a terrible economy in Florida and deep recession in the US, the chain saw its sales and profits increase modestly in fiscal 2009.

HISTORY

In 1925 William Davis borrowed $10,000 to open the cash-and-carry Rockmoor Grocery in Lemon City, Florida, near Miami. After a slow start, he had expanded his chain of Table Supply Stores to 34 by the time of his death in 1934. His four sons — A. D., J. E., M. Austin, and Tine — took over. In 1939 they purchased control of Winn & Lovett Grocery, which operated 78 stores in Florida and Georgia. The company, incorporated in 1928, was a leader in the 1930s in building new supermarket-type stores. The combined company settled in Jacksonville in 1944 and formally took the name Winn & Lovett.

After WWII the company, still controlled by the Davis family, acquired grocery chains throughout the South, including Steiden (Kentucky), Margaret Ann (Florida), Wylie (Alabama), Penney (Mississippi), King (Georgia), and Eden and Ballentine (South Carolina). The company consolidated with Dixie Home Stores of the Carolinas in 1955 and changed its name to Winn-Dixie Stores, Inc.

The most profitable company in the industry during the 1950s and early 1960s, Winn-Dixie continued to expand through acquisitions, adding Ketner and Milner (the Carolinas) and Hill (Louisiana and Alabama). Also in the 1960s Winn-Dixie entered the manufacturing, processing, and distribution arenas.

By 1966, under the leadership of chairman J. E. Davis, the company controlled so much of the grocery business in the South that, for antitrust reasons, the FTC imposed a 10-year moratorium on acquisitions. Winn-Dixie responded by growing internally and improving its existing stores. It also bought nine stores outside the US (in the Bahamas). When the expansion moratorium ended in 1976, the company bought Kimbell of Texas (sold 1979), adding stores and extensive support facilities in Texas, Oklahoma, and New Mexico.

William Davis' grandson Robert Davis took control as chairman of the company in 1983. After years of lackluster profits, Robert resigned in 1988 and was replaced by his cousin, Dano Davis. In the mid-1980s Winn-Dixie debuted a large combination store format called Marketplace, which offered services such as pharmacies and specialty shops. The company began replacing smaller stores with Marketplace stores; about 55 had been opened by the late 1980s.

In 1995 A. D., the only surviving son of the founder, died. In the first quarter of fiscal 1999, Winn-Dixie ended a 54-year streak of raising its dividends. The company settled a sex and race discrimination lawsuit filed by former and current employees for about $33 million in 1999.

The company also hired Allen Rowland, the former president of Smith's Food & Drug, as president and CEO.

In 2000 Winn-Dixie started a restructuring plan — cutting 8% of its workforce, closing more than 100 supermarkets, shuttering some manufacturing and warehouse facilities. By mid-2002 the company had exited the Texas (71 stores) and Oklahoma (five stores) markets entirely, laying off 5,300 workers.

In June 2003 Rowland retired from the company and was replaced by COO Frank Lazaran, previously president of Randall's Food Markets.

In August 2004 Winn-Dixie announced it had sold or closed 32 stores as part of its purge of underperforming assets, including nine stores in the Cincinnati area as well as stores in Kentucky, North and South Carolina, and Virginia.

Dano Davis retired as chairman in October 2004 after more than 35 years with the company. Davis was succeeded by Jay Skelton, president and CEO of DDI Inc., a diversified holding company owned by the Davis family. In December Lazaran was replaced (after only 18 months on the job) as CEO by Albertson's veteran Peter Lynch.

In February 2005 Winn-Dixie filed for Chapter 11 bankruptcy protection. Soon after, the supermarket chain sold 18 Georgia stores to Atlanta-based Wayfield Foods, All-American Quality Foods, and a partnership between holding company Alex Lee and Associated Wholesale Grocers, among other buyers. It also sold 81 supermarkets to various acquirers, including SUPERVALU. In August Winn-Dixie was hit by a storm of another sort: Hurricane Katrina, which caused property damage and inventory losses at about 110 of the 125 supermarkets operating in the New Orleans region.

In August 2006 Winn-Dixie completed the sale of a dozen stores operated by Winn-Dixie Bahamas to BSL Holdings Limited. Overall in 2006, the company closed or sold 374 stores. After 21 months in bankruptcy, Winn-Dixie emerged from Chapter 11 in late-November 2006.

In 2008 the company sold its two Florida dairies to Southeast Milk Inc.

EXECUTIVES

Chairman, President, and CEO: Peter L. Lynch, age 56
SVP Retail Operations: Frank O. Eckstein, age 62
SVP and CFO: Bennett L. Nussbaum, age 62
Group VP Information Technology:
Charles M. (Charlie) Weston, age 61
VP, Corporate Controller, and Chief Accounting Officer:
D. Michael Byrum, age 56
SVP and Chief Merchandising and Marketing Officer:
Daniel (Dan) Portnoy, age 52
SVP, General Counsel, and Secretary:
Laurence B. (Larry) Appel, age 48
SVP Human Resources: Anthony L. Austin, age 51
Regional VP Orlando: Daniel G. (Dan) Lafever
VP Maintenance, Energy, and Property Management:
Michael J. (Mike) Istre
VP, Delicatessen and Bakery: Nancy L. Gaddy
VP Development: Dan Tobin
VP Pharmacy: John Fegan
VP Real Estate: Peter J. Thomas
VP Center Store: Matt Gutermuth
Communications Manager: Dennis Wortham
Director Investor Relations: Eric Harris
Auditors: KPMG LLP

LOCATIONS

HQ: Winn-Dixie Stores, Inc.
5050 Edgewood Ct., Jacksonville, FL 32254
Phone: 904-783-5000   **Fax:** 904-370-7224
Web: www.winn-dixie.com

2009 Stores

	No.
Florida	353
Alabama	71
Louisiana	52
Georgia	23
Mississippi	16
Total	**515**

PRODUCTS/OPERATIONS

2009 Stores

	No.
Winn Dixie/Marketplace	505
SaveRite	10
Total	**515**

Selected Items Produced or Processed

Carbonated beverages
Cheese
Coffee
Cookies
Crackers
Cultured products
Eggs
Frozen pizza
Ice cream
Jams and jellies
Margarine
Mayonnaise
Meats
Milk
Peanut butter
Salad dressing
Snacks
Spices
Tea

COMPETITORS

Albertsons
ALDI
BI-LO
CVS Caremark
Dollar General
Farm Fresh
Harris Teeter
IGA
Kerr Drug
Kmart
Kroger
The Pantry
Publix
Sweetbay
Target
Walgreen
Wal-Mart

HISTORICAL FINANCIALS

Company Type: Public

Income Statement

FYE: Last Wednesday in June

	REVENUE ($ mil.)	NET INCOME ($ mil.)	NET PROFIT MARGIN	EMPLOYEES
6/09	7,367.0	39.8	0.5%	50,000
6/08	7,281.4	12.8	0.2%	50,000
6/07	7,201.2	300.6	4.2%	52,000
6/06	7,193.9	(364.9)	—	55,000
6/05	9,921.3	(832.6)	—	80,000
Annual Growth	**(7.2%)**	**—**	**—**	**(14.5%)**

2009 Year-End Financials

Debt ratio: 2.8%
Return on equity: 4.7%
Cash ($ mil.): 183
Current ratio: 1.45
Long-term debt ($ mil.): 24
No. of shares (mil.): 54
Dividends
Yield: 0.0%
Payout: —
Market value ($ mil.): 683

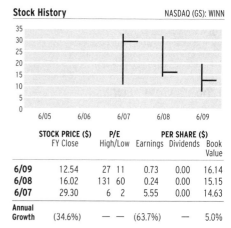

	STOCK PRICE ($) FY Close	P/E High/Low		PER SHARE ($) Earnings	Dividends	Book Value
6/09	12.54	27	11	0.73	0.00	16.14
6/08	16.02	131	60	0.24	0.00	15.15
6/07	29.30	6	2	5.55	0.00	14.63
Annual Growth	**(34.6%)**	**—**	**—**	**(63.7%)**	**—**	**5.0%**

World Fuel Services

You can't fuel all the people all the time, but World Fuel Services tries hard to do just that. The company provides fuel and services to commercial and corporate aircraft, petroleum distributors and ships at more than 2,500 locations around the world, 24 hours a day. The company estimates it holds more than 10% of the global marine fuels market. Its aviation fueling business focuses on serving small to medium-sized air carriers, cargo and charter carriers, and private aircraft. World Fuel Services also markets fuel and related services to petroleum distributors operating in the land transportation market. All told it operates 43 offices in 23 countries.

As part of its marine fueling services business, World Fuel Services arranges fueling for ships on a brokered basis and extends credit to a global customer base, which includes container lines, cruise ships, dry bulk carriers, fishing fleets, refrigerated vessels, and tankers. The company also provides financial credit for aviation fuels.

World Fuel Services maintains its competitive edge by offering a range of support services to its aviation and marine customers such as fuel market analysis, flight planning, ground-handling services, and weather reports.

The company is also growing through acquisitions. In 2007 the company acquired AVCARD, a leading provider of contract fuel sales and charge card services to the aviation industry, for $55 million.

In 2008 World Fuel Services acquired Texor Petroleum. In 2009 it bought wholesale motor fuel distributor TGS Petroleum. The company plans to combine TGS with Texor to expand World Fuel Services' presence as the largest independent wholesale motor fuel distributor in Illinois.

Expanding its UK market share, in 2009 the company acquired the Henty Oil Group of Companies a leading independent provider of marine and land fuels in the UK.

HISTORY

Neighbors Ralph Weiser and Jerrold Blair founded International Oil Recovery, an oil recycling company, in Florida in 1984. The company moved into aviation fueling by acquiring Advance Petroleum in 1986. Two years later International Oil Recovery diversified further, entering the hazardous waste market by buying Resource Recovery of America, a soil remediation company. In 1989 the firm acquired JCo Energy Partners, an aviation fuel company, and subsequently renamed its aviation fueling division World Fuel Services. The company set up International Petroleum in 1993 to operate a Delaware used-oil and water-recycling plant.

In 1995 the company changed its name to World Fuel Services Corporation. Also that year it nearly doubled its revenue base with the purchase of Trans-Tec, the world's #1 independent marine fuel services company. World Fuel also exited the environmental services business in 1995 to focus on its fuel services and oil recycling businesses.

The following year the company formed World Fuel International, a subsidiary based in Costa Rica that serves World Fuel's aviation customers in South and Central America, Canada, and the Caribbean. In 1998 it acquired corporate jet fuel provider Baseops International, which has offices in the UK and Texas.

In 1999 the company expanded its share of the marine fuel market with the acquisition of the Bunkerfuels group of companies, one of the world's top marine fuel brokerages.

To focus on its marine and aviation fueling businesses, World Fuel exited the oil recycling segment in 2000 when it sold its International Petroleum unit to waste services company EarthCare for about $33 million.

The company expanded into the United Arab Emirates with its 2001 acquisition of fuel services provider Marine Energy of Dubai. World Fuel acquired Rotterdam-based marine fuel reseller Oil Shipping Group in 2002.

In 2004 World Fuel Services acquired UK-based marine fuel reseller Tramp Holdings for $83 million.

EXECUTIVES

Chairman and CEO: Paul H. Stebbins, age 52, $6,089,643 total compensation
President, COO, and Director: Michael J. Kasbar, age 52, $6,095,665 total compensation
EVP and CFO: Ira M. Birns, age 46, $1,876,390 total compensation
EVP and Chief Risk and Administration Officer: Francis X. (Frank) Shea, age 68, $1,522,228 total compensation
SVP and Chief Accounting Officer: Paul M. Nobel, age 41
SVP International Sales, Trans-Tec Services: Charles E. Davies
SVP International Sales, Trans-Tec Services: Gregory Seremetis
SVP International Sales, Trans-Tec Services: Wade DeClaris
VP Human Resources: Ileana de Armas
VP Information Technology: Charles Salerno
VP Taxation: Richard White
VP Business Controls: Peter Soto
VP Global Tax and Legal Administration and Treasurer: Peter Tonyan
President, World Fuel Services, Inc.: Michael S. Clementi, age 47, $1,966,262 total compensation
Secretary and General Counsel: R. Alexander Lake
Auditors: PricewaterhouseCoopers LLP

LOCATIONS

HQ: World Fuel Services Corporation
9800 NW 41st St., Ste. 400, Miami, FL 33178
Phone: 305-428-8000 **Fax:** 305-392-5600
Web: www.wfscorp.com

2008 Sales

	$ mil.	% of total
US	8,462.5	45
Singapore	5,479.2	30
UK	3,286.5	18
Other countries	1,281.2	7
Total	**18,509.4**	**100**

PRODUCTS/OPERATIONS

2008 Sales

	$ mil.	% of total
Marine	9,915.3	54
Aviation	7,294.5	39
Land	1,299.6	7
Total	**18,509.4**	**100**

Selected Subsidiaries

Baseops Europe Ltd. (UK)
Baseops International, Inc.
Bunkerfuels Corp.
Bunkerfuels UK Ltd.
Casa Petro SA (Costa Rica)
Henty Oil Group of Companies (UK)
Marine Energy Arabia (United Arab Emirates)
PetroServicios de Costa Rica SA
Texor Petroleum
TGS Petroleum
Tramp Holdings Limited (UK)
Trans-Tec International SA (Costa Rica)
World Fuel International SA (Costa Rica)
World Fuel Services, Inc.
World Fuel Services, Ltd. (UK)
World Fuel Services (Singapore) Pte. Ltd.

COMPETITORS

BBA Aviation
BP Marine
Mercury Air Group
Sun Coast Resources

HISTORICAL FINANCIALS

Company Type: Public

Income Statement

FYE: December 31

	REVENUE ($ mil.)	NET INCOME ($ mil.)	NET PROFIT MARGIN	EMPLOYEES
12/08	18,509.4	105.0	0.6%	1,164
12/07	13,729.6	64.8	0.5%	916
12/06	10,785.1	63.9	0.6%	743
12/05	8,733.9	39.6	0.5%	647
12/04	5,654.4	28.6	0.5%	606
Annual Growth	**34.5%**	**38.4%**	**—**	**17.7%**

2008 Year-End Financials

Debt ratio: 1.6%
Return on equity: 19.2%
Cash ($ mil.): 314
Current ratio: 1.56
Long-term debt ($ mil.): 10

No. of shares (mil.): 30
Dividends
  Yield: 0.4%
  Payout: 4.1%
Market value ($ mil.): 1,096

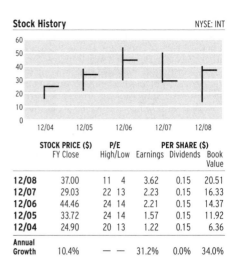

Stock History NYSE: INT

	STOCK PRICE ($) FY Close	P/E High/Low		PER SHARE ($) Earnings	Dividends	Book Value
12/08	37.00	11	4	3.62	0.15	20.51
12/07	29.03	22	13	2.23	0.15	16.33
12/06	44.46	24	14	2.21	0.15	14.37
12/05	33.72	24	14	1.57	0.15	11.92
12/04	24.90	20	13	1.22	0.15	6.36
Annual Growth	**10.4%**	**—**	**—**	**31.2%**	**0.0%**	**34.0%**

Worthington Industries

At least when it comes to steel, Worthington Industries may be considered a shape-shifter. One of the largest steel processors in the US, Worthington Industries shapes and processes flat-rolled steel for industrial customers, including automotive, appliance, and machinery companies. The company also forms flat-rolled steel to exact customer specifications, filling a niche not usually served by steelmakers and steel service centers with limited processing capabilities. Worthington's subsidiaries make products such as pressure cylinders, metal framing, and automotive panels. Through joint ventures, the company also makes steel products such as metal ceiling grid systems and laser-welded blanks.

Worthington's processed steel segment accounts for almost half of sales. The unit consists of Worthington Steel, which is an intermediate processor of flat-rolled steel. Worthington Steel is one of the largest flat-rolled steel processors in the US. Another unit, Gerstenslager, supplies automotive exterior body panels to North American automotive OEMs and other past model service businesses.

The company's metal framing unit, Dietrich Industries, reflects more than a quarter of sales. Dietrich designs and manufactures metal framing components and systems used in the US commercial and residential construction markets.

Worthington Pressure Cylinders, the company's pressure cylinder unit, makes pressure cylinders such as low-pressure liquefied petroleum gas, refrigerant gas cylinders, and high-pressure industrial gas cylinders. The cylinders are sold to automotive manufacturers, refrigerant gas producers and distributors, industrial forklift makers, and commercial and residential cookware producers.

Throughout much of this decade, Worthington has implemented an active acquisition and divestiture strategy, focusing on the processing of flat-rolled steel as the company's core business. During that time Worthington has invested more than $1 billion in several acquisitions and the modernization of its existing plants.

To expand its international presence and develop new products, Worthington has several joint ventures with companies such as ThyssenKrupp and United States Steel. In 2007 it bought 50% of Serviacero Planos to form another Mexican JV, called Worthington Serviacero. Worthington followed that move up with the formation of another joint venture, its first move into the European steel processing market. This JV is with Italian steel company Magnetto Group and will be based in Slovakia.

Back in the US it added Piper Metal Forming to its Worthington Pressure Cylinders unit in 2009. Piper operates through subsidiaries and manufactures and distributes cylinders for the medical, defense, and automotive markets.

HISTORY

In 1955 John H. McConnell, son of a steelworker, borrowed money on his car and started the Worthington Steel Company in the garage of his Worthington, Ohio, home. McConnell had noticed that large steel mills would not fill small, specialized steel orders — a market he decided to serve. Worthington posted an $11,000 profit its first year.

Worthington moved into its processing facility in Columbus, Ohio, in 1959 and continued to grow during the next decade. It went public in 1968.

The company bought Lennox's pressure-cylinder business and renamed itself Worthington Industries in 1971. Worthington continued to expand its profitable pressure-cylinder business through acquisitions. Its 1980 purchase of Buckeye International provided the framework for what would become Worthington's two other business segments: custom products and castings. The company further expanded operations with purchases of machine maker Capital Die, Tool and Machine Co. and recycled metals processing company I. H. Schlezinger & Sons.

Worthington formed a joint venture with U.S. Steel in 1986 for a specialty steel-processing plant; two years later it teamed with Nissen Chemitec and Sumitomo to make molded plastic parts for automakers. To ensure a steady supply of steel, Worthington purchased an interest in Rouge Steel in 1989 (sold in 2000).

In 1992 Worthington formed WAVE, a joint venture with Armstrong World Industries, to produce and sell suspended ceiling-grid systems in Europe. That year John P. McConnell, founder John H.'s son, became vice chairman of the company. He succeeded his father as CEO a year later.

Forging into new markets, Worthington formed a joint venture in 1994 with Mexico's Hylsa SA to operate a steel-processing facility in Monterey, Mexico. (In 2006 it sold its stake in the JV.) The company also entered new markets for existing product lines: Its 1996 purchase of metal-framing maker Dietrich Industries moved Worthington into the residential and commercial building markets, while in 1997 the company expanded its line of automotive parts by acquiring aftermarket body panel maker Gerstenslager in a stock swap worth about $113 million. Worthington also began constructing a new plant in Alabama designed to process one million tons of steel annually.

In 1998 Worthington expanded its international operations again by acquiring Austrian cylinder maker Joseph Heiser. That year the company sold its automotive metals unit, Worthington Precision Metals, to the investor group Veritas Capital Fund, and its share of London Industries (plastic parts for transplant automakers) to Japan-based partner Nissen Chemitec. In 1999

Worthington sold its Buckeye Steel Castings subsidiary to a management group that includes investment firm Key Equity Capital.

To increase its global presence, in 1999 the company bought Portugal-based Metalurgica Progresso de Vale de Cambra and a 51% interest in the Czech Republic's Gastec, both makers of pressure cylinders. Despite steady sales in fiscal 1999, profits fell by half, in part from low prices for cold-rolled steel, start-up costs at the company's new Alabama facility, and the General Motors strike.

Worthington acquired three independent galvanized steel producers in Pennsylvania — MetalTech, NexTech, and GalvTech — during 2000. Along the same vein, in 2002 the company purchased construction steel maker Unimast Incorporated (subsidiary of WHX Corporation).

In 2003 Worthington formed a joint venture with Ohio-based Viking Industries, an intermediate steel processor of hot-rolled steel coils.

John H. McConnell died in 2008.

EXECUTIVES

Chairman and CEO: John P. McConnell, age 58
President and COO: George P. Stoe, age 63
CFO: B. Andrew Rose, age 38
CIO: Robert (Rob) Richardson
SVP Manufacturing: Virgil L. Winland, age 61
SVP Marketing; President, Worthington Integrated Building Systems, LLC: Ralph V. Roberts, age 62
VP Communications: Catherine M. (Cathy) Lyttle
VP Administration, General Counsel, and Secretary: Dale T. Brinkman, age 56
VP Human Resources: Eric M. Smolenski
VP Purchasing: Robert A. Mowery
President, Worthington Cylinder: Harry A. Goussetis, age 55
President, Dietrich Industries (Dietrich Metal Framing): John E. Roberts, age 54
President, The Worthington Steel Company: Mark A. Russell, age 47
Auditors: KPMG LLP

LOCATIONS

HQ: Worthington Industries, Inc.
200 Old Wilson Bridge Rd., Columbus, OH 43085
Phone: 614-438-3210   **Fax:** 614-438-7948
Web: www.worthingtonindustries.com

2009 Sales

	$ mil	% of total
North America		
United States	2,395.4	91
Canada	66.5	3
Europe	169.4	6
Total	**2,631.3**	**100**

PRODUCTS/OPERATIONS

2009 Sales

	$ mil	% of total
Steel Processing	1,183.0	45
Metal Framing	661.0	25
Pressure Cylinders	537.4	20
Other	249.9	10
Total	**2,631.3**	**100**

Selected Subsidiaries

Dietrich Industries, Inc. (metal framing)
GalvTech (galvanized steel)
MetalTech (galvanized steel)
NexTech (galvanized steel)
The Gerstenslager Company (aftermarket body panels)
Worthington Cylinder Corporation (pressure cylinders)
Worthington Steel Company (steel processing)

Joint Ventures and Other Holdings

Spartan Steel Coating, LLC (52%, joint venture with Rouge Steel Coating; sheet steel)
TWB Company, LLC (45%, joint venture with ThyssenKrupp; laser-welded blanks for cars)
Worthington Armstrong Venture (50%, joint venture with Armstrong World Industries; suspended ceiling grid systems)
Worthington Specialty Processing (51%, joint venture with United States Steel; wide-sheet steel for the auto industry)

COMPETITORS

AK Steel Holding Corporation
Citation Corp.
Gibraltar Industries
Harsco
INTERMET
Nippon Steel
Nucor
O'Neal Steel
Reliance Steel
Russel Metals
Ryerson
Shiloh Industries
Steel Technologies
ThyssenKrupp Steel
United States Steel

HISTORICAL FINANCIALS

Company Type: Public

Income Statement

FYE: May 31

	REVENUE ($ mil.)	NET INCOME ($ mil.)	NET PROFIT MARGIN	EMPLOYEES
5/09	2,631.3	(108.2)	—	6,400
5/08	3,067.2	107.1	3.5%	6,900
5/07	2,971.8	113.9	3.8%	6,900
5/06	2,897.2	146.0	5.0%	8,200
5/05	3,078.9	179.4	5.8%	6,450
Annual Growth	**(3.9%)**	**—**	**—**	**(0.2%)**

2009 Year-End Financials

Debt ratio: 14.2%
Return on equity: —
Cash ($ mil.): 56
Current ratio: 1.61
Long-term debt ($ mil.): 100

No. of shares (mil.): 79
Dividends
 Yield: 4.9%
 Payout: —
Market value ($ mil.): 1,107

Stock History

NYSE: WOR

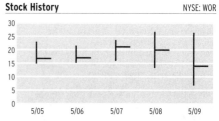

	STOCK PRICE ($) FY Close	P/E High/Low		PER SHARE ($) Earnings	Dividends	Book Value
5/09	13.99	—	—	(1.37)	0.68	8.93
5/08	19.94	20	10	1.31	0.68	11.19
5/07	21.11	18	12	1.31	0.68	11.83
5/06	17.03	13	9	1.64	0.68	11.95
5/05	16.76	11	7	2.03	0.65	10.38
Annual Growth	**(4.4%)**	**—**	**—**	**—**	**1.1%**	**(3.7%)**

W. R. Grace

W. R. Grace & Co. operates through two major units. Grace's Davison unit — which accounts for about two-thirds of sales — makes silica-based products, chemical catalysts, packaging sealants, and refining catalysts that help produce refined products from crude oil. Its Construction Products unit makes concrete and cement additives, and fireproofing chemicals. The company's customers include chemicals companies, oil refiners, and construction firms. Grace filed for bankruptcy protection in 2001 after an unexpected increase in asbestos litigation (injury claims nearly doubled in 2000); the company no longer makes such products.

The company is expanding manufacturing and sales operations in key regions (including China, India, the Middle East, Latin America, and Eastern Europe) to take advantage of growth. It is also pursuing global acquisitions to enhance its existing product offerings and penetrate desirable segments. In the last half of this decade Grace has aquired businesses in Venezuela and Sweden in addition to several in North America.

HISTORY

W. R. Grace & Co. grew from the businesses of Irishman William R. Grace, who fled the potato famine and moved to Peru in 1854 to charter ships trading guano fertilizer. In 1866 he moved his headquarters to New York and established shipping routes linking New York, South America, and Europe. The company traded fertilizer, agricultural products, and US manufactured goods.

Grace, mayor of New York City in the 1880s, died in 1904. His son Joseph became president in 1907, and he expanded the firm's business in South America and started the Grace National Bank in 1916. The company entered aviation in 1928 in a joint venture with Pan American Airlines, forming Pan American-Grace Airways (Panagra) to serve Latin America.

In 1945 Joseph's son Peter took the helm at age 32. He took the company public in 1953. The next year Grace expanded into chemicals, buying Davison Chemical and Dewey & Almy Chemical (sealants, batteries, and packaging). Peter then sold Grace National Bank (1965), Panagra (1967), and the Grace Line (1969).

Purchases during the 1960s and 1970s included American Breeders Service (1967), Herman's (56%, sporting goods, 1970; sold 1986), Baker & Taylor (wholesale books, 1970), Sheplers (western wear, 1976; sold 1986), El Torito-La Fiesta Restaurants (1976; sold 1995), and home-improvement store Handy City (1976). Grace sold its agricultural and fertilizer businesses in 1988 and added three European water-treatment firms to its holdings in 1990. In 1992 it sold Baker & Taylor and bought DuPont Canada's North American food-service packaging operations.

Peter Grace left in 1993 after nearly 50 years as CEO. J. P. Bolduc succeeded him but was brought down by a sexual harassment scandal two years later. Grace acquired Riggers Medizintechnik of Germany (dialysis products) and Florida-based Home Intensive Care and sold its oil field services and liquid storage and terminal businesses.

Grace began divesting businesses in 1995, selling its Dearborn business to Betz Laboratories

and the plant biotechnology portion of its Agracetus subsidiary to Monsanto. That year the company reclassified its health care business as discontinued; that move resulted in a dramatic drop in revenues. Albert Costello, a veteran executive from drug firm American Cyanamid, succeeded Bolduc.

In 1998 the company sold its biggest division, food packaging, to Sealed Air for about $4.9 billion in cash and stock (Grace shareholders wound up with more than 60% of Sealed Air). It also agreed to buy Imperial Chemical's Crosfield catalysts and silicas business but terminated the deal after US regulators raised antitrust issues. Grace relocated its headquarters to Columbia, Maryland, in 1999 and set up a $1 million financial education fund to settle an SEC lawsuit alleging the company socked away profits in the 1990s to mask poor earnings. The company upped its stake in Grace Chemicals K.K. (formerly Denka Grace), a Japanese joint venture to produce concrete admixture.

Also in 1999 Paul Norris, former president of AlliedSignal's specialty chemicals division, succeeded Costello as CEO. Early in 2001 Grace announced that it had filed for bankruptcy protection because of an unexpected 80% increase in asbestos-related litigation; previously, the company had managed to settle claims, which had come at a relatively manageable rate.

Grace continued to expand its presence in core markets in 2001; acquisitions included European companies Akzo-PQ Silicas (silica products) and Pieri S.A. (specialty construction chemicals). Also in 2001 Grace and Chevron Products (a unit of Chevron, formerly ChevronTexaco) formed catalyst developer Advanced Refining Technologies. In 2002 Grace acquired catalyst manufacturing assets from Sweden's Borealis A/S. The following year, Grace continued to expand internationally through the acquisition of German construction chemicals firm Tricosal Beton-Chemie.

In addition to acquisitions, Grace grew in 2002 and 2003 through improved sales for catalysts used in refining and increased volume at its Performance Chemicals unit, especially in the Asia/Pacific region.

In 2004 the company acquired Benelux firm Pieri N.V. It bought up sealants and adhesives maker Liquid Control later that year. It also acquired pharmaceutical chemical firm Alltech International as part of a strategy to build up its biotechnology and pharmaceutical customer base for silica-based products.

EXECUTIVES

Chairman, President, and CEO: Alfred E. (Fred) Festa, age 49, $5,579,588 total compensation
SVP and CFO: Hudson La Force III, age 44, $1,100,126 total compensation
CIO: Gloria L. Keesee, age 54
VP and Chief Human Resources Officer: Pamela K. Wagoner, age 45
SVP Administration: W. Brian McGowan, age 59
VP Public and Regulatory Affairs: William M. Corcoran, age 59
VP, General Counsel, and Secretary: Mark A. Shelnitz, age 50, $1,263,805 total compensation
VP; President, Davison Chemicals: Gregory E. (Greg) Poling, age 53, $2,198,849 total compensation
VP Operations: J. P. (Butch) Forehand
VP; President, Grace Construction Products: D. Andrew Bonham, age 48, $2,117,704 total compensation
Media Relations: Andrea Greenan
Investor Relations: Susette Smith
Auditors: PricewaterhouseCoopers LLP

LOCATIONS

HQ: W. R. Grace & Co.
7500 Grace Dr., Columbia, MD 21044
Phone: 410-531-4000 **Fax:** 410-531-4367
Web: www.grace.com

2008 Sales

	$ mil.	% of total
Europe/Africa	1,320.1	40
North America		
US	1,078.2	33
Canada & Puerto Rico	101.5	3
Asia/Pacific	582.9	17
Latin America	234.3	7
Total	**3,317.0**	**100**

PRODUCTS/OPERATIONS

2008 Sales

	$ mil.	% of total
Grace Davison	2,168.6	65
Grace Construction Products	1,148.4	35
Total	**3,317.0**	**100**

Selected Operations

Grace Davison
  Can and closure sealants
  Chemical catalysts
  Refining catalysts
  Silicas and absorbents

Grace Construction Products
  Air and vapor barriers
  Cement additives
  Coatings and sealants
  Concrete admixtures
  Fireproofing materials
  Masonry products
  Waterproofing materials

COMPETITORS

Albemarle
Ameron
BASF Catalysts
Cabot
Clariant
CRI/Criterion Catalyst
DuPont
Evonik Degussa
H.B. Fuller
UOP

HISTORICAL FINANCIALS

Company Type: Public

Income Statement				FYE: December 31
	REVENUE ($ mil.)	NET INCOME ($ mil.)	NET PROFIT MARGIN	EMPLOYEES
12/08	3,317.0	121.5	3.7%	6,300
12/07	3,115.2	80.3	2.6%	6,500
12/06	2,826.5	18.3	0.6%	6,500
12/05	2,569.5	67.3	2.6%	6,400
12/04	2,259.9	(402.3)	—	6,500
Annual Growth	10.1%	—	—	(0.8%)

2008 Year-End Financials

Debt ratio: —   No. of shares (mil.): 72
Return on equity: —   Dividends
Cash ($ mil.): 527   Yield: 0.0%
Current ratio: 2.81   Payout: —
Long-term debt ($ mil.): 1   Market value ($ mil.): 431

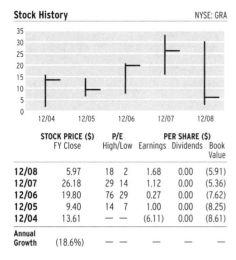
W.W. Grainger

Home, home on the Grainger is a well-stocked place. Through its three business segments — Grainger Branch-based, Acklands-Grainger, and Lab Safety Supply — W.W. Grainger distributes maintenance, repair, and service equipment, as well as components and supplies. It provides access to over 475,000 products such as compressors, motors, signs, lighting and welding equipment, and hand and power tools. The company has more than 600 branches and 18 distribution centers in the US, Canada, Mexico, Puerto Rico, Panama, and China. Its 1.8 million customers include contractors, service and maintenance shops, manufacturers, hotels, and government, health care, and educational facilities.

Grainger's Branch-based is the largest business segment, accounting for more than 80% of sales. The Industrial Supply unit distributes products for safety and security, lighting and electrical, power and hand tools, pumps and plumbing, and cleaning and maintenance industries. It encompasses about 435 branches located in all 50 states in the US, and international business units, which include Puerto Rico, Panama, and significant operations in Mexico and China. Almost 25% of sales consist of private label items with Grainger's trademark names, including Dayton (motors), Speedaire (air compressors), Dem-Kote (spray paints), Westward (tools), and Condor (safety products), to name a few. Grainger has begun a program in the US to enlarge the size of its branches and increase its staff in 25 metropolitan markets.

The company's Acklands-Grainger segment accounts for a little over 10% of sales and primarily focuses on distributing industrial and safety supplies. It leverages about 150 branches and six distribution centers located throughout Canada. In 2008 Acklands-Grainger spent $6.8 million to acquire Quebec-based Excel Industriel, which distributes maintenance, repair, and operations (MRO) supplies throughout the province. Also in 2008 the company paid over $5 million to acquire a little less than 50% interest in Asia Pacific Brands India, which is one of India's largest industrial and electrical wholesale distributors.

Lab Safety Supply markets safety products to businesses in both the US and Canada mostly through its branded catalogs. In 2009 the company will integrate the Lab Safety business into the Grainger Industrial Supply unit. Grainger's acquisitions of McFeely Square Drive Screws (woodworking) in 2007, and Highsmith (library equipment) for $27 million in 2008, will augment the integrated unit.

The company is attempting to increase sales by increasing its services. Grainger offers customers inventory management, energy audits, and purchasing analyses, which it hopes will help tempt customers to consolidate their spending with the company.

Senior chairman David Grainger, the founder's son, owns 9% of Grainger; director James Slavik owns 6%.

HISTORY

In 1919 William W. Grainger, a motor designer and salesman, saw the opportunity to develop a wholesale electric-motor sales and distribution company. He set up an office in Chicago in 1927 and incorporated the business a year later. With sales generated primarily through postcard mailers and an eight-page catalog called *MotorBook*, Grainger started shipping motors to mail-order customers.

Utilities and factories began to shift from direct-current to alternating-current power systems in the late 1920s. Uniform DC-powered assembly lines gave way to individual workstations, each powered by a separate AC motor. This burgeoning market opened the way for distributors such as W.W. Grainger to tap into segments that high-volume manufacturers found difficult to reach. In the early 1930s W.W. Grainger opened offices in Atlanta, Dallas, Philadelphia, and San Francisco; by 1936 it had 15 sales branches.

W.W. Grainger entered a boom period after WWII, and by 1949 it had branches in 30 states. The company continued to expand in the 1950s and 1960s, then went public in 1967.

William Grainger retired in 1968, and his son David succeeded him as CEO. The company expanded into electric motor manufacturing with the purchase of the Doerr Companies in 1969. Ten years later it opened its 150th branch.

Grainger's distribution became decentralized with the 1983 opening of its 1.4 million-sq.-ft. automated regional distribution center in Kansas City. The next year Grainger surpassed $1 billion in sales. The company sold its Doerr Electric subsidiary to Emerson Electric in 1986. It added 91 branches in 1987 and 1988.

After a 17-year hiatus, the company started making acquisitions again, buying Vonnegut Industrial Products in 1989; Bossert Industrial Supply and Allied Safety in 1990; Ball Industries, a distributor of sanitary and janitorial supplies, in 1991; and Lab Safety Supply in 1992. Grainger began integrating its sanitary supply business with its core activities in 1993.

For the first time in company history, no Grainger held the CEO position when president Richard Keyser was appointed in 1995, replacing David Grainger. That year the company moved its headquarters to Lake Forest, Illinois.

Getting wired in 1995, Grainger put its catalog on the World Wide Web. The next year it announced new supply agreements with American Airlines, Emerson Electric Co., Lockheed Martin, and Procter & Gamble. Also in 1996 the company

paid about $289 million for a unit of Canada's Acklands Ltd., distributor of automotive aftermarket products and industrial safety products. In 1998 Grainger won contracts, potentially worth more than $60 million over three years, to supply products to two health care organizations.

Grainger launched several online stores through its home page in 1999 (TotalMRO.com launched in 2000) and began negotiations in 2001 to split its Internet segment off as a separate entity (dubbed Material Logic). However, citing a slow economy, it later abandoned those plans and closed all Internet sites except FindMRO.com. Grainger took a $38 million writedown related to its Internet investments.

In 2002 Grainger was recognized by *FORTUNE* magazine as one of "America's Most Admired Companies," ranked fourth among the US's largest diversified wholesalers. The company completed the acquisition of Gempler's direct marketing division (tools and safety equipment) in 2003.

EXECUTIVES

Chairman, President, and CEO: James T. (Jim) Ryan, age 50, $5,474,528 total compensation
Chairman Emeritus: Richard L. (Dick) Keyser, age 66, $6,555,335 total compensation
Vice Chairman: P. Ogden Loux, age 66, $2,317,387 total compensation
SVP and CFO: Ronald L. Jadin, age 48
SVP Communications and Investor Relations: Nancy A. Hobor, age 62
SVP and General Counsel: John L. Howard, age 51, $1,730,233 total compensation
SVP Human Resources: Lawrence J. Pilon, age 56
SVP Enterprise Processes and Systems: Timothy M. Ferrarell, age 48
SVP and President, Grainger U.S.: Michael A. Pulick, age 44
SVP and President Grainger International: Court D. Carruthers, age 36
SVP Global Supply Chain: Donald G. MacPherson, age 41
SVP Sales and Marketing: Pat Davidson
VP Specialty Brands; President, Lab Safety Supply, Inc.: Larry J. Loizzo, age 54, $1,461,129 total compensation
VP and Controller: Gregory S. Irving, age 50
VP, Sales: Debra (Deb) Oler, age 52
Director, Investor Relations and External Communications: William D. Chapman
Auditors: Ernst & Young LLP

LOCATIONS

HQ: W.W. Grainger, Inc.
100 Grainger Pkwy., Lake Forest, IL 60045
Phone: 847-535-1000   **Fax:** 847-535-0878
Web: www.grainger.com

2008 Sales

	$ mil.	% of total
US	5,953.2	87
Canada	731.1	11
Other countries	165.7	2
Total	**6,850.0**	**100**

PRODUCTS/OPERATIONS

2008 Sales

	$ mil.	% of total
Grainger Branch-Based	5,675.3	83
Acklands-Grainger	727.8	11
Lab Safety	446.9	6
Total	**6,850.0**	**100**

Hoover's Handbook of

American Business

The Indexes

Index by Industry

INDUSTRY CATEGORIES

Aerospace & Defense	936
Agriculture	936
Automotive & Transport	936
Banking	936
Beverages	936
Business Services	936
Chemicals	936
Computer Hardware	937
Computer Services	937
Computer Software	937
Construction	937
Consumer Products Manufacturers	937
Consumer Services	937
Education	937
Electronics	937
Energy & Utilities	937
Environmental Services & Equipment	938
Financial Services	938
Food	938
Government	938
Health Care	938
Industrial Manufacturing	938
Insurance	939
Leisure	939
Media	939
Metals & Mining	939
Pharmaceuticals	939
Real Estate	939
Retail	939
Security Products & Services	939
Telecommunications Equipment	939
Telecommunications Services	940
Transportation Services	940

AEROSPACE & DEFENSE

Aerospace & Defense Parts Manufacturing
BE Aerospace 133
Goodrich Corporation 396
ITT Corporation 474
L-3 Communications 517
Lockheed Martin 540
Moog Inc. 596
Northrop Grumman 634

Aircraft Manufacturing
The Boeing Company 156
Textron Inc. 824

Weaponry & Related Product Manufacturing
Alliant Techsystems 65
General Dynamics 383
Raytheon Company 722

AGRICULTURE

Agricultural Support Activities & Products
Archer Daniels Midland 105
Cargill, Incorporated 188
CHS Inc. 217
Monsanto Company 595

Animal Production
King Ranch 507

Crop Production
Chiquita Brands International 216
Dole Food 298

AUTOMOTIVE & TRANSPORT

Auto Manufacturing
Ford Motor 364
General Motors 387

Auto Parts Manufacturing
ArvinMeritor 108
BorgWarner Inc. 160
Cummins, Inc. 269
Dana Holding 272
Federal-Mogul 350
Johnson Controls 488
Tenneco Inc. 816

Motorcycle & Other Small Engine Vehicle Manufacturing
Harley-Davidson 408
Polaris Industries 690

Pleasure Boat Manufacturing
Brunswick Corporation 174

Rail & Trucking Equipment Manufacturing
Trinity Industries 843

Recreational Vehicle Manufacturing
Thor Industries 828

Truck, Bus & Other Vehicle Manufacturing
Navistar International 611
Oshkosh Corporation 654
PACCAR Inc 657

Truck Leasing
Ryder System 742

BANKING

Custodial & Trust Services
Northern Trust 633

Money Center Banks
Bank of America 126
Bank of New York Mellon 128
Citigroup Inc. 227
JPMorgan Chase 493
Wells Fargo 906

Superregional Banks
BB&T Corporation 132
Comerica Incorporated 239
Fifth Third Bancorp 353
Huntington Bancshares 447
KeyCorp 502
PNC Financial Services 689
Regions Financial 723
SunTrust Banks 801
U.S. Bancorp 870
Zions Bancorporation 933

BEVERAGES

Alcoholic Beverages
Brown-Forman Corporation 173
Constellation Brands 250
E. & J. Gallo Winery 314
Molson Coors Brewing 593

Bottling & Distribution
Coca-Cola Enterprises 234
Pepsi Bottling Group 668
PepsiAmericas, Inc. 670

Nonalcoholic Beverages
The Coca-Cola Company 232
PepsiCo, Inc. 671

BUSINESS SERVICES

Affiliated Computer Services 47

Advertising & Marketing
IMS Health 455
Interpublic Group 467
Omnicom Group 650
Valassis Communications 875
Viad Corp 884

Auctions
eBay Inc. 320
Sotheby's 782

Commercial Cleaning & Facilities Management Services
ABM Industries 35

Commercial Printing
Cenveo, Inc. 203
Deluxe Corporation 285
R.R. Donnelley 741

Consulting
Accenture Ltd 36
McKinsey & Company 577
Watson Wyatt Worldwide 902

Information & Records Management Services
Iron Mountain 471

Legal Services
Baker & McKenzie 122
Skadden, Arps 775

Staffing
Administaff, Inc. 40
Automatic Data Processing 113
Hewitt Associates 428
Kelly Services 499
Manpower Inc. 551
MPS Group 600
Paychex, Inc. 664
Robert Half 732
Spherion Corporation 788
Volt Information Sciences 888

Uniform Rental & Laundry Services
Cintas Corporation 224

CHEMICALS

Agricultural Chemicals
Central Garden & Pet 201
Scotts Miracle-Gro 760
Terra Industries 820

Basic & Intermediate Chemical & Petrochemical Manufacturing
Air Products and Chemicals 52
FMC Corporation 361
Olin Corporation 648
Praxair, Inc. 695
Solutia Inc. 780
W. R. Grace 923

Chemical Distribution
Airgas, Inc. 53
Ashland Inc. 109
Sigma-Aldrich Corporation 773

Paints, Coatings & Other Finishing Product Manufacturing
PPG Industries 692
RPM International 740
Sherwin-Williams 771
The Valspar Corporation 877

Plastic & Fiber Manufacturing
A. Schulman 27
Dow Chemical 304
DuPont (E. I. du Pont de Nemours and Company) 311

Specialty Chemical Manufacturing
3M Company 26
Avery Dennison 117
Cabot Corporation 180
Cytec Industries 271
Eastman Chemical 316
Ecolab Inc. 321
International Flavors & Fragrances 463
The Lubrizol Corporation 545
Nalco Holding 605

COMPUTER HARDWARE

Computer Networking Equipment
Cisco Systems 225

Computer Peripherals
Imation Corp. 454
Lexmark International 530
Pitney Bowes 685
Western Digital 911
Xerox Corporation 926

Mass Storage Systems
EMC Corporation 327
NetApp, Inc. 617
Seagate Technology 763

Personal Computers
Apple Inc. 99
Dell Inc. 282
Hewlett-Packard 429

Specialized Computer Systems
Diebold, Incorporated 291
NCR Corporation 616

COMPUTER SERVICES

Computer Products Distribution & Support
Ingram Micro 458
ScanSource, Inc. 755
Tech Data Corporation 810

Information Technology Services
CACI International 182
Computer Sciences Corporation 242
International Business Machines 462
Perot Systems 674
SAIC, Inc. 746
Unisys Corporation 853

COMPUTER SOFTWARE

Accounting & Finance Software
Intuit Inc. 468

Database & File Management Software
Oracle Corporation 652

Development Tools, Operating Systems & Utilities Software
Microsoft Corporation 590

Engineering, Scientific & CAD/CAM Software
Autodesk, Inc. 112

Entertainment & Games Software
Activision Blizzard 38
Electronic Arts 324

Financial Services, Legal & Government Software
DST Systems 307

Health Care Management Software
Cerner Corporation 205

Multimedia, Graphics & Publishing Software
Adobe Systems 41

Networking & Connectivity Software
Novell, Inc. 636

Security Software
McAfee, Inc. 569
Symantec Corporation 804
VeriSign, Inc. 880

Storage & Systems Management Software
BMC Software 154
CA, Inc. 178

CONSTRUCTION

Construction & Design Services
Beazer Homes USA 134
Bechtel Group 135
Champion Enterprises 208
D.R. Horton 306
EMCOR Group 328
Fluor Corporation 360
Foster Wheeler 369
Hovnanian Enterprises 443
Jacobs Engineering 477
KB Home 496
Lennar Corporation 525
McDermott International 572
NCI Building Systems 615
NVR, Inc. 642
Peter Kiewit Sons' 677
Pulte Homes 712
The Ryland Group 744
The Shaw Group 770
Toll Brothers 837
URS 867

Construction Materials
Carlisle Companies 190
Lennox International 527
Martin Marietta Materials 560
Masco Corporation 561
USG Corporation 874
Vulcan Materials 888
Watsco, Inc. 900
Weyerhaeuser Company 913

CONSUMER PRODUCTS MANUFACTURERS

Apparel
Jones Apparel 489
Levi Strauss 529
Liz Claiborne 539
NIKE, Inc. 626
Phillips-Van Heusen 682
Polo Ralph Lauren 691
The Timberland Company 832
V.F. Corporation 882
Warnaco Group 895

Appliances
Whirlpool Corporation 914

Cleaning Products
Church & Dwight 219
The Clorox Company 229
S.C. Johnson 753

Consumer Electronics
Harman International 409

Hand Tools, Power Tools, Lawn & Garden Equipment
Black & Decker 151
Snap-on Incorporated 778
The Toro Company 839

Home Furniture
Furniture Brands International 376
La-Z-Boy 521
Leggett & Platt 524

Housewares
Newell Rubbermaid 620
Tupperware Brands 846

Jewelry & Watch Manufacturing
Fossil, Inc. 368
Tiffany & Co. 830

Mattress & Bed Manufacturers
Sealy Corporation 766

Office & Business Furniture, Fixtures & Equipment
Herman Miller 423
HNI Corporation 435
Steelcase Inc. 798

Personal Care Products
Alberto-Culver 58
Avon Products 120
Colgate-Palmolive 235
Estée Lauder 338
Kimberly-Clark 504
MacAndrews & Forbes 547
Procter & Gamble 701
Revlon, Inc. 728

Pet Products
PetSmart, Inc. 678

Photographic & Optical Equipment/Supplies Manufacturers
Eastman Kodak 317

Sporting Goods & Equipment
Quiksilver, Inc. 716

Tobacco
Alliance One International 64
Altria Group 67
Reynolds American 729
Universal Corporation 864

Toys & Games
Hasbro, Inc. 413
Mattel, Inc. 565

CONSUMER SERVICES

Car & Truck Rental
AMERCO 71
Avis Budget Group 118
Hertz Global Holdings 425

Death Care Products & Services
Service Corporation 769

Hair Salons
Regis Corporation 724

Rent-To-Own
Aaron's, Inc. 29
Rent-A-Center 726

Travel Agencies & Services
Carlson Wagonlit Travel 191

Carnival Corporation 193
priceline.com 698
Royal Caribbean Cruises 739

EDUCATION

Colleges & Universities
Apollo Group 98

ELECTRONICS

Contract Electronics Manufacturing
Benchmark Electronics 143
Jabil Circuit 475
Plexus Corp. 688
Sanmina-SCI 750

Electrical Products
Anixter International 92
A. O. Smith 94
Baldor Electric 124
Cooper Industries 255
Eaton Corporation 318
Exide Technologies 343
Thomas & Betts 827
WESCO International 909

Electronic Components
Arrow Electronics 107
Avnet, Inc. 119
Corning Incorporated 257
Molex Incorporated 592
QUALCOMM 713

Electronic Test & Measurement Instruments
Agilent Technologies 51
Itron, Inc. 472

Scientific & Technical Instruments
PerkinElmer, Inc. 673
Thermo Fisher Scientific 825

Semiconductor Equipment & Materials
Applied Materials 101
KLA-Tencor 508
Lam Research 519

Semiconductors
Advanced Micro Devices 43
Amkor Technology 87
Analog Devices 90
Broadcom Corporation 170
Intel Corporation 460
LSI Corporation 544
Maxim Integrated Products 566
Micron Technology 588
National Semiconductor 609
NVIDIA Corporation 641
SanDisk Corporation 749
Texas Instruments 823
Vishay Intertechnology 886
Xilinx, Inc. 927

ENERGY & UTILITIES

Electric Utilities
Allegheny Energy 60
Ameren Corporation 72
American Electric Power Company 75
CMS Energy 230
Consolidated Edison 249
Dominion Resources 299
DTE Energy 308
Duke Energy 309
Dynegy Inc. 312
Edison International 322
Entergy Corporation 332
Exelon Corporation 342
FirstEnergy Corp. 356

FPL Group 372
Northeast Utilities 632
NSTAR 638
Pepco Holdings 668
PG&E Corporation 681
Pinnacle West Capital 683
PPL Corporation 694
Progress Energy 703
Public Service Enterprise Group 709
SCANA Corporation 754
Southern Company 783
Westar Energy 910
Xcel Energy 925

Energy Trading & Marketing
Constellation Energy Group 251

Independent/Merchant Power Production
The AES Corporation 44
Calpine Corporation 184
NRG Energy 638

Natural Gas Utilities
CenterPoint Energy 200
National Fuel Gas 608
Nicor Inc. 625
NiSource Inc. 627
ONEOK, Inc. 651
Sempra Energy 768
Southern Union 784
Southwest Gas 787

Oil & Gas Exploration & Production
Anadarko Petroleum 89
Apache Corporation 96
Baker Hughes 123
BJ Services 149
Chesapeake Energy 214
Devon Energy 289
Diamond Offshore Drilling 290
ENSCO International 331
EOG Resources 334
Halliburton Company 403
Helmerich & Payne 421
Key Energy Services 502
Marathon Oil 553
Noble Corporation 628
Occidental Petroleum 644
Pioneer Natural Resources 684
Rowan Companies 738
Schlumberger Limited 756
SEACOR Holdings 762
Transocean Inc. 841
Weatherford International 903

Oil & Gas Refining, Marketing & Distribution
Adams Resources & Energy 39
AmeriGas Partners 84
Chevron Corporation 215
ConocoPhillips 245
Exxon Mobil 346
Ferrellgas Partners 353
Hess Corporation 427
Holly Corporation 436
Koch Industries 511
Sunoco, Inc. 800
Tesoro Corporation 821
UGI Corporation 851
Valero Energy 876
Williams Companies 917
World Fuel Services 920

Oil & Gas Transportation & Storage
El Paso Corporation 323
Enterprise Products Partners 333
Plains All American Pipeline 687

Water Utilities
American Water Works 82

ENVIRONMENTAL SERVICES & EQUIPMENT
Donaldson Company 302
Pall Corporation 658

Remediation & Environmental Cleanup Services
Tetra Tech 821

Solid Waste Services & Recycling
Republic Services 727
Waste Management 899

FINANCIAL SERVICES

Accounting
Deloitte Touche Tohmatsu 283
Ernst & Young Global 337
H&R Block 405
KPMG International 513
PricewaterhouseCoopers International 699

Asset Management
CalPERS (California Public Employees' Retirement System) 183
FMR LLC 362
Franklin Resources 373
Invesco Ltd. 470
Legg Mason 523
Principal Financial 700
State Street Corporation 797
T. Rowe Price Group 807
TIAA-CREF (Teachers Insurance and Annuity Association - College Retirement Equities Fund) 829
The Vanguard Group 879

Investment Banking
Goldman Sachs 395
Jefferies Group 481
Morgan Stanley 598

Investment Firms
Berkshire Hathaway 144
Fortune Brands 367

Lending
American Express 76
AmeriCredit Corp. 83
Capital One Financial 186
General Electric 384

Securities Brokers & Traders
Charles Schwab 209
E*TRADE Financial 339
Raymond James Financial 720
TD Ameritrade 809

Stock Exchanges
NASDAQ OMX Group 606
NYSE Euronext 643

Transaction, Credit & Collections
Dun & Bradstreet 310
Equifax Inc. 335
Fiserv, Inc. 357
MasterCard Incorporated 564
Total System Services 840
Visa Inc 885

FOOD
Kraft Foods 514

Candy & Confections
The Hershey Company 424
Mars, Incorporated 556

Canned & Frozen Foods
Campbell Soup 185
ConAgra Foods 244
Del Monte Foods 280

Dairy Products
Dean Foods 277
Land O'Lakes 520

Flavorings, Spices & Other Ingredients
McCormick & Company 571

Food Wholesale Distributors
Nash-Finch Company 607
Spartan Stores 787
United Natural Foods 854
Wakefern Food 890

Foodservice
ARAMARK Corporation 103
SYSCO Corporation 805

Grains
Flowers Foods 358
General Mills 386
Kellogg Company 497
Ralcorp Holdings 719
Sara Lee 751
Seaboard Corporation 761

Meat Products
Hormel Foods 441
Sanderson Farms 748
Smithfield Foods 777
Tyson Foods 848

Sauces & Condiments
H. J. Heinz Company 434
The J. M. Smucker Company 482

GOVERNMENT
Tennessee Valley Authority 817

HEALTH CARE

Health Care Products
Becton, Dickinson 137
Boston Scientific 161
C. R. Bard, Inc. 262
DENTSPLY International 288
Henry Schein 422
Hill-Rom Holdings 432
Hologic, Inc. 437
Invacare Corporation 469
Kinetic Concepts 506
Medtronic, Inc. 581
Owens & Minor 655
Patterson Companies 663
PSS World Medical 707
St. Jude Medical 747

Health Care Services
Aetna Inc. 46
CIGNA Corporation 221
DaVita Inc. 276
Express Scripts 345
HCA Inc. 415
Health Management Associates 416
Health Net 417
HealthSouth Corporation 418
Highmark Inc. 430
Humana Inc. 446
Kaiser Foundation Health Plan 494
Kindred Healthcare 505
Lincare Holdings 534
Magellan Health Services 549
Medco Health Solutions 580
Psychiatric Solutions 708
Quest Diagnostics 714
Sun Healthcare 799
Tenet Healthcare 815
UnitedHealth Group 863
WellPoint, Inc. 904

INDUSTRIAL MANUFACTURING
Ingersoll-Rand 456

Agricultural Machinery Manufacturing
AGCO Corporation 50
Deere & Company 279

Construction, Mining & Other Heavy Equipment Manufacturing
Caterpillar Inc. 196
Joy Global 492
Manitowoc Company 550
Terex Corporation 818

Fluid Control Equipment, Pump, Seal & Valve Manufacturing
Crane Co. 265
Parker Hannifin 661
SPX Corporation 790

Industrial Automation & Industrial Control Products Manufacturing
Danaher Corporation 274
Emerson Electric 329
Honeywell International 440
Rockwell Automation 734

Industrial Equipment Leasing
United Rentals 857

Industrial Machinery & Equipment Distribution
Applied Industrial Technologies 100
MSC Industrial Direct 601
W.W. Grainger 924

Industrial Machinery & Equipment Manufacturing
Briggs & Stratton 164
Dover Corporation 303
Illinois Tool Works 453
Kennametal Inc. 500
Lincoln Electric Holdings 535
Roper Industries 735
The Timken Company 834
United Technologies 861

Material Handling Equipment Manufacturing
NACCO Industries 603

Metal Fabrication
Commercial Metals 240
Precision Castparts 696

Packaging & Container Manufacturing
Ball Corporation 125
Bemis Company 142
Crown Holdings 266
Greif, Inc. 401
MeadWestvaco 578
Owens-Illinois 656
Rock-Tenn Company 733
Sealed Air Corp. 764
Sonoco Products 781
Temple-Inland 813

Paper & Paper Product Manufacturing
International Paper 465

Rubber & Plastic Product Manufacturing
Cooper Tire & Rubber 256
Goodyear Tire & Rubber 397

Textile Manufacturing
Mohawk Industries 591

Wire & Cable Manufacturing
Belden Inc. 140
CommScope, Inc. 241
General Cable 382

INSURANCE

Hartford Financial Services 412

Insurance Brokers

Aon Corporation 95
Marsh & McLennan 558

Life Insurance

Lincoln National 536
Massachusetts Mutual Life
  Insurance 563
MetLife, Inc. 585
New York Life Insurance 618
Northwestern Mutual Life
  Insurance 635
Protective Life 705
Prudential Financial 706
Torchmark Corporation 838

Property & Casualty Insurance

Aflac Incorporated 48
The Allstate Corporation 66
American Financial Group 77
American International Group 80
The Chubb Corporation 218
Cincinnati Financial 222
CNA Financial 231
Conseco, Inc. 246
Hanover Insurance 407
Liberty Mutual 531
Loews Corporation 542
Markel Corporation 554
Nationwide Mutual Insurance 610
Progressive Corporation 704
State Farm Mutual Automobile
  Insurance 796
Travelers Companies 842
Unum Group 865
USAA 872

Surety Insurance

Ambac Financial Group 70
MBIA Inc. 568

Title Insurance

The First American Corporation 355

LEISURE

Entertainment

Cinemark Holdings 223
Live Nation 537

Gambling

Boyd Gaming 162
International Game Technology 464
MGM MIRAGE 587

Lodging

Hilton Worldwide 433
Hyatt Hotels Corporation 448
Marriott International 555
Starwood Hotels & Resorts 794

Restaurants & Cafes

Bob Evans Farms 155
Brinker International 166
Burger King Holdings 176
The Cheesecake Factory 213
Cracker Barrel Old Country Store 264
Darden Restaurants 275
Denny's Corporation 287
DineEquity, Inc. 294
Domino's Pizza 301
Jack in the Box 476
McDonald's Corporation 573
Starbucks Corporation 793
Wendy's/Arby's Group 907
YUM! Brands 931

Sports & Recreation

Green Bay Packers 400

MEDIA

Cox Enterprises 261
Fox Entertainment 371
Hearst Corporation 420
News Corporation 623
Time Warner 833
The Walt Disney Company 893

Internet Content Providers

IAC/InterActiveCorp 450

Internet Search & Navigation Services

Google Inc. 399
Yahoo! 929

Music

Warner Music Group 896

Publishing

Advance Publications 42
American Greetings 79
E. W. Scripps 340
Gannett Co. 379
Hallmark Cards 404
John Wiley & Sons 485
Martha Stewart Living 559
McClatchy Company 570
McGraw-Hill 575
New York Times 619
Scholastic Corporation 758
Washington Post 897

Television

ABC, Inc. 32
CBS Corporation 198
Discovery Communications 296
NBC Television 613

METALS & MINING

Aluminum Production

Alcoa Inc. 59

Coal Mining & Processing

Arch Coal 104
CONSOL Energy 248

Copper Mining & Processing

Freeport-McMoRan Copper &
  Gold 374

Industrial Metals & Minerals

Cliffs Natural Resources 228

Precious Metals Mining & Processing

Newmont Mining 622

Specialty & Exotic Materials

USEC Inc. 873

Steel Production

AK Steel Holding 55
Allegheny Technologies 61
Carpenter Technology 194
Gerdau Ameristeel 391
Nucor Corporation 639
United States Steel 859

Steel Service Centers

Schnitzer Steel Industries 757
Worthington Industries 921

PHARMACEUTICALS

Biotechnology

Amgen Inc. 85
Baxter International 130
Covance Inc. 260
Genzyme Corporation 390
Gilead Sciences 392

Pharmaceuticals Distribution & Wholesale

AmerisourceBergen 84
Cardinal Health 187
McKesson Corporation 576
Omnicare, Inc. 649

Pharmaceuticals Manufacturers

Abbott Laboratories 31
Allergan, Inc. 62
Beckman Coulter 136
Bristol-Myers Squibb 168
Cephalon, Inc. 204
Eli Lilly 325
Forest Laboratories 366
Johnson & Johnson 486
Merck & Co. 583
Mylan Inc. 602
NBTY, Inc. 614
Perrigo Company 676
Pfizer Inc. 679
Watson Pharmaceuticals 901

REAL ESTATE

Commercial Property Investment

CB Richard Ellis Group 197

Commercial Real Estate Brokerage

Jones Lang LaSalle 491

Real Estate Investment Trusts (REITs)

Equity Residential 336
Simon Property Group 774

RETAIL

HSN, Inc. 444

Apparel & Accessories Retail

Abercrombie & Fitch 33
American Eagle Outfitters 73
AnnTaylor Stores 93
Brown Shoe Company 171
Charming Shoppes 210
Collective Brands 237
Foot Locker 363
The Gap 380
Guess?, Inc. 402
Limited Brands 533
Men's Wearhouse 582
Nordstrom, Inc. 629
Ross Stores 736
TJX Companies 835
Urban Outfitters 866

Auto Parts Retail

AutoZone, Inc. 115
Genuine Parts 388
The Pep Boys 666

Automobile Dealers

AutoNation, Inc. 114
CarMax, Inc. 192

Building Materials Retail & Distribution

Fastenal Company 349

Computer & Software Retail

Insight Enterprises 459
PC Connection 665

Consumer Electronics & Appliances Retail

Best Buy 146
RadioShack Corporation 718

Department Stores

Bon-Ton Stores 157
Dillard's, Inc. 292
J. C. Penney 480
Kohl's Corporation 512
Macy's, Inc. 548
Sears, Roebuck 767

Discount & Variety Retail

Big Lots 147
BJ's Wholesale Club 150
Costco Wholesale 259
Family Dollar Stores 347
Kmart Corporation 510
Target Corporation 808
Wal-Mart Stores 892

Drug Stores & Pharmacies

CVS Caremark 270
Rite Aid 731
Walgreen Co. 890

Gasoline Retailers

Casey's General Stores 195
The Pantry 660

Grocery Retail

A&P (The Great Atlantic & Pacific Tea
  Company, Inc.) 28
IGA, Inc. 452
The Kroger Co. 516
Publix Super Markets 711
Safeway Inc. 745
SUPERVALU INC. 803
Whole Foods Market 915
Winn-Dixie Stores 919

Hobby & Craft Retail

Jo-Ann Stores 484

Home Furnishings & Housewares Retail

Bed Bath & Beyond 139
Williams-Sonoma 918

Home Improvement & Hardware Retail

Ace Hardware 37
Home Depot 439
Lowe's Companies 543
True Value 845

Jewelry & Watch Retail

Zale Corporation 932

Music, Video, Book & Entertainment Retail

Amazon.com 69
Barnes & Noble 129
Blockbuster Inc. 152
Borders Group 158

Office Products Retail & Distribution

Office Depot 645
OfficeMax 647
Staples, Inc. 792
United Stationers 860

Toys & Games Retail

GameStop Corp. 378

SECURITY PRODUCTS & SERVICES

Security Products

Tyco International 847

Security Services

The Brink's Company 167

TELECOMMUNICATIONS EQUIPMENT

Telecommunications Equipment Distribution & Support

Brightpoint Inc. 165

INDEX BY INDUSTRY

Wireless Telecommunications Equipment

Harris Corporation 411
Motorola, Inc. 599
Palm, Inc. 659

Wireline Telecommunications Equipment

Tellabs, Inc. 812

TELECOMMUNICATIONS SERVICES

Cable & Satellite Services

Cablevision Systems 179
Charter Communications 212
Comcast Corporation 238
The DIRECTV Group 295
DISH Network 297

Data Services

EarthLink, Inc. 315
Global Crossing 393
Level 3 Communications 528

Fixed-line Voice Services Providers

AT&T Inc. 110
CenturyTel, Inc. 202
Frontier Communications 375
IDT Corporation 451
Qwest Communications 717

Wireless Communications Services

MetroPCS Communications 586
Sprint Nextel 789
Telephone & Data Systems 811
United States Cellular 858
Verizon Communications 881

TRANSPORTATION SERVICES

Airlines

AirTran Holdings 54
Alaska Air Group 57
AMR Corporation 88
Continental Airlines 252
Delta Air Lines 284
SkyWest, Inc. 776
Southwest Airlines 785
UAL Corporation 850
US Airways 869

Express Delivery Services

FedEx Corporation 351
United Parcel Service 855

Freight Forwarding Services

Expeditors International 344

Logistics Services

C.H. Robinson Worldwide 207
Hub Group 445

Postal Services

US Postal Service (United States Postal Service) 871

Railroads

Burlington Northern Santa Fe 177
CSX Corporation 268
Kansas City Southern 495
Norfolk Southern 631
Union Pacific 852

Trucking

Con-way Inc. 253
J.B. Hunt Transport Services 479
Werner Enterprises 908
YRC Worldwide 930

Lebanon
Cracker Barrel Old Country Store 264

Memphis
AutoZone, Inc. 115
FedEx Corporation 351
International Paper 465
Thomas & Betts 827

Nashville
HCA Inc. 415

TEXAS

Angleton
Benchmark Electronics 143

Austin
Temple-Inland 813
Whole Foods Market 915

Dallas
Affiliated Computer Services 47
AT&T Inc. 110
Blockbuster Inc. 152
Brinker International 166
Comerica Incorporated 239
Dean Foods 277
ENSCO International 331
Holly Corporation 436
Southwest Airlines 785
Tenet Healthcare 815
Texas Instruments 823
Trinity Industries 843

Fort Worth
AmeriCredit Corp. 83
AMR Corporation 88
Burlington Northern Santa Fe 177
D.R. Horton 306
RadioShack Corporation 718

Grapevine
GameStop Corp. 378

Houston
Adams Resources & Energy 39
Apache Corporation 96
Baker Hughes 123
BJ Services 149
BMC Software 154
Calpine Corporation 184
CenterPoint Energy 200
ConocoPhillips 245
Continental Airlines 252
Cooper Industries 255
Diamond Offshore Drilling 290

Dynegy Inc. 312
El Paso Corporation 323
Enterprise Products Partners 333
EOG Resources 334
Halliburton Company 403
Key Energy Services 502
King Ranch 507
Marathon Oil 553
McDermott International 572
Men's Wearhouse 582
NCI Building Systems 615
Plains All American Pipeline 687
Rowan Companies 738
Schlumberger Limited 756
Service Corporation 769
Southern Union 784
SYSCO Corporation 805
Transocean Inc. 841
Waste Management 899
Weatherford International 903

Irving
Commercial Metals 240
Exxon Mobil 346
Fluor Corporation 360
Kimberly-Clark 504
Pioneer Natural Resources 684
Zale Corporation 932

Kingwood
Administaff, Inc. 40

McKinney
Torchmark Corporation 838

Plano
Cinemark Holdings 223
J. C. Penney 480
Perot Systems 674
Rent-A-Center 726

Richardson
Fossil, Inc. 368
Lennox International 527
MetroPCS Communications 586

Round Rock
Dell Inc. 282

San Antonio
Kinetic Concepts 506
Tesoro Corporation 821
USAA 872
Valero Energy 876

Sugar Land
Noble Corporation 628

The Woodlands
Anadarko Petroleum 89

UTAH

Salt Lake City
Zions Bancorporation 933

St. George
SkyWest, Inc. 776

VIRGINIA

Arlington
The AES Corporation 44
CACI International 182
Watson Wyatt Worldwide 902

Falls Church
Computer Sciences Corporation 242
General Dynamics 383

Glen Allen
Markel Corporation 554
MeadWestvaco 578

McLean
Capital One Financial 186
Gannett Co. 379
Hilton Worldwide 433
Mars, Incorporated 556

Mechanicsville
Owens & Minor 655

Norfolk
Norfolk Southern 631

Reston
NVR, Inc. 642

Richmond
Altria Group 67
The Brink's Company 167
CarMax, Inc. 192
Dominion Resources 299
Universal Corporation 864

Smithfield
Smithfield Foods 777

WASHINGTON

Bellevue
PACCAR Inc 657

Federal Way
Weyerhaeuser Company 913

Issaquah
Costco Wholesale 259

Liberty Lake
Itron, Inc. 472

Redmond
Microsoft Corporation 590

Seattle
Alaska Air Group 57
Amazon.com 69
Expeditors International 344
Nordstrom, Inc. 629
Starbucks Corporation 793

WISCONSIN

Brookfield
Fiserv, Inc. 357

Green Bay
Green Bay Packers 400

Kenosha
Snap-on Incorporated 778

Manitowoc
Manitowoc Company 550

Menomonee Falls
Kohl's Corporation 512

Milwaukee
A. O. Smith 94
Harley-Davidson 408
Johnson Controls 488
Joy Global 492
Manpower Inc. 551
Northwestern Mutual Life
 Insurance 635
Rockwell Automation 734

Neenah
Bemis Company 142
Plexus Corp. 688

Oshkosh
Oshkosh Corporation 654

Racine
S.C. Johnson 753

Wauwatosa
Briggs & Stratton 164

Index of Executives

A

Aardsma, David A. 899
Aaron, Mark L. 831
Aaron, Roger S. 775
Abarca, Jessica 904
Abate, Peter 314
Abbott, Gay O. 802
Abbott, Michael 660
Abdelnour, Sam A. 915
Abel, Gregory E. 145
Abel, James E. 694
Abeles, Philippa 93
Aberle, Derek 714
Abernathy, Robert E. 504
Abernethy, Jack 371
Abi-Karam, Leslie R. 686
Abney, David P. 856
Aboaf, Eric 227
Abraham, Deborah 896
Abraham, Thomas R. 307
Abramowicz, Daniel A. 267
Abrams, Robert 775
Abshire, Richard B. 39
Abud, Joao Jr. 292
Acevedo, William 933
Achermann, Hubert 514
Ackart, Jennifer C. 721
Ackerman, Jeffrey C. 766
Ackerman, Melinda S. 448
Ackerman, Patricia K. 95
Ackerman, Paul R. 906
Ackerman, Philip C. 608
Acton, Elizabeth S. 239
Adam, Donald F. 143
Adamek, Mitch 672
Adams, Craig L. 342
Adams, D. Scott 706
Adams, Diana 71
Adams, J. Dann 335
Adams, J. Michael 61
Adams, Jimmie V. 518
Adams, K. S. Jr. 39
Adams, Katherine L. 440
Adams, Mark W. 589
Adams, Marvin W. 363
Adams, Mike 136
Adams, Rex D. 471
Adams, Robin J. 160
Adams, Thomas R. 730
Adams, Timothy M. 548
Adamson, Grant F. 814
Adderley, Terence E. 500
Addicks, Mark W. 386
Addison, Brian M. 288
Addison, James E. 755
Aderhold, Ronald K. 228
Adkerson, Richard C. 375
Adkins, Mark 420
Adkins, Rodney C. 462
Adler, Edward I. 833
Adler, Robert L. 322
Adornato, Theodore C. 788
Adrean, Lee 335
Adu-Gyamfi, R. Siisi 825

Advani, Vijay C. 374
Agar, Richard 406
Agnes, Pierre 716
Agnew, Dan 115
Agosta, Jeffrey A. 290
Aguirre, Fernando 216
Ahearn, Joseph 547
Ahlstrom, Lee M. 629
Ahmad, Shidah 52
Ahmed, Mumtaz 284
Ahuja, Lalit 808
Aijala, Ainar D. Jr. 284
Aiken, Robert S. 684
Ailes, Roger 371, 624
Ainsley, P. Steven 620
Aitken, Murray L. 456
Akin, Bruce A. 911
Akins, Nicholas K. 75
Akkad, Susan 339
Alapont, José Maria 351
Alario, Richard J. 502
Albanese, Gerard Jr. 554
Albani, Lisa 737
Albano, John J. 843
Albaugh, James F. 157
Alben, Jonah M. 641
Alber, Karen L. 434
Alber, Laura J. 918
Alberini, Carlos E. 403
Albers, Mark W. 347
Albert, James D. 601
Alberts, Shannon K. 57
Albrecht, William E. 645
Alderson, Christopher D. 807
Alderson, Deborah H. 747
Alderson, Jim 899
Aldrich, George E. 785
Alesio, Steven W. 311
Alexander, Anthony J. 357
Alexander, Bart 594
Alexander, Bradley K. 359
Alexander, Bruce K. 934
Alexander, David K. 601
Alexander, Forbes I. J. 476
Alexander, J. Rich 693
Alexander, Jimmy 38
Alexander, Penelope S. 374
Alexander, Robert M. 186
Alexander, Susan 783
Alfonso, Humberto P. 425
Alford, J. Philip 889
Alford, Sandra E. 123
Alger, Eugene V. 344
Alger, Montgomery 53
Allan, Graham D. 932
Allan, Michael J. 696
Allard, J 590
Allcott, Truitt 655
Alleman, James 241
Allen, Barry K. 408
Allen, Ben F. 558
Allen, Bradley D. 455
Allen, Bryan D. 407
Allen, David W. 281
Allen, Jay L. 210

Allen, John J. 612
Allen, Mark W. 40
Allen, Paul G. (Charter
   Communications) 212
Allen, Paul J. (Constellation Energy
   Group) 252
Allen, Richard W. 615
Allen, Samuel R. 280
Allen, Terri 665
Allendorph, Dave 612
Allison, Jeffrey J. 480
Allison, John A. IV 132
Allison, Robert J. Jr. 90
Allison-Putman, Andrea 406
Allmark, David 566
Allmond, Gracie H. 841
Almandoz, José 637
Almeida, Donald V. 699
Almogy, Gilad 102
Almond, Danny H. 838
Aloia, Albert A. 248
Alpert, Susan 581
Alphin, J. Steele 127
Alroy, Liore 451
Al-Saleh, Adel 456
Alseth, Becky 119
Alstead, Troy 794
Altabef, Peter A. 675
Alter, Jeffrey Donald 863
Altman, Steven R. 714
Altman, William M. 506
Altmeyer, John W. 190
Alton, Gregg H. 393
Altschul, Wayne 452
Alvarez, Ralph 574
Alves, Paget A. 790
Alving, Amy E. 747
Alvino, Guido 142
Alziari, Lucien 121
Amalfi, Peter 150
Amaral, Ricardo 739
Amble, Joan L. 77
Ambler, John O. 177
Ambrose, Adele D. 584
Ambrosio, Anthony G. 199
Amello, Jason A. 390
Amen, Robert M. 464
Ames, Marshall H. 526
Ames, Richard D. 193
Amick, Rebecca K. 145
Amoroso, Richard M. 72
Amos, Daniel P. 49
Amos, Paul S. II 49
Amundson, Joy A. 131
Anand, Naveen 232
Ancell, Christopher 718
Anderson, Aldon S. 934
Anderson, B. Chuck 645
Anderson, Bradbury H. (Best Buy) 146
Anderson, Bradley A. (Hewitt
   Associates) 428
Anderson, Bradley R. (Dell) 282
Anderson, Bruce 218
Anderson, Darcy G. 675
Anderson, David C. (PACCAR) 658

Anderson, David G. (HCA) 415
Anderson, David J. (Honeywell
   International) 440
Anderson, Douglas 191
Anderson, Gerard M. 308
Anderson, Harry L. 233
Anderson, John C. (Whirlpool) 915
Anderson, John L. (Hewitt
   Associates) 428
Anderson, Karie 342
Anderson, Marla 364
Anderson, Melissa H. 661
Anderson, Niall 394
Anderson, R. John 530
Anderson, Richard A. (AT&T) 111
Anderson, Richard H. (Delta Air
   Lines) 285
Anderson, R.J. 888
Anderson, Scott P. 664
Anderson, Stacia J. 808
Anderson, William T. 562
Anderson-Lehman, Ron 253
Andolino, Joseph F. 397
Andrada, Marissa 378
Andre, Erin M. 35
Andre, Kenneth B. III 401
Andreas, Philip B. 639
Andreotti, Lamberto 169
Andreu, Jordi 735
Andrew, T. Peter 171
Andrews, A. Michael II 518
Andrews, Audrey T. 815
Andrews, Charles E. 406
Andrews, Jeff 728
Andrews, Madhuri A. 844
Andrews, Steven R. 460
Anenen, Steven J. 114
Angel, Kathleen 282
Angel, Stephen F. 696
Angelakis, Michael J. 238
Angelastro, Philip J. 650
Angelini, Michael P. 407
Angelle, Evelyn M. 404
Angelo, Scott M. 292
Angerami, John 232
Angley, Ellen K. 639
Angove, Duncan B. 653
Anik, Ruby 481
Anselmi, Franco 370
Ansorge, Mark 897
Anstice, Martin B. 519
Anthony, Jeffrey H. 708
Anthony, Scott 235
Anton, Dianne Deering 66
Anton, Kevin J. 60
Antone, John A. 102
Antonellis, Joseph C. 797
Anzaldua, Ricardo A. 413
Apicerno, Kenneth J. 826
Apodaca, Steve 212
Appel, Andrew M. 96
Appel, Laurence B. 920
Appel, Matthew 933
Appelo, Willem T. 927
Applbaum, Lee 719

Canzano, Daniel A. 665
Cao, Ken J. 273
Capek, John M. 31
Capell, Peter J. 386
Capello, Jeffrey D. 162
Capezza, Joseph C. 418
Caplan, David L. 50
Capo, Brian 538
Capone, Michael L. 114
Cappelli, Gregory W. 98
Cappiello, Paul 397
Cappucci, Gabriel R. 580
Cappuccio, Paul T. 833
Captain, Lori 312
Capuano, Linda A. 553
Capus, Steve 613
Caputo, Lisa M. 227
Caracappa, Roger 339
Caracciolo, Anthony D. 393
Caragol, Richard 625
Carango, Keith T. 213
Carbonari, Bruce A. 367
Carbone, Richard J. 707
Carcaillet, Jean Claude 344
Card, Wesley R. 490
Cardillo, G. R. 333
Cardillo, James G. 658
Cardinale, Gerald P. 731
Cardona, Oscar 626
Cardoso, Carlos M. 501
Caresia, Eugene D. 353
Carey, Albert P. 672
Carey, Chase 371, 624
Carey, David R. 394
Carey, Jaime 130
Carey, Matt 439
Carges, Mark T. 320
Carioba, André M. 50
Caris, Phillip D. 257
Carius, J. R. 330
Carlini, Barbara D. 278
Carlotti, Carl M. 608
Carlson, David W. 378
Carlson, Gary E. (Lennar) 526
Carlson, Gary L. (HNI) 436
Carlson, Jennie P. 870
Carlson, LeRoy T. Jr. (Telephone & Data
  Systems, U.S. Cellular) 812, 858
Carlson, LeRoy T. Sr. (Telephone & Data
  Systems) 812
Carlson, Mark D. 748
Carlson, Peter M. 586
Carlson, Ria Marie 458
Carlson, W. Erik 298
Carlson, Walter C. D. 812
Carlton, Bob D. 604
Carlucci, David R. 456
Carman, Ronald T. 598
Carmean, Jeffrey B. 640
Carmichael, Clare M. 902
Carmichael, Greg D. 354
Carmichael, Martin 569
Carmine, Bryce D. 326
Carmody, Christine M. 639
Carmody, Cora L. 478
Carmola, John J. 397
Carmony, Robert F. 223
Carnett, John 502
Carney, Thomas D. 159
Carniaux, Bob 414
Caro, Antonio 236
Caro, Joseph 172
Carome, Kevin M. 471
Carosella, Debra B. 278
Carp, Daniel A. 285
Carp, Jeffrey N. 797
Carpenter, David E. 726
Carpenter, Randall R. (Briggs &
  Stratton) 164
Carpenter, Randy (HealthSouth) 419
Carpenter, Tod E. 302
Carpenter, W. Geoffrey 571
Carr, Edward 370
Carr, Gwenn L. 586
Carr, John 931

Carr, Terry 452
Carrabba, Joseph A. 228
Carrico, Kristin 888
Carrig, John A. 246
Carrig, Kenneth J. 238
Carrillo, Joseph R. 912
Carroll, Barbara 738
Carroll, Christopher F. 467
Carroll, David M. 906
Carroll, Melika D. 589
Carroll, Milton 200
Carroll, Teresa S. 500
Carroll, Thomas M. 742
Carruthers, Court D. 924
Carsky, Jack 886
Carson, John C. Jr. 724
Carson, Pamela A. 503
Carson, Robert A. 341
Carter, Brett C. 309
Carter, C. Michael 299
Carter, David W. 47
Carter, Dean 369
Carter, J. Braxton 587
Carter, Jerome N. 466
Carter, John D. (Schnitzer Steel) 758
Carter, Jonathan D. (Terex) 819
Carter, Marshall N. 644
Carter, Matthew E. 671
Carter, Michael G. 636
Carter, Paul 393
Carter, Robert B. 352
Cartner, James S. 360
Caruana, Ken 737
Carucci, Richard T. 932
Carullo, Anne 339
Caruso, Dominic J. 487
Caruso, Frank A. 237
Cary, Dennis M. 850
Cary, William H. 385
Casado, Jorge 822
Casale, Carl M. 596
Casale, Robert J. 563
CasaSanta, Daniel J. 160
Casazza, William J. 46
Cascella, Robert A. 438
Case, Gregory C. 96
Case, Joe 611
Casella, John A. 201
Casey, Donald M. Jr. 487
Casey, John P. 383
Casey, Mark J. 438
Casey, Phillip E. 392
Casey, Thomas M. 153
Cashman, Stacy A. 311
Casillo, Dave 460
Casper, John 407
Casper, Marc N. 826
Caspersen, Curt A. 356
Cass, Jim 557
Cassels, Scott L. 678
Castagna, Eugene A. 139
Castel, Carolyn 271
Castro-Wright, Eduardo 893
Cataldo, Robert 836
Catanese, George 721
Cates, James L. 30
Catlett, Pamela 626
Catmull, Edwin E. 894
Caton, Daniel 575
Caton, William A. 612
Catuna, Cornel 150
Catz, Safra A. 653
Caudill, James T. 152
Caudle, Darla 623
Causey, Bryan P. 348
Cava, Jeffrey M. 795
Cavalier, Lynn M. 357
Cavalier, Michael 223
Cavallaro, Len 537
Cavallo, Glen R. 800
Cavallo, Robert 894
Cavallucci, Eugene S. 411
Cavanagh, Michael J. 494
Cavanaugh, James W. 442
Cavanaugh, Lucille J. 347

Cavanaugh, Mark S. 201
Cavanaugh, Patrick W. 465
Cavanaugh, Robert B. 480
Cavaney, Red 246
Cave, Michael J. 157
Cavuoto, Dominick 854
Cazalot, Clarence P. Jr. 553
Cazenave, Bruce 201
Cazer, Michael J. 168
Cecchi, Suzanne 29
Cecchini, Robert L. 601
Cecere, Andrew 870
Cedar, Yoram 750
Cederoth, Andrew J. 612
Ceille, Kaye 119
Cejka, A. Timothy 347
Celentano, John E. 169
Celio, Richard C. 294
Cellino, Anna Marie 608
Cenac, Matthew 763
Cenk, William E. 910
Centrella, Roy R. 787
Ceratti, Gilberto 273
Cerenzia, Joseph A. 248
Cerepak, Brad M. 303
Cerf, Vinton G. 399
Ceron, Felipe 45
Cerrone, Stephen J. 752
Certosimo, Arthur 128
Cervone, Antonio B. 850
Cetti, Carlo E. 477
Chabraja, Nicholas D. 383
Chadwick, William S. Jr. 331
Chaffin, Janice D. 805
Chaffkin, Jeffrey 47
Chakmak, Paul J. 163
Challan, Peter 411
Chalmers, Steve 397
Chamberlain, E. Todd 724
Chamberlain, Glenda J. 916
Chambers, Chris 306
Chambers, John T. 226
Chambers, Lamar M. 110
Chambers, Norman C. 615
Chambers, Thomas P. 97
Chammah, Walid 598
Champion, Gina S. 755
Champy, James A. 675
Chancy, Mark A. 802
Chande, Amee 792
Chandler, Charles Q. IV 911
Chandler, Mark 226
Chandrasekaran, Srinivasan 913
Chandrasekher, Anand 461
Chang, Derek 295
Chang, Jason 34
Chao, Ed 587
Chapin, Christopher T. 148
Chaplin, C. Edward 568
Chapman, Barry J. 194
Chapman, David L. Sr. 771
Chapman, Neil A. 347
Chapman, Richard (Jo-Ann Stores) 484
Chapman, Richard E. (Kindred
  Healthcare) 506
Chapman, Steven M. 269
Chapman, William D. 924
Chappel, Donald R. 917
Chappell, Dave 653
Chappelle, George 752
Chariag, Belgacem 123
Charles, Marilyn R. 272
Charles, R. Lynn 291
Charles, Robert J. 903
Charlton, John S.N. 79
Charlton, Michael J. 817
Charlton, R. Scott 711
Charnas, Charles N. 430
Charness, Wayne S. 414
Charney, M. Jeffrey 49
Charreton, Didier 123
Charriau, Michel 476
Charron, Paul R. 185
Chase, Dana 203
Chase, Jacqueline A. 455

Chatillon, Devereux 759
Chattin, Angela 192
Chaudhri, M. Javade 768
Chavez, Christopher G. 748
Chaville, Bobbi 737
Chawla, Sona 891
Chazen, Stephen I. 645
Cheap, Richard A. 448
Cheatwood, Chris J. 685
Cheek, William E. 203
Cheeseman, Paul G. 344
Chelette, David N. 479
Chen, James L. M. 292
Chen, Thomas F. 31
Chenault, Kenneth I. 77
Chênevert, Louis R. 862
Chenevich, William L. 870
Cheng, Andrew 393
Cheng, Linda Y. H. 682
Chernicoff, Richard S. O. 750
Cherry, Dean E. 204
Cherry, Joseph A. 263
Chersi, Robert J. 363
Chesla, Mark 82
Chesnutt, Charles A. 389
Chessen, Robert M. 211
Cheviron, Mark J. 106
Chew, Lewis 610
Chiang, C. W. 246
Chiang, Hai Hwai 476
Chiarello, Guy 494
Chicles, Aris C. 474
Chidsey, John W. 176
Childress, Jan C. 249
Childs, Jeffrey J. 858
Childs, Russell A. 777
Chin, Moonhie K. 112
Ching, David T. 745
Chiodo, Stacey 603
Chirico, Emanuel 683
Chisolm, Steven 659
Chiu, Amy 768
Chmiel, Mark E. 287
Choate, Chris A. 83
Choate, William M. 96
Chochon, Michael D. 810
Chochoy, Gérard 351
Chodak, Paul III 76
Choksi, Sureel A. 529
Cholette, Kathleen A. 167
Chong, Arthur 170
Chou, John G. 85
Chouthai, Manoj S. 710
Chow, Joan K. 244
Chow Yee, Maria 902
Chowdhry, Uma 312
Chrispell, Cindy 800
Christ, Michael C. 831
Christal, Nancy R. 271
Christensen, Craig L. 822
Christensen, Eric D. 777
Christensen, Michelle 484
Christensen, Robert J. 658
Christensen, Troy 250
Christenson, James E. 423
Christenson, Michael J. 179
Christenson, Ronald L. 189
Christian, Kris 484
Christiansen, David A. 194
Christie, Anthony D. 394
Christie, Blair 226
Christie, Tod S. 765
Christopher, Eric 933
Christopher, William F. 60
Christopherson, Carol 716
Chu, Ronald J. 822
Chubb, Sarah 42
Chugg, Juliana L. 386
Chupein, Chuck 74
Churay, Daniel J. 931
Church, Douglas A. 181
Church, Steven C. 120
Churchill, Bruce B. 295
Churchill, David S. 51
Chwat, Anne 176

Cianci, Peter 308
Cicale, Ed 115
Ciccone, Christine M. 874
Cicconi, James W. 111
Cichocki, Andrew R. 54
Cieszko, Peter 363
Cimino, Julie 519
Cimino, Richard F. 261
Cimler, B. Melina 137
Cinquemani, Michael 124
Ciorciari, Anthony 465
Cipolla, John 600
Cipollone, Joseph B. 80
Cipriano, Giovanna 364
Ciprich, Paula M. 608
Cirelli, Joseph A. 667
Cirillo, Alexander C. Jr. 26
Cisarik, James A. 333
Cischke, Susan M. 365
Cisel, Scott A. 73
Ciskowski, Michael S. 877
Civgin, Don 67
Ckodre, Gary G. 583
Claflin, Bruce L. 44
Clancy, Celia 836
Clancy, John 472
Clancy, William M. 887
Clarey, Patricia T. 418
Clark, Alison 557
Clark, Carine 805
Clark, Celeste A. 498
Clark, Christopher T. (DENTSPLY) 288
Clark, Christopher W. (Goodyear Tire & Rubber) 398
Clark, David D. (Northwestern Mutual) 636
Clark, David W. (Macy's) 548
Clark, Frank M. Jr. 342
Clark, G. Edmond 352
Clark, Grant L. 880
Clark, Ian M. 842
Clark, Janet F. 553
Clark, Jerry S. 728
Clark, Mark T. 357
Clark, Matthew E. 213
Clark, Patrick M. 696
Clark, Randall L. 768
Clark, Richard B. (Monsanto Company) 596
Clark, Richard T. (Merck) 584
Clark, Roger 450
Clark, Steve 434
Clark, W. Edmund 810
Clarke, Charles J. 843
Clarke, E. V. 655
Clarke, Jeffrey W. 282
Clarke, Kim B. 502
Clarke, Mark C. 322
Clarke, Peter J. 632
Classon, Rolf A. 432
Claus, Christopher W. 873
Claus, Eric 29
Claxton, Robert C. 148
Clayton, R. Bruce 389
Cleary, James J. 324
Cleland, Jack H. 258
Clement, James H. Jr. 508
Clement, Philip B. 96
Clementi, Michael S. 921
Clemons, Billy Ray Jr. 708
Clemons, Tanya 680
Clendening, John S. 210
Cleves, Thomas A. 466
Cleys, Richard P. 755
Click, Betty J. 237
Clifford, John P. Jr. 843
Clifford, Mike 916
Clifford, Patricia A. 311
Clifton, Matthew P. 437
Cline, Stephanie E. 477
Clolery, Denise M. 154
Cloninger, Kriss III 49
Clontz, Steven T. 394
Clothier, Kevin C. 267
Cloud, Pamela 831

Clouse, Gregory R. 40
Clouser, Dennis R. 158
Cloutier, Ernest W. 472
Cloyd, Brian 798
Clurman, Sally 380
Clutton, Stan 566
Clyde, Robert W. 81
Coblens, Doug 297
Coblin, James M. 640
Coccagna, John S. 68
Cochran, John H. Jr. 495
Cochran, Mark D. 569
Cochran, Phyllis E. 612
Cochran, S. Robert 573
Cochran, Sandra B. 264
Cockrell, D. Michael 748
Cocozza, Keith 833
Cody, Thomas G. 548
Cody, William M. 704
Coe, Jeffrey A. 312
Cofoni, Paul M. 182
Cohen, Abby Joseph 395
Cohen, Alan M. 395
Cohen, Andrew (Jones Apparel) 490
Cohen, Andrew (Regis Corporation) 725
Cohen, Cory F. 497
Cohen, David L. 238
Cohen, Eran 237
Cohen, Eric I. 819
Cohen, Gary M. 138
Cohen, Harry D. 523
Cohen, Joan K. 406
Cohen, Jon R. 715
Cohen, Kenneth P. 347
Cohen, Larry 591
Cohen, Lyor 897
Cohen, Tod 320
Cohlmia, Melissa 511
Cohn, Beth 539
Cohn, Gary D. 395
Cohn, John D. 735
Cohn, Kenneth P. 668
Coker, Charles W. Jr. 781
Coker, Susan W. 262
Colalillo, Claudia J. 625
Colalillo, Joseph S. 890
Colavita, Michael 801
Colbert, Celia A. 584
Colby, Rob 716
Cole, Bruce A. 344
Cole, Daniel F. 73
Cole, David D. 203
Cole, Martin I. 36
Cole, Michael H. (Smithfield Foods) 778
Cole, Michael J. (A. O. Smith) 95
Cole, Thomas L. 548
Cole, Timothy A. 281
Coleman, Gary L. 838
Coleman, J. Edward 854
Coleman, James E. 314
Coleman, Kristin M. 175
Coleman, Richard E. 375
Coleman, Ronald F. 149
Coleman, Steven B. 334
Coleman Mayes, Michele 67
Colen, Fredericus A. 162
Coles, Martin 794
Colf, Richard W. 678
Colgan, Kevin E. 196
Colglazier, John 90
Colip, Randy L. 124
Coll, Denise M. 795
Coll, Mario M. III 90
Coll, Pierre 699
Collar, Gary L. 50
Colleran, Lisa N. 507
Collier, Doug 522
Collier, Earl M. Jr. 390
Collier, William L. III 375
Collier-Keywood, Richard 699
Collin, Dirk 646
Collingsworth, James M. 333
Collins, Betty L. 40

Collins, Cynthia 137
Collins, Daniel F. (Corning) 258
Collins, Daniel T. (Wendy's/Arby's Group, Inc.) 908
Collins, David M. 526
Collins, J. Barclay II 427
Collins, Jim 452
Collins, John 452
Collins, Karen J. 355
Collins, Kathy 406
Collins, Kevin J. 358
Collins, Michael D. 510, 767
Collins, Patrick T. 860
Collins, Valerie K. 276
Collis, Steven H. 85
Collum, Donald G. 844
Collupy, Ed 661
Colo, David J. 244
Colotti, Raymond L. 114
Colpo, Charles C. 655
Comas, Daniel L. 274
Combs, Gail 143
Combs, Stephen R. 900
Comey, James B. 541
Comfort, Stephanie G. 718
Competti, Eileen M. 573
Compton, Chuck 520
Compton, James E. 253
Compton, John C. 672
Comstock, Elizabeth J. 385
Conant, Douglas R. 185
Condon, John M. 420
Condrin, J. Paul III 532
Conger, Harry M. 375
Conish, Mark G. 220
Conklyn, Elizabeth D. 873
Conley, E. Renae 332
Conlon, Brad 306
Conlon, Michael W. 583
Connaughton, James L. 252
Connell, Tara J. 379
Connell, Thomas A. 398
Connelly, Margie 172
Connelly, Michael C. 925
Connelly, Peter W. 525
Connelly, Thomas M. Jr. 312
Conner, Penelope M. 639
Connery, Bruce L. 324
Connolly, John P. 284
Connolly, Patrick J. 918
Connolly, Timothy P. 860
Connor, Christopher M. 772
Connor, Frank T. 825
Conover, Donald E. 797
Conover, John W. IV 457
Conover, Pamela C. 193
Conrado, Eduardo 600
Conroy, Erin 172
Conroy, John J. Jr. 122
Considine, John R. 138
Constable, David E. 360
Constand, George T. 273
Constant, Guy J. 167
Conti, Corrado 883
Conti, Emanuele A. 311
Contreras, Mark G. 341
Convis, Gary L. 273
Conway, John W. 267
Conway, Mike 772
Conway, Paul D. 189
Cook, Beryl 624
Cook, Brian J. 875
Cook, Charles C. 313
Cook, Ian M. 236
Cook, Jeffrey L. 377
Cook, Neil 52
Cook, Richard W. 894
Cook, Scott D. 468
Cook, Steven M. 712
Cook, Susan J. 319
Cook, Timothy D. 99
Cook, William M. 302
Cooke, Roger A. 697
Cooley, Charles P. 546
Coolick, Gayle M. 211

Cooney, Wallace R. 898
Cooper, Frederick N. 837
Cooper, Gary 849
Cooper, H. Lee III 354
Cooper, Joe R. 148
Cooper, Marcia 818
Cooper, Nancy E. 179
Cooper, Rod 764
Cooper, Simon F. 556
Cooperman, Daniel 99
Coors, Peter H. 594
Cope, Donald G. 479
Copel, Marguerite 278
Copeland, Jananne A. 196
Copeland, Margot J. 503
Copley, David 329
Coppins, Kent G. 735
Copple, Robert D. 223
Coppola, Sue 800
Corbett, Jeffrey A. 703
Corbin, Tami 465
Corbusier, Drue 293
Corcoran, Maureen P. 797
Corcoran, William M. 923
Corcos, Helyn 805
Cordani, David M. 221
Cordeiro, Eduardo E. 181
Corkrean, John J. 321
Corless, Gary A. 708
Corley, Todd 34
Corn, Amy C. 686
Cornelio, Charles C. 537
Cornelison, Albert O. Jr. 404
Cornelius, James M. 169
Cornelius, Sigmund L. 246
Cornell, Brian C. 893
Corness, John B. 691
Cornew, Kenneth W. 342
Corona, George S. 500
Coronado, William J. 865
Correll, Donald L. 82
Corrigan, Mark 757
Corso, Clifford D. 568
Cortes, Joseph 204
Cortese, Steven J. 66
Cosgrove, Howard E. 638
Cosgrove, Stephen P. 445
Cosgrove, Tom 297
Coskey, Dave 163
Costa, Mark J. 316
Costello, Richard G. 413
Costlow, R. Lynn 858
Cote, David M. 440
Coticchia, Michael L. 101
Cotter, Ruth 44
Cottier, Gilles A. 773
Cottingham, William 783
Cottle, Karen O. 41
Cottrill, Scott A. 397
Cotty, Neil A. 127
Couch, David (Jabil) 476
Couch, David deS. (Spartan Stores) 788
Coughlan, Anthony G. 36
Coughlin, Catherine M. 111
Coughlin, Christopher A. (Timken) 835
Coughlin, Christopher J. (Tyco) 848
Coughlin, Philip M. 344
Coughran, W. M. Jr. 399
Coulton, Keiran 735
Council, Laverne M. 487
Courter, James A. 451
Courtois, Jean-Philipe 591
Courville, Arthur F. 805
Coury, Robert J. 603
Cousens, Ellis E. 486
Cousino, Mark 308
Couvillion, P. Doug 264
Covey, Steven K. 612
Coviello, Arthur W. Jr. 327
Covington, Alec C. 607
Cowan, Andrea F. 844
Cowan, Grace E.M. 247
Cowan, Keith O. 790
Cowden, Barbara 796

Fluegel, Bradley M. 905
Fluke, Kenneth W. 828
Flur, Dorlisa K. 348
Flynn, Edward B. III 114
Flynn, Timothy P. 514
Flynt, Jim D. 502
Foate, Dean A. 688
Foe, Bryan D. 207
Fogarty, James P. 211
Fogel, Arthur 538
Fogel, Glenn D. 698
Foggio, Richard S. 121
Fohrer, Alan J. 322
Foland, Jeffrey T. 850
Foley, Donald E. (ITT Corp.) 474
Foley, Donald H. (SAIC) 747
Foley, Joseph R. 866
Folkwein, Kristy J. 110
Folliard, Thomas J. 192
Follo, James M. 620
Fong, Ivan K. 188
Fong, Russell G. 184
Fontaine, R. Richard 378
Fontaine, Richard P. 560
Fontanes, A. Alexander 532
Foody, James G. 755
Foote, William C. 875
Ford, Beth E. 464
Ford, Jeffrey J. 456
Ford, Monte R. 89
Ford, Robert C. 195
Ford, Rollin Lee 893
Ford, Steven J. 190
Ford, Timothy A. 819
Ford, William C. Jr. 365
Forde, Richard H. 221
Forehand, J. P. 923
Foreman, Robert B. 791
Forese, James A. 227
Forester, Rich 295
Foresti, Ronaldo 531
Forkovitch, James K. 241
Forlenza, Vincent A. 138
Fornaro, Robert L. 55
Forrester, Craig W. 222
Forrester, Sean 292
Forstall, Scott 99
Forster, Kevin G. 190
Fortanet, Francisco 464
Forte, Deborah A. 759
Fortin, Daniel S. 232
Fortin, Mary Jane B. 81
Fortin, Raymond D. 802
Forward, Frank D. 150
Foschi, Pier Luigi 193
Foshee, Douglas L. 324
Foss, Eric J. 669
Foss, Karen 73
Foss, Linda L. 110
Fossel, Jon S. 866
Fossenier, Patrick J. 254
Foster, James 230
Foster, John 496
Foster, Mark 36
Foster, Mickey 352
Foster, Ronald C. 589
Foster, Scarlett Lee 596
Foster, W. Kim 362
Foster-Cheek, Kaye I. 487
Fostyk, Michael J. 74
Fouad, Sam 337
Foulkes, Helena B. 271
Fouracre, Jenny 301
Fowke, Benjamin G. S. III 925
Fowler, Richard G. 210
Fowler, W. Randall 333
Fox, Brad 746
Fox, Colin 819
Fox, Frank 641
Fox, Keith 575
Foxhall, Nene 253
Fracassa, Philip D. 835
Fradin, Roger 440
Fradin, Russell P. 428
Fradkin, Steven L. 633

Fraleigh, Christopher J. 752
Fraley, Robert T. 596
Framke, Gregory 340
Frampton, Brandon 661
Francis, Michael R. 808
Francis, Philip L. 679
Francis, Scott 897
Francisco, Daniel 589
Franck, John M. II 415
Frank, Alan 898
Frank, Alexander C. 598
Frank, Edward H. 171
Frank, Howard S. 193
Frank, Ronald C. 72
Frank, Ted 613
Frank, William P. 775
Franks, Brent J. 669
Franks, Martin D. 199
Franson, Arthur 729
Frantz, Gary N. 254
Frasch, Richard D. 189
Frascotti, Johnathan 414
Fraser, Cathy 815
Frasure, Jeff 560
Fratto, Fred 134
Frazer, Anne 159
Frazier, Brett 899
Frazier, Gregory A. 120
Frazier, Kenneth C. 584
Frechette, Peter L. 664
Freda, Fabrizio 339
Fredericksen, Gregory L. 654
Frediani, David R. 558
Freed, Vicki 739
Freedberg, Hugh R. 644
Freedman, Larry 193
Freeland, Richard J. 269
Freeman, Angela K. 207
Freeman, George C. III 865
Freeman, James I. 293
Freeman, Joshua 297
Freeman, Russell 675
Freeman, Thomas E. 802
Freer, Randy 371
Freidheim, Scott J. 510
Freitag, Randy 537
Freiwald, Gregory M. 305
French, Richard L. 281
Frenkel, Jacob A. 81
Frerichs, Robert N. 36
Frese, Calvin W. Jr. 198
Fretz, Deborah M. 801
Frey, Dennis J. 163
Frey, John W. 909
Freyman, Thomas C. 31
Frias, James D. 640
Fried, Ben 399
Fried, Samuel P. 533
Frieden, Sue 337
Friedery, John R. 126
Friedman, Adena T. 606
Friedman, Eric J. 775
Friedman, Neil B. 566
Friedmann, Lance 515
Friel, Robert F. 673
Friend, Stephen H. 584
Friendly, Ian R. 386
Friou, Phillip J. 49
Frisbie, Norman R. Jr. 374
Frisch, Steve 688
Frissora, Mark P. 426
Fristensky, Warren C. 486
Fristoe, David L. 744
Fritsch, Doug 452
Fritts, William 247
Fritz, Gregory A. 915
Fritze, Steven L. 321
Frizzell, Roger C. 89
Froesel, David W. Jr. 649
Froggatt, Chris N. 684
Froman, John W. 767
Fromm, Ronald A. 172
Frons, Brian S. 33
Frooman, Thomas E. 225
Fruchterman, Todd M. 507

Frutig, Ed 109
Frye, Julie 594
Frye, Kimberly R. 502
Fryfogle, James B. 687
Fu, Cary T. 143
Fuchs, James J. 696
Fuchs, Mark 399
Fuerst, Randall C. 182
Fugger, Edward F. Jr. 278
Fuller, Gary 437
Fuller, Rodger D. 781
Fuller, Ron 711
Fuller, Samuel H. 91
Fuller, Tony F. 726
Fuller, Wilford H. 537
Fulmer, Terry 124
Fulp, James A. 721
Fulton, Daniel S. 913
Fulton, J. Michael 239
Funk, Michael S. 855
Funnell, Colin 381
Furey, John J. 185
Furlow, Michael H. (Beazer Homes) 134
Furlow, Michael L. (Brinker) 167
Furman, Matthew 843
Fusaro, James 88
Fusco, Jack A. 184
Fussell, Stephen R. 31
Futcher, Jack 136
Futterman, Jeffrey C. 272
Fyrwald, J. Erik 605

G

Gabbard, Robert D. 694
Gabbert, Joseph P. 569
Gaberino, John A. Jr. 652
Gable, Greg 210
Gabos, Paul G. 534
Gaddis, Byron J. 697
Gaddy, Nancy L. 920
Gage Lofgren, Diane 495
Gagnon, David 176
Gaines, Bennett L. 357
Gaines, Laurie A. 167
Gaines, Phillip J. 931
Gajdos, Ludovit 241
Galanko, William A. 631
Galanti, Richard A. 259
Gale, William C. 225
Gales, Thomas A. 196
Galgano, Brenda M. 29
Galik, Jeffrey 169
Galindez, Antonio 305
Gallagher, Carolyn Lewis 872
Gallagher, Donald J. 228
Gallagher, Thomas C. (Genuine Parts) 389
Gallagher, Thomas F. (BJ's Wholesale Club) 150
Gallagher, Tim 193
Gallagher, William T. 267
Gallardo, Luis 284
Gallé, Rob 47
Gallegos, James H. 177
Gallett, Scott 160
Galligan, William (Kansas City Southern) 496
Galligan, William P. (US Postal Service) 872
Gallina, Bennett R. 121
Gallo, A. C. 916
Gallo, Joseph E. 314
Gallo, Robert J. 314
Gallo, Stephanie 314
Gallup, Patricia 666
Galovic, Scott 247
Galt, Helen M. 707
Galvin, Walter J. 330
Gamble, John W. Jr. 531
Gambrell, Michael R. 305
Gandolfo, Thomas J. 71
Gane, Steve 423

Gangwal, Rakesh 647
Gannaway, Michael T. 883
Ganser, Christopher D. 263
Gant, Douglas W. 56
Gant, Tony A. 39
Ganz, Peter J. 370
Ganzlin, Karen 810
Garascia, Jeff 760
Garceau, Dennis C. 106
Garceau, Mary L. 155
Garcia, Art A. 743
Garcia, Christian A. 404
Garcia, Daniel P. 495
Garcia, Elisa D. 646
Garcia, Fabian T. 236
Garcia, John A. 931
Garcia, Lillian D. 846
Gardiner, William J. 508
Gardner, Brian E. 405
Gardner, Hal 257
Gardner, Harold 308
Gardner, Heide 467
Gardner, Julie 512
Gardner, Timothy 453
Garland, Thomas J. 734
Garner, Jason 538
Garner, Shellene 88
Garnick, Murray 68
Garrard, V. Jane 846
Garraux, James D. 859
Garrett, Brian D. 242
Garrett, Kenneth R. 362
Garrett, Mark S. 41
Garrett, Michael D. 784
Garrett, Scott 137
Garrett, Thomas A. 908
Garriques, Ronald G. 282
Garrison, J. Daniel 770
Garrison, Robert K. 334
Garrison, Wayne 479
Garrity, Laurine M. 810
Garson, Gary W. 542
Garth, Matthew 60
Gartland, Thomas M. 119
Gartman, John A. 427
Garton, Daniel P. 89
Garvey, Mark 752
Gary, Marc 363
Gary, Michael 678
Gaskamp, Roger L. 40
Gasparovic, John J. 160
Gaspin, Jeff 613
Gass, John D. 215
Gass, Michelle 794
Gasser, Michael J. 401
Gast, Steven D. 931
Gaston, Douglas 238
Gaston, Patrick R. 882
Gates, R. Jordan 344
Gates, Stephen F. 246
Gates, William H. III 590
Gatfield, Stephen J. 467
Gatling, James Michael 131
Gatyas, Gary 456
Gaudiosi, Monica M. 785
Gauld, William B. 457
Gault, Polly L. 322
Gausman, William M. 668
Gaut, Steven K. 351
Gavagan, George R. 379
Gavenchak, Genie 624
Gavin, John F. 639
Gavrielov, Moshe 928
Gaw, James B. 445
Gawelek, Randolph J. 604
Gawronski, Grant L. 255
Gay, Charles 102
Gayner, Thomas S. 554
Gazioglu, Mary 726
Gearhart, Jeffrey J. 893
Gebert, Terry 735
Gebhart, Todd 569
Geckle, Timothy J. 744
Gedeon, Harvey 339
Gee, Carol R. 657

Gehl, Keith M. 348
Gehring, John F. 244
Geib, Sally L. 397
Geiger, Jeffrey S. 384
Geise, Laurel B. 355
Geisler, James E. 862
Geissler, Werner 702
Geist, Aaron 673
Gelbien, Lawrence J. 639
Geldmacher, Jay L. 330
Gellert, Jay M. 418
Gellert, John 763
Gelsinger, Patrick P. 461
Gelston, Tom 819
Geltzeiler, Michael S. 644
Gemunder, Joel F. 649
Genau, Michael 507
Gendreau, Ronald R. 413
Geneczko, Robert M. 694
Genho, Paul 508
Gennette, Jeffrey 548
Gentry, Jeffery S. 730
Gentz, Julie 917
Gentzkow, Paul F. 733
Gentzler, Roland G. 442
Genuario, Gina 204
George, Alan W. 336
George, Arthur L. 823
George, David C. 276
George, Philip J. 651
George, Richard 917
George, V. Carl 415
Georgens, Thomas 617
Gerber, William J. 810
Germain, Marc A. 563
German, Alston 351
Germano, Donald J. 510
Germanson, Christine 724
Germany, Rhonda G. 440
Germeroth, Gary M. 184
Gersh, Bruce 33
Gershenhorn, Alan 856
Gershman, Karen 808
Gershwind, Erik 602
Gerspach, John C. 227
Gerst, Robert 163
Gerstein, Richard 510
Gerstenberger, Tom 618
Gerstle, Mark R. 269
Gerstman, Ned I. 219
Geschke, Charles M. 41
Gestin, Denis M. 748
Gestrich, Thomas E. 466
Gfeller, Robert J. Jr. 543
Ghilardi, Emilio 44
Giacomini, Thomas 303
Gianopulos, James N. 371, 624
Gianos, Philip T. 928
Gibase, Christopher R. 163
Gibbons, Keith 571
Gibbons, Mary Anne 872
Gibbons, Peter D. 794
Gibbons, Thomas P. 128
Gibbs, Elizabeth L. 30
Gibbs, Nicki 286
Gibeau, Frank D. 325
Gibson, Charles S. Jr. 348
Gibson, Jed 837
Gibson, John W. (ONEOK) 652
Gibson, Jon R. (LSI Corp.) 545
Gibson, Phil 610
Gibson Brady, Holly E. 374
Gideon, Thomas F. 913
Giesler, Joseph D. 820
Gifford, Paul S. 397
Gifford, Robert K. 321
Gifford, William F. Jr. 68
Giga, Aziz S. 693
Gilbert, Andrew 714
Gilbert, E. Scott 558
Gilbert, James 162
Gilbert, Karen 849
Gilbert, Terrence M. 931
Gilkey, Glenn 360
Gill, Andy 210

Gill, Charles D. 862
Gillenwater, Neal 904
Gilles, Dennis J. 184
Gilles, Jean 280
Gillespie, Douglas 344
Gillett, Stephen 794
Gillette, Robert J. 440
Gilli, Erin 638
Gilligan, Edward P. 77
Gilligan, William R. 872
Gilliland, D. Gary 584
Gillingham, Lisa 698
Gillis, Michael L. 783
Gillis, Ruth Ann M. 342
Gillund, Laura 207
Gilmore, Dennis J. 355
Gilmore, Jay C. 287
Gimenez, Marcelo 394
Ginger, Andrew R. 779
Gingue, Denis F. 211
Ginsberg, Gary L. 624
Ginter, Matt 26
Gioja, Michael E. 665
Giordano, Thomas R. 902
Gips, Donald H. 529
Gipson, Jim 214
Girdwood, Amy 297
Gish, Stephen J. 237
Gisi, John J. 934
Gitlitz, Edward 119
Giuffre, Amy S. 409
Giuliano, Tony 647
Givens, Gregg W. 307
Gjesdal, Tamera 132
Gladden, Brian T. 282
Gladu, Debi 719
Glaser, Daniel S. 558
Glaser, Nancy 121
Glasgow, David M. 726
Glasgow, Gerald 314
Glass, Alex 91
Glass, Dennis R. 537
Glass, Holly P. 263
Glass, Robert W. 733
Glass, Sherman J. Jr. 347
Glass, William G. 341
Glasscock, Larry C. 905
Glasser, Elizabeth 45
Glassgow, Perry A. 409
Glassman, Hilary E. 376
Glassman, Karl G. 525
Gleason, Eric S. 61
Gleason, John J. 114
Glembocki, Jaroslaw S. 764
Glen, Douglas S. 587
Glendinning, Stewart 594
Glenewinkel, Arlen O. Jr. 821
Glenn, T. Michael 352
Glenn, William H. 77
Gliha, Lee Ann 538
Glisson, Britton 554
Glod, Pattie 533
Glover, R. Monty 771
Glowacki, John 243
Glueck, Ken 653
Gluski, Andrés R. 45
Glyer, Paul 137
Glynn, Meghan 516
Goachet, Pascal 351
Gochnauer, Richard W. 860
Gockley, John C. 858
Goda, Steven 301
Godbold, Francis S. 721
Goddard, Steve 154
Godich, Pete J. 286
Godridge, Leslie V. 870
Godwin, Benjamin B. 811
Godwin, Jerry H. 778
Goebel, Maryann 358
Goel, Manish 618
Goelzer, Paulo 452
Goeman, Donald D. 423
Goenaga, Domingo 382
Goerke, Brian 689
Goersch, Klaus 55

Goettel, Ralf 273
Goetz, Barbara M. 592
Goff, Gregory J. 246
Goff, Stacey W. 203
Goggins, Colleen A. 487
Goglia, Richard A. 722
Goh, Andrew 344
Goh, Charlie 144
Goings, E.V. 846
Goldberg, Glenn S. 575
Goldberg, Joel S 673
Goldberg, Neal L. 933
Goldberg, Paul E. 303
Golden, John 232
Golden, Ken 172
Golden, Michael 620
Golden, Robert C. 707
Golden, Stephen P. 472
Goldfinger, Solomon 619
Goldfrank, Jack C. 579
Goldman, Charles G. 363
Goldner, Brian 414
Goldner, Neal 422
Goldsmith, Rebecca 169
Goldstein, Abbe F. 729
Goldstein, Adam M. 739
Goldstein, Bruce 683
Goldstein, Don 198
Goldstein, I. Steven 830
Goldstein, Joanna 159
Goldston, David B. 484
Goldstone, Steven F. 244
Goldy, Susan E. 220
Golisano, B. Thomas 665
Golladay, Mark T. 615
Golsby, Stephen W. 169
Golub, Harvey 81
Gomez, Barbara M. 684
Gomo, Steven J. 617
Gonsalves, Rodney 52
Gonzalez, Edward A. 762
Gooch, James F. 719
Good, Kyle 759
Good, Lynn J. 309
Goodarzi, Sasan K. 469
Goodell, Elaine H. 539
Goodell, Timothy B. 427
Gooden, Clarence W. 268
Gooden, Linda R. 541
Gooden, William R. 242
Goodish, John H. 859
Goodman, Andrew 179
Goodman, Bruce J. 446
Goodman, Gregg M. 774
Goodman, Kim C. 77
Goodman, Richard A. 672
Goodman, Shira D. 792
Goodmanson, Richard R. 312
Goodrich, Donna C. 132
Goodson, Kenneth L. Jr. 423
Goodwald, Jerry A. 392
Goodwin, Michael W. 405
Goodwin, Scott J. 204
Gopal, Ajei S. 179
Gorbach, Pat 398
Gorder, Joseph W. 877
Gordon, Bancroft S. 556
Gordon, Beth G. 291
Gordon, David 213
Gordon, Deborah R. 438
Gordon, Derek A. 230
Gordon, Julie S. 428
Gordon, Michael 268
Gordon, Neil 611
Gordon, Robert A. 745
Gordon, Russell L. 741
Gordon, Susan C. 199
Gordon, Tim 698
Gore, Lisa 417
Goren, Isabella D. 89
Gorman, James P. 598
Gorman, Mark J. 481
Gorman, Richard T. 658
Gorman, Stephen E. 285
Gorman, Timothy W. 671

Gorsky, Alex 487
Gorsky, Dan 574
Gorup, Paul N. 206
Goshorn, Richard H. 880
Goss, Gavan 282
Gosselin, Stephen A. 196
Gossewisch, August 191
Gossin, Cheryl 250
Gottdiener, Charles E. 311
Gottesfeld, Stephen P. 623
Gottesmann, Patricia 180
Gottscho, Richard A. 519
Gottsegen, Jonathan M. 857
Gottung, Lizanne C. 504
Goturi, Rahul 780
Goubau, Gerald 501
Gough, Erin 613
Gould, Andrew 757
Gould, Michael 548
Gould, Robert L. 252
Goulden, David I. 327
Goulder, Michael L. 79
Goulding, Pete 188
Gouldthorpe, Hugh F. Jr. 655
Goulet, Ken R. 905
Gounelle, Patrick 337
Goussetis, Harry A. 922
Gove, Robert J. 589
Gozon, Richard C. 85
Graboff, Marc 613
Grabow, Karen 520
Grace, Claire S. 913
Grace, Mark 764
Gracey, Paul C. Jr. 625
Graddick-Weir, Miriam M. 584
Grady, John 611
Grady-Troia, Christopher 130
Graebner, Carol F. 406
Graf, Alan B. Jr. 352
Graf, Bob 546
Graf, Thomas J. 701
Grafe, Karl J. 78
Graff, Leslie J. 54
Grafton, Susan S. 146
Graham, Barry D. 242
Graham, Bruce L. 150
Graham, Donald E. 898
Graham, James 689
Graham, Jonathan P. 274
Graham, Steven B. 908
Graham, Terri F. 477
Grams, Blake M. 839
Gran, Alice N. 763
Grandinetti, Russell 69
Granneman, Thomas G. 720
Grant, Chris 495
Grant, Hugh 596
Grant, James W. 154
Grant, John 250
Grant, Robert E. 63
Grant, Tony 159
Grantham, Donald C. 429
Graphia, Gary P. 771
Grass, Keith B. 640
Graub, Jonathon 211
Graven, T.J. 173
Graves, Andrew E. 175
Graves, Chuck 655
Graves, Herbert IV 587
Graves, Kenneth A. 184
Gray, Carol J. 335
Gray, Jerry 419
Gray, John D. 726
Gray, Kimberly S. 456
Gray, Maria 374
Gray, Myron A. 856
Gray, Robert C. 431
Gray, Virginia C. 844
Greaves, Roger F. 418
Grebow, Peter E. 205
Greco, John R. 662
Greco, Joseph D. 641
Green, Anthony 688
Green, Dana I. 891

Green, Darryl E. 552
Green, George J. 420
Green, Jason W. 124
Green, Joe C. 597
Green, Judith 122
Green, Larry J. 126
Green, Michael W. 806
Green, Steven J. 686
Green, William D. 36
Greenan, Andrea 923
Greenberg, Lon R. 84, 851
Greenberg, Robert 50
Greene, Dale E. 239
Greene, Edward A. 264
Greene, Gregory F. 743
Greene, Richard S. 286
Greene, Robert E. 132
Greene, Russell S. 213
Greene, Stephen S. 874
Greene, Tom 236
Greenfield, David W. 501
Greenlee, Steve S.M. 347
Greenstein, Ira A. 451
Greenwald, Julie 897
Greenwell, Daniel D. 820
Greenwood, Charles F. 562
Greenwood, Greg A. 911
Greer, Alan W. 132
Greer, G. Bruce Jr. 648
Greffin, Judith P. 67
Gregg, Gary R. 532
Gregg, Kirk P. 258
Gregoire, Daniel N. 550
Gregory, E. Mark 239
Gregory, Michael J. 604
Gregory, Paul O. 635
Greifeld, Robert 606
Greig, Andy 136
Grein, Thomas W. 326
Greiner, Julie 548
Greiner, Mark T. 798
Grenell, Richard A. 277
Gresh, Philip M. Jr. 453
Gress, William J. 175
Grewcock, Bruce E. 678
Grewe, Wolfgang 284
Grey, Robert J. 694
Grey, Robin 529
Gri, Françoise 552
Grief, Stuart 825
Grier, Donna H. 312
Grier, Jeri 448
Grier, Mark B. 707
Grieshaber, Joseph A. Jr. 516
Griffin, Brian T. 580
Griffin, Christopher R. 875
Griffin, James R. 910
Griffin, Thomas J. 858
Griffith, G. Sanders III 840
Griffith, Geoffrey L. 39
Griffith, James W. 835
Griffith, John D. 808
Griffith, Michael J. 39
Griffith, Ray A. 38
Griffith, Susan P. 705
Griffith-Jones, John 514
Griffiths, William C. 209
Grigg, Richard R. 357
Griggs, Brent E. 706
Grigsby, Jennifer M. 214
Grillet, Robert J. 466
Grimes, James A. 749
Grimes, Kirk D. 360
Grimestad, Dwight E. 106
Grinney, Jay 419
Grippo, Michael J. 432
Griswold, Gary L. 26
Griswold, Scott A. 299
Groch, James R. 198
Grodzki, Kevin S. 175
Grohowski, Leo P. 128
Grollemund, Jean-François 38
Gromek, Joseph R. 896
Gronda, John D. 411
Gross, Bruce E. 526

Gross, Thomas S. 319
Grossman, Jeffrey W. 628
Grossman, Jennifer 299
Grossman, Marc A. 434
Grossman, Mindy 444
Grosso, Jon 512
Grove, Hannah 797
Grove, Janet E. 548
Grover, Fredrick W. 74
Groves, Ray J. 575
Grubbs, William J. 789
Grube, John P. 633
Grumbacher, M. Thomas 158
Grups, John M. 781
Grzybowski, Edward J. 830
Grzymkowski, Ron 34
Guarino, Gilbert B. 182
Guarino, Ludwig M. 888
Gubanich, Kathleen C. 879
Gubernick, Joseph 339
Gudbranson, Robert K. 470
Guenther, Cynthia S. 117
Guerrero, Juan 794
Guerrero, Scott 191
Guerton, Celine 191
Guglani, Sanjay 194
Guglielmo, Frank 467
Guifarro, Jan 236
Guild, Howard 757
Guiles, Edwin A. 768
Guldig, John F. 110
Guldin, Andreas 29
Guldner, Jeff 684
Gulley, Joan L. 689
Gulling, Mark V. 579
Gum, Barry E. 762
Gummer, Charles L. 239
Gunn, Timothy 539
Gunnell, Casey L. 184
Gunningham, Sebastian J. 69
Gunson, Douglas R. 640
Gunther, David T. 255
Guo, Karen 44
Guo, Patrick 817
Gupta, Anurag 165
Gupta, Ashwini 77
Gupta, Debashis 757
Gupta, Naresh 41
Gupta, Rahul 358
Gupta, Shailendra 458
Gurnari, Vincent J. Jr. 263
Gursahaney, Naren K. 848
Gustafson, Erick 558
Guthrie, Laura D. 184
Gutermuth, Matt 920
Gutierrez, David (Protective Life) 706
Gutierrez, David V. (Newmont Mining) 623
Gutiérrez, José M. 111
Gutierrez, Luis 261
Gutierrez, Maria G. 619
Gutierrez, Mauricio 638
Gutsch, James L. 762
Gutschewski, Bernard R. 852
Guttman, Tim G. 85
Guy, Betty 376
Guy, Stephan R. 652
Guyardo, Paul 295
Guyaux, Joseph C. 689
Guzowski, Michael S. 654
Guzzi, Anthony J. 329
Gwin, Robert G. 90
Gwyn, Susan E. 800

H

Haag, Joyce P. 318
Haak, Arne G. 55
Haaraoja, Brian 788
Hachigian, Kirk S. 255
Hack, Bruce L. 38
Hackenson, Elizabeth 45
Hacker, Todd M. 247
Hackett, David P. 122

Hackett, James P. (Steelcase) 798
Hackett, James T. (Anadarko Petroleum) 90
Hackett, Steven G. 697
Haddad, Emile 526
Hady, Todd 522
Haefner, Larry A. 232
Haeg, Lawrence P. 906
Haffner, David S. 525
Hagan, Annmarie T. 221
Hagan, Joseph J. 357
Hagan, Stacie 315
Hagedorn, Gene J. 124
Hagedorn, James 760
Hagel, Shawn R. 697
Hagelin, David M. 76
Hagemann, Robert A. 715
Hagen, Lisa B. 743
Hagen, Sue 299
Hager, David A. 289
Hager, Kenneth V. 307
Hagerman, Douglas M. 735
Haggai, Thomas S. 452
Haggerty, Gretchen R. 859
Haggerty, Joseph F. 603
Haggerty, Stephen G. 449
Hagopian, B. Kipling 567
Hahn, Eugene C. 57
Haire, John E. 42
Hairston, Peyton T. Jr. 818
Hajek, Josef 846
Hajj, Imad 828
Hajost, Michael A. 194
Hake, Kevin C. 443
Halbert, R. Keith 850
Halbouty, Thomas C. 685
Haldeman, Genevieve 805
Hale, Jerry 316
Hale, John A. 525
Hales, Michael T. 341
Haley, John J. 903
Haley, Roy W. 910
Hall, Bradley C. 851
Hall, Charles L. (Sprint Nextel) 790
Hall, Charles M. (General Dynamics) 383
Hall, Christopher S. 731
Hall, David (PC Connection) 666
Hall, David E. (Hallmark) 405
Hall, Donald J. (Hallmark) 405
Hall, Donald J. Jr. (Hallmark) 405
Hall, Edward 45
Hall, Frank W. 685
Hall, Jeffrey L. 345
Hall, John L. 653
Hall, Kenneth T. 679
Hall, Ladd R. 640
Hall, Miles 221
Hall, Nance 673
Hall, Neil F. 689
Hall, O. B. Grayson Jr. 724
Hall, Randal C. 889
Hall, Richard D. 155
Halla, Brian L. 610
Hallberg, Carl-Magnus 606
Haller, Heinz 305
Haller, Karen S. 787
Hallihan, Daniel G. 888
Halloran, Jean M. 51
Hallowell, Bryce 66
Hallowell, Harry H. 611
Halls, Ronald J. 364
Hally, Edward A. 242
Halnon, Bill 728
Halter, Hank 285
Halversen, David T. 846
Halvey, John K. 644
Halvorsen, Per-Kristian 468
Halvorson, George C. 495
Hamada, Richard 120
Hamaker, Donald W. 758
Hamblen, Don 767
Hambrick, James L. 546
Hamburg, Marc D. 145
Hamel, Dennis J. 57

Hamel, Matthew E. 173
Hames, Michael J. 823
Hamid, Wahid 672
Hamilton, Peter B. 175
Hammar, Margo 882
Hammer, Thomas E. 436
Hammergren, John H. 577
Hammett, Richard M. 648
Hammett, Suzanne 187
Hammond, Miriam 588
Hammond, Thomas R. 478
Hamp, Julie A. 672
Hamrah, Charlene M. 81
Hamrock, Joseph 76
Han, Bernard L. 298
Hance, James H. Jr. 790
Hance, Robert B. 31
Hancock, Peter D. 503
Hand, Hyune 311
Hand, Todd 464
Handley, Terry W. 195
Handley, Thomas W. 321
Handlon, Carolyn B. 556
Haney, James E. 408
Hanft, Noah J. 564
Hanks, Stephen G. 868
Hanley, T. Kathleen 194
Hanlon, Karen 764
Hanna, Steven R. 501
Hannan, Michael 884
Hannaway, Jennine 729
Hannes, William F. 685
Hannigan, Randy A. 84
Hannon, Michael J. 689
Hanor, Vicki 774
Hanrahan, Daniel J. 739
Hanrahan, Paul T. 45
Hansen, David 319
Hansen, Dennis J. 506
Hansen, Marka 381
Hansen, Michael 759
Hansen, Stephen W. 821
Hansen, Thomas J. 453
Hansen, William D. 547
Hanson, A. John 138
Hanson, Amy 548
Hanson, John N. (Joy Global) 492
Hanson, Jon F. (HealthSouth) 419
Hanson, Robert L. 530
Hanspal, Amar 112
Hansson, B. Thomas 752
Hanway, H. Edward 221
Hanzel, Kevin S. 334
Happe, Michael J. 839
Hara, Michael W. 641
Harant, Vaclav 605
Harari, Eli 750
Harber, Bill 193
Hardage, Ginger C. 786
Hardie, Warren N. 175
Harding, David P. 438
Harding, Jim 422
Hardis, Stephen R. 558
Hardman, Chris 529
Hardnock, Ronald L. 621
Hare, Stephen E. 908
Harford, Simon N. R. 121
Hargreaves, David D. R. 414
Hargrove, Randy 153
Hargrow, Ralph P. 594
Harig, Robert J. 264
Hariri, Abdi 519
Harjehausen, Edward A. 106
Harju-Jeanty, Tomas 370
Harker, Victoria D. 45
Harker, William R. 510, 767
Harlan, Joe E. 26
Harlan, M. Ann 483
Harlan, Robert E. 401
Harlow, Craig R. 778
Harmon, John F. 612
Harper, C. Gregory 200
Harper, Craig 479
Harper, John E. 675

Harper, Sean E. 86
Harrelson, Ryland L. 840
Harrigan, Edmund P. 680
Harrington, Anthony P.D. 699
Harrington, George W. 805
Harris, Allan D. 137
Harris, D. Russell 755
Harris, Eric 920
Harris, Frederick J. 384
Harris, H. Hiter III 689
Harris, Isaiah Jr. 221
Harris, Jeff M. 899
Harris, Jon 752
Harris, Kathryn J. 335
Harris, Margery M. 97
Harris, Patricia 574
Harris, Paul N. 503
Harris, Richard (Spherion) 789
Harris, Richard E. (Cummins) 269
Harris, Steven J. 388
Harrison, Caroline 42
Harrison, Dandridge 652
Harrison, John B. 514
Harrison, Kelly B. 911
Harrison, Lee 849
Harrison, Michael J. 832
Harrison, Robert E. 65
Harrison, Ronald 490
Harrison, Steve L. 527
Harrison, Thomas L. 651
Harrsen, Laurie 571
Harshman, Richard J. 62
Hart, Brett J. 752
Hart, Cathy J. 925
Hart, Craig J. 849
Hart, Linda W. 455
Hart, Michael A. (Gannett) 379
Hart, Mike (Regions Financial) 724
Hart, Patti S. 465
Hartenstein, James C. 908
Hartigan, Jim 434
Hartigan, John 624
Hartley, Cynthia A. 781
Hartley, David E. 105
Hartley, Jennifer A. 167
Hartley, John R. 747
Hartley, Thomas D. 596
Hartline, Alan 788
Hartman, Daniel M. 295
Hartman, William C. 319
Hartmann, Nancy F. 437
Hartnack, Richard C. 870
Harton, Don 223
Hartzog, Daniel A. 442
Harvey, Charles A. 489
Harvey, Christopher C. 637
Harvey, Connie 48
Harvey, David R. 773
Harvey, J. Brett 248
Harvey, Kent M. 682
Harvie, C. Thomas 398
Harvill, Barbara B. 192
Haser, H. William 817
Hasker, Rojon D. 746
Haskew, Kevin 109
Hassell, Gerald L. 128
Hassell, Stephen C. 330
Hassen, Ronald 606
Hassett, James A. 337
Hassey, L. Patrick 62
Hastings, John S. 377
Hatcher, Barbara A. 344
Hatcher, Michael J. 859
Hatfield, Gregory M. 738
Hatfield, James R. 684
Hatfield, Tinker 626
Hathcock, Bonita C. 446
Hatler, Patricia R. 611
Hatton, Vincent P. 258
Haub, Christian W. E. 29
Haubiel, Charles W. II 148
Hauck, Frank M. 327
Hauck, Walter S. III 311
Haude, Ellen 906
Haudrich, John 657

Hauenstein, Glen W. 285
Haugarth, Janel S. 803
Haugen, Janet 854
Haughie, Alan 351
Haun, Dallas E. 934
Haun, Patrick D. 822
Hausberg, Mark 367
Hauselt, Denise A. 258
Hauser, Paul R. 525
Hausrath, David L. 110
Havel, Kip 789
Havenstein, Walter P. 747
Haverkost, Ken 484
Haverty, Michael R. 496
Hawaux, André J. 244
Hawk, George W. Jr. 228
Hawkins, Amy 177
Hawkins, Jay L. 589
Hawkins, Joanne 450
Hawkins, Mark J. 112
Hawkins, William A. III 581
Hawley, Richard L. 625
Hawn, Steve 405
Hawthorne, Robert F. 142
Hay, Lewis III 372
Hay, Willard 794
Hayden, Mark 244
Haydukovich, Mark A. 72
Hayes, Gregory J. 862
Hayes, Jimmy W. 262
Hayes, John A. (Ball Corp.) 126
Hayes, John D. (American Express) 77
Hayes, Kenneth A. 150
Hayes, Peter B. 376
Hayes, Robert D. 436
Hayne, Margaret 867
Hayne, Richard A. 867
Hays, Eddie R. 233
Hayter, Robert L. 404
Haythornthwaite, Richard N. 564
Hayzlett, Jeffrey W. 318
Hazen, Samuel N. 416
Heacock, David K. 823
Healy, Kevin P. 55
Healy, Maureen 856
Healy, Thomas F. 662
Healy, William 438
Hearst, George R. Jr. 420
Heaslip, Steven J. 464
Heath, George E. 772
Heath, Ralph D. 541
Heath, Robert F. 164
Heatly, Danny J. 289
Heaton, Letha 554
Heavin, Jerry W. 496
Hebard, Douglas 144
Hebe, James L. 612
Hébert, Curtis L. Jr. 332
Hebert, Walter III 223
Heck, Sharon L. 145
Hecker, David 754
Heckes, Howard C. 878
Hedges, Barbara 212
Hedges, James L. 33
Hedlund, Steven B. 535
Heebner, David K. 383
Heekin-Canedy, Scott H. 620
Heffernan, Lee 560
Heffler, Mava K. 329
Hefner, Juanell 418
Hegi, Frederick B. Jr. 860
Heikkinen, Mika 813
Heim, James V. 201
Heim, Michael C. 326
Heimann, Sandra W. 78
Heimers, Edward F. Jr. 902
Hein, Leland J. 349
Heine, Kevin 128
Heine, Robert J. 326
Heinmiller, John C. 748
Heinrich, Daniel J. 230
Heinrich, Joseph D. 235
Heins, John D. 789
Heintz, Kenneth N. 635
Heintz, Michael J. 314

Heinz, Roger J. 813
Heise, Rita J. 189
Heiser, Thomas 327
Heitman, J. William 110
Heitman, Vicki C. 543
Heitmann, William F. 882
Helbing, Scott C. 111
Helck, Chester B. 721
Held, Jeffrey J. 903
Heldman, Paul W. 516
Heleniak, David W. 598
Helfer, Michael S. 227
Helfrich, Thomas E. 503
Heller, David 718
Heller, John S. 196
Heller, Paul 879
Hellickson, Mickey W. 508
Hellwig, Mark R. 522
Helm, Gordon K. 421
Helm, Robert W. 635
Helmbrecht, Steven M. 473
Helmerich, Hans 421
Helmerich, Walter H. III 421
Helms, Christopher A. 628
Helsel, Bruce E. 906
Helz, Terrance V. 255
Heminger, Gary R. 553
Hemingway, W. David 934
Hemme, Dennis Richard 232
Hemmer, J. Michael 852
Hemsley, Stephen J. 863
Hemus, Simon C. 846
Henderson, Frederick A. 388
Henderson, Jeffrey W. 188
Henderson, Mary E. 844
Henderson, Scott M. 516
Henderson, Susan 409
Henderson, Wendy E. 908
Hendricks, Christian A. 570
Hendricks, John S. 297
Hendricks, Kimberly A. 464
Hendrickson, David 491
Hendrickson, Gary E. 878
Hendrickson, John T. 676
Hendrix, Buck 794
Hendry, Andrew D. 236
Henebry, Timothy M. 658
Heneghan, James 212
Henkel, Herbert L. 457
Henley, Robert W. 642
Hennequin, Denis 574
Hennessy, Mark J. 462
Hennessy, Paul J. 698
Hennessy, Sean P. 772
Hennig, Jay K. 597
Henning, Gary S. 779
Hennon-Bell, Lori 707
Henrici, Peter G. 887
Henrikson, C. Robert 586
Henriques, George L. 664
Henry, Brian J. 819
Henry, Daniel T. 77
Henry, Peter 91
Henry, Robert K. 411
Henschel, Laurel E. 775
Hensel, Anthony D. 160
Hensgen, Heinz Ulrich 659
Hensley, Susan 314
Henson, Christopher L. 132
Herald, Alice A. 127
Herath, Kirk 611
Herbel, Vern D. 838
Herbert, C. Theodore 812
Herbert, Jeff 646
Herdman, Michael D. 126
Herglotz, Kevin 746
Herington, Charles M. 121
Herink, Daniel D. 40
Herkert, Craig R. 803
Herlihy, Donagh 121
Herman, Fred E. 726
Hermiz, Ramzi Y. 351
Hernandez, Carlos M. (Fluor) 360
Hernandez, Carlos M. (JPMorgan
  Chase) 494

Hernandez, Enrique Jr. 630
Hernandez, William H. 693
Hernowitz, Ira 414
Herpich, Richard P. 876
Herrema, Gregory J. 826
Herring, Joseph L. 261
Herringer, Maryellen C. 35
Herrington, Terri L. 466
Herrman, Ernie 836
Herrmann, Peggy A. 302
Herrmann, Susan 193
Herro, Leslee K. 34
Herschmann, Eric D. 785
Hershman, Lisa 120
Hertwig, James R. 268
Herzig, Bill 276
Herzog, David L. 81
Heske, Gerrit 126
Hess, Carl 903
Hess, David P. 862
Hess, John B. 427
Hesse, Chad F. 292
Hesse, Daniel R. 790
Hessels, Jan-Michiel 644
Hester, John P. 787
Hester, Troy L. 814
Hetterich, F. Paul 250
Hevelhorst, Richard P. 209
Hewitt, Dennis E. 651
Heyman, William H. 843
Heyse, Richard P. 910
Heystee, Susan 637
Hiatte, Patrick 177
Hibbard, Timothy A. 910
Hibbeler, Jeff 149
Hickerson, M. Neale 437
Hickey, Loughlin 514
Hickey, Michael A. 321
Hickey, Nancy W. 798
Hickey, William V. 765
Hickman, Rebecca L. 684
Hicks, Christie 795
Hicks, H. Thomas 868
Hicks, Kenneth C. 364
Hicks, Randall L. 155
Hicok, Gary 641
Hidalgo, Joaquin 626
Hidy, Richard J. 870
Hier-King, Jan 210
Higase, Edward T. 394
Higgins, Bryce 777
Hightman, Carrie J. 628
Higson, John Philip 121
Hilado, Tessa 672
Hild, Randy 716
Hildenbrand, Wilton 180
Hilf, Kristin 722
Hilfman, Dave 253
Hilger, James K. 277
Hill, Allen E. 856
Hill, Anne 117
Hill, Brian 623
Hill, Dan 342
Hill, David 624
Hill, Edwin J. 192
Hill, Elliott 626
Hill, George 646
Hill, Gregory P. 427
Hill, John (L-3 Communications) 518
Hill, John B. III (Calpine) 184
Hill, Kevin N. 665
Hill, Ralph A. 917
Hill, Susan E. 149
Hill, Terri L. 611
Hill, Willard I. Jr. 568
Hillegonds, Paul 308
Hilliard, R. Glenn 247
Hillman, Jeanne M. 913
Hillman, Lori A. 418
Hills, Stephen P. 898
Hillyer, Kim 810
Hilsheimer, Lawrence A. 611
Hilson, Joan Holstein 74
Hilton, Andy 474
Hilton, Bradley J. 708

Hilton, Michael F. 53
Hilton, Timothy T. 363
Hilton, William Barron 433
Hiltwein, Mark S. 204
Hilzinger, Matthew F. 342
Hinckley, Clark B. 934
Hindman, Craig A. 453
Hindman, James M. 63
Hine, C. Clarkson 367
Hinners, Billy 112
Hinrichs, Joseph R. 365
Hinrichs, Liane K. 573
Hinshaw, John 157
Hinshaw, Scott R. 301
Hinton, Leslie F. 624
Hinze, Brant 623
Hirokawa, Katsumi 593
Hirsberg, Josh 163
Hirsch, Didier 52
Hirsch, Elizabeth T. 696
Hirsch, Thomas J. 358
Hirschfeld, Marc 613
Hirschmann, James W. III 523
Hirst, Richard B. 285
Hissong, Cathy 257
Hitchery, Regina M. 60
Hite, Sharon 341
Hitz, David 617
Hixon, James A. 631
Hjelm, Christopher T. 516
Hoagland, Willard C. III 45
Hobbs, J. Neil 529
Hobbs, Laura Lopez 787
Hobbs, Steven A. 420
Hobor, Nancy A. 924
Hochberg, Elaine 366
Hochberg, Heather 898
Hochschild, Roger C. 599
Hodge, Harry 716
Hodges, Alexander W. 377
Hodges, Cheryl D. 649
Hodges, Mark S. 443
Hodges, Matt 378
Hodous, Brian 38
Hoekzema, Thomas K. 759
Hoeltzel, Mary T. 221
Hoesley, Joseph C 870
Hoffman, Aaron 752
Hoffman, Brad A. 410
Hoffman, Joyce Nixson 701
Hoffman, Margot 273
Hoffman, Michael J. 839
Hoffman, Randall G. 50
Hoffman, Richard W. 117
Hoffman, Stuart G. 689
Hoffman, Thomas F. 248
Hoffman, William 336
Hoffner, John F. 477
Hoffner, Warren E. 101
Hofmann, G. Michael 766
Hofmann, Herbert C. 542
Hogan, David M. 62
Hogan, Mike 378
Hogg, William F. Jr. 876
Hogge, Jerry 529
Hoglund, Raymond 303
Hoglund, Robert N. 249
Hoguet, Karen M. 548
Holbrook, Tom 716
Holcomb, Lee 541
Holden, Guy 489
Holden, Mark 511
Holder, Richard D. 319
Holder, William L. Jr. 293
Holifield, Mark 439
Holland, Christopher S. 104
Holland, David K. 226
Holland, G. Edison Jr. 784
Holland, Gregory D. 601
Holland, Kevin R. 216
Hollander, Gilbert P. 933
Holle, Oliver 880
Hollenbeck, John M. 356
Hollenbeck, Martin F. 222
Holleran, John W. 473

Holleran, Sandra J. 169
Holley, Charles M. Jr. 893
Holley, Jean K. 813
Holliday, Charles O. Jr. 312
Hollifield, Matthew V. 543
Holliman, Skipper 377
Hollinger, Mark 297
Hollinger, William R. 497
Holloman, J. Phillip 225
Holloway, Janet M. 596
Holman, Brad L. 716
Holman, Edwin J. 548
Holmberg, David L. 431
Holmes, David 507
Holmes, Jack A. 856
Holmes, Melanie 552
Holmes, Michael R. 345
Holmes, Tod C. 728
Holmquist, Lars 841
Holquist, Jeanine 798
Holschuh, Laurel A. 906
Holston, Michael J. 430
Holt, Bradford R. 777
Holt, Kevin R. 510, 767
Holt, Victoria M. 693
Holt, William M. 461
Holyfield, Jeff 231
Hölzle, Urs 399
Hombach, Robert J. 131
Homfray, Christopher C. 267
Honea, Adam 98
Hood, Henry J. 214
Hood, Mark E. 172
Hooda, Sheila 830
Hoogasian, Seth H. 826
Hoogenboom, Paul G. P. 740
Hooker, John T. 342
Hooley, Joseph L. 797
Hooley, Stephen C. 307
Hooper, Anthony C. 169
Hooper, John 913
Hooper, Ned 226
Hootkin, Pamela N. 683
Hoover, Joan 99
Hoover, R. David 126
Hope, James D. 806
Hopkins, Deborah C. 227
Hopkins, Frank E. 685
Hopkins, Henry H. 807
Hopkins, John L. 360
Hopkins, Thomas E. 772
Hopko, Kathleen M. 862
Hoplamazian, Mark S. 449
Hopmans, John 538
Hopp, Daniel F. 915
Hopper, James T. 101
Hopwood, Tony 191
Horan, Anthony J. 494
Horan, Douglas S. 639
Horiszny, Laurene H. 160
Horn, David C. 56
Horn, Randall C. 866
Hornbuckle, Mertroe B. 280
Hornbuckle, William J. 588
Horne, Chad 443
Horner, Digby 41
Horner, Jody 189
Horner, Kim 148
Horning, Roxanne V. 379
Hornstra, Peter E. 826
Horrell, Karen Holley 78
Horsch, James 313
Horton, Donald R. 306
Horton, Gary B. 72
Horton, Rick 306
Horton, Thomas W. 89
Horvath, Peter Z. 533
Hosking, Robert 733
Hoskins, John M. 818
Hostetter, Jerry 778
Houk, Keith D. 869
House, Beverly 34
House, Cecil R. 322
Householder, Joseph A. 768
Houston, Daniel J. 701

Houston, J. Wayne 889
Houston, Ken 502
Hove, R. Andy 654
Hover-Smoot, Scott 928
Hovnanian, Ara K. 443
Hovnanian, Kevork S. 443
Hovsepian, Ronald W. 93, 637
Howard, Bonnie L. 227
Howard, Christopher L. 709
Howard, Frank M. 389
Howard, Graeme 729
Howard, Jeffrey G. 860
Howard, Jerry 553
Howard, John L. 924
Howard, Kay L. 526
Howard, Kevin D. 212
Howard, Tim J. 829
Howe, Michael B. 331
Howe, Steve 337
Howell, J. Mark 165
Howell, Joseph M. III 529
Howell, Kevin T. 638
Howell, Mary L. 825
Howells, Jeffery P. 811
Howlett, C. A. 869
Hoyt, David A. 906
Hoyt, Rebecca A. 97
Hoza, Jeffrey S. 134
Hrabusa, John T. 711
Hrubiec, Robert T. 205
Hu, Mark K. 915
Huang, Claire 127
Huang, Jen-Hsun 641
Hubach, Joseph F. 823
Hubbard, Allan 774
Hubbard, Gary M. 742
Hubbard, Susan 393
Huber, Charles G. Jr. 720
Huber, Dennis G. 202
Huber, Gary E. 148
Huber, J. Kendall 407
Huber, Jeffrey T. 399
Huber, Maria Oh 52
Huber, Rudolph P. 60
Huber, Steven C. 807
Huck, Paul E. 53
Huckvale, Stephen A. 597
Hudson, Charles F. 838
Hudson, Paul B. 880
Hudson, R. Read 849
Hudson, William L. 764
Huebschen, Jeff 66
Huet, Jean-Marc 169
Huey, John W. 820
Huff, Brian 803
Huff, Heidi 452
Huff, Rolla P. 315
Huffman, Anne M. 703
Huffman, John U. 668
Huggins, Lois M. 752
Huggins, Stephen R. 397
Hugh, Yoon J. 299
Hughes, Alastair 491
Hughes, Dale 262
Hughes, Gregory W. 805
Hughes, James R. 242
Hughes, Jeff 728
Hughes, Timothy W. 262
Hulbert, Jay S. 671
Hulit, Barbara B. 274
Hull, David 551
Hull, Robert F. Jr. 543
Hull, Roger S. 355
Humber, Stephen W. 840
Humble, Rodney 325
Humes, William D. 458
Huml, Donald S. 401
Humphrey, John 736
Humphreys, Donald D. 347
Humphries, Brian 430
Humphries, G. Kent 806
Hund, Thomas N. 177
Hund-Mejean, Martina 564
Hung, Jim 395
Hunker, Chauncey J. 800

Huns, Adrian J. 220
Hunt, Edith 395
Hunt, Jack 508
Hunt, Kenneth C. 552
Hunt, Kevin J. 720
Hunt, Lisa K. 210
Hunt, Marsha L. 269
Hunter, Amber 777
Hunter, Jennifer 68
Hunter, Justin 419
Hunter, Larry D. 295
Hunter, M. Scott 292
Hunter, Mark 594
Hunter-Perkins, Paula 306
Hunziker, Leslie 426
Huonker, Donald C. Jr. 891
Hupfer, Charles J. 781
Hurd, Jeffrey J. 81
Hurd, Mark V. 429
Hurlburt, Terry L. 333
Hurley, J. Robert 137
Hurst, David B. 39
Hurst, Steve 146
Hurt, Linda J. 177
Hurwitz, Jeffrey S. 311
Huseby, Michael P. 180
Huspeni, Jeffrey R. 623
Husseini, Katherine 281
Husselbee, Brian J. 876
Hussey, John 91
Hussey, Walt 751
Huston, John J. 236
Hutcheson, Tad 55
Hutchinson, Blake 502
Hutchison, Larry M. 838
Hutchison, Philip A. 330
Hutterly, Jane M. 754
Huttleston, Timothy S. 29
Hutton, Donald R. 813
Hyde, Thomas D. 893
Hyle, Charles S. 503
Hyle, Kathleen W. 252
Hyne, Randy 369

I

Iaco, Steven 198
Ian, David 538
Iannarelli, John S. 84
Ianniello, Joseph R. 199
Iannucci, Patricia 659
Icahn, Carl C. 351
Ice, Carl R. 177
Ichord, J. William 768
Idiart, Roger A. 344
Idrovo, Javier H. 425
Iger, Robert A. 894
Igli, Kevin J. 849
Ignaczak, Edward 345
Ihrie, Richard W. 469
Ikeda, Donna S. 374
Ikeda, Douglas 438
Illig, Clifford W. 206
Imanse, Andrew 829
Immelt, Jeffrey R. 385
Ingersoll, Ellen M. 884
Ingoldsby, James J. 638
Ingram, Douglas S. 63
Ingram, Robert C. III 413
Ingram, Tony L. 268
Inman, Gordon E. 354
Inman, William J. 642
Innis-Thompson, Janice 830
Intraligi, Peter 471
Intrator, Tom 189
Ippolito, Gary 314
Irani, Ray R. 645
Ireland, Les H. 152
Irgang, Carole 515
Irick, Larry D. 911
Irizarry, Michael S. 858
Ironside, Colleen 538
Irvin, John W. 480
Irvin, Thomas R. 243

Irving, George W. 858
Irving, Gregory S. 924
Isaak, Richard R. 377
Isaman, Robert G. 819
Isbell, Jeri L. 531
Ismail, Alexandre 440
Ismail, Rashit 846
Isom, Robert D. Jr. 869
Israel, Craig M. 767
Israel, James A. 280
Istre, Michael J. 920
Itokazu, John T. 934
Ittel, Jeffrey 120
Ittycheria, Dev 154
Iuanow, Nicholas J. 344
Ive, Jonathan 99
Iverson, Gregory J. 98
Ivey, Craig S. 249
Ivey, Susan M. 730
Iwata, Jon C. 462
Iyer, Jay 750
Izumo, Seigo 393
Izzo, Ralph 710

J

Jabanoski, James R. 280
Jacko, John H. Jr. 501
Jackowski, Julie L. 195
Jackson, Alexander 235
Jackson, Deanna 716
Jackson, Jessica 435
Jackson, Jim 136
Jackson, Joleen 566
Jackson, Michael (IAC) 450
Jackson, Michael J. (AutoNation) 115
Jackson, Robert J. 759
Jackson, Russell M. 746
Jackson, Timothy E. 817
Jackson, William D. 658
Jacob, Beth M 808
Jacobs, David 122
Jacobs, Frances 863
Jacobs, Gary N. 588
Jacobs, Jeffrey A. 714
Jacobs, Joey A. 709
Jacobs, John L. 606
Jacobs, Lawrence A. 624
Jacobs, Paul E. 714
Jacobs, Philip C. 770
Jacobs, Steve D. 364
Jacobsen, Donald E. 629
Jacobsen, John S. 496
Jacobson, Douglas J. 214
Jacobson, Jeff A. 491
Jacobson, Michael R. 320
Jacobson, Mitchell 602
Jacobson, Paul A. 285
Jacobson, Richard J. (Cox
    Enterprises) 262
Jacobson, Rick (Fox
    Entertainment) 371
Jacoby, Lowell E. 182
Jacoby, Rebecca J. 226
Jacome, Jacobo 496
Jadin, Ronald L. 924
Jafa, Evan H. 355
Jaffe, Jeffrey M. 637
Jaffe, Jonathan M. 526
Jaffe, Seth R. 918
Jaffy, Stanley A. 142
Jain, Vivek 567
Jakeman, Brad 39
Jaksich, Daniel J. 145
Jakubek, John 294
Jakubik, Christopher M. 515
James, Charles A. 215
James, Courtland W. 721
James, Donald M. 889
James, Juanita T. 686
James, Kate 227
James, Kathi 134
James, Mark 440
James, Phyllis A. 588

James, Thomas A. 721
Jamesley, Karen C. 599
Jameson, John 904
Jamil, Dhiaa M. 309
Jamison, Joshua L. 212
Jan Vandenakker, Gert 189
Jandegian, Gary V. 868
Jandik, Dennis D. 302
Janeway, Dean 890
Jänisch, Christian 514
Jank, Michael J. 287
Janke, Kenneth S. Jr. 49
Janker, Franz 102
Jannausch, Julia P. 254
Jannini, Michael E. 556
Janov, Edward A. 787
Jansen, James C. 349
Janson, Julia S. 309
Janssen, Ann D. 334
Janssen, Vincent H. A. M. 752
Janzen, Peter S. 520
Jardine, Ian D. 826
Jarrault, Olivier M. 60
Jarrett, Charles E. 704
Jarrett, Madonna 284
Jarvis, Debbi 668
Jarvis, Stephen B. 57
Jasinowski, Isabel H. 398
Jassy, Andrew 69
Jastrem, John F. 884
Jastrzebski, Thaddeus J. 425
Jayaraman, Ranga 641
Jeffers, Mickey 855
Jeffery, W. Jeremy 49
Jeffries, Douglas C. 660
Jeffries, Michael S. 34
Jeffries, Telvin 512
Jelinek, W. Craig 259
Jellison, Brian D. 736
Jellison, William R. 288
Jemison, Steven W. 702
Jenkins, Charles H. Jr. 711
Jenkins, Dan 780
Jenkins, Ernest L. 668
Jenkins, James R. 280
Jenkins, John S. Jr. 848
Jenkins, Larry 199
Jenkins, Sharon K. 791
Jenness, James M. 498
Jennings, Thomas L. 583
Jensen, Brad 869
Jensen, James B. 777
Jensen, Joseph N. 75
Jensen, Keith A. 78
Jensen, Rick W. 469
Jeppesen, Jon A. 97
Jeppesen, Michael 237
Jermyn, Isadore 563
Jerzyk, Timothy P. 932
Jett, Ernest C. 525
Jewett, Joshua R. 348
Jewett, Patrick 120
Jha, Sanjay K. 600
Jimarez, Miguel 88
Jimenez, Frank R. 474
Jimenez, Richard 707
Jimenez, Roberto I. 262
Jobs, Steven P. 99
Jochumsen, Hans-Ole 606
Joerres, Jeffrey A. 552
Johannes, Gay M. 206
Johanneson, David 612
Johansson, Pertti 714
Johns, Christopher P. 682
Johns, John D. 706
Johns, Linda 371
Johns, Tammy 552
Johnsen, Constance R. 779
Johnsen, Kenneth L. 670
Johnson, Abigail P. 363
Johnson, Brian D. 442
Johnson, Bruce D. 725
Johnson, Carolyn M. 706
Johnson, Carver L. 516
Johnson, Charles B. 374

Johnson, Craig A. 68
Johnson, Curt G. 356
Johnson, David (Nalco) 605
Johnson, David A. (Jones Lang
    LaSalle) 491
Johnson, David D. (International Game
    Technology) 465
Johnson, David D. (Molex) 593
Johnson, David H. (Warner Music) 897
Johnson, Dick (Foot Locker) 364
Johnson, Edward C. III 363
Johnson, Ellen T. 467
Johnson, Galen G. 189
Johnson, Gerard 444
Johnson, Glenn S. 57
Johnson, Gregory E. 374
Johnson, H. Fisk 754
Johnson, Helen K. 460
Johnson, Henry P. 374
Johnson, James C. (Chesapeake
    Energy) 214
Johnson, James L. (Werner
    Enterprises) 909
Johnson, James L. Jr. (FMR) 363
Johnson, Jay L. 383
Johnson, John D. (CHS) 218
Johnson, John N. (Intel Corp.) 461
Johnson, Ken 911
Johnson, Kim 413
Johnson, M. Carl III 185
Johnson, Madeleine 786
Johnson, Margaret L. 714
Johnson, Mark E. 615
Johnson, Marsha S. 784
Johnson, Martha C. 110
Johnson, Michael A. 214
Johnson, Paul A. 926
Johnson, Phillip C. 389
Johnson, Preston H. Jr. 573
Johnson, R. Milton 415
Johnson, Raymond D. 377
Johnson, Richard J. (PNC
    Financial) 689
Johnson, Richard L. (Eastman
    Chemical) 316
Johnson, Rick L. (Cooper
    Industries) 255
Johnson, Robert H. (Sprint Nextel) 790
Johnson, Robert L. (Sprint Nextel) 790
Johnson, Rodney 784
Johnson, Roger 623
Johnson, Ronald B. 99
Johnson, Rupert H. Jr. 374
Johnson, Scott 754
Johnson, Stephen H. (Belden) 141
Johnson, Stephen L. (US Airways) 869
Johnson, Stephen M. (McDermott) 573
Johnson, Thomas D. 230
Johnson, Tyler 255
Johnson, W. Bruce 510, 767
Johnson, W. Donald 312
Johnson, Warren C. 597
Johnson, William D. (Progress
    Energy) 703
Johnson, William R. (Heinz) 434
Johnston, Elizabeth 285
Johnston, J. Bradley 814
Johnston, James W. 522
Johnston, Paul W. 900
Johnston, R. William 718
Johnston, Steven J. 222
Johnston, Thomas H. 79
Johnstone, Sherry 184
Joint, David 375
Jokinen, Tracy C. 878
Jolas, Paul M. 844
Joliet, Mariel A. 434
Jolliffe, Lynn 458
Jonas, Howard S. 451
Jonas, Jeff 462
Jonas, Thomas 579
Jones, Boisfeuillet 898
Jones, Charles E. 357
Jones, D. Michael 554
Jones, David A. Jr. 446

Jones, Derek 788
Jones, Douglas (MSC Industrial
    Direct) 602
Jones, Douglas L. (HNI) 436
Jones, Evon L. 539
Jones, Frances 132
Jones, George C. (Rowan
    Companies) 738
Jones, George S. Jr. (Exide) 344
Jones, Ginger M. 688
Jones, Gordon D. 306
Jones, Gregory 796
Jones, Hal S. 898
Jones, Ingrid Saunders 233
Jones, Jane D. 770
Jones, Janice M. 712
Jones, Jill 173
Jones, Joel 929
Jones, Jon C. 722
Jones, Joseph M. 311
Jones, Laura D. 65
Jones, Leslie 600
Jones, Linda 159
Jones, Mary S. 852
Jones, Maurice D. 551
Jones, Nicole S. 221
Jones, Paul W. 95
Jones, Randall T. Sr. 711
Jones, Robert G. 105
Jones, Sidney G. 389
Jones, Stephen J. 53
Jones, Tom 743
Jones, Wilson R. 654
Jonikas, Michael P. 691
Joos, David W. 231
Joppa, Sandra N. 302
Jordan, James L. 417
Jordan, Joe 904
Jordan, Lani 218
Jordan, Raymond 487
Jordan, Robert E. 786
Jordan, Ronald 644
Jorgensen, Blake J. 530
Joseph, Alex A. 274
Joseph, Pamela A. 870
Joseph, Thomas A. (Cincinnati
    Financial) 222
Joseph, Tommy S. (International
    Paper) 466
Josephson, Richard C. 758
Joshi, Vyomesh 430
Josiah, Timothy W. 722
Josuttes, Kenneth 209
Joumas, Greg 477
Jowers, Gaylon M. Jr. 840
Joyce, David L. 385
Joyce, Joseph M. 146
Joyce, Kenneth T. 88
Joyce, R. Todd 902
Joyce, Stephen P. 556
Joyce, Thomas P. (Public Service
    Enterprise Group) 710
Joyce, Thomas P. Jr. (Danaher) 274
Judge, Barry 146
Judge, James J. 639
Judge, Jonathan J. 665
Judge, Stephen 276
Juhlke, David P. 442
Julian, Paul C. 577
Juliano, David A. 238
Julien, David W. 773
Julien, Jeffrey P. 721
Jung, Andrea 121
Jurek, Richard 633
Juster, Andrew A. 774
Justice, Kelly P. 54
Justice, Richard J. 226

K

Kaafarani, Bilal 233
Kabat, Kevin T. 354
Kabureck, Gary R. 927
Kachmer, Mike 551

Noe, Gregory R. 280
Noel, Jeffrey 915
Noethen, Todd A. 148
Nolan, James W. 752
Nolan, Joseph R. Jr. 639
Nolan, Mike 514
Nolan, Paul 571
Nolan, Susan 675
Noland, Thomas J. Jr. 446
Nolden, Dean J. 551
Noll, Eric W. 606
Nollen, Margaret R. 435
Nolop, Bruce P. 340
Nolte, Reed 624
Nonnengard, James B. 724
Noonan, Cathy 594
Noonan, Thomas M. 266
Noonan, William J. 163
Nooyi, Indra K. 672
Norcia, Gerardo 308
Norcross, Jeanne 788
Nordeen, Jon K. 512
Nordin, Beth 218
Nordlund, D. Craig 51
Nordlund, H. Marty 909
Nordstrom, Blake W. 630
Nordstrom, Douglas A. 219
Nordstrom, Erik B. 630
Nordstrom, James F. Jr. 630
Nordstrom, Peter E. 630
Norfleet, Robert G. 478
Norman, John S. 141
Norman, Paul 498
Normile, Robert 566
Norrington, Lorrie M. 320
Norris, Gail 546
Norris, James M. 879
Norris, Jeff 187
Norris, Kim 180
Norris, Paul J. 766
Norris, Suzanne 539
Northenscold, Thomas R. 748
Nortman, Kara 450
Norton, David K. 620
Norton, Larry (Borders Group) 159
Norton, Larry C. (Temple-Inland) 814
Norton, Thomas F. 497
Norwood, Larry 546
Nosbaum, LeRoy D. 473
Nosbusch, Keith D. 735
Nothwang, Joseph R. 426
Novak, Barbara 109
Novak, David C. 932
Novakovic, Phebe N. 383
Novas, Paul D. 817
Novosel, Sarah 184
Nowe, Kevin G. 501
Nowlan, Kevin 109
Nugent, Alan F. 179
Nugent, Kellie 153
Nunez, Craig W. 404
Nunn, Thomas W. 57
Nussbaum, Bennett L. 920
Nussbaum, John L. 688
Nussbaum, Samuel R. 905
Nuti, William R. 616
Nyberg, Neil 498
Nye, C. Howard 561
Nygard, John R. III 526

O

Oakland, Steven T. 483
Oakley, Ronald W. 771
Obeney, Geoffrey J. 820
Oberfeld, Steven J. 772
Oberhelman, Douglas R. 196
Oberland, Gregory C. 636
Oberlander, Michael I. 172
Obermayer, Jeffrey L. 160
Oberton, Karleen 438
Oberton, Willard D. 349
Obrecht, Karl 729
O'Brien, David M. 431

O'Brien, Denis P. 342
O'Brien, Dermot J. 830
O'Brien, Hollis 44
O'Brien, James J. Jr. (Ashland Inc.) 110
O'Brien, James P. (Con Edison) 249
O'Brien, James W. (Vulcan
  Materials) 889
O'Brien, John F. 181
O'Brien, Katherine 619
O'Brien, Louise 327
O'Brien, Michael J. 650
O'Brien, Richard T. 623
O'Brien, Tom 236
O'Bryant, Daniel R. 117
O'Carroll, John 189
O'Connell, Brian 413
O'Connell, Christopher J. 581
O'Connell, Maureen E. 759
O'Connor, David P. 537
O'Connor, Deborah A. 647
O'Connor, Gerald P. 625
O'Connor, James E. 728
O'Connor, Thomas T. 476
O'Connor-Wente, Mary Kay 93
O'Day, Susan 894
O'Day, Terence L. 425
Odeen, Philip A. 45
O'Dell, Julie 405
Odell, Michael R. 667
Odenath, David R. 523
Odland, Steve 646
O'Donnell, James V. 74
O'Donnell, John A. 123
O'Donnell, Lawrence III 899
O'Donnell, Michael W. 628
O'Donnell, Nancy 621
O'Donnell, Terrence 825
O'Dowd, Sarah A. 519
Oehrig, Susan 71
Oesterle, Stephen N. 581
Ogden, Thomas D. 239
Ogilvie, Scott 136
Ogle, William 600
Ognjanov, Cindy J. 884
O'Grady, C. Thomas 255
O'Halleran, Michael D. 96
O'Hanley, Ronald P. 128
O'Hara, C. Scott 434
O'Herron, Felicity 718
Ohman, Daniel Laurence 863
Ohringer, Mark J. 491
Ojakli, Ziad S. 365
Okarma, Jerome D. 489
O'Keefe, Carolyn P. 294
O'Keefe, Colleen 637
O'Keefe, Edward 127
O'Keefe, Jeffrey T. 443
O'Keefe, Mary A. 701
Okeson, Nils H. 908
Okle, Debbie L. 241
Okura, Robert 213
Olanoff, Lawrence S. 366
O'Leary, Christopher D. 386
O'Leary, David C. 797
O'Leary, Edward J. 344
O'Leary, Joseph D. 679
O'Leary, Patrick J. 791
O'Leary, Richard A. 464
Oleksiak, Peter B. 308
Oler, Debra 924
Olin, John A. 408
Olivares, Jose 181
Oliver, David M. 803
Oliver, George R. 848
Oliver, H. Lynn 235
Oliver, Kirk R. 61
Oliver, Robert B. 380
Oliver, Walter M. 383
Olivera, Armando J. 373
Olivera, Chris 378
Olivier, Leon J. 632
Olivo, Maria 843
Olli, Amy F. 179
Olmsted, Peter J. 382
Olsen, Dave 794

Olsen, John J. 587
Olsen, Karla 911
Olsen, Michael S. 492
Olsen, Stephen 358
Olson, James 869
Olson, Jon A. 928
Olson, R. Casey 645
Olson, Robert E. 298
Olson, Tim 88
Olson, W. Kregg 97
Olsovsky, Jo-ann M. 177
O'Malley, James A. 173
O'Malley, Patrick J. 764
Oman, Mark C. 906
O'Mealia, Harry 523
O'Meara, Vicki A. 686
Omidyar, Pierre M. 320
Omtvedt, Craig P. 367
O'Neal, Leslie K. 814
O'Neale, Rosalyn T. 185
O'Neil, Scott M. 180
O'Neill, Finbarr J. 575
O'Neill, Jack 191
O'Neill, James R. 635
O'Neill, Sean P. 331
O'Neill, Thomas P. 537
O'Neill, Una 179
O'Neill Odum, Eileen 628
Onetto, Marc 69
Ong, Vincent 144
Onorato, Gianni 193
Onuscheck, Michael 162
Oosterveer, P.W.B. 360
Oppenheimer, Peter 99
Oprins, Michael 159
O'Quinn, William L. Jr. 65
Orcutt, Kim D. 192
Ordemann, William 333
O'Reilly, David J. 215
O'Reilly, James F. 274
Orlando, David 443
Ornstein, Lawrence H. 427
O'Rourke, Lori 539
Orr, M. Alan 421
Orr, Michael D. 389
Orr, Robert S. 491
Ortenstone, Susan B. 324
Orthwein, Peter B. 829
Osanloo, Michael 515
Osborn, William A. 633
Osborne, Robert S. 388
Osbourn, Joseph A. 811
O'Shanna, Richard J. 605
O'Shaughnessy, Lizbeth S. 798
O'Shea, John 811
O'Shea, William J. 185
Osterberg, Mark W. 55
Ostermann, Michael 344
Ostrander, Jane 817
O'Sullivan, Michael B. 737
Oswalt, David S. 762
Otellini, Paul S. 461
Otis, Clarence Jr. 276
Ott, Richard A. 334
Otte, Pat 589
Ottensmeyer, Patrick J. 496
Ottersgård, Lars 606
Otting, Joseph M. 870
Otty, Mark 337
Ouimette, Bern 878
Ouwerkerk, Mike 884
Overton, David 213
Overton, Richard S. 366
Owczarczak, Jack 720
Owen, Diane B. 435
Owen, John B. (Regions Financial) 724
Owen, John F. (Avon) 121
Owen, Kathleen L. 866
Owen, Marc E. 577
Owenby, Johnny A. 417
Owens, B. Craig 185
Owens, Betsy 767
Owens, Christine M. 856
Owens, George J. 770
Owens, Jack B. 314

Owens, James W. 196
Owens, Richard W. 503
Owens, Robert W. 801
Owens, Tom 223
Owens, William A. 202
Ownjazayeri, Vahid 771
Oyinlola, H. Sola 757
Ozan, Kevin M. 574
Ozzie, Ray 590

P

Pace, Louis M. 141
Pacheco, Brad W. 184
Pacheco, Maximo 466
Pacheco, Steve 352
Paci, Frank G. 661
Pacioni, Mark R. 593
Packebush, Steve 511
Packer, Karla L. 456
Padden, Preston 894
Padgett, Cindy M. 649
Padgett, Pamela 411
Padovani, Roberto 714
Pagano, James J. Jr. 474
Page, Ashley M. 452
Page, Gregory R. 189
Page, Larry E. 399
Pagnutti, Lou P. 337
Pai, Satish 757
Paiano, Robert 413
Pain, George H. 648
Paiva, Roger D. 392
Pajor, Charlie 605
Pajot, Gilles V. J. 456
Pakenham, Barry E. 61
Pakis, Val A. 546
Palacios, Fernando J. 520
Paladini, Lapo 673
Paladino, Steven 422
Palen, Gregory R. 691
Palensky, Frederick J. 26
Palermino, Debra A. 563
Palermo, James P. 128
Paliwal, Dinesh C. 410
Palkovic, Michael W. 295
Palm, Gregory K. 395
Palmer, Anthony J. 504
Palmer, Douglas 29
Palmer, James F. 635
Palmer, Kay J. 479
Palmer, Mark A. 806
Palmiere, Vince 606
Palmisano, Samuel J. 462
Palmore, Roderick A. 386
Palmquist, Mark 218
Palmucci, Mark 159
Paloian, John R. 742
Palumbo, John 85
Pambianchi, Christine M. 258
Pampel, Jochen 514
Panagos, Gregory S. 842
Panattoni, Lisa 297
Panayotopoulos, E. Dimitri 702
Pandit, Vikram S. 227
Panega, Andrew B. 742
Pangalos, Menelas 680
Pannier, David R. 457
Pant, Micky 932
Pantaleoni, Anthony D. 266
Paoletti, Stephen E. 405
Paolucci, Mike 430
Papa, John A. 487
Papa, Joseph C. 676
Papa, Mark S. 334
Papermaster, Mark 99
Papich, Kim 473
Pappacena, Edgardo 699
Pappas, Callie 758
Pappas, William D. 65
Pappert, Gerald J. 205
Paradie, Terrance M. 228
Paradiso, Dan 760
Paranicas, Dean J. 138

Pardee, Charles M. 342
Pardun, Thomas E. 912
Paren, Dennis A. 65
Parent, Louise M. 77
Parham, David J. 370
Park, Dennis S. 525
Park, Hyun 682
Park, John (IAC) 450
Park, John J. (Hewitt Associates) 428
Park, Laure E. 715
Parker, Dave 877
Parker, Herbert K. 410
Parker, James J. (Caterpillar) 196
Parker, James T. (WellPoint) 905
Parker, Jan 531
Parker, Jayne 894
Parker, John G. (Ford Motor) 365
Parker, John R. Jr. (Coca-Cola
    Enterprises) 235
Parker, Mark G. 626
Parker, P. W. 870
Parker, Patti 511
Parker, Ronald C. 672
Parker, Stuart 873
Parker, Todd 904
Parker, W. Douglas 869
Parkinson, Robert L. Jr. 131
Parlapiano, Donna 115
Parneros, Demos 792
Parodi, Dennis R. 74
Parrell, Mark J. 336
Parrish, Charles S. 821
Parrish, D. Michael 640
Parry, David C. 453
Parry, Matthew E. 909
Parry, Michael 329
Parry, Timothy R. 417
Parsky, Barbara J. 322
Parsons, Richard D. 227
Parsons, Steve 731
Parsonson, Greg 811
Parthasarathy, Rekha 458
Partridge, John M. (Visa Inc) 886
Partridge, John W. Jr. (NiSource) 628
Parulekar, Suneil V. 610
Parvarandeh, Pirooz 567
Pasha, Ahmed 45
Passa, Lester M. 268
Passerini, Filippo 702
Passig, Theodore O. 237
Passmore, Malinda G. 241
Pastor, Frederick Jr. 710
Pastore, Fred C. 568
Pate, Thomas R. 264
Patel, Ashvinkumar 929
Patel, Kalendu 146
Patel, Kiran M. 468
Patel, Manesh 751
Patel, Sanjay J. 813
Patel, Sunit S. 529
Paterson, John 462
Patineau, Paula J. 66
Patrick, George W. 82
Patrick, Stephen C. 236
Patricot, Hubert 235
Patsalos-Fox, Michael 578
Pattakos, Gregory 719
Pattee, Russell S. 697
Patterson, Chaka 342
Patterson, Dennis M. 802
Patterson, Douglas E. 678
Patterson, Elaine 648
Patterson, James 790
Patterson, Neal L. 206
Patterson, Samuel R. 689
Patterson, Suzanne D. 235
Patterson, Vernon L. 503
Patterson, William D. (American
    Water) 82
Patterson, William J. (Calpine) 184
Patton, Charles R. 75
Patton, Donald V. Jr. 31
Patton, Michael C. 401
Patton, Robert J. 531
Paugh, Laura E. 556

Paukovits, Timothy J. 694
Paul, Gerald 887
Paul, Matt T. 308
Paul, Steven M. 326
Pauley, Lisa A. 126
Paulin, Jan C. 638
Paull, Mitchell S. 30
Paulsen, Larry N. 685
Paulsen, Teresa 244
Pavelka, Darrel J. 237
Paver, Howard 427
Paver, Robert L. 476
Pavletich, Kristi 142
Pawl, Steve 621
Pawlowski, Brian 617
Paylor, Craig E. 654
Payne, James F. X. 136
Payne, Richard B. Jr. 870
Payne, Timothy D. 601
Payne, Tommy J. 730
Paz, George 345
Pazzani, John 832
Peace, N. Brian 543
Peach, Richard D. 758
Peacock, Russell M. 927
Peacock, S. Wayne 873
Pearce, Randy L. 725
Pearce, William D. 281
Pearl, Michael C. 90
Pearl, Suzanne J. 884
Pearson, Diana 560
Pearson, Harriet P. 462
Pease, Bob 610
Pease, Kendell M. 384
Peck, Arthur 381
Peck, Darcie 456
Peck, Patricia A. 364
Peck, Tom 530
Peckskamp, Daniel H. 664
Peconi, Maurice V. 693
Peden, Keith J. 722
Pedersen, Brandon S. 57
Pedersen, Robert J. 872
Pedowitz, Mark 33
Pedtke, Richard F. 457
Peebles, Robert M. 865
Peel, Michael A. 386
Peerman, Allyson 44
Peetz, Karen B. 128
Peevy, Mary DeClark 182
Pefanis, Harry N. 687
Pego, Margaret M. 710
Peigh, Terry D. 467
Peirez, Joshua L. 564
Peiros, Lawrence S. 230
Pekarsky, John R. 438
Peleo-Lazar, Marlena 574
Pelini, Richard A. 527
Pellegrino, Kathleen 446
Pellerito, Thomas J. 443
Pence, Robin 380
Pendergast, Rich 719
Pendergrass, Jennifer 294
Penegor, Todd 498
Peng, Victor 928
Penn, Loretta A. 789
Penner, Kim 511
Penno, Roberto 370
Penrose, Sheila A. 491
Pensabene, Gregory M. 90
Penzkofer, Brett 109
Peper, Cheri L. 97
Pepicello, William 98
Pepper, John E. Jr. (Disney) 894
Pepper, Jon L. (Hess Corporation) 427
Pepping, Karen K. 625
Pera, Antonio R. 85
Peranton, Richard L. 800
Pereira, Bill 451
Perello, Joseph 557
Perelman, Ronald O. 547, 729
Peressutti, Gian-Carlo 742
Perez, Arnaldo M. 318
Perez, Arnaldo 193
Perez, Derek 641

Perez, Peter M. 244
Perez, Roberto 659
Perez de Alonso, Marcela 430
Peribere, Jerome A. 305
Perich, Cecile K. 571
Perier, Francis I. Jr. 366
Periquito, Paulo F. M. O. 915
Perkins, Bruce 446
Perkins, David 594
Perkins, Jerry F. Jr. 889
Perkins, Kenneth J. 857
Perlin, Gary L. 186
Perlin, Jonathan B. 415
Perlitz, Thomas J. 266
Perlman, Beth S. 252
Perlmutter, David 461
Perlmutter, Roger M. 86
Peros, Jim 294
Perot, Ross Jr. (Perot Systems) 675
Perot, Ross Sr. (Perot Systems) 675
Perretta, Christopher 797
Perricone, Jaye D. 679
Perrin, Charles R. 896
Perrone, Frank 508
Perrott, Pam 554
Perry, Beverly L. 668
Perry, Dianne 926
Perry, James E. 844
Perry, Larry W. 173
Perry, M. Marnette 516
Perry, Marie L. 167
Perry, Mike 405
Perry, Scott R. 247
Pershing, John 146
Person, Steve 878
Perushek, Mary Lynne 302
Peruzzi, James 142
Pesce, William J. 486
Pesci, Robert A. 765
Pesicka, Edward A. 826
Petaja, Glen 659
Peter, Jennifer 410
Peters, Charles A. 330
Peters, Frank T. 592
Peters, Jill 213
Peters, Jon D. 683
Peters, Kevin A. 646
Peters, Lauren B. 364
Peters, Lisa B. 128
Peters, Mary Ellen 553
Peters, Robert 538
Peters, Scott 724
Peters, Susan P. 385
Peters, William E. 476
Peterson, Bruce D. 308
Peterson, Carl 201
Peterson, Eric (Home Depot) 439
Peterson, Eric H. (Blockbuster
    Inc.) 153
Peterson, Glen A. 764
Peterson, Greg 50
Peterson, Mark 242
Peterson, Randall B. 768
Peterson, Terry D. 286
Peterzalek, John T. 206
Petit, Marc 112
Petitt, Anthony B. 915
Petrakian, Raja 928
Petrarca, Mark A. 95
Petrella, Vincent K. 535
Petren, Carol Ann 221
Petrides, Yiannis 669
Petrolino, Michael 526
Petrovich, Dushan 557
Petruccelli, Charles 77
Petrucci, Laurie J. 364
Petruska, Steven C. 712
Petters, C. Michael 635
Petterson, David S. 259
Petterson, John S. 831
Pettet, Bruce 237
Pettus, Randy 749
Peugh, David B. 105
Pew, Robert C. III 798
Pezalla, Edmund J. 46

Pfaff, Mark W. 619
Pfanzelter, David 498
Pforzheimer, Harry 468
Phalen, James S. 797
Phelan, David C. 797
Phelan, William K. 510, 767
Phelps, R. Michael 678
Philbert, Rebecca 29
Philbin, Robert J. 841
Philips, Brian D. 352
Philips, Jeremy 624
Phillips, Barnet IV 775
Phillips, Brenda 554
Phillips, Charles E. Jr. 653
Phillips, Chip 271
Phillips, David P. 711
Phillips, Diana 783
Phillips, Doug 501
Phillips, Gregory A. 652
Phillips, Hank 115
Phillips, James M. 604
Phillips, John 491
Phillips, Nancy R. 354
Phillips, Randy E. 243
Phillips, Stephen R. 120
Philo, Ross 872
Phipps, P. Cody 860
Phipps, Scott 821
Piacentini, Diego 69
Piano, Phyllis J. 86
Piasecki, Matthew 886
Piatt, Rodney L. 603
Picard, Jean-Paul 284
Pichette, Patrick 399
Pick, Ted 599
Pickard, Frank C. III 883
Pickens, David T. 276
Pickering, Thomas R. 157
Piechoski, Michael J. 678
Pierce, Larry 788
Pierce, Leslie A. 292
Pierson, Alan 520
Pietrok, Gary 678
Piggott, Julie A. 177
Pignone, Marty F. 781
Pigott, Mark C. 658
Pike, Thomas H. 36
Pilch, Samuel H. 67
Pileggi, Dominic J. 828
Pileggi, Jennifer W. 254
Piligian, Georgette A. 586
Pillai, Hari 751
Pillsbury, Donaldson C. 783
Pilnick, Gary H. 498
Pilon, Lawrence J. 924
Pilon, Nathalie 828
Pimentel, Albert A. 569
Pimentel, Armando Jr. 372
Pimentel, Larry 739
Pinchuk, Nicholas T. 779
Pineci, Roy 645
Pinkston, Arnold A. 137
Pinneo, Jeffrey D. 57
Pinto, Mark R. 102
Pintoff, Craig A. 857
Pion, Jeffrey S. 198
Pipes, J. David 908
Pipes, Tommy 502
Piraino, Thomas A. Jr. 662
Pirog, Christine R. 139
Pirri, Sue 112
Pirro, Judith A. 93
Pisarczyk, Richard V. 347
Pistell, Timothy K. 662
Piszel, Anthony S. 355
Pittenger, John C. 511
Pitts, James F. 635
Pitts, Ronald E. 360
Pizzarro, Pedro J. 322
Pizzuto, Terri A. 445
Plack, Joseph 122
Plaeger, Frederick J. II 334
Plaisance, Melissa D. 746
Plaisance, Morrison R. 291
Plank, Roger B. 97

Shelnitz, Mark A. 923
Shelton, David E. 543
Shelton, Michael W. 329
Shelton, Todd 860
Shepard, Kathy 434
Shepard, Tom 886
Shephard, Daniel G. 561
Shepherd, Danny R. 889
Sherbin, Robert 641
Sheridan, Diane L. 53
Sheridan, Jerry E. 84
Sheridan, Joseph 890
Sheridan, Phil 733
Sheridan, William S. 783
Sherin, Keith S. 385
Sherman, Bethany 606
Sherman, Carol 716
Sherman, Jeffrey S. 138
Sherman, Scott A. 53
Sherr, Richard 836
Sherrard, Roger S. 662
Sherrill, Gregg M. 817
Sherry, Ann C. 193
Sherry, Peter J. Jr. 365
Sherwin, John E. 673
Sherwood, Michael S. 395
Shevchik, Joan O. 222
Shewmake, Charles W. 177
Shiba, Wendy C. 497
Shick, Eric J. 263
Shields, Brian J. 589
Shields, Gerald W. 49
Shields, Kenneth A. 721
Shields, Natalie A. 152
Shiely, John S. 164
Shiely, Vincent R. Jr. 164
Shilen, Thomas S. Jr. 752
Shilgalis, Joseph 813
Shilobrit, Tracy 552
Shin, Hak Cheol 26
Shipp, Earl 305
Shipps, David H.W. Sr. 315
Shirley, Brian M. 589
Shirley, Edward D. 702
Shivamber, Leon V. 411
Shivdasani, Raju M. 547
Shiver, Allen L. 359
Shivery, Charles W. 632
Shives, Paula J. 276
Shoaf, N.B. Forrest 264
Shoback, Robert G. 71
Shoemaker, Leslie L. 822
Shoemaker, Rodney A. 92
Shoen, Edward J. 72
Shoen, James P. 72
Shoen, Mark V. 72
Shoenfeld, David B. 872
Shoop, Randall A. 632
Shoquist, Debora C. 641
Shor, Michael L. 194
Shore, Brian K. 917
Short, Michael J. 115
Shoshani, Ziv 887
Shrader, Patricia B. 138
Shriner, Steven P. 802
Shroff, Jal S. 369
Shroyer, John L. 66
Shudtz, Peter J. 268
Shugar, Shelton 929
Shuler, Dennis W. 894
Shull, Dan 159
Shull, Dave 298
Shull, William 667
Shulman, Becky S. 406
Shultz, Martin L. 684
Shuma, Douglas D. 812
Shuman, Jeffrey S. 411
Shusterich, Fred L. 308
Siciliano, Daniel R. 465
Sickler, Doug 675
Sicree, Joseph R. 837
Siddall, David L. 90
Sidebottom, Peter 810
Siegel, Jay P. 487
Siegel, Kenneth S. 795

Siegel, Laurie A. 848
Siegel, Stephen B. 198
Siegmund, Jan 114
Siekierka, Nathan G. 243
Sievertsen, Jennifer 522
Sieving, Charles E. 372
Sigal, Elliott 169
Signorelli, Ivan 402
Sihilling, Calvin S. 607
Sihota, Bhupinder S. 152
Sikkel, J. Pieter 65
Silberman, Mitch 451
Silk, Arthur T. Jr. 150
Siluk, Linda M. 93
Silva, Brian A. 705
Silva, Ken 880
Silveira, William C. 583
Silver, Beth 560
Silverman, Barry J. 562
Silverman, Bruce 916
Silverman, Josh 320
Silverstein, Stanley P. 896
Silvestri, Scott 127
Sim, Judith 653
Simm, Daryl D. 651
Simmons, Harris H. 934
Simmons, Irina 327
Simmons, J. Matt Jr. 694
Simmons, Janelle N. 533
Simmons, Sabrina 381
Simmons, Wayne R. 715
Simon, Allen J. 201
Simon, David 774
Simon, Herbert 774
Simon, John R. 682
Simon, William S. 893
Simone, Thomas B. 855
Simonich, Pete 694
Simons, Doyle R. 814
Simonsen, Knut 308
Simpkins, Frank P. 501
Simpson, Murray L. 374
Simpson, Robert G. 899
Simpson, Shelley 479
Simpson, Stacy 450
Simpson, W. Marshall 655
Sims, Frank L. 189
Sims, John D. 62
Sims, Michael 216
Sims, Paula J. 703
Sims, Randy D. 206
Sinay, Jim 232
Sinclair, Charles L. 398
Sinclair, Robert P. Jr. 30
Sinegal, James D. 259
Singer, Bradley E. 297
Singer, Jim 722
Singer, Lowell 894
Singh, D. K. 244
Singh, Harmit J. 449
Singh, Kanwalinder 714
Singh, Manjit 216
Singh, Piyush K. 78
Singh, Vijay 694
Singleton, John A. 34
Siniscalchi, Patric 119
Sinkey, Jeffrey 34
Sipia, Joseph A. Jr. 220
Sipla, Gregory T. 656
Sipling, Philip J. 561
Siracusa, Paul A. 220
Sirkin, Allen E. 683
Sisco, Robby D. 181
Sisco, Robynne D. 880
Sisson, Kevin 766
Sistovaris, Violet G. 628
Siverd, Robert J. 382
Size, Robert J. 288
Sizemore, Carolyn T. 268
Skaggs, Robert C. Jr. 628
Skarie, David P. 720
Skelly, Peter G. 744
Skinner, James A. 574
Skirvin, Michael 836
Sklarsky, Frank S. 318

Skoog, Christopher R. 333, 652
Skornicki, Eliezer 241
Skove, David J. 705
Skowronski, Walter E. 157
Skredsvig, Janice 658
Skröder, Christian E. 846
Slabinski, Megan 733
Slacik, Charles P. 137
Slacik, Claudia 494
Slack, Henry R. 820
Slager, Donald W. 728
Slangen, Louis F. J. 470
Slark, Martin P. 593
Slater, Mark K. 458
Slater, Todd A. 648
Slavsky, Allan 902
Slevin, Eileen T. 619
Sleyster, Scott 707
Slifstein, Barry M. 741
Slight, Nikke 897
Slipsager, Henrik C. 35
Sloan, Carolyn C. 814
Sloan, Pat 650
Sloan, Robert D. 332
Slomann, Cheryl M. 213
Slone, Deck S. 105
Slone, Reuben E. 647
Sloup, Nicole R. 237
Slump, David 410
Slusser, Sarah 45
Sluzewski, James A. 548
Sly, Lynne D. 507
Sly, Patrick J. 330
Small, Clay G. 672
Smart, Gary 904
Smart, George M. 357
Smart, Jill B. 36
Smeltser, Jeremy W. 791
Smette, Darryl G. 289
Smid, Michael J. 931
Smiley, Keith R. 741
Smisek, Jeffery A. 253
Smit, Neil 212
Smith, Alan E. 390
Smith, Alfred J. III 55
Smith, Anthony H. 826
Smith, Arthur E. Jr. 628
Smith, Barbara R. 392
Smith, Bill 637
Smith, Brad D. (Intuit) 468
Smith, Bradford L. (Microsoft) 591
Smith, Bruce A. 821
Smith, Catherine R. 378
Smith, Craig R. 655
Smith, Daniel D. (Norfolk Southern) 631
Smith, Daniel L. (Raytheon) 722
Smith, David A. (PSS World Medical) 708
Smith, David F. (National Fuel Gas) 608
Smith, David J. (ADM) 106
Smith, Dennis I. 828
Smith, Donald G. (Family Dollar Stores) 348
Smith, Donnie (Tyson Foods) 849
Smith, Douglas G. (Tetra Tech) 822
Smith, Douglas H. (Timken) 835
Smith, Earl B. 820
Smith, Eli 771
Smith, Elizabeth (Perot Systems) 675
Smith, Elizabeth A. (Avon) 121
Smith, Frederick W. 352
Smith, Gordon A. 494
Smith, Gregory L. 244
Smith, Ike 502
Smith, Jack A. (Medco Health) 580
Smith, James L. (Adams Resources) 39
Smith, Jeffrey E. (BJ Services) 149
Smith, Jeffry S. (Brinker) 167
Smith, Jim (Cooper Tire & Rubber) 257
Smith, Joanne C. 432
Smith, John F. Jr. (General Motors) 388
Smith, Keith E. 163

Smith, Kenneth M. (Hilton Hotels) 433
Smith, Kenneth T. (Family Dollar Stores) 348
Smith, Larry T. 35
Smith, Lee 88
Smith, Linda J. 899
Smith, Lucinda B. 50
Smith, M. Lazane 854
Smith, Mark W. (Spherion) 789
Smith, Marschall I. (3M) 26
Smith, Matthew P. 649
Smith, Maura Abeln 466
Smith, Michael (CNA Financial) 232
Smith, Michael K. (NACCO Industries) 604
Smith, Michael R. (Publix) 711
Smith, Michelle 130
Smith, Mike (State Farm) 796
Smith, Paul 530
Smith, Peter C. 176
Smith, Quincy 199
Smith, Randy 849
Smith, Richard F. (Equifax) 335
Smith, Richard J. (Entergy) 332
Smith, Richard M. (CarMax) 192
Smith, Richard M. (Washington Post) 898
Smith, Rodney A. 92
Smith, Roger C. 838
Smith, Roland C. 908
Smith, Roy 272
Smith, Sandford D. 390
Smith, Sarah E. 395
Smith, Scott (Temple-Inland) 814
Smith, Scott C. (Genuine Parts) 389
Smith, Sherry M. 803
Smith, Stacy J. 461
Smith, Stephen F. (SYSCO) 806
Smith, Stephen J. (American Greetings) 79
Smith, Stephen M. (John Wiley) 486
Smith, Stephen P. (NiSource) 628
Smith, Susan T. (Hyatt) 449
Smith, Susette (W. R. Grace) 923
Smith, Tad 180
Smith, Timothy A. 278
Smith, Travis 484
Smith, W. David Jr. 828
Smithart-Oglesby, Debra 287
Smits, Jim 803
Smolenski, Eric M. 922
Smolik, Brent J. 324
Smoller, David A. 773
Smorey-Giger, Marcy 910
Smothers, Frederick W. 730
Smucker, Mark T. 483
Smucker, Richard K. 483
Smucker, Timothy P. 483
Smul, Spencer G. 339
Smyth, D. Edward I. 575
Smyth, Kevin 206
Smyth, Margaret M. 862
Smyth, Russell P. 406
Smyth, Thomas M. 54
Snape, Allan J. 367
Sneed, Norris P. 316
Sneed, Thomas K. 553
Snell, Mark A. 768
Snively, David F. 596
Snook, Jonathan D. 89
Snow, David B. Jr. 580
Snow, Marissa 777
Snowden, Joseph I. 697
Snyder, Burton H. 425
Snyder, Carole B. 357
Snyder, Daniel D. 730
Snyder, Gail G. 611
Snyder, Holly 611
Snyder, James C. Jr. 348
Snyder, Michael I. 837
Snyder, Tobi 490
Snyder, Troy 829
Snyder, William F. 442
Soares, Britaldo 45
Sobic, Daniel D. 658

Sobin, Carole 249
Socia, Robert E. 388
Sockwell, Allen 44
Socolow, Ellen 249
Soder, Christopher L. 698
Soderberg, Donald L. 787
Soderberg, Peter H. 432
Sodhani, Arvind 461
Soffe, Loretta 630
Sofio, Kenneth C. 258
Sohn, Harold L. 126
Sokolov, Richard S. 774
Sola, Jure 751
Solcher, Stephen B. 154
Soll, Bruce A. 533
Solomon, Darlene J. 51
Solomon, David F. 366
Solomon, Howard 366
Solomon, J. Stuart 76
Solomon, Joanne 88
Solomon, Larry 111
Solso, Theodore M. 269
Soltani, Peter K. 438
Somasegar, Sivaramakichenane 591
Somasundaram, Sivasankaran 303
Somerman, Mimi 155
Somers, Erin S. 550
Somers, John A. 830
Somma, Anthony D. 911
Sompolski, Timothy A. 467
Sondeno, Dudley J. 787
Sonders, Elizabeth Ann 210
Song, Jane J. 748
Soni, Paul J. 736
Sonkin, Mitchell I. 568
Sonnemaker, Scott A. 806
Sonnenberg, Steven A. 330
Sonsteby, Charles M. 167
Sood, Arvind K. 86
Sopp, Mark W. 747
Soranno-Keating, Valerie 77
Sorensen, Norman R. 701
Sorenson, Arne M. 556
Sorenson, Rob 192
Sorenson, Steven P. 67
Sorsby, J. Larry 443
Soto, Peter 921
Sotomayor, Jess 294
Sotos, Christopher S. 638
Soumbasakis, John 458
Southam, Arthur M. 495
Souvenir, Carole 583
Sova, Gary L. 728
Sovern, Michael I. 783
Sowder, Eric D. 543
Sowers, C. Martin 348
Sowinski, Ronald A. 101
Spafford, Jeffrey P. 649
Spagnoletti, Joseph C. 185
Spak, Deborah 131
Spangler, James K. 817
Spann, Carol 876
Sparby, David M. 925
Speak, Steven C. 272
Specter, Eric M. 211
Spector, Gerald A. 336
Spector, Joseph M. 164
Speer, David B. 453
Speese, Mark E. 726
Speidel, Stephen A. 460
Speirs, Jim 916
Spence, Jean E. 515
Spence, Kenneth F. III 843
Spence, Roy M. Jr. 650
Spence, William H. 694
Spencer, Jan B. 504
Spencer, Robert S. 122
Spencer, Stuart A. 219
Spencer, Terry K. 652
Spendlove, G. Scott 821
Sperling, John G. 98
Sperling, Peter V. 98
Spicer, Jim 848
Spierkel, Gregory M.E. 458
Spinella, Patricia A. 138

Spinelli, Francesca M. 679
Spinelli, Tony 335
Spinner, Steven L. 855
Spiro, Richard G. 219
Spitler, Kenneth F. 806
Splinter, Michael R. 102
Spornhauer, Tod P. 155
Spragg, Gregory E. 893
Sprague, Charles W. 358
Spratlen, Susan A. 685
Spratt, Randall N. 577
Spring, Shellee K. 206
Springer, Beth 230
Springman, Paul J. (Equifax) 335
Springman, Paul W. (Markel) 554
Sprinkle, Steve 314
Sproat, David P. 664
Sproule, Michael E. 619
Sprunk, Eric D. 626
Spurgeon, William W. 303
Squeri, Stephen 77
Squires, James A. 631
Squires, Nelson 53
St. Clair, Joyce 633
St. Dennis, Thomas 102
Stacey, John 410
Stacey, Neil H. 679
Stachiw, Mark A. 587
Stachtiaris, Alexander G. 826
Stadler, Mary K. 496
Staes, Charles W. 806
Stafford, Henry 74
Stafford, Raymond 366
Staggs, Thomas O. 894
Stakel, John 734
Staley, James E. 494
Stall, John A. 373
Stallings, Don T. 543
Stalnecker, Susan M. 312
Stam, Heidi 879
Stamps, Jeffrey M. 649
Stanage, Nick L. 273
Stanczak, William J. 84
Standefer, W. Steven 434
Standish, Thomas R. 200
Standke, Thomas 443
Standley, John T. 731
Stanislav, Martin T. 541
Stanley, Adam 96
Stanley, John 53
Stansik, James G. 301
Stanski, Bruce A. 360
Stanton, Jill 626
Stanton, Joe 250
Stanton, Matt 367
Stanutz, Nicholas G. 448
Staples, Cathy Odom 141
Staples, David M. 788
Starcher, Diana L. 906
Stark, Andrew R. 671
Stark, Arthur 139
Stark, David 596
Stark, Mark 414
Stark, Ronald J. 54
Starkey, Russell B. Jr. 874
Starkey, Talia 822
Starks, Daniel J. 748
Starling, David L. 496
Starnes, Clarke R. III 132
Starr, Loren M. 471
Starr, Rogers F. 478
Starrett, Dave 583
Stata, Ray 91
Staten, Reesa M. 733
Staton, Jimmy D. 628
Statton, Tim 136
Staub, Julie 115
Staubach, Roger T. 491
Stausboll, Anne 184
Stautberg, Timothy E. 341
Stavros, Christopher G. 645
Stawski, Ann 654
Stead, Tatiana 187
Steakley, Joseph N. 415
Stebbins, Paul H. 921

Stec, Stanley 491
Stecher, Esta E. 395
Stecher, Kenneth W. 222
Stecher, Paul W. 734
Stecher, Steven M. 247
Steed, Richard E. 734
Steele, C. David 105
Steele, Elisa 929
Steele, Gordon 621
Steele, John J. (Werner Enterprises) 909
Steele, John M. (HCA) 415
Steele, Milton 362
Steele, Robert A. 702
Steer, Robert L. 762
Steere, William C. Jr. 680
Steeves, Frank L. 330
Stein, Bradley 739
Stein, J. C. 427
Stein, Jay A. 438
Stein, Ken 162
Stein, Kevin M. 697
Stein, Laura 230
Stein, Mark J. 450
Steinberg, Gregory M. 80
Steinberg, Julian M. 546
Steiner, David P. 899
Steiner, Gerald A. 596
Steiner, Lisa P. 173
Steinhafel, Gregg W. 808
Steinhorn, Jeff L. 427
Steinke, Bruce 73
Steinkrauss, Mark A. 812, 858
Steinmetz, Mike 552
Steinour, Stephen D. 448
Stellato, Louis E. 772
Stenger, Edward J. 273
Stephan, Michael J. 115
Stephen, Craig A. 217
Stephens, Jay B. 722
Stephens, John J. 111
Stephens, Patrick A. 857
Stephens, Richard D. 157
Stephens, Thomas G. 388
Stephenson, Kent R. 313
Stephenson, Randall L. 111
Sterbenz, Douglas R. 911
Sterkenburg, Albert 288
Sterling, Tim 820
Stern, Colin D. 211
Stern, James F. 95
Stern, John 855
Stern, Michael 596
Stern, Rick 705
Stern, Robert E. 158
Stern, William 560
Sternad, Ken 856
Sternblitz, David H. 933
Sternschein, Evan 297
Sterrett, Stephen E. 774
Stetz, Gordon M. Jr. 571
Steuert, D. Michael 360
Steuterman, James M. 837
Stevens, Anne L. 194
Stevens, Charles R. 909
Stevens, Donald B. 659
Stevens, Matthew 316
Stevens, Robert J. 541
Stevens, Simon 863
Stevens, Thomas C. 503
Stevens, William J. 389
Steward, Larry E. 308
Stewart, James W. 149
Stewart, Jason 450
Stewart, Jonathan T. 561
Stewart, Julia A. 294
Stewart, Kenneth S. 322
Stewart, Laurie K. 53
Stewart, Marta R. (Norfolk Southern) 631
Stewart, Martha (Martha Stewart Living) 560
Stewart, Michael (McKinsey & Company) 578
Stewart, Michael K. (Marathon Oil) 553

Stewart, Michael R. (Perrigo) 676
Stewart, Shelley Jr. 848
Stewart, Timothy M. 712
Stice, J. Michael 214
Stickler, Randall G. 448
Stiehl, William G. 397
Stiles, Mark W. 844
Still, Debra W. 712
Still, Jay P. 685
Stinnett, Donald W. 415
Stinnett, Wayne D. 200
Stinson, Kenneth E. 678
Stinson, Mark 839
Stiritz, William P. 720
Stitt, Skip 48
Stobb, Patrick 398
Stock, Alan W. 223
Stock, Keith 830
Stockdale, Bryan K. 730
Stockdale, Caroline 897
Stockton, Bryan G. 566
Stockwell, Meri 188
Stoddart, William J. 654
Stoe, George P. 922
Stoeckert, George I. 311
Stoering, Mark 925
Stoessl, Michael A. 255
Stoffel, Robert E. 856
Stoffels, Paul 487
Stolar, Kathleen S. 474
Stolarczyk, Mark 588
Stoll, Mark R. 605
Stoller, Stuart P. 620
Stone, Carolyn J. 313
Stone, Douglas M. 820
Stone, Frank 141
Stone, Jeffrey M. 703
Stone, Larry D. 543
Stone, Mark A. 933
Stone, Rob 758
Stone, Steven M. 543
Stoneburner, Charles P. II 222
Stonestreet, Kate 122
Storey, Jeffrey K. 529
Stork, Hans 102
Stortz, Thomas C. 529
Story, Christopher A. 242
Story, Susan N. 784
Stotlar, Douglas W. 254
Stott, John 106
Stoupa, Ronald J. 667
Stouse, Mark 154
Stovall, Ron 77
Stover, Mitchell L. 808
Stowe, Martin 665
Strable, Deanna D. 701
Straka, Angeline C. 199
Strand, Jani 74
Strangfeld, John R. Jr. 707
Stransky, John E. 175
Strassler, Marc A. 731
Stratman, R. Joseph 640
Stratton, Jeffrey P. 574
Stratton, John G. 882
Straub, Terrence D. 859
Straube, David 36
Strauss, Christianne L. 386
Strauss, Mark F. 82
Strayer, Jacqueline F. 489
Streit, Paula 733
Strenkert, Arthur L. 329
Strianese, Michael T. 518
Strickland, D. Chad 30
Strickland, Robert L. (FMR) 363
Strickland, Robert S. (Wells Fargo) 906
Strigl, Dennis F. 882
Strobel, Russ M. 625
Stroh, Rosa C. 425
Strohm, Bruce C. 336
Strohmaier, Debra 402
Stromberg, William J. 807
Stromquist, Gary D. 531
Strong, Michael J. 198
Strong, Wendi E. 873
Stropes, David W. 177

Wolgemuth, Richard L. 169
Wolin, Neal S. 413
Wolpert, Stephen M. 175
Womack, C. Suzanne 537
Womack, Christopher C. 784
Womack, Michael A. 225
Wong, Arthur W. 805
Wong, Denise K. 891
Wong, Francis 788
Wong, Julie 610
Wong, K. Y. 44
Wong, Mike 750
Wood, Benjamin W. 736
Wood, Cliff 192
Wood, E. Jenner III 802
Wood, Elizabeth 896
Wood, Graham R. 362
Wood, Joseph W. 172
Wood, Michael J. 722
Wood, Roger J. 160
Wood, Stephen W. 298
Woodall, James C. 49
Woodall, Terry D. 738
Woodard, J. Timothy 573
Woodhead, Robin G. 783
Woodhouse, Michael A. 264
Woodruff, Bob 626
Woodruff, Mark E. 45
Woods, Andrew S. 708
Woods, Duane C. 899
Woods, M. Troy 840
Woods, Richard 187
Woodson, Gregory P. 236
Woodward, Eric 777
Woodward, Keith A. 386
Woodworth, John K. 26
Wooten, James H. Jr. 453
Wootton, Brook 629
Workman, John L. 419
Worley, R. Jay 54
Worraker, Simon 729
Wortham, Dennis 920
Worthington, John M. 512
Woteki, Catherine 557
Wotring, Randall A. 868
Woung-Chapman, Marguerite 324
Woys, James E. 418
Wozniak, Thomas P. 272
Wren, John D. 650
Wren, Topher 406
Wright, Donald P. 746
Wright, Elease E. 46
Wright, Fred 600
Wright, Gregory A. 821
Wright, James L. 242
Wright, Joseph C. (Briggs & Stratton) 164
Wright, Joseph R. Jr. (MacAndrews & Forbes) 547
Wright, Laura H. 786
Wright, Mary Ann 489
Wright, Phillip D. 917
Wright, W. Lance 874

Wright, William S. 739
Wright-Violich, Kimberly 210
Wu, Michael 928
Wuest, Michael J. 654
Wulf, Gene C. 142
Wulfsohn, William A. 693
Wunderlin, James F. 787
Wunning, Steven H. 196
Wunsch, Charles 790
Wurtzburger, Wendy 867
Wyatt, Frank B. II 242
Wyatt, J. Tom 381
Wyatt, John H. A. 152
Wyatt, Kenneth 203
Wyman, Peter L. 699
Wynne, Brian E. 235
Wynne, Diana S. 264
Wyshner, David B. 119
Wysolmierski, Jill 120
Wyzga, Michael S. 390

Y

Yabuki, Jeffery W. 358
Yaffa, Earle 775
Yaggi, W. Timothy 562
Yahalomi, Lior E. 887
Yahia, Laurance H. S. 532
Yahn-Urlaub, Patty 250
Yancey, Carol B. 389
Yang, Jerry 929
Yang, Silas S.S. 699
Yang, Taiyin 393
Yanos, Neal A. 817
Yardley, James C. 324
Yarrington, Patricia E. 215
Yates, Kathy 311
Yates, Lloyd M. 703
Yates, Richard L. 825
Yates, Stephen E. 503
Yazdi, Mahvash 322
Yeager, David P. 445
Yeager, Mark A. 445
Yeagley, Albert W. 483
Yearick, Molly 683
Yearwood, Carlton 899
Yeatman, Matthew C. 392
Yeatman, Perry 515
Yegnashankaran, Mohan 610
Yeh, Ying 318
Yelamanchili, Balaji 327
Yelvington, Lori 67
Yeomans, Janet L. 26
Yerbury, Robert J. 471
Yezbick, Gary L. 562
Yimoyines, John P. 605
Yohe, D. Scott 285
Yong, Paul 768
York, Conrad C. 636
Yospe, Joseph F. 35
Yost, C. Daniel 718

Yost, James A. 273
Yost, R. David 85
Yosufzai, S. Shariq 215
You, Harry L. 327
Young, Andrew F. 41
Young, Bernie 560
Young, Chester G. 891
Young, Chris 474
Young, Dennis 751
Young, Douglas L. 527
Young, James R. 852
Young, John S. 82
Young, Kevin 393
Young, Randall D. 307
Young, Ray G. 388
Young, Robert H. Jr. 54
Young, Ron 381
Young, Steven K. 309
Youngman, Michael L. 636
Young-Scrivner, Annie 672
Yousefi, Nariman 170
Yowan, David L. 77
Yslas, Stephen D. 635
Yu, Carrie 699
Yu, Louis W. 676
Yuckert, Gregory H. 913
Yuen, Teck Ping 476
Yun, William Y. 374
Yuse, Richard R. 722
Yuspeh, Alan R. 415
Yust, Paul F. 149
Ywaniw, Michael J. 659

Z

Zaccagnini, Steven M. 35
Zaccardo, Daniel A. 114
Zaccaria, Adrian 136
Zack, Michael 422
Zadeh, Mansour T. 778
Zaffino, Peter 558
Zagalo de Lima, Armando 927
Zaidi, Mohammad A. 60
Zakaria, Adel A. 280
Zalesky, Alexander 772
Zaman, Waheed 217
Zandman, Felix 887
Zandman, Marc 887
Zandman, Ruta 887
Zank, Dennis W. 721
Zapolsky, David 69
Zarges, Thomas H. 868
Zarin, Larry 345
Zarkin, Herbert J. 150
Zaslav, David M. 297
Zatkin, Steven 495
Zausner, Freeman M. 867
Zavada, Jeffrey J. 891
Zawoyski, Sara 671
Zebula, Charles E. 75
Zee, Frances B. L. 274

Zehnder, Anthony B. 247
Zehrer, Amy L. 34
Zeilstra, David C. 445
Zelenka, Thomas 758
Zeleny, Dennis 801
Zelisko, Judith P. 175
Zell, Samuel 92, 336
Zeller, Barbara A. 625
Zeller, Paul R. 455
Zelmanovich, Boris 348
Zelnak, Stephen P. Jr. 561
Zesch, Hal 877
Ziegler, David S. 38
Ziegler, Greg 222
Ziegler, Marie Z. 280
Zierhoffer, Carol J. 474
Zihlmann, Josef 773
Zimbalist, Michael 620
Zimmer, George 583
Zimmer, James E. 583
Zimmerman, Don 908
Zimmerman, J. Jeffrey 426
Zimmerman, John M. 115
Zimmerman, Lawrence A. 927
Zimon, Eugene J. 639
Zimpfer, Matthew J. 247
Zimpleman, Larry D. 701
Zinn, George 591
Zinsner, David A. 91
Zint, Erna 211
Ziskin, Ian V. 635
Zito, Robert T. 169
Zizzo, Lawrence F. Jr. 56
Zlatkus, Lizabeth H. 413
Znamierowski, David M. 413
Zoba, C. David 381
Zoellner, Hanns 241
Zollars, William D. 931
Zolnowski, Matthew J. 654
Zook, Dennis R. 259
Zopp, Andrea L. 342
Zore, Edward J. 636
Zovko, Gregory A. 859
Zozaya Delano, José G. 496
Zubretsky, Joseph M. 46
Zubrow, Barry L. 494
Zuckerman, Brian D. 667
Zuckerman, Mitchell 783
Zuehlke, Steve 223
Zukowski, Perry S. 647
Zulim, Thomas M. 333
Zulkey, Edward J. 122
Zumwalt, LeAnne M. 277
Zuraitis, Marita 407
Zurbay, Donald J. 748
Zurquiyah-Rousset, Sophie 757
Zurzolo, Debby R. 213
Zusi, Paula J. 93
Zwerner, Jeffrey S. 660
Zwicky, Erwin 53
Zygocki, Rhonda I. 215
Zylstra, Michael J. 264